THE READER'S
ENCYCLOPEDIA

William Rose Benét

THE READER'S ENCYCLOPEDIA

SECOND EDITION

Deluxe Library Binding
including eight portfolios
of full page illustrations

in two volumes

Volume One
A—L

THOMAS Y. CROWELL COMPANY

New York / Established 1834

Text Illustrations Editor: Robert H. Snyder, Jr.
Portfolio Illustrations Editor: Thomas C. Jones

Copyright © 1965 by Thomas Y. Crowell Company

Manufactured in the United States of America by The Riverside Press, Cambridge, Massachusetts
Library of Congress Catalog Card No. 65–12510

Publisher's Preface

The Thomas Y. Crowell Company has been publishing reference books since 1886. During those seventy-nine years, many of these books have passed through several editions, each of which has represented a significant improvement over the previous edition. In general, these changes were part of that continuing process of gradual revision which makes good reference books better. The second edition of *The Reader's Encyclopedia,* however, is much more than a revision. It is a new book built on the foundations of the old.

The Reader's Encyclopedia was first published in 1948, under the editorship of the late William Rose Benét. In 1955 a 28-page supplement was added. Almost immediately thereafter work was begun on a complete revision of the book.

The new *Reader's Encyclopedia* contains 19 per cent more material than the old. This expansion has been achieved by increasing the dimensions of the page, while retaining the old type size. The additional material falls into three classes:

1. New entries. These cover literary developments of the last fifteen years, and also earlier writings in areas and periods of growing interest to modern readers, such as the Orient, the Soviet Union, Latin America, and the Near East.

2. Expansion of old entries. This process has aimed at a well-balanced coverage of world literature, with emphasis on areas of special interest today. For example, the article on Camus has been increased by 65 per cent, that on Li Po by 87 per cent, those on Dostoevski, Gabriela Mistral, and Aeschylus by 600, 700, and 800 per cent, respectively.

3. Addition of illustrations. The inclusion of 148 line cuts of title pages, old woodcuts, and cartoons on literary subjects enhances the usefulness, as well as the appearance, of the book.

This special two-volume edition has been produced for those who like deluxe bindings and appreciate the type of illustrations in the eight portfolios, that help to acquaint the reader with the appearance of many of the literary personalities of the past.

Because a reference book is useful only in proportion to the accessibility of its information, special care has been taken with details of cross-referencing and the style of entry headings. Titles of non-English works, for example, are generally given both in English and in their original language, transliterated where necessary; Greek proper names appear in direct transliteration, as well as in their familiar latinized spellings. Basic data on authors and works are now included in the headings in uniform style.

The following persons contributed substantially to the present edition of *The Reader's Encyclopedia*:

JANE APTEKAR	PURSHOTAM LAL
DOLORES BAGLEY	THOMAS W. LOMBARDI
PATRICK A. BARRETT	MASON MARTENS
BENJAMIN K. BENNETT	JAMES MIROLLO
HARRIET A. BLUM	MARCIA NEWFIELD
SANDRA M-J BOSSY	ROBERT O'BRIEN
BETTY JO BROWN	GRAHAM PARRY
RICHARD J. CAREY	FREDERICK S. PLOTKIN
JOAN CENEDELLA	EDWARD QUINN
JON C. CHERUBINI	RICHARD C. ROBEY
CHRISTOPHER COLLINS	ARTHUR ROZEN
HELEN V. DELPAR	KENNETH SILVERMAN
KAREN S. EBBITT	ROBERT H. SNYDER, JR.
LEONORE FLEISCHER	DAVID STEPHENSON
JUAN FREUDENTHAL	EDWARD STEWART
ARTHUR G. HUDGINS	EDWARD TRIPP
PAUL R. JACKSON	DOROTHY J. TUCK
WALLACE B. KATZ	BETTE S. WEIDMAN
SUSAN KOTTA	PHILIP YAMPOLSKY

This book owes much to the work of Cyrena Jo Pondrom, Walter L. Hayward, and Charles F. Hollander, of the editorial and production staff.

A Note on Using This Reference Work

When a reader can find further information on a subject by consulting an additional entry, he is referred to it in one of two ways: by the use of SMALL CAPITALS (e.g.: He was associated with the GEORGIAN poets.) or by the word "see" (e.g.: **Golgotha.** See CALVARY.). The first word printed in small capitals is the one under which the cross reference is alphabetized. In general, readers are referred from one entry to another only when the second entry provides significant information relevant to the first. Cross-references are plentiful, however, in the entries on mythology, where it is often helpful to be able to trace a complex tale through two or more entries.

Entries are alphabetized without reference to definite or indefinite articles. Titles beginning with frequently met phrases such as *The History of* . . . or *The Adventures of* . . . are found under the first significant word. (E.g.: *Tom Sawyer, The Adventures of.*) Authors with pen names appear under the name by which they are best known: Marie Henri Beyle is found under his famous pseudonym, Stendahl, with a cross-reference under Beyle; Dickens appears under his own name, with a cross-reference under Boz. When the original title of a non-English work is commonly used by English speakers, its entry is found under that title, with a cross-reference under a well-known English title. (E.g.: **Would-be Gentleman, The.** See LE BOURGEOIS GENTILHOMME.) Works better known under English titles are found there, but with cross-references from their original titles, if these are frequently encountered. (E.g.: **A la Recherche du Temps Perdu.** See REMEMBRANCE OF THINGS PAST.)

The date of a play is that of its first production, when known, unless production was long delayed; otherwise the date is that of the first known printing.

Preface to the First Edition

At the end of the nineteenth century there died an English schoolmaster and clergyman whose life had spanned most of it. He was born in 1810. Two books in my father's library made me familiar, at an early age, with the Englishman's name. They were Brewer's *A Dictionary of Phrase and Fable* and Brewer's *The Reader's Handbook*. His full name was Ebenezer Cobham Brewer. Years later, when I was asked to edit a *Reader's Encyclopedia,* using *Crowell's Handbook for Readers and Writers* as nucleus, I discovered that, according to the preface of the first editor of that volume, it had originally owed much to the fascinating books of Dr. Brewer. (I always imagined him with a delightful beard—something like Edward Lear's—in which nested all the oddities of learning. Alas, I can boast no such receptaculum!) However, the *Handbook for Readers and Writers* had given his material extremely detailed revision, to say nothing of supplying a great deal that was new, relating to the Victorian era and to subsequent years, with especial attention to American literature and allusion. Since that time, of course, almost as many changes in taste, viewpoint, and interest have occurred as the handbook's editor found to have taken place between 1897 (when Dr. Brewer died) and 1925 (when the *Crowell Handbook* appeared). Twenty or more recent years have shown as many alterations as the previous thirty. And now, in the midst of the new Atomic Age, there are changes that even a modern editor could not have anticipated several years ago!

I wish immediately to acknowledge my indebtedness, not only to the editor of *Crowell's Handbook for Readers and Writers,* Miss Henrietta Gerwig, but also to an intermediate reviser, Miss Irene Hendry, whose knowledge of modern literature has proved indispensable to the present volume. Miss Gerwig's handbook was designed as "a dictionary of famous characters and plots in legend, fiction, drama, opera, and poetry, together with dates and principal works of important authors, literary and journalistic terms and familiar allusions." Miss Hendry's work, never before appearing in print, is incorporated here. But the original handbook is only one of several ancestors of the present work. Since the handbook's publication, so many people have contributed ideas and suggestions that the present volume has, in a sense, been composed for you by inquiring readers from all parts of the country. It is no mere revision, but veritably a new book.

Original entries on established authors of the past have been enlarged, with modern treatment. Full advantage has been taken of all the most modern reference books. More attention has been given to obscure works and figures in literature both of the distant and recent past. And, in line with the methodological advance in literary criticism of the past fifteen years or so, "whereby an author is interpreted not only in terms of the literal content of his works and the facts of his biography, but also in terms of the general intellectual forces of his time," entries have been chosen of significant figures, movements, and terms in aesthetics, science, philosophy, economics, and politics. Freud, Jung, Karl Marx, Lenin, The New Deal, the stream-of-consciousness tendency in fiction, and even futurism and surrealism have received due consideration. The fields of art and music are now extensively covered, incorporating important twentieth-century additions.

Such is the nature of an encyclopedia of this kind that one could go on almost indefinitely adding new information to that already accumulated. The limitations of such a volume are hard to establish. What is it that intelligent readers and writers do *not* wish to know? One simply has to set a term, and mark boundaries. Therefore, for this new book, much more grist has actually been gathered than has come through the mill. At that, it deserves to be called a one-volume literary encyclopedia.

I have endeavored carefully to check over what was already amassed, to expand, to fill up gaps, to carry on what was unfinished; to add bio-

graphical, historical, and other data that unfold-
ing world events made obligatory; to comb for
word, phrase, and allusion such reference works
as had been searched either superficially or not
at all; to discard the obsolete; to bring to light
the overlooked; and to play, in general, the role
of Argus-eyed modernizer. I am bound to have
made errors both of omission and commission.
But, with the able assistance of Dr. Alexander
Gode and the invaluable final rechecking of that
brilliant literary detective, Earle F. Walbridge, I
believe that this encyclopedia will now prove one
of the most complete and practicable in existence.
It will be found to cover an unusual range of information, to provide a reference to most allusions
occurring in your reading, to give all the important myths and legends and a great many of the
most important themes and characters in fiction
old and new, to include references that constantly
crop up in the critical writing of yesterday and
today, to furnish information as to literary schools,
trends, and movements past and present and biographical data on most "people of importance."
Likewise it will prove a real aid to the vocabulary
and allusiveness of writers, as well as providing
them with a genuine source book of ideas. As for
cross-word puzzlers, they will, of course, discover
it to be a necessity!

The curious mind inevitably stores up what it
has sometimes characterized as "much useless information." Yet, in literature, it is often these
peculiar bits of learning that serve most to adorn
and give flavor to a style. I have, however, endeavored to rid the book of all that is merely
archaic. I have tried to maintain balance and proportion between the modern world and the world

of antiquity. People used to speak of "dead languages." Yet, in English derivations, the dead
languages still live. In the same way, the mythology of the past constantly reappears in the
poetry of the present; and the classics may furnish
groundwork for the most modern fiction. (One
has only to think of *Ulysses*.) All of this such a
book as the one before you must comprehend. It
must also show itself thoroughly familiar with
modern literature and thought of all kinds, with
modern invention and science, with new art
media, with the continuity of history.

Either my memory is at fault or there is one
essay that neither Charles Lamb, William Hazlitt,
nor Christopher Morley ever wrote: one on Reference Books. The phrase for them, now cliché, has
been "mines of information." But a mine, at best,
is a rather dark and dreary excavation—not to say
dank, at times. I prefer to think of the book before
you as a cave like the famous one stumbled upon
by Aladdin. I might go on from there to describe
its revelation of treasure of so many varieties and
kinds, yet each in its own particular bin. For the
office of a reference book is, after all, to bring
some sort of order out of chaos. But it is also to
present to you a well-organized supplementary
memory, in one volume. The delights of such a
memory may be inexhaustible; the safaris of research it can initiate, endless; the urge to literary
creation which it can supply, present on every
page. And remember, that to enter this domain
of learning and imagination you have not even
to use that mysterious phrase, "Open Sesame!"

WILLIAM ROSE BENÉT

List of Full Page Illustrations

A

Aakjaer, Jeppe (1866–1930). Danish poet and novelist. As a novelist, Aakjaer was intensely concerned with social misery and the need for reform. *Vredens Børn* (*The Children of Wrath,* 1904) describes the oppressed existence led by servants on peasant farms. He is best known, however, for his lyric poetry, in which he celebrates the courage of the peasants and the beauties of his native Jutland. A merry simplicity characterizes the poetry of such collections as *Fri Felt* (1906), *Rugens Sange* (*Songs of the Rye,* 1906), and *Den Sommer og den Eng* (1910).

Aaron. In the Bible, the brother of Moses, the founder of the priesthood and the 1st high priest. He helped Moses in calling down the Ten Plagues and leading the Children of Israel out of Egypt (c. 1200 B.C.). Aaron directed the construction of the golden calf (made of gold earrings and other jewelry), which was idolatrously worshipped by the Israelites as the god of their deliverance, while Moses was receiving the Ten Commandments from Jehovah (Ex. 32). Aaron did not receive an inheritance in Canaan, as a punishment for doubting God's ability to bring water out of a rock.

Aaron's Rod. The name given to the rod of the tribe of Levi, used by Aaron during the 10 Plagues and the crossing of the Red Sea. When Aaron left his rod in front of the Ark, in the Tabernacle, it miraculously blossomed and bore almonds. This was interpreted as evidence of Jehovah's choice of Aaron as high priest (Num. 17:8).

Aaron. In Shakespeare's TITUS ANDRONICUS, the Moorish lover of the vengeful Tamora, with whom he plots the destruction of the Andronicus family. He flees Rome with the black child to whom Tamora gives birth, having substituted a white child and killed all witnesses, and is later condemned to death by Lucius.

Aaru. In Egyptian mythology, the fields of Aaru are the abode of the blessed dead and of the gods and goddesses.

Aasen, Ivar Andreas (1813–1896). Norwegian philologist. Aasen made from various dialects a Norwegian literary language called New Norwegian or *landsmaal,* in contrast to the Dano-Norwegian *rigsmaal.* In the poems of *Symra* (1863) he uses the *landsmaal* to describe peasant life and to voice his own subdued sadness.

Abaddon. The angel of the bottomless pit in *The Revelation of St. John the Divine.* Milton uses the name for the bottomless pit itself.

Abano, Pietro d'. Also **Petrus de Apono** (c. 1250–c. 1316). Italian philosopher, physician, astrologer. In his *Conciliator Differentiarum quae inter Philosophos et Medicos Versantur* ("reconciler of the differences among philosophers and doctors"), he advocated the systems of Averroes and other Arabic writers. He was so successful a scientist and physician that he was accused of black magic and heresy: brought twice before the Inquisition, he was acquitted once and died in prison before the second trial.

Abaris. A mythical Greek sage of the 6th century B.C. Surnamed "the Hyperborean," he is mentioned by Herodotus, Pindar, etc. Apollo gave him a magic arrow which rendered him invisible, cured diseases, gave oracles, and on which he could ride through the air. Abaris gave it to Pythagoras, who, in return, taught him philosophy.

Abbassids. The 2nd long dynasty (37 Caliphs, 750–1258) of the Muslim Empire. They claimed descent from Abbas (566–652), eldest uncle of Muhammad. Their reign was most firmly established and the court at Baghdad most splendid under HAROUN-AL-RASCHID, the Caliph described in the *Arabian Nights,* and his son Mamun (reigned 813–833).

Abbaye Group, the. A group of French writers and artists. They bought a house in Créteil near Paris, called it "L'Abbaye," and lived there communally for 14 months (1906–1907). After their separation they were influential in spreading the ideas of UNANIMISM, introduced to them by Jules Romains, a frequent visitor to the Abbaye. Among the group were René Arcos (1881–   ), Georges DUHAMEL, Luc Durtain (1881–1959), Pierre Jean JOUVE, Charles VILDRAC, and the cubist painter Albert Gleizes (1881–   ).

Abbé Constantin, L' (1882). A novel by Ludovic HALÉVY. This gentle tale, which owes its popularity to the simple, melodious grace of its author's style, tells of the effects of the sale of the largest chateau in the Abbé's parish. The ingredients of young love, charity, and fortune serve to placate the Abbé's fears for his parish and his godson.

Abbey Theatre. The famous Dublin home of the Irish National Theatre Society. It was established in 1901 for Irish actors in plays by Irish dramatists about Ireland; especially about her heroic past and peasantry. William Butler YEATS was influential in founding it. A. E. (q.v.), Lady GREGORY, and John Millington SYNGE wrote for it; and, in later years, so did Sean O'CASEY. See IRISH RENAISSANCE.

Abbot, The (1820). A novel by Sir Walter SCOTT centering on the escape from prison and flight to England of Mary, queen of Scots.

Abbot of Misrule or **Unreason.** See LORD OF MISRULE.

Abbotsford. The baronial mansion built by Sir Walter Scott on the Tweed near Melrose.

Abbott, George (1889–). American playwright and producer. He collaborated with James Gleason on *The Fall Guy* (1925), with Philip Dunning on *Broadway* (1926), with Ann Preston Bridgers on *Coquette* (1928), and with John Cecil Holm on *Three Men on a Horse* (1935). Thereafter, he turned to directing and producing. He is the author of a candid autobiography, *Mister Abbott* (1963).

Abbott, Lyman (1835–1922). American Congregational minister and editor. Abbott wrote a *Life of Henry Ward Beecher* (1903), but he is best known for his work as editor of the famous weekly THE OUTLOOK and of its immediate predecessor *The Christian Union* magazine. A liberal in theology and politics, Abbott exerted considerable influence on the American scene.

A B C Book or **Absey Book.** A primer or speller which used to be used as a child's first lesson book and contained merely the alphabet and a few rudimentary lessons often set in catechism form, as is evident from Shakespeare's lines:

> That is question now;
> And then comes answer like an Absey book.
> *King John,* i, 1

Abdera, Abderitan. Abdera was a maritime city of Thrace whose inhabitants were proverbial in ancient times for their stupidity. "Abderitan laughter" came to mean scoffing or incessant

The New England Primer (1727), an American A B C Book.

A — In *Adam's* Fall We Sinned all.

B — Thy Life to Mend This *Book* Attend.

C — The *Cat* doth play And after slay.

D — A *Dog* will bite A Thief at night.

E — An *Eagles* flight Is out of sight.

F — The Idle *Fool* Is whipt at School.

laughter. It was so called because Abdera was the birthplace of Democritus, the laughing philosopher, who is regarded as the greatest among the Greek physical philosophers.

Abderite, the. See DEMOCRITUS.

Abdiel (*Heb.,* "servant of god"). In Milton's PARADISE LOST, the faithful seraph who opposes Satan when he urges the angels to revolt.

Abednego. See SHADRACH, MESHACH, AND ABEDNEGO.

Abel. See CAIN.

Abélard, Pierre (1079–1142). French scholastic philosopher and theologian. He studied under Roscellinus (b. 1050), exponent of extreme NOMINALISM, then under William of Champeaux (1070–1121), supporter of realism. In this controversy of medieval theology Abélard evolved a middle position called *conceptualism,* holding that both particular objects and universal concepts are real. However, he angered the clergy, who emphasized faith rather than dialectic argument and proof, with his rationalistic approach to Church dogma, especially the dogma of the Trinity. Thus Saint BERNARD OF CLAIRVAUX persecuted him as a heretic, and Abélard died on his way to Rome to appeal to the Pope against a condemnation on this charge. Nevertheless, Abélard had been extremely popular as a lecturer; when he had to leave Notre Dame, his students followed him to various monasteries. His influence and his writings, such as SIC ET NON, increased the popularity of Aristotelian logic over that of Platonic theory.

His popular fame, however, resulted from his tragic love affair with HÉLOÏSE. Moved by his *Historia Calamitatum* (c. 1134), Héloïse wrote to him, and they exchanged their famous letters of love and suffering, including Abélard's advice on how she should conduct the convent he had turned over to her in 1129.

Abe Lincoln in Illinois (1938). A play by Robert E. SHERWOOD. Awarded a Pulitzer Prize, it deals with the life of Lincoln up to his election to the presidency; the dialogue contains selections from a number of Lincoln's own speeches and writings.

Abell, Kjeld (1901–1961). Danish playwright. The work of Abell is a provocative mixture of light, witty comedy and bitter satire. In 1937, *The Melody that Got Lost* (*Melodien, der blev Voek;* 1935), a clever play about the office proletariat, was produced in London; it was followed by *Eva aftjener sin Barnepligt* (*Eva Serves Her Time as a Child,* 1936). *Anna Sophie Hedvig* (1939), whose schoolteacher heroine murders her principal to save a child from persecution, is a violent protest against injustice.

Abencerrages (Sp. *Abencerrajes*). A family of Moors in Granada in the 15th century. They are famous in romance for their feud with the family of the Zegris (Sp. *Cegríes*). Chateaubriand wrote a novel called *The Last Abencerrage.*

abenteuerliche Simplicissimus, Der. See SIMPLICISSIMUS.

Abercrombie, Lascelles (1881–1938). English poet, critic, and writer of verse drama. He was associated with the GEORGIAN poets. His collections of poems include *Interludes and Poems* (1908) and *Twelve Idylls* (1928); *The Sale of St. Thomas* (1911) is a verse drama.

Abessa. See FAERIE QUEENE, THE.

Abhorrers. See PETITIONERS AND ABHORRERS.

Abie's Irish Rose (1922). A comedy by Anne Nichols. It had one of the longest records of performance (2,327) in the history of the theater. A Jewish boy and an Irish Catholic girl, fearing to tell their fathers that they are in love, are married by a Methodist minister. The play formed the basis for a novel (1927), a radio program (1942), and a movie (1946).

Abigail. In the Old Testament, the wife of Nabal and later of David (I Sam. 25:3). She referred to herself as the handmaid of David. In Elizabethan usage, the name came to signify a lady's maid. It is used in works by Marlowe, Beaumont and Fletcher, Swift, and Fielding. The name was further popularized by Abigail Hill (Mrs. Masham), the influential waiting-woman to Queen Anne.

Abnaki or Abenaki. An Algonquian Indian tribe. The English and French used the name to designate a loose confederacy of tribes occupying Maine and parts of New Brunswick and Quebec. The tribes fought as allies of the French until France lost its North American possessions.

abomination of desolation. An epithet, used in *Daniel* and in *Matthew*, referring to a pagan idol or statue set up in the temple at Jerusalem. The phrase is now used for anything very hateful or destructive.

Abou Ben Adhem. A short poem by Leigh HUNT. Because Abou begged to be written as "one who loves his fellowmen," his angel visitor

> . . . showed the names whom love of God had blest
> And lo! Ben Adhem's name led all the rest.

Abou Hassan. A young merchant of Baghdad, hero of the tale called "The Sleeper Awakened" in *The Arabian Nights*. While Abou Hassan is asleep, he is conveyed to the palace of HAROUN-AL-RASCHID where the attendants are ordered to do all they can to make him fancy himself the Caliph. He subsequently becomes the Caliph's favorite. See SLY, CHRISTOPHER.

Abra. A favorite concubine of Solomon. In his poem SOLOMON ON THE VANITY OF THE WORLD (1718), Matthew Prior describes her devotion in the celebrated lines:

> Abra was ready ere I called her name,
> And though I called another, Abra came.

Abrabanel or **Abarbanel, Judah León.** Known as **León Hebreo** (It., **Leone Ebreo**) or **Leo the Jew** (c. 1465–1535). A Jew expelled from Spain who came to Italy and practiced medicine while studying and writing philosophical material. His fame rests on the *Dialoghi d'Amore* (Dialogues of Love, 1535), a prose work that sets forth in a series of lively conversations Renaissance theories of love. The dialogues reveal the preoccupation in the Italy of the period with Neoplatonism and ancient learning in general.

abracadabra. A cabalistic charm, supposedly constructed from the initials of the Hebrew words Ab (Father), Ben (Son), and Ruach Acadasch (Holy Spirit), and once used as an antidote against various physical ills. From its role as charm it has come to be associated with any meaningless jargon and is a term frequently used by magicians. The word was originally written on parchment and suspended from the neck by a linen thread, in the following form:

```
A B R A C A D A B R A
 A B R A C A D A B R
  A B R A C A D A B
   A B R A C A D A
    A B R A C A D
     A B R A C A
      A B R A C
       A B R A
        A B R
         A B
          A
```

Abraham. The founder of the Hebrew people and its first patriarch. With his wife Sarah and his nephew LOT, he migrated from UR of Chaldees into the land of Canaan, where he settled and prospered. To test his faith, Jehovah commanded him to sacrifice his son ISAAC as a burnt offering; however, a ram caught in a thicket was provided instead, just when Abraham was about to draw the knife. The story of Abraham is told in Gen. 11–25 and in various Muslim legends.

Abrahamic covenant. God made a covenant with Abraham (Gen. 17) that He would be God to him and all his children and that they should inherit and dwell in the land of Canaan.

Abraham ben Meïr ibn Ezra (1092–1167). Spanish Jewish scholar. He wrote scientific treatises, biblical commentaries, and outstanding poems. He is the Rabbi ben Ezra of Browning's poem.

Abraham Lincoln. A biography by Carl SANDBURG. The first part, entitled *Abraham Lincoln: The Prairie Years,* was published in two volumes in 1926, and the second part, *Abraham Lincoln: The War Years,* was published in four volumes in 1939. For Sandburg, Lincoln was the archetypal figure of American democracy; the preparation of the biography, the second part of which won a Pulitzer Prize, occupied many years of the poet's life.

Abraham-man or **Abram-man.** A begging impostor, a pretended lunatic. In Tudor and early Stuart times, inmates of Bedlam who were not dangerously mad were kept in the "Abraham Ward," and allowed out from time to time in distinctive clothes, to supplement their scanty rations by begging. Richard Head, a writer of the latter part of the 17th century, says that many healthy rogues, imitating these TOM o' BEDLAMS, "used to array themselves with party-coloured ribbons, tape in their hats, a fox-tail hanging down, a long stick with streamers, and beg alms; but for all their seeming madness, they had wit enough to steal as they went along."

Abraham Newland. A bank note, so called from the name of Abraham Newland (1730–1807), the chief cashier of the Bank of England from 1782 to 1807, without whose signature no Bank of England notes were genuine.

Abraham's bosom. The repose of the happy in death (Luke 16:22).

abraxas. A cabalistic word. It was used by the Gnostics to denote the Supreme Being, the source of 365 emanations, the sum of the numbers represented by the Greek letters of the word totaling 365. It was frequently engraved on gems (hence known as *abraxas stones*) that were used as amulets or talismans. By some authorities the name is given as that of one of the horses of Aurora, the dawn goddess.

Absalom. In the Old Testament, the handsome and rebellious 3rd son of David, king of Israel, who "stole the hearts of the men of Israel" and plotted to become king in his father's stead (II Sam. 15:6). Riding on a mule in the decisive battle at Ephraim, Absalom was caught by his hair in an oak tree; finding him so suspended, one of David's army killed him despite previous commands of the king. David's lament, "O my son Absalom, my son, my son Absalom! would God I had died for thee, O Absalom, my son, my son!" has become a classic expression of paternal grief.

Dryden gave the name Absalom to the duke of Monmouth, Charles II's natural son, in his satire *Absalom and Achitophel* (1681).

Absalom, Absalom! (1936). A novel by William FAULKNER. The story centers on Thomas Sutpen, the son of a West Virginia poor white, and his attempts to fulfill his "grand design," to be accepted as a Southern aristocrat and founder of a wealthy family. He establishes himself in Jefferson, Miss., and at the climax of his career he is elected colonel of Jefferson's regiment in the Civil War. Returning to his estate, Sutpen's Hundred, after the war, he finds the plantation in ruins. His daughter's half brother and part-Negro lover has been killed by Sutpen's son, who has disappeared, and she has become a confirmed spinster. Sutpen's attempt to have another son by a poor-white girl ends in his murder by her grandfather. When the Sutpen saga comes to an end in 1910, all that is left of his dream is an idiot Negro, Jim Bond, Sutpen's only living descendant, howling in the ashes of the burned house.

In place of the sustained interior monologue Faulkner used in *The Sound and the Fury,* the story is projected by means of three narrators; their personalities and concerns are revealed as each tells the story of Sutpen. Miss Rosa COLDFIELD, Sutpen's sister-in-law, first tells the story to Quentin Compson shortly before his departure for Harvard; her story is supplemented by that of Quentin's father; and Quentin, in turn, relates the whole story with his own interpretation to his Harvard roommate, Shreve McCannon. See SUTPEN.

Absalom and Achitophel (1681). A political satire in verse by John DRYDEN. Written in heroic couplets, the poem attacks Puritan attempts to exclude the duke of York, the legitimate heir, from the throne of England because of his Catholicism. Using Biblical terminology, Dryden describes the efforts of Achitophel (the earl of Shaftesbury) to incite Absalom (the duke of Monmouth, illegitimate son of Charles II) to rebellion against his father. A second part, written by Nahum TATE and revised by Dryden, who added 200 lines, appeared in 1682.

Absentee, The (1812). A novel by Maria EDGEWORTH. The "absentee," Lord Clonbrony, allows his foolish wife to persuade him to leave his estate in Ireland and try to force a way into fashionable London society.

Absey Book. See A B C BOOK.

Absolute, Captain Jack. The hero of Sheridan's comedy THE RIVALS. The clever and gallant son of Sir Anthony Absolute, he is a rival of Bob Acres for the hand of Lydia Languish, to whom he is known only as Ensign Beverley.

Absolute, Sir Anthony. A character in Sheridan's comedy THE RIVALS. He is a testy, but warm-hearted old gentleman who imagines that he possesses a most angelic temper and that, when he quarrels with others, it is they, not he, who are out of sorts.

absurd. Modern philosophical term. Used by Albert CAMUS to describe the meaninglessness of human existence in the modern world, it is presented especially in his essay THE MYTH OF SISYPHUS (1942) and his novel THE STRANGER (1942). Jean-Paul SARTRE describes the absurdity of the human condition, which he makes a precondition for the philosophy of EXISTENTIALISM, in his novel NAUSEA (1938). The "Literature of the Absurd," however, usually refers to those works which deliberately violate or distort the conventions of the novel or the theater, grimly making them ridiculous in an attempt to show the absurdity of the human lives they represent. They often use either a barren setting or an emphasis on things —inanimate material objects—to express the a-human sterility of modern values. The tone may range from the broadly comic aspect of the absurd to the unsettling, the grotesque, or even the terrible. Alfred JARRY's UBU ROI (1896) is often considered the first direct ancestor of the movement, and Franz KAFKA's novels the first examples. The absurd shocked its way to widespread recognition in France with the novels and plays of Samuel BECKETT and the plays of Jean GENET and Eugène IONESCO. In America it finds expression in the work of the avant-garde playwrights Edward ALBEE and Jack GELBER, in England in the plays of Harold PINTER. The Swiss dramatist, Friedrich DÜRRENMATT, also writes in the absurd tradition.

Absyrtus. See the ARGONAUTS.

Abzu. In Sumerian mythology, the river that is supposed to surround the earth. The Abzu seems almost identical with the Greek Oceanus, the "river of ocean." In Babylonian mythology it is personified as Apsu, the fresh water, who has existed from the beginning of time with his wife Tiamat, the salt water; he plays an important role in the WAR OF THE GODS. The Sumerian ENKI and the Babylonian EA, almost identical gods of water and of wisdom, live in a palace in the Abzu, which was probably the Persian Gulf, the shores of which in early days may have reached northward to the city of Eridu.

academe. A place of study or instruction. It is so called from Plato's ACADEMY.

Académie française. The French Academy. Originating in secret meetings of men of literary taste in Paris around the year 1630, the Academy was established by order of the king and at the behest of Cardinal Richelieu in the year 1635. Made up of 40 members, supposedly the most distinguished living men of French letters, the Academy took as its purpose the protection and perfection of the French language and to that end began compiling its dictionary in the year 1639; the task has not yet been completed. The Academy also undertook the composition of definitive treatises on grammar, poetry and rhetoric. Ordered by Richelieu to censure Corneille's *Le Cid,* the Academy early adopted a policy of advocating old rules and traditions at the expense of innovation and change. In the late 18th century the *philosophes* gained a majority in the Academy and briefly lent it an influential voice. Inactive during the revolution, the Academy was reestablished in 1803 by Napoleon as part of the Institut de France and two years later took up headquarters in the Palais Mazarin, which it still occupies. Inevitably the Academy is a conservative body, reflecting the tastes of its membership—men, by definition, of age and secure reputation. Including many of the most significant names in past and present French literature, criticism, and philosophy, the membership list nonetheless reveals several surprising omissions, most regrettably that of Molière. In this century the Academy may be said to have fairly represented the cultural life of France and, in general, to have exercised a beneficent effect upon the preservation of the language.

Académie Goncourt. See Prix Goncourt.

Academy, the (Akademe). The name of Plato's school near Athens. It was named after a legendary hero, Hecademus or Academus. The school had a long history, continuing until Justinian suppressed the philosophic schools in 529 A.D.

Acadia. The old name for Nova Scotia, so called by the French from the river *Shubenacadie*. In 1621 Acadia was given to the Scot, Sir William Alexander, and its name changed; and in 1755 the old French settlers were driven into exile by George II. Many of them migrated to Louisiana, where their descendants are still known as "Cajuns" (Acadians). Longfellow has made this the subject of a poem in hexameter verse, Evangeline.

Acastus (Akastos). In Greek mythology, a son of Pelias. He sailed with the Argonauts and, after his father's death, became king of Iolcus. Believing the lie of his wife Cretheis that Peleus had made advances to her, he tried to kill him. Later Peleus conquered Iolcus and killed Acastus.

Accademia Della Crusca (It., "Academy of the Chaff"). Florentine literary academy founded in 1583 to purify Tuscan, the literary language of the Italian Renaissance. It was opposed to Tasso in the debate over the merits of his Gerusalemme Liberata. The first part of its official dictionary appeared in 1612 and the work is still in progress.

accent meter. (1) Accentual meter, that is, verse based on the alternation of accented and unaccented syllables. English prosody is based on accent meter as opposed to quantitative meter, or verse based on the alternation of long and short syllables, which is the basis of Greek and Latin prosody.

(2) Meter that depends only upon the number of accented syllables in the line and disregards the unaccented syllables. The feet that make up the line may be of any kind, including the monosyllabic foot. Accent verse has always been prevalent in popular ballads and songs, and it is often deliberately used in modern poetry. An example from *Sir Patrick Spens,* an early Scottish ballad of unknown authorship, is:

O lang, / lang, / may the la/dies stand
Wi thair gold / kems / in their hair,
Waiting / for thair / ain deir / lords,
For they'll / se thame / na mair.

Accolti, Bernardo (1458–1535). Italian poet and dramatist. Born in Arezzo, he is known as the Unique Aretine for his supposedly impromptu recitations of sonnets before the courts of Renaissance

Italy. His *Virginia,* a play drawn from Boccaccio's *Decameron* (*Gillette of Narbonne,* III, 9), was first performed in 1494. He is a prominent interlocutor in Castiglione's *Cortegiano.*

Accoramboni, Vittoria (1557?–1585). Her husband was murdered so that she might marry the Duke of Bracciano. After Bracciano's death in 1585, she was herself murdered by assassins hired by one of his relatives. She is a principal figure in Webster's play The White Devil, or Vittoria Corombona.

Account of My Hut, An (Hōjō ki). Japanese miscellany, a brief account of the personal experiences of Kamo no Chōmei (1153–1216). It details the natural disasters that visited Kyoto during the late Heian period (794–1185) and describes the life led by the author at his hermitage. It is strongly Buddhist in tone.

Aceldama (Gr., "field of blood"). A field in the Hinnon Valley near Jerusalem which, in Matthew (27:6–8), was purchased by the priests with the 30 pieces of silver ("the blood money") thrown down by Judas Iscariot after his betrayal of Jesus. It was used as Jerusalem's "potter's field" (so called because potters used such fields to obtain clay) for the burial of strangers. According to The Acts (1:18), Judas bought the field, fell into it, and "burst asunder." The usual version (Matt. 27:5) of Judas' death is that he hanged himself.

Acestes. In Vergil's Aeneid, the Trojan son of the river god Crimisus. During the funeral games held for Anchises in Sicily, where Acestes had established himself before the arrival of Aeneas, he discharges his arrow with such force that it takes fire from the friction of the air (Book V).

Acevedo Díaz, Eduardo (1851–1924). Uruguayan statesman and novelist. Trained as a lawyer, Acevedo Díaz was active in Uruguayan politics, spent part of his life in exile, and held several diplomatic posts. He described Uruguay's war for independence in an impassioned trilogy which he called "a hymn of blood": *Ismael* (1888), *Nativa* (1889–1890), and *Grito de gloria* (1894). His masterpiece is *Soledad* (1894), often considered the archetype of the gaucho novel. See gaucho literature.

Achard, Marcel (1899–   ). French dramatist. His characters are usually idealistic vagabonds and dreamers. His plays, such as *La Vie est belle* (1928), *Jean de la lune* (1929), *Domino* (1931), *Le Corsaire* (1938), and *Patate* (1957), are full of fantasy and the joy of life.

Achates. In Vergil's Aeneid, the constant companion of Aeneas. Thus, a *fidus Achates* is synonymous with a faithful companion and bosom friend.

Achelous (Acheloos). In ancient Greece, the large river that separated Aetolia from Acarnania, and the god thereof. This bull-headed god wrestled Heracles as a rival for Deianira, and lost one of his horns as well as the prize. When Alcmaeon, pursued by the Erinyes for the murder of his mother Eriphyle, sought a land that had not existed at the time of the murder, he found it in the delta of the Achelous, which was formed by new silt. Achelous gave his daughter Callirrhoe in marriage to Alcmaeon but she proved to be his death.

Acheron. (Gr., the River of Sorrows.) The river of the infernal regions into which Phlegethon and Cocytus flow; also, the lower world (Hades) itself.

Several actual Greek rivers, in addition, were given that name. See STYX.

Achilles. In Greek mythology, the son of PELEUS and the Nereid THETIS, and king of the MYRMIDONS, a Thessalian tribe. He is the hero of Homer's ILIAD and became the prototype of the Greeks' conception of manly valor and beauty. He took part in the Trojan War on the side of the Greeks as their most illustrious warrior, and slew the Trojan hero Hector. Achilles had been dipped in the STYX by his mother, which rendered him invulnerable except in the heel by which she held him. He was fatally wounded there by an arrow shot by Paris, Hector's younger brother, or, according to another version of the story, by the god Apollo who had assumed Paris' shape. The phrase *Achilles' heel* is used to describe the vulnerable point in the character of a man or nation.

Achitophel. In the Old Testament, David's traitorous counselor. He deserted to ABSALOM, who was trying to supersede his father, but hanged himself when his advice was disregarded (II Sam. 17). In his satire, *Absalom and Achitophel* (1681), Dryden used this name for the earl of Shaftesbury.

Acis (Akis). In classical legend, a handsome Sicilian youth, son of Faunus and the naiad Symaethis. The lover of Galatea, he was killed by his rival, the Cyclops POLYPHEMUS. The blood flowing forth from Acis' body changed into water and formed the river Acis. The story is the subject of an opera by Handel, *Acis and Galatea* (1721).

Acmeism. A movement in Russian poetry, active from about 1910 to 1917. The Acmeists, who belonged to a group known as the Poets' Guild, got their name from the high poetic standards they professed. They advocated concision in poetry, clear and concrete imagery, and precise use of words. The movement was a reaction against the mysticism and stylistic vagueness of the symbolist school of poetry, which had held sway in Russian literature from about 1895. The leading Acmeists were Nikolai GUMILIOV, Anna AKHMATOVA, and Osip MANDELSHTAM.

Acquainted with the Night (1928). A sonnet by Robert FROST. Written in *terza rima* and one of Frost's few poems set in the city, it is a mystical poem of loneliness and despair; "the time was neither wrong nor right," it declares.

Acrasia. See FAERIE QUEENE, THE.

Acres, Bob. A character in Sheridan's comedy THE RIVALS. A country gentleman, he is the rival of Captain Jack Absolute for the hand of Lydia Languish. He tries to ape the man of fashion, affects elaborate oaths, and blusters mightily, but when his courage is put to the test he proves himself an abject coward.

Acrisius. In Greek mythology, king of Argos and the father of Danae. An oracle declared that Danae would give birth to a son who would kill him, so Acrisius kept his daughter shut up in a brazen tower. Here she became the mother of Perseus by Zeus who appeared in the form of a shower of gold. The king of Argos now ordered his daughter and her infant to be put into a chest, and cast adrift on the sea, but they were rescued by Dictys, a fisherman. When grown to manhood, Perseus accidentally struck the foot of Acrisius with a quoit, and the blow caused his death, thus fulfilling the oracle.

acropolis (akropolis; Gr., high city). The citadel of a Greek city, generally situated on a hill. The Acropolis at Athens, a rocky plateau about 200 feet high, was the site of the ancient town. It was surrounded by walls which were destroyed by the Persians in 480 B.C., and later rebuilt by Themistocles. The Acropolis was the center of religious activity; many temples and statues of Athene were located there. The ERECHTHEUM, the PARTHENON and the Propylaea are among the best known of its monuments. The acropolis of Thebes was the Cadmeia; that of Corinth, the Acrocorinth.

acrostic. A composition, often in verse, in which a set or sets of letters (such as the first, middle, or last of each line) spell out a word, a word group, or part of the alphabet. 12 Psalms of the Old Testament are written acrostically, the 119th being an ingenious alphabetic acrostic. The Latin poets wrote acrostic verse, and the early English poet CYNEWULF signed his name to his works in acrostic runes. The Elizabethan Sir John Davies wrote 26 *Hymns of Astraea*, in which the first letters of the lines spell *Elisabetha Regina* 26 times. Edgar Allan Poe demonstrated skill in devising acrostics on the names of his loved ones. Charles Lamb devised a well-known acrostic conundrum spelling his name (*Lamb*) and pseudonym (*Elia*). Abecedarian hymns, designed to aid the memorizing of the alphabet, may be counted acrostics, and perhaps for this reason men of letters have held the form in low esteem as being little more than a childish riddle. The word "acrostic" is also applied to any word square which reads the same horizontally as vertically.

Actaeon (Aktaion). In Greek mythology, the son of Aristaeus and Autonoë. Having accidentally observed Artemis in her bath, while hunting on Mount Cithaeron, he was changed by the goddess into a stag and torn to pieces by his own hounds.

acte gratuite. See André GIDE.

Actes and Monuments. See John FOXE.

Actian games. The games celebrated at ACTIUM and in Rome in honor of Apollo. They were founded by Octavius Caesar to celebrate his naval victory over Antony in 31 B.C. and were held every four years.

Action Française, L'. A political group whose organ was the newspaper *L'Action Française,* founded in 1899. An extreme right-wing movement, it advocated monarchist, anti-Semitic, and Roman Catholic principles, serving as a focal point for rightist sympathies. Leon DAUDET and Charles MAURRAS were the chief editors of *L'Action Française;* its last issue was published on August 24, 1944 and spoke out in favor of Marshal Pétain.

Actium. A promontory in northwestern Greece at the mouth of the Ambracian Gulf. In a famous naval battle (31 B.C.) near here, Octavius (see AUGUSTUS) defeated the combined forces of ANTONY and Cleopatra, making himself master of the Roman world. During the battle Cleopatra's ships fled and, when Antony himself followed, his land forces surrendered to Octavius. See ACTIAN GAMES.

Act of Settlement. An act passed during the reign of William III (1701) in England, limiting the crown, after Queen Anne's succession, to members of the House of Hanover, provided they were Protestant. As a result of this act, the reign of the House of Stuart ended and that of Hanover began.

Act of Union. Specifically, the Act of 1706 declaring that on and after May 1, 1707, England and Scotland should have a united parliament. The two countries had been united under one sovereign since 1603. The term is also applied to the Act of 1536 incorporating Wales with England, and to that of 1800, establishing a legislative union of Great Britain and Ireland on and after January 1, 1801.

Acts of the Apostles. A book of the New Testament. It is the earliest contemporary history of the Christian Church in existence, beginning with Jesus' Ascension and ending with St. Paul's imprisonment. The best passages are written in a vivid first-person style by a traveling companion of Paul. It is thought that the author of *Acts* is Luke the physician, author of the Gospel bearing his name. The protagonist is St. Paul, who released Christianity from the conservative restrictions of Judaism and preached it as a new, universal religion.

Adad. The principal Babylonian storm-god. He took over this role after ENLIL, the Sumerian god of air and storms, and MARDUK, the Baal of Babylon, became more generalized in their functions.

Adam. In Shakespeare's As You LIKE IT, a faithful old family retainer who accompanies Orlando into the forest and offers to give him his savings. The well-known phrase "a faithful Adam" is based on this character.

Adam, Juliette. Born **Lamber.** Pen names: **Juliette Lamber; La Messine;** and Comte **Paul Vasili** (1836–1936). French novelist and editor. She founded and edited the periodical *La Nouvelle Revue.*

Adam, Paul [Auguste Marie] (1862–1920). French novelist. Originally associated with the symbolists, he was later concerned with the analysis of group action, as in mobs, in his novel series *Le Temps et la vie* (16 v., 1899–1903).

Adam and Eve. The first man and woman, according to the Old Testament. The initial chapters of Genesis tell the story of their creation, their sin in eating the FORBIDDEN FRUIT from "the tree of knowledge of good and evil" (Gen. 3:9), and their expulsion from Paradise, or the Garden of Eden, to thereafter "till the ground." Milton retells the story of "man's first disobedience" in *Paradise Lost* (1667). See LILITH.

the old Adam; the offending Adam. Adam, as the head of unredeemed man, stands for "original sin," or "man without regenerating grace."

the second Adam; the new Adam. Jesus Christ is so called.

Adam's ale. Water, because the first man had nothing else to drink; in Scotland, it is sometimes called *Adam's wine.*

Adam's apple. The protuberance in the forepart of the throat, the anterior extremity of the thyroid cartilage of the larynx; so called from the superstition that a piece of the forbidden fruit stuck in Adam's throat.

Adam's Peak. A mountain in Ceylon where, according to Muslim legend, Adam bewailed his expulsion from Paradise, standing on one foot for 200 years to expiate his crime; Gabriel then took him to Mount Arafat, where he found Eve.

Adamastor. The spirit of the stormy Cape (Good Hope). It is described by Camõens in the *Lusiad* as a hideous phantom that appears to Vasco da Gama

and prophesies disaster to all seeking to make the voyage to India.

Adam Bede (1859). A novel by George ELIOT. The highly principled Adam Bede loves Hetty Sorrel, a pretty, superficial girl. Although Adam tries to save her, she fancies herself the wife of the young squire, Arthur Donnithorne, who seduces her and then leaves her. In her grief she consents to marry Adam, but before they are wed she discovers that she is pregnant. She tries in vain to find Arthur, but in the end is found guilty of the murder of her child and is transported for life. Adam finally marries Dinah Morris, a young Methodist preacher.

Adam de la Hale (or Halle) (c. 1230–c. 1286). French poet and composer, author of the first known opera or play with music, *Li Gieus de Robin et Marion (The Play of Robin and Marion),* performed before the French court at Naples in 1275 or 1285.

Adamic, Louis (1899–1951). Yugoslav-born American writer. Adamic came to this country when he was 15. His own life as an immigrant is described in *Laughing in the Jungle* (1932). *The Native's Return* (1934) gives his impressions of revisiting Yugoslavia, and *Grandsons* (1935) is the saga of a Slovenian family in America. Always concerned with America as a melting pot, Adamic felt increasingly that the process was too slow; *My America* (1938) reflects this belief.

Adamites. The name for various heretical sects. Their belief was that they might attain to primitive innocence by rejecting marriage and clothing. There was such a sect in North Africa in the 2nd century; the *Abelites* were similar. The heresy reappeared in Savoy in the 14th century, and spread over Bohemia and Moravia in the 15th and 16th centuries. One Picard, of Bohemia, was leader in 1400, and styled himself "Adam, son of God." The paintings of Hieronymus Bosch are thought to have been influenced by his adherence to an Adamite sect.

Adamov, Arthur (1908–   ). Russian-born French dramatist. His *Ping-Pong* (1955) and *Paolo Paoli* (1957) are bitterly disillusioned satires of modern commercial society. Other plays include *L'Invasion* (1949), *Taranne* (1951), and *Les Âmes mortes* (1959).

Adams, Abigail [Smith] (1744–1818). Wife of John ADAMS, noted as a letter writer. The daughter of a Congregational minister, she married Adams in 1764. Her lively, perceptive letters, first published in 1840 in a selected form by her grandson Charles Francis Adams, mirror the affection and respect that existed between the Adamses and give a valuable picture of social and political life in the infant republic; they are included in their entirety in *Family Papers* (2 vols., 1963), the second series of *The Adams Papers* published by Harvard University.

Adams, Charles Francis, Jr. (1835–1915). American lawyer, railroad expert, and historian. This son of John Quincy and brother of Henry Adams was a successful businessman who in time became disgusted with the "low instinct" of money-getting, and turned to writing history. He was chiefly interested in the history of Massachusetts, and wrote *Three Episodes of Massachusetts History* (1892), and *Massachusetts: Its History and Historians* (1893). Earlier he had exposed corruption in railroads in *Chapters of Erie and Other Essays* (1871) and

Railroads: Their Origins and Problems (1878). He published lives of Richard Henry Dana (1891) and of his father (1900), as well as an *Autobiography* (1916).

Adams, Franklin P[ierce] (1881–1960). American columnist best known as **F.P.A.** He wrote a column, "The Conning Tower," which appeared in several New York newspapers from 1913 to 1941.

Adams, Hannah (1755–1831). American historian. The first professional woman writer in the United States, she wrote *Alphabetical Compendium of the Various Sects . . . from the Beginning of the Christian Era* (1784) and *A Summary History of New England* (1799).

Adams, Henry [Brooks] (1838–1918). American historian, scholar, and man of letters. A member of the famous Adams family of statesmen, Henry Adams was temperamentally fitted, not for political action, but for the equally arduous task of studying and writing history. Working for a time as a journalist, he became editor of the *North American Review;* at the same time, he held an assistant professor-

A page from Hannah Adams'
Alphabetical Compendium. . . .

NEW YORK PUBLIC LIBRARY

ENC   59

ánd made ufe of a book which they ftiled, *The gofpel according to the Hebrews.*

*Mofheim's Ecclef Hift vol. 1. p. 173. 174.
Hearnes Ductor Hiftoricus, vol. 2, p. 74.*

EICETÆ, A fect in the year 680, who affirmed, that in order to make prayer acceptable to God, it fhould be performed dancing.

Dufrefnoy's Chronological Tables. vol 1. p. 213.

EFFRONTES, So called from their fhaving their foreheads till they bleed, and then anointing them with oil, ufing no other baptifm but this.

They fay, the Holy Ghoft is nothing but a bare motion infpired by God in the mind ; and he is not to be adored.

Ro's View of all Religions, p. 233.

ELCESAITES, A fect, in the fecond century ; fo denominated from their prophet Elcefai, His fundamental doctrine was, that Jefus Chrift, who was born from the beginning of the world, had appeared from time to time under divers bodies.

Hiftory of Religion, vol. 4. [See Elcefaites]

ENCRATITES, or CONTINENTS, A name given to a fect in the fecond century, becaufe they condemned marriage, forbid the eating of flefh, or drinking of wine, and rejected, with a fort of horror, all the comforts and conveniencies of life. Tatian, an Affyrian, was the leader of this denomination. He regarded Matter as the fountain of all evil ; and therefore recommended, in a peculiar manner, the mortification of the body. He diftinguifhed the creator of the world from the Supreme
I   Being ;

ship of history at Harvard, where he taught medieval, European, and American history. Adams' first important book was the nine-volume study, *The History of the United States of America During the Administrations of Thomas Jefferson and James Madison* (1889–1891). Men, Adams deterministically argued, cannot change the course of history.

In 1872, Adams married Marian Hooper; after her suicide in 1885, he traveled to the Orient, and renewed an interest in science. His most important books, MONT-SAINT-MICHEL AND CHARTRES and THE EDUCATION OF HENRY ADAMS, reflect his lifelong quest for order and unity in a world he considered to be in the process of disintegration.

Adams' two novels, DEMOCRACY and ESTHER, reflect two of his absorbing concerns: corruption in a capitalistic government, and loss of religious faith caused by new scientific discoveries. Adams' letters, edited and published during the last 15 years, often reveal him at his best.

Adams, James Truslow (1878–1949). American historian. He won a Pulitzer Prize for *The Founding of New England* (1921), but is perhaps best known as the author of *The Epic of America* (1931), which has been translated into nine languages. Among his other works are *Revolutionary New England* (1923), *The March of Democracy* (2 vols., 1932–1933), *Building the British Empire* (1938), and *The American* (1943), an analysis of the American character. Adams was also the editor of the *Dictionary of American History* (6 vols., 1940).

Adams, John (1735–1826). Second president of the U.S. (1797–1801). A graduate of Harvard, Adams was admitted to the bar in 1758 and was carrying on a successful law practice when the Stamp Act crisis of 1765 drew him into politics. In a series of articles, later collected as *A Dissertation on the Canon and Feudal Law* (1768), he argued that the Stamp Act was contrary to the "inherent rights of mankind." He was a delegate to the first and second Continental Congresses and was an ardent advocate of the Declaration of Independence when it was presented to the congress.

In 1785, after several years' service as minister to France, Britain, and Holland, he began to write his *Defense of the Constitutions of Government of the United States of America* (1787–1788), in which he discussed the history of republican government. Elected vice president under Washington, he became president in 1797. He quarreled with Hamilton over a treaty with France in 1800, and the resulting split in the Federalist Party contributed to his loss to JEFFERSON in 1800. After his retirement from the presidency, he returned to his home in Quincy, Mass., and renewed his old friendship with Jefferson. Both men died within a few hours of each other on July 4, 1826.

Adams' essentially conservative political philosophy placed him between the extreme federalism of Hamilton and the agrarianism of Jefferson. His concept of republicanism was based on a "balance" of power that would prevent the power-hungry from gaining control, and his awareness of the weaknesses and vices of mankind led him to put his faith in the "natural aristocracy" of a few men, who, like himself, would use the power vested in them for the good of the people rather than for their private ends. The *Diary and Autobiography of John Adams* (4 vols., 1961) and *Family Papers* (2 vols., 1963) have been published as the opening sections of *The Adams Papers* by Harvard University Press. See Abigail ADAMS.

Adams, John Quincy (1767-1848). Sixth president of the U.S. (1825-1829). Adams accompanied his father, John Adams, to France in 1778, studied in European schools, and was graduated from Harvard in 1787. In 1791 in a series of 11 articles signed Publicola, he replied to Thomas Paine's *Rights of Man,* defending the rights of the minority in opposition to Paine's contention that the majority must prevail. After holding several diplomatic posts, Adams became secretary of state in 1817; he secured Florida from Spain in 1819 and was largely responsible for the promulgation of the MONROE DOCTRINE in 1823. In 1824 Adams, Andrew Jackson, and Henry Clay were among the four candidates for the presidency. Since no candidate received a majority of the electoral votes, the election was given to the House of Representatives. Clay threw his support to Adams, who was elected, and when Adams named Clay secretary of state, Jackson's followers cried "corrupt bargain." This charge, though undoubtedly baseless, hounded Adams during his term of office and contributed to his defeat in 1828. In 1830 he was elected to the House of Representatives, where he served for nearly 17 years, opposing the annexation of Texas and defending free speech in the face of efforts to stifle debate on the slavery question. Adams' diary, covering more than 60 years, was edited by his son, Charles Francis Adams, and published in 12 volumes as *The Memoirs of John Quincy Adams* (1874-1877).

Adams, Léonie [Fuller] (1899-). American poet. Her poems are marked by a deeply mystical view of nature, by vigorous metrics, and by a sense of song that lends delicacy to the packed meaning of her lines. Her books include *Those Not Elect* (1925), *High Falcon* (1929), *This Measure* (1933), and *Poems: A Selection* (1954).

Adams, Nick. The central character in most of the stories of IN OUR TIME, a collection by Ernest Hemingway. He appears also in the famous short story THE KILLERS.

Adams, Parson Abraham. The quixotic, vain, staunch friend of the hero of JOSEPH ANDREWS (1742), a novel by Henry Fielding. He is a guileless clergyman, totally ignorant of the ways of the world, always seeking the good of others. The element of paradoxical discussion that he introduces into the novel gives the book its truly comic character. He was drawn from Fielding's friend, the Rev. William Young, who edited Robert Ainsworth's *Latin-English Dictionary* (1752).

Adams, Samuel (1722-1803). American patriot and pamphleteer. Active in arousing public opinion against England before the American Revolution, he was responsible for the creation of a committee of correspondence to communicate Boston's grievances to other towns in Massachusetts and "to the World," and prepared for the committee a radical declaration, *State of the Rights of the Colonies* (1772). He was the leading spirit behind the Boston Tea Party and served in the Continental Congress (1774-1781), where he advocated immediate independence.

Adams, Samuel Hopkins (1871-1958). American writer. An effective member of the staffs of *McClure's* and *Collier's* magazines during the muck-raking days, Adams was active in exposing frauds, especially in the field of medicine, and was instrumental in bringing about the Pure Food and Drug Act (1906) He later wrote a long series of books dealing with the American background in fictional terms. He attacked dishonest journalism in his novel *The Clarion* (1914) and the scandals of the Harding administration in *Revelry* (1926). The latter book was supplemented by *The Incredible Era: The Life and Times of Warren Harding* (1939). He also wrote biographies of Daniel Webster and Alexander Woollcott.

Adams, William T. Pen name **Oliver Optic** (1822-1897). The author of various series of books for boys. He edited the journal *Our Boys and Girls,* founded in 1867 as a weekly, subsequently a monthly.

Addams, Jane (1860-1935). American leader in social work and the peace and women's suffrage movements. She is famous for her pioneering work at Hull House, a Chicago settlement house that she founded in 1889. In 1931 she, together with Nicholas Murray Butler, was awarded the Nobel Peace Prize. She wrote a number of books and articles on social problems, among them two autobiographical works: *Twenty Years at Hull House* (1910) and *The Second Twenty Years at Hull House* (1931).

Adding Machine, The (1923). A play by Elmer RICE. The dramatist uses expressionistic techniques to satirize the morality of the machine age. Mr. Zero loses his position when his employer installs adding machines. In a fit of temporary insanity, he murders the employer and is executed. Along with a co-worker, Daisy Diana Dorothea Devore, who has committed suicide to be with him, he finds himself in the Elysian Fields. Happily operating the celestial adding machine, Mr. Zero scorns the company of such men as Swift and Rabelais. He is finally reincarnated and returns to earth to continue evolving into the perfect soulless slave.

Addison, Joseph (1672-1719). English poet, essayist, and critic. In association with Richard STEELE, he perfected the essay as a literary form in his contributions to THE TATLER and THE SPECTATOR. His prose style was the model for pure and elegant English until the end of the 18th century; his comments on manners and morals were widely influential in forming the middle-class ideal of a dispassionate, tolerant, Christian world-citizen. *The Campaign* (1704), celebrating the victory at Blenheim, and his hymn *The Spacious Firmament on High* (1712) are his most famous poems. His musical play *Rosamond* (1705) was an attack on popular Italian operas, and his blank-verse tragedy *Cato* (1713) was enormously popular, combining an appeal to the party-spirit of the Whigs, and an avowed intention to purge the stage of immorality. Addison is bitterly attacked by Alexander Pope in EPISTLE TO DR. ARBUTHNOT (1735) in the character of Atticus. See Thomas TICKELL.

Address to the Deil (1786). A poem by Robert BURNS attacking the corrupt clergy of Scotland.

Ade, George (1866-1944). American humorist and playwright. Ade first achieved popularity in the columns of the Chicago *Record* with the creation of the brash but good-hearted Artie. Stories of a colored bootblack and a gentlemanly liar were added, the three becoming the titular heroes of *Artie* (1896), *Pink Marsh* (1897), and *Doc' Horne* (1899). In

1898 he began to write the stories that were collected as FABLES IN SLANG. He commenced his career as a playwright with a successful musical comedy, *The Sultan of Sulu* (1902), later writing *The County Chairman* (1903), a play directed against political corruption; THE COLLEGE WIDOW; and *Father and the Boys* (1908).

Adenauer, Konrad (1876–1967). First chancellor of the German Federal Republic (1949–1963), who led his country in its economic and political recovery after World War II. He was mayor of Cologne (1917–1933) but lost this position because of conflict with the Nazis. In 1945 he helped to found the Christian Democratic Union, his political party. He retired from public life in 1963.

Adler, Alfred (1870–1937). Austrian psychoanalyst. A disciple of Sigmund FREUD, he later rebelled against his master's teachings and held to a system of "individual psychology." In this he maintained that psychological differences among individuals—in behavior, attitude, and the like—were due to the differences in their means of attaining a feeling of superiority in their relations with society.

Adler, Felix (1851–1933). German-born American philosopher, teacher, and founder of the Ethical Culture movement. Adler came to America at the age of 16; he founded the New York Society of Ethical Culture while teaching at Cornell University in 1876. The society emphasized the need for a stronger morality, and advocated the moral education of children as well as various kinds of labor and social reforms. Adler established the first free kindergarten for the children of the poor in New York City; this later grew into a vocational school, the first to include manual training and ethical instruction in its curriculum. In 1884 Adler helped to establish the Tenement House Commission; he arranged for trained nurses to visit the poor, argued for parks and playgrounds in poor areas of the city, and opposed child labor. Ethical Culture societies have since sprung up in several cities of the United States and Europe. Among Adler's books are *The Moral Instruction of Children* (1892), *Marriage and Divorce* (1905), *What the Ethical Culture School Stands For* (1910), and *The Reconstruction of the Spiritual Ideal* (1923).

Admetus (Admetos). See ALCESTIS; ARGONAUTS.

Admirable Crichton, The (1902). A dramatic fantasy by J. M. BARRIE. The Earl of Loam, his family, and one or two friends are wrecked on a desert island, where the butler, the admirable Crichton, proves himself to be a man of infinite resource and power, far superior to the rest of the party. Barrie took the title from an epithet bestowed upon James Crichton (1560–1585?), Scottish traveler, scholar, and swordsman, by Sir Thomas Urquhart.

Admiral Hosier's Ghost (1739). A ballad by Richard GLOVER, based on the capture of Porto Bello by Admiral Edward Vernon in 1739. Admiral Francis Hosier (1673–1727) is sent with 20 ships to the Spanish West Indies to block up the galleons of that country. He arrives at the Bastimentos, near Porto Bello, but has strict orders not to attack and his men perish, not in battle, but from disease. Hosier dies of a broken heart. Upon Admiral Vernon's victory, Hosier and his 3,000 men rise from the dead and lament the cruel orders that forbade them to attack the foe, for "with 20 ships he surely could have achieved what Vernon did with only 6."

Adolphe (1815). A novel by Benjamin CONSTANT DE REBECQUE. Adolphe, the novel's young protagonist, has been influenced by his early relationship with a woman of strong intellectual convictions, and is unable to adopt the conventional masks of society. Having finished his studies, he sets out upon a period of travel in Germany and Poland. While visiting at a small German court, he establishes a liaison with Ellénore, mistress of Count P—. Adolphe, who began the affair out of pride rather than love, is deeply probed by the author who points out his inability to terminate the relationship as a result of his guilt, which leaves him desolate when Ellénore dies. The work, considered to be based in part on Constant's relationship with Mme. de STAEL, is a precursor of the modern psychological novel.

Adonai. See JEHOVAH.

Adonais (1821). A poem by Percy Bysshe SHELLEY. When Keats died in 1821, Shelley was moved to compose this elegy for his friend. He gave Keats the name of Adonais, probably in allusion to the mourning for Adonis. *Adonais* is considered one of the greatest elegies in the English language.

Adonis. In Greek mythology, a beautiful youth. Adonis was born of Myrrha (Smyrna) after she had been turned into a tree to escape her father, for whom she had an incestuous love. APHRODITE fell in love with Adonis when he was still a youth, but he was killed by a boar, which, according to some accounts, was Aphrodite's jealous lover Ares in disguise. From his blood sprang the anemone. According to another story, Aphrodite gave the infant Adonis in a chest to Persephone to take care of, but Persephone fell in love with him and would not return him. Zeus judged the case and ordered that Adonis should spend one third of the year with each goddess, the third where he chose. He chose to spend the extra third as well with Aphrodite.

This myth, the scene of which is laid in Asia, is one of the many in which a young god of vegetation dies and is resurrected. A part of the cult included the planting of "gardens of Adonis"—seeds in shallow soil which withered as quickly as they sprouted. The name of the god is derived from *adon* (lord), which appears in the Hebrew *adonai*, used as a substitute for the name of Yahweh (Jehovah). See TAMMUZ; VENUS AND ADONIS; ADONAIS.

Adramelech. One of the fallen angels. Milton has him overthrown by Uriel and Raphael in PARADISE LOST.

Adrasto (Adrastus). In the GERUSALEMME LIBERATA of Tasso, the commander of the Indian forces allied with other enemies of the crusaders. During the assault upon Jerusalem he is killed by Rinaldo at the final battle, which results in the fall of the city.

Adrastus (Adrastos). In Greek mythology, a king of Argos and leader of the expedition of the SEVEN AGAINST THEBES. He was the only member of the expedition to return alive.

Adrian or **Hadrian IV** (originally **Nicholas Breakspear**) (d. 1159). The only Englishman to be elected Pope (1154–1159). He crowned Emperor Frederick Barbarossa (1155), but soon entered a great conflict with him over the assertion of papal prerogatives. There is much historical controversy over his reputed gift of the feudal sovereignty of Ireland to Henry II of England.

Adriana. A character in Shakespeare's COMEDY OF ERRORS. She is the high-spirited and impatient wife of Antipholus of Ephesus and sister of Luciana.

Adullam. The cave in which David took refuge when he fled from King Saul. This stronghold attracted "every one that was in debt, and every one that was discontented" (I Sam. 22:1–2).

Advancement of Learning, The (1605). A treatise on philosophy by Francis BACON. Considered an excellent example of Renaissance thought, it extols the pursuit of learning and critically surveys the existing state of knowledge. Bacon later wrote a greatly expanded version, *De Dignitate et Augmentis Scientiarum* (1623), to form the first part of his projected INSTAURATIO MAGNA.

Advent (Lat. *adventus,* the coming to). The four weeks immediately preceding Christmas. It commemorates the first coming of Christ, and anticipates the second: the one to redeem, the other to judge the world. The season begins the Sunday on or nearest St. Andrew's Day (Nov. 30th). There is an old tradition of preaching on the "Four Last Things" on the Advent Sundays: Death, Judgment, Heaven, and Hell.

Adventists. Christian religious sects believing that the second coming of Christ and the end of the world are near at hand.

Adventures. For many titles beginning with the words *The Adventures of . . . ,* see the following proper names. For example, *The Adventures of Tom Sawyer* will be found under *Tom Sawyer, The Adventures of.*

Adventures of Philip, The (1862). A novel by William Makepeace THACKERAY. The hero, Philip Firmin, revolts against the hypocrisy of his father, Dr. George Brandon Firmin, whose sham marriage to Caroline Gann forms the subject of an earlier novel. As a boy he is befriended by Caroline, now known as Mrs. Brandon, or "the little Sister," and throughout the book he champions her cause. He is brought up in luxury, but, owing to his father's scheming, loses his money and is forced to earn a living as an editor. He marries Charlotte Baynes, the daughter of his guardian, whom his father had tricked to secure his fortune. After numerous difficulties, Philip comes into a fortune from Lord Ringwood, a wealthy relative. The novel is a sequel to *A Shabby Genteel Story* (1840), which is usually printed as its prologue.

Advice to the Privileged Orders (1792). A prose tract by Joel BARLOW. Barlow argues that the state exists not to protect property but to assure the political rights of the individual. The piece aroused a great deal of discussion and unfavorable criticism in England and was the subject of debate in the House of Commons. The Pitt ministry ordered it burned and Barlow jailed.

Æ or A.E. Pen name of **George William Russell** (1867–1935). Irish poet, painter, mystic, patriot of Irish Nationalism, and one of the organizers of the Irish Agricultural Co-operative movement. In 1886 he was associated, as was William Butler Yeats, with the founding of the Dublin Lodge of the Theosophical Society, for occult and Hermetic study.

His mystical poetry is based on visions, magic, and Eastern religious ideas; he writes about these interests in *The Candle of Vision* (1918). Among his collections of poetry are *Homeward: Songs by the Way* (1894), *The Earth Breath* (1897), and *House of the Titans* (1934). He also wrote *Deirdre* (1902), one of the first verse plays performed at the ABBEY THEATRE, and *The Living Torch* (1937), a collection of essays.

Aeacus (Aiakos). Greek mythological character. A son of Zeus and Aegina, king of Pythia, noted for his piety. He was the father of Telamon and Peleus by Endeis and of Phocus by Psamathe. The elder sons killed Phocus from jealousy and were banished. When all Greece was ravaged by drought because of PELOPS' murder of Stymphalus, Aeacus' prayers brought rain. At his death he became either a warder or a judge in Hades.

aedile. In ancient Rome, one of 4 magistrates whose duty it was to maintain order in the city and to take charge of public games and buildings. An aedile corresponds roughly to a modern commissioner of public works. His supervision of public games gave him great opportunities for gaining favor with the populace. Although a small sum was appropriated from the public treasury for these games, an aedile generally expended much more from his own purse to make the show magnificent and thus win votes for the next office in the CURSUS HONORUM, that of praetor.

Aeëtes (Aietes). See MEDEA.

Aegeon. In Shakespeare's COMEDY OF ERRORS, a merchant of Syracuse, the father of the two Antipholi and the husband of Aemilia. He is detained in Ephesus, pending ransom, because of the law barring Syracusans from the city.

Aegeon. See BRIAREUS.

Aegeus (Aigeus). A legendary king of Athens, father of THESEUS. Aegeus threw himself into the sea, thinking mistakenly that Theseus' expedition to Crete had failed. The Aegean Sea, according to tradition, was so named as a result of this event.

Aegipan (Aigipan). The god PAN. His horns, ears, and legs were goatlike. The name literally means goat Pan.

Aegis (Aigis). The shield or cuirass of Zeus. Made by HEPHAESTOS, it was the symbol of divine protection. An aegis was also worn by Athene. The word indicates that it was originally merely a goatskin.

Aegisthus (Aigisthos). See House of ATREUS.

Aegyptus (Aigyptos). In classic myth the father of 50 sons. They were married to the 50 daughters of his twin brother Danaus and all except one of them were murdered by their brides on the wedding night. See DANAIDES.

Aelfric, called **Grammaticus,** or **"the Grammarian"** (c. 955–c. 1020). English clergyman and scholar, a prolific writer in both Latin and Old English. He wrote a series of 120 homilies and saints' lives (990–998), then a treatise on the Old and New Testaments and a *Heptateuch,* a vernacular translation of portions of the first seven books of the Bible. His prose is alliterative and rhythmical, the finest in Old English. Concerned with the revival of learning, he wrote a Latin grammar and Latin-English glossary.

Aemilia. The virtuous mother of the twins, Antipholus of Ephesus and Antipholus of Syracuse, and the wife of Aegeon in Shakespeare's COMEDY OF ERRORS. When her family is lost to her in a storm, she becomes an abbess.

Aeneas. The hero of Vergil's AENEID. He was the son of the mortal ANCHISES and the goddess Aphrodite. According to Homer, he fought against the Greeks in the Trojan War and after the sack of Troy reigned in the Troad. Vergil, however, used another legend, according to which Aeneas carried his father Anchises on his shoulders out of the burning city and with a band of followers set out to establish a new nation; after wandering for many years, he is said to have arrived in Italy, where he founded the colony from which the Romans traced their origin. The epithet often applied to him is *pious*, i.e., devoted to the service of the gods and deeply aware of his obligations to his family and his country. See ASCANIUS.

Aeneas Silvius. See PIUS II.

Aeneid. An epic poem by VERGIL, composed of 12 books, in which the legendary Trojan origin of the Roman people is glorified. Vergil traces the lineage of the Julii from Iulus or ASCANIUS, the son of the Trojan hero AENEAS, down to Octavius Caesar (later Augustus), whose newly established principate the poem endorses. The poem was written at the request of the emperor and, though it was left unfinished at the sudden death of the poet (19 B.C.), it was greeted with enthusiasm by all educated Romans because of its nationalistic purpose.

In Book I, Aeneas and his Trojan followers are driven by a storm to the shores of Carthage and are hospitably entertained by Queen DIDO. In Book II, Aeneas tells the tale of the wooden horse and of the destruction of Troy. He describes his escape from the burning city with his father ANCHISES, his son Ascanius, and several followers. His wife was lost and died during their flight. The narrative is continued in Book III, in which Aeneas recounts the perils he encountered on the westward voyage from Troy and the death of his father. Book IV tells of Dido's love for Aeneas, his departure from Carthage, and her suicide and cremation on a great funeral pyre. In Book V, Aeneas and his followers reach Sicily and hold funeral games in honor of Anchises. (See ACESTES.) Aeneas visits Anchises in the underworld in Book VI, sees the future generations of Romans, and is told of their exploits. Here appear the much quoted lines of Anchises to Aeneas concerning the task of the Romans: "Roman, remember that you shall rule the nations by your authority, for this is to be your skill, to make peace the custom, to spare the conquered, and to wage war until the haughty are brought low."

In Book VII, LATINUS, king of the Latini, entertains Aeneas and promises his daughter LAVINIA to him in marriage; but Prince TURNUS, who has already been betrothed to her by her mother, raises an army to resist Aeneas. Book VIII tells of the preparations for war on both sides and of Aeneas' visit to Latium, the future home of the Romans. In Book IX, Turnus, in the absence of Aeneas, fires the Trojan ships and assaults their camp. The episode of NISUS AND EURYALUS occurs here. The war between Turnus and Aeneas is depicted in Book X. Here MEZENTIUS

and his son Lausas are slain by Aeneas. In Book XI, the battle continues. Book XII tells of the single combat between Aeneas and Turnus, and of the death of Turnus. See ACHATES; GYAS AND CLOANTHUS; HELENUS; PALINURUS.

Aeolus (Aiolos). In Greek mythology, the god of the winds, which he kept imprisoned in the Aeolian islands. He freed them at his own choice or the wish of other gods. In the *Odyssey*, Book X, he aided Odysseus in his homeward voyage by fastening the unfavorable winds in a leather bag and giving it into Odysseus' keeping, with a warning not to open it. While Odysseus slept, however, his seamen, thinking that he was secreting treasure from them, opened the bag and the ship was blown back to its starting point. Angrily Aeolus refused to cooperate further.

Aeolus (Aiolos). The grandson of Deucalion, the Greek Noah, and eponymous ancestor of the Aeolian Greeks.

Aerodrome, The (1941). A Kafkaesque social and political allegory by Rex WARNER. Its main character tries to impose his totalitarian system on a disorganized, easy-going village. The villagers successfully resist him.

Aeschylus (Aischylos) (525–456 B.C.). A Greek tragic dramatist. Aeschylus was born of an aristocratic family in Eleusis. In his youth, he fought against the Persians in the great battles of Marathon, Salamis, and Plataea. He seems to have been prouder of these feats than of his immense success as a playwright, which he did not even mention in the epitaph that, according to tradition, he wrote for himself. After 16 years of writing, he won his first prize for tragedy in 484 B.C.; he won his last with his masterpiece, the ORESTEIA, 25 years later. In 476 B.C. he had paid a successful visit to the court of Hiero I, Tyrant of Syracuse; three years before his death, he again went to Sicily, this time to Gela. According to a popular story, he was killed when an eagle dropped a tortoise on his bald head, mistaking it for a stone. The story is improved with the mention of an oracular prophecy that he would die of a blow from heaven.

Aeschylus wrote 90 plays, but only seven of them have survived: THE SUPPLIANT WOMEN, THE PERSIANS, the SEVEN AGAINST THEBES, PROMETHEUS BOUND, and the *Oresteia*, a trilogy. This last is the only extant example of the trilogies on related themes that were common in Aeschylus' day; it includes *Agamemnon*, The *Libation Bearers*, and the *Eumenides*. Aeschylus is noted for the grandeur of his language and of his subjects, which encompass not only the struggles between historical heroes (*The Persians*) and mythical (*Agamemnon*), but the grim conflict between the old laws and the new (*Eumenides*), and, in a sense, between man and gods (*Prometheus Bound*). Aeschylus' poetry is tense, closely packed, exciting, often somewhat rough, compared with the polished lines of Sophocles. His imagery is strong, startling, and sometimes forced, but always effective. The antithesis of Euripides' relatively colloquial speech, Aeschylus' dialogue is far from natural, but is well suited to the tragic immensity of his themes.

Aeschylus was a practical and imaginative man of the theater, as well as an inspired poet. He was the first to use a second actor in addition to the chorus;

this permitted for the first time dialogue between individuals. He also introduced elaborate costumes and the high-soled *cothurnoi* that gave his actors added stature. He seems to have enjoyed colorful effects; *The Persians* is filled with pageantry, and old Oceanus appears in *Prometheus Bound* riding on a sort of four-legged bird, perhaps the original of modern vaudeville's two-man horse. Tradition says that some of his costumes were so splendid that the hierophants at Eleusis copied them for their own vestments. The story is also told that his presentation in *Eumenides* of the chorus of Erinyes, hideous creatures with black skins and red tongues, so terrified the audience that women had miscarriages and children convulsions.

Aesculapius. See ASCLEPIUS; FAERIE QUEENE, THE.

Aesir. The collective name of the Norse gods who lived in heavenly ASGARD. There were said to be 12 gods and some 24 to 30 goddesses, but the number seems variable. The following may be mentioned: (1) Odin, the chief of the gods; (2) Thor, Odin's eldest son and god of thunder; (3) Tiu, another son, the god of wisdom; (4) Balder, the Scandinavian Apollo; (5) Bragi, god of poetry; (6) Vidar, god of silence; (7) Hoder the blind, slayer of Balder; (8) Hermoder, Odin's son and messenger; (9) Hoenir, a minor god; (10) Odnir, husband of Freya, the Scandinavian Venus; (11) Loki, the god of mischief; (12) Vali, Odin's youngest son.

Wives of the Aesir. Odin's wife was Frigga; Thor's wife was Sif; Balder's wife was Nanna; Bragi's wife was Iduna; Loki's wife was Siguna.

The important deities mentioned above are more fully treated under their names. See ASYNJA; VANIR.

Aesop. Greek fabulist. According to tradition, the author of *Aesop's Fables* was a Phrygian slave who probably lived from 620 to 560 B.C. It is inferable from Aristotle's mention of Aesop's acting as a public defender that he was freed from slavery, and Plutarch's statement that the Athenians erected a noble statue of him would tend to contradict the tradition that Aesop was deformed. There is little information on Aesop's life, and several scholars have consequently been led to doubt that he ever existed at all. The earliest extant collections of Aesop's stories were made by various Greek versifiers and Latin translators, to whose compilations were added tales from Oriental and ancient sources to form what we now know as *Aesop's Fables*. The majority of European fables, including those of LA FONTAINE, are largely derived from these succinct tales, in which talking animals illustrate human vices, follies, and virtues. Since some of Aesop's fables have been discovered on Egyptian papyri dating from 800 or 1,000 years before his time, it cannot be claimed that he was, by any means, the author of all the fables.

aesthetics. The branch of philosophy dealing with art and beauty. The term was first used by the German philosopher Alexander Baumgarten (1714–1762), though occidental preoccupation with problems of aesthetics goes back to the Greeks of the 4th century B.C.

Aetna. See ETNA.

Affair, The (1959). A novel by C. P. SNOW. It is a melodrama about an unpopular college teacher

with Communist sympathies. He is unjustly accused of forgery, but eventually justice prevails. The novel is part of the STRANGERS AND BROTHERS series.

Affliction (1633). A poem by George HERBERT. The author rebels against the way God has "deceived" him into abandoning his worldly hopes for His service, afflicted him with illness, loss of friends, a sense of uselessness. The poem concludes with the famous lines:

> Ah, my dear God! though I am clean forgot,
> Let me not love thee if I love thee not.

aficionado. See DILETTANTE.

Afinogenov, Alexander Nikolaevich (1904–1941). Russian dramatist. His plays describe the early struggles and problems of the Soviet regime. They include *At the Breaking Point* (1926), *The Crank* (1929), *Fear* (1931), *Distant Point* (1934), *Spain, Salute!* (1936), *The Mother of Us All* (1940), *Mashenka* (1941) and *On the Eve* (1941).

Afreet or **Afrit.** In Muslim mythology the second most powerful of the five classes of JINN or devils. They are of gigantic stature, very malicious, and inspire dread. Legend holds that King Solomon once tamed an Afreet, and made it submissive to his will.

African Farm, The Story of an (1883). A semi-autobiographical novel by Olive SCHREINER. She gives a vivid account of life on a Boer farm like her childhood home and describes the religious doubts and intellectual and emotional development of an ardent young feminist like herself.

African Queen, The (1935). A novel by C. S. FORESTER. It is the comic-heroic story of a missionary's sister and a timid Cockney engineer who try to blow up a German gunboat from their asthmatic steam launch, *The African Queen*.

After Many a Summer Dies the Swan (1939). A novel by Aldous HUXLEY. Centered around Jo Stoyte, a Californian oil magnate afraid of old age and death, it is a satire of some aspects of American life. Jeremy Pordage, working on some old English manuscripts, discovers that an 18th-century earl used the same rejuvenating system Stoyte is experimenting with. They go to England and find the earl, over 200 years old, a filthy ape. Old Mr. Propter is spokesman for Huxley's spiritual philosophy.

Afternoon of a Faun, The. See L'APRÈS-MIDI D'UN FAUNE.

Agadir Crisis (1911). An international incident precipitated by the arrival of a German gunboat at Agadir in French-controlled Morocco. German demands for African territory were repulsed.

Against the Grain, or **Against Nature (A Rebours;** 1884). A novel by Joris Karl HUYSMANS. Its subject is the quest of its DÉCADENT hero, Des Esseintes, for the rare and perverse in sensation. Restless and discontent, Des Esseintes seeks release from the ennui of existence in perfumes, music, painting, the love of circus acrobats, or the study of medieval Latin literature.

Agamedes. See TROPHONIUS.

Agamemnon. In Greek legend the king of Mycenae, son of ATREUS and leader of the Greeks at the siege of Troy. Homer makes him ruler over all Argos. He was the brother of Menelaus, the theft of whose wife Helen by Paris brought on the Trojan War. Before the expedition against Troy could sail, Agamemnon's daughter IPHIGENIA was sacrificed to Diana to appease that goddess for a sacred stag Agamemnon had killed. At Troy, Agamemnon's quarrel with Achilles cost the Greeks many lives and delayed the end of the war. (See ILIAD.) After the sack of Troy, Agamemnon returned home only to be murdered by his wife Clytemnestra, who was living as the paramour of Aegisthus.

Aganippe. Fountain of the MUSES, at the foot of Mount Helicon in Boeotia. Its waters were thought to inspire those who drank them.

agape. See LOVE FEAST; FAERIE QUEENE, THE.

Agapemone. A 19th-century English society. This communistic establishment of men and women was suspected of free-love practices.

Agassiz, Jean Louis Rodolphe (1807–1873). Swiss naturalist, teacher, and author. Agassiz came to the U.S. in 1846 as a lecturer with an established reputation; deciding to remain permanently, he became widely known as a professor at Harvard and curator of the Agassiz Museum at Cambridge. He was the founder of the Marine Biological Laboratory at Woods Hole, Mass. A fluent writer on geology and zoology, Agassiz showed an astonishing command of English. His major work is called *Contributions to the Natural History of the United States of America* (4 v., 1857–1862). An effective teacher of laymen and scientists, he epitomized his method in the directive: "Go to Nature; take the facts in your own hands; look, and see for yourself!" Opposed to the Darwinian theory of evolution, Agassiz did succeed in arousing interest in the natural sciences and establishing methods of study and classification. A member of the famous Saturday Club, he exchanged ideas with leading men of letters.

Agastya. In Hindu mythology, the legendary sage and pioneer in the epic age of the Aryanization of south India. Supposed to have been born in a jar, he is also known as Kumbhayoni, or "jarborn." Legend says that to his pupil Rama he presented the invincible bow and inexhaustible quiver of Vishnu. Another legend describes him as drinking the sea dry. As he was walking one day with Vishnu, the insolent ocean asked the god who the pigmy (the "jar-born" dwarf) was that strutted by his side. When Vishnu replied that it was the patriarch Agastya, who would restore earth to its true balance, the ocean contemptuously spat its spray in Agastya's face. Agastya, in revenge, drank it dry.

Agate, James Evershed (1877–1947). English dramatic critic. He wrote for the *Manchester Guardian*, the *Saturday Review*, and the *Sunday Times*.

Agathocles (361–289 B.C.). Tyrant of Sicily (316–304 B.C.). He was the son of a potter, and raised himself from the ranks to become general of the army. There is a story that he always kept an earthen pot at hand in memory of his origin. When he attacked the Carthaginians, he "carried the war into Africa" and "burned his ships behind him" that his soldiers might feel assured they must either conquer or die. Agathocles died of poison administered by his grandson. He is the hero of an English tragedy by Richard Perrington, a French tragedy

by Voltaire and a German novel by Caroline Pichler, all called by his name.

Agave (Agaue). In classic mythology, a daughter of Cadmus and mother of Pentheus, whom she tore to pieces in a mad fury under the illusion that he was a wild beast. This episode forms a part of Euripides' drama *Bacchae*. See BACCHANTS.

Agee, James (1909–1955). American novelist and film critic. Agee was raised in the Cumberland mountain area of Tennessee, the setting for his two novels. In 1936 he lived for a few weeks with several "typical" Alabama sharecropper families in order to write a magazine article on the plight of such people. Instead of a magazine article the result was the book *Let Us Now Praise Famous Men* (1941), with photographs by Walker Evans. During the 1940's Agee was a film reviewer. His work has been compiled as the first volume of *Agee on Film* (1958). After 1948 he worked almost exclusively for the motion pictures. The second volume of *Agee on Film* (1960) contains five of his screen plays. His first novel was *The Morning Watch* (1954). *A Death in the Family* was posthumously published in 1957 and was awarded a Pulitzer Prize. Dramatized by Tad Mosel as *All the Way Home* in 1960, the play too was a Pulitzer Prize winner. A collection of Agee's letters to Father Flye, an Episcopalian minister he had met as a youth, appeared in 1962.

Age of Anxiety, The (1948). A long poem by W. H. AUDEN. It concerns three men and a woman who meet by chance in a New York bar in wartime; all are suffering from the modern malaise, and feel guilty, isolated, and rootless. In a common dream they set out on a quest through a barren waste land. Hope in Christianity is presented as the solution to their problems. The title has frequently been used as a name to describe our age.

The Age of Anxiety is also the name of a ballet, danced to Leonard Bernstein's Second Symphony.

Age of Innocence, The (1920). A novel by Edith WHARTON. A satirical picture of social life in New York during the 1870's, it describes the marriage of Newland Archer to May Welland, who is bound by the tribal code of the elite. Although he is attracted to her unconventional cousin, Ellen Olenska, they are both too obedient to the code to seek happiness together.

Age of Reason, The (1794–1796). A controversial treatise by Thomas PAINE, expounding the deistic view of revealed religion. The work was widely denounced in America as immoral and atheistic.

Age of Reason, The. See ROADS TO FREEDOM, THE.

Agésilas (1666). A tragedy by Pierre CORNEILLE. Set in Ephesus in the time of Agesilaus, king of Sparta, it centers on the conflict between public opinion and the king's desire to marry a Persian. A compromise is effected, and he is finally able to marry the woman of his choice.

Aggravaine, Sir. In Arthurian legend, a son of MARGAWSE and a knight of the Round Table. In Malory's *Morte d'Arthur*, he is the brother of the knights Gawain, Gareth, Gaheris, and half brother of Mordred.

Agib. The third CALENDER in the *Arabian Nights*. He was wrecked on a loadstone mountain, lived for a year in the palace of the forty princesses, and lost an eye for his curiosity.

Agincourt, Battle of (1415). Battle in northern France. The English army defeated the more numerous, better armed French. It is the setting for Shakespeare's Henry V and Michael Drayton's *The Ballad of Agincourt* (c. 1605).

Aglaia. (1) One of the three Charites (Graces) of classic mythology.

(2) In Dostoevski's novel The Idiot, the fiancée of Prince Myshkin.

Aglaos. A poor Arcadian peasant. He was called by the Delphic oracle "happier than King Gyges of Lydia," because he was contented.

Agnès. In Molière's comedy L'Ecole des Femmes, the girl on whom Arnolphe tries out his educational experiments, with the aim of turning her into a perfect wife for himself. She has been brought up in a country convent and kept totally in ignorance of the difference between the sexes, conventional proprieties, the mysteries of marriage, and so on. When removed from the convent, she treats men like schoolgirls, playing with them and kissing them. An *Agnès* is therefore any naïve and innocent young girl. The French have the expression, *Elle fait l'Agnès,* that is, she is pretending to be wholly unsophisticated and ingenuous.

Agnes Grey (1847). A novel by Anne Brontë, published with her sister Emily's *Wuthering Heights.* It is a quiet account of the life of an ill-treated, lonely governess who eventually marries Mr. Weston, a curate.

Agni. The Hindu god of fire, sunlight, and lightning and lord of the gods of the earth. He is one of the more important deities described in the Vedas.

agnostic (Gr., *a,* not, *gignoskein,* to know). Thomas Huxley coined this term in 1869, alluding to the altar to "the Unknown God" mentioned in St. Paul's writings. Huxley meant to indicate the mental attitude of those who withhold their assent from whatever is incapable of proof, such as an unseen world, a First Cause, etc. Agnostics neither dogmatically accept nor reject such matters, but simply say *agnosco* (I do not know): they are not capable of proof.

Agramante (**Agramant**). The emperor of Africa who fights Charlemagne and the paladins in the Orlando poems of Boiardo and Ariosto. In the latter's poem he is killed by Oliviero (see Orlando Furioso).

Agrarians. A group of 20th-century American writers in the South. Among its members were Allen Tate, John Crowe Ransom, and Robert Penn Warren. Drawing their inspiration from the past, they favored agriculture as the economic base for the South; this would supposedly enable the South to return to its regional aristocratic heritage. These critics expressed their views in the symposium *I'll Take My Stand: The South and the Agrarian Tradition by Twelve Southerners* (1932). Many members of the original group have since abandoned their early position.

Agricane (**Agrican**). In Carolingian legend the King of Tartary who fights against the Christian forces of Charlemagne and his paladins. In the Orlando Innamorato of Boiardo, he besieges the lovely princess Angelica at Albracca, but is killed in combat by Orlando. Before he dies, he asks for and is given baptism.

Agrippa I (d. A.D. 44). A son of Herod. He was one of the Roman rulers before whom St. Paul was tried. His tribute, "Almost thou persuadest me to be a Christian" (Acts 26:28), is often quoted.

Agrippina. (d. A.D. 59). Daughter of Agrippina and Germanicus Caesar, sister of the emperor Caligula, and mother of the emperor Nero. She persuaded her husband the emperor Claudius, to name Nero, her son by a previous marriage, as his successor over his own son Britannicus; subsequently she had Claudius poisoned. After he became emperor, Nero, after many elaborate and thwarted attempts, finally succeeded in having Agrippina murdered.

Agrippina's mother was the granddaughter of Augustus, wife of Germanicus Caesar and mother of Caligula. She was banished by Tiberius to the isle of Pandatarra where she died (A.D. 33).

Aguecheek, Sir Andrew. In Shakespeare's Twelfth Night, a silly old fop with "3,000 ducats a year." Very fond of the table but with a shrewd understanding that "beef had done harm to his wit," Sir Andrew thinks himself "old in nothing but in understanding," and boasts that he can "cut a caper, dance the coranto, walk a jig, and take delight in masques," like a young man.

Ahab. (1) In the Old Testament, a king of Israel whose name has become a byword for wickedness. He is remembered especially for his hostility to the prophet Elijah and countenance of profane cults. At the instigation of his wife Jezebel, he executed Naboth on false charges in order to obtain possession of a vineyard which Naboth owned and refused to sell. His story is told in I Kings 16–22.

(2) The monomaniacal captain of the *Pequod* in Melville's Moby Dick (1851).

Ahasuerus. (1) In the Old Testament, king of the Medes and Persians, as related in the book of Esther.

(2) In medieval legend, one of the names given the Wandering Jew.

Ahi. In Vedic myth, the sky dragon that releases the rain when Indra's thunderbolt is hurled.

Ahmed, Prince. A character in the *Arabian Nights,* noted for the tent given him by the fairy Paribanou, which would cover a whole army but might be carried in one's pocket; he is also associated with the apple of Samarkand, which would cure all diseases.

Aho, Juhani. Pen name of **Johannes Brofelt** (1861–1921). Finnish novelist and short-story writer. Influenced by the realist movement, Aho depicted in his earlier work the daily lives of common people. He was not, however, motivated by a passion for social reform, but sought instead to paint a true portrait and to record his often humorous insights. In both *Papin Tytar* (*The Parson's Daughter,* 1885) and *Papin Rouva* (*The Parson's Wife,* 1893), he portrays the inner struggles of a young woman who is married to a man she does not love. A new strain appeared in Aho's work with the publication of the novel *Panu* (1897): national romanticism now colored his realism. In the short stories of *Lastuja* (*Chips,* 1891–1921), he shows himself a fine poet.

Aholah and **Aholibah**. In the Old Testament, the names of 2 harlots who symbolize the religious idolatry and pursuit of false faiths in Samaria and Jerusalem (Ezek. 23:4).

Aholibamah. In the Old Testament, the name of one of Esau's wives (Gen. 36:2) and of a duke, or leader, of Edom (Gen. 36:41). In Byron's poem, *Heaven and Earth* (1824), she is a proud, ambitious, queenlike beauty, the daughter of Cain's son and loved by the seraph Samiasa.

Ahriman or **Ahrimanes**. In the dual system of ZOROASTER, the spiritual enemy of mankind, also called Angra Mainyu and Druj (deceit). He has existed since the beginning of the world and is said to be in eternal conflict with Ahura Mazda or ORMUZD.

Ah Sin. The Chinese card player in Bret Harte's PLAIN LANGUAGE FROM TRUTHFUL JAMES.

Ahura Mazda. See ORMUZD.

Aïda. A spectacular opera by Giuseppe VERDI. The libretto by Camille du Locle was translated into Italian by Ghislanzoni and considerably reworked by Verdi himself. The story was based on a sketch by the French Egyptologist Mariette, who had originally thought of it as appropriate for ceremonies opening the Suez Canal. Verdi, however, did not consent to begin writing the opera until 1870, the year after the opening of the canal, and the only connection it retained with Mariette's original purpose was that the khedive of Egypt, who commissioned the opera, required that it should open in Cairo.

Aides, also **Aïdoneus.** See HADES.

Aiglon, L'. A drama by Edmond ROSTAND. It is based on the tragic career of Napoleon's son and heir, whom Victor Hugo called l'Aiglon (the eaglet).

Aiken, Conrad [Potter] (1889–). American poet. A graduate of Harvard, Aiken was influenced by Freud, Havelock Ellis, and William James, as well as by Edgar Allan Poe. Of his novels, perhaps the best known are THE BLUE VOYAGE and the autobiographical USHANT. He won a Pulitzer Prize in 1930 for his *Selected Poems* (1929). Among his volumes of poetry are *The Jig of Forslin* (1916), *The House of Dust* (1920), *Priapus and the Pool* (1922), *Serlin* (1925), *Time in the Rock* (1936), and *And in the Human Heart* (1940). *Costumes by Eros* (1928) is a collection of short stories. See KID, THE. His collected novels appeared in 1964.

Ainsworth, William Harrison (1805–1882). English historical novelist. From 1840 on he was editor of *Bentley's Miscellany, Ainsworth's Magazine,* and the *New Monthly.* He wrote 39 novels, including *Rookwood* (1834), *Jack Sheppard* (1839), *Old St. Paul's* (1841), *Windsor Castle* (1843), and *The Flitch of Bacon* (1854).

Airavata. In Hindu myth the holy elephant, Indra being its rider. He is supposed to have been created by seven chants from the mouth of Brahma.

Ajax (**Aias**). The most famous hero of the Trojan War after Achilles. He was king of Salamis, a man of giant stature, daring and self-confident, son of Telamon. When the armor of Hector was awarded to Odysseus instead of to himself, he turned mad from vexation and stabbed himself. His deeds are narrated by Homer and later poets. Sophocles wrote a tragedy called *Ajax,* in which "the madman" scourges a ram he mistakes for Achilles. His encounter with a flock of sheep, which he fancied in his madness to be the sons of Atreus, Agamemnon, and Menelaus, has been mentioned at greater or less length by several Greek and Roman poets. This Ajax is introduced by Shakespeare in his drama TROILUS AND CRESSIDA.

Ajax (**Aias**) **the Less.** In Greek legend, son of Oileus, king of Locris. The night Troy was taken, he offered violence to Cassandra, the prophetic daughter of Priam; in consequence, his ship was driven on a rock, and he perished at sea.

Akenside, Mark (1721–1770). English poet and physician to the queen (1761). He is the author of *The Pleasures of the Imagination* (1774), in blank verse, and of various minor poems.

Akhmatova, Anna. Pen name of **Anna Andreyevna Gorenko** (1888–1966). Russian poet. An outstanding member of the Acmeist school (see ACMEISM), she married the poet Nikolai GUMILIOV in 1910 and divorced him in 1918. Between 1912 and 1923 she published half a dozen volumes of poems, the best of which included *Evening* (*Vecher;* 1912) and *Anno Domini* (1922). Her poetry, principally intimate and personal love lyrics, is in the Acmeist tradition of clarity and sharpness of imagery. Akhmatova's abstinence from political themes led to an attack on her in 1946 by the Soviet cultural overseer, Andrei Zhdanov. She had published little since 1923 —being completely unpublished at all for one 17-year stretch—and after the attack issued only a few second-rate verses. In 1956, at the height of the Soviet thaw in the arts, two of her poems were reprinted in a Moscow literary journal.

Akins, Zoë (1886–1958). American dramatist. She won a Pulitzer Prize for her adaptation (1935) of Edith Wharton's THE OLD MAID. She also wrote such light romantic comedies as *A Royal Fandango* (1923) and *The Greeks Had a Word for It* (1930). In later years Miss Akins wrote screenplays, among them one for Edna Ferber's *Show Boat* (1926).

Aksakov, Sergei Timofeyevich (1791–1859). Russian writer. Born in Ufa, in the eastern steppes of Russia, Aksakov attended the University of Kazan and entered government service in Moscow. His early writing consisted mainly of essays and articles on the theatre. The novelist Gogol, who became a close friend of Aksakov's in the early 1830's, urged him to write the reminiscences of his early life in the steppe country. Aksakov produced three autobiographical works: *Semeinaya khronika* (*The Family Chronicle,* 1856), *Vospominaniya* (*Reminiscences,* 1856), and *Detskiye gody bagrova vnuka* (*Years of Childhood of Bagrov's Grandson,* 1858). In the *Chronicle* and *Years of Childhood,* Aksakov used fictitious names for his family. All three of these works, which are masterpieces of description and narration, have become classics in Russian literature. Aksakov's prose style is placed on a level with the best Russian prose writers, including Pushkin, Lermontov, and Turgenev. The love of the old patriarchal Russian way of life that is revealed in Aksakov's memoirs was passed on to his children. Two of his sons, Konstantin (1817–1860) and Ivan (1823–1886), became leading members of the SLAVOPHILES.

Akutagawa Ryūnosuke (1892–1927). Japanese short-story writer, noted for his novel subject matter, presented in a vivid and realistic style. Many of his stories have been translated into English. He committed suicide with an overdose of veronal.

Al Aaraaf (1829). A poem by Edgar Allan Poe. It is the title poem of his second collection, called *Al Aaraaf, Tamerlane, and Other Poems.* In Arabian folklore, Al Aaraaf is the region between Heaven and Hell, presided over by Nesace, a beautiful maiden. Poe's Al Aaraaf is a wondrous star, surrounded by four suns. The youth, Angelo, is brought there with the hope of entering Heaven; an earthly love prevents him from hearing Nesace's call.

Aladdin. One of the most celebrated characters in the *Arabian Nights,* hero of the story *Aladdin or the Wonderful Lamp.* The son of Mustafa, a poor tailor of China, Aladdin is a lazy, obstinate and mischievous boy when the tale opens. One day an African magician accosts him, pretending to be his uncle, and sends him into a cave to bring up a "wonderful lamp," giving him a "ring of safety." Aladdin secures the lamp but will not hand it to the magician till he is out of the cave; whereupon the magician shuts him up and departs for Africa. Wringing his hands in despair, Aladdin accidentally rubs the lamp and learns of its magic power as two genii appear to do his bidding. He asks to be delivered from the cave and is returned to his home. By means of this lamp, he obtains untold wealth, builds a superb palace, and marries BADROULBOUDOUR, the sultan's daughter. After a time, the African magician, offering new lamps for old, obtains the lamp from Aladdin's wife and causes the palace to be transported into Africa. Ultimately, however, Aladdin poisons the magician, regains the lamp and has his palace restored to its original place in China.

Aladino (Alandine). In the GERUSALEMME LIBERATA of Tasso, the aged king of Jerusalem who opposes the armies of the First Crusade led by Goffredo (Godfrey). He is killed in the final battle that precedes the Christian conquest of the holy city.

Alain. Pen name of **Emile Chartier** (1868–1951). French philosopher, essayist, and teacher. He took his pseudonym from the 15th-century poet Alain Chartier. Believing that to be alive is to be awake, Alain imbued a generation of disciples with the will to resist conformity. His writings were most often in the form of propos, short aphoristic essays much like fables or parables, which taught a practical lesson through imagistic narrative. Some of the many thousands of these propos have been collected in books about politics, his militant pacifism, psychology, philosophy, and literary criticism, including *Les Cent et un Propos d'Alain* (5 v., 1908–1929) and *Mars, ou la Guerre jugée* (1921).

Alain-Fournier. Pen name of **Henri Fournier** (1886–1914). French novelist. Alain-Fournier grew up in the beautiful countryside of La Chapelle-d'Angillon, in the department of Cher. The son of two schoolteachers, he wandered from the merchant marine, to military service, to a career in journalism. In 1914, Alain-Fournier died in action, leaving one work which alone secured his reputation as a significant French novelist: LE GRAND MEAULNES.

Alamanni, Luigi (1495–1556). Florentine poet and playwright. A leading Renaissance imitator of classical forms in the vernacular, his most substantial works are the *Coltivazione* (On Cultivation, 1546),

a didactic poem in imitation of Virgil's *Georgics* similarly dealing with the care of fields and gardens; and two epics: *Gyrone il cortese* (1548), which relates the adventures of the courteous knight Gyrone; and the *Avarchide* (1570), on the siege of Bourges (Lat., Avaricum) by King Arthur.

Alamo. A fortified mission in San Antonio, Texas. In 1836, during the Texas rebellion against Mexico, a force of Texans under William B. Travis was besieged there by a much larger Mexican army led by General Santa Anna. When the Mexicans succeeded in gaining entrance after a 13-day bombardment, every remaining defender was killed in hand-to-hand combat. Among those killed were Davy Crockett and James Bowie. "Remember the Alamo!" became a battle slogan of the Mexican War.

Alan-a-Dale or **Alin-a-Dale.** See ALLAN-A-DALE.

Alarcón, Pedro Antonio de (1833–1891). Spanish novelist. Alarcón's fame rests on his shorter works, particularly his humorous tale based on popular ballad tradition, *El sombrero de tres picos* (*The Three Cornered Hat,* 1874). His humor again raised him to prominence with the publication of the novelette *El capitán Veneno* (*Captain Venom* or *Poison,* 1881). Also well known is his full-length work, *El escándalo* (1875), which points out the redeeming effects of an innocent girl's love upon a quarrelsome aristocrat, and the novel *El niño de la bola* (1880).

Alarcón y Mendoza, Juan Ruiz de (c. 1581–1639). Mexican-born Spanish dramatist. Alarcón, who spent most of his life in Spain, studied at Salamanca and was appointed to the Council of the Indies in 1626. His humped back and touchy temperament made him a target for the gibes of rival dramatists, such as Lope de Vega.

A restrained and painstaking artist who paid close attention to style and characterization, he wrote 24 plays, most of which were published in 1628 and 1634. The best known of these are the "comedies of ethics," in which the comic element enforces a moral lesson: *Las paredes oyen,* a study of slander; *Mudarse por mejorarse,* which assails inconstancy in love; *La prueba de las promesas,* an attack on ingratitude; and LA VERDAD SOSPECHOSA.

A la Recherche du Temps Perdu. See REMEMBRANCE OF THINGS PAST.

Alaric. (370?–410). Gothic king and conqueror. As king of the Visigoths, he invaded Greece (395–396) and plundered Rome (410).

Alas y Ureña, Leopoldo. Also known as **Clarín** (1852–1901). Spanish novelist and critic. Though he exerted some critical influence during his period, his chief claim to fame lies in his two-volume novel *La Regenta* (1884–1885), considered one of the major works of European fiction in the 19th century. It applies a mixture of naturalism, akin to that of French writers, and psychological interpretation to Spanish provincial life, concentrating upon the plight of a heroine crushed by the boredom and malice present in her native town.

Albanact. Son of BRUTE, in Geoffrey of Monmouth's *History of the Kings of Britain.* According to Geoffrey, Albanact gave his name to Albany (Scotland).

Albany, duke of. In Shakespeare's KING LEAR, the gentle, wise, and courageous husband of the ruthless Goneril, eldest daughter of Lear. He is horrified at Goneril's behavior toward her father. At the play's end, he and Edgar are left to rule England.

albatross. The largest web-footed bird. It is the subject of many superstitions, especially among sailors. Coleridge's RIME OF THE ANCIENT MARINER is based on the belief that it is fatal to shoot an albatross.

Albee, Edward [Franklin] (1928–). American playwright. His first play, written in three weeks in 1958, was the one-act *Zoo Story,* performed first in German (W. Berlin, 1959). This was followed by *The Death of Bessie Smith,* a one-act play on the effects of racial discrimination in the lives of whites; it was produced on Broadway in 1961, paired with Albee's *The American Dream.* He also wrote two 15-minute plays: *The Sandbox,* a prelude to *The American Dream,* and *Fam and Yam,* a dialogue between playwrights. Albee's first three-act play was *Who's Afraid of Virginia Woolf?* (1962), a virulent unveiling of the relationship between a history professor and his wife, the daughter of the president of the college. In 1963 he dramatized Carson McCullers' novel *The Ballad of the Sad Café.*

Alberich. In Scandinavian and German legend, the dwarf who guards the treasure of the Nibelungs, owners of a magic ring. He plays a prominent part in both the *Völsunga Saga* and the *Nibelungenlied.* In Wagner's musical drama, *Der* RING DES NIBELUNGEN (1876), Loki and Wotan steal the ring and treasure, and Alberich's curse follows the ring wherever it goes.

Albers, Joseph (1888–). German artist. He taught at the BAUHAUS and, emigrating to the U.S., headed the art department of Yale University until 1958. His teaching has considerably influenced industrial design.

Albert, Prince. Full name **Albert Francis Charles Augustus Emmanuel of Saxe-Coburg-Gotha** (1819–1861). German husband of Queen VICTORIA and prince-consort of England, son of the Duke of Saxe-Coburg-Gotha. Through his tact and abiding interest in the arts and science, he overcame the initial distrust of the English people. It was largely through his work that the great Exhibition of 1851 was successful. His death left the queen and the nation in deep mourning.

Albertanus of Brescia. See MELIBEE.

Alberti, Leone Battista (1404–1472). Florentine humanist. He wrote poetry, plays, moral and philosophical essays, dabbled in painting and sculpture, and practiced architecture, designing the Rucellai Palace and Loggia and the facade of Santa Maria Novella in Florence. In Rimini, he redesigned the church of San Francesco for the tyrant Sigismondo Malatesta in 1445; one of the earliest examples of Renaissance classical style, it was called the *Tempio Malatestiano* because of its resemblance to pagan temples. In Rome, he was one of the early contributors to the architectural plans for Saint Peter's. He is particularly known for his treatises, on painting, *De pictura* (1435), on sculpture, *De statua* (1464), and on architecture, *De re aedificatoria* (1452, pub. 1485) in which he popularized Filippo Brunelleschi's innovations concerning the scientific study of vision and the use of ancient monuments as sources; he also described a system based on human proportions which allows the correct placement of figures within pictorial space.

From Alberti's *De statua,* showing human proportions.

Among his literary works are a play written in such perfect imitation of the Latin poets that Aldo Manutius thought it an original; an autobiography (1460); and his masterpiece, the treatise *On the Family* (*Della famiglia*), which uses the dialogue form to discuss his social philosophy, and presents a valuable portrait of life in his day.

Alberti, Rafael (1902–). Spanish poet and playwright. His early volumes, *Marinero en tierra* (1925), *La amanta* (1926), *El alba del alhelí* (1927), and *Cal y Canto* (1927), reveal his initial interest in folklore as an art motif. Later, as in his best-known work, *Sobre los ángeles* (1928), he shifted his focus, concentrating upon surrealist poetry. Alberti is also known for his popular plays *El hombre deshabitado* (1931), *El adefesio* (1944), and the tragedy *La Gallarda.*

Albertine disparue. See REMEMBRANCE OF THINGS PAST.

Albertine [Simonet]. The mistress of the narrator in Marcel Proust's REMEMBRANCE OF THINGS PAST. She refuses him when they meet at Balbec, but later comes to live with him in Paris, although secretly continuing to have affairs with other women. Tormented by his jealousy, she leaves him—only to be killed accidentally by being thrown from a horse.

Albert the Great. See ALBERTUS MAGNUS.

Albertus Magnus. (1206?–1280). German scholastic philosopher and churchman. His works include paraphrases of Aristotle's works, and he was very advanced for his day in his knowledge of experimental science. His teachings had great influence; Thomas AQUINAS was one of his students. He was canonized in 1932.

Albion. An ancient and poetical name for Great Britain. It is thought to have been so called from the white (Lat. *albus*) cliffs that face Gaul, but possibly from the Celtic *alp, ailp,* a rock, cliff, mountain. It was Napoleon who called England *Albion Perfide* (Perfidious Albion).

Albracca. In Boiardo's famous epic ORLANDO INNAMORATO, a fortress in Cathay to which ANGELICA retires in grief when Rinaldo fails to return her love. Here she is besieged by Agricane, king of Tartary, until Orlando kills him.

Albright, Ivan Le Lorraine (1897–   ). American painter. He spotlights, with microscopic realism, the pores, wrinkles, textures, and blemishes of humanity.

Alcaic verse or Alcaics. A Greek lyrical metre, so called from Alcaeus, a lyric poet. He is said to have invented it. Alcaic measure is little more than a curiosity in English poetry; probably the best example is Tennyson's:

O migh/ty-mouthed / in/ventor of / harmonies,
O skilled / to sing / of / Time or E/ternity.
God-gift/ed or/gan-voice / of Eng/land,
Milton, a / name to re/sound for / ages.

Alcalde de Zalamea, El (The Mayor of Zalamea, c. 1640). A tragic drama by Pedro CALDERÓN DE LA BARCA. This play was originally written by Lope de Vega, but Calderón re-adapted it, giving to the realism of the former master a more profound and intellectual outlook. Among the characters created by Calderón is the hero, Pedro Crespo, a farmer who is elected *alcalde,* or mayor, of Zalamea.

Don Álvaro, an army captain quartered in Pedro's home, violates his host's daughter and refuses to marry her; he does not believe that he has to answer to commoners for his conduct. After Pedro has Don Álvaro jailed, Don Lope, the captain's superior officer, demands his freedom, and King Philip II, who has arrived in Zalamea, agrees that Pedro has exceeded his authority. However, when Pedro reveals that the captain has been strangled in prison, the king, forced to admit that justice has been done, makes Pedro perpetual mayor of the town. This play, like many of Lope's works, is a protest against the capricious and despotic feudal nobility and upholds the dignity of the middle class.

Alceste. The hero of Molière's comedy LE MISANTHROPE. Alceste is disgusted with society. Courtesy seems to him the vice of fops, and the customary forms of civilized life no better than hypocrisy. He is in love with Celimène, a coquette who produces caustic "portraits" of her friends behind their backs and who embodies all the qualities with which he is most impatient.

Alcestis (Alkestis). The first extant play (438 B.C.) by EURIPIDES. It tells the story of Alcestis, a daughter of Pelias and wife of Admetus, king of Pherae. In gratitude for past kindnesses, Apollo had promised that Admetus might escape death if someone would consent to die in his place. When the time came, Admetus' aged parents refused to do so, but Alcestis voluntarily descended to Hades, from which Heracles soon rescued her. The drunken, comic Heracles makes this a tragicomedy; it was originally presented in lieu of a SATYR PLAY. By implication, it called into question the Athenian attitude toward women. In Gluck's opera *Alceste* (1767), the heroine is saved by the intervention of Apollo.

Alchemist, The (1610). A comedy by Ben JONSON. Subtle, a clever quack, and his whorish colleague, Doll Common, set up shop in the house of Lovewit while the latter is away. With the help of Lovewit's servant, Jeremy or Face, the "alchemists" succeed in tricking a whole series of gullible scoundrels, such as Abel Drugger, who seeks charms and advice on how to set up his tobacco shop for maximum good fortune; Dapper, a gambler in need of a familiar spirit (whom he is forced to await while bound in a privy with a gingerbread gag in his mouth); two sanctimonious Puritan Brethren, Ananias and Tribulation Wholesome, who hope to extend their philanthropies and their power by means of alchemy; and, most important, Sir Epicure Mammon, a miser and lecher who dreams of inordinate sensual pleasure. These and others, including Kastril, a young country fellow who wishes to learn to quarrel like a gallant, are adroitly fleeced by Subtle and his colleagues, until the return of Lovewit, who cleverly routs the quacks and takes advantage of their various accumulated gains.

Alcibiades (Alkibiades; c. 450–404 B.C.). An Athenian general and politician. Arrogant and ambitious, Alcibiades called democracy "acknowledged folly." He was brilliant but dissolute and ostentatious, earning both the admiration and the disgust of his fellow citizens. Alcibiades' courage and ambition won him an appointment as general. When Segesta appealed to Athens for aid against Selinus, Alcibiades spoke in favor of the ill-omened expedition. Spurred on by his speech, the Athenians sent him at the head of a huge fleet (415 B.C.). Just before the sailing he was implicated in a sacrilegious mockery of the Eleusinian mysteries. After the fleet had sailed he was recalled for trial, but escaped to Sparta. There, in revenge for the Athenians' confiscation of his property and sentencing him to death, he traitorously informed the Spartans of Athens' weak defenses. Sparta successfully cut off Athens' control over the farmlands through Decelea. Finally, he was forced to flee Sparta because of the jealousy of their leaders. When the Athenian democracy was overthrown, he was welcomed back to his native city. There, on the eve of a battle with Sparta, he was distrusted again. He fled to Persia, where on Sparta's orders he was killed. Alcibiades' return to Athens is incidentally treated in Shakespeare's *Timon of Athens;* he also appears in Plato's dialogues the *Phaedo* and the *Symposium,* and is caricatured in Aristophanes' *The Clouds.*

Alcina. The sister of Morgana and a personification of sensual pleasure in the Orlando poems of Boiardo and Ariosto. In the latter's poem, ORLANDO FURIOSO, she reigns, like Circe, over an island of oblivion filled with luring enchantments. She turns her lovers into trees, stones and wild beasts after tiring of them. RUGGIERO, one of her victims, stays with her until rescued by Melissa, who also restores Astolfo to himself after Alcina had turned him into a myrtle tree.

Alcinous (Alkinoos). See PHAEACIANS.

Alcione or **Alcyone.** See HALCYONE AND CEYX.

Alciphron (Alkiphron). A Greek rhetorician of the 2d or 3d century. He was the author of fictitious letters giving details of domestic life and manners of his time.

Alciphron, or the Minute Philosopher (1732). The title of a series of dialogues by Bishop BERKELEY, so called from the name of the chief speaker, a free-thinker.

Alcmaeon (Alkmeon or **Alkmaion).** In Greek mythology, a son of Amphiaraus and ERIPHYLE. As children, he and his brother Amphilochus were enjoined by their father to avenge him on his wife for the treachery that drove him into the fatal war as one of the SEVEN AGAINST THEBES. When Alcmaeon was grown, Eriphyle, bribed by Thersander, repeated her treachery by sending Alcmaeon too into war with Thebes. He led the EPIGONI to victory and, on his return, killed his mother. Dying, she laid a curse on any land that would shelter him, and the ERINYES drove him mad.

Alcmaeon wandered through many lands. Phegeus, king of Psophis, married him to his daughter Arsinoe and Alcmaeon gave her HARMONIA'S NECKLACE, with which his mother had been bribed. Eriphyle's curse brought famine on the land and Alcmaeon left Psophis. He wandered to the river Achelous. On its delta, which had not existed when the curse was laid, he was at last free from madness. The river god Achelous gave Alcmaeon his daughter Callirrhoe.

She bore him two sons, Acarnan and Amphoteros, but soon demanded the necklace for herself. Alcmaeon returned to Psophis and tricked Phegeus into giving him the necklace. As he was leaving, the trick was discovered and Alcmaeon was killed by Phegeus' sons. Callirrhoe, meanwhile, had been lending her favors to the amorous Zeus. At her request, he caused her sons by Alcmaeon to grow to manhood overnight. They killed Phegeus' sons and finally dedicated the necklace to Apollo at Delphi, where it was still shown in classical times.

Alcman (Alkman). A celebrated Dorian lyric poet of Sparta. He flourished in the first half of the 7th century B.C.

Alcmena or **Alcmene (Alkmena, Alkmene).** In Greek mythology, the mother of HERACLES by Zeus. Her cuckolded husband was AMPHITRYON.

Alcofribas. The pseudonym assumed by François RABELAIS in Books I and II of his GARGANTUA AND PANTAGRUEL. Alcofribas Nasier is an anagram of François Rabelais. Books III, IV, and V were all signed "M. Fran. (or Francoys) Rabelais, Docteur en Médecine."

Alcoran, see KORAN.

Alcott, [Amos] Bronson (1799–1888). American philosopher, teacher, and poet. After a period as itinerant peddler, Alcott organized an unorthodox school whose advanced methods and racially mixed enrollment caused public indignation. For a time he ran a cooperative experimental farm called FRUITLANDS. He then served as superintendent of schools in Con-

cord, Mass., but it was not until his daughter Louisa May ALCOTT succeeded as a writer that any measure of financial security was assured his family. In Concord he set up a school of philosophy with William T. Harris; together, they disseminated Alcott's benevolent philosophy. He published little but kept extensive journals; his most important published work includes *Tablets* (1868), *Observations on the Principles and Methods of Infant Instruction* (1830), and his contributions of ORPHIC SAYINGS to *The Dial.*

Alcott, Louisa May (1832–1888). American novelist and poet. Determined to write, she had to work to help support the family. Her father, Bronson ALCOTT, to whom the family was very devoted, kept them poor with a succession of philanthropic and educational schemes. Miss Alcott wrote her first book, *Flower Fables,* when she was 16; her first success was *Hospital Sketches* (1863), a volume based on the letters she wrote for soldiers as an untrained nurse in Georgetown Hospital, during the Civil War. Louisa May Alcott became famous in 1869, with the publication of LITTLE WOMEN. She continued with a series of books read by children and adults: *An Old-Fashioned Girl* (1870), *Little Men* (1871), *Eight Cousins* (1875), *Rose in Bloom* (1876), and *Under the Lilacs* (1878).

Her fiction is semiautobiographical and is still widely read; eight of the books are still in print.

Alcuin of York (735–804). English scholar. Trained at the cathedral school of York, set up by one of the Venerable Bede's students, he was invited to France by Charlemagne to aid in the revival of learning and ecclesiastical reform (see CAROLINGIANS). He established a school at the royal court and another at Tours, thus helping to return to the Continent the Christian learning and culture that had been preserved mainly in the English monasteries.

Aldanov, Mark. Pen name of **Mark Aleksandrovich Landau** (1886–1957). Russian *émigré* novelist. He is best known for his novel *The Fifth Seal (Nachalo kontza;* 1939), set during the Spanish Civil War.

Alden, John. See COURTSHIP OF MILES STANDISH, THE.

Aldigieri of Chiaramonte. In the MORGANTE MAGGIORE of Pulci and the Orlando poems of Ariosto and Boiardo a knight of Charlemagne's company who holds the castle of Agrismonte. In Pulci's poem he is killed by the traitorous Gano of Maganza.

Aldine editions. Editions of the Greek and Roman classics printed and published at Venice and elsewhere by Aldo Manuzio or Aldus Manutius (1450–1515) and his family from 1490 to 1597. Their handy octavo size and scholarly accuracy made them popular throughout Europe and helped promote Renaissance Humanism's ideal of reviving the classics. Aldo invented the type called *italics,* once called *Aldine,* and first used in a 1501 edition of Virgil.

Aldington, Richard (1892–1962). English poet, novelist, biographer, and translator. At one time married to the American poet Hilda DOOLITTLE, he was a member of the group that introduced IMAGISM. He was among those who, after World War I, found England barren and sterile. His collection of poems *Images of War* (1919) expresses his disgust with the war itself; *Soft Answers* (1932) is a collection of savage satires. His chief novels are DEATH OF A HERO and *All Men Are Enemies* (1933). His best-known biographies are *D. H. Lawrence: Portrait of a Genius, But . . .* (1950), and *Lawrence of Arabia* (1955). *Life for Life's Sake* (1941) is an autobiography.

Aldrich, Bess Streeter (1881–1954). American novelist. She is noted for her studies of pioneer life, especially *A Lantern in Her Hand* (1928), the story of a pioneer mother in Nebraska, and *Song of Years* (1939), a novel of pioneer Iowa. *Miss Bishop* (1933) is the story of a Middle Western teacher who misses marriage and brings up other women's children.

Aldrich, Thomas Bailey (1836–1907). American poet, editor, novelist, and dramatist. After an early career as journalist and war correspondent, Aldrich became the editor of *The Atlantic Monthly* in 1881. He later retired to devote himself to writing. Aldrich was a member of a brilliant literary circle in New York; although he was a man of great wit, his work is marred by excessive gentility and sentimentality. His most famous book is the novel, THE STORY OF A BAD BOY, based on his own childhood. His well-known short story, MARJORIE DAW, is included in the collection, *Marjorie Daw and Other People* (1873). Other popular works are *The Stillwater Tragedy* (1880), a collection of verse called *The Bells* (1855), and a series of plays.

Alecto (Allekto). In classic myth, one of the ERINYES (Furies).

Aleichem, Sholem or Shalom. Pen name of **Solomon J. Rabinowitz** (1859–1916). Russian-born Yiddish humorist. A noted author of tales in Yiddish, he was the son of Russian-Jewish storekeepers. For some years a rabbi, he escaped from the 1905 pogrom in Russia and, later, emigrated to the U.S. Sholem Aleichem's stories of Jewish life are noted for their combination of humor and pathos. Much of his large output has been translated into English, but the special quality of the Yiddish language, particularly in the uses of humor, loses a great deal in the translation, so that his reputation has failed to spread as far as it deserves.

Aleixandre [y Merlo], Vincente (1898–   ). Spanish poet. An emphasis upon the linking of strange metaphors, a favoring of free verse, and the presence of great technical skill are the main characteristics of his collected poems: *Ambito* (1928), *Espadas como labios* (1932), *Pasión de la tierra* (1935), *Sombra del paraíso* (1944), and *Mis poemas mejores* (1961). Aleixandre has had a profound influence upon younger, contemporary Spanish poets.

Alemán, Mateo (1547–after 1613). Spanish novelist. The son of a prison doctor, Alemán studied in Seville, Salamanca, and Alcalá and spent some 20 years as a government accountant. He was twice imprisoned for debt. In 1608 he went to Mexico in the company of Archbishop García Guerra, whose life he published in 1613.

Alemán is remembered chiefly as the author of GUZMÁN DE ALFARACHE, the second great picaresque novel after *Lazarillo de Tormes* (1554). The first part appeared in 1599 and, after Juan Jose Martí, a Valencian lawyer, produced a spurious sequel (1602), Alemán himself wrote a continuation (1604), in which he good-naturedly lampooned Martí. Alemán also wrote a biography of Saint Anthony of Padua (1604) and *Ortografía castellana* (1609), a treatise on spelling.

Alembert, Jean Le Rond d' (1717–1783). French mathematician and skeptical philosopher. He was the natural son of Mme. Claudine Guérin de TENCIN. As coeditor (1751–1759) with Diderot of the ENCYCLOPÉDIE, he wrote the *Discours préliminaire (Introduction)*, a veritable synthesis of human knowledge; numerous scientific, philosophical, and literary articles; and supervised all entries on mathematics. He was a member of the Academy of Science (1741), and the ACADÉMIE FRANÇAISE (1754), being secretary to the latter from 1772. He is best known for his *Traité de dynamique* (1743) and a history (1787) of the members of the French Academy who had died between 1700 and 1772.

Alencar, José Martiniano de (1829–1877). Brazilian novelist. Probably Brazil's finest romantic novelist, Alencar is known for his idealized portraits of Indians and for his deep feeling for the Brazilian landscape. His most popular novels are *O Guarani* (1857) and *Iracema* (1865), both of which deal with love between Indian and white.

Aleria. In the ORLANDO FURIOSO of Ariosto, an Amazon, one of ten married forcibly to GUIDONE SELVAGGIO (Guido the Savage) after he had killed the ten male champions of the Amazons who held him captive. Aleria, Guidone's favorite wife, helps him escape to join the armies of Charlemagne against the pagans.

Alete. In the GERUSALEMME LIBERATA of Tasso, an Egyptian ambassador who comes to the camp of Goffredo (Godfrey), the Christian commander, with Argante the infidel champion. He subtly tries to dissuade Goffredo from attacking Jerusalem, but when the attempt fails, he and Argante promptly declare war on the Crusaders.

Alexander (Aleksandros). The name given to Paris, son of Priam, by the shepherds who brought him up. Ironically, in view of its owner's character, the name means "protector of men."

Alexander VI, Pope. See BORGIA.

Alexander I (Aleksandr Pavlovich; 1777–1825). Czar of Russia (1801–1825). Alexander was given a liberal education by his grandmother Catherine the Great, and hopes were high in Russia that his reign would prove less despotic than that of his father, Paul I. However, Alexander showed little concern for reform. The invasion by Napoleon in 1812 and the subsequent years of war and political activity in Europe took up all of his attention. The renewed contact with Western political ideas, which the war brought about, once again stirred young Russians to thought and action. It was during this period that secret political groups were formed that finally made an unsuccessful attempt at a *coup d'état* in the DECEMBRIST REVOLT of 1825.

Alexander II (Aleksandr Nikolayevich; 1818–1881). Czar of Russia (1855–1881). Alexander II's reign was a period of major reform in Russia. In 1861 the long-awaited emancipation of the serfs took place. Three years later, elective assemblies (*zemstva*) were set up for local self-government. Judicial reforms, including public trial by jury, were also instituted. Despite these reforms, revolutionary activity increased. Several attempts were made on Alexander's life by the terrorist organization known as the People's Will (*Narodnaya volya*) before a successful attack on his life was made in March, 1881. Shortly before he was killed, Alexander had approved plans for an elective legislative assembly.

Alexander III (Aleksandr Aleksandrovich; 1845–1894). Czar of Russia (1881–1894). Alexander III was a conservative ruler, partially because of the influence of his former tutor and adviser, Konstantin POBEDONOSTZEV. Plans for constitutional government, which were begun by Alexander II, were dropped. Revolutionary agitation and terrorism continued, and the reign became a series of efforts by the regime to eradicate the revolutionaries and attempts on the latter on the life of the czar. A bomb plot in 1887 was squelched, and five of the conspirators were executed. Among these was Alexander Ulyanov, the older brother of Lenin, who reportedly swore vengeance for his brother's death.

Alexander, Sir William. Earl of **Stirling** (c. 1567–1640). Scottish poet. Alexander at one time held all of eastern Canada under royal grant, but died insolvent. A serious, plodding poet, he wrote sonnets, Senecan tragedies, and didactic poems. He is best known for *Doomsday* (1614), an epic poem in 12 books.

Alexander of Hales (c. 1175–1245). English theologian and scholastic philosopher, called "Doctor Irrefragabilis," a Franciscan after 1222. In his lectures at the University of Paris and in his Latin *Summa Universae Theologiae* he amalgamated the current Augustinianism of Christian doctrine with Aristotelian philosophy and the works of the Arabian commentators. His teaching greatly influenced St. Thomas Aquinas, St. Bonaventure, and others.

Alexander the Corrector. Self-assumed nickname of Alexander Cruden (1701–1770). A Scottish bookseller in London and compiler of the *Concordance to the Bible* (1737), he petitioned Parliament to constitute him "Corrector of the People." Confined on several occasions to an insane asylum, he developed a compulsion for carrying a sponge to wipe out licentious scrawls.

Alexander the Great (Alexander III of Macedon, 356–323 B.C.). The son of PHILIP OF MACEDON, and conqueror of the civilized world. He was appointed to his father's position as leader of the Greek confederation. He did away with his rivals to the throne, razing Thebes to the ground. He then began the invasion and conquest of Asia, and defeated Darius III, king of Persia. He marched through Syria, Egypt, Babylon, Susa, and Persepolis, founding the city of Alexandria in 331 B.C. Adopting the oriental customs of his captives, Alexander married a series of eastern princesses. On their way through India his exhausted troops rebelled, and Alexander was forced to begin the return to Macedon. He fell ill of a fever, and died after three days' illness at the age of 33. Alexander achieved the extension of Greek civilization into the East. His reign ushered in the Hellenistic Age. See BUCEPHALUS.

Admired for his courage and frequent generous and humane acts, Alexander figures in many English and French medieval romances. French heroic verse of six feet became known as the *Alexandrine*. Alexander's life is the subject of a tragedy by Racine (ALEXANDRE LE GRAND) and of Lyly's *Alexander and Campaspe* (1581).

Alexandre le Grand (Alexander the Great, 1665). A tragedy by Jean RACINE. Combining love and intrigue with historical details of Alexander's Indian campaign, the drama reaches its climax with Alexander's admiration for his betrayed enemy, the brave king Porus, and his consequent renunciation of the kingdom that he had conquered.

Alexandrian Library, the. The most famous library of antiquity. Located in Alexandria, it was, under the Ptolemies, the principal center of Hellenistic culture and contained hundreds of thousands of rolls. Among its earliest librarians were Callimachus and Apollonius of Rhodes. In his *Caesar and Cleopatra* G. B. Shaw treats humorously the burning of the library by Julius Caesar. It was burned and partly consumed in 391; and in 642, according to a dubious legend, the caliph Omar seized the city and used the library's books to "heat the baths of the city for six months." It is said that it contained 700,000 volumes, and the reason given by the Muslim destroyer for the destruction of the library was that the books were unnecessary in any case, for all knowledge that was necessary to man was contained in the Koran, and any knowledge contained in the library that was not in the Koran must be pernicious.

Alexandrian school. An academy of learning. It was founded about 310 B.C. by Ptolemy Soter, son of Lagus, and Demetrius of Phaleron; especially famous for its grammarians and mathematicians.

Alexandria Quartet, The. Four novels by Lawrence DURRELL: *Justine* (1957), *Balthazar* (1958), *Mountolive* (1958), and *Clea* (1960). The complex plot is made more complex by Durrell's attempt "to complete a four-decker novel whose form is based on the relativity proposition." Each novel presents a different point of view, and different truths about the same characters. Diaries and letters and novels-within-novels give still other views. *Justine* is about the love affair between the narrator, Darley, and the fascinating, enigmatic Justine. In *Balthazar* Darley learns, through Balthazar, a mutual friend, that Justine really loved his successful rival author, Pursewarden. Her apparently serene marriage to Nessim was really a cover for their illegal political activities—gun-running into British-held Palestine. *Mountolive* is a third-person novel (the "time" element in the relativity scheme) about a British diplomat in love with Nessim's mother but obliged to discover who is organizing the gun-running. *Clea,* narrated again by Darley, brings the threads of the story together and ends in an idyllic love between him and the serene painter, Clea.

Brilliant exotic and melodramatic episodes and a flamboyant poetical style enrich the works. Among the vivid characters are Melissa, a sad, lost night-club dancer; Narouz, a primitive, silent man who suddenly becomes a religious prophet; and Scobie, a comical old English homosexual. Durrell calls *The Quartet* "a big city poem." It is a wonderful evocation of Alexandria, an exotic and sordid city haunted by figures from its past, from the ancient alchemists to Antony and Cleopatra. *The Quartet* is also an investigation of modern love and a study of the growth of an artist.

Alexandrine. In prosody, a line of 6 iambic feet (iambic hexameter). The Alexandrine is the standard French heroic line, just as iambic pentameter is the standard line for English heroic verse. The name is thought to derive from *Li romans d'Alexandre*, a 12th-century French romance written in that measure relating the deeds of Alexander of Macedon. The Alexandrine was introduced in England by Michael Drayton and others in the 16th century, but never took root as a dominant measure in English poetry, perhaps because English, being an uninflected language, requires fewer syllables than French to express its meaning. However, the Alexandrine is used singly as the final line of the Spenserian stanza, where it affords a contrast to the predominant iambic pentameter.

Alexeyev, Konstantin Sergeyevich. See Konstantin STANISLAVSKI.

Alexis, Willibald. Pen name of **Wilhelm Häring** (1798–1871). German historical novelist. His early works *Walladmor* (1823) and *Schloss Avalon* (*Avalon Castle*, 1827) were strongly under the influence of Walter Scott and were even thought to be Scott's work in translation. Alexis' most famous later novel is *Ruhe ist die erste Bürgerpflicht* (*Quiet Is the First Civic Duty*, 1852), about the Napoleonic invasion of Germany.

Alexius Comnenus (1048–1118). Byzantine emperor (r. 1081–1118). He appealed to the West for military help against the Turks, giving impetus to the first of the CRUSADES. His daughter, **Anna Comnena** (1083–1148), wrote the *Alexiad* in Greek; although more a panegyric than a history of her father's career, it is an important source of information on this period.

Alfheim. In Scandinavian mythology, the region between heaven and earth inhabited by the elves.

Alfieri, Vittorio (1749–1803). Italian dramatist and poet. He wrote 19 tragedies (1775–1787) scrupulously observant of the classical unities and typified by a portrayal of the protagonist's struggle against moral and political tyranny. Among his dramas are *Cleopatra; Filippo,* whose protagonist is Philip II of Spain; *Antigone; Agamennone; Oreste; Virginia; Saul; Mirra;* and *Bruto Primo,* dedicated to George Washington, "the liberator of America," 1787. He also wrote sonnets and odes, five of which are grouped under the title *L'America Libera* (1781–1783) to celebrate the newly acquired independence of the U.S. In his lengthy and exciting *Vita* (*Autobiography*), he analyzed and exalted himself as a poet dedicated to the extirpation of all forms of political and intellectual bondage. His hatred of tyranny and love of freedom helped to revive the national spirit of Italy.

Alfonso X. Known as **El Sabio** ("The Sage" or "The Learned") (1221–1284). King of Castile and Leon (1252–1284), scholar, and poet. Alfonso is generally regarded as a political failure, his reign being marred by his futile attempts to capture the imperial crown and by a disastrous conflict with his second son, later Sancho IV. His true fame rests on his activities as a patron of art and learning. Scholars flocked to his court where, under his direction, they translated Arabic and Latin writings, copied manuscripts, and compiled historical, scientific, and legal works. Under his guidance, Castilian laws and customs were codified in *Las siete partidas,* begun about 1256, which presents a minute and accurate picture of 13th-century society. He was also responsible for

the compilation of the *Primera crónica general* or *Estoria de España,* a history of Spain from the deluge through the reign of Ferdinand III, Alfonso's father. Begun in 1270 and completed during the reign of Sancho IV, it is drawn from biblical, classical, and Arabic sources as well as from Spanish chronicles and epics, such as the *Poema de mio Cid.* Many scholarly and literary works are also ascribed to Alfonso's authorship, notably the charming *Cantigas de Santa María,* over 400 poems in Galician in honor of the Virgin.

Alfred, called **the Great** (c. 849–c. 900). King of Wessex in England (871–900). He began fighting against the Danes in 866 under his brother Aethelred, completing his first series of battles the year of his accession to the throne. He repulsed further attacks in 878 and between 893 and 897, when the Danes were defeated and retreated toward the north or into France.

Aside from his military successes, which made possible his successors' reconquest and unification of the rest of England, Alfred is known for the excellence of his domestic rule. He codified the laws and established a court school with scholars from abroad to promote the education of his people. He began a great translation project, determined to make available in Old English vernacular prose all the books he considered important, which then existed only in Latin. He himself translated Pope Gregory I's *Pastoral Care,* the world history by OROSIUS, and the *Consolation of Philosophy* by Boethius. His *Blostman* ("blossoms," i.e. "anthology") is largely culled from the *Soliloquies* of St. Augustine of Hippo. He had other scholars translate Gregory's *Dialogues* and Bede's *Ecclesiastical History of the English People,* and undertake the writing of the ANGLO-SAXON CHRONICLE. See also ASSER.

Algeciras Conference (1906). An international meeting at Algeciras, Spain. It was held largely at the urging of Kaiser Wilhelm II, who sought to curb French influence in Morocco. The conference members supported France.

Alger, Horatio, Jr. (1832–1899). American writer of books for boys. The oldest child of a Unitarian minister, Alger attended Harvard College and Harvard Divinity School, but fled to Paris as a rebellious bohemian. He was finally persuaded to return to the U.S. and became a minister. In 1866 he was made chaplain of a Newsboys' Lodging House, to which he devoted his time, money, and affection for the rest of his life.

Although Alger wished to write novels for adults, he actually turned out about 120 books for boys. Among the most popular were the *Ragged Dick Series* (1867), the *Luck and Pluck Series* (1869), and the *Tattered Tom Series* (1871). The heroes were bootblacks or newsboys whose virtue was invariably rewarded with riches and success. Alger also wrote juvenile biographies of famous men.

Algerine Captive, The (1797). An early American novel by Royall TYLER. It recounts the adventures of the hero, Updike Underhill, in his native New England backwoods, in Philadelphia where he meets Franklin, in London where he sees Tom Paine, and finally as a captive among the Algerines. The book is famed chiefly for its preface, which contained the first significant plea for native American fiction.

Algonquian or Algonkian. A linguistic family of widely distributed American Indian tribes whose territory stretched from Newfoundland to the Rocky Mountains. The tribes were mainly agricultural and sedentary.

Algren, Nelson (1909–   ). American novelist and short-story writer. Best known for his novel THE MAN WITH THE GOLDEN ARM, Algren is identified with the realistic school centered in Chicago; that city's west-side slums have been the principal inspiration of his work. His other works include *Somebody in Boots* (1935); *Never Come Morning* (1942); *The Neon Wilderness* (1947), a collection of short stories; *A Walk on the Wild Side* (1956); and *Who Lost an American?* (1963), a book of essays and travel pieces.

Alhambra. A citadel and palace at Granada, Spain, built by Moorish kings in the 13th century. Its name is derived from the Arabic *ḳal'-at al hamra* ("the red castle"). The buildings stand on a plateau some 35 acres in area and are surrounded by a reddish brick wall. Considered one of the finest examples of Moorish architecture in Spain, the palace consists largely of two rectangular courts:—the Court of the Pool or of the Myrtles and the Court of the Lions, —and their adjoining chambers. The latter court contains a famous central fountain, consisting of an alabaster basin supported by 12 lions of white marble. While he was an attaché at the American legation in Madrid, Washington Irving spent much time in the Alhambra and wrote a well-known volume of sketches and tales called *Legends of the Alhambra* (1832, 1852).

Ali Baba and the Forty Thieves. One of the most popular stories in the *Arabian Nights.* Hidden in a tree, the poor woodcutter Ali Baba sees a band of robbers enter a secret cave by saying the magic words, "Open Sesame." When they leave, he repeats the spell, gains access to the treasure, and becomes rich by carrying off gold from the stolen hoards. His brother, Cassim, also discovers the secret but forgets the word "Sesame" and cries "Open, Wheat! Open, Barley" to the door; he is killed by the thieves who find him trapped within the cave. Their captain tries several schemes to catch Ali Baba, but is always outwitted by the woodcutter's female slave, MORGIANA, who kills the whole band by pouring boiling oil into the jars where they have hidden themselves.

Alibert, François Paul (1873–   ). French poet. His works, primarily classical despite symbolist influence, include *L'Arbre qui saigne* (1907), *Odes* (1922), *Eglogues* (1923), and *Elégies romaines* (1923).

Alice Adams (1921). A novel by Booth TARKINGTON. It describes the disintegration of the middle-class Adams family in a small Midwestern town. The father, a minor employee in a drug company, has a nagging, ambitious wife and a shiftless son. Alice, his daughter, yearning for wealth and admiration and seeing herself always in a romantic role, almost deceives herself into believing that her fanciful explanations for the crudities of her family are valid. At the end of the book, her hopes doomed, she is seen bravely entering the stairway that leads to Frincke's Business College.

Alice's Adventures in Wonderland (1865). A whimsical story by Lewis CARROLL. The little girl Alice falls down a well into a strange country where everything happens with a fantastic illogicality. She finds that she can become a giantess or pygmy by nibbling alternate sides of a magic mushroom, and she has a series of remarkable adventures with the WHITE RABBIT, the CHESHIRE CAT, the MOCK TURTLE, the QUEEN OF HEARTS, the HATTER, the MARCH HARE, the DUCHESS, the DORMOUSE, and other strange characters. See THROUGH THE LOOKING-GLASS, and FATHER WILLIAM.

Alice W---n. The old love conjured up by Charles Lamb in his DREAM CHILDREN: A REVERIE as the mother of his imaginary children. She has been identified as the actress Frances Maria Kelly.

Alien and Sedition Acts (1798). 3 congressional acts that gave the president power to deport or imprison any alien considered dangerous to the nation, and to punish any person engaging in treasonable acts or issuing writings considered to be seditious. These measures were directed by the Federalists against propagandists for the French Revolution and the Democratic-Republican Party in the U.S.

Aljubarrota. A village in Portugal, some 40 miles north of Lisbon. It was the site of a battle (1385) between the forces of John I of Portugal and those of John I of Castile. The Portuguese routed the enemy, firmly establishing the independence that they had first won three centuries earlier.

Allah. The Arabic name of the Supreme Being, from *al,* the, and *illah,* god. *Allah il Allah,* the Muslim war cry, and also the first clause of the confession of faith, is a corruption of *la illah illa allah,* meaning "there is no God but the God."

The Garden of Allah. A novel by Robert Hichens (1904), the title of which refers to a region of the Sahara Desert.

Allan-a-Dale, Allin-a-Dale, or **Allen-a-Dale.** A minstrel in the Robin Hood ballads, who appears also in Scott's novel *Ivanhoe* (1820). He is assisted by Robin Hood in carrying off his bride when she is on the point of being married against her will to a rich old knight.

allegory. In literature, an extended METAPHOR in which characters, objects, incidents, and descriptions carry one or more sets of fully developed meanings in addition to the apparent and literal ones. John Bunyan's *Pilgrim's Progress,* for example, is apparently about a man named Christian who leaves his home and journeys to the Heavenly City. However, it is clear that Christian stands for any Christian man, and the incidents of his journey represent the temptations and trials that beset any Christian man throughout his life on earth.

Allegory has been a favorite form all over the world, and was particularly strong in Europe during the Middle Ages. Spenser's *Faerie Queene* (1590–1596), though late, is perhaps the best-known example.

In art, especially of the Middle Ages, allegory was also a favorite device: in particular it was used to depict good and evil engaged in symbolic action. See PERSONIFICATION.

Allegro, L' (1632). A poem by John MILTON, the title of which means literally the cheerful or merry one. It is a pastoral idyl, celebrating a mood

of gaiety and contrasting with the author's IL PEN-
SEROSO. The poem, like its companion piece, is written in Milton's early style, characterized by an Elizabethan freshness and vividness and a remarkable
command of verbal music.

Allen, Ethan (1738–1789). American Revolutionary soldier and hero of early Vermont. He commanded the Green Mountain Boys, a regiment originally raised by some Vermont settlers to fight a
claim on their land by Governor Tryon of New
York. With 83 of the Green Mountain Boys and
aided by Benedict Arnold, Allen seized Fort Ticonderoga in 1775. His own *Narrative of Captain
Ethan Allen's Captivity* tells of his capture by the
British after a rash attempt to take Montreal. He is
the hero of Daniel Pierce Thompson's novel *Green
Mountain Boys* (1839).

Allen, Frederick Lewis (1890–1954). American
editor and writer. On the editorial staffs successively
of the *Atlantic Monthly* and *Century Magazine*, he
joined *Harper's Magazine* in 1921 and later became
its editor in chief. He is also known for his lively social histories: *Only Yesterday* (1931), an account of
the 1920's in the U.S.; *Since Yesterday* (1940), a similar treatment of the 1930's; and *The Big Change*
(1952), an account of the transformation of the U.S.
from 1900 to 1950.

Allen, [William] Hervey (1889–1949). American historical novelist. He is best known for his first
novel, the long and phenomenally successful
ANTHONY ADVERSE. Allen began his career with several volumes of verse and also wrote *Israfel* (1926),
a biography of Edgar Allan Poe.

Allen, James Lane (1849–1925). American nov-
elist and short-story writer. He is noted for the
Kentucky setting of his books, among them A KEN-
TUCKY CARDINAL, *Aftermath* (1896), and *The Choir
Invisible* (1897), an historical romance of pioneer
Kentucky. *Flute and Violin* (1891) is a collection of
Kentucky short stories. Allen also wrote the sketches
of *The Blue-Grass Region of Kentucky* (1892).

Allen, Ralph (1694–1764). A noted English phi-
lanthropist, friend and benefactor of both Pope and
Fielding. Fielding may have depicted him as Squire
ALLWORTHY in *Tom Jones,* and Pope wrote of him:

> Let humble Allen, with an awkward shame,
> Do good by stealth, and blush to find it fame.

All for Love, or The World Well Lost (1678).
A tragedy in blank verse by John DRYDEN. In strict
observance of the classical unities, Dryden describes the last day on earth of Antony and Cleopatra. Simpler in plot, though less stirring than
Shakespeare's version of the famous story, Dryden's
play focusses on the conflict between Cleopatra, on
the one hand, and Antony's wife, Octavia, his general Ventidius, and his friend Dolabella on the
other, as they vie for possession of Antony's soul.

All God's Chillun Got Wings (1924). A play
by Eugene O'NEILL. White Ella Downey marries
Negro Jim Harris, who is struggling to become a
lawyer. The tragic consequences of her mental inferiority are intensified by the latent racial prejudice she shows in a desperate effort to gain superiority before lapsing into insanity and a regression to
childhood.

All Hallows' Day. See ALL SAINTS' DAY.

All Hallows' Eve. See HALLOWE'EN.

Allingham, William (1824–1889). Irish poet,
best known for light lyrics employing Irish folk
lore and dialect. He was briefly editor of *Fraser's
Magazine* (1874–1879) and much esteemed as a
critic by Dante Gabriel Rossetti and Coventry Pat-
more. He published over a dozen volumes of poetry,
perhaps the most famous of which is *The Fairies*
(1883).

alliteration. In poetry and prose, the repetition of consonants, especially initial consonants, as
in the sentence "Peter Piper picked a peck of pickled
peppers." Like ASSONANCE and CONSONANCE, alliteration tends to unify the passage or poem in which it
occurs, and in that function may be considered a
form of RHYME.

Alliterative Morte Arthur, The. See ARTHUR-
IAN LEGENDS.

alliterative verse. Form of versification of Old
English poetry such as *Beowulf,* similar to that of
some early medieval Continental poetry. In Old
English (or Anglo-Saxon) poetry, each line has
four accented syllables and a varying number of
unaccented syllables, divided into two halves of two
strong stresses each. There must be alliteration between at least one stressed syllable in the first half
and one in the second; preferably three, and sometimes all four, of the accented syllables in a line are
alliterative. The use of this form declined under the
influence of the strictly syllabic meters and rhyme
schemes in French and Italian poetry; it was revived,
however, during the 14th century in such works as
Piers Plowman and *Sir Gawain and the Green
Knight.* Poets of the late 19th and 20th centuries
have adapted alliterative verse in the trend away
from conventional toward accentual meters.

All Men Are Brothers. See SHUI HU CHUAN.

All Quiet on the Western Front (Im Westen
nichts Neues; 1929). A novel by Erich Maria
REMARQUE. It is the best known of the antiwar literature written during the period 1920–1939, expressing the horror and futility of war.

All Saints' Day or **All Hallows.** A feast in
honor of all Christian saints. Between 603 and 610
Pope Boniface IV changed the heathen temple called
the Pantheon into a Christian church, and dedicated
it to the honor of all the martyrs. The feast was first
observed on May 1, but in 834 it was changed to
November 1, and its use extended to the whole
Christian Church. It is a major feast of the Church.

The medieval English name *All Hallows* is derived from *halig,* Old English for holy (man), hence,
a saint. In France the day is called *Toussaint.* Much
folk lore and superstition are associated with the
eve of the day, called HALLOWE'EN.

All Souls' Day. The popular name for the
Commemoration of All the Faithful Departed. It
is observed by the Roman Catholic Church on November 2. It was instituted by Abbot Odilo of Cluny
in 993 and soon spread to the rest of the Western
Church. In many parts of Europe it is the custom
to place lighted candles on graves of friends and
family the previous evening.

All's Well that Ends Well (c. 1602). A comedy
by William SHAKESPEARE. After curing the king of
France of a malady, Helena, the daughter of a fa-

mous physician, is rewarded by the king's giving her in marriage to BERTRAM, the young count of Rousillon, whom she has long loved. He, however, scorns her and departs for the Florentine war, stating that until Helena obtains the ring on his finger and produces his child, he will not return nor can she call him husband. Disguised as a pilgrim, Helena follows Bertram to Florence, where she discovers that he is enamored of a young Florentine girl. She arranges an assignation and takes the girl's place, obtaining the ring and conceiving the child. Hearing false reports of Helena's death, Bertram returns to France. When she suddenly appears, having fulfilled his terms, she at last wins his love.

The plot is taken from Boccaccio's *Decameron* and was a familiar folk legend reworked by Shakespeare. See countess of ROUSILLON; PAROLLES.

All the King's Men (1946). A novel by Robert Penn WARREN. Jack Burden, a young intellectual, narrates the story of the rise and fall of Willie Stark, a Southern demagogue obviously modeled on the Louisiana politician Huey Long. Burden is forced to confront the problem of good and evil in Stark's career and at the end of the book is led to a new self-understanding. The novel won a Pulitzer Prize.

Allworthy, Squire [Thomas]. In Henry Fielding's TOM JONES, a wealthy justice of the peace, foster father to the foundling Tom Jones. One of the best-known characters in English fiction, he is a man of sturdy rectitude, modesty, and benevolence, completely disinterested as regards money and fame. He is strongly contrasted with his neighbor Squire WESTERN. Fielding's friend Ralph ALLEN is believed to have been the model for Squire Allworthy.

Bridget Allworthy. The sister of Squire Allworthy, who, as it turns out, is the mother of Tom Jones.

Alma. See FAERIE QUEENE, THE.

Almagest (Arab. article *al*, Gr. *megiste*, greatest). An astronomical treatise by the 2d century Alexandrian scholar PTOLEMY. The work was extensively used during the Middle Ages in an Arabic translation.

Almanach de Gotha. A European social register. A German periodical publication begun in 1763, it gives data on all royal or titled European families.

Almanack, Poor Richard's. See POOR RICHARD'S ALMANACK.

Almaviva, Count and Countess. Leading characters in Beaumarchais' comedies THE BARBER OF SEVILLE and THE MARRIAGE OF FIGARO and in the operas based upon them.

Almayer's Folly (1895). A novel by Joseph CONRAD. Almayer, an English trader in the (then) Dutch East Indies, is moved by two passions: the desire to find gold and love for his half-caste daughter. "Almayer's Folly" is an absurdly fine house he moves into after his daughter has gone away with a Malay prince. See OUTCAST OF THE ISLANDS, AN.

Alnaschar. In the story the "Barber's Fifth Night" in the *Arabian Nights,* the visionary character who invests all his money in a basket of glassware, which he fancies will bring him wealth and the vizier's daughter. As he dreams of the grand life he will lead, he grows angry with his supposed wife, upsets his basket, and smashes all the wares that have started his visions of wealth. Hence, an *Alnaschar dream* is counting one's chickens before they are hatched.

Alonso. The king of Naples and father of the innocent Ferdinand in Shakespeare's THE TEMPEST. Alonso's greed and enmity toward Prospero caused him to accept the tributes of Antonio, Prospero's brother, and to endorse the usurpation of Prospero's dukedom.

Alonso, Dámaso (1898–). Spanish poet and scholar. A translator of Joyce and Eliot, Alonso is known for his poetry, particularly the volumes *Poemas puros; poemillas de la ciudad* (1921) and *Hijos de la ira* (1944), the latter being a treatment of religion in the modern poetic idiom. As a scholar and literary critic he is known for his studies of the Spanish baroque poet Góngora, particularly *La lengua poética de Góngora* (1935).

Alonzo the Brave. A ballad by Matthew Gregory LEWIS which first appeared in his novel, THE MONK. It is a variant of the widespread traditional theme of the specter lover, popularized in the ballad *Lenore* by Gottfried August Bürger. Imogen was betrothed to Alonzo, but, during his absence in the wars, became the bride of another. At the wedding feast Alonzo's ghost sat beside the bride, and, after rebuking her for her infidelity, carried her off to the grave.

alpha and **omega.** The first and last letters of the Greek alphabet; hence the beginning and the end. In the Bible, Jesus says, "I am Alpha and Omega, the beginning and the end, the first and the last" (Rev. 22:13).

Alroy, David. A half-mythical Jewish medieval prince, local governor of his people under Muslim rule, with the title, Prince of the Captivity. He is the hero of Benjamin Disraeli's prose romance, *The Wondrous Tale of Alroy* (1833).

Alsop, Joseph [Wright] (1910–) and **Stewart [Johonnot Oliver]** (1914–). American journalists. From 1945 to 1958 the two brothers wrote "Matter of Fact," a syndicated newspaper column on politics. After 1958, when Stewart became a contributing editor and later Washington editor for the *Saturday Evening Post,* Joseph continued the column alone.

Alsop, Richard (1761–1815). American satirical poet, a member of the group known as the HARTFORD WITS. Alsop frequently collaborated with Theodore Dwight, Lemuel Hopkins, and others in the two series of Federalist verse satire known as *The Echo* (1791–1805) and *The Political Greenhouse* (1798).

Also sprach Zarathustra. See THUS SPAKE ZARATHUSTRA.

Altamira. Site near Santander, Spain, of a cave decorated with paleolithic mural paintings. It was discovered in 1879.

Altamirano, Ignacio Manuel (1834–1893). Mexican novelist and poet. A full-blooded Indian, Altamirano was an adherent of Benito Juárez and fought against the French intervention in Mexico. In 1869, he founded *Renacimiento,* a review to encourage literary activity, almost moribund after 15 years of turbulence. He became the mentor of the younger generation, to whom he advocated the importance of creating a literature rooted in national life. His poetry consists of a single volume of *Rimas* (1880), written before 1867 and notable for its description of the Mexican landscape. Altamirano's preoccupation with purely Mexican scenes and customs is also evident in the prose works for which he is best known: *Clemencia* (1869), a love story set against the background of the French intervention; *La navidad en las montañas* (1870), a novelette; and *El Zarco* (1901), a novel dealing with bandits in the state of Morelos.

Altamoro (Altamore). A fierce Saracen warrior in the GERUSALEMME LIBERATA of Tasso. He leads the Persian and African forces against the Christian armies at Jerusalem and is also a champion of Armida, who has sworn to give herself to any infidel knight who kills Rinaldo of Este. It is he who surrenders the remnants of the pagan armies to the Christian general Goffredo, signalling the final victory of the Crusaders at the holy city.

Alton Locke, Tailor and Poet (1850). A novel by the Rev. Charles KINGSLEY. This novel won for the author the title of The Chartist Clergyman (see CHARTISM) because of its picture of Alton Locke and his radical Chartist friends who move through the depressed regions of the London sweatshops. It was one of the first English novels to present a study of industrial conditions.

Altruria. See A TRAVELLER FROM ALTRURIA.

Alvarez, A[lfred] (1929–). English poet and critic, a follower of William EMPSON. *The Shaping Spirit* (1958) and *The School of Donne* (1962) are books of criticism.

Alvarez Quintero, Serafín (1871–1938) and **Joaquín** (1873–1944). Spanish dramatists, brothers who collaborated in their work. The brothers Álvarez Quintero are known for their light and amusing comedies; the best known of the more than 100 written are *Los galeotos* (1900), *El patio* (1900), *El amor que pasa* (1904), and *Doña Clarinés* (1909).

Alvaro, Corrado (1895–1956). Italian novelist, poet, essayist, and moralist. Alvaro was a world traveler who wrote several books of verse and travel, the latter noted for the author's keen perception and description of people, places, and customs. His numerous short stories have been collected in *Revolt in Aspromonte* (*Gente in Aspromonte;* 1930). For the most part these tales describe the hard, primitive life of Calabrian shepherds. His finest novels are *Man is Strong* (*L'Uomo E' Forte;* 1938) and *L'Età E' Breve* (1946), the first book of a three-novel cycle entitled *Memorie del Mondo Sommerso* describing Italian political and cultural life during the fascist period.

Alvaro, Don. (1) The husband of Mencia of Mosquera in Le Sage's GIL BLAS DE SANTILLANE.

(2) A character in Verdi's opera *La Forza del Destino*.

(3) A character in the romantic drama *Don Alvaro o La fuerza del sino* by Angel de Saavedra y Ramírez, duke of Rivas.

Alving, Oswald. The principal character in Ibsen's GHOSTS. A neurotic and dissipated young man, he becomes insane from congenital syphilis. His mother, embittered by her experiences, is in revolt against a society in which such conditions exist.

Amadís de Gaula (Amadis of Gaul). A 16th-century Spanish romance of chivalry. The first extant version (1508), consisting of four books, was compiled by Garci Ordóñez or Rodríguez Montalvo, a *regidor* of Medina del Campo, who stated that he was merely revising the original text; however, the fourth book is his own addition. The origin of the story is still obscure, though it was known in both Spain and Portugal at least as early as the 14th century.

The romance incorporates many details from the Breton cycle of the Round Table. Amadís, who exemplifies the chivalric ideals of valor, purity, and fidelity, is the illegitimate son of Perión, king of Gaul (Wales) and Elisena, princess of Brittany. Soon after birth he is abandoned by his mother, who puts his cradle in the sea; for this reason he is also known as *el Doncel del Mar,* or "Child of the Sea." He is rescued by the knight Gandalés and is educated in the court of the king of Scotland, where at the age of 12 he falls in love with Oriana, daughter of Lisuarte, king of England. Amadís then performs a series of incredible exploits, triumphing over sundry giants and monsters, but he always remains faithful to his lady-love. Other notable characters include Galaor, Amadís' brother; his cousin Agrajes; the Fairy Urganda, *la Desconocida,* or "the Unknown"; and Archeläus, a mischievous enchanter.

The work won enormous popularity throughout Europe and inspired numerous sequels and imitations, including Montalvo's *Las sergas de Esplandián* (1510) about the son of Amadís. The barber and priest in Cervantes' *Don Quixote* called it "the best of all the books of its kind," a verdict in which later generations have concurred.

Amado, Jorge (1912–). Brazilian novelist. In a series of novels beginning with *O País do Carnaval* (1931), Amado explores various aspects of life in his native state of Bahia. His works reflect his Marxist political views in their sympathy for the downtrodden and their keen awareness of social injustice. His best-known novels are probably *Terras do Sem Fim* (*The Violent Land,* 1942), about the cacao boom in the frontier districts of Bahia, and *Gabriela, Cravo e Canela* (*Gabriela, Clove and Cinnamon,* 1958), about social and political change in the

Illustration from a 1533 edition of *Amadis de Gaula.*

city of Ilheus in 1925–1926. Among his other novels are *Suor* (1934), *Jubiabá* (1935), and *Mar Morto* (1936).

Amahl and the Night Visitors. A one-act opera by Gian Carlo MENOTTI. It was written (1951) for production on television. Amahl, a crippled boy, adds his crutch to the gifts of the Magi and is cured.

Amaimon. One of the chief devils in medieval demonology. He is king of the eastern portion of hell; Asmodeus is his chief officer. He can be restrained from doing harm from the third hour until noon and from the ninth hour until evening.

Amalia (1851–1855). A novel by José Mármol (1817–1871), Argentine poet and novelist. Written while Mármol was in exile in Uruguay, the book is an impassioned denunciation of the barbarism and terror of the dictatorship of Juan Manuel de ROSAS. Although the plot is melodramatic and the principal characters are one-dimensional, Mármol's descriptions of life in Buenos Aires and of actual personages, such as the dictator himself, are vivid and convincing.

Amalthea. In Roman legend, the sybil who sold the sibylline books to Tarquin.

Amaltheia. The goat that suckled the infant Zeus in the cave in the Cretan mountain Dicte. Her horn became the *cornucopia*, the horn of plenty that has been a symbol of the earth's bounty since very ancient times.

Amanda. See PEREGRINE PICKLE.

Amants magnifiques, Les (The Magnificent Lovers, 1670). A COMÉDIE-BALLET in prose by MOLIÈRE. Written for the king and based on a subject chosen by him, the play recounts amid songs and dances the courtship of a princess by two princes and her preference for a lowly soldier.

Amaryllis. A rustic sweetheart. The name is borrowed from a shepherdess in the pastorals of Theocritus and Vergil. In Spenser's *Colin Clout's Come Home Again,* Amaryllis is intended for Alice Spenser, countess of Derby.

Amasis, ring of. Herodotus relates that Polycrates, tyrant of Samos, was so fortunate in everything that Amasis, king of Egypt, fearing such unprecedented luck boded ill, advised him to part with something which he highly prized. Polycrates accordingly threw into the sea a ring of great value. A few days afterwards, a fish was presented to the tyrant, in which the ring was found. Amasis now renounced friendship with Polycrates, as a man doomed by the gods; and not long afterwards, a Persian satrap put the too fortunate despot to death by crucifixion.

Amavia. See FAERIE QUEENE, THE.

Amazons (Amazones). A mythical race of women warriors. Ancient accounts differ as to where they lived; Herodotus places them in Scythia, north of the Black Sea; Apollonius Rhodius' *Argonautica* has them inhabiting a portion of the south shore. According to the legend, they were a hardy lot, burning off their right breasts in order that they might draw the bow better. They either destroyed or sent away any male children they had as a result of encounters with neighboring tribes. There are among the Greek myths many legends of encounters with them. HERACLES fought them in order to acquire the girdle worn by their queen, Hippolyta. He acquired it either by killing Hippolyta or by capturing her general, Melanippe, and holding her for ransom. Theseus also fought the Amazons and made one of them, either named HIPPOLYTA or Antiope, his wife. His son Hippolytus was their offspring. Hippolyta appears as the wife of Theseus, duke of Athens, in Shakespeare's *A Midsummer Night's Dream.*

Ambassadors, The (1903). A novel by Henry JAMES. The central character and first "ambassador," Lambert Strether, is sent to Paris by Mrs. Newsome, a wealthy widow whom he plans to marry, in order to persuade her son Chad to come home. Chad is deeply involved with a charming French woman, Madame de Vionnet, and the novel deals chiefly with Strether's gradual conversion to the idea that life may hold more real meaning for Chad in Paris than in Woollett, Mass. Strether comes to this conclusion in spite of his discovery that Chad and Mme de Vionnet are, in fact, more than just good friends. After the arrival of a second ambassador, Chad's sister Sarah, Strether decides to return to Woollett, urging Chad to remain in Paris. The essence of the novel is in Strether's remark, "Live all you can; it's a mistake not to."

ambiguous oath. A folklore motif, especially popular in medieval literature. An outstanding example may be found in the legend of TRISTAN AND ISEULT. Setting forth for the trial that is to determine whether she is guilty of a love affair with Tristan, Iseult sends word to Tristan to disguise himself as a poor pilgrim and meet her on the way. At her request, he then carries her across a stream so that she will not get wet. She is then able to swear at the trial that no one but King Mark (her husband) and "that poor pilgrim" who carried her across the stream has ever held her in his arms. She is subsequently absolved.

Ambler, Eric (1909–   ). English novelist and screenwriter. Ambler is best known for his realistic novels of espionage, usually dealing with ordinary Englishmen who find themselves enmeshed in a web of international intrigue. These include *Epitaph for a Spy* (1938), *The Mask of Dimitrios* (1939; U.S. title, *The Coffin of Dimitrios*), *Journey into Fear* (1940), *Judgment on Deltchev* (1951), and *Passage of Arms* (1959).

Ambrose. A tavern keeper. His name suggested the title for the celebrated NOCTES AMBROSIANAE, a series of imaginary conversations chiefly by Christopher North (John Wilson), published in *Blackwood's Magazine.* The blue parlor of Ambrose's Hotel in Edinburgh was in reality a rendezvous for Wilson and his friends, although the Ambrosian Nights were largely imaginary.

Ambrose, St. (c. 340–397). Bishop of Milan (374–397) and one of the Fathers of the Latin Church. A constant champion of the Church in its conflicts with paganism and the various early heresies, Ambrose was instrumental in driving the Arians out of Italy. He baptized Augustine of Hippo, who later became St. Augustine.

ambrosia (Gr. *a*, privative, *brotos,* mortal). The food of the gods. It is so called because it made them immortal. Anything delicious to the taste or fragrant in perfume is so called from the notion that whatever is used by the celestials must be excellent.

In actuality, ambrosia was probably the common and rather primitive cereal food of early Greece.

Ambrosio, or the Monk. See MONK, THE.

Amelia (1751). A novel by Henry FIELDING. Amelia, the idealized heroine, is the long-suffering, virtuous wife of Captain Booth, an impoverished army officer who has been unjustly thrown into prison. During his absence, his false friend Captain James makes overtures to Amelia, but her virtue prevails against him. In prison with Captain Booth is Miss Matthews, an adventuress who lures him into an affair, leaving him conscience-stricken. He is released from prison and Amelia forgives him, but soon after, he is thrown into debtor's prison for gambling. The situation is saved when Amelia receives an inheritance, and the two retire to the country to live a peaceful life.

Amélie. A character invented by Pierre Corneille in his tragedy CINNA. She encourages Cinna to lead a conspiracy against the emperor Augustus and is the cause of jealous friction between Cinna and his coconspirator MAXIME.

Amen, Ammon, Amun, or Amen-Ra. Among the ancient Egyptians, a deity usually represented as a man with a crown of two long plumes, and sometimes with a ram's head on a man's body. Originally a minor local deity of Thebes, he was brought into prominence about 2000 B.C. when his name was joined with that of RA, the sun god. As the composite figure Amen-Ra, he reigned as supreme King of the Gods; Amen appealed to the Theban patriot; Ra to the educated man. His oracle was in the Libyan oasis where Alexander the Great was told he was the son of Ammon. The Greeks identified Amen with Zeus.

America. Designation for both North and South America. Loose usage applies it chiefly to the U.S. Its origin is the name of Amerigo VESPUCCI, a Florentine merchant and traveler who claimed to have made a voyage in 1497 during which he discovered what is now the mainland of South America. His claim, although never proved, was perpetuated in the name given to the new continent in the West.

American, The (1877). A novel by Henry JAMES. Christopher Newman, a wealthy, self-made American in France, hopes to marry Claire de Cintré, a widowed daughter of the De Bellegardes, but that aristocratic old French family finally succeeds in circumventing him. Although Newman plans to retaliate by publishing proof that Claire's mother and brother were the virtual murderers of her father, he decides to give up his design because revenge is "really not his game." Both the contrast between the simple, innocent American and the sophisticated, corrupt European, and the necessity for renunciation later became common Jamesian themes.

American Academy of Arts and Letters. The inner circle of the National Institute of Arts and Letters. The latter, founded in 1898, created the smaller society to honor its more distinguished members. The first seven men elected to its membership were William Dean Howells, Augustus Saint-Gaudens, E. C. Stedman, John La Farge, Mark Twain, John Hay, and Edward MacDowell. The aim of the academy is to give "the stamp of its approval" to the

best in literature and art that both the past and the present have to offer.

American Caravan, The (1927-1936). An annual publication of American poetry and fiction. Its aim was to exhibit the best of contemporary literature, and its first editor was Van Wyck Brooks. He was followed by Lewis Mumford, Alfred Kreymborg, and Paul Rosenfeld. A number of well-known writers, including Ernest Hemingway, were represented in its pages.

American Civil War (1861-1865). A war between the U.S. and 11 Southern states which seceded from the Union and formed the Confederate States of America. The war was the result of longstanding social and economic differences between North and South that gradually became apparent after the War of 1812. Sectional conflict over such issues as the tariff and the extension of slavery was temporarily abated by the activities of men such as Henry CLAY and Daniel WEBSTER, but in the 1850's the position of each side became progressively more rigid; whether the war could have been averted is still a subject for discussion among historians.

Upon receiving the news of Abraham LINCOLN's election in 1860, South Carolina seceded, followed by 10 other Southern states, which then organized the Confederate government and elected Jefferson DAVIS president early in 1861; with the Confederate attack on Fort SUMTER, the actual fighting began. To the North, the principal objective was the preservation of the Union, though emancipation of the slaves became a secondary aim after 1862.

Although Union hopes for a quick victory were dashed by the rout at BULL RUN, it gradually became evident that, despite the brilliant leadership of such Confederate generals as Robert E. LEE and Thomas ("Stonewall") JACKSON, the superior human and industrial resources of the North would ultimately prevail. This was especially true after the Union victory at GETTYSBURG and Gen. GRANT's successful siege of Vicksburg (1863) ended Confederate hopes of securing foreign recognition and aid. In 1864, Grant, now supreme commander of the Union forces, turned to the conquest of Richmond, the Confederate capital, while W. T. SHERMAN undertook his famous march to the sea. After a gallant defense, Lee was forced to evacuate Richmond (April 2, 1865) and surrendered to Grant at Appomattox Courthouse, Va., on April 9.

With the possible exception of the Napoleonic Wars, no other conflict has produced more books. Among the most famous of the novels inspired by the war are Stephen Crane's RED BADGE OF COURAGE, Winston Churchill's THE CRISIS, and Margaret Mitchell's GONE WITH THE WIND. Other novelists who wrote about the war include Thomas Nelson PAGE, Mary JOHNSTON, Ellen GLASGOW, and MacKinlay KANTOR. Verse dealing with the war was written by such poets as Henry TIMROD, Paul Hamilton HAYNE, John Greenleaf WHITTIER, Walt WHITMAN, and Stephen Vincent BENÉT. Edmund Wilson's *Patriotic Gore* (1962) consists of essays about 19th-century Civil War literature.

See John BROWN; George B. McCLELLAN; SHILOH; ANTIETAM.

American Crisis, The. A series of 16 pamphlets written by Thomas PAINE between 1776 and

1783, widely distributed in the American colonies and touching on all of the important issues of the Revolution. The famous first *Crisis* paper, beginning, "These are the times that try men's souls," was ordered by Washington to be read to his troops on the eve of the battle of Trenton. In later *Crisis* papers, Paine called for a strong federal union.

American Democrat, The, or Hints on the Social and Civic Relations of the United States of America (1838). A political essay by James Fenimore COOPER, written on his return to New York, after a seven-year stay in Europe. Although a firm democrat, Cooper opposed a tyranny of the majority. Socially conservative, he favored an aristocracy of landowners; this cultured class would maintain stable values in American society. The book is Cooper's fullest statement of his beliefs, and is one of a series of volumes in which he criticizes the politics and manners of his countrymen. The other books are *A Letter to His Countrymen* (1834), *Homeward Bound* (1838), *Home as Found* (1838), and THE MONIKINS.

Cooper's outspoken criticism caused him to be denounced in the American press; acting as his own lawyer, he fought and won many libel suits. Although he lost most of his fortune, he helped to codify the libel laws of the U.S.

American Language, The (1919, 1921, 1923, 1936; *Supplement One*, 1945; *Supplement Two*, 1948). A treatise by H. L. MENCKEN. Believing at first that the American language and English were diverging, Mencken found that by 1923 American had become the more powerful tongue and was leading English along with it. He set out to examine the two streams of language and their differences in vocabulary, spelling, and pronunciation. He treated American slang, proper names, and non-English dialects in America. Ironically, his work won him a place among the scholars he had attacked and scorned.

American Mercury, The. An iconoclastic magazine founded in 1924 and edited by H. L. MENCKEN and George Jean NATHAN. For a decade, previously, both men had worked together as editors and part-owners of the *Smart Set*. Nathan retired as coeditor of the *Mercury* after a year, but remained as a departmental editor until 1930. Some departments were continued from the *Smart Set*, for example, the "Americana," a collection of absurdities in popular culture and cults, arranged geographically by states. But the magazine also contained articles on literary figures and other positive aspects of American culture. Among its contributors were Lewis Mumford, Sinclair Lewis, Carl Sandburg, and Vachel Lindsay. After Mencken's retirement in 1933, it was published as a pocket-size miscellany of conservative tendencies by Laurence E. Spivak. It eventually became a rightist organ of limited circulation, owned by millionaire J. Russell Maguire.

American Notes (1842). A volume of travel sketches by Charles DICKENS. The book was well received in England, but gave great offense in the U.S. Dickens, besides advocating the abolition of slavery, made many harsh and somewhat patronizing observations about the rawness and narrowness of life and manners in America.

American Revolution (1775–1783). The war for independence waged by the former British colonies in the present U.S. against the mother country. The conflict stemmed from the political and economic grievances of the colonists, especially after the FRENCH AND INDIAN WAR, when the British decided to end their former policy of "salutary neglect" toward the colonies by enacting such revenue-raising measures as the STAMP ACT and the Townshend Acts of 1767. Fanned by the writings of Samuel ADAMS and others, American resentment increased and erupted in such incidents as the BOSTON MASSACRE and the BOSTON TEA PARTY. The gathering of the first CONTINENTAL CONGRESS in 1774 was followed by the clash of British regulars and MINUTE MEN at LEXINGTON and Concord; Congress named George WASHINGTON commander-in-chief of its forces in 1775 and promulgated the DECLARATION OF INDEPENDENCE, largely the work of Thomas JEFFERSON, the following year. Important American leaders in the battles that followed were Ethan ALLEN, Benedict ARNOLD, Horatio GATES, George Rogers CLARK, Anthony WAYNE, Francis MARION, and John Paul JONES. The entry of France into the war against England in 1778 was a major factor in the final American victory; at the siege of YORKTOWN, a French fleet blockaded the harbor, while Washington was assisted by the forces of the Comte de ROCHAMBEAU and the Marquis de LAFAYETTE. The Treaty of Paris, signed after lengthy negotiations by John ADAMS, Benjamin FRANKLIN, and John JAY, ended the war.

The American struggle for freedom was accompanied by much literary activity, most of it political in nature, as seen in the works of Thomas PAINE, John TRUMBULL, and Francis HOPKINSON. Philip FRENEAU is sometimes called "the poet of the American Revolution."

See battle of BUNKER HILL; Patrick HENRY; Paul REVERE; John HANCOCK; Nathan HALE.

American Scene, The (1907). A travel book by Henry JAMES. The volume is mainly an examination of life in Saratoga, Newport, and other important American social and cultural centers, remembered as they were in the 1870's and 1880's and described as James saw them again in 1904, on a visit to the U.S.

American Scholar, The (1837). A Phi Beta Kappa address delivered by Ralph Waldo EMERSON at Harvard. Emerson called for a reliance on direct perception and native abilities, rather than a pale imitation of European culture. For the scholar, or Man Thinking, books must be secondary tools. O. W. Holmes called the address our "intellectual declaration of independence."

American Songbag, The (1927). A collection of folk songs and ballads made by Carl SANDBURG. In tours of the country, Sandburg himself sang many of these songs, accompanying them on his banjo or guitar. A number of them have been recorded by him, perhaps the best known being *The Boll-Weevil*.

American Tragedy, An (1925). A novel by Theodore DREISER. The author based his realistic and vivid study on the actual case of Chester Gillette, who in July, 1906, murdered Grace Brown at Big Moose Lake in the Adirondacks. Dreiser, who gave his protagonist the name Clyde Griffiths, at times faithfully follows the original facts; at other moments he transcends them with his own interpretations. Clyde Griffiths' boyhood, for example, reproduces some of the details of Dreiser's own earlier years.

In revolt against the poverty and piety of his Midwestern family, Clyde becomes a bellboy in a luxurious hotel and, after being involved in an automobile accident for which he is legally responsible, is employed by a distant relative, owner of a collar factory in upper New York State. There Clyde seduces Roberta Alden, an employee at the factory, but falls in love with Sondra Finchley, a girl of the local aristocracy, who symbolizes the wealth and glamor that he has been seeking. Clyde's relationship with Sondra is menaced when Roberta, now pregnant, demands that he marry her, and he carefully devises a plan to murder her. He lacks the courage to carry out his scheme, when he takes Roberta rowing on an isolated lake, but the boat accidentally overturns, and he allows Roberta to drown while he swims away. Clyde is accused of murder, and the remainder of the book is a powerful depiction of his subsequent trial, conviction, and execution. Although Clyde is portrayed as a weakling, Dreiser squarely indicts America's industrial society for dazzling persons like Clyde with the dream of an unattainable and meretricious luxury.

America the Beautiful (1895; rev. 1904, 1911). A poem by Katharine Lee Bates (1859–1929), best known as a patriotic song to the tune of Samuel A. Ward's hymn, *Materna*.

Amerika (1927). An unfinished novel by Franz KAFKA that was published posthumously. Less radically abstruse than his other two novels, *The Trial* and *The Castle,* it deals with the adventures of a European boy in an unreal, expressionistically depicted America. Its first chapter was completed and published separately in 1913 as *The Stoker (Der Heizer).*

Amethyst Ring, The (L'Anneau d'améthyste; 1899). A novel by Anatole FRANCE. The tale centers about the actions of its protagonist M. BERGERET.

Amfortas. Guardian of the GRAIL in medieval legend, grandson of TITUREL. Because he has sinned, he has been wounded by the sacred lance which wounded Christ and can only be cured by a blameless fool. See PARSIFAL and PARZIVAL.

Amidism, or **Pure Land Buddhism.** A Chinese and Japanese Buddhist salvationism. Its aim is rebirth in the Western Paradise of Amida (Sans. *Amitabha;* Ch. *A-mi-t'o*) Buddha. Stemming from northern India and Central Asia, it spread rapidly in China, incorporating many elements from popular folk religions. In the Ming period (1368–1644) it merged with Ch'an (Zen) Buddhism. In Japan Amida pietism sprang up at the Tendai Buddhist center of Mt. Hiei. Its leading exponents were Genshin (942–1017), Hōnen (1133–1212), founder of the Jōdo Sect, and Shinran (1173–1262), the first patriarch of the Shin Sect. Amidism developed during the Heian (794–1185) period and marks a shift from a Buddhism for the elite toward one with an appeal for the common people. Emphasis is placed on the recitation, with faith, of the *nembutsu,* or invocation of the Buddha's name, as the single requirement for rebirth in Amida's Paradise. Its single thought has had a lasting influence on both literature and the arts. The Shin was the first sect to allow its priests to marry. Shin and Jodo have the greatest number of adherents among Japanese Buddhist sects.

Amiel, Denys (1884–   ). French dramatist of the "school of silence" (see Jean-Jacques BERNARD). After *Le Voyageur* (1912, produced 1922), he collaborated with André Obey on *The Wife With the Smile (La Souriante Mme. Beudet;* 1921) and *La Carcasse* (1926). Other plays by Amiel include *Décalage* (1931), *Three and One* (1932), and *Café-Tabac* (1932).

Aminta. A famous Renaissance pastoral play by TASSO, written and first performed in 1573. The plot begins with the appearance of Venus' son Amor in the guise of a shepherd, determined to aim his arrows at the most obdurate nymph of Diana, Silvia, whose haughtiness has repulsed all lovers. Her friend Dafne (Daphne) tries to persuade her to fall in love with the shepherd Aminta, but she prefers the hunt; at the same time, Aminta spurns Amarilli, who loves him desperately. Aminta tells his friend Tirsi that there is no hope of gaining Silvia, as the wise Mopso has seen the future and confirmed the hopelessness of the pursuit. Now Satiro (the Satyr), also enamored of Silvia, decides to take her by force while she bathes. Aminta rescues her, but she flees from him. Later, believing Silvia dead, Aminta attempts suicide; but he survives to find Silvia convinced of his love and loving him in return. They wed and the play closes with the appearance of Venus, arrived to discover her unruly son and put an end to his mischief by taking him back to the Olympian court from which he had strayed.

Amis, Kingsley (1922–   ). English novelist and poet. His comic novels include the best-selling LUCKY JIM and *That Uncertain Feeling* (1955), *I Like It Here* (1958), and *Take a Girl Like You* (1960). *A Case of Samples* (1956) is a collection of intellectual, light-hearted poems. See ANGRY YOUNG MEN.

Amis and Amile. Also **Amys and Amylion** or **Amiloun.** French CHANSON DE GESTE based on an Oriental tale, made popular in 13th century French and English romance. The story celebrates an extraordinarily devoted friendship. Amis perjures himself to take Amile's place in a trial by combat, and is punished by leprosy. A vision reveals to Amile that only the blood of his children can cure his friend, so he kills them and effects the cure. But this generous sacrifice is miraculously rewarded: a visit to the children's dead bodies discovers them to be merely sleeping.

Amish. The Amish Mennonites, a strict sect of the 17th century, named from Jacob Ammann or Amen, a Swiss MENNONITE bishop.

Ammers-Küller, Johanna van (1884–   ). Dutch novelist. Her best-known novel is *The Rebel Generation* (1925), which was a best seller in Holland and widely translated.

Ammon. See AMEN.

Ammonius Saccas (c. 175–c. 242). An Alexandrian philosopher. The teacher of PLOTINUS, Ammonius made his students vow that they would not reveal his doctrines in writing. He was born a Christian but abandoned the faith.

Amores. See OVID.

Amoret. See FAERIE QUEENE, THE.

Amoretti (1595). Sonnet sequence by Edmund SPENSER.

Amorous History of the Gauls. See BUSSY-RAMBUTIN.

Amos. In the Old Testament, one of the Minor Prophets and the name of the oldest of the prophetic books in point of time. Amos had disquieting visions of the corruption of his city contemporaries. His pleas for personal and social righteousness are simply and movingly framed.

amour courtois. See COURTLY LOVE.

Amour médecin, L' (*Love, the Doctor,* 1665). A COMÉDIE-BALLET in prose by MOLIÈRE. By pretending to be a doctor, the hero Clitandre dupes the selfish Sganarelle into giving him the hand of his daughter and her dowry as well. See JOSSE; LUCINDE.

Ampère, André Marie (1775–1836). French physicist. Ampère made important discoveries in the fields of magnetism and electricity; these paved the way for the present-day study of electrodynamics. The *ampere,* the unit measure of intensity of an electric current, is named in his honor. Specific scientific orientation is less frequently found in his later work *Essai sur la philosophie des sciences* (1834–1844).

Amphiaraus. In mythology, the son of Oecles. It is not certain whether he was originally a man or god, although his name means "very sacred." Foreknowing the outcome of the expedition of the SEVEN AGAINST THEBES, Amphiaraus refused to take part in it until he was compelled to do so by his wife, ERIPHYLE. He attacked Thebes at the Homoloian Gate, but was driven off. While attempting to escape, he was swallowed up in a cleft in the ground made by Zeus's thunderbolt.

Amphion. A son of Zeus and Antiope. He became a famous musician and reigned, with his twin brother, in Thebes. Antiope, a daughter of Nycteus, the ruler of Thebes, lay with Zeus, but was driven from the city by her angry father. While fleeing to Sicyon, she gave birth to twins, Amphion and Zethus, on Mount Cithaeron. They were raised by shepherds and, on reaching manhood, learned of their mother's fate. Nycteus having died, his brother Lycus, now king, had brought Antiope back to Thebes, where he and his wife Dirce had long mistreated her. The twins went to Thebes, killed Lycus, and tied Dirce to the horns of a bull; she died at the Theban spring named for her.

Amphion and Zethus now shared the Theban throne and together built the city walls, though Amphion accomplished his part of the task by playing such ravishing music that the stones moved into place of their own accord. Amphion married NIOBE, but her arrogance led to the slaying by Apollo and Artemis of their many children and, according to some accounts, of Amphion himself. Zethus married Thebe, who gave her name to the city.

Amphitrite. In classic mythology, a goddess of the sea. She was the wife of Poseidon, daughter of Nereus and Doris, and mother of Triton.

Amphitryon. In Greek mythology, a king of Mycenae cuckolded by Zeus. The god assumed the likeness of Amphitryon for the purpose of visiting his wife, Alcmena, and gave a banquet at his house; but Amphitryon came home, and claimed the honor of being the master of the house. As far as the serv-ants and guests were concerned, the dispute was soon decided: "he who gave the feast was to them the host." Alcmena became the mother of HERACLES. This legend is the subject of three famous comedies by Plautus, Molière, and Dryden, all called *Amphitryon.* In 1929 there appeared a play entitled *Amphitryon 38,* meaning that it was the 38th treatment of the famous theme, by the French dramatist Jean Giraudoux (1882–1944).

Amphitryon (1668). A comedy by MOLIÈRE. It is derived from Plautus' treatment of the Amphitryon legend. Jupiter, smitten with Alcmène, assumes the appearance of her husband Amphitryon, the better to effect her seduction, while his attendant Mercury takes on the appearance of Amphitryon's servant Sosie. The play recounts the mounting confusion caused by the arrival of the real Amphitryon and Sosie. Eventually, Jupiter clears up the matter by explaining the deception.

Heinrich von KLEIST's *Amphitryon* (pub. 1808) is an adaptation of Molière's version, but concentrates much more on the tragic implications of the situation, especially for Alcmène.

amrita or **amreeta** (*Sans.,* without death). In Hindu mythology, the elixir of immortality, corresponding to the AMBROSIA of classical mythology. To the early Aryans, it was probably the juice of the soma plant, from which a sweet ritual wine was prepared.

Amun. See AMEN.

Amundsen, Roald (1872–1928). Norwegian polar explorer. Amundsen located the exact geographical position of the north magnetic pole on a voyage through the Northwest Passage (1903–1906). On December 14, 1911, he reached the South Pole and is known as its official discoverer. He flew across the North Pole with Lincoln Ellsworth in the dirigible *Norge* (1926). Amundsen disappeared (June, 1928) while on a flight to rescue the Italian explorer Nobile, who was lost returning from the North Pole. With Ellsworth and others he published *North West Passage* (1908), *South Pole* (1912), *Our Polar Flight* (1925), and *First Crossing of the Polar Sea* (1927).

Amusements sérieux et comiques d'un Siamois. See Charles Rivière DUFRESNY.

Amyclaean silence. Named for Amyclae, a Laconian town south of Sparta. Amyclae was ruled by the mythical TYNDAREUS. The inhabitants had so often been alarmed by false rumors of the approach of invading Spartans that they made a decree forbidding mention of the subject. When the Spartans actually came no one dared give the warning, and the town was taken. Hence the phrase "more silent than Amyclae."

Amys and Amylion. See AMIS AND AMILE.

An. The Sumerian god of heaven. Born of Nammu, the primeval sea, An and his sister-wife Ki (Earth) were originally joined as one, but their offspring ENLIL, the god of the air, separated them. An's place as head of the Sumerian pantheon was taken by Enlil. An is the same as the Babylonian god ANU.

Anabaptists. A general name for many Protestant sects which appeared in Germany during the 16th and 17th centuries. Although the various groups were usually in conflict with one another, most of them believed that they were restoring the purity of the primitive Christian church. Most practiced adult baptism, as described in the Bible, and several were involved with social and economic agitation. See MÜNSTER ANABAPTISTS.

Anabase (1924). A poem by St.-John PERSE. It was translated into English by T. S. Eliot in 1930. In this long work, the "upward journey" of the human spirit is portrayed through the expeditions of a Conqueror making his way across inhabited lands and deserts in Asia. He is loath to leave the pleasures and people of each successive city; yet restlessly he dreams of new travels and conquests and sets forth again.

Anabasis. See XENOPHON.

Anacharsis. The protagonist in a once celebrated historical romance entitled *Le Voyage du jeune Anacharsis en Grèce dans le milieu du IVe siècle avant l'ère vulgaire* (1788) by Jean Jacques BARTHÉLÉMY. The author, inspired by his archaeological research in Pompeii during a trip to Italy in 1755, seeks in this novel to bring alive classical antiquity in the time of Philip of Macedon and Demosthenes, and emphasizes particularly those aspects of science, art, and customs that history frequently neglects.

The real Anacharsis was a Scythian sage who, according to Herodotus, visited many countries in search of knowledge during the 6th century B.C.; Barthélémy's work, however, is completely original.

Anacreon (Anakreon). A Greek lyric poet. He wrote chiefly in praise of love and wine. He lived from about 563 to 478 B.C.

Anadyomene. An epithet of APHRODITE, alluding to her rising from the sea at birth.

anagoge. An elevation of the mind to things celestial. Specifically, the term is used to refer to exegesis that gives a mystical or spiritual meaning or application to the words of the Bible, as opposed to their literal, moral, or allegorical interpretation. See FOUR SENSES.

Anak. In the Old Testament, a giant of Palestine, whose descendants were terrible for their gigantic stature. The Hebrew spies said that they themselves were mere grasshoppers compared with the *Anakim*.

Analects (Lun-yü). One of the Chinese FOUR BOOKS. A brief, unsystematic collection of fragmentary writings attributed to Confucius and his school. Memorized until recently by every schoolboy, it is one of the most influential works in the history of Chinese thought. See Arthur Waley, *The Analects of Confucius* (1938).

Anand, Mulk Raj (1905–   ). Indian novelist writing in English. Educated in the Punjab and at Cambridge, he edited *Marg*, an art quarterly, and organized an Asian Writers' Conference in Delhi in 1956. His novels include *Coolie* (1936), *Two Leaves and a Bud* (1938), *Untouchable* (1947), and *Private Life of an Indian Prince* (1955).

Ananias. In the New Testament, an early Christian of Jerusalem. With his wife Sapphira, Ananias was struck dead for lying about the price of a piece of land they had sold in order to give the proceeds to their church (Acts 5). His name has since become a general term for one who lies.

anapest. In English prosody, a metrical foot consisting of three syllables, the first two unaccented and the third accented. The word "cig-a-RETTE" is an anapest. The METER made up of such units is called anapestic meter, and the following lines are a good example.

> i am MON/arch of ALL / i survey …
> i am LORD / of the FOWL / and the BRUTE.
> *Cowper, Alexander Selkirk*

Anarchiad, The (1786–1787). An American satirical epic poem, published anonymously in 12 installments of the New Haven *Gazette*. David Humphries, Lemuel Hopkins, Joel BARLOW, John TRUMBULL, and other HARTFORD WITS collaborated in its composition. It is chiefly an attack on French philosophy, paper money, Shays' Rebellion, and the condescending attitude of Europeans towards Americans.

Anat or **Anath.** Canaanite goddess, sister of Baal. A somewhat vengeful and violent deity, but loyal to her brother Baal, she has some characteristics in common with the Greek Artemis. She figures prominently in THE POEM OF BAAL and THE POEM OF AQHAT.

Anatol (1891). A play by Arthur SCHNITZLER. It presents several sentimental and erotic episodes from the life of a Casanovalike adventurer who constantly flits from one girl to another. Anatol's carefree and often shallow attitude toward life is contrasted with that of his more solid and sensible friend Max, but there is no real conflict, and the whole is pervaded with a light-hearted and sensuous humor. Hugo von Hofmannsthal wrote a preface in verse for the play.

Anatomy of Melancholy, The (1621). A prose work by Robert BURTON. Elaborately organized as a medical treatise, the *Anatomy* not only deals with various morbid mental states, their causes, symptoms, and cures, but is a compendium of notable utterances on the human condition in general, compiled from classical, scholastic, and contemporary sources. Melancholy, for Burton, embraced everything from raving lunacy to philosophical and occasional pessimism; as his quotations illustrate, it is "the character of mortality." The book is witty, pedantic, quaint, imaginative, inexhaustively rich, and, from Milton on, it has been pillaged by numerous authors.

Anaxagoras (500?–428 B.C.). A Greek philosopher, teacher of Pericles, Thucydides, Euripides, and possibly of Socrates. He believed in a dualistic universe, consisting of a chaotic mass of tiny particles or seeds that compose matter, and an ordering force that imparts motion. He called this force nous, or mind. Anaxagoras was also an astronomer, and correctly explained eclipses. He studied the size of the sun, the phases of the moon, and the behavior of meteors. Because his views conflicted with the state religion, Anaxagoras was charged with impiety and banished from the Athens he had made the center of philosophic argumentation. He is sometimes referred to as Anaxagoras of Clazomenae, after his birthplace in Asia Minor.

Anaximander (611?–547 B.C.). Greek philosopher of the MILESIAN SCHOOL, pupil of Thales. According to Anaximander, primary matter, which he called the *apeiron*, is eternal and indestructible. Motion and the separation of contradictory elements within this indefinite mass are the causes of plurality and variety in the universe. A practical scientist, Anaximander invented the sundial and was the first to prepare a map. He is known as the first Greek author to write in prose, although his philosophical treatise has perished.

Anaximenes (fl. 525 B.C.). Greek philosopher of the MILESIAN SCHOOL, associate of Anaximander. He believed that the condensation and rarefaction of air or *aether,* the primary substance, give rise to matter in all its forms.

Anaximenes of Lampsacus (c. 380–c. 320 B.C.). Greek rhetorician and historian, companion of Alexander the Great on his Persian expeditions. He wrote histories of Greece and biographies of Philip of Macedon and of Alexander. He is also thought to be the author of the only surviving work on rhetoric before Aristotle.

Anchises. In classic legend, a member of the royal house of Troy and the father of AENEAS by Aphrodite, who had fallen in love with him because of his beauty. According to Vergil, when Troy fell, Aeneas carried his aged father out of the burning city on his shoulders. Anchises died during Aeneas' wanderings and was buried in Sicily (AENEID, Book III).

Ancient Mariner, The Rime of the. See RIME OF THE ANCIENT MARINER, THE.

Ancient of Days. A scriptural title for the Deity (Dan. 7:9).

Ancients and moderns. See QUERELLE DES ANCIENS ET DES MODERNES.

Andersen, Hans Christian (1805–1875). Danish writer of fairy tales, poet, novelist, and dramatist. A skilled writer in all these genres, Hans Christian Andersen owes his worldwide fame to his fairy stories. Always popular with children, the 168 tales contain a mature wisdom together with gay whimsy. Andersen invested stories of folk and legendary origin with moral and symbolic significance. He could convey a fine perception of life's ironies while describing the fate of a tin soldier or a drab duckling. Among his best-known stories are *The Red Shoes, The Ugly Duckling, The Emperor's Clothes, The Tinder Box,* and *The Fir Tree.* The tales appeared from 1835 to 1872. Andersen's complete tales have been issued in several English editions.

Anderson, Marian (1902–   ). American contralto. She is the first Negro to have sung as a permanent member of the Metropolitan Opera Company in New York. She is greatly admired as a concert artist, especially in Europe, where she first established her reputation.

Anderson, Maxwell (1888–1959). American playwright. He is known for his experiments in verse drama, his insistence on the necessity of an inner moral struggle, and his success in the field of historical drama. After an early play, *White Desert* (1923), Anderson began collaborating with Laurence STALLINGS, the two producing WHAT PRICE GLORY?; *First Flight* (1925), about Andrew Jackson; and *The Buccaneer* (1925), a play about Sir Henry Morgan. In the late 1920's he wrote *Outside Looking In* (1925), based on Jim Tully's *Beggars of Life,* and *Saturday's Children* (1927), a domestic comedy. He then wrote with Harold Hickerson the first play to deal with the SACCO-VANZETTI case, *Gods of the Lightning* (1928). Anderson was to return later to this theme in his successful WINTERSET.

In the 1930's Anderson returned to historical drama, writing two plays dealing with 16th-century

themes, *Elizabeth the Queen* (1930) and *Mary of Scotland* (1933). *Valley Forge* (1934), a reinterpretation of Washington, followed. During the 30's, Anderson wrote better than a play a year; some of these are NIGHT OVER TAOS; BOTH YOUR HOUSES; *High Tor* (1937), which mingles real people and ghosts, past and present; *Knickerbocker Holiday* (1938), a musical with Kurt Weill; and *Key Largo* (1939), about a man who struggles to redeem himself for an act of cowardice committed during the Spanish Civil War.

World War II was reflected in several Anderson plays of the early 40's: *Candle in the Wind* (1941), an anti-Nazi play set in Paris; *The Eve of St. Mark* (1942); and *Storm Operation* (1944). After the war Anderson returned again to historical drama with *Joan of Lorraine* (1946); *Anne of the Thousand Days* (1948), a favorable interpretation of Henry VIII; and *Barefoot in Athens* (1951), a play about Socrates. Also noteworthy among Anderson's late dramas were *Lost in the Stars* (1949), a dramatization of Alan Paton's *Cry the Beloved Country,* and *The Bad Seed* (1955), the story of a grotesquely evil little girl, based on a novel by William March.

Anderson, Robert W[oodruff] (1917–   ). American playwright. He is the author of the successful play *Tea and Sympathy* (1953), the story of a preparatory school student unjustly suspected of homosexuality. He later wrote *All Summer Long* (1959) and *Silent Night, Lonely Night* (1959).

Anderson, Sherwood (1876–1941). American short-story writer and novelist. Born in Ohio, largely self-educated, Anderson worked at various trades and for several years was a copywriter in Chicago. There he met Midwestern writers associated with the Chicago literary renaissance, notably Theodore Dreiser and Carl Sandburg, and began his own literary career. His third book, WINESBURG, OHIO, a collection of related short stories dealing with individuals in a typical Midwestern town, brought him recognition as a leader in the revolt against established literary traditions.

Though his style has been decried by a later generation of writers and critics as artless and sentimental, it was for Anderson's time a significant breakthrough to an individual and original expression; not realistic in the sense of being an accurate reproduction of Middle Western speech, it has yet a kind of stylized realism that evokes the flavor of the Midwestern town, the pathos of lives trapped by conventionality and commercialism, the adolescent yearning to know and despair at discovery. Anderson was repelled by the industrial and commercial society he saw growing up all around him, and he frequently contrasted the contemporary scene with an earlier one devoted to craftsmanship and personal concern. For Anderson, modern society and the worship of materialistic success resulted in the erection of walls between people, a sterile sexuality, and a loss of skill in handicraft and the arts. Such walls, he believed, could only be broken down by love, creative human relationships, and a return to a personal involvement in one's craft.

Anderson never again equalled his achievement in *Winesburg, Ohio,* though his novel DARK LAUGHTER became a best seller. He was most at home in the short story, some of his best stories being *I'm a Fool, Death in the Woods,* and *I Want to Know Why.*

His stories are collected in THE TRIUMPH OF THE EGG and *Horses and Men* (1923). His novels include *Windy McPherson's Son* (1916), *Marching Men* (1917), POOR WHITE (1920), and *Many Marriages* (1923). A STORY TELLER'S STORY and *Tar: A Midwest Childhood* (1926) are autobiographical. His *Memoirs* (1942) and *Letters* (1953) were published posthumously.

Andō Hiroshige (1787–1858). Japanese painter and wood-block artist. He is famous for his *Tōkaidō Gojūsan-tsugi* (fifty-three stations along the Tōkaidō Highway), and as the last great master of the wood-block (*ukiyoe*) print. His work is said to have influenced Western painters, notably Whistler.

And Quiet Flows the Don. See QUIET DON, THE.

André, John (1751–1780). English army major to whom Benedict Arnold delivered the plans for the betrayal of West Point during the American Revolution. He was caught and hanged as a spy. He is the hero of *André* (1798), a play by William Dunlap.

Andrea del Sarto (1855). A poem by Robert BROWNING. Written in the form of a dramatic monologue, del Sarto, known as "the Faultless Painter," reveals his own character as he tells of the consuming passion for his beautiful, unscrupulous wife, Lucrezia, which prevented him from reaching the artistic stature of Raphael and Michelangelo.

Andreas Capellanus or **André le Chapelain** (late 12th–early 13th century). French chaplain at the court of Philip II. He wrote a Latin *Liber de Arte Honeste Amandi* (*Book on the Art of Loving Honestly*), a treatise on the art of love in the tradition of Ovid's *Ars Amoris*. It became a handbook of the theory and practice of COURTLY LOVE.

Andrew, St. One of the twelve disciples of Jesus; the brother of St. Peter. He is depicted in Christian art as an old man with long white hair and beard, holding the Gospel in his right hand, and leaning on a cross like the letter X, termed St. Andrew's cross. His day is November 30. It is said that he suffered martyrdom in Patrae (A.D. 70).

André Walter, Les Cahiers d' (1891). A short novelistic work by André GIDE. It purports to be the notebooks of a sensitive youth who is suffering romantic anguish because his beloved has obeyed her mother and married another. Its melodrama reveals the conflict between spiritual love and fleshly desire as irreconcilable. Gide also called his first book of poems *Les Poésies d'André Walter* (1892).

Andrews, Joseph. See JOSEPH ANDREWS.

Andrews, Pamela. See PAMELA, OR VIRTUE REWARDED.

Andreyev, Leonid Nikolayevich (1871–1919). Russian writer. Born in the province of Oriol, Andreyev studied law at the universities of St. Petersburg and Moscow, during which time extreme mental depression led to several suicide attempts. He graduated in 1897 but turned to writing instead of law for a living, receiving aid and encouragement from Maksim Gorki. Among the best of Andreyev's earlier works were *In the Fog* (*V tumanye*; 1902) and *Thought* (*Mysl*; 1902), the first dealing with awakened sexuality in a young boy, the second with insanity and murder. Such sensational themes were at this time still treated in a realistic manner by

Andreyev, but, from this period on, his work became increasingly complex, often strained in its search for sensational effect and symbolic import. This is especially apparent in a work such as *The Red Laugh* (*Krasnyi smekh;* 1904), a horrorific tale of the madness and terror of war. The same tendencies are evident in Andreyev's plays, which include HE WHO GETS SLAPPED, *The Black Maskers* (*Chiorniye maski;* 1908), *Anathema* (*Anatema;* 1909), and *The Life of Man* (*Zhizn cheloveka;* 1906).

Andrič, Ivo (1892–   ). Yugoslav novelist. Born in Bosnia of a family of artisans of very modest means, Andrič managed to secure an education in universities in several cities in what is now Yugoslavia, Poland, and Austria. He was active in the National Revolutionary Youth Organization before World War I, and after it served in the diplomatic service in Rome, Bucharest, Trieste, Graz, and Berlin. During the German occupation, he lived in retirement in Belgrade and wrote his major novels, all about Bosnia: *Miss; The Travnik Chronicle;* and THE BRIDGE ON THE DRINA. He was little known outside his own country until the last novel was translated into English. In 1961 he was awarded the Nobel prize for literature.

Androcles or **Androclus.** According to Aulus Gellius, Androcles was a Roman slave of the 1st century who removed a thorn from the paw of a lion. When Androcles was later thrown into the arena, the grateful beast began to caress him and they were both set free. George Bernard Shaw used this story as the basis of his play ANDROCLES AND THE LION.

Androcles and the Lion (1912). A play by George Bernard SHAW. Using the story of ANDROCLES as the basis of the plot, Shaw's play is about the early Christians' faith. The first act opens as a band of first-century Christians is being led to the arena in Rome to be martyred. Androcles, a meek tailor, whose fabled encounter with the lion has taken place in the prologue, is in the group. As they proceed toward Rome, they sing hymns and aver their faith. The two main characters are a Roman captain and Lavinia, a beautiful, young Christian. She enunciates the theme of the play: to make life worth living, one must have something to die for. In the arena one of the Christians fights so well that the emperor pardons them all, but one person must still be thrown to the lion to keep the crowd happy. Androcles volunteers and discovers that the lion is the same one that he had helped in the forest.

Andromache. In Homer's *Iliad*, the wife of Hector. She appears in Euripides' THE TROJAN WOMEN and is the heroine of his *Andromache* (430–424 B.C.). In the latter play, she has been carried off to Thessaly by Neoptolemus, Achilles' son; has borne him a child, and has been abandoned in favor of Hermione, the daughter of Menelaus and Helen. Her sufferings at their hands are the substance of the play, which, in portraying the Spartans as cruel and cowardly, served as an effective political indictment of the Athenians' enemies. Racine wrote a tragedy about Andromache entitled *Andromaque*.

Andromaque (1667). A tragedy by Jean RACINE. It is based on the Greek legend of ANDROMACHE but differs from it in several details of interrelation between the characters. The play is set in Epirus after the fall of Troy. Andromaque is loved by her captor

Pyrrhus whom she hates, but his action arouses the jealousy of his fiancée Hermione. Pyrrhus threatens to surrender Andromaque's son Astyanax to the Greeks if she will not yield to him. In exchange for his promise to protect her son, she agrees to marry Pyrrhus, but secretly intends to remain faithful to her dead husband Hector by killing herself after the wedding. The rejected Hermione persuades Orestes, the Greek ambassador, who has come to demand Andromaque's son, to murder Pyrrhus, and in exchange agrees to flee with him. But after the murder she reviles him and in her remorse commits suicide upon the funeral pyre of her adored Pyrrhus. Orestes goes mad. *Andromaque* is held by French critics to constitute the first representation in tragedy of the psychology of passion.

Andromeda. In Greek mythology, the daughter of Cepheus and Cassiopeia. Because her mother boasted that she was more beautiful than the Nereids, they induced Poseidon to send a sea-monster against Ethiopia, and an oracle declared that Andromeda must be sacrificed to it. Chained to a rock near Joppa, she was rescued by PERSEUS, who married her. He also killed Phineus, her former betrothed, and all his companions. She was placed among the stars upon her death.

Andromède (1650). A play by Pierre CORNEILLE. Based on the Andromeda legend, it exploited the most spectacular scenic effects of its day.

Andvari. King of the dwarfs in Scandinavian mythology, especially in the *Edda* and the *Völsunga Saga,* who gave up his treasure and magic ring to Loki in exchange for his liberty.

Anelida and Arcite (probably c. 1380 or 1381). An unfinished poem by Geoffrey CHAUCER, in 357 lines. Although Chaucer gives Statius as his authority, he apparently draws more on Boccaccio's *Teseida.* The story of how Arcite faithlessly leaves Queen Anelida for a new love is told in RHYME ROYAL. It introduces the better poetry of Anelida's song of complaint, written in stanzas of nine lines, except for two of sixteen.

angel (Gr., *angelos,* "messenger"). (1) In theology, a celestial being. In postcanonical and apocalyptic literature, angels are grouped in varying orders, and the hierarchy thus constructed was adapted to church uses by the early Christian Fathers. In his *De Hierarchia Celesti* the pseudo-Dionysius (early fifth century) gives the names of the nine orders; they are taken from the New Testament (Eph. 1:21 and Col. 1:16) and are as follows:

(i) SERAPHIM, Cherubim, and Thrones, in the first circle of the heavenly hierarchy.

(ii) Dominions, Virtues, and Powers, in the second circle.

(iii) Principalities, Archangels, and Angels, in the third circle.

The seven holy angels are Michael, Gabriel, Raphael, Uriel, Chamuel, Jophiel, and Zadkiel. Michael and Gabriel are mentioned in the Bible; the others appear in Apocryphal books.

Milton (*Paradise Lost,* Bk. 1, 392) gives a list of the fallen angels.

Muslims say that angels were created from pure, bright gems, the genii from fire, and man from clay.

(2) An obsolete English coin, current from the time of Edward IV to that of Charles I, bearing the figure of the archangel Michael slaying the dragon. Its value varied from 6s. 8d. in 1465 (when first coined) to 10s. under Edward VI. It was the coin presented to persons touched for the King's Evil.

Angelica. The bewitching heroine of the Orlando poems of Boiardo and Ariosto (see ORLANDO FURIOSO). A princess of Cathay, her arrival at the court of Charlemagne sows discord among the paladins, especially Rinaldo and Orlando. The latter goes mad for a time when he discovers that she has fallen in love with the simple Moorish youth Medoro and escaped to Cathay with him. By introducing her as the main plot impulse, Boiardo made the first important blending of the Carolingian legends with the amatory motifs of the Arthurian cycle.

Angelico, Fra [Giovanni]. Real name: **Guido di Pietro** (1387–1455). Italian painter. A Dominican friar of Fiesole, near Florence, he worked in Rome, Orvieto, and Florence. It was there that he completed the well-known series of frescoes for the monastery of San Marco, as a result of the patronage of Cosimo de Medici. In 1447, Fra Angelico was summoned to Rome by Pope Nicholas V for the purpose of painting several scenes from the life of Saint Lawrence, which were to be hung in the Vatican. A religious painter of grace and simplicity coupled with an admirable purity and delicacy of color, he did not share his contemporaries' enthusiasm for the new scientific naturalism of the day.

Angelo. (1) In Shakespeare's MEASURE FOR MEASURE, the puritanical lord deputy who governs Vienna in the absence of Duke Vincentio. Although he is widely known as "a man of stricture and firm abstinence," his austerity masks a violent inner nature.

(2) In Shakespeare's COMEDY OF ERRORS, a goldsmith who, having fashioned a gold chain for Antipholus of Ephesus, mistakenly gives it to Antipholus of Syracuse.

Angel Pavement (1930). A novel by J. B. PRIESTLEY. Set in London, it is the story of small businessmen and a grasping capitalist.

Angel Street (1942). A long-run mystery play (1295 performances) by the English playwright Patrick Hamilton (1909–1962).

Angelus. A Roman Catholic devotion in honor of the Incarnation. It is so called from the first words, *Angelus Domini* (The angel of the Lord). The prayer is recited three times a day at 6 A.M., noon, and 6 P.M., at the sound of a bell called the *Angelus.* Millet made a well-known painting with this title.

Angelus Silesius. Pen name of **Johann Scheffler** (1624–1677). German baroque poet. His most famous work, *Cherubinischer Wandersmann (The Cherubic Wanderer,* 1657) is a collection of religious epigrams of mystical character. Although he was a Catholic, Scheffler's thought is not unrelated to the earlier Protestant mysticism of Jakob Böhme and to the later movement of Pietism.

Anglo-Saxon Attitudes (1956). A satirical novel by Angus WILSON. The hero is an elderly medieval historian who decides to investigate a possible academic fraud with which he was once indirectly connected. In the process he discovers some truths about his family and himself.

Anglo-Saxon Chronicle, The [also called **Old English Annals**] (c. 891–924). An Old English history of England begun under the direction of

An. dcciiii. heꞃ æþelꞃeð penoinꞇ mꝥꞃc
na cꝥninꞇ onꝼenꞇ munuc hade. ꝥꝥ ꞃuce
heolo.xxix. pinꞇꝥa. ꝥþa ꝼenꞇ cenꝥeð to.

An. dccv. heꞃ aloꝼꝥið noꞃþan hꝥmbꞃa
cꝥninꞇ ꝼoꞃð ꝼeꞃðe on.xviii. k̄ ianꝥ. on
oꞃuꞃ ꝼeloa. þaꝼenꞇ oꞃ ꝥæð hiꞃ ꞃunu toꞃuce.

An. dccvi.

An. dccvii.

An. dccviii.

An. dccviii. heꞃ aloelm biꞃcop ꝼoꞃþ ꝼeꞃoe
ꞃeꝥæꞃ beꝥæꞃꞇan piðu biꞃcop. ꝥꝥæꞃ toðæleð on.
ꝼoꞃe ꝥeaꞃoum oantheleꞃ oaꞇum onꞇꝥa biꞃcop
Sciꞃe ꝥeꞃꞇ Seꞇꞃna laꞇoeꞃ. ꝥꞃꞇhiꞃꞇ ꝥæꞃ án.
oðeꞃ heolo oaniel. oðeꞃ aloohelm. æꞃtæꞃ alo
helme ꝼoꞃð heꞃe ꝼenꞇto. ꝥceolꝥeð ꝼenꞇ to
mꝥꞃcna ꞃuce. ꝥcenꝥeð ꝼoꞃ toꞃome. ꝥoꝼꝼa
moðhim. ꝥcenꝥeð ꝥæꞃ þæꞃ oð hiꞃ liꝼeꞃ enoe.
ꝥbꝥ ilcan ꞇeaꞃe pilꝼeꞃð biꞃcop ꝼoꞃð ꝼeꞃoe
inunoalum. ꝥhiꞃ licman læooe toꞃuꞃum.
heꝥæꞃ biꞃcop.xlv. pinꞇꝥa. þone ecꞃ ꝼeꞃð
cꝥninꞇ æꝥbe oꞃuꞃ toꞃome.

An. dccx. heꞃacca pilꝼeꞃioeꞃ ꝥꞃeoꞃ
ꝼenꞇ toþam biꞃcop oome þehe æꞃ heolo. ꝥ
þam ꝥlcan ꞇeaꞃe ꝼeahꞇ beoꞃhꞇ ꝼꝥið ealooꞃ.

The years 704–710 from *The Anglo-Saxon Chronicle*.

King ALFRED, still a major historical source. The early material is adapted from BEDE's work and from records kept by the monasteries. After the account of Alfred's wars against the Danes the *Chronicle* was officially kept up year by year until 924, after which the various extant manuscript copies of it show fragmentary continuations by different authors, one with entries as late as 1154.

Angry Young Men. A nickname coined by Fleet Street journalists for a group of English writers who came into prominence in the 1950's. The Angry Young Men, generally of working or middle-class origins, expressed the discontent and disillusion of a generation enfranchised and university-educated by British socialism but unable to effect an entrance into the restricted power circles of British politics, education, criticism, or literature. They expressed their suspicion and resentment of upper-class culture, manners, and snobbism and their disgust with Britain and with what they took to be British hypocrisy chiefly through the novel and the drama. They produced several works of undeniable power, won enormous press publicity and critical favor, and achieved an impressive commercial success which, in the opinion of several critics, has modified their fervor. The movement may be said to be in decline in the 60's. The leading Angry Young Men were John OSBORNE,

notable for the fury and bitterness of his plays, and Kingsley AMIS, remarkable among the group for the coherence and humor of his novels.

Animal Farm (1945). A satirical fable by George ORWELL. Some farm animals get tired of their servitude to man and start a revolution to run the farm as they want. They are betrayed, however, by their leaders, the pigs, into a worse servitude. The pigs' slogan is, "All animals are equal, but some animals are more equal than others." The book is a satire on the development of the Russian revolution under Stalin.

Animal Kingdom, The (1932). A play by Philip BARRY. It is the story of Tom Collier, who finds years of happiness with his mistress, Daisy Sage. After returning to his wife, he abandons her again for Daisy.

animal magnetism. See MESMERISM.

animals in heaven. The 10 animals which, according to Muslim legend, have been allowed to enter paradise. They are (1) Jonah's *whale;* (2) Solomon's *ant;* (3) the *ram* caught by Abraham and sacrificed instead of Isaac; (4) the *lapwing* of Balkis; (5) the *camel* of the prophet Saleh; (6) Balaam's *ass;* (7) the *ox* of Moses; (8) the *dog* Kratim or Katmir of the Seven Sleepers; (9) Al Borak, Muhammad's *ass;* and (10) Noah's *dove.*

Anker Larson, Johannes (1874–1957). Danish novelist and playwright. His novel *The Philosopher's Stone* (*De Vises Sten*, 1923) won the coveted Gyldendal prize and brought fame to the little-known writer. Anker Larson's absorbing interest in mysticism finds expression in all his novels, among them *Martha and Mary* (*Martha og Marie;* 1925), *With the Door Open* (*For aaben Dør;* 1926), and *Stranger in Paradise* (*Sognet, som vokser ind i Himmelen;* 1928).

Ann, Mother. See Ann LEE.

Annabel Lee (1849). A poem by Edgar Allan POE. Its subject, Poe's favorite, is the death of a beautiful woman.

Anna Christie (1922). A drama by Eugene O'NEILL. Anna is the daughter of Chris Christopherson, a Swedish captain who has come to regard all evil and misfortune as the work of "dat old davil sea." He had sent her away to be brought up in Minnesota, but in the play she turns up in port and falls in love with both the sea and with a brawny Irish seaman named Mat Burke. When she confesses to a shameful past in St. Paul, both her father and lover repudiate her. In the end, however, she is forgiven by them both. The play won a Pulitzer Prize in 1922. It was made into the musical comedy *New Girl in Town* (1957) by George Abbott.

Anna Comnena (1083–?1148). A daughter of the Byzantine emperor ALEXIUS COMNENUS. She wrote a history of her father's career entitled the *Alexiad.*

Anna Karenina (1873–1876). A novel by Count Leo TOLSTOI. The author's second great major novel, it is the story of a tragic, adulterous love. Anna meets and falls in love with Aleksei Vronski, a handsome young officer. She abandons her child and husband in order to be with Vronski. When he tires of her and leaves her to go to war, she kills herself by leaping under a train. The idea for the story reputedly came to Tolstoi after he had viewed the body of a young woman who committed a similar suicide. A subplot concerns the contrasting happy marriage of Konstantin Levin and his young wife Kitty. Levin's search for meaning in his life and his love for a natural, simple existence on his estate are reflections of Tolstoi's own moods and thoughts of the time. While working on the novel, Tolstoi began to experience the doubts and torments which he describes in *A Confession*.

Annales Cambriae (c. 955). A Latin history of Wales, importantly connected with the origins of ARTHURIAN LEGEND. It notes that at the battle of Mount Badon, a historical Arthur (prototype of King Arthur) wore a cross on his shield, and that Arthur and Medraut (a historical MORDRED) fell at the battle of Camlan in the year 537.

Anna Livia Plurabelle. In James Joyce's novel FINNEGANS WAKE, the personification of the Irish river, the Liffey, representing H. C. Earwicker's wife Anna. The initials A. L. P. are interwoven throughout the novel to represent the universal feminine principle.

Anna of the Five Towns (1902). A novel by Arnold BENNETT. The first of Bennett's novels dealing with the Potteries region, it is a naturalistic account of an ordinary woman's dull life. It is also a study of the repressive effects of Wesleyan religion. Anna is the daughter of Ephraim Tellwright, a miser and former preacher, who looks after the fortune Anna has inherited from her mother and forces her to extort high rent from her tenants. Anna becomes engaged to marry Henry Mynors, a pillar of the Church and a successful businessman, who is interested in her money. When she finds that she really loves Willie Price, son of a tenant her father has forced to ruin, she cannot break the habit of years of obedience and marries Henry. Old Mr. Price and Willie commit suicide.

Anne Boleyn (c. 1507–1536). Queen consort of HENRY VIII, mother of ELIZABETH I. A lady of honor to Henry's first queen, Catherine of Aragon, Anne soon attracted the attention of the king, to whom she was secretly married in January, 1533. Some months later Henry's first marriage was declared invalid, and Anne was crowned queen. After the disappointing birth of a daughter (the future Queen Elizabeth), a miscarriage, and a stillborn son, Anne lost favor with Henry. In 1536 she was made to stand trial for adultery, was condemned, along with five men accused of being her lovers, and executed.

Annenski, Innokenti Fiodorovich (1856–1909). Russian poet. A classical scholar and translator of Euripides and the French Parnassians, Annenski wrote lyric poems that were models of concision and exquisite finish. His small output of poetic work was published mainly in *Quiet Songs* (*Tikhiye pesni;* 1904) and *The Cypress Chest* (*Kiparisovskii laryetz;* 1910). Annenski was a potent influence on the poetry of the Acmeists and the early work of Boris Pasternak.

Anne of Austria (**Anne d'Autriche;** 1602–1666). Daughter of Philip III of Spain, consort of Louis XIII of France, and regent during the minority of her son Louis XIV.

Anne of Cleves (1515–1557). The fourth wife of HENRY VIII of England. Henry's marriage with Anne, a German, was arranged by Thomas Cromwell to create an alliance with the German Protestants.

Henry, however, disliked her, and after six months had the marriage declared null and void.

Anne of Geierstein, or The Maiden of the Mist (1829). A novel by Sir Walter SCOTT. Exiled Lancastrian supporters become involved with the defeat of Charles the Bold, duke of Burgundy, by the Swiss in the 15th century.

Anne of Green Gables. See L. M. MONTGOMERY.

Anniversaries, The. The general title of two long elegiac poems by John DONNE: *An Anatomy of the World* (1611) and *Of the Progresse of the Soule* (1612). Ostensibly written in memory of Elizabeth, young daughter of his patron, Sir Robert Drury, they are more concerned with the typical Donne themes of intellectual disorder and temporal decay.

anno Domini (*Lat.*). In the Year of our Lord; *i.e.,* in the year since the Nativity: generally abbreviated to A.D. It was Dionysius Exiguus who fixed the date of the Nativity; he lived in the early 6th century, and his computation is probably late by some three to six years. The custom of determining dates on this basis is said to be the result of the work of the Venerable Bede.

Annonce faite à Marie, L'. See TIDINGS BROUGHT TO MARY, THE.

Annual Register, The. A summary of the chief historic events of the year, first published by John and Robert Dodsley in 1758. It is still issued annually in England.

Annunciation, the Day of the. March 25, the day of the angel's (traditionally Gabriel's) announcement to the Virgin Mary of the forthcoming birth to her of the Messiah. It is also sometimes called Lady Day, which in medieval England was the first day of the legal year. The Annunciation was often represented in mystery plays, and is the subject of paintings by, among others, Fra Angelico, Andrea del Sarto, Titian, Tintoretto, and Murillo. The earliest authentic record of its celebration as a church festival is in 656.

Annus Mirabilis (*Lat.,* "year of wonders"; 1667). A poem by John DRYDEN. The poem describes the London fire and the Dutch war, the chief events of the year 1666. In a preface to the poem, Dryden discusses his conception of the poetic imagination.

Ann Veronica (1909). A novel by H. G. WELLS. It is the story of the heroine's struggle for independence, sexual freedom, and equality with men.

Anouilh, Jean (1910–   ). French dramatist and screen writer. *The Ermine* (1932) first presented his major recurrent theme, the "great thirst for purity." His plays, ANTIGONE (1942) and THE LARK (1953) for example, frequently oppose the freshness of youth to the staleness or even sordidness of age. Youth is embodied in the person of a young girl, poor but innocent and lovely; age is personified by a man who is usually wealthy and in a position of control. Allied to this contrast is the theme of the opposition between the poetry of fantasy or art and the sullying demands of practicality in the real world. The devices of play-within-a-play and disguised or pretended identity give symbolic expression to this conflict between artifice and actuality. Anouilh is never able to resolve these antitheses in an optimistic manner. The young and pure, however beau-

The Fox and Stork.

The Fox the Crane did Solemnly invite
Only to Tantalize her Appetite.
For nothing he but liquid Fare provides,
That spreading ore the table thinly glyds.
Of which his speare like beake could nothing sup
Whilst the sly Fox licks all vnkindly vp.

Thus Fraud t' Entangle fraud is oft design'd.

The Crane this false Imposture to requite
The Fox to new Carresses did invite
But a glass viall did her Cates conteyne,
Which only she w. length of bill could drayne.
The Fox thus foyld w. her more powerfull Arts,
To his owne Cell w. scorne & shame departs.

And falsehood is by falsehood Countermind.

An illustration by Francis Barlow from the first edition of *Aesop's Fables*,
published in London in 1666

John James Audubon, American naturalist and artist —
from an engraving after an original painting by Chappel

Jane Austen, English novelist — from an engraving after an original family portrait

Tower in which Balzac passed most of his time at College

Balzac's Birthplace, rue Royale, Tours

Honoré de Balzac, French novelist — from an engraving
by Nargeot after a drawing by Decaisne

Tower in which Balzac spent most of his time at college (above left)
Balzac's birthplace, rue Royale, Tours, France (above right)

Francis Beaumont, English dramatist — from an engraving by H. Robinson

Giovanni Boccaccio, Italian prose writer and poet —
from an engraving by W. Hopwood after a print by Cornelius Van Dalen

your faithful and affectionate humble servant James Boswell

James Boswell, Scottish writer, best known for his biography of Samuel Johnson—
from an engraving by Gimber after a sketch by Lawrence

An illustration by Botticelli for Dante's *Divine Comedy*

tiful, is fragile and unreal, compelled to face the inevitable bitterness and ugliness of actual human existence. The increasing bitterness and pessimism of his later work is half hidden beneath a veil of facile but charming satiric wit.

Anouilh's serious plays are often adaptations of well-known legends; the settings of his popular comedies range from castles to bourgeois domesticity. His plays published as *Pièces roses* (rosy plays) include *Thieves' Carnival* (*Le Bal des voleurs*, 1932) and *Time Remembered* (*Léocadia*, 1939). *Restless Heart* (*La Sauvage*, 1934), *Eurydice* (1941; also translated as *Legend of the Lovers* and *Point of Departure*), *Romeo and Jeanette* (1945), and *Medea* (1946) were published as *Pièces noires* (dark plays). *Pièces brillantes* (sparkling plays) were *Ring Round the Moon* (*L'Invitation au Chateau*, 1947; translated by Christopher Fry), *Cecile* (1949), *The Rehearsal* (*La Répétition*, 1950) and *Colombe* (1951). *Pièces grinçantes* (grating plays) include *Ardèle* (1948) and *The Waltz of the Toreadors* (1952). Anouilh's later plays are *L'Hurluberlu* (1959) and *Becket* (1959).

Anshar. Babylonian sky-god. Born of Lahmu and Lahamu, he fathered by his sister, Kishar, ANU, the god of heaven.

Anstey, Christopher (1724–1805). English poet. He became famous as the author of *The New Bath Guide* (1766), a series of verse letters supposedly written by Simpkin Blunderhead and other members of his family, describing the resort town of Bath. Tobias Smollett later used the same device in *The Expedition of Humphrey Clinker.*

Anstey, F. Pen name of **Thomas Anstey Guthrie** (1856–1934). English humorist, novelist, and playwright. Among his works are VICE VERSA, OR A LESSON TO FATHERS (1882), a satiric novel, and *The Man from Blankley's* (1901), a play very popular in its day.

Antaeus (Antaios). In Greek mythology, a gigantic wrestler, a son of Earth and Sea, Ge and Poseidon. His strength was invincible as long as he touched the earth; and when he was lifted from it, his strength was renewed on touching it again. It was Heracles who succeeded in killing this charmed giant by lifting him from the earth and squeezing him to death.

Antenor. A Trojan in Homer's ILIAD. It was he who advised that Helen return to Menelaus. He appears also in Chaucer's *Troilus and Criseyde* and in Shakespeare's *Troilus and Cressida.*

Anteros. In late Greek mythology, a son of Aphrodite and brother of Eros, the avenger of unreturned love. Or, according to some authorities, the opponent of Eros.

Anthony, St. First Christian monastic. He lived in the third or fourth century and founded a fraternity of ascetics who lived in the deserts of Egypt. The story of his temptations by the devil is a well-known subject of literature and art. It is the basis of Flaubert's novel, *La Tentation de Saint Antoine.*

Anthony, Susan Brownell (1820–1906). American reformer and teacher. She organized the Woman's State Temperance Society of New York, and was president of the National American Woman Suffrage Association (1892–1900). A firm abolitionist, she was among the first, after the Civil War, to support Negro suffrage. She conducted many lecture tours, and tested the suffrage law in the case of *United States vs. Susan B. Anthony.*

Anthony Adverse (1933). A historical novel by Hervey ALLEN. An enormous popular success, the book is set in the Napoleonic era and takes its hero all over the world in a series of rousing adventures. The enthusiastic response of readers to the book's great length surprised the publishing world and caused a trend, influencing numerous other works.

Anthony of Padua, St. (1195–1231). Franciscan friar, preacher, and theologian. He was born in Portugal, but spent his life teaching theology in France and Italy; he died in Padua, Italy. There is a legend that St. Anthony preached to a school of fishes that listened attentively until he was finished.

Antic Hay (1923). A satirical novel by Aldous HUXLEY. Comical and bitter, it is about a group of London intellectuals and their long, learned, futile conversations, in which everything seems valueless— God, love, art, learning, social reform, science. The central character is timid Theodore Gumbril, Junior, who gives up his job as a teacher to try to sell a new kind of trousers with built-in air cushion seats. He purchases a thick beard to help him act the part of a confident, aggressive man in business and in love. As in *Crome Yellow,* the general atmosphere of despair is deepened when the hero loses his girl.

Antichrist. Biblical term, occurring in the Epistles of John (I John 2:18), which refers to a "man of sin" (II Thess. 2:3) who denies the Father and Son and disowns the incarnation and messianic role of Jesus. Many legends are connected with the Antichrist, or deceiver, whose presence was supposed to precede the Second Coming of Christ and betoken the end of the world. Such stories are founded chiefly in II Thess. 2:1–12 and Rev. 8. The blasphemous beast with 7 heads and 10 horns, associated with the mystic numer 666, is identified with the Antichrist (Rev. 13–14). The early Christians associated the Antichrist with Caligula and Nero; Muhammad was also called Antichrist; and the name has since been applied figuratively to Hitler, Stalin, and other disturbers of world peace.

Antietam. A creek near Sharpsburg, Md., and the site of one of the bloodiest battles (Sept. 17, 1862) of the U.S. Civil War. Although the battle was a draw, the Union claimed victory because General Lee withdrew the Confederate troops to Virginia. General McClellan, the Union commander, was severely criticized for failing to pursue Lee and was soon replaced. See EMANCIPATION PROCLAMATION.

Antigone. In Greek mythology, the elder daughter of Oedipus. She is the heroine of Sophocles' tragedy ANTIGONE, and a principal character in his *Oedipus at Colonus* and Euripides' PHOENICIAN WOMEN. She appears briefly in the interpolated ending of Aeschylus' SEVEN AGAINST THEBES.

Antigone. One of the earliest extant tragedies of SOPHOCLES. After the defeat of the expedition of the SEVEN AGAINST THEBES, Creon, now king, decrees that the body of Polyneices shall lie unburied, in defiance of the rites due the dead. Antigone, OEDIPUS' daughter, gives her brother a token burial and, though she is affianced to his son Haemon, Creon condemns her to burial alive. Warned by TIRESIAS, he regrets his act too late; Antigone and Haemon kill themselves and Creon's wife Eurydice does the same on hearing the news.

Antigone (1942). A play by Jean ANOUILH first produced despite censorship as an allegory of France under the Vichy government.

Antigonus. A Sicilian lord and the beleaguered husband of the bold and strong-minded Paulina, in Shakespeare's WINTER'S TALE. When, at the command of King Leontes, he attempts to abandon the king's infant daughter in a deserted place, he is eaten by a bear.

Antilochus (Antilochos). In Greek legend, the son of Nestor and friend of Achilles. He was chosen to break to Achilles the news of Patroclus' death. Antilochus was killed by Memnon, the son of Aurora and Tithonus. The three friends, Antilochus, Achilles, and Patroclus were buried in the same mound. Odysseus saw them walking together in the underworld.

Antin, Mary. See PROMISED LAND, THE.

Antiochus. In Pierre Corneille's tragedy RODO-GUNE, the stepson of the wicked queen Cleopatra and the betrothed of Rodogune.

Antiope. (1) See AMPHION.

Antiope. (2) A queen of the AMAZONS. See THESEUS.

Antipholus of Ephesus and **Antipholus of Syracuse.** In Shakespeare's COMEDY OF ERRORS, the lost twin sons of Aegeon and Aemilia. Antipholus of Ephesus is the husband of Adriana. Antipholus of Syracuse comes to Ephesus in search of his lost brother and becomes enamored of Adriana's sister, Luciana.

Antiphon (c. 479–410 B.C.) A Greek Sophist and rhetorician. Against PROTAGORAS and the early Sophists, who believed in the supremacy of conventional law, he argued that men were by nature seekers after life, comfort, and unlimited pleasure, and that all law and restraint were consequently opposed to nature, which was for him the standard of right. He advised men to evade the law whenever possible; to obey it when expedient. Other Sophists developed the doctrine that might makes right from his work.

antipope. See POPE.

Antiquary, The (1816). A novel by Sir Walter SCOTT, and his own favorite among his works. It deals with the love of William Lovel for the daughter of Sir Arthur Wardour in the time of George III. See Jonathan OLDBUCK and Edie OCHILTREE.

Antisthenes. See CYNICS.

Antoine, André (1858–1943). French actor and theater director. Antoine is known for his directorship of the *Théâtre Libre* (1887–1894). A passionate love for the theater accompanied his desire to see more freedom and more possibility for experimentation on the French stage. Avant-garde in its bold unconventionality, the *Théâtre Libre* produced principally the plays of the naturalists, although it also played the works of contemporary Scandinavian, Russian, and German dramatists. Financial failure did not discourage Antoine, who opened another theater, the *Théâtre Antoine,* in 1897. He had already done much to revolutionize French theater, to encourage naturalness and to dispense with artificial stage conventions.

Antoinette, Marie. See MARIE ANTOINETTE.

Antonello da Messina (c. 1430–1479). Italian painter. After his early years at Messina, Sicily, he went to Naples; there he encountered the Flemish style of painting, particularly the use of oils, in such works as those of Jan van Eyck. In the years following 1475, both in Venice and other Italian cities, he became the chief sponsor of the new technique. His works, which favor the miniature still life, are noted for their handling of light and mastery of perspective. Among those considered his masterpieces are *Saint Jerome in his study* and the *Virgin Annunciate.*

Antonio. (1) The title character of Shakespeare's MERCHANT OF VENICE.

(2) The treacherous brother of Prospero in Shakespeare's THE TEMPEST. With the help of Alonso, the king of Naples, he has usurped Prospero's dukedom and cast him and his infant daughter adrift on a rotting bark. He is never troubled by conscience, but is, at last, forced to restore his brother's rightful position to him.

Antony, Mark or Marc. In Latin, Marcus Antonius (c. 82–30 B.C.). Roman triumvir and general. He was one of the tribunes who, in 49 B.C., supported Caesar and joined him before crossing the RUBICON. He was appointed consul in 44 and, after Caesar's death, swung the populace against the assassins to his favor with his eloquent oratory. It was at this time that CICERO delivered his famous Philippics (orations) against Antony. In 43, the Second TRIUMVIRATE of Antony, Octavian (later Augustus), and Lepidus was formed. Caesar's assassins, Brutus and Cassius, were defeated at Philippi in 42. From the year 40 on, Antony lived chiefly at Alexandria with CLEOPATRA, queen of Egypt, abandoning his wife Octavia, sister of Octavian. Open hostilities between Octavian and Antony broke out, and, in 31, the combined forces of Antony and Cleopatra were defeated by Octavian at ACTIUM. Antony committed suicide in Egypt after hearing a false report of Cleopatra's death (circulated, some say, by Cleopatra herself in an attempt to win Octavian's favor by causing Antony's death).

In Shakespeare's JULIUS CAESAR, he is portrayed as a devoted friend of Caesar. Though he is fond of revelry and amusements, he is also a shrewd strategist and capable general. After Caesar's death, he skillfully turns public opinion against the assassins by means of his funeral oration, which begins with the famous lines:

> Friends, Romans, countrymen, lend me your ears;
> I come to bury Caesar, not to praise him.
> The evil that men do lives after them,
> The good is oft interred with their bones;
> So let it be with Caesar.

Antony is depicted in Shakespeare's ANTONY AND CLEOPATRA as a declining hero, torn between his love for Cleopatra and his political ambitions. After his death, Agrippa utters a fitting epitaph:

> A rarer spirit never
> Did steer humanity; but you, gods, will give us
> Some faults to make us men.

Antony and Cleopatra (c. 1607). A tragedy by William SHAKESPEARE. Having given himself over to a life of sensual pleasure with CLEOPATRA in Egypt, Marc ANTONY returns to Rome upon hearing of his wife's death and of an attack on Italy by the forces of Sextus Pompeius. In Rome the differences between Antony and the two other triumvirs, Octavius CAESAR and Lepidus, are patched up by Antony's marriage to OCTAVIA, the sister of Octavius. When Antony, succumbing to Cleopatra's enticements, returns to Egypt, Octavius seizes upon the insult to his sister as a pretext for attacking his erstwhile ally. Octavius wins the naval battle of Actium when Cleopatra's fleet deserts. Antony, after unsuccessfully seeking to make terms with the victor, hurls defiance at him. Defeated in a later land battle and believing Cleopatra dead, the despairing Antony falls on his sword. Hearing that she is still alive, he is taken to her and lives long enough to lay his last kiss upon her lips. When Cleopatra learns that Octavius, now sole master of the empire, plans to lead her in triumph through Rome, the proud and imperious queen applies an asp to her bosom and joins her lover in death.

Shakespeare's source for the play was Sir Thomas North's translation (1579) of Plutarch's *Lives*. Dryden's drama *All for Love* (1678) also describes the last days of Antony and Cleopatra, and for many years was more frequently performed than the Shakespearean version. See Domitius ENOBARBUS.

Anu. The Babylonian god of heaven. A development of the Sumerian god AN, he was descended from Tiamat, the sea; his own parents were Anshar and Kishar. He was deposed and emasculated by KUMARBI, and replaced on his throne by his son Ea, the god of water and wisdom, who became far more important in the Babylonian pantheon than Anu himself.

Anubis. In Egyptian mythology, a deity who presided over funeral rites and insured the accuracy of the scales weighing the souls of the dead. He was the son of Osiris, the judge of the infernal regions, and was represented as a man with a jackal's head.

Anunnaki. The Sumerian deities of the underworld. Originally followers of the god of heaven, ANU, they somehow became gods of the underworld where they were inferior to its queen, ERESHKIGAL. Their demotion may have been punishment for some crime, or merely the result of Anu's displacement as principal god of the pantheon by Enlil.

Anville, Evelina. See EVELINA, OR THE HISTORY OF A YOUNG LADY'S ENTRANCE INTO THE WORLD.

Anzengruber, Ludwig (1839–1889). Austrian dramatist. He is best known for his dialect plays depicting rustic life, such as *Der Meineidbauer* (*The Farmer Forsworn*, 1872) and *Der Doppelselbstmord* (*The Double Suicide*, 1876). Because of his use of dialect and his treatment, especially in *Das vierte Gebot* (*The Fourth Commandment*, 1877), of family problems, he was important in the genesis of dramatic NATURALISM.

Aonian. Pertaining to Aonia, the region of Mts. Helicon and Cithaeron, in Boeotia. The Muses were supposed to live there. The Aonian fount was the fountain of Aganippe at the foot of Mt. Helicon.

Apache. The name of a nomadic and predatory tribe of North American Indians of Athapascan linguistic stock. They occupied what is now the southwestern U.S. The name is often applied to the hooligans of Paris; an *apache* dance is a violently acrobatic exhibition supposedly danced by a Parisian apache and his partner.

Apemantus. The churlish, cynical philosopher in Shakespeare's TIMON OF ATHENS. He foresees Timon's ruin and chides him for his pride, as great in ruin as it was in wealth. His hatred of mankind is paralleled and later surpassed by Timon's misanthropy.

Apes of God, The (1930). A novel by Wyndham LEWIS. It is an epic satire on the rich Bohemian artistic coteries which in Lewis's eyes reflected the social decay of the period. Among writers satirized are the Sitwell family, Gertrude Stein, James Joyce, and Virginia Woolf and the Bloomsbury group.

Aphrodite. The Greek goddess of erotic love and marriage. Although Homer calls her a daughter of Zeus and Dione, it was the more common story that she was born from the foam that gathered about the severed parts of the emasculated Uranus. She is said to have first stepped ashore on the island of Cythera, just off the coast of Laconia, hence her epithet Cytherea. Her name was identified by the Greeks with the word *aphros,* seafoam. As an Olympian deity, she was the wife of Hephaestus, but the lover of Ares. A familiar story about her tells how Hephaestus trapped her in bed with Ares by throwing a delicate golden net over them, and displayed their embarrassment to the other gods. In late Greek myth, Aphrodite was called the mother of EROS.

It is generally agreed that Aphrodite was originally an Asiatic goddess similar to ISHTAR. An ancient center of her worship was the island of Cyprus for which she was often called Cypris. In Rome, she was identified with Venus. See ADONIS.

Apicius, Marcus Flavius (fl., A.D. 14–37). A Roman epicure in the time of Tiberius. He wrote a book on the ways of tempting an appetite. Having spent a fortune in supplying rare delicacies for his table, and having only 10 million sesterces (about $400,000) left, he hanged himself, not thinking it possible to exist on such a wretched pittance. *Apicia* has become a stock name for certain cakes and sauces, and his own name is still proverbial in all matters of gastronomy.

Apis. In Egyptian mythology, the bull of Memphis, sacred to Osiris, of whose soul it was supposed to be the image; others said it was the union of divine and animal souls. The sacred bull had to have natural spots forming a triangle on the forehead and a half-moon on the breast. It was allowed to live only 25 years, when it was sacrificed and buried with great pomp.

apocalyptic literature (Gr., *apokalupsis,* "uncovering"). A type of prophetic literature common in ancient Hebrew and early Christian writing. It is filled with veiled symbolism (see FOUR HORSEMEN OF THE APOCALYPSE) and inspired by visions of the future triumph of the Messianic kingdom. THE REVELATION OF ST. JOHN THE DIVINE is often called the *Apocalypse*.

Apocrypha (Gr., *apokrupto,* "hidden"). Certain Old Testament books of doubtful authority. These books are included in the Greek (Septuagint) and Latin (Vulgate) versions of the Old Testament, but are usually regarded as noncanonical or of secondary value by other Christians and Jews. They are seldom printed in Protestant Bibles, but in the Authorized Version of 1611 they are given immediately after the Old Testament. The New Testament also has a large number of apocryphal books associated with it, consisting of later gospels, epistles, apocalypses and such fragments as the *Logia*. ORIGEN was the first to apply the term to books used by the church, to designate writings of a questionable character; it has come to signify false and heretical literature.

Apollinaire, Guillaume [born **Wilhelm Apollinaris de Kostrowitski**] (1880–1918). French poet and critic. In 1898, he met Alfred JARRY in Paris and was attracted to *l'esprit nouveau*, the new spirit in esthetic theory. A friend of Picasso, Braque, and other avant-garde artists, he wrote *Antitradition futuriste* and *The Cubist Painters* in 1913. The latter work first established CUBISM as a school of painting. The poems in *Alcools* (1913) combined free and classical verse forms; those in *Calligrammes* (1918) used words to draw lines, the controversial typography carrying poetry to its extreme limits. He called *Les Mamelles de Tirésias* (1903, pub. 1917) a "drame surréaliste," apparently the source of the name of the surrealist movement. It was made into an opera (1947) by Francis Poulenc, Apollinaire's other works include fiction: *L'Hérésiarque et Cie* (1910) and *The Poet Assassinated* (1916); the verse play *Couleur du Temps* (1918); and the posthumously published *Ombre de mon amour* (1948), poems, and *Tendre comme le souvenir* (1952), letters.

Apollo (Apollon). A Greek god, son of Zeus and Leto. Originally, perhaps, a god of flocks, he also became a god of healing, music, and archery. As Phoebus Apollo, he came to be the god of light, but not properly of the sun. He was born, with his sister Artemis, on the island of Delos, where his mother had taken refuge from the jealous Hera. At an early age, he killed the Python, the sacred snake of the DELPHIC ORACLE, and took charge of that oracle, which had previously belonged to a succession of earth godesses. Though implacable in anger, as the fates of MARSYAS and NIOBE show, he was surprisingly unsuccessful in love, to judge from the number of nymphs and mortals, such as DAPHNE and MARPESSA, who rejected his advances. Nevertheless, he has been called "the most Greek of Greek gods," speaking more than once for modern concepts of justice and human relations as opposed to the more primitive traditions. The most notable example of this tendency is his defense of Orestes on the Areopagus, dramatized in Aeschylus' *Eumenides*.

Apollodorus (Apollodoros). A Greek mythographer. Nothing is known of him, but his one extant work (if it is his), *The Library (Bibliotheke)*, is one of the most important sources of Greek mythology. Though it draws on the works of APOLLONIUS OF RHODES and the Athenian dramatists, it was largely based on a lost book by Pherecydes of Leros, dating from the early fifth century B.C.

Apollonian and Dionysiac. Terms used by Friedrich Nietzsche in THE BIRTH OF TRAGEDY to designate the two central principles in Greek culture. The Apollonian, which corresponds to Schopenhauer's *principium individuationis* ("principle of individuation"), is the basis of all analytic distinctions. Everything that is part of the unique individuality of a man or thing is Apollonian in character; all types of *form* or *structure* are Apollonian, since form serves to define or individualize that which is formed; thus, sculpture is the most Apollonian of the arts, since it relies entirely on form for its effect. Rational thought is also Apollonian since it is structured and makes distinctions.

The Dionysiac, which corresponds roughly to Schopenhauer's conception of "will," is directly opposed to the Apollonian. Drunkenness and madness are Dionysiac because they break down a man's individual character; all forms of enthusiasm and ecstasy are Dionysiac, for in such states a man gives up his individuality and submerges himself in a greater whole; music is the most Dionysiac of the arts, since it appeals directly to man's instinctive, chaotic emotions and not to his formally reasoning mind.

Nietzsche believed that both forces were present in Greek tragedy, and that true tragedy could only be produced by the tension between them. He used the names Apollonian and Dionysiac for the two forces because Apollo, as the sun-god, represents light, clarity, and form, whereas Dionysus, as the wine-god, represents drunkenness and ecstasy.

Apollonius of Rhodes (Apollonios Rhodios). An Alexandrian poet of the 3d-2d centuries B.C. According to tradition, he was a pupil of Callimachus, but quarreled with him and, when his youthful work the *Argonautica* proved unpopular, went to Rhodes. He later abridged this epic of the voyage of the ARGONAUTS; it won favor and he was appointed head of the Alexandrian Library.

Apollonius of Tyana or **Apollonios Tyanaios** (fl. A.D. 50). Greek Neo-Pythagorean philosopher. He studied in the temple of Asclepius at Aegae. An ascetic, he traveled through India, Babylonia, and Persia, absorbing mysticism. He had a school at Ephesus, and was credited with magical powers. Philostratus wrote a biography of Apollonius, recording his miraculous feats; the work is regarded as religious fiction.

Apologia pro vita sua, or a History of My Religious Opinions (1864). An autobiographical treatise by John Henry NEWMAN. In it the author outlines and defends the intellectual development that led to his conversion from the Anglican to the Roman Catholic Church. One of the most famous of English autobiographies, it is noted for its candor and intellectual passion, its subtle and musical prose style.

Apologie for Poetrie, An. An essay by Sir Philip SIDNEY, written during 1580–1583 in answer to an attack on poetry by the Puritan Stephen Gosson in THE SCHOOL OF ABUSE (1579). Sidney's essay defines as poetry all imaginative writing. In addition to defending its worth and replying to Puritan accusations against it, Sidney gives his own critical appraisal of the poetry and drama of the time. Two different editions of the essay, one titled *An Apologie for Poetrie*, the other *The Defense of Poesie*, were posthumously published in 1595.

Apology for Raymond Sebond (Apologie de Raimond Sebond). The longest of the ESSAYS of Michel de MONTAIGNE. It gives fullest expression to his skeptical philosophy. Montaigne's "defense" of the treatise of Sebond, a 15th-century Spaniard who attempted to demonstrate the existence of God by analogy with the hierarchy of nature in which man occupies the highest rung, was a pretense for demolishing the validity of reasoning altogether. Sebond's proof, asserted Montaigne, was no less credible than any other proof. Man vainly believes himself superior to the rest of creation by virtue of his reason, whereas in fact all his theorizing has not uncovered a single universal truth. Montaigne's skepticism was an affirmation of the relativity of knowledge and essentially a healthy reaction to the excessive faith in reason of the early Renaissance. It cleared his mind of preconceptions and prepared him for a search for wisdom based, not on intellectual speculation, but on his own experience.

Apology for the Life of Mrs. Shamela Andrews, An (1741). A novel by Henry FIELDING satirizing Samuel Richardson's PAMELA. Shamela is presented as a designing woman who deliberately tricks her master into marrying her.

Apolonio, Libro de. A Spanish heroic poem of the first half of the 13th century by an anonymous author, probably an Aragonese. Consisting of 2624 verses, it one of the oldest examples of CUADERNA VÍA. The story, based on a Greek legend, deals with Apollonius, prince of Tyre, who is separated from his wife, Luciana, and their daughter, Tarsia; after many adventures they are finally reunited. Other authors have utilized this theme, notably Shakespeare in *Pericles*.

Apophis. In Egyptian mythology, the power of darkness in the form of a serpent against whom the sun god Ra waged daily war.

aposiopesis. Deliberate failure to complete a sentence for rhetorical effect. As a figure of speech the form is often used to convey an impression of extreme exasperation or to imply a threat, as, for example, in "If you do that, why, I'll—" The rest of the sentence is understood.

apostles (Gr., *apostolos*, messenger, envoy). Jesus' 12 original disciples: PETER, ANDREW, JAMES THE LESS, JOHN, PHILIP, BARTHOLOMEW, THOMAS, MATTHEW, SIMON THE CANAANITE (also Simon Zelotes), JUDE (also Thaddaeus and Lebbaeus), JAMES THE GREATER, and JUDAS ISCARIOT. Jesus gave His message to these men personally and gave them the task of being his witness after His death. He shared with them the LAST SUPPER, which has become the fundamental sacrament of Christian worship.

To the apostles, Jesus entrusted the work of establishing the Church, with Peter to be the "rock" upon which it was built. Matthias was later chosen to take Judas Iscariot's place. All of the apostles met martyr's deaths except John and, of course, Judas Iscariot who committed suicide.

Beside Judas Iscariot, two other apostles have not been canonized: Philip and Simon the Canaanite. Paul, though not one of the original 12, is always classed as an apostle as is often Barnabas, Paul's companion in his first mission.

Apostolic Fathers. Christian authors born in the 1st century, when the apostles lived. John is supposed to have died about A.D. 99; Polycarp, the last of the Apostolic Fathers, born about 69, was his disciple. The *Five Apostolic Fathers* most referred to are Clement of Rome, Barnabas, Hermas, Ignatius, and Polycarp.

apostolic succession. A theological docu:ine first enunciated by Irenaeus (fl. 190). It maintains that the bishops of the church are direct spiritual descendants of the apostles and of the bishops consecrated by them, and that authority over the church's faith and discipline resides in them.

Apostolius, Michael (1422–1480). Greek scholar in Italy during the Renaissance. He defended Plato against the Greek Aristotelians.

apostrophe. A figure of speech using the direct address of a person or thing, usually absent, for rhetorical effect. The thing addressed is often personified, as in "Hence, loathed Melancholy!" which begins Milton's *L'Allegro*. The object of the apostrophe is frequently a real person, living or dead, as in "Milton, thou shouldst be living at this hour," the beginning of Wordsworth's sonnet on Milton.

Appian Way (Lat., *Via Appia*). The oldest and best preserved of all the Roman roads, it leads from Rome to Brundisium (Brindisi) by way of Capua. This "queen of roads" was commenced by Appius Claudius, the censor, in 312 B.C.

Appius Claudius. Roman decemvir (451–450 B.C.). He was one of 10 decemvirs appointed to draw up a code of Roman law. According to tradition, his passion for the beautiful plebian VIRGINIA caused an uprising, led by her father, which overthrew the decemvirate and established a tribunate.

apple of discord. In Greek mythology, the initial cause of the Trojan War. All the gods and goddesses except Eris (Discord) were invited to the wedding of Thetis and Peleus. In revenge, Eris threw among the guests a golden apple inscribed "For the fairest." Hera, Athene, and Aphrodite claimed it and were referred to Paris, the handsomest man in the world, for judgment. See the JUDGMENT OF PARIS.

Appleseed, Johnny. Nickname of **John Chapman** (1774–1845). American orchardist and folk hero. Born in Massachusetts, Chapman wandered westward to Pennsylvania, Ohio, Illinois, and Indiana. For 50 years he led a nomadic existence, preaching and distributing apple seeds to all he met. It is said that the orchards of the four states above owe their origin to Chapman's seeds.

Johnny Appleseed has become a favorite American folk hero, celebrated in many stories and poems. The poet Vachel Lindsay, who frequently referred to him, wrote a long poem called *In Praise of Johnny Appleseed* (1923).

apples of perpetual youth. In Scandinavian mythology, magical golden apples. They were in the keeping of Idhunn, daughter of the dwarf Svald and wife of Bragi. It is by tasting them that the gods preserve their youth.

apples of Sodom. Fruit which, in classical tradition, grew beside the Dead Sea. They are lovely in appearance, but full of ashes within. Josephus, Strabo, Tacitus, and others speak of them, probably referring to the gall-nuts produced by the insect *Cynips insana*.

Après-midi d'un faune, L' (The Afternoon of a Faun, 1876). A poem by Stephane MALLARMÉ. It presents the wandering thoughts of a faun on a drowsy summer afternoon. The poem inspired Debussy's *Prélude à l'Après-midi d'un faune* (1894), which was choreographed and danced by Nijinsky for Diaghilev's Russian Ballet in 1912.

Apsu. See ABZU.

Apsyrtus (Apsyrtos). See the ARGONAUTS

Apuleius, Lucius (fl., c. A.D. 155). Latin writer. He is best known today for his prose romance *Metamorphoses,* or THE GOLDEN ASS, the only Latin novel that survives in its entirety. Apuleius was born in North Africa. After studying in Carthage and Athens, he spent a number of years traveling and delving into the magic lore of the Mediterranean countries. He incorporated his vast knowledge and experience into the 11-volume *The Golden Ass.* Here, in a prose style as odd and fanciful as the tale itself, he narrates the story of a man who, transformed into a donkey, wanders from land to land observing the preposterous and brutal foibles of mankind. In one of the episodes, Apuleius recounts the famous story of Cupid and PSYCHE.

Aqhat. Hero of the Canaanite THE POEM OF AQHAT. The young son of the chieftain Danel, he is given a divine bow belonging to Anat. She kills him and he is eaten by eagles, but avenged by his sister Paghat. It is probable that in the lost final section of the poem, Aqhat revived.

Aquilante. In the Orlando poems of Boiardo and Ariosto he is the son of Oliviero and brother of Grifone (see ORLANDO FURIOSO). He is called *il nero* (the black) and his brother *il bianco* (the white) because each is protected by an enchantress of that color. The black enchantress had saved him from an eagle (hence his name) which had stolen him from his mother Ghismonda.

Aquinas, St. Thomas (c. 1225–1274). Italian scholastic theologian and philosopher, often called the Angelic Doctor (Lat., *Doctor Angelicus*). He came from a noble family, who strongly objected when he joined the Dominican Order in 1243 and forcibly detained him for over a year. He finally reached Paris and began his studies under ALBERTUS MAGNUS, whom he followed to Cologne in 1248. He began teaching at Paris in 1252, and thereafter taught alternately in Paris and in Italy. In 1254 he began his commentaries on the *Sentences* of Peter LOMBARD, on Boethius, and on the Bible, revealing Albertus Magnus and St. AUGUSTINE of Hippo as the greatest influences on his thought.

The treatises that followed were later incorporated into his two great *Summae,* or summaries of human knowledge. The *Summa [de Veritate Catholicae Fidei] contra Gentiles* (1259–1264) defends "the truth of the Catholic faith against the pagans" by making clear the distinction between the realms of reason and of faith: reason seeks knowledge from experimental and logical evidence, while faith seeks understanding through revelation, but uses the knowledge provided by reason. Thus they can never be in conflict, and both come from and reveal God as the source of all truth. The SUMMA THEOLOGICA, his greatest work, continues on this basis to summarize all that is known about God and man from the sources of both reason and faith.

Aquinas' followers were called *Thomists* in later scholastic disputes, especially with the Scotists (see John DUNS SCOTUS). His synthesis of theology and philosophy, known as Thomism, has since been officially recognized as a cornerstone in the doctrines of the Roman Catholic Church.

Arabian Nights' Entertainments, The, or **A Thousand and One Nights.** A collection of ancient Persian-Indian-Arabian tales, originally in Arabic, arranged in its present form about 1450, probably in Cairo. Although the stories are discrete in plot, they are unified by SCHEHERAZADE, the supposed teller; she postpones her execution by telling her husband, SCHAHRIAH, a story night after night, without revealing the climax until the following session.

The first European translation, into French, was Antoine Galland's 12-volume (1704–1717) free rendering of the oldest known manuscript of 1548. In 1840, E. W. Lane published a new scholarly English translation (three vols.); John Payne's translation appeared in nine volumes, 1882–1884; and Sir Richard Burton's monumental (10-vol.) English version was issued only to subscribers by the Kamashastra Society of Benares in 1885–1886. Among the more recent editions is a four-volume edition by Powys Mathers, completed in 1937. See ABOU HASSAN; ALADDIN; ALI BABA AND THE FORTY THIEVES; CALENDER; CARPET, MAGIC; HAROUN-AL-RASCHID; SINBAD THE SAILOR; Sidi NOUMAN.

Arachne. In Greek mythology, Arachne was a Lydian maiden. She challenged Athena to compete with her in needle tapestry. Athena metamorphosed her into a spider out of jealousy. *Arachnida* is the scientific name for spiders, scorpions, and mites.

Araf or **Al Araf.** In the Koran, the Islamic equivalent of purgatory, between heaven and hell. It is a place both for those neither morally good nor bad, and for those who, because their good and evil deeds were about equally balanced, must await their ultimate admission to heaven.

Edgar Allan Poe has a poem called AL AARAAF.

Arafat, Mount. A hill southeast of Mecca where, according to Muslim tradition, Adam met Eve after a punitive separation of 200 years during which time he was a wanderer on the face of the earth. He was conducted to its summit by the angel Gabriel.

Aragon, house of. A noble family of Spanish origin. Its members ruled in Sicily and later in southern Italy from the 13th through the 15th century. At Naples, the outstanding King Alfonso of Aragon (1385–1458), surnamed the Great, who ruled from 1443, was a celebrated patron of Humanists and poets. Under his inspiration, the men of letters gathered at his court founded the Neapolitan Academy, which included such men as Pontano and Sannazaro.

Aragon, Louis (1897–   ). French novelist, poet, and essayist. After brief associations with Cubism and DADAISM, Aragon wrote the novel *Le Paysan de Paris* (1926) as a participant in SURREALISM. He criticized the ideal of "pure poetry" in *Traité du style* (1928), however, and became a Communist in 1930, thereafter to devote his art to the ideal of social revolution. He was prosecuted for his poem *The Red Front* (1931), but responded with more poetry: *Persécuteur persécuté* (1931) and *Hourra l'Oural* (1934), and with leftist magazines. Social novels depicting "the real world," as the series is collectively titled include: *The Bells of Basel (Cloches de Bâle,* 1936) and *Passengers of Destiny (Les Voyageurs de l'impériale,* 1941; also trans. *The Century Was Young). Aurelien* (1944) and *Les Communistes* (1949) are autobiographical. Aragon abandoned current politics, however, in *Holy Week (La Semaine Sainte,* 1958), a panoramic epic of the flight of Louis XVIII at the beginning of Napoleon's 100 days in 1815.

His books of poetry include *Le Crève-Coeur* (1941), *Les Yeux d'Elsa* (1942), *Brocéliande* (1943), and *Le Nouveau Crève-Coeur* (1948). Many of these describe his participation in the Resistance and his love for his Russian-born wife **Elsa Triolet** (1896–   ), author of the novels *The White Charger* (1943) and *Fine of 200 Francs* (1945), as well as novels dealing with postwar social problems.

Aramis. One of the famous trio in Dumas' THE THREE MUSKETEERS, and a prominent character in its sequels TWENTY YEARS AFTER and THE VISCOUNT of BRAGELONNE. Aramis, always soberly garbed in black, regularly swore that he would soon forego his adventures for a pious life in a monastery.

Aranha, José Pereira de Graça. See José Pereira de GRAÇA ARANHA.

Ararat, Mount. See NOAH.

Araucana, La (1569–1590). An epic poem by Alfonso de Ercilla y Zúñiga (1533–1594), Spanish soldier and poet who went to Chile after the conquest and fought against the indomitable Araucanian Indians. The stubborn resistance of the Araucanians against Spanish rule is the theme of the poem. Ercilla stresses the nobility and valor of the Indians and of their leaders Lautaro and Caupolicán, who are drawn in Homeric proportions.

Arbante. In a tale from Ariosto's ORLANDO FURIOSO he is the son of King Cimosco of Frisia, the spouse of Olimpia, and the victim of the latter's unwillingness to marry him. Olimpia has him killed before they wed.

Arbaud, Joseph d' (1874–   ). Provençal poet and novelist. Recorder of the old language and traditions of the Provence region, Arbaud presented in *The Laurel of Arles* (*Lou Lausié d'Arle;* 1913) his philosophy that a tree—or a culture—must have deep roots to grow high. His works include poems: *Songs of the Marshes* (*Li Cant palustre;* 1919), *The Brazen Boughs* (*Li Rampau d'aram;* 1920), and *Vision of the North* (*La Visioun de l'Uba;* 1921). Among his novels are *The Beast of the Vaccares* (*La Bèstio dóu Vacarés;* 1924), *The Gypsy* (*La Caraco;* 1926). *Wild Animals* (*La Souvagino;* 1929) is a story collection.

Arber, Edward (1836–1912). English scholar. He was the editor of *Arber's English Reprints* (1868–1880) and other series of cheap, accurate editions of 15th-18th century works. He also edited *Transcript of the Registers of the Company of Stationers of London, 1554–1640* (1875–1894) and *Term Catalogues, 1668–1709* (1903–1906), basic sources for research in English literature and publishing.

Arbor of Amorous Devices, The. An anthology of Elizabethan lyric poetry. Published in 1597, it was one of many such published in England after the success of TOTTEL'S MISCELLANY. It was attributed by the printers to NICHOLAS BRETON, but it contains the work of other poets as well.

Arbuthnot, John (1667–1735). Scottish writer and court physician to Queen Anne. He was a close friend of Alexander Pope and Jonathan Swift and formed with them the SCRIBLERUS CLUB. His works include *The History of* JOHN BULL, which typified and fixed John Bull as the personification of England; *The Art of Political Lying* (1712), an essay; *Know Thyself* (1734), a philosophical poem; and *The Memoirs of* MARTINUS SCRIBLERUS (1741), an attack

THE ARBOR OF amorous Deuifes.

VVherin, young Gentlemen

may reade many plefant fancies, and fine deuifes: And
thereon, meditate diuers fweete Conceites, to court
the loue of faire Ladies and Gentlewomen
By N. B, Gent,

Imprinted at London by Richard Iohnes, dwelling at the
figne of the Rofe and Crowne, neere Saint Andrewes
Church in Holborne,
1597.

Title page of *The Arbor of Amorous Devices* (1597).

on pedantry. He is the addressee of Pope's EPISTLE TO DR. ARBUTHNOT.

Arcades ambo (Lat., "both Arcadians"). Two people with similar skills and tastes, such as CORYDON and THYRSIS in Vergil's *Seventh Bucolic,* who were "both in the flower of youth, both Arcadians and peers of pastoral song." When used ironically, the term implies that both are simpletons or scoundrels.

Arcadia (**Arkadia**). A district of the Greek Peloponnesus. According to Vergil, it was the home of pastoral simplicity and happiness. This notion was an early example of an illusion that has beset sophisticated intellectuals ever since: namely, that a simple, rustic life is not only idyllic, but somehow nobler than a more complex urban existence. The Arcadians were, as a matter of fact, the most backward of the Greeks, retaining to a relatively late date primitive, even savage customs that had long since died out elsewhere in Greece. Hence, to less poetically minded authors, the term Arcadian came to have a derogatory meaning.

The name Arcadia was taken by Sir Philip Sidney as the title of his famous pastoral romance (1590) and was soon generally adopted into English with much the old Virgilian significance. A 17th-century painting by Guercino, and a more famous one by Poussin of a slightly later date, show a shepherd's tomb on which is the inscription *Et in Arcadia ego* (Even in Arcadia am I), signifying presumably that death is present even in the most ideal earthly life.

Arcadian Academy (Accademia dell' Arcadia). An Italian literary academy founded at Rome (c. 1690) at the suggestion of Queen Christina of Sweden and headed by Giovanni Maria Crescimbeni, an historian of Italian poetry.

The academy's members proposed to counteract the fashionable mannerism of MARINISM by a return to the simple, unsophisticated pastoral motifs of the classical poets (hence the name Arcadia). Their program included the use of an unpretentious language, a close imitation of the classical poets, and a preference for short verse forms: the ode, sonnet, and canzonetta. Among its members were Carlo Frugoni (1692–1768), generally considered the most typical exponent of Arcadian ideals ("Frugoneria" describes his sonorous style); Paolo Rolli (1687–1765), lyric poet, librettist for Handel, and tutor at the English court; and METASTASIO.

The academy came under the special protection of the royal house of Sweden and was never formally disestablished. It still maintains a formal existence although its role as arbiter of Italian literary taste came to an end with romanticism. See LEO XIII.

archangel. A chief angel. In Judeo-Christian Scriptures and legend there are four: Michael, the warrior; Raphael, the healer; Gabriel, the herald; and Uriel, bringer of light. In the Koran, the four are Michael, the champion of the faith; Gabriel, the angel of revelations; Azrael, the angel of death; and Israfel, who sounds the trumpet of the resurrection. In the medieval hierarchy (see ANGEL) the archangels comprise the second order of the third division.

Archbishop of Granada. In Lesage's novel GIL BLAS DE SANTILLANE, a very rich, proud, and inflexible church dignitary. Gil Blas becomes his secretary and favorite. When he dares to criticize the archbishop's oratorical excellence, he is dismissed.

Archer, Isabel. The heroine of Henry James' THE PORTRAIT OF A LADY. A girl of great vitality, Isabel has an insatiable thirst for experience which causes her to reject the proposal of Lord Warburton, a wealthy and cultivated Englishman, and to marry the shadowy and sinister Osmond. At all times treated sympathetically by James, she comes to realize the danger of her American expansiveness. Nevertheless, she asserts her inner freedom by refusing to leave the man she married.

Archilochian bitterness. Ill-natured satire. It is so named from Archilochus, the Greek satirist (714–676 B.C.).

Archiloro. A Negro giant in an episode from the ORLANDO INNAMORATO of Boiardo. He is killed at the battle of Albracca by Agricane, the king of Tartary, who hopes to win the hand of Angelica, princess of Cathay.

Archimago. The enchanter in Books I and II of Spenser's FAERIE QUEENE, typifying hypocrisy and false religion.

Archimedes (c. 287–212 B.C.). Syracusan mathematician, astronomer, and inventor. Several of his treatises, including that on the sphere and the cylinder, are still extant. Archimedes discovered the principle of the displacement of water, which, by means of specific gravity, he used to test the amount of base metal in the crown of Hieron, ruler of Syracuse. He is said to have exclaimed "EUREKA," or "I have

found it," when the principle occurred to him as he stepped into his bath.

Archipenko, Alexander Porfirievich (1887–1964). Russian sculptor. Settling in the U.S. in 1923, he experimented with plastic materials and with the effects of transparency and reflection, tending toward abstraction in his sculpture.

Archpoet. See GOLIARDIC VERSE.

archy and mehitabel. The famous cockroach and cat created by Don MARQUIS in his newspaper column. Their stories were written at night in Marquis' deserted office by literary archy, who was obliged to write without capitalization because he could not operate the shift key on the typewriter. Archy often related the ribald adventures of the indomitable mehitabel, whose motto was "toujours gai." *The lives and times of archy and mehitabel* (1940) contains the original collection of the columns, *archy and mehitabel* (1927), and its sequels, *archy's life of mehitabel* (1933) and *archy does his part* (1935).

Arcita. See TESEIDA.

Arcite. (1) See ANELIDA AND ARCITE.

(2) See KNIGHT'S TALE.

Arcos, René. See ABBAYE GROUP, THE.

Arcturus. See GREAT BEAR.

Arendt, Hannah (1906–   ). German writer on political philosophy. Now resident in the U.S., she was educated at the universities of Marburg and Freiburg, and received her doctorate at the University of Heidelberg. In this country, she has taught at a number of universities, including those of California, Chicago, Princeton, and Wesleyan. Her best-known book, *Eichmann in Jerusalem: A Report on the Banality of Evil* (1963), is a study of the implications of the famous, emotionally charged trial of a high-placed Nazi official; it created a storm of controversy upon publication and was debated for months in literary journals. Her other books include *The Origins of Totalitarianism* (1951), *The Human Condition* (1958), *Between Past and Future: Six Exercises in Political Thought* (1961), and *On Revolution* (1963). She has also contributed to numerous publications, such as the *Partisan Review, Commentary, Review of Politics,* and *Journal of Politics.*

From 1944 to 1946, Miss Arendt was research director for the Conference on Jewish Relations, and 1949–1952 director of Jewish Cultural Reconstruction.

Areopagitica (1644). A famous pamphlet by John MILTON, written as an argument against restriction of freedom of the press. Probably Milton's best-known prose work because of the greatness of its cause and the eloquence of its rhetoric, it commands more interest than most of his other theological or political writings.

Areopagus (Areiopagos). The hill of Ares, located in Athens, west of the Acropolis. According to Greek myth, it was so named because it was there that Ares was tried for the murder of Halirrhothios, son of Poseidon. According to another story, the hill was named after an epithet of Athene, who had cast the deciding vote in the second trial of Orestes, supposedly held on this hill.

The name was also applied to a council of former *archons*, who assembled there. Under DRACO, the council had the duty of judging murderers, and exercised general administrative powers. Ephialtes and PERICLES reduced the scope of its function.

Ares. The Greek god of war, a son of Zeus and Hera. He was a lover of APHRODITE, by whom he had several children, but he also had various other mistresses. Probably Thracian in origin, Ares had no characteristics except belligerence, and, therefore, was rather disapproved of by the Greeks.

Aretino, Pietro (1492–1556). Italian Renaissance author. Aretino is famous throughout Europe for the volume and audacity of his writings. A self-styled Scourge of Princes, he aimed his satire at the powerful men of his day, but primarily at its social customs and literary pretensions. He was honored by princes and popes, and a friend of artists such as Titian, who painted Aretino's portrait. Among his many works— letters, dialogues, poems, comedies and tragedies— are both lascivious sonnets and a book on Christ. His best-known work is the comedy *La cortigiana* (*Life at Court*), written in 1525.

Arévalo Martínez, Rafael (1884–   ). Guatemalan novelist and poet. Though little is known of it, Arévalo's life has been apparently as bizarre as some of his writing; he was reported dead in 1920, only to turn up as director of Guatemala's National Library. He is best known as the creator of the "psychozoological" story. The most famous of these is *El Hombre que Parecía un Caballo* (1915), a Kafkaesque tale whose protagonist, modeled on a Colombian poet, resembles a splendid race horse, not only physically but, also, in his lack of moral sense. His other words include *Las Rosas de Engaddi* (1927), a collection of verse, and *El Mundo de los Maharachías* (1938), which deals with a shipwrecked traveller who finds himself in the land of the Maharachías, monkeylike beings superior to men.

Argalia. The brother of ANGELICA, the princess of Cathay who comes to sow discord in Charlemagne's court in the Orlando poems of Boiardo and Ariosto. In Boiardo's poem he is killed, but his horse Rabicane remains in the plot of Ariosto's version.

Argan. The hypochondriacal central character in Molière's comedy LE MALADE IMAGINAIRE. He attempts to marry his daughter Angélique to a doctor, in order to avoid the expense of apothecary's bills. At the conclusion of the play he is made a mock doctor in a burlesque ceremony of investiture, conducted in macaronic Latin.

Argante (Argantes). One of the two leading warriors among the infidels opposing the Crusaders in Tasso's GERUSALEMME LIBERATA. His death at the hands of Tancredi precipitates the conquest of the holy city by Goffredo (Godfrey), the commander of the Christian armies.

Argillano. In the Tasso epic GERUSALEMME LIBERATA an Italian Crusader among the Christian forces assaulting Jerusalem. When rumor reaches Argillano that the champion Rinaldo of Este is dead, he leads a revolt against the authority of Goffredo, the Christian commander who had caused Rinaldo to leave them in anger. Later, to amend for his rebellion, he plunges vigorously into battle and finds a noble death at the hands of Solimano, the Turkish king. Rinaldo eventually avenges Argillano's memory with the slaying of Solimano.

Argo. The galley, built by Argus, that carried Jason and the ARGONAUTS in search of the Golden Fleece. It was reputed to have been the first seagoing vessel.

Argonautica. See APOLLONIUS OF RHODES; ARGONAUTS.

Argonauts. A group of mythological heroes. They sailed to Colchis to recover the GOLDEN FLEECE. Jason had demanded the throne of Iolcos from Pelias, who had usurped it from his brother Aeson, Jason's father. Pelias agreed, if Jason would first return the Fleece to Greece. Those who joined Jason in this adventure included Heracles, Orpheus, Castor and Polydeuces, Peleus, Melampus, Mopsus, Meleager, Atalanta, Admetus, the winged sons of Aeolus, Calais and Zetes, the lynx-eyed Lynceus and his quarrelsome brother Idas, Telamon, Pelias' own son Acastus, and many others. Argus built their ship, the *Argo,* under Athene's direction, and Hera aided them throughout the voyage so as to punish Pelias for refusing to worship her.

Their first stop was Lemnos, where the women, lonely after having killed their husbands a year before, vainly entreated them to stay. They were hospitably received by the Doliones, but killed their king Cyzicus by mistake. In Mysia, when Heracles' beautiful young favorite Hylas was drowned in a spring by a love-struck naiad, Heracles would not give up the search for Hylas and had to be left behind. The Argonauts were challenged to box by Amycus, king of the Bebryces, who had killed many strangers in this manner. Polydeuces accepted the challenge and quickly killed Amycus. At Salmydessus they saw blind old King Phineus whose days were made miserable by the Harpies; they stole or befouled his food before he could eat—a punishment for his having revealed too much, as a seer, of the ways of Zeus. Zetes and Calais saved him by pursuing the Harpies until Iris promised that they would not return. In gratitude, Phineus gave the Argonauts much useful advice.

With the help of this advice and of Athene, they passed through the Clashing Rocks, which usually sprang together to crush ships between them. Later, shouts and the clashing of shields drove off the birds of Ares, which attacked them with a hail of sharp plumes. By a happy chance they saved the four sons of Phrixus from shipwreck and were led by them to their home, Colchis, where King Aeetes kept the Fleece. The cruel Aeetes promised to relinquish the Fleece if Jason could pass a test: he must plow a field with two fire-breathing bulls, sow dragon's teeth, and fight the armed men who would spring up (see also SPARTI). Jason succeeded with the secret aid of Aeetes' daughter MEDEA, who had fallen in love with him. Aeetes refused to honor his promise, but Medea lulled to sleep the dragon that guarded the Fleece and escaped with the Argonauts.

They were pursued, but escaped again when Jason and Medea treacherously slew her half-brother Apsyrtus and (according to some versions) flung pieces of his body from the ship. Zeus ordained that the Argonauts suffer many hardships for this outrage before reaching home. Making their way via the Danube, Rhine, and Rhone to the Mediterranean, they reached the island of Aea, where Circe, Aeetes' sister, purified Jason and Medea of murder. Thetis helped them past the Wandering Rocks; the singing of Orpheus got them safely past the SIRENS. While they were entertained by the Phaeacians, Queen Arete secretly arranged the marriage of Jason and

Medea and King Alcinous protected the Argonauts from pursuing Colchians.

Blown to the coast of Africa, they were marooned with their ship in the desert, but they were helped or encouraged by Libyan nymphs, by the Hesperides, and by the god Triton. As they neared Crete, the bronze giant Talus nearly crushed their ship with rocks, but was destroyed by Medea's sorcery. The Argonauts returned to Iolcos, where a trick of Medea's disposed of Pelias and, Aeson having died, Acastus became king. Jason returned the Fleece to the temple of Laphystian Zeus in Orchomenus.

Next to the Trojan War, the voyage of the *Argo* was the event most often celebrated in Greek epic. It is the subject in particular of the *Argonautica,* the masterpiece of Apollonius of Rhodes, which is notable for the psychological realism with which its characters are treated, its memorable picture of Medea, and its remarkably unheroic portrayal of its hero, Jason.

Arguedas, Alcides (1879–1946). Bolivian novelist, historian, and diplomat. Although Arguedas spent many years in Europe, especially in France where he was Bolivian consul, his best-known writings reflect his abiding concern with the problems of his homeland. He is remembered primarily for three works, each in a different field. *Pueblo enfermo* (1909) is a pessimistic and controversial analysis of Bolivian society. One of the most famous of the Indianist novels, *Raza de bronce* (1919) describes the exploitation of Bolivian Indians by inhuman landlords. Arguedas' most enduring work may be his five-volume *Historia de Bolivia* (1920–1929), which covers that country's history from 1809 to 1872.

Argus (Argos). A fabulous creature. According to Greek mythology, Argus had 100 eyes, for which he was called *Panoptes.* Hera set him to watch Io, of whom she was jealous. Hermes, however, acting under orders of Zeus, who had his eye on Io, charmed Argus to sleep and slew him. Hera changed Argus into a peacock, whose tail was full of eyes. "Argus-eyed," therefore, means jealously watchful.

Argus (Argos). The builder of the ship *Argo* for the Argonauts. He was assisted by Athene.

Argus (Argos). Odysseus' faithful dog, who, in the *Odyssey,* recognized his old master on his return to Ithaca.

Argyropoulos, Johannes (1410–1490). Greek scholar in Italy during the revival of classical studies. He taught at Florence and Rome, was a member of the Medici circle, and engaged in the translation and the editing of texts.

Ariadne. In Greek mythology, daughter of Minos, king of Crete. She gave Theseus a clew of thread to guide him out of the Cretan Labyrinth. Theseus married his deliverer, but when he arrived at Naxos forsook her. Later she became the wife of Dionysus. It is generally agreed that Ariadne was the name of a Cretan mother-goddess. Richard Strauss wrote an opera called Ariadne auf Naxos (1912).

Ariadne auf Naxos (1912; rev. 1916). An opera by Richard Strauss, with a libretto by Hugo von Hofmannsthal. It was originally intended as an interlude to be introduced into a performance of Molière's Le Bourgeois Gentilhomme. In it a serious drama about Bacchus and Ariadne is played simultaneously with the improvisations of a *commedia dell' arte* troupe. For the Vienna performance of 1916 Strauss wrote a long Prologue so that the opera could be performed independently of the play.

Arians. The followers of Arius, a presbyter of the church of Alexandria, in the 4th century. He maintained (1) that the Father and Son are distinct beings; (2) that the Son, though divine, is not equal to the Father; (3) that the Son had a state of existence previous to His appearance on earth, but not from eternity; and (4) that the Messiah was not real man, but a divine being in a case of flesh. The Arian tenets varied from time to time and also among their different sections. The heresy was formally anathematized at the Council of Nicaea (325), but the sect was not, and never has been, wholly extinguished. See also Athanasius.

Aridano. In the Orlando Innamorato of Boiardo a giant who guards the treasure of the witch Morgana at the bottom of a lake. Orlando kills him and seizes the treasure.

Ariel. A sprite in Shakespeare's The Tempest. Ariel has been freed by Prospero from a pine rift in which he was imprisoned by the evil witch Sycorax. Invisible at will, all light and spirit, he seems to symbolize man's imagination. After serving Prospero faithfully, Ariel is at last freed when his master renounces his magic.

Ariel (1900). An essay by José Enrique Rodó, which had a tremendous impact on Hispanic American intellectuals. Rodó appealed to the youth of Spanish America to aspire to the spirituality, idealism, and rationality symbolized by Shakespeare's Ariel and to reject the brutishness and sensuality represented by Caliban. Because Rodó censured U.S. materialism and utilitarianism in the essay, many readers erroneously assumed that he was pitting Anglo-Saxon crassness against Latin idealism. The essay is, however, a generalized guide for the future.

Arioch. In Milton's Paradise Lost, one of the fallen angels. The word means "a fierce lion"; Milton took it from Dan. 2:14, where it is the name of a man.

Ariodante (Ariodantes). The beloved of Ginevra in Ariosto's Orlando Furioso. The blame for his supposed suicide because of her infidelity is placed on her hands and she is doomed unless rescued by a champion. Rinaldo saves her and she is reunited with Ariodante, who is alive and arrives to defend her, when his identity is revealed.

Arion. A Greek poet and musician. He flourished about 700 B.C. According to legend, he was cast into the sea by mariners, but carried to Taenaros on the back of a dolphin.

Arion. A horse born of the union of Poseidon and Demeter. His magical swiftness saved his master Adrastus, the only one of the Seven Against Thebes to escape alive from the siege of Thebes.

Ariosto, Lodovico (1474–1533). Italian poet. He was born at Reggio, in Modena, and served the Este family of Ferrara for most of his life. His poems, satires, and learned plays were popular and respected in his day, but his masterpiece remains the Orlando Furioso (*Roland Mad*). A continuation of Boiardo's Orlando Innamorato (*Roland in Love,* 1495), it is a long narrative poem in octave stanzas dealing with the adventures of ROLAND and other knights of Charlemagne in wars against the Saracens.

Aristaeus (Aristaios). In classical mythology the son of Apollo and Cyrene. He was the god-hero protector of cattle and fruit trees. Aristaeus had offended the nymphs by pursuing Eurydice, the wife of Orpheus, who in her flight had been bitten by a serpent and died. In revenge the nymphs destroyed his bee hives, but, when he had propitiated them, new bees swarmed from a rotting carcass. He was the father of Actaeon by Autonoe.

Aristarchus (fl. 156 B.C.). Aristarchus of Samothrace, the greatest critic of antiquity and head of the Alexandrian library. His labors were chiefly directed to the *Iliad* and *Odyssey* of HOMER. He divided them into 24 books each, marked every doubtful line with an obelus, and every one he considered especially beautiful with an asterisk.

Aristides (Aristeides; 530–468 B.C.). An Athenian statesman and general. He is called "The Just" for his impartiality and honesty, which have become proverbial. According to tradition, an illiterate Athenian once came to Aristides, whom he did not recognize, and asked him to write the name of Aristides on a ballot demanding his ostracism from the state. The man explained that he had grown tired of hearing Aristides forever called "The Just." Without revealing his identity, Aristides wrote his own name.

Aristides of Miletus. See MILESIAN FABLES.

Aristippus (Aristippos; c. 435–c. 356 B.C.). Greek philosopher, pupil of Socrates. Aristippus founded the Cyrenaic School, named after his birthplace, Cyrene. This school, similar to the Epicurean, holds that pleasure is the goal of life, and that prudence should be exercised to avoid pain.

Aristophanes (445 B.C.–c. 380 B.C.). A Greek comic playright. Little is known of Aristophanes' life except that his first produced play won a second prize when he was only 18, and he continued to write fine comedies at a rate of about one a year for more than 20 years. His last two extant plays, *Ecclesiazusae* (392) and *Plutus* (388), were produced after the fall of Athens in 404 B.C. Perhaps because it was no longer possible for him to criticize the state freely, these comedies are considerably inferior to his earlier works.

Aristophanes was a brilliant if somewhat wide-swinging social satirist, who used the traditional freedom of OLD COMEDY to ridicule public figures, institutions, and even the gods. His favorite butts were the demagogue Cleon, whom he attacked in THE KNIGHTS and several other plays, and Euripides, who was lampooned in THE FROGS and THESMOPHORIAZU-SAE. Socrates is the victim in THE CLOUDS, in which Aristophanes inaccurately and unfairly makes him a wily sophist who teaches men to cheat others through cunning argumentation. It is apparent that the playwright was conservative in his views, disapproving of Euripides' humanizing of the gods and heroes, of modern trends in music and philosophy, and of the war with Sparta, whose rigid traditionalism he may even have admired. As a practical writer of comedy, however, he also knew that it is easier to draw laughter by ridiculing newfangled fads than by pointing out absurdities in modes of behavior that are generally accepted.

Another indication of the license permitted Old Comedy is the open but never prurient obscenity of the plays, a custom that began with their origin in one aspect of the fertility rites of Dionysus. (Aristophanes' eleven plays are the only surviving examples of the genre.) It is all the more striking that Aristophanes does not hesitate to make Dionysus, the patron of the dramatic festivals, an absurd figure in *The Frogs,* or to give men the upper hand over the gods in THE BIRDS.

Aristophanes was the most imaginatively original of the Greek playwrights, in that, while they wrote of (supposedly) historical figures, he invented not only completely new characters and situations but even entire worlds out of whole cloth. He was also a fine poet who wrote delicate and charming lyrics in his choral songs. His masterpiece, *The Birds,* is a remarkable example of both these outstanding qualities. In it he creates a delightfully improbable kingdom of birds and men, Cloudcuckooland, and his characters, both feathered and otherwise, sing one lovely lyric after another all through the play. Unfortunately for modern audiences, some of the qualities that make Aristophanes' comedies successful are difficult or impossible to reproduce in modern English: his poetry, his topical satire, and his knack for puns and garbled literary allusions. In spite of this, his comic genius was so universal that a great deal of the humor of his plays still comes through.

Aristophanes of Byzantium (fl. 195 B.C.). A leading critic, head of the Alexandrian library. He is known for his editing of the works of Homer, and for devising, or at least standardizing, the accents since used in the Greek language. These accents were intended for the benefit of foreigners learning Greek, a language that all educated people were expected to know in the days of the Roman empire.

Aristotelian unities. See UNITIES.

Aristotle (Aristoteles; 384–322 B.C.). Greek philosopher, born at Stagira. Brought up in a family of moderate wealth and position, Aristotle went at the age of 18 to Athens to study in Plato's Academy, where he remained for 20 years, until the death of his teacher. He moved to Assos, then to Mytilene, then to Macedon, whence he was invited by King Philip to tutor the young Alexander. Aristotle remained in Macedonia for eight years, until Philip was assassinated (336 B.C.) and Alexander succeeded to the throne. During the time he spent in Assos, Mytilene, and Macedon, much of Aristotle's work in natural history was done. On his return to Athens, he taught at the LYCEUM. Finally, in 323 B.C., at Alexander's death, Aristotle left Athens, where there was an upsurge of anti-Macedonian feeling, and retired to Chalcis, where he died a year later.

The works for which he was most widely known among the ancients have been lost, but fragments indicate that they were dialogues written in a highly polished rhetorical style. These are referred to as his exoteric writings, or those designed for the general public outside his school. A second class of writings, the esoteric, or those designed for use by the students of the Lyceum, has survived. These are called the acroamatic writings, and are known to us as the treatises of Aristotle. A third class of writings, the hypomnematic, or memoranda, have also been lost.

The treatises include first the logical works (*Categories, Topics, De Interpretatione, Prior Analytics, Posterior Analytics, Sophistical Refutations*) known as the *Organon*, or instrument. For Aristotle, logic was preparation for scientific knowledge, not knowledge itself. He was the first to insist on rigorous scientific procedure, and his method of demonstration. by the syllogism and by dialectic, or reasoning from the opinions of others, became standard philosophic method. Aristotle maintained that all human knowledge originates in sensible experiences, out of which the soul perceives the universal.

Aristotle's natural philosophy, contained in the eight books of the *Physics,* examines the physical universe. They include the important distinction between the substance (or essence) of a thing and its accidental properties. Other works in this group include *On the Heavens (De Caelo), On Coming into Being and Passing Away (De Generatione et Corruptione),* and *Meteorology (Meteorologic). Parva Naturalia* and *De Anima* are the titles of his works on psychology. He wrote an introduction to biology called *Historia Animalium,* in which he classified the animals, their methods of reproduction, and their evolution. In his treatises on metaphysics, known as *Metaphysica,* Aristotle discusses theology, or primary philosophy, which he considered the highest type of theoretical science. Unlike his teacher Plato he did not posit a separate world of perfect Forms or Ideas, but always finds form immanent in matter.

There are two Aristotelian ethical treatises, known as the *Nicomachean Ethics* and the *Eudemian Ethics.* According to the former, happiness is the goal of life. Pleasure, fame, and wealth, however, will not bring one of the highest happiness, which is achieved only through the contemplation of philosophic truth because it exercises man's peculiar virtue, the rational principle.

In Aristotle's *Politics* (eight books), the good of the individual is identified with the good of the city-state. The study of human good is thus a political inquiry, as it is in Plato. Aristotle discusses different types of government, finally preferring monarchy, an aristocracy of men of virtue, or constitutional government of the majority. Slavery is considered natural in Aristotle's politics, because some men are adapted by nature to be the physical instruments of others. Aristotle's *Rhetoric* treats methods of persuasion; the *Poetics* is his great contribution to literary criticism.

Called by Dante "the master of those who know," Aristotle mastered every field of learning known to the Greeks. His influence on St. Thomas Aquinas and the medieval world, through the translation of the Arabic scholar Averroes, was profound and enduring.

Arius (c. 256–336). Greek ecclesiastic. He lived and taught in Alexandria. His teachings on the nature of God constitute what is called the Arian heresy or Arianism. Arius felt that God is separate from the world, alone and unknowable. He taught that Jesus was a mortal, created being, not fully divine, and as such should be worshiped as secondary to God. At the church councils of Nicaea (325) and Constantinople (381), Arius and his followers were condemned as teachers of false doctrine. See ARIANS.

Arjuna (*Sans.,* the sinless). One of the five Pandava brothers and a hero of the great Hindu epic, the MAHABHARATA, especially prominent in the BHAGAVADGITA.

Ark of the Covenant. A wooden chest (possibly a model of a temple) overlaid with gold in which the presence of Jehovah was believed to dwell when communicating with Israel. The Ark was portable and was carried into battle. Its contents are thought to have been the stone tablets recording the law as given to Moses. It was installed in the Holy of Holies of Solomon's temple at Jerusalem. The fate of the original Ark is not known: it disappeared after the fall of Jerusalem in 586 B.C.

Arlen, Michael (1895–1956). Armenian-born English author. He is best known for a popular novel entitled THE GREEN HAT.

Arlequin. See HARLEQUIN.

Armada, Spanish. Also known as the **Invincible Armada.** The fleet assembled in 1588 by PHILIP II of Spain for the conquest of England. The armada, which consisted of some 130 ships and carried over 30,000 troops, set sail from Lisbon on May 29 under the command of the duke of Medina Sidonia. Its destination was the Netherlands, where the fleet was to pick up an army under Alexander Farnese, the duke of Parma, and transport it across the channel for an invasion of England.

After being forced by a storm to put in at Corunna for repairs, the armada was sighted by the English near Plymouth on July 29. Medina Sidonia, who was under orders to sail directly to the Netherlands, retired before the lighter and more maneuverable ships of the English fleet, suffering several losses, until he anchored at Calais on Aug. 6. Farnese's army, hemmed in by the Dutch fleet, was unable to stir. On Aug. 7, the English sent fire ships among the Spanish vessels, forcing them to flee. The following day the bitterest engagement of the campaign was fought off Gravelines, the Spaniards being bested by the gunnery of the combined English and Dutch fleets. A favorable change of wind enabled the armada to make for the North Sea and return to Spain by sailing around Scotland and Ireland, where severe storms caused further losses. The Spaniards lost over 63 ships and 9000 men in the campaign, and Spanish prestige suffered a severe blow.

Armado, Don Adriano de. A fantastical Spanish knight in Shakespeare's LOVE'S LABOUR'S LOST. A posturing, self-important fellow, given to absurd rhetoric, he is a satire on the popular Spanish knight of the Elizabethan era.

Armageddon. The name given in *The Revelation of St. John the Divine* (Rev. 16:16) to the site of the last great battle between good and evil before the Day of Judgment; hence, any great final struggle or conflict. Theodore Roosevelt popularized the term in connection with his break from the Republicans to form the Progressive Party in the presidential election of 1912. It has been frequently used in connection with the First World War.

arme Heinrich, Der. See HEINRICH, DER ARME.

Armida. In Tasso's GERUSALEMME LIBERATA, a beautiful sorceress, niece of the enchanter Idraote, sent by him to the Christian camp in hopes of sowing discord and confusion there. In the camp, she tells Goffredo, general of the Crusaders, a tearful story and requests ten of his knights to assist her in reclaiming her own lost kingdom. In the arguments that follow, Goffredo's leadership is severely tested, and more than ten of his most puissant knights fly after her. For a time she holds in her power the Christian champion Tancredi, who is rescued by Rinaldo of Este, himself soon a captive victim of her charms. When Rinaldo, whom she loves, is also rescued, Armida sets fire to her palace and flies in her chariot to the camp of the Egyptians, where she offers herself to any champion who will kill Rinaldo. In the final battle for Jerusalem she is put to flight by Rinaldo; she then tries to kill herself, but he persuades her to live and trust her future to him:

"Behold," she says. "thy handmaid; I obey:
Thy lips my future life, thy will my fortune sway!"
(XX, 136)

Armida's Garden. The enchantress Armida, of Tasso's GERUSALEMME LIBERATA, lives in a castle that contains a garden of gorgeous sensual delights, from lush flowers and fruits to alluring nymphs bathing in fountains. It symbolizes the attractions of the senses and their power over human reason. As such, it links Armida with Circe and Alcina and is the inspiration of Spenser's Bower of Bliss.

Armida's Girdle. The enchantress Armida, of Tasso's GERUSALEMME LIBERATA, wears a magical girdle of incomparable beauty and worth. The source of many of her powers, it enables her to know and do whatever she wills.

Arminianism. A religious heresy, opposed to Calvinism. It began in Holland in the early 17th century and then spread to England and the colonies in America. It denied the leading Calvinistic tenets that only the elect were to benefit by the sacrifice of Christ's death, and that the human will was powerless to reject or to forfeit divine grace once it had been received: it also opposed the doctrine of absolute predestination. Jonathan Edwards violently attacked Arminianism in America.

Arminius, probably the Latin form of **Hermann** (18 B.C.–A.D. 21). Hero-chieftain of the Germanic Cherusci tribe. Although he served in the Roman army for a while, he came home to find his people suffering under Roman dominion, and in A.D. 9 won a crushing victory over the Roman governor Varus. He was finally defeated by GERMANICUS in A.D 16. His exploits survive in popular legend and in plays such as G. F. Klopstock's *Hermanns Schlacht* (1769) and *Hermann und die Fürsten* (1784).

Armory Show. An exhibition of American and European modern art held in the 69th Regiment Armory, New York City in 1913. Among the organizers and contributors were Arthur Davies and John SLOAN. At this show Americans got their first look at the revolutionary work of such artists as Matisse, Kandinsky, Brancusi, Maillol, Picasso, and Braque. The painting that most attracted public attention was Marcel Duchamp's *Nude Descending a Staircase,* which one critic renamed "explosion in a shingle factory." In general, the conservative art critics were hostile to the show, especially to the foreign works that were much more extreme than those from the U.S. The public, however, flocked to the show: over 250,000 people paid to see the wild-looking European painting and sculpture. A few were conscious at once of what the Armory Show implied for art in America: modern art had arrived full-fledged from Europe, and it was in the U.S. to stay.

In the winter of 1963, the 50th anniversary of the Armory Show was celebrated in the same building. All of the works hung in the original show that could be traced were re-exhibited, most of those jeered at in 1913 being now considered masterpieces—or even outmoded.

Arms and the Man (1894). A play by George Bernard SHAW. Set in Bulgaria, it satirizes romantic attitudes about war. The title is taken from the first line of Vergil's *Aeneid: Arma virumque cano* (I sing of arms and the man). The libretto of the comic opera *The Chocolate Soldier* (1909) by Oskar Straus was unofficially based on the play.

Armstrong, John (1709–1779). Scottish poet and physician. He is noted for his didactic, blank-verse poem, *Art of Preserving Health* (1744).

Arnauld, Antoine (1612–1694). French writer and theologian. A Jansenist and a bitter opponent of all that he took to be false doctrine, Arnauld was a lifelong opponent of the Jesuits. A storm of controversy arose over his exposition of Jansenism in *La Fréquente Communion (The Frequent Communion,* 1643). *La Perpétuité de la foi de l'église catholique touchant l'Eucharistie (The Perpetuity of the Faith of the Catholic Church Regarding the Eucharist,* 1669–1676), written in collaboration with Pierre NICOLE, criticized the Calvinist conception of the Eucharist, and the *Traité des vraies et des fausses idées (Treatise on True and False Ideas,* 1683) demolished the pantheistical philosophy of Malebranche. *Lettre à un duc et pair (Letter to a Duke and Peer,* 1655), Arnauld's outspoken criticism of Jesuit practices in the confessional, brought about his condemnation by the Sorbonne, which in turn caused Pascal to write the *Lettres Provinciales.* Forced into hiding for almost 20 years of his life, Arnauld died in exile.

Arnauld-d'Andilly, Angélique. Known as **Mère Angélique de Saint Jean** (1624–1684). French nun and writer. Mistress of the novices at Port-Royal-de-Paris when the community was disbanded by order of the archbishop of Paris in 1664, she was moved to another convent and confined to a solitary cell without sacraments. She described her sufferings in the *Relation de Captivité (Account of Captivity,* 1760). From 1678 until her death she was abbess of Port-Royal-des-Champs.

Arndt, Ernst Moritz (1769–1860). German patriotic poet of great importance during Germany's wars of liberation from Napoleon (1813–1815). His most famous collection is *Lieder für Deutsche (Songs for Germans,* 1813), which includes the well-known song *Der Gott, der Eisen wachsen liess (The God Who Made Iron Grow).*

Arne, Thomas Augustine (1710–1778). English composer of operas, masques, and scores for plays. He wrote an English grand opera *Artaxerxes,* a score for Milton's COMUS, and songs for revivals of *As you like it* (1740) and *The Tempest* (1746). His patriotic song *Rule Britannia* is from the music for the masque *Alfred* (1740).

Arnim, Elisabeth ("Bettina") von, born **Brentano** (1785–1859). Wife of Achim von Arnim, sister of Clemens Brentano. In her youth she was a fervent admirer of Goethe, and her correspondence with the poet, *Goethes Briefwechsel mit einem Kinde* (*Goethe's Correspondence with a Child,* 1835) reveals the perfect emotional purity of her nature. Her *Dies Buch gehört dem König* (*This Book Belongs to the King,* 1843) is a naïve plea for royal assistance to alleviate poor economic and social conditions among the Silesian weavers.

Arnim, Ludwig Joachim ("Achim") von (1781–1831). German romantic poet. He was a close friend of Clemens Brentano, whose sister he married in 1811. With Brentano, he edited the folksong collection DES KNABEN WUNDERHORN. His unfinished novel *Die Kronenwächter* (*The Guardians of the Crown,* 1817), about 16th-century Germany, is important in the development of the German historical novel. See GERMAN ROMANTICISM.

Arnim, Gräfin von. See ELIZABETH, Countess Russell.

Arnold, Benedict (1741–1801). American army officer and traitor. Beginning his career as a patriot, Arnold led the attack with Ethan Allen on Fort Ticonderoga, N.Y. (1775), and he is now generally given credit for winning the important battle of Saratoga (1777). He was given command of the fort at West Point by Washington, but, embittered by repeated slights from Congress and other Americans, he arranged for its surrender to the British, and was made a brigadier general in the British army. After the war he sailed to England, where he died. He appears in William Dunlap's play *André* (1798) and in Kenneth Roberts' novel *Arundel* (1930). See John ANDRÉ; Horatio GATES.

Arnold, Sir Edwin (1832–1904). English poet, journalist, translator, and traveler. A student of Indian languages, Persian, and Turkish, Arnold traveled widely in the Orient. His best-known work, *The Light of Asia* (1879), is an epic poem on the life of Buddha; many of his other poems also deal with Eastern themes. He was the author of a number of translations of Oriental literature, including *The Indian Song of Songs* (1875) and *Indian Idylls* (1893).

Arnold, Matthew (1822–1888). English critic and poet. The son of Thomas ARNOLD, the clergyman who became headmaster of Rugby and made it one of England's most renowned public schools, young Arnold began his literary career as a poet, publishing *The Strayed Reveler and Other Poems* (1849); *Empedocles on Etna and Other Poems* (1852); *Poems* (1853); *Poems, Second Series* (1855); *Merope,* a dramatic poem (1858); and *New Poems* (1867). His poetry tends to be elegiac and brooding, and at its best is among the finest expressions of the plight of the sensitive Victorian caught between "two worlds, one dead,/ The other powerless to be born." His most famous poems are THE SCHOLAR-GIPSY, based on a legend of an Oxford student who, in poverty, joined a band of gypsies; *Stanzas from the Grande Chartreuse* (1855), in which the narrator, visiting a Carthusian monastery, mourns the loss of faith in the modern world; *Thyrsis* (1866), an elegy written on the death of Arnold's friend Arthur Hugh Clough, which Swinburne adjudged, after Milton's *Lycidas* and Shelley's *Adonais,* the finest elegy in the English language; and DOVER BEACH (1867), perhaps his best-known poem, which uses the image of the sea as a metaphor for the Sea of Faith, ebbing away from the naked shores of the world.

In 1857, Arnold was elected to the professorship of poetry at Oxford, and during the 10 years that he held this position he delivered many of the lectures that were to become part of his essays on criticism. The best-known collections of these are *On Translating Homer* (1861); *Essays in Criticism* (1st series, 1865; 2nd series, 1888); CULTURE AND ANARCHY (1869); and *Literature and Dogma* (1873). Seeing literature as both shaper and sustainer of the highest elements of culture, he urged that the great mass of the public—the "Philistine" middle class—be educated to improve its response to literature (and culture). He argued for high standards of literary judgment, using the "lines and expressions of the great masters . . . as a touchstone to other poetry." He believed that the English were too immersed in the spirit of "Hebraism," or strictness of conscience and rightness of conduct, and not sufficiently touched by the symmetry and spontaneity of "Hellenism"; he saw religious fundamentalism as one expression of this Hebraism, and attempted to interpret the Bible as literature and show that, as in all great poetry, the poetry of the Bible contained the moral and spiritual truths that were the essence of religion. He saw the task of the critic as "a disinterested endeavor to learn and propagate the best that is known and thought in the world." He is of importance as a shaper of both English and American criticism, up to the time of T. S. Eliot. See Arminius von THUNDERTENTRONCKH.

Arnold, Thomas (1795–1842). English educator, historian, and headmaster of Rugby (1828–1842). The father of Matthew ARNOLD, he is often referred to as "Arnold of Rugby," being chiefly remembered for his tenure there as headmaster, where he exerted great personal influence and set the modern pattern for the entire English public-school system. His literary works include a collection of sermons (1829–1834), an edition of Thucydides (1830–1835), a history of Rome (3 vols., 1838–1843), and *Lectures on Modern History* (1842).

Arnold of Brescia (c. 1100–1155). Italian theologian and reformer. He was persecuted by St. Bernard of Clairvaux as being a follower of Pierre ABÉLARD's Aristotelian philosophy. A preacher of asceticism, he railed against the wealth and temporal power of the clergy, and in 1145 encouraged a revolution in Rome against the Pope's civil authority. In 1155 the rebellion was suppressed and Arnold was hanged, then burned.

Arnolphe. In Molière's comedy, L'ECOLE DES FEMMES, a man of wealth with stern ideas on the proper training of girls to make good wives. He applies his educational methods to Agnès whom, in time, he intends to make his wife.

Arnothy, Christine (1928–). Hungarian-born French novelist. She won notice with the autobiographical *I am Fifteen and I Don't Want to Die* (1956), about a Hungarian family escaping the Russian siege of Budapest. The sequel, *It is Not So Easy to Live* (1957), moves through refugee camp experiences to marriage in Paris. Her novels include

God Is Late (1955), *The Charlatan* (1959), and *The Serpent's Bite* (1961).

Arnoux, Mme Marie. One of the main characters in the novel L'ÉDUCATION SENTIMENTALE by Gustave Flaubert. Frédéric Moreau suffers the passion of unrequited love for Mme Arnoux during the years of her marriage. In an ironic conclusion, when a middle-aged widow she comes to him, Frédéric rejects her offer of love.

Arouet, François Marie. See VOLTAIRE.

Around the World in Eighty Days (Le Tour du monde en quatre-vingt jours; 1873). A romance by Jules VERNE. The hero, Phileas Fogg, undertakes his hasty world tour as the result of a bet made at his London club. He and his French valet Passepartout meet with some fantastic adventures, but these are overcome by the loyal servant, and the endlessly inventive Fogg. The feat they perform is incredible for its day; Fogg wins his bet, having circled the world in only 80 days.

Arp, Hans. Also known as **Jean Arp** (1887–). German poet and sculptor. As a sculptor he is best known for his use of subtle, curved forms. With Hugo BALL and others he founded the DADA Cabaret Voltaire in Zürich (1916). A recent selection of his poetry is entitled *Wortträume und schwarze Sterne* (*Word-Dreams and Black Stars*, 1953).

Arrow of Gold, The (1919). A novel by Joseph CONRAD. It is a story of romance and adventure during the Second Carlist War. Conrad himself, when he was about 20, had been involved at the fringe of these events.

Arrowsmith (1925). A novel by Sinclair LEWIS. It follows the career of Dr. Martin Arrowsmith from his training under Max GOTTLIEB, through a small-town practice, the health department of a small city, an "institute" sponsored by a rich man and his wife, to an isolated West Indian island and an equally isolated Vermont farm. In his quest for pure science, Arrowsmith encounters meanness, corruption, and misunderstanding; he is often frustrated, and finally fails when he himself refuses to carry his principles to their logical extreme. Filled with medical lore, the details of which Lewis got from Paul DE KRUIF, the novel is frequently satiric and caused much controversy when it was first published.

'Arry and 'Arriet. Two characters from the pages of the English *Punch*. 'Arry, a good-natured but vulgar costermonger, and his wife 'Arriet were the creation of the *Punch* artist Edwin J. Milliken. 'Arry made his debut in *Punch's Almanac* of 1874 in *'Arry on 'orseback*.

Ars Amatoria, or Ars Amoris. See OVID.

Arsenal at Springfield, The (1845). A poem by Henry Wadsworth LONGFELLOW. A poem about peace, its theme was suggested by his wife.

Arsete (Arsetes). In the GERUSALEMME LIBERATA of Tasso, a eunuch, custodian of the warrior maid Clorinda. He had been given the child by her mother, the Ethiopian queen, who feared that its white complexion would arouse the suspicions of King Senàpo (Senapus). Arsete neglects to baptize her, despite her Christian parentage, but he tells her the story of her birth before the battle that results in her death at the hands of her beloved Tancredi. The latter baptizes her and receives her forgiveness as she dies in his arms.

Arsinoé. (1) The false prude of Molière's comedy LE MISANTHROPE.

(2) The scheming stepmother in Pierre Corneille's tragedy NICOMÈDE.

Ars Poetica (Lat., "the art of poetry"). A treatise by the Roman poet HORACE, laying down rules for the writing of poetry. English critics of the Renaissance and post-Renaissance periods were greatly influenced by this work.

Artabano (Artabane). In the GERUSALEMME LIBERATA of Tasso, a Saracen king who leads the African forces against the Crusaders during the battle for the holy city. His death at hands of the English baron Odoardo (Edward), takes place in the last canto of the poem.

Artagnan, Charles de Baatz d'. One of the famous guardsmen whose amazing adventures Alexandre Dumas narrates in THE THREE MUSKETEERS, TWENTY YEARS AFTER, and THE VISCOUNT OF BRAGELONNE. The works follow d'Artagnan through his various exploits to his death as Comte d'Artagnan, marshal of France. He is always the soldier—quick-witted, quick-tempered, and extraordinarily brave.

Artaud, Antonin (1895–1948). French dramatic theorist and producer. Artaud influenced many playwrights by urging that the theater should translate experience into universal and primitive images, as explained in *The Theater of Cruelty* (1935) and *The Theater and Its Double* (1938).

Artegal or **Arthgall.** See ELIDURE; FAERIE QUEENE, THE.

Artemidorus. In Shakespeare's JULIUS CAESAR, a teacher of rhetoric who tries to warn Caesar of the plot against him. He passes Caesar a note naming the conspirators, but Caesar fails to read it.

Artemis. Greek goddess of hunting and childbirth, daughter of Leto and sister of Apollo. Perhaps originally a Cretan goddess of fertility, she came to be regarded as a virgin, who demanded chastity from her female attendants, and even her male devotees, such as HIPPOLYTUS. Her attendants (who were either local goddesses or local versions of Artemis herself) included HECATE, CALLISTO, OPIS, BRITOMARTIS, and the mortal Iphigenia. She figures importantly in Euripides' plays HIPPOLYTUS and *Iphigenia in Aulis* (see IPHIGENIA).

Artemis of Ephesus, temple of. One of the SEVEN WONDERS OF THE ANCIENT WORLD. It contained a famous statue of the goddess—a cone surmounted by a bust covered with breasts—which was said to have fallen from Heaven. However, Minucius, in the second century A.D., described it as a wooden statue, and Pliny, a contemporary, claimed that it was made of ebony. As Diana of the Ephesians, this goddess, who bears a somewhat doubtful relationship to the Greek Artemis, appears in an episode in Acts 19:24-28.

art for art's sake. English equivalent of the French *l'art pour l'art,* which itself derives from Edgar Allan Poe in *The Poetic Principle:*

There neither exists nor can exist any work more thoroughly dignified . . . than the poem which is a poem and nothing more—the poem written solely for the poem's sake.

The doctrine which this represents, that the aim of art should be creation and the perfection of technical

expression rather than the service of a moral, political, or didactic end, had been evolving ever since
the romantic period. It was adumbrated by Coleridge
and given early expression by Poe in the above treatise, flowered among the French symbolist poets
and their English associate Walter Pater, and reached
its culmination in surrealism and the aesthetic theory of I. A. Richards. It was the dominant theory of
art and especially of poetry until the 1930's, when the
proletarian and Marxist movements in literature
threatened for a time to revive the 18th-century
didactic theories. After the beginning of World War
II in 1939, the latter movements began to lose much
of their influence.

Artful Dodger, the.   A young thief in Charles
Dickens' OLIVER TWIST, pupil of Fagin. He became
perfectly adept in villainy, and pickpocketing especially.

Arthur.   The hero of a great cycle of medieval
romance (see ARTHURIAN LEGEND). There was a
historical Arthur, a Celtic chieftain who lived in
Wales during the 6th century. Little is known of
him except that he was mortally wounded (according to the ANNALES CAMBRIAE) in the battle of
Camlan and was taken to GLASTONBURY where he
died. However, while elements of the historical
Arthur have been infused into the medieval romances, evidence indicates that there was an earlier,
mythical Arthur, possibly a Celtic deity, whose origins
are unknown. As they told and retold the story of
Arthur, and in attempting to produce a coherent
narrative out of diverse sources, the medieval romancers introduced Christian and other elements,
not originally Arthurian, thus further confusing its
origin. Despite the strong influence of Christianity in
the later versions of Arthur, scholars detect the Celtic
myth in which the GRAIL is a thinly disguised caldron of plenty and the opponents of Arthur and his
knights the last echoes of earlier long-displaced
deities.

By the time the Arthurian legends were given permanent shape in Malory's *Morte d'Arthur* (c. 1469),
the figure of Arthur as a legendary hero had become
fairly distinct. He was the natural son of UTHER

Arthur and his knights of the Round Table.
Frontispiece from the *History of Prince Arthur* (1634).

PENDRAGON and IGRAINE (see MERLIN), and was raised
by Sir Ector. By pulling the sword EXCALIBUR from
a block of stone, he proved his right to the throne
of England. He subdued 12 rebellious princes of
whom LOT, king of Norway, was chief, and won 12
great battles against the Saxon invaders. About his
ROUND TABLE he gathered a group of knights whose
deeds of daring and chivalry won his court high renown. Arthur himself became known far and wide
as a mighty warrior and a just and generous ruler.
His wife was GUINEVERE, his most valiant knight
LAUNCELOT. In the earlier romances the ruin that
finally overtakes Arthur was due entirely to Guinevere and the traiterous MORDRED; the story of her
illicit love for Launcelot and its demoralizing effect
on the court was added later. In distinct contrast
to Malory and the older romancers, who say that Arthur's sons were born out of wedlock, Tennyson in
his IDYLLS OF THE KING makes Arthur a man of the
highest morals, not only absolutely loyal to Guinevere but requiring that his knights "cleave to one
maiden only." The treason that brought an end to
Arthur's court was hatched while he was away on
conquest. After his return and defeat in a final,
terrible battle, the mortally wounded king was borne
away to the island of AVALON, where some accounts
say that he was buried while others say that he dwells
with his sister MORGAN LE FAY "till he shall come
again full twice as fair to rule over his people."

Arthur, Prince.   See FAERIE QUEENE, THE.

Arthur, Timothy Shay.   See TEN NIGHTS IN A
BAR-ROOM.

Arthurian legend.   A great body of literature
that revolves around the partly mythical, partly historical figure of King ARTHUR. It seems to have
neither traceable beginning nor foreseeable end, but
the earliest extant written references to Arthur are
found in Welsh literature of the 6th century.
Sources of information include the writings of the
historian GILDAS (c. 540); a poem entitled GODODIN
(c. 600); the work of the historian NENNIUS (c. 800);
the ANNALES CAMBRIAE (c. 955); THE SPOILS OF
ANNWN (10th century); and the very important
MABINOGION, a collection of tales which includes
Kulhwch and Olwen, perhaps the earliest, full-fledged
Arthurian romance.

In the 12th century the fame of Arthur spread to
England where it was noted by William of Malmesbury in his GESTA REGUM ANGLORUM. In Geoffrey
of Monmouth's Latin HISTORY OF THE KINGS OF
BRITAIN, Arthur attained full stature, becoming a
great national figure, the hero-king of marvelous
deeds accompanied by such figures as MERLIN, Guinevere, Gawain, and Mordred. Uther Pendragon also
made his appearance in context with the now traditional story of Arthur's conception, and there is what
may be the first mention of Arthur's departure, mortally wounded, for Avalon.

The Norman poet, Wace, transformed the work of
Geoffrey of Monmouth into an elegant verse chronicle, ROMAN DE BRUT. In this adaptation, the chivalric setting was expanded; the Round Table was
introduced for the first time; the death of Arthur
was further dramatized by the suggestion that he
had gone to Avalon to be healed of his wounds, with
the expectation of returning one day to Britain.

The innovations of the French poet CHRÉTIEN DE

TROYES involved, essentially, the unification of existing Arthurian materials into new narrative form. He wrote individual tales that highlighted the deeds of individual knights. The best known of these is *Lancelot,* a story that recounts the intensely enacted drama of Launcelot's adventures in the name of his great and undying love for Queen Guinevere, thus introducing into the stream of Arthurian legend that wondrous knight, Launcelot, and the important medieval theme of COURTLY LOVE.

The English priest Layamon (fl. 1198–1207) took the chronicle of Wace as his model and wrote THE BRUT—perhaps the first of the legends of Arthur to be composed in the English language. Layamon elaborated on the Round Table motif, effectively mixed native folk tradition with Norman elegance, and drew upon Celtic lore for a description of Arthur's journey to Avalon where Morgan le Fay waited to heal his wounds.

During the 13th century, the tales of Arthur enjoyed a period of popularity in Germany, which resulted in such works as those of GOTTFRIED VON STRASSBURG and WOLFRAM VON ESCHENBACH. In the 14th century, Arthurian legend saw an artistic revival that produced two especially important pieces of English literature: *The Alliterative Morte Arthur* (c. 1360) and SIR GAWAIN AND THE GREEN KNIGHT. In the first, an anonymous work, Gawain is the central figure, and it is his death, not Arthur's, that is the dramatic high point of the poem. Even his murderer, Mordred, weeps bitterly that it was his destiny to kill such a knight. The emphasis is on an early English kind of epic treatment, so that this version has an affinity more with *Beowulf* than with the customary form of Arthurian romance. Norman lightness and Celtic magic have no place in this work. When Arthur dies, he is carried to Glastonbury, not Avalon, for a Christian burial.

The second important poem of the 14th-century English revival, *Sir Gawain and the Green Knight,* is one of the most important examples of Arthurian literature; its unknown author ranks with Chaucer as one of the greatest of the Middle English poets. Part of the brilliance of this particular poem is found in its unusual imagery and dramatic effects. An excellent example of the latter is the sudden appearance of the Green Knight at the court of King Arthur, during New Year festivities, and his shocking challenge; Gawain accepts the challenge, and the story is essentially a testing and development of his character.

In the 15th century, the legends of Arthur were gathered together and given ultimate shape in Sir Thomas Malory's great English prose classic, LE MORTE D'ARTHUR. This rendition is, above all else, the work of a master story-teller. Malory utilized traditions other than those of Arthurian romance, elaborating most effectively on the GRAIL theme, and making good use of material from the TRISTAN AND ISEULT stories. The life of Arthur is recounted, including the story of his miraculous conception and birth, events leading to his coronation, various military exploits, and his ultimate death at the hands of Mordred. In this work, the mysterious Lady of the Lake stretches her arm from the depths of the lake and provides Arthur with the marvelous sword, Excalibur. There is an enchanted forest through

which disguised knights go galloping in search of odd beasts, the Holy Grail, perilous castles, ladies in distress, and behind almost any tree Morgan Le Fay may be waiting to capture passing knights of the Round Table. A villainous King Mark forever pursues the gallant Sir Tristram who is forever devoted to Queen Iseult. The exemplification of chivalry, Sir Launcelot, has many dramatic adventures in the name of love for Queen Guinevere or loyalty to King Arthur, while his son, the pure Galahad, is granted sight of the Holy Grail. *Le Morte d'Arthur* ends on the traditional, tragic note of Arthur's death and the dissolution of the Order of the Round Table.

Even in its own time, Malory's version of the Arthurian legend enjoyed considerable popularity. It was one of the works chosen for publication in 1485 by William Caxton, the first English printer, who gave it the title *Le Morte d'Arthur* and complained in a famous preface that Arthur was far better known and appreciated in other countries than his own. Caxton's complaint was subsequently more than answered as, one after the other, English poets dipped into Arthurian legend; the legend and the characters, however, changed, and the many versions reflect the changes in ideals, tastes, and preferences wrought by time. The Arthur in Spenser's *Faerie Queene* (1590, 1596, 1611), for example, is the ideal of manhood and bears little resemblance to earlier portraits of Arthur.

Perhaps the best-known modern retelling of the story of Arthur is Tennyson's IDYLLS OF THE KING (1859–1872). Like all the later romancers, Tennyson leaned heavily on Malory, but his approach is very different. The sin of Launcelot and Guinevere as the evil cause of the failure of the Round Table is strongly emphasized. Tennyson is often criticized for his shadowy, unreal, almost symbolic depiction of Arthur.

The story of Arthur has been told in the 19th and 20th centuries by such men as William Morris, Edwin Arlington Robinson, John Masefield, and Mark Twain, who burlesqued the romance of Arthur in *Connecticut Yankee in King Arthur's Court* (1889).

The popularity of the story of Arthur continues, being more recently retold, for example, by T. H. White in *The Once and Future King* (1958). This work has served to demonstrate once more the astonishing appeal of the legendary king, once a remote Celtic chieftain, whose name has already figured in literature for at least 1400 years.

Arthur Mervyn (Part I, 1799; Part II, 1800). A novel by Charles Brockden BROWN. The titular hero is a young man who becomes involved with a criminal, but later clears himself. The book is especially notable for its description of the yellow fever epidemic in Philadelphia in 1793.

Articles of Confederation and Perpetual Union. The constitution by which the United States was governed from 1781 until the ratification of the new CONSTITUTION in 1789. The central government created by the Articles lacked strength because each state remained sovereign and independent; there was no effective executive officer, and Congress lacked the power to levy taxes. To remedy these defects, a Constitutional Convention was called in 1787 and resulted in the writing of a new constitution.

Artzybashev, Mikhail Petrovich (1870–1927). Russian novelist and dramatist. His novel *Sanin* (1907) created a sensation because of its frank treatment and discussion of sex. His other works include *The Death of Lande* (1904) and *At the Brink* (1912).

Arundel (1930). A historical novel by Kenneth ROBERTS. The first of the author's stirring and authentic narratives, it deals with Benedict Arnold's expedition against Quebec. Arundel was the original name of Kennebunk, Me., Roberts' birthplace, and it had been his intention to give the history of Maine in a family chronicle, but he gave up the idea as he became more interested in the history of the country as a whole. Benedict Arnold's story is continued in RABBLE IN ARMS.

Arundhati. In Hindu legend, the wife of the great sage Vashishtha. Traditionally, she, along with Sita, represents the ideal Hindu wife.

Aruru. The Babylonian goddess who molded man, and later the hero Enkidu, out of clay. She appears in the *Epic of* GILGAMESH.

Arveragus. See FRANKLIN'S TALE.

Arviragus. (1) In Shakespeare's CYMBELINE, the valiant and noble younger son of Cymbeline, king of Britain. He is abducted by Belisarius as an infant and raised as his son under the name of Cadwal.

(2) In Chaucer's FRANKLIN'S TALE there is a character named Arviragus (or Arveragus). See GUIDERIUS.

Aryan language (from Sans. *arya*, noble). The Indo-European family of languages, from the name by which the Hindus and Iranians used to distinguish themselves from the nations they conquered. The place of origin of these languages is not definitely known, authorities differing so widely as between a locality enclosed by the river Oxus and the Hindu-Kush Mountains, and the shores of the Baltic Sea. The Aryan family of languages includes the Persian, Indic (Hindi, Sanskrit, etc.), Latin, Greek, and Celtic, with all the European except Basque, Turkish, Hungarian, and Finnic. It is sometimes called the Indo-European, sometimes the Indo-Germanic, and sometimes the Japhetic.

Aryan race. A term used by the German Nazis to designate, without any scientific basis, the original Indo-European race from which the German people were descended. They claimed that German superiority depended on the purity of the race, or in practical terms, on the extermination of the Jews. See Houston Stewart CHAMBERLAIN; Alfred ROSENBERG.

Ascalaphus (Askalaphos). In Greek mythology, an inhabitant of the underworld. When Hades gave Persephone permission to return to the upper world as she had eaten nothing, Ascalaphus said that she had partaken of a pomegranate. In revenge Persephone turned him into an owl by sprinkling him with the water of Phlegethon.

Ascalon, the Hermit of. In the GERUSALEMME LIBERATA of Tasso, a good wizard who helps Ubaldo and Guelfo break the power of Armida over the Christian champion Rinaldo of Este. With his help they are able to reach her castle on the Fortunate Isles and bring him to his senses. His return to the fray results in the final victory of the Crusaders.

Ascanius. Also known as **Iulus.** In classic legend, the son of AENEAS. He escaped with his father from Troy and later ruled over the kingdom in Italy which his father had secured. After Aeneas' death, Ascanius himself built its capital, Alba Longa. The gens Julia (or Iulia), to which Julius Caesar and Octavius Caesar belonged, supposedly derived its name from Ascanius' other name, Iulus, and accordingly sought to trace its lineage from the earliest ancestors of the Roman people. See AENEID; JULIAN EMPERORS.

Ascapart. A legendary giant conquered by Sir Bevis of Hamton. He was 30 feet high, and the space between his eyes was 12 inches. This mighty giant, whose effigy may be seen on the city gates of Southampton, could carry Sir Bevis and the latter's wife and horse under his arm with no difficulty.

Ascasubi, Hilario. See GAUCHO LITERATURE.

Ascent of F6, The (1936). A drama in verse and prose by W. H. AUDEN and Christopher ISHERWOOD. In a political crisis involving a border dispute in "British Sudoland," Sir James Ransom asks his brother Michael, a famous mountaineer, to lead a British expedition up F6, a mountain on the colony's frontier, which the Sudoland people believe to be haunted. Michael Ransom is reluctant to go, for he does not want to turn mountaineering into a political weapon, or to help his brother and his powerful, upper-class friends in their unscrupulous careers. But his mother urges him to go, to do a great deed; he agrees. The mountain is inhabited only by a strange order of monks, whose Abbot tells Ransom that the mountain is haunted in that each man meets his own demon there. The other climbers are killed one by one because of their particular obsessions or defects of character. At the top Ransom, delirious, goes through a nightmare trial scene with the other characters and finally sees *his* demon, his mother, and dies. As in Auden's other early work, the poet is concerned with both social and psychological diseases, and expresses himself through symbolism. Mr. and Mrs. A., ordinary English people, make up the chorus as they listen to the radio announcer's account of the expedition and comment on it. Benjamin Britten composed the music for the play.

Asch, Sholem (1880–1957). Polish-born American novelist. Asch, who wrote his books chiefly in Yiddish, is best known for his biblical novels: *The Nazarene* (1939), *The Apostle* (1943), and *Mary* (1949). These books reflect his conviction that Christianity should be considered the logical continuation of Judaism. *East River* (1946), a novel set in New York, illustrates the formation of the American character through the merging of diverse races and creeds. Asch's later works include *Moses* (1951), *A Passage in the Night* (1953), and *The Prophet* (1955).

Ascham, Roger (1515–1568). English prose writer and teacher, tutor to Elizabeth before her accession to the throne, later connected with her court as Greek preceptor. In his writings he urged the adoption of sports in an educational curriculum and defended English prose as a literary medium. His best known works are *Toxophilus* (1545), a treatise on archery, and *The* SCHOOLMASTER (1570), which expounds his pedagogical theories.

Aschenbach, Gustav von. See DEATH IN VENICE.

Asclepius (Asklepios). Greek god of healing, son of Apollo and Coronis. Apollo killed the mother for infidelity, but saved the unborn child, giving it into the care of CHIRON. Asclepius became extraordinarily proficient in medicine, but when he brought Hippolytus back to life, Zeus, thinking he had gone too far in interfering with divine prerogative, destroyed him with a thunderbolt. In revenge Apollo killed the Cyclopes. Asclepius was the father of Podalirus and Machaon, heroes at Troy, and of various daughters who were mere personifications of one form or another of healing.

Asem, An Eastern Tale, or A Vindication of the Wisdom of Providence in the Moral Government of the World (1759). A tale by Oliver GOLDSMITH concerning Asem, a hermit and misanthrope, who sees a vision of a world free from vice.

Asgard (from *as*, a god; *gard*[*h*], an enclosure, yard). The celestial dwelling place of the Scandinavian gods, equivalent to the Olympus of Greek mythology. It was said to be situated in the center of the universe and be accessible only by the rainbow bridge (*Bifrost*). Valhalla was the most famous great hall of its many regions and mansions, which also included Gladsheim, Vingolf, Valaskjalf, and Ydalir.

Ashcan School or The Eight. A term applied to a group of realistic American artists. They painted bars, prizefights, and street scenes rather than the pretty pictures fashionable at the turn of the 20th century. Their first exhibition in 1908 met with an uproar of disapproval that gave rise to the name of the group. Their members were Robert Henri (1865–1929), John SLOAN, Maurice Prendergast (1861–1924), Arthur B. Davies (1862–1928), George Luks (1867–1933), Everett Shinn (1873–1953), William Glackens (1870–1938), and Ernest Lawson (1873–1939).

Ashenden. The name W. Somerset MAUGHAM used for his own appearances in CAKES AND ALE and *The British Agent*.

Asherah or Asherat. The mother of the Canaanite gods, and consort of El. She lives in a palace in the north and exerts great influence over her husband. Even more than El himself, she seems hostile to the younger gods, such as Baal. Although her epithets refer to her as a sea-goddess, she fills a role in the Canaanite pantheon similar to that of Ge (Earth) in the Greek. See THE POEM OF BAAL.

Ashford, Daisy (1882–   ). English child author of the story THE YOUNG VISITERS. The book was published in 1919, wth a preface by J. M. Barrie claiming that the author, then a mature woman, was nine when she wrote it.

Ashkenazim. The middle and northern European Jews, as distinguished from the SEPHARDIM. It was originally the name of a people from Ashkenaz, near Ararat, mentioned in the Old Testament (Jer. 51:27). Ashkenaz is also the name of the eldest son of Gomer (Gen. 10:3).

Ashley, Lady Brett. The principal female character in Ernest Hemingway's novel THE SUN ALSO RISES. An Englishwoman, in Spain while she divorces her husband, she seeks to hide the emptiness of her life in friendship with the impotent Jake Barnes and an affair with the bullfighter Pedro Romero. She typifies the aimless pursuit of leisure of "the lost generation."

Ashnan. The Sumerian goddess of grain.

Ashtar. Canaanite god of artificial irrigation. During the period that the rain-god Baal spends in the underworld, he reigns on earth, but is not quite equal to the job. This role, clearly shown in THE POEM OF BAAL, is obviously an allegorical statement of the practical fact that irrigation cannot fertilize the earth as effectively as rain.

Ashton, Helen Rosaline (1891–1958). English novelist. She is the author of popular stories about doctors such as *Doctor Serocold* (1930), and fictional biographies such as *William and Dorothy* [Wordsworth] (1938) and *Parson Austen's Daughter* (1949).

Ashton, Lucy. See THE BRIDE OF LAMMERMOOR.

Ashton, Winifred. See Clemence DANE.

Ashtoreth. See ISHTAR.

Ashur. See ASSUR.

Ash Wednesday. The first day of Lent, so called from the ancient custom of sprinkling ashes on the heads of clergy and people. The ashes are prepared from the palms blessed on Palm Sunday the previous year.

Ash Wednesday (1930). A poem by T. S. ELIOT. The first of his poems to celebrate the peace found in orthodox Christianity, it is a poetic liturgy, meditation, and approach to mystical communion with God.

Asia. In classic mythology, one of the Oceanides, usually spoken of as wife of Iapetus and mother of Prometheus. In his PROMETHEUS UNBOUND, Shelley makes her play an important part as Prometheus' wife.

Asia. According to the Koran the wife of that Pharaoh who brought up Moses. Her husband tortured her for believing in Moses; but she was taken alive into paradise. Muhammad numbers her among the four perfect women.

As I Lay Dying (1930). A novel by William FAULKNER. It tells the story of the death of Addie Bundren and the ordeals her family undergo in carrying the body to Jefferson, Miss., for burial. Her husband, Anse; her four sons, Cash, Darl, Jewel, and Vardaman; her daughter, Dewey Dell; and several neighbors all reveal their relationships with Addie in the course of the story. A series of mishaps besets the family: in crossing a flooding river, the mules are drowned, Cash's leg is broken, and the coffin is upset and rescued by Jewel. Later, the family rests at a farmhouse, where Darl sets fire to the barn in an attempt to destroy the now-putrescent corpse; again the coffin is rescued by Jewel. The family finally reaches Jefferson, where Addie is buried; Darl is taken to the insane asylum, and Anse acquires a new wife.

In the course of the narrative it is revealed that Jewel was born of Addie's affair with Whitfield, a local preacher. Her relationship to Anse had been spiritually and emotionally barren, based on words alone. Significantly, Jewel is a silent man, active and passionate, while Darl is sensitive and perceptive, living in the world of his own mind.

The story unfolds in some 60 short sections, each labeled with the name of the character who narrates his thoughts and perceptions; as in *The Sound and the Fury*, Faulkner uses the stream-of-consciousness technique. A grim story of the ordeals of fire and water, the novel is often comic, ending with the new wife who is "duck-shaped" and popeyed.

Asimov, Isaac (1920–   ).   Russian-born American author known primarily as a science-fiction writer, Asimov has published more than 40 books interpreting science to the general public. *Building Blocks of the Universe* (1957) and *The Living River* (1959) both received awards for their excellence. *The Intelligent Man's Guide to Science* (2 vols., 1960) is an encyclopedic work for the layman. His books of science fiction written for those in high school are published under the pseudonym Paul French.

Asín Palacios, Miguel (1871–1944).   Spanish philologist and professor of Arabic studies. Author of the famous *La escatología musulmana en la Divina Comedia* (*Islam in the Divine Comedy*, 1919), which deals with the influence of Arabian authors, notably Aben Arabí, upon Dante, Asín Palacios was responsible for many of the discoveries pointing to the interrelationship between the Islamic and early Christian cultures. Also among his best-known works is the volume *El Islam cristianizado* (1931).

Asir.   See Aesir.

Ask or **Askr.**   In Norse mythology, the first man, created out of an ash tree by Odin, Vili, and Ve. The first woman was Embla.

Asmodée.   The devil-companion of Don Cléofas, in Alain René Lesage's picaresque novel *Le Diable Boiteux* (1707), sometimes entitled *Asmodeus* or *The Devil on Two Sticks* in English translations. He is an engaging little lame devil, with a great deal more gaiety than malice. He takes pleasure in showing his companion human ugliness and depravity by lifting the roofs off houses in Madrid.

Asmodeus.   The "evil demon" who appears in the Apocryphal book of *Tobit*. His business was "to plot against the newly wedded and . . . sever them utterly by many calamities." According to Hebrew mythology, Asmodeus fell in love with Sara, daughter of Raguel, and slew her seven husbands in succession, each on his bridal night. He was exorcised and driven into Egypt by a charm made by Tobias (on the advice of the angel Raphael) from the heart and liver of a fish burnt on perfumed ashes (Tobit 6:14; 7:2). In the Talmud, Asmodeus is called "king of the devils."

Aspasia.   A Milesian woman (fl. 440 B.C.) celebrated for her beauty and talents. She lived at Athens as mistress of Pericles, and her house became the center of literary and philosophical society; hence a fascinating and cultured courtesan. Walter Savage Landor wrote a series of imaginary letters, *Pericles and Aspasia* (1836).

Aspasia.   Titular heroine of Beaumont and Fletcher's drama, *The Maid's Tragedy* (1610). She is betrothed to Amintor but the King, wishing to provide a husband for his mistress Evadne, commands Amintor to marry her instead. Aspasia is a pathetic figure, the very type of ill-fortune and wretchedness, but she bears her fate with patience even when she becomes a jest and byword. Her tragic death gives the drama its name.

Aspects of the Novel (1927).   A literary study by E. M. Forster. Defining the novel as any work of prose fiction, Forster discusses not only plot and character, but also "fantasy," "prophecy" (or symbolism), and "pattern and rhythm" (writing of the structure of a novel as though it is, or should be, like a symphony).

Aspern Papers, The (1888).   A novelette by Henry James. According to passages in his notebook, James based *The Aspern Papers* on a story he had heard concerning the mistress of Byron, then living, who was in possession of several unpublished papers and letters of both Byron and Shelley. The narrator of *The Aspern Papers* learns that the former mistress of the romantic poet Jeffrey Aspern is still living in Venice and has in her possession a collection of the poet's papers which she will not permit to be published. In hope of gaining access to the papers, the narrator rents a room from the old lady and her middle-aged niece, but his plans are frustrated when, at the old lady's death, the niece demands marriage as the price of the papers.

Assassins.   A small Islamic sect. For two hundred years it terrified Europe with its secret murders. It was founded by Hassan-i-Sabbah near the end of the 11th century. From the nearly impregnable mountain stronghold of Alamut in Persia, and later from the Syrian stronghold of Masyad, the Assassins harried the Crusaders and their rival Islamic sects, remaining unbroken in power even by the great Saladin. They were finally destroyed in the 13th century by the Tatar prince Hulagu and, somewhat later, in Syria, by the Egyptian Sultan Baybars.

The name Assassins is derived from *hashish*, a drug made from hemp, with which, according to tradition, the victorious Assassins were rewarded upon their return from successful depradations. The secret of their long reign of terror was the absolute obedience that the young men of the sect were required to give to their leaders. The name of the sect soon came into the languages of Europe as a synonym for murderer.

Assembly.   During the French Revolution, a representative body which had three names: the National, Constituent, and Legislative. In 1789 the *tiers état* (third estate) declared itself to be the National Assembly and controlling body, and took the so-called Oath of the Tennis Court. Shortly thereafter, reinforced by a majority of clergy and a minority of nobles, it called itself the Constituent Assembly; in 1791 it framed and voted the first written constitution in French history. The Constituent Assembly was succeeded by the Legislative Assembly (1791), which voted the war against Austria and the imprisonment of Louis XVI, thus opposing the constitutional monarchy. In September, 1792 the Legislative Assembly was succeeded by the National Convention which immediately decreed the abolition of the monarchy. With this formality, the struggle among the various republican factions—Girondists, Jacobins, Cordeliers, adherents of Robespierre—began.

Asser (d. 909?).   Welsh monk, later bishop of Sherborne (after c. 900). About 885 King Alfred the Great invited him to his court as tutor and companion; he helped Alfred with his ambitious program of creating a center of popular learning. He wrote a biography of Alfred (c. 893), which includes a history of England from 849 to 887 and of Alfred's career until 887.

Assommoir, L' (The Dram Shop, 1877). One of the novels in the ROUGON-MACQUART series by Emile ZOLA. Written in the argot of the Paris streets, *L'Assommoir* is a study of the demoralizing effects of alcohol on the lives of working-class people. Although Zola had great compassion for these miserable people, his book was attacked as immoral because of the sordid nature of the subject.

assonance. In poetry and prose, the identity of vowel sounds, as in the words "scream" and "beech." Assonance is one of the many phonetic devices that serve to unify poetry and prose. In poetry it is frequently substituted for RHYME, and in this use is sometimes referred to as vowel rhyme. See CONSONANCE; ALLITERATION.

Assumption, Feast of the. August 15th, so called in honor of the Virgin Mary. In Catholic tradition, she was taken to heaven that day (A.D. 45) in her corporeal form, being at the time seventy-five years of age. There is a legend that the Virgin was raised soon after her death, and assumed to glory by a special privilege before the general resurrection.

Assumption of Hannele, The (Hanneles Himmelfahrt; 1893). A symbolic drama by Gerhart HAUPTMANN. It is the story of a maltreated girl who tries to drown herself and is taken to a wretched almshouse where she lapses into delirium. In her dreams she transforms the place and its dreary inhabitants into a fairy paradise of immense poetic beauty.

Assur or **Ashur.** The principal god of Assyria, which bears his name. The Baal of the Assyrian capital of Nineveh, he took over much of the dominant role that had been played by the Babylonian MARDUK.

Assur-bani-pal or **Ashurbanipal** (d. 626? B.C.). King of Assyria. The son of Esar-Haddon, he ruled Assyria, while his twin brother Samus-sum-yukin ruled Babylonia. Against great odds, Assur-bani-pal maintained his supremacy over Egypt and put down a Tyrian revolt. The most powerful of Assyria's rulers, he either subjugated or dominated the Manna, the Elamites, and the Cilicians. He also quelled a revolt by his brother in Babylonia, and harassed the northern Arabians. However, Assur-bani-pal had overreached himself and exhausted the resources of his own country to the extent that it collapsed completely not long after his death. He left behind him, however, a legacy of enormous importance for modern times: he had caused to be prepared for his royal library a large number of the most important literary works of the Near East; preserved on tablets, these were excavated in the middle of the 19th century in the ruins of Nineveh, his capital. Some characteristics of Assur-bani-pal are recognizable in the legendary SARDANAPALUS.

Astarotte. A fiend in Pulci's comic epic MORGANTE MAGGIORE. He takes Rinaldo from Egypt to the battle of Roncesvalles in a few hours by magic, discoursing on the way about theological questions. He has been regarded as Pulci's mouthpiece in the poem.

Astarte. See ISHTAR.

Astolfo. In medieval romance one of the twelve famous PALADINS of Charlemagne. An English duke, he joined the Emperor in his struggles against the Saracens. Known primarily for his great boasting, he was also generous, courteous, gay, and singularly handsome. In the *Morgante Maggiore* of Pulci and the Orlando poems of Boiardo and Ariosto he appears as Astolfo. In Ariosto, he rides a whale to the enchanted island of the witch Alcina and is detained by her until she tires of him. Transformed into a myrtle tree, he is rescued by MELISSA. Astolpho then journeys to the moon in search of Orlando's lost wits, which he brings back in a phial.

Astor, John Jacob (1763–1848). German-born American fur trader. Astor opened a fur store in New York City in 1786 and became the dominant figure in the fur trade of the Old Northwest. He later shifted his attention to the Far West, establishing Astoria, a trading post near the mouth of the Columbia River, in 1811. At his death he was the wealthiest man in the U.S. Washington Irving, on commission from the Astor family, wrote a laudatory account of ASTORIA.

Astoreth. See ISHTAR.

Astoria, or, Anecdotes of an Enterprise Beyond the Rocky Mountains (1836). A narrative arranged by Washington IRVING from material supplied by John Jacob Astor. Irving assumed the part of Astor's glorifier because he needed money, but parts of the work remain interesting as a record of life on the northwestern frontier. Astoria is a town established by Astor on the site of Fort Clatsop in Oregon, at the mouth of the Columbia River. Astor opened his fur-trading post there in 1811 and sold it to the British in 1812. It was subsequently returned to the U.S. by the treaty of Ghent (1814).

Astraea (Astraia). In classic mythology, the goddess of justice. She was generally said to be the daughter of Themis and Zeus. She was the last of the immortals to withdraw from the earth after the Golden Age. Afterward she became the constellation Virgo.

Astrate, Roi de Tyr (Astrate, King of Tyre, 1664). The most popularly successful tragedy of Philippe QUINAULT. The commoner Astrate loves Elise, queen of Tyre, but discovers that she has usurped the throne and that he is the lost son of the murdered king. The play aroused Boileau's harshest ridicule; the dilemmas of love, however improbable, are a recurring theme in Quinault's work.

Astrolabe, A Treatise on the (1391). An unfinished adaptation by Geoffrey CHAUCER of contemporary lore on astronomy and astrology. It is addressed to "little Lewis my son" (probably his own son, but possibly his godson Lewis Clifford), and explains the work of Messahala (eighth-century Arabian astronomer, known to Chaucer in Latin) in terms a child can understand. Of all Chaucer's prose works, it is the one that follows its model least closely, and therefore the best indication of Chaucer's own prose style.

Astrophel and Stella. A sonnet sequence by Sir Philip SIDNEY, written 1580-1584 and posthumously published in 1591. The "Stella" of the sonnets was Penelope Devereux. "Astrophel" (meaning star-lover) is a Greek pun on Sidney's name. After Sidney's death in 1586 his friend Edmund Spenser wrote an elegy called *Astrophel.*

Astyanax. See TROJAN WOMEN, THE.

Asur. See ASSUR.

Asura. In Hindu mythology, a demon, an opposer of the gods.

Asushu-Namir. In Babylonian mythology, a hermaphroditic creature. It was created by the god Ea to rescue ISHTAR from the underworld.

Asvins. In Hindu mythology, twin gods of light, the youngest of the gods. More than 50 hymns of the Rig Veda are addressed to them. See VEDAS.

Asynja. The goddesses of Asgard; the feminine counterpart of the AESIR.

As You Like It (c. 1600). A pastoral comedy by William Shakespeare. Duke FREDERICK has banished the rightful duke, who is his brother and Rosalind's father, to the Forest of Arden. Rosalind first meets ORLANDO after a contest in which he has felled Duke Frederick's wrestler Charles. Shortly afterwards, Orlando is forced to flee to the forest to escape the plots of his jealous brother Oliver. When Rosalind incurs her uncle's wrath and must also flee, Frederick's daughter CELIA and TOUCHSTONE the clown accompany her. In the forest of Arden, Rosalind, who has disguised herself as a youth by the name of Ganymede, meets Orlando and leads him through a series of episodes in which he unwittingly confides his love for her. Meanwhile, Oliver comes to the forest and, when Orlando saves him from death, the brothers are reconciled. In subsequent scenes, Touchstone woos the dull-witted AUDREY, Oliver woos Celia, the shepherd SILVIUS woos PHEBE, and Phebe woos the disguised Rosalind. At last, Rosalind reveals her identity, and the four pairs of lovers are united in the feast of Hymen before the banished duke and his followers. Rosalind's father is restored to his dukedom when Duke Frederick is converted by a monk and decides to enter a monastery. The story is based on Thomas Lodge's romance *Rosalynde: Epuphues' Golden Legacie* (1590). See JAQUES.

Atahualpa (1500?–1533). Inca emperor of Peru. Becoming ruler of the northern part of the Inca empire upon the death of his father Huayna Capac in 1527, Atahualpa wrested the southern portion from his half-brother Huascar. The dissension produced by this fratricidal conflict facilitated the Spanish conquest led by Francisco Pizarro, who captured Atahualpa in 1532. Although Atahualpa was promised his freedom in exchange for a huge ransom of gold and silver, Pizarro accused him of conspiring against the Spaniards and had him executed.

Atala (1801). A novel by François René de CHATEAUBRIAND. A melancholy tale of violent passion, set in the primeval woods of North America, it is generally cited as signalizing the beginning of the romantic movement in French literature.

Atalanta (Atalante). In Greek legend, a daughter of Iasus (some authorities say Zeus) and Clymene. She took part in the Calydonian boar hunt and drew first blood. Being very swift of foot, she refused to marry unless the suitor should first defeat her in a race. Melanion overcame her at last by dropping, one after another, during the race, three golden apples that had been given him for the purpose by Venus. Atalanta was not proof against the temptation to pick them up, and so lost the race and became a wife. In the Boeotian form of the legend Hippomenes takes the place of Melanion. In some legends, Atalanta was also one of the Argonauts. William Morris made this legend the subject of one of the tales in his *Earthly Paradise* and Swinburne wrote a dramatic poem *Atalanta in Calydon* on the same theme.

Atalanta in Calydon (1865). A tragedy by Algernon Charles SWINBURNE. It is based on the Greek legend of Atalanta and the Calydonian boar. It is remembered today chiefly for its choruses, particularly the *Hymn to Artemis*.

Atalide. In Jean Racine's tragedy BAJAZET, the princess beloved by the titular hero.

Ate. See FAERIE QUEENE, THE.

Atellanae, or **Atellan farces.** Low comedy interludes in the Roman theaters, introduced from Atella, in Campania. The characters of Macchus and Bucco are the forerunners of the modern Punch and Clown.

Athaliah. In the Old Testament (II Kings 11), the daughter of Ahab and Jezebel, and wife of Joram, king of Judah. After the death of her son Ahaziah, she gained the throne by murdering 42 princes of the house of David. She reigned six years, but in the seventh, Joash who had escaped the massacre was proclaimed the rightful king. Attracted by the shouts of the people at his coronation, Athaliah entered the temple where she was killed by the mob. Racine's last tragedy *Athalie* (1691) is based on this story.

Athalie (1691). A tragedy by Jean RACINE. It is based on the Old Testament story of Athaliah and Joash. Because it was written for the schoolgirls of St-Cyr, the play includes songs sung by a chorus of Levite maidens. *Athalie* was Racine's last work for the stage, and is considered by many critics the most perfect example of French classical tragedy.

Athamas. A mythological Greek king of Boeotia, son of Aeolus and brother of Sisyphus and Salmoneus. He married the phantom Nephele at Hera's command and by her had a son, Phrixus, and a daughter, Helle. The sacrifice of these children was prevented by the arrival of a ram with GOLDEN FLEECE. Athamas also fathered Learchus and Melicertes by INO.

Athanasius, St. Called Athanasius the Great (293?–373). A Greek father of the Church and lifelong opponent of the ARIANS. He is not the author of the Athanasian creed, which originated in the 5th or 6th century.

Atheist's Tragedy, The (1611). A tragedy by Cyril TOURNEUR. It presents the downfall of the self-seeking materialist D'Amville, whose early successes later turn to death and destruction.

Athene. The Greek goddess of war, handicraft, and wisdom. According to the most familiar story, she sprang fully armed from the head of Zeus when Hephaestus split it open with an axe. Zeus had previously swallowed his consort Metis, her mother, on learning that she would bear a child who would rule the gods. Another story, perhaps earlier, indicates that her birth was associated with some stream or lake; this may have been told of her as an ancient pre-Hellenic deity. In a dispute with Poseidon as to who should be patron of Athens, she won that distinction by bestowing on the Athenians the boon of the olive tree. The PARTHENON was dedicated to her.

In most myths, Athene was a virgin, though originally she may have been a mother-goddess. She appears in innumerable myths, but none better displays her unique intellectual qualities than her role in the ODYSSEY as the constant friend and adviser of the clever and imaginative Odysseus.

Athens. The capital of modern Greece and one of the chief city-states of ancient Greece, situated in Attica. Its name was synonymous with outstanding cultural achievement for centuries after its political ascendancy had ceased to exist with its defeat in the PELOPONNESIAN WAR.

Atherton, Gertrude [Franklin] (1857–1948). American novelist. Among her numerous books, the most famous are *The Conqueror* (1902), a fictional biography of Alexander Hamilton, and *Black Oxen* (1923), a novel about the rejuvenation of an older woman. Much of her writing deals with California, as in *The Californians* (1898) and *California: An Intimate History* (1914).

Athos. One of the famous friends and adventurers in Dumas' THE THREE MUSKETEERS. Athos also appears in the sequels TWENTY YEARS AFTER and THE VISCOUNT OF BRAGELONNE. He is unfailingly the gallant gentleman, quiet and reserved.

Atlante (Atlantes). A magician and sage in the Orlando poem of Boiardo and Ariosto. Atlante is the teacher of RUGGIERO the Saracen warrior destined to be converted and marry Bradamante.

Atlantic Monthly, The. An American magazine founded in Boston in 1857. Named by Oliver Wendell Holmes, it has been edited by a series of distinguished men: James Russell Lowell, James T. Fields, William Dean Howells, Thomas Bailey Aldrich, Horace E. Scudder, Walter Hines Page, Bliss Perry, Ellery Sedgwick, and Edward A. Weeks. Among its contributors are numbered the most outstanding writers in America. Since 1938, the magazine has been noted for greater breadth, international outlook, and increased interest in current affairs. Several collections have been issued, including *Atlantic Harvest* (1947) and *Jubilee* (1957), a selection from the magazine's first hundred years.

Atlantis. A mythic island of great extent, anciently supposed to have once existed in the western sea. It is mentioned by Plato (in the *Timaeus* and *Critias*), and Solon was told of it by an Egyptian priest, who said that it had been overwhelmed by an earthquake and sunk beneath the sea 9,000 years before his time. See LEMURIA; LYONNESSE; NEW ATLANTIS, THE.

Atlas. In Greek mythology, one of the TITANS, son of Iapetus and Clymene. He was condemned by Zeus for his share in the war of the Titans to uphold the heavens on his shoulders. He was stationed on the Atlas mountains in Africa, and the tale is merely a poetical way of saying that they prop up the heavens, because they are so lofty. The PLEIADES were Atlas' daughters.

The figure of Atlas with the world on his back was employed by the Flemish geographer Mercator (1512–1594, real name Gerhard Kremer), on the title page of his collection of maps in the 16th century. The name has since been used to mean a book of maps.

atman (Sans., "breath, self, soul"). In Hinduism the internal essence of the single individual. *Atman* can also be used to refer to the universal Self, the source of all other selves.

atomists. See LEUCIPPUS.

atonality. In music, the absence of tonality. Atonality negates the primacy of a keynote or tonic; the notion of a scale built upon the tonic, to which certain of the 12 notes of the chromatic scale belong and to which others are foreign; the building of harmonic combinations exclusively in thirds; and the distinction between consonant and dissonant combinations, especially the need to resolve dissonances into consonances.

Arnold SCHOENBERG is generally considered to have been the first composer of atonal music and the prime systematizer of its methods. He eventually elaborated a 12-tone method of composition in which the notes of the chromatic scale were organized into an inviolable order, or "row," so that no note might be emphasized at the expense of any other. While the term *atonal* first implied an experimental rebellion against the single tonal center, it eventually came to designate the systematic negation of tonality through absolute equality of all tones. The organizational methods by which such music has sought to preserve its atonality have proved to be of greater value to contemporary music than the somewhat negative doctrine of atonality itself. Theoreticians, including Schoenberg, have questioned whether it is not a contradiction in terms to speak of "atonal music," and many hold that true atonality is, in practice, impossible.

Atreus, the house of. The royal line of Mycenae, whose terrible story was a favorite source for the Athenian tragic dramatists. Atreus and Thyestes, sons of Pelops, became rivals for the throne of Mycenae, left vacant by the death of their brother-in-law Sthenelus and his son Eurystheus. Thyestes suggested that it should go to the possessor of the golden lamb. Atreus, who had previously hidden one in a chest, agreed, not knowing that his wife Aerope had given it to Thyestes, who had seduced her. Thyestes won the throne, but lost it when Atreus, with the aid of Zeus, made the sun move backward, an omen that proved Thyestes a usurper. Learning of the seduction, Atreus invited Thyestes to a banquet, served him his sons in a stew, then banished him, but not before Thyestes had cursed the house of Atreus.

Thyestes learned from the Delphic oracle that only by begetting a son by his own daughter Pelopia could he avenge himself. He ravished her at night, unrecognized. Atreus, having killed Aerope, the mother of Agamemnon and Menelaus, now married Pelopia, thinking her the daughter of King Thesprotus of Sicyon. Bearing Thyestes' child, she exposed it out of shame, but it was rescued by shepherds and named Aegisthus. Atreus learned of the child and believed it to be his own. Later he sent Aegisthus to kill Thyestes, but Thyestes revealed himself as Aegisthus' father. Pelopia killed herself in shame, but Aegisthus killed Atreus. Thyestes, avenged, became ruler of Mycenae again. Later, however, Atreus' son Agamemnon drove out Thyestes and killed his son Tantalus, married the latter's wife Clytemnestra, and became king of Mycenae.

Clytemnestra bore a son, Orestes, and three daughters, IPHIGENIA, ELECTRA, and Chrysothemis. She never forgave her husband for the sacrifice of Iphigenia, but, taking Aegisthus as a lover, conspired with him to kill Agamemnon. When he returned from the Trojan War, they slew him in his bath. They also slew his captive, CASSANDRA. Electra, however, had smuggled away Orestes for his safety to the Phocian king Strophius, who brought him up with his own son Pylades. Grown to manhood, Orestes returned and, with Electra's help, avenged his father by killing both his mother and Aegisthus.

For this crime, which had been approved in advance by the Delphic oracle, he was driven mad by the ERINYES (Furies) of his mother. Later he was tried for his crime on the Areopagus, with Apollo pleading his case. He did not regain his sanity, however, until, on the advice of Apollo, he recovered an image from the temple of Taurian Artemis. There his life was saved by Iphigenia, who had been transported thither by Artemis at the time of the supposed sacrifice. Returning to Mycenae, he killed the new king Aletes, Aegisthus' son, and ultimately ruled Argos and Sparta, as well. His friend Pylades, who had accompanied him to Tauris, married Electra. With the return of Orestes' sanity, Thyestes' curse on the house of Atreus—or that of Myrtilus on the seed of Pelops—was finally lifted.

The events from the return of Agamemnon to the trial of Orestes are told in the only extant trilogy of Greek tragedies, the *Oresteia* (458 B.C.) of Aeschylus: the *Agamemnon* recounts his murder; *The Libation Bearers* (*Choephori*), the vengeance of Orestes; the *Eumenides* his trial. Various parts of the story are also told in Sophocles' ELECTRA, Euripides' ELECTRA, ORESTES, and his plays on Iphigenia, and in Seneca's *Thyestes* and *Agamemnon*. Eugene O'Neill retold much of the story in modern terms in his MOURNING BECOMES ELECTRA. Jean-Paul Sartre adapted the story for his play THE FLIES.

Atropos. In Greek mythology, that one of the three FATES whose office it was to cut the thread of life with a pair of scissors.

Atticus, Titus Pomponius (109–32 B.C.). Roman man of letters. He left Rome in 88 B.C. and took up residence in Athens (hence his added surname Atticus), where he remained for 23 years. He was famed for his ability to keep on good terms with men of conflicting personalities and political views, such as Brutus, Marcus Antonius, and Cicero. In his Athenian villa, he kept a staff of slaves whose work was to make copies of contemporary writings. It was Atticus' publishing house which preserved the letters of Cicero, the *Epistulae ad Familiares* and the *Epistulae ad Atticum*, invaluable sources of information about behind-the-scenes politics in the last years of the Roman republic.

Attila (d. 453). King of the Huns. He is notorious for his attacks and inroads upon Europe during the final stages of the Roman Empire. He overran the Balkans (447–450) causing great destruction. In 451 he invaded Gaul, but was forced to withdraw after a series of defeats. He and his soldiers were feared for their cruelty and vandalism; Attila himself was called "the scourge of God." Pierre Corneille made him the hero of a tragedy *Attila* (1667). He appears in the *Nibelungenlied* under the name Etzel and in the *Völsunga Saga* as Atli.

Attila (1667). A tragedy by Pierre CORNEILLE. One of Corneille's least successful works, it recounts the villainy and death of the murderous king of the Huns.

Attucks, Crispus. See BOSTON MASSACRE.

Atwill, Lionel (1885–1946). English-born stage and screen actor. Famous for his roles in Ibsen plays, he supported Katharine Cornell and Helen Hayes and played opposite Nazimova. In the movies most of his parts were in horror pictures.

Atys or **Attis.** The Phrygian counterpart of the Greek Adonis and Phoenician TAMMUZ. He was beloved by Cybele, the mother of the gods, but out of jealousy, she drove him mad. He castrated himself, died at a pine tree, and violets sprang from his blood. Catullus wrote a poem in Latin on the subject, which has been translated into English by Leigh Hunt.

Aub, Max (1903–   ). Spanish author and dramatist. Aub, a prolific writer, is known for his ironic humor, revealed in his novels *Campo de sangre* (1945) and *Las buenas intenciones* (1954). He is also the author of a tragedy, *Deseada* (1950).

Auber, Daniel François Esprit (1782–1871). French composer of opera, especially comic opera. His best known work is FRA DIAVOLO. He was director of the Paris Conservatoire, 1842–1871.

Aubignac, Abbé d'. François Hédelin (c. 1604–c. 1673). French writer. Although Aubignac was a mediocre playwright, his *Pratique du Théâtre* (*Theatrical Practice*, 1657), urging the observance of the classical unities in drama, offers useful information on the French theater of the 17th century.

Aubigné, [Théodore] Agrippa d' (1552–1630). French poet and historian. A fervent supporter of the Protestant cause during the religious wars, he fought in numerous campaigns and, for 20 years, was the friend and adviser of Henry IV. *Les Tragiques* (1616), his great epic poem of the religious wars, combines satire, allegory, and invective. Composed of seven books, it describes the horrors of the war, the vice and corruption of the Valois kings and the courts of justice, the sufferings of the Protestant martyrs and concludes with a vision of the final judgment in Heaven. The use of the Alexandrine in *Les Tragiques* was influential in establishing it as the vehicle of elevated French poetry. The third volume of his *Histoire Universelle* (1616–1619), an account of the Protestant struggle in Europe from 1553 to 1601, was ordered burned by the Parlement of Paris.

Aubrey, John (1626–1697). English antiquary. His best-known work is the anecdotal *Minutes of Lives,* now commonly known as *Brief Lives,* which first appeared as part of Anthony à Wood's *Athenae Oxonienses* (1690). First published separately in 1813, it is a valuable source of information on the lives of important 17th-century figures.

Auburn. The name of the village in Oliver Goldsmith's poem THE DESERTED VILLAGE. It is an imaginary English village, but some of its features support Goldsmith's wistful recollections of his own youth in the Irish village of Lissoy where his father was pastor.

Aucassin and Nicolette (early 13th century). French *chante-fable* in alternating prose and verse, one of the best medieval love romances. Aucassin, son of the Provençal Count of Beaucaire, falls in love with Nicolette, a slave captured from the Saracens. The Count separates them by imprisonment, but Nicolette escapes and Aucassin follows, and they spend three years together until they are captured by Saracens. Aucassin is shipwrecked near home and, his father having died, becomes Count. Nicolette is carried to Carthage, where she is recognized as the king's daughter; but she flees an unwelcome marriage and finds her way to Beaucaire disguised as a minstrel, so that the lovers are happily reunited.

Auchincloss, Louis [Stanton] (1917–   ). American novelist and short-story writer. A member of a prominent family and a successful practicing lawyer himself, Auchincloss is known for his stories dealing with the upper echelons of society. *The Injustice Collectors* (1950) and *The Romantic Egoists* (1954), both thematically unified collections of short stories, won critical acclaim. His first novel, *The Indifferent Children* (1947), was published under the pseudonym Andrew Lee. Other novels include *Sybil* (1952), *A Law for the Lion* (1953), *The Great World and Timothy Colt* (1956), *Pursuit of the Prodigal* (1959), *Portrait in Brownstone* (1962), and *The Rector of Justin* (1964). *Powers of Attorney* (1963) is a collection of short stories.

Auden, W[ystan] H[ugh] (1907–   ). English poet and dramatist. His most influential work was written during the 1930's. He was the best known of the group of British writers of Marxist sympathies who hoped that socialism might be the answer to the economic and political problems of the period. The group included the poets C. Day-Lewis and Stephen Spender, and the dramatist and novelist Christopher Isherwood. Auden served in the Spanish Civil War. In 1938 he married Erika Mann, daughter of the novelist Thomas Mann. In 1939 he emigrated to the U.S. and later became an American citizen.

During World War II, Christianity took the place of socialism as Auden's central preoccupation, and the influence of Marx and Freud gave way to the influence of Kierkegaard and the modern Protestant theologians. In his early work Auden expressed the idea that civilization could be cured of its economic and political diseases by socialism, and from its psychological diseases by psychoanalysis, the general cure being love. The same themes appear in his later work but with an added spiritual dimension. Auden's indebtedness to T. S. Eliot is particularly evident in the imagery of his earlier poems. The poem *New Year Letter* (1941; U.S. title *The Double Man*) is an analysis of the poet's intellectual development and changing views. He edited and rewrote subsequent reprints of his poetry in order to omit what no longer suited his poetic, political, or religious ideas. He also wrote much verse in the popular music-hall tradition.

Auden's chief early works are *Poems* (1930), THE ORATORS, *Look Stranger* (1936; U.S. title *On this Island*), and *Another Time* (1940). For the GROUP THEATRE he wrote the Marxist and experimental plays *The Dance of Death* (1933) and, in collaboration with Christopher Isherwood, THE DOG BENEATH THE SKIN, THE ASCENT OF F6, and *On the Frontier* (1938). He collaborated with Louis MacNeice on the verse and prose work *Letters from Iceland*

(1937), and with Christopher Isherwood on *Journey to a War* (1939), about the war between Japan and China (it contains Auden's sonnet sequence *In Time of War*). The work of Auden's later period includes *The Quest* (1941), a sonnet sequence; FOR THE TIME BEING, a "Christmas Oratorio"; *The Sea and the Mirror* (1944), a "commentary" on *The Tempest;* and THE AGE OF ANXIETY. *Nones* (1951), *The Shield of Achilles* (1955), and *Homage to Clio* (1960) are collections of poetry. Auden collaborated on the libretto of Stravinsky's opera THE RAKE'S PROGRESS. *The Enchafed Flood* (1950) and *The Dyer's Hand* (1963) are critical works. He edited the *Oxford Book of Light Verse* (1938) and selections from Kierkegaard (1952, 1955).

Audiberti, Jacques (1899–1965). French novelist, poet, and dramatist. All his writing is characterized by verbal extravagance and imaginative exaltation of modern man. His works include poetry: *Race des hommes* (1937) and *Toujours* (1944); novels: *Abraxas* (1938) and *Carnage* (1941); plays: *Quoat-Quoat* (1946), *Le Mal court* (1947), *Les Femmes du Boeuf* (1948), and *La Hobereaute* (1956).

Audrey. In Shakespeare's As You LIKE IT, an awkward country wench who jilts William for TOUCHSTONE.

Audubon, John James (1785–1851). Haitianborn American naturalist and artist. Educated in France, Audubon came to the U.S. in 1806. He traveled widely in the U.S. and Canada in search of material for his study of animals, which he depicted in firm, detailed drawings tinted in clear watercolor. His drawings reveal a good sense of design in the placement of animals and in the suggestion of their setting. *The Birds of America,* published in England from 1827 to 1838, is his most famous work.

Aue, Hartmann von. See HARTMANN VON AUE.

Auerbach, Berthold (1812–1882). German novelist of Jewish background, known especially for his collection of stories about rustic life, *Schwarzwälder Dorfgeschichten* (*Village Stories from the Black Forest*, 1843–1854). His deep awareness of problems faced by the Jews led him to write both the essay *Das Judentum und die neueste Literatur* (*Judaism and Recent Literature*, 1836) and a novel *Spinoza* (1835–1837).

Aufidius, Tullus. In Shakespeare's CORIOLANUS, the Volscian general whom Coriolanus defeats in battle. Coriolanus refers to him as "a lion that I am proud to hunt." Although Aufidius is responsible for the death of Coriolanus, he is immediately remorseful and vows to honor his memory.

Aufstieg und Fall der Stadt Mahagonny. See RISE AND FALL OF THE TOWN MAHAGONNY.

Aufzeichnungen des Malte Laurids Brigge, Die. See NOTEBOOKS OF MALTE LAURIDS BRIGGE, THE.

Augean stables. The stables of Augeas (Augeias), a mythological king of Elis, in Greece. These stables, in which he kept 3,000 oxen, had not been cleaned for thirty years. One of the labors of Heracles was to clean them, which he did by causing two rivers to run through them. Hence the phrase *to cleanse the Augean stables* means to clear away an accumulated mass of corruption.

Augie March, The Adventures of (1953). A novel by Saul BELLOW. This modern picaresque novel about a Chicago youth who grows up during the depression years brought its author national recognition. Because he will not accept any defining role in life, Augie finds himself being swept along in a current of alternately hilarious and tragic events. Unlike his brother Simon, who marries the daughter of a wealthy Chicago coaldealer in order to rise from his lower-class Jewish environment, Augie refuses every opportunity for a settled existence. He suffers some hard knocks, but, as he says, there is an *"animal ridens* in me, the laughing creature, forever rising up."

Augier, Émile (1820–1889). French dramatist. Reacting against the extravagances of the romantic drama, Augier wrote comedies that affirmed respectable bourgeois values. His *Gabrielle* (1849) satirizes exaggerated sentiment, while *Le Fils de Giboyer* (1862) levels a sharp attack on current attempts to disregard the differences between politics and religion. Among his other works are *Le Gendre de Monsieur Poirier* (1854), *Les Effrontés* (1861), and *Maître Guérin* (1865).

Augustan age. The golden age of Roman literature which covered the reign of AUGUSTUS Caesar (27 B.C.–A.D. 14). The Augustan age has, also, come to describe the apogee of any national literature, as, for example, the age of Swift and Pope in 18th-century England, which is often called the Augustan age of English prose.

The imperial period of Roman history begins with the establishment (27) of the principate (a thinly disguised monarchy) of Augustus after his decisive defeat of Mark Antony at ACTIUM (31 B.C.). Unlike republican Rome (see CICERONIAN AGE), the long, dictatorial peace of Augustus was not a time of free public debate. Oratory was useless, for there was no one to be swayed by skillful argument: the senate was a rubber-stamp parliament, and the people were voiceless. Augustus alone steered the ship of state. Historians had to be wary of adhering too closely to the facts of recent history. Only LIVY, with his lofty, patriotic aim of reminding his contemporaries of the glories of their republican past, could survive as a practicing historian.

Poetry, however, was not so inhibited. Under the patronage of the emperor and his wealthy supporter MAECENAS, the period was the crowning epoch of Latin poetry. VERGIL, perhaps the greatest of the Roman poets, began his first successful work, the *Bucolics,* in the year of Cicero's death (43 B.C.). He soon found encouragement and patronage in the retinue of the young Octavius (Augustus). His subsequent works, the *Georgics* (30 B.C.) and the *Aeneid* (19 B.C.), were intended, at least in part, to support the large-scale reforms in public morality and public thinking instituted by Augustus.

Another great poet of the period, the satirist and lyricist HORACE, was very different from Vergil in style and subject. His great achievement was to give new life to Roman satire and to naturalize in Rome the metrical forms of the older Greek odes. Other poets of this period include TIBULLUS and PROPERTIUS, both writers of love elegies.

Although the Augustan Age was an age of poetry, the one great poet who was born at its beginning and who was, in certain ways, its popular spokesman, died in exile three years after the emperor's death. This poet was OVID, who wrote love elegies, mock didactics, and the phantasmagorical epic, *The Metamorphoses.* This poet's last, pathetic years on the bleak shores of the Black Sea bring to a close the Augustan Age of Roman literature.

Augustine, St. Lat., **Aurelius Augustinus** (354–430). Early Christian church father and philosopher. Born in Roman North Africa of a Christian mother and a pagan father, he received his early training primarily in Latin literature and earned his living as a teacher of rhetoric in Carthage, Rome, and Milan from 374 to 387. He joined the MANICHAEANS for a number of years, but was disillusioned and after a period of skepticism was converted to Christianity by St. AMBROSE and baptized in 387. He returned to Africa and established a monastic community; in 391 he had ordained a priest at Hippo, becoming bishop there in 395. His CONFESSIONS vividly record his spiritual experiences and development during this period.

For the remainder of his life he preached and wrote prolifically, defining points of Christian doctrine and engaging in theological controversy with the Manichaeans, the Donatists, and the Pelagians. He maintained the importance of a single, unified Church, and developed a theory of sin, grace, and predestination that became basic to the doctrines of the Roman Catholic Church, but that later was also used as the justification for the tenets of Calvin, Luther, and the Jansenists.

St. Augustine (Strassburg, 1490).

Other important writings include *On the Trinity* (*De Trinitate;* 400–416), THE CITY OF GOD, *On Nature and Grace* (*De Natura et Gratia;* 415), and the *Retractions* (*Retractationes;* 426), in which he revised some of the more exaggerated statements he had made earlier.

Augustine of Canterbury, St. (d. 604?). First archbishop of Canterbury. He was responsible for the Christianization of England and called "Apostle of the English." A prior of the Benedictine monastery of St. Andrew in Rome, he was sent by Pope Gregory I (c. 595) to lead a missionary group of 40 monks to England. When he landed at Thanet in 597, King Ethelbert of Kent received him hospitably; Ethelbert's Frankish wife Bertha was already a Christian, and he soon accepted baptism. Augustine went to Arles in France to be consecrated as "bishop of the English," then returned and with Ethelbert's support of his mission baptized 10,000 converts the same year. He was made archbishop of Canterbury in 601, consecrated Christ Church there in 603, and tried in vain to reconcile the Celtic bishops in the rest of England with the Roman Church.

Augustus. Original name, **Caius Octavius** (63 B.C.–A.D. 14). First emperor of Rome. After his adoption by his great-uncle Julius Caesar (about 45 B.C.), he called himself Caius Julius Caesar Octavianus. It was thus, as Caesar's lawful heir, that the 19-year-old Octavius, upon Caesar's assassination (44 B.C.), skillfully lured Caesar's legions over to his side and formed, with Mark ANTONY and Lepidus, the Second TRIUMVIRATE. He pressed the war against Caesar's assassins, Brutus and Cassius, and after helping to crush the rebels at PHILIPPI (42 B.C.) he successfully maneuvered Antony into accepting as his share of empire the eastern Mediterranean provinces. Between the years 40 and 31 B.C., Octavius consolidated his control over the West, that is, Italy, Gaul, and Spain. His "cold war" with Antony finally broke out into open hostilities at ACTIUM (31 B.C.) off the northwestern coast of Greece. There the combined naval forces of Antony and of CLEOPATRA, the ambitious queen of Egypt, met Octavius' well-trained armada and were decisively defeated.

After this victory, Octavius celebrated a splendid triumph: Rome greeted him as her savior and showed herself willing to accept his sole sovereignty for 44 years. In 28 B.C. he was made *princeps senatus* (first senator); on January 17 of the next year he received the honorary title Augustus (by which he was thenceforth known); and in a series of senatorial bequests, he was made consul, tribune, and proconsul. Despite this gradual assumption of complete dictatorial power, his avowed aim was the restoration of the Roman Republic and the purification of its social and religious life. Whatever reforms he did accomplish, however, he did so on his own, bypassing the Senate and the Comitia. (See PRINCEPS.)

The accomplishments of Augustus include the construction of public buildings (libraries, temples, monuments—he boasted that he had found Rome in brick and left it in marble); the revival of ancient religious rites; the restoration of the calendar (the month August was named after him); the reorganization of the political structure of the Empire; and the fostering of a native Roman literature. (See AUGUSTAN AGE.) His greatest accomplishment, however—the one that made all these others possible—was the long periods of peace he was able to maintain through his mastery of the art of statesmanship.

Octavius Caesar appears briefly in Shakespeare's JULIUS CAESAR. In Shakespeare's ANTONY AND CLEOPATRA, he is presented as a cold and puritanical man of relentless purpose, the "man of the future" as contrasted with the declining Antony.

Auld Hornie. An epithet for the devil in Scotland. Pan, with his horns, crooked nose, goat's beard, pointed ears, and goat's feet, was transformed by the Scottish into Satan. In Scotland and northern England, Satan is also *Auld Clootie, Auld Hangie, Auld Nick,* and *Auld Ane.* The use of *Auld* seems to imply that he can appear only as an old man.

auld lang syne. In the olden time, in days gone by. *Lang syne* is Scotch for long since. *Auld Lang Syne,* the song (1788, pub. 1796), usually attributed to Robert BURNS, is really a new version by him of a very much older song; in Watson's Collection (1711), it is attributed to one Francis Sempill (d. 1682), but it is probably even earlier. Burns, in a letter to James Thomson, writes that "It is the old song of the olden times, which has never been in print. . . . I took it down from an old man's singing." See Robert AYTOUN.

aulos. See GREEK MUSIC.

Auric, Georges (1899–   ). See LES SIX.

Aurispa, Giovanni (1376–1459). Sicilian scholar and teacher in several northern Italian cities. He is noted for his trip to Constantinople to obtain manuscripts for Italian patrons of the new learning in the Renaissance.

Aurora Leigh (1856). A narrative poem by Elizabeth Barrett BROWNING. The heroine, a talented girl who is left an orphan without financial resources, learns to support herself by her pen. She falls in love with and eventually marries her cousin, Romney Leigh, a man whose passion for social reform has involved him in strange and varied experiences.

Aus dem Leben eines Taugenichts (From the Life of a Ne'er-Do-Well, 1826). A story by Joseph von EICHENDORFF, about a lazy young man who picks up his fiddle one day and goes off to see the world. His light-hearted adventures carry him through Germany, Austria, and Italy, but finally he settles down and marries the girl of his dreams. The basic attitude of the book is summed up in the last words: "And everything, everything was good."

Auslander, Joseph (1897–1965). American poet. In collaboration with Frank Ernest Hill, he wrote *The Winged Horse* (1927), a history of poetry for young people. His own poetry employs conventional forms with varied themes. His collections include *Sunrise Trumpets* (1924), *Cyclops' Eye* (1926), *Riders at the Gate* (1938), and *The Unconquerables* (1943).

Austen, Jane (1775–1817). English novelist, often regarded as the greatest of women novelists. The seventh child of a country parson, Jane Austen passed her days, like many an English lady of the time, almost entirely within her family circle. The only dramatic event of her life was an attachment to a clergyman who died before they could become engaged, but this was an obscure and doubtful episode, producing little outward change in her life. She never married; had no contact with London literary life; spent all her time, when not writing, on ordinary domestic duties, among her numerous nephews and nieces. Out of the materials of such a narrow world, precisely by sticking scrupulously to that narrow world, she made great literature. Her completed novels, SENSE AND SENSIBILITY, PRIDE AND PREJUDICE, MANSFIELD PARK, EMMA, NORTHANGER ABBEY, and PERSUASION, are distinguished by their satirical wit and brilliant comedy, complex and subtle view of human nature, exquisite moral discrimination, and unobtrusive perfection of style. These qualities elevate her little world of struggling clerical families, husband-hunting mothers and daughters, eligible clergymen and landowners, country fools and snobs, into an enduring microcosm of the great world.

Austerlitz, battle of. Also called the **battle of the three emperors** (December 2, 1805). A famous battle taking place in Moravia (now Czechoslovakia) where Napoleon Bonaparte inflicted a heavy defeat upon the armies of Russia and Austria. The emperors of all three states were on the field, being in personal command of their forces.

Austin, William. See PETER RUGG, THE MISSING MAN.

Autobiography of Alice B. Toklas, The (1933). An autobiography by Gertrude STEIN, written as though the author were her secretary, Miss Toklas. Although the book provoked an attack by other Parisian writers and artists in *Testimony Against Gertrude Stein* (1935), it remains a fascinating account of expatriate life in the Paris of the period.

Autobiography of Benjamin Franklin, The. One of the most popular works of Benjamin FRANKLIN, translated into virtually every language. Covering only the period of his life up to his prewar stay in London as representative of the Pennsylvania Assembly, it was written at intervals beginning in 1771; the final segment was completed shortly before the author's death. Parts of the autobiography were published in France between 1791 and 1798, but the complete work did not appear until 1868. Franklin's many interests—philosophy, politics, religion, literature, and practical affairs—and his energetic pursuit of them have made his autobiography an American classic.

Autocrat of the Breakfast-Table, The (1858). A series of essays by the elder Oliver Wendell HOLMES. A heterogeneous collection of boarders gather around the table, providing an audience for the wit and philosophy of the Autocrat. The essays take the form of conversations that generally develop into monologues. Cleverly and epigrammatically, the Autocrat discourses on social, theological, and scientific topics. The book, seemingly disconnected, is unified by the recurring themes and personalities. Holmes includes several of his poems.

auto-da-fé (*Port.* act of faith). The ceremony accompanying the pronouncement of judgment by the Inquisition. It was followed by the execution of sentence by the secular authorities. This ceremony usually took the form of a procession through the chief streets of the city or town to the church where a sermon was preached on the true faith.

Autolycus (Autolykos). A notorious thief of Greek mythology. A son of Hermes, he taught Heracles to wrestle, but later sold him mares stolen from Eurytus. Traveling with Heracles to Amazon country, he was stranded in Paphlagonia, but rescued by the Argonauts. When he stole Sisyphus' cattle, changing their color by magic, he was detected by the owner, who seduced his daughter Anticleia in revenge. Thus he became the grandfather of Odysseus.

Shakespeare uses his name for the merry balladmonger and peddler in THE WINTER'S TALE, who "having flown over many knavish professions, . . . settled only on rogue." His songs, such as "When daffodils begin to peer," are justly famous.

Automedon. According to Homer, the companion and the charioteer of Achilles, but according to Virgil the brother-in-arms of Achilles' son, Pyrrhus. Hence, a coachman.

Autonoë. In Greek mythology, a daughter of Cadmus. She married Aristaeus and bore him Actaeon. Having joined with Ino and Agave in denying that the lover of their dead sister SEMELE had been Zeus, she was punished by the son of this union, Dionysus. Driven into a Bacchic frenzy by the god, she helped to kill her nephew, the Theban king Pentheus. See BACCHANTS, THE.

auto sacramental. A one-act religious drama popular in Spain from the 13th to the 18th century. Performed at Corpus Christi, these dramas were allegorical in character, dealing with historical, biblical, and mythological subjects by which the tenets of Catholicism could be expounded. The genre was perfected by CALDERÓN, who wrote over 80 *autos*. In 1736 Charles III prohibited their performance.

Avalon. (1) In ARTHURIAN LEGEND, the island to which King ARTHUR is taken after he has been mortally wounded in the terrible, final battle. One of the earliest mentions of the island occurs in the 12th-century Latin *History of the Kings of Britain* by Geoffrey of Monmouth. A short time later, in his *Roman de Brut,* Wace mentions that King Arthur expects to return from Avalon as "the hope of Britain" after his wounds have been healed. Later versions of this dramatic incident elaborate on and expand the whole considerably. In Malory's *Morte d'Arthur* (c. 1469), for example, the barge that comes to take Arthur to Avalon is signaled to by throwing the sword EXCALIBUR into the lake, and the barge itself is filled with the three mysterious and beautiful, other-world queens. See GLASTONBURY.

(2) A Celtic word meaning "the island of apples," and applied in Celtic mythology to the Island of Blessed Souls, an earthly paradise set in the Western seas.

Avanti. Another name for Ujjain, the capital of Malwa, often mentioned in classical Sanskrit literature.

Avare, L' (**The Miser,** 1668). A comedy by MOLIÈRE. It is derived from Plautus' *Aulularia.* HARPAGON, a wealthy miser, wishes to marry his daughter Elise to an old man, Anselme, since Anselme does not require a dowry. The miser himself wants to marry his son Cléante's beloved, Mariane. Cléante arranges the theft of his father's money box, and in order to regain his treasure Harpagon permits Cléante to marry Mariane. Elise is allowed to marry her beloved, Calère, when her father discovers him to be the son and heir of Anselme. A happy ending balances the grim picture of inhuman greed.

avatar (Sans., *avatara*, descent; hence, the incarnation of a god). In Hindu mythology the advent to earth of a deity in a visible form. The 10 avatars of VISHNU are the most celebrated. The word is used metaphorically to denote a manifestation or embodiment of some idea or phase.

Ave atque vale! (Lat., "Hail and farewell!"). The words of Catullus at his brother's tomb.

Ave Maria, or **Hail Mary** or **Angelic(al) Salutation.** A prayer to the Virgin Mary. Its first phrases are based on the angel's address to Mary (the Annunciation, Luke 1:28) and the greeting of her cousin Elizabeth (Luke 1:42). The present form of the prayer was fixed by Pope Pius V in the 16th century. It has appeared in many musical settings, the most popular of which are by Schubert and Gounod. The smaller beads of a rosary are often called *Aves* or *Hail Marys,* the longer ones *paternosters* or *Our Fathers.*

Avernus. A lake in Campania in central Italy. Its sulphurous and mephitic vapors gave rise in ancient times to the belief that it was the entrance to the infernal regions. Hence, Avernus is used as a synonym for hell or the infernal regions.

Averroes or **Averrhoes.** Arabic name: **Ibn-Rushd** (1126–1198). Spanish Muslim philosopher and scholar. He is best known for his commentaries on Aristotle, which had an important influence on medieval Christian scholasticism. He also wrote treatises on astronomy, medicine, and jurisprudence. All his works were written in Arabic, but became widely known through Hebrew and Latin translations.

Avesta. The sacred book of the Zoroastrians and Parsees, dating in its present form from the third and fourth centuries A.D., collected from the ancient writings, sermons, and oral traditions of Zoroaster before 800 B.C. The books are sometimes called the *Zend-Avesta* from a misunderstanding of the term *Avesta-Zend* (*Avesta* means the text and *zend* its interpretation; hence the latter name has been given to the ancient Iranian language in which the Avistak-va-Zand is written).

It is only a fragment and consists of five parts: (1) the Yasna, the chief liturgical portion, including Gathas, or hymns; (2) the Vispered, another liturgical work; (3) the Vendidad, which, like the biblical Pentateuch, contains the laws; (4) the Yashts, dealing with stories of the different gods; (5) the Khordah, a book of private devotions.

Avicenna (Arab. **Abn-Ali al-Husayn ibn-Sina;** c. 980–c. 1037). Arabian philosopher and physician. A Latin translation of his *Canon of Medicine* was used in Europe as the standard medical textbook until the 17th century. His *al-Shifa* (book of recovery), including sections on *Logic, Physics,* and *Metaphysics,* reveals his own adaptation of Aristotle's philosophy.

Avignon captivity, the (1309–1377). The period of the residence of seven popes at the palace of Avignon in Provence, under the control of French kings. During the papal schism two anti-popes resided there from 1378 to 1408. Clement VI bought the palace in 1348, and it remained a papal possession until 1791.

Avocat Pathelin, L'. See PATHELIN, LA FARCE DE MAISTRE PIERRE.

Avvakum, Archpriest (1621–1682). A leader of the OLD BELIEVER religious sect in Russia He is famous for his *Life* (*Zhitiye;* 1672–1675), written in a racy mixture of Church Slavonic, the old church language, and Russian vernacular.

Awake and Sing! (1935). A play by Clifford ODETS. It presents the various frustrations and tragedies of the Bergers, a lower-class Jewish family in the Bronx. The mother, with the best of intentions, browbeats her husband, forces her daughter to marry a man she doesn't love, and opposes her son's romance with a poor orphan. The results are disastrous but lead the one idealistic son to devote his life to the betterment of humanity.

Awkward Age, The (1899). A novel by Henry JAMES. It concerns the emergence of an English society girl from "the awkward age" into maturity and understanding. A rival of her mother in love for young Vanderbank, Nanda Brookenham is surrounded by older persons who are scheming and plotting. Vanderbank marries neither her nor her mother, and Nanda, disillusioned by her friends, goes to live in the country home of Mr. Longden, an older man who had once been in love with her grandmother.

Axe-Helve, The (1917). A poem by Robert FROST. Written in blank verse, it tells of a conversation between Frost and a neighbor, and then describes the poet's visit to the neighbor's home. Ostensibly the story of a craftsman who hates the inferior products of the machine age, the poem is reinforced by religious references which give it a deeper meaning.

Axis powers. See ROME-BERLIN AXIS.

Ayer, A[lfred] J[ules] (1910–). English philosopher. Approaching truth and logic through a study of the nature of language, he is a leading exponent of LOGICAL POSITIVISM; his best-known book is *Language, Truth, and Logic* (1936).

Aymé, Marcel (1902–). French fiction writer. His novels are usually sophisticated satire, such as *The Green Mare* (*La Jument Verte;* 1933), *The Secret Stream* (*Le Moulin de la Sourdine;* 1936), *The Miraculous Barber* (*Travelingue;* 1941), *The Second Face* (*La Belle Image;* 1942), *The Transient Hour* (*Le Chemin des Ecoliers;* 1946), and *The Barkeep of Blémont* (*Uranus;* 1948). His short stories are known for the wittily realistic development of fantastic or burlesque situations. English collections are *Across Paris and Other Stories* (1958), including *The Walker Through Walls* (*Le Passe-Muraille;* 1943), and *The Proverb and Other Stories* (1961). His children's books include *Les Contes du chat perché* (1939), *The Wonderful Farm* (1951), *Magic Pictures* (1954). *Clérambard* (1958) is a play.

Aymon, Four Sons of (Fr. **Les Quatre Fils Aymon**). French CHANSON DE GESTE. Aymon is the father of Guiscard, Alard, Richard, and Renaud de Montauban, who escape from Charlemagne's court after Renaud kills the emperor's nephew. Charlemagne forces a long war on them until his paladins urge a settlement, whereupon Renaud goes to Palestine to fight the Saracens. For Renaud's exploits in the Italian romances see RINALDO.

Aymot, Jacques (1513–1593). French humanist and translator. Tutor and then chaplain to Charles IX and Henry II, he later became bishop of Auxerre, which he made a center of humanism. He is best remembered for his translation (1559) of Plutarch's *Lives.*

Aytoun or Ayton, Sir Robert (1570–1638). Scottish poet and courtier. A friend of Ben Jonson, he was one of the first Scots to use English as a literary language. He is believed by some to be the author of the original version of AULD LANG SYNE.

Aytoun, William Edmonston (1813–1865). Scottish poet and teacher. His best work consists of parodies of Tennyson, the Brownings, and other poets, and ballads in the vein of Scott. The former are collected in *Bon Gaultier's Ballads* (1845, with T. Martin); the latter in *Lays of the Scottish Cavaliers* (1848) and *Ballads of Sotland* (1858). He is also known as the originator of the name SPASMODIC SCHOOL for P. J. Bailey and his followers.

Azazel. A Hebrew name symbolizing an evil spirit living in the wilderness. It is mentioned in connection with services held on the Day of Atonement (Yom Kippur), in which lots were cast on two goats; one for the Lord and the other for Azazel (Lev. 16). The goat for Azazel was referred to as the SCAPEGOAT. Milton uses the name for the standard-bearer of the rebel angels in *Paradise Lost* (1667).

Azeglio, Marchese d'. See Marchese Massimo Taparrelli D'AZEGLIO.

Azevedo, Aluízio (1857–1913). Brazilian novelist. The first exponent of naturalism in Brazil, Azevedo was a shrewd critic of contemporary society. His best-known work, *O Mulato* (1881), deals with the status of the mixed-blood in Brazil. He also wrote *Casa de Pensão* (1884), about the residents of a boarding house in Rio de Janeiro, and *O Cortiço* (1890), translated as *A Brazilian Tenement.*

Aziz, Dr. See PASSAGE TO INDIA, A.

Azorín. See José MARTÍNEZ RUIZ.

Azrael. In Muslim theology, the angel of death who watches over the dying and takes the soul from the body. He is one of the four highest angels at the throne of Allah, whom he serves as messenger. He will be the last to die, but will do so at the second trump of the archangel.

the Wings of Azrael. The approach of death; the signs of death coming on the dying.

Aztecs. A Nahuatl-speaking tribe of Indians who dominated much of Mexico at the time of the Spanish conquest (1519–1521) under Hernán Cortez. In the 12th century, the Aztecs moved into the valley of Anahuac from the northwest and gradually subdued neighboring tribes, turning them into tribute-paying vassals. The "emperor" of the Aztecs was chosen by a supreme council which represented the 20 clans that comprised the Aztec tribe. See TENOCHTITLÁN; MONTEZUMA II; CUAUHTÉMOC.

Azuela, Mariano (1873–1952). Mexican novelist. After participating briefly in the Mexican Revolution, Azuela moved to Mexico City in 1916 and devoted the rest of his life to his two professions, medicine and writing. In his 41 novels, which touch on virtually every aspect of Mexican life during the 20th century, Azuela revealed an abiding concern for social justice and human dignity as well as angry dismay at the cynicism and corruption that he so often found in all levels of society. Among his best-known works are *Mala yerba* (1909), an indictment of the powerful land-owning class; Los DE ABAJO, probably his finest novel; *Los caciques* (*The Bosses,* 1917), an attack on the political bosses of a small Mexican city; *Las moscas* (*The Flies,* 1918), a trenchant examination of political opportunism; *La Malhora* (1923), the story of a woman who is dogged by misfortune; and *Nueva burguesía* (1940), a bitter satire on the lower middle classes of Mexico City.

B

B., Mr. In Samuel Richardson's novel PAMELA, a gentleman of station who attempts to seduce Pamela, but ends by marrying her. Henry Fielding satirically expanded the initial "B" into "Booby" in *Shamela* (1741), his parody of *Pamela,* and in JOSEPH ANDREWS; some of the later editions of *Pamela,* however, attempted to avoid the implication by giving Mr. B. the name of Boothby.

Baal. An epithet for any of a number of ancient Semitic gods. A Semitic word meaning lord or possessor, it was usually applied to a god as lord of a city or other place. The title thus became applied to a great many local gods; even the Hebrew Yahweh was so referred to in earlier days by the ancient Israelites. Originally a sort of fertility demon, Baal became individualized in various localities, notably as the Babylonian BEL and the Canaanite Baal. As the storm-god, he plays the principal role in the Canaanite POEM OF BAAL. Variations of the name also occur in the Greek Belus and in such Carthaginian compounds as Hannibal. In Tyre, the local Baal was known as MELKARTH. The worship of Baalim was firmly established in Canaan at the time of the Israelites' entry. The Israelites adopted many of the Canaanite rites in their own worship of Jehovah. Moses, ELIJAH, and other prophets denounced this form of Baalim worship as heathenism; hence Baal came to mean a false god. Baal was also a nature god symbolizing generation whose appearance, along with that of Ashtoreth (ISHTAR), was considered a necessary prelude to spring.

Babar. The little elephant in a series of French children's books. Written and illustrated by Jean de Brunhoff (1899–1937), and translated into English, they proved very popular in the U.S.

Babbitt (1922). A satirical novel by Sinclair LEWIS. It presents a portrait of George Follansbee Babbitt, a middle-aged realtor, booster, and joiner in Zenith, the Zip City. He is unimaginative, self-important, and hopelessly middle class. Withal, he is vaguely dissatisfied and tries to alter the pattern of his life by flirting with liberalism and by entering a liaison with an attractive widow, only to find that his dread of ostracism is greater than his desire for escape. He does, however, encourage the rebellion of his son, Ted, saying "Don't be scared of the family. No, nor all of Zenith. Nor of yourself, the way I've been." The name of the book identified an American type and gave a new word to the language.

Babbitt, Irving (1865–1933). American critic, essayist. One of the founders of the NEW HUMANISM movement of the second decade of the 20th century, Babbitt taught at Harvard for many years and in many ways epitomized the "professors" against whom H. L. Mencken and other "literary radicals" railed for their conservatism and traditionalism. A theorist about criticism rather than a critic per se, he saw in a return to the classical concept of man a possible solution to the excesses of romanticism and naturalism, and urged the necessity of moral and ethical standards for the evaluation of literature. His books include *The New Laokoön* (1910); *The Masters of Modern French Criticism* (1912); *Rousseau and Romanticism* (1919); *Democracy and Leadership* (1924), an extension in the political realm of his theories about literature; and *On Being Creative* (1932).

Babel, Isaak [Emmanuilovich] (1894–?1939). Russian short-story writer. Babel was born in Odessa of a middle-class Jewish family. He developed an early interest in literature, particularly the works of Flaubert and Maupassant. His first published stories appeared in a journal edited by Maksim Gorki. The older writer recognized Babel's talent, but advised him to see more of life before doing more writing. During the civil war following the revolution, Babel was attached to the cavalry detachment of General Budenny fighting in Poland. He recorded his experiences in the volume of stories entitled RED CAVALRY. The next year he published ODESSA TALES about his early life in the port city. A memorable character of the Odessa stories is Benya Krik, the Jewish gangster leader.

The success of Babel's work was immense. His vivid descriptions of the brutality rampant during the war in Poland were rendered in short, exquisitely polished stories. A unique feature of his work was his habit of treating his romantic material in a sharply honed classical style, reminiscent of Maupassant at his most concise. Babel's knowledge of the powerful effect of concision in literature is revealed in a line from one of his stories: "There is no iron that can enter the human heart with such stupefying effect as a period placed at just the right moment." The effort it took to achieve his remarkable effects is revealed by Babel's friend, the writer Konstantin Paustovski in his reminiscences. Babel showed Paustovski a 200-page manuscript, which turned out to be 22 versions of one of Babel's short stories.

Babel's popularity waned in the 1930's. The chief reasons for this seem to have been his neglect of political themes in his work and a growing resentment, under Stalin, of the way he depicted the warriors of Budenny's regiment. He disappeared about 1938, apparently a victim of the purges then going on. He is reputed to have been executed or to have died in a concentration camp, but no real facts about his fate have been divulged.

Babel, Tower of. A structure erected after the Flood by the descendants of Noah when they reached Babylonia. According to Gen. 11, the plan was to build a tower that would reach to heaven; but Jehovah, to prevent its completion, "confounded their language" so they could not understand one another. Thus, a tower of Babel has come to signify a visionary scheme, while the word babel itself has become associated with a confused uproar in which nothing can be heard but hubbub.

Babes in the Wood. Characters in an old English ballad and nursery tale.

Babeuf, François Noël. Pen name of **Gracchus Babeuf** (1760–1797). French journalist during the French Revolution. His ideas anticipated present-day communistic theories. Accused of conspiring to overthrow the Directory and re-establish the constitution of 1793, he was guillotined.

Babington's conspiracy. A plot against the life of Elizabeth I. Anthony Babington (1561–1586), formerly a page to MARY, QUEEN OF SCOTS, was induced by the priest John Ballard to organize a conspiracy in 1586 to assassinate Queen Elizabeth, lead a Catholic uprising, and release Mary from confinement. The plot was detected and Babington and a dozen others were executed. A few months later Mary was beheaded, largely on the grounds of evidence of her complicity in the plot supposedly contained in letters between her and Babington.

Baboon, Lewis. A character in John Arbuthnot's political satire *The History of* JOHN BULL. He is meant to represent King Louis XIV of France and, in a larger sense, the French nation. Baboon is a play upon the word Bourbon.

Bacbuc. See ORACLE OF THE HOLY BOTTLE.

Bacchanalia. Festivals held in ancient Rome in honor of BACCHUS, the name under which the Greek god Dionysus was better known in Rome. Like the Greek Dionysia, the feast was eventually characterized by drunkenness, debauchery, and licentiousness of all kinds, so that the word *bacchanalian* came to mean wild and drunken.

bacchants (bakchoi). Followers of the Greek god DIONYSUS or Bacchus. Also known as *maenads*, they engaged in wild ritual dancing on wooded mountains, during which they tore apart and ate fawns and perhaps human victims. They are probably an oriental addition (see CYBELE) to the cult of the Thracian god Dionysus. Their revels on Mount Cithaeron are detailed in Euripides' drama *The Bacchants*.

Bacchants, The (Bacchae; 408–406 B.C.). A tragedy by EURIPIDES. It deals with the tragic punishment of Pentheus, king of Thebes, who imprisons DIONYSUS and is torn to pieces by his own mother, Agave, during a bacchanalian orgy. Gilbert Murray pointed out that this of all plays most closely resembles in form the Dionysian mysteries from which Greek tragedy sprang. (See BACCHANTS.)

Bacchelli, Riccardo (1891–   ). Italian critic, novelist, dramatist, and poet. A writer of historical novels, he has been compared to Alessandro Manzoni because of the serenity of his outlook on life, his congenial humor, serious scholarship, and preoccupation with language and style.

Bacchelli was an artillery officer in World War I and the editor of *La Ronda* (1919–1923), an influential literary review published in Rome. The review proposed that contemporary Italian literature reaffirm its classical traditions by drawing inspiration from the Renaissance, Leopardi, and Manzoni.

Bacchelli's best-known work is the 2,000-page historical novel, *Il Mulino del Po* (1935–1940; pub. 1948–1950), translated as *The Mill on the Po* and *Nothing New Under the Sun*. The novel is a saga of Italian life from the Napoleonic Wars to World War I. The principals are several generations of the Scacerni family, Lombard millers whose gristmill stands for over a century on the banks of the River Po. The author draws from their story the conclusion that life itself is an unebbing flow of pain and sorrow, as regular and rhythmic in its course as the river that runs alongside the mill. Another historical novel, *Il Diavolo di Pontelungo* (1927), narrates the attempts of the Russian anarchist Michael Bakunin to foment a revolution in Italy and concludes with a description of an unsuccessful socialist revolt in Bologna (1864). *Mal d'Africa* (1934) recounts the African travels of the 19th-century Italian explorer Gaetano Casati.

Bacchus. In Roman mythology, the god of wine. He was, in fact, a Greek god (Bakchos was one of the names of the Greek DIONYSUS), the Roman god of wine having been LIBER. Bacchus was worshipped in the annual, riotous festival called the BACCHANALIA, similar to the Greek Dionysia. However, the fat and drunken Bacchus familiar from so many paintings of the Renaissance period was a later concept, completely out of keeping with the classic view of Bacchus as a handsome young man and a powerful god. In the *Lusiad* (1572) of Camoëns, Bacchus is the guardian power of Islam and an evil demon of Zeus.

Bach, Johann Sebastian (1685–1750). Outstanding German composer of the late Baroque. He came of a family that produced many musicians in the 17th and 18th centuries. His vast output includes all types of music current at the time, except opera; he was also a violinist and a renowned organist. By the end of his life his compositions were considered old fashioned, even by his gifted composer sons. Though Bach's music attracted some attention from Mozart and others in the period 1750–1829, its modern revival may be said to date from Mendelssohn's revival, in the latter year, of the *St. Matthew Passion* (1729). Other large choral works are *St. John Passion* (1723), *Mass in B minor* (1733–1738), and *Christmas Oratorio* (1734). Bach also wrote 198 cantatas for various occasions of the church year, 23 secular cantatas, orchestral music, chamber music, and outstanding works for organ, harpsichord, and clavichord. For the organ, he wrote sonatas, fantasias, preludes, fugues, toccatas, and 143 chorale preludes based on Lutheran hymn tunes; for harpsichord or organ, French suites, English suites, partitas, the Italian concerto (1735), Goldberg variations (1742), and *Das wohltemperirte Clavier* (*The Well-tempered Clavier*, 1722 and 1744). The last is two monumental sets of preludes and fugues in each of the 24 major and minor keys, written to exploit the advantages of equal temperament or tuning, which made it possible to play equally well in all keys; up till then this had not been possible.

Bachaumont, François de (1624–1702). French writer. He is coauthor with Claude-Emmanuel Chapelle of *Voyage en Provence et Languedoc* (*Journey to Provence and Languedoc,* 1656), a humorous compilation in prose and verse of outrageous scenic and gastronomic descriptions, laced with literary satires and burlesques.

Bachelier de Salamanque, Le (1736). The last novel of Alain René LESAGE. It is the story of the adventures of a young Spanish bachelor of arts, Don Chérubin de la Ronda, who meets a vast number of people in his profession of tutor. The novel is a vehicle for a cynical satire of the ruling classes: the nobility, the bourgeoisie, and the clergy. The picaresque plot, though Spanish in setting, is merely an excuse to penetrate the thousand and one turpitudes of French society, in which those who have succeeded in life have done so only by intrigue.

Bacheller, Irving [Addison] (1859–1950). American newspaperman and novelist. His most popular novel was *Eben Holden* (1900); the story of a young man in the middle years of the 19th century, it sold over 1,000,000 copies. *D'ri and I* (1901) was a novel set at the time of the War of 1812. *A Man for the Ages* (1919) dealt with Lincoln. His other novels include *Keeping Up with Lizzie* (1911) and *A Candle in the Wilderness* (1930).

Bachofen, Johann Jakob (1815–1887). Swiss jurist and classical scholar, known for his recognition of a matrilineal principle in ancient societies. In *Das Mutterrecht* (*Matriarchal Right,* 1861), which has since been refuted, he claimed that the matriarchal stage precedes the patriarchal in the social development of all peoples.

Back to Methuselah (1922). A 5-play cycle by George Bernard SHAW. Extremely long and not very dramatically theatrical, this collection of plays is a satirical fantasy on the prolongation of life and the perfectibility of the human race. The scenes are laid in the Garden of Eden, in England at the time of the play's composition, and in successive stages of the future, until the span of life has been increased and man has become almost wholly intellect. This progress is accomplished, not through science, but through the strength of the human will engaged in creative evolution.

Bacon, Francis (1561–1626). English philosopher, statesman, and essayist. Having served as solicitor general and attorney general, he was appointed lord chancellor in 1618; he was created Baron Verulam in the same year and Viscount St. Albans in 1621. With the intention of becoming a "second Aristotle," he carried on scientific and philosophic investigations and planned to reorganize on an experimental basis the systems of thought and the practical methods of obtaining power over nature that were current in his day. He was violently opposed to reasoning from authority and the syllogistic quibbling to which scholastic philosophy had declined in the early 17th century, and argued always for clarity of observation and the development of keen critical faculties of mind.

Most of his work on philosophy and science was written in Latin. Bacon's most important writings are THE ADVANCEMENT OF LEARNING and NOVUM ORGANUM, which formed the first two parts of his projected INSTAURATIO MAGNA; *Sylva Sylvarum* (1627); and NEW ATLANTIS. He is best known in the field of literature for his series of ESSAYS. See BACONIAN CONTROVERSY.

Bacon, Frank (1864–1922). American actor and playwright. He is best known for his role of the amusing liar Lightnin' Bill Jones in LIGHTNIN', a play he wrote in collaboration with Winchell SMITH.

Bacon, Leonard (1887–1954). American poet and critic. Known for his satiric verse, he won the Pulitzer Prize with his book of poems, *Sunderland Capture* (1940). Other volumes of verse are *Ulug Beg* (1923), *The Legend of Quinebald* (1928), and *Day of Fire* (1944). *Semi-Centennial* (1939) is his autobiography.

Bacon, Nathaniel. See BACON'S REBELLION.

Bacon, Roger (c. 1214–1294). English philosopher and scientist. He was called "Doctor Mirabilis" or "the Admirable Doctor." His encyclopedic *Opus Majus* (1267) urged that in order to make the Roman Catholic Church the leader in the civilization of mankind, Christian studies should be expanded to include all the sciences; he placed great emphasis on the importance of mathematics and experimental science, disciplines practically ignored in the learning of the time. His writings indicate his own interest in optics, chemistry, and astrology, and he is credited with having foreseen the practical possibilities of the telescope, lenses to correct vision, gunpowder, and mechanical navigation and flight. His *Opus Minus* is an alchemical treatise; the *Opus Tertium* stresses the utility of scientific knowledge, saying that without it philosophy becomes absurd. In 1278 the Franciscans, whom he joined about 1250, declared his

Title page of *The History of Frier Bacon* (c. 1660).

THE

Famous History

OF

FRIER BACON.

Containing the wonderful things that he did in his Life ; Also the manner of his Death, with the Lives and Deaths of the two Conjurers *Bungey,* and *Vandermast.*

Very pleasant and delightful to be read.

London, Printed for W. Thackery, at the Angel in Duck-lane, and C. Bates next the Crown Tavern in West-smithfield.

works heretical, and he was imprisoned until 1292. He was working on a "compendium of theological studies" when he died.

Because of his advanced thinking on the need for experimental science and its practical possibilities, the popular imagination credited him with all sorts of magical achievements, supposedly the result of a league with the Devil. These legends began gathering at the beginning of the 14th century and appear in such works as Robert Greene's comedy *Friar Bacon and Friar Bungay* (1589).

Baconian controversy. An argument, first advanced in the mid-18th century, that William SHAKESPEARE did not write the plays attributed to him. The idea is based on the notion that Shakespeare, being a nobody from provincial Stratford, lacked the social background, education, and temperament to have written his masterpieces. The first claim for Sir Francis BACON as the true author was put forth by William Henry Smith in 1856; the following year Delia Bacon made an elaborate defense for Bacon's authorship in *The Philosophy of Shakespeare's Plays.* New "proof," in the form of a cryptogram of Bacon's signature in some of the plays, was offered by Ignatius Donnelly in *The Great Cryptogram* (1888) and by Mrs. E. W. Gallup in *The Bi-Lateral Cypher of Francis Bacon* (1900). Other writers, not satisfied that the evidence of authorship pointed to Bacon, attempted to prove the plays were really the work of Edward de Vere, earl of Oxford; or Roger Manners, earl of Rutland; or William Stanley, earl of Derby; or Henry Wriothesley, earl of Southampton; or Christopher Marlowe. There is no evidence that any of these men except Marlowe (who died in 1593 at the age of 29) ever wrote a line of blank verse. In orthodox Shakespearean scholarship, these controversies are ignored and it is assumed that Shakespeare wrote the plays.

Baconian philosophy. A philosophical system oriented toward experimental science and based on the principles laid down by the English philosopher Francis BACON in the second book of his NOVUM ORGANUM.

Bacon's Epitaph. 2 elegiac poems, first published in 1814, on the death (1676) of Nathaniel Bacon, the leader of Bacon's Rebellion, "made by his man." The poems are attributed to John and Ann Cotton of Queen's Creek, Va., and express opposed views of Bacon's character. Most critics consider them to be among the best early American poems. See BURWELL PAPERS.

Bacon's Rebellion (1676). An uprising of Virginia colonists, led by Nathaniel Bacon (1647–1676), a recent settler. Ostensibly the colonists wanted to quell Indian disturbances in the region, but they were actually protesting the dictatorial regime (1642–1676) of Governor William Berkeley (1606–1677). Although Bacon and his followers won some successes and burned Jamestown, his sudden death from fever resulted in the collapse of the rebellion.

Bactrian sage. A name given to ZOROASTER, or Zarathustra, the founder of the Perso-Iranian religion, which flourished in Bactria (the modern Balkh) before 800 B.C.

Badebec (*Fr.,* "open-mouthed"). In Rabelais' GARGANTUA AND PANTAGRUEL, the wife of Gargantua and mother of Pantagruel. The effort of giving birth

to Pantagruel, as well as to a train of mules, dromedaries, and camels laden with salted and smoked foods, costs Badebec her life.

Badon or **Mount Badon, battle of** (c. A.D. 520). In Arthurian legend, the place of King Arthur's great victories over the pagan Saxon invaders. See ANNALES CAMBRIAE.

Badroulboudour. In the *Arabian Nights,* the daughter of the sultan of China who becomes the wife of ALADDIN. Twice she nearly causes his death: by exchanging "the wonderful lamp" for a new copper one, and by giving hospitality to the false FATIMA.

Baedeker, Karl (1801–1859). German printer who began the publication of a widely known series of guidebooks. His name has since become almost synonymous with guidebook.

Baena, Cancionero de. See CANCIONERO DE BAENA.

Bagehot, Walter (1826–1877). English economist and critic. He was editor of the *Economist* (1860–1877) and is known for his lucid, highly readable, idiosyncratic works on political economy, history, and literature. His *The English Constitution* (1867) is a classic in its field; other works of note are *Physics and Politics* (1872) and *Literary Studies* (1879).

Baglioni. A notorious Italian family. It dominated the affairs of the city of Perugia during the medieval period and the early Renaissance. When they were not slaughtering the rival Oddi family and other enemies, they were kept busy by internal feuds.

Bagnold, Enid. Maiden and pen name of Lady Roderick Jones (1889–   ). English novelist and playwright. She is the author of the successful novels *Serena Blandish* (1925) and NATIONAL VELVET. In later life she wrote such plays as *The Chalk Garden* (1956) and *The Chinese Prime Minister* (1961).

Bahaism. The doctrines of the Bahais, emphasizing the spiritual unity of mankind, advocating universal peace, and imbued with mild Oriental mysticism. The Bahais succeeded the Persian religious sect of Babism. Bahaism was founded (1863) by Mizra Husayn Ali.

Bahr, Hermann (1863–1934). Austrian critic and playwright. Like the writers of German naturalism, he wished to see the growth of a literary movement which would take account of the peculiarities of the modern age; but in his *Die Überwindung des Naturalismus* (*The Overcoming of Naturalism,* 1891) he made it clear that he favored a more sophisticated style than that of naturalism. His best-known play is *Das Konzert* (*The Concert,* 1909), an urbane and witty comedy.

Baiardo. Also known as **Bajardo** or **Bayard.** Rinaldo's horse, of a bright bay color, once the property of Amadis of Gaul. He was found by Malagigi, the wizard, in a cave guarded by a dragon, which the wizard slew. According to tradition he is still alive, but flees at the approach of man, so that no one can ever hope to catch him.

In Boiardo's ORLANDO INNAMORATO, the pagan king Gradasso comes to Paris to fight Charlemagne's paladins in hopes of winning the horse and Orlando's Durindana, a sword supposed to have belonged to Hector of Troy.

Baïf, Jean Antoine de (1532–1589). French poet and member of the PLÉIADE, who is remembered not so much for his poetry as for his inexhaustible interest in experimentation. Besides writing love poetry—*Amours de Méline* (1552) and *Amour de Francine* (1555)—he tried his hand at scientific poetry in *Le Premier des Météores* (1567), championed a reform in spelling, and introduced his own metric form, *le vers baïfin.* Perhaps his most promising project was the short-lived *Académie de Poésie et de Musique,* which he persuaded Charles IX to found in 1570 in the interest of uniting the two arts.

Bailey, Nathan or **Nathaniel** (d. 1742). English lexicographer. His *Universal Etymological English Dictionary* (1721) marks the beginning of modern English lexicography in the sense of objective registration of the complete body of words in the language. It served as the point of departure for the famous dictionary of Samuel Johnson.

Bailey, Philip James (1816–1902). English poet. He wrote *Festus,* a long and heavily moralized version of the legend of FAUST which won fleeting critical esteem and enduring popularity throughout the 19th century. The poem alternates ratiocinative writing with bursts of nebulous rhapsody; the portions in the latter manner were imitated by the SPASMODIC SCHOOL of poets. *Festus* kept reappearing in new and larger editions, incorporating other works of Bailey, until by 1889 it had quadrupled in size (40,000 lines).

Bailly, Harry. See CANTERBURY TALES.

Bairam. The name given to two great Muslim feasts. The *Lesser* begins on the new moon of the month Shawwal, at the termination of the fast of RAMADAN, and lasts three days. The *Greater* is celebrated on the 10th day of the 12th month, Dhul Hijja, lasts for four days, and forms the concluding ceremony of the pilgrimage to Mecca. It comes 70 days after the Lesser Bairam.

Baisecul. See Lord KISSBREECH.

Bajardo. See BAIARDO.

Bajazet (1672). A tragedy by Jean RACINE. The play is purportedly based on actual events that took place in Constantinople in 1638. It depicts the imprisoned Bajazet's pretense of love for the sultana Roxane, who plans to free him in order to marry him and place him on the throne, which is to be seized from her husband. Discovering Bajazet's love for the princess Atalide, Roxane allows him to be executed; discovering her infidelity, the sultan orders Roxane's execution; and, discovering her lover's death, Atalide commits suicide.

Baker, Ray Stannard. Pen name, **David Grayson** (1870–1946). American journalist and authorized biographer of Woodrow Wilson. Baker joined the staff of *McClure's Magazine* during the muckraking days and continued his contributions to that movement as an editor of the *American Magazine.* (See MUCKRAKERS.) Under his pen name, he wrote a series of essays which first appeared in the latter magazine and were later published in book form as *Adventures in Contentment* (1907) and similar volumes.

baker, the. A name applied to LOUIS XVI of France. He was called "the baker" (*le boulanger*), his queen MARIE ANTOINETTE, "the baker's wife" (*la boulangère*), and the dauphin "the shop boy" (*le petit mitron*) by the rabble who, after besieging Versailles on Oct. 6th, 1789, escorted them to Paris. When the king learned from them that there was a bread famine in Paris, he ordered supplies of flour sent there. During the return to Paris, chariots loaded with wheat and flour preceded the king's carriage, and National Guards carried loaves of bread, or sausages, on the end of their bayonets.

Bakunin, Mikhail Aleksandrovich (1814–1876). Russian revolutionary and anarchist leader. Born into a cultured noble family, Bakunin was educated at a military school in St. Petersburg, and served for a short time as an army officer. He resigned from the army and moved to Moscow, where he met the radical journalists Vissarion Belinski and Alexander Hertzen and plunged into the study of German philosophy, which was in vogue with the Russian intellectuals of the time. In 1840, Bakunin went to Berlin to continue his studies. He befriended the novelist Ivan Turgenev, who was also studying in Berlin. Turgenev is reputed to have used Bakunin as the model for the idealistic hero of his novel *Rudin.* While in Berlin, Bakunin published one of his most important early articles, *Reaktziya v germanii* (*Reaction in Germany,* 1842). In the article is the phrase that was later adopted as an anarchist slogan: "The passion for destruction is also a creative passion."

Bakunin took part in revolutionary agitation in Germany, Austria, and France during 1848. He was arrested and extradited to Russia the following year. After being in prison for almost 10 years he was exiled to Siberia, from which he escaped in 1861, making his way to Europe via Japan and the U.S. He remained in Europe for the rest of his life, mostly in Geneva and London. By the late 1860's, Bakunin's anarchist views were fully formed, and he expounded them in the periodical *Narodnoe Delo* (*The People's Cause*), which he published in Geneva.

Bakunin was a tireless, if not always effective, revolutionary schemer. An observer of his activities during the Paris revolt of 1848 said of him: "On the first day of a revolution he is a treasure; on the second he ought to be shot." This kind of revolutionary zeal led to Bakunin's expulsion from the First INTERNATIONAL in 1872 on charges of opposing the leadership, headed by Karl Marx, and of setting up a rival revolutionary organization.

Balaam. In the Old Testament (Num. 22–23), a prophet of Pethor whom Balak, king of Moab, had persuaded to prophesy against the Israelites invading his territory. On the way to utter the curse, Balaam was forced three times to beat the ass upon which he was riding when it stopped short, blocked by God's angel. "Then Jehovah opened the eyes of Balaam and he saw the angel of the Lord standing in the way" (Num. 22:31). Balaam refused to curse Israel, but pronounced his blessing instead.

Balan. The name of a strong and courageous giant in many medieval romances. He was the father of Sir Fierabras, a paladin in Charlemagne's court. In the Arthurian cycle, he is brother of Sir BALIN.

balance of power. A policy of preventing one nation from gaining so much power that it will be in a position to threaten the security of other nations. It was formulated by Prince Metternich at the Congress of Vienna in 1815, and became a leading principle of the continental policy of Great Britain with regard to France and Germany. In European history after Napoleon it played an important part in the wars and shifting diplomatic alliances of the nations on the continent.

Balaustion. An imaginary character of ancient Greece in Browning's *Balaustion's Adventure* (1871) and *Aristophanes' Apology, including a Transcript from Euripides, being the last Adventure of Balaustion* (1875). *Balaustion's Adventure* is for the most part a free version of Euripides' drama ALCESTIS.

Balbec. The French seaside resort visited by the narrator in Marcel PROUST's *Remembrance of Things Past*. It is based on resorts of the Normandy coast, such as Trouville and Cabourg.

Balboa, Vasco Núñez de (1475-1517). Spanish explorer. Sailing to America in 1500, Balboa became leader of the small colony of Darien on the isthmus of Panama. In 1513, after an arduous trek across the isthmus with 190 picked companions, Balboa discovered the Pacific Ocean, which he named the "South Sea," and took possession of it in the name of Spain. He later incurred the enmity of Pedro Arias de Avila (known as Pedrarias), governor of Panama, who had him beheaded on a trumped-up charge of treason.

Balbuena or **Valbuena, Bernardo de** (1568-1627). Spanish-born Mexican poet and bishop of Puerto Rico. Balbuena is remembered mainly for two long poems, both examples of the baroque style in literature: *La grandeza mexicana* (1604), a patriotic description of Mexico City, and *El Bernardo* (1624), a fantastic epic of chivalry.

Balchin, Nigel (1908-). English novelist. He is the author of *The Small Back Room* (1943), a story of wartime scientific researchers, or "back room boys"; *Mine Own Executioner* (1945), a psychological thriller; and *Seen Dimly Before Dawn* (1962), a novel about a 15-year-old English schoolboy.

Balcony, The (**Le Balcon;** 1956). A drama by Jean GENET. Men who come to Madame Irma's brothel to enact their secret ambitions begin to fulfill the roles of the images they have been playing. All, however, find that active responsibility is less satisfying than their dream projections. The Chief of Police discovers that he cannot *become* the modern hero until a customer comes to enact a heroic image of him.

Balder or **Baldur.** In Norse mythology, the god of light, summer, innocence, and purity, called "the good." The son of Odin and Frigga, he dwelt at Breidhablik, one of the mansions of Asgard. He is said to have been slain by his rival Hoder while fighting for possession of the beautiful Nanna after Holder had obtained Miming's sword, by which alone Balder could be wounded. Another legend tells that Frigga bound all things by oath not to harm him, but accidentally omitted the mistletoe. Loki learned this and armed his blind brother Hoder with a mistletoe twig, with which, after all else had been tried, Balder was slain. His huge ship was used for his funeral pyre, where he was joined by his faithful wife Nanna. His death brought general consternation to the gods, and formed the prelude to their final overthrow. See VALI.

Among modern poems written around the Balder legend are Matthew Arnold's *Balder Dead,* William Morris' *Funeral of Balder,* Robert Buchanan's *Balder the Beautiful,* and Longfellow's *Tegner's Drapa.*

Balderstone, Caleb. In Scott's BRIDE OF LAMMERMOOR, the intensely loyal but tedious old butler of the master of Ravenswood. His ingenuity in concealing the signs of poverty is equaled only by the faithfulness with which he serves the impoverished Ravenswoods without hope of reward.

Baldovino Di Buglione (**Baldwin of Bouillon**). The brother of Goffredo (Godfrey of Bouillon), commander of the Crusaders in Tasso's epic GERUSALEMME LIBERATA. Baldovino, one of the best fighters in the Christian camp, staunchly defends his brother when the Crusaders rebel against Goffredo's leadership.

Bald Soprano, The (**La Cantatrice chauve;** 1948). An antiplay by Eugène IONESCO. It burlesques the nonsensical stuffiness of a middle-class English home by stringing together the clichés of a foreign language phrase-book.

Baldwin, Faith [Cuthrell] (1893-). American novelist. Miss Baldwin, who has been called a "circulating-library" novelist, has written with great popular success a steady stream of lightly sentimental books for the feminine audience. Her many titles include *Those Difficult Years* (1925), *Three Women* (1926), *Woman on Her Way* (1946), *Blaze of Sunlight* (1959), and *Testament of Trust* (1960).

Baldwin, James (1924-). American novelist and essayist. His first novel, *Go Tell It on the Mountain* (1953), tells of the religious awakening of a 14-year-old Negro boy living in the Harlem section of New York City, where Baldwin himself was born. With this book Baldwin established his reputation as a writer of deep insight. His nonfiction, which includes *Notes of a Native Son* (1955), *Nobody Knows My Name: More Notes of a Native Son* (1961), and *The Fire Next Time* (1963), contains a passionate and clearly articulate statement on the suffering of the American Negro and an angry indictment of a society that permits such conditions to exist. Many feel that Baldwin is more distinguished as an essayist than as a novelist, although both of his later novels have received critical praise. *Giovanni's Room* (1956), a novel about a homosexual relationship, is set in Paris, where Baldwin exiled himself for a number of years. *Another Country* (1961) is a powerful though uneven novel of personal relationships among Negroes and whites.

Baldwin, Stanley. 1st Earl of Bewdley (1867-1947). English statesman. Baldwin, who became a Conservative member of Parliament in 1908, served as prime minister in 1923-1924, 1924-1929, and 1935-1937. The abdication of Edward VIII (later the duke of WINDSOR) occurred during Baldwin's third term.

Bale, John (1495-1563). English author and prelate. He was one of the most outspoken and vituperative critics of Roman Catholicism at the time of the English Reformation. A protegé of Thomas Cromwell and under Cromwell's patronage, Bale produced a number of morality plays and interludes attacking the Catholic clergy. The most important of these is his *Kynge Johan* (c. 1548), considered the first example of the CHRONICLE PLAY later developed by Shakespeare. Bale is also noted for his *Illustrium Majoris Britanniae Scriptorum*

(1548; revised edition, 1557–1559), a valuable, although often inaccurate, catalogue of British writers
and their work.

Balfour, John, 3rd baron of **Burley** (d. 1688).
A character in Scott's *Old Mortality* (1816). Scott,
who depicted him as a bold and violent leader of
the COVENANTERS, confused him with John Balfour
of Kinloch.

Balfour Declaration (1917). An assurance by
Great Britain of protection for the Jewish settlement
of Palestine. After British forces had captured Palestine, the British Government declared its support
for limited Jewish immigration into the area. Arthur
James Balfour, the foreign secretary, drew up the
statement of policy, which thus acquired his name.
The Balfour Declaration formed the basis for British
policy on the mandate of Palestine for the next 30
years.

Balin, Sir. One of the knights of the Round
Table in Arthurian legend, brother of Sir Balan.
In Malory's *Morte d'Arthur* (c. 1469), the two
brothers unwittingly kill each other in single combat, neither recognizing the other until just before
death. At their request they are buried in one
grave by Merlin. Tennyson gives a much altered
version of the story in *Idylls of the King* (1859–
1872).

Balisand (1924). A novel by Joseph HERGES-
HEIMER. The story of a Federalist in tidewater
Virginia in the days of the Revolution and afterward, *Balisand* pictures the conflict between the
ideals of aristocracy and Jeffersonian democracy.

Balisarda. In the ORLANDO FURIOSO of Ariosto
a famous sword made in the garden of Orgagna by
the sorceress Falerina. It has the power to cut
through even enchanted substances and was given
to Ruggiero for the purpose of killing Orlando:

> He knew with Balisarda's lightest blows,
> Nor helm, nor shield, nor cuirass could avail,
> Nor strongly tempered plate, nor twisted mail.

Ball, Hugo (1886–1927). German writer and
actor. He was one of the founders of the DADA
movement in Zürich (1916). His *Hermann Hesse,
Sein Leben und sein Werk* (*Hermann Hesse, His
Life and Work,* 1927), a biography, stems from a
personal acquaintance with the novelist.

ballad. A narrative song, originally chiefly of
popular origin. Ballads fall into types according to
subject and include the domestic tragedy, concerning a murder or family feud; the historical ballad,
dealing with historical events; the outlaw ballad,
celebrating a popular rebel against established law,
such as Robin Hood or Jesse James; the Scottish
coronach, or lament ballad; and the folkloric ballad.
Among early ballads, coronach and historical ballads
and those involving romance elements were usually
composed by minstrels attached to noblemen's courts
and were written with a sense of literary values and
for a definite audience. The other types were popular products transmitted by oral tradition and had
much charm but little artistic finish. In the U.S.
many folk ballads are survivals or variants of the
old English ballads. However, there are a number
of indigenous types dealing with such subjects as
occupational pursuits (*Casey Jones*), the Negroes
and other national or ethnic groups (*John Henry*),

various sections of the country, famous battles, and
actual or legendary heroes.

English and Scottish ballads dating from the 14th
to the 16th century are found in Percy's RELIQUES
OF ANCIENT ENGLISH POETRY and Child's *English and
Scottish Popular Ballads*. Many literary ballads have
been written by later poets; among them may be
mentioned Campbell's *Lord Ullin's Daughter*, Scott's
Rosabelle, Rossetti's *Sister Helen*, and Stephen Vincent Benét's *Ballad of William Sycamore*.

ballade. A traditional verse form first appearing in Provençal literature. The ballade was developed in France and reached its height during the
14th century, when it first came into English. François Villon (15th century) probably wrote the best-
known ballades in literary history.

The ballade consists of three stanzas and an
envoi, and its distinguishing feature is a refrain
that appears as the last line of each stanza. The
stanza may be of seven, eight, or ten lines. The
ballade royal, written in RHYME ROYAL, has a fourth
stanza instead of an envoi. Only three or four
rhymes are used in all. The refrain adds to the
meaning of the poem in every occurrence; the envoi is usually addressed to the poet's patron or to
someone concerned with the subject of the poem.
Chaucer's *Ballade of Good Counsel* and Swinburne's *Ballad of Dreamland* are good examples in
English. See CHANT ROYAL.

Ballad of Dead Ladies, The (1869). An English translation by Dante Gabriel ROSSETTI of the
famous *Ballade des dames du temps jadis* of the
medieval French poet François Villon.

Ballad of Reading Gaol, The (1898). A poem
by Oscar WILDE. It is the study of a man condemned
to die and is drawn from the author's experiences
in the prison of the title.

ballata. An Italian dance song popular among
the folk as well as the learned during the Middle
Ages and the Renaissance. Derived from the Italian
word for dance (*ballo*), it was usually made up of
a stanza of varying length and a two-line refrain
intended for a soloist and a chorus of dancers. *Ballate*
were written by Boccaccio, Poliziano, Lorenzo de'
Médicis, and many others. Many were set to music by
such famous composers as Francesco Landini.

ballet. An art form combining music, dance,
and pantomime. Ballet originated in ancient Roman
pantomimic performances, and was a popular entertainment at the courts of the Italian princes. In the
17th century Catherine de' Médicis imported ballet
to France, where it acquired the *corps de ballet,*
elaborate sets and costumes, and dramatic plots,
often the work of leading poets and playwrights.
After the French Revolution, ballet in western
Europe became an adjunct to the opera, but survived in Russia in its classical form. The ballet of
the 20th century, largely the creation of the Ballet
Russe (Russian ballet) of Serge DIAGHILEV, is a
synthesis of classical dance with modern dance of
the sort pioneered by the American Isadora Duncan.
Contemporary ballet can range from pure dance,
without dramatic plot or incident, to danced drama,
with fully developed plot and characterization, lacking only speech. Balletic elements have infiltrated
and influenced opera, films, and stage plays.

balm. A curative. In the Bible, Jeremiah asks, "Is there no balm in Gilead?" meaning is there no medicine, or consolation (Jer. 8:22). "Balm" in this passage is the Geneva Bible's translation of the Hebrew *sori,* which probably means mastic, the resin yielded by the mastic tree, *Pistacia lentiscus,* which was formerly used in many medicines. In Wyclif's Bible the word is translated "gumme," and in Coverdale's "triacle." Balm of Gilead is also the name given to the black or balsam poplar.

Balmont, Konstantin Dmitriyevich (1867–1943). Russian poet. He was the first of the Russian SYMBOLISTS to become widely popular, primarily because of the musical quality of his poetry. His first work appeared in 1890, followed by other collections and translations, chiefly from English poetry. His favorite foreign poets were Shelley and Poe. Balmont emigrated after the revolution and lived in France until his death.

Balor. In the Gaelic mythological cycle, a FOMORIAN giant with an evil eye, which kills whomever it is turned on. In the tale BATTLE OF MOYTURA, he is slain by Lug who casts a stone from his sling into the eye of Balor, so that the eye comes "out through the back of his head."

Balsamo, Giuseppe. See Count Alessandro di CAGLIOSTRO.

Balthazar. (1) One of the three MAGI.

(2) In Shakespeare's COMEDY OF ERRORS, a merchant and friend of Antipholus of Syracuse.

(3) A servant to Don Pedro in Shakespeare's MUCH ADO ABOUT NOTHING.

(4) One of the four novels in Lawrence Durrell's ALEXANDRIA QUARTET.

Balue, Jean de la (1422–1491). French cardinal and politician. Accused of treason by Louis XI, he was imprisoned, it is said, in an iron cage. After 11 years he was freed as a result of papal intervention. Balue is a character in Scott's *Quentin Durward* (1823).

Baly or Bali. One of the great kings in the legends of India. He founded the city called by his name, redressed wrongs, upheld justice, was generous and charitable, so that at death he became one of the judges of hell. One day a dwarf asked the mighty monarch to allow him to measure three of his own paces for a hut to dwell in. Baly smiled and gave him permission. The first pace of the dwarf encompassed the earth, the second the heavens, and the third the infernal regions. Baly realized immediately that the dwarf was an incarnation of Vishnu and worshiped him. Vishnu made Baly king of hell and permitted him to revisit the earth once a year, on the first full moon of November.

Balzac, Honoré de (1799–1850). French novelist. Born at Tours, Balzac attended the Sorbonne where he acquired a passionate interest in literature. Unsuccessful experiments in the sensational novel and increasing debts marked his early years. At the age of 30, Balzac published his first successful novel, LES CHOUANS, and began the literary career that was to be as astoundingly prolific as it was important—he wrote more than 90 novels and tales. As in Stendhal and Flaubert, the romantic and the realistic coexist in both Balzac's character and his writings. Considered to be a founder of the realistic school, Balzac uses vast reams of meticulous detail

and faithfully depicts ordinary and undistinguished lives. Carefully documented, his novels are objective in their point of view and wide in their scope. Juxtaposed, however, with these realistic elements are the flagrantly romantic qualities of melodramatic plots, violent passions, and rhetorical passages. Balzac's characters are romantic in their extremism. Like the men and women of Dickens, they are painted in such bold strokes that they move away from human reality. Character traits, in such people as M. Grandet or Père Goriot, become heightened and exaggerated.

LA COMÉDIE HUMAINE is Balzac's tour de force, his masterpiece. The product of 20 years of creative labor, *La Comédie Humaine* is an attempt to present a complete social history of France in a thorough and scientific manner. The conception alone testifies to Balzac's almost superhuman energy and his unfailing vitality. Some of the finest novels in the series include EUGÉNIE GRANDET, LE PÈRE GORIOT, LA RECHERCHE DE L'ABSOLU, and CÉSAR BIROTTEAU. In style, Balzac's works are not graceful and polished. A strain of coarseness in the man and the work, a lack of concern with delicacy and subtlety, contributed to the clumsy strength of his prose. Balzac worked in breadth, not depth, and on his enormous canvas an unwieldly but intensely alive panoramic vision of France took shape.

Ban, King. In Arthurian legend (e.g., Malory's *Morte d'Arthur*), the king of Benwick and father of Sir Launcelot.

Bancroft, George (1800–1891). American diplomat and historian. A Democrat when most men of his background in Massachusetts were Whigs, Bancroft was named collector of the port of Boston as a reward for his party services in 1837. He later served as secretary of the navy and as minister to Great Britain and to Germany. He is best known, however, as the author of a 10-volume *History of the United States* (1834–1874), which he revised and cut to six volumes in 1876. A final revision (1883–1885) contained a volume on the *History of the Formulation of the Constitution.* Bancroft's historical work, which reflects his ardent faith in democracy and in the American people, has sometimes been compared to a Fourth-of-July oration. Although it is often considered outmoded, it is representative of 19th-century American nationalism.

Bandello, Matteo (1485–1561). Italian author. His *Novelliere* (1554), a collection of more than 200 short tales (see NOVELLA) which were translated into French and English, provided the basic plots for Shakespeare's *Romeo and Juliet, Much Ado About Nothing,* and *Twelfth Night.*

Banerjee, Tarashankar (1898–   ). Bengal's greatest living novelist. His writings are largely concerned with the decay of the landlord class and reveal his sympathetic attitude toward the oppressed peasants in Bengal's villages. *Rai Kamal* (1934) is considered his greatest work, but his enormously prolific output makes it difficult to assess the quality of his achievement.

Bang, Herman Joachim (1857–1912). Danish novelist and short-story writer. Acute sensitivity, loneliness, and compassion for those who suffer color all his work. After an abortive stage career, Bang turned to writing; his work is sometimes

marked, however, by a certain preciousness and affectation that recalls the actor. *Tine* (1889) is a critical account of the weakness shown by the Danes in the defeat of 1864. In the novel *Det hvide Hus* (*The White House*, 1898), he paints a vivid reminiscence of his childhood and of his mother, who died when he was 14. *Ved Vejen* (*By the Wayside*, 1886) and *Ludvigsbakke* (*Ida Brandt*, 1896) are both tragic idylls, which depict with sympathy the drab, gray lives of unhappy women. Although his subjects are naturalistic, Bang never attempts detachment, but views the world from the perspective of his own misery and isolation. His impressionistic style is delicate and graceful.

Bangorian controversy. A theological war of words. It was stirred up by a sermon preached March 31, 1717, before George I, by Dr. Hoadly, bishop of Bangor, on the text, "My kingdom is not of this world," the argument being that Christ had not delegated His power or authority to either king or clergy. Arguing against High Church prerogative, Hoadly denied virtually all independent political power to the Established Church. Hoadly was strongly attacked on this point by William Law. The sermon, which was printed by royal command, led to such discord in Convocation that this body was prorogued, and from that time till 1852 was allowed to meet only as a matter of form.

Banks, John (c. 1650–1706). English dramatist. He wrote the tragedies *Virtue Betrayed, or Anna Bullen* (1682) and *The Island Queens, or The Death of Mary, Queen of Scotland* (pub. 1684).

Banks' horse. A horse called Marocco trained to do all manner of tricks. It belonged to one Banks about the end of the reign of Queen Elizabeth. One of Marocco's supposed exploits was the ascent of the steeple of old St. Paul's. He is frequently mentioned in contemporary literature.

Bankside. The southern bank of the Thames River. In Elizabethan times it was outside the city limits of London and therefore suitable for the production of plays. (Puritan opposition to the theaters outlawed the presentation of theatrical events within the city.) Shakespeare's Globe was located on the Bankside.

Banquo. In Shakespeare's MACBETH, the thane of Lochaber and a general in the king's army. He is slain by order of Macbeth because the witches had foretold that his descendants would reign over Scotland. His ghost later appears to Macbeth at a banquet, though it is invisible to the others present. Described as having a "royalty of nature," a "dauntless temper of mind," and a "wisdom that doth guide his valor," he serves as a foil to the ambition-driven Macbeth.

The name Banquo is given in many old genealogies of the Scottish kings, but Shakespeare's character is not drawn from history. See FLEANCE.

banshee. The domestic spirit of certain Irish or Highland Scottish families. Banshees were supposed to take an interest in the welfare of the family, and to wail at the death of one of its members. The word is the Old Irish *ben side,* a woman of the elves or fairies.

Banville, Théodore de (1823–1891). French poet, dramatist, and man of letters. Banville was a contributor to the *Parnasse Contemporain* (1866).

His best collections of poetry are *Les Stalactites* (1846), *Le Sang de la coupe* (1857), and *Les Exilés* (1867). See PARNASSIANS.

banzai (Jap. *ban,* ten thousand; *sai,* year). A Japanese cheer of enthusiasm or victory.

Baptes. Priests of the goddess Cotytto. She was the Thracian goddess of lewdness, whose midnight orgies were so obscene that they disgusted even the goddess herself. They received their name from the Greek verb *bapto,* to wash, because of the so-called ceremonies of purification connected with her rites. (Juvenal, ii, 91.)

baptism. The rite of Christian initiation. It is performed by pouring or sprinkling water on a person, or by immersing him briefly in water, accompanied usually with the formula "I baptize thee in the name of the Father, and of the Son, and of the Holy Ghost." The rite is held to wash away the stain of ORIGINAL SIN and to make the recipient a member of the Christian church. Much controversy has surrounded the mode of administration, and the age at which baptism should be administered. See ANABAPTISTS; SACRAMENT.

Baptista. In Shakespeare's TAMING OF THE SHREW, a rich gentleman of Padua, the father of Katharina and Bianca.

Barabbas. The robber and insurrectionary leader whom Pilate released from prison instead of Jesus, according to the custom that, at the feast of Passover, one prisoner, by popular demand, should be freed (Matt. 27).

Various baptismal practices ridiculed in Daniel Featly's *The Dippers Dipt* (1660).

Barabbas (1950). A novel by Pär LAGERKVIST. The book tells the story of the fate of Barabbas, the criminal who was released instead of Christ, by Pilate. A reprobate, Barabbas is strangely affected by the Crucifixion and drawn, almost against his will, toward Christ's believers. Tortured by doubt, isolated from his fellow human beings, Barabbas seeks some certain meaning in existence. He dies with a cry of uncertainty still on his lips. Lagerkvist uses the biblical story to express his vision of man's anguish, his loneliness, and his desperate quest for meaning. He offers no simple, sure solution, but he does offer an intense compassion.

Barbara Allan (1724). A ballad by Allan RAMSAY, which appears in Percy's *Reliques*. Sir John Grehme is dying of love for Barbara Allan. Barbara goes to see him, and, drawing aside the curtain, says, "Young man, I think ye're dyan'." She then leaves him, but she has not gone more than a mile away when she hears the death-bell toll and bitterly repents what she has said.

Barbara Frietchie (1863). A poem by John Greenleaf WHITTIER. The central incident in the poem is the fictional encounter between Barbara Frietchie and Stonewall Jackson. He forbade his Confederate troops to harm her, when she prominently displayed a Union flag. Ninety-six years old, she stood at her window in Fredericktown:

> "Shoot, if you must, this old gray head,
> But spare your country's flag," she said.

Barbarossa (*It.,* "red-beard"). The surname attached to Frederick I (1123?–1190). King of Germany and Holy Roman emperor (1152–1190), he was a gifted ruler who helped unite Germany, but spent much of his time in the subjugation of Italy. He died on his way to the Third Crusade. There was a legend that he never died, but is still sleeping in the Kyffhäuser in Thuringia. There he sits at a stone table with his six knights, waiting the "fulness of time," when he will come from his cave to rescue Germany from bondage, and give her the foremost place of all the world. His beard has already grown through the table's slab, but must wind itself thrice round the table before his second advent. This legend originally grew up about Frederick's equally remarkable grandson, Frederick II.

Barbe-bleue. See BLUEBEARD.

Barberino, Andrea da (c. 1370–?1431). Tuscan *cantastorie* or minstrel and author of popular prose narratives of romantic material. *I Reali di Francia* (*The Nobility of France*) deals with the Carolingian heroes and feats; *Guerrino il Meschino* (*Guerrino the Wretched*) is his own creation of epic material, and is still popular today.

Barber of Seville, The (1775). The title of a comedy by BEAUMARCHAIS, and of two operas, one by Rossini (1816) and the other by Giovanni Paisiello (c. 1776), both based on the play. FIGARO, a rascal of a barber, aids his former master, Count Almaviva, to gain entrance to the house of Bartholo, so that the count can woo the latter's ward, Rosine, a beautiful young girl with whom Almaviva is in love. He succeeds with Figaro's help in marrying her in spite of old Bartholo's precautions.

barber's pole. A spirally painted pole, striped in red and white, displayed outside barber shops. A relic of the days when the callings of barber and surgeon were combined, it is symbolical of the winding of a bandage round the arm previous to blood-letting. The gilt knob at its end represents a brass basin, which is sometimes actually suspended on the pole.

Barbey d'Aurevilly, Jules (1808–1889). French novelist and critic. A minor romantic, Barbey d'Aurevilly is the author of two excellent novels, *L'Ensorcelée* (1854) and *Le Chevalier des Touches* (1864). Writing as literary or dramatic critic for such papers as the *Constitutionnel,* he produced reviews that were vigorous and perceptive, if somewhat prejudiced by his Royalist and Roman Catholic sympathies.

Barbizon school. The name given to a group of French landscape painters. Opposed to the classical teachings of the Academy, they withdrew and, from 1830 to 1870, made their center at Barbizon in the forest of Fontainebleau, seeking a new directness of observation from nature. Among them were Jean Baptiste Camille COROT, Jean François MILLET, Théodore Rousseau, and Charles Daubigny.

Barbour, John (1316?–1395). Scottish poet. He was archbishop of Aberdeen in 1375 and one of the auditors of the exchequer in 1372, 1382, and 1384. He is best known for his epic poem, THE BRUCE. Other poems, almost certainly his, include *Legend of Troy* and *Legends of the Saints,* both translations of works of Guido da Colonna.

Barbusse, Henri (1873–1935). French novelist and journalist. Barbusse is most famous for *Under Fire* (*Le Feu;* 1916), a brutally realistic picture of the absurdity of war. Other novels include *L'Enfer* (*The Inferno,* 1908), *Clarté* (*Light,* 1919), and *Les Enchaînements* (*Chains,* 1925).

Barchester Towers (1857). One of the best known of the novels of Anthony TROLLOPE in the BARSETSHIRE series. A sequel to *The Warden,* it is a novel of clerical intrigue showing the struggle between the trenchant Mrs. PROUDIE, the bishop's wife, and the insidious chaplain, Mr. Slope. Each wishes to become the dominant voice in the quiet cathedral town of Barchester. Mrs. Proudie eventually triumphs.

Barclay, Alexander (1475?–1552). English poet and divine. Barclay is famous for THE SHIP OF FOOLS (*The Shyp of Folys of the Worlde,* 1509), a satire on English life based on the German *Das Narrenschiff* by Sebastian Brant. He wrote a volume of *Eclogues* (1513?), which is considered to be one of the earliest examples of pastoral verse in English. He also translated some of the Latin poetry of Aeneas Silvius (1405–1464), who became Pope Pius II.

Barclay, Florence (1862–1921). English popular novelist. Her THE ROSARY was sensationally successful. Her ingredients were love, blood, tears, and purple religiosity.

Bard, The (1757). A Pindaric ode by Thomas GRAY, concerning a prophecy made by a Welsh bard to the invading King Edward I of England. It is based on Welsh legendary material and contains the famous line: "weave the warp and weave the woof." The central idea of the poem is that mankind from earliest times has been visited by the highest poetic inspiration.

Bardell, Mrs. In Charles Dickens' PICKWICK PAPERS, a widowed landlady of "apartments for single gentlemen" in Goswell Street. Long an admirer of Mr. Pickwick, she misinterprets some innocent remarks of his as a proposal of marriage and is induced by the unprincipled DODSON AND FOGG to sue for breach of promise. A verdict is obtained against Pickwick, but Mrs. Bardell is subsequently arrested for refusing to pay the costs of the trial and lodged in prison.

Bard of Avon. A popular epithet for William Shakespeare, who was born and buried at Stratford on Avon.

Bardolph. Sir John Falstaff's corporal in Shakespeare's HENRY IV: PART I and PART II and THE MERRY WIVES OF WINDSOR. In HENRY V he is promoted to lieutenant. He is a lowbred, drunken swaggerer whose red, pimply nose wins him the nickname "Knight of the Burning Lamp."

Barea, Arturo (1897–1957). Spanish novelist. Exiled as a result of the Spanish Civil War, he is best known for his autobiographical novel, *The Forging of a Rebel* (*La forja de un rebelde;* 1951), originally published in English in three parts: *The Forge* (*La forja*), *The Track* (*La ruta*), and *The Clash* (*La llama*). He also wrote the essay *Lorca, the Poet and his People* (*Lorca, el poeta y su pueblo;* 1944).

Barefoot Boy, The (1855). A poem by John Greenleaf WHITTIER. Its subject is the joy of a country childhood.

Baring, Maurice (1874–1945). English novelist, essayist, poet, and playwright. Until 1912 he worked as a journalist in Russia, and wrote several studies of Russian culture and literature. His interesting autobiography is entitled *The Puppet Show of Memory* (1922).

Barker, George (1913–   ). English poet. Like that of his contemporary, Dylan Thomas, his poetry is ecstatic, romantic, and violent, characterized by extravagant imagery and great technical dexterity in the use of puns, rhythms, and verbal devices. It is often also didactic, and concerned with moral and political issues. Collections of his poetry include *Poems* (1935); *Calamiterror* (1937), inspired by the Spanish Civil War; *Lament and Triumph* (1940); *Eros in Dogma* (1944); and *A Vision of Beasts and Gods* (1954).

Barker, Harley Granville-. See Harley GRANVILLE-BARKER.

Barker, James Nelson (1784–1858). American dramatist. In his plays, Barker, who held numerous public offices, expressed his ardent Americanism and his interest in politics. His best work is probably *Superstition* (1823), a blank-verse tragedy dealing with the English regicide Goffe and witchcraft trials in New England. He also wrote *The Indian Princess* (1808), in which Pocahontas figures prominently, and *Marmion* (1812), an adaptation of Scott's poem.

Barkis. In Charles Dickens' DAVID COPPERFIELD, the carrier who courts Clara PEGGOTTY by asking David to tell her "Barkis is willin'." Peggotty takes the hint and becomes Mrs. Barkis.

Barkley, Catherine. The heroine of Ernest Hemingway's novel A FAREWELL TO ARMS. An English nurse in an Italian hospital, she has a brief affair with the American lieutenant Frederic Henry but dies bearing his child.

Barlaam and Josaphat. An Eastern romance, probably written in the seventh century and popular in the Middle Ages, telling how Barlaam, an ascetic monk of the desert of Sinai, converted the Indian prince Josaphat to Christianity. It is believed to have been put in its final form by St. John of Damascus, a Syrian monk of the eighth century. Some authorities consider this a Christianized version of the story of Buddha. It includes the story of the three caskets which was used by Shakespeare in *The Merchant of Venice* (c. 1595).

A poetical version of the romance was written in the 13th century by the minnesinger Rudolf von Ems.

Barlach, Ernst (1870–1938). German dramatist and famous sculptor. His expressionistically tinged plays include *Der tote Tag* (*The Dead Day,* 1912) and *Die Sündflut* (*The Flood,* 1924).

Barleycorn, Sir John. An old song. As it was written down by Robert Burns, his neighbors vowed that Sir John should die, so they hired ruffians to "plough him with ploughs and bury him"; this they did, and afterward "combed him with harrows and thrust clods on his head," but did not kill him by these or by numerous other means which they attempted. Sir John bore no malice for this ill usage, but did his best to cheer the flagging spirits even of his worst persecutors. The song seems to recall fertility rites at corn-planting time.

Jack London wrote an autobiography called *John Barleycorn* (1913), which he described as his "alcoholic memories."

Barlow, Joel (1754–1812). American poet and diplomat, a leader of the anti-Federalist party, and one of the best-known of the HARTFORD WITS. In 1788 he left for Europe as a representative of some American business interests. He stayed abroad for 17 years and in 1795 was appointed American consul to Algiers. In Europe he shed his conservatism, became an ardent democrat, and befriended Thomas Paine.

Barlow's most popular poem was THE HASTY PUDDING; his most ambitious was *The Vision of Columbus,* first published in 1787, and later revised, lengthened, and reissued in epic form as THE COLUMBIAD. He was one of the authors of THE ANARCHIAD and also wrote ADVICE TO THE PRIVILEGED ORDERS, a controversial prose tract embodying his democratic ideals.

Barmecide feast. An imaginary feast where the dishes are empty; hence a reference to any appealing illusion. The allusion is to such a banquet given in jest for the poor Schacabac by a rich Barmecide prince in the *Arabian Nights'* story, "The Barber's Sixth Brother." The starving Schacabac pretends to eat and enjoy the empty dishes set before him, but when illusory wine is offered him, he feigns drunkenness and knocks the Barmecide down. The latter sees the humor of the situation, forgives Schacabac, and provides him with food to his heart's content.

Barnabas. In the New Testament, a companion of Paul and Mark. He accompanied them both on the first missionary journey. Barnabas was to go with Paul on his second journey and urged Paul to take

Mark, Barnabas' nephew, with them. Paul refused, however, since Mark had left them before the first journey was over. As a result, Paul took Silas with him and neither Mark nor Barnabas went. It is thought that Mark wrote his Gospel at the urging of Barnabas, perhaps under his direction.

Barnaby Rudge (1841). A novel by Charles DICKENS. The book revolves around the anti-Catholic GORDON RIOTS of 1780 in which the titular hero innocently participates for the pleasure of carrying a flag and wearing a blue bow. Barnaby is a half-wit, a fact mysteriously connected with the fact that his father murdered his employer and a fellow servant on the night of Barnaby's birth. Of conspicuous appearance, Barnaby is pale with long red hair; he dresses all in green and carries a large raven named Grip in a basket on his back. He is identified as a leading rioter and condemned to death, but is reprieved through the influence of Gabriel Varden. He spends the rest of his life with his mother in a cottage near Maypole, happily employed with his poultry and his garden.

Barnaby's father, Mr. Rudge, is mistakenly believed to have been murdered the same night as Mr. Haredale, his employer. After the murder, he is seen by many in the locality, but is thought to be a ghost. Years later he joins the Gordon rioters and is sent to Newgate, but makes his escape when it is burned down.

The plot of this book is one of Dickens' weakest, and the novel's chief interest lies in its depiction of the terrible riots. In exploring causes for the riots, Dickens finds the answer in a government that is heedless of the needs of its poor. A similar theme is dealt with in A TALE OF TWO CITIES.

Barnacle. The name given by Charles Dickens in LITTLE DORRIT to a "very high family and a very large family" active in governmental circles, nine of whom appear in the novel. They are bungling and incompetent. In all of them—particularly in Mr. Tite Barnacle, a permanent official in the CIRCUMLOCUTION OFFICE—Dickens satirizes governmental red tape.

Barnburners. The reform wing of the Democratic Party in New York during the 1840's. They were so called in allusion to the Dutch farmer who burned his barn in order to get rid of the rats. Led by Martin Van Buren, his son John, and Silas Wright, the Barnburners were opposed to the extension of slavery; in 1848 they bolted the Democratic Party and joined other antislavery elements to form the FREE-SOIL PARTY.

Barnes, Barnabe (1569?-1609). English poet. Barnes wrote *Parthenophil and Parthenophe, Sonnets, Madrigals, Elegies, and Odes* (1593) and *A Divine Century of Spiritual Sonnets* (1595).

Barnes, Djuna (1892-   ). American novelist and short-story writer. For many years a resident of Europe, Miss Barnes is the author of three experimental plays produced in 1919-1920 by the Provincetown Players: *Three from the Earth, An Irish Triangle*, and *Kurzy from the Sea. Ryder* (1928) and *Nightwood* (1936) are her best-known books. The latter, which has an introduction by T. S. Eliot, is a novel dealing with the Parisian artistic underground. *The Antiphon* (1958) is a surrealistic play in blank verse.

Barnes, Jake. The principal male character in Ernest Hemingway's novel THE SUN ALSO RISES. Made impotent by a war wound, he is hopelessly attracted to Lady Brett Ashley. Though in many ways his life is as aimless as the other "lost generation" characters, he lives by a code of behavior that gives him considerable stability.

Barnes, William (1801-1886). English poet and philologist. Of Dorsetshire yeoman stock, Barnes educated himself to such purpose that he became acquainted with some 60 languages, in addition to being a capable wood engraver, archaeologist, musician, and mathematician. He spent most of his life as a country schoolmaster and parson, publishing numerous philological works and composing the poems in Dorset dialect on which his fame rests. The poems are distinguished by simplicity and humor, fresh and vivid descriptions of nature, an unaffected and native pastoral quality. His works include *Poems of Rural Life in the Dorset Dialect* (1844, 1862), and *Poems of Rural Life in Common English* (1868).

Barnfield, Richard (1574-1627). English poet, author of *The Affectionate Shepherd* (1594), *Cynthia* (1595), and *The Encomium of Lady Pecunia* (1598). His fame, in large measure, rests on the fact that three of his lyrics, published (1599) in THE PASSIONATE PILGRIM, were long thought to be Shakespeare's.

Barnhelm, Minna von. See MINNA VON BARNHELM.

Barnum, Phineas T[aylor] (1810-1891). American circus man, impresario, and author. Barnum exhibited the midget, General Tom Thumb, in 1844, and brought Jenny Lind to America during 1850-1852. He entered into partnership with James A. Bailey, to present the famous Barnum & Bailey show; after Bailey's death in 1906, the show was absorbed by Ringling Brothers. Barnum's shows appealed to public curiosity, and the thirst for the sensational and the novel; the originator of this type of showmanship in America wrote *The Humbugs of the World* (1866) and possibly the *Life of P. T. Barnum, Written by Himself* (1855, frequently revised).

Baroja y Nessi, Pío (1872-1956). Spanish novelist. Known for his individualism and the cynical stoicism of his works, Baroja was a member of the GENERACIÓN DEL 98. His best-known work is the novel *El árbol de la ciencia* (*The Tree of Knowledge,* 1911). The tale is a study of Andrés Hurtado, a restless and selfless intellectual, who ends in suicide—thus reflecting the author's skepticism. Baroja is also the author of the trilogy *Tierra vasca* (1900-1909), *La sensualidad pervertida* (1920), and a novel dealing with Basque maritime life, *Las inquietudes de Shanti Andía* (*The Restlessness of Shanti Andia,* 1911).

baroque. A term applied to certain tendencies in European art in the latter 16th, the 17th, and the first half of the 18th centuries. Initially, and still primarily, the term referred to a free, exuberant style of architecture which supplanted the restrained and balanced style of the earlier Renaissance, but it was later applied to similar tendencies in painting, music, sculpture, and literature. The baroque style was dramatic, grandiose, ornate, full of motifs and forms expressive of conflict and energy. Originating in Italy and Spain, it spread throughout Europe, but is closely identified, especially in architecture, with Catholic Europe and was virtually the official style of the Counter Reformation. In literature the baroque spirit manifested itself in such movements as MARINISM in Italy, GONGORISM in Spain, and EUPHUISM in England. The word *baroque* has been used pejoratively, signifying a false, fantastic, over-emphatic style, but such a sense would be justified, if at all, only when applied to late baroque style such as ROCOCO.

Barr, Amelia E[dith] (1831-1919). English-born American novelist. She is noted for her highly romantic and sentimental works. Especially popular were *Jan Vedder's Wife* (1885); *The Bow of Orange Ribbon* (1886), a novel of early New York; and *Remember the Alamo* (1888).

Barr, Robert (1850-1912). Scottish editor and popular novelist. He concluded Stephen Crane's unfinished novel, *The O'Ruddy* (1903).

Barrack-Room Ballads (1892). A volume of poems by Rudyard KIPLING, celebrating the British soldier and army life throughout the Empire, in ballad meters and, frequently, cockney diction. See TOMMY ATKINS; GUNGA DIN; FUZZY WUZZY; MANDALAY.

Barrault, Jean Louis (1910-   ). French producer and actor. In 1947, Barrault founded the *Compagnie Jean-Louis Barrault–Madeline Renaud* with his actress wife. On the stage of their theater, the *Théâtre Marigny,* could be seen experimental productions, some of which Barrault describes in his two published works: *Reflexions sur le théâtre* (1945) and *Nouvelles Reflexions sur le théâtre* (1961).

Barren Ground (1925). A novel by Ellen GLASGOW. It is a realistic work of ingenious incidents and rich characterization in which Miss Glasgow touches successfully on many themes. The antithesis of the conventional romance, it is the story of Dorinda Oakley, a poor white who has been disappointed in love and turns her father's barren acres into a prosperous farm, but is less successful in her relations with the opposite sex.

Barrès, [Augustin-] Maurice (1862-1923). French novelist, journalist, and politician. His first novel trilogy, *Le Culte du moi* (1888-1891), portrayed the inner life of an egoist who in trying to develop his individual self discovers his need for others. The trilogy *Le Roman de l'énergie nationale* (1897-1903) is a social and philosophical commentary based on his own public life. Most famous of the nationalistic trilogy *Les Bastions de l'Est* (1905-1921) is *Colette Baudoche; The Story of a Young Girl of Metz* (1918). Barrès wrote other novels, including *The Sacred Hill (La Colline inspirée;* 1913), and many articles about World War I, collected in *L'Ame Française et la guerre* (11 vols., 1917-1922) and *Chronique de la Grande Guerre* (14 vols., 1920-1924).

Barretts of Wimpole Street, The (1930). A successful play by Rudolf Besier (1878-1942). It was produced in London and New York and based on the romance of Robert and Elizabeth Barrett Browning.

Barrie, Sir J[ames] M[atthew] (1860-1937). Scottish dramatist and novelist, known for the whimsy and sentimental fantasy of his work. His best-known plays are QUALITY STREET, THE ADMIRABLE CRICHTON, PETER PAN, *Alice Sit-by-the-Fire* (1905), WHAT EVERY WOMAN KNOWS, and *Dear Brutus* (1917). His outstanding prose works include *A Window in Thrums* (1889); MARGARET OGILVY, a biography of his mother; THE LITTLE MINISTER, a novel dramatized in 1897; and SENTIMENTAL TOMMY, a novel. See KAILYARD; THRUMS.

barring out. The closing of a schoolroom against a schoolmaster, a prank once common in British schools. *The Barring Out: or, Party Spirit* is the title of a novel by Maria EDGEWORTH.

Barrington, E. See Mrs. Lily Adams BECK.

Barrios, Eduardo (1884-   ). Chilean novelist and short-story writer. After wandering throughout Latin America and working at a variety of jobs, Barrios settled in Santiago, where he served as minister of education and director of the national library in the 1920's. Regarded as a master of the psychological tale, he excels in the portrayal of the hypersensitive personality. Such is the 10-year-old protagonist of the novelette *El niño que enloqueció de amor* (1915), who suffers physical and mental torment when he falls in love with Angélica, a friend of his mother, and ultimately loses his reason. In *Un perdido* (1917), the hero is an overwrought weakling who, unable to cope with reality, finds refuge in alcohol. Barrios' best work is probably *El hermano asno* (1922), which deals with the inner conflicts of two Franciscan monks: Brother Lázaro, who fears that he may violate his monastic vows, and Brother Rufino, who is disturbed by his reputation for sanctity.

Barry, Philip (1896-1949). American playwright. His work consists of sophisticated comedies and dramas of life among the wealthier classes, although he experimented with fantasy and mysticism in such plays as HOTEL UNIVERSE and *Here Come the Clowns* (1938). Notable among his plays are *You and I* (1922), *Paris Bound* (1927), *Holiday* (1929), THE ANIMAL KINGDOM, and THE PHILADELPHIA STORY.

Barrymore. The name of an American family of actors. Maurice Barrymore, whose real name was Herbert Blythe (1847-1905), and his wife Georgiana Drew (1856-1893), the daughter of the famous actor John Drew (1827-1862), were the initial users of the name. Their children were Lionel (1878-1954), Ethel (1879-1959), and John (1882-1942). Among them they scored many great stage and motion-picture successes. *The Royal Family* (1927), a play by George S. Kaufman and Edna Ferber, is considered a satire on the family. Gene Fowler's *Good Night, Sweet Prince* (1943) is mainly about John, but tells much about the others also.

Barsetshire, Chronicles of. A series of novels by Anthony TROLLOPE. Known also as the Cathedral Stories, they comprise *The Warden* (1855), BARCHESTER TOWERS, *Doctor Thorne* (1858), *Framley Parsonage* (1861), *The Small House at Allington* (1864), and *The Last Chronicle of Barset* (1867). In them Trollope disturbs the placidity of the cathedral town of Barchester with a series of agitations that ripple the clerical pools. The same characters reappear in most of them; among the best-known characters are Bishop and Mrs. PROUDIE, Archdeacon

Grantly, Rev. Septimus Harding, Rev. Mr. Crawley, the Thornes, Mr. Slope, Lady Arabella Gresham, and Signora Madeleine Neroni. Descendents of these families appear in the novels of Angela Thirkell.

bar sinister. In heraldry, a bar drawn in the reverse of the usual way. It was popularly but erroneously supposed to indicate bastardy. See BATON.

Bart, Lily. See HOUSE OF MIRTH, THE.

Bartas, Guillaume du (1544–1590). French poet, recognized throughout Europe in his time as the master of grave religious themes. Of a retiring and studious nature, he spent some time in the service of Henry IV during the religious wars. Despite his Protestant sympathies, his poetry was impartially Christian and appealed to Protestants and Catholics alike. His works include *Judith* (1573); *La Semaine* (1578), an account of the Creation; and the uncompleted *Seconde Semaine* (1584), in which he proposed to follow man from the Garden of Eden to the Last Judgment. Though frequently achieving eloquence and grandeur, his religious epic poetry lacked taste and abounded in the extravagant metaphors in vogue at the time. Soon outdated, it had dropped into obscurity by the 17th century.

Barthélemy, Jean Jacques (1716–1795). French orientalistist, man of letters, numismatist, and author. It was his erudition and love for antiquity that brought him, during the years 1757–1788, to write the historical romance *Le Voyage du jeune Anacharsis en Grèce, dans le milieu du IV*e* siècle avant l'ère vulgaire* (see ANACHARSIS). The book enjoyed a huge success and opened the doors of the French ACADEMY to Barthélemy in 1789.

Bartholdi, Frédéric Auguste. See Statue of LIBERTY.

Bartholomew, St. One of the 12 disciples of Jesus. The symbol of this saint is a knife, in allusion to the knife with which he was flayed alive. He is commemorated on August 24.

Bartholomew Anglicus (13th century). English scholar and Franciscan friar. His comprehensive Latin encyclopedia, *De Proprietatibus Rerum* (c. 1230–1250), was translated into all the European languages—into English by John de TREVISA—and remained in widespread popular use through the 16th century.

Bartholomew Fair (1614). A comedy by Ben JONSON. The enormous vitality of the fair, and not the plot, is the focus of attention. In this noisy and colorful play, Puritans and prostitutes, bumpkins and pickpockets, salesmen, rogues, gallants, and do-gooders rub shoulders and occasionally clash. Among the many incidents: a "reforming" but bungling justice constantly gets into trouble with the authorities and is carted off to the stocks; a foolish young man loses his fiancée through his own stupidity; and a crusading Brother loses a debate with a puppet on the morals of the theater. The exuberance of the play places it among Jonson's finest dramatic works.

Bartleby the Scrivener (1853). A long short story by Herman MELVILLE. The narrator, who operates a law firm on Wall Street, employs a scrivener, Bartleby, whose job it is to copy and proofread legal documents. Eventually he rejects these chores, stares blankly at an empty wall, and answers all entreaties with, "I should prefer not to." Unable to persuade Bartleby to work or to leave, the narrator moves to a new office, and the scrivener is taken to prison. Refusing all the privileges his former employer's vague sense of responsibility has bought for him, he dies of starvation.

Bartlett, John (1820–1905). American bookseller, editor, and publisher. Self-taught, Bartlett impressed the customers in the University Book Store in Cambridge, Mass. with the breadth of his learning. He was employed by Little, Brown & Co., becoming in time a partner (1865) and a senior partner (1878). His most famous book was the collection of *Familiar Quotations* (1855), which ran through nine editions in his lifetime. It has subsequently been revised and issued three more times. Bartlett also published *A New Method of Chess Notation* (1857), *A Shakespeare Phrase Book* (1882), and *A New and Complete Concordance to Shakespeare* (1894).

Bartók, Béla (1881–1945). Hungarian composer, pianist, and collector of folk songs. The folk songs of his native land provided material for a number of musical arrangements and scholarly treatises, but they also partly inspired the style of his original compositions, such as *The Castle of Duke Bluebeard* (1911), an opera with libretto by Balázs (see BLUEBEARD); *Allegro barbaro* (1911), a popular piano piece; a dance suite for orchestra (1923); *Music for String Instruments, Percussion and Celesta* (1937); *Mikrokosmos* (6 vols., 1926–1937), a famous pedagogical work for piano; string quartets; and piano concertos.

Bartolommeo, Fra. Real name, **Bartolommeo di Pagolo del Fattorino.** Familiarly, **Baccio della Porta** (c. 1472–1517). Italian painter. He worked in his native Florence, and at Venice and Rome. His style, strongly influenced by that of Leonardo da Vinci, is characterized by the employment of noble types and gestures, and by a relieflike clarity of outline. Among his masterpieces are the *Last Judgment*, the *Virgin and Child with Saints*, and the posthumous portrait of Savonarola, of whom he was an ardent follower.

Barton, Bernard (1784–1849). English poet known as the Quaker Poet. Barton is chiefly remembered as a close friend of Charles Lamb. A collection of his work, *Poems and Letters of Bernard Barton*, was published by his daughter Lucy in 1849.

Barton, Clara. Full name **Clarissa Harlowe Barton** (1821–1912). American philanthropist and founder of the American Red Cross. During the Civil War, although she had no official connection with any organization, she gathered and distributed supplies for the sick and wounded and ministered personally to casualties at the front. In 1882, as a result of her efforts, the U.S. joined the International Red Cross, and she became the first president of the American branch. Hers was the innovation whereby the Red Cross alleviates distress in peacetime disasters as well as in war.

Bartram, William (1739–1823). American botanist, explorer, and writer. He is best known for his *Travels Through North and South Carolina* (1791). His descriptions of tropical plants and animals were used as source material by a number of writers, including Wordsworth and Coleridge.

Baruch, Bernard M[annes] (1870–1965). American businessman and statesman. A graduate of the City College of New York, whose school of business administration is named after him, Baruch held several government posts connected with the war effort during World War I. In 1943 he became adviser to James F. Byrnes, war mobilization director, and was named U.S. representative to the UN Atomic Energy Commission in 1946. He is the author of *American Industry in the War* (1941), *A Philosophy for Our Time* (1954), *Baruch: My Own Story* (1957), and *Baruch: The Public Years* (1960). Long known as America's "elder statesman," he served for many years as a valued, if unofficial, adviser to presidents, his office a park bench opposite the White House.

Barzun, Jacques [Martin] (1907–   ). French-born American critic and educator. Dr. Barzun is now provost of Columbia University. He brings a scholarly point of view to the study of contemporary problems. Among his books are *Race: A Study in Modern Superstition* (1937), *Romanticism and the Modern Ego* (1943), *Teacher in America* (1945), *Berlioz and the Romantic Century* (2 vols., 1950), *God's Country and Mine* (1954), *The House of Intellect* (1959), and *Science: The Glorious Entertainment* (1964).

Basel, Council of (1431–1443). The last of the great reform councils of the 15th century. Beginning at Basel and continuing at Ferrara, Florence, and Rome, it brought about a temporary reunion of the Greek and Roman churches and further stimulated the REVIVAL OF LEARNING.

Bashō. See MATSUO BASHŌ.

Basic English. A simplified system of learning English from a selected vocabulary of the 850 most essential words. It was set up by C. K. OGDEN and propagated, also as an international auxiliary language, by the Orthological Institute, Cambridge, England. I. A. RICHARDS was one of its strongest advocates. Supporters claim that the system, which has no emotive words, encourages logical thought and expression; opponents say it destroys stylistic modulation, and they point to such examples as the translation into Basic of a famous phrase coined by Sir Winston Churchill: "Blood and eye-water and face-water."

Basile, Giambattista (c. 1575–c. 1632). Italian writer. He was the author of a collection of 50 stories in the Neapolitan dialect, called *Lo cunto de li cunti* (*The Story of Stories*). Because its storytelling is divided into five days and its general structure resembles that of the *Decameron,* it is also called *Il Pentamerone* (*The Pentameron*). Published posthumously in 1634, it is one of the first European books of folk tales, including such favorites as *Cinderella, Puss in Boots,* and *Beauty and the Beast,* which were later popularized by Perrault's *Contes des Fées* (1697). The Neapolitan was translated into Italian by Benedetto Croce and into English by Sir Richard Burton.

basilisk (Gr., *basileos,* a king). The king of serpents, a fabulous reptile, also called a COCKATRICE. It was alleged to be hatched by a serpent from a cock's egg. It was supposed to have the power of "looking any one dead on whom it fixed its eyes."

Bassani, Giorgio (1916–   ). Italian novelist and writer of short stories. His most noted novel, *Il Giardino dei Finzi-Contini* (1962), narrates the plight of an aristocratic Jewish family of Ferrara during the Fascist racial persecutions. His short stories are collected in *Cinque Storie Ferraresi* (1956). Bassani's writing describes his native Ferrara, and his fictional characters are seen as they experience the tensions of certain periods in history.

Bassanio. The impecunious and quick-witted friend of Antonio in Shakespeare's MERCHANT OF VENICE. He borrows 3,000 ducats from Antonio in order to woo Portia, a wealthy heiress of Belmont. In accordance with her father's will, Portia can marry only that one of her suitors who successfully chooses from among three caskets the one that contains her portrait. With the help of a hint from Portia, Bassanio rejects the gold and silver caskets and, selecting the leaden one, opens it to find "fair Portia's counterfeit."

Basse, William (c. 1583–c. 1653). English poet. A member of the SPENSERIAN SCHOOL, he was the author of *Sword and Buckler* (1602), *Three Pastoral Elegies* (1602), and *Great Britain's Sunset* (1613), an elegy on the death of Prince Henry, the elder son of James I.

Basselin, Olivier. A French song writer of the 15th century. He is especially known for his drinking songs.

Bassett, John Spencer (1867–1928). American writer and educator. He was a bold commentator on the Negro question, and, from 1906 on, a teacher at Smith College. Among his writings are *Anti-Slavery Leaders of North Carolina* (1898), *The Life of Andrew Jackson* (1911), and *Expansion and Reform* (1926).

Basso, Hamilton (1904–1964). American novelist. Basso is best known for *Sun in Capricorn* (1942), which depicts a demagogue thought to be modeled on Huey Long, and for *The View from Pompey's Head* (1954), a novel of the South and New York. His other works include *Courthouse Square* (1936), *The Light Infantry Ball* (1959), *A Quota of Seaweed* (1960), and the biography *Beauregard: The Great Creole* (1933).

Bastille (O. Fr., *bastir,* now *bâtir,* to build). A famous state prison in Paris. It was commenced by Charles V as a royal chateau in 1370, and was first used as a prison by Louis XI. It was seized and sacked by the mob in the French Revolution, July 14, 1789, a date that has become Bastille Day, which is celebrated much as is the American Fourth of July. The final demolition of the prison was commenced and the Place de la Bastille laid out on its site. A Bastille has come to mean a state prison for political offenders.

Bataille, [Felix-] Henry (1872–1922). French dramatist and poet. Bataille usually portrayed the psychological drama of morbidly passionate women in such plays as *Maman Colibri* (1904), *Poliche* (1906), *La Femme nue* (1908), and *La Vierge Folle* (1910).

Bates, Charley. In Charles Dickens's OLIVER TWIST, one of Fagin's pickpockets-in-training. He is always laughing uproariously and is almost equal in artifice and adroitness to the Artful Dodger.

Bates, H[erbert] E[rnest] (1905–   ). English writer of novels, novellas, and short stories. Bates is the author of *Fair Stood the Wind for France* (1944), *The Jacaranda Tree* (1948), *The Nature of Love* (1954), *When the Green Woods Laugh* (1960), and *The Day of the Tortoise* (1961). Always fond of a country setting, he uses it notably in *The Darling Buds of May* (1958) and in other novels about the comic, Rabelaisian farming family of Pop and Ma Larkin.

Bates, Miss. A character in Jane Austen's EMMA. An old maid, garrulous and a dreadful bore, she is nevertheless "a happy woman and a woman no one named without good will. . . . She loved everybody, was interested in everybody's happiness."

Bates, Ralph (1899–   ). English proletarian novelist. He described life in Spain and the Spanish civil war (1936–1939) in *Lean Men* (1934), *The Olive Field* (1936), and *Sirocco and Other Stories* (1939).

Bathsheba. In the Old Testament, the beautiful wife of Uriah the Hittite, sinfully loved by David who gave orders that Uriah, his captain, should be sent into the most dangerous part of the battle where he was slain. She was afterwards the wife of David and mother of Solomon (II Sam. 11:1–24).

baton. In heraldry, a bend or double line, from an upper corner of a shield to the opposite base point. When cut off at the ends, the baton indicated bastardy, as the bar or bend sinister was erroneously thought to have done.

Batrachomyomachia. See BATTLE OF THE FROGS AND MICE.

Battle Hymn of the Republic, The (1862). A patriotic song whose words were written by Julia Ward Howe. It was written in December, 1861, during the Civil War after a visit to a detachment of McClellan's army near Washington, D.C., when Dr. James Freeman Clark, a member of the party accompanying Mrs. Howe, urged her to write new words for the music of *John Brown's Body,* a song then popular with the Union soldiers. That night, towards dawn, Mrs. Howe awakened and found the words of a poem in her head, ready to march with the tune. She sprang out of bed, she relates, and without a light, in order not to awaken a baby who slept near her, wrote the *Battle Hymn.*

Battle of Britain. A term applied to bombing raids on Great Britain by German airplanes during World War II, especially during the summer of 1940.

Battle of Moytura, The. A 9th or 10th century Gaelic tale from the MYTHOLOGICAL CYCLE. It is a tale of battle between the TUATHA DÉ DANANN and the FOMORIANS. The principal figure of the Fomorians is BALOR whose evil eye is put out by LUG, thus turning the battle in favor of the Tuatha Dé Danann.

Battle of the Books, The (1704). A prose, mock-heroic satire by Jonathan SWIFT, written in 1697 and published with A TALE OF A TUB. It ridicules a literary squabble of the day as to the comparative merits of ancient and modern authors, touched off by Sir William TEMPLE's essay *Of Ancient and Modern Learning* and continued by Richard BENTLEY, among others. Swift showed his contempt for the entire controversy and, more broadly, for modern scholarship, criticism, and poetry by giving an account of a battle between modern and ancient books in St. James's Library, the outcome of which remains uncertain. The mock epic similes of the spider, signifying the moderns, and the bee, signifying the ancients, are among the most famous in all of literature.

Battle of the Frogs and Mice (Batrachomyomachia). A mock-heroic Greek poem of early date. War is caused by a frog's leaving his mouse friend to drown in the middle of a pond. When both sides are arrayed for battle, a band of gnats sounds the attack, and after a bloody battle the Frogs are defeated; but an army of land-crabs coming up saves the race from extermination, and the victorious Mice make their way home in terrible disorder. The name of the Mouse-king is Troxartes, probably a pun on *Tros,* a Trojan, and the poem is in many ways a burlesque of the *Iliad.* There is a 14th-century German skit on the same theme by G. Rollenhagen, a Meistersinger.

Battle of the Giants (1515). The battle of Marignano, in which Francis I of France won a complete victory over the duke of Milan and his Swiss allies. The battle is so called because the skill and obstinacy shown by the contenders on both sides.

Battle of the Herrings (Feb. 12, 1429). A battle during the siege of Orleans in the Hundred Years' War. The French attempted to intercept a supply of food being brought to the English by Sir John Fastolf, but the English repulsed them with barrels of herrings.

Battle of the Kegs, The (1778). A humorous ballad by Francis HOPKINSON. Composed to the tune of "Yankee Doodle," it tells of the alarm felt by the British over kegs charged with gunpowder which were floated down the Delaware.

Battle of the Lake Regillus, The. A ballad by Thomas Babington Macaulay in his LAYS OF ANCIENT ROME. Lake Regillus was the name of a small lake near Rome, traditional site of a Roman victory over the Latins (496 B.C.).

Battle of the Moat. A battle between Muhammad and Abu Sofian, chief of the Koreishites, before Medina. The Prophet had a moat dug before the city to keep off the invaders, and in it much of the fighting took place.

Battle of the Spurs. (1) A battle (1302) near Courtrai, Belgium, between a Flemish army and the French under Philip IV. The battle is so called because the victorious Flemings gathered from the field more than 700 gilt spurs worn by French nobles slain in the fight.

(2) A battle (1513) near Guinegate, France, between the English under Henry VIII and the French under Louis XII. The name is said to derive from the flight of the French cavalry.

Battle-Pieces and Aspects of the War (1866). A collection of poems by Herman MELVILLE. The tone of these 72 poems is elegiac rather than vengeful. Melville does not celebrate martial spirit in the best of his work; he mourns the early death of young men and the ruin of the country.

Baty, Gaston (1892–1952). French theater director and producer. His company, *Les Compagnons de la Chimère,* formed in 1922, performed such expressionistic plays as *Le Simoun* by Henri Lenormand and *Martine* by Jean Bernard. Noted for his splendid and imaginative settings, costumes, and lighting effects, Baty created drama in his *Théâtre Montparnasse* that joined stage magic and reality.

Baubo. In myth, an Eleusinian slave woman. In the allegory of Goethe's *Faust,* Part II, she symbolizes sensuality.

Baucis and Philemon. See PHILEMON AND BAU-
CIS.

Baudelaire, Charles Pierre (1821–1867). French
poet, one of the most important figures among the
French SYMBOLISTS. His typically DÉCADENT life was
ultimately tragic; his debauched, violent, and eccentric existence brought him to an early and painful death at the age of 46. In Paris he first began to
write as a critic and translator, introducing the
works of Edgar Allan Poe to Europe through translations that have since become French classics. Baudelaire published only a single volume of poetry, LES
FLEURS DU MAL. Stylistically, in its pure and carefully
classical form, his verse in some ways resembles that
of the Parnassians, but it is far more significant in
that it foreshadows the development of modern
poetry. Baudelaire's poems are filled with subtle
nuances and with almost painfully delicate sugges-
tiveness. The sensuous matter of a poem is conveyed
in beautifully striking images. He is famous for his
doctrine of correspondences, an exploration of the relationship of the various senses that lends a startling
newness to his work. Not only Baudelaire's technique but his subject matter—the beauty of the perverse or the morbid, and the probing analysis of
complex emotional states—has been reflected in 20th-
century poetry.

Bauhaus (*Ger.,* "house of architecture"). A
school of architecture and design, founded in Weimar, Germany, in 1919 by Walter GROPIUS. Its purpose was to unite the creative arts and the technology of modern mass production with 20th-century
architecture. In addition to more strictly architectural studies, courses in painting, handicrafts, the
theater, and typography were given by outstanding
artists, including Lyonel Feininger, Vassily Kandinsky, and Paul Klee. Functionalism, or the international style, in architecture and a number of examples of industrial design, such as tubular lighting
and steel furniture, were first developed at the
Bauhaus. In 1925 the school moved to the buildings
designed for it by Gropius in Dessau; three years
later, Mies van der Rohe became its director. During the rise of Hitlerian Germany, the Bauhaus came
increasingly under attack, and in 1933 it was forced
to close; but in Europe and the U.S., through its
masters and students, its great influence on modern
architectural thought continued.

Baum, L[yman] Frank (1856–1919). American
writer of children's books. He was the author of *The
Wonderful Wizard of Oz* (1900) and a subsequent
series of tales for young folk dealing with the mythical country of Oz. The later books did not match
the excellence of the first.

Baviad, The (1794). A biting verse satire by
William GIFFORD written to ridicule the DELLA-
CRUSCANS and their poetry. It was republished the
following year with a second part called *The Maeviad.* Bavius and Maevius were two minor poets
pilloried by Virgil in his *Eclogues,* and their names
are still used for inferior versifiers.

Bax, Clifford (1886–   ). English dramatist
and poet. Among his plays are *The Poetasters of
Ispahan* (1912), *The Rose without a Thorn* (1932),
and *Circe* (1948). His books include *Ideas and
People* (1936) and *Some I Knew Well* (1951).

Baxter, Richard (1615–1691). English divine.

A member of the Parliamentarian faction during the
English Civil War, he opposed the execution of
Charles I. He supported the Restoration, but suffered
imprisonment as a nonconformist under Charles II.
His *Saint's Everlasting Rest* (1650), a fervent appeal
for the Christian life, is a classic of English religious
writing.

Bayard (bay-colored). (1) The horse of the four
sons of Aymon. He grew larger or smaller as one or
more of the four sons mounted him. According to
tradition, one of his footprints may still be seen in
the forest of Soignes, and another near Dinant.

(2) The French name for Rinaldo's horse BAIARDO.

Bayard, Seigneur **de. Pierre du Terrail** (1473?–
1524). French knight and national hero, renowned
for his valor. Known as *le chevalier sans peur et
sans reproche,* he distinguished himself in the Italian
campaigns of Charles VIII, Louis XII, and Francis I.

Bayle, Pierre (1647–1706). French philosopher.
The son of a Calvinist minister, a convert to Catholicism and ultimately reconverted to Calvinism, he
held that neither faith nor reason can lead to certainty. He condemned superstition and advocated religious tolerance in *Pensées sur la comète* (*Thoughts
on the Comet,* 1682) and *Commentaire philosophique sur les paroles de Jésus-Christ* (*Philosophical
Commentary on the Words of Jesus Christ,* 1686).
The *Dictionnaire Historique et Critique* (*Historical
and Critical Dictionary,* 1697–1706), his most important work, treats its biographical, theological, and
philosophical subjects orthodoxly and reserves dissent
for the voluminous footnotes. Its directness pleased
the philosophes, and it influenced Diderot in the
compiling of the *Encyclopédie.*

Bay Psalm Book (1640). A metrical translation of the Biblical psalms by Richard MATHER,
Thomas Welde, John ELIOT, and 27 other ministers
of the Massachusetts Bay Colony. The book—the first
bound book printed in the English colonies—was
published by Stephen DAY in Cambridge in an edition of 1,700 copies. Its full title is *The Whole Booke
of Psalms Faithfully Translated into English Metre.*
(See title page on page 86.)

Bayreuth Festival. The musical festival at Bayreuth, Germany for the representation of Richard
WAGNER's operas.

Bazarov, Evgeni Vasil'yev. The central character of Ivan Turgenev's novel, FATHERS AND CHIL-
DREN. A representative of the young democratic generation rising in Russia about the middle of the 19th
century, Bazarov is a hard-headed materialist with
nothing but scorn for the old aristocratic order. He
is regarded as one of Turgenev's most successful
character portrayals.

Bazin, Hervé (1917–   ). French novelist,
grandnephew of René Bazin. In *Viper in the Fist*
(*Vipère au Poing;* 1947), he describes the psychological battle between a boy and his extraordinarily
hateful mother. His later novels describe various
kinds of love-hate relationships, usually in provincial
settings: *Head Against the Wall* (*La Tête contre
murs;* 1949); *Constance* (*Lève-toi et marche;* 1952);
In the Name of the Son (*Au nom du Fils;* 1960).

Bazin, René (1853–1932). French novelist. His
books concerned with the country life of rural
Catholics are *This, My Son* (*Les Noellet;* 1890),
Those of His Own Household (*Madame Corentine:*

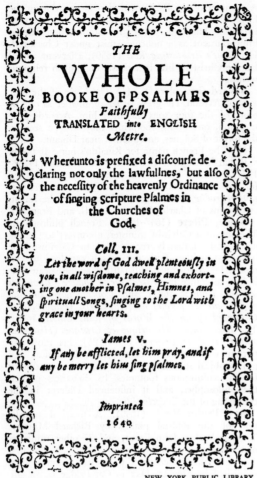

THE
VVHOLE
BOOKE OF PSALMES
Faithfully
TRANSLATED *into* ENGLISH
Metre.

Whereunto is prefixed a difcourfe declaring not only the lawfullnes, but alfo
the neceffity of the heavenly Ordinance
of finging fcripture Pfalmes in
the Churches of
God.

Coll. III.
*Let the word of God dwell plenteoufly in
you, in all wifdome, teaching and exhorting one another in Pfalmes, Himnes, and
fpirituall Songs, finging to the Lord with
grace in your hearts.*

Iames v.
*If any be afflicted, let him pray, and if
any be merry let him fing pfalmes.*

Imprinted
1 6 4 0

NEW YORK PUBLIC LIBRARY

Title page of the *Bay Psalm Book* (1640).

1893), and *Redemption* (*De toute son âme;* 1897). The problem of the desertion of the land for the cities is treated in *The Penitent* (*Donatienne;* 1903) and *The Coming Harvest* (*Le Blé qui lève;* 1907). Bazin discusses the political destiny of the disputed Alsace-Lorraine in *The Children of Alsace* (*Les Oberlé;* 1901).

BBC. See BRITISH BROADCASTING CORPORATION.

Beaconsfield, 1st earl of. See Benjamin DISRAELI.

Beacon Street. A famous street in Boston. It runs from Tremont Street along the Common and westward through the Back Bay district. Because of its residents, it became synonymous with wealth, social position, culture, and conservatism.

Bear, The. See Go DOWN, MOSES.

Beard, Charles A[ustin] (1874–1948). American historian. Having joined the faculty of Columbia University in 1904, Beard resigned in 1917 to protest the dismissal of two other professors for pacifism. Later he helped to organize the New School for Social Research.

Beard's best-known work is *An Economic Interpretation of the Constitution* (1913), in which he examined the backgrounds of the men who framed the U.S. Constitution and concluded that as property-owners they were interested chiefly in constructing a charter to protect their wealth. Beard, denied, however, that he was an economic determinist. He also wrote several books with his wife, Mary R[itter] Beard (1876–1958), notably *The Rise of American Civilization* (1927), *America in Midpassage* (1939), and *The American Spirit* (1942). In his later years, Beard became increasingly conservative and isolationist, expressing his views in such works as *American Foreign Policy in the Making* (1946) and *The Coming of the War* (1948). He also wrote *Economic Origins of Jeffersonian Democracy* (1915) and *The Economic Basis of Business* (1922).

Beardsley, Aubrey Vincent (1872–1898). English artist. Beardsley is known for his black-and-white drawings on fantastic and erotic subjects, chiefly as illustrations for books and periodicals representative of an English aesthetic movement during the 1890's.

Beatitudes. The sayings of Jesus in the opening verses of the SERMON ON THE MOUNT (Matt. 5:3–12), beginning "Blessed are the poor in spirit" and naming the virtues that make their possessor blessed.

beat movement. A part-social, part-literary phenomenon of the mid 1950's centered in Greenwich Village in New York, the North Beach district of San Francisco, and Venice West, a suburb of Los Angeles. Socially, the beat movement represented a rejection of middle-class values, of commercialism, and of conformity to a social norm; it advocated voluntary poverty, individualism, and release or "illumination" through jazz, sexual experience, and drugs. The term "beat" is meant to convey the usual connotations of worn-out and exhausted, but also to suggest beatitude or blessedness.

The chief spokesmen of the movement are Allen GINSBERG, Jack KEROUAC, Gregory Corso, William S. Burroughs, Lawrence Ferlinghetti, and Gary Snyder. Ginsberg was at least partially responsible for bringing the movement to national attention when his *Howl and Other Poems* (1956) was charged with obscenity and became something of a *cause célèbre*. Like Ginsberg, most of the beat writers are poets, and most work in loose structures and in the free-verse, incantatory tradition of Whitman. One of the more sensitive of the beat poets is Gary Snyder (1930–   ), whose poems of the Pacific Northwest, where he spent part of his childhood, are controlled and sometimes compelling. His books include *Riprap* (1959) and *Myths and Texts* (1960). Lawrence Ferlinghetti (1919–   ) is both poet and publisher (City Lights Books) and has published the work of many of the beat writers. His poetry includes *Pictures of the Gone World* (1955) and *A Coney Island of the Mind* (1958). Gregory Corso (1930–   ) tends to be provocative and impudent in his work, which is collected in *Gasoline* (1958) and *The Happy Birthday of Death* (1960).

Of the beat novelists the most widely known is Jack Kerouac, many of whose loosely constructed, picaresque works are set in beat environments. His books include *On the Road* (1957), *The Subterraneans* (1958), and *The Dharma Bums* (1960). William S. Burroughs (1914–   ), also a novelist, is known for *The Naked Lunch* (Paris, 1959; U.S.,

1962), a savage novel of the extremes of depravity experienced in dope addiction. Books on the beats include *The Beats* (1960), edited by Seymour Krim, and *A Casebook on the Beat* (1961), edited by Thomas Parkinson.

Beatrice. (1) The beloved of DANTE. He records the history of his love for her in LA VITA NUOVA, increasingly idealizing her until she becomes his spiritual inspiration. Thus, in the DIVINE COMEDY she is the symbol of divine revelation through faith, and guides him through Paradise. The original Beatrice was probably Beatrice Portinari (1266–1290), who married Simone de' Bardi.

(2) The high-spirited niece of Leonato in Shakespeare's MUCH ADO ABOUT NOTHING. Although she has sworn to have no man, she is attracted to Benedick, with whom she engages in a constant battle of wits. She is one of Shakespeare's most famous heroines.

Beattie, James (1735–1803). Scottish poet and philosopher. His opposition to the skeptical philosophy of Hume is set forth in his common-sense and orthodox reply, the *Essay on Truth* (1770). The essay contains what may be called an official doctrine of preromanticism. His best-known poem is THE MINSTREL; OR, THE PROGRESS OF GENIUS.

Beauchamp, Lucas. A character in William Faulkner's INTRUDER IN THE DUST and in his *Fire and the Hearth,* a short story in Go DOWN, MOSES. Lucas, the part-Negro grandson of Carothers McCaslin, is a dignified and independent man who lives on the borderline between the white and black worlds, thus causing a great deal of consternation among those white people who consider him arrogant and disrespectful.

Beauchamp, Mary Annette. See ELIZABETH, Countess Russell.

Beau Geste (1924). A best-selling novel by P. C. WREN about life in the French Foreign Legion. Beau Geste is the name the hero assumes.

Beauharnais, Joséphine de. Born **Marie Joséphine Rose Tascher de la Pagerie** (1763–1814). French empress. Born in Martinique, Josephine was first married to the vicomte Alexandre Beauharnais, who was executed as a counter-revolutionist in 1794. She had two children by this marriage, Eugène and Hortense, who became queen of Holland and mother of Napoleon III.

Josephine was a prominent figure in Parisian society when she met NAPOLEON BONAPARTE, then a comparatively obscure army officer whose reputation was on the rise. He fell passionately in love with her, as his letters testify, and they were married on March 9, 1796. At Napoleon's coronation she was crowned empress of France (Dec. 2, 1804). In 1809 Napoleon divorced his wife and empress as she had not provided him with an heir. She spent her last years in retirement at her lovely home in La Malmaison, occasionally receiving a visit from Napoleon.

Beaumarchais. Assumed name of **Pierre Augustin Caron** (1732–1799). French dramatist, courtier, and watchmaker to Louis XV. He is best known for his two comic masterpieces THE BARBER OF SEVILLE and *The Marriage of Figaro* (1784), both of which deal with the exploits of one of the world's cleverest servants, FIGARO. In addition to his

Mémoires (1774), he wrote three minor plays: *Eugénie* (1767), *Les Deux amis* (1770), and *La Mère coupable* (1792). He was also librettist of the opera *Tarare* (1787).

Beaumont and Fletcher. Beaumont, Francis (c. 1584–1616) and Fletcher, John (1579–1625), English dramatists. Their names are always linked together because of the plays on which they collaborated; these include such tragi-comedies as PHILASTER, *A King and No King* (1611), and THE MAID's TRAGEDY. In these and other plays, Beaumont and Fletcher foreshadowed and influenced Restoration drama. Other fruits of the collaboration include *The Nice Valour* (1606?), *Wit at Several Weapons* (1606), *The Captain* (c. 1611), *Love's Pilgrimage* (1615?), and *The Scornful Lady* (c. 1614).

In addition, Fletcher wrote a number of plays both alone and in collaboration with other dramatists. He was at his best when he could bring his lyric talents and sophistication to bear on such comedies of manners as THE WILD GOOSE CHASE, *The Scornful Lady* (c. 1614), *Wit without Money* (1614), and *Rule a Wife and Have a Wife* (1624). He also excelled at tragi-comedy, a form he and Beaumont had made their own. His unaided plays in this genre include *A Wife for a Month* (1624) and *The Humorous Lieutenant* (1619). Fletcher is the author of the famous pastoral play THE FAITHFUL SHEPHERDESS. In collaboration with Philip Massinger, he wrote *The Bloody Brother* (1615?), *The Tragedy of Sir John Van Olden Barnavelt* (1619), *The False One* (1620), and *The Double Marriage* (1620). He is said to have collaborated with Shakespeare on HENRY VIII and THE TWO NOBLE KINSMEN.

Beaumont also wrote several plays alone, two of which are noteworthy: THE KNIGHT OF THE BURNING PESTLE and *The Woman Hater* (c. 1606), a comedy of humors.

Beautiful Litigant, The. See François de BOIS-ROBERT.

Beauty and the Beast. A well-known fairy tale. Beauty saves the life of her father by consenting to live with the Beast. The Beast, being freed from a spell by Beauty's love, becomes a handsome prince, and marries her.

Beauvoir, Simone de (1908–   ). French novelist and essayist. She abandoned the teaching of philosophy with the publication of her first novel, *She Came to Stay* (*L'Invitée*, 1943), which, like THE MANDARINS, is important as a barely fictionalized document about Jean-Paul Sartre, his circle of leftist intellectuals, and their interpretations of EXISTENTIALISM. *The Blood of the Others* (*Le Sang des autres;* 1944) and *All Men Are Mortal* (*Tous les hommes sont mortels;* 1947) are novels that preach existentialist doctrines about human possibility in a world without God.

The long esssay *The Second Sex* (*Le Deuxième Sexe;* 1949) analyzes the difficult position of woman in the modern world; *The Long March* (1957) is a sympathetic description of Communist China. *Memoirs of a Dutiful Daughter* (*Memoire d'une jeune fille rangée;* 1958) is her autobiography to the age of 21; *The Prime of Life* (*La Force de l'âge*) continues it through the Resistance and records her close personal attachment to Sartre. Her other works include the essays in *Pyrrhus et Cinéas* (1944), the play *Les*

Bouches inutiles (1945), and the travel diary *America Day by Day* (1948).

Beaux' Strategem, The (1707). A comedy by George FARQUHAR. Thomas Aimwell and his friend Archer, the two beaux, having run through all their money, set out fortune-hunting and come to Lichfield as "master and man." Aimwell pretends to be very unwell, and as Lady Bountiful's hobby is tending the sick, she orders him to be removed to her mansion. Here he and Dorinda, daughter of Lady Bountiful, fall in love and finally marry. Archer falls in love with Mrs. Sullen, wife of Lady Bountiful's son Squire Sullen.

Beaver Coat, The (Der Biberpelz; 1893). A comedy by Gerhart HAUPTMANN. It recounts the machinations of the thieving washerwoman, Mrs. Wolff, and her poacher husband. She steals a beaver coat and then manages to escape detection by the stupid and officious magistrate, Wehrhahn. In fact, in the end she convinces him that she is the most virtuous and upright woman in the village.

Bebel, August (1840–1913). German socialist and member of the Reichstag. He was a very popular and influential leader of the German Social Democratic Party, which he and Wilhelm Liebknecht had helped to found in 1869, and was opposed to Bismarck's war policies.

Beccadelli, Antonio. See PANORMITA, I.

Beccari, Agostino (d. 1590). Italian poet. A native of Ferrara, he wrote the first Renaissance pastoral drama, the *Sacrificio* (1554). It influenced Tasso's *Aminta*.

Beccaria, Cesare (1735–1794). Italian economist and penologist. In his influential and humanitarian *Tratto dei Delitti e delle Pene* (1764) he opposed capital punishment and torture. He also was a contributor to the review IL CAFFÈ.

Becher, Johann Joachim. See PHLOGISTON.

Beck, Beatrix (1914–   ). French novelist, formerly secretary to André Gide. In *The Passionate Heart* (*Léon Morin, prêtre;* 1952) the narrator is converted by a beloved Catholic priest during the Occupation.

Beck, Mrs. **L[ily] Adams,** born **Moresby** (d. 1931). English popular romantic novelist and mystical Orientalist, who wrote under the pen names E. Barrington and Louis Moresby as well as under L. Adams Beck. As E. Barrington she wrote best-selling historical novels, including *The Divine Lady* (1924), about Nelson and Lady Hamilton, and *Glorious Apollo* (1925), about Byron.

Becker, Carl [Lotus] (1873–1945). American historian. A disciple of Frederick Jackson Turner and professor of history for many years at Cornell University, Becker published a number of important books, including *The Declaration of Independence: A Study in the History of Political Ideas* (1922), *Our Great Experiment in Democracy* (1924), *The Heavenly City of the Eighteenth-Century Philosophers* (1932), *Progress and Power* (1936), and *Modern Democracy* (1942).

Becket (1959). A drama by Jean ANOUILH about St. THOMAS À BECKET.

Beckett, Samuel (1906–   ). Irish-born French novelist and dramatist. A close friend of James Joyce, he settled in Paris in 1937. The novels *Murphy* (1938) and *Watt* (1944, pub. 1953) were written in English; in 1945 Beckett began writing first in French, then translating most of his own works into English. From 1947 to 1949 he wrote the novel trilogy composed of MOLLOY, MALONE DIES, and THE UNNAMABLE, and the play WAITING FOR GODOT. Later plays are ENDGAME, KRAPP'S LAST TAPE, *Happy Days* (1961), and *Play* (1963). *Krapp's Last Tape* and *Happy Days* were written in English.

Considered major works in the literature of the ABSURD, all Beckett's pieces present a comically pessimistic allegory of man's condition. Often the traditionally farcical gestures of the circus clown and the vaudeville actor are used to portray human weakness, frustration, and helplessness. Beckett's plays often parody past literary classics, or Cartesian rational thought. His characters typically advance through worsening stages of decrepitude or paralysis. Such human bonds as they form are the coupling of tyrant and victim, or at best of two pathetically groping dependencies. The only freedom they have exists within their own minds, where they invent characters whose existence becomes the proof of their own. Nevertheless, the freedom to invent is linked with the compulsive need to express, in the absence of anything to express or any meaningful language for expression. This need is the only force that maintains life in a world of progressive disintegration.

Other works include the English radio plays *All That Fall* (1957, translated as *Tous Ceux Qui Tombent*) and *Embers* (1960; translated as *Cendres*), and the French novel *Comment C'est* (1960).

Beckford, William (1760–1844). English man of letters. He is best known for VATHEK, AN ARABIAN TALE; an Oriental romance, it was written in French and translated into English probably by Samuel Henley in 1786. The associated *Episodes of Vathek* was translated from the French by Sir F. T. Marzials in 1912. Beckford's eccentric literary career and his penchant for the extravagant Gothic form in art and architecture (particularly his estate at Fonthill Abbey) place him in the tradition of Horace Walpole.

Beckmesser. The town clerk, a leading character in Wagner's opera, DIE MEISTERSINGER. He is the savage caricature of a contemporary critic named Hanslick, who had criticized Wagner's poetic accomplishments. The composer was dissuaded by his friends from naming the character Hans Lick.

Becque, Henri (1837–1899). French dramatist. Becque wrote plays that were naturalistic both in subject matter and in technique. In such dramas as *Michel Pauper* (1870), *Les Honnêtes Femmes* (1880), *Les Corbeaux* (*The Vultures,* 1882), and *La Parisienne* (1885), he presented realistic portraits of life, handicapped by a dearth of action and colorless characterization.

Bécquer, Gustavo Adolfo (1836–1870). Spanish poet. With the exception of some individual poems his works first appeared posthumously as *Rimas* (1871). Approximately 80 poems are to be found in this work, but though few in number, their quality established Bécquer's reputation as one of the major poets of the romantic era. With apparent simplicity, he created a delicately lyrical and deeply spiritual tone which infuses such poems as *Volverán las oscuras golondrinas* or *Del salón en el* *ángulo obscuro* and reappears in his prose treatments of legend, as in *Los ojos verdes.*

Beddoes, Thomas Lovell (1803–1849). English poet and playwright. An eccentric, melancholy man with a taste for the macabre, he wrote in the tradition of the Elizabethan poetic drama. He was a great admirer of Shelley and was in some degree influenced by him. His chief work, *Death's Jest Book, or The Fool's Tragedy,* was printed posthumously in 1850.

Bede. Called **the Venerable** [also **Baeda** or **Beda**] (c. 673–735). English historian and scholar. A monk at the Northumbrian monastery at Jarrow, he wrote over 30 works of history, grammar, science, theological commentary, etc. His best-known work is the Latin *Ecclesiastical History of the English People* (*Historia Ecclesiastica Gentis Anglorum;* 731), from the Roman invasion of England to 731, now a major source of historical and legendary information. It was translated into Old English under King ALFRED, and also provided the material for the early part of the ANGLO-SAXON CHRONICLE.

Bede, Cuthbert. See Edward BRADLEY.

Bedivere, Sir. In Arthurian legend, a dignitary of King Arthur's court. In Malory's *Morte d'Arthur* (c. 1469), it is he who, at the request of the dying Arthur, throws the sword Excalibur into the lake, and then bears the king to the barge that waits to carry him to AVALON.

bedlam. A lunatic asylum or madhouse. The word is a contraction of *Bethlehem,* St. Mary of Bethlehem being the name of a religious house in London that was converted into a hospital for lunatics in 1402. See TOM O' BEDLAM.

Bednyi, Demyan. Pen name of **Efim Alekseyevich Pridvorov** (1883–1945). Russian poet. A peasant by origin, Bednyi became the most popular Soviet poet in the early years of the regime, churning out topical verse in profusion. His pen name, Bednyi, means "poor" in Russian. His crude propaganda poetry earned him a prominent place in Soviet letters until 1936 when his opera libretto, *Epic Heroes (Bogatyri),* displeased the authorities because of its spoofing of the Russian epic tradition of folk poetry and of the introduction of Christianity to Russia. The old Bolshevik failed to realize that, at that point in history, the party viewed the epic tradition as a national treasure and the spread of Christianity as a progressive occurrence. Bednyi was reprimanded, and never regained his popularity.

Beebe, Lucius [Morris] (1902–   ). American journalist. Known also as a chronicler of café society, in 1952 he revived and became editor of the *Territorial Enterprise,* a weekly in Virginia City, Nev., for which Mark Twain once wrote. The colorful history of the paper is recounted in *Comstock Commotion, The Story of The Territorial Enterprise* (1954). He is also known for his books on trains, the latest of which is *Mr. Pullman's Elegant Palace Car* (1961).

Beecham, Sir Thomas (1879–1961). English conductor. Noted for the performance of works of Handel, Mozart, and Delius, whose works he championed, he is also remembered for his acid wit and pungent comments. He wrote an autobiography, *A Mingled Chime* (1944).

Beecher, Henry Ward (1813–1887). American clergyman, editor, and writer. The son of Lyman Beecher and brother of Harriet Beecher Stowe, he attended a school conducted by his sister Catherine in which he was the only boy among some 40 girls. He was graduated from Amherst College in 1834 and from Lane Theological Seminary in Cincinnati in 1837. An intensely emotional man, Beecher won a huge following with his sermons, in which he extolled the love of God and man; he also attacked slavery and advocated woman's suffrage and free trade. From 1861 to 1864 he was editor of *The Independent,* and from 1870 to 1881, of *The Christian Union.* In 1874 he was sued for damages by Theodore Tilton, who accused him of adultery with Mrs. Tilton. Although the jury could not reach a verdict and a council of Congregational churches found him innocent, Beecher's reputation was permanently damaged.

His *Seven Lectures to Young Men* (1844), a series of addresses on such topics as "Industry and Idleness" and "Gamblers and Gambling," was widely read. He also wrote a book of essays, *Plain and Pleasant Talk about Fruits, Flowers, and Farming* (1859) and *Norwood* (1868), a novel.

Beecher, Lyman (1775–1863). American preacher and author. Beecher became one of the outstanding preachers of his day; he was the father of a large family of which four children became famous: Catherine, Edward, Henry Ward, and Harriet Beecher Stowe. Opposed to Catholicism and the use of liquor, Beecher supported traditional Calvinism, and instituted drastic domestic discipline in his home. Even he, however, was accused of heresy, although he was finally acquitted by the synod. In addition to several pastorates in New England and New York, Beecher was president of the Lane Theological Seminary in Cincinnati (1832–1852). His sermons and articles were collected in *Works* (1852), and his *Autobiography* appeared in 1864. The Beecher household probably provided the details for Harriet Beecher Stowe's *Oldtown Folks* (1869).

Beelzebub. One of the "false gods" worshiped by the Israelites. He was originally a local Philistine god (or Baal) of Ekron, whose name meant "Lord of Flies." In this capacity, Baalzebub, as his name was properly spelled, probably had the power to send or protect from sickness, which was known to be carried by flies. Another Lord of Flies was Zeus Apomyios to whom the Greeks annually sacrificed at Actium. The Romans also sacrificed to flies in the temple of Hercules Victor. In the New Testament (Matt. 12:24) the Jews accuse Christ of driving out devils by the power of Beelzebub, called the Prince of Devils. In *Paradise Lost,* Milton makes Beelzebub one of the chief lords of Hell, next to Satan in power and rank.

Beer, Thomas (1889–1940). American writer. The author of three novels, *The Fair Rewards* (1922), *Sandoval* (1924), and *The Road to Heaven* (1928), Beer is better known for his book on Stephen Crane (1923) and for THE MAUVE DECADE, a study of the 1890's. *Hanna* (1929) dealt with the same decade. *Mrs. Egg and Other Barbarians* (1933) is a collection of short stories.

Beerbohm, Sir Max (1872–1956). English essayist and caricaturist. The half-brother of Sir Herbert Beerbohm-Tree, he was a brilliant figure in the London of the decadents and the Gay Nineties, contributing to the *Yellow Book*, and writing irreverent parodies (as in *A Christmas Garland*, 1895) and drawing brilliant caricatures under the signature "Max." His later works included the novel ZULEIKA DOBSON, essays such as those collected in the volume *In Defense of Cosmetics* (1922), and *Around Theatres* (1930). He remained a legend for his wit, brilliance, and powers of satire even after he had retired to live quietly in Italy during his middle and old age.

Beer-Hall Putsch (1923). A revolt in Munich led by Adolf HITLER and General Erich LUDENDORFF, who sought to overthrow the Bavarian government. Hitler was arrested and spent several months in prison, where he wrote MEIN KAMPF.

Beer-Hofmann, Richard (1866–1945). Austrian poet and playwright with neoromantic leanings. Active in Vienna and a friend of Hugo von HOFMANNSTHAL, he often treated Jewish themes, as in his plays *Jaakobs Traum* (*Jacob's Dream*, 1918) and *Der junge David* (*Young David*, 1933).

Beethoven, Ludwig van (1770–1827). German composer. A student of Haydn, he added the new, emotional qualities of romanticism to the tradition of formal precision that he inherited from the 18th-century masters of music. His nine symphonies are the most widely known among his works, although he wrote in a number of other musical forms, including chamber music, sonatas, and concertos. The most famous symphonies are the Third, called the EROICA, the Fifth (1808), the Sixth, or *Pastoral* (1808), and especially the Ninth, or *Choral* (1823). See FIDELIO.

Beggar on Horseback (1924). A fantastic comedy by George S. KAUFMAN and Marc CONNELLY, with music by Deems Taylor. A satire on business in the form of a dream, it is the story of a poverty-stricken composer, Neil McRae, who is persuaded to propose to a rich girl, Gladys Cady. In a dream he learns the horrible consequences of such a marriage; he is set to work in the Cady factory, murders the Cady family, and is thrown in prison. Upon awakening he is released from the engagement.

Beggar's Opera, The (1728). A ballad opera by John GAY, first produced at Lincoln's Inn Fields in London, a theater managed by John RICH. Very little escapes satiric treatment in this work; barbs are aimed at the elaborate, current Italian operatic style, at the prime minister Walpole, at marriage, at ladies and gentlemen, at lawyers, and at trade. The songs, many of them set to popular English and Scottish tunes, were arranged and scored by John Christopher Pepusch, who composed the overture.

The story concerns Peachum, a receiver of stolen goods. His biggest business is done with Captain Macheath, a highwayman with whom Peachum's daughter Polly has fallen in love. They marry secretly, and Peachum, now unable to use Polly in his business, gets his revenge by informing on Macheath and collecting the reward money. Macheath is taken off to Newgate prison which is run by the corrupt Lockit, who is in league with Peachum. Lockit's daughter Lucy falls in love with Macheath and helps him to escape. He is captured but saved from hanging by the mock intervention of a beggar and a player, since it would never do to let the fine

hero die. This happy ending satirizes the sentimental tragedy of the day. Bertold Brecht and Kurt Weill used *The Beggar's Opera* as the basis for their THREEPENNY OPERA.

Behan, Brendan (1923–1964). Irish playwright and wit. Born in Dublin at the time of civil strife in Ireland, Brendan Behan reflected in his life and works the zest, vitality, and macabre sense of humor of that tempestuous era. His early life was strongly influenced by the close association of his family with the Irish Republican Army, an association continued by Brendan who, at the age of 16, was arrested by English authorities for the possession of explosives with the intent of blowing up a battleship. He was found guilty and sentenced to three years in an English reform school, an experience he recounts with uninhibited gusto in the autobiographical *Borstal Boy* (1958). Behan subsequently served two more prison terms, the second of which resulted in his being deported to France. Having spent a good portion of his youth in jail, he utilized this experience as the basis of his two plays, *The Quare Fellow* (1956), a memorable exercise of "gallows humor," and *The Hostage* (1958). Despite his considerable reputation as a playwright, he was perhaps better known for his alcoholic exploits, accounts of which were featured prominently in the English and American press. For this reason he was dismissed by some critics as a buffoon, more interested in publicity than in playwrighting, and trading on a stereotyped conception of the wild young Irishman. For Behan, however, drinking was an essential expression of his approach to (and quarrel with) social reality. *Hold Your Hour and Have Another* (1964) is a collection of Behan's humorous pieces. A novel, *The Scarperer* (1964), was published posthumously.

Behemoth. The animal described in Job 40:15–24. If an actual animal were intended, it would seem to describe the hippopotamus; but modern scholarship tends to the opinion that the reference is purely mythological.

Behn, Mrs. Aphra (1640–1689). English novelist and dramatist. The first English female professional writer, she wrote a number of complicated comedies of intrigue, such as *The Rover, or The Banished Cavaliers: Parts I and II* (1677, 1680), *Sir Patient Fancy* (1678), and *The City Heiress, or Sir Timothy Treat-All* (1682). Her best-known novel is *Oroonoko, or the History of the Royal Slave* (c. 1678). She served Charles II as a spy in Antwerp.

Behrman, S[amuel] N[athaniel] (1893–   ). American playwright. He is especially known for his sophisticated comedies of ideas. *The Second Man* (1927) was his first play. Among his better-known later works are *Serena Blandish* (1928), a dramatization of a novel by the British novelist and playwright Enid Bagnold; *Biography* (1932), about a woman portrait painter and a journalist; *Rain from Heaven* (1934), one of the earliest anti-Nazi plays; END OF SUMMER; *Amphitryon 38* (1937), an adaptation from Jean Giraudoux; *Wine of Choice* (1938), on liberalism and its difficulties; No TIME FOR COMEDY; and *I Know My Love* (1949). Behrman is the author of two biographies: *Duveen* (1952), a work on the famous art dealer, and *Portrait of Max* (1960), a profile of Max Beerbohm. He has also written several film scripts. In 1958 he dramatized his autobiographical *The Worcester Account* (1954) as *The Cold Wind and the Warm.*

Being and Nothingness (L'Etre et le Néant; 1943). A long philosophical treatise by Jean-Paul SARTRE. Subtitled "an essay on phenomenological ontology," it is Sartre's major attempt to systematize his theoretical analysis of man's condition and consciousness which underlies EXISTENTIALISM. Postulating that for man existence precedes essence, he concludes that the very "nothingness" of man's essence in a world without God or meaning allows each person infinite potentialities in the shaping of his life, limited by the facts of the external world, but not by any *a priori* conditions of the so-called human nature.

Beith, Sir John Hay. See Ian HAY.

Bekenntnisse des Hochstaplers Felix Krull. See CONFESSIONS OF FELIX KRULL: CONFIDENCE MAN.

Bel. The supreme Babylonian god of the earth and atmosphere, called the god of lords. He is said to have created man and the universe and symbolizes male generative power. Bel is the same word as BAAL in Phoenician and Hebrew.

In the story *Bel and the Dragon,* an Old Testament Apocryphal book appended to the book of *Daniel,* Daniel exposes the trickery of the priest of Bel in Babylon and convinces the king that Bel is only an image and not an actual living deity.

Belarius. In Shakespeare's CYMBELINE, a noble and worthy lord banished by Cymbeline, king of Britain. He kidnaps Cymbeline's two sons and, using the name Morgan, raises them in a rustic region of Wales as his own sons. He is a spokesman for the pastoral life far from the deceit and intrigues of the court.

Belasco, David (1859–1931). American actor, theatrical producer, and dramatist. Belasco produced nearly 400 plays, many of them by native dramatists, and greatly influenced the American theater in the direction of greater emotionalism and more realistic stage properties. He developed the talents of many performers, such as David Warfield and Minnie Maddern Fiske.

His best-known plays include *The Heart of Maryland* (1895), a Civil War story inspired by Rose Hartwick Thorpe's poem *Curfew Must Not Ring Tonight!* (1867); THE GIRL OF THE GOLDEN WEST; and *The Return of Peter Grimm* (1911), a fantasy to which Cecil B. DeMille also contributed. Belasco also collaborated with other writers, notably with James A. Herne on *Hearts of Oak* (1879) and with John Luther Long on *Madame Butterfly* (1898).

Belcari, Feo (1410–1484). Florentine writer of sacred plays and a celebrated life of Giovanni Colombini. His *sacra rappresentazione* (mystery or miracle play) entitled *Abramo ed Isac* is one of the best of the genre, as well as the earliest by a known author.

Belch, Sir Toby. In Shakespeare's TWELFTH NIGHT, Olivia's riotous, bibulous uncle. He extracts drinking money from the foolish Sir Andrew Aguecheek by pretending to advance the latter's suit for Olivia.

Belfagor. A famous novella by Niccolò MACHIAVELLI about the adventures on earth of the archdevil Belfagor. He has been sent here from Hell to determine whether matrimony has been the principal cause of the damnation of its residents, as they all claim. In Florence, he poses as a Spaniard, Roderigo of Castile, and marries Onesta Donati, but the more he loves her the haughtier she becomes, until he is forced to flee from her. Later, faced with the possibility of living with her again, he prefers to return to Hell.

Belford, John. The libertine friend and correspondent of LOVELACE in Samuel Richardson's epistolary novel CLARISSA HARLOWE. Horrified by the rape of Clarissa, he reforms; he becomes Clarissa's executor and the editor of her voluminous correspondence.

Belgard. See FAERIE QUEENE, THE.

Belge. See FAERIE QUEENE, THE.

Belinda. The heroine of Alexander Pope's mock-heroic poem THE RAPE OF THE LOCK, who is described as the fairest of mortals:

> If to her share some Female Errors fall,
> Look on her Face and you'll forget 'em all.

Belinski, Vissarion Grigoryevich (1811–1848). Russian literary critic and journalist. Belinski gained prominence in literary circles for his *Literaturnye mechtaniya* (*Literary Reveries,* 1834), dealing with the development of Russian literature since the 17th century. He became the literary critic on the influential journal *Otechestvennye Zapiski* (*Fatherland Notes*), and, from 1846 to his death, on the *Sovremennik* (*The Contemporary*). The critical articles he wrote during these years, such as his annual surveys of Russian literature, were to have an overwhelming influence on the future course of Russian literary criticism. Belinski's ideas formed the theoretical basis for the NATURAL SCHOOL in Russian literature, which insisted that literature treat its subjects—especially poverty and exploitation of the people—realistically, with the aim of social reform. Although later critics exaggerated the social aspect of Belinski's literary doctrine, he was not entirely unaware of artistic quality. This fact is particularly evident in parts of the series of articles that he wrote from 1843 to 1846 on the work of Pushkin. But Belinski's fervent interest in social issues did occasionally blind him in regard to literary facts; he hailed Gogol as a great realist, and this erroneous label stuck to Gogol until the 20th century. Whatever confusion he introduced into Russian critical theory and practice, Belinski did, at least, serve Russian literature by insisting on its importance. He also encouraged the early efforts of some of Russia's finest writers, such as Lermontov, Gogol, Turgenev, and Dostoevski. Belinski's social bias has made him one of the ever quoted oracles of Soviet literary criticism.

Belinus. One of the kings in Geoffrey of Monmouth's HISTORY OF THE KINGS OF BRITAIN. According to the writer, Belinus founded CAERLEON, and, when he died, his ashes were put into an urn and then placed on top of a tower.

Belisarius (505–565). Byzantine general, responsible for the military success of Justinian I. Accused of conspiring against the life of the emperor, he was imprisoned in 562 and released in 563. Much later, an exaggerated version of his punishment made him a blind beggar, and this account was popularized by Jean-François Marmontel's philosophical novel *Bélisaire* (1767).

Belkin, Tales of (Povesti Belkina; 1830). A cycle of 5 short stories by Aleksandr PUSHKIN, with an introduction dealing with the life of the fictitious compiler of the tales, Ivan Petrovich Belkin. The tales are *Vystrel* (*The Shot*), *Metel'* (*The Snowstorm*), *Grobovshchik* (*The Undertaker*), *Stantzionnyi smotritel'* (*The Stationmaster*), and *Baryshnya-Krest'yanka* (*The Lady-Rustic*). The best known of the tales is probably *The Stationmaster,* which contains one of the first carefully drawn portraits in Russian literature of a character who is not a member of the nobility. The fictitious compiler of the tales, Ivan Belkin, whose rather commonplace life is recounted in the introduction, became famous as a literary character in his own right. Pushkin later wrote a prose fragment, *Istoriya sela Goryukhina* (*History of the Village of Goryukhin,* 1830), which purports to be an autobiography of Belkin. The extraordinary description of such an ordinary figure as Belkin is credited with being one of the first steps toward the realism which predominated in later 19th-century Russian literature.

Bell, Acton, Ellis, and **Currer.** The pseudonyms adopted by Anne, Emily, and Charlotte BRONTË respectively. In 1846 they published a volume entitled *Poems by Currer, Ellis, and Acton Bell.*

Bell, [Arthur] Clive [Howard] (1881–1964). English critic of art and literature. A member of the Bloomsbury group, he married Vanessa Stephen, the sister of Virginia Woolf. His major works of criticism include *Art* (1914), *Since Cézanne* (1922), *Proust* (1929), and *Account of French Painting* (1931). His son Julian (1908–1937), author of *Work for the Winter* (1936), a collection of poems, was fatally wounded while driving an ambulance for the Loyalists during the civil war in Spain.

Bell, Gertrude (1868–1926). English travel writer and authority on Arabia. Her books include *The Desert and the Sown* (1907). Her interesting *Letters* were published in 1927.

Bell, Laura. The heroine of William Makepeace Thackeray's PENDENNIS. As Mrs. Arthur Pendennis, she also appears in *The Newcomes* (1853–1855) and *The Adventures of Philip* (1862).

Bell, The (1958). A comic, philosophic novel by Iris MURDOCH. The story is set in a lay religious community attached to a convent and is concerned with the complex needs and self-deceptions that bind each member to the group. The bell, which represents the ideals of the community, precipitates the final scandal that forces the group to disband. The members regain their freedom, but not all are able to deal with it.

Bellamy, Edward (1850–1898). American novelist and reformer. He is best known for his popular utopian novel LOOKING BACKWARD: 2000–1887. Bellamy earlier wrote several romances, including *The Duke of Stockbridge* (1879), dealing with Shays's Rebellion, and two psychological studies, *Dr. Heidenhoff's Process* (1880) and *Miss Ludington's Sister* (1884). His short stories were collected in *The Blind Man's World and Other Stories* (1898).

Bellamoure, Sir. See FAERIE QUEENE, THE.

Bellay, Joachim Du. See Joachim DU BELLAY.

Bell, Book and Candle (1950). A play by John VAN DRUTEN. It is about a beautiful present-day witch who falls in love with a man and loses her powers as a sorceress.

Belle au bois dormant, La (**The Sleeping Beauty**). A charming nursery tale that first appeared in the CONTES DE MA MÈRE L'OYE of Charles PERRAULT. A magic spell confines a beautiful princess to a castle where she must sleep for 100 years. Only the kiss of a young prince brave enough to penetrate the dark wood which springs up about the castle can, and eventually does, awaken her from the enchanted sleep.

Belle Dame sans Merci, La (1819). A ballad by John KEATS. Its title and general theme are taken from an early French poem by Alain Chartier that was translated into English by Sir Richard Ros, and not by Geoffrey Chaucer, to whom it is often mistakenly attributed. Keats retains much of the medieval imagery of the French original.

Belle Plaideuse, La. See François de BOISROBERT.

Bellerophon or **Bellerophontes.** A grandson of Sisyphus. While living at the Argive court of King Proetus, he incurred the enmity of the queen, Antaea, by rejecting her advances. She falsely accused him to her husband, who sent Bellerophon with a letter to Iobates, the king of Lycia, his wife's father, recounting the charge, and praying that the bearer might be put to death. Iobates, unwilling to slay him himself, gave him many hazardous tasks (including the killing of the CHIMAERA), but as he was successful in all of them, Iobates made him his heir and gave him his daughter for a wife. Later Bellerophon is fabled to have attempted to fly to heaven on the winged horse Pegasus, but Zeus sent a gadfly to sting the horse, and the rider was overthrown. The revenge of Antaea is a familiar theme in folktale, found also in the stories of PHAEDRA and of Joseph and Potiphar's wife.

Bellerus. A giant, the legendary guardian of Lands End, England, once known as Bellerium.

Bell for Adano, A (1944). A novel by John HERSEY. It details the attempt of a sympathetic American officer to secure a new bell for an Italian village church which has been partially destroyed in World War II. Hersey won a Pulitzer Prize for the novel, which was later dramatized.

Bellini, Giovanni (c. 1430–1516). Venetian painter. The son of the artist **Iacopo Bellini** (c. 1400–c. 1470), both he and his brother **Gentile Bellini** (c. 1427–1507) were strongly influenced by their father's work and also by their brother-in-law, the painter Andrea MANTEGNA, during their early years at Padua. Within the context of the new medium of oil painting, however, Giovanni moved away from Mantegna's severity, towards a great richness and mellowness of color. His devoutly religious Madonnas and serene altarpieces also reveal a deep appreciation of landscape, and of the effect of light and color on atmosphere. His interest in light and color, when contrasted with the Florentine emphasis on line and modeling, was to become in the hands of Giorgione and Titian, his two greatest pupils, the glory of the Venetian school of painting. Among his masterpieces are *Christ Blessing,* the *Pietà,* and the *Agony in the Garden.*

His father Iacopo left few surviving works, but influenced his sons chiefly through his sketchbooks, which have entitled him to be called the initiator of the Venetian Renaissance in painting. His brother Gentile is noted for his ceremonial pageant pictures (especially the *Miracle of the Cross*) and for his portrait of Muhammad II, for whom he was court painter at Constantinople. Despite the Islamic prohibition of images, Gentile was cherished by the sultan because of his great artistry.

Bellini, Vincenzo (1801–1835). Italian opera composer. His works are characterized by elegance and lyrical charm. His principal operas are NORMA (his masterpiece), *I Puritani,* and *La Sonnambula.* Bellini was a close friend of Chopin, and his music is thought to have had some influence on the work of that composer.

Bellisant. The mother of the twins VALENTINE AND ORSON in French romance and the sister of the CAROLINGIAN king Pepin. Falsely accused of infidelity, she is banished to the forest for a while by her husband, Alexander of Constantinople.

Bello, Andrés (1781–1865). Venezuelan scholar and poet. As one of the most promising young men in Caracas, Bello studied classical literature, law, and philosophy; his interest in the natural sciences was stimulated by his meeting with Alexander von Humboldt, who greatly influenced him. In 1810, Bello was sent to England to seek support for the revolutionary junta of Caracas as part of a three-man delegation that also included Simón Bolívar. In England, where he remained for nearly 20 years, he began his famous edition of the *Poema del Cid,* based on the 12th-century text, and wrote his best-known poems: *Alocución a la Poesía* (1823), a declaration of literary independence in which he exhorts the Muse to abandon Europe for America, and *La agricultura de la zona tórrida* (1826), notable for its description of the plants of America in which realistic detail is combined with classical allusions. From 1829 until his death, Bello resided in Chile where he held important government posts, was a founder and first president of the University of Chile, and was the chief architect of the Chilean civil code. During this period, he published *La oración por todos* (1843), an adaptation of Hugo's *La prière pour tous* (1830) which is sometimes considered better than the original. His most enduring achievement, however, is probably his *Gramática de la lengua castellana* (1847), still the outstanding authority on Spanish grammar. See Domingo Faustino SARMIENTO.

Belloc, Hilaire. Pen name of **Joseph Hilaire Pierre Belloc** (1870–1953). English writer. Born in France, Belloc was a prolific author of light verse, essays, travel books, history, biography, works of Roman Catholic and conservative polemic, and fiction. Like G. K. Chesterton, with whom he had many attitudes in common, he engaged in a great deal of influential controversy attacking the ideas of H. G. Wells and Bernard Shaw; Shaw called the pair "the Chesterbelloc." He is now best remembered for his light, witty writing and for his verse for children. His humorous, mock-moral books for children include *The Bad Child's Book of Beasts* (1896), CAUTIONARY TALES, and *Cautionary Verses* (1941). His elegant, witty essays appeared in such volumes as *On Nothing* (1908) and *On Everything* (1909). *The Path to Rome* (1902) is a travel book strongly

flavored with humor and Catholic feeling; *Places* (1942) is a collection of short travel essays. He also wrote *History of England* (1925–1927) and biographies of Robespierre (1901), Wolsey (1930), and others. A collection of his letters was published in 1959.

Belloc Lowndes, Marie Adelaide. See Mrs. Belloc LOWNDES.

Bellona. In Roman mythology, the goddess of war and either wife or sister of Mars.

Bellow, Saul (1915–   ). American novelist. Best known for his picaresque ADVENTURES OF AUGIE MARCH, Bellow has a style that is rich, complex, and often comic. His first novel, *Dangling Man* (1944), is the story of a young man who is waiting to be inducted into the army. His second novel, *The Victim* (1947), deals with relations between Jew and Gentile. *Seize the Day* (1956) contains the excellent long story that entitles the volume, a play, and a shorter story, *Looking for Mr. Green.* The hero of *Henderson the Rain King* (1959) is a giant of a man with aspirations that match his bulk; the book departs from a realistically described American setting to a fantasy world where Henderson finds his destiny in a series of comic adventures that culminate in his becoming the rainmaker for a savage tribe. *Herzog* (1964), a novel about a college teacher, is highly autobiographical.

Bellows, George Wesley (1882–1925). American painter and lithographer. He is best known for his scenes of prizefights.

Bells and Pomegranates (1841–1846). A series of pamphlets containing poems by Robert BROWNING. They were issued by his publishers in an effort to popularize his work.

beloved disciple. John the evangelist, one of the 12 apostles.

beloved physician. Luke the evangelist. The beloved physician mentioned by St. Paul in *Colossians* (4:14) is presumed to be this Luke.

Beloved Returns, The (Lotte in Weimar; 1939). A novel by Thomas MANN. It is based on an imaginary incident in the life of Goethe: Charlotte ("Lotte") Buff, who was Goethe's sweetheart when he was young and who is thought to have been the model for the character Lotte in Goethe's THE SORROWS OF YOUNG WERTHER, comes to Weimar many years later and re-encounters the now old and established Goethe. Although in real life this incident never occurred, Mann has used it to make many intriguing explorations into Goethe's work and personality.

Beloved Vagabond, The (1906). A best-selling novel by William J. LOCKE. The vagabond is Paragot, a Bohemian philosopher and violinist, who wanders about Europe with a stray small boy (Anticot, who tells the story) and a homeless country girl.

Belphoebe. See FAERIE QUEENE, THE.

Belshazzar. The son of Nebuchadnezzar and the last of the Chaldaean dynasty, whose name means "may Bel protect the king." When his father fled the city of Babylonia after being defeated by Cyrus, Belshazzar assumed the throne in 539 B.C.; he was killed the next year in the sack of the city by Cyrus. According to scriptural narrative, he was warned of his coming doom by Daniel who interpreted the HANDWRITING ON THE WALL (Dan. 5:5–27).

Beltine (Cétshamain). May 1, one of the 4 great feast days of the ancient Celtic year. SAMAIN and Cétshamain (Beltine) are the feast days that divide the year into two halves, the hot and the cold seasons. See IMBOLC; LUGNASAD.

Belvidera. See VENICE PRESERVED.

Bely, Andrei. Pen name of **Boris Nikolayevich Bugayev** (1880-1934). Russian poet and novelist. One of the SYMBOLISTS, Bely, like Blok, was early in his career under the influence of the mystical ideas of the philosopher Vladimir SOLOVIOV. A student of philosophy and mathematics at the University of Moscow, Bely published his first poetry in 1901. He greeted the revolution enthusiastically with a long poem, *Christ Is Risen* (*Khristos voskrese;* 1918). Bely's best work is his prose, which includes the novels *The Silver Dove* (*Serebryanyi golub';* 1910), *Petersburg* (*Peterburg;* 1913), and *Kotik Letayev* (1918). Bely's prose style is rich, ornamental, and complex, often reminiscent of that of James Joyce in English. His later ideas had their source mainly in the anthroposophy of Rudolf Steiner, of whom Bely became a disciple. Bely left Russia in 1921, but returned in 1923, when he tried unsuccessfully to acclimate himself to the new society. His last years were spent writing his three volumes of memoirs which were published between 1929 and 1933: *On the Border of Two Centuries* (*Na rubezhe dvukh stoletii*), *The Beginning of a Century* (*Nachalo veka*) and *Between Two Revolutions* (*Mezhdu dvukh revolyutsii*). In his memoirs he included his reminiscences of Aleksandr Blok, his friend and fellow poet.

Bembo, Cardinal **Pietro** (1470-1547). Italian prelate and man of letters. Famed as a reformer and legislator of language and literature, he imposed classicist norms on the Tuscan tongue through his writings and inspired writers such as Petrarch to raise themselves to the level of classical models. Made a cardinal in 1539, he was a candidate for the papacy at the time of his death. His most famous works are the *Asolani* (1505), a group of dialogues on the nature of love which take their title from Asolo, the setting of the work, and the *Prose della volgar lingua* (*Essays on the Vernacular Tongue,* 1525).

Bemelmans, Ludwig (1898-1962). Austrian-born American writer and painter. Bemelmans' experiences in the hotel and restaurant business furnished material for his many entertaining stories and novels; he is also known for the charm of his books for children, especially *Madeleine* (1939). His work, written in a seemingly naïve though highly sophisticated style, was often illustrated by his own water colors and drawings. Among his many books are *Hansi* (1934), *My War with the United States* (1937), *Hotel Splendide* (1940), *Now I Lay Me Down to Sleep* (1944), *The One I Love Best* (1954), *The World of Bemelmans* (1955), *My Life in Art* (1958), and *Are You Hungry Are You Cold* (1960).

Benares or **Varanasi.** A holy city on the Ganges River in central India, famous as a place of pilgrimage.

Benassis, Dr. See COUNTRY DOCTOR, THE.

Benavente [y Martínez], Jacinto (1866-1954). Spanish playwright. Benavente was one of the leaders of Spanish drama during his day. He was a prolific writer whose works stress social satire or rural life. *Los intereses creados* (1907) is considered Benavente's masterpiece and is reminiscent of the Italian *commedia dell' arte*. His other well-known plays include *La mal querida* (*The Passion Flower,* 1913) and *Señora ama* (1908). In 1922 he was awarded the Nobel Prize for literature.

Ben Bolt. A popular song by Thomas Dunn English. It was first published in *The New Mirror* (1843). The heroine of George du Maurier's novel, *Trilby,* sings the song while hypnotized by Svengali. Several tunes have been used for English's lyrics, which begin "Oh, don't you remember sweet Alice, Ben Bolt?"

Benchley, Robert [Charles] (1889-1945). American drama critic, essayist, humorist, actor, and screenwriter. Highly successful in movies and on the radio, Benchley was admired for his short film *How to Sleep* (1935) and his famous sketch, *The Treasurer's Report* (1930). In his essays, Benchley portrayed his life as a series of frustrations and humiliations; his humor is based on the situation of the average American man, faced with the complexities of 20th-century life. Among his works are *20,000 Leagues under the Sea, or, David Copperfield* (1928), *From Bed to Worse* (1934), *My Ten Years in a Quandary* (1936), *Benchley Beside Himself* (1943), and the posthumous *Chips Off the Old Benchley* (1949). His son, Nathaniel, wrote a biography of him in 1955.

Benda, Julien (1867-1956). French philosopher and essayist. A violent defender of strict rationalism, he wrote a controversial attack on Bergsonism in 1912 and condemned the esthetics of contemporary literature for sensational emotionalism in *Belphégor* (1918). Benda is best known, however, for his attack on THE TREASON OF THE INTELLECTUALS. *The Yoke of Pity* (*L'Ordination;* 1912) is a novel.

bend sinister. In heraldry, two parallel lines from the upper right hand corner of a shield to the opposite base point. It was erroneously supposed to indicate bastardy. See BATON.

Benedick. In Shakespeare's MUCH ADO ABOUT NOTHING, a self-assured, cynical, and witty young nobleman of Padua. Although he has forsworn women, he constantly engages in repartee with the sharp-tongued Beatrice, with whom he is at last united through the conspiracy of their friends.

Benediktsson, Einar (1864-1940). Icelandic poet. Benediktsson was the leader of a nationalist movement that reacted against the bleakness and pessimism of the naturalist school. Active in political affairs, he published the newspaper *Dagskrá* for several years. In his verse, too, he expressed both optimism and patriotism, as well as his mystic beliefs. His volumes of poetry include *Sögur og Kvoeoi* (1897), *Hrannir* (1913), *Hvammar* (1930), and *Ljóomoeli* (3 vols., 1945).

Benelli, Sem (1877-1949). Italian dramatist. His best-known play is *La Cena delle Beffe* (1909), a melodrama set in Renaissance Florence, which was produced (1919) in New York as *The Jest* with John and Lionel Barrymore. He also wrote *La Maschera di Bruto* (1909) and *L'Amore dei Tre Re* (1910), which was the source of Italo Montemezzi's opera (1913) of the same name.

Beneš, Eduard (1884–1948). Czechoslovak statesman. Named foreign minister of Czechoslovakia when the republic was created in 1918, Beneš served for 17 years and was elected president in 1935. He held the post again after World War II, but resigned after the Communist coup d'etat of 1948.

Benét, Laura (1884?–   ). American poet and biographer. The sister of William Rose and Stephen Vincent BENÉT, she has published several books of verse, including *Fairy Bread* (1921) and *Is Morning Sure?* (1947), as well as a series of biographies for young people. Among her later books are *Coleridge, Poet of Wild Enchantment* (1952) and *Famous American Humorists* (1959).

Benét, Stephen Vincent (1898–1943). American poet and short-story writer. Known for his interest in fantasy and American themes, Benét also used his literary gifts as a novelist and writer for radio. His early collections of verse include *Five Men and Pompey* (1915), *Young Adventure* (1918), *Heavens and Earth* (1920), *The Ballad of William Sycamore* (1923), and *Tiger Joy* (1925). *King David* (1923) is a narrative poem about the biblical ruler. Benét's most famous poem, JOHN BROWN'S BODY, won a Pulitzer Prize. In *Litany for Dictatorships* (1935), he attacked totalitarian states. *Western Star* (1943), the first part of an American epic left incomplete at his death, was awarded a posthumous Pulitzer Prize.

Benét's first collection of short stories was *Thirteen O'Clock* (1937), which includes THE DEVIL AND DANIEL WEBSTER and *Sobbin' Women*. Other stories were collected in *Tales Before Midnight* (1939) and *The Last Circle* (1946). His novels include *Spanish Bayonet* (1926) and *James Shore's Daughter* (1934). Interested in the dramatic possibilities of radio, he wrote *They Burned the Books* (1942) and *A Child Is Born* (1942), a retelling of the birth of Jesus.

Benét, William Rose (1886–1950). American poet, critic, and editor. The elder brother of Stephen Vincent Benét, he wrote much poetry, collected in such volumes as *Merchants from Cathay,* (1913), *Starry Harness* (1933), *The Stairway of Surprise* (1947), and *The Spirit of the Scene* (1951). *Rip Tide* (1932) is a novel in verse. His verse autobiography, *The Dust Which Is God* (1941), won a Pulitzer Prize. One of the founders of the *Saturday Review of Literature,* he served on its editorial board and conducted the column of literary miscellany called "The Phoenix Nest" for many years. He was the original editor of *The Reader's Encyclopedia.*

Bengal Lancer. See Francis YEATS-BROWN.

Bengodi. (*It.,* "enjoy well.") The name of a "land of Cockaigne" in Boccaccio's DECAMERON (VIII, 3). This is the land where "they tie the vines with sausages, where you may buy a fat goose for a penny and have a gosling in the bargain; where there is also a mountain of grated Parmesan cheese, and people do nothing but make cheesecakes and macaroons." It occurs in the tale of *Calandrino and the Heliotrope,* and is described to Calandrino by his friends, who are trying to persuade him that he will find precious stones there. But since it is "farther away even than the Abruzzi," he decides not to go.

Bengtsson, Frans Gunnar (1894–1954). Swedish poet, historian, novelist, and essayist. *Legenden om Babel* (1925) is a collection of poems that express in polished verse a love of the heroic. His most famous work, the novel *Röde Orm* (*Red Orm,* 1943; *The Long Ships,* 1954) also deals with the heroic: it is a lusty and amusing account of Viking exploits.

Ben-Hur: A Tale of the Christ (1880). A novel by Lew WALLACE. The book grew out of a railroad car discussion that the author had with Robert Ingersoll, the free thinker. They discussed the divinity of Christ, and Wallace decided to study the life and times of Jesus. The book centers around Judah Ben Hur, a young aristocratic Jew, who is falsely accused of seeking to murder the Roman governor of Palestine. Sent to the galleys, he escapes, becomes a Roman officer, engages in a climactic chariot race with his betrayer, the false friend Messala, and is finally converted to Christianity. The book, highly popular, has been staged and twice made into a motion picture.

Benito Cereno (1856). A short story by Herman MELVILLE, collected in his volume PIAZZA TALES. Benito Cereno, the captain of a slave ship, appears to be in command; in reality, he is the prisoner of the slaves, who are led by Babo, a Senegalese posing as Cereno's valet. The story is narrated by Captain Amasa Delano, an innocent who can only suspect the presence of evil. Finally, the conspirators are undone, Cereno dies, and Babo is executed.

Benivieni, Girolamo (1453–1542). Florentine poet, member of the Medici circle. Benivieni is the author of a famous Renaissance poem, the *Canzone dell'Amor Divino* (*Song of Divine Love*), which summarizes the Platonic love theory of Ficino. The poem was the subject of an extensive commentary by Pico Della Mirandola, and influenced such writers as Bembo, Castiglione, and Spenser.

Benjamin. In the Old Testament, the youngest and favorite son of Jacob and Rachel, whose name means "son of the right hand." When, during the famine, Jacob sent his sons forth from Canaan to buy bread, he refused to let Benjamin go "lest peradventure mischief befall him" (Gen. 42:4). Jacob's son Joseph who was in charge of the granaries in Egypt told his brothers, without revealing his own identity, that they must bring Benjamin with them if they returned for more corn. When they did so, Joseph feasted them and gave them grain, but sent word after them that his silver cup was missing; when search was made it was found in Benjamin's sack, where it had been placed by Joseph's orders. Joseph then disclosed his identity and arranged for his father's migration to Egypt.

Benjamin's descendants formed the tribe of Benjamin; they were stalwart warriors and defenders of freedom. Israel's first king, Saul, came from this tribe as did the Apostle Paul.

Benn, Gottfried (1886–1956). German poet, short-story writer, and essayist. He was strongly influenced by Nietzsche. His early collections of expressionistic verse, *Morgue* (1912), *Fleisch* (*Flesh,* 1916), and *Schutt* (*Rubble,* 1919), are the best known.

Bennet, Elizabeth. See PRIDE AND PREJUDICE.

Bennett, [Enoch] Arnold (1867–1931). English novelist, playwright, and journalist. His finest novels are THE OLD WIVES' TALE and CLAYHANGER. Both are set in the industrial district in the English midlands where he was born, known as Five Towns in his novels. A humble clerk with literary ambitions, Bennett went to London at 21 (his autobiographical *A Man from the North* [1898] describes this period). He became a successful journalist, editing a woman's magazine, writing "Pocket Philosophies" such as *How to Live on 24 Hours a Day* (1908), and doing influential reviewing. In 1903 he went to live in Paris for some years and married a Frenchwoman. Influenced by the writings of Emile Zola, Bennett wrote naturalistic novels, studies of how his characters are the creatures of their environment. Among these are his two best novels, and ANNA OF THE FIVE TOWNS, *Whom God Hath Joined* (1906), *Hilda Lessways* (1911), *These Twain* (1915), *Riceyman Steps* (1923), *Lord Raingo* (1926), and *Imperial Palace* (1930). Among his collections of short stories are *Tales of the Five Towns* (1905) and *The Matador of the Five Towns* (1912). His successful comic novels are *A Great Man* (1904), BURIED ALIVE, THE CARD (*Denry the Audacious* in the U.S.), and *Mr. Prohack* (1922). He wrote, with Edward Knoblock, *Milestones* (1912), a successful drama about the rise of an industrial family. Bennett also wrote deliberate commercial fiction, such as *Sacred and Profane Love* (1905), for he wanted—and achieved—success, a famous-actress mistress, and a yacht.

Like the naturalistic novelists who were his contemporaries, his friend H. G. Wells and John Galsworthy, Bennett was attacked by the modernist Virginia Woolf, and is now somewhat neglected. His best work is distinguished by his rendering of the passage of time, his accurate descriptions of ordinary, apparently quite dull and unromantic lives, and his sympathetic portrayals of women.

Bennett, James Gordon (1795–1872). Scottish-born American newspaper editor. Bennett came to America in 1819 and settled finally in New York City, serving on the staff of *The Enquirer* and *The Courier*. On May 6, 1835, he founded the *New York Herald* and remained its editor until his retirement in 1867. It was an aggressive, widely read paper, notable for its extensive news coverage and lively editorials. According to Gerald W. Johnson, Bennett "filled his paper with vulgarity, vituperation, and scandal, but he got the news." His son, James Gordon Bennett (1841–1918), succeeded him as editor in 1867. The younger Bennett sent Stanley to Africa to find Livingstone and supported other expeditions to Africa and the Arctic. He was the founder of the Paris edition of the *Herald* (1887).

Benoît de Sainte-Maure or **Sainte-More** (12th century). Medieval French poet, attached to the court of Henry II of England from 1154 to 1189. He is said to be the author of the *Roman de Troie* (*Romance of Troy*, c. 1160), which gives the history of the Trojan War the atmosphere of medieval feudalism and the chivalric code; this seems to be the first appearance of the story of TROILUS and Cressida (here called Briseida). Benoît is also considered the author of the *Chronicle of the Dukes of Normandy* to 1135.

Benserade, Isaac de (1613–1691). French poet. A member of the Académie Française, Benserade specialized in writing masques and ballets, the popular court entertainments of his day. His sonnet on Job was so admired that a dispute arose whether this or Voiture's sonnet *Uranie* was better. Corneille had to call for an end to the quarrel, which had divided the literary world into *Jobelins* and *Uraniens.*

Benson, A[rthur] C[hristopher] (1862–1925). English scholar, best known as the author of volumes of essays, including *From a College Window* (1906). He wrote the words of the song *Land of Hope and Glory*. His father was archbishop of Canterbury; his brother, E[dward] F[rederic] Benson (1867–1940), wrote light novels, including *Dodo* (1893), which was supposed to be based on the character of the future Lady Oxford and created a sensation; a third brother, R[obert] H[ugh] Benson (1871–1914), became a Roman Catholic and wrote historical and contemporary novels with a strongly religious tone.

Benson, Sally (1900–   ). American short-story writer. She is the author of *Junior Miss* (1941), a best seller which was later made into a highly successful play, a movie, and a radio series. Among her other books are *People Are Fascinating* (1936), *Meet Me in St. Louis* (1942), and *Women and Children First* (1944).

Benson, Stella (1892–1933). English novelist and adventurous traveler. Her novels include *Tobit Transplanted* (1931), a retelling of the apocryphal story in a Korean setting.

Bentham, Jeremy (1748–1832). English philosopher of the utilitarian school. His social and philosophical ideas are to be found in his *Fragment on Government* (1776) and *Introduction to Principles of Morals and Legislation* (1789). His watchword was "the greatest good for the greatest number," and he tried to work out scientifically on a quantitative scale the values of pleasure and pain in moral motivation. See UTILITARIANISM.

Bentleman, Lawrence (1942–   ). Indian poet writing in English. He has worked for a commercial firm, a newspaper in Calcutta, and is currently a columnist for a New Delhi weekly. *Graffiti* (1962) is a collection of poems.

Bentley, E[dmund] C[lerihew] (1875–1956). English writer of detective stories and originator of a form of humorous biographical verse called CLERIHEWS. TRENT'S LAST CASE is a classic of detective fiction.

Bentley, Phyllis (1894–   ). English regional and historical novelist. Her Yorkshire novels include *The Inheritance* (1932) and *The House of Moreys* (1953). *O Dreams, O Destinations* (1962) is an autobiography.

Bentley, Richard (1662–1742). English classical scholar. His *Dissertation on the Letters of Phalaris* (1699) is one of the first studies to use philology as a test of authenticity. It sprang from a controversy (1695–1699) with Charles Boyle which Jonathan Swift continued in the BATTLE OF THE BOOKS. Swift, like other literary men of the day, saw nothing but modern pedantry in Bentley's painstaking scholarship. Bentley's Homeric studies are fragmentary, but historically important for showing that early Greek had a sound, later lost, which was represented by the letter *Digamma* and pronounced like the English *w*.

Benton, Thomas Hart (1782–1858). American statesman. From 1821 to 1851, Benton represented Missouri in the U.S. Senate, where he strongly favored Western interests. A vigorous supporter of Andrew Jackson, he fought the U.S. Bank, and was finally defeated for re-election because he championed the Union against the South. He wrote a well-known autobiography, *Thirty Years View* (2 vols., 1854, 1856). His daughter Jessie married John C. Frémont.

Benton, Thomas Hart (1889–   ). American painter and muralist. Born in Missouri, he became a leading advocate of regionalism, depicting in his work a contemporary view of life in the Middle West. He inveighed against all the European movements and is the author of *An Artist in America* (1937), which he also illustrated.

Benu. The Egyptian prototype of the Greek phoenix. It was a heronlike bird, the embodiment of Ra, worshiped under the composite form of Osiris with the head of a bird.

Benvolio. In Shakespeare's ROMEO AND JULIET, a nephew of Montague and Romeo's friend. Hoping that Romeo will be cured of his infatuation for the fair Rosaline, Benvolio persuades him to attend the Capulets' ball, so that he can compare her with the other beauties present. On several occasions he tries unsuccessfully to avert strife between the feuding Montagues and Capulets.

Beolco, Angelo (1502–1542). Italian dramatist. He is also known as *Ruzzante* (the Howler), after the chief peasant character in his dramas. They were performed by one of the first acting companies organized in Italy. The best of his seven comedies are the *Moschetta* (*Little Mosquito*, 1520) and the *Fiorina* (*Florin*, 1521).

Beowulf (early 8th century?). An Old English (Anglo-Saxon) epic of almost 3200 lines in ALLITERATIVE VERSE. It is the earliest extant written composition of such length in English, and indeed in all Teutonic literature. Its content was based on Norse legends merged with historical events of the early sixth century in Denmark; this oral tradition was carried to England by Danish invaders of the mid-sixth century, fused with the Christianity they absorbed there, and finally written down by a single but unknown poet shortly before or after 700.

Hrothgar, king of the Danes on the island of Zealand, has built the mead hall Heorot for feasting his warriors, but they abandon it because of the murderous ravages of the monster GRENDEL. Beowulf, nephew of King Hygelac of the Geats (on the coast of southern Sweden facing the Danes), comes with 14 warriors to challenge the monster, and is received by Hrothgar at a great feast. The Geats spend the night in the mead hall; Grendel comes, and in a mighty fight Beowulf with his bare hands wrenches the monster's arm from his shoulder, and mounts it as a trophy. The next day Hrothgar gives a triumphant feast in Heorot; but as they sleep that night, Grendel's mother comes to avenge her son, slaying a Dane and stealing the severed arm. Beowulf plunges into the demon-infested pond where the monsters live and wrestles with Grendel's mother. His own sword Hrunting proves of no use, but he

A page from a manuscript of *Beowulf*.

THE BRITISH MUSEUM

finds a sword crafted by the giants and beheads her. Then he severs the head of Grendel, who has died there of his wound, to bring back as a trophy. He and his Geats receive many gifts from Hrothgar when they leave, and from Hygelac when they reach home. Hygelac and his son both die in wars with the Swedes, so that Beowulf eventually becomes king of the Geats, ruling well for 50 years. Then a fire-breathing dragon, angered because a man has stolen a goblet from his hoarded treasure, begins to ravage the land. Beowulf goes out to slay it, but all his warriors fearfully desert him, except young Wiglaf. Although together they kill the dragon, Beowulf receives his own death-wound. Wiglaf berates his companions for cowardice, and Beowulf is given a stately burial.

The story is not told chronologically, however; events are often anticipated in prophecy or interpolated later in retrospect. Long speeches of celebration or lamentation, long descriptions of the feasts, and digressions into genealogy and history all give a colorful picture of life at that time. Memorable episodes not actually a part of the main action include Unferth's insult to Beowulf at the first feast and Beowulf's answering description of his swimming contest with Breca, and the tale of Finn and Hildeburh, sung by a minstrel at the second feast (see FINNSBURG).

Beppo (1818). A satirical poem by Lord BYRON. Beppo is the husband of Laura, a Venetian lady. He is taken captive at Troy, becomes a Turk, joins a band of pirates, grows rich, and, after several years' absence, returns to his native land, where he discovers his wife at a carnival ball with her *cavaliero servente*. He makes himself known to her, and they live together again as man and wife.

Béranger, Pierre Jean de (1780–1857). French folk poet. His songs, variously sentimental or witty, ribald or light-heartedly gay, assured him of fame during his lifetime. In such songs as *Le Roi d'Yvetot* (1813) he gave expression to popular feeling after the Napoleonic Wars when the French people, weary of the quest for glory, longed instead for comfort and for peace. His song *Le Marquis de Carabas* (1816) satirized the vain pretensions of nobles during the Bourbon restoration. Although *Chansons inédites* (1828), his collection of political verse celebrating Napoleon Bonaparte, won him a prison term, it earned him staunch popular approval.

Berceo, Gonzalo de (c. 1180–c. 1246). Earliest Spanish poet known by name. A secular priest at the Benedictine monastery of San Millán de la Cogolla, Berceo was a prolific writer of pious religious verse in the vernacular. His best-known poems are works dedicated to the Virgin, notably *Milagros de Nuestra Señora,* and lives of saints, such as *Vida de Domingo de Silos.* See MESTER DE CLERECÍA.

Berchtesgaden. A district in Bavaria, site of Hitler's country house. It was razed by Allied bombings in 1945.

Bercilak. See SIR GAWAIN AND THE GREEN KNIGHT.

Berdyayev, Nikolai Aleksandrovich (1874–1948). Russian religious philosopher. A Marxist in his youth, Berdyayev turned to religious views and played a large part in the renaissance of religious and philosophical thought in Russian intellectual life early in the 20th century. His writings, mainly aphoristic in form, often deal with the problem of freedom and man's relationship to the world in the light of this problem. His works include *The Spiritual Crisis of the Intelligentsia (Dukhovnyi krisis intelligentziya;* 1910), *The Philosophy of Freedom (Filosofiya svobody;* 1911), *The Meaning of Creativity (Smysl tvorchestva;* 1916), and studies of Dostoevski and of Russian religious and philosophical thinkers.

In 1922, with a number of other Russian intellectuals, Berdyayev was expelled from the Soviet Union. He went to Berlin and then to Paris in 1925 where he continued to write, edited a journal (*The Way;* Russian *Put'*), and worked for the Y.M.C.A. Press, a publisher of religious and philosophical works.

Bérénice (1670). A tragedy by Jean RACINE. The emperor Titus, newly acceded to the throne, learns that the Romans object to his marrying the foreigner Bérénice, queen of Palestine. Despite his love for her, he obeys the mandate of his people, and the lovers separate forever. Literary tradition holds that the duchesse d'Orléans arranged for Racine and Corneille to write plays on this subject, each in ignorance that the other was doing the same. In the resulting contest, Racine's play was judged the better. See TITE ET BÉRÉNICE.

Berenice (1835). A tale by Edgar Allan POE. Egaeus is in love with his epileptic cousin, Berenice.

Fascinated by her teeth, he draws them when she is presumed dead, after a fit. Berenice returns to life in a comic-horror climax.

Berenson, Bernard (1865–1959). Lithuanian-born American art connoisseur. A longtime resident of Italy, he was recognized by his generation as the greatest authority on Italian art from the 13th to the 17th century. Collectors and specialists alike have relied on his judgment. His *Italian Painters of the Renaissance* and other books and monographs remain classics in their field. *I Tatti,* his villa near Florence, with its magnificent library and superb art collection, has become, since his death, a European outpost of Harvard University. Excerpts from the diaries he kept from 1947 to 1956 were published as *The Passionate Sightseer* (1960).

Beresford, John Davys (1873–1949). English novelist. He was the author of *Jacob Stahl* (1911), a once popular story about a young man growing up.

Berezina. A river in western Russia. It flows into the Dnieper, and was the scene of battles in both 1812 when Napoleon's army retreated westward and in 1941 when the German army invaded the Soviet Union.

Bergamín, José (1894–   ). Spanish critic and dramatist. Bergamín directed (1933–1936) the critical review *Cruz y Raya* whose literary influence favored Spanish neo-Catholicism. He is also known for his dramas, which include *La hija de Dios* (1945), *Una mujer con tres almas* (1950), and for his collection of essays, *El cohete y la estrella* (1922).

Bergengruen, Werner (1892–   ). German novelist, known for his interest in historical subjects and for the humor of his style. Among his novels are *Der Grosstyrann und das Gericht (The Tyrant and the Court,* 1935), *Am Himmel wie auf Erden (In Heaven as on Earth,* 1940), and *Das Feuerzeichen (The Fiery Sign,* 1949).

Bergeret, M. The central figure in the four satiric novels that comprise Anatole FRANCE's *Histoire Contemporaine.* In the first volumes M. Bergeret holds an official position in a French provincial university. In the last two books, he is divorced from his wife and lives in Paris. These last books in the series deal extensively with the Dreyfus case, Bergeret serving as a vehicle for many of France's own feelings and convictions on the subject.

Bergman, Hjalmar Frederik (1883–1931). Swedish dramatist, novelist, and short-story writer. The son of a wealthy banker, Bergman did not develop his own unique literary qualities until his father's financial failure forced him to write for a living. Lively humor and ironic tenderness characterize Bergman's work; in both his novels and his plays the people are amusingly grotesque clowns. Among his novels and stories are *Hans nåds testamente* (1910), *Markurells i Wadköping (God's Orchid,* 1919) and *Chefen fru Ingeborg (The Head of the Firm,* 1924). His plays include *Marionettspel* (1917), *Swedenhielms* (1925), and *Patrasek* (1928).

Bergman, Ingmar (1918–   ). Swedish motion-picture director, writer, and producer. The son of a clergyman, Bergman has throughout his career been associated with A. B. Svensk Filmindustri; he first came to public attention with the script he wrote for *Torment* (1944). His own productions, made with a small company of devoted actors, are often concerned with questions of faith and belief; they include *Smiles of a Summer Night* (1955), *The Seventh Seal* (1956), *Wild Strawberries* (1957), *The Magician* (1958), *The Virgin Spring* (1959), *Through a Glass Darkly* (1960), *Winter Light* (1962), and *The Silence* (1963).

Bergotte. A famous author in Marcel Proust's Remembrance of Things Past. His work greatly influences the narrator, who admires the delicate, exquisite style of his writing.

Bergson, Henri (1859–1941). French philosopher. During his lifetime Bergson enjoyed wide popularity as a professor at the *Collège de France;* his lectures were always crowded and his books were eagerly read. His influence upon modern literature and thought has been of profound significance. Bergson's philosophy is complex, but the basic premise of his intellectual system is a faith in direct intuition as a means of attaining knowledge. To the experimental and rationalistic methods of science he opposed an antirational and mystical approach to understanding. Change or movement, Bergson believed, was the basis of all reality. Time should not be measured scientifically or mechanically, since for the human being time operates as a continuous flow in which past and present are inseparable to the consciousness and the memory. This theory of time in relation to the human self figures prominently in the long work of Marcel Proust, Remembrance of Things Past.

Bergson's interest in biological evolution led to the formulation of his theory of *élan vital,* a spirit of energy and life that moves all living things, and to the publication of his famous work *L'Evolution créatrice* (1907). His chief philosophical works are *Essai sur les données immédiates de la conscience* (1888; translated as *Time and Free Will*), *Matière et mémoire* (1896), *L'Energie spirituelle* (1919; translated as *Mind-Energy*), *Durée et simultanéité* (1922), *Les Deux Sources de la morale et de la religion* (1932), and *La Pensée et le mouvant* (1934). Of Jewish parentage, Bergson renounced the honors and posts awarded him by the French government in 1940, as a protest against hostile legislation passed by the Vichy government against the Jews.

Berkeley, George (1685–1753). Irish-born English bishop and philosopher. He was one of the earliest and most influential thinkers of the philosophic school of idealism. The exponent of a theory of philosophical immaterialism based on the proposition that to be is to be perceived, he maintained that material objects are ideas in our minds, with no independent existence, and that, therefore, the whole of reality consists of ideas in the mind of God. His chief works are Essay towards a New Theory of Vision; *Treatise concerning the Principles of Human Knowledge* (1710); *Three Dialogues between Hylas and Philonus* (1713); Alciphron, or The Minute Philosopher, a collection of popular pseudo-Platonic dialogues; *Theory of Vision* (1733); and Siris: A Chain of Philosophical Reflections and Inquiries Concerning the Virtues of Tar-Water. He was active in attacking the opinions of freethinkers, and was associated with a number of prominent 18th-century literary figures including Addison, Pope, and Swift. From 1728 to 1732, he lived in America, in the colony of Rhode Island, where he wrote *Alciphron* and founded the Literary and Philosophical Society and a college for the education of colonists and Indians.

Berkeley, Sir William. See Bacon's Rebellion.

Berlichingen, Götz von. See Götz von Berlichingen.

Berlin, Irving. Real name, **Israel Baline** (1888–   ). Russian-born American composer. He is known for his popular songs and lyrics, especially of a sentimental or patriotic nature, such as *Blue Skies* (1927), *God Bless America* (1939), and *White Christmas* (1942). He also wrote the scores for many musical comedies, including *As Thousands Cheer* (1933), *Annie Get Your Gun* (1946), and *Call Me Madam* (1954).

Berlioz, [Louis] Hector (1803–1869). French composer and conductor. His *Treatise on Modern Instrumentation and Orchestration* (1844) established a new concept of the symphony orchestra, and is still a basic text. His literary works give excellent descriptions of his musical environment, and have been collected in 10 volumes. His musical works are conceived almost entirely as musical embodiments of literary ideas. The *Symphonie Fantastique* (1830), subtitled *episode in the life of an artist,* is the first piece of sustained narrative music, the forerunner of the tone poems of Franz Liszt and Richard Strauss. Berlioz also invented the *idée fixe,* a basic theme that occurs in various forms in all movements of a work. *Harold en Italie* (1834) and *Roméo et Juliette* (1839) are two other programmatic symphonies. Other important works are the *Grande Messe des Morts (Requiem Mass),* the oratorio *L'Enfance du Christ (The Childhood of Christ),* and the gigantic opera *Les Troyens (The Trojans,* 1865–1869), which is based on the tragic love of Dido and Aeneas.

Berma. A great actress in Marcel Proust's Remembrance of Things Past. Partially modeled on Sarah Bernhardt, she is particularly famous for her roles in Racine's plays.

Bermoothes. An old name for Bermuda and the name of the island in Shakespeare's The Tempest. The adventures of Sir George Somers, who was shipwrecked there with a group of colonists in 1609, may have furnished some of Shakespeare's material for the play.

Bernabò of Genoa. A tale from Boccaccio's Decameron (II, 9). Bernabò makes a wager with a fellow merchant, Ambrogiuolo, that his wife Ginevra will not succumb to any man in his absence. Ambrogiuolo, stealing into Ginevra's room while she is asleep, removes some of her garments and observes that she has a mole under her breast. He then confronts Bernabò with the items he stole and his knowledge of the mole as proof of his having slept with Ginevra. Convinced he has truly lost his wager, and deeply grieved by his wife's supposed infidelity, he orders her death. But Ginevra persuades her executioner to show Bernabò her blood-stained garments and let her flee into exile. Disguising herself as a youth, Sicurano da Finale, Ginevra goes to sea with a Catalan merchant and reaches Alexandria, where the sultan takes her into his service. One day, she encounters Ambrogiuolo, who has come to sell his goods, including the garments taken from her room in Genoa that fateful night. Recognizing them, she asks to buy them and persuades him to tell how he got them. Knowing the truth at last, she sends for Bernabò and calls upon the sultan to judge Ambrogiuolo. She then startles all three of them by revealing herself as Ginevra. The sultan condemns Ambrogiuolo to death and sends Ginevra and Bernabò home, reconciled and joyous, to Genoa. The plot is that of Shakespeare's *Cymbeline*.

Bernadette of Lourdes, St. Real name, **Bernadette Soubirous** (1844–1879). French peasant girl canonized as a saint on Dec. 8, 1933. Bernadette was tending her sheep in February, 1858, when the Virgin Mary appeared to her several times in a vision and revealed the miraculous healing properties of the waters springing from the grotto in which she was standing. Lourdes, a town of the Gave de Pan in the department of Hautes-Pyrénées, is the site of the famous grotto which has become one of the principal Roman Catholic shrines and where many miraculous cures have been reported. Emile Zola drew inspiration from this story for his novel *Lourdes* (1894). THE SONG OF BERNADETTE is a similarly inspired historical novel by Franz Werfel.

Bernanos, Georges (1888–1948). French novelist and political writer. His novels reflect his fervent Catholicism and his intense concern with moral and spiritual problems. *Sous le Soleil de Satan* (*Under the Sun of Satan*, also translated as *The Star of Satan*, 1926), and DIARY OF A COUNTRY PRIEST both stress the heroism of sanctity in the struggles of rural clerics. His other novels include MONSIEUR OUINE and *Un mauvais rêve* (1951). In his political essays, Bernanos opposed parliamentary democracy because it did not provide enough protection from the greedy and the power mad, and urged a return to monarchy to institute a new moral order. *Les Grands Cimetières sous la lune* (*A Diary of My Times*, 1938) was inspired by his fury against Franco in the Spanish Civil War. His anti-Vichy writings of World War II are collected in *Lettre aux Anglais* (*Plea for Liberty*, 1942), *La France contre les robots* (1947), and *Le Chemin de la Croix des Ames* (1948). *Dialogues des Carmélites* (1949), a play, is the basis of Poulenc's opera of the same name.

Bernard. A leading character in Virginia Woolf's novel THE WAVES. He speaks the memorable final soliloquy.

Bernard, Jean Jacques (1888–   ). French dramatist, son of Tristan Bernard. A major exponent of the school of silence, he maintained that the theater is the art of "expressing what is unspoken," using delicate dialogue about trivia to capitalize on what is not said. Among his plays are *The Sulky Fire* (*Le Feu qui reprend mal;* 1921), *Martine* (1922), and *The Unquiet Spirit* (*L'Ame en Peine;* 1926).

Bernard, Tristan. Pen name of **Paul Bernard** (1866–1947). French dramatist and novelist. Bernard is best known for his popular traditional comedies, such as the two he wrote with A. Godferneaux: *Triplepatte* (1905), adapted by Clyde Fitch as *Toddles* (1908), and *Monsieur Codomat* (1907). His own comedies include *Le Petit Café* (1911), *Jules, Juliette, et Julien* (1929), and *Le Sauvage* (1931).

Bernard de Ventadour. See TROUBADOURS.

Bernardin de Saint-Pierre, Jacques Henri (1737–1814). French author and one-time civil engineer. He travelled extensively from 1761 to 1766 in western Europe, with the intention of promoting

a scheme to regenerate society. A malcontent like ROUSSEAU, he returned to Paris in 1770, where he became the former's disciple and intimate friend, sharing his love of nature and horror of civilization. In 1784 he published his *Etudes de la Nature,* a remarkable series of exotic descriptions of nature. Their object is to show the perfection of Nature, the work of a good God solicitous of man's welfare. The precision, charm, and mastery of the language, new to French literature, are marred at times by the infantilism of the author's reasoning and by his sentimentality; his "philosophy" is at times a caricature of Rousseau's. The fourth part of these *Etudes* comprises his most famous work, the short novel PAUL ET VIRGINIE. Stylistically, Bernardin de Saint-Pierre is a precursor of Chateaubriand in his vivid use of pictorial description.

Bernardino da Siena (1380–1444). Italian Franciscan friar. Famous for his sermons, he was a frequent subject for the artists of the time.

Bernardo. See MARCELLUS.

Bernard of Clairvaux, St. (1090–1153). French ecclesiastic. In 1113 he entered the Cistercian abbey of Citeaux; two years later he became the founder and abbot of a new Cistercian monastery at Clairvaux, a post he held until his death. His fame as a preacher soon spread, bringing crowds of pilgrims to Clairvaux, but Bernard refused all offers of ecclesiastical preferment. Nevertheless, his importance and prestige grew rapidly: through his work, the Cistercians became the greatest order in western Christendom, and he himself the greatest influence, at first in France and later throughout western Europe. He was instrumental in the success of Pope Innocent II's cause over the claims of the antipope, Cardinal Peter of Leon. In 1141 he secured an official condemnation of Pierre Abelard's works at the Council of Sens. In 1146 he summoned the people to join in a crusade, in the name of Pope Eugenius II, and Louis VII of France with many others was moved to organize the Second Crusade. He was canonized in 1173.

Bernard of Cluny or **Morlaix** (c. 1100–c. 1156). French Benedictine monk. He wrote a Latin poem *De Contemptu mundi,* famous through the English translation of John Mason Neale.

Berners, Lord. See John BOURCHIER.

Bernesque satire or **poetry.** See Francesco BERNI.

Berni, Francesco (c. 1498–1536). Florentine author of popular satires on contemporary social and literary conventions. His favorite forms were the extended or tailed sonnet, and the long poem in *terza rima* called *capitolo*. One of the latter, his *Capitolo al Fracastoro,* is widely admired for its vividly humorous description of a night's lodging in a vicarage, cast in the form of a letter to his friend Fracastoro. Bernesque satire, or the Bernesque style, refers to his treatment in a seriocomic way of such trivial subjects as eels, melons, peaches, or jelly. He is also noted for his rewriting of Boiardo's *Orlando Innamorato* in a pure Tuscan style.

Bernini, [Giovanni] Lorenzo (1598–1680). Italian sculptor and architect. The dominant influence on European sculpture for over a century, he was a typically baroque artist and did not shy away from whirling movement and illusionistic representation in stone. He is known for his consummate portrait busts and his fountains, particularly the fountain of Trevi, and, in Rome, the fountain of the Four Rivers. His religious works include the skillfully carved Saint Theresa group in Rome's Santa Maria della Vittoria, theatrically lit by a hidden overhead window, and the exuberant setting for the chair of Saint Peter. His best-known architectural achievement is the double colonnade of the Piazza of Saint Peter (1656–1668).

Bernstein, Eduard (1850–1932). German socialist. His *Die Voraussetzungen des Sozialismus und die Aufgaben der Sozialdemokratie (The Premises of Socialism and the Tasks of Social Democracy,* 1899) modified Marxist theory. He denied the necessity for a proletarian revolution, and urged the workers to improve their position through democratic activity.

Bernstein, Leonard (1918–   ). American conductor and composer. He is widely known for his television lectures on music, some of which were published as *The Joy of Music* (1959). He has written classical pieces, such as the Symphony No. 2 (1949), subtitled *The Age of Anxiety,* after W. H. Auden's poem, and musical comedies, such as *Candide* (1956) and *West Side Story* (1957). He succeeded Dimitri Mitropoulos as musical director of the N.Y. Philharmonic Orchestra in 1958.

Béroul (12th century). Medieval French poet. He wrote one of the early versions of the Tristan legend.

Berowne. See Biron.

Berryman, John (1914–   ). American poet and short-story writer. Berryman's *Poems* appeared in 1942, and was followed by *The Dispossessed* in 1948. *Homage to Mistress Bradstreet* (1956) is a long poem dealing with the 17th-century American poet Anne Bradstreet. Berryman has also written short stories and a biography of Stephen Crane (1950).

berserker. In Scandinavian mythology, a wild, ferocious, warlike being who was sometimes possessed of supernatural strength and fury. One account says the name originated from the grandson of the eight-handed Starkader, called *boer-serce* (bare of mail) because he went into battle unharnessed. Another holds that the name means simply men who have assumed the form of bears. The word is used in English both as an adjective denoting excessive fury, and a noun denoting one possessed of such.

Berthe aux grands pieds (*Fr.,* "Bertha with the large feet"). The title of a popular *chanson de geste* by the 13th-century minstrel Adenet le Roi. Historically, Berthe was the wife of Pepin the Short. She was influential at court in guiding the policies of her son Charlemagne (see Carolingians) until her death in 783.

Bertram. In Shakespeare's All's Well that Ends Well, the arrogant young count of Rousillon, who initially spurns the lovely Helena because she is a commoner.

Bertram, Edmund. See Mansfield Park.

Bertram, Harry. See Guy Mannering.

Bertran[d] de Born (c. 1140–c. 1215). Provençal warrior and troubadour. He is denounced in Dante's *Inferno* for having stirred up hostility between Henry II of England and his sons.

Berzelius, Baron Jöns Jakob (1779–1848). Swedish chemist. Founder of the present system of writing chemical symbols, Berzelius discovered selenium and thorium, and experimented in the field of electrolysis. A passage in his writings dealing with elective affinities in chemistry became the nucleus of Goethe's famous novel, *Die Wahlverwandtschaften. Larebok i Kemien* (1808–1828) is a handbook on chemistry.

Bes. The Egyptian god of pleasure.

Besant, Annie, born **Wood** (1847–1933). English author, theosophist, and political radical. A clergyman's wife, Mrs. Besant separated from her husband and became associated with Charles Bradlaugh in the free thought movement. An advocate of socialism and social reform, she was a member of the Fabian Society, an organizer of labor unions, a worker among impoverished and delinquent children. Later, after meeting Mme. Blavatsky, she became a leading theosophist in England. Interest in occult theology took her to India (1889) where she founded the Central Hindu College at Benares. Both in India and later back in England, she agitated for home rule in India. Among her best-known religious works are *Karma* (1895), *Four Great Religions* (1897), and *Wisdom of the Upanishads* (1906). Her other works include *Autobiography* (1893), *How India Wrought for Freedom* (1915), and *India, Bond or Free* (1926). See Theosophy.

Besant, Sir **Walter** (1836–1901). English novelist, historian, and critic. A prolific writer, Besant is best known for his novels dealing with social evils in East London, such as *All Sorts and Conditions of Men* (1882) and *Children of Gibeon* (1886). His interest in social reform led to his participation in the founding of The People's Palace in London (1887), an institution for the recreation and education of workingmen that ultimately developed into part of London University. He was also actively engaged in the improvement of copyright laws, and the betterment of the financial position of authors. His other works include historical novels and books on French literature and on the history of London, fields in which he was a noted authority. His *Autobiography* appeared in 1902.

Besier, Rudolf. See Barretts of Wimpole Street, The.

Bess, Good Queen. Elizabeth I of England.

Bessarion (1403–1472). Greek churchman and scholar. He came to Italy for the unity council of 1438–1439 and stayed to become a Roman Catholic cardinal. His scholarly activities influenced the revival of classical learning and Italian Renaissance Humanism generally. His collection of books became the nucleus of the Venetian Library of St. Mark's.

Bessie Bell and Mary Gray. A ballad by Allan Ramsay. Two young ladies of Perth, to avoid the plague of 1666, retire to a rural retreat called the Burnbraes, the residence of Mary Gray near Lynedock. A young man in love with both carries provisions to them. They all die of the plague and are buried at Dornock Hough.

bestiaries. Allegorical poems or books giving descriptions of various animals, or stories concerning them, with a Christian application or moral appended to each. Although the characteristics and habits assigned to each animal were largely legendary, the bestiaries were often treated during the

Cocodrillus (crocodile). From a 13th-century bestiary.

Middle Ages as treatises on natural history as well as moral instruction, and were highly popular.

The beast-fable, popular from Aesop to the medieval *Reynard the Fox,* was usually satirical and pragmatic in its moral; a fourth-century work in Greek was probably the first to turn animal descriptions into specifically Christian allegory, and its translations into Latin *Physiologi* were the basis of most English and Continental bestiaries. The best known are the Latin *Physiologus* (11th century) by the abbot Theobaldus, the *Bestiary* by the Anglo-Norman poet Phillippe de Thaün, and an anonymous Middle English *Bestiary* (c. 1250).

Besuch der alten Dame, Der. See VISIT OF THE OLD LADY, THE.

Bethany. A town of Palestine on the Mount of Olives. It was the home of Lazarus, brother of Mary and Martha, who was raised from the dead by Christ.

Bethgelert or **The Grave of the Greyhound** (1811). A ballad by William Robert Spencer (1769–1834) retelling a story common in Oriental and then in medieval European literature. In this version Gelert is a hound given by King John to Llewelyn the Great, who returns from the hunt one day to find his dog covered with blood and his infant son missing from an overturned cradle. Believing that Gelert has eaten the child, Llewelyn stabs him; but the hound's dying scream awakens the infant, who cries out from where he is hidden under a pile of coverings, and under the bed is found a huge wolf killed by Gelert.

Bethlehem. The ancient town in Judea, Palestine, where Jesus was born. Also the scene of Rachel's death, the home of Ruth and Naomi, and the city of David, it is mentioned frequently in both the Old and the New Testament.

Bethmann-Hollweg, Theobald von (1856–1921). Chancellor of the German Empire (1909–1917). He defended the German violation of Belgian neutrality (1914) at the beginning of World War I.

Betjeman, John (1906–   ). English poet and architectural authority. In satirical light verse, his poems celebrate the English countryside and ordinary provincial and suburban life. They nostalgically evoke the Victorian era and a past or passing English culture. Among collections of his poems are *Continual Dew* (1937), *New Bats in Old Belfries* (1945), *A Few Late Chrysanthemums* (1955), and *Summoned By Bells* (1960), a verse autobiography.

Betterton, Thomas (1635?–1710). English actor. The son of an under-cook in the service of Charles I, he joined Davenant's company at Lincoln's Inn Fields Theatre in 1661 and became its manager upon Davenant's death. The greatest actor on the Restoration stage, he excelled in Shakespearean roles, being equally adept in tragedy and comedy. His wife, Mary Saunderson, was a leading actress of the times.

Bettina. The name taken by Elisabeth Brentano, Countess von ARNIM (1785–1859), in her publication *Goethe's Correspondence With a Child* (1835) which purported to be her correspondence with Goethe.

Between the Acts (1941). A novel by Virginia WOOLF. It describes a pageant on English history, written and directed by Miss La Trobe, and its effects on the people who watch it. Most of the audience misunderstand it in various ways; a clergyman reduces its vision to a sermon. But, for a moment, Virginia Woolf implies, the pageant, or art, has imposed order on the chaos of human life.

Beulah, land of. In Bunyan's PILGRIM'S PROGRESS, that land of heavenly joy where the pilgrims tarry until they are summoned to enter the Celestial City; the paradise before the resurrection. The name occurs in the Bible (Isa. 62:4).

Beveridge, Albert [Jeremiah] (1862–1927). American historian and statesman. Elected to the U.S. Senate in 1899, Beveridge was defeated in 1911 when Old Guard Republicans refused to support him. He joined Theodore Roosevelt's Progressive Party and later turned to writing biographies. His *Life of John Marshall* (2 vols., 1916, 1919) won a Pulitzer Prize. At his death he was working on a biography of Lincoln, two volumes of which were published in 1928.

Beverley, Ensign. See CAPTAIN JACK ABSOLUTE.

Beverly, Robert (c. 1673–1722). American historian of the Virginia colony. His chief work is *The History and Present State of Virginia,* issued in London in 1705. It is one of the earliest self-consciously American works. "I am an Indian," Beverly wrote, "and don't pretend to be exact in my language."

Bevis of Hamton or **Southhampton, Sir.** A medieval chivalric romance. It has a slight connection with the Charlemagne cycle. In the English version, found in Michael Drayton's *Polyoblion,* (1622), the mother of Bevis slays his father and sells Bevis as a slave to Eastern merchants when he tries to avenge the murder. After many adventures, Bevis converts Josian, the daughter of the Soldan, to

Christianity and carries her off to England, where he finally revenges the death of his father. See ASCAPART.

Beyle, Marie Henri. See STENDHAL.

Beyond Good and Evil (Jenseits von Gut und Böse; 1886). A philosophical work by Friedrich NIETZSCHE in the form of a collection of aphorisms. In it, Nietzsche expresses his desire for a "transvaluation of all values." He contends that no human values are absolute; that all value distinctions (such as that between "good" and "evil") are artificial, the result of mere traditional prejudices; and that man should discard his old, outmoded values (such as "good" and "evil") in favor of ones more suited to contemporary cultural reality.

Beyond the Horizon (1920). A play by Eugene O'NEILL. The Mayo brothers love the same girl; Robert, who had wanted to seek adventure "beyond the horizon," stays home to marry the girl, and the prosaic Andrew goes to sea and later to the Argentine. In the end Robert dies embittered but happy "with the right of release—beyond the horizon." The play was awarded a Pulitzer Prize.

Bezukhov, Pierre. A central character in Count Leo Tolstoi's novel WAR AND PEACE. Like Prince Andrei Bolkonski, Pierre has a poor first marriage, but later falls in love with Natasha Rostova. After an attempt to assassinate Napoleon, Pierre is captured by the French and must take part in their disastrous retreat from Moscow. Released during a Cossack raid, Pierre learns of the death of his wife and of his great friend, Prince Andrei. Nearly overwhelmed by life, Pierre at last learns of the sheer joy of being alive. His eventual marriage to Natasha is a happy one for them both. Pierre represents to Tolstoi the triumph of a humanistic way of life.

Bhagavadgita (Sans., the song of God). An 18-part discussion between Krishna and Arjuna on the nature and meaning of life. It forms part of the MAHABHARATA. The dialogue takes place on the battlefield of Kurukshetra, the scene of the epic battle between the Kauravas and the Pandavas described in the Mahabharata. Arjuna, dejected and confused, refuses to fight his kinsmen, and Krishna counsels him on the "selfless act" performed within the context of duty, on the three ways to *moksha* or liberation (work, knowledge, and devotion) and on the three *gunas,* or qualities that constitute nature, human or otherwise. The *Gita* has profoundly influenced philosophers and creative writers in the West. It is paraphrased in Edwin Arnold's *Song Celestial* (1885). A readable contemporary version, *The Song of God* (1954), is by Christopher Isherwood and Swami Prabhavananda.

Bhagirath. In Hindu legend, the bringer of the Ganges River from heaven to earth after a 1,000-year penance. He wanted to cleanse the honor of his ancestors, who were cursed by the sage Kapila and burnt into cinders. The Ganges is sometimes known as the Bhagirathi.

Bharata. (1) In Hindu legend, the son of Dasharatha by Kaikeyi (in the epic, the RAMAYANA).

(2) The author of the NATYA-SHASTRA, a first-century treatise on drama.

(3) The name of the son of Dushyanta and Shakuntala in Kalidasa's play *Shakuntala.*

(4) The eldest son of the ancient sage Rishab-

hadeva. India, therefore, is sometimes called Bharata-varsha, or land of Bharata.

Bhasa (3rd century?). Sanskrit dramatist. His works show great skill in narration, exquisite poetry, and excellent stagecraft. *Svapna-Vasavadatta* (*The Dream of Vasavadatta*) is the most popular of the 13 Bhasa plays unearthed in 1912 in Trivandrum, South India, by Pandit Ganapati Sastri.

Bhattacharya, Bhabani (1906–   ). Indian novelist writing in English. Educated in India and at the University of London, he was for a time press attaché at the Indian embassy in Washington. He has published *So Many Hungers* (1948), *Music for Mohini* (1952), *He Who Rides a Tiger* (1954), and *A Goddess Named Gold* (1961).

Bhavabhuti (8th century). Sanskrit playwright. He is praised for subtle handling of poignant scenes. Two of his plays, *Mahavira Charita* (*Portrait of a Hero*) and *Uttara-rama-charita* (*The Later Story of Rama*), retell the *Ramayana* story in a highly dramatic and sometimes sentimentalized form; a third, *Malati and Madhava,* deals with a legendary tale.

Biadice. See GOLDEN FLEECE.

Bianca. (1) In Shakespeare's TAMING OF THE SHREW, the younger daughter of Baptista of Padua. She is as gentle and meek as her sister Katharina is violent and irritable.

(2) In Shakespeare's OTHELLO, the mistress of Cassio. She unwittingly aids Iago in his plot against Othello.

Bianchi and Neri (Whites and Blacks). Rival factions within the Guelph party in Tuscany about 1300 (see GUELPHS AND GHIBELLINES). The Bianchi wanted to maintain Florence as a democratic constitutionality independent of both emperor and pope; the Neri were willing to compromise with the pope to gain power against the emperor. See DANTE.

Bianchon, Horace. A tolerant and charitable Parisian physician who appears in many of the novels of Balzac's COMÉDIE HUMAINE. Bianchon is a member of Balzac's fictional CÉNACLE.

Biberius, Caldius Mero. The punning nickname of Tiberius Claudius Nero, the Roman emperor Tiberius who reigned from A.D. 14 to 37. Biberius means drink-loving; Caldius Mero, by metathesis is *calidus mero,* which means hot with wine.

Biberpelz, Der. See BEAVER COAT, THE.

Bible. The Christian sacred book. Actually a collection of books, the Holy Bible, as it is often called, is divided into two parts: the OLD TESTAMENT and the NEW TESTAMENT. The former contains 39 books according to the Protestants, with a supplement of 14 books known as the APOCRYPHA; other churches include either part or all of the Apocrypha in the Old Testament. The New Testament contains 27 books.

The word *bible* is from the Greek word *biblos,* which means book, and is derived from *byblos,* "papyrus."

The Old Testament was compiled from the 13th to the first century B.C. No original manuscripts have survived and present versions are based on two primary sources: the SEPTUAGINT, a Greek translation made from the Hebrew in Alexandria about 250 B.C., and the Massoretic Text, the work of a group of trained Jewish scholars, beginning in the sixth century after Christ, whose purpose was to correct and preserve the Hebrew versions then available. The Massoretic Text was completed by the end of the 10th century. The Septuagint became the accepted Christian version of the Old Testament, while the Massoretic Text has remained the Hebrew canon. Other important versions of the Old Testament are the Samarian Pentateuch, a fourth-century B.C. text preserved by the Samaritan community, and the VULGATE, a Latin translation by St. Jerome begun in A.D. 382. The Vulgate is still the authorized Roman Catholic version.

The New Testament was written, probably in Greek, during the first century; however, the earliest manuscripts date from the third and fourth centuries. There is no doubt that, in the years between the date of its original composition and those of extant manuscripts, numerous textual changes were made through poor copying and interpretive additions or subtractions. There are five general types of text identifiable in early manuscripts. When the New Testament canon was defined in 367, an attempt was made to standardize the texts. Of the 150,000 variants of New Testament text only 50 are significant, and no essential doctrine is affected by any of them.

The greatest number of New Testament texts are in Greek, but there are early Latin texts, parts of which were incorporated into the Vulgate. The New Testament is by far the best preserved document from the ancient world; there are about 175 papyri from the second to the fourth centuries and close to 3,000 manuscripts that date from before the invention of printing.

Bible, English versions. The principal versions of the English Bible are:

American Revised Version. A separate version published in 1901, the work of the American Committee on the Revised Version. It differs in a few particulars from the Revised Version (see below).

Authorized or *King James Version.* The version in general use in England. It was made by a body of scholars working at the command of King James I (hence sometimes known as the King James Bible) from 1604 to 1611, and was published in 1611. The modern Authorized Version is, however, by no means an exact reprint of that originally authorized by King James; a large number of typographical errors which occurred in the first edition have been corrected, the orthography and punctuation have been modernized, and the use of italics, capital letters, etc. altered. The Bishops' Bible was used as the basis of the text, but Tyndale's, Matthew's, Coverdale's, and the Geneva translations were also followed when they agreed better with the original. The King James Version became the Bible of almost all English-speaking Protestant sects, and its influence can be detected in nearly every subsequent version. It is still much in use and remains, in its simplicity and eloquence, the most beautifully written of all Bibles in the language. Its literary influence is inestimable; besides its direct effect on many important writers, it has been regarded as a major force in keeping English relatively unchanged since the 17th century. See HAMPTON COURT CONFERENCE.

Bishops' Bible. A version made at the instigation of Archbishop Parker (hence also called "Matthew Parker's Bible"), to which most of the Anglican bishops were contributors. It was a revision of the Great Bible (see below); it first appeared in 1568 and by 1602 had reached its 18th edition. It is this edition that forms the basis of the Authorized Version. See Treacle Bible (below).

Coverdale's Bible. The first complete English Bible to be printed. It was published in 1535 by Miles Coverdale. As Coverdale knew neither Hebrew nor Greek, his translation is from Latin and German sources, notably the Vulgate, another Latin version by Sanctes Pegninus (1527–1528), Luther's German version (1534), and the Swiss-German version of Zwingli and Juda (Zurich, 1527–1529). He used Tyndale's translations of the New Testament and the Pentateuch. The first edition was printed in Antwerp, but the second (Southwark, 1537) was the first Bible printed in England. Matthew's Bible (see below) is largely based on Coverdale's. See Bug Bible (below).

Cranmer's Bible. A name given to the Great Bible (see below) of 1540. It, and later issues of it, contained a prologue by Archbishop Cranmer, and on the title page a woodcut by Holbein shows Henry VIII seated while Cranmer and Thomas Cromwell distribute copies to the people.

Douay Version. A translation of the Vulgate made by English Catholic scholars in France. The New Testament was published in Rheims in 1582 and the Old Testament in Douay in 1609. It is sometimes called the Rheims-Douay Version. See Rosin Bible (below).

Geneva Bible. A revision of Tyndale and the Great Bible, undertaken by English exiles in Geneva during the Marian persecutions and first published in 1560. It was the work of William Whittingham (a brother-in-law of Calvin), assisted by Anthony Gilby and Thomas Sampson. Whittingham had previously published a translation of the New Testament (1557). The Genevan version, one of the most important in the history of the English Bible, was the first to be printed in roman type instead of black letter, the first in which the chapters are divided into verses (taken from Robert Stephan's Greek-Latin Testament of 1537), and the first in which italics are used for explanatory and connective words and phrases (taken from Theodore Beza's New Testament of 1556). It was immensely popular: from 1560 to 1616 no year passed without a new edition, and at least 200 are known. It was the Bible used by Shakespeare. In every edition the word "breeches" is used in Gen. 3:7; as a result this is popularly called the Breeches Bible (see below). See Goose Bible; Placemakers' Bible (below).

Great Bible. Coverdale's 1539 revision of his own 1535 edition collated with Tyndale and Matthew. It was made at the request of Thomas Cromwell. Its name comes from its large size (10 by 15 in.). The printing was begun by Regnault in Paris, halted by the Inquisition, and completed by Richard Graften and Edward Whitchurch in London. A second revision in 1540 is often called Cranmer's Bible (see above).

King James Bible. See Authorized Version (above).

Matthew Parker's Bible. The Bishops' Bible (above).

Matthew's Bible. A pronouncedly Protestant version published in 1537 as having been "truly and purely translated in English by Thomas Matthew," which was a pseudonym, adopted for purposes of safety, of John Rogers, an assistant of Tyndale. It was probably printed in Antwerp. The text is made up of the Pentateuch from Tyndale's version together with his hitherto unprinted translation of Joshua to II Chronicles inclusive and his revised edition of the New Testament, with Coverdale's version of the rest of the Old Testament and the Apocrypha. It was quickly superseded by the Great Bible (see above), but it is of importance as it formed the starting-point for the revisions which culminated in the Authorized Version. See Bug Bible (below).

Revised Standard Version. The newest American version which appeared in 1952; the New Testament was published in 1946. It employs a modern American idiom and has been widely accepted by Protestant churchmen.

Revised Version. A revision of the Authorized Version begun in 1870 by a body of 25 English scholars (assisted and advised by an American Committee). The New Testament was published in 1881, the complete Bible in 1885, and the Apocrypha in 1895.

Rheims-Douay Version. See Douay Version (above).

Taverner's Bible. An independent translation by a Greek scholar, Richard Taverner, printed in 1539 (the same year as the Great Bible) by T. Petit for T. Berthelet. It had no influence on the Authorized Version, but is remarkable for its vigorous, idiomatic English, and for being the first English Bible to include a third book of Maccabees in the Apocrypha.

Tyndale's Bible. The first printed English New Testament, translated by William Tyndale (Cologne, Worms, 1525). He followed it with the Pentateuch (Marburg, Hesse, 1530 or 1531), Jonah, Old Testament lessons appointed to be read in place of the Epistles, and a manuscript translation of the Old Testament to the end of Chronicles that was afterwards used in Matthew's Bible (see above). His revisions of the New Testament were issued in 1534 and 1535. Tyndale's principal authority was Erasmus' edition of the Greek Testament, but he also used Erasmus' Latin translation of the same, the Vulgate, and Luther's German version. Tyndale's version fixed the style and tone of the English Bible: about 90 per cent of his translation is retained in the Authorized Version. In 1535 he was arrested and put to death as a heretic the following year.

Wyclif's Bible. The name given to two translations of the Vulgate, one completed in 1380 and the other a few years later. Wyclif was neither the translator nor concerned with the translation of either of these. Nicholas of Hereford made the first version as far as Baruch 3:20; who was responsible for the remainder is not known. The second version has been ascribed to John Purvey, a follower of Wyclif. The Bible of 1380 was the first complete version in English, being a word-for-word translation of the Vulgate into a Midland dialect. The complete Bible remained unprinted until 1850, when the monumental edition of both versions was published by Forshall and Madden. Printings of the New Testament had appeared in the previous century.

Bible, specially named editions. The following Bibles are named either from typographical errors or archaic words that they contain, or from some special circumstance connected with them:

Adulterous Bible. The "Wicked Bible" (see below).

Bamberg Bible. The "Thirty-six Line Bible" (see below).

Bear Bible. The Spanish Protestant version printed at Basle in 1569; so called because the woodcut device on the title-page is a bear.

Bedell's Bible. A translation of the Authorized Version into Irish carried out under the direction of Bedell (d. 1642), bishop of Kilmore and Ardagh.

Breeches Bible. A name given to the Geneva Bible because Gen. 3:7 is translated, "The eyes of them bothe were opened . . . and they sowed figge-tree leaves together and made themselves breeches." This reading occurs in every edition of the Geneva Bible, but not in any other version though it is given in the then unprinted Wyclif manuscript ("ya sewiden ye levis of a fige tre and madin brechis"), and also in the translation of the Pentateuch given in Caxton's edition of Voragine's *Golden Legend* (1483).

Brother's Bible. The "Kralitz Bible" (see below).

Bug Bible. A name given to Coverdale's Bible (see above) of 1535 because Ps. 91:5 is translated, "Thou shalt not nede to be afrayed for eny bugges by night." The same reading occurs in Matthew's Bible and its reprints; the Authorized and Revised Versions both read "terror."

Complutensian Polyglot. The great edition, in six folio volumes, containing the Hebrew and Greek texts, the Septuagint, the Vulgate, and the Chaldee paraphrase of the Pentateuch with a Latin translation. It also includes Greek and Hebrew grammars and a Hebrew dictionary; it was prepared and printed at the expense of Cardinal Ximenes, and printed at Alcala (the ancient Complutum) near Madrid, 1513–1517.

Discharge Bible. An edition printed in 1806 containing *discharge* for *charge* in I Tim. 5:21, "I *discharge* thee before God, . . . that thou observe these things. . . ."

Ears to Ear Bible. An edition of 1810, in which Matt. 13:43 reads, "Who hath ears to *ear*, let him hear."

Ferrara Bible. The first Spanish edition of the Old Testament, translated from the Hebrew in 1553 for the use of the Spanish Jews. A second edition was published in the same year for Christians.

Forty-two Line Bible. The "Mazarin Bible" (see below).

Goose Bible. The editions of the Geneva Bible printed in Dort (or Dordrecht), Holland; the Dort press had a goose as its device.

Gutenberg Bible. The "Mazarin Bible" (see below).

He and *She Bible.* The two earliest editions of the Authorized Version (both 1611). In the first (now known as the "He Bible"), Ruth 3:15 reads, "and *he* went into the city"; the other (now known as the "She Bible") has the variant "*she*." "He" is the correct translation of the Hebrew, but nearly all modern versions—with the exception of the Revised Version—perpetuate the confusion and print "she."

Idle Bible. An edition of 1809 in which "the idole shepherd" (Zech. 11:17) is printed "the idle shepherd." In the Revised Version the translation is "the worthless shepherd."

Kralitz Bible. The Bible printed by the United Brethren of Moravia (hence, known as the Brother's Bible) at Kralitz (1579–1593).

Leda Bible. The third edition (second folio) of the Bishop's Bible published in 1572, and so called because the decoration to the initial in the Epistle to the Hebrews is a startling and incongruous woodcut of Jupiter visiting Leda in the guise of a swan. This, and several other decorations in the New Testament of this edition, were from an edition of Ovid's *Metamorphoses;* they created such a storm of protest that they were never afterwards used.

Leopolita Bible. A Polish translation of the Vulgate by John of Lemberg (ancient Leopolis) published in 1561 at Cracow.

Mazarin Bible. The first Bible to be printed (an edition of the Vulgate), and the first large book to be printed from movable metal type. It contains no date, but was probably printed in 1455, and was certainly on sale by the middle of 1456. It was printed at Mainz, but there is some question about who the printer was; it is now thought to have been either Johannes GUTENBERG or Fust and Schöffer. It is frequently called the *Gutenberg Bible.* By bibliographers it is usually known as the *Forty-two Line Bible* (having 42 lines to the page), to differentiate it from the Bamberg Bible of 36 lines. Its popular name is due to the fact that the copy found in the Mazarin Library, Paris, in 1760, was the first to be known and described.

Murderers' Bible. An edition of 1801 in which the misprint *murderers* for *murmurers* makes Jude 16 read, "These are murderers, complainers, walking after their own lusts . . ."

Old Cracow Bible. The "Leopolita Bible" (see above).

Ostrog Bible. The first complete Slavonic edition, printed at Ostrog, Volhynia, Russia, in 1581.

Pfister's Bible. The "Thirty-six Line Bible" (see below).

Place-makers' Bible. The second edition of the Geneva Bible, 1562; so called from the printer's error in Matt. 5:9, "Blessed are the placemakers [peacemakers], for they shall be called the children of God." It has also been called the "Whig Bible."

Printers' Bible. An edition of about 1702 which makes David pathetically complain that "printers [princes] have persecuted me without a cause" (Ps. 119:161).

Proof Bible (Probe-Bible). The revised version of the first impression of Luther's German Bible. A final revised edition appeared in 1892.

Rebecca's Camels Bible. An edition printed in 1823 in which Gen. 24:61 reads, "Rebecca arose, and her camels," instead of "her damsels."

Rosin Bible. A name sometimes given to the Douay Version of 1609, so called because it has in Jer. 8:22, "Is there noe rosin in Galaad." The Authorized Version translates the word by "balm," but gives "rosin" in the margin as an alternative. See Treacle Bible (below).

Sacy's Bible. A French translation, so called from

Louis Isaac le Maistre de Sacy, director of Port Royal, 1650–1679.

Schelhorn's Bible. A name sometimes given to the "Thirty-six Line Bible" (see below).

September Bible. Luther's German translation of the New Testament, published anonymously at Wittenberg in September, 1522.

She Bible. See He Bible (above).

Standing Fishes Bible. An edition of 1806 in which Ezek. 47:10 reads, "And it shall come to pass that the fishes [fishers] shall stand on it, . . ."

Thirty-six Line Bible. A Latin Bible of 36 lines to the column, probably printed by A. Pfister at Bamberg in 1460. It is also known as the Bamberg and Pfister's Bible, and sometimes as Schelhorn's, as it was first described by the German bibliographer J. G. Schelhorn in 1760.

Thumb Bible. An edition printed at Aberdeen in 1670; it measures one inch square by a half inch thick.

To-remain Bible. A Bible printed at Cambridge in 1805, in which Gal. 4:29 reads, "he that was born after the flesh persecuted him that was born after the spirit to remain, even so it is now." The words "to remain" were added in error by the compositor, the editor having answered a proofreader's query as to the comma after "spirit" with the penciled reply "to remain" in the margin. The mistake was repeated in the first 8vo edition published by the Bible Society (1805) and in their 12mo edition (1819).

Treacle Bible. A popular name for the Bishops' Bible (1568) because in it Jer. 8:22 reads, "Is there no tryacle in Gilead, is there no phisition there?" In the same Bible "tryacle" is also given for "balm" in Jer. 46:11, and Ezek. 27:17. Coverdale's Bible (1535) also uses the word "triacle." See Rosin Bible (above).

Unrighteous Bible. An edition printed at Cambridge in 1653, containing the printer's error, "Know ye not that the unrighteous shall inherit the Kingdom of God?" (I Cor. 6:9). It should read "shall *not* inherit." The same edition gave Rom. 6:13 as, "Neither yield ye your members as instruments of righteousness unto sin," in place of "*un*righteousness." This edition is sometimes known as the "Wicked Bible."

Vinegar Bible. An edition printed at the Clarendon Press, Oxford, in 1717 with the heading to Luke 20, "Parable of the Vinegar" instead of "Parable of the Vineyard."

Wicked Bible. An edition in which the word *not* is omitted in the seventh commandment, making it, "Thou shalt commit adultery." It was printed in 1632 in London by Barker and Lucas who were fined £300 for their unfortunate error. See Unrighteous Bible (above).

Wife-hater Bible. An edition of 1810 in which the word "life" in Luke 14:26 is printed "wife." It reads, "If any man come to me, and hate not his father . . . yea, and his own wife also. . . ."

Wuyck's Bible. The Polish Bible authorized by the Roman Catholics and printed at Cracow in 1599. The translation was made by the Jesuit Jacob Wuyck.

Zurich Bible. A German version (1530) composed of Luther's translation of the New Testament and portions of the Old, with the remainder and the Apocrypha by other translators.

Bible in Spain, The (1843). A travel book by George Borrow, considered one of the best in the English language. Supposedly based on the author's experiences in Spain as a colporteur for the Bible Society, it probably contains much material of his own invention. However, the book is thought to give a valid picture of Spanish life during the Carlist troubles.

Biblia Pauperum (*Lat.,* "the poor man's Bible"). A picture-book, widely used by the illiterate in the Middle Ages in place of the Bible. It was designed to illustrate the leading events in the salvation of man; later manuscripts as a rule had a Latin inscription to each picture. These *Biblia* were probably the earliest books to be printed, first from blocks and later with movable type.

Bibliotheke. See Apollodorus.

Bickerstaff, Isaac. A fictitious astrologer invented by Jonathan Swift to silence John Partridge, an almanac maker who had achieved a reputation as something of a prophet. In his almanac *Predictions for the ensuing year by Isaac Bickerstaff* (1708), Swift predicted Partridge's death on March 29. On March 30, he published a convincing account of the prophecy's fulfillment in *An Elegy of Mr. Partridge* (1708). The hoax was successful despite Partridge's protests that he was still very much alive. The joke was popular, and Richard Steele capitalized on Bickerstaff's fame by making him the supposed editor of the Tatler.

A page from a German *Biblia Pauperum* (1471).

Bickerstaffe-Drew, Monsignor Count **Francis Browning Drew** (1858–1928). English Roman Catholic clergyman and author. Under the pen name John Ayscough he wrote several novels, including *Dromina* (1909), *Mezzogiorno* (1910), and *Faustula* (1912).

Biddle, Nicholas (1786–1844). American financier. Named president of the Bank of the United States (1819), he opposed Andrew Jackson's contention that the bank charter was unconstitutional. His attempt to renew the national charter was defeated, and in 1836 the bank was renamed the Bank of the United States of Pennsylvania (1836); Biddle resigned in 1839.

Bidpai (also **Bidpay, Pilpay**), **Fables of.** Also known as **Kalilah and Dimnah** (c. 750). An Arabic version of a collection of Indian fables common to Buddhism and Brahminism. They were collected in the Sanskrit *Panchatantra* and translated into Persian about A.D. 55. *Bidpai* means court scholar, and the allegorical animal stories are told as a wise man's advice to a young Indian prince.

Biedermeier. In German literature, a tendency found most strongly in the period 1815–1848, during which most parts of Germany were governed by oppressive conservative regimes such as those of Prussia and Austria. It is often thought of as the antithesis of the *Jung Deutschland* (Young Germany) movement. Whereas the Young Germans stressed social criticism in thought, vigorous realism in style, and heroism in their characters, *Biedermeier* authors favored social conservatism in thought, didacticism in style, and a capacity for quiet resignation in their characters. The *Biedermeier* tendency is distinguished from romanticism by its emphasis on a sober, resigned attitude toward the world, as opposed to the romantics' highflown, fundamentally optimistic striving for the ideal. The late Swabian phase of German romanticism, however, nearly coincides with the *Biedermeier*. No major authors are purely and simply *Biedermeier*, but the three most important figures in whom the tendency is clearly marked are Grillparzer, Mörike, and Stifter.

Bienville, Sieur de. Jean Baptiste Lemoyne (1680–1768). French explorer of the lower Mississippi and Red River (1699). He was a lieutenant of the French king in Louisiana (1700) and governor of the colony (1701–1712; 1718–1725; 1733–1743). In 1718 he founded New Orleans.

Bierce, Ambrose [Gwinett] (1842–?1914). American journalist, short-story writer, and poet. Bierce had little education and was frankly ashamed of his sternly religious Ohio family; he fought bravely in the Civil War and left the federal army with the brevet title of major. Later coming to doubt the cause for which he had fought, he refused a large sum in back army pay, saying bitterly, "When I hired out as an assassin for my country, that wasn't part of the contract."

Bierce settled in San Francisco after the war, holding a variety of jobs. He published in local newspapers, *The Overland Monthly,* and his own newsletter; soon he became the literary dictator of the West Coast, his gibes determining the fate of books and authors. Bierce began to publish his stories, and with his friends, Joaquin Miller, Bret Harte, and Mark Twain, formed an important literary circle.

He married the daughter of a wealthy Nevada miner, whose wedding gift of $10,000 enabled the young couple to live abroad for four years. When Bierce returned from England, he had become witty and polished. Back in San Francisco, he wrote his famous column, "The Prattler," a mixture of literary gossip, epigrams, and short stories. Employed by the young William Randolph Hearst in Washington, he also wrote for *The Cosmopolitan* and prepared a collected edition of his works (12 vols., 1909–1912). Divorced from his wife in 1904, he broke off connections with his whole family. In 1913, tired of existence, he disappeared into Mexico. According to one story, he was killed in the war between Villa and Carranza.

Bierce's wit is cruel and brilliant; he was a clever epigrammatist and a forerunner of such American realists as Stephen Crane. His fame rests on three volumes in his collected works: In the Midst of Life, a collection of short stories; *Can Such Things Be?* (1893), a group of weird stories; and *The Devil's Dictionary* (1906). Bierce has been called a difficult genius who never attained full stature.

Bifrost (Icel., *bifa*, tremble; *rost*, path). In Scandinavian mythology, the rainbow bridge between Asgard, heaven, and Midgard, earth. The various colors of the rainbow were said to be reflections of its precious stones. Heimdall was keeper of the bridge, which was expected to collapse at Ragnarok under the weight of the onrushing sons of Muspelheim.

Big Ben. London's famous bell. It is attached to "the Westminster clock," standing in the Parliament tower, or St. Stephen's Tower. Big Ben weighs 13½ tons; it is named after Sir Benjamin Hall, chief commissioner of works in 1856, when the bell was cast.

Big Bertha. See Krupp.

Big Brother. A tyrannical political leader who assumes the role of protective elder brother. The term was invented by George Orwell. See 1984.

Bigelow, John (1817–1911). American writer and diplomat. Bigelow served as American consul-general at Paris and later as minister to France. He worked with William Cullen Bryant on the New York *Evening Post* and was secretary of state to the New York governor, Samuel J. Tilden. Out of these experiences he wrote two biographies, *William Cullen Bryant* (1893) and *Samuel J. Tilden* (1895). Bigelow's autobiography is called *Retrospections of an Active Life* (5 vols., 1909–1913). He is also the author of several historical works.

Big-Endians. In Jonathan Swift's Gulliver's Travels, a religious faction in the kingdom of Lilliput, who make it a matter of conscience to break their eggs at the big end. They are looked on as heretics by the orthodox party, who break theirs at the little end. The Big-Endians typify the Catholics, and the Little-Endians the Protestants.

Biggers, Earl Derr. See Charlie Chan.

Biglow Papers, The (1848). A series of poems and prose sketches by James Russell Lowell. A second series was issued during the Civil War and collected in 1867.

This work marks Lowell's first appearance as poet, abolitionist, and defender of American democracy. The first series is concerned with the Mexican War, while the second treats the Civil War; the poems are written in dialect, while the accompanying prose remains in standard English. There are three central characters: Hosea Biglow, a forthright commentator on current affairs; his friend, Birdofredom Sawin, a scoundrel; and the Reverend Homer Wilbur, used by Lowell as a foil for the first two characters. The series satirizes politicians and their doctrines, the cowardice of editors, and the follies of the wealthy, North and South. More significant than his satire is Lowell's use of language. His treatment of Yankee dialect is an important contribution to the literature of the American language. See Courtin', The.

Big Money, The (1936). A novel by John Dos Passos, the last book in the trilogy U.S.A. (q.v.). It portrays the extravagance and corruption of the 1920's, culminating in the stock-market crash of 1929 and in the personal tragedy or moral defeat of several of the leading characters. There are short interspersed biographies of such men as Henry Ford, Frank Lloyd Wright, William Randolph Hearst, and Rudolph Valentino.

Bildungsroman (*Ger.*, "novel of Education"). Also called **Entwicklungsroman** ("novel of development"). A type of novel common in German literature, which treats the personal development of a single individual, usually in youth. The definitive example of the form is *Wilhelm Meisters Lehrjahre* (*Wilhelm Meister's Apprenticeship*, 1795–1796; see Wilhelm Meister) by Goethe, which exercised an extremely strong influence on subsequent German novels. The *Bildungsroman* represents the culmination of a long tradition, but strictly speaking, the term may not be applied to any work earlier than *Wilhelm Meister*. Both Wolfram's *Parzival* (early 13th century) and Grimmelshausen's *Simplizius Simplizissimus* (1668 ff.), though treating individual development, are *primarily* concerned with depicting a Christian world order; and Wieland's *Agathon* (1766) concentrates more on philosophical ideas than on personal development as such. Among the greatest 19th-century *Bildungsromane*, all of which were influenced by *Wilhelm Meister*, are Novalis' *Heinrich von Ofterdingen* (1802), Eichendorff's *Ahnung und Gegenwart* (*Presentiment and the Present*, 1815), Stifter's *Der Nachsommer* (*Indian Summer*, 1857), and Keller's Green Henry. A 20th-century example is Mann's *The Magic Mountain* (1924), and among English novels Dickens' *David Copperfield* (1850) shows the general characteristics of the form. See Künstlerroman.

Billings, Josh. Pen name of **Henry Wheeler Shaw** (1818–1885). American auctioneer, real-estate agent, and humorist. After taking up many occupations, Shaw turned to writing humorous essays; when he studied the techniques of Artemus Ward and adopted cacography he became famous. He published volumes of *Sayings* (1865, 1866) and a series of *Allminax* (1869–1879). Among his other writings are *Josh Billings on Ice and Other Things* (1868), *Josh Billings' Struggling with Things* (1881), and *Josh Billings, His Works Complete* (4 vols., 1888). The Yankee humorist has been both highly praised and ignored; Charles H. Smith called him "Aesop and Ben Franklin, condensed and abridged."

Billingsgate. The site of an old passage through that part of the city wall that protected London on the river side. It was so called from the Billings, who were the royal race of the Varini, an ancient tribe mentioned by Tacitus. Billingsgate has been the site of a fishmarket for many centuries, and its porters and other workers were famous at least 300 years ago. Hence billingsgate became a synonym for vulgar and profane language.

Bill of Divorcement, A. A play by Clemence DANE.

Bill of Rights. The first 10 amendments to the CONSTITUTION OF THE UNITED STATES, guaranteeing civil liberties against infringement by the federal government. Among these rights are freedom of speech, of press, of religion, and trial by jury. The Bill of Rights became part of the Constitution on Dec. 15, 1791.

Billy Budd, Foretopman (post. 1924). A novella by Herman MELVILLE. Billy, innocently good, is cruelly antagonized by Claggart, the evil master-at-arms. Unjustly accused before the captain by Claggart, Billy, speechless with rage, strikes the schemer and kills him. Captain Vere, who loves Billy as his son, decides that he must hang the boy and uphold law. Vere's first obligation is the preservation of social welfare; justice, rather than mercy, must be administered to maintain order. Billy, understanding, mounts the yardarm willingly, crying "God bless Captain Vere."

Bimini. An island of the Bahama group. The FOUNTAIN OF YOUTH on Bimini, according to the legend, conferred eternal youth on all who drank its waters. Many journeys were made in search of it. See PONCE DE LEÓN.

Bing, Rudolf (1902-   ). Viennese-born American opera impresario. After important posts with various opera companies in Europe, he became general manager of the Metropolitan Opera House in New York in 1950.

Bingham, George Caleb (1811–1879). American painter. He is best known for scenes of life on the Mississippi and Missouri rivers. Their clear and strong composition is imbued with the poetry of subtle colors intensified by bright accents. The creator of political genre paintings, he became increasingly involved in politics, to the detriment of his painting.

Binyon, Laurence (1869–1943). English poet, dramatist, and art historian. His best-known work is his translation of Dante's *Divine Comedy* into English *terza rima*. His volumes of poetry include *The Burning of the Leaves* (1944), and his poetic dramas include *Attila* (1907).

Biographia Literaria (2 vols., 1817). A prose work by Samuel Taylor COLERIDGE. It contains essays on literary criticism and develops the author's distinction between FANCY and IMAGINATION. The book also contains a discussion of the distinction between reason and understanding, a trenchant critical analysis of Wordsworth's poetry, and detailed discussions of portions of the philosophies of Kant, Schelling, and Fichte.

Bion (2d century B.C.). Greek pastoral poet of Smyrna. A contemporary of Theocritus, he was best known for *Lament for Adonis*.

Biondello. In Shakespeare's TAMING OF THE SHREW, one of the servants of Lucentio, the future husband of Bianca.

Biondo, Flavio (1392–1463). Italian historian. He was the author of *Historiarum ab Inclinatione Romanorum Decades,* the first attempt at treating the "decline and fall" of the Roman empire.

Birch, Harvey. The hero of Cooper's THE SPY.

Birches (1916). A poem by Robert FROST. One of Frost's best-known poems, *Birches* describes the trees bent to the ground by ice storms; the poet imagines that they had been bent by a boy swinging on them, and wishes, when he himself is "weary of considerations," to climb toward heaven in a birch tree "till the tree could bear no more,/ But dipped its top and set me down again."

Bird, Robert Montgomery (1806–1854). American physician, dramatist, and novelist. Bird reputedly gave up his medical practice because of an unwillingness to collect fees. He sold several of his plays to an unscrupulous friend, actor Edwin Forrest, who allowed him only a tiny fraction of the profits, while refusing to let him publish his own work. The plays include *The Gladiator* (1831), *Oralloosa* (1832), and *The Broker of Bogota* (1834). Dr. Bird turned to novel writing, publishing NICK OF THE WOODS, his best book; *Calavar* (1834); *The Infidel* (1835); *The Hawks of Hawk Hollow* (1835); and others. Most of Bird's plays were included in *Life and Dramatic Works of Robert Montgomery Bird* (1919).

Birds, The (Ornithes; 414 B.C.). A famous comedy by ARISTOPHANES. Euelpides and Pithetaerus, fugitives from Athenian taxation and litigation, persuade the birds to found a city in the clouds, Nephelococcygia (Cloud-cuckooland). There they will be strategically placed to prevent the delightful smoke from the sacrifices of mortals from reaching the gods, unless the gods comply with the birds' demands. The plan is successful, the gods capitulate, and the birds and their two Athenian friends presumably live happily ever after. The comedy, filled with delightful fancies and lovely lyrics, is Aristophanes' masterpiece.

Bireno. In Ariosto's ORLANDO FURIOSO, the duke of Selandia. He is loved by Olimpia, whom he deserts after falling in love with the daughter of King Cimosco of Frisia.

Birkin, Rupert. The hero of D. H. Lawrence's novel WOMEN IN LOVE, in which he is Lawrence's spokesman.

Birmingham, George A. Pen name of **James Owen Hannay** (1865–1950). Irish clergyman and author. He wrote farcical novels of Irish life, the best of which was *Spanish Gold* (1908).

Biron or **Berowne.** One of the three lords of Navarre who take a three-year vow of celibacy and devotion to learning with King Ferdinand in Shakespeare's LOVE'S LABOUR'S LOST. Biron differs from the others in that, being a sensualist and a realist, he takes the oath only because he does not intend to be outdone by them.

Birrell, Augustine (1850–1933). English essayist and statesman. A lawyer, professor of law, parliamentarian, and one-time chief secretary of Ireland (1907–1916), Birrell is known for his essays on English authors and literature, OBITER DICTA, *Res Judicatae* (1892), *Collected Essays and Addresses* (1922), and *More Obiter Dicta* (1924). These are usually acute, judicious, and trenchantly witty. He also wrote the biographies, *Charlotte Brontë* (1885), *Hazlitt* (1902), and *Marvell* (1905).

Birth (1918). A novel by Zona GALE. Family and associates look upon Marshall Pitt as a tiresome nonentity. His wife leaves him, he fails in all his ventures, and finally dies trying to rescue a pet dog. His son recognizes his goodness and courage too late. *Mr. Pitt*, a dramatization of the novel by the author, appeared in 1924.

Birthmark, The (1846). A story by Nathaniel HAWTHORNE. Aylmer, a scientist, insists on removing a small birthmark from the cheek of his otherwise perfect wife, Georgiana. He succeeds, but Georgiana, no longer human, must die. In his attempt to master nature, Aylmer has "rejected the best the earth could offer."

Birth of Tragedy from the Spirit of Music, The (Die Geburt der Tragödie aus dem Geiste der Musik; 1872). A long philosophical essay by Friedrich NIETZSCHE. As a work of classical scholarship, it marks the final overthrow of WINCKELMANN's naïve conception of Greek culture as being perfectly static and blissful. Nietzsche sees in ancient Greece the tension and interaction of two opposed forces: the Apollonian, on one hand, which corresponds to Winckelmann's ideas, and the dark, mysterious Dionysiac, on the other. (See APOLLONIAN AND DIONYSIAC.) In particular, he attempts to trace the development of Greek tragedy from the original Dionysiac chorus and to show its decline as a result of Euripides' and Socrates' excessive Apollonian rationalism. The book ends with the hope that modern German music, specifically that of Richard Wagner, might give birth to a new tragic age. Nietzsche's early idolization of Wagner is still strong here, but in 1876 he broke with the composer and later polemicized frequently against him.

Bishop, Elizabeth (1911–   ). American poet. Winner of the Pulitzer Prize for poetry in 1956 for *Poems* (1955), Elizabeth Bishop writes mainly descriptive poems in the modern idiom with great stylistic subtlety. A regular contributor to periodicals, she brought out her first book of poems, *North and South*, in 1946. She was born in Worcester, Mass., and now lives in Petropolis, Brazil. She has held several fellowships, was a consultant at the Library of Congress 1949–1950, and was appointed honorary consultant in American letters in 1958.

Bishop, John Peale (1892–1944). American poet and essayist. Educated at Princeton, he was for a time managing editor of *Vanity Fair* and one of the American expatriates in Paris in the 1920's. Bishop is the author of several volumes of distinguished poetry, including *Green Fruit* (1917); *The Undertaker's Garland* (1922), with Edmund Wilson; *Now with His Love* (1933); *Minute Particulars* (1936); and *Selected Poems* (1941). After his return to the U.S., he wrote less poetry and produced some of his best work of criticism. *Many Thousands Gone* (1931) is a collection of short stories; *Act of Darkness* (1935) is a novel. His contributions both as poet and critic may be seen in the two volumes published after his death: *Collected Poems* (1948), edited with a memoir and preface by Allen Tate, and *Collected Essays* (1948), edited with an introduction by Edmund Wilson.

Bishop Blougram's Apology (1855). A poem in the form of a dramatic monologue by Robert BROWNING, originally published in his collection *Men and Women*. The speaker, Sylvester Blougram, confesses to intellectual skepticism yet continues to stand before the world as an exponent of doctrines he no longer holds. He justifies his position to Gigadibs, a young poet.

Bismarck, Prince **Otto von** (1815–1898). German statesman. As chancellor of Prussia (1862–1890) and the German Reich (1871–1890), he pursued a practical, opportunistic course that led to the formation of the German Reich in 1871. (See BLOOD AND IRON; EMS TELEGRAM; Count MOLTKE.) In the later years of his office he was respected for his conservative, responsible statesmanship. See DROPPING THE PILOT; KULTURKAMPF.

Bitter Sweet. (1) A long metrical narrative (1858), by Josiah Gilbert HOLLAND, at one time widely read.

(2) A popular operetta (1929), by Noel COWARD.

Bitzius, Albert. See Jeremias GOTTHELF.

Bizet, Alexandre César Léopold, called **Georges** (1838–1875). French composer. He is best known for his suite of incidental music to Alphonse Daudet's play *L'Arlésienne* (1872) and for his opera CARMEN. The latter was Nietzsche's favorite opera after he had turned his back on Wagner's music.

Björnson, Björnstjerne (1832–1910). Norwegian poet, novelist, and playwright. Björnson is known for his interest in his people and their history, first reflected in his "peasant novels" *Synnöve Solbakken* (*Trust and Trial*, 1857), *Arne* (1858), *A Happy Boy* (1860), and *The Fisher Maiden* (1868). For two years the manager-director of the National Theater at Bergen, he carried his interest in Norwegian history and legend over into his early plays, notably the trilogy of *Sigurd Slembe* (*Sigurd the Bastard*, 1862). A friend and rival of Henrik IBSEN, he also wrote plays of social realism which, though inferior to Ibsen's work, had greater popular success; the best of these are *The Editor* (1874), *A Bankruptcy* (1875), *The Gauntlet* (1883), and *Beyond Our Strength* (1883). Björnson published two volumes of poetry, *Poems and Songs* (1870) and *Arnljot Gelline* (1870), an epic. Interesting among his later novels are *Flags Are Flying in Town and Port* (1884) and *In God's Way* (1889), both of which are concerned with the problems of heredity and education. He was awarded the Nobel Prize in 1903.

Black and Tan. A member of the irregular force enlisted in England for service in Ireland as auxiliaries to the Royal Irish Constabulary during the disturbances of 1919–1922. The name arose because the original uniform of the force was the army khaki with the black leather accouterments of the R.I.C.

Black Beauty, The Autobiography of a Horse (1877). An imaginary autobiography of the horse, Black Beauty, by Anna SEWELL. In describing the ill treatment the horse receives from a series of owners, the author pleads for humane treatment of animals.

Black Book, The (1938). A novel by Lawrence DURRELL. Strongly influenced by Henry Miller's *Tropic of Cancer* (1934), the novel is a bizarre, erotic, surrealistic attack on "the English Death." The story is narrated by "Lawrence Lucifer." T. S. Eliot admired the book—understandably, since "the English Death" is Durrell's version of a sexually oriented waste land.

Blackburn, Thomas (1916–   ). English poet. Among his collections of mystical and visionary verse is *A Smell of Burning* (1961).

Black Dwarf, The (1816). A novel by Sir Walter SCOTT. It is the tale of an apparently malignant dwarf dwelling in seclusion in 18th-century Scotland, who proves ultimately to be of kind disposition. He finally reveals himself as Sir Edward MAULEY in order to prevent a forced marriage between Sir Frederick Langley and Isabella Vere.

black flag. The banner of a pirate ship. It usually was decorated with the skull and crossbones, and was known as the Jolly Roger.

Blackfriars. The name of 2 successive London theaters, both housed in the same building of an old Black Friars' monastery between Ludgate Hill and the Thames. The building was first leased as a theater (1576) by Sir William More to the Master of The Children of Windsor Chapel for the public performance of their plays before production at Court, and was used by them until 1584.

The second Blackfriars Theatre was housed in the same building after James Burbage's purchase (1596) of the property from More. After Burbage's death (1597) the property became his son Richard's, who leased it (1600) to Henry Evans and Nathaniel Giles for performances by the Children of the Chapel. Evans gave up his lease in 1608, and Burbage formed a company of owners consisting of himself, his brother Cuthbert, four of the King's Men (Shakespeare, Heminge, Condell, and Sly), and Thomas Evans. In 1609 the King's Men moved into their new theater, which became the center of the WAR OF THE THEATRES. Beaumont and Fletcher's plays and Shakespeare's last plays date from this time.

Blackfriars remained in operation as a theater until 1642, when all the theaters were closed. The building was dismantled in 1655. The site is now occupied by the offices of the London *Times*.

Black Hole of Calcutta. The punitive cell, measuring 14 ft. 10 in. by 18 ft., of the barracks at Fort William, Calcutta. In 1765, by order of Suraja Dowlah, 146 Europeans were thrown into it for a whole night; 23 survived to the next morning. Hence, a black hole is any lockup in military barracks.

Black Mass. See SATANISM.

Black Mischief (1932). A novel by Evelyn WAUGH. It is a farcical satire on various attempts to "civilize" a primitive country. The emperor himself introduces boots and contraceptives, which his subjects eat. The English and French try to take over the country; in the course of their efforts the hero, at a native banquet, is given some of his girl-friend to eat.

Blackmore, Richard Doddridge (1825–1900). English novelist. He wrote a number of novels of romance and adventure, of which LORNA DOONE is best known. His books are particularly notable for their secondary characters and for descriptions of England's West country, in which many of them are set. Among his other works are *Craddock Nowell* (1866), *Clara Vaughan* (1864), and *Christowell* (1882).

Blackmur, R[ichard] P[almer] (1904–1965). American critic and poet. In *The Double Agent* (1935) he analyzed modern poetry, arguing that form and content *together* comprise the poem's meaning. In the title essay of *Language As Gesture* (1952), Blackmur described linguistic gesture as "the outward and dramatic play of inward and imaged meaning." Among his other books are *The Expense of Greatness* (1940), *The Lion and the Honeycomb* (1955), and *Form and Value in Modern Poetry* (1957).

Black Prince. An epithet for Edward, prince of Wales (1330–1376), eldest son of King Edward III of England. Froissart says he was "styled black by terror of his arms." The appellation is sometimes thought to refer to the color of his armor, but usually to his martial deeds.

Black Riders and Other Lines, The (1895). A book of poems by Stephen CRANE. Partly inspired by the work of Emily Dickinson, the "other lines" of this collection are often epigrammatic parables written in free verse. The title poem comes from a boyhood experience in which Crane, after watching the waves beat against the shore, dreamed of black riders on black horses riding up, out of the water.

Black Shirt. One of the Italian Fascisti under Mussolini. The black shirt was the distinctive part of their uniforms. See S.S.

Blackstone, Sir William (1723–1780). English jurist. The famous *Commentaries* bearing his name for more than a century were fundamental in any study of English law. Hence Blackstone is synonymous with the law.

Black Tulip, The (La Tulipe Noire; 1895). An historical romance by Alexandre DUMAS. Set in Holland in the 17th century, the tale revolves about the struggle between two political factions.

Blackwood, Algernon (1869–1951). English writer of adventure stories and tales of the supernatural. *John Silence* is a series of stories about a psychical detective.

Blackwood's Magazine. A Scottish literary magazine, founded in 1817. It was strongly Tory in its political sympathies and violently opposed in its literary outlook to the so-called COCKNEY SCHOOL of poets. John Gibson Lockhart and James Hogg were well-known and influential members of *Blackwood's* staff.

Blagden, Isabella (1816–1873). English friend of the Robert Brownings. *Dearest Isa* (1951) is a collection of 154 letters written to her by Browning after his wife's death.

Blaine, James G[illespie] (1830–1893). American statesman. After serving in Congress (1862–1876), Blaine was a leading contender for the Republican presidential nomination in 1876 and was nominated in a famous speech by Robert G. Ingersoll, who referred to him as the "plumed knight," a designation with which he was henceforth associated. Blaine lost the nomination because of charges that he had used his political office for personal gain, but he became the candidate in 1884 against Grover Cleveland. Blaine's defeat is often ascribed to a remark by an overzealous supporter who described the Democratic Party as the party of "Rum, Romanism, and Rebellion," alienating Irish-American voters in the key state of New York. As secretary of state (1889–1892), he convened the first Pan-American Conference. The character of Sen. Ratcliffe in Henry Adams' DEMOCRACY is supposedly modeled on Blaine.

Blair, Eric. See George ORWELL.

Blake, Nicholas. The pen name under which C. DAY-LEWIS has written detective stories.

Blake, William (1757–1827). English poet, engraver, painter, and mystic. Apprenticed in 1771 to an engraver, he later illustrated his own work with copperplate engravings and water colors. He also illustrated Young's *Night Thoughts,* Gray's *Poems,* the Book of Job, and Dante's *Divine Comedy.* As a poet, he is known for his mysticism and complex, sometimes obscure symbolism. His visionary world is extremely important to his work. An antinomian, he bypasses the Church and experiences God directly; from boyhood on he had his visions, and from them created his personal mythology, of which URIZEN is a part. As his devoted wife remarked, "I have very little of Mr. Blake's company; he is always in Paradise." His works, in some of which both text and illustrations were engraved, include *Poetical Sketches* (1783); SONGS OF INNOCENCE and SONGS OF EXPERIENCE; and the so-called prophetic books including THE BOOK OF THEL, THE MARRIAGE OF HEAVEN AND HELL, *The Gates of Paradise* (1793), *The Visions of the Daughters of Albion* ([1793] see title page, below); *The Song of Los* and *The Book of Los* (1795). He also wrote JERUSALEM, *The Emanation of the Giant Albion* (1804), and MILTON.

Blanc, [Jean Joseph Charles] Louis (1811–1882). French socialist. Regarded as the father of state socialism, he founded (1839) the journal *Revue du Progrès* to promulgate his doctrines. One of the most prominent leaders of the abortive revolution of 1848, Blanc was forced to flee France that same year. His 12-volume *Histoire de la révolution française* (1847–1862) was written in England, where he lived until he returned to France in 1871.

A Blake title page designed and printed by the author.

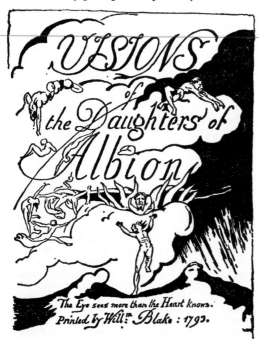

Blanchefleur or **Blancheflor.** See FLORES AND BLANCHEFLEUR.

Blanco Fombona, Rufino (1874–1944). Venezuelan novelist, short-story writer, poet, and essayist. Blanco Fombona was an exile during the long dictatorship of Juan Vicente Gómez, returning to Venezuela after the latter's death in 1935. His writing reflects his angry dismay at the stupidity, iniquity, and sordidness that he seemed to find everywhere. Accordingly his novels are weakened by bits of heavy-handed social satire and political propaganda. They include *El hombre de hierro* (1907), which depicts the triumph of evil over virtue; *El hombre de oro* (*The Man of Gold,* 1916), which exposes the venality and incompetence of Venezuelan politicians; and *La mitra en la mano* (1927), the story of an ambitious priest, who has been called a Venezuelan Elmer Gantry. *Cuentos americanos* (1904) and *Dramas mínimos* (1920) are his best-known collections of short stories. His poetry, which includes the collections *Pequeña ópera lírica* (1904) and *Cantos de la prisión y del destierro* (1911), shows the influence of MODERNISM. Among his other works are *Letras y letrados de Hispano-América* (1908) and *Grandes escritores de América* (1917), literary criticism; *La lámpara de Aladino* (1915), autobiographical sketches; and *El conquistador español en el siglo XVI* (1922), a study of the Spanish conquerors. He also edited the letters of Simon Bolívar, and edited and published several series of great American books.

Blandamour. See FAERIE QUEENE, THE.

Blanketeers. The name given to a body of Manchester workers who assembled in St. Peter's Field, Manchester, on March 10, 1817, with the purpose of marching to London to petition against what they considered unfair practices on the part of their employers. Each man was outfitted with provisions and a blanket. The leaders and some of the followers were arrested and imprisoned; the rest never got to London.

blank verse. In prosody, unrhymed verse. In English, the term usually means unrhymed iambic pentameter. In classical prosody, rhyme was not used at all; with the introduction of rhyme in the Middle Ages blank verse disappeared. It was reintroduced in the 16th century, and in England became the standard medium of dramatic poetry and frequently of epic poetry; Shakespeare's plays, for example, are written in blank verse.

Blanqui, Louis Auguste (1805–1881). French socialist. A fiery revolutionist who advocated the dictatorship of the proletariat, Blanqui served 46 years in prison for his efforts to bring about the overthrow of Louis Philippe.

Blarney Stone. A triangular stone in the wall of the castle at Blarney, Ireland, about 20 feet from the top and difficult of access. It contains the inscription "*Cormac McCarthy fortis me fieri fecit,* A.D. *1446.*" Tradition says that whoever can kiss this wins the power of being able to obtain all his desires by cajolery. As it is almost impossible to reach, a substitute has been provided by the custodians of the castle, and it is said that this is in every way as efficacious as the original.

Blas, Gil. See GIL BLAS DE SANTILLANE, HISTOIRE DE.

Blasco Ibañez, Vicente (1867–1928). Spanish novelist. His early, naturalistic novels, dealing with life in his native Valencia, are generally considered his best; these include *La barraca* (*The Cabin*, 1898) and *Cañas y barro* (*Reeds and Mud*, 1902). Later he wrote the novels that won him great popularity and financial rewards, perhaps at the expense of his literary reputation. Among these are *Los cuatro jinetes del Apocalipsis* (*The Four Horsemen of the Apocalypse*, 1916), a World War I story, and *Sangre y arena* (*Blood and Sand*, 1909).

Blast. A "little" magazine edited by Wyndham Lewis in association with Ezra Pound. In unconventional typography it advocated vorticism in art and literature.

Blatant Beast. See Faerie Queene, The.

blaue Blume. See blue flower.

Blaue Reiter, Der (The Blue Rider). A group of artists established in 1911 in Munich around Wassily Kandinsky and Franz Marc. Interested in an expressionistic use of color to convey emotion, the group organized exhibitions of the works of such painters as Henri Rousseau, Georges Braque, Pablo Picasso, Casimir Malevitch, and Paul Klee. Their 1912 yearbook contained articles on cubism and other artistic movements in France, Germany, and Russia, as well as an article dealing with the music of Arnold Schoenberg. The group dispersed in 1914, with the outbreak of the First World War. See Brücke, Die.

Blavatsky, Helena Petrovna, called **Mme. Blavatsky** (1831–1891). Russian-born spiritualist medium, magician, and occultist. She founded the Theosophical Society (see Theosophy). She wrote *Isis Unveiled* (1877) and *The Secret Doctrine* (1888), influential books of occult lore. She toured India, Europe, and the U.S., developing and preaching her doctrines. The poet William Butler Yeats was profoundly influenced by her work.

Bleak House (1852). A novel by Charles Dickens. The heroine is Esther Summerson, or rather Esther Hawdon, illegitimate daughter of Lady Dedlock and Captain Hawdon; Esther herself does not know her origins, and Lady Dedlock believes Esther to be dead. A ward of Mr. Jarndyce, Esther lives with him at Bleak House. Lord Dedlock's lawyer, Mr. Tulkinghorn, begins to suspect Lady Dedlock's secret past and unravels it; when Tulkinghorn is found dead, Lady Dedlock is suspected; she disappears and is later found dead. Tulkinghorn was actually killed by Lady Dedlock's maid. Esther ultimately marries Dr. Woodcourt. In the background of the novel is the interminable suit of *Jarndyce* vs. *Jarndyce*. Beginning as a dispute as to how the trusts under a Jarndyce will were to be administered, the suit drags on from year to year, from generation to generation. Two of the heirs are Richard Carstone and Ada Clare, his pretty cousin, who marry and live at Bleak House with John Jarndyce and Esther. When the case is finally settled, it is in Carstone's favor, but all the funds have been dissipated by the litigation. Carstone dies and Ada lives on at Bleak House with their son.

In this novel, Dickens attacks the delays and archaic absurdities of the courts, which he knew about firsthand from his frustrating and unprofitable experience of trying to sue the pirate publishers of *A Christmas Carol*. See Mr. Bucket; The Rev. Mr. Chadband; Miss Flite; Mrs. Jellyby; Jo; Krook; Harold Skimpole.

Blefescu. In Jonathan Swift's Gulliver's Travels, an island, northeast of Lilliput, inhabited by pygmies. It is supposed to represent France.

Bleibtreu, Karl (1859–1928). German author in the movement of naturalism. In his critical work, *Revolution der Literatur* (*Revolution of Literature*, 1886) he advocates what he calls "true romanticism," a genuine, heartfelt striving for human ideals. Among his creative works, *Dies Irae* (1882), the fictional diary of a French officer in the Franco-Prussian War, was most influential.

Blenheim, battle of (1704). During the War of the Spanish Succession, the battle in which John Churchill, duke of Marlborough, defeated Marshal Tallard at Blenheim on the upper Danube. It was the most resounding and decisive victory enjoyed by the British on the Continent since Agincourt. Louis XIV's schemes for pushing his frontiers up to the Rhine were thus thwarted and French prestige was badly shaken. The poem *The Battle of Blenheim* (1798) was written by Robert Southey.

Blenheim Steps. The site of an anatomical school on Bond Street in London, over which Sir Astley Cooper presided. Here "resurrectionists" were sure to find a ready mart for their gruesome wares, for which they received sums of money varying from £3 to £10, and sometimes more. Hence, *going to Blenheim Steps* means going to be dissected, or unearthed from one's grave.

Blessed Damozel, The (1850). A poem by Dante Gabriel Rossetti giving expression to the longing of the "blessed damozel" in heaven for her lover on earth.

Blessington, countess of. **Marguerite Power** (1789–1849). Irish writer. Her *Conversations with Lord Byron* (1834) are still interesting, but she is better known for her dramatic life. Sold by her father into marriage at 14, she fled from a brutal husband into a liaison with an English officer, who later gave her up (for £10,000) to the earl of Blessington. Her remarkable beauty, cleverness, and charm established her as a leading hostess of the day. After Blessington's death (1829), she became the companion, if not mistress, of Alfred, count d'Orsay, 12 years her junior, celebrated for his looks and accomplishments. To provide for "the last of the dandies" and her own luxurious tastes, she took to writing, but her novels and travel books failed to avert bankruptcy in 1849. She died a few months later, after following d'Orsay to France.

Blest Gana, Alberto (1830–1920). Chilean novelist. One of the outstanding realists of Latin-American fiction, Blest Gana, who spent many years in France, sought to be the Balzac of Chile. His best-known novel is *Martín Rivas* (1862). Dealing with the experiences of an impoverished provincial youth who falls in love with a girl of the aristocracy, the work gives an incisive, satirical view of Chilean society in the 1850's. Other works by Blest Gana include *Durante la Reconquista* (1897), an epic of Chile's struggle for independence, and *Los trasplantados* (1904), which depicts decadent Chilean émigrés in Paris.

Blifil, William. See Tom Jones.

Bligh, William (1754–1817). English admiral and master of the H.M.S. *Bounty*. Having sailed with Captain Cook on his second expedition when the breadfruit tree was discovered, Bligh was sent in 1787 on the *Bounty* to acquire specimens of the tropical tree for transplantation in the West Indies. His extreme severity led to mutiny, and Bligh, with 18 others, was set adrift. He succeeded in navigating nearly 4,000 miles of open sea and lived to carry out his original mission. His adventure is known from Byron's poem *The Island* and from a trilogy of novels by Charles Nordhoff and James Norman Hall, beginning with MUTINY ON THE BOUNTY.

Blind Bard or **Poet.** An epithet frequently applied to Homer. The tradition of Homer's blindness may possibly be related to that of DEMODOCUS, the blind rhapsode at the court of Alcinous in the *Odyssey*.

Blind Harry. See HENRY THE MINSTREL.

Bliss (1920). A short story by Katherine MANSFIELD. It describes a blissful afternoon and evening in the life of Bertha Young, who loves her husband, her baby and her home. In Mansfield's typically ironic ending, Bertha discovers that her husband is being unfaithful to her.

Blithedale Romance, The (1852). A novel by Nathaniel HAWTHORNE. Blithedale, a Utopian community, is modeled on BROOK FARM, the Transcendentalist experiment at West Roxbury, Mass., in which Hawthorne had participated 10 years before he wrote the novel. Miles Coverdale, the narrator, is a coldly inquisitive observer; in revealing his knowledge of the other members of the community, he reveals himself. Zenobia, a dark, queenly woman, is in love with Hollingsworth, an egoistic reformer who plans to convert Blithedale into an experiment in prison reform.

Priscilla, a pale innocent girl, fallen under the evil influence of the mesmerist Westervelt, has performed as the Veiled Lady. Taking refuge at Blithedale, she is revealed to be the half-sister of Zenobia. When Hollingsworth admits his love for Priscilla, Zenobia drowns herself. Hollingsworth, shocked by the experience, abandons his schemes, depending on Priscilla for strength. Coverdale, in the final chapter, admits that he, too, had always loved Priscilla. See Margaret FULLER.

Blitzkrieg (*Ger.*, "lightning warfare"). A form of large-scale surprise attack involving motorized forces with air support, developed by Germany in World War II.

Blitzstein, Marc (1905–1964). American composer and playwright. He is known for his experimentation with formal technique and his use of proletarian themes. *The Cradle Will Rock* (1937), an experimental play with music on the capital-labor theme, is his best-known work. He also wrote *I've Got the Tune* (1937), a radio song-play, *No for an Answer* (1941), and the libretto for the American adaptation of Bertolt Brecht and Kurt Weill's *Threepenny Opera*.

Blixen, Baroness **Karen.** See Isak DINESEN.

Bloch, Ernest (1880–1959). Swiss-born composer. Many of his works have a Hebraic flavor derived from traditional Jewish melodies and modes, such as his cello rhapsody, *Schelomo* (1916). His *Concerto Grosso No. 1* (1925) is a typical example of the return to old forms engendered by neoclassicism.

Bloch-Michel, Jean (1912–   ). French novelist. Active in the Resistance movement, Bloch-Michel worked on the journal *Combat* during the Liberation years. His novels are similar in spirit to the work of Albert Camus: sober, stoical, and grimly honest about the human condition. *Les Grandes Circonstances* (1949), *Journal du désordre* (1955), and *Un Homme estimable* (1956) are among his works.

Blok, Aleksandr Aleksandrovich (1880–1921). Russian poet. The greatest of the Russian SYMBOLISTS, he is generally ranked as one of the half-dozen major poets in Russian literature. Blok's early poems *Songs of the Beautiful Lady* (*Stikhi o prekrasnoi damye*; 1904) are hymns to a mystical vision of Sophia, a tendency originating with the philosopher Vladimir SOLOVIOV that played a large role in Russian symbolist poetry. Blok's loss of faith in his mystical experience of the eternal feminine was reflected in later poetry and plays, which grew increasingly bitter, gloomy, and ironic. In his lyrical drama, *The Puppet Show* (*Balaganchik;* 1905) he ridiculed his former beliefs. Another play, *The Stranger* (*Neznakomka*; 1906), depicts the former Beautiful Lady as a common prostitute. A poem of this title, written at the same time, expresses Blok's wish to escape the pain of his disappointment in drink. He also attempted to find solace in love affairs although toward the end of his life he claimed that he had had only two loves in his life: his wife Lyubov (a daughter of the scientist Mendeleyev) "and all the others."

Blok's masterpiece is his long poem THE TWELVE, an impressionistic picture of St. Petersberg during the early days of the revolution. Another well-known work is *The Scythians* (*Skify;* 1918), an address of both challenge and proffered friendship to the West from the new revolutionary Russia. Blok worked on a long autobiographical poem, *Retribution* (*Vozmezdiye*), from 1910 until his death, completing one chapter and parts of two others.

Blok's standing as one of the greatest Russian poets is based on a large body of lyrics, several excellent verse dramas, and his long poem *The Twelve*. His importance as an innovator in Russian prosody is also great. He created the new accentual verse in Russian known as *dolniki,* which is based only on the number of stresses per line, allowing any number of unstressed syllables between the stresses. This break with the classic prosody of syllabic-accentual verse, which took into account both stressed and unstressed syllables, introduced a new freedom into modern Russian poetry, which was used to good account by later poets such as Mayakovski, Esenin, and Anna Akhmatova.

Blood and Iron (*Ger.,* "Blut und Eisen"). A phrase used by BISMARCK at a meeting with members of the Reichstag (1862), to describe his political policies. He said, "The great questions of the day will not be settled by resolutions and majority votes, . . . but by blood and iron."

Blood Wedding. See Federico GARCÍA LORCA.

Bloody Assizes. The popular name for the trials conducted in England in 1685 by Lord Chief Justice George JEFFREYS after the collapse of Monmouth's Rebellion. Hundreds of both actual and presumed supporters of the duke of MONMOUTH were executed or sold into West-Indian slavery. The trials, which were brief, brutal, and flagrantly unjust, became a byword for relentless cruelty.

Bloody Mary. See MARY I.

Bloom, Hyman (1913–). Latvian-born American painter. He is known for his hypnotic, horrifying pictures.

Bloom, Leopold. The central character in James Joyce's novel ULYSSES. Bloom is an advertising canvasser of Jewish origin, living in Dublin. He is an unheroic but affirmative character, whose wanderings about Dublin are ironically contrasted with the epic voyage of Ulysses. Humane and generous, self-conscious and guilt-ridden, throughout the book his quest for love is frustrated and his best instincts are stifled. Only through his daydreams does Bloom find fulfillment as a social, political, and ethical human being. His rejection by Ireland may thus be seen as Joyce's indictment of a culture that is only artificially civilized. Symbolically, he is linked to a variety of literary and historical figures, among them, Elijah, Moses, and Christ.

Bloom, Molly. One of the three chief characters in James Joyce's novel ULYSSES. She is the wife of Leopold BLOOM, to whom she is unfaithful. A sardonic counterpart of Penelope in the *Odyssey*, she is a sensual, intuitive woman, for Joyce a symbol of the universal feminine principle. The final section of the novel consists of her famous stream-of-consciousness monologue: a single, uninterrupted sentence ending in an affirmative of life, "Yes."

Bloomsbury group. The name given to a group of English writers, artists, and philosophers who began to meet about 1906. They include the writers Virginia and Leonard WOOLF, E. M. FORSTER, and Lytton STRACHEY; the artists and art critics Roger FRY and Vanessa and Clive Bell; the economist John Maynard KEYNES; and the philosopher Bertrand RUSSELL. Bloomsbury was then an artistic, Bohemian section of London.

Blot in the 'Scutcheon, A (1843). A poetic drama by Robert BROWNING. Thorold, Earl Tresham, boasts that no blot has ever stained his noble family's escutcheon. Henry, Earl Mertoun, who is Thorold's neighbor, asks permission to marry Thorold's young sister Mildred. Thorold, unaware that Mertoun has already seduced Mildred, consents; but when he learns the truth he is beside himself with fury and shame. He kills Mertoun and poisons himself; Mildred dies soon after.

Bloudy Tenent, The (1644). A tract pleading for religious toleration, written by Roger WILLIAMS during a controversy with John COTTON. Its full title is *The Bloudy Tenent of Persecution, for Cause of Conscience, Discussed in a Conference between Truth and Peace*. It urges freedom of belief for Catholics, Jews, and pagans, as well as for Protestants. An advocate of democracy in government, Williams also declared that the "foundation of civill power lies in the people." Cotton wrote a reply entitled *The Bloudy Tenent, Washed, and Made White in the Bloud of the Lamb* (1647). Williams rejoined with *The Bloudy Tenent Yet More Bloudy by Mr. Cotton's Endeavour to Wash it White in the Bloud of the Lamb* (1652), in which he reaffirmed that each man must believe what his conscience tells him. Both writings are considered to be among the

most forceful and eloquent prose written in the American colonies in the 17th century.

Bloy, Léon [Marie] (1846–1917). French novelist and essayist. Bloy was a Catholic author who attacked contemporary society and prophesied an impending transformation in *Le Salut par les Juifs* (1892), *La Femme Pauvre* (1897), *Le Pélerin de l'absolu* (*Pilgrim of the Absolute*, 1914).

Bluebeard. The villain of the tale *Barbe-bleue* (1697) by Charles PERRAULT in his CONTES DE MA MÈRE L'OYE. Bluebeard entrusts the keys of his castle to each of his new brides in turn with the warning not to open a door behind which, unknown to them, are strewn the bodies of his previous wives. None can restrain her curiosity, and Bluebeard murders six wives for their disobedience before the seventh bride has the good fortune to escape him. Based on the crimes of the murderer Gilles de RETZ, the Bluebeard story has been the basis for numerous burlesques and dramatizations. Maurice Maeterlinck made it the subject of his *Ariane et Barbe-bleue* (1901).

Béla BARTÓK's opera *Duke Bluebeard's Castle* (1911) was composed to a libretto by Béla Balász in which the horrific elements of the tale were minimized and Bluebeard became a discontented, searching philosopher. Jacques OFFENBACH's operetta *Barbe-Bleue* (1866) was a rollicking burlesque, based only loosely on the Bluebeard theme.

blue flower (Ger., *blaue Blume*). A symbol in Novalis' novel HEINRICH VON OFTERDINGEN. It was later taken by a number of authors, including Heine in his *Die romantische Schule* (*The Romantic School*, 1833), as the representative symbol of all German romanticism. At the beginning of Novalis' novel young Heinrich is filled with a longing whose actual object he does not yet know, and the blue flower appears to him in a dream as the fulfillment of this longing. Thus, basically, it symbolizes the yearning for an ideal so distant that one does not yet know what it is, the romantic yearning for infinity. Novalis might have been thinking of the blue haze of distance when he chose the color of the flower.

Blue Hotel, The (1899). A short story by Stephen CRANE. First published in the volume *The Monster and Other Stories*, it is one of Crane's finest works. In the story, a Swede comes to a Nebraska hotel with his mind filled with the romantic violence of Western dime novels. Expecting the same violence, he finally causes a fight, leaves the hotel, and is killed in another argument in a bar. The story dramatizes the question of who was responsible for the Swede's death. Although one of the characters remarks, "Every sin is the result of a collaboration," the actual point of the story is not the moral complicity of the characters but rather the inexplicable mystery of a universe which, like the blizzard that rages throughout the story, cares nothing for the trials of mankind.

blue laws. The name given to all statutory regulations of personal conduct in matters of conscience. While the term has no technical legal meaning, it is also used to describe the severe laws passed at various times and places in colonial America, whose object was to stamp out "heresy," enforce a strict observance of the Sabbath, and even regulate kissing between husbands and wives. "Blue laws" may also refer to Puritan legislation in England. Connecticut, because of an especially rigid group of laws passed at New Haven in 1732, is sometimes called the *Blue Law State*.

blues. Negro folk songs, distinguished by certain expressive out-of-tune notes, called "blue notes," by their prevailing melancholy (though often ironically humorous), and by their unique poetic and musical form. The latter is as simple as it is effective: within each three-line stanza the first two lines are approximately the same; the third line resolves the tension caused by this repetition. Each line is followed by a brief musical interlude. Some poets have consciously imitated this form, notably Langston Hughes.

Blues and Grays. In the American Civil War, the Union and Confederate forces respectively, from the color of their uniforms. *The Blue and the Gray* (1867), a sentimental poem by Francis Miles Finch which was often recited at Memorial Day ceremonies, was inspired by women in Columbus, Miss., who strewed flowers over the graves of both Union and Confederate dead.

bluestocking. A female pedant, a woman of pretentious intellectual and literary interests. The term was originally applied (c. 1750) to meetings which took place at the home of Elizabeth MONTAGU, where literary discussions replaced cards and gossip. Among the guests was Benjamin Stillingfleet who always wore blue stockings (instead of the customary white for formal wear). It is in reference to him that the group—and later any group like it—came to be called derisively "the Bluestocking Club."

Blue Voyage, The (1927). A novel by Conrad AIKEN. It describes the people and incidents of a transatlantic voyage, largely in the stream-of-consciousness technique.

Blum, Léon (1872–1950). French statesman and political leader. Leader of the Socialist party (from 1919) and editor of its newspaper *Le Populaire*, Blum first served as premier in a Popular Front government (June 4, 1936–June 21, 1937). He carried through radical reforms in banking, labor, and agriculture. For brief periods in 1938 and 1946–1947, Blum again occupied the office of premier. Arrested by the Vichy government, he was imprisoned in a German concentration camp but released in 1945 by the Allies.

Blunden, Edmund (1896–   ). English poet and critic. Associated with the GEORGIAN poets, he served in World War I, receiving the Military Cross; *Undertones of War* (1928) is a major book of wartime reminiscence. His volumes of poems include *The Shepherd* (1922), *Shells by a Stream* (1944), and *A Hong Kong House* (1962).

Blunderhead, Simpkin. See Christopher ANSTEY.

Blunt, Wilfrid Scawen (1840–1922). English poet, author, diplomat, and explorer. Blunt traveled in a diplomatic and private capacity throughout Europe, the Near East, and India. He was bitterly opposed to 19th-century British policies of imperialism and exploitation, and once served a prison term for an inflammatory speech in Ireland. His best poems, a few lyrics from *Love Sonnets of Proteus* (1880) and *A New Pilgrimage* (1889), survive through their genuine force, pathos, and subtlety.

Blunt also wrote long political poems, such as *The Wind and the Whirlwind* (1883) and *Satan Absolved* (1899). Of his numerous prose works—mostly dealing with injustices of the British Empire—the most interesting are the famous *My Diaries, 1888-1914* (1920–1921), which were withdrawn by their publisher because of their revelations of British secret diplomacy. *The Poetical Works* (two volumes). appeared in 1914.

Blut und Eisen. See BLOOD AND IRON.

Bly, Nelly. See Elizabeth Cochrane SEAMAN.

Boadicea (d. A.D. 62). Celtic queen of the Iceni, Britons of Norfolk and Suffolk. Also known as the Warrior Queen, she rebelled against Roman rule, taking poison after being defeated in battle when the revolt was quelled.

Boanerges (Gr., "sons of thunder"). Christ's name (Mark 3:17) for his disciples James and John, because they wanted to call "fire to come down from heaven" to consume the Samaritans for not "receiving" Jesus (Luke 9:54).

Boar's Head Tavern. A London tavern. It was made immortal by Shakespeare in HENRY IV, as the favorite haunt of Prince Hal and Sir John Falstaff. The tavern was located in Eastcheap, on the site of the present statue of William IV, and was in existence until 1831.

Boaz. See RUTH.

Bobadil, Captain. A character in Ben Jonson's comedy EVERY MAN IN HIS HUMOUR. A military braggart, he is an ignorant, clever bully, completely cowardly, but thought by his dupes to be an amazing hero.

bobby. A London policeman. This slang word is probably derived from Sir Robert PEEL who was home secretary when the new Metropolitan Police Act was passed in 1828. Bobbies were also known as "peelers," a name originally applied to the Irish constabulary established by Peel.

Boccaccio, Giovanni (1313?–1375). Italian prose writer and poet. He was born at Certaldo (or possibly, as he hinted in one of his works, at Paris) and spent part of his youth at Naples (1329–1335). He enjoyed fashionable Neapolitan society, but not his father's merchant trade and the study of the law. From 1341 to his death he was mainly at Florence, where he pursued his chosen career as a man of letters. His prolific output, including many works of prose and poetry that were the first of their kind in Italian or European literature, entitle him to a place beside Petrarch as a founder of the Italian Renaissance. His scholarly works in Latin were written mainly towards the end of his life, when a spiritual crisis persuaded him to reject all vernacular writing as sinful. While not enjoying the popularity of his earlier efforts, these Latin works, with their interest in classical antiquity, were seminal in the growth of Humanism. Of the same order are his attempts to have Homer translated and made more accessible at a time when few knew Greek. On the recommendation of his close friend Petrarch, he supported an incompetent Greek scholar in his own home until a bad translation was completed. Still loyal to the vernacular tradition, he also lectured on Dante and wrote a eulogy of him during that final period.

His works and their chronological order are as

follows: *Caccia di Diana* (*Diana's Hunt*), the first
Italian hunting poem, in terza rima, written 1336–
1338; the prose romance FILOCOLO, including the
THIRTEEN QUESTIONS OF LOVE; the FILOSTRATO, a romance in ottava rima and the first of its kind written
by a man of letters; the TESEIDA, in octaves, the first
Tuscan epic; the *Ameto* (1341–1342), a prose romance with pastoral setting and characters; the
Amoroso Visione (1342–1343), an allegorical poem in
terzine; FIAMMETTA, a psychological romance whose
heroine may be a real woman (see MARIA D'AQUINO)
or the poetic equivalent of Beatrice and Laura; the
Ninfale Fiesolano (1346–1349), the first Italian idyll,
in octaves, the DECAMERON, his most famous work.
His last Italian works (1355–1375) were the *Corbaccio,* a satire against women; the eulogy of Dante;
and a commentary on the *Divine Comedy.* The
Latin works of the final period were *De Casibus
Virorum Illustrium* (*The Fate of Illustrious Men*);
De Claris Mulieribus (*On Famous Women*); and
De Genealogiis Deorum Gentilium (*Genealogies of
the Pagan Gods*), whose 13th book contains a defense of poetry.

Boccalini, Traiano (1556–1613). Italian satirist. His *Ragguagli di Parnaso* (*Dispatches from Parnassus,* 1612–1614), literary and political satires, were
popular and widely influential in 17th-century
Europe because of their literary topicality and their
anti-Spanish, prorepublican sentiments.

Bocksgesang. See GOAT SONG.

Bodenheim, Maxwell (1893–1954). American
poet and novelist. One of the most notorious of the
Bohemians who came to Greenwich Village during
the 1920's, Bodenheim in his early work was influenced by the romanticists and imagists, but later,
for example in his novel *Lights in the Valley* (1942),
he espoused various proletarian causes. Among his
volumes of poetry are *Introducing Irony* (1922),
Bringing Jazz (1930), and *Selected Poems, 1914–
1944* (1946). *Crazy Man* (1924), *Sixty Seconds*
(1929), and *Naked on Roller Skates* (1929) are
novels. Bodenheim carried on several feuds with his
literary contemporaries, the most famous one being
with Ben HECHT. In 1954 he and his third wife were
found murdered in a dingy, heatless room.

bodhisattva (*Sans.,* "being of wisdom"). In
Buddhism one who has attained the status of a
Buddha but who postpones his entry to Buddhahood
in order to assist others in their quest for the Truth.

Bodin, Jean (1530–1596). French lawyer and
political philosopher. He is noted for his *Six Books
of a Republic* (1576) and his *Method for the Easy
Comprehension of History* (1566). Almost alone
among 16th-century thinkers, Bodin attempted to
devise a comprehensive theory of political society.
He strove to discover some principle of order and
unity that would reconcile liberty and subjection,
yet satisfy conscience and reason, without regard to
divine or supernatural sanction. Two principles are
evident in his political philosophy. In the attempt
to find a principle of order, he defined political
sovereignty in terms of power, that is, he defined
the state in terms of a relation between political
inferiors and a political superior, and law as a command from the latter to the former. And in the
hope of resting this structure on grounds consonant
with conscience, he affirmed the principle of natural

law as an ethical and authoritative foundation for
political power: both the Sovereign, or political superior, and the subject, or political inferior, were
bound by natural law; the Sovereign to command
in accordance with justice, the subject to obey in
accordance with justice. These two tendencies in his
thought were, however, not adequately drawn together, and consequently, each strain was given separate and definitive formulation later. Bodin's theory
of sovereignty was systematically developed by
HOBBES; his conception of natural law as an ethical
foundation for the state, by GROTIUS and LOCKE.

Bodkin, Maud (1875–   ). English scholar.
She applied Jung's psychoanalysis to literary criti-
cism in her influential study, *Archetypal Patterns in
Poetry* (1934).

Bodleian library. A celebrated library at Oxford University in England. Projected by Sir Thomas
Bodly in 1598, it was opened in 1602. It is famous
for its collection of rare books and valuable manuscripts.

Bodmer, Johann Jakob (1698–1783). Swiss
scholar and critic. He was a translator of Milton
and a patron of Klopstock and Wieland. A strong
opponent of GOTTSCHED, he is most famous for his
editions of medieval German literature, such as
Parcival (the *Parzival* of Wolfram von Eschenbach,
1753) and *Fabeln aus dem Zeitpunkte der Minnesinger* (*Stories from the Time of the Minnesingers,*
1757), including the *Nibelungenlied.*

Body of Liberties, The (1641). A code of laws
for the government of the Massachusetts colony,
combining the common law of England with the
Mosaic law. Prepared by a committee led by Nathaniel WARD, it is ranked by some critics with the
Magna Charta and the Bill of Rights in its recognition of fundamental human rights. In 1648 an enlarged code was published under the title of *The
Laws and Liberties of Massachusetts.*

body snatcher. See RESURRECTION MAN.

Boece (probably 1381 or 1382). A prose translation by Geoffrey CHAUCER of the CONSOLATION OF
PHILOSOPHY by Boethius.

Boehme, Jakob. See Jakob BÖHME.

Boeotian. A rude, unlettered person; a dull
blockhead. The ancient Boeotians loved agricultural
and pastoral pursuits, so the Athenians used to say
they were as dull and thick as their own atmosphere.
On the other hand, Hesiod, Pindar, Corinna, Pelo-
pidas, Epaminondas, and Plutarch were all Boeotians.

Boer War (1899–1902). The usual name for the
war between Great Britain and the joint forces of
the Transvaal Republic and the Orange Free State.
The war was the culmination of a long-standing
conflict between the British and the Boers (South
Africans of Dutch descent), both of whom had interests in South Africa. The immediate cause of the
war was Great Britain's refusal to withdraw troops
stationed in Transvaal. The Boers had considerable
success in the beginning of the war, but soon gave
way to Britain's superior force. The war ended with
the fall of Pretoria (1900) and organized Boer resistance disappeared. Peace was not formally arrived at until 1902.

Boethius, [Anicius Manlius Severinus] (c. 480–
c. 524). Roman philosopher. Appointed in 510, he

served as consul under Theodoric the Great, until he was accused of treason and executed. Boethius is best known for his famous work, THE CONSOLATION OF PHILOSOPHY, written while he was imprisoned, awaiting final sentence. He also translated works by Aristotle and the neo-Platonist Porphyry, and wrote a number of philosophical treatises, especially on logic, which became textbooks for the Schoolmen of the Middle Ages and their major source of knowledge about the thinkers of antiquity.

Boffin, Nicodemus. In Charles Dickens' OUR MUTUAL FRIEND, the kindly "olden dustman," residuary legatee of John Harmon. He pretends that his inheritance has made him miserly and hardhearted, but actually he is keeping the fortune for young John Harmon, the rightful heir.

Bogan, Louise (1897–   ). American poet and critic. Miss Bogan's poetry, subtle and intellectual, shows the influence of the English metaphysical poets. Her work has appeared in *Body of This Death* (1923), *Dark Summer* (1929), *Sleeping Fury* (1937), and *Collected Poems* (a co-winner of the Bollingen Prize, 1954). A poetry reviewer for *The New Yorker,* Miss Bogan has also written the well-received *Achievement in American Poetry, 1900–1950* (1951) and *Selected Criticism: Poetry and Prose* (1955).

Bohème, La (1896). An opera by Giacomo PUCCINI. It is based upon Henri Murger's *Vie de Bohème* (1848). The story deals with the love affair of Rodolfo, a poet, and Mimi, a Paris seamstress, as well as with Rodolfo's penniless friends and the ups and downs of artist life in the Latin Quarter. Mimi is ill and finally dies.

Bohemian. A term applied to literary men and artists of loose and unconventional habits living on what they can pick up on their wits. Originally the name was applied to the gypsies, from the belief that before they appeared in Western Europe they had lived in Bohemia, or because the first who arrived in France came by way of Bohemia (1427). When they presented themselves before the gates of Paris they were not allowed to enter the city, but were lodged at La Chapelle, St. Denis.

Böhl de Faber, Cecilia. See Fernán CABALLERO.

Böhme or **Boehme, Jakob** (1575–1624). German mystic. His thought is often termed nature mysticism because of his belief in the unity of nature as a vehicle for immediate contemplation of the divinity and because of his concept of natural language (*lingua adamica*) as the language of the Holy Ghost. Böhme, who was a shoemaker by trade, thought of his ideas as a development of Protestantism, but found himself under attack by the Protestant as well as the Catholic clergy. His most famous works are *Aurora oder die Morgenröte im Aufgang* (*Aurora, or the Rising Dawn,* 1612), *Beschreibung der drei Prinzipien gottlichen Wesens* (*Description of the Three Principles of Divine Essence,* 1619), and *Mysterium Magnum* (1623). He was of great influence on subsequent German thought, especially in the movement of romanticism.

Bohn, Henry George (1796–1884). English publisher. His Bohn's Libraries of standard works at cheap prices became famous.

Boiardo or **Bojardo, Matteo Maria.** Count of **Scandiano** (1441–1494). Italian poet at the ducal court of Ferrara. While serving the Este family as their regent for Modena and Reggio, he composed love poems and his famous romantic epic, ORLANDO INNAMORATO (*Roland Enamoured*). It was left unfinished at his death, then taken up and continued by ARIOSTO in his ORLANDO FURIOSO (*Roland Mad*).

Boileau[-Despréaux], Nicholas (1636–1711). French poet and critic. He was one of the earliest and most characteristic of the neoclassicists, who urged prudence, moderation, common sense, and obedience to authority in the writing of literature. In his *Satires* (1666) he imitated Horace and Juvenal and attacked the social and literary foibles of his day, while his LE LUTRIN is a mock epic in the manner of Pope's *Rape of the Lock*. His chief work is *Art Poétique* (1674), in which he formulated in verse the literary principles that were dominant throughout the 18th century. Known as *le législateur du Parnasse* ("the legislator of Parnassus"), Boileau greatly influenced his friends and literary associates, who included Racine, Molière, and La Fontaine.

Bois de Boulogne. A large park west of Paris, France. It contains the famous race tracks of Longchamp and Auteuil. Parisians call it simply *le Bois.*

Bois-Guilbert, Sir Brian de. In Scott's IVANHOE, the violent preceptor of the Knights Templars, who first insults Rebecca, then rescues her from a burning castle. When Rebecca is charged with sorcery, she demands a trial by combat, and Sir Brian is appointed to sustain the charge against her, while Ivanhoe is her champion. Sir Brian is found mysteriously dead in the lists, and Rebecca is declared innocent.

Boisrobert, François de (1592–1662). French playwright. With the exception of *La Belle Plaideuse* (*The Beautiful Litigant,* 1654), a depiction of the Parisian life of the time, his comedies and tragicomedies are today largely forgotten. One of the original members of the Académie Française and one of Richelieu's *cinq auteurs,* he generously employed his influence with the cardinal to the advantage of other writers.

Boito, Arrigo (1842–1918). Italian poet, librettist, and composer. Strongly influenced by the romantic cult of the Middle Ages, he wrote verse which linked an antiquarian's interest in medieval lore with a moralist's preoccupation with the Faust-like struggle of good and evil in the individual. A member of the SCAPIGLIATURA group of writers, he published his collected verse in *Il Libro dei Versi* (1877). A legend in verse, *Re Orso,* was published the same year.

Boito wrote the music and libretti for *Mefistofele* (1868) and *Nerone,* first presented at La Scala in 1924. An admirer of Shakespeare, he wrote excellent libretti for Verdi's *Otello* (1885) and *Falstaff* (1893). He based his libretto for Ponchielli's *La Gioconda* (1879) on Hugo's *Angelo,* but used a pen name, apparently embarrassed over its old-fashioned melodrama.

Bojer, Johan (1872–1959). Norwegian novelist. A popular writer outside his own country, Bojer enjoyed a prolific literary career. His best known work in English translation is *The Great Hunger* (*Den store hunger;* 1916). More valuable for their artistic merit are his sensitive and powerful novels of peasant life: *Den siste viking* (1921) and *Folk ved sjøen* (*Folks by the Sea*, 1929).

Bok, Edward W[illiam] (1863-1930). Dutch-born American editor. Under his 30-year stewardship (1889-1919), the *Ladies' Home Journal* exerted great influence on the American home, and Bok made it the vehicle for his campaigns on behalf of world peace and against billboards and the common drinking cup. His autobiography, *The Americanization of Edward Bok* (1920), won a Pulitzer Prize.

Boldrewood, Rolf. See Thomas Alexander Browne.

Bolerium. In ancient geography, Land's End.

Boleyn, Anne. See Anne Boleyn.

Bolingbroke, Viscount. See Henry St. John.

Bolívar, Simón. Known as **El Libertador** (1783-1830). Venezuelan revolutionary leader and statesman. The scion of a wealthy Creole family, Bolívar was educated largely in Europe, where he absorbed the ideas of the Enlightenment and fell under the spell of Napoleon's reputation. During a visit to Rome, it is said, he vowed on the Aventine hill to free America from Spanish domination. Upon his return to Venezuela in 1810, he plunged into the separatist movement and emerged as its leader by 1813. Undismayed by numerous setbacks, he declared a war to extinction and won the independence of Colombia at the battle of Boyacá and that of Venezuela at the battle of Carabobo. The two regions, together with Ecuador, were incorporated in the republic of Gran Colombia with Bolívar as president.

After his famous meeting with San Martín at Guayaquil, Bolívar proceeded to Peru, most of which was still controlled by Spain. Bolívar's victory at Junín and that of his chief lieutenant, Antonio José de Sucre, at Ayacucho virtually ended Spanish resistance to the independence movement. He approved the creation of an independent republic, which was named Bolivia in his honor, in the region of Upper Peru and wrote a constitution for it embodying his republican, though authoritarian, principles. One of the first advocates of hemispheric solidarity, Bolívar sponsored a congress of American states in Panama (1826). Although unsuccessful, the congress is regarded as the forerunner of the contemporary Pan-American movement. Bolívar's last years were embittered by disputes with his former associates and by the disintegration of Gran Colombia; in 1828 he barely escaped assassination in Bogotá.

Because of the vigor and lucidity of his prose, Bolívar is considered an important figure in Latin-American literature. One of his best-known works is his letter from Jamaica (1815), an analysis of conditions in South America and a political program for the future. Another is his address to the congress of Angostura (now Ciudad Bolívar, Venezuela; 1818), in which he outlined a constitution for Gran Colombia that would provide order with freedom.

Bolkonski, Prince Andrei. One of the central characters of Count Leo Tolstoi's novel War and Peace. In his unhappy first marriage, Prince Andrei was arrogant and cynical. The loss of Natasha, whom he loves, causes him to take on a new fierceness in the war with Napoleon. He and Natasha fall in love again after she nurses his wounds received at Borodino, but he dies as a result of these wounds.

Böll, Heinrich (1917-   ). German novelist and short-story writer. Most of his writing was done after World War II. The religious and moral principles on which his critical attitude toward modern society is based are set forth in his *Brief an einen jungen Katholiken* (*Letter to a Young Catholic*, 1958). His best known novels are *Und sagte kein einziges Wort* (*And Did Not Say a Single Word*, 1953) and *Billard um halbzehn* (*Billiards at Nine-Thirty*, 1959).

Bollingen Prize. An annual award in poetry. First given in 1949 under the auspices of the Library of Congress, the award was supported by the Bollingen Foundation, a philanthropic trust created by Paul Mellon. A distinguished board of writers gave the first award to Ezra Pound for his Pisan Cantos, causing a lengthy and bitter controversy. The debate centered on whether the political and social views of a poet should affect an appraisal of his work, and thereafter the Bollingen Foundation canceled further prizes. In 1950, however, it was announced that the Bollingen Prize in poetry would be awarded by Yale University Library. Since then, distinguished living poets have been given the prize annually. Among the recipients are Wallace Stevens, Marianne Moore, E. E. Cummings, and Yvor Winters.

Bolshevik or **Bolshevist.** A member of the Russian revolutionary party headed by Lenin that seized power in October, 1917. The origin of the term was the congress of the Russian Social Democratic Party in London in 1903, when Lenin's radical wing of the party prevailed in a dispute, and the name *Bolshevik* was adopted by the group. The word comes from the Russian word *bolshe*, meaning "larger," while the name *Menshevik* adopted by the contending faction comes from *menshe*, "smaller."

Bona Dea (*Lat.*, "good goddess"). A Roman goddess of fertility and chastity, worshipped exclusively by women. She was the female counterpart of Faunus and was sometimes called Fauna. It was the rites of the Bona Dea that Clodius Pulcher profaned.

Bonaparte, Napoleon. See Napoleon Bonaparte.

Bonarelli, Guidobaldo (1553-1608). Italian dramatist. He wrote a famous pastoral play, *Filli di Sciro* (1607), which was translated into English as *Phyllis of Scyros*.

Bonario. A young soldier disinherited by his avaricious father, Corbaccio, in Jonson's comedy Volpone, or the Fox. His own blustering honesty proves to be his greatest disadvantage when he fights for his rights against such subtle rogues as Volpone and his own father.

Bonaventura. The pseudonym of the author of the German romantic novel *Die Nachtwachen des Bonaventura* (*The Night-Watches of Bonaventura*, 1805). The book is a witty and ironic account of the experiences of an ex-poet who has taken work as a town's night watchman in order to observe men without their deceptive, daytime façades. The author was probably Friedrich Gottlieb Wetzel (1779-1819), an otherwise insignificant poet.

Bonaventure or **Bonaventura, St.** Originally **Giovanni di Fidanza** (c. 1221-1274). Italian theologian, mystic, and scholastic philosopher, called the

"Seraphic Doctor." A Franciscan, he placed more emphasis on faith and less on reason than St. Thomas Aquinas, and is best known for his *The Journey of the Mind to God* (*Itinerarium Mentis ad Deum*). This, like his other works, explains that the direct contemplation of God is the goal of all the arts and sciences; philosophy's task is to discern intimations of God first in the external world, then in the soul itself, which is the image of God, and thus to prepare the mind for its ultimate mystic union with God. Bonaventure furthered the cult of the Virgin Mary, and wrote lives of Christ and St. Francis of Assisi, as well as the treatises *Breviloquium, Soliloquium*, and *De Reductione Artium ad Theologiam*.

Bond, James. The tough hero of popular novels of espionage by Ian FLEMING.

Bonhomme Richard. The French form of Benjamin Franklin's pseudonym, Richard SAUNDERS. It is also the name of John Paul JONES's famous man-of-war, a refitted French vessel, which was rechristened in Franklin's honor.

Bonjour Tristesse (1954). A short novel by Françoise SAGAN about teenage Cécile's jealous and tragic plot to prevent her father's remarriage by scheming with his mistress and her own lover.

Bonnard, Sylvestre. See CRIME OF SYLVESTRE BONNARD, THE.

Bonnefoy, Yves (1923–   ). French poet and critic. Bonnefoy is concerned with the mystic role of words in trying to immobilize experience in art. His poetry, imagistic and hermetic, includes *Du Mouvement et de l'immobilité de Douve* (1953), *Hier régnant désert* (1958), and *Pierre écrite* (1959).

bonnet rouge. The red cap of liberty worn in 1789 by the most fanatical French revolutionaries. It was officially adopted by the Commune in 1792, and is the emblem of red republicanism. The cap seems to have been derived from the Phrygian cap (see LIBERTY CAP) given to the freed slaves of Greece and Rome, and from the *bonnet rouge* worn by convicts. See CARMAGNOLE.

Bonnie Prince Charlie. See PRETENDER.

Bonnivard, François de (1495–1570). Genevan prelate and politician. He appears in idealized form as the hero of Lord Byron's THE PRISONER OF CHILLON.

bonsai. Japanese dwarf trees. Potted, they are stunted and trained, and attain great age.

bonseki. Japanese tray landscapes.

Bonus Army. A so-called army of unemployed U.S. World War I veterans. They came to Washington in 1932 to try to persuade Congress to vote immediate payment of the bonus due them in 1945 through the World War Adjusted Compensation Act of 1925. The men camped near the Capitol, picketed the Congressional buildings, and were finally dispersed with tear gas. The bonus was finally given in 1936.

bonze. The European name for the Buddhist clergy of the Far East, particularly Japan.

Booby, Lady. In Henry Fielding's novel JOSEPH ANDREWS, a vulgar upstart who tries to seduce her footman, Joseph Andrews. She is a foil to Parson ADAMS as well as a caricature of Samuel Richardson's PAMELA.

Book of Changes (I-ching). One of the Chinese FIVE CLASSICS. A divination manual adopted into the Confucian canon, it contains mystical speculations and is the subject of numerous commentaries. See Richard Wilhelm, *The I-ching or Book of Changes* (1950).

Book of Documents (Shu-ching). One of the Chinese FIVE CLASSICS. The first Chinese work of history, it contains speeches, pronouncements, and treatises dating to the Chou dynasty (1027–256 B.C.). The language is obscure and much of the text is of doubtful authenticity. See Bernhard Karlgren, *The Book of Documents* (1950).

Book of Marriage, The (1926). A symposium on the subject of marriage with Count Hermann Alexander KEYSERLING as editor and chief contributor. George Bernard Shaw declined to participate because he felt that no man can tell the truth about marriage while his wife is alive.

Book of Martyrs, The. The popular title given to John Foxe's *Actes and Monuments* (1563).

Book of Odes (Shih-ching). One of the Chinese FIVE CLASSICS. The first collection of poetry, it contains some 305 songs and was compiled around 600 B.C. See Arthur Waley, *The Book of Songs* (2d ed., 1954).

Book of Rites (Li-chi). One of the Chinese FIVE CLASSICS. A compilation of the first century B.C., it is composed of various older texts dealing with music, ritual practice, education, and other subjects. It is traditionally but inaccurately attributed to the disciples of Confucius.

Book of the Dead. A collection of magic incantations, prayers, and exorcisms, used in the religion of ancient Egypt as a guidebook for the dead on their journey through the underworld. Though not exactly such, it has been described by some as the Egyptian Bible.

Book of the Duchess, The (1369). A poem by Geoffrey CHAUCER, of 1335 lines in octosyllabic couplets. Based largely on French sources, particularly the *Roman de la Rose* and several works of Guillaume de Machaut, it was almost certainly written as an elegy on the occasion of the death of Blanche of Lancaster, first wife of Chaucer's patron, John of Gaunt. The poet reads the story of HALCYON AND CEYX until he falls asleep. Then he dreams of

A vignette from a *Book of the Dead*. The god Anubis weighs the dead man's tongue against his soul.

joining a hunt and meeting a knight in black, who laments the way Fortune has beaten him at the game of life by introducing him to a most perfect lady, letting him marry her and live with her in bliss, then snatching her away in death.

Book of Thel, The (1789). The first of William BLAKE's mystical writings known collectively as his prophetic books. Its theme is death, redemption, and eternity. It is written in free verse.

Boone, Daniel (1734–1820). American frontiersman. He is known for his exploration and settlement of Kentucky and has been celebrated by a number of American and English writers, including Cooper and Byron in *Don Juan* (1823). His adventures were popularized in the supposedly autobiographical account included in *Discovery, Settlement and Present State of Kentucky* (1784), written by John Filson, and have passed into American folklore.

Boötes (*Gr.,* "the ploughman"). The name of the constellation which contains the bright star, Arcturus. According to ancient mythology, Boötes invented the plough, to which he yoked two oxen, and at death, being taken to heaven with his plough and oxen, was made a constellation. Homer calls it the wagoner.

Booth, Amelia. See AMELIA.

Booth, Edwin [Thomas] (1833–1893). American actor, son of Junius Brutus BOOTH. One of the most noted of Shakespearean actors, Booth was the founder and first president of the Players Club. His letters were edited by Otis Skinner in a volume called *The Last Tragedian* (1939).

Booth, John Wilkes (1838–1865). American actor and assassin. The son of Junius Brutus Booth and brother of Edwin Booth, he was known for playing Shakespearean roles. During a performance of *Our American Cousin* at Ford's Theater in Washington on April 14, 1865, he shot President Lincoln and escaped, shouting *"Sic semper tyrannis! The South is avenged!"* Two weeks later he was trapped in a barn near Bowling Green, Va.; the barn was fired after he refused to surrender, and he probably shot himself.

Booth, Junius Brutus (1796–1852). English-born American actor. Coming to the U.S. in 1821, Booth toured the country playing in romantic dramas of violence and bloodshed. Junius Booth was the father of Edwin BOOTH, who also became famous as a tragedian, and of John Wilkes BOOTH.

Booth, William (1829–1912). English preacher, founder of the SALVATION ARMY (1865). He is noted for his work among the urban poor. He is the subject of a poem by Vachel Lindsay, GENERAL WILLIAM BOOTH ENTERS INTO HEAVEN.

Borachio. In Shakespeare's MUCH ADO ABOUT NOTHING, a villainous follower of Don John of Arragon.

Borah, William E[dgar] (1865–1940). American statesman. As U.S. senator from Idaho (1907–1940), he strongly opposed the World Court and American entry into the League of Nations. He was chairman of the powerful Senate Foreign Relations Committee from 1924 until his death, and was a leading isolationist in the period before World War II.

Borak, al. Muhammad's horse. It conveyed Muhammad from earth to the seventh heaven. It was milk-white, had the wings of an eagle and a human face, with horse's cheeks. Every pace it took was equal to the farthest range of human sight. The name is Arabic for "the lightning."

Bordeaux, Henry (1870–1963). French novelist and historical biographer. A Catholic writer of the Savoy region, Bordeaux is best known for the novels *The Will to Live* (*Les Roquevillard;* 1906), *Footprints Beneath the Snow* (*La Neige sur les pas;* 1912), and *The Gardens of Omar* (*Yamilé sous les cèdres;* 1923).

Borden, Lizzie (1860–1927). American woman indicted in a celebrated murder case. She was charged with having murdered (Aug. 4, 1892) her father and stepmother with an axe in their home in Fall River, Mass., and her trial was followed with eager interest all over the country. She was acquitted, but the murder became the theme of several ballads and poems that failed to accept the verdict, and of an anonymous but widely quoted quatrain: "Lizzie Borden took an ax/ And gave her mother forty whacks;/ When she saw what she had done,/ She gave her father forty-one." The crime has never been solved. Edmund Pearson, who wrote *The Trial of Lizzie Borden* (1937), was convinced of Lizzie's guilt, but she was ardently defended by Edward Radin in *Lizzie Borden: The Untold Story* (1961).

The case has been the subject of numerous literary works, notably the dramas *Nine Pine Street* (1933) by John Colton and *The Legend of Lizzie* (1959) by Reginald Lawrence; a one-act play, *Goodbye, Miss Lizzie Borden* (1947), by Lillian de la Torre; and a novel, *The Long Arm* (1895) by Mary E. Wilkins Freeman. *Fall River Legend* (1948) is a ballet by Agnes de Mille.

border-thief school. A term coined by Thomas Carlyle in his *Sartor Resartus.* He applied it to Sir Walter Scott and others who celebrated the achievements of freebooters and bandits like Rob Roy.

Boreas. In Greek mythology, the god of the north wind, and the north wind itself. He was the son of Astraeus, a Titan, and Eos, the morning, and lived in a cave of Mount Haemus in Thrace. He loved the nymph Orithyia and tried to be gentle with her. Since he could not speak soothingly or sing softly, he carried her off, true to his real character. He was by her the father of Zetes and Calais who both took part in the Argonauts' expedition.

Bores, The. See FÂCHEUX, LES.

Borges, Jorge Luis (1899–). Argentine short-story writer, essayist, and poet. Until about 1930, Borges devoted himself mainly to verse. His poems, such as those in *Fervor de Buenos Aires* (1923), *Luna de enfrente* (1925), and *Cuaderno de San Martín* (1929), are nostalgic and nationalistic treatments of Argentine themes. He also wrote concise and lucid essays on metaphysics, literature, and language. Later, however, as his failing eyesight and poor health made him a semi-invalid, he turned to the creation of the short fictional narratives for which he is best known today. Similar in some respects to the work of Kafka, Poe, and Valéry, these stories are fantastic and esoteric, reflecting the author's irony and skepticism. Among his work of fiction are *Historia universal de la infamia* (1935), *Ficciones* (1945, 1956), and *El Aleph* (1949). His collections of essays include *Inquisiciones* (1925),

El tamaño de mi esperanza (1926), *El idioma de los argentinos* (1928), and *Otras inquisiciones* (1952). In 1962 an English translation of some of his stories and essays appeared under the title *Labyrinths.*

Borgese, Giuseppe Antonio (1882–1952). Italian novelist, critic, poet, professor, and advocate of world unity. An outspoken opponent of fascism, he emigrated to the U.S. in 1931, where he became a citizen (1938) and taught at the University of Chicago. He wrote in excellent English his *Goliath* (1937), which describes the rise and consolidation of fascism and presents an intelligent analysis of authoritarian rule. He returned to Italy in 1948.

His best-known novel, *Rubé* (1921), is a fictionalized study of an idealistic generation's disillusionment and embitterment at the outbreak of World War I. Borgese also wrote the novel *I Vivi e I Morti* (1923). Collections of his short stories include *La Città Sconosciuta* (1924), *Le Belle* (1927), and *Il Sole Non E' Tramontato* (1929). Collections of verse include *La Canzone Paziente* (1910) and *Poesie* (1922). Noteworthy among his works written for the theater are *L'Arciduca* (1924) and *Lazzaro* (1925).

Borgia or **de Borja.** A Spanish family that rose to prominence in Italy during the Renaissance. It has since become a symbol of unbridled power, lust, and greed because of the legends it spawned. Its chief figures are

Alonso Borgia (1385–1458), who became Pope Calixtus III in 1455 and laid the foundation of his family's power and influence in Italy.

Rodrigo Borgia (1431–1503), who reigned as Pope Alexander VI from 1492. A nephew of Calixtus III and father of Cesare and Lucrezia, he exerted tremendous efforts in order to secure wealth and high station for his children.

Lucrezia Borgia (1480–1519), daughter of Rodrigo Borgia and sister of Cesare Borgia, one of the most famous (and infamous) women of history. A pawn in the designs of her father and brother, she was married three times. The first marriage was annulled; the second ended when her husband was murdered; the third, to Alfonso I of ESTE, duke of Ferrara, was a purely political match forced down the reluctant throats of the Estensi. Despite Lucrezia's exemplary life at Ferrara, gossip, scandal, rumors, and legends swirled about her and her family, so that she came down to posterity burdened with imputations of poisonings, incestuous relations with brother and father, illegitimate children, and generally whorish behavior. Thus Victor Hugo's play *Lucrèce Borgia* (1833), and Donizetti's opera *Lucrezia Borgia* (1833) tell the story of her natural son Gennaro, who turned against his mother before a final recognition and reconciliation, but there is no basis for the tale in fact. Modern scholars discount much, but not all, of her evil reputation on the grounds that as a Borgia and a Spaniard, as well as an illegitimate daughter of a pope, she became the target for the hatred stirred by her family's power and political activity in Italy. The praise heaped upon her by the poets Bembo and Ariosto is now regarded as more than mere flattery.

Cesare Borgia (1476–1507), son of Rodrigo, brother of Lucrezia and, for many, the very embodiment of Renaissance individualism in its sinister form.

The favorite of his father, he was made archbishop of Valencia in 1492 and a cardinal the following year. In 1498, released from ecclesiastical duties, he traveled to France as papal legate and was made duc de Valentinois by a grateful Louis XII (thereafter he was known as Valentino, or *il duca Valentino*). After a marriage to the sister of the king of Navarre, Cesare returned to Italy and became standard bearer of the Church as well as its captain general. Using his military skill and cunning, he proceeded to consolidate the states of the church and to carve out a principality for himself among the conquered territories, incidentally winning the admiration of Machiavelli, who found his swift cruelty and treachery appropriate to the goal envisioned. The death of his father and the accession to the throne of Peter by the hostile Julius II brought his brief but meteoric career to a halt, for he was unable to rally his forces in the midst of a serious illness and soon found himself compelled to leave Italy under guard. In Spain, where he managed to free himself from prison, he finally met his end in a skirmish at the age of 31. Like the other Borgias, he left behind a legend filled with murders, including that of his own brothers, incest with his sister, insatiable greed, and unbridled cruelty. Modern scholars doubt the incest and many of the murders, but cannot find evidence that the other ingredients of his reputation are mere fiction.

Borglum, [John] Gutzon [de la Mothe] (1871–1941). American sculptor. His most famous undertaking was the carving of the faces of Washington, Jefferson, Lincoln, and Theodore Roosevelt in gigantic scale on Mount Rushmore, South Dakota.

Boris Godunov (1825). An historical drama by Aleksandr PUSHKIN. It is based on the career of Boris Feodorovich GODUNOV when he was czar of Russia (1598–1605). In the play Boris is haunted by his guilt over the murder of the czarevich Dmitri. A false pretender to the throne who claims to be Dmitri but is actually an ambitious young monk invades Russia. Boris tightens his rule and prepares to defend his throne, but falls ill and dies, tortured by visions of the prince he murdered. The composer Mussorgski used this play as the basis of his opera (1869–1874) of the same name.

Börne, Ludwig (1786–1837). German journalist. He was an outspoken liberal and advocate of social and intellectual equality for the Jews. Like Heine, he entered voluntary exile in Paris (1830 on), but though many of his views were shared by Heine, the two constantly quarreled in print. His *Briefe aus Paris* (*Letters from Paris,* 1832–1834) were filled with criticism of Prussia and were prohibited by the government.

Borodin, Alexander Porphyrievich (1833–1887). Russian composer, one of "THE FIVE," also a chemist. He made use of Russian folk themes in much of his music and is considered to have influenced Debussy, Ravel, Stravinsky, and Sibelius. He wrote operas, symphonies, chamber music, and numerous songs. His best-known works are *In the Steppes of Central Asia* (1880), a tone poem, and the *Polovtsian Dances* from *Prince Igor,* an unfinished opera later completed by Rimski-Korsakov and Alexander Glazunov.

Borodino. The site of a decisive battle between Napoleon's forces and the Russian armies in September, 1812. The battle, which opened the way for Napoleon's entry into Moscow, has been dealt with in Russian literature. The most famous description is by Tolstoi in WAR AND PEACE.

Borrow, George (1803-1881). English traveler, philologist, and writer, noted for his works on gypsies. He wrote several volumes about his experiences as an agent of the Bible Society in Spain and Russia, including *The Zincali; or Account of the Gypsies in Spain* (1841), THE BIBLE IN SPAIN, LAVENGRO, and *The Romany Rye* (1857). Part autobiography and part fantasy, these works are exuberant, racy, and vivid in their description of scenes and incidents of vagabond life. As a philologist, Borrow is best known for his *Romano Lavo-Lil* (1874), a work on Romany, the gypsy language.

Bors, Sir. In Arthurian legend, one of the knights of the Round Table and uncle of Launcelot. In Malory's *Morte d'Arthur* (c. 1469), he is one of the three knights to be granted sight of the Holy Grail, the others being Percival and Galahad, who wins the quest.

Boru, Brian. See BRIAN BORU.

Bos, Charles Du. See Charles Du Bos.

Boscán Almogáver, Juan (c. 1498-1542). Spanish poet. A native of Barcelona, Boscán served as a soldier in Italy and a tutor to the duke of Alba. In 1526 he met Andrea Navagiero, the Venetian ambassador, who persuaded him to write Castilian poetry employing Italian forms and meters. Because of his efforts, he is remembered for having popularized Italianate verse in Spain. In 1543, the year after his death, his widow published his collected poetry. Included in this work are 92 sonnets and 11 *Canciones;* a long *Historia de Leandro y Hero* in unrhymed hendecasyllables; two *Epístolas,* one of which is addressed to Diego Hurtado de Mendoza; and *Octava Rima,* an allegory based on Bembo's *Stanze.* He also wrote an excellent prose translation (1534) of Castiglione's *Il Cortegiano* (1528). See GARCILASO DE LA VEGA.

Bosch, Hieronymus or **Jerome.** Real name, **Hieronymus van Aken** (1450?-1516). Flemish painter. Bosch, who was so named from his birthplace Hertogenbosch, Netherlands, painted religious pictures, scenes of heaven and hell, and allegories in which exquisite panoramas serve as background to the action of fantastic creatures and demons. His personal symbolism of sin and evil, dependent on contemporary literature, astrology, and popular beliefs, has led to contradictory interpretations, but the extreme delicacy, the refinement, and the richness of imagination displayed by his work is incontrovertible. After Bosch's death, a large portion of his work, including the famous *Gardens of Delight,* was brought to Spain by Philip II.

Bosco, Henri (1888-   ). French novelist of the Provence region. His stories, characterized by poetic fantasy, are filled with both sensual human warmth and a mystic Catholicism. Best known for *Le Mas Théotime* (*The Farm Théotime,* 1946, also translated as *Farm in Provence*), he has also written *L'Ane culotte* (1937), *Le Jardin Hyacinthe* (1940), *Monsieur Carré-Benoît in the Country* (1947), *Dark Bough* (*Un Rameau de la Nuit;* 1950), and *Barboche* (1958).

Bose, Buddhadeva (1908-   ). Indian poet and novelist in Bengali. Head of the comparative literature department of Jadavpur University, and visiting professor at New York University in 1959-1960, he has published over 100 volumes, the latest being a book of verse, *Je Andhar Alor Adhik.* He founded and edits *Kavita,* a poetry quarterly in Bengali.

Bosinney, Philip. In John Galsworthy's A FORSYTE SAGA, an architect, lover of Soames Forsyte's wife, Irene.

Boss, The (1911). A play by Edward SHELDON. The hero, Michael Regan, a corrupt contractor and politician, is based on James (Fingy) Connors of Buffalo, N.Y. He ultimately falls in love with a wealthy girl who marries him to save her father.

Bossuet, Jacques Bénigne (1627-1704). French prelate. A Roman Catholic bishop, educated by the Jesuits, Bossuet tutored the dauphin 10 fruitless years; it was for this apathetic pupil that he wrote his most important work, the *Discours sur l'histoire universelle* (*Discourse on Universal History,* 1681), a treatise on history from the Christian viewpoint. Turning to ecclesiastical duties, Bossuet preached sermons in which he united exposition of pure dogma with a simple, moving style. In his funeral orations for such personages as Anne of Austria and Marie Thérèse, wife of Louis XIV, he eloquently drew from the lives of the illustrious the "great and terrible lessons" which God teaches kings and men. Bossuet tirelessly defended the Catholic faith against Protestants and heretics; his *Relation sur le Quiétisme* (*Statement on Quietism,* 1698) is a criticism of the quietist movement.

Boston (1928). A novel by Upton SINCLAIR. Its central character is a lady of the Boston Brahmins who suffers pangs of social conscience and goes to work in a factory, where she meets Sacco and Vanzetti. She observes at close range the events following their arrest, appeal, and execution. Seething with indignation, the book partly follows the transcript of the trial.

Boston Hymn (1863). A poem by Ralph Waldo EMERSON. The poet celebrates freedom, denouncing kings and aristocrats. *Boston Hymn* is one of Emerson's most fervent expressions.

Bostonians, The (1886). A novel by Henry JAMES. James satirically portrays a strong-minded Boston feminist, Olive Chancellor, representing a new generation of "do-gooders," who thinks she has found a kindred soul in a beautiful and impressionable girl, Verena Tarrant. The plot turns on the domination of one woman by another and on the struggle between Olive and Basil Ransom for Verena. The theme was suggested by Alphonse Daudet's *Evangeliste* (1883), but James intended it to be at the same time "a tale very characteristic of our social conditions." Bostonians attacked the novel angrily as a false portrayal of their city, and many American critics censured James for his lack of local feeling. It was one of the first American novels to deal more or less explicitly with Lesbianism.

Boston Massacre (March 5, 1770). A clash between the townspeople of Boston and British troops. Sent to Boston to protect the customs commissioners, the soldiers fired on a mob of men and boys, killing five civilians. Further violence was averted by the withdrawal of the troops to some islands in the harbor. The slain leader of the mob was the Negro hero, Crispus Attucks (1723?–1770).

Boston News-Letter. The first newspaper published in the American colonies to have a permanent life. John Campbell, postmaster at Boston, published the first issue on April 24, 1704. The paper ran until 1776.

Boston Public Occurrences. The first newspaper to be published in the American colonies, appearing in 1690. It lasted only one day because its publisher failed to get a government license.

Boston Tea Party (Dec. 16, 1773). The destruction in Boston Harbor of 342 chests of tea by citizens disguised as Indians and led by Samuel Adams. The colonists were protesting an act of Parliament designed to save the East India Co. from bankruptcy at the expense of the colonists.

Boswell, James (1740–1795). Scottish man of letters and biographer. He is best known as a diarist and as the biographer of Dr. Samuel JOHNSON. He was called to the Scottish bar in 1766 and practiced law for 20 years. He met Dr. Johnson in 1763 and visited him yearly on vacations to London until he moved there. In 1786 he settled permanently in London, entered the English bar, but met with little success there. His literary fame and success began with *An Account of Corsica* (1768), a defense of Corsica's abortive struggle for freedom against the republic of Genoa. In 1773 he accompanied Dr. Johnson on a journey to Scotland; his account of the trip, *The Journal of a Tour to the Hebrides with Samuel Johnson, LL.D.*, appeared in 1785, by which time he was already working on THE LIFE OF SAMUEL JOHNSON, LL.D. Boswell was a man of great wit and charm; his personality was marked with fascinating turns of hypochondria and gaiety. He noted with amusement the fact that while he defended Corsican liberty abroad, he was opposed to further extensions of liberty at home. His papers are full of detailed plans for reform and admonitory addresses to himself such as, "Desperate. This day, *Easter* rouse. Be Johnson. You've done no harm. Be *retenu* [restrained], &c. *What* am I?" Occasionally he even took his own advice. See BOSWELL PAPERS.

Boswell Papers. The papers of James BOSWELL. Long believed to have been lost or destroyed, they constitute one of the most important literary finds of the 20th century. The discoveries include letters and manuscripts of Dr. Samuel JOHNSON and Sir Joshua REYNOLDS, as well as the manuscripts of THE LIFE OF SAMUEL JOHNSON, LL.D, *The Journal of a Tour to the Hebrides with Samuel Johnson, LL.D*, and Boswell's private journals. The bulk of the material was acquired by Yale University in 1949 and is in the process of being published in two series. The annotated "research edition" will run to at least 30 volumes A shorter "trade edition" is being published under the editorship of Frederick A. Pottle and others: *Boswell's London Journal, 1762–1763* (1950), *Boswell in Holland, 1763–1764* (1952), *Boswell on the Grand Tour: Germany and Switzerland, 1764* (1953), *Boswell on the Grand Tour: Italy, Corsica, and France, 1765–1766* (1955), *Boswell in Search of a Wife, 1766–1769* (1956), *Boswell for the Defense, 1769–1774* (1959), and *Boswell's Journal of a Tour*

to the Hebrides with Samuel Johnson, 1773 (1962), which was originally published in 1785. The Reynolds manuscript, *Portraits by Sir Joshua Reynolds*, was published by Yale in 1952.

Bosworth, battle of (Aug. 22, 1485). The concluding battle of the WARS OF THE ROSES. In the struggle, RICHARD III, the last Yorkist king, was slain, and the victor, Henry Tudor, became HENRY VII of England.

Botero, Giovanni (1540–1617). Italian political theorist. He defended church and monarchy in the *Ragion di Stato* (*Reason of State*, 1589), an anti-Machiavellian treatise which summed up the political thought of the Counter Reformation. Its title became a popular phrase in future political discussion.

Both Your Houses (1933). A play by Maxwell ANDERSON. A young congressman compiles evidence to prove political corruption, but finds that the father of the woman he loves is among those involved. It was awarded a Pulitzer Prize.

bo tree. The pipal tree or *Ficus religiosa* of India, related to the banyan tree. It was under one of these trees that Gautama attained enlightenment or perfect knowledge (Sans., *bodhi*) and so became the Buddha.

Botticelli, Sandro. Real name, **Alessandro di Mariano dei Filipepi** (1444–1510). Florentine painter. A pupil of Fra Lippo LIPPI, he depicted both religious and mythological subjects in a style dependent on the decorative patterns of flowing draperies and exquisite detail, on the graceful elongation of idealized figures, and on the swaying beauty of linear design. The *Primavera* (c. 1477) and *The Birth of Venus* (c. 1485), painted for the Medici and now in the Uffizi Gallery in Florence, are his masterpieces in this style. He also painted portraits of the Medici family and did some illustrations of Dante's *Divine Comedy*. At Rome he was commissioned to plan and execute with other artists the frescoes for the walls of the Sistine Chapel. His own contribution was the *Punishment of Korah, Dathan, and Abiram*. He became a follower of the religious reformer Savonarola during the last years of the 15th century and turned towards the illustration of allegories in a harsher, barer style.

Bottom. A weaver and the leader of the bumbling tradesmen-players who perform the tragedy of Pyramus and Thisbe for Duke Theseus in Shakespeare's MIDSUMMER NIGHT'S DREAM. He is a blustering, pompous, but lovable character who constantly misuses words and wants to enact every part in the play.

Bottom is finally persuaded to settle for the part of Pyramus in one of Shakespeare's funniest burlesques. Flute the bellows mender is chosen to play the heroine Thisbe, though he has "a beard coming." Snug the joiner, who is "slow of study," has the sole task of roaring like a lion. Snout the tinker, who is also given to bombast, takes the part of a most garrulous "Wall." Robin Starveling plays the Moon but "wanes" early, and Peter Quince, in bewildered fashion, essays the direction of the whole affair and speaks the prologue. Their combined efforts provide one of Shakespeare's greatest low comedy scenes.

Bottome, Phyllis. Pen name of **Mrs. Ernan Forbes-Dennis** (1884–1963). English novelist. A prolific writer, she is best known for two novels. *Private Worlds* (1934) is heavily influenced by the author's study with Alfred Adler, a prominent psychologist. In 1937 she published *The Mortal Storm,* an anti-Nazi novel written to warn the West. Phyllis Bottome also made several lecture tours in the U.S. before World War II. *Search for a Soul* (1948) is the first volume of an autobiography; the second, *Challenge* (1952), covers the years from adolescence to the early thirties. *Walls of Glass* (1958) is a book of short stories.

Bottomley, Gordon (1874–1948). English poet and poetic dramatist. Associated with the GEORGIANS, he dedicated himself to the revival of English verse drama; his works in this genre include *The Crier by Night* (1902), *King Lear's Wife* (1915), and *Gruach* (1921). Among his poems are *Chambers of Imagery* (1907 and 1912).

Boucher, François (1703–1770). French painter. His works include scenes, pastorals, portraits, and tapestry cartoons in the rococo style. He was very successful as a decorative artist in spite of a tendency toward the florid and sensual. His fashionable elegance made him a favorite of Madame de Pompadour and won him the title of court painter in 1765.

Boucicault, Dion. Original name, **Dionysius Lardner Boursiquot** (1820–1890). Anglo-Irish playwright, theatrical manager, and actor. Born in Ireland, he was educated in London and achieved success there, while still a minor, with the production of his play *London Assurance* (1841). In 1853, his reputation already established, he journeyed to New York City and became a leading figure on the U.S. stage. Boucicault dramatized Mayne Reid's novel *The Quadroon* (1856), which he rechristened THE OCTOROON, and he collaborated with Joseph Jefferson on the famous stage version of RIP VAN WINKLE, which began its long run in London in 1865. In his later years, he specialized more and more on plays with an Irish setting, among them *Arrah-na-Pogue* (1865) and *The Shaughraun* (1874). He has been described as "a director-playwright with a genius for theatrical effect."

Bouhours, Dominique. Known as **le père Bouhours** (1628–1702). French Jesuit and grammarian. In *Doutes sur la langue française* (*Doubts concerning the French Language,* 1674), Bouhours supported the reforms proposed by the Académie Française and aimed at raising the standard of the language. After the death of Claude Vaugelas, Bouhours became the leading grammarian of France.

Boulanger, Georges Ernest Jean Marie (1837–1891). French general. Boulanger, who enjoyed tremendous popular support, advocated militarism and revenge upon Germany after the Franco-Prussian War; the political movement Boulangism adopted his name and his aims. Elected deputy of the department of the Seine in 1889, Boulanger might have seized dictatorial powers; accused of conspiracy, he fled the country without awaiting trial. His popular cognomen, Man on Horseback, resulted from his habit of appearing mounted before Paris crowds.

Boulanger, Nadia (1887–   ). French conductor and composer. Herself once a pupil of Gabriel Fauré, she is famous as a teacher of composers, especially two generations of Americans, including Virgil Thomson, Aaron Copland, Roy Harris, Walter Piston, and Elliott Carter. She has also revived much old music, including works of Monteverdi.

Boulez, Pierre (1925–   ). French composer of extremely complex, pointillistic music. He is best known for *Le Marteau sans Maître* (1955), with a text by Réné Char.

Boulle, Pierre (1912–   ). French novelist. Like *The Bridge Over the River Kwai* (1952), most of his books are set amid the difficulties of war, international intrigue, or wilderness outposts. The novels satirize either the British code of conduct or the often ignoble origins of so-called heroism: *Not the Glory* (1950), *Face of a Hero* (1953), *The Test* (*L'Epreuve des hommes;* 1955), S.O.P.H.I.A. (1959), and *A Noble Profession* (*Un métier de seigneur;* 1960).

Bounderby, Josiah. In Charles Dickens' HARD TIMES, a vulgar banker and mill owner described as a "bully of humility." He is always boasting of his old ignorance and poverty, of an infancy passed in an "egg-box" under the care of his drunken grandmother. Actually, his parents doted on him, educated him at considerable sacrifice, and he now pays them a monthly stipend to keep out of sight. Bounderby marries Louisa Gradgrind, but later she separates from him.

bounds, beating the. An old custom, still kept up in many English parishes, of going round the parish boundaries on Holy Thursday, or Ascension Day. The schoolchildren, accompanied by the clergymen and parish officers, walked through their parish from end to end; the boys were switched with willow wands all along the lines of boundary, the idea being to teach them to know the bounds of their parish. Beating the bounds was called in Scotland *riding the marches* (bounds), and in England the day is sometimes called *gang-day.*

Bourbon. A French royal family whose line also formed ruling dynasties in Spain and Naples. The Bourbon kings of France were Henry IV, Louis XIII, XIV, XV, and XVI (1589–1793). It was said that the family "learned nothing and forgot nothing." Hence a Bourbon is anyone who fails to learn by experience. In the U.S., the name was given to the Democratic Party by its opponents.

Bourchier, John. 2nd Baron **Berners** (1467–1533). English translator, a high court official under Henry VIII. At the king's request he translated Froissart's *Chronicles* (2 vols., 1523, 1525), a classic of Tudor English prose, and the French romance *Huon de Bordeaux. The Golden Boke of Marcus Aurelius* and *The Castell of Love* were translated from French versions of Spanish works by Antonio de Guevara and Diego de San Pedro, and printed after his death.

Bourdaloue, Louis (1632–1704). French Jesuit priest and preacher. He delivered his first sermons in Paris in 1669, and till his death he was considered the greatest preacher of his era. Dealing chiefly with moral and practical questions, his sermons were as calm and rational as Bossuet's were emotional and stirring. Bourdaloue was a formidable opponent of the Jansenists.

bourgeois drama (**drame bourgeois**). A type of French play, developed from the COMÉDIE LARMO-

YANTE, which deals seriously with middle-class family relationships, problems, and duties. Representative plays of this type were often sentimental, morally edifying, melodramatic, mediocre, and humorless. The most famous of these plays are DIDEROT's *Le fils naturel* (1771) and *Le Père de famille* (1761); SEDAINE's *Le Philosophe sans le savoir* (1765); and Beaumarchais' *La Mère coupable* (1792). Diderot's theories about this type of drama were to have an influence on the social theater of Emile Augier and Dumas *fils*.

Bourgeois Gentilhomme, Le (The Would-be Gentleman, 1670). A COMÉDIE-BALLET by MOLIÈRE. M. JOURDAIN, a bourgeois and a boor, is determined to make a gentleman of himself and to that end studies dancing, fencing, and philosophy, allows himself to be fleeced by the unscrupulous nobleman DORANTE, and forbids his daughter's marriage to her beloved CLÉONTE or to any other commoner. The resourceful Cléonte disguises himself as the son of the Grand Turk and, babbling pseudo-Turkish, dupes M. Jourdain into granting him the girl's hand. A delightful comedy in its own right, the play has survived in the repertory for almost three centuries and has often served as a pretext for lavish ballets and *divertissements*.

Bourget, Paul Charles Joseph (1852–1935). French novelist and critic. Bourget's work occupies an important place in the development of the psychological novel, probing with new care and accuracy the state of the inner man. Among his finest novels are *Cruelle Enigme* (1885), *Le Disciple* (1889), *Cosmopolis* (1893), and *L'Etape* (1903). His critical works, such as *Etudes de Portraits* (1888) and *Pages de Doctrine et de Critique* (1912), use a similar analytical method. The tone of the later work, however, changed, becoming increasingly moralistic and didactic in such novels as *L'Emigré* (1907) and *Le Démon de midi* (1914).

Bourgh, Lady Catherine de. An overbearing "great lady" in Jane Austen's PRIDE AND PREJUDICE. An inveterate snob, she tries to prevent the marriage of Elizabeth and Darcy.

Bourjaily, Vance [Nye] (1922–). American writer. His first novel, *The End of My Life* (1947), was the story of a young man's mental and moral disintegration during World War II. Bourjaily was also an editor of *discovery*, a paperback periodical of the 1950's devoted to new authors. He has written several other novels and *The Unnatural Enemy* (1963), a book about the ethics of hunting.

Bourke-White, Margaret (1906–). American photographer. Known for her photographic studies of industry, social and economic conditions, and news personalities, she has worked in 34 countries, including the Soviet Union and the Arctic. She was a United Nations' war correspondent in Korea for *Life* magazine (1952) and was also associated with *Fortune* and *PM* as editor and photographer. She described her successful struggle against Parkinson's disease in her autobiography, *Portrait of Myself* (1963). See Erskine CALDWELL.

Bourne, Randolph [Silliman] (1886–1918). American literary critic and essayist. An early accident made Bourne a helpless cripple; he succeeded, however, in studying at Columbia University and abroad. He held radical views on education and politics and was an outspoken pacifist during World War I. He wrote for several publications, including *The Dial, The New Republic,* and *The Masses.* Among his books are *Youth and Life* (1913), *The Gary Schools* (1916), *Education and Living* (1917), and *Untimely Papers* (1919). After Bourne's death, Van Wyck Brooks edited *The History of a Literary Radical* (1920; reprinted 1956).

Bourrienne, Louis Antoine Fauvelet de (1769–1834). French diplomat, friend and secretary (1797–1802) to Napoleon. He wrote *Mémoires sur Napoléon* (10 vols., 1829), a vivid but untrustworthy work.

Boutelleau, Jacques. See Jacques CHARDONNE.

Bovary, Emma. The heroine of Gustave Flaubert's novel MADAME BOVARY.

bowdlerize. To expurgate a book. In 1818 an English physician, Thomas Bowdler (1754–1825), gave to the world a 10-volume edition of Shakespeare's works "in which nothing is added to the original text; but those words and expressions are omitted which cannot with propriety be read aloud in a family." Bowdler later treated Gibbon's *Decline and Fall* in the same way. Hence, we have the words *bowdlerist, bowdlerizer, bowdlerism, bowdlerization,* etc.

Bowen, Catherine [Shober] Drinker (1897–). American biographer. An accomplished musician who first wrote about music, Mrs. Bowen later turned to biography. Two early biographies were of musicians: Tchaikovsky (*Beloved Friend,* 1937) and Anton and Nicholas Rubinstein (*Free Artist,* 1939). These were followed by *Yankee from Olympus: Justice Holmes and His Family* (1944), *John Adams and the American Revolution* (1950), *The Lion and the Throne: The Life and Times of Sir Edward Coke* (1957), *The Adventures of a Biographer* (1959), and *Francis Bacon: The Temper of a Man* (1963).

Bowen, Elizabeth [Dorothea Cole] (1899–). Anglo-Irish novelist and short-story writer. She knew members of the Bloomsbury group and wrote in the tradition of sensibility, following Henry James and E. M. Forster. With satire, irony, and occasional melodrama she explores the relationships, emotional crises, and failures of feeling of her upper-middle-class characters. Her best-known novels are THE HOTEL, THE HOUSE IN PARIS, THE DEATH OF THE HEART, and THE HEAT OF THE DAY. Among her other books are *The Last September* (1929), *A World of Love* (1955), *A Time in Rome* (1960), and *The Little Girls* (1964). *Bowen's Court* (1942) studies the history of the Bowen family house in Ireland and 10 generations of the family. *Seven Winters & Afterthoughts* (1962) consists of two sections. The first, an autobiographical fragment, was first published in 1943; the second is a collection of critical essays. Among her collections of short stories are *The Cat Jumps* (1934), *Look at All Those Roses* (1941), and *The Demon Lover* (1945).

Bowen, John (1924–). English novelist. Among his satirical novels are *The Truth Will Not Help Us* (1956) and *After the Rain* (1958).

Bowen, Marjorie. See G. M. V. LONG.

Bower of Bliss. See FAERIE QUEENE, THE.

Bowers, Claude [Gernade] (1878–1958). American historian and diplomat. His historical works include *Jefferson and Hamilton* (1925) and *The Tragic Era: The Revolution after Lincoln*

(1929). In *My Mission to Spain* (1954), and *My Life* (1963), he described his experiences in politics and as ambassador to Spain and Chile.

Bowery. A district of New York City, now known as the last refuge for derelicts of all types. Bowery or *bouwerij* is the old Dutch word for farm; and Bowery Lane received its name because it led to the farm of Peter Stuyvesant, one of the Dutch governors of colonial days. It was for a long time the height of fashion to live on Bowery Lane, but with the growth of the city the character of the district underwent a radical change, becoming the site of dance halls and gambling resorts. *The Bowery,* a popular song by Charles H. Hoyt, gives an indication of the reputation of the district at the close of the 19th century.

Bowling, Lieutenant Tom. In Tobias Smollett's novel RODERICK RANDOM, the generous uncle of the hero. A man too frankly the product of the sea to be anything but ill at ease on land, he is careless of the niceties of life ashore.

Bowra, Sir [Cecil] Maurice (1898-   ). English classical scholar and author of criticism on ancient and modern European literature. Among his books are *Greek Lyric Poetry* (1936), *Heroic Poetry* (1952), and *Primitive Song* (1962).

Bow Street. A street near Covent Garden in London which contains the principal police court. The early police were called "Bow Street runners."

Box and Cox (1847). A farce by John Maddison Morton (1811–1891). It has been called "the best farce for three characters in the English language." The principal characters are Box and Cox; the third is the thrifty landlady who rents the same rooms to Box and Cox (one of whom is employed by night, the other by day) in the vain hope that her two tenants will remain ignorant of each other's existence. Hence, there developed the term a *Box and Cox arrangement.*

Boxer. A member of a secret society in China. This society took a prominent part in the rising against foreigners in 1900, which was suppressed by joint European action. The Chinese name was *gee ho chuan,* signifying "righteousness, harmony and fists," and implying training as in athletics for the purpose of developing righteousness and harmony.

Boy Bishop. St. Nicholas of Bari. He was so called because from his cradle he manifested marvelous indications of piety. The custom of choosing a boy from the cathedral choir on his day (December 6th), as a mock bishop, is very ancient. The boy possessed episcopal honor for three weeks, and the rest of the choir were his prebendaries. If he died during his time of office he was buried *in pontificalibus.* Probably the reference is to Jesus Christ sitting in the temple among the doctors while he was a boy. The custom was abolished in the reign of Henry VIII.

boycott. To refuse to have commerce of any sort with a person, group, or country for punitive or retaliatory reasons. The term is derived from the experience of Charles Cunningham Boycott (1832–1897). In his capacity of agent for a large landowner in County Mayo, Ireland, Captain Boycott was thus ostracized (even his servants left him) by the Irish agrarian insurgents of 1880.

Boyd, Nancy. A pen name of Edna St. Vincent MILLAY. It was used on the title page of a series of sketches, *Distressing Dialogues* (1924).

Boyle, Kay (1903-   ). American short-story writer and novelist. Miss Boyle was an expatriate for many years, living in France. As early contributor to "the little magazines," she is known for the stylish polish of her prose and psychological interest in character. Her books include *Wedding Day* (1931), *The White Horses of Vienna and Other Stories* (1936), *The Crazy Hunter* (1940), *American Citizen* (a poem, 1944), *1939* (1948), *His Human Majesty* (1949), *The Seagull on the Step* (1955), and *Generation without Farewell* (1959).

Boyle, Robert (1627–1691). Irish-born English physicist and chemist. Boyle's Law states that, if the temperature remains constant, the volume of a gas varies inversely with the pressure.

Boz. The pen name of Charles DICKENS. His *Sketches by Boz* (two series) appeared in 1836. "Boz, my signature in the Morning Chronicle," he tells us, "was the nickname of a pet child, a younger brother, whom I had dubbed Moses, in honor of [Goldsmith's] *The Vicar of Wakefield,* which, being pronounced Bozes, got shortened into Boz."

Brabançonne. The national anthem of Belgium, composed by Van Campenhout in the revolution of 1830. It is named from Brabant, of which Brussels is the chief city.

Brabantio. In Shakespeare's OTHELLO, a Venetian senator and father of Desdemona. When he learns of Desdemona's secret marriage to Othello, he accuses the Moor of having won his daughter by witchcraft. Since Desdemona insists on remaining with her husband, he is forced to accept the situation, but warns Othello:

> Look to her, Moor, if thou hast eyes to see:
> She has deceiv'd her father, and may thee."

Bracciolini, Poggio (1380–1459). Italian Humanist. He served as chancellor of Florence and papal secretary during a varied career that saw him spend four years in England and many others in search of lost manuscripts of classical writers in continental monasteries. Among the early Italian Renaissance humanists, he wrote the best Latin letters and dialogues and was especially known for his *De varietate fortunae (On the Vagaries of Fortune)*; a history of Florence; and a collection of jests and anecdotes, the *Liber facetiarum.*

Bracebridge Hall, or The Humorists (1822). A collection of tales and sketches by Washington IRVING. The book is a less successful sequel to *The Sketch Book of Geoffrey Crayon, Gent.*

Bracegirdle, Anne (1663?–1748). English actress. A protegée of Thomas Betterton, she was the intimate friend of Congreve and made her greatest successes as the heroines of his comedies, particularly as Millamant in *The Way of the World.* She retired in 1707, probably out of fear of being eclipsed by Mrs. Oldfield, a younger rival.

Brackenridge, Hugh Henry (1748–1816). American novelist and poet. One of the first writers to consider the native American scene valid material for literature, he collaborated with Philip Freneau on *The Rising Glory of America* (1772), a commencement ode at Princeton, and also wrote *The*

Battle of Bunker Hill (1776) and *The Death of General Montgomery* (1777), blank-verse dramas in the 18th-century style. His most important work is MODERN CHIVALRY, OR THE ADVENTURES OF CAPTAIN JOHN FARRAGO AND TEAGUE O'REGAN HIS SERVANT.

Bradamante or **Bradamant.** The warrior maiden of Carolingian legend, prominent in the Orlando poems of Boiardo and Ariosto (see ORLANDO FURIOSO) as the sister of Rinaldo and the beloved of Ruggiero. Known as the Virgin Knight, she wears white armor and a white plume; her spear magically unhorses any knight it touches. Her marriage to the Moor Ruggiero after his conversion, and the subsequent defeat of Rodomonte in single combat, form the subject of the last book of Ariosto's poem. The marriage of Bradamante and Ruggiero also enables Ariosto to flatter his noble patrons, the Este family, since it is said to be the forerunner of the future house of Este. She is also the title character of a play by Robert Garnier.

Bradamante (1582). A play by Robert GARNIER. It is derived from the Carolingian legend of BRADAMANTE and from Ariosto's *Orlando Furioso*. Centering on a combat between the knight Roger and the warrior-maiden Bradamante, with emphasis upon Roger's dilemma in choosing between the claims of love and duty, the play was the first of the French tragicomedies—an enormously popular genre in which romance and adventure led to a happy ending, the classical unities being freely disregarded.

Bradbury, Ray [Douglas] (1920–   ). American writer of science fiction. Bradbury is noted for his unearthly, fantastic tales, many of which have appeared in short-story anthologies. Among his books are *Dark Carnival* (1947), *The Martian Chronicles* (1950), *The Golden Apples of the Sun* (1953), *Dandelion Wine* (1957), and *A Medicine for Melancholy* (1959).

Bradby, Anne. See Anne RIDLER.

Braddock, Edward (1695–1755). English general. He led an ill-fated expedition against Fort Duquesne during the French and Indian War. Washington was one of his junior officers.

Braddon, Mary Elizabeth. Pen name, **Babington White** (1837–1915). English novelist. She is best known for her first (and one of her weakest) books, the melodramatic *Lady Audley's Secret* (1862). She was the author of some 80 other novels of a high-flown, romantic character, which, though ephemeral, were not devoid of quality.

Bradford, Andrew (1686–1742). American printer and publisher. On Dec. 22, 1719, he brought out the first number of the *American Weekly Mercury*, the earliest newspaper in Pennsylvania. It continued for more than 26 years. From 1713 to 1723 Bradford was the only printer in Pennsylvania.

Bradford, Gamaliel (1863–1932). American biographer. He is best known for his "psychographs," interpretative portraits concerned with depicting the subjective life of literary and historical figures. Perhaps the best of these are contained in *American Portraits* (1922), discussing Mark Twain, Henry Adams, Henry James, and others, and *Bare Souls* (1924), portraying Keats, Lamb, Voltaire, and other writers. *Damaged Souls* (1923), analyzing P. T. Barnum, Aaron Burr, and others, was perhaps his

most popular volume. His other books include *Types of American Character* (1895), *Confederate Portraits* (1914), *Portraits of Women* (1916), and *Elizabethan Women* (1936).

Bradford, Roark (1896–1948). American short-story writer and playwright. He is best known for the stories of OL' MAN ADAM AN' HIS CHILLUN. *John Henry* (1931), dealing with the legendary Negro, was dramatized in 1940. Other books by Bradford include *Ol' King David an' the Philistine Boys* (1930), *Let the Band Play Dixie* (1934), a collection of short stories; and *The Three-Headed Angel* (1937).

Bradford, William (1590?–1657). English-born American statesman. A leader in the founding of Plymouth, he was governor of the colony from 1621 to his death, except for five years during which he refused election. He was one of the authors of an account of the settlement of Plymouth known as MOURT'S RELATION, and is best known for his *History of Plimouth Plantation*, a chronicle of events in the colony from 1620 to 1646, which was not discovered and published until 1856.

Bradlaugh, Charles (1833–1891). English social and political reformer. Like Mrs. Annie BESANT, with whom he was associated, he was a free thinker. Although he was elected to Parliament for six years, he was not seated because as a free thinker he wished to affirm instead of swear on the Bible. Ultimately he won his point, and in 1886 was seated.

Bradley, Edward. Pen name, **Cuthbert Bede** (1827–1889). English clergyman and humorist. He wrote and illustrated *Adventures of Mr. Verdant Green, an Oxford Freshman* (1853–1856), *Tales of College Life* (1856), and other amusing, Dickensian accounts of Oxford life.

Bradstreet, Anne (1612?–1672). English-born poet of the Massachusetts Bay Colony. By birth an aristocrat, she was the daughter of one governor of the colony and wife of another. Although her verse in general alternates between scenes of domestic affection and conventional professions of piety, it shows a sensitivity to beauty not usually associated with the Puritans. THE TENTH MUSE LATELY SPRUNG UP IN AMERICA is the only edition of her poems published in her lifetime and the first volume of original verse to be written in America. She also wrote *Religious Experiences*, an autobiographical sketch, and *Meditations, Divine and Moral*, a collection of aphorisms for the instruction of her son. John Berryman wrote a remarkable poem, *Homage to Mistress Bradstreet* (1956), in which the sexual tenderness of Anne Bradstreet is set against the sternly chaste background of Puritan New England.

Brady, Cyrus Townsend (1861–1920). American clergyman and author. He wrote many books for boys and historical stories, biographies of Paul Jones, Andrew Jackson, and others.

Brady, Mathew B. (1823?–1896). American photographer. The first significant representative of his profession in the U.S., he is best known for his photographic record of the Civil War and for portraits of Abraham Lincoln and other outstanding personalities of the time.

Braes of Yarrow. See YARROW.

braggadocio. A braggart; one valiant with his tongue but a great coward at heart. The character is from Spenser's FAERIE QUEENE, in which Brag-gadochio appears as a kind of "Intemperance of the Tongue."

Bragi. In Scandinavian mythology, the son of Odin and Frigga, husband of Iduna, and god of poetry, eloquence, and song. He was represented as an old man with a long white beard. With Hermod, he received and welcomed to Valhalla all heroes who fell in battle.

Bragi's apples. An instant cure for weariness, decay of power, ill temper, and failing health. The supply was inexhaustible; after one was eaten another took its place immediately.

Bragi's cup. A cup which each new king had to drain and pledge by before he ascended the high seat of his fathers.

Bragi's story. A lengthy but interesting tale.

Bragmardo, Janotus de. In Rabelais' GARGAN-TUA AND PANTAGRUEL, a professor of theology sent by the Sorbonne to recover the bells of Notre Dame from Gargantua, who had taken them to hang around his mare's neck. Although he has already decided to return the bells, Gargantua listens to the sophist's harangue and is so amused by it that he sends him away amply rewarded.

Brahe, Tycho (1546–1601). Danish astronomer. He attempted to establish a system of astronomy mid-way between that of Copernicus and that of Ptolemy. The earth, he maintained, was motionless, and the five planets revolved around the sun, which circled the earth once every year. On Nov. 11, 1572, he discovered the celebrated "new star" in Cassiopeia, the first in a universe previously considered fixed for eternity, and his account of it, *De Nova Stella,* was published in 1573. He wrote a number of treatises on astronomy in Latin, the most important being *Astronomiae Instauratae Progymnasmata* (1602–1603), edited by Kepler, which dealt with the motions of the sun and the moon.

Brahma. In Hinduism, the Absolute, or God conceived as entirely personal. The theological abstraction was endowed with personality, and became the creator of the universe, the first in the divine TRIMURTI, or triad, of which the other partners were Vishnu the Preserver and Siva the Destroyer. The Brahmins claim Brahma as the founder of their religious system.

Brahma (1857). A poem by Ralph Waldo EMER-SON. In terms of Hindu philosophy, the poet expresses the pantheistic belief that God is everywhere and is found in the act of seeking.

Brahmin. A member of one of the four castes of Hinduism, representing the priestly and meditative order. See CASTE; BRAHMA.

Brahmo Samaj (*Bengali,* "the union of God"). A monotheistic offshoot of Hinduism. It was established in 1830 in Calcutta by Ram Mohun Roy (1774–1833), a wealthy and extraordinarily erudite Brahmin who wished to reform the ritualistic excesses of institutionalized Hinduism by founding an order free from idolatry and superstition. In 1844 the "church" was reorganized by Debendro Nath Tagore, and its reforming zeal and intellectual influence impressed sensitive Hindus everywhere, but especially in Bengal. The Samaj provided a spearhead of morally excellent people whose example succeeded in convincing even orthodox Hindus of the necessity of reform;

it also supplied an alert élite of educated Indians who did much for national autonomy, social reforms, and political independence. After 1947 its influence has gradually declined, partly because most of its ideas have been accepted and incorporated into the progressive sections of Hinduism.

Brahms, Johannes (1833–1897). German romantic composer. His works include four symphonies, concertos, chamber music, songs, and choral works, including the popular *Ein deutsches Requiem* (*A German Requiem,* 1867). He was the most successful of the romantic composers in reconciling the conflicting claims of lyricism and classical form, partly because of his study and editing of 16th-, 17th-, and 18th-century music.

Braille, Louis (1809–1852). French teacher of the blind. In 1829, Braille, who was himself blind from the age of three, developed an alphabetic system of raised points that enabled the blind to read.

Braine, John (1922–   ). English novelist. One of the ANGRY YOUNG MEN, he is author of the best-selling novel ROOM AT THE TOP. A sequel, *Life at the Top,* was published in 1962.

Brainworm. In Ben Jonson's comedy EVERY MAN IN HIS HUMOUR, the servant of Kno'well. A veritable Proteus in his metamorphoses, he appears first as Brainworm, then as Fitz-Sword, then as a reformed soldier whom Kno'well takes into his service, then as Justice Clement's man, and lastly as valet to the courts of law. By his various transformations he is able to play upon the same group of characters, and his rascalities serve as the catalyst to the comedy.

Braithwaite, William Stanley Beaumont (1878–1962). American poet and anthologist. He originated and edited for 17 years the *Anthology of Magazine Verse and Year Book of American Poetry.* Much of his own poetry appears in *Selected Poems* (1948).

Bramah, Ernest. See Ernest Bramah SMITH.

Bramante. Real name, **Donato d'Agnola** (c. 1444–1514). Italian architect and painter. Born in Urbino, he worked mainly at Milan, serving Lodovico Sforza, and then at Rome for the papacy, where he was consulted on all important architectural undertakings. One of his paintings, *Christ at the Column,* is considered a masterpiece, but his great fame rests on his achievements as an architect. One of the finest examples of his work is the *Tempietto,* the severely classical, small-scale, and perfect circular temple erected at Rome in 1502 on the spot where Peter allegedly was crucified. In 1506, he began to execute his design for the new basilica that eventually became the modern St. Peter's. Supposedly a rival of Michelangelo, he is thought to have secured for the latter the torturous and unwelcome task of decorating the ceiling of the Sistine Chapel.

Bramble, Matthew. The chief character in Tobias Smollett's novel HUMPHREY CLINKER. An irascible, eccentric, somewhat valetudinarian bachelor, he initiates the family expedition partly because of ill health and partly to distract the mind of his young niece Lydia Melford, who has fallen in love with a supposedly itinerant actor.

Tabitha Bramble. In the same book, the sister of Matthew Bramble, noted for her bad spelling. She is vain, prim, uncharitable, and in violent search for

a husband. She contrives to marry Captain LISMA-
HAGO, who is content to take her for the sake of
her £4,000.

Bramine's Journal, The. A journal kept by
Laurence STERNE and addressed to Mrs. Eliza Draper,
whom he met in London. It is dated from April,
1767, to August, 1767, after her departure for India.
See ELIZA.

Brancati, Vitaliano (1907–1954). Italian novelist
and essayist. He is noted for his satire of contemporary social manners and his ironic appraisals of fascist culture. His works include *Don Giovanni in
Sicilia* (1942), a light-hearted spoofing of anach-
ronistic Sicilian customs; *Il Vecchio con gli Stivali*
(1945), a humorous treatment of the Italian bourgeoisie's belief in fascist dreams of national glory;
and *Il Bell'Antonio* and *Paolo Il Caldo,* both political
satires. Brancati was essentially a realist of the school
of De Roberto. He freely employed dialect in his
fiction and, as a rule, used his native Catania as the
setting of his novels.

Branch, Anna Hempstead (1875–1937). American poet. Noted for her lyricism, she wrote *Nimrod,*
a narrative poem based on the biblical story. *The
Monk in the Kitchen* (1905) is perhaps her best-
known poem. Among her works are *The Heart of
the Road, and Other Poems* (1901), *The Shoes that
Danced* (1905), and *Sonnets from a Lock Box and
Other Poems* (1929).

Brancusi, Constantin (1876–1957). Romanian
sculptor, settled in France in 1904. He is known for
his simplified abstracted forms, executed in wood,
steel, stone, and bronze, and finished to a great
smoothness or polish. His best-known work in the
U.S. is *Bird in Space* (1919), a vertical swelling
shaft of highly polished metal.

Brand (1866). A verse drama by Henrik IBSEN.
The first of Ibsen's major plays, *Brand* deals with a
passionate and uncompromising idealist, a minister
who sacrifices the health and finally the life of his
child and his wife rather than violate his stern sense
of duty to his parish. Finally, Brand tries to lead
his parishioners to the greater Church of Life in the
mountains, but the people fall behind and abandon
him. In the symbolic closing scene on the mountain
Ice Church, Brand, about to be crushed by an ava-
lanche, calls out to God. He is answered by a voice
saying "God is Love."

Brand, Max. Pen name of **Frederick Faust**
(1892–1944). American writer. Although he published two books of verse under his own name, he
is best known for his Max Brand books, which are
old-style Westerns done with great storytelling
power. *The Untamed* (1918) is the first of this
lengthy series, while *Destry Rides Again* (1930) is
perhaps the most famous. He also wrote the books
and motion pictures about Dr. Kildare.

Brandan or **Brendan,** St. A semilegendary Irish
saint. He is said to have been buried at Clonfert (at
the age of about 94), in 577, where he was abbot over
3,000 monks. He is best known because of the very
popular medieval story of his voyage in search of the
EARTHLY PARADISE, which was supposed to be situated on an island in mid-Atlantic. The voyage lasted
for seven years, and the story is crowded with marvelous incidents, the very birds and beasts they
encountered being Christians and observing the fasts

and festivals of the Church. As late as 1755 St.
Brandon's Island, or the Island of San Borandan,
was set down in geographical charts as west of the
Canary group.

Brandeis, Louis D[embitz] (1856–1941). American jurist. Born in Louisville, Ky., Brandeis practiced
law in Boston, becoming known as the "people's attorney" because of his opposition to vested interests
and monopolies in every form. He was appointed to
the U.S. Supreme Court by President Wilson in
1916, his nomination being confirmed only after a
bitter struggle. Often joining Holmes and later
Cardozo in their dissents, Brandeis served on the
court until his retirement in 1939. He wrote several
books, including *Business, A Profession* (1914) and
The Curse of Bigness (1934). Brandeis University,
founded in 1948 in Waltham, Mass., is named after
him.

Brandes, Georg Morris Cohen (1842–1927).
Danish literary critic and scholar. Brandes exercised
great influence upon Scandinavian thought and literature, serving as leader of *Det moderne gennem-
bruch* ("the modern breaking-through"). In 1871 he
began to formulate the principles of a new realism
and naturalism, condemning abstract idealism and
fantasy in literature. Brandes was the author of several critical biographies, including a study of Henrik
Ibsen, who shared his literary goals, in his volume of
Critical Studies (1899). His other studies include
Søren Kierkegaard (1877), *Esaias Tegnér* (1878),
Wolfgang Goethe (1914–1915), and *François de Voltaire* (1916–1917). After spending several years in
Germany, Brandes came under the influence of Nietzsche's philosophy and disavowed democracy for an
aristocratic radicalism.

Brandimarte. In the Orlando poems (see OR-
LANDO FURIOSO) of Boiardo and Ariosto, the son of
king Monodante, brother of Origille, and the trusted
companion of Orlando, who had baptized him. He
is followed about continually by his faithful wife
Fiordiligi until Gradasso kills him.

Brandt, Margaret. In Charles Reade's historical
novel THE CLOISTER AND THE HEARTH, the heroine
and mother of Erasmus. Peter Brandt, her father, is
also a prominent character.

Brangwen, Ursula. The heroine of 2 novels by
D. H. Lawrence. In THE RAINBOW, her experience
as a teacher and rebel from her environment reflects
Lawrence's own; in the sequel, WOMEN IN LOVE,
she is based more on Lawrence's wife, Frieda LAW-
RENCE.

Brant, Joseph. Indian name, **Thayendanegea**
(1742–1807). Mohawk Indian chief. During the
American Revolution, he commanded the Indian
forces cooperating with the British and ravaged the
Mohawk Valley of New York. An earnest Christian,
he also translated the Book of Common Prayer into
the Mohawk tongue.

Brant, Sebastian (1458–1521). German didactic
poet and satirist. Most famous for THE SHIP OF
FOOLS, Brant was a highly conservative, even hide-
bound thinker. Although he is often classified as a
humanist, he was very much afraid of change in
any form, and cannot properly be so called.

Brantôme, Seigneur **de. Pierre de Bourdeilles**
(1540?–1614). French soldier, adventurer, and me-
morialist. His two chronicles, *Vies des hommes il-*

Das Narren Schyff.

Gen Narragonien.

Hi funt qui defcendunt mare in nauibus
faciétes opationem in aquis multis.
Afcendüt vfcp ad celos / & defcédunt vfcp
ad abyffos: aia eorü in malis tabefcebat ∿
Turbati funt & moti funt ficut ebrius: &
omnis fapientia eorü deuorata eft .
.Pfalmo .Cvi.

Title page of Sebastian Brant's *Ship of Fools* (1494).

lustres et grands capitaines français and *Vies des dames galantes* (1665–1666), reveal him as credulous and uncritical, impressed by spectacle and fascinated by trivialities and gossip, but they survive as an interesting portrait of French-Renaissance manners.

Braque, Georges (1882–1963). French painter, associated with Pablo Picasso in the development of CUBISM. His subjects were chiefly still lifes. In 1952 he began a series of designs of birds which bring to a culmination of simplicity his elegance of line and precision of color.

Brass, Sampson. In Charles Dickens' OLD CURIOSITY SHOP, a knavish, servile attorney, affecting great sympathy with his clients but in reality fleecing them without mercy.

Sally Brass. Sampson's sister, and an exaggerated edition of her brother.

Brave New World (1932). A satirical novel by Aldous HUXLEY. Set in the year 632 AF (After Ford), it is a grim picture of the world which Huxley thinks our scientific and social developments have already begun to create. Human embryos are developed in bottles and conditioned to collectivism and passivity. A "savage" is found in New Mexico and imported as an experiment. He has educated himself by reading Shakespeare and believes in spirituality and moral choice; in the new world he soon goes berserk and kills himself. The title, which is highly ironic, is from Shakespeare's *The Tempest*.

brazen head. A theme of many legends. The legend of the wonderful head of brass that could

speak is common in early romances, and is of Eastern origin. In *Valentine and Orson,* a gigantic head kept in the castle of the giant Ferragus of Portugal tells those who consult it whatever they require to know, past, present, or to come. The most famous brazen head in English legend is that fabled to have been made by Roger Bacon. It was said if Bacon heard it speak he would succeed in his projects; if not, he would fail. His familiar, Miles, was set to watch, and while Bacon slept the head spoke thrice. "Time is"; half an hour later it said, "Time was." In another half-hour it said, "Time past," fell down, and was broken to atoms. References to Bacon's brazen head are frequent in literature.

Bread and Wine (Pane e Vino; 1937; revised, 1962). A novel by Ignazio SILONE. The hero, Pietro Spina, returns to his native Abruzzi after 15 years of exile to continue his antifascist agitation. As he travels through the country, disguised as a priest, he sees the inroads made upon the Italian character by Mussolini's rule. Finding that the underground movement is in chaos and doubting the validity of his old revolutionary slogans, he eventually flees to avoid certain arrest. Other important characters include the devout Cristina and Don Benedetto, a priest who is an uncompromising opponent of the regime and who is poisoned by the sacramental wine he drinks as he celebrates mass. In the 1962 version of the novel, the Italian title was changed to *Vino e Pane.*

Break, Break, Break (1842). A poem by Alfred TENNYSON, one of those inspired by the death of his friend Arthur HALLAM.

Break of Noon (Partage de Midi; 1906). A poetic drama, revised in 1948, by Paul CLAUDEL. Mesa, struggling with his devotion to God, suddenly falls in love with Yse, mysterious and fecund wife of his friend De Ciz, and acknowledges her as the necessary complement of his own being. However, when she senses that Mesa still secretly feels their human love is a barrier to spiritual love, Yse abandons him and her De Ciz children and takes Mesa's child to rejoin her former lover Amalric. When Mesa comes to woo her back, their child is dead, and they recognize the necessary impossibility of their earthly happiness.

Breasted, James Henry (1865–1935). American historian and archaeologist. He is noted for his many books on ancient Egyptian history. His *Ancient Times: A History of the Early World* (1916) was reissued as *The Conquest of Civilization* (1926).

Brecht, Bertolt (1898–1956). German dramatist. Despite his explicit commitment to Marxist dogma, his plays have been immensely popular in the West. His early plays, such as *Trommeln in der Nacht* (*Drums in the Night,* 1922), *Im Dickicht der Städte* (*In the Jungle of Cities,* 1924), and *Mann ist Mann* (*Man Is Man,* 1927), are closely related in technique to the movement of EXPRESSIONISM, and though they are permeated by the cynical and critical irony toward modern society that appears in all his works, they do not yet systematically advocate any political doctrine. Brecht's decisive turn to Marxism, however, came shortly afterward in THE THREEPENNY OPERA and RISE AND FALL OF THE TOWN MAHAGONNY. It is also in these plays that his mature technique is first fully exemplified, the technique of the EPIC THEATER that was to dominate his subsequent production. In 1933, Brecht was driven from Germany by the rise of Nazism, and began a 14-year exile in Denmark, Sweden, Finland and, from 1941 to 1947, in the U.S. The plays written during this exile include direct attacks on Nazism, such as THE PRIVATE LIFE OF THE MASTER RACE and *Schweyk im Zweiten Weltkrieg (Schweyk in the Second World War*, written 1944–1945); plays with historical settings such as LIFE OF GALILEO and MOTHER COURAGE AND HER CHILDREN; and two Chinese parables, THE GOOD WOMAN OF SEZUAN and THE CAUCASIAN CHALK CIRCLE. In 1947, Brecht returned to Zürich and went from there to East Berlin in 1948 where he founded his own company; his works of the last period consist almost entirely of adaptations.

Breck, Alan. In Robert Louis Stevenson's novel KIDNAPPED, a high-spirited, courageous, and slightly unscrupulous supporter of the Stuart claimant to the throne. After being shipwrecked, he and David Balfour, the young hero of the book, travel through Scotland. His full name is Alan Breck Stewart (or Stuart) and he is very proud to bear the name of a king. He appears in Stevenson's *Catriona* (1893) also.

Bregendahl, Marie (1867–1940). Danish novelist. A regionalist writer, she described peasant life in her native Jutland with quiet skill and sober sympathy. Her most important works are *En Dødsnat (A Night of Death*, 1912) and *Sødalsfolkene* (7 vols., 1914–1923).

Breitmann, Hans. The hero of a series of ballads written in German-American dialect; also, the pen name of his creator, Charles Godfrey Leland (1824–1903). The first and most famous of the ballads is *Hans Breitmann's Party*, published in *Graham's Magazine* (May, 1857), of which Leland was then editor. Leland's published collections about Breitmann, a jovial Pennsylvania Dutchman, include *The Breitmann Ballads* (1871), *Hans Breitmann in Tyrol* (1894), and *Hans Breitmann's Ballads* (1914).

Bremond, Henri (1865–1933). French literary critic and historian. Bremond left the Jesuit order for a literary career, but his principal work, *Histoire littéraire du sentiment religieux en France* (1916–1933), is an 11-volume study of religious elements in French literature.

Brennius. One of the kings in Geoffrey of Monmouth's HISTORY OF THE KINGS OF BRITAIN. He struggled with Belinus for the kingdom, but ultimately made a treaty with him.

Brentano, Clemens Maria (1778–1842). German romantic poet. He was the brother of Bettina von Arnim. In his lyrics, he had a genius for capturing the folk spirit, and it was he who invented the so-called folk legend of the LORELEI, in a poem that appeared in his novel *Godwi* (1800–1801). But he was also capable of highly sophisticated poems, especially on religious subjects, as in his unfinished *Romanzen vom Rosenkranz (Romances of the Rosary*, written 1810 ff.). With his friend (and later brother-in-law) Achim von Arnim, he edited DES KNABEN WUNDERHORN, a collection of folk songs; and his private collection of folk books (see VOLKSBUCH) provided the material for Görres' treatise on the subject. Brentano's short narrative works include the novella *Geschichte vom braven Kasperl*

und dem schönen Annerl (Story of Upright Casper and Lovely Annie, written 1816, pub. 1838), and numerous MÄRCHEN. See GERMAN ROMANTICISM.

Brest-Litovsk, Treaty of (1918). A treaty between Germany and the Russian Bolshevik government, signed in the Polish city of the same name. Russia withdrew from World War I and ceded vast territories in eastern Europe.

Brethren of the Common Life. A group of mystics in Germany and the Low Countries during the 14th and 15th centuries. It was founded by Gerard Groote (1340–1389), a Dutchman. The Brethren lived together communally and through their schools assisted greatly in establishing reforms in education and religion. Erasmus and Martin Luther were at one time their pupils, and the *Imitation of Christ* was one of the products of the influence of the sect's brand of mysticism.

Breton, André (1896–1966). French poet, novelist, and essayist. He was greatly influenced by his reading of Arthur Rimbaud's poetry, his studies of Freudian theory, and his own work in psychiatry. His friendship (1916–1919) with Jacques Vaché (1895–1919), who committed suicide as a deliberate mark of his contempt for modern society, also made a deep impression. In 1919 Breton met Tristan Tzara and led a group of friends into the DADA movement. By 1921, however, he had rejected Tzara's nihilistic use of the irrational as a mockery of reason in favor of a serious research into the subconscious as the autonomous source of truth and beauty. The results of his experiments in automatic writing were published as *Les Champs magnétiques* (1921), written with Philippe Soupault.

In 1924 he founded SURREALISM; his three manifestoes (1924, 1930, 1942) are the most important theoretical statements of the movement. Other critical essays in its defense include *Les Pas perdus* (1924), *Légitime Défense* (1926), *Le Surréalisme et la peinture* (1928), and *What Is Surrealism?* (1934).

A growing interest in the study of dreams and psychic states led to the novel NADJA and *Les Vases communicants* (1932), a study of dreams. Breton joined the Communist Party in 1927, but left it in 1935 after trying unsuccessfully to identify surrealism as the artistic representative of social revolution.

His poems exalting love include those in *Le Revolver à Cheveux Blancs* (1932), *L'Amour Fou* (1937), *Fata Morgana* (1941), and *Arcane 17* (1945).

Breton, Nicholas (1545?–1626). English poet, author of numerous prose pamphlets, moral, religious, and lyric verse. He is known primarily as a pastoral poet, and the best examples of his verse can be found in *England's Helicon* (1600). He is represented in *Breton's Bower of Delights* (1591) and *The Arbor of Amorous Devices* (1597); though both of these books were assigned to him by the printers, the work of other poets is also included.

Bréton de los Herreros, Manuel (1796–1873). Spanish playwright. The clarity of the work of this prominent social satirist makes up for the lack of bitter irony in his comedies of middle-class life. His classic, *Marcela o ¿cuál de las tres? (Marcela*, 1831), deals with the problems of a widow beset by three suitors: one arrogant, another loud, and the third melancholy. Among his best-known dramas are *La* *escuela del matrimonio, A Madrid me vuelvo,* and *Muérete y verás.*

Breton lais or **lays.** Rhymed stories popular in England in the 14th century. They usually deal with Celtic themes and often use Arthurian material. The origin of this literary form is unknown, but it was perfected in the 12th century by MARIE DE FRANCE who wrote, among others, the lai *Sir Launfal.* The Franklin in Chaucer's *The Canterbury Tales* (1388) speaks of the old Bretons who rhymed their tales and sang them to the accompaniment of a musical instrument. *Sir Orfeo* is one of the best-known English Breton lais.

Breton's Bower of Delights. See Nicholas BRETON.

Brett, Dorothy (1891–   ). English painter and friend of D. H. Lawrence. She is the author of *Lawrence and Brett* (1933), a book of reminiscences.

Brian Boru, Boroimhe or **Borumha** (926–1014). Irish king (after 1002) and national hero. His victory over the Danes at Clontarf (1014) put a permanent end to their sovereignty over Ireland, but he was murdered in his tent after the battle.

Briareus (Briareos). In classic legend, a huge monster with 100 arms and 50 heads. With his brothers, Cottus and Gyges, he conquered the Titans by hurling at them 300 rocks at once. Thetis called him to the aid of Zeus when Hera, Athene, and Poseidon rebelled against him. He was also called Aegeon (Aigaion).

Bricklayer, the. A nickname for Ben JONSON, from his stepfather's trade.

Bricks Without Straw (1880). A novel by Albion W. TOURGÉE. This book, a sequel to the earlier A FOOL's ERRAND, is one of the earliest to deal with racial problems in the postwar South. The novel has as its hero a New England schoolteacher in the South who sympathizes with the Negroes.

Bride Comes to Yellow Sky, The (1898). A short story by Stephen CRANE. Published in the collection *The Open Boat and Other Tales of Adventure,* it deals with the conflict between Sheriff Jack Potter and Scratchy Wilson, one of the old frontier gunfighters. Potter brings his new wife to Yellow Sky and encounters Scratchy, who is looking for a fight. When Scratchy realizes that Potter has no gun, he realizes that the old days are gone forever.

Bridehead, Sue. See JUDE THE OBSCURE.

Bride of Abydos, The (1813). A poem by Lord BYRON. The heroine is Zuleika, daughter of Giaffer, pasha of Abydos. She is the plighted bride of Selim; but Giaffer shoots him, and Zuleika dies of a broken heart.

Bride of Lammermoor, The (1819). A historical novel by Sir Walter SCOTT, set in the reign of William III. The titular heroine is Lucy Ashton, daughter of Sir William Ashton, an unscrupulous man who has made great gains in fortune and position by bringing the estate of Lord Ravenswood to ruin through legal trickery. Though he has sworn vengeance, Ravenswood's son Edgar falls in love with Lucy; the lovers plight their troth at the Mermaid's Fountain, but while Edgar is away, Lucy is forced by her parents to marry the unpleasant, dissolute Frank Hayston, laird of Bucklaw. Deranged with grief, Lucy stabs and critically wounds her bride-groom; she dies in convulsions the following day. Edgar, hearing of the marriage and taking it as Lucy's rejection of him, is on his way to a duel with her brother when he is lost in the quicksand of Kelpies Flow, fulfilling an ancient prophecy. The novel is based on historical incident.

In Donizetti's opera *Lucia di Lammermoor* (1835), which is based on the novel, Bucklaw dies of the wound inflicted by his bride, and Edgar, heartbroken at Lucy's death, stabs himself. See Caleb BALDERSTONE.

Bride of the Sea. Venice. The city was so called from the ancient ceremony of the wedding of the sea by the doge, who threw a ring into the Adriatic, saying, "We wed thee, O sea, in token of perpetual domination." This took place each year on Ascension Day, and was enjoined upon the Venetians in 1177 by Pope Alexander III, who gave the doge a gold ring from his own finger in token of the victory achieved by the Venetian fleet at Istria over Frederick Barbarossa, in defense of the pope's quarrel. See BUCENTAUR.

Brideshead Revisited (1945). A novel by Evelyn WAUGH, subtitled *The Sacred and Profane Memories of Captain Charles Ryder.* As an undergraduate Ryder met Sebastian Marchmain and later visited him and his family at Brideshead, their home. Billeted there during World War II, Ryder recalls the members of this family and their individual responses to their Catholic faith.

Bridewell. An ancient London prison in Bridge Street, Blackfriars. It was built as a hospital on the site of a former royal palace over a holy well of medicinal water, called St. Bride's (Bridget's) Well.

Bridge, The (1930). A long poem by Hart CRANE. In this, his most important work, Crane attempted to synthesize a picture of modern America by the use of symbols from its past and present, centered about Brooklyn Bridge as a chief symbol of man's aspiration and achievement. Written in several sections, the poem makes use of such figures from the American past as Columbus, Whitman, Poe, and Emily Dickinson; they themselves function as bridges, connecting and fusing the disparate elements of American life into an organic whole. Not only past and present, but time and eternity are fused, the latter bridge being furnished by the Mississippi River.

Bridge of San Luis Rey, The (1927). A novel by Thornton WILDER. The winner of a Pulitzer Prize, it tells of the collapse of a bridge in Peru in 1714. Five travelers on the bridge are killed, and the accident is witnessed by Brother Juniper, a Franciscan friar. The priest wonders whether it really was an accident or a deliberate plan of the Almighty, and it is his subsequent investigation into the lives of the five people that forms the core of the book.

Bridge of Sighs. An enclosed bridge in Venice, connecting the Doge's Palace with the state prisons. According to popular tradition, prisoners were conveyed across this bridge from the judgment hall to the place of execution.

Bridge on the Drina, The (Na Drini Ćuprija; 1945). A chronicle by Ivo ANDRIĆ. This long narrative, which its author appropriately called a chronicle, relates in a series of episodes the history of a bridge near the Bosnian town of Višegrad. That history covers three and a half centuries, through much of which the Bosnians lived under Turkish overlords. This is probably the most important of Andrić's several novels about his native Bosnia.

Bridge Over the River Kwai, The. See Pierre BOULLE.

Bridge Perilous. See FAERIE QUEENE, THE.

Bridges, Robert (1844–1930). English poet, appointed British poet laureate in 1913. His poetry is classical in spirit and in diction (he advocated a return to the diction of the 18th century and was a co-founder of the SOCIETY FOR PURE ENGLISH). His prosody is mildly experimental. He did important work in metrics, including a study of *Milton's Prosody* (1893). *His Poetical Works* was published in 1912, and THE TESTAMENT OF BEAUTY in 1929. *A Passer-by* is his finest lyric. He also wrote plays, chiefly on classical subjects, and critical essays. Bridges was a friend of Gerard Manley Hopkins, and published his poetry in 1918.

Bridie, James. Pen name of **Osborne Henry Mavor** (1888–1951). Scottish playwright. His plays are famous for their wit and fancy. *The Anatomist* (1930) and *The Sleeping Clergyman* (1933) are dramatizations of well-known criminal cases. *Storm in a Teacup* (1936) is set in Scotland. *One Way of Living* (1939) is autobiographical.

Bridlegoose, Judge. An anglicism for Juge Bridoie, the judge in Rabelais' GARGANTUA AND PANTAGRUEL who decides the cases brought before him by a throw of dice. He explains to Pantagruel that he had never made a mistake until his eyesight began to fail. The dice-throwing and Bridlegoose's insistence that volumes of documents are necessary to allow a case to mature properly are a lively satire on legal procedures.

Beaumarchais in the *Marriage of Figaro* (1784) named his judge "Bridoison," but his magistrate, a slave to legal procedure, bears little resemblance to Rabelais' character.

Bridoie, Juge. See Judge BRIDLEGOOSE.

Bridoison. See Judge BRIDLEGOOSE.

Brieux, Eugène (1858–1932). French dramatist. Brieux's early works—*Ménages d'Artistes* (1890) and *Blanchette* (1892)—were first produced at Antoine's Théâtre Libra. In *Les Trois Filles de M. Dupont* (1899), Brieux, at heart a moral and social reformer, leveled violent criticism at parents who seek to manipulate the lives of their children. *La Robe Rouge* (1900) demands that criminal law be reformed; *La Femme Seule* (1913) staunchly defends women's rights. Although Brieux did not possess the depth necessary for excellent drama of ideas, he did possess a large fund of sympathy and a vigorous sense of protest.

Briffault, Robert Stephen (1876–1948). English anthropologist. He was the author of the once widely read study *The Mothers* (1927).

Brigge, Malte Laurids. See NOTEBOOKS OF MALTE LAURIDS BRIGGE, THE.

Bright, John (1811–1889). English statesman and orator. A liberal, he was strongly opposed to the CORN LAWS and the Crimean War and favored the North in the U.S. Civil War. He is the author of *Speeches on Parliamentary Reform* (1867), *Speeches*

on *Questions of Public Policy* (1869), and *Speeches on Public Affairs* (1869).

Brighton Rock (1938). A novel by Graham GREENE. Set in an English seaside resort, it is the story of Pinkie, a teen-age criminal gang leader and murderer. The novel has elements of a detective story, psychiatric case history, and essay on moral theology.

Brigliadoro (Golden Bridle). Orlando's horse in the poems of Boiardo and Ariosto (see ORLANDO FURIOSO).

Brihat-kathasaritsagara. See KATHASARITSAGARA.

Brillat-Savarin, Anthelme (1755–1826). French politician and gourmet. His *Physiologie du goût* (1825) is a famous work on gastronomy.

Brimming Cup, The (1921). A novel by Dorothy Canfield FISHER. In this story set in Vermont, Mrs. Fisher tells how a man of the world, mature and selfish, seeks to win Marise Crittendon from her husband, Neale. The latter is too honorable to seek to hold her, but events convince her that she needs his integrity more than Vincent Marsh's passion. *Rough-Hewn* (1922) tells of Neale and Marise earlier in their lives.

Brinnin, John Malcolm (1916–). American poet and editor. He was the editor of various avant-garde periodicals and later published several volumes of poetry, including *The Garden Is Political* (1942), *The Lincoln Lyrics* (1942), and *The Sorrows of Cold Stone* (1951). After inviting Dylan Thomas to give readings in the U.S., he wrote *Dylan Thomas in America* (1955) and edited *A Casebook on Dylan Thomas* (1960).

Brinton, [Clarence] Crane (1898–). American historian, biographer, and educator. A teacher at Harvard since 1923, Brinton has written numerous books, among them *The Political Ideas of the English Romanticists* (1926), *The Jacobins* (1930), *Nietzsche* (1941), and *The Shaping of the Modern Mind* (1953).

Brinvilliers, Marquise de. Born **Marie Madeleine d'Aubray** (1630–1676). Notorious French poisoner and a favorite subject for writers. Mme. de Sévigné describes Brinvilliers' execution in her letters.

Briscoe, Lily. A painter, a leading character in Virginia Woolf's novel To THE LIGHTHOUSE.

Briseida. The beloved of TROILUS in the *Roman de Troie* of BENOÎT DE SAINTE-MAURE. In later versions of the story she is known as Criseida or Cressida.

Briseis. The daughter of Briseus. She was the subject of the quarrel in the ILIAD between Agamemnon and Achilles; when the former robbed Achilles of her, Achilles refused any longer to go to battle, and the Greeks lost ground daily.

Brissot [de Warville], Jacques Pierre (1754–1793). French revolutionist and journalist. His antimonarchical pamphlets, inspired by the ideas of Rousseau, caused him to be exiled. He traveled in the Netherlands, Switzerland, England, and the U.S. Returning to France in 1789, he became editor of the newspaper *Le Patriote français* until his death; he was a leader of the GIRONDISTS, and the paper became their organ. Brissot's humanitarian interests led him to advocate penal reform in France, and later to found the society of the "Amis des noirs" in 1788, dedicated to the abolition of slavery. An ad-

Charlotte Brontë, English novelist—
from an engraving after an original painting by Chappel

Lord Byron

Lord Byron, English poet—from an engraving by Edwin for the *Analectic Magazine*

Miguel de Cervantes, Spanish novelist, dramatist, and poet—
from an engraving by E. Mackenzie after a Spanish print engraved by D. F. Selma

James Fenimore Cooper, American novelist—
from an engraving by W. E. Marshall after a painting by C. L. Elliott (above)

Otsego Hall, his residence in Cooperstown, New York—from an engraving (below)

William Cowper, English poet—
from an engraving by T. Gimbrede after a drawing by T. Laurence

Cromwell dissolving the Long Parliament: Oliver Cromwell—from engravings

Cartoons by George Cruikshank, English illustrator and caricaturist

Death mask of Dante Alighieri, Italian poet, by Kenyon Cox—
from an engraving by J. H. E. Whitney

mirer of the U.S., he founded the Gallo-American Society; he wrote *Considerations on the Relative Situation of France and the United States* (1788, in English) and *The Commerce of America with Europe* (1794, in English). When the JACOBINS overthrew the Girondists, Brissot was guillotined.

Bristol Boy, the. An epithet for the poet Thomas CHATTERTON. He is so called because his chief poetic works deal with the imagined 15th century antiquities of the port city of Bristol.

Britannia. A personification of the British Empire. The first known representation of Britannia as a female figure sitting on a globe, leaning with one arm on a shield, and grasping a spear in the other hand, is on a Roman coin of Antoninus Pius, who died A.D. 161. The figure reappeared on the English copper coin in the reign of Charles II, 1665.

Britannicus. Original name, **Claudius Tiberius Germanicus** (c. A.D. 41–55). Son of Messalina and the emperor Claudius, heir apparent to the throne. Through the scheming of his stepmother, AGRIPPINA, he was denied succession to the throne. It is believed that Nero, his half brother, poisoned Britannicus at a banquet. The name Britannicus was given to him by the senate because the conquest of Britain took place at about the time of his birth. He is the subject of a tragedy (1669) by Racine.

Britannicus (1669). A tragedy by Jean RACINE. The material of the play is derived from Tacitus. Smitten with Junia, the beloved of his half brother Britannicus, the emperor Nero attempts to win her; unsuccessful, he causes Britannicus to be arrested and poisons him. Junia escapes from the palace and becomes a vestal virgin. The play abounds in political subplot and marks Racine's first challenge of Corneille on the older playwright's homeground: political drama.

British Broadcasting Corporation. Called the **BBC.** The government-owned radio and television broadcasting body in Great Britain. The three radio networks are called the Light Programme, the Home Service, and the Third Programme. It is the last that is famous for its extremely erudite programming. The BBC was established in 1927.

Britomart. In Spenser's FAERIE QUEENE (Books III and IX), a lady knight, the personification of chastity.

Britomartis. A Cretan goddess, later an attendant of Artemis. Loved by King Minos, she hid from him for nine months and finally flung herself into the sea to escape him. She was saved by being caught in, or hiding under, fishermen's nets.

Brittain, Vera. Pen name of **Mrs. George Edward Gordon Catlin** (1896–   ). English essayist and novelist. She wrote *Testament of Youth* (1933), an autobiography, and *Testament of Friendship* (1940), a memorial to her friend Winifred Holtby. *Testament of Experience* (1957) is a companion piece to her earlier autobiography and covers the years from 1925 to 1950.

broadside ballads. Popular songs and poems, written in doggerel. They were printed in black letter on a single sheet of paper, decorated with woodcuts, with the name of the tune to which the ballads in question were to be sung, and sold for a penny or two on the street corners of England in the late 16th and early 17th centuries. Their subject

The Revvard of Murther,

In the Execution of *Richard Smith*, for murthering *Mary Davis* widdow, to whom hee made a promise of Marriage after he had gotten her with Childe : she was found drownd in a Pond neare More Fields, the 27. of *November* last, and the said *Richard Smith*, executed this present Saterday, being the 12. of *December*, 1640. for the same fact.

To the tune of, *Ned Smith*.

An English broadside ballad (1640).

matter was taken from political events, battles or wars, murders, strange happenings, executions, freakish births, domestic quarrels, and the like, and also included moral exhortations and religious propaganda.

Broadway. The main street of New York City, extending from near the lower tip of Manhattan northward through the length of Manhattan and the Bronx to beyond the city line. Though famous in its own right, the street is mainly known today for its association with the theater: since nearly all commercial drama originates in New York City, the term Broadway is practically synonymous with the American theater. Most of the major theaters in the city are not more than a block or two from Broadway. In a more general sense, Broadway denotes the gay night life of the American metropolis in a quasi-legendary conception.

In the 1950's, the term Off Broadway became prominent in referring to the growing number of small theaters in other parts of Manhattan which offered theater fare considered commercially unprofitable for Broadway. These theaters were often tiny, grubby, and impoverished, but some of them gave fine performances of experimental plays or classical revivals that could not otherwise have been seen. In time, the Off-Broadway theater became highly popular, and, with rising costs, was beset by many of the financial ills of Broadway. However, it also attracted first-class actors and even some outstanding playwrights, such as Tennessee Williams, who consented to have new works performed off Broadway.

Brobdingnag. The country of giants 12 times the size of man in Jonathan Swift's satire GULLIVER'S TRAVELS. Told by Gulliver of European customs and institutions, the king observes, "I cannot but conclude the bulk of your natives to be the most pernicious race of little vermin that nature ever suffered to crawl upon the earth." The inhuman nobility of this view contrasts with the meanness and pettiness of the people of LILLIPUT. See GLUMDALCLITCH.

Broch, Hermann (1886–1951). Austrian novelist. He is best known for his *Der Tod des Vergil* (*The Death of Vergil*, 1945) in which mythical and penetrating psychological elements are blended in an original and powerful manner that has excited comparisons with such writers as James Joyce and Thomas Mann. His most famous earlier work, more directly concerned with social and historical problems, is *Die Schlafwandler* (*The Sleepwalkers*, 1931–1932), a trilogy of novels. Broch, whose widely varied background influenced his writing, studied philosophy and mathematics, was active in the textile industry, wrote numerous sociological and literary essays in addition to his novels, and died while engaged in research on mass psychology at Yale University. He had left his homeland after being imprisoned by the Nazis.

Brocken. The highest peak of the Harz range in Saxony. On the eve of May Day, i.e., the feast of Walburga (Walpurgis) or Walpurgis Night, the Brocken was the scene of a famous witches' Sabbath. It is also known for the specter of the Brocken, an optical illusion, first observed on the Brocken, in which shadows of the spectators, greatly magnified, are projected on the mists about the summit of the mountain opposite. In one of De Quincey's opium dreams there is a powerful description of the Brocken specter.

Brod, Max (1884–   ). Austrian writer. He is best known for his edition of the works of his friend Franz Kafka, who bequeathed him all his unfinished manuscripts. He also wrote a fine biography entitled *Franz Kafka* (1937) and several critical works on the same author. He now lives in Tel Aviv, and his own lyric and narrative writing deals largely with Jewish themes.

Brofelt, Johannes. See Juhani Aho.

Broken Heart, The (c. 1629). A tragedy by John Ford. The feud between the Spartan families of Crotolon and Thrasus was to have been ended by the marriage of the former's son Orgilus to the latter's daugher Penthea. However, Thrasus dies, and his son Ithocles gives Penthea to the jealous old merchant Bassanes. Meanwhile, Ithocles' friend Prophilus has fallen in love with Orgilus' sister Euphranea. He marries her, and the breach between the two families seems to have been healed. Orgilus even intercedes as an arbiter in Ithocles' suit for the hand of Calantha, the king's daughter. Soon her loveless marriage is too much for Penthea. She loses her mind and, shortly thereafter, dies. On a visit to her bier, Orgilus avenges himself by stabbing Ithocles to death. Apprehended, Orgilus is allowed to open a vein and bleed to death. Calantha dies of a broken heart.

Broken Jug, The (**Der zerbrochene Krug**; written 1803, pub. 1811). A one-act comedy by Heinrich von Kleist. The plot revolves around the figure of a Dutch village judge named Adam who, on the very day that his court is being observed by a government inspector, finds that he must hear a case in which he himself is the guilty party. By his swift inventiveness, he manages to keep the truth hidden for a while, but is finally discovered.

Brome, Alexander (1620–1666). English attorney and royalist poet. Noted for his drinking songs and satirical verse, he was the author of *The Cun-*

ning Lovers (1654), a comedy, and *Songs and Poems* (1661).

Brome, Richard (d. 1652). English dramatist known for his realistic and satirical comedies of life in London. His best plays are A Jovial Crew *The City Wit, or The Woman Wears the Breeches* (c. 1628), *The Weeding of Covent Garden* (1632), and *The Sparagus Garden* (1635). He was the last of the comic dramatists of the Tudor-Stuart period.

Bromfield, Louis (1896–1956). American writer. Bromfield established his reputation with his early novels, the four books of a tetralogy called *Escape:* The Green Bay Tree, *Possession* (1925), *Early Autumn* (1926), and *A Good Woman* (1927). He also received praise for his factual and descriptive accounts of the 1,000-acre Ohio farm he purchased and turned into a productive showcase: *Pleasant Valley* (1945), *Malabar Farm* (1948), *Out of the Earth* (1950), and *From My Experience* (1955). One of his numerous other novels, *The Rains Came* (1937), is set in Malabar, the coastal region of India after which his farm was named.

bromide and sulphite. Words coined by Gelett Burgess in his humorous essay *Are You a Bromide, or The Sulphitic Theory* (1907). In it he explains the terms bromide and sulphite as applied to psychological rather than chemical analysis. The bromide, according to Burgess, "does his thinking by syndicate. He follows the main-traveled roads, he goes with the crowd." The sulphite, on the other hand, is unconventional, original, everything that the bromide is not.

Bronnen, Arnolt (1895–1959). German dramatist in the movement of expressionism. His violently emotional works include *Vatermord* (*Parricide,* written 1915, performed 1922), and *Katalaunische Schlacht* (*Catalaunian Battle,* 1924). Bronnen was a socialist and friend of Brecht until the two parted company when Bronnen turned to Nazism.

Bronstein, Lev Davidovich. See Leon Trotsky.

Brontë family. An English family, originally of Irish descent, that produced three 19th-century novelists: Charlotte, Emily, and Anne. On the death of his wife in 1821, the Reverend Patrick Brontë, a curate, sent for his sister-in-law to help him bring up his six children. A few years later all the girls except Anne were sent to board at the Clergy Daughters' School at Cowan Bridge; conditions at the school were dreadful, and worsened by the administration's belief that physical discomfort was spiritually edifying. The two eldest girls died at the school in 1825, and Charlotte and Emily were returned home. Lowood School in Jane Eyre was based on Charlotte's unhappy memories of Cowan Bridge. During much of their childhood, the four remaining Brontë children were free to roam and play in the Yorkshire moors, giving free reign to their imaginations. Charlotte, with the help of her brother Branwell, created Angria, a vast African empire, and wrote of the lives and adventures of its inhabitants. At the same time Emily kept a journal, the *Gondal Chronicle,* on the wars and intrigues of the Royalists and Republicans in a mysterious North country.

In 1831, *Charlotte* (1816–1855) was sent to Roe Head School, where she returned to teach from 1835–1838. She worked for a time as a governess and then, in 1842, went with Emily to Brussels to study at the school of Constantine Héger, where she taught the following year. Many of the scenes of VILLETTE are based on Charlotte's experiences at the school and on her deep but frustrated emotional attachment to Héger. In 1845, Charlotte made the accidental discovery that Emily and Anne had been writing verse. She herself had composed many poems, and she collected them all into a volume (1846) of poetry signed by Currer (Charlotte), Ellis (Emily), and Acton (Anne) Bell, pseudonyms that they retained throughout their later work. The book, published at their expense, was unsuccessful, selling only two copies. Charlotte soon submitted her first novel, *The Professor*, to a number of publishers, and it was rejected so many times that she finally withdrew it. She nevertheless set to work to complete *Jane Eyre*, which was published and achieved spectacular success.

On the strength of her one novel, WUTHERING HEIGHTS, and the best of her poems, **Emily** (1818–1848) is generally considered to be of greater genius than her sisters. Her mysticism is reflected in her work, especially in her extraordinary novel and in such poems as *The Prisoner, Remembrance, The Old Stoic,* and *The Visionary*. Some skeptics have maintained that *Wuthering Heights* was actually the work of her dissipated brother, **Patrick Branwell** (1817–1848), on the grounds that no woman, let alone one who led such a circumscribed life, could have written such a turbulent and passionate book. But Branwell, who was tubercular and addicted to alcohol and possibly to opium, had no literary talent. He died in 1848, and Emily, who caught cold at his funeral, died a few months later.

Anne (1820–1849), the least talented of the sisters, wrote two novels, AGNES GREY and THE TENANT OF WILDFELL HALL. It is possible that neither of these books would be remembered today if she were not the sister of Charlotte and Emily.

After her sisters' death Charlotte devoted herself to the care of her father, who was going blind. She completed SHIRLEY, which was well received, as was *Villette,* her last novel. These were years of social lionization, and in London and elsewhere she met Thackeray, Matthew Arnold, Mrs. Gaskell, Harriet Martineau, and others. She married Arthur Bell Nichols, her father's curate, in 1854 and died the following year. *The Professor* was published posthumously in 1857, and *Emma,* a fragment, appeared in 1860.

Bronze Horseman, The (Mednyi Vsadnik; 1833). A long poem by Aleksandr PUSHKIN. Its theme is the conflict between the desires of an ordinary individual, represented by the poor clerk Evgeni, and the demands of a powerful state, represented by Peter the Great. A flood inundates St. Petersburg, the capital city built on the Neva River at Peter's orders, and drowns Evgeni's fiancée. Demented by his grief, Evgeni stands before the imposing statue of the emperor and curses Peter's inhuman willfulness, which he blames for his fiancée's death. In a hallucination, he imagines that Peter is chasing him through the streets of the city. After this, Evgeni is cured of his rebelliousness. Whenever he passes the statue of the emperor, his manner once again shows respect and fear.

The poem displays one aspect of Pushkin's attitude toward Peter the Great. Pushkin also recognized that, however much Peter's sometimes cruel power was to be deplored, the emperor had done Russia great service. In the long poem, *Poltava* (1828–1829), Pushkin extolled Peter for his service to the country.

Bronzino, Il. Real name, **Agnolo di Cosimo Allori** (1503–1572). Florentine portraitist. A pupil of the mannerist Pontormo, he was strongly influenced by Michelangelo's religious paintings. His best-known works include the *Portrait of Ugolino Mantelli* and the *Portrait of Eleonora of Toledo with her Son*.

Brooke, Dorothea. The idealistic heroine of George Eliot's MIDDLEMARCH. Her sister Celia and their uncle, Squire Brooke, with whom they live, are also prominent characters.

Brooke, Frances [Moore] (1724–1789). English-born Canadian novelist. The wife of a clergyman, Mrs. Brooke followed her husband to Canada, where he was chaplain to the garrison at Quebec. Her four-volume *History of Emily Montague* (1769) had a Canadian setting and is often considered the first Canadian novel. However, Mrs. Brooke's work was based on English models and had no perceptible effect on Canadian literature, though it does give a vivid picture of social life in 18th-century Quebec.

Brooke, Henry (1703–1783). Irish poet and novelist. His best known works are *Universal Beauty* (1735–1736), a philosophical poem dealing with physical and theological concepts; *Gustavus Vasa* (1739), a play; and THE FOOL OF QUALITY, a novel.

Brooke, Rupert (1887–1915). English poet. He was widely known and admired for his war poetry, especially the series of sonnets called *1914;* it expressed the patriotic idealism of the early years of World War I. He died in service during the war, of septicaemia. He was a traditional, GEORGIAN poet; *Grantchester* and *The Great Lover* are well-known examples of his early work. Later he was influenced, like T. S. Eliot, by his study of 17th-century poetry (he published a study of John Webster in 1916), and began to write such witty, original poems as *Heaven* and *Dust.* St. John Ervine is said to have drawn the hero of his novel *Changing Winds* from Rupert Brooke.

Brook Farm. A utopian community established in 1841 at West Roxbury, Mass. The members of the Brook Farm Institute of Agriculture and Education, led by George RIPLEY, shared equally in work, benefits, and remuneration; among those associated with the community were Theodore Parker, William Henry Channing, Nathaniel Hawthorne, Margaret Fuller, Charles A. Dana, G. W. Curtis, and Albert Brisbane. The group, later influenced by FOURIERISM, changed its name to the Brook Farm Phalanx; in 1846, when the "Central Phalanstery" burned down, it disbanded. Emerson viewed this experiment made by his fellow Transcendentalists with skepticism; he called Brook Farm "the Age of Reason in a patty-pan." Hawthorne, who came to West Roxbury in the hope of finding an economical way to live and write, soon found communal living unattractive. He modeled the community in THE BLITHEDALE ROMANCE on Brook Farm.

Brook Kerith, The (1916). A novel by George MOORE. A presentation of the life of Jesus, the author follows the customary account as far as the Crucifixion, but later Joseph of Arimathea finds Jesus still alive. For 30 years afterward He lives as a shepherd by the Brook Kerith. He has rejected his early belief in himself, which he considers blasphemy, and when he finally meets Paul the Apostle and hears his version of the story, he is horrified and plans to go to Jerusalem and reveal the truth. Paul, however, forces him to realize that his story would not be believed.

The ravens fed Elijah by this brook of Palestine, called Cherith in the Bible.

Brooks, Cleanth (1906–   ). American literary critic and educator. Brooks became associated with the NEW CRITICISM when he coedited (1935–1942) THE SOUTHERN REVIEW with Robert Penn WARREN. He wrote two college textbooks: *Understanding Fiction* (1943), in collaboration with Warren, and *Understanding Drama* (1945), with Robert Heilman. In these texts, and in his own volumes, *Modern Poetry and the Tradition* (1939) and *The Well-Wrought Urn* (1947), he influenced contemporary methods of teaching literature. Brooks's approach to literature emphasizes close reading and structural analysis; he tends to look for and favor in poetry the central qualities of wit, irony, paradox, symbolism, and dramatic structure. Since 1947, he has taught at Yale University; with Warren he has written *Modern Rhetoric* (1949), and with W. K. Wimsatt, Jr., *Literary Criticism: A Short History* (1957). *William Faulkner: The Yoknapatawpha Country*, the first of a proposed two-volume study, appeared in 1963.

Brooks, Van Wyck (1886–1963). American critic and biographer. His early writings, such as *The Wine of the Puritans* (1908), were critical of the narrowness and insularity of the Puritan heritage and urged a broader, more unified cultural ideal for the nation. In the five volumes of the "Makers and Finders" series, Brooks created the first composite picture of American cultural and literary development. The best-known volumes of the series are *The Flowering of New England, 1815–1865* (1936), which was awarded a Pulitzer Prize, and *New England: Indian Summer, 1865–1915* (1940). Brooks also wrote *America's Coming of Age* (1915), *The Ordeal of Mark Twain* (1920), *The Pilgrimage of Henry James* (1925), and *The Life of Emerson* (1932).

Broteas. In Greek mythology, an extremely ugly son of Tantalus and brother of Pelops who flung himself onto a pyre because of his ugliness or blindness. He was said to have carved a still existing statue of Rhea on the side of Mount Sipylus.

Brother Jonathan. The generic name for a New Englander, hence for Americans and America. One account of its origin tells how, when Washington was in want of ammunition, he called a council of officers, but no practical suggestion could be offered. "We must consult Brother Jonathan," said the general, meaning His Excellency Jonathan TRUMBULL, governor of the state of Connecticut. This was done, and the difficulty was remedied. "To consult Brother Jonathan" then became a set phrase, and Brother Jonathan became a name for the typical shrewd Yankee. He appears as a character in *The Contrast* (1787), a play by Royall Tyler.

Brothers Karamazov, The (Brat'ya Karamazovy; 1879–1880). A novel by Feodor DOSTOEVSKI. Considered his best work, it is one of the outstanding novels in literature. The main plot involves Feodor Pavlovich Karamazov and his four sons: Dmitri, Ivan, Alyosha, and the bastard Smerdyakov (see KARAMAZOV). Feodor Pavlovich, a depraved buffoon, is Dmitri's rival for the affections of the local siren, GRUSHENKA. Violent quarrels over her and over Dmitri's disputed inheritance ensue until Feodor Pavlovich is murdered. Dmitri is arrested and brought to trial for the crime. This basic line of action is complicated throughout the novel by a host of other factors masterfully linked to the main plot. The second son, Ivan, a tortured intellectual, gradually realizes that he has secretly wished for his father's death and may have transmitted this wish to Smerdyakov, a grotesque caricature of the brilliant Ivan. Dmitri's relations with his ex-fiancée, KATERINA IVANOVNA, also prove to have a bearing on his involvement in the crime and his unwillingness to defend himself against the charges. The youngest son, Alyosha, plays no direct part in the crime, but acts throughout the book as a religious foil to the depraved Feodor Pavlovich, the passionate Dmitri, and the rationalistic Ivan. By means of Alyosha, the elder ZOSIMA, who expresses the author's religious views, is introduced into the novel.

Balancing, or perhaps outweighing, Zosima's religious message is the expression of unbelief enunciated by Ivan. His attitude is forcefully conveyed in the famous "Legend of the GRAND INQUISITOR," a parable of his own invention which he relates to Alyosha. Essentially a pessimistic look at man's religious possibilities, the Legend has been regarded by some critics as evidence of Dostoevski's own religious doubts.

Besides being a story of crime and a novel of religious and ethical ideas, the book is, in part, a social document. The intellectual and political ideas current in 19th-century Russia are introduced by Ivan and the careerist Rakitin, while the Legend may be read as a critique of the socialist utopia as well as of religious orthodoxy. The judicial reforms of the later 19th century and the effects they had are revealed during the trial of Dmitri.

The literal, religious, social, and ethical levels of the novel are buttressed by the psychological probings for which Dostoevski is well known. The book abounds in instances of the author's mastery in this area, from the portrayal of the corrupt yet shameful Feodor Pavlovich, to the mental disintegration of the brilliant Ivan, to the painful adolescence of Kolya Krasotkin.

Broun, Heywood [Campbell] (1888–1939). American journalist and novelist. Known for his liberal sympathies and opposition to social injustice, Broun wrote for several New York newspapers and magazines. He was equally well known and loved as a kindly, unpunctual fellow whose huge bulk and untidy appearance led him to be called a "one-man slum." The Newspaper Guild, which Broun helped found, has established an annual award for reporting done "in the spirit of Heywood Broun." A *Collected Edition* of his writings appeared in 1941.

Brown, Charles Brockden (1771–1810). American novelist and editor. Regarded as the first American professional author, he introduced the Indian into U.S. fiction and was among the first Americans to win a hearing abroad. Brown anticipated the later deep interest in psychotic characters, foreshadowing Poe's interest in the horrifying. His fame rests on six Gothic romances: WIELAND, *Ormond* (1799), ARTHUR MERVYN, EDGAR HUNTLY, *Clara Howard* (1801), and *Jane Talbot* (1801).

Brown, Ford Madox (1821–1893). English painter. He represented historical or social and moralizing subjects with accurate draftsmanship characterized by repeated areas of color. He was never a member of the PRE-RAPHAELITE BROTHERHOOD, but there was a reciprocal influence between that group and himself.

Brown, John (1800–1859). American abolitionist. In the 1850's Brown, an abolitionist since his youth, became obsessed with the idea of freeing the slaves by force. In 1855 he and five sons went to Kansas, then a battleground between pro- and antislavery forces. The following year, with his approval, a small band, including four of his sons, murdered five settlers near Potawatomi Creek during an antislavery raid. Later he and 40 men resisted an attack on Osawatomie by proslavery men.

Now nationally known as "Old Brown of Osawatomie," he made plans to foment a slave insurrection in the South. On Oct. 16, 1859, he attacked Harper's Ferry, Va. (now West Va.) with 21 men and seized the U.S. arsenal and armory there. A detachment of marines under Col. Robert E. Lee defeated and captured Brown. During his trial for treason, he conducted himself with dignity, maintaining that he had been an instrument in the hands of God. He was convicted and hanged on Dec. 2, a martyr in the eyes of abolitionists.

His career inspired the Civil War marching song *John Brown's Body Lies A-Mouldering in the Grave* and numerous literary works, notably Stephen Vincent Benét's narrative poem, *John Brown's Body* (1928).

Brown, John (1810–1882). Scottish physician and author. He is famous for his dog story RAB AND HIS FRIENDS and his essay on *Marjorie Fleming* (1863), the 10-year-old prodigy and pet of Sir Walter Scott.

Brown, Thomas. See John FELL.

Brown, Tom. See TOM BROWN'S SCHOOL DAYS.

Brown, William Hill (1765–1793). American novelist, poet and dramatist, probably the author of THE POWER OF SYMPATHY. Born in Boston, Brown also wrote a series of verse fables, a tragedy, a comedy, and another short novel of incest and seduction, *Ira and Isabella* (1807).

Browne, Charles Farrar. See Artemus WARD.

Browne, Hablot Knight. See PHIZ.

Browne, Sir Thomas (1605–1682). English writer and scholar. Browne was a successful physician who, except for his years of schooling at Oxford and in Europe, spent his life in the town of Norwich. He was knighted in 1671 by Charles II as a steadfast Royalist famous for his antiquarian scholarship. As Browne himself knew, he had a curiously mixed nature: by temperament melancholy, mystical, and credulous, he was by training a scientist and philosophical skeptic. He was also a lover of language and classical learning, and his sonorous, stirringly cadenced prose style, rich in exotic coinages and striking images, is one of the most remarkable accomplishments in English literature. He is most brilliant when he treats themes that allow the full display of his personality, such as religion in RELIGIO MEDICI and morality and oblivion in HYDRIOTAPHIA OR URN BURIAL. His other works are *Pseudodoxia Epidemica,* also called VULGAR ERRORS; *The Garden of Cyrus* (1658); and *Christian Morals,* edited in 1756 by Samuel Johnson.

Browne, Thomas Alexander. Pen name, **Rolf Boldrewood** (1826–1915). Australian novelist who wrote some 30 novels of adventure. His best-known book is *Robbery Under Arms* (1888), which depicts life in the Australian gold fields.

Browne, William (c. 1591–?1643). English poet. The most influential member of the early 17th-century SPENSERIAN SCHOOL of pastoral poets, he was the author of *Two Elegies* (1613) on the death of Prince Henry, the elder son of James I, and of *Britannia's Pastorals* (1613, 1616). His poems were also published in *The Shepherd's Pipe* (1614), a book of eclogues in which George Wither and Sir John Davies, prominent Spenserians, were also represented. *Britannia's Pastorals* is said to have influenced Milton and Keats.

brownie. The house spirit in Scottish superstition. At night he is supposed to busy himself in doing little jobs for the family over which he presides. Farms are his favorite abode. Brownies are brown or tawny spirits, in opposition to fairies, which are fair ones. In the U.S. the adventures of the brownies were popularized by a series of *Brownie Books* by Palmer Cox.

Browning, Elizabeth Barrett (1806–1861). English poet, wife of Robert BROWNING. In childhood she suffered a spinal injury and, until her meeting with Browning, seemed to be doomed to invalidism and seclusion from the world. The Brownings' courtship under the eyes of Elizabeth's jealous, tyrannical father, their elopement, and subsequent happy married life in Italy form one of the most celebrated of literary romances. Hawthorne described Mrs. Browning as "a pale, small person scarcely embodied at all," and this ethereality of her physical appearance is reflected by the palpitating fervor, the unworldly tenderness and purity of her work. Often, however, these qualities decline into stridency, diffuseness, and confusion. Her themes were dictated by her broad humanitarian interests; a deep if unorthodox religious feeling; her affection for her adopted country, Italy; and, of course, her love for Browning. Her greatest work, SONNETS FROM THE PORTUGUESE, a sequence of love sonnets addressed to her husband, remains an extraordinary and living achievement. Her other works include *Essay on Mind, With Other Poems* (1826), a translation of Aeschylus' *Prometheus Bound* (1833), *The Seraphim And Other Poems* (1838), *Poems* (1844), CASA GUIDI WINDOWS, AURORA LEIGH, *Poems Before Congress* (1860), and *Last Poems* (1862). See CRY OF THE CHILDREN, THE; LADY GERALDINE'S COURTSHIP.

Browning, Robert (1812–1889). English poet. The son of a bank clerk, Browning was long unsuccessful as a poet and financially dependent upon his family until he was well into adulthood. When in his teens, he discovered Shelley and adopted Shelleyian liberalism in opinion and confessionalism in poetry. Accordingly, his first poems—*Pauline* (1833), PARACELSUS, SORDELLO,—were long, personal, and self-consciously poetic,—though the latter two supposedly had as their subject actual historic personages. All three works were considered failures, and, from 1837 to 1846, Browning attempted to write verse drama for the stage, again unsuccessfully. In 1845 he met Elizabeth Barrett, then considered one of the outstanding poets of the day, and married her the following year. Partially because of her ill health and partially because of her father's opposition to the marriage, Browning took his wife to Italy, and remained there until her death in 1861. The story of their love has been dramatized by Rudolf Besier in THE BARRETTS OF WIMPOLE STREET.

PIPPA PASSES, a dramatic poem included in the collection BELLS AND POMEGRANATES, was among Browning's first significant works; Pippa, a little Italian girl, passes by singing, and unwittingly influences the lives of four groups of people. During the next 25 years Browning published many volumes of poetry, all of which sold badly: *Dramatic Lyrics* (1842), which contained *Porphyria's Lover*, MY LAST DUCHESS, *Soliloquy in a Spanish Cloister*, and *The Pied Piper of Hamelin*; *Dramatic Romances and Lyrics* (1845), which included How THEY BROUGHT THE GOOD NEWS FROM GHENT TO AIX and *The Bishop Orders His Tomb at St. Praxed's Church*; *Christmas Eve and Easter Day* (1850), a long poem; and *Men and Women* (1855), which contained many of his best-known poems: FRA LIPPO LIPPI, ANDREA DEL SARTO, BISHOP BLOUGRAM'S APOLOGY, *Two in the Campagna*, and *A Grammarian's Funeral*. In the collection *Dramatis Personae* (1864) were RABBI BEN EZRA and PROSPICE.

After 40 years of poetic obscurity, Browning abruptly came into his own with the publication of the massive THE RING AND THE BOOK. The story, which Browning found in an old manuscript, deals with a 17th-century murder case; in the poem, each of 12 characters presents his view of the action in a long dramatic monologue.

Though his philosophy is now considered less profound than it was at the height of his success, Browning is notable for his psychological insight into character and motivations, his sometimes abrupt but forceful colloquial English, his perfection of the form of the dramatic monologue in which a speaker tells something of himself and reveals more than he intends or realizes, his learning, and his predilection for Italian Renaissance subjects. See Elizabeth Barrett BROWNING; BLOT ON THE 'SCUTCHEON, A; LURIA; RETURN OF THE DRUSES.

Browning Version, The (1948). A one-act play by Terence RATTIGAN. It is set in an English boys' school. An old teacher, universally disliked by the students, has his hard exterior cracked by a sympathetic and understanding boy. *The Browning Version* was made into a motion picture with a fine performance by Michael Redgrave as the teacher.

Brownism. The teachings of Robert Browne (1550?–1633), an English divine. He first formulated the principles of Congregationalism.

Brownshirts. See S.A.

Brownson, Orestes Augustus (1803–1876). American writer on theology and philosophy. Brownson was a New Englander so thoroughly individualistic that he could not agree long with anybody—even with himself. Raised as a strict Puritan, he became successively a Presbyterian, a Universalist, and a Unitarian; in 1844 he was converted to Roman Catholicism but was severely criticized when he tried to promulgate his own American form of Catholicism. His political views were similarly varied; at first, he was a Utopian socialist, an admirer of Robert Owen; later, he helped to organize a Workingmen's Party. He then became active in Democratic Party politics, until he lost faith in the intelligence and integrity of the common people.

To spread his beliefs, Brownson established the *Boston Quarterly Review* (January, 1838), which in 1842 was merged with the *United States Democratic Review;* in 1844 it became *Brownson's Quarterly Review*, continued until 1865, was revived in 1872, and terminated in 1875. His writings include *New Views of Christianity, Society, and the Church* (1836); a semiautobiographical novel, *Charles Elwood, or The Infidel Converted* (1840); and *The Convert* (1857), an autobiography.

Bruce, Robert. Called **the Bruce** (1274–1329). Scottish national hero, king of Scotland from 1306. Though at first he swore fealty to Edward I of England as king of Scotland (1296), Robert Bruce soon followed the popular leader Sir William WALLACE and raised arms against Edward in a struggle to gain Scottish independence. In July, 1297, however, he signed the capitulation of Irvine whereby Scottish lords were pardoned in return for their allegiance. Bruce took no part in Wallace's continued struggle and final downfall, but remained, to all outward appearances, loyal to the English. He was appointed co-regent of Scotland together with William Lamberton and John Comyn; he entered into a secret agreement with Lamberton binding him to uphold the patriotic cause.

After the execution of Wallace, Bruce murdered (1306) Comyn, an enemy of long standing, and was thenceforth openly committed to the Scottish cause. He was crowned Robert I of Scotland at Scone in 1306; he then set about to win his kingdom. He suffered defeat at Methven, took refuge on the coast of Ireland, was outlawed, and was excommunicated by the pope. After the death of Edward I and Edward II's accession to the throne, Bruce faced an easier opponent. He returned to Scotland and in a series of engagements, wrested most of Scotland from the English; his crusade finally culminated in the treaty (1327) by which Edward III recognized Scotland as independent and Bruce as her sovereign. Bruce died in 1329 of leprosy, barely enjoying the fruits of his own achievement. See BRUCE, THE; BRUCE AND THE SPIDER.

Bruce, The (c. 1375). An epic poem by John BARBOUR. The poem, a mixture of anecdote and accurate history, concerns the deeds of Robert BRUCE, James DOUGLAS, and the struggle for Scottish independence.

Bruce and the spider. It is said that when Robert BRUCE was forced by the English to retreat to Ireland, he took heart from a spider: one day he watched the spider try six times to fix its web on a beam in the ceiling. "Now shall this spider," said Bruce, "teach me what I am to do, for I also have failed six times." The spider's seventh effort was successful, whereupon Bruce left Ireland, collected 300 followers, landed at Carrick, and at midnight, surprised the English garrison at Turnberry Castle. In *Tales of a Grandfather*, Sir Walter Scott tells us that in remembrance of this incident, it has always been deemed a foul crime in Scotland for any of the name of Bruce to harm a spider.

Brücke, die (The bridge). A group of German painters, formed in 1905 in Dresden. In rebellion against impressionism, they aimed to found a truly expressive school of German painting. Ernst Ludwig Kirchner and Eric Heckel were among the leaders of the group, whose members were influenced by the art of Africa and the South Seas and by primitive German religious art. Using color in an expressionistic manner, these artists painted dramatic landscapes and nudes, mystical and visionary compositions, and depicted the anguish and loneliness of the street, the circus, and the *café dansant. Die Brücke* was incorporated into the BLAUE REITER movement in 1912.

Bruckner, Anton (1824–1896). Austrian organist and composer of church and symphonic music. A friend of Richard Wagner, he taught theory and organ at the Vienna Conservatorium from 1868 to 1891. His style is a mixture of homely simplicity and Catholic mysticism. His works include nine symphonies, three masses, and numerous shorter works for the church.

Bruegel or **Brueghel** or **Breughel, Pieter** (1525?–1569). Flemish painter. He painted scenes from peasant life, fantastic recreations of biblical subjects such as the tower of Babel, and landscapes composed of closely observed details combined to form an immense panorama in which small figures enact religious dramas and perform common tasks. His splendidly composed and brightly colored, realistic paintings are noted for their keen and often humorous observation of nature and mankind. Bruegel had two sons, Pieter the Younger (1564?–1637?), who often copied his father, and Jan (1568–1625), called "Velvet Bruegel," who painted landscapes, allegorical pictures, and still lifes.

Brueys, L'Abbé David-Augustin de. See BATHELIN, LA FARCE DE MAISTRE PIERRE.

Bruin, Sir. See REYNARD THE FOX.

Bruller, Jean. See VERCORS.

Brumaire. The 2nd month in the French REVOLUTIONARY CALENDAR. It began Oct. 22, 23, or 24, depending on the year, and ended Nov. 21, 22, or 23. The name comes from *brume* (*Fr.,* "fog"), and was used because this season was often marked by foggy weather. The celebrated 18th Brumaire (Nov. 9, 1799) was the day on which the Directory was overthrown and Napoleon established his supremacy.

Brunanburh, battle of (10th century). An Old English poem of 73 lines in ALLITERATIVE VERSE, included in the *Anglo-Saxon Chronicle*. It celebrates the victory (937) of the English under King Aethelstan over the invading Vikings and Scots.

Brunelleschi, Filippo (1377–1446). Florentine architect and goldsmith. He used his knowledge of Gothic and Romanesque architecture in spanning the immense space covered by his dome for the cathedral of Florence, while in such buildings as the Pazzi Chapel, the Church of San Lorenzo, the Pitti Palace (1446), the Hospital of the Innocenti (1419), and the Church of the Santo Spirito (1435), he introduced the classical elements—columns, arches, ornamental details—that form such an integral part of Renaissance architecture. His classicism was spurred by a trip made to Rome in 1433 with his friend DONATELLO for the purpose of studying the Roman ruins. Along with Donatello and other Florentine artists, he shared the patronage of Cosimo de' Medici. He also invented linear perspective: the mathematical device for the construction of a rational space, with depth and interval, as seen from a single point of view.

Brunello. In the Orlando poems of Boiardo and Ariosto, a cunning dwarf and expert thief who steals Angelica's magic ring and then loses it to Bradamante, who needs it to free her beloved RUGGIERO from the enchanter Atlante.

Brunetière, Vincent de Paul Marie Ferdinand (1849–1906). French literary critic. Conservative and neoclassical in his tastes, Brunetière opposed the naturalistic school because he deplored its lack of moral purpose. Dogmatic in his beliefs, he applied the principles of Darwinian evolution to the development of literature. Among his most important works are *Le Roman Naturaliste* (1883), *Etudes critiques sur la littérature française* (1880–1907), *Evolution des genres* (1890–1894), and *Histoire de la littérature française classique* (1904–1907), which was begun in 1904 and left unfinished at the time of the author's death.

Brunetto Latini. See Brunetto LATINI.

Brunhild. See VÖLSUNGA SAGA; NIBELUNGENLIED; Wagner's RING DES NIBELUNGEN.

Bruni, Leonardo (1374–1444). Italian humanist and historian. Also known as Leonardo Aretino, from his birthplace at Arezzo, he was a chancellor of Florence, his adopted city and a papal secretary. One of the outstanding early Italian Renaissance Humanists, he wrote in Latin, Greek, and Italian, and did translations and other scholarly works. His *History of Florence* (*Historiarum Florentinarum libri xii;* 1610) is sometimes described as the first modern history because of its break with medieval methods of narrating past events.

Bruno, Giordano (1548–1600). Italian philosopher. Bruno is sometimes referred to as the Nolan from his birthplace at Nola, near Naples. After studying at the university of Naples and entering the Dominican order, he fled from his vows and his native land in 1576 in order to begin his career as an itinerant teacher of controversial philosophical subjects. In 1582, at Paris, he wrote his first literary work, the comedy *Il Candelaio*. While in England during the next few years, he met Sir Philip Sidney and Fulke-Greville, debated at Oxford, and produced several philosophical dialogues in Italian. *La cena de le ceneri* (*Ash Wednesday Supper*, 1584) defended the Copernican system and Bruno's notion of the infinite universe, while *De la causa, principio e uno* (*On Cause, Principle, and Unity,* 1584) and *De l'infinito universo e mondi* (*On the Infinite Universe and Its Worlds*, 1584) offered an anti-Aristotelian metaphysics grounded largely in mystical Neoplatonism and Pantheism. The *Spaccio della bestia trionfante* (*Banishment of the Triumphant Beast,* 1584), dedicated to Sidney, deals largely with ethics; the *Cabala del cavallo pegaseo* (*Cabala of the Pegasean Steed*), also written during this period, is a satire against pretentious ignorance and obscurantism, in the form of an ironic praise of asininity that recalls a similar "praise of folly" by Erasmus. *De gli heroici furori* (1585), also dedicated to Sidney, deals with heroic enthusiasms, such as the aspirations of the intellectual mind and the inspirations of poetry. The discussion revolves about a group of poems by Bruno himself and by Luigi Tansillo, who is an interlocutor in the dialogue.

Between 1585 and 1591, Bruno wandered through France, Switzerland, and Germany, everywhere encountering opposition to his unorthodox ideas and irascible personality. In 1591, at Frankfurt, he published a group of Latin works in which he continued to expound his philosophy. In scope these works range from mnemonics and monism to the atom and the monad, from the pre-Socratic philosophers to Nicholas of Cusa and Copernicus. The most important of the works is *De immenso et innumerabilis seu de universo et mundis* (*On Immensity and Innumerability, or on the Universe and Its Worlds*), consisting of verse, prose commentary, and diagrams. In 1592, he was betrayed to the Inquisition at Venice; a year later he was in a Roman prison, where he languished for seven years. His refusal to recant earned him condemnation as a heretic and execution at the stake on February 17, 1600.

Despite the difficulty of his style and the obscurity of his thought, Bruno influenced contemporaries such as Spenser. Among modern authors, his influence is present in Joyce's *Finnegans Wake.* In philosophy he anticipated Leibniz and other subsequent thinkers.

Brush, Katharine [Ingham] (1902–1952). American novelist, short-story writer, and columnist. She is known for her successful works of fiction appearing in *Cosmopolitan* and other magazines. An annalist of "the jazz age," she is the author of a number of novels, including *Glitter* (1926), *Young Man of Manhattan* (1930), and *Red-Headed Woman* (1931). Collections of her short stories are *Night Club* (1929) and *Other Women* (1932).

Brut, The (c. 1205). A Middle English verse rendition by the English priest Layamon (fl. 1189–1207) of Wace's Norman French ROMAN DE BRUT. A mixture of alliteration and rhyme, it is the first long poem in Middle English with any claim to literary quality, and marks the first appearance of the story of King Arthur in English. It relates the mythical history of Britain from its founding by BRUTE, a descendant of Aeneas, to the year 689. It contains versions of the stories of King LEIR (Lear), CYMBELINE, and other legendary kings of Britain. See ARTHURIAN LEGEND.

Brute (Brutus). In Geoffrey of Monmouth's HISTORY OF THE KINGS OF BRITAIN, a mythical ancestor of the British. According to Geoffrey, he is the great-grandson of the Trojan Aeneas. After an adventurous life, he lands in England, which—says the writer—he calls Britain after his own name. His three sons are ALBANACT, CAMBER, and LOCRINE.

Brutus, Decius. In Shakespeare's JULIUS CAESAR, a conspirator against Caesar. By flattering Caesar's pride, he persuades him to attend the Senate despite Calpurnia's pleas.

Brutus, Lucius Junius. Roman CONSUL (509 B.C.). One of the first two consuls in Rome's history, he is known as "the founder of the Roman Republic." According to legend, he feigned idiocy in order to escape the fate of his father and brother who were killed by his uncle Tarquinius Superbus, king of Rome. When Sextus, son of Tarquinius Superbus, ravished LUCRETIA, Brutus, casting off his feigned simple-mindedness, swore vengeance; he led an insurrection which expelled the Tarquins from Rome and changed the magistracy of kings to that of consuls. Brutus and Tarquinius Collatinus, husband of Lucretia, were chosen consuls.

Brutus, Marcus Junius (c. 85–42 B.C.). Roman politician and general. He was known for his devotion to the ideals of the republic, and, in the civil struggle between CAESAR and Pompey, he supported the latter, who had legality on his side. After the battle at Pharsalus (48 B.C.), which ended in the defeat of Pompey, Caesar pardoned Brutus and made him one of his companions. Caesar appointed him governor of Cisalpine Gaul (46) and praetor (44). His love for Caesar notwithstanding, Brutus was persuaded by CASSIUS to murder Caesar; he was deluded into thinking that this act would recall the ideals of the republic which had disintegrated under Caesar's dictatorship. Accordingly, Caesar was murdered on the IDES of March in 43 by a group of conspirators under Brutus and Cassius. Mark ANTONY turned public opinion against the conspirators in his oration at Caesar's public funeral, and Brutus and Cassius fled Rome. Both raised armies, and Antony and Octavius, Caesar's lawful heir (later Augustus), temporarily suspended their struggle for power and marched against them. In the first engagement at Philippi (42) Brutus was victorious over Octavius while Cassius, overwhelmed by Antony's forces, committed suicide. In the second engagement, Brutus' forces were surrounded by those of Octavius, and Brutus committed suicide. According to Plutarch, when Antony found Brutus' body, he wrapped it up in his own robe for burial and had the ashes sent to Servilia, Brutus' mother. Another story, however, says that Antony had Brutus' head cut off and flung it at the feet of a statue of Caesar. See ET TU, BRUTE.

In Shakespeare's JULIUS CAESAR, Brutus is depicted as an idealist, "high in all the people's hearts," who joins the conspiracy out of love of country. Antony's eulogy is famous:

> This was the noblest Roman of them all;
> All the conspirators save only he
> Did that they did in envy of great Caesar;
> He only, in a general honest thought,
> And common good to all, made one of them.

Bryan, William Jennings. Known as the **Great Commoner** and the **Boy Orator of the Platte** (1860–1925). American political leader and orator. Having been twice elected to Congress (1890, 1892), Bryan became editor of the Omaha *World-Herald* after an unsuccessful Senate bid in 1894. In 1896 he won the Democratic presidential nomination when, as an advocate of the free coinage of silver, he electrified the convention with the famous "Cross of Gold" speech that ended, "You shall not press down upon the brow of labor this crown of thorns, you shall not crucify mankind upon a cross of gold." After a strenuous campaign, in which he won the support of Southern and Western agrarians, he lost to William McKinley by fewer than 600,000 votes. In 1901 he founded a weekly newspaper, the *Commoner,* which he edited until 1913. Again an unsuccessful presidential candidate in 1900 and 1908, he was named secretary of state by President Wilson, but he resigned in 1915 when he felt that the president's policies might involve the U.S. in World War I. After the war his fundamentalist religious beliefs led him to take part in a movement to prevent the teaching of evolution in American schools; in 1925 he served as prosecutor in the celebrated Scopes Trial.

Bryan was one of the most popular lecturers on the Chautauqua circuit; best loved of all his talks was one on *The Prince of Peace,* which he repeated innumerable times until 1924. Vachel Lindsay paid tribute to Bryan in his poem *Bryan, Bryan, Bryan: The Campaign of 1896, as Viewed at the Time by a 16-Year-Old* (1919), but he was pilloried in H. L. Mencken's *In Memoriam: W. J. B. (Prejudices,* 5th Series, 1926).

Bryant, William Cullen (1794–1878). American poet, critic, and editor. Bryant's early beliefs were Calvinist; his politics were Federalist and his tastes, classical. During his life, he moved from these attitudes to almost opposite beliefs, finally achieving a balanced view.

After beginning at the law, he achieved early fame when his poems were published in 1817. In 1825, he went to New York from his native Massachusetts to work on the New York *Evening Post.* Later he became its editor, and a leading democrat; he supported Lincoln, encouraged liberal causes, and espoused a less severe religion. Throughout his life he continued to write poetry, but rarely achieved the quality of his earliest work, Thanatopsis, To a Waterfowl, and Inscription for the Entrance to a Wood. Bryant's important works include early political satire in *The Embargo* (1808), collected *Poems* (1832), *The Fountain* (1842), and *The Flood of Years* (1876). He translated the *Iliad* (1870) and the *Odyssey* (1871).

Bryce, James. Viscount **Bryce of Dechmont** (1838–1922). English statesman and historian. Ambassador to the U.S. from 1907 to 1913, he was one of the founders of the League of Nations. His best-known writings are *The Holy Roman Empire* (1862) and *The American Commonwealth* (1888), both highly regarded studies in history and political science. He wrote a number of other books on travel, biography, jurisprudence, and political science.

Bryher. Pen name of **Winifred Bryher** (1894–   ), English historical novelist. She authentically and poetically recreates Greece and Rome in *Gate to the Sea* (1958) and *Roman Wall* (1954). English historical scenes are portrayed in *Ruan* (1960), the Celts; *The Fourteenth of October* (1952), the battle of Hastings; and *The Player's Boy* (1953), early seventeenth century. *Heart to Artemis* was published in 1962 and *Coin of Carthage* in 1963.

Brynhild. See Völsunga Saga; Nibelungenlied; Wagner's Ring des Nibelungen.

Bryusov, Valeri Yakovlevich (1873–1924). Russian poet. One of the founders of the symbolist movement, Bryusov established in 1904 a journal *The Scales (Vesy),* which became an important showcase for the symbolist work of the next five years. Bryusov was heavily influenced by the French symbolists and transmitted this influence into the Russian movement. His major collections of verse are *Urbi et Orbi* (1903) and *Stephanos* (1905). Bryusov accepted the Bolshevik regime, and as a consequence his work, while not as politically oriented as the Soviets would like, is at least accepted and reprinted in the Soviet Union.

Bubastis. The Greek name of Bast, or Pasht, the Artemis of Egyptian mythology. She was the daughter of Isis and sister of Horus, and her sacred animal was the cat.

Buber, Martin (1878–1965). Jewish theologian, philosopher, and writer. He has contributed to the modern development of Hasidism and has devoted much of his life to winning recognition of the cultural value of Judaism. His writings include *Moses, The Revelation and the Covenant* (1946), *The Prophetic Faith* (1949), *Two Types of Faith* (1951), *Eclipse of God* (1952), and *Tales of the Hassidim* (1961).

bucentaur (Gr., *bous,* "ox"; *centaurous,* "centaur"). A gaily ornamented ship or barge, from the name of the Venetian state galley employed by the doge on Ascension Day when he went to wed the Adriatic (see Bride of the Sea). It was probably so called from the galley's figurehead, a man's head with an ox's body.

Bucephalus (Gr., *boukephalos,* "bull-headed"). The favorite horse of Alexander the Great. Philip II had determined to destroy the high-spirited horse no one could mount, but allowed his son to try his skill first. Observing that the horse was terrified by its own shadow, Alexander turned its eyes into the sun, and was able to mount. By taming him Alexander fulfilled an oracle concerning the succession to the throne of Macedon.

Buchan, Sir John. 1st Baron **Tweedsmuir** (1875–1940). Scottish writer and governor general of Canada. He wrote many romantic adventure stories with idyllic natural settings. His first successful book was *Prester John* (1910), a romance of South Africa. The Thirty-Nine Steps, *Greenmantle* (1916), and *The Three Hostages* (1924) are adventure and spy novels whose hero is Richard Hannay. Other stories, such as *Huntingtower* (1922), are about a group of Scottish slum boys called the Gorbals Die-Hards. *John Macnab* (1925) is about poaching, hunting, and fishing in Scotland. Buchan's biographies include a life of *Cromwell* (1934) and a life of Cromwell's Scottish contemporary, *Montrose* (1928). *Memory-Hold-the-Door* (1940) is an autobiography.

Buchanan, Robert Williams (1841–1901). Scottish poet, dramatist, critic, and novelist. He is remembered for his cruel literary attack, entitled The Fleshly School of Poetry, which began a literary and personal quarrel that lasted several years. He was a prolific and successful dramatist, and his

Poetical Works (1901) contains a number of poems of interest.

Büchner, Georg (1813–1837). German dramatist. He is known especially for the brilliant imagination and theatrical skill with which he treats social, human, and metaphysical problems in the plays DANTONS TOD and WOYZECK. Inspired in his student days by the ideals of the French Revolution of 1789, he became a political radical and, in 1834, publicized a militant socialist program in his *Der hessische Landbote* (*The Hessian Messenger*), a tract which violently attacked the oppressive archduchy of Hesse. As a dramatist, he reinforced his socialist sympathies with a brutally stark, realistic style that caused him to be regarded as a forerunner of naturalism. But he was also a master of metaphysical symbolism, and his works contain passages of the highest poetic beauty. Other products of his short career are the comedy *Leonce und Lena* (written 1836) and the fragmentary novella *Lenz* (1879) about the life of the poet Reinhold Lenz.

Buck, Pearl [Sydenstricker] (1892–   ). American novelist. The daughter of American missionaries, Mrs. Buck was raised in China and is best known for her books about Chinese life. Part of her purpose has been to make the East known to the West. She was awarded a Pulitzer Prize in 1932 for THE GOOD EARTH, the first novel in a trilogy called *The House Of Earth,* finished in 1935. She received the Nobel Prize for Literature in 1938.

Mrs. Buck is the author of many other novels about the Far East, including *Dragon Seed* (1942), *Pavilion of Women* (1946), and *The Living Reed* (1963), and of two autobiographical works, *My Several Worlds* (1954) and *A Bridge for Passing* (1962). She also translated a Chinese classic under the title *All Men Are Brothers* (1933) and wrote several novels with an American setting under the pseudonym John Sedges.

Bucket, Mr. A shrewd detective in Charles Dickens' BLEAK HOUSE. He discovers that Hortense, the French maid of Lady Dedlock, murdered Mr. Tulkinghorn. Speaking of the detectives of fiction, Swinburne calls Bucket "that matchless master of them all."

Buckingham, 1st duke of. George Villiers (1592–1628). English nobleman, whose erratic political and military policies caused continual friction with Parliament and foreign powers. The profligate favorite of James I, he was known for his good looks, and his face at death was described as "the face of an angel." He was assassinated by John FELTON. He was used as a character by Scott in *The Fortunes of Nigel* (1822) and by Dumas in *The Three Musketeers* (1844).

Buckingham, 2nd duke of. Henry Stafford (1454–1483). English nobleman, a staunch supporter of Richard III in the early part of his reign. He later rebelled against Richard and was captured and executed. In Shakespeare's RICHARD III, he is depicted as the crafty "second self" of the king, but he balks at Richard's demand that he kill the two sons of Edward IV.

Buckingham, 2nd duke of. George Villiers (1628–1687). English nobleman and writer. The son of the 1st duke of Buckingham and a favorite of Charles II, he was a member of the court clique known as the CABAL, his name furnishing the third letter of the famous acronym. With Samuel Butler, Thomas Sprat, and others, he wrote *The Rehearsal* (1671), a burlesque tragedy satirizing Dryden. He is a character in Scott's *Peveril of the Peak* (1822) and *Woodstock* (1826) and in Dryden's *Absalom and Achitophel* (1681).

Buckle, Henry Thomas (1821–1862). English historian. He is known chiefly for the first volume of his *History of Civilization in England* (1857), which caused a sensation in England and the U.S. because of its bold thinking. Buckle's special theory was that climate, soil, food, and other aspects of nature play a large role in the intellectual progress of mankind. A second volume of his *History* appeared in 1861, but was generally considered inferior to the first.

Bucolics (Bucolica). Also known as **Eclogues (Eclogae).** Ten pastoral poems by VERGIL, written in the years 43–37 B.C. Though based on the idyls of Theocritus, the *Bucolics* are sophisticated tours de force and subtle allegories of contemporary events and persons. As Vergil's first notable achievement, they mark the beginning of his writing career and his entry into the literary circle of Augustus and Maecenas.

The first bucolic portrays the anguish of a shepherd forced to leave his ancestral lands. This is a reference to the threatened confiscation of Vergil's lands by Mark Antony in 43. The second is the love song of CORYDON for the boy Alexis. An amoebaean contest, i.e., a singing contest in which one shepherd sings an impromptu couplet to which the other must reply with a variation of tone and subject matter, composes the third poem. Interwoven into this rustic game of wits are references to Vergil's

Woodcut of Vergil's first *Bucolic* (Strassburg, 1502).

patrons and to the farm which, through their influence, was restored to the poet.

The fourth poem is perhaps the most famous bucolic of all. In it, Vergil predicts a new age of peace for the world which will be ushered in by the birth of a child. Often called the *Messianic Eclogue,* this poem has been variously interpreted as a natal poem for an expected child (either that of Mark Antony and Octavia or of Octavius Caesar and Scribonia) and as an inspired prophecy of the birth of Christ. It was because of this poem that medieval Christians revered Vergil as a pagan prophet whom God had chosen to prepare the world for the coming of the Prince of Peace.

The fifth poem is an elegant exchange of songs by two shepherds; its subject is elegaic—the death of a young shepherd, Damon—but it actually refers to the death of Julius Caesar. The sixth is the "Song of Silenus," a capsule cosmogony which seems to show Vergil's acquaintance with Lucretius' *De Rerum Natura.* The seventh poem is another amoebaean singing contest.

The eighth bucolic contains two love elegies, in both of which the singers use magical refrains. The poem is sometimes called *Pharmaceutria* (sorcery). The ninth is a gracious exchange of songs between a young man and an old man in which there are many oblique references to the death of Caesar, the Roman civil wars, and the confiscations.

The final bucolic is dedicated to Gallus, a leading patrician and writer of elegies who was an early protector of Vergil. This poem is in the form of a consolation sent to Gallus, who is brokenhearted over the infidelity of his mistress. Many authorities now claim that this artificial piece is a clever pastiche of Gallus' own love lyrics.

Vergil's *Bucolics* were the principal influence on pastoral tradition after the Renaissance, and it was their calm elegance that became the dominant tone of pastoral verse. The refrain "Sweete Themmes, runne softly, till I end my song" in Spenser's *Prothalamion* is an echo of the recurrent refrain in the eighth *Bucolic: Incipe Maenalios mecum, mea tibia, versus;* and the opening of Milton's *Lycidas,* "Yet once more, O ye laurels, and once more, / Ye myrtles brown . . . / I come to pluck" is an adaption of *Et vos, o lauri, carpam te, proxima myrte. (Bucolic* II).

Budd, Lanny. See Upton SINCLAIR.

Buddenbrooks (1901). A novel by Thomas MANN. It treats the decline of a prosperous North German commercial family. Both Johann Buddenbrook, Sr., the patriarch when the novel opens, and his son Johann, Jr. (Consul Buddenbrook) are exemplary bearers of the family's solid and rational tradition. But symptoms of decadence appear in the consul's children: Toni, the daughter, is an aimless personality; Christian is an outright ne'er-do-well; and Thomas, who takes over the family business, has a repressed potential for decadence, which shows itself in his occasional attraction to art and philosophy and in his inability to keep the family fortune from declining. In Thomas' son Hanno, finally, the symbolic connection between art and decadence and the symbolic antithesis between art and life culminate. Hanno is frail and sickly, fond of music and filled with creative longings; he dies as a boy, bringing the family line to an end.

Buddha (*Sans.,* "the enlightened"). Real name, Siddhārtha GAUTAMA. Also known as **Shākyamuni.** The founder of BUDDHISM. He is traditionally said to have died in 544 B.C.

Buddhism. The system of religion inaugurated by the Buddha in India in the 6th century B.C. The four sublime verities of Buddhism, the "Four Aryan or Noble Truths," are as follows:

(1) Pain exists.

(2) The cause of pain is "birth sin." The Buddhist supposes that man has passed through many previous existences, and all the sins accumulated in these previous states constitute man's "birth sin."

(3) Pain is ended only by NIRVANA.

(4) The way that leads to nirvana is the "Eightfold Path": right faith, right judgment, right language, right purpose, right practice, right obedience, right memory, and right meditation.

The abstract nature of the religion, together with the overgrowth of its monastic system and the superior vitality and energy of Brahminism, caused it to decline in India itself; but it spread rapidly to the surrounding countries and took so permanent a hold that it has millions of adherents in India, Ceylon, Tibet, China, and Japan.

Early Indian Buddhism (Theravāda or Hīnayāna) emphasized personal salvation; later Mahāyāna Buddhism developed, promising salvation for all. Mahāyāna Buddhism spread to Central Asia, China, and Japan and is the principal Buddhism in these countries. Hīnayāna is still practiced in Ceylon. Numerous sects and variant teachings exist, ranging from highly academic and abstruse doctrines to simple salvationism.

Budé, Guillaume (1468–1540). French scholar and humanist. Secretary and librarian to Francis I, he translated Greek texts into Latin and published them with critical analyses of the works themselves, rather than of previous commentaries on the works as had been done previously. In correspondence with humanists like Erasmus, More, and Rabelais, he zealously advocated classical studies, not only to gain erudition, but to cultivate the mind and regain classical wisdom. Along with others close to Francis I, he was instrumental in the founding of the COLLÈGE DE FRANCE (1530), where for the first time Greek and Hebrew were taught in addition to Latin.

Buffalo Bill. See William F. CODY.

Buffon, Comte **Georges Louis Leclerc de** (1707–1788). French naturalist, curator of the Jardin du Roi from 1739. He is best known for his *Histoire naturelle* (36 vols., 1749–1788), continued in eight volumes by his assistants and published in 1804; his *Epoques de la nature* (1779); and *Théorie de la Terre* (1749). His works deal with the earth, minerals, animals, and man. He helped lay the foundations for 19th-century work in natural science, especially in zoology and comparative anatomy, and was the first to write a history of the earth in terms of a series of successive geologic stages. His theories (*e.g.,* his development of geographic zoology) anticipated those of Lamarck and Darwin. The *Discours sur le style,* his inaugural address to the French ACADEMY in 1753, reflects his concern with literary style: "Style is the man himself" is a famous quotation from it. His writing is vivid, eloquent, and majestic.

Building of the Ship, The (1849). A poem by Henry Wadsworth LONGFELLOW. Often considered his best ode, the poem describes the building of a ship, interweaving the details with those of the approaching marriage of the builder's daughter and the owner's son. The ship is used as a symbol for life itself, and at the end, for the Union.

Bukharin, Nikolai Ivanovich (1888–1939). Russian Communist leader and editor. He joined the Bolsheviks in 1906 and was a leader in the movement by 1912 when, with Lenin, he co-edited the party organ, *Pravda*. In 1916 he was the editor of the revolutionary paper *Novy Mir* (*The New World*) in New York. The head of the Third International (1926–1929), he was expelled from the party only to be reinstated. Suspected of being a supporter of Trotsky, he was arrested and executed in the purges of 1938.

Bulba, Taras. See TARAS BULBA.

Bulfinch, Thomas (1796–1867). American teacher and writer. Bulfinch held a business post throughout his life, devoting his leisure to writing. His *Age of Fable* (1855) is still used in American schools as an introduction to Greek, Roman, Scandinavian, and Celtic mythology. *The Age of Chivalry* (1858), another straightforward, expurgated popularization of mythology, has pleased many young readers.

Bulgakov, Mikhail Afanasevich (1891–1940). Russian dramatist. He is best known for his DAYS OF THE TURBINS and for his dramatizations of Gogol's *Dead Souls* (1932) and Cervantes' *Don Quixote* (1940).

Bull, Olaf Jacob Martin Luther (1883–1933). Norwegian poet, short-story writer, and playwright. Love for the bare beauty of sea and mountain and pine forest, characteristically Norwegian, finds expression in Bull's poetry. In 1918 he spoke out violently against the destructive impact of German militarism on all fineness and beauty in life. A painstaking craftsman, Bull wrote intellectual, highly introspective verse. His collections include *Digte* (1909), *Digte og Noveller* (1916), *Stjernerne* (1924), *De hundrede aar* (1928) and *Oinos og Eros* (1930).

Bull, The Sacred. See APIS.

Bulldog Drummond. The hero of stories by Sapper (pen name of H. C. McNEILE). Drummond is a patriotic Englishman and a modern Robin Hood.

Bullitt, William C[hristian] (1891–   ). American diplomat. He was ambassador to Russia (1933–1936), to France (1936–1941), and ambassador-at-large (1941–1942). He wrote one novel, *It's Not Done* (1926), in addition to such nonfiction as *Report to the American People* (1940) and *The Great Globe Itself* (1946).

Bull Run. A brook in Virginia and the site of two battles during the U.S. Civil War. In the first battle of Bull Run (July 21, 1861), Union forces, confident of an easy victory that would enable them to push on to Richmond, were initially successful. But the stand of the Confederate brigade led by Thomas Jackson, which won him the nickname "Stonewall," and the arrival of reinforcements turned the apparent Union victory into rout. The second battle of Bull Run (Aug. 30, 1862) also ended in defeat for the Union. These battles are sometimes known as the battles of Manassas from nearby Manassas Junction.

Bulwer-Lytton, Edward George Earle Lytton. 1st Baron Lytton (1803–1873). English novelist and dramatist. A member of Parliament for 15 years, Bulwer-Lytton served as colonial secretary from 1858 to 1859 and was created a peer in 1866. Among his notable historical novels are EUGENE ARAM, THE LAST DAYS OF POMPEII, *Rienzi* (1835), *Leila* (1838), THE LAST OF THE BARONS, and *Harold* (1848). Scholarly in their historical detail and often heavy, but just as often thrilling in their narrative, these books held the interest of several generations of readers. In addition, Bulwer-Lytton wrote the supernatural tales ZANONI and *A Strange Story* (1862), the long poem *King Arthur* (1849), and numerous dramas, including *Richelieu* (1839) and *Money* (1840)—the latter reflecting his occasional attraction to social themes. See CAXTONS, THE.

Bumble, Mr. In Charles Dickens' OLIVER TWIST, a minor official in the workhouse where Oliver is brought up. He is a cruel, fussy man with mighty ideas of his own importance. He has given to the language the word "bumbledom," for the officious arrogance and conceit of the petty dignitary. After marriage to Mrs. Corney, the high and mighty Bumble is sadly henpecked.

Bumppo, Natty. The central figure in THE LEATHERSTOCKING TALES, a series of novels by James Fenimore COOPER. Called by many names in the novels, among them Leatherstocking, Hawkeye, Deerslayer, Pathfinder, and *La Longue Carabine*, Natty remains the uncorrupted natural man. Companioned by Chingachgook, a Mohican chief, Natty prefers the moral code of the Indian to the selfish exploitation of nature by white settlers. Superior to the Indians in woodcraft, he is loyal and courageous, a voluntary outcast who follows the wilderness westward.

Bunch, Mother. A noted London alewife of the late Elizabethan period, nominal source of many jests and anecdotes, and often mentioned in Elizabethan drama. The "Epistle to the Merrie Reader" in *Pasquil's Jests, mixed with Mother Bunches Merriments* (1604) gives the following description of her:

> She spent most of her time in telling tales, and when she laughed, she was heard from Aldgate to the Monuments at Westminster, and all Southwarke stood in Amazement. . . . She dwelt in Cornhill, neere the Exchange, and sold strong Ale . . . and lived an hundreth, seventy and five years, two days and a quarter, and halfe a minute.

Other books were named after her, such as *Mother Bunch's Closet newly Broke Open* (1609), "containing rare secrets of art and nature, tried and experienced by learned philosophers, and recommended to all ingenious young men and maids, teaching them how to get good wives and husbands."

Bundren, Addie. The principal character in William Faulkner's novel As I LAY DYING. Although she dies near the beginning of the story, much of the action of the characters is determined by their relationships with the dead woman.

Bungay or **Bongay, Friar.** A famous necromancer of the 13th century. His story is much overlaid with legend. It is said that he "raised mists and vapors which befriended Edward IV at the battle of Barnet." In the old prose romance, *The Famous History of Friar Bacon,* and in Greene's *Honourable History of Friar Bacon and Friar Bungay* (1591), he appears as the assistant to Roger Bacon (d. 1294) in his diabolical scientific experiments; he also appears in Bulwer-Lytton's novel *Last of the Barons* (1843).

Bunin, Ivan Alekseyevich (1870-1953). Russian novelist, short-story writer, and poet. He was the first Russian to win the Nobel Prize for literature (1933). Bunin emigrated from Russia in 1918 and lived in France until his death. He is famous chiefly for his prose works, which had a closer kinship with the prose of the 19th-century masters than with the modernist experiments of his own period. His novels, *Derevnya* (*The Village,* 1910) and *Sukhodol* (*Dry Valley,* 1912), written in the restrained "classical" style of Turgenev, Goncharov, or Chekhov, depict the stagnation of life in provincial Russia. His short story, *Gospodin iz San-Frantzisko* (*The Gentleman from San Francisco,* 1916), is world famous. Bunin's poetry is less highly esteemed than his prose, but he did a number of successful translations in Russian, notably of the works of Longfellow and Byron.

Bunker Hill, battle of (June 17, 1775). The first great battle of the American Revolution. To control the high ground overlooking Boston, American troops built a redoubt on nearby Breed's Hill. Under General Howe, 2,400 British troops assaulted the hill but were repulsed twice with heavy losses. After the third assault, the Americans, their powder exhausted, retreated to Bunker Hill, where nearly a fourth of them were slain or wounded.

Bunner, H[enry] C[uyler] (1855-1896). American short-story writer, poet, novelist, and editor of *Puck,* a weekly humor magazine. Bunner wrote such novels as *The Midge* (1886), a story about a bachelor and his orphan ward, but he is best remembered for his short short stories, especially *Short Sixes: Stories to Be Read While the Candle Burns* (1891). He also published *Made in France: French Tales with a United States Twist* (1893) and other books. The best of his *vers de société* appeared in *Airs from Arcady and Elsewhere* (1884).

Bunsen, Robert Wilhelm [Eberhard von] (1811-1899). German chemist. His many contributions to experimental science include the method of spectrum analysis, developed with Gustav Kirchhoff, and the bunsen burner, a heating apparatus.

Buntline, Ned. See E. Z. C. JUDSON.

Bunyan, John (1628-1688). English writer and preacher. The son of a Bedfordshire tinker, Bunyan adopted his father's trade and served in the Parliamentary army from 1644 to 1646. In 1648 or 1649 he married a woman whose dowry included two devotional books which, he later said, first turned his thoughts to religion. After a period of intense spiritual struggle, he joined the Baptist church at Bedford and later became a lay preacher. His refusal to bow to royal edicts banning nonconformist preaching led to his imprisonment from 1660 to 1672. During these 12 years he devoted himself to study of the Bible and Foxe's *Book of Martyrs* and wrote many of his books, including his autobiography,

GRACE ABOUNDING TO THE CHIEF OF SINNERS. Upon his release he became minister of the nonconformist church at Bedford, a position which he held for the rest of his life. In 1675 he was again imprisoned for a few months, during which time he wrote his most celebrated work, PILGRIM'S PROGRESS.

His other writings, all religious in character, most of them allegorical, include *The Holy City, or the New Jerusalem* (1665), *A Confession of My Faith, and a Reason of My Practice* (1672), THE LIFE AND DEATH OF MR. BADMAN, and THE HOLY WAR. An outstanding narrative genius, he wrote in a style that has been highly praised for its simplicity, vigor, and concreteness.

Bunyan, Paul. A legendary lumberjack of the American northwestern forests. A comic folk hero, he is frequently the subject of "tall tales," in which each storyteller strives to surpass the others. It is said that the dragging of Bunyan's pick cut out the Grand Canyon. When he builds a hotel, he has the "last seven stories put on hinges so's they could be swung back for to let the moon go by."

The legend of Paul Bunyan may have first appeared in Quebec, or northern Ontario; James Stevens traced him to a French-Canadian logger named Paul Bunyon, who won a reputation as a prodigious fighter in the Papineau Rebellion against England in 1837, and later became famous as the boss of a logging camp. Paul Bunyan's first appearance in print seems to be in an advertising pamphlet, *Paul Bunyan and His Big Blue Ox* (1914), published by the Red River Lumber Company. Written and illustrated by W. B. Laughead, it immediately became popular and was reissued many times. Among those who have retold the Bunyan stories are Virginia Tunvey, Esther Shepard, James Stevens, Glen Rounds, Dell J. McCormick, and Acel Garland. Daniel Hoffman studied the legend in his book, *Paul Bunyan: Last of the Frontier Demigods* (1952).

Burbage, Cuthbert. See Richard BURBAGE.

Burbage, James (d. 1597). English actor and theater-builder. In 1576 Burbage leased land in Shoreditch and built on it the first theater in England specifically intended for stage performances. It was known simply as "The Theater." In 1596 he acquired a house in Blackfriars which, being roofed over, was used for plays during the winter months. After Burbage's death his sons tore down The Theater and re-erected it in Bankside, where it became the GLOBE Theater. See Richard BURBAGE.

Burbage, Richard (1567?-1619). English actor, son of James Burbage. Richard and his brother Cuthbert Burbage inherited a share in their father's two playhouses, The THEATER and the BLACKFRIARS. Because of difficulties about the lease of the site of The Theater, they transported the building to a location in Bankside, where it was reassembled as the GLOBE Theater. Richard, one of the chief actors of his day, acted every major part in the plays of Shakespeare, as well as in those of Ben Jonson and Beaumont and Fletcher, and was particularly celebrated for his roles in tragedy. He was also a painter of some note, and the Felton portrait of Shakespeare is sometimes ascribed to him.

Burbank, Luther (1849-1926). American plant breeder. Born in Massachusetts, Burbank took up the profession of market gardening at the age of 21.

There he produced his first new creation, the Burbank potato. Moving to California, he settled down in Santa Rosa in a nursery garden and greenhouse. His aim, the cultivation of "better fruits and fairer flowers," did not include theoretic formulation; in 1905, the Carnegie Institute persuaded him to accept a salary and allow them to gather the data his experimenting accumulated. The arrangement was unsuccessful, and soon ended. By importation of foreign plants, hybridization to eliminate undesirable characteristics, and selection, Burbank was able to create new varieties of plums, berries, lilies, roses, apples, peaches, quinces, nectarines, potatoes, tomatoes, corn, asparagus, and innumerable others. His acknowledged master and the source of his earliest inspiration, Burbank wrote, was Charles Darwin.

Burchiello. Real name **Domenico di Giovanni** (1404–1448). Florentine barber, author of humorous sonnets. He influenced Berni and other Renaissance satirical writers. One of the verses in his *Sonetti* (1757) is a debate between Poetry and his Razor, concerning the amount of time that the barber spends on each. He was called *il Burchiello* (It., "canal barge or wherry"), possibly because of a sign in his shop.

Burckhardt, Jakob Christoph (1818–1897). Swiss historian of art and culture. His best-known work is *The Civilization of the Renaissance in Italy* (*Die Kultur der Renaissance in Italien;* 1860), for many years the classic analysis of the Renaissance. According to Burckhardt, Italy's unique political organization, based on the city-state rather than feudalism, had fostered the individualism upon which the Renaissance spirit rested. Thus, Italy was the cradle of the Renaissance and of modern man.

Burd, Ellen. In Scotch legend, a sister of CHILDE ROWLAND. She is rescued by him from the fairies who had shut her up in a castle in Elfland.

Bürger, Gottfried August (1747–1794). German poet of the STURM UND DRANG, close to the GÖTTINGER HAIN group. Under Herder's influence, he wrote ballads in folk style, the most famous of which is LENORE.

Burgess, [Frank] Gelett (1866–1951). American humorist and illustrator. He was the author of *Goops and How to Be Them* (1900), *Are You a Bromide* (1907), *Look Eleven Years Younger* (1937). He also wrote the famous nonsense quatrain beginning "I never saw a purple cow." See BROMIDE AND SULFITE.

Burgess, Thornton Waldo (1874–1965). American author of *Bedtime Stories,* a syndicated series of animal stories for children. Beginning in 1912, they appeared daily in numerous newspapers throughout the U.S. He also published a large number of his stories in book form.

Burghley or **Burleigh,** Baron. **William Cecil** (1520–1598). English statesman, the chief adviser to Elizabeth I.

Burgoyne, John (1722–1792). English army officer and dramatist. While commander-in-chief of the northern army, he was forced to surrender to the Americans at Saratoga in 1777. He later took part in the impeachment of Warren Hastings. Garrick produced his *Maid of the Oaks* (1775) and *The Heiress* (1786), which was enormously popular. He figures prominently in George Bernard Shaw's *The Devil's Disciple* (1900) and in Kenneth Roberts' *A Rabble in Arms* (1933).

Buried Alive (1908). A humorous novel by Arnold BENNETT. Priam Farll, a famous but shy painter, allows his rascally valet, Henry Leek, to be buried in Westminster Abbey under his name. Farll attends his own funeral, posthumously marries the splendid, comfortable Alice Chalice, and is accused of forging his own paintings. The book contains much satire of the London art world.

Burke, Edmund (1729–1797). Irish-born English statesman and author, known for his orations in the House of Commons. He was sympathetic toward the American colonies and the Irish Catholics, and was a strong enemy of the French Revolution. Among his most famous speeches are ON AMERICAN TAXATION, ON CONCILIATION WITH THE COLONIES, and *On the Nabob of Arcot's Private Debts* (1785), in which Burke discusses the great prosecution of Warren HASTINGS and tries to make him the scapegoat for all the abuses connected with the regime of the East India Company. His published works include *A Vindication of Natural Society* (1756), an ironic attack on deism; *A Philosophical Inquiry into the Origin of Our Ideas of the Sublime and Beautiful* (1756), a pioneer study in the psychological basis of aesthetic enjoyment; *Observations on the Present State of the Nation* (1769); *Thoughts on the Cause of the Present Discontents* (1770), in which Burke declares that politics deals with men and nations in actuality, never in bloodless abstractions; *Letter to the Sheriffs of Bristol* (1777); REFLECTIONS ON THE FRENCH REVOLUTION; and *Letters on the Proposals for Peace with the Regicide Directory of France* (1796–1797). He was associated with Samuel Johnson and Sir Joshua Reynolds in 1764 in forming the LITERARY CLUB. His influence on early 19th century German national economists is particularly pronounced.

Burke, Kenneth [Duva] (1897–). American literary critic, philosopher, and translator. Burke's translations of the German authors Thomas Mann, Emil Ludwig, Oswald Spengler, and Hugo von Hofmannsthal contributed greatly to making them known in the U.S. Among Burke's own writings are *Philosophy of Literary Form—Studies in Symbolic Action* (1941), *A Grammar of Motives* (1945), and *Rhetoric of Motives* (1950).

Burke, Thomas (1886–1945). English novelist and essayist. He wrote romantic, melodramatic stories about the Limehouse slum district in London. They include *Limehouse Nights* (1916) and *Abduction* (1939).

Burlador de Sevilla y el convidado de piedra, El (The Libertine of Seville and the Stone Guest, pub. 1630). A play by TIRSO DE MOLINA. It gave to world literature one of its most enduring character types, Don Juan. Based on a 14th-century Sevillan chronicle, Tirso's play relates how Don Juan Tenorio, a dissolute young rake, kills Don Gonzalo Ulloa, father of one of his lady loves, in a duel. Later Don Juan pulls the beard of a stone effigy of Don Gonzalo and invites the figure to dinner. The statue accepts and returns the hospitality by inviting Don Juan to an entertainment at his tomb, where he is strangled by the stone figure and his soul is carried off to hell.

Tirso's Don Juan, the first in a long line of successors, ignores the conventions of honor; he seeks only to secure his pleasure. At the same time he is profoundly religious and noble, exemplifying the conflict between the morality inherited from the Middle Ages and the libertinism fostered by the Renaissance. Among the most notable of later works in which Tirso's character appears are Byron's DON JUAN, Mozart's DON GIOVANNI, Zorrilla's DON JUAN TENORIO, and Shaw's MAN AND SUPERMAN.

Burlingame, [William] Roger (1889–1967). American writer. After being associated with Charles Scribner's Sons from 1914 to 1926, he turned to writing as a full-time occupation. In addition to several novels, including *You Too* (1924), a satire on advertising, Burlingame has written a number of books showing his knowledge and interest in the history of technology in the U.S.

Burnand, Sir Francis Cowley (1836–1917). English playwright and editor of the periodical *Punch* (1880–1906). He wrote many burlesques including *Cox and Box* (1867), with music by Sir Arthur Sullivan. *Happy Thoughts* (1866), originally a series for *Punch*, has been widely read. He also wrote *The Incompleat Angler* (1887).

Burne-Jones, Sir Edward Coley (1833–1898). English painter. A member of the PRE-RAPHAELITE BROTHERHOOD, he was accorded wide public adulation. He painted classical, religious, medieval, literary, and symbolic scenes, marked by mysticism, emotion, and exotic decoration.

Burnet, Gilbert (1643–1715). English historian and churchman, bishop of Salisbury. Deeply involved in the religious and political controversy of the times, a confidential adviser to William and Mary, Burnet found time to write two important histories: *A History of the Reformation of the Church of England* (1679–1714) and the *History of His Own Time* (1724–1734). These books, based on original documents or personal experience, are early models of scientific historical research.

Burnet, Thomas (1635?–1715). English clergyman and author. He is known for his chief work *Telluris Theoria Sacra* (1681), translated as *The Sacred Theory of the Earth*, a prose exploration into the origin and development of the cosmos.

Burnett, Frances Eliza Hodgson (1849–1924). English-born American author of popular romances and books for children. Her works include LITTLE LORD FAUNTLEROY, *Sara Crewe* (1888), and *The Secret Garden* (1911).

Burnett, W[illiam] R[iley] (1899–   ). American writer. A leading exponent of HARD-BOILED FICTION, Burnett made his fortune with *Little Caesar* (1929), a story of gangsters in the prohibition era. Turned into a movie, it made Edward G. Robinson a star. Among his later books are *Iron Man* (1930), *Dark Hazard* (1933), *Nobody Lives Forever* (1944), *The Asphalt Jungle* (1949), *Pale Moon* (1956), and *Underdog* (1957).

Burney, Fanny [Madame d'Arblay] (1752–1840). English author. The daughter of a prominent musician and keeper of robes in the queen's household, she is chiefly known for her *Diaries and Letters, 1778–1840* (1842–1848), *Early Diary, 1768–1778* (1889), and her novels EVELINA, OR THE HISTORY OF A YOUNG LADY'S ENTRANCE INTO THE WORLD;

CECILIA, OR MEMOIRS OF AN HEIRESS; *Camilla;* and *The Wanderer, or, Female Difficulties* (1814). She was one of the first novelists to deal with the experiences of a young girl coming in contact with the social world, and may be regarded as a link between Samuel Richardson and Jane Austen in the history of the novel.

Burning Babe, The (written c. 1593, pub. 1595). A mystical religious poem by Robert SOUTHWELL in which the poet has a vision of the suffering infant Christ on Christmas day.

burning bush. In the Old Testament, a bush burning with fire and not consumed (Ex. 3:2). It was out of this bush that the voice of God spoke to Moses on Mount Horeb, telling him that the Children of Israel were to be delivered from the oppression of the Egyptians and brought, under the leadership of Moses, into the land of Canaan. Because of its scriptural connotation and in commemoration of its early history of persecution, the burning bush became an emblem of the Presbyterian Church.

Burning Bush, The. See Sigrid UNDSET.

burning ghat. A Hindu cremation place. One of the best known is at Kalighat in Calcutta.

Burns, John Horne (1916–1953). American novelist. Burns is best known for his first book, *The Gallery* (1947), a series of connected sketches about American and British soldiers in Naples during World War II. He also wrote *Lucifer with a Book* (1949) and *A Cry of Children* (1952).

Burns, Robert (1756–1796). Scottish poet, generally considered the greatest of his nation. Self-educated, the son of a humble cotter and a farm laborer himself, Burns became a social as well as a literary sensation with the publication of his early poems in 1786. He is best known for his lyrics, written in the Scottish vernacular, on nature, love, patriotism, and peasant life. Among the most famous of these last are those addressed to a clergyman with whose theology he disagreed and against whom he had a personal grudge: THE HOLY FAIR, *Holy Willie's Prayer, Address to the Unco Guid,* and ADDRESS TO THE DEIL. He also wrote *To a Mouse, To a Mountain Daisy, Sweet Afton, Ye Flowery Banks, A Red, Red Rose,* SCOTS, WHA HAE, *John Anderson My Jo,* AULD LANG SYNE, and *A Man's a Man for a' That,* which expresses Burns's democratic opinions. His longer poems include THE COTTER'S SATURDAY NIGHT, TAM O'SHANTER, and THE JOLLY BEGGARS.

Like Chaucer and Byron, Burns was a master of the technique of using conversational rhythms in poetry. He almost always wrote to an old tune for which he sought appropriate words: "These old Scottish airs are so nobly sentimental that when one would compose for them, to *south* the tune, as our Scotch phrase is, over and over, is the readiest way to catch the inspiration, and raise the bard into that glorious enthusiasm so strongly characteristic of our old Scotch poetry." See SYLVANDER; HIGHLAND MARY; MARY CAMPBELL.

Burnt Njal. The hero of one of the best known of the early Icelandic sagas, *The Story of Burnt Njal.* The plot concerns the grim blood feud between the families of two well-to-do landowners, Njal and Gunnar, who are personal friends. Hallgerda, the spiteful and selfish wife of Gunnar, is the instigator of the feud, which progresses with a regular alternation of murders between the two sides until it culminates in the burning of Njal's home and his death within.

Burnt Norton. See FOUR QUARTETS.

Burnt-Out Case, A (1960). A novel by Graham GREENE. Set in a leper colony in the Congo, it is the story of a famous architect who is a spiritual leper and "burnt-out case."

Burr, Aaron (1756–1836). American politician. After distinguishing himself in the American Revolution, Burr served in the U.S. Senate (1791–1797) and organized a strong Democratic machine in New York through the previously nonpolitical Tammany Society. He was vice president (1801–1805) under Jefferson, whom he had tied in electoral votes in the election of 1800. Burr's long-standing enmity with Alexander Hamilton culminated in a duel (1804), in which Hamilton was killed and which ruined Burr personally and politically. In 1806 he became involved in a conspiracy in the Old Southwest, the nature of which has never been fully clarified, and was tried and acquitted of treason. Burr appears as a character in several novels, including H. B. Stowe's *The Minister Wooing* (1859), Gertrude Atherton's *The Conqueror* (1902), and Kenneth Roberts' *Arundel* (1930).

Burroughs, Edgar Rice. See TARZAN.

Burroughs, John (1837–1921). American naturalist, essayist, and poet. A farm boy who deeply loved nature, Burroughs was for a time a treasury clerk in Washington, D.C., where he met Walt Whitman. They became close friends, and Burroughs made the first biographical study of Whitman, *Notes on Walt Whitman as Poet and Person* (1867), a considerable portion of which was written by Whitman himself. Later the book was expanded into *Walt Whitman: A Study* (1896).

After working as a bank examiner (1873–1884), Burroughs settled at Riverby on the Hudson River, and the fame he acquired by his numerous essays on nature and his natural history collections attracted many visitors. He became a national figure, with his snowy white beard and his broad forehead and benign expression. He became a close friend of Theodore Roosevelt.

Reading Burroughs is for many people almost like actually seeing what he describes, so vivid, concrete, and pleasant is his writing. As he expressed it in *The Summit of the Years* (1913), "I go to books and nature as a bee goes to a flower, for a nectar that I can make into my own honey." His best-known collections include *Wake-Robin* (1871), *Riverby* (1894), *Ways of Nature* (1905), and *Leaf and Tendril* (1908).

Burroughs, William S. See BEAT MOVEMENT.

Burt, [Maxwell] Struthers (1882–1954). American novelist and short-story writer. Burt combined his personal knowledge of Philadelphia society and Wyoming ranches in his novel *The Delectable Mountains* (1927). He also wrote *John O'May and Other Stories* (1918), *The Interpreter's House* (1924), and several other volumes, including some poetry.

Burton, Sir Richard Francis (1821–1890). English explorer and writer of travel books. His *First Footsteps in Eastern Africa* (1856) is an account of his travels with John Speke (1827–1864). In 1858 the two went to East Africa again where Burton discovered Lake Tanganyika and Speke discovered Lake Victoria. As British consul, Burton traveled in West Africa, Brazil, Damascus, and Trieste. He published more than 30 narratives on his travels. He also made a literal translation of the *Arabian Nights*.

Burton, Robert (1577–1640). English churchman and prose writer. Burton entered Oxford as a student in 1593, later becoming vicar of St. Thomas, Oxford, and keeper of his college library. Thereafter he never left the little university town. He was a passionate scholar with a consuming curiosity about every phase of learning: medicine, history, literature, science, and theology. He possessed, moreover, an extraordinary memory, a great power of systematizing facts, and the gifts of eloquence, sympathy, and dry wit. Except for a few minor Latin pieces, he left only one work, THE ANATOMY OF MELANCHOLY, into which he poured a lifetime's hoard of classical and curious learning.

Burwell Papers. An account of Bacon's Rebellion, written around 1676 near Williamsburg, Va., by a planter named John Cotton. It was first printed in 1814 from an 18th-century copy owned by the Burwell family of Virginia. The lost original was the source for a verse history of the rebellion by Ebenezer Cook. The two epitaphs on Bacon contained in the Burwell Papers have been called the finest poems written in colonial America. See BACON'S EPITAPH. The account is also known as *The History of Bacon's and Ingram's Rebellion,* the title of the 1866 edition.

Bury the Dead (1936). A one-act play by Irwin SHAW. A pacifist fantasy, it deals with six men, killed in World War I, who refuse to be buried and at last persuade their living fellow soldiers to join them in a revolt against war.

busby. A tall headdress of fur worn in the British Army by hussars, artillerymen, and engineers. A bag of the same color as the facings of the regiment hangs from the top on the right.

Busch, Niven (1903–). American writer. A successful writer of popular fiction, Busch uses backgrounds that range from the Old West to 20th-century Europe. *Duel in the Sun* (1944), a novel of the Southwest in the 1880's, is perhaps his best-known work. He is also the author of *The Carrington Incident* (1941), *Day of the Conquerors* (1946), *The Furies* (1948), *The Hate Merchant* (1953), *The Actor* (1955), and *California Street* (1959).

Busch, Wilhelm (1832–1908). German humorous poet and illustrator. His well known book of verses, *Max und Moritz* (1865), illustrated by himself, is a veiled but sometimes bitter satire of average bourgeois complacency. "Max und Moritz" is still a common phrase in German, used in reference to mischievous children in general.

Buscón, Vida del (1626). A PICARESQUE novel by Francisco de QUEVEDO. Probably written about 1607, it is witty, cruel, and cynical, devoid of any feeling for humanity. Its full title is *Historia de la vida del Buscón, llamado Don Pablos, ejemplo de vagamundos y espejo de tacaños.* It relates the career of Pablos, the son of a Segovian barber and a woman of loose morals, who enters the service of a young gentleman, Don Diego Coronel. They both lodge at a boarding house in Salamanca, whose keeper, the avaricious Licenciado Cabra, was probably the prototype of Dickens' Squeers. After numerous unsavory adventures, Pablos emigrates to America, where he hopes to improve his fortunes.

bushidō (*Japanese*, "way of the warrior"). The code of ethics formerly adopted by the military leaders and feudal clan rulers of Japan. Not a written code, its provisions varied with the times, but the general emphasis was on loyalty and duty. Also involved was a certain aesthetic sensitivity and an attachment to ZEN discipline.

Busirane. See FAERIE QUEENE, THE.

Busiris. A mythical king of Egypt, who, in order to avert a famine used to sacrifice to the gods all strangers who set foot on his shores. Hercules was seized by him; and would have fallen a victim, but he broke his chain, and slew the inhospitable king. He is the titular hero of a blood-and-thunder tragedy (1719) by Edward Young.

Buson. See TANIGUCHI BUSON.

Bussy D'Ambois (c. 1604). A tragedy by George CHAPMAN. Bussy, a poor countryman who has gained the patronage of Monsieur, the king's brother, finds favor at the court of Henri III, despite the enmity of the duke of Guise, whose wife Bussy has been courting. Soon, however, his attentions turn to Tamyra, countess of Montsurry, and he becomes Monsieur's rival for the lady's affections. Where Monsieur fails, Bussy succeeds and becomes Tamyra's lover. Eventually, Count Montsurry forces Tamyra, his wife, to write a letter to Bussy imploring him to come to her. Bussy falls into the trap and is killed by Montsurry.

Bussy-Rambutin, Comte de Bussy. **Roger de Rambutin** (1618–1693). French soldier and writer. His *Histoire amoureuse des Gaules* (*Amorous History of the Gauls*, 1665), a collection of anecdotes libeling ladies of the court and presenting a disagreeable portrait of his cousin Mme. de Sévigné, earned him 17 years' exile and brought his military career and royal favor to a dismal end. Not surprisingly, the book enjoyed a wild popularity. Bussy-Rambutin was elected a member of the Académie française.

Butler, Joseph (1692–1752). English bishop and philosopher. He is known for his defense of revelation, *The Analogy of Religion* (1736). Unlike the optimistic deists, who found sufficient evidence of God's perfection and of His moral government in nature and in the heart of man, Butler stressed the imperfection of nature and of man. Accordingly, he argued that if nature, even with all its defects, furnished proof of Divine Creation, then the revealed religion of Scripture, with *analogous* defects, might also be considered the work of God.

Butler, Rhett. The rugged and free-living hero of Margaret Mitchell's historical novel, GONE WITH THE WIND.

Butler, Samuel (1612–1680). English poet, most famous for HUDIBRAS, a mock-epic satirizing the Puritans. Butler's work is distinguished by its relentless exposure of cant, hypocrisy, and human absurdity, its arresting figures of speech, odd rhymes, and witty parade of learning. His *Genuine Remains in Verse and Prose* (1759) contains a set of *Characters* in the manner of THEOPHRASTUS and THE ELEPHANT IN THE MOON, a verse satire on the Royal Society.

Butler, Samuel (1835–1902). English satirist, novelist, Homeric scholar, and translator. Son of a clergyman and grandson of Bishop Samuel Butler, whose biography (1902) he wrote, Butler too was destined for the church; upon graduation from Cambridge, however, religious doubts caused him to abandon it and he emigrated to New Zealand (1859–1864) where he accumulated a small fortune in sheep farming.

A brilliant amateur biologist, Butler was immediately attracted to Darwin's theory of evolution, but, believing Darwin had excluded mind from the life process, he subsequently took exception to certain aspects of it in a series of criticisms which he elaborated throughout his life. His essay *The Deadlock in Darwinism* and his books on evolution—*Life and Habit* (1877), *Evolution, Old and New* (1879), *Unconscious Memory* (1880), and *Luck or Cunning?* (1887)—are still very readable.

His satiric masterpiece, EREWHON, attacked contemporary attitudes in social morals, religion, and science. *The Fair Heaven* (1873) is a subtle, ironic attack on revealed religion presented in the guise of a convincing defense of the gospels, yet in fact undermining them. *Erewhon Revisited* is a continuation of his attack on revealed religions.

Butler also wrote *The Authoress of the Odyssey* (1897), in which he seriously defends his conviction that the *Odyssey* was written by a woman; *Shakespeare's Sonnets Reconsidered* (1899); and THE WAY OF ALL FLESH, a novel, and perhaps his best-known work. He was an extremely versatile, original, and brilliant writer, one of the most searching critics of his age.

Butor, Michel (1926–   ). French novelist and essayist of the NEW WAVE. *A Change of Heart* (*La Modification*, 1957; also translated as *Second Thoughts*) and *Passing Time* (*L'Emploi du Temps;* 1956) are experimental novels showing the effect of the passage of time on human relationships. His other novels, too, deal symbolically with psychological rather than objective time and memory: *Passage de Milan* (1954) and *Degrees* (1960). He explained his literary theories in *Le Génie du Lieu* (1958) and the autobiographical *Repertoire* (1960).

Buzfuz, Serjeant. In Charles Dickens' PICKWICK PAPERS, the pleader retained by DODSON AND FOGG for the plaintiff in the celebrated case of *Bardell* v. *Pickwick*. Serjeant Buzfuz is an able orator, who proves that Mr. Pickwick's innocent note about "chops and tomato sauce" is a declaration of love, and that his reminder "not to forget the warming-pan" is only a flimsy cover to express the ardor of his affection.

Byles, Mather (1707–1788). American clergyman and poet. The son of a Boston saddler, and nephew of Cotton Mather, Byles graduated from Harvard in 1725. His two chief collections were *Poems on Several Occasions* (1744) and *The Conflagration* (1755), verse greatly influenced by Alexander Pope with whom Byles corresponded. A sort of official greeter for New England, Byles was the most noted wit of 18th century America.

byliny. The epic poems of the Russian peasantry in song form. A number of specific heroes reappear throughout these songs. Their feats are fantastic and are often engagingly ingenuous. Many of the *byliny* are divided into cycles, such as the cycle of Kiev, the cycle of Novgorod, the cycle of Ivan the Terrible, and others. They range in time from the earliest mythological periods to the 18th century.

Bynner, [Harold] Witter (1881–   ). American poet. Bynner early wrote *An Ode to Harvard* (1907) and later did editorial work for *McClure's Magazine*. In 1916 he was involved with Arthur Davison Ficke in the SPECTRA hoax. In 1922 he published *A Book of Plays*. Interested in the art of China and India, he published *The Jade Mountain* (1929), a translation of Chinese poetry; *Indian Earth* (1929), a volume of verse; and *The Way of Life According to Laotzu* (1944). Among his other books are *Journey with Genius* (1951), an account of time spent with D. H. Lawrence, and *New Poems* (1960).

Byrd, Richard E[velyn] (1888–1957). American polar explorer. A descendant of the Virginia planter William Byrd, he flew by airplane over the North Pole (1926) and the South Pole (1929), and took part in three expeditions to Antarctica (1928–1930, 1933–1935, 1939). He described his adventures in *Skyward* (1928), *Little America* (1930), and other books.

Byrd, William (1543?–1623). English composer. Known in 16th-century Europe as the "Father of Music," he wrote much church music, chamber and instrumental music, and a number of songs and madrigals on texts by Sir Philip Sidney, Ovid, Ariosto, and other famous poets. He is considered to have originated the solo song with string accompaniment. Although he wrote music for the Anglican Church, Byrd remained a devout Catholic.

Byrd, William (1674–1744). American historian of the Virginia colony, scholar, explorer, and member of the Royal Society of London, one of the most cultivated men in colonial America. His best-known works are *The History of the Dividing Line,* concerning the dispute over the boundary between Virginia and North Carolina; *A Journey to the Land of Eden;* and *A Progress to the Mines*. They are included in a collection of his papers, known as *The Westover Manuscripts,* first published in 1841. Diaries which Byrd kept in shorthand as a hobby for several years were discovered nearly 200 years after his death and published as *The Secret Diary of William Byrd of Westover* (1941) and *Another Secret Diary* (1942).

Byrne, Donn. Original name, **Brian Oswald Donn-Byrne** (1889–1928). Irish-American novelist and short-story writer. Best known for his novel MESSER MARCO POLO, Donn Byrne always tried to hide the fact that he had been born in Brooklyn. A romantic imagination, the use of fantasy, and a graceful style mark his writing. *Blind Raftery* (1924) is a novel about the Gaelic poet Anthony Raftery (1745?–1835). His many stories were collected in *The Changeling* (1923), *Rivers of Damascus* (1931), and *The Woman of the Shee* (1932).

Byron, George Gordon [Noel]. 6th baron **Byron of Rochdale.** Called **Lord Byron** (1788–1824). English poet. In both his works and his life he created the "Byronic hero"—a defiant, melancholy young man, brooding on some mysterious, unforgivable sin in his past. Whatever Byron's sin was, he never told, but neither did he deny the legends of wildness, evil, and debauchery that grew up about his name. The heroes of Byron's poems are gen-

erally swashbuckling brigands who perform heroic feats. Byron himself, however, was short, somewhat stout, and limped from a club foot.

His profligate father died when Byron was three years old, and he was raised in Scotland by his mother. He was educated at Harrow and at Trinity College, Cambridge, receiving an M.A. from the latter in 1808. In 1809 he took his seat in the House of Lords, having come into the family title and estates through the death of his great-uncle in 1798. His first published work, HOURS OF IDLENESS, a collection of poems, was given a devastating, although accurate, review by the *Edinburgh Review*. This review was answered by Byron in the virulent satire, ENGLISH BARDS AND SCOTCH REVIEWERS. After a very short time in Parliament, Byron and his friend J. C. Hobhouse left England for a tour of the Mediterranean that took them from Spain to the Near East. The trip fired Byron's romantic nature with tantalizing views of the Orient and supplied material for many of his later works.

Following his return to England (1811), Byron published the first two cantos of CHILDE HAROLD'S PILGRIMAGE, a fictionalized account of his trip. *Childe Harold* was an immediate success; as Byron put it, he woke up one morning to find himself famous. In the next two years he published *The Giaour* (1813), THE BRIDE OF ABYDOS, THE CORSAIR, and *Lara* (1814).

Byron was much admired by women and had been involved in several intrigues before he married Anne Isabella MILBANKE in 1815. However, his promiscuous behavior after the marriage completely destroyed his reputation. Shortly after the birth of their daughter (1815), Lady Byron separated from her husband. Byron later spoke bitterly of the marriage, referring to their honeymoon as a "treaclemoon," and once a deed of separation had been signed he left England, never to return.

He traveled to Switzerland, where he lived with the Shelleys at Lake Geneva. Byron began a liaison with Clara CLAIRMONT, but moved restlessly on, arriving in Venice in November, 1816, in the company of his friend Hobhouse. He spent the next six years in Italy, always championing and often taking part in the Italian nationalist movement. In 1819, Byron met and fell in love with the 17-year-old countess Theresa GUICCIOLI, and critics have attributed much of the poet's enthusiasm for Italy to her influence. With Leigh Hunt, Byron edited *The Liberal* (1822), but after the collapse of the *Carbonari* movement they were left without a cause. The next year, following the death of Shelley, Byron outfitted a ship and sailed to Greece to take part in the battle for Greek independence. He died, fever-stricken, at Missolonghi in January, 1824. After being given full military honors in Greece, his body was shipped back to England for burial at Newstead Abbey, his baronial seat.

Byron's poetic output was never slowed down by his political and personal adventures. While in Italy he finished *Childe Harold* (1816, 1817) and wrote THE SIEGE OF CORINTH, PARISINA, and THE PRISONER OF CHILLON, all poetic narratives. In 1817 he wrote his first poetic drama, MANFRED, which was followed by MARINO FALIERO, *Cain, a Mystery* (1821), *Heaven and Earth* (1822), WERNER, and THE DEFORMED TRANSFORMED. Among Byron's most accomplished works are his satires, such as BEPPO, THE VISION OF

JUDGEMENT, in which he answers the attack on him by the poet Robert Southey; *The Age of Bronze* (1823); and his masterpiece, DON JUAN. *Don Juan,* begun in 1819, was still unfinished when Byron died. This 16,000 line poem in 16 cantos was continually added to by the poet, and as such it can be read as a contemporaneous account of the author's moods and feelings. Byron used *Don Juan* as a platform to express many of his sardonic opinions of people and events. The protagonist is, of course, Byron himself, only thinly disguised as the famous Spanish rake.

As a poet and especially as one of the English romantics, Byron has found less favor than Keats or Shelley; he is looked on as the embodiment of romanticism rather than its spokesman. The bizarre aspects of Byron's life have somewhat overshadowed his technical virtuosity as a poet: the man has been more closely examined than his work. However, at its best Byron's poetry shows an extraordinary rhyming ability combined with a free-flowing, dynamic style. His work rarely has the profundity found in that of Shelley or Keats, but his opus as a whole is a forceful expression of the majesty and desolation of history, the vanity of pomp, and the fleeting quality of fame. His work has always been more popular in Europe, especially Germany, than in England and the U.S. See DESTRUCTION OF SENNACHERIB, THE.

Byron, Harriet. See SIR CHARLES GRANDISON.

Byrsa. The citadel of Carthage. It was built, according to legend, by DIDO, who was told by the local ruler that she might purchase as much land as could be enclosed within a bull's hide. By cutting the hide into narrow strips, she obtained a sizable piece of land. The hide (Gr., *byrsa*) supposedly gave the place its name; historically, the name comes from a Phoenician word meaning *citadel.*

Byzantine Empire. The eastern or Greek division of the Roman Empire, sometimes called the Later or Eastern Roman Empire. For the purposes of administration, DIOCLETIAN (r. 284–305) divided the rule of the empire among four emperors, an experiment that led to 20 years of civil strife after his abdication. The empire was reunited in 324 when CONSTANTINE THE GREAT, defeating all his rivals, became sole ruler of the whole empire.

The Byzantine Empire may be dated from Constantine's creation of a second capital, modeled on Rome, at BYZANTIUM which he renamed Constantinople (now Istanbul). From the establishment of this city as a second Rome the division of east from west was formalized, and the east soon emerged as the dominant half. More important, unlike Rome with its pagan history, Constantinople was, from the very first Christian, and it was Greek, thus dividing east from west still further. As Rome declined and finally fell (476), the Byzantine Empire flourished: it was a major, if not the major, power in Europe up to the mid-11th century. Politically, it played the highly significant role of protecting Europe, through the Middle Ages, against invasions from western Asia. The absolute monarchy, with the monarch elected by God, instituted by Constantine the Great remained largely unchanged throughout the long life of the empire, which fell at the hands of the Turks in 1453. See JUSTINIAN.

The iconography of the Byzantine Empire developed out of Christian symbolism. Its chief features are the circle, dome, and round arch; its chief symbols are the lily, cross, vesica, and nimbus. Saint Sophia at Constantinople and Saint Mark's at Venice are fine exemplars of Byzantine architecture and decoration.

Byzantium. A city on the European shore at the mouth of the Thracian Bosporus. It was first established by Megarian colonists (c. 657 B.C.). In the sixth century B.C. it came under Persian rule and then alternately under Spartan and Athenian rule in the fifth and fourth centuries. After its revolt from the second Athenian League (357), it was independent and became an ally of Rome at the time of the Third Macedonian War. It subsequently came under Roman rule and was chosen by Constantine the Great for his new capital; he renamed it CONSTANTINOPLE, and it is now called Istanbul, a major city in Turkey.

Byzantium appears as a central symbol in the poetry of William Butler YEATS. It occurs in *Sailing to Byzantium* and *Byzantium,* where it represents the richness of an artistic civilization and the triumph of art over time and death.

C

Caaba or **al Caaba.** See KAABA.

Cabal. In English history, an influential clique of ministers at the court of Charles II from 1667 to 1674. The group derived its name from the initials of its members (Clifford, Ashley, Buckingham, Arlington, and Lauderdale), who were notorious for their intrigues and corruption. The word *cabal*, which is now used to signify a body of political intriguers, was probably popularized by the activities of the English Cabal, but it had long been associated with secrecy and magic. See CABALA.

cabala or **kabbalah.** The oral traditions of the Jews, said to have been delivered by Moses to the rabbis and handed down through the centuries by word of mouth. The word comes from *qabbalah*, the Hebrew word for "tradition," and in the Middle Ages was a popular term for the Jewish theosophy describing the World of Souls. The rabbis, or cabalists, who were the guardians of the cabala were feared as possessing secrets of magical powers.

Caballero, Fernán. Pen name of **Cecilia Böhl de Faber** (1796–1877). Spanish novelist. Of Spanish descent, Fernán Caballero was born in Switzerland but emigrated to Spain in 1813. The appearance of her first novel, *La Gaviota* (*The Seagull*, 1849) marked the beginning of the regional school in Spanish literature. The tale relates the progress of a low-born singer who marries a German surgeon, becomes a well-known opera star, has an affair with a bull-fighter, and after marrying again, returns to her native province. Set in Andalusia, the novel is noted for its colorful descriptions of life in that province. She also wrote *Clemencia* (1852) and *La familia de Alvareda* (1856).

Cabbages and Kings (1904). A volume of 19 connected stories by O. HENRY. The stories are set in a fictional country called Coralio in Central America. The title, from the ballad of the Walrus and the Carpenter in Lewis Carroll's *Alice in Wonderland,* announces the intention "to talk of many things." The picture of life presented is one of mingled romance and realism.

Cabell, James Branch (1879–1958). American novelist and essayist. Cabell belonged to an old Virginian family, and some of his most laborious writings are concerned with the genealogies of his own and other families. His first book, *The Eagle's Shadow,* appeared in 1904. While writing his second book, *Gallantry* (1907), Cabell became irritated by having to describe a scene he had never visited. As a result, he created his own mythical country, the medieval French province of Poictesme, the name of which is probably a compound of Poitiers and Angoulême. In a long series of symbolic and satirical

novels, he traced the history of the imaginary province from 1234 to 1750, describing in great detail its laws, easy sexual morality, courtly manners, legends, and habits. (See Dom MANUEL).

It was not until the publication of JURGEN in 1919 that Cabell received any popular success, and his acceptance was due largely to the attempt to suppress the book on the grounds of immorality. In the 18-volume *Storisende Edition* (1927–1930), Cabell arranged the Poictesme novels in sequence of action rather than in the order in which they were published. Among the books in the series are *Beyond Life* (1919), *The Soul of Melicent* (1913; revised as *Domnei*, 1920), *Chivalry* (1909), *Jurgen, Gallantry* (1907), THE CREAM OF THE JEST, *The Silver Stallion* (1926), and *Something about Eve* (1927). Cabell also wrote numerous books of poetry and nonfiction.

When asked how to pronounce his name, Cabell rhymed, "Tell the rabble my name is Cabell."

Cabeza de Vaca, Alvar Núñez (c. 1490–c. 1557). Spanish explorer and governor. Cabeza de Vaca saw military action in Italy and Spain before joining an ill-fated expedition (1528) to Florida under Pánfilo da Narváez, during which he and a few companions were marooned on Galveston Island near Texas. After spending six years as a merchant among Indian tribes in the area, Cabeza de Vaca began his long journey back to civilization. During a period of captivity among the natives, he met two other Spaniards and a Negro slave, also survivors of the Narváez expedition; the four of them managed to escape and headed for Mexico, winning the favor of Indians along the way by healing the sick. They reached Culiacán on the Pacific coast of Mexico in 1536. Cabeza de Vaca himself described his adventures in *Naufragios* (1542).

In 1540 he was appointed governor of the province of La Plata in South America. After an unsuccessful attempt to reach the legendary city of Manoa, he was deposed by a revolt in Asunción, supposedly because he was usurping royal authority, but probably because he insisted on decent treatment for the Indians.

Cable, George Washington (1844–1925). American short-story writer and novelist. He is known for his tales dealing with the Creoles of New Orleans; Cable was part of the local color movement of the late 19th century, and a master of the various dialects of his native city. His first literary success was OLD CREOLE DAYS, a collection of stories to which *Madame Delphine* (1881) was added in later editions. THE GRANDISSIMES, a complex novel of social forces and his most widely read work today, showed Cable to be an important writer whose treatment of race relations and violence was to foreshadow such later Southern writers as William Faulkner and Robert Penn Warren. *Dr. Sevier* (1884) attacked the corruption of New Orleans in the period before the Civil War.

An enemy of slavery and a reformer, Cable published *The Silent South* in 1885. This argument for better treatment of Negroes and for prison reform increased the animosity of the Creoles toward Cable, forcing him to move to Massachusetts, where he continued to write on social problems in *The Negro Question* (1888) and *The Southern Struggle for Pure Government* (1890). Cable's later fiction is thought to be inferior to his earlier work. It includes *Strong Hearts* (1899), *"Posson Jone'" and Père Raphaël* (1909), and *Gideon's Band* (1914).

Cabot, John (1450–1498) and **Sebastian** (c. 1476–1557). Outstanding Italian navigators and explorers. The senior Cabot traveled to the Orient in 1480 in hope of improving the spice trade. While there he became impressed with the need for a northwest passage to Cathay: this was to become the ruling passion of his career and that of his son. Cabot traveled to England, settling in Bristol, where he received a patent of discovery from Henry VII and set sail in 1497 accompanied by his son on a voyage of discovery. He reached Baffin Land and cruised along the Newfoundland coast, which he thought to be Asia; a second voyage in 1498 carried him to the Delaware Capes and Hatteras. He is generally credited with the discovery of the North American continent.

His son Sebastian, an expert cartographer as well as explorer, made an unsuccessful attempt to locate the Northwest Passage in 1509. He was then commissioned by the Spanish to explore the possibility of a southwest passage to the Pacific and from 1526 to 1529, he was in South America, following the River Plate. In 1533 he became the governor of a joint stock Company of Merchant Adventurers whose aim was to find a northeast passage to China; their expedition reached Russia and opened trade possibilities instead. Sebastian died wealthy and famous, but he never realized his elusive goal.

caccia. A poem in free verse, employing mainly short lines. Popular during the Italian Renaissance, *caccia* are generally used to portray hunting scenes or any outdoor experience, serving to provide the necessary shouts, exclamations, and conversational examples that form the body of the poem. The literal meaning of the word *caccia* is the hunt or chase. Many poems cast in this form appeared, usually anonymously, between 1350 and 1450; these were set to music but few have survived.

Caccini, Giulio (1546–1618). Italian musician and composer. Caccini was a member of the Florentine *Camerata,* a group of theorists and composers, including V. Galilei, Peri, Rinuccini, and Monteverdi, who created the first operas. He wrote the music, not extant, for Chiabrera's *Rapimento di Cefalo,* performed in 1600.

Cacus. In Roman mythology, a famous robber son of Vulcan. He is represented as three-headed, and vomiting flames; he lived in Italy, and was strangled by Hercules. It is thought that, with his sister Caca, Cacus was actually a primitive god of the hearthfire.

Cadalso y Vázquez, José (1741–1782). Spanish poet, essayist, and soldier. Once described as a man who wrote classicism and lived romanticism, Cadalso is best known for such satirical works as *Los eruditos a la violeta* (1772), directed against superficial learning, and *Cartas marruecas* (1793), essays notable for their acute analysis of Spanish decadence. *Noches lúgubres* (1792) are prose dialogues in which he described an attempt to disinter the body of his dead mistress. His best poetry appears in *Ocios de mi juventud* (1773).

Cade, Jack [originally **John**] (d. 1450). Irishborn English rebel who assumed the name of Mortimer and claimed York kinship. He led an insurrection, usually called "Cade's Rebellion," of about 30,000 heavily armed Kentishmen protesting oppressive taxation and unjust administration of the government under King Henry VI. They defeated a royal army and occupied London (July, 1450) for two days, executing two of the king's ministers. On the third day, however, their plundering turned the citizenry against them. Cade tried to make a stand, but a promise of pardon dispersed most of his army, and he was pursued into Sussex and slain. He appears in Shakespeare's Henry VI: Part II, and in R. T. Conrad's tragedy *Jack Cade* (1835), rewritten as *Aylmere* (1852) and very popular in 19th-century America.

Cadenus. One of Swift's many pseudonyms, an anagram of *decanus* (Lat., "dean"). It appears in *Cadenus and Vanessa* (1713, pub. 1726), one of Swift's best poems, which gives an account of his relationship with Esther Vanhomrigh and was written to dispel her passion for him. The poem also reflects Swift's zeal for improving the minds of young ladies, which had begun with his tutorship of Esther Johnson. At the request of Esther Vanhomrigh, *Cadenus and Vanessa* was published after her death.

Cade's Rebellion. See Jack Cade.

Cadignan, Diane de. The Duchess of Maufrigneuse, afterwards Princess of Cadignan. One of Balzac's most heartless and brilliant women, the Princess is the mistress of many of the men who appear in the novels of La Comédie Humaine. She is the heroine of Les Secrets de la Princesse de Cadignan.

Cadmus (Kadmos). In Greek mythology, a son of Agenor and Telephassa. Sent from their Phoenician home to seek their sister Europe, he and his brothers were told not to return without her. The Delphic oracle advised him to give up the search and to found a city where a cow with a moon-shaped mark lay down to rest. This he did at Thebes in Boeotia. Killing a dragon sacred to Ares, he sowed its teeth and armed men sprang up from the ground (see also Sparti). When he flung a stone among them, they killed each other, except for five who became his allies.

At a wedding attended by the gods Cadmus married Harmonia, daughter of Ares and Aphrodite; she bore him a son, Polydorus, and four daughters, Autonoë, Ino, Agave, and Semele. He fortified the Theban acropolis, the Cadmeia. In his old age he resigned the throne to his grandson Pentheus, after whose early death Cadmus and Harmonia migrated to Illyria and ultimately became serpents. Through Polydorus, Cadmus fathered the ill-fated dynasty that ended with Oedipus' grandsons. He appears in Euripides' tragedy *The Bacchae* as a follower of Semele's son Dionysus. (See BACCHANTS, THE.)

Cadou, René Guy (1920–1951). French poet. The best of his deceptively simple and sentimental poetry is collected in *Poèmes Choisies* (1950) and *Hélène; ou, le règne végétal* (1952).

Caduceus. An ancient Greek herald's wand (*kerykeion*) entwined with snakes or ribbons. Perhaps originally associated in Greek religion with fertility *daimones* (see DAEMON) it became especially identified with Hermes, the herald of the gods, and ASCLEPIUS (Aesculapius), the demigod of healing. Through the latter, it became a symbol of the physician's profession, as it is today.

Caedmon (d. 680?). Old English religious poet. According to Bede he was an illiterate herdsman who received divine inspiration in a dream to write religious poetry. He entered a monastery and made narrative poetry in ALLITERATIVE VERSE of the scriptural histories told to him. Actually, there is only one hymn which he certainly composed; the rest of the "Caedmonian manuscript" is the work of several different authors. The first "book" has adaptations of Genesis, Exodus, and Daniel. The second, called *Christ and Satan,* is of much later date, perhaps even ninth century (see CYNEWULF).

Caeneus (Kaineus). See LAPITHS.

A page from a manuscript of *Caedmon's Hymn.*

Caerlon (Welsh, "city of legions"). A place name prominent in Arthurian legend as the seat of King Arthur's court. The most noted early references to Caerlon in connection with Arthurian literature occur in the writings of the Welsh historians. From Geoffrey of Monmouth (12th century), for example, we learn that Caerlon was situated on the river Usk, that it was founded by Belinus, and that it became the archbishopric for Cambria (Wales). See CAMELOT; CARDUEL.

Caesar, [Caius] Julius (100–44 B.C.). Roman general and statesman. After a brilliant early career in politics, where he distinguished himself in oratory, and in generalship which he displayed in Spain (61–60 B.C.), Caesar was elected consul in 59. In the same year he joined with Pompey and Crassus in the First TRIUMVIRATE. After his consulate, as was customary, he was allotted the governorship of a province: his choice was GAUL. For nine years (58–49) he pushed back the boundaries of Roman Gaul until he had conquered all of central Europe from the Rhine to the Pyrenees. In 49, Pompey and the leaders of the Senate, fearing the prestige of Caesar and the strength of his fanatically loyal legions, ordered him to resign his command and return to Rome without his army. This he refused to do; "The die is cast," he is reported to have said as he led his army across the RUBICON into Italy. Pompey fled together with many members of the senatorial party, including Cicero and Cato the Younger. Following his opponents to Thessaly in northern Greece, Caesar defeated them in the battle of Pharsalus (48). In subsequent campaigns, he secured his firm hold on the empire in several ways: he placed CLEOPATRA on the throne of Egypt (47); he defeated the king of Pontus at the Battle of Zela (47); he crushed the remainder of the senatorial army at Thapsus in North Africa (46). His return to Rome in the spring of 46 was marked by lavish public festivals. He was hailed as a demigod; the name of the fifth month (*Quintilis*) in the Roman calendar was changed to *Julius* (July) in his honor. During the year that followed, Caesar made many reforms in the senatorial system and in the general management of the empire. His most durable reform, however, was his revision of the calendar. With the help of an Alexandrian astronomer, he established the Julian calendar which, with minor changes, is the one we use today. It went into effect on January 1, 45 B.C.

Opposition to Caesar on the part of the aristocratic party was still seething beneath the surface of Roman politics. On March 15, 44 (the IDES of March), a group led by CASSIUS Longinus and Marcus Junius BRUTUS assassinated Caesar, thus bringing to a sudden end uncompleted plans for the reorganization of Rome and the empire.

Caesar was one of the foremost orators of his age; only Cicero was esteemed the more persuasive of the two speakers. He also found time to record some of the history that he himself helped to make. His COMMENTARIES ON THE GALLIC WAR (51) and his *Commentaries on the Civil War* (45), which was unfinished, show him as a clear and vigorous prose stylist.

Even in his lifetime, the name *Caesar* represented the Roman *Imperium.* By the time of Christ—75 years later—it was used to connote civil government.

When Diocletian, at the end of the third century, split the empire into East and West, he appointed two Caesars as vice-regents. Through the Middle Ages to the present day, Caesar's name has survived as Kaiser and Czar. (See JULIAN EMPERORS.)

Caesar appears in many historical dramas, notably in Shakespeare's JULIUS CAESAR and George Bernard Shaw's CAESAR AND CLEOPATRA. In *Julius Caesar,* Brutus is actually the main interest of the play while Caesar is drawn as a weakling and a braggart. This characterization has often been criticized as untrue to history.

Caesar's famous dispatch *"Veni, vidi, vici"* (I came, I saw, I conquered) was written to the senate to announce his overthrow of Parnaces, king of Pontus.

Caesar's wife must be above suspicion. When Pompeia's name became linked with Clodius', Caesar divorced her, not because he believed her to be guilty, but because the wife of Caesar must not even be suspected of crime. See CALPURNIA.

Caesar and Cleopatra (1906). A play by George Bernard SHAW. A wise, unsentimental Caesar is the center of a loose plot about political intrigue in ancient Egypt. Shaw gives unfamiliar personalities to both Caesar and Cleopatra. Not Shakespeare's "serpent of the old Nile," this Cleopatra is a giddy teen-ager, convinced the Romans are monsters. Under Caesar's tutelage she loses her charm and becomes a precocious adult. Caesar, balding and practical, is amused by Cleopatra, history, and himself. Shaw's plot is taken directly from Plutarch's *Parallel Lives.*

caesura. In prosody, a break or pause in the flow of a line of poetry for rhetorical effect. The caesura is as related to meaning as to verse technique, since it must be occasioned by a sense pause such as the end of one sentence and the beginning of another. Formerly subject to the strict rules of classical prosody, the caesura is now used freely and naturally to vary the music of the line and thus of the entire poem.

Caffè, Il (*Ital.,* "The Coffeehouse"). An Italian literary gazette (1764-1766). Although carrying some articles of a purely literary nature, it was mainly concerned with promoting economic, social, and political reform on the basis of ideas formulated by the luminaries of the French Enlightenment. The review's founders and chief contributors were the economist Pietro Verri (1728-1797), his brother Alessandro, and the penologist Cesare Beccaria. Voltaire and d'Alembert praised its efforts to familiarize the Italian public with French rationalist thought.

Cagliostro, Count **Alessandro di.** Real name: **Giuseppe Balsamo** (1743-1795). Italian charlatan. He traveled throughout Europe with his wife, posing as a man of rank and duping the credulous with his feats of magic and alchemy. Later the couple founded a secret masonic sect which gained many adherents. Implicated in the DIAMOND NECKLACE AFFAIR in 1785, he was imprisoned in the Bastille. In Rome he was condemned to death by the Inquisition for heresy, but the sentence was commuted to life imprisonment.

Cahan, Abraham (1860-1951). Russian-born American novelist and editor. Cahan came to America in 1882, joined the staff of Yiddish journals in New York City, and became a founder and editor-in-chief of the *Jewish Daily Forward.* His best-known

novel is THE RISE OF DAVID LEVINSKY, dealing with the archetypal immigrant experience. Other works include *Yekl, a Tale of the New York Ghetto* (1896) and *The Imported Bridegroom and Other Stories of the New York Ghetto* (1898).

Cahiers de la quinzaine. See Charles PÉGUY.

Caiaphas. In the New Testament, a high priest before whom Jesus was brought to trial. He was a member of the SANHEDRIN.

Cain. In the Old Testament, the son of Adam and Eve and murderer of his brother Abel. Cain killed his brother out of jealousy when Abel's sacrifice of the firstlings of his flock proved more acceptable to Jehovah than his own sacrifice of the fruit of the ground. Then Jehovah, to signify his disapproval cast his curse upon him and made Cain "a fugitive and a vagabond in the earth." The rivalry of a shepherd for the approval of a deity is as old as Sumerian literature (see DUMUZI).

According to Muslim tradition, Cain refused to follow his father's desire that he marry Abel's twin sister, Jumella, and instead married his own twin sister Aclima. God rejected Cain's sacrifice to signify his disapproval of this marriage.

Byron wrote a dramatic poem *Cain, a Mystery* (1821) based on the Bible narrative. Coleridge's prose poem *The Wanderings of Cain* (1798) is on the same subject.

Cain, James M[allahan] (1892-   ). American novelist. Cain established a reputation as a writer of hard-boiled fiction with his first novel, *The Postman Always Rings Twice* (1934). It is the story of a young hobo who has a love affair with the wife of the owner of a roadside stand and plots with her to murder her husband and collect his insurance. Later novels include *Serenade* (1937), *Mildred Pierce* (1941), *Past All Dishonor* (1946), and *Mignon* (1955).

Caine, [Sir Thomas Henry] Hall (1853-1931). English novelist. His books were phenomenally successful and earned him a fortune. Among the best known are *The Manxman* (1894), *The Eternal City* (1901), and *The Prodigal Son* (1904). As a young man he served as secretary to D. G. Rossetti, and published his *Recollections* of the poet in 1882.

Caine Mutiny, The (1951). A novel by Herman WOUK. It takes place aboard the *Caine,* a World War II mine sweeper, whose officers rebel against the cowardly and inefficient Captain Queeg. A book of sustained and gripping narrative power, it had a tremendous impact on the American reading public. A section of it was later equally effectively dramatized by the author as *The Caine Mutiny Court Martial* (1953).

Ça Ira (Fr. "it will go"). Name and refrain of a popular patriotic song (1790) of the French Revolution. The rallying cry was borrowed from Benjamin Franklin, who used to say in reference to the American revolution, *"Ah! ça ira!"* ("we'll succeed!")

Caius, Dr. An irascible French physician in Shakespeare's MERRY WIVES OF WINDSOR. His courtship of Anne Page has the backing of her mother, Mrs. Page.

Cakes and Ale (1930). A novel by W. Somerset MAUGHAM. It is a satire of English literary life in which ASHENDEN and Kear (a popular novelist based on Hugh Walpole) re-examine the life of the great

Victorian writer Driffield. Driffield was said to be based on Thomas Hardy, but Maugham vigorously denied it. The central character is Rosie, Driffield's first wife, an exuberant, promiscuous barmaid.

Calais (Kalais). See ARGONAUTS.

Calamity Jane. The nickname of **Martha Jane Burke** (1852?–1903). Born in a Montana mining community, she was a well-known frontier character, pony-express rider, and scout. She became the heroine of *Deadwood Dick on Deck, or Calamity Jane the Heroine of Whoop Up,* one of a series of dime novels by Edward L. Wheeler that began in 1884. The name has come to be a synonym for one who is always predicting misfortune, one who puts the worst possible interpretation on any turn of events.

Calamus (1860). A group of poems in Walt Whitman's LEAVES OF GRASS. Intended as a complementary section to *Children of Adam,* the poems celebrate "the manly love of comrades." Calamus is a hardy and aromatic kind of grass or rush, often called sweet flag.

Calandrino and the Heliotrope. A tale from Giovanni Boccaccio's THE DECAMERON. It tells of the simpleton Calandrino and his belief that there is a stone called the heliotrope that can make him invisible. Imagining he has found it, he eludes his friends Bruno and Buffalmacco and returns home. When his wife scolds him for bringing home so many stones, he beats her, convinced that she has destroyed the virtues of his find. Only when his friends confess the jest, is he persuaded not to beat her again. Calandrino appears in several of the *Decameron* stories.

Calder, Alexander (1898–   ). American artist. He is known for his constructed mobiles.

Calderón de la Barca [y Henao], Pedro (1600–1681). Spanish dramatist, one of his country's great literary figures. Born in Madrid of a prosperous family of the lower aristocracy, Calderón was educated at the Jesuit college there and attended the university at Salamanca. Beginning his literary career about 1620, he was a soldier as well as a successful playwright. In 1651 he became a priest. After his ordination he wrote only AUTOS SACRAMENTALES and command plays for the court theater.

Calderón brought to the theater a fine power of reasoning, an intellectual outlook, a keen dramatic instinct, and a delicate imagination. He was a typical writer of the Baroque period, frequently given to metaphors and artificially imposed symbols. His philosophy was influenced by such stoics as Epictetus and Seneca and by St. Augustine and St. Thomas Aquinas. His pessimism can be traced to a biblical origin in the Book of Job and Ecclesiastes. Most of the *comedias* and *autos* written at the end of his life proclaim the vanity of life and the emptiness of human existence.

Calderón wrote more than 120 plays and some 70 *autos;* there are, in addition, about 20 short pieces, such as *entremeses* and *zarzuelas.* Among the best-known works of Calderón's early period, in which he gave vent to his rebellious and restless personality, are EL ALCALDE DE ZALAMEA, considered one of his finest plays; *La devoción de la cruz (Devotion to the Cross),* which shows how devotion to the cross can negate even the most heinous crimes; *El cisma de*

Inglaterra, dealing with Henry VIII and Anne Boleyn; *La niña de Gómez Arias;* and *Luis Pérez el Gallego.*

Like other dramatists of Spain's Golden Age, Calderón wrote several dramas based on *pundonor,* or the point of honor, a theme with which he is often associated. The concept in this case is limited to conjugal honor. According to the code, apparently condoned by Calderón, the barest rumor of a wife's infidelity gave her husband the right to take her life. Plays in this vein include EL MÉDICO DE SU HONRA, *A secreto agravio, secreta venganza,* and *El pintor de su deshonra.*

Calderón also wrote intricate, ingenious *comedias de capa y espada,* or cloak-and-sword comedies, filled with duels, secret hiding places, and veiled women. Among the best of these are *Hombre pobre todo es trazas, El astrólogo fingido,* and *La dama duende.* In the more philosophical epoch of Calderón's career, the following plays are noteworthy: LA VIDA ES SUEÑO, often considered his masterpiece; EL MÁGICO PRODIGIOSO; *En esta vida todo es verdad y todo es mentira;* and *Saber del bien y del mal.*

Calderón is regarded as the outstanding writer of *autos sacramentales,* a genre which he perfected. His *autos* include EL GRAN TEATRO DEL MUNDO, LA CENA DE BALTAZAR, and *El divino Orfeo.*

Caldwell, Erskine [Preston] (1903–   ). Amerian novelist and short-story writer. A native of the Deep South, Caldwell is noted for his vivid studies, earthy or starkly tragic, of life among Southern sharecroppers and Negroes in Georgia's back country. In spite of its implied plea for social justice, Caldwell's work has often been attacked on the grounds of immorality. TOBACCO ROAD is his best-known novel, though GOD'S LITTLE ACRE has also been tremendously popular.

Caldwell began his career with some powerful short stories, notably *Country Full of Swedes* (1933). He collaborated with Margaret Bourke-White, his former wife, on three picture-and-comment documentaries, including *You Have Seen Their Faces* (1937). During World War II, they were in Russia as war correspondents, an experience which produced his *All Out on the Road to Smolensk* (1942) and other works. *Call It Experience* (1951) is a literary autobiography. Other works of fiction include *Trouble in July* (1940); two volumes of short stories, *Jackpot* (1940) and *The Sure Hand of God* (1947); *A Place Called Estherville* (1949); another volume of stories, *The Courting of Susie Brown* (1952); and *Claudelle Inglish* (1959).

Caldwell, [Janet Miriam] Taylor (1900–   ). English-born American novelist. Miss Caldwell's career, during which she produced a long succession of best sellers, began with *Dynasty of Death* (1938), a story of two families who control a huge munitions trust. This story was continued in *The Eagles Gather* (1940) and *The Final Hour* (1944). *The Earth Is the Lord's* (1941) is a romance about Genghis Khan, and *The Turnbulls* (1943) describes the life of an English cotton industrialist. She again dealt with families of wealth and power in *This Side of Innocence* (1946). Other books include *Dear and Glorious Physician* (1959) and *Your Sins and Mine* (1961). Miss Caldwell has occasionally used the pseudonym Max Reiner.

Caleb. In the Old Testament, a Hebrew leader at the time of the conquest of Canaan. He was one of the 12 spies sent by the Israelites to appraise the strength of Canaan and to judge whether the Israelites were strong enough to invade it. Because he and Joshua were the only ones who reported favorably, they were the only ones of their generation permitted to enter the Promised Land.

Caleb Williams, The Adventures of, or Things as They Are (1794). A novel by William GODWIN. Highly suspenseful, it anticipates, in some respects, detective fiction, and is a social commentary on the relative positions of the privileged and lower classes. Caleb Williams is a young man in the service of Falkland, an aristocrat who values his good name above everything else. Quite accidentally, Caleb discovers that Falkland has committed a murder for which an innocent person has been executed. Although Caleb would never reveal his master's crime, Falkland has him imprisoned on false charges. Caleb then escapes from prison, but is relentlessly tracked down by the suspicious Falkland. As a last resort, Caleb tells the truth and Falkland is forced to confess. Caleb suffers terrible self-reproach at having caused his master's ruin. This novel was dramatized by George Colman, the younger, under the title of *The Iron Chest.*

Caledonia. Scotland; the ancient Roman name, now used only in poetry and in a few special connections.

calender (from Persian *galandar*). A member of a begging order of dervishes, founded in the 13th century by Qalandar Yusuf al-Andalusi, a native of Spain, who obliged its members to be perpetual wanderers. This feature has made the calenders prominent in Eastern romance. The story of the Three Calenders in the *Arabian Nights* is well known; they are three royal princes, disguised as begging dervishes, each of whom has lost his right eye.

Tale of the First Calender. No names are given. This calender was the son of a king, and nephew of another king. While on a visit to his uncle, his father died and the vizier usurped the throne. When the prince returned, he was seized and his right eye pulled out. The uncle died and the usurping vizier made himself master of this kingdom also. The hapless young prince assumed the garb of a calender, wandered to Baghdad, and being received into the house of "the three sisters," tells his tale in the hearing of the Caliph HAROUN-AL-RASCHID.

Tale of the Second Calender. No names given. This calender, like the first, was the son of a king. On his way to India he was attacked by robbers, and though he contrived to escape, lost all his possessions. In his flight, he came to a large city where he encountered a tailor who gave him food and lodging. In order to earn a living, he became a woodsman and accidentally discovered an underground palace in which a beautiful lady was kept confined by an evil genius. Intent on liberating her, he kicked down the talisman; the genius killed the lady and turned the prince into an ape. As an ape he was taken on board ship and transported to a large commercial city where he was made vizier to the sultan. The sultan's daughter undertook to disenchant him, but to accomplish this she had to fight with the malignant genius. She succeeded in killing

the genius and restoring the enchanted prince, but received such severe injuries in the struggle that she died, and a spark of fire that flew into the right eye of the prince destroyed it. The sultan was so heartbroken at the death of his only child that he insisted on the prince's quitting the kingdom without delay. He assumed the garb of a calender and being received into the hospitable house of the three sisters, tells his tale before Caliph Haroun-al-Raschid.

Tale of the Third Calender. This calender, King Agib, was wrecked on the loadstone mountain which drew all the nails and iron bolts from his ship; but he overthrew the bronze statue on the mountaintop, the cause of the mischief. Agib then visited ten young men, each of whom had lost his right eye, and was carried by a roc to the palace of 40 princesses, with whom he stayed a year. The princesses were then obliged to leave for 40 days, but entrusted him with the keys of the palace, with free permission to enter every room but one. On the 40th day, curiosity finally induced him to open this room, where he saw a horse which carried him through the air to Baghdad. The horse then deposited him, and knocked out his right eye with a whisk of its tail, as it had done to the 10 young men whom it had previously met.

calends. The first day of the Roman month. See IDES; NONES.

Calhoun, John C[aldwell] (1782–1850). American statesman. A native of South Carolina, Calhoun was elected to Congress in 1810 and became one of the "war hawks" who advocated war with Great Britain. He was secretary of war (1817–1825) and vice president under J. Q. Adams and Andrew JACKSON. After the passage of the protectionist "Tariff of Abominations," Calhoun wrote his *South Carolina Exposition* (1828), defending state sovereignty and the right of NULLIFICATION, a doctrine he elaborated in a letter (1832) to Governor Hamilton of South Carolina. Breaking with Jackson over nullification and other issues, Calhoun resigned the vice presidency in 1832 and was elected to the U.S. Senate the same year. Except for a brief term as secretary of state, he sat in the Senate until his death, the leading spokesman for the minority interests of the South.

A political theorist of considerable originality, some of whose ideas anticipated those of Karl Marx, he was austerely intellectual; it is said that on one occasion he tried to write a poem, produced the single word "Whereas," and never repeated the attempt.

Caliban. In Shakespeare's THE TEMPEST, the deformed, half-human slave of Prospero. The son of the witch Sycorax and a devil, Caliban symbolizes mankind's primitive urges.

Robert Browning's poem, *Caliban upon Setebos, or Natural Theology in the Island,* is an attempt to express for such a creature as Caliban his crude philosophy of God and the universe. Percy MacKaye wrote a poetic drama, *Caliban* (1916), showing the regeneration of Caliban through love for Miranda.

Caliban by the Yellow Sands (1916). A masque by Percy MACKAYE. In this poetic drama, drawn in part from Shakespeare's *Tempest*, Caliban is seen as "that passionate child-curious part of us all," who is regenerated through Prospero's wisdom and his own love for Miranda.

Calidore, Sir. See FAERIE QUEENE, THE.

Caligorante. In the ORLANDO FURIOSO of Ariosto, a huge sea monster defeated by Astolfo with his magic horn, given to him by the good witch Logistilla. Astolfo ties the monster in its own net and goes from city to city, dragging the monster behind him in order to display the great victory he has achieved.

Caligula. Original name, **Caius Caesar** (A.D. 12–41). Roman emperor (37–41). Son of Agrippina and GERMANICUS CAESAR, he was brought up among the legions in Germany where the soldiers gave him his nickname, Caligula, because he wore the soldier's boot (*caliga*). He was held high in the emperor Tiberius' favor, and on Tiberius' death, which was either caused or helped along by Caligula, he succeeded to the throne. Caligula was at first revered by the people as the son of Germanicus, but after a serious illness, he appeared very much changed and behaved like a madman. His wild extravagance led him to extortion and plunder. He was finally murdered and was succeeded by his uncle Claudius. He is the main character in the play CALIGULA by Albert Camus.

Caligula (1944). A play by Albert CAMUS. The author makes the Roman emperor a sensitive man horrified by what Camus calls elsewhere the absurd condition of human life. Caligula adds to the senselessness by arbitrary acts of violence, obeying the mistaken logic that he can escape the condition of man by severing all his ties with humanity and thus by asserting his own freedom achieve the impossible. His seemingly mad complicity in his own assassination symbolizes his failure.

Calisto y Melibea, La tragicomedia de. See CELESTINA, LA.

Callaghan, Morley [Edward] (1903–   ). Canadian novelist and short-story writer. After meeting Ernest Hemingway in Toronto in the 1920's, Callaghan went to Paris, where he became acquainted with the American expatriates there and contributed to *This Quarter, transition,* and similar periodicals. His novels, which are noted for their "hard-boiled" realism, include *Strange Fugitive* (1928), *The Loved and the Lost* (1951), *The Many Colored Coat* (1960), and *A Passion in Rome* (1962). *Now That April's Here* (1936) and *Stories* (1959) are collections of short stories. His years in Paris are recounted in *That Summer in Paris* (1963).

Callimahcus (Kallimachos; born c. 310 B.C.). Greek poet, born in Cyrene. According to tradition he was head of the ALEXANDRIAN LIBRARY, and was highly regarded in his own time, and thereafter, for his short poems. He is said to have engaged in a literary feud with APOLLONIUS OF RHODES.

Calliope (Kalliopeia). The Muse of epic poetry, and chief of the MUSES. She was the mother of Orpheus by Apollo or King Oeagrus.

Callirrhoe (Kallirrhoe). See ALCMAEON.

Callirrhoe (Kallirrhoe). The lady-love of Chaereas in Chariton's Greek romance, the *Loves of Chaereas and Callirrhoe.* It was probably written in the 6th century A.D.

Callisto and **Arcas (Kallisto, Arkas).** Callisto was an Arcadian nymph metamorphosed into a she-bear by ARTEMIS for not remaining a virgin like her other attendants. Her son Arcas, having met her in the chase, would have killed her, but Zeus converted him into a he-bear, and placed them both in the heavens, where they are recognized as the Great and Little Bear. Arcas was the eponymous ancestor of the Arcadians.

Call of the Wild, The (1903). A novel by Jack LONDON. This famous story tells how the dog Buck is stolen from his comfortable home and pressed into service as a sledge dog in the Klondike. At first he is abused by both men and doge, but he learns to fight ruthlessly and finally finds in John Thornton a master whom he can respect and love. When Thornton is murdered, Buck breaks away to the wilds and becomes the leader of a pack of wolves. See WHITE FANG.

Calpe. See PILLARS OF HERCULES.

Calpurnia. Third wife of Julius CAESAR. They were married in 59 B.C. On the night before he was assassinated she dreamed that a templelike gable, dedicated in his honor, smashed to the ground and that Caesar lay dying in her arms. She is a character in Shakespeare's JULIUS CAESAR; she begs Caesar not to attend the Senate. Caesar's first two wives were Cornelia and Pompeia.

Calvary or **Golgotha** (Lat., *calvaria,* Aram., *gŭlgŭtha,* "skull"). The place outside the wall of Jerusalem where Jesus was crucified. Its exact location is unknown; tradition ascribes it to the present site of the Church of the Holy Sepulcher.

Calverley, Charles Stuart (1831–1884). English poet and parodist. He wrote light verse, parodies, and translations, including *Verses and Translations* (1862); *Theocritus Translated into English Verse* (1869); and *Fly Leaves* (1872).

Calvin, John. Adapted form of **Jean Cauvin** (1509–1564). French Protestant reformer. His theological doctrines had tremendous influence, particularly in the Puritan religion of England, Scotland, and later America.

Calvin had an early background of humanism, being a student of Latin and Greek and familar with the writings of Plato, Seneca, and St. Augustine. Because of the radical Protestant views expressed in a public speech he wrote in 1533 to be delivered at an inaugural ceremony at the University of Paris, Calvin was forced to flee the capital and soon France as well. He establshed himself in Geneva, where eventually he became an absolute dictator, strictly enforcing his theological doctrines and rules of conduct. His greatest work is INSTITUTES OF THE CHRISTIAN RELIGION.

Calvinism as a religious system recognized only the Bible as a source of knowledge and authority in questions of belief. Its chief principles were (1) the total depravity of man as a result of Adam's fall; (2) the absolute power of the will of God; (3) the superiority of faith to good works, since man has no will of his own; (4) salvation by grace from God rather than by any act of the will of man; and (5) the divine predestination of those to be saved, or the Elect, although, since no one can tell whether he is a member of the Elect, all must lead holy and pious lives, acknowledging God's supreme power and obeying His commands.

Calydonian boar. A creature of Greek legend.

Oeneus, king of Calydon, in Aetolia, having neglected to sacrifice to Artemis, was punished by the goddess' sending a ferocious boar to ravage his lands. A band of heroes collected to hunt the boar, which was eventually slain by MELEAGER after he had been first wounded by Atalanta. A dispute over the boar's head led to a war between the neighboring tribe of Curetes and the Calydonians. This was one of the most famous sagas of Greece, but is not recorded in any outstanding single work.

Calypso (Kalypso). In Homer's ODYSSEY, the nymph of the island of Ogygia. She detains the shipwrecked Odysseus there seven years. Loyal to Penelope, he refuses her offer of immortality if he stays, and at last, at Zeus's command, she helps him to continue on his way toward Ithaca.

Cama. See KAMA.

Cambel. See FAERIE QUEENE, THE.

Camber. In Geoffrey of Monmouth's HISTORY OF THE KINGS OF BRITAIN, a son of BRUTE, and the person after whom Wales (Cambria) was said to be named.

Cambina. See FAERIE QUEENE, THE.

Cambrai, League of. A league formed in 1508 by the Papacy, France, Spain, and the Holy Roman Empire against Venice. The War of the League of Cambrai (1508–1510) resulted in the defeat of the Venetians.

Cambridge, Richard Owen (1717–1802). English man of letters who wrote the famous mock-epic *Scribleriad* (1751). He was an intimate of Samuel Johnson.

Cambridge critics. A group of influential 20th-century English critics. They were centered at the University of Cambridge. They rejected the traditional method of studying literature in the light of its historical period, the author's biography, and other external influences. They preferred to make a detailed, quasi-scientific analysis of the work itself. This method had its best results when applied to complex poetry, and these critics praised symbolistic, metaphysical, witty, and modern poetry at the expense of more traditional verse. I. A. RICHARDS and William EMPSON were pioneers in the study of exact meanings in poetry. See LOGICAL POSITIVISM; F. R. LEAVIS; SCRUTINY; NEW CRITICISM.

Cambridge Platonists. A group of English liberal philosophic-religious thinkers of the latter half of the 17th century, whose general aim was to effect a reconciliation between reason and mystical religiosity. Their mode of thought and terminology were taken chiefly from Plato and the Neoplatonists. They were vehemently opposed to Hobbes's materialism, their most important doctrine being the absolute existence of right and wrong. The outstanding members of the group were Ralph Cudworth (1617–1688), Nathaniel Culverwel (1618–1651), Joseph GLANVILL, Henry MORE, Benjamin Whichcote (1609–1683), and John Smith (1616–1652). Their thought may be summarized in Smith's words: "To follow reason is to follow God."

Cambuscan or **Cambyuskan.** See SQUIRE'S TALE.

Cambyses II (d. 522 B.C.). A Persian ruler. He succeeded his father Cyrus the Great, reigning from 529 to 522 B.C. Reputed to be tyrannical, he conquered Egypt and made that country part of the Persian Empire. His throne was assumed by an impostor, and he died while returning to Persia to defend it.

Camelot. A place name prominent in Arthurian literature, one of the spots where King ARTHUR held court. In many of the legends, we find both Camelot and CAERLEON as court capitals, each being appropriate, apparently, to certain times of the year. For example, Caerleon is sometimes found to be the place where King Arthur and his court celebrated Pentecost and Camelot the place where the court went for the celebration of Christmas. See CARDUEL.

Camilla. In Vergil's Aeneid, a warrior maiden who fought fearlessly against the Trojans in their war with TURNUS, and was killed in battle. She was so speedy, says Vergil, that she could run across a field of corn without bending a single blade or cross the sea without even wetting her feet.

Camille. See DAME AUX CAMÉLIAS, LA.

Camille. In Pierre Corneille's tragedy HORACE, the sister of Horace and the fiancée of Curiace, Horace's opponent in combat. When Horace kills Curiace, Camille curses Rome, and her infuriated brother slays her.

Camillo. An honorable and faithful counsellor to Leontes, king of Sicilia, in Shakespeare's WINTER'S TALE. Commanded by Leontes to poison Polixenes, he leaves his beloved country rather than commit the crime. When he at last returns, he marries the bold and courageous PAULINA.

Camino Galicia, León Felipe. See León FELIPE.

Camisards. The Calvinists of Cevennes who in 1703 rebelled against Louis XIV after his revocation of the Edict of Nantes. Their leader, Jean Cavalier (1680–1740), escaped to England and became governor of Jersey. The word *camisard* refers to the insurgents' white shirts.

Camlan, Battle of. See ANNALES CAMBRIAE.

Camões or **Camoëns, Luis Vaz de** (1524?–1580). Portuguese poet. After being banished from court because of his romance with Caterina de Ataíde (the "Natercia" of his poems), a lady-in-waiting to the queen, Camões served in North Africa, where he lost his right eye in an engagement with the Moors. In 1552 he was imprisoned for wounding a court official in a street brawl. Sailing to India in 1553 as a common soldier, he was later named official trustee for the property of the dead and absent in Macao and was briefly imprisoned for allegedly embezzling government funds. After numerous hardships, he managed to return to Lisbon in 1570.

Camões' best-known work is his epic poem, Os LUSIADAS, notable for its synthesis of national, religious, and humanistic themes. He is also regarded as one of Portugal's greatest lyric poets, largely because of his sonnets and *canções*. His other works include three plays: *Os anfitriões,* which was inspired by Plautus' *Amphitruo; El-Rei Seleuco,* based on an episode in Plutarch; and *Philodemo.*

Campagna di Roma. Territory of Old Latium surrounding Rome, about 30 by 100 miles in extent. It is usually simply called the Campagna and is not to be confused with ancient Campania, the territory directly south of Latium.

Campanella, Tommaso (1568–1639). Italian philosopher. Born in Calabria, he spent most of his life in the prisons of Naples, Padua, and Rome because of his interest in astrology, naturalistic philosophy, and radical political schemes. After his final imprisonment in Rome, he fled to France in 1634, where he died. A prolific writer, he produced many Italian lyrics, a critical treatise on poetry, and his masterpiece, *La città del sole* (*Civitas Solis* or *City of the Sun*, 1623). Written in 1602 during his imprisonment, and based on Plato and Thomas More, it describes his utopia, a society organized communistically and ruled by a priest-philosopher. His Latin works, dealing largely with metaphysics and theology, also include a treatise on the Spanish monarchy and an apology for Galileo.

Campaspe. Also called **Pancaste.** A beautiful woman, the favorite concubine of Alexander the Great. Apelles, it is said, modeled his Aphrodite Anadyomene from her. According to Pliny, Alexander gave her up to Apelles, who had fallen in love with her while painting her likeness. John LYLY produced, in 1583, a drama, *Alexander and Campaspe.*

Campbell, Joseph (1879–1944). Irish poet. He published some of his work under his Gaelic name, Seosamh MacCathmhaoil. His works include *Rushlight* (1906), and *Irishry* (1913).

Campbell, Mary. One of the women loved by Robert BURNS. She died of fever in 1788, and the poem *To Mary in Heaven* (1789) was written on the first anniversary of her death. See HIGHLAND MARY.

Campbell, Mrs. Patrick, born **Beatrice Stella Tanner** (1865–1940). English actress who played important roles beginning with the title role in Pinero's *The Second Mrs. Tanqueray.* She originated the part of Eliza Doolittle in Shaw's *Pygmalion,* written expressly for her.

Campbell, Roy (1902–1957). South African poet. A neofascist and disciple of Wyndham Lewis, he wrote satires and poems of colorful nature description. He was converted to Catholicism in about 1935. He fought on the fascist side on the Spanish Civil War; *Flowering Rifle* (1939) is a long satiric poem celebrating Franco's victory. Among his collections of poems are *The Flaming Terrapin* (1924), *Adamastor* (1930), and *Talking Bronco* (1946). He has done translations of the poems of St. John of the Cross, and written two autobiographies: *Broken Record* (1934) and *Light on a Dark Horse* (1952).

Campbell, Thomas (1777–1844). Scottish poet, best known for his literary ballad LORD ULLIN'S DAUGHTER. He also produced some notable martial lyrics, including *Ye Mariners of England* (1800); *Hohenlinden* (1802); and *The Battle of the Baltic* (1809). Of his longer narrative works only GERTRUDE OF WYOMING retains interest. Campbell was an editor (*The New Monthly Magazine*) and anthologist of some influence in his day. See LOCHIEL.

Campbell, Walter Stanley. Pen name, **Stanley Vestal** (1887–1957). American writer. An authority on the Old West, under his own name he has edited documents and books relating to Indians and explorations. Under his pen name he has written such books as *Fandango, Ballads of the Old West* (1927), *Kit Carson* (1928), *Mountain Men* (1937), *Queen of Cowtowns: Dodge City* (1952), and *Joe Meek* (1952).

Campbell, [William] Wilfred (1861–1918). Canadian poet and novelist. After studying at the Episcopal Divinity School in Cambridge, Mass., Campbell was ordained in 1885 and was given a parish in West Claremont, Mass. In 1891 he resigned from his church offices, feeling that their formality and dogmas restricted him. His books of poetry include *Snowflakes and Sunbeams* (1888), *Lake Lyrics* (1889), and *Beyond the Hills of Dream* (1899). He also wrote historical novels, notably *Ian of the Orcades* (1906) and *A Beautiful Rebel* (1909).

Campbell, William Edward March. See William MARCH.

Campbells Are Coming, The. A famous song composed in 1715. The earl of Mar raised the standard for the Stuarts against George I. John Campbell was commander-in-chief of His Majesty's forces and the rebellion was quashed.

Campion, Thomas (1567–1620). English poet and musician. He is famous for his songs written to music of his own composition, collected in such volumes as *A Book of Airs* (1601), *Two Books of Airs* (c. 1613), and *The Third and Fourth Books of Airs* (c. 1617). His lyrics possess rare charm and freshness, as well as a melodiousness and metrical variety that reflect their musical origin. He was also the author of *Observation in the Art of English Poesy* (1602), an argument for the use of classical, quantitative meters in English verse, which prompted Samuel Daniel's *Defence of Ryme* (1602).

Campistron, Jean Galbert de (1656–1723). French soldier and playwright. An admirer and imitator of Racine, he wrote several tragedies characterized by their melancholy treatment of classical subjects, among them *Arminius* (1684) and *Andronic* (1685). His greatest successes were the tragedy *Tiridate* (1691), which depicted the denobling power of passion, and the comedy *Le Jaloux désabusé* (*The Jealous Man Undeceived,* 1709).

Campo, Estanislao del. See GAUCHO LITERATURE.

Campoamor, Ramón de (1817–1901). Spanish poet. His best-known work may be sampled in the volumes *Doloras* (1846), *Humoradas* (1872), and *Pequeños Poemas* (1872–1874). These are filled with poems in the style favored by Campoamor: philosophical epigrams expressing a humorous point of view.

Campus Esquilinus. The burial place for the lowest classes, just outside the Servian Wall of Rome.

Campus Martius. The field of Mars. A grassy plain along the east bank of the Tiber in ancient Rome, used for elections, martial exercises, public games, and the like.

Camus, Albert (1913–1960). Algerian-born French philosopher, novelist, dramatist, journalist. After studying philosophy at Algiers, Camus organized (1935) the Théâtre de l'Equipe, a young avant-garde dramatic group, and worked with it until 1938. Then, until the beginning of World War II, he worked both in North Africa and in Paris as a journalist. It was between 1937 and 1941 that he wrote the works that made him famous upon their publication during the war: the novel THE STRANGER, the essay THE MYTH OF SISYPHUS, and the play CALIGULA. He also sketched THE MISUNDERSTANDING, which he finished in 1943. All four present the feeling of the ABSURD, the plight of man's need for clarity and rationality in confrontation with the unreasonable silence of the universe, and various tragedies of man's failure to assume proper consciousness of his condition, or, if he does, to find the human values by which he can shape his life.

After the occupation of France by the Germans in 1941, Camus became one of the intellectual leaders of the Resistance movement. He helped found the underground newspaper *Combat* in 1943, was its chief editor during the war, and continued to write for it until 1946, when it began open publication after the liberation of France. Camus was a close associate of Jean-Paul SARTRE and his circle; although they cooperated in Resistance activities, however, the differences between their philosophical positions became more and more apparent. Camus has sometimes been classified among the existentialists, but he himself refuted their position in many of his writings (see EXISTENTIALISM).

His refusal to take solace in a concept of divine or cosmic meaning for human life did not conflict with Camus' humanistic attitude that man is capable of a certain degree of dignity in honestly facing his solitary condition and trying to find and assert the human values, such as the maximum possible individual freedom, intercommunication, and even love, within the limitations of that condition. His commitment to this humanistic attitude, and consequently to humanitarian causes, is reflected in the novel THE PLAGUE, about men doing the futile best they can in the face of disaster. The short novel THE FALL more bitterly comments on the difficulty of finding a mode of active life compatible with total consciousness both of the absurd and of one's inescapable solidarity with other human beings.

During the late 1950's, Camus renewed his active interest in the theater, writing and directing stage adaptations of William Faulkner's *Requiem for a Nun* and Dostoevski's *The Possessed*. He was awarded the Nobel Prize for literature in 1957.

THE REBEL gives a book-length statement of his philosophical attitudes. In *Actuelles I-III* (1950, 1953, 1958) are essays on political, social, and literary questions collected from *Combat* and elsewhere; *Resistance, Rebellion, and Death* (1961) is an English selection from these. Other works include the early essays *L'Envers et l'endroit* (1937) and *Noces* (1939), mostly sympathetic sketches of North Africa; *Letters to a German Friend* (*Lettres à un ami allemand;* 1945), written during the war; the plays *State of Siege* (*Etat de Siège;* 1948) and *The Just Assassins* (*Les Justes;* 1950); and the six short stories in *The Exile and the Kingdom* (*L'Exil et le Royaume;* 1957).

Canaan. An ancient region of vague boundaries. It lay roughly between the Jordan River and the Mediterranean Sea. This "Promised Land" of the Israelites was actually rather infertile. A mixture of Semites and Indo-Europeans lived there until the Israelites conquered much of the area. The Semites, worshippers of *baalim* (see BAAL), had a fairly rich culture, many evidences of which have been uncovered in the 20th century at UGARIT and elsewhere. Most of them were under the domination of Egypt or, for a time, of the Hittites. The civilization of Phoenicia was to a considerable extent a continuation of that of Canaan.

The rabbinical tradition that Canaan, a son of

Ham, was the first of the seven sinners who made idols for the heathens, reflects the regrettable history of Israelitish backsliding into the baal-worship of their Canaanite neighbors. For Canaanite literature see the POEM OF BAAL and the POEM OF AQHAT.

Canace. See FAERIE QUEENE, THE.

Canacee. See SQUIRE'S TALE.

Canaletto or **Canale, Antonio** (1697-1768). Venetian painter, known for his broad views of Venice. He rendered architectural detail with great precision and flawless perspective, and bathed his scenes in a clear light of sharp contrasts. Bernardo Bellotto (1724-1780), his nephew and pupil, is also sometimes called Canaletto.

Canby, Henry Seidel (1878-1961). American literary critic, biographer, editor, and teacher. Canby served as literary editor of the New York *Post,* helped to found and edit the *Saturday Review of Literature* (1924), and acted as chairman of the Book-of-the-Month Club (1926-1954). He taught at Yale University for more than 20 years. Among his many volumes are *The Short Story* (1902), *Thoreau: A Biography* (1939), *Walt Whitman: An American* (1943), and *Turn West, Turn East: Mark Twain and Henry James* (1951). *American Memoir* (1947) is an autobiography.

Cancer. One of the twelve signs of the zodiac (the Crab, June 21st to July 23rd). It appears when the sun has reached its highest northern limit, and begins to go backward toward the south; but, like a crab, the return is sideways.

According to fable, Hera sent Cancer against HERACLES when he combated the HYDRA of Lerna. It bit the hero's foot, but Heracles killed the creature, and Hera set it in the sky.

Cancionero de Baena. An anthology of 576 poems compiled in 1445 by Juan Alfonso de Baena (1406-1454) for John II of Castile. The poems, lyrics of the courtly, aristocratic school, show the development of Spanish poetry in the 14th and 15th centuries. The works of over 50 authors are included, notably Alfonso Alvarez de Villasandino, a representative of the Galician-Portuguese school, and Micer Francisco Imperial, who was influenced by Dante.

Candida (1903). A play by George Bernard SHAW. This is one of Shaw's most theatrically successful works; its subject is marriage. Candida Morell's husband is a hearty, popular Christian Socialist clergyman. Eugene Marchbanks is an 18-year-old rhapsodic, visionary poet who is in love with Candida. Forced to choose between them she remains with her husband when she realizes that he needs her, being the weaker of the two men. The plot of *Candida* shows the influence of Ibsen's *A Doll's House*. Shaw, however, has reversed the roles of puppet and master: Morell's seeming strength wholly rests on Candida's dignity and character.

Candide, ou L'Optimisme (1759). VOLTAIRE's most popular philosophical novel. It satirizes the optimistic creed of LEIBNIZ: "All is for the best in this best of all possible worlds." Dr. PANGLOSS, tutor to the hero, Candide, is the embodiment of this theory, maintaining it through thick and thin, despite the most blatant evidence to the contrary. Misadventures begin when young Candide is kicked out of the castle of Thunder-ten-tronckh for making love to the baron's daughter, Cunégonde. Thereafter, he, Cunégonde, and Pangloss embark—sometimes singly, sometimes together—on a long series of disastrous adventures. After being impressed into the Bulgarian army, Candide is beaten nearly to death; he deserts and flees to Holland where he learns that Cunégonde and her family have been massacred. He and Pangloss go to Lisbon, arriving in time for the historic earthquake (1755); there they are condemned by the Inquisition, and Pangloss is hanged. But Cunégonde —alive, after all—saves Candide, who later finds it necessary to kill a Jew and an Inquisitor to discourage them from pursuing Cunégonde. Still hunted by the Inquisition, Candide leaves Cunégonde and, with his valet Cacambo, flees to safety among the Jesuits, who are warring on Spain and Portugal. Candide kills their general, a Jesuit who is none other than Cunégonde's brother. He flees to El Dorado, but because he misses Cunégonde, leaves, loaded with riches. He returns to France, where he is threatened with imprisonment and cheated out of his fortune by swindlers. He travels to Portsmouth and then to Venice, where he learns that Cunégonde has been captured by pirates and is washing towels in Constantinople. On the ship to Turkey, Candide discovers that two of the galley slaves are none other than Cunégonde's brother, whom he did not kill, and Pangloss, who had not been properly hanged. He finally finds Cunégonde, now very ugly, and marries her against his will. All of them finally settle down on a little farm. Pangloss insists that all these calamities happened for the best. Candide replies, *"Il faut cultiver notre jardin"* (*Fr.,* "We must cultivate our garden"). All the disasters in the novel have historical precedents, and we may conclude from Candide's last remark either that work is far more profitable than vain speculation, or that work is the antidote to man's unhappy lot.

Candlemas Day. The popular name for the Feast of the Purification of the Virgin Mary, February 2. On this day Christ was presented by her in the Temple. The feast is so called from the custom of blessing on this day all the candles which will be used in a church throughout the year. They symbolize Christ as "the light of the world" and "a light to lighten the Gentiles," phrases spoken of Jesus at the time of his Presentation by the aged Simeon. There is also a weather legend associated with the day. See GROUNDHOG DAY.

Canfield, Dorothy. See Dorothy Canfield FISHER.

Canidia. A Neapolitan, beloved by the poet HORACE. When she deserted him, he held her up to contempt in certain of his epodes and satires as an old sorceress who could by magic spell unsphere the moon.

Canidius. In Shakespeare's ANTONY AND CLEOPATRA, the lieutenant general of Antony's land forces. Canidius vainly advises Antony against engaging Octavius Caesar in naval battle and later defects to the enemy.

Cannae. The battlefield in southeast Italy where HANNIBAL defeated the Romans under Varro and L. Aemilius Paulus with great slaughter in 216 B.C. Any fatal battle that is the turning point of a great general's prosperity may be called his Cannae. Thus, Moscow was the Cannae of Napoleon.

Cannery Row (1945). A novel by John STEINBECK. In this episodic work, Steinbeck returns to the style of *Tortilla Flat* to produce a rambling account of the adventures and misadventures of workers in a California cannery and their friends. One character, Doc, was reportedly modeled on the marine biologist Edward F. Ricketts (1896–1948), with whom Steinbeck collaborated on *The Sea of Cortez* (1941).

Canonization, The (1633). A poem by John DONNE in which he claims that the reciprocal love between him and his mistress is so deep and unworldly as to make them saints of love. It is a fine example of the vehemently colloquial and ingeniously conceited style typical of Donne.

Canon's Yeoman's Tale, The. One of the CANTERBURY TALES of Geoffrey CHAUCER. In the *Prologue* a Canon and his Yeoman overtake the pilgrims. The Host asks if the Canon can tell a story, and the Yeoman begins to reveal his master's craftiness as a fraudulent alchemist. The Canon bids him be silent, but he has decided to leave the alchemist's service, so he continues his vituperative report, and the Canon rides off to avoid shame. The Yeoman bitterly describes the apparatus and processes of the "cursed craft" of alchemy, and all the money and labor lost in searching for the elixir to turn base metals into gold. Then he tells a tale about a canon, not his ex-master, who pretends to take a priest into his confidence and let him help in the conversion of quicksilver and copper to silver. The canon effects the exchange by sleight of hand, but the duped priest believes in the actual transmutation of the metal and asks to buy the formula. The canon accepts forty pounds, making him think it a bargain price, and can never be found by the priest again.

Canossa, Count **Ludovico** of (1476–1532). Italian courtier and prelate. He is noted for his diplomatic missions and his participation in the dialogues of THE COURTIER by his kinsman Castiglione.

cantari. See CANTASTORIE.

cantastorie. Tuscan minstrels, or singers of tales, of the 14th century who composed and performed, usually in the public places of Italian towns and villages, *cantari,* long narrative poems in *ottava rima.* Although the preferred subject was the Carolingian legends, especially the loves and battles of Orlando (Roland), Christian and classical material also helped to form the repertoire of the *cantastorie.* Though many of their works died with the anonymous singers, some survived to influence the later Renaissance *romanzo* (romantic epic) of Pulci, Ariosto, and Boiardo.

Cantatrice Chauve, La. See BALD SOPRANO, THE.

Canterbury Tales, The (c. 1387–1400). Poetic work by Geoffrey CHAUCER. Although unfinished, it is his longest and his finest work, written in decasyllabic couplets except as noted in the entries for individual tales. The *General Prologue* establishes the framework for the stories: the poet has joined with 30 others (although the *Prologue* says 29) to make the usual April pilgrimage to Becket's shrine at Canterbury; he describes each of his companions, who are of widely varying classes and occupations. Their host at the Tabard Inn, Harry Bailly, proposes to come with them and serve as judge in a story-telling contest to occupy the long hours of the journey;

⁋ The tale of the chanons yeman

⁋ And begynneth the tale

With this chanon I dwelt þþ yere
And of his science am I neuer the ner
Al that I had I haue lost ther by
And god woot so haue mo than I
There as I was wont to be right fressh & gay
Of clothynge and of other good aray
Now may I were an hose vp on myn hed
And where my colour was both fressh & red
Now it is wan and of a ledyn hewe
Who so it vseth sore shal he it rewe
And of my swynk yet blent is myn eye
Lo suche auauntage it is to multiplye
That sledyng science hath made me so bare
That I haue no good where that euer I far
And yet I am endetted so sore therby,
Of gold that I borowed trulye

*From Caxton's 2nd edition of the
Canterbury Tales (1483).*

each pilgrim is to tell two stories on the way to Canterbury, two on the way back, and the teller of the best tale will get a free dinner at the Tabard upon their return. Chaucer only wrote 24 tales, however: 21 are told by characters described in the *Prologue,* one is told by the Canon's Yeoman, who joins the group after they have already started, and Chaucer himself begins one tale, and when interrupted tells a second. In addition to the characters who do narrate tales (see below) Chaucer describes the Knight's Yeoman, two Priests accompanying the Prioress, a Haberdasher, a Carpenter, a Weaver, a Dyer, a Tapicer (weaver of tapestry), and a Plowman.

Although such "frame stories" were common in Chaucer's day, Chaucer was an innovator in his choice of such a diverse assembly of narrators, in the concomitant diversity of style of their tales (from chivalric romance to bawdy *fabliau,* from folk tale to sermon), and in the way he develops the drama of the interaction of his characters' personalities. With a few exceptions, where Chaucer obviously had not thoroughly worked out his scheme, the tales and the manner of their telling (except for the convention of being in verse) are completely suited to the nature of their tellers. And between the actual narratives are interludes in which the characters talk—often argue—with each other and with the host, revealing much about themselves. These episodes usually occur in the "prologues" to the tales, and each is described in connection with the tale it accompanies. See:

CANON'S YEOMAN'S TALE (the fraudulent alchemist)
CLERK'S TALE (patient Griselda)
COOK'S TALE (Perkin)
FRANKLIN'S TALE (Dorigen, Arveragus, and Aurelius)
FRIAR'S TALE (the summoner and the Devil)
KNIGHT'S TALE (Palamon and Arcite)
MANCIPLE'S TALE (the tell-tale crow)
MAN OF LAW'S TALE (Constance)
MELIBEE (told by Chaucer)
MERCHANT'S TALE (January and May)
MILLER'S TALE (Nicholas, Alison, and Absolon)
MONK'S TALE (the falls of illustrious men)
NUN'S PRIEST'S TALE (Chauntecleer and Pertelote)
PARDONER'S TALE (the revellers who seek Death)
PARSON'S TALE (sermon on Penitence)
PHYSICIAN'S TALE (Virginia)
PRIORESS'S TALE (the murdered boy who sings)
REEVE'S TALE (the miller's family and the students)
SECOND NUN'S TALE (Life of St. Cecilia)
SHIPMAN'S TALE (the miserly merchant, his wife, and the monk)
SQUIRE'S TALE (Cambuscan and Canacee)
SUMMONER'S TALE (Thomas and the friar)
THOPAS, SIR (told by Chaucer)
WIFE OF BATH'S TALE (the knight and the hag)

Canth, Minna (1844–1897). Finnish playwright and novelist. In Finland she was the pioneer of the new naturalism, depicting drab lives and indicting the upper classes with passionate fervor for their neglect of such misery. In the plays *Työmiehen Vaimo (The Laborer's Wife,* 1885) and *Papin Perhe (The Parson's Family,* 1891) she speaks against restriction and limitation of the human being, whether by unjust social laws or by the narrow prejudices of the older generation.

Cantos. An incomplete epic poem by EZRA POUND. It was published in separate sections: *Cantos I-XVI* (1925), *A Draft of XXX Cantos* (1930), *Eleven New Cantos XXXI-XLI* (1934), *Fifth Decad of Cantos* (1937), *Cantos LII-LXXI* (1940), *Cantos* (1948), PISAN CANTOS, SECTION: ROCK DRILL 85-95 DE LOS CANTARES, *Thrones: 96–109 de los Cantares* (1959). The earliest of the *Cantos* were published in magazine form as early as 1917. One of the most important 20th-century works of poetry, the *Cantos* have a loose musical structure and were once described by Pound himself as a ragbag. Central to their conception is the use of Odysseus as a man in search of a culture and of Ovid's *Metamorphoses* as a touchstone of individual and cultural transformation. Pound quotes widely from the literary and historical documents of the ancient Greeks, the medieval Provençal poets, writers of the Italian Renaissance, and American statesmen of the Jeffersonian period. His economic beliefs, especially regarding usury, play an important part throughout the work; they appear particularly in large sections devoted to American politics and to the Chinese.

Canty, Tom. The beggar boy in Mark Twain's PRINCE AND THE PAUPER. He changes places with Prince Edward VI.

Canute or **Knut** (c. 944–1035). Danish king who finally became King of England (after 1016) as well, taking an English wife and maintaining peace and security. A 12th-century legend describes how he rebuked his flatterers by commanding the waves to stand still—in vain, of course—to show the limits of his power. *The Song of Canute* is an early 12th-century lyric in Middle English, supposedly composed by Canute while rowing past the abbey of Ely and hearing the music of the services.

canzone. Italian lyric form of verse, popular during the Middle Ages and the Renaissance. Derived from the Provençal *canso,* it normally consisted of from five to seven stanzas, each echoing the first in number of lines and in rhyme scheme. A final short stanza (the *congedo,* or *commiato*) follows the pattern of the Provençal *tornada* or the French *envoi* in addressing the poem itself or in directing it on a mission to some personage. The subject matter is usually amatory, but might also be political, satiric, or humorous. *Canzoni* were written at the Sicilian court of Emperor Frederick II in the 13th-century and later by Dante, Petrarch, Boccaccio, and the leading poets of the Renaissance. In English, an example of the canzone form is Spenser's marriage hymn, the *Epithalamion.*

Capaneus (Kapaneus). In Greek mythology, one of the SEVEN AGAINST THEBES. He was struck dead by a thunderbolt for declaring that not Zeus himself should prevent his scaling the city walls. Evadne, his wife, threw herself into the flames while his body was burning.

Čapek, Karel (1890–1938). Czech dramatist, novelist, and essayist. Čapek's early scientific training enabled him to devise convincing backgrounds for his plays and novels dealing with the scientific and fantastic. An ardent defender of and worker for the short-lived Czech republic, he was simultaneously founder and director of the Vinohradsky Art Theater, an editor on a Prague newspaper, and a creative writer. In his essays he reveals himself politically an idealist and optimist, while in his fiction and stage works he emerges a highly imaginative moralist and ironist. His best known play is R.U.R. (q.v.); other plays include *The Life of the Insects* (1922); *The Makroupolos Secret* (1925), dealing with the scientific prolongation of life; *Power and Glory* (1938); and *The Mother* (1939). *Money and Other Stories* (1929) is a collection of short stories; *War with the Newts* (1937) and *The Cheat* (1941) are novels. His essays include *President Masaryk Tells His Story* (1934) and *The First Rescue Party* (1939).

Capetians. The third dynasty of the kings of France (reigned 987–1328). Their feudal domain was Ile de France; its central location facilitated their consolidation of power and administration. The succeeding Valois and Bourbon dynasties were branches of the Capet family.

Capital (*Das Kapital;* 1867–1894). A systematic critical study of capitalist economy by Karl MARX, based on the ideas which he formulated, with Friedrich ENGELS, in *The Communist Manifesto.* Volume one appeared in 1867; volumes two and three were completed by Engels from Marx's notes (1885–1894).

Capitoline geese. Sacred geese kept on the Capitoline Hill of Rome. According to tradition, when the Gauls invaded Rome, a detachment in single file clambered up the hill of the capitol so silently that the foremost man reached the top without being challenged. When he was striding over the rampart, some geese, disturbed by the noise, began to cackle, and awoke the garrison. Marcus Man-

lius rushed to the wall and hurled the fellow over the precipice. To commemorate this event (390 B.C.) the Romans carried a golden goose to the capitol every year.

Capitoline Hill. Of the seven hills on which ancient Rome was built, the one which held the capitol.

capitolo. The Italian word means, literally, chapter, but its literary usage refers to any lengthy poem in TERZA RIMA. During the Renaissance, it was predominantly the vehicle for satirical verse of the kind written by Francesco Berni, although *capitoli* were also composed on sacred subjects and sometimes used as the form for verse epistles.

cap of liberty. See LIBERTY CAP.

Caporetto. A town in Yugoslavia, formerly belonging to Italy. It was the scene of a disastrous defeat (1917) sustained by Italian forces under General Cadorna during World War I. The subsequent Italian retreat is vividly described in Hemingway's FAREWELL TO ARMS.

Capote, Truman (1924–   ). American novelist and short-story writer. Although he was born in New Orleans, Capote does not consider himself primarily a Southern writer. His concern with the Gothic romance, however, does provide a link with the Southern literary tradition. His special mark is the exploration of the dividing-line between dream and reality.

Capote's first novel was OTHER VOICES, OTHER ROOMS. *The Grass Harp* (1951) deals with a young orphan who goes to live with two aunts, Dolly and Verena Talbo, who respectively represent an imaginative view of life and a grasping sense of reality. *Breakfast at Tiffany's* (1958) is the story of Holly Golightly's search for identity in New York. Capote's other works include *Local Color* (1950), a book of essays and travel sketches, and *A Tree of Night* (1956), a collection of short stories.

Capri. An island off the coast of Italy not far from Naples. During the last years of Tiberius' reign, the emperor spent most of his time there. It is now a popular tourist resort, known especially for its Blue Grotto, with phosphorescent waters.

Captain Bonneville, The Adventures of (1837). A narrative prepared by Washington IRVING from the documents of Captain Benjamin L. E. de Bonneville (1796–1878). Bonneville explored the Northwest during his career in the army, and met Irving while the latter was at work on *Astoria.* Irving agreed to do Bonneville's story as a sequel. Irving, sympathetic to the Indians, condemns the treatment they received at the hands of the white trappers.

Captain Brassbound's Conversion (1900). A play by George Bernard SHAW. Lady Cecily Waynflete talks Brassbound out of his plan for revenge on his uncle. Set in Morocco, using the U.S. Navy as a *deus ex machina,* and written in a variety of dialects, this is one of Shaw's less dramatically successful plays. It was written for the actress Ellen Terry, who said it was "more fitted for the closet than the stage."

Captain Craig (1902). The title poem of a book of verse by Edwin Arlington ROBINSON. One of the author's long and characteristic narratives, it describes a picturesque and talkative old vagabond, Captain

Craig, who preaches the doctrine that "God's humor is the music of the spheres" and that one must "laugh with God."

Captain of Köpenick, The (Der Hauptmann von Köpenick; 1931). A satirical comedy by Carl ZUCKMAYER. It caricatures the narrowness of Prussian militarism and bureaucracy. Wilhelm Voigt, a penniless cobbler who, because he is an ex-convict, can obtain neither a work permit nor a passport to leave the country, gets possession of an army captain's uniform. By taking advantage of people's slavish respect for the military, he arrests the mayor of Köpenick and robs the town hall. What he really wants is a passport, but all he finds is money. In the end, when he gives himself up, the authorities refuse to believe that as silly-looking a character as he could have been the impostor.

Captain's Doll, The (1923). A short story by D. H. LAWRENCE. In it he puts forward some of his ideas about marriage. A German countess makes and sells a puppet of her lover, who is a captain in a Scottish regiment. He says that romantic love always makes a doll of its object, and that their marriage must be based instead on her vows to "honor and obey" him.

Captain Singleton (1720). The hero and shortened title of *The Life, Adventures and Piracies of the famous Captain Singleton,* a first-person narrative of piracy and buccaneer raids on the African coast written by Daniel DEFOE.

Captive, The. See REMEMBRANCE OF THINGS PAST.

Capuana, Luigi (1839–1915). Italian novelist and critic. The champion of Zolaesque realism in Italy, he began his literary career as drama critic for the noted Florentine newspaper *La Nazione.* A member of the SCAPIGLIATURA group of writers, Capuana was a fervent admirer of the psychological novels then popular in France, England, and Russia. They influenced his later novels and short stories in which a detailed investigation into the psychological behavior of exceptional, pathological individuals is joined by a scrupulous regard for realistic descriptions and a precise, unadorned style. Capuana's theorization of Zolaesque realism laid the foundation for *verismo,* its Italian counterpart.

Capuana's first novel, *Giacinta* (1879), is perhaps the best example of his "pseudo-scientific" technique. The plot is in itself unimportant for it only serves to give an insight into the protagonist's peculiar behavior. Giacinta takes a lover on the day of her marriage to a man whom she despises yet whom she wanted as her husband. The lover's eventual feeling of repugnance for her causes her to commit suicide. The author explains her behavior in terms that reflect a psychoanalysis of her personality and suggest Freudianism *avant la lettre:* Giacinta inherited a sexually promiscuous appetite from her mother and was traumatically affected by being raped at the age of 14.

Il Marchese di Roccaverdina (1901) traces the life of the marquis of Roccaverdina from the time he murders his mistress' husband to his own suicide, brought about by feelings of guilt although he is never suspected by his mistress or by the police.

The novel *Profumo* (1890) describes the unreasoning hysteria of a woman whose nervous condition causes her body to emanate an odor of orange blossoms.

Among Capuana's many works are collections of short stories, depicting the customs and landscape of Sicily, and critical essays: *Le Novelle Appassionate* (1893), *Le Novelle Paesane* (1894), *Fausto Bragia* (1897), *Lo Sfinge* (1897), *Il Decameroncino* (1901), *Coscienze* (1905), and *La Voluttà di Creare* (1906).

Capulet and **Montague.** The English names of the Capelletti and the Montecchi, two noble families of legends of 14th-century Verona. The feud between the two houses has been immortalized by Shakespeare's ROMEO AND JULIET.

Old Capulet, Juliet's father, is an irascible, unimaginative man who loves his daughter but is incensed when she refuses to marry Paris, the husband he has chosen for her. Upon hearing of the death of the two lovers, he is reconciled with Lord Montague, Romeo's father, who vows to erect a golden statue to the "true and faithful Juliet."

Caracalla. Full Latin name, **Marcus Aurelius Antonius** (A.D. 188–217). Roman emperor (211–217). He was nicknamed Caracalla after the long, hooded tunic worn by the Gauls, which he wore after he became emperor. He and his brother Geta succeeded to the throne after their father's death, but Caracalla had his brother assassinated, along with several of the most distinguished statesmen in the country. His reign was marked by cruelty and treachery. He was murdered by the praetorian prefect.

Caractacus or **Caradoc.** A legendary king of the Silures in Britain. He withstood the Roman armies for nine years; but he was finally betrayed by Carthismandu, queen of the Brigantes, and led captive to Rome in A.D. 51. He is a prominent figure in the Welsh *Triads* and in Michael Drayton's *Polyolbion* (1622).

Caractères de Théophraste traduits du grec, avec les caractères ou les Moeurs de ce siècle. See Jean de LA BRUYERE.

Caravaggio, Michelangelo Merisi da (1569–1609). Italian painter. Reacting against MANNERISM and idealism, he introduced a powerful realism into his paintings of biblical scenes by employing crude peasant types and dramatizing them by means of harsh light and violent contrasts. His naturalistic method earned him much opposition in his day, but his influence was important for such later painters as George de la Tour, Velasquez, and Rubens. Typical of his best work is the masterpiece *Christ at Emmaus.*

Carbonari (*Ital.,* "charcoal burners"). The name given to a secret political association that flourished in Italy and France early in the 19th century. The group first came into being during the reign (1808–1815) of Joachim Murat in Naples. The movement originally sought to free Italy from foreign domination, but democratic and republican sentiments later arose as well. After the failure of several uprisings, the Carbonari were absorbed by MAZZINI's Young Italy society. The movement gained prominence in France after 1820.

Carco, Francis. Pen name of **François Marie Alexandre Carcopino-Tusoli** (1886–1958). French poet, novelist, and critic. He is a recorder of the charms of Montmartre in such poetry as *La Bohème* *et mon coeur* (1912) and *Poèmes en prose* (1948). Carco's argot-filled novels of bohemian life and morals include *Perversité* (1925, translated by Ford Madox Ford), *Rue Pigalle* (1927), and *The Hounded Man* (*L'Homme traqué;* 1921, also translated as *The Noose of Sin*). He is also known for his memoirs *The Last Bohemia* (*De Montmartre au Quartier Latin;* 1927), and for his biographies of Villon (1927) and Verlaine (1939).

Card, The (1911). A humorous novel by Arnold BENNETT. The card is a good-humored, comic, smart young man called Denry. He earns a living by playing ruthless, remunerative tricks on Five Towns citizens.

Cardano, Girolamo (1501–1576). Italian philosopher. Skilled in medicine and mathematics, Cardano was familiar with many of the intellectual centers of the Italian Renaissance. His *Ars magna* (*Great Art,* 1545) was an important and influential mathematical treatise embodying many of his achievements.

Cardinal, The (1641). A tragedy by James SHIRLEY. Duchess Rosaura, a rich young widow, is betrothed to the heroic Don Columbo, nephew of the mighty cardinal, despite her preference for the Count d'Alvarez. While Columbo is away at war, she breaks the engagement and prepares to marry Alvarez. Columbo, after winning a great victory, returns and kills Alvarez. Rosaura then promises to marry Colonel Hernando, an officer who hates Columbo, if he will avenge her. When Columbo is killed, suspicion falls on Hernando, and the cardinal cleverly arranges to become Rosaura's guardian. He plans to rape and poison her, but Hernando, returning just in time, stabs first the cardinal and then himself. The cardinal confesses his crimes, pretends to have poisoned Rosaura, and offers her an antidote, which is actually poison. Thus, the dying cardinal has his revenge.

Cardozo, Benjamin Nathan (1870–1938). American jurist and associate justice of the U.S. Supreme Court (1932–1938). A liberal who believed that law should reflect social change, Cardozo wrote five important books: *The Nature of the Judicial Process* (1921), *The Growth of the Law* (1924), *The Paradoxes of Legal Science* (1928), *The Law and Literature* (1931), and *Law Is Justice* (1938). For both style and content his legal opinions are regarded as classics.

Carducci, Giosuè (1835–1907). Italian poet and literary critic. Self-proclaimed antiromantic classicist, patriot, liberal, and freemason, he was professor of Italian literature at the University of Bologna from 1860 to 1904. The aims and struggles of the *Risorgimento* are reflected in such works as *Juvenilia* (1860), *Levia Gravia* (1868), *Giambi ed Epodi* (1879), and *Rime Nuove* (1887), while *Odi Barbare* (1877–89) and *Rime e Ritmi* (1898) reveal his predilection for classical motifs and meters and archaic language; throughout, there is a positive endorsement of liberal ideology. *The Hymn to Satan* (*L'Inno a Satana,* 1863; pub. 1870) is a vigorous manifesto of rebellion in which the obscurantism and asceticism of traditional religion are denounced while human achievement in material progress is praised. Awarded the Nobel Prize for literature (1906), he is considered the national poet of modern Italy.

Carduel. In the Breton lai *Sir Launfal* by MARIE DE FRANCE, the place in which King Arthur holds his court at Pentecost. See CAMELOT; CAERLEON.

Carêmeprenant. See KING LENT.

Carew, Thomas (c. 1595–c. 1639). English poet. One of the SONS OF BEN, he was the first and probably best of the CAVALIER POETS. A courtier of Charles I, Carew was a sensualist and libertine who, it is said, repented on his deathbed. His work shows the influence of Donne as well as of Jonson: not only are there phrases, cadences, and themes reminiscent of Donne, but Carew's poetry has a richness of conceit and a play of intellect rare in Cavalier verse. In their essential spirit, however—their melody, grace, and polish—his poems reflect the art of Jonson. Carew wrote numerous songs and light love lyrics, such as the song *Ask Me No More Where Jove Bestows* and *Mediocrity in Love Rejected,* and a number of more serious pieces distinguished by their perspicacity, tact, and feeling, such as the lovely epitaph on Maria Wentworth. His collected poetry appeared in the posthumous volume *Poems* (1640), and he was also the author of a masque *Coelum Britannicum* (1633).

Carey, Henry (1687?–1743). English poet and composer. He wrote farces, burlesques, songs, and often accompanying music for the stage. His best-known ballad is SALLY IN OUR ALLEY (1729). His other works include *Namby Pamby* (1725), a poem, the title of which he also gave as a nickname to Ambrose PHILIPS; CHRONONHOTONTHOLOGOS (1734), a burlesque tragedy; *The Dragon of Wantley* (1737), a burlesque opera relating the tale of the slaying of a dragon; and *The Honest Yorkshire Man* (1735), a ballad-farce. There was a rumor that Carey was also the author of *God Save the King.*

Carey, Mathew (1760–1839). Irish-born American editor and author. He founded the *American Museum* (1787–1792), one of the first successful American literary periodicals, which printed works by Francis Hopkinson, Benjamin Franklin and the Hartford Wits. For a time Carey also edited the COLUMBIAN MAGAZINE. As a writer he is best known for *The Porcupiniad* (1796), an attack on William Cobbett for the latter's criticism of America, and *The Olive Branch* (1814), a plea for Anglo-American reconciliation after the War of 1812.

Cariteo or **Chariteo. Benedicto Gareth** (c. 1450–1514). Italian poet. Born in Barcelona, Cariteo spent most of his life at Naples in the service of the house of Aragon and as a member of the Neapolitan literary academy. His fellow academicians, noting the resemblance between his Catalan name Gareth and the Greek *Charites* (the Graces), addressed him with the Latinized form, *Chariteus;* the Italian equivalent, Cariteo, or Chariteo, then became standard. His lyrics, to which he gave the title *Endimione* (Endymion) because in them the object of his love is called Luna (the Moon), were published in 1506. These are essentially Petrarchan in style, but more exuberant and daring in the choice of metaphors (see CONCEIT), and were influential in establishing a style that contrasted with the purer Petrarchism championed by Bembo. His imitators were and are sometimes called Chariteans.

Carker, James. In Charles Dickens' DOMBEY AND SON, the business manager of the firm of Dombey. He not only brings the firm to bankruptcy, but he elopes with Dombey's second wife Edith. Edith leaves him at Dijon, and Carker, returning to England, is accidentally killed by a railway train.

Carlo Magno. The Italian form of Charlemagne and the name used to designate him in the three great Italian poems on the Carolingian material: the *Morgante* of Pulci and the Orlando poems of Boiardo and Ariosto.

Carlos, Don (1545–1568). Spanish prince. The son of Philip II by his first wife, Mary of Portugal, Don Carlos was mentally and physically unsound and was subject to fits of maniacal rage. He was betrothed to Elizabeth of Valois, but Philip married her himself. Later he conceived a bitter hatred for his father, hindering his policies whenever possible. When he laid plans to leave Spain secretly, he was imprisoned at Philip's orders and died a few months later. Although he probably died of natural causes, it was widely rumored that he had been murdered at his father's instigation. The unlucky prince was the subject of Schiller's tragedy DON CARLOS and of dramas by Thomas Otway and Vittorio Alfieri. Verdi based one of his finest operas, *Don Carlo* or *Don Carlos* (1867) on Schiller's play.

Carlota or **Charlotte** (1840–1927). Belgian-born empress of Mexico. The daughter of King Leopold I of Belgium, she was the wife of the ill-fated MAXIMILIAN, whom she urged to accept the Mexican crown offered by Napoleon III of France. In 1866, when Maximilian's empire seemed on the verge of collapse, she went to France in a futile attempt to persuade Napoleon not to withdraw his troops from Mexico. During a visit to the Vatican, she lost her mind and never fully regained her sanity.

Carlovingians. See CAROLINGIANS.

Carlyle, Thomas (1795–1881). Scottish-born English prose writer. He is remembered for his explosive attacks on sham, hypocrisy, and excessive materialism; his distrust of democracy and the mob; and his highly romantic belief in the power of the individual, especially the strong, heroic leader. During much of his own life he struggled courageously, though hardly quietly, with poverty and "dyspepsia" (probably painful gastric ulcers). He was influenced in his early career by German literature, which he helped to popularize in England, being a particular admirer of Schiller and Goethe.

Carlyle's best-known book is the THE FRENCH REVOLUTION. Of his public lectures, the famous *On Heroes, Hero-worship, and the Heroic in History* (1841) best expresses his cult of the leader. His hatred of *laissez faire* policies, fears of the destruction of personality by the machines of industrialism, and his distrust of social legislators are to be found in the essays *Chartism* (1839), *Past and Present* (1843), and *Latter Day Pamphlets* (1850). Among his biographies are *Life of Schiller* (1823–1824), *Cromwell* (1845), *The Life of Sterling* (1851), and *History of Frederick II of Prussia, Called Frederick the Great* (1858–1865). SARTOR RESARTUS, called a spiritual biography, is one of his most characteristic works and aroused violent protest when published. Carlyle's style is savage and apocalyptic; it is marked by unusual words and figures of speech, agitated and mounting rhythms, and expressions influenced by the German language. See Jane WELSH; CRAIGENPUTTOCK.

Carmagnola, Count of. **Francesco Busone** (1390–1432). The famous Italian CONDOTTIERE who fought for the Visconti of Milan and the republic of Venice until the latter, fearing his successes, had him killed.

carmagnole. (1) Costume of French Revolutionists: wide-collared jacket, wide, black pantaloons, red cap (see BONNET ROUGE), and scarlet or tricolored waistcoat. The jacket was adopted from that worn in the south of France by the Piedmontese workmen of Carmagnola.

(2) A Red Republican song and dance of the time of the French Revolution, with the refrain:

> *Dansons la Carmagnole,—Vive le son, vive le son—*
> *Dansons la Carmagnole,—Vive le son du canon!*

Carman, [William] Bliss (1861–1929). Canadian poet, essayist, and lecturer. He is best known for his collaboration with Richard HOVEY on *Songs from Vagabondia* (1894) and its sequels. In 1928, Carman was made Poet Laureate of Canada. Among his other volumes are *Low Tide on Grand Pré* (1893), *Behind the Arras* (1895), and *The Rough Riders and Other Poems* (1909).

Carmelites. An order of mendicant friars. It was founded at Mt. Carmel by the Crusader Berthold in the 12th century. Expelled from the Holy Land by the Saracens in the 13th century, they came to Europe. The order of Carmelite nuns dates from 15th century, the greatest being the Spanish mystic Saint Teresa of Avila, who organized the austere branch of the discalced (shoeless) Carmelites in contrast to the traditional Carmelites of the mitigated rule.

Carmen (1875). An opera by Georges BIZET based on Mérimée's novel of the same name. Carmen, a gypsy, flirts with the young Spanish officer Don José, and he lets her escape arrest for stabbing another girl. She persuades him to desert and cast in his lot with a band of gypsy smugglers. Soon, however, she forgets José in her interest in the torero Escamillo. When she refuses to return to him, José stabs her.

Carmer, Carl [Lamson] (1893–). American writer. While teaching at the University of Alabama, Carmer composed the popular *Stars Fell on Alabama* (1934), a volume of Alabama folklore. He has also written a similar volume in the folklore of New York, his native state, *Listen for a Lonesome Drum* (1936). His other books include *The Hudson* (1939); *Genesee Fever* (1941), a novel; *Windfall Fiddle* (1950), a distinguished juvenile; and *The Susquehanna* (1955).

Carmilhan. A legendary phantom ship of the Baltic. The captain of this ship swore he would double the Cape, whether God willed it or not. For this impious vow he was doomed to abide for ever and ever captain in the same vessel, which always appears near the Cape, but never doubles it. The kobold of the phantom ship, named Klaboterman, helps sailors at their work, but beats those who are idle. When a vessel is doomed, the kobold appears smoking a short pipe, dressed in yellow, and wearing a nightcap. See also FLYING DUTCHMAN.

Carmina Burana. See GOLIARDIC VERSE.

Carné, Marcel (1906–). French film director and producer. Representative of the early portion of Marcel Carné's career are *Quai des Brumes* (1938) and *Le Jour se Lève* (1939), realistic studies of tragic lives with an emphasis on character and milieu. His later work is characteristic of the French cinema during the five years of German occupation. Like Cocteau, he took refuge in the romantic allegory touched with fantasy and mysticism. His most renowned works of this period, produced in collaboration with Jacques PRÉVERT, are *Les Visiteurs du Soir* (1942) and *Les Enfants de Paradis* (1945).

Carnegie, Andrew (1835–1919). Scottish-born American industrialist and philanthropist. Starting as a bobbin boy in Pennsylvania at $1.20 a week, Carnegie achieved a commanding position in the steel industry through his organizing ability and acumen as a judge of men. After selling his steel interests to the U.S. Steel Corp. for $250 million in 1901, he devoted himself to philanthropy, providing funds for numerous public libraries and for such institutions as the Carnegie Endowment for International Peace. His philanthropy was inspired by his conviction that men who amassed great wealth were morally obligated to use it for the public good. He first expressed this doctrine, known as "the gospel of wealth," in an article, *Wealth,* in 1889. His other writings include *Triumphant Democracy* (1886), *The Gospel of Wealth and Other Timely Essays* (1889), and an *Autobiography* (1920).

Caro, Annibale (1507–1566). Italian diplomat and humanist. He wrote Petrarchan verse, comedies, and letters. His most famous work was his verse translation (1563–1566) of Vergil's *Aeneid* and his prose version of Longus' *Daphnis and Chloe.*

Carolingians or **Carlovingians.** Second dynasty of Frankish kings. They held the office of "mayor of the palace" under the weak later Merovingian kings, but they were the virtual rulers, particularly CHARLES MARTEL and his son Pepin the Short (c. 714–768), who finally deposed the nominal ruler in 751 and was anointed king of the Franks by the Pope in 754. His two sons jointly inherited the crown, but when Carloman (751–771) died, CHARLEMAGNE became sole king. His battles greatly enlarged his territory to include most of France, Germany, and northern Italy, and in 800 Pope Leo III crowned him Emperor of the Holy Roman Empire, thus identifying his temporal power with the interests of Christianity. He was an effective administrator, especially known for his attempt to revive learning and culture, sometimes known as the *Carolingian Renaissance.* To re-educate the clergy, he established schools and imported scholars from abroad, including ALCUIN of York. After his death, however, internal divisions weakened the empire, and the reign of his successors ended in Germany in 911 and in France in 987.

The *Carolingian legends* are the romances of medieval and Renaissance Europe dealing with the supposed adventures of Charlemagne's PALADINS. See especially those associated with ROLAND.

Caron, Pierre Augustin. See BEAUMARCHAIS.

Carpaccio, Vittore (c. 1450–c. 1526). Venetian painter. A student of the Bellini brothers, he is noted for his ceremonial and narrative pictures, which abound in colorful detail. His masterpiece is the series of canvases that relate the *Story of St. Ursula.* His most important student and disciple was Veronese.

Carpenter, Edward (1844–1929). English poet and writer. Originally a clergyman, Carpenter's socialist views caused him to leave the church and earn his living as lecturer, farmer, and sandal-maker. A disciple of Walt Whitman, whose poetry his own verse closely resembles, he was also a partisan of democracy and apologist for homosexual love. His best-known prose works are *England's Ideal* (1887), *Civilization: Its Cause and Cure* (1889), and *Love's Coming of Age* (1896). Collections of his poetry include *Narcissus* (1873), *Toward Democracy* (1883–1905), and *Sketches from Life in Town and Country* (1908).

carpet, magic. In Eastern wonder tales and romances, a stock device for transporting a character to any place he wished to go. It is sometimes termed *Prince Housain's carpet* because of the role it plays in the well-known story of Prince Ahmed in the *Arabian Nights.* The most popular magic carpet, however, was that of King Solomon which, according to the Islamic legend related in the Koran, was of green silk. When he traveled, his throne was placed on it, and it was large enough for all his forces to stand upon; in order to screen his party from the sun, the birds formed a canopy over them with their wings.

carpetbagger. In U.S. history, a derisive epithet applied to Northerners who went south to take part in Reconstruction governments. To disgruntled Southerners, the carpetbags these men carried were indicative of their transience and lack of property interests in the South.

Carr, John Dickson. Pen names, **Carter Dickson, Carr Dickson** (1906–   ). American writer of detective and mystery stories. Many of Carr's books are set in England, where he lived for many years, and feature the astute sleuthing of the corpulent Dr. Gideon Fell. Carr emphasizes the puzzle element in the solutions of his mysteries, occasionally adding a touch of the macabre, and often using authentic historical backgrounds. Among his many books are *The Bride of Newgate* (1950), *Behind the Crimson Blind* (1952), *Cut-Throat* (1955), *The Dead Man's Knock* (1958), and *The Men Who Explained Miracles* (1963).

Carracci, Annibale (1560–1609). Italian painter. With his brother **Agostino** (1557–1602) and his cousin **Lodovico** (1555–1619), he founded an academy in Bologna, in 1582, where artists followed a course of study that served as a model for later academies. Based on the principle of eclecticism, it combined elements from the art of the Venetian school and that of Correggio, Raphael, and Michelangelo in an effort to achieve classical beauty. Annibale Carracci's religious pictures and large decorative schemes, notably his frescoes in the Farnese Gallery in Rome, reveal that he was the most talented member of this artistic family. His leading disciples were Domenichino and Guido Reni.

Carranza, Venustiano (1859–1920). Mexican political leader. An associate of Francisco Madero in the revolutionary movement of 1910, Carranza became provisional president in 1915 and was elected president in 1917. His administration saw the promulgation of the nationalistic Constitution of 1917, still in force today, but he ignored its provisions for social and economic reform. Despite U.S. recognition of the Carranza government in 1915, the border raids of Pancho VILLA and American agitation against "godless and socialistic Mexico" brought the two countries to the verge of war. When it became apparent that Carranza planned to name his own successor, revolt broke out; attempting to flee with a trainload of loot, Carranza was murdered at the hands of his own men.

Carrillo y Sotomayor, Luis (1583?–1610). Spanish poet and soldier. Considered a forerunner of Góngora, he wrote difficult, latinate verse, such as *Fábula de Acis y Galatea*. In his *Libro de la erudición poética,* he argued that Spanish should be latinized and that poetry should be cultivated only by the learned. His works were first published in 1611.

Carroll, Lewis. Pen name of **Charles Lutwidge Dodgson** (1832–1898). English author, mathematician, and photographer. A lecturer in mathematics at Christ Church, Oxford, Carroll was shy and stammering, reputedly a boring lecturer, whose mathematical writings include *An Elementary Treatise on Determinants* (1867), *Euclid and His Modern Rivals* (1879), *Curiosa Mathematica* (1888), and *Symbolic Logic* (1896). He was ordained as a deacon but never preached, and was a talented portrait photographer. His principal enthusiasm, however, was for little girls, for whom he created many amusing games and puzzles and for one of whom, Alice Liddell, he wrote his famous ALICE'S ADVENTURES IN WONDERLAND and THROUGH THE LOOKING GLASS. These became highly popular among adult readers; theorists of surrealism in the 20th century seriously interpreted Carroll's works as early embodiments of their own principles; and Freudians have made much of the symbolism of the Alice books. Carroll's other works of fantasy and nonsense include *The Hunting of the Snark, An Agony in Eight Fits* (verses, 1876), *Sylvie and Bruno* (1889), and *Sylvie and Bruno concluded* (1893). Through these works run veins of satire, parody, masterfully inverted logic, and extremely suggestive symbolism. See Sir John TENNIEL.

Carryl, Charles Edward (1842–1920). A New York financier and writer of children's books of a type reminiscent of those of Lewis Carroll, as *Davy and the Goblin* (1886); *The Admiral's Caravan* (1892). They contain some brilliant nonsense verse.

Carson, Christopher. Known as **Kit Carson** (1809–1868). American trapper and guide. Carson crossed the Mohave Desert in 1830 and served as a guide for Frémont's first western expedition (1842). He took an important part in the conquest of California during the Mexican War and fought in New Mexico during the Civil War, rising to the rank of brigadier general. Joaquin Miller's poem *Kit Carson's Ride* (1871) tells how Carson rescued his Indian bride from a prairie fire on their wedding day. Carson also appears in numerous dime novels and folk legends.

Carson, Rachel L[ouise] (1907–1964). American writer and scientist. Miss Carson's *The Sea Around Us* (1951) and *The Edge of the Sea* (1956) are known as works of literary as well as scientific merit. She maintained her impeccable style and aroused far more discussion and controversy with *The Silent Spring* (1962), in which she contended that the indiscriminate use of weed killers and insecticides constitutes a hazard to wildlife and to human beings.

Carstone, Richard. See BLEAK HOUSE.

Carswell, Mrs. **Catherine** (1879–1946). Scottish novelist and critic. Her biography of D. H. Lawrence, a close friend, was suppressed as libelous.

Cartaphilus or **Kartaphilos.** The doorkeeper of the Judgment Hall under Pontius Pilate in the variant of the WANDERING JEW legend told by the historians of St. Albans, Roger of Wendover (d. 1236) and Matthew PARIS. They reported that an Armenian archbishop, visiting St. Albans in 1228, said that he had recently dined with a man named Joseph who as Cartaphilus had been rude to Christ and had consequently become the Wandering Jew. The Flemish chronicler Philip Mousket (13th century) wrote a similar version about 1243.

Carte de tendre. See CLÉLIE, HISTOIRE ROMAINE.

Carter, Nick. A fictional American detective who has appeared in over 1,000 stories. He was apparently invented by John R. Coryell (1848–1924), who worked in a writing team with Thomas Chalmers Harbaugh (1849–1924) and Frederick Van Rensselaer Dey (1861?–1922); Nick made his first appearance in *The Old Detective's Pupil* (1886). The Nick Carter dime novels were extremely popular, and other writers continued the series in stories, movies, and radio plays.

Carteret, Philip (1639–1682). English colonial governor of New Jersey (1664–1676) and, after division of the colony, of East New Jersey (1676–1682). He came into conflict with Sir Edmund Andros, governor of New York, who challenged his right to collect duties on goods entering Jersey ports.

Carthage. Ancient city and state in North Africa. Founded in the ninth century B.C. by Phoenicians from the kingdom of Tyre, it was located on a peninsula near the site of modern Tunis. According to Roman legend, it was founded by DIDO. It became dominant among Phoenician cities in North Africa, founded several colonies in Africa, and held sway over the native agricultural population of a large region. Carthage carried on considerable trading activities along the coasts of the Mediterranean and founded colonies in Spain, Sardinia, and Sicily. There existed between Rome and Carthage a number of treaties restricting Rome from interfering with Carthaginian trade. These treaties governed the relations between Rome and Carthage until the PUNIC WARS. Carthage was ultimately burned to the ground by the Romans in the Third Punic War (149–146 B.C.).

Carthago delenda est. (Lat., "Carthage must be destroyed.") This is the phrase with which CATO THE ELDER ended all his speeches in the senate.

Carthusians (from *Chartreuse,* near Grenoble in France). An order of monks. It was founded in 1084 by St. Bruno. They were sworn to perpetual silence, continuous wearing of hair shirts, and eating of only one meal a day.

Cartier, Jacques (1491–1557). French navigator. During the second of his three voyages to America, he sailed up the St. Lawrence River, which he discovered, to an Indian village called Hochelaga, the site of modern Montreal, and named it Mount Royal.

Carton, Sydney. The hero of Charles Dickens' A TALE OF TWO CITIES. He is a dissipated young man whose temperament is contrasted with that of Charles Darnay; the great physical resemblance of the two is an important factor in the plot. Carton loves Lucie Manette, but, knowing of her attachment to Darnay, never attempts to win her. His love for her, however, brings out his nobler qualities, and ultimately brings him to die on the guillotine in place of Darnay. His last thoughts are the famous lines, "It is a far, far better thing that I do, than I have ever done; it is a far, far better rest, that I go to, than I have ever known." See Bully STRYVER.

Cartwright, William (1611–1643). English preacher, dramatist, and poet. Highly regarded by his contemporaries, Cartwright was one of the sons of Ben, or poets influenced by Ben Jonson. His best-known plays are *The Ordinary* (1634) and *The Royal Slave* (1636), which were first presented at Oxford University.

Caruso, Enrico (1873–1921). Italian dramatic tenor of worldwide popularity. The tremendous power and brilliance of his voice combined with an impassioned delivery and dynamic personality earned him many admirers, but also partially caused his death from overwork and strain. He was especially famous in the lead roles in *Pagliacci, Aïda, La Bohème,* and *Tosca.*

Carvajal, Micael or **Miguel de** (c. 1480–c. 1560). Spanish dramatist. He is best known for his *Tragedia Josefina* (c. 1535), a tragedy in four acts about Joseph and his brethren.

Carver, John (c. 1576–1621). 1st governor of the Plymouth Colony. He also hired and outfitted the *Mayflower,* and helped obtain financial backing for the voyage.

Cary, Joyce (1888–1957). Anglo-Irish novelist. He is the author of two trilogies, the first consisting of *Herself Surprised* (1941), *To Be a Pilgrim* (1942), and THE HORSE'S MOUTH, and the second of PRISONER OF GRACE, *Except the Lord* (1953), and *Not Honour More* (1955). The semiautobiographical *A House of Children* (1941) gives an impression of his Irish childhood. Trained as an artist, he brought his knowledge of a painter's problems to his best-known novel, *The Horse's Mouth.* From 1913 to 1920 Cary worked for the Nigerian political service. All his first novels are set in Africa and are about Africans, interracial problems, and the duties of government and law. His African novels are *Aissa Saved* (1932), *An American Visitor* (1933), *The African Witch* (1936), and MISTER JOHNSON. Cary's later books are Dickensian in their humor and wealth of characters, and are concerned with English social history. In this group are *Charley Is My Darling* (1940), *The Moonlight* (1946), *A Fearful Joy* (1949), *The Captive and the Free* (1959), and the trilogies. A celebrant of the power of the creative imagination, Cary presents it in many forms—in an African clerk (*Mister Johnson*), an artist (*The Horse's Mouth*), and a politician (the *Prisoner of Grace* series).

Casabianca. A poem by Felicia HEMANS celebrating the heroic death of Giacomo Jocante Casabianca, the little son of a French naval captain. The boy was set by his father on watch. The ship caught fire, and his father was burnt to death. As the flames spread, the boy called to his father, but stood by his post until the ship blew up.

Casa de Bernarda Alba, La. See Federico GARCÍA LORCA.

Casa Guidi Windows (1851). A long poem by Elizabeth Barrett BROWNING, written on behalf of the national aspirations of the Florentines.

Casals, Pablo or **Pau** (1876–). Spanish cellist and conductor. His mastery of interpretation and technique on the cello is now legendary; he has extended his profound musical insight to his teaching and conducting. Since the defeat of the Spanish Loyalists in 1939, Casals has chosen voluntary exile: first in Prades, France, where he established an annual music festival, later in Puerto Rico, where the festivals continued. *Conversations with Casals* (1956), by J. M. Corredor, surveys Casals' life and thought.

Casanova [de Seingalt], Giovanni Jacopo (1725–1798). Italian adventurer. After his expulsion from a Venetian seminary for scandalous misconduct, Casanova commenced a lively career as charlatan, gambler, and lover that took him to all the capitals of Europe. His fortunes fluctuated widely: in 1755, for example, he was imprisoned in Venice for impiety and magic, but after making a daring escape, he turned up in Paris, where he enjoyed temporary affluence as director of the state lottery and came in contact with such luminaries as Louis XV and Mme. de Pompadour. In 1785 he was made librarian at Count Waldstein's castle of Dux in Bohemia, where he remained until his death. His famous *Mémoires* (12 vols., 1826–1838) are no doubt unreliable as to his own career but are of great interest historically.

Casaubon, Rev. Mr. See MIDDLEMARCH.

Casca. In Shakespeare's JULIUS CAESAR, a conspirator against Caesar. He is known for his blunt, unadorned language.

Casey Jones. American ballad about a train wreck. It is probably based on the wreck in 1900 of the "Cannonball Express," whose driver, John Luther Jones (1864–1900), was born in Cayce, Kentucky, hence the nickname "Casey." Two railroad men, T. Lawrence Seibert and Eddie Newton, published the song in 1909 and may have been the authors.

casket letters, the. Eight letters and a series of poems supposedly written by MARY, QUEEN OF SCOTS to James, Earl of Bothwell. At least one of these was held to prove her complicity with Bothwell in the murder of her husband, Henry, Lord Darnley. The letters were found in a casket that fell into the hands of the Earl of Morton in 1567, four months after Darnley's death and a few days after Mary's surrender to the rebelling Scottish lords. The following year the letters were used as evidence in the investigation of the charges brought against Mary by the rebels. All trace of the original letters disappeared after 1584, and their authenticity is still a matter of dispute.

Casona, Alejandro. Pen name of **Alejandro Rodríguez Alvarez** (1903–). Spanish playwright. Spanish audiences received his *La Sirena Varada* (1934) and *Nuestra Natacha* (1936) with great acclaim. Since 1939, Casona has resided in Argentina where his *La Dama del Alba* (1944) and *Los Arboles Mueren de Pie* (1949) have been similarly well received.

Casperl. See GASPAR.

Cassandra (Kassandra). In Greek mythology, a daughter of Priam and Hecuba. She was gifted by Apollo with the power of prophecy. However, when she refused the god's advances he ordained that no one would believe her predictions, although they were invariably correct. She was carried off to Argos by Agamemnon and was killed with him by Clytemnestra and Aegisthus. She appears prominently in Euripides' *The Trojan Women* and Aeschylus' *Agamemnon*, as well as in Shakespeare's *Troilus and Cressida*. Her name has become synonymous with all prophets of doom.

Cassatt, Mary (1845–1926). American painter and print maker. She resided most of her life in France, where she was associated with Edgar Degas and the impressionists. She treated the theme of maternity with objectivity and an interest in simple everyday gestures, but she derived her style of clear lines, flat colors, and unusual composition from Japanese art.

Cassim Baba. See ALI BABA AND THE FORTY THIEVES.

Cassio, Michael. In Shakespeare's OTHELLO, the handsome young Florentine whom Othello appoints as his lieutenant. Iago, jealous of the preference shown to Cassio, encourages his weakness for drink and involves him in a brawl, causing his dismissal. Iago then convinces Othello that Cassio is Desdemona's lover. When Iago's plot is uncovered, Othello reinstates Cassio and asks his pardon before committing suicide.

Cassiopeia (Kassiopeia). In Greek mythology, the wife of Cepheus, king of Ethiopia, and mother of ANDROMEDA. In consequence of her boasting of the beauty of her daughter, she was sent to the heavens as the constellation Cassiopeia, the chief stars of which form the outline of a lady seated in a chair and holding up both arms in supplication.

Cassius. Full Latin name, **Caius Cassius Longinus** (d. 45 B.C.). Roman general and politician. During the civil war between CAESAR and Pompey, Cassius allied himself with Pompey. After Pompey's defeat at Pharsalus (48 B.C.), Caesar pardoned Cassius and made him praetor (44). Unlike BRUTUS, however, Cassius never ceased to be Caesar's enemy, in spite of the favor shown him. It was Cassius who conceived the plot against the dictator's life, and he who persuaded Brutus to join the conspiracy. After Caesar's murder, public opinion turned against the conspirators, and they fled from Rome. Cassius and Brutus met the forces of Octavius and Antony at Philippi (42), and during the first engagement Cassius, overwhelmed by Antony's forces, precipitately committed suicide, not knowing that Brutus had driven Octavius from the field. Brutus' forces were defeated some days later.

In Shakespeare's JULIUS CAESAR, Cassius is depicted as the instigator of the plot to assassinate Caesar. Grasping and ambitious, he urges the reluctant Brutus to join the conspiracy, pointing out, in a famous speech, that each man controls his own destiny:

> The fault, dear Brutus, is not in our stars,
> But in ourselves, that we are underlings.

Caesar says of him:

> Yon Cassius has a lean and hungry look;
> He thinks too much: such men are dangerous.

At Philippi, rashly assuming that Brutus has been defeated, Cassius commits suicide and thus helps turn Brutus' initial victory into overwhelming defeat.

Cassola, Carlo (1917–). Italian novelist. Inspired by Italy's fascist experience, his novels include *Fausto and Anna (Fausto e Anna;* 1952), *I Vecchi Compagni* (1953), *La Casa di Via Valadier* (1956), *Un Matrimonio del Dopoguerra* (1958), *Bebo's Girl (La Ragazza di Bubé;* 1960), and *Un Cuore Arido* (1961), which depicts the love life of a Tuscan seamstress in prewar Italy.

Interested in sociopolitical problems of postwar Italy, Cassola has written a notable polemical study about the conditions of Tuscan miners, *I Minatori della Maremma* (1956).

Castalia. A fountain of Parnassus sacred to the Muses. Its waters had the power of inspiring with the gift of poetry those who drank of them.

Castaway, The (1803). A tragic poem, his last, by William COWPER. It was based on an incident described in *A Voyage Round the World* (1748), by Admiral George Anson (1697–1762), a celebrated seaman of the eighteenth century. It tells of a lonely death at sea and compares this with the poet's own in a mood of despairing prophecy.

caste (Port. *casta,* race). One of the hereditary classes of society in India. The four great Hindu castes are the *Brahmin* (the priestly and meditative order), the *Shatriya* or *Kshatriya* (soldiers and rulers), *Vaishya* (husbandmen and merchants), and *Sudra* (peasants and laborers). The untouchables or outcastes form a fifth group, to whom the religious books are sealed; they are held cursed in this world, and without hope. Mahatma Gandhi and the present Indian government have done much to improve the position of this last group.

Castelar, Emilio (1832–1899). Spanish statesman and orator. A professor of history at Madrid university, he became president of the first Spanish republic in 1873. His speeches, which may be studied in his *Discursos* (1871), raised him to the position of Spain's greatest orator and exerted an influence upon European affairs. He is also the author of *Fra Filippo Lippi* (1877) and an account of his travels in Italy, *Recuerdos de Italia* (1872).

Castelo Branco, Camilo (1825–1890). Portuguese novelist. Castelo Branco was a prolific writer whose works reflect his own turbulent existence. Born out of wedlock, he had numerous love affairs, briefly contemplated entering the priesthood, and in 1861 was imprisoned for adultery. During his incarceration he wrote his best-known novel, *Amor de Perdição* (1862), a semiautobiographical tale of thwarted passion. Considered an outstanding prose stylist, he later turned toward realism, particularly in *Novelas do Minho* (1875), studies of rural life, and *A Brasileira de Prazins* (1882). He also wrote *Onde Está a Felicidade?* (1856), *Um Homem de Brios* (1857), and *Eusébio Macário* (1879), a parody of Zolaesque realism.

Castelvetro, Lodovico (1505–1571). Italian Renaissance literary critic. He is noted for his commentary (1570) on Aristotle's *Poetics;* its influence was felt in Europe through the 18th century.

Castiglione, Baldassare (1478–1529). Italian diplomat, writer, and courtier. One of the most important and influential authors in Europe during the Renaissance, he was born at Mantua, where he served the Gonzaga family, then moved to Urbino and the service of its duke, Guidobaldo da Montefeltro. In 1506, he was in England to receive the Order of the Garter for his master from Henry VII. In 1524, he went to Spain as papal envoy and died there in 1529, universally mourned. Although he wrote poetry in various genres, his chief work is *Il Libro del Cortegiano* (*The Book of the Courtier*), known simply as *Il Cortegiano* (THE COURTIER). Finished in 1518, the book sets forth in a series of dialogues the author's conception of the ideal courtier and the norms of courtesy in a cultured society. Castiglione's portrait, done by his friend Raphael, is one of the masterpieces of the Louvre museum.

Castillejo, Cristóbal de (1490?–1550). Spanish poet. A Cistercian monk, he spent most of his life in the service of Archduke Ferdinand, later king of the Romans. His poems, which were published in 1573, include *Sermón de Amores; Diálogo de la Vida de Corte,* a satire on court life; and *Contra los que Dejan los Metros Castellanos,* a diatribe on poets who adopted Italian meters.

Castillo y Solórzano, Alonso de (1584–c. 1648). Spanish novelist and dramatist. He is best known for his numerous picaresque novels, notably *Las Harpías en Madrid* (1631), *Aventuras del Bachiller Trapaza* (1637), and *La Garduña de Sevilla* (1642).

Castle, Egerton (1858–1920). English novelist. In collaboration with his wife Agnes (d. 1922), he wrote a series of popular romantic novels including *The Pride of Jennico* (1898), *The Bath Comedy* (1900), and *The Secret Orchard* (1901). Several of his books were dramatized.

Castle, Joyous. See FAERIE QUEENE, THE.

Castle, The (Das Schloss; 1926). An unfinished novel by Franz KAFKA, published posthumously. In its bare essentials, it is the story of a man against a bureaucracy and in this is similar to THE TRIAL. The hero, a land surveyor known only as K., is constantly frustrated in his efforts to gain entrance into a mysterious castle, which is administered by an extraordinarily complicated and inaccessible bureaucratic hierarchy. The book invites allegorical interpretation; K.'s striving has been seen as the human quest for comprehension of the ways of an incomprehensible God and his frustration has been seen as symbolic of the actual human condition. But apart from any exact interpretation, the novel clearly reflects Kafka's convictions about the problematic nature of human existence, as well as his stylistic mastery and frequent ironic humor.

Castle Dangerous (1832). A novel by Sir Walter SCOTT. Castle Dangerous or the PERILOUS CASTLE of James DOUGLAS was so called because it was taken from the English three times between 1306 and 1307. In the novel Black Douglas promises to release his prisoner, Lady Augusta, if the castle is surrendered to him. Sir John de Walton consents, gives up the castle, and marries the lady.

Castle Garden. A large circular building at the Battery, New York City. It was built as a fort in 1807. It became a concert hall where Jenny Lind gave a famous concert. Later an immigrant station, than an aquarium, it has been restored to its original form and is a federal monument.

Castle of Indolence (1748). A poem in Spenserian stanzas by James THOMSON. The castle of the poem is situated in the land of Drowsiness, where every sense is steeped in enervating delights. The owner is an enchanter who deprives all who enter his domains of their energy and free will. In Canto II, Selvaggio, the Knight of Arts and Industry, breaks the spell cast by the wizard Indolence. It is considered Thomson's best work by many critics.

Castle of Otranto, The (1764). A GOTHIC NOVEL, the first of that genre in English, by Horace WALPOLE. The villain, Manfred, prince of Otranto, inhabits the castle of Otranto and rules the realm unlawfully; his grandfather had poisoned Alfonso, the rightful ruler, and it had been cryptically prophesied that the usurpers would prevail so long as the castle was big enough to hold the rightful ruler. Manfred plans to marry his son Conrad to Isabella, daughter of the marquis of Vicenza, but in one of many supernatural events, Conrad is crushed to death by a gigantic helmet in the courtyard. Manfred then determines to marry Isabella himself in the hope that she will present him with another heir, whom he needs in order to maintain control of the realm. Isabella, terrified of Manfred, is aided by the handsome young peasant Theodore in her escape. In fulfillment of the prophesy, Alfonso's ghost, grown too large for the castle, tears it down and rises from the ruin, proclaiming Theodore, future husband of Isabella, the true heir to Otranto.

Castle Rackrent (1800). A novel by Maria EDGEWORTH depicting the dissolute life of Irish landlords of the 18th century. A succession of irresponsible members of the Rackrent family, watched by their ineffectual tenantry, dissipate their fortunes until they reach the verge of destitution.

Castor (Kastor) and Polydeuces (Polydeukes, Pollux). In Greek mythology, sons of Leda and Tyndareus or Zeus, called the **Dioscuri**. Beginning with their births, their lives and adventures are told in many versions. Both may have been the mortal sons of Tyndareus, or both immortal sons of Zeus; but the commonest tale makes Castor mortal. They sailed with the Argonauts, and it was Polydeuces, a great boxer, who killed Amycus, the brutal Bebrycian king, in a boxing match. Later, they quarreled with another pair of twins, Lynceus and Idas, and in the ensuing fight, all but Polydeuces were killed. Polydeuces begged his father Zeus to let him share his immortality with his brother. This wish being granted, they either spend one day together in heaven, the next in Hades, or they alternate in spending a day in each.

Castor and Polydeuces became patron gods of mariners, appearing in St. Elmo's fire. In late myth they were identified as the constellation Gemini. Their cult became highly popular in Rome, where Polydeuces was known as Pollux.

Castorp, Hans. The central figure in Thomas Mann's novel THE MAGIC MOUNTAIN. He is a young marine engineer of middling talents, the son of a Hamburg merchant family. He is described early in the book as an "unwritten sheet of paper," by which Mann means that his personality has yet to take shape. He is essentially passive and reflects the characters and events about him, more than he acts upon them.

Castro, Inés de (c. 1310–1355). Spanish noblewoman. She was the mistress of Dom Pedro, eldest son and heir of King Alfonso IV of Portugal. Pedro married her after the death of his first wife, and Alfonso, fearful that she and her powerful family constituted a threat to the dynasty, had her put to death. Upon his accession to the throne in 1357, Pedro had her body exhumed and placed upon a throne, forcing his courtiers to render her the homage denied her in life. Her remains were later taken to Alcobaça, where a magnificent mausoleum was built. Many writers have retold her tragic story, notably Camões in Os Lusiadas and Luis Vélez de Guevara in *Reinar Después de Morir*.

Castro Alves, Antônio de (1847–1871). Brazilian poet. The chief representative of the *condoreira* school of poets, so called because their poetic flights resembled those of the Andean condor, Castro Alves was strongly influenced by Victor Hugo, whom he acclaimed as "master of the world." A handsome, dashing youth, he was "discovered" by José de Alencar and Machado de Assis, who were impressed by his *Gonzaga* (1867), a prose drama about an abortive revolution in 18th-century Minas Gerais. After a shooting accident resulted in the loss of a foot, Castro Alves was stricken by tuberculosis, which caused his death at the age of 24. He spent his last months in the preparation of *Espumas Fluctuantes* (1870), his best-known collection. Effectively combining the ideals of romanticism with social criticism, his poetry is characterized by great verbal opulence and emotional force, though critics point out that it is often overwrought and bombastic. He is affectionately remembered by his countrymen as "the poet of the slaves," because of the ardent abolitionist sentiments he expressed in such poems as *Vozes d'Africa* and *O Navio Negreiro,* both included in the 1921 edition of *Os Escravos,* the first to follow the author's plan.

Castro y Bellvís, Guillén de (1569–1631). Spanish dramatist. A soldier turned writer, Castro was a disciple of Lope de Vega. His fame rests largely on *Mocedades del Cid* and its sequel, *Hazañas del Cid,* which were derived almost entirely from popular ballads about the medieval hero. These plays were the direct source of Corneille's *Le Cid* (1636).

Casuarina Tree, The (1926). A collection of short stories by W. Somerset MAUGHAM. Maugham successfully dramatized the title story as *The Letter* in 1927; it is the story of a white woman in Malaya who shoots her lover when he confesses that he is now in love with a Chinese woman.

cat. A domesticated feline to which many curious beliefs have adhered. It was called a "familiar," from the medieval superstition that Satan's favorite form was a black cat. Hence witches were said to have cats as their familiars.

In ancient Rome the cat was a symbol of liberty. The goddess of Liberty was represented as holding a cup in one hand, a broken scepter in the other, with a cat lying at her feet. No animal is more an enemy to all constraint than a cat.

In Egypt the cat was sacred to Isis, or the moon. It was held in great veneration and was worshiped with great ceremony as a symbol of the moon not only because it is more active after sunset but from the dilation and contraction of its pupils, symbolical of waxing and waning. The goddess Bast (Bubastis), representative of the life-giving solar heat, was portrayed as having the head of a cat, probably because that animal likes to bask in the sun. Diodorus tells us that whoever killed a cat, even by accident, was by the Egyptians punished by death, and according to Egyptian tradition, Artemis assumed the form of a cat, and thus excited the fury of the giants.

catachresis. (1) The wrong use of one word for another, as in "his action was most affective" instead of "effective."

(2) The use of an especially far-fetched figure of speech such as one involving literal impossibility or paradox, as in a mixed metaphor.

Catcher in the Rye, The (1951). A novel by J. D. SALINGER. It deals with two days in the life of Holden Caulfield, who has run away from his prep school just before the start of the Christmas vacation; unwilling to go home, he drifts about in New York, getting himself into a series of wryly humorous adventures. The sophistication and amazing but credible articulateness of this slightly unbalanced adolescent uniquely convey contemporary youth's dissatisfaction with adult society.

Catchpoles. An anglicism for the Chicanous in Rabelais' GARGANTUA AND PANTAGRUEL, who live on the Isle of Procuration. They make their living by offering to be beaten for a fee. Through these strange creatures Rabelais satirized the legal officers whose unpleasant task it was to deliver court summonses.

Câteau-Cambrésis, Treaty of. See DISASTROUS PEACE.

categorical imperative. See CRITIQUE OF PRACTICAL REASON.

Cather, Willa [Sibert] (1876–1947). American novelist. As a child, Willa Cather, who was born in Virginia, was taken to Nebraska, which later provided her with the setting for much of her finest work. After working as a newspaperwoman in Pittsburgh and as a teacher in Allegheny, Pa., she joined the staff of *McClure's Magazine* in New York City.

Miss Cather's first novel was *Alexander's Bridge* (1912), the story of an engineer, Bartley Alexander, torn between love for his wife and an actress he had known in his youth. She then wrote three excellent novels dealing with the life of the immigrant settlers in the Middle West: O PIONEERS!, THE SONG OF THE LARK, and MY ÁNTONIA. Two later novels, ONE OF OURS and A LOST LADY, are concerned with the Midwest and their characters' relation to its pioneer past. With THE PROFESSOR'S HOUSE and DEATH COMES FOR THE ARCHBISHOP, Miss Cather turned to the Southwest. Her interest in Roman Catholicism shown in the latter book was continued in SHADOWS ON THE ROCK, a novel about 18th-century Quebec. Other novels by Miss Cather are *My Mortal Enemy* (1926), *Lucy Gayheart* (1935), and *Sapphira and the Slave Girl* (1940). Her short stories and novelettes were collected in *The Troll Garden* (1905), YOUTH AND THE BRIGHT MEDUSA, *Obscure Destinies* (1932), and *The Old Beauty and Others* (1948).

In time Miss Cather's high regard for the courage and industry of the pioneers seemed to become a deep hatred for the modern world. She was, according to Maxwell Geismar, "an aristocrat in an equalitarian order, an agrarian writer in an industrial order, a defender of the spiritual graces in the midst of an increasingly materialistic culture."

Catherick, Anne. See THE WOMAN IN WHITE.

Catherine de Médicis (1519–1589). Italian-born queen of France. The great-granddaughter of Lorenzo the Magnificent, she married the future Henry II of France in 1533, and was the mother of Francis II, Charles IX, and Henry III. As regent during the minority of Charles, she intrigued with both the Huguenots and the Roman Catholic party and in 1572 persuaded him to order the MASSACRE OF ST. BARTHOLOMEW.

Catherine Parr (1512–1548). The sixth and last wife of HENRY VIII of England. Catherine took Henry as her third husband in 1543. An accomplished scholar and a woman characterized by piety and kindness, she was undoubtedly a wholesome influence on the king. She brought Mary and Elizabeth, who had been regarded as illegitimate for many years, back to court and treated them as princesses. She also tried to lessen the religious persecutions of the time. Shortly after Henry's death she married Sir Thomas Seymour, a former suitor and the uncle of the new king, Edward VI. She died after the birth of her first child in 1548.

Catherine the Great or **Catherine II** (**Ekaterina Alekseyevna;** 1729–1796). Empress of Russia (1762–1796). Her reign was marked by increased contact with the West. At that time, French culture was predominant in Europe and the empress herself took part in the intellectual life of the continent, corresponding regularly with Voltaire, Baron von Grimm, and Diderot. The beginning of Catherine's reign promised a liberalization of the regime in Russia. She intended to reform the legal code of the country, for this purpose composing a *Nakaz* (*Instruction*) on which the reforms were to be based. Much of the material in the *Nakaz* came from such liberal thinkers as Montesquieu and Beccaria. Catherine's liberal attitude changed as a result of the peasant uprising (1773–1774) led by Emelyan PUGACHEV and the French Revolution in 1789. The change in attitude led to the banning of satirical journals in Russia, which the empress had encouraged for a time. The primary target of the ban was Nikolai Ivanovich Novikov, whose criticism of Russian society was becoming too sharp for Catherine's taste. Novikov was imprisoned in 1791 and was freed after her death. Another victim of the empress's conservatism was Aleksandr Nikolayevich RADISHCHEV, who published his now famous *Puteshestviye iz peterburga v moskvu* (*A Journey from Petersburg to Moscow*) in 1792. Radishchev's criticisms of Russian life incensed Catherine and the author was exiled to Siberia.

Catherine's chief political achievements were the acquisition of land in the Ukraine that had been long held by Poland and the establishment of Russia's frontier on the coast of the Black Sea. Her dream of conquering Constantinople from the Turks was unfulfilled and was later taken up by other nationalist political thinkers.

Cathleen Ni Houlihan (1904). A one-act play by William Butler YEATS. It concerns a young Irish peasant who leaves his home and fiancée in order to follow a poor old woman. She is Cathleen Ni Houlihan, symbol of Ireland, who promises fame to those who help her recover her land from the strangers (the English) who have taken it. The part was written for Maud GONNE.

Cathos. One of the 2 ridiculous snobs in Molière's comedy LES PRÉCIEUSES RIDICULES.

Catiline. Full Latin name, **Lucius Sergius Catilina** (d. 62 B.C.). Roman conspirator. An able but unscrupulous patrician, Catiline organized a conspiracy of similarly desperate men to overthrow the Roman government by force. The plot was discovered by CICERO, who exposed it in his four eloquent orations: *In Catilinam*. Driven from Rome by Cicero's first speech, Catiline later fell in battle against the Roman army. He is the subject of a tragedy (1611) by Ben Jonson.

Catlin, George (1796–1872). American artist. He lived with Indians in the Middle West and in Central and South America, taking notes, gathering material, and picturing their life. His collection was placed in the National Museum in Washington and proved of great documentary value. He is the author of several books, including *Life Amongst the Indians* (1861).

Cato, Marcus Porcius. Known as **Cato the Elder** (234–149 B.C.). Roman statesman. His long public career was a constant struggle against enemies of the state abroad and moral laxity at home. As censor, Cato became the stern arbiter of Roman manners and did his utmost to suppress all innovations in thought and behavior. All that did not fit his severe code of moral rectitude he labeled "un-Roman." Despite the decisive defeat of Carthage in 202 B.C., he still regarded it as Rome's persistent enemy, and he would end each of his speeches in the Senate with the phrase *Carthago delenda est* ("Carthage must be destroyed"). In 146, Cato, at the age of 85, had his wish granted: Carthage was evacuated and burnt, and its rubble was leveled with ploughs and oxen.

Except for his treatise *De Re Rustica* (also known as *De Agri Cultura*), Cato's writings, including his great work on Roman history *Origines,* are now lost. His prose style was admired for its vigor and terseness.

Cato, Marcus Porcius. Known as **Cato the Younger** (95–46 B.C.). Roman statesman. The great-grandson of Cato the Elder, he is often considered the last of the Romans of the old school. Unwilling to win an election by bribing the populace, he lost it but gained the admiration of the Roman nobility. In Caesar's conflict with Pompey, Cato backed the latter and, after Pompey's defeat at Pharsalus, went with him into exile. When Caesar's legions defeated the army of the nobility in North Africa, Cato—then at Utica—took his own life. The conservative Senatorial Party went on to revere him as a saint and renamed him *Cato Uticensis* ("Cato of Utica") for his last stoic act of defiance. Of him, Lucan wrote: *Victrix causa diis placuit, sed victa Catoni!* ("The gods were pleased with the cause that won—Cato with the cause that lost!"). His death is described in Addison's tragedy *Cato* (1713).

Cat on a Hot Tin Roof (1955). A play by Tennessee WILLIAMS. It deals with the neurotic Pollitt family living in the Mississippi Delta. "Big Daddy" Pollitt is dying of cancer; Gooper, the oldest son, and his wife plot to gain the father's property. Brick, the younger son, an alcoholic ex-football star, and his wife, Maggie ("the cat"), are driven apart when Brick accuses Maggie of being responsible for his friend's death. In a confrontation with his father, Brick admits his failings and Maggie untruthfully announces that she is pregnant in an attempt to help her husband gain his inheritance. At the end of the play, the audience is left with a hope of reconciliation between Brick and Maggie. The play was awarded a Pulitzer Prize.

Cattle-Raid of Cooley, The. In Gaelic literature, an 8th-century epic tale from the ULSTER CYCLE. It is perhaps the most important of the early Irish sagas. Queen MEDB brings war against the Ulstermen, and CÚ CHULAINN alone defends the territory against her army for a long period. The most poignant moment in the tale is the combat between Cú Chulainn and his own foster brother, Ferdiad, whom he ultimately kills. This tale had considerable influence on the writers involved in the 19th-century Irish Renaissance.

Catton, Bruce (1899–   ). American historian and journalist. After working for various newspapers in Cleveland, Boston, and Washington, Catton entered government service in 1942 and later served as director of information for the War Production Board. From this experience came *The War Lords of Washington* (1948). He became deeply interested in the American Civil War, but it was not until 1952 that he began devoting his full time to writing Civil War history. His works in this field include *Mr. Lincoln's Army* (1951), dealing with the early years of the war; *Glory Road* (1952), relating the campaigns of 1862–1863; *A Stillness at Appomattox* (1953), which won a Pulitzer Prize; and *Grant Moves South* (1959). *The Coming Fury* (1961) and *Terrible Swift Sword* (1963), the first two volumes of his centennial history of the war, cover events from the Democratic convention at Charleston in April, 1860, to the fall of 1862.

Catullus, Gaius Valerius (87–?54 B.C.). Roman lyric poet. Born in Verona, he went to Rome as a young man. Through his charm and precocious brilliance he gained easy admittance to the refined and prodigal society of the day; through his ardent susceptibility he fell disastrously in love with a young Roman matron who became the "Lesbia" of his poems. She was the beautiful, gifted, and unscrupulous Clodia, sister of the notorious Clodius Pulcher (see CICERO). She became the dark muse of his poetry, and her life and personality are closely intertwined with the life and lyrics of Catullus.

At 30, Catullus found himself bankrupt, emotionally as well as financially, and in 57 B.C., after his final break with Clodia, he traveled to Asia with his friend Gaius Memmius, who was taking the post of propraetor of Bithynia. On his way back to Rome, a year later, he passed his brother's grave near Troy. Here he probably wrote the famous ode which ends *Frater, ave atque vale* (Brother, hail and farewell). He died himself not long afterwards, at the age of 30, or 33 at the most.

Of his poems, 116 composed in a number of lyric meters are extant. Among them are such celebrated love lyrics as *Vivamus, mea Lesbia, atque amemus* and *Odi et amo;* the mock threnody on the death of Lesbia's parrot; the *Lament of Atthis;* the miniature epic on the marriage of Peleus and Thetis; and a host of stinging epigrammatic attacks on his personal enemies.

Catullus brought many Greek rhythms into Latin literature, and was the first Roman poet to exploit fully the classical lyric meters. He exerted wide influence on subsequent poets, such as Tibullus, Propertius, Ovid, and Horace and Martial. In English literature his influence can be traced in the Elizabethan wedding odes and in the Caroline lyrics.

Caucasian Chalk Circle, The (Der kaukasische Kreidekreis; 1944–1945). A play by Bertolt BRECHT. Based on a Chinese fable (see THE CIRCLE OF CHALK), it concerns the conflict between a rich, powerful woman who has abandoned her baby son and a peasant girl who has brought him up. Both women claim the child, and the judge before whom the case is brought instructs each of them to take one of the child's hands and attempt to pull him out of a circle chalked on the floor, to show the strength of their love. The rich woman yanks with all her might and succeeds, because the peasant girl, afraid of hurting the boy, lets go. The judge, however, awards the child to the peasant girl, for he recognizes that she has shown the greater love.

Caudine Forks. A narrow pass in the mountains near Capua, now called the valley of Arpaia. It was here that the Roman army, under the consuls T. Veturius Calvinus and Sp. Postumius, fell into the hands of the Samnites (321 B.C.) and was made to pass under a yoke made up of three spears, two stuck into the ground parallel to each other and the third placed above them. The army was then allowed to depart in ignominy.

Caudwell, Christopher. Pen name of **Christopher St. John Sprigg** (1907–1937). English literary critic and writer of detective stories. His Marxist literary criticism was influential during the leftist 1930's: *Illusion and Reality* (1937). He was killed fighting with the International Brigade in the Spanish Civil War.

Cautionary Tales (1907). Verses for children by Hilaire BELLOC. They are mock-moral anecdotes about the fearful fates of children who Chew String, Tell Lies, or Bang Doors.

Cauvin, Jean. See John CALVIN.

Cavafy, Constantine P. Pen name of **C. P. Kavafis** (1863–1933). Greek poet. Though Greek culture and the Greek past is the subject of much of his finest verse, Cavafy lived most of his life in Alexandria, where he was born. During his lifetime he published only one small book of poems, which he later revised. Most of his poems were distributed only among his personal friends. They were scarcely known to readers of English until some of them were translated in 1952. Esteemed by critics as one of the finest modern Greek poets, Cavafy's work was brought to wider notice by their admiration.

There are two main classes of Cavafy's poems: narrative poems of events in the Greek past, and personal lyrics often concerned with homosexual love. In both the author's remarkable capacity for objectivity shows itself. The first, far from being heroic, are ironic in tone; the second are straightforward and unsentimental. The style and tone of Cavafy's work, expressed in simple, almost dry language, is peculiarly his own. *The Complete Poems of Cavafy*, translations by Rae Dalven, was published in 1961.

Cavalcade. See Noel COWARD.

Cavalcanti, Guido (1250–1300). Italian poet. He was one of the STILNOVISTI group and a close friend of Dante. Most of his "love songs," the *Canzone d'amore,* were addressed to a French lady named Mandetta. They were translated by Dante Gabriel Rossetti (1861) and by Ezra Pound (1911).

Cavalier, Jean. See CAMISARDS.

Cavalier of the Rose, The. See ROSENKAVALIER, DER.

Cavalier poets. English lyric poets associated with the court of Charles I, chief of whom were Robert HERRICK, Thomas CAREW, John SUCKLING, and Richard LOVELACE. They are best known as writers of frank, high-spirited, gracefully fanciful love poems and songs. See SONS OF BEN.

Cavalleria Rusticana (Rustic Chivalry). An opera by Pietro MASCAGNI (1890) based on a novella by Giovanni VERGA.

Cavender's House (1929). A narrative poem by Edwin Arlington ROBINSON. It tells how Cavender, who pushed his wife off a cliff because he suspected her of infidelity, is still uncertain of her guilt 12 years later.

Cavendish, Margaret. Duchess of Newcastle (1624?–1674). English noblewoman, one of the outstanding writers of her sex in the 17th century, known for her eccentricity of dress and behavior. She wrote prolifically, producing 13 printed books. Her best-known work is her *Sociable Letters* (1664), presenting a vivid picture of her times. She also wrote *The Life of William Cavendish* (1667), a biography of her husband, the duke of Newcastle, who had been a devoted follower of both Charles I and Charles II.

Caves du Vatican, Les. See LAFCADIO'S ADVENTURES.

Cavour, Conte Camillo Benso di (1810–1861). Italian statesman. Named prime minister of Sardinia in 1852, he devoted himself to the cause of Italian unification. His efforts saw fruition in 1861 when Victor Emmanuel II of Sardinia became king of all Italy excepting Rome and Venetia.

Cawdor, and Other Poems (1928). A collection of poems by Robinson JEFFERS. *Cawdor,* the title poem, is based on the story of Phaedra and Hippolytus; it deals with the desire of Fera Cawdor for her stepson, Hood, who rejects her advances. Cawdor, suspecting the boy has seduced Fera, kills him. Later Cawdor learns that Hood was innocent, and suffers from his inability to expiate his guilt.

Cawein, Madison [Julius] (1865–1914). American poet. He is best known for his *Kentucky Poems* (1902), a selection published in England with a laudatory introduction by Edmund Gosse. He wrote more than 30 books, including *Blooms of the Berry* (1887) and *The Cup of Comus* (1915).

Caxton, William (c. 1422–1491). The first English printer, also an important translator. He moved to Bruges, where he established himself as a dealer in textiles, remaining active in commerce until about 1470, even serving as governor (1465–1469) of the English Association of Merchant Adventurers in the Low Countries. Between 1469 and 1471 he translated a French romance about the Trojan War, then, to meet the great demand for the book, set about learning the new art of printing, probably with Colard Mansion at a press in Bruges. In 1474 or 1475 his *Recuyell of the Historyes of Troye* became the first book ever printed in English. The second was *The Game and Playe of the Chesse* (1475), which he had also translated from the French.

Caxton established a printing press in Westminster when he moved to England in 1476, and thereafter printed nearly 80 books, including the *Mirrour of the World* (1481), *The Golden Legend* (1483), Malory's *Morte d'Arthur* (1485), and the works of Boethius, Geoffrey Chaucer, and John Gower. Many of the books were his own translations from the French, including a great many of the Carolingian and Arthurian romances. What Caxton chose to print naturally became the staple reading matter for the English reading public of his time. His assistant Wynkyn de Worde became his successor after his death, reprinting many of Caxton's most popular titles.

Caxtons, The (1849). A novel by Edward BULWER-LYTTON. Along with its sequels, *My Novel* (1853) and *What Will He Do with It* (1858), it narrates the history of an upper middle-class English family. The story is supposed to be written by

Caxton's advertisement, which he printed in 1477. It is thought to be the earliest English broadside.

Jf it plefe ony man fpirituel or temporel to bye ony pyes of two and thre comemoracios of falifburi vfe enpryntid after the forme of this prefet lettre whiche ben wel and truly correct, late hym come to weftmonefter in to the almonefrye at the reed pale and he fhal haue them good chepe .·.·

Suplico ftet cedula

Pisistratus Caxton. His father, Austin Caxton, is an impractical philosopher and scholar, lost in vague dreams and plans for his proposed masterpiece on *The History of Human Error.* The launching of this magnum opus is finally made possible by the money that Pisistratus brings back from Australia. Others of the Caxton family are the gay, irresponsible Uncle Jack, who is an inveterate and not too lucky promoter; the fine old soldier, Captain Roland, also an uncle of Pisistratus; and Roland's son Herbert, a wild young man with gypsy blood in his veins, who dies a heroic death in India.

Cayrol, Jean (1911–   ). French poet and novelist. The novel trilogy *Je vivrai l'amour des autres* (1947–1950) depicts a Lazarus figure, a wandering beggar who assumes the miseries of the world. This theme is continued in the essay *Lazare parmi nous* (1950) and in many of his poems, such as *Pour tous les temps* (1955). Other works include *Poèmes de la Nuit et du Brouillard* (1945) and *Passetemps de l'homme et des oiseaux* (1947).

Cecchi, Giovanni Maria or **Giammaria** (1518–1587). Florentine notary and wool merchant who was also one of the first professional Italian playwrights. He wrote some 50 comedies, farces, and religious plays, his best being the comedy *L'Assiuolo (The Horned Owl).*

Čech, Svatopluk (1846–1908). A Czech epic poet and satirist. He celebrated Slavic traits and democratic ideals in his epic poems, though his novels were mildly satirical. Perhaps his best work, however, was in his lyrics.

Cecil, Lord [Edward Christian] David [Gascoyne] (1902–   ). English literary critic and biographer. Among his urbane studies are *Early Victorian Novelists* (1934); *The Young Melbourne* (1939); *Lord M.* (1954), the second part of his biography of Melbourne; and *The Fine Art of Reading* (1957).

Cecil, William. See William Cecil BURGHLEY.

Cecilia, St. A Roman lady who underwent martyrdom in the 3d century. She is the patron saint of the blind, being herself blind; also patroness of musicians, and inventor of the organ. According to tradition an angel fell in love with her for her musical skill, and used nightly to visit her. Her husband saw the heavenly visitant, who thereupon gave to both a crown of martyrdom, which he brought from Paradise. Dryden and Pope have written odes in her honor, and both speak of her charming an angel by her musical powers. See SECOND NUN'S TALE.

Cecilia, or Memoirs of an Heiress (1782). A novel by Fanny BURNEY. In order to keep her fortune, Cecilia Beverly, an heiress of somewhat inferior birth, must marry a man who will adopt her name. Mortimer Delvile loves her, but his family is proud of its antiquity and only he can perpetuate its name. Their love is thwarted by this and other obstacles, particularly the schemes and prejudices of those who wish to make use of Cecilia for their own ends. The two finally marry secretly, but further misunderstanding separates them until Delvile locates her by placing an advertisement in the "agony column" of the daily newspaper.

Cecrops (Kekrops). The traditional founder of Athens and first king of Attica. Supposed to have sprung from the ground, he was represented as half man, half serpent.

Cela, Camilo José (1916–   ). Spanish novelist. *La familia de Pascual Duarte* (1942), his first novel, was a huge success both in Spain and abroad. The tale, an example of the TREMENDISMO technique, presents the self-narrated account of the life of a murderer awaiting execution. Cela is also known for his social satire *La colmena* (*The Hive,* 1951) and is considered one of the most able of contemporary Spanish writers.

Celebrated Jumping Frog of Calaveras County, The (1865). A story by Mark TWAIN. It is based on an actual event reported in the California newspapers. Jim Smiley, a miner, bets that his frog, Dan'l Webster, can outjump any other. A stranger accepts the dare; while Jim is distracted, he pours quail shot into Dan'l. The story, reprinted many times, appeared in Clemens' first book, a collection of tales called *The Celebrated Jumping Frog* (1867).

Celestial City. See PILGRIM'S PROGRESS.

Celestina, La (1499). The popular title of *La tragicomedia de Calisto y Melibea,* a Spanish novel in dialogue by an anonymous author. The oldest known edition, dating from 1499, contains 16 acts which were increased to 21 in a 1502 edition. There is some doubt as to the author of the first act and of the 1502 additions, but it is generally agreed that Acts 2–16 were written by Fernando de Rojas, a lawyer and converted Jew from Toledo who served as *alcalde mayor,* or chief magistrate, of Talavera.

The plot deals with the noble young Calisto and his love for Melibea. When she proves cold to his advances, he enlists the aid of Celestina, an unscrupulous, self-seeking crone, who persuades Melibea to relent. Just when the romance is progressing smoothly, Calisto is killed by a fall from a ladder. In despair, Melibea flings herself from a tower to her death.

Most of the interest in the novel centers about the demonic figure of the go-between Celestina. Although the young lovers move in a world of idealized passion, Celestina and the servants, prostitutes, and other low-life characters who surround her give a coarse but vivid picture of the common people of 15th-century Spain.

Unsuitable for the stage because of its length, the *Celestina* strongly influenced Spanish writers, notably Lope de Vega. It was widely translated, the English version (1631) by James Mabbe being especially well known. See Juan RUIZ.

Celeus (Keleos). In Greek legend, a king of Eleusis, husband of Metanira. He sheltered DEMETER when she was wandering in search of her daughter. In return, Demeter wished to give his son Demophon immortality. When Metanira objected to her placing the infant in the fire to immortalize him, Demeter angrily revealed herself as a goddess. She instituted the famous ELEUSINIAN MYSTERIES and bestowed on Celeus' other son TRIPTOLEMUS the honor of being mankind's teacher in the use of the plough.

Celia. The very virtuous, naïve young wife of Corvino in Jonson's comedy VOLPONE, OR THE FOX. Inexperienced in the ways of the world, she is victimized by the lecherous Volpone, by the jealous Lady Politick Would-Be, and above all by her own greedy husband.

Celia. Rosalind's cousin, daughter of Duke Frederick, in Shakespeare's As You Like It. She is a merry young lady who cheerfully follows her cousin into banishment for the sake of their friendship and eventually weds Oliver.

Célimène. In Molière's comedy Le Misanthrope, a coquette courted by Alceste, the misanthropist. Hence, the name has become a synonym for any flagrant coquette.

Céline, Louis-Ferdinand. Pen name of the doctor **Louis-Ferdinand Destouches** (1894–1961). French novelist. Celine is known for the misanthropic invective of Journey to the End of the Night (1932) and Death on the Installment Plan (Mort à crédit; 1936), which expose almost everything as either evil or insane. He looked to communism, but after a trip to Russia renounced it in Mea Culpa (1937). He turned to fascism with the violently anti-Semitic diatribe Bagatelles pour un massacre (1937) and the attack on the "degenerate" French in Ecole des cadavres (1938). When he returned from his exile in Germany, he wrote D'un chateau l'autre (1957) and Nord (1960).

Cellini, Benvenuto (1500–1571). Florentine goldsmith, sculptor, and author of one of the world's great autobiographies. First published in 1730, the work was actually begun in 1558, when Cellini started dictating his memoirs to an apprentice. It tells of his adventures in Italy and France, his relations with popes and kings and with fellow artists, his production of works like the Perseus statue. A fairly complete picture of the times emerges from the work, though exaggerated by the author's distortion of his own role in events. Its realism, vivid descriptions, racy style, and, above all, its portrait of a genuine personality have exerted a strong influence on historians of the Renaissance, as Burkhardt, who see it as confirming the view that the key to the period is the emergence of modern individualism. Goethe's translation and Berlioz' musical interpretation are examples of its continuing impact on other artists.

Cement (Tzement; 1925). A novel by Feodor Vasilvevich Gladkov. The book was one of the first to deal with the problems of reconstruction and industrialization in Russia after the civil war. It is now ranked as one of the early Soviet classics.

Cénacle. In 19th-century France, the name of a literary and political group meeting in the salon of Charles Nodier and, later, the name of a similar group led by Victor Hugo. Honoré de Balzac made use of this designation in some of the novels of his La Comédie Humaine; among the most active members of this fictional cénacle were Daniel d' Arthez, Henri de Marsay, and Horace Bianchon.

Cena de Baltazar, La (Belshazzar's Feast). An auto sacramental by Pedro Calderón de la Barca. Heedless of the prophet Daniel's call to repentance, Belshazzar, king of Babylon, revels with his wives Vanity and Idolatry and his jester, Thought. He is finally struck down by Death.

Cenci, Beatrice (1577–1599). A historical personage. She is known as the Beautiful Parricide, from a famous portrait in Rome's Barberini palace attributed to Guido Reni. She was the daughter of Francesco Cenci (1549–1598), a choleric, cruel, and vice-laden Roman nobleman. With her mother and two brothers, Beatrice successfully plotted the death of her father at the hands of hired bravos. It is possible, however, that the immediate provocation of the murder was Francesco's discovery of his daughter's intimacy with one of the family's stewards.

The plot was revealed by one of the bravos, and the conspirators were brought to trial. Great sympathy was aroused by the plight of the young, beautiful Beatrice, and her attorney attempted to play upon this by falsely claiming that Francesco had tried to commit incest with her. However, Pope Clement VIII refused the sought-for pardon and on September 11, 1599 Beatrice was beheaded. Her story has been a favorite theme of poetry and art, the most famous use being Shelley's tragedy The Cenci (1819), in which she is treated sympathetically.

Cendrars, Blaise (1887–1961). French poet and novelist. An innovator in his verse forms, he was lyrical even in his prose, especially in the autobiographical L'Homme foudroyé (1945). His novels of adventure include Le Panama ou les Aventures de mes sept oncles (Panama, or, The Adventures of my Seven Uncles, 1919), L'Or (Sutter's Gold, 1925), Moravagine (1926), Rhum (1930), and Bourlinguer (1948).

censor. In ancient Rome, a magistrate of high rank. His duty was to take the census, see that Senate vacancies were filled, take inventory on government finances, allot government contracts for public works, and investigate and, if necessary, correct the state of public morality. Originally, two censors were elected for a five-year period, called a lustrum; in 433 B.C., the term of office was shortened to 18 months. As a distinct office, the censorship disappeared in the reign of Domitian (84 A.D.).

Centaurs (Kentauroi). In classic mythology, beings who were half horse and half man. They fought with the Lapiths at the marriage feast of Pirithous, were expelled from their country, and took refuge on Mount Pindus. Chiron was the most famous of the centaurs. Both Lapiths and Centaurs are thought to have been actual Thessalian tribes.

Centlivre, Mrs. Susannah (1667–1723). English dramatist and actress. She wrote a number of comedies of intrigues such as The Busy Body (1709), The Wonder, a Woman Keeps a Secret (1714), and A Bold Stroke for a Wife (1718).

Cent nouvelles nouvelles, Les (1462). A collection of prose tales by an unknown member of the court of Philip of Burgundy. Modeled on Boccaccio's Decameron (1353) and Poggio's Facetiae (early 15th century), the stories are comic, often licentious, anecdotes purportedly told by the members of the court.

cento (Lat., a patchwork). A literary composition, especially a poem, of lines or parts from the writings of established authors, and with a meaning and message different from the original. Centos were freely produced during the decadent period of Greece and Rome; Ausonius (c. 310–395), who put together the scandalous Cento Nuptialis with lines taken from Vergil, enunciated rules concerning their composition. Among well-known examples are the Homerocentones, taken by Byzantine compilers from Homer, the Cento Vergilianus by Proba Falconia (4th century), which used Vergil to relate Biblical history, and the Christian hymns devised by the monk

Metellus (12th century) from the works of Vergil and Horace.

Central Powers. In World War I, Germany and her allies: Austria-Hungary, Bulgaria, Turkey.

Century of Louis the Great, The. See Charles PERRAULT.

Cephalus (Kephalos) and Procris. In classic legend, Cephalus was Procris' husband. She deserted him, out of jealousy. Searching for her, he rested a while under a tree. Procris, knowing of his whereabouts, crept through some bushes to ascertain if a rival was with him; and he, hearing the noise and thinking it to be made by some wild beast, hurled his javelin into the bushes and slew her. When the unhappy man discovered what he had done, he slew himself in anguish of spirit with the same javelin.

Cerberus (Kerberos). In Greek mythology, the three-headed dog, keeper of the entrance of the infernal regions. Heracles dragged the monster to earth to show him to Eurystheus, and then took him back. The Sibyl who conducted Aeneas through the lower world threw the dog into a profound sleep with a cake seasoned with poppies and honey (*Aeneid* vi, 417–425). The phrase *give a sop to Cerberus* therefore means to give a bribe, to quiet a troublesome person.

Ceres. An Italian goddess of fertility, later identified with the Greek DEMETER.

Cerf, Bennett [Alfred] (1898–   ). American publisher and editor. In 1925, with Donald S. Klopfer, Cerf bought the Modern Library series of inexpensive reprints of the classics from Boni and Liveright. He made the series a tremendous success and added many new titles over the years. In 1927 he and Klopfer founded Random House, which merged with Harrison Smith and Robert Haas in 1936 and has published many noted writers. Cerf has compiled and edited a number of books, many of them anthologies of humor.

Cernuda, Luis (1904–   ). Spanish poet. His early works include *Perfil del aire* (1927), and *La invitación a la poesía* (1933). These have been described as romantic, but possess a strain of hardy intellectualism. Cernuda left Spain during the revolution, traveling to the continent and later to England. In 1947 he was a member of the faculty of Mount Holyoke College. His recent work includes the prose poem *Ocnos* (1943) and *Tres narraciones* (1948).

Cervantes [Saavedra], Miguel de (1547–1616). Spanish novelist, dramatist, and poet. Born in Alcalá de Henares, Cervantes came from a good though impecunious family. Little is known of his education except that in 1568 he was a student of the Madrid humanist Juan López de Hoyos, who edited an elegaic volume on the death of Queen Isabel de Valois to which Cervantes contributed some verses. In 1569 he went to Italy, became a soldier, and fought in the battle of Lepanto (1571), in which he acquitted himself with distinction and lost the use of his left hand; he was extremely proud of his role in the famous victory and of the nickname he had earned, *el manco de Lepanto*. As Cervantes was returning to Spain with his brother on the galley *El Sol* in 1575, the ship was captured by Barbary pirates, and the two brothers were taken to Algiers as slaves. Miguel remained in captivity for five years, during which he made several romantic if futile efforts to escape. His

ransom of 500 ducats was finally paid by the Trinitarian friars.

Having returned to Spain, Cervantes married Catalina de Salazar y Palacios in 1584, fathered an illegitimate daughter, and in 1587 secured employment as a purchasing agent for the navy. In this capacity he traveled throughout the country, often becoming involved in disputes with communities reluctant to part with their crops; on one occasion he was excommunicated for seizing grain that belonged to the church. Twice he was imprisoned for debt.

In 1605 Cervantes and his family, who were then living in Valladolid, were accused of complicity in the death of a young nobleman. They were later absolved, but the records of the case give evidence of the poverty and wretchedness of Cervantes' mode of existence at the time. His position improved considerably, however, after the publication of the first part of DON QUIXOTE in the same year. Although Cervantes' previous literary efforts had met with little success, *Don Quixote* immediately caught the fancy of the reading public. Moving to Madrid, he devoted his last years to writing.

Cervantes' reputation as one of the greatest writers in history rests almost entirely on *Don Quixote* and on the 12 short stories known as the NOVELAS EJEMPLARES. His literary production, however, was considerable. *La Galatea* (1585), a pastoral romance, was his first long work; similar in form and content to other novels of this type, it received little contemporary notice and is remembered largely because of its authorship. Cervantes repeatedly promised to write a continuation, but it never appeared.

He next turned his attention to the stage and wrote between 20 and 30 plays in the years immediately following 1585. Two extant dramas of this period are *El trato de Argel* and *La Numancia,* both of which were first printed in 1784. The former, dealing with the life of Christian slaves in Algiers, is of interest only because of its autobiographical details. The latter, which recounts the siege and capture of Numantia by the Romans under Scipio Africanus, has won wider approbation, partly because of some powerful scenes and partly because of its expressions of patriotism. In 1615 Cervantes published his *Ocho comedias, y ocho entremeses nuevos.* Only one of the full-length plays, *Pedro de Urdemalas,* has met with critical favor, but the *entremeses,* or interludes, are highly regarded for their sprightly and realistic pictures of Bohemian life.

Cervantes himself realized that he was deficient in poetic gifts, a judgment confirmed by later generations. Aside from his plays, his most ambitious work in verse is the *Viaje del Parnaso* (1614), an allegory which consists largely of a rather tedious though good-natured review of contemporary poets. *Los trabajos de Persiles y Sigismunda* (1617) is a verse romance in the manner of Heliodorus, which Cervantes thought would be either the worst or the best book in the Spanish language. Though some critics have boggled at the fantastic geography of its early scenes and the incredible adventures of its characters, others have praised its polished style.

Regardless of its merits, the *Persiles* will be remembered, if only for its dedication and prologue. Addressed to the conde de Lemos, the dedication was signed on April 19, 1616, just four days before Cervantes' death. Quoting an old ballad, *Puesto ya el pié en el estribo* ("One foot already in the stirrup"), Cervantes takes leave of his patron and of the world with the same gallantry and grace that characterized both his life and his work.

César Birotteau, Histoire de la grandeur et de la décadence de (1837). A novel by Honoré de BALZAC. The title character is a perfume dealer who is admitted to the Legion of Honor. Dazzled by the honor, he gives a lavish ball to celebrate the event. This necessitates the complete remodeling of his home, and as a result of all this expense and of several unwise investments, he is completely ruined. Within three years he is able to pay his debts, but, ironically, he dies soon afterward. The novel, which forms part of LA COMÉDIE HUMAINE, is said to reflect Balzac's own unhappy experiences in business.

Cesbron, Gilbert (1913–). French novelist, essayist, and dramatist. His novels usually have moral and social themes. *Saints in Hell* (*Les Saints vont en enfer;* 1952) concerns the struggles of worker-priests in Paris, and *Lost Children of Paris* (*Chiens perdus sans collier;* 1954) is about juvenile delinquency. Other works include the novels *The Innocents of Paris* (1944), *La Tradition Fontquernie* (1947), *Avoir Eté* (1960), and the play *No Plaster Saint* (*Briser la statue;* 1952).

Céspedes, Alba de (1911–). Italian writer. Her novels sympathetically explore the position of the modern Italian woman. Her best-known novel, *Il Quaderno Proibito* (*The Secret,* 1954), concerns the gradual deterioration of a marriage; it is written in the form of a diary kept secretly by the wife.

cestus (kestos). (1) The girdle of Aphrodite, made by her husband Hephaestus. It was reputed to possess magical power to move to ardent love. By a poetical fiction, all women of irresistible attraction are supposed to be wearers of Aphrodite's girdle, or the *cestus.* It is introduced by Spenser in *The Faerie Queene* as the girdle of Florimel. It gave to those who could wear it "the virtue of chaste love and wifehood true," but if any woman not chaste and faithful put it on, it "loosed or tore asunder." (2) The *cestus* in Roman games was a covering for the hands of boxers, made of leather bands and often loaded with lead or iron.

Cézanne, Paul (1839–1906). French painter. The great master of postimpressionism and perhaps the greatest figure in modern French painting, Cézanne was born in Aix-au-Provence, the son of a banker. His early works were low in key and heavy in medium, but after 1870 he began to paint out of doors and allied himself with the impressionists. By 1876 he had already begun to accentuate mass, rather than light, in an effort to achieve a better illusion of volume. Cézanne's statement that "Nature must be treated through the cylinder, the sphere, the cone," summarizes his desire "to make of impressionism something as solid and durable as the painting in the museums." This search led him to displace visual planes, to raise the horizon, to construct his paintings in such a way that each departure from nature would increase the impression of form and depth. He retained the pure colors of impressionism, but used them to build up volume through the contrast of tones. He spent much of his life as a recluse in Provence, painting the famous still lifes, landscapes,

and portraits, that were then unknown except to a few of his contemporaries. It was not until the last decade of the century that his reputation began to grow. Cézanne is said to have been in the mind of Emile Zola, his former schoolmate and friend, during the composition of *L'Œuvre* (1886); Zola represents his hero as a restless painter and failure.

Chaadayev, Piotr Yakovlevich (1794–1856). Russian philosophical thinker. He is famous for his *Philosophical Letters* which unfavorably compared Russia's past and present condition to that of the Western nations. The publication of the first letter in 1836 brought down a storm of abuse and police persecution on Chaadayev, who was officially declared insane and put under house arrest for a time.

Chadband, Rev. Mr. In Charles Dickens' BLEAK HOUSE, a typical, canting hypocrite "in the ministry."

Chagall, Marc (1889–). Russian-born French painter. From his earliest paintings, scenes of Russian village life, he developed an individualistic style of great poetry, fantasy, and brightness, typified by his pair of lovers floating over, or nesting in, large bouquets of flowers. With World War II, he introduced social and religious elements in his art, painting numerous crucifixions. He designed theatrical scenery and stained-glass windows, and illustrated Nikolai Gogol's *Dead Souls* (1948) and the *Fables* of La Fontaine (1952).

Chairs, The (Les Chaises; 1951). A tragic farce by Eugène IONESCO. It presents a Kafka-like image of modern man. An old lighthouse keeper, preparing to die, invites a group of guests to a gathering where his final words of wisdom will be delivered. In a scene that is both a dramatic and a symbolic *tour de force,* he and his wife rush desperately about to seat an enormous crowd of imaginary guests. The bare, empty stage juxtaposed with the frenzied human effort offer an absurd image of modern man, isolated, frustrated, and unable to order the chaos of life. A final irony, ludicrous and bitter, is the audience's discovery that the orator can neither read nor write.

Chakravakas. Sanskrit for red geese or sheldrake, favorite symbols with classical Indian writers. In legend, these birds were supposed to be ideally happy during the daytime, but at night a curse separated them and they bewailed each other's absence from the opposite banks of a river.

Chalciope (Chalkiope). See GOLDEN FLEECE, THE.

Chalcondyles, Demetrius (d. 1511). Greek editor of classical texts. He prepared early and influential editions of Homer (1488) and Euripides (1493). Also a scholar and teacher at Padova, Florence, and Milan, he numbered among his students Castiglione, Reuchlin, Trissino, and the future Pope Leo X.

Chaliapin, Feodor Ivanovitch (1873–1938). Russian basso, famed for his acting as well as his singing, especially in the title role of *Boris Godunov.* He wrote two volumes of memoirs: *Pages from My Life* (1926) and *Man and Mask* (1932).

Challenger, Professor. An adventurous, iconoclastic, rather opinionated scientist of imposing girth who appears in Conan DOYLE's *The Lost World* (1912). Doyle regarded him as his most amusing character.

Chambered Nautilus, The (1858). A poem by Oliver Wendell HOLMES. The sea creature that enlarges its shell as it grows is an example to the human being:

> Build thee more stately mansions, O my soul,
> . . . .
> Leaving thine outgrown shell by life's unresting sea!

Chamberlain, Houston Stewart (1855–1927). British-born political philosopher who became a German citizen in 1916. His *Foundations of the Nineteenth Century (Die Grundlagen des neunzehnten Jahrhunderts;* 1899), a historical defense of the superiority of the Germanic race, contains anti-Semitic theories that were later developed by the NAZIS. See ARYAN RACE.

Chamberlain, Neville (1869–1940). Conservative prime minister of England from 1937 to 1940. He is remembered chiefly for his role in the Munich meeting with Hitler in September, 1938, in which he pursued a policy of appeasement. For a time, his name became synonymous with betrayal in the writing of Marxists and liberals, who considered that he had delivered Czechoslovakia into the hands of the Nazis. He was succeeded in office by Winston Churchill.

Chamber Music (1907). A volume of poems, mainly love lyrics, by James JOYCE. They show the influence of the Elizabethan poets and of the early William Butler Yeats and his circle.

Chambers, Charles Haddon (1860–1921). Australian playwright. His best comedy, *The Tyranny of Tears* (1902), was produced by Charles Wyndham.

Chambers, Sir E[dmund] K[erchever] (1866–1954). English literary scholar. His books on *The Medieval Stage* (1903), *The Elizabethan Stage* (1923), and *William Shakespeare* (1930) are among the standard works on the subjects.

Chamisso, Adalbert von (1781–1838). German poet and botanist. He is famous for his ballads and the story, PETER SCHLEMIHLS WUNDERSAME GESCHICHTE. He was one of the first poets to turn away from the unswerving idealism of earlier GERMAN ROMANTICISM, and to write with a genuine love for the common people; for example, he wrote poems about beggars and washerwomen. He was appointed botanist to a Russian ship and published a diary of his expedition around the world. He was custodian of the botanical gardens in Berlin.

Champion, or British Mercury, The (1739–1741). A tri-weekly periodical edited by Henry FIELDING under the pseudonym of Captain Hercules Vinegar. Modeled on Richard Steele's *Tatler,* it was predominantly a vehicle of opposition to the government of Sir Robert Walpole.

Champlain, Samuel de (1567–1635). French explorer. He discovered and explored Lake Champlain and in 1608 founded the colony of Quebec.

Champollion, Jean François (1790–1832). Famous French Egyptologist. As a result of his study of the Rosetta Stone, he obtained a clue for deciphering Egyptian hieroglyphics.

Chamson, André (1900–   ). French novelist and essayist. At first a regional writer of the Protestant Cévennes area—he has written poems in Provençal—he became famous for his novels *Roux le Bandit* (1925), *Les Hommes de la route* (1927),

and *Le Crime des Justes* (1928), all translated by Van Wyck Brooks. As a result of his widening interest in ethical and political problems he wrote *La Galère* (1939); *Le Puits des miracles* (1945), an account of life during the German Occupation; *L'Homme qui marchait devant moi* (1948); *La Neige et la fleur* (1951); and *Le Chiffre de nos jours* (1954).

Chan, Charlie. A shrewd Chinese detective living in Hawaii who appears in several stories by Earl Derr Biggers (1884–1933). Given to wise, philosophical reflections, Chan acts on the assumption that if he can understand a man's character, he can predict his actions in any given circumstance. He first appeared in *The House Without a Key* (1925). Later Chan stories include: *The Chinese Parrot* (1926); *Behind That Curtain* (1929); *Charlie Chan Carries On* (1930); *Keeper of the Keys* (1932).

Chanakya (3rd century B.C.). Author of the Sanskrit *Chanakya-niti* or *The Laws of Chanakya* and the well-known *Artha-shastra,* an elaborate explanation of the science of national economics and statecraft. He was the minister of Emperor Chandragupta Maurya and is sometimes called Vishnugupta or Kautilya.

Ch'an Buddhism. Japanese ZEN. The Meditation School in China. Meditation was widely used in all forms of BUDDHISM in India and China, but Ch'an was the first to put almost exclusive emphasis on it. Traditionally Bodhidharma (fifth century) is given as the founder in China, and the sixth patriarch, Hui-neng (d. 713), is honored as the developer of the sect as a religion. The actual history is unclear, but by the T'ang Dynasty (618–906) Ch'an had gained great popularity and there were numerous teachers throughout China. Ch'an advocates "direct seeing into one's own mind" and realizing Buddhahood in oneself. It emphasizes the teacher-disciple relationship and transmission from mind to mind rather than through written words. After the persecutions of Buddhists (845) it became the dominant school in China. By the Sung period (960–1279) it had split into various sects and an organized church had been developed. It was the Ch'an of this time that was transmitted to Japan, together with the elaborate KOAN system. The two principal branches are Lin-chi (Japanese *Rinzai*) and Ts'ao-tung (Japanese *Sōtō*), both of which flourish in Japan today. By the Ming period (1368–1644) Ch'an had lost its vitality and became mixed with the Pure Land School, or Amidism.

Chance (1913). A novel by Joseph CONRAD. Flora de Barral marries Captain Roderick Anthony, and she and her father put to sea with him on the *Ferndale.* Flora fears that her husband has married her only out of pity, because her father is a broken man, a financier just out of prison for fraud. She is a tortured soul, suffering from an obsessional relationship with her father. Finally De Barral's attempt to poison Anthony, discovered and thwarted by mere "chance," clarifies the situation. Most of the story is told by MARLOW.

Chance Acquaintance, A (1873). A novel by William Dean HOWELLS. Kitty Ellison falls in love with Miles Arbuton, a young Bostonian, while they travel on the St. Lawrence River. They become engaged, but Miles, meeting some fashionable and snobbish friends, ignores Kitty. She breaks the engagement, knowing she cannot be happy with a Boston Brahmin.

Chancellor, Olive. See BOSTONIANS, THE.

Chancellorsville, battle of (May 2–4, 1863). In U.S. history, a Civil War battle near Fredericksburg, Va., in which the Union army under Gen. Joseph Hooker was defeated by Confederate forces under Gen. Robert E. Lee. Thomas ("Stonewall") Jackson, the Confederate general, was accidentally shot by his own men during the battle and died of pneumonia on May 10. This battle is said to have furnished the background for Stephen Crane's *Red Badge of Courage* (1895).

Chand, Prem. Pen name of Nawab Rai (1880–1936). Greatest short-story writer and novelist in Hindi. His early work was written in the Urdu language, but lack of a sufficiently large audience made him write his best novels in Hindi. *Seva-Sadan* (1907) describes the predicament of an innocent wife forced into prostitution. *Premashran* (1922) depicts the conflicting interests of tenant and landlord. *Nirmala* (1923) deplores the evils of the dowry system. *Ranga-bhumi* (1924) attacks the depredations of capitalists. *Karma-buhmi* (1925) is a strong indictment of British colonial rule in India. Prem Chand's work, loaded with social content, finds its best expression in his last novel, *Godan* (*The Cow-Gift;* 1936), a harrowing tale of the difficulties of the life of the Indian peasant. To critics who complained of the propagandistic "realism" in his writings, he explained that he wrote with "a touch of humanity, a poetic nuance. These make a story. All else fails."

Chandala (*Sans.,* outcaste). In India the child of a Sudra father and a Brahmin mother. See CASTE.

Chandler, Raymond (1888–1959). American detective-story writer. A master of the hard-boiled, though literate, crime story, Chandler was the creator of the private detective Philip Marlowe. His best-known novels include *The Big Sleep* (1939), *Farewell, My Lovely* (1940), and *The Long Goodbye* (1954). *The Simple Art of Murder* (1950), a collection of short stories and novelettes, contains an excellent and well-known essay on the writing of crime fiction.

Changeling, The (c. 1623). A tragedy by Thomas MIDDLETON and William ROWLEY. Beatrice Joanna, a young noblewoman betrothed to Alonzo De Piracquo, falls in love with Alsemero, a Venetian gentleman. After postponing the wedding she calls in Deflores, the ugly servant of her father whom she has always despised, and enlists his aid in killing Alonzo. After Deflores, who adores Beatrice Joanna, has dispatched Alonzo, he claims her person as his reward. Horrified, she refuses, but Deflores, a desperate man, swears to tell all unless she becomes his mistress. Trapped, she agrees. She marries Alsemero but, fearful of exposure, substitutes her virginal servant Diaphanta in the bridal bed. When Diaphanta lingers too long, Deflores sets fire to the house and kills the girl in her burning chamber. But by this time, Beatrice Joanna and Deflores have been found out. Confronted by Alsemero, they confess, and Deflores kills both Beatrice and himself.

Channing, Edward Tyrell (1790–1856). American editor and teacher. One of the famous Channings of New England, Edward Tyrell Channing practiced law and helped to found and edit the *North American Review* (1815), one of the most important American review magazines. As Boylston Professor of Rhetoric at Harvard, he had great influence on literature; among those he guided were Emerson, Thoreau, Holmes, Lowell, Edward Everett Hale, and R. H. Dana, Jr. Dana edited Channing's *Lectures* (1856). These reveal that he taught his students to dispense with ornament in style.

Channing, William Ellery (1780–1842). American clergyman. An ordained Congregational minister, he came to reject Calvinism, especially its emphasis on the depravity of mankind. At the ordination of Jared Sparks in 1819, he delivered a sermon that led to the formal emergence of Unitarianism, and he became the apostle of the movement. An advocate of abolition and other social reforms, he was one of the leading propagandists of the era. His ideas are believed to have contributed to the development of Transcendentalism.

cha-no-yu. Japanese tea ceremony. It arose during the Muromachi period (1333–1600) and was brought to its highest refinement by Sen no Rikyū (1521–1591), a Zen priest. There are many schools of tea ceremony, and during the Tokugawa period (1600–1868) it was greatly refined and elaborated. It consists of the drinking of thick green tea served in tea bowls, often of great artistic merit, under an elaborate ceremonial etiquette supervised by a tea master. Simplicity, harmony, and quietude form its basic spirit.

Chanson de Roland. See ROLAND.

chansons de geste (*Fr.* songs of deeds). The medieval French metrical romances celebrating the heroic deeds of historical and legendary knights. The epics of the 11th and early 12th centuries were divided into lays (*Fr.,* *laiss*) or stanzas of irregular length, usually with 10-syllable lines united by assonance or a single rhyme. They glorified the code of chivalric honor in battle and gave little place to women. By the 13th and 14th centuries the role of women and romantic love became more important, regular rhyme schemes were introduced, and the alexandrine (12-syllable line), which later became the standard for French classical verse, became popular.

Most of the *chansons de geste* were written by TROUVÈRES about the PALADINS of Charlemagne or the knights who were his enemies, and arranged in cycles according to the ancestor of each group of heroes. They were sung by JONGLEURS and court minstrels.

One of the earliest and best was the *Chanson de Roland.* Other groups center on Charlemagne's childhood, his wars in Spain, his pilgrimage to Jerusalem. There is an important cycle about *Garin de Monglane* and his descendants, including the chanson *Girard de Viane,* which describes Roland's meeting with OLIVIER. Another is the *Geste de* DOON DE MAYANCE, grouping the traitors and the families at war with Charlemagne.

Chanticleer. See under NUN'S PRIEST'S TALE.

chanties. See SHANTIES.

chant royal. An elaboration of the BALLADE form. The chant royal was developed in medieval France and used for serious and stately themes. It was not introduced in England until the latter part of the 19th century during the revival of interest in French forms. It is a 60-line poem having 5 stanzas of 11 lines and an envoi of 5 lines, each ending with the refrain, as in the ballade.

Chaos. In Greek mythology, the original void. Out of Chaos, according to Hesiod, came Earth, Tartarus, Eros (Love), Erebus (Darkness), and Nyx (Night). The Orphics (see ORPHISM) claimed that Chaos, Night, and Darkness coexisted, and Love came from an egg laid by Night; Eros parthenogenetically produced the first generation of gods.

Chapayev. See Dmitri FURMANOV.

chapbook. Originally one of the books carried about for sale by *chapmen* (tradesmen, *chap* meaning purchase or bargain). Hence, any book of a similar nature, a tract, small collection of ballads, or the like.

Chapelain, Jean (1595–1674). French critic and man of letters. For 20 years he labored at an epic poem, *La Pucelle* (the first part was published in 1656), generally reckoned to be a failure. He was a regular visitor at the Hôtel de Rambouillet, where his advocacy of classical forms in literature and especially of the three unities in drama had considerable influence. Conservative and a founding member of the Académie française, he conceived the plan of the Académie's dictionary, and at Richelieu's request he drafted that institution's censure of Corneille: *Sentiments de l'Académie sur Le Cid* (1638).

Chapelle, Claude Emmanuel Luillier (1626–1686). French poet. An intimate of Boileau, Molière and Racine, Chapelle was coauthor with François de BACHAUMONT of the entertaining *Voyage en Provence et Languedoc* (1656) and an enthusiastic admirer and exponent of the philosophy of Pierre GASSENDI.

Chaplin, Charlie. Real name, **Charles Spencer Chaplin** (1889–   ). English-born motion-picture actor, director, writer, producer, and composer. He is internationally famous as the creator of the inimitable tramp character Charlie. The tramp wears baggy pants, oversized shoes, and a derby hat; he carries a bamboo cane and has an awkward walk. His naïve approach invariably involves him in dangerous situations from which he extricates himself effortlessly by sheer good will. The tramp has enormous trust and affection for all men, and the ludicrous predicaments into which these lead him are resolved as if by divine grace. Chaplin made his screen debut with Mack Sennett's Keystone Company in 1914. In the next few years he appeared in *Tillie's Punctured Romance, The Count, Easy Street,* and *The Cure.* In 1918 he became an independent producer with his own company, First National Films, and in 1923 he was one of the founders of United Artists. Among his most notable films are *The Kid* (1919), *The Gold Rush* (1926), *City Lights* (1931), *Modern Times* (1936), *The Great Dictator* (1940), *Monsieur Verdoux* (1947), and *Limelight* (1952). He has published *My Autobiography* (1964).

Chapman, George (1559?–1634). English poet, scholar, and playwright. Chapman is best remembered today for his translation of the works of Homer, which began with his *Seven Books of the Iliad* in 1598. In 1611 he published the entire *Iliad,* in 1615 the *Odyssey,* and in 1616 *The Whole Works of Homer.* The translation, in rhymed couplets, often departs from and expands upon the original, but it is a notable poetic achievement in its own right. It was praised by Lamb and Coleridge, and most

memorably by Keats in his sonnet *On First Looking into Chapman's Homer.* Among Chapman's poems are *The Shadow of Night* (1594) and *Ovid's Banquet of Sense* (1595). He completed Christopher Marlowe's unfinished *Hero and Leander* (1598), and wrote a number of plays, of which the best known are the tragedies BUSSY D'AMBOIS (c. 1604) and its sequel, *The Revenge of Bussy D'Ambois* (c. 1610). However, some scholars feel his best plays were his romantic comedies, such as *All Fools* (c. 1599) and *May Day* (c. 1602). His other plays include *The Blind Beggar of Alexandria* (1596); *An Humorous Day's Mirth* (1597); *The Gentleman Usher* (c. 1602); *Monsieur D'Olive* (1604); and *Charles, Duke of Byron,* I & II (1607–1608).

Chapman, John. See Johnny APPLESEED.

Chaque Homme dans sa nuit (Each in His Darkness, 1960). A novel by Julian GREEN. The hero Wilfred Ingram, a Catholic, moves in a sordid, carnal world. He is not able to deny his faith, however, but suffers in his knowledge of his own sin. When he is dying, Ingram's face is transformed by an expression of joy and peace: his faith, in spite of sin, has transcended death. Characteristically, Green's vision remains hopeful, although he probes the depths of human evil and misery.

Char, René (1907–   ). French poet of the Midi region. The poems he wrote while associated with the surrealistic movement are collected in *Le Marteau sans maître* (1934). Like his poetry of the Resistance, *Seuls Demeurent* (1945) and *Feuillets d'Hypnos* (1946), included in the English *Hypnos Waking: Poetry and Prose* (1956), Char's later poetry tends to be brief and hermetic. It reveals a close communion with nature and seeks a humanistic exaltation of man.

character writers. A school of English prose writers in the first half of the 17th century. They wrote sketches of men and women—either as individuals or types—in descriptive, analytical, or satirical form as observed in the life of their time. Many of them were influenced by the work of Theophrastus, the Athenian Peripatetic philosopher, who wrote studies of 30 types of personality, such as the Flatterer and the Grumbler, under the title of *Characters.* The best-known English character writers are Joseph HALL, Owen FELLTHAM, Sir Thomas OVERBURY, and John EARLE.

Chardin, Jean (1643–1713). French writer and traveler. He is the author of *Voyage en Perse et aux Indes Orientales (Journey to Persia and to the East Indies,* 1711).

Chardin, Jean Baptiste Siméon (1699–1779). French painter. He is known for his calm still lifes, domestic scenes, and portraits. His paintings of kitchen utensils, game, and fruit are painted with great subtlety and richness of color, animated by bright flashes of light, and unified by reflections of tone. Chardin's sure sense of form and harmonious composition has made his work become a source of study for later artists, notably Edouard MANET and Georges BRAQUE.

Chardonne, Jacques. Pen name of **Jacques Boutelleau** (1884–   ). French novelist. Chardonne, who writes in the classical tradition about the spiritual problems of married life, is best known for his trilogy *Les Destinées sentimentales* (1934–1936).

Other novels include *L'Epithalame* (1921), *Eva* (1930), and *Chimériques* (1948).

Charge of the Light Brigade, The. A poem by Alfred TENNYSON celebrating the famous "death charge of the 600" at Balaclava in the Crimea, Sept. 20, 1854. A British brigade, knowing the folly of their orders, charged the Russian line and was virtually annihilated:

> Theirs not to make reply,
> Theirs not to reason why,
> Theirs but to do and die.
> Into the valley of Death
>   Rode the six hundred.

Chariclea (Charicleia). The lady-love of Theagenes. She appears in the exquisite erotic Greek romance called ETHIOPICA, the story of Theagenes and Chariclea, by Heliodoros.

Charis. According to Homer, one of the Graces and wife of HEPHAESTUS. In later times the name was applied to any of the three Graces (Charites).

Charites, the. See GRACES, THE.

Charlemagne or **Charles the Great** (742–814). Frankish king, crowned Holy Roman Emperor in 800. See his history under CAROLINGIANS. He and the knights said to be his paladins became the center of a number of *chansons de geste,* or medieval epic romances, most having very little basis in fact except for the defeat of the rear guard at RONCESVALLES. Famous versions of these legends include the French *Chanson de* ROLAND and in Italian Pulci's MORGANTE MAGGIORE, Boiardo's ORLANDO INNAMORATO, and Ariosto's ORLANDO FURIOSO.

Charles. In Shakespeare's As You LIKE IT, a wrestler in Duke Frederick's court, whom Orlando challenges and defeats.

Charles I (1600–1649). Stuart king of England (1625–1649) and 2nd son of James I. The first years of his reign were marked by disputes with Parliament over matters of finance, religion, and foreign policy. In 1629 he dissolved Parliament and ruled alone for 11 years, but in 1640 he was compelled to recall Parliament to deal with the problems of the Scottish rebellion and a growing lack of money. From this point on, the conflict between King and Commons became more intense; the former's stubbornness and duplicity and the latter's insistence on its rights and its generally anti-Anglican (Puritan) character led to the CIVIL WAR and Charles's beheading in 1649. In his private personality, Charles was a virtuous, deeply pious, and courageous man, as his deportment at his trial and execution revealed; but his public character was marred by double-dealing, obstinacy, ingratitude to friends, and a lack of political intelligence. Charles is a prominent character in Dumas' *Twenty Years After* (*Vingt Ans Après,* 1845). See EIKON BASILIKÉ; PETITION OF RIGHT.

Charles II (1630–1685). Stuart king of England (1660–1685). He was proclaimed king in Scotland after the death of his father Charles I, but it was only after 11 years of exile, struggle, and disappointment that he assumed the throne of England. This restoration was brought about by compromise and Parliament's invitation, not by force of arms, and throughout Charles's reign, he was obliged to intrigue and maneuver for parliamentary support. A brother of the openly Catholic James, he was anxious to obtain a wider measure of religious tolerance in England and also to strengthen the monarchy and ensure the succession of James. He failed in his first goal and attained only a very partial and transient success with the latter. His reign was disturbed by shifting alliances, several wars, numerous actual and fictitious conspiracies, the Great Plague (1665), and the Fire of London (1666), but was productive of much in literature, science, and architecture. Charles II was an easygoing, intelligent, pleasure-loving, witty man, notorious for the number of his amours and illegitimate offspring. He is an important character in Scott's *Peveril of the Peak* (1823) and *Woodstock* (1826). See Nell GWYNN.

Charles VII (of France). See DAUPHIN.

Charles, Duc d'Orléans (1391–1465). French poet, son of Louis d'Orléans (brother of King Charles VI) and father of King Louis XII. In 1415 he was taken captive to England, where he wrote most of his graceful *ballades* and *rondeaux.* After his ransom in 1460 he established a miniature court at Blois as a patron of the arts, entertaining François Villon and others.

Charles V. Also known as **Charles I** of Spain (1500–1558). Holy Roman Emperor. The son of Philip the Fair of Flanders and Joanna the Mad of Spain, Charles inherited Burgundy and Flanders upon his father's death (1506) and, because of his mother's insanity, acceded to the throne of Spain after the demise of his grandfather, Ferdinand II, in 1516. Spanish resentment against the Flemish-born youth was heightened when he secured election as Holy Roman Emperor in 1519 at great expense and without consulting the *cortes,* or parliaments, of Spain. During Charles's absence in Germany, this resentment erupted in the revolt of the *comuneros,* or townsmen, in which nobles and commoners were at first arrayed against the monarchy but later turned into a class struggle. Other rebellions broke out in Valencia and among the *Moriscos,* or converted Moors, of Spain.

After the suppression of these revolts, Spain enjoyed internal peace and prosperity while Charles devoted himself to foreign affairs. There were several wars with France, whose ruler, FRANCIS I, feared Hapsburg domination of Europe. (See PAVIA.) Challenging Turkish designs in the Mediterranean and in central Europe, Charles captured Tunis in 1535 but failed to take Algiers in 1541. He also attempted to suppress Lutheranism in Germany.

Disillusioned by the frustration of his hopes for religious and political peace in Europe and burdened by debt, Charles decided to give up his many crowns, assigning the imperial title to his brother Ferdinand and his hereditary possessions to his son Philip. In 1556 he retired to the Hieronymite convent of Yuste in Estremadura, where he lived in seclusion until his death.

Charles, Nick. A detective created by Dashiell HAMMETT. He first appeared in *The Thin Man* (1932). A witty and debonair man, he was a striking contrast to Hammett's other famous detective, Sam Spade.

Charles Martel or **Charles the Hammer** (689?–741). Frankish ruler, grandfather of Charlemagne. See CAROLINGIANS. He is famous for his victory over the Moors near Tours in 732.

Charles's Wain, Charles' Wain. An old popular name for the Great Bear. The constellation forms the rough outline of a wheelbarrow or rustic wagon, and the "Charles" stands for Charlemagne. One possible etymology suggests that King Arthur (Lat., *Arturus*) became identified with *Arcturus,* a bright star in Boötes, the constellation which seems to be directing the wagon. Confusion between the legendary cycles of romance connected with Arthur and Charlemagne established the name Charles's Wain in the popular mind.

Charles the Great. See CHARLEMAGNE.

Charleston School. A group of American men of letters. They supported the Southern position in the years before the Civil War. The group, including Paul Hamilton HAYNE, William Gilmore SIMMS, and Henry TIMROD, had its headquarters in Charleston, South Carolina.

Charlot, André Eugène Maurice (1882–1956). British theatrical manager and producer. He was born in Paris and was well known for *Charlot's Revue.*

Charlotte Temple (pub. in England, 1791; U.S., 1794). An early American novel by Susannah Haswell ROWSON. Originally entitled *Charlotte, a Tale of Truth,* it has run through more than 100 editions and is still occasionally read. The heroine is lured from her English home and deserted in New York by a British officer named Montraville, who later repents. Mrs. Rowson wrote a sequel *Charlotte's Daughter,* better known as *Lucy Temple,* published posthumously in 1828.

Charlus, Baron **Palamède [Mémé] de.** An important aristocrat in Marcel Proust's REMEMBRANCE OF THINGS PAST. One of the GUERMANTES, he cultivates his reputation as a virile woman-chaser, but is secretly a homosexual.

Charmian. In Shakespeare's ANTONY AND CLEOPATRA and Dryden's ALL FOR LOVE, a gay, kindhearted attendant on Cleopatra. After the queen's death, she kills herself by applying one of the asps to her own arm.

Charnwood. 1st baron **Godfrey Rathbone Benson** (1864–1945). English biographer. He is best known for his *Abraham Lincoln* (1916).

Charon. In classic myth, the ferryman of the STYX. Charon's toll was a coin, about equal to a penny, placed in the mouth or hand of the dead by the ancient Greeks to pay Charon for ferrying the spirit across the river Styx to ELYSIUM.

Charpentier, Gustave (1860–1956). French composer. He is mainly known for his opera *Louise* (1900), which had a striking success at the time of its premiere. Its realistic libretto deals with the lives and loves of working-class Parisians.

Charpentier, Marc Antoine (1634–1704). Most important French-born composer of the 17th century. Charpentier is known principally for his church music and his oratorios. He was unable to write for the Opéra until after Lully's death, for that composer enjoyed a monopoly of the musical stage, but his one opera, *Medée,* was finally produced in 1693. Because of Lully's quarrel with Molière, Charpentier wrote the elaborate musical score for Molière's last play, *Le Malade Imaginaire.*

Charrière, Isabelle de. See ZÉLIDE.

Charterhouse of Parma, The (La Chartreuse de Parme; 1839). An historical novel by STENDHAL. In essence the tale is a chronicle of the adventures of its young hero, Fabrizio del Dongo. Set in the post-Napoleonic era, this remarkable analysis of ROMANTICISM leads us through the battle of Waterloo, life and intrigue in a small Italian court, romantic love, imprisonment, the priesthood, and finally terminates in a Carthusian monastery.

Charteris, Leslie (1907–   ). English novelist. The son of a Chinese surgeon and an Englishwoman, he was originally named Leslie Charles Bowyer Lin. A naturalized American citizen, Charteris is known for his very popular stories about a gentleman burglar nicknamed THE SAINT.

Chartier, Alain (c. 1390–c. 1435). French poet, prose writer, and diplomat under Charles VII. In his first poem, the *Livre des quatre dames.* (1415), four ladies lament the death of their lovers in the French defeat by Henry V at Agincourt. He described the confused condition of France in the years that followed in his best-known prose work, the *Quadrilogue Invectif* (1422). His prose style, modeled on that of the Latin orators, marked the revival of classicism in French literary style. The title and theme of his popular poem *La Belle Dame sans merci* (1424) were used by John KEATS. Other works include the poem *Bréviaire des nobles* (c. 1424) and the prose *Traité de l'espérance* (c. 1428).

Chartier, Emile. See ALAIN.

Chartism (1838–1849). The political movement and program of the group of English reformers known as Chartists. Their main target of criticism was the Reform Bill of 1832, which had failed to extend the vote to the workingman. Their principal demands, published in "the People's Charter," were for universal manhood suffrage and for the annual election of parliament, abolition of property qualifications and payment to its members, vote by ballot, and equal representation in electoral districts. Members of the group were mostly industrial workers led by radical intellectuals. Chartism disappeared from the political scene after 1849, but all the Chartists' aims, with the exception of annual parliaments, were ultimately realized.

The Chartist Clergyman. Charles KINGSLEY, so called because of his sympathy with the Chartists and other working-class movements.

Charybdis. See SCYLLA AND CHARYBDIS.

Chase, James Hadley. Pen name of **René Raymond** (1906–   ). English author of crime and adventure fiction. His most widely read novel was *No Orchids for Miss Blandish* (1939).

Chase, Mary C[oyle] (1907–   ). American playwright. She is best known for her Pulitzer Prize-winning play HARVEY. Her earlier plays had achieved little success, but two later plays were well received: *Mrs. McThing* (1952) and *Bernardine* (1952). *Midgie Purvis* was produced on Broadway in 1961.

Chase, Mary Ellen (1887–   ). American novelist and teacher. Miss Chase is noted for her regional novels dealing with the Maine seacoast, her native setting. Of these, *Mary Peters* (1934) and *Silas Crockett* (1935) are perhaps her best. The latter, chronicling the fortunes of a Yankee family through four generations, has as its theme the hardships inflicted on the old clipper sailors by the introduction of steamships. Other novels are *The Plum Tree* (1949) and *The Edge of Darkness* (1957). For many years professor of English literature at Smith College, Miss Chase has also written stories for young people, including Mary Christmas (1926) and *Gay Highway* (1933), and several volumes of nonfiction, most notably *The Golden Asse; and Other Essays* (1929), *This England* (1936), and *Psalms for the Common Reader* (1962). Her autobiography, *A Goodly Heritage* (1932), and its sequel, *A Goodly Fellowship* (1939), deal with her experiences as a teacher.

Chase, Stuart (1888–   ). American economist and semanticist. Under the influence of Henry George, Chase became interested in social problems, especially those relating to conservation, consumer education, semantics, and labor. Among his books are *The Tragedy of Waste* (1925), *Your Money's Worth* (in collaboration with F. L. Schlink, 1927), *A New Deal* (1932), *The Tyranny of Words* (1938), and *Live and Let Live* (1960).

Chastelard (1865). A tragedy by Algernon Charles SWINBURNE, the first of a trilogy on Mary Queen of Scots. It is based on the life of Pierre de Boscosel de Chastelard, a French poet who was executed for his love for Mary. The other dramas in the trilogy are *Bothwell* and *Mary Stuart*.

Chastellain, Georges. See RHÉTORIQUEURS, LES GRANDS.

Chateaubriand, Vicomte **François René de** (1768–1848). French writer, forerunner of the romantic movement. The work of Chateaubriand is characterized by egotistical melancholy, impassioned emotion, and a love of untamed nature. His interest in Roman Catholicism and the Middle Ages, in exotic countries and primitive tribes, foreshadows typically romantic concerns (see ROMANTICISM). Chateaubriand is famous for his fictional portrayal of America. His novels ATALA, RENÉ, and LES NATCHEZ all deal with North America and the North American Indians. *Les Martyrs* (1809) and *L'Itinéraire de Paris à Jérusalem et de Jérusalem à Paris* (1811) are concerned with Greece, the Holy Land, and the Near East. Other works include LE GÉNIE DU CHRISTIANISME and MÉMOIRES D'OUTRE-TOMBE. Chateaubriand's political career was a stormy one. He favored the Bourbon monarchy and served it as ambassador to England, Italy, and Germany, and as minister of foreign affairs.

Châtelet, Marquise **du. Gabrielle Emilie Le Tonnelier de Breteuil** (1706–1749). French mathematician and   physicist. Mistress of VOLTAIRE, she lived with him at Montjeu and at her château at Cirey (in Lorraine). The liaison lasted 14 years until her death. The marquise had an intense interest in the theories of Leibniz and Newton and propagated the latter's ideas in France. She wrote *Traité sur le bonheur* (1749) and *Traduction des principes de Newton* (1756). See EMILIE.

Chats-Fourrés. See FURRY LAWCATS.

Chatterley, Lady. See LADY CHATTERLEY'S LOVER.

Chatterton, Thomas (1752–1770). English poet. His literary fabrications are distinguished by their poetic genius. While still a mere boy, living in Bristol, he wrote a number of poems couched in elaborately archaic spelling that he declared to be the work of one Thomas Rowley, a nonexistent monk, poet, and

antiquarian of the 15th century. In this way, Chatterton evolved a romance of Bristol centering around William Canynges, a merchant who became lord mayor. Notable poems in this series are: *Bristowe Tragedie: or, the Dethe of Syr Charles Bawdin* (1772) and *An Excelente Balade of Charitie* (1777). His deception was successful for awhile, although it was exposed in 1777–1778 by Thomas Tyrwhitt and Thomas Warton. Chatterton also wrote *Apostate Will* (1764), a satire, and *The Revenge* (1770), a successful burlesque opera. In despair at his poverty, after moving to London, he killed himself at the age of 17 by taking poison. A volume of his collected works was published in 1803. Chatterton was a favorite figure of the English Romantic poets, becoming for them the prototype of the neglected genius. See MARVELLOUS BOY; BRISTOL BOY, THE.

Chaucer, Geoffrey (c. 1343–1400). English poet and public servant, by far the most important writer of Middle English and considered one of the finest poets in literature. His family had been in the royal service, and in 1357 Chaucer is known to have been already in the service of the wife of Prince Lionel, and to have met John of Gaunt, another of the King's sons, who became one of his most important patrons. He joined the English army's invasion of France in 1359, was captured, and was ransomed by King Edward III in 1360. His activities for the next six years remain unknown: he may have been with Lionel in Ireland, he may have attended law school, he may already have entered the King's service. About 1366 he married Philippa, one of the Queen's

A page from William Morris'
Kelmscott Chaucer (1896).

attendants and the sister of Katherine Swynford, later John of Gaunt's mistress, then wife, Philippa apparently gave him two sons, "little Lewis" (see *Treatise on the* ASTROLABE) and Thomas, highly successful in public service in the 15th century. There may have been one daughter, or perhaps two, but the evidence is uncertain.

In 1367 Chaucer was given a life pension by the King, and apparently remained in the royal service thereafter, going abroad on a number of more or less secret diplomatic missions between 1368 and 1378, mostly to France. The two trips into Italy (1372–1373) and 1378) proved extremely important in his literary development because of his discovery of the works of Dante, Boccaccio, and Petrarch, which greatly influenced his own; it is probable that he read all their major works except Boccaccio's *Decameron*, and he knew many of those tales through Petrarch and French translations.

In 1374 he was given a house of his own and made Controller of Customs on wools, skins, and hides; in 1382 he was also given control of Petty Custom on wines and other goods. About 1385 he established his residence in Kent, where he was elected justice of the peace and briefly (1386) a member of Parliament. After his wife died in 1387, his financial fortunes worsened, possibly through political retaliation for his opposition to the Gloucester cause in the years of Richard II's minority following Edward's death in 1377. At any rate, soon after Richard came of age, he appointed Chaucer Clerk of the King's Works (1389), in charge of the maintenance and repair of public buildings, parks, bridges, etc. Chaucer resigned this position in 1391, and was appointed deputy forester of a royal forest in Somerset. He retained his residence at Kent and his activities in London, however. In 1394 Richard awarded him another life pension, Chaucer having resigned the first one in 1388. He seems to have been in attendance (1395–1396) on Henry Bolingbroke, John of Gaunt's son, who deposed Richard in 1399, and as Henry IV increased Chaucer's annuity.

Chaucer's early work is heavily influenced by the French tradition of the poetry of love. It includes the BOOK OF THE DUCHESS and the *Romaunt of the Rose* (probably c. 1370; a translation, of which only the beginning is now extant, of the French ROMANCE OF THE ROSE), both in octosyllabic couplets. *Saint Cecilia*, later used as the SECOND NUN'S TALE, was probably written about 1373, most of the tragedies incorporated into the MONK'S TALE about 1374.

The HOUSE OF FAME and ANELIDA AND ARCITE, written about six years later, are considered transitional works, for they begin to show the influence of Italian literature, although still essentially in the French tradition. Soon afterward Chaucer translated as *Boece* the CONSOLATION OF PHILOSOPHY by Boethius. About the same period he wrote the PARLIAMENT OF FOWLS and within a few years *Palamon and Arcite*, later adapted as the KNIGHT'S TALE, as well as TROILUS AND CRISEYDE and the LEGEND OF GOOD WOMEN. This is called his period of Italian influence.

His period of maturity is considered to begin in 1387 with the writing of the *General Prologue* to the unfinished CANTERBURY TALES. He certainly worked on them through 1394, and probably until his death. In addition, he revised some of his earlier work and

wrote the *Treatise on the Astrolabe*. There are also 16 short poems, written at various periods in his career in different stanzaic forms, and 5 poems of doubtful authorship.

In the early 1370's Chaucer began to abandon the octosyllabic couplets of his early works—although he used the form once more in the *House of Fame*—largely in favor of RHYME ROYAL, although he also tried eight- and nine-line stanza forms. In the mid-1380's he first began to use the decasyllabic couplet, probably in *Palamon and Arcite* (although it was possibly first written in stanzaic form and then adapted for the *Knight's Tale*) and certainly in the *Legend of Good Women*. This is the first known English use of the decasyllabic couplet, which Chaucer then used for most of the *Canterbury Tales*, and which evolved into the heroic couplet.

Chaucerian roundel. A variation of the French RONDEL form, first written by Chaucer. The Chaucerian roundel is characterized by the repetition of the first as a refrain at the end of the second and third stanzas. It has 10 lines and its rhyme scheme is: A-b-b, a-b-A, a-b-b-A (A being the refrain).

Chauchat, Clavdia. In Thomas Mann's novel THE MAGIC MOUNTAIN, a Russian tubercular patient with whom Hans CASTORP falls in love and whose presence is a major cause of his remaining at Haus Berghof. Her fingernail-biting, careless dress, and door-slamming reflect the lax and decadent way of life she represents.

Chauncey, Charles (1705–1787). American clergyman. He is best known for his opposition to the revivals and conversions of the "GREAT AWAKENING," which he attacked in such works as *Seasonable Thoughts on the State of Religion* (1743), a reply to Jonathan Edwards' *Some Thoughts Concerning the Present Revival of Religion* (1742). Chauncey's *Salvation of All Men*, published anonymously in 1782, marked the beginning of Universalism in New England. An ardent patriot before and during the Revolution, he also wrote a number of political tracts.

Chauntecleer. See under NUN'S PRIEST'S TALE

chauvinism. Blind and pugnacious patriotism of an exaggerated kind; unreasoning jingoism. Nicholas Chauvin, a soldier of the French Republic and Empire, was madly devoted to Napoleon and his cause. He was introduced as a type of exaggerated bellicose patriotism into a number of plays, including Scribe's *Le Soldat laboureur*, Cogniard's *La Cocarde tricolore*, Bayard and Dumanoir's *Les Aides de camps*, and Charet's *Conscrit Chauvin*. The term *chauvinism* spread quickly into a great number of languages.

Chávez, Carlos (1899–). Outstanding Mexican composer and conductor of the century. He was director of the National Conservatory in Mexico City, and conductor of the Orquesta Sinfónica de México from 1928 to 1952. His music, principally orchestral, makes considerable use of elements from Mexican Indian folk music.

Cheapside. A London street running east from St. Paul's Churchyard. Formerly it was noted for its shops. Before the Great Fire of 1666, it was an open square, called The Cheaps, where markets and fairs were held.

Cheeryble brothers. In Charles Dickens' novel NICHOLAS NICKLEBY, two brothers, Ned and Charles.

Wealthy, self-made London merchants, they are ever ready to help those struggling against the buffets of fortune.

Cheever, John (1912–   ). American short-story writer and novelist. Subtle, ironic attacks on suburbia characterize most of Cheever's writing. His stories, many of which originally appeared in *The New Yorker*, have been collected in such books as *The Enormous Radio and Other Stories* (1953), *The Housebreaker of Shady Hill and Other Stories* (1958), and *Some People, Places and Things That Will Not Appear in My Next Novel* (1961). *The Wapshot Chronicle* (1957) was a best-selling novel. Its sequel *The Wapshot Scandal* appeared in 1964.

Cheka. In early Soviet Russian history, the secret police body established in 1917 to guard against counterrevolutionary activity. The name is an abbreviation for "Extraordinary Commission for the Combat of Counterrevolution, Sabotage and Breach of Duty by Officials." In 1922 it was replaced by the GPU, or Gay-Pay-Oo (State Political Administration), which shortly thereafter became the OGPU (United State Political Administration). In 1934 secret policy duties were taken over by the NKVD (People's Commissariat of Internal Affairs). In 1946 this body was changed to the MVD (Ministry of Internal Affairs). After 1946, the Soviet security service was placed in the hands of the KGB (Committee of State Security), which employed less terror than its predecessors.

Chekhov, Anton Pavlovich (1860–1904). Russian short-story writer and playwright. Noted for his masterful short stories and lyrical dramas, Chekhov was born in Taganrog in the south of Russia, the third of six children. He was the son of a merchant and the grandson of an ex-serf who had purchased his freedom. Chekhov attended secondary school in Taganrog, and in 1879 enrolled in the School of Medicine at the University of Moscow. He graduated in 1884. While at the university, Chekhov had to earn money to help support the large family. Following the example of his older brother, Aleksandr, he began contributing short sketches, stories, and jokes to humorous journals and papers. Many of these early stories were published under such pen names as Antosha Chekhonte, Anton Ch., and The Doctor Without Patients. *Skazki Mel'pomeny* (*Tales of Melpomene*, 1884), was the first volume of Chekhov's stories published. Other early collections of tales were *Piostrye rasskazy* (*Motley Tales*, 1886) and *V sumerkakh* (*In the Twilight*, 1887).

Chekhov's work attracted the attention of the writer Dmitri Grigorovich, who encouraged the young author to continue writing and introduced him to Alexei Suvorin, publisher of *Novoye Vremya*, a leading St. Petersburg daily. The more secure financial position offered by this connection enabled Chekhov to pay more attention to improving the quality of his stories. The number of stories written each year fell steadily, but the artistic quality of the work improved, and Chekhov's reputation grew.

In 1890, Chekhov made a trip to the prison island of Sakhalin in the Far East. His observations and experiences were related in *Ostrovo sakhalina* (*Sakhalin Island,* 1893). The trip was made despite Chekhov's weakened condition from the tuberculosis that had appeared while he was still a student at the university. The whole of Chekhov's short life was a constant struggle against the steady advance of the disease. After his return to Russia, Chekhov took part in relief work during the 1892 famine. He then bought a small estate at Melikhovo, not far from Moscow, and moved there with his family. While living at Melikhovo, Chekhov created some of his best-known works, including the tales WARD No. 6, *Uchitel' slovestnosti* (*The Teacher of Literature,* 1894), MY LIFE, and PEASANTS. During this period he also produced two of his major plays, THE SEA GULL and UNCLE VANYA. *The Sea Gull* was first performed in St. Petersburg in 1896. It was so badly received that Chekhov vowed to give up playwriting. Two years later, however, the drama was put on with great success by the newly formed Moscow Art Theatre. Chekhov's play was so important in establishing the reputation of the new repertory theater that the directors made a gull the company's emblem.

His failing health forced Chekhov to move in 1898 to the milder southern climate of Yalta in the Crimea. Here he often met with the writers Maksim Gorki and Count Leo Tolstoi. From this time until the end of his life, Chekhov's creative activity was concerned mainly with drama. The few major stories of these later years were *Dama s sobachkoi* (*The Lady with the Dog,* 1898), IN THE RAVINE, *Arkhiyerei* (*The Bishop,* 1902), and *Nevesta* (*Betrothed,* 1903).

In 1901, Chekhov married Olga Knipper, a Moscow Art Theatre actress. The couple lived apart much of the time, because Chekhov's ill health forced him to remain in the warmer climate at Yalta. During this period Chekhov wrote for the Art Theatre his two famous plays, THE CHERRY ORCHARD and THE THREE SISTERS.

Chekhov's failing health induced his doctors to send him to the health resort at Badenweiler, Germany, in 1904. He died there in July.

The main theme of Chekhov's prose fiction is life's pathos, caused by the inability of human beings to respond to or even to communicate with one another and the pervading mood of sadness and hopelessness arising from this situation. This characteristic theme is clearly seen in A DREARY STORY, which is usually regarded as the first work of Chekhov's mature period, that is, after his comic and satirical stories. Chekhov was equally adept at creating a lyrical atmosphere, engendered by man's response to nature and untouched by the pain of relations as they exist between people. His most successful story of this type is *Step'* (*The Steppe,* 1888), describing a long trip across the plains as experienced by a young boy on his way to school in a distant town.

Chekhov is famed as a master of the short story. Even though some of his best prose pieces are almost novel-length, these stories, as well as his better-known short works, achieve their effect with the minimum of artistic means. All of his best work is an illustration of Chekhov's dictum: "Conciseness is the sister of talent."

Chekhov's plays deal with the passing of the vitality of the Russian landed gentry. His characters, helpless before the changes taking place in 19th-century Russia, take refuge in elaborate, improbable dreams of renewed prosperity. His plots are simple, mere outlines for the creation of atmosphere and delineation of character at which he excels. The result is a group of plays, combining comedy, pathos, anti-climax, and digression in a wholly natural effect that seems to belie the careful workmanship of the dramatist. *Ivanov* (1887) and the four major plays already mentioned are among the finest in the modern repertory. His shorter plays include *Medved'* (*The Bear*, 1888), *Tragik ponevole* (*A Tragedian in Spite of Himself*, 1889), *Svadba* (*The Wedding*, 1889), *Na bolshoi doroge* (*On the High Road*, 1884), *Zhubilei* (*The Jubilee*, 1891), *Predlozheniye* (*The Proposal*, 1888), and *Lebedinaya pesnya* (1887).

Chemins de la liberté, Les. See ROADS TO FREEDOM, THE.

Chénier, André Marie de (1762–1794). French poet, often considered the greatest of 18th-century France. His *Bucoliques* and, to a lesser extent, his *Elégies* reflect his early love and remarkable understanding of Greek antiquity. At first sympathetic with the French Revolution, he was later horrified at the excesses of the Jacobins and wrote denunciatory pamphlets. He was arrested by order of Robespierre, whom he had attacked. During his imprisonment and before he was guillotined, he wrote, on bits of smuggled paper, his satiric and bitter *Iambes* against his persecutors, and his last, most famous ode *La Jeune captive*, inspired by a fellow victim. His philosophical poetry (e.g., *L'Invention*) gives poetic expression to the scientific ideas of his age. Most of his works were published posthumously in 1819. His life inspired Giordano's opera *Andrea Chénier* (1896).

Chernyshevski, Nikolai Gavrilovich (1828–1889). Russian critic and editor. For three years after graduation from the university at St. Petersburg, Chernyshevski was a schoolteacher in his native Saratov. In 1853 he returned to St. Petersburg and began his journalistic career on the *Sovremennik* (*The Contemporary*), which he turned into the period's leading radical publication. Chernyshevski became the chief spokesman for the radical wing in literature; he and his younger colleague Dobrolyubov in their critical writings gave further emphasis to the social aspect of literature, which the renowned critic BELINSKI had brought to light. Chernyshevski supplied an example of the literature he praised in his didactic novel, *Chto Delat'*? (*What Is To Be Done?*; 1863). In the novel, he expounded his ideas of how the true revolutionary should think and behave. Though the work is more of an ideological tract than a novel, it suited the mood of the times and attained wide popularity. It is now regarded in the Soviet Union as a revolutionary classic. Chernyshevski was arrested in 1862 for revolutionary activities; he was sentenced to 7 years at hard labor with 20 years of exile in Siberia. In 1883, he was permitted to leave Siberia because of his health; he returned to Russia and lived out his life in Saratov.

Cherry Orchard, The (*Vishnovyi sad*; 1904). A play by Anton CHEKHOV. Its four acts portray the declining fortunes of the Ranevskis, a landowning family, who are about to lose their estate and beloved cherry orchard. Poor management, neglect, and impracticality have brought the family to the point of bankruptcy, but no one is able to act to head off the disaster. The suggestion of the practical businessman Lopakhin that the family chop down the orchard and build houses on the land is met with horror. For the Ranevskis, the orchard represents the pleasant past, before the mysterious forces of the changing times threatened their idyllic existence. The estate is finally sold from under the hapless family. Lopakhin buys the land and proceeds to carry out his plan to destroy the orchard and erect houses. As the family sadly prepares to depart, the sound of an ax chopping down a cherry tree is heard off stage.

The play, regarded as one of Chekhov's finest dramatic works, is both a penetrating study of the changing way of life in Russia at the end of the 19th century and a vivid depiction of what the change means to the people involved. The stage portraits of the Ranevskis, with their inability to do anything to save themselves, and of Lopakhin, the representative of a new rising class in society, are masterpieces of dramatic creation.

Cherubim, Don. See BACHELIER DE SALAMANQUE, LE.

Cherubini, [Mario] Luigi [Carlo Zenobio Salvatore] (1760–1842). Italian composer. He settled in Paris in 1788. His principal works are his operas, of which he wrote 24. *Medée* (1787) has recently been revived with great success. He was the favorite composer of Napoleon, and was much admired by Beethoven.

Cheshire cat. In Lewis Carroll's ALICE'S ADVENTURES IN WONDERLAND, a creature that has the ability to vanish at will, its grin being the last thing to go.

Chesnutt, Charles W[addell] (1858–1932). American novelist. Chesnutt, who is sometimes called the first Negro novelist, was a teacher, newspaperman, and lawyer. His first story, *The Goophered Grapevine*, appeared in the *Atlantic* in 1887. His first book, *The Conjure Woman* (1899), centered about Uncle Julius McAdoo, a character not unlike Uncle Remus. His later books dealt with race prejudice: *The Wife of His Youth and Other Stories of the Color Line* (1899), *The House Behind the Cedars* (1900), *The Colonel's Dream* (1905). In 1928, Chesnutt received the Spingarn gold medal for his pioneer work in depicting the struggles of the American Negro.

Chester, George Randolph. See GET-RICH-QUICK WALLINGFORD.

Chester Cycle. A series of 24 medieval English MYSTERY PLAYS performed by the guilds of Chester at Whitsuntide (13th to 16th centuries).

Chesterfield, 4th earl of. Philip Dormer Stanhope (1694–1773). Statesman and man of letters. A friend of Alexander Pope and an important patron of letters, Lord Chesterfield was unsuccessful in his belated attempt to patronize Samuel Johnson's DICTIONARY OF THE ENGLISH LANGUAGE after it had been completed. Johnson's rebuke is famous:

Is not a patron, My Lord, one who looks with unconcern on a Man struggling in the water and when he has reached ground encumbers him with help?

Johnson's comment on Chesterfield's *Letters* to his natural son Philip Stanhope is equally well known: "They teach the morals of a whore, and the manners of a dancing master." The judgment is too severe. Written between 1737 and 1768, Lord Chesterfield's *Letters to his Son* (1774) form one of the classic portraits of an ideal 18th-century gentleman.

Chesterton, G[ilbert] K[eith] (1874–1936). English journalist, essayist, novelist, and poet; author of biography, history, literary criticism, and polemical works. Like his friend, Hilaire BELLOC, he was a propagandist of his Catholicism and his conservative political views (the two were referred to as Chester-belloc). Chesterton became a Catholic in 1922, but had always been a traditionalist, admiring the Victorians, romanticizing the Middle Ages, and attacking H. G. Wells and Bernard Shaw. He is best remembered for his essays, such as *On running after one's hat* (1908), which are gay and witty, and for such poems as *Lepanto* (1911), which are full of gusto. Sometimes he conveyed his serious ideas in fantastic novels, as in THE NAPOLEON OF NOTTING HILL, THE MAN WHO WAS THURSDAY, and a series of detective novels, beginning with *The Innocence of Father Brown* (1911), in which the priest Father Brown is sleuth. Chesterton wrote a good history of *The Victorian Age in Literature* (1913). Among his polemical works are *Heretics* (1905), *Orthodoxy* (1908), *What's Wrong with the World?* (1910), and *The Everlasting Man* (1925), an outline of history.

Chettle, Henry (c. 1560–?1607). English dramatist. The only extant play solely his work is *The Tragedy of Hoffman* (1602). He also collaborated with John Day, Thomas Dekker, and Anthony Munday.

Chevalier à la mode, Le (1687). A comedy of manners by Florent DANCOURT. It recounts the exploits of an impudent and imprudent chevalier who almost succeeds in his simultaneous courtship of two rich widows and the niece of one of them. The play gives a lighthearted but not inaccurate picture of the French society of Dancourt's day.

Chevallier, Gabriel (1895–   ). French novelist whose *Clochemerle* (1934) is a grotesquely comic caricature of village life. His other novels include *Sainte-Colline* (1937) and *The Euffe Inheritance* (1945).

Chevy Chase. One of the oldest ballads in English. There is some evidence that it may have grown out of the Battle of Otterborne, and a Scottish version exists earlier than 1549. It is included in Percy's *Reliques* (1765).

Cheyney, Peter (1896–1951). English writer of tough, adventurous crime fiction. He wrote *Dames Don't Care* (1937) and numerous other novels.

Chiabrera, Gabriello (1552–1638). Italian lyric poet and satirist. He is noted for his numerous *canzonette;* 30 satirical *Sermoni;* the pastoral poem *Alcippo* (1604); and odes in imitation of Horace, Pindar, and Anacreon. Wordsworth admired him greatly and translated several of his epitaphs.

Chiang Kai-shek (1886–   ). Chinese statesman and general. An early follower of SUN YAT-SEN, he studied in Russia and on Sun's death in 1925 became leader of the Nationalist movement. In 1927 he broke with the Russian communists in China. After several years of civil war between the communists and the Nationalists, a truce was reached in 1936 so that a united China led by Chiang might face the threat of Japanese aggression. Upon the outbreak of war with Japan in 1937, Chiang became commander of China's forces and was named provisional president in 1943. Elected president in 1948, he was forced to abandon the mainland of China in the face of communist military successes and in 1949 settled on the island of Taiwan (Formosa), which

he maintained, with extensive American aid, as the last stronghold of the republic of China. He was reelected president in 1954 and in 1960.

Chiang Mei-ling (1898–   ). American-educated, Christian Chinese wife of CHIANG KAI-SHEK. She became known throughout the world for her activities in the administration of the national affairs of her country, for her influence on the policies of her husband, and for her importation of Western ideas and methods into China. *China Fights for Her Life* (1938), *China in Peace and War* (1940), and *This Is Our China* (1940) are books by Mme. Chiang written in English.

Chicago Group or **Chicago Renaissance.** A group of American writers. From about 1912 to about 1925, Chicago seemed well on its way to becoming the literary capital of the U.S. Although many of the writers dealt with Middle Western subjects, the literary activity also had a cosmopolitan scope, especially through such literary magazines as Harriet Monroe's POETRY: A MAGAZINE OF VERSE and Margaret Anderson's *Little Review*. The term is variously used to include such writers as H. B. FULLER, Theodore DREISER, Ben HECHT, Sherwood ANDERSON, Edgar Lee MASTERS, and Carl SANDBURG.

Chicanous. See CATCHPOLES.

Chichen-Itza. An ancient city of Yucatán, Mexico, with well-preserved ruins of the Mayan civilization.

Chichikov, Pavel Ivanovich. The central character of Nikolai Gogol's DEAD SOULS. Plump and prosperous-looking, appearing as respectable as he claims to be, Chichikov is actually an unctuous swindler. A totally mediocre man, whose only abilities are a knowledge of social form and a talent for flattery, he almost succeeds in his dishonest scheme because he allows the people he is swindling to believe they are swindling him.

Ch'ien-lung. Name of Chinese era (1736–1795). A period of great literary and academic ferment.

Chikamatsu Monzaemon (1653–1725). Japanese dramatist. Composer of puppet plays (*joruri*) and *kabuki* drama. He is famous for both his historical spectacles (*jidaimono*) and domestic plays (*sewamono*) many of which are still performed today. Cf. *Major plays of Chikamatsu* (1961) by Donald Keene.

Child, Francis James (1825–1896). American philologist. Professor of Middle English at Harvard, he was an authority on Chaucer and his contemporaries. For many years Child occupied himself with the collection in eight volumes of *English and Scottish Popular Ballads* (1857–1858). It was revised from 1883 to 1898, and issued in 10 volumes. This most authoritative work in its field printed 305 distinct English and Scottish ballads, as many as possible from manuscript sources, with varying versions and exhaustive critical comment and notes.

Childe. A medieval title of honor. In times of chivalry, noble youths who were on probation as candidates for knighthood were called *infants, valets, damoysels, bacheliers,* and *childe.*

Childe Harold's Pilgrimage (Cantos I & II published 1812; Canto III, 1816; Canto IV, 1818). A long narrative poem in Spenserian stanzas by Lord BYRON. The romantically melancholy hero, Childe Harold, disillusioned with a life devoted to the pursuit of pleasure, embarks on a solitary pilgrimage through Portugal, Spain, the Ionian Islands, Albania, Greece, Belgium, the Rhine valley, the Alps, and the Jura. The poet evokes the events and people associated with each place: Rousseau and Julie, Napoleon, the battles of Waterloo and Spain, the bondage of Greece. In the fourth canto Byron drops the device of the hero to speak directly to the reader, describing the great men and historical associations of the Italian cities. The poem satisfied the popular craving for descriptive travel literature of Byron's day and did much to establish the poet's fame.

Childermass, The. See HUMAN AGE, THE.

Childe Rowland (sometimes spelled **Roland**). Younger brother of "the fair Burd Ellen" in the old Scottish ballad. Guided by the enchanter Merlin, he undertakes to bring back his sister from Elfland, whither the fairies have carried her, and succeeds in his perilous exploit. See BURD ELLEN.

Childers, Erskine (1870–1922). Anglo-Irish writer, soldier, and politician. He is best known for his novel *The Riddle of the Sands* (1900), which describes an imaginary German plot to invade Britain. He devoted himself to Irish republicanism and was captured and executed in its cause.

Childhood (Detstvo; 1913–1914). 1 volume of an autobiographical trilogy by Maksim GORKI. The other two volumes are *In the World* (*V lyudakh;* 1916) and *My Universities* (*Moi universitety;* 1923). Of the three volumes, *Childhood* is the richest in insight and incident, chiefly because of the memorable portrait in it of Gorki's grandmother, Akulina Ivanovna Kashirina.

Childhood, Boyhood, Youth (Detstvo, Otrochestvo, Yunost'; 1852, 1854, 1857). An autobiographical trilogy by Count Leo TOLSTOI. *Childhood* was the first of Tolstoi's works to receive wide attention. The descriptions of life on a provincial estate are among the best depictions of nature in Russian literature.

Children of Adam (1860–1867). A group of poems in Walt Whitman's LEAVES OF GRASS. The poems praise physical love and procreation; Whitman claims that Adam's children have lost the Garden of Eden through the degradation of their senses. Body and soul are not separate, but one. "Lusty, phallic," Whitman is the unashamed "chanter of Adamic songs."

Children of Heracles, The (Heracleidae; 427? B.C.) A tragedy by EURIPIDES. Eurystheus, the cruel king of Argos who had forced HERACLES to perform the 12 labors, has continued to persecute the hero's children after his death. Led by old Iolaus, Heracles' trusted friend, they win the protection of Demophon, king of Athens. Iolaus, made young again for one day, fights with the Athenians against the Argives. Eurystheus is captured and put to death.

Written at the height of the Peloponnesian War, the play praises Athens as a champion of freedom and points out that Sparta, now her enemy, should be grateful to the city that had defended the children of Heracles, from whom the Spartans claimed descent.

Children of the Ghetto (1892). A novel by Israel ZANGWILL. It consists of a number of episodes in the lives of the poor, striving people in London's Jewish community. Zangwill paints vivid portraits of his characters.

Children of the Soil (1894). A novel by H. SIENKIEWICZ. It gives a vivid and comprehensive picture of Polish life.

Children's Hour, The (1860). A poem by Henry Wadsworth LONGFELLOW. It is devoted to his three daughters, whose mother was Mary Potter, the poet's first wife.

Childs, Marquis W[illiam] (1903–). American journalist and writer. Childs writes a syndicated political column and is the author of a number of books of nonfiction, including *Sweden: The Middle Way* (1936) and *Eisenhower, Captive Hero* (1958). *The Cabin* (1944) and *The Peacemakers* (1962) are novels.

Child's Garden of Verses, A (1885). A small collection of verses by Robert Louis STEVENSON. Written expressly for children and from a child's point of view, they have nevertheless delighted adults as much as children since they were written. Among the favorite titles are *My Shadow* and *The Lamplighter*.

Chillingsworth, William (1602–1644). English writer. Although he was at one time a Roman Catholic, he is best known for his *Religion of the Protestants a Safe Way to Salvation* (1638).

Chillingworth, Roger. The vengeful husband of Hester Prynne in Hawthorne's THE SCARLET LETTER.

Chillon. See PRISONER OF CHILLON, THE.

Chimaera (Chimaira). One of the monstrous offspring of TYPHON and ECHIDNA. It is generally represented as having the head of a lion, the body of a goat, and the tail of a serpent. It was killed by BELLEROPHON, mounted (in most versions) on the winged horse Pegasus.

Ch'in. The first Chinese empire (221–207 B.C.). It saw the country unified for the first time. A canal system and the Great Wall were constructed, and the various writing styles reduced to one. The thought of the LEGALIST SCHOOL prevailed during this brief but important dynasty.

Chinatown. The Chinese quarter of a city, especially of New York or San Francisco in the U.S. Until recently, the Chinatowns in these two cities were famous for their gambling dens, vice, and opium trade. These illegal activities were under the control of the TONGS, and were the cause of murderous tong wars and feuds. Once the power of the tongs was broken, Chinatowns began a new prosperity in the tourist trade. As a result of the trade embargo on Communist Chinese goods, most souvenirs now for sale in Chinatowns are of Japanese origin. The Chinese quarter of London is called Limehouse.

Chinese literature. Two varying literary streams may be found in the first historical records (11th-3d centuries B.C.) left by the Chinese: the shamanistic, represented by the divination inscriptions on oracle bones used in scapularmancy, and the official, found in the inscriptions on bronzes, which generally contain information concerning the king's relationships with his ministers. Both of these types of inscriptions are written in an archaic form of writing, whose stylization attests to a long period of development. Among ancient texts, the BOOK OF DOCUMENTS, which represents the official tradition, contains speeches and proclamations of a historical nature, and the ELEGIES OF CH'U, although of dubious authenticity, contains material relating to shamanism, as does the first poetry collection, the BOOK OF ODES. After the eighth century B.C. a period of incessant warfare among rival feudal principalities disrupted the nation and there arose from the sixth century on a variety of philosophical systems that sought to propound solutions to the political and ethical problems of the times. Confucius, an unsuccessful would-be advisor to the government of his state, spread his moral and political teachings; they were later elaborated upon by his disciples and further developed by Mencius and other philosophers. The passive, yielding doctrines of Taoism found much favor, and came into conflict with Confucianism. For a brief period during the Ch'in Dynasty (221–207 B.C.) the Legalist School of ruthless and practical expediency gained the upper hand, and a vast number of books were destroyed by governmental order. By the second century B.C., however, the scattered texts had been reassembled (although not without many accretions and much tampering with the originals) and Confucianism had established itself as a political and ethical system which was to endure, with modifications, until the 20th century. The Han Dynasty (202 B.C.-A.D. 220) found the writing of history established as a major literary form. SSU-MA CH'IEN's *Shih chi*, covering the whole span of Chinese history, set the pattern for the later DYNASTIC HISTORIES, 24 in number, which detailed the events of each dynasty as viewed by the regime that replaced it. As governmental compilations they reflect the official Confucian doctrine. The third to sixth centuries A.D. saw the introduction of Buddhism from India and Central Asia. Missionaries and later Chinese priests undertook the translation of Buddhist texts, frequently using Taoist terminology to approximate the meaning of newly introduced philosophical concepts. All forms of Indian Buddhism were imported indiscriminately, and a number of highly complex philosophical systems developed, each based on Indian texts or interpretations of them. There was a gradual sinicization of this new religion with many purely Chinese works being added to the canon; although Confucianism continued its hold, many emperors and high officials became zealous converts to Buddhism. During the T'ang Dynasty (618–906) Ch'an (Zen) Buddhism gained wide acceptance; the vast temple complexes and land holdings of the other sects placed a severe economic burden on the nation, leading to the persecution of 845, from which Ch'an emerged as the dominant Buddhist sect. The revival of Confucianism in the 12th century and the gradual introduction of Amidist beliefs into Ch'an accounted for the decline in importance of this type of Buddhism from the 14th century on. The T'ang Dynasty was noted for a great revival of poetry as a popular literary form. Poetry, philosophical works and their commentaries, essays, and histories had always been the principal forms of Chinese literary expression: with the writings of Po CHÜ-I, LI PO, WANG WEI, TU FU and others, poetry gained heights hitherto unattained. The origins of Chinese fiction can be traced to the Han Dynasty, but official disapproval of such literature worked against its preservation. Some early works of fiction from the T'ang Dynasty have been found among the documents unearthed at TUN-HUANG. Written in colloquial language, they are tales of the supernatural, Buddhist stories, and prose romances, many deriving from the oral tradition. HSI YU CHI, stemming from this tradition, reached its final form in the 16th century and details the fantastic adventures of the priest Hsüan-tsang and his companions. The SHUI HU CHUAN and the CHIN P'ING MEI are major novels whose popularity continues unabated. The HUNG LOU MENG, characterized by a sensitivity and depth of character development not found in other works, has been described as the greatest Chinese novel. Novels have frequently been the subject of suppression and censorship, particularly during the Ch'ing Dynasty (1644–1912), when officials found them too critical of existing conditions. The Ch'ing period saw great literary activity, with enormous collectanea, encyclopedias, and works in all fields of scholastic and scientific endeavor being compiled. In the 20th century much fiction, notably short stories, has been produced, the writings of LU HSUN being of particular importance. See CIRCLE OF CHALK.

Ch'ing or **Manchu** Chinese dynasty (1644–1912). An alien dynasty. It replaced the Ming, and became gradually sinicized. Ineffectual in the face of the Western nations, the Ch'ing dynasty was eventually destroyed by the Chinese themselves with the establishment of the Republic in 1912.

Ching-t'u Buddhism. See AMIDISM.

Chin P'ing Mei. Chinese novel of the Ming Dynasty (1368–1644). It details the history of Hsi Men and his six wives. Highly satirical, it is set in the declining years of the dynasty and has been frequently banned and censored for its sexual detail. See *Chin P'ing Mei, The Golden Lotus* (1940). Introduction by Arthur Waley.

Chios. One of the seven cities claiming to be the birthplace of HOMER. Two different lists of these cities exist in Greek epigram: *Smyrna, Chios, Colophon, Salamis, Rhodos, Argos, Athenae;* or, *Smyrna, Chios, Colophon, Ithaca, Pylos, Argos, Athenae.*

Chirico, Giorgio di (1888–). Italian painter. His important work, from 1911 to 1920, greatly influenced surrealism. He is known for enigmatic landscapes in which solitary figures and elements of classical architecture create a feeling of premonition by means of exaggerated perspective, lengthened shadows, and lonely sense of space. During the 1920's, when he was associated with surrealism, he painted faceless figures suggestive of dummies, but later reverted to academism.

Chiron (Cheiron). A learned centaur. He taught music, medicine, and hunting to Achilles, Hercules, Asklepios, Jason, and many other heroes. A son of Cronos and Philyra, he is often spoken of as a king or leader of the Thessalian centaurs. Accidentally wounded by one of Heracles' poisoned arrows, Chiron gave up his immortality to Prometheus in order to find relief from the unbearable pain in death.

chivalry. The system of customs and conventions connected with knighthood in the Middle Ages. Derived from the French word *chevalier*, meaning horseman or knight, it was originally associated with the business of recruiting knights for the purpose of making war. It came to include the curriculum of training the young knight to fight, to hunt, to serve his lord, to govern his own vassals, and ultimately it evolved into that courtly ideal in which the true knight was not only courageous and skillful in war but also generous, pious, and courteous. When the championing of the weak began to be emphasized as part of the ideal, chivalry became as important in peace as in war, and, among other things, the tournament flourished. Another component of the chivalric code was the ideal of COURTLY LOVE, an element that further refined the knight by requiring that he be poet and musician and that he be dedicated to some lady of his choice.

Chivers, Thomas Holley (1809–1858). American poet and physician. The son of a wealthy landowner, Chivers preferred writing verse and joining the cults of his day to practicing medicine systematically. He published several volumes of verse, including *The Lost Pleiad and Other Poems* (1845), *Eonchs of Ruby, A Gift of Love* (1851), *Memoralia* (1853), and *Virginalia* (1853). Sometimes his extraordinary combinations of words resulted in exquisite melody; at other times, they became sheer nonsense.

A friendly rival of Edgar Allan Poe, Chivers offered his less fortunate friend a permanent haven on his estate. After Poe's death, he charged that Poe had plagiarized from him. Chivers' influence has also been traced in the work of Rossetti and Swinburne.

Chloe. The shepherdess beloved by Daphnis in the pastoral romance of Longus, entitled DAPHNIS AND CHLOE. Hence Chloe has become a generic name among romance writers and pastoral poets for a rustic maiden, not always of the artless variety.

Chloe. See STREPHON.

Chocano, José Santos (1875–1934). Peruvian poet. Considered the outstanding exponent of MODERNISM in Peru, Chocano led a colorful life as revolutionary and political agitator; he was murdered while riding a streetcar in Chile. He early revealed his concern with American themes in *La epopeya del morro* (1899), written when he was 20, which describes the suicide of a group of Peruvian soldiers who threw themselves into the sea rather than surrender during the so-called War of the Pacific (1879–1883). His subsequent poetry glorified the Indian, the tropical landscape, and the legacy of Spain. In *La epopeya del Pacífico,* which appears in his best-known collection, *Alma América* (1906), he expressed his misgivings about the power of the U.S. Although he could be simple and spontaneous, his style tended to be florid and, at times, grandiloquent.

Chopin, Frédéric [François] (1810–1849). Composer and pianist. Born near Warsaw of a French father and Polish mother, he was resident in France for most of his career. He was the outstanding pianist and composer for the piano in the Romantic era. Nearly all his compositions are for piano: preludes, scherzos, sonatas, waltzes, ballades, études, polonaises, mazurkas, nocturnes, etc. Chopin was a close friend of the painter Delacroix and was admired by the composer Schumann. For several years he was associated with George SAND, the novelist, in an unhappy affair which ended in a quarrel and estrangement. Chopin died of tuberculosis of the larynx, a disease that had caused him much weakness and suffering.

Chopin, Kate [O'Flaherty] (1851–1904). American short-story writer and novelist. She is known for her portrayal of Creole life in Louisiana. Her best works were included in two collections of short stories: *Bayou Folk* (1894) and *A Night in Acadie* (1897). Her novel, *The Awakening* (1899), a tale of extramarital love and miscegenation, created a storm of criticism when it was first published.

Choquette, Robert (1905–   ). U.S.-born Canadian poet. Although Choquette wrote a long radio series, *Métropole,* and some rural novels, his greatest achievement is his poetry. In his first book of poems, *A Travers les Vents* (1925), he showed a passionate feeling for the north country, more lyrical and less morbid than much Canadian writing about that region. The poems in his second book, *Metropolitan Museum* (1931), contrast the serene art in the museum with the frantic life of the city around it. His other works include *Poésies Nouvelles* (1933) and *Suite Marine* (1953).

choragos. An earlier term in Greek classical drama, for the leader of the chorus. See CORYPHAEUS.

Chou. The second Chinese dynasty (c. 1027–256 B.C.). The classic age of Chinese civilization, which saw the development of a feudal state and society. The *Book of Odes* is a product of this age, as well as the thought of Confucius, the Taoist religious system, and other important philosophical concepts. The Chou kings held actual power only briefly, and the period was marked by almost incessant warfare among rival principalities.

Chouans, Les (1829). A historical novel by Honoré de BALZAC. His first literary success, it now forms part of LA COMÉDIE HUMAINE. The heroine is the beautiful spy Marie de Verneuil, and the hero is the marquis de Montauran, a Royalist leader. The Chouans themselves were French peasant insurgents, supporters of the royalist cause at the time of the Revolution. Jean Cottereau, their first leader, was nicknamed *Chouan*—a corruption of the French *chatuant* (a screech owl)—because of his secret call in times of danger.

Chou En-lai (1898–   ). Premier of Communist China. Educated in Japan and France, he was one of the founders of the Communist party in China. Joined Sun Yat-sen (1924); became active in the Red Army (1931); founded Chinese Soviet Republic (1931); began all-out military operations against Chiang Kai-shek (1947). Premier of Communist China (1949–   ).

Chou Shu-jen. See LU HSUN.

Chrétien de Troyes (fl., 1160–1190). French poet at the court of Marie de Champagne and Philip of Flanders. He wrote some of the earliest Arthurian romances including EREC ET ENIDE, *Cligés,* and YVAIN, OU LE CHEVALIER AU LION. Two of his most important works are *Lancelot, ou le chevalier de la charrette* (*Launcelot, or the Knight of the Cart*) and *Perceval, ou le conte du Graal* (*Percival, or the Story of the Grail*), which were left incomplete at his death. *Lancelot* deals with the adventures of the Arthurian LAUNCELOT, and *Perceval* (see PERCIVAL) is the earliest literary version of the Grail legend. *Guillaume d'Angleterre,* a version of the life of St. Eustace, has been attributed to him by some scholars.

Christabel (1816). A fragmentary poem by Samuel Taylor COLERIDGE. It is known for its interesting metrical form and its distinctive effects of the super-natural, which are often compared with THE RIME OF THE ANCIENT MARINER. Christabel's purity and innocence are threatened by the wicked enchantress, Lady Geraldine.

Christian. (1) A follower of Christ. The first use of the word occurred at Antioch (Acts 11:26).

(2) The pilgrim hero of Bunyan's PILGRIM'S PROGRESS. His journey from the City of Destruction to the Celestial City forms the substance of Part I.

Christian, Fletcher. The leader of the mutinous sailors in the novel MUTINY ON THE BOUNTY by Charles Nordhoff and James Norman Hall.

Christian Hero, The (1701). A pamphlet by Richard STEELE, written when the author was in the British army, and perhaps occasioned by a duel in which Steele was wounded. It is an attack on dueling and the code of honor.

Christian Science. A religious movement whose teaching is that healing is done by spiritual means rather than by surgery or medicine. It preaches spiritual confidence in the face of disaster, and by an understanding of God as the impersonal, infinite Mind. Christian Science, founded by Mary Baker EDDY in 1866, has spread throughout the U.S., the British Empire, Germany, and the rest of Europe. The First Church of Christ, Scientist, in Boston, Mass., has more than 3,000 branches. Mrs. Eddy's book, *Science and Health with Key to the Scriptures* (1875) contains the teachings of the religion. Mark Twain wrote a savage attack on the cult in *Christian Science* (1907).

Christian Socialism. A religious political movement founded in England in the 1840's under the leadership of Frederick Denison MAURICE. Its aim was to remedy the condition of the laboring class by a program of education and legislative reform, and by encouraging the propertied class to practice Christian ethics in their dealings with the poor. The movement opposed the heartless individualism and competitiveness of 19th-century capitalism. Aside from Maurice, one of the chief adherents of the movement was Charles KINGSLEY. The movement was influenced by the work of William Godwin and Thomas Carlyle.

Christie, Agatha (1891–). English detective-story writer and playwright. She is the prolific author of consistent best sellers. Her detective hero is usually Hercule Poirot, a Belgian. *The Murder of Roger Ackroyd* (1926) is generally considered to be her most ingenious book. In addition to her many mystery stories, she has written "straight" novels under the pen name of Mary Westmacott. Among her numerous books are *The Pale Horse* (1962), a mystery story with a supernatural theme, and *Double Sin and Other Stories* (1961), a collection of short pieces. Her mystery play, *Witness for the Prosecution* (1953), was successful in both London and New York.

Christie Johnstone (1855). A novel by Charles READE. It is primarily the story of the titular character, a Scottish fishergirl, and her artist lover, Charles Gatty. Gatty's mother opposes the match, but when Christie saves Charles' life Mrs. Gatty relents. The subplot concerns the Viscount Ipsden, whose health has been impaired by his cousin Barbara Sinclair's refusal to marry him. He meets Christie while following his doctor's prescription to mingle with humble folk and "relieve one fellow creature a day." Eventually Barbara marries the viscount.

Christina (1626–1689). A queen of Sweden, daughter of Gustavus Adolphus (1594–1632). She was given the education of a man and made her court a center of intellectual activity to which she invited distinguished foreign scholars, artists, and philosophers. The French philosopher Descartes died while in Christina's employ as tutor. Before she came of age, the affairs of state, troubled by the Thirty Years' War, were conducted by Axel Oxenstierna. She herself reigned for ten years (1644–1654) and abdicated in favor of her cousin Charles X. She embraced Roman Catholicism (1655) and died in poverty in Rome.

Christina de Pisan (c. 1364–c. 1430). Italian-born French poet and scholar. She turned to writing at 25 when she was left a widow with three children, and was probably the first woman since antiquity to earn her livelihood as an author. Her poetry includes love lyrics, a patriotic glorification of Joan of Arc, and three longer philosophical poems. Her prose works include *La Cité des dames* (*The City of Ladies*), largely adapted from Boccaccio's *De Claris Mulieribus,* treatises on education and history; and two defenses of women (1399, 1400) against the satirical accusations in Jean de Meung's *Roman de la Rose* (see ROMANCE OF THE ROSE).

Christmas, Joe. The protagonist of William Faulkner's LIGHT IN AUGUST. The illegitimate child of Milly Hines and a man supposedly Mexican, Joe is placed in an orphanage by his fanatically religious grandfather, who believes him to be part-Negro. He is adopted by a strict Calvinist couple, who know nothing of his origins. After wandering over the Southwest for several years, Joe arrives in Jefferson, Miss., where he has an affair with a white woman, kills her, and becomes the object of a manhunt. At home in neither the world of the whites nor that of the Negroes, Joe continually alienates himself from both worlds and rushes to castration and death at the hands of a mob.

Christmas Carol, A (1843). A Christmas story by Charles DICKENS. The subject is the conversion of Scrooge, "a grasping old sinner," by a series of visions of Christmases past, present, and to come. Scrooge has glimpses of his life as a schoolboy, apprentice, and young lover; of the joyous home of Bob CRATCHIT, his underpaid clerk; of what his lot would be if he were to die now, heartless and despised. These visions wholly change his nature, and he becomes benevolent and cheerful, loving all and by all beloved. Although Dickens wrote the story partly for the income it would bring, he said afterwards that he laughed and cried over it as he did over no other story.

Christmas Day. The popular English name for the Feast of the Nativity of Jesus Christ, December 25. This date was first set in 336, by the Roman Church, the Eastern Churches having earlier settled on the date of January 6 as the Feast of the EPIPHANY. December 25 was observed in pagan Rome as the festival *Natalis Invicti Solis* (Birth of the Unconquered Sun), sacred to the sun god Mithras. Christmas became a great popular festival in the Middle Ages, which led to objections by some of the Reformers. The observance was forbidden in England under the Commonwealth (1644–1660), and in Calvinist New England.

Christophe, Henri (1767–1820). Negro king of Haiti. Christophe served as lieutenant to Toussaint L'Ouverture in the revolution against the French (1791). He succeeded DESSALINES as head of the government under the title Henri I. In 1820 a rebellion of his subjects caused him to commit suicide, with a legendary silver bullet.

Christopher, St. A saint of the Greek and Latin churches. Legend relates that St. Christopher was a giant who one day carried a child over a brook, and said, "Child, thou hast put me in great peril. I can bear no greater burden." To this the child answered, "Marvel thou nothing, for thou hast borne all the world upon thee, and its sins likewise." As Christopher sank beneath his load, the child told the giant He was Christ, and Christopher resolved to serve Christ and Him only. He died three days afterward and was canonized. The Greek and Latin churches look on him as the protecting saint against floods, fire, and earthquake.

Christopher Robin. The son of A. A. MILNE, for whom he wrote the POOH books. Christopher Robin is the only human character in a world of small animals.

Christ Stopped at Eboli (**Cristo Si E Fermato a Eboli;** 1945). An autobiographical work by Carlo LEVI. It is an eloquent and moving description of the life the author shared for a year with the peasants of a remote area of Italy, where he was exiled for his political views during the fascist regime.

Christy Minstrels. A troupe of Negro minstrels organized in New York (c. 1842) by Edwin P. Christy (1815–1862). Some of Stephen C. FOSTER's music was written for them.

Chronicle, The Anglo-Saxon. See ANGLO-SAXON CHRONICLE.

Chronicle of the Kings of England. See GESTA REGUM ANGLORUM.

Chronicle play. A play employing—sometimes very loosely—historical events as the basis of its action. The earliest example in English is John Bale's *Kynge Johan* (c. 1548). The finest examples are Shakespeare's Richard II and Henry IV plays (1594–1598) and Christopher Marlowe's *Edward II* (1592).

Chronicles, I and II. Two Old Testament canonical books, originally one book in Hebrew, which follow II Kings. The author, known only as "the chronicler," parallels the epochs described in II Samuel and II Kings. He stresses certain aspects to present a colorful picture of the traditions and attitudes of the time.

Chronicles of England, Scotland, and Ireland (1577). A history by Raphael HOLINSHED. The *Chronicles* was the source of much of the material used in Shakespeare's *Macbeth, King Lear,* and *Cymbeline.* The section concerning the history of Scotland is said to be chiefly a translation of *Scotorum Historiae* (1527) by Hector Boece. In 1587 a second and expanded edition was published, but parts of it did not please Queen Elizabeth, and she tried to have it suppressed.

Chrononhotonthologos (1734). A burlesque of contemporary drama by Henry CAREY, subtitled "the

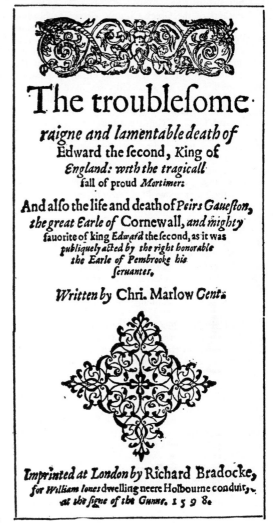

The troublesome·
raigne and lamentable death of
Edward the second, King of
England: with the tragicall·
fall of proud *Mortimer:*

And also the life and death of *Peirs Gaueston,*
the great Earle of Cornewall, *and mighty·*
fauorite of king *Edward* the second, as it was
publiquely acted by the right honorable
the Earle of Pembrooke *his·*
seruantes,

Written by Chri. Marlow *Gent.*

Imprinted at London by Richard Bradocke,
for William Iones *dwelling neere* Holbourne conduit,
at the signe of the Gunne. 1 5 9 8.

Title page of Marlowe's chronicle play
Edward II (1598).

Most Tragical Tragedy that was ever Tragedized by any company of Tragedians." The title is the name of th. King of Queerumania, the pompous main character, and is used for any bombastic person who delivers inflated address. The play is noted for its frank criticism of the theater of its day.

Chryseis. In Homer's ILIAD, daughter of Chryses, a priest of Apollo. She was famed for her beauty. During the Trojan War, Chryseis was taken captive and allotted to Agamemnon, king of Argos. When he refused to accept ransom, Chryses evoked a plague and Agamemnon was forced to let her go.

Chrysippus (Chrysippos). See PELOPS.

Chrysoloras, Manuel (d. 1415). Greek scholar. He was invited to Florence to teach in 1396, the first of many who came to Italy to foster the revival of classical studies during the Renaissance. His teaching and scholarly activities did not prevent him from traveling widely in Italy and throughout Europe, as well as his native Constantinople.

Chrysostom, St. John (c. 345–407). One of the Fathers of the Greek Church, elected archbishop (patriarch) of Constantinople in 398. He stressed asceticism and knowledge of the Scriptures in religion, as well as charity, social justice, and reform within the Church; he established the basis of the present liturgy of the Orthodox Eastern Church. Many of his sermons and addresses have been preserved, including *On Priesthood, On the Statues,* and a great deal of Biblical exegesis.

Chuang Tzu. A Chinese Taoist text attributed to Chuang Chou (369?–286? B.C.). The first Chinese work to deal solely with spiritual subjects, it advocates the transcending of the physical world and calls for a union with the Tao, the mysterious and indescribable first principle of the universe. Witty and imaginative, it is a work of exceptional literary distinction. See H. A. Giles, *Chuang Tzu* (1926). See TAOISM.

Chubb, Thomas Caldecot (1899–   ). American poet and biographer. In addition to such volumes of verse as *Ships and Lovers* (1933), *Cliff Pace and Other Poems* (1936), and *Cornucopia* (1953), Chubb's work includes a biography of Boccaccio (1930) and one of Aretino (1940). *The Months of the Year* (1960) contains translations of Italian poems.

Chu Hsi (1130–1200). Chinese Confucian scholar, largely responsible for the Confucian revival (Neo-Confucianism) in the Sung Dynasty. He synthesized, reorganized, and reinterpreted the teachings, adopting elements from Buddhism and Taoism, to form a new Confucian system that became the orthodox philosophy until the establishment of the Republic in 1912. His teachings were of considerable importance in Japan, particularly during the Tokugawa period, when they were adopted as the official state philosophy. See also CONFUCIANISM.

Ch'un-ch'iu. See SPRING AND AUTUMN ANNALS.

Chung-yung. See MEAN, THE.

Church, Benjamin (1639–1718). American soldier known as one of the outstanding guerilla fighters in the wars between the New England colonists and the Indians. From his notes his son Thomas Church (1673–1748) wrote *Entertaining Passages Relating to Philip's War* (1716), an account of the elder Church's experiences.

Church, Richard [Thomas] (1893–   ). English poet, novelist, and literary critic. His books of poetry include *Collected Poems* (1948), *The Inheritors* (1957), and *North of Rome* (1960). Among his prose works are *Over the Bridge* (1955) and *Calm October* (1961).

Church, Thomas. See Benjamin CHURCH.

Churchill, Charles (1731–1764). English poet and clergyman, known for his biting satiric verse. His major works are *The Rosciad* (1761), an attack on London actors and acting which is often ranked with Pope's *Dunciad; The Ghost* (1762), an account of the notorious COCK LANE GHOST episode ridiculing Samuel Johnson for his interest in it; THE PROPHECY OF FAMINE, A SCOTS PASTORAL, a verse satire voicing English distrust of Scotland; *The Duellist* (1764), a poem defending the political position of John Wilkes and attacking all his detractors, particularly Smollett; *Gotham* (1764), a verse epistle setting forth the "idea of a patriot king" (see Henry

ST. JOHN); and *The Candidate* (1764), a poetic attack on the conservative political policies of Cambridge University.

Churchill, John. See 1st duke of MARLBOROUGH.

Churchill, Sarah (1914–   ). English actress. The daughter of Sir Winston Churchill, she married Vic Oliver (Viktor Samek) in 1936 (divorced 1945) and Anthony Beauchamp in 1949. She has appeared on the American stage in *Gramercy Ghost* (1951) and on television.

Churchill, Winston (1871–1947). American novelist. He is noted for his enormously successful historical romances. Although his first novel, *The Celebrity* (1898), supposedly a satire on Richard Harding Davis, was moderately popular, it was with his second, RICHARD CARVEL, that he established his literary reputation. THE CRISIS, THE CROSSING, CONISTON, and *Mr. Crewe's Career* (1908), a story about the control of state politics by railroad interests, followed. Churchill was interested in social questions and religion, and his later books reflect these preoccupations. *The Inside of the Cup* (1913) deals with the relations of religion and modern society. Other books are *A Far Country* (1915), a story of a modern prodigal son; *The Dwelling Place of Light* (1917), an account of a New England factory strike; and *The Uncharted Way: The Psychology of the Gospel Doctrine* (1940).

Churchill, Sir Winston [Leonard Spencer] (1874–1965). English statesman and author. A political Conservative, he held many important governmental offices between 1911 and 1955. He is best remembered, however, as Prime Minister during World War II. He became popular both in England and in the U.S. because of his personality and his confidence in the capacity of Britain to survive against odds. He was noted for the eloquence of his speeches and his capacity for making memorable phrases. He has written many books, including a history of World War II, in six volumes, and *A History of the English-Speaking Peoples,* in four volumes. He was awarded the Nobel Prize for Literature (1953).

Churchyard, Thomas (1520?–1604). English poet and soldier. Churchyard is best remembered for the verse accounts of Cardinal Wolsey and Jane Shore in *The Mirror for Magistrates. Shore's Wife* is considered his best work. Some of his poems and ballads appeared in broadsheets or in popular Elizabethan miscellanies. His works, primarily autobiographical, appeared as *Churchyard's Chips* (1575), *Churchyard's Choice* (1579), *Churchyard's Charge* (1580); *Churchyard's Challenge* (1593); etc.

Chūshingura. Japanese *joruri* and *kabuki* play by Takeda Izumo (1691–1756). Known in English as the *League of the Loyal Ronin,* it concerns the revenge taken by 47 loyal retainers whose master was forced to take his life. After attaining their objective, all 47 likewise commit *harakiri.* It is based on a historical incident.

Chute, La. See FALL, THE.

Ch'u Tz'u. See ELEGIES OF CH'U.

Ciappelletto, Ser. The hero of a tale from Giovanni Boccaccio's THE DECAMERON. He makes a false confession about his wicked life before his death and soon becomes a legendary paragon of virtue, St. Ciappelletto.

Ciardi, John (1916–   ). American poet, teacher, and critic. Ciardi's essays on the art of reading and enjoying poetry are notable for their lively wit, perception, and common-sense attitudes. Among his collections of critical writings are *How Does a Poem Mean?* (1959) and *Dialogue with an Audience* (1963). His poetry tends to be ironic but is not without muted depths and power. His earliest collection, *Homeward to America* (1940), was followed by *Other Skies* (1947), *As If* (1955), *I Marry You* (1958), *39 Poems* (1959), *In the Stoneworks* (1961), and *In Fact* (1962). He translated Dante's *Inferno* (1954) in *terza rima* and in idiomatic English to recall Dante's use of the vernacular. His translation of the *Purgatorio* appeared in 1961.

Cibber, Colley (1671–1757). English dramatist, poet, and actor. He is best known for the sentimental comedy *The Careless Husband* (1704), and such others as *Love's Last Shift* (1696), *She Would and She Would Not* (1702) and *The Provoked Husband* (1728), an adaptation of Molière's *Tartuffe*. He also wrote a famous description of the Restoration and early 18th-century theater, *Apology for the Life of Mr. Colley Cibber, Comedian* (1740). Cibber was poet laureate for 27 years from 1730, was generally considered one of the worst poets to hold the office, and even admitted that he was granted the post for being a good Whig.

Cicero, Marcus Tullius (106–43 B.C.). Roman orator, statesman, and man of letters. After carefully preparing himself for a career in law, Cicero made his oratorical debut under the dictatorship of Sulla, his first public success occurring in 80 B.C. The next two years he spent in Greece and Rhodes, where he continued his study of philosophy and rhetoric. After his return to Rome, he was elected quaestor (76) and aedile (70). In the year of his aedileship he was asked by the Sicilians to be their attorney against their former governor Verres. Even though his opponent was Hortensius, the most famous orator of the day, Cicero was able to amass such a convincing array of evidence of the dishonesty and cruelty of Verres that the defendant took the first chance to slip into voluntary exile. In 67 Cicero was overwhelmingly elected praetor, and as such came out in favor of the Manilian Law, the proposal that would confer on Pompey complete command in his war with Mithradates. Thus, in his first purely political oration, Cicero registered himself on the side of Pompey and the aristocratic party.

Cicero himself, however, was of equestrian rank; he was a parvenu, or *novus homo,* whose family had never been distinguished by holding public office. Although he was a member of the aristocratic party, he was looked down upon by many members of his own faction. Nevertheless, in 64 he succeeded in being elected consul of Rome. It was this year of his consulate (63) that marked his greatest success: the almost singlehanded foiling of the conspiracy of CATILINE. His four brilliant orations against Catiline (*In Catilinam*) show that Cicero was not only a master of the Roman art of pleading but also a master of the equally Roman art of politics; he emerges as a beleaguered patriot protecting himself from paid assassins, a shrewd chief of state gathering the means to overcome a civil criminal, and a clever propagandist presenting himself to the people as one greater than Romulus, for Romulus merely founded Rome while Cicero was its savior. Catiline and his army were defeated, and the principal conspirators were summarily executed.

Soon afterward, however, Cicero's influence waned. His enemies became more outspoken. Finally, in 58, CLODIUS PULCHER had a bill passed which declared that anyone who had executed a Roman citizen without trial should be declared an outlaw. In the face of growing popular indignation, Cicero voluntarily retired to Greece. The sentence of banishment was pronounced *in absentia,* his properties destroyed or confiscated, and his wife and daughter harassed.

Through the influence of his friends, he was, within a year and a half, recalled from exile and entirely restored to his former rank within the commonwealth, but he found himself obliged to spend the next six years defending these same friends from their political enemies. His orations in defense of Sestius, Plancius, and Milo date from this period. In the 50's he also found time for study and for writing. He returned to the two great enthusiasms of his youth: philosophy and the art of rhetoric. Between the years 54–51 he wrote *De Re Publica,* a six-book work on political philosophy of which about one third is extant. In 55 he wrote his great treatise on oratory, *De Oratore.* Written in the form of a dialogue, this treatise deals with the proper training for an orator, the style and treatment appropriate to particular themes, and the manner of delivery most apt to sway an audience.

But there was no longer a place for oratory in the Roman world. The senate was dwarfed by the figures of Julius Caesar and Pompey, and these two giants called for war. In 49, after long hesitation, Cicero left Italy and pledged his life and fortune to the cause of Pompey. In the next year, when Caesar crushed Pompey in the battle of Pharsalus, Cicero realized that the cherished traditions of republican Rome were crumbling. Even though the victorious Caesar pardoned him and welcomed him back to Rome, Cicero, shaken and disillusioned, remained aloof from politics. He retired to his villa in the mountains of Tuscany and sought out what he called *otium cum dignitate* (leisure with dignity). Between the years 47 and 44, he wrote the five books of the *Tusculanae Disputationes,* on the subject of happiness; his works on theology and augury, *De Natura Deorum* and *De Divinatione;* his two dialogues on old age and friendship, DE SENECTUTE and DE AMICITIA; and his handbook on Stoic morality, *De Officiis.*

In 44, with the death of Caesar, Cicero, then in his 63rd year, saw his chance to re-enter politics and to save Rome from demagoguery and chaos. He hoped to play the role of the elder statesman and to serve as guardian to the young Octavius. Accordingly, he attacked Mark Antony in 14 orations known as Philippics. But Octavius turned against his would-be ally and, joining Antony and Lepidus in the Second TRIUMVIRATE, declared Cicero an outlaw. He tried to escape to Greece but was overtaken by a mob of bounty hunters; his head and right hand were presented to his enemy Antony, who had them placed on the rostrum in the Forum, where the orator had first won his glory.

Cicero was not only Rome's greatest orator; he was

perhaps its most articulate philosopher. Through his philosophical treatises, he helped to make Latin a strong, yet surprisingly flexible, vehicle for logical speculation. Through his mastery of Latin prose, he transformed Latin from a blunt utilitarian language —one most fit for merchants, generals, and lawyers —to a rich chromatic language that rivaled Greek in its capacity to convey at the same time the gamut of feelings and the fine distinction of ideas.

Cicero's prose style is rhetorical, in the best sense of the word; it is intended to persuade. It has always been contrasted with the style of Tacitus and Sallust, who both preferred a tight, tersely emphatic prose to the symphonic sonorities of Cicero. These two stylistic schools continued in conflict into the 16th and 17th centuries when in England the Tacitean style of Francis Bacon was contrasted with the Ciceronian style of Jeremy Taylor. See ATTICUS; CICERONIAN AGE.

Ciceronian age. In its intellectual aspects, the last years of republican Rome are often referred to as the Ciceronian age, or the age of CICERO, dating from the emergence of Cicero (80 B.C.) to the empire under Augustus (27 B.C.). The prose—as well as the politics—of the late republic was dominated by Marcus Tullius Cicero. Like Cato the Elder, Cicero was a versatile writer-statesman, but where Cato was representative of the sharp, straightforward, vernacular Latin style, Cicero was the creator and pre-eminent representative of the smooth and rhetorically powerful Hellenized style. A master of oratory, Cicero was also a thoughtful and thorough student of literary criticism, a foremost authority on Stoic philosophy, and a brilliant letter writer. Other prose writers of the period include the historians Julius CAESAR and SALLUST, both of whom set a high standard of excellence for all subsequent Roman historians, and Terentius VARRO, reputedly the most learned and productive scholar of his time.

Although the Ciceronian age is conspicuously an age of prose, it also embraces LUCRETIUS and CATULLUS, two of the most significant poets in Latin literature. Lucretius wielded the dactylic hexameter of Ennius in his long and passionate poem on Epicurean science, *De Rerum Natura*. Catullus was the first truly successful writer of Latin lyric poems. These he modeled on the literary forms of the Alexandrine school of Hellenistic Greek literature.

With the murder of Cicero (43), the last great voice of Roman republicanism was stilled. The transition to the imperial period had begun and its dominant figure was to be the young Octavius Caesar, later Augustus. In his struggle with Mark Antony, from the death of Julius Caesar (44) to its culmination at ACTIUM (31), Rome leaves behind her old republican ideals to become an empire, and the Ciceronian age gives way to the AUGUSTAN AGE.

Cid, Le (The Cid, 1637). A tragedy by Pierre CORNEILLE. One of Corneille's most powerful tragedies, *Le Cid* is considered by many critics to mark the beginning of modern French drama. The playwright borrowed from Guillén de Castro's treatment of the subject, but compressed the material into a swiftly moving play.

Cid, Poema del or **Cantar de mio.** An epic poem in Spanish, written about 1140 by an unknown Castilian bard. The poem has survived only in a single manuscript copy from which several pages are missing, made in 1307 by one Per Abbat. It was first published in 1779 by Tomás Antonio Sánchez.

The poem is based on the exploits of Rodrigo or Ruy Díaz de Bivar (c. 1043–1099), who was known as *el Cid* (from Arabic *Sidi,* "lord"). Born near Burgos, he was named chief marshal, or *alférez,* of the royal army by Sancho II of Castile and later served under Sancho's brother and successor, Alfonso VI, who banished him because of personal differences. The Cid fought both for and against the Moorish rulers who at that time controlled much of the Iberian peninsula. A highlight of his career was his conquest of Valencia (1094), which halted Almoravid expansion in Spain. In 1074 he married Doña Jimena Díaz, a niece of Alfonso. He was also known as *el Campeador* ("the Champion").

Consisting of 3735 lines, the poem is divided into three parts, or *cantares.* The first deals with the Cid's exile and concludes with his defeat of the count of Barcelona. A famous episode describes his entry into Burgos, where no one will speak to him until a little girl explains that King Alfonso has warned the people to refuse him lodging. In the second part, the Cid captures Valencia, is reconciled with the king, and marries his two daughters, Doña Elvira and Doña Sol, to two nobles, the *infantes,* or heirs, of Carrión. The third part recounts the outrageous conduct of Rodrigo's sons-in-law, who beat and abandon their wives. The Cid avenges himself by defeating them in a trial by combat and then arranges the marriage of his daughters to the princes of Navarre and Aragon.

Similar in form to the *Chanson de Roland,* the poem is notable for its simplicity and directness and for its exact, picturesque detail. Despite the inclusion of much legendary material, the figure of the Cid, who is depicted as the model Castilian warrior, is not idealized to an extravagant degree.

The Cid appeared in many other medieval poems, among them the epic *Cantar de Rodrigo,* which was written about 1400 and is based almost entirely on legend. Later authors also made use of this theme, notably Juan de la Cueva, Lope de Vega, Guillén de CASTRO, and Juan Eugenio Hartzenbusch. Castro's *Mocedades del Cid* was the direct source of Corneille's LE CID. Present knowledge about the historical character and the *Poema de mio Cid* is derived largely from the exhaustive investigations of Ramón Menéndez Pidal, who published a three-volume critical edition (1908–1911).

Cimabue, Giovanni. Real name, **Cenni di Pepo** (c. 1240–c. 1302). Florentine painter. Tradition celebrates him as "the father of Italian painting" and the teacher of GIOTTO. He was himself taught by Byzantine artists, so that several iconlike Madonnas and Crucifixions have been attributed to him, but there are no extant works that can be positively established as his. His renown among his contemporaries is attested to by Dante, who describes him in the *Purgatorio,* as having "held the field" until surpassed by Giotto.

Cimber, Metellus. In Shakespeare's JULIUS CAESAR, a conspirator against Caesar. After he unsuccessfully appeals to Caesar to revoke a decree banishing his brother from Rome, he and the other conspirators fall on Caesar and stab him to death.

Cimetière marin, Le (The Graveyard by the Sea, 1920). A poem by Paul VALÉRY. Written in decasyllabic six-line stanzas, it describes the dazzling noon of the Mediterranean coast, where Valéry spent his boyhood. The narrator ironically contrasts the attractive clarity of timeless intellectuality with the inevitable decay of all that lives in reality. He concludes, however, that for a mortal being "It is necessary to try to live."

Cimmerians (Kimmerioi). A legendary tribe. Homer placed them beyond Oceanus, in a land of never-ending gloom. Immediately beyond was Hades. Pliny placed Cimmeria near the Lake Avernus, in Italy, where "the sun never penetrates." The phrase "Cimmerian darkness" signifies intense darkness.

Historically, the name Cimmerians is given to a nomad tribe from the Crimean region who, under pressure from the Sarmatians and Scythians, overran Asia Minor in 635 B.C.

Cimosco. In the ORLANDO FURIOSO of Ariosto, the King of the Frisians. His son Arbante is supposed to wed the unwilling Olimpia. When the latter causes the death of Arbante, Cimosco plans to take revenge on her lover, Bireno. But while in captivity, Bireno falls in love with Cimosco's daughter and deserts Olimpia for her.

Cincinnatus, Lucius Quinctius. An early Roman hero. According to tradition, he was appointed DICTATOR in 458 B.C. and sent to rescue a Roman army besieged by the Aequians on Mount Algidus. Cincinnatus routed the Aequians and, after a dictatorship of 16 days, renounced public life and returned to his farm.

Cinderella. The heroine of an ancient fairy tale. Her name (Fr., *Cendrillon;* Ger., *Aschenbrötel*) means literally the little cinder girl. The story, probably of Eastern origin, was mentioned in 16th-century German literature and was popularized in Perrault's *Contes de ma mère l'oye* (1697). Cinderella is the drudge of a household while her elder sisters go to balls. At length, a fairy godmother enables Cinderella to go to the Prince's ball. The Prince, of course, falls in love with her, and she is later rediscovered by him by means of a glass slipper that she has dropped, and that will fit no foot but her own. The details of the complete story, not found in most children's books, are somewhat gruesome. Rossini's delightful opera *La Cenerentola* (1817) is based on a considerably modified version of the story.

Cinna. In Shakespeare's JULIUS CAESAR, a young poet. After Caesar's murder, he is mistaken for Cinna the conspirator by the irate Roman citizens.

Cinna (1640). A tragedy by Pierre CORNEILLE. It is based on an episode in Roman history recounted in Seneca's *De Clementia*. Though trusted by the emperor Augustus, Cinna leads a conspiracy to overthrow him, encouraged by his beloved Amélie who desires to avenge the death of her father. Maxime, a fellow conspirator also in love with Amélie, betrays the plot, hoping to cause Cinna's arrest. The last act focuses on Augustus' struggle to choose between mercy and revenge. Ultimately, he pardons the lovers as well as the treacherous Maxime. The play reflects Corneille's interest in political subjects.

cinq auteurs (*Fr.,* "five authors"). The French playwrights BOISROBERT, COLLETET, CORNEILLE, L'Estoile, and ROTROU, who were hired by Cardinal RICHELIEU to write plays under his supervision conforming to his strong views on the drama. A man with literary ambitions of his own, Richelieu occasionally chose the subject matter with which his authors were to deal, but more frequently merely dictated the treatment. Few of the plays he commissioned are remembered, though several were performed for the king.

cinquain. In prosody, a quintet or five-line stanza. The term is also used to designate the five-line poem of two, four, six, eight, and two syllables respectively; this form was invented by Adelaide Crapsey who was greatly influenced by the Japanese HAIKU and TANKA.

> Just now,
> Out of the strange
> Still dusk—as strange, as still—
> A white moth flew. Why am I grown
> So cold?
>
> Adelaide Crapsey, *The Warning*

cinquecento (*It.,* the five hundreds). Italian designation of the 16th century. This is the age of the high RENAISSANCE—of Ariosto and Castiglione, Machiavelli and Aretino. In art history, the age of Raphael, Leonardo da Vinci and Michaelangelo, and of the advent of Mannerism and the proto-Baroque.

Cipolla, Brother. A friar in one of the tales from Giovanni Boccaccio's THE DECAMERON. He specializes in duping villagers with fake relics. Planning to display a feather from the wings of the archangel Gabriel, he discovers that some coals have been substituted for it; quickly, he recovers his poise and announces that they are from the brazier on which Saint Lawrence met his death.

Circe (Kirke). A sorceress of Greek mythology. She lived in the island of Aeaea. When Odysseus landed there, Circe turned his companions into swine, but he resisted this metamorphasis by virtue of a herb called *moly,* given him by Hermes.

Circe was Aetes' sister and the aunt of Medea. She purified Jason and Medea for the murder of Absyrtus and gave them advice on their homeward journey.

Circle of Chalk, The. A Chinese classical play of the Yuan dynasty (1259–1368), sometimes attributed to Li Hsing-Tao. The lovely Chang-hi-tang is sold to a teahouse by her destitute family and is bought by Mr. Ma, the tax collector, to whom she bears a son. Jealous for her position as head wife and heir, Mrs. Ma poisons her husband's tea and bribes witnesses to prove that Chang-hi-tang has murdered him and that the concubine's child is really her own. The new emperor, who has ordered all cases involving the death penalty retried before him, listens to the evidence; he then places the child in a chalk circle and directs Mrs. Ma and Chang-hi-tang each to take hold of one of the baby's arms and, thus, gain the child by pulling him out of the circle. When Mrs. Ma wins this contest, for Chang-hi-tang is unwilling to hurt the child by pulling at all, the emperor decides that the concubine is the rightful mother and Mrs. Ma the murderess, and he leaves it to Chang-hi-tang to pronounce justice. She orders Mrs. Ma to make herself a cup of tea and to let her conscience decide what sort of tea it ought to be. In later adaptations additional symbolic chalk circles and a love affair between the emperor and Chang-hi-tang were added. Bertolt Brecht used the play as the basis of his *Caucasian Chalk Circle,* in which the stagecraft is purportedly modeled on the classical Chinese convention and moralistic and socio-economic didacticisms replace the subtlety and beautifully lyric verse that distinguish the original.

A very similar story is told in the Bible of a wise judgment of SOLOMON.

circumlocution (literally, talking around). A deliberately roundabout and wordy way of saying something. Frequently it represents an evasion of a plain but perhaps unpalatable truth.

Circumlocution Office. A term applied in ridicule by Charles Dickens in LITTLE DORRIT to public offices in England, because each person tries to shuffle off every task onto someone else. Hence, routine formality and the red tape of bureaucracy.

Ciriaco [Pizzicolli] D'Ancona (1391-1455). Italian archeologist and scholar. One of the genuine enthusiasts for antiquity in the Italian Renaissance, he roamed widely in search of inscriptions, monuments, and ruins. He is reported to have said of his journeys, "I go to awake the dead!"

Cithaeron (Kithairon). A mountain range between Attica and Boeotia. Near to both Thebes and Athens, it was the scene of many events of Greek mythology. Perhaps most notable of these were the death of Pentheus at the hands of his mother Agave and her BACCHANTES, and the exposing of both the infant Oedipus and the twins Amphion and Zethus.

Cities of the Plain. See REMEMBRANCE OF THINGS PAST.

Citizen of the World, The (1762). An epistolary novel by Oliver GOLDSMITH. In almost colloquial prose, it is supposedly written by a Chinese philosopher, LIEN CHI ALTANGI, who visits England and reports on it to his friends in the East. The letters were published with the subtitle *Letters from a Chinese Philosopher Residing in London to his Friends in the East.* In these "Chinese Letters," Goldsmith is typical of his day in his praise of simplicity. Here the main catchword is Nature's "simple plan." The philosopher's observations are supplemented by those of his friend, the MAN IN BLACK, by Beau TIBBS, and by Lady Betty TEMPEST. The letters are linked by a subplot, in which the philosopher's son rescues the Man in Black's daughter from captivity in Persia, brings her to England, and marries her. The novel first appeared as a series of essays in Newbury's *Public Ledger* (1760-1761) under the title, *The Chinese Letters.* This device of the Oriental traveler was perfected in Montesquieu's *Lettres Persanes* (1721).

City, The (La Ville; 1890). A poetic drama, revised in 1897, by Paul CLAUDEL. It presents in allegorical form the building, the destruction, and the salvation of the City of Men.

City in the Sea, The (1831). A poem by Edgar Allan POE. The poet evokes a grim landscape in melodic lines. His description of the shrine includes the well-known lines:

> Whose wreathèd friezes intertwine
> The viol, the violet and the vine.

City of Destruction. In Bunyan's PILGRIM'S PROGRESS, the world of the unconverted. Bunyan makes Christian flee from it and journey to the

Celestial City, thereby showing the "walk of a Christian" from conversion to death.

City of Dreadful Night, The (1874). A long poem by the Victorian poet James THOMSON, published in *The City of Dreadful Night, And Other Poems.* It describes an imaginary city of misery and horror created out of the author's own sense of despair as, afflicted with insomnia, he walked at night through the streets of London.

City of God, The (De Civitate Dei; 22 vols., 413-426). A long treatise by St. AUGUSTINE. It is an apology for Christianity against the accusation that the Church was responsible for the decline of the Roman Empire. It interprets human history as a conflict between the City of God (*Civitas Dei*), which includes the body of Christians belonging to the Church, and the Earthly City (*Civitas Terrena*), composed of pagans and heretical Christians. Augustine foresees that through the will of God the people of the City of God will eventually win immortality, those in the Earthly City destruction.

city of refuge. A sacred area. Moses, at the command of God, set apart three cities on the east of Jordan, and Joshua added three others on the west, whither any person might flee for refuge who had killed a human creature inadvertently. The three on the east of Jordan were Bezer, Ramoth, and Golan; the three on the west were Hebron, Shechem, and Kedesh (Deut. 4:43; Josh. 20: 1-8).

Medina, in Arabia, where Muhammad took refuge when driven by conspirators from Mecca, is known as the *city of refuge.* He received a warm welcome when he entered Medina in A.D. 622.

Civil Disobedience (1849). An essay by Henry David THOREAU. Its major premise is "that government is best which governs least." Thoreau asserts that a man's first loyalty is to his own nature; true to himself, he may then be true to a government. The essay influenced Gandhi's doctrine of passive resistance.

Civil War, American. See AMERICAN CIVIL WAR.

Civil War, English, or **Great Rebellion.** A civil war brought on by conflict between CHARLES I and the LONG PARLIAMENT over economic, political, and religious issues. The war had two phases. The first (1642-1646) was fought between the Royalist party, which included most of the nobles and gentry and adherents of the Church of England, and the Parliamentary party, which was supported by Presbyterians and other dissenters and the middle classes in general. In 1643 the Scottish COVENANTERS joined the Parliamentary cause. After initial Royalist successes, this phase ended with Parliamentary victories at MARSTON MOOR and NASEBY.

The second phase, which lasted from about 1648 to 1652, followed the acquisition of power by the Parliamentary army and more radical dissenters, or INDEPENDENTS, led by Oliver CROMWELL. The struggle was now between this group and the king, who was executed in 1649, conservative members of Parliament, Irish Royalists, and the Scots, now allied with Charles II. In the Preston campaign (1648), the Irish War (1649-1650), and the battles of Dunbar (1650) and Worcester (1651), Cromwell emerged victorious. See GRAND REMONSTRANCE; John HAMPDEN; NEW MODEL ARMY; PRIDE'S PURGE; and John PYM.

Clair, René (1898–   ). French film director and producer. From his first effort in 1923, *Paris qui dort,* René Clair revealed a unique sense of the absurd, especially as embodied in the French bourgeois. His talent culminated during the silent era in the *Italian Straw Hat* (1927), a witty film version of Eugène Labiche's famous 19th-century farce of the same name. With the introduction of sound, Clair began new experimentation. His famous trilogy, *Sous les toits de Paris* (1929), *Le Million* (1931), and *A nous la liberté* (1931), is characterized by an ingenious mingling of music and dialogue with silent film techniques. In 1934 he went to work for the British and American film industry, later returning to France.

Clairmont, Clara Mary Jane. Known as **Claire** (1798–1879). Stepdaughter of William Godwin and mother of Lord BYRON's daughter Allegra. She was a friend of the Shelleys.

Clan-na-Gael. An Irish secret organization. It was founded in Philadelphia in 1881, and was successor to the Fenian brotherhood (1856). Its avowed object was to secure "the complete and absolute independence of Ireland from Great Britain, and the complete severance of all political connection between the two countries, to be effected by unceasing preparation for armed insurrection in Ireland." See FENIANS.

Clare, Ada. See BLEAK HOUSE.

Clare, Angel. See TESS OF THE D'URBERVILLES.

Clare, John (1793–1864). English poet. Clare was born into a barely literate, impoverished Northamptonshire peasant family, had little formal education, and long supported himself as a farm laborer. After the appearance of his first book (*Poems Descriptive of Rural Life and Scenery,* 1820), he became famous as a peasant poet, the curiosity of one London Season. Thereafter, however, he was plagued by ill-health, neglect, poverty, and finally, madness. In 1837 he was committed to a mental asylum and died in confinement. Much of Clare's voluminous verse lacks distinction, but his best poems possess a startling originality and directness of vision, ranking high among English nature poetry. Aside from his first volume, his works include *The Village Minstrel* (1821); *The Shepherd's Calendar* (1827); and *The Rural Muse* (1835). The recent edition of *Selected Poems of John Clare* (1950) by Geoffrey Grigson includes many poems written in madness.

Clarel: A Poem and a Pilgrimage in the Holy Land (1876). A long poem by Herman MELVILLE. Clarel, a young theological student, oscillates between faith and doubt. In love with Ruth, a Jewish girl, he leaves her to join a group of pilgrims traveling from Jerusalem to Gethsemane, the Dead Sea, and Bethlehem. The pilgrims, conversing with Clarel, represent almost every persuasion. They are: Nehemiah, a saintly old man who knows the time of the Second Coming; Vine, a seclusive aesthete resembling Melville's friend, Nathaniel Hawthorne; Derwent, an Emersonian optimist; Mortmain and Ungar, cynical pessimists; Margoth, a materialist; a Dominican friar, and many others. When Clarel returns, he finds that Ruth has died; he is left alone to face reality, the possessor of new wisdom. Melville asks if civilization can survive, after science has caused a loss

of faith. His poem, though technically weak, has considerable intellectual strength.

Clarence, 3rd duke of. George (1449–1478). English noble, son of Richard Plantagenet, duke of York. He originally took up arms against his brothers Edward (IV) and Richard (III), but was later reconciled with them. Convinced that Clarence was plotting against him, Edward had him imprisoned, and it is said that he was drowned in a butt of malmsey wine. In Shakespeare's RICHARD III, he is depicted as the victim of Richard's machinations and is arrested when Richard revives an old prophecy that "G of Edward's heirs the murderer shall be." He also appears in Shakespeare's *Henry VI: Part III.*

Clarendon, 1st earl of. Edward Hyde (1609–1674). English historian and statesman. An influential adviser to Charles I and lord chancellor under Charles II, he was falsely accused of treason and banished in 1667. In France he wrote his *Life* (1759) and completed his chief work, *The History of the Rebellion and Civil Wars in England* (1702–1704). The *History* is best known for Clarendon's perceptive and tolerant character sketches of the leading personages of the time. His daughter Anne married the duke of York, later James II, and bore two daughters who became Queen Mary and Queen Anne.

Clarendon Press. A printing establishment connected with Oxford University, England. It was founded partly with the profits from the 1st earl of Clarendon, Edward Hyde's *History of the Rebellion.*

Clares, Poor. See POOR CLARES.

Claretie, Jules (1840–1913). French journalist and writer. Claretie served as director of the COMÉDIE FRANÇAISE in 1885. His 20-volume work *La Vie à Paris* (1881–1911) is a piece of facile, clever writing.

Claribell. See FAERIE QUEENE, THE.

Clarín. See Leopoldo ALAS Y UREÑA.

Clarissa Harlowe (1747–1748). An epistolary novel by Samuel RICHARDSON, generally considered to be his masterpiece. Its original title is *Clarissa, or, The History of a Young Lady.* It is the longest novel in the English language, totaling about one million words. It is noted for its subtle and penetrating psychological treatment of character. Clarissa has been coldly commanded by her tyrannical family to marry Mr. Solmes, a man she despises. She refuses, even though it pains her to defy her parents. Locked in her room, isolated from family and friends, Clarissa corresponds secretly with Robert LOVELACE, a suitor disapproved of by her family; she finally throws herself upon his protection and flees with him. It soon becomes clear to her, however, that Lovelace's sole aim is to seduce her. Her virtue is so great that Lovelace becomes obsessively absorbed in breaking it down; convinced finally that she will never yield to him, he becomes desperate, drugs and rapes her. He then proposes marriage, but Clarissa refuses, retires to a solitary dwelling, and dies of grief and shame. Lovelace, whose heart the reader never really knows, is killed in a duel with Colonel Morden, Clarissa's cousin. Rousseau was greatly influenced by *Clarissa Harlowe* in his novel, JULIE, OU LA NOUVELLE HÉLOÏSE. See John BELFORD; Anna HOWE.

Clarisse. See Anne LENCLOS.

Clark, George Rogers (1752–1818). American Revolutionary frontier leader. His victories over the

British at Kaskaskia and Vincennes (1778–1779) assured American control of the Old Northwest.

Clark, Walter van Tilburg (1909–   ). American novelist and short-story writer. Although he was born in Maine, Clark lived most of his life in the Far West, and it is with this region that his talents are almost entirely identified. He is best known for *The Ox-Bow Incident* (1940), his forceful first novel that tells of the lynching of three supposed cattle rustlers just as word arrives that they are innocent. He is also the author of two other novels: *City of Trembling Leaves* (1945) and *The Track of the Cat* (1949). *The Watchful Gods* (1950) is a collection of short stories.

Clarke, Austin (1896–   ). Irish poet and writer of verse plays and novels. His work is inspired by the Irish countryside, legends, and history. His *Collected Poems* appeared in 1936, and *Collected Later Poems,* in 1961. *The Singing Men at Cashel* (1936) and *The Sun Dances at Easter* (1952) are novels. *Collected Plays* appeared in 1963.

classical. (1) Usually, a term referring to the classics, or to the period of greatest power among the Greeks and Romans, especially their culture.

(2) In literature and art in general, a term used to express, with reference to a single work as well as to an entire age, dominance of form over content; technical precision over emotional expressiveness; clarity, restraint, and rationality over ambiguity, extravagance, and free play of the imagination. It is opposed to ROMANTICISM. See NEOCLASSICISM.

(3) In music, the term is applied to work that accepts certain basic conventions of form and structure as the natural framework for the expression of ideas, as distinguished from music that is more concerned with the expression of individual emotions than with the achievement of formal unity. The term is usually restricted to music from 1750 to 1830, the period marked by the rise of the symphony and the composers HAYDN and MOZART. BEETHOVEN stands as a transitional figure to the Romantic era. The term is also used commonly to denote all serious or art music, as distinguished from all popular and folk music.

classics. The Romans were divided by Servius into five classes. Any citizen who belonged to the highest class was called *classicus;* the rest were said to be *infra classem,* that is, beneath the class. Accordingly, authors of the best or first class were termed *classici auctores* (classic authors). The term has come to describe any work or body of works of the first or highest order; thus we have English classics, French classics, and so on.

Claudel, Paul [Louis Charles Marie] (1868–1955). French dramatist, poet, and diplomat. After spending his boyhood in a small village, Claudel came with his family to Paris. He believed he had lost the conventional Catholic faith of his parents, but at 18 he rediscovered in the prose poems of Arthur Rimbaud's *Les Illuminations* and *Une Saison en Enfer* the revelation of the supernatural; that Christmas Eve during a service at Notre Dame Cathedral he suddenly felt himself permanently converted to fervent faith. He spent four years discovering the literature which was to influence him most, including the Bible, Aeschylus, Vergil, and Dante, and attending Mallarmé's salons.

In 1890 he published TÊTE D'OR and wrote THE CITY, both showing much symoblist influence. In 1893 he began his career as a foreign diplomat and came as a consul to Boston and New York; he wrote *The Exchange* (*L'Echange;* 1893), a play set on the east coast of the United States, and translated the *Agamemnon* of Aeschylus into French. In 1895 he went to China, which he describes in the prose poems of *The East I Know* (*Connaissance de l'Est;* 1900). Thereafter he traveled widely, serving in the Far East, Germany, Italy, Brazil, and again in the U.S. until 1935, after which he lived in retirement, primarily at a country home in France. *L'Arbre* (1901), a collection of all his plays to that date, includes *La Jeune fille Violaine,* which Claudel later adapted as the well-known THE TIDINGS BROUGHT TO MARY. He published BREAK OF NOON in 1906, and THE HOSTAGE in 1909, soon followed by the last two plays of the Coûfontaine trilogy. In 1916 he completed the translation of the last two plays of Aeschylus' *Oresteia* trilogy. Between 1919 and 1924 he wrote the long play THE SATIN SLIPPER, greatly influenced by the Nō theater of Japan (he went to Tokyo as ambassador in 1921). Among his later works the best known are the dramatic oratorios *The Book of Christopher Columbus* (*Le Livre de Christophe Colomb;* 1927), with music by Darius Milhaud, and *Jeanne d'Arc au Bûcher,* with music by Arthur Honegger.

Claudel's plays, as well as his lyric poems, are written in poetic "versets" of irregular length, often of several lines, without rhyme or conventional meter; the dynamic, vigorous rhythm often resembles that of biblical verse. His inspiration is primarily religious, but he writes as passionately and eloquently of the physical world as of the spiritual; for him all things are manifestations of God, fulfilling His designs and redounding to His glory. The plays describe the conflict in men between their earthly desires and needs—to plow and reap, to explore and conquer, to delight in sensual pleasures, to love one another—and their eventual spiritual destination. The harmony of the physical cosmos, which he presents with sweeping magnificence, represents for Claudel the grandeur of God; similarly, the energy men bring to their human passions becomes the medium through which they can come to an intimation of divine love; and the greater the capacity of a character's soul for intense passion of any kind, the greater the value and the joy of its final mystic surrender to God.

Shorter lyrical poems include *Cinq Grandes Odes* (1910), *Corona benignitatis anni Dei* (1914), and *Ode jubilaire* (1921), about Dante. His prose includes discussions of his own poetic form and of poetry in general, religious meditations as in *A Poet Before the Cross* (*Un Poète regarde la Croix;* 1932), and much biblical commentary.

Claudine. Heroine of four semiautobiographical novels by COLETTE: *Claudine at School* (*Claudine à l'école;* 1900), *Claudine in Paris* (*Claudine à Paris;* 1901), *Claudine Married* (*Claudine en ménage;* 1902), and *The Innocent Wife* (*Claudine s'en va;* 1903).

Claudio. The brother of the virtuous Isabella in Shakespeare's MEASURE FOR MEASURE. He is the pivotal character in the play, embodying humanity's weakness and standing between the strict purity of Isabella and the cruel austerity of Angelo.

Claudio. In Shakespeare's MUCH ADO ABOUT NOTHING, a handsome young Florentine lord, who has served with distinction in the army of Don Pedro. He falls in love at first sight with Hero.

Claudius I. Full Latin name, **Tiberius Claudius Drusus Nero Germanicus** (10 B.C.-A.D. 54). Roman emperor (A.D. 41–54). He was excluded from public affairs by Caligula, his predecessor and nephew. When Caligula was murdered in A.D. 41, Claudius was proclaimed emperor by the praetorian guard. He was persuaded by AGRIPPINA, his second wife, to set aside his own son BRITANNICUS and adopt her son by a former marriage, Lucius Domitius (later NERO), as his successor. When Claudius, too late, repented this move, he was poisoned by Agrippina. Claudius was noted for his writing, but none of his work is extant. He is the principal character in two historical novels, *I, Claudius* (1934) and *Claudius the God* (1934), by Robert Graves.

Claudius. In Shakespeare's HAMLET, the uncle of Hamlet. He has poisoned his brother, the king of Denmark, married his widow, and ascended the throne before the play opens. Shakespeare depicts him as a sensual though able ruler whose lust for power fails to be tempered by the gnawing of his conscience.

Claudius, Matthias (1740–1815). German poet, known for his simple, sincere Christianity and his love for the common people and nature. His works include *Tändeleien und Erzählungen (Triflings and Stories,* 1763) and a periodical that he edited, *Der Wandsbecker Bothe (The Wandsbeck Messenger,* 1771–1775).

Claudius the God (1934). A novel by Robert GRAVES. A sequel to *I, Claudius,* it is an unusual historical and psychological novel, written in the form of the autobiography of the Emperor Claudius. It does not present the traditional view of Claudius as a despicable weakling.

Claus, Peter. See KLAUS, PETER.

Claus, Santa. See SANTA CLAUS.

Claussen, Sophus (1865–1931). Danish poet and essayist. Influenced by the French symbolist movement, and particularly by the work of Baudelaire, Claussen was Denmark's leading symbolist poet. His poetry, woven of esoteric imagery and intricate paradox, expresses a sensuous joy in life. In a romantic manner he worshiped the creative vitality of nature, likening it to the vigorous creativity of the poet figure. Among his collections are *Naturbørn* (1887), *Frøken Regnvejr* (1894), *Pileflöjter* (1899), *Danske vers* (1912), *Heroica* (1925), and *Hvededynger* (1930).

Claveret, Jean (1590–1666). French playwright and author. In *Traité du poème dramatique,* Claveret challenged the classical rule restricting the action of a drama to a 24-hour period. His play *L'Esprit fort* (1630), which ridicules a man who pretends to be of strong character and independent judgment but who is actually a moral coward, is notable as the first French comedy of manners.

Clavers, Mrs. Mary. See Caroline KIRKLAND.

Clavileño. In Cervantes' DON QUIXOTE, the wooden horse on which the knight and his squire make a fantastic journey through the air. It is governed by a wooden pin in its forehead. The horse is a well-known figure in European and Near Eastern folklore.

Clay. A short story in James Joyce's DUBLINERS (1914). It is about a very ordinary, ineffectual, pitiful spinster called Maria who goes to the family party of a man to whom she was nurse when he was a child. The story, which has little action, is largely a character study of Maria. During a blindfold party game the children play a trick on her, making her put her fingers in a dish of wet clay. The clay is a symbol of her character; she herself is a symbol of Ireland.

Clay, Henry (1777–1852). American statesman, often called "The Great Pacificator." As a member of Congress from Kentucky, he was Speaker of the House (1811–1820, 1823–1825) and a leader of the "war hawks" who urged war with Great Britain before 1812. After running unsuccessfully for the presidency in 1824, he was named secretary of state by John Quincy ADAMS. He later served in the U.S. Senate (1831–1842, 1849–1852), where he espoused an "American System" of internal improvements and protective tariffs to strengthen the national economy. In 1832 and 1844 he was the unsuccessful Whig candidate for president; he is credited with saying, "I would rather be right than be President." Devoted to the preservation of the Union, he was largely responsible for the enactment of the COMPROMISE OF 1850. See John RANDOLPH.

Clayhanger (1910). The 1st novel in a series by Arnold BENNETT. Under the domination of his unimaginative puritanical father, Edwin Clayhanger is forced to give up his ambition to become an architect and enters the family printing business. He falls in love with Hilda Lessways, but his father will not give him enough money to marry, and he learns that Hilda is already married. Hilda's husband, George Cannon, is found to be a bigamist, old Clayhanger dies, and Edwin and Hilda are married. The novel has notable descriptions of Five Towns life, the conflict between father and son, and the son's own inner conflicts. In *Hilda Lessways* (1911) the same events are narrated from Hilda's point of view; *These Twain* (1916) is a study of the couple in married life; and *The Roll Call* (1918) is about Hilda's son, George.

Clea. See ALEXANDRIA QUARTET, THE.

Cléante. The name given by Molière to 3 of his characters. (1) In LE MALADE IMAGINAIRE, the lover of Angélique, the daughter of Argan.

(2) In L'AVARE, the son of Harpagon.

(3) In LE TARTUFFE, the brother-in-law of Orgon.

Cleisthenes (Kleisthenes; fl. 507 B.C.). Athenian statesman, considered the second founder of the democracy. Cleisthenes saw that the divisiveness of the clans would forever keep SOLON's government from working well. Cleisthenes' organization aimed to do away with local political influence. Taking the natural divisions of the *demes* as the basis for the Athenian state, he divided the country into three regions: the city, the coast, and the inland area. Each of the regions was divided into ten *trittyes,* a total of 30. From the 30 *trittyes,* Cleisthenes formed ten groups of three, so that none of the ten groups had two *trittyes* from the same region. Each group, though it was based on artificial geography, was known as a tribe. Local political action was ended, and all citizens worked for the general good. Cleisthenes replaced Solon's Council of 400 (based on the four clans) with a Council of 500, fifty from each tribe. The operation of the Council shows that the Athenians understood representative government. Cleisthenes is also supposed to have initiated the practice of ostracism.

Clelia. See CLOELIA.

Clélie, Histoire Romaine (1654–1660). A novel in 10 volumes by Madeleine de SCUDÉRY. Derived and enormously elaborated from the Roman legend of Cloelia, the novel recounts the tribulations endured by Clélie as hostage of Sextus Tarquinus and climaxes with her swimming of the Tiber and her long-sought reunion with her lover Aronce. Rich in digressions, the novel includes the *carte de tendre,* an imaginative map of the amorous sentiments, drawn up by Madeleine de Scudéry with the aid of her salon.

Clemenceau, Georges (1841–1929). French statesman. During the Civil War Clemenceau served as a correspondent with Grant's army. He was an ardent supporter of Dreyfus and agitated for a new verdict in the case. Serving first as a senator (1902–1920), then as Minister of the Interior (1906), Clemenceau became premier of the Third Republic (1906–1909). Premier again in 1917, he led France to victory in World War I and headed the French delegation to the Peace Conference at Versailles.

Clemens, Samuel Langhorne. See MARK TWAIN.

Clement VII, Pope. See MEDICI.

Clementina della Porretta, The Lady. In Samuel Richardson's novel SIR CHARLES GRANDISON,

a devout young Catholic deeply in love with Sir Charles.

Cléofas Pérez Zambullo, Don. The high-spirited hero of two picaresque novels: *Le Diable boiteux* (1707) by Alain René LESAGE; the other (on which Lesage modelled his novel), *El Diablo cojuelo* (1641) by Louis Vélez de Guevara. In both books Don Cléofas uncorks the little devil ASMODEUS from a bottle, and as a reward, the latter shows him the vices of Madrid.

Cleon or **Kleon** (d. 422). Athenian demagogue and leader of the war party during the Peloponnesian War. He is chiefly remembered today as one of the favorite butts of Aristophanes, particularly in his comedy THE KNIGHTS.

Cléonte. In Molière's LE BOURGEOIS GENTILHOMME, the suitor for the hand of M. Jourdain's daughter. Since he is a commoner and M. Jourdain will have none but a nobleman for son-in-law, Cléonte is forced to disguise himself as the son of the Grand Turk in order to win her hand.

Cleopatra. In the chronology of Egyptian queens, **Cleopatra VII** (69–30 B.C.). Last Macedonian queen of Egypt. From 51 to 49 B.C. she was joint ruler with and wife of her brother Ptolemy XIII, in accordance with Egyptian tradition. She was driven from the throne by her brother, but reinstated by Julius CAESAR in 48; this gave rise to a war between Caesar and Ptolemy XIII in which the latter was killed, and his younger brother Ptolemy XIV ascended the throne and married Cleopatra. Cleopatra lived with Caesar in Rome from 46 to 44 and had by him a son, Ptolemy XV, who was later put to death

The *carte de tendre* from an English edition of *Clélie*. In the form of a map, it outlines the course of love.

by Augustus. Returning to Egypt after Caesar's assassination, Cleopatra gave her support to the Second Triumvirate of ANTONY, Octavius (later Augustus), and Lepidus against the republicans Brutus and Cassius. Mark Antony, who had been appointed to rule over Asia and the East, succumbed completely to her charms and abandoned his wife Octavia to live with Cleopatra. They had three children. After the defeat of Antony and Cleopatra at ACTIUM, Antony killed himself on hearing a false report of her death; some say she spread the report herself to gain favor with Octavius by causing Antony's death. When she heard that Octavius planned to exhibit her triumphantly in Rome, she committed suicide by applying a poison asp to her bosom. Famed for her extraordinary charm and beauty, she was also highly cultivated.

The capricious and imperious queen is one of the most complex and fully developed of Shakespeare's female characters. In his ANTONY AND CLEOPATRA, she is a wildly erratic, jealous, and avaricious woman, but withal sincerely in love with Antony. The famous speech of Enobarbus aptly describes her:

> Age cannot wither her, nor custom stale
> Her infinite variety; other women cloy
> The appetites they feed, but she makes hungry
> Where most she satisfies; for vilest things
> Become themselves in her, that the holy priests
> Bless her when she is riggish.

She also appears in Dryden's ALL FOR LOVE OR THE WORLD WELL LOST and Shaw's CAESAR AND CLEOPATRA.

Cleopatra's Needle. Either of two obelisks, one in Central Park in New York City, the other on the Thames Embankment in London. They were erected by Thothmes III, a pharaoh of the 18th dynasty, in Heliopolis. Augustus had them removed to Alexandria about 9 B.C. They antedated Cleopatra by many centuries.

clerihew. A form of verse invented by Edmund Clerihew BENTLEY. It consists of two couplets that humorously characterize a person whose name is one of the rhymes.

Clerk's Tale, The. One of the CANTURBURY TALES of Geoffrey CHAUCER, written in RHYME ROYAL and based on a Latin adaptation by Petrarch of the 100th tale in Boccaccio's *Decameron* (see GRISELDA). The people of Saluzzo urge their Marquis Walter to marry and provide a successor. He chooses Griselda, the virtuous, lovely, and hard-working daughter of the poorest man in town. She promises that she will always willingly obey him, proves well gifted for helping him rule, and is much beloved by the people, but he insists on trying her steadfast devotion to the extreme. He takes both of their children away from her shortly after birth, telling her that he must kill them because the people feel that his heirs must not share her lowly ancestry. Finally he divorces her, sending her home, then recalling her to supervise the preparation of the palace and the reception of a new bride. She does everything willingly, until finally Walter reveals that the supposed bride and her brother are Griselda's own children, secretly raised by Walter's sister, and all live in affectionate happines thereafter. Chaucer implies humorously that the story cannot literally mean that Griselda's behavior, any more than Walter's, is worthy of emulation, but rather is an allegory of the constancy all men should show in unavoidable adversity.

Cleveland, [Stephen] Grover (1837–1908). 22d and 24th president of the U.S. (1884–1888, 1892–1896). Having served as mayor of Buffalo, N.Y., and as governor of New York, Cleveland was elected to the presidency on the Democratic ticket in 1884, defeating James G. BLAINE. In 1886 he married Frances Folsom in the first presidential wedding held in the White House. He ran for a second term in 1888 and was defeated by Benjamin Harrison, whom he in turn defeated in 1892. During the Panic of 1893 he secured the repeal of the Sherman Silver Purchase Act to end a drain in U.S. gold reserves. In 1894 he alienated labor by sending troops to Illinois to prevent interference with the mails during the Pullman Strike. He also invoked the Monroe Doctrine to help settle a boundary dispute between Venezuela and British Guiana. The hero of Paul Leicester Ford's THE HONORABLE PETER STIRLING is supposedly modeled on Cleveland.

Cleveland or **Clieveland, John** (1613–1658). English METAPHYSICAL POET. A reader in rhetoric at Cambridge and a Royalist during the English Civil War, he wrote satire in both verse and prose against the Puritans. In his poetry the metaphysical CONCEIT was carried to its point of greatest extravagance, degenerating often to a kind of witty ornamentation. He was very popular in his day and was imitated by numerous lesser poets. The most complete and authentic volume of his work was *Clievelandi Vindiciae, or Cleveland's Genuine Remains* (1677).

Cliff Dwellers, The (1893). A novel by Henry B. FULLER. Fuller, a pioneer in the depiction of city life, perhaps originated the term "cliff dwellers" to describe the denizens of huge apartment houses and skyscrapers. A Chicago skyscraper is the central locale of the book, which explores the subject of wealth and its effects on a large number of characters.

Clifford, Mrs. Lucy, born Lane (?–1929). English novelist and playwright, best known for her literary associations—with Leslie Stephen, George Eliot, James Russell Lowell, and Henry James. Her most successful novel was *Mrs. Keith's Crime* (1885), the story of parents who are tried for ending the misery of their hopelessly ill and suffering child.

Cligés. See CHRÉTIEN DE TROYES.

Clinker, Humphrey. See HUMPHREY CLINKER.

Clinton, Sir Henry (1738?–1795). English general in the American Revolution. Named commander in-chief of all British forces in America, he captured Charleston, S.C. (1780). His delay in sending reinforcements to Cornwallis contributed to the British surrender at Yorktown.

Clio. In classic mythology, one of the nine MUSES, the inventor of historical and heroic poetry.

Addison adopted the name as a pseudonym, perhaps because many of his papers in the *Spectator* are signed by one of the four letters in this word, probably the initial letters of Chelsea, London, Islington, Office.

Clitandre. The impostor-hero of Molière's *comédie-ballet* L'AMOUR MÉDECIN. Also, a tragicomedy by Pierre CORNEILLE (1632).

Clitus. In Shakespeare's JULIUS CAESAR, a servant of Brutus. When Brutus asks Clitus to kill him, he refuses, saying that he would rather kill himself.

Clive, Robert. Baron **Clive of Plassey** (1725–1774). Founder of the empire of British India and governor of Bengal (1764), who obtained for the East India Company sovereignty over the whole province. On his return to England in 1767, he met a storm of obloquy and inquiries into his actions, and although he was acquitted, he later committed suicide.

Clodius Pulcher, Publius (d. 52 B.C.). Roman patrician and tribune. He was known as a profligate and as a bitter enemy of CICERO. Cicero had disproved Clodius' alibi when the latter was accused of profaning the rites of the BONA DEA by attending them in disguise, and, though through bribery Clodius was acquitted, he hated Cicero and harassed him from then on. It was Clodius who passed a bill exiling anyone who put a Roman to death without right of appeal—a measure directed against Cicero who had members of the Cataline conspiracy executed—and thus sent Cicero into exile (58). Clodius was the brother of the notorious Clodia, the "Lesbia" of Catullus' poetry.

Cloelia or **Clelia.** In the legendary history of Rome, a Roman maiden, one of the hostages given to Lars Porsena. She made her escape from the Etruscan camp by swimming across the Tiber. She was sent back by the honorable Romans; Porsena, however, not only set her at liberty in recognition of her courage but also released her fellow hostages. Mlle. de Scudéry took this story as the framework for her celebrated romance *Clélie*, published in 10 volumes (1654–1660).

Cloete, [Edward Fairly] Stuart [Graham] (1897–). South African novelist. His novels, such as *Turning Wheels* (1937), are often set in South Africa and are usually historical, about the early Boer settlers. *West with the Sun* (1962) is a travel book.

Cloister and the Hearth, The (1861). A historical novel by Charles READE. The action takes place on the Continent in the latter years of the 15th century. Among the historical characters of note whom Reade introduces into the narrative are Froissart, Gringoire, Deschamps, Luther, Villon, and—as a child—Erasmus. The story centers around the tragically thwarted love of Erasmus' parents: Gerard, a talented young writer, and the red-haired Margaret, daughter of Peter Brandt. A forged letter convinces Gerard of Margaret's death; and, after a period of despair and wild living, he becomes a monk of the Dominican order, unaware that Margaret has given birth to Erasmus, his son. When after many adventures and misadventures the pair meet again, Gerard is unable, because of his vows, to live with his family. He manages, however, to settle nearby. Margaret soon dies of the plague, and the heartbroken Gerard dies shortly thereafter.

Clootie, Auld. See AULD HORNIE.

Cloridano. In the ORLANDO FURIOSO of Ariosto, a Moorish soldier, companion of Medoro, who goes with the latter to retrieve from the battlefield the body of their king Dardinello, after he had been killed by Rinaldo at the siege of Paris. Surprised by Zerbino, he leaves the body to Medoro and flees, but later dies defending his friend.

Clorinda. In the GERUSALEMME LIBERATA of Tasso, a pagan warrior maid from Persia. She is the daughter of King Senapo (Senapus) of Ethiopia, but when she was born, her mother the queen, fearful that the child's white complexion would arouse the suspicions of the king, substitutes a Negro child for her and gives her up to the care of the eunuch Arsete. At one point, Arsete loses her and she is suckled by a tiger. Later, he finds her again and takes her to the East, where she grows up skilled in arms. At the battle of Antioch, to which she comes to fight the knights of the First Crusade, she meets briefly and falls deeply in love with TANCREDI (Tancred), one of the leading Crusaders. When she offers her arms to the king of Jerusalem, Aladino, in exchange for the lives of Sofronia and Olindo, she finds herself once again in combat with her beloved. Unwittingly, Tancred wounds her in a night attack. Before she dies in his arms, she seeks baptism, having learned from Arsete of her Christian parentage. Tancred, in desperate grief, grants her wish and receives her forgiveness. Later, he has a vision of her in heaven.

Closterman, Pierre (1921–). French novelist. The work of Closterman, a World War II aviator, has risen to popularity in France with the work of other explorers and adventurers, among them Maurice Herzog who writes of mountain climbing, and Alain Bombard who writes of the sea. Testaments to man's courage and to his powers of endurance, Closterman's works include *Le Grand Cirque* (*The Big Show*, 1948) and *Feux du ciel* (*Flames in the Sky*, 1951).

Cloten. In Shakespeare's CYMBELINE, the son of the second wife of Cymbeline by a former husband. He is an arrogant, vindictive lout who does, however, display some good sense. Cloten is the rejected lover of Imogen.

Clotho. See the FATES.

Cloud, The (1820). A poem by Percy Bysshe SHELLEY. A lyrical description by a cloud of its cyclical journey from the sky to the earth and back once more to the sky, it expresses the poet's pantheism and his idea of nature's eternal alteration, rebirth, and recurrence.

Cloud-cuckoo-land (Gr., **Nephelococcygia**). A Utopian city built in the sky by the birds in Aristophanes' comedy *The Birds*. It has come to refer to visionary schemes in general.

Clouds, The (Nephelai). A comedy by Aristophanes (423 B.C.). This clever satire unfairly equates Socrates with the Sophists, noted for their capacity to use argument cunningly to prove whatever point they wished to make, whereas the actual Socrates seriously criticized them, believing that argument was useful only if it arrived at truth. A dishonest farmer, Strepsiades encourages his son Phidippides to enroll in Socrates' school, the Thinkery, where he can learn to evade his numerous creditors through shrewd argument. Strepsiades is delighted with his son's immense success until the young man turns his new talent against his father. At this point the old man regrets turning away from the old virtues and ends by setting fire to the Thinkery.

Clouet, François (c. 1510–c. 1572). French painter. Appointed court painter by Francis I, he is known for his soberly accurate portrait drawings and paintings. His father, Jean (c. 1486–1541), who served in a similar capacity, was a noted miniaturist.

Clovis I. *Ger.* **Chlodwig**, equivalent to later *Fr.* Louis (c. 466–511). King of the Salian Franks (after 481) who reunited the kingdom of his grandfather Merovée and firmly established the MEROVINGIAN dynasty. He married a Christian princess and had himself and all his people baptized, thus securing the political backing of the Roman Catholic Church.

cluricaune. In Irish folklore, an elf, particularly one guarding secret treasure.

Clutton-Brock, Arthur (1868–1924). English critic and essayist. He is highly regarded for his style. He wrote studies of Shelley (1909) and William Morris (1914). He was a Fabian socialist.

Clymene (Klymene). In Greek mythology, the daughter of Oceanus and Thetis, wife of Iapetus, and mother of Atlas, Prometheus, and Epimetheus. Clymene is, also, the name of many other heroines in Greek mythology and legend, especially that of the mother of Phaethon.

Clytemnestra (Klytaimnestra or Klytaimestra). In Greek legend, the daughter of Tyndareus and Leda. She became the wife of Agamemnon, whom she and her paramour Aegisthus murdered after his return from Troy. She was slain by her son Orestes. See the House of ATREUS.

Clytie (Klytie). In classical mythology, an ocean nymph, in love with the Sun-God. Her love passed unnoticed, and she was changed into the heliotrope, or sunflower, which, traditionally, still turns to the sun, following him through his daily course.

Coates, Robert M[yron] (1897–   ). American writer and art critic. During the 1920's Coates was an expatriate in Europe, where he wrote his first novel, *The Eater of Darkness* (1929). He later became art critic for *The New Yorker*. He is also the author of *The Outlaw Years* (1930), a history of the Natchez Trace pirates, and *Wisteria Cottage* (1948) and *The Farther Shore* (1957), two fictional studies of criminal psychology.

Cobb, Humphrey (1889–1944). American novelist. He is best known for *Paths of Glory* (1935), his powerful World War I novel belonging to the school of Remarque. It was made into a successful play by Sidney Howard and into an excellent movie.

Cobb, Irvin S[hrewsbury] (1876–1944). American writer, humorist, and newspaperman. Noted especially for his Judge PRIEST stories, Cobb earlier was a newspaperman for the New York *Sun* and the *World*. He later wrote for *The Saturday Evening Post* and, from 1922 to 1932, for *Cosmopolitan*. Cobb was in the main stream of American humor and was a direct follower of Artemus Ward and Mark Twain. The number of books and stories he wrote was immense. His first book was *Back Home* (1912). In addition to the Judge Priest books, Cobb wrote humorous skits, travel books, such as *Europe Revised* (1914), and an autobiography, *Exit Laughing* (1941).

Cobbett, William (1762–1835). English writer and journalist. He is best known for his pro-British pamphlets written in the U.S. under the pseudonym Peter Porcupine, and for his newspaper *Cobbett's Political Register,* published in England beginning in 1802. He became a member of Parliament in 1832. *Rural Rides* (1830), descriptions of life and agricultural conditions in the English countryside, remains his most interesting work today.

Cobden, Richard (1804–1865). English statesman and publicist. He is especially known as an advocate of free trade and peace. He was a member of Parliament most of the time from 1841 to his death, but refused party affiliation and opportunities to become a cabinet minister. He was a leader, with John Bright, of the Anti-Corn Law League (see CORN LAWS) and earned some unpopularity for his opposition to the Crimean War. He was an adherent of the North in the U.S. Civil War. His *Political Writings* were published in 1867 and his *Speeches on Questions of Public Policy* in 1870.

Cobweb. See PEASE-BLOSSOM.

Coccioli, Carlo (1920–   ). Italian-born writer who now publishes in French. In 1946 Coccioli published his first novel, *Il Migliore et l'Ultimo. Le Ciel et la Terre* (1952, translated from the Italian) is the story of the struggles of a parish priest, Don Ardito Piccardi. In its concern with spiritual problems it reveals a marked kinship with the work of Georges Bernanos. *La Ville et le Sang* (1955), *Manuel le Mexicain* (1956), and *La Table Ronde* (1957) were written in French.

cockatrice. A fabulous and heraldic monster with the wings of a fowl, tail of a dragon, and head of a cock. It was so called because it was said to be produced from a cock's egg hatched by a serpent. According to legend, the very look of this monster would cause instant death. In consequence of the crest with which the head is crowned, the creature is called a basilisk. Isaiah (King James version) says, "The weaned child shall put his hand on the cockatrice' den" (xi, 8), to signify that the most obnoxious animal should not hurt the most feeble of God's creatures.

Cock Lane Ghost. The ghost of one Mrs. Kent; she appeared as a "luminous lady" and was supposedly responsible for mysterious noises. This fraud, perpetrated in Cock Lane, Smithfield, London by a man and his 11-year-old daughter, was exposed in 1762. Samuel Johnson took an interest in the ghost and was satirized for believing in it by Charles CHURCHILL in his poem *The Ghost;* Johnson's interest, of course, did not stem from credulity, but from a determination to expose the fraud.

Cockney School. An epithet applied by John Gibson LOCKHART to the group of writers that included Leigh Hunt, Hazlitt, Shelley, and Keats. The group was largely composed of Londoners, and Lockhart, who was a devoted partisan of the LAKE POETS and a fierce enemy of writers whose aims or principles varied from his own, sneeringly referred to Hunt as "the Cockney Homer" and to Hazlitt as "the Cockney Aristotle."

Cocktail Party, The (1949). A poetic drama by T. S. ELIOT. On one level the play is a contemporary drawing-room comedy; on another it is a profound religious work concerned with universal themes. The cocktail party is a trivial affair at which ordinary Edward tries to hide from his friends the fact that his wife, Lavinia, has just left him. Edward and Celia are lovers, and Celia urges Edward to take the opportunity, divorce his wife, and marry her. However, Edward suddenly feels he needs his wife most. An unidentified stranger at the party warns Edward that his decision has set in motion events that he may not be able to control. When Lavinia returns the couple go together to a psychiatrist, Sir Henry Harcourt-Reilly, who turns out to be the stranger who was at the party. He reconciles the couple, telling them there are two kinds of good life, the acceptance of ordinary day-to-day duties, such as they have chosen, and the way of self-dedication and self-sacrifice, which Celia has finally chosen; Celia's choice is the best. Two years later, at another cocktail party, the guests learn that Celia has been martyred on a tropical island. The psychiatrist and Julia, a meddling old woman, are god and guardian-angel figures, and put forward Eliot's Christian point of view. The verse, characterized by passages of incantation and repetition, is written in the rhythms of conversation.

Cocteau, Jean (1889–1963). French poet, novelist, dramatist, essayist, film writer, and director. In the vanguard of almost every experimental artistic movement of the century, especially cubism and surrealism, Cocteau did much to promote the work of such innovators as Picasso, Chirico, Stravinsky, and the Groupe des six. Through all his works runs the theme of the poet-angel, defier of Destiny and guardian of the divine in man. The poet can be glimpsed in children and legendary heroes, but he risks being lost in the disorder of the modern world.

The most famous of his modernistic ballets are *Parade* (1916), music by Erik Satie, scenery by Picasso; *Le Boeuf sur le toit* (1920), music by Darius Milhaud; and *Les Mariés de la tour Eiffel* (1921), music by the Groupe des six.

His poetic novels are *Thomas the Impostor* (1923), set in World War I, *The Grand Ecart* (1923), and LES ENFANTS TERRIBLES (1930).

For the theater Cocteau adapted a number of myths and legends: *Antigone* (1922), *Romeo et Juliette* (1924), *Orphée* (1926), *Oedipus Rex* (1928; a libretto for an opera by Stravinsky), THE INFERNAL MACHINE (1934; also on the Oedipus myth), *Les Chevaliers de la Table Ronde* (1937), and *Bacchus* (1951). Original plots include those of *The Human Voice* (1930; made into an opera by Francis Poulenc), *Intimate Relations* (*Les Parents terribles;* 1938), *The Typewriter* (*La Machine à écrire;* 1941), and *The Eagle Has Two Heads* (*L'Aigle a Deux Têtes;* 1946).

His most famous films include the surrealistic *The Blood of a Poet* (*Le Sang d'un Poète;* 1932), *The Eternal Return* (1944), *Beauty and the Beast* (*La Belle et la Bête;* 1945), *Les Parents terribles* (1948) and *Les Enfants terribles* (1950).

In addition to a number of volumes of poetry his works include the cartoons, verse, and prose of *Le Potomak* (1913, pub. 1919); the critical essays of *A Call to Order* (1926); the personal account *Opium: A Diary of a Cure* (1930); and the autobiography *Portraits-Souvenir* (1935).

Cocu imaginaire, le. See SGANARELLE.

Cocytus (Kokytas). One of the five rivers of hell in Greek mythology. The word means the river of lamentation. The unburied were doomed to wander about its banks for 100 years. It flows into the river Acheron. See STYX.

Code of Justinian. See JUSTINIAN I.

Cody, William F[rederick]. Known as **Buffalo Bill** (1846–1917). American scout, showman, and folk hero. An expert horseman and marksman, Cody was a rider for the pony express, a frontier scout,

and a hunter of buffalo. After 1883 he toured the U.S. and Europe in his "Wild West Show." Cody's career was popularized by the dime novels of E. Z. C. JUDSON (Ned Buntline), who claimed that he had given Cody his sobriquet.

Coffin, Robert P[eter] Tristram (1892–1955). American poet. Coffin is noted for his writings dealing with his native state of Maine. A Pulitzer Prize winner in poetry for *Strange Holiness* (1935), he wrote many volumes of verse, including *Golden Falcon* (1929), *Maine Ballads* (1938), and *People Are Like Ballads* (1946). He also wrote several prose works about Maine and the volume called *The Kennebec* (1937) for the Rivers of America series. Positive and optimistic (America, he said, "is promises—promises kept"), both his prose and poetry are marked by a frank colloquialism.

Coghill, Nevill (1899–   ). English literary scholar. He is best known for his translation of Chaucer's *The Canterbury Tales* into modern English (1951).

cogito ergo sum. The axiom of DESCARTES. It was formulated as the starting place of his system of philosophy. It means "I think, therefore I exist." Descartes, at the beginning, provisionally doubted everything, but he could not doubt the existence of the *ego,* for the mere fact that *I* doubt presupposes the existence of the *I:* in other words, the doubt could not exist without the *I.*

Cohan, George M[ichael] (1878–1942). American actor, song writer, playwright, and producer. As a child Cohan acted in vaudeville in a family theatrical group, "The Four Cohans." The first play that he wrote, produced, and acted in was *The Governor's Son* (1901). He followed this with *Little Johnny Jones* (1904), in which he played a role always thereafter associated with him, "the Yankee Doodle Boy." Among his musicals and dramas were *Forty-Five Minutes from Broadway* (1906); GET-RICH-QUICK WALLINGFORD; *Broadway Jones* (1912), a play and musical about a young spendthrift; and *Seven Keys to Baldpate* (1913), based on a novel by Earl Derr Biggers. In the course of his career, Cohan wrote many songs which have remained American favorites: *Over There, I'm a Yankee Doodle Dandy, Grand Old Flag, Give My Regards to Broadway,* and *Mary Is a Grand Old Name.*

Cohen, Octavus Roy (1891–1959). American writer of short stories and detective fiction. Best known for his stories about stereotyped Negro characters, he was the creator of Florian Slappey and Epic Peters. They appeared in such books as *Florian Slappey Goes Abroad* (1928), *Epic Peters, Pullman Porter* (1930), and *Florian Slappey* (1938).

Coignard, Jérôme. A character created by Anatole France. Coignard is an irreverent, licentious abbé who also manages to be a wise and witty philosopher. The chief personage in AT THE SIGN OF THE REINE PÉDAUQUE and *Les Opinions de Jérôme Coignard* (1893), Coignard is one of France's most popular characters. Many of the author's own beliefs and opinions are voiced by him.

Colbert, Jean Baptiste (1619–1683). French statesman. After hastening the downfall of Fouquet, Colbert was made controller general of finance by Louis XIV in 1665. Although Colbert initiated many wise reforms, the costs of the king's wars and courtly extravagances defeated his plans to increase national prosperity. Colbert founded several academies and was a patron of men of letters.

Colchis (Kolchis). In Greek mythology, a city at the eastern end of the Black Sea on the River Phasis. It was ruled by Aeetes, from whom the Argonauts stole the GOLDEN FLEECE.

Cold Comfort Farm (1932). A novel by Stella GIBBONS. A brilliant parody of the novel of rustic pessimism, such as those written by Mary WEBB and other writers in the Hardy tradition, it virtually put an end to a widely popular genre.

Coldfield, Rosa. A narrator and important character in William Faulkner's novel ABSALOM, ABSALOM! Her empty life centers in her hatred of Thomas Sutpen, her brother-in-law, whom she sees as a monster, though he has long been dead.

Cole, King. Legendary English king best known as the "Old King Cole" of the nursery rhyme. He is sometimes identified with the Coel who according to Geoffrey of Monmouth made himself king of the Britons in the third century, was the father of St. Helena, and thus the grandfather of the Emperor Constantine the Great. He appears often in literature, as in John Masefield's poem *King Cole* (1921).

Cole, Thomas. See HUDSON RIVER SCHOOL.

Coleridge, Samuel Taylor (1772-1834). English poet, essayist, and critic. The son of a Devonshire clergyman, Coleridge was a precocious, dreamy boy; he attended Christ's Hospital school where he met Charles Lamb and formed a friendship that was to last a lifetime. He attended Cambridge (1791-1793, 1794), but did not receive a degree. In 1794 he

Program of Coleridge's lectures on Shakespeare (1808).

met Robert Southey at Oxford, and the two developed their plan, called PANTISOCRACY, to establish a small, ideal community in the U. S. Unable to finance their project, they had to abandon it. In the meantime, because marriage was an essential factor in the pantisocratic scheme, Coleridge became engaged to Sarah Fricker, sister of Southey's fiancée, only to discover, too late, that his love for Mary Evans was reciprocated. His unfortunate marriage (1795) to Miss Fricker ended in separation some seven years later.

In 1796, Coleridge published his first volume of poetry and in the same year began the publication of *The Watchman,* a liberal political periodical, which lasted only 10 issues. He was by now in great financial difficulty and was considering entering the Unitarian ministry when the brothers Josiah and Thomas Wedgwood granted him an annuity of 150 pounds, thus enabling him to pursue his literary career.

In 1797, Coleridge formed a friendship with Wordsworth, a friendship that stimulated Coleridge's finest achievements in poetry, including THE RIME OF THE ANCIENT MARINER, KUBLA KHAN, and the first part of CHRISTABEL. Wordsworth and Coleridge together published LYRICAL BALLADS, and subsequently traveled to Germany where Coleridge studied philosophy at Göttingen University and mastered the German language. On their return to England (1799), Coleridge translated Schiller's *Wallenstein.* Afflicted by the damp climate of the Lake District, where he had settled in order to be near Wordsworth, Coleridge took up opium as a remedy and swiftly became addicted. After writing the second part of *Christabel* and *Dejection: An Ode,* Coleridge wrote very little poetry from then on. Hoping to improve his health, he sailed to Malta in 1804 but returned to England in 1806 without improvement. From 1808 to 1819 he gave seven series of lectures on Shakespeare and other literary subjects, which were brilliant if disorganized. During the years 1809 and 1810 he published a politico-philosophical review, *The Friend,* and a revised version of his tragedy *Osorio* (written 1797) was successfully produced in 1813. Three years later Coleridge took up residence with a doctor, in order to control his opium addiction. In 1817 he republished his earlier poems and BIOGRAPHIA LITERARIA, which contains a good deal of information on Wordsworth as well as much of Coleridge's finest literary criticism. Although his poetic achievement was small in quantity, Coleridge was without a doubt the most perceptive English critic of his time and virtual intellectual spokesman for the English romantic movement.

Colette. Pen name of **Sidonie Gabrielle Colette** (1873-1954). French novelist. The CLAUDINE books, written with her husband, were published under his pseudonym Willy. After their collaboration ended in 1904 and until 1916, she used the name Colette Willy, then Colette. She became a music-hall dancer and mime, and wrote *La Vagabonde* (1910), *L'Envers du music-hall* (1913), and *Mitsou* (1919). Remarried twice, she continued to write wry, penetrating novels of the demimonde and the feminine heart: often the older one, as in *Chéri* (1920) and *La Fin de Chéri* (1926). Her best-known works include *Gigi* (1945); her childhood reminiscences in *La Maison* *de Claudine* (1922) and *Sido* (1929); her description of German Occupation in *Paris de ma fenêtre* (1944); and her late memoirs published in *L'Etoile Vesper* (1946) and *Le Fanal Bleu* (1949).

Colette Baudoche. See Maurice BARRÈS.

Coligny, Gaspard de (1519–1572). French admiral. During the reign of Charles IX he was leader of the Huguenots and made several attempts to establish colonies for French Protestants in America. He was a victim of the MASSACRE OF ST. BARTHOLOMEW.

Colin and Lucy. A tragic love ballad by Thomas TICKELL (1720). It was called by Oliver Goldsmith "the best ballad in our language." Colin was betrothed to Lucy but forsook her for a bride "thrice as rich as she." Lucy was sad, but was present at the wedding; when Colin saw her, "the damps of death bedewed his brow, and he died." Both were buried in one tomb, and many betrothed maidens came there "to deck it with garlands and true-love knots."

Colin Clouts Come Home Againe (1595). A long allegorical pastoral poem by Edmund SPENSER. The shepherd Colin Clout describes to his fellow-shepherds his journey with the Shepherd of the Ocean (Sir Walter Raleigh) to the land of the beautiful shepherdess Cynthia (Queen Elizabeth). Colin Clout also appears in THE SHEPHEARDES CALENDER.

Collar, The (1633). A poem by George HERBERT, in which the author, after rebelling against his profitless service of God, is abruptly and totally reconciled. The poem makes use of irregular line-lengths and rhymes to achieve a remarkable dramatic effect. The collar is the clerical collar, emblem of servitude to God.

Collean, May. The heroine of a Scottish ballad. "Fause Sir John" carried her to a rock in order to throw her down into the sea; but May outwitted him and subjected him to the fate he had designed for her.

Collection, The (1962). A one-act play by Harold PINTER. It is about a homosexual who is accused of making love to another man's wife. The husband enters into a strange, aggressive relationship with the homosexual, perhaps in an attempt to enrage the homosexual's partner as he himself feels outrage and injury.

The Collection was first produced on BBC television (1961).

Collège de France. An institution of higher learning in Paris. Founded by Francis I in 1530 at the instigation of Guillaume BUDÉ, it represented an attempt to place humanistic studies on an equal footing with the theological studies provided at the Sorbonne. Hebrew and Greek were taught for the first time, thus earning it the plaudits of enthusiastic humanists such as Rabelais and Ronsard. First known as the Collège des Lecteurs royaux, it has been called the Collège de France since the Revolution.

College Widow, The (1904). A comedy of college life by George ADE. In the play, the daughter of the college president is asked to use her charms on a certain halfback to induce him to play for the right team. Extremely popular in its day, it has continued to be produced.

Colleoni, Bartolommeo (1400–1475). A famous Italian CONDOTTIERE. Following a brilliant military career highlighted by his tactical genius with artillery, Colleoni lived in pleasant retirement as lord of Bergamo; most of his fellow *condottieri* met violent ends. The statue made of him by the sculptor Verrocchio, still to be seen in Venice, is the major prop of his present-day fame.

Colletet, Guillaume (1598–1659). French poet and playwright. One of the original members of the Académie and one of Richelieu's CINQ AUTEURS, Colletet is less remembered for his plays than for his poems, which include *Divertissements* (1631–1633), *Banquet des Poètes* (1646), and *Epigrammes* (1653).

Collier, Constance. Stage name of **Laura Constance Hardie** (1880–1955). English actress. Once an Edwardes Gaiety Girl, she appeared in *Peter Ibbetson* (1917), *Our Betters* (1923), which had 548 performances, and many other plays. *Harlequinade* (1929) is her autobiography.

Collier, Jeremy (1650–1726). English clergyman, known for his *Short View of the Immorality and Profaneness of the English Stage* (1698), an attack on the licentiousness of the Restoration theater. His work drew an angry reply from CONGREVE, whom he had signaled out for censure, along with Dryden, D'Urfey, and Vanbrugh.

Collier, John (1901–   ). English-born American short-story writer and novelist. Collier's first novel, *His Monkey Wife: Or Married to a Chimp* (1930), was written in the sardonic and fantastic vein that characterized his later work. His other novels include *Epistle to a Friend* (1931), *Full Circle* (1933), and *Defy the Foul Fiend* (1934). Best known for his numerous short stories, which are witty, satiric, grotesque, often macabre, and graced with a delicate and impeccable style, he is often compared to Saki. Among his short-story collections are *No Traveller Returns* (1931), *Green Thoughts* (1932), *The Devil and All* (1934), *Variations on a Theme* (1935), *A Touch of Nutmeg* (1935), and *Presenting Moonshine* (1941). Many of the stories in these collections, as well as previously unpublished works, were reprinted in *Fancies and Goodnights* (1951).

Collin, Jacques. The consummate villain of Honoré de Balzac's LA COMÉDIE HUMAINE. Collin plays a part in many of the novels. In LE PÈRE GORIOT, under the name and disguise of Vautrin, he makes love to the landlady and eats her cheap scanty food until the spiteful Mlle Michonneau gives him up to the police. Collin also appears in *Les Splendeurs et misères des courtisanes* (1843) and *La Dernière incarnation de Vautrin* (1847) as a Spanish priest and philosopher.

Collingwood, R[obin] G[eorge] (1889–1943). English philosopher. He wrote on art, history, religion, and science; among his best-known books are *Principles of Art* (1937), *The Idea of History* (1945), and *The Idea of Nature* (1946). He also published an *Autobiography* (1939).

Collins, Mr. In Jane Austen's PRIDE AND PREJUDICE, a self-important clergyman, very much the toady and prig. Elizabeth Bennet refuses his proposal of marriage, and he marries Charlotte Lucas instead.

Collins, [William] Wilkie (1824–1889). English novelist, best known as the author of THE WOMAN IN WHITE and THE MOONSTONE. He is considered by some to have been the first English author of *bona fide* detective and mystery novels. Collins was a good friend of Charles Dickens, a contributor to Dickens' magazines and occasional collaborator. The two men reciprocally admired and influenced one another, and though their talents are in other respects unequal, Collins occasionally rivaled Dickens in the creation of character and mood, excelled him in handling plot. Among Collins' other books are *The New Magdalen* (1873), *The Haunted Hotel* (1879), and *Heart and Science* (1883).

Collins, William (1721–1759). English poet. One of the preromantics of the eighteenth century, Collins wrote only a small quantity of poetry, consisting chiefly of odes on nature subjects in a quiet, melancholy vein, distinguished by their smoothness and their skillful use of sound-effects. Such work, centering about a personified abstraction, came to be called the "descriptive" or "allegorical" ode. His best-known poems, many of which were published in *Odes on Several Descriptive and Allegorical Subjects* (1746), are *Ode to Evening* (1746); *How Sleep the Brave* (1746); *Dirge in Cymbeline* (1744); and *Ode Occasioned by the death of Mr. Thomson* (1749), commemorating his significant literary relationship with the poet James Thomson. Collins' view of poetry, as set forth in his *Ode on the Poetical Character*, is that it is essentially imaginative, divine in origin, and wild and impassioned in method and insight. All his life Collins suffered from poverty and illness, and he was insane before his death.

Collodi. See PINOCCHIO, THE ADVENTURES OF.

Colman, George. Known as **Colman the elder** (1732–1794). English dramatist. He is best remembered for such comedies as *The Clandestine Marriage* (1766), written with David Garrick, and *The Jealous Wife* (1761).

Colman, George. Known as **Colman the younger** (1762–1836). English playwright known for *The Heir at Law* (1797) and *John Bull* (1803), both comedies. See DELLA-CRUSCANS.

Coloma, Luis (1851–1915). Spanish priest and author. He is best known for the satiric novel *Pequeñeces* (*Currita, Countess of Albornoz,* 1891). This vigorous and realistic work was widely enjoyed during the period at the expense of the real personages so easily identifiable with its characters.

Colonel Jack (1722). The hero and shortened title of *The History of the Most Remarkable Life and Extraordinary Adventures of the truly Hon. Colonel, Jacque, vulgarly called Colonel Jack,* written in the form of an autobiographical novel of a convicted pickpocket, by Daniel DEFOE. The colonel (born a gentleman and bred a pickpocket) goes to Virginia, and passes through all the stages of colonial life, from "slave" to slave owner and landowner, while his haunting sense of guilt and wrong-doing gradually vanishes.

Colonna, Francesco (1432?–?1527). Italian author and Dominican monk. He created one of the most beautiful and mystifying books of the Italian Renaissance, the *Hypnerotomachia Poliphili* (*The Strife of Love in a Dream with the Lover of Polia*); written in 1467, it was published by Aldus in 1499 with nearly 20 woodcuts. In two books and in a Latinized Italian prose, the author tells of the dream-journey of Poliphilus and of his love for Polia. Beneath the surface of its allegorical and romantic plot are various esoteric meanings and devices, such as the fact that the initial letters of its chapters spell out the author's name and address. An anonymous Elizabethan translation spread its influence then; but its appeal extended to modern times, as in Charles Reade's *Cloister and the Hearth.*

Colonna, Vittoria (1492–1547). Italian poet. She was a friend of Michelangelo, who addressed several of his poems to her. Her own poems include sonnets on her dead husband, Ferrante d'Avalos, and upon religious themes. They were published in her *Canzoniere* (*Song Book,* 1538).

Coloquio de los perros, El. One of the stories in Cervantes' NOVELAS EJEMPLARES. In this PICARESQUE tale, the dog Berganza is given the power of speech for one night and describes to another dog his experiences under various masters, satirizing human behavior in the process.

Colossians, The Epistle of Paul the Apostle to the. A book of the New Testament. It is a letter written by Paul, while he was in prison, to the early Christians of Colossae, the ancient city of Phrygia in Asia Minor. He urges them to ignore the syncretic ideas then common in the Near East.

Colossus of Rhodes. A gigantic statue of HELIOS on the island of Rhodes. Completed about 280 B.C., this famous statue commemorated the successful defense of Rhodes against Demetrius Poliorcetes in 304 B.C. One of the Seven Wonders of the World, it stood 105 feet high, and is said to have been made from the warlike engines abandoned by Demetrius. It was designed and built by the sculptor Chares, a pupil of Lycippus. The story that it destroyed the harbor arose only in the 16th century.

Colum, Mary (1886?–1957). Irish-American literary critic; wife of Padraic Colum. *From These Roots* (1937) is a book of criticism and *Life and the Dream* (1947) is an autobiography that throws light on the literary life of Ireland in the early 20th century.

Colum, Padraic (1881–   ). Irish poet and dramatist; later resident in the U.S. and president of the Poetry Society of America. He was associated with the IRISH RENAISSANCE and the Irish National Theater, in company with William Butler Yeats, A. E., Lady Gregory, and John Millington Synge. *The Fiddler's House* (1907) and *Thomas Muskerry* (1910) are earthy, Ibsenish plays. *Wild Earth* (1907) is a collection of poems about Irish country life. Many of his lyrics have been set to music and are familiar as near-folk songs. He also wrote books on travel and folklore. *The Poet's Circuits* appeared in 1960.

Columba, St. (Ir., *Colum;* 521–597). An Irish saint. After establishing several churches and monasteries in Ireland, the nobly born Columba converted the Picts in northern Scotland, where he founded more monasteries.

Columban, St. (543–615). An Irish saint. Most of his life was devoted to the founding of monasteries in France, Switzerland, and Italy. Several of his erudite writings are extant.

Columbiad, The (1807). An epic poem by Joel BARLOW, first published in briefer form as *The Vision of Columbus* (1787). Columbus is taken by Hesper, the spirit of the Western World, to the Mount of Visiton and there foresees the future of the North American continent.

Columbian Magazine. An early American literary magazine, founded in Philadelphia in 1786.

Among its editors were Mathew Carey and Francis Hopkinson. It ran until 1792 and featured an unusual amount of American fiction.

Columbine. A stock character in old Italian comedy. She first appeared about 1560 and was shortly thereafter transplanted to English pantomime. She is the daughter of PANTALOON and the sweetheart of HARLEQUIN. Like Harlequin, she is supposed to be invisible to mortal eyes. See PIERROT.

Columbus, Christopher (*Sp.* **Cristóbal Colón;** *It.* **Cristoforo Colombo;** 1451–1506). Discoverer of America. The son of a Genoese wool weaver, Columbus went to sea as a youth, becoming a skilled navigator. He conceived a plan to reach Asia by sailing westward, but was rebuffed at the English, French, and Portuguese courts; in 1492 Ferdinand and Isabella of Spain finally agreed to sponsor the voyage, naming him Admiral of the Ocean Sea, Viceroy, and governor of the lands he might discover.

Columbus set sail from Palos, Spain, on Aug. 3, 1492, with a fleet of three ships: the *Niña*, the *Pinta*, and the flagship *Santa María*—and some 90 officers and men. On October 12 he made his first landfall at an island in the Bahamas, probably Guanahuani, which he called San Salvador. Ignorant of the fact that he had discovered a new world, Columbus then reached Cuba and Hispaniola (Santo Domingo), where he established a settlement called Navidad, and sailed for Spain.

During his second voyage (1493–1496), Columbus discovered Puerto Rico and Jamaica. However, he began to have difficulties with the Spaniards on Hispaniola, who chafed at his iron discipline. Returning to America in 1498, he touched Trinidad and sailed along the coast of Venezuela. Meanwhile, the trouble on Hispaniola continued, and Francisco Bobadilla, who had been sent as royal commissioner to investigate complaints against Columbus, ordered him back to Spain in chains. Though none of his political powers were restored, Columbus was permitted to undertake a fourth voyage (1502–1504), during which he explored the coast of Central America. After being marooned on Jamaica for over a year, he returned to Spain, where he died in poverty and neglect. Both Seville and Santo Domingo claim to possess his remains.

The best known of Columbus' writings is the journal of his first voyage. Washington Irving wrote a biography, *History of the Life and Voyages of Columbus* (1828), based on material he gathered while serving as an attaché at the American legation in Madrid. Poems about the great discoverer include James Russell Lowell's *Columbus* (1847), Walt Whitman's *The Prayer of Columbus* (1874), and Joaquin Miller's *Columbus* (1896). Paul Claudel wrote a dramatic oratorio, *The Book of Christopher Columbus* (1927), with music by Darius Milhaud.

Columbus, History of the Life and Voyages of (1828). A multivolume biography by Washington IRVING. He gathered the material while serving in the U.S. embassy at Madrid. The book includes some of the documents made available by the duke of Veraguas, a descendant of Columbus. Although Irving idealized the explorer, the book remains readable. He later added a volume called *The Companions of Columbus* (1831).

Combat. See Albert CAMUS.

Combray. A French village in Marcel PROUST's *Remembrance of Things Past*. The narrator's family visit relatives there, and it is the scene of many of his childhood memories, including the walks along the Méséglise Way and the Guermantes Way. Based on the village of Illiers, southwest of Chartres on the Loire River, it includes some details from Proust's birthplace in the Parisian suburb Auteuil.

comedia de capa y espada (Sp., "cloak-and-sword play"). A form of Spanish drama, dealing with the upper middle classes and deriving its name from the typical street costume of these groups. Stressing incident rather than characterization, these plays have complex and romantic plots that employ such devices as mistaken identities, disguises, and mutual misunderstandings. Lope de VEGA and CALDERÓN wrote excellent examples of this type of play.

comédie-ballet. A theatrical form, originally devised by MOLIÈRE for the entertainment of Louis XIV, consisting of comedy with ballet inserted between the acts. The *comédie-ballet* was one of the most popular entertainments of 17th-century France.

Comédie-Française. French national theater, now known as the *Théâtre-Français* and housed in a Paris theater of that name. A troupe of MOLIÈRE's actors, established at the *Théâtre de Petit-Bourbon* in 1658, became the core of a new theater formed in 1681 by the union of several theatrical companies and titled officially the *Comédie-Française*. The company was often called *La Maison de Molière*. After the Revolution, the *Comédie-Française* was renamed the *Théâtre-Français* (1791) and given the theater where its performances are still held today.

Comédie Humaine, La (The Human Comedy). The title given by Honoré de BALZAC in 1841 to the whole body of his work, including both completed and projected novels. The vast canvas of the work is France itself, seen from a variety of perspectives and peopled by more than 2,000 characters. Individuals of all social classes are depicted with accuracy and massive detail. A forerunner of such naturalistic works as those of Zola and the Goncourt brothers, *La Comédie Humaine* is divided into three main areas of study: manners, philosophy, and marriage. The first group is subdivided into scenes of private life, provincial life, Parisian life, country life, political life, and military life. Among the best known of these novels are LES CHOUANS, EUGÉNIE GRANDET, LE PÈRE GORIOT, LA RECHERCHE DE L'ABSOLU, CÉSAR BIROTTEAU, *Le Curé de village* (1839), LA COUSINE BETTE, THE COUNTRY DOCTOR, and COUSIN PONS.

comédie larmoyante (Fr., *"tearful comedy"*). A popular French 18th-century type of sentimental comedy in which the exaggeratedly pathetic situations of the characters made the audience weep. Concern with the triumph of virtue afforded playwrights the opportunity of moralizing to excess. Examples of this type of play are to be found in LA CHAUSSÉE's *La Fausse antipathie* (1733), *Le Préjugé à la mode* (1735), and *Mélanide* (1741); in Voltaire's *L'Enfant prodigue* (1736) and *Nanine* (1749); and in DESTOUCHES' *Le Glorieux* (1732). The comédie larmoyante was to develop into the BOURGEOIS DRAMA.

Comedy of Errors, The (c. 1594). A comedy by William SHAKESPEARE. AEMILIA, wife of AEGEON, has twin sons, both named ANTIPHOLUS, who shipwrecked in infancy have been carried, one to Syracuse, the other to Ephesus. The play represents An-tipholus of Syracuse going in search of his brother; and to make the confusion of identities more absurd, the brothers each have a slave named DROMIO, and the Dromios are also indistinguishable twins. ADRI-ANA, the wife of the Ephesian, mistakes the Syra-cusan for her husband and later has her real hus-band arrested as a madman. Great confusion results, but ultimately the matter is brought into court. Not only do the brothers recognize each other at last, but their mother Aemilia, now an abbess in whose priory the Syracusan had taken refuge during the excite-ment, and their father Aegeon, who had come to Ephesus to search for his son, appear in court, and the entire family is reunited. The sources of the plot are the *Menaechmi* and the *Amphitruo* of Plautus, both written in the second century B.C.

Come Hither (1923). An anthology of verse and prose compiled by Walter DE LA MARE. It has be-come a classic book for children.

Come into the Garden, Maud. Well-known first line of Alfred Tennyson's MAUD.

Comendador de Ocaña, El. See PERIBÁÑEZ O EL COMENDADOR DE OCAÑA.

Comical History of the States and Empires of the Moon and **Comical History of the States and Empires of the Sun.** See CYRANO DE BERGERAC.

comic relief. The relaxation of the audience's tension by means of an interpolated comic episode in a serious play. Its function is to permit a stronger renewal of the emotional surge. A good example is the grave-diggers' scene in *Hamlet*. Some critics hold that the function of such scenes is not relief but in-creased tension through senseless and ironical juxta-position of opposites.

Comines (also **Commines** or **Commynes**), **Philippe de** (c. 1446–1511). Flemish-born French chronicler and diplomat, in the service of Charles the Bold, then Louis XI, then Charles VIII. The largest part of his *Memoirs* (written 1489–1490) describes the reign of Louis XI; the last part (writ-ten 1497–1498) concerns the Italian expedition of Charles VIII. The *Memoirs* are more serious and im-partial than any European history written up until that time; and they were the basis for Scott's novel QUENTIN DURWARD.

Coming Struggle for Power, The (1932). The chief work of John STRACHEY. It predicts a close and final conflict between capitalism and Communism, and the doom of capitalism.

Cominius. In Shakespeare's CORIOLANUS, the Ro-man general under whom Coriolanus serves in the battle against the Volscians. He has a judiciousness and humility which Coriolanus lacks.

Comintern. See INTERNATIONAL.

comitia. In ancient Rome, an assembly of the people that had the authority to act on certain mat-ters submitted to them through official channels. They met at the foot of the Capitol at a place called *Comitium.*

Commager, Henry Steele (1902–   ). Amer-ican historian. A native of Pittsburgh, Pa., Com-mager was educated at the University of Chicago. From 1939 to 1956 he was professor of history at Columbia University; in the latter year he joined the faculty of Amherst College. His writings are popular among both scholars and the general public.

His works include *The Growth of the American Republic* (1930), written with S. E. Morison and subsequently revised and expanded; *Theodore Parker* (1936); *The Heritage of America* (1939), with Allan Nevins; and *The American Mind* (1950). He also edited *Documents of American History* (1934).

Commander of the Faithful. A title of the Caliphs, first assumed by Omar I (581, 634–644).

commedia dell'arte (*It.,* comedy of the profes-sion or of skill). Italian dramatic genre dating from the mid-16th century, when professional theatrical companies, especially the famous *Gelosi* (*The Jealous Ones*) began to include in their repertoire a new form of comedy characterized by improvisation upon a bare outline of plot (*scenario*), and the use of stock characters, some wearing masks, that combined features of the learned as well as the popular drama. It is this testing of the actor's virtuosity and skill that gave the genre its name, not an association with a professional craft or guild. Among the famous and enduring stock characters were "the beautiful young lady," an ingenue with a name such as Julia or Lucinda; her "lover," handsome but impecunious, sometimes called Octavio; Pantalone, a Venetian merchant as foolish as he is wealthy; the Doctor, sometimes called Graziano, who is a hopeless pedant; a braggart captain, later called SCARAMUCCIA; and a collection of servants who provide anything from sparkling wit to acrobatics as they move in and out of the story, sometimes helping, at other times hinder-ing the affairs of their masters and mistresses. The oldest of the wily or blundering manservants is Zanni (a dialect version of Gianni or Giovanni); later the word was used to designate a whole troupe of come-dians. Following variations of the type included Arlecchino or Harlequin, famous for his particolored costume (derived from the original patched garments he wore); he is sometimes called Truffaldino or Mezzetino; Tartaglia, noted for his eyeglasses and his comic stuttering; Brighella, the usual companion of Arlecchino; and Pulcinella, who speaks in Nea-politan dialect, has a tremendous nose, and is al-ways hungry—he survives in the PUNCH AND JUDY shows of the puppet theater. The *commedia dell'arte* was popular in Italy and throughout Europe (thanks to traveling companies) for several hundred years; it strongly influenced the development of European comedy and of individual writers such as Molière, Goldoni, and Gozzi.

Commemoration Ode (1865). A poem by James Russell LOWELL, more accurately entitled *Ode Re-cited at the Harvard Commemoration*. It was writ-ten on request in honor of the Harvard students who had died in the Civil War. In its published form, Lowell added 66 lines, beginning with the famous "Such was he, our Martyr-Chief."

Commentaries on the Gallic War (c. 58–44 B.C.). An historical work in 7 books by Julius CAESAR. Written in a brisk, straightforward third person, each book covering one year, it narrates the campaigns, starting in 58 B.C., by which Caesar made Gaul a permanent part of the empire. Though not intended as polished literature, the work is valued as a masterpiece of clear, concise Latin and historical accuracy. Caesar, who had never lost a campaign or left the field before the enemy, had no reason to exaggerate or misrepresent; perhaps the only subjective note in the *Commentaries* is introduced in his justification of the war.

Commines or **Commynes, Philippe de.** See COMINES.

Committee of Public Safety (*Comité de salut public*). Formed on April 6, 1793, it assumed direction of the government during the French Revolution from 1793 to 1795. Although theoretically subordinate to the Constitutional Convention, this committee soon concentrated all power in its hands and instituted the REIGN OF TERROR. Its most famous members were ROBESPIERRE, Antoine Saint-Just, Georges Couthon, Lazare Carnot, and Bertrand Barrère.

Commodus, Lucius Aelius Aurelius (A.D. 161–192). Roman emperor (180–192). He succeeded to the throne on the death of his father Marcus Aurelius. His reign was marked by his prodigality, self-indulgence, and violence. He prided himself on his gladiatorial skill and was strangled by an athlete in a conspiracy.

Common, Doll. The mistress and assistant in charlatanry of Subtle in Jonson's THE ALCHEMIST.

Common Sense (1776). A political treatise by Thomas PAINE, urging immediate separation from England. In a few months more than 100,000 copies were published in America. The work was influential in bringing about the Declaration of Independence.

Commune of Paris. The revolutionary government established in Paris during 1792 by the representatives of the communes, the smallest administrative districts of France. It led to the period known as the Reign of Terror. More commonly, the term is applied to the insurrectionary government that took possession of Paris (March 18–May 28, 1871), after the withdrawal of the Prussian troops.

Communist Manifesto, The (*Das Kommunistische Manifest;* 1848). A pamphlet by Karl MARX and Friedrich ENGELS, the classic document of communist theory. It analyzes history in terms of class conflict, predicts the imminent overthrow of the ruling bourgeoisie by the oppressed proletariat, and envisions a resulting classless society in which personal property would be abolished. The *Manifesto* calls upon the proletariat of the world to unite and strengthen itself for this final revolution.

Company of Jesus. See JESUITS.

Compensation (1841). An essay by Ralph Waldo EMERSON. The writer claims that evil is balanced by good, that "every sweet hath its sour; every evil its good." The doctrine of compensation, precluding the necessity for an afterlife, caused Emerson to be criticized by the religiously orthodox, as well as the liberals who considered his view too naïve.

Compleat Angler, The, or the Contemplative Man's Recreation (1653). A treatise on fishing by Izaak WALTON. It takes the form of a dialogue in which Piscator (an angler) tries to convince Venator (a hunter) that fishing is the superior sport. Their friend Auceps, a fowler, is silenced early in the work. Charles COTTON wrote a continuation which appeared in the fifth edition (1676).

Compromise of 1850. In U.S. history, a collective name for five acts of Congress which attempted to settle the controversy over the extension of slavery into the territory recently acquired from Mexico. In the Senate, Henry Clay and Daniel WEBSTER supported compromise measures, while John C. Calhoun pleaded for equal rights for the South, and William Seward argued that "a higher law" forbade constitutional safeguards for slavery. The compromise bills provided for the admission of California as a free state and for the establishment of territorial governments in New Mexico and Utah without restrictions regarding slavery; in addition, the Fugitive Slave Law was strengthened, and the slave trade was abolished in the District of Columbia.

Compson. A family in THE SOUND AND THE FURY and other works by William FAULKNER. One of the old, aristocratic families of YOKNAPATAWPHA County, the Compsons trace their American ancestry back to the early 18th century, but by the early 20th century the family is decaying. In the 1930's the family property is sold and the last male Compson is a childless bachelor. The family includes Benjamin, the idiot of *The Sound and the Fury;* Candace (Caddy), a girl whose checkered career includes a seduction, a marriage to a banker and another to a motion-picture executive, and who is last seen in Paris during the German occupation; Jason Lycurgus Compson I, the first of the family to settle in Mississippi; Jason II, a brigadier general in the Civil War to whom Thomas Sutpen of ABSALOM, ABSALOM! tells part of his story; Jason III, an intelligent but ineffectual lawyer who first sells some of the family property; Jason IV, a shrewd and selfish storekeeper who sells the remaining property; Quentin Compson, the illegitimate daughter of Caddy; Quentin MacLachan Compson, an introspective young man who commits suicide at Harvard in 1910.

In addition to *The Sound and the Fury,* the Compson family appears in the short story *That Evening Sun,* and Quentin MacLachan Compson is one of the three narrators in *Absalom, Absalom!*

Compton-Burnett, Ivy (1892–   ). English novelist. A pitiless observer of human cruelty and lust for power, she writes witty and terrifying social comedies of family life—all in dialogue. Her wit, irony, and malice are like a fiercer Jane Austen's. All her novels follow the same form. They are set in large country houses, between 1885 and 1901, and consist almost entirely of polite, mannered, aphoristic dialogue between the members of the ingrown household. The background story concerns a struggle for power between a tyrant and his victim (often servants or precocious children), and a murder or some other melodramatic event. Some of her titles are *Pastors and Masters* (1925), *Brothers and Sisters* (1929), *A House and Its Head* (1935), *Elders and Betters* (1944), *Manservant and Maidservant* (1947, U.S. title, *Bullivant and the Lambs*), *Two Worlds and Their Ways* (1949), *Mother and Son* (1955), and *The Mighty and Their Fall* (1962).

Comte, [Isidore] Auguste [Marie François] (1798–1857). French philosopher. Known as the founder of positivism, Comte sought to apply the methods of observation and experimentation used in the sciences to philosophy, social science, and even religion. He hoped that through the use of such methods, rather than through idealistic appeal to absolute principles, social reform might be achieved. The philosophy of positivism only admits knowledge gained by the scientific method as real or positive.

Cours de philosophie positive (6 vols., 1830–1842) is Comte's basic formulation of the doctrine. Comte had a significant influence on the thought of his time. Both Taine and John Stuart Mill show the effect of his ideas in their own philosophical writings.

Comus (1634). A MASQUE by John MILTON. In late Roman mythology, Comus was the god of sensual pleasure, son of Bacchus and Circe. The name is from the Greek *komos* meaning "revel." In the masque, a young lady is left in the woods by her two brothers who have gone to find food for her. She falls into the hands of Comus, who tries to persuade her to become his consort, queen of his band of riotous monsters. She resists, is almost rescued by her brothers aided by an attendant spirit, but a spell has been cast upon her, which is broken by the power of Sabrina, nymph of the river Severn.

The masque was first performed in the Ludlow castle of the earl of Bridgewater, whose three children played the parts of the brothers and sister. Its theme is the struggle between chaste temperance and sensual pleasure; both causes are eloquently represented, and its richness of language and fancy make it one of the greatest works of its kind.

Conan Doyle. See Sir Arthur Conan DOYLE.

conceit. A whimsical, ingenious, extended META-PHOR. In a conceit an object, scene, person, situation, or emotion is presented in terms of a simpler analogue, usually chosen from nature or a context familiar to author and reader alike. First developed by Petrarch, the conceit became a standard stylistic device in poetry and spread to England in the 16th century.

The METAPHYSICAL POETS, by extending the range of poetic analogy into the realms of science, religion, learning, and practical life, produced a distinct and arresting kind of conceit. Their aim was to startle the reader by showing a very exact correspondence between a thought or emotion and some particular aspect of a seemingly alien and inappropriate object. A famous example is found in these lines from Donne's *A Valediction: Forbidding Mourning* in which, parting from his mistress, he uses the figure of a drawing compass to describe the bond between their souls:

> If they be two, they are two so
> As stiffe twin compasses are two,
> Thy soule the fixt foot, makes no show
> To move, but doth, if th'other doe.
>
> And though it in the center sit,
> Yet when the other far doth rome,
> It leanes, and hearkens after it,
> And growes erect, as that comes home.

Here the conceit is adapted as the best means of expressing a complicated thought; its exactitude and naturalness give it force. With the later metaphysical poets, like John Cleveland and Abraham Cowley, the conceit becomes more fanciful, less exact, at best a kind of witty ornament, at worst absurdity, as when Cleveland speaks of his mistress' hand:

> So soft, 'tis air but once removed,
> Tender as 'twere a jelly gloved.
> Cleveland, *Fuscara*

conceptism or **conceptismo** (from Sp., *concepto*, "a conceit"). A 17th-century Spanish stylistic form which sought to express clever and penetrating ideas by means of verbal devices such as puns, antitheses, and epigrams. Often, however, originality and wit were achieved at the expense of thought and common sense. Conceptism is best exemplified in the works of Baltasar GRACIÁN, whose *Agudeza y arte de ingenio* (1648) exhaustively describes every type of literary conceit. See GONGORISM.

Conciliatore, Il. An Italian semiweekly published in Milan (1818–19). Edited by Silvio PELLICO, it adopted a liberal, progressive position on political, social, and literary questions and, accordingly, favored the romantic movement just then emerging in Italy. It was suppressed by the Austrian police because of its politically liberal point of view.

Concord, Battle of. See LEXINGTON.

Concord Hymn (1836). A poem by Ralph Waldo EMERSON. Written at the completion of the Concord Monument, the poem includes the famous lines:

> Here once the embattled farmers stood
> And fired the shot heard round the world.

Condenado por desconfiado, El (pub. 1635). A religious drama by TIRSO DE MOLINA, dealing with the problem of free will and predestination. Paulo is persuaded by the devil to leave his hermitage and seek Enrico, whose fate, he is told, will be the same as his. Discovering that Enrico is a cheat and a bully, Paulo becomes a bandit in despair. An angel disguised as a shepherd asks him to repent and trust in God, but Paulo refuses. Enrico, however, repents before he dies and is saved. Unwilling to believe in Enrico's salvation, Paulo refuses to confess his sins and is damned for his pride and lack of faith.

Condensed Novels and Other Papers (1867). A series of parodies by Bret HARTE. The book imitates such writers as Dickens, Cooper, Simms, Hawthorne, and Irving. Not all travesties, some of the sketches reflect Harte's admiration and respect for writers who influenced him.

Condillac, Etienne Bonnot, Abbé (1715–1780). French philosopher. He contributed articles on philosophy to the ENCYCLOPÉDIE. In his *Essai sur l'origine des connaissances humaines* (1746) and *Traité des sensations* (1754), he shows, as a disciple of Locke, that thought is not innate, but is derived from sensations and experience. He exerted considerable influence on the IDÉOLOGUES.

Condition humaine, La. See MAN'S FATE.

Condorcet, Marquis de. **Marie Jean Antoine Nicolas Caritat** (1743–1794). French philosopher and mathematician. He advocated the theory of the "infinite perfectibility of man" in his *Esquisse d'un tableau historique des progrès de l'esprit humain* (1794). In this work, Condorcet traces human development through 9 epochs, and predicts that man will become perfect in the 10th. Arrested as a member of the GIRONDIST faction, he died in prison.

condottiere (It.). A professional soldier of fortune who leads or conducts a band of mercenaries. During the Italian Renaissance, these captains were commissioned to fight wars in support of the city states and petty duchies. Some of them, such as the Sforza, eventually became nobles themselves; others (the Gonzaga and Montefeltro families) sold their armed services even though they were already nobles in possession of states and petty principalities. Foreigners, such as the famous Sir John Hawkwood, an English captain, numbered among their ranks. Their legendary cruelty is captured by Verrocchio in his statue of Bartolommeo Colleoni, which still frightens tourists in Venice.

Confessio Amantis (1386/1390). Poem in Middle English by John GOWER, of over 30,000 lines in octosyllabic couplets. The narrator is an unhappy lover who appeals to Venus and is sent to confess to her priest Genius, who instructs him concerning the seven deadly sins against Love; each lesson is embellished with one or more stories from Biblical or classical legend. Chaucer had certainly read this work when he wrote the *Man of Law's Tale* and the *Wife of Bath's Tale,* although Gower was not his only source for the stories. The tale of Apollonius of Tyre also was a source for Shakespeare's *Pericles, Prince of Tyre.*

Confession, A (Ispoved'; 1879–1881). An account by Count Leo TOLSTOI of the spiritual crisis leading to the formation of the religious and philosophical ideas he preached in his later years. The work records Tolstoi's growing discontent with life as he experienced it in civilized society, and his gradual conclusion that a life close to nature was requisite for the ideal life. *A Confession* is regarded as one of Tolstoi's most powerful nonfiction works because of its effective depiction of the intense spiritual struggles of one of the world's great geniuses.

confessions. A form of autobiography or simulated autobiography. Intimate and possibly guilty matters not usually disclosed are "confessed," presumably to serve some sort of didactic purpose. Confessions constitute a literary genre which began with the *Confessions of St. Augustine.* They reached the height of their development in the era of romanticism, when they already began to show symptoms of narcissistic decadence. Among the most famous confessions in literature are Rousseau's *Confessions* and De Quincey's *Confessions of an English Opium Eater.*

Confessions. An autobiography by Jean Jacques ROUSSEAU. Written between 1766–1770, it was published posthumously (Books I–VI in 1781, Books VII–XII in 1788). In this work, Rousseau "frankly and sincerely" reveals the details of his erratic and rebellious life. Scholars find, however, that his unconscious motivation was to justify himself in the eyes of his supposedly numerous persecutors. The autobiographical account given in *Confessions* is supplemented by the three dialogues written in 1775–1776: *Rousseau juge de Jean-Jacques, Rêveries du promeneur solitaire,* and *Correspondance.* They inaugurated a fashion in literature for confessions, but Rousseau's successors, such as Chateaubriand, Lamartine, George Sand, and Renan lack his openness.

Confessions of an English Opium Eater (1822). A largely autobiographical work by Thomas DE QUINCEY. It gives an account of the poet's early life and describes the growth and effects of his habit of taking opium.

Confessions of a Thug. See Philip Meadows TAYLOR.

Confessions of Felix Krull: Confidence Man (Bekenntnisse des Hochstaplers Felix Krull; 1954). A novel by Thomas MANN. In its adventurous and episodic quality, it is his closest approach to the picaresque novel. Krull, like many of Mann's characters, represents the artist, and his profession indicates the symbolic connection in Mann's mind between the artist and the actor or charlatan.

Confessions of Harry Lorrequer, The (1839). A novel by Charles LEVER. It relates the scrapes and adventures of the high-spirited young Irish hero, Harry Lorrequer. The first part of the book is concerned with his part in Wellington's campaigns.

Confessions of Saint Augustine, The (397–401). A spiritual autobiography by St. AUGUSTINE. He describes his devoutly Christian mother, Monica, his life with the concubine who gave him his son Adeodatus (371–389), his exploration of Manichaeism and neo-Platonism, and his conversion to Christianity. Designed to show the details of the soul's progress, from enjoyment of the beauties outside itself to a study of its own nature and finally to joy in the knowledge of God, the work was the first in literature to be concerned entirely with an introspective analysis of the author's own spiritual and emotional experiences.

Confidence-Man, The: His Masquerade (1857). A novel by Herman MELVILLE. The scene is a Mississippi River boat, ironically named the *Fidele.* A plotless satire taking place on April Fool's Day, the book is filled with characters difficult to distinguish from one another; most of them are different manifestations of the confidence man. A sign hanging on the door of the *Fidele's* barbershop expresses the theme: "No Trust." The confidence man, king of a world without principle, succeeds in gulling men by capitalizing on false hopes and offering false pity. At the end of the book, the flickering light hanging above the table where an old man reads the Bible goes out completely.

Confucianism. Chinese political and moral philosophy based on the teachings of CONFUCIUS. Originally one of the several rival teachings during the Chou Dynasty (1027–256 B.C.), it found little favor at first, but by the second century B.C. had become the official creed of China. Essentially a guide for statecraft and a moral teaching, it was enlarged upon and developed by MENCIUS, often regarded after Confucius as the second Chinese sage. In the third century B.C. the HSÜN TZU further elaborated and organized the teachings, and by the Han Dynasty (202 B.C.–A.D. 220) it was the orthodox teaching, dominating Chinese political and ethical thought until the early 20th century. During the Han Dynasty many extraneous elements, such as the YIN AND YANG theory, were introduced, attempts were made to deify Confucius, and to use Confucian doctrines as justification for the absolute right of the emperors. Throughout its history Confucianism came into frequent conflict with Buddhism and Taoism, but it retained its position as the official state philosophy, largely because of the Imperial University and the examination system for government employees that perpetuated its power. The Sung Dynasty (960–1279) witnessed a great Confucian revival under the leadership of CHU HSI and his school. Known as Neo-Confucianism, the teachings were reorganized; a minute examination of the precepts of the Confucian sages as well as of all external phenomena was called for, and the FOUR BOOKS became the basis for all education. Neo-Confucianism had great influence in Japan, where it became the basis on which the Tokugawa government was organized.

Confucius (551?–497? B.C.). Chinese political and ethical philosopher and would-be reformer. Failing to achieve personal ambitions and success, he taught a large number of disciples who carried on, developed, and greatly altered his teachings, so that by the second century B.C. they formed the dominant philosophy in China. Confucius advocated a this-worldly, rational philosophy, which emphasizes humanity (*jen*), reverence for the ancient sages, and government by personal virtue.

Congo, The: A Study of the Negro Race (1914). A poem by Vachel LINDSAY. He attempted to represent Negro ragtime rhythms in verse by means of various verbal effects. It falls into three sections: "Their Basic Savagery," "Their Irrepressible High Spirits," and "The Hope of Their Religion."

Congregationalist. A member of the Congregational Church. Its doctrines, known as evangelical or orthodox, include autonomy tempered by co-operation and fellowship of the individual congregations.

Congreve, William (1670–1729). English dramatist, usually considered the greatest master of the Restoration comedy of manners. The son of an English army officer stationed in Ireland, Congreve was educated at the Kilkenny School, where Swift was a schoolmate, and at Trinity College, Dublin. His

Confucius in court costume.

first play, *The Old Bachelor* (1693), which was produced under Dryden's auspices, was widely acclaimed. It was followed by three other comedies: *The Double Dealer* (1693), LOVE FOR LOVE, and his masterpiece, THE WAY OF THE WORLD. In these plays Congreve revealed a genius for urbane, scintillating wit that rivalled Molière's. He also wrote a tragedy, *The Mourning Bride* (1697), remembered chiefly as the source of such oft-quoted phrases as "Music hath charms to soothe a savage breast." The same year he engaged in controversy with the Reverend Jeremy COLLIER, who attacked the lewdness of the English stage, and was apparently bested in the exchange. After 1700, Congreve gave up writing for the theater and spent the rest of his life in the company of such friends as Swift, Steele, and Pope, who dedicated his translation of the *Iliad* to him; the visiting Voltaire, however, regretted that the "writer" had turned into a "gentleman." See Anne BRACEGIRDLE.

Coningsby, or the New Generation (1844). A novel by Benjamin DISRAELI. It contains many of his political opinions on the social issues of his day. There appear in the book several prominent contemporary figures, thinly disguised, and much of the book's popularity may be credited to the interest in identifying them. Gladstone is said to be depicted as Millbank, the Marquis of Hertford as the Marquis of Monmouth, and Coningsby may represent either Lord Littleton or Lord Lincoln. A notable character is the Jew, Sidonia, said to be drawn partly from Baron Alfred de Rothschild, partly from the author himself.

Coniston (1906). A historical novel by Winston CHURCHILL. Churchill became interested in the politics of New Hampshire, where he lived for many years, and to some extent embodied his observations and conclusions in this story, laid in the years between the administrations of President Jackson and President Grant. His chief character is Jethro Bass, an able but corrupt Vermont politician whose quest for power leads him to break with the woman he loves. Bass was modeled on Ruel Durkee, a New Hampshire political boss.

Conjectures on Original Composition, in a Letter to the Author of Sir Charles Grandison (1759). An essay by Edward YOUNG which undertakes to defend originality against slavish imitation. Young restates many of the arguments in the old controversy between the Ancients and Moderns (see BATTLE OF THE BOOKS), and concludes that, in the long run, it is in the nature of man and the universe that the future shall surpass the past and that the progress of art is basically the result of the efforts of the original genius.

Connecticut Wits. See HARTFORD WITS.

Connecticut Yankee in King Arthur's Court, A (1889). A novel by Mark TWAIN. A blow on the head conveys the superintendent of a Hartford arms factory back to the days of King Arthur. When the Yankee's ingenuity and know-how encounter the world of medieval superstition, Mark Twain takes the opportunity to satirize the Old World, chivalry, kings, and the church. Many of the Arthurian knights are seen through the unimpressed eyes of the Yankee. He marries and has a child, but another blow restores him to his own time.

Connell, Norreys. See Conal O'RIORDAN.

Connelly, Marc[us Cook] (1890–   ). American playwright. Connelly collaborated with George S. KAUFMAN on several plays: DULCY; *To the Ladies* (1922), a study in illusions; *Merton of the Movies* (1922), a dramatization of Harry Leon Wilson's satiric novel about Hollywood; and BEGGAR ON HORSEBACK. By himself he wrote *The Wisdom Tooth* (1926), a clerk's futile but pleasant dream of how he defies his employer; THE GREEN PASTURES; *The Farmer Takes a Wife* (1934), with characters taken from Walter D. Edmonds' *Rome Haul* (1929); and *A Story for Strangers* (1948), a parable about a talking horse.

Connelly, Cyril (1903–   ). English essayist, critic, and novelist. He ran the magazine *Horizon* (1940–1949). His best-known book is *The Unquiet Grave* (1945), a collection of melancholy pensées, aphorisms, and quotations. It was published under the pen name **Palinurus** (Connelly thinks Palinurus fell into the sea through a typically modern will to failure). His other works are his partly autobiographical *Enemies of Promise* (1938); *The Condemned Playground* (1946), a collection of essays and literary criticism; the novel *The Rock Pool* (1936); and *The Missing Diplomats* (1953).

Conquest of Canaan, The. (1) A 9,000-line epic poem (1785) by Timothy DWIGHT, based on the Old Testament Book of Joshua and called by its author "the first American epic." Joshua, who in the poem represents George Washington, was the leader under whom the Jews entered the Promised Land of Canaan and defeated the inhabitants. In the poem, one critic has remarked, 18th-century Americans with Hebrew names talk like Milton's angels and fight like prehistoric Greeks.

(2) A novel (1905) by Booth TARKINGTON. Canaan is a town in Indiana where intolerance and narrow-mindedness hold sway. Joe London, making his way against great obstacles, wins out against the townspeople, marries a beautiful heiress, Ariel Tabor, and becomes the town's mayor.

Conquistador (1932). A narrative poem by Archibald MacLEISH. Awarded the 1933 Pulitzer Prize in poetry, it is based on an eye-witness account of the Spanish expedition led by Hernando Cortez to Mexico in the 16th century written by Bernal DÍAZ DEL CASTILLO. Heroic and realistic, it emphasizes the love of individual men for adventure, rather than official plans for expansion, as the real motive for the expedition.

Conrad. The hero of Lord Byron's poem THE CORSAIR. He is said to have been partly modeled on Jean Lafitte, the famous pirate who assisted Andrew Jackson at the Battle of New Orleans.

Conrad, Joseph (1857–1924). Polish-born English novelist, whose original name was Teodor Jósef Konrad Korzeniowski. Best known in his own time as a writer of sea stories, he is now more admired as a novelist of moral exploration and a master of narrative technique. He was influenced by the technique of Henry James. (See MARLOW.) NOSTROMO, HEART OF DARKNESS, and LORD JIM are regarded as his greatest works. His earliest novels, including ALMAYER'S FOLLY and AN OUTCAST OF THE ISLANDS, are full of romantic description, with a mysterious, mystical atmosphere and much analysis and brooding. YOUTH, TYPHOON, and THE SHADOW-LINE—and, indeed, in

some respect, most of his tales—describe men's characters being tested in conditions of extreme danger and difficulty. Almost all his mature novels are concerned with moral dilemmas, isolation, and the psychology of men's inner urges. Among these are THE NIGGER OF THE NARCISSUS, THE SECRET AGENT, UNDER WESTERN EYES, CHANCE, VICTORY, THE ARROW OF GOLD, and THE RESCUE. THE SECRET SHARER is a remarkable short story. Conrad collaborated with Ford Madox Ford on the novels *The Inheritors* (1901) and *Romance* (1903). He also wrote *The Mirror of the Sea* (1906), *Some Reminiscences* (1912, U.S. title, *A Personal Record*), and *Notes on Life and Letters* (1921).

The son of a Polish nobleman, writer, and militant nationalist, Conrad had an adventurous youth. (See *Arrow of Gold* and, for an account of his smuggling days, *Mirror of the Sea*.) From 1878 to 1894 he worked at sea on British merchant ships, rising to the rank of captain. As a boy he had educated himself by reading widely in Polish and French, but he began to learn English only when he became a seaman. He was a naturalized British citizen. In 1895 he published his first novel, *Almayer's Folly*, left the sea, married, and settled down near London to write. Conrad is regarded as a major 20th-century novelist and a distinguished stylist in the English language.

Conradi, Hermann (1862–1890). German author and radical exponent of NATURALISM. In the preface to the anthology *Moderne Dichtercharaktere* (*Modern Figures in Poetry,* 1884) edited by him, he expresses the desire for a "modern" poetic movement, meaning timeliness and sincerity, as opposed to formal polish and artificiality. Among his own works are a collection of prose sketches, *Brutalitäten* (*Brutalities,* 1886), and a novel *Adam Mensch* (*Adam Man,* 1889).

Conrart, Valentin (1603–1675). French grammarian and man of letters. An original member of the ACADÉMIE FRANÇAISE, he was appointed perpetual secretary of that organization and enormously influenced its policies on grammar and style. Not a prolific author, he is remembered chiefly for the extant fragments of his *Mémoires* (1824), which include an account of the FRONDE.

Conscience, Hendrik (1812–1883). Flemish novelist. *In't Wonderjaer 1566* (*In the Year of Marvels, 1566*), published in 1837, was his first novel and the first book to be published in modern Flemish. *De Leeuw van Vlaanderen* (*The Lion of Flanders*) of 1838 is the one of his more than 100 books that is likely to continue to be read.

conscience clause. A clause in an act of Parliament. It relieves persons with conscientious scruples from certain requirements in the act in which it appears. It generally has reference to religious matters, but came into wider prominence with the English Compulsory Vaccination Act of 1898, and with the introduction of conscription in the First World War.

conscript fathers. (Lat., *Patres conscripti.*) The senators of ancient Rome. Romulus instituted a senate consisting of 100 elders, called *Patres*. After the Sabines joined the state, another hundred were added. Tarquinius Priscus, the fifth king of Rome, added a third hundred. When Tarquinius Superbus, the seventh and last king of Rome, was driven out by Junius BRUTUS, several of the senate followed him. Brutus appointed new men to the vacancies. The new members were enrolled in the senatorial registry and called *Conscripti;* the entire body was then addressed as *Patres et Conscripti,* or *Patres conscripti.*

conservation of energy. See Julius Robert MAYER.

Consolation of Philosophy, The (De Consolatione Philosophiae; c. 524). A philosophical work by BOETHIUS. Written while Boethius was in prison awaiting execution, it consists of a dialogue in alternating prose and verse between the author, lamenting his own sorrows, and a majestic woman who is the incarnation of his guardian Philosophy. She develops a modified form of Neoplatonism and Stoicism, demonstrating the unreality of earthly fortunes, then proving that the highest good and the highest happiness are in God, and reconciling the apparent contradictions concerning the existence of evil, if God is all-good and all-powerful, and the existence of man's free will, if God has foreknowledge of everything. The work became very popular; it inspired many translations, including English ones by King Alfred, Chaucer, and Queen Elizabeth.

consonance. In poetry and prose, the identity of consonants, as in the words "leaves" and "lives." Like ASSONANCE and ALLITERATION, consonance may be considered a form of RHYME since it involves degrees of identity of sound and serves to unify a poem.

Constable, Henry (1562–1613). English poet. A convert to Catholicism, Constable lived much of his life on the Continent. He wrote sonnets and pastoral poems, which are represented in *England's Helicon* (1600) and other anthologies. His sonnet sequence *Diana* was published in 1592 and expanded in 1594. A series of religious sonnets, *Spiritual Sonnets to the Honor of God and His Saints* (published 1815) is attributed to him.

Constable, John (1776–1837). English landscape painter. Mostly self-taught, he repeatedly sketched the same scenes, notably Salisbury cathedral, under varying conditions. In order to impart to his naturalistic landscapes the impression of moving clouds and changing light, he used looser, less blended brushstrokes than were usual at his time. He painted more finished exhibition pieces, yet gained little recognition in England. In France, however, Eugène Delacroix learned much from his brighter colors, the BARBIZON SCHOOL was influenced by the directness of his observation, and later, the Impressionists admired his temporary effects of light.

Constance. See under MAN OF LAW'S TALE.

Constance, Council of (1414–1418). The church council that brought about the end of the GREAT SCHISM, which had seen rival French and Roman popes reigning at the same time, each claiming supreme authority.

Constant de Rebecque, Henri Benjamin. Known as **Benjamin Constant** (1767–1830). Swiss-born French politician, journalist, novelist, best remembered for his short novel ADOLPHE. His famous liaison with Mme. de STAËL began in 1794 and lasted for 17 years. From 1816 he devoted himself to his brilliant political career, writing political and religious treatises, including a pamphlet attacking Napoleon. His journals are of great interest.

Constantine I. Called **the Great** (A.D. 272–337). Roman emperor (306–337). On the death of his father, Constantine laid claim to part of the empire and was acknowledged as master of the countries beyond the Alps. He defeated Maxentius, who had possession of Italy, in the battle of the Milvian Bridge (312), where, according to legend, a cross appeared to him in the sky bearing the words *in hoc signo vinces* ("by this sign you will conquer"). He was converted to Christianity in 313. He defeated Licinius (323), who had gained possession of the East, and thus became sole emperor of the whole empire. He called the great COUNCIL OF NICAEA (325) where the NICENE CREED was adopted. Constantine chose Byzantium as his capital and renamed it CONSTANTINOPLE after himself. See BYZANTINE EMPIRE.

Constantinople. The Christian capital of the Roman empire founded by CONSTANTINE THE GREAT and dedicated in A.D. 330 on the site of ancient Byzantium. It remained the center of the BYZANTINE EMPIRE, the successor to the Eastern Roman Empire, until 1453 when it fell to the Turks. Constantinople is now the Turkish city of Istanbul.

Constant Nymph, The (1924). A consistently popular novel by Margaret KENNEDY. It concerns the family and friends of Albert Sanger, an eccentric musician who is the father of numerous children. His children, both legitimate and illegitimate and all talented, are known collectively as Sanger's circus. The nymph is 15-year-old Teresa Sanger, who has to deal with adult problems of love and fidelity.

Constitution. A 44-gun frigate, U.S. Navy, launched in 1797. The *Constitution* took part in the Tripolitan War against the Barbary corsairs of North Africa. Later, in the War of 1812, under the command of Isaac Hull (1773–1843), she forced the surrender of the British frigate *Guerrière* off Cape Race, Newfoundland (Aug. 19, 1812), and was victorious in seven other encounters. When the *Constitution* was ordered dismantled, Oliver Wendell Holmes wrote the poem *Old Ironsides* (1830), which prompted her rebuilding. She is now permanently moored at Boston and houses a museum.

Constitution of the United States of America. The fundamental law adopted in 1787 and in effect since March, 1789, supplanting the ARTICLES OF CONFEDERATION signed in 1781. The Constitution established a republican form of government for the U.S., with separate executive, legislative, and judicial branches. Twenty-four amendments to the original instrument have been adopted. The 24th amendment, ratified in 1964, forbids the collection of poll taxes as a requirement for voting in presidential and congressional elections. See BILL OF RIGHTS.

Consuelo (1842). A novel by George SAND. The title character, a gypsy girl raised in the streets of Venice, is discovered by the maestro Porporo and becomes a successful opera singer. She eventually marries a Bohemian count and travels with Joseph Haydn to Vienna. Her adventures end in Berlin, where she is feted and admired by Frederick the Great. *La Comtesse de Rudolstadt* (1843–1845) is a sequel.

consul. One of the two chief magistrates of the ancient Roman republic chosen annually in the CAMPUS MARTIUS. In the early ages of Rome they were chosen by noble families, but in 367 B.C. the people were extended the privilege of electing one from among themselves. The consuls were the highest civil authority; they commanded the army and presided over the senate. At the expiration of one year of office, the consul was sent to govern a province and was then called a proconsul. The office continued under the empire and, although almost entirely stripped of its power, was a coveted position until A.D. 534. The original consulate was established in 509 B.C. when the people chose Tarquinius Collatinus and Lucius Junius BRUTUS as consuls, after Brutus had driven Tarquinius Superbus, seventh and last of the Roman kings, out of Rome.

Consul, The (1950). A three-act tragic opera by Gian Carlo MENOTTI about a woman who desperately needs to leave her country and is frustrated by bureaucratic red tape.

Contes de ma mère l'Oye (Mother Goose Tales, 1697). A book of fairy tales by Charles PERRAULT. Drawing upon popular folk stories, Perrault collected the tales into a single volume and gave them the simple and graceful form in which they are known today. The *Contes* included LA BELLE AU BOIS DORMANT (*The Sleeping Beauty*), *Le Petit Chaperon Rouge* (LITTLE RED RIDING-HOOD), *La Barbe-Bleue* (BLUEBEARD), *Le Maître-chat ou le chat botté* (*Puss-in-Boots*), *Les Fées* (*The Fairies*), *Cendrillon ou la petite pantoufle de verre* (*Cinderella, or The Little Glass Slipper*), *Riquet à la houppe,* and *Le Petit Poucet* (*Tom Thumb*).

Contes Drôlatiques (Droll Stories, 1832–1837). A collection of tales by Honoré de BALZAC. Written in the style of the medieval *fabliaux*, these frequently gross tales are related with verve and gusto.

Contes et nouvelles en vers (1664–1674). A collection of tales derived from Ariosto, Boccaccio, Machiavelli, Petronius, and others by Jean de LA FONTAINE. Though set in graceful verse and popular in their day, the tales have often been criticized for their ribaldry, and upon his religious conversion, in 1692, La Fontaine publicly disavowed them.

Continental Congress. The congress of representatives from the British colonies of North America, first convened in Philadelphia in 1774 to consider grievances against the mother country. The Second Continental Congress adopted the Declaration of Independence, organized the Revolutionary Army, and conducted diplomatic negotiations with foreign nations. After the ratification of the Articles of Confederation (1781), it functioned as the central governing body of the new republic under the title, "The United States in Congress Assembled."

Contrast, The (1787). A play by Royall TYLER. Opening at the John Street Theater in New York City on April 16, 1787, it marked the true beginning of American drama. The plot involves the romantic affairs of Billy Dimple, a wealthy Anglophile, whose engagement to the clever Maria does not prevent him from flirting with other women. He eventually loses Maria to the staid but attractive Captain Manly, a Revolutionary officer. The most notable character, however, is Manly's servant Jonathan, first of the innumerable stage Yankees of American drama, whose plain practicality and wisdom make him a symbol of rural virtue.

Conversation at Midnight (1937). A long poem by Edna St. Vincent MILLAY. Eight men, assembled after dinner in a Washington Square house, discuss controversial social, political, and aesthetic issues of the time.

Conversations with Goethe. See Johann Peter ECKERMANN.

Convidado de piedra, El. See BURLADOR DE SEVILLA, EL.

Conway, Thomas. See CONWAY CABAL.

Conway Cabal (1777). A faction that tried unsuccessfully to remove Washington and make General Gates commander-in-chief of the American forces. Doubt still exists as to the nature and extent of the plot, but General Thomas Conway (1735–c. 1800), the man for whom it is named, probably did not play the leading role.

Cook or **Cooke, Ebenezer** (c. 1672–1732). American colonial poet, self-styled "Poet-laureate of Maryland." What little is known of Cook's life derives from his long satiric poem, *The Sot-Weed Factor* (1708), a diatribe against the crudities of life in the New World by one forced to live there because of "Friends unkind, and empty Purse." A revised edition of the poem appeared in 1731, with changes presenting a less harsh picture of colonial life. In the same volume, Cook published a verse history of Bacon's Rebellion based upon the *Burwell Papers*. Published by William Parks, the volume is entitled *The Maryland Muse* and is the first volume of American poetry published in the South. In 1960, John Barth published *The Sot-Weed Factor,* a satirical novel based on Cook's life.

Cook, George Cram (1873–1924). American novelist and playwright. Although Cook wrote *Roderick Taliaferro* (1903), a story of Montezuma's empire, and *The Chasm* (1911), a socialist novel, he is best known for his association with the American little theater movement. Cook and his wife, Susan GLASPELL, organized the PROVINCETOWN PLAYERS in 1915 in Provincetown, Mass. There, under Cook's direction, the early plays of Eugene O'Neill were firs. produced. Re-established in New York in 1916, the group continued to produce O'Neill's plays. *Suppressed Desires* (1915) was a one-act comedy on a Freudian theme by Cook and his wife. His play *The Spring* was produced in New York in 1921. After the success with the Provincetown Players, Cook, who had no interest in competing with commercial theater, gave up the project and sailed in 1921 for Greece, where he lived until his death.

Cook, James. Known as **Captain Cook** (1728–1779). English navigator and explorer who discovered New Caledonia and the Sandwich (Hawaiian) Islands. He was murdered by the natives in revenge for a flogging administered to one of them for stealing a boat.

cook one's goose. To ruin one's prospects. According to legend, Eric, king of Sweden, came to a certain town with very few soldiers. The enemy, in mockery, hung out a goose for him to shoot at. Finding, however, that the king meant business, and that it would be no laughing matter for them, they sent heralds to ask him what he wanted. "To cook your goose for you," he replied.

Cook's Tale, The. An unfinished fragment in the CANTERBURY TALES of Geoffrey CHAUCER. Roger the Cook laughs at the *Reeve's Tale* and offers to tell a similarly bawdy jest. He begins a story about the apprentice Perkin, a reveller too fond of dice and women for his master's taste. A metrical romance sometimes called *The Cook's Tale of Gamelyn* has been erroneously attributed to Chaucer, who probably at one time intended to adapt it. See GAMELYN.

Coolidge, [John] Calvin (1872-1933). 30th president of the U.S. (1923-1929). Coolidge first won national attention when, as governor of Massachusetts, he broke the Boston police strike of 1919, declaring that there was "no right to strike against the public safety by anybody, anywhere, any time." In 1920 he became the Republican vice-presidential nominee and, succeeding to the presidency on the death of Warren G. Harding, was elected in his own right in 1924. In 1928 he announced that he did not "choose to run" for the presidency again. An uncompromising Republican, noted for his taciturnity and frugality, Coolidge wrote an *Autobiography* (1929). He was the subject of a well-known biography by William Allen White, *A Puritan in Babylon* (1938).

Cooper, Anthony Ashley. See 1st earl of SHAFTESBURY.

Cooper, James Fenimore (1789-1851). American novelist. James Fenimore Cooper, a son of the wealthy landowner Judge William Cooper, who founded Cooperstown, N.Y., was born in Burlington, N.J. After his expulsion from Yale, he became a sailor; in 1811, he married Susan DeLancey, and occupied himself as a gentleman farmer. At the age of 31 he wrote his first novel. Although *Precaution* (1820) was a failure, Cooper continued to write. In 1823, he wrote THE PIONEERS and THE PILOT, both works of signal importance in American literature. *The Pilot* is the first American novel of the sea, and *The Pioneers* introduces the character of Natty BUMPPO, the natural man uncorrupted by civilization. Natty has taken on mythic significance in the history of the American imagination. Cooper's audience demanded that he be revived in THE LAST OF THE MOHICANS, THE PRAIRIE, THE PATHFINDER, and THE DEERSLAYER.

From 1826 to 1833 the Coopers lived abroad. Turning out novels at a prolific rate, Cooper returned to Jacksonian America dismayed to discover that the democracy he had defended abroad had turned to mobocracy. He was outspoken in his criticism, and was denounced in the American press. In the 1840's, while involved in numerous lawsuits, he wrote an Antirent trilogy, THE LITTLEPAGE MANUSCRIPTS, in which he defended the existence of a landed gentry as a stabilizing force in democracy. SATANSTOE, with its lively portraits of contrasting Yankee, Middle Colony, and Dutch manners in colonial New York, is one of Cooper's most successful books.

Although Cooper's literary craftsmanship can rarely be admired, his 50-odd volumes, in their use of the American landscape and their unique creation of Leatherstocking, constitute the foundation of American literature. See LEATHERSTOCKING TALES, THE; SPY, THE; MONIKINS, THE; AMERICAN DEMOCRAT, THE.

Cooper, Peter (1791-1883). American industrialist and philanthropist. The owner of a Baltimore iron works, Cooper designed and built the first American steam locomotive, popularly known as "Tom Thumb," in 1830. In 1857 he founded Cooper Union, an educational institution in New York City dedicated to the "advancement of science and art." He ran for the presidency in 1876 as the candidate of the Greenback Party.

Cooper, Samuel (1725-1783). American clergyman, known for his revolutionary writings against British rule in the colonies. He was the author of sermons, pamphlets, and articles for the *Boston Gazette*. His most famous work is *The Crisis* (1754), a pamphlet attacking the currently proposed bill for excise taxes in America. Cooper also worked prominently in support of the alliance with France (1778) made by Benjamin Franklin.

Copeau, Jacques (1879-1949). Theatrical producer and critic. From 1904 to 1910, Copeau wrote as a drama critic; his essays are collected in *Critiques d'un autre temps* (1923). With Gide and Rivière, he helped to found the *Nouvelle Revue Française* in 1909, and later became its editor in chief (1912-1914). Best known for his theatrical career, Copeau opposed the realism of Antoine and Lugné-Poë. With Charles Dullin and Louis Jouvet, he directed the *Théâtre du Vieux-Colombier,* an experimental playhouse that sought to bring poetry and subtle evocation back to the theater. Dullin and Jouvet eventually left to begin their own theaters; Copeau spent some years training young actors and from 1936 to 1941 served as a producer of the *Comédie Française.*

Copernicus, Nicolaus. Latinized form of **Niklas Koppernigk** (1473-1543). Polish astronomer. It was Copernicus who laid the foundations for modern astronomy by upsetting the Ptolemaic system of astronomy, which had prevailed since the second century. PTOLEMY placed the earth at the center of the universe; Copernicus advanced the theory that the earth and all the other planets revolved around the sun in individual orbits while spinning on their axes. He finished his treatise on this subject, *De Revolutionibus Orbium Coelestium* (*On the Revolutions of Heavenly Bodies*), in 1530, but it was not published until 1543, when its author lay dying. Opposition to his theories was theological as well as scientific: not only had Copernicus ignored the wisdom of the ancients, he had displaced man from the center of the universe.

Cophetua. A mythical king of Africa. Of great wealth, he fell in love with a beggar girl, Penelophon (Zenelophon in Shakespeare's *Love's Labour's Lost,* IV, i.), and married her. He is the hero of a ballad in Percy's *Reliques,* and Tennyson versified the tale in *The Beggar-Maid.*

Copland, Aaron (1900-   ). American composer. He is probably the best known representative of American nationalism in music. His most popular works employ American subjects and styles, often modeled on jazz or folk music, for example, in *Music for the Theatre* (1925), *El Salón México* (1937), and *Appalachian Spring* (1944, a ballet). Since the 1930s he has been concerned with improving general understanding of modern music by organizing concerts and writing such books as *What to Listen for in Music* (1939), *Our New Music* (1941), and *Music and the Imagination* (1952).

Copley, John Singleton (1738-1815). American painter. He began his career as a portrait painter in Boston; in 1775, he settled in England, where he turned to historical painting. He is best known for his early portraits, sharply observed and executed in a severe and uncompromising manner.

Coppard, A[lfred] E[dgar] (1878–1957). English short-story writer and poet. *Adam and Eve and Pinch Me* (1921) was his first collection of short stories. Ranging from realism to fantasy, his stories are marked by pathos and gentle irony, and possess the direct narrative interest of the folk tale. His *Collected Tales* were published in 1951 and *Lucy in Her Pink Jacket* in 1954; his *Collected Poems* appeared in 1928.

Coppée, François Edouard Joachim (1842–1908). French poet and playwright. Coppée was a contributor to the *Parnasse Contemporain* (1866). His poetic works include *Le Reliquaire* (1866), *Intimités* (1868), *Les Humbles* (1872), *Le Cahier Rouge* (1874), and *Les Récits et les Elégies* (1878).

Copperheads. In U.S. history, Northerners, mainly Democrats, who during the Civil War favored the Confederate cause and advocated a negotiated peace.

Copts. Christian Egyptians who hold that St. Mark founded their church at Alexandria. They belong to the Jacobite branch of the Eastern Orthodox Church and, since the Council of Chalcedon in 451, have possessed the patriarchal chair of Alexandria. The word is probably derived from Coptos, the metropolis of the Thebaid. The Copts conduct their worship in a dead language called "Coptic," derived from ancient Egyptian but written in Greek capital letters. St. Anthony (c. 250–350), the founder of Christian monachism, was a Copt.

copyright. The exclusive right to reproduce, publish, and sell works of literature, music, or art. The first copyright act in England was that of 1709, subsequently subject to various modifications and additions. In 1842 a new act was passed granting copyright for 42 years after publication or until 7 years after the author's death, whichever should be the longer period. This act was superseded by the Copyright Act of 1911, under which the period of protection was extended to 50 years after the death of the author, irrespective of date of publication. This act also deals with copyright in photographs, engravings, architectural designs, musical compositions, and phonograph records.

The first copyright act in the U.S. was enacted by the states of Connecticut and Massachusetts in 1783, following vigorous agitation by Noah Webster. The first national statute, passed in 1790, was modelled upon the then existing British law. Additional acts were passed in 1846, 1856, 1859, and 1865. At present, U.S. copyrights may be secured under the Act of March 4, 1909 (as amended), for a period of 28 years; a 28 year renewal period is allowed, bringing the maximum period of copyright to 56 years.

Influenced by lobbyists for book manufacturers reluctant to extend U.S. copyright to books manufactured abroad, the U.S. did not sign the Berne International Copyright Convention (1886), and thus, until the formulating of the Universal Copyright Convention under the auspices of UNESCO, a certain confusion existed in the field of U.S.-international copyright. Though the U.S. and most of the members of the Berne convention have signed the Universal Copyright Convention, a worldwide international copyright does not at the moment exist, the Soviet Union preferring in general to remain outside copyright conventions.

A common-law copyright, secured to the author by the act of creation and requiring no formality, is recognized in the U.S. and in England.

Coq d'or, Le (**The Golden Cockerel**, 1909). A satirical opera by Rimsky-Korsakov, flaying the foibles of royalty.

Coquette, The (1797). An American novel by Hannah Webster Foster. It is a *roman à clef* in epistolary form, in which the heroine is seduced by an army officer and is later deserted by a minister who had once wooed her. Inconclusive attempts have been made to identify her as the daughter of a prominent Yale trustee, and her seducer as Aaron Burr or as the son of Jonathan Edwards.

Corbaccio (Carrion Crow). A miserly Venetian in Jonson's comedy Volpone, or the Fox. He disinherits his own son in a vain attempt to inherit the wealth of Volpone. His desperate attempts to acquire more wealth than he has already are the more ironic in that Corbaccio himself is so old and decrepit that he will be unable to enjoy it.

Corbacho, El. See Alfonso Martínez de Toledo.

Corbet, Richard (1582–1635). English churchman and poet, known for his joviality. Although he served as bishop of Oxford and of Norwich, he was too convivial and tolerant to be an efficient prelate; his success was mainly due to his reputation as an anti-Puritan and his assiduous courtship of the powerful. A friend of Ben Jonson, he was popular at the Mermaid Tavern because of his skill at extemporizing poetry. Of his written works the best known is *The Fairies' Farewell* (1647), a humorous lament for the departure of England's merrier fairies, which Corbet blames on Puritanism.

Corbière, Edouard Joachim. Known as **Tristan Corbière** (1845–1875). French poet. Associated with the symbolist school, in his *Gens de mers* (published in *Les Amours jaunes*, 1873), Corbière treats the world of those who live upon the sea in a realistic and forceful manner. See symbolists.

Corbin, Alice. See Alice Corbin Henderson.

Corceca. See Faerie Queene, The.

Corday, Charlotte (1768–1793). French patriot who stabbed Jean Paul Marat to death in his bath. She was an adherent of the Revolution and sympathized with the Girondists, but was repelled by the excesses of the Reign of Terror. She was guillotined on July 17, 1793.

Cordelia. In Shakespeare's King Lear, the youngest daughter of Lear. She is disinherited by Lear because she lacks the "glib and oily art" of flattery. Her simplicity and sincerity move the king of France to marry her despite her disinheritance. It is of her that Lear speaks the famous lines: "Her voice was ever soft, gentle and low, an excellent thing in woman."

Cordelier (*i.e.* cord-wearer). A Franciscan friar of the strict rule. In the Middle Ages they distinguished themselves in philosophy and theology. Duns Scotus was one of their most distinguished members. The traditional origin of the name is that in the reign of St. Louis they repulsed an army of infidels, and the king asked who those *gens de cordelics* (corded people) were.

Cordeliers, the. French Revolutionary club of 1790 known officially as *La Société des Amis des Droits de l'Homme et du Citoyen*. MARAT, DANTON, and ROBESPIERRE were among the speakers at its meetings. The club played an active part in overthrowing both the monarchy and the GIRONDISTS. It ceased to function in 1794 when its leading members were guillotined. The name "Cordeliers" comes from the old (Franciscan) Cordelier monastery, where the club held its meetings.

Corelli, Archangelo (1653–1713). Italian violinist and composer. He had a wide European reputation, and was the first to establish a characteristic style of writing for the violin. His best-known work is a set of variations on the Spanish dance *La Folía*.

Corelli, Marie. Pen name of **Mary Mackay** (1855–1924). English romantic novelist. She was sensationally popular at the end of the 19th century. At first ambitious to be a musician, she turned to literature after a "psychical experience." Her first novel, *A Romance of Two Worlds* (1886), like most of her later books, was about "spirit power and universal love." She also wrote *Vendetta* (1886), *Barabbas* (1893), *The Sorrows of Satan* (1895), *The Master Christian* (1900), and many other novels.

Corin. In Shakespeare's As You Like It, a philosophical old shepherd who assuages Silvius' romantic grief and befriends Rosalind.

Corinna's Going A-Maying (1648). A poem by Robert HERRICK, in which the poet implores his late-sleeping mistress to rise and join the May Day festivities. Against a background of spring freshness and picturesque country rite, he sings of life's shortness, urging love and "the harmless folly of the time."

Corinne, or Italy (1807). A romantic novel by Mme. de STAËL. Oswald Nevil, an English lord, recuperating in Rome, meets the famous poetess Corinne, who, half-English and half-Italian, has exiled herself from her native England; they fall in love. Nevil wishes to marry Corinne, but she hesitates, fearing the rigidity of the English life she once knew; her present unconventional life is too dear to her. Oswald, forced to return to England, later gives in to the pressures of his social milieu and marries the wholly English Lucile, half sister of Corinne. When she learns of the marriage, Corinne dies of grief. Idealistic and passionate, *Corinne* is a psychological study of two tormented souls, and a celebrated description of Italian civilization and mores.

Corinthians, The First Epistle and **The Second Epistle of Paul the Apostle to the.** Two books of the New Testament. They are letters written by Paul to the troubled Christian church in the cosmopolitan Greek city of Corinth. The two canonical letters incorporate parts of two other letters. The Christians in Corinth were exposed to the very worldly, licentious atmosphere of this city. Paul tells them to ignore these influences; he also deals with a crisis over internal dissension and local authority. These two books are of particular historical interest because of the insight they offer into first-century Christians' problems with the pagan world. The 13th chapter of I Corinthians contains Paul's beautiful discourse on Christian love, one of the most noteworthy chapters in the Bible.

Coriolanus, The Tragedy of (c. 1608). A tragedy by William SHAKESPEARE. Caius Martius, an honorable but haughty patrician, defeats the Volscians under Tullus AUFIDIUS at Corioli and is given the name of Coriolanus. He is then persuaded to seek election to the consulship, though the thought of currying favor with the masses repels him. When Brutus and Sicinius, two unscrupulous tribunes, incite the populace against him, Coriolanus angrily denounces the plebeians for their fickleness and ingratitude and is driven from the city. Enraged by the treatment he has received, he joins the forces of Aufidius, who is preparing another attack on Rome. As the Volscian army menaces Rome, MENENIUS and COMINIUS, two old friends, unsuccessfully plead with Coriolanus to spare the city, but he remains obdurate until VOLUMNIA, his mother, and Virgilia, his wife, add their appeals to the others. Coriolanus raises the siege and tries to explain his conduct to the Volscians. Aufidius, envious of the Roman's prestige, accuses him of treachery, and as the Volscians hurl abuse at him, Coriolanus is murdered by agents of Aufidius.

The direct source of the play is Thomas North's translation (1579) of Plutarch's *Lives*, which records the career of the legendary patrician.

Cornaro, Luigi (1467–1566). Italian author. He wrote four *Discorsi della vita sobria* (*Discourses on the Life of Moderation*). His work was translated by George Herbert and admired by many subsequent authors, including Addison.

Corneille, Pierre (1606–1684). French dramatist. Son of a lawyer, he abandoned a career at the bar in order to write for the theater, initially under the patronage of Richelieu as one of the cardinal's CINQ AUTEURS. *Mélite* (1629), his first play and a comedy of manners, was successfully produced in Paris. There followed the tragicomedy *Clitandre* (1632), seven comedies of only moderate interest, and his first tragedy, MÉDÉE (1635). Although LE CID (1637) won an enormous popular success, Richelieu persuaded the Académie française to censure the play's violation of the dramatic unities as well as its emotional style. Madame de Rambouillet's salon also expressed doubt concerning the play's merit. For three years, chastened and disturbed, Corneille wrote nothing for the theater. He finally broke his silence with the tragedies HORACE, CINNA, POLYEUCTE, RODOGUNE, HÉRACLIUS, LA MORT DE POMPÉE, NICOMÈDE, ANDROMÈDE, and a comedy, LE MENTEUR. With *Le Cid,* these tragedies marked Corneille's brief leadership of the French stage. After the failure of *Pertharite* (1651), Corneille withdrew to Rouen. In 1659 he returned to the theater with OEDIPE, only to find that during his absence the public had come to prefer the directness and simplicity of Racine to the complexity of his own late style. The plays of Corneille's decline include the tragedies *La Toison d'or* (*The Golden Fleece,* 1660), *Sertorius* (1662), *Sophonisbe* (1663), *Othon* (1664), AGÉSILAS, ATTILA, *Suréna* (1674), and the comedies TITE ET BÉRÉNICE (1670) and *Pulchérie* (1672). Corneille eventually retired from the theater and translated *The Imitation of Christ* into French verse.

Corneille can be considered the prime shaper of the French classic theater. While earlier writers had attempted a tragedy of actions, Corneille sought tragedy in the depiction of the human soul, thus substituting an interior drama for the exterior drama of his predecessors. Borrowing the greater part of his subjects from classical mythology and history, Corneille excelled in the creation of tragic protagonists: men and women of heroic dimension caught in the conflict of reason, will, or duty with an all-powerful love or hatred. Propelled by the highest sentiments and gifted with an enormous will to triumph over the obstacles of destiny, his characters are drawn in large, bold strokes and sometimes, in the magnificence of their deeds and language, exceed the bounds of humanity and rise to the superhuman.

Corneille, Thomas (1625–1709). French playwright and brother of Pierre Corneille. A skilled technician and an accomplished imitator, he kept the French theater stocked with workmanlike though not highly original plays during the interval between Pierre Corneille's great tragedies and those of Racine. Notable among his works are the romantic tragedy *Timocrate* (1656), based on an episode in La Calprenède's *Cléopâtre,* and the heroic tragedy *Ariane* (1672), based on the Ariadne legend.

Cornelia. See GRACCHI.

Cornelius. See VOLTIMAND.

Cornford, Frances Crofts (1886–1960). English poet. The granddaughter of Charles Darwin and wife of Francis Macdonald Cornford, she usually wrote restrained poems about nature; her best-known poem is the ironic *To a Fat Lady Seen from the Train.* Her *Collected Poems* appeared in 1954.

Cornford, Francis Macdonald (1874–1943). English scholar. He wrote *From Religion to Philosophy* (1912), an anthropological study, and *The Origin of Attic Comedy* (1914), in which he traces comedy back to the Dionysian fertility rites.

Cornhuskers (1918). A collection of poems by Carl SANDBURG. It includes such well-known poems as *Cool Tombs, Prairie, Caboose Thoughts, Wilderness, Chicago Poet, Testament,* and *Haunts.*

corn laws. Laws passed at various times in English history, from 1436 to 1842, regulating the domestic and foreign grain trade of England. The most controversial corn laws were those of the 19th century, which levied a high duty on imports and raised domestic prices, causing great hardship among the poor of England, especially in the manufacturing districts. Feeling against the laws ran high and when the Corn Law of 1815 was passed in order to counteract the post-Napoleonic depression, there were riots. In 1839, an Anti-Corn Law League was formed to bring about repeal of the laws. Richard COBDEN and John BRIGHT were the leading orators associated with the Anti-Corn Law League. The grain tariff was reduced in 1849 and entirely abolished in 1862.

Cornucopia. The horn of plenty, an ancient symbol of the bounty of growing things. Often identified with the horn of Amaltheia, the goat that had suckled the infant Zeus, it was frequently shown in art as an attribute of various forms of a fertility DAEMON.

Cornwall, duke of. In Shakespeare's KING LEAR, the grasping, ruthless husband of Lear's daughter Regan. When Gloucester shelters Lear, Cornwall piucks Gloucester's eyes out in revenge. A servant, horrified at the cruel deed, kills Cornwall and is in turned killed by Regan.

Cornwallis, Charles, 1st marquis (1738–1805). English major general in the American Revolution. He defeated General Greene at Guilford Courthouse, N.C., but was forced to surrender at Yorktown shortly thereafter. He later served as viceroy of Ireland and governor-general of India.

Coronado, Francisco Vásquez de (1510–1554). Spanish explorer. In 1540 Coronado left Mexico as commander of an expedition to conquer the Seven Cities of Cibola in present New Mexico, which earlier explorers had described in glowing terms. After undergoing extreme hardships and traversing Arizona, New Mexico, Texas, Oklahoma, and Kansas, Coronado returned to Mexico empty-handed and disillusioned. One of his men, García López de Calderón, discovered the Grand Canyon on a side expedition.

Corot, Jean Baptiste Camille (1796–1875). French landscape painter. The least realistic of the BARBIZON SCHOOL, his style evolved from the influence of contemporary classicism to the poetic rendition of landscapes in which a silver-grey haze envelops and harmonizes perfectly balanced figures and trees. Corot's work also includes historical subjects and figure paintings, the latter being only less prized than his landscapes today.

Corpus Juris Civilis. See under JUSTINIAN I.

Correggio, Antonio Allegri da (c. 1489–1534). Italian painter. He is known for his use of chiaroscuro and blurred outlines in mythological paintings. These have a sensuous, almost seductive, sweetness and reveal his use of light and trompe l'oeil to create the illusion of church ceilings opening up into the heavens. His mythological paintings—*Antiope, Jupiter and Io, Ganymede*—strongly influenced French painting during the 18th century. His frescos on the octagonal cupola of the cathedral at Parma was a leading source of later baroque ceiling decoration in Italy and throughout Europe.

Corsair, The (1814). A narrative poem by Lord BYRON. The pirate chief CONRAD disguises himself as a dervish, in order to enter the palace of Sultan Seyd. He is discovered and imprisoned, but Gulnare, queen of the harem, releases him, and he returns to the pirates' isle, only to find that Medora, his true love, has died in his absence. He, therefore, returns to his native Greece, where he heads a rebellion and is shot. Upon his death, his page Kaled is discovered to be Gulnare in disguise. *Lara* (1814), another narrative poem, deals with Conrad's last adventures in Spain, where he has returned as Lara. He lives a strange and secluded life until he is recognized and killed. Conrad and Lara are prototypes of the Byronic hero, extravagant, romantic, and mysterious. See Sir EZZELIN.

Corso, Gregory. See BEAT MOVEMENT.

Cortez or **Cortés, Hernando** or **Hernán** (1485–1547). Spanish conqueror of Mexico. Cortez arrived in the New World in 1504 and was mayor of Santiago, Cuba, when he was ordered by Governor Velázquez to lead an expedition to Mexico. Velázquez later tried to halt the voyage, but Cortez had already set sail (1519). Reaching the mainland, he was fortunate in acquiring the services of two interpreters, one of whom was the famed Malinche or Doña Marina, daughter of an Aztec chieftain, whom the Maya had enslaved; she became Cortez' mistress as well as his confidante.

After founding the city of Vera Cruz, Cortez moved against the Aztec capital at Tenochtitlán, forming alliances with other Indian tribes, such as the Tlaxcalans, who hated the Aztecs. When some of the more faint-hearted Spaniards spoke of returning to Cuba, Cortez ordered their ships to be destroyed.

Although MONTEZUMA, the Aztec chief at Tenochtitlán, was outwardly friendly, Cortez captured him and held him as a hostage. Upon hearing that Velázquez, in an attempt to reassert his authority over Mexico, had dispatched another expedition under Pánfilo de Narváez, Cortez returned to the seacoast and persuaded Narváez' men to desert their commander and join him. Back in Tenochtitlán, he found that the actions of Pedro de Alvarado, his deputy, had incited the Indians to revolt and that Montezuma had been killed. During the disastrous *noche triste,* or "sad night" (June 30, 1520), the Spaniards were forced to flee with the loss of many men. Cortez immediately began to plan another campaign against Tenochtitlán, which was captured the following year. Though he was granted many honors and was created marquis of the Valley of Oaxaca, Cortez gradually lost his political power in Mexico and was supplanted in 1535 by the first viceroy, Antonio de Mendoza.

Cortez himself gave a vivid description of the conquest of Mexico in five letters he wrote to Charles V of Spain. The best-known account, however, is the history of Bernal DÍAZ DEL CASTILLO, which Archibald MacLeish used as the basis of his poem *Conquistador* (1932). Novels laid in this period include Lew Wallace's *The Fair God* (1873) and Samuel Shellabarger's *Captain from Castile* (1945). See CUAUHTÉMOC.

Corvino (It., "Raven"). A greedy merchant in Jonson's comedy VOLPONE, OR THE FOX. Though very jealous of his innocent young wife, Celia, he willingly offers her to the lecherous Volpone in the hope of inheriting some of his money.

Corvo, Baron. See Frederick ROLFE.

Cory, William Johnson (1823–1892). English poet, classicist. Cory published a single volume of verse, *Ionica* (1858), in which is found the famous translation from Callimachus, *Heraclitus,* beginning "They told me, Heraclitus, they told me you were dead."

Coryate or **Coryat, Thomas** (1577?–1617). English traveler and buffoon at court. *Coryate's Crudities* (1611) is a curious account of his travels on foot through France, Savoy, Italy, and other countries.

corybantes (korybantes). See CYBELE.

Corydon. A conventional name for a rustic or shepherd; a brainless, love-sick youth derived from the shepherd in Vergil's *Bucolic* II. See ARCADES AMBO.

Corydon (1924). An essay in dialogue form by André GIDE. Written during the years 1911–1920, it maintains that the homosexual is not unnatural, nor harmful either to himself or to society. It provoked violent criticism, directed less toward the book than toward Gide himself.

Coryell, John R. See Nick CARTER.

coryphaeus (koryphaios). The leader of the chorus in Greek classical drama. An earlier term for the same office was *choragos.* Both words have been used figuratively to apply to the leader of any group, or, more especially, its most active member.

Cosette. In Victor Hugo's novel LES MISÉRABLES, the daughter of Fantine and the adopted daughter of Jean Valjean.

Cosimo, Piero di (1462–1521). Florentine painter. He is noted for the lyric quality of his paintings and his penchant for the fantastic and the strange. In his religious works or in his mythological scenes, harshness alternates with tender melancholy. VASARI says he boiled his eggs with the varnishes, 50 at a time, in order to devote every minute to his work. His best-known works include the *Death of Procris,* the *Passage of the Red Sea* (one of the Sistine Chapel frescoes), and the *Memorial Portrait of Simonetta Vespucci,* the celebrated Florentine beauty used by Botticelli as a model for his *Primavera* and *Birth of Venus.*

Cossacks, The (Kazaki; 1863). A novel by Count Leo TOLSTOI. The central character, Olenin, tired of life in civilized society, attempts to find happiness among the wild, free-living Cossacks of the Caucasus. The portraits of the old Cossack Eroshka and the native girl Maryana are especially successful. Critics generally cite this short work as the finest book written by Tolstoi before *War and Peace.*

Costain, Thomas B[ertram] (1885–1965). Canadian-born American writer. Costain came to the U.S. in 1920 and became fiction editor of *The Saturday Evening Post.* He is best known for his historical novels, notably *The Black Rose* (1945), which is set in medieval England and China, and *The Silver Chalice* (1953), a biblical tale woven around the chalice of Antioch. Costain also wrote *Joshua* (1943), a biography of the biblical hero, and several volumes of popular history, including *The Three Edwards* (1958) and *The Last Plantagenets* (1962). *Son of a Hundred Kings* (1950) is a semiautobiographical novel about a Canadian boy.

Costard. In Shakespeare's LOVE'S LABOUR'S LOST, an unlettered clown who tries to imitate the learned court wits of Elizabethan times. He uses the word "honorificabilitudinitatibus" and speaks of the "contempts" of a letter.

Coster, Charles de (1827–1879). A Belgian writer. His best-known work, *La Légende de Thyl Ulenspiegel et de Lamme Goedzak* (1868), succeeds in making of Tyll Eulenspiegel a delightful incarnation of the Flemish folk spirit.

Côté de chez Swann, Du. See REMEMBRANCE OF THINGS PAST.

Côté de Guermantes, Le. See REMEMBRANCE OF THINGS PAST.

Cotter's Saturday Night, The (1786). A sentimental poem in Spenserian stanzas by Robert BURNS, famous for its description of Scottish peasant life and for the story of Jenny.

Cotton, Charles (1630–1687). English poet and translator. Cotton is best known for his translation 1685) of Montaigne's *Essays,* a clear, faithful, and vigorous version which is often preferred to the earlier Florio translation. An intimate friend of Izaak Walton, he wrote a treatise on fly-fishing which was included in the fifth edition (1676) of THE COMPLEAT ANGLER. Cotton was also the author of several other translations from the French, some rather scurrilous burlesques of Vergil and Lucian, and a number of poems on fishing, country life, and related subjects, which have a certain homely charm and fidelity to the rural scene. These last, collected in *Poems on Several Occasions* (1689), were admired by Wordsworth, Coleridge, and Lamb.

Cotton, John (1584–1652). English-born Puritan clergyman and writer. Dissatisfied with conditions in England, Cotton, who was already a famous clergyman, emigrated to Boston in 1633 and became one of the colony's most influential leaders. Known for his tireless scholarship and aristocratic political views, he wrote numerous works including *The Keys of the Kingdom of Heaven* (1644); *Milk for Babes* (1646), a children's catechism; and *The Bloudy Tenent Washed* (1647), part of a celebrated controversy with Roger Williams (see BLOUDY TENENT, THE). Cotton Mather was his grandson.

Cotton, Sir Robert Bruce (1571–1631). English antiquary, collector of books, manuscripts, coins, medals, etc. He was the founder of the famous Cottonian Library, now in the British Museum, which contained many otherwise unobtainable manuscripts saved from destroyed monasteries, including those of *Beowulf*, *The Pearl*, and *Gawain and the Green Knight*. The identifying titles of the manuscripts were derived from the busts of Roman emperors which adorned the bookcases holding these collections; thus, the *Beowulf* manuscript is called "Cotton Vitellius A XV" from the Emperor Vitellius, and the manuscript of *The Pearl* is known as "Cotton Nero A X" from the Emperor Nero.

Cotton allowed the free use of his library to leading scholars of his time and presented manuscripts from his collection to the Bodleian Library when it was founded. His library was bequeathed to the English nation on the death of his grandson in 1701.

Cotytto. The Thracian goddess of fertility, worshiped at Athens with licentious rites. See BAPTES.

Council of Nicaea (325). The first ecumenical council of the Christian Church. Called by CONSTANTINE THE GREAT, it was held in Nicaea, a small town in Bithynia, Asia Minor. The major undertaking of the council was a discussion of the views of ARIUS, who held that Jesus was the most exalted human of all time, but had not been created out of nothing nor was he eternally existent, and that he was capable of right and wrong in his own free will. The council's decision was against Arius, ascribing a purely divine nature to Jesus (see TRINITY).

The council published a confession of faith called the Nicene Creed (from the Latin *credo,* "I believe"). It was based on an older creed that had been used in Caesarea, but carefully defined the orthodox doctrine of the Trinity. The Nicene Creed is used (with minor changes) in the liturgies of the Roman, Greek, and Anglican churches, and its doctrinal teachings have been accepted by most Protestants.

Counterfeiters, The (Les Faux-Monnayeurs; 1926). A novel by André GIDE. The novelist Edouard keeps a journal of events in order to write a novel about the nature of reality. The intrigues of a gang of counterfeiters symbolize the "counterfeit" personalities with which people disguise themselves to conform hypocritically to convention or to deceive themselves. The adolescent boys Bernard Profitendieu and Olivier Molinier, having left home in order to be free to find and develop their true selves, encounter many varieties of hypocrisy and self-deception in human relationships and barely escape falling into such poses themselves. Both begin by seeking a close emotional tie with Edouard. Each, however, comes to recognize that Edouard is inadequate as an ideal for emulation, particularly when the novelist cannot recognize the psychological reality of the schoolboy Boris' useless suicide, which is an indirect result of the counterfeiters' machinations.

Counter Reformation. A term used to describe the Roman Catholic reaction to the Protestant Reformation of the 16th century. Beginning with the Council of Trent, and later through the efforts of the INQUISITION and the JESUITS, the Roman church sought to consolidate its position and win back its former adherents. Literature and the other arts became involved as vehicles for the renewal of faith and the propagandizing of Roman Catholic dogma. Artists were bound by conscience and external pressure to help or at least not hinder the cause. The so-called Counter-Reformation style in literature, sometimes identified with or considered a part of the baroque style, flourished during the latter half of the 16th century and the first half of the 17th century. It was characterized by the use of rhetoric, a straining after the ironic, the paradoxical, and the witty, attempts to render reality as well as the world of the spirit in concrete and highly sensuous imagery, especially in religious verse. Though its leading practitioners in Italy, Spain, France, and England, poets such as Tasso, Marino, Ceppède, Góngora, Lope de Vega, Southwell, and Crashaw were Catholics, the style left its mark on such Protestant poets as D'Aubigné and Donne in their use of the metaphysical conceit.

Countess Cathleen, The (1891). A poetic drama by William Butler YEATS. It describes how the countess Cathleen sells her soul to the devil in exchange for the souls of the starving Irish peasants. In her wanderings through Ireland the Countess Cathleen is accompanied by Oona, an old nurse, and Aleel, a poet who loves her in vain. The part of the countess was written for Maud GONNE. The play was one of the first produced by the company that was later to become the ABBEY THEATRE company. At its first production it provoked a riot by Catholics offended at what they considered Yeats's theological irregularity in having God save the heroine's soul at the end.

Count of Monte Cristo, The (Le Comte de Monte Cristo; 1844). A romance by Alexandre DUMAS. The hero, Edmond Dantès, is about to begin a blissful existence as captain of his vessel and husband of his sweetheart, when a false political charge condemns him to life imprisonment. He escapes, in a highly dramatic manner, and flees to the island of Monte Cristo. With the aid of a treasure he unearths, Dantès becomes a powerful and darkly mysterious figure. Eventually, all who wronged him suffer his revenge.

Country Doctor, The (Le Médecin de campagne; 1833). A novel, part of LA COMÉDIE HUMAINE, by Honoré de BALZAC. The title character is Dr. Benassis, whose kindly spirit and indefatigable efforts on behalf of the people of his village make him universally beloved.

Country House, The (1907). A novel by John GALSWORTHY. It is a naturalistic social study of the traditions and attitudes of the English landed aristocracy. These traditions are threatened in the Pendyce family when the dashing young son, George Pendyce, becomes involved in a divorce scandal. Eventually, through the coercion of his father and the sentimental persuasions of his mother, George is extricated. Thus

Galsworthy ends by supporting the values of country house life and reassuring his conservative readers that they need not take his satire and criticism too seriously.

Country of the Pointed Firs, The (1896). A book of tales and sketches by Sarah Orne JEWETT. Thinly bound together by a faint thread of plot, the entire series describes a Maine seaport town from the point of view of a summer resident. The portraits of the townspeople are sympathetically drawn. Willa Cather thought so well of the book that she placed it beside *Huckleberry Finn* and *The Scarlet Letter*.

Country Wife, The (1675). A comedy by William WYCHERLY. Pinchwife, an overly jealous husband, brings his simple country wife, Margery, to London for the marriage of his sister Alithea to the credulous Sparkish. Despite Pinchwife's efforts, Margery soon becomes familiar with the fashionable ways of the city and ends by cuckolding him with the libertine Horner, who has spread the rumor that he is a eunuch to facilitate his access to willing wives. Thus, Pinchwife's jealousy leads his wife to infidelity while Sparkish eventually loses Alitha because of excessive confidence in her loyalty.

In 1766 Garrick rewrote the play as *The Country Girl*, modifying some of its bawdiness.

Couperus, Louis Marie Anne (1863–1923). Dutch novelist. He is known as the outstanding writer of the Dutch realist school of fiction. His most important works chronicle the lives of insignificant people with great insight and attention to detail. THE SMALL SOULS, the first of a tetralogy, is the best example of this preoccupation, though *Old People and the Things That Pass* is probably his outstanding single novel. He wrote more than 30 novels.

couplet. In prosody, a pair of lines forming a unit. This is usually because they are either set off as a separate stanza or because they rhyme. The best known couplet is the so-called HEROIC COUPLET.

Courbet, Gustave (1819–1877). French painter. Spokesman of realism, he painted straightforward and unembellished, oversized scenes of everyday life and autobiographical events. Although he was decried by his conservative contemporaries, he rejected harmonious composition and color in his desire to express truth, and achieved a forceful expression, especially in his landscapes.

Cours de Philosophie Positive. See Auguste COMTE.

Courtier, The (Il Cortegiano; 1528). A Renaissance courtesy book by Baldassare CASTIGLIONE. Written in 1518, its four books of dialogues describe the conversations held at the court of Urbino on four successive evenings in 1507. The main interlocutors are Federico Fregoso, Lodovico Di Canossa, Bernardo Bibbiena, Giuliano de' Medici, Pietro Bembo, Ottaviano Fregoso, and Emilia Pia, who along with the hostess, Elisabetta Gonzaga, acts as moderator. In the first book, the ideal courtier is said to require noble birth, skill in arms, courage, a handsome appearance, and dexterity in swimming, hunting, dancing, and the arts. He must be able to write and speak well, but above all without affectation. The manner of doing these things must be nonchalant and natural (*sprezzatura*).

The second book is devoted to language, the kind and the occasion of speech as well as the manner of

Title page of Hoby's translation of
The Courtier (1577).

addressing oneself to princes and friends. Bibbiena dominates the discussion with a long treatment of jests and witticisms. The third book features Giuliano de' Medici's discourse on the *donna di palazzo*, the court lady, who is required to maintain her femininity while displaying a knowledge of letters, the arts, and how to entertain the court. She must be morally superior, an injunction that produces a lengthy debate on the chastity of women and the problems of amatory relationships at court.

The fourth book deals with the final and true role of the ideal courtier: to guide his prince in matters of government and state. After further discussion of the education of the prince and the best forms of political organization, Bembo concludes the book with a rhapsodic explanation of Platonic Love, the union of beauty and goodness in the ascent to God.

Not long after its publication, the book was translated into French, German, Spanish, and Russian. The English version of Sir Thomas Hoby (1561) insured its popularity in England, where it influenced the writings of Spenser and Sidney, the plays of Shakespeare, and the educational and social theory and practice of the English Renaissance. With the courtesy books of Guazzo and Della Casa, it formed a trio of crucial landmarks in the development of English attitudes towards the requirements of being a gentleman.

Courtin', The (1867). A poem by James Russell LOWELL. Written in Yankee dialect, it was originally published in the second series of THE BIGLOW PAPERS. This tale of rural courtship was introduced as a diversion from the discussions of politics with which the rest of the *Biglow Papers* are concerned. The poem is still valued as a fine example of native American humor and sentiment.

courtly love or *(Fr.)* **amour courtois.** A medieval code of attitudes toward love and of the highly conventionalized conduct considered suitable for noble lords and ladies. It postulates the adoration and respect of a gallant and courageous knight or courtier for a beautiful, intelligent, lofty-minded noblewoman who usually remains chaste and unattainable. He performs noble deeds for her sake, but suffers terribly because she remains indifferent or, even if she favors his devotion, because her purity and his respect for it prevent the consummation of their love. Often he must keep secret the name of his beloved, although he carries her scarf or glove into battle or celebrates her beauty in song, for the lady is usually married to someone else; a basic tenet of the code is the incompatibility of love with marriage. Nevertheless, the lover welcomes the suffering of his passion, for it ennobles him and inspires him to great achievements.

The tradition of courtly love seems to have first been popularized by the Provençal TROUBADOURS of southern France in the 11th century. Through ELEANOR OF AQUITAINE's patronage of the troubadours, the convention spread to the royal courts of northern France, of England, and then of Germany (see MINNESINGERS). Eleanor's daughter Marie de Champagne urged her chaplain Andreas Capellanus to write a treatise on the art of love; and the "court of love," in which a group of court gentlefolk gather to debate specific theoretical problems of conduct in the interpretation of the code, became popular as a social pastime and a literary convention. The principles of courtly love were embodied in the first part of the allegorical ROMANCE OF THE ROSE, and in medieval romances such as the cycles concerning King Arthur, Tristan and Iseult, and Troilus and Cressida, most notably in the version of the Launcelot legend by Chrétien de Troyes.

In Italy the STILNOVISTI of the late 13th century adapted the tradition in a "sweet new style," which further idealized the role of woman in the spiritual elevation of the man who adores her. This worship of the beloved thus became fused with the cult of the Virgin Mary, and with the concept of the ideal in Platonism. By the 16th century courtly love had become only one aspect of the code governing the entire bearing and conduct of the courtier and his lady. The most famous handbook of courtly behavior was Castiglione's THE COURTIER, translated into English by Sir Thomas Hoby in 1561. This and the Stilnovistic works of Dante and Petrarch, all identifying physical beauty and social decorum with moral and ultimately with spiritual worth and the approach to a Platonic ideal, greatly influenced much Elizabethan writing, such as that of Sir Philip Sidney and Edmund Spenser. The exaltation of a worthy woman because of the elevating aspect of courtly love is especially prominent in Spenser's *Four Hymns.*

Courtship of Miles Standish, The (1858). A long narrative poem by Henry Wadsworth LONGFELLOW. The captain of the Plymouth settlement, Miles STANDISH, sends his friend John Alden to woo Priscilla Mullins for him. Despite his honest pleas for the older man, Priscilla prefers John as a husband.

When Miles is reported killed, the lovers plan their marriage. On the eve of the wedding Standish returns to give his blessings to the young couple.

Cousin, Victor (1792–1867). French philosopher and teacher. A professor of philosophy at the Sorbonne, Cousin delivered brilliant lectures, helping to increase the reputation of the university. A student of German philosophy, he met both Hegel and Schelling. Not a philosophical creator, but a synthesizer who drew upon former systems, Cousin is considered the founder of the Eclectic school. Among his published works are *Cours d'histoire de la philosophie moderne* (1841–46) and *Fragments pour servir à l'histoire de la philosophie* (1865).

Cousine Bette, La (1846). A novel, part of LA COMÉDIE HUMAINE, by Honoré de BALZAC. The title character, Lisbeth Fischer, is a harsh old spinster who masks frustration and bitterness behind a facade of good will. Driven by fierce jealousy, she deliberately destroys a romance between her young niece and a Polish sculptor.

Cousin Pons, Le (1847). A novel, part of LA COMÉDIE HUMAINE, by Honoré de BALZAC. The hero, Silvain Pons, is a musical composer who squanders most of his income on works of art. Ugly and lonely, he becomes a glutton and social parasite as he grows older.

Cousins, Norman (1912–). American journalist and editor. Cousins became editor of the SATURDAY REVIEW in 1942. A decade later he dropped the words "of Literature" from the title and broadened the magazine's scope to reflect his interest in world affairs and arts of communication other than literature. Cousins has also written books on world federalism and foreign policy, including *Modern Man Is Obsolete* (1945) and *In Place of Folly* (1961).

Cousteau, Jacques-Yves (1910–). French underwater explorer and writer. Inventor of the Aqua-Lung and other devices for submarine investigation, he records many of his experiments and discoveries in *The Silent World* (1953) and *The Living Sea* (1963).

Covenanters. A term applied, during the 16th and 17th centuries, to the Scottish Presbyterians who banded together in a series of agreements, or covenants, to defend their religion against royal encroachments. In 1643 the English Parliament and the Scots drew up a Solemn League and Covenant that provided for changes in the English church in conformity with Presbyterian principles; in return, the Covenanters agreed to join the Parliamentary struggle against Charles I.

Coventry Cycle. A cycle of MIRACLE PLAYS. Supposedly they were performed at Coventry, England. They are among the best of the surviving plays of this genre.

Coverdale, Miles (1) (1488–1568). An English priest, converted to Lutheranism and translator of the first complete Bible in English (1535). See BIBLE, ENGLISH VERSIONS.

(2) The narrator of Hawthorne's BLITHEDALE ROMANCE and a leading character in the story.

Coverley, Sir Roger de. The simple, good, and altogether delightful country squire created by Richard STEELE as a chief character in the imaginary club that supposedly wrote THE SPECTATOR. He was further developed by Joseph ADDISON, and it is to

Addison that we are indebted for this portrait of a perfect English gentleman in the reign of Queen Anne. Roger de Coverley is the name of a country-dance similar to the Virginia Reel and it was Addison's fiction that Sir Roger's great-grandfather invented the dance.

Covetous Knight, The. See LITTLE TRAGEDIES.

Coxey's Army. A group of about 400 unemployed who marched on Washington, D.C., in 1894 during a period of economic distress. Led by Jacob S. Coxey (1854–1951), they demanded federal legislation to create jobs and increase the amount of money in circulation. The army disbanded after Coxey and two other leaders were arrested for trespassing on the grounds of the Capitol. Coxey led another army in 1914.

Coward, Noel [Pierce] (1899–   ). English actor, composer, and playwright. He is best known for his witty, brittle, and sophisticated comedies of the British "leisure class." His works for the theater, in addition to musical revues, include *The Vortex* (1925), a serious drama; *Bitter Sweet* (1929), an operetta; *Private Lives* (1930), his most successful comedy; *Cavalcade* (1931), a patriotic play on the British Victorian tradition in the history of a single family; and *Blithe Spirit* (1941). *Present Indicative* (1937) is an autobiography; *Pomp and Circumstance* (1960) is a novel. He wrote, directed, and acted in a war movie *In Which We Serve* (1942). The second volume of his autobiography *Future Indefinite* was published in 1954; it describes his experiences as an entertainer in the second World War. His costume piece *Quadrille* (1952), starring the Lunts, had long runs in both London and New York. He has appeared on television and in night clubs.

cowboy. A Western cattle herder. The name was originally applied to Tory raiders during the American Revolution who plundered neutral land. The Western version is a breed that learned much of its way of life from the Mexican *vaquero.* Dime novels did much to make the cowboy a popular folk figure in the U.S., and the tradition has been carried on with apparently untiring success by the motion pictures and, later, by television.

Cowley, Abraham (1618–1667). English META-PHYSICAL POET and essayist. His conceits were fantastic and extreme, popular in his own day, but regarded with disfavor by the time of Dryden. He was also famous as the originator of the English Pindaric ode. Cowley published his first volume, *Poetical Blossoms* (1633), at the age of 15; later works include DAVIDEIS, his best-known poem.

Cowley, Mrs. Hannah (1743–1809). English dramatist. One of the earliest English female playwrights, she wrote a number of comedies of manners touched with sentimentality. Among the best are *The Belle's Stratagem* (1780) and *A Bold Stroke for a Husband* (1783).

Cowley, Malcolm (1898–   ). American critic and poet. A member of the American colony in France during the 1920's, Cowley discussed expatriate psychology in *Exile's Return: A Narrative of Ideas* (1934; rev., 1951). His other works include two volumes of poetry, *Blue Juniata* (1929) and *The Dry Season* (1942), and *The Literary Situation* (1954), an analysis of the writer's place in American society. He wrote an influential study of William Faulkner's

works as the introduction to the *Viking Portable Faulkner* (1946), which he edited.

Cowper, William (1731–1800). English pre-romantic poet. From the time he was 24, Cowper suffered from a religious mania and was subject to fits of despair—he was convinced that he was excluded from salvation—and intermittent attacks of insanity. After his first breakdown, he went to Huntingdon to board with Morley Unwin until Unwin's death (1767). He then moved, with the widowed Mary Unwin, to OLNEY and continued to live with her until her death (1796). His poetic career began late in life, with the production of hymns, didactic verse, nature lyrics, and religious poetry. His best-known poem is THE TASK. Others, also well known, include *Truth, The Progress of Error, Expostulation, Hope, Charity, Conversation,* and *Retirement,* all published in 1782, *The Diverting History of* JOHN GILPIN, a humorous ballad published with *The Task,* and the *Olney Hymns* (1779). He also translated Homer (1791) and on his death left many letters and introspective autobiographical writings. Cowper was interested in freeing English verse from the facility of the followers of Pope. "Give me a manly rough line," writes Cowper, "with a deal of meaning in it, rather than a whole poem full of musical periods, that have nothing but their oily smoothness to recommend them." See THE CASTAWAY; STRICKEN DEER.

Cowperwood, Frank Algernon. The central character in a trilogy of novels by Theodore DREISER. Patterned after the life of Charles T. Yerkes, Cowperwood is a man with an overweening desire for power, which drives him on to ruthless pursuit of financial dominance but fails to bring him happiness. The three novels are THE FINANCIER, THE TITAN, and *The Stoic.*

Coyle, Kathleen (1886–1952). Irish novelist. *A Flock of Birds* (1930) is a sensitive novel about the Irish revolution. In *Immortal Ease* (1939), the character Victoria Rising is supposed to be based on Elinor Wylie.

Cozzens, James Gould (1903–   ). American novelist. His *S.S. San Pedro* (1931), a novel based on the sinking of the *Vestris* in 1928, was the first of his works to attract wide attention. *Guard of Honor* (1948), which received a Pulitzer Prize, deals with soldiers and civilians at a Florida air force base during World War II. *By Love Possessed* (1957) became a best seller and was highly praised by many critics. Perhaps because it was so highly praised, a critical reaction set in, and Cozzens' work was attacked, most notably by Dwight Macdonald in *Commentary* in an article called "By Cozzens Possessed." Other novels by Cozzens include *The Last Adam* (1933), *Men and Brethren* (1936), and *The Just and the Unjust* (1942).

Crabbe, George (1754–1832). English poet. He escaped extreme poverty through the financial assistance of Edmund Burke. Considered a transitional figure between neoclassicism and romanticism, Crabbe wrote in the heroic couplet; his sympathies were humanitarian but opposed to sentimentality. His best-known poem is THE VILLAGE, a realistic answer to Oliver Goldsmith's *The Deserted Village.* Other poems by Crabbe, similar in theme to *The Village,* include *The Newspaper* (1785), *The Parish Register* (1807), and *The Borough* (1810). *Peter Grimes,* one of the most powerful tales in *The Borough,* is the subject of a tragic opera, first produced in 1945, by Benjamin Britten.

Crabbed Age and Youth. An anonymous Elizabethan lyric (1599), presenting a series of antitheses between youth and age.

Crabtree, Cadwallader. In Tobias Smollett's novel PEREGRINE PICKLE, an embittered and misanthropic old Welshman, who assists the hero in his satiric exposés of society's folly.

Craddock, Charles Egbert. See Mary Noailles MURFREE.

Craig, [Edward] Gordon (1872–   ). English actor, stage designer, producer, and writer on subjects related to the theater. He organized and published a journal, *The Mask* (1908), and founded a theatrical school at the Arena Goldoni in Florence, Italy. He is the son of Ellen Terry and Edward Goodwin.

Craigenputtock. A lonely farm near Dumfries, Scotland, owned by Jane WELSH, the wife of Thomas CARLYLE. The couple lived there from 1828 to 1834, and it was there that Carlyle wrote much of his best work. Ralph Waldo Emerson visited the Carlyles at Craigenputtock in 1833.

Craigie, Pearle Mary Teresa. Pen name **John Oliver Hobbes** (1867–1906). American-born English novelist and dramatist. Her best-known work— such as her play *The Ambassadors* (1898) and the novels *Some Emotions and a Moral* (1891) and *The Herb-Moon* (1896)—is marked by sophistication and satirical wit. Though a devout, even mystical Catholic, Mrs. Craigie was very much a woman of the world, active in the fashionable life of London.

Craig's Wife (1925). A play by George KELLY. It is a study of a selfish, narrow woman, more interested in her house than in her husband; by the end of the play everyone has left her and she is alone with the house. It was awarded a Pulitzer Prize.

Craik, Dinah Maria Mulock (1826–1887). English novelist, author of over 40 volumes including novels, tales for children, books of travel, and poetry. Her only novel of note is JOHN HALIFAX, GENTLEMAN. Most of her work is characterized by a note of rather tedious piety and sentimentality.

Cranach or **Kranach, Lucas** (1472–1553). German painter and engraver. He owes his fame to his altarpieces and to his portraits of Martin Luther and other German reformers. As court painter to the elector of Saxony, he also painted a number of biblical and mythological scenes.

Crane, [Harold] Hart (1899–1932). American poet. One of the first to attempt to express the spirit of a mechanized 20th century in valid and appropriate poetic terms, Crane is known for his unique, imaginative, and powerful creative talent. Strongly influenced by such poets as Arthur Rimbaud and T. S. Eliot, he nevertheless created his own distinctive style of dramatic rhetoric and extremely complex, compact imagery. In constant revolt from a father who had little appreciation for his poetic gifts, Crane often used elements from his own life for the stuff of his poetry. As a young man he came to New York from Ohio, worked at various jobs, and wrote poetry which was finally published in *Poetry,* the *Little Review,* and other little magazines. In 1926 he published his first collection of verse, *White Buildings,* contain-

ing an inscription from Rimbaud, whose influence is clear.

Crane reacted strongly to the poetry of T. S. Eliot, recognizing the power of the verse at the same time that he rejected the negative view of modern culture found especially in *The Waste Land.* THE BRIDGE was, in part, an answer to Eliot, an attempt to evoke the "myth of America," to write a poem that would fuse American culture, past, present, and future, into one ecstatic whole. (This rejection of cultural pessimism was not new to Crane; it infused several of the poems in *White Buildings,* notably *For the Marriage of Faustus and Helen.*) The poem remains one of the major achievements of 20th-century poetry.

Always torn by personal difficulties, in the throes of despair over what he considered his failing literary powers, Crane committed suicide by jumping overboard from the ship bringing him back from Mexico, where he had gone on a Guggenheim fellowship to write a poem on the Spanish Conquest.

After his death, a volume of poems collected for publication, *Key West: An Island Sheaf,* was found. This group, together with other unpublished poems, was included in *Collected Verse* (1933). See Samuel GREENBERG.

Crane, Ichabod. A character in Washington Irving's tale, THE LEGEND OF SLEEPY HOLLOW. Crane is a gawky schoolmaster, described as resembling "some scarecrow eloped from a field."

Crane, Stephen [Townley] (1871–1900). American novelist, short-story writer, poet, and war correspondent. In his short life, Crane managed to produce work that assured him a permanent place in American literature. Best known for his novel THE RED BADGE OF COURAGE, he has been variously described as an impressionist, a realist, and a symbolist. Ignored by critics in the years immediately after his death, he has since been the subject of much critical controversy, but his importance as a writer is indisputable.

Crane was born in Newark, N.J., the son of a Methodist minister and writer of religious tracts. His mother was also a writer, for a time editor of the *Christian Advocate.* After one semester each at Lafayette College and Syracuse University, he gave up formal schooling and devoted himself to journalism and literature.

His first novel was MAGGIE: A GIRL OF THE STREETS. Although published by Crane at his own expense and ignored by reviewers, this realistic study brought him the respect of Hamlin Garland and William Dean Howells. In 1895, Crane published both *The Red Badge of Courage,* which brought him immense prestige, especially in England, and his first volume of poems, THE BLACK RIDERS. GEORGE'S MOTHER appeared the following year.

Sent to cover a filibustering expedition to Cuba, Crane was on board the *Commodore* when it sank on New Year's Day, 1897. From this experience came THE OPEN BOAT, the short story that has been called one of the finest in the English language. Meanwhile, Crane had fallen in love with Cora Taylor, whom he had met in Florida, and together they went to Greece as war correspondents, an experience responsible for the novel *Active Service* (1899). At the close of the war, they established themselves in England.

During the Spanish-American War, Crane went to

Cuba as a reporter for the New York *World* and the New York *Journal*. Plagued by ill health and financial difficulties, he returned for the last year of his life to England, where among his close friends was Joseph Conrad, who greatly admired his writing. Of the work of his last years, the stories THE BRIDE COMES TO YELLOW SKY and THE BLUE HOTEL may be singled out for special praise, the latter being included in the collection *The Monster and Other Stories* (1899). Other works include *The Little Regiment and Other Episodes of the American Civil War* (1896), *The Third Violet* (1897), WAR IS KIND, WHILOMVILLE STORIES, *Wounds in the Rain* (1900), *Great Battles of the World* (1901), *Last Words* (1902), *The O'Ruddy* (1903), and *Sullivan County Sketches*, compiled by Melvin Schoberlin in 1949.

Cranford (1853). A story by Mrs. GASKELL dealing with the life of the peaceful little English village of Cranford, inhabited chiefly by old ladies who practice elegant economy and a quaint social decorum under the leadership of the Honorable Mrs. Jamieson. The chief characters are the two Miss Jenkyns: Miss Deborah and Miss Mattie.

Cranmer, Thomas (1489–1556). Archbishop of Canterbury. Cranmer first came to the attention of HENRY VIII through his suggestions regarding Henry's divorce from Catherine of Aragon. He was made Archbishop in 1533, and contributed substantially to the progress of the English Reformation by encouraging the circulation of the Bible in English, in the preparation of the First and Second Prayer Books of Edward VI, and in the formulation of the 42 (now 39) Articles of Religion. In 1553 he was persuaded to sign the dying request of Edward VI to give the crown to Lady Jane GREY. After Lady Jane's brief reign and the accession of the Catholic Mary, Cranmer was sent to the Tower. He was burned at the stake for heresy in 1556.

Crapsey, Adelaide (1878–1914). American poet. A teacher at girls' schools and at Smith College, Miss Crapsey wrote her poetry in the last year of her life, developing her own form, the CINQUAIN, derived from Japanese poetry. Her work resembles that of the imagists in its firmness and concentration. Her poetry was posthumously published in *Verse* (1915). See Jean WEBSTER.

Crashaw, Richard (1612–1649). English META-PHYSICAL POET. Although Crashaw's father was a Puritan preacher, the poet became a convert to Catholicism in his early 30's. From the beginning of the English Civil War until his death, he lived in exile on the continent, first in Paris and later attached to the household of Cardinal Palotto and to the shrine of Loreto in Italy.

Crashaw is best known for his religious verse, though he wrote a good deal of secular verse and much Latin poetry. Even before his conversion, his religious poems reflected a straining, passionate mysticism and a love of lush, sensuous imagery and ornate conceits in the manner of the Marinist Italian poetry of the 16th and early 17th centuries. Although he was partly inspired to write religious verse by his reading of George Herbert's *The Temple* (1633), Crashaw's work is distinguished by a luxuriance and high-keyed emotiveness alien to Herbert. His style is highly individual and uneven: he is capable of an ardor and brilliance hardly surpassed in literature, but he can also be overwrought and tasteless.

In 1646 Crashaw published *Steps to the Temple*, a collection which contains his well-known secular poems MUSICS DUEL and WISHES TO HIS SUPPOSED MISTRESS, and his religious poems to Sts. Theresa and Mary Magdalene. *The Flaming Heart*, a hymn to St. Theresa, which deals with her precocious piety and mystic transports, shows Crashaw at his strongest; but *St. Mary Magdalene, or The Weeper*, in which he describes her penitential tears in a series of extended and extravagant images, contains overelaborate conceits and bathetic passages. Other works by Crashaw are *Epigrammatum Sacrorum Liber* (1634) and *Carmen Deo Nostro* (1652).

Crassus, Marcus Licinius. Surnamed **Dives**, i.e., "the Rich" (115?–53 B.C.). Roman financier and politician. Shortly after the civil war of Marius and Sulla, Crassus came into political prominence by defeating the slave army of SPARTACUS in 71. After this military victory, he turned his talents to business and by shrewd speculation was able, within 10 years, to amass a vast fortune. In 59 he joined Caesar and Pompey in the First TRIUMVIRATE and was allotted the command of Asia Minor. He was killed fighting the Parthians at Carrhae.

Cratchit, Bob. In Charles Dickens' A CHRISTMAS CAROL, the clerk of Ebenezer Scrooge. Though Cratchit has to maintain nine dependents on meager wages, his home, unlike his employer's, is filled with happiness and love.

Tiny Tim Cratchit. The little lame son of Bob Cratchit, a winsome and beloved child. In the ordinary course of events he was doomed to an early death, but Scrooge, after his change of character, makes Tiny Tim his special care.

Crawford, F[rancis] Marion (1854–1909). American novelist. He is best known for popular romances with historical backgrounds and glamorous depictions of life in cosmopolitan society. His first novel, MR. ISAACS, achieved enormous popularity. Novels with a contemporary setting include those of the SARACINESCA series, *Dr. Claudius* (1883), and *The White Sister* (1909). His historical novels include *Via Crucis* (1898) and *In the Palace of the King* (1900).

Crawford, Mary and **Henry.** See MANSFIELD PARK.

Crawley, Captain Rawdon. The husband of Becky Sharp in Thackeray's VANITY FAIR. Separated from his wife, he ends his days as governor of Coventry Island.

Sir Pitt Crawley. Rawdon's father. A rich, vulgar baronet, he is "a philosopher with a taste for low life." On the death of his second wife, Sir Pitt proposes to Becky Sharp, but she has already married his son.

Mr. Pitt Crawley. Sir Pitt's eldest son. He inherits fortunes from his father and from the aunt who disowned Crawley for his marriage to Becky.

Mr. and Mrs. Bute Crawley. A "tall, stately, jolly, shovel-hatted rector," brother of Sir Pitt, and his politic little wife.

Crayon, Geoffrey. A pen name of Washington IRVING. He published THE SKETCH BOOK and *The Crayon Miscellany* (1835) under this pseudonym.

Crazy Jane. A beggar, the spokesman and heroine of a series of poems by William Butler YEATS.

Advocating the natural joys of life, she flouts conventional morality, especially in *Crazy Jane and the Bishop*.

Creakle. In Charles Dickens' DAVID COPPERFIELD, a hard, vulgar schoolmaster to whose charge David is entrusted and in whose school he first makes the acquaintance of STEERFORTH. The portrait of Creakle is Dickens' protest against the harsh treatment meted out to children by schoolmasters.

Cream of the Jest, The (1917). A novel by James Branch CABELL. This "comedy of evasions" is the story of an author, Felix Kennaston, who by means of a hieroglyphic disk escapes into a dream world where he pursues a changing yet always similar image of his beloved. She turns out to be his wife.

Creasey, John (1908–   ). English writer of crime fiction. One of the ablest and most prolific practitioners of his craft, Creasey is perhaps best known for his documentary novels about George Gideon of Scotland Yard, which he writes under the pseudonym of J. J. Marric. These include *Gideon's Day* (1955), *Gideon's Week* (1956), *Gideon's Staff* (1959), and *Gideon's Risk* (1961). Creasey also uses other pen names, including Michael Halliday, Gordon Ashe, and Jeremy York.

Creasy, Sir **Edward Shepherd.** See FIFTEEN DECISIVE BATTLES OF THE WORLD.

creation myths. The earliest known myth of the creation is from Sumer of the third millennium B.C. First was the goddess Nammu, the primeval sea; she gave birth to An, the sky-god, and Ki, the earth-god —earth and sky, both solid elements, being joined together. Their offspring Enlil, the god of air, separated them. He lighted his realm by begetting Nanna, the moon-god, who in turn fathered Utu, the sun-god. Enlil next impregnated Ki, who gave birth to Enki, the god of water and of wisdom. Enki ordered the universe, but was unable to create man—a task that the goddess Nintu accomplished by molding him of clay.

In the Babylonian creation myth of the WAR OF THE GODS (*Enuma elish*), Marduk forms man out of the blood and bones of Kingu, a henchman of the defeated Tiamat. An Egyptian belief was that the original sun-god, Atum, standing on a mound in the midst of the slowly receding primeval waters, gave birth parthenogenetically to the other gods and to those parts of the universe which they embodied. According to the familiar biblical story in the first chapter of Genesis, the universe and man were created by Yahweh in seven days, beginning with light and ending with man and woman. In the second chapter appears a variation on the creation of man, which is older and closer to folk tale; woman is created of a rib detached from Adam while he sleeps. Christian theology added that the Son and the Holy Ghost existed with Yahweh from before the creation. The Eastern branch of the Church, however, denied that Jesus had existed from the beginning and the resulting *"filioque* controversy" was the ostensible cause of the split between Eastern and Western churches in 1054.

The first Greek description of creation, in the *Theogony,* attributed to Hesiod, seems to have been a theological elaboration of genuine myth. First to exist was Chaos, from which came Earth, Tartarus, Love, Darkness, and Night. Night and Darkness gave birth to Day and the upper air (Aether). Earth parthenogenetically produced Heaven, Mountains, and Sea. After this prelude, the Hesiodic version proceeds with nearly universal mythic elements that are probably far older. Uniting with Heaven (Uranus), Earth (Ge) gave birth to Oceanus and the Titans. The last of these was Cronus, who overthrew and emasculated his father, only to be supplanted in turn by his son Zeus (see KUMARBI). A highly artificial myth current in the doctrines of Orphism claimed that Chaos, Night, and Darkness existed at the beginning; Love (Eros) sprang from an egg laid by Night and himself gave birth to the other gods. The creation of man seems not to have interested the Greeks very deeply; of various versions, the most prominent made Prometheus their creator—he having molded them of clay.

In Vedic mythology, creation began with Aditi, celestial space. Sky and Earth were sometimes regarded as the first goddesses, sometimes as the original male and female elements, which are known to so many other mythologies; later the sky was personified as Varuna. The first man was Manu; his daughter-mate Ida was born of the food that he offered as a sacrifice to Vishnu in gratitude for being saved from the flood.

Crébillon, Claude Prosper Jolyot de (1707–1777). French author and son of Prosper Jolyot de CRÉBILLON. His novels, tales, and dialogues reflect the moral laxity of his day. *Le Sopha* (1745), for example, tells the experiences of a man transformed by metempsychosis into a sofa, and the scandalous adventures which take place on it. His other works include *L'Ecumoire* (1733) and *La Nuit et le moment* (1755). He was, like his father, one of the dramatic censors of the French government.

Crébillon, Prosper Jolyot de (1674–1762). French dramatist. His tragedies rely more on violence and horror than on grandeur. Nicolas Boileau called him a "drunken Racine." His best play, *Rhadamiste et Zénobie* (1711), whose subject was taken from a novel of Jean Segrais, enjoyed considerable popularity; his other plays did not. He was elected to the French ACADEMY in 1731, and became one of the official dramatic censors of the time. Though he considered himself a literary descendant of Racine, he is merely a precursor of the romantic melodrama.

credo (*Lat.,* "I believe"). A creed or confession of faith. The most important historical Christian creeds are the *Apostles'* and the *Nicene* (both 4th century), and the *Athanasian* (5th century). Later credal statements of importance are found in the *Decrees of the Council of Trent* (1563), the *Augsburg Confession* (1530), and the *Westminster Confession of Faith* (1647).

Creevey, Thomas (1768–1838). English diarist of the Georgian era. His journals and correspondence covering a period of 36 years were published in 1903 as the *Creevey Papers.*

Cremona. A fine violin made in Cremona, in Lombardy. There, in the 17th and early 18th centuries, lived violin makers of worldwide renown, such as Andrea Amati (c. 1520–c. 1610), Nicolò Amati (1596–1684), Antonio Stradivari (1644–1737), and numerous members of the Guarneri family, especially Giuseppe (1687–1744).

Creon (Kreon). (1) In Greek mythology, a king of Thebes. The brother of Jocasta, he served as regent after the death of her husband Laius, and became king after the death of Eteocles in the War of the SEVEN AGAINST THEBES. He condemned Oedipus' daughter ANTIGONE to death and, repenting too late, lost his own son Haemon as a consequence.

(2) A king of Corinth, whose daughter Glauce married Jason and met her horrible fate through the jealousy of MEDEA. He appears in Euripides' tragedy *Medea.*

Crepuscolari, I (*Ital.,* "the twilight poets," a name coined by the critic G. A. Borgese). A group of Italian poets of the early 20th century whose work is notable for its use of musical and mood-conveying language and its general tone of despondency. Their attitude represents a reaction to the content-poetry and rhetorical style of CARDUCCI and D'ANNUNZIO, favoring instead the unadorned language and homely themes typical of PASCOLI. An affinity existed with the French SYMBOLISTS (Valéry, Rimbaud, and Mallarmé). Guido GOZZANO was the most competent exponent of the movement.

Cressida. See CRISEYDE.

Cretheis. See ACASTUS.

Crétin, Roger Auguste. See Roger VERCEL.

Creusa (Kreousa). (1) See ION.

(2) In the *Aeneid,* the daughter of Priam and Hecuba and wife of AENEAS.

Crèvecœur, Michel Guillaume Jean de. Pen name **J. Hector St. John** (1735–1813). French author, agronomist, traveler and settler in America from 1754 to 1780. After having traveled through Canada, the Great Lakes region, and Pennsylvania, he settled on a farm in the colony of New York. Here, between 1770 and 1781, he wrote LETTERS FROM AN AMERICAN FARMER, an extremely popular series of essay-letters. On his return to the U.S. to serve as French consul in 1783, he did much to improve Franco-American relations. More letters, found in 1922 and published as *Sketches of Eighteenth Century America* (1925), give informative and accurate descriptions of colonial American rural life. He also wrote *Voyage dans la haute Pennsylvanie et dans l'état de New York, par un membre adoptif de la nation Onéida* (1801), an account of his early travels and of the American Indians, which he pretended to have translated from an original manuscript. Selections from *Voyage* were translated and published under the title *Crèvecœur's Eighteenth-Century Travels in Pennsylvania and New York* (1961) by Percy G. Adams.

Cricket on the Hearth (1845). A Christmas tale by Charles DICKENS. In the happy home of John Peerybingle and his wife Dot, the cricket on the hearth chirps when all is well and is silent when unhappiness pervades. They take in an elderly boarder whom John soon discovers is a young man in disguise. His suspicions are aroused when he sees this man with his arm around Dot. The cricket takes things in hand, counseling John not to find fault. Soon, the young man, who turns out to be Edward Plummer, bursts in with his young bride May Fielding. He explains all: after his long absence he came back disguised so that he could ascertain whether May truly loved Tackleton, the man she was to marry. Happiness returns to the house and Edward

is reunited with his father Caleb and his blind sister Bertha.

Crillon, Louis des Balbis de Berton de (1541–1615). French general, known as *L'Homme sans peur* (*Fr.,* "the man without fear"). He fought against the Huguenots in the French religious wars and took part in the battle of Lepanto. He later entered the service of Henry IV, who called him "bravest of the brave," and fought at the battle of Ivry.

Crime and Punishment (Prestupleniye i nakazaniye; 1866). A novel by Feodor DOSTOEVSKI. The poor student Raskolnikov, after a long period of brooding over his poverty and the helpless position of his mother and young sister, plans and carries out the murder of an old woman pawnbroker. Surprised in the act, he has to kill the old woman's sister, also. His motives for the murder are then re-examined. Raskolnikov, whose name is derived from the Russian word for *schismatic,* has claimed that he needed the money to help his family, that with the money he could raise himself and become a benefactor to mankind, and finally that by transgressing the law he showed a boldness that put him in the same category as a Napoleon. One by one Raskolnikov's motives are proven false, as his conscience works on him. He instinctively feels disgust for his act, and is unable to bring himself to use the money he has stolen. The torments of conscience he endures prove to him that he lacks the qualities of an amoral superman. He turns for sympathy to SONYA Marmeladova, a young girl forced into prostitution to support her drunken father, his wife, and three small children. Sonya urges him to confess his crime. The police inspector Porfiri Petrovich, an astute psychologist, already strongly suspects Raskolnikov and simply waits for the confession he is sure will come. Raskolnikov finally does break down, although he stubbornly refuses to admit sorrow for having killed the old pawnbroker. He is sentenced to Siberia, where Sonya devotedly follows him, and there he gradually begins to achieve the peace and humility necessary for his sincere repentance.

The novel, the first of Dostoevski's five large works, reveals the mastery of psychological observation and analysis for which the author is hailed. Beside the depiction of Raskolnikov's anguished mind before, during, and after his crime, there are vivid studies of the profligate SVIDRIGAILOV, the saintly Sonya, and her drunken father, MARMELADOV.

Crimean War (1854–1856). A war between Turkey with its allies (England, France, and Sardinia) and Russia. It succeeded for the time being in shattering Russia's ambitions of leadership in southeastern Europe. The chief battles were at Alma, Balaklava, Inkerman, and the famous siege of Sevastopol. The result was the Treaty and Declaration of Paris (1856), in which the integrity of Turkey was guaranteed, the Black Sea neutralized, and Danubian navigation declared free. An event in this war was celebrated by Tennyson in his poem *The Charge of the Light Brigade.* It was also the scene of Florence Nightingale's heroic activities as a nurse.

Crime of Sylvestre Bonnard, The (Le Crime de Sylvestre Bonnard; 1881). A novel by Anatole FRANCE. Sylvestre Bonnard is a kind-hearted, absent-minded old archeologist. The aged scholar's crime is the kidnapping of Jeanne Alexandre, the orphaned daughter of his former love, from a school in which she is abused and unhappy. Threatening complications result, but when it is discovered that Jeanne's guardian is an embezzler, she is made the legal ward of M. Bonnard.

Criseida. The heroine of Giovanni Boccaccio's romance FILOSTRATO and the prototype of Chaucer's heroine in his *Troilus and Criseyde*.

Criseyde. Beloved of Troilus in Geoffrey Chaucer's TROILUS AND CRISEYDE. She is more complicated than her prototype in Boccaccio's *Il Filostrato;* although a practical opportunist, she is genuinely affectionate, not the heartlessly fickle girl she becomes in Shakespeare's *Troilus and Cressida*.

Crishna. See KRISHNA.

Crisis, The (1901). A historical novel by Winston CHURCHILL. The action centers in St. Louis during the controversy over slavery. The hero, Stephen Brice, is a Yankee; the heroine, Virginia Carvel, a Southerner. The novel shows the inevitability of the Civil War, yet stresses the fact that neither side wanted it. The book includes a notable portrait of Lincoln.

Criterion, The (1922-1939). A quarterly literary review. It was edited in London by T. S. ELIOT and reflected his opinions.

Critical Fable, A (1922). Amy LOWELL's imitation of her kinsman James Russell Lowell's FABLE FOR CRITICS. For a time the poem was thought to have been written by Leonard Bacon, an attribution encouraged by Miss Lowell. The poem consists of a dialogue with the earlier Lowell, during the course of which many poets of the 1920's are discussed.

critical philosophy. See Immanuel KANT.

Criticón, El (1651, 1653, 1657). A philosophical novel by Baltasar GRACIÁN. Divided into three seasons (the spring of childhood, the autumn of manhood, and the winter of old age), it describes the encounter on a desert island of the wise and noble Critilo with the savage Andrenio. Critilo brings Andrenio in contact with civilization, acting as his guide to human society. The pessimistic conclusions of both men probably explain at least part of the admiration that Schopenhauer felt for the book.

Critique of Judgment (Kritik der Urteilskraft; 1790). A philosophical work by Immanuel KANT. It contains Kant's aesthetic philosophy. He believed that the representation of a thing in art constitutes a partial understanding of the thing in itself (*Ding an sich*).

Critique of Practical Reason (Kritik der praktischen Vernunft; 1788). A philosophical work by Immanuel KANT. Kant constructed a philosophy of ethics based on practical reason, or the free will of man. Since the moral law itself is unconditional and universal, it is called the categorical imperative; its basic formulation is "Act only on that maxim whereby you can at the same time will that it should become a universal law." Our knowledge of God is obtained through our moral feelings, not through pure reason.

Critique of Pure Reason (Kritik der reinen Vernunft; 1781). A philosophical work by Immanuel KANT, in which he maintained that all sense experience must be inherently rational, and therefore, that rational knowledge about experience is possible. But although reason can understand a thing considered as an object of experience, reason cannot understand the thing-in-itself (*Ding an sich*).

Crito (Kriton; fl. 400 B.C.). An Athenian friend and follower of Socrates. Plato wrote a dialogue called *Crito* in which his friend attempts to persuade Socrates to escape from prison. Socrates refuses to break the law of Athens. His well-known last words were, "Crito, I owe a cock to Aesculapius."

Croce, Benedetto (1866-1952). Italian philosopher, literary critic, and historian. A prolific writer of encyclopedic range, Croce set forth his philosophical system, in which the influence of German idealism is discernible, in the four volumes of his *Filosofia dello Spirito: Estetica Come Scienza dell'Espressione e Linguistica Generale* (1902), *Logica Come Scienza del Concetto Puro* (1905), *Filosofia della Pratica, Economica, ed Etica* (1908), and *Teoria e Storia della Storiografia* (1916). He was perhaps most influential as an aesthetician, emphasizing the intuitive nature of art.

He also wrote numerous works of literary criticism, including *La Poesia di Dante* (1920) and the six-volume *Letteratura della Nuova Italia* (1914-1940). Among his other works are *Materialismo Storico ed Economia Marxista* (1900), *Breviario di Estetica* (1913), and *Storia d'Italia dal 1871 al 1915* (1927). For 27 years he edited *La Critica,* a bimonthly magazine.

A staunch liberal during the fascist regime, he was a member of the post-World War II Committee of Liberation, a delegate to the constitution-making Italian Parliament (1945-1947), and president of the Italian Liberal Party until 1947.

Crockett, David or **Davy** (1786-1836). American frontiersman, public official, and folk hero. After serving as a scout under Andrew Jackson in the Creek War of 1813-1814, Crockett became a justice of the peace in Tennessee; he later boasted that none of his decisions, which were based on "natural-born sense instead of law learning," was ever reversed. He was also a prodigious hunter of bears and claimed to have killed over 100 in eight or nine months. A humorous suggestion that he run for Congress led him to undertake the race, and he was elected for three terms (1827-1831, 1833-1835), becoming known as the "coonskin Congressman." His opposition to the policies of President Jackson endeared him to the Whigs but cost him his seat, and he decided to go to Texas, where he died fighting heroically at the ALAMO. He was speedily made into an American folk hero who could talk the language of animals, ride the lightning, lie with extravagant grandeur, and whip his weight in wildcats.

Several books have been attributed to Crockett, notably *A Narrative of the Life of David Crockett* (1834). He may also have had a hand in some of the *Crockett Almanacs,* which appeared from 1835 to 1856. They contained the usual meteorological and astronomical data, as well as tall tales involving such figures as Crockett, Daniel Boone, and Kit Carson.

Crockett, Samuel Rutherford (1860-1914). Scottish novelist. Abandoning the ministry for a literary career, he participated in the romantic revival. A member of the KAILYARD school of writers, he wrote *The Stickit Minister* (1893) and many fine and exciting historical novels.

crocodile. A symbol of deity among the ancient Egyptians. According to Plutarch, it is the only aquatic animal that has its eyes covered with a thin transparent membrane, by reason of which it sees and is not seen, as God sees all, Himself not being seen. To this, he adds: "The Egyptians worship God symbolically in the crocodile, that being the only animal without a tongue, like the Divine Logos, which standeth not in need of speech" (*De Iside et Osiride*). Achilles Tatius says, "The number of its teeth equals the number of days in a year." Another tradition is that during the seven days held sacred to Apis, the crocodile will harm no one. See TROCHI-LUS.

crocodile tears. Hypocritical tears. The tale is that crocodiles moan and sigh like a person in deep distress to allure travelers to the spot, and even shed tears over their prey while in the act of devouring it. Shakespeare refers to this in the second part of *Henry VI* (1592).

Crocus. In classic legend, a young man enamored of the nymph Smilax. She did not return his love. The gods changed him into the crocus flower, to signify unrequited love.

Croesus (**Kroisos;** fl. 550 B.C.). King of Lydia famous for his wealth. According to a story recounted by Herodotus, Croesus was once visited by SOLON, who, instead of calling Croesus the happiest of mortals, as the vain ruler had expected, said, "Account no man happy before his death." Croesus indignantly dismissed Solon, but the Greek proved to be right. Later, misinterpreting an oracle from Delphi that war with Persia would cause the fall of a great empire, Croesus attacked Cyrus, king of Persia, in 546 B.C. The kingdom to fall turned out to be his own. Sentenced to death by fire, Croesus called the name of Solon, recalling too late his wisdom. Cyrus, upon inquiry, learned the story of the interview, and countermanded the death sentence. Instead he made Croesus one of his trusted advisers.

Unfortunately for the story, it is chronologically impossible, since the dates of Croesus and Solon did not coincide. The remark attributed to Solon was a popular proverb; it appears as the final lines of Sophocles' *Oedipus Tyrannos,* among other places.

Crofts, Freeman Wills (1879–1957). Anglo-Irish writer of detective stories and creator of Inspector French. *The Cask* (1920) is one of his cleverest novels.

Crome Yellow (1921). A satirical novel by Aldous HUXLEY. It is concerned with the odd, learned conversations and comic adventures of a group of people gathered at a country house party: Mrs. Wimbush, who believes in spiritualism; Mr. Wimbush, who reads aloud portions of his absurd history of his house, Crome; Mr. Scogan, who is planning a "Rational State" much like the one Huxley describes in *Brave New World;* and other eccentrics. The central character is Denis Stone, an ineffectual young poet whose banal verse is included in the novel. His one decisive action takes him away from the girl he shyly and secretly loves.

Crommelynck, Fernand (1885–). Belgian dramatist. *Le Cocu magnifique* (1920) is the best known of his poetic, sardonic farces. Among his other plays are *Le Sculpteur de masques* (1908), *Tripes*

d'or (1925), and *Chaud et Froid ou L'Idée de monsieur Dom* (1934).

Crommyonian sow. In Greek mythology, a dangerous wild pig. This animal roamed the land of Crommyon on the Isthmus of Corinth. Theseus killed it.

Cromwell, Oliver (1599–1658). English Puritan leader and Lord Protector of the Realm (1653–1658). As commander of the famous cavalry regiment called Ironsides, he contributed to the Parliamentary victories at Edgehill and Marston Moor and, as joint commander of the NEW MODEL ARMY, defeated the Royalists at Naseby. After the execution of Charles I, he led an army against the rebellious Roman Catholics of Ireland, whom he persecuted so relentlessly that his name is still regarded there with odium. Although he refused the title of king, his powers as lord protector were such that he was able to rule as virtual dictator. An efficient administrator, he permitted religious toleration and pursued a vigorous foreign policy. His son, Richard, trained to be his successor, alienated both the army and Parliament and was dismissed in 1659.

Cromwell, Thomas, Earl of Essex (1485?–1540). English statesman. In 1524 Cromwell was employed by Cardinal Wolsey to survey some of the smaller monasteries with a view to their suppression. He was attached to Wolsey until the latter's fall from royal favor in 1529, after which time Cromwell himself rose steadily in power. According to Cardinal Pole, Cromwell urged HENRY VIII to proclaim himself head of the church and thereby make unnecessary a papal dispensation for his divorce from Catherine of Aragon. When in 1534 the Act of Supremacy established the king as head of the Church, Cromwell's policy was made law, and he became Henry's chief adviser in ecclesiastical matters. He became Lord Chamberlain in 1539, but the following year incurred Henry's disfavor over the king's marriage to Anne of Cleves, which Cromwell had fostered in the hope of gaining the support of German Protestants. He was accused of treason by his enemies, and executed in 1540.

Cronin, A[rchibald] J[oseph] (1896–). Scottish novelist and physician. Many of his bestselling novels are about the medical profession. Among his best-known books are *Hatter's Castle* (1931), *Three Loves* (1932), *The Citadel* (1937), *The Stars Look Down* (1935), *The Keys of the Kingdom* (1941), *The Spanish Gardener* (1950), and *The Judas Tree* (1961).

Cronos (**Kronos**). One of the TITANS of Greek mythology, and father of Zeus. Born of Uranus (sky) and Ge (earth), he married his sister-titan Rhea. Learning from Ge that his son would dethrone him, he swallowed their children, Hestia, Demeter, Hera, Hades, and Poseidon, but Rhea and his sons rescued Zeus. This son did indeed dethrone Cronos, as had been predicted.

Cronos is believed to have been an ancient pre-Hellenic god of fertility. The sickle with which he is depicted in art probably was his attribute as a god of crops, though the Greeks explained that this was the sickle with which he had castrated his father Uranus. The Romans identified Cronos with their equally vague deity SATURN.

cross. An ancient symbol of many uses. Long before the birth of Christ, it was used in Carthage for ornamental purposes. Runic crosses were set up by the Scandinavians as boundary marks, and were erected over the graves of kings and heroes. According to Cicero, the staff with which the Roman augur marked out the heavens was in the shape of a cross. The Egyptians employed it as a sacred symbol, and two buns marked with crosses were discovered at Herculaneum. It was a sacred symbol among the Aztecs long before the landing of Cortez. It was worshiped in Cozumel and Palenque; in Tabasco, it symbolized the god of rain. It was also the emblem of Quetzalcoatl as lord of the four cardinal points and their respective winds.

There are many legends about the cross of the crucifixion. It is said to have been made of four kinds of wood: palm, cedar, olive, and cypress, signifying the four quarters of the globe. Another legend says that Solomon cut down a cedar and buried it on the spot where the pool of Bethesda later stood. Shortly before the crucifixion, the cedar floated to the surface of the pool, and was used as the upright of the cross. During the Middle Ages, enough fragments of the "true cross" were sold as relics to account for an entire forest of crosses. According to legend, the Emperor Constantine, on his march to Rome, saw a luminous cross in the sky, with the motto *"In hoc signo vinces"* (by this sign conquer). The night before the battle of Saxarubra (312) a vision appeared to the emperor in his sleep instructing him to inscribe the cross and the motto on the shields of his soldiers. He obeyed the voice and the vision, and won the battle. A very similar legend has been applied to various other conquerors, however. The cross generally associated with the crucifixion in art is a Latin cross, or *crux immissa.* St. Andrew's cross, the *crux decussata,* is shaped like an X; the *tau* cross, or *crux commissa,* is a very ancient symbol of a T shape, thought to have been originally a phallic emblem.

The *tau* cross with a circle at the top, the *crux ansata,* was common to various Egyptian deities, including Isis and Osiris. The circle signifies the eternal preserver of the world. The *tau* is the monogram of Thoth, the Egyptian Hermes, the god of wisdom.

Crossing, The (1904). A historical novel by Winston CHURCHILL. It deals mainly with the settlement of Kentucky and with the conquest of the Northwest Territory by George Rogers Clark during the American Revolution. The hero, a youth named David Ritchie, takes part in Clark's campaign.

Crossing Brooklyn Ferry (1856). A poem by Walt WHITMAN. The poet is one with all those who cross from shore to shore. Regardless of time and space, he shares the experience of life itself.

Crossing the Bar (1889). A famous poem by Alfred TENNYSON, which uses, as a metaphor for death, a description of putting out to sea on a calm evening. Before his death the author instructed his publishers to insert it at the end of each section of his works.

Crossman, R[ichard] H[oward] S[tafford] (1907–). English writer on politics, economics, and philosophy; journalist and leftist politician. He is best known as editor of THE GOD THAT FAILED, a collection of essays by ex-Communists.

Cross Purposes. See MISUNDERSTANDING, THE.

Crotchet Castle (1831). A novel by Thomas Love PEACOCK. A delightful satire on romantic themes, being a humorously erudite discussion of various curious topics. The central one is an argument to determine the most desirable period of history, with the Rev. Folliott contending for Athenian Greece, Mr. MacQuedy for contemporary Scotland, and Mr. Chainmail for the Middle Ages.

Crothers, Rachel (1878–1958). American playwright. She is interested in the place of women in the modern world. *Susan and God* (1937) is a play about a woman who masks her selfishness under a new-found religious zeal. Among her plays: *Nice People* (1921), *Let Us Be Gay* (1929), and *When Ladies Meet* (1932).

Crouse, Russel (1893–1966). American journalist, playwright, and theatrical producer. Crouse early wrote the libretto for the musical *The Gang's All Here* (1931) and published two books on 19th-century American life: *Mr. Currier and Mr. Ives* (1930) and *It Seems Like Yesterday* (1931). With Howard LINDSAY he dramatized LIFE WITH FATHER and *Life with Mother* (1948), based on the books by Clarence Day; *State of the Union* (1945), a Pulitzer Prize-winning satire on American politics; *Call Me Madam* (1950), a musical comedy; and *Tall Story* (1959). Also with Lindsay he produced Joseph Kesselring's comedy *Arsenic and Old Lace* (1940), the story of two old ladies who poison people for their own good. Crouse wrote the book on which *The Sound of Music* (1960) was based.

Crowdero. In Butler's HUDIBRAS, one of the rabble leaders encountered by Hudibras at a bearbaiting. The original was one Jackson or Jephson, a milliner.

Crowe, Captain. In Tobias Smollett's novel *The Adventures of Sir LAUNCELOT GREAVES,* the attendant of Sir Launcelot in his peregrinations to reform society. Sir Launcelot is a Georgian Don Quixote; Captain Crowe is his Sancho Panza.

Crowley, [Edward] Aleister (1875–1947). English poet and author of books on magic and occult lore. He was a legendary figure, notorious for his celebrations of Black Magic rites. He wrote such books as *Songs of the Spirit* (1898) and *The Diary of a Drug Fiend* (1922). He is the subject of Somerset Maugham's novel *The Magician.*

Crowne, John (c. 1640–c. 1703). English dramatist, best known for his lively comedy *Sir Courtly Nice, or It Cannot Be* (1685). His other plays include the heroic drama *The Destruction of Jerusalem by Titus Vespasian* (1677), *The Country Wit* (1675), *The English Friar* (1689), *The Married Beau* (1694), and a string of meretricious tragedies.

Crowninshield, Frank [Francis Welch] (1872–1947). American editor. Associated with various magazines, including *The Bookman,* he is best known as the editor of *Vanity Fair* (1914–1935). A witty after-dinner speaker, he was one of the founders of the Museum of Modern Art and wrote such books as *Manners for the Metropolis* (1908) and *The Bridge Fiend* (1909).

Crucible, The (1953). A play about the Salem, Mass., witchcraft trials of 1692 by Arthur MILLER. Raising the question of freedom of conscience, it provided a parallel to McCarthyism in America during the early 1950's.

Cruden, Alexander. See ALEXANDER THE CORRECTOR.

Cruikshank, George (1792–1878). English illustrator and caricaturist. He is famous as the illustrator of Dickens (*Sketches by Boz* and *Oliver Twist*) and Scott, and as a social and political satirist.

Crummles, Mr. Vincent. See NICHOLAS NICKLEBY.

Cruncher, Jerry. A minor character in Charles Dickens' A TALE OF TWO CITIES. He works in a bank by day and is a RESURRECTION MAN by night. His wife is continually saying her prayers, which Jerry terms "flopping."

Crusades. Wars undertaken in late medieval times by Christians against the Turks and Saracens for the recovery of the Holy Land and, nominally at least, for the honor of the cross. The word is derived from *Lat.* crux, "cross."

Crusoe. A self-reliant solitary man who adjusts himself to the primitive conditions he finds, from the tale ROBINSON CRUSOE by Daniel Defoe.

Crusts. See HOSTAGE, THE.

Cruz, Sor Juana Inés de la. See JUANA INÉS DE LA CRUZ, SOR.

Cruz Cano y Olmedilla, Ramón de la (1731–1794). Spanish dramatist. His humorous one-act plays, or *sainetes,* form the body of his work. These may be described as classical only insofar as their satiric mirroring of 18th-century Spanish life remains didactic in nature. The most famous of his portrayals of middle-class mores are *La pradera de San Isidoro, El rastro por la mañana, Le Plaza Mayor por Navidad,* and *El fandango del candil.*

Cry of the Children, The (1843). A poem by Elizabeth Barrett BROWNING, expressing intense sympathy for the victims of child labor in the English mines and factories of her day and indicting those who were responsible for their exploitation.

Cry, The Beloved Country (1948). A widely read and influential novel by Alan PATON. It is the moving story of a Zulu country parson who comes to Johannesburg to find that the environment has forced his sister to become a prostitute and his son a murderer. The language is Biblical and poetic. The novel was made into a musical play entitled *Lost in the Stars* (1949), with words by Maxwell Anderson and music by Kurt Weill.

cuaderna vía. A form of medieval Spanish versification. The stanza consists of four 14-syllable lines with a single rhyme, and each line is divided into two equal hemistichs. *Cuaderna vía* was always used for poetry written in the style known as MESTER DE CLERECÍA.

Cuauhtémoc (1495?–1525). Last Aztec emperor of Mexico. The nephew and son-in-law of Montezuma, Cuauhtémoc became emperor after the latter's death and led the Indian resistance to the Spaniards after they had been driven out of Tenochtitlán. He was seized by Cortez after the capital had been taken and was put to torture when he refused to reveal the location of a supposedly fabulous Aztec treasure. Forced to accompany Cortez on an expedition to Honduras, he was accused of inciting the Indians to revolt and was executed.

cubism. An artistic movement begun in 1907 in Paris. It was influenced by the structural simplifications of African sculpture and by CÉZANNE's concepts of geometry in the visual representation of objects. Cubism is characterized by a reduction of objects, figures, and occasionally of landscapes to their basic geometric forms. This effect is achieved by flattening and superimposing planes without the use of perspective or light. Analytical cubism (1910–1912) increased the breakdown of forms and simultaneously represented various aspects of the same object. Monochromatic and austere, this phase led to the inclusion on the canvas of such materials as sand, glass, newspaper, and cloth. With synthetic cubism (1913–1914) the planes grew larger and more varied, form and color reappeared, and reality was represented in its most general terms. Pablo PICASSO and Georges BRAQUE were the founders of cubism in the visual arts, and its most outstanding representatives.

In literature, the poets Guillaume APOLLINAIRE, Max JACOB, Pierre REVERDY, and André SALMON helped to form cubist doctrines and collaborated on the cubist bulletins, although they preferred the term *l'esprit nouveau* (new spirit) to cubism. They experimented with cubistic poetry, arranging apparently imagistic lines in clear-cut blocks. The results were the immediate precursors of surrealistic poetry: Apollinaire's *Alcools* (1913) and *Calligrammes* (1918); Jean Cocteau's *Ode à Picasso* (1917); Jacob's *Le Laboratoire central* (1921); Reverdy's *Les Ardoises du toit* (1918) and *Cravates de chanvre* (1922); and Salmon's *Prikaz* (1919).

Cú Chulainn. Also known as **Cuculain, Cuchullin, Cuchulain,** and **Cu Cullin;** original name **Setanta.** In Gaelic literature, chiefly the ULSTER CYCLE, an Irish warrior of pagan times, a great hero of legendary feats. He is sometimes described as "the Achilles of the Gael." Ostensibly of mortal parentage, Cú Chulainn is represented to be in fact the son of the sun god Lugh. When, as a mere child, he is attacked by a ferocious hound, he kills it; when he sees the grief of its owner, Culain, he takes on the role of watchdog until a hound can be found to replace the one he killed. He is thereafter known as "the hound of Culain," or Cú Chulainn. As a young man he receives training at arms from the woman warrior Scathach on the isle of Scathach, now Skye. When Scathach is attacked by Aoife, another female warrior, Cú Chulainn subdues Aoife and makes love to her; when leaving the island, he instructs her to send their son Conlaoch to Ireland when he comes of age, under a vow to let no man stop him or force him to reveal his name. Conlaoch arrives in Ireland years later and kills so many warriors that he becomes embattled with Cú Chulainn who kills him, learning his identity too late. In one version, they kill each other; in another, Cú Chulainn, in his grief, does battle with the sea and finally sinks, exhausted, into it.

In the most widely known version of the Cú Chulainn story, Cú Chulainn singlehandedly deters the invading army of Queen Maeve until the Red Branch warriors of Ulster awaken from an enchantment. In this version Cú Chulainn duels with his foster brother, Ferdiad. (See CATTLE-RAID OF COOLEY.) Some years later, MEDB gathers an army for the express purpose of killing Cú Chulainn and succeeds by creating, with the help of magic, an imaginary host with whom he fights to exhaustion. Fatally wounded, Cú Chulainn binds himself to a pillar and dies standing and facing the enemy. Emer, his widow to whom he had returned after being seduced by Fand, the wife of the sea god Mananaan, throws herself into his grave and dies. During the Irish Renaissance, Cú Chulainn became a favorite subject for poets, notably William Butler Yeats, who describes his central exploit in *On Baile's Strand*.

cuckold. The husband of an adulterous wife. The name derives from *cuckoo*, the chief characteristic of this bird being to deposit its eggs in other birds' nests. Dr. Johnson explained that "it was usual to alarm a husband at the approach of an adulterer by calling out Cuckoo, which by mistake was applied in time to the person warned." The cuckold was traditionally supposed to wear horns as the attribute of his condition. The usage is ancient; the Romans used to call an adulterer a cuckoo.

Cudworth, Ralph. See CAMBRIDGE PLATONISTS.

Cueva de Garoza, Juan de la (1550?–?1610). Spanish dramatist and poet. Cueva was one of the first playwrights to compose dramas dealing with events in Spanish history, such as *Los siete infantes de Lara* and *Cerco de Zamora*. For, as he maintained in his *Exemplar poético* (1606), he believed that dramatists should use native themes and meters instead of blindly imitating Greek and Latin models. The principal character of his comedy *El infamador* is considered a forerunner of Tirso's Don Juan. Cueva's poems include *Coro febeo de romances historiales* (1587), a collection of old ballads, and *La conquista de la Bética* (1603), an epic about the conquest of Andalusia.

Cuff, Sergeant. See MOONSTONE, THE.

Cullen, Countee (1903–1946). American poet. Known for his poetry on Negro themes, Cullen established his reputation with his first book, *Color* (1925). In addition to a novel, *One Way to Heaven* (1931), he published several other collections of verse including *The Ballad of the Brown Girl* (1928), *Copper Sun* (1927), *The Black Christ and Other Poems* (1929), and *The Medea and Some Poems* (1935). *The Lost Zoo* (1940) and *My Lives and How I Lost Them* (1942) are children's books.

Culloden, or **Drummossie Moor.** A heath in Scotland where the duke of Cumberland defeated Prince Charles Edward Stuart (the Young PRETENDER) on April 27, 1746. The old Scottish ballad of Culloden begins "Drummossie Moor, Drummossie Day!" See Flora MACDONALD.

Culprit Fay, The. See Joseph Rodman DRAKE.

Culture and Anarchy (1869). A collection of essays on political and social conditions by Matthew ARNOLD. In these are found some of his most famous arguments for the role of literary culture in the spiritual life of England. The collection includes the famous essay HEBRAISM AND HELLENISM.

Culverwel, Nathaniel. See CAMBRIDGE PLATONISTS.

Cumberland, Richard (1732–1811). English dramatist. He is the author of a number of sentimental domestic comedies such as *The West Indian* (1771), *The Jew* (1794), *The Fashionable Lover* (1772) and *The Brothers* (1769).

Cumberland Road. The first main road to the American West, begun in 1811 and built for the most part with Federal money. It ran from Cumberland, Md., over the mountains to Wheeling and Zanesville on the Ohio and finally to Vandalia, Illinois. When completed it was about 600 miles long, 60 feet wide, and had a paved strip 20 feet wide in the middle. Over this National Pike ran the Western mails.

Cummings, E[dward] E[stlin] (1894–1962). American poet. One of the most gifted and independent poets of his era, Cummings was born in Cambridge, Mass., and was educated at Harvard. He is known for the eccentricity of his typography and punctuation, which he employed to indicate the rhythmic pattern and interwoven meaning of his poems. Until the 1930's he preferred the lower case e. e. cummings.

His work includes lyrical love poems, humorous character sketches, and bitter satires on the foibles and institutions of his time. Tough characters of the sort well publicized in the U.S. in the 1920's frequently appear in his poems, along with contemporary slang and dialect and the rhythms of jazz. Cummings' first published work was THE ENORMOUS ROOM, a novel based on his experiences in a French prison in World War I. This was followed by the first of his many volumes of poetry, *Tulips and Chimneys* (1923). His other volumes of verse include *XLI Poems* (1925), *&* (1925), *Is 5* (1926), *ViVa* (1931), *No Thanks* (1935), *50 poems* (1940), *1 × 1* (1944), *Poems 1923–1954* (1954), and *Ninety-five poems* (1958). He also published two plays, HIM and *Santa Claus* (1946), a book of drawings and paintings called *CIOPW* (1931); a travel book, EIMI; a satirical ballet, *Tom* (1935); and *i, six nonlectures* (1953).

Cummins, Maria Susanna. See LAMPLIGHTER, THE.

Cunctator (*Lat.*, "the delayer"). Epithet for Quintus Fabius Maximus (d. 203 B.C.). He was the Roman general who harassed Hannibal by avoiding direct engagements, and wore him out by marches, countermarches, and skirmishes from a distance. The English FABIAN SOCIETY was so named in honor of his policy.

Cunégonde. See CANDIDE.

Cunha, Euclides da. See SERTÕES, Os.

Cunningham, Allan (1784–1842). Scottish poet, essayist, and biographer. Many of his poems are in Scottish dialect or are adaptations of traditional lyrics. His *Songs of Scotland* (1825) includes the well-known *A Wet Sheet and a Flowing Sea*. Other verse collections by Cunningham are *Songs* (1813) and *Songs and Poems* (1847). He is also known for his *Lives of the Most Eminent British Painters, Sculptors, and Architects* (1829–1833) and for his *Memoirs of Burns* (1834).

Cunninghame-Graham, Robert Bontine (1852–1936). Scottish-Spanish travel and story writer and historian. At different times he was an adventurer in South America, a Labour member of Parliament, and a friend of W. H. Hudson, Joseph Conrad, and Bernard Shaw. He wrote *Mogreb-el-Acksa, or Journey in Morocco* (1898); *Scottish Stories* (1914) and other collections of short stories; and many biographical and historical works on South America, including *The Conquest of New Granada* (1922).

Cunstance. See MAN OF LAW'S TALE.

Cupid. In Roman mythology, the god of love, son of Venus and Mercury, and counterpart of the Greek Eros. He is usually represented as an exquisite boy with wings, bearing a bow and quiver of arrows, and is often described as blind or blindfolded. The bow is used to shoot the arrows, which are invisible and which cause the one shot to fall irrevocably in love. Originally depicted as a young man, as in the myth of Cupid and Psyche, Cupid later developed into the familiar cherubic but mischievous little boy.

Curate of Meudon. See François Rabelais.

Curel, François de (1854–1928). French dramatist. Curel's career began in 1892, when Antoine, director of the *Théâtre Libre,* accepted some of his plays, among them *Les Fossiles* and *L'Envers d'une sainte.* A landed aristocrat who did not depend on the theater for his living, Curel wrote erratically. His work may be seen, however, in terms of a gradual dramatic evolution. The early plays, *Sauvé des eaux* (1889, later produced as *L'Amour brode* [1893]), and *La Danse devant le miroir* (1913), *L'Invitée* (1893), and *L'Envers d'une sainte* (1892), are dramas of passion that portray a conflict between some desired ideal and a brutal reality. The next group of plays, *La Nouvelle Idole* (1895), *Le Repas du lion* (1897), *La Fille Sauvage* (1902), are rather weighty dramas of ideas, although the emphasis still falls on inner turmoil. His last plays, among them *L'Ame en folie* (1919), *Ivresse du sage* (1922), and *Orage mystique* (1927), are characterized by a biting gaiety and contain more autobiographical elements than the earlier work.

Curetes (Kouretes). In Greek mythology, sons of Rhea. They protected the infant Zeus from Cronos by covering his cries with the clashing of their shields as he grew up in a cave on Mount Dicte in Crete. They were regularly associated with the rites of Zeus' mother Rhea, and were identified by the Greeks with the Corybantes, who performed a similar function in the rites of Cybele. Jane Harrison, in her *Themis,* suggests that both were minor divinities who had originally been the young men (*kouroi*) who took children from their mothers at puberty and initiated them in noisy rites into manhood and full membership in the tribe. (The Curetes were also a tribe who were neighbors of the Calydonians.)

Curiace. In Pierre Corneille's tragedy Horace, the opponent of Horace in the combat between the cities of Rome and Alba. Although Curiace is the fiancé of Horace's sister Camille, Horace must kill him for the honor and safety of his native city, Rome.

Curiatii, the. In legendary Roman history, the three brothers who engaged in combat against the three Horatii.

Curie, Marie Sklodowska (1867–1934). Polish scientist. She is best known for her discovery, with her husband, Pierre Curie, of radium. With A. H. Becquerel, they were awarded the Nobel Prize for physics (1903) for this discovery. She again won the Nobel Prize for chemistry in 1911. *Madame Curie* (1937) is a biography written by her daughter Eve Curie. Another daughter, Irène Curie-Joliot (with her husband Frédéric Joliot) won the Nobel Prize for chemistry (1935).

Curran, John Philpot (1750–1817). Irish orator and magistrate. He is noted for his defense of the leaders of the Irish insurrection of 1798, for his defense of parliamentary reform, and for his support of Catholic emancipation.

Currier and Ives. Nathaniel Currier (1813–1888) and **James Merritt Ives** (1824–1895), American lithographers. In 1835 Currier began to sell lithographs of notable current events and later (1857) he formed a partnership with Ives, his former bookkeeper. The firm published lithographic prints illustrating scenes of farm life, sports, famous disasters on land and sea, and all the mechanical and technical innovations of the age. Drawn in great detail by a number of artists, these prints were soon supplanted by photography, but they are a valuable record of the middle and latter part of the 19th century.

Curry, John Steuart (1897–1946). American painter. He is known for his portrayals of rural life in his native Kansas.

Curse of Kehama, The (1810). An epic poem by Robert Southey. Kehama is the mighty raja of the world. To save his daughter Kailyal from the advances of Kehama's son, Ladurlad kills him. In retaliation Kehama curses Ladurlad, charming his life so that, while he cannot be harmed by disease, weapons, or age, neither can he eat or drink. The curse turns out to be a blessing, for Ladurlad is able, through his immunity, to save his daughter from countless dangers. Eventually, Kehama tries to take over hell and, drinking a potion of immortality, finds he has drunk of immortal death and is forever condemned to hell as a supporter of the lord of hell. Kailyal also drinks the potion and is brought to immortality in the Bower of Bliss, while Ladurlad dies and awakes in heaven. The background of the poem is Hindu folklore and mythology.

Cursor Mundi (c. 1300). Anonymous religious poem in a northern dialect of Middle English, of about 24,000 lines largely in rhyming couplets. Very popular in its day, it describes the "course of the world" in seven ages from the creation to doomsday; its history is based on the Old and New Testaments, interspersed with numerous legends and saints' lives from medieval lore, and told in a style resembling that of the chivalric romances.

cursus honorum (*Lat.,* "course of honors"). In ancient Rome, the steps up the ladder of political success. In order of influence, the magistrates whose offices were generally included in the *cursus honorum* were the tribune, the quaestor, the aedile, the praetor, and the consul. By the time he reached the consulate, the Roman politician had usually made his fortune and was ready to be assigned the comfortable governorship of a conquered province.

Curtain Theatre. Famous Elizabethan playhouse. It was located in Shoreditch and used as an "easer" (an annex to accommodate overflow crowds) to the neighboring Theatre. Shakespeare's company, the Lord Chamberlain's Men, occupied the Curtain between the closing of the Theatre in 1597 and the opening of the Globe in 1599. Some scholars believe it to be the "wooden O" referred to in Shakespeare's *Henry V.*

Curtis, George William. See Potiphar Papers.

Curtis, Jean-Louis (1917–   ). French novelist. *The Forests of the Night* (1947) analyzes young participants in the Resistance; *The Side of the Angels*

(*Les Justes Causes;* 1954) does the same for members of postwar intellectual movements. Acute insights into the ideals and habits of his generation shape other works such as *Chers Corbeaux* (1951), *L'Echelle de soie* (1956), and *La Parade* (1960).

Curtius, Marcus. Legendary Roman hero of 4th century B.C. He is said to have leaped in full armor on horseback into a chasm that had been opened in the Forum at Rome by an earthquake; in so doing he fulfilled a soothsayer's proclamation that the sacrifice of Rome's chief treasure, which Curtius interpreted to mean a brave man, would close the fissure.

Cusa, Nicholas of (Nicholas Krebs or Krypffs). Also known as **Nicolaus Cusanus** (1401–1464). Born at Cusa (Kues) near Trier in Germany, he became a cardinal, an ecclesiastical statesman, and a theologian, but was also an outstanding humanist, philosopher, and mathematician. Known mainly as an early forerunner of the Copernican theory, he was more famous in his day as a brilliant student at Padua, a papal legate at the age of 25, and an influential figure at the Council of Basel (1433). His trip to Constantinople a few years later brought about the Council of Ferrara (1438), which led to the temporary union of the Eastern and Western churches and brought many Greek scholars to Italy (See REVIVAL OF LEARNING and HUMANISM). As deputy to his friend Pope Pius II, he was able to write philosophical works in peace and deal in them with esoteric and subtle ideas. He intuited notions later explored by Copernicus and BRUNO (the infinity of the universe, the cosmological relevance of mathematics, the coincidence of opposites). His most famous work, *De docta ignorantia* (*On Learned Ignorance*), insists on the simplicity of truth against the Aristotelian weaving of abstractions and verbal webs.

Custer, George Armstrong (1839–1876). American general. Custer is best known for his "last stand" (1876) at the Little Big Horn River in Dakota Territory when he and his troops were overwhelmed and annihilated by Sioux warriors under Crazy Horse. Custer's wife, Elizabeth Bacon Custer (1843–1933), described their life together in *Boots and Saddles* (1885). See SITTING BULL.

Custom of the Country, The (1913). A novel by Edith WHARTON. The heroine is Undine Spragg, a ruthless social climber who, through several marriages and divorces, samples the pleasures of money and aristocratic titles before finding her own level and marrying the youth from her home town who has become a millionaire.

Cutty Sark. A witch in Robert BURNS' poem TAM O'SHANTER. The term means "short shirt" (*cutty* being the Scottish word for short, *sark* being Scottish for shirt), and Burns uses it jocularly to describe the witch that catches Tam's eye. *Cutty* is also used to describe a short, plump woman and, by extension, is used playfully to describe a hussy.

Cuvier, Baron **Georges Léopold Chrétien Frédéric Dagobert** (1769–1832). French zoologist and paleontologist. Cuvier was instrumental in founding the sciences of comparative anatomy and paleontology. He published a series of lectures on his findings, *Leçons d'anatomie comparée* (1800–1805), and a work entitled *Recherches sur les ossements fossiles* (1821–1824).

Cuzco, El. A city in Peru, once the capital of the Inca empire. According to one Inca legend, it was founded about 1100 by the first emperor, Manco Capac, who was given a golden staff by the sun god and told to establish a city on the spot where the staff sank into the ground.

Cybele (Kybele or Kybebe). An ancient Asian goddess identified by the Greeks with RHEA. Originally a bisexual earth goddess, she was made a female by the gods. Jealously in love with the beautiful youth Attis, who was preparing to marry a nymph, she drove him to madness, in which he castrated himself and died. She mourned for him thereafter. Cybele was celebrated in orgiastic rites by eunuch priests.

In her rites she was always associated with the corybantes, a group of young men who dance and play musical instruments. Because these rites were similar to those of Rhea and her attendant CURETES, which were also widely practiced in Phrygia, the two became identified. Cybele, one of whose names was the Great Mother, became an important goddess in Rome, where she was known as *Magna Deum Mater.*

Cyclic poets. Epic poets. For some centuries after Homer, the Cyclics continued to write narratives filling out the story of the Trojan War and a cycle of poems about Thebes. In spite of various traditions, little is known about either the poems or their authors. Undoubtedly, however, they supplied later mythographers with a great deal of their material.

cyclopean masonry. The gigantic old Pelasgic ruins of Greece, Asia Minor, and Italy, such as the Gallery of Tiryns, the Gate of Lions at Mycenae, the Treasury of Athens, and the Tombs of Phoroneus and Danaos. They are composed of huge blocks fitted together without mortar, with marvelous nicety, and are fabled to be the work of the CYCLOPS. The term is also applied to similar structures in many parts of the world.

Cyclops (Gr., *kyklops,* circular eye). Any of a group of giants, offspring of Ge and Uranus. Hesiod listed three of them, named Brontes, Steropes, and Arges, who forged Zeus's thunderbolts. Each had only one eye, which was set in the middle of his forehead.

The most famous of the Cyclopes, however, was Polyphemus, whose cannibal welcome to Odysseus and his sailors is related both in the *Odyssey* and in Euripides' satyr play *Cyclops.*

Cygne, Le (The Swan). A poem by Stéphane MALLARMÉ. The swan serves as a symbol representing the cold and sterile solitude of the poet, who lives in a world set apart from that of ordinary men. Images of whiteness, ice, and snow are used to create the poem's atmosphere.

Cymbeline. One of the kings in the 12th-century HISTORY OF THE KINGS OF BRITAIN written by Geoffrey of Monmouth. When Caesar invaded the British island, he forced the Britons to pay tribute and took Cymbeline with him as a hostage. Cymbeline was brought up in Rome as a Roman. When he became king of Britain, he lived peacefully with the Romans. After his death, his sons Guiderius and Arviragus refused to pay tribute, and a new Roman invasion ensued. Some five centuries later, he became the central, titular figure of Shakespeare's play *Cymbeline*.

Cymbeline (c. 1610). A play by William SHAKE-SPEARE. Upon hearing of the secret marriage between his daughter IMOGEN and POSTHUMUS LEONATUS, a gentleman of his court, Cymbeline, king of Britain, banishes Posthumus, who goes to Rome. There he meets the cynical IACHIMO, who makes a wager that, going to Britain, he will cause Imogen to be unfaithful. When Imogen scorns his advances, Iachimo resorts to subterfuge. He gains access to her bedroom in the dead of night, steals her bracelet, and convinces Posthumus that he has won the wager. The outraged husband orders his servant PISANIO to murder Imogen, but the kindly fellow allows her to escape dressed as a boy. In the wilds of Wales she comes upon the banished lord BELARIUS, who is living with Cymbeline's two sons, GUIDERIUS and ARVIRAGUS, whom he had abducted as infants. Eventually Iachimo's villainy is exposed, Imogen and Posthumus are reconciled, and Cymbeline is reunited with his sons.

The historical source of the play is Holinshed's *Chronicles* (1577), but the theme of the wager is taken from Boccaccio's *Decameron*. Although the highly complicated plot often seems to be a parody of the extravagance of Elizabethan drama, the play itself contains much beautiful and moving poetry, "Hark! hark! the lark" and "Fear no more the heat o' the sun" being famous examples.

Cymocles. See FAERIE QUEENE, THE.

Cymodoce. A sea nymph and companion of Venus, in Vergil's *Georgics* and *Aeneid*. See FAERIE QUEENE, THE.

Cynara. The lady to whom the best-known poem of Ernest Dowson is addressed. Each stanza closes, "I have been faithful to thee, Cynara, in my fashion." The poem has a Latin title: *Non sum qualis eram bonae sub regno Cynarae.*

Cynewulf or **Cynwulf** (early 9th century). Old English religious poet. His identity is known because he wove RUNES spelling his name into the ends of four poems in ALLITERATIVE VERSE: *The Fates of the Apostles*, the *Ascension*, *Juliana*, and *Elene*, the story of St. Helena and her son Constantine. In the EXETER BOOK the *Ascension* is preceded by the *Incarnation* and followed by the *Last Judgement*, also attributed to Cynewulf, the three poems being commonly known as *Christ*. The more than 80 "riddles" in the *Exeter Book* were long attributed to Cynewulf, but he probably wrote very few of them. His work probably influenced the unknown authors of *Christ and Satan* (see under CAEDMON), *Andreas*, and the remaining "riddles," which are short poems of descrip-

tion, some simple, some very obscure. See VERCELLI BOOK.

Cynics. A Greek school of philosophy. It was founded at Athens by Antisthenes (c. 455–c. 360 B.C.), a pupil of Socrates. Antisthenes held that happiness is only to be attained by freedom from desires. The principles of the Cynics were illustrated in the life of DIOGENES. The school may have been named after Antisthenes' school in the gymnasium at Cynosarges, or it may have been derived from *kyon* (dog), Diogenes' nickname. The views of the Cynics were later adopted and modified by the Stoics under Zeno.

Cynthia. The moon; a surname of ARTEMIS or Diana. The Roman Diana, who personified the moon, was so called from Mount Cynthus in Delos, where she was born.

Cyprian, St. Full name **Thascius Caecilius Cyprianus** (c. 200–258). The first Christian bishop to suffer martyrdom. The son of a wealthy patrician family, he was converted to Christianity (246), made bishop of Carthage (248), and there beheaded as a martyr (258). His *Letters* are an important source of information about the early Christian church.

Cyrano de Bergerac, Savinien (1619–1655). French author and playwright. In his fantasies *Histoire comique des états et empires de la lune* (*Comical History of the States and Empires of the Moon*, 1656) and *Histoire comique des états et empires du soleil* (*Comical History of the States and Empires of the Sun*, 1661) Cyrano recounts his imaginary visits to the moon and sun; his descriptions of their people and institutions are broadly satirical of the society and politics of his own day. He also composed the comedy *Le Pédant joué* (*The Pedant Tricked*, 1654) and the tragedy *La Mort d'Agrippine* (*The Death of Agrippina*, 1653), both still recognized as poetic and remarkable works. A freethinker and a soldier, famed for his skill in duels as well as for his inordinately long nose, Cyrano served as inspiration for the central character in Edmond ROSTAND's play *Cyrano de Bergerac* (1897).

Cyrenaic School. See ARISTIPPUS.

Cyrus the Great (d. 529 B.C.). The founder of the Persian Empire. Cyrus dethroned his grandfather Astyages, and conquered Lydia and Babylonia. He permitted the exiled Jews to rebuild Jerusalem, as recorded in the Old Testament and treated generously the conquered Lydian king CROESUS. Legends surrounding his birth are related by Herodotus.

Cytherea (**Kytherea**). An epithet of APHRODITE. It resulted from her first setting foot on the island of Cythera after her birth from seafoam.

D

Dabit, Eugène (1898–1936). French novelist of the working class. Like *Hôtel du Nord* (1929), his other novels treat sympathetically the life of the laborer: *Villa Oasis* (1932), *Faubourgs de Paris* (1933), and *Le Mal de Vivre* (1939).

dactyl. In English prosody, a metrical foot consisting of three syllables, the first accented and the second and third unaccented. The word "won-der-ful" is a dactyl. The METER made up of such units is called dactylic meter. The six-foot dactylic line was the epic verse of Latin and Greek poetry and was used by Homer and Vergil. An example in English is: "THIS is the/ FOREST pri/MEVAL, the MURMuring/ PINES and the /HEMlocks . . ." from Longfellow's *Evangeline*.

Dactyls (Daktyloi). Sacred smiths vaguely connected with the worship of RHEA in Crete and sometimes identified with the CURETES and the Corybantes (see CYBELE). The idea that they were possessed of magical powers is related to the ancient notion that all smiths were magicians.

Dada or Dadaism. A literary and artistic movement founded in 1916 and devoted to the negation of all traditional values in philosophy and the arts. Its form was a protest against what its leaders felt to be the insane destruction of civilized life and thought during World War I. Organized in Zurich by Tristan TZARA, with Hans ARP, the German poet Hugo Ball, and medical student Richard Huelsenbeck, the movement produced the *Dada* review. This review proclaimed its intention to replace logical reason in thought with deliberate madness, and to substitute intentionally discordant chaos for established notions of beauty or harmony in the arts. Dada meetings turned into riots; art exhibits were mocking hoaxes. The former cubist painter Francis Picabia, who had been leading a similar movement in New York with Marcel DUCHAMP, joined Tzara's group in 1918. The next year they joined in Paris with André BRETON, who with Louis ARAGON, Paul ELUARD, and Philippe SOUPAULT founded the ironically named review *Littérature*. While Tzara continued his sensational efforts at pure negation, the Germans adapted the revolt to the service of Communism. Breton and his group became interested in the subconscious, breaking with Tzara in 1921 and officially founding SURREALISM in 1924. Dadaism revived in the 1930's in England and America, as a revolt against traditional artistic values.

Daedalus (Daidalos). In Greek mythology, a fabulously cunning artisan. An Athenian, the son of Metion and descendant of Hephaestus, he was exiled from Athens for murdering his apprentice Talus or Perdix. Fleeing to Crete, he earned a questionable distinction by constructing the wooden cow in which Minos' queen PASIPHAË was able to satisfy her passion for a bull. He was then faced with the necessity of providing a place to keep their offspring, the Minotaur; for this purpose he built the famous LABYRINTH.

Having made himself so useful to Minos, he was imprisoned in his own Labyrinth so that he could not leave the king's service. Making wings of wax and feathers for himself and his son Icarus, he flew away to Sicily. Icarus, however, disobeying his father's instructions, flew too close to the sun; the wings melted and he fell to his death in the sea.

daemon (daimon). A minor divinity in ancient Greece. Originally beneficent spirits of the dead who insured fertility and often had animal as well as human forms, certain daemones became more individualized in function and ultimately developed into heroes or gods. Dionysus retained most clearly the character of a fertility daemon.

daemonic (Ger., das Dämonische). In a special sense, a quality of certain characters in Goethe's works, such as the heroes of GÖTZ VON BERLICHINGEN and EGMONT. The daemonic figure is endowed with a powerful, uncannily attractive individual force that sweeps other people along in its violent destiny. In FAUST, it is Mephistopheles rather than Faust himself who exemplifies this quality. In his famous poem *Urworte, Orphisch* (*Primal Orphic Words*, 1817), Goethe defines the basic elements in human destiny as Daemon, Chance, Love, Necessity, and Hope, Daemon referring to each man's unique, inborn, developmental force, the unalterable law of his own individual growth.

Daffodils, The (1807). A famous nature poem by William WORDSWORTH. The poem is characteristic of English romanticism in its appreciation of an object of nature for its own sake.

Dagon. A god of the Philistines. He was supposed (from very uncertain etymological and mythological indications) to have been symbolized as half man and half fish. He is mentioned by Milton in *Paradise Lost* and *Samson Agonistes*.

Dahl, Roald (1916–   ). Welsh-born American short-story writer. Dahl popularized the mythical gremlins in his book *The Gremlins* (1944). In 1946 he published *Over to You*, 10 stories of flying and fliers. Moving to the U.S., he began publishing stories in *The New Yorker* and soon became known for his mastery of the macabre. His books include *Some Time Never* (1948), *Someone Like You* (1953), *Kiss, Kiss* (1960), and *James and the Giant Peach* (1961), a juvenile book.

Dahn, Felix (1834–1912). German author, best known for his "professorial novels," so called because of the antiquarian and scholarly exactness that destroys their artistic value. The most famous is *Ein Kampf um Rom* (*A Struggle for Rome,* 1876).

Daiches, David (1912–   ). Scottish literary critic. He wrote *The Novel and the Modern World* (1939), *Virginia Woolf* (1942), *Robert Burns* (1951), *Willa Cather* (1951), and *A Critical History of English Literature* (1960). *Two Worlds: An Edinburgh Jewish Childhood* (1956) is an autobiography.

daimyō (*Jap.,* "great name"). Feudal lord. It was used chiefly in reference to the clan heads and owners of large fiefs during the Tokugawa period (1600–1868).

Daisy Miller (1878). A novelette by Henry JAMES. It deals with an unsophisticated, "strikingly, admirably pretty" girl from Schenectady who runs athwart the conventions of a group of Europeanized Americans who enforce the rules with unthinking severity.

Daladier, Edouard (1884–   ). Premier of France three times: in 1933, 1934, 1938–1940. With the English prime minister Neville Chamberlain, Daladier was responsible for signing the Munich pact with Hitler in 1938. In 1939 Daladier signed the declaration of war against Germany; he resigned as premier just before the German invasion and the surrender of France. Daladier was arrested, first by the Vichy regime, and was later imprisoned in Germany. After the war he was elected to a seat in the National Assembly.

Dalai Lama. See LAMA.

Dalcroze. See JAQUES-DALCROZE.

Dali, Salvador (1904–   ). Spanish painter and etcher. He is best known for his paintings of irrational subjects done in a meticulously realistic style. Long a disciple of SURREALISM, he has also experimented with pointillism, scientific cubism, futurism, constructivism, and bulletism. The last-named involves shooting a 16th-century blunderbuss filled with graphite at a blank etching plate and printing the resulting pattern. Many critics and a great deal of the public dismiss Dali as merely an artistic prankster; however, his work has been purchased and displayed by the Museum of Modern Art (New York) and the Metropolitan Museum of Art (New York). Perhaps his most famous painting is *Persistence of Memory* (1931), a desolate landscape with limp, melting watches sagging over cliffs and leafless trees.

Dalinda. The servant of the calumnied Ginevra in an episode of the ORLANDO FURIOSO of Ariosto. Her revelations to Rinaldo expose the villain Polinesso, the slanderer of her mistress, and he is then denounced and killed in a duel.

Dalloway, Mrs. See MRS. DALLOWAY.

Daly, Arnold (1875–1927). American actor and producer. In 1903 he produced Shaw's *Candida* and thereafter appeared exclusively in Shaw's dramas. His arrest, trial, and acquittal after the first performance of MRS. WARREN'S PROFESSION (1905) is a famous case. The play caused a sensation because Mrs. Warren's profession is prostitution.

Daly, T[homas] A[ugustine] (1871–1948). American newspaperman and poet. He is best known for his poems in Italian and Irish dialect, especially *Mia Carlotta.* Among his books are *Canzoni* (1906),

Carmina (1909), *Madrigali* (1912), and *McAroni Ballads* (1919).

Damascus. A city in Syria on the edge of the desert. Famous for its silks and steel, it is generally considered the oldest city to have continuing existence in the world. It is frequently referred to in the Old Testament (Gen. 14:15; 15:2). Its role in the history of Paul's conversion is told in the New Testament, Acts 9.

Damayanti. See NALA.

Dame aux Camélias, La (Camille, 1852). A play by Alexandre DUMAS, *fils.* The work, which was first published as a novel (1848), met with great success, both at home and abroad. The heroine Marguerite Gauthier, known in America as Camille, is a beautiful courtesan who has become part of the fashionable world of Paris. Scorning the wealthy Count de Varville who has offered to relieve her debts should she once more become his mistress, she escapes to the country with her penniless lover Armand Duval. Here Camille makes her great sacrifice. Giving Armand whom she truly loves the impression that she has tired of their life together, but actually at the request of his family, she returns to Paris and her life of frivolity. The tale concludes with the ultimate tragic reunion of Armand and the dying Camille. This sentimental story, dealing with a real moral and social problem, is also the basis of Verdi's opera *La Traviata.*

Damien de Veuster, Joseph. Known as **Father Damien** (1840–1889). A Belgian Roman Catholic missionary. He is noted for his work with the lepers in a government hospital on Molokai Island in the Hawaiian group, where he contracted leprosy and died. Robert Louis Stevenson wrote a famous essay, *Father Damien: An Open Letter to the Rev. Dr. Hyde* (1890).

Damkina. In Babylonian mythology, the wife of MARDUK.

Damnation of Theron Ware, The (1896). A novel by Harold FREDERIC. The main character, an earnest young clergyman, suffers emotional conflict when he realizes the deficiencies of the church. The book, suggesting the disintegration of religious orthodoxy, was sensational at the time of its publication.

Damocles' sword. A symbol of anxiety. Damocles, a sycophant of Dionysius the Elder, of Syracuse, was invited by the tyrant to try the felicity he so much envied. Accepting, he was set down to a sumptuous banquet, but overhead was a sword suspended by a hair. Damocles was afraid to stir, and the banquet was a tantalizing torment to him.

Damoetas. A herdsman. Theocritus and Vergil use the name in their pastorals.

Damon and Pythias. Two inseparable friends of Greek legend. They were Syracusans of the first half of the fourth century B.C. Pythias, condemned to death by Dionysius the tyrant, obtained leave to go home to arrange his affairs on condition that Damon agree to take his place and be executed should Pythias not return. Pythias was delayed, Damon was led to execution, but his friend arrived just in time to save him. Dionysius was so struck with this honorable friendship that he pardoned both of them.

Dämonische, das. See DAEMONIC.

Dampier, William (1652–1715). English navigator and buccaneer. Perhaps the first Englishman to see Australia, he discovered and named New Britain Island in the Pacific, and Dampier Archipelago, off the coast of Australia, is named after him. During a voyage around the world, he marooned Alexander Selkirk, the prototype of Robinson Crusoe, on the Juan Fernandez Islands near Chile, and subsequently was the pilot of the privateering company that rescued Selkirk in 1709. He wrote several accounts of his experiences, the best known of which is *A New Voyage Round the World* (1697).

Damrosch, Walter [Johannes] (1862–1950). German-born conductor and composer. He championed the cause of Wagner in the U.S., and was the originator of educational radio concerts. *My Musical Life* (1923) is his autobiography. His father, Leopold Damrosch (1832–1885) and his brother, Frank [Heino] Damrosch (1859–1937), were also conductors.

Dana, Charles Anderson (1819–1897). American journalist. Reformer and editor, Dana became assistant secretary of war under Stanton. After the Civil War he bought the New York *Sun*, which soon became one of the leading newspapers in the U.S. Although he competed with Godkin's *Post* in sensationalism, Dana surrounded himself with the best newspaper writers of the day. H. L. Mencken said that he "produced the first newspaper on earth that was decently written." Dana discussed his craft in *The Art of Newspaper Making* (1895).

Dana, Richard Henry, Jr. (1815–1882). American lawyer and writer. During his student days, Dana had serious difficulty with his eyes; he shipped out as a common sailor to improve his health. Dana might have traveled as a passenger, but chose the more strenuous course of working on the *Pilgrim* on a voyage around Cape Horn in 1834. He returned home in 1836, his health much improved. From the journal he had kept, he wrote the American sea classic, Two Years Before the Mast. The same year, he finished law school and was admitted to the bar; his experiences at sea led him to become a sailor's lawyer. He wrote a manual for sailors, *The Seaman's Friend* (1841), which became an authority on naval law. His sympathy for the downtrodden did not allow him to amass wealth as a lawyer, nor did it leave him much time for writing. He did collect the lectures of a famous teacher, Edward Tyrell Channing (1856).

Dana, Richard Henry, Sr. (1787–1879). American poet, editor, and lecturer. A founder of the *North American Review,* he also published his own journal, called *The Idle Man* (1821–1822). In 1833, his work was collected in the two-volume *Poems and Prose Writings* (enlarged, 1850).

Danaë. The daughter of King Acrisius of Argos. Because the Delphic oracle predicted that his death would come at the hands of his daughter's son, Acrisius built a tower of brass and shut Danaë in it. But Zeus visited her as a shower of gold and made her the mother of Perseus. Acrisius then set mother and son adrift in a chest, but they were saved by Zeus.

Danaides. The 50 daughters of Danaos. They were punished in Hades for having murdered their husbands on their wedding night by having to draw water everlastingly in sieves from a deep well. The reason for their gory deed was told in a trilogy of plays by Aeschylus, of which only The Suppliant Women remains.

dance of death. An allegorical representation of the triumph of Death over people of every age and class, reminding men of their mortality. Originating in the Middle Ages as a morality play, it became even more popular as a subject for pictures, such as the woodcuts by Hans Holbein. Closely related is the *danse macabre,* in which the dead themselves lead the dance, rather than an abstract personification of Death.

Goethe used "dance of death" for the title of his ballad *Todtentanz;* W. H. Auden's *The Dance of Death* (1933) is a dramatic poem satirizing the decline of the English middle class.

Dance of Death, The (1901). A double play by August Strindberg. One of Strindberg's most powerful plays, *The Dance of Death* is characterized by intense psychological realism in its presentation of a love-hate relationship between husband and wife. Alice has been virtually imprisoned by Edgar, her tyrannical husband, for 25 years; now he is gravely ill, and the conflict focuses on his attempts to maintain his domination of his wife and her attempts at retaliatory torture.

Dance to the Music of Time, A. A sequence of novels by Anthony Powell. It includes *A Question of Upbringing* (1951), *A Buyer's Market* (1952), *The Acceptance World* (1955), *At Lady Molly's* (1957), *Casanova's Chinese Restaurant* (1960), and *The Kindly Ones* (1962). The novels describe the narrator's schooldays, youth, and maturity, and the lives of his various friends. Though primarily satiric in tone, they are indebted to Marcel Proust for the underlying sadness they express about life and time.

Dancourt, Florent Carton. Known as Sieur d'Ancourt (1661–1725). French comic playwright. Jesuit-educated and intended for the law, Dancourt married an actress and devoted himself to acting and playwriting instead. His prose comedies are informal in style and often reveal their hasty composition, but rollicking satire and topical subject matter redeem such works as Le Chevalier à la mode, *La Loterie* (*The Lottery,* 1697), *Le Notaire obligeant* (*The Obliging Notary,* 1685), *Les Bourgeoises à la mode* (1692), *Le Mari retrouvé* (*The Rediscovered Husband,* 1698), *Les Bourgeoises de Qualité* (1700), and *Les Agioteurs* (*The Stock-Speculators,* 1710), in which Dancourt lampooned decadent aristocracy, social climbers, financial fraud, speculation, judicial inefficiency, and other vices and foibles of his day.

Dandaka. In Hindu legend, a king of the solar dynasty (Raghu), who raped the daughter of his *guru.* He was punished by having his kingdom turned into the forest known as Dandakaranya, often mentioned in classical Indian writing (Sans. *aranya,* forest).

Dandin. The mad magistrate and central figure of Jean Racine's comedy Les Plaideurs. Locked up in the house by his son and prevented from judging in court, he hears farcical cases involving neighbors, household servants, and pets.

Dandin. See Perrin Dendin.

Dane, Clemence. Pen name, taken from the church of St. Clements Dane in London, of **Wini-**

fred **Ashton** (1888–1965). English novelist, dramatist, and poet. Her best-known play *A Bill of Divorcement* (1921) made the reputation of Katharine Cornell; she adapted it for the stage from her novel *Legend* (1919). Her other well-known novels are *Regiment of Women* (1917) and *Broome Stages* (1931), about a theatrical family whose history parallels that of the Plantagenet family. Her other plays include *Will Shakespeare* (1921); *Naboth's Vineyard* (1925), a play about Jezebel; *Come of Age* (1934), a poetic play about Thomas CHATTERTON; and *Till Time Shall End* (1961).

Danel or **Daniel.** Father of the young hero in the Canaanite THE POEM OF AQHAT. Danel is a powerful but pious chieftain, who is granted a son by El only to lose him at the hands of Anat.

Dangeau, Marquis **de. Philippe de Courcillon** (1638–1720). French courtier and favorite of Louis XIV. His ill-written but scrupulously detailed *Mémoires,* a record of court affairs from 1684 to 1720, are an invaluable historical source and aided SAINT-SIMON in the composition of his own *Mémoires.*

Dangerfield, Thomas. See MEAL-TUB PLOT.

Dangerous Corner (1932). A play by J. B. PRIESTLEY. A chance remark at a party is the "dangerous corner" which leads to embarrassing revelations about those present. At the end of the play the opening conversation is renegotiated, this time successfully.

Daniel. A biblical hero whose deeds and prophecies are recorded in the Old Testament book of his name. For continuing to pray to his own God while a captive in Babylon, he was cast into a den of lions, but divinely delivered. Especially gifted with "understanding in all visions and dreams" (Dan. 2:17), he successfully exercised this gift by interpreting Nebuchadnezzar's disquieting dreams, as well as the mysterious handwriting on the wall which disturbed the revelry of Belshazzar (Dan. 5:5).

Nothing is known of Daniel except what appears in his book. The first half of the book tells the story of the Hebrew prophet living in Babylon during the exile; the second half is his prophetic vision.

It is now thought that *Daniel* was written c. 164 B.C. instead of in the sixth century B.C., that Daniel's "predictions" were history by the time of writing.

Daniel, Arnau[l]t (12th century). Provençal TROUBADOUR, for a while attached to the court of Richard the Lion-hearted. He invented the SESTINA, and was greatly praised by Dante and Petrarch for the technical virtuosity of his versification.

Daniel, Samuel (c. 1562–1619). English poet and dramatist. Daniel is known for the purity of his diction, the smoothness and grace of his verse: he was called "well-languaged Daniel" by contemporaries. His works include the famous sonnet sequence, *Delia* (1592, with numerous later "augmented" editions); *The Complaint of Rosamund* (1592), a first-person narrative of the sort found in the MIRROR FOR MAGISTRATES; *The Civil Wars* (1595–1609), a verse history of the Wars of the Roses; *A Defense of Rime* (1603), an essay answering Thomas CAMPION's attack on English rhymed and accentual verse; and *The Vision of the Twelve Goddesses* (1604), the first masque to be written for the new court of James I. He wrote two tragedies in the style of Seneca, *Cleopatra* (c. 1593) and *Philotas* (1604).

Daniel Deronda (1874–1876). The last novel of George ELIOT. The heroine, Gwendolyn Harleth, marries Henleigh Grandcourt in order to avoid impending destitution of herself and her mother; this she does in spite of a previous promise not to, made to the mother of his illegitimate children. Grandcourt turns out to be a tyrannical, selfish man, bent on breaking Gwendolyn's high-spiritedness. When Grandcourt drowns in a moment of delay before Gwendolyn throws him a rope, she blames herself. In her distress she turns to Daniel Deronda, a man of fine character whom she has long admired. His sympathetic advice and her suffering, caused by the realization that he will never marry her, serve to develop her finer qualities. Deronda, a man of the highest ideals, has been brought up by his rich guardian as a Christian, but learns that he is a Jew. He marries Mirah Cohen whom he had saved from suicide. In Mordecai, who turns out to be Mirah's lost brother, he finds a friend who inspires him with the cause of Jewish nationalism. After Mordecai's death he and Mirah go to Palestine to live.

Daniello, Bernardino (d. 1565). Italian critic from Lucca. He wrote the first Italian Renaissance treatise on the art of poetry, *La poetica* (1536).

Daniels, Jonathan [Worth] (1902–   ). American journalist and writer. The son of Josephus Daniels, he succeeded his father as editor of the Raleigh, N. C., *News and Observer*. From 1943 to 1945 he was an administrative assistant to President Roosevelt. *Frontier on the Potomac* (1946) describes the Washington scene during those years. He also wrote *A Southerner Discovers the South* (1938), *Tar Heels: A Portrait of North Carolina* (1941), and *The End of Innocence* (1954).

Daniels, Josephus (1862–1948). American journalist and statesman. Born in Washington, N. C., Daniels was editor of the Raleigh *Times and Observer* from 1884 until his death. He served as secretary of the navy (1913–1921) and as ambassador to Mexico (1933–1941). His autobiographical volumes are of great historical interest: *Editor: In Politics* (1940), *The Wilson Era* (2 vols., 1944, 1945), and *Shirt Sleeve Diplomat* (1947).

Daniel the Stylite. See STYLITES.

Daninos, Pierre (1913–   ). French novelist. His experience as liaison officer with the British army inspired the character of Marmaduke Thompson. Thompson first appeared in a newspaper in 1943, then in the ironically humorous novels *The Notebooks of Major Thompson* (1954) and *The Secret of Major Thompson* (1956). *Un Certain Monsieur Blot* (1960) shows Daninos as the amused philosophical observer of his time. Other novels include *Les Carnets du Bon Dieu* (1947), *L'Eternel Second* (1949), and *Sonia, les autres, et moi* (1952).

Dannay, Frederic. See Ellery QUEEN.

D'Annunzio, Gabriele (1863–1938). Italian poet, novelist, dramatist, and soldier. He was an exceptionally prolific writer whose principal artistic aim seems to have been the detailed and verbally precise analysis of passion. His position as a decadent results from the absence of any real concern for morality, conscience, and thought in his work, so that the well-exercised pleasures of the senses alone give meaning to life. His heroes are unfettered by the bourgeois ethic; their refined ability to enjoy sensual pleasure and to experience "perfect passion" make them a law to themselves, suggestive of Nietzsche's superman.

The D'Annunzian hero first appeared in the novel *Il Piacere* (*The Child of Pleasure,* 1889) in the person of the amoral sybarite Andrea Sperelli. His other novels include *Giovanni Episcopo* (*Episcopo & Company,* 1892), *L'Innocente* (*The Intruder,* 1892), *Il Trionfo della Morte* (*The Triumph of Death,* 1894), and THE FLAME OF LIFE, based on his celebrated liaison with Eleonora DUSE. Among his best-known dramas are *La Città Morta* (*The Dead City,* 1898), LA GIOCONDA, *Francesca da Rimini* (see PAOLO AND FRANCESCA), and *La Figlia di Jorio* (*The Daughter of Jorio,* 1904). His finest lyric poems are probably included in *Le Laudi* (1903–1912), particularly in the third book, *Alcione.* He also wrote short stories describing peasant life in his native Abruzzi: *Terra Vergine* (1882), *Libro delle Vergini* (1884), and *San Pantaleone* (1886).

An ardent nationalist, he led an expedition into the city of Fiume in 1919 and held it for 15 months in defiance of Italy's obligations under the Treaty of Versailles. He later supported the chauvinistic Fascist Party.

danse macabre. See DANCE OF DEATH.

Dante. Full name, **Dante** (or **Durante**) **Alighieri** (1265–1321). Italian poet. The first important author to write in Italian and one of the greatest poets in all literature, he was born in Florence, where he became thoroughly educated in both classical and Christian literature. As a young man, Dante joined actively in both the politics and the actual fighting in the wars between the GUELPHS

Dante entering the woods (*Inferno* Canto I). Frontispiece from a 1506 edition of *The Divine Comedy.*

AND GHIBELLINES. He belonged to the BIANCHI, one of the rival factions within the Guelph party, and when the Neri finally achieved power late in 1301, Dante and many others were sentenced (1302) to perpetual banishment, condemned to death by burning should they be caught again in Florence. The Bianchi soon made an alliance with the Ghibelline party and attempted several unsuccessful attacks on Florence. Their hopes ended with the death (1313) of the emperor Henry VII, who they had hoped would reunite Germany and Italy. Thereafter, Dante spent most of his time writing his *Commedia* (see THE DIVINE COMEDY) under the patronage of Ghibelline leaders, one in Verona, then one in Ravenna. The exact period of the composition of the *Commedia* is unknown. Dante may have begun it as early as 1300, more probably 1307, but the major part of the writing was almost certainly done after 1315, and the last section completed shortly before his death.

Dante had first met BEATRICE in 1274 when he was nine; their second meeting was nine years later. After her death in 1290 he wrote LA VITA NUOVA, which reveals the significance of his idealized love for her as the inspiration for most of his works. He finally married Gemma Donati (1292?), by whom he had two sons and one or two daughters; she did not, however, accompany him into exile in 1302.

Dante's early works include a number of amatory lyrics in the form of the CANZONE and the sonnet, many of which appear in *La Vita Nuova* and in the unfinished *Il Convivio* or *Convito* (*The Banquet,* 1304–1307), which consists of three long commentaries, encyclopedic in scope, each on one of his own *canzoni* (see STILNOVISTI).

De vulgari eloquentia (1304–1306) is a Latin treatise "on the vernacular tongue." In opposition to the general assumption of his day that Latin must be used for all important writing, Dante urges that the courtly Italian used for amatory lyrics be enriched with the best from every spoken dialect and established as a serious literary language, thus unifying the separated Italian territories by the creation of a national culture. He also analyzes several Italian dialects, anticipating the much later science of linguistics, and considers various problems of literary style and specific poetic forms, especially the *canzone.* In fact, Dante used his native Tuscan for the *Commedia* and *La Vita Nuova,* and thereby established that dialect as the ancestor of modern Italian.

In the Latin treatise *De Monarchia* (*On Monarchy,* usually translated as *On World Government,* c. 1313) Dante presents the political perspective that also becomes a major theme in the *Commedia.* He believes that a unified temporal authority, the Holy Roman Empire, is necessary, but deplores the rivalry for supreme political power currently raging between the emperors and the papacy. He prophesies that peace will only be achieved when the universal monarchy of the empire is established and recognized as being dependent only on God, although reverent toward the spiritual authority of the Church. Then Church and State will be allies with separate responsibilities in guiding mankind to peaceful happiness on earth and bliss in heaven.

Other works include two *Eclogues* (c. 1319) in Latin verse; the *Quaestio de aqua et terra* (1320), a scholastic treatise on physics; and 13 Latin *Epistles*, including both personal and political letters.

Dantès, Edmond. See COUNT OF MONTE CRISTO.

Danton, Georges Jacques (1759–1794). French lawyer, orator, and leader of the FRENCH REVOLUTION. He became a leader of the CORDELIERS early in the Revolution, a member of the Legislative ASSEMBLY in 1792, and was a major figure in the storming of the Tuilleries. In the new republic he was the minister of justice. He instituted the Revolutionary Tribunal (Mar. 10, 1793). Now a partisan of peace, he came into increasing conflict with ROBESPIERRE, who later charged him and his followers with a conspiracy to overthrow the government. His trial was a mockery and he was guillotined. His death is the subject of a dramatic poem, *Dantons Tod* (Ger., *Danton's Death*, 1835) by Georg Büchner. In a speech (Sept. 2, 1792) inspired by the dangers of the European alliance against revolutionary France, Danton uttered the famous words: *"Il nous faut de l'audace, encore de l'audace, et toujours de l'audace, et la France est sauvée."* (Fr., "We must dare and dare, and dare again—and France is saved.").

Dantons Tod (Danton's Death, 1835). A drama by Georg BÜCHNER, depicting with convincing psychological perception and frequent ironic humor the steps leading up to the execution of George Jacques DANTON. The play is starkly realistic; Danton first appears in it as a tired, apathetic, somewhat licentious, and rather unrevolutionary character. But this, by contrast, only increases the effectiveness of his idealistic commitment when he finally defies Robespierre.

Daphne. In Greek mythology, the daughter of a river-god, loved by Apollo. She fled from the amorous god, and escaped by being changed into a laurel, thenceforth the favorite tree of Apollo.

Daphnis. In Greek mythology, the Sicilian shepherd who invented pastoral poetry. Though the son of Hermes and a nymph, and a half-brother of Pan, he was unfortunate in love, being blinded by a nymph for a not very clear reason. He made up sad but lovely songs on the subject, and was eventually taken up to heaven by Hermes. On the other hand, Theocritos, the human inventor of the pastoral, claims in his first idyl that Daphnis died of unrequited love, a punishment from Aphrodite for having refused the love of women.

Daphnis and Chloë. A Greek pastoral poem, generally ascribed to the sophist Longus (fourth or fifth century A.D.). It tells the story of the tender love of Daphnis and Chloë, the children of a goatherd and a shepherd. It owes its fame in modern times to the French version by Amyot (1559). Major works in its later tradition are Tasso's *Aminta*, Montemayor's *Diana*, and Saint-Pierre's *Paul et Virginie*. Maurice Ravel made two highly popular orchestral suites from his ballet music for *Daphnis and Chloe* (1912).

Da Ponte, Lorenzo (1749–1838). Italian librettist and poet. Appointed poet to the Italian Theater in Vienna, he was commissioned by Mozart to write the librettos for *Le Nozze di Figaro* (1786; see FIGARO), DON GIOVANNI, and *Così Fan Tutte* (1790). In 1805 he emigrated to the U.S., where he was appointed professor of Italian literature at Columbia

University. His colorful memoirs, *Memorie*, first appeared in 1823.

Da Porto, Luigi (1486–1529). Italian soldier and courtier. Da Porto took a story by Masuccio and turned it into *Giulietta e Romeo* (see ROMEO AND JULIET), first published in 1530. Although it reached Shakespeare through such intermediary sources as Bandello and English translators, it was Da Porto who first gave it its definitive plot and characters.

Dapper. A character in Ben Jonson's comedy THE ALCHEMIST (1610). A lawyer's clerk, he goes to Subtle, the "alchemist," to be supplied with a familiar to make him win in horse-racing, cards, and all games of chance.

Darby and Joan. A designation for a loving, old-fashioned, virtuous married couple. The names appear in a ballad called *The Happy Old Couple*, probably written by Henry Woodfall, and the original characters are said to have been John Darby of Bartholomew Close, who died in 1730, and his wife. Woodfall served his apprenticeship as a printer to John Darby. Some authorities attribute the ballad to Matthew Prior. It was originally distributed as a broadside ballad in 1748.

Darcy. See PRIDE AND PREJUDICE.

Dardanelles. The ancient HELLESPONT, a strait between Europe and Asiatic Turkey. During World War I the Allies attacked the Turks here, and suffered defeat. In 1941 it was the gateway to Russia from the Mediterranean but Turkey, as neutral, refused passage of it. Its fortifications were so strong that no attempt on it was made by sea.

Dardinello. In the ORLANDO FURIOSO of Ariosto, the King of Zumara in Africa, son of Almonte, and one of the leading pagan warriors besieging the forces of Charlemagne at Paris. He is killed by Rinaldo.

Dare, Virginia (1587–?). The first child of English parents born in America. She and her parents were among the settlers who disappeared from the "lost colony" at Roanoke Island.

Dares Phrygius. In Homer's *Iliad*, the priest of Hephaestus in Troy. He allegedly wrote a poem on the siege of Troy. A Latin poem of the fifth century after Christ, *De Excidio Troiae Historia*, allegedly a translation of Dares Phrygius' work. The translation is attributed to Cornelius Nepos because it is prefaced by a forged letter from him to Sallust claiming to have found the old manuscript written in Phrygian characters. Although now known to be a literary forgery, the decidedly inferior poem was one of the versions by which the story of Troy was known to the Middle Ages. See DICTYS CRETENSIS.

Darío, Rubén. Pen name of **Félix Rubén García** (1867–1916). Nicaraguan poet and essayist, famed as the founder and high priest of MODERNISM. Raised by relatives, Darío wrote verse as a child and was known in Central America as "the boy poet." In 1886, he went to Chile, where he published his first major work, *Azul* (1888), a collection of verse and prose sketches that bore the imprint of French PARNASSIANISM and revealed the fondness for lush, exotic imagery that was to characterize his work. In 1890, he returned to Central America, where he embarked on the first of his two unhappy marriages, and, after a short visit to Spain in 1892, moved to Buenos Aires. The appearance of *Prosas profanas* (1896), in which the influence of French SYMBOLISM is fused with that of the Parnassians, marked the highpoint of the modernist movement. In 1898, Darío went to Spain as a correspondent for *La Nación,* a Buenos Aires newspaper with which he was long associated. He was acclaimed by the intellectuals of Spain's "generation of '98," who, like Darío, were profoundly affected by the outcome of the Spanish-American War. *Cantos de vida y esperanza,* generally regarded as his best work, appeared in 1905. Not only does it show the technical excellence and lyric beauty of his earlier poetry, but there is greater freedom and a new feeling for native themes, which he had previously rejected. Darío's concern for "our America" is also evident in "A Roosevelt," a poetic diatribe against the U.S. motivated by the seizure of Panama in 1903, and in *Canto a la Argentina* (1910). Darío's later work also reveals a deepening disillusionment and despair. Although he was named Nicaraguan minister to Spain in 1908, Darío's last years were marred by financial difficulties and poor health due in part to his heavy drinking. In 1915, after an unsuccessful lecture tour of the U.S., he was stricken by pneumonia in New York and died soon after his return to Nicaragua. Darío's influence on Spanish poetry can be measured by the statement of Pedro Henríquez Ureña that "of any poem written in Spanish it can be told with certainty whether it was written before or after him."

Darius I. Known as **Darius the Great** (c. 550–486 B.C.). King of Persia. A member of a younger branch of the royal family, Darius assumed the throne in 521 after quelling a rebellion led by the magician Gautama, who claimed to be Bardiya, brother of the dead king Cambyses. Darius was an excellent administrator, extended the boundaries of the Persian Empire, and built an imposing capital at Persepolis. His exploits are recorded on the famous monument at Behistun in Iran.

According to legend, Darius was one of seven Persian princes who agreed that he should be king whose horse neighed first; his was the first to do so when he tethered a mare near it.

Darius III. Surnamed **Codomannus** (c. 380–330 B.C.). Last king of Persia. Defeated by Alexander the Great at the Granicus river, at Issus, and at Arbela, he was killed by one of his own satraps.

Legend relates that when Alexander succeeded to the Macedonian throne, Darius sent to him for the traditional tribute of golden eggs, but Alexander answered, "The bird which laid them is flown to the other world, where Darius must seek them." The Persian king then sent him a bat and ball, in ridicule of his youth; but Alexander told the messengers that with the bat he would beat the ball of power from their master's hand. Lastly, Darius sent him a bitter melon as emblem of the grief in store for him; but the Macedonian declared that he would make the shah eat his own fruit.

Dark Ages. The earlier centuries of the MIDDLE AGES. Roughly, it encompasses the era between the death of Constantine and the close of the Carolingian dynasty. It was so termed because of the intellectual darkness supposedly characteristic of the period, but nowadays few writers dare to use the term without the qualification "so-called."

Dark Laughter (1925). A novel by Sherwood ANDERSON. It deals with the escape of John Stockton, a Chicago newspaperman, from a life he regards as sterile and oppressive, ruled by the machine. In conscious imitation of Mark Twain's Huckleberry Finn, Stockton travels by boat down the Mississippi River. Eventually, he takes a job as a laborer, under the name of Bruce Dudley, in a factory in his former hometown in Indiana, and there he and Aline Grey, the wife of his employer and a woman similarly dissatisfied with a mechanical life, fall in love and elope. The "dark laughter" of the title is that of the American Negro, who, uncorrupted by white civilization and white morality, is alone still capable of a simple, uninhibited joy.

Darkness at Noon (1941). A novel by Arthur KOESTLER. Analyzing various kinds of Communist psychology, it is an account of the moral struggles of an idealistic revolutionary who is persuaded by his superiors to confess to crimes against the state which he did not commit.

Darley, George (1795–1846). Irish-born English poet, mathematician. In his use of symbols to express abstract ideas, he anticipates the symbolist school of poetry. He first earned a living writing mathematical textbooks and, but for a severe speech impediment, might have been an eminent professor of that subject. Later he wrote astute, if harsh, criticism of drama and art. His work includes the verse drama *Sylvia* (1827), and the collections *Errors of Ecstacie* (1822) and *Nepenthe,* published posthumously in 1876.

Darling, Wendy, Michael, and **John.** See PETER PAN.

Darnay, Charles. In Charles Dickens' A TALE OF TWO CITIES, a teacher of languages who loves Lucie Manette and marries her. He is a French aristocrat, nephew of the Marquis de St. Evrémonde, and has changed his name, emigrating to England in rebellion against his family, who have committed grave injustices against peasants. Because of his family, he is considered an enemy of the revolution and when he returns to Paris to help an old servant unjustly imprisoned, he himself is arrested and sentenced to the guillotine; he is saved by the self-sacrificing intervention of Sydney Carton.

Darnel, Aurelia. See LAUNCELOT GREAVES.

Darnley, Henry Stuart, Lord (1545–1567). Great-grandson of Henry VII, and the second husband of MARY, QUEEN OF SCOTS. Displeased at not receiving the crown matrimonial from Mary, Darnley became jealous of David Rizzio, one of her favorite counselors, and was an accomplice in his murder. Shortly thereafter Darnley himself was murdered—possibly with Mary's knowledge—at Kirk o' Field, a solitary house near Edinburgh; the house was blown up with gunpowder, and Darnley's body, apparently strangled, found nearby.

Darrow, Clarence [Seward] (1857–1938). American lawyer, lecturer, and writer. A well-paid railroad lawyer, Darrow viewed the cases he defended unsympathetically. In the famous Eugene DEBS case, Darrow resigned his position with the railroads and won a national reputation for his defense of Debs. Later he defended Nathan Leopold and Richard Loeb, who murdered a young boy (1924), and saved them from execution. He was the chief counsel for J. T. Scopes, who was accused of violating Tennessee law by teaching evolution in a public school. (See SCOPES TRIAL.) Although Darrow lost the case, he destroyed the reputation of the prosecuting attorney, William Jennings Bryan.

Darrow wrote two novels, *Farmington* (1904) and *An Eye for an Eye* (1905). Among his other volumes are *Crime: Its Cause and Its Treatment* (1922); *Infidels and Heretics* (with Wallace Rice, 1929), an anthology; and *The Story of My Life* (1932). He appears as a character in *Inherit the Wind* (1955), a play based on the Scopes trial, by Robert E. Lee and Jerome Lawrence, and in Meyer Levin's book *Compulsion* (1956), based on the Loeb-Leopold case.

D'Artagnan. See Charles de Baatz d'ARTAGNAN.

Darwin, Charles Robert (1809–1882). English naturalist, grandson of Erasmus DARWIN. An original expounder of the theory of evolution by natural selection, since known as Darwinism, he was to have a profound influence on human concepts of life and the universe. Although he studied medicine at Edinburgh and prepared for the ministry at Cambridge, his abiding interest was natural history, and it was as naturalist that he sailed on the *Beagle* (1831–1836) on an expedition to southern islands, South American coasts, and Australia. On his return to England he published *Zoology of the Voyage of the Beagle* (1840). As secretary of the Geological Society (1838–1841), he came into contact with the noted geologist Sir Charles Lyell (1797–1875), who urged him to write on his experiments in inbreeding and his theory of evolution by natural selection. He received (1858) from Alfred Russel Wallace (1823–1913) an abstract outlining an identical theory of natural selection, independently arrived at. He published Wallace's essay along with his own, written in 1844, in 1858. In 1859 he published his ORIGIN OF SPECIES; it is said that the first edition sold out in one day, and immediately a raging controversy arose. Within one year, the book's importance, still felt today, as the leading work in natural philosophy in the history of mankind, was recognized. Darwin's later important works include *The Movements and Habits of Climbing Plants* (1865), *The Variation of Animals and Plants under Domestication* (1868), *The Descent of Man* (1871), and *Selection in Relation to Sex* (1871). See SCOPES TRIAL.

Darwin, Erasmus (1731–1802). English physician, botanist, and poet. He is the author of *The Botanic Garden* (1789, 1791), a didactic poem in heroic couplets discoursing on plants and flowers according to the theories of Linnaeus. Darwin's *Zoönomia* (1794–1796) is a treatise on evolutionary development, not, however, in the sense that his grandson Charles Robert DARWIN was to assign to that term.

Das, Deb Kumar (1936–   ). Indian poet writing in English; also a research scientist. He published *The Night Before Us* (1960).

Dasharatha. In Hindu legend, a king of the solar dynasty; in the Ramayana, father of Rama. He had three chief queens, and when the sage Rishyasringa performed a special sacrifice for him, Rama was born to Kaushalya, Lakshmana and Shatrughna to Sumitra, and Bharata to Kaikeyi. His daughter was Shanta. After he ordered Rama into fourteen years' exile in order to keep a promise he had made to the evil-minded Kaikeyi, he died of a broken heart.

Dashwood, Elinor and **Marianne.** See SENSE AND SENSIBILITY.

Dashwood, Elizabeth Monica. See E. M. DELAFIELD.

Datta, Sudhindranath (1901–1960). Indian poet and critic in Bengali. He was a leader of the modernist movement in Bengali and translated European poetry. His best-known work is *Orchestra.*

Daudet, Alphonse (1840–1897). French novelist of the naturalist school. Daudet is noted for his keen observation, his sympathetic portrayal of character, and his vivid presentation of incident. His novels deal with life in Provence, his birthplace, and with the various social classes of Paris. The Provençal stories (see TARTARIN), vigorous and good-humored, include LETTRES DE MON MOULIN, *Tartarin de Tarascon* (1872); *Tartarin sur les Alpes* (1885), and *Port-Tarascon* (1890). Daudet's novels of Parisian manners include *Le Nabob* (1877), NUMA ROUMESTAN, *Les Rois en exil* (1879), and *Sapho* (1884).

Daudet, Léon (1868–1942). French journalist and writer. The son of Alphonse Daudet, he gave up medicine to devote himself to political journalism. His intemperate, antidemocratic articles, polemical essays, and diatribes at first appeared in *Le Gaulois, Le Figaro,* and the fanatically anti-Semitic *La Libre Parole;* then, in 1908, Daudet became coeditor with Charles Maurras of the ultraroyalist Catholic journal L'ACTION FRANÇAISE. For 20 years the force of his invective was feared, and he wielded a political influence that enabled him to be elected to the Chamber of Deputies, where he served from 1919 to 1924. His influence was, however, insufficient to sustain a murder charge which he had brought against the chauffeur in whose cab his son had committed suicide. The chauffeur prosecuted him, and, following a noisy trial, he was sentenced to prison for defamation. With royalist help he escaped and fled to Belgium in 1927. Daudet wrote the novels *L'Astre noir* (*The Black Heavenly Body,* 1893), *Les Morticoles* (1894), and *Sylla et son destin* (1922). His nonfiction books include *L'Avant-guerre* (1913), *Souvenirs* (1914), *L'Hérédo* (1916), *Le Monde des images* (1919), and *Le Stupide XIX*ᵉ *siècle* (*The Stupid XIXth Century,* 1922).

Daumier, Honoré (1808–1879). French painter and caricaturist. On the staff of *La Caricature* and *Charivari,* he produced an enormous number of powerful lithographs commenting with bitter humor, scathing satire, or tragic seriousness upon the faults of the bourgeoisie, the corruption of the law, and the injustices of his age. His direct, economically stated paintings with their superb handling of light and shade remained unappreciated until after his death.

Dauphin. The heir to the French crown under the Valois and Bourbon dynasties. Guy VIII, count of Vienne, was the first so styled, apparently because he wore as his emblem a dolphin. The title descended in the family until 1349, when Humbert III ceded his *seigneurie,* the Dauphiné, to Philippe VI (du Valois), one condition being that the heir of France assume the title of *le Dauphin.* The first French prince so called was Jean, who succeeded Philippe; the last was a Duc d'Angoulême, son of Charles X, who renounced the title in 1830. The

Dauphin remembered in connection with JOAN OF ARC was Charles VII (1403–1461), the son of the feeble-minded Charles VI. The early part of his reign was wasted in internal dissensions within the court which the weak Dauphin was unable to put down. Thanks to the efforts of Joan, he was crowned in 1429, but it was not till some years later that a group of more vigorous councillors than he had previously had were able to make the new king take a firm policy. Eventually, partly due to the influence of his remarkable mistress Agnes Sorel, Charles became a fairly strong monarch. Apparently embarrassed over his lack of support for Joan during her lifetime, he arranged for her rehabilitation about 25 years later.

The so-called Lost Dauphin was Charles, son of Louis XVI and Marie Antoinette, called after his father's death Louis XVII by French loyalists. According to official accounts he died in prison two years later, but the secrecy surrounding his death inevitably led sympathizers to believe that he had actually escaped. In later years, innumerable pretenders appeared who claimed to be the Lost Dauphin.

Davenant or **D'Avenant**, Sir **William** (1606–1668). English dramatist and poet, thought by some to be an illegitimate son of Shakespeare. His SIEGE OF RHODES, a heroic tragedy with "musical recitative," is considered the first English opera. Though his writing was very popular in his time, his only outstanding work is *Gondibert* (1651), a heroic poem formed on the aesthetic theories of Hobbes and anticipating Dryden's style.

Davenport, Marcia (1903–   ). American novelist. Mrs. Davenport is the daughter of the famous singer Alma Gluck, and her first book was a life of Mozart (1932; rev. 1956). She followed this with several highly popular novels, including *Of Lena Geyer* (1936), *The Valley of Decision* (1942), *East Side, West Side* (1947), *My Brother's Keeper* (1954), and *Constant Image* (1960).

David. The shepherd-king of the Old Testament and the reputed author of many of the Psalms. The youngest son of Jesse, he was secretly anointed king by the prophet Samuel while Saul was still on the throne. Stories of his early life are concerned with his immortal friendship for Saul's son Jonathan, and with Saul's growing jealousy. Though he charmed away the black moods of Saul with his harp (I Sam. 16:23), he was, for many years, forced to flee from Saul's anger. When no one else would venture to respond to the giant's challenge, he killed Goliath, the huge champion of the Philistines, with only his slingshot and some stones (I Sam. 17).

After the death of Saul and Jonathan, David became the second king of Israel (c. 1000–c. 960 B.C.). His latter years were concerned with his guilty love for BATHSHEBA, and his grief over the revolt of his son ABSALOM.

David, St. (*fl.* 6th century A.D.). The patron saint of Wales. Legend relates that he was son of Xantus, Prince of Cereticu, now called Cardiganshire; he was brought up a priest, became an ascetic in the Isle of Wight, preached to the Britons, confuted Pelagius, and was preferred to the see of Caerleon or Menevia (i.e., *main aw,* narrow water or firth). Here the saint had received his early education, and when Dyvrig, the archbishop, resigned his see to him, St. David removed the archiepiscopal residence to Menevia, which was henceforth called St. David's. The waters of Bath "owe their warmth and salutary qualities to the benediction of this saint." The leek

David and Bathsheba. From a German Bible (1483).

worn by Welshmen on *St. David's Day* is in memory of a complete victory obtained by them over the Saxons (March I, 640). This victory is ascribed to the prayers of St. David, and his judicious adoption of a leek in the cap, that the Britons might readily recognize each other. The Saxons, having no badge, not unfrequently turned their swords against their own supporters.

David, [Jacques] Louis (1748-1825). French painter. An accomplished realist, he lent the precision of his drawing to the formulation of a measured and heroic art inspired by the antiquity of republican Rome, and became the indubitable leader of French classicism. During the French Revolution, he supported Robespierre and produced one of his masterpieces, *The Death of Marat* (1793); he then became court painter on the accession of Napoleon. The figures of his historical paintings are sharply lit and sculptural in quality, but often harshly colored and theatrically posed. His exactitude was more suited to the art of portraiture, of which he has given us some admirable examples.

David Copperfield (1849-1850). A novel by Charles DICKENS, admittedly autobiographical. As a mere boy, after his mother's death, David is sent by his cruel stepfather Mr. Murdstone to London to make his living; here he pastes labels on bottles in a warehouse by day and is the single lodger of the poverty-stricken though optimistic Mr. MICAWBER and his family. David finally runs away to his great-aunt Betsey TROTWOOD, who becomes his guardian. After a period of school life in CREAKLE's school, he settles down to work with Mr. WICKFIELD, a lawyer, and finds a warm friend in Wickfield's daughter Agnes. Unaware of Agnes's deep devotion to him, David marries Dora SPENLOW, a rattlebrained childlike woman, who dies soon after. Neither his literary success nor his marriage has brought him the peace and happiness he yearns for, and David turns to Agnes with the realization that he has always loved her. She is involved in extricating her father from the deceits of the unctuous Uriah HEEP, who has gained a financial hold over them. With the help of Mr. Micawber, Uriah Heep is foiled; David marries Agnes and together they find happiness.

David Copperfield is a devastating exposé of the inhuman treatment of children in 19th-century England. Among the well-known secondary characters in the book are BARKIS, the PEGGOTTY family, STEERFORTH, and Tommie TRADDLES.

Davideis (1656). An epic poem in four books by Abraham COWLEY, describing the troubles of King David of the Hebrews. The poem is incomplete.

Davidson, Jo (1883-1952). American sculptor. He was a portraitist of eminent personalities, such as Franklin D. Roosevelt and Georges Clemenceau.

Davidson, John (1857-1909). Scottish poet, playwright, and author. Known in his day as the poet of Anarchy from the gloomy, pessimistic philosophy expressed in his long poetic *Testaments* (1901, 1902, 1908), Davidson survives through a few lyrics such as *The Ballad of Hell* (1894) and *A Runnable Stag* (1906). Collections of his verse include *Fleet Street Eclogues* (1893, 1896) and several volumes of *Ballads* (1894, 1897, 1899). He also wrote successful plays, several novels, translations, and criticism.

Davidson, Lawrence H. The pen name under which D. H. LAWRENCE published *Movements in European History* (1921).

Davie, Donald (1922-   ). English poet and critic. A witty, antiromantic poet like other followers of William Empson, he published *New and Selected Poems* in 1961.

Davies, Sir John (1569-1626). English poet of the SPENSERIAN SCHOOL. The author of epigrammatic and ingenious poetry and treatises in verse, he is known for the vigor and intelligence of his writing. Among his works are *Orchestra* (1596), a treatment in poetry of the dance; *Hymns to Astraea* (1599), a collection of acrostic hymns praising Queen Elizabeth; and *Nosce Teipsum* (1599), a philosophical poem on the immortality of the soul.

Davies, W[illiam] H[enry] (1871-1940). Welsh-born English poet. He wrote simple, Wordsworthian poems on nature, and was associated with the GEORGIANS. Until he was over 30, he was a hobo and peddler by choice. His best-known book is his prose *Autobiography of a Super-tramp* (1908).

Daviot, Gordon. See Elizabeth MACKINTOSH.

Davis, Clyde Brion (1894-1962). American newspaperman and novelist. Davis worked on many newspapers from coast to coast, but he is best known for his novel *"The Great American Novel"* (1938), the story of a newspaperman whose roving life is spent in dreaming about the great American novel he expects to write. *The Anointed* (1937) is the story of a sailor who thinks he is divinely inspired. Davis also wrote *The Arkansas* (1940) for the Rivers of America series, and over 15 other novels with American settings.

Davis, Elmer [Holmes] (1890-1958). American journalist and radio commentator. Born in Indiana, Davis worked for the New York *Times* and wrote a history of the newspaper (1921). Having joined the staff of CBS in 1939, he interrupted his work there to head the Office of War Information (1942-1945), then returned to radio work. Known for his fearless interpretation of the news, he attacked Senator McCarthy in a collection of essays called *But We Were Born Free* (1954). Davis also wrote several works of fiction, notably *Giant-Killer* (1928), a novel telling the story of King David from a rationalist viewpoint.

Davis, H[arold] L[enoir] (1896-1960). American novelist. He became well known for his realistic historical novel *Honey in the Horn* (1935), a story of frontier life in Oregon. He is also the author of *Harp of a Thousand Strings* (1947), a narrative dealing with the French Revolution; *Beulah Land* (1949) and *Winds of Morning* (1951), both frontier novels; *Team Bells Woke Me* (1953), a collection of short stories; and *Distant Music* (1957), a family chronicle set in southeastern Oregon.

Davis, Jefferson (1808-1889). American statesman. A graduate of West Point, Davis was wounded at the battle of Buena Vista in the Mexican War. In 1847 he became U.S. Senator from Mississippi and later served as secretary of war under Franklin Pierce. Again elected to the Senate in 1857, he resigned when Mississippi seceded and was chosen president of the Confederacy in 1861. His policies, however, aroused much controversy within Confederate ranks. After the Civil War, he was captured and imprisoned; in 1866 he was indicted for treason, but was never tried.

Davis, Owen (1874–1956). American playwright. He is the author of numerous popular melodramas, the most celebrated of which are *Nellie, the Beautiful Cloak Model* (1906) and *The Nervous Wreck* (1923). He won a Pulitzer Prize for *Icebound* (1923), the story of a family who greedily wait for the mother to die. Davis successfully dramatized *Ethan Frome* (1936) and a number of other novels.

Davis, Rebecca [Blaine] Harding (1831–1910). American author and mother of Richard Harding DAVIS. She was one of the earliest American realists, known for her attempts to deal in fiction with the life of industrial workers, the problem of the Negro, and political corruption. Her early success was the "muckraking" *Life in the Iron Mills,* published in *The Atlantic Monthly* in April, 1861. This was followed by *Margaret Howth* (1862), a novel set in an Indiana milltown. *Waiting for the Verdict* (1868) was a story about racial bias; *John Andross* (1874) was a tale of political corruption.

Davis, Richard Harding (1864–1916). American journalist and novelist. The son of novelist Rebecca Harding Davis, he covered wars all over the world, and his vivid, dramatic dispatches made him the leading reporter of his day. Aided by his good looks and sartorial elegance, he became equally famous as a personality, the embodiment of "the mauve decade" of the 1890's. Although his fiction is considered somewhat slick and superficial, he was a skillful storyteller and created several memorable characters, notably Gallegher, the enterprising office boy, and Cortland Van Bibber, the Robin Hood of the social set. Davis' works of fiction include *Gallegher and Other Stories* (1891), *Van Bibber and Others* (1892), *Soldiers of Fortune* (1897), *Captain Macklin* (1902), and *The Bar Sinister* (1903). He also wrote more than 20 plays, including *The Dictator* (1904).

Davis, Stuart (1894–1964). American painter. He evolved a meticulous language of abstract symbols and intense color.

Davis, Thomas Osborne (1814–1845). Irish poet. Davis founded, with John Blake Dillon and Charles Gavan Duffy, *The Nation* (1842), in its day the most influential organ of Irish nationalism. He is best known for his ballads, collected in *Poems* (1846).

Davy Jones. A sailor's name for the evil spirit of the sea. The term seems to be a corruption of *Duffy* or *Duppy Jonah,* the word *duffy* or *duppy* standing, among the Negroes of the West Indies, for "a haunting spirit or ghost." Jones is a corruption of Jonah, the prophet who was thrown into the sea. "He's gone to Davy Jones' locker" is the nautical way of saying that a messmate is dead and has been buried at sea.

Day, Clarence [Shepard], Jr. (1874–1935). American writer. He was best known as the author of two unique collections of humorous sketches based on recollections of his parents: LIFE WITH FATHER, and *Life with Mother* (1936). Day also wrote *This Simian World* (1920), *God and My Father* (1932), and *Scenes from the Mesozoic* (1935).

Day, John (1522–1584). English printer. He printed the first church music book in English (1560)

and the first English edition of John Foxe's *Actes And Monuments* (1563).

Day, John (c. 1574–c. 1640). English dramatist. He is best known for *The Parliament of Bees* (1608) and part one of *The Blind Beggar of Bethnal Green, or Thomas Strowd* (1600), written with Henry Chettle. His other plays include *The Isle of Gulls* (1606) and *The Travels of Three English Brothers* (1607). He also collaborated with Thomas Dekker.

Day or **Daye, Stephen** (1594?–1668). The first printer in New England. He brought out the *Bay Psalm Book* (1640), the first book printed in the English colonies. The town of Cambridge, Mass., granted him 300 acres of land for "being the first that sett upon printing."

Day-Lewis, C[ecil] (1904–). Irish-born English poet and author of detective stories under the pen name Nicholas Blake. Associated during the 1930's with the Marxist poets W. H. Auden and Stephen Spender, he, like them, wrote much didactic verse, and used the imagery of industrial society. His later poetry is more personal and reflective. Among his collections of poetry are *From Feathers to Iron* (1931), *The Magnetic Mountain* (1933), *A Time to Dance* (1935), and *An Italian Visit* (1953). *A Hope for Poetry* (1934) and *Revolution in Writing* (1935) are critical essays on the aims of the Marxist poets. He has made good verse translations of Vergil's *Georgics* (1941) and *Aeneid* (1952), and has also written children's books. Among his detective novels is *The Worm of Death* (1961).

Day of Atonement or **Yom Kippur.** The most solemn Jewish fast. It culminates the 10 days of penitence at the beginning of the Jewish New Year, falling on the 10th day of the 7th month (*Tishri*). In ancient times, a priest made atonement for the whole community, a bullock was sacrificed; its blood sprinkled on the Ark of the Covenant; and a SCAPEGOAT selected to carry the poeple's sins "into a solitary land." It involved abstinence from all labor, food or drink and the recitation of penitent prayers for forgiveness.

Day of Doom, The (1662). A celebrated poem by Michael WIGGLESWORTH. It describes the Day of Judgment and the sentencing to punishment in Hell of sinners and of infants who died before baptism. So popular was the poem that no first or second edition of it exists; the copies were apparently thumbed to shreds. It is estimated that one out of every 20 persons in the Bay colony bought a copy, making it the first American best seller.

Day of the Locust, The (1939). A novel by Nathanael WEST. Set in Hollywood, the book deals with the failure of the American dream. The central character is Homer Simpson, who arrives in California only to find monotony and boredom. The book culminates in a surrealistic riot at a movie premiere.

Day of the Rabblement, The (1901). An attack by James JOYCE on the parochial nationalism of the Irish Literary Theatre (see ABBEY THEATRE). He accused this theater movement of neglecting true art in trying to appease the people, or Irish rabblement.

Days (1852). One of the best poems by Ralph Waldo EMERSON. It expresses this thought from his essay, *Works and Days:* "He only is rich who owns the day."

Days of the Turbins (Dni Turbinikh; 1926). A drama by Mikhail BULGAKOV. It gives a well-balanced account of the conflict during the Russian Revolution between the Czarist White Guard and the forces of the Red Army.

Dazai Osamu. Pen name of **Tsushima Shuji** (1909–1948). Japanese novelist, author of pessimistic works, widely read in the postwar period. He died with a woman in a suicide pact. Several of his works have appeared in translation: *Shayō* (*The Setting Sun,* 1947) and *Ningen Shikaku* (*No Longer Human,* 1948), both translated by Donald Keene.

D'Azeglio, Marchese. **Massimo Taparrelli** (1798–1866). Italian patriot and writer of historical novels which were inspired by the Italian struggle for national independence (the RISORGIMENTO). Most noted are *Ettore Fieramosca* (1833) and *Niccolò de' Lapi* (1841). He is also known for his polemical writings and for his memoirs, *I Miei Ricordi* (1867).

Deacon's Masterpiece, The, or, The Wonderful "One-Hoss Shay" (1858). A poem by Oliver Wendell HOLMES. The deacon built his shay so sturdily that it would never break down; based on logic, it lasted a hundred years. The shay never did break down; it simply fell apart all at once: "Just as bubbles do when they burst." Clearly Holmes was satirizing Calvinist dogma, or any inflexible though highly logical system designed for permanence.

Dead, The. The last and most famous of the short stories in James Joyce's DUBLINERS (1914). It concerns Gabriel Conway, an Irish college teacher. Gabriel and his wife Gretta spend the evening at his elderly aunts' Christmas dance, a rather moribund affair; one incident after another makes Gabriel feel more and more a social failure. Seeing his wife look radiant after hearing an old song, he takes her home in a romantic mood. She tells him the song reminded her of a boy called Michael Furey, who was once in love with her, but who died when he was 17. In a famous last paragraph Joyce describes Gabriel looking at the snow and thinking of his aunts who will soon be dead, of himself who is spiritually almost dead, and of his wife's dead lover.

Dead End (1935). A play by Sidney KINGSLEY. It depicts life in New York's slums by means of typical scenes taking place in a dead-end street.

Dead Sea Scrolls (also called **Qumram manuscripts**). The fragmentary remains of a large library of the ancient Jewish sect of Essenes. They were discovered in 1947 in a cave around the Qumram Valley of the Dead Sea. Thousands of fragments of manuscripts comprise the archaelogical discovery; over 100 scrolls of Old Testament books—all except the book of Esther—have appeared. The oldest texts date from 200 B.C., 1,000 years older than any previously existing documents.

Dead Souls (Myortvye Dushi; 1842). A novel by Nikolai GOGOL. It relates the adventures of an archswindler, Pavel I. CHICHIKOV. The hero, who has already been in trouble for shady deals when he appears on the scene, has conceived a weird scheme for making his fortune anew. He intends to buy from landowners all of their serfs who have died since the last census was taken. These serfs are still alive according to government records, and the landowner has to pay taxes on them until the next census strikes them off the list. Chichikov's plan is to pay the owner a small sum, assume the burden of the taxes on these "dead souls" himself, and become the rightful owner of them. Then he intends to mortgage them and to acquire a real estate of his own in eastern Russia. The novel follows Chichikov as he makes friends with the right people in town and visits the local landowners, to each of whom he gently puts his strange proposition. He neglects to tell them, however, what he plans to do with the dead souls once he has them. The description of the landowners he visits, their reactions to his proposal, and Chichikov's reactions to their reactions make up some of the finest scenes in the novel. Eventually rumors spread through the town about Chichikov's deals with the landowners MANILOV, SOBAKEVICH, KOROBOCHKA, and PLYUSHKIN. The obnoxious NOZDRYOV adds lies of his own invention to the rumors, and Chichikov finally wings away from the town in his troika.

Gogol was working on a second part to the novel in which Chichikov was to be reformed and become a genuinely respectable citizen. The author destroyed most of the manuscript shortly before his death and only fragments of it have survived.

Dead Souls has been unanimously acclaimed as one of the greatest novels in the Russian language, for its characterizations, humor, and style. The perpetual question of whether Gogol was a realist or a fantasist has created differences of opinion, however, about just what kind of novel Gogol wrote. The influential critic Vissarion Belinski accepted Gogol's fiction as being truthful to Russian life. This view, retained by later radical critics, is the official Soviet doctrine on Gogol. Other critics have stressed the many fantastic elements in Gogol's work: the grotesque caricatures of real people that compose his characters, the extravagance of his imagery, and use of hyperbolic language.

De Amicis, Edmondo (1846–1908). Italian educator, moralist, and essayist. De Amicis is noted for the sentimental and moral tenor of his writings. An admirer of Manzoni and politically a moderate socialist, he was chiefly interested in the pedagogical and social problems of post-Risorgimento Italian society. His fiction—*Le Novelle,* a collection of short stories (1872); *Gli Amici* (1884); and *Il Cuore* (1886)—is candidly didactic. *La Vita Militare* (1869) recounts his experiences as an infantry officer in the Italian army during the Austro-Prussian War (1866). *Romanzo di Un Maestro* (1890) and *Idioma Gentile* (1905) are interesting essays in practical pedagogy: the former discusses state-run public schools; the latter treats informally the correct spoken and written usage of the Italian language.

A world traveler, De Amicis was one of the first men of letters to write carefully detailed accounts of the places he visited: *Londra* (1874), *Spagna* (1873), *Olanda* (1874), *Marocco* (1876), *Constantinopoli* (1878), and *Parigi* (1879). In his later years he devoted himself to improving the lot of the impoverished Italian proletariat. His *Sull'Oceano* (1889) vividly narrates the plight of Italian emigrants to the Americas.

De Amicitia (44 B.C.). A dialogue on the subject of friendship by CICERO. The chief interlocutor is Gaius Laelius Sapiens. Hence the essay is also known as the *Laelius.*

Dear Judas, and Other Poems (1929). A collection by Robinson JEFFERS. The title poem is an attempt to rehabilitate the reputation of Judas. He is presented as a man who loves Jesus but finds him grown too fond of power. Judas therefore betrays him in the belief that he will be jailed for a few days and then released, escaping later execution as a rebel.

Death and the Fool. See TOR UND DER TOD, DER.

Death Comes for the Archbishop (1927). A novel by Willa CATHER. It describes the missionary efforts of the French bishop Jean Latour and his vicar, Father Joseph Vaillant, to establish a diocese in the territory of New Mexico. The novel is based on the lives of the two eminent French clerics, Bishop Jean Baptiste Lamy (1814–1888) and Father Joseph Machebeuf. They prevail over all adversities to build a cathedral in the wilderness.

Death in Venice (Der Tod in Venedig; 1913). A novella by Thomas MANN. Gustav von Aschenbach, the hero, is a successful author, proud of the self-discipline with which he has ordered his life and work. On a trip to Venice, however, he becomes aware of mysterious decadent potentialities in himself, and he finally succumbs to a consuming love for a frail but beautiful Polish boy named Tadzio. Though he learns that there is danger of a cholera epidemic in Venice, he finds he cannot leave the city, and eventually he dies of the disease. The story is permeated by a rich and varied symbolism with frequent overtones from Greek literature and mythology.

Death of a Hero (1929). A novel by Richard ALDINGTON. It expresses the author's disillusionment with the idealistic patriotism of World War I. The "hero" is so disgusted by a corrupt and wasteful English society, neurotic parents, and the complications in his love life, that he invites his own death.

Death of a Salesman (1949). A play by Arthur MILLER. A bitter indictment of American values, it is the story of Willy Loman, a traveling salesman, who experiences a profound sense of failure as he discovers signs of aging in himself and takes stock of his accomplishments. The play ends in his suicide.

Death of Ivan Ilyich, The (Smert' Ivana Ilyicha; 1886). A story by Count Leo TOLSTOI. It concerns the thoughts on life and death of a dying man. An ordinary man who had never particularly bothered himself about large questions, Ivan is forced into his contemplation by the discovery that he will soon die of cancer. The problems he ponders are similar to those that acutely occupied Tolstoi himself when he went through the spiritual crisis described in *A Confession*. Ivan's acceptance of death as part of the natural order of things recalls a similar conclusion reached by Prince Andrei Bolkonski in *War and Peace*.

Death of Pompey, The. See MORT DE POMPÉE, LA.

Death of Seneca, The. See François L'HERMITE.

Death of the Heart, The (1938). A novel by Elizabeth BOWEN. It is the story of Portia, an illegitimate 16-year-old girl who comes to live with her half brother when her mother dies. To escape from the arid, artificial, unfeeling social world of her London relatives she falls in love with ordinary, insensitive Eddie—who is soon found holding hands with someone else. Innocence and idealism die in Portia's heart, but she also grows up into an acceptance of the world as it is.

Death of the Hired Man, The (1914). A poem by Robert FROST. It narrates the argument between a farmer and his wife over whether or not to keep a defeated old hired hand, who, in his last hours, has returned to them. When the farmer seeks out the man he finds him dead. The poem contains the kind of folk wisdom that made Frost popular, but also has an almost mystical undercurrent giving layers of meaning beyond the obvious debate.

Débâcle, La (The Downfall, 1892). A novel in the ROUGON-MACQUART series by Emile ZOLA. The characters in *La Débâcle* are dwarfed by Zola's realistic and thoroughly detailed account of the Franco-Prussian War.

de Barral, Flora. The heroine of Joseph Conrad's novel CHANCE. She is torn between her husband and her father.

De bello Gallico. See COMMENTARIES ON THE GALLIC WAR.

Deborah. In the Old Testament, a Hebrew prophetess and judge of Israel (Judg. 4:4). She summoned Barak to fight against the tyranny of Jabin, prophesied success, and accompanied him in battle against Sisera, captain of Jabin's army. After their victory over the Canaanites, she sang a famous song of triumph (Judg. 5), considered by scholars to be one of the oldest pieces of writing in the Old Testament.

Debrett, John (1752–1822). English publisher and original compiler of the *Peerage of England, Scotland, and Ireland* (1802) and the *Baronetage of England* (1808).

Debs, Eugene V[ictor] (1855–1926). American socialist leader. Founder of the Social Democratic Party and its leader during the period of its greatest influence (1897–1916), Debs was a candidate for the presidency five times, and was renowned for his campaign oratory. He came to prominence as a leader of the famous Pullman strike in Chicago (1894) and was imprisoned for his participation. (See Clarence DARROW.) A powerful figure in American politics, he always insisted on the primacy of democratic procedures. His *Writings and Speeches* were collected in 1948 by Arthur M. Schlesinger, Jr.

Debussy, Claude [Achille] (1862–1918). French composer. He is identified with musical impressionism, although he preferred to call himself simply *musicien français*. Certain revolutionary characteristics of his work, such as unresolved discords, exotic scales, and free forms, prepared the way for many developments of modern music. His best-known pieces include *Suite Bergamasque*, a piano suite containing the famous *Clair de Lune; Prélude à l'après-midi d'un faune* (1894), a tone poem inspired by Mallarmé's eclogue *L'Après-midi d'un faune (Afternoon of a Faun*, 1876); *Pelléas et Mélisande* (1902), his only opera, composed to Maeterlinck's play; *La Mer* ("The Sea," 1905), a tone poem; *Children's Corner Suite* (1908), a piano suite; and *Jeux* ("Games," 1913), a ballet.

décadents. A term applied narrowly to the group of French poets whose leaders were Rimbaud, Verlaine, and Mallarmé (see SYMBOLISTS). Broadly and more popularly the term *décadents* is applied to the poets and prose writers, chiefly French, of the postromantic period. Morbid and perverse tastes, unconventional and often sensational social behavior, and hyperaesthetic temperaments characterize the *décadents*. In their writings, they placed emphasis upon creative self-expression, advancing the ideal of pure art. In his novel AGAINST THE GRAIN (*A Rebours*), J. K. Huysmans creates a hero who is the epitome of the *décadent*. Oscar Wilde is the leading figure in the English counterpart of this French phenomenon.

Decalogue. See TEN COMMANDMENTS.

Decameron, The. A collection of tales by Giovanni Boccaccio, written 1351–1353. The title (from Gr., *deca*, ten, and *hēmera*, day) refers to the frame story: in the year of the black death, 1348, seven young ladies and three young gallants meet in a Florentine church and decide to escape from the city to the hills of Fiesole. There they spend the time in telling stories on 10 days. The 100 novelle, ranging from anecdotes and fabliaux to folk tales and fairy tales of ancient lineage, include many that became famous and influential in European literature: *Ser Ciappelletto*, BERNABÒ OF GENOA, GILLETTE OF NARBONNE, THE REVENGE OF TANCRED, ISABELLA, OR THE POT OF BASIL, THE EATEN HEART, BROTHER CIPOLLA, A GARDEN IN JANUARY, CALANDRINO AND THE HELIOTROPE, TITUS AND GISIPPUS, THE PATIENT GRISELDA. It is unlikely that Chaucer knew the book, though he used similar stories; but the tales have appeared in the works of other English and European writers in a steady stream up to modern times. They have also been used for plays, operas, and paintings.

De Casseres, Benjamin (1873–1945). American newspaperman, poet, and biographer. An innovator and radical individualist, he wrote flamboyant essays for the New York papers. His books include *The Shadow-Eater* (1915), *Black Suns* (1936), and *Don Marquis* (1938).

Decatur, Stephen (1779–1820). American naval officer. He commanded the squadron that sailed to Algeria in 1815 to impose upon the British a peace on American terms. On his return, he uttered this famous toast at a banquet: "Our country! In her intercourse with foreign nations may she always be in the right; but our country, right or wrong!"

Decembrist revolt. A short-lived, unsuccessful uprising in Russia in December, 1825. Led by young nobles of some of Russia's oldest families, the Decembrists wanted to institute a constitutional form of government and deny the throne to Nicholas I following his accession on the death of Alexander I. The insurgents were arrested; 5 were executed, and over 100 exiled to Siberia. The revolt was the first such uprising led by members of the aristocracy. The event has been a constant point of reference for Russian revolutionaries and writers as an example of a courageous bid for freedom. The Decembrists included many friends of the poet Pushkin, but he was never proved to have been involved in the affair.

De Civitate Dei. See CITY OF GOD, THE.

Declaration of Independence. The public act by which the Second Continental Congress, on July 4, 1776, declared the 13 North American colonies to be free and independent of Great Britain. New York alone did not ratify the act until July 9. It was signed on Aug. 2, 1776, by the representatives of all 13 colonies. The document was nominally the work of a drafting committee, but actually Thomas Jefferson wrote it practically in its entirety.

Declaration of the Rights of Man (La Declaration des droits de l'homme et du citoyen). In French history, a document setting forth the principles of the FRENCH REVOLUTION. Consisting of a preamble and 17 articles, it was modeled on the American Declaration of Independence and was voted by the Constituent ASSEMBLY on August 27, 1789.

Decline and Fall (1928). A bitter, farcical, satiric novel by Evelyn WAUGH. Paul Pennyfeather, the unfortunate hero, is unjustly expelled from Oxford and turns to teaching at an appalling boys' school. He falls in love with the mother of one of his pupils, and is arrested and imprisoned for unknowingly working in her white slave trade business. Finally he returns to Oxford to study theology.

Decline and Fall of the Roman Empire, The History of the (1776–1788). A history by Edward GIBBON. Although later scholarship has superseded much of the information in this work, it has taken its place among the classical works of historical literature in the English language. The work is divided into three periods and covers a total of 13 centuries: from the rule of Trajan and the Antonines to the decay of the Western Empire; from the era of Justinian in the Eastern Empire to the founding of the Holy Roman Empire in the west under Charlemagne; and from the restoration of the Western Empire to the capture, in 1453, of Constantinople by the Turks. Gibbon's point of view is best expressed in his observation that history is a record of "little more than the crimes, follies, and misfortunes of mankind."

decorum. The ideal of propriety, or appropriateness. Stemming from classical authors, it was defined and put into practice as a literary principle by the neoclassicists of the latter part of the 17th and the 18th centuries. In accordance with this principle, literature, especially poetry, was required to be polished, dignified, clear, rational, moderate, conventional, and "elevated"; in order to achieve elegance, Latinized diction and generality and abstraction in figurative language were preferred elements of style. Wide use of the epithet was one result of the latter tendency. Leading exponents of the principle of decorum were Boileau, Pope, and Samuel Johnson. See NEOCLASSICISM.

Woodcut from a 1518 edition of *The Decameron*.

Decoud, Martin. A character in Joseph Conrad's novel Nostromo. A cynic with no inner resources, he kills himself when he is stranded on an isolated island.

decretals. The name of ecclesiastical historians for the second part of the canon law. It contains the decrees and decisions of the early popes on disputed points.

The false or forged decretals were designed to support the claim of the popes to temporal as well as spiritual authority, and purport to be the decisions of some thirty popes of the first three centuries.

The ninth century forgery known as the *Donation of Constantine* is among the false decretals. This purports to relate how Constantine the Great, when retired to the Bosporus in 330, conferred all his rights, honors, and property as Emperor of the West on the Pope of Rome and his successors. It is said, also, to have been confirmed by Charlemagne.

Dedalus, Stephen. The hero of James Joyce's novel A Portrait of the Artist as a Young Man and one of the three chief characters in his novel Ulysses. Stephen's character, background, and life history are closely modeled on Joyce's own. His name is clearly symbolic of the creative artist (see Daedalus).

Portrait concerns Stephen's struggle to gain his identity as an artist by freeing himself from his family ties, the narrowness of his Catholic upbringing, and the cultural aridity and frenzied nationalism of Ireland. The book ends on an affirmative note as Stephen is about to leave Dublin for Paris. In *Ulysses*, however, Stephen has returned to Ireland, defeated and undeceived. Still emotionally involved with the cultural and religious values his intellect rejects, Stephen is paralyzed as an artist. In the earlier book Stephen is portrayed fairly straightforwardly; his adolescent sense of superiority and colossal pride are presented with no trace of irony. But Joyce's detached portrayal of Stephen in *Ulysses* stands in ironic contrast to his earlier vision.

Dedlock, Lady. See Bleak House.

Dee, John (1527–1608). English mathematician and astrologer. A magician who had practiced at various European courts, Dee was imprisoned in England soon after the accession of Mary Tudor on the charge of having practised sorcery against her life. He was released in 1555, and later enjoyed the favor of Elizabeth, whom he instructed in astrology. He wrote numerous works on astrology and mathematics.

Deeping, [George] Warwick (1877–1950). English novelist. He is the author of Sorrell and Son and other popular novels.

Deerslayer, The (1841). A novel by James Fenimore Cooper. Although it was the last of The Leatherstocking Tales to be written, *The Deerslayer* is the novel of Natty Bumppo's youth. The scene is Lake Otsego, N. Y., called Glimmerglass in the story. Young hunters, Natty and his friend Hurry Harry March live with the Delaware Indians. They fight the Hurons with the aid of the British. Part of the story deals with the fruitless attempts of Judith Hutter to interest Natty romantically. Chingachgook, the Delaware chief who becomes Natty's companion in other volumes, enters the hero's life in this book.

Defarge, M. In Charles Dickens' A Tale of Two Cities, a revolutionist, keeper of a wine shop in the Faubourg St. Antoine, in Paris. He is a rough, bull-necked, implacable-looking man.

Mme Defarge. M. Defarge's wife, a harsh, remorseless woman and a revolutionary fanatic. It is her sister whom St. Evrémonde attacks and in her revenge she is instrumental in having Charles Darnay sentenced to the guillotine because he is related to the marquis. She has compiled a list of aristocrats and enemies of the Revolution, encoded in the stitches of her knitting. Knitting incessantly while watching the daily executions at the guillotine, she is a perfect example of the tricoteuses.

Defender of the Faith (Fidei Defensor). Henry VIII of England. A title given to him by Pope Leo X in 1521, for a Latin treatise *On the Seven Sacraments.*

Défense et Illustration de la Langue française (1549). A treatise on poetry by Joachim Du Bellay which served as the doctrine of the French poets of the Pléiade. It contained two main propositions: (1) that the French language be "defended" as a mode of poetic expression against those who were trying to rival the classic poets by writing in Latin; (2) that in order to attain its full potential of expression, French must be "illustrated" or embellished by borrowing from Greek and Latin and by the use of archaic, dialectal, and technical words. "Illustration" also included the imitation of literary formulas discovered by the ancients and the adoption of poetic forms such as the classical ode and the Italian sonnet. None of these ideas was new with Du Bellay, who sought to raise poetry to the eminence it had enjoyed in ancient times, but by fitting them into a coherent system, he gave form to the revolutionary aims of the Renaissance poets.

Defense of Poesie, The. Alternate title of An Apologie for Poetrie by Sir Philip Sidney.

Deffand, Marquise du. Marie de Vichy-Chamrond (1697–1780). Witty and cynical French noblewoman, leader in Parisian social life and literary and philosophical circles. Her salon was frequented by Turgot, d'Alembert, Marivaux, Baron de Grimm, and others. When she lost her sight in 1754, she engaged Julie Lespinasse as a companion; a violent quarrel between the two broke up the salon. Her correspondence with Voltaire, Montesquieu, Horace Walpole, and others documents 18th-century society.

Déficit, Madame. Contemptuous name given to Marie Antoinette because she was always demanding money of her ministers and never had any. See Baker.

Definition of Love, The (1681). A poem by Andrew Marvell, dealing with exalted passion and the impossibility of its fulfillment.

Defoe, Daniel (1660–1731). English novelist, pamphleteer, journalist, and political agent. He is celebrated for his frank and dramatic realism in fiction, and the accuracy, vigor, and lucidity of his journalism. Defoe was born Daniel Foe, son of a London tallow-chandler (he added the genteel "De" when over forty years of age). He is best known for his novels Robinson Crusoe and Moll Flanders, and for his Journal of the Plague Year, a historical reconstruction. Others of his works include *The True-Born Englishman* (1701), a rugged, satirical poem on English hatred of foreigners when, in fact, there is no true-born Englishman; *The Shortest Way with the Dissenters* (1702), satirizing ecclesiastical intolerance in the extreme right of the Church of England by ironically proposing that all Non-Conformist preachers be hanged—and for which he was imprisoned and pilloried; *A Tour Thro' the Whole Island of Great Britain* (1724-1727), in three volumes, an important source for early English economic life; and several novels other than his most famous, including *Memoirs of a Cavalier* (1720), a romance concerning the Cavalier's service under Gustavus Adolphus, King of Sweden; CAPTAIN SINGLETON; COLONEL JACK; and *Roxana, or, the Fortunate Mistress* (1724), which purports to be a true account of a strumpet flourishing among the aristocracy. Defoe edited, from 1704 to 1713, *The Review*, a newspaper which anticipated the *Tatler* and the *Spectator,* though it laid much greater stress on discussions of commerce and the news than did the others. He supported King William III and was later a secret agent in the pay of the moderate Tories under Robert Harley (1705). Defoe was also the first author of ghost-stories in modern English literature, an example of which is *A True Relation of the Apparition of One Mrs. Veal.* See Mrs. VEAL.

De Forest, John William (1826-1906). American novelist and memoirist. At the outbreak of the Civil War, De Forest joined the Union army; after Lee's surrender he served as the head of the Freedman's Bureau in South Carolina. His best-known novel, MISS RAVENEL's CONVERSION FROM SECESSION TO LOYALTY, includes a realistic treatment of war; also based on his Southern experience is *Kate Beaumont* (1872). Among De Forest's other books are the novels *Witching Times* (1856), *Seacliff* (1859), *Overland* (1871), and *Honest John Vane* (1875). His posthumously published memoirs are included in *A Volunteer's Adventures* (1946) and *A Union Officer in the Reconstruction* (1948). An early American realist, De Forest was admired by William Dean Howells, and is considered a forerunner of Stephen Crane.

Deformed Transformed, The (1824). An unfinished poetic drama by Lord BYRON. The hero Arnold hates life because he is horribly deformed, but when he is by magic transformed into the shape of his own choosing, he goes forth a young Achilles, bent on adventure. He joins the besieging Bourbon army at Rome and attempts to rescue the beautiful but disdainful Olimpia; here the drama breaks off.

Degas, [Hilaire Germain] Edgar (1834-1917). French painter. Associated with the impressionists, although he was not interested in landscape, Degas is noted for his mastery of motion, his superb line and color, and the veracity of his observation. He painted, drew, made lithographs, etchings, and modeled clay figures, but his favorite medium was pastels. He portrayed ballet dancers at work or in the glare of spotlights, milliners, laundresses, and women at their toilet, with scientific attention to the strained, even ungraceful, momentary positions of unobserved movement and transfigured his subjects. It was from the Japanese, whose prints became known in France about 1860, that Degas derived much of the intimacy of presentation, originality of composition, and heightened decorative quality that marks his painting.

de Gaulle, Charles [André Joseph Marie] (1890–   ). French general and statesman. After the surrender of France to German forces in 1940, de Gaulle rallied his countrymen to the cause of a Free France, refusing to accept the terms of the armistice with Germany. Court-martialed in absentia and condemned to death (August, 1940), he appointed himself leader of the Free French and established his headquarters in England. At the Casablanca Conference with Winston Churchill and Franklin D. Roosevelt he represented France. After the war de Gaulle served as head of a provisional government, from November, 1944 to January, 1946. During twelve years of retirement from political life he wrote and published his three-volume memoirs, *Mémoires de guerre* (1954-1959). In English the books are titled *The Call to Honour (1940-1942)*, *Unity (1942-1944)*, and *Salvation (1944-1946)*. In June 1958, at the height of the Algerian crisis, de Gaulle became the last premier of the Fourth Republic. A new constitution, providing for a much strengthened executive branch, was drafted and de Gaulle was elected the first President of the French Fifth Republic in December, 1958.

Degée, Olivier. See Jean TOUSSEUL.

Dehmel, Richard (1863-1920). German lyric poet influenced by Nietzsche. His early work, like that of his friend Liliencron, shows characteristics of naturalism, but he quickly developed an ecstatic subjective style similar to that of expressionism. His best-known volumes include *Erlösungen (Salvations,* 1891), *Weib und Welt (Woman and the World,* 1896), and *Schöne wilde Welt (Beautiful Wild World,* 1913).

Deimos. See PHOBOS.

Deiphobus (Deiphobos). In classic legend, one of the sons of Priam. Next to Hector, he was considered the bravest and boldest of all the Trojans. On the death of his brother Paris, he married Helen; but Helen betrayed him to her first husband, Menelaus, who slew him. He appears in the *Iliad* and *Aeneid,* and also in Shakespeare's *Troilus and Cressida.*

Dei plenus. Full of the god. Inspired, or possessed by frenzy as the Maenads in Greco-Roman mythology, who celebrated the orgiastic rites of DIONYSUS or the CORYBANTES dancing to Cybele.

Deirdre. The heroine of the greatest love story in Irish legend, found in the ULSTER CYCLE. Like the elopement tale PURSUIT OF DIARMAID AND GRÁINNE, the story of Deirdre is an early parallel to episodes in the Tristan and Iseult legend. The story has many versions, but, in general, Deirdre is the daughter of Felim, storyteller to Conchobar, king of Ulster. When she is born it is prophesied that she will be the most beautiful woman of Ireland and that she will bring bloodshed and death. To avert the prophecy, Conchobar determines to marry her when she comes of age. She is raised by the nurse Lavarcham in a secluded house in the woods where she sees no one but a few servants. Lavarcham's stories about Noisi, nephew of Conchobar and son of Usnech, fire her young imagination, and her constant pleas finally persuade Lavarcham to bring him to the house. Deirdre falls in love with him, and the two with Noisi's two brothers flee to Alba, or Scotland, to avoid the wrath of Conchobar. Ultimately they are persuaded to return and, betrayed, the sons of Usnech are killed. In some versions Deirdre kills herself at the grave of Noisi; in others, finding herself a captive of Conchobar, she dashes her brains against a rock. Synge's play *Deirdre of the Sorrows* (1910) is based on this legend, as is Yeats's *Deirdre* (1907).

deism. A belief in the existence of a personal God who is manifested neither supernaturally in history nor immanently in nature. Deism has been called "natural religion"; it is based on reason as opposed to revelation. It sprang up with the spread of scientific knowledge during the Renaissance and reached its height in the 18th century. Notable adherents of deism included Lord Herbert of Cherbury, the 3d earl of Shaftsbury, and Henry St. John in England, and Voltaire and the Encyclopedists in France. Their views affected literature—for example, Pope's ESSAY ON MAN—and the views of nature entertained by Wordsworth, Coleridge, and others.

De Jong, David Cornel (1905-). Dutch-born American writer. *Belly Fulla Straw* (1934) tells the story of a Dutch immigrant family. *Domination of June* (1944) is a volume of poetry. *Snow-on-the-Mountain* (1946) contains some of his short stories. *With a Dutch Accent* (1944) describes his own experiences. *The Desperate Children* (1949) and *Two Sofas in the Parlor* (1952) are both novels.

Dekker, Thomas (1572?-?1632). English dramatist. He was one of the Henslowe group who worked long and hard to produce the quantities of plays needed by that company. Consequently, his plays are often hastily constructed but brightened by charming verse and Dekker's warm, easy feeling for people. Among his best are THE SHOEMAKER'S HOLIDAY, THE HONEST WHORE: PARTS I AND II, and the allegorical OLD FORTUNATUS. Most of his plays, however, were written in collaboration: THE ROARING GIRL, with Thomas Middleton; *The Virgin Martyr* (c. 1620), with Philip Massinger; *The Witch of Edmonton* (1621), with John Ford and William Rowley; and *The Sun's Darling* (1624), with Ford.

De Kooning, Willem (1904-). Dutch-born American artist. He began in 1948 a series of large paintings entitled *Woman*, whose unrestrained color and violent emotional brushwork immediately impressed many younger painters.

De Koven, Reginald (1857-1920). American composer of light operas (*The Begum*, 1887; *Robin Hood*, 1890; *Student King*, 1906) and the grand opera *Canterbury Pilgrims* (1917), with a libretto by Percy MACKAYE. He is also known for his musical setting for Kipling's *Recessional*.

de Kruif, Paul (1890-). American bacteriologist and popular writer on science and medicine. De Kruif (whose name rhymes with *knife*) collaborated with Sinclair Lewis on much of the medical background for *Arrowsmith*. His own books on great figures and events in medical history are written in a lively style and have been very popular. Among them are *Microbe Hunters* (1926); *The Hunger Fighters* (1928); *Men Against Death* (1932); *Yellow Jack* (1934), a play written in collaboration with Sidney Howard; *The Fight for Life* (1938); *Man Against Insanity* (1957). His autobiography, *The Sweeping Wind*, appeared in 1962.

Delacroix, [Ferdinand Victor] Eugène (1799-1863). French painter. Leader of the romantic movement, he opposed the fire of his vision to the clarity of Ingres. He often used for his compositions past historical subjects, but he was also involved in contemporary struggles as evidenced by two of his most famous paintings: *The Massacre of Chios* (1824) and *Liberty Leading the People* (1831). A visit to North Africa, in 1832, furnished him with further subjects, notably hunting scenes, which he continued to paint throughout his life. Delacroix stressed movement and color for emotive and dramatic purposes. His vibrant palette, heightened by the juxtaposition of complementary colors, and his observation that shadows have color anticipated the discoveries of the impressionists. His famous *Journals* (1893-1895) are a distinguished contribution to literary and artistic criticism.

Delafield, E. M. Pen name of **Elizabeth Monica Dashwood** (1890-1943). English novelist. She wrote ironic comedies of manners, among them DIARY OF A PROVINCIAL LADY and *The Provincial Lady in America* (1934).

De la Mare, Walter (1873-1956). English poet, novelist, and anthologist. He was a romantic writer whose work expressed his interest in childhood, nature, dreams, and the uncanny. Much of his writing is nominally for children. Among his collections of poetry are *The Listeners* (1912), the title poem of which is his most famous and successful lyric; *Peacock Pie* (1913); and *Collected Poems* (1942). His prose writings include the novels *Henry Brocken* (1904), THE RETURN, and MEMOIRS OF A MIDGET; *Crossings, a Fairy Play* (1921), *Early One Morning* (1935), a book about children; and short stories. Among De la Mare's fine anthologies are COME HITHER and *Behold, This Dreamer!* (1939).

Deland, Margaret [ta Wade Campbell] (1857-1945). American novelist and short-story writer. Often associated with the local colorists, she was the creator of the Pennsylvania town of Old Chester, home of Dr. Lavendar, a kindly rector who appears in many of her stories. The town is the setting for *Old Chester Tales* (1898); *The Awakening of Helena Richie* (1906), a novel about a woman who must choose between her lover and her adopted son; and its sequel, *The Iron Woman* (1911). Other novels by Mrs. Deland include *John Ward, Preacher* (1888), about an orthodox minister married to a woman of liberal religious views, and *Philip and His Wife* (1894), about the conflict of an artist and his wife over the rearing of their only child.

Delaney, Shelagh (1936-). English playwright. She writes with wit and bawdy humor about the English lower class into which she was born. Her first play, *A Taste of Honey* (1958), was written when she was 18. The heroine is pregnant with the illegitimate child of a Negro sailor. She is helped by the companionship of her friend, a homosexual artist. Delaney's second play, *The Lion in Love* (1960), is the story of an impecunious street peddler and his extravagant wife. As with her first play, this work is filled with an extraordinary collection of vivid, unique characters.

de la Roche, Mazo (1879-1961). Canadian novelist. Miss de la Roche's novels of the Whiteoak family of Jalna, an estate in southern Ontario, have sold over two million copies. Among the many titles in the series are *Jalna* (1927), *Whiteoaks of Jalna*

(1933), *Young Renny* (1935), *Whiteoak Harvest* (1936), *Whiteoak Heritage* (1940), *Return to Jalna* (1946), *The Whiteoak Brothers* (1953), *Centenary at Jalna* (1958), *Morning at Jalna* (1960). *Ringing the Changes* (1957) is an autobiography.

Delectable Mountains. See PILGRIM'S PROGRESS.

Deledda, Grazia (1875–1936). Italian novelist. She is noted for her many novels and short stories depicting the peasantry of her native Sardinia. An incidental rather than deliberate realist, she was concerned chiefly with the inner experiences of her characters. Among her best known works are *Racconti Sardi* (1894), *Anime Oneste* (1895), *Elias Portolu* (1903), *Cenere* (1904), *L'Edera* (1908), and *La Madre* (*The Mother*, 1920), which was made into a motion picture with Eleonora Duse. She was awarded the Nobel Prize for literature in 1926.

Delia. The name of many ladies addressed in poetry. She was a shepherdess in Vergil's *Eclogues*, the lady love of Tibullus, and the lady to whom Samuel Daniel addressed his sonnets. The Delia of Pope's satires is the second Lady Delorraine of Ledwell Park.

Delias. The Delian ship (i.e. the ship of Delos) that according to legend, Theseus made; it carried him to Crete when he slew the Minotaur. In memory of this it was sent every fourth year with a solemn deputation to the Delian Apollo. During the festival, which lasted 30 days, no Athenian could be put to death, and as Socrates was condemned during this period his death was deferred till the return of the sacred vessel. The ship had been so often repaired that not a stick of the original vessel remained at that time.

Delibes, Léo (1836–1891). French composer. While he is most famous for his ballets, Delibes is also the composer of LAKMÉ, a staple of the French repertory of opera. His ballets include *La source* (1866), *Coppélia* (1870), *Jean de Nivelle* (1880), and *Kassya*, which was finished by Massenet after the composer's death.

Delight in Disorder (1648). A poem by Robert HERRICK. He pleads for "a sweet disorder in the dress" on the grounds that the little imperfections in a lady's dress are particularly beguiling.

Delilah. A Philistine woman in the Old Testament who was mistress of SAMSON and betrayed him. When she discovered that Samson's strength lay in his hair, she cut it off so that he was able to be captured by the Philistines (Judg. 16). Her name has come to be associated with any fascinating and deceitful woman.

Dell, Ethel M. Maiden name and pen name of **Ethel Mary Savage** (1881–1939). English novelist. She was the author of such novels as *The Way of an Eagle* (1912) and *Sown Among Thorns* (1939).

Dell, Floyd (1887–   ). American novelist, playwright, and editor. Early associated with the CHICAGO GROUP of writers, Dell moved to New York in 1914 and became an associate editor of the leftist periodicals *The Masses* and the *Liberator*. He later became known for a number of novels dealing with postwar disillusion, youth in the jazz age, and the Bohemian life current at the time in Greenwich Village. His most popular novel is MOON-CALF. *The Briary-Bush* (1921) is a sequel. *Janet March* (1923) and *Runaway* (1925) are other novels similar in

theme and treatment. His most successful play was the comedy *Little Accident* (1928), based on his novel *The Unmarried Father* (1927). In 1927 he edited with Paul Jordan Smith an excellent edition of Burton's *Anatomy of Melancholy*. *Love in the Machine Age* (1930) is a reasoned statement of his attitudes toward sex. *Homecoming* (1933) is an autobiography.

Della Casa, Giovanni (1503–1556). Florentine cleric and author of the popular courtesy book, *Il Galateo,* written 1551–1555. Unlike *The Courtier* of Castiglione, it is realistically concerned with minor problems of good manners in polite, rather than courtly, society. It was translated by Peterson in 1576, in time to influence Elizabethan concepts of courtesy. To this day, *sapere il galateo* ("to know the *Galateo*") is a popular Italian phrase signifying that one is polite.

Della-Cruscans. A clique of English poets who met originally in Florence in the latter part of the 18th century. Their sentimental, affected work, which appeared in the periodical magazines the *World* and the *Oracle*, created for a time quite a furore, but was

Title page of Della Casa's *Il Galateo* in Robert Peterson's translation (1576).

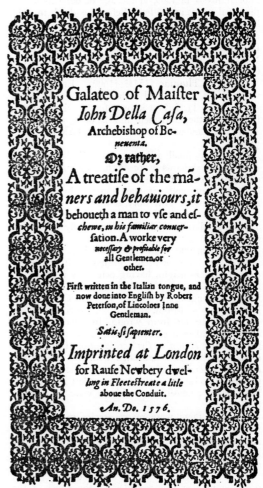

mercilessly gibbeted in THE BAVIAD and *The Maeviad* of William Gifford. The clique took its name from the famous Academia della Crusca (literally, "Academy of Chaff") which was founded in Florence in 1582 with the object of purifying the Italian language —sifting away its "chaff"—and which published an important dictionary in 1611. Members of the clique included Robert Merry, who signed himself "Della Crusca," Mrs. Hannah Cowley, who signed herself Anna Matilda, James Cobb, a writer of farces, James Boswell, Thomas Morton, George Colman, and Mrs. Elizabeth Robinson.

Della Porta, Giambattista (1535-1615). Neapolitan author and amateur scientist. Della Porta wrote some 30 comedies as well as books on various scientific subjects. His plays were known in England by such dramatists as Middleton, and his *Magia naturalis* (1589) gained popular attention in its translation as *Natural Magic.*

Della Rovere. Italian family prominent during the Renaissance.

Francesco della Rovere (1414-1484) became Pope Sixtus IV in 1471. The famous Sistine Chapel of the Vatican bears his name.

Giuliano della Rovere, nephew of Francesco, became Pope Julius II in 1503, at the age of 60; still he led the papal forces in the field. Before his death in 1513, he had founded the Vatican Museum, begun the construction of St. Peter's, and employed Raphael, Bramante, and Michelangelo in various projects. In 1506, the Della Rovere became dukes of Urbino when Guidobaldo of Montefeltro died leaving no heir.

Deloney, Thomas (1543?-?1600). English prose writer, a silk-weaver and author of numerous BROADSIDE BALLADS. He is best known for his vivid tales of life among the craftsmen and laborers of London. The most famous of these is THE GENTLE CRAFT (1597).

Delos. A small island in the Cyclades where Apollo and Artemis were born. Having been the only place to accept Leto when she was ready to give birth to these gods, it was honored by becoming sacred to Apollo. This story is told in the *Homeric Hymn to Delian Apollo.* Delos was said to have been a floating island, which Poseidon finally made fast to the bottom of the sea.

Delphic oracle. An ancient oracle at Delphi, on the southern slope of Mount Parnassus. It was of extremely ancient origin, having originally belonged to a chthonic deity. Aeschylus' claim in the *Eumenides* that it belonged successively to Ge, Themis, and Phoebe—two of whom, at least, were earth goddesses —may not be far from wrong. In later times, the oracle was taken over by Apollo, who, according to the *Homeric Hymn to Pythian Apollo,* killed the python, a sacred snake associated with the oracle. The oracular utterances were made by the Pythia, a priestess who sat on a tripod over a cleft in the rock. Her incomprehensible mouthings were interpreted by a priest.

Although there were many oracles in the Greek world, the Delphic oracle was regarded as a final authority in religious matters. A great many of the most famous Greek myths involve the working out of oracles that issued from Delphi.

Associated with the shrine was the *omphalos,* a sacred stone that was regarded as the navel of the world, though various other centers made the same claim. Some authorities believe that the *omphalos* was the phallic cap of a tomb, possibly that of the python, since many oracles were associated with the tombs of heroes. In the first part of the *Eumenides,* Orestes clings to the *omphalos* in seeking sanctuary from the Erinyes or Furies.

Delphine (1802). Epistolary romantic novel by Mme de STAËL. It is the story of unfulfilled love between Delphine and Léonice (a character inspired by Benjamin CONSTANT DE REBECQUE). In the end he is shot as a traitor and she poisons herself. The book is one of the first feminine autobiographies in French literature. See Mme de VERNON.

Deluge, The. The second in a trilogy of historical novels by Henryk SIENKIEWICZ. See WITH FIRE AND SWORD.

De Marchi, Emilio (1851-1901). Italian novelist. Like Manzoni, he believed that the novel could be used legitimately as a guide to moral living. He was also influenced by the SCAPIGLIATURA and by the prose style of Verga and Capuana. His three best-known novels—*Demetrio Pianelli* (1889), *Arabella* (1892), and *Giacomo L'Idealista* (1897)—reflect his interest in contemporary social and moral problems. His protagonists are defeated by evil forces operating in society, yet their defeat awakens in them an attitude of resignation and purposeful self-sacrifice that seem to the writer the final victory of the human spirit. Demetrio Pianelli, for example, is an unassuming government clerk who realizes a capacity for love and self-sacrifice through a succession of tragic events.

An interesting example of De Marchi's narrative skill is *Il Cappello del Prete* (1888), which describes the hallucinating experiences of a priest's murderer. The scene is Naples, and the action centers on the Neapolitans' proverbial passion for the national lottery, a theme exploited by Matilda Serao in *Il Paese della Cuccagna* (1891).

Demeter. The Greek goddess of corn. Her principal myth concerned the abduction of her daughter Persephone by Hades, which took place in Sicily. When the young goddess, called also simply Kore (daughter), plucked a certain flower, the earth opened and Hades snatched her away to the underworld in his chariot. Demeter, bearing torches, sought her all over the world until Helios told her what had happened. She left Olympus in anger that the gods had permitted the abduction, and the earth grew desolate. Appearing as an old woman in the village of Eleusis, she was hospitably received by King Celeus and his wife Metaneira. She tended their son Demophoon, and would have immortalized him in the fire had not Metaneira seen her doing so and screamed. The goddess thereupon revealed her true identity and commanded that her rites should be celebrated at Eleusis.

Disturbed at the blight on the earth, Zeus approached Hades to bring about a reconciliation. Because Persephone had eaten pomegranate seeds in the underworld, she was not allowed to leave permanently, but it was arranged that she should spend two thirds of every year with her mother. In gratitude for Eleusinian hospitality, Demeter gave a bag of seeds to Celeus' son Triptolemus and sent him in a chariot by winged dragons throughout the world to plant corn and teach its culture. Demeter was very widely worshiped, but her most important cult center remained Eleusis, her major festival the ELEUSINIAN MYSTERIES. For other legends of Demeter see PELOPS and IASION.

Demetrius. In Shakespeare's MIDSUMMER NIGHT'S DREAM, a young man betrothed to Hermia by her father's decree. When she escapes to the forest with her lover Lysander, he pursues them and is pursued in turn by Helena, his jilted sweetheart.

De Mille, Cecil B[lount] (1881–1959). American motion-picture producer and director. De Mille began his long association with Hollywood when he went there in 1913 with Jesse L. Lasky and Samuel Goldwyn and directed *The Squaw Man,* one of the first full-length movies ever made. In 1921 he became president of Cecil B. De Mille Productions and began to produce the monumental motion-picture extravaganzas so identified with his name. Among the best-known of these are *The Ten Commandments* (1923; remake, 1956), *The King of Kings* (1927), *The Sign of the Cross* (1932), *The Plainsman* (1936), *Union Pacific* (1939), and *The Greatest Show on Earth* (1952).

Demiurge (Demiourgos). Any power or personality creating a world, real or imaginary. From the Greek for "worker of the people." The modern meaning goes back to Plato's use of the word for the inferior god who created the world.

Democracy (1880). A novel by Henry ADAMS, first published anonymously. A social and political satire based on the corruption of the second Grant administration, the book includes characters modeled on President Hayes and James G. Blaine. A charming and intelligent young widow, Madeleine Lee, moves to Washington "to touch with her own hands the massive machinery of society." She finally rejects an offer of marriage from a senator who has compromised his moral integrity for political advantage.

Democratic Vistas (1871). An essay by Walt WHITMAN. The poet, alarmed by the "hollowness of heart" in post-Civil War America, sees a decline in vigor and moral consciousness. Although the U.S. has enjoyed "unprecedented materialistic advancement," it has become increasingly superficial in social, moral, and intellectual spheres. "We live," says Whitman, "in an atmosphere of hypocrisy throughout."

Turning to the future, he envisions, in an America disburdened of foreign imitation, the rise of a group of artists. These men and women are needed, for "the work of the New World is not ended, but only fairly begun."

Democritus (Demokritos; c. 460–c. 370 B.C.). A philosopher, also called the Abderite and the Laughing Philosopher. He was born in ABDERA and traveled widely. He adopted the atomistic theory of LEUCIPPUS, holding that the universe is composed of atoms that move about in space and form themselves into bodies. Atoms are eternal, while bodies perish; the soul is a form of fire, which animates the human body. Democritus also held that pleasure, along with self-control, was the goal of life. His cheerful disposition won him the epithet of the Laughing Philosopher. He is supposed to have put out his eyes in order that he might think without outside disturbances.

Demodocus (Demodokos). A minstrel. According to Homer (ODYSSEY viii), he sang the amours of Ares and Aphrodite in the court of Alcinous while Odysseus was a guest there.

Demogorgon. A terrible deity, whose very name was capable of producing the most horrible effects. He is first mentioned by the 4th-century Christian writer, Lactantius, who, in so doing, is believed to have broken the spell of a mystery, for *Demogorgon* is supposed to be identical with the infernal Power of the ancients, the very mention of whose name brought death and disaster, to whom reference is made by Lucan and others. Hence Milton speaks of "the dreaded name of Demogorgon" in *Paradise Lost.* According to Ariosto, Demogorgon was a king of the elves and fays who lived on the Himalayas, and once in five years summoned all his subjects before him to give an account of their stewardship. Spenser, in *The Faerie Queene,* says that he dwells in the deep abyss with the three fatal sisters. Shelley so calls eternity in *Prometheus Unbound.*

De Morgan, William (1839–1917). English novelist. A retired manufacturer, De Morgan achieved immediate success at the age of 67 with his somewhat old-fashioned, Dickensian first novel, *Joseph Vance* (1906). *Alice-for-Short* (1907) and other successful novels followed.

Demosthenes (384–322 B.C.). The most famous of Greek orators. Opposed to the encroachment of Philip II of Macedon, Demosthenes delivered the first *Philippic* in 351 B.C. Five years later he was sent as an ambassador, with nine others, to conclude a peace with Philip. Dissatisfied with the agreement, Demosthenes refused to honor its terms. When Philip broke the treaty shortly afterward, the Greek patriotic party chose Demosthenes as its leader. After Philip's assassination in 336 B.C., Demosthenes was one of the leaders of the anti-Macedon uprising. Alexander demanded his arrest, but he was spared. When Harpalus, the Macedonian treasurer, fled to Athens, the 700 talents he had stolen from Alexander were placed in a vault to be returned; later, Demosthenes was accused of having accepted part of the money as a bribe. He was forced into exile, though the patriotic party recalled him at the death of Alexander. In 322 B.C. the joint rulers of Macedon, Antipater, and Craterus captured Athens, and Demosthenes took poison to escape arrest. His major orations are the three *Philippics* (351, 344, 341 B.C.), three *Olynthiacs* (349, 349 B.C.), *On the Peace* (346 B.C.), *On the Embassy* (344 B.C.), *On the Affairs of the Chersonese* (341 B.C.), and *On the Crown* (330 B.C.). Demosthenes is traditionally supposed to have overcome speech defects by speaking over the roar of the sea with pebbles in his mouth. He rigorously applied himself to the development of a fine style, combining great rhetorical skill with simplicity and directness of language. His arguments were designed to appeal to a popular audience. Sixty-one speeches have come down to us under his name, although some are not considered genuine. He influenced, among others, Cicero, Quintilian, Burke, Fox, and Pitt.

demotic writing. An Egyptian hieroglyphic script, developed in the 5th century B.C. A simplified form of *hieratic* writing, running from left to right in horizontal lines, it was first used mainly for social and business purposes, but later for religious and literary purposes as well; it continued to be employed by the priests of Isis as late as A D. 452.

Dendin or **Dandin, Perrin** (*Fr.,* "Ninny"). In Rabelais' GARGANTUA AND PANTAGRUEL, an old man whom Judge BRIDLEGOOSE cites for the extraordinary number of disputes he settles, though he is not a judge by profession. When his son, Tenot Dendin, attempts to carry on his practice, he fails to settle a single quarrel because, as his father explains, he always intervenes at the very beginning of the dispute when the litigants are still averse to compromise. Perrin's secret is to wait until both parties are so tired of their dispute that they will welcome any judgment that will bring an end to their wrangling.

Racine gave the name "Dandin" to a character with a mania for judging in his comedy *Les Plaideurs* (1668). In La Fontaine's *Fables* (1678–1679), "Perrin Dandin" settles the dispute between two pilgrims over an oyster by eating it himself.

Denham, Sir John (1615–1669). Irish-born English poet. He was an architect by profession and was for a time surveyor general of works, with the young Christopher Wren as his assistant. Denham was famous in his own day for *The Sophy* (1642), a melodramatic tragedy, and *Cooper's Hill* (1642), a didactic poem. The latter was praised by Dryden, and imitated by Pope in *Windsor Forest* (1713). See George WITHER.

Denikin, Anton Ivanovich (1872–1947). Russian general. In 1917, he supported Kornilov's attempt to overthrow the Bolshevik regime. After Kornilov's death, during the civil war, he succeeded him as supreme commander of the White armies, and led the anti-Bolshevik forces in southern Russia until General Wrangel took over the command in 1920. Denikin then fled to Constantinople and, in 1926, went to live in France.

Dennis, Nigel (1912–   ). English novelist. He is the author of *Cards of Identity* (1955), a fantastic, nightmarish satire about modern man's loss of his sense of identity.

dénouement (*Fr.,* "the untying"). In drama and fiction, the final unwinding of the tangled elements of the plot which ends the suspense; it follows the climax. The word is also applied to the final solution of complicated sets of actions in life.

Denry the Audacious. See CARD, THE.

Deor's Lament or **The Complaint of Deor** (9th century?). Old English poem of 42 lines in ALLITERATIVE VERSE. The poet describes the misfortunes of Germanic heroes, which overshadow his own sad luck in being ousted by his lord in favor of another minstrel; there are seven unequal stanzas with the recurring refrain that as "that has passed, this will too."

de profundis (*Lat.* "out of the deep;" hence, an extremely bitter cry of wretchedness). Ps. 130 is so called from the first two words in the Latin version. It forms part of the Roman Catholic burial service. Oscar Wilde's letter to Lord Alfred Douglas, a personal essay of confession and reminiscence written in prison bore the title *De Profundis* (1905).

De Quincey, Thomas (1785–1859). English essayist and critic. He is famous for CONFESSIONS OF AN ENGLISH OPIUM-EATER, a fascinating memoir distinguished by great imaginative power and prose that

is splendid and elaborate without stiffness. These qualities are also present in his personal and fugitive essays such as *Suspiria de Profundis* (1845), *The English Mail Coach* (1849), and *Murder Considered as One of the Fine Arts* (1827, 1839). One of the major critics of the romantic movement, he had clear, judicious taste and remarkable insight, and was learned and original though sometimes prolix and vague. He was closely associated with Wordsworth and Coleridge, residing for a time in the Lake Country, and was also acquainted with Lamb, Hazlitt, Hood, and other literary figures. Much of his work appeared in such journals as *Blackwood's Magazine* and was collected by himself in the 24-volume *Writings* (1851–1859).

Derain, André (1880–1954). French painter. He was an original member of the FAUVES and was closely associated with Matisse and Vlaminck. He exhibited at the first Fauve show in 1905 at Paris. By 1913 he began to evolve a more distinctive style in his work, influenced by primitive sculpture, cubism, and the works of van Gogh, Gauguin, and Seurat.

De Rerum Natura. See LUCRETIUS.

Derleth, August [William] (1909–   ). American novelist. He is best known for his *Sac Prairie Saga,* a group of regional novels depicting life in a Wisconsin community (modeled on Sauk City) from 1830 to the present; included in the series are *Still Is the Summer Night* (1937), *Wind Over Wisconsin* (1938), and *Restless Is the River* (1939). His *Wisconsin Saga* includes *Bright Journey* (1940) and *The Hills Stand Watch* (1960). He is also the author of *Still Small Voice* (1940), a biography of Zona Gale; *Selected Poems* (1944); *Sac Prairie People* (1948) and *Wisconsin Earth* (1948), collections of short stories; and several volumes of detective and science fiction.

De Roberto, Federico (1866–1927). Italian novelist. He is known as a leading exponent of the precisely realistic fiction produced by the *verismo* literary movement (see Luigi CAPUANA). A member of the Milanese circle of naturalistic writers among whom were G. VERGA and G. ROVETTA, De Roberto gave an objective, scholarly description of contemporary Italian society in his two major historical novels: *The Viceroys* (*I Vicerè;* 1894) and *L'imperio* (1929). *The Viceroys* is a lengthy account of the political fortunes of an aristocratic Sicilian family, the Uzedas of Francalanza, in the period between the collapse of the Bourbon dynasty and the proclamation of Italian unity (1859–1861). De Roberto's interest centers on a detailed study of character types, and his purpose is to show the determining influence of inherited family traits in the Uzedas' reaction to a critical moment in history.

L'imperio continues the study of the Uzeda family describing the fortunes of the youngest member, Count Consalvo, when he becomes a deputy to the new Italian parliament.

De Roberto began his writing career as a literary and art critic for the Milanese newspaper *Corriere della Sera.* A devoted friend of Verga at a time when the author of *The Malavoglias* was unfavorably received by the critics, De Roberto wrote his biography (which was never completed).

His minor novels are *Ermanno Raeli* (1889), *L'Illusione* (1891), *La Sorte* (1891), and *Spasimo* (1897).

Derzhavin, Gavril Romanovich (1743–1816). Russian poet. Though his verse is less polished than that of such poets as Pushkin and Tyutchev, Derzhavin's work can bear comparison with any Russian poetry for power and vividness. His best-known works are *Bog* (*Ode to God,* 1784), *Na smert' knyazya Meshcherskogo* (*On the Death of Prince Meshcherski,* 1779), and *Felitza* (*Felitsa,* 1782). This last is an ode to Catherine the Great, whom Derzhavin served as court poet and administrator.

Desai, Anita (1937–). Indian novelist writing in English. Born of Indian-German parentage, she was educated in Delhi. Her novel, *Cry the Peacock* (1963), reveals fine craftsmanship and subtle, delicate feeling.

De Sanctis, Francesco (1817–1883). Italian literary critic. Minister of education in the first Italian cabinet (1861) and professor of comparative literature at the University of Naples (1871–1877), he is noted as the founder of modern literary criticism in Italy. Influenced by Hegel, he formulated an aesthetic theory which maintains that an artist's formal expression is intrinsically linked to his idea-content; this theory, in turn, influenced Benedetto Croce. De Sanctis wrote critical essays such as *Saggi Critici* (1865) and *Nuovi Saggi Critici* (1872), and a celebrated *Storia della Letteratura Italiana* (1870–1871).

Descartes, René (1596–1650). French mathematician and philosopher. Father of the modern scientific method, he is also known as the originator of analytic geometry and progenitor of modern physiological psychology. Seeking absolute certainty in the application of "methodical doubt" to all received opinions, Descartes challenged the metaphysical view of the universe in his principal works, *Discours de la Méthode* (*Discourse on Method,* 1639) and *Principia philosophiae* (*Principles of Philosophy,* 1644), in which he divided the universe into mutually exclusive but interacting spirit and matter, the spirit subject to reason and the matter subject to mechanical laws. The resulting philosophy is called *Cartesianism* after its creator. Descartes formulated the principle Cogito, ergo sum (I think, therefore I am) and held it to be a model of certainty. See Nicolas Malebranche.

descent to the underworld. The motif of numerous stories in the mythology and folk lore of all peoples. The descent is usually made to rescue someone either abducted or rightfully dead, to find the answer to a question or discover a secret from the ruler of the underworld, or to seize some treasure. To partake of the food of the dead (or of fairyland in later folk lore) prevents the visitor from ever returning. Among the most famous descent stories are the Greek myths of Orpheus and Eurydice, Demeter and Persephone, and Heracles' bringing of Cerberus up from Hades and his rescue of Alcestis. Also well known are the Babylonian story of Ishtar's descent to rescue Tammuz, the Norse myth of Hermod's journey to Hel to bring back Balder. There are similar tales in Hindu, Chinese, and Japanese writings, and among the Ainus, Melanesians, North American Indians, and Eskimos. Descents to Hell are common also in early Christian literature.

Deschamps, Eustache (c. 1346–c. 1406). French poet and diplomat. He wrote a great number of bitterly satirical *ballades* and *rondeaux* about the political situation in France and the wars with England, and the first known critical treatise on the writing of poetry in French. His long, unfinished poem *Miroir de mariage* is a satire against women, including the prototype of the mother-in-law of French farce.

Desdemona. The innocent, artless, and lovely heroine of Shakespeare's Othello. She is the daughter of Brabantio.

De Senectute (44 b.c.). An essay on old age by Cicero, written in the form of a dialogue. Its main speaker, Cato the Elder, discourses to his younger friends on the advantages of a serene old age. From his name, it is often called the *Cato Major.*

Deserted Village, The (1770). A poem by Oliver Goldsmith, portraying the rural depopulation of the latter half of the eighteenth century. He attributes it to the increase in luxury, foreign trade, the enclosure of open pastures by absentee landowners, and the cancerous growth of London. The poem is dedicated to Sir Joshua Reynolds. See Auburn.

De Sica, Vittorio (1902–). Italian motion-picture director and actor. He made his screen debut in *What Rascals Men Are* (1932); he directed his first motion-picture, *Red Roses,* in 1939. He is best known for his highly distinguished films: *Shoe Shine* (1946) and *The Bicycle Thief* (1949).

Desire Under the Elms (1924). A tragedy by Eugene O'Neill. Set in New England, it deals with Ephraim Cabot and his new young wife, Abbie. Abbie seduces Eben, the youngest son of Ephraim, hoping to bear a son she can claim is Ephraim's. When it appears to Eben that Abbie has used him only for her own ends, he threatens to expose her infidelity; to prove her love for him she smothers the child. The play exemplifies O'Neill's interest in Freudian psychology and in the conflict between a repressive Calvinism and Dionysian surrender.

Desmarets de Saint-Sorlin, Jean (1596–1676). French poet, novelist, and playwright. An original member of the Académie française and holder of an administrative post by virtue of his intimacy with Richelieu, Desmarets opposed the Jansenists of Port-Royal in religious controversies and vehemently objected to Boileau's condemnation of national and Christian themes as subjects for epics, deriving his own epics *Clovis ou la France Chrestienne* (*Clovis, or Christian France,* 1657) and Esther (1673) from French history and the Bible respectively. His novel *Ariane* (1632) evokes the Rome of Nero, and his comedy *Les Visionnaires* (*The Visionaries,* 1637) ridicules the extravagances of certain fashionable ladies of his day, with cutting reference to Madame de Rambouillet. The play served Molière as model for *Les Femmes Savantes.*

Desmoulins, Camille (1760–1794). French journalist, pamphleteer, and collaborator with Mirabeau during the French Revolution. He was called *Procureur de la lanterne* (Fr., "agent of the lantern") for his anti-aristocratic pamphlet *Le Discours de la lanterne aux Parisiens.* As deputy to the Convention (1792), he had a small rôle to play, and two years later he was executed with Danton by Robespierre.

Desnos, Robert (1900–1945). French poet. At first associated with surrealism, he later turned to simple lyrics, like the love song *Poème à la mystérieuse* (1926) and other poems of love and liberty in *Corps et Biens* (1930) and *Fortunes* (1942). His

30 *Chante-fables pour les enfants sages* (1944) are animal fantasies in a singsong rhythm.

de Soto, Hernando or **Fernando** (1500?–1542). Spanish explorer. Having served with Pizarro in Peru, de Soto won permission from Charles V to conquer Florida, where he landed in 1539 with some 600 men. For the next three years he wandered through present Georgia, the Carolinas, Alabama, Mississippi, Arkansas, and Louisiana; though he found no gold, he is credited with discovering the Mississippi River in 1541. He died on the banks of the Mississippi, and his body was sunk in the river by his men.

Despair. See FAERIE QUEENE, THE.

Desportes, Philippe (1546–1606). Foremost French poet at the court of Henry III and successor to the Pléiade poets. Solely concerned with pleasing his protectors, he confined himself to writing love poetry so impersonal as to be applicable to any occasion (*Premières Oeuvres* [1573] and *Dernières Amours* [1583]) and to translating the *Psalms* (1591) to flatter the piety of Henry III. He cultivated the modish Petrarchan theme of idealized love and imitated the elaborate metaphors dear to the Italian poets. Clarity, suppleness, and harmony still lend charm to his poetry, otherwise lacking in substance.

Dessalines, Jean Jacques (1758–1806). Negro revolutionary leader and emperor of Haiti. As leader of the insurgent slaves, Dessalines fought alongside of Toussaint L'Ouverture and aided by the English, he succeeded in driving out the French in 1803. In 1804, Dessalines established the republic of Haiti, and the following year, under the title Jacques I, he became the country's emperor (1805–1806). His cruel reign led rapidly to his assassination by Henri CHRISTOPHE and Pétion.

Destouches, Louis Ferdinand. See Louis Ferdinand CÉLINE.

Destouches, Philippe. Pen name of **Philippe Néricault** (1680–1754). French dramatist. Famous for *Le Philosophe marié* (1727), *Le Glorieux* (1732) and other sentimental comedies, Destouches sought to make comedy morally edifying. His plays are early forerunners of the COMÉDIE LARMOYANTE.

Destruction of Sennacherib, The (1815). A well-known poem by Lord BYRON. It vividly portrays the annihilating plague that struck down the invading army of the Assyrian king Sennacherib in Palestine during the seventh century B.C.

Deucalion's Flood. The Deluge of Greek legend. Deucalion (Deukalion) was son of Prometheus and Clymene, and was king of Phthia, in Thessaly. When Zeus sent the deluge, Deucalion built a ship, and he and his wife, Pyrrha, were the only mortals saved. The ship at last rested on Mount Parnassus, and Deucalion was told by the oracle of Themis that to restore the human race he must cast the bones of his mother behind him. The two cast the stones of their mother Earth as directed. Those thrown by Deucalion became men, those thrown by his wife became women.

Bayard Taylor has a lyrical drama entitled *Prince Deukalion* (1878), in which he takes Deukalion and Pyrrha over all the earth and through all ages of history.

deus ex machina. A theatrical device used in Greek tragedy. In several plays of Euripides, a god appears at the last moment to provide the solution to the tangled problems of the main characters. The god is let down from the sky on a sort of crane. The phrase has come to refer to a playwright's use of external means to solve the problems of his characters—a practice generally frowned upon.

Deuteronomy. A book of the Old Testament, the last book of the Pentateuch. It reiterates the Mosaic law and, ending with the death of Moses, contains the final episodes in his life. It was probably written during the reign of Manasseh (c. 698–643 B.C.). Either suppressed or forgotten for a generation, the book was discovered in 621 B.C. hidden in the temple. It has been expanded by later writers. The original parts (most of chaps. 5–26 and 28) are thought to be the first book ever canonized as divine law.

Deutsch, Babette (1895–   ). American poet and critic. Her poems, which often have social implications, have been collected in many volumes, from *Banners* (1919) and *Honey out of the Rock* (1925) to *Animal, Vegetable, Mineral* (1954) and *Coming of Age: New and Selected Poems* (1959). *Potable Gold* (1929) and *This Modern Poetry* (1935), enlarged as *Poetry in Our Time* (1952, 1956, 1962), are critical works. Among her other books is one on Whitman (1941) and *Poetry Handbook* (1957; rev., 1961). Miss Deutsch is also a translator of German and Russian verse, usually in collaboration with her husband, Avrahm Yarmolinsky.

Deval, Jacques (1894–   ). French playwright of popular comedies. Best known for *Tovaritch* (1934), about a group of Czarist emigrés in France, Deval also wrote the play *Mademoiselle* (1932).

de Valera, Eamon (1882–   ). Irish statesman. De Valera was born in New York City of a Spanish father and an Irish mother. President of the Irish home rule party Sinn Fein from 1917 to 1926, he became the leading statesman of the Irish Free State, as prime minister and later as president.

de Vere, Aubrey Thomas (1814–1902). Anglo-Irish poet, essayist. A friend of Cardinal Newman, de Vere was a convert to Catholicism; his poetry found its inspiration in religion and in the myths and legends of Ireland, a country that he also defended in such prose works as *English Misrule and Irish Misdeeds* (1848). Three-volume editions of his poetry (*Poetical Works*) and criticism (*Critical Essays*) were published between 1884 and 1889. His *Recollections* (1897)—he was a friend of Tennyson, Browning, Carlyle—are interesting.

devil. In Jewish and Christian theology, an apostate spirit. The name is also given to the chief of devils, known as *the Devil*, who is the supreme spirit of evil, the adversary of God, the enemy and tempter of man, and the ruler of Hell. In the Bible and Apocrypha the Devil or devils are variously referred to as SATAN, ASMODEUS, BEELZEBUB, SAMAEL, and, according to the Church Fathers, as LUCIFER. Devils' names in literature and popular usage include MEPHISTOPHELES, Auld Nick, AULD HORNIE, Auld Ane, Clootie, and Hangie.

The Devil and devils are frequently represented with a cloven foot, since rabbinical writers refer to them as *seirizzim* (goats). As the goat is the prototype of uncleanliness, the prince of unclean spirits is aptly represented under this emblem.

Devil and Daniel Webster, The (1937). A short story by Stephen Vincent BENÉT. First published in the *Saturday Evening Post,* it was adapted as an opera (1938) with music by Douglas Moore, and later was made into a play. In it, a New England farmer, Jabez Stone, sells his soul to the Devil for material prosperity, but is saved from paying his debt by the oratorical eloquence of Daniel Webster before a demonic jury.

Devil and Tom Walker, The (1824). A story by Washington IRVING. It first appeared in his collection, TALES OF A TRAVELLER. The story concerns the devil's attempt to hold Tom to his bargain. Despite Tom's wiles, the devil succeeds.

Devils, The. See POSSESSED, THE.

Devil's Advocate. The *advocatus diaboli,* a man appointed to attest the claims of a candidate for canonization before a papal court. He advances all arguments he can against the candidate, who is defended by the *advocatus dei* (God's advocate), who says all he can in support of the proposed canonization. By extension, the term is used of a destructive critic, or one who deliberately searches for flaws in order to bring out the whole truth.

Devil's Disciple, The (1897). A play by George Bernard SHAW. It is set in America during the Revolution. Dick Dudgeon, a reprobate, allows himself, to his own surprise, to be arrested by the English and sentenced to death in place of Parson Anderson. The parson, too, finds a new side to his personality, when he leads an armed band to fight the British and rescue Dick. Shaw's thesis is that convention and circumstance fix a person's life, but under crisis people make startling discoveries about themselves. An exciting and brilliant play, *The Devil's Disciple* makes particular fun of the military.

Devil's General, The (Des Teufels General; 1946). A play by Carl ZUCKMAYER. It depicts the inner struggle of a Nazi *Luftwaffe* general who, though in principle opposed to Nazism, manages to rationalize his position as a servant of the regime. But when he is confronted by a saboteur, a man true to his principles, who is doing his best to hamper the German war effort, the general recognizes the untenability of his own compromise and deliberately flies off to his death in a sabotaged plane.

De Vinne, Theodore Low (1828–1914). American master printer and historian. He founded and managed Theo. L. De Vinne & Co., later the De Vinne Press, and became widely known for the excellence of his printing and engravings. He was the founder and sixth president of the Grolier Club (1884), a society of bibliophiles in New York City. Among his books are *The Invention of Printing* (1876), and *The Practice of Typography* (4 v., 1900–1904).

Devoción de la cruz, La. See Pedro CALDERÓN DE LA BARCA.

Devotions upon Emergent Occasions (1624). A series of meditations on the "Variable, and therefore miserable condition of Man" by John DONNE. The work was ostensibly written during a long, grave illness. Its style is highly metaphorical and complex. It contains the famous passage from which Ernest Hemingway drew the title of *For Whom the Bell Tolls* (1940):

No man is an Iland, intire of it selfe; every man is a peece of the Continent, a part of the maine; if a Clod bee washed away by the Sea, Europe is the lesse, as well as if a Promontorie were . . . ; any mans death diminishes me, because I am involved in Mankinde; And therefore never send to know for whom the bell tolls; It tolls for thee.

De Voto, Bernard [Augustine] (1897–1955). American historian and critic. De Voto first gained public attention with his *Mark Twain in America* (1932), a rebuttal to Van Wyck Brooks's *Ordeal of Mark Twain* (1920). He also taught at Harvard, filled "The Easy Chair" of *Harper's* from 1935 to 1955, and wrote several novels, including *The Crooked Mile* (1924) and *Mountain Time* (1947). The work that he himself rightly regarded as his most important was his historical writing, principally *The Year of Decision: 1846* (1943); *Across the Wide Missouri* (1947), which won a Pulitzer Prize; and *The Course of Empire* (1952).

Devushkin, Makar Alekseyevich. The hero of Feodor Dostoevski's short novel, POOR FOLK. Devushkin is a timid clerk, desperately in love with Varvara Alekseyevna Dobroselova, and acutely conscious of the impossibility of his love because of his greater age and extreme poverty. His condition is sharply brought home to him when he reads Nikolai Gogol's short story, *The Overcoat,* which portrays a downtrodden clerk too much like Devushkin himself. He complains about writers dealing with such subjects in one of his letters to Varvara.

Dewey, George (1837–1917). American naval officer. As commander of the Asiatic Squadron during the Spanish-American War, Dewey moved his fleet into Manila Bay and in a seven-hour battle destroyed the Spanish naval force in the Far East. He then blockaded Manila Bay, enabling General Wesley Merritt to land his troops and effect the conquest of the Philippines.

Dewey, John (1859–1952). American teacher, philosopher, and educational reformer. A believer in William James's PRAGMATISM, Dewey employed the principles of that philosophy in his progressive movement in education. He advocated "learning by doing," rejecting traditional methods of teaching by rote. Although his principles have been adopted by many, not all of Dewey's disciples are restrained by his common sense. Among his many books are *The School and Society* (1900; rev. 1908, 1932), *Interest and Effort in Education* (1913), *Democracy and Education* (1916), *The Quest for Certainty* (1929), *Art as Experience* (1934), and *The Problems of Man* (1946).

Dewey, Melvil (1851–1931). American librarian. Dewey invented his decimal system of library classification while still a student librarian at Amherst College (1874–1876). Referred to as the DEWEY DECIMAL SYSTEM, it is widely used in the U.S. Dewey later became the librarian of Columbia University, and there founded the first school of library science (1887). He was director of the New York State Library from 1889 to 1906.

Dewey decimal system. A system of book classification for library cataloguing. It was devised by Melvil DEWEY in 1876. The system divides books into 10 main groups, represented by figures, as in the following example:

800–899 Literature (novels, plays, poetry, criticism). Each of the main classes is then further subdivided. When the distinctions between books become fine, decimals are used; this gave the system its name. Unusually large libraries have abandoned the Dewey system for that used by the Library of Congress, but approximately 85% retain it.

Dexter, Timothy (1747–1806). American merchant and eccentric. Becoming enormously wealthy as the result of a series of transactions that should logically have proved disastrous, he named himself "Lord Timothy Dexter" and built a great mansion in Newburyport, Mass. He wrote an admiring and amusing account of his own exploits in *A Pickle for the Knowing Ones, or Plain Truths in a Homespun Dress* (1802). The book had no punctuation, but Dexter satisfied his critics by including a page full of various punctuation marks in a second edition, inviting his readers to "peper and solt it as they plese." John P. Marquand wrote a biography, *Lord Timothy Dexter*, in 1925, which he revised in 1960 as *Timothy Dexter Revisited*.

Dey, Frederick Van Rensselaer. See Nick CARTER.

dharma (*Sans.*, "that which binds"). An ethical code, way of life, social conscience, truth, the natural order. To a Hindu, *sva-dharma* (*sva,* self) would mean one's right to perform the duties dictated by one's nature and conscience. In Buddhism *dharma* is the law of the Buddha.

Dhôtel, André (1900–   ). French novelist. In such tales as *Faraway* (*Le Pays où l'on n'arrive jamais*, 1955), Dhôtel creates a poetic atmosphere of magic and suspense.

Diablo cojuelo, El. See Luis VÉLEZ DE GUEVARA.

Diafoirus. The name of 2 quack doctors, father and son, in Molière's comedy LE MALADE IMAGINAIRE. As their name suggests, they are obsessed with the liver.

Diaghilev, Sergei Pavlovitch (1872–1919). Art critic, impresario, and founder (1909) and director of the Russian Ballet in Paris. He encouraged new ideas and techniques, first as an art critic, later in his ballets, which provided an audience for experiments in the various arts of music, painting, costume design, and dance. As a result, he attracted the talents of such composers as Claude Debussy, Maurice Ravel, Igor Stravinsky, and the members of Les Six; such artists as Pablo Picasso, Leon Bakst,

The punctuation from Dexter's *A Pickle*, etc.

[Note to Dexter's Second Edition.]

founder mister printer the Nowing ónes complane of my book the fust edition had no stops I put in A Nuf here and thay may peper and solt it as they plese

,,
,,
::
::
...............!!!!!!!!!!!!!!!!!!!...............
...............!!!!!!!!!!!!!...............
...............!!!!!!...............
...............!...............
,,
,,,,,,,,,,,, mmmmmmmmmmmmmmmmmm ....

Henri Matisse, and Georges Braque; such dancers and choreographers as M. M. Fokine, Anna Pavlova, Vaslav Nijinsky, and Léonide Massine. Many studies of Diaghilev and his ballet have been written.

Dial, The. A magazine founded in New England in 1840. The organ of the Transcendentalist movement, its founders were Theodore PARKER, Bronson ALCOTT, Orestes BROWNSON, Margaret FULLER, and Ralph Waldo EMERSON. Miss Fuller served as editor from 1840 to 1842, and Emerson, with Thoreau's help, took over until 1844, when the magazine ceased publication. During its short history, it wielded a great deal of influence in literary, philosophic, and religious thought. In addition to publishing the work of its founders, *The Dial* published the poetry of Jones Very and William Ellery Channing.

Since 1844, three other magazines have taken the same name. Moncure Conway founded the second *Dial* in 1860, in Cincinnati. In 1880, a conservative group founded the third *Dial* in Chicago. When it moved to New York in 1918, it became the outstanding literary review of its time. Until 1920, with the aid of Conrad AIKEN, Randolph BOURNE, and Van Wyck BROOKS, it published articles by leading radical thinkers including John Dewey and Thorstein Veblen. After 1920, it was devoted to the encouragement of *avant-garde* authors. Marianne MOORE became editor in 1926. The magazine ceased publication three years later.

The present *Dial,* a literary quarterly, was founded in 1959. It is edited by James Silberman.

Dialogues des morts. See Bernard le Bovier de FONTENELLE.

Dialogues of the Dead. See Bernard le Bovier de FONTENELLE.

Diamond. See FAERIE QUEENE, THE.

diamond jousts. Jousts instituted by King Arthur, "who by that name had named them, since a diamond was the prize." The story, as embroidered by Tennyson in his *Launcelot and Elaine* from Malory, is that Arthur found nine diamonds from the crown of a slain knight and offered them as the prize of nine jousts in successive years. Launcelot had won them all, but when he laid them before the queen, Guinevere, in a fit of jealousy—the result of believing false rumors about Launcelot and Elaine—flung them into the river a moment before the corpse of Elaine passed in the barge.

Diamond Necklace Affair. A famous scandal in French history (1783–1785). The jewelers Böhmer and Bassenge had originally made the necklace, containing 500 diamonds, for Mme Du Barry; but, after the death of Louis XV, they were unable to dispose of it. To recoup their investment, they repeatedly but unsuccessfully pressed MARIE ANTOINETTE to buy it. The scheming, so-called Comtesse, Jeanne de La Motte, a high-class courtesan, knowing that Cardinal de Rohan, a rich, profligate churchman, wished to ingratiate himself with the queen—partly because he fatuously believed he could become her lover, and partly to regain royal favor—fraudulently persuaded him that Marie Antoinette secretly wished to buy the necklace, convincing him that the queen had chosen him to negotiate with the jewelers on her behalf. He agreed to act as intermediary and to deliver the necklace to Mme de La Motte who, in turn, would deliver it to Marie Antoinette. To lend credibility to her ruse, Mme de La Motte arranged for a young modiste and woman of the streets to impersonate the queen at a short garden meeting with Rohan; she also forged several letters which fanned the cardinal's infatuation and confirmed his role as go-between. He made a down payment on the necklace and delivered it to Mme de La Motte who, with her young accomplice and lover Rétaux de Villette, took it apart, sold the individual diamonds in England and Paris, and kept the money herself. Böhmer tried to collect the balance from the Queen, insisting that she had authorized Rohan to purchase it. The Queen, indignant at being accused of dishonesty, reported the affair to her husband, Louis XVI, who caused a sensation by having the cardinal arrested publicly. At the ensuing trial, Rohan was exonerated, but exiled to the country by the king, who still believed him guilty; Marie Antoinette was cleared of any duplicity; Mme de La Motte was publicly branded, whipped, and sentenced to life imprisonment. She later escaped to England where she wrote her memoirs, accusing the queen.

Diana. An ancient Italian and Roman divinity, later identified with the Olympian goddess ARTEMIS.

Diane de Poitiers (1499–1566). Mistress of Henry II of France. She wielded immense power over Henry, who was 10 years her junior, until his death in 1559. She spent her last years at her château at Anet, which had been designed for her by Philibert Delorme, a celebrated architect.

Dianora. See GARDEN IN JANUARY, A.

Diary of a Country Priest, The (Journal d'un curé de campagne; 1936). A novel by Georges BERNANOS. It describes the struggles of a young priest with his diseased body and his ineffective parish projects. He is uncertain about whether his intervention in the affairs of the Count's family is true service to God.

Diary of Anne Frank. See Anne FRANK.

Diary of a Provincial Lady (1930). A novel, in diary form, by E. M. DELAFIELD. A phlegmatic husband, disconcerting children, temperamental servants, and dreadful neighbors are the problems of ordinary upper-middle-class domestic life of the period.

Diary of a Scoundrel, The (Na vsyakogo mudretza dovolno prostoty; 1868). A comedy by Aleksandr OSTROVSKI. A clever rogue, Glumov takes advantage of the foibles of society to advance himself. He is discredited by the discovery of his diary, in which he ridicules the pretensions and stupidity of his associates, but he brazenly confronts the discoverers and triumphs.

Diary of a Writer, A (Dnevnik pisatelya; 1873, 1876–1877, 1880–1881). A series of collected articles and short sketches published in the form of a journal by Feodor DOSTOEVSKI. He began the project as a section in Grazhdanin (The Citizen), a weekly newspaper he edited in 1873–1874. The so-called diary was concerned mostly with political and social questions, although Dostoevski did publish in it a few of his short stories, including Krotkaya (The Meek One, 1876), and Son smeshnogo cheloveka (The Dream of a Ridiculous Man, 1877). In 1880, the Diary contained Dostoevski's famous speech at the Pushkin celebration in Moscow.

Díaz, Porfirio (1830–1915). Mexican dictator. An erstwhile supporter of Juárez, Díaz seized power in 1876 and ruled Mexico for 35 years. Although his regime brought political and fiscal stability, only a handful of politicians, landowners, and foreign capitalists prospered, while the rural masses lived in virtual servitude. Díaz was ousted in 1911 and died in exile in Paris.

Díaz de Bivar, Rodrigo or **Ruy.** See CID, POEMA or CANTAR DE MIO.

Díaz del Castillo, Bernal (1496–1584). Spanish soldier and historian. Díaz was one of the 400 soldiers who took part in the Spanish conquest of Mexico; he later settled down on an estate in Guatemala. Piqued by an official history of the conquest which he felt unduly glorified the achievements of Cortez, Díaz, then an octogenarian, attempted to tell what really happened in his Historia verdadera de la conquista de la Nueva España (True History of the Conquest of New Spain, 1632), perhaps the best popular history in the Spanish language. With a plethora of minute yet vivid detail, Díaz celebrates the exploits of the common soldiers who accompanied Cortez in a style remarkable for its homely vigor. An intensely personal document in which Díaz does not minimize his own achievements and depicts Cortez as a very fallible human being, the work gives an excellent picture of the individuality and tenacity that characterized the 16th-century conquistadors.

Dichtung und Wahrheit (Poetry and Truth, 1811–1814). An autobiography by Johann Wolfgang von GOETHE. It is not so much a simple recounting of the events of his life as an attempt to explain the major strains of his inner development and set forth the essential principles on which his poetic activity was based.

Dickens, Charles (1812–1870). English novelist, the most popular and considered by many the greatest of his country. Like that of the children in many of his novels, Dickens' childhood was a difficult and unhappy one; his father, a navy clerk, was constantly in debt and was thrown into debtors' prison, and Dickens was sent to work in a blacking factory at the age of 12. Most bitter for him was his parents' failure to educate him. He reacted to this indifference by working hard, a lifelong characteristic. He became an office boy in a law firm, then a county reporter, and finally a reporter of debates in Parliament for the Morning Chronicle in 1835. His Sketches by Boz, satires on daily life, were serialized in the Old Monthly Magazine (1833–1835). Immediately asked to do another series, he wrote The Posthumous Papers of the Pickwick Club, better known simply as PICKWICK PAPERS; these were illustrated by Phiz (H. K. Browne) and made Dickens successful at 24. With OLIVER TWIST, Dickens began his indictment of the society of his place and time, a society that grossly mistreated and abused the poor, especially children, driving them to crime. While working on Twist, his wife Catherine's sister died; his deep grief and lifelong utterances of love for this sister-in-law underline his less profound relationship with his wife, from whom he was separated in 1858. They had 10 children.

NICHOLAS NICKLEBY, like Oliver Twist, was serialized in Bentley's Miscellany. The next two, BARNABY RUDGE and THE OLD CURIOSITY SHOP, were serialized in Dickens' own, new weekly periodical, Master Humphrey's Clock; they were his least successful novels. In 1842, Dickens made a trip to the U.S. where he trod on native sensibilities by urging the abolition of slavery and the establishment of an international copyright. Back in England, he published his insulting AMERICAN NOTES and MARTIN CHUZZLEWIT, a powerfully satiric novel of selfishness, hypocrisy, and financial speculation as it bloomed in insular England and the open spaces but narrow minds of the U.S. Dickens met with sensational success with the publication of A CHRISTMAS CAROL and he followed it in consecutive years with other Christmas books including A CRICKET ON THE HEARTH. His next novel, DOMBEY AND SON, was written in Switzerland.

In 1850 Dickens founded the weekly *Household Words*, and in 1859 another weekly, *All the Year Round*, both of which he kept until his death; most of his later works were published in these periodicals.

With DAVID COPPERFIELD, his more mature works begin. Autobiographical, it was Dickens' own favorite. In BLEAK HOUSE, an exposé of political corruption and court delay, Dickens displays a gloomy lack of faith in the ability of governmental institutions, held together with red tape and filled with archaic practices, to benefit the people. HARD TIMES is a protest against utilitarian lack of feeling and imagination and is perhaps Dickens' most single-minded social novel. Further disillusionment came in LITTLE DORRIT, which included memories of Dickens' father in debtors' prison. Next came his dramatic novel A TALE OF TWO CITIES. This was soon followed by GREAT EXPECTATIONS, considered by many as his finest work. OUR MUTUAL FRIEND is highly regarded by some critics; but others find it humorless, diffuse, and contrived. In 1858, Dickens began to give public readings, which he continued on his second visit to the U.S. in 1867–1868. He died in England while working on his novel *The Mystery of* EDWIN DROOD. He was buried in Westminster Abbey.

No other English writer has created a world of characters so distinctively cruel or suffering, comic or repugnant as Dickens has; no other writer has written so convincingly of the wrongs inflicted on children by adults in the 19th century. Attacks on Dickens' sentimentality and tendency to caricature have detracted little from his stature as a great humorist and creator of characters; these he brought to life with a wealth of meaningful detail, a myriad of odd gestures, expressions, speech patterns, and physiognomies. As a social critic he focused sharply on the iniquities and inequities of his environment. See Boz.

Dickens, Monica (1915–   ). English novelist, great-granddaughter of Charles Dickens. Her popular early books were entertaining accounts of her experiences in new jobs—as a cook in *One Pair of Hands* (1939) and nurse in *One Pair of Feet* (1942). Other books include *Man Overboard* (1958), *The Heart of London* (1961), and *Cobbler's Dream* (1963).

Dickinson, Emily (1830–1886). American poet. One of the three children of Edward Dickinson, lawyer and treasurer of Amherst College, she shared a cultivated family life. After attending Amherst Institute and Mount Holyoke Female Seminary, she retired to her home; later, dressing only in white, she rarely came down from her room to meet her guests.

Her father, a stern Calvinist who served a term in Congress, dominated his daughter's life. Among the other men who influenced her were the Reverend Charles Wadsworth, whose trip to California is cryptically referred to in the poetry; Samuel Bowles, editor of the *Springfield Daily Republican*, where one of her poems appeared; Benjamin F. Newton, a short-lived scholar and lawyer, who introduced her to the works of Emerson; T. W. HIGGINSON, soldier and critic; and Judge Otis P. Lord, a family friend.

Throughout her adult life Emily Dickinson wrote poetry; only two of the almost 2,000 poems she wrote were published in her lifetime. Uniformly short, consisting usually of four-line stanzas, the poems are written in a terse, aphoristic style. Although she personally rejected Calvinist theology, Emily Dickinson was influenced by the philosophy of Jonathan Edwards; like Emerson, she found that spirit manifested in nature. Physically isolated, she belongs in the tradition of American poetry that includes Whitman and Robert Frost.

Dickinson, Goldsworthy Lowes (1862–1932). English philosopher, essayist, and worker for international peace. *The Greek View of Life* (1896) is among his books.

Dickson, Carter or **Carr.** See John Dickson CARR.

Di Costanzo, Angelo (1507–1591). Italian Renaissance sonneteer and historian of his native city, Naples. He was important in the development of Petrarchism and Marinism because of his attempts at bringing to the sonnet the witty effects of epigrams. He was especially popular in the 18th century, among the Arcadians. His *Rime* (*Verses*) were not published until 1709.

dictator. In ancient Rome, the temporary supreme commander. In times of great national danger, the senate would call upon the consuls to appoint a dictator who would hold office for no longer than six months. See CINCINNATUS.

Dictator of Letters. Epithet for VOLTAIRE (François Marie Arouet), who was also called "the Great Pan."

Dicte (Dikte). A Cretan mountain where, in a cave, the infant Zeus was tended by nymphs and the CURETES and suckled by the goat Amaltheia. An actual cave on this mountain has proved through excavation to have been a center of an important Minoan cult centering about a young child.

diction. Word choice in verbal expression with all that such choice implies in questions of correctness, clarity, and style. The *mot juste*, or exactly right word, is the ideal of good diction. Popularly, it is often confused with enunciation.

Dictionary of the English Language (1755). A monumental work by Samuel JOHNSON, which made his reputation and was the standard dictionary until Noah Webster's. In 1747, Johnson applied to Lord CHESTERFIELD for patronage and was refused; upon completion of the work, Chesterfield made a belated offer, which Johnson then refused in a famous letter. In his preface to the *Dictionary*, addressing critics, Johnson wrote, ". . . and it may repress the triumph of malignant criticism to observe, that if our language is not here fully displayed, I have only failed in an attempt which no human powers have hitherto completed."

Dictys Cretensis. Reputed author of an alleged, eye-witness account in Latin of the siege of Troy, which was one of the versions of the Troilus legend known to the Middle Ages. Both Dictys Cretensis and DARES PHRYGIUS are names mentioned by Homer.

didactic poetry. Poetry to teach factual information or moral lessons. Didactic verse has since time immemorial combined the mnemonic virtues of rhyme and rhythm with information to be memorized, as in the nursery rhyme "Thirty days hath September." In the view of some philosophers, the underlying aim of all literature is at least in part didactic; but aside from such an underlying aim, purely didactic poetry is no longer written. Some examples of didactic poetry in literary history are: Lucretius's *De Rerum Natura*, Vergil's *Georgics*, Erasmus Darwin's *Botanic Garden*, and Pope's *Essay on Man*.

Diderot, Denis. Nicknamed **Pantophile Diderot** (1713-1784). French encyclopedist, materialistic philosopher, novelist, satirist, dramatist, and art critic. Until recently, he was famous mainly for having compiled and edited, with d'ALEMBERT and others, the ENCYCLOPÉDIE OU DICTIONNAIRE RAISONNÉ DES SCIENCES, DES ARTS ET DES MÉTIERS (28 vols., 5 suppls., 2 index vols.). Among his philosophic works are *Pensées philosophiques* (1746), which is deistic in thought and a defense of human passions; *Lettre sur les aveugles . . .* (1749), a study of how the blind learn, containing his view on materialism (he was imprisoned for three months because of this work); *Lettre sur les sourds et les muets* (1749), one of the first studies on the deaf and dumb, as well as an inquiry into aesthetics; *Pensées sur l'interprétation de la nature* (1753), containing ideas which foreshadow discoveries in biology, the theory of transformism, and natural selection. Diderot's audacity and profundity in scientific thought are strikingly illustrated in his *Le Rêve de d'Alembert* (1769, pub. 1830), one of his three dramatic dialogues in which he presents surprising insights into the physical, moral, and social universe; in it is found the first modern conception of the cellular structure of matter. His novels include *Les Bijoux indiscrets* (1748); *La Religieuse* (written 1760, pub. 1796), an attack on life in convents; LE NEVEU DE RAMEAU, a dialectical satire on contemporary society and conventional morality; and the satirico-philosophical JACQUES LE FATALISTE, in which Diderot poses the problem of freedom versus predeterminism, and at the same time experiments with the form of the novel. Among Diderot's plays, the most famous are *Le Père de famille* (1758) and *Le Fils naturel* (1757). Moral in tone, and rather mediocre, they illustrate his theories on the drama and became prototypes for the BOURGEOIS DRAMA. Diderot's theories on the drama, which he developed in several essays, e.g., *Paradoxe sur le comédien* (1773-1778, pub. 1830), were put into practice by Emile Augier and Dumas fils, in their moralistic, social-minded plays. In the *Salons*, written for Baron de Grimm's *Correspondance littéraire, philosophique et critique*, Diderot inaugurated art criticism as a literary genre. His *Lettres à Sophie Volland* attest to his genius as a letter-writer.

Dido. Also known as **Elissa.** The name given by Vergil in his AENEID to the founder and queen of Carthage. According to Roman legend, she fled from Phoenicia to North Africa after her brother Pygmalion, king of Tyre, had murdered her husband, Sychaeus, for his wealth. (See BYRSA.) The name Dido was also an epithet of the Phoenician goddess Astarte.

In Vergil's poem, she hospitably receives Aeneas and the Trojans when they are shipwrecked on her shores. Through the plotting of the goddess Venus, she falls in love with Aeneas and tries to persuade him to settle in North Africa and share Carthage with her. But when the will of the gods is announced to him by their messenger Mercury, Aeneas yields, half against his will: he must abandon Dido and found his own nation in Italy. After his departure, Dido, in grief, takes her life by the sword, and is cremated on a great funeral pyre which Aeneas, now far out to sea, beholds burning on the shore.

Ovid's *Heroides* contains a letter, supposedly written by Dido to Aeneas, in which she reminds him of all she has done for him and begs him to remain. Other works dealing with the unfortunate queen include Nash and Marlowe's tragedy *Dido, Queen of Carthage* (1594), Purcell's opera *Dido and Aeneas* (1689), and Piccinni's opera *Didon* (1783).

Diego [Cendoya], Gerardo (1895-). Spanish poet and scholar. His well-known earlier collections, *Imagen* (1922), *Manual de espumas* (1924), and *Versos humanos* (1925), reveal a style which relates the growth of a poem to that of a living organism. His recent work includes the volume *Romancero de la novia* (1944).

Diego, San. A modification of Santiago (*Span.*, St. JAMES, patron saint of Spain).

Dies Irae (*Lat.*, Day of Wrath). A famous medieval hymn on the last judgment, probably composed by Thomas of Celano, a native of Abruzzi, who died in 1255. It is derived from the Vulgate version of Joel 2:31, and used in the Mass for the Dead and on All Souls' Day.

Dietrich of Bern. See THEODORIC THE GREAT.

Digby, Sir **Kenelm** (1603-1665). English naval commander, diplomat, writer, and council member of the Royal Society. He discovered the necessity of oxygen for plant life. Among his works are *A Treatise of the Nature of Bodies* (1644), *A Treatise Declaring the Operations and Nature of Man's Soul* (1644), and his allegorical *Memoirs* (1827).

dilettante (from Italian; literally, one who takes delight in a thing). Like *amateur*, which means literally, one who likes a thing, the term *dilettante* is especially applied with reference to the fine arts. Since mere fondness of an art guarantees neither knowledge nor ability, *amateur* as well as *dilettante* have come to mean one who dabbles in a given subject. The Spanish word *aficionado*, popularized in English with the flurry of interest in bullfighting, carries the sense of the knowledgeable enthusiast that the other two words have nearly lost.

Dill Pickle, A (1920). A short story by Katherine MANSFIELD. A pair of lovers meet by chance in a restaurant after they have been separated for six years. In the half hour they spend together she rediscovers his charm and regrets ever leaving him, then rediscovers his faults and leaves him sitting in the restaurant. A sour dill pickle in an anecdote he tells functions as a symbol for the whole experience.

Dillon, George (1906–   ). American poet, translator, and editor. Editor of POETRY from 1937 to 1950, Dillon earlier published his own poetry in *Boy in the Wind* (1927) and *The Flowering Stone* (1931). The latter won a Pulitzer Prize. In collaboration with Edna St. Vincent Millay, he published a translation of Baudelaire's *Les Fleurs du Mal* (1935).

dimeter. In prosody, a line of verse containing two metrical feet. It may be in any meter, usually identified together with the name of the meter, as iambic dimeter, trochaic dimeter, etc.

Dimmesdale, Arthur. The guilty minister in Hawthorne's THE SCARLET LETTER.

Dinarzade. Sister of SCHEHERAZADE in *The Arabian Nights*.

Dindenault. See DINGDONG.

Dindymus. In ancient geography, a mountain range between Phrygia and Galatia, sacred to Cybele, the Great Mother of the Gods, often also called Dindymene.

Dîners Magny. A restaurant in Paris, the scene of informal meetings held by an inner circle of French novelists between 1862 and 1875. Among the men who gathered there, for dinner and discussion, were Edmond and Jules de Goncourt, Théophile Gautier, Alphonse Daudet, Ernest Renan, Gustave Flaubert, and Charles Sainte-Beuve.

Dinesen, Isak. Pen name of Baroness **Karen Blixen**, born **Dinesen** (1883–1962). Danish short-story writer. Married to her cousin Baron Blixen, Isak Dinesen lived from 1914 to 1931 on a coffee plantation in British East Africa, now Kenya. *Out of Africa* (1937), published simultaneously in English and Danish, is a sensitive account of her experiences. Her first book, *Seven Gothic Tales* (1934), was published in English and received immediate critical acclaim; *Winter's Tales* (1942) is another well-known collection. During the German occupation of Denmark, Isak Dinesen published a symbolic critique of the conquerors, *Gengoeldelsens Veje (The Angelic Avengers,* 1947) under the name of Pierre Andrézel. A delicate subtlety of both mood and expression characterizes her acutely perceptive, often mysterious stories.

Ding an sich. See CRITIQUE OF PURE REASON; CRITIQUE OF JUDGMENT.

Dingdong. An anglicism for Dindenault, the sea-going sheep trader in Rabelais' GARGANTUA AND PANTAGRUEL who sells PANURGE a ram for an exorbitant price. Panurge punishes Dingdong by heaving the ram overboard, thus causing the whole herd to stampede into the sea, dragging the trader with them. Panurge declares that such good sport was well worth the price he had paid for the ram.

Dinggedicht (*Ger.,* "thing poem"). A lyric poem about an objective entity which, though it is most often a material thing, may also be a person or situation. The poet seeks not so much to describe from his own point of view as to recreate the intrinsic essence of the object in question, to get inside the object, as it were. Ideally, the reader should react to the poem as though he were reacting, on a deeper and more perceptive level than usual, to the thing itself. In many poems of this type, those by Eduard Mörike and Conrad Ferdinand MEYER for example, the sub-ject is a work of art; but Rainer Maria RILKE, with whom the term *Dinggedicht* is most often associated, expanded the technique to include such subjects as living animals, human situations, and common household objects. The *Dinggedicht* is recognized in German literary criticism as a distinct poetic form.

Dinmont, Dandie. An eccentric and humorous farmer in Scott's GUY MANNERING. He owns two terriers, Mustard and Pepper, reputedly the progenitors of the Dandie Dinmont breed.

Diocletian [Gaius Aurelius Valerius] (A.D. 245–313). Roman emperor (284–305). He inaugurated the period of the Partnership of Emperors. He ruled with Maximian from 285, and divided the empire again (293) to include Constantius Chlorus and Galerius as rulers. Diocletian governed the eastern portion. At the instigation of his colleague Galerius, he began a terrible 10-year persecution of the Christians in 303. Diocletian abdicated (305) and retired to his native Dalmatia, where he spent the last years of his life.

Diogenes (c. 400–c. 325 B.C.). Greek CYNIC philosopher, pupil of Antisthenes. According to Seneca, he lived in a tub. The ascetic Diogenes is said to have searched in daylight with a lantern for an honest man. He exposed the vanity and selfishness of men. Diogenes' contempt for worldly goods is indicated by his reply to Alexander the Great, when the latter asked if he could do the philosopher any favor. Diogenes answered, "Yes, move out of my sunshine." Diogenes' nickname was *kyon*, or dog, a comment on his mode of living.

Diogenes Laertius (c. 200–250). A Greek author. Nothing is known of this writer's life. He wrote *Lives and Opinions of Eminent Philosophers,* of unknown date. He included the biographies of 82 Greek thinkers from Thales to Epicurus, which he compiled from the works of earlier writers. Diogenes chiefly records anecdotes to illustrate the viewpoint or character of his subject. The greatest value of the book is its preservation of three epistles and the maxims of Epicurus.

Diomedean swap. An exchange in which all the benefit is on one side. The expression is based on an incident related by Homer in the *Iliad*. During the proscribed exchange of credentials before a fight to the death, the Greek hero Diomedes and the Trojan hero Glaucus discover that their families had been allied. Forgetting their quarrel, they exchange armor, but Glaucus' armor is pure gold, while Diomedes' is only brass. Homer remarks that Zeus must have addled Glaucus' wits.

Diomedes. In Shakespeare's ANTONY AND CLEOPATRA, an attendant of Cleopatra. He brings word to Antony that Cleopatra, whom he has been told is falsely dead, is actually still alive.

Diomedes or **Diomed.** In Greek mythology, a king of Argos. He is described as one of the bravest warriors at the siege of Troy. He survived the siege, but on his return home, found his wife living in adultery, and saved his life by living in exile in Italy. See also DIOMEDEAN SWAP.

Dione. A titaness and consort of Zeus to whom, according to one Greek myth, she bore Aphrodite. Her name was later occasionally applied to Aphrodite.

Dionysiac. See APOLLONIAN AND DIONYSIAC.

Dionysus (Dionysos). Also known as **Bacchus** in Roman mythology. The Greek god of wine and fertile crops, the son of Zeus and Semele. Saved from his dead mother, the unborn child was sewed into Zeus's thigh. After his birth, he was torn to pieces by the Titans at the jealous Hera's instigation. Revived by Rhea, he was transformed into a kid and raised by nymphs. As a young man, he invented wine and introduced the vine to many lands, accompanied everywhere by a troop of maenads and suitors. Those who opposed his orgiastic rites were driven mad or otherwise destroyed. He married Ariadne, whom Theseus had deserted in the island of Naxos. Later he took the place of Hestia as one of the twelve Olympians and raised his mother from Hades under the name of Thyone.

The important festivals, among them the Eleusinian Mysteries and the Athenian Antestheria, celebrated the cult of Dionysus as the DAEMON of reviving vegetation in the spring. An influential development of this cult was Orphism, which in turn influenced the philosophies of Pythagoras and Plato. Euripides' play THE BACCHANTS (408–406 B.C.) tells the story of Dionysus' gory triumph over Pentheus, king of Thebes. It is generally acknowledged that drama, especially tragedy, developed out of the traditional ceremonies performed at Dionysian festivals to celebrate the death and resurrection of the god.

Dioscuri (Gr. *Dios kouroi,* sons of Zeus). See CASTOR AND POLYDEUCES.

Diotima. An Arcadian prophetess, the teacher of Socrates. She is quoted by him in Plato's *Symposium.*

Dircaean Swan. PINDAR; so called from Dirce (see AMPHION), a fountain in the neighborhood of Thebes, the poet's birthplace.

Dirce (Dirke). See AMPHION.

Directory, the. The name of the executive body of government in France created by the Constitution of 1795 during the FRENCH REVOLUTION; it lasted from October, 1795 to November, 1799. The Directory consisted of five men elected by the Council of 500 and the Council of the Elders (or *Anciens*). Ineffective because of internal dissensions, corruption, and bankruptcy, it was overthrown by Napoleon.

Dirty Hands (Les Mains sales; 1948). A drama by Jean-Paul SARTRE. The play, translated into English, was produced on Broadway under the title *Red Gloves.* Louis' faction of the Proletarian Party consider Hoederer's policies inexpedient. To kill him, the young intellectual Hugo is sent to Hoederer's house as a secretary, accompanied by his wife Jessica. Hugo delays his murder, however, increasingly impressed by Hoederer. He finally shoots him when he finds Hoederer kissing Jessica, but he does it with no definable motive, neither jealousy nor political conviction. The Party eventually switches to Hoederer's policies, and, after his prison term Hugo is examined to see if he is "salvageable" for further Party work; if not, he will be shot. In despair because Hoederer's death now has no public meaning, as the act of killing had no private meaning for him, Hugo tries to claim the significance of both by refusing to be "salvageable." The play dramatizes the dilemma that, in order to accomplish anything, a man must

Dionysus riding in a chariot drawn by a satyr, who carries a wine storage jar. Dionysus is crowned with grape leaves.

be willing to have "dirty hands"—that is, apparently, to accept the argument that the end justifies the means. Hoederer, who does so, seems most "real" as a person to Hugo and Jessica; idealistic Hugo suffers when he discovers that he cannot.

Dis. A name for HADES and hence the lower world.

Disastrous Peace, the (La Paix malheureuse). A name given to the Treaty of Câteau-Cambrésis (1559). It followed the battle of Gravelines. It was signed by France, Spain, and England, and by it France ceded the Low Countries to Spain, and Savoy, Corsica, and 200 forts to Italy.

Discours de la méthode. See René DESCARTES.

Discours sur l'histoire universelle. See Jacques Bénigne BOSSUET.

Disenchanted, The (1950). A novel by Budd SCHULBERG. The central character is Manley Halliday, a famous alcoholic novelist of the 1920's, based on F. Scott Fitzgerald. Schulberg had known the senior writer, and the book—a fictional re-creation of his personal experiences—is a melodrama approximating the tragedy of Fitzgerald's own life in Hollywood. The book was dramatized in 1958.

disestablishment. The act of withdrawing from a church its established position or privileges in relation to the state. The Irish Church was disestablished by an act of Parliament in 1869. The Church of England was disestablished in Wales by several acts in 1920.

Dismas or **Dysmas.** The usual name in the apocryphal gospels for the penitent thief. He was crucified with Jesus. He became the patron saint of thieves. The impenitent thief is commonly known as *Gesmas* or *Gestas*. Longfellow, in his *Golden Legend*, calls the penitent Titus and his fellow thief Dumachus.

Disney, Walt[er Elias] (1901–   ). American pioneer in animated cartoons and motion-picture producer. Disney studied at the Chicago Academy of Fine Arts and later became a commercial artist. In 1923 he went to Hollywood and began to create the first of his famous animated cartoons. His series of films featuring Oswald the Rabbit won wide favor, after which came those featuring Mickey Mouse and Donald Duck, his almost universally known creations. Disney made *The Three Little Pigs* in 1933 and, thereafter, turned his attention to making full-length pictures in this technique; *Snow White and the Seven Dwarfs* (1938), *Fantasia* (1940), and *Dumbo* (1942) are among the best known of these. *The Living Desert* (1953) was the first of a number of documentary films on wild life and nature that Disney subsequently produced.

Disraeli, Benjamin. 1st earl of **Beaconsfield** (1804–1881). English statesman and novelist. A member of Parliament, leader of the opposition in Commons, thrice chancellor of the exchequer, and twice prime minister, Disraeli was created a peer in 1876. It was by his initiative that Britain acquired the Suez canal in 1875, and he was responsible for having Queen Victoria proclaimed "Empress of India" and for negotiating "peace with honor" at the Congress of Berlin. As a young man, Disraeli had hesitated in deciding between a political and a literary career; his best novels, written at this time, are marked by acute wit, sharp realism, and a totally individual and often fantastic style. They include VIVIAN GREY, *The Young Duke* (1831), his two earliest works; *Contarini Fleming*, a psychological romance (1832), and *The Wondrous Tale of Alroy*, a historical novel (1832), both of which reveal the pride which Disraeli, a baptized Anglican, felt in his Jewish ancestry, a pride which he was to retain throughout his life; *Henrietta Temple*, a love story (1836); *Venetia* (1837), which presented in fictionalized form episodes from the lives of Byron and Shelley; CONINGSBY, OR THE NEW GENERATION, first in a projected political trilogy; SYBIL, OR THE TWO NATIONS, the second in the series, a depiction of the Chartist movement with such a frank portrayal of labor conditions that it was instrumental in provoking factory reform; TANCRED, OR THE NEW CRUSADE, the last novel in the trilogy, an implicit proposal that English politics and church seek a revitalizing inspiration from Semitic sources; and two political novels dating from late in his political career, LOTHAIR (1870) and *Endymion* (1880). Disraeli's nonfictional works are now chiefly of historical interest, but like his novels they exemplify his conservative convictions, his disdain for the theories of abstract rights and the a priori systems of the utilitarians, his trust in democratic Toryism, his acceptance of the duty of social reform, and his pride in empire and crown.

D'Israeli, Isaac (1766–1848). Father of Benjamin DISRAELI. Isaac's father, Benjamin D'Israeli, was a Jewish merchant descended from a family of Spanish refugees who came to England in 1748. Isaac had several works published anonymously, including *Curiosities of Literature* (6 vols., 1791–1834) and *Amenities of Literature* (3 vols., 1841).

Dissertation on Roast Pig, A. One of the most famous of Charles LAMB's *Essays of Elia*, it is a humorous account of the "accidental discovery" of the process of cooking pork.

Dissertation upon Parties (1735). A well-known political pamphlet by Henry ST. JOHN, Viscount Bolingbroke, which rejects the notion of divine right of kings and sets forth the idea of a king, free from the restrictions of party factionalism, who would assume leadership and preserve both a balanced government and traditional civil liberties.

dissociation of sensibility. A phrase coined by T. S. Eliot in *The Metaphysical Poets* (1921). According to Eliot, the 17th-century poets could "feel their thought as immediately as the odour of a rose," but after them a "dissociation of sensibility" set in and poets became either intellectual or emotional, but not both. Like the French symbolists, Eliot was trying to recapture that lost fusion of thought and feeling.

distich. The classical designation of a unit of two lines in a strophic poem for choral recitation. The term is used in English only in relation to or in translations of poetry from other languages. The elegiac distich of classical times consists of a hexameter followed by a pentameter, a form also used by the German poets Goethe and Schiller in poetic aphorisms. An example by Schiller, which is a characterization of the distich, reads, in Coleridge's translation:

In the hexameter rises the fountain's silvery column,
In the pentameter aye falling in melody back.

dithyramb (Gr., *dithyrambos*, a choric hymn). Originally a wild, impetuous kind of Dorian lyric in honor of Dionysus. It was traditionally ascribed to Arion of Lesbos (about 620 B.C.), who was thereafter called *the father of dithyrambic poetry*. It was said to be the origin of drama.

Ditzen, Rudolf. See Hans FALLADA.

Dive Bouteille, Oracle de la. See ORACLE OF THE HOLY BOTTLE.

Diverting History of John Bull and Brother Jonathan (1812). A satire by James Kirke PAULDING, under the pseudonym of Hector Bullus. The book relates the settling of Jonathan's farms (the U.S.) and their revolt from Bullock Island (England). Violently anti-British in tone, the story was continued in a sequel, *The History of Uncle Sam and His Boys* (1835).

Diverting History of John Gilpin, The. See JOHN GILPIN.

Divine Comedy, The (**Commedia**, completed 1321; called **Divina Commedia** after the 16th century). An epic poem by DANTE, his major work. It has 100 cantos in TERZA RIMA, divided equally (after an introductory canto in the first section) into three sections of 33 cantos each. The poet finds himself lost in the wood of Error on Good Friday, 1300. He is met by the spirit of Vergil, the great classical poet whom Dante considers the incarnation of the highest knowledge attainable by the human mind. Vergil conducts him through Hell to free him of the temptation to sin; then on Easter morning they begin the ascent of the mountain of Purgatory to purify Dante's soul of even the capacity for error. Vergil must leave Dante at the top of the mountain, for man alone, without grace, can go no further; but in the Earthly Paradise there Dante meets BEATRICE, who represents divine revelation, and she conducts him through Paradise to God. For details of each section see INFERNO; PURGATORIO; PARADISO.

The cosmology, angelology, and theology of the work are based firmly on the system of St. Thomas AQUINAS, but Dante considered the Church of his time a "harlot" no longer serving God—he meets seven popes in the Inferno, for instance—and was therefore frequently considered a heretic. The characters whom Dante meets on his journey are drawn largely from ancient Roman history and from recent and contemporary Italian history, including Dante's personal friends and enemies; their vivid portraiture and the constant allusions to human affairs make the work, although in structure a description of the Beyond, actually a realistic picture and intensely involved analysis of every aspect of earthly human life. Dante's literal journey is also an allegory of the progress of the individual soul toward God, and the progress of political and social mankind toward peace on earth; it is a compassionate, although moral, evaluation of human nature and a mystic vision of the Absolute toward which it strives. Thus the universality of the drama and the lyric vigor of the poetry are far more important than the specific doctrinal content.

Divine Pagan. See HYPATIA.

Divinity School Address, The (1838). An address by Ralph Waldo EMERSON. Delivered before the graduates of the Harvard Divinity School, the address shocked Boston's conservative clergymen.

Emerson stressed the divinity of man and the humanity of Christ. He denied miracles and did not quote scripture. Evil was represented as possessing a negative character; instead of a positive force, it became a vacuum into which good would easily flow. Further, he upheld intuition, rather than ritual, as a means of knowing God.

Dix, Dorothy. Pen name of **Elizabeth Meriwether Gilmer** (1870–1951). American newspaper writer. She is known as the author of a widely syndicated column of advice on domestic problems, which was first published in 1896 in the New Orleans *Picayune*.

Dixie. A nostalgically regarded American paradise in the South. It is also the popular name of a song, originally entitled *I Wish I Was in Dixie's Land*, composed by Daniel Decatur Emmett in 1859. A great favorite in the South, it was taken up by the soldiers in the Confederate army. Fanny Crosby wrote a Union version of the text in 1861, known as *Dixie for the Union*.

The origin of the word Dixie is obscure. It has been suggested that it is related to the Mason and Dixon line; others believe that a Louisiana bank, printing its pre-Civil War bills in French with a big Dix (ten) in the middle of the 10-dollar notes, made the South the land of "dixies." A further, and ironic derivation is from the name of a slaveholder on Manhattan Island in the late 18th century; so benevolent was he that when his slaves were moved down south, they pined for "Dixie's land" up north.

Dixon, Jim. In Kingsley Amis's novel LUCKY JIM, a young university teacher beset by comic misfortunes.

Djinnestan. See JINNISTAN.

Dobell, Sydney (1824–1874). English poet and critic. Probably the most estimable member of the SPASMODIC SCHOOL, Dobell wrote such long poems as *The Roman* (1850) and *Balder* (1854) and many ballads and sonnets. While there are numerous fine passages and striking lines in the former, Dobell was an uneven writer and his reputation rests largely on shorter works, such as the ballad *Keith of Ravelston* (1857).

Dobie, J[ames] Frank (1888–1964). American teacher, historian, and folklorist. Dobie, who is especially identified with the University of Texas, has taught in a number of universities. He was a visiting professor at Cambridge University and from this experience came a book of observations, *A Texan in England* (1945). Among the books of this cultural historian of the Southwest are *Coronado's Children* (1931), *Tales of the Mustangs* (1936), *Apache Gold and Yaqui Silver* (1939), *Guide to Life and Literature in the Southwest* (1943; revised and enlarged, 1952), *The Mustangs* (1952), and *I'll Tell You a Tale* (1960).

Döblin, Alfred (1878–1957). German novelist and essayist, known as a leading representative of EXPRESSIONISM. His major novel, however, *Berlin Alexanderplatz* (1929), is less expressionistically tendentious, more scer.ic and realistic than his earlier works, and shows the influence of John Dos Passos and James Joyce. Döblin, a physician, emigrated from Germany in 1933 and became a French citizen.

Dobrée, Bonamy (1891–   ). English authority on Restoration drama. Dobrée is the author of

Restoration Comedy (1924) and *Restoration Tragedy* (1929).

Dobrolyubov, Nikolai Aleksandrovich (1836–1861). Russian journalist and literary critic. After graduation from the St. Petersburg Pedagogical Institute in 1857, Dobrolyubov began his brief career on the journal *Sovremennik* (*The Contemporary*). Like his colleague CHERNYSHEVSKI, Dobrolyubov emphasized the social usefulness of literature. The best-known of his critical essays are *Tiomnoye Tzarstvo* (*The Kingdom of Darkness,* 1859), a study of Ostrovski's drama *The Storm; Chto takoye oblomovshchina?* (*What is Oblomovshchina?* 1859), on Goncharov's novel *Oblomov;* and *Kogda zhe prediot nastoyashchi den'?* (*When Will the Real Day Come?* 1860), on Turgenev's novel *On the Eve*. Belinski, Chernyshevski and Dobrolyubov formed the triumvirate of 19th-century critics most often cited in Soviet literary criticism.

doctor. A scholastic or honorary title conferred by a university. Today the word is commonly synonymous with physician, from the degree M.D., Doctor of Medicine. In the medieval universities doctors were advanced students who were usually also teachers. The Schoolmen, or theologians who lectured in the cloisters and cathedral schools, were also called doctors.

Doctor. For titles beginning with *Doctor,* see also under Dr.

Doctors of the Church. Certain early Christian Fathers, especially four in the Greek (or Eastern) Church and four in the Latin (or Western) Church.

Eastern Church. St. Athanasius of Alexandria (d. 373), who defended the divinity of Christ against the Arians; St. Basil the Great of Caesarea (d.? 379) and his co-worker St. Gregory of Nazianzus (d.? 389); and the eloquent St. John Chrysostom (d. 407), Archbishop of Constantinople.

Western Church. St. Jerome (d. 420), translator of the Vulgate; St. Ambrose (d. 397), bishop of Milan; St. Augustine (d. 430), bishop of Hippo; and St. Gregory the Great (d. 604), the pope who sent St. Augustine, the Apostle of the Anglo-Saxons, to England.

Doctor Zhivago (Doktor Zhivago; 1957). A novel by Boris PASTERNAK. This famous book centers around the experiences of a member of the intelligentsia during the Russian Revolution. The story's hero, Yuri Zhivago, is a young doctor with a mild interest in the coming revolution and a great interest in literature. He composes poems, mostly with religious overtones; 25 of his verses form the last part of the novel. Zhivago's discussions with his uncle Kolya and his friends contain most of the explicit anti-Marxist passages that offended Soviet censors. The novel was refused publication in the Soviet Union, but was published abroad, bringing down the wrath of Soviet officialdom on Pasternak's head. Soviet authorities were as much bothered by the religious spirit pervading the novel as they were by the outspoken opposition to Marxism. Pasternak's opposition is implied throughout the book in the frequent contrast between the revolution's attempt to order men's lives rationally and the free, living spirit Zhivago finds in nature and in such characters as his mistress, Lara. Zhivago's, and the author's, sympathies are always obviously with life as opposed to the ideas about life held by the Marxists. The poetic spirit of the book is enhanced by the language in which it is written. In the original Russian, the lines often fall into the cadences of verse and almost always strike the reader with the intense force usually expected from well-written poetry.

Doctrine and Discipline of Divorce (1644). A famous prose argument by John MILTON on the religious justifications and legality of divorce. It may have been prompted, in part, by his own marital difficulties with his first wife, Mary Powell.

Dodd, William E[dward] (1869–1940). American historian and diplomat. Dodd was ambassador to Germany from 1933 to 1937, when he resigned to lecture against Nazism. His *Ambassador Dodd's Diary* (1941) contains his reactions to Nazism. Earlier he had written several books on American history, including *Statesmen of the Old South* (1911), *Lincoln or Lee* (1928), and *The Old South* (1937).

Doderer, Heimito von (1896–   ). Austrian novelist. Influenced by Robert Musil, he was known for his critical attitude toward what he regarded as the militaristic orientation of the 20th century. His best known novel is *Die Strudelhofstiege* (1951), which takes its title from the name of a stone stairway in Vienna.

Dodge, Mary Mapes (1831–1905). American writer and editor of *St. Nicholas Magazine* (1873–1905). Her books for children, *Hans Brinker, or the Silver Skates* (1865) and *Donald and Dorothy* (1883), are classics.

Dodgson, Charles Lutwidge. See Lewis CARROLL.

Dodona. A famous oracle in the village of Dodona in Epirus, and the most ancient of Greece. It was dedicated to Aeus, and the oracles were delivered from the tops of oak and other trees, the rustling of the wind in the branches being interpreted by the priests. Also, brazen vessels and plates were suspended from the branches, and these, being struck together when the wind blew, gave various sounds from which responses were concocted. Hence the Greek phrase Kalkos Dodones (brass of Dodona), meaning a babbler, or one who talks an infinite deal of nothing.

According to tradition, two black pigeons took their flight from Thebes, in Egypt; one flew to Libya, and the other to Dodona. On the spot where the former alighted, the temple of Zeus Ammon was erected; in the place where the other settled, the oracle of Zeus was established, and there the responses were made by the black pigeons that inhabited the surrounding groves. This fable is probably based on a pun upon the word *peleiai,* which usually meant "old women," but in the dialect of the Epirots signified pigeons or doves.

Dodsley, Robert (1703–1764). English poet, playwright, and the most important publisher and bookseller of the eighteenth century. With the aid of Alexander Pope, he opened his bookshop at the sign of Tully's Head in Pall Mall, London, and was soon publishing the works of Pope, Samuel Johnson, Edward Young, William Collins, and many others. His publication of poetry culminated in *A Collection of Poems by several hands* in 6 volumes (1748–1758); his chief connection with English fiction was the London edition of *Tristram Shandy*. Dodsley was also the editor of a collection of *Old Plays* (12 vols., 1744), beginning with a morality play, which went through several revised and enlarged editions.

Dodson and Fogg, Messrs. In Charles Dickens' PICKWICK PAPERS, two unprincipled lawyers who undertake on speculation to bring an action against Mr. Pickwick for breach of promise, and file accordingly the famous suit of *Bardell* v. *Pickwick*. The names Dodson and Fogg are frequently used as synonymous with unscrupulous or dishonest solicitors.

Dodsworth (1929). A novel by Sinclair LEWIS. Samuel Dodsworth, a rich automobile manufacturer in the Midwestern city of Zenith, retires and goes to Europe with his frivolous wife, Fran. Fran becomes involved in several love affairs with European adventurers, and Dodsworth, lonely and unhappy, meets Edith Cortwright, an American widow who teaches him to appreciate the traditions of Europe. He eventually leaves his wife for the more mature companionship of Edith. The novel was dramatized in 1934 by Sidney Howard.

dog. An animal that in medieval art symbolizes fidelity. A dog is represented as lying at the feet of St. Bernard, St. Benignus, and St. Wendelin; as licking the wounds of St. Roch; as carrying a lighted torch in representations of St. Dominic. In monuments the dog is placed at the feet of women to symbolize affection and fidelity, as a lion is placed at the feet of men to signify courage and magnanimity. Many of the Crusaders are represented with their feet on a dog, to show that they followed the standard of the Lord as faithfully as a dog follows the footsteps of his master.

Dog Beneath the Skin, The (1935). A satiric drama in prose and verse by W. H. AUDEN and Christopher ISHERWOOD. Parodying traditional fairy-tale themes and the technique of the popular 20th-century musical comedy, it concerns the quest for Sir Francis Crewe, a missing English heir.

Dogberry. A pompous but comical constable in Shakespeare's MUCH ADO ABOUT NOTHING. He has a habit of confusing his words, sagely remarking, for example, that "comparisons are odorous." He and his crony Verges take Borachio into custody as a suspicious character and ask Leonato to question him. Leonato fails to comprehend their garbled story, however, and Don John's plot against Hero and Claudio nearly succeeds.

doggerel. Originally, loose and irregular verse, often comic or burlesque. It gave the impression of having been quickly and casually composed, as in *Hudibras,* Butler's satirical epic. A pejorative meaning has now become attached to the word, connoting triviality of subject matter and inexpertness of technique, as in "mere doggerel."

Dog Star. Sirius, the brightest star in the firmament. Its influence was supposed in ancient times to cause great heat, pestilence, etc. It was called Dog Star (Caniculus) because it belongs to the constellation *Canis Major* (larger dog).

Doktor Faustus (1947). A novel by Thomas MANN. In it the intense and tragic career of the hero Adrian LEVERKÜHN, a composer, is made to parallel the collapse of Germany in World War II. To achieve this end, Mann employs the device of having another character, Serenus ZEITBLOM, narrate Leverkühn's story from memory, while the war is going on, and

intersperse his narrative with remarks about the present situation. In this way, it is implied that it is the same demonic and always potentially destructive energy inherent in Leverkühn's music that is also, on a larger scale, behind the outburst of Nazism. Mann thus suggests that the violent FAUSTIAN drive, when it is not diverted into art, or when there is no single artistic genius to harness it into creative process, will be perverted and result in grossly subhuman degradation. Thus, Mann is concerned here with his favorite theme, the artist's isolation in the world; but whereas earlier treatments such as TONIO KRÖGER had shown the artist attempting to get along with the world's values, here the world is seen attempting to cope with a force that is proper only to art.

Dolce, Lodovico (1508–1566). Italian dramatist. He wrote Senecan tragedies in the modern manner of Giraldi, which influenced the Elizabethan drama. His best-known work is the *Marianna* (1565).

dolce stil nuovo. See STILNOVISTI.

Dolet, Etienne (1509–1546). French scholar and printer. From his printing press at Lyons he issued works by Rabelais, Clément Marot, and others, as well as his own *Commentarii linguae Latinae* (1536–1568), a philosophical study. Convicted of heresy and blasphemy, he was hanged and then burned in Paris.

Dolgoruki, Arkadi Makarovich. The hero of Feodor Dostoevski's novel, A RAW YOUTH. Arkadi is the illegitimate son of Versilov.

Makar Ivanovich Dolgoruki. The nominal father of Arkadi, Makar is an old former serf who has become a religious pilgrim. He preaches humility and love and a striving for seemliness in relations among men. He has often been compared to a similar peasant philosopher, Platon Karatayev in Tolstoi's *War and Peace.*

Dolittle, Dr. The animal-loving doctor hero of children's stories by Hugh LOFTING.

Dollfuss, Engelbert (1892–1934). Chancellor of Austria (1932–1934). He was assassinated in a Nazi *Putsch.*

Dolliver Romance, The (1876). An unfinished novel by Nathaniel HAWTHORNE. It was supposed to have been published serially in *The Atlantic Monthly,* but the author died before his plans were realized. Dr. Dolliver attempts to prepare an elixir of life so that he might live to care for his granddaughter, Pansie. In contrast to the selfless Dolliver, Colonel Dabney demands the elixir for purely selfish reasons. Dabney finally dies, ironically, of an overdose of the elixir.

Doll's House, A (1879). A play by Henrik IBSEN. Sheltered, petted, and expected to behave like an amiable nitwit by first her father and then her husband, Nora Helmer has committed forgery in order to get money to save her husband's life. Though she has repaid the money, her husband finally finds out about her act. His behavior makes Nora realize that in their eight years of marriage he has never looked on her as a human being, but only as a doll, and she leaves him in order to learn to become a person in her own right.

Dolopathos. See THE SEVEN WISE MASTERS.

Dombey and Son (1848). A novel by Charles DICKENS. The proud, unfeeling Mr. Dombey has but one ambition in life: to have a son that his firm might

be called Dombey and Son. When his son Paul is
born he promises to fulfill this ambition, which over-
rides even grief at the death of Mrs. Dombey. Young
Paul, a delicate, sensitive boy, is quite unequal to the
great things expected of him; he is sent to Mr.
Blimber's school and gives way under the strain of
the discipline. In his short life he wins the love of
all who know him. Mr. Dombey is embittered by
Paul's death. Florence, his daughter, lives on with him
trying desperately to win his love, but she has succeeded only in incurring his hatred because she lives
while her brother died. Dombey marries again, but
his second wife, Edith Granger, runs off with Mr.
CARKER, his business manager. Florence marries the
kind young Walter Gay. Dombey's firm fails, and
alone and miserable, he finds himself longing for
the sweet and kind daughter whom he treated so
coldly. The two are reconciled, and Dombey tries to
expiate his past through his grandchildren.

The novel is noted for its complex structure. The
symbolism of death as the sea and life as the flow
of the river into the sea, used often in his later novels,
is first used here.

Dom Casmurro (1900). A novel by Joachim
Maria MACHADO DE ASSIS. The narrator, a middle-
aged lawyer nicknamed Dom Casmurro (roughly,
"Mr. Peevish") because of his difficult disposition,
reflects on his adolescence and on his youthful romance with Capitú, whom he later married. An aura
of uncertainty and ambiguity hovers over the book
—not even the question of Capitú's adulterous relationship with Escobar, her husband's best friend, is
fully settled. Written in a limpid, wryly humorous
style, the novel is largely plotless and is frequently
interrupted by the narrator's asides.

Domdaniel (Lat. *domus*, house or home; *Danielis*,
of Daniel). A fabled abode of evil spirits, gnomes,
and enchanters, "under the roots of the ocean" off
Tunis, or elsewhere. It first appears in Chaves and
Cazotte's *Continuation of the Arabian Nights* (1788–
1793), was introduced by Southey into his *Thalaba*,
and used by Carlyle as synonymous with a den of
iniquity.

Domenichino, il. Real name, **Domenico Zam-
pieri** (1581–1641). Italian painter. A product of
the eclectic academy of the CARRACCI at Bologna, he
is noted for his religious and mythological works, including the *Last Communion of St. Jerome* (1614)
and several fresco and easel treatments of the life of
St. Cecilia, patroness of music.

Domesday or **Doomsday Book** (1086). Latin
record of a census and survey of most of England. It
was compiled at the order of William the Conqueror.
All property is described and evaluated in detail,
along with a census of its inhabitants and its domestic
animals, as of (1) the time of Edward the Confessor,
(2) the time of William's bestowal of the estates on
their new owners, and (3) the time of the survey and
future potential. *Domesday* means "day of judgment,"
and the records were probably so named because they
were the final authority for property litigation; they
served as the basis for tax assessments until 1522.
Other similar records were often called the *Domesday Book* of a given locality; E. L. Masters used the
title for a collection of verse (1920).

Dominic, St. (1170–1221). Spanish-born Roman
Catholic priest and founder of the Dominican order.

An important church official in his native Spain, he
went to Languedoc in 1205 to preach orthodox doctrine to the Albigenses, but, contrary to the tradition, he was not an "inquisitor," nor did he take
a personal part in the bloody massacre of the Albigenses, who held to the Manichaean heresy. In 1215,
he organized his band of followers into the Dominican order, or Preaching Friars, devoted to missionary
work.

Dominicans. The popular name for the Order
of Preachers founded by St. Dominic in 1215. The
most famous member of the Order was a theologian,
St. Thomas AQUINAS. The Dominicans early acquired
the punning sobriquet *Domini canes* (*Lat.*, "dogs of
the Lord") because of their swift and vigorous penetration into the life of the Church over all of Europe.
In England they were formerly called Black Friars
from their black dress, and in France Jacobins, because their mother establishment in Paris was in the
rue St. Jacques.

**Dom Juan ou le Festin de Pierre (Don Juan
or the Stone Guest,** 1665). A prose comedy by
MOLIÈRE. It is derived from the play EL BURLADOR DE
SEVILLA Y EL CONVIDADO DE PIEDRA of Tirso de Molina.
The rake DON JUAN abducts Elvire, marries her, and
abandons her—not the first time he has so mistreated
a woman. He then ironically invites the statue of a
man he has murdered to dinner; the statue accepts
and returns the invitation, and as it takes Don Juan
by the hand a fiery chasm opens and swallows him.
Molière added the character Elvire as well as many
characteristic touches to this grim tale. There are
scenes of sparkling comedy; the valet Sganarelle is
timidity incarnate, and Don Juan assumes the traits
common to the libertine nobility of Molière's day.
Perhaps for this reason the play, though enormously
popular, was suppressed. It was later put into verse
by Thomas Corneille.

Domus Aurea (*Lat.*, "golden house"). A palace
of the emperor Nero, at or near the site of the Colos-
seum. It was the scene of many banqueting orgies.

Doña Bárbara (1929). A novel by Rómulo GAL-
LEGOS. The central character Doña Bárbara, as her
name implies, symbolizes barbarism. Believing herself possessed of supernatural powers, she rules a vast
domain on the Venezuelan *llanos* and bends men to
her will through bribery, intimidation, and murder.
Some saw in Doña Bárbara's rapacity and ruthless-
ness a resemblance to the practices of Juan Vicente
Gómez, Venezuelan dictator when the book was published.

Donalbain. In Shakespeare's MACBETH, the
younger son of Duncan, the murdered king, and the
brother of Malcolm. He flees to Ireland after his
father's death.

Don Alvaro o la fuerza del sino (1835). A
romantic tragedy in prose and verse by Ángel
Saavedra, duque de RIVAS. Don Alvaro, in love with
Doña Leonor, accidentally kills the girl's father, then
slays her two brothers in a duel. Before he dies, the
younger brother kills Doña Leonor in the mistaken
belief that she is the paramour of his father's murderer. Stricken with grief, Don Alvaro leaps to his
death. This play was the basis of Verdi's opera *La
Forza del Destino* (1862).

Donatello. Real name, **Donato di Niccolò dei
Bardi** (1386–1466). Florentine sculptor. An associate

Charles Dickens, English novelist, at the ages of 31, 47, and 56—
from sketches appearing in *Charles Dickens by Pen and Pencil*
by Frederick G. Kitton (above)

The parlor of the Leather Bottle, Cobham, mentioned in *Pickwick Papers* (below)

Gustave Doré, French illustrator and painter—
from an engraving after a drawing by Tonnard

ALL FOR LOVE:

OR, THE

World well Loft.

A

TRAGEDY,

As it is Acted at the

THEATRE-ROYAL;

And Written in Imitation of *Shakespeare's* Stile.

By *John Dryden*, Servant to His Majesty.

Facile est verbum aliquod ardens (ut ita dicam) notare : idque re-
stinctis animorum incendiis irridere.   Cicero.

In the SAVOY:

Printed by *Tho. Newcomb*, for *Henry Herringman*, at the Blew An-
chor in the Lower Walk of the *New-Exchange.* 1678.

Title page from the first edition of John Dryden's greatest play, *All for Love*

THE LAST SUPPER
(1523)

The Last Supper from an engraving by Albrecht Dürer, German painter and engraver

Ralph Waldo Emerson, American poet, essayist and philosopher, at the age of 56—
from an engraving by T. Johnson

Johann Wolfgang von Goethe, German poet, playwright, and novelist—from an engraving by Hinchliff after a portrait by Dawe (left)

Oliver Goldsmith, English poet, playwright, and novelist—from an engraving by J. B. Longacre after a painting by Sir Joshua Reynolds (right)

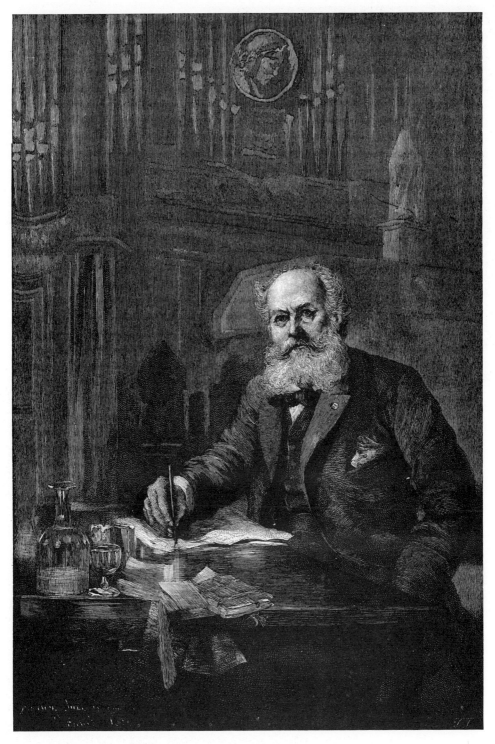

Charles François Gounod, French composer —
from an engraving by T. Johnson after a life drawing by A. J. Goodman

William Hogarth, English painter and engraver—
from an engraving by J. Mollison after a self-portrait by Hogarth

of Filippo Brunelleschi and Lorenzo Ghiberti, he studied antique sculpture but rejected the serenity of its idealized beauty in favor of a more vigorous style. In stone and bronze, in reliefs and in free-standing statues admirably integrated with their architectural setting, he stressed power of expression and dramatic action. His masterpieces include *The Boy David*, the first large bronze free-standing nude since classical times, and the bronze equestrian statue of GATTAMELATA, also the first of its kind since antiquity.

Donation of Constantine. See DECRETALS.

Donatus. In full, **Donatus de octibus partibus orationis.** The most famous Latin grammar. It was named after its author Aelius Donatus, Roman grammarian of the fourth century, who was one of the instructors of St. Jerome.

Don Carlos (1787). A play by Friedrich SCHILLER, based on the life of the son of the Spanish king Philip II. Don CARLOS' libertarian idealism is shared by the older and more experienced Marquis Posa, and the two plot against the tyrannical king. The prince, however, is suspected, and in order to save him, Posa contrives to draw all suspicion upon himself and is murdered by the king. Carlos is then offered his freedom, but in a last, unconsidered burst of idealism, he defies the king, and is turned over to the Inquisition for execution. The play is the basis of Verdi's opera *Don Carlos* (1867).

Don Flows Home to The Sea, The. See QUIET DON, THE.

Don Giovanni (1787). An opera by Wolfgang Amadeus MOZART, with a libretto by Lorenzo DA PONTE. It deals with the adventures of the Spanish libertine DON JUAN. After he and his servant Leporello have committed one piece of villainy after another, the statue of a nobleman Don Giovanni has murdered appears and takes him off to the infernal regions. It is regarded as one of the supreme works of art.

Doni, Anton Francesco (1513–1574). Florentine author and unfrocked priest. He is noted for his dialogues *I Marmi* (*The Marble Steps*) and *I Mondi* (*The Worlds*). The latter was influenced by the *Utopia* of Thomas More, the first example of an English Renaissance work stirring Italian imitation. Doni's work was, in turn, utilized by Campanella in his utopia, *The City of the Sun*.

Donizetti, Gaetano (1797–1848). Prolific Italian composer of operas. The best known are *Don Pasquale* (1845), *Lucrezia Borgia* (1833), LUCIA DI LAMMERMOOR, and *La Favorita* (1840).

Don Juan. A legendary profligate. The origin of the central theme of his widespread legend—that of a statue of a dead man who accepts a libertine's invitation to dinner—is not known. Its first appearance in any literary form was in Tirso de Molina's EL BURLADOR DE SEVILLA (1630), which gave the hero the identity that he has retained ever since: Don Juan, a young nobleman of Seville. It also suggested the internal complications of his nature that have endlessly fascinated writers and composers. The name of Tirso's hero quickly became a synonym for an obsessive and unscrupulous pursuer of women.

The basic plot of this play soon reached France, by way of Italy, and was used in several plays, most notably Molière's DOM JUAN OU LE FESTIN DE PIERRE,

which introduced the figure of Elvire, Don Juan's wife. The attempts of English writers to treat Don Juan, such as Shadwell's *The Libertine* (1676), were unimpressive until G. B. Shaw included his "Don Juan in Hell" scene in MAN AND SUPERMAN. The only significant one of several Spanish versions of the legend after *El Burlador de Sevilla* was DON JUAN TENORIO (1844), by José Zorrilla y Moral. Among the French versions after Molière's day were stories and plays by Prosper Merimée, Dumas père, Alfred de Musset, Balzac, and Flaubert. Pushkin wrote a short verse drama that closely followed the Don Juan legend, *The Stone Guest* (see LITTLE TRAGEDIES).

The most famous of all forms of the story is undoubtedly Mozart's great opera DON GIOVANNI, written to a libretto by Lorenzo da Ponte, although there were several slightly earlier operatic versions. Another outstanding musical work inspired by the Don Juan legend is Richard Strauss's tone poem *Don Juan*.

Don Juan (1819–1824). An unfinished epic satire by Lord BYRON. Byron's DON JUAN only slightly resembles the legendary Spanish rake. He begins his adventures in Spain, but is sent abroad at the age of 16 by his mother, Donna INEZ. His ship is wrecked and he is cast up on a Greek island, where he is nursed back to health by the beautiful HAIDÉE. Lambro, the girl's father, discovers the lovers together, captures Juan, and sells him as a slave to GULBEYAS, the sultana of Constantinople. However, Juan then falls in love with DUDU, a beautiful girl in the harem, and so arouses the jealousy of Gulbeyas that he barely escapes with his life. His next adventure takes him to Russia, where as a soldier he attracts the favor of the Empress Catherine. She sends Juan to England as a courier. The poem breaks off with Juan in England.

Don Juan is sprinkled with long digressions in which Byron, through his hero, gives his views on wealth, power, society, chastity, poets, diplomats, and England. It is written in *ottava rima* and even in its incomplete state contains 16,000 lines in its 16 cantos.

Don Juan in Hell. See MAN AND SUPERMAN.

Don Juan Tenorio (1844). A drama in verse by José ZORRILLA Y MORAL. In Zorrilla's version of the DON JUAN legend, the hero falls in love with the virtuous Doña Inés, repents of his sins, and is saved by her prayers on his behalf. Though Zorrilla himself deprecated his work, it is one of Spain's most popular plays and is regularly performed during the first week in November.

Donnay, Maurice (1859–1945). French playwright. Donnay began his dramatic career with humorous short pieces which he wrote for the Montmartre cabaret *Le Chat Noir*. A gay, quick wit characterizes his comedies, the best of which also contain psychological insight: *Amants* (1895), *La Douloureuse* (1897), *L'Autre Danger* (1902), and *Paraître* (1906). His problem plays, marked by a perceptive wit, include *La Clairière* (1900) and *Les Eclaireuses* (1913), a study of feminism.

Donn-Byrne, Brian Oswald. See Donn BYRNE.

Donne, John (1572?–1631). English poet, first and greatest of the METAPHYSICAL POETS. Donne was of good family, bred as a Roman Catholic, well educated in theology and law, and in his youth a lover of company and elegant women. In 1614, after a long period of hardship following his secret marriage to Anne More, and as his hopes of secular preferment waned, he was converted to Anglicanism. Ordained in 1615, he became dean of St. Paul's Cathedral six years later and possibly the most influential preacher in England.

Donne's best-known poetry falls into two classes, the early ironic and erotic verse and the later religious poems. In his verse satires and in such lyrics as Go And Catch a Falling Star (often entitled *Song*) and *Woman's Constancy,* Donne makes a witty display of worldliness, skepticism, and fickleness. Other poems, such as *The Extasie,* The Anniversaries, The Canonization, and Twicknam Garden, are moving expressions of passion or grief. Donne's love poetry is remarkable for its close analysis of the nature and psychology of love; in its emotional sophistication and highly personal tone, it differs markedly from the conventional courtly love poetry of Donne's day. The later religious poems powerfully express the yearning for union with God of a man obsessed with death, oppressed by his sense of human limitation and sin, by an almost invincible doubt of salvation. Among the most famous of these poems are the sonnets, *Death Be Not Proud* and *Batter My Heart; Three Person'd God;* and the *Hymne to God the Father.*

Donne also wrote numerous elegies, epigrams, and verse letters, many sermons, and the Devotions, an extraordinary series of meditations on the theme of sickness and mortality. This last prose work, together with *The Anniversaries,* reveals his preoccupation with the themes of mutability and death, the paradoxical human union of spirit and matter, themes which are crucial even in the love poems.

Donne's poetry is marked by intellectual power, deep learning, and intense emotion. His imagery, to which the adjective "metaphysical" was chiefly applied, is powerful and striking; it was drawn from Scholastic philosophy, the science of the day, trades and professions, and the simple, commonplace things of everyday life. His meter is irregular and dramatic, preserving the cadence and immediacy of ordinary speech.

Donne's poems were published in 1633 and were very popular and widely imitated during the next generation. He was almost unknown, however, during the 18th century and was disapproved of by Samuel Johnson. A few of the Romantics liked him, but it was only in the 20th century that interest in him was revived to any considerable extent. See conceit.

Donnithorne, Arthur. See Adam Bede.

Donnybrook Fair. A fair held near Dublin in August from the time of King John till 1855. It is noted for its bacchanalian orgies and light-hearted rioting. The name has become proverbial for a disorderly gathering.

Don Pasquale (1845). The title of a comic opera by Gaetano Donizetti.

Don Quixote (de la Mancha, El ingenioso hidalgo) (1605, 1615). A novel by Miguel de Cervantes Saavedra. Alonso Quijano is a gaunt country gentleman, kindly and dignified, who lives in the province of La Mancha. His mind is so crazed by reading romances of chivalry that he believes himself called upon to redress the wrongs of the whole world. Changing his name to Don Quixote de la Mancha, he is knighted by an innkeeper whose miserable hostelry he mistakes for a castle. As his lady love he chooses a peasant girl named Aldonza Lorenzo whom he transforms into Dulcinea del Toboso. Don Quixote now sallies forth into the world but after several mishaps, including a beating administered by some merchants whom he challenges to a passage at arms, he returns to his home. Undaunted, he asks Sancho Panza, an ignorant rustic, to be his squire and promises to reward him with the governorship of the first lands they conquer. Riding Rocinante, a nag as bony as himself, Don Quixote sets out a second time, accompanied by Sancho on his ass Dapple.

During his travels Don Quixote's overexcited imagination invariably blinds him to reality: he thinks windmills to be giants, flocks of sheep to be armies, and galley-slaves to be oppressed gentlemen. Toward the end of the novel, Sancho is named governor of the isle of Barataria, a mock title given to him by some noblemen whose only aim is to make sport of the squire and his master. After being bested in a duel with the Knight of the White Moon, in reality a student of his acquaintance in disguise, Don Quixote, tired and disillusioned, returns to La Mancha, and shortly before his death, renounces books of knight-errantry.

The first part of *Don Quixote,* which may have

Title page of the first edition of *Don Quixote* (1605).

EL INGENIOSO
HIDALGO DON QVI-
xote de la Mancha.

Compuesto por Miguel de Ceruantes Saauedra.

DIRIGIDO AL DVQVE DE
Bejar, Marques de Gibraleon, Conde de Benalcaçar, y Bañares, Vizconde dela Puebla de Alcozer, Señor de las villas de Capilla, Curiel, y Burguillos.

Impresso con licencia, en Valencia, en casa de Pedro Patricio Mey, 1605.

A costa de Iusepe Ferrer mercader de libros, delante la Diputacion.

been conceived while Cervantes was in prison, was first printed in 1605 in Madrid by Juan de la Cuesta. In 1614 a second part was published by an unknown author who used the pseudonym Alonso Fernández de Avellaneda. This bit of plagiarism, though not an unusual practice at the time, spurred Cervantes to complete his own sequel, which appeared the following year and is usually considered superior to the first part.

Although it is generally agreed that Cervantes meant his novel to be a satire on the exaggerated chivalric romances of his time, some critics have interpreted it as an ironic story of an idealist frustrated and mocked in a materialistic world. Others have seen it as a veiled attack on the Catholic church or on contemporary Spanish politics. To many, the contrasting figures of Don Quixote and Sancho Panza, the visionary idealist and the practical realist, symbolize the duality of the Spanish character. With its variegated assortment of minor characters, shepherds, innkeepers, students, priests, and nobles, the novel also gives a panoramic view of 17th-century Spanish society. At the same time its essential humanity has made it a universal favorite. See CLAVILEÑO.

Don Ramón. In D. H. Lawrence's THE PLUMED SERPENT, a scholarly Mexican, the political, religious, and sexual hero of the novel.

Don Segundo Sombra (1926). A novel by Ricardo Güiraldes (1886–1927), Argentine novelist and short-story writer. Güiraldes was a wealthy cosmopolite who travelled widely, but *Don Segundo Sombra* reveals his native roots and draws on his childhood experiences at *La Porteña*, his family's ranch in Buenos Aires province. The narrator of the novel is a boy who runs away from the aunts who have raised him and attaches himself to Don Segundo Sombra, an itinerant ranch worker. During their five-year odyssey, Don Segundo not only teaches him to be an expert cowboy and horseman, but also shows him how to live with courage and honor, according to the gaucho code. After discovering that he is the illegitimate son of a wealthy rancher who has left him his estate, the narrator, by now a young man, acquires a measure of formal culture. Don Segundo, feeling that there is no longer need for his tutelage, goes on his lonely way. In this novel, considered the outstanding fictional example of GAUCHO LITERATURE, Güiraldes captured the essence of the gaucho myth in his scenes of life on the pampas and, above all, in the idealized figure of Don Segundo.

Dooley, Mr. See Finley Peter DUNNE.

Doolittle, Hilda. Pen name, **H.D.** (1886–1961). American poet. Miss Doolittle went to Europe in 1911 where she became acquainted with poets practicing IMAGISM, the movement with which her own name and work are primarily identified. She married the English poet Richard Aldington and thereafter lived abroad. Her work shows the influence of the Greek classics and is distinguished for its simple, clear, and precise visualizations of scenes, images, and objects. *Sea Garden* (1916), her first book of poetry, was followed by *Hymen* (1921); *Heliodora and Other Poems* (1924); *Collected Poems* (1925 and 1940); *Hippolytus Temporizes* (1927), a verse tragedy; and *The Flowering of the Rod* (1946). *Helen in Egypt* (1961), a book-length poem, was published

posthumously. She also wrote fiction, usually dealing with historical themes, as in *Palimpsest* (1926) and *Hedylus* (1928).

Doomsday Book. See DOMESDAY BOOK.

Doon. A river in Ayrshire, Scotland, celebrated in the poems of Robert BURNS.

Doon de Mayence. A medieval cycle of CHANSONS DE GESTE about the heroes opposed, at least part of the time, to Charlemagne. They include the histories of GANELON, OGIER THE DANE, and the *Four Sons of* AYMON.

Doppelgänger (Ger., *doppel*, double; *gänger*, walker). The ghostly or spiritual double of a living being, the appearance of which supposedly presages that person's imminent death. The *Doppelgänger* theme is a favorite with German romantic authors and has been treated by E. T. A. Hoffmann and Heinrich Heine; the latter's poem, *Der Doppelgänger*, was set to music by Franz Schubert.

Dora. See Dora SPENLOW.

Doralice. In the Orlando poems of BOIARDO and Ariosto, the daughter of King Stordilano of Granata and the betrothed of Rodomonte, whom she deserts for Mandricardo, thus causing a fatal discord in the camp of the pagan warriors opposed to Charlemagne and his paladins.

Dorante. The unscrupulous nobleman in Molière's LE BOURGEOIS GENTILHOMME. He fleeces the social-climbing M. Jourdain of a great deal of his wealth under the pretext of offering him social advancement.

Doré, [Paul] Gustave (1833–1883). French illustrator and painter. He is famous for masterly and imaginative illustrations of such classics as the works of Rabelais, Balzac, Dante, Cervantes, and the Bible.

Doria, Andrea (c. 1468–1560). Genoese admiral; called "Father of Peace" and "Liberator of Genoa." In 1951 his name was given to a luxury liner of the Italian Line, that sank (July 25, 1956) during a transatlantic crossing after having been rammed by the S.S. *Stockholm*. The name is also that given to one of the main characters in Schiller's *Fiesko*.

Dorian or **Doric.** Pertaining to the Dorians, traditionally the last of the groups of tribes who invaded Greece in pre-Classical times. The so-called Dorian invasion, probably from the North, early in the 12th century B.C., put an end to the Mycenaean era and was long thought to have caused a protracted Dark Age, although the process is now considered to have been much less clear-cut and complete than was formerly supposed.

In Classical times, Doric attitudes were identified with solidity and simplicity, as in the "Doric order" of architecture characterized by plain, chaste forms. The "Dorian mode" in music, a scale that may be reproduced by playing all the white notes from one D to the next on a piano, was regarded by Plato as being conducive to sobriety and other virtues needed by the citizen of an ideal state. See GREEK MUSIC.

Dorigen. See FRANKLIN'S TALE.

Dormouse, the. The mouse in ALICE'S ADVENTURES IN WONDERLAND. He is thrust into a teapot by the Hatter and the March Hare. The word dormouse probably means "sleeping mouse" (from Fr., *dormir*, "to sleep").

Dorotea, La (1632). A prose romance in dialogue by Lope de VEGA. He called it "the most beloved of my works." The novel is partly autobiographical, and the Dorotea of the title is the actress Elena Osorio, with whom Lope had an affair and whom he called Filis in other works. He wrote the book at an early age but revised it years later, including details of his liaison with Marta de Nevares. *La Dorotea* was influenced by LA CELESTINA, whose main character is reincarnated in Lope's work by Gerarda.

Dorothea, St. A martyr under Diocletian about 303. She is represented with a rose branch in her hand, a wreath of roses on her head, and roses with fruit by her side; sometimes with also an angel carrying a basket with three apples and three roses. The legend is that Theophilus, the judge's secretary, scoffingly said to her, as she was going to execution, "Send me some fruit and roses, Dorothea, when you get to Paradise." Immediately after her execution, while Theophilus was at dinner with a party of companions, a young angel brought to him a basket of apples and roses, saying, "From Dorothea in Paradise," and vanished. Theophilus, of course, was a convert from that moment. The story forms the basis of Massinger's tragedy, *The Virgin Martyr* (1622).

Dorr Rebellion (1842). A rising in Rhode Island led by Thomas Wilson Dorr (1805–1854) to revise the state constitution, which severely restricted suffrage. In 1842 Dorr was elected governor by the reformers, while Samuel King was chosen at the regular elections; thus the state had two separate governments, Dorr basing his authority on the power of the people. The movement collapsed after Dorr's attempt to seize the state arsenal was frustrated by King, who had declared martial law. A constitution providing for nearly universal suffrage was adopted in 1843.

Dorset, Thomas Sackville, earl of. See Thomas SACKVILLE.

Dory, John. See JOHN DORY.

Dos Passos, John (1896–   ). American novelist. Best known for his trilogy *U.S.A.* (q.v.), Dos Passos was one of the group of Harvard writers who graduated shortly before World War I. With E. E. Cummings, who had also gone to Harvard, and Ernest Hemingway, who had not, Dos Passos joined the Norton-Harjes Ambulance Service during the war. From this experience came his first important novel, THREE SOLDIERS.

After the war he was a newspaperman and free-lance writer. His next novel, MANHATTAN TRANSFER, was a major step toward the technical perfection of his later trilogy. The work also reveals the conflict between Dos Passos' concern for individual liberty and his social conscience which was to remain characteristic of his work as a writer. In the late 1920's, he turned to the theater with three plays noted for their "movie" technique: *The Moon Is a Gong* (1926), *Airways, Inc.* (1928), and *Fortune Heights* (1933).

In 1930, Dos Passos published THE 42ND PARALLEL, the first novel of his trilogy. *1919* (q.v.) and THE BIG MONEY completed the series, which was published as *U.S.A.* in 1938. A massive achievement, the trilogy is noted for its technical brilliance and mastery of language. Combining such special devices as the "news-reel" and the "camera eye" with many short, well-written biographies and the narrative proper, *U.S.A.* is a vast panorama of American life; indeed, the country itself is its subject and protagonist.

Dos Passos began a new trilogy, which was later published under the single title *District of Columbia* (1952), with ADVENTURES OF A YOUNG MAN. This saga of the Spottswood family also includes *Number One* (1943) and *The Grand Design* (1949). This trilogy and THE GROUND WE STAND ON mark a change in Dos Passos' social and political attitudes; always concerned with the freedom of the individual, he became much more conservative during this period. His books of nonfiction include *State of the Nation* (1944), *Tour of Duty* (1946), *The Prospect Before Us* (1950), *Chosen Country* (1951), *The Theme Is Freedom* (1956), *The Great Days* (1958), *Prospects of a Golden Age* (1959), and *Midcentury* (1961).

Dostoevski, Feodor Mikhailovich (1821–1881). Russian novelist. One of the most outstanding and influential writers of modern literature, Dostoevski was born in Moscow, the son of a doctor and the second of eight children. When he was 16 years old, Dostoevski's mother died. A year later, he was enrolled in the Military Engineering School in St. Petersburg. His elder brother Mikhail had also applied, but was turned down by the medical examiners. Young Dostoevski was left alone, in an atmosphere uncongenial to his nature, without Mikhail, his closest friend, and with what he considered an insufficient allowance. His letters to his father begin to sound a note that is to be heard often in his later correspondence: his desperate need for more money. Another problem was his work at the school; drawing plans for military fortifications interested him far less than reading literature. Before his graduation (1843), Dostoevski had already decided that his career would not be that of a military engineer. He remained in the army's service just a little over a year after graduation; he then resigned and took up his lifelong occupation as a writer.

Dostoevski's first publication (1844) was a translation of Balzac's novel *Eugénie Grandet*. Meanwhile, he was working on a novel of his own, a work in epistolary form entitled POOR FOLK. The manuscript reached the leading critic of the day, Vissarion BELINSKI, probably by way of Dostoevski's friend Dmitri Grigorovich and the poet Nikolai Nekrasov. Belinski read the work and launched into ecstatic praise of it. *Poor Folk* perfectly fulfilled his idea of what literature should be; it showed compassion for the poor and downtrodden and succeeded in stirring the reader's humanitarian feelings. Belinski's approval was enough to insure Dostoevski's reputation as a talented new writer. The novel was published (1846) in the *Petersburg Miscellany* (*Petersburgski sbornik*), edited by Nekrasov. A few weeks later Dostoevski's second work, THE DOUBLE, appeared. This short novel, a study of a poor clerk's mental disintegration, was less pleasing to both critics and public. In 1846, Dostoevski also published a short story, *Gospodin Prokharchin* (*Mr. Prokharchin*). The critical acclaim at first given Dostoevski's work was now absent: *The Double, Mr. Prokharchin,* and *Khozayka* (*The Landlady,* 1847) were all failures in Belinski's estimation. The adverse criticism strained Dostoevski's relations with Belinski and the circle of young writers surrounding him, including Nekrasov and Ivan TURGENEV—the feud with Turgenev becoming a lifetime preoccupation of Dostoevski.

A more serious problem than bad reviews or literary feuds began at about this time for the young author: the onset of the epileptic attacks that were to plague him throughout his life. Some writers, including Sigmund Freud, have speculated that these attacks actually began earlier, about the time Dostoevski's father was murdered by his serfs (1844). This theory holds that the attacks were a form of self-punishment for Dostoevski's suppressed wish for his father's death and that his later gambling mania was similarly caused. The preoccupation with the theme of parricide in Dostoevski's last novel, THE BROTHERS KARAMAZOV, is also evidence of Dostoevski's feeling of guilt, according to this view.

In 1848, Dostoevski published three short stories: Slaboye serdtze (A Faint Heart), Chestnyi vor (The Honest Thief), and Belye nochi (White Nights). In the last of these stories, the emphasis on the unreal, miragelike quality of St. Petersburg foreshadows a theme that was developed further in some of his later works. At this time, Dostoevski was also working on a novel, Netochka Nezvanova, but he never completed it. It was during this year that he became involved with a group of young intellectuals headed by Mikhail Vasilyevich Petrashevski (1819–1867). The Petrashevski circle, as the group was known, met to read and discuss the works of the French Utopian socialists and other political and social topics forbidden open discussion by the Czarist regime. In 1849 the members of the group were arrested. They were charged, among other things, with having read the banned Belinski letter to Nikolai GOGOL and of having conspired to set up a secret printing press. After eight months in prison, during which time he wrote another short story, Malenkyi geroi (The Little Hero), Dostoevski was taken with his alleged fellow conspirators to the site of their execution. At the very last moment, they were informed that their sentence was actually to be exile and imprisonment in Siberia. The shattering experience of the near execution never left Dostoevski. He used the episode in his novel THE IDIOT, and mentioned it in his journalistic writings.

Dostoevski was sentenced to four years in the labor camp at Omsk, after which he was obliged to enlist for a four-year term in the army, most of which time he served at Semipalatinsk. These years have been described by Dostoevski as vitally important ones for his development as a writer. His enforced contact with the convicts at Omsk gave him a knowledge of the Russian lower classes, possessed by no other Russian author. During his prison term the only book allowed him was the New Testament, which he read constantly and which directed his thought toward the religious view of life so prominent in his novels. The fruits of his observations and thought in the Omsk prison were contained in his THE HOUSE OF THE DEAD.

While serving his army term, Dostoevski met and, after a hectic courtship, married (1857) the widow Marya Dmitrieyevna Isayeva. In 1859 he was allowed to resign from the army and to return to European Russia, settling first in Tver and then returning to

St. Petersburg. While still in Siberia, he had begun writing again, and he arrived in St. Petersburg with two short novels: Dyadushkin son (Uncle's Dream) and A FRIEND OF THE FAMILY, both published in 1859. In 1861 his brother Mikhail began to publish the journal Vremya (Time). In this periodical Dostoevski published the novel THE INSULTED AND INJURED in which one of his major ideas, the beneficial effects of suffering, was first enunciated. He also serialized his House of the Dead in the journal.

In the summer of 1862, Dostoevski made his first trip to Europe, visiting Paris, London, and Geneva. His impressions of what he saw were contained in Zimnye zametki o letnikh vpechatleniyakh (Winter Notes on Summer Impressions, 1863).

The journal Vremya was suppressed by the government in 1863, because of an unfortunate article on the Polish rebellion of that year. Dostoevski, who had been editing the publication, made his second trip abroad at this time. This time, however, he had a companion, Apollinariya (Polina) Suslova, a young woman who had contributed a short piece to Vremya in 1861. Dostoevski's relations with his wife had been strained for some time. Whether Polina was a cause or a result of this situation is unclear. It is certain, however, that Polina was a torment to him. She was reputedly Dostoevski's model for "the infernal woman" whom he depicted in his later novels. On the trip through Europe, Dostoevski visited the gambling houses at Wiesbaden, Germany, where he gave in to the mania that, for some years, was to continue to trouble him.

Returning to Russia (1864), Dostoevski became editor of the new journal published by his brother. In this periodical, Epokha (Epoch), appeared NOTES FROM UNDERGROUND, the work that is generally cited, because of its artistic excellence and psychological acuteness, as the first of Dostoevski's mature writings. Dostoevski wrote the work while tending his dying wife, who was, at last, succumbing from consumption which had long afflicted her. Shortly after her death, Dostoevski had another blow: the death of his brother Mikhail. Left with the care of Mikhail's family as well as with that of his own stepson, he labored desperately to make Epokha a successful publication. The conservative political slant he gave the journal lessened its popularity, however, and in 1865 the venture had to be abandoned. Dostoevski made another trip to Europe where he again met Polina, did some gambling, and worked on a novel he hoped would pull him out of his financial predicament. This work, CRIME AND PUNISHMENT, was published in 1866. In the same year Dostoevski published a short novel, THE GAMBLER. The deadline for this work was fast approaching, and the novelist had to hire a stenographer to take down the work in shorthand and transcribe it. The girl hired for this job, Anna Grigoryevna Snitkina, became Dostoevski's second wife in 1867. The couple went abroad to escape creditors the following year. They lived in Dresden, Baden-Baden, and Geneva, always in financial straits made worse by Dostoevski's intermittent gambling sprees. On the trip to Geneva, they stopped off in Basle where Dostoevski saw Holbein's painting Dead Christ in the museum. The strong impression of the work prompted Dostoevski to include a discussion of it in the novel he was then writing. This work, published in serial form in 1868, was *The Idiot*. The effort involved in attempting to portray the saintly Myshkin in the novel was made more agonizing by the death of his infant daughter Sonya, who died at the age of three months.

During 1869, Dostoevski and Anna moved restlessly about Europe, from Switzerland, to Italy, to Austria, and finally to Dresden again. There a second daughter, Lyubov, was born. Dostoevski was at work during this period on one of his best short novels, THE ETERNAL HUSBAND. At the same time he was making preliminary notes for a massive work, to be contained in several novels, that would deal with the religious problems which had been the center of his thought for some years. The work was to be "the life of a great sinner," tracing his early growth, his falling away from faith, and his ultimate redemption. The broad scope of ideas contained in the plan was to include all of Dostoevski's late novels. STAVROGIN, the sinister hero of THE POSSESSED, could be taken as a depiction of the great sinner who had lost his faith, as could IVAN KARAMAZOV. Arkadi, the young hero of A RAW YOUTH, in some respects resembles the nascent sinner, who has not yet set out on the journey through the "furnace of doubt" that leads to religious faith. The idea of the movement into the world and back to faith is also present in *The Brothers Karamazov*.

After his return to Russia (1871), Dostoevski again entered journalistic work, editing the weekly *Grazhdanin (The Citizen)*, in 1873–1874. In 1876 he published the first part of his DIARY OF A WRITER. This publication, which was also issued in 1877 and in 1880–1881, contained articles on political, social, and literary topics, as well as some original short stories, including *Krotkaya (A Gentle Spirit*, 1876) and *Son smeshnogo cheloveka (The Dream of a Ridiculous Man*, 1877). These last years of Dostoevski's life were financially the easiest ones he had known. Professionally, he was also at his peak, especially after the publication of *The Brothers Karamazov*. The climax of his long career came with his speech at the Pushkin celebration in Moscow in 1880, in which he cited the poet as a model of his own ideas about the unique, all-embracing universality of the Russian character. In January, 1881, Dostoevski died in St. Petersburg.

Since his death Dostoevski's reputation has steadily grown as one of the greatest writers in literary history. The acuteness of his psychological perceptions and analyses have amazed later experts in psychology, including Freud. Dostoevski's philosophical profundity has provided a rich field of investigation and imitation for writers and philosophers. His range of philosophical ideas and approaches has led to his being claimed as a forerunner by such diverse groups as Russian Orthodox thinkers and atheistic existentialist writers. With TOLSTOI Dostoevski ranks as a supreme master of the realistic novel which is Russia's major contribution to literature. Dostoevski's artistic methods have until recently received less attention than his psychological and philosophical ideas. That he was above all a master artist has been attested by readers the world over and, perhaps more convincingly, by other great novelists who have an intimate knowledge of the craft of fiction.

In his own country, Dostoevski has less public recognition than he has in other countries. His well-known animus toward socialism, his emphasis on religion and on the irrationalism in the psychological processes of the individual mind have made him unattractive to the rulers of Soviet literary opinion, particularly during the most rigid periods of intellectual censorship under Stalin. As better ways are found to explain away embarrassing aspects of Dostoevski's work, Soviet publishers will undoubtedly tend to reprint his novels more often.

Dotheboys Hall. See NICHOLAS NICKLEBY.

Double, The (Dvoinik; 1846). A short novel by Feodor DOSTOEVSKI. *The Double* is a fantastic tale, similar in style and manner to some of Gogol's work, particularly to *Diary of a Madman*, which also depicts the mental disintegration of the hero. Yakov Petrovich GOLYADKIN, the hero of *The Double*, is a lowly civil servant who awkwardly and unsuccessfully pursues the daughter of his employer. After some cruel rebuffs, a strangeness enters Golyadkin's world and another Golyadkin, his absolute double, appears on the scene. Where the old Golyadkin had fumbled, the young Golyadkin is adroit. He is soon a favorite in exactly the way the first Golyadkin yearned to be. The nightmare ends when Golyadkin is taken away from his phantoms to the madhouse.

At the time of its publication, *The Double* aroused no enthusiasm in the critics. They were more interested in work which made some kind of social comment, such as Dostoevski's *Poor Folk*, than they were in depictions of the processes of psychological breakdown. The influential critic Belinski was especially displeased with the work and began to rue his earlier high praise of the author.

Doubting Castle. See PILGRIM'S PROGRESS.

Doughty, Charles Montagu (1843–1926). English traveler and writer. He is best known for his *Travels in Arabia Deserta* (1888), an account of two years of tribulation and wandering in Arabia notable for its vivid picture of Bedouin life and its curious, intriguing style, which combines English words and phrases with many Arabic expressions. Doughty also wrote a number of poems—which share some of the peculiarities of his prose—of which the best known is the lengthy *The Dawn in Britain* (1906).

Douglas. A family in Scottish history, legend, and romance. There were two branches: the *Black Douglases*, or senior branch, and the *Red Douglases*, who came to the fore later. They are prominent in Sir Walter Scott's novels, notably the following:

(1) *Sir James*, the first of the Black Douglases. See James DOUGLAS.

(2) *Archibald the Grim*, natural son of "the Good Sir James." He is prominent in *The Fair Maid of Perth*.

(3) *James Douglas*, earl of Morton, one of the Red Douglases. He figures prominently in THE MONASTERY and THE ABBOT.

(4) *Ellen Douglas*. Heroine of Scott's narrative poem, *The Lady of the Lake*.

Douglas, Lord Alfred (1870–1945). English poet, noted as a sonnet writer. His relationship with Oscar Wilde provoked his father, Lord Queensberry, to action that led to Wilde's conviction for homosexual practices. See DE PROFUNDIS.

Douglas, Gawain or **Gavin** (1474?–1522). Scottish poet, bishop of Dunkeld. He was the author of *The Palace of Honor* (printed c. 1553) and *King*

Hart (first printed in 1786), two allegorical poems, and a translation of the *Aeneid* (completed 1513), which is called the earliest translation of a Latin classic into English. Douglas was a member of the group called the Scottish Chaucerians.

Douglas, James. Called **Black Douglas** (1286–1330). In the days of Robert Bruce and Edward II, Douglas invaded England and plundered many towns and villages in the North. In his *History of Scotland*, Scott writes: "It was said that the name of this indefatigable and successful chief had become so formidable that women in the northern countries, used to still their froward children by threatening them with the Black Douglas." He destroyed an English garrison three times, and it is on one of these incidents that Scott based his novel CASTLE DANGEROUS.

Douglas, Lloyd C[assel] (1877–1951). American novelist. A clergyman, Douglas was over 50 when he published his first book, *Magnificent Obsession* (1929), and thereafter he published several best-selling novels of a piously didactic, inspirational character. Perhaps the best known of these is *The Robe* (1942), the story of what happened to Christ's robe after the Crucifixion. Other novels are *Precious Jeopardy* (1933), *Green Light* (1935), *White Banners* (1936), *Disputed Passage* (1939) and *The Big Fisherman* (1948).

Douglas, [George] Norman (1868–1952). English novelist and travel writer. Best known for the novel SOUTH WIND, Douglas lived for many years on the island of Capri and in Italy and other Mediterranean countries, and made these the settings for his books. An art lover and a scholar (biologist, geologist, archaeologist, and classicist), he was also a hedonist and a skeptic. His interests are uniquely blended in his books. In *Siren Land* (1911), his first book, he established his style. It is a traveler's lively description of Sorrento and Capri, interspersed with learned, fantastic, and lightly satirical essays. *Fountains in the Sand* (1912) is about Tunisia, and *Old Calabria* (1915), considered his best travel book, is about southern Italy. The novels *They Went* (1920) and *In the Beginning* (1927) are fantasies about mankind's early history. Among Douglas's other books are *London Street Games* (1916); *Birds and Beasts of the Greek Anthology* (1927); *Some Limericks* (1928); *How About Europe?* (1929), a claim that Christianity is causing the decay of our society, and *Looking Back* (1933), a fragmentary autobiography.

Douglas, Stephen A[rnold] (1813–1861). American statesman, known as the "Little Giant." After holding several state offices in Illinois, Douglas was elected to Congress in 1843 and to the U.S. Senate in 1847. He introduced the KANSAS-NEBRASKA ACT, which incorporated the principle of popular sovereignty, but lost the support of Southern Democrats when he opposed the proslavery Lecompton constitution for Kansas, which he claimed violated popular sovereignty. During his famous debates (1858) with Abraham Lincoln when both were candidates for the Senate, Douglas formulated his "Freeport doctrine," maintaining that the people of a territory might admit or exclude slavery because slavery could not exist unless it was supported by local police regulations. Although Douglas won the Senate seat, the Freeport doctrine further alienated Southerners and probably cost him their backing for the 1860 Democratic nomi-nation. In 1860 Douglas was the presidential candidate of Northern Democrats and lost to Lincoln.

Douglas, William O[rville] (1898–   ). American jurist and author. Beginning as a high-school teacher in Yakima, Wash., Douglas then studied law, practiced in New York City, and taught at Columbia and Yale universities. He entered government service in 1929 and was appointed to the U.S. Supreme Court by President Roosevelt 10 years later.

Several of his books, based on trips abroad, give expert reports on political conditions and vivid depictions of foreign scenes; these include *Strange Lands and Friendly People* (1951), *Beyond the High Mountains* (1952), and *North from Himalaya* (1953). Douglas, an outdoor man and a lover of nature, also wrote *My Wilderness: The Pacific West* (1960). Among his other works are *An Almanac of Liberty* (1954), *America Challenged* (1960), *A Living Bill of Rights* (1961), and *Mr. Lincoln and the Negroes* (1963).

Douglass, Frederick (1817?–1895). American abolitionist, orator, and journalist. The son of a Negro slave and a white father, Douglass escaped to the North in 1838. A speech he delivered at an anti-slavery convention in Nantucket in 1841 made such an impression that he was soon in great demand as a speaker. Mobbed and beaten because of his views, he described his experiences in an outspoken *Narrative of the Life of Frederick Douglass* (1845). After a two-year stay in Great Britain, where he earned enough money to buy his freedom, he founded *The North Star*, a newspaper which he published for 17 years, advocating the use of Negro troops during the Civil War and civil rights for freedmen. He held various public offices after the war.

Doukhobors. See DUKHOBORS.

Dove Cottage. The house where Dorothy and William WORDSWORTH made their home, from 1799 to 1807, at Grasmere in the English Lake District. See LAKE POETS.

Dover Beach (1867). A poem by Matthew ARNOLD expressing his pessimism with regard to the future of the modern world and advocating personal fidelity and love as the rather desperate substitute for the ebbing "sea of faith":

> Ah, love, let us be true
> To one another! for the world, which seems
> To lie before us like a land of dreams,
> So various, so beautiful, so new,
> Hath really neither joy, nor love, nor light. . . .

Dowden, Edward (1843–1913). Anglo-Irish essayist, poet, and critic. He is known chiefly for his numerous books on Shakespeare such as *Shakespeare, His Mind and Art* (1875), *A Shakespeare Primer* (1877), and *Introduction to Shakespeare* (1893). He was also the author of a notable *Life of Shelley* (1866).

Dowland, John (1563–1626). Composer and lutenist. Dowland was born in Ireland and died in London, but spent much of his life in France, Germany, and Denmark. He ended his days as lutenist to the King of England. A man of melancholy temperament, Dowland is accounted the greatest lutenist the world has ever known, and his compositions for lute, and for voice and lute, are the finest of their type.

Downing Street. Figuratively, the British government in power (because the Prime Minister lives at No. 10, and his cabinet usually meets there) or the foreign office (which is also located there). It is in Westminster.

Dowsabell. A common name for a sweetheart, especially an unsophisticated country girl, in poems of Elizabethan times. It is from the French *douce et belle*, sweet and beautiful. Michael Drayton wrote a poem called *The Ballad of Dowsabell* (1606).

Dowson, Ernest [Christopher] (1867–1900). English poet. Dowson is best known for his poem CYNARA, properly entitled *Nom Sum Qualis Eram Bonae Sub Regno Cynarae*.

Doyle, Sir Arthur Conan (1859–1930). English novelist, known chiefly for his series of tales concerning Sherlock HOLMES. Also noteworthy are his historical novels, *Micah Clarke* (1888) and THE WHITE COMPANY, and his imaginative fantasy *The Lost World* (1912). The Holmes stories, conceived to augment Doyle's income from an unsuccessful medical practice, quickly made their author famous. At one point, tiring of the detective, Doyle attempted to exterminate him in *The Memoirs of Sherlock Holmes* (1894), but the clamor of his admirers forced him to resurrect Holmes for several further volumes, and his popularity has waned little since. Doyle was much interested in the occult, and wrote a *History of Spiritualism* (1926). Among his finer characters are Professor CHALLENGER and Brigadier GERARD.

Drachenfels (*Ger.* dragon-rock). The home of the dragon slain by Siegfried in the NIBELUNGENLIED.

Drachman, Holger (1846–1908). Danish poet. At first, Drachman joined the "Modern Awakening" movement led by Georg Brandes and wrote poems of passionate sympathy for suffering laborers. Among his early collections are *Doempede Melodier* (1875), *Ungdom i Digt og Sang* (1879), *Ranker og Roser* (1879), and *Princessen og det halve kongerige* (1878). In the 1880's, however, he turned his lyric gifts to new ends and produced the romantic, patriotic verse of such collections as *Dybe Strenge* (1884), *Sangenes Bog* (1889), and *Unge Viser* (1892).

Draco (Drakon; fl. 650 B.C.). An Athenian legislator. In 621 B.C. he was given extraordinary power to codify the laws of Athens for the first time. His work was designed to replace individual revenge with public justice. His code was known for its severity, and was said to have been written in blood, rather than ink. The death penalty was prescribed for several crimes, and cases of murder were to be tried by the AREOPAGUS. Under Draco's Code, debtors could be claimed as slaves. SOLON abolished the Code except for the law relating to murder.

dragon. A mythical beast. Found in the mythology and folklore of innumerable peoples, it was commonly conceived of as a kind of large serpent of hostile disposition. In its earliest forms, it was a monster sea serpent, perhaps suggested to the primitive mind by the undulating surface and unruly habits of rivers and seas. The first known example is the Sumerian KUR, though its precise appearance is not clear from the three extant myths in which he or she appears. Kur, like all dragons, seems to have existed mainly to be killed by a hero; the Sumerian champions who accomplished this feat were ENKI, NINURTA, and the goddess Inanna.

The basic theme of the sea dragons slain by a hero was developed further by the Babylonian conquerors of Sumeria in the story of the WAR OF THE GODS, in which the primeval sea, TIAMAT, the mother of the gods, is regarded as a dragon; she is killed by the hero Marduk. Among the Canaanites it is Baal, the storm god, who subdues YAM, the dragon of the sea. The Hebrew Yahweh is similarly credited with the destruction of the leviathan, of Rahab, and of simply "the dragon." Several Greek heroes slay dragons that are also associated with water and with the Near East. PERSEUS rescued Andromeda from a sea monster in Canaan; the Canaanite CADMUS killed a dragon that guarded a spring at Thebes. The HYDRA, as the name implies, was also a water creature, and Heracles had many Near Eastern connections. Even the famous feat attributed to St. GEORGE is an echo of the Perseus myth, for George killed his dragon at Lydda very near to Joppa, where Perseus' dragon ravaged the land.

Another common class of dragons guarded sacred places. This notion may have sprung from the widespread belief that the dead returned as serpents (Cadmus, himself, became one) and were often venerated as such. Sacred snakes were associated with many oracles, including that at Delphi, and for such religious festivals as the Thesmophoria at Athens. Dragons (Gr. *drakon*, snake) guarded the apples of the HESPERIDES and the GOLDEN FLEECE. The less benevolent dragons of northern Europe guarded hoards of treasure, which were wrested from them by such heroes as BEOWULF and Sigurd (SIEGFRIED).

The dragons of the Chinese and Japanese mythology are totally different from the hostile varieties. Powerful spirits of air, sea, and earth, they are generally benevolent and are responsible to a considerable degree for the orderly functioning of natural phenomena.

Among the many Christian saints who are usually pictured with dragons may be mentioned St. Michael; St. Margaret; St. Sylvester, the pope; St. Samson, archbishop of Dol; St. Donatus; St. Clement of Metz; St. Romain of Rouen, who destroyed the huge dragon, La Gargouille, which ravaged the Seine; St. Philip the Apostle, who killed another at Hierapolis, in Phrygia; St. Martha, who slew the terrible dragon, Tarasque, at Aix-la-Chapelle; St. Florent, who killed a dragon that haunted the Loire; St. Cado, St. Maudet, and St. Pol, who did similar feats in Brittany; and St. Keyne of Cornwall.

Among the ancient Britons and Welsh the dragon was the national symbol on the war standard; hence the term, PENDRAGON for the *dux bellorum*, or leader in war (*pen* = head or chief). See FAFNER; GRENDEL.

Dragontina. In the ORLANDO INNAMORATO of Boiardo, an enchantress who rules the Island of Forgetfulness. At one point in the story, Orlando is her prisoner until rescued by Angelica, who needs him to defend her fortress at Albracca.

Drake, Sir Francis (1540?–1596). First English circumnavigator of the globe. After sailing as a privateer against Spanish vessels in the West Indies, Drake in December, 1577, set off on his round-the-world voyage. He passed through the Straits of Magellan, up the coast of South America, and as far as 48° north latitude along the North American coast, which he named New Albion and claimed in the name of Elizabeth. He then sailed to Celebes, around the Cape of Good Hope, and back to England, returning in October of 1580. He fought against the Spanish Armada in 1588, and died in the course of an expedition to the West Indies.

Drake, Joseph Rodman (1795–1820). American poet and satirist. Drake studied medicine but after obtaining his degree opened a pharmacy in New York City. His early death from tuberculosis prevented his full development as a poet. With Fitz-Greene HALLECK, Drake composed the witty *Croaker Papers;* he is best known for the posthumously published tale in verse called *The Culprit Fay* (1835). A nature fantasy, the poem tells the story of a fay who loved a mortal maiden. Another well-known poem is the eulogy, *The American Flag* (1819). Drake is buried in the New York City park that was named in his honor.

Drake, Temple. A character in William Faulkner's SANCTUARY and REQUIEM FOR A NUN. A 17-year-old college student in *Sanctuary*, Temple is a provocative and irresponsible girl who invites by her actions the rape she half fears and half desires. Playing the part of the victim, she subsequently allows herself to be kept at a brothel by POPEYE and perjures herself at the murder trial of an innocent man, less out of malice toward the accused than out of indifference. In *Requiem for a Nun*, she persists in her former attitudes by refusing, until the very end, to see herself as anything but a respectable woman wronged by circumstance.

dramatic irony. A theatrical device, consisting in the conscious production by the author of an ironical situation, i.e., a marked incongruity between a character's words and the action; as for instance in Schiller's *Wallenstein* when the hero (not aware of the plot on his life of which the audience has been informed) says before going to bed: "I intend to take a long rest." The understanding of the unintentional play on words imparts to the audience for a moment the role of "an omniscient god of the drama."

dramatic unities. See UNITIES.

Drapier's Letters (1724–1725). A series of pamphlets by Jonathan SWIFT, purporting to be from the pen of a linen draper, "M. B. Drapier." They attack a patent for coining halfpence granted to William Wood by King George I and Sir Robert Walpole without the consent of the Irish Parliament, and advise the Irish not to accept the coinage. Although Wood's halfpence were certified a sound coinage, the scheme was defeated after severe riots by the Dublin mob.

Draupadi. In Hindu legend, daughter of king Drupada and wife of the five Pandava brothers (in the MAHABHARATA). In the epic, she is a strong-willed, proud character, whose outrage at being disrobed in the palace hall by Duryodhana is one of the major factors in leading up to the battle of Kurukshetra, when the Pandavas take revenge on Duryodhana.

Draupnir. In Scandinavian mythology, a magic ring, the symbol of fertility, made for Odin by the dwarfs. Every ninth night it dropped eight rings equal in size and beauty to itself.

Drayman Henschel (Fuhrmann Henschel; 1898). A drama by Gerhart HAUPTMANN. A man

has promised his late wife to be faithful to her memory. However, he is trapped into marriage by the machinations of his ambitious housekeeper. Oppressed and bullied by her, he finally commits suicide.

Drayton, Michael (1563–1631). English poet. Born in the same county (Warwickshire) as Shakespeare, he matched the master in the range, if not the quality, of his poetic achievement. Always experimenting and continually revising, Drayton wrote sonnets, dramas, odes, mythological poems, satires, pastorals, and historical verse narratives. His works include *Idea, the Shepherd's Garland* (1593); *Idea's Mirror* (1594), a sonnet sequence; *England's Heroical Epistles* (1597); POLYOLBION, a poetical survey of the topography of England; NIMPHIDIA, a charming minor epic set in a fairy atmosphere; *Idea*, a completely revised version of his earlier sonnet sequence; and *The Muses Elyzium* (1630). Drayton also wrote a number of plays that have not survived. According to one tradition, it was as a result of a "merry meeting" with Drayton and Ben Jonson that Shakespeare contracted the illness that resulted in his death.

Dream Children: A Reverie (1822). One of the best-known essays of Charles LAMB, prompted by the death of the author's brother James. In it, Lamb describes an imaginary conversation held with the children he has never had. See ALICE W—N.

Dream of Gerontius, A. A poem by John Henry NEWMAN in which Gerontius makes his last journey

Title page of Drayton's satire *The Owle* (1604).

to God, carried by his guardian angel through a world of good and evil spirits. *A Dream of Gerontius* has been set to music in the form of an oratorio by Sir Edward Elgar (1900).

Dream of the Red Chamber. See HUNG LOU MENG.

Dream of the Rood, The. Old English religious poem, one of the finest, of 156 lines in ALLITERATIVE VERSE. A fragment of it is inscribed (early eighth century) on a stone cross in Scotland, and the VERCELLI BOOK has a complete version (late ninth century). The poet lyrically describes dreaming that the Rood, or True Cross, speaks to him about its own history and urges him to promote its cult. Then he tells how the dream has changed his life, alluding to Christ's life in his own prayer for heavenly reward.

dreams, the gates of. Two gates in Hades, one of ivory and one of horn. Dreams that delude pass through the ivory gate, those that come true pass through the gate of horn. This fancy depends upon two puns: ivory in Greek is *elephas*, and the verb *eliphairo* means to cheat with empty hopes; the Greek for horn is *keras*, and the verb *karanoo* means to accomplish. Anchises dismissed Aeneas through the ivory gate, on quitting the infernal regions, to indicate the unreality of his vision.

Dreary Story, A (Skuchnaya istoriya; 1889). A story by Anton CHEKHOV subtitled *From the Notebook of an Old Man.* The story is usually regarded as the starting point of Chekhov's mature writings. In it he introduces the theme of the difficulty of real communication between people, which he was to take up in so many of his later works. The old man of the tale, Professor Nikolai Stepanovich, realizes as his life draws to a close that he has lived his years without a unifying ideal to make a whole of his personal, professional, and social relationships. As he reviews it, his life seems fragmented, aimless, and worthless. The same kind of despair is experienced by his young ward Katya. Because neither can really communicate with the other, both the professor and Katya are left to endure their agonies singly.

Dred Scott decision (1857). A U.S. Supreme Court decision in the case of Dred Scott (1795?–1858), a Negro slave who had been taken by his master from Missouri to Illinois and Wisconsin, where slavery was prohibited. After his return to Missouri, Scott sued for his liberty on the basis of his residence in free territory. Deciding against Scott, the court held that he was not a citizen of the U.S. and therefore could not bring suit in a federal court, and that the MISSOURI COMPROMISE, which forbade slavery in Wisconsin, was unconstitutional because it deprived persons of their property (i.e., their slaves) without due process of law. The decision was bitterly attacked by Northern abolitionists because it declared in effect that slavery could not be barred from the territories.

Dreigroschenoper, Die. See THREEPENNY OPERA, THE.

Dreiser, Theodore [Herman Albert] (1871–1945). American novelist. Dreiser is known as one of the principal exponents of American NATURALISM; though many critics have inveighed against the clumsiness and crudeness of his style, the power and importance of his work cannot be denied.

The son of a highly religious father and a sensitive and loving mother, Dreiser knew poverty from an early age and was later to react strongly against organized religion. After a year at the University of Indiana and a career as a newspaperman in Chicago, St. Louis, Pittsburgh, and New York, he submitted his first novel, SISTER CARRIE, to Doubleday, Page & Co. Read by Frank Norris, who was very enthusiastic, the novel was accepted for publication, only to be withdrawn later after only 1,000 copies had been printed (but not distributed) when Doubleday himself objected to the book's frankness and its lack of conventional moral viewpoint.

Despondent about *Sister Carrie,* Dreiser contemplated suicide, but was guided by his brother Paul into a very lucrative position with the Butterick publications; in a few years he had become head of the firm. After a 10-year interval, Dreiser published JENNIE GERHARDT. Like *Sister Carrie,* it is an absorbing study of a fallen woman. THE FINANCIER began "the trilogy of desire," the story of a captain of high finance, Frank Cowperwood. Influenced by the evolutionary theories of Herbert Spencer and by Nietzsche's concept of the superman, Dreiser still managed to combine with these ideas a poetic sense of the mystery and beauty of the universe. While these ideas are subordinate in *The Financier* and THE TITAN, in the final work of the trilogy, *The Stoic* (1947), they assume great importance.

THE "GENIUS," the most autobiographical of all Dreiser's novels, is generally considered one of his least successful works. During this period Dreiser also published three autobiographical books: *A Traveler at Forty* (1913), *A Hoosier Holiday* (1916), and *A Book About Myself* (1922; later republished as *Newspaper Days*). *Hey-Rub-a-Dub-Dub: A Book of the Mystery and Terror and Wonder of Life* was published in 1919.

In 1925 came AN AMERICAN TRAGEDY, a book based on the famous case of Chester Gillette's murder of Grace Brown. In 1927, Dreiser visited Russia, publishing after his return the two books that marked his acceptance of socialism and the rejection of his former despairing emphasis on fate and determinism: *Dreiser Looks at Russia* (1928) and *Tragic America* (1931). From this point on Dreiser concerned himself more and more with socialism and left-wing politics.

The Bulwark, which was begun as early as 1910, was published posthumously in 1946, and *The Stoic,* the last of the Cowperwood trilogy, in 1947. Both show the influence of the mystic strain which, although present in Dreiser's character from the beginning, became pronounced in his last years. Other works include *Plays of the Natural and Supernatural* (1916), *Free and Other Stories* (1918), *The Hand of the Potter* (1919), *Twelve Men* (1919), *The Color of a Great City* (1923), *Moods* (1926), *A Gallery of Women* (1929), *Fine Furniture* (1930), and *Epitaph* (1930).

Drepane. See PHAEACIANS.

Dressler, Marie (1873–1934). The stage name of Leila Koerber, a Canadian-born American comedienne. She had great success on the stage and in motion pictures, mainly in broad comic roles that were lifted out of mediocrity through the honesty and warmth of her personality. She made famous a song, *Heaven Will Protect the Working Girl.*

Dreyfus, Alfred (1859–1935). Central figure in the famous Dreyfus case which divided France for almost four years. An officer in the French artillery of Jewish descent, Captain Dreyfus was accused and convicted of having betrayed military secrets. In 1894 he was sent to Devil's Island to serve a life imprisonment sentence. Evidence attesting to the innocence of Dreyfus and to the guilt of a Major Esterhazy was uncovered but suppressed by the military. Dreyfus was finally pardoned in 1906 by the *Cour de Cassation*. He transcended, however, his individual significance, becoming a symbol of injustice for liberal intellectuals who vigorously opposed right-wing reactionary forces such as the military and the church. Emile Zola wrote the letter J'ACCUSE, and many other men of letters were ardent Dreyfus supporters. In *A la recherche du temps perdu,* Marcel Proust gives an excellent picture of the alignment of French opinion on the controversial case.

Dr. Faustus, The Tragical History of (first performed in 1588; first published in 1604). A play by Christopher MARLOWE. The yearning for the infinite that characterizes Marlowe's heroes is embodied in Dr. Faustus, the seeker after power through knowledge. The legend of the scholar who sells his soul to the Devil becomes a powerful portrait of a man torn by conflicting desires. In a scene that borrows from earlier morality drama, a good and bad angel, external representations of inner conflict, battle over the soul of Faustus. Despite the moral at the end, which advises the wise to heed the awful fate of Faustus, Marlowe's attitude throughout is one of sympathy and understanding for the boundless longings of his hero. See FAUST.

Drinkwater, John (1882–1937). English poet, dramatist, and biographer. His poetry belongs to the GEORGIAN school. He wrote historical and biographical plays, such as *Abraham Lincoln* (1918) and *Mary Stuart* (1921). *Inheritance* (1931) and *Discovery* (1932) are autobiographical volumes.

driver of Europe (Fr., *cocher de l'Europe*). The designation the empress of Russia used for the duc de Choiseul (1719–1785), minister of Louis XV, because he had spies all over Europe, and thus ruled its political cabals.

Dr. Jekyll and Mr. Hyde. See STRANGE CASE OF DR. JEKYLL AND MR. HYDE, THE.

Dromio of Ephesus and **Dromio of Syracuse.** In Shakespeare's COMEDY OF ERRORS, the merry identical twins who are the servants of the identical twins Antipholus of Ephesus and Antipholus of Syracuse. The twin Dromios are roundly beaten and sent hither and yon in the confusion which results when they and their masters, unbeknownst to each other, end up in the same city.

Dropping the Pilot. The title of a political cartoon in the English magazine *Punch* by Sir John Tenniel. It dramatized the resignation of Bismarck after his disagreement with Kaiser Wilhelm II in 1890. Bismarck, as the old pilot, solemnly leaves his ship while the youthful emperor, now in sole command, watches.

Droste-Hülshoff, Annette von (1797–1848). German poetess. She is remembered especially for ballads in which she combines vivid renderings of natural scenes from her Westphalian homeland with a swift, subtle narrative gift and a compact use of language. Another side of her nature, deeply religious, is seen in the collection *Das geistliche Jahr* (*The Spiritual Year,* 1851). Her famous novella, *Die Judenbuche* (*The Jews' Beech Tree,* 1842), though set in a simple rustic atmosphere, is psychologically deep and succeeds in evoking a powerful sense of mystery about the workings of fate.

Drugger, Abel. A character in Ben Jonson's comedy THE ALCHEMIST (1610). A seller of tobacco, he is artless and gullible in the extreme. He is building a new house, and comes to Subtle the "alchemist" to know on which side to set the shop-door, how to dispose the shelves so as to ensure most luck, on what days he may trust his customers, and when it will be unlucky for him to do so.

Druid. A member of the ancient Gaulish and British order of priests, teachers of religion, magicians, or sorcerers. The word is the Lat. *druidae,* or *druides* (always plural), which was borrowed from the Old Irish *drui* and Gaelic *draoi.* Practically our only literary sources of knowledge of the druidic cult are Pliny and the *Commentaries* of Caesar, which say that the rites of the Druids were conducted in oak groves and that they regarded the oak and the mistletoe with peculiar veneration; that they studied the stars and nature generally; that they believed in the transmigration of souls, and dealt in "magic." Their distinguishing badge was a serpent's egg (see DRUID'S EGG), to which powerful properties were credited. The order seems to have been highly organized, and, according to Strabo, every chief had his druid, and every chief druid was allowed a guard of thirty men.

In Samuel Butler's *Hudibras* there is an allusion to the

> Money by the Druids borrowed,
> In t'other world to be restored.

This refers to a legend recorded by one Patricius (St. Patrick?) to the effect that the Druids were wont to borrow money to be repaid in the life to come.

Druid's egg. A fabled egg hatched by the joint labor of several serpents, and buoyed into the air by their hissing. The person who caught it had to ride off at full speed, to avoid being stung to death; but was sure to prevail in every contest, and to be courted by those in power. Pliny says he had seen one of them, and that it was about as large as a moderate-sized apple.

Drummond, William Henry (1854–1907). Irish-born Canadian poet and physician. Drummond is best known for his verse in French-Canadian dialect about rural life in Quebec. These poems are a mingling of humor and sentiment, at times slightly satirical. Collections of his work include *The Habitant and Other French-Canadian Poems* (1897) and *Johnnie Courteau and Other Poems* (1901).

Drummond of Hawthornden, William (1585–1649). Scottish poet. Owner of an extensive library and ardently Royalist in politics, he translated French and Italian lyric poetry, especially the works of Ronsard, Passerat, and Desportes. His own verse, which includes *Flowers of Zion* (1623), is known for its grace and smoothness. He also left interesting notes on Ben Jonson's conversation during the latter's visit to Hawthornden in 1618.

Drums Along the Mohawk (1936). A historical novel by Walter D. EDMONDS. The bitter struggle in the Mohawk Valley between the supporters of the American Revolution and their British foes is vividly portrayed. Stress is laid on the destructiveness of the Tories and their Indian allies. The novel is based on the kind of careful research that Edmonds describes in *How You Begin a Novel* (*Atlantic Monthly*, Aug., 1936).

Druon, Maurice. Pen name of **Maurice Kessel** (1918–   ). French novelist. *The Curtain Falls* (*La Fin des hommes*) is a detailed chronicle of the moral and commercial corruption of two bourgeois families between the world wars. The work includes *The Magnates* (*Les Grandes Familles;* 1948; first translated as *The Rise of Simon Lachaume*), *Feet of Clay* (*La Chute des corps;* 1950), and *Rendezvous in Hell* (1951). *The Accursed Kings* (6 vols., 1956–1961) is a series of historical novels about the French monarchy of the 14th century. *The Glass Coffin* (1963) is a collection of short stories.

Drury Lane. A street in London named after Drury House, which was built by Sir William Drury in the time of Henry VIII. The street has been the site of several theaters of the same name, the first of which was built by Thomas Killigrew in 1663 as the Theatre Royal and was described by Samuel Pepys. After it was destroyed by fire in 1672, a new theater, designed by Christopher Wren, was erected on the site of the present Drury Lane Theatre and was opened in 1674.

Druses. A people and sect of Syria living south of Damascus near the mountains of Lebanon and Anti-Libanus. Their unitarian faith combines Moslem, Christian, Jewish, and Sufist ideas. They offer devotions both in mosques and churches, worship the images of saints, and observe the fast of RAMADAN. Their name is probably derived from that of their first apostle, Ismail Darazi or Durzi (11th century A.D.).

Browning wrote a tragedy, *Return of the Druses* (1841).

dryad. In Greek mythology, a tree nymph. Originally, the dryads were specifically oak-nymphs (*drys*, oak), but the name came to be applied to all tree nymphs. Nature spirits who died with the trees they inhabited, they were also called *hamadryads*. The most famous of them, perhaps, was Eurydice, the wife of Orpheus.

Dryden, John (1631–1700). English poet, dramatist, and critic. He was the outstanding figure in letters during the Restoration and literary dictator of his age.

Dryden came from a good, but impecunious, country family with a Parliamentarian and Church of England background. In his middle 20's he went to London, where his gifts were quickly recognized in intellectual circles, though he had to struggle for years to earn a respectable living by means of his plays and translations. Dryden made several radical shifts in his religion and politics: in 1659 he eulogized Cromwell in the *Heroick Stanzas;* a year later he celebrated Charles II in *Astraea Redux;* in 1682 he published RELIGIO LAICI, a defense of Anglicanism; five years later THE HIND AND THE PANTHER revealed him as an ardent partisan of Catholicism and Catholic James II. In 1688, however, he refused to take an oath of allegiance to William and Mary, remaining loyal to James II at the cost of important offices, including the laureateship of England.

Dryden's earliest work, such as his elegy *Upon the Death of Lord Hastings* (1650), is in the extravagant late metaphysical vein of Cowley. Soon he developed a more restrained and natural style, close to normal cultivated speech and employing the heroic couplet to emphasize its finish and point. This was to be the dominant poetic style for a century, though perhaps never again more forceful and various than it was in Dryden's hands. It was a vehicle particularly well-adapted to satirical and didactic works, such as ABSALOM AND ACHITOPHEL, THE MEDAL, MACFLECKNOE, *Religio Laici,* and *The Hind and the Panther*. Dryden also used it in his translations of Virgil and other Latin poets and in a number of his plays, although his greatest play, ALL FOR LOVE, is written in blank verse. His prose writings are also of great importance: the orderly, lucid, and masculine style which distinguishes his prefaces and critical essays, such as the ESSAY OF DRAMATIC POESY, became one of the chief models for modern prose. These works reveal Dryden as an acute and extraordinarily sensible critic.

In addition to those referred to above, the following poems by Dryden also deserve mention: the lyrics *To Mrs. Killegrew* (1686), *A Song for St. Cecilia's Day* (1687), and *Alexander's Feast* (1697); a number of longer poems, such as ANNUS MIRABILIS; and his paraphrases and translations of Chaucer, Boccaccio, Ovid, Juvenal, Lucretius, and Homer. Other memorable plays by Dryden are *The Indian Emperor* (1665), *Almanzor and Almahide, or The Conquest of Granada* (1670), *Aurengzebe* (1675), and *Don Sebastian* (1690). See John SHEFFIELD.

Dryope. In Greek legend sister of Iole and wife of Andraemon. For having plucked inadvertently the lotus into which the nymph Lotis had been changed, Dryope herself was changed into a lotus.

Dry Salvages, The. See FOUR QUARTETS.

Duat. In Egyptian mythology, one of the abodes of the dead in the underworld through which the sun passed by night.

Du Barry, Comtesse. **Mari Jeanne Bécu** (1743–1793). Adventuress and mistress of Louis XV from 1768 to his death (1774). She ruled both king and court, and was famous for her prodigality as a patron of artists and men of letters. She was guillotined on Dec. 7, 1793.

Du Bellay, Joachim (1522–1560). French poet. A companion of Ronsard at the Collège de Coqueret in Paris, Du Bellay was one of the founders of the PLÉIADE and author of its poetic program: DÉFENSE ET ILLUSTRATION DE LA LANGUE FRANÇAISE. His melancholy nature easily lent itself to the Petrarchan type of idealized love then in vogue, a tendency reflected in his first work, *L'Olive* (1549), the first French collection of sonnets. Yet the following year he produced *A une Dame*, a biting satire of this very convention. In 1553, ailing and downcast at his failure to win royal favor, he accompanied his cousin Cardinal Du Bellay to Rome as his secretary. He approached Rome with the reverence of a confirmed Latinist and left it four years later greatly disillusioned. Upon his return to France in 1558, he published four volumes: the *Poemata*, written in Latin in the style of the Italian humanists; *Les Antiquités de Rome,* in which he exalted ancient Rome; *Les Regrets,* in which he bitterly satirized the mediocrity of contemporary Rome and expressed his regrets over his self-imposed exile; and the *Divers jeux rustiques,* in which he freed himself from his cares and relaxed into pastoral pieces and sensual love poems. The *Poète courtisan* (1559) was a last embittered satire on the court poets.

Second only to Ronsard in the eyes of his contemporaries and posterity, Du Bellay could not reconcile himself to this position and harbored a jealousy which he did not always attempt to hide.

Dubliners (1914). A collection of short stories by James Joyce. By dealing successively with incidents in the childhood, adolescence, maturity, and public life of Dubliners, Joyce provides a picture of the paralyzing world from which he fled. Most of the characters and scenes are mean and petty, sometimes tragic; they are drawn from ordinary Catholic middle-class life. The style is simple and moving, more in the manner of Anton Chekhov than in that of the author's more famous works. In all the stories, Joyce uses a device he named the EPIPHANY, having a sudden remark, symbol, or moment that epitomizes and clarifies the meaning of a complex experience. Among the best known of the stories are THE SISTERS, Counterparts, CLAY, IVY DAY IN THE COMMITTEE ROOM, and THE DEAD. Several of the characters introduced in *Dubliners* reappear in *Ulysses.*

Joyce had difficulty in finding a publisher for his book, and it did not appear until many years after it had been written. It was severely attacked because the names of actual persons and places in Dublin are mentioned in it.

Du Bois, William E[dward] B[urghardt] (1868–1963). American writer, editor, and teacher. The descendant of a French Huguenot and an African slave, Du Bois was trained as a sociologist and did much to promote greater understanding of Negroes. *The Souls of Black Folk* (1903), a collection of essays, is his best-known work. He wrote many other works, among them *The Negro* (1915), *Black Folk: Then and Now* (1930), *Color and Democracy* (1945), *In Battle for Peace* (1952), and *The Black Flame, A Trilogy,* which consists of *The Ordeal of Mansart* (1957), *Mansart Builds a School* (1959), and *Worlds of Color* (1961).

Du Bos, Charles (1882–1939). French critic. Du Bos combined Catholicism with the influence of Walter Pater to become a leading commentator on the literary production of his time. Much of his thought is collected in *Approximations* (7 vols., 1922–1937) and his *Journal Intime* (8 vols., 1946–   ).

Duccio di Buoninsegna (c. 1260–1319). Italian painter. He was the founder of the Sienese school of painting and is noted for the refinement and delicacy of his style. His masterpiece is the *Virgin in Majesty,* (1311), a panel in the cathedral of Siena; equally celebrated scenes from the life of Christ are to be found on its reverse side.

Duchamp, Marcel (1887–   ). French painter of the DADA movement. His *Nude Descending a Staircase* (1912) caused a sensation at the ARMORY SHOW. His brother, Raymond Duchamp-Villon (1876–1918), was a cubist sculptor.

Duchess, the. A character in Lewis Carroll's ALICE'S ADVENTURES IN WONDERLAND. The duchess wallops her baby till it howls and sings this lullaby to it:

> Speak roughly to your little boy,
>   And beat him when he sneezes;
> He only does it to annoy,
>   Because he knows it teases.

Duchess of Malfi, The (c. 1613). A tragedy by John WEBSTER. The last of the great Elizabethan dramas, it deals movingly with the disastrous marriage of a noblewoman and a commoner. The duchess, the widowed sister of Ferdinand, duke of Calabria, and of the cardinal, offends them by marrying her steward, Antonio. The lovers are forced to separate: Antonio flees, and the duchess is kept prisoner in her house, where she is subjected to mental torture. Bosola, the cardinal's henchman, strangles the duchess and her children and later murders Antonio. The play is based on William Painter's *The Palace of Pleasure* (1566–1567).

Duclos, Charles Pinot (1704–1772). French historian, moralist, and man of letters. On succeeding Voltaire as historiographer of France in 1750, he wrote *Mémoires pour servir à l'histoire des moeurs du XVIII° siècle* (1751). He also wrote novels and short stories, including *Histoire de la baronne de Luz* (1741), and *Les Confessions du comte de . . .* (1741). As secretary of the French ACADEMY, he supervised the 1762 edition of its famous dictionary.

Du côté de chez Swann. See REMEMBRANCE OF THINGS PAST.

Dudintzev, Vladimir (1918–   ). Russian novelist. His novel, NOT BY BREAD ALONE, created a sensation with its criticism of the Soviet bureaucracy. Dudintzev was attacked by Soviet critics in violent terms until Khrushchev, in May, 1959, finally put an end to the prolonged controversy by declaring that Dudintzev was not an enemy of the regime, but had merely erred in his efforts to criticize some aspects of Soviet society. Since that time Dudintzev has issued only a short work entitled *A New Year's Tale* (*Novogodnaya skazka*), which Western critics have hopefully interpreted as another anti-Soviet jibe. The work, however, is obscure, and Dudintzev's intention cannot easily be discerned.

Dudley, John, duke of **Northumberland** (1502?–1553). Protector of Edward VI. In an attempt to transfer the crown from the Tudor dynasty to his own family Northumberland persuaded the dying Edward VI to will the succession to Lady Jane GREY, Northumberland's daughter-in-law. After the attempt to place Queen Jane on the throne failed, he was executed.

Dudley, Robert, earl of **Leicester** (1531–1558). Favorite of Elizabeth I. The brother of Guildford Dudley (the husband of Lady Jane GREY), Robert Dudley was condemned to death after the attempt to place Lady Jane on the throne had failed. He was pardoned by ELIZABETH I and became Master of Ordnance and one of her chief favorites at court. She made him a Knight of the Garter, created him earl of Leicester, and gave him a castle at Kenilworth. His wife, Amy Robsart, died under somewhat suspicious circumstances, but there is no proof that her death—which freed Leicester to marry Elizabeth if she would have him—was anything but accidental. He is a main character in Sir Walter Scott's novel *Kenilworth.*

Dudone. One of the paladins of Charlemagne in the Carolingian stories centered about Orlando. He also appears in the MORGANTE MAGGIORE of Pulci and the poems of Orlando of Boiardo and Ariosto. In the latter's ORLANDO FURIOSO he is given the command of a complete navy magically created by Astolfo. Dudone's new fleet then routs the pagan army sailing with Agramante their leader to fight the Christians. In the GERUSALEMME LIBERATA of Tasso, he is Dudone of Consa (Contz), one of the adventurers among the crusading knights. When he is killed by the pagan warrior Argente, the Crusaders withdraw from battle to honor his corpse.

Dudu. In Lord Byron's narrative poem DON JUAN, one of the beauties of the harem into which Juan has been admitted in female attire. Next day, the sultana, out of jealousy, orders that both Juan and Dudu be stitched in a sack and cast into the sea; but, by the connivance of Baba, the chief eunuch, they effect their escape.

Duessa. An evil enchantress in Spenser's FAERIE QUEENE (Books I, II, and V), representing variously the Roman Catholic Church, Mary Tudor, and Mary, Queen of Scots.

Dufay, Guillaume (c. 1400–1474). Flemish (Belgian) composer. He lived and worked in Italy, Savoy, Burgundy, and Flanders. At the end of his life, Dufay was the most highly regarded composer in Europe. His finest music was written for the church. It was he who first established the practice of having polyphonic music sung by a chorus; hitherto each part had been performed by a single voice or instrument.

Dufresny, Charles Rivière (1648–1724). French playwright and novelist. His *Amusements sérieux et comiques d'un Siamois* (*Serious and Comic Amusements of a Siamese*, 1699), which criticized French institutions by the then novel device of recounting the reactions to Paris of a visiting Siamese, did much to set the fashion and establish the pattern for similar works, notably Montesquieu's *Lettres Persanes*. Among his plays, *Le Chevalier Joueur* (*The Gambling Knight*, 1697), which dealt realistically with the gambling mania, and the comedies *L'Esprit de Contradiction* (*The Spirit of Contradiction*, 1700) and *Le Double Veuvage* (*The Double Widowing*, 1702) were the most successful.

Dufy, Raoul (1877–1952). French artist, painted still lifes, harvest, street, and racetrack scenes. He developed a distinct style of briefly drawn details and fresh colors.

Duhamel, Georges. Pen name **Denis Thévenin** (1884–1966). French dramatist, novelist, critic, and poet. A leading member of the ABBAYE GROUP, Duhamel then turned to the theater and wrote *The Light* (1911), *In the Shadow of Statues* (1912), and *Combat* (1913). He also published *The New Book of Martyrs* (1917) and *Civilisation,* stories of World War I. Duhamel's works also include two long novel series, the cycle of SALAVIN (5 vols., 1920–1932) and the PASQUIER CHRONICLES (10 vols., 1933–1945). His essay *The Heart's Domain* (*La Possession du monde;* 1919) urges, as do his novels, the cultivation of the inner life on which is based the fraternity of mankind. He won the Prix Goncourt in 1918 for *Civilisation.*

Duino Elegies (**Duineser Elegien;** 1923). A series of poems by Rainer Maria RILKE. They are elegiac in mood, though not, strictly speaking, in form and meter. In them, Rilke develops his own, highly personal solution to some of the human problems posed by Existentialism, without, however, committing himself as a follower of that school of philosophy and poetry. "Duino" is the name of a castle near Trieste where Rilke, in 1911–1912, was a guest of the Princess Marie von Thurn und Taxis, to whom he presented the poems.

Dujardin, Edouard (1861–1949). French writer. A poet and a distinguished editor, he allied himself with the symbolists. He is known for his influential novel LES LAURIERS SONT COUPÉS, the first example of interior monologue.

Dukhobors or **Doukhobors** (Russ. *Đukhobortsi,* "spirit wrestlers"). A religious sect that arose among Kharkov peasants in the mid-18th century. Guided by "inner light," they rejected the authority of Church and State, and led communal lives under "inspired" leaders. Their beliefs have been compared to those of Quakers. Internal dissensions and resistance to military service subjected them to a series of forced migrations and dispersals.

Thousands removed to western Canada in 1898, where they founded prosperous if turbulent settlements as the "Christian Community of Universal Brotherhood." Their sporadic protests against taxes and compulsory education (especially those led by the violent "Sons of Freedom") have taken the form of fires, bombings, and marches in the nude, which abated in the late 1950's after a new threat of expulsion.

Dulce et Decorum Est (1920). A poem by Wilfred OWEN, bitterly denouncing war. The title is ironic, being a quotation from Horace: *Dulce et decorum est pro patria mori* (It is sweet and fitting to die for one's country).

Dulcinea del Toboso. The lady love of DON QUIXOTE in Cervantes' novel. Her real name is Aldonza Lorenzo, but the knight dubs her Dulcinea del Toboso. "Her flowing hair," says the knight, "is of gold, her forehead the Elysian fields, her eyebrows two celestial arches, her eyes a pair of glorious suns, her cheeks two beds of roses, her lips two coral portals that guard her teeth of Oriental pearl, her neck is alabaster, her hands are polished ivory, and her bosom whiter than the new-fallen snow." According to Sancho Panza, she is "a stout-built sturdy wench, who could pitch the bar as well as any young fellow in the parish."

Dulcy (1921). A comedy by George S. KAUFMAN and Marc CONNELLY. It is based on a character created by the columnist Franklin P. Adams. In the course of her well-meaning, self-appointed task of helping her husband put through an important business deal, Dulcy makes one blunder after another, but her efforts unexpectedly turn out all right.

Dull, Anthony. A dull-witted constable in Shakespeare's LOVE'S LABOUR'S LOST. He becomes the butt of the pedantic wit of Holofernes and Sir Nathaniel and understands absolutely nothing of what they say.

Dullin, Charles (1885–1949). French actor, director, and producer. Associated with Jacques COPEAU in the *Théâtre de Vieux-Colombier,* Dullin founded his own company at the *Théâtre de l'Atelier* in 1921. He stressed poetry and fancy on the stage, rather than a naturalistic portrayal of reality. Dullin produced plays by a wide variety of playwrights, among them Marcel Archard, Stève Passeur, Armand Salacrou, Jules Romains, and Pirandello.

Duma. Russian parliamentary body created in 1905. Its function was to advise Czar Nicolas II in matters of legislation. It was overthrown by the Russian Revolution (1917).

Dumachus. See DISMAS.

Dumain. In Shakespeare's LOVE'S LABOUR'S LOST, one of the three young lords who join the king of Navarre in an oath of celibacy and study. He becomes enamored of Katherine.

Dumas, Alexandre. Known as **Dumas fils**, or the younger (1824–1895). French dramatist. The natural son of Alexandre Dumas the novelist, the younger Dumas became an extremely popular playwright during the Second Empire. In technique his plays were realistic; for subjects he chose moral and social problems, depicting the adulterous intrigues and financial scandals of the upper social classes. Among Dumas's most successful works were: LA DAME AUX CAMÉLIAS, *Le Demi-Monde* (1855), *La Question d'argent* (1857), *Un Père Prodigue* (1859), *L'Ami des Femmes* (1864), *Les Idées de Mme Aubray* (1867). Heavy-handed didacticism characterized his later dramas.

Dumas, Alexandre. Known as **Dumas père** (1802–1870). French novelist and dramatist. Alexandre Dumas has become almost legendary for his prolific literary output (almost 300 volumes), and the rollicking gusto with which he lived and wrote. Dumas maintained a corps of collaborators—whom he termed his factory—who were engaged in searching through earlier memoir writers for suitably exciting plots. Accused of altering historical fact to suit his fictional purposes and of pilfering unscrupulously from other writers, Dumas remained supremely indifferent to such charges. His historical romances, all of the swashbuckling variety, include such favorites as THE COUNT OF MONTE CRISTO, THE THREE MUSKETEERS, THE BLACK TULIP, THE VISCOUNT OF BRAGELONNE, and TWENTY YEARS AFTER. Critics point quickly, and rightly, to the excessive melodrama of Dumas' work, to his lack of psychological perception, and to his careless style, but the color and drama of his novels continue to insure their popularity. In France Dumas is noted for his plays: *Henri III et sa cour* (1829), *Napoléon Bonaparte* (1831), *Antony* (1831), and *La Tour de Nesle* (1832).

du Maurier, Daphne (1907–). English novelist and short-story writer. Her popular novels, compounded of melodrama, romance, the scenery of Cornwall, and some history, include *Jamaica Inn* (1936), *Rebecca* (1938), *Frenchman's Creek* (1942), *Hungry Hill* (1943), *The King's General* (1946), *My Cousin Rachel* (1951), and *The Glass-Blowers* (1963). She is a granddaughter of George du Maurier and daughter of the actor Sir Gerald du Maurier (1873–1934). Her *Gerald, A Portrait* (1934) is a biography of her father.

du Maurier, George [Louis Palmella Busson] (1834–1896). English novelist and illustrator. He illustrated the work of Thackeray, Hardy, James, and Meredith, and was famous for his caricatures in *Punch*. His novels, PETER IBBETSON, the highly successful TRILBY, and *The Martian* (1896), are tinged with social satire and colored with the memories of the author's days as an art student in Paris. He also wrote light verse in English and French, which was popular in its day.

Dumbwaiter, The (1960). A one-act play by Harold PINTER. The two characters are assassins waiting in a hotel room for their victim to arrive. When an order for a Chinese meal is sent to them on the dumbwaiter they assume that their room was once a restaurant. They fill the order as best they can with candy and biscuit. They are deluged with orders for food from an unknown person who they feel is testing them. As the time approaches for the killing one of the assassins, a questioning, childish person, starts to feel remorse for their other victims. He leaves the room; when he returns, his partner kills him.

Dumuzi. A Sumerian shepherd-god, known elsewhere as TAMMUZ. He was loved by INANNA (Ishtar). Although he does not appear in the extant Sumerian myth of her descent into the underworld, the close parallel with Ishtar's search for Tammuz makes it highly likely that that was the purpose of Inanna's descent.

Dumuzi also is a central figure in a myth in which he, a shepherd, disputes with the farmer god Enkimdu for the favor of Inanna. Although Dumuzi is elsewhere her lover, she here prefers the farmer. This is one of several Sumerian myths with an obvious parallel to the story of CAIN and Abel.

Dunbar, Paul Laurence (1872–1906). American poet. Dunbar is noted for his highly skilled use of Negro themes and dialect. Writing at a time when literary regionalism was in vogue, he was undoubtedly influenced by Thomas Nelson Page. Although he was the son of a slave, his poetry is sentimental and lacks the bitterness of the work of later Negro writers. *Lyrics of Lowly Life* (1896) is his most famous collection. It was followed by *Lyrics of the Hearthside* (1899), *Lyrics of Love and Laughter* (1903), and *Lyrics of Sunshine and Shadow* (1905). He also wrote novels, including *The Uncalled* (1898) and *The Sport of the Gods* (1902).

Dunbar, William (1465?–?1530). Scottish poet. For a time he was a Franciscan friar and later a diplomatic agent for James IV of Scotland. His works include *The Thrissel and the Rois* (*The Thistle and the Rose,* 1503), a political allegory; *The Dance of the Sevin Deidly Sinnis* (1503–1508), a religious dream vision; *The Goldyn Targe* (c. 1508), an allegory in the tradition of *The Romance of the Rose; Lament of the Makaris* (i.e., poets; c. 1508), an elegy on the death of great poets of the past that has been compared to the poetry of François Villon; and *The Two Marryit Women and the Wedo* (c. 1508), a satire on women. Dunbar is considered one of the greatest of the SCOTTISH CHAUCERIANS.

Duncan. In Shakespeare's MACBETH, the generous and gracious king of Scotland whom Macbeth murders to attain the crown. When prodded by his wife to do the deed, even Macbeth protests against it, extolling Duncan's virtues:

> Besides, this Duncan
> Hath borne his faculties so meek, hath been
> So clear in his great office, that his virtues
> Will plead like angels trumpet-tongued against
> The deep damnation of his taking-off.

Duncan, Isadora (1878–1927). American dancer. She was acclaimed in London, Paris, and on the Continent, and established a German school of dancing near Berlin in 1904 and later one in Moscow. In 1926–1927, she wrote her autobiography, entitled *My Life.* She choreographed compositions by Tchaikovsky and Chopin. She was strangled in an automobile accident when her scarf was caught in a wheel.

Duncan, Robert [Edward] (1919–   ). American poet. At one time an editor of the *Experimental Review* and of *Phoenix,* Duncan has been influential among the younger poets both as an artist and a theorist. His work is highly distinctive and is characterized by lyricism, irony, and intensity. Collections of his poetry include *Selected Poems* (1959) and *The Opening of the Field* (1960).

Dunciad, The (1728; final version, 1743). The "dunce-epic," a satire in heroic couplets by Alexander POPE. The first version, in three books, was written under the influence of Swift; it attacked all critics of Pope's works, poetasters, publishers, and pedants. In 1729 this version, with changes, was republished as *The Dunciad Variorum.* A fourth book, *The New Dunciad,* appeared in 1742 and the final version, *The Dunciad in Four Books,* was published a year later. In the first book, the leading role was initially given to Lewis THEOBALD, but in the final version it is Colley CIBBER who is named king of the Dunces, his rule extending over the empires of Emptiness and Dullness. The second book, a burlesque of the account of funeral games for Anchises in Vergil's *Aeneid,* depicts Cibber's coronation; it is celebrated with games and contests, and as everyone drowses off to sleep, poetry-reading. In the third book, Cibber falls asleep and sees, in his dreams, the past, present, and future; in all three, Dullness prevails. In the fourth book, Dullness reigns supreme over scholarship, art, and science. The goddess of Dullness, thus firmly entrenched, gives directions to her several agents to encourage foolish and trifling pursuits and to discourage thought, and night and chaos are finally restored. *The Dunciad* is considered by many to be among Pope's crowning achievements, and, in spite of its topicality, its satire is still fresh and biting.

Dunne, Finley Peter (1867–1936). American journalist and humorist. Dunne worked for several newspapers in his native Chicago, writing his first "Mr. Dooley" essays for the *Evening Post.* Later he became part owner of the *American Magazine,* to which he contributed a pungent department entitled "In the Interpreter's House," and was editor of *Collier's* (1918–1919).

Dunne's fame rests entirely and solidly on his creation of Martin Dooley, an imaginary Irishman who presided over a small saloon on Chicago's West Side. Dooley was modeled, Dunne said, on a saloon-keeper named James McGarry. In his earlier pieces Dunne called his philosophic barkeeper Col. McNeery, but when McGarry objected to the too-ready identification, Dunne changed the name to Dooley.

From the days of the Spanish-American War to World War I, Mr. Dooley reviewed public men and affairs with a wit and wisdom that made him a national institution. He made his remarks to his faithful friend and customer, Malachi Hennessey. Possibly Mr. Dooley's most famous utterance was, "Whether th' Constitution follows th' flag or not, th' Supreme Court follows th' illiction retarns." "There's only one thing," said Dooley elsewhere, "that would make me allow mesilf to be a hero to the American people, and that is it don't last long."

Dunne wrote more than 700 essays about Mr. Dooley, some of which were collected in *Mr. Dooley in Peace and War* (1898), *Mr. Dooley in the Hearts of his Countrymen* (1899), and other books. *Mr. Dooley Remembers: The Informal Memoirs of Finley Peter Dunne* (1963) was edited by his son Philip Dunne.

Dunne, John William (1875–1949). English author of *An Experiment with Time* (1927) and *The New Immortality* (1938). These books of popular philosophy purported to demonstrate, through mathematics, the immortality of the soul and the principle of serialism (that the individual passes through a single sequence of time as he lives, but all other times and places exist simultaneously always). His books influenced J. B. PRIESTLEY and others.

Dunsany, Lord. Edward John Moreton Drax Plunkett (1878–1957). Irish dramatist and poet. A member of the Anglo-Irish gentry, he was educated at Eton. After service in the Boer War (1899–1902), he became active in the newly founded ABBEY THEATRE. In 1909 his play *The Glittering Gates* was produced at the Abbey by William Butler Yeats and won quick acclaim. This was followed by a number of other successes, many of them one-act plays, the best known of which are *A Night at an Inn* (1916), his finest play; *The Laughter of the Gods* (1916); and *If* (1922). Superficially his work appears to be merely the naive expression of Celtic whimsy with the usual assortment of fairies and other supernatural creatures. Dunsany, however, employed this background to satirize human behavior with a disarmingly simple, seemingly unconscious, wit.

Duns Scotus, John (c. 1265–c. 1308). Scottish scholastic theologian, known as the "Doctor Subtilis." He joined the Franciscans and was a teacher at Oxford, Paris, and Cologne, becoming famous for his defense of the dogma of the Immaculate Conception, and his description of man's free will as a horse capable of throwing off grace, its rider. Declaring that the existence of God or the immortality of the human soul cannot be proved by human reason, he thus challenged the harmony of faith and reason, of theology and philosophy, so important in the system of St. Thomas Aquinas. For centuries his followers, called *Scotists,* disputed with the Thomists over this and other doctrinal questions. Eventually Scotism was modified until it resembled Thomism on most issues.

Duns Scotus' theories are formulated in his metaphysical treatises *De Rerum Principio, Quaestiones, Opus Oxoniense,* and the commentaries on the *Sentences* of Peter Lombard. Although he had tried to urge philosophy's greater dependence on divine revelation by showing the limitations of human reason, the controversy had the opposite effect of lessening philosophy's concern with theology. His opposition to classical studies led in the Renaissance to the use of his name (Duns, Dunse, or Dunce) for a pedantic sophist incapable of real learning, and thence to the current meaning of *dunce* as a stupid, dull-witted person.

Dunstable, John (c. 1370–1453). The most important English composer of the 15th century; also a mathematician and astronomer. He infused beauty and grace into the rigid and angular English music of the 14th century, and had an influence on French music.

Duomo. See GIOTTO'S TOWER.

Dupes, Day of (*Journée des Dupes*). November 11, 1630, when Marie de Médicis and Gaston, Duc d'Orléans extracted from Louis XIII the promise that he would dismiss his minister Cardinal Richelieu. The cardinal went immediately to Versailles, the king repented, and Richelieu became more powerful than ever. Marie de Médicis and Gaston, the dupes, paid dearly for their short triumph.

Dupin, Aurore Amantine Lucille. See George SAND.

Dupin, C. Auguste. An amateur detective created by Edgar Allan POE. Appearing in the three stories Poe called his ratiocinative tales, Dupin works solely by deductive method. His unofficial status, bewildered friend, and cold logic have become familiar characteristics of the literary detectives modeled on him. See MURDERS IN THE RUE MORGUE, THE; PURLOINED LETTER, THE.

Du Pont, Eleuthère Irénée (1771–1834). American gunpowder manufacturer, son of Pierre Samuel DU PONT DE NEMOURS. He came to the United States in 1799 and founded, in Wilmington, Del., the gunpowder and textile firm of E. I. Du Pont de Nemours & Co. (1802–1804). In 1822, he was appointed director of the Bank of the United States.

Du Pont de Nemours, Pierre Samuel (1739–1817). French economist, friend and disciple of FRANÇOIS QUESNAY, the PHYSIOCRAT. He was imprisoned during the French Revolution and emigrated to the United States in 1799. At Jefferson's request he prepared a scheme for national education which, although never adopted in the U.S., influenced the French educational code. He returned to France (1802–1815), but again emigrated to the U.S. two years before his death.

Durandal, Durendal, Durandana, or **Durindana.** The magic sword of ROLAND (Orlando). Once used by Hector, it was given to Roland by Charlemagne in some stories, by MALAGIGI the magician in others.

Durant, Asher. See HUDSON RIVER SCHOOL.

Durant, Will[iam] [James] (1885–   ). American teacher, philosopher, and historian. Durant, perhaps the greatest popularizer of philosophic ideas in American publishing history, originally wrote *The Story of Philosophy* (1926) as a lecture series; the book was so popular that it was translated into a dozen languages and soon sold over a million copies. Durant then began a series on *The Story of Civilization: Our Oriental Heritage* (1935), *The Life of Greece* (1939), *Caesar and Christ* (1944), *The Age of Faith* (1950), *The Renaissance* (1953), *The Reformation* (1957), and *The Age of Reason Begins* (1961) and *The Age of Louis XVI* (1963), both written with his wife, Ariel Durant.

Duras, Marguerite (1914–   ). French novelist who usually presents events in terms of their psychological significance, most often to a woman, as in *Sea Wall* (*Un Barrage contre le Pacifique;* 1950), *Le Marin de Gibraltar* (1952), and *The Square* (1955). Other works include the film scenario *Hiroshima mon amour* (1959) and the novels *La Vie tran-*

quille (1944) and *Moderato Cantabile* (1958). She adapted *Moderato Cantabile* for the screen.

Durbeyfield, Tess. See TESS OF THE D'URBERVILLES.

Dürer, Albrecht (1471–1528). German painter and engraver. Travels in Italy in 1494 and 1505 familiarized him with Italy's search for clarity in art. At first he followed the German Gothic tradition of linear unrest and vehemence, but this style gradually gave way to greater breadth and simplicity, until he achieved a classical art of great expressiveness. Acutely aware of his own importance as an artist and increasingly interested in the teachings of Martin Luther, he sought to reconcile the strictness of the Reformation with the humanistic aspects of the Renaissance and its classical conern with ideal beauty. In the process he created the greatest expression of German Renaissance art. He painted a number of famous religious works and self-portraits, but he is particularly renowned for his numerous woodcuts and engravings depicting Apocalyptic visions, allegories, the Passion of Christ, and the life of the Virgin. The delicacy and strength of his hand is also demonstrated by portrait and landscape drawings and by minute studies of animals and details of nature. During his last years he wrote theoretical works on geometry and perspective, and on anatomy and human proportion.

D'Urfey, Thomas or **Tom** (1653–1723). English dramatist and song writer. He is known for such comedies as *Love for Money* (1691), *The Marriage-*

A Dürer woodcut for Brant's *Ship of Fools* (1494).

Hater Matched (1692), and *The Comical History of Don Quixote: Parts I, II, and III* (1694–1696). There is also a six-volume collection of his songs: *Wit and Mirth* (1719–1720).

Durga. The wife of Shiva. She is also known as Uma, Parvati, and KALI. The *Durga Puja* is Bengal's greatest religious festival, usually taking place in September or October.

Durrell, Gerald [Malcolm] (1925–   ). English zoologist and writer about animals. The brother of Lawrence Durrell, he is the author of *My Family and Other Animals* (1956). Other books include *A Zoo in My Luggage* (1960) and *The Whispering Land* (1961).

Durrell, Lawrence [George] (1912–   ). Anglo-Irish novelist, poet, and playwright. He is best-known for THE ALEXANDRIA QUARTET, a series of novels set in Egypt. Most of Durrell's other works are set on Mediterranean islands or in Europe, where he has spent most of his life. Henry Miller helped him to publish his first prose work, THE BLACK BOOK, in France in 1938. Employed by the British Council and the British Foreign Office in Egypt, Argentina, Belgrade, and Cyprus, Durrell wrote boys' adventure stories, humorous sketches of diplomatic life, and novels and travel books about Mediterranean islands. His Aegean books are *Prospero's Cell* (1945), *The Dark Labyrinth* (1947), *Reflections on a Marine Venus* (1953), and *Bitter Lemons* (1957), about life in Cyprus during the Turkish-Greek-British struggles. Like Norman Douglas, Durrell compares Anglo-Saxons unfavorably with Southern Europeans, who have, he thinks, a better sense of history and art, and more sexual freedom.

Durrell's poems have been appearing consistently since 1938. Usually on Mediterranean and classical subjects, they are romantic, taut, and sometimes humorous. *The Death of General Untebunke* (1938) is an ironic biography. Durrell's *Collected Poems* appeared in 1956. His poetic dramas are *Sappho* (1950) and *Acte* (1961).

Dürrenmatt, Friedrich (1921–   ). Swiss playwright. Dürrenmatt, who writes in German, is especially known for his mastery of the bizarre and for the penetrating irony with which he comments on both the contemporary world and the helplessness of the human situation in general. His two most significant works are both tragicomedies: *Die Ehe des Herrn Mississippi* (*The Marriage of Mr. Mississippi*, 1952), a grotesque depiction of what has happened to moral and social values in our day, and the famous THE VISIT OF THE OLD LADY, which is an ironic modern counterpart to classical tragedy, treating the theme of the death of one man for the sake of the community. His other well-known plays include *Romulus der Grosse* (*Romulus the Great*, 1949) and *Ein Engel kommt nach Babylon* (*An Angel Comes to Babylon*, 1954). In his stage technique Dürrenmatt, like his countryman Max Frisch, follows Brecht's lead by frequently disrupting the stage-illusion in order to make the audience think in a more direct way about the ideas being presented. Besides his plays he has also written several detective stories with overtones of deeper meaning, including *Der Verdacht* (*Suspicion*, 1953), and a well-known essay entitled *Theaterprobleme* (*Problems of the Theater*, 1955), treating the subject of modern drama.

Durtain, Luc. See ABBAYE GROUP, THE.

Durvasas. In Hindu legend, one of the 7 great sages. In Kalidasa's play SHAKUNTALA, he is an ancient ascetic who curses Shakuntala because she neglects to serve him when he visits Kashyapa's *ashram* (hermitage).

Du Ryer, Pierre (c. 1600–1658). French playwright. Du Ryer's output was of wide range and included the pastoral *Les Vendages de Suresne* (*The Grape Harvests of Suresne*, 1635), unorthodox in the realism of its setting, the Seine of his own day; the romantic tragedy *Alcionée* (1640); the biblical tragedies *Saul* (1642) and *Esther* (1644); and historical tragedies, which are considered his best work. Of these, *Scévole* (1647), based on the legend of Mucius Scaevola, is generally reckoned his masterpiece.

Duse, Eleonora (1859–1924). Italian actress. Descended from a theatrical family, she scored her first great success when, aged 14, she played Juliet in Verona. Later she was acclaimed for her Camille and her interpretations of Ibsen's heroines. In 1895, she and Sarah Bernhardt, both appearing in London in Sudermann's *Magda,* invited the critics to choose between them; George Bernard Shaw was among those who preferred Duse. When she was in her late 30's, she entered into an artistic and romantic liaison with Gabriele D'ANNUNZIO, playing the title roles in his *La Gioconda* and *Francesca da Rimini.* An actress of great emotional power, she was noted for her great simplicity and lack of theatrical artifice.

Dutch Courtezan, The (1603). A drama by John MARSTON. Freevil, in love with the gentle Beatrice, wishes to break off his old relationship with Franceschina, the Dutch courtesan. To twit his upright friend Malheureux, he takes him to Franceschina's house where the young man falls under the courtesan's spell. Discovering the facts about Freevil's forthcoming marriage, Franceschina turns to Malheureux and promises to give herself to him when he brings her Freevil's ring as a token that the latter is dead. Malheureux informs Freevil of her offer, and the two stage a mock quarrel. Malheureux hurries to Franceschina with the ring and then finds that she has betrayed him to the authorities. As Malheureux is about to be executed, Freevil appears and reveals the subterfuge.

Dutchman's Fireside, The (1831). A novel by James Kirke PAULDING. A faithful depiction of Dutch life in 18th-century America, the book follows the adventures of Sybrandt Nestbrook in the French and Indian Wars. The hero, reported dead, returns in time to win the hand of Catalina Vancour.

Dutch Wars. Three wars fought between England and the United Provinces (Holland) in 1652–1654, 1664–1667, and 1672–1674. The first two were inspired by commercial rivalry and consisted largely of naval engagements and raids upon shipping and colonies. Among these was the British raid on New Amsterdam in 1664 which brought about the cession of that colony. The third war, very unpopular in England, was brought about by the desire of Charles II's ally, Louis XIV of France, to seize the Spanish Netherlands, and French land campaigns were important. Overall the wars were to England's advantage, but the Dutch were able to preserve the integrity of their home territory and government.

Dutourd, Jean (1920–   ). French novelist and essayist. Dutourd is the satirical humorist of such works as *A Dog's Head* (*Une tête de chien;* 1950), *The Best Butter* (*Au Bon Beurre;* 1952, also translated as *The Milky Way*), and *Five A. M.* (*Doucin;* 1955). *The Taxis of the Marne* (1956) is an autobiographical and political essay.

Duun, Olav (1876–1939). Norwegian novelist. In both subject and style Duun is a regionalist writer. *Juvikfolke* (*The People of Juvik,* 6 vols., 1918–1923), a novel series and his finest work, is set in his native Namdalen. He writes in *landsmaal,* the spoken language of Norway, and not in the traditional literary Dano-Norwegian *riksmaal.*

Duval, Claude. A highwayman, famed in legend and ballad. He was hanged at Tyburn in 1670 and provided with an epitaph beginning: "Here lies Du Vall: Reader, if male thou art look to thy purse, if female, to thy heart."

Duveneck, Frank (1848–1919). American portrait painter and etcher. The Ashcan School was influenced by his direct presentation and by the vigorous brushwork, learned in Munich, Germany, with which he defined the planes of a face on the canvas.

Du Vergier de Hauranne, Jean. Abbé de Saint-Cyran (1581–1643). French theologian. A man of austere and unshakable religious conviction, Du Vergier defended the rights of bishops against the Jesuits in his pamphlets *Petrus Aurelius* (1632–1633). Appointed director of Port-Royal in 1635, he introduced into the convent the moral and theological convictions of JANSENISM, which he had acquired from his teacher and friend Cornelius Jansen. In 1638, Richelieu became uneasy at Du Vergier's enormous religious influence and ordered him sent to prison where he remained till the year of his death.

Dvořák, Antonin (1841–1904). Czech composer. He was director of the National Conservatory of Music in New York City (1892–1895), and head of the Conservatory in Prague (1901). He wrote many operas and symphonies (among these the *New World Symphony*), symphonic poems, overtures, rhapsodies, nocturnes, scherzos, concertos, and choral works.

dwarf. A tiny, often misshapen person. Dwarfs have figured in the legends and mythology of nearly every race, and Pliny gives particulars of whole races of them, possibly following travelers' reports of African Pygmies. Among the Teutonic and Scandinavian peoples, dwarfs held an important place in mythology. They generally dwelt in rocks, caves, and recesses of the earth, were the guardians of its mineral wealth and precious stones, and were very skilful in the working of these. They had their own king, as a rule were not inimical to man, but could, on occasion, be intensely vindictive and mischievous. They play an important role in Wagner's RING DES NIBELUNGEN.

Dwight, Theodore (1764–1846). American lawyer and writer. Like his brother Timothy, he was one of the HARTFORD WITS and wrote satirical verse in collaboration with Richard ALSOP. He also wrote a pro-Federalist *History of the Hartford Convention* (1833).

Dwight, Timothy (1752–1817). American poet and educator, a grandson of Jonathan Edwards, and leader of the Hartford Wits. A Calvinist in religion and Federalist in politics, Dwight was president of Yale (1795–1817), whose staff and curricula he brilliantly developed. His most popular poems were THE CONQUEST OF CANAAN, *The Triumph of Infidelity* (1788), and *Greenfield Hill* (1794). A clergyman as well, Dwight served as a chaplain in the Revolutionary army and wrote many sermons, 173 of which were collected as *Theology, Explained and Defended* (1818–1819).

Dyer, Sir Edward (1540?–1607). English poet of the Elizabethan period. A friend of Sir Philip Sidney, Fulke Greville, and Edmund Spenser. He was best known for his lyric beginning "My mind to me a kingdom is."

Dyer, John (1699–1757). English poet and painter. He was a member of a literary coterie which included James Thomson and Richard Savage, and studied painting with Jonathan Richardson. His first major poem GRONGAR HILL is in Pindaric form and deals with the tradition of evening contemplation which was popularized by Milton's *Il Penseroso.* Other important poems are *The Ruins of Rome* (1740) and *The Fleece* (1757), a didactic account of sheep-raising and the wool trade in supposed imitation of the pastorals of Vergil and Alexander Pope.

dynastic histories. Chinese historical works detailing the history of the various ruling houses. They begin with the Han Dynasty (202 B.C.–A.D. 220) and continue until the Ch'ing or Manchu (1644–1912). There are altogether 24 such histories, each composed by writers of the dynasty following one which had fallen.

Dynasts, The. See Thomas HARDY.

Dysmas. See DISMAS.

Dzhugashvili, Iosef Visarionovich. See Joseph STALIN.

E

Ea. The Babylonian god of water and of wisdom. Developed from the Sumerian ENKI, he was one of the most important gods in the pantheon. It was he who, to a considerable extent, established the orderly functions of earth, sky, and sea, especially as they affect man, though specific functions such as irrigation or the growth of grain were in the hands of lesser gods. It was he whose wisdom or cunning often saved the universe and the other gods from disaster. He disposed of the stone monster of KUMARBI when it threatened heaven; he alone of the gods found the means to save ISHTAR from the underworld; and he saved mankind from the flood by warning Utnapishtim to build his ark, as explained in the *Epic of* GILGAMESH.

Each and All (1839). A poem by Ralph Waldo EMERSON. Written on the occasion of a seashore walk, it is an expression of faith in the oneness of the universe. The poet praises the "perfect whole" in which all parts are interdependent. *Each and All* was later collected in Emerson's *Poems* (1847).

eagle. A large, powerful predatory bird. It is used in many lands and ages as an emblem symbolizing strength and swiftness. The Romans used it from the time of Marius as the ensign of a legion. The French under the Empire assumed the same device. The golden eagle and the spread eagle, devices of the emperors of the East, adapted from the ensigns of the ancient kings of Babylon and Persia, of the Ptolemies and the Seleucides, came to commemorate the Crusades. In Christian art, the eagle is emblematic of St. John the Evangelist, because, like that bird, he looked on "the sun of glory." St. Augustine, St. Gregory the Great, and St. Prisca are also often shown with an eagle.

When Charlemagne was made leader of the Holy Roman Empire, he joined the German eagle, which faces right, to the Roman eagle, which faces left. The resulting double-headed eagle thus became the emblem of the Holy Roman Empire and of the Austrian Empire which regarded itself as its successor. In Russia, the same emblem symbolizes the Eastern or Byzantine Empire and the Western or Roman Empire, supposedly combined under the Russian Ivan Vasilyevich when, in 1472, he married Sophia, the niece of Constantine XIV, the last emperor of Byzantium. The phrase in Psalm 103, "Thy youth is renewed like the eagle's," refers to an ancient superstition that every ten years the eagle soars into the fiery region and plunges thence into the sea, where, molting its feathers, it acquires new life. See PHOENIX.

Eakins, Thomas (1844–1916). American painter. He studied anatomy in Philadelphia, where he settled, making dissections and taking casts. A realistic painter, he made full use of this knowledge in scenes of sports, especially rowing. Experimenting in various directions, he painted genre scenes, did some sculpture, and is known for penetrating, uncompromisingly objective portraits such as *The Clinic of Dr. Gross*.

Earhart, Amelia (1898–1937). American aviator. She was the first woman pilot to cross the Atlantic Ocean in an airplane (June 17, 1928). She was married to George Palmer Putnam, the publisher, and was herself the author of several books, notably *Last Flight* (1938), edited by her husband. In July, 1937, she was lost in an attempt to fly across the Pacific.

Earle, John (1601?–1665). English prose writer and prelate. His *Microcosmography* (1628) is considered one of the best works by the 17th-century CHARACTER WRITERS; it is a miniature human comedy, both witty and contemplative.

Earnshaw, Catherine. See WUTHERING HEIGHTS.

Earthly Paradise, the. A place of perfect beauty, peace, and immortality, widely believed in the Middle Ages to exist on earth in some as yet undiscovered land or island. It was sometimes identified with the Biblical Garden of Eden and located in the Near East; sometimes it was situated in the Far East, as in a legendary letter from PRESTER JOHN, which locates it within three days' journey of his kingdom, or in *The Travels of Sir John* MANDEVILLE; other maps and reports place it variously in the Atlantic, Pacific, and Indian Oceans. See ST. BRANDAN.

William MORRIS' *The Earthly Paradise* (4 vols., 1868–1870) is a long collection of narrative poems modeled on Chaucer's. The prologue tells how a band of Norse sailors flee the Black Death and go in search of the Earthly Paradise. They finally come to rest in "a nameless city in a distant sea." Then follows a series of banquets at which 24 tales are told; each month one of the Norsemen tells a medieval saga or romance, and one of the hosts relates a classical myth. In between are lyric interludes describing the changing landscape, a poem for each month.

Earwicker, Humphrey Chimpden. The protagonist of James Joyce's novel FINNEGANS WAKE. Literally a middle-aged Irish tavern keeper with a guilty conscience, he represents all sinful mankind. His initials, HCE, are interwoven throughout the book.

East Coker. See FOUR QUARTETS.

Easter. The Christian Paschal festival. The name was adopted from A.S. *eastre,* a heathen festival held at the vernal equinox in honor of the Teutonic goddess of dawn, called by Bede *Eostre* (cognate with L. *aurora* and Sanskrit *ushas,* dawn). On the introduction of Christianity it was natural for the name of the heathen festival to be transferred to the Christian, since the two fell at about the same time.

Easter Day is the first Sunday after the 14th day of the Paschal moon. The Paschal moon is the first moon whose 14th day comes on or after the vernal equinox (March 21). Consequently, Easter Sunday cannot be earlier than March 22, or later than April 25. This was fixed by the council of Nicaea, A.D. 325. It was formerly a common belief that the sun danced on Easter Day.

Easter Rebellion (1916). An abortive revolution staged on Easter Monday, 1916 in Dublin by the revolutionary Fenian organization attempting to secure Irish independence from England. Frustrated by the English delay in granting home rule, the FENIANS —under the leadership of Patrick Pearse (1879–1916) and James Connolly (1870–1916)—seized the general post office and a number of other locations in Dublin, proclaiming an Irish republic. The rebels, about 2000 in number, held their positions for six days before succumbing to the overwhelming superiority of the English forces. The ruthless behavior of the British soldiers, coupled with the execution of all the rebel leaders, led to a wave of violent anti-English sentiment, and the rebellion became a rallying point for all Irishmen. The events were celebrated in a number of literary efforts, notably in Yeats's *Easter Sunday* and, with considerable irony, in O'Casey's play *The Plough and the Stars*.

Easter Wings (1633). A poem by George HERBERT. The two stanzas of the poem are composed of lines that become progressively shorter, then longer, creating a shape resembling a pair of wings. The sense of the poem, which deals with the Fall and man's participation in Christ's Resurrection, fits perfectly in this form.

Eastlake, Sir **Charles Lock** (1793–1865). English painter and art critic. He made sketches of Napoleon as a prisoner aboard H.M.S. *Bellerophon*, from which he developed two large portraits. He served as keeper of the National Gallery (1843–1847) and became its director in 1855. He is known for his pictures of Italian banditti and for several paintings of episodes in the life of Christ.

East Lynne (1861). A novel by Mrs. Henry WOOD which was immensely popular, particularly in a dramatic version. Its heroine, Lady Isabel Vane, after running off with another man, returns to her remarried husband disguised as a nurse to care for her own children. After keeping up this pretense for a considerable time, she is at last reconciled to her husband.

Eastman, Max [Forrester] (1883–   ). American critic, poet, and essayist. Eastman began his career as a teacher of philosophy and psychology at Columbia University. During this period he was occupied with aesthetics and wrote *The Enjoyment of Poetry* (1913). When the First World War broke out, Eastman turned to political and social controversy. He became a Marxist, but opposed the Stalinist development of Soviet Russia. Eastman helped to found two important magazines, THE MASSES and *The Liberator* (1917); he was tried for sedition when *The Masses* was suppressed for antiwar writings in 1917. Some of Eastman's other books are *Marxism: Is It Science?* (1940); *Heroes I Have Known* (1942); *Lot's Wife* (1942), a narrative poem; *Enjoyment of Living*

(1948); *Poems of Five Decades* (1954); *Reflections on the Failure of Socialism* (1955); and *Great Companions—Critical Memoirs of Some Famous Friends* (1959).

East of Eden (1952). A novel by John STEINBECK. Based on the biblical story of Cain and Abel, the book centers on the lives of Adam Trask and his two sons, Cal and Aron. Adam settles in the Salinas Valley in California with his wife, Cathy, who bears the two boys, leaves her husband, and becomes a prostitute. Adam, who favors Aron, is at first unable to forgive Cal when he drives Aron to his death by telling him that their mother is a prostitute.

Eaten Heart, The. A tale from THE DECAMERON of Giovanni Boccaccio. In this story, William of Roussillon gives to his wife the heart of her lover. When she discovers that she has eaten the heart, she kills herself and is buried with her lover.

Eaton, Margaret or **Peggy O'Neale** (1796–1879). Wife of John H. Eaton, U.S. secretary of war (1829–1831). The daughter of a Washington tavern-keeper, Peggy was the wife of John B. Timberlake, a navy purser, when Andrew JACKSON and his friend Eaton lodged at her father's inn in 1823. After Timberlake's death, Eaton married the pretty widow in 1829 amid rumors that he had been overly familiar with her while her husband was alive. When Jackson named Eaton secretary of war in 1829, the wife of Vice President Calhoun and the wives of other Cabinet members refused to call on her. The president, however, remained loyal to his friends, perhaps remembering the social abuse to which the recently deceased Mrs. Jackson had been subjected. The feud eventually turned into a political issue, resulting in the resignations of Eaton, Secretary of State Van Buren, and other Cabinet members, and widened the growing rift between Jackson and Calhoun.

Eberhart, Richard (1904–   ). American poet and teacher. Eberhart's first collection was *A Bravery of Earth* (1930). Among his later works are *Song and Idea* (1942), *Burr Oaks* (1947), *Undercliff; Poems, 1946–1953* (1953), *Great Praises* (1957), and *Collected Poems, 1930–1960* (1960). His poetry is characterized by short lines, few rhymes, and the use of simple, homely things from which the poet draws a parallel to some metaphysical truth. He was a founder of the Poets' Theater at Cambridge, Mass.; his verse play *The Apparition* was first produced there (1951). His *Collected Verse Plays* appeared in 1962.

Ebers, Georg (1837–1898). German novelist and Egyptologist. He is known for his pedantic "professorial novels," such as *Eine ägyptische Königstochter* (*An Egyptian Princess*, 1874) and *Kleopatra* (1894).

Ebert, Friedrich (1870–1925). German statesman. He was the first president of the Weimar Republic (1919–1925) and leader of the Social Democrats.

Eblis. In Muslim legend, the Devil, called Azazel before the fall, who rules over the evil genii or JINN. When Adam was created, Allah commanded all the angels to worship him, but Azazel replied, "Me thou hast created of smokeless fire, and shall I reverence a creature made of dust?" Allah was angry at this insolent answer, and turned the disobedient angel into a Sheytan (devil) and he became the father of devils. Another Muslim tradition has it that before life was breathed into Adam, all the angels came to look at the shape of clay, among them Azazel, who, knowing that Allah intended man to be his superior, vowed never to acknowledge him as such and kicked the figure until it rang.

Eblis had five sons: *Tir,* author of fatal accidents; *Awar,* the demon of lubricity; *Dasim,* author of discord; *Sut,* father of lies; *Zalambur,* author of mercantile dishonesty.

Ebuda. In the ORLANDO FURIOSO of Ariosto an island of the Hebrides, west of Scotland. Here Angelica and later Olimpia are exposed to the cruel sea monster called the Orc. Ruggiero rescues Angelica and Orlando rescues Olimpia from the beast.

Eça de Queiroz, José Maria (1845–1900). Portuguese novelist and short-story writer. Considered Portugal's greatest novelist, he is best known for *O Crime Do Padre Amaro (The Sin of Father Amaro,* 1876), a naturalistic satire directed against clerical corruption which was based on his observations as a municipal official in the province of Leiria. His gift for ironic social criticism was further revealed in *O Primo Basilio (Cousin Basilio,* 1878), a study of a middle-class Lisbon family, and *Os Maias* (1880), about upper-class life. He also wrote a fanciful short novel, *O Mandarim* (1880); the novel *A Relíquia (The Relic,* 1887); *A Cidade e as Serras (The City and the Mountains,* 1901); short stories; *Prosas Bárbaras* (1905), a collection of articles and stories; and *Cartas de Inglaterra* (1945), letters about Victorian England, where he lived from 1874 to 1888.

Ecbasis Captivi. Full title **Ecbasis cuiusdam Captivi, per Tropologiam (The Escape of a Certain Captive, with Allegorical Significance,** usually called **The Escape of the Calf,** c. 940). A Latin tale about a calf running away from his stable, only to be threatened by a wolf until rescued by a fox. It probably represents a monk running from his vows and his monastery, and in danger of great sin until rescued by discipline. Its importance, however, is in the development of the beast-epic, for some of the animals and events reappear in the clerical satire *Ysengrimus* (1148), direct ancestor of REYNARD THE FOX.

Ecclesiastes. A book of the Old Testament. It was formerly ascribed to Solomon because of its opening verse, "The words of the Preacher, the son of David, king in Jerusalem," but it is now generally assigned to an unnamed author of the third century B.C. The book's refrain is "vanity of vanities; all is vanity." (Eccl. 1:2).

Ecclesiastical History of the English People. See BEDE.

Ecclesiazusae (Ekklesiazousai). See ARISTOPHANES.

Echegaray [y Eizaguirre], José (1832–1916). Spanish dramatist. His works, which enlarge upon the romantic theme of melancholic passion, are noted for their high degree of technical skill. The best known of his fustian compositions are *O locura o santidad* (1877), in which a Quixotic hero is accused of folly for attempting to pass along his fortune to its rightful owners, and EL GRAN GALEOTO. This last mentioned work relates the transformation of the three virtuous and honorable members of a triangle situation, society being blamed for their corruption. In 1904 Echegaray received the Nobel Prize.

Echeverría, Esteban (1805–1851). Argentine poet. During a five-year stay in Paris, Echeverría absorbed the tenets of French romanticism which permeate his works of poetry, especially *Elvira, o la novia del Plata* (1832), *Consuelos* (1834), and *La cautiva* (1837), notable for its depiction of the Argentine pampa and its inhabitants. Echeverría's opposition to dictator Juan Manuel de Rosas led him and other idealistic youths to form the *Asociación de Mayo,* a secret revolutionary group dedicated to liberal, democratic principles. His hatred for Rosas also inspired him to write EL MATADERO, the work for which he is probably best known today.

Echidna. A monster of classical mythology, half woman, half serpent. By Typhon she was mother of the CHIMAERA, the many-headed dog Orthos, the hundred-headed dragon of the Hesperides, the Colchian dragon, the Sphinx, Cerberus, Scylla, the Gorgons, the Lernaean hydra, the vulture that gnawed away the liver of Prometheus, and the Nemean lion.

Spenser makes her the mother of the Blatant Beast in the *Faerie Queene* (1596).

Echo. A nymph of Greek mythology. There are several stories of why she seemed to be merely a disembodied voice. Perhaps the commonest is that she pined away from unrequited love for NARCISSUS until only her voice remained. According to another story, Hera, annoyed at Echo's babbling while she was trying to spy on Zeus, took away the nymph's speech, allowing her only to echo others. Yet a third version explains that Pan, furious that she could not love him, maddened some shepherds until they tore her into such tiny pieces that nothing was left but her voice.

Eckermann, Johann Peter (1792–1854). A friend and literary assistant to Goethe. He helped Goethe prepare the *Ausgabe letzter Hand* (final edition) of his works. His *Gespräche mit Goethe* (English edition, *Conversations with Goethe,* in 3 vols., 1836–1848) are daily records of Goethe's personal talks with Eckermann and constitute in their remarkable authenticity a monument to the ideal amanuensis.

eclectic (from *Gr.* "ek-legein," to choose, select). Selectiveness as a way of living. The name given to those who do not attach themselves to any special school (especially philosophers and painters), but pick and choose from various systems, selecting and harmonizing those doctrines and methods that suit them.

eclogue. Specifically, a pastoral dialogue in verse. The speakers, usually two shepherds or a shepherd and his mistress, discuss topics ranging from the state of their hearts to that of the nation, from the management of sheep to that of verse. Loosely, any short poem with pastoral elements may be called an eclogue. See BUCOLICS.

Ecole des femmes, L' (The School for Wives, 1662). A verse comedy by MOLIÈRE. ARNOLPHE has arranged for his beloved AGNÈS to be raised in total innocence, in order that she may never prove unfaithful when he marries her. Because of her unsophistication, Horace is able to win her affections and persuades her to run away with him. Unaware of Arnolphe's relation to the girl, Horace asks him to hide her. Arnolphe is about to spirit her away to a convent when it is revealed that Agnès' father, the rich Enrique, has arranged with Horace's father for their children to be married. The play was criticized for supposed moral as well as literary flaws, and Molière replied to his critics in two works: *La Critique de l'Ecole des Femmes* (1663) and *L'Impromptu de Versailles* (1663).

Ecole des femmes, L'. A novel trilogy by André GIDE about the position of women in the modern world. It includes *The School for Wives* (1929), *Robert* (1929), and *Geneviève* (1936).

Ecole des maris, L'. See SGANARELLE (2).

Ector, Sir. In Malory's *Morte d'Arthur* (c. 1469), the foster father of King Arthur and father of Sir KAY.

Edda. The name given to two Icelandic collections of early Scandinavian mythology. The manuscripts comprising the *Elder* or *Poetic Edda* (written 9th to 12th century) were discovered about 1643 by the Icelandic Bishop Brynjolf Sveinsson (1605–1675), who erroneously attributed them to Saemund Sigfusson (1056–1133) and called the work *The Edda of Saemund.* The 34 lays, or poems, tell the mythological stories of the Old Norse gods and heroes.

The *Younger* or *Prose Edda,* also called the *Snorra Edda* (early 13th century), was written by SNORRI STURLUSON. In five parts, it includes a prefatory account of the creation of the world and of pagan poetry; the stories of early Scandinavian mythology; further legends of the gods, given as the "sayings of Bragi," god of poetry; the *Skalda,* a detailed account of the rules of ancient prosody; and the *Hattatal,* a technical analysis of meters. Other linguistic treatises and a list of poets were added after Sturluson's death.

Eddy, Mary Baker (1821–1910). American religious leader, editor, and author. The founder of CHRISTIAN SCIENCE, Mrs. Eddy published *Science and Health* (1875) as an exposition of her ideas and as the official statement of the organization she headed. In this book and others of her *Miscellaneous Writings* (1896) she taught that pain, disease, old age, and death were "errors." She founded the Church of Christ, Scientist, in Boston (1879), and the newspaper, *The Christian Science Monitor* (1908). Mrs. Eddy was influenced by Transcendentalism, and particularly, by the work of Ralph Waldo Emerson. Toward the end of her career, she was attacked by the New York *World, McClure's Magazine,* and Mark Twain, who wrote a book on *Christian Science* (1907) ridiculing her beliefs. The doctrines of Christian Science are summarized in the first sentence of Mrs. Eddy's *Science and Health:* "The Prayer that reforms the sinner and heals the sick is an absolute faith that all things are possible to God."

Edel, Leon (1907–   ). American critic and biographer. A professor of English at New York University, Edel has edited much of the work of Henry James. *Henry James: The Untried Years, 1843–1870* (1953) is the first volume of a proposed four-volume biography. For *Henry James: The Conquest of London, 1870–1881* and *Henry James: The Middle Years, 1882–1895* (both published in 1962), Edel was awarded the Pulitzer Prize and the National Book Award. His other books include *James Joyce: The Last Journey* (1947); *Willa Cather, A Critical Biography* (1953), written with E. K. Brown; and *The Psychological Novel, 1900–1950* (1955).

Eden. Paradise, the country and garden in which ADAM AND EVE were placed by God (Gen. 2:5). The word means delight, pleasure; it has often been used metaphorically to describe a place of charming scenery.

Edgar. In Shakespeare's KING LEAR, the legitimate son of the earl of Gloucester. He is disinherited because of his bastard brother Edmund's lies. After Gloucester has been blinded and ousted from his castle by Regan and Cornwall, Edgar finds him and saves him from suicide. He then kills the treacherous Edmund.

Edgar Huntly; or, Memoirs of a Sleep-Walker (1799). A novel by Charles Brockden BROWN. Really a detective story, the plot involves a supposed murder, an attempted murder, and a real murder. The Indians, who turn out to have committed the crime, are not idealized; the novel had a great influence on James Fenimore Cooper.

Edgeworth, Maria (1767–1849). An Irish novelist, best known for her novel CASTLE RACKRENT. Many of her other works have their setting in Irish life, among them *Belinda* (1801), THE ABSENTEE, *Vivian* (1812), and *Ormond* (1817). She wrote in the tradition of the novel of manners in which Jane Austen excelled, but was also very sensitive to local atmosphere, and portrayed national character with great sympathy. In this respect she exercised a fair influence on her friend Sir Walter Scott. Her letters as well as her novels are still highly readable.

Edict of Nantes. See NANTES, EDICT OF.

Edison, Thomas A[lva] (1847–1931). American inventor. Born in Ohio, Edison was educated at home by his mother and at the age of 12 was a newsboy on the railroad; later he became a telegraph operator. Edison patented over 1000 inventions, including the incandescent electric lamp, the microphone, the phonograph, and the Edison accumulator. In 1913 he produced talking motion-pictures. He is credited with the definition of *genius* as 2% inspiration and 98% perspiration.

Editions de Minuit, Les. See VERCORS.

edle Einfalt und stille Grösse. See Johann Joachim WINCKELMANN.

Edmonds, Walter D[umaux] (1903–   ). American historical novelist. Edmonds made his native region of northern New York as much his own literary property as it is possible for an author to do. The Black River, the Black River Canal, and the Erie Canal dominated his imagination. His books are authentic in research and setting, vivid in their style and narrative. They include *Rome Haul* (1929), *Erie Water* (1933), DRUMS ALONG THE MOHAWK, *Chad Hanna* (1940), *In the Hands of the Senecas* (1947), and *The Wedding Journey* (1947). He has also written *The First Hundred Years* (1948), *They Fought With What They Had* (1951), *Uncle Ben's Whale* (1955), and a number of juveniles.

Edmund. In Shakespeare's KING LEAR, the bastard son of the earl of Gloucester. He instigates the disinheritance of his half-brother Edgar, betrays his father, and schemes with Lear's daughter Goneril to poison her husband, Albany. Mortally wounded by Edgar, the repentant Edmund tries unsuccessfully to save Cordelia, Lear's youngest daughter, from execution.

Edo. See TOKYO.

Edo period. See TOKUGAWA.

Education of Henry Adams, The (privately printed, 1907; posthumously published, 1918). An autobiographical work by Henry ADAMS. Subtitled *A Study in 20th-Century Multiplicity*, it complements MONT-SAINT-MICHEL AND CHARTRES. Adams' book, written in the third person, might have been an account of the experience of any sensitive man; he uses himself as a model of modern man, searching for coherence in a fragmented universe. Adams considers his education a failure, for it had not prepared him for the conflicts to be faced.

The book is not a complete autobiography; it omits any mention of the 13 years of Adams' marriage, and the seven years following his wife's suicide. It does, however, present a vivid picture of places and people the author knew. In the chapter, "The Virgin and the Dynamo," Adams compares two eras; the dynamo, symbol of mechanistic force, acts on passive man in the 20th-century "multiverse," while the Virgin, symbol of unity, correspondingly stands for the 13th-century concept of an ordered universe.

Education sentimentale, L' (Sentimental Education, 1869). A novel by Gustave FLAUBERT. Flaubert presents a picture of life among French dilettantes, intellectuals, and revolutionaries at the time of the decline and fall of Louis Philippe's monarchy and the Revolution of 1848. The events of the Revolution and the establishment of the Second Empire, carefully documented, provide a further background for the main action. The novel's protagonist, Frédéric Moreau, is an egotistical and ambitious young man who comes to Paris from the provinces determined to pattern his life upon literature's romantic hero. He undergoes the romantic passion of unrequited love for MME ARNOUX, but does not forego involvement in several less ideal and ultimately disillusioning affairs. Like the desires of Emma Bovary (see MADAME BOVARY), his dreams are pathetic and sometimes contemptible. Like Emma, too, Moreau is a wholly real person, whom Flaubert draws with truly objective detachment and complete artistic mastery.

Edward. A medieval English ballad which has many versions. In most of these, a young man named Edward explains to his mother that he has killed his father. In some variations, there is the suggestion that the mother encouraged the murder. A modern version of this "domestic tragedy" ballad may be found in a poem by Robinson Jeffers: *Such Counsels You Gave To Me* (1937).

Edward II (1284–1327). King of England (after 1307). He is the subject of a play by Christopher MARLOWE.

Edward VI. Edward Tudor (1537–1553), King of England (1547–1553). The son of Henry VIII and his third wife, Jane Seymour, Edward became king when he was only nine years old. He was under the Protectorate first of his uncle, Edward Seymour, lord Somerset, and then of John Dudley, duke of Northumberland. Largely through Northumberland's machinations, Edward signed a deposition willing the crown to his second cousin, Lady Jane GREY, who was also Northumberland's daughter-in-law.

Edward VIII. See duke of WINDSOR.

Edwardian. Pertaining to English life and letters in the early years of the 20th century, a period corresponding roughly to the reign (1901–1910) of Edward VII. In general, the era witnessed a relaxation of Victorian conservatism and complacency, together with a questioning and criticism of authority and accepted social values. G. B. Shaw, Arnold Bennett, and H. G. Wells were among the writers who reflected these tendencies. The term is also used to refer to the opulence and elegance of the period. Victoria Sackville-West described the era in her novel *The Edwardians* (1930).

Edwards, Harry Stillwell (1855–1938). American lawyer, editor, public official, and writer. Edwards won the Chicago *Record* $10,000 prize (1896) for his novel, *Sons and Fathers*. When he was 64 years old, he wrote the book for which he is well known: *Eneas Africanus* (1919). It is the story of a Negro slave who becomes separated from his master in 1865; for eight years he wanders through the South on a humorous pilgrimage in the wilderness until he and his master are reunited. Edwards also wrote *Eneas Africanus, Defendant* (1921).

Edwards, Jonathan (1703–1758). American theologian and philosopher. In his early youth Edwards was a precociously brilliant scholar, showing a keen interest in scientific observation. His early philosophical thought tended toward Idealism under the influence of Locke, and many of his ideas resembled those of George Berkeley, whose work at that time he did not know.

Edwards' theology was more basically Calvinistic than that of earlier Puritan divines, who emphasized the covenantal relation between God and man, rather than the absolute supremacy of a God bound by no contract. He believed "that the essence of all religion lies in holy love" and that sin was a "property of the species," which both justified God's punishment of man and made possible mercy and redemption. His sermon on *Sinners in the Hands of an Angry God* (1741), so horrifying to later readers, was in fact an exhortation on the necessity of salvation, as well as a reminder of the torments that awaited the unregenerate. His beliefs on the place of the emotions in religious experience led him to champion the "GREAT AWAKENING," in which he saw dramatic conversions as evidence of the "peculiar and immediate" manifestation of God. Among his works are *A Faithful Narrative of the Surprising Work of God in the Conversion of Many Hundred Souls* (1737) and *A Careful and Strict Enquiry into Freedom of the Will* (1754).

Edwards, Richard (1523?–1566). English dramatist and poet. Edwards' only extant play is *Damon and Pythias* (published 1571). Some of his poems appeared in THE PARADISE OF DAINTY DEVICES (1576).

Edwin Drood, The Mystery of (1870). An unfinished novel by Charles DICKENS. The orphans Edwin Drood and Rosa Bud have been betrothed by their fathers, and are to marry when Edwin is 21, though the obligatory nature of the agreement has in fact made love between them impossible. Rosa arouses the admiration of two men: Edwin's ostensibly devoted Uncle Jasper, a disagreeable hypocrite who loves her passionately, and Neville Landless, a youth who detests Edwin for his mistreatment of the young girl. At their last meeting before they are to be wed, Edwin and Rosa acknowledge that they can never be happy together and break their engagement. The same night Edwin mysteriously disappears, and Jasper, who has done all he can to aggravate the enmity between Edwin and Neville, accuses the latter of murdering his nephew. Rosa's guardian notices

Jasper's displeasure on learning that the engagement had been broken before the disappearance. Neville is arrested, but, since no body can be found, he is released untried. Jasper, however, continues to connive against Neville and to pursue the terrified Rosa, while a mysterious Mr. Datchery appears on the scene to frustrate Jasper's intrigues. At this point the novel breaks off. In the absence of any solution left by Dickens, it has been a favorite puzzle of literary detectives to attempt to solve the mystery. The most convincing proposed solutions generally hinge on two questions: whether or not Edwin is actually dead, and what Mr. Datchery's true identity is. Some have held that Datchery is actually Edwin.

Egeria. In Roman legend, the nymph who instructed NUMA POMPILIUS, 2nd king of Rome, in his wise legislation. Hence, a woman counselor, especially a woman who advises and influences a statesman.

Egeus. In Shakespeare's MIDSUMMER NIGHT'S DREAM, the stern father of Hermia. He forces her betrothal to Demetrius despite her love for Lysander, who is just as desirable a suitor.

Eggleston, Edward (1837-1902). American novelist and clergyman. He is known for regional fiction dealing with Indiana, and especially for THE HOOSIER SCHOOLMASTER. An ardent reformer, Eggleston wrote several other novels of importance, including *The Circuit Rider* (1874), a book describing the impact of Methodism on the frontier; *Roxy* (1878), the story of the trials of a young woman in frontier Indiana; and *The Graysons* (1887), a novel introducing Lincoln as a young lawyer.

Egil. The brother of Wieland or Volund, the Vulcan of Norse mythology. Egil was a famous archer; in the Saga of Thidrik there is a tale about him which is the counterpart of the famous story of WILLIAM TELL and the apple.

Eglamour, Sir. In Shakespeare's TWO GENTLEMEN OF VERONA, a chivalrous old knight who helps Silvia escape from Milan to find her beloved Valentine.

Egmont (publ. 1788). A tragedy by Johann Wolfgang von GOETHE. It is based on the downfall of a historical Count Egmont (1522-1568) who was executed in connection with the Netherlandic revolt against Spain. Like Goethe's earlier GÖTZ VON BERLICHINGEN, Egmont is upright and straightforward in his striving for freedom, but unable to survive in an atmosphere of subtle political machinations. Though Goethe was already working on the play in 1776, in his STURM UND DRANG period, he did not finish it until his second year in Italy, when his ideas had already taken a strong turn toward the classical. This change is reflected in the play's relative polish of form and language as compared with *Götz*. Beethoven wrote his famous *Egmont* music for Goethe's play. See DAEMONIC.

Egoist, The (1879). A novel by George MEREDITH. The "egoist" is Sir Willoughby Patterne of Patterne Hall, possessed of good looks, wealth, and all the virtues except humility and a sense of humor. He invites his fiancée, Clara Middleton, and her father, a clergyman who loves good food and wine, to spend a month at the Hall, where he is the idol of his two old aunts. Clara—"a rogue in porcelain" as Mrs.

Mountstuart Jenkinson, the clever widow who regulates the social life of the countryside, pronounces her—is soon longing to extricate herself from the attentions of her self-centered lover. She is thankful for the diversion of Patterne's gay Irish guest, De Craye, who makes violent love to her, but gives her confidence to Vernon Whitford, Patterne's cousin and secretary. Patterne, who has had a sad experience previously, is in mortal dread of being jilted by Clara, and to preserve his dignity he proposes to his former worshiper Laetitia Dale, whom he had made use of for this same purpose before. Many complications arise, but Vernon and Clara finally confess their love, and Patterne is forced to plead with the now thoroughly disillusioned Laetitia to become the mistress of Patterne Hall.

Egoist, The. An English little magazine. Originally founded as a feminist periodical in 1911, it became the chief organ of imagist poetry (see IMAGISM). Ezra POUND, T. S. ELIOT, Hilda DOOLITTLE, Richard ALDINGTON, Rebecca WEST, and Harriet Weaver were associated with its publication.

Egyptian, The. See Mika Toimi WALTARI.

Ehrenburg, Ilya Grigoryevich (1891-   ). Russian novelist, poet, and journalist. Much of his early life was lived in Paris where he published his first book of poems (1911). He covered the Spanish Civil War for Soviet papers in 1936-1937 and during World War II spent some years in Paris. His first important novel, *The Extraordinary Adventures of Julio Jurenito* (*Neobyknovennoye priklyucheniya Julio Jurenito;* 1922), is a satire on modern European civilization. His other novels include *The Fall of Paris* (*Padeniye Parizha;* 1941), dealing with the war in Western Europe before Russia's involvement; *The Storm* (*Burya;* 1948), a war novel; and *The Thaw* (*Ottepel';* 1954, 1956), an outspoken work about shortcomings under Stalin's regime which gave its name to the period of greater relaxation after Stalin's death.

In installments during 1961-1963, Ehrenburg published his memoirs, entitled *People, Years, and Life* (*Lyudi, gody, zhizn*), which contain interesting revelations about the maneuverings of Soviet intellectual life. Ehrenburg himself has often been accused of being an opportunist who knew too well how to avoid purges in the literary world. He has, however, been a fairly persistent advocate of greater intellectual freedom in Soviet letters and has been a rallying point for Soviet admirers of Western culture.

Eichendorff, Joseph Freiherr von (1798-1857). German romantic poet. He is most famous for his many poems that treat idyllically the unspoiled woods of his Silesian homeland, and for the long story AUS DEM LEBEN EINES TAUGENICHTS. His novel *Ahnung und Gegenwart* (*Presentiment and the Present,* 1815), a BILDUNGSROMAN, reflects Eichendorff's Catholicism in that the hero ends by renouncing this world and entering a monastery. During his career, Eichendorff was a friend of many of the German romantics (see GERMAN ROMANTICISM), including F. Schlegel, Arnim, and Brentano, and later in life he wrote a number of works on literary history, for example, *Über die ethische und religiöse Bedeutung der neueren romantischen Poesie in Deutschland* (*On the Ethical and Religious Importance of Recent Romantic Poetry in Germany,* 1847).

Eichmann, Adolf (1906–1962). German Nazi, in charge of the execution of Jews (1942–1945). He escaped capture after the war, but in 1960 was apprehended by Israeli security forces in Argentina. Worldwide controversy was aroused during his trial (1961) by an Israeli court, which condemned him to death for crimes against humanity.

Eiffel Tower. An iron tower 984.25 feet high. It was built for the Paris Exposition of 1885 on the Champ de Mars. It was named for the engineer Alexandre Gustave Eiffel (1832–1923) who also built the framework for the Statue of Liberty and designed the locks for the Panama Canal. Its sections were prefabricated and assembled on the spot.

Eikon Basiliké (*Gr.*, "royal image"; 1649). A book purporting to be the spiritual autobiography of CHARLES I. Published at the time of Charles's execution, it contains his meditations and prayers during his political troubles as well as his advice to his son. Its authorship is often attributed to John Gauden (1605–1662), an Anglican clergyman who became bishop of Worcester. The book was so popular that Parliament authorized Milton to write an official reply, his *Eikonoclastes* (*Gr.*, "image-breaker"; 1649).

Eimi (1933). A narrative of travel in Russia by E. E. CUMMINGS. Written in a stream-of-consciousness style, including puns, parodies, and typographical innovations, the book is an impressionistic study of what Cummings himself had seen, heard, and felt. The title (pronounced to rhyme with Mamie) is Greek and means *I am.*

Ein' feste Burg (*Ger.* A mighty fortress). The first words of Martin LUTHER's metrical version of Psalm 46. It is used in the opera *Les Huguenots* by MEYERBEER.

Einstein, Albert (1879–1955). German-Swiss-American physicist. Einstein is best known for his theory of relativity, first enunciated in 1905, which made possible the modern concept of the atom. In 1921 he won a Nobel Prize. Einstein left Germany after the rise of the Nazis and settled in the U.S., where he worked at the institute for Advanced Study in Princeton, N.J., until 1945.

Eisenhower, Dwight D[avid] (1890–   ). American general and 34th president of the U.S. (1953–1961). Born in Denison, Texas, Eisenhower graduated in 1915 from the U.S. Military Academy at West Point. In 1942 he was made commander of the Allied forces landing in North Africa. He became a full general in February 1943, was appointed Supreme Commander of the Allied Expeditionary Forces in Europe, led the Normandy invasion, and directed the overthrow of the Nazis (1944–1945). He later became chief of staff in Washington and told his own story of the European war in *Crusade in Europe* (1948). He was president of Columbia University from 1948 to 1952, taking a leave of absence to serve as Supreme Allied Commander in Europe and to set up the forces of the North Atlantic Treaty Organization.

Eisenhower was eyed by both Republicans and Democrats for the presidential nomination in 1952. He accepted the Republican bid and defeated Adlai E. Stevenson in the election. As president he generally took a middle road in his policies, continuing foreign aid and advocating a balanced budget while he opposed government control in private enterprise.

He was reelected in 1956, again defeating Stevenson. *Mandate for Change, 1953–1956,* the first volume of Eisenhower's account of his administrations, *The White House Years,* appeared in 1963.

Eisenstein, Sergei M[ikhailovich] (1898–1948). Russian motion-picture director. Acclaimed as one of the greatest of all film directors, whose methods of cutting and mounting film to gain the effects of montage and dynamic progression have been widely imitated, Eisenstein was trained as a civil engineer and as an architect, then served in the Bolshevik army as a volunteer (1918–1920). His first film, *Strike* (1924), was notable for its skillful handling of crowd movement. Several remarkable scenes in *Potemkin* (1926) were even more significant as milestones in the development of cinematic technique. Among his other famous films are *Ten Days That Shook the World* (1928), the never-completed epic *Que Viva Mexico* (1931–1932), *Alexander Nevsky* (1928), and *Ivan the Terrible* (*Part I,* 1941; *Part II,* 1946), which was originally planned as a trilogy.

Eisteddfod. The Welsh national congress of bards. It had its origin in an extremely old Welsh assembly called the Gorsedd; in its present form it probably began in the twelfth century. Eisteddfod means literally "a session." Minstrelsy has been an important part of Welsh culture from the earliest days, and the present purpose of the Eisteddfod is to maintain an interest in the ancient traditions.

El. The supreme god of many ancient Semitic races in the Near East. He was represented in the form of a bull. The golden calf of the Old Testament probably was sacred to one of his offspring. See THE POEM OF BAAL and THE POEM OF AQHAT.

Elaine. In Arthurian romance, the name given to two ladies, both of whom love LAUNCELOT. In Malory's *Morte d'Arthur* (c. 1469), the first Elaine is the daughter of King Pelles. Falling in love with Sir Launcelot, she takes on for a night the likeness of Queen Guinevere, in order to deceive him. As a result, a son is born to them, and he is given the name of GALAHAD.

The second Elaine, known as the "lily maid of Astolat" is the Elaine of Tennyson's *Lancelot and Elaine* in his *Idylls of the King,* in which he recasts Malory's version of the story. This Elaine loved Launcelot "with that love which was her doom." Her love is so great that she dies of it. According to her request, her dead body is then placed on a barge, a lily in her right hand and a letter, avowing her love and showing the innocence of Launcelot, in her left. The barge, steered by an old servitor, moves down the river, and, when it stops at the palace entrance, Arthur orders the body borne in. The letter is read, and Arthur directs that the maiden shall be buried like a queen, with her sad story blazoned on her tomb. Tennyson has also told her story in his *The Lady of Shalott.*

Elba. An island in the Mediterranean to which Napoleon Bonaparte was banished when he abdicated power in 1814. After 10 months, he escaped from Elba and returned to France for the Hundred Days that ended at WATERLOO.

El Dorado (*Sp.,* the gilded). A legendary king. El Dorado was the supposed King of Manoa, a fabulous city of immense wealth localized by early explorers on the Amazon. He was said to be covered with oil and then powdered with gold dust. This operation had been performed so many times that he was permanently, and literally, gilded. Many expeditions, from both Spain and England (two of which were led by Sir Walter Raleigh), tried to discover El Dorado, and the name was later transferred to his supposed territory. Hence, the term refers to any place or realm of fabulous richness.

Eleanor of Aquitaine (c. 1122–1204). Queen of Louis VII of France (1137–1151), then of Henry II of England (1152–1204), mother of Richard I and King John. Because she was heiress of Aquitaine, about half of southern France, England claimed possession of the region, thus precipitating about 400 years of wars between France and England. She backed the rebellion of her sons against Henry II (1173), for which she was imprisoned (1174–1189). Richard released her after his accession to the throne, and when he went on his crusade, she protected his interests against John. Later she reconciled the brothers and continued to be politically important during John's reign. An ardent patron of the Provençal TROUBADORS, she was influential in bringing them and their works to her courts.

Elective Affinities, The. See WAHLVERWANDT-SCHAFTEN, DIE.

Electra (**Elektra**). (1) In Greek mythology, a daughter of Agamemnon and Clytemnestra, and sister of Orestes. Her tragic story (see House of ATREUS) was told by each of the three great Athenian dramatists, Aeschylus in his *Oresteia* trilogy, Sophocles and Euripides in their plays called *Electra*. Richard Strauss wrote an opera of a version of Sophocles' play by Hugo von Hofmannsthal (1903). *Mourning Becomes Electra* (1931), a trilogy of plays by Eugene O'Neill, is a retelling of the *Oresteia* story set in 19th century New England. Jean Giraudoux also adapted the story for his play *Electre* (1937).

(2) One of the PLEIADES, daughter of Atlas, mother of Dardanus. She is known as "the lost Pleiad," for it is said that she disappeared a little before the Trojan war, that she might be saved the mortification of seeing the ruin of her beloved city. She showed herself occasionally to mortals, but always in the guise of a comet.

Electra (**Elektra**; 414? B.C.). A tragedy by SOPHOCLES (414? B.C.). It deals with the return of Orestes to Argos and the murder of Clytemnestra. Electra is the heroine; as in the *Philoctetes* and the *Oedipus at Colonus,* Sophocles isolates his tragic hero in order to emphasize the qualities of heroism and tragic endurance. As a consequence, the murder of Clytemnestra and Aegisthus is left to the very end; the climax of the play is the long recognition scene between Orestes and Electra. Also, in order to develop the character of Electra to the fullest extent, Sophocles leaves Orestes almost blank; he is the avenger, a paragon of virtue, and nothing more. Thus the recognition scene is the fitting climax, since Electra's trials are now over. Clytemnestra is the real enemy, and Aegisthus is no threat. Euripides reverses this emphasis in order to make Clytemnestra's death more unnecessary and more horrible; Sophocles' determination to represent the murder as an example of "natural recoil" necessitates a strong character for the queen.

Electra (**Elektra**; 413 B.C.). A drama by EURIP-IDES (413 B.C.). Aegisthus has forced Electra to marry a kindly old farmer so that she cannot enter into a dangerous marriage with some great prince. Electra has no power to avenge her father as the wife of a peasant; her only hope is Orestes. The play opens in the peasant's small hut in the mountains. The peasant speaks the prologue, after which Orestes and Pylades enter furtively. Various devices lead gradually to the recognition of brother and sister, which comes about through the summoning of the old servant of Agamemnon who rescued Orestes as a baby. In this play the murder of Aegisthus precedes that of Clytemnestra. Aegisthus is portrayed as the real force behind the usurpation; Clytemnestra is represented as being to some degree the victim of circumstances. In this way the play leads up to the murder of Clytemnestra, who is summoned to the peasant's hut on the pretext that Electra has just had a child. Clytemnestra goes inside, to be met by Orestes and Electra. Euripides' presentation is designed to inspire the utmost horror at the act and great pity for the victim. The play ends with the beginning of the madness of Orestes, brought on by the Erinyes.

Elegies of Ch'u (**Ch'u Tz'u**). Chinese poetry anthology attributed to Ch'ü Yüan of the Chou Dynasty (1027–256 B.C.). It contains 17 poem cycles, dealing with the virtues, largely unrecognized, and the misfortunes of the poet. Also included are nine poems of shamanistic import. The text is corrupt and contains many Han Dynasty accretions. See Arthur Waley, *The Nine Songs: a Study of Shamanism in Ancient China* (1956); David Hawkes, *Ch'u Tz'u: The Songs of the South* (1959).

elegy. In classical prosody a poem in elegiac distichs, in modern prosody a lyrical poem of plaintive content and mood, especially a poem of lament for someone or something departed. Thought to be among the greatest elegies in English are Milton's *Lycidas,* Shelley's *Adonais,* Tennyson's *In Memoriam,* and Matthew Arnold's *Thyrsis,* all poems of mourning, and Gray's *Elegy Written in a Country Churchyard* in a more general plaintive vein.

Elegy Written in a Country Churchyard. A poem by Thomas GRAY (1742?–1750, pub. 1751), probably the most popular—and often considered the greatest—poem written in the eighteenth century. Its familiar theme deals with rural life combined with the tragic dignity inherent in man. This pastoral idealization and meditation on death is made even more subjective at the end by the introduction of "The Epitaph."

Elephant in the Moon, The. A satire on the Royal Society by Samuel BUTLER. In it, an elephant discovered on the face of the moon is revealed to be only a mouse imprisoned in the telescope. The work was first published in a posthumous collection of Butler's *Genuine Remains in Verse and Prose* (1759).

Eleusinian Mysteries. Ancient Greek religious rites. They were performed in honor of DEMETER and her daughter Persephone (Kore) at Eleusis in Attica. Begun probably in late Mycenaean times, with the introduction of the worship of Demeter to Eleusis, these rites became the most famous mysteries in the Greek or Roman world, and continued to be celebrated well into the Christian era. The secret of the rites was so successfully guarded that, in spite of their tremendous importance, no one can say precisely what they were. It is known, however, that they centered about the abduction of Persephone by HADES, her return, and the subsequent reconciliation of Demeter and Hades. In short, they celebrated the revival of corn in the springtime. Also connected with the rite in some way was a youthful godling Iacchus, about whom almost nothing is known, except that he was later identified with Dionysus.

Elgar, Sir Edward (1857–1934). English composer. His most notable compositions include the oratorios *Dream of Gerontius* (1900), *The Apostles* (1903), and *The Kingdom* (1906); *Pomp and Circumstance,* a march (1902); *Enigma Variations* (1899). He also wrote symphonies, songs, and sonatas.

Elgin marbles. A collection of Greek sculptures, mainly of the Phidian school (see PHIDIAS). It includes the bulk of the surviving sculptural decoration of the Parthenon. The works were removed from Athens (1803–1812) by Lord Elgin and were purchased by the British government in 1816. The collection now resides in the British Museum in London.

Elia. See Charles LAMB.

Elidure. Legendary king of England. According to Geoffrey of Monmouth he became king after his elder brother Artegal (or Arthgall) was presumed dead. When Artegal returned after a long exile, Elidure nobly resigned the throne to him. The story appears in John Milton's *History of Britain* and William Wordsworth's poem *Artegal and Elidure.*

Elihu. A name given to several Old Testament characters, the most notable being found in the book of Job. Here, Elihu attempts to reason with Job about his troubles, after the three false comforters have spoken (Job 32).

Elijah. In the Old Testament, a Hebrew prophet who lived during the ninth century B.C. in the reign of Ahab. During the great drought which he foretold, he was fed miraculously by ravens near the stream Cherith, and by Zarephath's widow whose dead son he restored to life. He opposed the prophets of Baal and challenged them to a dramatic contest on Mount Carmel where two altars were built, one to Baal and one to Jehovah. Baal was deaf to the repeated cries of his prophets, but Jehovah answered Elijah by sending fire from heaven. The story of Elijah's discouragement under the juniper tree is well known (see I Kings 19:4). He did not die but was carried up to heaven in a whirlwind (II Kings 2:11). He cast his mantle on Elisha whom he had anointed prophet in his stead; hence, the phrase *Elijah's mantle* signifies succession to any office.

Eliot, Charles William (1834–1926). American teacher and chemist. President of Harvard from 1869 to 1909, he helped to make that school one of the best known in the world. In 1894, Eliot helped to establish Radcliffe College for women. Introducing the elective system, he influenced college education everywhere in the U.S. He improved the graduate and professional schools at Harvard, attracting great scholars to the faculty. Believing that "All the books needed for a real education could be set on a shelf five feet long," he was persuaded to edit the famous Harvard Classics, a 50-volume set.

Eliot, George. Pen name of **Mary Ann** or **Marian Evans** (1819–1880). English novelist. Of the first rank among Victorian novelists, George Eliot was the daughter of a Warwickshire land agent, a man of strong Evangelical Protestant feeling. Her severance from her father's religion was a great source of conflict for her and distress for him. Early in the 1840's she became acquainted with the new and "advanced" biblical and theological scholarship of Germany and translated D. F. Strauss's *Leben Jesu (Life of Jesus,* 1846). After her father's death, she began to associate with a group of rationalists in London; one of them, John Chapman, took her on as assistant editor for the *Westminster Review,* a post she held from 1851 to 1854. She became a friend of Herbert Spencer and through him met George Henry LEWES. Although Lewes was separated from his wife, he could not obtain a divorce, and, in 1854, George Eliot entered into an irregular union with him that lasted until his death (1878); they lived as man and wife and were accepted as such by their friends.

George Eliot was on the verge of middle age before she wrote her first fiction. In 1857 (when she assumed her pen name) her first works of fiction—three short stories—appeared in *Blackwood's* and were published later that same year as the volume *Scenes of Clerical Life.* ADAM BEDE, her first full-length novel, followed soon after, and in 1860 came two more novels: THE MILL ON THE FLOSS and SILAS MARNER. Inspired by a trip to Florence, she did a great deal of painstaking research in the Italian Renaissance and produced her only historical novel, ROMOLA in 1863. Turning again to the contemporary scene in England she wrote FELIX HOLT, THE RADICAL and MIDDLEMARCH, generally considered her finest work. Her last novel, DANIEL DERONDA, is peopled with characters who illustrate her moral philosophy. In 1880, two years after Lewes's death, she married J. W. Cross, a clergyman; she died later that same year.

George Eliot's fiction is a vehicle for the serious discussion of social and moral problems of her time; her purpose is primarily didactic. She presents, on a vast scale and crowded with detail, a beautifully observed world of peasants and townsfolk. Her greatest preoccupation is with moral problems, and, more particularly, with the moral development of her characters, many of whom strive with the difficulty of arriving at an individual and mature view of life. See SPANISH GYPSY, THE.

Eliot, John (1604–1690). English-born American teacher, missionary, and linguist. Emigrating to Massachusetts in 1631, Eliot devoted himself to converting the Indians to Christianity; he established 14 colonies of "Praying Indians" and translated the Bible into the dialect of the Naticks, an Algonquian tribe, in 1663. Most of his work was destroyed during King Philip's War. Eliot also wrote *The Christian Commonwealth* (1659), in which he advocated a society based entirely on obedience to the Scriptures. The book was suppressed by Massachusetts authorities for fear of angering the restored monarchy in England. See BAY PSALM BOOK.

Eliot, Lewis. The hero and narrator of the STRANGERS AND BROTHERS novels by C. P. Snow.

Eliot, Sir Thomas. See Sir Thomas ELYOT.

Eliot, T[homas] S[tearns] (1888–1965). American-born English poet, critic, and dramatist. He lived in England from 1914 and became a British subject in 1927. Universally recognized as one of the major

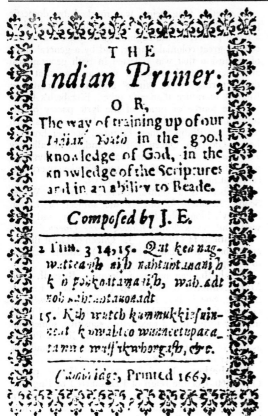

THE
Indian Primer;
OR,
The way of training up of our
Indian Youth in the good
knowledge of God, in the
knowledge of the Scriptures
and in an ability to Reade.

Composed by J. E.

2 Tim. 3 14,15. Qut kea nag-
wutteauh aih nahtuntuuanih
k u pohkouttamaiih, wah adt
tou nihtautauoaadt
15. Kah wutch kummukkiefuin-
eeat kuwabtuo wunneetupata_
tamne wuffukwhongaih, &c.

Cambridge, Printed 1669.

Title page of John Eliot's *Indian Primer* (1669).

poets of the 20th century, Eliot's reputation grew to almost mythic proportions during his own lifetime. Because of its radical innovations in poetic technique and subject matter, his poetry revolutionized the literary conventions bequeathed by the Romantics and Victorians and gave expression to the spirit of the post-World War I world.

Eliot was born in St. Louis, Missouri. He was educated at Harvard, where his flair for eclectic scholarship and his keen sensitivity to the social-psychological currents of the day were already marked characteristics, according to the reminiscences of his fellow students. Realizing that the poetry of his own day could be of little use to him as literary models, he turned to the poetry of other nations and epochs. The English Jacobeans and the French Symbolists were a revelation to him; his indebtedness to Laforgue and Baudelaire is already apparent in his undergraduate poems. After doing graduate work at Harvard, the Sorbonne, and Oxford, Eliot settled in London in 1915. There he came under the influence of Ezra Pound, who recognized Eliot's genius at once, and criticized and encouraged his work. Pound was also largely responsible for getting the early poems into print; he saw to the publication of THE LOVE SONG OF J. ALFRED PRUFROCK in *Poetry* in 1915 and introduced Eliot to Harriet Weaver, who published his first volume of verse, *Prufrock and Other Observations,* in 1917. With his early work in print, Eliot's reputation quickly grew. By the time THE WASTE LAND appeared in 1922, his position was firmly established among the avant garde, and he had become the recognized leader of younger poets.

In technique, as in subject matter, Eliot's poetry broke with the literary conventions of his day, conventions that he felt were inadequate to express the experience of the modern world. In order to capture the spirit of a new age he believed it was necessary to create new poetic forms and a new poetic language, which, in turn, might break up current modes of perception and change contemporary attitudes. Perhaps his most important technical innovations were twofold: instead of "poetic diction" Eliot used the idiom and natural rhythms of speech, and instead of relying on abstractions he expressed himself solely through sense impressions (see OBJECTIVE CORRELATIVE and DISSOCIATION OF SENSIBILITY). The subject matter of his early poems also reflected the world about him. For material, he drew upon his own social background as well as the surrounding squalor of an industrial age. In such poems as *Prufrock,* PORTRAIT OF A LADY, GERONTION, the SWEENEY poems, *The Waste Land,* and THE HOLLOW MEN, he depicts the emotional impoverishment, boredom, and spiritual emptiness common to both the dying genteel world of devitalized social rituals and the new urban materialistic world. Eliot's later poetry reflects his conversion to the Anglican Church in the late 1920's. In poems such as ASH WEDNESDAY, *The Journey of the Magi,* and *Marina,* he portrays alternating stages of despair, skepticism, hope, and joy in the soul's struggle for renewal. FOUR QUARTETS is generally acknowledged to be the major work of this latter period. It is a series of four long meditative poems in which Eliot weaves together his complex thoughts on the irreconcilable tension between man's position in the space-time world and his desire to escape its dimensions. He has also written poems in a lighter vein, such as THE HIPPOPOTAMUS and OLD POSSUM's *Book of Practical Cats* (1939).

In an early essay, TRADITION AND THE INDIVIDUAL TALENT, Eliot propounded the doctrine that poetry should be impersonal, transmuting private feelings into general truths. This view is closely connected with his belief in the indebtedness of the poet to the tradition of the past and the necessity for incorporating the experience of the past into the poetry of the present. His early critical essays were collected in *The Sacred Wood* (1920), a volume that established his reputation as a critic and had an enormous impact on contemporary literary taste. By exalting the Elizabethan dramatists, metaphysical poets, Dante, and the French poets of the 19th century, and attacking Milton and the Victorian and Romantic poets, he effected a general change in literary values. Among his critical works are *The Use of Poetry and the Use of Criticism* (1933) and *The Classics and the Man of Letters* (1942). After joining the church, Eliot devoted much of his prose writing to cultural problems, particularly the place of religion in society. *After Strange Gods: A Primer of Modern Heresy* (1934), *The Idea of a Christian Society* (1939), and *Notes Towards a Definition of Culture* (1948), are books of social criticism. In *For Lancelot Andrewes,* a collection of essays published in 1929, Eliot declared himself "an Anglo-Catholic in religion, a classicist in literature, and a royalist in politics," and the labels stuck, despite his changing opinions. For from his earlier exploratory essays in literary values to his later essays, in which he frequently reversed or modified his previous positions, Eliot's judgments have often been taken to be dogmatic, though in fact he has always viewed them as tentative.

In *Poetry and Drama* (1951) Eliot discusses the problems he faced in attempting to revive poetic drama for the modern stage. His first play, MURDER IN THE CATHEDRAL, is generally considered to be his best. It was followed by THE FAMILY REUNION, THE COCKTAIL PARTY, *The Confidential Clerk* (1954), and *The Elder Statesman* (1958).

Eliot was long associated with Faber & Faber, Ltd., British publishers, and was a director of the firm at his death. He received the Nobel Prize in 1948.

Elise. The illicit queen of Tyre in Quinault's tragedy ASTRATE, ROI DE TYR. Elise is also the name of the miser's daughter in Molière's comedy L'AVARE.

Elisha. In the Old Testament, a Hebrew prophet. He was selected by ELIJAH to be his successor. In contrast to his predecessor, Elisha was urbane and sophisticated. His ministry lasted for 50 years during which time he was counselor to four kings of Israel (c. 850–790 B.C.). His work (which included many civic projects) and his prophecies are recorded in II Kings.

Elissa. See DIDO; FAERIE QUEENE, THE.

elixir of life. The potion of the alchemists to prolong life indefinitely. It was imagined sometimes as a dry drug, sometimes as a fluid. *Elixir* (*Arabic*, a powder for sprinkling on wounds) also meant among alchemists the philosopher's stone, the tincture for transmuting metals, and the name is now given to any sovereign remedy for disease, especially one of a quack character.

Eliza. A character in Harriet Beecher Stowe's UNCLE TOM'S CABIN.

Eliza. Eliza Draper, wife of an official of the East India Company, to whom Laurence Sterne addressed THE BRAMINE'S JOURNAL and the *Letters of Yorick to Eliza* (1775). The letters are a sentimental account of their passionate but Platonic love affair in 1766. *The Letters of Eliza to Yorick* (1775) and *Letters supposed to have been written by Yorick and Eliza* (1779) are forgeries.

Elizabeth I. Elizabeth Tudor (1533–1603). Queen of England (1558–1603), daughter of HENRY VIII and ANNE BOLEYN. Elizabeth was proclaimed queen by Parliament on the death of her elder half-sister, Mary Tudor. She re-established Protestantism and the supremacy of the English ruler over the Pope, ended foreign religious and political domination, and helped, with her claim of being "mere English" and her refusal to take a foreign consort, to strengthen England's growing sense of nationality and unity. Among the major political events of her reign was the execution of Mary, Queen of Scots, for complicity in a Catholic plot against the life of Elizabeth. The death of the Catholic queen may have been the final stroke that moved Philip of Spain to action; the following year, in 1588, he sent the "invincible Armada" against England, and was soundly defeated.

Elizabeth's long reign was marked by domestic peace and prosperity, by the growth of England as a naval power, by the beginnings of what was to become a great colonial empire, and by a general spirit of expansion that was reflected in both geographical and literary exploration; it was an age that produced perhaps more "firsts" and more "greats" in English literature than any other. Elizabeth's Court was the source of much of the lyric poetry of the time, and she numbered among her courtiers such men as Sir Philip Sidney. Edmund Spenser honored her as Gloriana, Queen of Fairyland, in his allegory *The Faerie Queene*. She was fond of plays and pageants, and many of Shakespeare's plays were presented at her Court. See ELIZABETHAN.

Elizabeth is a central character in Sir Walter Scott's *Kenilworth*. She is the subject of Lytton Strachey's biography *Elizabeth and Essex,* and Maxwell Anderson's drama *Elizabeth the Queen*.

Elizabeth II (1926–   ). Queen of Great Britain and Northern Ireland (1952–   ). She is married to Philip, duke of Edinburgh.

Elizabeth. Pen name of Countess **Russell**, born **Mary Annette Beauchamp** (1866–1941). English novelist. She is best known for *Elizabeth and Her German Garden* (1898), a semiautobiographical novel in diary form; it is a meditative, sensitive, sometimes satirical account of the author's trying life in Prussia as wife of Count von Arnim. Her second husband was a brother of Bertrand Russell.

Elizabethan. Pertaining to the 45-year period (1558–1603) of the reign of ELIZABETH I of England, sometimes considered the English renaissance. In both literary and political history her reign divides itself into two distinct phases: an early, seemingly undistinguished period in which Elizabeth's tenuous hold on royal authority and the Elizabethan writer's experimental probing of his language (which had hitherto been regarded as an inferior, even barbaric tongue) were gradually becoming consolidated; and a later, dazzlingly brilliant and enormously successful era. This began, in the political realm, with the execution of Mary Stuart (MARY QUEEN OF SCOTS) in 1587, and in literature with the publication of Edmund Spenser's THE SHEPHEARDES CALENDAR (1579). It is this latter quarter of a century that is generally identified as Elizabethan. (In drama the term is often used to embrace all activity relative to the stage until the closing of the theatres in 1642.) Nevertheless, it was in the early period that the groundwork was laid for the later, great achievements.

The first two years of Elizabeth's reign were marked by two events in literature, insignificant in themselves but representative of interests, attitudes, and linguistic developments that were to bear fruit near the close of the century. These were the publication of the first full translation of Vergil's *Aeneid* into English and of the first extant edition of A MIRROR FOR MAGISTRATES. These two works, both of which were extremely popular throughout the reign, reflected the two chief sources of the Elizabethan inheritance: classical humanism, with its grand and noble conception of the dignity of man, and in the case of *A Mirror for Magistrates,* the medieval tragic sense of life, with its intense concentration on the fact of death. From these diverse sources, the later Elizabethans managed to fuse a picture of man and the universe that was sweeping and heroic, and at the same time circumscribed by the overwhelming sense of human mortality. One of the most comprehensive portrayals of this conception is Christopher Marlowe's Dr. Faustus. Surely the finest expression of this vision is Hamlet's apostrophe on man:

What a piece of work is a man! how noble in reason! how infinite in faculty! in form and moving how express and admirable! in action how like an angel! in apprehension how like a god! the beauty of the world! the paragon of animals! And yet, to me, what is this quintessence of dust?

Although the greatest literary achievement of the Elizabethans lies in drama, their accomplishments in the other genres are only slightly less substantial. To the development of English the Elizabethans contributed, on one level, the ornate, rhetorical, expansive prose derived from Cicero and culminating in the massive dignity of Richard Hooker's *Laws of Ecclesiastical Polity*. On another level, the Elizabethans enriched the language through the racy colloquialism that characterizes the prose pamphlets of the period, written by such men as Robert Greene, Thomas Nashe, and the pseudonymous "Martin Marprelate." (See Marprelate controversy.) Probably the finest prose achievement in this latter category is John Florio's magnificent translation of the *Essays of Montaigne*.

In poetry the great monument of the Elizabethan era (as well as being in tone and style a very representative poem) is Edmund Spenser's The Faerie Queene. In the six elaborately constructed, enormously detailed allegorical books comprising the poem, he attempted to write a great moral epic that would glorify Elizabeth and England as Vergil had glorified Augustus Caesar and Rome. Spenser also contributed to another significant Elizabethan poetic development: the sonnet sequence. But here both Spenser, in his Amoretti, and Sir Philip Sidney, in his pioneering sequence Astrophel and Stella, were overshadowed by the mysterious, unorthodox, untitled collection we know as the Sonnets of Shakespeare. Other well-known sequences were Samuel Daniel's *Delia* and Michael Drayton's *Idea*.

It is in the drama of the period, however, that the vitality, splendor, and diversity we identify as Elizabethan is exuberantly displayed. Emerging from the primitive morality plays and interludes of the earlier part of the century, Elizabethan drama, possibly as a result of the new upsurge of national identity and patriotic fervor that followed the victory over the Spanish Armada, began to attract a new school of playwrights. Chief of these was the titanic figure of Christopher Marlowe, defying all moral and metrical conventions as he attempted to capture the spirit of the age in his portraits of the "overreachers" in such plays as Tamburlaine, The Jew of Malta, and *Dr. Faustus*. The instrument of Marlowe's expression was blank verse, a new and staid meter that he transformed into a thundering drum roll, later characterized by Ben Jonson as "Marlowe's mighty line." At the same time the drama was developing in lesser keys. George Peele and John Lyly experimented to combine light fantasy and romantic comedy in such plays as *The Arraignment of Paris* and *Endymion* to the delight of the Court, the agency which stood as

a buffer between the acting companies and the growing militance of the Puritan opposition to the stage. This opposition forced the players to set up their theaters outside London proper in a suburb on the south side of the Thames. Playgoing became increasingly popular among the non-Puritan population. Plays such as Thomas Kyd's The Spanish Tragedy enjoyed an unparalleled success and the Theatre (the first public theater, built in 1576 by James Burbage) became so popular that by 1585 a second playhouse, the Curtain, was being used to accommodate the overflow.

Into this heady atmosphere stepped the man whom many regard as the supreme literary artist of all time. In 1588 William Shakespeare was 24 and, like the nation itself, newly conscious of his powers and of the capacity of the English language as a fit vehicle to serve those powers. He capitalized on the revolutionary treatment that Marlowe had given blank verse, achieving a greater range and flexibility than his predecessors had been capable of, and he responded to the newly developing national mood with a series of chronicle plays (the Histories). These plays helped to articulate a sense of national self-identity best epitomized by John of Gaunt's speech in Richard II:

> This royal throne of kings, this sceptred isle,
> This earth of majesty, this seat of Mars,
> This other Eden, demi-paradise,
> This fortress built by Nature for herself
> Against infection and the hand of war,
> This happy breed of men, this little world,
> This precious stone set in the silver sea,

This glorification of the nation proved, however, to be the least of his contributions. He managed to run the gamut of comic potential, ranging from the slapstick farce of The Merry Wives of Windsor through the romantic fantasy of A Midsummer Night's Dream to the dark satire of Measure for Measure. Finally he produced in his tragedies those explorations of the human condition that are familiar to everyone.

By 1600, three years before the death of Elizabeth, the Elizabethan vision had begun to fade, and the literature that mirrored the life of its time underwent a change (see Jacobean). The literature of the 1590's, a literature rich in harmony, profuse and expansive in detail, and essentially affirmative in its vision of life, had lost its vitality and splendor and had already begun to be parodied. The old queen, now almost 70, and childless, had not designated an heir. The earl of Essex, whose brilliance and daring epitomized the era, had suffered a humiliating defeat in the Irish campaign, and insurrection was in the air. The Renaissance in England was over and the "counter-Renaissance" had begun.

Elizabeth of Hungary, St. Patron saint of queens, being herself a queen. She died in 1231 at the age of 24, and her day is November 19. She gave so bountifully to the poor that she starved her own household. One day her husband met her going out with her apron filled with something heavy, and demanded of her what she was carrying. "Only flowers, my lord," said Elizabeth, and to save the lie God converted the loaves of bread into flowers. She is the heroine of Kingsley's dramatic poem *The Saint's Tragedy* (1846).

Elle et Lui (He and She, 1859). A novel by George SAND. The author describes in retrospect her version of the love affair with Alfred de Musset. Musset had died two years earlier, but his brother Paul published *Lui et Elle* as a protest against Miss Sand's interpretation of the affair and its complexities.

Elliott, Anne. See PERSUASION.

Elliott, Ebenezer (1781–1849). English poet called the Corn-Law Rhymer because much of his verse consisted of invective against the CORN LAWS, so ruinous to England's laboring classes. These poems were forceful and cogent enough to play a significant part in the repeal of the laws. He wrote *The Village Patriarch* (1829); *Corn Law Rhymes* (1831); *The Splendid Village* (1833–1835); and many miscellaneous poems.

Ellis, [Henry] Havelock (1859–1939). English psychologist, essayist, and art critic. He is best known for his pioneering and at that time scandalous studies in sexual psychology, including *Man and Woman* (1894), *Studies in the Psychology of Sex* (6 vols., 1897–1910), and *The Erotic Rights of Women* (1918). *The Dance of Life* (1923), in which the dance is made to symbolize the vital rhythm of the universe, was his most popular book. He also wrote essays on art and literature, *Little Essays of Love and Virtue* (1922, 1931), and *My Life* (1939), a revealing autobiography. He was a close friend of the novelist Olive Schreiner.

Ellison, Ralph [Waldo] (1914–   ). American writer. Ellison, who studied at Tuskegee Institute, has lectured at a number of colleges and published work in various periodicals in both the essay and short-story form. His impressive first novel, INVISIBLE MAN, which won a National Book Award, was hailed as an outstanding work on the Negro in America.

Ellwood, Thomas (1639–1714). English Quaker and writer. Milton's friend and Latin reader, he is said to have suggested the writing of *Paradise Regained* (1671). His books include a *Sacred History of the Old and New Testaments* (1705–1709) and an *Autobiography* (1714).

Elmer Gantry (1927). A novel by Sinclair LEWIS. It deals with a brazen ex-football player who enters the ministry and, through his half-plagiarized sermons, his physical attractiveness, and his unerring instinct for promotion, becomes a successful evangelist and later the leader of a large Middle Western church. Carefully researched, the novel was realistic enough to shock both the faithful and unfaithful.

Elmire. In Molière's comedy LE TARTUFFE, the wily wife of Orgon. By a clever ruse she unmasks the hypocrite Tartuffe and finally convinces her husband of his duplicity.

Elm Tree on the Mall, The (L'Orme du Mail; 1897). A novel by Anatole FRANCE. The tale centers about the actions of its protagonist M. BERGERET.

Elohim. See JEHOVAH.

Elohistic and Jehovistic Scriptures. Elohim and Jehovah (Yahwe) are the most common of the many names given by the ancient Hebrews to the Deity. The fact that they are both used with interchangeable senses in the Pentateuch gave rise to the widely held theory that this group of five books was written in two different periods. The Elohistic paragraphs, being more simple, more primitive, more narrative, and more pastoral, are held to be the older. The later Jehovistic paragraphs, which indicate a knowledge of geography and history, seem to exalt the priestly office, and are of a more elaborate character, were subsequently woven into the Elohistic narrative.

This theory was originally stated by Jean Astruc, the French scholar, in his *Conjectures sur les mémoires originaux, dont il paroit que Moyse s'est servi pour composer le livre de la Genèse* (1753), a book that formed the starting point for all modern criticism of the Pentateuch.

Elpenor. In Homer's *Odyssey*, a member of Odysseus' crew. He falls from a roof during their stay with Circe and is killed. He is the first man Odysseus meets when visiting Hades, and he asks that his body be buried.

Elsie Dinsmore. Title of one of the 26 Elsie Books by Martha Finley (real name, Martha Farquharson, 1828–1909). The books deal with the trials and adventures of Elsie Dinsmore. Elsie is a pious little prig who remains a paragon of all the virtues, although she is persecuted by associates, relatives, and even her father. Her story proved so popular with 19th-century girl readers that the series was continued until long after Elsie had become a grandmother.

Elsie Venner: A Romance of Destiny (1861). A novel by Oliver Wendell HOLMES. Elsie, whose mother was bitten by a snake while carrying her, has distinctly serpentine qualities. Isolated from other human beings, she never removes the heavy gold necklace that presumably hides an unsightly and revealing mark. Although she falls in love with Bernard Langdon, the young schoolteacher, her strange and repellent nature forbids the return of affection. Only her Negro mammy understands Elsie's mystery. In the attempt to humanize herself, the girl dies. Through Elsie Venner, Holmes opposes the Calvinist belief that a human being may be held morally responsible for an inherited flaw. He considered the doctrine of Original Sin a barbarism. For Holmes, the physician or psychologist, not the preacher, should treat the morally diseased.

Elsinore. The English name of Helsingör, a city in Denmark on the island of Zealand. It is the site of Kronberg Castle, the traditional scene of Shakespeare's HAMLET.

Elstir. A great painter in Marcel Proust's REMEMBRANCE OF THINGS PAST. His work is an idealized composite of that of a number of French impressionist painters, particularly of Claude Monet's.

Eluard, Paul. Pen name of **Eugène Grindel** (1895–1952). French poet. After his interest in DADAISM Eluard became, with André Breton, one of the founders of SURREALISM. *Les Nécessités d'une vie et les conséquences des rêves* (1921) gave flashes of the "living reality" of dreams; *Mourir de ne pas mourir* (1924) built a bridge of pure and passionate poetry between dream and reality. Then Eluard became the poet of the couple, of loving communion with the other as well as with the universe of nature: *Capitale de la douleur* (1926), *L'Amour, la poésie* (1929), *La Rose Publique* (1934), and *Les Yeux fertiles* (1936). Deeply moved by the Spanish Civil War and World War II, Eluard extended this communion to the fraternity of mankind in *Livre ouvert*

(1940, 1941), *Poésie et Vérité* (1942), *Au Rendez-vous allemand* (1944), *Poèmes politiques* (1948), and *Le Dur Désir de Durer* (translated by Stephen Spender, 1950).

Elvire. In Molière's DOM JUAN OU LE FESTIN DE PIERRE, the woman whom Juan abducts and marries, only to abandon.

Elyot or **Eliot**, Sir **Thomas** (1499?–1546). English humanist, diplomat, and prose writer. Elyot is best known for *The Book Named the Governor* (1531). The first treatise on education published in English, it is regarded as one of the important 16th-century contributions to the development of English prose. He also wrote *Of the Knowledge Which Maketh a Wise Man* (1533); *The Castel of Helth* (1534), a popular treatise on medicine; and the first complete Latin-English dictionary (1538). His many translations from Latin and Greek helped to spread the reading of the classics throughout the educated classes of England. Elyot is said to be an ancestor of the 20th-century American-born poet T. S. ELIOT, in whose poem *East Coker* (1940) are quotations from the work of Sir Thomas.

Elysium (Elysion). The abode of the blessed in Greek mythology. Hence the Elysian Fields, the Paradise or Happy Land of the Greek poets. Elysian means happy, delightful.

Elzevir. A family of Dutch publishers and printers flourishing in the 17th century. A style of type was named *Elzevir* after this family. Books of their printing are of special value. The best are editions of classical and French authors. The Elzevir imprint is found in 1213 books: 968 Latin, 44 Greek, 126 French, 32 Flemish, 22 Oriental, 11 German, 10 Italian.

Emancipation Proclamation (Jan. 1, 1863). A proclamation issued by President Abraham Lincoln declaring that all slaves in areas still in rebellion against the U.S. were henceforth to be free. The proclamation did not affect slaves in the border states nor in territory under U.S. military occupation. A preliminary proclamation had been issued on Sept. 22, 1862 after the Union success at Antietam had bolstered the likelihood of ultimate victory over the Confederacy. Slavery was not completely abolished until the adoption of the 13th amendment to the Constitution in 1865.

Embla. The first woman, in Norse mythology, created out of an elm by the gods Odin, Vili, and Ve. The first man was Ask.

emblem books. Originally a symbolic picture illustrating a moral idea, but during the Renaissance and baroque periods, when emblems were immensely popular, the picture was always accompanied by a motto or pungent phrase and a short poem (epigram, sonnet, etc.) expanding upon the moral significance of the scene depicted (see IMPRESA). The illustration is commonly called the *cor* (heart), and the accompanying poetry the *anima* (soul) of the emblem. An example would be a depiction of Hercules standing between a bearded sage representing wisdom and a satanic figure representing vice. The motto above says, "When Vice and Vertue Youth shall wooe,/ Tis hard to say, which way 'twill go." Below the picture is a stanza in which the idea is treated at greater length (from George WITHER's *A Collection of Emblemes*, 1635). A famous European collection, or

Fruſtra quis ſtabilem figat in Orbe Gradum.

This changing World no lasting Joys can give,
The slipp'ry Ground your Footsteps will deceive.

An 18th-century reprint of an emblem
by Francis Quarles.

emblem book, was that of the Italian Andrea Alciati; in England, Francis QUARLES' *Emblems, Divine and Moral* (1635) was immensely popular. Emblems and emblem books, the latter's appeal boosted by the development of engraving, influenced many poets in their choice and treatment of subject matter and descriptive detail.

Emerald Isle. Ireland. This term was first used by Dr. William Drennan (1754–1820), in the poem *Erin*. It refers to the bright verdure of the island.

Emerson, Ralph Waldo (1803–1882). American poet, essayist, and philosopher. After a studious but undistinguished career at Harvard, and a brief period of teaching, Emerson entered the ministry. He was appointed to the Old Second Church in Boston, his native city, but soon became an unwilling preacher. Unable in conscience to administer the sacrament of the Lord's Supper, he resigned his pastorate at the death of his young wife, Ellen Tucker. The following year, 1832, he sailed for Europe. Visiting Landor, CARLYLE, and Coleridge, he began to formulate his own philosophy. Emerson's friendship with Carlyle was both lasting and significant. The insights of the British thinker helped him to reconcile some of his own confusions. Two other trips to England followed, in 1847 and 1872, but neither was as vital as the first.

On his return to New England, Emerson became known for the challenges to traditional thought in his essays and lectures. His first book, NATURE, summarized his major ideas. In 1835, he married Lydia Jackson and settled in Concord, Mass. The center of a literary circle, "the sage of Concord" became the chief spokesman for TRANSCENDENTALISM. Other members of his group included Margaret Fuller, Bronson Alcott, Henry Thoreau, and W. E. Channing.

Among Emerson's best work are ESSAYS, FIRST AND SECOND SERIES, *Poems* (1847), REPRESENTATIVE MEN, ENGLISH TRAITS, and THE CONDUCT OF LIFE (1860). His best-known addresses are THE AMERICAN SCHOLAR and THE DIVINITY SCHOOL ADDRESS. For two years, 1842–1844, Emerson edited the Transcendentalist journal, THE DIAL.

Emerson's philosophy is characterized by its reliance on intuition as the only way to comprehend reality. His conception of life as "spiritual vision" owes much to the work of Plotinus. He was influenced, too, by Swedenborg and Boehme. Like Thoreau and Whitman, he was attracted to mystical Indian literature and philosophy.

Emerson's unit of thought is the epigrammatic sentence. His prose style is not clearly organized or easy to follow, but has moments of great brilliance. Emerson wrote a poetic prose; intuitive rather than logical in form, the essays are ordered by recurring themes and images. His poetry, on the other hand, is often called harsh and didactic; he knew himself to be a "husky singer."

A believer in the "divine sufficiency of the individual," Emerson was a steady optimist. His refusal to grant the positive existence of evil caused Melville, Hawthorne, and Henry James, Sr., among others, to doubt his judgment. In spite of skepticism, Emerson's beliefs—that each man shares in the Over-Soul, or God; that Nature is a manifestation of Spirit; and that man possesses, within himself, the means to all knowledge—expressed in his memorable sentences, are of central importance in the history of American culture. See BOSTON HYMN; BRAHMA; CONCORD HYMN; DAYS; EACH AND ALL; MERLIN; THRENODY; Jones VERY.

Emesh and **Enten.** The brothers in Sumerian mythology who were created by the god of the air, Enlil. Each was assigned special duties connected with fertility; they quarreled, however, over which was the more important, and Enlil decided in favor of Enten, who thereafter was designated the god of farmers. This tale may have been a forerunner of the story of Cain and Abel.

Emilia. (1) In Shakespeare's OTHELLO, Iago's sharp-tongued wife and faithful waiting-woman to Desdemona. When she publicly denounces Iago's villainy, he stabs her, and she dies at her mistress' feet.

(2) Heroine of Boccaccio's TESEIDA.

Emilia Galotti (1772). A tragedy by Gotthold Ephraim LESSING in which Emilia, a middle-class girl, unwittingly arouses the passion of a prince, who has her bridegroom murdered and hopes to make her his mistress. In the end, to preserve her honor, her father stabs her to death.

Emile, ou l'Education (1762). An educational romance by Jean Jacques ROUSSEAU. It describes, in loose, story form, the bringing up of the boy Emile according to what Rousseau calls the principles of nature. He emphasizes character formation, learning by experience and observation, physical exercise, the mastery of useful trades, judgment, and hard work. One of the dominant principles of Rousseau's theory

is that the child is not an adult and should not be treated as such until he is ready. Hitherto education was usually inconsiderate of the various psychic stages of a child's development; Rousseau deserves credit for showing that the object and the methods of education should change with these stages. In Book IV, Emile's moral and religious education is summarized in the *Profession de foi du vicaire* SAVOYARD. The natural religion that Rousseau advocates in this section led to his persecution by the church authorities. Book V deals with the education of Sophie, a girl intended for Emile's wife. Her unique purpose is to please men, and to be charming, modest, virtuous, and submissive. (Curiously enough, in his sequel *Emile et Sophie*, Rousseau relates the infidelity of Sophie and the breakup of their marriage.) The work had a notable influence on pedagogical theory in France, Germany, and England. It was immediately translated into English. The thinking of educators of the 19th century, Friedrich Wilhelm August Froebel, Johann Heinrich Pestalozzi, and Johann Friedrich Herbart, is derived directly from Rousseau.

Emilie. The "divine Emilie," to whom VOLTAIRE wrote verses, was Marquise du CHÂTELET, with whom he lived at Cirey from 1734 to her death in 1749.

Emireno (**Emirene**). In the GERUSALEMME LIBERATA of Tasso, a Christian convert to the Islamic faith and the chief of the allied forces of the infidels against the Crusaders. He is killed by Goffredo, the Christian commander, during the final battle for the holy city.

Emma (1816). A novel by Jane AUSTEN. Charming, wilful Emma Woodhouse has no responsibilities other than the care of an indulgent father. To amuse herself she plays with other people's affairs, planning their lives the way she sees fit. Her first project is pretty, vapid Harriet Smith, a parlor-boarder at a nearby school and the natural daughter of an unknown person. Encouraging her to aspire to the hand of Mr. Elton, a young clergyman, Emma prevents Harriet's accepting the offer of the far more appropriate Robert Martin, a young farmer. Emma's plans go awry: the snobbish, ambitious Elton first aspires to Emma's hand, and, haughtily rejected, chooses instead the crass, pretentious daughter of a wealthy family for his bride. Other moves, notably Emma's interference in the courtship of Jane Fairfax and Frank Churchill, are not any more successful. When Harriet shows signs of attachment to Knightly, a somewhat dictatorial but frank and generous gentleman, Emma appreciates the folly and thoughtlessness of her meddling; she discovers that her long friendship with Knightly has grown into love. Propriety and common sense prevail: Emma marries Knightly, Harriet her first love, Robert Martin. The book is much concerned with the themes of self-delusion and notions of class and decorum fundamental to English society. See Miss BATES.

Emmanuel, Pierre. Pen name of **Noël Mathieu** (1916–   ). French poet and essayist. Both the style and the symbolism of much of his poetry were inspired by the Bible and Greek mythology: *Tombeau d'Orphée* (1942), *Sodome* (1946), and *Babel* (1951). The volumes *Jours de Colère* (1942) and *La Liberté guide nos pas* (1945) are poetry of the Resistance. *Cantos* (1944), *Chansons du dé à coudre* (1947), and *Versant de l'age* (1958) represent elaborate attempts to express the mystery of existence. *Poésie raison ardente* (1947), *Qui est cet homme?* (1947), and *L'Ouvrier de la onzième heure* (1954) are prose essays.

Emmet, Robert (1778–1803). Irish patriot. The son of a liberal-minded, well-to-do physician, Robert became involved, while still in college, in the cause of the UNITED IRISHMEN; the latter fought, sometimes with violence, for the rights of Irish Catholics who had been deprived of their land under Cromwell. In 1803, Emmet was part of an insurrection that was put down by the British. Although he could have escaped, he remained in Dublin to protect his followers and the girl he loved, Sarah Curran. He was tried for treason, and executed at the age of 25 by hanging and decapitation.

Empedocles (**Empedokles**; fl. 444 B.C.). A Greek philosopher, interested in biology, medicine, and physics. In his work called *On Nature,* an epic poem in hexameters, Empedocles identifies four immutable elements in the universe: earth, air, fire, and water. The things of this world are produced by the association and dissociation of these elements. Empedocles called the two opposing forces love and strife. In another poem, called *Purifications,* Empedocles approves of the doctrine of transmigration. According to Greek tradition, Empedocles threw himself into the crater of Mt. Etna. In his poem *Empedocles on Etna,* Matthew Arnold found the philosopher a figure expressive of his own pessimism.

Emperor Jones, The (1920). A play by Eugene O'NEILL. Set on an island in the West Indies, the play deals with a former Pullman porter, Brutus Jones, who has set himself up as emperor. When the play begins the natives are beginning to revolt, and Jones is forced to flee. As he rushes through the jungle the tom-toms beat steadily, and he becomes more and more the victim of his own terror. Jones retrogresses on the evolutionary ladder, becoming a participant in a slave auction and finally the victim of his—and mankind's—aboriginal fears. In the end he is killed by the natives who use the silver bullets Jones had said were necessary. A sensation as a play, *Emperor Jones* was also successful as an opera (1933) by Louis Gruenberg, with a libretto by Kathleen de Jaffa.

empirics. An ancient Greek school of medicine founded by Serapion of Alexandria (2nd century B.C.). He contended that it is not necessary to obtain a knowledge of the nature and functions of the body in order to treat diseases, but that experience is the surest and best guide (Gr. *empeiros,* experienced, from *peira,* trial). The empirics were opposed to the dogmatic school founded by HIPPOCRATES, which made certain dogmas or theoretical principles the basis of practice. Now, any quack or pretender to medical skill is called an *empiric.*

empyrean. In Ptolemaic philosophy, the last of the 5 heavens. It was made of pure elemental fire and was the seat of the deity. Called the empyrean from the Gr. *empyros,* fiery, it was employed in Christian angelology—for instance, by Dante in his *Divine Comedy*—as the abode of God and the angels.

Empson, William (1906–   ). English poet and critic. A mathematician before he became a poet, Empson wrote verse characterized by scientific references and by wit, ingenuity, and obscurity. The poet's complicated notes on his verse add to the crossword-puzzle effect. His poems are restrained in technique, often being written in such traditional forms as the VILLANELLE and TERZA RIMA. They are sometimes humorous. *Poems* appeared in 1935 and *The Gathering Storm,* in 1940. Although he has published little poetry, his work had a great effect on the young English poets of the 1950's such as Kingsley Amis, A. Alvarez, Donald Davie, Thom Gunn, and John Wain.

Empson's criticism has also been influential. A leading CAMBRIDGE CRITIC, he has been influenced by the ideas of I. A. Richards. His critical works include *Seven Types of Ambiguity* (1930), *Some Versions of Pastoral* (1935), *The Structure of Complex Words* (1951), and *Milton's God* (1962), a controversial attack on Christianity, denouncing it as a cruel religion.

Ems telegram (1870). The report of an interview between King Wilhelm of Prussia and the French ambassador at the resort of Ems, originally sent to Bismarck. Bismarck condensed the text so that it appeared to report a diplomatic insult, and then released it to the press. The resulting international furor incited declaration of the Franco-Prussian War, just as Bismarck had planned.

Encina or **Enzina, Juan del** (1468?–?1529). Spanish dramatist and poet. Encina took minor orders as a youth, was in the service of the duke of Alba, and later lived in Rome. In 1519 he visited the Holy Land, where he was ordained and said his first mass. Often called "the father of Spanish drama," he is best known for his dramatic pieces, usually called *églogas* or "eclogues," which were published in various editions of his *Cancionero* (1496). Most of these plays have religious themes and were performed before aristocratic audiences; the characters, however, are usually Spanish peasants, realistically and humorously portrayed, who speak a rustic dialect, *sayagués,* that became a stock theatrical device. Among his most famous works in this genre are the two eclogues in which Pascuala, Mingo, and the squire Gil appear; the Carnival *Egloga de Antruejo,* and the farcical *Auto del repelón,* dealing with a brawl between peasants and Salamanca students. After his stay in Rome, Encina wrote three plays which reveal the influence of Italian pastoral poetry and represent an attempt to elevate the drama; these are *Egloga de Plácida y Victoriano, Egloga de tres pastores,* and *Egloga de Cristino y Febea.* He also wrote numerous *villancicos,* or Christmas carols, which were used at the end of most of his plays.

Encyclopédie, ou Dictionnaire raisonné des sciences, des arts et des métiers (**Methodical Dictionary of the Sciences, Arts, and Trades,** 1751–1780). A French encyclopedia. Based originally on an idea to translate the English *Cyclopaedia* of Ephraim Chambers, the work's whole scope was greatly expanded by DIDEROT, and his coeditors d'ALEMBERT and Louis de Jaucourt. The contributions of such famous *encyclopédistes* (also called *philosophes*) as CONDILLAC, HELVÉTIUS, MONTESQUIEU, ROUSSEAU, QUESNAY, TURGOT, and Diderot himself helped make it the great literary monument of the 18th century, even though many of the articles were written by hack writers under the direction of Jaucourt. The work mirrors that French brand of 18th-century philosophical skepticism and scientific determinism which was derived from Bacon, Locke, and Descartes among others. Its spirit of inquiry led it to combat superstition; the supernatural; religious authority, intolerance, and persecution; unequal distribution of wealth; fiscal privileges; and abuses of justice. Attention was paid to the latest scientific discoveries, particularly in the natural sciences. Reforms in government, education, and commerce were prudently advocated, also. One new feature of the encyclopedia was the inclusion of articles and plates on the mechanical trades (weaving, paper-making, printing, etc.). An ingenious system of cross references often led the reader to another article that ridiculed the contradictions accepted in the theological discussion of the first article; hence, the Jesuits opposed it, causing the encyclopedia to be temporarily suppressed in 1752 and 1759 by the government, and condemned by the pope in 1759. Though the history of the suppression of this work is generally recounted as one of energetic and efficacious persecution by the government and the church, in fact this is not so. The relatively few attempts at suppression were half-hearted on the part of the government and had little or no effect on its final publication. Mme. de POMPA-DOUR along with several government officials, among whom was Chrétien-Guillaume de MALESHERBES, an enlightened administrator and director of *la librairie* (the governmental censoring body), did everything in their power to encourage its publication for the public good. Diderot, with the help of Jaucourt, worked tirelessly to bring out the "clandestine" edition in Paris, which appeared in 17 volumes (plus 11 volumes of plates) between 1751 and 1772. Diderot had no hand in the five-volume supplement (1776–1777), or in the two analytical index volumes (1780). Other editions followed. In spite of its imbalance (for example, six lines devoted to *Alpes* and one column to artichoke recipes), errors, and unacknowledged plagiarism, it was a highly successful business venture. At one point there were 4,000 subscribers, and the profit is said to have been 300 per cent.

Endgame (**Fin de partie**; 1957). A play by Samuel BECKETT. The blind chair-bound autocrat Hamm, whose parents Nagg and Nell are confined to ashcans, learns from his servant Clov of the disappearance of objects and the deaths of people in a disintegrating world.

Endicott or **Endecott, John** (1589?–1665). English-born governor of the Massachusetts Bay Colony. He served as the first governor of the colony (1628–1630) until the arrival of John Winthrop. A zealous Puritan, he persecuted Quakers and the followers of Thomas Morton. He is the title character of *Endicott and the Red Cross* (1837), a short story by Nathaniel Hawthorne, and of one of Longfellow's *New England Tragedies* (1868).

End of Summer (1936). A play by S. N. BEHRMAN. Set in a summer home in Maine, it includes a brilliant portrait of a psychiatrist.

Endor, witch of. See WITCH.

Endymion. In Greek mythology, a beautiful youth, sometimes a shepherd. As he slept on Mount Latmus he so moved the cold heart of Selene, the moon goddess, that she came down and kissed him and lay at his side. He woke to find her gone, but the dreams that she gave him were so strong and enthralling that he begged Zeus to give him immortality and allow him to sleep perpetually on Mount Latmus. Other accounts say that Selene herself bound him by en enchantment so that she might come and kiss him whenever she liked. There are, in fact, innumerable explanations in myth of Endymion's sleep. Keats used the story as the framework of his long allegory, *Endymion* (1817), and it forms the basis of Lyly's comedy, *Endimion, the Man in the Moone* (1585).

Enfants Terribles, Les (1929; also translated as **The Holy Terrors**). A novel by Jean COCTEAU about the fantasy-world rituals and fierce amoral passions of a group of children.

Engels, Friedrich (1820–1895). German socialist and collaborator of Karl MARX, whom he met in Paris in 1844. Together they wrote THE COMMUNIST MANIFESTO, although Engels gave Marx the credit for its theoretical formulation. Engels completed CAPITAL after Marx's death.

England, rulers of. Egbert, originally king of the West Saxons, conquered the other English realms, making himself master of all England.

SAXONS	
Egbert	829– 839
Ethelwulf	839– 858
Ethelbald	858– 860
Ethelbert	860– 866
Ethelred I	866– 871
Alfred the Great	871– 899
Edward the Elder	899– 924
Athelstan	924– 940
Edmund I	940– 946
Edred	946– 955
Edwy	955– 959
Edgar	959– 975
Edward the Martyr	975– 978
Ethelred II	978–1016
Edmund II	1016

DANES	
Canute	1016–1035
Harold I	1035–1040
Hardecanute	1040–1042

SAXONS	
Edward the Confessor	1042–1066
Harold II	1066

HOUSE OF NORMANDY	
William I	1066–1087
William II	1087–1100
Henry I	1100–1135
Stephen	1135–1154

HOUSE OF PLANTAGENET	
Henry II	1154–1189
Richard I	1189–1199
John	1199–1216
Henry III	1216–1272
Edward I	1272–1307
Edward II	1307–1327
Edward III	1327–1377
Richard II	1377–1399

HOUSE OF LANCASTER	
Henry IV	1399–1413
Henry V	1413–1422
Henry VI	1422–1461

HOUSE OF YORK	
Edward IV	1461–1470
HOUSE OF LANCASTER	
Henry VI	1470–1471
HOUSE OF YORK	
Edward IV	1471–1483
Edward V	1483
Richard III	1483–1485
HOUSE OF TUDOR	
Henry VII	1485–1509
Henry VIII	1509–1547
Edward VI	1547–1553
Lady Jane Grey	1553
Mary I	1553–1558
Elizabeth I	1558–1603
HOUSE OF STUART	
James I	1603–1625
Charles I	1625–1649
COMMONWEALTH	
Council of State	1649–1653
Oliver Cromwell (Lord Protector)	1653–1658
Richard Cromwell (Lord Protector)	1658–1659
HOUSE OF STUART	
Charles II	1660–1685
James II	1685–1688
William III	
and Mary II (d. 1694)	1689–1702
Anne	1702–1714
HOUSE OF HANOVER	
George I	1714–1727
George II	1727–1760
George III	1760–1820
George IV	1820–1830
William IV	1830–1837
Victoria	1837–1901
HOUSE OF SAXE-COBURG	
Edward VII	1901–1910
HOUSE OF WINDSOR	
George V	1910–1936
Edward VIII	1936
George VI	1936–1952
Elizabeth II	1952–

England's Helicon (1600). One of the miscellanies (see TOTTEL'S MISCELLANY), or collections of poetry, published in the Elizabethan period. It is distinguished by the good taste shown in the selection of its contents, and unique in that the editors deliberately limited the book to pastoral poetry. It contains work by Shakespeare, Sidney, Spenser, Drayton, Lodge, among others.

English Bards and Scotch Reviewers (1809). A long verse satire by Lord BYRON. Neoclassical in flavor and written in heroic couplets, it was occasioned by the harsh reception given to Byron's first book of poems, *Hours of Idleness* (1807), by the *Edinburgh Review*. In the poem, Byron not only attacks his critics but the older generation of English romantic poets as well, including Wordsworth, Coleridge, Scott, and Southey.

English Traits (1856). An analysis of the English people by Ralph Waldo EMERSON. The book grew out of a series of lectures delivered by Emerson after two visits to England. He discusses some of his English contemporaries, Wordsworth, Carlyle, and Coleridge. Amused by English pomp, the American is impressed by the practical sense of the English and by their writers.

English Woman's Love Letters, An. See Laurence HOUSMAN.

Engstrom, Albert (1869–1940). Swedish author and artist. Engstrom's fame rests upon his perceptive cartoons and on the illustrated stories that depict life in Småland and on the Stockholm archipelago. Among his collections of tales are *Samlade berättelser* (1915–1934), and *Nationalupplaga* (*Twelve Tales*, 1934). As editor of the comic journal *Strix* from 1924 to 1940, he revealed a keen but kindly satirical wit.

Enki. The Sumerian god of water and of wisdom. He lived near the ancient city of ERIDU in his watery palace in the ABZU—probably the Persian Gulf. This god, like his later Babylonian counterpart EA, was principally responsible for ordering the functions of the elements that affect life on earth. Cleverest of the gods, he provided the land with sweet water, fathered Uttu, the goddess of plants, found a way to rescue Inanna from the underworld, and saved mankind from extermination in the great flood. He was not, however, infallible. While in his cups, he let the seductive goddess slip away with his "divine decrees," which would give supremacy to her favored city of Erech instead of to Eridu. His attempt to create man was a pathetic failure, and it was left to the goddess NINTU to mold of clay a satisfactory human being.

Enkidu. A friend of Gilgamesh in the *Epic of* GILGAMESH. Molded of clay, and at first a wild man who lives with the beasts, he becomes a hero who first defeats Gilgamesh in wrestling, then becomes his fast friend. They share various adventures together, but Enkidu is condemned to death by the gods for his part in slaying the storm bull of heaven. Gilgamesh's search for the secret of eternal life is the result of his grief over Enkidu's death. He appears also in Sumerian mythology.

Enkimdu. A Sumerian farmer god. He disputed with the shepherd god DUMUZI for the favor of Inanna and won it.

Enlightenment, the. The 18th century. This period is variously called the Age of Reason and, in France, *Le Siècle des Lumières* because its writers as a whole applied reason to religion, politics, morality, and social life. Aside from purely historical events, the 18th century does not lend itself to a chronological view; its unity lay not in a coherent development or progression of ideas, but rather in the intellectual energy and enthusiasm which characterized its writers. Intensely aware of their heritage and dependency upon the ancients, these men clarified, sifted, and developed this heritage.

The rule of Louis XIV had been an oppressive one, and the somber religious tone which it took before the Sun King's death caused the reaction to it to be all the greater. The government, continued by the monarchies of Louis XV (1715–1774) and Louis XVI (1774–1793), fell ever deeper into discredit. The failure of John Law's MISSISSIPPI BUBBLE (June, 1720), the increasing national debt due to royal prodigality, and the repeated hiring and dismissal of incapable finance ministers—and even of capable ones like Cardinal Fleury, Turgot, and Necker—all contributed to the economic instability of France. The necessity for reform became clear. The century culminated in the FRENCH REVOLUTION, a crisis that reflected these economic and social ills; the application of reason to the human situation, so typical of the 18th century, perhaps made it clear to the middle class that the old order did not have to prevail. In most aspects of French culture, the influence of the increasingly economically independent bourgeoisie was to replace that of the aristocracy.

The Enlightenment began by breaking down the older forms of metaphysical and philosophical knowledge; Cartesianism, with its spirit of systems (*esprit de système*), was replaced by a systematic spirit (*esprit systématique*)—the a priori by the a posteriori. In contrast to the 17th century, in which reason represented tradition, authority, stability, the 18th century saw reason as a tool, a means to authority. Questions were no longer envisaged under the aspect of pure thought, but were examined from a social and practical point of view. This preoccupation with the useful caused men to turn to the physical world; writers like VOLTAIRE, DIDEROT, d'ALEMBERT, and MONTESQUIEU made literature out of the natural sciences, astronomy, law, travel, philosophy, politics, and education. The investigation into natural and social phenomena, what we would today broadly designate as science, was called philosophy in the 18th century. The *philosophe* represented an ideal, as did the *honnête homme* in the 17th century, or as the universal man characterized the Renaissance. The philosophers of this age were in search of a concrete anthropology, a knowledge of man in general. This common goal by no means implied a homogeneous point of view: one has only to compare the differences between Voltaire and ROUSSEAU, BUFFON and CONDILLAC, Diderot and HELVÉTIUS.

It is perhaps CONDORCET who, in his *Sketch for a historical picture of the progress of the human mind* (written in 1793-1794) best summarizes the optimism and faith in human reason so characteristic of the age. In tracing man from the dawn of history, Condorcet first emphasized the liberation of mankind from ignorance, tyranny, and superstition by means of his science and his reason; he then sketched a hopeful future in which mankind would be free, equal in wealth, in education, and with sexual equality; he finally envisaged the moral, intellectual, and physical improvement, indeed perfection, of humanity that would arise through better instruction, laws, and institutions.

Enlil. The Sumerian storm-god of the air. He was born of the union of An (heaven) and Ki (earth), who were regarded as joined together. Enlil separated them—the element air may have been thought to separate the vault of heaven from earth by its own expansion. Enlil married Ninlil, who bore him three gods of the underworld (Nergal, Ninazu, and an unknown god) and Nanna, the moon, who in turn became the father of Utu, the sun. Next Enlil impregnated his mother Ki and produced NINTU, another earth goddess. Enlil became more important in the pantheon than his father An, and in turn he was himself to a degree supplanted from his place as principal god by ENKI. Enlil was the chief god of the Sumerian city of Nippur. In the Baby-

lonian period, MARDUK took on many of his attributes, and Adad became the storm-god.

ennead (from Gr. *ennea,* nine). A group of 9 units, as, for example, the 9 gods found in the pantheon of the ancient Egyptians.

The title *The Enneads* was given to the works of the neo-Platonist Plotinus because each of the six books contains nine chapters.

Ennius, Quintus (239-?169 B.C.). Latin poet. The earliest of the great epic poets of Rome, he is regarded as one of the founders of Latin literature. His successful use of Greek meters in his dramas and epic poetry ushered in a new era in the development of literary Latin. As an epic poet, employing the Greek dactylic hexameter in Latin, he is a precursor of Vergil, Rome's greatest poet.

Enobarbus, Domitius. In Shakespeare's ANTONY AND CLEOPATRA, a trusted officer of Antony. He deserts Antony after Actium, but when the latter magnanimously sends him his treasure, he is so remorseful that he commits suicide. His astute and witty observations on the behavior of Antony and Cleopatra make him one of Shakespeare's most engaging secondary characters.

Enoch Arden (1864). A narrative poem by Alfred TENNYSON. Arden is a seaman who has been wrecked on a desert island, and returning home after a long absence finds his wife married to another. Seeing her happy and prosperous, he resolves not to make himself known, so he leaves the place and dies of a broken heart. Hence, any story that involves a long-lost mate returning to discover his spouse remarried is often described as having an Enoch Arden plot.

Enormous Room, The (1922). An autobiographical novel by E. E. CUMMINGS. It describes a period of imprisonment in a French military concentration camp near Paris (1917-1918), where the author was incarcerated on a false charge of treason. Cummings' own experiences and the personalities of the various other prisoners are presented with their individual psychological reactions to the injustices of their treatment. Ironically structured on John Bunyan's *Pilgrim's Progress,* the book is highly vivid, often even lyrical, in its bitter attack on man's inhumanity to man.

Enquiry Concerning Political Justice, An (1793). A political and philosophical treatise by William GODWIN with the subtitle "its influence on General Virtue and Happiness." The author examines the systems of government, law, and religion of his day, and concludes that monarchy is corrupt and all government, in fact, an obstacle to the development of mankind. It urges the abolition of all social and political institutions created by man, including government, law, wealth, and marriage, and places total confidence in the fundamental perfectibility of man. This treatise was regarded with horror by the conservative elements of the day, and had a great influence on the English Romantic poets, particularly Shelley.

Enten. See EMESH.

entente; *entente cordiale* (Fr.). A cordial understanding between nations; not quite amounting to an alliance, but something more than a *rapprochement.* The term is not new, but is now usually applied to the *entente* between England and France that was arranged largely by the personal endeavors of Edward VII in 1906.

Triple Entente. A friendly alliance between Great Britain, France, and Russia before World War I. During the war Great Britain, France, and Italy were referred to as the *Entente.*

Little Entente. An alliance between Czechoslovakia, Yugoslavia, and Romania entered into after the signing of the Treaty of the Trianon (1920), with the avowed purpose of defeating any Hungarian plan for a restoration of the Hapsburgs.

Entwicklungsroman. See BILDUNGSROMAN.

Enumaelish. See WAR OF THE GODS.

Envy (Zavist'; 1927). A novel by Yuri OLIOSHA. A notable work of fiction, it portrays the struggle of the individual against the encroachments of the growing collectivist society in Soviet Russia. This hackneyed theme is rendered fresh by Oliosha's imaginative use of images and language and by his creation of the memorable characters Ivan Babichev and Nikolai Kavalerov. Both are disaffected with the society, though for different reasons: Babichev because he sees the danger of human feelings being destroyed, and Kavalerov because he yearns for personal glory and envies the less talented people who can adjust and make their way in the new system. Babichev's brother, Andrei, is a representative of the adjusted man. He is a director of a Soviet food combine, briskly going about his business, which consists of planning new, cheap cafeterias to feed the masses. Whether Andrei actually does triumph over his good-for-nothing brother Ivan is, at the book's end, a moot point. This fact apparently began to worry Soviet critics who praised the novel at first and then began to criticize it severely.

Eos. In Greek mythology the goddess of the dawn. She is the daughter of Hyperion and Thea and drives across the sky in a chariot drawn by two horses. It was Eos who asked Zeus to give TITHONUS immortality; however, she forgot to have Tithonus made eternally youthful.

Eothen, or Traces of Travel Brought Home from the East. See Alexander William KINGLAKE.

Epée, Charles Michel de l' (1712–1789). French abbé. He was a pioneer in the development of a system of manual communication for the deaf and dumb.

Epeios. Builder of the TROJAN HORSE. He was the principal craftsman with the Greek forces at Troy.

Ephesian letters. Characters assumed to be of a mystic nature by the Ephesians, a people greatly addicted to magic. Magic characters were marked on the crown, cincture, and feet of Diana. At the preaching of Paul in Ephesus, many converts who had used "curious," or magical, books burned them (Acts 19:19).

Ephesians, The Epistle of Paul the Apostle to the. A New Testament book. Traditionally ascribed to Paul, this letter was probably written by some one who used his name and borrowed freely from his epistle to the COLOSSIANS for its content. Consisting of two parts, it first explains God's plan to unite all humanity in Christ and then shows the role of the Church in the working of this plan.

Ephialtes. See OTUS.

Ephyre. A prehistoric Greek city. It was identified in Classical times with Corinth. Founded by Sisyphus, it was later ruled by Jason. Indeed, since no significant Mycenaean remains have been found at Corinth, it is likely that most myths involving Corinth should be referred to Ephyre, which was probably one of the many Mycenaean towns unearthed on the Isthmus near the present Corinth.

epic. A very long narrative poem presenting adventures on a grand, heroic scale organically united through a central figure of heroic proportions. The adventures are made up of episodes which contribute to the formation of a race or nation. The earliest epics were formed from various works of unknown poets. Among the best-known of these folk epics are the *Iliad* and *Odyssey* (attributed to Homer), the Anglo-Saxon *Beowulf*, the East Indian *Mahabharata*, the Spanish *Cid*, the Finnish *Kalevala*, the French *Song of Roland*, and the German *Nibelungenlied*.

The so-called classical or art epic is distinctly the work of a single author. Influenced largely by Vergil, it developed certain almost universal characteristics. These include beginning *in medias res,* the invocation of the muse, and the statement of the epic purpose. Other conventions, usually observed by writers of epic, are descriptions of warfare and the use of the supernatural. Familiar classical epics include Vergil's *Aeneid,* Dante's *Divine Comedy,* Tasso's *Jerusalem Delivered,* Spenser's *Faerie Queene,* and Milton's *Paradise Lost.*

Epicasta (Epikaste). The name given to Jocasta in the *Iliad* and some other Greek works. See OEDIPUS.

Epic Cycle. The name given a series of very early (c. 800–500) epic poems by authors other than Homer or Hesiod, all of which are lost, but which are recounted in later synopses. They deal with events connected with the Trojan War not included in the *Iliad* or the *Odyssey.* Poems of the Epic Cycle include the *Theogonia* and *Titanomachia,* on the creation and early history of the world; *Cypria,* on the theft of Helen; *Aethiopis, Ilias Parva, Iliu Persis,* and *Nostoi,* continuations of the *Iliad;* and *Telegonia,* on the death of Odysseus. There are other cyclic poems, such as those on Thebes and on heroes such as Heracles, Theseus, and the Argonauts; strictly speaking, however, the term "Epic Cycle" refers to the Trojan stories alone.

Epicene, or The Silent Woman (1609). A comedy by Ben JONSON. A gentleman named Morose has resolved to disinherit his nephew, Sir Dauphine, by marrying and producing an heir. A man who can bear no noise, he has discovered a perfect mate, a woman who "spends but six words a day." But just after the wedding, Epicene, the silent woman, turns into a shrill harpy who belabors her husband mercilessly. Alarmed, Morose tries mightily to break the match, even going so far as to offer Sir Dauphine a generous allowance and his inheritance if he will take the lady off his hands. Sir Dauphine complies immediately by plucking off Epicene's wig, revealing that "she" is a boy whom Dauphine has carefully trained and employed.

Epic of Creation, Babylonian. See WAR OF THE GODS.

Epictetus (Epiktetos; fl. A.D. 100). A Greek Stoic philosopher. An emancipated slave, Epictetus taught in Rome until A.D. 94, when Emperor Domitian banished all philosophers from the city. He moved to Nicopolis, where he established a school. No written works survive, but his pupil Arrian preserved his essential doctrines in a manual. Epictetus counseled men to wish for nothing that is not under their control. He advocated a serene life, free from unfulfilled desires, and calm in the face of death. He said that a man should behave in life as he would at a banquet, taking only a polite portion of what is offered. See STOICISM.

Epic Theater. A term used by Bertolt BRECHT to designate his own style of playwriting as opposed to the style of conventional drama. In conventional drama, suspense is created by means of a tightly woven plot, which constantly develops and welds the play together into a unity; in the Epic Theater, suspense is deliberately avoided, and the play consists of a loose sequence of virtually independent scenes (just as the individual scenes of an epic poem are usually less dependent on one another than those of a conventional drama). Conventional drama attempts to capture the audience's emotions, to create a powerful and continuous illusion in which the audience will become emotionally involved; the Epic Theater, on the other hand, deliberately avoids playing on the audience's emotions, seeks rather to make the audience emotionally detached, and attempts to convey its meaning entirely on an intellectual plane. One specific technique often used by Brecht for achieving the effect of the Epic Theater consists in having a character step to the front of the stage and directly address the audience, thereby breaking the illusion and inviting the audience to regard the play intellectually.

Epicurus (Epikouros, c. 340–c. 270 B.C.). Greek philosopher, founder of the Epicurean School. The school is often referred to as the Garden, after the place in which Epicurus taught in Athens. Only fragments remain of his work, but his biographer DIOGENES LAERTIUS gives the texts of three epistles and forty maxims, which indicate that Epicurus advocated reliance on the senses. In order to reduce man's anxiety, he posited a materialistic physics, in which the universe consisted of Democritean atoms and void. He tried to eliminate superstition and the dread of death. Pleasure, by which Epicurus meant freedom from pain, is the highest good. Serenity, the harmony of mind and body, is best achieved, he said, through virtue and simple living. The current usage of the term *epicure* to describe one devoted to sensual pleasures, reflects a misunderstanding of the philosophy of Epicurus.

epicycles. See PTOLEMY.

Epigoni (Epigonoi). In Greek mythology, the sons of the SEVEN AGAINST THEBES. They were led by ALCMAEON, a son of Amphiaraus, who had demanded that his sons avenge his death at Thebes. Alcmaeon might have forgotten this vow, but Thersander, the son of Polynices, bribed his mother, Eriphyle, to urge him on, as she had earlier urged Amphiaraus. TIRESIAS had warned the Thebans that the city would fall when the last of the Seven died. The only one to survive the earlier siege had been Adrastus, king of Argos. On learning that his son, Aegialeus, one of the Epigoni, had been killed in the new siege, Adrastus died of grief.

Tiresias then advised the Thebans to flee the city at once, which they did, under cover of night. Tiresias, who had lived through seven generations of Theban rulers, at last died. The escaping Thebans continued as far as Hestiaea, where they founded the city. The Epigoni razed Thebes.

epigram. A brief, pithy, pointed, and witty piece of poetry or prose. The epigram was especially popular as a literary form in classic Latin literature and in European and English literature of the Renaissance and neoclassical periods. Coleridge wrote of it:

> What is an epigram? A dwarfish whole,
> Its body brevity, and wit its soul.

epilogue. (1) The final part of a work of literature (except a play), completing and rounding it off; the opposite of preface. (2) After a play, the speech (frequently in verse) addressed by an actor or group of actors to the audience; the opposite of prologue. (3) In rhetoric, the last of the five divisions of a model oration. (4) In music, the final section of a composition, the coda. A free use of the term occurs in Goethe's *Epilogue to Schiller's Bell* (*Epilog zu Schillers Glocke*), written in commemoration of the younger poet's death.

Epimenides (7th century B.C.). A Cretan poet and philosopher. According to Pliny (*Natural History*) he fell asleep in a cave when a boy, and did not wake up for 57 years, when he found himself endowed with miraculous wisdom.

Epimetheus. In classic myth, the brother of Prometheus and husband of PANDORA. The name signifies afterthought, in contrast to Prometheus, forethought.

Epinay, Louise Florence Pétronille de la Live d' (1726–1783). French author. She is well known on account of her friendship with Diderot, d'Alembert, Baron d' Holbach, Baron de Grimm, and others. For Rousseau she built a cottage in the garden of her château near Montmorency. About her *Mémoires et correspondance* (1818), Sainte-Beuve has written: "The memoirs of Mme d'Epinay are not a work, they are an epoch."

Epinicia (Epinikia). Odes of victory in national games, as the Olympic, Pythian, Delphic, Nemean, and Isthmian games. There are among PINDAR's extant works 44 Epinicia.

Epiphany (Gr. *epiphaneia*, appearance or manifestation). The feast on January 6, commemorating the showing of Christ to the nations, at the time of the visit of the MAGI. One of the oldest of Christian festivals, it originally was the feast of the birth of Christ, as it still is in the Eastern Churches. In England it was called Twelfth Day, from which comes TWELFTH NIGHT.

epiphany. A term coined by James JOYCE for the sudden revelation of the essential nature of a thing, person, or situation. It is the moment in which "the soul of the commonest object . . . seems to us radiant," and may be manifested through any chance word or gesture. Among Joyce's earliest works were little sketches or prose poems, which attempted to record such moments; he called them epiphanies. Some are incorporated in his novel *Stephen Hero;* in this novel he also gives the clearest explanation of what he means by epiphany.

Epipsychidion (1821). A poem by Percy Bysshe SHELLEY. The title, a word coined by Shelley from Greek, means "this soul out of my soul." Of over 700 lines, the poem is addressed to Emilia VIVIANI, whom Shelley regarded as an embodiment of the ideal love and beauty that he constantly sought. Along with an allegorical history of the poet's soul, the poem includes rapturous praise of Emilia Viviani, a famous justification of free love, and a glowing vision of an Edenic isle in the Aegean.

Epistle to Dr. Arbuthnot (1735). A satiric poem by Alexander POPE in the form of a dialogue between the poet and Dr. John ARBUTHNOT, a physician and man of letters who was a friend of Pope. The poem gives Pope's judgment on his own work and pitilessly attacks his contemporaries, especially Joseph ADDISON, who is characterized as "the jealous Atticus," and Lord John HERVEY who is satirized as the effeminate "Sporus."

Epistolae Obscurorum Virorum (Letters of Unknown Men, 1515, 1517). A satire on scholasticism. It is directed specifically at the reactionary University of Cologne, in the form of letters supposedly written by various church figures to a Cardinal Ortwinus. The book parodies a collection of letters that Ortwinus himself had published under the title of *Epistolae Clarorum Virorum (Letters of Famous Men)*. The *Epistolae Obscurorum Virorum* are a central document of German humanism, and implicitly support Johann REUCHLIN in his struggles with the renegade Jew Pfefferkorn. The authors are not known, but it is quite likely that Ulrich von HUTTEN wrote part of the book.

Epithalamion (1595). Lyric poem by Edmund SPENSER. It was written to celebrate his marriage. It has been called his highest poetic achievement.

E Pluribus Unum (*Lat.,* One From Many). A motto of the seal of the U.S. First proposed on Aug. 10, 1776, by a committee composed of Franklin, John Adams, and Jefferson, it appeared officially for the first time on a coin in New Jersey in 1786.

Epstein, Sir Jacob (1880–1959). American-born British sculptor. Epstein settled in London after studying in Paris under Rodin. He made no attempt at realism in his figures; as a result his work has been criticized as unpleasantly grotesque. Among Epstein's best known figures are *Mother and Child, Rima, Day, Night, Adam, Genesis, Ecce Homo, Venus.* He has also done portrait busts of prominent statesmen and artists, including Churchill, Bernard Shaw, Joseph Conrad, and Lady Gregory. He wrote an autobiography called *Let There Be Sculpture* (1940).

Equicola, Mario (1470?–1525). Italian man of letters and courtier who served the Este family at Ferrara. He wrote a history of Mantua, but was noted in his time for an influential book, *De natura de Amore (On the Nature of Love,* 1525). It was one of several philosophical treatises on love that spread Neoplatonic doctrine among such Renaissance writers as Ficino, Benvieni, and Castiglione.

Erasmus, Desiderius (1466–1536). Dutch scholar and philosopher, noted for his satire, *The Praise of Folly.* Erasmus called his religious outlook "the philosophy of Christ," yet his thought was influenced by varied tendencies, some Christian, some secular. He was affected by the German religious tradition,

which stressed personal piety in religion, as well as by the work of Italian humanists such as Pico della Mirandola. He adhered to the view of German pietism that religion was less a matter of ceremony and doctrine than of morality and rational piety, and his classical education and the influence of Pico and other humanists tended to stimulate in him a skeptical, critical attitude toward superstition, clericalism, and excessive religious zeal. He tried to combine the critical, rational, and secular attitude of classical antiquity and Italian humanism with the religious piety of the German Middle Ages. Aware of ecclesiastical corruption, and hostile to the intolerant dogmatism of the Church of his time, he was at first sympathetic to the Reformation and the attempts of Luther to reform the Church. Yet, humane and moderate at a time when the Reformation was fanning religious conflict, war, and hatred, he was forced finally to oppose the extremism of Luther and become an enemy of the Reformation.

Erato. In Greek mythology, the muse of love poetry. She is usually represented holding or playing a lyre.

Ercilla y Zúñiga, Alonso de. See ARAUCANA, LA.

Erda. In Wagner's RING DES NIBELUNGEN, the earth goddess NERTHUS.

Erebus (Erebos). In Greek mythology, the son of CHAOS and brother of Night; hence darkness personified. His name was given to the gloomy cavern underground through which the Shades had to walk in the course of their passage to Hades.

Erec et Enide. The earliest Arthurian romance in French, written in the 12th century by CHRÉTIEN DE TROYES. It tells of Erec, a knight at the court of King Arthur, who goes out in search of adventure and stays overnight at a run-down castle; here he meets Enide, the beautiful daughter of the baron who is master of the castle. Erec asks for her hand, marries her, and then retires from the active life of a knight in order to enjoy the pleasures of domestic life. His reputation soon begins to suffer from this, however, and one day he overhears his wife bemoaning the situation. The knight thereupon blames her for the state of affairs in which they find themselves, and sets out once more in search of adventure, forcing Enide to accompany him. They have amazing adventures in which Erec proves himself to be of prodigious strength and valor, although he is harsh in his treatment of his wife. Eventually she is kidnaped by a robber baron while the knight lies in an apparent state of death. He revives in time to rescue her, and at length they are reconciled.

Erech or **Uruk.** An ancient Sumerian city. It is best known as the capital of the hero GILGAMESH. It was also the favored city of INANNA, who tricked the god Enki into giving it preference over his own city of Eridu.

Erechtheum (Erechtheion). A temple of the tutelary deities of Athens in the ACROPOLIS of Athens. It derived its name from King Erechtheus.

Ereshkigal. The Sumerian queen of the underworld. She is said to have been carried off by KUR into the underworld; the god Enki then went out to do battle with Kur, but the outcome is unknown. Later, however, Ereshkigal reigns in the underworld and appears as a baleful figure in the myth of

INANNA's descent. Her role bears a striking resemblance to that of the Greek Persephone, who was carried off by Hades and thereafter reigned—at least, part of the year—in the underworld. The further parallel of the rivalry of Persephone and Aphrodite for the love of ADONIS suggests that Inanna may have descended to the underworld in search of her lover TAMMUZ; the closely related myth of ISHTAR and Tammuz supports this conclusion.

Erewhon (1872). A satirical novel by Samuel BUTLER about a UTOPIA. In the institutions of Erewhon (an anagram of "Nowhere") Butler satirizes contemporary English attitudes towards religion, science, crime, etc. *Erewhon* is probably the most brilliant specimen of 19th century Utopian novels. A sequel, *Erewhon Revisited,* was published in 1901.

Ericson (also **Ericsson, Erikson, Eriksson**), **Leif** (fl. 1000). Norse explorer, son of Eric the Red. According to legend he was returning from Norway to Greenland (c. 1000) when a storm drove his ship to a shore he called *Vinland* (also *Vineland, Wineland*), variously said to have been Labrador, Newfoundland, or New England. Thus it is asserted that he, not Columbus, was the first European to discover North America.

Eric the Red (c. 950–c. 1000). Norwegian explorer, father of Leif Ericson. He fled Norway, then Iceland, to escape murder charges. He named Greenland, which had been discovered 100 years before, and founded its first colony about 985.

Eridu. An ancient Sumerian city. In ancient times it was probably on the shores of the Persian Gulf, which no longer extends so far northward. It was the cult center of the god Enki and of his Babylonian counterpart, Ea.

Erifilla. A giantess in the ORLANDO FURIOSO of Ariosto, who guards the entrance to Alcina's enchanted castle. She is defeated by Ruggiero, who then falls prey to Alcina's subtle enchantments for a time.

Erigena, Johannes Scotus. See JOHANNES SCOTUS ERIGENA.

Erinyes. The Furies of Greek mythology. Snakyhaired and hideous women who sprang from the blood of Uranus when he was castrated by his son Cronos, they lived in the underworld, from which they issued to pursue and drive mad those who had committed such heinous crimes as patricide. They appeared prominently in Aeschylus' *Eumenides,* where, after relentlessly harassing Orestes for the murder of his mother (see the House of ATREUS), they give up vengeful insistence on the ancient law of blood for blood and are thenceforward worshiped in Athens as the Eumenides (Kindly Ones). In some accounts there were three, named Tisiphone, Alecto, and Megaera.

Eriphile. The slave girl in Jean Racine's tragedy IPHIGÉNIE EN AULIDE who, infatuated with Achilles, betrays the plot to save Iphigénie from being sacrificed to the gods. Far from winning Achilles or achieving her rival's death, her treachery seals her own doom, for the priests demand her sacrifice instead.

Eriphyle. In Greek mythology, the sister of Adrastus and wife of Amphiaraus. In a quarrel, the two men agreed henceforth to let Eriphyle decide their differences. Later, POLYNICES persuaded Adrastus

to help him attack Thebes, but Amphiaraus, a seer, opposed the expedition of the SEVEN AGAINST THEBES, foreseeing that only Adrastus would survive it. Polynices won the support of the vain and greedy Eriphyle by bribing her with HARMONIA's NECKLACE. Amphiaraus, bowing to his wife's will because of his vow, joined the expedition, but enjoined his young sons, ALCMAEON and Amphilochus, to avenge his death on his mother and on the Thebans.

On growing to manhood, Alcmaeon might have forgotten his mother's crime had she not repeated it at his own expense. Bribed by Thersander, Polynices' son, she urged Alcmaeon to lead the EPIGONI against Thebes. Alcmaeon returned from the war victorious and, learning of his mother's double treachery, killed her. Like Orestes, he was pursued by the ERINYES through many tragic events.

Eris. The goddess of discord, sister of Ares. He flung the APPLE OF DISCORD. See JUDGMENT OF PARIS.

Erlking or *Ger.* **Erlkönig,** king of the alders (a mis-translation of the Danish *eller-konge,* king of the elves). A malevolent goblin of the Black Forest who lures people, especially children, to destruction. Never actually a part of medieval German folk tradition, he was first popularized by Goethe in his famous ballad *Der Erlkönig.* One of Franz Schubert's most famous songs is a setting of Goethe's poem.

Erminia. In the GERUSALEMME LIBERATA of Tasso, a Syrian maiden whose life was spared by the Crusader Tancredi (Tancred) at the battle of Antioch. Though she loves him, he is enamored of Clorinda, the warrior maid from Persia. At one point Erminia, learning that Tancredi lies wounded, goes to him in Clorinda's armor; but both he and the other Christian knights pursue her in the belief that she is Clorinda. Taking pleasant refuge in a beautiful wood, she is cared for by an old shepherd, who extolls the virtues of the pastoral life. Later, in the camp of the Egyptian armies, she informs Vafrino, the shield-bearer of Tancredi sent as a spy, of a plan to disguise a group of infidel warriors in Crusaders' dress so that they can close with and kill Goffredo, the Christian general. On the way to Jerusalem with Vafrino she encounters the wounded Tancredi and nurses him tenderly back to health. After she takes him back to the camp outside the holy city, she disappears from the plot and Ariosto says nothing further of her fate.

Ermonide. In the ORLANDO FURIOSO of Ariosto, a Dutch knight who is killed by the Scottish warrior Zerbino when he attempts to slay the old hag Gabrina, an ancient enemy of his family.

Ernst, Max (1891–). German painter. A member of the surrealists and the earlier Dadaists, Ernst originally studied philosophy while at the universities of Cologne and Bonn. He was drawn into art with no formal training through his friendship with André Breton and Louis Aragon. He has written for the surrealist publication *Literature and the Surrealist Revolution.* His paintings include *The Chaste Joseph* and *Max Ernst showing a Girl his Father's Head.*

Eroica. BEETHOVEN's Symphony No. 3. Its first title was *Sinfonia grande Napoleon Bonaparte.* When he learned about Napoleon's accession to the imperial throne of France (May 18, 1804), Beethoven changed it in a fit of rage to *Sinfonia eroica com-*

posta per festiggiare il sovvenire d'un grand'uomo (*Heroic symphony composed to celebrate the memory of a great man*).

Eros. The Greek god of love. According to the accounts in Hesiod, Eros was one of the earliest gods, born of Chaos at the same time as Mother Earth. He came to be the patron god of beautiful young men. Only in late myth did he become a child, the naughty son of Aphrodite, as he appears in the *Argonautica* and elsewhere. It was in this form that he was identified with the Latin CUPID.

Eros. In Shakespeare's ANTONY AND CLEOPATRA, a faithful soldier of Antony. Commanded by Antony to kill him, he commits suicide rather than take his master's life.

Erostratus or **Herostratus.** The Ephesian who set fire to the temple of Artemis on the day that Alexander the Great happened to be born (356 B.C.). This he did to make his name immortal; and, in order to defeat his object, the Ephesians forbade his name ever to be mentioned.

Erra-Pater. The assumed name of the author of an almanac published about 1535 as *The Pronostycacion for ever of Erra Pater: A Jewe born in Jewery, a Doctour in Astronomye and Physycke.* It is a collection of astrological tables, rules of health, and the like, and is arranged for use in any year. It is occasionally referred to in contemporary literature.

Title page of Erra-Pater's almanac (c. 1535).

THE BRITISH MUSEUM

[He] had got him a suit of durance, that would last longer than one of Erra Pater's almanacks, or a constable's browne bill.—Thomas Nashe, *Lenten Stuffe* (1599)

The almanacs were frequently reprinted, and nearly a hundred years later Samuel Butler says of William Lilly, the almanac maker and astrologer:

> In mathematics he was greater
> Than Tycho Brahe or Erra Pater.
> *Hudibras,* i, 1 (1663)

Error. See FAERIE QUEENE, THE.

Erymanthian boar. In Greek mythology, a devastating boar. It had its haunt on the mountain range of Erymanthus between Arcadia and Achaia. It was finally killed by HERACLES.

Erysichthon. In classic myth, an impious person. He profaned a grove sacred to Demeter by cutting down a great oak. He was punished by terrible, incessant hunger.

Erythraean main. Literally, the Red Sea. In ancient geography, the Erythraean Sea was the Indian Ocean including the Red Sea and the Persian Gulf.

Esau. In the Old Testament, the eldest son of Isaac and Rebekah. The name itself means in Hebrew "rough" or "covered with hair." In return for a mess of pottage, it was Esau who sold his birthright to his twin brother JACOB (Gen. 25:33–34). In another story, Jacob put on a hairy animal skin and secured the blessing that his blind father had intended for Esau (Gen. 27).

Escalus. In Shakespeare's ROMEO AND JULIET, the prince of Verona. He orders the feuding Montagues and Capulets to end their public brawls on pain of death and later banishes Romeo from Verona for killing Tybalt.

Escamillo. The toreador in Bizet's opera CARMEN.

Escorial or **Escurial, El.** A royal palace some 25 miles northwest of Madrid, built (1563–1584) by PHILIP II. Dedicated to St. Lawrence, on whose feast day the battle of St. Quentin was fought in 1557, the building is in the shape of a gridiron, in commemoration of the gridiron on which St. Lawrence was martyred, and is famed for its artistic and bibliographic treasures. It also contains a monastery with a celebrated art collection and library, a church, and a mausoleum where the kings of Spain lie buried.

Escosura [y Morrogh], Patricio de la (1807–1878). Spanish novelist and dramatist. Escosura is best known as the author of romantic historical novels, patterned on the Waverley novels of Sir Walter Scott. The most famous of these is *Ni Rey ni roque* (1835), whose value lies in its portrayal of the native Spanish landscape.

Escragnolle, Alfredo d'. See Viscount TAUNAY.

Esenin, Sergei Aleksandrovich (1895–1925). Russian poet. Born of peasant parents, Esenin used the theme of the passing of rural Russia in his poetry. One of the finest lyric poets of the early Soviet period, he was for a time connected with a literary group called the Imaginists, founded in 1919, which, like the English and American Imagists, stressed the importance of the image in poetry. His growing popularity went hand in hand with an increasingly wild life. For a chaotic year (1922–1923), he was married to the dancer Isadora Duncan. His drinking bouts grew in length, and he died, having slashed his wrist in a hotel room in Leningrad and written a farewell poem with his blood, by hanging himself. His suicide was attributed by the Soviet regime to his mental instability, and Esenin's works have not been suppressed as have those of other disaffected literary figures. His four volumes of lyrics, with their glowing pictures of the Russian countryside, are still popular in Russia.

Esmeralda. A beautiful gypsy girl, the heroine of Victor Hugo's novel THE HUNCHBACK OF NOTRE DAME.

Esmond, Henry or **Harry.** The hero of Thackeray's novel HENRY ESMOND.

Francis Esmond. The supposed heir to the Castlewood estate. He brings up Henry with his own children but allows him to believe he is an illegitimate son of the dead viscount to whom the estate belonged.

Rachel Esmond (Lady Castlewood). The wife of Francis. After his death she marries Henry Esmond.

Frank Esmond. The son of Francis and Rachel. Like Henry, he is an ardent supporter of the Pretender.

Beatrix Esmond. The daughter of Francis and Rachel; a beautiful coquette. After numerous affairs, notably one with James Edward Stuart, the Pretender, which destroys his chances for the throne, she marries Tusher, her brother's tutor, and succeeds in having him made bishop. "She was imperious," says the author, "she was light-minded, she was flighty, she was false. She had no reverence for character and she was very, very beautiful."

esoteric (Gr.). Those within, as opposed to *exoteric,* those without. The term originated with Pythagoras, who stood behind a curtain when he gave his lectures. Those who were allowed to attend the lectures, but not to see his face, he called his exoteric disciples; but those who were allowed to enter the veil, his esoterics.

Aristotle adopted the same terms; those who attended his evening lectures, which were of a popular character, he called his exoterics; and those who attended his more abstruse morning lectures, his esoterics.

Espina [de la Serna], Concha (1880–1955). Spanish novelist. Her works include *La esfinge maragata* (1913), a regional novel, and *El metal de los muertos* (1920), which deals with the plight of Spanish mine workers. She is known for her feminine sensitivity and the thoroughness of her narration.

Esprit des lois, De l'. See SPIRIT OF LAWS, THE.

Esprit Fou, L'. See Jean CLAVERET.

Espronceda y Delgado, José (1808–1842). Spanish poet. Espronceda was a romantic in word and in deed. An early conspiracy left him with no choice but to flee Spain; later he was an ardent supporter of liberalism in Holland, while in 1830 he joined the revolutionary cause in Paris. His work stresses patriotic and Byronic themes. His most famous short poems, which appeared in his *Poesías* (1840), include *A Jarifa en una orgía, El verdugo, El mendigo,* and *A la patria.* However, his reputation rests upon two longer works: *El estudiante de Salamanca* (1839), which deals with the adventures of Félix de Montemar, a typical romantic hero who witnesses his own funeral, and the long dramatic

poem *El diablo mundo* (1840–1841), considered his masterpiece, which resembles Byron's *Don Juan* and contains a famous *Canto a Teresa,* dealing with the poet's lost love.

Esquemeling, Alexander Olivier (1645?–1707). A Dutch buccaneer. His book, *De Americaensche Zeerovers* (*The Buccaneers of America,* 1678), has become an important source for the history of piracy.

Essay Concerning Human Understanding, An (1690). A treatise by John LOCKE dealing with the origin and scope of human knowledge. Its basic premise is the empirical origin of ideas, which can be described as the raw material with which the mind works. The mind of man at birth, Locke claimed, is like a blank sheet of paper and possesses no "innate ideas." Man acquires knowledge through experience, which is made up of sensation, impressions of the external world derived through the senses, and reflection, the internal operation of the mind. Knowledge stems from the perception of relationships among ideas. Locke's essay contributed greatly to the growth of 18th-century rationalism and, through its impact on the work of Hume, Kant, and others, influenced modern theories of knowledge.

Essay for the Recording of Illustrious Providences, An (1684). A pseudoscientific treatise by Increase MATHER. The work is a collection of reports involving supernatural incidents in New England, which Mather examines in an attempt to prove and illustrate the intervention of God in human affairs. The book was republished twice in the 19th century as *Remarkable Providences.*

Essay of Dramatic Poesy (1668). A famous critical essay by John DRYDEN. It is in the form of a conversation among four Englishmen who have ventured out on the Thames in a barge in hope of witnessing an engagement between the Dutch and English fleets. They discuss Greek, French, and English drama, the merits of several dramatists, and the use of blank and rhymed verse in plays.

Essay on Criticism, An (1711). A didactic poem in heroic couplets by Alexander POPE, written when he was 21 or younger. It is a discussion, based on neoclassical doctrines, of literary taste and style, principles of verse structure and of criticism, and gives a brief history of criticism. Standards of taste are to be derived from the order found in nature:

> Those rules of old discovered, not devised,
> Are nature still, but nature methodized.

The poem is sprinkled with well-known couplets:

> A little learning is a dangerous thing;
> Drink deep, or taste not the Pierian spring.

> True wit is nature to advantage dressed,
> What oft was thought, but ne'er so well expressed.

> Good nature and good sense must ever join;
> To err is human, to forgive divine.

Essay on Man, An (1733–1734). The best-known poem of Alexander POPE. Written in heroic couplets, it is divided into four Epistles dealing respectively with man's relation to the universe, to himself, to society, and to happiness. The poem is addressed to, and was inspired by Henry St. John, Lord Bolingbroke; it expresses a deistic philosophy (see DEISM) loosely derived from Leibniz, being intended to set forth a coherent scheme of the universe, to "vindicate the ways of God to man" and to declare that "whatever is, is right." It is optimistic and shows the characteristic neoclassical faith in reason and respect for tradition and authority.

Essays (Essais; 1580, 1588). The masterpiece of the French moralist Michel de MONTAIGNE, creator of the personal discursive essay. Loosely constructed, they ramble at will over any number of subjects like a spirited conversation. The order in which the chapters appear and the division into three books had no logical significance. However, the order in which Montaigne actually wrote has been established and reveals a certain progression in his thought from a classic stoic attitude to one of skepticism (see APOLOGY FOR RAYMOND SEBOND) to a final affirmation of the possibilities in human nature. He found that the knowledge he sought resided in man alone, of which he was a representative. To extract knowledge, therefore, he must learn to know himself, as his great model Socrates had taught. In the *Essays*, he delved into his own experience, gleaned the lessons it held for him, and gradually filled out his "self-portrait." The ideas he expressed on such topics as death, friendship, virtue, suffering, education, politics, freedom, nature, and man are peculiarly his own. At the same time they are universal, since the truth Montaigne found is rooted in human nature itself. Montaigne was highly original in turning attention from academic learning and intellectual theorizing to man himself. Freed from the prejudices of his time, he cleared the way for the consideration of morality, politics, and justice as separate disciplines, independent of religious dogma, whose successful practice was closely related to an understanding of human nature. He has endured because every reader has found not only the portrait of Montaigne in the *Essays*, but glimpses of his own image.

Essays or Counsels, Civil and Moral, The. A collection of brief essays by Francis BACON, published in three editions during his lifetime: a first edition of 10 essays (1597); a second of 38 (1612); and a third of 58 (1625). Generally, they deal with questions of personal or public conduct and philosophical or religious matters. They are written in a witty, pithy, widely metaphorical, and highly original style.

Essays, First and Second Series (1841; 1844). Two collections of essays by Ralph Waldo EMERSON. The *First Series* includes the essays called *History*, SELF-RELIANCE, COMPENSATION, *Spiritual Laws, Love, Friendship, Prudence, Heroism*, THE OVER-SOUL, *Circles, Intellect*, and *Art*. The *Second Series* includes *The Poet, Experience, Character, Manners, Gifts, Nature, Politics*, and *Nominalist and Realist*.

Essays in Idleness (Tsurezure gusa). Japanese miscellany of the Muromachi Period (1333–1600) by Yoshida Kenkō (1283–1350), a court official and Buddhist monk. The 243 passages, of varying length, are mainly sketches, comments, and anecdotes, which reflect both a cynical worldliness and a rather shallow Buddhistic outlook.

Essay towards a New Theory of Vision (1709). A philosophical treatise dealing with the doctrine of immaterialism by George BERKELEY.

Establishment. Popular name for those who, wielding power in Britain, are sometimes humorously and sometimes resentfully considered to form an ex-clusive society that runs the country. The Establishment is conceived of as an arm of the British upper class, dedicated to preserving the values, rights, and powers of that class, generally at the expense of the rest of the population. Its membership includes virtually all royalty, nobility, money, power, and influence in British life, from debutante to prime minister, from playwright to press baron. The Establishment periodically assimilates to its bosom all competition or opposition that can be ingratiated or bought off and squashes the rest. It is, consequently, self-preserving, self-perpetuating, and unbeatable.

Este. Italian noble family, lords of the province of Ferrara from the 13th through the 16th century, who took their name from the city of Este (hence also *Estensi*). Their influence on literature and the other arts was especially great during the Renaissance, when their court was a center of activity in the drama and devoted to the romanzo, or romantic epic. The most famous recipients of their patronage were the poets Boiardo, Ariosto, and Tasso. Among the outstanding Estensi were:

Leonello d'Este (1407–1450). Marquis of Ferrara, man of letters, patron of such artists as Alberti, and himself a minor poet of some ability.

Ercole I d'Este (1431–1505). Duke of Ferrara (1471–1505). Patron of Boiardo, father of two celebrated Renaissance women: Beatrice d'Este (1475–1497), wife of Lodovico Sforza of Milan; and Isabella d'Este (1474–1539), wife of Francesco Gonzaga of Mantua and one of the most learned and cultivated women of her time.

Alfonso II d'Este. Duke of Ferrara (1559–1597). Patron of Tasso, who was forced to confine the poet in an asylum after a mental breakdown. Alfonso's sister Eleonora d'Este (1537–1581) was once thought to have been the object of Tasso's love, and the reason for his confinement, but this is now considered a fiction.

Ippolito d'Este. Cardinal (1479–1520). Friend of Leonardo da Vinci and patron of the poet Ariosto.

Luigi d'Este (1538–1586). A cardinal and patron of the poet Tasso until 1572, when the latter entered the service of Duke Alfonso.

Estébanez Calderón, Serafín (1799–1867). Spanish statesman and author. His most famous work is the colorful *Escenas andaluzas* (1847), which deals with the picturesque life, customs, and dress of the inhabitants of the province of Andulasia.

Estensi. See ESTE.

Esterhazy, Marie Charles Ferdinand Walsin (1847–1923). French army officer. Esterhazy confessed in 1899 that he had forged the documents that led to the conviction of Alfred DREYFUS. He spent the remainder of his life in exile in England.

Esther. The name of an Old Testament heroine (in Hebrew, *Hadassah*) whose story is told in the book bearing her name. In place of Queen Vashti, King Ahasuerus chose the beautiful Jewish maiden Esther as his queen. She kept her religion secret, on the advice of her uncle and guardian Mordecai, until the evil Haman conceived a plot to destroy all Jews in the kingdom. As queen, she made a courageous plea for her people to Ahasuerus, and Haman was hung on the gallows he intended for Mordecai. Orthodox Jews still celebrate the feast of Purim to commemorate this deliverance.

Esther (1673). An epic by Jean DESMARETS DE SAINT-SORLIN, based on the Old Testament Book of Esther.

Esther (1689). A tragedy in 3 acts by Jean RACINE. Based on the Book of Esther and relating the story of Esther and Ahasuerus, the play was written for the schoolgirls of St.-Cyr at the request of Mme. de Maintenon; the nature of the commission explains the unorthodox interpolation of songs by a chorus of Israelite maidens.

Esther (1884). A novel by Henry ADAMS. Esther Dudley, a free-thinking young painter, falls in love with the clergyman Stephen Hazard, but, hostile to his church and alienated by his orthodox views, she breaks their engagement. The character of Esther is thought to be modeled after that of Adams' wife Marian. The artist Wharton, a character in a romantic subplot, may have been drawn from the sculptor Augustus St. Gaudens, who created the impressive memorial to Mrs. Adams in the Rock Creek Cemetery in Washington.

Esther Waters (1894). A novel by George MOORE. It is the story of an English servant and her long struggle to bring up her illegitimate son. The boy's father, William Latch, who had been footman in the household where Esther had her first position, finally turns up as a bookmaker and innkeeper and marries her, but her happy married life is only an interlude in a distressed and melancholy existence.

Estienne, Henri (1531–1598). French humanist, printer, and philologist. The son and grandson of illustrious printers, he lived in Geneva, but he also spent much time among the humanists of Paris. His publication of the works of Anacreon (1554) and of other Greek authors exercised a great influence on the Pléiade poets. An admirer of Greek, which he considered the only worthy predecessor to French, he published a *Thesaurus graecae linguae* (1572) and five works on the French language. His most important work in French, *Apologie pour Hérodote* (1566), is a satire on his age; *Dialogues du nouveau françois italianisé* (1578), a satire, laments the corruption of the French language by Italian influences.

Estrées, Gabrielle d' (1573–1599). Mistress of Henry IV of France. The daughter of the marquis of Cœuvres, she won the affection of Henry when he visited the castle of Cœuvres and became his mistress in 1592, bearing him several children, who were legitimized. Henry's plans to marry Gabrielle after his divorce from Margaret of Valois were cut short by her death.

Estrildis. See LOCRINE.

Etaples, Jacques Lefèvre d' (1453–1536). French theologian. He was one of the first French theologians to reject medieval scholasticism in favor of the humanism of the Renaissance. Rather than teach from commentaries on the classics, as had been done previously, he taught from his own editions of the texts, such as Aristotle's *Physics* (1492–1494), *Ethics* (1494), and *Politics* (1506). Under the influence of Erasmus, he wrote his Latin commentaries (1522) on the New Testament, which led him to reject the body of Church dogma and to consider Scripture as the only sound basis of Christianity. He thus became one of the forerunners of the Protestant reform movement.

Eteocles (Eteokles). In Greek legend, a son of OEDIPUS and Jocasta. See SEVEN AGAINST THEBES.

Eteoclus (Eteoklos). See SEVEN AGAINST THEBES.

Eternal City, the. Rome. The epithet occurs in Ovid, Tibullus, and other writers, and in many official documents of the Empire. In Vergil's *Aeneid,* Jupiter tells Venus that he would give to the Romans *imperium sine fine* (an eternal empire).

eternal feminine. A phrase from the last lines of Goethe's FAUST, "Das Ewig-Weibliche/Zieht uns hinan" ("The eternal feminine/Draws us onward"). Goethe symbolizes this idea in the Virgin Mary at the end of *Faust,* and both GRETCHEN and HELEN are manifestations of it, but its full meaning is more general. Whereas Mephistopheles represents nihilism, the complete lack of upward striving, the eternal feminine is the goal of all upward striving, of all man's attempts, however futile or misguided, to improve himself or his world.

Eternal Husband, The (Vechnyi muzh; 1870). A short novel by Feodor DOSTOEVSKI. It is a brilliant psychological study of the relations between a cuckolded husband and his wife's ex-lover. The husband, Pavel Pavlovich Trusotzki, torments himself as well as the lover, Aleksei Ivanovich Vel'chaninov. He hints to Vel'chaninov that the daughter his wife bore before she died was actually Vel'chaninov's. Trusotzki horribly mistreats the little girl who loves him, nevertheless, and who falls ill and dies when she is separated from him. Vel'chaninov hopes he has seen the last of Trusotzki, but the half-mad little man turns up again, urging Vel'chaninov to come and meet his prospective second wife, as if inviting cuckoldry all over again.

Ethan Brand (1851). A short story by Nathaniel HAWTHORNE. Brand, setting out to discover the Unpardonable Sin, finally finds it in his own heart. For this "sin of an intellect that triumphed over the sense of brotherhood with man and reverence for God," he destroys himself.

Ethan Frome (1911). A short novel by Edith WHARTON. In a typical New England village, the title character barely makes a living out of his stony farm and exists at odds with his wife Zeena, a whining hypochondriac. When Mattie, Zeena's cousin, comes to live with them, love develops between her and Ethan. They try to end their hapless romance by steering a bobsled into a tree; but both end up cripples, tied to a long life of despair with Zeena. Zeena, however, is transformed into a devoted nurse while Mattie becomes the nagging invalid.

Etherege, Sir George (1634–1691). English dramatist. He is noted for such brilliant, if licentious, comedies as *The Comical Revenge, or Love in a Tub* (1664), *She Would If She Could* (1668), and THE MAN OF MODE.

Ethiopians (*Gr.* burnt-faces). A legendary race of people in Greek mythology. The country of the Ethiopians lay south of Egypt, close to the stream of Ocean. Cepheus, husband of Cassiopeia and father of Andromeda, was one of their kings. Memnon, the son of Aurora and Tithonus who fell in the Trojan War, was another. In Greek drama mention is often made of various gods being off in Ethiopia, meaning they were a great distance removed from the action of the play.

Ethiopica. The story of the loves between Theagenes and Chariclea, by Heliodoros (Heliodorus), Greek romance writer and later bishop of Tricca, in Thessaly, in the 4th century. The book, considered the earliest of extant Greek romances, was formed by 10 volumes, largely borrowed from by subsequent novelists, and especially by Madeleine de SCUDÉRY, TASSO, Guarnini, and D'Urfé.

Etna or **Aetna.** The famous Sicilian volcano. In the Aeneid, Vergil ascribes its eruption to the restlessness of Enceladus, a giant who lies buried under the mountain, where the Greek and Latin poets also placed the forges of Vulcan and the smithy of the Cyclopes.

Etourdi, L' (The Scatterbrain, 1665). MoLIÈRE's 1st comedy. In the play, which is set in Messina, Lélie has fallen in love with Clélie but has not the money to buy her. His servant Mascarille contrives a series of maneuvers for obtaining the girl, but the hare-brained Lélie fumbles them all. Nonetheless, he finally obtains Clélie.

Etranger, L'. See STRANGER, THE.

Etre et le Néant, L'. See BEING AND NOTHINGNESS.

Etruria. See ETRUSCANS.

Etruscans. An ancient non-Italic race which established itself in northern Italy some time before the 7th century B.C. Modern Tuscany is roughly the center of what was their kingdom, Etruria. The Tusci, as they were called by the Romans, gained great power in Italy and the western Mediterranean, and held sway over Rome until 509 B.C. when the last Etruscan king was expelled from that city. The Romans feared and hated them for many years thereafter, although they were finally absorbed both politically and culturally into the Roman state. Their art shows influences from Greece, Egypt, Syria, Cyprus, and Mesopotamia, and it, in turn, influenced Roman art. Their language remains undeciphered and their origin a mystery, although the Greek historian Herodotus asserts that they came from Lydia in Asia Minor.

Ettrick Shepherd, the. See James HOGG.

Et tu, Brute. According to SUETONIUS in his Lives of the Caesars, Julius Caesar on being stabbed by Marcus Junius BRUTUS, whom he had counted among his trusted friends, exclaimed: Et tu, Brute fili ("You also, O Brutus, my son"). Shakespeare, in his play JULIUS CAESAR, immeasurably heightened the effect of the passage by adding to it an expression of utter despair at such betrayal: "Et tu, Brute! Then fall, Caesar!" The phrase is currently used as an expression of amazement at a sudden revelation of treachery or ingratitude.

Etzel. The name given ATTILA of the Huns in German legends such as the NIBELUNGENLIED. He is known as Atli in the VÖLSUNGA SAGA.

Eucharist (from Gr. eucharistein, to give thanks). The sacrament of the Lord's Supper (see LAST SUPPER).

Euclid (Eukleides; fl. 300 B.C.). A Greek mathematician. He lived and taught at Alexandria. His Elements (of geometry) in 13 books became the basis of future geometry. He is celebrated in Edna St. Vincent Millay's well-known line, "Euclid alone has looked on beauty bare."

Eugene Aram (1832). A novel by Edward BUL-WER-LYTTON, founded on a famous murder case. The real Eugene Aram (1704–1759) was a Knaresborough schoolmaster convicted of murdering a shoemaker, Daniel Clarke, to whom he owed money. Bulwer-Lytton makes the youthful Aram commit murder to secure money to further his own idealistic purposes. He goes free for a time, falls in love, all unknowingly, with a relative of the murdered man, and is in his wedding clothes when he is accused of the crime.

Eugene of Savoy, Prince (1663–1736). French aristocrat who served the Austrian Hapsburgs as military commander and administrator. He drove the invading Turks out of Hungary in 1697.

Eugene Onegin (Evgeni Onegin; 1831). A novel in verse by Aleksandr PUSHKIN. For the influence it had on later Russian literature and in its own right, Eugene Onegin is probably Pushkin's most important work. The novel relates the experiences of its Byronic hero, Eugene. Bored with the social life in St. Petersburg, he visits his country estate and meets Tatyana, a young girl who falls in love with him and naïvely offers herself to him. The bored Eugene is not interested and rather bluntly tells Tatyana this. For lack of any other amusement, he then provokes a duel with Lenski, a young romantic poet who has become his friend. Lenski is killed, and Onegin goes back to the world of society. After his departure, Tatyana visits Eugene's country manor, browses through his library, and begins to realize how hollow and artificial he is.

A few years later when Eugene meets Tatyana, who is now the wife of a prince and a prominent member of St. Petersburg society, her beauty and charm, and perhaps her eminence in society, turn his head. He announces his love to her in a letter, as Tatyana had to him in years before. Tatyana admits she still loves him, but refuses him because of her duty to her husband.

Pushkin's novel has been a rich source of character types for Russian writers. His use of an ironic narrator to tell the story has perhaps been equally influential. This narrative device was especially well developed by Dostoevski. The libretto for Tchaikovsky's opera Eugene Onegin (1879) was faithfully adapted from Pushkin's tale by the composer's brother Modeste.

Eugénie, Empress. Full name, Eugénie Marie de Montijo de Guzmán. Comtesse de Téba (1826–1920). Wife of NAPOLEON III, and empress of the French (1853–1871). A leader of fashion, her feminine charm added brilliance to the French court. Her influence upon her husband reveals her lack of interest in liberal and democratic ideas. After the downfall of the empire, she fled to England, where she was befriended by Queen Victoria.

Eugénie Grandet (1833). A novel, part of LA COMÉDIE HUMAINE, by Honoré de BALZAC. Félix Grandet, the embodiment of greed and domestic tyranny, destroys the romance of his daughter Eugénie with her cousin Charles, condemning her to a futile, joyless existence.

Eulenspiegel or **Ulenspiegel, Till** or **Tyll.** Called in English **Tyll Howleglas** or **Owlglass.** A German peasant popular in legend as a player of pranks. Tradition makes him a native of Brunswick who died in 1350. The stories associated with his name tell of the often brutal tricks and practical jokes he

LA VIE
JOYEUSE ET RECRÉATIVE
DE
THIEL-ULESPIÉGLE,

*De fes faits merveilleux & fortunes qu'il a eu;
lequel par aucune rufe ne fe laiffa pas tromper.*

A TROYES,
Chez A P F. ANDRÉ. Imp Lib. & Fabricant de
Papier, Grand·rue, v s à·vis la Relle·Croix.

A 16th-century French edition of *Till Eulenspiegel*.

played, mostly on innkeepers and other tradespeople, but sometimes on priests or noblemen. The first written account was probably a Low German one of about 1483, the next a High German text of 1515. The satire of these seems to emphasize the tricks as the revenge of the peasant upon the townsmen who scorn him as inferior. The rogue's adventures, highly popular and adapted in translations all over Europe, had been printed in England by 1560. Charles de Coster wrote a modernized version in 1867, and Richard Strauss used the theme musically in his tone poem *Till Eulenspiegel's Merry Pranks* (1894).

eulogy. A formal piece of writing or an oration in praise of a person or thing; by extension, it has come to mean any general expression of praise.

Eumaeus (Eumaios). The faithful slave and swineherd of Odysseus in the ODYSSEY.

Eumenides. See ERINYES.

Euphorion (*Gr.,* well-bearing). In late classical tradition, the son of the shades of Achilles and Helen of Troy.

In Part II of FAUST, Goethe makes him the son of Faust and Helen and uses him as an allegory for Lord Byron's career. Euphorion lives only for the joy of the moment and, like Icarus, finally flings himself too high, only to fall and die. Helen follows him to the underworld, leaving Faust behind.

Euphrasia. The heroine of Arthur MURPHY's tragedy *The Grecian Daughter* (1772). She nurses her starving father Evander, King of Syracuse, with milk from her own breast when he is imprisoned by Dionysius the younger. The incident is not historical, but is related of other heroines of legend.

Euphrosyne (*Gr.* Joy). In classic mythology, one of the three Charites, or GRACES.

Euphues. The chief character of John LYLY's *Euphues, The Anatomy of Wit* (1579) and *Euphues and his England* (1580). Euphues is a witty, pleasure-loving young Athenian who, sojourning in Naples, attempts to win Lucilla, fiancée of his friend Philautus. This procedure estranges him from Philautus, but when Lucilla chooses a third lover, the unworthy Curio, the two friends are united in disillusionment. There is little plot in either romance; the interest lies chiefly in long philosophic discussions and in the elaborate and affected style that gave rise to the terms EUPHUISM and *euphuist*. This style, marked by ingenious antitheses, alliteration, exempla, complicated figures, and skillfully balanced sentences, was for a while in great vogue. It was frequently parodied, however, and by 1590 a reaction in favor of a more masculine, pithy style had set in.

euphuism. An artificial style of English speech and writing popular in the late Elizabethan and Jacobean periods. It derived its name from *Euphues: The Anatomy of Wit* (1579) by John LYLY, who either invented the style or derived it from translations of certain works of a Spanish writer, Antonio de GUEVARA. It was characterized by exaggerated Baroque refinement and artificiality of style, with plentiful references to mythical birds and beasts, constant alliteration, and the frequent use of unduly neat antitheses. The intent of this elaborate elegance was to woo feminine readers by seeming to edify them, while avoiding scholarly solemnity. The attempt was so successful that even Queen Elizabeth began to affect the euphuistic style. The fashion lasted for half a century, and Lyly had many imitators, notably Robert GREENE and Thomas LODGE. (See EUPHUES.)

eureka (*Gr.,* more correctly *heureka,* I have found it). An exclamation of delight at having made a discovery. Originally that of ARCHIMEDES, the Syracusan philosopher, when he discovered how to test the purity of Hiero's crown. The tale is that Hiero, a famous tyrant of Syracuse, delivered a certain weight of gold to a smith to be made into a votive crown, but, suspecting that the gold had been alloyed with an inferior metal, asked Archimedes to test it. The philosopher did not know how to proceed, but in stepping into his bath, which was quite full, observed that some of the water ran over. It immediately struck him that a body must remove its own bulk of water when it is immersed; silver is lighter than gold, therefore a pound weight of silver will be more bulky than a pound weight of gold, and would consequently remove more water. In this way he found that the crown was deficient in gold. Vitruvius says: "When the idea flashed across his mind, the philosopher jumped out of the bath exclaiming, '*Heureka! heureka!*' and, without waiting to dress himself, ran home to try the experiment."

Eureka (1848). An essay on the material and spiritual universe by Edgar Allan POE. Under the influence of Laplace and Newton, Poe presented his view of the universe as a mystic and material unity. An interesting contribution to scientific and philosophic thought, the piece indicates that Poe saw the possibility of non-Euclidean geometry. Many of his notions are surprisingly in agreement with the latest theories of cosmic origin.

Euripides (480?-405 B.C.). A Greek tragic playwright. A slightly younger contemporary of Aeschylus and Sophocles, and less honored in his time, Euripides is now admired for his remarkably modern attitudes and his profound insights into psychology. In spite of Aristophanes' taunt that his mother had sold vegetables, he was actually high born and well educated. He was twice married, both times unhappily. Although he wrote between 80 and 90 plays, Euripides won prizes only four times. In 409 B.C., he left Athens and died at the court of King Archelaus of Macedonia.

According to tradition, Euripides was withdrawn and bookish, and his plays reveal a sharply inquiring mind that must have made him many enemies in Athens. He was cruelly lampooned by Aristophanes in two comedies, THE CLOUDS and the THESMOPHORIAZUSAE. The slanders against him and the relative unpopularity of his plays may account for his leaving Athens when he was still at the height of his powers; yet Sophocles dressed his chorus in mourning when news of Euripides' death reached Athens.

Seventeen tragedies by Euripides remain, beginning with the ALCESTIS in 438 B.C., and ending with THE BACCHANTS in about 405 B.C. He also wrote the fragmentary SATYR PLAY CYCLOPS about 424-423 B.C., and may have written another existing tragedy, *Rhesus,* of which the date is unknown. Although called a tragedy, the *Alcestis* has a strong comic element that relates it more closely to the satyr plays.

Three qualities in Euripides' plays have especially attracted modern readers: his biting social criticism, his subtle psychological analyses of his characters, and their humanity, as compared to the larger-than-life remoteness of the heroes and heroines of Aeschylus and Sophocles. Euripides attacked, at least by implication, many attitudes accepted by the Athenians: the subordinate position of women (*Alcestis*), and foreign women in particular (MEDEA); the unjust treatment of illegitimate children (*Hippolytus*); above all, the glory of war (THE TROJAN WOMEN). His own attitude toward his home city of Athens seems to have changed strikingly in the decade between his ANDROMACHE and *The Trojan Women.* The earlier play bitterly attacks the Spartans as cruel and cowardly, and seems to imply that the Athenians would never behave in such a manner. In *The Trojan Women,* however, they behave in much the same way to the defeated Trojans, killing the child Astyanax out of fear that the line of Hector will be perpetuated. This play reflected Euripides' disillusionment and outrage over the massacre by Athenians of the inhabitants of Melos, because they had remained neutral in the PELOPONNESIAN WAR. This disgust with war is evident also in the IPHIGENIA IN AULIS, one of his last plays. Even as early as the *Andromache,* however, it was clear that Euripides found no glory in war, but only needless suffering and inhumanity.

Some of the irony of the *Alcestis,* in which Admetus gallantly allows his wife to die for him, may have been lost on the Athenians, who considered men's lives more valuable than those of women. But in the *Medea* the sharp-tongued heroine makes his criticism of the treatment of women abundantly clear. Medea, like Electra and Phaedra (in the *Hippolytus*), is drawn with extraordinarily acute insights into her emotions. They are queens, yet they are extremely human women, rather than heroic personages of tragedy. It was in this reduction of tragic figures to human proportions that Euripides laid the groundwork for the New Comedy that was to come. Euripides' characters speak a much more colloquial language than that of the other tragedians, but it is still poetry of a high order, especially in the choral odes.

Euripides' other plays include ION, IPHIGENIA in TAURIS, HELEN, ELECTRA, ORESTES, HECUBA, and THE SUPPLIANT WOMEN.

euroclydon. A tempestuous northeast wind of the Mediterranean. Also called *gregale,* i.e., the wind from Greece. The first part of Euroclydon is the word *eurus,* the east wind of classical antiquity; the second *clydon,* a wave. The word occurs in the New Testament (Acts 27:14) and may be a popular adaptation of the manuscript variant (now preferred) *Euraquilo,* in which the second part is *Aquilo,* the north wind.

Europa (Europe). In classic myth, a daughter of Agenor, or, according to the *Iliad,* daughter of Phoenix. She was famed for her beauty. Zeus in the form of a white bull carried her off and swam with her to the island of Crete. She was the mother of Minos, Rhadamanthus, and Evandros or Sarpedon, and, according to some forms of the legend, of the Minotaur.

Europeans, The (1878). A novel by Henry JAMES. The plot centers about the visit of "the Europeans," Felix Young, an artist, and his sister Eugenia, the morganatically married Baroness Muenster whose husband is about to repudiate their marriage, to the farm of their New England relatives, the Wentworths. The Europeans hope to gain much from their American cousins; the baroness futilely tries to make a wealthy marriage, and Felix paints portraits of the Bostonians he meets, eventually marrying a kinswoman who is eager to escape from her bleak environment. James tends to treat his themes here comically, and although he portrays the Wentworths' moral solidity with respect, he nevertheless calls attention to their provincialism and timidity.

Euryanassa. See TANTALUS.

Eurydice. See ORPHEUS.

Eurylochus (Eurylochos). In classic myth, the only companion of Odysseus whom CIRCE was unable to change into a hog.

Eurystheus. In Greek mythology, a king of Mycenae, and cousin of HERACLES. On the urging of Hera, or for some other reason, he imposed upon that hero his twelve famous labors.

Eurytion. (1) A centaur. In Greek legend, at the marriage feast of Pirithous, King of the LAPITHS, with Hippodamia, he became intoxicated and offered violence to the bride, thus causing the celebrated battle of the Lapiths and Centaurs.

(2) Eurytion was also the name of the giant guarding Geryon's castle slain by HERACLES.

Eusebius of Caesarea (260?–?340). A theologian, called the "father of ecclesiastical history." He wrote a Christian Church history in 10 books and also a universal history.

Eustace and Hilda. A trilogy by L. P. Hartley, consisting of *The Shrimp and the Anemone* (1944, U.S. title *The West Window*), *The Sixth Heaven* (1946), and *Eustace and Hilda* (1947). In the first book Eustace, as a little boy, tries ineffectually to rebel against his emotionally dominating elder sister. In *The Sixth Heaven,* as a student at Oxford, he tries to rid himself of Hilda by encouraging a romance between her and one of his schoolfellows. In the last book, after Hilda has been seduced, deserted, and has had a mental breakdown, Eustace restores her to health at the cost of his own life. Their relationship is emphasized by symbolic imagery. As a child Eustace is shown watching a sea anemone (Hilda) devouring a shrimp (himself); the shrimp struggles free, carrying the anemone's entrails with him.

Eustace Diamonds, The (1873). A novel by Anthony Trollope. It is the story of the beautiful, mendacious Lady Elizabeth Eustace who tries to keep a valuable diamond necklace she had from her husband before he died. Since it is a family heirloom, the Eustace family tries to retrieve it. Lady Elizabeth fails in her attempt to keep it, is humiliated, and marries the dubious Mr. Emilius, an apparent bigamist.

Eustazio (Eustache of Bouillon). In Tasso's epic poem Gerusalemme Liberata, the younger brother of Goffredo (Godfrey), the Christian commander. He opposes his brother, urging the Crusaders to help the enchantress Armida regain her kingdom. Later he becomes her slave until released by Rinaldo of Este.

Euterpe. One of the 9 Muses, the inventor of the double flute. She was the muse of Dionysiac music, patroness of joy and pleasure, and of flute-players.

Evadne. (1) In Greek legend, wife of Capaneus. She threw herself on the funeral pile of her husband, and was consumed with him.

(2) Name of one of the principal characters of Beaumont and Fletcher's drama, *The Maid's Tragedy* (1610). The sister of Melantius, Aminotor was compelled by the King to marry her, although he was betrothed to Aspasia, the "maid" whose death forms the tragic event of the drama.

Evangeline, A Tale of Acadie (1847). A narrative poem by Henry Wadsworth Longfellow. The lovers, Gabriel Lajeunesse and Evangeline Bellefontaine, are separated when the British expel the Acadians from Nova Scotia. He is carried to Louisiana, and she to New England. The two spend years searching for one another. Nursing the sick in an epidemic in Philadelphia, she recognizes him as the dying man in her care. Now an old woman, Evangeline also dies, and the two are buried together.

Evan Harrington (1860). A novel by George Meredith. The hero, Evan Harrington, is the son of Melchisedec Harrington, the tailor, "the great Mel." Mel, who is ambitious, has succeeded in marrying his three daughters into good society, and with their assistance proposes to make a gentleman of Evan. Through the scheming manipulations of his sister the Countess de Saldar, "the most consummate liar in literature," Evan is introduced under false pre-

tenses among the guests at a house party at the home of the high-born Rose Jocelyn. Evan and Rose fall in love; she half suspects the truth; he tries to confess it. Meantime "the great Mel" has died, leaving huge debts, and the sensible and forthright Mrs. Mel makes every effort to persuade her son to assume the business. The truth comes out at last, but the romance survives the shock.

Evans, Caradoc (1883–1945). Welsh novelist, playwright, and journalist. He wrote scathing satires on Welsh life: *My Neighbors* (1919), *Nothing to Pay* (1930), *Wasps* (1933) and *This Way to Heaven* (1934).

Evans, Mary Ann. See George Eliot.

Evans, Maurice (1901–   ). English-born American actor. He scored a great success in performances of Shakespeare's plays directed by Margaret Webster, and in Shaw's *Man and Superman*. Though usually at his best in roles calling for great vitality, he was particularly moving as Richard II.

Evans, Nathaniel (1742–1767). Colonial American poet. Born in Philadelphia, where he attended a Moravian boarding school, Evans later went to England, where he was ordained a minister in the Society for the Propagation of the Gospel. Settling in Haddonfield, N.J., he wrote gifted Spenserian and Miltonic verse, collected after his death and published in 1772 as *Poems on Several Occasions*. He was a protégé of William Smith and a close friend of Thomas Godfrey, to whom he dedicated some poems.

Evans, Sir Hugh. In Shakespeare's Merry Wives of Windsor, a pedantic Welsh parson and schoolmaster of extraordinary simplicity and native shrewdness.

Evans, William (d. 1632). An English giant, nearly 8 feet tall. A porter of Charles I, he carried Sir Jeffrey Hudson, the queen's dwarf, in his pocket. Sir Walter Scott wrote of him in *Peveril of the Peak* (1823).

Eve (from Heb., *hawwāh*, life). The 1st woman, the wife of Adam, and "the mother of all living" (Gen. 3:20). Because Eve persuaded Adam to eat the forbidden fruit in the Garden of Eden, her name is often used as a synonym for a temptress. See Adam and Eve.

Evelina, or The History of a Young Lady's Entrance into the World (1778). A novel by Fanny Burney. After having been brought up in the country by Reverend Arthur Villars, a friend of her grandfather, Evelina Anville is sent to live in London with Villars' friend Lady Howard. Here Evelina is introduced to the ways of society. Though courted by Sir Clement Willoughby, whom she recognizes for the rake that he is, she prefers the gentlemanly Lord Orville. However, they are kept apart by numerous misunderstandings and by the mystery and stigma surrounding Evelina's birth; she turns out to be the daughter of Sir John Belmont and all ends happily.

Evelyn, John (1620–1706). English diarist and miscellaneous writer. A man whose interests ranged from gardening to numismatics, Evelyn held a number of offices under Charles II and was a prominent member of the Royal Society. His varied background and participation in the political events of his day lend interest and importance to his *Diary* (1818) which covers the years from 1640 to 1706.

Eve of St. Agnes, The (1819). A poem by John KEATS. It is based on the legend that on the Eve of St. Agnes, young maidens are allowed a glimpse of their future husbands. Porphyro thus comes to Madeline on St. Agnes' Eve and soon they depart into the timeless world of love. Some of Keats's most striking sensuous imagery is found in this poem.

Eve of St. John, The (1800). A ghostly romantic ballad by Sir Walter SCOTT.

Everdene, Bathsheba. See FAR FROM THE MADDING CROWD.

Everlasting Mercy, The (1911). A narrative poem by John MASEFIELD. It describes the redemption of a drunken villager. It was a popular success and influenced other poets. The GEORGIAN poets were influenced by its rural setting, and younger, experimental poets admired its sometimes harsh and colloquial language and its occasional use of oaths.

Ever Victorious Army, the. See Charles George GORDON.

Everyman (c. 1500). Most famous of the MORALITY PLAYS, probably translated into English from the Dutch *Elckerlijk* (1495). When Everyman receives a summons from Death, he tries vainly to persuade his friends Fellowship, Kindred, Worldly Goods, Beauty, and others to journey with him; but only Good Deeds remains faithful, although so weak because of Everyman's neglect that Knowledge and

Title page of the morality play *Everyman* (c. 1500).

Confession must renew his strength so that he can accompany Everyman to the grave. The subtitle reads "A Treatise how the hye Fader of Heven sendeth Dethe to somon every creature to come and gyve a counte of theyr lyves in this Worlde."

Hugo von HOFMANNSTHAL's *Jedermann* (1911) is a reworking of the play into German verse.

Every Man in His Humour (1598). A comedy by Ben JONSON. A familiar classic plot is used as a vehicle for the study of a series of characters, each of whom is possessed by a particular HUMOUR or dominating characteristic. The plot, which is rife with incident and misunderstanding, concerns the efforts of Young Kno'well and Wellbred to escape or contain the displeasure of their father and brother-in-law respectively. The characters to whom the title applies are: Captain Bobadil, whose humour is bragging of his brave deeds and military courage, and who is thrashed as a coward by Downright; Kitely, whose humour is jealousy of his wife and who is befooled and cured by a trick played on him by Brainworm; Stephen, whose humour is verdant stupidity and who is played on by everyone; Kno'well, whose humour is suspicion of his son; Dame Kitely, whose humour is jealousy of her husband, but she, like him, is cured by a trick devised by Brainworm.

The play exists in two versions, the first of which uses Italian names and places. A sequel, *Every Man Out of His Humour* (1599), has even less coherency of plot but presents a rich collection of the foibles of the time.

Everyman's Library. A series of books, popularly priced, including, among its hundreds of titles, most of the best works of the greatest authors of the past. The idea of the library was conceived by Ernest Rhys, and the first fifty titles appeared in 1905.

Evil May Day. The name given to the 1st of May, 1517, when the young apprentices in London rioted against the French residents of the city. A serious riot, it was put down only with difficulty. Sir Thomas More, and the earls of Shrewsbury and Surrey were among those helping to quell the riot. Of the thousands of apprentices involved, 278 were arrested, and 15 were hanged, drawn, and quartered. The incident forms the basis of an anonymous Elizabethan play, *Sir Thomas More*.

Ewald or **Evald, Johannes** (1743–1781). A Danish national lyric poet and dramatist. He was the author of the first original Danish tragedy *Rolf Krage* (1770) and the national festival drama, *The Fishers* (1779), containing the song, *King Christian Stood by the Lofty Mast,* which has become a Danish national song.

Ewig-Weibliche, Das. See ETERNAL FEMININE.

Excalibur (OFr., *Escalibor*). The sword of King ARTHUR in Arthurian romance. It is called *Caliburn* by Geoffrey of Monmouth, and *Caledvwlch* in the *Mabinogion*. There is in Irish legend a famous sword called *Caladbolg,* a name that is thought to mean "hard belly," i.e., capable of consuming anything; this and the name Excalibur are probably connected.

The way that Arthur gains the sword is variously told in Arthurian legend. In some versions, Excalibur is the sword, magically fixed in a stone, that can be withdrawn only by one who is the rightful king of England, and Arthur proves to be the only knight that can pull the sword from the stone. In Malory's

Morte d'Arthur (c. 1469), Excalibur is a gift to Arthur from the LADY OF THE LAKE. After the last battle, when Arthur lies mortally wounded, he commands Sir Bedivere to return Excalibur to the lake. Sir Bedivere throws it into the water, and an arm, clothed in white samite, appears to receive it.

Excursion, The. A long didactic poem by William WORDSWORTH, forming part of *The Recluse* (1814). It includes discussions of virtue, religious faith, the industrial revolution and its social effects, and the education of children.

Exemplary Novels. See NOVELAS EJEMPLARES.

Exeter Book (Codex Exoniensis; c. 975). Collection of manuscripts of Old English poetry, presented to Exeter Cathedral (c. 1070) by Leofric, its first bishop. It includes WIDSITH, THE SEAFARER, THE WANDERER, DEOR'S LAMENT, and a number of poems attributed to CYNEWULF, including *Christ, Juliana,* and the "riddles."

Exiles (1918). A play by James JOYCE. The central character is Richard Rowan, who, like Joyce himself, is an Irish writer who has spent much of his life abroad and feels estranged from Irish society on his return to Dublin. The action concerns various love entanglements between Richard, his common law wife, Bertha, and his friends. It is a naturalistic play, indebted to the work of Ibsen, whom Joyce greatly admired. Only moderately successful on the stage, *Exiles* is chiefly important for the light it throws on the development of Joyce's ideas about the artist's alienation from society.

existentialism. A contemporary movement in philosophy. Although it grew out of the development of the philosophical tradition all over Europe, it was highly popularized in France in the 1940's and is usually associated with the theories expressed by Jean-Paul SARTRE. The beginnings of existentialism are found in the writings of the Danish Søren KIERKEGAARD, the German Friedrich NIETZSCHE, and the Russian Feodor DOSTOEVSKI, although none of them formulated a logical system. The works of the Germans Martin HEIDEGGER and Karl JASPERS were the most immediate influence on Sartre's thinking, along with the method of approach of the phenomenologist Edmund HUSSERL.

All existentialists are concerned with ontology, the study of being. The point of departure is human consciousness and mental processes. In contrast to most previous philosophical systems, which maintain that an *a priori* essence precedes or transcends the individual existence of people or of objects, the existentialists conclude that existence precedes essence. The significance of this for human beings is that the concept that a man has an essential self is shown to be an illusion. A man's self is nothing except what he has become; at any given moment, it is the sum of the life he has shaped until then. The "nothing" he begins with is thus the source of man's freedom, for at each moment it is man's will that can choose how to act or not to act. However, each such decision affects the future doubly: a man is or should be responsible for the consequences of his actions; and each action necessarily excludes the other potential actions for that moment, and their consequences, and thus at least partially limits the potentialities for future actions.

By what standards, then, should man make his decisions? Man's mind cannot discern any meaning for this existence in the universe; when he abandons his illusions, he finds himself horrified by the absurdity of the human condition. The question of the existence of God (or some cosmic purpose) is irrelevant, according to Sartre and the atheistic existentialists, because even if He does exist (which they usually deny), He does not reveal to men the meaning of their life. Thus man must create a human morality in the absence of any known predetermined absolute values. Honesty with oneself is perhaps the major value common to existentialist thinking; all their writings describe the emotional anguish of trying to achieve it. Sartre calls the "man of good faith" one who understands the human condition described above and fully accepts the responsibility of the freedom it entails. The "man of bad faith" accepts illusion, is deliberately hypocritical, or tries to use the excuse of "good intentions" to escape responsibility for the consequences of his actions, the ramifications of which always involve other people. The man of good faith judges a potential action by estimating the result if everyone, not just himself, were to perform it. Yet despite the difficulty of choice, he does not withdraw from life, but is *engagé,* actively engaged in the business of living with himself and with other men.

The Christian existentialists agree that man can never know God's purpose, but they affirm that it exists and that through a "leap of faith" man can establish his values in accordance with it. However, they too describe the anguish and the responsibility of honest action, for a man can never be certain that his decision is actually based on an intuition of the divine and not on the disguised temptation of evil.

Other writers in the existentialist tradition are Gabriel MARCEL, leader of Christian existentialism in France, the Spaniards Miguel de UNAMUNO and José ORTEGA Y GASSET, and the Jewish mystic Martin BUBER.

Albert CAMUS is often classified with the movement, but he considers many of Sartre's postulates as much an unjustifiable "leap of faith" as that of the religious existentialists. His "man of the Absurd" resembles Sartre's "man of good faith" in that both acknowledge man's lonely condition in the face of the silence of the universe; both reject despair and commit themselves to the anguish and responsibility of living as best one can; and both consider the exercise of one's own freedom inseparable from the opportunity for all men to exercise theirs, which is contingent on their freedom from poverty, political oppression, and other avoidable external limitations. However, Camus' writings do not attempt to constitute an organized philosophical system of ontology, as do Sartre's.

exodos. In classical Greek drama, the last choral passage in a tragedy or comedy, recited or sung as the chorus left the orchestra. See PARODOS.

Exodus (*Gr.,* a going out). The escape by the Jews from their bondage in Egypt (c. 1200 B.C.). Led by Moses, they crossed the Red Sea and wandered for 40 years in the Sinai wilderness, finally reaching Canaan. During this time God revealed His name, His laws, and the destiny of Israel. The covenant between God and Israel promised Israel a "land flowing with milk and honey" in return for homage and reverence.

The book of Exodus is the second volume of the Pentateuch. It gives the account of Moses' birth, the Israelites' departure from Egypt, and the beginning of their long journey to Palestine. The 20th chapter of Exodus contains the Ten Commandments.

Exodus is the title of a novel by Leon Uris (1958) about the establishment of the modern state of Israel.

ex pede Herculem. From this sample we may judge of the whole. Literally (*Lat.*), Hercules [may be drawn] from his foot. Plutarch says that Pythagoras calculated the height of Heracles (*Gr.* for the *Lat.* Hercules) by comparing the lengths of various stadia in Greece. A stadium was 600 feet in length, but Heracles' stadium at Olympia was much longer; therefore, said the philosopher, the foot of Heracles was proportionately longer than an ordinary foot; and as the foot bears a certain ratio to the height, so the height of Heracles can be easily ascertained. *Ex ungue leonem* (a lion [may be drawn] from its claw) is a similar phrase.

expressionism. In European art, a movement beginning about 1900, in which strong expression of the artist's subjective feelings becomes all important. The expressionist artists sought to portray, not what they perceived from without, as the impressionists did, but only what they felt from within themselves. Moreover, they rejected harmony and beauty as criteria of art, and used violent distortion, instead, in order to represent intense emotions, especially terror, pathos, or agony. The movement flourished mainly in Germany, where it was developed by such groups as *Der* BLAUE REITER (The Blue Rider) and *Die* BRÜCKE (The Bridge). Major expressionist artists include the Norwegian painter Edvard Munch (1863–1944); the German sculptor Ernst Barlach (1870–1938); and the Austrian painter Oskar Kokoschka (1886–   ). The roots of expressionistic style may be found in earlier European art, for example, the turbulent lines and violent colors used by van Gogh, the fantastic caricatures in Goya's graphic work, and the contorted forms of Grünewald's religious art.

In reference to literature, expressionism denotes a movement, from about 1910 to 1925, closely akin to the corresponding movement in art. Basically, the expressionists tended to stress the individual's *will* and the *expression* of purely internal visionary experience, as opposed to the emphasis in impressionism and symbolism upon the individual's more or less passive *reception* of experience, and the emphasis in naturalism upon thorough objectivity. Expressionism made its first major breakthrough in the field of lyric poetry with such figures as Georg Trakl, Georg Heym, Franz Werfel and Ernst Stadler, whose verses are fired with an ecstatic, hymnlike quality and written in a language that seeks to compress as much concentrated meaning in as small a space as possible. Expressionist drama, likewise, takes compression as one of its principal goals: everything not immediately necessary for expressing the play's central idea is omitted; the external world is merely sketched in; the dramatis personae are not characters but types, without fully developed personalities and often without names; the successive scenes are often connected only by ideas, not by any continuity of action; and the dialogue is often compressed into a "telegram-style." Major playwrights include Georg Kaiser, Reinhard Sorge, Walter Hasenclever, Ernst Toller, Fritz Unruh, Ernst Barlach, and Bertolt Brecht in his earlier work. Narrative prose, finally, did not come into its own as an expressionist medium until after the movement had passed its peak. Major figures are Leonhard Frank, Alfred Döblin, and again, Franz Werfel. In terms of history and politics, expressionism may be seen as a continuation of the satirical rejection of complacent bourgeois values begun by such writers as Sternheim and Frank Wedekind; then, with the coming of World War I, most of the expressionists took a strong pacifistic stand. After the war, several of the most powerful figures, including Kaiser, Toller, and Brecht, came out for social revolution; but by the mid-20's, revolutionary fervor had, for the most part, given way to a resigned skepticism or even outright cynicism, and expressionism was past.

Expurgatory Index. See INDEX, THE.

Eyck, Hubert van (1366?–1420) and **Jan van** (1390?–1441). The founders of the Flemish school of painting. The brothers van Eyck are reputed to have originated the modern process of oil painting. The only known authentic work by Hubert's hand is the celebrated altarpiece, the *Adoration of the Lamb* at Ghent, which was completed by Jan. A polyptich containing over 20 panels, it is generally considered one of the great masterpieces of Western art, in its magnificence of color, skillful handling of light and atmosphere, and deeply religious tone. Both men were artists of keen observation, rendering with vigorous realism and infinite detail the world they saw around them, whether the beauty of flowers, trees, and common objects or the richness of materials and jewels. Through the artistic genius of their religious paintings and portraits and their technical innovations, the brothers van Eyck exerted an enormous influence, revolutionizing painting in northern Europe by breaking with the Gothic tradition and instituting a new realistic vigor.

Eyeless in Gaza (1936). A novel by Aldous HUXLEY. It is about Anthony Beavis, a weak-minded man who spends most of his life behaving badly in a meaningless, valueless world. In middle age he is converted to Huxley's own mystical doctrines. Sunbathing with his mistress on the roof of his house, he is bespattered with blood when a dog falls from a passing plane. Beavis goes to Mexico and meets a mystical anthropologist who converts him to pacifism, vegetarianism, and Eastern mysticism, thereby reshaping his character. The title is from John Milton's *Samson Agonistes,* who was

> Eyeless in Gaza, at the mill, with slaves.

Eyre, Simon (d. 1459). English shoemaker. According to tradition he enjoyed a fast-rising political career and became Lord Mayor of London in 1445. He appears in Thomas Deloney's *The Gentle Craft* and in Thomas Dekker's THE SHOEMAKER'S HOLIDAY.

Ezekiel (6th century B.C.). A Hebrew prophet during the Babylonian Exile. His sermons to Israel are found in the Old Testament book bearing his name. He stresses the moral responsibility of the Jews for their captivity and calls for a return to godliness and faith.

Ezekiel, Nissim (1926–   ). Indian poet writing in English. Editor of *Quest,* an influential "little magazine" (1954–1960), he became associate editor of *Imprint*, a Bombay literary monthly. His books of poetry include *A Time to Change* (1951), *Sixty Poems* (1953), *The Third* (1959), and *The Unfinished Man* (1960).

Ezra. In the Old Testament, a Jewish priest who led a band of 1,500 Jews back to Jerusalem from their captivity in Babylon (c. 390 B.C.). The Old Testament book of Ezra, grouped with Nehemiah in early Hebrew canon, tells about the journey and Ezra's attempts to re-establish the temple and morally purify the Jewish community.

Ezzelin, Sir. In Lord Byron's *Lara* (1814), a gentleman who recognizes Lara as the corsair Conrad. A duel ensues, resulting in the death of Ezzelin. See CORSAIR, THE.

F

Fabian. In Shakespeare's TWELFTH NIGHT, a sharp-witted servant of Olivia and a participant in the merry pranks on Malvolio.

Fabian Society. An association of socialists founded in 1884 by a small group of middle-class intellectuals, including George Bernard Shaw and Sidney Webb. The name is derived from Quintus Fabius (275–203 B.C.), a Roman general who won his way against Hannibal by wariness and caution rather than violence and defiance. See CUNCTATOR.

fable. A short tale, usually epigrammatic, with animals, men, gods, and even inanimate objects as characters. The action of a fable illustrates a moral which is usually (but not always) explicitly stated at the end. This moral often attains the force of a proverb. The fable form appears early in man's cultural development, being a common part of the oral folk literature of primitive tribes. It appeared in ancient Egyptian papyri of c. 1500 B.C., and in Greece a recognizable fable was included in the works of Hesiod in the 8th century B.C.; by far the most famous fables are those attributed to AESOP, a Greek slave who lived about 600 B.C. In India the fable also appeared early, the great Indian collection, the *Panchatantra,* having been composed in the 3rd century. Modern fables have been in the main dominated by the genius and style of LA FONTAINE, the great French fabulist of the 17th century, who wrote fables in polished and witty poetry that have been almost universally translated and imitated. Among the best-known modern fabulists are Gay (England, 17th century); Lessing (Germany, 18th century); and James Thurber (U.S., 20th century).

Fable, A (1954). A novel by William FAULKNER. Set in France during World War I, *A Fable* is both an allegory of the passion of Christ and a study of a world that has renounced individualism and chosen submission to authority and the secular values of power and chauvinism. The novel centers on a young corporal, born in a cow-shed, who enlists in the French army, incites a mutiny, and is eventually executed for cowardice. When the gravesite is struck by an enemy shell, his body disappears. The characters of the novel tend to be either personifications of abstractions or modern versions of biblical figures.

Fable for Critics, A (1848). A long verse satire by James Russell LOWELL. The fable of Apollo and his dealings with an American critic is of little interest; the poem's value is in the witty profiles in verse of leading writers. Among the writers satirized in pungent and accurate sketches are Emerson, Longfellow, Hawthorne, Poe, Cooper, Whittier, Holmes, and Lowell himself. The poet makes the important assertion that American literature has come of age.

Fables choisies, mises en vers (Selected fables, set in verse, 1668, 1678–1679, 1694). A collection of verse fables by Jean de LA FONTAINE. Though freely derived from ancient and modern sources, the fables are stamped with La Fontaine's own gently ironic view of life and society. In colorful and ingenious free verse, by means of animal symbols and spirited dialogues, the author propounds a philosophy of sense and moderation, drawing practical lessons from the tribulations of crows, mice, ants, and the like and holding his fellow men up to affectionate ridicule. The fables, however, are not primarily moralistic in intent, but graceful and worldly stories told for the pleasure of telling.

Fables in Slang (1899). A collection of sketches by George ADE that first appeared in the Chicago *Record.* Humorous tales illustrating the common sense of ordinary people, the *Fables* won attention for their rendering of contemporary American speech. Ade's "slang," however, is not slang, but a picturesque prose with numerous racy colloquialisms and many luxuriant figures of speech.

fabliaux (12th–14th centuries). Short humorous tales, often ribald or scurrilous. Highly popular in the Middle Ages, they are situation comedies burlesquing the weaknesses of human nature; women, priests, and gullible fools are often the butts of the buffoonery, which sometimes becomes savagely bitter. The material derives from the oral folk tradition of bawdy anecdotes, practical jokes, and clever tricks of revenge, but the term *fabliau* was first specifically applied to a medieval French literary form, a narrative of 300–400 lines in octosyllabic couplets. About 150 of these are still extant. Similar prose tales became popular all over Europe, as in Boccaccio's *Decameron.* Apparently only a few narratives in the style of the *fabliau* were written in England; the most notable are the ones Chaucer included in his *Canterbury Tales,* such as the tales told by the Miller, the Reeve, the Friar, the Summoner, and the Shipman.

Fabre, Jean Henri (1823–1915). French naturalist. Fabre is the author of *Souvenirs entomologiques* (1879–1907), a 10-volume work on insect life. After his death, his laboratory became a national museum.

Fabriano, Gentile da (c. 1370–1428). Italian painter. His is a delicate and richly patterned style, Gothic in its attention to detail and incident, but Renaissance in its assimilation of contemporary themes and techniques. His best-known works include *The Flight into Egypt* and the *Adoration of the Magi.*

Fabricius, Gaius (d. c. 270 B.C.). Roman hero, famed for his honesty and incorruptibility. In Rome's struggle with King Pyrrhus of Epirus, he was sent as envoy to the enemy camp for the exchange of prisoners. There he was offered casks of gold and jewels if he would divulge state secrets. When bribery failed, the king ordered a flap of his tent opened, revealing a gigantic elephant only inches from the Roman envoy. Through both trials, Fabricius stood undismayed. When he departed, he left Pyrrhus with a striking example of Roman honor and bravery.

Fâcheux, Les (**The Bores**, 1661). The first COMÉDIE-BALLET by MOLIÈRE. Written in haste for a royal fete, it is based on satires of Horace and Régnier. The play depicts the maddening interruptions of the hero's courtship by an endless variety of bores, most of them drawn from the author's own observation. The production was enormously successful and started the fashion for *comédie-ballet*.

factotum (Lat., *facere totum*, to do everything). One doing for his employer all sorts of services. Sometimes called a *Johannes Factotum*. Formerly the term meant a busybody, or much the same as our Jack-of-all-trades, and it is in this sense that Robert GREENE used it in his famous reference to Shakespeare:

There is an upstart Crow beautified with our feathers, that with his *Tygers hart wrapt in a Players hyde*, supposes he is as well able to bumbast out a blanke verse as the best of you: but being an absolute *Johannes fac totum*, is in his owne conceit the onely Shake-scene in a countrie. (*Groatsworth of Wit*, 1592)

Facundo (1845). The popular title of a book by Domingo Faustino SARMIENTO. Its full title is *Civilización y barbarie, Vida de Juan Facundo Quiroga*. One of the classics of Hispanic-American literature, the book is partly an attack on the dictatorship of Juan Manuel de ROSAS, partly a somewhat fanciful biography of Facundo, an Argentine political boss, and partly a sociological analysis of Argentine society. Argentina's troubles, Sarmiento believed, stemmed from the conflict between the civilization of the Europeanized urban classes and the barbarism of the ignorant, untamed gauchos, as exemplified by Rosas and Facundo. Written in a vigorous, spontaneous style, the work is also famous for its description of the Argentine pampas and of gaucho types, such as the outlaw and the tracker. *Facundo* was first translated into English by Mary Tyler Mann, wife of Horace Mann, who was a good friend of Sarmiento.

Fadeyev, Aleksandr Aleksandrovich (1901–1956). Russian novelist. His early novel, *The Rout* (*Razgrom;* 1927), also translated as *The Nineteen*, reintroduced the psychological realism of the 19th-century novel into Soviet literature. Fadeyev's novel came after a number of so-called proletarian works, which often were little more than tedious documentation of socialist construction without human characters or concerns. His story of a band of Red partisans fighting in the Far East contains both excitement and psychological portraits of the characters that make them vivid to the reader. Fadeyev's next work, *The Last of the Udegs* (*Poslednyi iz Udege;* 1928–1936), also set during the Civil war in the Far East sector of the fighting front, was not as successful. His third work, *The Young Guard* (*Molodaya gvardiya;* 1945), depicted underground resistance

of young Communists living under the German occupation. The book was criticized for not stressing the leading role of the Communist Party in the resistance; and Fadeyev dutifully revised the work. From 1939 to 1953, he was secretary of the Union of Soviet Writers, a post from which he was moved after Stalin's death. Fadeyev committed suicide in 1956.

Faerie Queene, The (Books I–III, 1590; IV–VI, 1596). An allegorical epic poem by Edmund SPENSER. *The Faerie Queene* was conceived as a work of 12 books, each of which was to have portrayed, in the person of its leading knight, one of the 12 private moral virtues; the work as a whole was to be unified by the figure of Prince Arthur, the "image of a brave knight," in whom all these virtues were perfected. In the prefatory letter to Sir Walter Raleigh, Spenser indicated that, if the first 12 books were well received, he would go on to "frame the other part of politic virtues" in Arthur after he became king. However, only 6 books of 12 cantos each and 2 additional cantos on Mutability (publ. 1609) were published, the other books, if they existed, possibly having been burned in the fire that destroyed Spenser's castle at Kilcoman in 1598.

Gloriana, the Faerie Queene, signifies both the abstract concept of Glory and Queen Elizabeth in particular. Drawing heavily from the chivalric romances, Spenser has Prince Arthur see her in a vision and

The Red Cross Knight (*The Faerie Queene*, 1598 ed.).

determine to "seek her out in Faeryland." Gloriana is holding her annual 12-day feast, on each day of which one of the 12 adventures which were to form the 12 proposed books was to begin. Following the traditional epic form, *The Faerie Queene* begins not with the scene of the feast and the begging of the first knight for a boon, but *in medias res,* with the knight already setting out on his adventure.

As a religio-political allegory of the times, *The Faerie Queene* presents aspects of Roman Catholicism in the evil figures of the false Duessa and the wicked enchanter Archimago (Bks. I and II), and attacks the Catholic emperor Philip of Spain, England's greatest enemy, as the tyrant Grantorto (Bk. V); Duessa, executed by Queen Mercilla (Elizabeth) in Book V, here figures as the Catholic Mary, Queen of Scots. The moral allegory is explored in the trials and temptations undergone by the knights representing the virtues. The spiritual allegory of man's quest for salvation is carried on throughout by the structure of the chivalric quest-motif. In each book, the leading knight is associated with a particular virtue.

Book I: The Legend of the Red Cross Knight, or of Holiness. The RED CROSS KNIGHT (Holiness), having put on the Christian armor mentioned by St. Paul, is sent by Gloriana to rescue the parents of the virgin UNA (Truth), who have been imprisoned and their kingdom laid waste by a Dragon. With Una the Knight comes to the den of Error, a monster half woman and half serpent; after a dreadful battle Error is vanquished. They then meet with ARCHIMAGO (Hypocrisy), a seemingly pious, aged man, and spend the night in his hut. There the Red Cross Knight is subjected to dreams that make him believe Una false, and he abandons her. He comes upon the Saracen knight Sansfoy, accompanied by his lady Fidessa (DUESSA, Falsehood). The Red Cross Knight slays the Saracen and is beguiled by the lies of Fidessa. Thinking to make a garland for her head he plucks a branch from a tree, which bleeds, and which reveals itself to be Fradubio (the Doubter), who had been transformed into a tree by Duessa. Meanwhile Una, following her Knight, meets a Lion, who afterward attends her. She spends the night in the hut of Abessa (Superstition), daughter of Corceca (Blind devotion). Kirkrapine (Churchrobber) comes to bring his plunder to his mistress Abessa, but is slain by the Lion. Una travels on, followed by Archimago in disguise as the Red Cross Knight. He overtakes her and they meet Sansloy, who attacks the disguised Archimago and exposes him, and takes Una off to a wild forest. The real Red Cross Knight, by this time, has come with Duessa to the House of Pride, magnificent in appearance but built on a foundation of sand, and ruled by Queen Lucifera (Pride, and chief of the Seven Deadly Sins). Sansjoy arrives and does battle with the Red Cross Knight, who would have killed him but for the magic intervention of Duessa, who causes Sansjoy to disappear and carries him in the car of Night to the Infernal regions, where he is healed of his wounds by Aesculapius. Meanwhile Una, being attacked by Sansloy, is rescued by a troop of fauns and satyrs. Sir Satyrane (Natural Chivalry) finds her and accompanies her on her journey. They meet Archimago disguised as a pil-grim, who tells them that the Red Cross Knight is dead.

Duessa, having returned from her journey to the Underworld, persuades the Red Cross Knight to drink from an enchanted pool, which robs him of his strength. He is taken captive by the giant Orgoglio (Arrogant pride), who also makes Duessa his mistress. Una learns of her hero's plight, and meeting by chance Prince Arthur, persuades him to go to the Knight's rescue. Arthur slays the giant, strips Duessa of her rich robes and reveals her as a loathsome hag. The Red Cross Knight and Una travel on and soon meet Despair, who tempts the Knight to end his life. He is rescued by Una, who brings him to the house of Holiness to be healed. After this he and Una journey to Eden, the land of her captive parents, and after a three-day battle the Knight slays the Dragon. He and Una are betrothed, but before the marriage can take place Archimago, disguised as a messenger, brings a letter from Duessa, who claims that the Knight is betrothed to her. Their falseness is revealed, Archimago is captured and bound in prison, and Una and her Knight are married.

Book II: The Legend of Sir Guyon, or of Temperance. Archimago, having escaped from his confinement, meets Sir Guyon (Temperance) and a Palmer (Sobriety or Prudence), and tells them that the Red Cross Knight has shamefully attacked a virgin; to insure the desired effect, he has disguised Duessa as a weeping virgin and placed her beside the road, and she complains of her dreadful treatment at the hands of the Knight. They travel on and soon they meet the Red Cross Knight, with whom Sir Guyon almost comes to blows before each recognizes the Christian emblem on the other's shield.

Sir Guyon and the Palmer discover the dying Amavia, who tells them how her dead husband, Sir Mordant, had succumbed to the wiles of the enchantress Acrasia (Intemperance), who lives in the Bower of Bliss on the Wandering Island. Amavia dies, and Guyon swears vengeance. They come to a castle in which live three half-sisters, Medina (Golden Mean), Perissa (Excess), and Elissa (Deficiency). Sir Guyon entrusts to Medina Amavia's infant, which he has named Ruddymane because its hands are stained with its mother's blood. He then meets raging Furor and his mother, the hag Occasion; he silences Occasion, whose constant ranting spurs Furor to anger, by putting a lock on her tongue, and binds Furor with a hundred iron chains. Phaon (or Phedon), the young squire whom Furor had been tormenting, tells how through jealousy and rage he had slain his innocent sweetheart, Claribell, and poisoned Philemon, the friend who deceived him. Pyrocles (Fiery anger) arrives, and he and Sir Guyon fight. Brought to his knees, Pyrocles begs for mercy, and is spared. He unbinds Occasion and Furor, but soon falls a victim to them himself.

Cymocles (Loose living), hearing that his brother Pyrocles is dead, leaves the Bower of Bliss and his mistress Acrasia and travels to find Sir Guyon. He is ferried into the Idle Lake by Phaedria (Wantonness), whose dalliance with him soon makes him forget about revenge. Taking him to the Floating Island, she lulls him to sleep, and returns to the strand where she encounters Sir Guyon seeking a ferry. They meet the awakened and enraged Cymocles, who attacks Guyon, but Phaedria stops their battle. Meanwhile Pyrocles, inflamed by Furor, tries to end his torments by drowning himself in the Idle Lake, but is saved and healed of his fiery wounds by Archimago.

Sir Guyon comes to the den of Mammon, who takes him to the House of Riches, which adjoins Hell. He tries to tempt Guyon to covet his treasure, but the knight refuses all temptations, and asks to be taken back to earth. He is found in a trance by the Palmer just before Pyrocles and Cymocles arrive, bent on vengeance. Thinking him dead, they are about to strip him of his armor when Prince Arthur appears. After a dreadful battle in which both Pyrocles and Cymocles are killed, Guyon revives from his trance and he and Arthur travel to the castle of Alma (the Soul), besieged by the enemies of Temperance. The leader of this rabble is Maleger, the incarnation of evil passions; his twelve troops typify the seven deadly sins and the lusts of the five senses. Arthur gives him terrific battle, but each time Maleger is cast to the ground he rises up even more powerful. Finally Arthur remembers that Earth is Maleger's mother, and restores him each time he falls; so Arthur squeezes the life out of him and throws him in a lake.

After a perilous sea journey Sir Guyon and the Palmer arrive at the Bower of Bliss, where they capture Acrasia in a net, destroy the Bower, and restore to their normal shape the lovers whom Acrasia had transformed into beasts.

Book III: The Legend of Britomart, or of Chastity. Sir Guyon sends the captive Acrasia to the Faery Court, and he and Arthur travel on in search of adventure. Meeting an unknown knight, Guyon charges, but is unhorsed, for the strange knight is the lady Britomart (Chastity), who wields an enchanted lance. When Arthur and Guyon go off to rescue the fair Florimell, pursued by a lustful forester, Britomart remains behind, and soon comes to the Castle Joyous, where she finds six knights attacking one. She learns that the lady of the castle demands the love of every knight who comes that way, and if he loves another he is forced to do battle with the six knights. She subdues them and enters the castle, where Queen Malecasta (Lust), thinking her a man, tries to seduce her.

Meanwhile Arthur's squire, Timias, separated from his master, is ambushed by the lustful forester and his brothers, whom he kills in a bloody battle. Badly injured himself, he is discovered by the virgin huntress Belphoebe. She cures his wounds with herbs, but he pines away from love of her. Florimell, fleeing the forester, comes to the cottage of a wicked witch, whose churlish son lusts after the fair virgin. Again she flees, pursued by a monster sent by the witch, and reaching the sea escapes in a boat in which a fisherman is sleeping. The witch, however, then creates a counterfeit Florimell, who is borne away one day by Braggadocchio, only to have her taken from him by another knight. The true Florimell, out on the sea, resists the advances of the lustful fisherman; her cries bring the help of Proteus, who takes her to his bower at the bottom of the sea.

Meanwhile Sir Satyrane meets the libertine Sir Paridell, and they come to the castle of Malbecco (Jealousy), an aged miser, and his beautiful young wife Hellenore. A cunning seducer, Paridell soon persuades Hellenore to run away with him, but before leaving her husband she steals part of his money and sets fire to the rest. Malbecco, torn between pursuing his wife and rescuing his burning money, knows not what do to. Finally he sets off in search of Hellenore, whom Paridell has by now abandoned and who has gone to live with the satyrs. After watching the satyrs with Hellenore Malbecco is consumed with jealousy, and tries to persuade her to return to him, but she refuses. He returns to his buried treasure, only to find that it has been stolen by the servant of Braggadocchio. Mad with jealousy and fury, he casts himself from a cliff—but he is so consumed by wrath that there is nothing left of him but an airy sprite. He crawls into a cave, where he dwells forever in misery.

Britomart comes upon Scudamore (Shield of Love), who is prostrated with grief that his beloved Amoret is a captive of the enchanter Busirane, who torments her because she will not renounce her love for Scudamore. Britomart promises to rescue Amoret, and she and Scudamore ride to Busirane's enchanted castle, which is guarded by a fire through which only Britomart is able to pass. Having found in the empty but lavishly decorated castle an iron door that will not open, she waits; and at midnight the door flies open and a strange Masque of Cupid passes through it. When the door opens at midnight the next night, she rushes in, finding the room empty save for Amoret, bound to a pillar, and Busirane. The enchanter and Britomart fight, and Busirane is subdued. He is forced to undo his enchantments and restore Amoret to health, and is himself bound in chains.

Book IV: The Legend of Cambel and Triamond, or of Friendship. Amoret and Britomart, in search of Scudamore, meet the knights Blandamour and Paridell, accompanied by Duessa and Ate (Dissension), a foul old hag. Later, Blandamour and Paridell come upon Scudamore, and Paridell attacks him but is badly beaten. Ate lyingly tells Scudamore that she has seen Amoret false to him with Britomart. At this point arrives Sir Ferraugh with the false Florimell he had taken from Braggadocchio. Blandamour, desiring the lovely false Florimell, rides against her knight and captures her. Paridell, egged on by envy and the querulous counsel of Ate, demands that Blandamour share Florimell with him, and the two erstwhile friends come to blows. Later, they come upon the knights Cambel and Triamond and their ladies Cambina and Canace. Canace, a fair and modest lady loved by many, had refused to love any of her suitors; in order to end the strife among her would-be lovers, her brother Cambel agreed to do battle with the stoutest three, the victor to have his sister. The three bravest and boldest were the triplets Priamond, Diamond, and Triamond, sons of Agape. Cambel, protected by a magic ring, was able to slay both Priamond and Diamond; however, their fairy mother had been granted by the Fates that the spirits of the first of her two sons to die would enter the body of the third, so that when Cambel gave the death-stroke to Triamond it failed to kill him. Neither knight could kill the other, and finally their battle was ended by the appearance of the triplets' sister Cambina, who brought peace. Canace was married to Triamond, and Cambina to Cambel.

Together, all agree to go on to the Tournament held by Sir Satyrane in honor of the lost Florimell, whose golden girdle he had found and now offers as a prize to the lady judged the loveliest. The false Florimell is acclaimed the fairest, but the magic cestus, which will girdle only the waists of the virtuous, will not stay fastened.

Meanwhile Scudamore meets Artegal disguised, and both swear vengeance on Britomart, whom they believe has wronged them. They meet her but are both quickly unhorsed. Artegal, fighting her on foot, strikes off her helmet, and seeing her face falls into a rapture of love. Britomart recognizes Artegal's face as the image of her true love she had seen in her magic mirror, and they become betrothed.

The true Florimell, imprisoned in a dungeon by Proteus, still rejects his advances and is true to her beloved Marinell—who has no use for women, and is still suffering from a wound given him by Britomart. Finally his wound is cured by Tryphon, and he and his mother Cymodoce go to the house of Proteus for a great banquet. Marinell chances to overhear Florimell's complaint of her love of him from her dungeon, suddenly falls in love with her, and ultimately has her released.

Book V: The Legend of Artegal, or of Justice. Irena (Ireland) goes to the court of the Faerie Queene to complain of the tyrant Grantorto (Great wrong), who withholds her inheritance. Gloriana sends Artegal (Justice) and with him her own groom Talus (Iron Man). On their journey Artegal kills Pollente, a Saracen who stations himself on the Bridge Perilous and kills and robs travelers, bestowing the spoils on his daughter Munera. Talus then forces his way into the castle stronghold, casts Munera over the wall and into the river, burns the spoils, and destroys the castle utterly. On their way to the wedding of Florimell and Marinell, Artegal and his groom meet Braggadocchio and the false Florimell. Artegal changes armor with Braggadocchio and wins the tournament thus clad. Later, wearing his own armor as victor of the tournament, Braggadocchio presents the false Florimell; Artegal then proclaims Braggadocchio a fraud and confronts the false Florimell with her true image. The false Florimell promptly melts away and vanishes.

Artegal and Talus rescue Terpine from a band of Amazons about to hang him, and besiege the Amazon city. Radigund, the Queen, offers to meet Artegal in single combat, the winner to become the servant of the loser. Artegal, struck with pity at the sight of Radigund's beautiful face, surrenders to her, and is made her thrall. Talus, however, escapes and brings news of Artegal's plight to Britomart, who kills Radigund and frees Artegal. Traveling on, Artegal meets Prince Arthur rescuing Samient, handmaiden to Queen Mercilla (Mercy). On their way to the Queen they encounter the robber Malengin (Guile), who tries to escape by turning himself into various animals, but is captured and killed by Talus. Arriving at the palace, the knights find Queen Mercilla about to dispense justice; Duessa is brought to the bar and charged with having tried to usurp Mercilla's crown, judged guilty, and executed. At this time appear at the palace two sons of Belge, whose land is held by the tyrant Geryoneo, asking Mercilla for aid. Prince Arthur goes off to rescue Belge, slays the

monster, and restores her to her rightful kingdom. Artegal completes his original quest, and frees Irena and conquers Grantorto.

Book VI: The Legend of Calidore, or of Courtesy. Sir Calidore (Courtesy) in pursuit of the Blatant Beast (Slander), finds the fair Pastorella, the foster-daughter of a shepherd, and falls in love with her. Finally he rescues her from brigands and takes her to castle Belgard, ruled by Sir Bellamoure and his wife the fair Claribell. Calidore leaves Pastorella there and continues on his quest for the Beast. Through a distinctive birthmark Pastorella is revealed to be the long-lost daughter of Bellamoure and Claribell. Calidore conquers the Blatant Beast and binds it in chains.

Fafner. In Wagner's DER RING DES NIBELUNGEN, one of the giants who built Valhalla for Wotan. He and his brother Fasolt accept Alberich's golden ring in place of Freya, the price originally agreed on. Fafner kills Fasolt and changes himself into a dragon to guard the hoard which is now his. He is killed by Siegfried. In the Norse sources, Fafnir (not Fafner) has no brother and is guarding Andvari's gold as a venom-breathing dragon from the start.

Fagin. In Charles Dickens' OLIVER TWIST, a villainous old Jew who leads a gang of thieves, mostly boys. These he trains to pick pockets and pilfer. Fagin assumes a suave and fawning manner but is grasping, tried, and full of cruelty. He is ultimately arrested, tried, and condemned to death. Fagin is one of Dickens' most famous characters.

Faguet, Emile (1847–1916). French literary critic and professor of literature at the Sorbonne. Faguet published several volumes of French literary history and several critical studies as *Les Grands Maîtres du XVII siècle* (1885).

Fahrenheit, Gabriel Daniel (1686–1736). German physicist who devised the thermometer scale that bears his name. On the Fahrenheit thermometer, the freezing and boiling points of water are designated as 32° and 212° above the zero of its scale.

Fairfax, Edward (d. 1635). English poet and translator. Fairfax is remembered as the author of the first complete translation of Tasso's *Jerusalem Delivered*. Published in 1600, it was called *Godfrey of Bulloigne, or the Recoverie of Jerusalem,* and was written in heroic couplets and characterized by rich and imagistic language. Fairfax also wrote eclogues, most of which have never been published.

Fairfax, Thomas. 3rd Baron **Fairfax of Cameron** (1612–1671). English military leader and statesman. As commander-in-chief of the Parliamentary forces, he organized the New Model Army and defeated Charles I at Naseby. Less able in civilian affairs, he became an instrument in the hands of stronger men and reluctantly acquiesced to the execution of the king. He later participated in negotiations for the Restoration and headed the commission dispatched to Charles II at The Hague.

Fair God, The (1873). A historical novel by Lew WALLACE. The book is set in Mexico during the conquest by Cortez, when Montezuma futilely tried to resist the Spaniards. The fair god is Quetzalcoatl, Aztec god of the air. The result of 30 years of research and writing, the book went through 20 editions in 10 years.

Fair Maid of Perth, The (1828). A novel by Sir Walter SCOTT set in the 14th century. The Fair Maid is Catherine Glover, daughter of a glovemaker of Perth, who kisses Henry Smith, the armorer, in his sleep on St. Valentine's Day. Smith proposes marriage, and although Catherine refuses at first, she becomes his wife at the end of the novel. The concurrent plot is the romance of Prince James, son of Robert III of Scotland, and LOUISE, THE GLEE-MAIDEN.

Fair Maid of the West, The: Parts I and II (c. 1631). A romantic drama by Thomas HEYWOOD. It deals with the love of Bess Bridges, a gallant and virtuous barkeep, for Spencer, an adventurer about to embark for the Azores. Hearing that he is dead, she outfits a ship and sails off to bring his body home. She captures a Spanish vessel on which Spencer is being held prisoner, and the two sail for Morocco where the dark King Mullisheg is much taken with the white girl. However, Bess manages to gain the king's consent to her marriage with Spencer.

In Part II, the king tries to seduce Bess but she and Spencer escape, are recaptured, are released, then shipwrecked and separated. Penniless, Bess is rescued by the duke of Florence who tries to make love to her. Eventually though, Spencer turns up and the lovers are reunited.

Faithful Shepherdess, The (1609). A pastoral play by John FLETCHER. (See BEAUMONT AND FLETCHER.) Clorin, the faithful shepherdess, tends the grave of her dead lover and gathers medicinal herbs to benefit mankind. To her is drawn Thenot, who adores her for her loyalty and pines for her so long as she remains indifferent to his pleas. At the opposite pole of behavior are the lusty Amarillis and Cloe, for whom no lover is too forward, and the conniving lechery of the Sullen Shepherd. After many complications in which all the shepherds' and shepherdesses' reactions are tested in various situations, virtue and chastity triumph;—lust and lechery are repudiated.

fakir. In Arabic-speaking Muslim lands, a religious beggar or mendicant. Many are wanderers who attract attention and alms by performing such acts of austerity as lying on beds of nails: others perform menial offices connected, for example, with burials and the cleaning of mosques.

Falerina. In the ORLANDO INNAMORATO of Boiardo, a witch who presides over the enchanted garden of Organga. Here Orlando finds a book that teaches him how to break Falerina's enchantments, and as a result she is forced to do his bidding for a time.

Falerno. An Italian sweet wine. It was grown in what the ancients called *Falernus Ager*, a fertile district some 20 miles north of Naples. It was celebrated by Horace.

Faliero, Marino. See MARINO FALIERO.

Falkberget, Johan Petter (1879–   ). Norwegian novelist. The novel cycle *Christianus Sextus* (6 vols., 1927–1935), his most important work, is set in the mining town of Röros. Although his own early experiences in the mines gave Falkberget an understanding of hardship and suffering, his work is marked by Christian faith and a firm optimism.

Falkenhayn, Erich von (1861–1922). Chief of the German General Staff (1914–1916). The suc-cessor to Helmuth von Moltke, he was dismissed after the unsuccessful attack at Verdun and replaced by Paul von Hindenburg.

Falkner, John Meade (1858–1932). English novelist and antiquarian. *The Lost Stradivarius* (1895) is a story of demoniacal possession in a musical setting. *Moonfleet* (1898) is a boys' adventure tale about smugglers. *The Nebuly Coat* (1903) is a romance in which all Falkner's interests—music, architecture, church history and heraldry—are skillfully combined.

Fall, The (La Chute; 1956). A short novel by Albert CAMUS. A former Parisian lawyer explains to a stranger in an Amsterdam bar his current profession of judge-penitent. His bitter honesty prevented him first from winning his own self-esteem through good deeds, then from exhausting his own self-condemnation through debauchery. Knowing that no man is ever innocent, he is still trying to forestall personal judgment by confession, by judging others, and by avoiding any situation demanding action.

Falla [y Matheu], Manuel [Maria] de (1876–1946). Spanish composer. Spain's first major composer of instrumental music since the 17th century, Falla studied in Paris, was influenced by the impressionist technique of Debussy, and developed a brilliant and individual style of orchestration. Aside from *Noches en los Jardines de España* (Nights in the Gardens of Spain, 1915) and the *Concerto for Harpsichord* (1926), his best known music, all of it Andalusian in coloring, was written for the stage. His operas include *La Vida Breve* (Life is Short, 1905) and EL RETABLO DE MAESE PEDRO (*Master Peter's Puppet Show*, 1923); his ballets include *El Amor Brujo* (Love, the Magician, 1915) and *El Sombrero de Tres Picos* (The Three-Cornered Hat), the latter based on a comedy of Alarcón. Falla's dramatic cantata *Atlántida* was posthumously completed and performed in 1963.

Fallada, Hans. Pen name of **Rudolf Ditzen** (1893–1947). German novelist. Inclined toward EXPRESSIONISM in his youth, he later became known as a sympathetic depictor of the lower classes. He wrote the best-selling *Kleiner Mann—was nun?* (*Little Man, What Now?*, 1932), a novel about Germany during the depression of the 1920's and 1930's.

Fallersleben, Hoffmann von. See August Heinrich HOFFMANN.

Fall of the House of Usher, The (1839). A tale by Edgar Allan POE. A friend visits Roderick Usher in his old family mansion. The two read together, the friend attempting to dispel Roderick's gloom. Usher plays strange music of his own composition and shows his friend one of his paintings. Although his twin sister, Madeline, has been placed in the family vault dead, Usher is convinced she lives. When she suddenly appears in her blood-stained shroud, brother and sister fall dead together. The visitor, hurriedly departing, turns to see the house split asunder and sink into the tarn.

Falls of Princes. A very long poem by John LYDGATE, written in rhyme royal between 1430 and 1438, and first printed in 1494. Based on Boccaccio's *De Casibus Virorum Illustrium*, the poem deals with great men from the time of Richard II (1377–1399) and their rise to and decline from fame and power, subject to the fluctuations of fortune. The ghost of each appears before the poet and relates his sufferings.

Falstaff, Sir John. The most famous comic character created by Shakespeare. He appears in HENRY IV: PARTS I and II, and THE MERRY WIVES OF WINDSOR, and his death is given some attention in *Henry V.* Falstaff is a monumentally self-indulgent braggart, the culmination of a line that can be traced back to Plautus' *Miles Gloriosus* and the *capitano* of the *commedia dell'arte.* Falstaff is totally unapologetic: he revels in his lechery and chicanery, lies without scruple and, when caught in a lie, unabashedly seeks to turn everything to his own advantage. But his knavery is so engaging and his lust for life so keen that he has become one of the favorite characters of dramatic literature. He holds forth at the Boar's Head Tavern with a rascally crew that includes Bardolph, Nym, Peto, Pistol, and Prince Hal's companion Poins. Later, commissioned by the king to recruit for the army, he assembles the following company: Ralph Mouldy, Simon Shadow, Thomas Wart, Francis Feeble, and Peter Bull-calf.

familiar. A spirit bound to its master's service by a supernatural tie. It is usually represented in the form of a small animal such as a cat, mouse, or poodle.

Family Reunion, The (1939). A drama in verse by T. S. ELIOT. Combining elements of social comedy and Greek tragedy, it deals with the return of Harry, Lord Monchensey, to his English family home for the birthday of his old mother, Amy. The family think Harry is behaving oddly. Only his wise aunt, Agatha, understands that he has murdered his wife and is seeing the Eumenides, or avenging furies. She tells him that when he was born his father wanted to kill his mother, and would have done so if Agatha had not dissuaded him. Harry is bound to suffer from the family curse, especially in the decaying old family house. Agatha presides over Harry's flight; over the disintegration of the rest of the family; and over Amy's death. Like Sir Henry Harcourt-Reilly and Julia in *The Cocktail Party,* she serves as Eliot's mouthpiece.

fancy. In English romantic aesthetic theory, the clever, playful faculty of mind that combines sensations, observations, impressions—the various materials of art—and brings them to bear in a work of art. It is distinguished from IMAGINATION, notably by S. T. Coleridge in his BIOGRAPHIA LITERARIA, in that fancy does not transcend its material to produce truly inspired literature.

Faneuil Hall. A market house containing an assembly hall in Boston, Mass., given in 1742 to his fellow citizens by the merchant and slave trader Peter Faneuil (1700–1743). After the fire of 1761, it was rebuilt by the city and became the meeting place of American patriots during the Revolution. It is now remembered as "the cradle of liberty."

Fangen, Ronald August (1895–1946). Norwegian novelist, playwright, and critic. In all his work Fangen speaks eloquently and soberly of a Christian solution to the world's problems; he rejects belief in the communist and materialist doctrines popular between the wars. Among his plays are *Synde fald* (1920), *Den forjoettede dag* (1926), and *Som det kunde ha gått* (1925). His novels include *Nogen*

unge mennesker (1929), *Duel* (1932), *På bar bunn* (1936), and *En lysets engel* (*Both are My Cousins,* 1945).

Fanshawe (1828). A novel by Nathaniel HAWTHORNE, published anonymously. Fanshawe, a pale, serious student, falls in love with Ellen Langdon, the ward of Dr. Melmoth, president of Harley College. Rescuing her from an attempted seduction, Fanshawe gives Ellen up to the man he knows she loves, and soon dies. The college and its environs are modeled on Hawthorne's *alma mater,* Bowdoin College, in Maine. Influenced by Scott and the Gothic novel, *Fanshawe* illustrates Hawthorne's developing technique.

Fantine. One of the principal characters in Victor Hugo's novel LES MISÉRABLES. She is the mother of Cosette.

Faraday, Michael (1791–1867). English chemist and physicist. As a journeyman bookbinder he heard a lecture by Sir Humphry Davy who impressed him so deeply that he resolved to turn all his attention to the natural sciences. He became one of the greatest chemists of his time and a pioneer in the young science of electricity. His publications are numerous. His monograph on candles deserves to rank as a classic in popular scientific literature.

Farange, Maisie. See WHAT MAISIE KNEW.

farce. An exaggerated type of comedy, full of ludicrous incidents and expressions. The word is the OFr. *farce,* stuffing (from Lat. *farcire,* to stuff); originally meaning a passage in the vernacular inserted in a Latin text or liturgy, the farce in medieval France came to resemble the earlier FABLIAUX, but specifically for dramatic representation. Like *La Farce de maistre Pierre* PATHELIN, the most famous, most farces were written in octosyllabic couplets, and burlesqued the foibles and vices of ordinary life, setting the pattern for future French comedy.

Farewell Address (Sept. 17, 1796). The address prepared by George WASHINGTON just before his retirement from the presidency. Probably written with the aid of Hamilton and Madison, it was never delivered publicly. In it Washington explained his reasons for refusing to run for a third term and warned against the dangers of the party system. He advised the U.S. to avoid permanent alliances with foreign nations and to trust to "temporary alliances for extraordinary emergencies." It did not contain the phrase "entangling alliances," with which it is often associated and which appeared in Jefferson's first inaugural address.

Farewell to Arms, A (1929). A novel by Ernest HEMINGWAY. It deals with the romance of Frederic HENRY, an American lieutenant in the Italian ambulance service during World War I, and Catherine Barkley, an English nurse. She becomes pregnant, and after the disastrous Italian retreat from Caporetto (superbly described by Hemingway), Henry deserts, joins Catherine, and escapes with her to Switzerland, where she dies in childbirth. This is one of the best-known novels depicting the tragedy and destruction of World War I.

Far from the Madding Crowd (1874). A novel by Thomas HARDY. Bathsheba Everdene is loved by Gabriel Oak, a young farmer who becomes bailiff of the farm she inherits; by William Boldwood, who owns a neighboring farm; and by Sergeant Troy, a handsome, inconsiderate young adventurer. She marries Troy, who mistreats her and squanders her money. When he leaves her and is presumed drowned at sea, Bathsheba becomes engaged to Boldwood. Troy however reappears, and is murdered by Boldwood, who goes mad as a result of his action and is sent to an institution instead of being sentenced. Bathsheba then marries Gabriel, the steadiest and most faithful of her three suitors.

Fargue, Léon-Paul (1876–1947). French poet. His early works reflect the influence of Mallarmé's symbolist salons. Fargue moves through a surrealist concern with the reality of the dream world to an eerily melancholy expression of the poetry of modern city life. His style varies from regular verse to poetically rich prose in such works as *Tancrède* (1911), *Espaces* (1921), *D'après Paris* (1931), and *La Piéton de Paris* (1939).

Farigoule, Louis. See Jules ROMAINS.

Farinelli (real name **Carlo Broschi**; 1705–1782). Italian castrato soprano, the most famous singer of the 18th century.

Farmer George. King George III of England (1738–1820), who reigned from 1760 to his death; so called from his farmerlike manners, taste, dress, and amusements.

> A better farmer ne'er brushed dew from lawn.
> —Byron, *Vision of Judgment*

Farnol, [John] Jeffery (1878–1952). English writer of popular historical romances, such as *The Broad Highway* (1910) and *The Amateur Gentleman* (1913).

Farquhar, George (1678–1707). English comic dramatist of the early 18th century. His plays reveal the growing taste for sentiment, which was beginning to replace the brilliance and wit of the Restoration. His best-known plays are THE BEAUX' STRATAGEM, *The Recruiting Officer* (1706) and *The Constant Couple* (1699).

Farrago, Captain. See MODERN CHIVALRY.

Farrar, Geraldine (1882–). American dramatic soprano. She knew many roles but was most famous as Carmen and Madama Butterfly. She acted in several silent films. *Such Sweet Compulsion* (1938) is her autobiography.

Farrell, James T[homas] (1904–). American novelist. Known for his lengthy studies of lower-middle-class Irish-Catholic life, Farrell was born in the South Side section of Chicago, which forms the background for his own works. His stories dealing with STUDS LONIGAN began to appear in 1932; they aroused heated controversy, for Farrell practiced a frankly naturalistic mode of writing that did not hesitate to unveil the crudities of life among the people of his novels. The characters of the novels, which sometimes use a stream-of-consciousness technique, are presented with what is often a sociologist's objectivity. The emphasis is on poverty, religious bigotry, economic inequality, individual frustration, vice, and the destructive influence of environment. Some critics assert that the very dreariness and turgidity of Farrell's style has defeated the author's aim, but others praise the powerful, cumulative effect of personal tragedy that distinguishes Farrell's most famous work; the Studs Lonigan trilogy, which is comprised of *Young Lonigan, The Young Manhood of Studs*

Lonigan, and *Judgment Day.* Five other novels concern Danny O'NEILL. Farrell's *Note on Literary Criticism* (1936) is one of the most important literary statements of the "proletarian" point of view of the 1930's. *The Silence of History* (1963) also deals with an Irish-American youth in Chicago in the 1920's.

fasces. In ancient Rome, a symbol of authority. They were bundles of birch or elm rods fastened together by a red strap with the blade of an ax projecting from the bundle. The *fasces* were carried by the left hand, on the left shoulder by the LICTORS who accompanied magistrates. The rods and the ax represented the king's authority to punish or execute criminals. Within the city of Rome, the ax was removed in recognition of the accused's right to appeal to the people in the matter of life and death.

Benito Mussolini's Fascist Party, which controlled Italy from 1922 to 1944, used the *fasces* as its emblem. Fasces have appeared on U.S. coins and adorn many government buildings.

fascism. An authoritarian and totalitarian political system characterized by aggressive nationalism and the absolute sovereignty of the state over individual rights and interests. Its principles were put into practice by Benito MUSSOLINI and his Fascist Party in Italy. See Vilfredo PARETO; NAZI.

Fasolt. See FAFNER.

Fast, Howard (1914–). American novelist and short-story writer. Born in New York City, he is known for his vivid historical novels, many of which espouse radical political causes. *Citizen Tom Paine* (1943) and *Freedom Road* (1944) avowedly grew out of his association with the Communist Party. Fast later broke with communism, describing his disillusionment in *The Naked God* (1957). Among his better-known novels are *The American* (1946), a sympathetic treatment of Governor John Peter Altgeld of Illinois, and *Spartacus* (1958), a portrayal of the Roman revolutionary leader.

Fastnachtsspiel (*Ger.,* Shrovetide-play). A form of simple, often slapstick, comedy with a clear moral message, current in Germany in the 15th and 16th centuries. The earliest example, however, comes from the 13th century, and the origins of the form are thought to go back to spring fertility rites among the Germanic tribes. Hans SACHS is considered to have perfected the form.

fata (*It.,* a fairy). A female supernatural being introduced in Italian medieval romance, usually under the sway of DEMOGORGON. In ORLANDO INNAMORATO we meet with the "Fata Morgana" (see MORGAN LE FAY); in Boiardo, with the "Fata Silvanella," and others.

Also called *Fata Morgana* is a sort of mirage in which objects are reflected in the sea, and sometimes on a kind of aerial screen high above it. It is occasionally seen in the neighborhood of the Straits of Messina, and named from Morgan le Fay, who was fabled by the Norman settlers in England to dwell in Calabria.

fatal raven. The emblem on the Danish standard, *Landeyda*, which was consecrated to the war god Odin. It was said to have been woven and embroidered in one noontide by the daughters of Regner Lodbrok, son of Sigurd. If the Danish arms were destined to defeat, the raven hung his wings; if victory was to attend them, he stood erect and soaring, as if inviting the warriors to follow.

Fates, the (*Gr.*, moirai; *Lat.*, parcae or fata). In Greek mythology, 3 daughters of Nyx (Night). They controlled the destinies of men. Originally birth-goddesses, the Fates came to be represented as three old women who spun the thread of life. They were identified by Hesiod as Clotho (or Kloto), who spun the thread; Lachesis, who measured it out; and Atropos, who cut it. Generally, even Zeus himself is subject to their decisions.

Father, The (1887). A play by August STRINDBERG. Dealing with the psychological antagonism between men and women, *The Father* centers on the Captain and his inability to prevent the female members of his family from subjugating him. His wife, Laura, torments him by leading him to suspect that Bertha is not his daughter, spreads rumors that he is insane, and finally succeeds in driving him mad and to his death.

Father Brown. A Catholic priest and detective, hero of a series of stories by G. K. CHESTERTON.

Fathers and Children or **Fathers and Sons** (Ottzy i deti; 1862). A novel by Ivan TURGENEV. it portrays the conflicts between the older aristocratic generation and the new democratic intelligentsia in Russia during the 1860's. The chief character is the nihilist BAZAROV, who espouses a strictly materialistic attitude toward life. His chief adversary is Pavel Petrovich KIRSANOV, an uncle of Bazarov's friend Arkadi, who upholds the aristocratic traditions in the face of Bazarov's ridicule. The novel, which is considered one of Turgenev's finest works, originally aroused widespread controversy in Russia, with both radicals and conservatives denying the accuracy of the portrayal of Bazarov. One side considered it slandered the younger generation; the other accused Turgenev of presenting too favorable a picture of the nihilist. Only Dmitri Pisarev among the radicals accepted the portrayal of Bazarov as accurate.

Father William. A humorous ballad by Lewis CARROLL appearing in ALICE'S ADVENTURES IN WONDERLAND; it is a parody of *The Old Man's Comforts* (1799), a poem by Robert Southey.

Fatima. (1) According to the Koran, the daughter of Muhammad, and one of the 4 perfect women. The other three are Khadijah, the prophet's first wife; Mary, daughter of Imran; and Asia, wife of the Pharaoh drowned in the Red Sea.

(2) The name usually given to the last wife of BLUEBEARD.

(3) A female hermit in the *Arabian Nights* (1548) who was murdered by the African magician as a part of his schemes against Aladdin.

Faulconbridge, Philip. In Shakespeare's KING JOHN, the natural son of Richard I (Coeur de Lion). Leader of John's forces, he is a blunt, fiercely patriotic Englishman who sums up his philosophy in his final speech:

> This England never did, nor never shall,
> Lie at the proud foot of a conqueror,
> But when it first did help to wound itself.
> . . . Nought shall make us rue,
> If England to itself do rest but true.

Faulkner, William (1897–1962). American novelist and short-story writer. Faulkner, who was awarded the Nobel Prize in 1949, is generally recognized as a great American novelist. In his novels, many of them set in the imaginary YOKNAPATAWPHA COUNTY, he created a complex social structure within which he explored the burden of the Southern past, the inability of the Southern aristocracy to meet the demands of modern life, the relations between Negro and white, and the alienation and loneliness that so beset 20th-century man. But more than this he drew an immense gallery of characters, vivid and unforgettable.

Faulkner came from an old Mississippi family, and elements of the family past appear in his books. His great-grandfather Col. William C. Faulkner (who later spelled his name Falkner) wrote a popular romance, *The White Rose of Memphis* (1880). His violent death in 1889 furnished his great-grandson with material for SARTORIS and THE UNVANQUISHED, in which Colonel John SARTORIS is modeled on Colonel Falkner. In 1918, William Faulkner enlisted in the Canadian Air Force but did not see active service. After the war he briefly attended the University of Mississippi and worked at many odd jobs. He published a book of verse, *The Marble Faun*, in 1924 and, with the help of Sherwood Anderson, secured the publication of his first novel, *Soldier's Pay*, the following year. Neither this book nor his second novel, *Mosquitoes* (1927), are considered among Faulkner's best.

In *Sartoris* (1929), Faulkner created Yoknapatawpha County, which was to be the setting for most of his subsequent works. In the same year appeared THE SOUND AND THE FURY, usually considered among Faulkner's masterpieces. Although the styles of the two books are radically different—*The Sound and the Fury* owes much to James Joyce and the stream-of-consciousness technique—both deal with the breakup of old aristocratic Southern families. In As I LAY DYING, Faulkner relates a terrifyingly comic story of a ritualized burial journey. But it was not until SANCTUARY that Faulkner created a sensation and achieved anything like popular success. Faulkner himself did much to mislead the reaction to this novel by suggesting that it was hurriedly written as a mere potboiler. It is true that *Sanctuary* is often grotesquely shocking, but it is, nevertheless, a book of great craft, allegorical in intent.

It was followed by LIGHT IN AUGUST, which relates the agonizing story of Joe Christmas, and the equally brilliant ABSALOM, ABSALOM!, considered by Cleanth Brooks to be Faulkner's best book.

For many critics, *Absalom, Absalom!* marks a high point in Faulkner's development. While *The Unvanquished* has occasionally been highly praised, it is generally considered one of Faulkner's weaker books. THE HAMLET is the first part of the trilogy that now includes *The Town* (1957) and *The Mansion* (1959).

The collection Go DOWN, MOSES AND OTHER STORIES contains the justly famous story *The Bear*. INTRUDER IN THE DUST and REQUIEM FOR A NUN, in some ways a sequel to *Sanctuary*, are generally not thought to be Faulkner at his best. The same judgment has been made of A FABLE, in which Faulkner left Yoknapatawpha County for the French army in World War I. Other works are THESE THIRTEEN, *A Green Bough* (verse, 1933), *Doctor Martino and Other*

Stories (1934), *Pylon* (1935), THE WILD PALMS, KNIGHT'S GAMBIT, and *Big Woods* (stories, 1955).

In the 1930's, many critics saw only the melodramatic violence in Faulkner's writing. It was not until Malcolm Cowley's introduction to *The Portable Faulkner* in 1946 that the continuity and consistency in Faulkner's work, as well as his concern with "the tragic fable of Southern history," were really seen and understood.

Faunus. In Roman mythology, a rural deity, grandson of Saturn and father of Lavinia's father Latinus. He, as well as Silvanus, came to be more and more identified with the Greek PAN, with whom he had many traits in common. His priests were the Luperci, his main festival the LUPERCALIA. When not viewed as an individual, he appeared in the multiformity of the fauns, possibly under the influence of the Greek pans, satyrs, and sileni in their relation with Pan. The fauns were satyrlike beings with tails, horns, goats' legs and feet, and furry, pointed ears. Two festivals called *Faunalia* were held on February 13 and December 5.

Hawthorne wrote a novel, *The Marble Faun* (1860), in which it is hinted that the hero is a faun. It was suggested by the statue of a youthful faun by Praxiteles, now in the Capitoline Museum in Rome. The same title is used by William Faulkner for a collection of verse (1924).

One of the best-known poems of Stéphane Mallarmé is his *L'Après-midi d'un faune* (*Afternoon of a Faun*). Debussy's orchestral tone poem *Prélude à l'après-midi d'un faune* (*Prelude to Afternoon of a Faun*, 1892) became the firm foundation of its composer's fame.

Fauré, Gabriel [Urbain] (1845–1924). French composer, organist, and teacher. He became choir director at the Madeleine in Paris in 1877, and organist in 1896, taught composition at the Paris Conservatoire from 1896, and was its director from 1905 to 1920. His best-known works are the *Requiem Mass* (1887), and many songs, which include settings of poems by Verlaine, Rimbaud, Baudelaire, and Sully Prudhomme. Maurice Ravel was a pupil of his.

Faust. A legendary figure, the subject of many literary works. The historical personage behind all the various Faust legends seems to have been a German necromancer named Georg Faust (1480?–?1538). Bits of his life are known from contemporary testimony, including that of Philipp Melanchthon, but it is impossible to make a complete biography of him. His career was not without success, for he sometimes gained influence in powerful ecclesiastical and worldly courts. The power he enjoyed, combined with the boasting for which he was famous, captured the imagination of many after his death, and various altered and exaggerated versions of his exploits soon began to appear in print (see FAUSTBUCH). The name Johann, given him in the folk books and by Marlowe in DR. FAUSTUS, probably results from confusion with a different magician.

Johann Wolfgang von GOETHE was first attracted to the Faust legend by the *Faustbuch* and a Faust puppet-show he saw in his youth. But it was not until 1808 that the completed play, *Faust, Der Tragödie erster Teil* (*Faust, The First Part of the Tragedy*) first appeared. It is in this Part I that Goethe develops the character of Faust as the old scholar who yearns to comprehend not so much all knowledge as all

experience, but finds that in order to do so he must promise his immortal soul to the destructive tempting spirit, MEPHISTOPHELES. The latter helps rejuvenate Faust, who then falls in love with and seduces a young girl named GRETCHEN. She bears him a child, but panics and drowns it, and the last scene of Part I is set in the dungeon where, awaiting execution for her crime, she refuses to flee with Faust and puts her trust in God.

In Part I, Mephistopheles promises to show Faust both "the small world" of personal feeling and experience, and "the great world" of history, politics, and culture. This distinction neatly parallels the difference between the two parts. In Part II (1832), which is much longer and more allegorical than Part I, Goethe took the opportunity to develop many of his ideas on mythology, cultural development, art, statesmanship, war, courtly life, economics, natural science, and religion, to the extent that the plot is sometimes lost from view. Toward the end, Faust attempts to justify his existence by reclaiming land from the sea in order to found an ideal society, but the plan fails. Faust's soul is finally rescued by a choir of angels who speak the motto *Wer immer strebend sich bemüht, / Den können wir erlösen* ("He who exerts himself in constant striving, / Him we can save"). See URFAUST; WAGNER; WALPURGISNACHT; MOTHERS, THE; HOMUNCULUS; HELEN; EUPHORION; ETERNAL FEMININE.

Thomas Mann, in his DOKTOR FAUSTUS, does not directly treat the Faust legend, but uses it as a parallel to the fall of his own hero, Adrian Leverkühn.

The Faust legend has inspired several operas, including Boïto's *Mefistofele* (1866), Berlioz' *La damnation de Faust* (1893), and Busoni's *Doktor Faust* (1925). The most famous of these is Charles Gounod's *Faust* (1859), which is based on Goethe's play.

Faust, Frederick. See Max BRAND.

Faustbuch, Das (Ger., "Faust-book"). A term referring to any of the several German folk books (VOLKSBUCH) which relate the career of Dr. Johann FAUST. The first such book was printed by Johann Spies in 1587, and many variations appeared shortly afterwards. Goethe's main sources, however, seem to have been a much later version by Nikolaus Pfitzer (1674) and an abridgment of Pfitzer's book which appeared in 1725.

Faustian. Of or pertaining to either the historical FAUST or any of his fictional counterparts. From this basic meaning the term has broadened until, in modern usage, it is often used when characterizing any unswerving and unquenchable will to possess all of human knowledge or experience.

Faustina [Annia Galeria]. The name of 2 Roman empresses. Faustina the Elder was married to the emperor Antoninus Pius, and died in A.D. 141. Faustina the Younger, her daughter, was married to the emperor Marcus Aurelius, the adopted son and successor of Antoninus, and died in 175. Both were notorious for their evil lives, though Marcus Aurelius professed to believe his wife the best of women. Swinburne's poem *Faustine* was written with these empresses in mind.

Fauves, les. A group of French artists (ROUAULT, DERAIN, DUFY, VLAMINCK, etc.) who grouped around Matisse and exhibited together from 1905 to 1907. The movement is characterized by the use of violent

THE
HISTORIE
OF
THE DAMNABLE
LIFE, AND DESERVED
DEATH OF DOCTOR
IOHN FAVSTVS.

Newlyprinted, and in conuenient places, imperfect
matter amended : according to the true Copie printed
at Frankfort; and tranflated into Englifh,
By P. R. Gent.

Printed at London for Iohn Wright, and are to be fold at the Sign of the
Bible in Gilt-fpur-Street without Newgate. 1636.

An English translation of a German *Faustbuch* (1636).

color and the rejection of modeling. The outraged contemporary reaction gave their name to *les Fauves,* the wild beasts.

Faux-Monnayeurs, Les. See COUNTERFEITERS, THE.

Favonius. In Roman mythology, a personification of the west wind. He is a promoter of vegetation, identical with the Greek Zephyrus.

Favorite, The (Les Personnages; 1961). A novel by Françoise MALLET-JORIS showing that even Cardinal Richelieu was only an instrument in the hands of Destiny rather than a maker of history.

Fawkes, Guy. See GUNPOWDER PLOT.

Fawley, Jude. See JUDE THE OBSCURE.

Fearing, Kenneth [Flexner] (1902–1961). American poet and novelist. He is noted for his satiric attacks upon the mechanized society of America, often using such elements as the comic strip and advertising as symbols of that society. Fearing published several volumes of poetry, including *Poems* (1935), *Dead Reckoning* (1938), *The Afternoon of a Pawnbroker and Other Poems* (1943), and *New and Selected Poems* (1956). *The Hospital* (1939) is a serious novel. He also wrote mystery novels, the best known being *The Big Clock* (1946), the story of a manhunt in which the quarry must track himself down. *The Crozart Story* appeared in 1960.

Feast During the Plague, The. See LITTLE TRAGEDIES.

Feast of Fools. A kind of Saturnalia, popular in the Middle Ages. Its chief object was to honor the ass on which Jesus made his triumphant entry into Jerusalem. This blasphemous mummery was held on the Feast of the Circumcision (Jan. 1). The office of the day was chanted in travesty, then a procession was formed and all sorts of foolery was indulged in. An ass was an essential feature, and from time to time the whole procession imitated braying, especially in the place of "Amen."

Feast of Lanterns. A popular Chinese festival. It is celebrated at the first full moon of each year. Tradition says that the daughter of a famous mandarin fell into a lake one evening. The father and his neighbors went with lanterns to look for her, and happily she was rescued. In commemoration thereof, a festival was ordained, and it grew in time to be the celebrated Feast of Lanterns.

Federalist, The (1787–1788). A series of 85 papers or essays written to urge New York voters to approve the U.S. Constitution. About 50 of the series are said to have been written by Alexander HAMILTON, the others by James MADISON and John JAY. The essays were intended to show how the proposed constitution would create an effective national government in conformity with republican principles. They are now considered outstanding studies in the practical application of political theory.

Fedin, Konstantin Aleksandrovich (1892–   ). Russian novelist. After serving in the Red Army during the civil war, Fedin became connected with the SERAPION BROTHERS and published his first story, *The Orchard* (*Sad*) in 1920. The theme of the story, which recurs in several of his later works, is the conflict between the old and new in changing Soviet society. His first novel, *Cities and Years* (*Goroda i gody;* 1924), also uses this theme, contrasting the vacillating Andrei Startzov, a type of SUPERFLUOUS MAN, with the devoted Communist, Kurt Wahn, who eventually kills Startzov as a traitor to the cause. The novel constituted a departure from the style then prevalent in Russian fiction. Instead of the wildly romantic treatment of its subject, rendered in vivid and exotic language, found in the work of Pilnyak, Vsevolod Ivanov, and other young writers, Fedin used the calm, objective description and sober psychological probing typical of the 19th-century Russian novel. He departed from it, however, in his complicated handling of the chronological sequence of the narrative, beginning with the novel's denouement, and flashing back and forth in time to tell his story.

Fedin's second novel, *The Brothers* (*Bratya;* 1928), treated the same theme of an individual's acclimation to the revolution in a manner even closer to the classical Russian novel's realism. His next large work, *The Rape of Europe* (*Pokhishcheniye evropy;* 1934–1935), concerned relations between the West and the new Soviet society.

After the war Fedin published two more novels, which are considered his best works: *First Joys* (*Pervye radosti;* 1945–1946) and *Unusual Summer* (*Neobyknovennoye leto;* 1948). Both portray life in the Volga region of Saratov shortly before World War I and during the revolution.

Feininger, Lyonel [Charles Adrian] (1871–1956). American artist. Of German descent, and associated with the BAUHAUS throughout its existence, he became a leader of the nonrepresentational movement in painting. In his landscapes of sea or city he divides forms and space into segmented planes, limited by straight lines. His son Andreas Feininger (1906–), a talented photographer, has published *The World As I See It* (1963).

Feisi or **Feiyasi, Abul Feis ibn Mubarak** (1547–1595). Indo-Persian poet and scholar, crowned king of poesy (c. 1572) by the Mogul Emperor Akbar the Great. He translated parts of the *Mahabharata* into Persian.

Félibrige. An association of Provençal poets. It was founded near Avignon (1854) for the cultivation of Provençal as a literary language. The school's first leader was Joseph Roumanille, and its membership included Frédéric MISTRAL, Rémy Marcellin (1832–1908), Jean Brunet (1823–1894), Paul Giéra (1816–1861), Anselme Mathieu (1828–1925), Alphonse Tavan (1833–1905) and Théodore Aubanel (1829–1886).

Felipe, León. Pen name of **León Felipe Camino Galicia** (1884–). Spanish poet. He is best known in Spain for his early work, *Versos y oraciones del camino* (1920), and abroad for the larger volume *Antología rota, 1920–1947* (1947). His poetry, simple and direct, reveals the influence of Walt Whitman whom Felipe has translated.

Felix Holt the Radical (1866). A novel by George ELIOT. Felix Holt is an ardent young man of strong social convictions who attempts, by living as a watchmaker among the lower classes in his area, to encourage them to better themselves. Against him is set Harold Transome, who is running for Parliament as a radical, yet possesses none of the social sense of Felix. Felix finds himself in love with Esther, imagined to be the daughter of the local curate, Rufus Lyon. Eventually, Esther has to choose between Felix and Transome. As a complication, Felix, in his efforts to prevent the workers from rioting on Election Day, has accidentally killed a man and is on trial. His trouble brings Esther to the realization that she loves him, and when he is pardoned she becomes his wife. Running through the novel are the legal problems concerning the inheritance of the Transome property, and the attending mystery surrounding Esther's birth.

Felix Krull. See CONFESSIONS OF FELIX KRULL: CONFIDENCE MAN.

Fell, Dr. See John FELL.

Fell, John (1625–1686). English scholar and prelate, subject of the well-known quatrain by Thomas Brown (1663–1704):

> I do not love thee, Dr. Fell,
> The reason why I cannot tell;
> But this I know, and know full well,
> I do not love thee, Dr. Fell.

Brown is said to have composed these lines when Fell, who was dean of Christ Church, Oxford, promised to remit a sentence of expulsion if the youth could make an impromptu translation of Martial's 33rd epigram:

> Non amo te, Sabidi, nec possum dicere quare;
> Hoc tantum possum dicere non amo te.

Fellini, Federico (1920–). Italian motion-picture director and writer. He appeared as an actor for a short time before 1940, when he began his career as a script writer and director. Among the films for which he has received international acclaim are *La Strada* (1956), *La Notta di Cabiria* (1957), *La Dolce Vita* (1960), and *8½* (1963).

Felltham or **Feltham, Owen** (1602?–1668). English essayist, poet, and CHARACTER WRITER. His two major works are *Resolves, Divine, Moral, and Political* (1628) and *A Brief Character of the Low Countries* (1652). An ardent Royalist, he once referred to Charles I as "Christ the Second."

Felton, John (1595?–1628). English soldier and assassin. In 1628 he assassinated the Duke of Buckingham, who had refused him the command of a company, and was hanged at Tyburn. He appears in Dumas' *The Three Musketeers* (1844).

Femmes savantes, Les (**The Learned Ladies,** 1672). A comedy by MOLIÈRE. It satirizes women who devote themselves to women's rights, science, and philosophy to the neglect of domestic duties and wifely amenities. Philaminte, who is capable of discharging a servant for employing bad grammar, wants to marry Henriette, her daughter, to Trissotin, a man whose tastes and opinions match her own. Her daughter Armande advocates Platonic love and science, and her sister Bélise is a self-styled philosopher who imagines that everyone is in love with her. Henriette, who has no sympathy with the lofty flights of her female relatives, is in love with Clitandre, but is prevented from marrying him until her father loses his property through the "savant" proclivities of his wife and Trissotin withdraws his suit of the girl. Clitandre and Henriette are thereupon united, Clitandre declaring his beloved the "perfect" or thorough woman—in distinction, Molière implies, to the rest of her family.

Fénelon, François de Salignac de la Mothe- (1651–1715). French prelate and writer. Fénelon's success in tutoring the duc de Bourgogne, grandson of Louis XIV, won him an appointment to the Académie française, the title of archbishop, and a favored position at court. He lost favor embracing the unorthodox doctrines of Quietism, and upon publication of his epic TÉLÉMAQUE, which in offering political advice to the dauphin indirectly reproved the policies of the king, Fénelon was exiled to his diocese. Liberal in his political and educational theories, Fénelon expressed his convictions in *De l'Education des filles* (*Concerning the Education of Girls,* 1687) and *Table de Chaulnes* (1711).

Fenian cycle. In GAELIC LITERATURE, a group of tales revolving around the deeds of FIONN MAC CUMHAIL and his son Oisín, or OSSIAN. The term *Fenian* comes from "fian," a band of warriors. The chief Fenian text is the *Colloquy of Old Men,* a discussion between St. Patrick and Ossian; also important is THE PURSUIT OF DIARMUID AND GRÁINNE. Paganism is somewhat modified in the Fenian cycle, Christianity reaching Ireland in the old age of Ossian.

Fenians or **Fenian Brotherhood.** An anti-British, secret association of disaffected Irishmen founded in New York in 1857 with a view to securing the independence of Ireland. The movement spread over the U.S. and through Ireland (where it absorbed the pre-existing Phoenix Society); several attempts at insurrection in Ireland were made as well as an invasion of Canada from the U.S. Eleven "national congresses" were held by the Fenian Brotherhood in the U.S. between 1863 and 1872, after which it continued as a secret society. It was a forerunner to the Irish Republican Brotherhood. The name Fenian is derived from Fionn mac Cumhail, the name of the great, semimythological hero of Ireland. See CLAN-NA-GAEL; SINN FEIN; YOUNG IRELAND; EASTER REBELLION.

Fenollosa, Ernest Francisco (1853–1908). American poet, art critic, and Orientalist. After living in Japan and teaching for 12 years at the University of Tokyo, Fenollosa returned to the U.S.; he became curator of the Boston Museum of Fine Arts and was a widely received lecturer. He later returned to Japan, and finally moved to England, where he died. His collected poems appeared as *East and West* (1893). *Epochs of Chinese and Japanese Art* (2 v., 1912), his greatest art book, was published posthumously. During the Westernization of Japan, Fenollosa saved many ancient art treasures from mishandling and destruction. His private collection formed the nucleus of the Fenollosa-Weld Collection in the Boston Museum. After his death, Fenollosa's wife turned his notes and papers over to the poet Ezra Pound. From Fenollosa's work, Pound made the celebrated translations from Li Po that appear in his *Cathay* (1915), as well as the versions of classical Japanese drama found in *Certain Noble Plays of Japan* (1916).

Fenrir or **Fenris-wolf.** In Scandinavian mythology, the wolf of Loki and brother of Hel, typifying the goading of a guilty conscience. It was said that when he gaped, one jaw touched earth and the other heaven. Odin sought vainly to chain him but the wolf was expected to swallow Odin at the day of doom. Percy MacKaye wrote a dramatic poem entitled *Fenris the Wolf* (1905).

Fenton. In Shakespeare's MERRY WIVES OF WINDSOR, a young gentleman who woos and finally wins "sweet Anne Page." He had formerly been a companion of Prince Hal.

Ferber, Edna (1887–). American novelist and short-story writer. Edna Ferber started her long career as a highly successful writer of fiction with several collections of short stories. Her best-selling novels include *The Girls* (1921); *So Big* (1924), which was awarded a Pulitzer Prize and which deals with the struggles of the widowed Selina DeJong to support herself and her son Dirk; SHOW BOAT; and *Cimarron* (1930), a story of the spectacular land rush of 1889 in Oklahoma. In collaboration with George S. Kaufman, Miss Ferber wrote several popular plays: *Minick* (1924), based on one of her best short stories; *The Royal Family* (1927), which exhibited the Barrymores in a humorous vein; *Dinner at Eight* (1932), about a fashionable dinner party; and *Stage Door* (1936). Among her many later novels are *Giant* (1952) and *Ice Palace* (1958).

Ferdinand. (1) The young king of Navarre who takes an oath with three friends to make his court "a little Academe, still and contemplative in living art" in Shakespeare's LOVE'S LABOUR'S LOST.

(2) The son of Alonso, king of Naples, in Shakespeare's THE TEMPEST. Untouched by worldly corruption, he falls in love at first sight with Prospero's daughter Miranda and willingly undergoes the labors Prospero imposes to test his love for her.

Ferdinand II of Aragon or **Ferdinand V** of Castile (1452–1516). King of Spain. In 1469 Ferdinand married Isabella of Castile and, upon her accession to the throne in 1474, the two great kingdoms of Spain were permanently united. During their reign Ferdinand and Isabella sought to consolidate royal power and to assure the racial and religious purity of Spain. The first aim they accomplished by destroying the privileges of the unruly Castilian nobility and by limiting the once-considerable independence of the towns. The second aim was achieved by the establishment of the Spanish INQUISITION (1478) and by the conquest (1492) of Granada, the last Moorish kingdom in Spain. In the same year the Jews of Spain were ordered to become Christians or face expulsion; the same alternatives were offered to the Moors of Castile in 1502. Perhaps the most important event of their reign was the discovery of America in 1492 by Christopher Columbus, whose voyage was made possible by Isabella. Ferdinand expanded Spanish power in Europe as well, acquiring Naples in 1503 and the kingdom of Navarre in 1512. Upon the death of Isabella in 1504, he ruled Castile as regent for their demented daughter, Joanna the Mad. In 1506 he took a second wife, Germaine de Foix.

Ferdinand Count Fathom, The Adventures of (1753). A novel by Tobias SMOLLETT. The titular hero, son of a harridan mother, is an amoral Machiavellian rogue who nearly succeeds in destroying Monimia, the fiancée of his master and friend, Count de Melvil. Reduced to ignominy and disgrace when his schemes miscarry, he is finally rehabilitated by the benevolent Melvil, and reforms under an assumed name. The novel professes to terrify the iniquitous into virtue through an appeal to the "impulses of fear." Fathom, completely reformed and prosperous, reappears as a character in *The Expedition of* HUMPHREY CLINKER.

Fergus. A famous warrior in the ULSTER CYCLE of Gaelic literature. Fergus also appears in James Joyce's *Ulysses* (1922).

Ferlinghetti, Lawrence. See BEAT MOVEMENT.

Fernández de Avellaneda, Alonso. See DON QUIXOTE.

Fernández de Lizardi, José Joaquín (1776–1827). Mexican novelist and journalist. Fernández de Lizardi is often called *El Pensador Mexicano* (*Sp.,* the Mexican Thinker), the name of a newspaper he established in 1812 as a vehicle for his ideas on morality and patriotism. It is, however, as a novelist that he is best known, notably for EL PERIQUILLO SARNIENTO, often considered the first Hispanic-American novel, and for *La quijotita y su prima* (1818–1819), which was inspired by Rousseau's theories of education.

Fernández de Moratín, Leandro. See Leandro Fernández de MORATÍN.

Fernández Flórez, Wenceslao (1886–). Spanish writer. The journalistic style of his early newspaper career reappears in the ironic humor of his novels, including *Valvoreta* (1917), *Las siete columnas* (*The Seven Pillars,* 1926), and *Los que no fuimos a la guerra* (1930).

Fernández y González, Manuel (1821–1888). Spanish novelist and dramatist. He is known for his prolific output of historical novels patterned on the works of the English romanticists. His best-known novels are *Los siete infantes de Lara* (1853), *El cocinero de Su Majestad* (1857), and *Historia de un murciélago* (1857). He also wrote the drama *Cid Rodrigo de Vivar* (1858).

Ferney, the patriarch or **philosopher of.** Epithet for VOLTAIRE (François Marie Arouet). Ferney is the name of the estate that Voltaire bought near Geneva in 1758 and where he spent the last 20 years of his life. He is known as the patriarch of Ferney because of his fatherly interest in the management of the estate and in his staff of servants. For them and for the local inhabitants, Voltaire built a pottery factory and a church. His grand manner of entertaining his numerous famous visitors also explains this epithet. Secure from political and religious interference at Ferney, because of its geographical location, Voltaire poured forth innumerable vitriolic pamphlets attacking just about everyone who disagreed with him.

Ferragù, Ferrau, Ferracute, or **Ferragus.** In Ariosto's ORLANDO FURIOSO, a Saracen knight, son of Lanfusa. Having lost his helmet in a river, he vowed to wear none other than Orlando's. In the ORLANDO INNAMORATO of Boiardo, he was supposed to wed Angelica, as her brother Argaglia wished; but she fled from him. In the Ariosto continuation, he is finally killed by Orlando when wounded in the navel, his only vulnerable part.

Ferrar, Nicholas (1592–1637). English theologian. With several members of his family he established a religious colony at LITTLE GIDDING in Huntingdonshire that was renowned for its piety. Ferrar translated religious works, wrote the *Story Books of Little Gidding*, first published in 1899, and was responsible for publishing the work of George Herbert, his friend. The last of T. S. Eliot's *Four Quartets* (1943) is entitled *Little Gidding*, the poet using Ferrar's community as an example of achieved spiritual life.

Ferrars, Edward. See SENSE AND SENSIBILITY.

Ferraugh, Sir. See FAERIE QUEENE, THE.

Ferrex and Porrex. Sons of King Gorboduc in the HISTORY OF THE KINGS OF BRITAIN by Geoffrey of Monmouth. The king divided his kingdom between them, but Porrex drove his brother from Britain. When Ferrex returned with an army he was slain, but Porrex was shortly after put to death by his mother, whose favorite was Ferrex. The story forms the basis of the Tudor drama GORBODUC (1592), the first English tragedy by Norton and Sackville.

Ferumbras. See FIERABRAS.

Feste. Olivia's clown in Shakespeare's TWELFTH NIGHT. He takes part in the pranks against Malvolio, and he also sings the well-known song, "O mistress mine!"

Festin de pierre, Le. See DOM JUAN OU LE FESTIN DE PIERRE.

Festus. See Philip J. BAILEY.

Fet, Afanasi Afanasyevich (1820–1892). Russian lyric poet. Fet was the illegitimate son of Afanasi Shenshin, a landowner, and a German woman named Foeth (Fet in Russian). He retained the name Fet throughout his literary career. His first volume of poems (1840) received little notice. With the publication of two more books of verse in 1850 and 1856, however, Fet's reputation was established as a

lyric poet whose work was unexcelled in its melodic quality, his chief themes being love and nature. The quality and the concerns of Fet's work were not palatable to the utilitarian critics of the 1860's. They cited his poetry as an example of the sterility of "art for art's sake." One of their favorite targets for ridicule was a short poem by Fet, *Shopot, robkoe dykhan'e* (*Whispering, timid breathing*). An impressionistic description of the break of dawn, the poem contains no verbs. The unfriendly critical reception of his work induced Fet to stop publishing poetry for more than 20 years. He lived quietly on his estate near the home of his friend, Leo Tolstoi. In the 1880's, several more volumes of Fet's poems were published.

Feuchtwanger, Lion (1884–1958). German novelist. He was noted for his treatment of historical and political themes, and for his application of psychoanalytic ideas to the development of character. Among his novels are *Die hässliche Herzogin Margarete Maultasch* (*The Ugly Duchess,* 1923), *Jud Süss* (1925, translated as *Power*), *Der jüdische Krieg* (1932, translated as *Josephus*), and *Der Wartesaal* (*The Waiting Room*), a trilogy including *Erfolg* (*Success,* 1930), *Die Geschwister Oppenheim* (1933, translated as *The Oppermanns*), and *Exil* (1939, translated as *Paris Gazette*). Feuchtwanger was active as a pacifist and a socialist, and was forced into exile by the rise of Nazism. He was a friend of Bertolt Brecht and collaborated with him on several plays including *Leben Eduards II von England* (*Life of Edward II of England,* 1923), and adaptation of *Edward II* by Marlowe. See Arnold ZWEIG.

feudalism or **feudal system.** The system of distribution of land and political allegiance prevalent throughout Europe during the Middle Ages. According to its purest form, the king owns all the land over which he rules, but gives portions of it as inheritable fiefs to his vassals, in exchange for loyalty and a specified amount of military service. These feudal lords similarly divide their land among their followers, and the subdivision continues, forming a pyramidal hierarchy in which each nobleman has an obligation to the lord above him and authority over those below him. At the base of the pyramid are the serfs, the farmers who belong to the land they work, owing most of its produce to its lord and changing masters when the land changes hands through gift or marriage alliances or wars.

The feudal system was dominant from the 9th to the 14th century, when the rise of the merchant class and the growing importance of the towns began to change the social structure. Some feudal elements, however, such as the hierarchy of the propertied class of nobles, continued through the 19th century.

Feuerbach, Ludwig (1804–1872). German philosopher. He analyzed religion from a psychological and anthropological viewpoint in *Das Wesen des Christentums* (*The Essence of Christianity,* 1841) and *Das Wesen der Religion* (*The Essence of Religion,* 1845). Denying the traditional antithesis of the divine and the human, he maintained that divinity is man's projection of his own human nature. Love and morality, the basis of human relations, are the essence of religion. This tendency toward secularization of religion in the mid-19th century is also found in the work of David Friedrich Strauss and Ernest Renan.

Feuillants, Le Club des. A French political club born of a schism between members of the JACOBIN Club in July, 1791. They were more moderate than the Jacobins in their wholehearted support of the constitutional monarchy provided for by the Constitution of 1791, and in their distrust of the political influence of the Parisian mob. The Feuillants came to power early in 1792, but were soon replaced by the GIRONDISTS over the question of war with Austria. Their political power rapidly waned and they were suppressed by the Jacobins after the fall of the monarchy in September, 1792. The club's members met in the old convent of the Feuillants, a branch of the Cistercian Order, hence their name.

Feuillet, Octave (1821–1890). French author and playwright. One of the most appreciated, popular writers of his period, Feuillet is the author of the sentimental novel *Roman d'un jeune homme pauvre* (1858). The young hero of this tale refuses to marry his wealthy beloved and later destroys the proof which would enable him to take possession of her family fortune. His honor does not go unrewarded, however, for he soon inherits an even larger fortune and is at last united with his love. Feuillet's dramas, which received the same approval as his novels, include *La Belle au bois dormant* (1867) and *La Partie de dames* (1883).

feuilleton. The section of a French newspaper devoted to tales, serials, light literature, and criticism. The title of this early 19th-century phenomenon is derived from the French *feuille* (a leaf) as the first feuilletons were printed on the detachable, lower portion of the page. The word is now applied to pamphlets, generally of a political nature, that are distributed on the street.

Few Figs from Thistles, A (1920). A collection of poems by Edna St. Vincent MILLAY. The second of her collections, this volume differs from the earlier *Renascence and Other Poems* (1917) in its greater tone of sophisticated flippancy. Seeming to epitomize youthful Bohemianism, the poems were widely quoted in Greenwich Village, among the best known of them being *First Fig, Recuerdo,* and *The Philosopher.*

Fiammetta. The lady celebrated by Giovanni BOCCACCIO in his verse and prose works. The literal meaning of her name, flickering or darting fire, suggests his passion for her. *Fiammetta* is also the title of a psychological romance written by Boccaccio in 1344–1346, in which she is the heroine describing her abandonment by Panfilo and her subsequent grief. Since she is also called Maria, it was once assumed that Fiammetta was really MARIA D'AQUINO. Modern scholars now hold that she was purely fictional, a Boccaccian equivalent of LAURA and other ladies of the lyric tradition.

Fichte, Johann Gottlieb (1762–1814). German philosopher and political thinker. An important force in the development of GERMAN ROMANTICISM, in his *Grundlage der gesammten Wissenschaftslehre (Foundation of the Complete Theory of Knowledge,* 1794), he developed the distinction made earlier by Kant between phenomenal reality and the thing-in-itself (see CRITIQUE OF PURE REASON). He maintained that the essence of the universe is ego—mind, that is, or spirit—and that the ego itself posits the material world by a process called productive imagination.

Man's ideas do not come from experience of the material world, for his mind is part of the universal creative ego and finds fulfillment in self-conscious unity with it. Fichte's main political work is *Reden an die deutsche Nation (Addresses to the German Nation,* 1808), in which his earlier enthusiasm for the French Revolution is replaced by a stern condemnation of Napoleon. Fichte, who believed in the nobility of the German spirit, hoped that Germany would unite and free Europe from French rule.

Ficino, Marsilio (1433–1499). Italian philosopher and scholar. The first and most influential Platonist of the Renaissance, as a child he was taken into the Florentine household of Cosimo de' Medici for the express purpose of learning the philosophy of Plato and his followers, the Neoplatonists. He soon became the center of a group of intellectuals, including Angelo Poliziano and Pico della Mirandola, loosely called the Florentine Academy. He translated Greek works into Latin, wrote such commentaries as the famous one on Plato's *Symposium* (in Latin and Italian), and composed original treatises. His main impulse seems to have been the desire to reconcile Platonism (actually Neoplatonism) with the tradition of Christian thought, as in his *Theologia platonica de immortalitate animorum (The Platonic Theology of the Immortality of Souls).* Among the many European and English writers influenced by his writings are Benvieni, Pico della Mirandola, Bembo, Castiglione, Spenser, and Chapman. Among the poets who read and used him, it was frequently the Platonic theory of spiritual or philosophic love that appealed rather than theological or cosmological theory.

Ficke, Arthur Davison (1883–1945). American poet and critic. Ficke's interests were divided between art—especially Japanese art—and poetry. In the former field he published *Twelve Japanese Painters* (1913) and *Chats on Japanese Prints* (1915). As a poet he was noted for his sonnets; his two interests combined in *Sonnets of a Portrait Painter* (1914). He was involved with Witter BYNNER in the SPECTRA hoax.

Fiddler's Green. The Elysium of sailors; a land flowing with rum and lime juice; a land of perpetual music, mirth, dancing, drinking, and tobacco; a sort of Dixie Land or land of the leal.

Fidei Defensor. See DEFENDER OF THE FAITH.

Fidelio (1805). An opera by Ludwig von Beethoven, based on Bouilly's *Lenore.* The hero is Don Fernando Florestan, a state prisoner in Spain, and the heroine his faithful wife Leonora, who disguises herself as a man and under the name Fidelio becomes the jailer's servant in order to protect her husband and bring about his release. It is the only opera Beethoven wrote. Beethoven composed four overtures for *Fidelio* that are often performed in concert.

Fidessa. See FAERIE QUEENE, THE.

Field, Arthur William (1888–). Australian novelist. Born in Gosport, England, Field was sent as a boy to Australia where his early literary influences were Charles Dickens, Sir Arthur Conan Doyle, and Alexandre Dumas. He led an adventurous life as a sheepherder, cowhand, gold miner, fur trapper, and soldier. Many of his actual experiences are vividly related in his books: *House of Cain* (1929), *Murder Down Under* (1937), *The Devil's*

Steps (1940), *The New Shoe* (1951), *Death of a Love* (1954), *The Sinister Stones* (1954).

Field, Eugene (1850–1895). American poet and journalist. Expelled from three colleges because of his pranks, Field turned to journalism. He settled in Chicago, where he wrote a column, "Sharps and Flats," for the *Daily News*. Collecting his newspaper verses into several books, he published *The Tribune Primer* (1882), *A Little Book of Western Verse* (1889), *Love Affairs of a Bibliomaniac* (1896), and several other volumes. He wrote many popular and sentimental poems for children, including *Little Boy Blue* (1889).

Field, Michael. Joint pen name of **Katharine Harris Bradley** (1846–1914) and **Edith Emma Cooper** (1862–1913). English authors, they collaborated (from 1884) on lyric poetry and poetic closet dramas. Their lyrics—their best work—are represented by *A Selection From the Poems of Michael Field* (1923).

Field, Nat[han] or **"Nid"** (1587–?). English actor and dramatist. He became one of the Children of the Chapel Royal in 1600, remaining with that company until 1613, when he was absorbed into the Lady Elizabeth's Players. Two years later he joined the King's Men. He was apparently an excellent actor, generally playing the part of young lovers. His name comes 17th on the list of 26 actors in the 1623 Shakespeare folio. He was the author of two comedies, *A Woman Is a Weathercock* (1609?) and *Amends for Ladies* (pub. 1618), and is believed to have collaborated with Philip Massinger, John Fletcher, and Francis Beaumont.

Fielding, Henry (1707–1754). English novelist and playwright, an important figure in the development of the English novel. His career as a dramatist has been eclipsed by his career as a novelist, and all that is remembered today of his plays is TOM THUMB, a brilliant farce, and *Pasquin* (1736) and *The Historical Register for 1736* (1737), two social and political satires. Robert Walpole's Licensing Act of 1737 ended the use of the stage for political satire, and so terminated this phase of Fielding's career. Turning to the study of law, he was admitted to the bar; in 1749 he became London's first police magistrate and, with the organization of the Bow STREET Runners, a pioneer in the detection of crime.

In the meantime his literary career continued. From 1739 to 1741 he edited the periodical CHAMPION. When Richardson's PAMELA was published, Fielding was moved to parody it, first in APOLOGY FOR THE LIFE OF MRS. SHAMELA ANDREWS, and once again, more brilliantly, in JOSEPH ANDREWS. In 1743 he published three volumes of *Miscellanies*, which included his ironic satire JONATHAN WILD. TOM JONES, his greatest novel, and AMELIA, an early example of social realism, appeared soon after. In 1754, in an attempt to restore his failing health, he made a trip to Portugal and wrote an account of it in A JOURNAL OF A VOYAGE TO LISBON. He died at Lisbon.

Field of the Cloth of Gold. A plain near Guisnes, France. There Henry VIII (of England) had his interview with Francis I (of France) in 1520; so called from the splendor and magnificence displayed there on that occasion.

Fierabras or **Ferumbras.** One of Charlemagne's PALADINS in medieval French and English romances. A Saracen giant, son of King Balant of Babylon, he has conquered Rome and taken the holy relics. But Olivier defeats him in a duel, and he becomes a Christian knight. His sister Floripas is also baptized and marries Guy of Burgundy.

Fiesole. A village near Florence, Italy, chiefly famous for a Dominican monastery decorated by Fra Angelico.

Fiesole, Mino da (1431–1484). Tuscan sculptor. His tombs, particularly that of Pope Paul II (1473), portrait busts, and reliefs, are known for their finish, delicacy of detail, and strongly devotional aspects.

fifteen, the. The JACOBITE rebellion of 1715, when James Edward Stuart, "the Old PRETENDER," with the Earl of Mar, made a half-hearted and unsuccessful attempt to gain the throne of England. The reference is to the year of the attempt, to distinguish it from the forty-five (1745) revolt of "the Young Pretender," Charles Edward Stuart.

Fifteen Decisive Battles of the World (1851). A historical work by Sir Edward Creasy (1812–1878). The author discusses those battles which in his opinion have effected some great and permanent political changes in Western history. The battles under discussion are Marathon; Syracuse; Arbela; Metaurus; Teutoberg Forest; Chalons; Tours; Hastings; Orléans; the defeat of the Spanish Armada; Blenheim; Poltava; Saratoga; Valmy; Waterloo.

Title page of Field's *Amends for Ladies* (1639 ed.).

AMENDS FOR LADIES.

With the merry prankes of Moll Cut-Purse: Or, the humour of roaring:

A Comedy full of honeft mirth and wit.

As it was Acted at the *Blacke-Fryers*, both by the PRINCES Servants, and the Lady ELIZABETHS.

By *Nath. Field.*

LONDON,

Printed by *Io. Okes*, for *Math. Walbaneke*, and are to be fold at his Shop, at *Grayes-Inne* Gate 1639.

fifth column. Enemy sympathizers engaged in sabotage. The term was first used during the Spanish Civil War (1936-1939) by General Mola, who stated in a broadcast that he had four columns of soldiers advancing on Madrid and a fifth column of sympathizers within the city who would arise to attack the defenders from the rear. It was made the title of a play (1938) by Ernest Hemingway; the term came into wide use during the German invasion of Holland, Belgium, Luxembourg, and France in 1940, when fifth columnists were active. During World War II, the term applied to a systematic organization of spies penetrating the civilian life of the enemy country to acquire information, obstruct military preparations, alarm, confuse, and divide the populace, and assist or join the invading army. It was also applied to citizens who were enemy sympathizers. The fifth column, in fact and in rhetoric, is the modern equivalent of the Trojan Horse.

Fifth Monarchy Men. A fanatical sect of millenarians in England at the time of the Commonwealth, who maintained that the fifth monarchy, when Christ should reign on earth 1,000 years, was near at hand and that they must establish it by force. They listed Assyria, Persia, Greece, and Rome as the preceding four monarchies. Their uprisings (1657 and 1661) came to nothing.

Figaro. The rascally hero of two comedies by BEAUMARCHAIS: THE BARBER OF SEVILLE and its sequel *Le Mariage de Figaro, ou La folle journée* (1784). The complicated plot of the latter play concerns Count Almaviva, who is tired of his wife Rosine and tries to find solace elsewhere. Figaro, now the count's doorkeeper, loves Suzanne, Rosine's maid. Almaviva, himself taken with Suzanne, is in favor of the marriage between Figaro and Suzanne, provided he can exercise his feudal rights over Suzanne. His attempts to achieve his ends are constantly thwarted by various conspiracies, rendering him constantly ridiculous. His infidelity to Rosine is exposed, and Figaro, having outwitted his master, finally marries Suzanne. Beaumarchais' bitter criticisms of the ruling classes caused the play to be suppressed for three years; he was even imprisoned five days for his audacity; but the public demanded its performance, and its success was possibly the greatest any play has ever had in the history of French theater. In Figaro's famous, daring monologue (Act V, scene 3), he says: "What have you [the nobility] done to deserve such wealth? You took the trouble to be born, and nothing else." Mozart composed an opera based on this play: *Le Nozze di Figaro* (*The Marriage of Figaro,* 1786), in which the political implications are absent.

Filarete, Il. Real name, **Antonio Averlino** (c. 1400-1470). Florentine sculptor and architect. He worked for the Sforza family in Milan, where he built the Ospedale Maggiore (1457) and the Medici bank. In Rome, he carved the bronze doors for the old St. Peter's, which were retained for the present structure. His treatise on architecture, *Trattato dell' architettura* (1464), was described by VASARI as "perhaps the most stupid book ever written;" it contains plans for what he called *Sforzinda,* an ideal, wholly symmetrical city.

Filelfo, Francesco (1398-1481). Venetian diplomat and scholar. Like other Humanists of the Italian Renaissance, he wrote Latin verse and translated from Greek, which he had studied at Constantinople (see HUMANISM). His activities as teacher and scholar centered in the university at Florence and the court of Milan.

Filicaia, Vincenzo da (1642-1707). Italian lyric poet. A member of the ARCADIAN ACADEMY, he is known for his odes and sonnets on religious and patriotic themes. His most famous sonnet, *Italia,* was translated by Byron in *Childe Harold's Pilgrimage* (Canto III, 1. 110).

Filioque controversy. An argument that long disturbed the Eastern and Western branches of the Christian Church. The difference of opinion still forms one of the principal barriers to their fusion. The point was: Did the Holy Spirit proceed from the Father *and* the Son (*filio-que*), or from the Father only? The Western Church maintains the former position and the Eastern the latter.

Filippovna, Natasha. In Feodor Dostoevski's novel THE IDIOT, the beautiful, tormented woman whose proud nature is continually exacerbated by the memory of a shameful seduction in her youth. Prince Myshkin tries to help her, but is able only to offer her his pity. She finally runs away with the passionately jealous ROGOZHIN, who kills her.

Filocolo, Il. A lengthy prose romance by Giovanni Boccaccio. Its title, a Greek coinage meaning *Love's Labor,* refers to the travails of its leading characters, Florio and Biancofiore. Derived from the French tale FLORES AND BLANCHEFLEUR, it was filled with many episodes and digressions by Boccaccio which later were used by European and English writers. The most famous of these digressions is the THIRTEEN QUESTIONS OF LOVE.

Filostrato, Il. A romance in octaves by Giovanni Boccaccio, whose title means "a man overwhelmed by love." The man is Trojan Troiolo (Troilus), who loves and wins Criseida with the help of her cousin and his friend Pandaro (Pandarus). But when she leaves the Trojan camp to return to her father on the Greek side, she quickly betrays Troiolo's trust, leaving him stunned by grief. Boccaccio drew the plot from the *Roman de Troie* of Benoît de Sainte-More, then supplied Chaucer with the story of his *Troilus and Criseyde.* See GUIDO DELLE COLONNE.

Filumena, St. (Philomena). A saint unknown till 1802. A grave was discovered in that year in the catacomb of St. Priscilla on the Salarian Way (leading from Rome to Ancona), with this inscription on tiles: *"lumena paxte cymfi,"* which, being rearranged, makes *Pax tecum Filumena.* Filumena was at once popularly accepted as a saint, though never canonized, and so many wonders were worked by her that she has been called *La Thaumaturge du Dix-neuvième Siècle.* In 1961, the Vatican officially prohibited her further veneration.

Financier, The (1912). A novel by Theodore DREISER. It is the first volume in the trilogy that includes THE TITAN and *The Stoic* (1947). All three deal with a typical industrial and financial magnate of the late 19th century. Dreiser admitted that he based his central character, Frank Algernon Cowperwood, on the figure of Charles T. Yerkes (1837-1905), who gained control of the Chicago street-railway system. The book begins with a famous scene in which Cowperwood as a young boy in Philadelphia watches a lobster devour a squid, this act becoming for him a symbol of what life really is. Working his way upward, the hero is caught in a stock-market crash and receives a prison sentence for illegal dealings. At the end of the book, when he is released, he marries and goes to Chicago to begin his climb again.

Fin de partie. See ENDGAME.

Fingal, An Ancient Epic (1761). An epic poem by James MACPHERSON. Purportedly a translation from Gaelic, the poem was attributed by him to OSSIAN, son of Fingal, and told of the adventures of the legendary hero Fingal or FIONN MAC CUMHAIL.

Finnabair. In Gaelic literature, the Irish GUINEVERE, daughter of MEDB and Ailill. One of the figures in the Ulster cycle, she appears in such tales as the *Cattle-Raid of Cooley* and *Fled Bricrenn*.

Finnegans Wake (1939). The last and most revolutionary experimental novel by James JOYCE. It is almost inaccessible to readers who have not done some special study; a great many volumes of explication have been published since the novel's first, controversial appearance. The main difficulty is in the language. Joyce uses an elaborate language of his own devising, made up of puns, portmanteau words, and words from foreign languages, with endless philological variations. He incorporates literary, historical, and philosophical allusions; names of people and places in Dublin; Irish references; slang; phrases from newspapers, popular songs, art, and the world of sport; and words and syllables from every other imaginable source. By means of this complex language and its rich connotations, Joyce is able to relate his slight, rather obscure central story to the whole historic, psychological, religious, and artistic experience of mankind. Critics relate Joyce's difficult linguistic method to the scholasticism he encountered during his strict Catholic education, and his presentation of different levels of meaning simultaneously to the influence of medieval allegory.

Most literally, the novel presents the dreams and nightmares of H. C. Earwicker and his family as they lie asleep at night. Their anxieties, secret thoughts, unexpressed desires, and the events of the past day recur in their minds. Humphrey Chimpden Earwicker, a Protestant Irishman of Scandinavian descent (and thus, like Bloom of *Ulysses*, an outsider) is the middle-aged keeper of a tavern in Dublin. He has a wife, Anna, and three children: Isobel, a daughter now in her teens, and twin sons, Kevin and Jerry. At some time in the past Earwicker has accosted someone in Phoenix Park, but it is never made clear whether this was a young girl or a man; he still feels guilty and fears investigation by the authorities. In his dream Earwicker's personal guilt is related to various religious taboos and legends, and he is associated with Lucifer, Adam, Humpty Dumpty, and other figures. Another sexual taboo and guilt complex in Earwicker's dream concerns his daughter Isobel, whom he substitutes as a love object for his wife; however, to avoid incest he transforms her into Iseult the Fair and himself into Tristram. He also imagines himself as Jonathan Swift, the Irish writer who loved two women. Because of the similarity in names, Earwicker is also associated with earwigs (see Persse O'REILLY). Earwicker represents Everyman and general maleness. His initials, HCE, are interwoven throughout the book, particularly in the recurrent phrases Here Comes Everybody and Haveth Childer Everywhere. Anna, his wife, like Molly Bloom of *Ulysses*, resents the universal feminine principle, and becomes identified with the River Liffey, personified in the novel as Anna Livia Plurabelle. The Anna Livia Plurabelle sections are among the most remarkable in the novel, being triumphs of Joyce's poetic prose. Eventually all the women in the novel merge into this figure as the river merges into the sea. Earwicker's two sons are complementary opposites. Jerry, who appears as Shem the Penman, is a rebellious, introverted artist of the type of Stephen Dedalus, and Kevin, or Shaun the Postman, is a man of action and an average, extroverted citizen.

In structure the novel is entirely circular, ending in an unfinished sentence which is completed by a half sentence at the beginning. The history of mankind and the river-to-sea progression of time and individual life are also seen as circular. In Christian thought the fall of man is followed by the resurrection; Earwicker's mysterious misdeed took place in Phoenix park, and the title of the novel refers both to the Irish hero Finn MacCool, who was supposed to return to life some day to be the savior of Ireland, and to Tim Finnegan, the hero of a music hall ballad about a man who jumped up indignantly in the middle of his own wake. Joyce used the ideas of cyclical repetition of Giambattista Vico; Freud's dream psychology; Jung's theory of a collective unconscious; and Giordano Bruno's theory of the complementary but conflicting nature of opposites (Shem and Shaun).

Joyce began writing *Finnegans Wake* in 1922. During the 17 years of its composition the novel was known as *Work in Progress*, and several parts of it were published separately as they were completed; the whole work was revised before publication.

Finn MacCool. See FIONN MAC CUMHAIL.

Finnsburg (or **Finnesburh**), **The Fight at** (8th century?). Old English (Anglo-Saxon) poem, of which only a 50-line fragment is extant. In the version of the story incorporated in BEOWULF, King Finn of the Frisians has married Hildeburh of the Danes, but treacherously attacks her brother Hnaef and his followers while they are his guests. The following spring the Danes under Hengest kill Finn and carry Hildeburh back to Denmark.

Fionn mac Cumhail. Also known as **Finn mac Cumhail, Finn MacCool.** Legendary Irish hero, hero of the FENIAN CYCLE, and leader of the Fenians, a band of warriors. He is now believed to have an historical basis, dating back to the third century B.C. The Fenians and Fionn himself were famous for their remarkable strength and stature, their fearlessness, and their extraordinary feats. As a child, Fionn was educated in the forest by a poet. His profound wisdom came from his having tasted the salmon of knowledge which fed on the hazelnuts of wisdom. His life is one of countless adventures with giants and hags; in the service of the high king at Tara, he performs many deeds, and it is for the king that he organizes the Fenians, or Fianna. His life knows two great loves: his first wife, Sedb, mother of his son Oísin, or OSSIAN, and his second wife, Gráinne, who betrays him with his kinsman Diarmuid. THE PURSUIT OF DIARMUID AND GRÁINNE is the best known of the stories of Fionn. Fionn is the hero of James Macpherson's poem FINGAL, AN ANCIENT EPIC, a spurious translation from the Gaelic.

Fiordiligi or **Fiordelisa.** In the Orlando poems of Boiardo and Ariosto, the daughter of King Dilistone. As a child she was stolen from her parents and brought up with BRANDIMARTE, a knight whom she loves and follows everywhere on his adventures. Eventually, the revelation of her royal birth enables them to marry, but Brandimarte is killed soon after. She builds a tomb for him and encloses herself within it to await her own death.

Fiorentino, Ser **Giovanni.** The Italian author of a collection of 50 *novelle* in imitation of the *Decameron* of Boccaccio, entitled by later readers *Il Pecorone (The Numbskull).* The author, about whom nothing is known, says he finished the tales in 1385. One of the stories, "Giannetto and the Lady of Belmont," provided Shakespeare with the pound of flesh and other details of *The Merchant of Venice.*

Firbank, Ronald (1886–1926). English novelist. Heir of the decadents of the 1890's, and a Catholic, Firbank was an escapist who created fantastic, elegant wish-fulfilment myths, and a wit who was master of brilliant dialogue. Gaily vicious, his characters are society ladies, ecclesiastics, lesbians, kings, nuns, and Negroes. The mid-century is seeing a revival of interest in his work, with a successful musical-comedy adaptation of VALMOUTH. *The Flower Beneath the Foot* (1923) is a romance and a saint's life. *Prancing Nigger* (1924) is a sympathetic account of a Negro family in Haiti who leave their village to educate their daughters—disastrously—in the big city. *Concerning the Eccentricities of Cardinal Pirelli* (1926) describes that dignitary's death in pursuit of a pretty choirboy through the cathedral.

Fir Bolg. In Gaelic literature, the 3rd race to invade and inhabit Ireland. They were defeated by the fourth race of invaders, the TUATHA DÉ DANANN.

Firdousī or **Firdusī** or **Firdausī.** (Born **Abul Qāsim Mansur** or **Hasan;** ?941–1020). Persian epic poet. His major work is the epic SHAH-NAMA. It was written at the request of the Sultan Mahmud ibn Sabuktagin who wanted a history of Persia. Its completion required 35 years. When it was finished in 1010, the sultan did not send the promised reward of a thousand gold pieces for every thousand couplets (60,000 in all), but substituted silver instead. In anger Firdousī gave the silver away, wrote a bitterly scurrilous satire that he sent to the sultan, and fled to exile. In Baghdad he wrote a long poem, *Yusuf and Zuleikha,* on the Koranic version of the loves of Joseph and Potiphar's wife, a popular theme in Persian literature. After nine years he returned to his birthplace of Tūs, Persia, where he died shortly thereafter.

Firenzuola, Angelo (1493–c. 1548). Florentine author. His best-known work is the dialogue *Della bellezza delle donne* (1541) concerning the beauty of women. This work is a study of the Renaissance conception of the ideal female type familiar in the paintings of the period.

Fire of London, Great. A fire that broke out in a baker's shop in Pudding Lane in 1666 and burned for three days and three nights. Much of the city was destroyed, including the old Gothic cathedral of St. Paul's. In his *Diary,* Samuel Pepys described how the fire spread "in corners and upon steeples, and

between churches and houses as far as we could see . . . in a most horrid malicious bloody flame."

First-Born. See GIANTS.

First Folio. The first collection of the plays of William SHAKESPEARE. It was compiled by his fellow actors John Heminges and Henry Condell, and published in 1623, seven years after his death. It contained 36 plays (omitting *Pericles,* but otherwise including all the plays now considered to be authentic) arranged under the headings of comedies, histories, and tragedies. It was dedicated to two literary patrons, the earl of Pembroke and the earl of Montgomery, and for many years was considered to be a more authoritative text than the earlier quarto editions of individual plays. Several editions appeared, the third of which (second issue, 1664) included seven additional plays of which only one, the sometimes-disputed *Pericles,* is considered to be the work of Shakespeare. A facsimile edition of the First Folio was published by the Oxford University Press in 1902, and by Yale University Press in 1954.

Fischer, Lisbeth. See COUSINE BETTE, LA.

Fischer, Louis (1896–   ). American writer and journalist. Fischer is especially known for his keen interest in modern political developments in Russia and India. His books include *The Soviets in World Affairs* (1931), *Men and Politics, An Autobiography* (1941), *Gandhi and Stalin* (1947), *The Life and Death of Stalin* (1952), *Russia Revisited* (1957), and *Russia, America and the World* (1961). He also edited *Mahatma Gandhi* (1950), the autobiography of the great Indian leader whose personal disciple Fischer became.

fish. As a symbol for Christ it was used by the early Christians. The letters of the Greek word for fish, ICHTHYS, formed an acrostic of the words Jesus Christ, Son of God, Saviour.

Fisher, Dorothy Canfield [formerly **Dorothy Canfield**] (1879–1958). American novelist and short-story writer. Mrs. Fisher was a kindly but discriminating interpreter of American life, especially in New England, from the beginning of her career. Among her most widely read novels are THE SQUIRREL-CAGE, *The Bent Twig* (1915), THE BRIMMING CUP, *Rough Hewn* (1922), *Her Son's Wife* (1926), and *The Deepening Stream* (1930). In *Four-Square* (1949) 17 of her short stories were collected. The best of her nonfiction work is *Vermont Tradition; The Biography of an Outlook on Life* (1953).

Fisher, [Alvero] Vardis (1895–   ). American novelist. Fisher first became known with his tetralogy of novels dealing with the life of Vridar Hunter, an autobiographical hero who is carried through childhood, adolescence, and maturity in a quest for the meaning of life: *In Tragic Life* (1932), *Passions Spin the Plot* (1934), *We are Betrayed* (1935), and *No Villain Need Be* (1936). His novel about the early Mormons, *Children of God* (1939), won the Harper Prize Novel award. With *Darkness and the Deep* (1943) he began a series of stories portraying the development of primitive man, which he called *Testament of Man. Peace Like a River* (1958), *My Holy Satan* (1959), and *Orphans in Gethsemane* (1960) are part of this series. Two later books are *Love and Death* (1960) and *Suicide or Murder: The Strange Death of Meriwether Lewis* (1962).

Fisherman's ring. The Pope's signet ring for attesting papal briefs. It bears his name encircling a figure of Peter, a fisherman and first bishop of the Roman Church. A new ring is made for each Pope and is destroyed at his death, to avoid forged documents.

Fitz Boodle Papers, The (1842–1843). A series of sketches and tales by William Makepeace THACK-ERAY. The principal character is a lazy young noble-man, George Savage Fitz Boodle, with a flair for Bohemian life.

FitzGerald, Edward (1809–1883). English trans-lator, man of letters. During his lifetime, FitzGerald was known only (and by few) for his wit and per-sonal sweetness; he was "dear old Fitz" to such as Thackeray and Tennyson. His *Six Dramas of Cal-deron* (1853) was poorly received when published, though later acclaimed as great translation. His fa-mous translation of the RUBÁIYÁT OF OMAR KHAY-YÁM was ignored until discovered by Dante Gabriel Rossetti and others after FitzGerald's death. His reputation is largely founded on this poem, so free in rendition as to be virtually an original work, and masterful in its concentration, music, and command of tone. FitzGerald's *Letters and Literary Remains* (ed. W. A. Wright, 1899) are also of much interest.

Fitzgerald, F[rancis] Scott [Key] (1896–1940). American novelist and short story writer. One of the most gifted writers of his generation, Fitzgerald be-came known for his novels and stories of the 1920's; he called it the "Jazz Age" and described it as "a new generation grown up to find all Gods dead, all wars fought, all faiths in man shaken." As a spokes-man for the Jazz Age, Fitzgerald created glittering characters, cynical and irresponsible, trying to turn life into an endless, gay party; as the moralist he felt himself essentially to be, he infused his novels and stories with the sense that something was desperately wrong.

Fitzgerald was born in St. Paul, Minnesota, where his mother's well-to-do middle class family had its roots; he was named after the author of *The Star-Spangled Banner*, an ancestor of his father. He at-tended Princeton, but did not receive his degree; here it was that he began his lifelong friendship with Edmund Wilson. He served in the army, but never saw action, and in fact spent most of his time work-ing on his first novel THIS SIDE OF PARADISE. Pub-lished in 1920, it was a spectacular success both fi-nancially and critically. In the same year he married the beautiful Zelda Sayre and together they embarked on a life that reads like one of his novels, commuting between the plush hotels and better speakeasies of the U.S. and the fashionable resorts of Europe, where they mingled with other wealthy, sophisticated ex-patriates. They made homes on the Riviera, and in Paris, New York, Long Island, and Washington. It was a glamorous life that was to end tragically with Zelda's incurable mental illness and Fitzgerald's break-down.

Fitzgerald followed his first success with a collec-tion of short stories *Flappers and Philosophers* (1920), and a second novel *The Beautiful and Damned* (1921), in which he describes the pervading goal of his day as "the final polish of the shoe, the ultimate dab of the clothes brush, and a sort of intellectual There!" *Tales of the Jazz Age* (1922) and *The*

Vegetable (a play; 1923) were followed by THE GREAT GATSBY, often considered his finest work. As was his custom, he immediately followed the novel with another collection of short stories, *All the Sad Young Men* (1926).

From this point on in his career, Fitzgerald had an increasingly difficult time in keeping abreast of the enormous financial and emotional demands be-setting him. His next novel, TENDER IS THE NIGHT, was not published until 1934, its progress having been constantly interrupted with attempts to meet his expenses by writing stories for magazines. The strain of Zelda's severe mental illness and of trying des-perately to bring her back to health contributed to his own personal crisis which he described in *The Crack-Up* (1936). His determined, and to some ex-tent, successful efforts to put the pieces of his life back together and to devote himself to writing ended with his early death. His last novel, *The Last Tycoon* (1941), incomplete at his death, is considered by many critics to be his best.

Fitzgerald was also a master of the short story form; among his finest are *The Rich Boy, The Dia-mond as Big as the Ritz,* and *Babylon Revisited.*

Fitzgerald has been the subject of a great number of biographical and critical works; the central char-acter of Budd Schulberg's novel *The Disenchanted* (1950) is modeled closely on Fitzgerald in his de-clining years. His *Letters*, edited by Andrew Turn-bull, appeared in 1963.

Fitzgerald, Robert David (1902–). Aus-tralian poet. His work is noted for its vitality and metaphysical content. His *Essay on Memory* won the Australia-wide competition that took place during the 150th anniversary celebration. His writings in-clude *The Greater Apollo: Seven Metaphysical Songs* (1927), *To Meet the Sun* (1929), *Moonlight Acre* (1938), *This Night's Orbit* (1953), *Between Two Tides* (1952), and *The Wind at Your Door* (1959).

Fitzmaurice-Kelly, James (1857–1923). English authority on Spanish literature. He wrote authorita-tive works in his field and was editor of *The Oxford Book of Spanish Verse* (1913).

Five, The. A group of late 19th-century Russian composers who, fervent nationalists, hoped to develop an indigenous school of music. It consisted of Mily Balakirev (1837–1910), who was leader, César Cui (1835–1918), MUSSORGSKY, BORODIN, and RIMSKY-KORSAKOV.

Five Classics. Works in the Confucian canon. They are: BOOK OF ODES, BOOK OF CHANGES, BOOK OF RITES, BOOK OF DOCUMENTS, and the SPRING AND AUTUMN ANNALS. Together with the *Four Books*, they served as the basis of Chinese education until recent times.

Five-Foot Shelf. A popular name for the HAR-VARD CLASSICS.

Five Nations. (1) A confederation of five re-lated tribes of the Huron-Iroquois linguistic stock: the Mohawks, Oneidas, Onondagas, Cayugas, and Senecas. See IROQUOIS LEAGUE.

(2) The Five Civilized Nations or Tribes were the Cherokee, Chickasaw, Choctaw, Creek, and Seminole, so called because they had gone far in absorbing the civilization of the white settlers.

Five-Year Plan. A period of industrial construc-tion and consolidation in the Soviet Union. The first plan lasted from 1928 to 1932. At the instigation of the literary group RAPP, many novels, stories, and plays were produced depicting the time. Among the best were works by Valentin Katayev (*Time, Forward!*) and by Leonid Leonov.

Flaccus, Quintus Horatius. See HORACE.

Flag Day. June 14, celebrated in the U.S. as the anniversary of the formal adoption of the Stars and Stripes in 1777, though not a legal holiday.

Flagellants. Members of religious associations who hold that the wrath of God can be appeased only by self-flagellation. The first wave of this movement spread over Europe, starting from Italy, about the year 1260. Scenes of public processions with the exhibition of bloody self-castigation were repeated on a larger scale at the time of the plague called the black death (about 1348). For a modern group with similar tenets see PENITENTES.

Flagstad, Kirsten (1895–1962). Norwegian dramatic soprano. She was famous for her Wagnerian interpretations, especially in the role of Isolde. Her autobiography, *The Flagstad Manuscripts* (1952), was narrated to the music critic, Louis Biancolli.

Flaherty, Robert Joseph (1884–1951). Canadian explorer, writer, and pioneer documentary motion-picture director. From 1910 to 1916, he led a number of expeditions into the subarctic regions of eastern Canada. Among his classic documentary films are *Nanook of the North* (1922), *Moana of the South Seas* (1925), *Tabu* (1931), *Man of Aran* (1934), *Elephant Boy* (1935), and *Louisiana Story* (1948). He wrote the autobiographical *A Film-Maker's Odyssey* (1939) and the novels *The Captain's Chair* (1938) and *White Master* (1939).

Flame of Life, The (Il Fuoco, 1900). A novel by Gabriele D'ANNUNZIO. It deals with the love affair of La Foscarina, a great tragic actress in her prime, and Stelio, a young poet. Inspired by the author's liaison with Eleonora DUSE, the novel caused a scandal upon publication.

Flaminio, Marcantonio (1498–1550). Venetian lyricist. He is noted for his prolific output of secular and religious verse in Latin during the Renaissance. Especially noteworthy is the *Lusus Pastorales* (*Pastoral Fancies*, 1552), eight books of bucolic verse.

Flanders, Moll. See MOLL FLANDERS.

Flaubert, Gustave (1821–1880). French novelist. Born at Rouen in Normandy, Flaubert is one of the great literary artists of the 19th century. Although his name is associated with the naturalist movement, his artistic beliefs and ideals may not be so neatly summarized. Victor Hugo, Chateaubriand, and Gautier were the writers whom Flaubert most admired. A deep strain of romanticism in his own nature, which found expression in lyricism and vivid imaginings, was resolutely curbed in the service of his theories of art. Like Gautier, Flaubert believed in perfection of form and in the absolute value of art: *l'art pour l'art* ("art for art's sake"). In technique, his work is marked by exactness and accuracy of observation, extreme impersonality and objectivity, and extraordinary balance and precision of style. But his precise, careful portrayal of object and event, although naturalistic in method, was not naturalistic in aim. Flaubert's concern was to create reality through the art of exact selection and the chiseled perfection of his style. Beset by ill health and by per-

sonal misfortune, he led a solitary life of rigid discipline. His obsession with the writer's craft is legendary. Hour after hour, he would labor over the rhythm or the music of a particular sentence, seeking *le mot juste*. He wrote MADAME BOVARY, SALAMMBÔ, L'EDUCATION SENTIMENTALE, *Tentation de Saint-Antoine* (*The Temptation of Saint Anthony*, 1874), and the unfinished *Bouvard et Pécuchet* (1881). The short stories *Un Coeur Simple* (A SIMPLE HEART), *La Légende de Saint-Julien-l'Hospitalier*, and *Hérodias* appeared in the single volume *Trois Contes* (1877); these masterful tales revealed Flaubert's great command of this genre.

Flavius. In Shakespeare's TIMON OF ATHENS, the "true and honest" servant of Timon. His loyalty to Timon never wavers, even when his master is reduced to ruin. Flavius shares his savings with Timon's other servants and offers to give Timon the remainder.

Flavius and **Marullus.** In Shakespeare's JULIUS CAESAR, two tribunes, supporters of the defeated Pompey. They bitterly reproach the Roman masses for their fickleness, reminding them that they had once paid Pompey the same homage that they now give to Caesar.

Fleance. In Shakespeare's MACBETH, the son of Banquo. After the assassination of his father, he escapes to Wales. From him, according to legend, proceeded in a direct line the Stuart line of Scotland, thus fulfilling the witches' prophecy that Banquo's descendants would be kings.

Flecker, James Elroy (1884–1915). English poet and dramatist. He is known for his iconoclastic manner, his interest in Greece and the Orient, and the pictorial richness of his writing. His poetic works include *The Bridge of Fire* (1908), *The Golden Journey to Samarkand* (1913), *The Burial in England* (1915), and *Collected Poems* (1916). His plays are *Don Juan*, produced in 1925, and HASSAN, which was widely celebrated in the 1923 production. He wrote one novel, *King of Alsander* (1914). Flecker was called "the last of the Parnassians."

Flecknoe, Richard. See MacFLECKNOE.

Fleet marriages. Clandestine marriages that were performed without banns or license by needy chaplains, in Fleet Prison, London. As many as thirty marriages a day were sometimes celebrated in this manner. This practice was suppressed and declared null and void in 1774.

Fleet Street. A street in London now synonymous with English journalism and newspaperdom. It was a famous thoroughfare centuries before the first newspaper was published there at the close of the 18th century. The name derives from the old stream, the Fleet, now subterranean, which flowed nearby.

Fleming, Henry. The hero of Stephen Crane's novel THE RED BADGE OF COURAGE and of his short stories *Lynx-Hunting* and *The Veteran* (see WHILOMVILLE STORIES). In the novel, Fleming learns the meaning of fear and later, almost accidentally, of courage.

Fleming, Ian (1908–1964). English author of crime and adventure fiction. The hero of most of his novels is James Bond, a secret agent for British Intelligence. Among Fleming's works are *From Russia With Love* (1951), *Casino Royal* (1954), *Dr. No* (1959), *Goldfinger* (1959), and *Thunderball* (1961).

Fleming, Paul (1609–1640). German baroque poet. Although a close follower and admirer of Martin Opitz, he shows more depth of personal feeling in his verse. A complete edition of his works, *Teutsche Poemata* (German Poems, 1642), appeared posthumously.

Fleming, Peter (1907–   ). English travel writer and novelist. Among his books are *Brazilian Adventure* (1933); *News from Tartary* (1936); *Operation Sea Lion* (1957), dealing with a projected invasion of England during World War II; *Siege at Peking* (1959), about the Boxer Rebellion; and *Bayonets to Lhasa* (1961), an account of a British invasion of Tibet in 1904.

Fleshly School of Poetry, The (1871). An article in the *Contemporary Review* by Robert Buchanan. It is a vitriolic diatribe against the poetry of the Pre-Raphaelite Brotherhood, particularly that of Dante Gabriel Rossetti. These writers were accused of morbidity, nastiness, perverted sensuality, and indifference to larger and more exalted concerns of poetry. Buchanan, who wrote the piece over the signature Robert Maitland, at first denied authorship, but was later obliged to admit it. Swinburne became involved in the celebrated quarrel that followed, and his trenchant reply is to be found in *Under the Microscope* (1872). *The Fleshly School of Poetry* was reprinted in the volume *Notorious Literary Attacks* (1926), edited by Albert Mordell. See Stealthy School of Criticism.

Fletcher, Giles, the younger (1588?–1623). English poet. He is best known for Christ's *Victorie and Triumph in Heaven and Earth* (1610), a religious poem modeled on the work of DuBartas and Spenser, which is thought to have had a great influence on Milton's *Paradise Regained* (1671). He was the son of Giles Fletcher, the elder (1549?–1611), who wrote *Licia* (1593), an early book of sonnet sequences.

Fletcher, John. See Beaumont and Fletcher.

Fletcher, John Gould (1886–1950). American poet and critic. First associated with imagism and later with the Agrarians, he felt that modern poetry needed new patterns and new subject matter. His *Selected Poems* (1938) won a Pulitzer Prize. *Irradiations: Sands and Spray* (1915), his first volume of poetry, was followed by such other collections as *Goblins and Pagodas* (1916), *Breakers and Granite* (1921), *The Black Rock* (1928), and *XXIV Elegies* (1935). His prose works include a book on Gauguin (1921), *John Smith—Also Pocahontas* (1928), *The Two Frontiers: A Study in Historical Psychology* (1930), and the autobiography *Life Is My Song* (1937).

Fletcher, Phineas (1582–1650). English poet. The brother of Giles Fletcher the younger, he was a follower and imitator of Spenser. He is best known for *The Purple Island* (1633), an allegorical poem on man in terms of the topography and settlement of an island. Among his other works are *Locustae* (1627), an anti-Jesuit poem in Latin, its paraphrased English title being *The Apollyonists*; *Britain's Ida* (1627), a mythological poem in the manner of Spenser and first published as the work of Spenser; *Piscatory Eclogues and Other Poetical Miscellanies* (1633). Milton's Satan is believed to have been suggested by the Lucifer of *The Apollyonists*.

fleur-de-lis. See Lily of France.

Fleurs du mal, Les (The Flowers of Evil, 1857). A volume of poetry by Charles Baudelaire. Faced with the conflict of good and evil, Baudelaire discards the conventional distinctions and seeks beauty or good in the perverse, the grotesque, and the morbid. His sensibility, painfully alive to all emotions and sensations, lends unity to the various poems.

Flies, The (Les Mouches; 1943). A play by Jean-Paul Sartre. The plot is an adaptation of Aeschylus' story of Orestes. Zeus shares with Aegistheus "the bitterness of knowing men are free," although the townsfolk are content to let their king shoulder their decision-making along with their responsibility for guilt. Orestes is the dangerous man who knows that he is free, and that "human life begins on the far side of despair." To teach his people to be free and responsible, Orestes kills Aegistheus and takes with him the crowd of repulsive flies, the Furies of the Greek drama, who symbolize conscious acceptance of the consequences of one's acts. When it was first produced during the Occupation, the play had overtones of a call to resistance to the Vichy government's collaboration with the Nazis.

Flint, F[rank] S[tuart] (1885–1960). English imagist poet (see imagism) and translator. His collections of poetry are *In the Net of the Stars* (1909), *Cadences* (1915), and *Otherworld* (1915).

Flirtatious Mother, The. See Philippe Quinault.

Flite, Miss. In Charles Dickens' Bleak House, a pathetic old woman, demented because of the delay of her suit in chancery.

Floating Island. See Faerie Queene, The.

Flodden or **Flodden Field, Battle of.** A battle in Northumberland on Sept. 9, 1513. James IV of Scotland was defeated and killed by the forces of the earl of Surrey, who was in charge of the action in the absence of Henry VIII. The battle, in which there were up to 10,000 Scottish dead, among them all Scotland's leaders, was made the subject of poems by John Skelton, Thomas Deloney, and others. The battle is described in the 6th canto of Sir Walter Scott's *Marmion, A Tale of Flodden Field.*

flood myths. A very widespread theme in mythology is the destruction of the world by a flood and the survival of one human being, often with his family, thanks to the good will of a god. The most famous flood narrative, that of Noah, is based closely on the far older Babylonian story of Utnapishtim, told in the *Epic of* Gilgamesh. This in turn was based on the Sumerian legend of Ziusudra. In Hindu mythology, Vishnu appears to Manu, the first man, as a fish and warns him of the coming flood; the god himself leads Manu's ship to a safe mooring in the mountains of the North. In the Greek myth, Deucalion (see Deucalion's Flood), the son of Prometheus, is the hero who, with his wife Pyrrha, is saved and repopulates the earth. The Hittite Noah was Ullush. Stories of a great flood are also found in many parts of Asia, in Australia, and in North and South America, though they are uncommon in Europe. It has been suggested that these myths arose either from traditions of local floods or from attempts to explain striking configurations of the landscape.

Flora. In Roman mythology, goddess of flowers. Hence, in natural history all the flowers and vegetable productions of a country or locality are called its *flora.*

Flora. See TURN OF THE SCREW, THE.

Flores (or Floris) and Blanchefleur (*Fr.* Floire et Blancheflor). A medieval metrical romance in French and English. Flores and Blanchefleur are a Christian prince and princess who are brought up together and fall in love. Before Blanchefleur is carried off as a slave by the Saracens, she gives Flores a ring that will tarnish when she is in danger. It warns him, and he pursues her through many adventures to an Oriental Emir's harem, which he enters concealed in a basket of roses. When he is discovered, the lovers are sentenced to death, but are pardoned by the Emir because of the beauty of their love for each other. Boccaccio adapts this tale in his IL FILOCOLO.

Florian, Jean Pierre Claris de (1755–1794). French dramatist, novelist, and fabulist, admitted to the French ACADEMY in 1788. His comedies, such as *Les Deux billets* (1799) and *Le Bon ménage* (1782), depict bourgeois life in which Arlequin appears as a sentimental character. Marie Antoinette called Florian's novels "milk soup," such was their insipidity; among these are *Galatée* (1783, adapted from Cervantes) and *Numa Pompilius* (1786, a feeble imitation of Fénelon's *Télémaque*). His fame rests on his agreeable, limpid *Fables,* which are similar to those of La Fontaine, though much less pessimistic.

Florimell. See FAERIE QUEENE, THE.

Florio, John (1553–1625). English lexicographer and translator. The son of an Italian Protestant refugee, Florio compiled an Italian-English dictionary, *A Worlde of Words* (1598), revised as *Queen Anne's New World of Words* (1611); he is best known, however, for his famous and enduring translation of Montaigne's *Essays* (1603).

Floris. See FLORES AND BLANCHEFLEUR.

Florismart. One of Charlemagne's PALADINS in medieval romances, a close friend of Roland.

Florizel. The son of Polixenes, king of Bohemia, in Shakespeare's WINTER'S TALE. During a hunting expedition, he sees Perdita, supposedly the daughter of a shepherd, falls in love with her, and courts her under the assumed name of Doricles. When Polixenes objects to the match, Florizel flees with her to Sicilia, where it is revealed that she is the long-lost daughter of that country's king, Leontes.

Flower and the Leaf, The (15th century). Anonymous allegorical poem of about 600 lines in rhyme royal, for a long time erroneously attributed to Geoffrey Chaucer. The knights and ladies of the Flower, fond of frivolous sports and amusements, are given shelter from a shower by the more serious company of the Leaf.

flower arrangement, Japanese. See IKEBANA.

Flowering Judas (1930). A collection of short stories by Katherine Anne PORTER. Originally printed in a limited edition, it was later reprinted with four stories added. It was the first major work to establish its author's reputation.

Flower of Chivalry. An epithet. It was often applied to Sir Philip Sidney, statesman, poet, and soldier (1554–1586) and to the Chevalier de Bayard, *le Chevalier sans Peur et sans Reproche* (1476–1524).

Fluellen. A pedantic Welsh captain in Shakespeare's HENRY V. He attempts to draw a comparison between Henry and Alexander the Great, but after he points out that one was born at Monmouth and the other at Macedon, both of which begin with the same letter, and that there is a river in both cities, he finds that he has exhausted his parallelisms.

Flute. See BOTTOM.

Flutter, Sir Fopling. See MAN OF MODE, THE.

Flying Dutchman. A legendary spectral ship. Supposedly, it can be seen in stormy weather off the Cape of Good Hope; it is considered an omen of ill luck. Sir Walter Scott, in his note to *Rokeby,* says that the ship was originally a vessel laden with precious metal, on which a horrible murder was committed; then plague broke out among the crew, and no port would allow the vessel to enter. The ill-fated ship still wanders about like a ghost, doomed to be sea-tossed, never more to enjoy rest. Captain Marryat's novel *The Phantom Ship* (1839) tells of Philip Vanderdecken's successful but disastrous search for his father, the captain of the *Flying Dutchman.* WAGNER's opera *The Flying Dutchman (Der Fliegende Holländer;* 1843) embodies the legend in a different form. An old Dutch captain, in the midst of a struggle with the elements, has sworn an impious oath to round the Cape even if it takes an eternity to do it. The curse, which is laid on him for centuries, will only be lifted if he finds a wife willing to sacrifice everything for his sake. The opera deals with the lifting of the curse by the Norwegian maiden Senta.

Foch, Ferdinand (1851–1929). Marshal of France, made supreme commander of the Allied forces in 1918, the last year of World War I.

Fogazzaro, Antonio (1842–1911). Italian novelist and poet. A representative of liberal Catholicism, he attempted to reconcile traditional dogma with modern science. His finest novel, *Piccolo Mondo Antico (The Patriot,* 1896), dramatizes the antithetical attitudes toward religion held by Franco Maironi, a rigid Catholic, and his wife Luisa, a rationalist. Only a shared tragedy succeeds in reconciling their mutual antagonism in favor of a trusting Christian faith. Other major novels include *Malombra* (1881), *The Politician (Daniele Cortis;* 1885), *Piccolo Mondo Moderno* (1901), *Il Santo* (1906), and *Leila* (1911). They describe a curious symbiosis of exalted mysticism and impassioned sensuality, suggestive of symbolist influence. *Il Santo* was judged heretical by church authorities. See Piero MAIRONI.

Fogg, Phileas. Hero of AROUND THE WORLD IN EIGHTY DAYS by Jules Verne.

Földes, Jolán, Anglicized as **Yolanda** (1903–). A Hungarian novelist, permanently established in London. Her novel *The Street of The Fishing Cat* was awarded the All-Nations Novel prize in 1936.

Folengo, Teofilo or **Girolamo** (1496–1544). Italian satiric poet and Benedictine monk. He is famous for his mock epic poem, *Baldus.* Published in two parts totaling 25 books, the poem was written in Macaronic Latin, a mixture of the classical tongue with Italian. In its satire it was influenced by earlier writers like Erasmus, Pulci, and Boiardo; its chief impact was on Rabelais, who used several of its characters and incidents. It has sometimes borne the title *Macaronicae,* and Folengo, also, has been known by the pseudonym he affixed to the poem, Merlin Cocai.

Folk book. See VOLKSBUCH.

Folle de Chaillot, La. See MADWOMAN OF CHAILLOT, THE.

Fomorians. In Gaelic literature, a race of giants who periodically came from the sea to raid prehistoric Ireland and inevitably tangled with whoever happened to be inhabiting the island at the time. See BATTLE OF MOYTURA, THE.

Fontaine, Jean de la. See Jean de LA FONTAINE.

Fontainebleau. A town 37 miles southeast of Paris. Its palace was from the Middle Ages a favorite residence of the royal families of France. Several treaties were signed there. The forest of Fontainebleau is considered the most beautiful in France. It was the resort of the Barbizon school of painters, also known as the Fontainebleau or Fontainebleau-Barbizon school.

Fontane, Theodor (1819–1898). German novelist, perhaps his country's greatest master of the social novel. In his youth, he was primarily a ballad writer but is not highly regarded as such; and it was not until the 1870's that he turned to novel writing. His style is realistic and witty, and he uses a great deal of dialogue to recreate the atmosphere of the society he depicts. Without being excessively gloomy, he is constantly skeptical of men's ability to rise above the foolishness they have inherited from the past. Most of his novels treat the decline of the Prussian nobility and the rise of the bourgeois, and most of his plots concern either persons who are living in the past or those who unsuccessfully try to transcend traditional values. His best-known novels are *Irrungen, Wirrungen* (*Mistakes, Confusions,* 1888), about a nobleman who finally chooses a socially acceptable bride over the girl he loves; *Frau Jenny Treibel* (1892), about *nouveau riche* families who jockey for social position by marrying their children to the right persons; and *Effi Briest* (1895), his greatest work, about a middle-class girl who is obliged by her family to marry the old baron who had once been her mother's sweetheart. As a critic, Fontane was one of the first to appreciate the young authors of naturalism, particularly Gerhart Hauptmann.

Fontanne, Lynn (1887?–   ). British-American actress. She is married to the actor Alfred LUNT, with whom she has starred in many stage productions, mainly light comedies. One of her finest performances was as the old lady in Dürrenmatt's *The Visit of the Old Lady.*

Fontenelle, Bernard le Bovier de (1657–1757). French man of letters. *Entretiens sur la pluralité des mondes* (*Conversations on the Plurality of Worlds,* 1686), the best known of his writings, discusses the solar system in terms easily grasped by the general reader. In *Dialogues des morts* (*Dialogues of the Dead,* 1683), historical figures conduct imaginary and witty dialogues on a variety of philosophical subjects. Ostensibly opposing the pagan belief in oracles and upholding the scientific method, the *Histoire des oracles* (*History of Oracles,* 1686) levels a subtle attack at religious orthodoxy and blind obedience to authority. In *Digressions sur les anciens et les modernes* (*Digressions upon the Ancients and the Moderns,* 1688) Fontenelle sides with the moderns,

predicting unlimited progress in the arts and sciences.

Fonvizin, Denis Ivanovich (1745–1792). Russian satirical dramatist. He is best known for two classic comedies: *The Brigadier* (*Brigadir;* 1769) and *The Minor* (*Nedorosl';* 1782). The second play, considered his masterpiece, satirizes the barbaric habits of the semieducated gentry of the time.

Fool, Lear's. In Shakespeare's KING LEAR, the strangely wise companion in motley who travels in the storm with Lear, commenting on the behavior of mankind and peppering his words with song. The character is enigmatic in intent, "a pestilent gall" to Lear because of his bitter, mocking wit. He disappears at that point in the play at which Cordelia returns to help Lear, and he is believed in some way to represent truth, a trait also reflected in Cordelia, sometimes referred to by Lear as his "fool."

Fool of Quality, The (1765–1770). A long novel by Henry BROOKE, describing the education of young Harry Moreland, destined to become earl of Moreland and to marry a princess of Morocco. It presents, as Charles Kingsley remarked, "the education of an ideal nobleman by an ideal merchant prince"; and it teaches that "all virtues, even justice itself, are merely different forms of benevolence."

fools. Attendants at court. From medieval times until the 17th century licensed fools or jesters were commonly kept at court, and frequently in the retinue

Will Sommers, the court jester of Henry VIII.

of wealthy nobles. Thus we are told that the regent Morton had a fool, Patrick Bonny; Holbein painted Sir Thomas More's jester, Patison, in his picture of the chancellor; and as late as 1728 Swift wrote an epitaph on Dickie Pearce, the fool of the earl of Suffolk, who died at the age of 63 and is buried in Berkeley Churchyard, Gloucestershire. Dagonet, the fool of King Arthur, is also remembered.

Among the most celebrated court fools are: Rayère, of Henry I; Scogan, of Edward IV; Thomas Killigrew, called "King Charles jester" (1611–1682); Archie Armstrong (d. 1672), and Thomas Derrie, jesters in the court of James I; James Geddes, to Mary Queen of Scots; his predecessor was Jenny Colquhoun; Patch, the court fool of Elizabeth, wife of Henry VII, Will Sommers (d. 1560), Henry VIII's jester, and Patche, presented to that monarch by Cardinal Wolsey; and Robert Grene, jester in the court of Queen Elizabeth I.

The fools of Charles V of France were Mitton and Thévenin de St. Léger; Haincelin Coq belonged to Charles VI, and Guillaume Louel to Charles VII. Triboulet was the jester of Louis XII and Francis I (1487–1536); Brusquet, of whom Brantôme says "he never had his equal in repartee," of Henri II; Sibilot and Chicot, of Henri III and IV; and l'Angély, of Louis XIII.

The guild fools of medieval times played an important part in the spread of literature and education. They formed a branch of the Troubadour organization, a force that permeated Europe.

Fool's Errand, A (1879). A novel by Albion W. Tourgée. This book, published anonymously by "one of the fools," was admired by the public and the critics. The fool's errand was the attempt to rebuild the South, after the Civil War, in the image of the North. The novel concludes that Reconstruction is a failure. Tourgée discusses such groups as the new Ku Klux Klan in the passages of social history interwoven with the story. The story of a Union colonel from Michigan who moves to a Southern plantation after the war, the novel is semiautobiographical.

foot. See METER.

Foote, Samuel (1720–1777). English playwright and actor known for his sensational and libelous plays. In *The Minor* (1760), Foote satirizes METHODISM and George Whitefield; in *The Maid of Bath* (1761), he derides the suitors of the famous singer Elizabeth Linley, then wife-to-be of Richard SHERIDAN. His "scandal-chronicle" comedies gave Foote an opportunity to display his remarkable mimicry and to caricature mercilessly his enemies. Foote's other popular "noonday-skits" include *The Diversions of the Morning* (1747), *An Auction of Pictures* (1748), and *Taste* (1752). His biting wit earned him the epithet "the English Aristophanes."

Forbes, Esther (1894?–   ). American historical novelist. Miss Forbes's favorite setting is New England. Among her books are *O Genteel Lady!* (1926); *A Mirror for Witches* (1928), a powerful novel of a 17th-century girl accused of witchcraft; *The General's Lady* (1938); *Johnny Tremaine* (1943); *The Running of the Tide* (1948); and *Rainbow on the Road* (1954). *Paul Revere and the World He Lived In* (1942) was awarded a Pulitzer Prize.

Forbes, Kathryn. Pen name of **Kathryn Anderson McLean** (1909–1966). American writer. Miss Forbes's short stories about her maternal grandmother, a Norwegian immigrant, were collected as *Mama's Bank Account* (1943). *I Remember Mama*, a dramatization of the book by John Van Druten, appeared the following year. Miss Forbes is also the author of *Transfer Point* (1947), the story of a 10-year-old girl and a San Francisco trolley car, and *Dog Who Spoke to Santa Claus* (1956), a collection of Christmas stories.

Forbidden City. The city of LHASA in Tibet. It was so called because of the hostility of the lamas to visitors other than pilgrims. Also the section of Peking with the Imperial palace, which was formerly closed to the general public.

forbidden fruit. Figuratively, unlawful indulgence, from the fruit of the tree of the knowledge of good and evil eaten by ADAM AND EVE in disobedience of God's command. According to Muslim tradition, the forbidden fruit was the banana or Indian fig, because fig leaves were employed to cover the disobedient pair when they felt shame as the result of sin.

Forced Marriage, The. See SGANARELLE (3).

Ford, Ford Madox. Original name, **Ford Madox Hueffer** (1873–1939). English novelist and editor. His mother was the daughter of Ford Madox Brown, the Pre-Raphaelite painter, and sister-in-law of William ROSSETTI. Violet HUNT was Ford's mistress for some time. His best novels, THE GOOD SOLDIER and the tetralogy PARADE'S END, are studies of the emotional relationships in marriage and adultery. The early novels *The Inheritors* (1901) and *Romance* (1903) were written in collaboration with Joseph Conrad, whose oblique narrative method Ford admired and imitated. He wrote critical studies of Conrad (1924) and of Henry James (1913). An important literary editor, Ford founded the *English Review* in 1908 and edited the *Transatlantic Review,* from Paris, from about 1924. He "discovered" D. H. Lawrence (see MIRIAM) and was a friend of James Joyce and Ezra Pound. Among his volumes of autobiography and memoirs are *No Enemy* (1929), *Return to Yesterday* (1931), and *It Was the Nightingale* (1933). During the 1950's, Ford began to be increasingly recognized as a major 20th-century writer.

Ford, Henry (1863–1947). American industrialist. Founder of the Ford Motor Co. (1903), he is famous for introducing the principles of mass production to the manufacture of inexpensive automobiles. The Ford Foundation, established in 1936, has done much toward furthering peace, improving college salaries, and protecting freedom of speech, even though Ford himself was often extremely conservative in his social outlook. With Samuel Crowther he wrote several books, among them *My Life and Work* (1923).

Ford, John (1586–c. 1640). English dramatist. He is known for his portrayal of passion and for his concentration on incest and other sexual abnormalities, as revealed in such works as 'TIS PITY SHE'S A WHORE and THE BROKEN HEART. These characteristics are less apparent in PERKIN WARBECK. His other plays include *The Lovers' Melancholy* (1628), *The Lady's Trial* (1638), *The Fancies, Chaste and Noble* (c. 1635), *Love's Sacrifice* (1630), *The Sun's Darling* (1624), and *The Witch of Edmonton* (c. 1623), written with William Rowley and Thomas Dekker.

Ford, Paul Leicester (1865–1902). American novelist and historian. His fame rests principally on two novels: THE HONORABLE PETER STIRLING and JANICE MEREDITH. With his brother, Worthington Ford, he issued some important bibliographies, *Winnowings in American History* (15 v., 1890–1891). Among his various historical and biographical works are *The True George Washington* (1896) and *The Many-Sided Franklin* (1899).

Forester, C[ecil] S[cott] (1899–1966). English novelist, creator of Horatio HORNBLOWER. He is best known for his Hornblower books, but he also wrote the successful *Payment Deferred* (1926), a crime novel; *The Gun* (1933), and THE AFRICAN QUEEN. His recent works include *The Naval War of 1812* (1957) and *Hunting the Bismarck* (1959).

Forest Lovers, The (1898). A popular historical romance by Maurice HEWLITT. Set in the Middle Ages, it is the story of the colorful adventures of Prosper le Gai. Out of pity he marries a waif who turns out to be the Coutess Isoult of Morgraunt.

Forever Amber. See Kathleen WINSOR.

formalism. A movement in Russian literary theory and criticism during the 1920's. It was characterized by its members' interest in aesthetic as opposed to social aspects of art. Although they lost the dominant place in Soviet literature to the advocates of proletarian and socialist art, the movement did inject a healthy interest into Russian literary criticism in the nature of literature and the problems of literary craft. Such interests had been generally subordinate to social concerns since the 19th-century critic Vissarion Belinski set the tone and direction of Russian criticism with his socially-oriented analyses and evaluations. The leading formalist theorists and critics were Victor Shklovski, Boris Eikenbaum, Yuri Tynyanov, Victor Zhirmunski, Boris Tomashevski, and Victor Vinogradov.

Forman, Harry Buxton (1842–1917). English critic and editor. He was responsible for painstaking editions of the works of Keats (1890) and Shelley (1876) and was a supporter of Rossetti, Morris, Meredith, and other contemporary poets.

Fornovo, battle of. In 1495, the French troops of King Charles VIII fought an army of Italian and mercenary troops and safely extricated themselves from defeat. However, a year later, at Atella, they were defeated; for the Italians, it was a major victory against the foreigner; and the basis of the fame of their leader, Francesco Gonzaga.

Fors Clavigera. See John RUSKIN.

Forster, E[dward] M[organ] (1879–   ). English novelist, short-story writer, and essayist. He is known for his liberal humanism, notably exemplified in his greatest novel, A PASSAGE TO INDIA, which is a study of the prejudices and injustices of the English rule over colonial India. With quiet irony, in all his novels he reveals the moral and emotional deficiencies of English middle-class life. HOWARDS END is based on his well-known motto "Only connect." Forster believes that people of different races and classes should "connect" with one another, and that within themselves individuals should "connect the prose with the passion"—be imaginative, mystical, and sensitive to nature as well as practical. Like Norman Douglas and D. H. Lawrence, Forster believes that middle-class English people tend to lack the capacity for passion and intuition, and must learn it from other countries, especially Southern Europe, and perhaps from the lower-class English. The novels WHERE ANGELS FEAR TO TREAD and A ROOM WITH A VIEW, both set in Italy, revolve about this theme. Forster's novels are technically enriched by the symbolic and structural devices discussed in his critical work ASPECTS OF THE NOVEL.

Brought up in the country in the house he later celebrated as Howards End, Forster was educated at King's College, Cambridge and continued to live there and in the village of Abinger. His novel THE LONGEST JOURNEY gives a picture of Cambridge life. Abinger is celebrated in *Abinger Harvest* (1936). In Cambridge and London Forster was associated with the BLOOMSBURY GROUP. He traveled to Europe and India, and lived in Alexandria for a while, writing about it in *Pharos and Pharillon* (1923), a collection of essays. He also wrote a number of short stories, chiefly of an allegorical kind, which he published in *The Celestial Omnibus* (1911) and *The Eternal Moment* (1928).

After an early burst of creative activity, Forster wrote no more novels. After 1924 he published only collections of literary and sociological essays such as *Abinger Harvest* and *Two Cheers for Democracy* (1951), biographies, and books of literary criticism. One of the great English novelists of our time, Forster has sometimes been underestimated because all his work belongs to the first quarter of the century.

Förster-Nietzsche, Elisabeth (1846–1935). Sister of Friedrich Nietzsche. In her additions to the works he left unfinished when he went insane, especially *Der Wille zur Macht* (*The Will to Power*, 1901), she distorted his views to make him appear a racist.

Forsyte Saga, The. A series of novels by John GALSWORTHY. Galsworthy continued to write novels about the Forsyte family throughout his life, but strictly the *Saga* consists of *The Man of Property* (1906), *In Chancery* (1920), and *To Let* (1921). The whole work was published with two additional "interludes," *Indian Summer of a Forsyte* and *Awakening,* in 1922. The Forsytes are a large upper-middle-class London family of conventional, materialistic businessmen. When the *Saga* opens, 10 members of the oldest generation are still alive. Most of the novels are concerned with two members of the second generation, Soames Forsyte and Young Jolyon, and their children.

The "man of property" of the first and best-known novel is Soames Forsyte, a typical member of the Forsyte family. His wife Irene, whom he regards as just another piece of property, falls in love with Philip Bosinney, a young architect. Soames devotes all his money and power to punishing them, and Philip is killed in an accident. *In Chancery* tells of the Forsytes' divorce. Irene marries Young Jolyon, the only sensitive member of the Forsyte family, and Soames marries a French girl, Annette. In *To Let,* Soames' daughter Fleur falls in love with Jon, the son of Young Jolyon and Irene; when the young couple learn the truth about their parents Jon draws back in order to remain loyal to his mother.

A Modern Comedy (1929) is a second series of novels about the Forsytes; it consists of *The White*

Monkey, The Silver Spoon, Swan Song, and two "interludes." This series carries the story up to Galsworthy's own day and is full of descriptions of the contemporary scene—toward which the aging author was unsympathetic. Most of the novels are about Fleur, her husband Michael Mont, and their friends. *End of the Chapter* (1933) is a little-read trilogy which is also concerned with Fleur and her friends. The Forsytes recur in many of Galsworthy's short stories and even in novels centered about other families.

In *The Forsyte Saga* itself Galsworthy satirizes Soames Forsyte and his materialistic values and champions the artist, the rebel, and the underdog. But in later novels he praises Soames' solid traditionalism, preferring him to the members of the modern young generation.

Fort, Paul (1872–1960). French poet and dramatist. In 1890 he reacted against the naturalist *Théâtre Libre* of ANTOINE by founding the *Théâtre d'art,* which became the influential *Théâtre de l'Oeuvre* under the director LUGNÉ-POË. Fort wrote a number of symbolic plays with historical subjects for the new theater, among them *La Petite Bête* (1890), *Ysabeau* (1924), and *Les Compères du Roi Louis* (1927). A native of central France, he celebrated her history and culture in forty volumes of *Ballades françaises* and *Chroniques de France* (1897–1951), versified poetry usually printed as prose paragraphs.

For the Time Being (1944). A Christmas oratorio in verse and prose by W. H. AUDEN. It retells the Nativity story in contemporary idiom, with modern allusions, and with some comic, music-hall ballads as well as lyrical choruses. Auden equates the bad political and spiritual condition of the world just before the birth of Christ with the contemporary situation.

Fortinbras. In Shakespeare's HAMLET, the prince of Norway. A man of action unlike the introspective Hamlet, he has planned to invade Denmark but, deterred by his uncle and Claudio, marches on Poland instead. When Hamlet dies, Fortinbras arrives to claim the Danish throne and to restore order to the kingdom.

Fortuna. In Roman mythology, the goddess of fortune or chance. She was identified with the Greek Tyche, and she was often depicted with a rudder, as the pilot of destiny, with wings, or with a wheel. The wheel of fortune was a widely used symbol in medieval art and literature, forming the concept on which Lydgate's *Falls of Princes* (1494) and Chaucer's *Monk's Tale* from the *Canterbury Tales* (1387–1400?) were based.

Fortunate Islands. Also called **Islands of the Blessed** or the **Happy Islands.** Imaginary islands in the ocean. Here the souls of the good lived in eternal bliss. The name was later applied to Canary and Madeira Islands.

Fortunatus. A hero of medieval European legend. A native of Cyprus, he meets the goddess of Fortune, who offers him any one of her gifts: wisdom, long life, riches, and the like. He chooses riches, and she gives him a purse that refills itself whenever he draws from it. On his travels he steals a magic wishing cap from the sultan of Cairo. These apparent treasures, however, eventually prove the ruin of him and his two sons, pointing the moral that

worldly goods do not bring happiness. The story first appears in print in a German collection of 1509. It was dramatized by Hans Sachs in 1553, Thomas DEKKER in 1660, and J. L. TIECK (*Phantasus,* 1812–1816). See SCHLEMIHL, PETER.

Fortunes of Nigel, The (1822). A novel by Sir Walter SCOTT set in the period of James I, in which James himself is a character. It relates the attempts of Lord Nigel Olifaunt to secure his properties and a wife.

forty. A number of frequent occurrence in Scripture. Hence it was formerly treated as, in a manner, sacrosanct. Moses was 40 days in the mount; Elijah was 40 days fed by ravens; the rain of the flood fell 40 days, and another 40 days expired before Noah opened the window of the ark; 40 days was the period of embalming; Nineveh had 40 days to repent; Jesus fasted 40 days; He was seen 40 days after His resurrection.

St. Swithin betokens 40 days' rain or dry weather; a quarantine extends to 40 days; 40 days, in the Old English law, was the limit for the payment of the fine for manslaughter; the privilege of sanctuary was for 40 days; the widow was allowed to remain in her husband's house for 40 days after his decease; a knight enjoined 40 days' service of his tenant; a stranger, at the expiration of 40 days, was compelled to be enrolled in some tithing; Members of Parliament were protected from arrest 40 days after the prorogation of the House, and 40 days before the House was convened; a new-made burgess had to forfeit 40 pence unless he built a house within 40 days.

The ancient physicians ascribe many strange changes to the period of 40; the alchemists looked on 40 days as the charmed period when the philosopher's stone and elixir of life were to appear.

forty-five, the, sometimes **'45.** The second rebellion of the JACOBITES which occurred in 1745 and failed. Prince Charles, "the Young PRETENDER," had to escape to France with the aid of Flora MACDONALD. See FIFTEEN, THE.

42nd Parallel, The (1930). A novel by John Dos Passos, 1st book in the trilogy later called *U.S.A.* (q.v.). Set in the period immediately before World War I, the novel interweaves episodes from the lives of several characters with the "newsreel" and "camera eye" devices and with biographies of Eugene Debs, Luther Burbank, William Jennings Bryan, Andrew Carnegie, Edison, and others.

The characters, some of whom appear in other parts of the trilogy, include Fainy McCreary ("Mac"), who eventually joins the Mexican Revolution; the ruthless J. Ward Moorehouse; Eleanor Stoddard, with whom he has an affair; and Charley Anderson, who later becomes a war hero and airplane manufacturer. These various interlocking strands are designed to show the U.S. on the eve of the First World War, rather than the development of particular individuals. Although the book is sometimes confusing, it is, nevertheless, a powerful presentation of a vast canvas of human nature and history.

forty stripes save one. A punishment. The Jews were forbidden by the Mosaic law to inflict more than 40 stripes on an offender, and for fear of breaking the law they stopped short of the number. If the scourge contained three lashes, 13 strokes would equal forty save one.

Forty Thieves. See ALI BABA AND THE FORTY THIEVES.

For Whom the Bell Tolls (1940). A novel by Ernest HEMINGWAY. Set against the background of the Spanish Civil War (1936–1939), it tells the story of Robert Jordan, an idealistic American college professor, who has come to Spain to fight with the Republican army. He has been assigned to a band of guerrillas led by Pablo and his wife, Pilar, a powerful peasant woman. Jordan's task is to blow up a bridge of strategic importance. He falls in love with Maria, a young Spanish girl who has been raped by the Fascists, and, during the three days they are together, they try to forget the impending event in their passion for each other. There is jealousy and distrust among the peasant members of the guerrilla company, several are killed, and the inefficiency and jealousies of the Communist leaders are revealed, but Jordan carries out his mission. He blows up the bridge successfully, but is wounded and left on the hillside to die. The title of the novel is taken from one of the best-known passages in the DEVOTIONS of John Donne.

Foscari, Francesco (1373–1457). Famous *doge* (leader) of the Venetian republic. His long service to his city ended tragically with his expulsion from office. The story of how his enemies used the weaknesses of his son to humiliate him attracted the interest of Lord Byron, who immortalized the affair in his *Two Foscari*.

Foscolo, Ugo (1778–1827). Italian novelist, poet, and patriot. He was the author of *Le Ultime Lettere di Jacopo Ortis* (1802), the first Italian novel in the modern sense of the word. Influenced by Goethe's *Werther,* and told in the form of exchanged letters, it relates the story of the futile love of the young student Ortis for a married woman; Ortis' sufferings, compounded of fruitless passion and frustrated patriotism, eventually drive him to suicide. Foscolo's best-known poem, *I Sepolcri* (1807), reveals his dual poetic personality in its romantic spirit and neoclassical style.

A zealot for the cause of Italian national unity, he fought with Napoleon's Italian army and went into voluntary exile when Austria regained possession of Venetia and Lombardy. While in England (1816–1827), he wrote critical essays on literary, historical, linguistic, and political topics relating to Italy.

Foster, Hannah Webster (1759–1840). American novelist, author of THE COQUETTE. She wrote one other book, *The Boarding School* (1798), a series of didactic lectures on "female deportment."

Foster, Stephen Collins (1826–1864). American song writer and popular composer. Among his best-known songs are MY OLD KENTUCKY HOME, OLD FOLKS AT HOME, *Old Black Joe,* and *Jeanie with the Light Brown Hair.* His OH! SUSANNA appeared in 1848 and, becoming extremely popular with the gold-rush "forty-niners," established his success. Many of his songs were used by the Negro minstrel troupes popular at the time and have become genuine American folk songs. Foster died, almost destitute, in the charity ward of Bellevue Hospital in New York.

Fouché, Joseph. Duke of **Otranto** (1763–1820). French minister of police. A master of political in-

trigue, Fouché was renowned for his espionage system. He served in turn as minister of police, senator, minister of the interior, and again as minister of police. In 1816, Fouché was exiled from France. Stefan Zweig has written a biographical study entitled *Joseph Fouché.*

Fountainhead, The (1943). A novel by Ayn RAND. The hero of this widely sold book, who is supposedly modeled on Frank Lloyd Wright, is an architect of enormous conceit who nevertheless succeeds in justifying his faith in the permanent values of honest design.

Fountain of Youth. In popular folk tales, a fountain supposed to possess the power of restoring youth. Expeditions were fitted out in search of it, and at one time it was supposed to be in BIMINI. See PONCE DE LEÓN.

Fouqué, Friedrich von. Baron de la Motte (1777–1843). German author of fantastic tales and sentimental romances. He was prominent in the movement of GERMAN ROMANTICISM. His most famous work is the tale UNDINE.

Fouquet, Jean (c. 1420–c. 1480). French painter. The leading representative of French 15th-century painting, he was deeply influenced by both the work of the early Florentine school and the Flemish tradition of the Van Eycks. The court painter of Louis XI, he is known equally as a miniaturist and portrait painter.

Fouquet or **Foucquet, Nicolas** (1615–1680). French superintendent of finance under Cardinal Mazarin. At best a haphazard financier, Fouquet bestowed generous favors upon men of letters and incurred the disfavor of King Louis XIV. Arrested by royal order in 1661, he was tried for speculation and sentenced to life imprisonment. He died after 19 years in prison.

Fouquier-Tinville, Antoine Quentin (1746–1795). French revolutionist. He was a public accuser of unexampled ferocity before the Revolutionary Tribunal (March 1793–July 1794). He wrote articles of accusation against Marie Antoinette and ROBESPIERRE, who was once his benefactor.

Fourberies de Scapin, Les. See SCAPIN.

Four Books. The four principal works in the Confucian canon. They are: The ANALECTS, the GREAT LEARNING, The MEAN, and the MENCIUS. Except for the *Analects,* these were relatively unimportant works until raised to an exalted status by Chu Hsi during the Sung Dynasty (960–1279). From this time they were used as the primary textbooks in the Chinese educational system and served as the basis for civil service examinations until 1905. See the FIVE CLASSICS.

Four Horsemen of the Apocalypse. The personifications of the evils of war who appear in the Revelation of St. John the Divine (Rev. 6). They are Conquest, Slaughter, Famine, and Death, and are seen on white, red, black, and pale horses, respectively. The Spanish novelist Vicente Blasco-Ibáñez entitled his widely read novel of World War I *The Four Horsemen of the Apocalypse (Los cuatro jinetes del apocalipsis;* 1916); it has twice been produced as a motion picture.

four hundred, the. The inner circle of New York society, the élite. The term originated in 1892 when only 400 guests were invited to a ball given by

Mrs. William Astor since her ballroom had space for only that number. See FOUR MILLION, THE.

Four Hymns to Love and Beauty (1596). A set of poems by Edmund SPENSER. The first two, *A Hymn in Honor of Love* and *A Hymn in Honor of Beauty,* were written in Spenser's youth. According to his introductory note, he desired to "amend" his youthful praise of natural love and beauty, and so wrote the second two hymns to heavenly love and beauty. All four poems, however, partake strongly of the Platonist and neo-Platonist ideas that mark much of his work, and there is little ideological conflict between the two sets of hymns.

Fourierism. The social system advanced by François Marie Charles Fourier (1772–1837), French reformer and economist. In order that men might live in the harmony to which they were naturally predisposed and which could be developed under proper conditions, Fourier envisioned a society in which economic activities would be carried on by phalanxes, groups consisting of some 1600 persons, who would live in common buildings called phalansteries. Products would be divided among the members of each phalanx, with labor receiving the largest share; private property, however, would not be abolished. A republican form of government, with elective officials, would be established. Fourier outlined his ideas in several works, including *Théorie des quatre mouvements* (1808), *Traité de l'association domestique agricole* (1822), and *Le Nouveau Monde industriel* (1829–1830). A number of Fourieristic communities and periodicals were founded in France, and several novels by George Sand show the influence of his ideas. Introduced into the U.S. in 1842 by Albert Brisbane, Fourierism was adopted by the members of BROOK FARM.

Four Million, The (1906). A collection of 25 short stories by O. HENRY. The title, referring to the actual population of New York City at the time, was selected as a rebuttal to Ward McAllister's famous remark that "there are only about 400 people in New York society." The book contains O. Henry's famous story, THE GIFT OF THE MAGI, although perhaps its best piece is *An Unfinished Story.* O. Henry's favorite characters—shop girls, tramps, the humble and lowly in general—people these tales and give utterance to the author's unique brand of gently ironic sentimentality.

Fournier, Henri. Real name of ALAIN-FOURNIER.

Fournier, Pierre. See Pierre GASCAR.

Four P's, The (performed c. 1520; published 1544). An INTERLUDE by John HEYWOOD. It is a debate among a Palmer, a Pardoner, and a Potecary, with a Pedlar acting as judge, as to who can tell the biggest lie. The Palmer, who asserts that he never saw a woman out of temper, wins the prize.

Four Quartets (1936–42). A long poem by T. S. ELIOT. Considered by many critics to be Eliot's major poetic achievement, it is an elaborate, allusive meditation on time and eternity, consisting of four poems named for four different places. The first (published in 1936), is set in *Burnt Norton,* a house with a rose garden in which children are playing. The second is *East Coker* (1940), the village in England from which Eliot's 17th-century ancestor set out for the New World. *The Dry Salvages* (1941) is a group of rocks off the coast of Massachusetts, where Eliot lived

as a boy; the poem also has descriptions of the Mississippi, St. Louis having been his childhood home. The last poem (1942) is inspired by LITTLE GIDDING and its chapel. It is a wartime poem; there are references to the bombing in London alongside references to the English Civil War. The whole work is as elaborately constructed as a piece of music, with its recurrent imagery, series of symbols (the separate poems are concerned, respectively, with air, earth, water, and fire), and literary, historical, and Christian references. Each poem ends with some words about the poet's craft and the problems of creating a work of art.

Four Saints in Three Acts (1927). An opera by VIRGIL THOMSON to a libretto by GERTRUDE STEIN, first produced in 1934 with an all Negro cast. The text exemplifies Miss Stein's unique style: repetitive, sonorous, contradictory, and obscure. The opera is actually divided into four acts, with about a dozen saints, some historical and others fictitious. One famous line is "Pigeons on the grass alas."

four senses. The 4 varieties of Scriptural interpretation: 1. historical or literal, 2. allegorical, 3. moral, 4. anagogical. "Jerusalem is *literally* a city in Palestine, *allegorically* the Church, *morally* the believing soul, *anagogically* the heavenly Jerusalem."

fourteener. (1) In English prosody, a line containing 14 syllables, usually 7 iambic feet. It was widely used in English verse about the middle of the 16th century. See POULTER'S MEASURE.

(2) A poem of 14 lines, a sonnet or any other variation of this length, is now sometimes referred to as a fourteener.

Fourteen Points. A statement of American peace aims during World War I. It was made by President Woodrow WILSON in an address to Congress on Jan. 8, 1918. Briefly abridged, the Fourteen Points are as follows:

(1) Open covenants of peace, openly arrived at.

(2) Freedom of navigation upon the seas, except by international action.

(3) Removal of economic barriers and establishment of equality of trade conditions.

(4) Adequate guarantees of reduction of national armaments to the lowest point consistent with domestic safety.

(5) An impartial adjustment of all colonial claims with fair consideration for the interests of populations and governments concerned.

(6) Full cooperation in obtaining for Russia an unhampered opportunity for the independent determination of her own political development.

(7) The evacuation of Belgium.

(8) The restoration of Alsace-Lorraine to France.

(9) The readjustment of Italian frontiers on clearly recognized lines of nationality.

(10) Autonomous development for the peoples of Austria-Hungary.

(11) The relations of the Balkan states to be determined along historically established lines of allegiance and nationality.

(12) Autonomous development for other nationalities under Turkish rule; freedom of the Dardanelles.

(13) The establishment of an independent Polish state.

(14) The establishment of a general association of nations for the purpose of affording mutual guaran-

tees of political and territorial integrity to great and small alike.

In Nov., 1918, the other Allies reluctantly accepted the Fourteen Points, with reservations, as the basis for an armistice. The treaty of VERSAILLES, which ended the war, incorporated several of Wilson's points, including the covenant of the League of Nations.

fourth estate. The daily press. It is reputed to be the most powerful of all, the others being the Lords Spiritual, the Lords Temporal, and the Commons. Edmund Burke, referring to the Reporters' Gallery, is credited with having said, "Yonder sits the fourth estate, more important than them all," but it does not appear in his published works.

Fourth of July. An American national holiday in celebration of the Declaration of Independence, July 4, 1776, which declared the 13 colonies free and independent and absolved of all allegiance to Great Britain. It is also called *Independence Day.*

Fowler, Gene. Real name, **Eugene Devlan Fowler** (1890–1960). American writer. Born in Denver, Colo., Fowler had a successful career both as a newspaperman and script-writer. He is best known, however, for his lively biographies of picturesque contemporaries whom he knew personally. The first of these, *The Great Mouthpiece* (1931), was about a New York lawyer. It was followed by *Timberline* (1933), an account of two Denver editors. His best book is *Good Night, Sweet Prince* (1943), a biography of John Barrymore. Other books include *Beau James* (1949), the story of Jimmy Walker; *A Solo in Tom-Toms* (1946); and *Schnozzola: The Story of Jimmy Durante* (1951).

Fowler, Henry Watson (1858–1933). English lexicographer. With his brother F. G. Fowler (1870–1918), he wrote *The King's English* (1906). Fowler compiled a number of dictionaries based on the great *Oxford English Dictionary.* His most famous work is *A Dictionary of Modern English Usage* (1926), a remarkable compilation of learning, wit, humor, and good taste.

Fox, Charles James (1749–1806). Celebrated English statesman and orator. He was a Tory member of Parliament at the age of 20, and two years later became lord of the admiralty under Lord North. Removed from his post at the insistence of King George III, who disliked him both for his personal independence and for the dissoluteness of his life, Fox led the opposition to North's coercive measures against the American colonies. He was foreign secretary (1782–1783), first under Rockingham and then in Portland's coalition ministry, the latter being turned out of office by the king's intervention against Fox's India reform bill. He was kept out of office by the king until 1806 when William Pitt the younger died and he again held the portfolio of foreign secretary in the so-called All-The-Talents ministry during the last year before his own death. Fox once gave a toast: "Our Sovereign, the people." He urged abolition of slavery, favored the French Revolution, and objected to English participation in continental wars. He loved literature and made one venture into authorship with *History of the Early Part of the Reign of James II* which, unfinished, was published two years after his death.

Fox, George (1624–1691). The founder of the Society of Friends, or QUAKERS. The son of a weaver, and an apprentice to a cobbler, he became an itinerant lay preacher. He was an unusual combination of mystic and highly practical man, a fact that led him to denounce social evils in forthright terms that nine times landed him in prison. Nevertheless, he was very widely respected and loved for his remarkable personal qualities. He traveled as a missionary to the West Indies and America, and to Holland and Germany. Beginning about 1650, many persons had been so attracted to his teachings that they were organized in the Society of Friends, who were nicknamed Quakers. Because of his limited education, his writings were inelegantly though often effectively expressed.

Fox, John [William], Jr. (1863–1919). American writer of fiction. He achieved enormous popularity with his two best-selling novels, THE LITTLE SHEPHERD OF KINGDOM COME and THE TRAIL OF THE LONESOME PINE. An earlier novel, *The Kentuckians* (1898), contrasts the prosperous inhabitants of Kentucky's bluegrass region with its impoverished mountaineers. Fox's short stories and sketches were collected in *A Cumberland Vendetta* (1895), *Hell for Sartain* (1897), *Blue Grass and Rhododendron* (1901), and *Christmas Eve on Lonesome, and Other Stories* (1904).

Foxe, John (1517–1587). English martyrologist. Educated at Oxford, Foxe was made a Deacon in 1550. He was exiled between 1554 and 1559, the years of the reign of the Catholic Mary I, during which time he wrote a first Latin draft of his great work on martyrs. A revised and longer version was published in English in 1563 as *Actes and Monuments of These Latter Perilous Days* (commonly known as *The Book of Martyrs*). Two volumes, enlarged further, appeared in 1570. The *Actes and Monuments* was tremendously influential, being used practically as a companion-volume to the Bible in English churches and households for many years. The work is of interest historically for its many accounts of the deaths of contemporary Protestant martyrs.

F.P.A. See Franklin Pierce ADAMS.

Fracastoro, Girolamo (1483–1553). Veronese physician and poet. He is noted for his Latin verse,

Burning Anne Askew (1546). From Foxe's *Actes and Monuments.*

𝔗𝔥𝔢 deſcription of Smythfielde witn tue order end maner of certayne of tlje Councell, ſyttng there at the burnyng of Anne Aſkewe and Laceis witf the others.

especially the *Syphilis sive de morbo gallico* (*Syphilis or the Gallic Disease*), a combined mythological and scientific treatment of the subject. He is also the author of an important critical treatise, the *Navigerius*, which uses the dialogue form to discuss Renaissance literary problems and theories.

Fra Diavolo (1830). A highly popular comic opera by D. F. E. AUBER. It is founded on the exploits of Michele Pezza (1771?–1806), a celebrated brigand and renegade monk, who evaded pursuit for many years amidst the mountains of Calabria. The libretto is by Scribe.

Fradubio. See FAERIE QUEENE, THE.

Fragonard, Jean Honoré (1732–1806). French painter. A versatile imitator of Antoine Watteau and Giambattista Tiepolo, he painted and drew landscapes, mythological love-scenes, and fashionable outdoor gatherings. With verve and charm, he extended the popularity of rococo up to the time of the French Revolution.

Fra Lippo Lippi (1855). A poem in the form of a dramatic monologue by Robert BROWNING. The painter, speaking to street guards of Florence who have come upon him in the midst of a night adventure, gives his biography and his views on life and art. See Fra Lippo LIPPI.

Framley Parsonage, The. See BARSETSHIRE, CHRONICLES OF.

France, Anatole. Pen name of **Jacques Anatole François Thibault** (1844–1924). French novelist, poet, and critic. An eminently civilized man of letters, Anatole France occupied the chief position in the French literary world for many years. In 1872, he published *Les Poèmes dorés,* a volume of poetry in the manner of the PARNASSIANS—pure in form and classical in spirit. A poetic drama *Les Noces corinthiennes* was published in 1876. France's career as a critic began in 1888, when he was appointed literary editor of *Le Temps,* a popular daily. His criticism is avowedly impressionistic and subjective, the imaginative play of a finely developed mind and cultivated sensibility responding to and revealing his world and age. Elected to the French Academy in 1896, he reached the peak of his fame during the turn of the century. By the time of his election he had published his famous novels THE CRIME OF SYLVESTER BONNARD; THAÏS, made into an opera by Massenet (1894); AT THE SIGN OF THE REINE PÉDAUQUE; THE RED LILY; and a volume of short stories, *L'Etui de Nacre* (*The Mother-of-Pearl Box,* 1892). Highly allusive in nature, France's subtle and ironic work displays an urbane cynicism and tolerant mockery. His style, like the tone of his writing, is sophisticated, delicate, and graceful. His later novels include PENGUIN ISLAND, THE GODS ARE ATHIRST, and the REVOLT OF THE ANGELS. *Histoire Contemporaine* (1896–1901) is a collection of four satirical novels: THE ELM TREE ON THE MALL, THE WICKERWORK WOMAN, THE AMETHYST RING, and *M. Bergeret à Paris.* France's autobiographical works include *Le Livre de mon ami* (*My Friend's Book,* 1885), *Pierre Nozière* (1899), *Le Petit Pierre* (*Little Pierre,* 1918) and *La Vie en Fleur* (*The Bloom of Life,* 1922). The relaxed detachment of many of France's writings may be juxtaposed with his passionate interest in the Dreyfus case. France's character, like his career, is interesting for its many facets. He was awarded the Nobel Prize for literature in 1921.

France, king of. In Shakespeare's KING LEAR, the husband of Cordelia, Lear's youngest daughter. Recognizing her virtues, he marries her although she has been disowned by her father.

France, rulers of. Like earlier members of his house, Pepin the Short ruled the domain of the Franks as mayor of the palace on behalf of the ineffectual MEROVINGIANS; the Carolingian dynasty began when Pepin set aside the last of the "do-nothing kings" and had himself crowned in 751.

THE CAROLINGIANS	
Pepin the Short	751 – 768
Charlemagne	768 – 814
Louis I	814 – 840
Charles I	840 – 877
Louis II	877 – 879
Louis III	879 – 882
Carloman	882 – 884
Charles II	884 – 888
Eudes (Odo)	888 – 898
Charles III	898 – 922
Robert I	922 – 923
Rudolf	923 – 936
Louis IV	936 – 954
Lothair	954 – 986
Louis V	986 – 987

THE CAPETS	
Hugh Capet	987– 996
Robert II	996–1031
Henry I	1031–1060
Philip I	1060–1108
Louis VI	1108–1137
Louis VII	1137–1180
Philip II	1180–1223
Louis VIII	1223–1226
Louis IX	1226–1270
Philip III	1270–1285
Philip IV	1285–1314
Louis X	1314–1316
John I	1316
Philip V	1316–1322
Charles IV	1322–1328

HOUSE OF VALOIS	
Philip VI	1328–1350
John II	1350–1364
Charles V	1364–1380
Charles VI	1380–1422
Charles VII	1422–1461
Louis XI	1461–1483
Charles VIII	1483–1498
Louis XII	1498–1515
Francis I	1515–1547
Henry II	1547–1559
Francis II	1559–1560
Charles IX	1560–1574
Henry III	1574–1589

HOUSE OF BOURBON	
Henry IV	1589–1610
Louis XIII	1610–1643
Louis XIV	1643–1715
Louis XV	1715–1774
Louis XVI	1774–1792

FIRST REPUBLIC	
National Convention	1792–1795
Directory	1795–1799
Napoleon (Consul)	1799–1804

FIRST EMPIRE

Napoleon I	1804–1814

HOUSE OF BOURBON

Louis XVIII	1814–1824
Charles X	1824–1830

HOUSE OF ORLÉANS

Louis Philippe	1830–1848

SECOND REPUBLIC

Louis Napoleon	1848–1852

SECOND EMPIRE

Napoleon III	1852–1870

THIRD REPUBLIC—PRESIDENTS

Thiers, Louis Adolphe	1871–1873
MacMahon, Marshal	1873–1879
Grévy, Jules	1879–1887
Carnot, Sadi	1887–1894
Casimir-Périer, Jean Paul	1894–1895
Faure, François Félix	1895–1899
Loubet, Emile	1899–1906
Fallières, Armand	1906–1913
Poincaré, Raymond	1913–1920
Deschanel, Paul	1920
Millerand, Alexandre	1920–1924
Doumergue, Gaston	1924–1931
Doumer, Paul	1931–1932
Lebrun, Albert	1932–1940

VICHY GOVERNMENT

Pétain, Henri Philippe	1940–1944
Laval, Pierre	1942–1944

PROVISIONAL GOVERNMENT—PRESIDENTS

de Gaulle, Charles	1944–1946
Gouin, Félix	1946
Bidault, Georges	1946
Blum, Léon	1946–1947

FOURTH REPUBLIC—PRESIDENTS

Auriol, Vincent	1947–1954
Coty, René	1954–1959

FIFTH REPUBLIC—PRESIDENT

de Gaulle, Charles	1959–

Francesca, Piero della. Real name: **Piero dei Franceschi** (1420?–1492). Italian painter and mathematician. Born in Umbria, he came in contact with the monumental tradition of Masaccio and the scientific studies of Brunelleschi and Alberti during a stay in Florence. His own work, in which an almost abstract simplification of forms is fused with a sensitive observation of light effects, creates a world of great solidity, simplicity, and calm. He wrote two mathematical treatises on perspective and on the five regular solids, and was the first to treat optics and perspective with a purely scientific method. Among his masterpieces are *The Legend of the Holy Cross,* a series of frescoes in the sanctuary of the church of St. Francis at Arezzo; the *Portrait of Federigo da Montefeltro; The Resurrection;* and the *Brera Madonna,* his last work. His leading pupils were Melozzo da Forlì and Luca Signorelli.

Francesca da Rimini. See PAOLO AND FRANCESCA.

Francis I (1494–1547). King of France (1515–1547). After conquering Milan by his victory at Marignano (1515), Francis tried unsuccessfully to be

elected Holy Roman Emperor and waged four wars against his victorious rival Charles V, who advanced claims to the French duchy of Burgundy and also to Milan. The first war (1521–1525) came to an end when Francis was defeated and taken prisoner at Pavia. In the second war (1527–1529) he lost his hold on Italy by the treaty of peace signed at Cambrai for him by his mother Louise of Savoy and known as the *Paix des Dames.* The third war (1536–1538) led to a truce. The fourth war (1542–1544) was terminated with the peace of Crespy which left Francis in possession of Burgundy while Charles retained Milan. Francis' reign is marked by the Renaissance in France. He himself was a patron of the arts. His sister was the celebrated Margaret of Navarre.

Franciscans. Also called **Friars Minor, Minorites,** and **Grey Friars.** A Catholic religious order. It was founded by Saint FRANCIS OF ASSISI (1209) simply as a confraternity and approved informally by Pope Innocent III (1210). The members made the usual vows of obedience, chastity, and a strict poverty permitting no possessions and dependent solely on the offerings of the faithful. Honorius III confirmed (1223) a new set of rules (including the requirement of a novitiate, etc.) for the now numerous order; but administrative struggles over the conviction of some that the order should be permitted to own the buildings it used and other necessaries eventually split the order (1415) into the Conventuals, following the modified rules, and the more traditional Observants. About 1528 even stricter reforms were instituted by a third branch, the Capuchins. About 1214 Francis had instituted a second order for nuns, called Poor Clares from their leader St. Clara; and about 1221 he organized the Brothers and Sisters of Penance as a third order of laymen, hence called Tertiaries. This important innovation was soon imitated by other religious orders.

Francis Ferdinand (1863–1914). Archduke of Austria, nephew of Francis Joseph and heir to the imperial throne of Austria. His assassination at Sarajevo, Bosnia, by Gavrilo Princip, a member of a Serbian secret society, precipitated the outbreak of World War I.

Francis Joseph I or **Franz Josef** (1830–1916). Emperor of Austria (1848–1916). He succeeded to the throne upon the abdication of his uncle, Ferdinand I, during the revolution of 1848 in Vienna. Throughout his reign he opposed the forces of liberalism and maintained a traditional imperial court. There was much tragedy in his personal life: he was the brother of the ill-fated MAXIMILIAN of Mexico; his wife Elizabeth was assassinated in 1898; his only son Rudolf committed suicide; and the assassination of his nephew and heir, Archduke Francis Ferdinand, precipitated World War I.

Francis of Assisi, St. Originally **Giovanni Francesco Bernardone** (1181 or 1182–1226). Italian monk, founder of the Order of FRANCISCANS. The son of a prosperous merchant, he turned at about 26 to a life of asceticism and mysticism, devoting himself to the care of the poor, the sick, and the leprous, as well as to prayer. Feeling a divine call to imitate Christ's life and to preach, he gathered about him a small group of followers and drew up (1209) the rules of life for the monastic order called the Friars Minor, later known as the Franciscans. They journeyed to Rome in 1210 and received verbal confirmation from the Pope. Francis joined a pilgrimage to Palestine (1219–1220), then resigned his leadership of the now numerous Friars Minor because of internal disputes about administration.

Francis' approach to religion was characterized by its joyousness and its love of nature; he called both animate and inanimate creations his brothers and sisters, and his preaching to the birds has become a popular subject for artists, as has the episode when two years before his death he is said to have received on his body the *stigmata* resembling Christ's wounds after 40 days of fasting on Mount Alverno. He was canonized as a saint in 1228, two years after his death; and about a century later the legends and anecdotes about his life, along with his sermons and sayings, were collected as the *Little Flowers of St. Francis Fioretti di S. Francesco d'Assisi*).

Franck, César Auguste (1822–1890). Belgian-French organist and composer. Among his works are the *Symphony in D minor* and the *Mass for Three Voices,* from which comes the familiar *Panis Angelicus.* His style is romantic and expansive, full of chromatic harmony and restless modulation. Among his pupils were Alexandre Guilmant, Vincent d'Indy, and Charles Bordes. These three founded a school, the *Schola Cantorum* (1894) to perpetuate their master's influence and methods.

Franco, Francisco (1892–   ). Spanish political leader. Chief of staff of the Spanish army at the beginning of the Civil War (1936–1939), Franco became leader of the insurgents after the death of generals José Sanjurjo and Goded. With the help of Germany and Italy, favored by British and American "nonintervention," he consolidated his position and assumed dictatorial powers shortly after the fall of Madrid (March 28, 1939). He is sometimes known as *el Caudillo* ("the leader").

Franco, Matteo (1447–1494). Florentine poet and priest. A partisan of the Medici, he wrote verse concerning the behavior of his parishioners, and exchanged sonnets with Pulci in a bitter literary feud. The *Sonetti* were first published in 1759.

Franco, Niccolò (1515–1570). Italian poet. Born in Benevento, he was the author of a group of dialogues and verses entitled *La Filena* (1537–1542). He was at first a friend and partisan, then a bitter enemy of Aretino.

Franco-Prussian War. Also known as the **Franco-German War** (1870–1871). A war between France, then ruled by Napoleon III, and Prussia, whose prime minister at the time was Otto von Bismarck. Relations between the two powers deteriorated when Bismarck supported the candidacy of Prince Leopold Hohenzollern-Sigmaringen, a relative of King William of Prussia, to the vacant throne of Spain. Prince Leopold eventually withdrew, but Bismarck, who wanted war, edited the famous EMS TELEGRAM describing an interview between William and the French ambassador in such a way as to make it seem that the king had insulted France, which retaliated by declaring war on July 19, 1870. The French were overwhelmed by the well-trained, well-organized Prussian forces, and a large part of the French army and Napoleon himself were forced to surrender at Sedan. A republic was then proclaimed in Paris, which was besieged by the Prussians and

capitulated on Jan. 28, 1871. By the treaty of Frankfort, France lost the provinces of Alsace and Lorraine and agreed to pay an indemnity of five billion francs; an army of occupation would remain in France until the indemnity was paid. Bismarck used the victory to complete German unification, and after the states of Bavaria, Baden, and Württemberg had joined the German Confederation, King William was proclaimed German emperor on Jan. 18, 1871 in the Hall of Mirrors at Versailles.

Frank, Anne (1929–1944). German-Jewish girl who hid from the Nazis with her parents and several friends in an Amsterdam warehouse from 1942 to 1944. Her diary, covering the years of hiding, was found by friends and published as *Het Achterhus* (*Du.,* "the annex"; 1947); it was later published in English as *The Diary of a Young Girl* (1952). Against the background of the mass-murder of European Jewry, the book presents a vivid picture of a group of hunted people forced to live and survive together in almost intolerable proximity. Written with humor as well as insight, it offers an extraordinary picture of a girl growing up and conveys all the preoccupations of adolescence and first love. The diary ends three days before the Franks and their friends were discovered by the Nazis. Anne died in the extermination camp at Bergen-Belsen in 1944. The book was dramatized as *The Diary of Anne Frank* and performed the world over.

Frank, Bruno (1887–1945). German novelist and playwright. He was influenced by Thomas Mann and noted for his historical and psychological realism. His best-known works are *Zwölftausend* (*Twelve Thousand,* 1927), a play, and *Cervantes* (1934), a story.

Frank, Leonhard (1882–1961). German playwright and novelist with socialist leanings. He is best known for his short novel *Karl und Anna* (1926, dramatized 1929).

Frank, Waldo [David] (1889–1967). American writer. Frank has been noted for his criticism of contemporary civilization, often from the point of view of political liberalism. Novels of his that attracted attention were *The Dark Mother* (1920), *Rahab* (1922), *Holiday* (1923), *The Death and Birth of David Markand* (1934), *The Bridegroom Cometh* (1938), *Summer Never Ends* (1941), *The Invaders* (1948), and *Not Heaven* (1953). His works of nonfiction include *Virgin Spain* (1926), *Dawn in Russia* (1932), *Chart for Rough Water* (1940), *Bridgehead: The Drama of Israel* (1957), *The Rediscovery of Man* (1958), and *Cuba: Prophetic Island* (1961).

Frankau, Gilbert (1884–1952). English popular novelist, author of *World Without End* (1943).

Frankau, Pamela (1908–   ). English novelist, daughter of Gilbert Frankau. Among her novels is *A Wreath for the Enemy* (1954), the story of a girl growing up.

Franken, Rose (1895–   ). American novelist and playwright. She is best known for the Claudia series of novels, dealing with the happy domestic life of a girlish heroine. A stage version of *Claudia* (1929), the first novel in the series, was produced in 1941. Her other plays include *Mr. Dooley, Jr.* (1932) and *Another Language* (1934).

Frankenstein, or the Modern Prometheus (1818). A romance by Mary Wollstonecraft SHEL-

LEY. Frankenstein, a young student, animates a soulless monster made out of corpses from churchyards and dissecting rooms by means of galvanism. Longing for sympathy and shunned by everyone, the creature ultimately turns to evil and brings dreadful retribution on the student for usurping the Creator's prerogative, finally destroying him. Several movies have been based on the novel. Mrs. Shelley gave no name to the monster, but he is commonly called Frankenstein after his creator, the student. This, of course, is an error.

Frankfurter, Felix (1882–1965). Austrian-born American jurist and teacher. After a brief career practicing law, Frankfurter taught at Harvard Law School (1914–1939) and engaged in various governmental pursuits until his appointment to the U.S. Supreme Court (1939–1962). He wrote many legal textbooks as well as *The Case of Sacco and Vanzetti* (1927), *The Public and Its Government* (1930), *Mr. Justice Holmes and the Supreme Court* (1939), and *Law and Men* (1956). *Felix Frankfurter Reminisces,* edited by Harlan B. Phillips, appeared in 1960.

Frankie and Johnny. One of the most famous of American folk ballads. It relates Frankie's pursuit and murder of her unfaithful sweetheart, Johnnie. The refrain is: "He was her man, but he done her wrong." It inspired a series of paintings by Thomas Hart Benton, another by John Held, Jr., and several dramas.

Franklin, Benjamin (1706–1790). American statesman, author, inventor, printer, and scientist, sometimes called "the wisest American." The son of a Boston tallow chandler, Franklin was apprenticed at 12 to his brother James, a local printer, to whose newspaper he contributed a series of Addisonian essays, the *Dogood Papers* (1722). In 1723 he ran away to Philadelphia, where he set up his own newspaper, published POOR RICHARD'S ALMANACK, and with intense energy established a subscription library, a philosophical society, a fire company, a hospital, a militia, became postmaster of Philadelphia, proposed the University of Pennsylvania, devised bifocal spectacles, a stove, and a water-harmonica. He later performed electrical experiments leading in 1752 to his invention of the lightning rod, which earned him election to the Royal Society in London, the compliments of Louis XV of France, and several honorary degrees. Active for the colonies throughout the Revolution, he helped draft and was a signer of the Declaration of Independence. He concluded an alliance with France (1778) and was one of the diplomats to negotiate the treaty of peace with Great Britain (1783). In 1787 he attended the Federal Constitutional Convention. His AUTOBIOGRAPHY is considered one of the classics of the genre. Herman Melville introduced him into *Israel Potter* (1855), and he also appears in Irving Bacheller's *In the Days of Poor Richard* (1922).

Franklin Evans, or The Inebriate (1842). A novel by Walt WHITMAN. In this conventional temperance tract, a country boy suffers degradation and torment when he falls under the influence of alcohol in New York City. Finally reforming, he lives an honorable life.

Franklin's Tale, The. One of the CANTERBURY TALES of Geoffrey CHAUCER. Apparently it is based on a tale in Boccaccio's *Il Filocolo* and similar to his tale of a GARDEN IN JANUARY in the *Decameron,* although Chaucer attributes it to a Breton *lay.* The Franklin opposes the views in the WIFE OF BATH'S TALE, saying that love flies when constrained by sovereignty. In his tale, Dorigen accepts her husband Arveragus (or Arviragus) as her servant in love but her lord in marriage. When Arveragus goes off to war, she refuses the advances of the squire Aurelius, playfully promising that she will be his when he removes all the rocks from the coast of Brittany. Arveragus returns, and Aurelius pines until a magician succeeds in making it appear that the rocks have disappeared. Aurelius reminds Dorigen of her promise. She decides she should rather kill herself than dishonor her marriage; but when Arveragus learns the story, he says she must keep her promise, and sends her to meet Aurelius. The squire meets this display of nobility by releasing her from her promise, and the magician, not to be outdone, releases the squire from his 1000-pound debt, since the magic did not achieve its purpose.

Fraser, G[eorge] S[utherland] (1915–   ). Scottish poet and critic. Associated with the NEW APOCALYPSE movement, he wrote *Vision and Rhetoric* (1960) and works on Dylan Thomas and Ezra Pound.

Fraunhofer lines. The dark lines in the solar spectrum, caused by the passage of light through certain gases in the atmosphere. They were named after the Bavarian physicist Joseph von Fraunhofer (1787–1826), who was the first to classify them. See Gustav Robert KIRCHHOFF.

fravashi. In Persian religion, a spiritual protector or guardian angel of each individual, especially of the believer. It is the pre-existing archetype of every man in the presence of ORMUZD and corresponds to the Roman GENIUS.

Frazer, Sir James George (1854–1941). Scottish scholar and anthropologist. He is best known for his famous work THE GOLDEN BOUGH, which is noted for its important contributions to the study of early religion and anthropology. Other works include *Totemism* (1887); *Folk-lore in the Old Testament* (1918); and numerous translations of such classical writers as Ovid, Pausanias, and Apollodorus.

Fréchette, Louis [Honoré] (1839–1908). Canadian poet and journalist. He is best known for *La légende d'un peuple* (1887), a series of epic poems inspired by the leading events and personages in French-Canadian history. In 1880 the French Academy honored two other poetic works by Fréchette, *Les fleurs boréales* (1879) and *Les oiseaux de neige* (1880), and he became Canada's first poet laureate.

Frederic, Harold (1856–1898). American novelist and journalist. He is known for realistic portrayals of small-town and rural life. His most popular novel, THE DAMNATION OF THERON WARE, was a pioneering work in the development of psychological realism. Frederic is credited with helping to prepare the way for the works of Stephen Crane and Theodore Dreiser. *Seth's Brother's Wife* (1887) is a story of a triangular love affair. *In the Valley* (1890) is a historical novel dealing with the battle at Oriskany in 1777.

Frederick II, known as **Frederick the Great** (1712–1786). King of Prussia (1740–1786). He was an enlightened despot who built up the Prussian state through vast territorial acquisitions and domestic reforms. An enthusiastic amateur of music he composed and played chamber music. He was a patron of the arts, friend of Voltaire. He wrote voluminously, almost always in French. He built the palace of Sans Souci (1747) near Potsdam. During his later years he was known as *der Alte Fritz* (Old Fritz).

Frederick, Duke. The uncle of Rosalind and father of Celia in Shakespeare's As You Like It. "Of rough and envious disposition," he has usurped his older brother's dukedom, but he is finally converted by a monk and enters a monastery.

Frederick the First. See BARBAROSSA.

Frederick the Great. See FREDERICK II.

Free Kirk. The church organized by those who, in 1843, left the national Church of Scotland (thereafter often referred to as the Auld Kirk), in order to be free from state control in spiritual matters. In 1929 the United Free Church of Scotland was reunited with the established Church of Scotland, thus bringing together the large majority of all Scottish Presbyterians.

Freeman, Douglas Southall (1886–1953). American historian. An editor of the Richmond *News Leader,* Freeman won a Pulitzer Prize for his exhaustive *Robert E. Lee* (4 vols., 1934). He continued his studies with *Lee's Lieutenants* (3 vols., 1942–1944) and then went further back in American history with a seven-volume life of *George Washington* (1948–1957), the last volume of which was completed by his assistants, J. A. Carroll and M. W. Ashworth.

Freeman, Mary E[leanor] Wilkins (1852–1930). American novelist and short-story writer of the local-color school. She is known for her use of dialect and her character studies of the frustrated and decadent New Englanders left after the Western expansion. Among the collections of her short stories, the genre in which she did her best work, are *A Humble Romance and Other Stories* (1887), A NEW ENGLAND NUN AND OTHER STORIES, and *The Wind in the Rose Bush* (1903). Her novels include *The Revolt of Mother* (1890), *Jane Field* (1893), and *The Portion of Labor* (1901).

Freeman, Richard Austin (1862–1943). English scientific detective-story writer. His detective hero is the physician Dr. John Thorndyke.

Freemasons. A fraternal organization claiming, without basis, to trace its origins to Hiram of Tyre and the Temple of Solomon. The modern secret fraternity had its origin in England in the 18th century, and its connection with masons, the workers in stone, arises from the fact that the founders adopted many of the practices of the old masonic guilds as being most suitable to their purpose. These medieval guilds consisted of workmen who, by the nature of their calling, had to move from place to place, and their secret passwords and other rituals were adopted so that when on their travels they could prove without difficulty that they were actually Free and Accepted Masons, and so secure the comradeship of their brother masons as well as get employment. In each district where cathedrals and churches were being built, lodges were created, much as a branch of a trade union would be today, and these had their masters, wardens, and other officials.

Free-Soil party. An American political party op-

posed to the extension of slavery. It was formed in 1848 by antislavery Democrats and Whigs and by members of the Liberty party. In 1848 Martin Van Buren, their presidential candidate, failed to carry a single state and, by splitting the Democratic vote in New York, helped win the election for Zachary Taylor, the Whig nominee. In 1854 the Free-Soilers were part of the coalition that formed the Republican party. See BARNBURNERS.

free verse or **vers libre.** In prosody, verse free of the rules of versification. Free verse is composed in lines cadenced according to meaningful stress rather than the mechanical alternation of accent and nonaccent; the starts, stops, and pauses of line division play an important part in its rhythm.

The term *vers libre* was coined by the French poets of the Symbolist movement (see SYMBOLISM), notably Jules Laforgue and Gustave Kahn, to describe their verse technique. Whitman, of course, had written such verse before them, as had the ancient Hebrew poets of the Psalms and other parts of the Bible.

Free verse became the prevailing poetic form for a brief time in the 1920's, and subsequently in the 20th century has continued as one of the main prosodic streams alongside traditional and modernist traditional forms. Poets who have worked substantially in free verse in English include: H. D. (Hilda Doolittle), Robinson Jeffers, D. H. Lawrence, Amy Lowell, Edgar Lee Masters, Ezra Pound, Carl Sandburg, Wallace Stevens, and William Carlos Williams.

Fregoso, Federico (1480–1541) and **Ottaviano** (d. 1524). Genoese noblemen. The nephews of Guidobaldo of Montefeltro, they appear as interlocutors in THE COURTIER of Castiglione. Federico was later made archbishop of Salerno by Pope Julius II; Ottaviano became doge of Genoa in 1513, and later served as governor when it fell to Francis I.

Freiligrath, Ferdinand (1810–1876). German liberal political poet, a revolutionary during the 1840's and later a strong admirer of Bismarck. His most famous volume is the *Glaubensbekenntnis (Declaration of Faith,* 1842) that led to his break with the Prussian government.

Freischütz (*Ger.* "free-shooter"). Legendary marksman popular in German folk lore of the 14th to 16th century. The Devil gives him seven bullets, six of which will infallibly hit what the marksman aims at, but the last will be directed by the Devil. The account in Apel's *Gespensterbuch* (book of ghosts, 1810–1815) suggested WEBER's opera *Der Freischütz* (1821), libretto by Friedrich Kind (1768–1843). The woodsman Max must win a sharpshooting contest to win the hand of Agathe. Because his marksmanship is not perfect, he allows his colleague Caspar, already a servant of the Devil, to arrange for him to make a pact with the Black Huntsman for the magic bullets. The seventh shot, aimed at a dove, would have killed Agathe, but her bridal wreath deflects it, and Caspar dies instead.

Frémont, John C[harles] (1813–1890). American explorer, soldier, and politician. Frémont, an officer in the U.S. Topographical Corps, made three important expeditions to the Far West, and his *Report of the Exploring Expedition to the Rocky Mountains* (1843), which he wrote with the help of his wife, Jessie, daughter of Thomas Hart Benton, was widely read. During the Mexican War, he played a controversial role in the conquest of California; he was later found guilty of mutiny and disobedience by a court-martial and although President Polk remitted his sentence, he resigned from the army. In 1856 he ran for the presidency on the anti-slavery platform of the newly formed Republican Party. After the outbreak of the Civil War, Frémont was given a command in the Department of the West, but was removed because of his radical antislavery policies. From 1878 to 1883 he was territorial governor of Arizona. Irving Stone's *Immortal Wife* (1944) is a biographical novel about the Frémonts.

Fremstad, Olive (1871–1951). Swedish-born American dramatic soprano. Although she began singing as a contralto, she soon proved herself a foremost interpreter of soprano roles in both German and Italian opera. Thea Kronborg, the heroine of Willa Cather's novel, *The Song of the Lark* (1915), was modeled after her.

French, Alice. Real name of **Octave Thanet** (1850–1934). American novelist and short-story writer. Miss French's stories, laid mostly in the villages of rural Arkansas, are part of the LOCAL-COLOR school. Her special interest was the labor problem; she advocated cooperatives rather than labor unions. Among her books are *The Man of the Hour* (1905), *Knitters in the Sun* (1887), and *The Heart of Toil* (1893).

French Academy. See ACADÉMIE FRANÇAISE.

French and Indian War (1754–1763). The last, most decisive conflict in the 150 years' struggle between France and England for possession of the North American continent. It was the American phase of the SEVEN YEARS WAR and ended with the cession of Canada to Great Britain in the Treaty of Paris (1763).

French Renaissance. The French Renaissance roughly encompasses the 16th century.

Fervor for the Italian Renaissance took hold of the French court following the military campaigns of Charles VIII, Louis XII, and FRANCIS I in Italy. As traffic between Italy and France increased, French art, architecture, and most particularly literature felt the effects. Clément MAROT introduced the Italian sonnet into French poetry. Queen MARGARET OF NAVARRE wrote the first collection of French tales modeled on the *Decameron* of Boccaccio. However, the Italian influence in this period was more intellectual than artistic. French writers developed a new critical spirit and moral sense from reading Greek and Latin literature, which had been rediscovered in Italy. They were humanists, interested in the full development and enjoyment of man's capacities, and they cultivated a taste for the refinements of Italian Renaissance society.

The influence from the north affected particularly the scholars. It was characterized by a philosophical questioning of the long-entrenched dogmas of the Church. French scholars became avid for knowledge as the old taboos fell and the flood of printed matter opened up formerly neglected fields of learning. Francis I engaged Guillaume BUDÉ as his librarian and, at Budé's instigation, founded the COLLÈGE DE FRANCE, where Greek and Hebrew were taught for the first time. The Collège soon became a rallying point for the "Evangelists," those who sought the basis for faith in the Scriptures themselves, rather than in papal bulls and church decrees.

The two currents of new ideas from the north and from the south merged in the short-lived marriage between humanism and Evangelism which marks the first flowering of the French Renaissance around 1530. The writers of this period shared in differing degrees the general excitement, and all participated in the burst of intense optimism, feverish activity, and exaltation. François RABELAIS emerges as the most important literary figure of the period. While his GARGANTUA AND PANTAGRUEL is largely a continuation of the medieval fabliaux in form, it fairly breathes the new spirit in its rich multilingual vocabulary and its sheer amassing of detail in every field of knowledge.

The second half of the century saw a distinct change in the tenor of the French Renaissance. The glorious reign of Francis I was followed by the rule of four ineffective kings (Henry II, Francis II, Charles IX, and Henry III), the last three more or less subservient to their mother, CATHERINE de Médicis. After the publication of John CALVIN's *Institutes* in French in 1541, the happy alliance between humanism and Evangelism had been irrevocably ruptured. The early Evangelists were succeeded by militant Protestant reformers who not only challenged Roman Catholicism, but menaced the very basis of French royal authority as well, thereby losing its protection. Henceforth, the Protestant Reformation and humanism went their separate ways. The universal exuberance of the first humanism gave way to a notion of a distinctly French art nourished by Italian and classical example but proudly asserting French genius in the French language. Joachim DU BELLAY gave the clarion call of this new artistic consciousness with his DÉFENSE ET ILLUSTRATION DE LA LANGUE FRANÇAISE in 1549. The *Défense* signaled the formation of the PLÉIADE, a group of poets led by Pierre de RONSARD, whose mission was to raise French poetry to the eminence of Italian and ancient poetry. A parallel group of poets at Lyons, headed by Maurice SCÈVE and Louise LABÉ, had no declared mission, but its poetry was so personal in tone that it too contributed to the liberation of the French literary idiom.

Meanwhile, the rise of Protestantism led to civil war. The country became a bloody battleground of the contending Protestant and Catholic ideologies. Eventually these wars produced their own poets, notably the impassioned Agrippa d'AUBIGNÉ. His narrative poem, *Les Tragiques* (1616), recounting the horrors suffered by the Protestant martyrs and the divine retribution to come, introduced into French literature the visions of a soul possessed.

The end of the century saw the birth of a new spirit which was to develop into the classicism of the 17th century. Primitive attempts at a new drama distinct from the popular mystery plays and passion plays of the Middle Ages produced the tragi-comedies of Robert GARNIER, from which Corneille would later draw inspiration. The political chaos resulting from the religious wars brought the realization that national stability depended upon a strong central government free from religious ideology. King HENRY IV established absolute rule which Louis XIV was later to consolidate. The great literary figure of the period was Michel de MONTAIGNE, friend and unofficial counselor to Henry IV. In his ESSAYS, a genre which he invented, Montaigne reflected the general disillusionment over the first period of humanistic optimism and over the ensuing bloody conflicts of the religious wars. He called for a rejection of ideologies in the interest of the first priority, man himself. His greatest concern was the requirements imposed by human nature for its proper development. To learn these requirements nothing less was needed than a rigorous search for the lessons of individual experience. In turning inward to study human psychology as the source of knowledge, Montaigne gave a new and modern meaning to the term "humanism," which extended beyond France to affect all of Europe. He was the great precursor of the ideal *honnête homme* of the 17th century.

French Revolution. The world-famous revolution in France of the THIRD ESTATE against the clergy and nobility, which formally began in May, 1789, and ended in December, 1799, with Napoleon's dictatorship. Until this time, France had been ruled as a monarchy with two privileged classes: the nobility and the clergy. Under this old order there was no place for either the new class of economically independent bourgeois or the new class of industrial workers. They, as well as the peasants, bore the brunt of excessive spending on the part of the nobility. Heavy taxes, *corvées* (obligatory services to the king), military service, backward agricultural methods, and internal tariff barriers—all medieval feudal institutions still existing in 18th-century France—were also contributory causes to the revolution; they had been systematically attacked by the major writers of this Age of Reason, particularly by the PHYSIOCRATS. The badly needed economic reform which these latter advocated failed because of the unwillingness of the ruling classes to relinquish any of their privileges. France's national debt was also increased by her participation (which she could ill afford) in the American Revolution. On May 5, 1789, the States-General (the assembly of the three Estates of the Realm) was convoked by LOUIS XVI and NECKER in an effort to obtain a general fiscal reform. The third estate, constituting a majority against the

ruling classes, defiantly proclaimed itself the National Assembly on June 17, and later, when Louis XVI closed their meeting place, adjourned to an indoor tennis court and took the OATH OF THE TENNIS COURT. The king, on June 27, yielded and legalized this assembly, but at the same time dismissed Necker, at MARIE ANTOINETTE's insistence, and surrounded Versailles with his troops. On July 14, a Paris mob led by DESMOULINS, stormed the Bastille. Louis then recalled Necker and recognized the legal existence of the Constituent Assembly (as the new National Assembly was called). The Assembly adopted the DECLARATION OF THE RIGHTS OF MAN, proclaiming the fundamental principles of the revolution, and drafted a new constitution creating a limited monarchy. In addition, church lands were nationalized and religious orders suppressed. Meanwhile, radical political clubs, especially the JACOBINS, were gaining power in Paris.

Louis XVI finally accepted the constitution and on October 1, 1791, a new Legislative Assembly was convened. In the same year Louis tried to flee France, as many nobles had already done, but was brought back a prisoner to Paris. The Legislative Assembly consisted of members of various political clubs, more or less radical, like the FEUILLANTS, and the CORDELIERS. During this era some of the leaders of the revolution wore the BONNET ROUGE, and "Liberty, Equality, and Fraternity," was their motto. At first, foreign governments were sympathetic to the revolution, but because both the king and French émigrés were inciting European monarchs to intervene on behalf of French royalty, they began to be frightened by the progress of the lower classes. Austria and Prussia issued threats, and on April 20, 1792, war was declared on Austria, and three months later Prussia declared war on France. This war began the succession of foreign wars which in turn led to the Napoleonic Wars. The repeated defeats of the Revolutionary armies were attributed to Royalist treason and on September 2 and 3, 1792, the people invaded the prisons and massacred 1,200 prisoners (the September Massacres). In Paris, the National Convention, headed by MARAT and DANTON, succeeded the Legislative Assembly, and its first act was to abolish the monarchy; the king was tried for treason and beheaded on Jan. 21, 1793. The Convention tried to continue the war, which by now included England, Spain, and most of the other European countries, but it was torn by internal dissention among the GIRONDISTS, the Montagnards, and the Cordeliers. The Convention established the COMMITTEE OF PUBLIC SAFETY which ruled France. ROBESPIERRE, now in control of the Jacobins, joined the Committee at the insistence of SAINT-JUST, and, as its leader, established a virtual dictatorship. The period following is known as the REIGN OF TERROR, which, because of its excesses, was eliminated by the Convention's coup of 9 THERMIDOR. Once Robespierre was executed, a period of reaction set in, and a new constitution (1795) set up the DIRECTORY. The incompetence, corruption, and intrigues of the Directory, and the military reverses of the army brought France to the brink of disaster. Napoleon Bonaparte, hero of the Italian Campaign, returned from Egypt, and with the help of the army and his supporters, overthrew the Directory on 18 BRUMAIRE, and established the Consulate. He was the

Contemporary woodcut of Parisians celebrating the fall of the Bastille (July 14, 1789).

ruler of France until 1814 when the Bourbon kings were restored to power.

French Revolution, The (1837). A history in 3 parts by Thomas CARLYLE. Critics have preferred to call it a drama or a prose epic rather than a history. The central motif is the nemesis that follows upon the oppression of the poor. The work established Carlyle's reputation as a historian and remains widely read to this day.

Freneau, Philip [Morin] (1752–1832). American poet. One of the first American poets to achieve renown for his verse in the U.S., he is best known for his political poems, most of them written at the time of the American Revolution: *A Poem on the Rising Glory of America* (1772), written in collaboration with Hugh Henry Brackenridge on their graduation from Princeton; *American Liberty* (1775); *General Gage's Confession* (1775); and *The British Prison-Ship* (1781), an account of his experiences as a prisoner of war after capture at sea near the West Indies. His poems on nature and on the Indian, considered precursors of the romantic movement in America, include: *The Wild Honey Suckle* (1786), *The Indian Burying Ground* (1788), *On a Honey-Bee Drinking from a Glass of Wine* (1809).

Freneau was anti-Federalist in his politics and a deist in religion. Admired by Jefferson, he edited the *National Gazette* from 1791 to 1793, in which he attacked Alexander Hamilton.

Fréquente Communion, La. See Antoine ARNAULD.

Frere, John Hookham. Pen name **William and Robert Whistlecraft** (1796–1846). English diplomat, satirist, translator. After holding several important offices Frere became ambassador to Spain at the outbreak of the Spanish insurrection against Napoleon. Dissatisfaction with his part in early English defeats in the Peninsular War forced his replacement and retirement from diplomacy. His articles for the *Anti-Jacobin* (1797), an antiradical weekly, are good examples of his satirical writing. His famous translations of Aristophanes (1839) and other writing is collected in his *Works* (1872).

Freud, Sigmund (1856–1939). Austrian psychologist, the originator of PSYCHOANALYSIS. Freud was trained as a medical doctor at the University of Vienna. He graduated in 1881, but never practiced internal medicine. He soon became interested in neuropathology and studied hypnotism and cerebral anatomy.

He became dissatisfied with hypnotism as a treatment for hysterical patients. However, he had noticed that some patients had fallen into reveries in which they had talked about their problems and afterwards had felt better. From these observations he began to formulate his theory of "free association" which is the kernel of psychoanalysis. In Freudian practice, patients under the guidance of an analyst attempt to recall emotional episodes that aggravated conflicts, and thus recognize and release frustrated emotions. Freud used dream interpretation as one of his basic tools in analysis. The patient's dreams were analyzed for their symbolic content and were used as a guide to the patient's internal life. Freud viewed dreams as a person's means of expressing repressed emotions, and repression was seen as the source of neurotic behavior.

Freud postulated the existence of three internal forces that govern a person's psychic life: (1) the *id*, the instinctual force of life—unconscious, uncontrollable and isolated; (2) the *ego*, the executive force that has contact with the real world; (3) the *superego*, the governing force, or moral conscience, that seeks to control and direct the ego into socially acceptable patterns of behavior.

As his theories began to take concrete form, Freud started to publish his findings. *The Interpretation of Dreams* (1900) was one of the first reports on his independent studies of the subconscious. By this time his work had begun to attract attention outside his native Vienna, and others took up his cause. In 1908 the first International Congress of Psychoanalysis met in Vienna. Many young doctors, some of them now famous in their own right, attended this meeting; among them were Alfred ADLER, A. A. Brill, Ernest Jones, and Carl JUNG.

From the beginning the very nature of his work made Freud the center of controversy. His theories about sex have been, in general, misunderstood by the public and in varying degrees rejected by many of his followers. Freud maintained that the primary motivating factor in human psychology and human behavior is sexual, but he did not limit this to its purely erotic connotations. The sexual instinct, as Freud saw it, has many of the aspects ordinarily referred to as "social." He found elements of strong sexuality among children and ascribed most neuroses to the repressive influence of social and individual inhibitions on sex.

While many of Freud's ideas have been superseded he is still considered the great innovator in the field of psychiatry, and is almost worshiped in some circles. The work of only one other man in this century, Albert Einstein, has had as great an impact on man's way of thinking and acting. Freud's influence has been especially strong on artistic expression, both the fine arts and literature. Such authors as Thomas Mann and James Joyce have embodied much of his thought in their works.

Among Freud's important works are *Three Contributions to the Theory of Sex* (1910), *Wit and Its Relation to the Unconscious* (1916), *Leonardo da Vinci: A Psychosexual Study of an Infantile Reminiscence* (1916), *Totem and Taboo* (1918), *The Ego and the Id* (1927), and *Moses and Monotheism* (1939).

Freud, a Jew, was forced to flee from the Nazis in 1938. He and his family moved to England where he died, an honored and respected man.

Frey or **Freyr.** The Scandinavian god of peace and fertility, the dispenser of rain, and the patron god of Sweden and Iceland. The son of Niörd and husband of Gerda, he was originally one of the Vanir but was received among the Aesir after the war between the two. Among his treasures was a magic ship, *Skithbathnir*, which could be folded up like a tent, a golden helmet with the crest of a wild boar, *Gullinbursti*, and his horse *Blodighofi* (Bloody hoof).

Freya. The Norse goddess of love, fecundity, and death. She was the wife of Odin, but he deserted her for Frigga because she loved finery better than her husband. One account says that she flies through the air with the wings of a falcon, another that she rides in a chariot drawn by two cats. The chief legends concerning Freya relate the efforts of the giants to carry her off. In one instance Thor, dressed as a veiled bride, impersonates Freya in order to recover his hammer from the giant Thrym.

She is also known as *Frea, Frija, Frigg, Frige,* and the like, and it is from her that our Friday is named. In Teutonic mythology, Freya and Frigga are the same.

Freyre, Gilberto [de Mello] (1900–   ). Brazilian sociologist, anthropologist, and social historian. Freyre is best known for *The Masters and the Slaves (Casa-Grande e Senzala;* 1933) and *The Mansions and the Shanties (Sobrados e Mucambos;* 1936), brilliant studies of Brazilian patriarchal society from the 16th to the 19th centuries. In these and later books, notably *Brazil: An Interpretation* (1945), revised and expanded as *New World in the Tropics* (1959), he has maintained that the fusion of diverse ethnic and cultural elements—Portuguese, Amerindian, and African—has resulted in a distinctively Brazilian civilization. The Portuguese settlers in Brazil, he claims, were particularly suited for creating this new tropical culture because of their racial tolerance and previous colonial experiences in India and Africa.

Freytag, Gustav (1816–1895). German novelist and playwright, known for his detailed realism in both style and choice of subject matter. He was a political liberal and was strongly interested in the problems of his day, as is seen in his comedy *Die Journalisten (The Journalists,* 1854), which deals with international politics, and his novel *Soll und Haben (Should and Have,* 1855) about commercialism. But he always attempted to see his own time in the light of the past, as in *Die Ahnen (The Ancestors,* 1873–1880), a series of six novels covering most of German history, and *Bilder aus deutscher Vergangenheit (Scenes from the German Past,* 1859 ff.), a historical study.

friar (Lat., *frater,* brother). A monk, especially one belonging to one of the four great mendicant orders: FRANCISCANS, DOMINICANS, Augustinians, and CARMELITES.

Friar John. An anglicism for Frère Jean des Entommeures (Fr., *entamer,* to carve the first slice, hence Friar John of the Hearty Eaters or Trenchermen), a major character in Rabelais' GARGANTUA AND PANTAGRUEL. As Gargantua's comrade in arms in Book I, he is the hero of the war against PICROCHOLE. At the end of the war Gargantua gives him the abbey of THÉLÈME as a reward for his bravery. Friar John has all the faults of monks but none of their vices. Ignorant, unclean, and gluttonous, he is also frank, lusty, and courageous. Rabelais clearly had great affection for Friar John and created in him one of his most picturesque characters.

Friar Laurence. See Friar LAURENCE.

Friar Rush or **Bruder Rausch** (*Ger.* "intoxication"). In late medieval German legend, a demon disguised as a friar. He leads monks and friars into wickedness by all sorts of devious and generally amusing devices. He appears in the English prose *History of Friar Rush* (1568) and several minor tales and plays.

Friars Major (Lat. *fratres majores*). The Dominicans.

Friars Minor (Lat. *fratres minores*). The Franciscans.

Friar's Tale, The. One of the CANTERBURY TALES of Geoffrey CHAUCER. The Friar and the Summoner reveal their enmity, and the Summoner promises to retaliate after the Friar tells his tale. The Friar describes an extremely lewd and dishonest summoner who meets the Devil disguised as a bailiff. The two swear friendship and gossip about their respective techniques of extortion. They pass a carter cursing his horse and cart and hay for being stuck in the mud, his words consigning them to the Devil. But the Devil explains to the Summoner that he cannot take them because the carter does not really mean the curse. Then the Summoner decides to extort money from an innocent woman by threatening her with a summons to the archdeacon for adultery. He ignores her words that send him to the Devil, but the Devil ascertains that she really means them, and gleefully carries the Summoner off to Hell.

Friar Tuck. A fat, jovial vagabond friar in the ROBIN HOOD ballads and a character in the May-day plays. His costume consists of a russet habit of the Franciscan order, a red corded girdle with gold tassel, red stockings, and a wallet. He appears in Sir Walter Scott's novel *Ivanhoe* (1820) as the "holy clerk of Copmanhurst."

Fricka. In Wagner's RING DES NIBELUNGEN, the goddess of marriage and wife of WOTAN. See FRIGGA.

Fricker, Sara. See Samuel Taylor COLERIDGE.

Friday. The sixth day of the week. It is named for the goddess FREYA. In the Romance languages it is named for the corresponding Roman goddess Venus. Friday is traditionally the day when Adam was created, when he was expelled from Paradise, when he repented, when he died, when Christ was crucified, when the dead will rise for the last judgment. In many Christian churches Friday is a fast day. To spill salt on Friday is a bad omen. It used to be the day for the execution of capital punishment and is often called hangman's day.

Frieda. See Frieda von Richthofen LAWRENCE.

Friend of the Family, The, or **The Village of Stepanchikovo (Selo Stepanchikovo;** 1859). A short novel by Feodor DOSTOEVSKI. It portrays the horrible spectacle of a petty and talentless ex-toady, Foma Fomich Opiskin, ruling a household by playing on the guilt feeling he induces in the master of the house. Foma, with his immense aptitude for hypocritical self-righteousness, is a sort of Russian Tartuffe.

Frigga or **Frigg.** The supreme Norse goddess of Asgard, and wife of Odin. She presided over marriages and may be identified with the Roman Juno. In Teutonic mythology, she is identified with Freya.

Frisch, Max (1911–   ). Swiss playwright and novelist, writing in German. He is noted for his ironic and original treatments of the problems of man in the age of technology. Among his plays, which show the influence of Bertolt Brecht, are *Als der Krieg zu Ende war (When the War Was Over,* 1949), and *Don Juan oder Die Liebe zur Geometrie (Don Juan or The Love of Geometry,* 1953). His two best-known novels, both of which treat the problem of human identity in the modern world, are *Stiller* (1954) and *Homo Faber* (1957).

Frison-Roche, Roger (1906–   ). French novelist. He has produced adventure stories such as *First on the Rope* (*Premier de cordée*, 1943), *Grand Crevasse* (1948), and *The Lost Trail of the Saharas* (1950).

Frobisher, Sir Martin (1535?–1594). English navigator. Frobisher led three expeditions in search of the Northwest Passage between 1576 and 1578, and discovered Frobisher Bay. He commanded the *Triumph* against the Spanish Armada, was vice-admiral under Sir Francis Drake in his expedition to the West Indies (1586), and vice-admiral in Sir John Hawkins' expedition to the Portuguese coast in 1590.

Fröding, Gustaf (1860–1911). Swedish poet. A writer of lyric and religious verse, Fröding's first collection of poems, *Guitarr och dragharmonika* (1891), revealed his unique poetic gifts; he achieves a blend of irony, melancholy, and humor. Other early collections were *Nya dikter* (1894), and *Stank och flikar* (1896). The poem "En Morgondröm" in the latter volume was branded pornography and led to a court case. Acquitted, but shaken and deeply disturbed, Fröding suffered a mental breakdown and was confined to an asylum in 1898. Although he left the asylum, the remaining years of his life were marked by ill health. *Gralstänk* (1898) contains a series of religious poems expressing a faith in the divinity of all things in the world.

Frog, Nicholas. A character in John Arbuthnot's *The History of* JOHN BULL who represents the Dutch people.

Frogs, The (Batrachoi, 405 B.C.). A comedy by ARISTOPHANES. In it, Dionysus, the patron of the drama, having grown weary of the lack of inspiring dramatists in Athens, decides to go down to Hades to bring back Euripides. Knowing that Heracles has already been there, he borrows his famous lion skin as a disguise, and sets off with his slave Xanthias. When he arrives in Hades, he discovers that Heracles, who had once stolen the guardian dog Cerberus, is not popular there, and hastily changes costume with Xanthias. After further confusion over which of the two is actually Dionysus, the god finds Euripides. However, having listened to an argument between him and his rival playwright Aeschylus, he decides to return to earth with Aeschylus instead, because he is the weightier playwright. Besides being a charming comedy, the play is a striking example of the freedom of speech allowed the writer of Old Comedy. Dionysus is made an absurd figure, though he was the patron of the festivals at which the comedy was performed.

Froissart, Jean (1337?–?1410). French poet and historian. He enjoyed the patronage of Queen Philippa of England from 1361 until her death in 1369, and then the protection of two French noblemen. He traveled widely throughout western Europe seeking firsthand accounts of the events of the Hundred Years' War. His *Chronicles* (1369–c. 1400) give a vivid picture of Europe from 1325 to 1400, although dates and geography are often inaccurate, and the history is often distorted by perspective, the first volume sympathizing with the English, the last three espousing the French cause. The description of events until 1356 is largely a revision of the chronicle by Jean le Bel (c. 1290–c. 1370).

Froissart also wrote a number of graceful lyrics and a long verse romance, *Méliador*.

Frollo, Claude. The villain of Victor Hugo's novel THE HUNCHBACK OF NOTRE DAME. Frollo is an archdeacon whose reputation for sanctity is seriously undermined by his base passion for Esmeralda.

From Here to Eternity (1951). A novel by James JONES. It is a story of life in the regular army before the Japanese attack on Pearl Harbor in 1941. A sprawling (861 pages), powerful, occasionally vulgar book, it caused a sensation at its publication. Jones's writing is vigorous, vivid, and fluent. The title is taken from the well-known phrase "damned from here to eternity," a quotation from *Gentlemen Rankers*, Kipling's poem of British army life.

Fromm, Erich (1900–   ). German-born American psychoanalyst and philosopher. Fromm came to the U.S. in 1934 and has worked for the National Institute for Social Research in New York City and taught at various universities. His books have done much to elucidate and popularize many current philosophical and psychological ideas. His works include *Escape from Freedom* (1941); *Man for Himself: An Inquiry into the Psychology of Ethics* (1947), its sequel; *Psychoanalysis and Religion* (1950); *The Forgotten Language: An Introduction to the Understanding of Dreams, Fairy Tales, and Myths* (1951); *The Art of Loving* (1956); *May Man Prevail? An Inquiry into the Facts and Fictions of Foreign Policy* (1961); *Beyond the Chains of Illusion: My Encounter with Marx and Freud* (1962); and *The Dogma of Christ, and Other Essays on Religion, Psychology, and Culture* (1963).

From Morn Till Midnight (Von Morgens bis Mitternachts; 1916). A play by Georg KAISER. The hero, a bank teller, attempts to break out of his pitifully circumscribed existence by embezzling a large sum of money. He embarks on a wild spree, spending money by the fistful in a frantic pursuit of pleasure that is to give meaning to his life, but is finally disillusioned and commits suicide.

Fronde. An insurrectionary French political party during the minority of Louis XIV and the ministry of Cardinal Mazarin. The Fronde revolted against the crown (1648–1652), but, though successful in temporarily holding the capital, were unable to achieve their aim of curbing royal power. Members were called *frondeurs* by the Court Party, who likened them to boys slinging stones in the streets and scampering away at the approach of authority.

Frondeurs. See FRONDE.

Front de Boeuf, Sir Reginald. A vicious opponent of IVANHOE, in Scott's novel. He dies at the siege of his castle at Torquilstone.

Frontino. A fiery steed in the ORLANDO FURIOSO of Ariosto. Formerly belonging to Sacripante, it was stolen by the dwarf Brunello and given to the warrior Ruggiero.

Frost, Robert (1874–1963). American poet. Although he was born in San Francisco, he is best known for his verse dealing with New England life and character. Frost moved east in 1885, attended Dartmouth and Harvard for brief intervals, and held various odd jobs. From 1900 to 1905 he farmed in New Hampshire. But poetry was his real vocation, and in 1912, after his failure to be published in the U.S., he went to England, where for three years he wrote poetry, talked with poets, and published two collections, *A Boy's Will* (1913) and *North of Boston* (1914). The latter book contains several of Frost's best-known poems, including MENDING WALL, THE DEATH OF THE HIRED MAN, *Home Burial,* and *A Servant to Servants.*

Back in America in 1915, Frost began to gather a reputation, following the American publication of *North of Boston.* Maintaining his own creative independence, aloof from the poetic movements of the day, he next published *Mountain Interval* (1916), a volume containing THE ROAD NOT TAKEN, *An Old Man's Winter Night,* and BIRCHES. With *New Hampshire* (1923), there is the first indication of Frost's awareness of himself as poet; as he says in the title poem, he is "a creature of literature." There is also present a tone of irony that had earlier been muted. THE AXE-HELVE, STOPPING BY WOODS ON A SNOWY EVENING, and *Two Witches* appear in this volume.

A FURTHER RANGE saw the introduction of contemporary concerns in Frost's poetry and the beginning of his later tendency toward abstract philosophizing, which was to result in the two verse dramas *A Masque of Reason* (1945) and *A Masque of Mercy* (1947). Frost's other collections include WEST-RUNNING BROOK, *A Witness Tree* (1943), *Steeple Bush* (1947), *Complete Poems* (1949), and *In the Clearing* (1962).

Frost is often seen as opposed to the main tendencies of modern poetry. He is the clear, simple, moral poet who sings of rural, democratic joys and who is, above all, the lover of nature. But although Frost is perhaps most closely akin to Emerson and Emily Dickinson, he clearly learned much from modern poetic movements. If he is the positive poet of rural America, he is also the chronicler of the dark night of the human soul, the sophisticated poet, full of irony and ambiguity. He wrote in traditional verse forms, but within the poems he created a tension of thought and feeling, reinforced by tension between colloquial speech and traditional metrics, that is unmatched in American poetry. The poem, as he said in *The Figure a Poem Makes,* is "a momentary stay against confusion."

Frost was awarded the Pulitzer Prize in 1924, 1931, 1937 and 1943 for *New Hampshire, Collected Poems, A Further Range,* and *A Witness Tree.*

Froth, Master. In Shakespeare's MEASURE FOR MEASURE, a foolish gentleman, too shallow for great crime and too light for virtue. See Mistress OVERDONE.

frottola. An Italian verse form popular among both folk and learned poets during the early Renaissance. It is characterized by a long discursive style, chiefly in short lines, that comments on topical as well as literary subjects. Its nearest English analogue is the so-called Skeltonic verse practiced by John SKELTON.

Froude, James Anthony (1818–1894). English historian. He wrote a *History of England from the Fall of Wolsey to the Defeat of the Spanish Armada* (1856–1870). As executor of Thomas Carlyle he wrote *Reminiscences of Carlyle* (1881) and a *Life of Thomas Carlyle* (1884). With his brother, Richard Hurrell Froude (1803–1836), who contributed to

TRACTS FOR THE TIMES, Froude was associated for a time with the Oxford Movement.

Fruitlands. An experimental cooperative community (1842–1843) founded by Bronson ALCOTT at Harvard, Mass. Its plan included vegetarianism, farming, and teaching. Alcott's daughter, Louisa May Alcott, described the colonists with gentle humor in *Transcendental Wild Oats* (1876), a fictional sketch.

Fruits of the Earth, The (Les Nourritures terrestres; 1897). A poetic work by André GIDE. It is a hymn in prose and poetry to the beauty of all experience, exhorting youth to prepare itself for receiving all the joy of life by casting off all that is artificial or merely conventional. In the 1920's a generation of restless youth welcomed the work as a popular handbook of self-liberation.

Fry, Christopher (1907–   ). English dramatist. He was born Christopher Harris, but took his mother's name. His plays are most often in verse forms; they are witty and full of poetic conceits. The heroine of *The Lady's Not for Burning* (1949) is a young witch. Among his other plays are *A Phoenix Too Frequent* (1949); *A Sleep of Prisoners* (1951), designed to be produced in churches; *Venus Observed* (1950); *Ring around the Moon* (1950), a translation of *L'Invitation au Château* by Jean Anouilh; *The Dark is Light Enough* (1954); and *Curtmantle* (1961).

Fry, Elizabeth (1780–1845). English Quaker philanthropist, noted as promoter of wide-ranging prison reforms, particularly in the treatment of female prisoners. Her *Memoirs* were published in 1847.

Fry, Roger (1866–1934). English art critic and painter. A member of the BLOOMSBURY GROUP, he was a pioneer in introducing the work of Cézanne and other POST-IMPRESSIONIST painters. He was at one time curator of paintings at the New York Metropolitan Museum. Among his books are *Vision and Design* (1920), *Transformations* (1926), *Cézanne: A Study of his Development* (1927), and *Reflections on British Painting* (1934). He also edited *Sir Joshua Reynolds' Discourses* (1905). Virginia Woolf wrote his biography (1940).

Fudge Family. A family whose adventures are related in Thomas MOORE's satire *The Fudge Family in Paris* (1818). Each member of the family writes letters to friends back home in England; they are meant to satirize the *parvenu* English abroad.

Fuenteovejuna (The Sheep Well, c. 1619). A drama by Lope de VEGA. Based on actual historical records, the story takes place during the reign of Ferdinand and Isabella. Commander Fernán Gómez, the lascivious lord of Fuenteovejuna, violates Laurencia, a peasant girl of the community. She tells her misfortune to the townspeople who, enraged by her words, storm the commander's castle and put him to death. The king sends a judge to discover the identity of the murderer, but all the villagers, even under torture, will say only that Fuenteovejuna killed him. Impressed by the heroic behavior of the people, the king pardons them and puts the village under the crown's protection.

Führer, der (*Ger.,* "Leader"). A title assumed by Adolf HITLER, who claimed to be the true representative of the German people. It was also used by leaders of subdivisions within the Nazi Party.

Fuhrmann Henschel. See DRAYMAN HENSCHEL.

Fujiwara. See HEIAN.

Fujiyama. More correctly **Fuji-no-Yama,** but commonly called **Fujisan.** The sacred mountain of Japan. The mountain, Japan's highest (12,394 feet), is in the province of Suruga, 60 miles southwest of Tokyo. It is a snow-capped volcano, inactive since 1708, a resort of pilgrims and prominent in Japanese art.

Fuller, Henry B[lake] (1857–1929). American novelist. Fuller won success with his first novel, *The Chevalier of Pensieri-Vani* (1890), written under the pseudonym Stanton Page, but his best-known book is THE CLIFF DWELLERS, the first successful novel about an American city. Working as a book critic for Chicago newspapers, he was active in Chicago's literary circles, especially those engaged in making POETRY the most important magazine of its kind in the country. Fuller himself issued two collections of verse: *The New Flag* (1899) and *Lines Long and Short* (1917).

Fuller, [Sarah] Margaret. Marchesa **Ossoli** (1810–1850). American editor, essayist, poet, and teacher. A brilliant and well-educated women, Miss Fuller edited *The Dial* for two years. She had a gift for languages, and translated Goethe, spreading enthusiasm for his work. She held Saturday "conversations" regularly, and wrote critical articles for the New York *Tribune*. Unfavorably criticizing Longfellow and Lowell, she alienated the Boston Brahmins from the Transcendentalists. In 1846, Miss Fuller went abroad; visiting Italy, she mingled with leading authors, and became involved in Italy's struggle for freedom. She met Giovanni Angelo, Marquis Ossoli, who was 10 years younger than she, and became his mistress. They had a son, and were later married. Miss Fuller became very active in the hospitals when fighting began in Italy; she started to write a book on Giuseppe Mazzini and the war of liberation. In May, 1850, the family set sail for New York; their vessel was shipwrecked off Fire Island. The body of the infant son washed ashore, but the others were never recovered.

Margaret Fuller published a number of books, among them *Summer on the Lakes* (1844), *Woman in the Nineteenth Century* (1845), and *Papers on Literature and Art* (1846). She was attacked in James Russell Lowell's A FABLE FOR CRITICS, and Hawthorne is said to have modeled his character, Zenobia, in THE BLITHEDALE ROMANCE, on the dynamic and paradoxical figure of Margaret Fuller.

Fuller, Roy (1912–   ). English poet. His early poems were sociological, in the manner of W. H. Auden, and his later poems more romantic and mythological. His collections include *Poems* (1939) and *The Ruined Boys* (1959).

Fuller, Thomas (1608–1661). English clergyman and writer. One of the most popular preachers and authors of his day, Fuller was appointed chaplain to Charles II after the Restoration. His writing is remarkable for its wit, tolerance, and common sense. Among his works are *The History of the Holy War* (1639), an account of Palestine during the Crusades; *The Holy State and the Profane State* (1642), a series of character sketches; *Good Thoughts in Bad Times* (1645), brief essays on contemporary religious conflicts; and *The History of the Worthies of England* (1662), a collection of biographical sketches.

Fulton, Robert (1765–1815). American inventor. After working as an artist and draftsman, Fulton went to Europe in 1786 where he remained for 20 years, devoting himself to science and mechanics. Although he made several important inventions, he is best known for his applications of steam to navigation. He designed the first commercially successful steamboat, the *Clermont*, which traveled from New York to Albany (Aug. 17–22, 1807) in 62 hours of operating time.

Fulvia (d. 40 B.C.). A Roman matron married successively to the demagogue Clodius Pulcher, Curio, and Mark Antony. It is said that when Cicero was murdered by Antony's orders, his head was brought to Fulvia who drove a needle through his tongue in revenge for the things he had said against her husband in his famous Philippics.

Funeral Oration. See PERICLES.

Furcht und Elend des Dritten Reiches. See PRIVATE LIFE OF THE MASTER RACE.

Furies. See ERINYES.

Furmanov, Dmitri Andreyevich (1891–1926). Russian novelist. He is the author of the much-praised Soviet classic *Chapayev* (1923). A story of the civil war, it contrasts the characters of an emotional, haphazard guerilla leader, General Chapayev, and a cool, detached, and efficient Bolshevik commissar, who was Furmanov himself.

Furness, Horace Howard (1833–1912). American Shakespearian scholar. In 1871 he began to edit the *New Variorum* edition of Shakespeare's works. It was carried to completion by his son, **Horace Howard Furness** (1865–1930). The elder Furness' treatment of the text of Shakespeare's plays is considered conservative; his edition includes abstracts of previous criticism as well as variant readings. His son's work reveals less scholarship and judgment. On the latter's death, he bequeathed his great Shakespearian library to the University of Pennsylvania.

Furnivall, Frederick James (1825–1910). An English philologist. He was the founder of innumerable English literary societies, including the Early English Text Society (1864), the Chaucer Society and the Ballad Society (1868), the New Shakespeare Society (1873), the Browning Society (1881), the Wyclif Society (1882), and the Shelley Society (1885). He edited the *Six-Text Print of Chaucer's Canterbury Tales* (1868–1875) and began a dictionary for the Philological Society that developed into the *Oxford English Dictionary*.

Furor. See FAERIE QUEENE, THE.

Furphy, Joseph. Pen name **Tom Collins** (1843–1912). Australian novelist. A perfect example of late literary blooming, Furphy was 60 when his novel *Such is Life* (1903) was published. And though, as a youth, he showed great promise with a prize-winning poem on the death of Abraham Lincoln, he published only some verses and sketches in the next 20 years, during which period his brilliant style developed. *Such is Life* caught the notice of only a small group upon its publication. Later, however, the book proved to be a starting point for the longer form of Australian novel. Furphy, a self-educated man, flouted all the rules, and in this way wrote a novel of complete

Washington Irving, American essayist, biographer, and historian, at the age of 67—
from an engraving by T. Johnson after a daguerreotype by Plumb

Thomas Jefferson, third President of the United States, distinguished author,
philosopher, and college president—from an engraving

Life mask of John Keats, English poet—from an engraving by T. Johnson

An illustration for *Candide* by Paul Klee, Swiss painter

Emma Lazarus, American poet and linguist —
from an engraving by T. Johnson after a photograph by W. Kurtz

Sylvester Brounorver ad vivum delin.   P. Vanderbanck sculp:

Mr John Locke. 1695

John Locke, English author and philosopher—
from an engraving by P. Vanderbanck after a life drawing by Sylvester Brounorver

Henry Wadsworth Longfellow, American poet, linguist, and professor, in his later years—
from an original photograph

Martin Luther, German religious reformer —
from an engraving after a woodcut by Lucas Cranach

originality. *Such is Life* has recently been recognized as one of the best frontier novels in English.

Furry Lawcats. An anglicism for the Chats-Fourrés, who inhabit the Wicket, where Pantagruel and his friends are arrested in Rabelais' GARGANTUA AND PANTAGRUEL. The Furry Lawcats, so called in allusion to the ermine-bordered robes worn by judges, are a rapacious breed who use their incomprehensible subtleties to devour everything. Among them, vice is deemed virtue, and evil passes for good; though they plunder the universe, their authority is unquestioned. Pantagruel and his companions are released only when Panurge, after answering a riddle posed by Graspall, or Grippeminaud, archduke of the Furry Lawcats, tosses them a bag full of gold coins. This episode was Rabelais' most violent satire on the courts of justice.

Furtado, R. de L. (1922–). Indian poet writing in English, currently Professor of English in Delhi University. *The Centre*, poems, appeared in 1955; *Shelley*, literary criticism, in 1958; *The Oleanders and Other Poems* in 1960.

Further Range, A (1936). A collection of poems by Robert FROST. It contains several humorous and satirical pieces and a group of epigrams called *Ten Mills*. The longest poem in the book, *Build Soil*, reflects the poet's concern with contemporary political developments. Also included in the collection are *Desert Places, Neither out Far Nor in Deep, Design*, and *Provide, Provide*.

futurism. A radical movement in literature and art initiated in 1909 by the Italian poet and novelist Filippo Tommaso Marinetti (1876–1944). His *Manifeste du Futurisme* (1909) called for a revolutionary attitude toward life and art in general, exalting such aspects of contemporary life as speed, machinery, and war. The special manifesto on literature (1912) insisted on courage, audacity, and rebellion as the essential elements of poetry; it advocated freedom for the word (*parole in libertà*), the abolition of syntax, and similar anarchic, "liberating" tendencies. In the field of art, futurism produced its most interesting works before World War. In their effort to portray dynamic movement and force, futurist painters often presented a moving object in successive stages of motion. Among the representatives of futurist art were the painters Giacomo Bella and Gino Severini and the

sculptor Umberto Boccioni. The movement won for a time the endorsement of the Italian fascists.

Futurism influenced modern European literature and art and was also a forerunner of cubism, dadaism, expressionism, and surrealism. Its most immediate effect was felt in Russia where futurists attempted to do away with what they regarded as stale and hackneyed in Russian poetry, especially the kind of work written by the symbolist poets. The chief members of the Russian futurists were Velemir Khlebnikov and Vladimir Mayakovski. The Fauvist attitude of the futurists was revealed in their manifesto, *A Slap in the Face of Public Taste* (*Poshchiochina obshchestvennomu vkusu;* 1912), which voiced their demand: "Throw Pushkin, Dostoevski, Tolstoi . . . overboard from the steamship of modernity." The search for new poetic techniques led Khlebnikov to experiment with "trans-sense language" (Russ., *zaumnayi yazik* or *zaum*), in which words are shorn of their meanings and used only for their sound values. One of Khlebnikov's experiments consisted of a poem, written in 1910, made up of neologisms derived from the word *smekh* ("laughter"). Mayakovski, the greatest poet of the group, was more successful in developing a new kind of poetry. Its chief features were a rhetorical style, original rhymes, powerful rhythms, and an emphasis on the individual word, rather than the line, as the basis of poetic organization.

Although revolutionary in temper and tone, the work of the futurists was too literary for the Soviet cultural overseers. To propagate their views, the futurists formed the organization known as LEF (Left Front of the Arts) in 1923 and published a journal under that name. The journal failed in 1925, and was revived briefly in 1927–1928 as *Novyi LEF* (*New LEF*), but eventually the project died. By this time the proletarian trend in literature, advocated by RAPP (q.v.), was dominant.

Fuzzy Wuzzy (1892). Title of one of Rudyard Kipling's BARRACK-ROOM BALLADS celebrating the bushy-haired warriors of the Sudan who fought Gordon and Kitchener.

> So 'ere's to you, Fuzzy Wuzzy, at your 'ome in the Soudan;
> You're a pore benighted 'eathen but a first-class fightin' man.

G

Gaboriau, Emile (1835–1873). A literary pioneer who popularized the detective story in France. Gaboriau created the memorable hero MONSIEUR LECOQ.

Gabriel. One of the archangels who appears in the Jewish, Christian, and Muslim systems of belief. In Hebrew mythology, he is sometimes regarded as the angel of death, the prince of fire and thunder, but more frequently as one of the Deity's chief messengers and the only angel who can speak Syrian and Chaldee. In the Talmud, he appears as the destroyer of Sennacherib's armies, as the man who showed Joseph the way, and as one of the angels who buried Moses.

Christians hold that Gabriel was the angel of the Annunciation who appeared to the Virgin Mary; he also announced to Zacharias the future birth of John the Baptist. It is he who is to blow the trumpet on Judgment Day.

The Muslims call Gabriel the chief of the four favored angels and the spirit of truth. He was the angel who, according to the Koran, revealed the sacred laws to Muhammad.

Milton, in his *Paradise Lost* (1667), makes Gabriel chief of the angelic guards placed over Paradise.

Gabriel Conroy (1876). A novel by Bret HARTE. The longest of his fictional writings, it gives a vivid picture of mining conditions during the early days of the California gold rush. Among the best-drawn characters is the professional gambler, Jack Hamlin.

Gabrieli, Giovanni (1555–1612). Venetian composer, pupil of his uncle, Andrea Gabrieli (c. 1515–1586), also a composer of note. From 1576 to 1580 he was in Munich with Orlando de Lassus. He was a teacher of Michael Praetorius and Heinrich Schütz. Long associated with the Cathedral of St. Mark's in Venice, Gabrieli brought to its peak the Venetian style of polychoral writing (pieces for two or more groups of instruments or voices in different parts of the building). He is also important as a bridge between the Renaissance and Baroque styles in music.

Gabrina. In the ORLANDO FURIOSO of Ariosto an old hag whose ugliness evokes laughter in anyone who looks at her, but prompts quarrels among the knights who defend her. When the warrior maiden Marfisa, her protectress, defeats the Scottish knight Zerbino, the latter is compelled to keep Gabrina's company and follow her. He saves her from her enemy Ermonide, but she ungraciously charges him with the death of Pinabello. Zerbino, rescued by Orlando, later punishes the false knight Oderico by compelling him to keep Gabrina's company. Eventually, Oderico hangs her.

gadfly. A fly that bites or annoys cattle. In Greek mythology, Hera sent a gadfly to torment the white-horned cow in whose shape Zeus tried to protect his beloved Io from his wife's jealousy. A gadfly also bit Pegasus and caused him to send BELLEROPHON plunging to the earth.

Gaelic League. An organization founded in Dublin in 1863. Its purpose is to preserve and extend the vernacular use of the Gaelic language, the native tongue of Ireland.

Gaelic literature. The literature of Gaelic-speaking Ireland and Scotland. Irish literature is usually divided as follows: Old Irish (up to 900); Middle Irish (up to 1350); Late Middle, or Early Modern, Irish (up to 1650); and Modern Irish (from 1650). Up until the 12th century, Gaelic literature was entirely oral; it was committed to memory by bards and transmitted orally from generation to generation. In the middle period, a few monks began to set it down lest it be entirely forgotten.

Old Irish literature survives in medieval manuscripts, which are copies of older manuscripts; among the most important of these are *Lebor na Huidre* (*The Book of the Dun Cow*), *The Book of Leinster*, *The Yellow Book of Lecan*, *The Book of Ballymote*, and *The Speckled Book*. The romances and sagas contained in these books have been grouped according to characters and subject matter. The major groupings of these hero sagas are three: the MYTHOLOGICAL CYCLE, the ULSTER CYCLE, and the FENIAN CYCLE. The mythological cycle relates various traditions about the early settlement and conquest of Ireland. The Ulster cycle deals with Irish heroes, the greatest of whom is Cú Chulainn. The Fenian cycle deals with a much later period and extends into the Christian era which comes in the extreme old age of Oisin or Ossian, poet of the Fenians. The cycles are prose narratives interspersed with poetic dialogue.

The later Middle Irish literature written in Gaelic is generally less significant than that of the older periods; unlike the earlier literature, the bulk of which is anonymous, the later medieval literature was written by known poets, several of whom are worthy of mention. The chief bards of the 13th through 15th century are Gilbride Albanach McNamee (13th century), the religious poet Donough Mor O'Daly (13th century), and Teig Og O'Higgins (15th century). To this late medieval period also belongs the celebrated Gaelic narrative collection *The Three Sorrows of Story Telling*. The 16th and 17th centuries saw a great poetic revival and the rise of Modern Irish prose. As England conquered Ireland and as Protestantism became firmly established in England, Gaelic literature evinced fiercer patriotism and affirmed Catholicism. The decline of bardic poetry, however, was already under way before Cromwell's arrival (1649) in Ireland. The prose of the 16th and 17th century is transitional; the religious writings and monumental history of Ireland of Geoffrey Keating (1570–c. 1650) is the very foundation of Modern Irish literature. The number of Gaelic-speaking Irish declined somewhat after the arrival of Cromwell and the settling of English in Ireland; however, the potato famine of 1847 dealt the most severe blow, for, in the consequent depopulation of the country, the Gaelic west was hardest hit and the proportion of Gaelic speakers in Ireland dropped in three short years from three fourths to one quarter.

In the later 19th century, through the efforts of Irish scholars, there came the great Gaelic literary revival that continued into the 20th. See GAELIC LEAGUE; IRISH RENAISSANCE.

Gaheris, Sir. See MARGAWSE, QUEEN.

Gainsborough, Thomas (1727–1788). English painter. He rivaled Sir Joshua REYNOLDS as a fashionable portraitist, but his work shows greater simplicity and a lighter, rapid, and vibrant touch. One of the first painters to depict English scenery, he painted landscapes for his own pleasure and liked to portray his sitters in the open, but he allowed his art to be limited by the fashion of the day, which rejected landscape as a minor genre. Among his delightful portraits is the well-known *Blue Boy*.

Galafrone. In the ORLANDO INNAMORATO of Boiardo, the king of Cathay. He sends his daughter Angelica and his son Argalia to Paris to fight against Charlemagne and his paladins, the one using her beauty, the other his enchanted arms.

Galahad, Sir. In the later legends of King Arthur, the purest and noblest knight of the Round Table. Best known from Malory's *Morte d'Arthur* (c. 1469), he is the illegitimate son of Sir Launcelot and the princess ELAINE and the last descendant of Joseph of Arimathea. He alone is qualified to fill the SIEGE PERILOUS at the Round Table, and he alone achieves the quest for the Holy GRAIL. His career ends in Sarras, after he has completed the quest. Later writers, particularly of the romantic period, wrote newer versions of Sir Galahad into the Arthurian legend. Among these are Tennyson and Mark Twain. The name of Sir Galahad has become, in fact, synonymous with the chivalrous, the perfect knight.

Galápagos Islands. An archipelago of volcanic islands on the equator, west of Ecuador. It is noted for its large tortoises (Sp. *galápago,* tortoise), elephant seals, and other species that exist nowhere else. It was investigated by Darwin during his voyage in the *Beagle,* later by William Beebe. It is the setting of Melville's short story *The Encantadas.*

Galatea (Galateia). (1) A Nereid; see ACIS. (2) See PYGMALION.

Galatians, The Epistle of Paul the Apostle to the. A New Testament book. It is a letter from Paul to the various Christian churches in Galatia. Paul argues for the universality of the Christian faith, and tries to save it from becoming merely a Judaistic sect.

Galba (5 B.C.?–A.D. 69). Roman emperor (A.D. 68–69). He was made emperor after Nero's death by the Praetorian guard, but was killed after a few months because he was unwilling to fulfill the expectations of his followers.

Gale, Zona (1874–1938). American novelist and short-story writer. Born in Wisconsin, Miss Gale is best known for her work dealing with small-town life in the Middle West. She joined the staff of the New York *World* in 1901, but soon left to devote her time to writing. Her first novel, *Romance Island,* was published in 1906. The sentimentality that characterized Miss Gale's early writing was evident in her popular series of stories about the mythical Friendship Village. But despite their one-sided view, the author's talent for accurate observation gave them an aura of reality.

During World War I Miss Gale was again living in Wisconsin. Her pacifist views brought her the enmity of her neighbors, and her views of village life were greatly altered. This change of attitude is reflected in BIRTH and in her short novel MISS LULU BETT, which was an immediate success. In the same realistic vein were *Faint Perfume* (1923), which pitted the sensitivity of her heroine against the crassness of middle-class life, and two collections of short stories, *Yellow Gentians and Blue* (1927) and *Bridal Pond* (1930). A strain of mysticism, hinted at in earlier work, was apparent in *Preface to a Life* (1926) and in much of her later writing.

Galen (Klaudios Galenos, 2d century). A famous Greek physician and philosopher. For centuries he was the supreme authority in medicine; hence, any physician.

Galeoto or **Galeotto.** The Italian name of Gallehault, one of the forms of GALAHAD, which has attached to itself a quite divergent meaning. Its modern connotations come from a passage in Dante's *Inferno* telling how PAOLO AND FRANCESCA read of a guilty kiss between Launcelot and Guinevere and yielded to the suggestion. Gallehault was the knight who had brought Launcelot and the queen together, and he performed the same office for Paolo and Francesca, for "Galeoto was the book and he who wrote it. That day we read no more." Hence, though far from the character of Galahad, Galeoto has become a term for a panderer in Italy and Spain. In José Echegaray's tragedy EL GRAN GALEOTO, gossip is the "Galeoto."

Galiana. A Moorish princess, whose father, King Gadalfe of Toledo, reputedly built a palace for her on the Tagus River. It was so splendid that the phrase, a palace of Galiana, became proverbial in Spain.

Galilei, Galileo. Known as Galileo (1564–1642). Italian astronomer, physicist, and philosopher. Galileo's achievements led to a new physical and mathematical concept of nature. He discovered the isochronism of the pendulum (1583), hydrostatic balance (1586), Jupiter's satellites (1610), sun spots (1610), the moon's libration (1637), among other accomplishments. A staunch advocate of COPERNICUS, he found himself in difficulties with the Church, but was not unduly harassed until the publication of his *Dialogo dei due massimi sistemi (Dialogue on the Great World Systems,* 1632). The following year he was tried before the INQUISITION on charges of proclaiming and defending the Copernican system, which had been denounced as heretical. Unwilling to sacrifice his remaining years and his work to a fruitless heroism, he recanted his views. Legend has it that after doing so, he muttered *"Eppur si muove!"*

(And yet it moves!), in quiet insistence on the earth's motion. During his remaining years he was under close watch, in virtual house arrest, but he was widely acclaimed and revered. The *Dialogue* was the first scientific treatise written in Italian, the layman's language, rather than in the customary Latin. He is the subject of Brecht's play THE LIFE OF GALILEO.

gall. Bile; the very bitter fluid secreted by the liver. The word is used figuratively as a symbol of anything of extreme bitterness. The phrase "gall and wormwood" compounds the bitterness.

The gall of bitterness means the bitterest grief; extreme affliction. The ancients taught that grief and joy were subject to the gall as affection was to the heart, knowledge to the kidneys, and the gall of bitterness means the bitter center of bitterness, as the heart of hearts means the innermost recesses of the heart or affections. In the Acts it is used to signify the sinfulness of sin, which leads to the bitterest grief. According to tradition, pigeons have no gall, because the dove sent from the ark by Noah burst its gall out of grief, and none of the pigeon family has had a gall ever since.

Gall, Franz Joseph (1758–1828). German physician and phrenologist. His major scientific treatise is *Anatomie et physiologie du système nerveux en général* (*Anatomy and Physiology of the Nervous System in General*, 1810–1819). See PHRENOLOGY.

Gallegos [Freire], Rómulo (1884–   ). Venezuelan novelist, educator, and political leader. When lack of funds forced Gallegos to abandon his legal studies, he turned to teaching and, from 1912 to 1930, was director of various educational institutions. The publication of DOÑA BÁRBARA, Gallegos' best-known novel, aroused the hostility of Juan Vicente Gómez, Venezuela's dictator, who tried to silence the author by offering him a seat in the senate. Gallegos chose voluntary exile instead, living in the U.S. and Spain, where he was an employee of the National Cash Register Co. Returning to Venezuela, after the death of Gómez in 1935, he served briefly as minister of education, directed motion-picture versions of several of his novels, and was an unsuccessful presidential candidate in 1942. In 1945 a coup engineered by Acción Democrática, a liberal political party of which Gallegos had been a founder, overthrew the government, and he was elected president of Venezuela for the term 1948–1952. Late in 1948, however, Gallegos was deposed by a military junta and remained in exile until the overthrow of Marcos Pérez Jiménez in 1958.

As a novelist, Gallegos is famed for his interpretation of the people and customs of the Venezuelan *llanos*, or tropical prairies. Besides *Doña Bárbara*, his best-known novels are *La trepadora* (1925), a psychological study of an illegitimate son who seeks his family's acceptance; *Cantaclaro* (1934), which relates the adventures of a wandering minstrel on the *llanos;* *Canaima* (1935), a story laid in the tropical forest where the evil spirit "canaima" dwells; and *Pobre negro* (1937), which describes slavery and mulatto life in 19th-century Venezuela.

Gallehault. The name for GALAHAD in the old French romance *Lancelot du Lac*. See GALEOTO.

Gallic Wars. See COMMENTARIES ON THE GALLIC WAR.

Gallup, George H[orace] (1901–   ). American public-opinion statistician. Having founded the Institute of Public Opinion (1935) and spent some time measuring public reactions by means of polls, Gallup began to forecast the results of such reactions, particularly in the realm of political elections. He is the author of *The Pulse of Democracy: A New Technique for Measuring Reader Interest* (1940) and numerous articles on public opinion.

Galotti, Emilia. See EMILIA GALOTTI.

Galsworthy, John (1867–1933). English novelist and playwright, known for his portrayals of the British upper classes and for his social satire. His most famous work is his novel series beginning with THE FORSYTE SAGA (1906–1922); Galsworthy continued to write novels about the Forsyte family throughout his life. His plays are remarkable realistic and satirical studies based on various different social problems. Like Bernard Shaw and other contemporary writers of dramas of ideas, Galsworthy was influenced by the drama of Henrik Ibsen.

Born into an upper-middle-class family like the ones he usually wrote about, Galsworthy was trained as a lawyer and his legal knowledge colors many of his novels and plays. He turned to literature after he had met Joseph Conrad on a voyage. A passionate romance with Ada Galsworthy, his cousin's wife, who encouraged his writing, led to their marriage some 10 years later, in 1905. Galsworthy's earliest works, written under the pseudonym of John Sinjohn, were volumes of short stories and two novels influenced by Turgenev: *Jocelyn* (1898) and *Villa Rubein* (1900). He came to artistic maturity in 1906, with the publication of his novel *The Man of Property* (the first installment of *The Forsyte Saga*) and the production of his play *The Silver Box*. In the work of this early period Galsworthy attacked the smug conventionality and self-righteous hypocrisy of the middle classes, and championed the artist, the rebel, and the underdog (see his play JUSTICE). He became less satirical and more sentimental and traditional in the later Forsyte novels, such as THE COUNTRY HOUSE and THE PATRICIAN, and the plays *The Skin Game* (1920) and *Loyalties* (1922). He refused knighthood in 1918 but accepted the Order of Merit in 1929 and the Nobel Prize in 1932.

Galuppi, Baldassare (1706–1785). Italian composer, principally of opera. The work that inspired Browning's poem *A Toccata of Galuppi's* is thought to have been the *Toccata in A major* by the Italian composer Pietro Domenico Paradies or Paradisi (1707–1791).

Gálvez, Manuel (1882–   ). Argentine novelist. Gálvez is best known for his naturalistic novels in which he mercilessly exposed Argentina's social evils, revealing a Dickensian sympathy for the downtrodden. *La maestra normal* (1914), often considered his best work, is a tale of seduction notable for the author's depiction of the pettiness and monotony of life in the provincial city of La Rioja. Córdoba is the setting for *La sombra del convento* (1917), which describes the conflict between conservative clericalism and liberalism. Gálvez' most popular novel was *Nacha Regules* (1919); although its plot is melodramatic, dealing with the redemption of a fallen woman through true love, the novel gives a chilling portrait of conditions in a Buenos Aires brothel and among the poor in general.

Gama, Vasco da (c. 1460–1524). Portuguese explorer. The first European to discover a sea route to the East, he rounded the Cape of Good Hope on Nov. 22, 1497, sailed along the coast of Africa, and crossed the Indian Ocean to reach Calicut on May 20, 1498. He made a second trip to the East in 1502–1503 and was named viceroy of India in 1524. He is the hero of Camões' LUSIADAS, and Meyerbeer's opera *L'Africaine*.

Gambara, Veronica (1485–1550). Italian poet. She wrote sonnets on Petrarchan love themes and on the political events of her day. Her *Rime* (*Verses*) and *Lettere* were published in 1759.

Gambetta, Léon (1838–1882). French lawyer and statesman. Violently opposed to Napoleon III, he served as a member of the new government of National Defence (September, 1870). In a futile attempt to organize national resistance, Gametta made a spectacular balloon escape during the Prussian siege of Paris. He served as president of the Chamber of Deputies (1879–1881) and as premier of France (1881–1882), during the Third Republic.

Gambler, The (Igrok; 1866). A short novel by Feodor DOSTOEVSKI. The gambling mania of the tale's hero, Aleksei Ivanovich, is a reflection of the author's own tendency. The heroine of the story, Polina, is based on Polina Suslova, Dostoevski's lover in 1862–1863.

Gamelin, Evariste. Chief character in the novel THE GODS ARE ATHIRST by Anatole France. A young artist, Gamelin becomes an avid member of the revolutionary tribunal. Ironically, he himself is put to death by the guillotine.

Gamelyn, The Tale of. A metrical romance in Middle English. Often called **The Cook's Tale of Gamelyn**, it has been erroneously attributed to Chaucer (see COOK'S TALE). Gamelyn is the youngest of three brothers. The eldest robs him of his share of their father's property, and after a series of successes and reverses in reclaiming it, Gamelyn takes to the forest and eventually becomes chief of a band of outlaws. The second brother tries to help him and winds up in chains, but Gamelyn returns to overthrow their wicked brother, now sheriff, as well as the dishonest judge and jury. Thomas Lodge adapted the story in his romance *Rosalynde* (1590), a major source for Shakespeare's As You Like It.

Gamesmanship. A term popularized by Stephen POTTER through his humorous book *Theory and Practice of Gamesmanship, or the Art of Winning Games without Actually Cheating* (1947).

Gammer Gurton's Needle (1566). The second oldest English comedy. It was first performed at Cambridge in 1566, and published in 1575. It was formerly ascribed to John Still (1543?–1607), Bishop of Bath and Winchester, but the claim of William Stevenson (d. 1575?) is now generally favored. A coarse and vigorous comedy, it deals with the housewife Gammer Gurton's loss of her needle as she is mending her servant Hodge's breeches; it closes with the painful but farcical discovery of the missing needle in the seat of Hodge's pants.

Gamp, Sarah, usually called **Sairey.** A disreputable nurse in Charles Dickens' MARTIN CHUZZLEWIT, famous for her bulky umbrella and perpetual reference to Mrs. Harris, a purely imaginary person

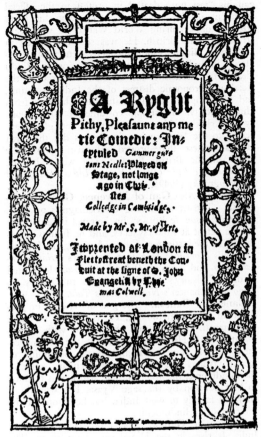

Title page of *Gammer Gurton's Needle* (1575).

whose opinions always confirm her own. She is fond of strong tea and more potent stimulants.

Hence, a regular Gamp came to signify a low-class, drink-sodden, uncertificated maternity nurse, and an umbrella, especially a large, badly rolled cotton one, came to be called a gamp.

gandharva (*Sans.*, celestial musician). In the Hindu tradition, marriage by the mere exchange of garlands, a love union, recognized by Manu, the Hindu law codifier, as one of the eight acceptable types of marriage.

Gandhi, Mohandas Karamchand, called **Mahatma** (great-souled) **Gandhi** (1869–1948). Hindu nationalist leader. He is considered the architect of Indian independence and self-rule. He studied law in England and practiced in India. In 1893 he went to South Africa to help in the struggle of Indian settlers to gain political rights; it was here that Gandhi first used the technique of passive resistance that later became his chief weapon against the British in India. After returning to India in 1914, he supported the British in World War I, but in 1919 he formed the Satyagraha, a politico-religious movement of non-cooperation with the British, which caused him to be imprisoned for "civil disobedience." In 1924 he became president of the Indian National Congress, a position he held until 1934. He urged the boycott of all English goods in 1932, the same year that he began his "fast unto death" in protest to the official treatment of the untouchables. He won his point after six days. During World War II he was again arrested by the British. He was shot and killed in 1948 by a Hindu Nationalist. His tremendous popularity in India was due to his devotion to Hindu ideals, his asceticism, his efforts to overcome the social and economic distress of the Indian peasants, and his campaign to eliminate untouchability from Hindu society. His simple costume of white worn by the wrinkled old man in the plain steel glasses appealed to the Western imagination as did the form of his protest that proved effective against the might of the British Empire. His works include *Indian Home Rule* (1922), *Young India* (1924) and *Autobiography* (1949).

Ganelon. Also **Gan of Mayence, Gano of Maganza.** The traitor among Charlemagne's paladins. In the *Chanson de* ROLAND his betrayal is responsible for the defeat at RONCESVALLES, and he figures prominently as the instigator of discord among the knights in Pulci's *Morgante Maggiore,* Boiardo's *Orlando Innamorato,* and Ariosto's *Orlando Furioso.* He is cited as one of history's notorious traitors in Dante's *Inferno* and Chaucer's *Nun's Priest's Tale.*

Ganesh or **Ganesa.** The god of wisdom or prudence in Hindu mythology. He is the son of Shiva and Parvati, and is always represented with an elephant's head. He is propitiated at the commencement of important work and at the beginning of sacred writings because he is the legendary scribe of the Hindu epic, the *Mahabharata,* which was dictated to him nonstop by the sage Vyasa. His worship is confined largely to west India, but he is one of the most popular Hindu deities.

Ganges or **Ganga.** The most sacred river of India. It rises in the Himalayas, flows about 1500 miles, and empties into the Bay of Bengal by many mouths. It is also known as the Bhagirathi. Its source, in Hindu legend, lies at the feet of Brahma, and its descent to the earth was through the matted locks of Shiva, the king of *yogis* or ascetics; hence the ritual necessity for orthodox Hindus to bathe in the holy river on certain days in order to be rid of their imperfections. See BHAGIRATH.

Ganivet, Angel (1865–1898). Spanish philosopher and critic. His most famous work is the philosophical inquiry into the Spanish national character entitled *Idearium español* (1898), which points the way toward the *Generación del 98* in its analysis of abulia, a lack of will in the Spanish people. Ganivet is also the author of two novels, considered semiautobiographical in nature, *La conquista del reino de Maya* (1897) and *Los trabajos del infatigable creador Pío Cid* (1898).

Ganor, Ganora, Geneura, Ginevra, Genievre, Guinevere, Guenever. Various ways of spelling the name of King Arthur's wife. She is called Guanhumara or Guanhumar by Geoffrey of Monmouth, but Tennyson made GUINEVERE the popular English form.

Gant, Eugene. The central character in Thomas Wolfe's autobiographical novels LOOK HOMEWARD, ANGEL and OF TIME AND THE RIVER. Gant is a young man of robust energies and intense emotion; he feels "different" from others, and has vast, romantic yearnings toward love, adventure, personal achievement, and a semimystical, unknown goal which carries him on a virtual pilgrimage through the U.S. and Europe. Other characters with the same family name are likewise drawn from life: Oliver Gant, Eugene's father; Eliza Gant, his mother; and Ben Gant, his older brother.

Ganymede (Ganymedes). In Greek mythology, the cup-bearer of Zeus, successor to Hebe, and a type of youthful male beauty. The son of Tros, an early king of Troy, he was carried off by Zeus on the back of an eagle because of his unusual beauty.

García de la Huerta, Vicente (1734–1787). Spanish playwright. His work is thought to have anticipated romanticism while preserving neoclassical principles. His most successful work is the verse drama *Raquel* (1778), dealing with the love between Alfonso VIII and a Jewish girl from Toledo, a theme previously treated by Lope de Vega and by Mira de Amescua.

García del Castañar. See Francisco de ROJAS ZORRILLA.

García Gutiérrez, Antonio (1813–1884). Spanish dramatist. The most popular of his many plays is *El trovador* (1836), a romantic historical tragedy that was the basis of Verdi's opera IL TROVATORE. He also wrote *Venganza catalana* (1864) and *Juan Lorenzo* (1865), sometimes considered his masterpiece.

García Lorca, Federico (1898–1936). Spanish poet and playwright. He is considered the most deeply appreciated Spanish poet, both at home and abroad. Born in Madrid, he began his career with the study of law; however, he abandoned this for verse and travel. After a period of great initial creativity revealing an even greater promise, García Lorca was brutally murdered by Falangists during the Civil War. His tragic death created a vacuum in Spanish literature, which present-day poets are still seeking to fill.

García Lorca's first poetic venture, *Libro de poemas* (1921), met with little success, but revealed his poetic bent. His next work, *Romancero gitano* (1928), breathing new life into the old tradition of the Spanish ballad, skyrocketed Lorca to fame. The work is a collection of Andalusian ballads, each containing the intense strains of the native gypsy songs (*cante-jondo*) of the area. One of the best-known of the ballads is *Muerte de Antonito el Camborio.* The poet's preoccupation with death is apparent in the title of his most famous poem, *Llanto por Ignacio Sánchez Mejías* (*The Death of a Bullfighter,* 1935). This work is considered to be the greatest elegy in modern Spanish poetry. García Lorca's well-known collections also include *Poeta en Nueva York* (*The Poet in New York,* 1940), which contains the poem *El rey de Harlem,* and *El diván del Tamarit* (1936).

García Lorca has an equally merited reputation as a dramatist. His plays, which have been translated into several languages, are among the most popular in Spanish literature. The most famous of his tragedies are *Bodas de sangre* (*Blood Wedding,* 1933), which relates the story of a young bride who runs off with a previous lover—he is subsequently murdered by her husband; *Yerma* (1934); and *La casa de Bernarda Alba* (*The House of Bernarda Alba,* 1936), the story of a brutal woman bent on a course of action which results in anguish and suicide for her daughters.

García Lorca was also an accomplished musician and amateur painter.

Garcilaso de la Vega (1501?–1536). Spanish poet and soldier. Garcilaso spent much of his brief life in Italy, where he lived, as he himself wrote, "Now using the sword, now the pen" (*Tomando, ora la espada, ora la pluma*). Often called "the Spanish Petrarch" because of his successful imitation of Italian poetry, he was a close friend of Juan Boscán, whose widow published his works with those of her husband in 1543. Garcilaso wrote 38 sonnets, five *canciones*, five odes, two elegies, and one *epístola* or "epistle," which are notable for their technical excellence and delicacy of sentiment. His first eclogue, dealing with the unhappy loves of the shepherds Salicio and Nemoroso, is generally considered his masterpiece.

Garcilaso de la Vega. Known as **El Inca** (1539–1616). Peruvian historian. The son of a Spanish knight and an Inca princess, Garcilaso is often regarded as the first spokesman for the South American mestizo. After fighting in European wars for 30 years, he settled in Spain, was ordained a priest, and devoted himself to history. His masterpiece is the *Comentarios reales* (*Royal Commentaries*, 1609), in which he described the Inca Empire and its conquest by Spain. Although some critics have claimed that it gives too fanciful and idealized a picture of Inca civilization, it is still considered a major source of information about pre-Columbian America. Garcilaso also wrote *Florida del Inca* (1605), an account of De Soto's explorations in what is now the southern U.S.

Garden, Mary (1877–). Scottish-born operatic soprano. Noted for the dramatic qualities of her singing, she was chosen over Maeterlinck's mistress to sing the first Mélisande in Debussy's opera, which estranged the poet from the composer. She wrote *Mary Garden's Own Story* (1951) with Louis Biancolli's help.

Garden, The (1681). A poem by Andrew MARVELL. It was written while he was a tutor at the country estate of the Cromwellian general Thomas Fairfax. The poet dwells on the contrast between the innocence, peace, and beauty of the garden and the stress and trouble of the outside world. At the height of his contemplation of the garden, his mind performs a typically Marvellian transformation:

> Annihilating all that's made
> To a green thought in a green shade.

Garden in January, A. A tale from Giovanni Boccaccio's THE DECAMERON. Dianora tells Ansaldo, an unwelcome suitor, that he can have her if he can make her garden as gay with flowers in January as it is in May. With the help of a magician, to whom he promises a generous reward, Ansaldo succeeds. Dianora's husband, learning of her plight, agrees to the fulfillment of the pact, whereupon Ansaldo matches his generosity by releasing Dianora from the pledge. The magician, too, joins in the general display of courtesy by refusing his reward. This is essentially the *Franklin's Tale* of Chaucer.

Garden Party, The (1922). A short story by Katherine MANSFIELD. While a wealthy woman and her daughters are preparing for their garden party, a poor laborer is killed in an accident. Young Laura is sent to take the widow and orphans the cakes left over from the party; the experience makes her see her own life in a new light for a moment. The reality of the outer world has intruded suddenly and violently upon the delicate artifice she has known as life.

Gardner, Erle Stanley (1889–). American writer of detective stories. One of the most successful writers of crime detection in the history of American publishing, Gardner, who has written over 100 books, usually employs two sleuths: the lawyer Perry Mason, hero of a long series that began with *The Case of the Velvet Claws* (1933), and Douglas Selby, who appears in *The D.A. Calls It Murder* (1944). Using the pseudonym A. A. Fair, Gardner has also created the engaging Donald Lam and Bertha Cool, who are featured in *Pass the Gravy* (1959) and other works.

Gareth, Sir. In Arthurian legend, one of the knights of the Round Table. In Malory's *Morte d'Arthur* (c. 1469) he is the youngest son of King Lot and MARGAWSE. His mother, to deter him from entering Arthur's court, says jestingly that she will consent to his doing so only if he conceals his name and goes as a scullion for 12 months. He agrees to this, and Sir Kay, the king's steward, nicknames him "Beaumains," because his hands are unusually fine and large. At the end of the year he is knighted, and obtains his first quest when Linet begs the aid of some knight to liberate her sister Liones held prisoner by Sir Ironside in Castle Perilous. Linet treats Sir Gareth with great contempt, calling him a washer of dishes and a kitchen knave, but he overthrows five knights and frees Liones, whom he marries. Tennyson retells the story in *Gareth and Lynette* in his *Idylls of the King* (1859–1872).

While rescuing Queen Guinevere from death at the stake, Sir Launcelot unwittingly kills Sir Gareth, who is standing guard, and thus evokes the vow of revenge from Gareth's brothers that ultimately effects the downfall of King Arthur's court and the end of the Round Table. See Sir GAWAIN.

Gargamelle. In Rabelais' GARGANTUA AND PANTAGRUEL, the daughter of the king of the Parpaillos (*Fr.*, "butterflies"), wife of Grandgousier and mother of Gargantua. In the eleventh month of her pregnancy she goes into labor as a result of eating too much tripe and, after taking an astringent, gives birth to Gargantua through her left ear.

Gargantua (*Sp.*, "gullet"). The name of a giant-hero in medieval folk literature, whom Rabelais made the father of Pantagruel in his satire GARGANTUA AND PANTAGRUEL. He figures in four of the five books, but as a major character only in *La Vie inestimable du grant Gargantua, père de Pantagruel* (1534), which is now known as Book I.

Son of GRANDGOUSIER and GARGAMELLE, Gargantua miraculously enters the world through Gargamelle's left ear, shouting "Drink, drink, drink!" The narrative continues in a similar vein, recounting his extraordinary childhood and adolescence; his trip to Paris on his famous mare, whose tail switches so violently that she fells the entire forest of Orléans; his lawsuit over stealing the bells of Notre Dame Cathedral to hang around his mare's neck; his encyclopedic course of studies in Paris; his defense of his father's lands against the assaults of PICROCHOLE; and his founding of the abbey of THÉLÈME at the war's end. Apart from the buffoonery, the work also provides a biting and realistic satire on various aspects of contemporary society—monasticism, scholastic education, the legalistic pedantry of the theologians at the Sorbonne—and on the causes and effects of tyrannical power. It vividly describes student life in the Latin Quarter of Paris, and provincial life and manners in Rabelais' native Chinon. It contrasts antiquated educational programs with the humanistic studies that were just coming into prominence; despotism with intelligent, humane government; and oppressive monasticism with healthy living.

Gargantua and Pantagruel (1532-1564). The English title for a 5-part satirical work by François RABELAIS. Derived in part from the medieval fabliaux, it was published as follows:

Les Horribles et espovantables faictz et prouesses du tres renommé Pantagruel, Roy des Dipsodes, fils du grant géant Gargantua (1532), later known as Book II, recounts the life of PANTAGRUEL up to the war against the Dipsodes in UTOPIA.

La Vie inestimable du grant Gargantua, père de Pantagruel (1534), which is now known as Book I, describes the life of GARGANTUA through the founding of the abbey of THÉLÈME.

Le Tiers Livre des faictz et dictz heroiques du noble Pantagruel (Book III, 1546) presents a discussion of the problem faced by Pantagruel's companion PANURGE, who cannot decide whether or not to marry. Pantagruel accompanies Panurge as the latter consults a sibyl, a mute, a poet, an astrologer, a theologian, a physician, a philosopher, and a madman, none of whom can provide a solution. Panurge then persuades Pantagruel and his friends to embark on a voyage to the ORACLE OF THE HOLY BOTTLE for the answer. The book is rich in humanistic learning in the fields of divination, botany, and moral philosophy; at the same time it satirizes poets, judges, fortune-tellers, etc.

Le Quart Livre (Book IV, 1552), which relates the departure for the Holy Bottle in Cathay, reflects the keen interests of the period in the great voyages of discovery. Although in Book II, Pantagruel had reached Utopia by sailing around the Cape of Good Hope, this time the voyagers follow the North Atlantic route taken by the French explorer Jacques Cartier. Pantagruel and his companions visit several islands, where they meet the PAPIMANIACS, the POPE-FIGS, and other peoples who serve as targets for Rabelais' satirical thrusts against contemporary society. Like its predecessors, this book was condemned by the Sorbonne for its attacks on the Church.

The posthumous *Cinquième et dernier livre* (Book V, 1564), which includes L'ISLE SONANTE, is probably not entirely of Rabelais' authorship. Most modern scholars believe it was published by an imitator who developed sketches and drafts left by Rabelais. As the voyage to Cathay continues, Rabelais launches into a violent satire on religious and legal institutions. (See FURRY LAWCATS.) At last Pantagruel and his friends arrive at the temple of the Holy Bottle, where the oracle answers Panurge's question by a single word, "Drink!" This reply has been taken to mean that each man must eventually solve his own problems and that life's aim is a never-ending quest for knowledge, from which comes wisdom.

Rabelais was a man of his time who delighted in satirizing the religious, political, legal, and social institutions and practices of 16th-century France. He displayed a characteristically Renaissance thirst for erudition, but he also exalted the development of all human faculties, in accordance with his basic belief that human nature is fundamentally good. His universal genius reached far beyond his own century and has influenced numerous later writers, including La Fontaine, Molière, Voltaire, Swift, Balzac, Hugo, and Gautier.

Garibaldi, Giuseppe (1807-1882). Italian patriot. An ardent republican and associate of Mazzini, he was forced to flee from Italy because of his political activities and lived in South America (1834-1848). On his return he served in the army of the short-lived Roman Republic and upon its defeat made a dramatic retreat through central Italy. He escaped to the U.S. (1850-1854), where he became a naturalized citizen and worked for a while as a candlemaker on Staten Island. Returning to his native land, in order to secure the unification of Italy, he swore allegiance to King Victor Emmanuel of Sardinia. After taking part in the war against Austria, he invaded the so-called Kingdom of the Two Sicilies with his famous band of 1,000 men known as the Red Shirts. After the conquest of Sicily, he crossed to the mainland and drove Francis II from Naples. When the Sicilian king capitulated and Victor Emmanuel was proclaimed king of Italy (1861), Garibaldi withdrew to his farm in Caprera. He later led two unsuccessful expeditions of liberation against Rome and fought on behalf of the French republic in the Franco-Prussian War. On his statue on the Janiculum overlooking Rome is engraved his famous cry, *Roma o Morte* ("Rome or Death").

Garigliano, battle of (1503). The meeting at which the Spanish forces defeated the French armies in a struggle over possession of the kingdom of Naples, to which both laid claims.

Garland, [Hannibal] Hamlin (1860-1940). American short-story writer and novelist. Garland is best known for his realistic studies of the hardships and frustrations of farm life in the Middle West. Born in Wisconsin, Garland went to Boston and became a friend of William Dean Howells and others in the Boston literary circle. In 1887 he returned to the Midwest, where the barren and difficult lives of the farmers impressed him as being the stuff of fiction. Influenced by the realism of Howells and the single-tax ideas of Henry George, he began to write the stories and sketches published in MAIN-TRAVELLED ROADS. Other stories were collected in *Prairie Folk* (1892) and *Wayside Courtships* (1897), later published under the single title, *Other Main-Travelled Roads* (1910). Always interested in social reform, Garland's novels of the period center around political corruption: *Jason Edwards* (1892), *A Member of the Third House* (1892), and *A Spoil of Office* (1892).

In 1894 Garland issued his literary manifesto, *Crumbling Idols,* a group of essays calling for the repudiation of any imitation of past masters. Garland called his brand of realism "veritism," a concern for truth which emphasized local color, impressionism, and an art which is basically "sociologic." Although he was seldom able to live up to his own precepts, Garland influenced other writers, notably Stephen Crane.

A Little Norsk (1892) and *Rose of Dutcher's Coolly* (1895) both dealt with the drudgery of farm life. Garland then turned to writing novels about the Indians and the Far West. *The Captain of the Gray-Horse* (1902), which contains an appeal for justice to the Indians, is the most famous of these. *Cavanaugh, Forest Ranger* (1910) was also very popular. Garland also wrote four autobiographical narratives, the first two of which were A SON OF THE MIDDLE BORDER and the Pulitzer Prize-winning *A Daughter of the Middle Border* (1921).

Garneau, François Xavier (1809–1866). Canadian historian and poet. Garneau is best known for his four-volume *Histoire du Canada* (1845–1852), the first major literary achievement by a French-Canadian author.

Garnett, Constance. See Edward GARNETT.

Garnett, David (1892–   ). English novelist, son of Edward and Constance Garnett. He wrote fantasies, including LADY INTO FOX and *A Man at the Zoo* (1924), and the delicate, odd love story, *Aspects of Love* (1955). Garnett also published autobiographies which include accounts of his father's Bloomsbury life, beginning with *The Golden Echo* (1953). He also edited *The Letters of T. E. Lawrence* (1938) and *The Essential T. E. Lawrence* (1951). Other recent works include *A Shot in the Dark* (1958), *A Net for Venus* (1959), and *The Familiar Faces* (1962).

Garnett, Edward (1868–1937). English critic, biographer, and essayist. He was the son of Richard GARNETT. The best-esteemed publisher's reader in London, he encouraged and helped to publicize such writers as Joseph Conrad, John Galsworthy, and D. H. Lawrence. His wife, Constance Garnett (1862–1946), was renowned for her translations of Dostoevski and other Russian authors, much of whose work she made available to English readers for the first time.

Garnett, Richard (1835–1906). English librarian, literary historian, poet, critic, biographer, chief keeper of printed books at the British Museum (1890–1899). Garnett edited *Relics of Shelley* (1862) and contributed to the *Encyclopædia Britannica* and the *Dictionary of National Biography*. He also wrote poetry, numerous biographies, translations, essays, and an excellent collection of original fables, *The Twilight of the Gods* (1888). He was the father of Edward GARNETT.

Garnier, Robert (1544–1590). French dramatist. A fervent Catholic, he was concerned with restoring morality and faith during the religious wars. His own conviction expressed itself in the most lyrical and successful tragic verse dramas written in France before the great period of 17th-century French tragedy. His tragi-comedy BRADAMANTE and tragedy *Les Juives* (1583) are the high points of French Renaissance theater.

Garratt, the mayor of. Garratt is in England, near Earlsfield, Wimbledon; the first "mayor" was elected in 1778. He was really the chairman of an association of villagers formed to put a stop to encroachments on the public common, and as his election coincided with a general election, the society

made it a law that a new "mayor" should be chosen at every general election. These elections gave rise to several satirical *Addresses by the Mayors of Garratt,* and Samuel Foote wrote a farce on the subject entitled *The Mayor of Garratt.*

Garrick, David (1717–1779). English actor and theater manager. He was educated in Lichfield and went to London with Samuel Johnson, his teacher and friend. He and his brother started a wine business, but were unsuccessful. Garrick turned to acting and his quick success enabled him to buy part of the patent for Drury Lane; his career as manager began in 1747. He did much to revive Shakespeare's popularity and wrote many theater pieces himself—largely farces and light comedies.

Garrison, William Lloyd (1805–1879). American abolitionist. In 1831 Garrison founded *The Liberator,* a weekly newspaper in which he denounced slavery and slaveholders with such vehemence that he was nearly killed by a Boston mob in 1835. He sought complete and immediate freedom for the slaves and demanded that the North repudiate its ties with the South, condemning the Constitution as "a convenant with death and an agreement with hell." *The Liberator* ceased publication in 1865 after the passage of the 13th amendment to the Constitution, which abolished slavery.

Garter, the Most Noble Order of the. The highest order of knighthood in Great Britain, instituted by Edward III on April 23, 1349. St. George is considered its special patron, and it is sometimes called the Order of St. George. Originally limited to 25 knights in addition to the king, it was reorganized and expanded in 1831 to include the Prince of Wales and to provide for the admittance of other members of the royal family, as well as of foreign royalty. The emblem of the order is a blue garter bearing the words *Honi soit qui mal y pense.*

The story is that Joan, countess of Salisbury, while dancing with the King, let fall her garter, and the gallant Edward, perceiving a smile on the faces of the courtiers, picked it up, bound it round his knee, and exclaimed, *"Honi soit qui mal y pense."* ("Evil to him who evil thinks.") The blue garter and the motto of the order are thus accounted for.

Garth, Sir Samuel (1661–1719). English physician and poet. His best-known work is *The Dispensary* (1699), a mock-heroic poem satirizing apothecaries. He was also a member of the KIT-CAT CLUB.

Garuda. In Hindu mythology, a supernatural being, half man and half bird, with golden body and red wings. Vishnu rides on Garuda.

Gary, Romain (1914–   ). Russian-born French novelist and diplomat. Gary is best known for *A European Education* (1945), about the Polish resistance in World War II, and THE ROOTS OF HEAVEN. Almost all of his novels satirize men's weaknesses and condemn many specific modern types, yet point hopefully to the potential dignity of man. His works include *The Company of Men* (*Le Grand Vestiare;* 1949), *The Colors of the Day* (1952); *Lady L.* (1958). *Promise at Dawn* (*La Promesse de l'aube;* 1960) is an autobiographical account of his youth.

Gas. The general name given to a loose trilogy of plays by Georg KAISER: *Die Koralle* (*The Coral,* 1917), *Gas I* (1918) and *Gas II* (1920). Taken together, they constitute a monumental indictment of the overmechanization in modern society.

The hero of *The Coral,* who is called the Billionaire, has risen to the highest possible position in industry, but is nonetheless constantly tormented by memories of his unhappy childhood. In an attempt to escape himself, he murders the Secretary, who is his double, and acquires the little piece of coral that symbolizes the latter's identity. Though he is executed for the crime, he still feels a kind of exhilaration at having broken clear of his rut. In *Gas I,* the Billionaire's son has taken over the plant which is now producing the gas that drives all other industry. The machinery fails, however, and there is a huge explosion that brings the son to his senses and prompts him to offer the workers land instead of a new gas plant, to offer them mastery over themselves rather than new enslavement to the machine. But the Engineer persuades the workers to rebuild the plant, and the Billionaire's son is killed in an ensuing riot. In *Gas II,* the final drama, the state has taken over the gas plant and is using it to fight a war. The workers attempt to make peace with the enemy, but fail; and the Great Engineer then persuades them to produce and use his new superweapon, a gas bomb. The device is detonated, and the play ends in a vision of total annihilation.

Gascar, Pierre. Pen name of **Pierre Fournier** (1916–   ). French fiction writer, journalist. His prisoner-of-war experiences inspired the cruel realism of his short novel *The Season of the Dead.* The novel was published with the six brutal allegories of *The Animals* (both 1953) in *Beasts and Men.* His travels as a journalist, which produced the reports *Chine ouverte* (1955) and *Voyage chez les vivants* (1958), also inspired the novel *The Coral Barrier* (1958), set against the racism and colonialism of Italian Somaliland. *The Seed* (1955) recalls his own boyhood in a provincial factory town.

Gascoigne, George (1525?–1577). English poet, playwright, and prose writer. Gascoigne was educated at Cambridge, studied law, and was elected a member of Parliament (1557/59). In 1566 he produced at Gray's Inn *The Supposes,* a prose adaptation of Ariosto's comedy *Gli Suppositi,* and the first prose comedy in English. This was followed by the blank-verse tragedy *Jocasta,* written in collaboration with Francis Kinwelmersh and adapted from a play by Euripides. Military adventures took Gascoigne away from England for three years, during which time a collection of his verse and other writings appeared. Called *A Hundred Sundry Flowers* (1572) and published without his permission, it caused a mild sensation, and Gascoigne himself published an enlarged edition in 1575. The same year appeared his "tragical comedy" *A Glass of Government.* In July of 1575 he accompanied the party of Queen Elizabeth visiting Kenilworth Castle, where he was commissioned by Leicester to write verses and masques for entertainment. *The Princely Pleasures at the Court of Kenilworth* (1576) contains some of his writings for that occasion. His blank verse satire *The Steel Glass* (1576) is one of the first satires in English; it was prefixed by a commendatory sonnet by Sir Walter Raleigh—the first of his poems to appear in print. In 1577 Gascoigne dedicated to Elizabeth a collection of moral elegies called *The Grief*

of Joy. He was the stepfather of Nicholas Breton, and is considered one of the leading men of letters during the period before Spenser and after Wyatt and Surrey.

Gaskell, Elizabeth Cleghorn, born **Stevenson** (1810–1865). English novelist. She is known for her depictions of English country life and for her pioneering studies of conflicts between capital and labor in Victorian industrialism. In the former class are the novels CRANFORD and *Wives and Daughters* (1864–1866), which show a fine degree of observation and characterization. Her social novels, chiefly MARY BARTON and *North and South* (1855), are notable for their sympathetic portrayal of the oppressed laboring classes in mid-19th-century England. She herself lived mainly in Manchester, a center of the depressed regions. Mrs. Gaskell was the friend of many literary figures in England, including Charlotte Brontë, whose biography she wrote in 1857, and George Eliot, whose work she influenced. Among her other books *Ruth* (1853) and *Sylvia's Lovers* (1863) are worthy of notice.

Gaspar or **Caspar** (the white one). One of the three MAGI. His offering to the infant Jesus was *frankincense,* in token of divinity. At some point in medieval dramatic presentations of the nativity, he became a comic figure. He soon degenerated in Germany into Casperl, a popular comic servant who appeared in puppet shows, notably the Faust play, in which he is Faust's servant.

Gaspé, Philippe Aubert de (1786–1871). Canadian novelist. Gaspé was high sheriff of the district of Quebec for many years until forced to withdraw from public life because of business difficulties and debts. At the age of 76 he published *Les anciens canadiens* (*The Canadians of Old,* 1863), a historical romance considered a classic of French-Canadian literature. His *Mémoires* (1866) is a collection of notes and hints for historians.

Gassendi, Pierre (1596–1655). French philosopher and mathematician. An opponent of the mechanistic world view of Descartes and an advocate of the atomistic theory of Epicurus, Gassendi wrote works on mathematics and philosophy, as well as lives of the astronomers Copernicus, Regiomontanus, and Tycho Brahe. Appointed professor of mathematics at the Collège de France in 1645, he achieved influence in learned and literary circles, and is said to have numbered Molière and Chapelle among his disciples.

Gaster. See MESSER GASTER.

gate of horn and ivory gate. In Greek mythology, the two gates of the abode of Sleep. Through them dreams come forth. Those passing through the gate of horn are true.

Gates, Horatio (1728?–1806). American general. At the time he was given credit for repulsing Burgoyne's army at Saratoga (1777), though modern historians maintain that the victory was due at least as much to Benedict Arnold. After suffering a serious defeat at Camden, S.C. (1780), Gates was relieved of his command. See CONWAY CABAL.

Gatomaquia (The Battle of the Cats, 1634). A mock-heroic poem by Lope de VEGA. Notable for its biting irony and wit, this burlesque of the Italian epic deals with the romantic affairs of the cat

Zapaquilda and her two suitors, Marramaquiz and Micifuf.

Gattamelata (It., *Honeyed Cat*). The popular cognomen of a notorious Italian CONDOTTIERE, Erasmo da Narni, who fought mainly for the Venetian republic and died in 1443. His equestrian statue, the work of Donatello, still stands before the church of Saint Anthony in Padua.

gaucho literature. A term used to describe literary works dealing with the gaucho, or outlaw cattle hunter, of the Rio de la Plata region of South America. In many works of this type he is treated realistically, and some writers, notably Sarmiento in his FACUNDO, decried his influence on the national life of Argentina and Uruguay. Elsewhere, however, he emerges as a romantic symbol of a pure and uncomplicated past.

The literary manifestations of gaucho folklore sprang from the extemporaneous songs of the gaucho minstrels known as *payadores*. One of the first writers to compose a literary work on the gaucho theme was Hilario Ascasubi (1807–1875), author of *Santos Vega* (1851; 1872), a poem narrated by the *payador* Santos Vega, a familiar figure in gaucho legend. The work is notable for the author's careful description of rural life and setting and for his use of authentic gaucho terminology. *Fausto* (1866) by Estanislao del Campo (1834–1880) is a mock-epic in which a gaucho who has witnessed a performance of *Faust* describes the action in his own crude language. The outstanding example of gaucho poetry is probably MARTÍN FIERRO, whose title character is drawn in heroic proportions.

Among the first prose writers to concentrate on the gaucho was Eduardo Gutiérrez (1853–1890) whose "thrillers," especially *Juan Moreira* (1880), demonstrated the vitality of the genre. Gutiérrez' dramatization (1884) of his work was extremely successful, and the gaucho soon became a familiar theatrical character, notably in the plays of Florencio SÁNCHEZ.

Soledad (1894) by Eduardo ACEVEDO DÍAZ is generally considered the prototype of later gaucho novels. Other novelists concerned with the subject were the Uruguayans Javier de Viana (1872–1926), author of the naturalistic *Gaucha* (1899), and Justino Zavala Muniz (1897–   ) and the Argentine Benito LYNCH, whose *Romance de un gaucho* (1930) is written entirely in gaucho idiom. Güiraldes' DON SEGUNDO SOMBRA, an able synthesis of American material and European technique, is widely regarded as the finest gaucho novel.

Gaudeamus igitur (Lat. "Therefore let us rejoice"). The first words of a Latin student song of German origin. The words date from 1267, the tune is 18th century. It is quoted by Brahms in the *Academic Festival Overture.*

Gauden, John. See EIKON BASILIKÉ.

Gauguin, [Eugène Henri] Paul (1848–1903). French painter. One of the most remarkable figures in modern painting, in 1883 he abandoned his job as a brokerage clerk, and the support of his family, in order to devote himself to painting. Poor and restless, he traveled, visiting Vincent Van Gogh in Arles and finally setting out for Tahiti in 1891. He returned to France only once and spent the rest of his life in the South Pacific, living among the natives. Gauguin developed a very decorative, highly original, personal style consisting of simplified forms and generally flat planes limited by a sinuous line and the use of brilliant, pure, unmixed color exaggerated to the point at which a reddish tinge in the foliage becomes pure vermillion, sand pink, and tree trunks blue. Gauguin's painting, especially his color, had great influence on later artists, notably on Henri MATISSE and the expressionists. He himself left an autobiographical account of his life on Tahiti, *Noa Noa* (1897), while W. Somerset Maugham's novel *The Moon and Sixpence* (1919) is a reconstruction in fictional terms of the whole of Gauguin's life.

Gaul (Lat., *Gallia;* hence, the English adjective *Gallic*). In classical geography the territory that comprises modern France and Belgium and part of northern Italy. *Cisalpine Gaul,* that is, Gaul on *this* (the Italian) side of the Alps, extended almost as far south as Florence. *Transalpine Gaul,* that is, Gaul beyond the Alps, included all the Gallic, German, and Celtic tribes from the Rhine to the Pyrenees. Gaul has been used as a literary name for modern France.

gauntlet, to run the. To be attacked on all sides, to be severely criticized. The word came into English at the time of the Thirty Years' War as *gantlope,* meaning the passage between two files of soldiers, and is the Swedish *gata,* a way, passage and *lopp* (connected with our *leap*), a course. The reference is to a punishment formerly common among soldiers and sailors; the company or crew, provided with rope ends, were drawn up in two rows facing each other, and the delinquent had to run between them, while every man dealt him as severe a chastisement as he could.

"To throw down the gauntlet" means to challenge. The custom in the Middle Ages, when one knight challenged another, was for the challenger to throw his gauntlet on the ground, and if the challenge was accepted the person to whom it was thrown picked it up.

Gautama. The personal name of Buddha. His family name was Siddhartha, his father's name Suddhodana, and his mother's Maya. *Buddha* means the enlightened, the one who knows. He assumed this title at about the age of 36, when, after seven years of seclusion and spiritual struggle, he believed himself to have attained the perfect Truth.

Gauthier, Marguerite. See DAME AUX CAMÉLIAS, LA.

Gautier, Théophile (1811–1872). French poet and novelist. The early poems and prose tales of Gautier move in the realm of the fantastic and the macabre. In his later poetry, however, Gautier stresses perfection of form and achieves a carefully polished beauty. His emphasis on form and his doctrine of *l'art pour l'art* (art for art's sake) make him a forerunner of the Parnassian school. Gautier's poetry includes *Poésies* (1830); *Albertus* (1832), a fantastic narrative poem; *La Comédie de la Mort* (1833), another long poem dealing with the sensual and the ideal; and *Émaux et Camées* (1852), considered the best example of his pure, minutely chiseled style (see PARNASSIANS). Among Gautier's novels and tales are *Les Jeune-France* (1833), *Mlle. de Maupin* (1835), *La Jettatura* (1856), and *Le Captaine Fracasse* (1861-1863).

Gawain, Sir. In Arthurian legend, one of the knights of the Round Table, nephew (in some versions, cousin) of King Arthur, and probably the original hero of the Grail quest. One of the earliest figures in the legends of Arthur, he appears in the Welsh *Triads* and the *Mabinogion* as Gwalchmei. He is the central figure in two major 14th-century English works: *The Alliterative Morte d'Arthur* and Sir Gawain and the Green Knight. He is known as "the Courteous" and is first represented as the flower of chivalrous knighthood, but later writers (including Malory) downgraded him. In Malory's *Morte d'Arthur* (c. 1469) he is the son of King Lot and Queen Margawse. He is King Arthur's favorite cousin and one of the most outstanding of the Round Table knights. He avenges the death of his father by killing King Pellinore, kills Sir Lamerok, who is the lover of his mother, and kills his cousin Sir Uwayne, who is the son of Morgan Le Fay. Then, when Sir Launcelot unwittingly kills his youngest brother, Sir Gareth, Sir Gawain swears revenge. Twice he challenges Sir Launcelot to single combat at the siege of Benwick, and the second time is fatally wounded by that great knight who so unwillingly fought him. Returning to Britain, Sir Gawain dies, but not before repenting and writing a letter of reconciliation to Sir Launcelot.

Gay, John (1685–1732). English poet and playwright. A friend of Alexander Pope, he is known for his pungent satire and contemporary realism. The Beggar's Opera, a satire of Sir Robert Walpole and the court of George II, won him enduring fame. Among his other works are *Rural Sports* (1713), a poem dedicated to Pope; *The Shepherd's Week* (1714), six pastorals written partly to parody the pastorals of Ambrose Philips; *Trivia, or the Art of Walking the Streets of London* (1716), a humorous but realistic depiction of the grotesque aspects of 18th-century London; Polly, a sequel to *The Beggar's Opera*, which was suppressed until 1777 because of the virulence of its political satire; and *Fables* (1727–1738) a collection of 66 tales, the last 16 of which were published posthumously. In the 18th century, these last rivalled *The Beggar's Opera* in popularity. See John Rich.

Gay-Lussac, Joseph Louis (1778–1850). French chemist and physicist. Gay-Lussac made the first balloon ascent for purposes of scientific investigation. He discovered hydrosulphuric and oxychloride acids, and his name is associated with the law of volumes, or Gay-Lussac's law, concerning the proportions in which gases combine.

Gay Science. A translation of *gai saber,* the old Provençal name for the art of poetry. A guild called the *Gai Saber* was formed at Toulouse in 1323 with the object of keeping in existence the dying Provençal language and culture. Its full title was "The Very Gay Company of the Seven Troubadors of Toulouse."

Gaza, Theodore (d. 1475). Greek scholar. Born in Salonika, he was one of the first Greek scholars to arrive in Italy to help stimulate the revival of classical studies during the Renaissance. He taught at Ferrara and in Rome, under the patronage of Pope Nicholas V.

Ge or **Gaea.** In Greek mythology the personification of the Earth. She is the offspring of Chaos, or at least comes into being after it. Uranus is both her child and husband. Their children, besides such things as seas and mountains are the Titans and Cyclopes. After her separation from Uranus she bore the Erinyes and Giants, being fertilized by the blood from his castration. Later she gave birth to Typhon, whose father was Tartarus.

Geb. In Egyptian religion, the god of earth, represented in human form, with beard and staff and a goose on his head. He was the husband of his sister Nut, the sky goddess, with whom he fathered Isis and Osiris.

Geber or **Jabir** (*Arab., Jabir ibn Hayyan; fl.* 721–776). An Arabian alchemist, born at Thous, in Persia. He wrote in the usual mystical jargon of the period several treatises on the art of making gold, which led to the creation of the word gibberish in imitation of his name.

Geburt der Tragödie aus dem Geiste der Musik, Die. See Birth of Tragedy from the Spirit of Music, The.

Geddes, Norman Bel (1893–1958). American stage and industrial designer. He made his reputation with his first production, *Nju,* in 1916. Thereafter he designed well over 200 theatrical productions; his settings for Max Reinhardt's *The Miracle* (1923) attracted particular attention. He also produced designs for ships, offices, and furniture, and devised a scheme for automobile highways described in his book *Magic Motorways* (1940).

geese, Capitoline. See Capitoline geese.

Gehenna. The New Testament name for the Valley of Hinnom surrounding Jerusalem. It is the place of eternal torment, the "valley of slaughter" (Jer. 19:6) where sacrifices to Baal and Moloch were offered. See Tophet.

Geibel, Emanuel (1815–1884). German poet, capable of classicistic elegance in style, but not known as a creator or innovator. Besides lyrics, he produced several dramas, including a tragedy *Brunhild* (1858).

Geijerstam, Gustaf af (1858–1909). Swedish novelist and playwright. Such early novels as *Grakallt* (1882), *Fattigt folk* (1884), and *Erik Grane* (1885) were gloomy naturalistic studies that delved into abnormal psychology. In his later works, however—*Minapojkar* (*My Boys,* 1896) and *Boken om lille-bror* (*The Book About Little Brother,* 1900), for example—Geijerstam waxed sentimental and domestic. His popular folk plays include *Svärfar* (1888), *Aldrig i lifvet* (1891), and *Per Olsson och hans käring* (1894).

Geisel, Theodor Seuss. Pen name, **Dr. Seuss** (1904–   ). American comic draughtsman and writer and illustrator of immensely popular humorous children's books.

geisha. A Japanese professional singing and dancing girl. Hence, especially in Western misconception, a licensed prostitute.

Gelber, Jack (1932–   ). American playwright. His first play, *The Connection* (1959), with its minutely realistic depiction of drug addiction, its stretches of obscenity and junkie argot, and its improvised jazz assault upon the audience, came to be regarded as an important expression of the generation who grew up in the 1950's. Gelber's second play, *The Apple* (1961), carried the attack on conventional dramaturgy and on the spectator even further and was received with mingled admiration and distaste. As in *The Connection,* the actors mingled with the audience between the acts, a device pioneered by Eugene O'Neill in *Marco Millions.*

Gelée, Jacquemart. See under REYNARD THE Fox.

Gelli, Giambattista (1498–1563). Florentine shoemaker and amateur moral philosopher. Gelli's aim in writing his treatises was to popularize learning for his fellow artisans. His *Circe* (1549), in 10 dialogues, had already been translated into English by 1570. He also wrote 20 short lives of Florentine artists and gave lectures on Dante and Petrarch at the Florentine Academy.

Gemara (Aram., "complement"). The 2nd part of the TALMUD. It consists of annotations, discussions, and amplifications of the MISHNAH, which is the first part. The Mishnah is the interpretation of the written law, the Gemara is the interpretation of the Mishnah. There is a Babylonian Gemara and a Palestinian Gemara. The former, which is the more complete, is by the academies of Babylon, and was finished by the sixth century; the latter, compiled in Palestine, was completed at the close of the fourth century.

Generación del 98. A group of Spanish writers of the early 20th century. Profoundly affected by the outcome of the Spanish American War (1898), they probed deeply into Spanish life and institutions in order to find the reasons for their country's disastrous defeat. Members of the group included José MARTÍNEZ RUIZ, Eduardo MARQUINA, Antonio MACHADO, Ramón PÉREZ DE AYALA, Juan Ramón JIMÉNEZ, Jacinto BENAVENTE, the brothers ALVAREZ QUINTERO, Ramón del VALLE-INCLÁN, Pío BAROJA, and Miguel de UNAMUNO. Their goal was betterment of Spanish life through education and opposition to bossism and to clericalism. In literature the movement advocated simplicity of style, the discarding of exaggeration, international rather than purely Spanish inspiration, the exalting of the countryside, and a contempt for patterns—it was felt that the pattern of life itself should be sought by playwrights and novelists.

General William Booth Enters into Heaven (1913). A poem by Vachel LINDSAY. Written after the death of the leader of the Salvation Army, it was first published in *Poetry.* It is written in the rhythmic drumbeats of a Salvation Army band, and is intended to be sung to the music of *Washed in the Blood of the Lamb.*

Genesis (Gr., "origin"). The 1st book of the Old Testament. In Hebrew, it is called *Bereshith,* "In the beginning," from the initial words of the text.

The first 11 chapters deal with the early days of the creation of the world; the remaining (12–50) are an account of the patriarchs of Israel: Abraham, Isaac, Jacob, and Joseph.

Genêt, Edmond Charles Edouard (1763–1834). French diplomat in the U.S. As minister of the First Republic, "Citizen" Genêt hoped to draw the U.S. into France's war against England and Spain. Attacking the government for its policy of neutrality, he sought to create a change of presidential attitude through popular agitation. He also commissioned privateers in American ports to prey upon English ocean commerce. He was recalled on the insistence of Washington, but meanwhile the Girondists—his

faction of moderate republicans ruling the First Assembly—had fallen from power, and he lived for the rest of his life on Long Island.

Genêt, Jean (1910–   ). French dramatist, and essayist. A professional thief who had served a number of jail sentences, he was freed by the intervention of Jean-Paul Sartre and Jean Cocteau. His plays reveal a concern with the illusory nature of reality, particularly with the ambiguous definitions of good and evil in a society characterized by repression and hypocrisy. Of all the dramatists of the ABSURD, Genêt probes most deeply into the inner self: its dreams, illusions, deceptions, and bitterly frustrated longings. Among his stylized, lurid, and nightmarishly disillusioning plays are: THE MAIDS, *Deathwatch* (*Haute Surveillance;* 1949), THE BALCONY, and *The Blacks* (*Les Nègres;* 1958). His other works include the prose *Our Lady of the Flowers* (*Notre-Dame des Fleurs;* 1949), *The Thief's Journal* (*Journal de voleur;* 1949, with a preface by Sartre), and *Poèmes* (1948).

Geneva. The capital of the Swiss canton of Geneva. Situated on the Lake of Geneva, or Lac Leman, it was a center of the Reformation under Calvin (1536–1564). It was also the birthplace of Jean-Jacques Rousseau. It served as the seat of the League of Nations after World War I.

Geneva Bible. See BIBLE, ENGLISH VERSIONS.

Geneva convention. An agreement made by the European powers at Geneva (1864; supplemented 1868). It established humane regulations for the treatment of disabled soldiers in war. It was revised and brought into accord with modern methods of warfare in 1906 and has since been ratified by almost every country.

Genevieve (earlier **Genovefa**) **of Brabant.** Heroine of an old German folk tale, wife of Count Palatine Siegfried of Trèves. Their majordomo Golo falsely accuses her of infidelity during the absence of Siegfried, who orders her killed. But the executioner allows her to escape into the forest, where she lives with her infant son, nourished by a doe. Siegfried learns of his error, and six years later, when he discovers the hiding place by chance while pursuing the doe, they are reunited.

Genghis (**Jenghiz**) **Khan** (1162–1227). A Mongol emperor. Named **Temujin,** by his father, who died when the boy was 13 years old, he took the title by which he is commonly remembered, and which means "perfect warrior." Genghis, with the aid of his mother, quickly regained the supremacy of the allied tribes who had defected after his father's death, and then proceeded to extensive conquests. He took vast territories in north China, then moved westward through Iran and Iraq, subduing nations wherever he passed. He pillaged considerable sections of India as well. Genghis' generals ravaged considerable parts of Russia before returning to their homeland.

Barbarously cruel, Genghis was one of the most brilliant generals of history. His successors, however, could not hold his vast empire together, and it lasted only a fairly short period. (See TAMERLANE.) His conquests, nevertheless, had far-reaching effects on history, for they set in motion a chain of events that led to the westward invasions of the Turks and helped to establish the Ottoman Empire. See KUBLAI KHAN; GOLDEN HORDE.

Génie du Christianisme, Le (The Genius of Christianity, 1802). A treatise on Christianity by François René de CHATEAUBRIAND. The author extols Christianity, describing it as the great force that develops the soul of man, and citing it as the chief source of progress in the modern world. This work, not only won great popular approval for Chateaubriand, but also earned him the good will of Napoleon.

genii or **ginn.** See JINN.

Genius (pl. *Genii*). In Roman mythology, the spirit that presides over the birth of every man and attends him throughout his life. (Women had no individual Genii, but were under the general protection of Juno.) The Genius, as the individual life-principle, was especially honored on a man's birthday; considered as one's higher self, it was also called to witness a man's oath. There were also corporate Genii: Genii of the family, the tribe, and the nation. Under the empire, the Genius of the emperor was worshiped throughout the Roman World. Moral philosophers, seeking to explain moral conflict within human nature, posited an opposing, evil Genius. In Christian times these two Genii became the guardian angel and his diabolical counterpart.

"Genius," The (1915). A novel by Theodore DREISER. The hero of this semiautobiographical work is Eugene Witla, a Middle Western artist, who becomes the art director of a large magazine corporation, has numerous love affairs, attains financial and social success, and marries Angela, who dies in childbirth. Witla himself suffers a breakdown but recovers his health and devotes himself thereafter to painting and to the care of his daughter. According to Helen Dreiser, in her book *My Life with Dreiser* (1951), Witla is a composite of three real persons: the artist Everett Shinn, an art editor whom Dreiser knew, and Dreiser himself.

Genji, The Tale of. See TALE OF GENJI, THE.

Genovefa. See GENEVIEVE OF BRABANT.

Genroku. The name of a Japanese era (1688–1703). The greatest flowering of Japanese literature and culture during the Tokugawa period (1600–1868) occurred during this era. See CHIKAMATSU MONZAEMON, MATSUO BASHŌ, and IHARA SAIKAKU.

genteel tradition. A term first used by George SANTAYANA. In *The Genteel Tradition at Bay* (1931), he applied it to those American writers at the close of the 19th century who upheld traditional social, moral, and literary standards, emphasizing correctness and conventionality. Among these writers were Richard Henry STODDARD, Bayard TAYLOR, Edmund Clarence STEDMAN, and Thomas Bailey ALDRICH. Santayana associated the term with New England, and attacked the later flowering of the genteel attitude in Paul Elmer MORE, Irving BABBITT, and the NEW HUMANISM.

Gentle Craft, The. A tale by Thomas DELONEY (1597), celebrating shoemakers and their craft. Part I deals with St. Hugh, the patron saint of cobblers, and St. Winifred. Part II tells of St. Crispin and St. Crispinian, also patron saints of cobblers. Part III, the best-known section of the story, gives an account of Simon EYRE, the shoemaker Lord Mayor of London.

Gentleman from Indiana, The (1899). A novel by Booth TARKINGTON. The hero is John Harkless, the young editor of a country newspaper in Indiana, who fights courageously against political corruption and is eventually elected to Congress.

Gentleman's Magazine, The. An English periodical, founded in 1731 by Edward Cave, a printer at St. John's Gate, Clerkenwell. It was the first periodical to call itself a "magazine." The publication was at first a miscellany of essays extracted from weekly journals, together with a systematic chronicle of current news. Samuel JOHNSON was a regular contributor and an editor in the early 1740's, and, under his direction, the extracts were largely replaced by original matter. The magazine was issued until 1914.

Gentlemen Prefer Blondes (1925). A humorous novel by Anita Loos. Subtitled "The Illuminating Diary of a Professional Lady," it tells the story of Lorelei Lee, a good-looking but not very intelligent girl, who manages to do very well for herself with Mr. Gus Eisman, the Button King. A satire on "the gold-diggers" of Hollywood, the book had an enormous vogue, though rumor has it that some fraction of its popularity may be ascribed to the fact that it was taken seriously by girls who thought it a useful handbook on how to get rich.

Geoffrey of Monmouth (c. 1100–c. 1155). Medieval English historian. A canon at Oxford, he wrote the important Latin prose HISTORY OF THE KINGS OF BRITAIN (*Historia Regum Britanniae*), one of the sources of the ARTHURIAN LEGEND and of considerable literary influence. He is considered to be the creator of the heroic image of King Arthur.

George, St. The patron saint of England since about the time of the institution of the Order of the Garter (c. 1348). He was "adopted" by Edward III. He is commemorated on April 23. St. George had been popular in England from the time of the early Crusades, for he was said to have come to the assistance of the Crusaders at Antioch (1089), and many of the Normans (under Robert, son of William the Conqueror) then took him as their patron.

That St. George is a historical character is beyond all reasonable doubt. He is now believed to have been

St. George. Woodcut from a broadside ballad.

a Cappadocian official in Diocletian's army, martyred April 23, A.D. 303. There are various versions of his *Acta*, one saying that he was a tribune and that he was asked to come and subdue a dragon that infested a pond at Silene, Libya, and fed on the dwellers in the neighborhood. St. George came, rescued a princess (Sabra) whom the dragon was about to make its prey, and slew the monster after he had wounded it and the princess had led it home in triumph by her girdle.

The legend of St. George and the dragon is in part a universal folk theme (see ANDROMEDA), in part an allegorical expression of the triumph of the Christian hero over evil, which St. John the Divine beheld under the image of a dragon. Similarly, St. Michael, St. Margaret, St. Sylvester, and St. Martha are all depicted as slaying dragons; the Saviour and the Virgin as treading them under their feet. A snake or a dragon biting its tail was sometimes an attribute of Father Time in Renaissance art.

The legend forms the subject of an old ballad given in Percy's *Reliques*. Spenser introduces St. George into his *Faerie Queene* as the Red Cross Knight. See KALYB.

George, Henry (1839–1897). American economist and reformer, known for his study of the problems of poverty. His most famous theory is that of the single tax, or a tax on land, which was the most important form of wealth in his day, set forth most persuasively in PROGRESS AND POVERTY. Other works are *The Irish Land Question* (1881), *Social Problems* (1884), *Protection and Free Trade* (1886), and *Science of Political Economy* (1897). The Fabian Society in England and later movements for economic reform in the U.S. were influenced by George's theories. He died while campaigning for the office of mayor of New York (for the second time) as an independent Democratic candidate.

George, Stefan (1868–1933). German poet. Strongly influenced by Nietzsche in his youth, he adopted an aristocratic doctrine of the poet as a chosen being, from which he never entirely departed; but later in his career, under the impact of World War I, he became more concerned with political reality and developed a conception of the poet as priest, with a duty not only to himself and his art, but also to his people. The poet, he believed, must preserve traditional spiritual values and prevent his people from succumbing to the excitement of wartime brutality and regarding war as an end in itself. Despite his development toward an idealistic patriotism, George's cultural interests were always international in scope. He was a prolific translator (e.g., Baudelaire, Dante, Shakespeare, the English Pre-Raphaelites) and came into personal contact with the French symbolist poets Verlaine and Mallarmé, by whom he was strongly influenced. Of his own works, the following collections of poems are most famous: *Das Jahr der Seele* (*The Year of the Soul*, 1897), *Der Stern des Bundes* (*The Star of the League*, 1914), and *Das neue Reich* (*The New Kingdom*, 1928). His style abounds in esoteric mythical allusions and archaic linguistic forms, and his works are rendered still less accessible by innovations in punctuation and typography. The "George-circle," a small group of literary apostles whom he collected about himself, is credited with a major role in the critical "rediscovery"

of such important German writers as Friedrich Hölderlin and Jean Paul Richter, whose works had fallen into neglect around the turn of the century. See Hugo von HOFMANNSTHAL; Friedrich GUNDOLF; Karl WOLFSKEHL.

George's Mother (1896). A novelette by Stephen CRANE. This is the story of the mother of George Kelsey, who battles unsuccessfully against the lures of the city for her son's allegiance. A religious woman, she dies still believing in her idealized view of George, not knowing that she has really lost. The story was early hailed for its social realism and its artful manipulation of common people and everyday events.

Georgians. A group of English poets, whose style dominated the early years of the 20th century, and who wrote poetry of nature and rustic life in the traditional manner of Wordsworth. The trend was inaugurated by John Masefield's THE EVERLASTING MERCY and A. E. HOUSMAN's Shropshire ballads; it was turned into a movement by Edward Marsh, who published the biennial anthology *Georgian Poetry* (1912–1922). The name reflects the accession of King George V in 1910. The chief Georgian poets were Lascelles ABERCROMBIE, Edmund BLUNDEN, Gordon BOTTOMLEY, Rupert BROOKE, W. H. DAVIES, John DRINKWATER, W. W. GIBSON, Ralph HODGSON, Harold MONRO, T. Sturge MOORE, Robert NICHOLS, J. C. SQUIRE, Edward THOMAS, and Francis Brett YOUNG.

Georgia Scenes, Characters and Incidents, &c., in the First Half Century of the Republic (1835). A collection of 18 humorous sketches by Augustus Baldwin LONGSTREET. In this popular book, Longstreet alternates Addisonian essays with excellent tales of the folkways of Georgia. A pioneer regionalist, he faithfully reproduced Georgia's language.

Georgics (Georgica). A didactic poem in 4 books on the subject of agriculture, composed in 37–30 B.C. by VERGIL. As Vergil's *Bucolics* were based on Theocritus' *Idyls*, so his *Georgics*, also, had a classical Greek precedent: Hesiod's *Works and Days*. Although the work was conceived and executed within the classical genre of the simple didactic, it is more than an agricultural handbook: it is the subtle and profound work of a philosopher-poet. Like the *De Rerum Natura* of Lucretius, to which it is in many ways a reply, Vergil's *Georgics* is built upon a solid didactic foundation from which it rises naturally to peaks of impassioned eloquence.

Book I contains advice on farming in general. After giving an account of the ills that followed the assassination of Julius Caesar, the poet prays that the Roman blood spilled at PHARSALUS and PHILIPPI may be sufficient to expiate the nation's ancestral guilt and that the young Octavius Caesar will save the world from civil war.

In Book II, Vergil concerns himself with grape vines and fruit trees, though he again rises above mere instruction. This book also contains a famous paean to the crops and heroes of Italy.

At the beginning of Book III, the poet rededicates himself to his work. He takes up the care and propagation of livestock, and at the end of the book describes the effect of a plague which killed all living things.

Unlike Lucretius, who ends his poem with a similar scene of a plague in Athens, Vergil passes directly into the sunny Book IV of his *Georgics* and tells a tale of miraculous regeneration. The book is formally concerned with the raising of honey bees, but its most important sections deal with two myths of death and resurrection, one within the other. The bees of Aristaeus, god of beekeeping, have suddenly died. His mother, the sea divinity Cyrene, advises him to consult Proteus, who tells Aristaeus that his bees have been killed by the dryads. The nymphs were avenging the death of Eurydice who, while being pursued by Aristaeus, stepped on a snake and died of its bite. Proteus then relates the pathetic tale of Orpheus and Eurydice. At his mother's suggestion, Aristaeus sacrifices four bulls and four heifers to the shades of Orpheus and Eurydice. After he has let their carcasses rot for nine days, he beholds a swarm of living bees issuing forth from the decaying bellies of the cattle.

Geraint, Son of Erbin. A medieval Welsh tale from the MABINOGION in which King Arthur figures. This story has a parallel in the tale EREC ET ENIDE of Chrétien de Troyes. Tennyson drew his characters Geraint and Enid in his *Idylls of the King* (1859–1872) from the same source.

Gerard, Brigadier. An egotistical, swashbuckling, braggart Napoleonic soldier, hero of a series of tales by Sir Arthur Conan DOYLE.

Gerhardi, William Alexander (1895–   ). English novelist. A disillusioned satirist, he wrote *Futility* (1922), *The Polyglots* (1925), and *Resurrection* (1934). His other works include the novels *Of Mortal Love* (1936) and *My Wife's the Least of It* (1938), the plays *I Was a King in Babylon* (1948) and *Rasputin* (1960), *The Romanoffs: An Historical Biography* (1940), and *The Life and Times of Lord Beaverbrook* (1963).

Géricault [Jean Louis André] Théodore (1791–1824). French painter. The exhibition in 1819 of his masterpiece *The Raft of Medusa*, a realistic and dramatic indictment of death and suffering, caused a storm of protest, and marked the beginning of the struggle between the classical and romantic schools of painting. A powerful draftsman and superb colorist, Géricault is equally known for his paintings of animal life and vivid historical scenes.

Germ, The. This "little magazine" was published from January to April, 1850, by the PRE-RAPHAELITE BROTHERHOOD. In its pages the Pre-Raphaelites printed poems, reproductions of their paintings, and expositions of their artistic ideas.

Germanicus Caesar (15 B.C.–A.D. 19). Roman general. He was adopted by his uncle, the emperor Tiberius and received command of the legions in Germany. He scored a huge success in his campaign against the Germans (A.D. 11–16), but just when he was about to conquer the whole country between the Rhine and the Elbe, Tiberius, alarmed at his strength, recalled him to Rome. It was believed by many that Germanicus was poisoned, possibly at Tiberius' bidding. Germanicus had nine children by Agrippina, among whom were the notorious Caligula and AGRIPPINA, mother of Nero.

German romanticism. Romanticism in Germany was not one movement but a series of separate ones. The first of these, called Jena romanticism after

the small university town where most of the writers met, flourished around 1798–1802 and centered about the brothers F. and A. W. SCHLEGEL. The Schlegels, however, did not regard themselves as the founders of a romantic movement for, in their definition, romantic meant simply modern (from the Middle Ages on), as opposed to classical (Greek and Latin). As romantic authors, they wished to go beyond the classics, but *not* to deny them; in fact, they were very much a part of the philhellenic tradition that also produced WEIMAR CLASSICISM.

But they did set out in new directions. F. Schlegel urged writers to strive for a progressive universal poetry, by which he meant that romantic poetry must constantly develop, that it must not cease to be progressive, and that its ultimate goal must be universal, a synthesized comprehension of the entire world; these ideals of dynamism and universality were opposed to the Weimar classical ideals of balance and limitation. NOVALIS and Wackenroder strove for a new synthesis of art and religion. And Tieck and Novalis made new advances in the characteristically romantic form of the MÄRCHEN, which was later developed by BRENTANO and E. T. A. Hoffmann.

The second of Germany's romantic movements, which flourished in Heidelberg around 1804–1808, was less urbane than Jena romanticism and tended more to stress the beauties of unspoiled nature. It was also in Heidelberg romanticism that the romantic interest in German history and folklore, which had begun with Wackenroder and Tieck, first really took root. Major figures in this phase were Achim von Arnim, Brentano, Görres, Eichendorff, and the brothers Grimm.

But in the atmosphere of growing nationalism that culminated in the wars of liberation against Napoleon (1813–1815), German literature took a turn toward realism, and it is mainly this which characterizes the work of the Berlin group of about 1808–1813, although in their idealism and their frequent use of the *Märchen*-form they are still recognizably romantic. Major figures were E. T. A. Hoffmann, Fouqué, Chamisso, Heinrich von Kleist, and again, Arnim and Brentano.

Finally, after the wars of liberation, under the conservative Prussian and Austrian regimes of 1815–1848, German romanticism again followed the tenor of the times. The Swabian School, which Heine attacked vigorously in his *Die romantische Schule* (*The Romantic School*, 1833) and which included Uhland, Kerner, Lenau, Hauff and Schwab, was a primarily conservative group, interested in the preservation of tradition, and was already very like the postromantic BIEDERMEIER movement.

Disparate though it was, there is a unifying principle inherent in German romanticism. In the 18th century, some voices had already been heard against the prevailing rationalism of the age: Hamann, Herder, Jacobi, Klopstock, the poets of the STURM UND DRANG and of Weimar classicism. In very general terms, German romanticism may be seen as the culmination of all these movements, the final overthrow of the enlightenment, and the definitive redirection of 19th-century literature into nonrationalistic areas of experience. The philosophers most closely associated with German romanticism were Fichte and Schelling. See romantic IRONY.

Germinal (1885). A novel by Emile ZOLA, one of the ROUGON-MACQUART novels. *Germinal* is a study of the bitter sufferings of workers in the French mines. Zola's intense sympathy for the lower classes and his pleas for social reform find powerful expression in this careful portrait of life in the mines.

Germinie Lacerteux (1869). A novel by the GONCOURT brothers. Based on the sordid life of one of the Goncourts' own servants, and composed with attention to realistic detail, this work is naturalistic in both its form and subject matter.

Gernando of Norway. In the GERUSALEMME LIBERATA of Tasso, a Christian knight who is the rival of Rinaldo of Este for the command vacated as a result of the death of Dudone. When the quarrel results in his death, Rinaldo is charged with the crime by Goffredo, the Christian general. Like Achilles, Rinaldo stalks off in anger and leaves the Crusaders without one of their leading warriors.

Geronimo. Indian name: **Goyathlay** (1829–1909). American Apache chieftain. In 1885–1886 he led an attack on white settlers; he was captured by General George Crook (1829–1890), escaped, and later surrendered to General Nelson A. Miles (1839–1925). He finally settled down with members of his tribe on farmland and ranches at Fort Sill, Okla. There he joined the Dutch Reformed Church in 1903, and dictated an account of his life to Stephen M. Barrett; it was published as *Geronimo's Story of His Life* (1906). A town in Arizona is named for the Indian chief. During World War II, American parachutists would often begin their jump by yelling "Geronimo." The reason for their adoption of the Indian name is unknown.

Géronte. The name of the old man who is a stock figure in early French comedy. By Molière's time the character had taken on the unpleasant traits exemplified by the Géronte of LE MÉDECIN MALGRÉ LUI.

Gerontion (1920). A poem by T. S. ELIOT. Spoken by "an old man in a dry month," it is a despairing poem about old age, aridity, the spiritual decay of the world, and the need and unlikelihood of salvation.

Gerontius, The Dream of. See DREAM OF GERONTIUS, THE.

Gershwin, George (1897–1937). American composer. He began his career by composing popular songs, soon combined them into musical comedies, such as *George White's Scandals* (1920–1924), *Funny Face* (1927), and *Of Thee I Sing* (1931; the first musical to win a Pulitzer Prize). However, his chief importance resulted from his ability to bring jazz and popular styles into the realm of classical music, especially with the internationally famous works, *Rhapsody in Blue* (1924) and *Porgy and Bess* (1935; see PORGY). His songs have been collected in *George Gershwin's Song Book* (1932). His brother Ira Gershwin (1896–) was a popular Broadway lyricist who wrote lyrics for many of George's shows.

Gerson, Jean Charlier de (1363–1429). French theologian. Court preacher to Charles VI, he was famous for his sermons in both Latin and French. Gerson was a prominent scholar, the chancellor of the University of Paris, and a delegate to the councils of Pisa and Constance where he strove for church unity and ecclesiastical reforms. He was one of the leading opponents of the *Romance of the Rose*, which he condemned to be burned (1399) as a threat to morality. The authorship of the *Imitation of Christ* is sometimes attributed to Gerson, instead of to Thomas à Kempis.

Gertrude. In Shakespeare's HAMLET, the queen and mother of Hamlet. A weak-willed woman, who has married her husband's brother and murderer, she draws from Hamlet the cry: "Frailty, thy name is woman!"

Gertrude of Wyoming (1809). A poem by Thomas CAMPBELL. The setting is in the wilds of the Wyoming Valley in Pennsylvania. The heroine, Gertrude, is the daughter of the patriarch Albert; the hero is Henry Waldegrave, who as a boy spends three years in the patriarch's home and later returns to marry Gertrude. The settlement is attacked by a mixed army of Indians and British and both Albert and Gertrude are shot. Henry then joins the army of Washington.

Gerusalemme liberata (Jerusalem Delivered). The celebrated romantic epic by Torquato TASSO. Written during the Italian Renaissance, some time between 1559 and 1575, it was published in a definitive version of twenty cantos in 1581. The whole work had been translated into English by 1600, the accomplishment of Edward Fairfax. Unlike other Renaissance romances, it was based on the historic events of the First Crusade (1096–1099) and utilized several historical characters. The plot begins with the fictional war in its sixth year and the election of Goffredo (Godfrey) as the chief of the Christian armies encamped on the plains of Tortosa. As they prepare to attack Jerusalem, its king Aladino learns from the enchanter Ismeno that the city will not fall if a statue of the Virgin is removed from a Christian church and placed in a mosque. Finding the statue stolen, Aladino plans revenge on the Christian community of the city, but a young Christian maiden, Sofronia, offers to take the blame, as does her beloved, Olindo, who hopes thereby to save her. Aladino promptly orders both put to death, and they are saved only by the timely appearance of the warrior maiden Clorinda, who offers her sword in return for their lives. Now the pagan warrior Argante (Argantes), having failed to dissuade Goffredo from the attack, declares war upon the Crusaders. When the Christians attack the holy city, Argante kills their champion Dudone and the Christians withdraw to do him honors. Heeding the infernal decree of Plutone (Pluto), the enchanter Idraote sends his beautiful niece Armida to confound the Christian camp. She tells Goffredo of her need for ten knights to retake the city of Damascus; he is unwilling, but many more than ten Crusaders follow her away, among them the most puissant in the Christian army. Rinaldo also departs in anger because Goffredo has denounced him for the murder of Gernando, his rival for the command vacated because of the death of Dudone. Argante now challenges the Christian knights and kills Ottone, but his ferocious duel with Tancredi (Tancred) is interrupted when Erminia, who loves the latter, lures him away by disguising herself as his beloved Clorinda. Goffredo's depleted forces now face the challenge of Solimano (the Soldan, or Solyman), leader of the Arabs, but the archangel Gabriel intervenes to save tnem. Solimano soon joins forces with Aladino. in the renewed assault by the Crusaders, Tancredi unknowingly wounds Clorinda, who forgives him and is baptized before dying. Goffredo, learning from a vision that only Rinaldo can break the enchantments of Ismeno and free the armies to continue their assault upon the city, sends Guelfo and Ubaldo to bring him back. Dallying with Armida, Rinaldo is finally disenchanted and persuaded to return. With his return, the Crusaders are soon victorious. The unyielding Argante is killed by Tancredi, but the Egyptian forces, spurred by Armida, try to renew the battle. Rinaldo administers the final defeat to the infidels by killing Solimano and subduing Armida. With Aladino dead and the Egyptian king killed by Goffredo, the Crusaders can enter the great city at will. There, at dawn, led by Goffredo, they worship at the sepulcher of Christ.

Gervaise. One of the principal characters in the novels of Emile Zola's ROUGON-MACQUART series. She first appears in L'ASSOMMOIR.

Geryon. In Greek mythology, a monster with three bodies and three heads. His oxen ate human flesh and were guarded by Orthrus, a two-headed dog. HERACLES slew both Geryon and the dog.

Geryoneo. See FAERIE QUEENE, THE.

Geschichten Jaakobs, Die. See JOSEPH AND HIS BROTHERS.

Gesmas. The impenitent thief. He was crucified with Jesus. In the apocryphal *Gospel of Nicodemus,* he is called Gestas. The penitent thief was DISMAS.

Gespräche mit Goethe. See Johann Peter ECKERMANN.

Gestapo. The abbreviated name of the Nazi *Geheime Staatspolizei* (Secret Political Police), taken from the initial syllables of the words. Formed by Goering (1933), it became under HIMMLER the state's arm of terror.

Gesta Regum Anglorum (Chronicle of the Kings of England, c. 1120–1128). Latin history by WILLIAM OF MALMESBURY. It covers the history of England from 449 to 1128, including an account of Arthur, which indicates that the legends surrounding the hero were already prevalent in England.

Gesta Romanorum ("Deeds of the Romans"). Latin collection of tales, many of them of Oriental origin, very popular in the Middle Ages. It may have been compiled in England in the late 13th century; it was printed in 1473 and frequently thereafter, different versions including about 100 to 200 tales. The episodes are usually arbitrarily assigned to the reign of a Roman emperor, but there is little real history; similarly, a "moral" or "application" follows each tale, purportedly for the use of preachers, but it is not a religious work. Chaucer, Shakespeare, and later English writers have drawn frequently on the tales for plot material.

Gestas. See GESMAS.

Gesualdo, Carlo (c. 1560–1613). Italian composer and Prince of Venosa, near Naples. One of the most curious composers in musical history, Gesualdo was responsible for the brutal murder of his first wife (his first cousin) and her lover. His often experimental madrigals and other compositions are harmonically daring, filled with constant chromatic modulation, and nervously restless. He was a close friend of the poet Torquato Tasso, whose poems he set. Tasso's name has been linked with that of Leonora d'Este, Gesualdo's second wife.

Gethsemane. An olive grove or garden on the western slope of the Mount of Olives. It was here that Jesus went to pray after the Last Supper, and that Judas Iscariot betrayed him to the Roman soldiers (Mark 14:32–43; Matt. 26:36–49). Centuries-old olive trees growing on the site are today tended by monks of the Greek, Armenian, Russian, and Roman Churches.

Get-Rich-Quick Wallingford (1908). A group of related stories by George Randolph Chester (1869–1924). Wallingford, whose name has become part of American folklore, is a company promoter. With his satellite Blackie Daw, he engages in many dubious enterprises, but always manages to escape the hand of the law. Chester continued his adventures in several other books: *Young Wallingford* (1910), *Wallingford and Blackie Daw* (1913), *Wallingford in His Prime* (1913). George M. Cohan made a successful dramatization of the stories in 1910.

Gettysburg. A town in southern Pennsylvania and the site of a major battle (July 1–3, 1863), often considered the turning point of the American Civil War. The Confederates under Gen. Lee were defeated by numerically superior Union troops under Gen. George Meade. Casualties are estimated at about 23,000 for the Union Army, about 28,000 for the Confederates. Though Lee's retreat into Virginia was temporarily blocked by the flooding of the Potomac, Meade's failure to attack permitted the Confederates to escape on July 13 after the river fell.

Gettysburg Address (Nov. 19, 1863). An address prepared and delivered by President Abraham Lincoln at the dedication of the national cemetery at Gettysburg battlefield. Lincoln's brief address, which followed a two-hour oration by Edward Everett, the principal speaker of the day, is perhaps the most moving and eloquent statement of the American creed. Mary Raymond Shipman Andrews wrote "a sentimental footnote to history" in *The Perfect Tribute* (1906), a fictional account of the delivery and effects of the address.

Ghebers or **Guebres.** PARSEES, or followers of the ancient Persian religion, Zoroastrianism. The name, bestowed upon them by their Arabian conquerors, is now applied generally to fire worshipers.

Ghelderode, Michel de (1898–1962). Belgian dramatist. In the 1920's he wrote plays for marionettes, and his later works often use a similar stylization. Sometimes the human actors are masked to resemble puppets, for his characters are often the grotesque caricatures of farce and fantasy. Ghelderode was inspired by the flamboyance of Shakespeare and the Golden Age of Spain, the satiric realism of the Flemish painters, and the allegories of traditional folklore. His plays, mingling the burlesque and the mystical, did not begin to be widely known until 1946. They include *Christopher Columbus* (1927), *Escurial* (1928), *Barabbas* (1928), *The Women at the Tomb* (1928), *Chronicles of Hell* (*Fastes d'enfer,* 1929), *Pantagleize* (1930), *Sire Halewyn* (1934), *Hop, Signor!* (1935), and *School for Buffoons* (*L'Ecole des bouffons;* 1937).

Ghéon, Henri. Pen name of **Henri Vangeon** (1875–1944). French dramatist, essayist, and critic.

Ghéon was associated with the *Nouvelle Revue française* and published in it a series of critical articles: *Nos Directions: réalisme et poésie* (1911). He is best known for the religious plays that he wrote after his conversion to Catholicism, especially *Le Pauvre sous l'Escalier* (1920).

Ghibellines. See GUELPHS.

Ghiberti, Il. Real name, **Lorenzo di Cione di Ser Buonaccorso** (1378–1455). Florentine sculptor. His style combines tradition and innovation: the grace of medieval sculpture and a vivid pictorial quality, unparalleled elsewhere, caused by the use of perspective and the manipulation of planes in relief. He executed the famous north and east doors of the baptistry of Florence (1402–1422 and 1427–1452, respectively), which are elaborately decorated with panels in gilt bronze relief. Toward the end of his life he wrote three *Commentaries* (*I Commentarii*) on art, which survive in very imperfect form and include his autobiography and the first account of the lives of the artists of the 14th century.

Ghirlandaio, Il. Real name, **Domenico di Tommaso Bigordi** (1449–1495). Florentine painter. He was noted for his religious easel pictures and his narrative frescoes. Influenced by Fra Lippo Lippi, he in turn influenced the young Michelangelo, who worked in his studio. Among his best-known works are the frescoes behind the high altar of Santa Maria Novella in Florence, especially *The Birth of the Virgin;* portraits of Florentine humanists of the Medici circle; the touching *Portrait of an Old Man and a Boy;* the *Adoration of the Shepherds in the Uffizi;* and the wall frescoes of the Sistine Chapel, done with Botticelli.

Ghismonda. See TANCRED, THE REVENGE OF.

Ghosts (1881). A play by Henrik IBSEN. Ten years after her husband's death, Mrs. Alving is about to open an orphanage dedicated to his memory. Her son, Oswald, has just come home from abroad. She reveals to the moralistic Pastor Manders, who many years before had advised her against leaving her husband, that the late Captain Alving had lived and died drunken and profligate, and that Regina, the serving-girl, is actually his daughter. Oswald is beginning to go insane from hereditary syphilis, a legacy from his father; and Mrs. Alving realizes that, in basing her actions on duty rather than love, she has been indirectly responsible both for her husband's dissoluteness and her son's incipient insanity. The "ghosts" of the title are the dead conventions and beliefs that prevented Mrs. Alving from living for "the joy of life."

Giacometti, Alberto (1901–   ). Swiss painter and sculptor. His fleshless, elongated, gloomy figures display his interest in surrealism. He works and lives in Paris.

Giacosa, Giuseppe (1847–1906). Italian dramatist, poet, librettist, and short-story writer. Giacosa is considered the leading Italian playwright of the late 19th century. The themes of his dramas undergo an observable change paralleling the changing literary tastes of the public for whom he wrote. Initially (c. 1870–1890) he composed graceful, charming verse plays reflecting the romantic cult of the Middle Ages and naturalistic interest in scientifically precise descriptions of character and setting. To this period belong *La Partita a Scacchi* (1873), *Il Trionfo d'Amore*

(1875), *La Signora di Challant,* written for Sarah Bernhardt (1891). Subsequently he wrote serious social dramas influenced by the problem plays of Henrik Ibsen and the popularity of French, Russian, and English psychological novels. Among his plays of social criticism are *Tristi Amori* (1888), *I Diritti dell'Anima* (1900), *Come Le Foglie* (1900), and *Il Più Forte* (1905). In collaboration with Luigi Illica, he wrote the libretti for Puccini's *La Bohème* (1896), *La Tosca* (1900), and *Madama Butterfly* (1904).

Giacosa's nondramatic writings include *Novelle e Paesi Valdostani* (1886), short stories set against the background of his native Val d'Aosta (Piedmont), and a collection of travel essays on America.

Giafar, or **Jaffar the Barmecide.** Vizier of the Caliph Haroun-al-Raschid and companion of his adventures. He appears frequently in the *Arabian Nights.*

Giall. In Scandinavian mythology, the river on the frontiers of Niflheim or hell, equivalent to the Greco-Roman Styx. Over it pass the doomed on a golden bridge.

Giambullari, Pier Francesco (1495–1555). Florentine historian. His history of Europe, *Istoria d'Europa,* covering the years 887–947, was published posthumously (1566) in its unfinished state. It was one of the first Humanist (see HUMANISM) histories to look at the past from the wider viewpoint of the Empire, rather than from the narrower interest of one city or state.

Gian ben Gian. In Arabic legend, a king of the JINN and founder of the Pyramids. He was overthrown by Eblis, the Muslim Lucifer.

Giant Despair. See PILGRIM'S PROGRESS.

Giants (Gigantes) or **Earth-Born (Gegeneis).** In Greek mythology, offspring of Ge (earth), impregnated by blood from the castrated URANUS (sky). They were in most accounts of human form, but with serpents' tails instead of feet. They warred on the gods, hurling whole trees and giant rocks. They were finally defeated only with the aid of HERACLES. Immortal, they were buried alive under mountains—generally volcanoes. Possibly oriental in origin, they are thought to have been personifications of the violent forces in nature. They should not be confused with the HUNDRED-HANDED or OTUS AND EPHIALTES.

Giants in the Earth: A Saga of the Prairie (1924–1925 in Norwegian; 1927 in English). A novel by Ole E. RÖLVAAG. The first volume of a trilogy that includes *Peder Victorious* (1929) and *Their Father's God* (1931), it is a stark and realistic work describing the hardships, both mental and physical, of a small group of Norwegian farmers who set out from Minnesota with their families in 1873 to settle in the then unopened Dakota Territory. The novel centers on Per Hansa, his devotion to the land, the growing religious fanaticism of his wife, Beret, and his final disappearance in a blizzard.

The hero of the two succeeding novels is Peder Victorious Holm, Per Hansa's youngest son, who marries a devout Irish Catholic, Susie Doheny, and later quarrels with her over the raising of their son, Petie.

Giants in the Earth was successfully dramatized (1928) by Thomas Job and made into an opera (1951) by Douglas Moore

giaour. Among the Muslims, a term used contemptuously for one, especially a Christian, who does not adhere to their faith.

Byron wrote a poem, *The Giaour* (1813). In it, Leilah, the beautiful concubine of the Caliph Hassan, flees with a Giaour to her destruction; the Giaour later becomes a monk and tells his story while on his deathbed.

Gibbon, Edward (1737-1794). English historian, noted for his masterpiece *The History of the* DECLINE AND FALL OF THE ROMAN EMPIRE. He formed the plan for this great work during a tour of Italy (1764) while "musing amidst the ruins of the Capitol." He entered Parliament in 1774 and was made commissioner of trade and plantations. The first volume of his "History," which appeared in 1776, was very well received, though his chapters on Christianity provoked severe criticism from some quarters. Succeeding volumes were not as warmly received as the first. Gibbon's *Memoirs,* put together by Lord Sheffield, were published in 1796.

Gibbon, Lewis Grassic. See James Leslie MITCHELL.

Gibbons, Stella (1902–   ). English novelist and poet. Her best-known book is COLD COMFORT FARM, a brilliant parody of the novel of rustic pessimism.

Gibbs, A[rthur] Hamilton (1888-1964). English-born American novelist. The youngest of three writing brothers, he wrote best-selling novels, including *Soundings* (1925), *Chances* (1930), *The Need We Have* (1936), and *Obedience to the Moon* (1956).

Gibbs, Cosmo Hamilton. See Cosmo HAMILTON.

Gibbs, Sir **Philip [Hamilton]** (1877-1962). English journalist and novelist. The second of three writing brothers, he was knighted for his work as a frontline correspondent during World War I. His books of essays and social commentary include *Realities of War* (1920), *Now It Can Be Told* (1920), and *The New Elizabethans* (1953).

Gibraltar. A famous rock fortress at the western entrance to the Mediterranean Sea.

Gibson, Charles Dana (1867-1944). American illustrator. The creator of "the Gibson Girl," he modeled his drawings on his wife, the beautiful, dignified, and fashionable Irene Langhorne. Nearly every woman during the gay 90's imitated her clothes, looks, and manners. Gibson also illustrated many books, most notably the stories of Richard Harding Davis.

Gibson, W[ilfred] W[ilson] (1878-1962). English poet, associated with the GEORGIAN group. His most successful poems are about the grim, industrial lives of working people, as in *Daily Bread* (1910) and *Thoroughfares* (1914).

Gide, André (1869-1951). French writer and editor. Brought up in an austere Protestant household, Gide reacted passionately against the prohibitions of revealed religion. Yet his search for self—the underlying theme of his more than 80 published works—remained essentially a religious search, and Gide is as well known for his influence as a moralist and a thinker as for his contributions to literature.

At 18 he met Pierre Louÿs and other aspiring writers and artists, and attended the literary salons of José-María de Hérédia and Stéphane Mallarmé. In 1891 he published *Les Cahiers d'*ANDRÉ WALTER, reflecting his spiritual love for his cousin Madeleine and his conviction that physical desire must be suppressed. He published his first poems the next year, but by 1900 he had practically abandoned this form of writing. Gide shared Paul Valéry's fascination with the myth of Narcissus as a symbol of man's hopeless and misdirected yearning for perfection. His friends read the essay *Le Traité du Narcisse* (1891) as a definition of symbolism, but its theories were actually quite differently intended, and Gide soon separated from the group.

With his first trip to North Africa in 1893, Gide broke with his entire past. He rejected mortification of the flesh, believing that harmony of body and soul was possible only if both were satisfied, and deliberately sought sensual experience. His discovery of his homosexual leanings troubled him, but the tolerance of the North Africans and the open encouragement of Oscar Wilde in 1895 freed him of embarrassment. THE FRUITS OF THE EARTH is a hymn to the joy of the search for experience.

Gide considered himself a disturber of youth, ever urging individual self-cultivation, while paradoxically warning against a narcissistic concern with self. His fiction is autobiographical only to the extent that each major figure is an exaggerated personification of one aspect of his own character. Thus, THE IMMORALIST and STRAIT IS THE GATE were conceived as companion pieces to show the unhappy consequences of amoral hedonism in the first and of equally selfish self-abnegation and asceticism in the second.

Always concerned with motivation and the function of man's will, Gide was influenced by Dostoevski (his translations and analyses did much to make the Russian novelist popular in France) and agreed that there are both good and evil impulses, not traceable to common motives such as love, hate, or self-interest. He was fascinated by examples of the apparently disinterested *acte gratuit,* or gratuitous act, and concluded that it is motivated solely by a personal need to assert one's individuality and thus the only human act that reveals one's essential character; LAFCADIO'S ADVENTURES presents a murder as such an act.

Gide was twice tempted to find self-development in commitment to something outside himself. His correspondence with his friends Francis Jammes (pub. 1948) and Paul Claudel (pub. 1949) reveal their unsuccessful attempt to convert him to Catholicism. Then on a trip to French Equatorial Africa in 1925 he was horrified by the French treatment of the natives. He expressed his views on the subject in *Travels in the Congo* (*Voyage au Congo;* 1927, and *Le Retour du Tchad;* 1928), and began to advocate the reform of social institutions, becoming an admirer of the ideal of Communism and its practical experiment in the Soviet Union. But he could not accept the party's orthodox dogma without the right to question, and in 1936 was disillusioned by a visit to the Soviet Union, described in *Return from the USSR* (*Retour de l'URSS;* 1936) and *Afterthoughts on the USSR* (*Retouches à mon retour de l'URSS;* 1937).

The novel THE COUNTERFEITERS exposes the hypocrisy and self-deception with which people try to avoid sincerity. Gide's own obsessive concern with personal and public honesty often led him to face public scandal—especially with his insistence that the bounds of the natural include homosexuality. When CORYDON drew violent criticism, Gide answered with IF IT DIE. . . . He pursued this ideal of perfect frankness in his comprehensive private, literary, and philosophical *Journals* (1939–1950), omitting only the details of his marriage with his cousin Madeleine. After her death (1938) he wrote the painful account of their mutual love and unhappiness, published posthumously as *Et nunc manet in te* (1951), translated as *Madeleine* (1952).

Gide was one of the most influential editors of LA NOUVELLE REVUE FRANÇAISE. In 1947 he was awarded the Nobel Prize for his varied contributions to literature.

Other important works by Gide, available in English, include the satires *Paludes* (1895) and *Le Prométhée mal enchaîné* (1899), collected as *Marshlands and Prometheus Misbound* (1953); the plays *Philoctète* (1899), *Le Roi Candaule* (1901), *Saül* (1903), *Bethsabé* (1912), and *Perséphone* (1934), collected as *My Theater* (1951); the play *Oedipe* (1931) and the tale *Thésée* (1946), collected as *Two Legends: Theseus and Oedipus* (1950); and the tales *Isabelle* (1911) and THE PASTORAL SYMPHONY, included in *Two Symphonies* (1931). See ECOLE DES FEMMES.

Gideon. In the Old Testament, a Hebrew liberator, reformer, and one of the judges of Israel for 40 years. With a company of 300 men, he delivered his people from the Midianites. The army was purposely reduced to 300 by eliminating all who were afraid and all who drank from a stream instead of lapping the water from their hands. To give the impression of being a huge army, they made a great noise by breaking pitchers and blowing trumpets (Judg. 7:16–20).

Gielgud, Sir **[Arthur] John** (1904–   ). English actor. He has appeared in plays by Wilde, Shakespeare, and Sheridan as well as contemporary works. He has been seen on the movie and television screen in both England and America.

Gifford, William (1756–1826). English literary critic and poet, first editor (1809–1824) of the *Quarterly Review*. He edited Elizabethan plays and wrote the verse satires THE BAVIAD and *The Maeviad* (1795).

Gift of the Magi, The (1906). A short story by O. HENRY. Containing perhaps the most famous of O. Henry's trick endings, this Yuletide narrative tells how a nearly penniless young husband and wife are each determined to buy the other a suitable Christmas present. He sells his watch to buy her a set of combs; she has her beautiful hair cut off and sells the tresses to buy him a watch fob. The tale was included in THE FOUR MILLION.

Gilbert, Sir **Humphrey** (1539?–1583). English navigator. The half-brother of Sir Walter Raleigh, Gilbert made a voyage with him in 1578. He wrote a *Discourse of a Discoverie for a new passage to Cataia* (published 1576, written and circulated earlier), in which he urged exploration for the discovery of a northwest passage (see NORTHEAST PASSAGE). His arguments probably influenced Sir Martin Frobisher's voyages in search of such a passage in 1576–1578. He established the first British colony in North America

at St. John's, Newfoundland (August 5, 1583), but went down with his ship on the return voyage to England.

Gilbert, Sir **William S[chwenck]** (1836–1911). English dramatist and writer of humorous verse. He is best remembered as librettist of the GILBERT AND SULLIVAN comic operas. Among his other dramatic pieces are *The Palace of Truth* (1870), *Pygmalion and Galatea* (1871), and *Engaged* (1877). Several of the Gilbert and Sullivan operas owe their origin to Gilbert's collection of humorous ballads, *Bab Ballads* (1866–71), which show his great facility in versifying. He had a penchant for whimsicality, nonsense, and topical satire.

Gilbert and Sullivan operas, also called **the Savoy Operas.** A series of comic operas, text by William Schwenck GILBERT and music by Arthur Seymour SULLIVAN, originally produced (1881 et seq.) at the Savoy Theatre in London by Richard D'Oyly Carte. An outstanding achievement in music collaboration, the titles are *Thespis or The Gods Grown Old* (1871), *Trial by Jury* (1875), *The Sorcerer* (1877), H. M. S. PINAFORE (1878), THE PIRATES OF PENZANCE OR THE SLAVE OF DUTY (1880), PATIENCE OR BUNTHORNE'S BRIDE (1881), IOLANTHE OR THE PEER AND THE PERI (1882), *Princess Ida or Castle Adamant* (1884), THE MIKADO OR THE TOWN OF TITIPU (1885), *Ruddigore* (1887), THE YEOMEN OF THE GUARD (1888), *The Gondoliers* (1889), *Utopia, Limited* (1893), and *The Grand Duke* (1896). The first of these operas, and the last two, written after a serious quarrel between Gilbert and Sullivan, are almost never performed. Highly satiric, the operas poke fun at contemporary Victorian life. The Gilbert and Sullivan following, called Savoyards after the name of the theater, is still considerable.

Gilberte. The first girl beloved by the narrator in Marcel Proust's REMEMBRANCE OF THINGS PAST. Daughter of Charles SWANN and ODETTE DE CRÉCY, she repudiates her Jewish background when her mother remarries, and eventually marries Robert de SAINT-LOUP.

Gil Blas de Santillane, Histoire de (1715, 1724, 1735). A PICARESQUE novel in four volumes by Alain René LESAGE. The extraordinary number of episodes in this novel render any coherent plot summary impossible. The setting is Spanish, but the society depicted is really French. The hero, Gil Blas, leaves home at 17 to try his fortune at Salamanca; in his journeys he meets a large number of people—adventurers, thieves, valets, actors, authors, doctors, clergymen, and noblemen. Lesage has very little good to say about any of them. Gil Blas himself, though full of good intentions, is a singularly weak character. One critic (Lester G. Crocker) says that Gil Blas goes through the three stages of innocence, corruption, and the triumph of virtue. Among the more famous portraits in the novel are the ARCHBISHOP OF GRANADA, DON ALVARO, and DR. SANGRADO. (See also THE SOUL OF PEDRO GARCIAS.) From the literary historical view, Lesage continues the traditions of the realistic novels written in the 17th century by Charles Sorel, Antoine Furetière, and Paul Scarron. This novel also affords a good example of the evolution of the French language between the 17th and 18th centuries, in that an increase in the concision of narrative style is apparent.

Gildas (c. 500). An early Welsh historian who wrote about the battle of Mount Badon. This battle was later hailed as the greatest triumph of an historical Arthur who may be the prototype of the literary King Arthur. There is no mention of the name in Gildas' work, however. See ARTHURIAN LEGEND.

Gilded Age, The (1873). A novel by Mark TWAIN and Charles Dudley WARNER. Colonel Beriah Sellers, a schemer who always fails, persuades his friend, Squire Hawkins, to join him in an ill-fated land speculation scheme in Missouri. Hawkins' adopted daughter is seduced by Colonel Selby, whom she later murders. All the characters are modeled on real people; among them are William Weed and his political gang, based on the Tweed Ring in New York. The phrase "gilded age" has been adopted as a description of the hectic post-Civil War period.

Gilder, Richard Watson (1844–1909). American newspaper and magazine editor and poet. He edited Scribner's Monthly (1870–1881) and The Century Magazine (1881–1909). Among his volumes of poetry are The New Day (1876) and Five Books of Songs (1900). Gilder's refusal to receive Robert Louis Stevenson, because rumors had led him to doubt the latter's respectability, has gained him a degree of notoriety.

Gilderoy. Real name: Patrick Macgregor (d. 1636). Scottish cattle-stealer and highwayman. According to an old ballad, he robbed Cardinal Richelieu in the presence of the king, picked Oliver Cromwell's pocket, and hanged a judge. He was hanged in Edinburgh.

Gildippe. In Tasso's GERUSALEMME LIBERATA, the wife of Odoardo (Edward). Having accompanied her husband on the crusade, this capable fighter deals the infidels many stout blows before being killed by Solimano, their leader.

Giles, St. Patron saint of cripples. The tradition is that Childeric, king of France, accidentally wounded a hermit in the knee when hunting; and the hermit, that he might better mortify the flesh, refused to be cured, remaining a cripple for life. His day is September 1, and his symbol a hind, in allusion to the "heaven directed hind" which went daily to his cave near the mouth of the Rhone to give him milk. He is sometimes represented as an old man with an arrow in his knee and a hind by his side. Churches dedicated to St. Giles were usually situated in the outskirts of a city, and originally without the walls because some cripples and beggars were not permitted to pass the city gates.

Gilgamesh. A mythical hero of Sumer and Babylonia. Though he is best known from the famous Babylonian EPIC OF GILGAMESH, he was originally a Sumerian hero, the king of the ancient city of Erech. In a Sumerian myth, he comes to the aid of the goddess INANNA who is distressed because she is unable to cut down the Huluppu tree in the garden, in order to have furniture made of it: a snake, a dangerous bird, and Lilith have all taken up residence in it. When Gilgamesh chases them away and chops down the tree, Inanna gives him (untranslatable) gifts, but he accidentally drops them into the underworld. His companion Enkidu undertakes to go after them, but fails to observe the precautions essential in such ventures and cannot return. His ghost, however, is permitted to come back long

UNIVERSITY MUSEUM, PHILADELPHIA

Sumerian shell inlay of Gilgamesh taming two monsters.

enough to carry on a lengthy conversation with Gilgamesh. The ending of the myth is unknown from the fragmentary tablets on which it was found.

Gilgamesh, Epic of. A Babylonian poem (c. 2000 B.C.). One of the oldest and most important major epics in literature, it was first discovered on clay tablets in the library of ASSUR-BANI-PAL (668–626 B.C.). Like the ILIAD and the ODYSSEY, it is composed of far earlier elements of myth and folklore that have been joined into a single poem through a process of gradual accretion. Also, like Homer's epics, it enjoyed immense popularity for centuries; passages from it were frequently quoted in later literature. The epic includes stories, originally separate, of GILGAMESH, a legendary king of Sumerian origin; ENKIDU, a sort of primeval man; Utnapishtim, the Babylonian Noah; and several other tales.

Gilgamesh was a mighty, part-immortal king of Erech whose subjects eventually prayed for relief from his tyranny. Taking pity on them, the lord of heaven ordered the goddess Aruru to mold out of clay a hairy wild man named Enkidu. This monstrous creature lived with and ate like the beasts, whom he saved from the snares of hunters. Learning of his existence, Gilgamesh sent a young woman to seduce him, after which the animals would have no more to do with him. The woman told him of Gilgamesh's tyranny, and Enkidu resolved to challenge his power. This he did at the New Year's festival, but when he had defeated Gilgamesh in wrestling, the two became fast friends.

The first exploit that they undertook together was to cut down a cedar in the sacred wood guarded by the monster Humbaba, who breathed fire and plague and had one eye that could turn men to stone. They felled the cedar and Humbaba came roaring to the attack, but the sun-god (at the plea of the goddess Ninsun, Gilgamesh's mother) saved them by blinding the monster with hot winds. After the friends defeated and beheaded Humbaba, the goddess ISHTAR endeavored to seduce Gilgamesh, but he reminded her bluntly how she had treated TAMMUZ and other lovers, turning many of them into beasts. Furious, she belabored the lord of heaven with threats until he sent the storm bull of heaven against them, but the two youths promptly killed it and offered its heart to the sun-god. Enkidu now had a series of dreams which revealed to him that the gods, outraged at this act, had decreed his death. Lying on his bed, he gradually grew weaker until he died.

Grief-stricken, Gilgamesh determined to learn the secret of eternal life by seeking out the sage Utnapishtim, the only mortal ever to have escaped death. In spite of many trials and warnings, Gilgamesh reached the ocean of death and was rowed across it by the ferryman Urshanabi into the presence of Utnapishtim. The old man told him of how, in the early days of the earth, a great flood had destroyed his fellow men. He, warned by EA, the god of wisdom, had saved himself and his family by building an ark in which they had floated for seven days and nights until the ark grounded on a mountain. Utnapishtim had then sent out a dove, a swallow, and a raven; and, when the last of these having found dry land did not return, he and his family had offered thanks to the gods for their safety. Utnapishtim and his wife, thereafter, had been sent to the island at the end of the earth where they now lived, and where they had become immortal.

Gilgamesh now understood that this immortality was a special gift of the gods, and that neither Utnapishtim nor any other mortal would ever learn the secret of eternal life. The sage told him, however, of a herb growing at the bottom of the sea that would restore his youth. Taking leave of the old man, Gilgamesh tied stones to his feet, dived into the sea, and found the plant. After he had gone a long way on his journey home to Erech, he stopped to rest and bathe in a spring, laying the plant on the ground. A snake quickly appeared and made off with it; tasting the plant, it cast off its old skin and was made young again. Gilgamesh wept. Now he understood that no human being can escape old age and death. Resigned to the fate that he shared with all men, he returned to his homeland, where he died.

Gillette of Narbonne. The heroine of a tale from Giovanni Boccaccio's THE DECAMERON. As a reward for curing the king of France, she obtains the right to marry Bertrand of Roussillon. The reluctant bridegroom flees angrily to Florence, where he loves a young woman, until discovering that he has slept with his own wife thinking she was his mistress, and that she has borne him two sons, he is finally reconciled. This is essentially the story of Shakespeare's play *All's Well That Ends Well.*

Gil y Zárate, Antonio (1793–1861). Spanish playwright. He is well known for his abandonment of neoclassic principles; this is apparent in his *Carlos II, el hechizado* (1844), a moderate romantic drama which attacks reactionary political views. He is also the author of *Guzmán el Bueno* (1847).

Giménez Caballero, Ernesto (1899–). Spanish writer and academician. Giménez is the founder of the avant-garde publication *La Gaceta Literaria* (1927). His best-known writings include *Notas marruecas de un soldado* (1923); *Yo, inspector de alcantarillas* (1928), a surrealistic novel; and

Genio de España (1931), which is considered his best work.

Ginevra. In Ariosto's ORLANDO FURIOSO, a Scottish princess unjustly accused by LURCANIO of causing the death of his brother and her beloved, Ariodante (Ariodantes). Doomed to die unless a champion appears to fight Lurcanio, she tells her story to Rinaldo, who, having learned from her maid Dalinda that Ginevra was betrayed by Polinesso, denounces the latter before the king and then kills him in a duel. Ariodante, who is actually alive and present to defend Ginevra, reveals himself and wins her hand.

Ginsberg, Allen (1926–). American poet. A leading poet of the BEAT MOVEMENT, Ginsberg writes an incantatory, loosely structured line reminiscent of Whitman. *Howl and Other Poems* (1956) is a violent lament for what society has done to his generation; it became something of a *succès de scandale* when it was charged with, and subsequently cleared of, obscenity. Ginsberg has also written *Kaddish and Other Poems* (1961) and *Empty Mirror: Early Poems* (1961).

ginseng. A Chinese herb valued as a medicine. Its root, often forked, explains why it corresponds in Chinese folk lore to the Western MANDRAKE.

Ginza. Street in Tokyo, running from Shimbashi to Kyobashi. It is the center of a high-class shopping and entertainment district.

Gioconda, La. A portrait by LEONARDO da Vinci. One of the most famous of paintings, it is better known as the Mona Lisa. Its subject was a Neapolitan noblewoman, Madonna (Mona) Lisa del Giocondo. The portrait, which hangs in the Louvre, is especially noted for the lady's smile, which inspired *The Gioconda Smile,* one of Aldous Huxley's best-known short stories. It has been pointed out, however, that similar enigmatic smiles were a popular feature of portraits for this period.

Gioconda, La (1876). An opera by Amilcare Ponchielli based on Victor Hugo's *Angelo the Tyrant of Padua.* The libretto was written by Arrigo Boïto under the pseudonym Tobia Goria—presumably through embarrassment over its melodramatic plot.

Gioconda, La (1898). A drama by Gabriele D'ANNUNZIO. The title character is a model for a brilliant young sculptor, Lucio Settala. Out of loyalty to his devoted wife Silvia, he tries to resist the fascination that Gioconda exercises over him. Eventually, however, he leaves Silvia for Gioconda, who he feels is the real inspiration of his art. Eleonora Duse, to whom the play is dedicated, scored a great success in the title role.

Giocondo. Hero of an episode in the ORLANDO FURIOSO of Ariosto, his name is better known in its French paraphrase Joconde.

Giono, Jean (1895–). French novelist of the Provence region. This countryside is presented with sensuous realism in such early works as *Hill of Destiny (Colline; 1928), Lovers Are Never Losers (Un de Baumugnes; 1929), Harvest (Regain; 1930),* and the semiautobiographical *Blue Boy (Jean le bleu; 1932).* Preferring a Hellenistic pantheism and the earthy life of the peasant to Christianity and modern civilization, he expressed his love of life in *The Song of the World (Le Chant du monde; 1934)* and *Joy of Man's Desiring (Que ma joie demeure; 1935).* Although he fought in the First World War, he went to prison rather than serve in the Second, upholding the principles of his pacifist essay *Refus d'obéissance* (1937). His other works include the short story *La Femme du boulanger* (1935, filmed as *The Baker's Wife*, 1939) and the plays *Lanceurs de graines* (1937) and *Le Bout de la Route* (1941). Among his novels are *Le Grand Troupeau* (1931), *Les Grands Chemins* (1951), and *The Malediction* (*Le Moulin de Pologne;* 1952).

Giorgione, Il. Real name, **Giorgio da Castelfranco** (c. 1478–1510). Little is known of his life and scarcely a half dozen paintings can be safely ascribed to him, yet this young and influential student of Giovanni Bellini is known as the chief master of the Venetian school of his day. He is celebrated for the sensuous and poetic grace of his work and for his introduction of a new range of subject matter:— idyllic scenes of pastoral love that depend for their effect on the golden color harmony which unifies the whole. Among his authenticated works are the enigmatic *Tempest* (1506), the *Fête Champêtre*, the *Castelfranco Madonna*, and *Sleeping Venus*.

Giotto [di Bondone] (1266?–1337). Florentine painter. The greatest Italian painter of the pre-Renaissance, he was, according to tradition, a pupil of CIMABUE and a friend of Dante. VASARI acclaimed him for breaking with the rigid Byzantine tradition of his time by introducing the direct observation of nature, and recounted that, when asked by the pope for a sample of his work, the artist sent only a perfect circle painted with a free movement of his arm from the elbow. His monumental work brought a new strength and force to art. He created architectural and landscape backgrounds for his massive, sensitively drawn figures, while his subdued colors and masterly compositions contribute to the expressive power of each scene. The quality of his genius is best seen in the series of 38 frescoes in the Scrovegni (Arena) Chapel in Padua, depicting the life of Christ and other Biblical subjects (1304–1306); the extent of his actual contribution to the earlier frescoes in the Church of St. Francis at Assisi is debatable. He also frescoed the Bardi and Peruzzi chapels of the Church of Santa Croce in Florence and is said to have done frescoes and mosaics for the old St. Peter's in Rome. In 1334, Giotto became the official architect of Florence. He is generally considered to have begun the construction of the separate *campanile,* or bell tower, of the Florence cathedral; it is likely that he also carved some of its reliefs with Andrea Pisano.

Giotto's tower. The campanile of the Duomo (the church of Santa Maria del Fiore) in Florence. It was designed by GIOTTO, and the construction begun in 1334. However, much of the final form of the building may be due to Giotto's successor Andrea Pisano. The Duomo, begun in 1298, was not completely finished until 1888.

Giovannitti, Arturo (1884–1959). Italian-born American poet. A crusader for social and economic change, he was jailed during the Lawrence, Mass., textile strikes, an experience which caused him to write *The Walker* and several other prose poems. In 1917, he wrote *When the Cock Crows,* a poem inspired by the lynching of the labor leader Frank Little. His principal collection of verse is *Arrows in the Gale* (1914).

Giovio, Paolo (1483–1552). Italian Renaissance historian. He wrote a history of his own times; a group of lives of famous men; the *Elogia virorum illustrium,* a series of prose and verse inscriptions for the portraits collected in his private museum; and a treatise on IMPRESE, or devices, which was translated by Samuel Daniel in 1585.

Gipsy. See GYPSY.

Giraldi, Giambattista Cinzio or **Cinthio** (1504–1573). Ferrarese scholar, teacher, and author of *novelle*, plays, and literary criticism. His collection of 100 *novelle,* called *Gli Ecatomiti,* was a plot source of Shakespeare's *Othello* and *Measure for Measure.* In his tragedies, Giraldi followed the style of Seneca and was influential in popularizing tragedies filled with horror and bloodshed. He also used happy endings for some of his plays, thus becoming a pioneer of the tragi-comedy. His critical discourses were also important in Renaissance discussion of literary types, and imitation of the ancient writers.

Giraudoux, [Hippolyte] Jean (1882–1944). French dramatist, novelist, essayist, and diplomat. All Giraudoux's works are characterized by a verbal extravagance, an elegance and virtuosity of imagery and style that verges on poetic fantasy; even in a serious play like TIGER AT THE GATES, it masks the horror of the apparent inevitability of tragedy.

The novel *My Friend from Limousin* (*Siegfried et le Limousin;* 1922) was transformed into the play *Siegfried* (1928), portraying the Franco-German conflict. The plot of the novel *Bella* (1926) centers in an antithesis within French politics, that of *Eglantine* (1927) in the social antithesis of a simple-minded country gentleman and a rich Jewish banker. These two and especially the earlier novels *Suzanne and the Pacific* (1921) and *Juliette Visits the Land of Man* (*Juliette au pays des hommes;* 1924) show Giraudoux's predilection for charming young girl characters who represent the candid innocence of divinity, of nature, of ideal Truth. To grow up or to fall in love is to enter the "terrible convent of human beings" with its heartache, disillusion, and even tragedy; his treatment of the UNDINE tale in the play *Ondine* (1939) has the same theme. Giraudoux has a humanistic and compassionate view of the adult world; nevertheless, he delights in escaping from it in extravagant comedies like THE MADWOMAN OF CHAILLOT.

Many of his plays are based on Greek myth or the Bible, but make very free with the legends; for instance, his *Judith* (1931) falls in love with Holofernes before she kills him. Among his other adaptations—besides the above-mentioned *Siegfried* and *Tiger at the Gates*—are *Amphitryon 38* (1929), *Electre* (1937), *The Apollo of Bellac* (1942), and *Sodome et Gomorrhe* (1943).

Other works include *Amica America* (1918), about his stay in the United States; *Adorable Clio* (1920), vignettes from World War I; the plays *The Enchanted* (*Intermezzo;* 1933) and *The Virtuous Island* (*Supplément au voyage de Cook;* 1935); the novels *The School for Indifference* (*L'Ecole des indifférents,* 1911), *Simon the Pathetic* (1918), *The Adventures of Jérôme Bardini* (1930), and *The Chosen One* (*Choix des élues;* 1938).

Girl of the Golden West, The (1905). A play by David BELASCO. The heroine is a courageous saloonkeeper in a Western mining camp who falls in love with an outlaw. The play was the basis of Puccini's *La Fanciulla del West* (1910), the first grand opera written on an American theme.

Girondists, or the Gironde, or the Girondins. A middle class political party during the FRENCH REVOLUTION (1791–1793). They were so named because many of their members were from the department of the Gironde. Their point of view was republican: they advocated overthrow of the monarchy, an agressive foreign policy, and were anticlerical. Although the most powerful party for a time, they were overthrown in June, 1793, because of their attempt to soften the ever-rising spirit of fanaticism among the more extreme revolutionists. Among their ranks were Jacques Pierre BRISSOT (their leader, and after whom they were sometimes called *Brissotins*), CONDORCET, and the adherents of Madame ROLAND.

Gironella, José María (1917–   ). Spanish novelist. His works, which have been very popular in translation, include *Un hombre* (*The Soil was Shallow,* 1946), his initial success; the well-known *Los cipreses creen en Dios* (*The Cypresses Believe in God,* 1951), a tale of events leading up to the Spanish Civil War; and its sequel, *Un millón de muertos* (1961).

Girty, Simon (1741–1818). American soldier, known as "the Great Renegade." He deserted from the Revolutionary Army (1778) and later led British and Indian raiding expeditions. Although he is said to have saved the life of Simon Kenton, Girty was widely known for his brutality. He is the title character of Elinor Wylie's poem, *Simon Girty* and also appears in Stephen Vincent Benét's *The Devil and Daniel Webster* (1937).

Gish, Lillian (?1896–   ). American stage and screen actress. After her first success in *Birth of a Nation,* she played in many other films, including *The Scarlet Letter, Broken Blossoms, Orphans of the Storm,* etc. She appeared on stage in *Camille, Uncle Vanya, The Star Wagon,* and others. Her sister Dorothy is also well-known as an actress.

Gissing, George [Robert] (1857–1903). English novelist, critic, and essayist. Gissing's brilliant academic career was cut short when, attempting to reform and support a young prostitute, he was caught stealing money from classmates. He was expelled and imprisoned; soon after he spent a year of privation and wandering in the U.S., then returned to England. He married the prostitute, entering a life of misery and poverty, and when she died, he remarried, again unhappily.

Gissing's love of the classics, the hardships of his life, and his mixed idealism and pessimism, are reflected in his best-known novels *The Nether World* (1881) and NEW GRUB STREET. These books are characterized by their realism and psychological acuteness, and by the subtlety, grace, and subdued passion of their style. Other aspects of his temperament and talent are exhibited in THE PRIVATE PAPERS OF HENRY RYECROFT and his fine *Charles Dickens: A Critical Study* (1898). Other novels include *Demos* (1886), *Thyrza* (1887), *A Life's Morning* (1888), *Born in Exile* (1892), *The Odd Women* (1893), and *In the Year of Jubilee* (1894).

Giusti, Giuseppe (1809–1850). Italian satiric poet. His clever satires held up to ridicule the so-called "humaneness" of the guillotine (*La Guigliotina a Vapore,* 1833), foreign domination of Italy (*Lo Stivale,* 1836), and many other aspects, both important and trivial, of 19th-century society.

Giustinian, Leonardo (1388–1446). Venetian scholar and poet. Giustinian wrote and composed the music for popular songs in Venetian dialect. He excelled in *strambotto, canzonetta,* and *laude,* so much so that variations and adaptations of such of his poems as *Se li arbori sapessen favellare* (If the trees could speak) are still heard in the Italy of today.

Gjellerup, Karl (1859–1919). Danish writer long resident in Germany. His interest in German art and music found expression in *Richard Wagner i hans Hovedvaerk* (*Richard Wagner in his Chief Work, the Ring of Nibelung,* 1890). His novels include *En Idealist* (1878), *Germanernes Laerling* (1882), and *Der Pilger Kamanoto* (*The Pilgrim Kamanoto,* 1906), a novel set in India and the only novel by Gjellerup to be translated into English. In 1917 he shared the Nobel prize for literature with another Danish writer, Henrik Pontoppidan.

Gladkov, Feodor Vasilyevich (1883–1958). Russian novelist. He is famous as the author of CEMENT, one of the first proletarian novels of Soviet literature, which had an immense success with Soviet critics. In 1932–1938, Gladkov published *Energy* (*Energiya*), describing the building of Dneprostroi dam during the Five-Year Plan. One of his best works is his autobiography, *Story of My Childhood* (*Povest' o detstve;* 1949), reminiscent of Gorki's autobiography in style and quality.

Gladstone, William Ewart. Called the **Grand Old Man** (1809–1898). English statesman, financier, and orator. His high abilities were early recognized by his party (Whig), and during the short-lived administration of Sir Robert Peel (December 1834–April 1835), he was made first junior lord of the treasury and then undersecretary for the colonies. During his brilliant career he was chancellor of the exchequer (1852–1855), leader of the Liberal Party (1867), and Prime Minister four times (1868–1874; 1880–1885; 1886; 1892–1894). Milestones in his career are the disestablishment of the Irish Church, two Home Rule bills for Ireland (1886, 1893), both defeated, and the denunciation of Turkish atrocities in Bulgaria. The most prominent man in politics of his time, he was rivaled only by his Tory opponent, Benjamin Disraeli. In spite of his full career, he found time for considerable writing. His works include *The State in its Relations to the Church* (1838), *Letters on the State Persecutions of the Neapolitan Government* (1851), *Studies on Homer and the Homeric Age* (1858), *Juventus Mundi* (1869), and pamphlets on *Bulgarian Horrors* (1876, 1877), *Homeric Synchronism* (1876), and *Gleanings of Past Years* (1879).

Glanvill, Joseph (1636–1680). English clergyman and philosopher, one of the CAMBRIDGE PLATONISTS. Although he was a scientist and a skeptic who supported the Royal Society in his *Plus Ultra, or the Progress and Advancement of Knowledge since the time of Aristotle* (1668), in other works he defended the pre-existence of souls and belief in witchcraft. His best-known book *The Vanity of Dogmatizing* (1661) contains the theme of Matthew Arnold's poem *The Scholar Gypsy* (1853).

Glasgow, Ellen [Anderson Gholson] (1874–1945). American novelist. One of her country's greatest regional writers, Ellen Glasgow confined her work to the study of the South as typified in Virginia, her native state. In all, she wrote 19 novels, and Henry Seidel Canby has said, "she was a major historian of our times, who, almost singlehandedly, rescued Southern fiction from the glamorous sentimentality of the Lost Cause."

Although her early books, such as *The Battle-Ground* (1902), were in the tradition of the Southern romance, she was already in revolt against what she called the "sanctified fallacies" of the South, and the growth of her art may be measured by contrasting these with VIRGINIA, a characteristic study of a woman in a particular time and place. The years following World War I saw the appearance of what was probably her most distinguished work, the novels BARREN GROUND, THE ROMANTIC COMEDIANS, *They Stooped to Folly* (1929), and *The Sheltered Life* (1932). As she grew older, she became more conservative, rejecting the work of such Southerners as William Faulkner and regretting the loss of manners that the modern world had brought.

Her later works include *Vein of Iron* (1935) and *In This Our Time* (1941), which was awarded a Pulitzer Prize. *A Certain Measure: An Interpretation of Prose Fiction* (1943) is a valuable statement on her art as well as a helpful account of the grand design of her novels. *The Woman Within* (1954), her autobiography, and *Letters of Ellen Glasgow* (1958) were published after her death.

Glaspell, Susan (1882–1948). American novelist and dramatist. Miss Glaspell early wrote short stories and, in 1909, a novel, *The Glory of the Conquered*. With her husband, George Cram COOK, she organized the PROVINCETOWN PLAYERS, an experimental theater designed to combat the commercialism of Broadway. For its opening, she and her husband wrote the satiric one-act play, *Suppressed Desires* (1915). Miss Glaspell wrote several other novels: *Fidelity* (1915), *Brooks Evans* (1928), and *Judd Rankin's Daughter* (1945). Among her plays are *The People* (1917), *Bernice* (1919), *The Verge* (1921), and *Alison's House* (1930), which was based on the life of Emily Dickinson and awarded a Pulitzer Prize. *The Road to the Temple* (1926) is a biography of her husband.

Glasperlenspiel, Das. See MAGISTER LUDI.

Glass, Montague [Marsden] (1877–1934). English-born American writer of fiction. He is best known as the creator of the titular heroes of POTASH AND PERLMUTTER (1910).

Glass Menagerie, The (1944). A play by Tennessee WILLIAMS. With Tom Wingfield narrating both the introduction and the conclusion, the play is set in memory. It takes place shortly before Tom left home for the merchant marines and focuses on his mother, who constantly imagines scenes of the "gentlemen callers" of her girlhood, and on his sister Laura, a partial cripple who has withdrawn from the real world into the private universe of her glass animals. The mother insists that Tom bring home a gentleman caller for Laura, and when he does the friend breaks the horn on Laura's glass unicorn, making the animal less of a freak and allowing her momentarily to break out of the world of her menagerie.

However, after kissing Laura, the friend admits that he is already engaged; Laura's emergence from her fragile world is left in doubt.

Glastonbury. An ancient town in Somerset, England, dating from Roman times. It is traditionally associated with Arthurian legend and with the Holy Grail. It is at Glastonbury that JOSEPH OF ARIMATHEA is said to have established the first Christian Church in England and, earlier, to have planted his staff, which took root and became the Glastonbury thorn that burst into blossom every Christmas eve. Local legend has it that Arthur and Guinevere are buried there, and it has been recorded of the historical Arthur that he was buried there. Most of the Arthurian romances, however, place Arthur in AVALON after his death.

Glaucus (Glaukos). Once a fisherman of Boeotia. He became a sea-god endowed with the gift of prophecy and instructed Apollo in the art of soothsaying.

Glaucus (Glaukos). In ancient Greek myth, a son of Sisyphus and father of Bellerophon. Because he would not allow his horses to breed, Aphrodite maddened them until they killed him.

Glaucus (Glaukos). A mythical leader of Lycian troops in the Trojan War. For the story of his meeting with Diomedes, see DIOMEDEAN SWAP.

Glaucus (Glaukos). In ancient Greek myth, a son of Minos. He drowned in a vat of honey. Minos ordered the seer Polyidos, once he had found the child, to revive him. The CURETES told Polyidos to find the most pat simile for a cow of three colors. When Polyidos mentioned the fruit of the dog rose, he saw a snake and killed it. The snake's mate restored the first snake with a herb, which Polyidos promptly used on Glaucus with success. Later, however, Polyidos was angry with Minos for confining him to the palace. He had taught the art of divination to Glaucus, but on finally leaving Crete, he made Glaucus spit into his mouth and the boy forget everything he had learned.

Gleizes, Albert. See ABBAYE GROUP, THE.

Glencoe or Glen Coe. The valley of the river Coe in western Scotland. It was the scene of the massacre of Glencoe (1692), in which governmental troops led by a member of the clan of Campbell treacherously murdered 38 members of the Macdonald clan because of their Jacobite sympathies.

Glinka, Mikhail Ivanovich (1804–1857). The first important Russian composer. He wrote *Ivan Susanin*, or *A Life for the Czar*, the first Russian national opera, in 1836; *Russlan and Ludmilla*, after a poem by Pushkin, in 1842; and overtures, symphonies, and orchestral suites.

Globe, The. Elizabethan playhouse built in 1599 by Richard and Cuthbert Burbage on the Bankside south of the Thames. It became the permanent home of the Lord Chamberlain's (later King's) Men, Shakespeare's company, and it was here that his greatest plays, including *Hamlet, Macbeth, King Lear,* and *Othello,* were first presented. The Globe was unquestionably the most popular theater in London and its design—about which there is considerable controversy among scholars—became the model for the numerous theaters that sprang up in the early years of the 17th century. In June, 1613, the Globe was consumed by fire during a presentation of Shakespeare's *Henry VIII*. The theater was rebuilt in 1614 and remained standing until 1644, when it was pulled down to make room for residences.

Gloriana. The Queen of Faeryland in Spenser's Faerie Queene.

Glorious Revolution. The name given by English Whigs to the movement (1688–1689), in which James II was driven from the throne and the crown was offered to William of Orange and his wife Mary, eldest daughter of James. Carried out by those who opposed James's attempts to impose Catholicism on the country and to restore absolute monarchy, the revolution established the supremacy of Parliament. Although there was little opposition to the revolution in England, James had many supporters in Scotland and Ireland. James's Scottish adherents won the battle of Killiecrankie (1689), but James himself was defeated at the battle of the Boyne in Ireland (1689). See Right, Declaration of.

gloss. (1) An explanation or interpretation, the rendering of an obscure expression. The term is especially used to denote a marginal or interlinear note, of the kind abounding in medieval literature where Latin, Greek, or Hebrew words had to be rendered in the vernacular Teutonic, Romanic, and Celtic tongues. These special glosses are philologically very important and represent the oldest rudiments of bilingual dictionaries.
(2) A running commentary amplifying and explaining a difficult text.
(3) In prosody, a poetic composition which is a variation on a theme. A "texte" is chosen from some poetic work, and succeeding stanzas use a line or a couplet of the texte as the last line or lines until it has all appeared in the composition.

Gloucester, earl of. In Shakespeare's King Lear, the faithful old lord who shelters Lear from the storm. His aid to Lear is betrayed by his bastard son, Edmund, and his eyes are plucked out by Lear's daughter Regan and her husband, Cornwall. Evicted from his castle and bent on suicide, Gloucester is saved by his loyal son, Edgar, whom he had previously disinherited.

Glover, Richard (1712–1785). English poet, author of the ballad Admiral Hosier's Ghost, which was published in Percy's Reliques of Ancient English Poetry. His chief work *Leonidas* (1737; enlarged in 1770 to 12 books), probably the most discussed blank-verse epic poem of the half-century, was translated into French and German and owed its success in part to the use Robert Walpole's opponents could make of it, for it was chiefly written in support of the Opposition Party.

Glubdubdrib. The island of sorcerers and magicians off the coast of Balnibarbi in Jonathan Swift's Gulliver's Travels, where Gulliver is shown Homer, Aristotle, Vergil, and other famous men of antiquity.

Gluck, Christoph Willibald [von] (1714–1787). Austrian opera composer. In *Orfeo* (1762; see Orpheus) he created a new style of Italian opera. Conventional virtuosity was abandoned in favor of dramatic truth and a moving simplicity of expression, and the use of chorus and ballet was adopted from French opera. His adoption of this style was largely due to his librettist, Raniero de' Calzabigi. Later "reform" operas were *Alceste* (1767), *Paride e Elena*

(1770), *Iphigénie en Aulide* (1774), *Armide* (1777) and *Iphigénie en Tauride* (1779).

Gluckists. The supporters of Gluck in a foolish rivalry in Paris (1774–1780) between the admirers of that composer, an Austrian, and those of Piccini, an Italian. Marie Antoinette was a Gluckist, and consequently Young France favored the rival claimant. In the streets, coffee-houses, private houses, and even schools, the merits of Gluck and Piccini were canvassed, and all Paris was ranged on one side or the other.

Glumdalclitch. In Jonathan Swift's Gulliver's Travels, a girl, nine years old, 40 feet high, who is Gulliver's nurse in Brobdingnag.

Glyn, Elinor (1864–1943). English novelist. Replete with tiger skins and violent passion, her best-selling romantic novels were once considered daring and slightly scandalous. *Three Weeks* (1907), *It* (1927), and *Romantic Adventure: The Autobiography of Elinor Glyn* (1936) are among her best known works.

gnome. According to the Rosicrucian system, a misshapen elemental spirit. It dwells in the bowels of the earth and guards the mines and quarries. The word seems to have been first used (perhaps invented) by Paracelsus, and to be derived from Gr. *ge-nomos*, earth-dweller.

Gnomic poets. Greek poets, such as Theognis of Megara and Solon, the lawgiver, whose writings are gnomic or aphoristic, containing maxims.

Gnostics (Gr. *gnosticos*). *Knowers*, as opposed to *believers;* various sects in the first six centuries of the Christian era. They tried to accommodate Christianity to the speculations of Pythagoras, Plato, and other Greek and Oriental philosophers. They taught that knowledge, rather than mere faith, is the true key of salvation. In the Gnostic creed Christ is esteemed merely as an eon or divine attribute personified, like Mind, Truth, Logos, Church, etc., the whole of which eons made up this divine pleroma or fullness. St. Paul, in several of his epistles, speaks of this "fullness [pleroma] of God."

Go and Catch a Falling Star (1633). The first line of a famous lyric by John Donne, often entitled *Song*. A series of impossible feats are declared to be less difficult than the task of finding a woman "true and faire."

goat. An animal associated from very early times with the idea of sin (see Scapegoat) and with devil lore. It is an old superstition in England and Scotland that a goat is never seen during the whole of a twenty-four-hour period, for once a day it pays a visit to the devil to have its beard combed. Formerly the devil himself was frequently depicted as a goat; and the animal also typifies lust and lechery.

Goat Song (Bocksgesang; 1921). A play by Franz Werfel. It deals with the elemental frenzy of a group of peasants in revolt who worship a monster, half man and half ram, that has appeared out of the woods. The revolt is suppressed, and the monster killed; but one of the peasant girls bears its child, which symbolizes the continued existence of a chaotic potential in man.

Gobbo, Old. In Shakespeare's Merchant of Venice, the "sand-blind, high-gravel blind" father of Launcelot Gobbo. He encounters his son after an absence in an amusing scene of reconciliation.

Launcelot Gobbo. A clownish servant, the son of Old Gobbo. He leaves Shylock's service for shorter hours, more pay, and more sleep in the service of Bassanio.

Go-Between, The (1953). A novel by L. P. HARTLEY. A tragic love triangle is observed by an uncomprehending 13-year-old schoolboy, who carries messages between the adult characters.

Gobineau, Comte Joseph Arthur de (1816–1882). French diplomat, writer, and Orientalist. His best-known work, the sociological treatise *Essai sur l'in-égalité des races humaines* (1853–5), advanced an early form of the theory of Aryan, or Teutonic, racial superiority. His skillful Oriental tales, such as *Akrivie Phrangopaulo* (1872), *Mademoiselle Irnois* (1847), or *Adélaïde* (1913), represent Gobineau's best writing. He also published works concerning the Italian Renaissance, and Oriental religions and philosophies.

goblin. A familiar demon. It lived, according to popular belief, in private houses and chinks of trees; in many parts miners attribute those strange noises heard in mines to them. The word is the Fr. *gobelin*, probably a diminutive of the surname *Gobel*, but perhaps connected with Gr. *kobalos*, an impudent rogue, a mischievous sprite, or with the Ger. KOBOLD. As a specimen of forced etymology, it may be mentioned that Johnson, in his *Dictionary*, records that

this word some derive from the *Gibellines*, a faction in Italy; so that *elfe* and *goblin* is *Guelph* and *Gibelline* because the children of either party were terrified by their nurses with the name of the other.

Godden, Rumer. Pen name and maiden name of Mrs. **Rumer Haynes Dixon** (1907–). English novelist. Her novels *Black Narcissus* (1939) and *The River* (1946) are both set in India. *Take Three Tenses* (1945) is an experiment in the handling of time. Other successes are *Kingfishers Catch Fire* (1953), *An Episode of Sparrows* (1955), *The Greengage Summer* (1958), and *The Battle of the Villa Fiorita* (1963). She also wrote books for children, including *Miss Happiness and Miss Flower* (1961).

Godey, Louis Antoine. See GODEY'S LADY'S BOOK.

Godey's Lady's Book. An American magazine of the mid-19th century. Famous for its hand-colored fashion plates and its art reproductions, *Godey's Lady's Book* found its way into 40,000 homes. Louis A. Godey (1804–1878) founded the magazine in 1830, and was its sole editor for six years; he then bought Sarah Josepha Hale's *Ladies' Magazine* and shared his editorship with her. Mrs. Hale (1788–1879), the author of *Mary Had a Little Lamb* (1830), was an advocate of women's rights and leader of the movement for a national Thanksgiving Day. Mrs. Hale retired in 1877, Godey died the following year, and the magazine continued publication only until 1898.

Godferneaux, A. See Tristan BERNARD.

Godfrey, Thomas (1736–1763). American poet and dramatist. The son of a Philadelphia glazier, Godfrey was apprenticed to a local watchmaker at 13. Wholly self-educated, he wrote songs and Chaucerian adaptations which attracted the attention of William Smith and the young poets at the College of Philadelphia. He died while on military duty in North Carolina. Two years later his friend Nathaniel Evans collected and published his poems as *Juvenile Poems*

on Various Subjects. The volume included Godfrey's PRINCE OF PARTHIA, often called the first American play.

Godfrey de Bouillon. See GOFFREDO.

Godiva, Lady (11th century). English benefactress, wife of Earl Leofric of Mercia. According to tradition, she asked her husband to relieve Coventry of certain burdensome taxes (c. 1040), but he jested that he would do so only if she would ride naked through the marketplace at midday. She did, covered only by her long hair, and Leofric kept his promise. In some versions, she had previously requested all the townspeople to stay indoors at the appointed hour, and not to look at her; one tailor, since known as "Peeping Tom of Coventry," looked through his window, for which a miracle struck him blind. The legend appears as one of Walter Savage Landor's *Imaginary Conversations* (1829), Alfred Tennyson's poem *Godiva, A Tale of Coventry* (1842), and a number of other literary works.

Godkin, Edwin Lawrence (1831–1902). Irish-born American journalist, editor, and author. In 1865 Godkin helped to found *The Nation* and became its first editor. When the magazine became the weekly edition of the New York *Post* (1881), Godkin became associate editor of that newspaper, and later, editor-in-chief (1883–1900). Among his achievements was the establishment of higher standards for book reviewing. His published works include *Reflections and Comments, 1865–95* (1895), and *The History of Hungary and the Magyars* (1853).

Gododin (c. 600). A poem by the Welsh bard Canu Aneurin (fl., c. 600). It is important in connection with ARTHURIAN LEGEND because it contains the first known reference to an Arthur. The poem is about the battle of Cattraeth (603) in which the tribe of the Gododin was defeated by the Saxons.

Go Down, Moses (1942). A collection of short stories by William FAULKNER. Set in Faulkner's mythical YOKNAPATAWPHA COUNTY, the stories are unified by a common theme, the ritual of the hunt—whether it be a hunt for Old Ben in *The Bear*, for the lovesick Negro in *Was*, for buried gold in *The Fire and the Hearth*, or for the Negro killer in *Pantaloon in Black*. All but the last deal with the members, black and white, of the complicated McCASLIN family, beginning with the second generation in *Was* and ending with the sixth in *Delta Autumn*. There is, in addition, an underlying theme of initiation into manhood and the responsibility of carrying out the social traditions.

The Bear, the most famous of the stories and possibly Faulkner's best, deals mainly with the hunt for Big Ben, an enormous and elusive bear. A shorter but equally important section tells how Isaac McCaslin, through the discovery of his grandfather's Negro offspring, rejects his claim to the McCaslin plantation and the guilt of slavery with which it is stained.

Godoy Alcayaga, Lucila. See Gabriela MISTRAL.

Gods Are Athirst, The (**Les Dieux ont soif;** 1912). An historical novel by Anatole FRANCE. It deals with the French Revolution. See Evariste GAMELIN.

God's Determinations Touching His Elect. A long poem on the Puritan theory of Grace by Edward

TAYLOR, begun around 1685 but unpublished until 1939. It combines elements of the cycle of lyric poems and of the medieval morality play. The imagery is alternately regal and homely, using 11 different verse forms. While not a play, the poem is cast as a drama. The first act traces man's predicament since the Fall; the second shows Christ and Satan battling for man's soul; the third describes the difficulties of the Christian life and the soul's fear of unworthiness; the last shows the soul entering the royal coach of Grace and flying to the feast of love in heaven.

God's Little Acre (1933). A novel by Erskine CALDWELL, dealing with shiftless and amoral Georgia mountaineers. The protagonist has set aside one acre of his land the income of which is to go to the church, but he constantly shifts the acre's location according to his own momentary plans and needs.

gods of classical mythology. The deities of the Greeks and Romans. The Romans identified many of their own deities with those of the Greeks. Since Greek mythology was far richer and more imaginative, the characteristics of the Greek gods tended to dominate those of the Roman deities. However, in later ages, knowledge of Greek mythology was generally gained through Roman sources, and the Roman names of the gods—and even the Latinized spelling of the Greek names—were more widely known. Those Greek and Roman deities who, in later times, were regarded as equivalent are as follows:

GREEK	ROMAN
Zeus	Jupiter
Apollon	Apollo
Ares	Mars
Hermes	Mercury
Poseidon	Neptune
Hephaestus	Vulcan
Hera	Juno
Demeter	Ceres
Artemis	Diana
Athena	Minerva
Aphrodite	Venus
Hestia	Vesta

These were the 12 chief gods, the Olympians of Greek mythology. Other well-known gods were:

Dionysus (Bakchos)	Bacchus
Eros	Cupid
Hades (Plouton)	Pluto
Kronus	Saturn
Persephone	Proserpina

A Greek hero equally popular with the Romans was Heracles, whose Latin name is Hercules.

For the chief deities of Scandinavian mythology, see AESIR and VANIR.

God that Failed, The (1950). A collection of essays edited by R. H. S. CROSSMAN. Written by persons who were attracted to Communism in the 1930's and were later disillusioned, it is an important document on a phase of modern history and thought. The contributors are Arthur Koestler, Ignazio Silone, Richard Wright, André Gide, Louis Fischer, and Stephen Spender.

Godunov, Boris Feodorovich (1552–1605). Russian czar (1598–1605). After the death of Ivan IV (Ivan the Terrible) in 1584, Godunov became regent for the imbecile Feodor I. He was elected to the throne on the death of Feodor. The mysterious death of the czarevich Dmitri (1591) is presumed to have been caused by Boris to clear his path to the throne. As regent he brought new vitality to the Russian nation, regaining land in Sweden and colonizing Siberia. After he became czar he lost the support of the nobility; his prestige was weakened by the appearance of a pretender claiming to be the murdered Dmitri. Boris died shortly after the false Dmitri invaded from Poland, but before the two men had confronted each other.

The poet Pushkin wrote a play called BORIS GODUNOV, which was the basis of Mussorgski's opera of the same name.

Godwin, William (1756–1836). English novelist and political theorist. A leading radical of the 18th century, he believed that it is impossible to be rationally persuaded and not act accordingly, and that therefore, man could live in harmony without law and institutions; he believed in the perfectibility of man. He was influenced by the ideas of ROUSSEAU and the French Encyclopedists, and in turn had a great influence on the English Romantics, particularly Wordsworth, Coleridge, Shelley, and Byron; Shelley's *Preface* to his *Revolt of Islam* is an excellent exposition of Godwin's ideas. Among Godwin's works are AN ENQUIRY CONCERNING THE PRINCIPLES OF POLITICAL JUSTICE, AND ITS INFLUENCE ON GENERAL VIRTUE AND HAPPINESS; *The Adventures of CALEB WILLIAMS, OR THINGS AS THEY ARE*, a novel; *St. Leon* (1799) a supernatural tale; and a *History of the Commonwealth* (1824–1828). Godwin's wife was the feminist Mary WOLLSTONECRAFT, and his daughter, Mary Wollstonecraft SHELLEY, was Shelley's second wife.

Goebbels, Paul Joseph (1897–1945). Minister of propaganda in Nazi Germany. After the collapse of Germany in World War II he poisoned himself and his family.

Goering, Hermann Wilhelm (1893–1946). Minister of aviation in Nazi Germany. Captured by the Allies (1945), he committed suicide before his scheduled execution.

Goes, Hugo van der (1440–1482). Flemish painter. Belonging to the school of the van Eycks, his religious scenes are known for their vigorous personalization of figures, strength of color, and tension in attitudes and spatial conception.

Goethe, Johann Wolfgang von (1749–1832). German poet, playwright, and novelist. Besides writing, he held an important cabinet post at the ducal court in Weimar, directed the theater in that city, and carried on extensive research in science, especially plant biology, on which he wrote *Die Metamorphose der Pflanzen* (*The Metamorphosis of Plants*, 1790), and optics, the subject of his *Zur Farbenlehre* (*On the Theory of Colors*, 1810). In his scientific studies, he always attempted to see the individual phenomenon as part of an organic, developing whole, in opposition to the categorizing science of his time. His poetic works, too, are characterized by this interest in the natural, organic development of things, rather than in any idealistic schemes.

In his early career (1769–1776), Goethe was recognized as a leading figure in the STURM UND DRANG. His well-known poem *Prometheus* (written 1774?), with its insistence that man must believe not in gods but in himself alone, might be seen as a motto for the whole movement. HERDER's strong influence upon his thinking during these years is reflected, for example, in his essay *Von deutscher Baukunst* (*On German Architecture,* 1773). The plays GÖTZ VON BERLICHINGEN, *Clavigo* (1774), *Stella* (1774), and EGMONT belong to this initial phase of his development, as do the earliest Faust sketches and the short novel THE SORROWS OF YOUNG WERTHER.

Goethe's youth was emotionally hectic to the point that he sometimes feared for his reason, but in 1775, after a relaxing trip to Switzerland, he made a decisive break with his past and left his native Frankfurt am Main for the small city of Weimar. It was there that he first assumed serious governmental responsibility; and it was there that he met the woman he was to worship for a decade, Charlotte von STEIN. These years, until 1786, were not very productive for Goethe the writer, but they did contribute much to the characteristic personal balance that appears in his later work.

Goethe spent the years 1786–1788 in Italy, a trip that he later described in his *Italienische Reise* (*Italian Trip,* 1816) and which significantly influenced his growing commitment to a classical view of art. In Italy, he completed his play IPHIGENIA IN TAURIS, which, along with his *Römische Elegien* (*Roman Elegies,* 1788–1790, pub. 1795) and the play TORQUATO TASSO, is customarily taken as the beginning of WEIMAR CLASSICISM.

From this point on, Goethe's life was relatively settled and though he traveled much, his base was always Weimar where he was, in effect, the court's cultural director. But his poetic development was by no means finished. In 1794 began his close and fruitful friendship with SCHILLER, and the ensuing years saw his work expand into new directions, as in the epic poems REINEKE FUCHS and HERMANN UND DOROTHEA, and the novel WILHELM MEISTER. He was also in contact with the founding figures of GERMAN ROMANTICISM, especially the brothers Schlegel, but marked romantic tendencies do not begin to appear in his work until later: for example, in the novel DIE WAHLVERWANDTSCHAFTEN or in *Der West-östliche Divan* (*The West-Eastern Divan,* 1819), a lyric cycle that shares the romantics' interest in the Orient; and in Part II of FAUST.

In a sense, Goethe's development came full circle. At the beginning of his so-called classical period (1788–1805) he had repudiated the emotionalism of his own *Werther;* but as time went on, he tended back toward his earlier attitudes. In his lyric *Trilogie der Leidenschaft* (*Trilogy of Passion,* 1824), one poem, addressed to the character Werther, shows the extent of his regained understanding and sympathy for his own youthful works.

At times, Goethe was grossly insensitive to the merits of such great authors as Hölderlin, Kleist, and Heine, but with himself he was never less than honest; despite the extraordinary length of time spanned by his career, he never stagnated, but was always learning and expanding, seeking to grasp more of what he regarded as the poet's proper domain, the entire world.

Valuable material about his life and personality may be found in his autobiographical DICHTUNG UND WAHRHEIT and in Johann ECKERMANN's *Gespräche*

mit Goethe (*Conversations with Goethe,* 1836). See also DAEMONIC; MÄRCHEN; Johann LAVATER.

Goffe, William (1605?–?1679). English regicide. One of the judges at the trial of Charles I, he fled to America in 1660 with his father-in-law, Edward Whalley (1616?–?1675). Their mysterious wanderings in New England, where they lived for many years, turned them into semilegendary figures. Goffe appears in numerous literary works, notably Scott's *Peveril of the Peak* (1823), Cooper's *The Wept of Wish-Ton-Wish* (1829), and J. K. Paulding's *The Puritan and His Daughter* (1849).

Goffredo (Godfrey de Bouillon). The principal character of Tasso's romantic epic GERUSALEMME LIBERATA. When the poem was first translated by Thomas Carew in 1594, and completed by Edward Fairfax in 1600, its English title was *Godfrey of Bullogne.* Godfrey, duke of Lorraine, was the chosen commander of the allied Crusaders who assaulted Jerusalem in the year 1099. He was also for a time king of Jerusalem. In Tasso's poem, though divinely appointed, he must contend with infidel forces, enchantments, infernal spirits, and division in his ranks; but he finally leads the triumphant Christian army into the city. In worship at the sepulcher of Christ, he hangs his arms in fulfillment of his vow to recover the holy city.

Gog. In the Bible (Ezek. 38:39), the king of Magog, a northern land whose fierce hordes were to invade Israel. Scholars sometimes identify Gog with Gyges, a ruler of Lydia in Asia Minor. In Revelation 20:7, Gog and Magog symbolize the enemies of the kingdom of God, in this case Gog being associated with Magog, a son of Japheth (Gen. 10:2). Elsewhere (I Chron. 5:4), Gog is a descendant of Reuben, eldest of the 12 sons of Jacob.

In British legend, Gog and Magog are the sole survivors of a monstrous brood, the offspring of the 33 infamous daughters of the Emperor Diocletian, who murdered their husbands and, being set adrift in a ship, reached Albion, where they fell in with a number of demons. Their descendants, a race of giants were extirpated by Brute and his companions, with the exception of Gog and Magog, who were brought in chains to London and were made to do duty as porters at the royal palace, on the site of the London Guildhall, where their effigies have been at least since the reign of Henry V. The old giants were destroyed in the Great Fire of 1666, and the present ones, 14 feet high, were carved in 1708 by Richard Saunders.

Gogarty, Oliver St. John (1878–1957). Irish physician and writer of memoirs, essays, and poetry. He was said to be the original of Malachi (Buck) Mulligan in James Joyce's *Ulysses.* His exuberant memoirs are full of reminiscences of his friends, including Joyce, William Butler Yeats, and other Irish writers. Among his books of memoirs are *As I Was Going Down Sackville Street* (1937) and *I Follow St. Patrick* (1938).

Gogol, Nikolai Vasilyevich (1809–1852). Russian novelist, dramatist, and short-story writer. Gogol was born in the Ukraine in the province of Poltava. His father, a member of the petty nobility, had a small estate and was an amateur playwright. Gogol used some lines from his father's plays as epigraphs for his early stories in the collection *Vechera na* *khutore bliz Dikan'ki (Evenings on a Farm Near Dikanka*; 1831–1832). After attending school in the Ukraine, Gogol went to St. Petersburg where he worked as a government clerk and as a teacher, for a short while lecturing in history at St. Petersburg University. His first attempt at literary work, a short poem called *Italia* (1829) was mildly successful. This encouraged Gogol to try a long narrative poem, *Hanz Keuchelgarten* (1829), which turned out to be a disaster. In 1831, Gogol met Pushkin and established a friendship that lasted until the great poet's death. Pushkin was impressed with Gogol's Dikanka tales, which were largely based on Ukrainian folklore with an admixture of Gogol's own fantasy. Even these early tales reveal some features characteristic of Gogol's mature style: a rich mixture of vulgarisms and high-flown rhythmical rhetoric with often sharp juxtapositions between the two levels.

Gogol's next published work was *Arabeski (Arabesques*, 1835), containing a collection of essays and three of his St. Petersburg stories: *Nevski prospekt (Nevski Prospect*), *Portret (The Portrait*), and *Zapiski cumashedshego (Diary of a Madman*). The last story is a remarkable depiction of the mind of the lunatic Poprishchin, a civil servant who comes to believe that he is the king of Spain. In the same year Gogol published a collection of Ukrainian stories entitled *Mirgorod,* including *Starosvetskiye pomeshchiki (Old-world Landowners*), Taras Bulba, *Vii,* and *Povest' o tom, kak possorilsya Ivan Ivanovich s Ivanom Nikiforovichem (The Story of How Ivan Ivanovich Quarreled with Ivan Nikiforovich*). Two more stories, *Kolyaska (The Carriage*) and *Nos (The Nose*), appeared in 1836. *The Nose* is another example of Gogol's predilection for fantasy, a story about a man whose nose abruptly leaves him and gads about town, wearing clothes and riding in a fine carriage. In April, 1836, the first performance of Gogol's satiric comedy The Inspector General was given. The mixed reaction to the play upset the author, who was always extremely sensitive about the public's attitude to his work. He left Russia for Europe, traveled in Italy, Germany, Switzerland, and France, and finally settled down in Rome. Except for short visits to Russia in 1839–1840 and 1841–1842, he was abroad for 12 years. Gogol had taken with him from Russia a few chapters of his novel, Dead Souls, which was completed in Rome and published in 1842 in a four-volume edition of his works. Also in the edition was his famous story The Overcoat and all his previously published work.

After the publication of the first part of *Dead Souls,* which was well received in Russia, Gogol began writing to friends and publishing requests for material to use in the planned second part of the work. Whether he felt his creative power failing or whether he really believed that accounts of daily life from amateur correspondents would be useful is obscure. In ill health and increasingly obsessed with a religious mania, Gogol aimlessly traveled about Europe, took a pilgrimage to Palestine, and eventually returned to Russia in 1848. His reception in his homeland was cool, at least among the radical intelligentsia. Two years before his return, Gogol had published a didactic work entitled *Vybrannye mesta iz perepiski c druz'yami (Selected Passages from Correspondence with Friends,* 1846) in which he upheld the autocratic

Czarist regime and the patriarchal Russian way of life and advised landowners to allow their peasants to read only the Bible lest they pick up dangerous ideas. The book stirred up a storm of protest among the radicals and elicited a violent letter from the critic Vissarion Belinski, which became at least as well known in Russia, though it was banned from print, as the book that caused it to be written. What Belinski and the other radicals failed to notice was that Gogol himself had never explicitly criticized the social system in Russia. His critics merely assumed that previously such was the implication of his writings.

From 1848 until his death (1852), Gogol fell more and more into melancholia, aggravated by his fears of spiritual damnation. Shortly after burning some of his manuscripts, including the second part of *Dead Souls,* he took to his bed and died.

Gogol is recognized as one of the greatest writers in Russian literature from the point of view of the imaginativeness and stylistic richness of his work. No Russian author has handled the wealth of the Russian language so well. Gogol's choice of everyday life as the basis of much of his work had a profound effect on future Russian literature, although the degree and the purposes of his realism as interpreted by Belinski and later radical critics are doubtful. Whether he intended it or not, Gogol's work was held up as a model for later Russian writers, who turned their attention to a sympathetic observation and realistic description of the lower levels of Russian society.

Despite his later evidences of conservatism and religiosity, Gogol is viewed by Soviet critics, as he was early in his career by Belinski, as a realist who used his work to point out social evils with the aim of bringing about reform. His development in the last years of his life, including the *Selected Passages,* is regarded officially as the result of mental aberration.

Gokak, V. K. (1909–   ). Indian poet, playwright, essayist, and critic writing in Kannada. Currently professor of English at the Karnatak University, he was president of the Karnatak Poets' Conference (1934). His publications include *The Poetic Approach to Language* (1948) in English; *Pavana,* poems, and *Sahityadalli Pragati,* criticism, in Kannada.

Gold, Michael. Pen name of **Irving Granich** (1894–   ). American writer. One of the major figures in American "proletarian literature," Gold was the first to define the term clearly in his article *Towards Proletarian Art* published in *Liberator* magazine (Feb. 1921), while his later novel *Jews Without Money* (1930) became a model for aspiring proletarian novelists.

Goldberg, Isaac (1887–1938). American writer. He is known for his interest in language, which resulted in *The Wonder of Words* (1938), and for his books introducing Latin-American literature to the American public: *Studies in Spanish-American Literature* (1920) and *Brazilian Literature* (1922). Other works include a book on William S. Gilbert and the Gilbert and Sullivan operettas (1913), *Tin Pan Alley* (1930), and biographies of H. L. Mencken (1925) and Havelock Ellis (1926).

Gold Bug, The (1843). A story by Edgar Allan Poe. William Le Grand accidentally discovers a cipher giving the location of buried treasure. Unraveling its instructions, he drops the beetle, or gold bug, through one eye of a skull, and unearths a fortune. The story takes place on Sullivan's Island off South Carolina.

Golden Apple. See APPLE OF DISCORD; ATALANTA.

Golden Ass, The (2nd century). The common, alternative title of the *Metamorphoses*, a satirical romance, by Lucius APULEIUS. It is narrated in the first person by Lucius, a licentious young man with insatiable curiosity about people and things. While visiting a sorceress in Thessaly, he induces a maid to steal a magic potion which will turn him into an owl. He takes the wrong potion and turns into an ass instead. In this disappointing form he wanders throughout Greece, passing through the hands of a series of owners who mistreat him. Interspersed throughout the narrative are lively stories of intrigue, witchcraft, and love, most famous of which is Cupid and PSYCHE. Lucius is finally restored to his human form with the help of the goddess Isis.

Ever since its first appearance, *The Golden Ass* has enjoyed an unusually sustained popularity. The book's influence has been considerable and can best be seen in such writers as Boccaccio, Cervantes, and Rabelais. Apuleius borrowed his stories and plots from Greek predecessors; he may have based his book on the same work by Lucius of Patrae that inspired LUCIAN's novel *Lucius, or the Ass*.

Golden Bough, The (1890–1915). A comprehensive work on comparative religion and mythology by Sir James George FRAZER. The general title of the 12 volumes refers to the branch broken from a sacred tree by Aeneas before his descent into the underworld. Although many of his conclusions have been discredited, Frazer's book was a seminal work in its field, and most subsequent scholarship recognizes a great debt to it. In its single-volume condensation, it has become a popular classic. *The Golden Bough* had a significant influence on the literary world, and played an important part in the conception of *Finnegans Wake* by James Joyce and of *The Waste Land* by T. S. Eliot. See KING OF THE WOOD.

Golden Bowl, The (1904). A novel by Henry JAMES. The heroine, Maggie Verver, the daughter of an American millionaire, marries the impoverished Prince Amerigo. Her old school friend, Charlotte Stant, who has had an affair with the prince, later marries Adam Verver, Maggie's father, and continues her relationship with her lover. The second part of the novel deals with Maggie's discovery of the liaison and with her reaction to it. This is generally considered to be James's most difficult work.

golden calf. An image of worship made of gold earrings and other jewelry by the Hebrews under the direction of Aaron, while Moses was receiving the Ten Commandments (Ex. 20) on Mount Sinai. When Moses returned with the two stone tablets on which were written the laws and found his people adoring the image (a form of BAAL-worship), he destroyed the tablets and threw the powdered dust of the calf into the spring of Marah. After he had led his people in repentance, he returned to the mount and received two new tablets.

Golden Dog, The (unauthorized, 1877; auth. ed., 1896). A novel by William Kirby (1817–1906), English-born Canadian novelist and editor. This was the first Canadian novel to achieve widespread popularity. The story, set in old French Quebec, served as a model for numerous Canadian historical romances in the 19th century and later.

Golden Fleece, the. In Greek mythology, the fleece of pure gold, taken from a miraculous winged ram. Athamas, a son of Aeolus and ruler of Boeotia, married the phantom Nephele (see IXION), who bore him a son Phrixus and a daughter Helle. He also became the father of Learchus and Melicertes by Cadmus' daughter INO. Jealous of Nephele, Ino persuaded the Boeotian women secretly to parch the seed wheat, then caused a false oracle to be brought from Delphi: only the sacrifice of Phrixus and Helle would save the crops. At the last moment, a winged, golden ram was sent by Hermes, and Phrixus and Helle escaped on its back. As it flew, Helle fell and was drowned in the Hellespont, the straits thereafter named in her honor. Phrixus reached Colchis at the eastern end of the Black Sea; he gave the ram to King Aeetes, who nailed its fleece to an oak in the grove of Ares, and married Aeetes' daughter Chalciope, who bore him four sons. The fleece was later seized by the ARGONAUTS and returned to Iolcus.

Golden Horde. A body of Mongol Tartars of the 13th century. They overran eastern Europe, and were so called from the magnificent tent of Batu Khan, grandson of Genghis Khan. The kingdom of the Golden Horde at its height reached from the Dniester to central Asia. It was overthrown by Ivan III of Russia (1480), and broke up into a number of smaller khanates with that of Astrakhan representing the Golden Horde.

Golden Legend, The (1483). A compilation of lives of the saints and other ecclesiastical commentaries, one of the most popular books published by William Caxton. It drew on the material in the Latin *Legenda Aurea* of Jacobus de Voragine (1230–1298), but was based mostly on French and English versions.

Golden Legend, The (1872). A poem by Henry Wadsworth LONGFELLOW. It is the second part of a trilogy called *Christus: A Mystery*. The theme is a variant of the Faust legend, reflecting the attitudes of the Middle Ages toward Christian truths.

Golden Rose, the. The annual custom whereby the Pope bestowed upon a worthy individual or place an exquisite rose made of gold. In 1494, Pope Alexander VI presented the rose to King Charles VIII of France in hope of dissuading him from invading Italy—to no avail.

Golden Treasury of the Best Songs and Lyrical Poems in the English Language, The (1861; second series 1897). An anthology of poetry from the 16th to mid-19th century by F. T. PALGRAVE. A monument to late romantic taste (particularly in its predilection for the short lyric), it was one of the most influential of English anthologies.

Golding, Louis (1895–1958). English novelist. Among his novels of Jewish life in a large industrial town are *Magnolia Street* (1932) and *Five Silver Daughters* (1934).

Golding, William (1911–   ). English novelist. He is the author of *The Inheritors* (1955), LORD OF THE FLIES, PINCHER MARTIN (U.S. title *The Two Deaths of Christopher Martin*), *Free Fall* (1959), *The Inheritors* (1962), and *The Spire* (1964). Golding calls his books fables and uses them to express his rather grim view of the world—the view that most men are basically evil and life is a tooth-and-claw

Ðre beginneth the hystorye of Noe the first conday in Seragesme //

NEW YORK PUBLIC LIBRARY

Noah in the ark. From Caxton's
Golden Legend (1484).

affair. His World War II experiences in the navy and his years spent teaching small boys have helped to shape his philosophical attitudes. Master of strange situations and ironic surprise twists, Golding also enriches his books with symbols and literary, mythological, and Christian allusions.

Goldoni, Carlo (1707–1793). Italian dramatist. Born in Venice, he wrote some 150 comedies through which he became the creator of the modern Italian comedy in the style of Molière, superseding the traditional COMMEDIA DELL'ARTE, then vigorously defended by Carlo Gozzi. His comedies, written in Italian and in the Venetian dialect, depict the foibles of the middle and lower classes of Venice and offer a true-to-life portrayal of character and action absent in the older *commedia* technique of improvisation carried out by stock characters. His finest comedies appeared in the years 1748–1760. Among them are *La Bottega del Caffè, La Locandiera, La Vedova Scaltra, La Famiglia dell'Antiquario,* and the dialect plays *I Rusteghi* and *Le Barufe Chiozote*. In his *Mémoires* (trans., 1877), which like his last plays were written in French, he described his verbal warfare with the traditionalists of the theater and stated: "The secret of the art of a writer of comedies is to cling to nature and never to leave her." A writer for the Italian theater in Paris and pensioned by Louis XIV, he was impoverished as a result of the French Revolution.

Goldsmith, Oliver (1731–1774). Irish-born Eng-lish poet, playwright, and novelist. Educated in Ireland, he left for Edinburgh in 1752, and never returned. He studied medicine for a while at Leyden in 1754, then made the Grand Tour of the Continent, returning to England in 1756, where he became engaged in literary hackwork, and, for a time, was employed by Samuel Richardson, the printer and novelist. His literary fame began with THE TRAVELLER, a didactic poem surveying national modes of happiness, which was praised by Samuel Johnson and other members of the LITERARY CLUB. His major works include *An Enquiry into the Present State of Polite Learning in Europe* (1759), a prose essay attributing the decline of polite learning to the inferiority of poets; *The Bee* (1759), a periodical containing perhaps his most famous tales—REVERIE AT THE BOAR'S HEAD TAVERN and ASEM, AN EASTERN TALE; THE CITIZEN OF THE WORLD, a satiric epistolary novel in imitation of Montesquieu's *Lettres Persanes* (1721); THE VICAR OF WAKEFIELD, a novel; THE DESERTED VILLAGE, a poem; and THE GOOD NATUR'D MAN and SHE STOOPS TO CONQUER, comedies. A beloved member of Dr. Johnson's circle, he was noted for his comic verbal *faux-pas,* though it seems that Goldsmith buffooned purposely on occasion without his friends ever suspecting it. At the end of his life he retorted to their raillery in a series of brilliant caricatures, *The Retaliation* (1774). See GOLDY; GOODY TWO-SHOES; HERMIT, THE.

Goldy. The pet name given to Oliver GOLDSMITH by Dr. Samuel Johnson. David Garrick said of Goldsmith, "He wrote like an angel and talked like poor Poll."

Golgotha. See CALVARY.

Goliardic verse. The light Latin verse of 12th- and 13th-century Germany, France, and England by university students and wandering clerics, minstrels, and *jongleurs*. This poetry was of two types: scurrilous satire defying all kinds of civil and ecclesiastical authority, including the Pope; and gay, nonchalant, ribald celebrations of nature, women, and wine, including some drinking songs still popular. The Goliards, as the authors were called, often referred to a mythical Golias as their leader and patron, ironically dignifying him with the titles of "Bishop" (*episcopus*) and "Archpoet" (*archipoeta*). He is sometimes identified with Primus, a 12th-century scholar from Orleans. The *Confession of Golias,* as well as much other Goliardic verse, was once attributed to Walter MAP. A large collection of this poetry was published in Germany as *Carmina Burana* (1847), some of which J. A. Symonds translated in his *Wine, Women, and Song* (1884). Carl Orff set *Carmina Burana* to music in 1935.

Goliath. See DAVID.

Golovlyov Family, The (Gospoda Golovlyovy; 1872–1876). A novel, written under the pen name N. Shchedrin by Mikhail SALTYKOV. It depicts the dissolution of a Russian provincial landowning family. Arina Petrovna, the rapacious mother of the family, dominates her husband and alienates her four children, caring only for adding to her estates. The land eventually passes to her son Porfiri, who is nicknamed IUDUSHKA (Little Judas). He proves to be just as grasping and unloving as his mother had been, driving away his own children. The gloomy chronicle comes to an end with the unctuous Iudushka sinking into ruin and death through drink. The novel is one of the classics of 19th-century Russian realism.

Golyadkin, Yakov Petrovich. The hallucination-ridden hero of Feodor Dostoevski's short novel, THE DOUBLE.

Gomberville, Marin le Roy, Sieur de (1600–1674). French novelist. An original member of the ACADÉMIE FRANÇAISE, Gomberville wrote novels of heroic adventure, usually set in exotic lands and historical periods with which the author had little familiarity. *La Caritie* (1621), *Polexandre* (1629–1637), and *La Cythérée* (1640) lushly evoked an imagined Central America and North Africa. *Polexandre,* the author's most important work, was the five-volume tale of a beautiful island queen and the travels of her knight Polexandre around the world; it included the first description of seascape and tempest to be found in French literature. Upon his conversion to Jansenism in 1651, Gomberville published *La Jeune Alcidiane,* a Christian sequel to *Polexandre,* with the intention of counteracting what he supposed to be the nefarious effect of the earlier book.

Gómez de la Serna, Ramón (1888–   ). Spanish writer. A prolific author, he is known for his biographies, which range in scope from Goya to *Oscar Wilde* (1929) and include *Lope de Vega* (1945), El Greco, Azorín, and Valle-Inclán. His major achievement, however, is his invention and subsequent use of *greguería,* a strange literary form which joins humor with the metaphoric conceit in a startling manner: "the pillows resting on the window sill are *pulcinellas* tired of the night's performance," or "Bottle, wine's coffin." This style forms the basis of such works as *El torero Caracho* (1926), *La malicia de las acacias* (1927), and *La Nardo* (1934).

Gomorrah. See SODOM AND GOMORRAH.

Gompers, Samuel (1850–1924). English-born American labor leader. Arriving in the U.S. in 1863, Gompers joined the Cigarmakers' Union and became its president in 1877. He played an important role in the organization of the American Federation of Labor, which he headed from 1886 until his death (except for the year 1895). Devoted to practical ends, such as improvements in wages and hours, he believed that unions should avoid political alliances.

Gonçalves Dias, Antônio (1823–1864). Brazilian poet and ethnologist. Perhaps Brazil's first truly national poet, Gonçalves Dias was a fervent patriot who wrote verse glorifying the Indian and the tropical landscape. His best-known poem is *Canção do Exilio* (*Song of Exile,* 1846), whose first lines—"There are palm trees in my homeland, where the sabiá sings"—are familiar to every literate Brazilian.

Goncharov, Ivan Aleksandrovich (1812–1891). Russian novelist. Born in Simbirsk (now Ulyanovsk), Goncharov spent his childhood on the family estate. The richness and comfort of the old patriarchal way of life he experienced there was later immortalized in his major novel, OBLOMOV. Goncharov's idyll in the country ended in 1822, when he was sent to Moscow to complete his education. He was miserable in the city and consoled himself by reading extensively, forming an interest in literature that led him to enroll in Moscow University's faculty of letters. He graduated in 1834 and entered the civil service. Goncharov's first important novel, *Obyknovennaya istoriya* (*A Common Story,* 1844), dealt with the

loss of idealistic dreams when a young provincial encounters life in the city. The theme was later to be touched on in *Oblomov.* The critic Vissarion Belinski called *Obyknovennaya istoriya* "a terrible blow to romanticism, dreaminess, sentimentality, and provincialism."

In 1849, Goncharov had already completed the first chapters of his masterpiece. He published one of the chapters, "Oblomov's Dream," in that year. Work on the novel was interrupted by a world cruise he took as secretary for a Russian expedition on the ship *Pallada* from 1852 to 1855. He published a description of the journey in *The Frigate 'Pallada'* in 1858. The following year, *Oblomov* appeared.

Goncharov retired from government service in 1867 and completed his third novel, *Obryv* (*The Precipice,* 1869), on which he had been working for almost 20 years. The novel contrasted the materialist views of the socialists with those of the old Russian patriarchal world. Goncharov's unmistakable preference for the conservative way of life scandalized the radicals. During the remaining years of his life, Goncharov lived a secluded life in his St. Petersburg apartment, occasionally pulling himself free from his mental depression and illnesses to take a trip abroad. His writings during this period consisted mainly of sketches, articles, and reminiscences. The best known of these works is *Mil'on terzani* (*A Million Torments,* 1872), an essay on *Woe from Wit,* the classic Russian comedy by Aleksandr S. Griboyedov.

Goncourt, Edmond (1822–1896) and **Jules de** (1830–1870). French writers known as the **Brothers Goncourt,** who collaborated in their work. Early leaders in the movement of NATURALISM, the Goncourt brothers are forerunners of Emile Zola. Such novels as GERMINIE LACERTEUX and *Madame Gervaisais* (1869) are studies of pathological or degenerate subjects. *La Fille Elisa* (1877), written by Edmond alone, is a realistic description of prostitution. The Brothers Goncourt went to great lengths in order to depict a subject with precision and accuracy. To write *Sœur Philomène* (1861), for example, they went into hospitals, studying the exact conditions. Their work is episodic in form and impersonal in tone. In addition to their naturalistic novels, the Goncourts wrote several studies of 18th-century costumes, art, and furniture. They were also avid collectors of objets d'art and are thought to have been the first to introduce Japanese art into France. See PRIX GONCOURT.

Goneril. In Shakespeare's KING LEAR, the eldest daughter of Lear. The instigator of the cruelties perpetrated on Lear, she refuses to house her father's large entourage. Later she plots with Edmund to kill her husband, the duke of Albany, poisons her sister Regan, who also loves Edmund, and finally stabs herself when the plot is discovered.

Gone with the Wind (1936). A historical novel by Margaret MITCHELL, an American. At the time of the author's death, it had won a Pulitzer Prize and had sold more than 8,000,000 copies; a motion picture version (1939) was equally successful. The heroine of this, her only book, is Scarlett O'Hara, a fiery Southern belle, whose love for Ashley Wilkes is frustrated when he marries gentle Melanie Hamilton; after being widowed twice, Scarlett weds Rhett Butler, who proves more than a match for her. The novel also depicts, from a Southern viewpoint, the tumult and suffering caused by the Civil War and Reconstruction.

Góngora y Argote, Luis de (1561–1627). Spanish poet. A native of Córdoba, Góngora studied at Salamanca and though he probably had little vocation for the priesthood, he took minor orders, becoming prebendary of Córdoba's cathedral. In 1617 he was ordained and was named chaplain to King Philip III. After suffering an apoplectic stroke in 1626, he retired to Córdoba, where he died.

Góngora's literary career had two distinct phases. Initially, as a disciple of Fernando de Herrera, he wrote verse that was relatively simple and remarkable for its exuberance, charm, and wit. These early poems include Italianate sonnets; *romances* or ballads (*Amarrado al duro banco, Servía en Orán al rey, Angélica y Medoro*); and *letrillas* or songs (*Aprended, flores de mí*).

After 1600, however, Góngora deliberately cultivated the abstruse style to which he gave his name, Gongorism, and for which his enemies dubbed him *Príncipe de las Tinieblas* ("Prince of Darkness"). Written for the intellectual elite, his poems in this manner, particularly the *Fábula de Polifemo y Galatea* and the *Soledades*, caused a sensation. Though many, including Cervantes, hailed Góngora's innovations, others, notably Lope de Vega and Quevedo, bitterly attacked him.

Góngora's works were first collected by Juan López de Vicuña in 1627. A more complete collection, including the play *Las firmezas de Isabela* and fragments of two other dramas, was issued in 1633 by Gonzalo de Hozes y Córdoua.

Gongorism (Gongorismo). A Spanish literary style, sometimes called *cultismo* or *culteranismo*, used by Luis de Góngora and other 17th-century poets. Designed to appeal to the cultivated (*los cultos*), it is characterized by an emphasis on Latin terms and syntax, by frequent allusions to classical mythology, and lavish use of tropes, metaphors, hyperbole, and antitheses. Gongorism can also be considered as a purely stylistic variant of the contemporaneous literary trend known as conceptism, which appeared mainly in prose. It had counterparts in the Marinism of Italy and the Euphuism of England. Although Góngora used the style to enhance the sonority and richness of his verse, in the hands of lesser poets it became mere affectation, and Gongorism later became synonymous with bad writing.

Gonne, Maud (1866–1953). Irish patriot and philanthropist. In 1903 she married Major MacBride, an Irish patriot who was executed (1916) by the British after the Easter Rebellion. She was the first diplomatic emissary (1921) of the Irish Free State to Paris. Famous for her beauty and known as an actress, painter, and linguist, she is the heroine of several poems and plays by William Butler Yeats. *A Servant of the Queen,* her autobiography, was published in 1940.

Gonzaga. Italian noble family of Mantua. It was famed during the Renaissance for its cultural patronage. Outstanding were:

Lodovico Gonzaga (1414–1478), the marquis who employed the painter Mantegna, the architect Alberti, the scholars Pico della Mirandola and Poliziano, and the educator Vittorino da Feltre.

Federico Gonzaga (1440–1484) continued his father's patronage, was skilled in diplomacy, and excelled as a condottiere.

Francesco Gonzaga, son of Federico (1466–1519), married the famous Isabella d'Este and was a military commander during the period.

Elisabetta Gonzaga, his sister (1471–1526), married Duke Guidobaldo of Urbino (see Montefeltro) and became the duchess of Castiglione's *Cortegiano* (*The Courtier*).

Federigo Gonzaga, (1500–1540), Francesco's son continued the family tradition by employing Giulio Romano and Pietro Aretino. He was the first duke of Mantua, having received the title from Emperor Charles V.

González Prada, Manuel (1848–1918). Peruvian essayist and poet, famed as a polemicist. A member of a distinguished Peruvian family, González Prada fought in the so-called War of the Pacific (1879–1883), in which Peru suffered a humiliating defeat at the hands of Chile. In a famous speech (1886), he uttered the phrase "old men to the tomb, young men to work," which became the battle cry of those who sought changes in the established order. Uncompromising and incorruptible, he devoted his life to exposing his country's ills in scathing but highly polished prose, hurling his most impassioned invective at the politicians and at the Roman Catholic Church. He became the intellectual mentor of several generations of Peruvian reformers and revolutionaries. Some of his best-known articles and speeches are collected in *Páginas libres* (1894) and *Horas de lucha* (1908). He also wrote several volumes of poetry, the best of which is probably *Baladas peruanas* (1935), which gives a realistic portrayal of Indian life.

Gonzalo. In Shakespeare's The Tempest, the kindly old counsellor who peppers his words with wisdom and is mocked for his garrulity by Alonso and Antonio. His ministrations helped save Prospero's life.

Goodbye, Mr. Chips (1934). A best-selling short novel by James Hilton. It deals sentimentally with the life of an English schoolmaster.

Good Companions, The (1929). A novel by J. B. Priestley. Good humored, and filled with comic characters and varied scenes from English life, it is the story of a group of oddly assorted people who run a touring music-hall company called The Good Companions.

Good Earth, The (1931). A novel by Pearl Buck. It describes the rise of Wang Lung, a Chinese peasant, from poverty to the position of a rich landowner, helped by his patient wife, O-lan. Their vigor, fortitude, persistence, and enduring love of the soil are emphasized throughout. Generally regarded as Pearl Buck's masterpiece, the book won universal acclaim for its sympathetically authentic picture of Chinese life.

Good Friday. The Friday preceding Easter Day, the anniversary of Jesus' Crucifixion. "Good" here means *holy;* Christmas, as well as Shrove Tuesday, used to be called "the good tide." According to old superstition, those born on Christmas Day or Good Friday have the power of seeing and commanding spirits.

Good Natur'd Man, The (1768). A comedy by Oliver Goldsmith. The story concerns Honeywood, a likeable young man prone to extravagance. His uncle, in order to demonstrate that his friends will abandon him if he has no money, has Honeywood arrested for debt. Honeywood is in love with the beautiful, wealthy Miss Richland. When he is released from prison he assumes that a friend of his in the government is responsible for his freedom, though actually it is Miss Richland who is responsible. In the end Honeywood's uncle arranges a match with Miss Richland.

Good Queen Bess. ELIZABETH I of England.

Goodrich, Samuel Griswold (1793–1860). American publisher, editor, author of children's books, and memoirist. Adopting the pseudonym of Peter Parley, Goodrich published a series for children beginning with *The Tales of Peter Parley About America* (1827). For about 30 years he wrote volumes of history, geography, science, and travel for children, with the help of several collaborators, including Hawthorne. His best book is considered *Recollections of a Lifetime* (1856).

The patron of many American authors, he introduced Nathaniel Hawthorne to the public in his magazine *The Token* (1828–1842); some of the best of the *Twice-Told Tales* first appeared there. Goodrich's *Parley's Magazine* (1833–1844) also had some distinguished contributors.

Good Samaritan. See SAMARITAN, GOOD.

Good Soldier, The (1915). A novel by Ford Madox FORD. The narrator discovers that for the past nine years his wife has been the mistress of his best friend, Captain Ashburnham, the apparently honorable "Good Soldier" of the title. Conventional appearances and bitter truth are ironically juxtaposed.

Good Soldier Schweik, The (Osudy Dobrého Vojáka Švejka za Světové Války, 1920–23; Eng. translation, 1930). A novel by Jaroslav HAŠEK. The author originally planned this gargantuan satire on the military bureaucracy of Austria and on war in general as a six volume work, but lived to complete only four volumes. The novel chronicles the laughable misadventures of the kindhearted Schweik, which by their very absurdity point up the stupidity of war. The book has been variously hailed as a brilliant lampoon, as an epic defense of pacifism, and as a Czech *Don Quixote*.

Good Women, The Legend of. See LEGEND OF GOOD WOMEN.

Good Woman of Sezuan, The (Der gute Mensch von Sezuan; 1938–1940). A play by Bertolt BRECHT. Three gods come to earth to find a "good man," and the only person in the town of Sezuan who will give them shelter is the prostitute Shente. With the money they give her, she opens a tobacco shop, but her own natural charity soon brings her to bankruptcy. She disguises herself as a "male cousin," Shui Ta, and by ruthless business policies gains back the money she had benevolently given away. Basically, the play criticizes the social order in which a good person must pretend to be bad in order to survive.

Goody Blake and Harry Gill (1798). A poem by William WORDSWORTH. Gill is a farmer who forbids old Goody Blake to carry home a few sticks of firewood which she has picked up from his land. She curses him for his meanness, saying that he will never from that moment cease from shivering with cold, and from that hour, a-bed or up, summer

or winter, at home or abroad, his teeth "chatter, chatter, chatter still."

Goody Two-shoes (1765). A nursery tale written for the publisher John Newbery by Oliver GOLDSMITH. Goody Two-shoes is a very poor child, whose delight at having a pair of shoes is so unbounded that she cannot forbear telling everyone she meets that she has "two shoes"; whence her name. In time, she acquires knowledge and becomes wealthy.

Googe, Barnabe (1540–1594). English poet and translator, best known for his volume of *Eclogues, Epitaphs and Sonnets* (1563), regarded as containing some of the earliest examples of pastoral poetry in English. His work is considered representative of English poetry between the period of WYATT and SURREY and that of SPENSER. It is particularly marked by alliteration and the use of the FOURTEENER, an iambic line of seven feet.

Gookin, Daniel (1612?–1687). English-born American author and colonial administrator. Known for his humanitarian interest in the Indians, in 1656 he was appointed superintendent of all the Indians who acknowledged the government of Massachusetts. He wrote *Historical Collections of the Indians in New England* (1792) and *An Historical Account of the Doings and Sufferings of the Christian Indians in New England* (1836).

Goose, Mother. A mythical character famous as giving the name to *Mother Goose's Nursery Rhymes*. This name seems to have been first used in English in *Songs for the Nursery, Or Mother Goose's Melodies for Children*, published by T. Fleet in Boston, Mass., in 1719. PERRAULT's *Contes de ma mère l'oye* (*Tales of my Mother Goose*) had appeared in 1697.

Goose Bible. See BIBLE, SPECIALLY NAMED EDITIONS.

goose step. A step formerly used in the Prussian army on ceremonial occasions. At each pace the thigh had to be brought to a right angle with the erect body. It was supposed to look extremely dignified when carried out by a well-drilled body of men, but it was unmercifully ridiculed by the Allies during World War I.

Gorboduc, or Ferrex and Porrex (produced 1561, published 1565). A play by Thomas Sackville and Thomas Norton, the first Senecan tragedy in English, the first English play to be written in blank verse, and one of the first to use English historical material. The story is based on the legendary history of England of Geoffrey of Monmouth. Gorboduc, a British king, has two sons, Ferrex and Porrex. He divides his kingdom between them, but they quarrel, and Porrex kills his brother. Soon afterward, Porrex himself is murdered in his bed by his mother, who loved Ferrex better. The people, horrified, rebel and kill both the old king and queen. The nobility then kill many of the rebels. Soon, since there are no heirs to the throne, the country falls into civil war and is laid waste.

Gorbodug. One of the kings in Geoffrey of Monmouth's HISTORY OF THE KINGS OF BRITAIN. He reappears in the pre-Shakespearean tragedy GORBODUC by Sackville and Norton.

Gordian knot. An intricate problem. Gordias, a peasant, was chosen king of Phrygia, and dedicated his wagon to Zeus. The wagon yoke was fastened to a pole so cleverly that it was said that whoever undid the knot would reign over the empire of Asia. Alexander cut the knot with a single stroke of his sword. "Cutting the Gordian knot" became proverbial for the decisive and bold completion of a complicated action.

Gordon, Caroline (1895–   ). American novelist and short-story writer. Miss Gordon received both critical and popular acclaim for her first novel, *Penhally* (1931), the story of three generations on a Kentucky plantation. Her other books include *Aleck Maury* (1934); *The Garden of Adonis* (1936); *None Shall Look Back* (1937), a fictional study of the Confederate general Nathan Bedford Forrest; *Green Centuries* (1941); *The Forest of the South* (1945), a collection of 17 skillfully written short stories; *The Women on the Porch* (1946); *The House of Fiction* (1950), a textbook written with Allen Tate; *The Malefactors* (1956); and *Old Red and Other Stories* (1963).

Gordon, Charles George. Known as **Chinese Gordon** and **Gordon Pasha** (1833–1885). English soldier. In 1860 he was attached to a British force operating against China, and commanded a Chinese force, called the Ever Victorious Army, against the Taiping rebels (1863–1864). He quelled the rebellions after 33 engagements and resigning his command, was presented by the emperor with the yellow jacket and peacock's feather of a mandarin of the first class. He was governor (1874–1876) of the equatorial provinces of central Africa in the service of the khedive of Egypt and in 1877 was created pasha by the khedive. As governor-general (1877–1879) of the Sudan, Darfur, the equatorial provinces, and the Red Sea littoral, he suppressed slave trade. Sent by the British government in 1884 to the Sudan to assist the khedive in withdrawing the garrisons of the country, which could no longer hold out against the Mahdi, he was besieged by the Mahdi at Khartoum and killed in the storming of the city. There is a fine biographical sketch of Gordon in Lytton Strachey's *Eminent Victorians* (1918).

Gordon Riots. The riots that occurred in London in 1780, fomented by Lord George Gordon, to compel the House of Commons to repeal the bill passed in 1778 for the relief of Roman Catholics. Charles Dickens has given a very vivid description of these riots in Barnaby Rudge.

Gorgias (c. 483–375 B.C.). A Greek philosopher, Sophist, and teacher of rhetoric. He exercised a great influence on the development of classical Greek style: Plato's dialogue on rhetoric is called *Gorgias.* His lost work, *On Nature or the Non-existent,* is believed to be a refutation of Presocratic argument for a fundamental principle of unity in the universe which underlies all appearances.

Gorgons (Gorgones). Monsters of classical myth. With golden wings and claws of brass, their hair was a mass of live serpents and their aspect was so terrible that all who looked at them were turned to stone. There were three: Stheno, Euryale, and Medusa, daughters of Keto and the aged sea-god Phorcys and sisters of the Graiae, who guarded them. Medusa, their chief, and the only mortal one, was slain by Perseus. The Gorgon's head was a favorite subject in ancient Greek art; because they believed that its power would terrify the enemy, the Greeks carved it on shields and armor and even on city walls. It was also used as an amulet to protect against enchantment.

Goriot, Père. See Père Goriot, Le.

Gorki, Maksim. Pen name of **Aleksei Maksimovich Peshkov** (1868–1936). Russian writer. Gorki was the first great Russian writer to emerge from the ranks of the proletariat. Born in Nizhni Novgorod (now named Gorki), he was orphaned at an early age and lived for a brief time with his grandparents. Financial difficulties soon forced the boy at the age of nine to go into the world to make his own way. He was a dishwasher on a Volga steamer, bakery-shop worker, fisherman, railroadman, and clerk, as well as a down-and-outer, before he began to write. His hard life drove him to a suicide attempt in 1887. His pen name, Gorki, is the Russian equivalent of "the bitter one." His first published story, *Makar Chudra* (1892), appeared in a Tiflis newspaper. His stories, sketches, and articles were published in local newspapers in provincial towns, until they finally attracted the notice of the writer and journalist Vladimir Korolenko, who helped him get his first stories placed in journals in St. Petersburg. The first story to appear was *Chelkash* (1895). This was followed by a stream of stories, and in 1898 two volumes of Gorki's stories and sketches were issued. By then the one-time tramp was famous all over the country. Gorki's work of this period drew heavily on the kind of life he had himself experienced, which of necessity meant that most of his characters and themes were taken from the lowest level of Russian society. Gorki both depicted the wretched lives of this class of "creatures that once were men" and infused his stories with a heavy dose of protest against the society that allowed such wretchedness to exist. His most successful story of this period was Twenty-six Men and a Girl.

Gorki's popularity and financial success allowed him to embark on a longer work: his first novel, *Foma Gordeyev* (1899), a study of a declining bourgeois merchant family in a Volga town. In the meantime, he had moved to St. Petersburg and founded a publishing house, *Znaniye (Knowledge)*, that was later to publish such well-known writers as Andreyev, Kuprin, and Bunin. He also joined the Social-Democratic Party and contributed much of his literary earnings to furthering the Marxist revolutionary movement. This activity displeased the government, and, when he was elected an honorary member of the Russian Academy of Sciences in 1902, the government vetoed the choice. The authors Anton Chekhov and Vladimir Korolenko promptly resigned their memberships in protest.

Gorki's formerly romantically tinged realistic pictures of lower-class life became increasingly grim and angry. The most forceful expression of his attitude is the drama The Lower Depths, his second play, regarded as his dramatic masterpiece. Gorki's first play was *The Petit-Bourgeois (Meshchanye;* 1901), an indictment of the philistinism of that class.

For his Bolshevik activities in the revolution of 1905, Gorki was arrested. Public indignation forced his release and he went abroad, visiting Europe and the U.S. and settling on Capri. In 1907, he issued his didactic novel about the revolutionary movement, Mother. Although artistically weak, the book's message has made it a favorite with Soviet literary hucksters. *Tales of Italy (Skazki ob Itali;* 1911–1912) depicted the lives of the Italian working classes. The next years saw the production of one of Gorki's best works, his autobiographical trilogy. The first part, CHILDHOOD, appeared in 1913–1914. The second part, *In the World (V lyudakh),* came out in 1916, and the third volume, *My Universities (Moi universitety),* in 1923.

Gorki had been allowed to return to Russia in 1913. His former sympathy with the Bolsheviks had abated somewhat. He saw unbridled violence as a threat to the existence of what had been worthwhile in the cultural life of the past. When the advocates of proletarian Marxism attempted to sweep away the cultural past, Gorki did what he could to save it. He organized the publishing venture, *Vsemirnaya literatura (World Literature),* which helped many writers earn enough bread to stay alive during the chaotic months following the revolution. He also helped establish a "House of Arts" (*Dom iskusstv*) and a "House of Scholars" (*Dom uchonykh*), which offered writers a place to stay and, more important, a place to work. This aspect of Gorki's activity has caused him to be called a bridge between the old classical culture of Russia and the new Soviet culture.

The influence Gorki had with the Bolshevik leaders was often used to good advantage to help writers who were down and out or in trouble with the new regime. He, also, was active in discovering and encouraging new writers, such as Vsevolod Ivanov and Konstantin Fedin. Thus, he helped both to preserve the old culture and foster the new.

In 1921, Gorki, weakened by his strenuous work load, went abroad for a rest. He remained in Italy until 1928. During this period, beside the third volume of his autobiography, he wrote two novels—*The Artamonov Business (Delo Artamonovykh;* 1925) and *The Life of Klim Samgin (Zhizn Klima Samgina;* 1927–1936)—and two plays produced after his return to Russia—*Yegor Bulychov and Others (Yegor Bulychov i drugiye;* 1931) and *Dostigayev and Others (Dostigayev i drugiye;* 1932). The plays and *The Artamonov Business* all deal with the same theme, the decay of merchant families. *The Life of Klim Samgin,* a huge work of which four volumes were finished, also treats the decline of a particular class, the intelligentsia.

After his return to the Soviet Union, Gorki helped develop the literary doctrine of SOCIALIST REALISM, which was formed in 1932. His own ideas about what he meant by socialist realism differed somewhat from official doctrine as it was later interpreted.

Gorki died in 1936, while undergoing medical treatment. In the 1937–1938 purge trials, the ex-secret police chief Yagoda confessed that Gorki's death was ordered by him as part of a so-called Trotskyite plot. The real truth of the matter is still unknown.

Gorki's fictional work generally suffers from lack of a controlled style and a tendency to overindulge in philosophical discourse. His place in Russian literature is secure, however, for his autobiographical trilogy and for his *Reminiscences (Vospominaniya;* 1919) of Tolstoi, Chekhov, and Andreyev, which are full of sharp insights and interesting anecdotes.

Gorky, Arshile (1904–1948). Armenian-born American painter. A native of Turkish Armenia, Gorky came to the U.S. in 1920. A precise draftsman, he combined rich color and nongeometric forms derived from nature to create increasingly surrealistic works of art.

Görres, Joseph von (1776–1848). German scholar and political writer. He was a friend of BRENTANO and Arnim. His best-known scholarly work is *Die deutschen Volksbücher (The German Folk-books,* 1807), in which the word VOLKSBUCH was first used in its present sense. Politically, he was violently anti-Napoleonic during the French domination of Germany and expressed his views in the newspaper *Rheinischer Merkur (Rhenish Mercury)* which he founded in 1814. After Napoleon's defeat, however, he came into conflict with the Prussian government and was forced into exile in 1816.

Gospels. See MATTHEW, THE GOSPEL ACCORDING TO ST.; MARK, THE GOSPEL ACCORDING TO ST.; LUKE, THE GOSPEL ACCORDING TO ST.; JOHN, THE GOSPEL ACCORDING TO ST.

Gösta Berlings saga (1891). A novel of Swedish life by Selma LAGERLÖF. It relates the adventures of the impulsive and temperamental young hero, whose magnetic personality inevitably draws people to him. His turbulent passions just as inevitably involve him, and those attracted to him, in misfortune. Eventually he marries the Countess Elizabeth, whose husband has divorced her. Through Elizabeth's influence and his own efforts, he is able to begin a life that more nearly approximates his ideals.

Gotham, wise men of. Fools, wiseacres. The legend is that King John, on his way to Lynn Regis, intended to pass through Gotham, in Nottinghamshire, with his army, and sent heralds to prepare his way. The men of Gotham were resolved, if possible, to prevent this expense and depredation, so they resolved to play the fool. Some raked the moon out of the pond; some made a ring to hedge in a bird; others did equally foolish things. The king then abandoned his intention, and "the wise men" of the village cunningly remarked, "We ween there are more fools pass through Gotham than remain in it."

A collection of popular tales of stupidity was published in the reign of Henry VIII as *Merie Tales of the Mad Men of Gotham, gathered together by A.B. of Phisike, Doctour.* Since that date many other tales have been attached to the inhabitants of Gotham. The old nursery rhyme is well known:

> Three wise men of Gotham
> Went to sea in a bowl;
> If the bowl had been stronger
> My story had been longer.

The name *Gotham* was given to New York City by Washington Irving in his satirical *Salmagundi Papers* (1807) and has remained in current use.

Gothic novel. A type of novel characterized by horror, violence, supernatural effects, and a taste for the medieval, usually set against a background of Gothic architecture, especially a gloomy and isolated castle. The genre originated in England with Horace Walpole's CASTLE OF OTRANTO. In its early forms, and even as late as THE MYSTERIES OF UDOLPHO by Mrs. Ann Radcliffe, the supernatural is given a naturalistic explanation, the aim being to produce a "correct," i.e. probable, medieval romance. Even so, its excesses produced a satirical reaction as in Jane Austen's NORTHANGER ABBEY, while conversely, in William Beckford's VATHEK, where Gothic terrors merge with the terrors of an Oriental despotism, the very monstrosities themselves seem to verge on parody. Matthew Lewis' THE MONK marks a new departure: its horrors are frankly supernatural, but psychologically symbolic. This development culminates in MELMOTH THE WANDERER by Charles Robert Maturin, and, in America, in novels by Charles Brockden BROWN, Nathaniel HAWTHORNE, and Edgar Allan POE. A similar development took place on the Continent, especially in Germany. In the 20th century, the movement of SURREALISM claimed the Gothic novel as one of its forerunners.

Götterdämmerung. See RAGNAROK.

Gottfried von Strassburg (early 13th century). German minnesinger or court poet. His handling of the Tristan and Iseult legend (c. 1210) was one of the best court epics in Germany; it was the major source for Wagner's opera *Tristan und Isolde* (1865).

Gotthelf, Jeremias. Pen name of **Albert Bitzius** (1797–1854). Swiss novelist, writing in German, known especially for his conservative, didactic piety which is, however, sometimes lightened by humor. He was a well-established Protestant pastor for more than a decade before beginning to write his many novels about peasant life, such as *Der Bauernspiegel* (*The Peasants' Mirror*, 1837), *Wie Uli, der Knecht, glücklich wird* (*How Uli, the Servant, Becomes Happy*, 1841), and *Elsi, die seltsame Magd* (*Elsie, the Strange Maid*, 1850). His novella *Die schwarze Spinne* (*The Black Spider*, 1842) is a masterful treatment of the occult.

Göttinger Hain (Göttingen Grove). An association of German poets formed in 1772, most of whose members were students at the University of Göttingen. The name Hain (grove) was drawn from a poem by Klopstock, whom the young poets took as their model. Some members were Voss, Hölty, and the brothers Stolberg. Bürger was close to the group, but not a member. The tendencies of the group, which dispersed in 1774, were related to those of the STURM UND DRANG movement.

Gottlieb, Max. In Sinclair Lewis' ARROWSMITH, an old, disillusioned, but dedicated scientist who helps to train Arrowsmith in research methods. Gottlieb may have been modeled on Jacques Loeb (1859–1924), the great biophysiologist on the staff of the Rockefeller Institute for Medical Research (1910–1924).

Gottsched, Johann Christoph (1700–1766). German aesthetician and dramatist of the enlightenment, under the influence of French neo-classicism. He was strongly opposed by such figures as Bodmer and Lessing, who advocated artistic directions less dependent upon foreign models. His most famous play is *Der sterbende Cato* (*The Dying Cato*, 1732).

Götz von Berlichingen (1773). A play by Johann Wolfgang von GOETHE, freely adapted from the life of Götz von Berlichingen (1480–1562), a German knight. In Goethe's treatment, Götz becomes a typical STURM UND DRANG hero, a powerful individual personality, unwaveringly committed to his own straightforward conception of justice, but in the end not able to escape the subtle maneuverings of his political adversaries. Formally, Goethe wished to emulate Shakespeare, in opposition to the prevailing style of neoclassicism, and the play is written in a powerful, rough-and-ready prose, with short pithy scenes and constant changes of setting between them. See DAEMONIC.

Goudge, Elizabeth (1900–   ). English novelist. Her popular novels sensitively evoke the English countryside, English history, and the world of children. Among them are *A City of Bells* (1936), *Towers in the Mist* (1938), *Green Dolphin Street* (1944), *Gentian Hill* (1950), *The Rosemary Tree* (1956), and *The Scent of Water* (1963). *The Little White Horse* (1947) is a book for children.

Gould, Charles. A central character in Joseph Conrad's novel NOSTROMO, the owner of a silver mine in South America. Doña Emilia is his gentle wife.

Gounod, Charles François (1818–1893). French composer. His best-known operas are *Faust* (1859) and *Roméo et Juliette* (1867). He at first wrote sacred music; among his songs is the famous *Ave Maria* based on Bach's first prelude of the *Well Tempered Clavier*.

Gourmont, Rémy de (1858–1915). French literary critic and novelist. In his early years as a critic, Gourmont wrote perceptive, sympathetic articles on the symbolist poets, published in *Le Livre des masques* (1896) and *Promenades littéraires* (1904–1913). His novels, rather chilly in tone, emphasize the biological origins of all human behavior. They include *Les Chevaux de Diomède* (1897), *Le Songe d'une Femme* (1899), *Une Nuit au Luxembourg* (1906), and *Un Cœur Virginal* (1907). Among his essays are *L'Esthétique de la Langue Française* (1899), *Le Problème du Style* (1902), and *Physique de l'Amour* (1903). These are marked by irony, an interest in the sensual, and a quick, probing intelligence. Disfigured by a skin disease, Gourmont spent much of his life in seclusion.

Gower, John (1325?–1408). English poet, a friend of Chaucer, well known at the courts of Richard II and Henry IV. He wrote serious poetry of the allegorical and didactic type common in his day, urging moral and social reforms. His principal works are the French SPECULUM MEDITANTIS, the Latin Vox CLAMANTIS, and the English CONFESSIO AMANTIS, as well as some lighter short poems in all three languages.

Goya y Lucientes, Francisco José de (1746–1828). Spanish painter and etcher. He worked for the Royal Workshop as a designer of cartoons and became Royal Painter in 1786. After the death of Charles III he went on to serve his son, Charles IV, portraying the king, his family, and the nobility in brilliant, often cruelly truthful paintings which rank among the most discerning in the world of art. A severe disease left him deaf at 47, yet the following years mark the peak of his fame. The injustice and inhumanity of the period of the Spanish War of Independence against Napoleon's occupation (1808–1814) and of Ferdinand VII's reign (1814–1820) elicited a tortured reaction from him. He painted scenes of disasters, madness, and satanism, and executed the series of etchings entitled *The Disasters of War*, in which he indicted violence and murder with bitter realism and censured the moral dishonesty of those who would not rebel against human misery.

In 1823, Goya left for Bordeaux, in France, where

he continued to paint with unshaken confidence and originality. He left an extensive production: portraits, religious paintings, scenes of the Inquisition, of crime, of the people's everyday work, engravings of war and the bullfight. The paintings were little known outside Spain until 1896, and *The Disasters of War* were not published till 1863, yet Goya exerted a profound influence on modern art. Eugène Delacroix, Honoré Daumier, and Edouard Manet were among the first to be influenced by his visionary representation of the world and by his approach to art, from which he banished all academic conceptions of composition and draftsmanship in order to give color the double role of unifying loosely constructed paintings and of defining the forms.

Gozzano, Guido (1883–1916). Italian poet. Afflicted by poor health throughout his short life, Gozzano is best known for his lyric poetry, collected in *I Primi e gli Ultimi Colloqui* (1927). Although he was originally influenced by D'Annunzio, his work reveals a melancholy, passive attitude toward life that aligns him with the CREPUSCOLARI poets.

Gozzi, Count Carlo (1720–1806). Italian playwright. A member of the Granelleschi Society, whose purpose it was to preserve Tuscan literature from foreign influences, Gozzi ignored theatrical innovation and produced charming and witty plays, many of them dramatized versions of fairy tales. Goethe and Mme. de Staël, among others, were admirers of his work. His play *Re Turandot* (*King Turandot*, 1762) was translated into German by Schiller, and became the basis for operas by Weber, Busoni, and Puccini. *Fiaba dell' amore delle tre melarancie* (*Fable of the Love of Three Oranges*, 1761), which was derived from Basile's *Cunto delli Cunti* and presented the two rival dramatists Goldoni and Chiari under the satirical guises of a fairy and a magician, revived the stock characters of the Italian comedy of masks and enjoyed a huge popular success. Almost a century and a half later, it was used by Prokofiev as the basis for his opera *The Love of Three Oranges*. A portion of Gozzi's output was modeled on Spanish plays, and his later works include tragedies in which he experimentally introduced comic elements.

Gozzoli, Benozzo, or **Benozzo di Lese** (1420–1497). Italian painter. One of the leading figures of the early Florentine Renaissance, he was a pupil of Fra Angelico and strongly influenced by Gentile da Fabriano. His forte was the large-scale narrative fresco, in which he combined Italian realism and Gothic fantasy in a delightful way. For his patrons, the Medici, he decorated the chapel of their palace in Florence and included portraits of the family in his masterpiece, *The Journey of the Magi*. He is also known for his Old Testament scenes painted at the *campo santo* of Pisa, especially the *Story of Noah*.

Grabbe, Christian Dietrich (1801–1836). German playwright, known especially for the ironic, often pessimistically cynical and disillusioned attitude that permeates his works. His style is an early example of the 19th-century turn toward realism, away from the idealism of such dramatists as Schiller. Among his works are *Scherz, Satire, Ironie und tiefere Bedeutung* (*Joke, Satire, Irony and Deeper Significance,* pub. 1827) and *Don Juan und Faust* (1829).

Graça Aranha, José Pereira de (1868–1931). Brazilian diplomat, novelist, and man of letters. A champion of nationalism in literature, Graça Aranha is best known for *Canaan* (*Chanaan;* 1902). A novel of ideas, it consists largely of a conversation between two Germans, newcomers to Brazil, who discuss the development of the Brazilian nation.

Gracchi. A prominent family of republican Rome. Its most famous members were **Tiberius Sempronius Gracchus** (163?–133 B.C.) and his brother **Gaius Sempronius Gracchus** (d. 123 B.C.). As tribune (133), Tiberius secured the enactment, despite much opposition, of an agrarian reform law that would grant public lands to the impoverished Italian peasantry. When, in defiance of custom, he sought a second term as tribune, he and 300 of his followers were killed in an election riot.

His work was carried on by Gaius who, as tribune in 123 and 122, sought to regulate the price of grain in Rome and proposed extension of the franchise. Like his brother, he was killed at the instigation of the senate.

The mother of the Gracchi brothers was the famous Cornelia, daughter of SCIPIO AFRICANUS, who was considered the ideal Roman matron. According to tradition, she was once visited by a wealthy woman who displayed her jewels and asked to see Cornelia's. Pointing to her sons, Cornelia replied, "These are my jewels."

Grace Abounding to the Chief of Sinners (1666). An autobiography by John BUNYAN. Written while he was in prison, it describes his spiritual struggles and the development of his religious convictions.

Graces, the. In Roman mythology, the Gratiae, goddesses who embodied beauty and charm. Called by the Greeks the Charites, they were, by some accounts, named Aglaia (Brilliance), Thalia (the Flowering), and Euphrosyne (Joy), though their names and even their number varied. Although they were probably very early spirits of vegetation, they did not in classical times have any cult of importance. They are best known from their many appearances in art.

Gracián, Baltasar (1601–1658). Spanish prose writer and Jesuit priest. The outstanding exponent of CONCEPTISM, Gracián has been variously regarded as a moral philosopher of considerable depth and as an unoriginal intellectual poseur. His best-known works are EL CRITICÓN, an allegorical novel, and *Agudeza y arte de ingenio* (1642, 1648), a manual of conceptism, in which he defined the numerous varieties of literary *agudeza* ("fine distinction, ingenuity"). In *El Héroe* (1637), he drew a portrait of the ideal Christian hero. *El Discreto* (1646) discusses the 25 *realces,* or "adornments," which make up the well-bred gentleman, while the *Oráculo manual o arte de prudencia* (1647) is a collection of 300 maxims that offer a distillation of worldly wisdom.

gracioso. A comic servant in Spanish drama. Although the character appeared under the name of *simple* or *bobo* in the works of earlier dramatists, such as Torres Naharro and Lope de Rueda, Lope de Vega is often regarded as its creator.

Gracq, Julien. Pen name of **Louis Poirier** (1910–). French novelist and playwright. His works share a haunting mood partly Gothic, partly surrealistic, and an impressionistic, symbolic style. His novels include *The Castle of Argol* (1945), *A Dark Stranger* (*Un beau ténébreux;* 1945), and *Balcony in the Forest* (1958).

Gradasso. Oriental monarch who besieges Charlemagne at Paris in Boiardo's ORLANDO INNAMORATO; in Ariosto's ORLANDO FURIOSO, he is killed by Orlando and the other paladins in a battle to which he had challenged them.

Graeae (Graiai). Literally, the gray-haired women. In Greek myth, the sisters and guardians of the GORGONS. They owned only one eye and one tooth among them, which they shared in turn. PERSEUS, robbing them of these, forced them to show him the way to the Gorgons, and to give him their winged sandals, magic wallet, and cap of invisibility. Hesiod mentions only two Graeae, Enyo and Pephredo; later legends add a third, Deino.

Graham, Stephen (1884–   ). English travel-writer. He traveled mostly in Russia, writing about his experiences and the history and literature of the country in such books as *Undiscovered Russia* (1913) and *Summing Up on Russia* (1951). He tramped the American West with Vachel Lindsay and wrote *Tramping with a Poet in the Rockies* (1922).

Grahame, Kenneth (1859–1932). English author of children's books and essays. He wrote THE WIND IN THE WILLOWS, *The Golden Age* (1895), and *Dream Days* (1898).

Graham of Claverhouse, John. 1st Viscount **Dundee.** Known as **Bloody Claverse** and **Bonny Dundee** (1649?–1689). Scottish soldier. He was dubbed "Bloody Claverse" by the Scottish COVENANTERS, whom he persecuted with great severity for 20 years. In 1689 he raised an army of Highlanders to fight for James II and won the battle of Killiecrankie, but was mortally wounded. To Jacobites he became known as "Bonny Dundee," a semilegendary hero. He is a character in Scott's novel *Old Mortality* (1816).

Grail, Holy Grail, or **Sangreal (Sangraal).** A famous talisman (variously represented as a chalice, dish, stone, and cup into which a lance drips blood), the center around which a huge corpus of medieval legend, romance, and allegory revolve. The precise origin and nature of the Grail is unknown and has been the subject of countless scholarly researches; these have attempted to sort out the features of ancient fertility cults, Celtic myth, and Christianity in the Grail romances. The Grail is best known as the object of a quest on the part of the knights of the ROUND TABLE in Arthurian legend. It brings healing and food to those who touch it and can be found only by one absolutely pure.

The best-known accounts of the Grail are those that give it a Christian origin and generally run along the following lines: It is the vessel from which Christ drank at the Last Supper and that afterwards came into the possession of JOSEPH OF ARIMATHEA who caught in it some of the blood that flowed from the wounds of the crucified Saviour. He carried it with him to England, and it provided him with food, drink, and spiritual sustenance for the rest of his life. It was handed down to his successor and thence from generation to generation, GALAHAD, in Malory's *Morte d'Arthur* (c. 1469), being Joseph's last descendant. In some accounts it disappears after Joseph brings it to England. In still others, it is the

dish out of which Christ and his disciples ate the paschal lamb at the Last Supper. The theory of a Christian origin of the Grail, however, has been abandoned. Many now hold that the Grail was originally a female sex symbol used with the bleeding lance mentioned in Chrétien de Troyes' early account in ancient fertility rites. Jessie L. Weston's discussion of this theory in *From Ritual to Romance* (1920) was the source used by T. S. Eliot for his poem *The Waste Land* (1922), where the Grail theme occurs in this symbolic form.

The mass of literature concerning the Grail cycle, both ancient and modern, is enormous. The chief sources of the principal groups of legend are the *Peredur* in the *Mabinogion,* which is one of the most archaic forms of the story; the unfinished *Perceval, ou le conte du Graal* by Chrétien de Troyes, in which the Grail is a hollow dish, accompanied by a bleeding lance (see PERCIVAL); Wolfram von Eschenbach's PARSIFAL (c. 1210), the best example of the story as transformed by ecclesiastical influence; a chivalric version by Gottfried von Strassburg; the 13th-century French *Percival le Gallois* (founded on earlier English and Celtic legends that had no connection with the Grail), showing Percival in his later role as an ascetic hero, translated by Dr. Sebastian Evans (1893) as *The High History of the Holy Grail;* and the *Quête du St. Graal,* which, in its English dress, is found in Malory's *Morte d'Arthur.* It was the French poet Robert de Boron (fl., c. 1215), who, in his *Joseph d'Arimathie ou Le Saint Graal,* first definitely attached the history of the Grail to the Arthurian cycle and first mentioned the Grail as a chalice containing Christ's blood. The framework of Tennyson's *Holy Grail* in his *Idylls of the King* (1859–1885), is taken from Malory.

Gráinne. See PURSUIT OF DIARMUID AND GRÁINNE, THE.

Grand Canal. The chief water thoroughfare of Venice, Italy.

Grande Demoiselle, La. See Duchesse de MONTPENSIER.

Grandet, Eugénie. See EUGÉNIE GRANDET.

Grandgousier (*Fr.,* "great gullet"). In Rabelais GARGANTUA AND PANTAGRUEL, the king of Utopia, husband of Gargamelle, and father of Gargantua. Grandgousier, a just and peace-loving patriarch who lives at the Devinière, the house where Rabelais was born, has been identified with the latter's own father.

Grand Inquisitor, The Legend of the. In Feodor Dostoevski's THE BROTHERS KARAMAZOV, the parable related by Ivan to Alyosha, expressing the former's religious doubts. The tale relates how Christ returns to earth in Seville during the Inquisition, how He is recognized by the people, and immediately arrested by the Inquisition leaders. The Grand Inquisitor, a menacing old churchman, visits Christ's cell and upbraids Him for returning, saying that the Church no longer needs Him, that He has misapprehended man's nature and has burdened man with too much freedom. The Church, says the Inquisitor, understands that man does not want the burden of free choice but wants to be led. The Church's allegiance has been shifted to the Other, to the Devil, the Inquisitor claims, and Christ is now only an unwanted distraction. Henceforth, he says, man will be cared for by the few leaders of the Church who are strong enough to take on themselves the burden of freedom and to guide the weak masses. At the end of his tirade, the Inquisitor throws open the cell door and orders Christ to leave and never return. Christ, who has been silent throughout the interview, answers the old man with a kiss on the cheek before leaving, presumably an expression of His love even for the unbeliever.

The Grand Inquisitor is the most famous single section of the novel and is often excerpted as an independent piece for anthologies, although its thematic connections with the novel as a whole are strong. The ideas it expresses have been considered formulations of Dostoevski's own religious doubts.

Grandison, Charlotte. In Samuel Richardson's last novel, SIR CHARLES GRANDISON, the witty and inconsiderate sister of the hero, and major correspondent of Harriet Byron. Her flippant treatment of her husband Lord G., at once amusing and shocking, is in studied contrast to Harriet's serious affection for Sir Charles.

Grandison, Sir Charles. See SIR CHARLES GRANDISON.

Grandissimes, The: A Story of Creole Life (1880). A novel by George W. CABLE. It is set in New Orleans in the period of the Louisiana Purchase. An outside observer, Frowenfeld, learns of the family feuds, especially those between the De Grapions and the Grandissimes, the race feuds, and the struggle between the new order and the old. The book is filled with vivid characters, notably the Creole mother and daughter Nancanou, and the African king Bras Coupé, who allows himself to be tortured to death rather than be a slave.

Grand Meaulnes, Le (1913; translated as **The Wanderer** and **The Lost Domain**). The novel that won ALAIN-FOURNIER his reputation. Le Grand Meaulnes, the young hero, has a curious adventure at Christmastime. In the middle of the woods he discovers a gay party and a beautiful girl both hidden in an old house. His love for the girl, Yvonne, and his friendship with her brother, Franz, shape his life, bringing him intense joy and intense sorrow. The uniqueness of the novel lies in its delicate combination of fantasy and realism. Actuality and the dream world mingle indistinguishably in the experience of a young boy coming to manhood.

Grandonio of Volterra. In the ORLANDO FURIOSO of Ariosto, a pagan knight from Spain, noted for his rude and discourteous manner. He is defeated by the warrior maiden Bradamante.

Grand Remonstrance. In English history, the protest passed by the House of Commons on Nov. 22, 1641. It listed the unconstitutional acts of Charles I and demanded reform.

Gran Galeoto, El (The Great Galeoto, 1881). A tragedy by José ECHEGARAY, in which spiteful gossip is the "GALEOTO" of the title. The heroine is suspected by the spying public and finally by her husband, Julian, of improper relations with his young secretary, Ernest. They are innocent, but are powerless to convince Julian, who dies from a wound received in a duel for his wife's honor.

Grani (gray-colored). Siegfried's horse, of marvelous swiftness.

Granich, Irving. See Michael GOLD.

Grant, Ulysses S[impson] (1882–1885). Ameri-

can soldier and 18th president of the U.S. (1869–1877). A graduate of West Point and a veteran of the Mexican War, Grant later engaged unsuccessfully in farming and business. He entered the Union army in 1861 and after capturing Forts Henry and Donelson in Tennessee (1862), was promoted to major-general; he led the Union forces at SHILOH and captured Vicksburg (1863), splitting the Confederacy in half. Appointed commander-in-chief of the Union army in 1864, he moved against Richmond, the Confederate capital, in a slow and costly but ultimately successful campaign and accepted the surrender of General Lee at Appomattox Courthouse. His two presidential terms were marred by extensive graft and corruption that involved such highly placed officials as Secretary of War W. W. Belknap and O. E. Babcock, Grant's private secretary. After his retirement, Grant was left penniless through the failure of a brokerage firm, but his *Personal Memoirs* (1885), which he completed while dying of throat cancer, brought his family nearly $500,000.

Gran teatro del mundo, El (The Great Theater of the World). An AUTO SACRAMENTAL by Pedro CALDERÓN DE LA BARCA. It deals with the world in terms of a theatrical allegory. The Author (God) presents a performance in which a beggar, a rich man, and other figures, including personifications of vices and virtues, play out their roles. The play demonstrates that the things of this world pass away and only God is eternal.

Grantly, Archdeacon. See BARSETSHIRE, CHRONICLES OF.

Grantorto. See FAERIE QUEENE, THE.

Granville-Barker, Harley (1877–1946). English critic, dramatist, director, and actor. Before World War I, Granville-Barker was noted both as an actor, specializing in Shavian roles, and as the author of such plays as THE VOYSEY INHERITANCE and THE MADRAS HOUSE. In 1911–1913 his staging of *The Winter's Tale, A Midsummer Night's Dream,* and *Twelfth Night* effected a radical change in Shakespeare production. Today Granville-Barker is best known for his critical works, such as his *Prefaces to Shakespeare* (1923–1947), which analyze the plays from a director's point of view, and *A Companion to Shakespeare Studies* (1934), which he edited with G. B. Harrison.

Grapes of Wrath, The (1939). A novel by John STEINBECK. Awarded the Pulitzer Prize in 1940, this moving and highly successful proletarian novel tells of the hardships of the Joad family. "Okie" farmers forced out of their home in the Oklahoma dust-bowl region by economic desperation, they drive to California in search of work as migrant fruitpickers. The grandparents die on the way; on their arrival the others are harassed by the police and participate in strike violence, during which Tom, the Joad son, kills a man. At the conclusion of the novel, throughout which descriptive and philosophical passages alternate with narrative portions, the family is defeated but still resolute.

Graspall. See FURRY LAWCATS.

Gratiae. See GRACES, THE.

Gratiano. (1) In Shakespeare's MERCHANT OF VENICE, a friend of Antonio and Bassanio. He "speaks an infinite deal of nothing, more than any man in all Venice." Gratiano marries Nerissa, the waiting-gentlewoman of Portia.

(2) In Shakespeare's OTHELLO, the brother of Brabantio and uncle of Desdemona.

Grattan, Henry (1746–1820). Irish orator and statesman. He was a persistent advocate of Irish independence and Catholic emancipation. In 1782, when the legislative independence of Ireland was gained by Grattan and the "Protestant Volunteers," the British Parliament gave up the right to pass laws binding upon Ireland.

gratuitous act. See André GIDE.

Grau [Delgado], Jacinto (1877–1958). Spanish playwright. His output, though small, is appreciated both at home and abroad, and includes *El conde Alarcos* (1917), *El hijo pródigo* (1918), *Don Juan de Carillana* (1919), and *El señor de Pigmalión* (1930).

Grau, Shirley Ann (1929–   ). American short-story writer and novelist. Born in New Orleans and raised in Alabama, Miss Grau writes subtly and realistically of Southerners, black and white, in *The Black Prince and Other Stories* (1955). *The Hard Blue Sky* (1958) and *The House on Coliseum Street* (1961) are novels.

Graustark (1901). A romantic novel by George Barr McCUTCHEON. Subtitled *The Story of a Love Behind the Throne,* this enormously popular melodrama tells how an American named Grenfall falls in love with the Princess Yetive in the highly colorful kingdom of Graustark. McCutcheon's first novel, it was sold outright for $500 to a publisher who subsequently reaped a fortune from it. It was followed, however, by the sequels *Beverly of Graustark* (1904) and *The Prince of Graustark* (1914), which were equally and more equitably profitable.

Graves, Alfred Perceval (1846–1931). Irish man of letters and poet. The father of Robert GRAVES, he was a leader in the Irish literary renaissance. Among his works are *Songs of Killarney* (1872) and *Irish Songs and Ballads* (1879).

Graves, Morris (1910–   ). American artist. Deeply influenced by the spirituality of the Far East, he is known chiefly for his somber expressionistic paintings of birds.

Graves, Robert (1895–   ). English poet, novelist, and critic. His individualistic poems are polished and dryly humorous; often they make cosmic statements through quaint personal myths. Among his many collections of poetry are *Fairies and Fusiliers* (1917), *Collected Poems* (1959), *More Poems* (1961), and *New Poems* (1962). *Goodbye to All That* (1929) is a striking autobiography covering his experiences fighting in World War I.

Graves's historical novels are scholarly and mischievous; he often interprets his characters in psychologically convincing ways that are quite different from the conventional, traditional view. *I, Claudius* (1934), CLAUDIUS THE GOD, *Wife to Mr. Milton* (1943), *The Golden Fleece* (1944), *King Jesus* (1946), and *Homer's Daughter* (1955) are novels of this kind. Among his books of literary criticism are *A Survey of Modernist Poetry* (1927), with Laura Riding as co-author; THE WHITE GODDESS; and *Oxford Addresses on Poetry* (1962). *The Long Week-End* (1940) is a social history of the interwar years in England. *The Nazarene Gospel Restored* (1953), with Joshua

Podro as co-author, is a bold, scholarly reinterpretation of the origins of Christianity. He translated and commented on *The Greek Myths* (1955). Graves was a friend of T. E. Lawrence and Laura Riding, and encouraged the young English writer Alan Sillitoe. After having lived in Majorca for many years, he returned to England in 1961 to become professor of poetry at Oxford University.

Graveyard by the Sea, The. See CIMETIÈRE MARIN, LE.

graveyard school. A preromantic movement in English poetry of the 18th century, composed chiefly of followers and imitators of Edward YOUNG and Robert BLAIR. It is so named because of the meditative, melancholy tone of the characteristic verse of the school, the scene of which was often laid in graveyards and cemeteries, and because of the moral and religious reflections inspired by their thoughts of impending death.

Gray, Asa (1810–1888). American botanist and teacher. A professor at Harvard, he published a series of scientific studies of American flora and several textbooks. Among these are *Elements of Botany* (1836), *Manual of Botany of the Northern U.S.* (1848), and *How Plants Grow* (1858). Highly regarded by scholars, Gray made Harvard a center of botanical research in America.

Gray, Thomas (1716–1771). English poet and noted letter-writer. He was one of the forerunners of the romantic movement in England. His most important correspondence was with Horace Walpole, Thomas Wharton, and William Mason. His works, largely meditative lyrics and Pindaric odes are marked by love of nature and melancholy reflection. His poetry includes *Ode to Spring, Hymn to Adversity,* and *Ode on a Distant Prospect of Eton College* (1742); *Sonnet on the Death of Richard West* (1775), which contains the well-known lines ". . . where ignorance is bliss, 'Tis folly to be wise"; *Ode on the Death of a Favorite Cat, Drowned in A Tub of Gold Fishes* (1748), light verse in the neoclassic manner; ELEGY WRITTEN IN A COUNTRY CHURCHYARD, his most famous work; *The Progress of Poesy,* on the power of music; THE BARD; *The Fatal Sisters* and *The Descent of Odin* (1761), both in imitation of early Welsh and Norse verse. The biography published by his friend and correspondent William Mason, in 1775, contains many of his famous letters.

Gray expressed his poetic ideal thus: "Extreme conciseness of expression, yet pure, perspicuous, and musical, is one of the grand beauties of lyric poetry. This I have always aimed at, and never could attain." See STOKE POGES.

Grazzini, Anton Francesco (1503–1584). Florentine apothecary and author of stories and plays. He was also a founder of the Academy of the *Umidi,* in which his academic name was *Il Lasca* (the Roach). One of his plays, *La Spiritata* (*The Possessed*), has been translated into English under the title of *The Bugbears.*

Great Awakening. A religious revivalist movement (1740–1750) which swept through the American colonies and was marked by violent and sensational public repentance and conversion. It began in Massachusetts under the influence of the preaching of Jonathan EDWARDS and of the English evangelist George Whitefield. The movement was opposed by

S I N N E R S
In the Hands of an
Angry G O D.
A S E R M O N

Preached at *Enfield*, *July* 8th 1 7 4 1.

At a Time of great Awakenings ; and attended with remarkable Impreffions on many of the Hearers.

By *Jonathan Edwards*, A. M.

Paftor of the Church of CHRIST in *Northampton*.

Amos ix 2, 3. *Though they dig into Hell, thence fhall mine Hand take them ; though they climb up to Heaven, thence will I bring them down. And though they hide themfelves in the Top of Carmel, I will fearch and take them out thence ; and though they be hid from my Sight in the Bottom of the Sea, thence I will command the Serpent, and he fhall bite them.*

The Second Edition.

? T O N : Printed and Sold by S. KNEELAND ". GREEN in Queen-Street over againft the 1 7 4 2.

A popular sermon published during the Great Awakening.

---

a liberal group led by Charles CHAUNCEY whose ideas led in time to the doctrine of Unitarianism.

Great Bear and **Little Bear** (**Ursa Major** and **Ursa Minor**). Constellations. In Greek legend, Callisto, a nymph of Artemis, had a son by Zeus. His wife Hera (or Zeus himself) changed Callisto into a bear. When she was about to be shot by her son Arcas, Zeus converted mother and son into constellations. The name given to the two constellations considered as a single group, is Arctos.

The Greek word *arktos*, a bear, is still kept in the names Arcturus (the bear-ward, from *ouros*, guardian), and Arctic. The Sanskrit name for the Great Bear is from the verb *rakh*, to be bright, and it has been suggested that the Greeks named it *arktos* as a result of confusion between the two words. Arcturus was once the name given to the Pole Star.

Encompassed within Great and Little Bear are star formations popularly known as the Big Dipper and the Little Dipper; the latter contains the North Star, which is also known as the Pole Star, Polaris.

Great Bible. See BIBLE, ENGLISH VERSIONS.

Great Cham of Literature. A sobriquet for Dr. Samuel JOHNSON first used by Smollett in a letter to Wilkes. *Cham* is an obsolete word, synonomous with *Khan*, applicable to the ruler of the Tartars, the Mongols, and the emperor of China.

Great Divide, The (1906). A drama by William Vaughn MOODY. Originally entitled *The Sabine Woman,* the play has as its theme the conflict between Puritan New England and the American West. Ruth Jordan, from Massachusetts, is attacked by three men while alone in her brother's cabin in Arizona; she saves herself by agreeing to marry one of them and, eventually, after many trials, comes to love him and his Western independence.

Great Expectations (1860–1861). A novel by Charles DICKENS. The novel traces the growth of Philip Pirrip, called Pip, from a boy of shallow dreams to a man of depth and character. Pip is reared by his sister and her husband Joe Gargery, a blacksmith. In his youth he is influenced by the eccentric Miss HAVISHAM, who was jilted on her wedding night and who has brought up her adopted niece Estella to hate men. As a young man, Pip is informed that an unknown benefactor has provided money for his education and expects to make him his heir. Forsaking his humbler friends—particularly the faithful Joe—he sets off to London with the firm intention of becoming a gentleman and realizing his "great expectations." He soon learns that his patron is Abel MAGWITCH, a transported convict, whom Pip had helped years earlier; Magwitch also turns out to be Estella's father. With this knowledge Pip's dreams fade; he returns home after Joe saves him from imprisonment for debt, and sets himself to honest work. He marries Estella after her husband, Bentley Drummle, dies. Among the gallery of characters in the book are Biddy, who becomes Joe's second wife; the Pocket family; Uncle PUMBLECHOOK; Dolge Orlick, the murderer of Pip's sister; and Mr. JAGGERS.

The novel is regarded by many as Dickens' greatest achievement, although the happy ending, which according to Dickens' biographer John Forster was written on the advice of Bulwer-Lytton, detracts from the work somewhat.

Great Gatsby, The (1925). A novel by F. Scott FITZGERALD. The mysterious Jay Gatsby lives in a luxurious mansion on the wealthy Long Island shore, entertaining hundreds of guests at lavish parties that have become a legend on the island. Nick Carraway, the narrator, lives next-door to Gatsby, and Nick's cousin Daisy and her crude but wealthy husband Tom Buchanan live in the house directly across the harbor from Gatsby's. Gatsby reveals to Nick that he and Daisy had a brief affair before the war and her marriage to Tom; born Jay Gatz of a poor midwestern family, he has accumulated enormous wealth through shady transactions solely to make himself the kind of man he thinks Daisy admires: his one dream, and the reason he bought his house and gives his parties, is to win her back. He persuades Nick to bring him and Daisy together again, but ultimately he is unable to win her from her husband. Daisy, driving Gatsby's car, runs over and kills Tom's mistress Myrtle, unaware of the woman's identity. Myrtle's husband traces the car and shoots Gatsby, who has remained silent in order to protect Daisy. Gatsby's friends and business associates all desert him, and only Nick, Gatsby's father, and one habitué of the parties attend the funeral. The novel's power derives not from its violent plot, but from its sharp and antagonistic portrayal of wealthy society in America and from the exposure of the "Jazz Age," Fitzgerald's favorite subject, in all its false glamour, cultural barrenness, moral emptiness, and desperate boredom. Yet the novel transcends its own bitter view and is probably Fitzgerald's most humane work. It has enjoyed continuous popularity since its first publication, and, written in a fully-developed and easy style, it is now considered one of the chief texts of American literature of the post-World War I period.

Great God Brown, The (1926). A play by Eugene O'NEILL. Masks are used to symbolize the varying personalities of the characters as they are and as they appear to other people. The "great god Brown" is a successful businessman, devoid of inner resources; he eventually takes the mask of Dion Anthony (as his name suggests, a Dionysian character), a frustrated artist who dies. With Dion's mask, Brown is accepted by Dion's wife as the real Dion, for she has known and loved only her husband's mask, not his true self.

Great Learning, The. One of the Chinese FOUR BOOKS. Originally one chapter from the BOOK OF RITES, it was elevated to importance in the Confucian educational and philosophical system during the Sung Dynasty (960–1279). It emphasizes self-cultivation.

Great Mother, the. A nature goddess of ancient Anatolia. Her names and appellations include CYBELE, the mountain mother, the Idaean mother, and still others. In Greek mythology, Cybele is generally associated with Rhea.

Great Theater of the World, The. See GRAN TEATRO DEL MUNDO, EL.

Greaves, Sir Launcelot. See LAUNCELOT GREAVES.

Greco, El. Sobriquet of **Kyriakos Theotocopoulos** (c. 1541–1614). Greek-born Spanish painter. Having mastered the technique of icon painting in Crete, he went to Italy where he studied the work of Titian and Tintoretto. In 1577 he settled in Toledo, Spain, where, isolated from artistic influences, he developed a highly personal style which retains the movement of baroque drawing while suppressing the very spatial depth which baroque art sought to create. He painted intense portraits, mystic saints, and deeply expressive religious scenes. His use of such effects as discordantly contrasted cool colors, elongated distortions of the human frame, bright illumination, and flashing accents was misunderstood by contemporaries, and the significance of his art was not recognized until the 19th century. His best-known works include *Assumption of the Virgin* (1577), *Burial of the Count of Orgaz* (c. 1584), *Pentecost* (1604–1614), and *View of Toledo* (1600–1610).

Greek Anthology, The. A collection of several thousand poems, songs, gravestone inscriptions, epigrams, epitaphs, and the like, by numerous Greek writers, known and anonymous, from the 5th century B.C. to the 6th century A.D. Its original form was a collection called the *Garland of Meleager* (c. 60 B.C.), to which continuous additions were made. A number of the poems in *The Greek Anthology* have become famous. The Elizabethan poetic miscellany (see TOTTEL'S MISCELLANY) was a spiritual descendant of *The Greek Anthology.*

Greek epic poetry. Greek epic, a development from oral tradition. The earliest extant examples are the ILIAD and the ODYSSEY of HOMER. The functions of the Mycenaean rhapsode (*rhapsodos*) or minstrel are clearly shown in the character of Demodocus, the blind bard who entertained Odysseus and other guests at the court of the Phaeacian king Alcinous in the *Odyssey*. It was his duty to sing of the great heroes of past and present in order to entertain and please the kings and lords who could afford such a luxury. Unlike Demodocus, most bards probably traveled from court to court. Wherever they stopped, they would find it expedient to recite events that were especially gratifying to the local lord; his own exploits or those of heroes he claimed as forebears, much as Vergil later made the myths of Aeneas a paean to the glory of Rome and of his personal patron, Augustus. To this end the bard would often fabricate a connection between his patron of the moment and some great event or hero, such as the sack of Troy or the deeds of Heracles. This custom accounts in part for the apparent ubiquity of Heracles and Theseus and, more important, for the process of gradual accretion which, over a period of centuries, culminated in such epics as the *Odyssey,* in which a great mass of originally unrelated myths and folk tales adhered to the story of one hero.

An itinerant bard had to be able not only to recall an enormous number of tales, but to recite them in the dactylic hexameters which, by the time of Homer, had already been the traditional language of epic for centuries. Since writing, if it was used at all for literary purposes, must have been only a kind of shorthand, a bard was called upon to perform prodigious feats of memory. At the same time, in adjusting his tales to the requirements of the immediate situation, he had to be able to improvise at length.

The structure of the great Greek epics, even in the relatively literary form in which they have been preserved, show clearly their oral origins. One of their most striking characteristics is the great number of repeated phrases (for example, epithets such as "wine-dark sea" or "shepherd of the people") which are applied more or less indiscriminately to a variety of places or people. Every bard memorized a vast repertory of these formulae, which he could then apply on the spur of the moment in an appropriate spot in a poem according to the demands of the meter. It was probably this patchwork approach to poetry that earned him the name of rhapsode: "stitcher."

The repetition of stock phrases inevitably tends to monotony, especially when those phrases must, for practical reasons, be kept general enough in tone to be largely interchangeable. It is a measure of the genius of Homer, whoever he may have been, that he was able, within these traditional limitations, to achieve considerable individuality in his characters and to overcome monotony with sheer dramatic and poetic power.

Greek music. The music of ancient Greece. Music was extensively cultivated and studied in ancient Greece, and was considered important to the state, because of its supposed control of human passions and morals. Only fragments of the actual music have survived, but many important theoretical treatises still exist, and have had an important influence on music ever since. The principal modes (or scales) in which Greek music was written are: Phrygian, brisk and spirited; Dorian, bold and grave; Lydian, full of soft pathos; Mixolydian, dirgelike.

The principal instruments used in Greek music were the *aulos* and the *kithara*. *Auloi* is a generic name for wind instruments of the flute and oboe type; the *kithara*, and its close relative the *lyra* or lyre, was a plucked string instrument with 3 to 15 strings.

Greek Passion, The (Ho Christós Xanastauronetai; 1951). A novel by Nikos KAZANTZAKIS. Set in modern Anatolia, it is a story of the persecution of the Greek inhabitants of an impoverished village by their Turkish overlords and, worse, by each other. At the beginning, several of the villagers are chosen for roles they are to play eight months later in a local passion play. By the time Passion Week comes, the play has been forgotten in a succession of violent events—and the villagers have played out their assigned roles in real life. A powerful modern morality play, the novel reveals the darker passions in men's lives that deeply concerned Kazantzakis.

Greeley, Horace (1811–1872). American journalist and political leader. As a newspaper printer and editor in New York, Greeley advocated many reform movements including abolition. He served in Congress (1848–1849) and supported the candidacy of Lincoln for president. Averse to the Republican policy of revenge on the South following the Civil War, he ran unsuccessfully against Grant in 1872. Greeley supported the agrarian movement and worked for a liberal policy for settlers; one of his favorite sayings was "Go West, young man." In sympathy with the laboring classes in New York City, he also favored "magnanimity in triumph," a policy of universal amnesty and universal suffrage after the Civil War. His willingness to put up bail for Jefferson Davis brought him much abuse, but he never allowed his subscribers' threats to modify his editorial views.

Green, Anna Katharine (1846–1935). American novelist and short-story writer. She is especially remembered for *The Leavenworth Case* (1878), said to be the first detective fiction written by a woman. Other works include *The Hand and the Ring* (1883) and *The Filigree Ball* (1903).

Green, Anne (1899–). American novelist. Shortly after her birth, her family moved to Paris where her father was in business, and Miss Green, whose brother is Julian GREEN, has described the household in her volume of reminiscences: *With Much Love* (1948). Her novels include *The Selbys* (1930), *A Marriage of Convenience* (1933), *Fools Rush In* (1934), *The Silent Duchess* (1939), *Just Before Dawn* (1943), and *The Old Lady* (1947).

Green, Frederick Lawrence (1902–1953). Irish novelist, best known for his *Odd Man Out* (1945), a novel about a young Irish revolutionary.

Green, Henry. Pen name of **Henry Yorke** (1905–). English novelist and manufacturer. All his novels have extremely brief titles, such as *Blindness* (1926); *Living* (1929), a compassionate proletarian novel; *Party Going* (1939); LOVING, his best-known novel; *Back* (1946), an account of a man's return from the war; *Concluding* (1948), a satire on a future bureaucratic state; *Nothing* (1950); and *Doting* (1952). His novels, written almost entirely in realistic dialogue, are elegant and witty but ambiguous comedies of manners. Often two forces are brought into conflict, such as the old and the young,

the past and the present, the employer and the servant. Though the novels are apparently simple, even naïve, they have mysterious symbolical overtones (see *Loving*). *Pack My Bag* (1939) is a collection of reminiscences.

Green, Julian or **Julien** (1900–). French novelist of American parentage. He is the brother of Anne GREEN. Green is as much influenced by his Puritan heritage as by the Catholicism to which he was converted. His novels, originally written in French, reflect his obsessive sense of sin, his terrible consciousness of the violence and sadism of which men are capable, his fascination and fear of madness and death. Depicting a varied yet constant battle between good and evil, Green's works include *Avarice House (Mont-Cinère;* 1926), *The Closed Garden (Adrienne Mesurat;* 1927), *The Dark Journey (Leviathan;* 1929), *The Dreamer (Le Visionnaire;* 1934), *Then Shall the Dust Return (Varouna;* 1940), MOÏRA, and CHAQUE HOMME DANS SA NUIT. *Sud* (1953), *L'Ennemi* (1954), and *L'Ombre* (1956) are plays; *Personal Record 1928–1939* (1939) and *Memories of Happy Days* (1942) are autobiographical volumes.

Green, Paul E[liot] (1894–). American playwright and teacher. He is best known for dramas portraying life in the South, often set in his native state of North Carolina. His most important plays are *In Abraham's Bosom* (1927), a Pulitzer Prize-winning drama about a mulatto who tries to establish a school for Negroes in a North Carolina town; *The Field God* (1927), concerning poor whites; *The House of Connelly* (1931), dealing with the contrast between aristocratic Southern landowners and the tenant farmers; and a dramatization (1940) of Richard Wright's *Native Son*. Green wrote scripts in Hollywood during the 30's, eventually returning to teach at the University of North Carolina. His later plays deal with folk customs and beliefs; among them are *The Lost Colony* (1937), a historical pageant dealing with the first settlement on Roanoke Island; *The Common Glory* (1947), set at the time of the Revolution; *Wilderness Road* (1955); and *The Stephen Foster Story* (1959).

Green, Thomas Hill (1836–1882). A British philosopher, noted for his *Prolegomena to Ethics* (1883) and *Principles of Political Obligation* (1895). Against Social Darwinists such as Spencer, who argued that man was determined by natural forces such as evolution, Green followed Hegel in asserting that man was a free and rational being who acted in relation to rational moral ideals; that the highest moral ideal revealed by reason was the ideal of the perfect state, that man's most important duties were therefore political. Freedom was not the ability to do as one liked, but the power to identify one's self with the highest rational good, i.e., the ideal of the perfect state, and the responsibility to criticize and reform the existing social order in accordance with this ideal.

Green Bay Tree, The (1924). A novel by Louis BROMFIELD. It tells the story of Lily Shane who begins life in a Middle Western industrial town and goes to Paris to bear an illegitimate child. Bromfield's first novel, it is also the first novel in the tetralogy entitled *Escape*.

Greenberg, Samuel (1893–1917). Austrian-born American poet. Greenberg, who came to the U.S. as a child, began writing poetry in a hospital for the tubercular. None of his poems was published during his lifetime, but, after his early death, Hart CRANE found his manuscripts. Crane was deeply impressed by the strange imagery and flights of intense imagination, and some of Greenberg's phrases are recognizable in Crane's own poems. *Poems: A Selection from the Manuscripts* was published in 1947, with a preface by Allen Tate.

Green Carnation, The (1894). A novel by Robert S. Hichens (1864–1950). It satirizes the decadence of the period at the end of the 19th century; in particular, it is intended as a lampoon on Oscar Wilde. The "green carnation" of the title is "the arsenic flower of an exquisite life." The hero, Lord Reginald Hastings, "too modern to be reticent," is put in his place by a heroine who, when he complains that she is almost ordinary, replies that she is glad of it and flatly refuses to marry him.

Greene, Graham (1904–   ). English novelist, short-story writer, and playwright. He is an ardent convert to Catholicism, and all his writings reflect his religious views. Greene's novels are unusual combinations of psychological studies, adventure thrillers, and essays on moral and theological dilemmas. Among the best known of his works are BRIGHTON ROCK, THE POWER AND THE GLORY (first published in the U.S. as *The Labyrinthine Ways*), THE HEART OF THE MATTER, and A BURNT-OUT CASE. He also wrote a number of lighter novels in which the thriller element predominates, but which are still about problems of good and evil. Some of these "entertainments," such as THE THIRD MAN, have made excellent movies.

Greene's settings are varied: Sweden in *England Made Me* (1935), wartime London in *The Ministry of Fear* (1943) and *The End of the Affair* (1951), Mexico, Africa, or an English seaside town. The place, however, is always in a state of seedy decay and the people in a state of spiritual and psychological chaos. Greene has a journalist's sense of topicality. Many of his novels were set in unusual places just before they became international crisis spots: *The Quiet American* (1955), about a fumbling idealist in cold-war Viet Nam; *Our Man in Havana* (1958), a Cuba spy-story "entertainment"; and *A Burnt-Out Case* (1960), set in the Congo. Greene has also written *Twenty-One Stories* (1954), a collection of short stories, meditative travel books such as *Journey without Maps* (1936), and plays such as *The Living Room* (1953), *The Potting Shed* (1956), and *The Complaisant Lover* (1959).

Greene, Robert (1560?–1592). English prose writer and dramatist. Greene traveled in Europe, took his M.A. degree from both Oxford and Cambridge, and then appeared in London, where he became known as a University Wit and a writer of rogue literature. During his brief life he was a remarkably prolific writer, having 38 publications—prose romances, pamphlets, dramas—to his credit at the time of his death. His early prose works, showing the influence of John LYLY and the Euphuistic style (see EUPHUISM), include *Mamilla* (1583); *The Myrrour of Modesty* (the story of Susanna, 1584); *Alcida, Greene's Metamorphosis* (1588). *Euphues, His Censure of Philautus* (1587), is a continuation of Lyly's work. *Pandosto, the Triumph of Time* (1588)

is a prose romance which provided Shakespeare with the plot for *A Winter's Tale*. *Menaphon* (1589, reprinted as *Greene's Arcadia*) is a pastoral romance modeled after Sir Philip Sidney's *Arcadia*.

All Greene's plays were performed posthumously. They include *The Comical History of Alphonsus, King of Arragon* (c. 1587); *Friar Bacon and Friar Bungay* (c. 1589, acted 1594), a comedy that may have been inspired by Marlowe's *Dr. Faustus*, dealing with the legendary alchemical pursuits of Roger Bacon and Thomas Bungay; *Orlando Furioso* (acted 1592), a free adaptation of Ariosto; *The Scottish History of James IV* (c. 1591); and, with Thomas Lodge, *A Looking Glass for London and England* (c. 1590, acted 1592). It is possible that Greene was in part responsible for the original plays dealing with HENRY VI, which Shakespeare allegedly revised and rewrote. In his last pamphlet, A GROATSWORTH OF WIT, Greene gives the first contemporary mention of Shakespeare in a warning to his fellow-playwrights to beware the upstart actor who, with his "tiger's heart wrapped in a player's hide," is encroaching on their territory and writing plays himself.

As one of the writers hired to reply to the Puritan pamphlets in the Martin MARPRELATE CONTROVERSY, Greene was attacked by Richard Harvey in *Plaine Percevall and the Peace-maker of England* (1590). Greene answered with *A Quip for an Upstart Courtier* (1592), directed against Harvey and his two brothers. By the time Gabriel HARVEY retaliated in *Foure Letters and Certaine Sonnets*, Greene was dead "of a surfeit of pickled herring and Rhenish wine," and his defense was taken up by Thomas NASHE; however, it is Gabriel Harvey who wrote an account of Greene's last days.

Greene's repentance pamphlets, while in part autobiographical, should probably not be taken entirely as documents of personal repentance and confession. They include *Greene's Mourning Garment* (1590); *Never Too Late* (1590); *Farewell to Folly* (1591); and *A Groatsworth of Wit Bought with a Million of Repentance* (1592), which contains the allusion to Shakespeare. His "cony-catching" pamphlets (1591–92) are realistic descriptions of London low-life and underworld activity; they include *A Defense of Cony-Catching; Disputation between a He-Cony-Catcher and a She-Cony-Catcher; The Black Book's Messenger;* and *A Notable Discovery of Cozenage*.

Green-eyed monster. Iago's term for jealousy in Shakespeare's *Othello*. A greenish complexion was formerly held to be indicative of jealousy; and as cats, lions, tigers, and all the green-eyed tribe "mock the meat they feed on," so jealousy mocks its victim by loving and loathing it at the same time.

Green Hat, The (1924). A best-selling novel by Michael ARLEN. Its popularity was largely due to the way in which it captured the licentious, disillusioned spirit of the time. With a self-sacrificing heroine and a husband who kills himself on his wedding night because he has syphilis, the novel is a sentimental account of sexual license among the wealthy.

Green Henry (Der grüne Heinrich; first version, 1854; second, 1879–1880). A largely autobiographical novel by Gottfried KELLER in the tradition of the BILDUNGSROMAN. Heinrich Lee, the hero, called green because of his youthful naïveté, wishes to become a great painter and expends a great deal of time and energy at this pursuit before he finally discovers that he can never achieve more than moderate competence. In the course of his adventures, however, he neglects his widowed mother, and it is in this aspect of the story that the novel's two versions diverge. In the early version, Heinrich assumes all the blame for his mother's eventual death; his attacks of conscience break both his spirit and body, and he dies. In the later version, however, Heinrich's guilt is not stressed, and he successfully adjusts himself to a life of civic service as a government official.

Green Knight. See SIR GAWAIN AND THE GREEN KNIGHT.

Green Mansions (1904). A romance of the South American tropics by William Henry HUDSON. The hero, Mr. Abel, tells the tragic story of his love for the bird girl, Rima, an ethereal maiden whose jungle upbringing has brought her close to the powers and beauty of nature. Abel has just succeeded in awakening the human emotion of love in the half-wild girl when she is killed by a band of savages.

Green Mountain Boys, The (1839). A novel by Daniel Pierce Thompson (1795–1868), American lawyer, novelist, and historian. The book's central character is the hero Ethan Allen. Immensely popular, the novel was the most successful of Thompson's attempts to preserve romantic episodes in early Vermont history and gives a vivid picture of Revolutionary times in Vermont.

Green Pastures, The (1930). A play by Marc CONNELLY, based on the sketches in Roark Bradford's OL' MAN ADAM AN' HIS CHILLUN. This famous play, which was awarded a Pulitzer Prize, presents reverent though humorous versions of Old Testament stories as they are told by an old Southern Negro preacher in terms of the lives of his congregation.

Greenwich Village or **The Village.** A section of New York City west of Washington Square. It was noted during the early 20th century and the years immediately preceding and following World War I as the haunt of Bohemian artists, writers, and radicals, who originally chose it as a place to live because of its cheapness. In former days it had been a quaint, small village reached from the city in lower Manhattan by stage coach.

By the time of the 1930's, Greenwich Village was chiefly a residential district for young business and professional couples, who could pay higher rents than their predecessors the Bohemians, and the artists and writers had moved to Brooklyn or to the Connecticut suburbs. Among the well-known personalities who have lived and worked in Greenwich Village at one time or another are: Floyd Dell, Gelett Burgess, Max Eastman, Emma Goldman, William Vaughn Moody, Eugene O'Neill, Edna St. Vincent Millay, William Rose Benét, Katherine Anne Porter, E. E. Cummings, Carson McCullers, and James Baldwin; among the little magazines published there were *The Little Review*, *The Masses*, and *The Seven Arts*. Several novels of Floyd Dell deal with the life in Greenwich Village in its heyday.

Greg, Sir W[alter] W[ilson] (1875–1959). English bibliographer and literary scholar. A pioneer in the use of scientific bibliography in literary criticism, he wrote *Pastoral Poetry and Pastoral Drama* (1906) and *A Bibliography of the English Printed Drama to the Restoration* (2 vols., 1939, 1951).

Gregorian chant. The ritual plain song, or *cantus firmus*, a kind of unison music in the eight church modes. A collection of these, edited by Pope Gregory I, has come down to us. It is still used in the services of the Roman Catholic Church and Greek Catholic Church.

Gregorian year. The civil year, according to the correction introduced by Pope Gregory XIII in 1582. The equinox, which occurred on March 25 in the time of Julius Caesar, fell on March 11 in the year 1582. This was because the Julian calculation of 365¼ days to a year was 11 min. 10 sec. too much. Gregory suppressed ten days, so as to make the equinox fall on March 21, as it did at the Council of Nice, and, by some simple arrangements prevented the recurrence in future of a similar error.

The New Style, as it was called, was adopted in England in 1752, when Wednesday, September 2, was followed by Thursday, September 14.

This gave rise to a double computation: Lady Day, March 25, Old Lady Day, April 6; Midsummer Day, June 24, Old Midsummer Day, July 6; Michaelmas Day, September 29, Old Michaelmas Day, October 11; Christmas Day, December 25, Old Christmas Day, January 6.

Gregory I. Called **Gregory the Great**, St. (c. 540–604). Benedictine monk elected Pope (590–604). He established the temporal power of the papacy, reformed monastic discipline, and sent AUGUSTINE with 40 monks to England. According to tradition it was he who established the liturgical music known as GREGORIAN CHANT.

Gregory VII, St. Original name, **Hildebrand** (c. 1020–1085). Italian pope (1073–1083). As pope he pursued a policy of establishing the papacy as the supreme office in the Church and of protecting the Church from the civil states in Europe. He issued a decree (1075) that prohibited lay investiture of the clergy, that is, clergy could no longer be appointed to office by civil authorities. He called Henry IV of Germany to Rome to answer charges of oppression of the Church and sacrilege. Henry was outraged at Gregory's play for authority and tried to depose him. Gregory responded by excommunicating Henry. Henry did penance in the snow before Gregory's palace at Canossa and gained conditional absolution (1077). In 1078, Gregory renewed the excommunication, and Henry declared war. He appointed Clement III as antipope (1080) and captured Rome in 1084. Gregory was rescued from the castle Sant' Angelo, and died in exile at Salerno the next year.

Gregory, Horace [Victor] (1898–). American poet, critic, and translator. Much of his poetry criticizes middle-class life and presents dramatic monologues or character studies of petty racketeers and gangsters and people of the city slums. Among his books are *Chelsea Rooming House* (1930), *No Retreat* (1933), *Chorus for Survival* (1935), *Poems: 1930–1940* (1941), *The Shield of Achilles: Essays on Poetry and Beliefs* (1944), *Selected Poems* (1951), and *Medusa in Gramercy Park and Other Poems* (1961). In 1931 he translated the poems of Catullus; in 1958 Ovid's *Metamorphoses*. He also wrote *Pilgrim of the Apocalypse* (1933), a study of D. H. Lawrence; *A History of American Poetry, 1900–1940* (1946), with his wife, Marya ZATURENSKA; and critical biographies of Amy Lowell (1958) and James Mc-Neill Whistler (1959).

Gregory, Lady **Isabella Augusta** (1852–1932). Irish dramatist. The first 40 years of Lady Gregory's life were from a literary viewpoint extremely un-eventful, with little if any thought given to the sub-ject. With the death of her husband, Sir William Gregory, in 1892, however, she developed a strong interest in Irish literature and history, and in 1898, when she met William Butler Yeats, she was ready to lend her talent, wealth, and position to the slowly developing sense of national consciousness that was to burgeon into the Irish literary renaissance. The major focus of her energy was directed to the Irish National Theatre, which later evolved into the Abbey Theatre and which she served as a director. In 1914 she wrote a history of the movement, *Our Irish Theatre.*

Her own literary efforts were primarily designed to reawaken the Irish national consciousness through translations and collections of ancient Celtic legend and folklore. She is best known, however, for her one-act plays, which were originally designed as "fillers" for the Abbey program. Among these the best known are *Spreading the News* (1904) and *The Rising of the Moon* (1907).

Her beautiful estate at Coole in western Ireland is celebrated in Yeats's lovely poem, *The Wild Swans at Coole.* See IRISH RENAISSANCE.

greguería. See Ramón GÓMEZ DE LA SERNA.

Greif, Andreas. See Andreas GRYPHIUS.

Gremio. In Shakespeare's TAMING OF THE SHREW, a rich old gentleman, suitor to Bianca. He con-siders himself an ideal mate because of his advanced years.

Grendel. The monster in BEOWULF. He is de-scribed as a giant in human shape, a descendant of Cain who lives in a murky pond with his mother among other strange and vicious sea-beasts. For 12 years mother and son come to land occasionally and devour human victims, until Beowulf comes to kill them.

Grenfell, Sir **Wilfred** (1865–1940). English medical missionary and writer, widely known as Grenfell of Labrador. He wrote adventure tales and books of a religious nature, including *A Labrador Doctor* (1919) and others.

Grenville, Sir **Richard** (1541?–1591). English naval commander. The cousin of Sir Walter RALEIGH, Grenville commanded a fleet of seven of Raleigh's ships carrying colonists who were attempting to settle on Roanoke Island, off the coast of North Carolina (1585). When in 1591 his ship, the *Revenge,* was isolated by a fleet of fifteen Spanish ships off Flores, Grenville fought off the Spaniards for fifteen hours. His heroic battle is celebrated in Tennyson's ballad *The Revenge.*

Gresset, Jean Baptiste Louis (1709–1777). French poet and dramatist. He is noted for his poem *Vert-Vert* (1734), relating the adventures of a parrot, and a successful comedy *Le Méchant* (1745), which satirizes contemporary salon society.

Gretchen (German diminutive for Margarete). In Part I of Goethe's FAUST, the young and simple, lower-class girl whom Faust seduces with the aid of Mephistopheles' magic. She reappears as a penitent

spirit at the end of Part II and greets Faust's salvation with joyful song. See ETERNAL FEMININE.

Grettir the Strong. A hero of *The Grettisaga,* a 14th-century Icelandic tale. Concerned with a histori-cal hero of the late 10th and early 11th century, the story is of unusual interest because of resemblances to parts of the 8th-century Old English epic *Beowulf.* There is a translation of it by William Morris.

Grettisaga, The. See GRETTIR THE STRONG.

Greuze, Jean Baptiste (1725–1805). French painter. He was greatly admired by his contempo-raries for his narrative genre scenes of morality, such as *The Paralytic tended by his Children* and *A Father's Curse: the Ungrateful Son.* Today these overdramatic, insincere, and sentimental paintings are found inferior to his portraits.

Greville, Sir **Fulke.** 1st Baron **Brooke** (1554–1628). English courtier and diplomat. Greville's epi-taph reads: "Servant to Queen Elizabeth—Councillor to King James—and Friend to Sir Philip SIDNEY." It is in this last capacity that he is best remembered, and for his *Life* (1652) of Sidney. Greville had a dis-tinguished career in government, becoming chancel-lor of the exchequer under James I. He was a patron of the arts and learning, and a fair poet in his own right.

Grey, Lady **Jane** (c. 1537–1554). The great-granddaughter of Henry VII and for nine days queen of England. At 16 she was married to Lord Guild-ford Dudley, whose father, the earl of Northumber-land, was Protector of Edward VI. As part of a plan to change the succession of the crown from the Tudors to the Dudleys, Northumberland persuaded the dying Edward to settle the crown on Lady Jane and bypass the claims of Mary and Elizabeth. Lady Jane was proclaimed Queen on June 10, 1553, but by the 19th Mary had gathered powerful supporters, de-feated the forces of Northumberland, and was pro-claimed Queen by the Lord Mayor. Lady Jane and her husband were imprisoned and finally executed.

Grey, Zane (1875–1939). American writer of Westerns and articles on outdoor life. In 1904, Grey made up his mind that writing rather than dentistry was to be his career. A first-rate storyteller, he won enormous popular success with *Riders of the Purple Sage* (1912) and a long succession of later novels. Possibly his best books are *The Last of the Plainsmen* (1908) and the nonfiction collection *Tales of Fishing* (1925).

Grey Friars. Franciscans. Black Friars are Do-minicans, and White Friars, Carmelites.

Griboyedov, Aleksandr Sergeyevich (1795–1829). Russian dramatist. His satirical masterpiece, WOE FROM WIT, is one of the classics of Russian drama. For most of his career, Griboyedov was a civil servant. His death was spectacular: serving as Russian minister to Persia, he was cut to pieces by a raging mob that sacked the Russian embassy in Tehran. Griboyedov was the subject of an interesting fictionalized biography entitled *The Death of Vazir-Mukhtar (Smert' Vazir-Mukhtara;* 1929) by the So-viet writer Yuri Nikolayevich Tynyanov (1894–1944).

Grieg, Edvard [Hagerup] (1843–1907). Nor-wegian composer. The rhythmic and melodic pat-terns of his work capture the spirit of his homeland. Grieg wrote operas, choral works, dances, songs, and concertos for various instruments; his PEER GYNT suite, written as incidental music to accompany Ibsen's play, is well known. His songs and chamber music employ subtle and delicate harmonies.

Grieg, [Johan] Nordahl [Brun] (1902–1943). Norwegian poet, novelist, and playwright. The vigor and the adventurous spirit that marked Grieg's life and his writings manifested itself first during his student days. A voyage as a seaman on a Norwegian freighter produced the realistic account *Skibet går videre* (*The Ship Sails On*, 1924); he also traveled through Europe living with tramps. Although he wrote plays during the 1920's, it was not until Grieg's trip to Russia (1933–1935) that his work acquired real force and dramatic vitality. Study of the Russian theater strengthened his sympathy for the working classes and led him to write his plays about controversial social issues. *Vår oere og vår makt* (*Our Honor and Our Might*, 1935) treats the greed of Norwegian ship owners during World War I; *Men imorgen* (*But Tomorrow—*, 1936) presents a conflict between labor and Nazism. In Spain during the civil war as a journalist with republican sympathies, Grieg published a novel, *Men ung må verden ennu voere* (*But Young the World Must Be*, 1938) based on his experiences in Russia, Spain, and Norway. He went to England with the Norwegian government in exile at the time of the German invasion, and flew missions over Germany in American bombers. Before his death, he wrote several war lyrics that express a deepened love for his country and an undaunted courage. *Flagget* (1945), *Friheten* (1945), and *Habet* (1946) are his posthumous collections of poetry.

Grierson, Francis. See Benjamin Henry Jesse Francis SHEPARD.

Grierson, Sir Herbert J[ohn] C[lifford] (1866–1960). Scottish scholar, critic, and editor who, in such books as *The First Half of the 17th Century* (1906), *Poems of John Donne* (1912), and *Metaphysical Poets from Donne to Butler* (1921), helped to bring about the current revival of interest in the Metaphysical poets.

Grieux, le Chevalier des. See MANON LESCAUT.

Grieve, Christopher Murray. See Hugh MACDIARMID.

griffin. A mythical monster. Also called *griffon*, *gryphon*, and similar names. It is fabled to be the offspring of the lion and eagle. Its legs and all from the shoulder to the head are like an eagle; the rest of the body is that of a lion. This creature was sacred to the sun, and kept guard over hidden treasures. The griffins were in perpetual strife with the Arimaspians, a people of Scythia, who rifled the gold mines for the adornment of their hair. The belief apparently grew out of the stylized animal commonly represented in Scythian art, originally perhaps a chicken.

Griffith, D[avid Lewelyn] W[ark] (1875–1948). American motion-picture director and producer. One of the pioneers in the early days of the film, he is especially known for his mobile and imaginative use of the camera and for having developed such techniques as the closeup, the long shot, the flashback, and the fadeout. After a period as actor and script writer, he became a director for the Biograph Company. Later he began to produce motion pictures independently, and in 1923 he was one of the founders of United Artists. Among his famous films are *The Birth of a Nation* (1915), *Hearts of the World*

(1917), *Broken Blossoms* (1919), *Way Down East* (1920), and *Orphans of the Storm* (1921).

Grifone (Gryphon). In the Orlando poems of Boiardo and Ariosto, the son of Oliviero and brother of AQUILANTE. He is called *il bianco* (the white) and his brother *il nero* (the black), because each of them is protected by an enchantress of that color. The white enchantress rescued him from a griffin (hence his name), which had stolen him from his mother, Ghismonda.

Grigorovich, Dmitri Vasilyevich (1822–1899). Russian novelist and short-story writer. Grigorovich's father died when he was a child, and he was raised by his French mother and governess. Not until he attended school in Moscow did he learn to read and write Russian. In 1836 he entered the military engineering school in St. Petersburg. One of his fellow students was the future novelist Feodor Dostoevski. During his four years at the school, Grigorovich developed a strong interest in literature. He made the acquaintance of such leading figures as the critic Vissarion Belinski, the poet Nikolai Nekrasov, and the novelist Ivan Turgenev. About this time the NATURAL SCHOOL in Russian literature, originating from Belinski's literary doctrines, was in the ascendancy. Grigorovich became one of the leading members of this movement. His first contribution was *Peterburgskiye sharmanshchiki* (*Petersburg Organ-grinders*, 1844), a sketch realistically depicting the lives of organ-grinders in the capital. The piece appeared in *Fiziologiya Peterburga* (*Physiology of Petersburg*, 1845), an anthology devoted to an examination of life in St. Petersburg.

Grigorovich's best works were published in the following two years. *Derevnya* (*The Village*, 1846) was one of the first literary works to deal extensively with peasant life. It was followed by another study of the peasantry: *Anton-Goremyka* (1847). Although they were criticized as presenting a somewhat idealized picture, both these stories did much to make peasant life acceptable material for literature.

Grigoryev, Apollon Aleksandrovich (1822–1864). Russian poet and literary critic. Grigoryev grew up in the conservative middle-class section of Moscow, ZAMOSKVARECHYE, which Ostrovski often used as the setting for his dramas. After graduating from Moscow University, Grigoryev began a wandering career as literary critic for a series of journals. One of his most important associations was with the *Moskvityanin* (*The Muscovite*), where his contacts with Ostrovski and other supporters of an independent Russian culture had a great effect on his own literary theories. In 1856, Grigoryev went abroad for two years. On his return he wrote for the journal *Vremya* (*Time*), published by the novelist Feodor Dostoevski and his brother Mikhail Dostoevski. These men, together with the philosopher Nikolai Nikolayevich Strakhov (1828–1896), shared Grigoryev's views that Russian culture must be an organic growth rooted in Russian life, rather than an imitation of Western culture. Russian literature and art, they maintained, must grow from Russian soil (*pochva*). The ideas of the *pochvenniki*, as the group was known, were set forth by Grigoryev in his article *Paradoxy organicheskiye kritisizma* (*Paradoxes of Organic Criticism*). At about the same time, he wrote the autobiographical work, *Moi literaturniye i nravst-*

venniye skitalchestva (*My Literary and Moral Wanderings*), in which he describes his intellectual development and, also, gives vivid sketches of life in Zamoskvarechye.

Grigoryev's poetry has received less attention than his critical writings. Taking Lermontov and Byron as his poetic masters, Grigoryev wrote mainly romantic lyrics describing his unfortunate love affairs. His narrative poem *Vverkh po volge* (*Up the Volga*, 1857) describes his unsuccessful attempt to rehabilitate a prostitute. A cycle of poems also published in 1857, *Bor'ba* (*The Struggle*), contains some of his best lyrics, reputedly inspired by gypsy songs. Aleksandr Blok, who edited a collection of Grigoryev's verse in 1915, acknowledged the influence of some of these lyrics on his own work.

Grigson, Geoffrey (1905–   ). English poet, essayist, and critic. His volumes of poetry include *Several Observations* (1939) and his prose works include *Essays from the Air* (1951). He edited the periodical anthology *New Verse* (1933–1939).

Grillparzer, Franz (1791–1872). Austrian dramatist whose work is modeled on the dramas of Shakespeare and Calderón. Though his plays often show a deep, sentimental melancholy about the impossibility of reconciling reality with the ideal, his thought never degenerates into mere romantic lamentation and, like the writers of the BIEDERMEIER movement, he believes that a rewarding life is still possible for the man who recognizes and remains within the salutary limits of his nature. His early plays, which are more emotionally extravagant than his later ones, include *Die Ahnfrau* (*The Ancestress*, 1817), a fatetragedy not unlike those of Zacharias Werner, and a tragedy (1818) about the Greek poetess Sappho. But with the trilogy *Das goldene Vliess* (*The Golden Fleece*, 1822), on the story of Jason and Medea, and with the historical tragedy *König Ottokars Glück und Ende* (*King Ottocar's Success and Downfall*, 1825), he hit his dramatic stride, and these plays are among his greatest. His works were not generally wellreceived, however, and after the dismal failure of *Weh dem, der lügt* (*Woe to Him Who Lies*, 1838) he became completely discouraged and never published another play. Still, he continued writing, and among the dramas he left behind at his death are two of his most famous: *Die Jüdin von Toledo* (*The Jewess of Toledo*, completed 1855) and *Ein Bruderzwist in Habsburg* (*A Fraternal Struggle in the House of Hapsburg*, written c. 1855). His well-known novella *Der arme Spielmann* (*The Poor Minstrel*, written 1831) is a sentimental but carefully constructed masterpiece.

Grimald, Nicholas (1519–1562). English poet, scholar, and clergyman. Grimald is best known for his 40 poems, most of them translations from Latin, which appeared in the first edition of TOTTEL's MISCELLANY (1557). He also wrote two Latin plays and translated Cicero's *De Officiis* (1553).

Grimm, Jacob Ludwig Carl (1785–1863) and his brother **Wilhelm Carl** (1786–1859). German scholars, considered the founders of Germanic philology as a systematic study. Among the works on which they collaborated are *Deutsche Sagen* (*German Legends*, 1816) and the famous collection of *Kinder- und Hausmärchen* (lit., "Children's and Household Tales," 1812 ff.) known as *Grimm's Fairy-Tales* (see

MÄRCHEN). For the latter, they got most of their material not from written documents but from peasants whom they interviewed; Wilhelm, who tended more toward literary criticism and appreciation than his brother, did most of the transcription. Jacob, more the scholar, wrote a *Deutsche Grammatik* (*German Grammar*, 1819 ff.) in which he formulated "Grimm's Law," the first attempt to explain the consonantal differences between Greek and Latin words and their cognates in the Germanic languages. It was also Jacob who did most of the work on the definitive *Deutsches Wörterbuch* (*German Dictionary*, 1852 ff.), begun by the brothers and still in progress.

Grimmelshausen, Hans Jakob Christoffel von (1610?–1676). German novelist, strongly influenced by the tradition of the picaresque novel in France and Spain. Although contemporary with baroque poets such as Andreas Gryphius, Grimmelshausen used a less ornamented style, which was more accessible to the people. His most famous work is the novel SIMPLICISSIMUS.

Grindel, Eugène. See Paul ELUARD.

Grippeminaud. See FURRY LAWCATS.

Griselda or **Grisilda** (**The Patient**). The heroine of the final tale of Giovanni Boccaccio's THE DECAMERON. Her husband, the marquis of Saluzzo, chooses her from among the peasantry, then decides to test her fidelity. First, he pretends their two children are dead by his hand; then he feigns boredom and pretends he has married again, using his own daughter as the supposed new love. Turned out of the house, she endures her sufferings nobly and remains constant until Saluzzo relents; she is then restored to her home and children, having won the love and admiration of her husband and his people.

Basically the Job story in modern dress, the tale was known to Boccaccio from a French source; it was in turn translated into Latin by Petrarch. From this Latin version rather than from the Italian source Chaucer drew the CLERK's TALE, to which he supplied his own ironic comment on the credibility of the tale:

> Grisilde is dead, and eek her pacience,
> And both at once buried in Italie.

Groatsworth of Wit Bought with a Million of Repentance, A (1592). A pamphlet written by Robert GREENE, supposedly while he was dying. It is in part a repentance tract and a warning to his fellow-playwrights to eschew evil and thus avoid his own bitter end. It contains the famous reference to SHAKESPEARE as "an upstart crow, beautified with our feathers, that . . . supposes he is as well able to bombast out a blank verse as the best of you; and being an absolute *Johannes fac totum*, is in his own conceit the only Shake-scene in a country." See illustration on page 426.

Grongar Hill (1726). A poem by John DYER imitative of the early poems of Milton. It presents a picturesque, contemplative, and melancholy landscape in sharp contrast to its lively companion poem *The Country Walk*.

Groote, Gerard (1340–1384). A Dutch reformer and founder of the society of BRETHREN OF THE COMMON LIFE.

Gropius, Walter [Adolf] (1883–   ). German architect. The organizer and head of the BAUHAUS

GREENES, GROATS-VVORTH

of witte, bought with a
million of Repentance.

Deſcribing the follie of youth, the falſhood of make-
ſhifte flatterers, the miſerie of the negligent,
and miſchiefes of deceiuing
Courtezans.

Written before his death and publiſhed at his
dyeing requeſt.

Fælicem fuiſſe infauſtum.

LONDON
Imprinted for William Wright.
1 5 9 2.

Title page of Greene's *A Groatsworth of Wit* (1592).

until 1928, he has been established in the U.S. since 1937. His influence in the field of education continued on this continent when he became chairman of the department of architecture at Harvard (1938–1953). His conception of architectural teamwork led to the formation of The Architects' Collaborative (TAC), designers of Harvard's Graduate Center. It has attracted commissions on the scale of a civic center for Tallahassee, Fla., and the new U.S. Embassy in Athens.

Grosseteste, Robert (c. 1175–1253). English prelate and scholar, bishop of Lincoln (after 1235). He is known for his determined struggle to protect the English clergy against both King Henry III and Pope Innocent IV, particularly as to the right of making ecclesiastical appointments. Also important to medieval intellectual life were his voluminous writings on everything from philosophy and theology to husbandry, largely in Latin, but also including *Le Château d'Amour* (*The Castle of Love*), a French poem of religious allegory.

Grossi, Tommaso (1790–1853). Italian poet and novelist. A member of the romantic school, he is the author of a novella in octaves entitled *Ildegonda* (1820), and a 15-canto epic poem *I Lombardi alla Prima Crociata* (1826). His novel *Marco Visconti* (1834), which follows Manzoni's model for the historical novel, is noted for its illustration of the theme of Italian independence. Verdi based the libretto for his opera *I Lombardi alla Prima Crociata* (1843) on the epic poem.

Grosz, George (1893–1961). German artist. He is known for his venomous satirical drawings which he used to attack militarism, the bourgeoisie, and capitalists. Greatly effected by the first World War, he participated in the Dada movement. When he was exiled to the U.S. after Hitler came to power, his satire became less aggressive.

Grote, George (1794–1871). English historian, educator. Active in the liberal and humanitarian movements of his day, Grote was, with John Stuart Mill and Henry Brougham, a founder of the University College, London. He was an advocate of parliamentary reform and higher education for women. He is best known for his *History of Greece* (1845–1856), for many years the definitive English work in its field, though now superseded by later scholarship. He was also the author of *Plato and the Other Companions of Socrates* (1865) and *Aristotle* (1872).

Grotius, Hugo. Latinized form of **Huig de Groot** (1583–1645). A Dutch jurist and statesman. His *De Jure Belli et Pacis* (1625), written after his escape to France as leader of the Remonstrants, is regarded as the real beginning of the science of international law. His voluminous writings include a number of tragedies.

Groto, Luigi (1541–1585). Italian dramatist and poet. Known as *Il Cieco d'Adria* (the Blind Poet of Adria) after his infirmity and his birthplace near Venice, he was the author of lyrics, comedies, and tragedies. One of the latter, *La Hadriana*, retells the story of *Romeo and Juliet*, but far more popular and influential were his epigrams and madrigals, mainly imitations of the *Greek Anthology*. He was also a diplomat and, at times, an actor, as when he performed the role of Tiresias in Sophocles' *Oedipus Rex* at the famous theatre of Vicenza built by Palladio.

ground-hog day. February 2. On that day, according to popular legend, the ground hog, or woodchuck, emerges from the hole in which he spent the winter, but if he sees his shadow he goes back to hibernate for six weeks more, and winter lasts that much longer. See CANDLEMAS DAY.

Ground We Stand On, The (1941). A collection of biographical sketches by John Dos Passos. Dos Passos in his novels had been passionately critical of contemporary American life. In these sketches he turned to the past to affirm the American Dream as it appeared exemplified in the philosophy of men who had made or influenced our earlier era, such as Roger Williams, Sam Adams, Tom Paine, Jefferson, Joel Barlow, and Hugh Henry Brackenridge.

Group Theatre, The. A London theater and acting company. It flourished during the 1930's, performing Marxist, labor-sympathizing, and experimental plays. W. H. AUDEN and Christopher ISHERWOOD wrote plays for this theater.

Groussard, Serge (1920–   ). French novelist and journalist. His novels are a kind of fictionalized reporting of the contemporary scene: *Pogrom* (1948), about the Jews in Tripolitania, *Woman With No Past* (*La femme sans passé;* 1954), and *German Officer* (*Un officier de tradition;* 1954).

Grove, Sir George (1820–1900). English engineer and writer on music. He built the first iron lighthouse at Jamaica (1841). He is remembered chiefly as the editor of the standard *Dictionary of Music and Musicians* (1879–1886). He served as director of the Royal College of Music at Kensington from 1882 to 1894.

Grove, Lena. A character in William Faulkner's LIGHT IN AUGUST. Although not central to the main action of the story, Lena Grove offers an important and implicit contrast to the violence and death present in the plot. Her confinement symbolically re-enacts the confinement of Joe CHRISTMAS' mother, and her placidity and animal unconcern make her a minor kind of Earth Mother, carrying out her natural function of reproduction in a context that seems, but for her, hostile to life and growth.

Growth of the Soil, The (**Markens Grøde;** 1917). Nobel prize-winning novel by Knut HAMSUN. Hamsun describes an elemental existence in the rough open country of Norway. Isak and Inger, the hero and heroine of the novel, are individuals, yet they possess a simple, hardy vitality that makes them personifications of pioneer life.

Grub Street. The former name of a London street (now Milton Street). Dr. Johnson says that it was "Much inhabited by writers of small histories, dictionaries, and temporary poems; whence any mean production is called *grubstreet.*" The word is used allusively for needy authors, literary hacks, and their work. George Gissing wrote a novel entitled NEW GRUB STREET.

Grumio. The clownish, punning servant of Petruchio in Shakespeare's TAMING OF THE SHREW. With his good-humored playfulness, he is a perfect foil for the lusty and vigorous Petruchio.

Grundtvig, Nicolai Frederik Severin (1783–1872). Danish poet, historian, and linguist. Until the death of his father, a clergyman, in 1813, Grundtvig served as a country curate. His prolific writing career began in Copenhagen where he published poems and articles; he also made several translations into Danish, including *Beowulf* (1820). After a term as vicar (1821–1826) that terminated in violent theological controversy, Grundtvig spent two years in England studying Anglo-Saxon manuscripts. He returned to Copenhagen where he became a bishop in 1861. As a historian, he practiced a romantic approach, treating Scandinavian mythology in *Nordens Mythologi* (1808). A religious reformer and educationalist as well, Grundtvig was a figure of great influence in Denmark.

Grundy, Mrs. *What will Mrs. Grundy say?* What will our very proper and strait-laced neighbors say? A phrase from Tom Morton's English comedy *Speed the Plough* (1800). In the first scene Mrs. Ashfield shows herself very jealous of neighbor Grundy, and farmer Ashfield says to her: "Be quiet, wull ye? Always ding, dinging Dame Grundy into my ears. What will Mrs. Grundy say? What will Mrs. Grundy think? . . ."

grüne Heinrich, Der. See GREEN HENRY.

Grünewald, Matthias (1480?–1528). German painter. He is generally regarded as the last and greatest representative of the German Gothic school. His work has great power and originality, its distortion in drawing, heavy chiaroscuro, and rich color adding to its emotional intensity. The complex, many-winged altarpiece—now in the Colmar Museum—is his masterpiece.

Grushenka. In Feodor Dostoevski's THE BROTHERS KARAMAZOV, the beautiful young woman loved by Dmitri and pursued by his father, Feodor Pavlovich. Although her past is checkered and her reputation not the best, Grushenka is as large-hearted in her way as Dmitri himself. Often referred to in the novel as a kitten and a cat, she shows both sets of qualities, being playful and soft at times and crafty and malicious at others. Her love for Dmitri grows, regenerates her, and at the end of the novel she prepares to follow him to his Siberian imprisonment.

Gryll Grange (1860). A novel by Thomas Love PEACOCK. The action, such as it is, takes place during a house party in an English country mansion. There is a great deal of witty and erudite conversation, while most of the events are of a cheerfully preposterous character, such as the simultaneous marriage of nine couples that ends the book.

Gryphius, Andreas. Pen name of **Andreas Greif** (1616–1664). German baroque poet and dramatist. Gryphius, like Grimmelshausen, was deeply affected by the Thirty Years' War. His works frequently deal with the theme of the vanity of human life and of petty human ambitions, and it is characteristic that in his two most famous historical tragedies, *Katharina von Georgien* (*Catherine of Georgia,* 1657) and *Carolus Stuardus* (*Charles Stuart,* 1657), the hero dies a martyr's death. Gryphius' tragic style was strongly influenced by Seneca and by the Dutch drama of his time, but his own originality is felt in such works as *Cardenio und Celinde* (1657), which has been called the first "bourgeois tragedy" in German, and in his comedies, the most famous of which is *Absurda Comica oder Herr Peter Squentz* (1663). In his lyrics he often combines religious subject matter and classical forms.

gryphon. See GRIFFIN.

Guanhumara. See GUINEVERE.

Guard, Theodore de la. See Nathaniel WARD.

Guardi, Francesco (1712–1793). Venetian painter, pupil of Antonio Canaletto. Using muted tones animated by dabs of bright color and a sketchy touch to suggest details and highlights, he painted intimate, poetic scenes of Venice, its courtyards, canals, and piazzas.

Guardian Angel, The (1867). A novel by Oliver Wendell HOLMES. Myrtle Hazard, an orphan brought from the tropics to live in an austere New England home, is descended from a line of ancestors of widely differing natures. Excitable and uncontrolled, she runs away; when she is returned to New England, she becomes ill and hysterical. Under the intelligent guardianship of Professor Gridley, she is restored to health and falls in love with the young sculptor, Clement Lindsay. During the Civil War, she goes with him to the front, and nurses the wounded. Proper treatment and environment overcoming heredity, her mental balance is restored.

Guarini, Giambattista (1538–1612). Ferrarese poet. He wrote one of the most popular and influential of Renaissance dramas, IL PASTOR FIDO. A pastoral tragicomedy in imitation of TASSO's AMINTA, it was translated into English by Sir Richard Fanshawe in 1647. In John Fletcher's *The Faithful Shepherdess* (1610), Guarini's faithful shepherd has changed sex, and the plot has been altered, but the English play is based upon the Italian. As a critic, Guarini defended his mixture of tragedy and comedy, and generally argued for greater freedom from classical rules in literary genres.

Guarino of Verona (1374–1460). Italian educator. Teaching mainly at the Ferrara court school, he used methods, based on Greek ideals, intended to educate the pupil completely. Both he and VITTORINO OF FELTRE exercised great influence on their pupils and on future educational theory.

Guarneri. See CREMONA.

Guazzo, Stefano (1530–1593). Italian diplomat and man of letters. His *La civile conversazione* (1574), is a courtesy book composed of four books of dialogues which offer a model for the would-be gentleman to follow in polite discourse. In England, the translation (1581–1586) by George Pettie and Bartholomew Young placed it beside THE COURTIER and the *Galateo* of Della Casa as indispensable reading.

Gudrun. (1) A German epic poem written about 1210 by an unknown Austrian, apparently in imitation of the *Nibelungenlied*. Its many sea settings are unusual among German tales. Of its three sections, the first concerns Hagen, king of Ireland, and the second describes Hetel's courtship of Hagen's daughter Hilde. In the third part, their daughter Gudrun is engaged to Herwig of Seeland, but is abducted by Hartmut of Normandy. She refuses to marry her captor, so for 13 years she is forced to do menial servant's work. At last Herwig, accompanied by Gudrun's brother, comes to her rescue; and the lovers are happily married.

(2) Sigurd's wife in the VÖLSUNGA SAGA, better known as Kriemhild in the NIBELUNGENLIED and Gutrune in Wagner's tetralogy of operas, DER RING DES NIBELUNGEN.

(3) The heroine of the Icelandic LAXDALE SAGA, and daughter of Queen Grimhild. She was a selfish, independent, forceful woman, married successively to Thorwald, Thord, and Bolli, and in love with Kjartan, whose death she caused.

(4) One of the two leading women characters in D. H. Lawrence's novel WOMEN IN LOVE. She is believed to have been based on Katherine Mansfield.

Guebres. See GHEBERS.

Guedalla, Philip (1889–1944). English historian and biographer who wrote in the manner of Lytton Strachey. Among his biographies are *Palmerston* (1926) and *The Duke* (1931), which is about Wellington.

Guelfo (Guelph) or **Carlo (Charles) of Denmark.** In the GERUSALEMME LIBERATA of Tasso, the Christian knight who narrates the death of Sveno in a massacre which he alone survived. He is also one of the two knights (the other, Ubaldo) sent by Goffredo the Christian general to bring back Rinaldo of Este. He and Ubaldo complete their mission with the aid of the Hermit of Ascalon, who shows them where to find Rinaldo and how to extricate him from the enchantments of Armida.

Guelphs (or Guelfs) and Ghibellines. Names of the rival political parties in 12th-century Germany, adopted by 13th- and 14th-century Italian parties. The Ghibellines were the supporters of the Holy Roman Emperor, at that time a German; the Guelphs were his opponents, usually supported by the papacy. At the time of DANTE the Guelphs of Tuscany were bitterly divided into two factions: see BIANCHI AND NERI.

Guérin, Georges Maurice de (1810–1839). French poet. His prose poem *Le Centaure* was published posthumously by George Sand in *Revue des Deux Mondes* (1840). His sister Eugénie Guérin (1805–1848) is famous for her *Journal*, a posthumously published diary.

Guermantes, de. A large family of the French aristocracy, in Marcel Proust's REMEMBRANCE OF THINGS PAST. Duc Basin, called the Prince de Laume before his father's death, is the elder brother of Baron de CHARLUS and of Mme de Marsantes, the mother of Robert de SAINT-LOUP. Basin's wife, Oriane, the Duchesse de Guermantes is even more of an aristocrat in her own right, being a descendant of the eighth-century Geneviève de Brabant and a cousin of many of the members of European royalty. She is represented as the most important hostess in French society, and the narrator in his youth goes through a period of worshiping her extravagantly. There are also the Prince and Princesse de Guermantes, and various other relatives by blood and marriage.

Guermantes Way, The. See REMEMBRANCE OF THINGS PAST.

Guerrazzi, Francesco Domenico (1804–1873). Italian novelist. He was a prolific author of historical novels with patriotic themes in keeping with the struggle for Italian independence. His best-known work is *L'Assedio di Firenze* (1836).

Guerre de Troie n'aura pas lieu, La. See TIGER AT THE GATES.

Guest, Lady Charlotte Elizabeth (1812–1895). Welsh writer. Her MABINOGION (1838–1849, 1877), a collection of tales translated from the Welsh, is a classic of Celtic folklore.

Guest, Edgar A[lbert] (1881–1959). English-born American writer of verse. At the age of 20, Guest began to conduct a daily column of verse in the Detroit *Free Press*. His sentimental, folksy, moralistic doggerel was widely syndicated, extremely popular, and known throughout the U.S. Among his collections are *A Heap o' Livin'* (1916), *Just Folks* (1917), and *Life's Highway* (1933).

Guevara, Antonio de (c. 1480–1545). Spanish historian and Franciscan monk. He wrote *The Dial of Princes* (*Libro Llamado Relox de Principes, en el Qual Va Encorporado el Muy Famoso Libro de Marco Aurelio;* 1529), a didactic novel giving an imaginary life of Marcus Aurelius, and a series of *Epístolas Familiares* (1539–1545), often called the *Golden Letters* because of their supposed worth. These works, translated into English by Thomas North and Edward Hellowes, may have been the inspiration for Lyly's *Euphues*. See EUPHUISM.

Guggenheim fellowships. Annual awards provided by the John Simon Guggenheim Memorial Foundation. Each year, 40 or 50 fellowships are given to Americans in the fields of literature, stagecraft, art, music, history, philosophy, and science. Among the writers who have received the award are John Dos

Passos, W. H. Auden, Jacques Barzun, Theodore Roethke, and Lewis Mumford.

Guicciardini, Francesco (1483–1540). Florentine historian and diplomat. Guicciardini's public career was spent in the service of the Medici and the papacy. Though critical of his contemporary, Machiavelli, he shares with him a realistic approach and a modern historical sense in his *Storia d'Italia* (*History of Italy*) and other writings. Passages of the *Storia*, translated into English by Geoffrey Fenton from a French version, appeared in the *Chronicles* of Holinshed, thus exerting an important influence on English writers like Raleigh and Bacon.

Guiccioli, Countess **Teresa** (1801?–1873). Italian noblewoman, known for her long-lasting liaison with Lord BYRON. She was still a very young girl, married to a much older man, when in 1819 their relationship began; a year later she left her husband and became Byron's openly acknowledged mistress. The attachment, which lasted the rest of Byron's life, is considered to have had a steadying influence on the poet and to have contributed to his increasing literary skill and facility during his years in Italy. She wrote *My Recollections of Lord Byron* (1868).

Guiderius. In Shakespeare's CYMBELINE, the elder son of Cymbeline, king of Britain. He is abducted by Belarius as an infant and raised as his son under the name of Polydore. He and his brother Arviragus are "as gentle as zephyrs blowing below the violet . . . and yet as rough, their royal blood enchaf'd, as the rud'st wind."

Guidiccioni, Giovanni (1500–1541). Italian papal official. He is noted for his sonnets on Italian affairs during the crucial years 1526–1530, when the Spanish were gaining domination over Italy and the Papacy. His *Rime* (*Verses*) were published in 1557.

Guido delle Colonne (13th century). Sicilian poet. He is known for his *Historia Troiana* (c. 1285), a Latin work in which he embodies the Troilus story adapted from the *Roman de Troie* of Benoît de Sainte-Maure. Guido is considered to have been the source of Boccaccio's *Il Filostrato*. He visited England in the retinue of Edward I when the latter returned from the Crusades.

Guidone Selvaggio (Guido the Savage). In the ORLANDO FURIOSO of Ariosto, a younger brother of Rinaldo and kinsman of Astolfo. Having been shipwrecked on the coast of the Amazons, he is doomed to fight their ten male champions. He slays them all, but must then marry ten of the Amazons. With the help of his favorite wife, Aleria, and Astolfo, who uses his magic horn to scatter the Amazons, he escapes and joins the forces of Charlemagne against the pagan armies.

Guildenstern. See ROSENCRANTZ AND GUILDENSTERN.

Guillaume de Lorris (early 13th century). French poet famous for having written the first part of the ROMANCE OF THE ROSE.

Guillaume Tell. See William TELL.

Guillén, Jorge (1893–   ). Spanish poet and academician. Born in Valladolid, Guillén began a teaching career that took him from Seville to Wellesley and then to Harvard University. His cold, intellectual poetry reveals the influence of Paul Valéry; it appears in the volume *Cántico* (1928), which is enlarged with every new edition. Other recent volumes include *Maremágnum* (*Clamor*, 1957) and *Viviendo y otros poemas* (1958).

guillotine. A decapitating machine much used during the French Revolution. A similar device was already in use in the 16th century in the south of France and in Italy, where it was called *mannaia* and was used exclusively for beheading nobility. Joseph Ignace Guillotin (1738–1814), member of the Constitutional Assembly, proposed in 1789 that a uniform method of capital punishment be established and that a machine, surer and swifter than the headsman's hand, be devised to carry it out. Dr. Antoine Louis, then secretary of the French College of Surgeons, was the actual designer of the guillotine, and it was at first called *louison* or *louisette*. It was first used on April 25, 1792. It is still the legal method of execution in France.

Guinevere. In Arthurian legend, the wife of King ARTHUR. In the many versions in which she appears, her name is spelled a variety of ways. (See GANOR.) She is, for example, the Guanhumara of Geoffrey of Monmouth, the early Irish Finnabair, the Welsh Gwenhwyvar. In many of the romances, she is said to be the daughter of King Leodegrance who, when Arthur and Guinevere are married, gives to Arthur the famous ROUND TABLE.

Like her classical counterparts, Helen of Troy and Persephone, Guinevere is one of those legendary heroines who is always being abducted and whose beauty brings betrayal, war, disaster. In Geoffrey of Monmouth's *History of the Kings of Britain* (1137), she is seduced by Arthur's nephew (or son), MORDRED, thus ultimately bringing about the death of Arthur and an end to many others. In most versions, however, it is Sir LAUNCELOT with whom Guinevere is illicitly involved. In *Lancelot* (c. 1180) by Chrétien de Troyes, it is that ideal knight who must go to the rescue of Guinevere when she is kidnapped by an unknown knight.

In Malory's *Morte d'Arthur* (c. 1469), Sir Launcelot is not only often the rescuer of Guinevere, but also her abductor. Here also, however, it is Mordred who, in the absence of Arthur, has usurped the kingdom and wishes to seduce and marry Guinevere. Thus begins the closing tragedy that culminates in the death of Arthur and the end of the order of the Round Table. Arthur hastens back from his expedition against Leo, king of the Romans; Guinevere flees, and a desperate battle is fought in which Mordred is slain and Arthur mortally wounded. Guinevere renounces Launcelot after the death of Arthur and takes the veil at Almesbury, where later she dies. But even at the end, Launcelot must go to carry her away once more. In a vision one night, he is told that Queen Guinevere is dead. Sadly, he goes for her, carries her body to Glastonbury, and places it beside the body of King Arthur.

Tennyson, in his *Idylls of the King* (1859–1885) makes Guinevere guilty only in her passion for Launcelot, and not a party to Mordred's treachery.

Guinicelli or **Guinizelli, Guido** (c. 1240–c. 1276). Italian poet, founder of the STILNOVISTI school of poetry. Only a few of his sonnets and lyrics have survived; the most famous is the *canzone* called *Al Cor Gentil*, translated as *The Gentle Heart* (1861) by Dante Gabriel Rossetti.

Guinness, Sir Alec (1914–   ). English stage and screen actor. He was a member of the Old Vic (1936–1939), afterward touring Europe. He appeared on the stage in New York in Eliot's *The Cocktail Party* (1950). He is best known in America as a film actor for his outstanding, subtle comic roles in *Man in the White Suit*, *Kind Hearts and Coronets*, *The Lavender Hill Mob*, and *The Horse's Mouth* (for which he wrote the screen play). As a dramatic actor his depiction of Fagin in *Oliver Twist* so aroused the ire of pressure groups that the film was banned in the U.S. for several years.

Güiraldes, Ricardo. See Don Segundo Sombra.

Guise. A French ducal house, a branch of the house of Lorraine. The Guise family acquired great political influence upon the accession (1559) of Francis II, who had married Mary, Queen of Scots, granddaughter of Claude, first duke of Guise. Henry, third duke of Guise (1550–1588), was known, like his father, as *le Balafré* (*Fr.*, "the scarred") because of a battle scar on his face. He became the leader of the Roman Catholic party in French politics and organized the Holy League. The idol of the Parisian mob, Henry probably aspired to the French throne and was murdered at the instigation of Henry III. The league, subsequently under the leadership of the duke of Mayenne, brother of the third duke, was crushed before the end of the 16th century. The direct line of the house of Guise became extinct in 1675. See also Henry IV (of France).

Guiterman, Arthur (1871–1943). American poet. A deft light versifier, Guiterman, who was born in Vienna of American parents, first attracted attention with his *Rhymed Reviews* in *Life* magazine. He made an adaptation of Molière's *L'Ecole des Maris* in rhymed verse for the Theatre Guild (1933), and wrote the libretto and lyrics for Walter Damrosch's opera, *The Man Without a Country* (1937). *Betel Nuts* (1907), *The Laughing Muse* (1915), *Ballads of Old New York* (1920), and *Lyric Laughter* (1939) are among the collections of his verse.

Guitry, Sacha [Alexandre Pierre Georges] (1885–1957). French actor and dramatist, son of the actor Lucien Guitry (1860–1925). Extremely popular between the world wars for his light sparkling comedies, he wrote over 130 plays, such as *Le Page* (1902), *Sleeping Partners* (1916), *Mariette* (1928), and *Where There's a Will* (1934). Some, such as *Deburau* (1918), *Pasteur* (1919), and *Mozart* (1926), were historical biographies.

Guizot, François Pierre Guillaume (1787–1874). French historian and statesman. A professor of history at the Sorbonne during the earlier years of his career, Guizot published historical works that comprise a voluminous body of writing. He became involved in politics during the July Monarchy (see July Revolution) and served in various ministerial capacities under Louis Philippe (1830–1848).

Gulbeyas. The sultana in Lord Byron's Don Juan. Having purchased Juan at the slave market and introduced him into the harem in female attire, she is outraged to find that he prefers Dudu, one of the attendant beauties, to herself. She attempts to have them drowned in the Bosphorus, but they escape.

Gulistan (Pers., *Rose Garden*, 1285). A collection of lyrics by the Persian poet Sa'di. Polished and accomplished, full of moral reflections, both witty and sweet, it contains sections on kings, dervishes, contentment, love, youth, old age, and social duties, together with many stories and philosophical sayings.

Gulliver's Travels (1726). Best-known title of *Travels into Several Remote Nations of the World*, *by Lemuel Gulliver*, a satiric masterpiece written in the form of a journal by Jonathan Swift. Lemuel Gulliver, a ship's physician, makes four voyages: to Lilliput, whose inhabitants are six inches tall; to Brobdingnag, a land of giants; to the flying island of Laputa, an empire of "wise men"; and to Houyhnhnmland, inhabited by Houyhnhnms and Yahoos. Swift's bitterest work, *Gulliver's Travels* satirizes man's abuse of human reason as reflected in his political, social, and academic institutions; at best, man is foolish; at worst, he is nothing more than an ape. A multifarious book, it is various in its appeal: it is enchantingly playful and fantastic, and is often read by children; it is a witty, allegorical depiction of the political life and values of Swift's time; it is a bitter denunciation of mankind; finally it is Swift's reflections on man's corruption of his highest attribute, reason.

Gull's Hornbook, The (1609). A prose satire by Thomas Dekker. In the form of a mock hornbook, or primer, it attacked the manners of emptyheaded dandies (gulls) through ironic instructions in the kind of behavior that would attract attention at the theater, the tavern, the gambling house, and other public places.

Gumiliov, Nikolai Stepanovich (1886–1921). Russian poet. Gumiliov was one of the founders of the Acmeist movement. His early travels in Africa were reflected in the exoticism of his poetry. Between 1910 and 1918, he was married to the poet Anna Akhmatova, also a member of the Acmeist group. After the revolution, Gumiliov openly expressed his opposition to the Bolsheviks, and was executed for conspiracy in 1921. See Acmeism.

Gundolf, Friedrich. Pen name of **Friedrich Gundelfinger** (1880–1931). German literary historian, critic, and biographer. In his youth he was a member of the circle about Stefan George. His works include *Shakespeare und der deutsche Geist* (*Shakespeare and the German Spirit*, 1911); *Shakespeare in deutscher Sprache* (*Shakespeare in German*, 1908), a 10-volume translation done in collaboration with George; and works on the German romantics.

Gunga Din (1892). One of Rudyard Kipling's Barrack-Room Ballads, in praise of a Hindu watercarrier for a British Indian regiment.

> An' for all 'is dirty 'ide
> 'E was white, clear white, inside....
>   ... You're a better man than I am, Gunga Din.

Gunn, Thom[son William] (1929–   ). English poet. His verse, stylistically influenced by William Empson, often deals with violent, contemporary subject matter. Among his publications is *My Sad Captains* (1961).

Gunnar. See Gunther.

Gunnarsson, Gunnar (1889–   ). Icelandic novelist, poet, and playwright. Born into a farming family and largely self-educated, Gunnarsson celebrated in his work the courage and dignity of humble people in his native land. During his extended stay in Denmark (1910–1939), he published a nostalgic novel series, *Borgsloegtens Historie* (4 vols., 1912–1914). A longer novel series, planned as a narration of Iceland's history, includes *Edbrødre* (*The Sown Brothers*, 1918) and *Salige er de Enfoldige* (*Seven Days' Darkness*, 1920).

Gunpowder Plot. In English history, a conspiracy of a few Roman Catholics led by Robert Catesby to murder James I and the members of both houses of Parliament. The date selected for the attempt was Nov. 5, 1605, when James was to appear in person at the opening of Parliament. The plot was foiled when Guy Fawkes (1570–1606), who had undertaken to fire the gunpowder for the explosion, was arrested in the cellar under the House of Lords on November 4. The failure of the plot is still celebrated in England on November 5 as Guy Fawkes Day.

Gunther. Burgundian king who courts Brunhild in the NIBELUNGENLIED and Wagner's RING DES NIBELUNGEN, known as Gunnar in the VÖLSUNGA SAGA. He is probably partially based on Gundahar, a historical ruler overthrown by the Huns in 436.

Günther, Johann Christian (1695–1723). German poet admired by Geothe. His style is halfway between the mannerism of the late Baroque and the more personal lyric that developed in the 18th century. His works include a tragedy, *Die Eifersucht* (*Jealousy*, 1715).

Gunther, John (1901–   ). American journalist and writer. With *Inside Europe* (1936) Gunther established his reputation as a careful researcher and colorful writer. *Inside Asia* (1939), *Inside Latin America* (1939), *Inside U.S.A.* (1947), *Inside Africa* (1955), and *Inside Russia Today* (1958) followed, and a quarter century later, he came full circle with *Inside Europe Today* (1961). He is also the author of *Death Be Not Proud* (1949), a moving memorial on the death of his son, and *Roosevelt in Retrospect* (1950). Gunther described how and why he wrote the "Inside" books in *A Fragment of Autobiography* (1962).

guru. (Sans., "venerable"). In Hinduism one's personal spiritual teacher and religious guide. *Guru* was the title taken by the succession of SIKH spiritual and temporal leaders from 1469 to 1708.

Gustavus II, known as **Gustavus Adolphus** (1594–1632). A king of Sweden, the Lion of the North, or the Snow King. Supporting the Protestant cause in the Thirty Years' War (1630–1632), he won the battle of Lützen against Wallenstein, but was mortally wounded. One of the greatest generals of all times, he saved Protestantism in Germany. His death left Sweden under a regency with his six-year-old daughter CHRISTINA as nominal queen.

gute Mensch von Sezuan, Der. See GOOD WOMAN OF SEZUAN, THE.

Gutenberg, Johann (c. 1400–c. 1468). German printer, usually considered the inventor of movable metal type. Documents dating from 1439 indicate that he was involved in various secret operations employing a press and a device presumed to be a type mold. In 1455 at Mainz he entered into a partnership with Johann Fust, a moneylender. The partnership was dissolved five years later when Gutenberg defaulted on the loan and Fust seized Gutenberg's equipment and stock and continued the operation himself with the help of Peter Schöffer. It is generally accepted that the so-called *Gutenberg Bible* —more properly called the *Mazarin Bible* from its discovery in 1760 in the library of Cardinal Mazarin in Paris (see BIBLE, SPECIALLY NAMED EDITIONS)— was issued from the press that Gutenberg established and Fust took over. Whether Gutenberg alone was responsible for this edition is uncertain. None of the work ascribed to him bears his name.

After he lost his press to Fust, Gutenberg came under the patronage of Conrad Humery, a counselor of Mainz, and continued to print books. The *Catholicon* of 1460 is a fine example of his later work.

Gutiérrez, Eduardo. See GAUCHO LITERATURE.

Gutiérrez Nájera, Manuel (1859–1895). Mexican poet and journalist. Generally considered a precursor of MODERNISM, Gutiérrez Nájera was strongly influenced by the French Parnassians and symbolists. His verse is graceful, subjective, and elegiac, distinguished by elegance of style and perfection of form. His best-known poems, such as *Tristissima Nox,* *Serenata de Schubert,* and *Non omnis moriar,* were written after 1880; his poetry remained scattered until 1896 when a collection of his *Poesías* appeared with a preface by Justo Sierra. Gutiérrez Nájera is also remembered as the founder of the *Revista Azul,* Mexico's first modernist review.

Gutrune. See KRIEMHILD.

Gutzkow, Karl (1811–1878). German novelist and dramatist in the movement of JUNG DEUTSCHLAND (Young Germany). His early novel *Wally, die Zweiflerin* (*Wally, a Doubting Girl,* 1835) aroused a storm of protest because of its extensive treatment of such generally avoided subjects as atheism and free love, and he was jailed for three months as a result. His later social novel, *Die Ritter vom Geiste* (*The Knights of the Spirit,* 1850–1851), though not as sensational as *Wally,* is more competent as a work of art. Among his dramas, the best known is *Uriel Acosta* (1846), which depicts the struggle of a Jew for intellectual freedom.

Guy Mannering (1815). A novel by Sir Walter SCOTT, set in Scotland at the time of George III. Guy Mannering, a young Englishman traveling in Scotland, stops overnight at the home of the laird of Ellangowan. A son is born to the laird that night and Mannering, a student of astrology, predicts two crises in the boy's life in his fifth and 21st years. He then goes on his way. Some time later, the son, Harry Bertram, disappears at the age of five. His mother dies of shock and the laird lives on only for a few years, leaving his daughter Lucy in the care of Dominie SAMPSON, a friend and schoolteacher, on his death. Mannering, returned from India after years of living there, invites Lucy and Dominie to live with him and his daughter, Julia. He is followed from India by a Captain Brown whom he erroneously suspects of loving his wife and with whom he has dueled. Brown is actually in love with Julia. In the climax of the book, Brown is recognized by a gypsy; he is Harry Bertram, although he did not know it, and was spirited off by the unscrupulous lawyer Glossin who got Harry's father's estate for himself since the heir had disappeared. All is restored to Harry and he wins the friendship of Mannering and the hand of Julia. The book is noted not so much for its plot, which brims with coincidences, as for

the creation of such notable characters as Meg MER-
RILIES and Dandie DINMONT.

Guy of Warwick (c. 1300). The title of a Middle English romance and the name of its hero. The
exploits and adventures of Guy of Warwick are typical of the heroes of non-Arthurian romance, such
as Bevis of Hampton, Havelock, and King Horn.
To obtain Phelis (Felice) as his wife, Guy of Warwick undertook many knightly deeds. He rescued the
daughter of the emperor of Germany, and went to
fight against the Saracens, slaying the doughty Col-
dran, Elmaye King of Tyre, and the soldan himself.
Then he returned and wedded Phelis, but in 40 days
went back to the Holy Land, where he slew the
giant Amarant, and many others. Having achieved
all this he became a hermit near Warwick. Daily he
went in disguise to his own castle and begged bread
of his wife Phelis; but on his death bed he sent her
a ring, by which she recognized him, and went to
close his dying eyes.

Guyon, Sir. See FAERIE QUEENE, THE.

Guzmán, Martín Luis (1887–   ). Mexican essayist and novelist. During the Mexican Revolution,
Guzmán was an adherent first of Venustiano Carranza, then of Pancho Villa. From 1923 to 1936 he
lived in Spain, where he wrote the books that
brought him immediate renown. Guzmán's best-
known work is *El águila y la serpiente* (*The Eagle*

Guy of Warwick killing the giant.
From the 1560 edition.

and the Serpent, 1928), an autobiographical collection of sketches describing scenes and personages of
the revolution. *La sombra del caudillo* (1929) is a
roman à clef exposing the cynicism and intrigue that
characterized Mexican politics in the 1920's. In the
four-volume *Memorias de Pancho Villa* (1938–1940),
Guzmán gives an account of the deeds and sayings
of the revolutionary hero.

Guzmán de Alfarache, Vida del Pícaro (1599,
1604). A PICARESQUE novel by Mateo ALEMÁN. The
book is supposedly the autobiography of a Sevillian
rogue who composes it while in forced retirement in
the galleys, where he has been sent for defrauding
a rich widow. After relating each of his adventures,
the narrator adds a long moral; these passages are
outstanding for their superb prose and good sense.
The book also contains numerous subsidiary tales,
such as the famous story of Ozmin and Daraja. Alemán's original title for the work was *Atalaya de la
vida* (*Watch-tower of Life*), but his contemporaries
insisted on calling it *El Pícaro*.

Gwendolen or **Guendolene.** See LOCRINE.

Gwenhwyvar. See GUINEVERE.

Gwyn or **Gwynne, Eleanor.** Known as **Nell
Gwyn** (1650–1687). English actress and mistress of
Charles II. She is said to have begun her career as
an orange-vendor in a London theater. As an actress,
she was noted for her skill in comedy roles, and her
gaiety and good nature made her a great favorite
with the public. She became Charles's mistress in
1668 and bore him two sons, one of whom was later
made Duke of St. Alban's. According to tradition,
the King's dying request to his brother was "Let not
poor Nelly starve."

Gyas and Cloanthus. In Vergil's AENEID, two
companions of Aeneas, generally mentioned together
as "fortis Gyas fortisque Cloanthus." The phrase has
become proverbial for two very similar characters.

gypsy. A member of a dark-skinned nomadic
race. Gypsies first appeared in England about the
beginning of the 16th century, and, as they were
thought to have come from Egypt, were named
Egyptians, which soon became corrupted to *Gypcians*,
and so to its present form. They call themselves
Romany (from Gypsy *rom*, a man, husband), which
is also the name of their language: a debased Hindu
dialect with large additions of words from Persian, Armenian, and many European languages. It is thought
that early gypsies migrated from Northern India.

The name of the largest group of European gypsies
is *Atzigan;* this, in Turkey and Greece, became
Tshingian, in the Balkans and Romania *Tsigan*, in
Hungary *Czigany*, in Germany *Zigeuner*, in Italy
Zingari, in Portugal *Cigano*, and in Spain *Gitano*.
The original name is said to mean dark man. See
BOHEMIAN.

There is a legend that the gypsies are waifs and
strays on the earth because they refused to shelter
the Virgin and her child in their flight to Egypt.

H

Habakkuk. An Old Testament book bearing the name of its author. It is a short, cogitative book written just before the fall of Jerusalem in 586 B.C. The author questions the actions of a god who uses a wicked enemy to punish his sinful people. Habakkuk resolves his problems by foreseeing a final triumph over evil by the forces of righteousness and faith.

Habington, William (1605–1654). English poet. He was the author of the lyrical collection *Castara* (1634), a series of elegant poems praising the chastity of his mistress and muse.

Hachette, Louis Christophe François (1800–1864). French publisher, founder of the Paris firm of Hachette et Cie (1826). The firm is noted for its carefully annotated, classical texts, its educational books, and dictionaries.

Hacker, Louis M[orton] (1899–   ). American historian and teacher. Interested in the impact of economics on American politics, public policy, and social and individual behavior, Hacker wrote *A Short History of the New Deal* (1934), *The Triumph of American Capitalism* (1949), *American Capitalism* (1957), and other books. He joined the faculty of Columbia University in 1934 and later became dean of the university's School of General Studies.

Hades (Haides, Aidoneus). The place of the dead. In Homer, the name of the god, also called Plouton (Pluto), who reigns over the dead. In later mythology, the name was also applied to the abode of the departed spirits, a place of gloom, but not necessarily, like the Christian Hell, a place of punishment and torture. As the state or abode of the dead it corresponds to the Hebrew *Sheol,* a word which the translators of the Authorized Version frequently replaced with the misleading *Hell.* Hence Hades is often used as a euphemism for Hell.

Hadith (Arabic, "a saying or tradition"). The traditions about the prophet Muhammad's sayings and doings. This compilation, made in the 10th century by the Muslim jurists Moshin and Bokhari, forms a supplement to the Koran as the Talmud does to the Jewish Scriptures. The *Hadith* was originally not allowed to be committed to writing, but the danger of the traditions being perverted or forgotten led to their being placed on record.

hadji. A pilgrim; specifically, a Muslim who has completed the required pilgrimage or *hadj* to Mecca. The word is often prefixed to a name as an epithet of honor. See ISLAM.

Hadrian. Full Latin names **Publius Aelius Hadrianus** (A.D. 76–138). Roman emperor (117–138). As part of his policy of consolidation and of renouncing conquest, he established the Euphrates as the Eastern boundary of the Roman Empire. He effected the construction in Britain of Hadrian's Wall (120–123) from Solway Firth to the south of Tyne as a protection against the Picts and Scots. He profoundly admired Greek culture and did much to beautify Athens with new buildings. His tomb at Rome and his villa at Tibur are remarkable structures. Hadrian was a learned man, an amateur architect, and a writer of genuine gifts. His reign was one of the finest ages in Roman history, and it continued for many years longer through his foresight in choosing as his successors Antoninus Pius and Marcus Aurelius. Marguerite Yourcenar wrote a thoughtful fictional biography of Hadrian, which she called a "meditation on history," in *Mémoires d'Hadrien* (*Memoirs of Hadrian;* 1951).

Hadzhi Murad (1911). A novel by Count Leo TOLSTOI. A short book, written in 1904, it is set during a Cossack uprising in the Caucasus. Replaced as a leader by a rival, Hadzhi deserts to the Russians. He later changes his mind and, pining for his own people, decides to go back to them, even though he knows they will kill him for his desertion. The novel is generally considered one of the most artistic works of Tolstoi's later period.

Haeckel, Ernst (1834–1919). German zoologist and philosopher who popularized the ideas of Darwin. In *The Riddle of the Universe* (*Die Welträtsel;* 1899) he applied the doctrine of evolution to philosophy and religion.

Haemon (Haimon). See ANTIGONE.

Hāfiz. Pen name of **Shams-ud-din Muhammad** (c. 1300–1388). Persian poet. A student of both poetry and theology, Hāfiz became a dervish, a member of the Sūfi, an Islamic sect, and a professor of Koranic studies; his pen name, Hāfiz, "one who remembers," was the Persian term applied to a scholar who knew the Koran by heart. The *Divān of Hāfiz* is a large collection of odes (*ghazals*) written in 5 to 15 couplets (*distichs*) each. The second lines of the couplets rhyme throughout and the last couplet always introduces the poet's name. An example of a final couplet is: "The laughing wine, the sweet girl's tumbled tresses,/ Were more than even Hāfiz could deny!" The odes are arranged alphabetically in the book according to their rhymes. The subjects of the odes include love, wine, birds, flowers, the instability of all things human, and Allah and the prophets. Beside their apparent content, the odes have religious meaning in the mystical terms of the Sūfi.

Best known for his odes, Hāfiz also wrote in other forms, especially the *rubáiyát* (rhymed quatrains).

Hagar. In the Old Testament, the Egyptian serv-ant of Abraham's wife Sarah. When she bore Abra-ham a son ISHMAEL, she grew haughty towards her mistress, who remained childless; but after the birth of Sarah's son Isaac, Hagar and Ishmael were cast out into the wilderness. On one occasion, when they were perishing of thirst, an angel of the Lord pointed out a spring of water in the desert, thereby saving the lives of Hagar and Ishmael (Gen. 21).

Hagen or **Hagan.** Murderer of Siegfried in German legend. A retainer of the Burgundian kings in the NIBELUNGENLIED, he is their half-brother (son of ALBERICH) in Richard Wagner's four-part opera RING DES NIBELUNGEN.

Haggadah. The portion of the MIDRASH that contains rabbinical interpretations of the historical and legendary, ethical, parabolic, and speculative parts of the Hebrew scriptures. The portion devoted to law, practice, and doctrine is called the *Halachah*. They were begun in the 2nd century and completed by the 11th.

Haggai. A book of the Old Testament named for its author. The prophet Haggai's main concern was with the correct and speedy rebuilding of the temple in Jerusalem after the return from exile in Babylon (c. 530 B.C.). He also expresses the Mes-sianic hope.

Haggard, Sir [Henry] Rider (1856–1925). Eng-lish novelist, whose tense, mysterious stories usually occur in some exotic African setting. His most effec-tive novels are *King Solomon's Mines* (1885), *Allan Quartermain* (1887), SHE (1887), and its sequel *Ayesha* (1905). Many of his books, notably *She* and *King Solomon's Mines*, have been dramatized and made into motion pictures.

Hagia Sophia. See SANTA SOPHIA.

Hague Tribunal. An international court of arbi-tration meeting at The Hague. It arose out of the Hague Congress on disarmament in 1899 and has been superseded by the Permanent Court of Inter-national Justice.

Hahn, Otto (1879–). German chemist. He has done highly important work in radiology and atomic fission. In 1938, with Lise Meitner and Fritz Strassman, he split the uranium atom. He won the Nobel Prize for chemistry in 1944.

Haidée. In Lord Byron's DON JUAN, the beauti-ful Greek girl who finds Juan when he is cast ashore on one of the Cyclades. She hides him in a cave, and the two soon fall in love. When her father, Lambro, a rich Greek pirate, returns from an expe-dition, the romance is discovered. Juan is exiled, and Haidée goes mad and dies after a lingering illness. There is also a Haidée who figures in Dumas' *Count of Monte Cristo*.

haikai. See HAIKU.

haiku. A form of Japanese poetry, composed of seventeen syllables (in 5, 7, 5 pattern), giving a complete impression or mood. Its greatest practitioner was MATSUO BASHŌ, who established the rules for the content of the poems and the allusions permitted. It developed from *haikai*, a form of linked verse (composed by various poets) popular in the 16th and 17th centuries. *Hokku* is the opening verse in a series of linked verse; *haiku* is a separate poem of the

haikai school. The three terms are frequently con-fused. An example of *haiku* by Matsuo Bashō:

> This road:
> no one walks along it.
> Dusk in autumn.

See TANKA.

Haile Selassie (1891–). Name assumed upon coronation by Ras **Tafari,** emperor of Ethiopia (1930). Called the Lion of Judah, he was driven from Ethiopia by Italian conquest in 1936–1941, but re-stored to his throne in 1941.

Hairy Ape, The (1922). A play by Eugene O'NEILL. An expressionistic drama, it tells of a crude stoker on a transatlantic liner. Yank, who feels that he "belongs" in the depths of the ship, becomes disillusioned with his life when he and the men are inspected by a society girl. His attempt to climb the evolutionary ladder fails in New York City, where he finally goes to the zoo; realizing that the ape is his nearest kin in spirit, he releases the animal from its cage and is crushed to death by the beast.

Hajar-al-Aswad. In the Muslim faith, a famous black stone, irregularly oval, about seven inches in breadth and surrounded with a circle of gold, which is found in the northeast corner of the KAABA. Ac-cording to legend, when Abraham wished to build the Kaaba, the stones came to him of their own ac-cord and he commanded all the faithful to kiss this one. The stone was supposed to have been whiter than milk when it first came from Paradise, but be-came black through the sins of the millions that had kissed it. On the Day of the Resurrection, it is be-lieved, the stone will have two eyes by which it will recognize all those who have kissed it, and a tongue with which it will bear witness to Allah.

The stone is probably an aerolite, and it was wor-shiped long before Muhammad's day. In the second century A.D. Maximus Tyrius spoke of the Arabians paying homage to it, and Persian legend states that it was an emblem of Saturn.

Hajji Baba of Ispahan, The Adventures of (1824). A PICARESQUE romance by James MORIER, dealing with life in Persia. The hero is a sort of Per-sian Gil Blas whose roguery takes him into all spheres of Persian society. In a satiric sequel, *Hajji Baba in England* (1828), he visits England as a government official, seeing familiar customs with a foreign eye.

Hajji Khalfah. Original name **Mustafa ibn-Abdallah** (1600?–1658). A Turkish historian and bibliographer. He compiled a bibliographical lexicon, with memoirs of the authors, of more than 25,000 books in Arabic, Turkish, and Persian.

Hakluyt, Richard (1553–1616). English scholar and clergyman. As a boy Hakluyt became interested in maps and explorations, and devoted his life to compiling and editing accounts of English voyages of discovery. In 1582 he published his first compilation, *Divers Voyages touching the Discovery of America.* This was followed in 1589 by *Principal Navigations, Traffics, Voyages, and Discoveries of the English Nation,* which was greatly enlarged to three volumes in 1598–1600. Called "the prose epic of the modern English nation," it contains accounts of the voyages of Raleigh, of the Cabots, of Drake's circumnavigation, of Martin Frobisher's search for the Northwest Passage, and the like. His work, which reflects the great exploring spirit of the Elizabethan age, gave additional impetus to English exploration, conquest, and colonization.

Halachah. The division of the MIDRASH that deals with the interpretation of the law, points of doctrine, etc. See HAGGADAH.

Halbe, Max (1875–1944). German dramatist in the movement of NATURALISM. He is best known for his early works, which include *Ein Emporkömmling* (*An Upstart*, 1889), a village tragedy; and *Die Jugend* (*Youth*, 1893), a lovers' tragedy of the Romeo and Juliet type, which also treats the conflict between modern personal values and traditional religious ones.

halcyon days. A time of happiness and prosperity. Halcyon is the Greek for a kingfisher, compounded of *hals*, the sea, and *kyo*, to brood on. The ancient Sicilians believed that the kingfisher laid its eggs and incubated them for 14 days before the winter solstice on the surface of the sea. During this time the waves of the sea were always unruffled.

Halcyone and Ceyx. A story told by Ovid and his medieval adapters, and used by Chaucer (spelled Alcione and Seys) as an introduction to his BOOK OF THE DUCHESS. Halcyone is often the daughter of Aeolus. She learns in a dream of the death of Ceyx, her husband, who has been drowned in a shipwreck. Next morning she finds his body cast up by the sea, and three days later she dies, usually by casting herself into the sea in grief.

Hale, Edward Everett (1822–1909). American clergyman and author. He is best known for his realistic story THE MAN WITHOUT A COUNTRY. He also wrote whimsical tales, historical romances, and scholarly works, and was the founder of *Old and New* (1870–1875), a magazine later absorbed by *Scribner's*. *A New England Boyhood* (1893, enlarged, 1900) and *Memories of a Hundred Years* (2 v., 1902) are autobiographical.

Hale, Nancy (1908–). American novelist and short-story writer. Born in Boston, the granddaughter of Edward Everett Hale, she is the author of a number of novels, among them *The Young Die Good* (1932), *Never Any More* (1934), *The Prodigal Women* (1942), and *The Sign of Jonah* (1950). Her perceptive short stories are collected in *The Earliest Dreams* (1936), *Between the Dark and the Daylight* (1943), and *The Empress' Ring* (1955). *A New England Girlhood* (1958) is her autobiography embroidered by fancy. She also wrote *The Pattern of Perfection* (1960) and *The Realities of Fiction: A Book About Writing* (1962).

Hale, Nathan (1755–1776). American hero in the Revolutionary War. He was sentenced by the British to be hanged as a spy and went to his death with the words, "I only regret that I have but one life to lose for my country." He is the hero of a drama by Clyde Fitch entitled *Nathan Hale* (1898).

Hale, Sarah Josepha. See GODEY'S LADY'S BOOK.

Halévy, Elie (1870–1937). French historian. A student of English social and political history of the 19th century, Halévy published a comprehensive study: *Histoire du peuple anglais au XIXᵉ siècle* (1912–1923, 1926–1932). His other works include *L'Angleterre en 1815* (1912), *Du Lendemain de Waterloo à la veille du Reform Bill* (*1815–1830*)

(1923), *De la crise du Reform Bill à l'avènement de Sir Robert Peel* (*1830–1841*) (1923).

Halévy, Ludovic (1834–1908). French dramatist and novelist. With Henri Meilhac (1832–1897), Halévy wrote gay, spirited librettos for the light operas of Offenbach, including *La Belle Hélène* (1865), *La Vie parisienne* (1867), and *La Grande Duchesse de Gérolstein* (1867). The partners also produced the libretto for Bizet's CARMEN and the two light, witty comedies *Froufou* (1869) and *La Petite marquise* (1874). Writing alone, Halévy enjoyed success as a novelist, his best-known work being the charming L'ABBÉ CONSTANTIN.

Half Moon. See Henry HUDSON.

Haliburton, Thomas Chandler (1796–1865). Canadian humorist. In 1856, Haliburton, a lawyer and judge, retired and went to England, was welcomed into literary and political circles, and was elected to the House of Commons. A fanatic conservative, he was critical of the U.S., frequently expressed contempt for what he called "the lower orders," and became an avowed enemy of democracy. In 1835 Haliburton began writing in the newspaper *The Novascotian* humorous sketches about Sam SLICK, an itinerant Yankee clockmaker. This lampoon on Americans was apparently primarily intended to make Nova Scotians appreciate their own country and British institutions, but also to contrast Nova Scotian indolence with Yankee industry and shrewdness. The first sketches, with others added, were collected in *The Clockmaker, or, The Sayings and Doings of Samuel Slick of Slickville* (1837). This series was followed by several others, including *Sam Slick's Saws and Modern Instances* (1853). The books became very popular, first in Canada, then in the U.S. and England. Sam Slick became the best-known character in the field of Yankee humor and had many imitators. A shrewd, ruthless trader, ready to trick his customers at every opportunity, Sam is full of wise saws and has an unfailing supply of humorous stories. Some of his sayings gained wide currency, such as: "Politics makes a man as crooked as a pack does a peddler; not that they are so awful heavy either, but it teaches a man to stoop in the long run."

Halifax Law. A severe penalty peculiar to this English town. By this law, whoever committed theft in the precinct of Halifax was to be executed on the Halifax gibbet, a kind of guillotine. Hence the expression *go to Halifax.*

Hall, Donald (1928–). American poet and editor. At one time the poetry editor of the *Paris Review*, Hall has done much to make the younger contemporary poets more widely known by collecting their work in several anthologies. *The New Poets of England and America* (1957), compiled with Robert Pack and Louis Simpson, was an excellent representative collection of poets born between 1917 and 1935; it was followed by *The New Poets of England and America #2* (1962), with Robert Pack; *The Poetry Sampler* (1962); and *Contemporary American Verse* (1962). Hall's collections of his own poetry include *Exiles and Marriages* (1955) and *The Dark Houses* (1958).

Hall, James Norman (1887–1951). American novelist and short-story writer. Hall was coauthor with Charles Bernard NORDHOFF of the remarkably successful trilogy: MUTINY ON THE BOUNTY, *Men Against the Sea* (1933), and *Pitcairn's Island* (1934). During the First World War, Hall flew with the Lafayette Escadrille, an experience which provided him with material for subsequent books written both independently and with Nordhoff. Among the books on which they collaborated were *Lafayette Flying Corps* (1920), *Falcons of France* (1929), *The Hurricane* (1936), and *Botany Bay* (1941).

Hall, Joseph (1574–1656). English clergyman, satirist, poet, and CHARACTER WRITER. Named successively bishop of Exeter and of Norwich, he is known for his satires, such as *Virgidemiarum* (1597), in which he attacked contemporary institutions and individuals, and *Mundus Alter* (1605), directed against Roman Catholics. His *Characters of Virtues and Vices* (1608) is in the direct tradition of Theophrastus, except that its emphasis is on moral, rather than social, virtues and evils.

Hall, Radclyffe (1886–1943). English novelist and short-story writer. Her novel *The Well of Loneliness* (1928) caused a sensation because it treated with sympathy sexual perversion among women. It was banned in England and suspended in the U.S.

Hallam, Arthur Henry (1811–1833). English poet and essayist whose early death caused Tennyson to write IN MEMORIAM. Hallam, who was a close friend of Tennyson's and the fiancé of his sister Emily, was touring the Continent when he suddenly died in Vienna. His death was a profound shock to Tennyson and the cause of deep conflict between doubt and faith in the poet's life.

Halleck, Fitz-Greene (1790–1867). American poet, banker, and secretary to John Jacob Astor. Literature was Halleck's avocation. With his friend, Joseph Rodman DRAKE, he wrote the lively *Croaker Papers* (1819) for New York newspapers. Halleck's *Poetical Works* appeared in 1847. He is best known for his elegy (1820) written at Drake's death, beginning "Green be the turf above thee," and for his popular poem, *Marco Bozzaris* (1825).

Hallelujah (Heb., *halelu-Jah*, praise ye Jehovah). An exclamation used in songs of praise and thanksgiving.

Hallelujah lass. A name given, with a humorously contemptuous import, to female members of the Salvation Army in its early days.

Haller, Harry. The hero of Hesse's STEPPENWOLF. Part of the novel's vitality stems from the fact that Haller's experiences, like his initials, are patterned on Hesse's own.

Halley, Edmund (1656–1742). English astronomer. A friend of Newton, whose *Principia* (1687) he published at his own expense, Halley is best known for his study of comets. He concluded that the comets of 1531, 1607, and 1682 were in reality a single body and accurately predicted its return in 1758. The comet has since been known as Halley's Comet.

Hallowe'en. October 31, in the old Celtic calendar the last day of the year. Its night was the time when all the witches and warlocks were abroad and held their wicked revels. At the introduction of Christianity it was taken over as the eve of ALL SAINTS. It is still devoted to all sorts of games in which the old superstitions can be traced. See SAMAIN.

Halper, Albert (1904–   ). American novelist and short-story writer. He is chiefly known for his graphic studies of workingmen in large U.S. industries and of slum life, especially in his native Chicago. His style is naturalistic, and he is considered a writer of the proletarian school of the 1930's. *Union Square* (1933), though his first published work, was his fourth novel. His other works include *Sons of the Fathers* (1940), *The Little People* (1942), *The Golden Watch* (1953), and *Atlantic Avenue* (1956).

Hals, Frans (1580?–1666). Dutch portrait and genre painter. His sitters represent every class of society, from officers, burgomasters, and merchants to fishwives and itinerant entertainers. He represented them in animated and momentary attitudes, capturing a casual glimpse with quick and broad brushstrokes. His work is known for its vitality and, during his later period, for its gray and black tonal harmonies.

Ham. In the Old Testament, one of the three sons of NOAH, his brothers being Shem and Japheth. According to legend, Ham was the ancestor of the Hamitic races which populated Africa; their black skins were the result of Ham's iniquity in viewing his father drunk and naked, while his brothers walked backwards, with averted eyes, to cover Noah (Gen. 19: 22–23). One of his sons was Canaan.

Haman. See ESTHER.

Hamann, Johann Georg (1730–1788). German philosopher and aesthetician. In his *Des Ritters von Rosencreuz letzte Willensmeinung über den göttlichen und menschlichen Ursprung der Sprache* (*The Knight of Rosencreuz's Last Will, on the Divine and Human Origin of Language*, 1772), he contended that language is basically irrational, and thus he opposed the rationalism of enlightenment thought. He was influenced by pietism and was a teacher of Herder. See STURM UND DRANG.

Hamelin, Pied Piper of. See PIED PIPER OF HAMELIN.

Hamilcar Barca (270?–228 B.C.). Carthaginian general, father of HANNIBAL. He was appointed to the command of the Carthaginian forces in Sicily, in the 18th year of the First PUNIC WAR, in 247 B.C. After the defeat of the Carthaginians in 241, Hamilcar crossed over into Spain and, within nine years, obtained possession of a considerable portion of Spain for Carthage. He was drowned during a campaign.

Hamilton, Alexander (1757–1804). American statesman and chief author of THE FEDERALIST essays. He served as the first secretary of the treasury (1789–1795) and recommended fiscal measures, such as the creation of a national bank, that reflected his belief in a strong, centralized government. Distrusting the capacity of the common man, he advocated government by the elite. He was killed in a duel by Aaron Burr, whose political ambitions he had thwarted. He is the subject of Gertrude Atherton's "dramatized biography" *The Conqueror* (1902).

Hamilton, Anthony (1646–1720). Irish-born French writer. His brilliant style and humor are at their best in his short novel *Les Mémoires du Chevalier de Grammont* (1713), which recounts the adventures and amorous exploits of his brother-in-law and depicts scandals at the court of Charles II of England. He also wrote some short stories in imitation of *The Arabian Nights,* and some mordant poems.

Hamilton, Cosmo. Pen name of **Cosmo Hamilton Gibbs** (1872–1942). English popular novelist, dramatist, and short-story writer, eldest of the Gibbs brothers. *Mrs. Skeffington* (1910), a drawing-room comedy, is his best-known work.

Hamilton, Edith (1867–1963). American classical scholar. She is distinguished for her books translating for modern readers the meaning of Greek and Roman life. Her most famous works include *The Greek Way* (1930), *The Roman Way* (1932), *The Prophets of Israel* (1936), and *The Echo of Greece* (1957).

Hamilton, Lady Emma, born **Lyon** (1761?–1815). Wife of Sir William Hamilton, mistress of Horatio NELSON. Of humble birth but of great beauty, she became the mistress of Hamilton's nephew, Charles Greville, who sold her to the elderly diplomat in exchange for payment of his debts. She attained great popularity and influence at the court of Naples, where Hamilton was envoy, and there met Nelson, becoming his mistress in 1798. The lovers were extremely open about their relationship, and the birth of Nelson's daughter, Horatia (1801), gave further cause for scandal. After Nelson's death, her extravagance caused her to be imprisoned for debt (1813); she was released a year later and died in poverty in France.

Hamilton, Patrick. See ANGEL STREET.

Hamlet, The (1940). A novel by William FAULKNER, the 1st book of a trilogy that also includes *The Town* (1957) and *The Mansion* (1959). Spanning almost 50 years in time, the trilogy is centered on the innumerable and vicious members of the SNOPES family, the first of whom invades YOKNAPATAWPHA COUNTY early in the 20th century. In the hamlet of Frenchman's Bend, Flem Snopes begins as a clerk in Will Varner's store; through usury, connivance, and thrift, he becomes part-owner of the store and husband of Eula VARNER, Will's daughter. In Jefferson, Flem works his way into Colonel Sartoris' bank, finally becoming vice-president. In order to enrich himself still further, he drives the bank president, Manfred De Spain, from town. In *The Mansion,* Flem moves into the now-vacant De Spain mansion, one of the largest and oldest houses in Jefferson. Flem has no human feelings of any kind, caring only for money and for the outward appearance of respectability. He imports a number of cousins—Mink, I.O., Lump, Ike, Eck—whom he installs in various positions in the community, until the local citizens feel that they are overrun with Snopeses.

The novels are loosely episodic, humorous, and ironic. *The Hamlet* is made up of material dealing alternately with horse-trading and love—economic life vis-à-vis emotional life. *The Town* continues this contrast on a more sophisticated level, centering on the hopeless and almost comic love of Gavin STEVENS, first for Eula Varner Snopes and then for her daughter Linda, and on the machinations used by Flem to acquire more money. *The Mansion* departs from this scheme, dealing primarily with the attempts of Mink Snopes to return to Jefferson and murder Flem, and with the relationship between Gavin and Linda. Each of the novels is made up of sections narrated mainly by characters who observe the action rather than take part in it, such as V. K. RATLIFF, the ubiquitous sewing-machine salesman, and Chick MALLISON, the young nephew of Gavin Stevens.

Hamlet of A. MacLeish, The (1928). A poem by Archibald MACLEISH. In this dramatic monologue, the poet contrasts Hamlet's situation with that of modern man, symbolized by the poet himself. He attempts to show that the sensitive man today has no knowledge of the evil he tries to fight.

Hamlet, Prince of Denmark (c. 1601). A tragedy by William SHAKESPEARE. It is his most famous play and one of the most fascinating in world literature.

Hamlet, prince of Denmark, falls into melancholia after the death of his father, the king. CLAUDIUS, his father's brother, has assumed the throne and married Hamlet's mother, GERTRUDE, within two months of the king's death. His father's ghost appears to Hamlet, accuses Claudius of murdering him, and demands revenge. Hamlet then resolves to feign madness in order to disguise his intentions. His rejection by OPHELIA, to whom he has shown attention, leads her father, POLONIUS, to the conclusion that love has driven the prince mad. Unable to bring himself to action and beset by doubts as to the truth of the ghost's words, Hamlet persuades some traveling players to re-enact the death of his father. Claudius' violent reaction to the play convinces Hamlet of his uncle's guilt. Later, in his mother's chamber, the prince kills the eavesdropping Polonius, mistaking him for Claudius. Using this murder as a pretext for disposing of the prince, Claudius sends Hamlet to England with ROSENCRANZ AND GUILDENSTERN, who

Title page of the first quarto of *Hamlet* (1603).

THE HUNTINGTON LIBRARY

THE
Tragicall Hiſtorie of
HAMLET
Prince of Denmarke

By William Shake-ſpeare.

As it hath beene diuerſe times acted by his Highneſſe ſeruants in the Cittie of London : as alſo in the two Vniuerſities of Cambridge and Oxford, and elſe-where

At London printed for N.L. and Iohn Trundell.
1603.

bear secret letters to the king of England, advising him to put the prince to death. But Hamlet discovers the plot and manages to return to Denmark. Ophelia, driven mad by Hamlet's rejection and the death of her father, commits suicide. Her brother, LAERTES, who has been studying in Paris, returns for her funeral, intent upon revenging himself for the deaths of his father and sister. Inciting him further, Claudius arranges for a duel between Laertes and Hamlet, in which Laertes will be provided with a poisoned sword. To insure Hamlet's death, Claudius also prepares a cup of poisoned wine. During the duel, Laertes nicks Hamlet with the poisoned sword, while the queen accidentally drinks the poisoned wine and dies. Having unwittingly seized the poisoned rapier in the scuffle, the dying Hamlet kills both Laertes and Claudius. See FORTINBRAS.

Although *Hamlet* is a play of revenge, its greatness lies in the unique and thoughtful nature of the prince, whose temper is philosophical rather than active. He does not so much pursue his revenge as he is swept to it through the events of the play. His preoccupation with the nature and consequences of man's actions has led critics to call him "the first modern man." The complexity and richness of the play have furnished critics and performers with material for hundreds of interpretations.

The earliest source of the play is a story which first appeared in *Historia Danica* (1514) by the Danish chronicler Saxo Grammaticus, and was later translated in *Histoires Tragiques* (1570) by Pierre de Belleforest. An earlier version of the play (c. 1589), now lost, is referred to as "Ur-Hamlet," or source Hamlet.

Hammarskjöld, Dag (1905–1961). Swedish statesman. Hammarskjöld worked first in the field of public finance, serving as undersecretary of state in the Swedish department of finance from 1936 to 1946, and subsequently as financial advisor to the Swedish government. In 1953 he was chosen secretary-general of the United Nations; the diligence, imagination, and courage with which he performed his job earned him worldwide respect and admiration. Greatly concerned with the emerging African nations, Hammarskjöld was on his way to attempt some peaceful solution for the problems of the troubled Congo when he lost his life in a plane crash over Northern Rhodesia. In 1961 the Nobel Prize for peace was awarded to him posthumously. *Markings* (1964) is a collection of poems and entries from his personal journal which he called "a sort of white-book concerning my negotiations with myself and God."

Hammerstein, Oscar (1895–1960). American musical comedy librettist and producer. A talented and prolific theatrical craftsman, Hammerstein wrote, in collaboration or singly, the book and lyrics for 18 musicals, including *Rose Marie* (1924), *The Desert Song* (1926), *Show Boat* (1927), *New Moon* (1928), *Sweet Adeline* (1929), *Music in the Air* (1932), *May Wine* (1935), *Oklahoma* (1943), *Carmen Jones* (1943), *Carousel* (1945), *South Pacific* (1949), *The King and I* (1951), *Me and Juliet* (1953), *Flower Drum Song* (1958), and *The Sound of Music* (1959). He also wrote six screen plays, and with Rodgers produced five Broadway hit shows. Hammerstein collaborated with the best light composers of his day, including Romberg, Kern, and Rodgers.

Hammett, [Samuel] Dashiell (1894–1961). American writer of detective stories and movie scripts. An excellent craftsman, Hammett was the founder of the so-called hard-boiled school of detective fiction (see HARD-BOILED FICTION). In THE MALTESE FALCON he first presented his famous "private eye," Sam Spade. Of his many detective books, Hammett's favorite was *The Glass Key* (1931). *The Thin Man* (1932) offered another sleuth, Nick CHARLES, who was to become as well known as Sam Spade. Hammett's work was highly regarded by some European critics, notably André Gide.

Hammurabi. King of Babylon, 2067–2025 B.C. One of the greatest rulers of antiquity, he is chiefly remembered for his remarkable code of laws, which no doubt accounted in part for the success with which he governed much of Mesopotamia.

Hampden, John (1594–1643). English statesman. He became a popular symbol of resistance to royal tyranny when he fought the attempts of Charles I to collect ship-money from the inland counties without the consent of Parliament. At the outbreak of the Civil War he raised a regiment for the Parliamentary army and was mortally wounded at Chalgrove Field.

Hampden [Dougherty], Walter (1879–1955). American actor. One of the most distinguished on the American stage, he appeared in a number of Shakespearean roles and in *Cyrano de Bergerac, An Enemy of the People, Our Town,* and many other plays, as well as many motion pictures.

Hampton Court Conference (1604). A conference held under James I at Hampton Court, a royal palace on the Thames, to settle the differences between the Puritans and the High Church party of the Church of England. Although the Puritans failed to win their objectives, it was here that the first suggestion was made for the revision of the Bible that resulted in the King James or Authorized Version of 1611.

Hamsun, Knut Pederson (1859–1952). Norwegian novelist and playwright. Born of a farming family, Hamsun spent the years of his young manhood in poverty, wandering from one incongruous job to another. Two steamer voyages to the U.S. yielded positions as street-car conductor, dairyman, and finally as fisherman off the Grand Banks of Newfoundland. In 1890 his novel *Sult* (*Hunger,* 1899) appeared, establishing Hamsun's reputation as a significant author. He focused on the inner turmoil of his young hero, abandoning the current literary concern with social problems. In style, too, the work was original and provocative: the author experimented with the possibilities of the Norwegian *riksmaal.* In his writings, Hamsun both affirms and attacks. Such novels as *Pan* (1894), *Victoria* (1898), and *En Vandrer spiller med Sordin* (*With Muted Strings,* 1909) express a mystical feeling for nature. Other novels—*Segelfoss By* (1915) and *Konerne ved Vandposten* (*The Women at the Pump,* 1920), for example—contain angry criticism of modern life. In 1920 he received the Nobel prize for *Markens Grøde* (THE GROWTH OF THE SOIL). An influential figure in the modern literary world, Hamsun lived during the latter part of his life in isolation from society, at Nøerholmen near the sea which he loved.

Han. Chinese dynasty (202 B.C.–A.D. 220). The Chinese imperial age, which witnessed great developments in science, literature, and the arts. Confucian thought was systematized and established as the dominant ethical and political philosophy. The *Shih chi*, the first historical annal, was composed during this period.

Hancock, John (1737–1793) American statesman. He served as president of the Continental Congress (1775–1777) and was the first signer of the Declaration of Independence. From the bold legibility with which he signed that document, there developed the expression a "John Hancock," meaning an autographed signature.

Handel, George Frideric (1685–1759). German-born composer, with Bach the greatest figure of the late Baroque in music. After study in Germany and Italy (1706–1709), he settled permanently in England in 1712, and became a naturalized British subject in 1726. Handel's works are nearly all in two genres, Italian opera and English oratorio and odes. Notable among his 39 operas are: *Giulio Cesare* (1724), *Rodelinda* (1725), *Sosarme* (1732), *Orlando* (1733), *Alcina* (1735), and *Atalanta* (1736). Full of beautiful music, these works for various reasons have been little performed since the 18th century, but in the last generation there have been many revivals, which still continue. His oratorios and odes, usually on Biblical subjects, are the outstanding large choral works in the English language. Most were written after 1738, when Handel faced financial ruin because of the failure of his operatic ventures. The best of the oratorios are: *Saul* (1739), *Israel in Egypt* (1739), *Messiah* (1742), *Belshazzar* (1744), *Hercules* (1744), *Solomon* (1748), and *Jephtha* (1751). The other secular choral works are: *Acis and Galatea* (1720), *Alexander's Feast* (1736; text by Dryden), *Ode for St. Cecilia's Day* (1739; text by Dryden), and *L'Allegro, il Penseroso ed il Moderato* (1740; text of the first two acts by Milton). He also wrote church music, chamber music, and harpsichord suites, but the best known of his other works are 12 *concerti grossi* for orchestra (1739), 12 organ concertos (1738–1740), the *Water Music* (1715–1717), and the *Fireworks Music* (1749), the last two being suites for orchestra.

Handful of Dust, A (1937). A novel by Evelyn Waugh. Satirical in its treatment of upper-class English society, it is a comic novel about Tony Last, owner of a Gothic mansion which he loves. His old-fashioned values, however, cannot support him in the changing modern world. Deserted by his wife, he becomes an explorer in Brazil and is captured and enslaved by a mad old man who forces him to read Dickens aloud every afternoon.

Handlyng Synne ("handbook of sins," c. 1303). Religious poem by Robert Mannyng, of 12,630 lines in octosyllabic couplets. It is a Middle English adaptation of the *Manuel des Pechiez*, written in Anglo-French by William of Wadington (late 13th century), a treatise on the ten commandments, the seven deadly sins, and the seven sacraments. However, Mannyng illustrates his homilies with legendary tales and contemporary anecdotes that give a lively and vivid picture of the customs of his time.

handwriting on the wall. An announcement of some coming calamity, or the imminent fulfilment of some doom. The allusion is to the handwriting on Belshazzar's palace wall announcing the loss of his kingdom. See Daniel.

Handy Andy (1842). A novel by Samuel Lover. The book's Irish hero, Andy Rooney, "had the most singularly ingenious knack of doing everything the wrong way." Despite his blunders Handy Andy finally wins his cousin, Oonah, and is declared heir to Lord Scatterbrain's title and wealth.

Han Fei Tzu. Chinese politico-philosophical work of the Legalist School. The author, Han Fei Tzu (d. 233 b.c.) was a scholar and political adviser. Harsh, practical, and cynical, it propounded an anti-Confucian philosophy of government. Its teachings were put into practice during the short-lived Ch'in Dynasty (221–207 b.c.). See W. K. Liao, The *Complete Works of Han Fei Tzu* (1939, 1960).

Hanging Gardens of Babylon. One of the Seven Wonders of the Ancient World. According to Diodorus Siculus, the garden was 400 ft. square, rising in a series of terraces from the river in the northern part of Babylon. It was provided with earth to a sufficient depth to accommodate trees of a great size. According to tradition, it was built by Nebuchadnezzar to gratify his wife Amytis, who was weary of the flat plains of Babylon and longed for reminders of her native Median hills.

Hanley, James (1901–   ). English novelist. A merchant seaman at one time, Hanley writes most of his realistic novels about ships, sailors, and the sea. Among his works are *The Furys* (1934), *The Closed Harbour* (1952), *The Welsh Sonata* (1954), and *Levine* (1955). *At Bay* (1943), *Crilley* (1945), and *A Walk in the Wilderness* (1950) are collections of short stories.

Hannah. In the Old Testament, the wife of Elkenah and mother of the prophet Samuel. She made and kept a vow that if the Lord gave her a child, she would give him to the service of the temple (I Sam. 1:2).

Hannay, James Owen. See George A. Birmingham.

Hannay, Richard. In John Buchan's The Thirty-Nine Steps and its sequels, a South African mining engineer who becomes a British general and an energetic spy-catcher.

Hanneles Himmelfahrt. See Assumption of Hannele, The.

Hannibal (247–183 b.c.). Carthaginian general, son of Hamilcar Barca. As a child he was taken to Spain by his father and made to swear eternal enmity to Rome, an oath he never forgot. His whole life was a struggle against the Romans. At the onset of the Second Punic War, he invaded Italy from Spain, crossing the Alps with elephants by way of the Little St. Bernard, and plunged Rome into immediate danger through his victory at Cannae (216). He was ultimately defeated by Scipio Africanus and recalled to Africa. Years later, he escaped extradition to Rome by committing suicide.

Hanno. Carthaginian navigator who led a colonizing expedition down the west coast of Africa (5th century b.c.).

Hanno the Great. Carthaginian politician of 3rd century b.c. He favored peaceful relations with Rome, in opposition to Hamilcar Barca and Hannibal.

Han of Iceland (Han d'Islande; 1823). A romance by Victor Hugo. Rich in elements of the macabre and the grotesque, it is a tale of 17th-century Norway. The title character is a bloodthirsty individual who boasts descent from the monster Ingulph the Exterminator. His career is a long succession of crimes and horrors.

Hansards. Official reports of Parliamentary proceedings in England, named after Luke Hansard (1752–1828), the printer of the House of Commons journals (from 1774). Hansard was also the printer for Robert Dodsley, the prominent publisher and bookseller. Thomas Curson Hansard, his eldest son, published *Typographia* in 1825.

Hans Brinker or The Silver Skates (1865). A well-known story for children by Mary Mapes DODGE. The hero is a Dutch boy, and the book gives an interesting picture of life in Holland.

Hanseatic League. A confederacy begun in the 13th century among towns of northern Germany for mutual defense, particularly of their trade routes. During the 14th century it expanded to include most German and Dutch cities, and reached the height of its political and commercial power, making trade agreements with other countries as a unit. The need for the League declined in the 16th century, and the last meeting was held in 1669.

Hänsel and Gretel. An opera for children by Engelbert HUMPERDINCK (1893) based on the well-known fairy tale by the brothers Jacob and Wilhelm GRIMM. It portrays the adventures of Hänsel and Gretel, the broom-maker's children, with the Sand Man, the Dew Man, and the terrible Crunch Witch.

Hanuman. In the RAMAYANA, the monkey helpful to Rama in constructing a bridge from India to Ceylon. With his followers, he enabled Rama to rescue his wife Sita from the stronghold of Ravana, the demon-king of Ceylon. In some parts of India he is worshiped as a deity.

Hapsburg. A royal Central European family. Germanic in origin, the family derived its name from the ancient castle of Hapsburg (hawk's castle) in what is now Switzerland. Counts of Hapsburg were known as early as the 11th century, and it is their descendants who occupied the thrones of Germany, Austria, Hungary, Bohemia, Spain, etc., and for nearly 400 years were the rulers of the Holy Roman Empire. The still current phrase, "a Hapsburg lip," refers to the familial characteristic of a protruding lower lip observable in 18 generations of Hapsburgs.

Hara. Another name for SHIVA, the destroying aspect of the Hindu *Trimurti.*

harakiri (Japanese *hara* abdomen, *kiri* cutting). More commonly called *seppuku* in Japan, the Sinico-Japanese reading of the same characters in reverse order. Harakiri is a method of suicide by disembowelment, which began to be used in the Kamakura period (1185–1333). Frequently a form of protest, it was also a type of death penalty imposed during the Tokugawa period (1600–1868) on criminals of high rank.

Harbaugh, Thomas Chalmers. See Nick CARTER.

Harbor, The (1915). A novel by Ernest POOLE. The changes of New York harbor over the years become symbolic of the changes in the hero's mind. An artist, he is divided between the vewpoint of his father-in-law, who helps to build the harbor into a great commercial center, and that of a col-

lege friend, who presents the side of the workers. In time he chooses the latter standpoint.

Harcourt-Reilly, Sir Henry. A gin-drinking psychiatrist and god-figure in T. S. Eliot's verse-drama THE COCKTAIL PARTY.

hard-boiled fiction. A type of detective or crime story current in 20th-century American literature. A sense of realism is generated by laconic and often vulgar dialogue, through the depiction of cruelty and bloodshed at close range, and the use of sordid environments. The genre was closely associated with the magazine *Black Mask* (founded 1919) and with its editor Joseph T. Shaw, who compiled *The Hard-Boiled Omnibus: Early Stories from Black Mask* (1946). Among the writers of hard-boiled fiction are Dashiell HAMMETT, Raymond CHANDLER, George Harmon Coxe, and W. R. BURNETT. At first, such fiction was a serious attempt not dissimilar in aim to the work of such major writers as Ernest HEMINGWAY and John Dos PASSOS; later, it tended to degenerate into the sensationalism and undisguised sadism of writers like Mickey SPILLANE.

Hard Cash. See LOVE ME LITTLE, LOVE ME LONG.

Hardenberg, Friedrich Leopold Freiherr von. See NOVALIS.

Harding, Warren G[amaliel] (1865–1923). 29th president of the U.S. (1921–1923). Originally the editor and publisher of a newspaper in Marion, Ohio, Harding served as lieutenant governor of the state and was elected to the U.S. Senate in 1915. In 1920 he became the Republican candidate for president after his nomination had been decided upon by a handful of party leaders "in a smoke-filled room." Harding waged a front-porch campaign, promising a "return to normalcy" that appealed to war-weary Americans and won him 404 electoral votes while his Democratic opponent, James M. Cox, received only 127. His administration, one of the least distinguished in American history, is remembered largely for the corruption that flourished as Harding's cronies, especially the notorious "Ohio gang," helped themselves at the federal till. (See TEAPOT DOME.) While returning from a trip to Alaska, Harding became fatally ill in San Francisco. Embolism was listed as the cause of death. *Revelry* (1926), a novel by Samuel Hopkins Adams, and *The Gang's All Here* (1959), a play by Jerome Lawrence and Robert E. Lee, are based on Harding's administration.

Hard Lot, A (Gorkaya sud'bina; 1859). A drama by Alexei PISEMSKI. Dealing with the tragic conflicts caused by a love affair between an estate owner and the wife of one of his serfs, the play is regarded as one of the most powerful realistic tragedies in Russian drama.

Hardouin, Jean (1646–1729). French Jesuit priest and scholar. Librarian to Louis XIV, Hardouin was so skeptical that he questioned the truth of all received history and denied the authenticity of the *Aeneid* of Vergil and the *Odes* of Horace. He thus came to epitomize the doubting philosopher.

Hard Times (1845). A novel by Charles DICKENS. Thomas Gradgrind, a fanatic of the demonstrable fact, has raised his children Tom and Louisa in an atmosphere of grimmest practicality. Louisa marries the banker Josiah BOUNDERBY partly to protect her brother who is in Bounderby's employ, partly because her education has resulted in an emotional atrophy that makes her indifferent to her fate. Tom, shallow and unscrupulous, robs Bounderby's bank and contrives to frame Stephen Blackpool, an honest and long-suffering mill hand. Meanwhile, Louisa's dormant emotions begin to awaken, stimulated by disgust for the vulgar Bounderby and the attentions of the charming, amoral James Harthouse. When she runs away to her father and when Tom's guilt is discovered, Gradgrind realizes how his principles have blighted his children's lives. Ultimately Louisa secures a separation from Bounderby and Tom flees the country. The novel is Dickens' harshest indictment of practices and philosophical justifications of mid-19th-century industrialism in England.

Hardwick, Nan. See TRAGEDY OF NAN, THE.

Hardy, Alexandre (c. 1569–1632). French playwright. A prolific author, Hardy wrote literally hundreds of plays and published 34 of them, including the biblical tragedy *Marianne,* in the years 1623–1628. An innovator with a sure theatrical flair, Hardy enlivened dramatic movement by omitting the chorus, pruning soliloquies and monologues, introducing confrontations between main characters, and permitting violence on stage. Though poetically and rhetorically inferior to much of his predecessors' work, Hardy's plays achieved an enormous popularity in their time and performed the invaluable service of bridging the gap between the French drama of the Middle Ages and Renaissance and that of the 17th century.

Hardy, René (1911–). French novelist. Known for his studies of men in war, Hardy wrote such novels as *The Sword of God* (*Le fer de Dieu;* 1953), set in Indo-China, and *Bitter Victory* (*Amère Victoire;* 1955).

Hardy, Thomas (1840–1928). English novelist and poet. Hardy was born in Dorsetshire, the region that he later called Wessex in his novels. He trained as an architect and began to practice in 1867, though he soon became disillusioned and sought another medium for expression. He had been writing poems for several years, but he could find no publisher for his verse; he attempted a novel, but his first book, *The Poor Man and the Lady,* was rejected. *Desperate Remedies* (1871) was published anonymously, as was *Under the Greenwood Tree* (1872). In 1873 he published A PAIR OF BLUE EYES under his own name; the book was successful, and he began a full-time literary career. In the next 24 years, he produced 11 novels: FAR FROM THE MADDING CROWD, *The Hand of Ethelberta* (1876), THE RETURN OF THE NATIVE, *The Trumpet-Major* (1879), *A Laodicean* (1881), TWO ON A TOWER, THE MAYOR OF CASTERBRIDGE, *The Woodlanders* (1887), TESS OF THE D'URBERVILLES, JUDE THE OBSCURE, and *The Well-Beloved* (1897). Hardy's view of life, particularly as shown in his major novels, was one shaped by the prevalent materialistic and deterministic theories of 19th-century science, which saw man as subject to forces he could neither understand nor control; a naturalist, Hardy wrote forceful studies of life in which his characters are continually defeated in their struggle against their physical and social environment, against their own impulses, and against

the malevolent caprices of chance. Though his style is often awkward, it has a harsh power that contributes to the almost tragic intensity of his best work.

Hardy's first volume of verses, *Wessex Poems,* appeared in 1898, though it contained poetry he had written since the 1860's. Abandoning the novel, probably because of the shocked public reaction to *Jude the Obscure,* he continued to write poetry, publishing six more volumes of lyrical verse, which were gathered together in the *Collected Poems* of 1931, and one later volume, *Winter Words in Various Moods and Meters* (1928). Sometimes colloquial, uneven, and ragged, Hardy's verse is highly original, and has a wide variety of metrical styles and stanza forms, and a wide scope of tone and attitude, as is apparent from the ironically humorous ballad on *The Ruined Maid,* the pensive *Darkling Thrush* or the simple but moving *She Hears the Storm.* Hardy's most ambitious poetic work, *The Dynasts* (1903, 1906, 1908), is an epic drama on the Napoleonic wars.

hare. According to tradition, it is unlucky for a hare to cross one's path, because witches transform themselves into hares. In medieval science, the hare was a most melancholy beast, and ate wild succory in the hope of curing itself. Its flesh was supposed to generate melancholy in any who partook of it.

Another superstition was that hares are sexless, or that they change their sex every year. Among the Hindus the hare is sacred to the moon because, as they affirm, the outline of a hare is distinctly visible in the full disk. The idea that a March hare is mad derives from the fact that hares are unusually shy and wild in March, their rutting season. Erasmus, however, says "Mad as a marsh hare," and adds, "hares are wilder in marshes from the absence of hedges and cover."

Hari. Another name for VISHNU, the preserving aspect of the Hindu *Trimurti.*

Häring, Willibald. See Willibald ALEXIS.

Harington or **Harrington, John** (1561–1612). English satirist and miscellaneous writer. A godson of Queen Elizabeth, he translated Ariosto's *Orlando Furioso* into English (1591) at her command. He was banished from court because of some of his ribald satires, such as *The Metamorphosis of Ajax* (1596), a history of water closets. He also wrote many pamphlets and epigrams.

Harleian Library. The celebrated library of rare books, papers, and documents collected by Robert HARLEY and his son Edward (1689–1741). The Harleian manuscripts were acquired by the British government for the British Museum. A selection of Harleian pamphlets was published as *The Harleian Miscellany* (1744–1746).

Harlem. A section of New York City. It is inhabited largely by Negroes and Latin Americans. It was popular among intellectuals and society people of the 1920's because of its cabarets and SPEAKEASIES and its jazz. During the latter 1930's it also became a center of attraction for devotees of swing and boogie-woogie music. Harlem is the scene of *Naked on Roller Skates,* by Maxwell Bodenheim; *All God's Chillun Got Wings,* by Eugene O'Neill; *Nigger Heaven,* by Carl Van Vechten, and *The Cool World,* by Warren Miller. The character of its residents is depicted in the works of such Negro writers as Countee Cullen, Langston Hughes, W. E. Du Bois,

Ann Petry (author of *The Street* [1946]) and James Baldwin.

Harlequin or **Arlequin.** Originally *Arlecchino,* a stock character of Italian comedy (possibly from the name of a medieval demon or goblin), Harlequin became the buffoon of French and then of English pantomime. He has a shaven head, wears a mask and particolored tights, and carries a wooden sword. Often invisible to all but COLUMBINE, he is a rival of PIERROT or some other Clown for her love. His character is adapted to the *opéra-comique* and the *comédie bourgeoise* by such writers as Jean-Pierre de FLORIAN, Pierre de MARIVAUX, and Alexis PIRON.

Harleth, Gwendolyn. See DANIEL DERONDA.

Harley, Robert. 1st earl of **Oxford** (1661–1724). English Tory statesman and politician who was chancellor of the exchequer and leader of the Tory ministry (1710). See HARLEIAN LIBRARY.

Harley Street. A street in London known for its many specialist physicians' and surgeons' offices.

Harlowe, Clarissa. See CLARISSA HARLOWE.

Harmon, John, alias **John Rokesmith.** See OUR MUTUAL FRIEND.

Harmonia's Necklace. An unlucky possession; something that brings evil to all who possess it. In classic mythology, Harmonia was the daughter of Ares and Aphrodite. On her marriage with Cadmus, she received a necklace that proved disastrous to all who possessed it after her. See ERIPHYLE; ALCMAEON.

Haroot and Maroot. Angels in medieval angelology. In consequence of their want of compassion to man, they were susceptible to human passions, and were sent upon earth to be tempted. They were kings of Babel, and teachers of magic and the black arts.

Haroun-al-Raschid or **Harun-Al Rashid.** *Aaron the Upright.* Fifth caliph of Arabia (785–809). He entertained friendly relations with Charlemagne, whom he resembled in his patronage of the arts and learning. He was idealized as the splendid caliph of the ARABIAN NIGHTS' ENTERTAINMENTS, where everything curious, romantic, and wonderful is associated with his name and reign. See ABOU HASSAN; CALENDER; GIAFAR.

Harpagon. The central character in Molière's comedy L'AVARE. Nothing in life, not even his children, is more important to him than his hoard of money. Both Harpagon and his son Cléante desire to marry Mariane; but when the former, having lost a casket of money, is asked which he prefers—the money or Mariane—he says that he prefers the money, and Cléante marries the lady. Harpagon imagines that everyone is out to rob him, and when his casket is stolen he seizes his own arm in a frenzy. He proposes to give his daughter Elise in marriage to an old man named Anselme, because no dowry will be required. When Elise's lover Valère cites reason after reason against the unnatural alliance, the miser makes but one reply: "sans dot" (without dowry). On another occasion, Harpagon solicits Jacques to tell him what people say about him; when told that he is called a miser and a skinflint, he becomes helplessly enraged and beats poor Jacques in his terrible passion.

Harpagus (Harpagos, 6th century B.C.). A Median general. According to legend, the Median king Astyages chose him to expose the infant CYRUS. He gave the task to a herdsman, who kept the infant alive. Astyages punished Harpagus by serving to him at a banquet the flesh of his own son. Harpagus afterward became Cyrus' most trusted general.

Harpers Ferry. A town in West Virginia. The arsenal of Harpers Ferry was raided on Oct. 16, 1859, by the abolitionist, John BROWN. Lee took it from a large Union force on Sept. 15, 1862.

Harper's Magazine. An American magazine founded in 1850 as *Harper's New Monthly Magazine.* It was called *Harper's Monthly Magazine* after 1900, and after 1925, simply *Harper's Magazine.* During the 19th century it was devoted to literature, and frequently published serials of English authors, including Dickens, Bulwer-Lytton, Trollope, Thackeray, and George Eliot. The department of comment called "The Easy Chair" was conducted by a series of distinguished editors, among them W. D. Howells and G. W. Curtis. Howells also published articles on the new realistic fiction in a department called the "Editor's Study," which he began in 1885. Later contributors were Mark Twain, Booth Tarkington, Frank R. Stockton, and Woodrow Wilson. After World War I, economic, social, and political problems received more emphasis in the magazine.

harpies (harpyai). In Greek mythology, predaceous birds with women's faces. They were

Cover of the first issue of *Harper's Magazine* (1850).

daughters of the titaness Electra and sisters of Iris. They are most familiar from the story that they regularly snatched away the food from the blind king PHINEUS until they were pursued and frightened away by the ARGONAUTS CALAIS and Zetes, winged sons of Boreas. They seem to have combined the primitive concepts of wind spirits and predatory ghosts with actual characteristics of carrion birds.

Homer mentions only one harpy. Hesiod gives two, and later writers three. Their names were Ocypeta (rapid), Celeno (blackness), and Aello (storm).

Harpocrates (Harpokrates). The Greek form of the Egyptian Heru-P-Khart (Horus the Child). He is represented as a youth. As he has one finger pointing to his mouth, he was adopted by the Greeks as the god of silence.

Harp-Weaver and Other Poems, The (1923). A collection of poems by Edna St. Vincent MILLAY. This volume, which was awarded a Pulitzer Prize in poetry, was especially praised for the excellence of the 39 sonnets included, especially for the one beginning "Euclid alone has looked on Beauty bare."

Harraden, Beatrice (1864–1936). English novelist. Her greatest success was the novel *Ships That Pass in the Night* (1893) which sold over a million copies. Miss Harraden's other books include *In Varying Moods* (1894); *Interplay* (1908), and *Rachel* (1926). She was a leader in the woman's suffrage movement in England.

Harrington (1811). A novel by Maria EDGEWORTH. The titular hero is a Jew, and the novel was one of the first deliberate attempts to portray a Jew in fiction in a favorable light. As such it is worthy of note, but the character of Harrington is generally dismissed as wooden and oversentimentalized.

Harrington or Harington, James (1611–1677). English political theorist. A republican, though a good friend of Charles I, he is best known for his controversial political romance, *The Commonwealth of Oceana* (1656). Harrington's analysis of politics was distinguished by its emphasis on the idea that the form of government possible for a country depends on the distribution of property, especially land.

Harris, Joel Chandler (1848–1908). American journalist and author. He is famous for his humorous adaptations of native Negro folk legends in the Uncle Remus stories. His tales, marked by simple humor and authentic Negro dialect, are undoubtedly the greatest in the school of Negro folk literature. He wrote many of his stories first for the Atlanta *Constitution* and later collected them into such works as UNCLE REMUS: HIS SONGS AND HIS SAYINGS, *Nights with Uncle Remus* (1883), and several other collections. They dealt chiefly with animals such as Brer Rabbit, and illustrated such maxims as the ability of intelligence to win out over brute force. Harris also wrote local-color stories of Southern life; these include *Mingo and Other Sketches in Black and White* (1884), which contrasts the aristocracy and the middle class, and the novel *Gabriel Tolliver* (1902), set in the Reconstruction period. *On the Plantation* (1892) is largely autobiographical. See TAR BABY.

Harris, John Beynon. See John WYNDHAM.

Harris, Roy [really **Leroy**] (1898–   ). American composer. Many of his works have been inspired by American folk music, for example, the Symphony No. 4 (*Folksong Symphony;* 1940) and *American Ballads* (piano piece; 1942).

Harrison, William Henry. See TIPPECANOE AND TYLER TOO; Martin VAN BUREN.

Hart, Heinrich (1855–1906) and his brother **Julius** (1859–1930). German poets who were the leading theoreticians of early NATURALISM. In their periodically published *Kritische Waffengänge* (*Critical Passages-at-Arms;* 1882–1884), they stated that they wanted a naturalism in literature like the "naturalness of Goethe's poems," as opposed to any classicistic artificiality. Heinrich's best-known volume of verse is *Weltpfingsten* (*Whitsuntide of the World;* 1872); Julius' is *Homo sum* (*I Am a Man;* 1889).

Hart, Moss (1904–1961). American playwright and librettist. Hart began his career with *The Hold-Up Man* (1925), but his first real success came with *Once in a Lifetime* (1930), the first of a long series of plays written in collaboration with George S. KAUFMAN. Together they wrote *Merrily We Roll Along* (1934), the Pulitzer Prize-winning YOU CAN'T TAKE IT WITH YOU, *I'd Rather Be Right* (1937), *The American Way* (1939), THE MAN WHO CAME TO DINNER, and *George Washington Slept Here* (1940). Hart wrote the libretto for Irving Berlin's *Face the Music* (1933) and for Kurt Weill's *Lady in the Dark* (1941). He also wrote *Winged Victory* (1943), *Light Up the Sky* (1948), and *The Climate of Eden* (1952). Hart won the Antoinette Perry Award for his direction of the musical *My Fair Lady.* His autobiography, *Act One* (1959), became a best seller.

Harte, [Francis] Bret[t] (1836–1902). American short-story writer, novelist, editor, and poet. Harte left school early and went to San Francisco, where he mined, taught school, and finally became a journalist. He began his literary career with humorous sketches, attracted some attention with his verses, and achieved great fame through his short stories.

Editing the OVERLAND MONTHLY during the late 60's, he published a collection of his poetry, *The Lost Galleon and Other Tales* (1867), and his satirical CONDENSED NOVELS.

It was during this period that he wrote his best-remembered stories: THE LUCK OF ROARING CAMP and OUTCASTS OF POKER FLAT. His PLAIN LANGUAGE FROM TRUTHFUL JAMES, a comic verse narrative, was written in 1870.

During the 1870's, Harte was unable to continue writing at this level; he lost popularity and a contract to write for the *Atlantic Monthly.* Neither the novel GABRIEL CONROY nor the play *Ah Sin* (1877), written with Mark Twain, helped to restore his finances. Later he became a consul in Germany and Scotland, and was a favorite in European literary circles. His last work was a second series of *Condensed Novels* (1902).

Harte's work is marked by sentimentality, humor, and a penchant for showing thieves, vagabonds, and miners as more admirable than conventional and law-abiding folk. He is remembered for his pioneering work in Western local color writing. See M'LISS.

Hartford Convention (1814). A secret meeting of New England Federalists who were opposed to the War of 1812 to discuss revision of the Constitution. The delegates adopted several resolutions designed to preserve the influence of New England in the federal government. The news of the peace treaty with Great Britain and of Andrew Jackson's victory at New Orleans made the delegates a target for public ridicule, and they were accused, without evidence, of sedition and treason.

Hartford Wits. The name given to a group of 18th-century American poets, including Timothy DWIGHT, John TRUMBULL, and Joel BARLOW. The group was also known as the Connecticut Wits and the Yale Poets. Other members of the group, not all of them Yale men, were Lemuel Hopkins (1750-1801), David Humphries (1752-1818), Theodore DWIGHT, and Richard ALSOP. Except for Barlow, the Wits were Federalist in politics and Calvinist in religion. See ANARCHIAD, THE.

Hartley, David (1705-1757). English philosopher. He is best known for his study of human psychology, the *Observations on Man* (1749). Inspired by Newton's principle of gravitation, which had bound all physical bodies in a harmonious unity, Hartley endeavored to find some principle which would similarly unite moral phenomena. Following Locke, he developed the principle of association of ideas, by which simple ideas "run into complex ones by means of Association." According to Hartley, the moral sense was not innate, but acquired through the association of pleasurable sensations with ever loftier and wider objects: the child began by loving the tree; the man, through association, learned to love its Creator. With the proper education, Hartley contended, every man might learn to associate pleasure with the right objects, and thus the perfectibility of man was conceivable.

Hartley, L[eslie] P[oles] (1895-   ). English novelist and short-story writer. He wrote the trilogy EUSTACE AND HILDA, *The Boat* (1949), *My Fellow Devils* (1951), THE GO-BETWEEN, *A Perfect Woman* (1955), and *Facial Justice* (1961). Hartley is a perceptive and ironic observer of the social scene, who gives his novels depth through his skillful use of symbolism.

Hartmann von Aue (c. 1170-c. 1215). German court poet. His epic romances *Erec* and *Iwein*, free adaptations of the work of Chrétien de Troyes, introduced the Arthurian legends into Germany. However, his most popular work was the much shorter *Der arme Heinrich*, the only one based on German legend. See HEINRICH, DER ARME.

Hartzenbusch, Juan Eugenio (1806-1880). Spanish dramatist. His best-known work, *Los amantes de Teruel* (*The lovers of Teruel*, 1837), is considered one of the major Spanish romantic dramas because of its successful fusion of intense passion, melancholy, and medieval romance. The play deals with the amatory relationship between Diego Marsilla and Isabel Segura and culminates in the tragic death of both lovers. Hartzenbusch also wrote *La jura de Santa Gadea* (1845), dealing with the Cid, and two plays of magic, *La redoma encantada* (1839) and *Los polvos de la madre Celestina* (1841).

Harvard, John (1607-1638). An English clergyman, the son of a butcher, for whom Harvard University is named. He settled at Charlestown, Mass., and became the first benefactor of the college at New Towne, bequeathing to it his library of 300 volumes and half his estate, valued at £800. The college was renamed Harvard College in his honor in the year of his death, the third year of its existence.

Harvard Classics (1909-1910). A 50-volume set of books, containing selections from the literature of the world. It was edited by Charles W. Eliot, president emeritus of Harvard University, and published by P. F. Collier & Son. The original idea for the set can be traced to a chance remark of Eliot: "All the books needed for a real education could be set on a shelf five feet long!" From this remark and its physical make-up, the set is also known as "the Five-Foot Shelf."

Harvey (1944). A play by Mary C. CHASE. Harvey is a six-foot rabbit who appears only to the amiable drunkard who is the play's protagonist. The comedy turns on the futile attempts of eminent psychiatrists to dispel Harvey forever. The play had a long success on Broadway and was awarded a Pulitzer Prize.

Harvey, Gabriel (1545?-1630). English poet and satirist. A friend and possibly the tutor of Edmund Spenser, Harvey is thought to be the "Hobbinol" of Spenser's *Shepheardes Calender* (1579). Some of the correspondence between the two men appears in *The Letter-Book of Gabriel Harvey, A.D. 1573-80* (published 1884). Harvey, a literary conservative and something of a pedant, tried to introduce classical meters into English poetry and considered himself to be the "father of English hexameter." He is best known, however, for his acrimonious pamphlet-battle with Robert GREENE and Thomas NASHE. In connection with the Martin MARPRELATE CONTROVERSY, Harvey's brother Richard attacked Greene and, as a side issue, Nashe. Greene replied, and a literary feud began which ultimately narrowed down to a duel of words between Harvey and Nashe. Harvey's contributions to this dispute include *Foure Letters, and Certaine Sonnets, especially touching R. Greene* (1592); *A New Letter of Notable Contents* (1593); and *The Trimming of T. Nashe* (1597). Finally, in 1599, the Archbishop of Canterbury put an end to the quarrel by ordering the Harvey-Nashe tracts burned and forbidding them to be reprinted.

Harvey, William (1578-1657). English physician, physiologist, and anatomist. The discoverer of the theory of the circulation of the blood, Harvey announced his theory to the College of Physicians in 1616, but did not publish his treatise on it until 1628 (*Exercitatio Anatomica de Motu Cordis et Sanguinis in Animalibus*). He also studied the reproductive functions of animals, and in his *Exercitationes de generatione animalium* (1651) theorized that both parents, not only the male, contribute to the form of the offspring.

Hašek, Jaroslav (1883-1923). A Czech novelist and short-story writer. His major work, THE GOOD SOLDIER SCHWEIK (English translation, 1930), is a satire in four volumes (planned as six), which has been compared with the creations of Rabelais and Cervantes.

Hasidism. The tenets of the Hasidim, a Jewish sect founded about 300 B.C. in protest against Hellenistic innovation. Its members, unlike many of their brethren, strictly observed the ritual of purification and separation, as commanded by Jewish law. In the middle of the 18th century, in reaction against growing Jewish secularism and intellectualism, the Polish rabbi Israel Ben Eliezer founded a Hasidic sect devoted to mysticism, a revival of the earlier Hasidim. Modern Hasidism is characterized by a wariness of secularism in religion and of intellectualism and rationalism pursued for their own sake. Its members continue the strict observation of ritual law of their predecessors and do not recognize the state of Israel, holding that Israel can be returned to the Jews only by the Messiah himself. A world-famous Yeshiva, or school for Talmudic study, has been established by the Hasidim in the Williamsburg section of Brooklyn, N.Y.

Hassan (1923). A romantic play by James Elroy Flecker. Hassan is a poetic confectioner of Baghdad. He becomes the caliph's favorite but has to leave the court when he denounces the caliph's execution of young lovers. The play was spectacularly produced with ballets by Fokine and music by Delius.

Hassgesang. See Hymn of Hate.

Hastinapur. The ancient site of Delhi, often referred to in classical Indian writing. It was situated on the Ganges, about 30 miles east of modern Delhi.

Hastings, Battle of (1066). Battle near Senlac in Sussex, England, where Harold II died defending his claim to the English throne against the Norman William the Conqueror. William was crowned shortly afterward, thus effecting the "Norman Conquest," which greatly influenced English history, language, and literature.

Hastings, Warren (1732–1818). English statesman and administrator of India. He went to Calcutta in the East India Company's service in 1750, becoming successively a member of the Calcutta council, governor of Bengal, and governor-general of India. He was impeached in 1788 for corruption and cruelty, chiefly because of his conduct in regard to the zamindar of Benares whom he deposed and the begum of Oudh whose treasures he had allegedly confiscated. Although he was prosecuted by Edmund Burke, among others, his famous trial resulted in acquittal in 1795. Hastings is the subject of a famous essay by Thomas Babington Macaulay.

Hasty Pudding, The (1796). A mock-heroic poem by Joel Barlow, describing the making and eating of the celebrated New England mush. It was one of the most popular of Barlow's works.

Hasty Pudding Club. A Harvard undergraduate organization that gave the first of its annual dramatic productions in 1844. The plays produced are burlesques. Some of the university's most eminent graduates have taken part in these performances, from George Santayana to Robert Benchley. At early meetings hasty pudding, made of corn meal, was served.

Hatchway, Lieutenant Jack. In Tobias Smolletts' novel Peregrine Pickle, a retired naval officer on half pay, the friend and companion of Commodore Hawser Trunnion, and an abettor of the hero's mischief.

Hathaway, Anne. The wife of William Shakespeare.

Hathor. The Egyptian sky goddess, worshiped under several forms, in whom the sun was supposed to rise and set. As the personification of the sky, she was the female counterpart of Osiris and was represented as a cow with a disc and two plumes. Like Isis, she was a goddess of love, mirth, and joy,

corresponding to the Greek Aphrodite. Her temple at Denderah still exists.

Hatter, The. A character in Lewis Carroll's Alice's Adventures in Wonderland. During the course of a mad tea party he puts a riddle to Alice, "Why is a raven like a writing desk?" to which there is no answer. He has a watch that tells the day but not the time, and his eccentric behavior includes pouring hot tea on the Dormouse in order to wake him. The character is a burlesque of the rather illogical expression, "Mad as a hatter."

Hauff, Wilhelm (1802–1827). German romantic poet. He is well known for ballads and for narratives in Märchen style, such as the famous Phantasien im Bremer Ratskeller (Fantasies in the City Hall Tavern of Bremen, 1826). His novel Lichtenstein (1827), which was influenced by Walter Scott, is a closely documented work about 16th-century Germany and, along with the works of Willibald Alexis, is important in the genesis of the German historical novel. See German romanticism.

Hauptmann, Gerhart (1862–1946). German dramatist. Though he wanted at first to be a sculptor, he turned early to writing and produced a romantic epic entitled Promethidenlos (The Lot of the Promethides, 1885). But in accordance with the literary tenor of the times, he soon turned to realism in the story Bahnwärter Thiel (Trackwalker Thiel, 1887), and then, in his first play, Vor Sonnenaufgang (Before Sunrise, 1889), he developed a naturalistic style. This play, dedicated to "the consistent realist Bjarne P. Holmsen" (see Arno Holz) and influenced by Ibsen, treats the dangers of alcoholism in a starkly down-to-earth manner; it aroused a storm of critical controversy at its first performance, and marked the establishment of German naturalism as a recognized literary movement. Hauptmann himself wrote several more plays in a similar style, such as Das Friedensfest (The Celebration of Peace, 1890) and The Weavers; but in Hanneles Himmelfahrt (Hannele's Ascension, 1893) it became clear that his development was taking him away from naturalism. Though there are many naturalistic elements in this play, a large portion of it is taken up by an ecstatic, mystical vision of the heaven into which a dying girl is about to enter. Other plays, such as Fuhrmann Henschel (Coachman Henschel, 1898), Rose Bernd (1903), and Und Pippa tanzt (And Pippa Dances, 1906), also show this mixture of basically naturalistic style and subject matter with deeply symbolic overtones or insertions. And finally, in such plays as The Sunken Bell and Der Arme Heinrich (Poor Henry, 1902), he does away with naturalistic elements altogether.

After becoming established, Hauptmann was long regarded as the patriarch of modern German literature, but none of his later works had the same immediate appeal or aroused the same stormy controversy as his earlier ones. And yet his later period was by no means barren, and among its notable products are Der Narr in Christo Emanuel Quint (The Fool in Christ, Emanuel Quint, 1910) and Im Wirbel der Berufung (In the Confusion of Vocation, 1936), both novels; Der Ketzer von Soana (The Heretic of Soana, 1918), a story; and an epic Till Eulenspiegel (1928). Among his late plays are Vor Sonnenuntergang (Before Sunset, 1932) and a monumental treatment of the story of the house of Atreus in his *Atriden-Tetralogie* (*Atrides Tetralogy*), which includes *Iphigenie in Delphi* (1941), *Iphigenie in Aulis* (1944), *Agamemnons Tod* (*Agamemnon's Death*, 1948) and *Elektra* (1948). He was awarded the Nobel Prize for literature in 1912. See Till EULENSPIEGEL.

Hauptmann von Köpenick, Der. See CAPTAIN OF KÖPENICK, THE.

Hauser, Kaspar (1812?–1833). German foundling who appeared as a youth of about 16 in Nuremberg. He showed no signs of ever having been in contact with other humans but displayed normal intelligence. He is the subject of the novel *Caspar Hauser* (1908) by Jakob WASSERMANN.

Haushofer, Karl (1869–1946). German geographer. He used geopolitical theories to justify German expansion in Europe, and his claim that Germany needed *Lebensraum* ("living space") had a strong influence on Nazi ideology.

Havelok the Dane. A hero of medieval romance. The orphan son of the Danish king Birkabegn, he is exposed at sea through the treachery of his guardians. When the raft drifts to the coast of Lincolnshire, a fisherman, Grim, finds the young prince and brings him up as his own son. Believed to be a peasant, he is united with a princess who is to be degraded because she stands in the way of certain ambitious nobles. But Havelok, having learned the story of his birth, obtains the aid of an army of Danes to recover his wife's possessions, and in time becomes the king of Denmark.

Havisham, Miss. In Charles Dickens' GREAT EXPECTATIONS, a rich, eccentric, old recluse who lives in a decaying mansion. Years before she was jilted on the eve of her wedding and has since worn a wedding dress, complete with veil, white satin shoes, and bridal flowers in her hair. She has adopted Estella with the design of using her as an instrument of vengeance on the male sex; this she does by educating Estella to hate and torture men. She repents of her schemes just before her death caused by shock and burns when her ancient gown catches fire.

Estella Havisham. Miss Havisham's ward, later revealed to be the daughter of Abel MAGWITCH. She is a beautiful, self-possessed girl, convinced of her own heartlessness. Pip loves her, but she marries Bentley Drummle, knowing that they will torture each other. After Drummle's death and the misery of her marriage, she is at last ready for Pip's love.

Hawes, Stephen (d. 1523?). English poet. Hawes became a member of the household of Henry VII, to whom he dedicated *The Pastime of Pleasure* in 1506. Printed by Wynken de Worde in 1509, it is a long and elaborate allegorical poem, influenced by the poetry of LYDGATE and anticipating in some of its aspects Edmund Spenser's FAERIE QUEENE. Hawes wrote several other pieces, among them *A Joyful Meditation,* written for the coronation of Henry VIII in 1509, and the allegorical poem *The Example of Virtue* (printed 1512).

Hawk, Sir Mulberry. See NICHOLAS NICKLEBY.

Hawkes, Jacquetta (1910–). English archeologist and writer, wife of J. B. PRIESTLEY. *A Land* (1951) is a poetic account of the physical and human evolution of Britain.

Hawkins, Sir Anthony Hope. Pen name **Anthony Hope** (1863–1933). English novelist, author

First page of Hawes's *A Joyful Meditation* (1509).

of THE PRISONER OF ZENDA (1894), its sequel, *Rupert of Hentzau* (1898), and *The Dolly Dialogues* (1894).

Hawkins, Jim. See TREASURE ISLAND.

Hawkins, Sir John (1532–1595). English navigator and naval commander. With the expeditions of his nephew Sir Francis Drake, Hawkins' privateering voyages to the Spanish-American coast helped bring about the break between England and Spain. As Rear Admiral, Hawkins helped defeat the Spanish Armada in 1588. He died at sea as second in command under Drake on an expedition to the West Indies.

Hawkwood, Sir John (1320–1394). A celebrated captain of mercenaries. He was knighted by Edward III for his services against the French. He organized a band of professional soldiers, called the White Company, and went to Italy. Known to the Italians as Giovanni Acuto (thus Machiavelli refers to him), he enjoyed great success as a CONDOTTIERE.

Hawthorne, Nathaniel (1804–1864). American novelist and short-story writer. Born into an old New England family, Hawthorne was very much aware of his ancestors. The Hathornes (as they spelled it) participated in the Salem witch trials in the 17th century, and later in the Quaker persecutions. The writer, reflecting on the past, always felt a sense of guilt and made this a theme in his work.

The son of a sea captain, Hawthorne was educated at Bowdoin College, where he knew Franklin Pierce and Henry Wadsworth Longfellow. For 12 years, after his graduation in 1825, he lived in his mother's house in Salem; in virtual retirement, he wrote sketches and stories for annuals and newspapers. In 1828, he anonymously published a novel, FANSHAWE, based on his college life. Suddenly ashamed of his work, he withdrew most of the copies and burned them. Devoting his energies to short fiction, he explored the nature of sin. Hawthorne's first important book was a collection of short tales and sketches called TWICE-TOLD TALES.

In Boston as surveyor of the Customs House, Hawthorne renewed his acquaintance with Longfellow and the literary world. He invested his savings in the Transcendentalist experiment at BROOK FARM in 1841, and married Sophia Peabody the following year. Having found communal living unattractive, Hawthorne brought his bride to the Old Manse in Concord, Mass. The Manse, owned by the Ripleys, had been the home of Ralph Waldo Emerson. Here the author enjoyed three and a half happy years, during which his first daughter, Una, was born. He published his second collection of stories, MOSSES FROM AN OLD MANSE; this volume was brilliantly reviewed by Herman Melville, establishing an important friendship between the two men.

Later the Hawthornes moved to Salem, where the writer served again as surveyor in a Customs House. Removed from duty in 1849 as a result of political maneuvering (see Charles Wentworth UPHAM), Hawthorne began to write his masterpiece, THE SCARLET LETTER. The book brought him fame and some degree of financial independence. Although collections of early short pieces appeared after 1850, the year marked the end of Hawthorne's dedication to short fiction. He turned to the composition of novels and a few books for children. Living in Lenox, Mass., near Melville, Hawthorne wrote THE HOUSE OF THE SEVEN GABLES and THE BLITHEDALE ROMANCE. He collected the tales and sketches of THE SNOW IMAGE AND OTHER TWICE-TOLD TALES and wrote a campaign biography for his friend Franklin Pierce. When Pierce was elected president, he appointed Hawthorne consul at Liverpool and Manchester (1853–1857). After 1857, Hawthorne traveled through Europe for three years, completing his last published novel, THE MARBLE FAUN, in England.

On his return, Hawthorne collected a series of sketches about England called OUR OLD HOME. During the last decade of his life he wrote only sporadically. At his death, four unfinished novels were found among his notes. Among these were SEPTIMUS FELTON and THE DOLLIVER ROMANCE.

Turning to the historical past, Hawthorne found Puritan New England a congenial setting for his work. Claiming the privileges of the romancer, he deplored the lack of material for the artist in contemporary America, a land of shadowless daylight. His precise, almost classic prose style and his use of symbol and allegory made a great impression on his contemporary, Herman Melville, and on the later American writers, Henry James and William Faulkner. See TANGLEWOOD TALES.

Hay, Ian. Pen name of Sir **John Hay Beith** (1876–1952), English novelist, dramatist, and soldier. His light, humorous novels are often about the life and ethos of English boys' boarding schools. The best known is *A Safety Match* (1911). Hay dramatized stories by his friend P. G. Wodehouse, and collaborated on a number of plays including *Admirals All* (1934) and *Housemaster* (1936). *The First Hundred Thousand* (1915) was a popular account of Kitchener's army.

Hay, John [Milton] (1838–1905). American statesman and man of letters. Hay was assistant to John G. Nicolay, President Lincoln's private secretary, and they later collaborated on the 10-volume *Abraham Lincoln: A History* (1890). After the Civil War, Hay held several diplomatic posts and wrote for the New York *Tribune*. In 1898 he became President McKinley's secretary of state, a position he continued to hold under Theodore Roosevelt, helping to effect the Open Door policy in China and the negotiations for the Panama Canal.

As a writer, Hay is best known for his *Pike County Ballads* (1871) in western dialect; included in the collection was *Jim Bludso of the Prairie Belle,* a poem about a steamboat engineer who sacrifices himself to save his passengers when his boat catches fire. *Castilian Days* (1871) is a travel book of observations on Spanish civilization. Hay also wrote an anonymous novel, *The Breadwinners* (1884), in which he defended the propertied classes against the "dangerous" demands of labor.

Hayakawa, S[amuel] I[chiye] (1906–). Canadian-born American semanticist and teacher. Hayakawa taught at various universities before becoming a professor of language arts at San Francisco State College. A follower of Alfred Korzybski, he adapted and popularized Korzybski's principles of general semantics in *Language in Action* (1941). The book was extensively revised as *Language in Thought and Action* in 1949. In 1943 he became one of the founders and editors of the magazine *ETC., A Review of General Semantics.* He has edited *Language, Meaning and Maturity* (1954) and *Our Language and our World* (1950), both collections of articles that originally appeared in *ETC.*

Haydn, Franz Joseph (1732–1809). Austrian composer. He was kapellmeister of the Esterhazy family at Esterhaz (Eisenstadt) in Hungary (1760–1790), where he wrote some of his greatest music. In England (1791–1792; 1794–1795) he wrote and conducted twelve symphonies. In Vienna (from 1795), he wrote his last six masses, his finest chamber music, and the two great oratorios, *The Creation* and *The Seasons.* His total output includes 104 symphonies, concertos, about 20 operas, 12 masses, other church music, 84 string quartets, much other chamber music, 52 piano sonatas, and songs. Haydn's music shows much development during his long creative life. In the beginning he was under the influence of a rather superficial group of Viennese composers, but in the long years in the country in Hungary, as Haydn himself says: "There was no one about me to confuse and torment me, and I was compelled to become original." In later years, important influences were the young Mozart and the choral works of Handel, which he heard in England; these inspired the writing of the oratorios and left their mark on the late masses.

Haydon, Benjamin Robert (1786–1846). English painter. He is noted for his works on historical subjects. His writings include *Lectures on Painting and Design* (1844–1846). Wordsworth and Keats addressed sonnets to him.

Hayes, Alfred (1911–   ). English-born American novelist and poet. Hayes grew up in New York City, and *The Big Time* (1944), his first book of poems, extensively uses the city background in its imagery. During World War II, he served in the army in Italy, an experience which provided material for his two novels *All Thy Conquests* (1946) and *The Girl on the Via Flaminia* (1949). His later work includes the novels *Shadow of Heaven* (1947) and *In Love* (1953). *Welcome to the Castle* (1950) is a book of poems.

Hayes, Helen (1900–   ). American actress. A native of Washington, D.C., Miss Hayes gave her first public performance at the age of six. Later she scored great successes in such plays as *Mary of Scotland* and *Victoria Regina,* and in 1932 won an Academy Award for her acting in the motion picture *The Sin of Madelon Claudet.* In 1928 she married playwright Charles MacArthur. A Broadway theater is named in her honor.

Haymarket. The name of a street in London. It is between Pall Mall and Piccadilly Circus and is the center of London's theater district. The Haymarket Theatre is the second oldest London playhouse still in use. The original building was erected in 1720, the current one dates from 1820.

Haymarket Square riot (May 4, 1886). A riot that occurred in Chicago's Haymarket Square when the police tried to disperse a labor protest meeting, organized by anarchists, and a bomb was thrown, killing 7 policemen and wounding 70 others. The trial of eight anarchist leaders followed; seven were sentenced to death, one to 15 years in prison. When petitions protesting the verdict were circulated by William Dean Howells and other prominent persons, the sentences of two of the prisoners were commuted to life imprisonment, but four others were executed in 1887. In 1893, Governor John Peter Altgeld freed the three men still in jail. The incident was a temporary setback to the labor movement in general.

Hayne, Paul Hamilton (1830–1886). American poet. Hayne contributed to the *Southern Literary Messenger* and collected his *Poems* in 1855. Two years later, he founded *Russell's Magazine,* named after the bookstore in Charleston where Hayne and his friend Henry Timrod often met. Ardently patriotic, he wrote fervent poems on the Civil War; one of these is *The Battle of Charleston Harbor.* During Sherman's march to the sea, Hayne's mansion was destroyed. He moved to Georgia, where he supported his family entirely from his writings. Among these are *Legends and Lyrics* (1872), *The Mountain of the Lovers* (1875), and *The Broken Battalions* (1885). His work is chiefly distinguished for its landscapes of the South, as in *Aspects of the Pines* and *The Cottage on the Hill.* Hayne edited the poems of his friend Timrod in 1873.

Hayston, Frank. See BRIDE OF LAMMERMOOR, THE.

Hazard of New Fortunes, A (1890). A novel by William Dean Howells. Dryfoos, a Pennsylvania German who has recently risen to great wealth, brings his family to New York. Hoping to dissuade his son, Conrad, from joining the ministry, he purchases a magazine, *Every Other Week,* making Conrad the publisher. Dryfoos is also the father of two girls who, with their newly acquired fortune, are striving to enter high society. Basil March, editor of the magazine, is faced with a moral problem when Dryfoos demands the dismissal of Lindau, an old German socialist, from the magazine's staff. Lindau resigns, and later, participating in a strike of streetcar drivers and conductors, he is beaten to death. Conrad, also present at the strike, attempts to defend the old man and is killed by a stray bullet. Dryfoos sells the magazine to March, and takes his daughters to Europe, so they may continue their social climbing.

Hazlitt, William (1778–1830). English essayist and literary critic. At first dedicated to a career as a painter, he realized his talent was insufficient and turned to writing. Hazlitt became known for his studies and lectures on contemporary authors and the Elizabethan playwrights. His firm political liberalism estranged him from his friends Wordsworth, Coleridge, and Southey because he felt they had betrayed the liberalism of their youth. He went to London in 1808 and became a contributor to newspapers and periodicals, notably the *Edinburgh Review* and the *Examiner.*

After Coleridge, Hazlitt is probably the most penetrating and erudite of the early romantic critics, and is still eminently readable. Among his important works are: *The Characters of Shakespeare's Plays* (1817); *The Round Table* (1817, with Leigh Hunt); *A View of the English Stage* (1818); *Lectures on the English Poets* (1818); *Lectures on the English Comic Writers* (1819); *Lectures on the Dramatic Literature of the Age of Elizabeth* (1820); *Table Talk* (1821–1822); *Liber Amoris* (1823), an account of an unhappy love affair; and *The Spirit of the Age* (1825). He is considered one of the greatest masters of English prose.

H.D. See Hilda DOOLITTLE.

Headlong Hall (1816). A novel by Thomas Love Peacock. A brilliantly witty piece, it presents the mildly philosophic opinions on life exchanged by Mrs. Foster, the optimist, Mr. Escot, the pessimist, and Mr. Jenkinson, the status-quo-ite. It is a satire on the idealistic aspirations of romanticism.

Heard, [Henry Fitz] Gerald (1889–   ). English writer, resident in the U.S. since 1937. He has written about mystical religion and science and was a commentator on popular science for the British Broadcasting Corporation. Many of his books prove through anthropology and psychoanalysis man's need for religion, and describe his own mystical, oriental-style faith. Among his books are *The Ascent of Humanity* (1929), *Code of Christ* (1941), *Gabriel and the Creatures* (1952), and *Human Venture* (1955). His ideas greatly influenced Aldous Huxley; Christopher Isherwood and Huxley have been associated with him in California in the study of Eastern religion. He has written detective novels under the name of H. F. Heard.

Hearn, [Patricio] Lafcadio [Tessima Carlos] (1850–1904). American journalist and author. Of Greek and English-Irish parentage, he was born in the Ionian Islands. He is noted for the poetic prose style of his exotic and fantastic tales; he dedicated himself to "the worship of the Old, the Queer, the Strange, the Exotic, the Monstrous." After some early publication, including translations of stories by Théophile Gautier (in *One of Cleopatra's Nights,* 1882),

Hearn achieved success in works set in Louisiana and the Caribbean. *Chita* (1887) is a novel about a young girl who survives a tidal wave on a small island; YOUMA is concerned with a slave insurrection.

Hearn's search for the exotic led him to Japan in 1890, where he spent the rest of his life teaching and writing about the Japanese scene. He married and became a Japanese citizen under the name of Koizumi Yakumo. He published several books on Japan, including *Kokoro* (1896), *In Ghostly Japan* (1899), and *Japan: An Attempt at Interpretation* (1904). But his best work was his first, *Glimpses of Unfamiliar Japan* (1894).

Hearst, William Randolph (1863–1951). American newspaper publisher. Beginning his career on the San Francisco *Daily Examiner* in 1887, Hearst acquired a vast newspaper and magazine empire, which he ruled from his estate, San Simeon, in California. His name early became synonymous with "yellow journalism," and his skill in the methods of mass communications helped magnify a Cuban insurrection into the Spanish-American War. A staunch isolationist, Hearst served in Congress (1903–1907) and later made an unsuccessful bid for the governorship of New York.

Heartbreak House (1920). A play by George Bernard SHAW. A complex, allegorical work in which Shaw indicts apathy, confusion, and lack of purpose as the causes of the world's problems. The characters —all larger than life and with symbolic names—are gathered at the home of an eccentric sea captain; they each represent an evil in the modern world. Into their midst comes young Ellie Dunn, whose search for a husband Shaw treats as a new generation searching for a way of life. While the play is essentially a pessimistic one, it ends on a note of optimism: The first bombs of a war caused by the old order kill Boss Mangan, the avaricious capitalist, and Ellie selects as her spiritual husband the eccentric old owner of Heartbreak House, who represents common sense.

Heart of Darkness (1902). A long short story by Joseph CONRAD. MARLOW tells his friends of an experience in the (then) Belgian Congo, where he once ran a river steamer for a trading company. He describes the cruel colonial exploitation there. Fascinated by reports about the powerful white trader Kurtz, Marlow went into the jungle in search of him, expecting to find in his character a clue to the evil around him. He found Kurtz living with the natives and brought him away, dying; Kurtz's last words were "The horror! The horror!" The "heart of darkness" is the jungle, and the primitive, subconscious heart of man.

Heart of Midlothian, The (1818). A novel by Sir Walter SCOTT. The title alludes to the old jail at the center of Edinburgh, where the novel opens with scenes of the Porteous riots in 1736, when the commander of the Civic Guard, Captain Porteous, was lynched by a mob of incensed citizens after he had fired on a crowd. The plot concerns Effie Deans, a farmer's daughter, who is seduced by George Staunton, and who is tried and sentenced to death for murdering their child. Her loyal half-sister Jeanie determines to walk to London to seek a pardon from George II, and in spite of all obstacles, actually accomplishes her task. Effie marries Staunton, but shortly afterward he is shot by a gypsy boy, in reality his il-

legitimate son, who had not died after all. Jeanie marries Reuben Butler, a Presbyterian minister. The novel has a factual basis.

Heart of the Matter, The (1948). A novel by Graham GREENE. Set in West Africa, its hero is Scobie, an English Roman Catholic who is torn between his adulterous love for a young girl and his duty to his wife and his religion.

Heathcliff. The central character of Emily Brontë's novel WUTHERING HEIGHTS. Spurned by his childhood love, Catherine, he is obsessed with a desire for revenge that not only poisons her life and his but very nearly taints their children. Heathcliff is a romantic, almost demonic figure drawn on a heroic scale.

Heathen Chinee, The. See PLAIN LANGUAGE FROM TRUTHFUL JAMES.

Heat of the Day, The (1949). A novel by Elizabeth BOWEN. Set in wartime London, it is a melodramatic but sensitive story of espionage, counterespionage, and suicide, and of the emotions of the people involved.

heaven (AS, *heofon*). The word properly denotes the abode of the Deity and his angels; also the upper air.

In the Ptolemaic system the heavens were the successive spheres of space enclosing the central earth at different distances and revolving around it at different speeds. The first seven were those of the so-called planets, the Moon, Mercury, Venus, the Sun, Mars, Jupiter, and Saturn; the eighth was the firmament containing all the fixed stars; the ninth was the crystalline sphere, invented by Hipparchus (second century B.C.), to account for the precession of the equinoxes. These were known as *The Nine Heavens*; the 10th—added much later—was the *primum mobile*.

According to the Muslims, there are seven heavens. *The first heaven* is of pure silver, and here the stars, each with its angel warder, are hung out like lamps on golden chains; it is the abode of Adam and Eve. *The second heaven* is of pure gold, and is the domain of John the Baptist and Jesus. *The third heaven* is of pearl, and is allotted to Joseph. Here Azrael, the angel of death, is stationed, and is forever writing in a large book the names of those just born and blotting out those of the newly dead. *The fourth heaven* is of white gold, and is Enoch's. Here dwells the Angel of Tears, whose height is "500 days' journey," and he sheds ceaseless tears for the sins of man. *The fifth heaven* is of silver, and is Aaron's. Here dwells the Avenging Angel, who presides over elemental fire. *The sixth heaven* is composed of ruby and garnet, and is presided over by Moses. Here dwells the Guardian Angel of heaven and earth, half snow and half fire. *The seventh heaven* is formed of divine light beyond the power of tongue to describe, and is ruled by Abraham. Each inhabitant is bigger than the whole earth and has 70,000 heads, each head 70,000 mouths, each mouth 70,000 tongues, and each tongue speaks 70,000 languages, all forever employed in chanting of the Most High.

To be in the seventh heaven is to be supremely happy. The cabalists maintained that there are seven heavens, each rising in happiness above the other, the seventh being the abode of God and the highest class of angels. See PARADISE.

Heaven and Hell (1956). An essay by Aldous HUXLEY. It describes the effects the drug mescalin has on the mind, and compares the ecstatic and depressed states it produces with mystics' accounts of heaven and hell. Huxley had described his own experiments with mescalin in *The Doors of Perception* (1954).

Hebbel, [Christian] Friedrich (1813–1863). German dramatist, known especially for the philosophical and historical theories which, though they sometimes enhance his works, often mar the dramatic effect. Almost all his plays take place at historical turning points, in accordance with ideas that he formulates in *Mein Wort über das Drama* (*My Word on the Drama*, 1843) and in the preface to his tragedy MARIA MAGDALENA. Among his plays are also a tragedy (1841) about the Biblical heroine JUDITH; *Herodes and Mariamne* (1850), which treats the Herod in whose reign Christ was born (see MARIAMNE); *Agnes Bernauer* (1855), a tragedy of love between a prince and a commoner; *Gyges und sein Ring* (*Gyges and His Ring*, 1856), based on the story of Candaules; and *Die Nibelungen* (1862), a trilogy based on the story of the Nibelungenlied. In style, Hebbel's plays are considered realistic, as opposed to the idealism of the classical and romantic authors of the earlier 19th century.

Hebe. In Greek mythology, goddess of youth. She was the cupbearer of the immortals before GANYMEDE superseded her. She was the wife of Heracles and had the power of making the aged young again.

Hebraism and Hellenism (1869). A well-known essay by Matthew ARNOLD. It appeared in the collection *Culture and Anarchy*. It analyzes and contrasts the Hebrew and the Greek cultures, the two strongest influences on British culture. Arnold maintains that the "uppermost idea" of Hellenism is "to see things as they really are," while that of Hebraism is "conduct and obedience."

Hebreo or **Ebreo, León.** See Judah León ABRABANEL.

Hebrews, The Epistle of Paul the Apostle to the. A New Testament book. Scholars place its date of writing around A.D. 100, but have been unable to identify its author; it is generally agreed that Hebrews is not an actual Pauline epistle. One of the most eloquent books in the New Testament, it stresses the powerful role of Jesus as the highest priest of God whose personal sacrifice was made for all men.

Hecate (Hekate). One of the TITANS of Greek mythology. The only one who retained her power under the rule of Zeus, she was the daughter of Perses and Asteria, and became a deity of the lower world after taking part in the search for Persephone. She taught witchcraft and sorcery, and was a goddess of the dead. As she combined the attributes of, and became identified with, Selene, Artemis, and Persephone, she was represented as a triple goddess and was sometimes described as having three heads: one of a horse, one of a dog, and one of a lion. Her offerings consisted of dogs, honey, and black lambs, which were sacrificed to her at crossroads.

In Shakespeare's MACBETH, she appears as the queen of witches. After berating the three "weird sisters" for having made prophecies to Macbeth without her knowledge, she joins them in completing his destruction.

Hecht, Ben (1893–1964). American journalist, playwright, and novelist. Born in New York City, Hecht began his career in Chicago, where he worked as a reporter and took part in that city's "literary renaissance." His first novel, *Erik Dorn* (1921), the story of an intellectual who throws over both wife and mistress for the excitement of European revolution, was based on his experiences as Berlin reporter for the Chicago *News*. *Count Bruga* (1926) and *A Jew in Love* (1930) are lampoons of Maxwell BODENHEIM, who had drawn an unflattering portrait of Hecht in *Ninth Avenue* (1926). Hecht's play *Winkelberg* (1958) is also about Bodenheim. A prolific writer, Hecht wrote numerous short stories during his Chicago days, many of them being included in *The Collected Stories of Ben Hecht* (1945).

Hecht collaborated with Charles MacArthur on two plays: *The Front Page* (1928), a fast-paced portrayal of newspaper life, and *Twentieth Century* (1933). He also wrote the scenarios for several films. Hecht attacked anti-Semitism in *Guide for the Living* (1944) and advocated an extreme form of Zionism at the time Israel was being formed. *Perfidy* (1961) is a polemical attack on some of the leaders of the Israeli government. *A Child of the Century* (1954) is his frank, entertaining, and unconventional autobiography.

Hector (Hektor). Eldest son of Priam, the noblest and most magnanimous of all the Trojan chieftains in Homer's ILIAD. After holding out for ten years, he was slain by Achilles, who lashed him to his chariot, and dragged the dead body in triumph thrice round the walls of Troy. The *Iliad* concludes with the funeral obsequies of Hector and Patroclus.

In modern times his name has somewhat deteriorated, for it is used today for a swaggering bully, and "to hector" means to browbeat, bully, bluster.

Hecuba (Hekabe). In Homer's *Iliad*, the wife of Priam and mother of Hector. She is a tragic figure in Euripides' THE TROJAN WOMEN. In his HECUBA, her grief has made her a kind of Fury. In revenge for the murder of her son Polydorus, she blinds the Thracian king Polymestor, after killing his children. According to myth (perhaps through confusion with Hecate), she was transformed into a fiery-eyed hellhound. In Shakespeare's *Hamlet*, the Player King is deeply moved by his own speech about her, and Hamlet marvels, "What's Hecuba to him, or he to Hecuba?"

Hecuba (?425 B.C.). A tragedy by EURIPIDES. Hecuba, queen of Troy, has seen all of her 50 children die except her daughter Polyxena and POLYDORUS, her youngest son, whom she sent to King Polymestor in Thrace at the beginning of the war. As the play begins, she lies exhausted in front of her tent in Chalcidice, where the Greek expedition has taken her. A messenger comes to announce the decision of the Greeks in council: Polyxena must die to assuage the shade of Achilles. Polyxena goes to her death with dignity; soon after, the body of Polydorus is brought onto the stage. When Hecuba learns which of her children this is, she yearns for revenge. She lures Polymestor to her tent, blinds him, and kills his sons. Polymestor is reduced to an animal state as he crawls and gropes his way out of the tent. The closing scene shows Polymestor and Hecuba arguing their cases before Agamemnon. When Agamemnon decides for Hecuba, Polymestor breaks into prophecy and foresees the murder of Agamemnon and the horrible death of Hecuba, who will bark like a dog.

Many critics, approaching the *Hecuba* as a drama of character, have found contradictions in the plot, which is divided into two parts: the death of Polyxena and the blinding of Polymestor. Hecuba is involved in both of them, and her character changes through the play, but Euripides' tragic conception concerns more than Hecuba. The theme of the play is the brutality of suffering. Though Hecuba is the principal actor, the climactic speech is the prophecy of Polymestor, which displays Polymestor and Hecuba at the same bestial level. The key to Euripides' purpose is his use of myth; the old tales of Agamemnon's murder and Hecuba's animal metamorphosis become the climax to the long series of brutalities in the play.

Hedda Gabler (1890). A play by Henrik IBSEN. Hedda, a ruthless, neurotic woman, is bored with her dull, scholarly husband, repelled by the idea of her possible pregnancy, and concerned that she may have to forgo certain luxuries if her husband fails to be appointed a professor at the university. She learns that meek Thea Elvsted has helped reform the brilliant but dissipated Eilert Lövberg, who had once been in love with Hedda, and that the success of Lövberg's new book has made him her husband's rival for the professorship. Determined to show her power over Lövberg and thwart Thea's good influence, she lures him back into dissipation. She finds the missing manuscript of a second book, far more important to Lövberg than the first, but lets him believe that it is lost beyond recall. When, in despair, he threatens to end his life, she gives him a pistol and urges him to "die beautifully." He dies quite horribly, and Hedda finds herself in the power of Judge Brack, who knows that Hedda gave Lövberg the pistol and intends to use his knowledge to make her his mistress. Hedda finds this situation unbearable and "dies beautifully" by putting a bullet through her head.

Hedin, Sven Anders von (1865–1952). Swedish geographer and explorer in Central Asia, China, and India. Accounts of his journeys include *Through Asia* (1898), *Central Asia and Tibet* (1904), *Overland to India* (1910), and *The Silk Road* (1936).

Heep, Uriah. In Charles Dickens' DAVID COPPERFIELD, a clerk of Mr. WICKFIELD. One of the most famous characters in fiction, he is a detestable sneak, who is everlastingly forcing on one's attention that he is "'umble." Actually, Uriah is designing and malignant and he becomes a blackmailing tyrant over Mr. Wickfield. His infamy is brought to light by Mr. Micawber.

Hegel, Georg Friedrich Wilhelm (1770–1831). German philosopher. He greatly influenced the study of history and metaphysics in that he saw reality as a dynamic process, rather than as a reflection of static ideals. The process of reality, he maintained, is governed by the dialectical law: every thesis implies its own contradiction, or antithesis, and their conflict ends in a synthesis which again brings forth its antithesis. History, understood in terms of the dialectic, is produced by the conflicting impulses and interests of men, but at the same time shows the progressive self-realization of human reason and freedom. Great men are those whose personal aims coincide with the aim of the historical process; and in the later years of

his life, Hegel used this concept of history to justify support of the Prussian state. His concept of the dialectic was developed by many subsequent philosophers, notably Marx and Engels; but the latter discarded Hegelian idealism and applied the dialectic to a materialistic view of history. Hegel's works include *The Phenomenology of the Spirit* (*Die Phänomenologie des Geistes;* 1807) and *The Philosophy of Right* (*Grundlinien der Philosophie des Rechts;* 1821). He was a close friend of both Hölderlin and Friedrich Schelling, with whom he held many ideas in common.

Heggen, Thomas [Orlo] (1919–1949). American novelist. Heggen, who was a member of the staff of the *Reader's Digest,* used his wartime experiences in the navy to write MISTER ROBERTS, an extremely successful novel, later adapted for the stage by Joshua Logan.

hegira or **hijira** (Arabic, "the departure"). The flight of MUHAMMAD from Mecca to MEDINA when he was expelled by the magistrates, July 16, 622. In 639, the Caliph Omar decreed that the Muslim calendar would date from this event.

Heian. The second Japanese historical period (794–1185). It saw the development of an exquisitely refined culture under the Imperial Court at Kyoto (Heian). Literature and the arts were marked by an extreme elegance, strongly influenced by Buddhist and Chinese thought. The *Tale of Genji* and the *Pillow-book of Sei Shōnagon* are products of this age. It was dominated by the Fujiwara family and is also known as the Fujiwara period.

Heiberg, Gunnar Edvard Rode (1857–1929). Norwegian playwright and essayist. A clever satirist, Heiberg mocked the absurd pettiness of Norwegian political life and treated other current concerns in such plays as *Kong Midas* (1890), *Gerts have* (1894), and *Det store lod* (1895). In *Balkonen* (*The Balcony,* 1894) and *Kjoerlighedens tragedie* (*The Tragedy of Love,* 1904), he turns his lyric powers to an analysis of the primitive force of sexual passion.

Heidegger, Martin (1889–   ). German philosopher, influenced by Kierkegaard, whose ideas form the basis of the existentialist movement. In *Sein und Zeit* (*Being and Time,* 1927), he distinguishes between two types of being: human existence (*Dasein*) and nonhuman presence (*Vorhandensein*), such as that of physical objects. Human existence is characterized by personal consciousness and accompanied by feelings of insecurity and dread (*Angst*). *Angst* is not fear of anything specific, but a general dread of nothingness.

Heidenstam [Carl Gustaf] Verner von (1859–1940). Swedish poet and novelist. An aspiring painter, Heidenstam turned to another art form with the publication of his first collection of poetry, *Vallfart och vandringsår* (1888). The vigorous modern rhythms and exuberant mood of the poems had a significant effect on young writers who were rebelling against naturalism. *Dikter* (1895) and *Nya Dikter* (1915) revealed Heidenstam's lyrical gifts. After 1890 he became chiefly a prose writer; in 1916 he received the Nobel Prize for literature.

Heidi. A children's story of life in the Swiss Alps by Johanna Spyri (1827–1901).

Heifetz, Jascha (1901–   ). Russian-born American violin virtuoso. He was a child prodigy;

his technique and artistry continued to amaze people as he matured. He settled in the U.S. after the Russian Revolution and became one of the most popular violinists of the century.

Heike monogatari, see TALES OF THE HEIKE, THE.

Heimat, Die. See MAGDA.

Heimdall. One of the gods of Scandinavian mythology, son of the nine virgin daughters of Aegir and called the White God with the Golden Teeth. As watchman of Asgard, he dwelt on the edge of heaven, guarded the rainbow bridge Bifrost, and possessed a mighty horn whose blast could be heard throughout the universe. It was said that he could see for 100 miles by day or night, that he slept less than a bird, and could hear the grass grow. When Ragnarok, the twilight of the gods, comes, he will sound his Gjallarhorn to assemble the gods and heroes. See LOKI.

Heimskringla. The most important prose collection in Old Norse literature, containing 16 sagas of Norwegian history through 1177, sketched through the medium of biography, with a compendium of ancient Scandinavian mythology and poetry. Its name comes from its opening words, *Kringla heimsins,* the circle of the world. The authorship is attributed to SNORRI STURLUSON.

Heine, Heinrich. Name at birth: **Chaim Harry Heine** (1797–1856). German poet, satirist, and journalist of Jewish origin. His ambiguous attitude toward Germany, combining a sincere sentimental love for the land and the people with biting irony about many German institutions, customs, and literary trends, appears in the early *Reisebilder* (*Travel-Sketches,* 1826 ff.), one of which is *Die Harzreise* (*Trip in the Harz Mountains,* 1826), his first major literary success. Gradually, however, he began to realize that the conflict between his liberal political views and the oppressive conservative regime in Prussia would make it impossible for him to remain in Germany. His attention was specifically drawn to Paris, where both the political ferment of the July Revolution (1830) and the growth of Saint-Simonianism attracted him; in 1831 he went there and remained for the rest of his life. In Paris, he was primarily active as a journalist and critic, writing in both German and French, and much of his work was intended to promote better understanding between his native and adopted lands: for example, *Französische Zustände* (*The Situation in France,* 1833); *Zur Geschichte der Religion und Philosophie in Deutschland* (*On the History of Religion and Philosophy in Germany,* 1834), which was also published in French; and *Die romantische Schule* (*The Romantic School,* 1833). In 1835, a Prussian edict prohibited his writings in Germany, naming him as a leader in the JUNG DEUTSCHLAND (Young Germany) movement with which he had, however, been only peripherally associated.

In his early poems, notably the *Buch der Lieder* (*Book of Songs,* 1827 ff.), which includes his famous ballad on the LORELEI-theme, Heine stands close to GERMAN ROMANTICISM. But though romantic elements remain in his later verse, especially the collection *Romanzero* (1851), there is also a strong tendency toward irony about romanticism, as in the narrative poems *Atta Troll* (1843) about the death of a trained bear, and *Deutschland, ein Wintermärchen* (*Ger-*

many, a Winter Tale, 1844) a political and literary satire. See PLATEN, BÖRNE.

Heinrich, Der arme (Poor Heinrich) (early 13th century). A narrative poem by HARTMANN VON AUE, based on German legend. The nobleman Heinrich is told he will not be cured of his leprosy until a virgin is willing to die for him. As he cannot wish such a sacrifice, he gives away most of his possessions and goes to live with one of his tenant farmers. This man's daughter learns how the cure must be effected and offers herself as the victim. This is enough to cause an instant cure, and Heinrich marries her. Heinrich becomes Prince Henry of Hoheneck in H. W. Longfellow's *The Golden Legend* (1851), and the tale is retold in Gerhart Hauptmann's drama *Der arme Heinrich* (1902).

Heinrich von Ofterdingen. Legendary German minnesinger, or medieval court poet. See under WARTBURG. NOVALIS uses his name for the title and hero of an unfinished symbolic novel (pub. 1801) in which the BLUE FLOWER represents the union of the dream world and the real world for the poet. The novel treats the imaginary development of Heinrich from a completely naïve young man into an accomplished poet. Wagner makes him one of the competing minstrels in TANNHÄUSER.

Heinse, Johann Jakob Wilhelm (1749–1803). German novelist. His justification of immoralism on aesthetic grounds is related to the tendencies of the STURM UND DRANG. His critical works on art, especially Italian painting, are significant, and his interest in this field may also be seen in the novel *Ardinghello oder Die glückseligen Inseln* (*Ardinghello or The Isles of the Blessed,* 1787), which is important in the growth of the BILDUNGSROMAN (novel of education).

Hekatoncheires. See the HUNDRED-HANDED.

Hel or **Hela.** The daughter of LOKI in Scandinavian mythology, who was queen of the dead and goddess of the lower regions. Here she was cast by Odin to dwell beneath the roots of the sacred ash, Yggdrasil. The region of Hel was also the home of the spirits of those who had died in their beds, as distinguished from Valhalla, the abode of heroes slain in battle.

Heldenbuch, Das (book of heroes). Name given to several collections of medieval German epics. The

Woodcut from a German *Heldenbuch* (c. 1500).

earliest extant manuscript is from 1472, the first printed version about 1477, although the poems were probably composed in the 13th century. The episodes are grouped in two cycles, one concerning Dietrich of Bern (see THEODORIC THE GREAT), the other about the brothers ORTNIT and Wolfdietrich.

Helen (Helene). In Greek mythology, the daughter of Zeus and Leda and wife of Menelaus. Her abduction by Paris led to the Trojan War. In the ILIAD of Homer and The TROJAN WOMEN of Euripides, she appears as a shallow and self-centered woman, unconcerned with the havoc her infidelity has wrought. Throughout literature from Greek times to the present, she has been a symbol of womanly beauty and sexual attraction. As such she has appeared in many dramas, including Marlowe's *Doctor Faustus,* Goethe's *Faust,* and Jean Giraudoux' *Tiger at the Gates.* Euripides' HELEN, however, tells another version of the story. The Helen at Troy was a phantom created by Hera to cause war. Menelaus' faithful wife, kidnapped by Hermes, remained in Egypt throughout the war, but they were finally reunited, despite the attempt of the Egyptian king Theoclymenus to marry her by force. This story of the false Helen was attributed to the poet STESICHORUS, who was said by Plato to have been blinded by Helen (who was also a goddess) for maligning her in verse. He redeemed her reputation, and his own sight, by writing the story of the phantom. Gluck wrote an opera on the traditional Helen, *Paride ed Elena* (1770). At the imperial court in Part II of Goethe's *Faust,* Faust makes Helen and Paris appear in a magical vision but, forgetting that it is an illusion, falls violently in love with Helen and causes an explosion by his rash attempt to take her from Paris. In the classical WALPURGIS NIGHT, however, he finds the real Helen, and the two of them enjoy a brief idyll that symbolizes the romantic ideal (see the brothers SCHLEGEL) of a synthesis between Nordic and classical cultures. See EUPHORION; ETERNAL FEMININE.

Helen (Helene; 412 B.C.). A play by EURIPIDES. Following Stesichorus' version of the story of HELEN of Troy, the play opens in Egypt. Hermes has brought her there after Paris has abducted from Troy not Helen but a phantom created in her likeness by Hera. She has been kindly treated by King Proteus, but he has died and his son Theoclymenus, who hates the Greeks, wants to marry her. Teucer arrives and tells of the destruction of Troy seven years before. Thousands have died because of the woman they all believe is Helen; her own mother and brothers have killed themselves in shame at her conduct; Menelaus and his ships are lost.

Menelaus arrives, however, and, recognizing his wife—the phantom having vanished—bitterly realizes that the TROJAN WAR has been fought for nothing. Pretending that Menelaus is dead, Helen borrows a ship to hold obsequies for him at sea. Together they escape from Theoclymenus and sail for home.

Helena. (1) In Shakespeare's MIDSUMMER NIGHT'S DREAM, a young Athenian lady in love with Demetrius. She pursues him despite his love for Hermia and is at last rewarded when Puck anoints him with a love potion.

(2) The persistent and loving heroine of Shakespeare's ALL'S WELL THAT ENDS WELL. She loves the haughty Bertram despite his scorn for her.

Helen of Kirconnell. A famous Scottish ballad. Helen is the lover of Adam Flemming. One day, while they are standing on the banks of a river, a rival suitor points his gun at Adam. Helen throws herself in front of him and is shot. The two rivals then fight, and the murderer is slain. Wordsworth embodies the same story in his poem *Ellen Irwin.*

Helenus. In Vergil's AENEID, a Trojan prince and prophet, the only son of Priam to survive the fall of Troy. He falls to the share of Pyrrhus (Neoptolemus) when the captives are awarded, and eventually marries Andromache, his brother Hector's widow. In some versions of the legend he is said to have deserted to the Greeks, and in others he is said to have been captured by Odysseus.

Helicon (Helikon). A Boeotian mountain. It was known by the Greeks as the home of the Muses. It contained the fountains of Aganippe and Hippocrene, connected by "Helicon's harmonious stream." The name is used allusively of poetic inspiration.

Heliogabalus. Full Latin name, **Varius Avitus Bassianus** (204–222). Roman emperor (218–222). He began as a priest in the temple of the sun god Elagabalus (hence his name as emperor). He was put forward as the son of CARACALLA and proclaimed emperor by the soldiery. Giving himself up to infamous debauchery, he left affairs of state to his mother. He was killed by the Praetorian Guard.

Helios. The Greek sun god. He rode to his palace in Colchis every night in a golden boat furnished with wings. He appears principally in the myth of PHAËTON, though his cattle are important in the ODYSSEY. His cult was important on the island of Rhodes; the famous COLOSSUS OF RHODES was a statue of Helios. See HERACLES.

heliotrope (Gr., "turn-to-sun"). The sun god loved Clytie, but forsook her for her sister Leucothoe. On discovering this, Clytie pined away; and the god changed her at death to a flower, which, always turning toward the sun, is called heliotrope.

The bloodstone, a greenish quartz with veins and spots of red, used to be called heliotrope, the story being that if thrown into a bucket of water it turned the rays of the sun to blood color. This stone also had the power of rendering its bearer invisible.

Helle. See GOLDEN FLEECE, THE.

Hellen. In Greek legend, a king of Phthia, eponym of the Hellenic race.

Hellenore. See FAERIE QUEENE, THE.

Hellespont. The ancient name of the Dardanelles, named for Athamas' daughter Helle (see THE GOLDEN FLEECE). In the classical romance, Leander used to swim the Hellespont to visit Hero, a priestess of Sestos. Lord Byron prided himself upon duplicating this feat.

Hell-fire Club. See MEDMENHAM ABBEY.

Hellman, Lillian (1905–   ). American dramatist. She is noted for her plays of psychological conflict. *The Children's Hour* (1934) dealt with a young girl who starts the rumor that the two heads of her school are Lesbians. THE LITTLE FOXES and THE WATCH ON THE RHINE are two of Lillian Hellman's most successful dramas. Others include *The Searching Wind* (1944) and *Toys in the Attic* (1960).

Hellström, Gustaf (1882-1953). Swedish writer. A career as foreign correspondent gave a foreign flavor to his novels, which are set in such world capitals as New York, London, and Paris. Among his works are *Ungkarlar* (1904), *Kuskar* (1910), *Bengt Blancks sentimentala resa* (1917), *Snormakare Lekholm far en idé* (*Lacemaker Lekholm has an idea,* 1927), and the autobiographical series *En man utan humor* (1921-1944).

Helmholtz, Hermann Ludwig Ferdinand von (1821-1894). German physicist who developed the theory of the conservation of energy, first formulated by Julius Robert MAYER.

Héloïse (1101-1164). Niece of the Canon Fulbert of Notre Dame Cathedral, famous as the beloved of Pierre Abélard. He was her tutor when he fell in love and seduced her (1118). They were secretly married after the birth of their son Astrolabe, although Héloïse tried to dissuade him, fearing the marriage would ruin his career. And in fact, when the marriage became known, Fulbert had Abélard emasculated; Héloïse became a nun and Abélard a monk. Their famous exchange of letters (see under ABÉLARD) made their story popular as a romantic tragedy, and in 1817 their bodies were reburied in one grave.

helot. A serf of ancient SPARTA. Possibly members of the earlier population of the area enslaved by their Dorian conquerors, they constituted the lowest class in the city-state. According to tradition, Spartan fathers used to ply their helot slaves with liquor on occasion so that their sons might learn by their disgusting example to detest drunkenness.

Helper, Hinton Rowan (1829-1909). American writer. Helper, who was born in North Carolina and was raised on a plantation, is best known for *The Impending Crisis of the South: How to Meet It* (1857), in which he argued that the South was economically and culturally far behind the North because of its slave labor. He held that slavery should be taxed out of existence and that all Negroes should be sent back to Africa. The book was an immediate success in the North, but it became illegal in most parts of the South even to own a copy.

Helvétius, Claude Adrien (1715-1771). French materialistic philosopher and encyclopedist. In his most famous work, *De l'Esprit* (1758), he asserts that human minds at birth are uniformly blank and that general progress and well-being therefore depend upon education, institutions, and laws. Utilitarian in his thinking, he states that religion has failed in becoming the framework for morality and that the only real basis for morality and for law is the public interest, i.e., that which is good for the greatest number. For this heretical doctrine the Sorbonne, the Pope, and the *Parlement* had the work condemned and burned. Jeremy Bentham and James Mill acknowledge his influence.

Hemans, Felicia Dorothea, born **Browne** (1793-1835). English poet, best known for her lyrics, *The Landing of the Pilgrim Fathers* and CASABIANCA. Mrs. Heman's work was much admired in its day for what was deemed nobility and pathos. She was also famous for her beauty and learning. Her *Poetical Works* were edited by W. M. Rossetti in 1873.

Hemingway, Ernest [Miller] (1899-1961). American novelist and short-story writer. Starting his writing career as a newspaperman and foreign correspondent, Hemingway was a meticulous literary craftsman whose terse, economic style, dramatic understatement, and superb dialogue have been extremely influential on modern prose writers. Sometimes erroneously dismissed as being sentimentally obsessed with violence, Hemingway clearly portrays in his work the sensitivity of a man hurt by the violence which he sees as a characteristic of our time.

Hemingway's first published volume was *Three Stories and Ten Poems* (1923); it contained the stories *Up in Michigan, Out of Season, My Old Man,* and six poems which had been previously published in *Poetry* (January, 1923). The author's first major work, IN OUR TIME, was a collection of 15 stories, many of them dealing with the early biography of Nick Adams, whose boyhood was to be a prototype for those of later Hemingway heroes. His first novel, *The Torrents of Spring* (1926), with its burlesque of Sherwood Anderson, is significant only as a declaration of his literary independence. It was with the appearance of THE SUN ALSO RISES that Hemingway's reputation became widely established. Often considered his best work in this form, it depicts "the lost generation" and the disillusionment that followed World War I.

MEN WITHOUT WOMEN, a collection that includes the famous stories THE KILLERS and *Fifty Grand,* continued Hemingway's early success. For those critics who consider Hemingway at his best in the short-story form, this volume and the later *Winner Take Nothing* (1933) rank high indeed. Hemingway next wrote A FAREWELL TO ARMS, a romantic, vivid, and impeccably written novel whose genesis was derived from material published in the earlier volume *In Our Time*. Two works of nonfiction followed: *Death in the Afternoon* (1932), with its eulogy of ritualized bullfight, and *Green Hills of Africa* (1935).

In 1937, Hemingway's early dissociation from political questions gave way to a position of greater involvement. To HAVE AND HAVE NOT, with its dying hero gasping, "One man alone ain't got . . . no chance," was the first to mark this change. That same year, deeply sympathetic with the Loyalist cause, he went to Spain as a war correspondent during the Civil war. *The Fifth Column* (1938), a play presenting "the nobility and dignity of the cause of the Spanish people," continued this concern as did his novel FOR WHOM THE BELL TOLLS.

During the next decade, Hemingway was almost silent. Taking part in World War II as a correspondent and waging his own irregular war at the head of a make-shift corps of his own, he did not publish another novel until 1950 when *Across the River and into the Trees* appeared. This novel, in which an aging hero revisits the scene of his World War I wounding, was almost unanimously rated as inferior work. But in 1952 came THE OLD MAN AND THE SEA, a novelette that was widely acclaimed and awarded the Pulitzer Prize. In 1954, Hemingway was given the Nobel Prize in literature. He published nothing more of significance before his self-inflicted death in 1961.

The author's short stories were collected in *The*

Short Stories of Ernest Hemingway (1938). *A Moveable Feast* (1964), published posthumously, is a reminiscence of the author's early years in Paris. See SHORT HAPPY LIFE OF FRANCIS MACOMBER, THE; SNOWS OF KILIMANJARO, THE.

Hemlock and After (1952). A novel by Angus WILSON. The hero is a middle-aged writer who is trying to reconcile his high-minded ideals with his failures and homosexual impulses. Wilson's attitude toward his many characters is both satirical and diagnostic.

Hémon, Louis (1880–1913). French novelist. Although Hémon spent only a short time in Canada, he is best known for *Maria Chapdelaine* (1916), a novel of farm life in Quebec, which became very popular after its posthumous publication.

Henchard, Michael. See MAYOR OF CASTERBRIDGE, THE.

Henderson, Alice Corbin (1881–1949). American poet and editor. With Harriet MONROE, she founded the magazine POETRY, and served as its associate editor (1912–1916). Her own poetry was collected in *The Spinning Woman of the Sky* (1912), *Red Earth* (1920), and *The Sun Turns West* (1933). She also compiled with Miss Monroe, *The New Poetry: An Anthology* (1917).

Hengist and **Horsa.** Two brothers in Geoffrey of Monmouth's *History of the Kings of Britain*. They were Jute invaders of England (c. 449), whose aid in war against the Picts was enlisted by the ancient British king VORTIGERN. Horsa is said to have been killed in battle in 455, Hengist to have ruled the kingdom of Kent, which they founded, until 488.

Henley, William Ernest (1849–1903). English poet, dramatist, and editor. As editor of the *National Observer* (1889–1894) and the *New Review* (1898–1903), Henley was a revolutionary force in English literature, publishing and defending early works of such writers as Barrie, Hardy, Kipling, Wells, Shaw, and Conrad. In his own work he was a pioneer in the use of free verse (*In Hospital,* 1888) and wrote a number of poems of merit and technical accomplishment. Unfortunately, aggressive jingoism mars much of such volumes as *The Song of the Sword* (1893) and *For England's Sake* (1900) and Henley has had the ill-luck to be known, generally, as the author of a single poem, the meretricious INVICTUS. His collected *Poems* appeared in 1912. He also collaborated with his friend R. L. Stevenson on three plays, and was the author of numerous critical essays (*Works,* 1908).

Hennepin, Father **Louis** (1640–?1701). Belgian-born Franciscan friar and explorer. He accompanied La Salle through the Great Lakes (1679) and joined a party that explored the Upper Mississippi Valley. While a captive of the Sioux, he discovered the Falls of St. Anthony, near present-day Minneapolis. In France he published *Description de la Louisiane* (1683) and other, somewhat exaggerated, accounts of his experiences. His claim that he descended to the mouth of the Mississippi has since been shown to be false.

Henriade, La (1723, republished in 1728 with revisions). An epic poem in 10 cantos by VOLTAIRE. It recounts the struggle of Henry of Navarre (later HENRY IV of France) to obtain the throne. Voltaire depicts the assassination of Henry III and the religious wars with the HOLY LEAGUE, and by implication condemns civil strife and religious fanaticism.

Henrietta Maria (1609–1669). Queen consort (1625–1649) of Charles I of England and mother of Charles II and James II. The daughter of Henry IV of France, she was a Roman Catholic. Forced to flee to France (1644), she returned to England after the Restoration.

Henriques, Robert (1905–   ). English soldier and novelist. Among his works are *No Arms, No Armour* (1939), *Home Fires Burning* (1945), *Through the Valley* (1950), and *A Stranger Here* (1953).

Henry IV. Also known as **Henry Bolingbroke** and **Henry of Lancaster** (1367–1413). King of England (1399–1413), the 1st monarch of the house of Lancaster. The son of John of Gaunt and the grandson of Edward III, he was banished by RICHARD II in 1398. The following year he invaded England, overthrew Richard, and assumed the crown himself. He is a central character in Shakespeare's HENRY IV: PART I and PART II, and also appears in RICHARD II. The surname Bolingbroke refers to the castle in which he was born.

Henry V (1387–1422). King of England (1413–1422). The son of Henry IV, he invaded France in an attempt to reconquer England's former possessions there, winning an important victory at Agincourt (1415). Subsequent military successes and astute diplomacy resulted in the treaty of Troyes (1420), by which Henry was to marry Catherine of Valois, daughter of Charles VI, king of France, and inherit the French crown upon Charles's death. See HENRY V, THE LIFE OF KING.

Henry VII. Also known as **Henry Tudor** (1457–1509). King of England (1485–1509), the 1st monarch of the Tudor dynasty. As earl of Richmond and the principal representative of the Lancastrian claim to the throne of England, he defeated Richard III at Bosworth Field in 1485. His subsequent marriage to Elizabeth, daughter of Edward IV, marked the end of the WARS OF THE ROSES. Later he successfully suppressed a rebellion by the Yorkist pretender PERKIN WARBECK. He was succeeded by his son Henry VIII.

Henry VIII. Henry Tudor (1491–1547). Second of the Tudor kings, king of England (1509–1547). At the beginning of his reign Henry married Catherine of Aragon, his brother's widow; because of some ecclesiastical protest about the validity of such a union, he was forced to acquire a Papal dispensation. When, nearly twenty years later, Catherine had not borne him a son, personal and political reasons moved him to consider divorce. The Pope was unwilling, doubly so since Rome was in the hands of the Emperor Charles V, Catherine's nephew. Various delays occurred, and finally Henry chose the expedient of overthrowing papal jurisdiction, thus at one fell swoop making possible his divorce, channeling the revenues from monasteries and Church lands away from Rome to the Crown and, almost incidentally, and for political far more than religious reasons, initiating the English Reformation. Early in 1533, before any kind of divorce had been granted, he secretly married ANNE BOLEYN, and a few months later had his first marriage declared void and his second declared valid. This was followed by an Act of Succession, giving the right of succession to the throne to offspring of Anne and denying it to Mary (later MARY I), Catherine's daughter, on the grounds of her illegitimacy. To both this and the Act of Supremacy, by which Henry was made head of the Church, subjects were required to give an oath of acceptance, a thing that no devout Catholic could do, and in default of which Sir Thomas More, formerly Lord Chancellor, was executed for high treason.

Anne, like Catherine before her, bore only one child that lived, and that a daughter, the future ELIZABETH I. In 1536 Anne was dispatched on a charge of adultery, and Henry married Jane Seymour, who died bearing him the much-desired son, destined to become the boy-king Edward VI. In 1540 Henry married the German princess Anne of Cleves, but disliked her and divorced her almost immediately. Catherine Howard, the next of his wives, was soon charged with adultery and beheaded. His last wife was Catherine Parr, a patroness of the arts, who survived him. Before his death Henry fixed the succession in his will, giving it to Edward, Mary, and Elizabeth (though both of his daughters had previously been declared illegitimate), who succeeded him in that order.

Henry IV. Also known as **Henry of Navarre** and **Henry the Great** (1553–1610). King of France (1589–1610), the first of the Bourbon dynasty. Raised as a Calvinist, Henry became leader of the French Huguenot party in 1569 after the death of the first prince of Condé. He succeeded to the throne of Navarre as Henry III and married MARGARET OF VALOIS, sister of Charles IX of France, in 1572. When the death of the brother of Henry III, the reigning king of France, made Henry of Navarre heir presumptive, the refusal of the HOLY LEAGUE to recognize his title led to the conflict known as the War of the Three Henrys (Henry III of France, Henry of Navarre, and Henry, duke of GUISE). After the assassination of the king of France, Henry's victory over the league at Ivry and his conversion to Catholicism enabled him to secure the crown. One of France's ablest monarchs, Henry initiated a program to hasten recovery from the religious wars. He issued the Edict of NANTES and, in foreign affairs, followed a policy of opposition to the Hapsburgs. He was assassinated by François Ravillac, a Roman Catholic fanatic. See Gabrielle d'ESTRÉES; duc de SULLY; and HENRIADE, THE.

Henry IV (1050–1106). Holy Roman emperor. On the death of his father, Henry III, in 1056, he succeeded to the kingdoms of Germany, Italy, and Burgundy. In 1065 Henry was declared of age and assumed the throne. His reign was marked by the great struggle between empire and papacy over the question of lay investiture. Hitherto the emperors had filled the ecclesiastical positions within their dominions at their pleasure. But Pope GREGORY VII decided to claim this power for the papacy, and in 1075 he issued a decree forbidding lay investiture. Almost immediately, Henry responded by filling several sees in Italy with bishops of his own choosing. When Gregory threatened excommunication, Henry called together the German bishops and answered: "I, Henry, king by the grace of God, together with all our bishops, say unto thee, come down, come

down from thy throne and be accursed through all the ages." Gregory forthwith deposed the bishops, excommunicated Henry, and declared the thrones of Italy and Germany vacant. Henry was then faced with a revolt in his territories, as his vassals gave him notice that a new emperor would be chosen within the year if he did not relent. Accordingly, the emperor went in 1077 to meet the pope at Canossa. There, outside the castle, Henry garbed as a penitent waited for three days in the snow before Gregory would receive him and grant conditional absolution. When Henry returned to Germany, he found that the princes had elected a new emperor in spite of his penance. Gregory remained neutral for a time, then renewed the excommunication. After Henry had defeated and killed his rival Rudolf, duke of Swabia, he marched on Rome. An attempt at compromise through the convocation of a synod failed, and in 1083 Henry deposed Gregory and installed Clement III, who promptly crowned Henry emperor. Meanwhile, the German princes had chosen a new king, Hermann of Luxemburg, and Henry was compelled to renew the struggle. By 1088 he had restored his authority throughout Germany. He survived conspiracies by his second wife and his eldest son Conrad, only to be defeated by his second son Henry, later Henry V, who declared he owed no allegiance to an excommunicated father. In 1105 a diet in Mainz forced Henry IV to abdicate. After escaping to Cologne, he began negotiations with England, France, and Denmark. He was engaged in organizing an army when he died in 1106.

Henry IV: Part I (c. 1597–1598). A historical play by William SHAKESPEARE, depicting early years of the reign of England's HENRY IV. After defeating rebellious Scottish barons, Henry PERCY, the famous Hotspur, eldest son of the powerful earl of Northumberland, refuses to yield his prisoners to the king unless his kinsman Edmund Mortimer, captured by the rebellious Welshman Owen Glendower, is ransomed. Since Mortimer is pretender to the throne, Henry refuses his ransom. Angered, the Percy family joins the rebels. Meanwhile, the king's son and heir, Prince Hal, continues to annoy his father by keeping company with the band of revelers led by Sir John FALSTAFF. But, hearing of the uprising, Hal takes command of a part of his father's forces, helping to defeat the rebels at the battle of Shrewsbury (1403). Hal saves his father's life and kills Hotspur.

Henry IV: Part II (c. 1597–1598). A historical play by William SHAKESPEARE, completing the description of the reign of HENRY IV. Despite the death of Hotspur, the rebellion continues, under the leadership of the earl of Northumberland. Meanwhile, Hal has returned to the riotous company of FALSTAFF. Upon Northumberland's desertion, the rebels negotiate with the king's second son, John of Lancaster, who promises to redress their grievances if they will disband. They accept and are promptly killed by the treacherous prince. News of his enemies' defeat reaches the king on his deathbed. Hal is named king (Henry V) and promptly repudiates his misspent youth by banishing Falstaff from his presence. Shakespeare's source for both plays about Henry IV is Holinshed's *Chronicles* (1577).

Henry V, The Life of King (c. 1598–1599). A historical play by William SHAKESPEARE. Shortly after his coronation, HENRY V decides to press his claims to the French throne and leads an army into France. He defeats a vastly larger French army at Agincourt (1415), wins the hand of the French princess, Catherine of Valois, and is recognized as heir to the French throne. Against this background, Shakespeare reveals Henry's rapport with the doughty English soldiers. The death of FALSTAFF is also reported in the play.

In HENRY IV: PART I and PART II and in *Henry V*, Shakespeare chronicles Henry's life from his days as a profligate youth under the influence of Sir John Falstaff to his victory at Agincourt as king of England. His character is used by Shakespeare as a study in statesmanship. Although Henry steeps himself in the revels and schemes of Falstaff, part of him always remains aloof. For, as he explains:

> I know you all, and will awhile uphold
> The unyok'd humour of your idleness:
> Yet herein will I imitate the sun,
> Who doth permit the base contagious clouds
> To smother up his beauty from the world,
> That when he please again to be himself,
> Being wanted, he may be more wonder'd at.

Henry VI: Part I (c. 1590–1592). The 1st play of a historical trilogy by William SHAKESPEARE, depicting the early years of Henry's reign up to his marriage with MARGARET OF ANJOU. After the death of Henry V, the realm of the child king, Henry VI, falls under the control of his uncles, the regents John, duke of Bedford, and HUMPHREY, duke of Gloucester. War has broken out anew in France; under JOAN LA PUCELLE, the French begin to drive the English out. Meanwhile, Richard Plantagenet, having successfully pressed his claims to the title of the duke of York, quarrels with the powerful Beaufort family of the house of Lancaster, setting the stage for the Wars of the Roses. After a temporary reconciliation of Yorkists and Lancastrians, a marriage is arranged between Henry and the daughter of the French earl of Armagnac in order to seal a truce between England and France. However, at the urging of the earl of Suffolk, Henry chooses Margaret of Anjou to be his queen.

Henry VI: Part II (c. 1590–1592). The 2nd play of a historical trilogy by William SHAKESPEARE, covering the early years of the Wars of the Roses. After his marriage to Margaret, Henry is dominated by the queen and the duke of Suffolk, who plot the overthrow of the lord protector, Humphrey, the duke of Gloucester, by convicting Humphrey's wife, the duchess of Gloucester, of sorcery, and thus forcing his shameful retirement. Meanwhile, Richard Plantagenet, having convinced the earl of Salisbury and Richard Neville, earl of Warwick, of his right to the throne, waits for the opportunity to seize it. Before leaving to suppress a revolt in Ireland, he encourages Jack CADE to launch a rebellion in his absence. Subsequently, Richard returns to England and meets and defeats the king's forces at St. Albans (1455).

Henry VI: Part III (c. 1590–1592). The 3rd play of a historical trilogy by William SHAKESPEARE, covering the downfall of Henry and the victory of the house of York in the person of Edward IV. After the defeat of his forces at St. Albans, Henry begs Richard Plantagenet to allow him to reign during his lifetime. Richard agrees, but Margaret, Henry's queen, is set on destroying Richard. At Wakefield,

she defeats him and puts him to death. But Richard's sons, Edward (IV) and Richard (III), triumph over Margaret at Towton, and Edward becomes king. Henry, who has fled, returns to England and is imprisoned in the Tower of London. Edward sends Warwick to France to arrange a marriage with Bona, sister of Louis XI. In his absence, Edward marries Lady Elizabeth Grey, and Warwick, annoyed, goes over to Margaret. After several reverses, Edward defeats Margaret at Tewkesbury (1471) where Henry's son, Edward, prince of Wales, is killed. Shortly thereafter, Richard (III) murders Henry in the Tower. The principal sources for the trilogy about Henry VI were Holinshed's *Chronicles* (1577) and Edward Hall's *Union of The Noble and Illustrious Families of Lancaster and York* (1547).

Henry VIII, The Famous History of the Life of King (1613). A historical play by William SHAKESPEARE. John Fletcher (see BEAUMONT AND FLETCHER) may have written parts of the play.

The drama begins with the return of HENRY VIII from the Field of the Cloth of Gold. Edward Stafford, duke of Buckingham, is about to warn the king of the growing power of Cardinal Wolsey when he is falsely accused of treason and executed. Meanwhile, Henry who has met Anne Bullen becomes concerned with the legal aspects of his marriage to Katharine of Aragon. Through Wolsey, he negotiates with the pope for a divorce. But when Wolsey discovers that the king plans to marry Anne, he tries to stop the divorce, is found out, and, while under arrest for treason, dies. Henry's marriage is annulled by Thomas Cranmer, archbishop of Canterbury, and the king marries Anne. Katharine dies, commending her daughter, Mary, to Henry's protection. The nobles, jealous of Cranmer's growing influence, try to discredit him but Henry protects the archbishop and makes him godfather of the infant Elizabeth. The principal source of the play is Holinshed's *Chronicles* (1577); the portions dealing with Cranmer are derived from Foxe's *Book of Martyrs* (1563).

Henry, Frederic. A principal character in Ernest Hemingway's novel A FAREWELL TO ARMS. An American lieutenant in the Italian ambulance service during World War I, he falls in love with an English nurse, Catherine Barkley. He deserts to be with her, but she dies in childbirth.

Henry, John. A legendary Negro hero of American ballads and folk tales. Born supposedly in the "Black River country," he was employed in the building of railroads or as a roustabout on river steamboats. John Henry is a man of prodigious strength; in one well-known tale he dies from overexertion, after winning a contest against a steam drill. The tales are apparently based on the exploits of a giant Negro who worked on the Chesapeake & Ohio Big Bend Tunnel in the early 1870's. In 1931, Guy B. Johnson made a collection of varying ballads in *John Henry: Tracking Down a Negro Legend*. In the same year Roark Bradford based a novel, *John Henry*, on several tales. Bradford's novel was later dramatized with music by Jacques Wolfe (1931).

Henry, O. Pen name of **William Sydney** [earlier spelled **Sidney**] **Porter** (1862–1910). American short-story writer. An extremely popular and prolific writer during his lifetime, O. Henry is noted for his sentimental, semirealistic stories dealing with the lives of modest people and his mastery of the surprise ending, which came to be known as the "O. Henry ending" and has been widely imitated in commercial fiction. Born in North Carolina, he later went to Texas, where he became the editor and publisher of a humorous magazine THE ROLLING STONE. Charged with embezzling funds from a bank, he fled to Central America, subsequently the scene of CABBAGES AND KINGS. He later returned and, although there has been much debate over his actual guilt in the matter, served over three years in the federal penitentiary at Columbus, Ohio. While in prison, he published the first of his stories signed O. Henry— *Whistling Dick's Christmas Stocking* (1899)—in *McClure's Magazine*. The pen name is presumed to be the abbreviation for the name of a French pharmacist, Etienne-Ossian Henry, found in the *U.S. Dispensatory*, a reference work Porter used when he worked as prison pharmacist.

In prison O. Henry heard many stories that were the germs of his later narratives, among them the tale of Jimmy Connors, the thief who became the hero of A RETRIEVED REFORMATION. But his work is most identified with New York City, where he subsequently lived and to which he gave the name "Bagdad-on-the-Subway." In his own lifetime numerous collections of O. Henry's stories were published, including THE FOUR MILLION, and others appeared after his death. *Works of O. Henry* (2 vols., 1953) includes all of his stories and some of his poems. In 1918, the O. Henry Memorial Awards were established. These are given to the best stories published each year in American magazines, the prize stories and the leading contenders then being published together in an annual collection. See GIFT OF THE MAGI, THE; LAST LEAF, THE.

Henry, Patrick (1736–1799). American statesman and orator. As a member of the Virginia House of Burgesses, he offered a series of resolutions against the Stamp Act (1765). He later served in the Continental Congress and as governor of Virginia. Famous passages from his speeches include:

Caesar had his Brutus; Charles the First, his Cromwell; and George the Third—*may profit by their example.* If *this* be treason, make the most of it. (Virginia House of Burgesses, 1765)

Is life so dear, or peace so sweet, as to be purchased at the price of chains and slavery? Forbid it, Almighty God! I know not what course others may take; but as for me, give me liberty, or give me death! (Virginia Convention, 1775)

Henry Esmond, Esquire, The History of (1852). A historical novel by William Makepeace THACKERAY. It is written in the first person, supposedly by Henry ESMOND. He is brought up by Francis Esmond, heir to the Castlewood estate with Francis' own children, Beatrix and Frank, and grows up in the belief that he is the illegitimate son of Thomas Esmond, the deceased viscount of Castlewood. On his deathbed, Francis confesses to Henry that he is the lawful heir, but Henry keeps the information secret. He and Frank Esmond are ardent supporters of James Edward, the (Old) Pretender, who falls in love with Beatrix and ruins his chances for the throne. When Beatrix joins the prince abroad, Henry, who has been in love with her, renounces the Pretender;

he marries her mother, Rachel, Lady Castlewood, instead and takes her to America. The story of their descendants is related in Thackeray's THE VIRGINIANS.

Henryson, Robert (1430?–1506). Scottish poet, one of the group of SCOTTISH CHAUCERIANS. His works include *Tale of Orpheus* (printed 1508); *Testament of Cressid* (printed 1593), a treatment of the TROILUS legend, attributed to Chaucer until the 18th century; and *Moral Fables of Aesop the Phrygian* (printed 1621).

Henry the Minstrel, also known as **Blind Harry** (fl. 1470–1492). Scottish bard. His epic poem *Wallace* (c. 1482) celebrates the Scottish hero Sir William Wallace. The poem, which was widely popular, shows the influence of Chaucer.

Henry the Navigator (1394–1460). Portuguese prince. The younger son of John I, he planned and directed a campaign of exploration and discovery that subsequently led to Portugal's extensive conquests in the Orient and the New World. From his residence at Sagres, which became the foremost center of navigation in Europe, he dispatched several vessels each year into the uncharted seas to the south and west, meeting only failure until 1434 when Cape Bojador was rounded. On later voyages Madeira and the Azores were discovered.

Henschke, Alfred. See KLABUND.

Hephaestus (Hephaistos). In Greek mythology, the god of fire and metal-working. Later he was identified with the Roman VULCAN. Hephaestus was either the son of Zeus and Hera, or produced by Hera alone. Homer related that Hera threw her lame son out of heaven, ashamed of his deformity. In revenge, Hephaestus wrought a golden throne from which Hera could not arise. In another story, Hephaestus took the part of Hera against Zeus, who then hurled him from heaven. He fell for nine days and was finally picked up, lamed for life, on the island of Lemnos.

Married to the unfaithful APHRODITE, he became known as the special patron of cuckolds. Hephaestus (or Prometheus) delivered ATHENE from the head of Zeus with the stroke of an ax.

Heptaméron (1559). An unfinished collection of 72 tales by MARGARET OF NAVARRE. Modeled on the *Decameron* (1353) of Boccaccio, the work is otherwise original. All but one of the tales were probably based on her own experiences. Though weak in literary style, the work is distinguished for its psychological perception and its didactic quality.

heptameter. In prosody, a line of verse containing seven metrical feet in any METER. It is usually identified together with the name of the meter: for example, iambic heptameter.

Hera. A Greek goddess, daughter of Cronos and Rhea, and both sister and wife of Zeus. She appears most often in myth as a jealous wife who persecutes her husband's many mistresses (Semele, Io, Leto, and others) or their children (Dionysus, Heracles). Her worship, however, antedated that of Zeus in Greece, where she had important shrines at Argos and elsewhere. The Heraean Games for women were celebrated at Olympia long before the famous Olympic Games for men. She was the patroness of the ARGONAUTS.

Heracles (Herakles) (Lat. *Hercules*). A mythical Greek hero of fabulous strength. Heracles was the son of Zeus and Alcmena, who had caught Zeus' notice when her husband AMPHITRYON was away from Thebes. Amphitryon, however, returned the same night that Zeus had visited her, and in good time she gave birth to twins, Heracles and Iphicles, who was merely the son of Amphitryon. HERA, who had done everything possible to prevent the birth, did not give up. She sent two snakes to attack the twins, but Heracles strangled them in his crib. Heracles married the Theban king's daughter Megara, but, driven mad by Hera, he killed Megara and all their children. When he returned to his senses, he went into exile and bound himself to serve his cousin Eurystheus, the king of Mycenae, for 12 years. At the end of this time he would become immortal. Although he traveled far and wide for many of the famous Labors, Heracles' own home seems to have been at Tiryns. His Labors were as follows:

1. Killing the NEMEAN lion. This frightful beast, sent by Hera to ravage the Nemean plain and to annoy Heracles, he killed by clubbing and strangling it, although it was supposedly invulnerable. Henceforward he wore its skin.

2. Killing the HYDRA. This tremendous snake, one of the many delightful monsters spawned by Echidna, inhabited the Lernaean swamps. As soon as one of its numerous heads was lopped off, others grew in its place. Heracles persuaded his friend Iolaus to burn the stumps before the heads could grow and thus they disposed of the beast, as well as a crab sent by Hera to help it out. This crab became the constellation of Cancer.

3. Capturing the ERYMANTHIAN BOAR. Heracles brought this redoubtable beast back to Eurystheus and nearly scared him out of his wits.

4. Capturing the Hind of ARTEMIS. Heracles succeeded in capturing this sacred animal after a year's search and Artemis permitted him to carry it off to Argos if he promised to let it go, which he did.

5. Killing the man-eating Stymphalian birds. Heracles chased them from their hiding in the woods by banging a bronze rattle, then shot them down one by one.

6. Cleansing the AUGEAN STABLES. These stables, belonging to King Augeas of Elis, had never been cleaned. Heracles accomplished the task in a day by redirecting a river through them.

7. Capturing the Cretan Bull. This bull, which may have been the father of the Minotaur, was taken alive and shown to Eurystheus, like the Hind, then released.

8. Capturing the horses of Diomedes, son of Cyrene and Ares. These horses were fed on human flesh by their owner, the king of the Bistonians. They suddenly became tame when Heracles fed their master to them. He then took them back to Eurystheus and dedicated them to Hera.

9. Capturing the girdle of Hippolyta. Either alone or with an army, Heracles defeated the AMAZONS and either killed Hippolyta or secured the girdle by holding one of her generals, Melanippe, for ransom.

10. Killing the monster Geryon. Heracles threatened Helios with his bow until the god gave him his golden cup, in which Heracles sailed the river Oceanus to the far west. There, after disposing of the herdsman Eurytion and the ferocious dog Orthrus, he killed Geryon himself, stole his cattle, and returned with them, either in the cup or by a long and arduous route through Spain, France, and Italy.

11. Capturing Cerberus. Heracles made his way down to HADES, dragged up Cerberus, the three-headed dog that watches the gates, showed him to Eurystheus, and duly returned him to his proper place. According to one story Heracles actually fought with and wounded Hades himself.

12. Stealing the apples of the HESPERIDES. These apples grew on a tree guarded by a terrible dragon and belonging to the Hesperides, daughters of Night, who lived near the Atlas Mountains. There are various tales as to how Heracles plucked the apples: He either killed the snake or put it to sleep and took the apples himself, or he sent Atlas for them, holding the sky on his shoulders meanwhile.

Heracles had innumerable other adventures, either separately or incidentally to his main labors. He eventually died after donning the poisoned shirt dipped in the blood of the centaur NESSUS, which his wife Deianira had given him. He built himself a funeral pyre on Mount Oeta and persuaded Poeas with the gift of his bow and arrows to set it afire. After this he ascended to Olympus and married Hebe.

The last three labors of Heracles seem to indicate that he achieved immortality by his feats. A very considerable number of his adventures were added to his saga to explain the many places in which his cult flourished. Some authorities believe that the root of the Heracles saga is the adventures of an actual Mycenaean king of Tiryns who performed mighty feats at the bidding of his overlord, the high king of Mycenae. His feats were a favorite subject of art among the Greeks and in the Renaissance.

Heracles appears in two tragedies by Sophocles, *The Trachinian Women* (*Trachiniai*) and *Philoctetes,* in two by Euripides, *Alcestis* and *The Madness of Heracles* (*Herakles Mainomenos*); and in Seneca's *Hercules Furens.* Euripides' *The Children of Heracles* (*Herakleidai*) tells of the final defeat of Eurystheus, who had continued to persecute Heracles' family after his death.

Heracles Mainomenos. See HERACLES.

Heraclitus (Herakleitos; fl. 500 B.C.). A Greek philosopher, belonging to one of the ruling families of Ephesus. Over a hundred fragments of his work have survived. The style is oracular, striving to indicate a truth rather than explicate it. Referred to as the dark philosopher, Heraclitus' best-known statement is "all things change." He considered the basic stuff of the universe to be fire.

Héraclius (1647). A tragedy by Pierre COR-NEILLE. It is derived from the annals of Baronius. Héraclius, son of the murdered emperor of the East, has been raised by a loyal nurse as the son of the usurper Phocas; this masquerade, which has saved Héraclius' life, has been accomplished at the sacrifice of the nurse's own son. For political reasons, Phocas wishes Pulchérie, daughter of the former emperor, to marry Héraclius, supposedly his own son, who in reality are brother and sister. When Phocas learns the truth he almost kills Héraclius, but a conspiracy ends his life, and Héraclius becomes emperor. The play is further complicated by additional characters, disguises, and misunderstandings.

Herakleidai. See HERACLES.

Herbert, Sir **A[lan] P[atrick]** (1890–). English humorist, poet, and member of Parliament. He is known for his work in securing a modification of the English divorce laws; divorce is the subject of his novel *Holy Deadlock* (1934). He also campaigned for the improvement of English canals and waterways, which provide the setting for his novel *The Water Gipsies* (1930). His volumes of witty and humorous essays include *Light Articles Only* (1921), and his collections of light verse include *Less Nonsense* (1944).

Herbert, Edward. 1st Baron **Herbert of Cherbury** (1583–1648). English soldier, diplomat, and philosopher, brother of George Herbert. His attempts, in such works as *De Veritate* (1624) and *De Religione Gentilium* (1663), to discover a rational and universally self-evident basis for religion make him the first of the English deists. He also wrote an interesting *Autobiography,* which was discovered and published by Horace Walpole in 1764, and poetry in the metaphysical vein.

Herbert, George (1593–1633). English poet of the METAPHYSICAL SCHOOL. Herbert, who was a brother of Lord Herbert of Cherbury, came from a Welsh family famous for its soldiers and statesmen. For a long time he aspired to a government career, but a growing sense of religious vocation and the death of James I and other patrons led him to become an Anglican priest. In 1630 he was given the rural living of Bemerton, where he died a few years later, esteemed almost as a saint.

All of Herbert's poetry is religious, even that written during his period of secular ambition. In fact, a major theme of his work, revealed in poems like THE COLLAR and AFFLICTION (I), is the conflict between his calling and his ambition, his pride in his descent and his attainments. Other poems, such as THE SACRIFICE, deal with every facet of religious life: the vicissitudes of a believer's hopes and fears; the nature of God, with emphasis on His love and suffering for man; the festivals, institutions, and doctrines of the Church. Herbert often expresses deep religious anxiety, but his characteristic mood is one of sweetness and equilibrium, a trusting, intimate friendliness with God. Technically, his work is marked by simple diction, striking colloquial rhythms, and the use of symbols and images from ecclesiastical ritual, farming, the trades, science, and everyday household pursuits. He is also known for his extraordinary metrical inventiveness and his occasional "pattern poems": poems whose lines are arranged to form a given shape like an altar or wings or a cross, such as the well-known EASTER WINGS.

Herbert wrote one volume of poems, THE TEMPLE; a treatise on the life and duties of a country parson, *A Priest to the Temple* (1652); and several collections of proverbs. His work was highly popular in its day, but attacked in the later 17th century as overelaborate in conceit and perversely ingenious. He had some admirers in the 19th century, but it was not until the 20th century, with the general revival of interest in metaphysical poetry, that his work was once more appreciated.

Herbert, Victor (1859–1924). Irish-American conductor and composer. He was the conductor of the Pittsburgh Symphony, 1898–1904. He wrote some 30 operettas, including *Babes in Toyland* (1903);

Mlle. Modiste (1905); *The Red Mill* (1906); *Naughty Marietta* (1910). He also wrote a cello concerto, other orchestral music, and two grand operas.

Herbst, Josephine [Frey] (1897–). American novelist. Associated with the so-called proletarian novelists, she was born in Iowa and early became an advocate of radical political and social change. Three of her novels—*Pity Is Not Enough* (1933), *The Executioner* (1934), and *Rope of Gold* (1939)—were designed as a trilogy to portray the decay of capitalistic society. Her more recent books include *Somewhere the Tempest Fell* (1947), *New Green World* (1954), and *The Watcher with the Horn* (1955).

Hercules. See HERACLES.

Hercules Furens. See HERACLES.

Herder, Johann Gottfried (1744–1803). German philosopher, historian, and critic. He is known as the most prominent representative of 18th-century irrationalism. His interest in the folk spirit (see VOLKSGEIST) was not confined to Germany, and his collection of *Volkslieder* (*Folk Songs,* 1778–1779), which was prompted by Percy's *Reliques of Ancient English Poetry,* included Nordic, English, and Romance songs, as well as German. His ideas about the value of intuition in both creation and criticism were taken up and developed by Goethe, with whom he was closely associated, and by German romanticism. His other works include *Von deutscher Art und Kunst* (*On German Character and Art,* 1773), *Auch eine Philosophie der Geschichte zur Bildung der Menschheit* (*Another Philosophy of History for the Education of Mankind,* 1774), and *Briefe zur Beförderung der Humanität* (*Letters for the Furtherance of Humanity,* 1793–1797). See HAMANN; STURM UND DRANG.

Heredia, José María de (1803–1839). Cuban poet. Exiled at 20 for revolutionary activity against the Spanish regime in Cuba, Heredia imbued his poetry with the disillusion and frustration that was the lot of many Cuban intellectuals of his generation. After spending two unhappy years in the U.S., he settled in Mexico, where, except for a brief trip to Cuba in 1836, he remained for the rest of his life. Although Heredia's poetry is classical in form, he has been called the first romantic poet of Hispanic America because of the subjectivity and intensity that characterize his verse. The two poems generally considered his best are *En el teocalli de Cholula* (1820), in which Heredia reflects on the impermanence of all earthly endeavor, and *Niagara* (1824), in which the poet describes the scene in a style as torrential as the falls itself, and then laments his solitude, so far from home.

Hérédia, José Maria de (1842–1905). Cuban-born French poet. A pupil of Leconte de Lisle, Hérédia was one of the first PARNASSIANS. His finest poetry is contained in the 118 sonnets of *Les Trophées* (1893), which are remarkable for the richness of their imagery, the sonorousness and cadence of their language, and the evocative character of their historical impressions.

Hereward the Wake (1865). A historical novel by Charles KINGSLEY. The titular hero is a reckless young Saxon who for a time successfully opposes the Norman conquest. He plunders and burns the abbey of Peterborough, establishes his camp in the Isle of Ely where he is joined by Earl Morcar, is blockaded for three months by William I, but makes his escape with some of his followers.

Hergesheimer, Joseph (1880–1954). American novelist and short-story writer. A skillful popular writer, Hergesheimer won considerable acclaim with his novels *The Three Black Pennys* (1917), JAVA HEAD, and BELISAND. He is also known as the author of *Tol'able David,* a short story about a Virginia mountain boy who triumphs over great odds, which was first published in his collection of short stories, *The Happy End* (1919). His other works include the novels *Linda Condon* (1919), *Cytherea* (1922), *The Bright Shawl* (1922), and *The Party Dress* (1930).

Hermann. See ARMINIUS.

Hermann und Dorothea (1797). An idyllic epic in hexameters by Johann Wolfgang von GOETHE, set during the French invasions of Germany that followed the French Revolution. Goethe explicitly avoids the heroic and concentrates on the bourgeois honesty and simplicity of the love between his two main characters, which he sees as a balance to the unrest of the times.

hermaphrodite. A plant or animal containing both male and female organs of reproduction. The word is derived from the Greek myth of Hermaphroditus, son of Hermes and Aphrodite as told in Ovid's *Metamorphoses.* The nymph Salmacis became enamored of him, and prayed that she might be so closely united that "the twain might become one flesh." Her prayer was answered, and the nymph and boy became one body.

Hermes. Divine herald of Greek mythology. This ancient Arcadian deity was also a god of flocks, of roads, of trading, and of thieves, the inventor of the lyre, and the guide of souls on the way to Hades. The son of Zeus and Maia, he grew miraculously in both size and cunning, on the first day inventing the lyre and stealing Apollo's flocks. He was widely worshiped in the form of the herm, a phallic pillar. The amusing story of his exploits on the day of his birth was told in the fourth Homeric hymn and in Sophocles' satyr play, *Ichneutai.* The Romans identified him with Mercury (Mercurius), their god of tradesmen.

Hermes Trismegistus (*Gr.,* the thrice-great Hermes). A name applied by the Neoplatonists to the Egyptian god Thoth. He was almost identical to the Greek god Hermes.

The name was also applied, from about the third century, to the supposed author of a body of alchemic, occult, and mystical writings. Until the 17th century he was thought to have been a contemporary of Moses, and his writings were considered Christian and almost as sacred as the Bible. Actually the Hermetic books were composed by a group of teachers who lived in Alexandria in the first two centuries B.C. or A.D.; they were a composite of Egyptian magical writings, Jewish mysticism, and Platonism. The 20th century is seeing a revival of interest in the Hermetic writings, notably in the work of the French symbolists and the occult system of William Butler Yeats.

hermeticism. A name applied to a 20th-century school of Italian poets. It was first used by the noted Italian critic Francesco Flora to characterize the difficult, "occult-meaning" verse of a group of Italian poets headed by Salvatore QUASIMODO, Giuseppe UNGARETTI, and Eugenio MONTALE.

The verse of these poets originated in the French symbolist school of "pure poetry" as practiced by Mallarmé and Valéry. Decadent poetry entered Italy through the CREPUSCOLARI poets, and it is from them that "the hermetics" have evolved.

Typical of hermetic poetry is a deliberate rarefaction of poetic language; this is the result of the poet's attempt to verbalize a personal impression that seems to transcend common experience in a language that conveys it with the maximum fidelity and immediacy. The hermetics reject rhetoric and the stylistic mechanics of formal traditional poetry. They adopt instead a vocabulary that is extremely personal, idiosyncratic, and, to the uninitiated, abstruse and often meaningless.

Hermetic writings. See HERMES TRISMEGISTUS.

Hermia. In Shakespeare's MIDSUMMER NIGHT'S DREAM, the daughter of Egeus of Athens, who escapes to the woods with Lysander rather than marry her father's choice, Demetrius.

Hermione. (1) In Greek legend, the only daughter of Menelaus and Helen. She became the wife of Neoptolemus, son of Achilles, but Orestes assassinated him and married Hermione, who had already been betrothed to him. She appears in Euripides' ANDROMACHE as the cruel persecutor of the heroine.

(2) The virtuous and uncomplaining wife of Leontes, king of Sicilia, in Shakespeare's WINTER'S TALE.

Hermit, The (1721). See Thomas PARNELL.

Hermit, The (1765). A ballad by Oliver GOLDSMITH. The hero and heroine are Edwin and Angelina. Angelina is the daughter of a wealthy lord "beside the Tyne"; her hand is sought in marriage by many suitors, among whom is Edwin, "who had neither wealth nor power, but he had both wisdom and worth." Angelina loves him, but "trifles with him"; and Edwin, in despair, leaves her and retires from the world. One day, Angelina, in boy's clothes, seeks refuge at a hermit's cell; it is not long before she discovers that the hermit is Edwin, and from that hour they never part again. Goldsmith has been accused of borrowing his story from the ballad *The Friar of Orders Gray.*

Hermod or **Hermodr.** In Scandinavian mythology, the son of Odin and messenger of the gods. It was he who journeyed unsuccessfully to Hel to bring back Balder, killed by his blind brother Hoder. With Bragi, Hermod received and welcomed to Valhalla all heroes who fell in battle.

Hernández, José. See MARTÍN FIERRO.

Herndon, William Henry (1818–1892). American lawyer. The son of an Illinois tavern keeper, Herndon studied law with Abraham LINCOLN and became his law partner in 1844. Idealistic and well read, he is said to have influenced Lincoln's views on slavery. In the biography he wrote with Jesse Weik, *Herndon's Lincoln: The True Story of a Great Life* (1889), Herndon stated that Ann Rutledge had been the only woman Lincoln had ever loved; Mrs. Lincoln retaliated by labeling Herndon a drunkard and a ne'er-do-well. Regardless of the accuracy of these particular charges, the work contributed much valuable information about Lincoln's early life.

Herne, James A. Original name **James Ahearn** (1839–1901). American actor and dramatist. A capable actor whose daughters Julie and Crystal also attained prominence on the stage, Herne developed as a writer into an impressive realist. His best-known works include *Hearts of Oak*, written with David Belasco (1879), an adaptation of an English melodrama that was later revised as *Sag Harbor* (1899); *Margaret Fleming* (1890), a frank treatment of adultery that shocked contemporary audiences; *Shore Acres* (1892), a realistic study of Maine life; and *The Reverend Griffith Davenport* (1899), about a Southern Methodist circuit rider during the Civil War.

Herne's Egg, The (1938). A poetic drama by William Butler YEATS. Full of the symbolism and philosophy of Yeats's own occult system, it is the story of two warring Irish kings, their theft of the eggs of the sacred Great Herne and raping of the priestess of the Great Herne, and their death under a curse.

Hero. In Shakespeare's MUCH ADO ABOUT NOTHING, the greatly maligned daughter of Leonato, governor of Messina. She is of a quiet, serious disposition, and thus forms a contrast to the gay and witty Beatrice, her cousin.

Hero and Leander. Hero and heroine of a romantic Greek legend. Leander, who lived in Abydos, swam across the HELLESPONT every night to court Hero in *Sestos*. When he was drowned in a storm, she flung herself into the sea. They are well known from Marlowe's *Hero and Leander* (pub. 1598) and Byron's *The Bride of Abydos* (1813).

Herod Antipas. Son of HEROD THE GREAT, tetrarch of Galilee and Peraea (4 B.C.–A.D. 39). He married his niece Herodias, who had been the wife of his half brother Herod Philip. This incestuous marriage was loudly denounced by JOHN THE BAPTIST and brought about John's beheading at the request of Herodias' daughter SALOME. It was before this Herod that Pontius Pilate sent Christ; Herod "set him at nought, and mocked him, and arrayed him in a gorgeous robe, and sent him again to Pilate" (Luke 23:7–15). Herod was ultimately banished to Gaul in A.D. 39; Herodias voluntarily accompanied him.

Hérodiade (1869). A dramatic poem by Stéphane Mallarmé. The heroine soliloquizes upon the isolation of her existence. As is LE CYGNE she is a symbol of the chill sterility that characterizes the aesthetic life.

Herodias. See SALOME.

Herodotus (Herodotos; c. 480–c. 425 B.C.). A Greek historian, often called the Father of History. He was born at Halicarnassus, in Asia Minor, and traveled widely, living first at Samos and later at Athens. Herodotus was the first to carry on research into the events of the past and to treat them in a rational rather than a mythical manner. Although he lacked the political sense of Thucydides, his relation of incidents and anecdotes is extremely readable. His history of the Persian invasion of Greece until 479 B.C. is divided into nine books, named after the nine Muses. He is criticized for credulity, but admired for the charm of his narrative. The relation of the battles of Thermopylae, Salamis, and Plataea in Books VII, VIII, and IX is vivid, and his object, to perpetuate the memory of "great and wonderful deeds," is fully realized.

Herod the Great (73?–4 B.C.). King of Judea

Herodotus: a woodcut of the Gardens of Babylon reconstructed from his description. From the *Histories* (1592).

under the Roman regime (37–4 B.C.). The birth of Jesus Christ took place in the last year of his reign (an error in chronology first assigned it to A.D. 1), and it was he who ordered the Massacre of the INNOCENTS.

Herod had his wife Mariamne (and later their two sons) put to death because he suspected her of adultery, a suspicion which was without foundation. The story of Herod and Mariamne has been the subject of several tragedies including Voltaire's *Mariamne* (1724) and Friedrich Hebbel's *Herodes und Mariamne* (1850). The expression "to out-herod Herod" means to surpass the worst of tyrants in violence and wickedness and refers to Herod the Great's tyrannical nature. He was the father of HEROD ANTIPAS.

On Heroes, Hero Worship, and the Heroic in History. See Thomas CARLYLE.

heroic couplet. In English prosody, a rhymed couplet written in iambic pentameters, the English heroic (or epic) line. The neoclassical rules of the 17th and 18th centuries in England required that the heroic couplet express a complete thought and allowed no enjambment between the lines; it was a "closed" couplet. These requirements, however, were a phenomenon of that period, and both before it, as in Chaucer's and Shakespeare's work, and after, from the romantics on, the construction of sentences has been allowed to carry over from line to line and couplet to couplet; such couplets are called "open" or "run-on" couplets.

Hero of Our Time, A (Geroi nashego vremeni; 1840). A novel by Mikhail LERMONTOV. It portrays a young aristocrat during the reign of Czar Nicholas I in the 1830's. The hero, Grigori Aleksandrovich Pechorin, faces the dilemma of all the young men of his time: to serve the state or to remain inactive. All other outlets for the talents and energies of the Russian aristocracy were closed. The willful and morbid

Pechorin reacts to this situation by assuming the pose of a world-weary Byronic wanderer. His sinister air, however, is no pose. His aimless willfulness is a real threat to all who come near him. Serving as an army officer in the Caucasus, he has a love affair with a native girl which indirectly leads to her death, briefly becomes involved with a band of smugglers which almost leads to his death, and kills another young officer in a duel. Exciting as the adventures are, the most notable thing about the novel is the revelation and analysis of Pechorin's personality as rendered by his old army companion Maksim Maksimych, by a fictional narrator who meets Pechorin, and by the hero himself in his journal, which make up the last three sections of the book. The portrayal is one of the best studies of the character of the SUPERFLUOUS MAN in 19th-century Russian literature. Lermontov's novel is ranked beside the works of the later great Russian novelists, whose narrative techniques and acute psychological analysis he anticipated.

Herrera, Fernando de (1534?–1597). Spanish poet. Herrera spent his uneventful life in his native Seville, disturbed only by his platonic passion for Doña Leonor, countess of Gelves, to whom he addressed elegant Petrachan sonnets. Known to his admiring contemporaries as *el Divino*, he sought to enrich and elevate Spanish lyric verse by the use of loftier themes and by verbal innovations. He unfolded his esthetic doctrines in his controversial *Anotaciones a las obras de Garcilaso de la Vega* (1580). His finest poems were inspired by patriotic sentiment. Among these are the song celebrating the Christian victory over the Turks at Lepanto; the ode to Don Juan of Austria, on the occasion of a Moorish revolt in the Alpujarras (1571); and the elegy on the death of King Sebastian of Portugal, killed at Alcázar Kebir in 1578. His other extant works include an account of the Cyprus war and the victory at Lepanto (1572) and a eulogy on the life and death of Thomas More (1592).

Herrera y Reissig, Julio (1875–1910). Uruguayan poet. A representative of the "baroque" or extravagant wing of MODERNISM, Herrera y Reissig was the leader of a Bohemian literary group that met in the attic of his father's home in Montevideo. His poetry, designed to appeal to the few, is characterized by experimentation in vocabulary and by unusual imagery, though his themes were often drawn from everyday life. His poems, which were not collected until after his death, include *Desolación absurda* and *Julio*.

Herrick, Robert (1591–1674). English poet, known for his pastoral and love lyrics. Herrick, though a clergyman, was a lover of London's society of poets and wits and, at first, regarded his appointment to a rural Devonshire living as bitter exile. However, his interest in country life produced contentment and much of his best poetry. A Royalist, Herrick lost his parish during the English Civil War. He lived happily in London until the Restoration when he regained his old living and there spent the rest of his days.

Herrick was a CAVALIER POET, one of the sons of Ben, or poets who followed the tradition of Ben Jonson. Like his master, he was strongly influenced by the Latin poets, but his classicism is devoid of pedantry, rooted in a natural spiritual affinity to the Latin lyricists. At its best, Herrick's poetry has an unaffected simplicity, a gracefulness compatible with robustness and humor, vivid pictorial fancy, and unfailing command of form and feeling. Many of his short poems make ideal song lyrics: his famous To THE VIRGINS, To MAKE MUCH OF TIME became one of the most popular songs of the 17th century. Herrick writes of rustic rites and superstitions, flowers, fairies, country content, wine, the making of verse, and a number of imaginary mistresses and their clothing, as in DELIGHT IN DISORDER. He also wrote some excellent religious verse in the *Noble Numbers* section of his collection HESPERIDES.

Herrick is essentially a happy poet. While such poems as *To the Virgins,* CORINNA'S GOING A-MAYING, and *To Daffodils* deal with the inevitability of age and death, the theme is treated with a gentle Epicurean melancholy which invites one to enjoy life's fleeting beauty. His love poems do not suggest passion's tragic possibilities, and his religious verse does not repudiate his secular poems in any absolute way. Poems dealing with aspects of religious anxiety, such as To HIS ANGRY GOD, are honest and touching, but not cries from the depths. More characteristically, he expresses gratitude or simple piety.

Herrick published only one volume of verse, *Hesperides,* which—in spite of the popularity of some of his songs—was quickly forgotten. Only near the end of the 18th century was his work rediscovered and appreciated.

Herrick, Robert (1868–1938). American teacher and novelist. While teaching at the University of Chicago, Herrick sought to describe and analyze the problems of modern industrial society, especially the corruption of the middle-class soul by commercialism. He himself drew a distinction between those of his novels that were realistic and a limited group that were, as he said, idealistic, manifesting a kind of broadminded Puritanism. His most widely read book was *The Master of the Inn* (1908), the story of a physician who cures mental illness. *The Common Lot* (1904) depicts the fashion in which a young Chicago architect succumbs to commercialism. Other novels by Herrick include *One Woman's Life* (1913), about a selfish socialite, and *Chimes* (1926), which gives an unfavorable picture of a large university, presumably the University of Chicago.

Herries Chronicle, The. A series of novels by Hugh WALPOLE. Set chiefly in the English Lake District, *Rogue Herries* (1930), *Judith Paris* (1931), *The Fortress* (1932), and *Vanessa* (1933) comprise the series. They form a romantic historical family saga, from the 18th century to the present day.

Herrings, Battle of the. See BATTLE OF THE HERRINGS.

Herriot, Edouard (1872–1957). French statesman. Leader of the Radical Socialist party, Herriot served twice as premier in 1924–1925 and in 1932. He held numerous public offices: among them, Senator, Minister of State (1934–1935), President of the Chamber of Deputies (1925–1926; 1936–1940, under the Popular Front), and President of the National Assembly (1947).

Herrnhuter. See MORAVIAN BRETHREN.

Herschel, Sir William. Originally **Friedrich Wilhelm Herschel** (1738–1822). English astronomer who discovered a new planet (1781) which he called

Georgium Sidus in honor of King George III. It is now known as Uranus. He also discovered moons of Saturn and Uranus and was a pioneer in sidereal science. His studies were continued by his son Sir John Frederick William Herschel (1792–1871).

Hersey, John [Richard] (1914–   ). American novelist and journalist. Hersey's early books of non-fiction, *Men on Bataan* (1942) and *Into the Valley* (1943), are direct reflections of his experiences as a war correspondent. His novel A BELL FOR ADANO, which won a Pulitzer Prize, was based on Hersey's careful observation of the American occupation of Italy. In 1946, Hersey visited Hiroshima and wrote an objective and horrifying account of the impact of the atomic bomb blast on six survivors. Appearing in *The New Yorker* magazine in 1946, it was reprinted in book form as *Hiroshima* (1946). Man's inhumanity and courage are also the themes of Hersey's most ambitious novel, THE WALL, the story of the extinction of the Warsaw ghetto by the Germans. Later novels include *A Single Pebble* (1956), *The War Lover* (1959), and *The Child Buyer* (1960). *Here to Stay* (1963) is a collection of biographical sketches illustrating human courage and tenacity.

Hertha. See NERTHUS.

Hertz, Heinrich Rudolf (1857–1894). German physicist, known for his experiments with electromagnetic waves. His identification of radio waves (sometimes called "hertzian waves") led to the development of wireless telegraphy.

Hertzen or **Herzen, Aleksandr Ivanovich** (1812–1870). Russian journalist ad political thinker. The illegitimate son of a nobleman, Hertzen very early interested himself in social and political problems. At Moscow University he became the leader of a group of students also interested in politics. Such activity led in 1834 to his arrest and exile to the provinces. He was allowed to return to the capital in 1836, but was again exiled in 1840. Finally, in 1847, he obtained permission to emigrate from Russia and never returned. He witnessed the 1848 revolutions in western Europe with some disappointment and finally settled in London in 1852.

In 1857, Hertzen began to publish his famous revolutionary periodical, *Kolokol* (*The Bell*), which had a large readership in Russia even though it had to be smuggled into the country. Czar Alexander II himself was reputed to be a regular reader of the publication. In the journal Hertzen carried on a spirited criticism of the social order in Russia and a constant advocacy of the necessity for Russia to adopt Western socialism.

Hertzen's major works are *S togo berega* (*From the Other Shore*, 1850), a series of articles on socialism and revolution, and *Byloe i Dumy* (*My Past and My Thoughts*, 1852–1855), an autobiography that describes the intellectual atmosphere of the 1850's.

Hervey, John. Baron **Hervey of Ickworth** (1696–1743). English politician and lord privy seal (1740–1742). He is the author of *Memoirs of the Court of George II.* Hervey was attacked by Alexander Pope, because of his well-known effeminacy, as "Sporus" in the EPISTLE TO DR. ARBUTHNOT: "that thing of silk, Sporus, that mere white curd of ass's milk."

Herwegh, Georg (1817–1875). German political poet. He is most famous for his *Gedichte eines Le-*bendigen (*Poems of a Living Man*, 1841 ff.), which were directed against the reactionary regimes in Prussia and Austria and were part of the growing revolutionary sentiment that led to the upheavals of 1848. Later in life, he polemicized against Bismarck.

Herzog, Emile. See André MAUROIS.

Hesiod (*Hesiodos*, 8th century B.C.). A Greek poet known as the Father of Greek didactic poetry. The most important works ascribed to him are *Works and Days* and *Theogony*. The first consists of moral maxims and precepts on farming. It is a rich source of information on primitive beliefs concerned with everyday life. The *Theogony* is an account of the origin of the world and of the gods.

If the statements made in the *Works and Days* are authentic, Hesiod lived most of his life as a farmer in Boeotia. His father was an impoverished farmer who had taken to the sea to make ends meet. The *Works and Days* was addressed to Hesiod's brother, supposedly a wastrel who had cheated Hesiod of much of his share of the family property.

Hesione. In Greek legend, a daughter of Laomedon, king of Troy, and sister to PRIAM. Her father exposed her to a sea-monster in order to appease the wrath of Apollo and Poseidon, but she was rescued by Heracles who made the stipulation that he should receive a certain reward. Laomedon did not keep his promise, so Heracles slew him, took Troy, and gave Hesione to Telamon, by whom she became the mother of TEUCER. The refusal of the Greeks to give her up to Priam is given as one of the causes of the Trojan War.

Hesperia. From Greek *hesperos*, evening. Italy was so called by the Greeks, because it was to them the land of the setting sun and the evening star. The Romans, for a similar reason, transferred the name to Spain.

Hesperides. Three sisters who guarded the golden apples that Hera received as a marriage gift. They were assisted by the dragon Ladon. HERACLES, as the last of his twelve labors, slew the dragon and carried some of the apples to Eurystheus. Many poets call the place where these golden apples grew the garden of the Hesperides. The apples are thought to have been a symbol of immortality.

Hesperides is the title of Robert HERRICK's collected poetry (1648), in allusion to the idyllic, pastoral character of most of his poems.

Hess, Rudolf (1894–   ). German Nazi and close friend of Hitler, whom he met in 1920. (See MEIN KAMPF.) In 1941 Hess flew to Scotland, presumably for private negotiations, but was held as a prisoner of war. At the Nuremberg Trials he was sentenced to life imprisonment.

Hesse, Hermann (1877–1962). German novelist. He was known especially for his burgeoning imagination, as well as for the accuracy of his psychological and cultural observations. As the title of his verse collection *Romantische Lieder* (1899) reveals, in his early career he was strongly influenced by GERMAN ROMANTICISM, especially by the writings of Novalis, and several Romantic traits remained with him throughout his life: his intense interest in music, for example, and his tendency to combine the ideas of widely varying times and cultures into a single whole. But the mature Hesse was by no means dependent upon any school of writing; his later works are characterized by a highly individualized style and a strikingly original view of man and culture which combines, among other things, ideas from psychoanalysis and Asian religion. His most famous novels are *Demian, Die Geschichte einer Jugend* (*Demian, A Story of Youth*, 1919), STEPPENWOLF, *Die Morgenlandfahrt* (*Trip to the Orient*, 1932) and *Das Glasperlenspiel* (literally, *The Glass-Bead Game*, 1943), translated as MAGISTER LUDI. Hesse's style is lively and engaging, rich in human sympathy, imagination, and ironic humor. He was a Swiss citizen from 1921 to his death, and was awarded the Nobel Prize in 1946. His essays include *Zarathustras Wiederkehr* (1920) and *Blick ins Chaos* (*In Sight of Chaos*, 1920). His poetry was collected in *Gesammelte Dichtungen* (1952).

Hessian. One whose services in politics or war can be easily bought; so called from the German mercenaries, primarily from Hesse-Cassel and Hesse-Darmstadt, who fought for England in the American Revolution.

Hestia. A Greek goddess, later identified with Vesta, the Roman goddess of the hearth. Originally one of the twelve Olympians, she resigned her place to Dionysus.

Hesychasts (Gr., *hesychos*, still, calm). A sect of mystics or quietists in the Eastern Church, who lived on Mount Athos in the 14th century. By contemplating their navels, they aimed to attain perfect serenity and supernatural insight, which would enable them to feel, diffused through them, the uncreated but communicable divine light that shone on Mount Tabor at the transfiguration of Christ.

hetaera (hetaira). Literally, a female companion or comrade. In ancient Greece, a courtesan of the better class. Some hetaeras were freed women or even women of free birth. LAIS and PHRYNE are the most famous ones.

He Who Gets Slapped (To, kto poluchayet poshchiochini; 1914). A drama by Leonid ANDREYEV. The play's central character is a disenchanted intellectual who seeks refuge as a clown in a circus. The clown, famed for the number of slaps he can endure, apparently symbolizes intellect being buffeted for the amusement of the coarse, uncomprehending mob.

Hewlett, Maurice (1861–1923). English historical novelist. His very popular books were THE FOREST LOVERS, a romance set in the Middle Ages; *Richard Yea-and-Nay* (1900), about Richard Coeur de Lion (King Richard I); and *The Queen's Quair* (1904), a romance founded on the life of Mary Queen of Scots (see KINGIS QUAIR).

Hexam, Lizzie. In Charles Dickens' OUR MUTUAL FRIEND, heroine of the subplot. She is the daughter of a Thames waterman, and finally marries Eugene Wrayburn, whose life she has saved.

hexameron. Six days taken as one continuous period; especially the six days of the Creation.

hexameter. In prosody, a six-foot line. The word usually refers to the dactylic hexameter line which was the epic verse of classical poetry, whereas the French epic line of iambic hexameter is usually called the ALEXANDRINE. The hexameters of the ancients have been imitated in English in Longfellow's *Evangeline*, Clough's *Bothie*, and Kingsley's *Andromeda*. The Authorized Version of the Bible furnishes a number of examples of "accidental" hexameters; the following are well known:

How art thou fallen from Heaven, O Lucifer son of the Morning.
Why do the heathen rage and the people imagine a vain thing?
God is gone up with a shout, the Lord with the sound of the trumpet.

Hexapla (Gr., "sixfold"). The collection of Old Testament texts collated by ORIGEN. It contains in parallel columns the Hebrew text in Hebrew and in Greek characters, the SEPTUAGINT (with emendations), and the versions of Aquila, Theodotion, and Symmachus.

Hexateuch. The first 6 books of the Old Testament. It contains the PENTATEUCH plus Joshua, which relates the final settlement of the Jews in the Promised Land.

Heyer, Georgette (1902–   ). English popular novelist, author of romantic swashbuckling historical novels and detective stories. *The Grand Sophie* (1950), *The Reluctant Widow* (1947), and *Friday's Child* (1946) are among her works.

Heym, Georg (1887–1912). German poet. Very influential in early EXPRESSIONISM, he himself was under the influence of Baudelaire, Rimbaud, and Stefan George. His works include *Der Athener Ausfahrt* (*The Athenians' Sally*, 1907), a tragedy, and *Der ewige Tag* (*The Eternal Day*, 1911), a collection of poems.

Heyse, Paul (1830–1914). German novelist, immensely popular in his time but not highly regarded today. His technical mastery of the novella form, however, is undisputed; the most effective among his numerous novellas is *L'Arrabbiata* (*The Angry Girl*, 1855), a love story set in Italy. He also outlined a theory of the novella in the preface to the collection *Deutscher Novellenschatz* (*Treasury of German Novellas*, 1871 ff.), which he edited. Among his novels, *Kinder der Welt* (*Children of the World*, 1873) is respected; but his plays and lyric poetry are of little value. He received the Nobel Prize in 1910.

Heyst, Axel. A misanthropic but generous man, hero of Joseph Conrad's novel VICTORY.

Heyward, DuBose (1885–1940). American novelist, poet, and dramatist. He is best known for PORGY, his first novel, which became a successful play and served as the basis for George Gershwin's opera *Porgy and Bess. Mamba's Daughter* (1929) was another novel of Charleston Negro life, and it was also successfully dramatized (1939). Heyward's other novels include *Peter Ashley* (1932), a story set in the Civil War, and *Star-Spangled Virgin* (1939), about the Virgin Islands and the New Deal. Heyward began his career as a poet, publishing *Carolina Chansons* (1922) with Hervey Allen. He later published two more volumes of verse.

Heywood, John (1497?–1580?). English poet, a friend of Sir Thomas MORE, and a court musician and entertainer under Henry VIII, Edward VI, and Queen Mary. He made popular the court INTERLUDES that later became an important part of entertainment for royalty and the nobility in Elizabethan and Jacobean times. THE FOUR P's is his most famous work of this type. He also wrote epigrams and proverbs included in his *Works* (1562) and a satirical allegory on religion, *The Spider and the Fly* (1556).

Heywood, Thomas (c. 1570–1641). English dramatist. One of the Henslowe group, he wrote plays remarkable for their pictures of English domestic life. Among the best are A WOMAN KILLED WITH KINDNESS, THE FAIR MAID OF THE WEST: PARTS I AND II, *The Wise Woman of Hogsden* (c. 1604), *The Captives* (1624), and the masque *Love's Mistress* (1634). His other plays include *A Maidenhead Well Lost* (c. 1633), *A Challenge for Beauty* (c. 1635), *King Edward IV* (c. 1599), *The Royal King and the Loyal Subject* (c. 1602), *The English Traveller* (c. 1624), and a series of dramatizations of classical myths: *The Golden Age* (c. 1610), *The Silver Age* (c. 1610), *The Brazen Age* (c. 1610), and *The Iron Age: Parts I and II* (1610).

Hezekiah. In the Old Testament, a king of Judah for 29 years. He was noted for his efforts to abolish idolatry, which had flourished under his father Ahaz, and to restore the worship of Jehovah. The famous destruction of the Assyrian army under Sennacherib occurred during his reign (II Kings 18).

Hiawatha (1855). A long narrative poem by Henry Wadsworth LONGFELLOW. Hiawatha, an Ojibway Indian, is reared by his grandmother, Nokomis, daughter of the Moon. After detailing the hero's accumulation of wisdom, the poet recounts the deeds of Hiawatha in revenging his mother, Wenonah, against his father, the West Wind. Hiawatha eventually becomes the leader of his people, teaching peace with the white man. When his wife, Minnehaha, becomes ill, he goes with her to the land of the Northwest Wind. The poem has been endlessly parodied. See Henry Rowe SCHOOLCRAFT.

Hichens, Robert Smythe (1864–1950). English novelist. *The Green Carnation* (1894) is a novel satirizing Oscar Wilde. Among his popular successes were *The Garden of Allah* (1904) and *Bella Donna* (1909), both set in North Africa.

Hickok, Wild Bill [James Butler] (1837–1876). American soldier, scout, and U.S. Marshal. Hickok fought in many Civil War, frontier, and Indian battles. As marshal at Hays City and later in Abilene, Kan., he faced some of the toughest men on the frontier, killing only in self-defense or in the line of duty. In 1872, he toured the east with Buffalo Bill (William Cody). Four years later, he was murdered by the notorious Jack McCall, and was buried in Deadwood, S.D. He became a legend during his lifetime, and after his death, a folk hero. Hickok's friend, the poet scout Captain Jack Crawford, dedicated a ballad to him, called *The Burial of Wild Bill*. See PONY EXPRESS.

Hicks, Edward (1780–1849). American folk artist. A coach and sign painter, he was also a Quaker minister in Newton, Pa. He painted landscapes and allegorical scenes, notably *The Peaceable Kingdom* in which the lion and the calf, the wolf, the tiger, and the lamb rest together in toylike simplicity. The background opens up to reveal a historical antecedent of this hoped-for peace—William Penn signing his peace treaty with the Indians.

Hicks, Granville (1901–   ). American author and literary critic. He was known during the 1930's for his Marxist interpretations of literature; works from this period are *The Great Tradition* (1933), *John Reed* (1936), *I Like America* (1938), and *Fig-*

ures of Transition (1939). In 1939, after the non-aggression pact between the U.S.S.R. and Nazi Germany, Hicks resigned from the Communist Party. He edited *The Letters of Lincoln Steffens* (with Ella Winter, 1938) and *Proletarian Literature in the U.S.* (1935). His three novels are *Only One Storm* (1942), *Behold Trouble* (1944), and *There Was a Man in Our Town* (1952). Hicks conducts a column of fiction criticism in the *Saturday Review*.

Hidalgo y Costilla, Miguel (1753–1811). Mexican priest and revolutionary leader. Banished to the village of Dolores for his unorthodox views and irregular personal life, Hidalgo became the representative of the lower classes in Mexico's struggle for independence from Spain. On Sept. 16, 1810, in the parish church, he uttered the *grito de Dolores*—"Long live Our Lady of Guadalupe, death to bad government, death to the Spaniards!"—which became the battle cry of the insurgents. At the head of an ill-kempt army of Indians and mestizos, Hidalgo won victories at Guanajuato and Guadalajara but, perhaps because of a lack of ammunition, failed to attack Mexico City. In March, 1811, he was captured by the Spaniards and shot. Mexicans now celebrate Sept. 16 as their Independence Day.

hieratic (*Gr.*, "holy"). Consecrated to sacred uses. The Greeks applied the term to an Egyptian cursive form of hieroglyphic writing which, though originally used for all literature, came to be reserved for religious texts when DEMOTIC writing was adopted for secular use.

Hieronimo. The central character in Thomas Kyd's SPANISH TRAGEDY.

Higden, Ranulf (c. 1299–c. 1364). English chronicler, a Benedictine monk. His *Polychronicon*, a Latin history of the world from its creation to 1327, was continued by others through 1357 and popularized in English by John de TREVISA.

Higgins, F[rederick] R[obert] (1896–1941). Irish poet, editor, and director of the ABBEY THEATRE from 1935. His work includes *Salt Air* (1924) and *The Gap of Brightness* (1940).

Higginson, Thomas Wentworth (1823–1911). American Unitarian clergyman, soldier, editor, and writer. A New England abolitionist, Higginson led the first Negro regiment in the Civil War (1862–1864). He related his experience in *Army Life in a Black Regiment* (1870). A friend of many prominent writers, he told of them in *Cheerful Yesterdays* (1898). Emily Dickinson sent him several of her poems, and carried on a correspondence; after her death, Higginson and Mabel Loomis Todd edited her *Poems* (1890). A believer in women's rights, Higginson wrote a book called *Common Sense About Women* (1881). He published biographies of Margaret Fuller (1884), his ancestor Francis Higginson (1891), Longfellow (1902), and Whittier (1902). He also wrote essays, literary histories, a novel and some verse; his *Writings* were collected in seven volumes in 1900, and his *Letters and Journals* were published in 1921.

High Church. An unofficial division of the Church of England and the Episcopal Church in America. It is distinguished by the importance it places upon the priesthood, the sacraments, and, in general, the outward forms and ceremonies of liturgical ritual.

higher criticism. The name applied to modern textual criticism of the Bible, treating such problems as authorship, authenticity, dates of composition. By those who accept the doctrine of the literal inspiration of the Bible, the term is used in a pejorative sense. The phrase was first used in 1787 in Eichhorn's *Einleitung in das Alte Testament.*

Higher Pantheism, The. A poem by Alfred TENNYSON, written in 1869, in which the poet urges a belief that God not only is found in the world (pantheism) but also that He transcends it. Swinburne wrote a parody of this in *The Higher Pantheism in a Nutshell.*

Highland Mary. The most shadowy of Robert BURNS's sweethearts, but the one to whom he addressed some of his finest poetry, including *My Highland Lassie, O, Highland Mary, Thou Ling'ring Star* and—perhaps—*Will ye go to the Indies, my Mary?* She is believed to have been Mary CAMPBELL.

high tea. A meal served by the British at the usual teatime. Besides tea, it includes fish, cold meats, pastry, and many other delicacies.

High Wind in Jamaica, A (1929, first published in U.S. as *The Innocent Voyage*). A novel by Richard HUGHES. A family of children living in Jamaica in the 19th century are sent to England after a hurricane has partly destroyed their home. Amiable pirates capture them by mistake, and the children bring about the pirates' ruin; one girl becomes a murderess. The irrationality and impenetrability of a child's amoral world and the horror of the whole situation are brilliantly conveyed.

Hiketides. See THE SUPPLIANT WOMEN (1) and (2).

Hilda Lessways. A novel by Arnold Bennett. See CLAYHANGER.

Hildebrand. (1) Hero of German legend, a follower of Theodoric the Great. In the *Hildebrandslied* (c. 800), a short poetic fragment, he is challenged to single combat by a young warrior. He discovers that the young man is his son Hadubrand, whom he has not seen for 30 years, and tries to stop the fight. Hadubrand, unbelieving, accuses him of a coward's evasive lie and insists on the battle, only to be slain by the older and better warrior. See the *Nibelungenlied* for Hildebrand's role there.

(2) The original name of Pope GREGORY VII.

Hillary, Richard (1919–1943). English fighter-pilot, who wrote a moving account of his experiences in *The Last Enemy* (1942, U.S. title *Falling Through Space*).

Hillyer, Robert [Silliman] (1895–1961). American poet and teacher. The winner of a Pulitzer Prize for his *Collected Verse* (1933), Hillyer also wrote critical essays, several novels, and made a rendering of the Egyptian *Book of the Dead* called *The Coming Forth by Day* (1923). His volumes of poetry include *Hills Give Promise* (1923), *Pattern of a Day* (1940), *The Death of Captain Nemo* (1949), *The Relic and Other Poems* (1957), and *Collected Poems* (1961).

Hilton, James (1900–1954). English novelist. His two best-selling books were GOODBYE, MR. CHIPS, and *Lost Horizon* (1933), a novel about the mythical land of SHANGRI-LA. He also wrote *Random Harvest* (1941), about a man suffering from amnesia.

him (1927). A play by E. E. CUMMINGS. Taking hints from the German expressionists, James Joyce,

and other literary pioneers, Cummings produced an extraordinary conglomeration of techniques and effects in this "phantasmagoria." It was produced by the Provincetown Players in 1928.

Himmler, Heinrich (1900–1945). High-ranking official in Nazi Germany. One of the founders of the party, he organized the S.S. (q.v.) (1929) and GESTAPO (1933) and became supreme police commissioner (1936). He poisoned himself after his capture by the Allies.

Hinayāna. See BUDDHISM.

Hind and the Panther, The (1687). A poem by John DRYDEN in defense of the Catholic religion. The hind is the Church of Rome, and the panther is the Church of England. James II is the lion which protects the hind from the bear (Independents), the wolf (Presbyterians), the hare (Quakers), the ape (Freethinkers), the boar (Anabaptists), and the fox (Arians). One of Dryden's most celebrated works, the poem is notable for its wit, the brilliance of its argument, and its passages of rare eloquence and power.

Hindemith, Paul (1895–1963). German-born composer and violinist. One of the most prolific and versatile composers of his day, with an individual style that is generally dissonant and contrapuntal. *Mathis der Maler* (1938; text by Hindemith) is probably his best known opera; other works include *Das Marienleben* (1923, song cycle to poems by Rilke), *Ludus Tonalis* (piano pieces, 1943), and diverse chamber music. He also wrote several theory texts.

Hindenburg, Paul von (1847–1934). German general and statesman. He succeeded Falkenhayn as chief of the High Command during World War I and served as president of the Weimar Republic (1925–1934). In 1933 he was forced to make Hitler chancellor. See Eric LUDENDORFF.

Hind Horn. See HORN, KING.

Hindle Wakes. See William Stanley HOUGHTON.

Hindu calendar. This year is divided into 12 months. An intercalary month occurs after every month in which there are two new moons, which is once in every three years. This inserted month takes the name of the month preceding it. The months, the first of which begins about April 11, are Baisakh, Jeth, Asarh, Sawan, Bhadon, Asin (Kuar), Katik, Aghan, Pus, Magh, Phagun (Phalgun), and Chait.

Hinduism. The religious and social system of India, organically interrelated by DHARMA. Hinduism is based on birth and conduct, and because it has no founder or creed, tends to be nondogmatic. *Dharma* involves belief in *karma* or the principle of cause as affecting a future existence. Past *karma* can be "burnt away" and future *karma* annihilated by the performance of the "pure act" (selfless, detached, dedicated action), which leads to its by-product *moksha* or liberation (in Buddhism called NIRVANA), a state of release from the painful dualities, polarities, and ambivalences of the phenomenal world. Many techniques are prescribed for the attainment for *moksha:* worship, pilgrimage, *yoga,* many ascetic practices, and respect for a spiritual teacher or *guru.* If any of these are performed for the satisfaction of one's ego, the act becomes "impure" or tainted by *karma,* and falls under the category of the good or bad deed, leading to good or bad rebirth. The ultimate goal is serenity, not ecstasy or agony. The numerous sects of Hinduism implicitly recognize these principles, and their monistic or pantheistic philosophy is derived from the Vedas or the Upanishads, which were organized into a metaphysical framework known as Vedanta by the seventh century philosopher Shankaracharya, sometimes called the "Aquinas of India."

Hindus, Maurice [Gershon] (1891–). Russian-born American writer. Coming to the U.S. in 1905, Hindus has been principally concerned in his work with the land of his birth, which he has revisited many times. His numerous books on the subject include *Russian Peasant and Revolution* (1920), *Broken Earth* (1926), *Humanity Uprooted* (1929), *Red Bread* (1931), *Mother Russia* (1943), *The Cossacks* (1945), and *Crisis in the Kremlin* (1953). He is also the author of *To Sing with the Angels* (1941), a novel about the Nazi occupation of a small Czechoslovakian community, and *Green Worlds* (1938), an account of his youth.

Hinkson, Mrs. Katherine. See Katherine TYNAN.

Hinnom, the Valley of. See GEHENNA; TOPHET.

Hippalca, or Ippalca. In the ORLANDO FURIOSO of Ariosto, the maidservant of the warrior maiden Bradamante and a messenger between her mistress and the knight Ruggiero, Bradamante's beloved.

Hippius, Zinaida Nikolayevna (1867–1945). Russian poet. One of the Russian SYMBOLISTS, she was the wife of the author and critic Dmitri MEREZHKOVSKI. Her poetry, lyrical and introspective exercises, holds less interest than her reminiscences of the greater poets, such as Blok, Bryusov, and Sologub, whom she received in her St. Petersburg salon. In 1919 she and her husband emigrated to France.

hippocampus. In Greek mythology, a fabulous sea horse; head and forequarters of a horse and tail of a dolphin. It was represented as attached to chariots of Poseidon and the tritons. Paintings of hippocampi were found in Pompeii.

Hippocrates (Hippokrates; 460?–?377 B.C.). A Greek physician born on the island of Cos; known as Father of medicine. According to tradition, he devised a code of medical ethics that imposed on his disciples the oath still administered to men about to enter medical practice and known as the Hippocratic Oath. Eighty-seven treatises are attributed to him.

Hippocratic oath. An oath of allegiance to ethical professional standards. It is administered to M.D. candidates at each commencement at Columbia, Cornell, and other universities. Its original version is attributed to HIPPOCRATES. The form now commonly used is:

I do solemnly swear by that which I hold most sacred:
That I will be loyal to the profession of medicine and just and generous to its members;
That I will lead my life and practice my art in uprightness and honor;
That into whatsoever house I shall enter, it shall be for the good of the sick to the utmost of my power, I holding myself aloof from wrong, from corruption, and from the temptation of others to vice;
That I will exercise my art solely for the cure of my patients, and will give no drug, perform no operation for a criminal purpose, even if solicited, far less suggest it.
That whatsoever I shall see or hear of the lives of men which is not fitting to be spoken, I will keep inviolably secret.
These things I do promise, and in proportion as I am faithful to this my oath may happiness and good repute be ever mine—the opposite if I shall be forsworn.

Hippocrene (*Gr.* "hippos," horse; "krene," fountain). The fountain of the Muses on Mount HELICON, produced by a stroke of the hoof of PEGASUS; hence, poetic inspiration.

Hippodamia (Hippodameia). (1) The bride of Pirithous (see LAPITHS).
(2) The wife of PELOPS.

hippogriff (Gr. *hippos,* a horse, and *gryphos,* a griffin, thus a winged horse). The flying steed whose father was a griffin and mother a filly. In Ariosto's ORLANDO FURIOSO, it carries Ruggiero away from his beloved Bradamante to the island of the enchantress Alcina. It also takes Astolfo to Ethiopia, from whence he ascends to the moon to retrieve Orlando's lost wits. Further mention is made of the hippogriff in Milton's *Paradise Regained.*

Hippolyta (Hippolyte). An Amazon queen. When Eurystheus demanded her girdle, Heracles went to fetch it. He succeeded either by killing her, or by holding her general Melanippe for ransom. This queen, or another of the same name, attacked Attica and was defeated with her Amazons by Theseus. He married her and she bore him Hippolytus. Some, however, call her Antiope.

In Shakespeare's MIDSUMMER NIGHT'S DREAM, she is the proud and sophisticated woman who is betrothed to Theseus, duke of Athens. The play of the artisans is presented as a part of the celebration of the wedding.

Hippolyte. In Jean Racine's tragedy PHÈDRE, the stepson of Phèdre and the object of her guilty passion. He rebuffs her advances, but his father, King Theseus, is convinced of his guilt and brings about his death by invoking Neptune against him.

Hippolytus (Hippolytos, 428 B.C.). A tragedy by EURIPIDES. Aphrodite, angry at Hippolytus, the illegitimate son of Theseus by the Amazon Hippolyta, because he scorns the love of women, avenges herself on him by causing Theseus' wife Phaedra to fall in love with him. Though wasting away of her passion, Phaedra will not tell Hippolytus, but, during Theseus' absence, her nurse gives the story away. Hippolytus is horrified, but will say nothing to Theseus. Humiliated, Phaedra hangs herself, leaving a message for Theseus claiming that Hippolytus has tried to violate her. Theseus returns and, refusing to listen to Hippolytus' denials, lays on him one of three unfailing curses given him by his father Poseidon. Hippolytus is soon killed when a bull rising from the sea frightens his horses. Artemis, whose faithful servant Hippolytus has been, now reveals the truth to Theseus, who is grief-stricken over Hippolytus' death and his own guilt, although Hippolytus frees him of this guilt with his dying words.

This story was also told in Racine's masterpiece PHÈDRE, and in such lesser works as Seneca's *Phaedra,* Robinson Jeffers' dramatic poem *The Cretan Woman* (1954), and Mary Renault's novel *The Bull from the Sea* (1962).

Hippomedon. See SEVEN AGAINST THEBES.

Hippopotamus, The (1920). A rhyming, comic poem by T. S. ELIOT. It is about the "True Church."

Hiraoka Kimitake. See MISHIMA YUKIO.

Hirohito (1901–). Emperor of Japan (1926–). The name of his reign is Shōwa.

Hiroshige. See ANDŌ HIROSHIGE.

Hiroshima. The Japanese city which was the target of the first atomic bomb used in warfare (August, 1945). The bomb was dropped by the U.S. at the close of World War II. Hiroshima was largely destroyed by that attack, and afterward rebuilt. *Hiroshima,* by John Hersey (1946), gave a factual and devastating account of the event. Since then, Hiroshima has become a symbol of the tragic division and possible reconciliation between people.

Hirschfeld, Georg (1873–1935). German playwright. As a writer, Hirschfeld is identified with the movement of NATURALISM. His two best-known plays, both of which deal with women under extraordinary conditions of social pressure, are *Die Mütter* (*The Mothers,* 1896) and *Agnes Jordan* (1898).

His Family (1917). A novel by Ernest POOLE. A study of the results of immigration, depicting the contrasting ideals of two generations in New York City, this is the story of a father and his three daughters. One daughter is devoted to the welfare of her five children; another, a principal of a high school, sacrifices herself to the interests of young people; the third is a devotee of pleasure. The novel was awarded a Pulitzer Prize.

Histoire amoureuse des Gaules. See BUSSY-RAMBUTIN.

Histoire comique des états et empires de la lune and **Histoire comique des états et empires du soleil.** See Savinien CYRANO DE BERGERAC.

Histoire des oracles. See Bernard le Bovier de FONTENELLE.

Historia Ecclesiastica Gentis Anglorum. See BEDE.

History. For many titles beginning with the words *History of . . . ,* see the following proper names. For example, *The History of Tom Jones, a Foundling* will be found under *Tom Jones, a Foundling, The History of.*

History of New York from the Beginning of the World to the end of the Dutch Dynasty, A (1809). A satire by Washington IRVING. The book is presented as the work of a fictional character called Diedrich Knickerbocker. Beginning with a chapter on the creation of the world, the format of the volume mocks the pretensions of early historians. The burlesque became more pointed as Irving included many facts about the colony. The book contains lively descriptions of Dutch manners and morals. It was frequently reprinted after Irving expurgated racier passages, which offended descendants of the Dutch.

History of the Kings of Britain, The (Historia Regum Brittanniae; 1137). A Latin prose chronicle in 12 books by GEOFFREY OF MONMOUTH. The work is of special importance in relation to the development of ARTHURIAN LEGEND, and also as a source book (partly by way of Holinshed's *Chronicles*) for Elizabethan dramatists. It purports to be a true account of events involved in the founding of the English nation, but is a mixture of fact and fantasy. It begins with the arrival in England of the mythical BRUTE, or Brutus, great-grandson of the Trojan Aeneas. In subsequent pages, there are accounts of such ancients as HENGIST AND HORSA, VORTIGERN, King LEAR, FERREX AND PORREX, CYMBELINE, GORBODUG, many of whom turn up again in later literature, notably in the plays of Shakespeare.

The strongest influence of Geoffrey's work on other writers has been in the area of Arthurian legend. With the introduction of Merlin the magician, Uther Pendragon, and the building of Arthur into a towering national figure who conquers large chunks of Europe, the legends of Arthur achieved new impetus. Translations and adaptations of the *History of the Kings of Britain* soon appeared in other countries, the most notable of these being the French *Roman de Brut* (1155) of Wace.

Though Wace cautiously expressed doubts about the truth of Geoffrey's "history," the work was not seriously questioned by Englishmen for several centuries. Indeed, in the 16th century one claim to the throne was considerably strengthened by the popular belief that the claimant was directly descended from King Arthur. See BELINUS; BRENNIUS; LUD.

Histriomastix. An anonymous play satirizing the stage, probably written in part by John MARSTON in about 1599. It was answered by Ben Jonson in EVERY MAN OUT OF HIS HUMOUR (1599). See WAR OF THE THEATERS.

Hita, arcipreste of. See Juan RUIZ.

Hitler, Adolf (1889–1945). German NAZI and FÜHRER of the THIRD REICH (1933–1945), whose talents as popular orator and political tactician were the foundation of his demogogic power. Appointed chancellor (1933) by President HINDENBURG and granted temporary dictatorial powers by the legislature, he was given complete executive power by a plebiscite following Hindenburg's death (1934). Hitler promised to avenge the shame suffered by Germany after World War I and to reestablish the grandeur of the ARYAN RACE. His annexation of Austria and Czechoslovakia (1938) and invasion of Poland (1939) brought on World War II. Although Hitler was an absolute dictator, much of his strength was based on the efficient administration of subordinates such as Goebbels, Goering, Himmler, Ribbentrop, and Schacht. It is thought that Hitler committed suicide after the collapse of Germany in 1945. See BEER-HALL PUTSCH; MEIN KAMPF.

H. M. Pulham, Esq. (1941). A novel by John P. MARQUAND. Unlike the title character in Marquand's *The Late George Apley,* Pulham partially escapes from his New England background by way of World War I and falls in love with a girl in New York; but like Apley he weds the girl his family selects for him. The book goes on to explore the price of conformity for both Pulham and his wife.

Hobbema, Meindert (1638–1709). Dutch painter. After Ruisdael, with whom he studied, Hobbema is considered the finest landscapist of the Dutch school. His works are distinguished by subdued colors, careful details, and the invariable presence of a water mill.

Hobbes, John Oliver. See Pearle Mary Teresa CRAIGIE.

Hobbes, Thomas (1588–1679). English philosopher. Hobbes spent most of his long life as tutor and companion to the Cavendish family (the earls of Devonshire), though he once tutored Charles II in mathematics. He also spent a number of years in Europe, where he became acquainted with such thinkers as Galileo and Descartes. In England, his friends included Harvey, Ben Jonson, Cowley, and

John Selden. An ardent Royalist, Hobbes defended secular monarchy in his best-known work, LEVIATHAN, OR THE MATTER, FORM, AND POWER OF A COMMONWEALTH, but its anticlericalism made his position difficult in Restoration England.

Hobbes has been called the father of materialism: his system reduces all events, even those of thought and memory, to some species of physical motion. He was a pioneer of modern political science, a forerunner of associational psychology, and a leader of modern rationalism, insisting on the complete separation of philosophy and theology. He was, in addition, the master of an unusually forceful and lucid prose style. His other works include *Elements of Law* (1651, 1655) and *Philosophical Rudiments* (1651), treatises on human nature and government.

Hobbit. A gnomelike creature, invented by the novelist J. R. R. TOLKIEN.

hobgoblin. An impish, ugly, and mischievous sprite, particularly Puck or Robin Goodfellow. The word is a variant of *Rob-Goblin*, i.e., the goblin Robin, just as Hodge is the nickname of Roger.

Hobson, Laura Z[ametkin] (1900–). American novelist. She is best known for her novel, *Gentleman's Agreement* (1947), which deals with anti-Semitism in the U.S. Mrs. Hobson worked for various magazines and newspapers until 1935, when she began to write short stories. Her first novel, *The Trespassers* (1943), dealt with the problems of refugees denied entrance to the United States because of the immigrant quota system. She has also written *The Celebrity* (1951) and *First Papers* (1964).

Hoby, Sir Thomas (1530–1566). English diplomat and translator, famous for his translation of *Il Cortegiano* (THE COURTIER) by Baldassare Castiglione. The book became a manual for English courtiers, and influenced the writings of Wyatt, Surrey, Sidney, and Spenser.

Hoccleve, Thomas. See Thomas OCCLEVE.

Hoder, Hodur, or Höthur. The Scandinavian god of darkness, called the blind old god, as opposed to his brother BALDER, the god of light. According to fable, Loki urged Hoder to kill Balder with an arrow made of mistletoe. Hoder was in turn slain by Vali, the guardian of justice.

Hodgson, Ralph (1871–1962). English GEORGIAN poet. His best-known poems, such as *The Bells of Heaven* and *The Bull*, are passionate protests against cruelty to animals.

Hoffmann, August Heinrich (1798–1874). Pen name: **Hoffmann von Fallersleben.** German political poet of libertarian sympathies. He wrote *Deutschland, Deutschland über alles* (*Germany, Germany, Over All*, 1841), a song that later (1919) became Germany's national anthem. Since the Nazi era in Germany, it has become popular belief that the poet wanted Germany to conquer all other nations; but in fact, Hoffmann was simply pleading for a single unified Germany to take precedence over all the numerous states into which the land was divided at the time.

Hoffmann, E[rnst] T[heodor] A[madeus] (1776–1822). German author, known especially for his fantastic and often humorous tales, two collections of which are the *Fantasiestücke* (*Fantasy-pieces*, 1814–1815) and the *Nachtstücke* (*Night-pieces*, 1817). His MÄRCHEN style represents a new departure in roman-

tic writing, for he weaves the fantastic world closely into the real world—as opposed, for example, to Novalis, whose idealistic *Märchen* have nothing of the real world in them. Thus, Hoffmann may be said to stand between romanticism and the realism of the later 19th century. The same mixture of fantasy and realism characterizes his two novels, *Die Elixiere des Teufels* (*The Devil's Elixirs*, 1816) and the unfinished *Kater Murr* (*Tom-Cat Murr*, 1820). The latter, which is the fictional autobiography of a cat, also includes the story of Hoffmann's most famous character, a composer named Johannes Kreisler who is a typical example of ZERRISSENHEIT. Hoffmann himself was a composer as well as an author, and wrote the music for the opera UNDINE based on a story by his friend Fouqué. See TALES OF HOFFMANN.

Hofmann, Hans (1880–). German abstract painter. Settling in the U.S. in 1932, he has exerted great influence through the schools he founded in New York and in Provincetown, Mass.

Hofmannsthal, Hugo von (1874–1929). Austrian playwright, poet, and essayist. His early writings (pre-1901) are typical of the movement of IMPRESSIONISM. Most of his lyric poetry, for example, was written during this period, and, like that of his friend Stefan George, it combines mysticism and exoticism in content with delicate balance in form and a style full of innuendoes that suggest more than they state. Among his most famous poems are *Manche freilich . . . (Many, it is true . . .)*, about the mystical unity of all human destinies, and *Vorfrühling (Pre-Spring)*, which suggests the feeling of the wind on a night just before spring. The short plays that he wrote during this period, including *Der Tod des Tizian* (*Titian's Death*, 1892), *Das kleine Welttheater* (*The Small World-Theater*, 1897), and DER TOR UND DER TOD, are very much like his lyrics; in them, the emphasis is not on action but on the poetic expression of a mystical mood, which permeates the situation.

The essay *Brief des Lord Chandos* (*Letter of Lord Chandos*, 1901), however, marks a clear turning point in Hofmannsthal's career. In it, he states that he no longer finds language adequate as a means of expression; even the word *apple*, he says, has so many different connotations for different people that one is never certain of exactly communicating one's meaning with it. He had become discouraged with the lyric as an expressive medium, and, in many of his post-1901 dramas, he attempts to compensate for the inadequacies of language by turning to traditional and mythical subject matter, that is, he attempts to communicate more directly with his audience by treating material that is part of everyone's cultural heritage. Examples of this tendency in his works are *Elektra* (1903), an adaptation of Sophocles' tragedy; *Ödipus und die Sphinx* (1906), on the story of Oedipus; *Jedermann* (EVERYMAN, 1911), an adaptation of the medieval morality play; *Das Salzburger grosse Welttheater* (*The Great World-Theater of Salzburg*, 1923), based on Calderón's *El gran teatro del mundo;* and *Der Turm* (THE TOWER, 1925), a free adaptation of Calderon's *Life Is a Dream*. Also, in these later plays, he makes more extensive use of dramatic action and stage arrangements for expressive purposes, rather than relying on language alone. Finally, his search for better means of communication led him to combine his art with music in the opera librettos he wrote for Richard Strauss, which include *Der* ROSENKAVALIER and *Die Frau ohne Schatten* (*The Woman with No Shadow*, 1919).

In his later period, Hofmannsthal became deeply interested in the structure and problems of culture, both in Austria and in Europe in general. Besides his dramatic works, he produced several essays on cultural questions, including the well known *Das Schrifttum als geistiger Raum der Nation* (*Letters as the Spiritual Environment of the Nation*, 1927).

Hofmann von Hofmannswaldau, Christian (1617–1679). German poet. His style is characterized as "late baroque" or "manneristic," because of the self-conscious richness, sometimes highly overloaded, of his imagery and language. His writing does not have the stoic, ascetic quality that is found in Gryphius' works, but he was nonetheless a religious man, and the influence of German mysticism is felt in his verse. A characteristic poem is his sonnet *Auf den Einfall der Kirchen zu St. Elisabeth* (On the Collapse of the Church in St. Elizabeth), in which a rich, detailed picture of the ruined building is given, followed by a moral comparing it to the religion of the time.

Hofstadter, Richard (1916–   ). American historian. A member of the faculty of Columbia University, Hofstadter won a Pulitzer Prize for *The Age of Reform: From Bryan to F.D.R.* (1955), an unsentimental analysis of populism and progressivism, which he viewed as the precursors of modern conservatism rather than of the New Deal. His other works include *Social Darwinism in American Thought* (1944); *The American Political Tradition* (1948), essays emphasizing the continuity in American politics; *The Development of Academic Freedom in the United States* (1955), in collaboration with Walter P. Metzger; and a study of the causes and manifestations of *Anti-Intellectualism in the United States* (1963).

Hogarth, William (1697–1764). English painter and engraver. Generally regarded as the greatest pictorial satirist of England, his reputation was established through the plates for Samuel Butler's *Hudibras* (1726). He then did a series of satirical paintings, *The Harlot's Progress* (1731), engravings of which he distributed the following year by subscription. They achieved a tremendous success and Hogarth went on to do other series of narrative paintings which he afterwards engraved. *The Rake's Progress* was distributed in 1735, *Marriage à la Mode* in 1745. Hogarth's fame rests on these satirical series, in which he expressed the hard morality of his age with sharpness and humor; however, his admirable portraits, with their strong sense of color and direct, free handling of paint, also make a claim to artistic greatness. His engravings are said to have furnished Henry Fielding with prototypes for his characters, and inspired the libretto of W. H. Auden and Chester Kallman for Stravinsky's opera *The Rake's Progress* (1951).

Hogg, James. Known as **the Ettrick Shepherd** (1770–1835). Scottish poet. He was so called because he was born in Ettrick and inherited the occupation of shepherd from his family. Largely self-educated, he is known for his verse celebrating Scottish rural scenes and pursuits and for his treatments of the Celtic folklore tradition. He was encouraged by Sir

Fencing master's advertisement engraved by Hogarth.

Walter Scott and in his later life was associated with *Blackwood's Magazine*.

Hogg, Thomas [Jefferson] (1792–1862). English lawyer, intimate friend and biographer of Shelley. At the request of Shelley's widow and family, Hogg undertook Shelley's biography, the first two volumes of which appeared in 1858. Dissatisfied with the results, Shelley's family denied him further access to the materials necessary to complete the work. Although what he did write was often more about Hogg than Shelley, the two volumes remain an accurate, valuable, and loyal account of the poet's early years.

Hōjō ki. See ACCOUNT OF MY HUT, AN.

hokku. See HAIKU.

Hokusai. See KATSUSHIKA HOKUSAI.

Holbein, Hans, the younger (1497–1543). German painter. His father (c. 1460–1524), after whom the son was named, was also a distinguished painter, noted for his altar-pieces. The younger Holbein studied and worked in Basel and was led by the artistic depression ensuing from the Reformation to undertake a trip to England (1526–1528), and finally to settle there in 1530. He executed smoothly finished, carefully detailed, precisely drawn, and richly colored portraits and religious paintings. His formal portraits preserve the features of Erasmus, Sir Thomas More and his family, Thomas Cromwell, and Henry VIII, in whose services he spent his last years.

Holcroft, Thomas (1744–1809). English dramatist. His *Tale of Mystery* (1802) has been called "the first English melodrama." His other plays include the sentimental drama *The Road to Ruin* (1792), the comedy *Love's Frailties* (1794) and translations of Beaumarchais' *Le mariage de Figaro* and Destouches' *Le glorieux*. He was a member of the DELLA-CRUSCANS.

Holda. See HULDA.

Hölderlin, Friedrich (1770–1843). German poet. In his predominant use of classical verse forms and syntax he was a follower of Klopstock, but his language is more compressed and powerful than the older poet's. He was not directly affilated with either of the two major literary movements of his time, Weimar classicism or romanticism, but his thought has elements in common with both. He shares the classicists' love of balance and repose, but couples it with a romantic yearning for complete oneness with nature and for a religion that could combine pantheism, Greek religion, and Christianity. Schelling and Hegel, friends of his since their school days, expressed similar ideas at times.

Hölderlin's life was never settled or happy. He lacked both money and recognition, and these strains, combined with that of his entirely platonic but socially suspect love affair with a married woman (Susette Gontard, whom he calls "Diotima" in his poems), drove him insane in 1803, so that his actual career lasted only about a decade. Neither Schiller nor Goethe recognized Hölderlin's greatness, but his lyric poetry and his novel HYPERION ODER EREMIT IN GRIECHENLAND are now counted among the greatest literary achievements in the language. Some of his finest lyrics (written 1800–1803) are *Brod und Wein* (*Bread and Wine*), an elegy celebrating both Christ and Dionysus; *Der Archipelagus*, an ode in which it is hoped that modern Germany will tend toward the character of ancient Greece; *Heidelberg* and *Der Rhein*, odes on the city and the river, respectively; and the patriotic ode *Germanien*.

Holger Danske. National folk hero of Denmark, usually identified with OGIER THE DANE. He supposedly still sleeps under Elsinore, waiting to arise when Denmark needs him.

Holgrave. The young daguerreotypist in Hawthorne's THE HOUSE OF THE SEVEN GABLES.

Holinshed or **Hollingshead, Raphael** (d. c. 1580). English historian. Holinshed is famous as the author of the CHRONICLES OF ENGLAND, SCOTLAND, AND IRELAND (1578). A massive history of the world had been begun by Reginald Wolfe; when Wolfe died in 1573 Holinshed took over the project and, with the assistance of Richard Stanihurst and William Harrison, completed it on a somewhat smaller scale as a history of England. The work is memorable primarily as a source of plots for Elizabethan dramatists, particularly Shakespeare.

Holland, Josiah Gilbert (1819–1881). American editor and writer. His early writings appeared under the pseudonym of Timothy Titcomb. He was popular in his period for his sentimental didacticism. Among his novels are *Arthur Bonnicastle* (1873), a partly autobiographical book, and *Sevenoaks* (1875), the story of an unscrupulous New England millionaire. Holland also wrote poetry and was especially well known for BITTER SWEET. In 1870 he became co-founder and co-editor of *Scribner's Monthly*.

Holley, Marietta. Pen name, **Josiah Allen's Wife** (1836–1926). American writer of humorous stories. While relating the adventures of Josiah Allen and his wife Samantha, the author—an ardent advocate of temperance and women's suffrage—often propagandized her own beliefs in her stories. *Samantha at the Centennial* (1877) and *Samantha in Europe* (1895) were two of her most popular books.

Hollow Men, The (1925). A poem by T. S. ELIOT. Mixing nursery rhyme and liturgy, it presents his view of the spiritual emptiness and doom of the 20th century through the symbol of a scarecrow (the guy of Guy Fawkes night; see GUNPOWDER PLOT). Its epigraph is from Joseph Conrad's *Heart of Darkness*.

Holm Saxe. See Helen Hunt JACKSON.

Holmes, Oliver Wendell, Sr. (1809–1894). American physician, professor, man of letters. By his own definition, he was a New England Brahmin, a man of cultivated family and sufficient fortune. Holmes earned local recognition as a youth with the poem OLD IRONSIDES.

A member of the Harvard Class of '29, Holmes frequently celebrated his classmates in topical verse. After graduation he spent two years in Paris (1833–1835) studying medicine. In 1836, a year typical of his active life, Holmes, at the age of 25, took a medical degree at Harvard, began his practice, became a member of the Massachusetts Medical Society, wrote a *Dissertation on Intermittent Fever in New England,* won the Boylston Prize, wrote the Phi Beta Kappa poem, and published his first volume of verse. The book contained two of his best-loved poems, "The Last Leaf," and "The Moral Bully." In 1847, the doctor accepted a Harvard professorship of anatomy and physiology and turned out another volume of verse. He was a witty and popular teacher, until his resignation in 1882 at the age of 73.

When THE ATLANTIC MONTHLY began publishing under James Russell Lowell, Holmes gave it its name, and contributed THE AUTOCRAT OF THE BREAKFAST-TABLE, a series that combined fiction, essay, conversation, drama, and verse. The *Autocrat*, modeled on the work of Addison and Steele, made Holmes famous for wit and originality. THE CHAMBERED NAUTILUS, his most frequently anthologized poem, appeared there. He continued the essays in two further series: *The Professor* . . . (1859), and *The Poet* . . . (1872).

A conversationalist in the tradition of Dr. Johnson, Holmes was in great demand as a guest and speaker. He was a familiar figure at the dinners of the Saturday Club, of which Emerson, Longfellow, Whittier, Lowell, Agassiz, and Motley were members.

Holmes always rebelled against his Calvinist upbringing. As an enlightened scientist, he urged that criminals be educated rather than punished. His poem THE DEACON'S MASTERPIECE is a satire on tightly constructed dogmas. Holmes's "medicated" novels, ELSIE VENNER, THE GUARDIAN ANGEL, and A MORTAL ANTIPATHY continue his attack on Calvinist theology.

Holmes was not only ahead of his time in social thought, but his essay on *The Contagiousness of Puerperal Fever* anticipated Semmelweis. In 1884, Holmes produced a biography of Emerson, and in 1888, wrote the series *Over the Teacups,* for the *Atlantic.* He was honored at Cambridge, Edinburgh, and Oxford during his 1886 trip to Europe. He was the father of the great jurist Oliver Wendell Holmes, Jr.

Holmes, Oliver Wendell, Jr. (1841–1935).
American jurist. Son of the celebrated physician and
author of the same name, Holmes graduated from
Harvard University and served in the Union army
for three years during the Civil War; he was wounded
three times, twice severely. He was lost to sight for
a while, and the elder Holmes reported his adventures in search of him in *My Hunt After "The Captain" (Atlantic Monthly,* November, 1862).

Holmes began to practice law in Boston in 1867, on
his return from the first of many trips to England,
and began to teach at the Harvard Law School in
1870. His lectures on *The Common Law* (1881) became classics. In 1882 he was appointed to the Supreme Judicial Court of Massachusetts and became
chief justice in 1899. In 1902 he was appointed to
the Supreme Court by President Theodore Roosevelt,
and after a notable series of opinions and dissents
was regarded as the leading exponent of law in Anglo-
Saxon countries. He retired in 1932.

Known as "the great dissenter," he had certain
fixed ideas, the chief of which was that the law was
made for society, not society for the law. He held
that the life of the law was not logic but experience,
that law was not an absolute "but what the courts
will enforce," and that "the first call of a theory of
law is that it should fit the facts." It was an axiom
of his that "certainty generally is an illusion, and
repose is not the destiny of man." He said, "The best
test of truth is the power of thought to get itself accepted in the market." His dissents often had great
influence, and in time many of his views were accepted as good law, such as his pronouncements,
always based on the Constitution, on the plenary
power of Congress over commerce, on the taxing
power of Congress, on the meaning of "police power,"
and on the provisions of the Bill of Rights, especially
the first amendment.

In addition to *The Common Law,* Holmes published in his own lifetime *Speeches* (1891; rev. 1913)
and *Collected Legal Papers* (1920). His correspondence with Sir Frederick Pollock and with Harold J.
Laski has also been published.

Holmes, Sherlock. The most famous detective
of fiction, a creation of Sir Arthur Conan Doyle,
who introduced him in his *Study in Scarlet* (1887).
His adventures are continued in *The Sign of the
Four* (1889); *The Adventures of Sherlock Holmes*
(1891); *The Memoirs of Sherlock Holmes* (1893);
The Hound of the Baskervilles (1902); *The Return
of Sherlock Holmes* (1904); *The Valley of Fear*
(1915); *His Last Bow* (1917); and *The Case Book
of Sherlock Holmes* (1927). Holmes has such brilliant analytical faculties and indefatigable interest in
any detective problem that he regularly puts Scotland Yard to shame. He is abrupt in manner, master
of the violin and a dozen obscure sciences, and a
victim of the cocaine habit. His admiring friend, Dr.
Watson, usually records his triumphs. Holmes's inveterate enemy is the malevolent Moriarty.

Holmsen, Bjarne P. See Arno Holz.

Holofernes. A tedious, pedantic schoolmaster in
Shakespeare's Love's Labour's Lost. Holofernes and
Sir Nathaniel are described as "arts-men" who "have
been at a great feast of languages and stolen the
scraps."

Holofernes. See Judith.

Holt, Felix. See Felix Holt, the Radical.

Holtby, Winifred (1898–1935). English novelist. Her best book was her last, *South Riding* (1936),
a novel about Yorkshire life. See Vera Brittain.

Hölty, Ludwig Heinrich Christoph (1748–1776).
German poet, member of the Göttinger Hain group.
Along with Bürger, he contributed much to the 18th-
century revival of the German ballad. His *Gedichte
(Poems,* 1783) were edited posthumously by Friedrich
Stolberg and Johann Heinrich Voss.

Holy Alliance. A league formed by Russia,
Austria, and Prussia in 1815. It was designed to regulate the affairs of Europe after the fall of Napoleon
"by the principles of Christian charity." This meant
that every endeavor would be made to stabilize the
existing dynasties and to resist all change. It lasted
until 1830, and was joined by all the European
sovereigns except those of England and Turkey, and
the Pope.

Holy Bible. See Bible.

Holy City. That city considered by the followers of a given faith to be sanctified by its connections
with that faith. Allahabad is the Holy City of the Indian Muslims; Benares, that of the Hindus; Cuzco,
of the ancient Incas; Fez, of the Western Arabs;
Jerusalem, of the Jews and Christians; Kairwan,
near Tunis, containing the Okbar Mosque in which
is the tomb of the prophet's barber, that of North
African Muslims; Mecca and Medina, of all Muslims; Moscow and Kiev, of the Russians, the latter
city having been the cradle of Christianity in Russia.

Holy Cross or **Holy Rood Day.** September 14,
the day of the Feast of the Exaltation of the Cross.
Called by the Anglo-Saxons "Roodmass-day," it is
kept in honor of the exposition of a portion of the
true Cross in the basilica erected at Jerusalem by the
Empress Helen (c. 326). Another event connected
with it is the recovery of the piece of the Cross
which had been stolen from Jerusalem in 614 by
Chosroes, king of Persia, and by Heraclius in 629.

Holy Fair, The (1786). A poem by Robert
Burns ridiculing the Holy Fair at Mauchline. Three
"sisters"—Fun, Superstition, and Hypocrisy—visit the
Fair and view scenes of immorality.

Holy Family. The infant Jesus, Mary and Joseph.
Anne, the mother of Mary, Elizabeth, and the infant John the Baptist are often also present in pictures of the Holy Family.

Holy Grail. See Grail.

Holy Land. Any land held to be holy by the
devotees of a particular faith. The Christians call
Israel the Holy Land, because it was the site of
Christ's ministry. To Muslims, Mecca, the birthplace
of Muhammad, is the Holy Land. The Chinese
Buddhists regard India as holy because it was the
native land of the Buddha. The Greeks considered
Elis holy because it was the site of the temple of
Olympian Zeus, near which the Olympic Games were
held every four years.

Holy League, the. (1) Designation for an agreement arranged by Pope Julius II among the Italian
and European powers. It was directed against France.
The War of the Holy League (1511–1513) put an
end to French plans for the domination of Italy. Another league, called the Second Holy League, was
an agreement among the Papacy, France, and the
Italian powers directed against Spain. The War of

the Second Holy League (1526–1529), won by Spain, insured her control of Italy and the Papacy thereafter.

(2) An association formed in 1576 under the auspices of Henry, duke of GUISE, to defend the Roman Catholics against French Protestants and to win the French throne for the Guises. The league, which was subsidized by Philip II of Spain, was defeated by Henry IV of France at Arques and Ivry and lost its influence after his conversion to Catholicism.

Holy Living and Dying. A religious work by Jeremy TAYLOR. It was originally published in two parts: *The Rule and Exercise of Holy Living* (1650) and *The Rule and Exercise of Holy Dying* (1651).

Holy of Holies. The innermost quarter of the Jewish temple. In it the Ark of the Covenant was kept. Into this place only the high priest was allowed to enter, and that but once a year, on the Day of Atonement. The term, or its Latin equivalent, *sanctum sanctorum,* has been applied to any haven kept sacred from the world in general.

Holy Roman Empire. A loose confederation of German states ruled by various royal German houses who claimed the imperial authority of ancient Rome. The butt of generations of joking students ("it was neither Holy, Roman, nor an Empire"), the Holy Roman Empire lasted in name for over 1,000 years (800–1806). It began when Charlemagne was crowned emperor by Pope Leo III and ended when Francis II (Francis I of Austria) abdicated. While the power of the emperor and the cohesion of the empire always existed more in theory than in practice, the Holy Roman Empire did give a certain unity to the many German states.

The first German emperor was Henry the Fowler who was crowned in 919. Since the title was not hereditary, the emperor being elected by seven electors, the crown was held at various times by nearly all the royal German houses. The uninterrupted line of Hapsburg emperors began in 1438. The power and prestige of the Austrian Hapsburgs reflected on the empire as well. Under Maximilian I and Charles V the empire had its greatest strength. After Charles relinquished the crown in 1556, there began the steady decline that ended in 1806 with the empire's extinction.

Holy Sepulcher. The rock-hewn tomb in a garden outside the walls of Jerusalem, traditionally the burial place of the body of Christ after the Crucifixion. Although the site of the tomb has never been precisely identified, rumor has fixed it in a cave under the edifice known as the Church of the Holy Sepulcher in Jerusalem, which was begun by Constantine the Great in the fourth century, destroyed and rebuilt—once during the Crusades—and reconsecrated in 1810 after extensive repairs.

Holy Trinity. See TRINITY.

Holy War. A war in which religion plays or purports to play a considerable part. The Crusades, the Thirty Years' War, the wars against the Albigenses, and many others have been so called. A holy war launched by Muslims against Christians was known as a *jehad.*

Holy War, The (1682). An allegory by John BUNYAN, depicting the salvation of the soul of man. The city of Mansoul is captured by Diabolus, but is later liberated by the forces of Emmanuel, son of the builder of the city. Although the city falls into evil and is again assaulted by Diabolus, Emmanuel is ultimately victorious. It is thought that Bunyan's experiences in the English Civil War may have contributed to the military and political allegory in this work.

Holz, Arno (1863–1929). German author. A few of his poems appeared in Hermann Conradi's anthology *Moderne Dichtercharaktere (Modern Figures in Poetry,* 1884); in these, as well as in his own volume *Das Buch der Zeit, Lieder eines Modernen (The Book of the Time, Songs of a Modern Man,* 1886), he showed himself an exponent of the early, idealistic phase of German NATURALISM. But during 1888–1890, when he became a friend of Johannes SCHLAF, he turned strongly toward what he called consistent realism, and attempted to reproduce everyday reality in his writing. At the same time, he turned away from lyric poetry to narrative and drama, and with Schlaf, co-authored the two starkly realistic works: *Papa Hamlet* (1889), a collection of prose sketches which appeared under the pseudonym Bjarne P. Holmsen, advertised as a translation from the Danish, and the play *Die Familie Selicke (The Selicke Family,* 1890) about the troubles of a poor Berlin family. Shortly afterward, he wrote a theoretical work, *Die Kunst, ihr Wesen und ihre Gesetze (Art, Its Essence and Its Laws,* 1891), in which he strongly disputed the claim that art is a metaphysical absolute. The difference, he said, between a child's crude drawing and a true work of art is entirely relative; the artist simply has more skill in reproducing his perception of nature. Holz himself, however, turned away from naturalism and back to lyric poetry in his *Phantasus* (1898 ff.), and in a theoretical work *Revolution der Lyrik (Revolution of Lyric Poetry,* 1899) he defended the use of completely free verse.

Home, Daniel Dunglas (1833–1886). A Scottish spiritualist medium who was the subject of Robert Browning's poem, *Sludge the Medium* (1864). He conducted séances at courts and in public in the U.S., England, France, and Prussia and was the author of *Incidents of my Life* (1863).

Home, John (1722–1808). English playwright, known for his drama *Douglas* (1756) and for his friendship with David Hume and William Collins.

Homer. Ionian poet. To him the ILIAD and the ODYSSEY are traditionally attributed. As early as the Hellenistic period, a few scholars insisted that the epics were the work of different authors. Orthodox opinion, however, claimed that Homer had composed both works, and numerous biographies were written of him. Eight of these are extant, but their dates and authors are unknown and they are regarded as largely invention. There was a further firm tradition that Homer was blind. A measure of the reliable information about Homer known to the ancients is the fact that seven cities claimed to have been his birthplace: Chios, Colophon, Smyrna, Rhodes, Argos, Athens, and Salamis. The fact is that nothing whatever is known about Homer the man, including the crucial point of whether he existed.

Nevertheless, modern scholars have learned a great deal about the works that the Greeks attributed to Homer. These were not only the *Iliad* and the *Odys-*

sey, but also the BATTLE OF THE FROGS AND THE MICE and the HOMERIC HYMNS, and certain epics from the EPIC CYCLE, known today only in brief fragments. It has long been accepted as certain that of these only the first two can be considered as genuinely "Homeric," although the Homeric hymns were clearly written in imitation of Homer's style. Today even most "unitarians," who believe the *Iliad* and the *Odyssey* each to be the work of a single author, do not consider them the work of the same author. The diction and language of the *Odyssey* show it to be a somewhat later work.

All scholars are aware that GREEK EPIC POETRY of the Homeric age was the end product of a long period of gradual accretion during which historical events, legends, and folk tales were stitched together by many generations of rhapsodes or bards. In the case of the *Iliad* and the *Odyssey*, this process probably covered four centuries, from shortly after the series of events known as the TROJAN WAR in the early 13th century B.C. to the mid-ninth century, which seems the most likely date for Homer. The "analytic school" of Homeric scholars believe that this process continued up to the sixth century B.C., when PISISTRATUS had the epics arranged for regular recitation at the Panathenaic festivals. This would mean that the epics were compiled and edited from bits and pieces rather than composed to a significant extent by a single individual.

Although analytic theories tended to dominate Homeric studies after the pioneer work of F. A. Wolf in 1795, there has been in recent years a strong resurgence of the unitarians. The most widely held position today is that, although both the *Iliad* and the *Odyssey* are made up of traditional materials, each bears the unmistakable imprint of a single artistic intelligence. This belief is supported by the remarkable structural, dramatic, and stylistic unity achieved in both epics, in spite of numerous and obvious anachronisms and other discrepancies. The *Odyssey*, in spite of—or perhaps in part because of—its broader scope and greater variety, evidences more clearly than the *Iliad* the work of a single poet. It is remarkable for its extraordinarily modern structure, which employs the techniques of the "flash-back" and parallel lines of action common in the novel.

The *Iliad* and the *Odyssey* as they are known today are based on the texts edited in the sixth century B.C. for use in Athens. A considerable amount of tampering with the *Iliad* was done by the Athenians in order to increase their role in its events and the texts were further edited in the second century B.C. by two distinguished scholars in Alexandria: Aristarchus of Samothrace and Aristophanes of Byzantium. The extant texts are substantially those of Aristarchus.

Homer, Winslow (1836–1910). American painter. Beginning as an illustrator, he was special correspondent during the Civil War for *Harper's Weekly*. About 1880 he gave up illustration for painting. A realist, he presented the shooting of rapids or scenes from hunting and fishing with great directness. He settled on the Maine coast about 1884. His themes became the everyday life of fishermen, and the power of sea and wind. Maine and the West Indies, which he subsequently visited, inspired him to do superb watercolors, striking for their breadth of handling and economical suggestion of moving sea and air.

Homeric hymns. Poems in the epic style composed by poets known as Homeridae or sons of Homer. Modelled after the works of Homer, these hymns or Preludes were presented by the Homeridae before their recitation of Homer at public festivals. Thirty-three poems are extant, among them hymns to Demeter, Pan, Apollo, and others.

Home, Sweet Home. A popular song with lyrics by John Howard PAYNE. It was written to a tune by Sir Henry Rowley Bishop (1786–1855) and first sung in his opera, *Clari, or, the Maid of Milan* (1823).

Homme Révolté, L'. See REBEL, THE.

Homunculus (*Lat.*, "little man"). In Part II of Goethe's FAUST, a miniature man in a vial who is artificially created by WAGNER in an attempt to raise man above his dependency on sex for reproduction. Homunculus leads Faust and Mephistopheles to the classical WALPURGIS NIGHT.

Honegger, Arthur [Oscar] (1892–1955). French composer, member of LES SIX. His best-known works include *Pacific 231* (1924; an orchestral imitation of a steam locomotive) and two cantatas: *Le Roi David* (*King David;* 1921; text by René Morax) and *Jeanne d'Arc au Bûcher* (*Joan of Arc at the Stake;* 1938; text by Paul Claudet).

Honest Whore, The: Parts I and II (1604, 1605). A comedy by Thomas DEKKER. Hippolito, in love with Infelice, the daughter of the duke, believes that she is dead, and is inconsolable. Actually, she has been sent to a convent to separate her from Hippolito. Meanwhile, the constant Hippolito has been taken to the home of the courtesan Bellafont, whose advances he resists. She, however, falls madly in love with him and embarks on a life of chastity. Soon, Hippolito discovers that Infelice is alive and rushes to the convent to marry her. The duke arrives too late to prevent the match and becomes reconciled to the union. Bellafont, by order of the duke, is married to her first lover, Matheo. The subplot revolves around Candido, a linen draper, whom nothing perturbs. He is so mild and serene that his wife, in desperation, has him committed to an asylum. At the end, he is released, his brow gently furrowed with concern for his wife's sanity.

In Part II, the honest Bellafont's worthless husband Matheo is in prison, and she seeks help from Hippolito, who is struck by her beauty. When Matheo is released from prison, her sorrows only increase. Her husband stoops at nothing, even suggesting that she return to her old profession to provide money; Hippolito presses her with his unwanted attentions. Meanwhile, Orlando Friscobaldo, Bellafont's father, has disguised himself and become Matheo's servant, in order to watch over his daughter. Soon, Bellafont is falsely arrested for prostitution, and Matheo accuses her of infidelity with Hippolito. However, her father revealing himself, establishes her innocence, and Matheo is sternly warned to repent. Again the patient Candido appears, this time in the process of taming his second shrewish wife.

Honorable Peter Stirling, The (1894). A novel by Paul Leicester FORD. Its hero, an honest and fearless politician in New York City, is said to represent the young Grover Cleveland; this was denied by the author. The book is valued as an accurate picture of ward politics in the urban America of the 1890's.

Hood, Robin. See ROBIN HOOD.

Hood, Thomas (1799–1845). English poet and humorist. Hood suggested as his epitaph "Here lies one who spat more blood and made more puns than any man living." His actual epitaph reads "He sang the Song of the Shirt." Together they suggest something of the contradictory nature of his life and art: the long struggle with illness and poverty maintained with courage and gaiety, his unique standing as a poet both humorous and serious. He earned a livelihood through his light verse, which ranges from the penetrating but good natured satire of Miss KILMANSEGG to such pun-filled buffoonery as *Faithless Nelly Grey* (1834):

> O Nelly Grey! O Nelly Grey!
> Is this your love so warm?
> The love that loves a scarlet coat,
> Should be more uniform.

Among his serious works, his poems of social protest, such as *The Song of The Shirt* (1843), are most famous, but he wrote a wide variety of lyrics and ballads. Some of his collections are *Odes and Addresses to Great People* (1825), *The Midsummer Fairies* (1827), *Whims and Oddities* (1826, 1827).

Hooker, [William] Brian (1880–1946). American librettist and poet. He wrote the librettos for two operas composed by Horatio Parker: *Mona* (1911) and *Fairyland* (1915). With W. H. Post, he wrote the libretto for *The Vagabond King* (1925), an operetta based on Justin H. McCarthy's *If I Were King* (1901), with music by Rudolph Friml. Hooker's greatest success, however, is his translation (1923) of Edmond Rostand's *Cyrano de Bergerac*, which was first produced on Broadway with Walter Hampden in the title role. He also published a collection of *Poems* (1915).

Hooker, Richard (1554?–1600). English theologian. Hooker took holy orders in 1581. As a result of a controversy with a strict Calvinist, he attempted to clarify the position of the Church of England and wrote his great work, *The Laws of Ecclesiastical Polity* (1593–1597). The treatise treats church government from a philosophical and logical point of view, and anticipates the "common consent" grounds for government of Locke and Rousseau.

Hooper, J. J. See Captain Simon SUGGS.

Hoosier Schoolmaster, The (1871). A novel by Edward EGGLESTON. A widely read, realistic story of frontier life in the Middle West, it deals with the life of a schoolmaster in the days before the Civil War. It was followed by *The Hoosier Schoolboy* (1883).

Hoover, Herbert [Clark] (1874–1964). 31st president of the U.S. (1929–1933). After a successful career as a mining engineer and businessman, Hoover won an international reputation during World War I when he served as chairman of the American Relief Committee, as chairman of the Commission for Relief in Belgium, and as U.S. Food Administrator. As secretary of commerce (1921–1928), he organized his department in order to make it serve business interests more efficiently. In the 1928 presidential election he defeated Al Smith, the Democratic candidate, becoming the first Republican to crack the "Solid South." Faced by the great depression of 1929 soon after he entered the White House, Hoover, an advocate of self-help, was reluctant to use the power of the federal government to revive the economy, though he supported the Reconstruction Finance Corporation (1932) to extend loans to banks and other business enterprises. In 1932 he sought reelection but was defeated by Franklin D. Roosevelt. From 1947 to 1949 he headed a bipartisan commission to study ways of simplifying and improving the structure of the executive branch of the federal government. Hoover's books include *American Individualism* (1922), *The Challenge to Liberty* (1934), *Memoirs* (3 vols., 1951–1952), and *The Ordeal of Woodrow Wilson* (1958).

Hope, Anthony. See Sir Anthony Hope HAWKINS.

Hopkins, Arthur [Melancthon] (1878–1950). American producer and playwright. His producing career started with *The Poor Little Rich Girl* (1913) and closed with *The Magnificent Yankee* (1946). He put on plays by Shakespeare, Ibsen, and O'Neill, and was the author of several plays and books.

Hopkins, Gerard Manley (1844–1889). English poet and Jesuit priest. He is known for his small number of brilliant poems on religion and nature, and for his revolutionary innovations in poetic technique. His poetry is distinguished by an intricate type of rhythm, which he called SPRUNG RHYTHM; by puns, internal rhymes, and intricate patterns of wordplay; and by an extremely individual technique of elliptical phrasing and compound metaphor capable of great concentration of meaning. His work is thought to be indebted to Old English alliterative verse, to the METAPHYSICAL poets, especially George Herbert, and to traditional Welsh poetry.

Hopkins was a member of a large, artistically gifted family, and was himself talented in drawing and music as well as in poetry. He loved sensuous beauty; his earliest poems are lush and Keatsian, and for many years he kept diaries describing the beauties of nature. At Oxford University he was a student of Walter Pater and wrote a Platonic dialogue *On the Origin of Beauty*. He also came under the influence of Benjamin Jowett and Cardinal Newman. Converted to Roman Catholicism in 1866, he was inducted into the Jesuit order in 1868. He received his theological training in North Wales. Hopkins tried to compensate for his sensuous nature by entering on an extremely ascetic course of life. It was not till 1875 that, at the wish of his Rector, he broke a seven years' poetic silence and wrote THE WRECK OF THE DEUTSCHLAND, his first great poem. Subsequent poems celebrated the beauty and INSCAPE of God-made nature, and reflected his personal experience as a priest and his concern about social conditions and industrial materialism. He became a professor of Greek in Dublin University in 1884. His last poems include his "terrible" sonnets, which express his sense of alienation from God—a state commonly experienced by mystics.

Hopkins' poems were very much in advance of his time and none were published during his lifetime. He sent them, with long letters, to the poet Robert Bridges, his friend from Oxford days; Bridges published them in 1918. Because of the originality of his poetry and the date of its publication Hopkins tends to be regarded as a leading modern poet rather than as a Victorian. His techniques influenced a number of 20th-century British and American poets, notably W. H. Auden and Dylan Thomas. Hopkins' letters, notebooks, and papers were published in four volumes from 1935 to 1938. These contain details of his metrical and aesthetic theories, accounts of his spiritual progress, and many descriptions of nature. Among Hopkins' best-known individual poems are *The Windhover, Pied Beauty, The Caged Skylark, Felix Randall, Spring and Fall,* and *The Leaden Echo and the Golden Echo.*

Hopkins, Lemuel. See HARTFORD WITS.

Hopkinson, Francis (1737–1791). American politician, writer, and musician. Devoted to the cause of the American colonies, he wrote *A Pretty Story* (1774), an allegorical satire describing the quarrel between America and England, and THE BATTLE OF THE KEGS, his best-known work. He was also a signer of the Declaration of Independence. His *Seven Songs* (1788) was the first book of music published by an American composer. See also COLUMBIAN MAGAZINE.

hop-o'-my-thumb. A pigmy or midget. The name has been given to several dwarfs, as well as being commonly used as a generic term.

Hopper, Edward (1882–   ). American painter. His stark scenes of austere New England architecture are relieved by a crystalline light.

Horace. Full Latin name, **Quintus Horatius Flaccus** (65–8 B.C.). Roman lyric poet and satirist. The son of a freed slave, Horace was born at Venusia in southern Italy. His father, a tax collector, spared no effort or expense to provide his son with the best possible education; he took Horace to Rome to study under the best Roman grammarian. To complete his education, Horace, then a young man of 20, enrolled at the University of Athens (45 B.C.). While he was there, word came that Caesar had been assassinated. Like many Roman intellectuals, Horace rallied to the cause of revolution and liberty, and, when Brutus appeared at Athens, he followed him, entering the senatorial army as a military tribune. After the defeat of Brutus at Philippi (42), Horace returned penniless to Rome and managed to get a job with the Roman civil service as a clerk.

Here he began writing his first successful poetry: a group of clever satires and a mélange of iambic poems after the manner of Greek lyrics. These poems won him the admiration of Vergil who, in 38, introduced Horace to the influential patron MAECENAS. Thus began a lifelong friendship between the patron and the young poet, and, in 33, Maecenas gave Horace a small estate in the Sabine Hills. There he polished his satires (*The Sermones*) and his iambic poems (*The Epodes*); he published them in 30.

His great poetic work was his four-book collection of odes (*The Carmina*), the first three books of which appeared in 23. In them he displayed what Petronius termed a "painstaking felicity" of expression. Horace was the finished master of stanzaic meters, just as Vergil was the incomparable master of the larger and more sonorous dactylic hexameter. Horace's hexameters, as he used them in his satires and in his epistles (*The Epistulae,* composed 22–8), were deliberately unmajestic; they employed everyday diction, interspersed with occasional slang, and

were written in a conversational tone in which whole passages, nevertheless, have the feeling of elegant, musical prose. Throughout his poetry, his personality, though seldom obtrusive, is always evident. His poetry is, indeed, his own most vivid biography. Here we sense the presence of a sly but never ungenerous man, a sometimes aloof lover of independence who was also the devoted friend of the emperor Augustus, of Maecenas, and of Vergil; an epicurean in good times and a stoic in adversity; an artist and a country gentleman who had learned the advantages of cultivating his own garden in poetry as well as in politics.

Among Horace's other works are the *Carmen Saeculare,* a liturgical hymn composed for the secular games held at Rome in 17, and the ARS POETICA (*Art of Poetry*) which was adapted as a handbook on style by the neoclassicists of the 16th and 17th centuries. Horace died in 8, only a few months after the death of his friend and supporter Maecenas, beside whose grave he was buried. See CANIDIA.

Horace (1640). A tragedy by Pierre CORNEILLE. The material of the play is derived from Livy. Horace and his two brothers are chosen to represent Rome, Curiace and his two brothers to represent Alba, in a combat that will decide the war between the two cities. When his brothers are killed, Horace pretends to flee and thus contrives to kill each adversary separately. His sister Camille, the betrothed of Curiace, curses Rome. Infuriated, Horace kills her and is summoned before the king. Curiace's sister Sabine begs to be executed in Horace's place. His father pleads for him, and in view of his brave deed the king pardons Horace.

Horace. The young lover of Agnès in Molière's comedy L'ECOLE DES FEMMES.

Horatian Ode upon Cromwell's Return from Ireland, An (1650). A poem by Andrew MARVELL. It celebrates Cromwell as a kind of fated and elemental force, but with elements of pity for Charles I and strong suggestions of uneasiness about a future with Cromwell in supreme power.

Horatii, the three. In Roman legend, three brothers of the Horatia gens, or clan. They are celebrated for their combat with the three Curiatii, brothers from Alba Longa, to determine whether Rome or Alba was supreme. Two of the Horatii fell, while the Curiatii, though each was severely wounded, stood their ground. The surviving Horatius, unhurt, feigned flight. The Curiatii pursued him at unequal distances because of their wounds, and Horatius turned and killed them severally. He returned home in triumph bearing the bodies of the three Curiatii. His sister Horatia, recognizing one of the bodies as her betrothed, began to weep. Angered by her tears in his moment of triumph, Horatius plunged his sword into her breast, exclaiming: "So perish every Roman woman who bewails a foe." Horatius was condemned to death for this murder, but was acquitted with a token punishment: a beam symbolizing a yoke was erected across the street and Horatius passed under it with covered head, thus showing submission to Roman law. The beam came to be known as "sister's gibbet."

Horatio. In Shakespeare's HAMLET, the loyal friend and confidant whom the dying Hamlet adjures:

If thou didst ever hold me in thy heart,
Absent thee from felicity awhile,
And in this harsh world draw thy breath in pain,
To tell my story.

Horatius Cocles. Legendary hero of ancient Rome. When Lars PORSENA attacked Rome in the 6th century B.C., Horatius and two companions defended a bridge across the Tiber against the entire Etruscan army while the bridge behind them was destroyed by the Romans. Horatius then swam the river safely. In his honor a statue was erected and he was given as much land as he could plow in a day. Another version has Horatius fighting alone and drowning in the Tiber.

Horatius' exploits are the subject of the poem *Horatius* in Macaulay's book of poems, *The Lays of Ancient Rome* (1842).

Horn, King. Hero of a 12th-century French metrical romance and a 13th-century English one. Son of the king of Sudenne, he is set adrift by the Saracen pirates who kill his parents. He comes to Westernesse, where he is brought up by the king and becomes the lover of the princess Rymenhild (or Rimel). A companion betrays the affair, and Horn is banished. As a disguised adventurer he defeats a Saracen invasion in Ireland, but declines the reward of marriage to the princess and returns to Westernesse to free Rymenhild from the threat of an unwelcome marriage, proving his identity by a magic ring she had given him. He leaves to recapture Sudenne from the Saracens, returns to release Rymenhild from a second unwelcome marriage, and finally takes her home to rule happily as king and queen of Sudenne. *Horn Childe* is a 14th-century English imitation with some variations. *Hind Horn* is a ballad describing Horn's return to Rymenhild disguised as a palmer.

Hornblower, Horatio. The courageous but sensitive hero of a series of popular novels by C. S. FORESTER. The novels, notable for their authentic historical background, follow Hornblower's naval career from midshipman to admiral in the wars against Napoleon. The character appeared in *The Happy Return* (1937), *Lord Hornblower* (1946), *Mr. Midshipman Hornblower* (1950), and other books.

Horn Childe. See HORN, KING.

Hornie, Auld. See AULD HORNIE.

Horn of Fidelity. A horn sent by Morgan le Fay to King Arthur. No lady could drink out of it who was not "to her husband true"; all others were sure to spill the contents. The horn was carried to King Mark, and "his queene with a hundred ladies more" tried the experiment. Only four ladies present managed to "drinke cleane." Ariosto's enchanted cup possessed a similar spell. See MANTLE OF FIDELITY.

Horn of Plenty. See CORNUCOPIA.

Horns of Cuckoldry. See CUCKOLD.

Hornung, Ernest William (1866–1921). English novelist and short-story writer. He created RAFFLES, hero of *The Amateur Cracksman* (1899) and other books, and wrote novels about Australia. Hornung was the brother-in-law of Sir Arthur Conan Doyle.

Horsa. See HENGIST.

Horse Sacrifice. In Hindu history, the *Ashvamedha*. This ritual was performed in ancient times by the absolute ruler of India in order to show his complete control over the land.

Horse's Mouth, The (1944). A novel by Joyce CARY, the third in his first trilogy. It is the story of Gulley Jimson, passionate artist and exuberant, rascally, comic old man, whose hero is William Blake.

Herself Surprised (1941) is about one of Gulley's mistresses, the fascinating, down-to-earth Sara Monday. She is successively cook, fine lady, housekeeper, thief, and respectable middle-class wife. *To Be a Pilgrim* (1942) is the story of Sara's other lover, the religious, near senile lawyer, Mr. Wilcher. The central character of each book tells his own story in his own distinctive idiom.

Hortensio. A friend to Petruchio and unsuccessful suitor to Bianca in Shakespeare's TAMING OF THE SHREW. It is at Hortensio's suggestion that Petruchio sets out to win the shrewish Katharina. Hortensio, rejected by Bianca, marries a rich but unmanageable widow.

Horus. A major god of the ancient Egyptians, the son of Osiris and Isis, sometimes referred to as the god of silence. The Greeks called him Harpocrates and portrayed "Horus the Child" as a boy with a finger in his mouth. As one of the solar deities, he was represented by a hawk, or as a hawk-headed man; his emblem was the winged sun disk.

Hosea. An Old Testament book named for its author, an 8th-century (B.C.) prophet. The book is in two distinct parts. The first, a personal history of the prophet's home life with an errant wife, can be read as an allegory of God's trials with a sinful Israel. The second part is a catalogue of Israel's wickedness.

Host (Lat. *hostia,* an animal offered as a sacrificial victim). Bread consecrated in the Eucharist. It is so called in the Latin Church because it is considered a real victim of flesh, blood, and spirit, offered up in re-creation of Christ's sacrifice. At the service of Benediction, or when carried in procession, it is exposed in a vessel called a *monstrance. The elevation of the Host* refers to that moment when the celebrant of the Mass lifts up the Host immediately after its consecration, so that it may be seen by the people.

Hostage, The (L'Otage; 1909). A poetic drama by Paul CLAUDEL. It is the first of the plays, which with *Crusts* and *The Humiliation of the Father* form a trilogy, about the aristocratic Coufontaine family during the 19th century. Sygne de Coufontaine saves the pope by marrying her former servant Toussaint Turelure, an opportunist now become the most powerful man in France. However, she cannot complete her sacrifice by ceasing to hate her husband and their new-born son; consequently, when the cousin she loves tries to shoot Turelure, she intercepts the bullet and dies. In *Crusts* (*Le Pain Dur;* 1914) the son Louis causes his father's death and marries a Jewish woman, Sichel. *The Humiliation of the Father* (*Le Père humilié;* 1916) describes the love between their blind daughter Pensée and the brothers Orian and Orso de Homodarmes.

Hostos, Eugenio María de (1839–1903). Puerto Rican educator and man of letters. Hostos was educated in Spain where he wrote *La peregrinación de Bayoán* (1863), a political novel, and fought for the short-lived republic of 1868. His hopes that Puerto Rico might be granted autonomy with Santo Domingo and Cuba in a confederation of the Antilles were dashed by the imperialist attitude of the Spanish republicans. Hostos continued, however, to work for this goal in Santo Domingo, where he lived until

1889, establishing its first normal school. After a 10-year stay in Chile, he returned to Santo Domingo in 1900, bitterly disappointed at the results of the Spanish-American War, which finally doomed his dream of Antillean federation.

Hostos is remembered, not only as a patriot, but also as an enlightened teacher, dedicated to progress and truth. His best-known work, *Moral social* (1888), is a guide to ethical social conduct which was designed as a school text. He also wrote a famous essay (1872) on *Hamlet*.

Hotel, The (1927). A novel by Elizabeth BOWEN. She satirizes the empty social round of idle middle-class English people in a Riviera hotel. The heroine, Sydney Warren, passes through a period of devotion to a sophisticated older woman, a brief engagement to a clergyman, and then emerges from the hotel to freedom.

Hotel Universe (1930). A play by Philip BARRY. Stephen Field's experience of life and the depth of his philosophy enable the old man to act as a sort of mystic psychiatrist for a number of guests in his home in southern France.

Hotson, Leslie (1897–). American scholar. One of the most indefatigable of 20th-century Shakespearean scholars, Hotson has established a reputation as a literary detective, largely as a result of his exhaustive research among unpublished records. His discoveries include the details of Christopher Marlowe's murder (*The Death of Christopher Marlowe*, 1925); the uncovering of new records related to Shakespeare's life (*I, William Shakespeare*, 1937; *Shakespeare versus Shallow*, 1931); an extraordinarily well-documented account of the first performance of *Twelfth Night* (*The First Night of "Twelfth Night"*, 1954) and a highly controversial theory that Shakespeare's Globe was actually a theatre in the round (*Shakespeare's Wooden O*, 1959).

Houdon, Jean Antoine (1741–1828). French sculptor. He is famous for his animated, vigorously conceived yet delicately executed busts. He portrayed, among others, Voltaire, Diderot, Mirabeau, Jean Jacques Rousseau, George Washington, and Benjamin Franklin.

Hough, Emerson (1857–1923). American novelist. He is known especially for *The Mississippi Bubble* (1902), about the 18th-century French speculation in Louisiana. His other novels include *The Covered Wagon* (1922), about a train of 200 wagons moving westward in 1848, and *North of Thirty-Six* (1923), a story of herding on the Chisholm Trail.

Houghton, William Stanley (1881–1913). English dramatist. He became famous and made a fortune from one work, *Hindle Wakes* (1912). Within a year of the first performance in London, the play had been acted 2,000 times in London, Manchester, New York, and Chicago. It deals with the cotton mills districts of Lancashire. Houghton had begun his career in the business of his father, who was a cotton merchant.

Hougron, Jean (1923–). French novelist. His first six novels, including *Reap the Whirlwind* (*Tu récolteras la tempête;* 1950) and *Blaze of the Sun* (*Soleil au ventre;* 1952), describe aspects of the hatred caused by the war in Indo-China. Later books are psychological suspense stories, such as *Question of Character* (*Je reviendrai à Kandara;* 1955).

Hound of Heaven, The (1893). The best-known poem of Francis THOMPSON. In startling cosmic imagery, arresting cadences, it presents the "autobiography" of a fugitive from God's redemptive love.

houris. Black-eyed damsels said to be the reward of the faithful in the Muslim Paradise. Possessed of perpetual youth and beauty, they can renew their virginity at pleasure and are always equal in age with their husbands. According to the Koran, every believer will have 72 of these *houris* in Paradise and, depending on his wish, his intercourse may be fruitful or otherwise; if an offspring is desired, it will grow to full estate in an hour.

Hours, The (Horai). Greek goddesses of the seasons. In Greek, the word implied seasons, rather than hours, and these goddesses varied in number according to various concepts of the number of seasons in the year. Hesiod named them Eunomia, Dike, and Irene (Eirene).

Hours of Idleness (1807). The 1st book of poems published by Lord BYRON. He was only 19 at the time, and some of the poems were written years earlier. The severe criticism in the *Edinburgh Review* brought forth the satire ENGLISH BARDS AND SCOTCH REVIEWERS, Byron's first mature work.

House in Paris, The (1935). A novel by Elizabeth BOWEN. A story of complex love affairs, infidelities, and tragedy is revealed largely through two children who meet by chance at a house in Paris for a day. The boy Leopold, the illegitimate issue of his mother's early love affair, is finally taken home to his mother and her new husband.

House of Fame, The (probably 1379 or 1380). An unfinished poem by Geoffrey CHAUCER, of 2158 lines in octosyllabic couplets. It begins as a love-vision of the French type, but draws more on the works of Ovid, Vergil, and Dante. In the first "book" the poet introduces his dream and describes finding himself in the Temple of Venus. Here he finds engraved Vergil's story of Dido and Aeneas. In the second book he conducts a lively conversation with a great shining eagle who carries him to the House of Fame, presumably to learn more about love. But the third section shows lady Fame in her house distributing fame and slander among some of her applicants and denying any renown to others, all with arbitrary capriciousness. Then the poet is taken to the House of Rumor, inhabited by shipmen, pilgrims, couriers, and other gossips, who increase the falsity of their tidings with each retelling.

House of Life, The. A sonnet sequence by Dante Gabriel ROSSETTI, written during the period between 1848 and 1881. Chiefly autobiographical, it was inspired by Elizabeth SIDDAL, the author's wife. The title refers to the house of human life in astrology.

House of Mirth, The (1905). A novel by Edith WHARTON. Lily Bart, an orphan, tries to secure a wealthy husband, rejecting Lawrence Seldon, whom she loves but who lacks a fortune. Lily becomes involved with another man who tries to blackmail her, and is falsely accused of an intrigue with another woman's husband. Her fortunes become progressively worse until she becomes a milliner and eventually takes an overdose of sleeping pills. The intention of the novel was to satirize and reveal the weaknesses of New York society.

House of Pride. See FAERIE QUEENE, THE.

House of Riches. See FAERIE QUEENE, THE.

House of the Dead, The (Zapiski iz myortvogo doma; 1861–1862). An account of life in a Siberian prison by Feodor DOSTOEVSKI. The work is based on Dostoevski's own experiences in the Omsk prison (1850–1854), to which he was sentenced for having belonged to the Petrashevski circle, a study group interested in French Utopian socialism.

House of the Seven Gables, The (1851). A novel by Nathaniel HAWTHORNE. Iron-willed, grasping Colonel Pyncheon obtained the desirable land on which he built the pretentious House of the Seven Gables by accusing its humble owner, one Matthew Maule, of witchcraft. Old Maule, hanged for his crime, cursed the Colonel, saying "God will give him blood to drink." That curse, reverberating down the generations, affects the whole family.

At the time of the story, the withered old spinster, Hepzibah Pyncheon, and her brother Clifford live in the house. Desperately poor, Hepzibah must open a cent-shop in order to refuse aid from Judge Jaffrey Pyncheon, the intellectual and moral heir of the old colonel. Clifford has just returned from an extended imprisonment for the murder of an uncle. The murder, in reality committed by Jaffrey, enabled the latter to gain control of the Pyncheon fortune. Clifford, a weak-willed aesthete, has been destroyed by the 30-year sentence.

Phoebe, a visiting Pyncheon country cousin, and Holgrave, the young daguerreotypist boarding in the house, fall in love. Holgrave, a descendent of Matthew Maule, breaks the family curse, refusing to betray Phoebe by exercising his mesmeric powers. Hawthorne, in treating the weight of past guilt, once again reveals an unpardonable sin: the violation of another's soul.

Housman, A[lfred] E[dward] (1859–1936). English poet and Latin scholar. He is best known for his collection of poems called A Shropshire Lad (1896). These lyrics, set against a background of the English countryside and showing the influence of traditional English ballads and classical verse, are marked by their spirit of irony, and by their melancholy sense of youthful disillusionment, the transitoriness of youth and love, and the sadness of life. Their tone is ascribed to the author's disappointment at his mediocre performance at his final examinations at Oxford and to his passionate love for a college friend, Moses Jackson. Jackson is referred to in the poems by the classical name of Terence. In later years Housman became a professor of Latin, edited Manilius' Astronomica, and published Last Poems (1922). These poems, and those collected posthumously by his brother, Laurence Housman, in More Poems (1936), were mostly written during the same period as A Shropshire Lad. Shropshire is an English county. Two of Housman's best-known poems are Loveliest of trees, the cherry now . . . and Terence, This [poetry] is Stupid Stuff. . . .

Housman, Laurence (1865–1959). English novelist, dramatist, and illustrator. He was the brother of A. E. Housman. His first—almost his only—popular success came by accident. He published anonymously An Englishwoman's Love Letters (1900). They were accepted by the public as genuine. With 32 of his plays censored in one way or another, he has been called "England's most censored playwright,"

but his Victoria Regina (1934), with Helen Hayes, was an enormous success in America. His work is brilliantly versatile: he was a beautiful draughtsman, a fine poet, and a delightful writer of fantastic stories.

Houssain. The brother of Prince Ahmed in one of the Arabian Nights stories. He possesses a piece of carpet or tapestry of such wonderful power that anyone has only to sit upon it and be transported in a moment to any place he desires. See CARPET, MAGIC.

Houston, Sam[uel] (1793–1863). American soldier and statesman. Settling in Texas in 1833, Houston became a champion of Texan independence from Mexico. As commander-in-chief of the Texan army, he decisively defeated General Santa Anna at San Jacinto (1836) and served as president of the new republic (1836–1838, 1841–1844). After Texas was admitted to the Union in 1845, he became one of the first two senators from the state. He was elected governor in 1859 but was deposed when he refused to approve the entrance of Texas into the Confederacy.

Houyhnhnmland (pronounced whinnimland). The country of Gulliver's fourth voyage in Jonathan Swift's GULLIVER'S TRAVELS, inhabited by Houyhnhnms, a race of horses. The Houyhnhnms, an embodiment of all that is good in mankind, are endowed with virtue and reason and live an idyllic existence. They hold in subjection the YAHOO, an inferior race whom Gulliver closely resembles. The Houyhnhnms consider Gulliver inferior, but he learns from them—so much so that, when he returns finally to his own country, he finds his fellow man so repellent that he becomes a confirmed misanthrope.

Hovey, Richard (1864–1900). American poet and dramatist. Hovey studied painting, became a candidate for priest's orders (never completed), and finally turned to newspaper work. Known for his exaggerated behavior, he adopted the costume of Oscar Wilde. He was impressed by Mallarmé and Maeterlinck, translating several of the latter's plays into English. In 1892, he and his friend Bliss Carman went to Nova Scotia and New Brunswick; the two then published Songs from Vagabondia (1894). Hovey's best-known poems include Men of Dartmouth, Eleazar Wheelock, and Stein Song.

Howard, Leslie (1893–1943). English actor. He was popular in the U.S. as both a stage and screen performer, appearing in Berkeley Square, Hamlet and The Petrified Forest. He died in an airplane accident in World War II (his plane was probably shot down).

Howard, Sidney [Coe] (1891–1939). American dramatist. Howard early did adaptations from foreign plays and collaborated with Edward Sheldon on Bewitched (1924). His first original play to attract attention was the Pulitzer Prize-winning THEY KNEW WHAT THEY WANTED. Best known of his later plays are THE SILVER CORD and Yellow Jacket (1934), a documentary dealing with the conquest of yellow fever, written with Paul de Kruif. Howard also wrote Lucky Sam McCarver (1925); Ned McCobb's Daughter (1926); Salvation (1928), with Charles MacARTHUR; Lute Song (1930), with Will Irwin; and Dodsworth (1934), with Sinclair Lewis.

Howards End (1910). A novel by E. M. FORSTER. It deals with an English country house called Howards End and its influence on the lives of the materialistic Wilcoxes, the cultured and idealistic Schlegel sisters, and the poor bank clerk Leonard Bast. The Schlegels try to befriend Bast. Mr. Wilcox, whom Margaret Schlegel later marries, gives him financial advice which ruins him. Helen Schlegel becomes his mistress for a short time and bears his son; thereupon Charles Wilcox thrashes and accidentally kills him. The house passes from intuitive, half-mystical Mrs. Wilcox to her husband's second wife, Margaret Schlegel, to Margaret's nephew, Leonard Bast's son. Illustrating Forster's motto "Only connect," the house brings together three important elements in English society: money and successful business in the Wilcoxes, culture in the Schlegels, and the lower classes in Leonard Bast.

Howe, Anna. In Samuel Richardson's novel CLARISSA HARLOWE, the friend and correspondent of Clarissa. She treats Clarissa with loyalty and affection, but more in the spirit of worldly prudence than with understanding. She is unable to save Clarissa, despite her sound and practical common sense.

Howe, E[dgar] W[atson] (1853–1937). American editor and novelist. He is known for his first novel, *The Story of a Country Town* (1883), one of the early examples of realism in American fiction. Howe wrote other novels of less importance and several collections of editorials and aphorisms, including *Lay Sermons* (1911), *Ventures in Common Sense* (1919), and *The Indignations of E. W. Howe* (1933).

Howe, Julia Ward (1819–1910). American poet and reformer. In 1843 she married Samuel Gridley Howe, the noted humanitarian and teacher of the blind, and soon came to know many of New England's distinguished men and women. After her husband's death she continued his work and lectured on woman suffrage, prison reform, and international peace. Although she is remembered chiefly for THE BATTLE HYMN OF THE REPUBLIC, she wrote several collections of verse, including *Passion Flowers* (1854) and *Later Lyrics* (1866), and is the author of *Sex and Education* (1874), *Modern Society* (1881), and *Reminiscences* (1899).

Howe, M[ark] A[ntony] DeWolfe (1864–1960). American biographer and editor. Howe was associated with several magazines, especially the *Atlantic Monthly*. Although his books have a wide range, he was preeminent in the field of biography. He wrote biographies of Phillips Brooks (1899), Charles Eliot Norton (1913), Barrett Wendell (1924), for which he was awarded a Pulitzer Prize, John Jay Chapman (1937), and several others. He also edited the series *Beacon Biographies* (31 vols., 1899–1910) and wrote several volumes of verse. *A Venture in Remembrance* (1941) is his autobiography.

Howe, Samuel Gridley (1801–1876). American physician, teacher, and humanitarian. After receiving a medical degree from Harvard in 1824, he sailed to Greece, where he spent six years aiding the Greeks in their struggle for independence from Turkey. In 1831 he was named director of the school for the blind in Boston that later became the Perkins Institute; his best-known patient was the blind deaf-mute Laura Bridgman (1829–1889), whom he trained by means of a raised type that he had devised and by other methods that later proved successful with Helen Keller. He was also interested in helping other handicapped persons. Active in the antislavery clause, he

founded, with his wife, Julia Ward HOWE, an abolitionist newspaper, *The Commonwealth*. He subsequently returned to Europe to help the Cretans in their revolt against the Turks. His best-known work is *Historical Sketches of the Greek Revolution* (1828). Mrs. Howe wrote a *Memoir* (1876) of her husband's life.

Howell, James (1594?–1666). Welsh-born English author. He is best known for his *Epistolae Hoelianae: Familiar Letters* (1645–1655), most of which were written while he was imprisoned as a Royalist sympathizer during the Civil War. He also compiled a *Lexicon Tetraglotton* (1660), a polyglot dictionary of English, French, Italian, and Spanish.

Howells, William Dean (1837–1920). American novelist, editor, critic, and poet. Born and raised in Ohio, he had little schooling, but regularly contributed poems and tales to newspapers. Howells wrote of his boyhood and youth in the autobiographical *A Boy's Town* (1890) and *Years of my Youth* (1916). By the time he was 23, he had published a book of poems, *Poems of Two Friends* (1860), and a campaign life of Abraham Lincoln. In 1860, he made a literary pilgrimage to Boston, where he was received by Lowell, Holmes, and Fields.

The reward for his campaign biography was the consulship in Venice, where Howells spent the war years. On his return, he published *Venetian Life* (1866), a series of travel letters and impressions. He worked for several magazines, finally becoming the editor of THE ATLANTIC MONTHLY in 1871. A firm friend of Mark Twain, he also encouraged another admirer, the young Henry James.

Howells' most important contribution to literary criticism is his theory of realistic fiction. He shared with George Eliot a literary interest in the commonplace, and defined realism as "nothing more or less than the truthful treatment of material." Howells' bias is revealed, however, when he chooses Jane Austen as the most truthful of writers. Among his own books, THEIR WEDDING JOURNEY, A MODERN INSTANCE, and THE RISE OF SILAS LAPHAM illustrate his theory best.

Leaving the *Atlantic,* Howells wrote a column for *Harper's;* influenced by Tolstoy and the American socialist Laurence Gronlund, he supplemented his realism with liberal views. A HAZARD OF NEW FORTUNES and A TRAVELLER FROM ALTRURIA are studies of American social institutions. Later in life, his militant liberalism subsiding, Howells continued to write realistic novels. Among them, *The Landlord at Lion's Head* (1897) and *The Kentons* (1902) approach his best earlier work in quality. He issued a number of reviews and articles collected from magazines, the most important of which is *My Mark Twain* (1910).

Howells' reputation continued to grow; known as the dean of American letters, he was president of the American Academy of Arts and Letters. Although he praised the posthumously published poems of Emily Dickinson, and encouraged Stephen Crane and Frank Norris, he was regarded as a genteel sentimentalist by Sinclair Lewis, H. L. Mencken, and Theodore Dreiser. Modern evaluation, restoring his reputation, grants him unquestioned historical importance in the development of American literature. See A CHANCE ACQUAINTANCE; THE LADY OF THE AROOSTOOK; INDIAN SUMMER.

How Green Was My Valley (1940). A popular novel by Richard LLEWELLYN. Written in a lyrical style, it tells the story of a Welsh mining family.

Howleglas or **Owlglass, Tyll.** See EULEN-SPIEGEL.

How They Brought the Good News from Ghent to Aix (1845). A ballad by Robert BROWNING. Noted for its onomatopoetic effects, it describes a purely imaginary incident.

How to Write Short Stories (1924). A collection of 10 stories by Ring LARDNER. The sardonic preface discloses that the purpose of the volume is to discuss the art of short-story writing, the stories that follow being "samples." Among them are such classic Lardner tales as *Alibi Ike* and *Champion.*

Hrosvitha or **Hrotsvitha.** See ROSWITHA.

Hrothgar. See BEOWULF.

Hsi Yü Chi (Journey to the West). Chinese novel of the Ming Dynasty (1368-1644) by Wu Ch'eng-en (c. 1500-1580). Describes the adventures of the priest Hsüan-tsang during his pilgrimage to India in search of the scriptures, accompanied by Monkey and other creatures. Humorous, satirical, and absurd, it has enjoyed continued popularity. Partially translated by Arthur Waley, *Monkey* (1943).

Hsün Tzu. Chinese Confucian work attributed to Hsün Ch'ing (c. 300 B.C.). It exerted considerable influence during the Han period (202 B.C.–A.D. 220). The first Confucian text in expository form, it contradicts the *Mencius* by saying that man is by nature evil, and attacks superstition, extolling rationalism in its stead. It places great emphasis on the need for education.

Huang Ti. A legendary emperor of China (c. 2600 B.C.). He is credited with the invention of bricks, musical instruments, etc. His name means yellow emperor.

Hubbard, Elbert (1856-1915). American businessman, printer, and writer. At the age of 36, Hubbard stopped selling soap and toured Europe. Highly impressed by the Kelmscott Press of William Morris, he returned to East Aurora, New York, and founded the Roycroft Press. He issued many "arty" books and magazines, and produced such household objects as pottery, metal and leather work, and furniture. He wrote a series of 170 *Little Journeys* to the homes of notable men and women, and published two magazines, *The Philistine* (1895-1915) and *The Fra* (1908-1917), largely filled with his own writings. Himself a self-conscious aesthete, Hubbard was known as "Fra Elbertus" or "the Fra." His most successful publication was A MESSAGE TO GARCIA, an exhortation to fidelity and enterprise that became enormously popular among businessmen; they distributed copies to their employees to provide "inspiration." Hubbard appeared on the vaudeville stage, and attracted many people to East Aurora. He died when the *S. S. Lusitania* was sunk in the Irish Sea by a German submarine.

Huch, Ricarda (1864-1947). German novelist, poet, and essayist. She was especially noted for her historical sense as expressed, for example, in the novels of her Garibaldi cycle: *Die Verteidigung Roms* (*The Defense of Rome,* 1906), *Der Kampf um Rome* (*The Struggle for Rome,* 1907) and *Das Leben des Grafen Frederigo Confalonieri* (*Life of Count Frederigo Confalonieri,* 1910). Her essays on German romanticism are also well known.

Huckleberry Finn, The Adventures of (1884). A novel by Mark TWAIN. Huck escapes from the lonely cabin in which his drunken, brutal father had imprisoned him; on Jackson's Island he meets Jim, a runaway slave. Together they float down the Mississippi River on a raft, occasionally stopping at the banks. In these brief episodes Huck participates in the lives of others, witnessing corruption, moral decay, and intellectual impoverishment. He learns from Jim of the dignity and worth of a human being. Life on the river comes to an end when Jim is captured; Huck, reunited with TOM SAWYER, helps him to escape, subordinating society's morality to his own sense of justice and honor. When Tom's Aunt Sally says she wants to adopt Huck, he decides to head westward to avoid being "sivilized."

Hudibras (1663, 1664, 1678). A long satirical poem in three parts by Samuel BUTLER, directed against the hypocrisy and intolerance of the Puritans. Its hero Hudibras, modeled after various Presbyterian worthies of the Commonwealth, is a country justice who sets out with his squire Ralpho, an Independent, to reform abuses and enforce the laws for the suppression of popular amusements. Like Don Quixote, Hudibras is of comical appearance, humpbacked and potbellied, with an untidy yellow-red beard. He, too, rides a broken-down nag and receives much punishment in the performance of his exploits. The poem, written in jingling, doggerel couplets, gave rise to the adjective *hudibrastic,* meaning mock-heroic or in the style of *Hudibras.*

Hudson, Henry (died after 1611). English navigator and explorer. Engaged by the Dutch East India Co. to find a Northwest Passage to the Orient, he sailed to America on the *Half Moon* and explored the river that now bears his name, reaching as far as Albany (1609). On a later voyage he was set adrift by his own men.

Hudson, Sir Jeffrey (1619-1682). English dwarf, at one time page to Queen Henrietta Maria. When he was 30 years old, he was under two feet high, but later reached a height of about three feet nine inches. He was a cavalry captain in the Royalist army during the Civil War. Afterwards he was captured by pirates and sold as a slave in Barbary, but managed to escape. He is a character in Scott's *Peveril of the Peak* (1823). See William EVANS.

Hudson, Stephen. Pen name, **Sidney Schiff** (1869-1944). English novelist and translator. Most of his novels are about a single group of persons and include *Tony* (1924), *Richard, Myrtle, and I* (1926), and *A True Story* (1930). Hudson completed Scott Moncrieff's translation of Proust's *Remembrance of Things Past.*

Hudson, William Henry (1841-1922). English naturalist and novelist, born in Argentina of American parentage. He became a naturalized British subject in 1900. He is best known for his writings on nature subjects, especially those with an Argentine background. His books include *The Purple Land* (1885), *Argentine Ornithology* (1888-1889), *Nature in Downland* (1900), *El Ombú* (1902), *Little Boy Lost* (1905), and *A Shepherd's Life* (1910). He is best remembered for GREEN MANSIONS and his autobiographical *Far Away and Long Ago* (1918).

"Hudibras Catechized." An engraving by Hogarth for Samuel Butler's *Hudibras*. (1726).

Hudson River School. The name given to a group of 19th century U.S. artists who painted rural scenes, especially in the Catskills, after 1830. Realistic, poetic, or fantastic interpretations were given to these landscapes, which were popularized by Thomas Cole (1801–1848) and Asher B. Durant (1796–1886). Cole, the leader of the movement, painted both visionary and more factual views, while Durant represented large scenes with patiently accurate draftsmanship.

Hudson's Bay Company. A joint stock company chartered in 1670 by Charles II for the purpose of purchasing furs from the Indians. Its territory, the Hudson's Bay Territory or Rupert's Land, included all the streams flowing into Hudson Bay. It was sold to the British government (1869) and incorporated with the Dominion of Canada (1870).

Hueffer, Ford Madox. See Ford Madox FORD.

Huerta, Vicente García de la. See Vicente GARCÍA DE LA HUERTA.

Hughes, Charles Evans (1862–1948). American jurist and public official. Hughes's distinguished legal career led to his being elected governor of New York in 1906 and 1908. In 1910 he was appointed to the Supreme Court by President Taft, but resigned to run against Woodrow Wilson for the presidency in 1916. Defeated by a narrow margin, he returned to law practice, but served as secretary of state from 1921 to 1926 when he became a member of the courts of international arbitration and justice at the Hague. In 1930 President Hoover appointed him chief justice of the Supreme Court; he served until 1941. Mod-

erately conservative in his views, he supported many of the measures proposed by President Roosevelt, although he fought the president's court reorganization plan and opposed government agencies that usurped the functions of courts.

Hughes, Hatcher (1881–1945). American dramatist and teacher at Columbia University. He is best known for the Pulitzer Prize-winning *Hell-Bent for Heaven* (1923), a play about a religious fanatic among the North Carolina mountaineers. With Elmer Rice he wrote *Wake Up, Jonathan* (1921), and alone he wrote several other successful plays.

Hughes, [James] Langston (1902–). American poet. Marked by the use of the rhythms of the blues and the ballad, often documentary in tone, his poems deal with the trials and joys of the American Negro. He has published volumes of verse from *Weary Blues* (1926) and *The Dream Keeper* (1932) to *Ask Your Mama* (1961). From his own poem, *Cross*, he made the play *Mulatto* (1935); this in turn was produced in a musical version called *The Barrier* (1950). He is also known for his humorous sketches, written originally for a Negro newspaper, which are collected in *Simple Speaks His Mind* (1950) and *The Best of Simple* (1961). His other works include the novel *Not Without Laughter* (1930) and *The Ways of White Folks* (1934), a short-story collection.

Hughes, Richard (1900–). English novelist and dramatist. The novel A HIGH WIND IN JAMAICA is generally considered to be his greatest achievement.

Hazard (1938) is a sea story. *The Fox in the Attic* (1961) is the first part of a long historical novel to be entitled *The Human Predicament*. Described by its author as a study of his own times, the novel opens in 1923 and is to close with the Second World War.

Hughes, Thomas (1822–1896). English jurist, reformer, and author. He wrote Tom Brown's School Days and its sequel, *Tom Brown at Oxford* (1861). He was associated with Christian Socialism, and worked ardently to improve the conditions of the poor.

Hugh of Lincoln, St. (c. 1246–1255). English boy said to have been tortured and murdered by the Jews of Lincoln, a number of whom were hanged in consequence. Legends of miracles gathered around his name, such as the story that he spoke to his mother, though dead, and identified his murderer. His tragedy appears in Chaucer's Prioress's Tale, *Alphonsus of Lincoln* (1459), Marlowe's *The Jew of Malta* (1589), and a number of ballads such as *Sir Hugh, Hugh of Lincoln, The Jew's Daughter*.

Hugh Selwyn Mauberley (1920). A poem in several sections by Ezra Pound. Although there has been much discussion on the exact relationship between Pound and his persona Mauberley, the poem represents Pound's farewell to London and is a vehement denunciation of a civilization marked by war, the commercialization of the arts, and a general and sexual sterility. The artist either prostitutes his art as did Arnold Bennett ("Mr. Nixon") or he manages to barely exist in a solitary and destitute state as did Ford Madox Ford (the "stylist"). Mauberley himself is finally capable of only a refined and delicate art in such a corrupt civilization. It has been suggested that Mauberley represents the poet Pound would have become had he remained the simple imagist, unconcerned by the cultural and economic problems that from this point on were to occupy him.

Hugin and Munin. In Scandinavian mythology, the two ravens, typifying Thought and Memory, which sat on Odin's shoulders and brought him news from earth.

Hugo, Victor [Marie] (1802–1885). French poet, novelist, dramatist, and leader of the romantic movement in France. Like Chateaubriand, the literary figure he so admired, Hugo played an active part in political life. Serving first as a peer under the monarchy of Louis Philippe, he transferred his loyalties to the republicans in 1848 and was elected to the popular assembly. Deeply disturbed by the restoration of the Second Empire, in 1851 Hugo fled France, living in exile for 18 years in the Channel Islands. His last public office was held under the Third Republic, in which he served as a senator. His love of liberty and his hopes for mankind were regarded, however, as a poet's dream, and Hugo had little real political influence during this period. If he lacked political influence, Hugo's influence upon French literature of the 19th century was unrivaled. In each genre he revealed himself as a romantic par excellence (see romanticism). The voice of his poetry is always musical, often highly personal, reflective, and sometimes characterized by gentle melancholy. Often considered France's greatest lyric poet, Hugo experimented with language and with rhythm, displaying a fine sensitivity to the sound and color of

words. *Les Feuilles d'Automne* (1831) and *Contemplations* (1856), both describe the moods and emotions of the poet in richly sonorous verse. In other volumes, however, such as *Les Châtiments* (1853) which attacked Napoleon III or *Les Chants du Crépuscule* (1835), Hugo conceived of the poet's role as public and prophetic. The poet should lead and guide the people, rather than express his own responses to nature's beauty or personal sorrow. This same strain appears again in Hugo's long novels which reveal a humanitarian interest in the problems and suffering of the common man. Stylistically the novels are marked by violent melodrama, panoramic sweep, and the colorful use of language. These novels, best known of Hugo's work to the English audience, include Han of Iceland, The Hunchback of Notre Dame, Les Misérables, Toilers of the Sea, The Man Who Laughs, and Ninety-Three. In the drama his preface to *Cromwell* (1827) became a manifesto adopted by the romantic dramatists. Hugo asserted the playwright's independence from the rigid rules of classicism. He suggested such innovations as a mixture of the comic and the tragic, colloquial dialogue, new freedom in meter and from the traditional unities of time and place. His own plays, historical melodramas filled with rather wooden typically romantic personages, include *Hernani* (1830), *Ruy Blas* (1838) and *Les Burgraves* (1843). Some of these are better known today as sources for operatic librettos, notably *Hernani* and *Le Roi S'amuse* (1832; *Rigoletto*), both set to music by Verdi, and *Angelo* (1835), which became Ponchielli's *La Gioconda*.

Huguenots. A term applied to French Protestants during the religious wars of the 16th and 17th centuries. The name was first applied to citizens of medieval Geneva who resisted the claims of the dukes of Savoy over the city; it is probably an adaptation of *Eidgenossen* (*Ger.,* "confederates"). See Nantes, Edict of.

Huis Clos. See No Exit.

Hulda. Old German goddess of marriage and fecundity who sent bridegrooms to maidens and children to the married. The name means "the Benignant," and is an euphemistic appellation.

Hull, Edith Maude. See Sheik, The.

Hull, Isaac. See Constitution.

Hull, Hell, and Halifax. An old beggars' and vagabonds' "prayer." As quoted by Taylor, the Water Poet (early 17th century), it was:

> From Hull, Hell, and Halifax,
> Good Lord, deliver us.

Hell was probably the least feared as being farthest from them; Hull was to be avoided because it was so well governed that beggars had little chance of getting anything without doing hard labor for it; and Halifax, because anyone caught stealing in that town was beheaded without intermediate proceedings.

Hulme, Thomas Ernest (1883–1917). English critic and philosopher. He is noted for *Speculations* (1924) and *Notes on Language and Style* (1929). He was killed in World War I, but his ideas were later widely popularized by T. S. Eliot and Ezra Pound. Hulme distinguished classicism, which he considered true and "realistic," from humanism and romanticism, both of which he judged false and "unrealistic." Humanism, he claimed, erroneously described man as "naturally" good and capable of perfection; classicism, on the contrary, truthfully depicted man as "intrinsically bad or limited, but disciplined by order and tradition to *something fairly decent*." Humanistic (and romantic) art, further, was undisciplined and imprecise, he concluded, while classic art was "clean, clearcut, and mechanical." See IMAGISM.

huma. A fabulous Oriental bird always on the wing. It is said that every head over which its shadow passes will wear a crown.

Human Age, The. A satirical prose epic by Wyndham LEWIS. It consists of *The Childermass* (1928), and *Monstre Gai* and *Malign Fiesta* (1955). The subject is a surrealistic journey to a nightmare heaven. The description is macabre and imaginative; the language is obscure—full of allusion, word-play, and parody.

Human Comedy, The. See COMÉDIE HUMAINE, LA.

Humanism. An attitude of the mind that accompanied the flowering of the RENAISSANCE. The term refers to several varied literary and scholarly activities inspired by the study of antiquity but differing in aim and scope. Humanism in the Renaissance took its name from the *studia humanitatis*, those studies (grammar, rhetoric, poetry, history, and moral philosophy) that were thought to possess human value: the ability to make man a fully realized human creature, elevated and distinct from the lower animals. The ancient writers of Greece and Rome were particularly revered, as it was felt that they had excelled in such studies and would thus be of value in teaching the modern Christian how to attain the perfections of life. This aspect of Humanism, sometimes called the REVIVAL OF ANTIQUITY, includes the study of the classics; editorial and philological work on ancient texts; the search of enthusiasts for unknown but extant manuscripts, statues, medals, and coins; the writing of modern works in classical Latin; and the teaching of the classics in universities and to the children of the nobility.

Our English term *humanists*, used to designate the participants in the above-mentioned activities, is derived from the Italian word *umanista*, which was first used in the late 16th century to describe a university teacher of the humanities. Renaissance humanists include scholars and poets such as Petrarch, often called the first humanist; instigators of "the revival" such as the Greek scholar Chrysoloras; the philologists Valla and Erasmus; archaeologists and antiquarians such as Poggio and Ciriaco; the educators Vittorino of Feltre and Guarino of Verona; philosophers, historians, and men of letters such as Pius II and Leonardo Bruni; and a host of secretaries, chancellors, legates, and other royal advisors who, having imbibed the spirit of the period, used their mastery of eloquence in practical labors. Outstanding English humanists during the Renaissance were More, Colet, Elyot, and Ascham.

The origins of Humanism have been found to lie in the introduction of Greek studies into Italy by refugee and other visiting scholars from the Byzantine world; and in the economic flowering of the Italian city-states, which provided the necessary wealth and leisure for cultural activities. From Italy, Humanism spread north to France, England, the Netherlands, and Germany as well as Spain. By the time of its arrival in the northern countries, however, the purely cultural aims gave way to the needs of the Reformation; theological disputation and educational theory assumed greater importance than the study and imitation of pagan authors and text. In succeeding centuries, the influence of Humanism persisted mainly in the school curricula.

Modern Humanism (see NEO-HUMANISM) only vaguely resembles the Renaissance brand, and is primarily a secular philosophy devoted to the propagation of a self-sufficient system of human values.

Humbaba. A one-eyed monster in the *Epic of* GILGAMESH. This gorgon-faced giant, whose eye can strike men dead, who breathes fire and plague, and who speaks in a whirlwind, is the guardian of the forest of the gods. He is killed by Gilgamesh and Enkidu, with the help of the sun-god, who blinds him with searing winds.

Humboldt, Baron **Alexander von** (1769–1859). German naturalist. With Aimé Bonpland, a French botanist, he traveled throughout Latin America (1799–1804), studying physical geography and meteorology; in the Andes, he determined the relationship between altitude and temperature, and he also discovered the cool Peruvian current that now bears his name. The volumes in his *Voyage aux régions équinoxiales du Nouveau Continent* (1807 ff.) greatly influenced later explorers and give an excellent picture of political and economic conditions in Latin America on the eve of independence. His main work is *Kosmos* (1845–1862), a description of the physical universe. He was the brother of Wilhelm von Humboldt.

Humboldt, Wilhelm von (1767–1835). German philologist, statesman, and educator. The brother of Alexander von Humboldt, he was a friend of both Geothe and Schiller. His most important work is *Über die Kawisprache auf der Insel Jawa* (*On the Kawi Language of the Island of Java*, 1836–1840). See WEIMAR CLASSICISM.

Hume, David (1711–1776). Scottish philosopher and historian. His empirical outlook is clearly seen in his *Natural History of Religion* (1757), *Dialogues concerning Natural Religion* (1779), in which anthropomorphism is assailed, and in his essay *On Miracles* where he asserts that "no testimony for any kind of miracle has ever amounted to a probability, much less a proof." His philosophical skepticism, often referred to as Humism, restricts human knowledge to the experience of ideas and impressions, and has been of extraordinary importance in the history of modern metaphysical thinking. Hume was the author of many treatises and essays, and of a history of England during the reigns of James I and Charles I. His best-known work is *Philosophical Essays Concerning Human Understanding* (1748), later issued as *An Enquiry Concerning Human Understanding*.

Humevesne. See Lord SUCKFIST.

Humiliation of the Father, The. See HOSTAGE, THE.

humor. An obsolete medical term for the supposed four principal humors or liquids of the body. In medieval times, these were supposed to be blood, phlegm, yellow bile, and black bile. They were thought to correspond to the four principal temperaments: the sanguine, the phlegmatic, the choleric, the melancholic. This idea was still popular in Elizabethan days. Ben Jonson's comedy, *Every Man in His Humour,* makes his characters stereotyped with one ruling temperament for each. Albrecht Dürer is said to have thought of the four temperaments and humors in connection with his paintings of the four evangelists.

Humperdinck, Engelbert (1854–1921). German composer. A friend of Richard Wagner, he is best known for his fairy-tale opera HÄNSEL UND GRETEL (1893). He also composed incidental music for Shakespeare and for Maeterlinck's play *The Blue Bird.*

Humphrey. Duke of **Gloucester** and earl of **Pembroke** (1391–1447). English noble. The youngest son of Henry IV, he was known as a patron of learning and donated his library to Balliol College, Oxford. Upon the death of his brother Henry V, he served as protector for the young Henry VI. His first marriage having been annulled in 1428, he married his mistress, Eleanor Cobham, whose dabblings in sorcery contributed to his downfall in 1447. He appears in Shakespeare's HENRY IV: PART II, HENRY V, and HENRY VI: PART I and PART II.

Humphrey Clinker, The Expedition of (1771). An epistolary novel by Tobias SMOLLETT. The letters are written by Matthew BRAMBLE, his sister Tabitha, their niece, their nephew, and their maid Winifred JENKINS. Each correspondent has a highly individual style and caricatures himself unwittingly. The titular hero of this comic masterpiece, who plays a lesser role than the Brambles, is a workhouse lad who enters into their service by chance and who later becomes a Methodist preacher. He falls in love with Winifred, and is eventually found to be the natural son of Mr. Bramble. The "expedition" of the title is a family tour through England and Scotland, during which the correspondents express surprisingly varied reactions to the same events. Of particular note is the picture of Hot Wells (a sobriquet for the city of Bath), a fashionable watering place. See Captain LISMAHAGO.

Humphries, David. See HARTFORD WITS.

Hunchback of Notre Dame, The (*Notre Dame de Paris*) (1831). A romance of medieval times by Victor HUGO centering about the life of the great Parisian cathedral. The principal characters are Esmeralda, the gypsy dancer in love with Captain Phoebus, Claude Frollo, the hypocritical archdeacon, whose evil passion for Esmeralda causes him to denounce her as a witch, and Quasimodo, the "Hunchback of Notre Dame," a deformed bellringer, whose devotion saves Esmeralda for a time when she seeks protection from the mob in the belfry of the Cathedral. Esmeralda is finally executed, and Quasimodo throws Frollo from the heights of Notre Dame.

Hundred Days. The days between March 20 and June 28, 1815. On March 20, Napoleon reached the Tuileries after his escape from Elba; June 28 was the date of the second restoration of Louis XVIII. Napoleon left Elba February 26; landed near Cannes, March 1; entered Paris, March 20; and signed his abdication June 22, three days after the fateful battle at WATERLOO.

Hundred-Handed, The (Hekatoncheires). In Greek mythology, three hundred-armed giants, off-spring of Ouranus and Ge. They assisted Zeus in his war against the Titans. Their names were Cottus (Kottos), Briareus (also called Aegaeon), and Gyes.

Hundred Years' War (1337–1453). The long series of wars between France and England, beginning in the reign of Edward III and ending in that of Henry VI.

The first battle was a naval action off Sluys, and the last the fight at Castillon. The war originated in English claims to the French crown, and resulted in the English being expelled from the whole of France, except Calais.

Huneker, James Gibbons (1860–1921). American critic and man of letters. Although Huneker's greatest area of concentration was music, he is known for his impressionistic criticism in all fields of art. *Iconoclasts* (1905) called attention to many European playwrights up to that time little known in the U.S. Other collections of critical and biographical pieces were *Mezzotints in Modern Music* (1899), *Chopin* (1900), *Overtones* (1904), *Egoists* (1909), and *New Cosmopolis* (1915). He also published two collections of short stories, *Melomaniacs* (1902) and *Visionaries* (1905), and one novel, PAINTED VEILS. *Steeplejack* (2 vols., 1919), his autobiography, contains many of his views on art.

Hungerford, Margaret Wolfe. Born **Hamilton** (1855?–1897). Irish novelist. She wrote more than 30 novels, of which the best-known is *Molly Bawn* (1878). Most of her books were signed "The Duchess."

hunger strike. The refusal of a prisoner or a prominent person to take any food until he has been released or secures some desired concession. The practice seems to have originated in Russia, but was widely employed by suffragette prisoners in England during the early years of the 20th century and later by Irish political prisoners. The hunger strike was used to particular effect by Mohandas K. GANDHI, the Indian nationalist, in his struggle with the British.

Hung Lou Meng. Chinese novel by Tso Hsueh-chin of the Ch'ing Dynasty (1644–1912). Autobiographical in nature, it details the decline in fortune of the Chia family, giving a vivid picture of the social life of the times. Written in the colloquial, it has had an enduring popularity. See Chi-chen Wang, *Dream of the Red Chamber* (1958).

Hunt, Henry. Called **Orator Hunt** (1773–1835). A persuasive orator who presided over the meeting in St. Peter's Field, Manchester, at the time of the PETERLOO MASSACRE (1819). Yeomen and soldiers charged upon the reform meeting, and the news of this outrage so aroused the poet Shelley in Italy that he wrote *The Masque of Anarchy.* Orator Hunt was sentenced to two years' imprisonment. Later he became a member of Parliament (1830–1833), and published his memoirs in 1820.

Hunt, [William] Holman (1827–1910). English painter. With John Everett Millais and Dante Gabriel Rossetti, Holman Hunt founded the PRE-RAPHAELITE BROTHERHOOD. In 1905 he published his two-volume *Pre-Raphaelitism and the Pre-Raphaelite Brotherhood;* in the same year he was awarded the Order of Merit.

Hunt, [James Henry] Leigh (1784–1859). English journalist, essayist, poet, and political radical. For years, in the face of poverty, vilification, and official persecution, Hunt edited a series of one-man journals.

From 1813 to 1815 he was imprisoned for attacking the future George IV in his *Examiner,* becoming a hero of the radicals. He is most important as an essayist and critic, early champion of Shelley and Keats. Byron was briefly Hunt's patron, but the two were unable to get along; Hunt's *Lord Byron and Some of His Contemporaries* (1828) reflects some bitterness. Though much of his prose is perspicacious and graceful, his poetry tends to be slight and sentimental. A few shorter poems, such as ABOU BEN ADHEM (1834) and *Jenny Kissed Me* (1844), and parts of *The Story of Rimini* (1816), are still of interest. Among his other works are: *Critical Essays* (1807); *The Round Table* (1817, with William HAZLITT); *The Months* (1821); *Men, Women and Books* (1847); *Autobiography* (1850).

Hunt, Violet (1866–1942). English biographer and novelist. She was daughter of the Pre-Raphaelite painter Alfred William Hunt and for some years mistress of Ford Madox FORD. Her autobiography *I Have This to Say* (1926) and her biography *The Wife of Rossetti* (1932) are valuable because she knew so many of the literary people of her day. Miss Hunt wrote garish novels, such as *White Rose of Weary Leaf* (1908), and macabre stories, such as *Tales of the Uneasy* (1910).

Hunter, Evan (1926–   ). American novelist. His first novel, *Blackboard Jungle* (1954), which grew out of his own experiences as a teacher, is a sensational exposé of the brutal underworld of a big-city high school. In *Strangers When We Meet* (1958), Hunter investigated marital infidelity in suburbia. He is also the author of *Matter of Conviction* (1959), and *Mothers and Daughters* (1961).

Hunter, Mr. and Mrs. Leo. In Charles Dickens' PICKWICK PAPERS, a celebrity-hungry couple who invite Pickwick and his friends to their house. Mrs. Hunter is the author of "Ode to an Expiring Frog," generally considered a masterpiece.

Huon de Bordeaux (early 13th century). French CHANSON DE GESTE, popularized through a prose version (1454) and the English translation by Lord Berners, *Huon of Burdeuxe* (c. 1540). Huon kills Charlot in self-defense, ignorant that his attacker is Charlemagne's son. His death sentence is suspended on condition that he go to the court of the Emir of Babylon, kill his most important knight, and kiss his daughter Esclairmonde three times. OBERON, king of the fairies, meets and befriends Huon, helping him to succeed in all his adventures and marry Esclairmonde. The tale was used by Christoph Martin Wieland in his epic poem *Oberon* (1780), and from there adapted by Weber for his opera *Oberon* (1826).

Hurd, Richard (1720–1808). English bishop, and author. His *Letters on Chivalry and Romance* (1762) set forth a historical approach to the study of the medieval romance in which the Gothic is contrasted with the classical art of Greece. Hurd's enthusiasm for the medieval and Gothic forms added greatly to the vogue of medievalism demonstrated in the poetry of James Macpherson, Thomas Chatterton, Thomas Percy, and others. Other works include an edition of the works of Horace (1749) and *Moral and Political Dialogues* (1759), which represents Joseph Addison and John Arbuthnot discussing feudalism amidst the ruins of Kenilworth.

Hurst, Fannie (1889–   ). American novelist and playwright. She began her long and successful career with such works as *Humoresque* (1919), a collection of stories about Jewish life in New York City. The title story tells of a poor boy who became a great violinist. *Lummox* (1923), the story of a servant girl whose greatness of soul shines amid her sordid surroundings, is one of her best-known novels. Her other books include *Star-Dust* (1921), *Back Street* (1931), *Imitation of Life* (1933), and *God Must be Sad* (1961). *Anatomy of Me* (1958) is her autobiography.

Hurstwood, George. A leading character in Dreiser's novel SISTER CARRIE. A wealthy man at the beginning of the novel, he helps Carrie in her rise to success but is himself destroyed in the process.

Hurtado de Mendoza, Diego (1503–1575). Spanish historian and poet. A member of one of Spain's noblest families, Hurtado was a humanist who read Greek, Hebrew, and Arabic as well as a distinguished diplomat who represented the king in Venice, Rome, and at the Council of Trent. A quarrel with another noble in 1568 led to his exile from Madrid. He retired to Granada, where he wrote his masterpiece, the *Guerra de Granada* (1627), a vivid history of the Morisco uprising of 1568–1571 which was modeled on the works of Tacitus and Sallust. His poetry is of two types: his sonnets and the *Fábula de Adonis, Hipómenes y Atalanta* reveal the influence of classical and Italian verse, but he was more successful with Spanish forms, as is shown by his witty, sometimes cynical, *redondillas*. The authorship of LAZARILLO DE TORMES has also been attributed to him. At his death he left all his books and manuscripts to the library of the Escorial.

Hu Shih (1891–1962). Ambassador to U.S. (1938–1942). President of Academia Sinica. One of modern China's greatest scholars, he wrote widely on philosophy, literature, and history. Author of *China's Place in the Present World Struggle* (1942).

Huss, John or **Jan Hus** (1369–1415). A Bohemian religious reformer. Rector of the University of Prague, he was condemned and burned at the stake for propagating a reform doctrine influenced by Wycliffe. His followers, the Hussites, organized a religious and political party and waged a fierce civil war (1419–1434). Their radical wing, the Taborites, became merged with the Bohemian Brethren. The conservatives or Calixtines later turned Lutheran or Roman Catholic.

Husserl, Edmund (1859–1938). German philosopher. He was a leader in the development of PHENOMENOLOGY as the basis for a new philosophical method. His work has had much influence on the existentialists, especially Jean-Paul Sartre, who studied under him from 1933 to 1934. His works include *Logical Inquiries (Logische Untersuchungen;* 1900–1901) and *Thoughts toward a Pure Phenomenology and Phenomenological Philosophy (Ideen zu einer reinen Phänomenologie und phänomenologischen Philosophie;* 1922).

Hussonet. A character in Gustave Flaubert's novel L'EDUCATION SENTIMENTALE. A friend of the hero Frédéric Moreau, Hussonet is an opportunistic journalist and editor. He voices firm support of the principles of 1848, but after Louis Napoleon's successful coup d'état he rapidly became an ardent supporter of the empire.

Hutchinson, Anne (1591–1643). English-born American religious teacher. Her assertion that salvation could come only through personal intuition of God's grace, and not through good works, conflicted with the beliefs of many clergymen in the Massachusetts Bay Colony and produced a bitter controversy that divided the entire settlement. In 1637 she was tried and banished from the colony "for traducing the ministers and their ministry." She and her family moved to Rhode Island, then to New York, where they were killed by Indians.

Hutchinson, A[rthur] S[tuart-]M[enteth] (1879–). Popular English novelist. He is author of IF WINTER COMES. Later works include *The Uncertain Trumpet* (1929), *He Looked for a City* (1940), and *Bring Back the Days* (1958).

Hutchinson, John. See Lucy HUTCHINSON.

Hutchinson, Lucy (1620–1675). English prose writer. She is known for her biography of her husband, Colonel John Hutchinson (1615–1664), an outstanding Puritan leader and soldier during the English Civil War. The work, entitled *Memoirs of the Life of Colonel Hutchinson*, was written after 1664 and published in 1806. It is considered noteworthy because of its character analysis of its subject, its defense of the Puritan character in general, and its picture of a 17th-century English Puritan household.

Hutchinson, R[ay] C[oryton] (1907–). English novelist. He has written many serious, sensitive books, including *The Answering Glory* (1932), *Recollection of a Journey* (1952), and *The Stepmother* (1955).

Hutten, Ulrich von (1488–1523). German humanist writer. Luther's most vigorous defender among the nobility, he was a progressive in religion and politics and wished to see Germany freed from the yoke of Rome, as is clearly expressed in his Lucianlike dialogue *Inspicientes* (*The Onlookers*, c. 1521). In matters of social change, however, he was conservative and opposed the rise of the cities. He has been suspected of writing the second half of the EPISTOLAE OBSCURORUM VIRORUM, but this is not certain.

Huxley, Aldous (1894–1963). English novelist, essayist, and satirist. He was the grandson of Thomas Huxley, great-nephew of Matthew Arnold, brother of Julian Huxley, and half-brother of Andrew Huxley (winner of the 1963 Nobel prize for physiology). Huxley's early work differs sharply from that of his later years, the break reflecting his conversion to mysticism. His early novels are witty, despairing evocations of society in the 1920's, satirizing the intellectual pretensions and poses of the era. Among the novels of this period are CROME YELLOW, *Antic Hay* (1923), *Those Barren Leaves* (1925), and POINT COUNTER POINT. Huxley's early short stories were collected in *Mortal Coils* (1922). In the 1930's Huxley's work began to reflect his growing preoccupation with occult studies. Among his later novels are EYELESS IN GAZA, AFTER MANY A SUMMER DIES THE SWAN, *Time Must Have a Stop* (1944), and *Island* (1962). Huxley is noted for his interest in science; his forty-fifth and last book, *Literature and Science* (1963) is an essay on both. BRAVE NEW WORLD, one of his best-known books, expresses his concern over the dangers of scientific progress; *Ape and Essence* (1948) is a satire about the world after an atomic war. His most important essays are *Music at Night* (1931), *Beyond the Mexique Bay* (1934), *The Perennial Philosophy* (1946), *The Doors of Perception* (1954), HEAVEN AND HELL, and *Brave New World Revisited* (1958).

Huxley studied medicine, but was prevented from practicing by a disease of the eyes that temporarily blinded him. He was associated with J. Middleton Murry and Katherine Mansfield in editing the *Athenaeum*. A friend and admirer of D. H. Lawrence, Huxley edited his letters in 1932; it was Lawrence who encouraged him to begin to search for spiritual values when he was in despair. In 1947 he settled in California, where he became associated with the Ramakrishna Mission in Hollywood and pursued various occult studies.

Huxley, Julian [Sorell] (1887–). English biologist and writer, brother of Aldous Huxley. He is the author of *Essays of a Biologist* (1923), *The Science of Life* (with H. G. and G. P. Wells, 1929), *What Dare I Think?* (1931), *The Captive Shrew and Other Poems* (1932), *Evolution: the Modern Synthesis* (1942), *New Bottles for New Wine* (1957), *The Humanist Frame, 1961*.

Huxley, Thomas Henry (1825–1895). English biologist and teacher. He is known for his defense of the theory of evolution held by Darwin, and for his lectures and writings popularizing science. His books include *Man's Place in Nature* (1863), *The Physical Basis of Life* (1868), *Lay Sermons, Addresses, and Reviews* (1870), *Science and Morals* (1886), *Essays upon Some Controverted Questions* (1892), and *Ethics and Evolution* (1893). Huxley was called "Darwin's Bulldog" and engaged in a controversy with the English statesman Gladstone on the question of scientific evolutionary theories as opposed to Biblical lore. He was the grandfather of Aldous and Julian HUXLEY.

Huysmans, Joris Karl (1848–1907). French novelist. Of Dutch ancestry, Huysmans was born, lived, and died in Paris, where after a prolonged spiritual struggle, he became a convert to Roman Catholicism. His neurasthenia and perverse tastes mark Huysmans as a typical DÉCADENT. Stylistically, his work is characterized by vivid and concrete figures, fantastic description, and a gift for portraying the grotesque. Among his novels are *Marthe, Histoire d'une Fille* (1876), a naturalistic account of a young prostitute's life; AGAINST THE GRAIN; *Là-Bas* (1891), part of a spiritual autobiography; and *La Cathédrale* (1898).

Hyacinth (Hyakinthos). In Greek mythology, a beautiful youth loved by Apollo. Zephyr, the jealous west wind, spoiled Apollo's aim when he was throwing the discus; it struck Hyacinth and he died. From his blood sprang the hyacinth (not the modern flower), bearing on its petals the cry of grief, AI. Hyakinthos was, in fact, a pre-Hellenic local deity in Amyclae, antedating Apollo's appearance in Greece.

Hyde, Douglas (1860–1949). Irish poet, scholar, and statesman. The first president of Eire (1938–1945), he wrote much of his work in Gaelic and devoted himself to the restoration of Irish culture. He was one of the founders of the ABBEY THEATRE and wrote many books on Irish history, literature, and folk lore. His *Love Songs of Connaught* (1894) is a classic compilation. His other works include *Answer to Communism* (1949), and *I Believed* (1950), an autobiographical account of how he came to join the Communist party, grew disillusioned with it, and became a convert to Catholicism.

Hyde, Edward. See earl of CLARENDON.

Hyde, Mr. See STRANGE CASE OF DR. JEKYLL AND MR. HYDE, THE.

Hyde Park (1). A large park in west-central London. It has become a symbol of freedom of speech, for the many speakers who hold impromptu meetings there are traditionally allowed to say anything they please, however critical it may be of the government.

(2) A village in New York State, overlooking the Hudson and famous as the residence of Franklin D. Roosevelt and his family. It now contains a museum devoted to mementoes of Roosevelt's presidency.

Hydra. A monstrous serpent of Greek mythology. It was born of TYPHON and ECHIDNA. Living in the swamps of the river Lerna, it had many heads; when one was cut off, another grew in its place. HERACLES finally killed it by having his friend Iolaus burn the stumps with torches as soon as the heads were removed. Heracles poisoned his arrows with its blood. See CANCER.

Hydriotaphia, or Urn Burial (1658). An essay by Sir Thomas BROWNE. In part a scientific report on some Roman burial urns that had recently been unearthed in Norfolk, the essay becomes a moving meditation on mortality and oblivion. The famous last chapter on death is considered an example of nearly flawless English prose.

Hymettus. A mountain E. and SE. of Athens, famous for its honey and for a marble used in building ancient Athens.

Hymir. In Scandinavian mythology, a giant with a frosty beard who personified the inhospitable sea. He owned the kettle in which the gods brewed their ale, and it was he who took Thor in his boat and robbed him of his prey when the latter god sought to kill the Midgard serpent.

Hymn of Hate (Hassgesang). A German poem popular during World War I by Ernst Lissauer (1882–1937). Its refrain "Gott strafe England" ("God punish England") was the source of the English verb "to strafe."

Hypatia (c. 370–415). Member of the Neoplatonic School of philosophy at Alexandria, in the 5th century A.D. A daughter of Theon, the mathematician, Hypatia was murdered by the Alexandrine mob. Her story is told in the historical novel HYPATIA (1853), by Charles Kingsley. She is also known as the *Divine Pagan*.

Hypatia (1853). A historical novel by Charles KINGSLEY, a romance of 5th-century Alexandria. The hero, a young monk named Philammon, leaves his monastery for a more active struggle with the brilliant pagan life of the great city. He is strongly drawn to Hypatia, a lecturer on Greek philosophy and a woman of rare spiritual charm, and is much moved by her discussions. But the fanatical Christians of the city cannot tolerate her teachings, and she is torn to pieces by an angry mob. Philammon then recedes into the desert to meditate upon tolerance.

hyperbole. In rhetoric, a figure of speech consisting of exaggeration or extravagance of statement. It is used deliberately for effect and not meant to be taken literally, as in "the waves were mountains high," or "I was fainting from hunger."

Hyperboreans. A happy people of early Greek legend. They were supposed to dwell on the other side of the spot where the North Wind had its birth, and therefore to enjoy perpetual warmth and sunshine. They were said to be the oldest of the human race, the most virtuous, and the most happy, dwelling for some thousand years under a cloudless sky, in fields yielding double harvests, and in the enjoyment of perpetual spring.

Later fable held that they had not an atmosphere like our own, but one consisting wholly of feathers. Both Herodotus and Pliny mention this fiction, which they say was suggested by the quality of snow observed to fall in those regions.

Hyperion. In Greek mythology, one of the TITANS, son of Uranus and Ge, and father of Helios, Selene, and Eos (the Sun, Moon, and Dawn). The name is sometimes given by poets to the sun itself. One of the best-known works of John KEATS is his "poetical fragment" of this name (1820).

Hyperion (1839). A romance by Henry Wadsworth LONGFELLOW. Paul Flemming travels in Europe, falling in love with Mary Ashburton. She scorns him, and he continues his search for the mythical blue rose of German legend, the symbol of the unattainable. Often called Longfellow's *Wilhelm Meister,* the book is studded with old legends.

Hyperion oder Der Eremit in Griechenland (Hyperion or the Hermit in Greece, 1797–1799). An epistolary novel by Friedrich HÖLDERLIN. It is set in modern Greece, but expresses an elegiac longing for the human and artistic perfection of ancient Greece.

Hypermnestra. In Greek legend, the wife of Lynceus and the only one of the fifty daughters of Danaus who did not murder her husband on their bridal night. See DANAIDES.

Hypnos. In Greek mythology, the god of sleep.

Hypocrite, The. See TARTUFFE, LE.

Hypsipyle. In Greek legend, a queen of Lemnos. When the women of her island killed their husbands to a man for infidelity, she saved her father Thoas, who escaped in a boat. When the ARGONAUTS arrived on their way to find the Golden Fleece, she and her women were so hospitable that they repopulated the island. Later, however, Hypsipyle was sold into slavery for having saved Thoas, and was the nursemaid who permitted the child OPHELTES to be fatally bitten by a snake.

I

Iacchus (Iakchos). An obscure Greek deity. A young man associated with the worship of Demeter and Persephone in the ELEUSINIAN MYSTERIES, he was later identified with DIONYSUS.

Iachimo. In Shakespeare's CYMBELINE, a Roman courtier who wagers with Posthumus Leonatus that he can seduce the latter's wife Imogen. A worldly and affected libertine, he has no redeeming qualities.

Iago. In Shakespeare's OTHELLO, the "ancient," or ensign, who is driven by bitterness against his master for having chosen Cassio as his lieutenant. Though outwardly the epitome of "honesty and trust," he causes the downfall and near-death of Cassio and weaves the Machiavellian plot that plants in Othello's mind the false suspicion of his wife's infidelity with Cassio.

Ironically, one of Shakespeare's most famous speeches on honor is delivered by Iago:

Good name in man and woman, dear my lord,
Is the immediate jewel of their souls:
Who steals my purse steals trash; 'tis something, nothing;
But he that filches from me my good name
Robs me of that which not enriches him
And makes me poor indeed.

His also is the famous phrase:

O, beware, my lord, of jealousy;
It is the green-eyed monster, which doth mock
The meat it feeds on.

iamb (or iambus). In English prosody, a metrical foot consisting of two syllables, the first unaccented, the second accented. The word "beTRAY" is an iamb. The METER made up of such units is called iambic meter, and the following lines are a good example:

As NIGHT/ drew ON,/ and, FROM/ the CREST
Of WOOD/ed KNOLLS/ that RIDGED/ the WEST,
The SUN,/ a SNOW/-blown TRAV/eller, SANK
From SIGHT/ beNEATH/ the SMOTH/ering BANK.
                    Whittier, *Snow-Bound*

Iambic meter is the most common English measure; insofar as one can generalize, it is the prevailing meter of natural English speech.

Ianthe. A poetic name much in use in the 19th century. The Ianthe to whom Byron dedicated his *Childe Harold* was Lady Charlotte Harley, only 11 years old at the time. He borrowed it from Walter Savage Landor, who had thus etherealized the middle name of his early sweetheart, Sophia Jane Swift. Landor wrote many poems in her praise. Shelley gave the name to the maiden to whom the fairy queen appears in *Queen Mab*.

Iapetus. In classical mythology, a TITAN son of Uranus and Ge, father of Atlas, Prometheus, Epimetheus, and Menoetius, and ancestor of the human race.

Iasion. According to a Greek myth, a mortal who was united with Demeter and made her the mother of Plutus. He was killed for his presumption by Zeus' lightning. The myth probably symbolizes the fertilization of the fields.

Ibarbourou, Juana de (1895–   ). Uruguayan poet, often known as "Juana de América." Married at 18, she led a quiet life as a wife and mother. She is best known for the poems in *Las lenguas de diamante* (1918) and *Raíz salvaje* (1922); simple, sensuous, and earthy, they are characterized by a subjectivity that has been described as narcissistic.

Iberia. Spain; the country of the Iberus, the ancient name of the river Ebro.

Iberville, Sieur d'. Pierre le Moyne (1661–1706). French-Canadian commander and explorer. Born in Montreal, Iberville served in the French navy and took part in successful engagements with the English in the Hudson Bay area. In 1699 he organized and led an expedition which located the mouth of the Mississippi. In 1702 he established colonies at Biloxi and Mobile.

ibis. A sacred bird of the ancient Egyptians. It was especially associated with the god Thoth who, in the guise of an ibis, escaped the pursuit of Typhon. Its white plumage symbolized the light of the sun, its black neck the shadow of the moon, its body a heart, and its legs a triangle. It was said to drink only the purest of water and to be so fond of Egypt that it would pine to death if transported elsewhere. The ibis was encouraged to make its nest in temples and was often mummified.

Ibraham. The Abraham of the Koran.

Ibsen, Henrik [Johan] (1828–1906). Norwegian poet and playwright. The son of a middle-class family that suffered severe financial reverses when he was a boy, Ibsen was apprenticed to a druggist in his teens, began to study medicine, but soon found his way into the theater. In 1851 he was appointed manager and official playwright of the new National Theater at Bergen, for which he wrote four plays based on Norwegian folklore and history, notably *Lady Inger of Östrât* (1855), dealing with the liberation of medieval Norway. He left the Bergen theater for the post of manager of the Norwegian Theater at Christiania (now Oslo), remaining there until the theater failed in 1864. To this period belong *The Vikings of Helgoland* (1858) and *The Pretenders* (1864), historical dramas; and *Love's Comedy* (1862), a satire. With the aid of a traveling scholarship,

Ibsen began a period of self-imposed exile from his homeland, living until 1891 in various cities on the Continent, primarily Rome, Munich, and Dresden. In 1891 he settled in Christiania, where he lived until his death in 1906.

Ibsen's first two major plays, both in verse, were the symbolic tragedy BRAND and the mock-heroic fantasy PEER GYNT. *The League of Youth* (1869), a political satire, was his first modern prose drama. It was followed by *Emperor and Galilean* (1873), a historical play in two parts on Julian the Apostate. *Pillars of Society* (1877) deals with the shady acts of a wealthy and hypocritical businessman. A DOLL'S HOUSE, a social drama on marriage, was alternately vilified and praised for its sympathy with woman's rights and the questions raised when Nora Helmer slammed the door on her doll's house and her duties and went out in the world to learn how to be a human being. GHOSTS touched on the forbidden subject of "social disease" and attacked social conventions and duty as destroyers of life and happiness. In *An Enemy of the People* (1882), Ibsen contrasted the enlightened and persecuted minority with the ignorant, powerful majority; Dr. Stockman is voted an "enemy of the people" because he insists that the town's famous and prosperous baths are dangerously polluted and must be shut down for expensive repairs. The play was followed by the poetic and symbolic drama THE WILD DUCK; ROSMERSHOLM, another play on the problems of idealism; *The Lady from the Sea* (1888), a play with supernatural overtones and a happy ending. HEDDA GABLER, one of Ibsen's greatest plays, is a striking study of a modern neurotic woman. THE MASTER BUILDER deals symbolically with the plight of the artist. *Little Eyolf* (1894) concerns parental responsibility. Ibsen's last two works, the realistic JOHN GABRIEL BORKMAN and the highly symbolic WHEN WE DEAD AWAKEN, both deal with men who are dead spiritually because they have sacrificed love.

Called the father of modern drama, Ibsen discarded the Scribean formula for the well-made play that had ruled the 19th-century theater. He brought the problems and the ideas of the day onto his stage, emphasized character rather than ingenious plots, and created realistic plays of psychological conflict. Throughout all his works, the social dramas as well as the symbolic plays, run the twin themes that the individual, not the group, is of paramount importance, and that the denial of love is the one unforgivable sin, tantamount to a denial of life.

Ibycus (Ibykos, 6th century B.C.). A Greek lyric poet. According to legend, he was murdered with only a passing flock of cranes as witnesses. In the presence of a large crowd one of the murderers betrayed himself, when he saw a flock of cranes pass overhead, by exclaiming: "The cranes of Ibycus!" This phrase signifies hence "unsuspected witnesses to a crime."

Icarius (Ikarios). In Greek legend an Athenian who was taught the cultivation of the vine by Dionysus. He was slain by some peasants who had become intoxicated with wine he had given them, and who thought they had been poisoned. They buried the body under a tree; his daughter Erigone, searching for her father, was directed to the spot by the howling of his dog Maera, and when she discovered the

Icarus and Daedalus (Freiburg, 1493).

body she hanged herself for grief. Icarius became the constellation *Boötes*, Erigone the constellation *Virgo*, and Maera the star *Procyon*, which rises in July, a little before the dog star.

Icarus (Ikarus). In Greek mythology, son of DAEDALUS. He flew with his father from Crete; but the sun melted the wax with which his wings were fastened on, and he fell into the sea, hence called the Icarian.

Iceland Fisherman, An. See PÊCHEUR D'ISLANDE.

I-ching. See BOOK OF CHANGES.

ichthys (*Gr.*, "fish"). An early symbol of Christ. The word is an anagram of the phrase *I*esous *CH*ristos, *TH*eou *Y*ios, *S*oter, "Jesus Christ, Son of God, Saviour." This word, and the ichthys symbol, two facing curved lines which overlap at one end, are found on many early Christian seals, rings, urns, and tombs.

icon. In the Eastern Church, an image or representation of Christ, a saint, or an angel. Icons are sacred and honored with relative worship (kissing, incense, light) but not with supreme worship, which is due to God alone. They range from elaborate works of art in the church buildings to humble enamel and niello objects carried by the peasantry.

iconoclasts (*Gr.*, "image breakers"). Reformers who rose in the Eastern Church in the seventh and eighth centuries, beginning under Emperor Leo III, the Isaurian. They destroyed sacred images or ICONS in the churches because they feared such visual representation would lead to pagan idol worship. The iconoclasts' crusade continued for 120 years under Constantine Copronymus, Leo the Armenian, Theophilus, and other Byzantine emperors, known as the *Iconoclast emperors*. Eventually, images were used in the Western Church, but in the Eastern Church sculptures are still excluded, though pictures are allowed.

A person who criticizes or seriously questions ideas and attitudes previously accepted as correct, just, and valuable by convention and tradition, rather than by independent examination and judgment, is also called an *iconoclast*.

Milton attacked the royal image of Charles II in his prose pamphlet *Eikonoclastes* (1649).

Idaean Mother. CYBELE, who had a temple on Mount Ida, in Asia Minor.

Idalian. Pertaining to Idalium, an ancient town in Cyprus, or to Aphrodite, to whom the place was consecrated.

Idas. In Greek legend, the son of Arene by Poseidon and brother of LYNCEUS. See ARGONAUTS.

Idea of a Patriot King (1749). A pamphlet by Henry ST. JOHN. It expressed the doctrine that the ideal government is without party and thus anticipated the actual political program of George III and strongly influenced the 19th-century Tory political ideology.

idéologues. A group of materialistic and pragmatic philosophers and psychologists of the late 18th century. They included disciples of CONDILLAC, CONDORCET, Pierre Jean Georges Cabanis, and Antoine Louis Claude Destutt de Tracy. Liberal and antireligious, they believed that ideas originate in physical sensation and that morality is therefore physical in origin; they proclaimed the self-sufficiency of man. Their literary influence is found in the works of Benjamin Constant and Stendhal, and in the literary criticism of Taine and Renan.

ides. In the Roman calendar, the 15th of March, May, July, and October, and the 13th of all the other months. The ides always fell eight days after the NONES.

According to Plutarch, Julius Caesar ignored a soothsayer's warning to beware the ides of March, the day on which he was slain.

Idiot, The (1868). A novel by Feodor DOSTOEVSKI. It is concerned with the effect of the saintly Prince Myshkin on worldly society in St. Petersburg. Myshkin's gentle, childlike nature and his refusal to take offense at anything have earned him the nickname of "the idiot." He himself admits to having been virtually an idiot for several years while under medical care in Switzerland. On the death of his benefactor, he returns to Russia to find himself heir to a large fortune. Almost immediately the trustful Myshkin is entangled in the affairs of the corrupt world of society. On the trip back to Russia he has already met the violently passionate ROGOZHIN who is obsessed by the beautiful Natasha FILIPPOVNA, the victim in her youth of an older man who brought her up as his mistress. The shame Natasha feels has driven the proud girl to degrade herself even more. Only when she meets Myshkin does she feel she has encountered a sympathetic being. This feeling eventually drives her to greater self-torment, when she realizes that Myshkin's apparent love is, in fact, pity.

Myshkin becomes involved with another woman, young Aglaya Epanchin, to whom he also cannot give the normal passionate love she wants, although he does ask her to marry him. His pity for Natasha, however, overcomes whatever love it is he feels for Aglaya, and he goes off to try again to redeem her. His vacillations manage only to hurt both women and, finally, to enrage the jealous Rogozhin to the point of murder. The latter tries unsuccessfully to kill Myshkin and, at the end of the novel he murders Natasha. Confronted with the scene, Myshkin relapses into idiocy.

Dostoevski's announced intention with the character of Myshkin was to portray a truly good man. The attempt has been viewed by critics as only partially successful, not only because Myshkin wreaks havoc with most of the characters he influences, but also because of the abstract, bloodless quality of the characterization itself. A more successful effort of this type is ALEXEI KARAMAZOV, in whose portrayal Dostoevski managed to blend harmoniously both human and Christlike attributes.

Dostoevski acknowledged that *The Idiot* was not completely successful, but insisted that the book was nevertheless his personal favorite among his works. Besides the figure of Myshkin, the author included in the novel many of his ideas on the superiority of Orthodoxy to Western religion and on the connections between Roman Catholicism and socialism.

Idiot's Delight (1936). A play by Robert E. SHERWOOD. Several travelers are detained at an Alpine resort hotel just before the outbreak of a second world war. They include a honeymooning English couple, a German scientist, a French munitions manufacturer, and a troupe of American actors. Harry Van, promoter of the troupe, recognizes Irene, the Russian mistress of the munitions manufacturer, as a woman he once knew slightly in Omaha. The outbreak of the war is announced, and "the little people" in and around the hotel become patriotic and join the army; they all leave but Irene, who has renounced her arms manufacturer and consequently lost her passport. Harry decides to remain with her; they are trapped in the hotel during an air raid. The play was awarded a Pulitzer Prize.

Idle Lake. See FAERIE QUEENE, THE.

Idler, The (1758–1760). A series of essays by Samuel JOHNSON. Published in the *Universal Chronical, or Weekly Gazette,* they are lighter in tone than the RAMBLER and incline to the satiric portrait and Oriental tale.

Idomeneus. King of ancient Crete, an ally of the Greeks at Troy. Part of his tale is told in the ILIAD. After the city was burned he made a vow to sacrifice whatever he first encountered, if the gods granted him a safe return to his kingdom. It was his own son that he first met. He offered him up to fulfill his vow, but a plague followed, and the king was banished from Crete as a murderer. See also JEPHTHAH; ISAAC.

Idraote (Idraotes). In the GERUSALEMME LIBERATA of Tasso, a wizard commissioned by Satan to prevent the Christian capture of Jerusalem. He sends his niece, Armida, to the Christian camp to use her seductive charms in sowing confusion there; she succeeds admirably.

Iduna, Idun, or **Ithunn.** In Scandinavian mythology, the goddess who kept in Asgard the golden apples eaten by the gods to preserve their eternal youth. The daughter of the dwarf Svald and wife of Bragi, she personified the year between March and September, when the sun was north of the equator. When the sun descended below the equator, Loki was said to carry her off to Giant-Land and steal her apples. When the sun rose again above the equator in March, Iduna made her escape in the form of a sparrow.

idyll. (1) A pastoral poem, usually brief, describing the picturesque in country life and conveying a mood of peace and contentment. The most celebrated idylls of antiquity are those of Theocritus and Vergil. Idylls may also be narrative poems, sometimes of epic stature, as in Tennyson's *Idylls of the King.*

(2) Any bucolic, peaceful, romantic episode or period in life or literature which might be a suitable subject for an idyll.

(3) In music, a romantic pastoral composition.

Idylls of the King (1859–1885). A series of poems in 10 books by Alfred TENNYSON. Based on ARTHURIAN LEGEND, they comprise *The Coming of Arthur, Gareth and Lynette, Geraint and Enid, Merlin and Vivien, Lancelot and Elaine, The Holy Grail, Pelleas and Etarre, The Last Tournament, Guinevere,* and *The Passing of Arthur.* In interpreting the Arthurian legend, Tennyson focuses on the introduction of evil into the hitherto unblemished Camelot through Lancelot's sin of adulterous love for Guinevere. Because of this approach, some commentators have found Tennyson's conception of Arthur lacking in substance.

If It Die . . . (Si le grain ne meurt; 1926). An autobiographical work by André GIDE. Written in 1920, it records Gide's experiences during his trips to North Africa in 1893 and 1894–1895. In part a confession of homosexuality, the book was intended to force public discussion of an issue then normally avoided.

If Winter Comes (1920). A once popular novel by A. S. M. HUTCHINSON. Bearing a thematic resemblance to the work of Warwick Deeping, it tells the story of Mark Sabre, unhappily married, who befriends a pregnant girl and is suspected of being the father of her illegitimate child. Sabre discovers that the real culprit is the idolized son of his business associate. When the boy's death at the front is reported, he knows that he will never be able to clear himself of the charges. Despite such misfortunes, the novel ends happily with Sabre's divorce and his remarriage to a woman he has always loved. The title is taken from the last line of Shelley's *Ode to the West Wind:* "If Winter comes, can Spring be far behind?"

Ignatius of Loyola, St. See St. Ignatius of LOYOLA.

Igraine, Igerne, or **Ygerne, Queen.** In Arthurian literature the mother of King ARTHUR. In many versions, she is the virtuous wife of Gorlois, duke of Tintagel, and she is innocently seduced by King UTHER PENDRAGON when the magic of Merlin gives him the appearance of her husband. In other versions, Uther and Gorlois fight, and the latter is slain. Uther then besieges Tintagel Castle, takes it, and compels Igraine to become his wife. Nine months afterwards, Uther dies, and on the same day Arthur is born.

Ihara Saikaku (1642–1693). Japanese novelist. He wrote erotic stories and tales of merchant class life. His writings reflect the new bourgeois culture centering in Osaka. His works enjoyed immense popularity and are still widely read. See *The Life of an Amorous Woman* (1962) by Ivan Morris.

I.H.S. The first three letters of the Greek form of Jesus, and a widely used Christian symbol. In time, the long "e" (H) was mistaken by people of Latin culture for a capital H, and various phrases arose that used these letters as initials, such as *Jesus Hominum Salvator* (Jesus, Savior of men) and *In hac salus* (safety in this, i.e., the Cross).

ikebana. Japanese flower arrangement. It was developed as an art during the Muromachi period

(1333–1600), where it was used in conjunction with the tea ceremony. In the Tokugawa period (1600–1868) it became highly formalized, and a large number of schools arose, each with its own specialized techniques, most of which are still extant.

Ikeda Hayato (1899–1965). Japanese politician. In 1960 he became head of the Liberal Party and Prime Minister.

Ikshvaku. In Hindu legend, the first king of the solar dynasty. He is known as Raghu.

Ilf and Petrov. Pen names of the Soviet humorists **Ilya Arnoldovich Ilf** (1897–1937) and **Yevgeni Petrovich Katayev** (1902–1942). Their two comic novels, TWELVE CHAIRS and *The Little Golden Calf (Zolotoi telionok,* 1931), recount the hilarious machinations of the master con-man, Ostap Bender. The two writers also collaborated on a satirical account of their visit to the U.S., *One-Storied America (Odnoetazhnaya Amerika;* 1936). Ilf died of tuberculosis in 1937; Petrov was killed during the war in 1942.

Iliad. Greek epic poem (8th century B.C.?) attributed to HOMER. In 24 books of dactylic hexameter verse, it details the events of the few days near the end of the TROJAN WAR, focusing on the withdrawal of Achilles from the contest and the disastrous effects of this act on the Greek campaign. The plot is as follows:

Book I. AGAMEMNON, commander-in-chief of the Greek forces, refuses to return his captive Chryseis to her father Chryses, a priest of Apollo. An ensuing pestilence is divined to be the result of this unseemly act, and the Greeks insist that Agamemnon relinquish Chryseis. He grudgingly does so, but takes ACHILLES' captive Briseis in her place. Furious, Achilles refuses to fight with the Greeks. His mother, THETIS, persuades Zeus to turn the tide of battle so that the Greeks will see how much they need Achilles.

Book II. A false dream sent by Zeus leads Agamemnon to plan a battle. He tests his men by suggesting that they return home. To his dismay, they start to rush for the ships, and are only restrained when ODYSSEUS beats their leader Thersites. The "Catalogue of Ships" lists the combatants and their forces.

Book III. PARIS, whose abduction of HELEN from Sparta was the cause of the war, now engages in single combat with her husband, MENELAUS. About to be killed, Paris is spirited away by APHRODITE.

Book IV. ATHENA, who favors the Greeks, causes the Trojan PANDARUS to break the truce by treacherously shooting Menelaus, and the battle is joined.

Book V. DIOMEDES is the hero of the day, killing Pandarus and many others and even wounding Aphrodite and (with Athena's help) Ares, who are helping the Trojans.

Book VI. HECTOR, the Trojan leader, returns to Troy, bids the women pray to Athena, and bids farewell to Andromache, his wife, and his infant son in a touching scene. On the battlefield, Diomedes and GLAUCUS, finding that their godfathers were friends, refrain from fighting and exchange armor, Glaucus accepting bronze for gold.

Book VII. After an indecisive battle between the Trojan leader Hector and Great AJAX, there is a pause. Under pressure from the Trojans, Paris, though refusing to give up Helen, promises to make handsome restitution. The Greeks refuse his offer and build a wall to protect their ships.

Book VIII. Zeus orders the other gods not to interfere in the war. HERA and Athena at first defy him, but are chastened. The war turns in the Trojans' favor.

Book IX. Desperate, Agamemnon offers to return Briseis to Achilles and make further restitution. Odysseus, Ajax, and Phoenix, Achilles' old tutor, bear the offer to Achilles, but he indignantly refuses it and vows to start for home the next day.

Book X. Odysseus and Diomedes spy on the Trojans, and kill Dolon and the Thracian king, Rhesus.

Book XI. Agamemnon worries the Greeks, but he, Odysseus, Diomedes, and others are wounded. Achilles sends Patroclus to inquire about the course of the fighting. Nestor urges him to beg Achilles to fight or to send Patroclus with Achilles' MYRMIDONS.

Book XII. The Trojans under Hector break through a gate in the Greek walls.

Book XIII. In spite of Zeus's commands POSEIDON rallies the Greeks under Idomeneus and the Ajaxes.

Book XIV. Hera amorously deceives Zeus and puts him to sleep, while Poseidon helps the Greeks. The Trojans are driven back and Hector is wounded.

Book XV. When Zeus awakes, Poseidon is forced to cease aiding the Greeks and APOLLO rouses Hector to lead the Trojans as far as the Greek ships, where he tries to burn them. Patroclus meanwhile begs Achilles to fight.

Book XVI. Achilles gives Patroclus his armor and tells him to repel the Trojan advance, but no more. Patroclus drives the Trojans to the walls of Troy, killing SARPEDON and Hector's charioteer; but there Hector kills him, with the aid of Apollo.

Book XVII. Hector takes Achilles' armor, but, in a violent fight, Menelaus and the Greeks recover Patroclus' body.

Book XVIII. In spite of Thetis' warnings that he is fated to die, Achilles determines to avenge Patroclus in battle. Hephaestus makes him a new shield, richly engraved with many scenes.

Book XIX. Achilles announces that he will fight. Agamemnon makes amends. Achilles' immortal horses, Xanthus and Balius, warn him that this is the last time they will bear him safely from the field. Knowing that he is soon to die, Achilles goes into battle.

Book XX. Since Zeus's promise to Thetis now is fulfilled, the other gods are free to join in the war. Aligned with the Greeks are Athena, Hera, Poseidon, Hephaestus, and Hermes; with the Trojans, Apollo, Ares, Artemis, Aphrodite, and Leto. Aeneas fights with Achilles, but is rescued by Poseidon; similarly Hector is saved by Apollo.

Book XXI. Achilles routs the Trojans, killing many in the river Xanthus, which fights against him. Only Apollo saves the Trojans from destruction.

Book XXII. Hector waits alone outside the walls of Troy to meet Achilles. At first he flees from him three times about the city but then turns to fight. Abandoned by Apollo he is tricked by Athena and killed by Achilles, who drags his body behind his chariot to the ships, while his family and all Troy lament on the city walls.

Book XXIII. Achilles holds a great funeral for

Patroclus, burning 12 Trojan youths with his body. Games are held in his honor.

Book XXIV. For days Achilles continues to heap indignities on the corpse of Hector, until Zeus warns him through Thetis that the gods will be angered. The Trojan king, PRIAM, begs the body from Achilles, who recognizes in him a fellow-sufferer, and consents. A funeral is held for Hector.

The Trojan war is now known, thanks to the discoveries of SCHLIEMANN and his successors, to have been a historical event of the 13th century B.C., though hardly the glorious contest described in the *Iliad*. About that event there grew up a vast number of legends, which, during the succeeding centuries, were told and retold by the bards in accordance with the traditions of GREEK EPIC POETRY until a certain amount of order was imposed on the many variant strands. It was probably about four centuries after the war that a particular group of these myths were modeled into the dramatic and stylistic unit that became known as the *Iliad*. This work was attributed to an Ionian poet called Homer.

Controversy still rages on whether Homer was a single poet or many, but there is little question of the essential unity of concept that makes the *Iliad* a great poem. In spite of the monotonous similarity between one hand-to-hand combat and the next and in spite of the epithets and other bardic formulas that can apply as well to one hero as to another, the *Iliad* is far more than a vast, highly formalized panorama of battle. Many of the principal figures are considerably individualized; Achilles, Agamemnon, Nestor, Paris, Hector, Thersites, Dolon. There are amusing touches: the ignominious flight of the Greeks when Agamemnon tests their loyalty, Glaucus giving his gold armor in an access of hospitality; there are moving scenes: Hector's infant son frightened by the plume on his father's helmet, Achilles going into battle in spite of his horse's warning, Priam and Achilles weeping together over their mutual loss. All these scenes give the story a human significance that deeply involves the reader in its events. One of the most impressive qualities of the poem is the dramatic impact that the poet achieved by concentrating his attention not on the siege of Troy, but on the tragic results of one man's anger. In spite of Achilles' implacable and (to modern readers) childish resentment of a slight on his honor, he is a genuinely noble figure who knowingly embraces certain death rather than live a long life without glory.

The *Iliad* is written in the poetic line regularly associated with Greek epic, the dactylic hexameter. The dialect of the poem is primarily Ionic, with a strong subsoil of Aeolic, which had been the language of the earlier inhabitants of the part of Ionia from which Homer traditionally came. However, the language of the *Iliad*, or of epic in general, was more a traditional poetic diction than an actual speech.

The world of the Trojan War was very imperfectly remembered in the Homeric poem, written centuries later. Some of the traditional material, inherited and faithfully passed on by Homer, must have been incomprehensible to him: for example, the use of the Mycenaean full-length rectangular shield, which had long been obsolete. As a result, the soldiers in the *Iliad* are sometimes described as bearing the round bronze shield of the poet's day, whereas elsewhere they carry the ancient long shield. Such discrepancies as these have aided scholars in sorting out old and new material in the work. Other anachronisms are the result of deliberate tampering, in order to increase the role of Athens in the war and to diminish that of her enemies. This process may well have taken place in the days of PISISTRATUS, when the recitation of Homer became a regular part of the Panathenaic festival. The fact that certain barbarous customs, such as human sacrifice, torture, and mutilation, scarcely appear in the *Iliad* is probably also due to later expurgation.

I'll Take My Stand: The South and the Agrarian Tradition by Twelve Southerners. See AGRARIANS.

illuminism. A pseudoscientific movement of mystics and visionaries in the 18th century which influenced literature in the 19th century. A wave of mysticism, whose origins date from the Middle Ages, came from Germany, Switzerland, and Sweden, and reached France, forming a freemasonry of illuminists or mystics. At first inspired by Christian doctrines, they sought to live according to the Gospel and to regenerate their souls by direct contact with the divine. They also, however, believed in spiritism, magnetism, alchemy, and magic and professed to invoke the invisible and the arcane. Among the more famous illuminists were Swedenborg, who conversed with the dead; Lavater, a believer in black magic, who thought to contact God by magnetism; Claude de Saint-Martin ("the unknown philosopher"), who sought to hasten the coming of Christ by meditation and prayer; Mesmer; the Comte de Saint-Germain, who pretended to be several hundred years old and to possess the elixir of eternal life; Gall; and the famous Cagliostro, who evoked spirits. An almost instinctive reaction against 18th-century rational philosophies, illuminism under many names (e.g., millenarism, syncretism, neopaganism, pythagorism, theosophy, etc.) influenced some writers of the romantic period. It revived a sense of religious exaltation and mystery and created, or re-created, a need for the infinite, a belief in man's inner nature and a feeling for the mysteries of nature and of love. Among the writers who were influenced in the 19th century were Joseph de Maistre, in his *Soirées de St. Petersbourg;* Charles Fourier; the Christian philosopher Pierre-Simon Ballanche; Charles Nodier, in his fantastic tales; Balzac; and Gérard Nerval.

Illusionists, The (Le Rempart des béguines; 1950). A novel by Françoise MALLET-JORIS about a girl of fifteen who becomes the Lesbian lover of her father's mistress.

Ilmarinen. A smith in the KALEVALA, inventor of the SAMPO. He created one of his wives out of gold and silver and brought her to life, but she was so cold that whatever came near her would probably freeze.

Ilsan the Monk. A boisterous friar in the 13th-century German epic the *Rosengarten* (*The Rose Garden at Worms*). He brings home 52 garlands from an expedition against the garden, and presses their thorns into the flesh of his fellow friars until they consent to pray for the forgiveness of his sins.

Imaginary Cuckold, The. See SGANARELLE.

Imaginary Invalid, The. See MALADE IMAGINAIRE, LE.

imagination. In romantic aesthetic theory, the creative function of the intellect by which separate elements of experience are synthesized in a new whole differing from and transcending any of its original parts. S. T. Coleridge set forth the distinction between it and fancy in his BIOGRAPHIA LITERARIA. He said that imagination was the "shaping and modifying" power while FANCY was the "aggregative and associative" power; imagination "struggles to idealize and unify" while fancy is merely "a mode of Memory emancipated from the order of time and space."

imagism. A theory of poetry adopted about 1910 by a number of English and American poets who followed the leadership of T. E. HULME and Ezra POUND. The movement confessed to several predecessors—e.g., medieval philosophy, the aesthetics of Henri Bergson, and Japanese poetry—but it was primarily a reaction against the stultified form and diction of Georgian verse. It demanded absolute precision in the presentation of the individual image; in metrics it proposed the cadence of "the musical phrase," by which was meant a controlled free verse. Generally speaking, imagist poems were short, pointed observations, often no more than four or five lines in length and usually balanced on a single radically original metaphor.

Pound and Hulme were joined by a number of other poets, notably Hilda DOOLITTLE, Richard ALDINGTON, William Carlos WILLIAMS, and later, Amy LOWELL. They called themselves *Imagistes*. In 1912 Pound edited the first imagist anthology, *Some Imagiste Poets*. Meanwhile, he and the others propagandized vigorously for their beliefs, and Pound, who had become foreign editor of Harriet Monroe's POETRY magazine, published therein a number of manifestoes as well as his own and his friends' poems. Pound later abandoned the movement and with Wyndham Lewis went on to vorticism; though Amy Lowell carried on for a few years, by 1917 or 1918 the movement, as an institutional device, had expired. It had, however, exerted an enormous influence on the development of modern poetry and had provided the break with the immediate past which was necessary before a new literature could appear. Some of imagism's most enduring monuments have been translations such as those made by the English poet Arthur Waley from Chinese poetry and by Francis Densmore from American Indian poetry.

Imbolc. February 1, one of the 4 great feast days of the ancient Celtic year. See SAMAIN; BELTINE; LUGNASAD.

Imhotep. In the mythology of ancient Egypt, the god of learning in general, and a physician later deified as god of medicine. He corresponds to the Greek Asclepius.

Imitation of Christ (De Imitatione Christi; 1426). A religious treatise commonly ascribed to THOMAS A KEMPIS. It has been said that this book has had more influence on Christianity than any other book except the Bible. It is mystical in tone as it explores the inner life and the value of contemplation, yet remarkably clear in its simplicity. Other candidates for the authorship of this work are the brilliant chancellor of the University of Paris, Jean Gerson, and a Jean Gersen, who is only identified as the abbot of Vercelli.

Imlac. In Samuel Johnson's novel RASSELAS the son of a rich merchant of Goiama, a city near the mouth of the Nile. Imlac is a great traveler, philosopher and poet, who accompanies Rasselas on his journey and returns with him to the Happy Valley. Imlac, the moralistic spokesman for Johnson himself, teaches that man should make the most of what order and reason he can find, but that it is folly to stake one's hopes on a facile discovery of divine order in the world.

Immaculate Conception. The belief that the Virgin Mary, from the moment of her conception, was free from the stain of ORIGINAL SIN. The belief has been widespread among Christians as a pious opinion, but has also had many opponents, especially St. Thomas Aquinas in the 12th century. In 1854, in the bull *Ineffabilis Deus,* Pope Pius IX proclaimed it a dogma, making the belief binding for Roman Catholics. The feast is observed on December 8.

Immermann, Karl Lebrecht (1796–1840). German novelist and playwright. His *Die Epigonen* (*The Late-Comers,* 1836) is one of the earliest German social novels. It is set in the Germany of the 1830's when, partly because of the stultifying political conservatism of Austria and Prussia, there was a widespread feeling of having been born too late for the great and exciting ages of humanity. His later novel *Münchhausen* (1838–1839) is quite a daring experiment in form. It consists of two main stories developed in alternating episodes; though connected, they are independent enough to be separated, and one, entitled *Der Oberhof* (*The Upper Manor*), is often printed alone. *Der Oberhof* is a rustic village story reflecting the BIEDERMEIER tendency, whereas the remainder of the novel, a variation on the adventures of Baron Munchhausen, is an urbane document of social criticism. Immermann's best-known drama *Merlin* (1832) is more romantic than either of the novels.

Immoralist, The (*L'Immoraliste;* 1902). A tale by André GIDE. Michel takes his bride Marceline to North Africa, where he develops tuberculosis and becomes hyperconscious of physical sensations, particularly of his attraction to young Arab boys. Back on his French estate after being cured, he is encouraged by his friend Ménalque to rise above conventional good and evil and give free rein to all his passions. When Marceline falls ill with the tuberculosis she caught while nursing him, he takes her south. He neglects her demands on him more and more, however, in order to keep himself free, since his new doctrine demands that the weak be suppressed if necessary for the preservation of the strong. She dies, and he, guilt-ridden and debilitated by his excesses, tries to justify his conduct to a group of friends.

Imogen. In Shakespeare's CYMBELINE, the daughter of Cymbeline and the tender, faithful wife of Posthumus Leonatus. Attempting to find her husband, who erroneously believes that she has betrayed him, she disguises herself as a page and assumes the name of Fidele.

Impending Crisis of the South, The. See Hinton Rowan HELPER.

Importance of Being Earnest, The (1895). A comedy by Oscar WILDE. It is noted for its witty lines, its clever situations, and its satire on the British nobility and clergy. It deals with the aspirations of Jack Worthing to the hand of Gwendolen Fairfax, daughter of Lady Bracknell. Lady Bracknell objects to the marriage because of the obscurity of Worthing's background; he was found in a handbag in Victoria Station and has no information as to who his parents were. Eventually matters are straightened out by the revelation that Worthing is actually the son of Lady Bracknell's sister and was left in the handbag as an infant through the absentmindedness of a governess. His name is actually Ernest John Moncrieff and he is the brother of his friend Algernon Moncrieff. Worthing is particularly happy that his name turns out to be Ernest since he has created an imaginary younger brother of that name for the benefit of his ward Cecily Cardew (who eventually marries Algernon); this "Ernest," a purportedly rakish fellow whom Worthing had constantly to get out of scrapes, was Worthing's excuse for absenting himself from his country estate, where Cecily lived under the tutelage of Miss Prism, to go to London to see Gwendolen.

impresa. The Italian word for heraldic device or personal motto. Its literal meaning of enterprise suggests its key idea: an expression of the soul of an individual, his goal or chief characteristic. *Imprese,* very popular during the Renaissance and baroque eras in Europe, could be a single pungent phrase or a few lines, accompanied by illustration or used alone. The fact that many were collected and commented upon relates them to the popular EMBLEM BOOKS, which are, however, a somewhat different device. In English literature, an example is Spenser's *Shepheardes Calender,* in which each of the eclogues is prefaced by a motto appropriate to the character involved, as in Colin's *"Anchóra speme"* (Still I hope), inaccurately termed an emblem by Spenser.

impressionism. A term applied originally to the work of a group of 19th-century French painters in Paris. Associated with naturalism, rebelling equally against the academic and romantic schools, the impressionists attempted to convey in painting the impression gained from the direct observation of nature. Concerned principally with the study of light and its refractions, they used only the colors of the spectrum, and did much of their work out of doors, thus continuing the tradition of their forerunners, the BARBIZON SCHOOL. Claude Monet, Renoir, and Alfred Sisley are the most typical representatives of impressionism in its purest form, other important members of the group being Manet, Degas, Pissarro, and Cézanne. In 1874, when the work of several of these artists was rejected by the Salon, they organized their own separate exhibition, but for an entire generation their work was generally ignored or derided. Gradually the group began to disintegrate, each artist developing in his own manner, yet a vast spiritual unity continued to mark their work.

Impressionism had an enormous effect on the subsequent history and development of painting both in and outside of France. Among American-born painters its influence can be seen in the works of James McNeill Whistler, John Singer Sargent, Mary Cassatt, and Maurice Prendergast.

In German literature of the late 19th and early 20th centuries, impressionism denotes the style of writing characterized by extreme precision in language and emphasis on accurately rendering, in all their vagueness and complexity, subjective impressions of unique, individual experiences. Impressionism is therefore most commonly found in lyric poetry, especially that of Liliencron, Dehmel, the early George, Hofmannsthal, and the early Rilke; but it is also clearly an element in Thomas Mann's early prose style, especially in *Buddenbrooks,* and in the dramatic writing of Arthur Schnitzler. The subjectivity of impressionism constitutes a reaction against both the materialism of mid-19th-century philosophy and the programmatic objectivity of naturalism; but naturalism and impressionism still had much in common, particularly the wish to make words more precise and the tendency to concentrate on specific human situations, so that several major writers, including Hauptmann, Holz and Schlaf, were active in both movements. See EXPRESSIONISM.

In music, impressionism stresses sonorous effects for their own sake, i.e., the use of harmonies and instrumental timbres as musical "colors" that blend and change without clear direction or purpose other than the evocation of a general mood. Most impressionistic pieces have literary or pictorial titles; the programmatic implications are generally more important than form or structure. Claude Debussy, Maurice Ravel, Ottorino Respighi (1879–1936), and Charles Tomlinson Griffes (1884–1920) are among those composers associated with impressionism.

Im Westen nichts Neues. See ALL QUIET ON THE WESTERN FRONT.

Inanna or Ininni. A Sumerian goddess of erotic love and of war. She was a prototype of the goddess ISHTAR who, under various names but with remarkably consistent nature, was the chief female goddess of the Near East for 3,000 years. Many of her attributes caused her to be later identified with Artemis, Aphrodite, and other Greek goddesses. The most important of the many myths in which she figures is that of her descent into the underworld, whose queen is her dire sister Ereshkigal. Parallel myths of Ishtar make it likely that this dangerous journey was undertaken to rescue her lover DUMUZI or TAMMUZ. Inanna first orders her herald Ninshubur, if she does not return in three days, to notify the assembled gods. She then goes down into the underworld. As she approaches the queen's palace, her robes and ornaments are removed one by one until she is finally led naked before Ereshkigal. As Inanna had expected, she is killed by glances of death from the queen and the Anunnaki, judges of the underworld, and her body is hung from a stake.

On his mistress's instructions, Ninshubur begs the gods for aid, but only ENKI is willing to help. He sends two creatures to the underworld bearing the food and water of life, which they sprinkle on Inanna's body. Reviving, she returns to earth; but the dead swarm up out of the underworld and accompany her wherever she goes. The remainder of the myth has not been discovered.

In Camera. See NO EXIT.

Incas. A Quechua-speaking people who dominated pre-Columbian Peru. The name *Inca* was also given to their kings, absolute monarchs who were worshiped as descendants of the sun. From their capital at CUZCO, they gradually conquered neighboring regions, especially after 1438 when Pachacuti and his son, Topa Inca, extended Inca rule as far

north as Quito and as far south as northern Chile. See ATAHUALPA; Francisco PIZARRO; GARCILASO DE LA VEGA.

incunabula (Lat., "a cradle"). Works of art or industry of the infant stages in the development of a given field. In the history of bookmaking, books printed before 1500. They are sometimes called cradle books or fifteeners. In this sense the singular "incunabulum" can be used.

Independents. In the English CIVIL WAR, the radical wing of the Parliamentary party. It consisted of Puritans and other independent dissenters who were opposed to the Presbyterian faction. They came to power with the RUMP PARLIAMENT and were the dominant party during the rule of Oliver Cromwell.

Index, The. Official list of books that Roman Catholics are not allowed to read. The Roman Index includes both the *Index Librorum Prohibitorum* and the *Index Expurgatorius.* The former contains a list of such books as are absolutely forbidden to be read by faithful Catholics. The latter contains such books as are forbidden till certain parts are omitted or amended. The lists are made out by a board of cardinals called the *Congregation of the Index.*

Indiana (1832). A novel by George SAND. In this violently romantic work, which served as a springboard to establish George Sand's literary reputation, the events bear a provocative resemblance to those in the author's own life. Its heroine, a Creole named Indiana, abandons her old husband for a fascinating young lover.

Indian Summer (1886). A novel by William Dean HOWELLS. Theodore Colville, a journalist of 40, meets a childhood acquaintance, the widow Mrs. Lina Bowen, in Florence. He becomes engaged to her young ward, Imogene Graham. When Imogene

Incunabula: printing in the 15th century.

admits that she is in love with a younger man, Colville finally recognizes the more mature love he feels for Mrs. Bowen.

Indra. Also called **Mahendra** (from Sans., *maha, great*). The chief god in the Hindu pantheon of lower deities. In Hindu myth, he is also the god of heaven and ruler over thunder, lightning, and storm. He molested Ahalya and was cursed by her husband, the sage Gautama. See AHI; AIRAVATA; MATALI.

In Dubious Battle (1936). A novel by John STEINBECK. It deals with the problem of labor organization among the migrant fruit-pickers in California. Mac, the leading character, is a veteran organizer for the Communist Party who allows nothing to interfere with his service to the cause, not even the murder of his friend Jim Nolan. Another important character is Doc Burton, an uncommitted sympathizer who helps the striking workers.

Industrial Workers of the World. Called the **IWW.** A federation of industrial unions established at Chicago in 1905. Dedicated to the overthrow of capitalism by direct means, it called general strikes and resorted to sabotage. Many "wobblies," as members were called, refused to fight in World War I, claiming that it was a struggle between capitalists. The IWW became increasingly unpopular during the war, when ultrapatriotic feeling swept the U.S. In 1918 the U.S. government arrested, tried, and convicted its leaders, and by 1925 its influence had ended.

Inez, Donna. In Byron's poem DON JUAN, the mother of Juan. After worrying her husband, Don José, to death by her prudery and want of sympathy, Donna Inez endeavors to raise Juan by the strictest rules of propriety and make him a model of all the virtues. Unfortunately, he is seduced by her best friend, the equally proper and intellectual Donna Julia.

infantes de Lara, Cantar de los siete. See LARA, CANTAR DE LOS SIETE INFANTES DE.

Infant Phenomenon, The. The stage name of the allegedly 10-year-old Ninetta Crummles in Charles Dickens' NICHOLAS NICKLEBY. Actually, she is at least 15 and her low stature results from being kept up late every night and "an unlimited allowance of gin and water."

Infernal Machine, The (La Machine infernale; 1934). A tragedy by Jean COCTEAU. It uses the story of Oedipus as an example of a cosmic joke, "one of the most perfect machines constructed by the infernal gods for the mathematical annihilation of a mortal." Oedipus, who possesses the intuitive, imaginative qualities of Cocteau's ideal poet figure, is brutally crushed by a hostile external world.

Inferno (Hell). Part I of the DIVINE COMEDY by DANTE. Vergil conducts Dante through the region of damnation, where the souls suffer eternal punishments appropriate to their sins. In the anteroom are those who did nothing in life, neither good nor evil. Then follow nine levels of Hell, descending conically into the earth. The first is Limbo, where are the blameless but unbaptized spirits, including the great men of pagan antiquity. The circles of the sins of incontinence, least terribly punished, include the carnal sinners (see PAOLO AND FRANCESCA), the gluttons, the misers and the spendthrifts, the wrathful and the sullen. With the sixth circle, that of the

heretics, begin the horrible torments of the City of Dis, generally fiery. The seventh circle contains the violent against others (murderers), against self (suicides), and against God and Nature (blasphemers, perverts, and the like). The eighth level includes 10 categories of the fraudulent (seducers, sorcerers, thieves, hypocrites, and various kinds of liars and evil counselors). The most odious of the fraudulent, the traitors, are frozen in the ice of the ninth circle: the betrayers of their own relatives or country (see UGOLINO) and, at the very center of the earth, Lucifer with three heads gnawing on Brutus and Cassius, the betrayers of Julius Caesar, and Judas Iscariot, the betrayer of Jesus Christ. Turning around at Lucifer's waist, Dante and Vergil emerge through a tunnel into the opposite hemisphere, which is covered with water, to approach the island of the mountain of Purgatory.

Informer, The (1925). A novel by Liam O'FLAHERTY. It is a psychological melodrama describing the last day of Gypo Nolan, a destitute Irish revolutionary who turned a comrade in to the police for 20 pounds.

Inge, William (1913–   ). American playwright. He is known for his dramas dealing with average people of the Midwest. His first play, *Farther Off from Heaven* (1947), was produced by Margo Jones in her Dallas theater. *Come Back Little Sheba* (1950) won the George Jean Nathan and the Theatre Time awards; *Picnic* (1953) won the Pulitzer Prize and was later made into a movie. *Bus Stop* (1955) was a successful play and was also later made into a movie, as was *The Dark at the Top of the Stairs* (1957). *A Loss of Roses* was produced in 1960. Inge is also the author of a successful screenplay, *Splendor in the Grass* (1961).

Ingemann, Bernard Severin (1789–1862). Danish poet and novelist. Ingemann was the author of a series of popular historical novels set in the Danish middle ages. A schoolteacher in the old town of Sorø, he acquired a lively sense of the past and a love for the ancient chivalric values. Among his novels are *Valdemar Seier* (*Waldemar, surnamed Seir, or the Victorious,* 1826), *Erik Menveds Barndom* (*The Childhood of King Eric Menved,* 1828) and *Kong Erik og de Fredløse* (*King Eric and the Outlaws,* 1833). *Morgensange for Børn* (1837) and *Morgen og Aften sange* (1839) are collections of simple delicate lyrics that express a naïve vision of the world.

Ingénu, L' (1767). A satiric romance by VOLTAIRE. The hero, l'Ingénu, returns to France after having been brought up by the primitive Huron Indians in Canada. His simple, frank, and naturally good qualities are violently contrasted by Voltaire with the conventional mores and religious convictions of the civilized world. The story is a criticism of highly placed officials during Louis XV's time, a protest of the abuse of power, and a satire of the absurdities of society's conventions. See NOBLE SAVAGE.

Ingersoll, Robert G[reen] (1833–1899). American lawyer, public official, and orator. He was known as "the Great Agnostic" for his defense of free-thinking in religious matters. An active Republican, he became a sought-after orator when he eloquently nominated James G. BLAINE for the presidency (1876). Influenced by Voltaire and Paine, Ingersoll is known for such aphorisms as these: "Many people think they have religion when they are merely troubled with dyspepsia"; "With soap, baptism is a good thing"; and "An honest God is the noblest work of man." Among Ingersoll's books are *The Gods* (1872), *Some Mistakes of Moses* (1879), and *Why I Am an Agnostic* (1896). After his death appeared *The Works of Robert G. Ingersoll* (12 v., 1900). See BEN-HUR.

Ingmars, the. A Swedish family whose struggles and adventures are narrated in the short stories that comprise Selma Lagerlöf's JERUSALEM.

Ingres, Jean Auguste Dominique (1780–1867). French painter. The acknowledged leader of the classical school, he painted many religious, historical, and mythological subjects. These are less appreciated today than his portraits, but he is noted for the strong, refined purity of his drawing and the abstract grace of his form and line.

Iniquity, the. See VICE, THE.

In Memoriam (Lat., "in memory of"). A long poem written between the years 1833 and 1850 by Alfred TENNYSON, in memory of his friend Arthur HALLAM, who died in 1833. It is considered one of the great English elegies and, on the whole, the poet's most impressive longer work. The poem not only deals with Hallam's death and Tennyson's enduring sense of loss, but also attempts to grapple with many of the intellectual and religious problems of the mid-19th century: the decline of faith, the rise of skepticism and scientific materialism.

inner light. Spiritual illumination. Specifically, in QUAKER doctrine, the term designates a divine presence in the soul of every man, the light of Christ that gives moral guidance and religious and spiritual assurance to all who are willing to receive it.

Inner Temple and Middle Temple. See INNS OF COURT.

Innes, Hammond. Pen name of Ralph Hammond-Innes (1913–   ). English novelist, writer of thrillers with backgrounds marked by unusual accuracy of detail. Among his works are *The White South* (1949), *Naked Land* (1954), *Land God Gave to Cain* (1958), *Doomed Oasis* (1960), and *Harvest of Journeys* (1960), an autobiography.

Innes, Michael. The pen name under which J. I. M. STEWART writes his detective stories.

Inness, George (1825–1894). American landscape painter. The English landscapists and the BARBIZON SCHOOL influenced his portrayal of familiar landscapes in their varying moods. In his last years he allowed an increasing poetic vagueness to blur the delicately toned landscapes he created from memory.

Innocents, Massacre of the. The slaughter of the male children of Bethlehem "from two years old and under," when Jesus was born (Matt. 2:16). This was done at the command of Herod the Great in order to cut off "the babe" who was destined to become "King of the Jews." The Feast of the Holy Innocents commemorating this event is December 28.

In British parliamentary phraseology, the phrase denotes the withdrawal of the bills which there has not been time to consider and pass before the close of the session.

Innocents Abroad, The, or, The New Pilgrim's Progress (1869). A travel book by Mark TWAIN. It is based on a series of letters he wrote from Europe as a roving correspondent. The book bur-

lesques the sentimental travel book popular in the mid-19th century. Admiring the leisure of Europeans, Clemens criticized some American manners.

Innocent Voyage, The. See HIGH WIND IN JAMAICA.

Innommable, L'. See UNNAMABLE, THE.

Inns of Court. The four legal societies that have the exclusive right of calling candidates to the English bar, and maintain instruction and examination for that purpose. They are all in London, and are the Inner Temple, the Middle Temple, Lincoln's Inn, and Gray's Inn. Each consists of a legal faculty governed by a board of "benchers."

Ino. In Greek mythology, a daughter of Cadmus and consort of ATHAMAS, by whom she had two sons, Learchus and Melicertes. Ino's jealousy drove the children of Athamas' first wife Nephele to the sacrificial altar, but they were saved by the GOLDEN FLEECE. Because Ino and Athamas helped Zeus to save the infant Dionysus from Hera's wrath, Hera revenged herself by driving them mad. Athamas killed Learchus, mistaking him for a stag; Ino escaped with Melicertes and flung herself into the sea, but Zeus, grateful because she had protected Dionysus, transformed her into the sea goddess Leucothea. He transformed Melicertes into the sea god Palaemon, and, under those names, both watch over storm-tossed sailors.

In Our Time (1924). A collection of short stories by Ernest HEMINGWAY. First published in France and the following year in the U.S., many of the stories deal with the development of young Nick Adams, who bears some resemblance to the author himself. In *Indian Camp*, Nick is introduced to the violence of life when he accompanies his doctor father; *Big Two-Hearted River* shows his mental state after he has been wounded in World War I. The stories alternate with imagistic "chapters" that give glimpses of the war and of bullfighting. See KILLERS, THE.

In Parenthesis (1937). A book by David JONES. It is a modernistic, poetic account of infantry life in the First World War. Realistic description is mixed with Celtic mythology, Arthurian legend, and Christian allusion.

In Praise of Johnny Appleseed (1921). A poem by Vachel LINDSAY. It follows the career of John Chapman over the Appalachians, his wanderings among the Indians and in the wilderness, and his vigorous old age.

Inquisition. A court commonly called the Holy Office. It was instituted to inquire into offenses against the Roman Catholic religion, and fully established by Gregory IX in 1235. Torture, as a means of extracting recantations or evidence, was first authorized by Pope Innocent IV in 1252, and those found guilty were handed over to the secular arm to be dealt with according to the secular laws of the land. This was followed by the founding of the *Congregation of the Inquisition* in Rome, 1542. The Inquisition was only once introduced into England (viz., at the trials of the Templars, who were suppressed in 1308); it was most active in southern Europe, and flourished sporadically in Spain until the 19th century. In the Provençal region of France, where the Inquisition fostered the rise of militant monastic orders designed to stamp out mass heretic movements, the Dominican order played a crucial role in the Albigensian Crusade; the Inquisition was suppressed in France in 1772.

Inquisition, Spanish. A tribunal for suppressing heresy in Spain, established by Pope Sixtus IV in 1478 at the request of Ferdinand and Isabella. The first Inquisitor-General was Tomás de Torquemada (c. 1420–1498), a Dominican monk whose name has become a byword for cruelty and severity.

Though nominally under papal control, the Inquisition was actually an agency of the crown, which often used it for political purposes. The principal victims of the Inquisition in Spain were the converted Muslims and Jews, known respectively as *Moriscos* and *Marranos.* It also investigated crimes against morality, such as polygamy and rape. Its procedures were secret, and suspects were not told the identity of their accusers; torture was sometimes used. Penalties, which were announced at solemn public gatherings called *autos de fé,* ranged from reprimand and warning to "relaxation," i.e., being delivered to the secular authorities to be burned at the stake. The Inquisition was suppressed in 1808 and its successor, the Tribunal of the Faith, was abolished in 1834.

Insarov. The hero of Ivan Turgenev's novel, ON THE EVE. A Bulgarian revolutionary who lives only to free his country from Turkish oppression, the dedicated Insarov inspires love in the young Russian Elena STAKHOVA.

inscape. A term coined by the poet Gerard Manley HOPKINS. Usually applied to an object or scene in nature, it means essential, intrinsic quality and oneness that is composed of a number of separate characteristics. *Instress* is the force that creates and maintains *inscape.*

Inscription for the Entrance to a Wood (1817). A poem by William Cullen BRYANT. The poet finds solace in the woods for the guilt and misery of the world.

Inspector General, The (Revizor; 1836). A comic drama by Nikolai GOGOL. It is regarded as one of the best plays in Russian dramaturgy. The action revolves about a case of mistaken identity. The central character Khlestakov, a run-of-the-mill civil servant from St. Petersburg, is stranded in a small provincial town. The corrupt officials of the town, hearing that a government inspector is on the way there, convince themselves that Khlestakov is the man. Khlestakov quickly catches on and goes along with the error, bragging of his high connections in the capital, taking bribes, and wooing the mayor's daughter and wife. He is unmasked when a gloating letter he has writen to a friend in St. Petersburg is read by the inquisitive postmaster, but before he is found out, Khlestakov has prudently left town. While the town officials are fuming about the ruse, the real inspector general arrives.

The play was taken as a social satire at the time of its production and that view has remained the standard one in Russian criticism. There are, however, many fantastic aspects to the comedy, particularly in Khlestakov's inane chattering.

Instauratio Magna (*Lat.,* "great renewal"). A projected work by Francis BACON, designed to be a comprehensive survey of the principles, methods, and accomplishments of the "new philosophy," or experimental science. Only two of six parts were completed: THE ADVANCEMENT OF LEARNING and NOVUM ORGANUM.

Institute of France (Institut de France). A national French society, established in 1795 by the Republican Convention "to advance the sciences and arts of research . . . and to prosecute those scientific and literary labors which shall have for their end general utility and the glory of the republic." The organization includes five academies: L'ACADÉMIE FRANÇAISE, *L'Académie des Inscriptions et Belles-Lettres, L'Académie des Sciences, L'Académie des Beaux Arts,* and *L'Académie des Sciences Morales et Politiques.*

Institutes of the Christian Religion (Institution de la religion chrétienne; 1536). The principal work of John CALVIN. It first appeared in Latin in 1536, and a French translation, made by Calvin himself, was published in 1541. Designed as a reply to attacks on Protestantism and as a guide to Scripture, the work states, with passionate conviction, the essential doctrines of the new religion.

Insulted and Injured, The (Unizhennye i oskorblyonnye; 1861). A novel by Feodor Dostoevski. The first of his full-length novels, it is also the first of his works clearly to express Dostoevski's characteristic ideas about the purifying function of suffering. The book has a conventional, melodramatic plot, with Ivan Petrovich (Vanya), who is in love with Natasha Ikhmeneva, trying to aid her in her wooing of Alyosha Valkovski. Ivan, a young writer who bears some resemblance to the young Dostoevski, engages in philosophical duels with the cynical Prince Valkovski, Alyosha's father, an early sketch of the "predatory type" more fully developed in SVIDRIGAILOV in *Crime and Punishment* and STAVROGIN in *The Possessed.*

The sentimental atmosphere of the novel is heightened by the presence of a young girl, Nelly. Taken obviously from Dickens, she undergoes harrowing experiences at the hands of the prince before she is rescued.

interior monologue. See STREAM OF CONSCIOUSNESS.

interlude. A form of dramatic entertainment, originating during the reign of Henry VIII of England and popular at the Tudor court. The exact nature of the interlude is not known, but it is believed to have originated as a brief skit between the courses of a banquet. Court interludes, of which John HEYWOOD was the outstanding author, were usually lively and realistic and devoted chiefly to entertainment. Heywood's THE FOUR P's is a typical example. There were also educational interludes, didactically teaching an edifying moral; these were usually written in Latin, using type characters and situations, and were performed at public schools, such as Eton. The interlude is considered a transitional form between the miracle plays and MORALITY PLAYS of the Middle Ages and fully developed Elizabethan drama.

International. The name of 3 successive international associations, or congresses, designed to unite the working classes of all nations and promote Marxist socialism.

First International. The International Working Men's Association was founded in London in 1864 under the leadership of Karl MARX and Friedrich Engels. It had some success for the next five years, lending its support to aggrieved workers in England and in Europe, but, when the Russian anarchist Bakunin joined in 1869, a rift opened up between his followers and the less radical Marxists. Bakunin's group was expelled in 1872, but the organization lost the support of the nationalistic trade unions being formed at this time, and the last congress was held in Philadelphia in 1876.

Second International. Formed in 1889, the Second International followed the same Marxist theories as the First. After repeated attempts to avoid war, the movement lost most of its force when the First World War broke out and most of the members supported the war as national subjects, instead of opposing it as internationalists.

Third International. Also called the *Communist International* or *Comintern.* Established in Russia in 1919 as a result of the revolution, this International was formed to help spread Communist revolution throughout the world. The hostility of the Communists to the more moderate Socialists in the rest of Europe led to a revival of the Second International in the 1930's to provide a united Socialist front. The Third International was dissolved in 1943 by Stalin.

A so-called Second-and-a-half International was formed in Vienna in 1919; its attempt to reconcile the Socialists and Communists ended in total failure in 1922. Trotsky formed a Fourth, or Anti-Comintern, International in 1937 from his exile in Mexico, but it had little influence.

In the American Grain (1925). A volume of essays by William Carlos WILLIAMS. Attempting to discover the essential qualities of the American character, it includes sketches of such figures as Columbus, Poe, and Franklin, but it stresses minor figures of a less heroic nature. The book shares Van Wyck Brooks's search for a "usable past," and was used by Hart Crane in his attempt to create the myth of America in THE BRIDGE.

In the Midst of Life (1891). A collection of 26 stories by Ambrose BIERCE. In these tales of horror, Bierce implies that life is subject to accident and coincidence. The stories have twist endings rarely surpassed in literature. Ten of the tales deal with soldiers, and in every case, the young men die. Bierce's characters are generally abstractions, interesting not for their individuality but for their tragic fate. The mood of horror, established by realistic detail, is further exaggerated by the author's sardonic humor. Among the most famous of the stories are *An Occurrence at Owl Creek Bridge, A Horseman in the Sky, The Man and the Snake,* and *The Eyes of the Panther.*

In the Ravine (V ovrage; 1900). A long story by Anton CHEKHOV. A study of the brutal lives of the peasantry in a small provincial town, this work has long been considered one of Chekhov's best prose pieces. On its publication, it was unanimously acclaimed one of the outstanding works of Russian literature. The story's central characters are the shopkeeper Tzybukin, his two sons, and their wives, Aksinya and Lipa. Aksinya is a rapacious creature who eventually takes over the household and shop, drives out the old man, and causes the death of Lipa's small son.

Intruder in the Dust (1948). A novel by William FAULKNER. Lucas BEAUCHAMP, an aging Negro who has long nettled the townsfolk of Jefferson by his refusal to adopt the Negro's traditionally servile attitude, is wrongfully accused of murdering a white man and is threatened with violent death at the hands of a mob. Through the efforts of 16-year-old Chick MALLISON, Aleck Sander, Chick's Negro friend, and 70-year-old Miss Eunice Habersham, Lucas' innocence is proved and the real murderer captured. Because of his relationship with Lucas, Chick comes into manhood able to recognize other human beings as individuals, regardless of their color.

Invictus (*Lat.,* unconquered). The title of a well-known poem (usually deplored by critics) written in a tuberculosis hospital, by William Ernest HENLEY. Its last lines read:

> It matters not how strait the gate
> How charged with punishment the scroll,
> I am the master of my fate,
> I am the captain of my soul.

Invincibles, the Irish. An Irish secret society. It was founded in Dublin in 1881 with the object of doing away with the English tyranny. Members of this society were responsible for the Phoenix Park murders in 1882.

Invisible Man (1952). A novel by Ralph ELLISON. This unusual first novel is the record of a Negro boy's progression from youthful affirmation to a sense of total rejection; his final invisibility—that is, his loss of social identity—gives him a point of view often compared with that of the hero of Dostoevski's *Notes from the Underground.* Ellison's unnamed protagonist at first has a rather unrealistic trust in the motives of others. He is dismissed from a Negro college for showing one of the founders how Negroes actually live in the South. In New York City he plays a political role for the Communists, until he realizes that they are merely using him as a symbol of the Negro; as a person he is as invisible to them as to everyone else. During a surrealistic Harlem riot, he comes to the realization that to affirm his identity he would have to contend with both white people and the leaders of his own race.

Io. In Greek mythology, a priestess of Hera. Zeus seduced her, then transformed her into a cow to save her from Hera's wrath. Hera, however, sent a gadfly which drove Io over Greece and much of Asia. In Egypt she finally regained human form and gave birth to twins, Belus and Agenor, who fathered many dynasties of Greece, Crete, and Asia Minor. She appears in Aeschylus' PROMETHEUS BOUND.

Iolanthe; or, The Peer and the Peri (1882). An opera by GILBERT AND SULLIVAN. Iolanthe is a fairy banished because she married a mortal. Her son, Strephon, is a fairy down to the waist, but his legs are mortal. This leads to complications when he wishes to marry Phyllis, a shepherdess. The opera satirizes the House of Lords and the Courts of Chancery.

Iolcus or **Iolcos** (Iolkos). A city in Thessaly, the modern Volo, point of embarkation of the ARGONAUTS.

Ion (418 B.C.). A drama by Euripides. It treats the legend of Ion, son of Creusa and Apollo. He ultimately became king of Athens and ancestor of the Ionian race. It is one of Euripides' most dramatic plays. It has been interpreted by some as a skeptical drama that questioned the sanctity of Apollo and the honesty of his Delphic oracle.

Ionesco, Eugène (1912–   ). Romanian-born French dramatist of the ABSURD school. His earlier works are characterized by deliberate *non sequiturs,* the logic of nightmares, and strange metamorphoses. The stage is cluttered with inanimate or rotting things that proliferate until any remnant of the human is pathetically stifled. Nevertheless, these grimly grotesque farces remain essentially comic, because Ionesco is essentially sympathetic to the human attempt, however pitifully inadequate, at communication and love. THE BALD SOPRANO, *The Lesson* (1950), *Jack, or the Submission* (1950), THE CHAIRS, *Victims of Duty* (1952), and *Amedée* (1953) are all tragicomic in tone. Although the compassionate satire and the atmosphere of the fantastic remain, with *The Killer* (*Tueur sans gages;* 1958), Ionesco's plays begin to employ a more explicit symbolic technique and a more straightforward plot line. THE RHINOCEROS is almost a conventional allegory.

Iphiclus (Iphiklos). See MELAMPUS.

Iphigenia (Iphigeneia). In Greek mythology, the eldest child of Agamemnon and Clytemnestra. She was sacrificed by her father in order to gain favorable winds for the Greek fleet on its way to Troy (see IPHIGENIA IN AULIS). Her mother used this act as an excuse for murdering Agamemnon on his return. Their son Orestes, driven mad after killing Clytemnestra, went to the savage land of Tauris and there found his sister, whom Artemis had spirited away from her funeral pyre. Iphigenia saved Orestes and his friend, Pylades, and sailed away with them (see IPHIGENIA IN TAURIS).

Iphigenia in Aulis (Iphigeneia he en Aulidi; c. 405 B.C.). A tragedy by EURIPIDES. The seer Calchas has predicted that only the sacrifice of Iphigenia will save the Greeks from remaining trapped in the harbor at Aulis by unfavorable winds. Agamemnon has already sent for his daughter, pretending that she is to marry Achilles. He regrets his decision, but is dissuaded from altering it by the scorn of Menelaus. When Iphigenia arrives, with her mother Clytemnestra and her brother Orestes, even Menelaus relents, but Agamemnon orders the sacrifice, sure that Odysseus will force his hand in any case. Clytemnestra begs her husband to free his daughter, and Achilles, who has known nothing of the plot, offers to save her, but Iphigenia agrees to sacrifice herself for the Greeks.

The play was finished by Euripides' son after the playwright's death. An ending in which Iphigenia is saved when Artemis carries her off and substitutes a deer on the altar is thought to be a later interpolation. An altered version of this story was made into an opera by Gluck, *Iphigénie en Aulide* (1772).

Iphigenia in Tauris (Iphigeneia he en Taurois; c. 414–412 B.C.). A tragedy by EURIPIDES. After murdering his mother Clytemnestra (see ORESTEIA), ORESTES has been pursued by the Furies and Apollo has said he will be cured of madness only if he rescues the statue of Artemis from the savage inhabitants of Tauris (the Crimea), who kill all Greeks they find in their country. With his faithful friend Pylades, Orestes arrives in Tauris. The two are promptly captured and are brought to the high priestess to be ritually prepared for their sacrifice. The priestess is Iphigenia, who had been transported to Tauris by Artemis (see IPHIGENIA IN AULIS). In a moving scene, she and Orestes recognize each other. After each of the friends has offered to die for the other, she manages by a ruse to save both and escape with them in a boat. They are driven back by the wind, but saved when Athena appears and orders Thoas, the Taurian king, to let them leave. A version of this story was made into an opera by Gluck, *Iphigénie en Tauride* (1779).

Iphigenia in Tauris (Iphigenie auf Tauris; prose version, 1779; final version in verse, 1787). A play by Johann Wolfgang von GOETHE after Euripides' play of the same title. Iphigenia, whom her father Agamemnon had wished to sacrifice in order to get good weather for the Greeks' voyage to Troy, has been snatched away by Artemis and left in Tauris as a priestess. Her brother Orestes, tormented by the Furies, then comes unwittingly to Tauris, is joyfully reunited with his sister, and both sail home. Goethe, however, does away with Euripides' *deus ex machina* and makes the play's resolution arise from what he later called pure humanity, the inner core of emotional sympathy that unites men, transcends all boundaries of nationality or religion, and ultimately assuages all guilt. See WEIMAR CLASSICISM; Charlotte von STEIN.

Iphigénie en Aulide (1679). A tragedy by Jean RACINE. Its material is freely drawn from the play by Euripides. An oracle declares that only the sacrifice of Iphigénie can release the Greek fleet from Aulis, where unfavorable winds have stranded it. Priests force Agamemnon to send his daughter word that Achilles, her betrothed, desires her at Aulis for an immediate marriage. Achilles is incensed to learn of the ruse, but Iphigénie obediently awaits her fate. Remorseful, Agamemnon arranges for his daughter to escape, but the slave-girl ERIPHILE (a character invented by Racine), who loves Achilles, reveals the plan. The priest Calchas declares Eriphile the victim the gods require, for her name at birth was Iphigénie. Eriphile kills herself on the altar, and Iphigénie is spared.

I.R.A. See IRISH REPUBLICAN ARMY.

Iras. In Shakespeare's ANTONY AND CLEOPATRA, the second lady-in-waiting to Cleopatra. She dies shortly before her mistress.

Ireland, William Henry (1777–1835). English forger of Shakespearean manuscripts and documents. His own blank verse play, *Vortigern and Rowena,* which he attributed to Shakespeare, was a complete failure on the stage (1796) and led to the exposure of the forgeries, and shortly thereafter Ireland wrote *An Authentic Account of the Shaksperian MSS.* He also published several ballads, poems, novels, memoirs, and translations.

I Remember Mama (1945). A play by John VAN DRUTEN. A dramatization of Kathryn Forbes' *Mamma's Bank Account* (1943), it is the amusing and tender story of a Norwegian mother and father raising their children in America in the early days of the 20th century. The situation later became the basis of a successful television serial starring Peggy Wood.

Irena. See FAERIE QUEENE, THE.

Irene. In John Galsworthy's Forsyte Saga, the sensitive, passionate heroine. Wife of Soames Forsyte, she falls in love with Philip Bosinney, is divorced, and marries Young Jolyon Forsyte.

Ireton, Henry (1611–1651). English general and statesman. The husband of Oliver Cromwell's daughter Bridget, he was a cavalry commander at the battle of Naseby. He became a member of Parliament in 1645 and was one of the judges at the trial of King Charles I.

Iriarte, Tomás de (1750–1791). Spanish fabulist and poet. His best-known work is the collection of fables, 76 in all, entitled *Fábulas literarias* (1782), which satirizes contemporary literature in a series of apologues including *El burro flautista* and *El oso y el mono.* Iriarte also completed a verse translation of Horace.

Iris. The Greek goddess of the rainbow, or the rainbow itself. In classic mythology, she is called the messenger of the gods when they intended discord, and the rainbow is the bridge or road let down from heaven for her accommodation. When the gods meant peace they sent Hermes.

Irish Renaissance. A term used to describe the outburst of creative activity at the turn of the last century, which grew out of the attempt to awaken the Irish people to the wealth and value of their native culture. The movement, which had been developing very slowly in the latter half of the 19th century, achieved its major impetus from the political martyrdom of the Irish leader Charles Stewart Parnell, an event which caused many thoughtful Irishmen to abandon the attempt to achieve a national identity within an English framework. The Gaelic culture with which the movement identified itself had been, prior to the English invasion in the 12th century, among the richest and most advanced in Europe, particularly distinguished by the enormous prestige with which it invested the tribal bard or storyteller.

The movement itself had two major developments: the activities of the Gaelic League, an organization founded in 1893 by Douglas Hyde to restore Gaelic as the official language of Ireland; and the formation of the Irish National Theatre Society in 1901, out of which grew the famous Abbey Theatre Company. The leading figures of this latter movement were William Butler Yeats, Edward Martyn (1859–1927), George Moore, Lady Gregory, and the actors William (1872–1947) and Frank (1870–1931) Fay. The Abbey Theatre soon became (and remained for the next 30 years) a storm center, the result of the brilliant but, at the time, controversial plays of Yeats, John M. Synge and Sean O'Casey. Riots and vigorous protestations greeted the productions of Synge's *Playboy of the Western World,* Yeats's *Countess Cathleen* and O'Casey's *The Plough and the Stars* (1926) and *Juno and the Paycock.* Despite the protests at home, the Abbey soon developed an international reputation, and the players, featuring such performers as Sara Allgood (1883–1950) and Barry Fitzgerald (1888–1961) enjoyed their greatest success, ironically enough, on tour in England. Other significant Abbey dramatists were Padraic Colum, Lennox Robinson, and Paul Vincent Carroll. Although the Abbey's greatest days are now past, its impact on the modern theatre is still felt and its legacy may be seen in the work of two recent Irish

dramatists of note, Brendan Behan and Samuel Beckett.

In nondramatic literature, the revival was sparked by the poetry of Yeats and A.E., the fanciful and charming re-creations of Irish legends in the novels and poems of James Stephens, the more realistic treatment of contemporary life in the novels and short stories of Liam O'Flaherty, Sean O'Faolain and Frank O'Connor. The irony that marks so much of the Irish Renaissance—its great achievement lies, not in the restoration of Irish culture, but in the immeasurable enrichment of English literature—is nowhere so pronounced as in one of its greatest products: James Joyce, who so steadfastly refused to be associated with the revival and yet whose work is saturated with Irish life.

Irish Republican Army (I.R.A.). A secret organization founded to work for Irish independence from England. It continued to exist even after the Republic of Ireland was established in 1937.

Iroldo. A character in Boiardo's Orlando Innamorato whose friend Prasildo falls in love with his wife Tisbina. He generously gives her up and leaves, but later Prasildo rescues him and they fight together.

Iron, Ralph. See Olive Schreiner.

iron crown of Lombardy. The crown of the ancient Longobardic kings. It was used at the coronation of Agilulph, king of Lombardy, in 591, and among others who have since been crowned with it are Charlemagne, as king of Italy (774); Henry of Luxemburg (the emperor Henry VII), as king of Lombardy (1311); Frederick IV (1452); and Charles V (1530). In 1805, Napoleon put it on his head by his own hand.

In 1866, at the conclusion of peace, the iron crown was given up by Austria to Italy and was replaced in the cathedral at Monza, where Charlemagne had been crowned, and whence it had been taken in 1859. It is so called from the fact that there is within it a narrow band of iron, said to have been beaten out of one of the nails used at the Crucifixion. According to tradition, the nail was given to Constantine by his mother, St. Helena, who discovered the true cross. The outer circlet is of beaten gold, and set with precious stones.

Iron Heel, The (1907). A novel by Jack London. Prophetically, it describes events from 1912 to 1918 when a fascistic organization, the Iron Heel, seizes power in the U.S. The hero is Ernest Everhard, a socialist who fights the Iron Heel.

Iron in the Soul. See Roads to Freedom, The.

Iron Mask, Man in the. See Man in the Iron Mask.

Ironsides. A name given to the cavalry troops that fought under Oliver Cromwell in the English Civil War, especially after the battle of Marston Moor (1644). Earlier, the name was applied only to a famous cavalry regiment led by Cromwell.

irony. In rhetoric, a deliberate dissembling for effect or to intensify meaning. An example is subtle sarcasm or language meant to be understood only by the initiated. Irony often takes the form of pretended ignorance as a device to lead on and eventually to confound an opponent, as in Socratic irony. Dramatic irony is the theatrical device of making a speaker utter words which have a hidden meaning intelligible to the audience but of which he himself is unconscious, as when Oedipus, in Sophocles' *Oedipus Tyrannus,* calls down curses upon the slayer of Laius, not knowing that they will fall upon his own head. In life, an occurrence or series of occurrences are said to be ironical that are quite the reverse of what might have been expected, as if fate had intended to be ironical in the rhetorical sense; "the irony of fate" expresses this meaning more explicitly.

irony, romantic. A literary technique first specifically defined by Friedrich SCHLEGEL. Romantic irony is basically the introduction of paradox into a literary work, as, for example, when the hero of a novel suddenly announces that the author of the novel has died and that he, the hero, will carry on the work, a situation that occurs in Brentano's *Godwi* (1800–1801). Another common ironic technique is for statements *about* a literary work to be included *within* the work. Examples of this are Tieck's play *Puss in Boots* (*Der gestiefelte Kater,* pub. 1797), in which a fictitious audience is put on the stage to criticize the play, and Schlegel's own novel *Lucinde* (1799), which embodies a theory of the novel.

Iroquois League. A confederacy of Iroquoian-speaking Indian tribes organized about 1570 in what is now western New York. The members of the league, who called themselves "People of the Long House" because they dwelt together in harmony, were the Mohawks, Oneidas, Onondagas, Cayugas, Senecas (and later the Tuscaroras). During the 17th century they warred against the French and other Indian tribes. Most of the Iroquois supported England in the American Revolution, and many settled in Canada after peace was concluded. Hiawatha, the Mohawk chief whose name was immortalized in Longfellow's *Song Of Hiawatha* (1855), played an important part in creating the League.

Irus (Iros). In Greek legend, the beggar of Ithaca. He ran errands for Penelope's suitors. When Odysseus returned home dressed as a beggar, Irus challenged him, and Odysseus broke his jaw with a blow. (See ODYSSEY.)

Irving, Sir Henry (1838–1905). English actor. He played successfully various roles and in 1874, with his performance of Hamlet, won real distinction. He took over the management of the Lyceum Theatre in 1878 and made many tours to the U.S. with his company, which included Ellen TERRY. He was the first actor to be knighted (1895), and was buried in Westminster Abbey.

Irving, Washington (1783–1859). American essayist, biographer, and historian. Although he prepared to be a lawyer, Irving was physically delicate, and his indulgent family allowed him to lead the life of a man of letters. His first published writing was a series of newspaper sketches appearing under the pseudonym of Jonathan Oldstyle, Gent. In 1807, in collaboration with his brother William, and James Kirk Paulding, Irving wrote the SALMAGUNDI papers; these humorous and satirical pieces modeled on Addison brought him local renown in New York. His first book, A HISTORY OF NEW YORK FROM THE BEGINNING OF THE WORLD TO THE END OF THE DUTCH DYNASTY, supposedly by Diedrich Knickerbocker, created the character of the phlegmatic Dutchman. A quaint and humorous figure, Knickerbocker is a familiar byword, particularly in New York.

After the death of his fiancée, Irving sailed for

Europe, where he remained for 17 years. His best-known book, THE SKETCH BOOK OF GEOFFREY CRAYON, GENT., was published there in 1820, followed by BRACEBRIDGE HALL and TALES OF A TRAVELLER. For financial reasons, Irving accepted a position in the U.S. embassy in Madrid. Fascinated by Spain, he enthusiastically wrote four works: HISTORY OF THE LIFE AND VOYAGES OF COLUMBUS, *The Conquest of Granada* (1829), *Companions of Columbus* (1831), and THE LEGENDS OF THE ALHAMBRA. He returned home, and journeyed across the prairies, recording his trip three years later in A TOUR ON THE PRAIRIES. He contracted with John Jacob Astor to write the history of ASTORIA and produced a sequel, *The Adventures of* CAPTAIN BONNEVILLE. From 1842 to 1846 Irving served as U.S. minister to Spain. He then retired to Sunnyside, his home in Tarrytown, N.Y. As an old man, he wrote biographies of Goldsmith and Mahomet, and completed a five-volume biography of George Washington (1855–1859) shortly before his death.

Irving took as his models Scott, Addison, and Goldsmith, never attempting to develop an original idiom. Though he rarely manifests moral or intellectual awareness, the charm, delicacy, and pictorial quality of his writing give it lasting value. Irving proved to skeptics at home and abroad that the world would read an American book. Further, among the delightful tales and sketches are a few that have become part of American folklore. See WOLFERT'S ROOST.

Irwin, Wallace [Admah] (1875–1959). American newspaperman, writer of humorous verse and fiction. Irwin won national fame with *The Love Sonnets of a Hoodlum* (1902), a remarkable collection of Petrarchan verses in the American vernacular. He is also known for creating the character of Hashimura Togo, a Japanese schoolboy, under whose name he wrote epistolary stories for at least 20 years. The first collection of these was *Letters of a Japanese Schoolboy* (1909). He also wrote *Mr. Togo, Maid of All Work* (1913); *The Rubaiyat of Omar Khayyam Jr.* (1902); *Seed of the Sun* (1921), a serious novel about the problems of the Japanese living in California; and *Yankee Doctor in Paradise* (1941), in collaboration with Dr. Sylvester Lambert.

Is. See Ys.

Isaac. In the Old Testament, the only son of ABRAHAM and Sarah, the husband of Rebekah, and the father of JACOB and ESAU. He was nearly offered as a sacrifice to prove his father's faith, but at the last moment God intervened and told Abraham to slay a ram instead (Gen. 24–28).

Isaacs, Jorge. See MARÍA.

Isabella. In the ORLANDO FURIOSO of Ariosto, the Saracen princess, daughter of the king of Galicia and beloved of the Christian knight Zerbino. After the latter is killed by Mandricardo, she lets herself be slain by Rodomonte, who in grief builds a shrine to commemorate the unfortunate lovers.

Isabella. The beautiful and intensely virtuous religious novice who is the heroine of Shakespeare's MEASURE FOR MEASURE. She is finally united with the introverted, philosophical Vincentio, duke of Vienna.

Isabella I. Known as la Católica ("the Catholic") (1451–1504). Queen of Castile. The daughter of John II of Castile, she married FERDINAND II of Aragon in 1469. Her accession to the throne of Castile upon the death of her brother Henry IV in 1474 led to the permanent union of the two great kingdoms of Spain.

Isabella, or The Pot of Basil (1820). A poem by John KEATS, adapted from a tale by Boccaccio. Set in Florence, it tells of Isabella's love for Lorenzo. Her brothers, discovering this love, revenge themselves by murdering Lorenzo in a forest. The ghost of Lorenzo appears to Isabella and tells her of the crime; she goes to the forest, digs up his head, and plants it in a pot of basil, keeping it by her and watering it with her tears. Her brothers discover her grotesque secret and steal the pot, leaving Isabella to die of grief.

Isaiah. A prophetical book of the Old Testament. In its present form it is the work of at least three distinct authors in three successive stages of Jewish history from c. 750 to c. 450 B.C. The first part is strongly political, the author having been a counselor of the Judaean kings. Urging peace with Israel's enemies, he can still foresee the coming tragedy of the Babylonian Exile. The middle chapters of Isaiah (40–55) were written after 586, when Jerusalem fell. They call on Israel not to lose faith in its god and prophesy the return of his loving care. The last part reflects the period of Nehemiah's return to Jerusalem and the rebuilding of the city and temple (c. 450). It is nationalistic and stresses the ritualistic side of Judaism.

All three parts of Isaiah are filled with Messianic hope. The life of the Messiah is told in Isaiah.

Ischia, battle of (1464). The Neapolitan fleet of the Aragonese monarchs defeated the French navies in this battle, thus ending the efforts of the Angevins to regain the throne of Naples, lost to Alfonso of Aragon in 1442.

Isenbras or **Isumbras, Sir** (14th century). Hero of a Middle English verse romance. Strong and prosperous but arrogant, he is offered the choice of suffering either in youth or in old age. Choosing the former, he is beset by great misfortunes, which humble him. After performing many deeds of generosity and bravery for 21 years, he is restored in happiness to all he had lost.

Isengrim. See REYNARD THE FOX.

Iseult. The name of the heroine in the medieval cycle TRISTAN AND ISEULT. There are many other versions and parallels of this cycle, beginning with early Irish tales (see THE PURSUIT OF DIARMUID AND GRAINNE) and appearing in the modern world in such forms as the music drama of Richard Wagner; Iseult's name appears in various forms: Isolde, Isolt, Ysolt, etc. In general, Iseult the Fair is an Irish princess, wooed and won by TRISTAN for his uncle, King MARK of Cornwall. But in the process of journeying to the court of King Mark, both Iseult and Tristan drink a magic potion that causes them to fall in love with one another, a love which is completely binding, even in the face of death. The major part of this cycle is concerned with the adventures of the pair, after the marriage of Iseult to King Mark, in the name of their great love. Ultimately Tristan is banished and goes to Brittany where he marries another, Iseult of the White Hands. When he is about to die, he sends for his love, Iseult the Fair, but she arrives too late. Lying beside the body of Tristan, she too dies. When the two lovers are buried next to one another, a briar grows up from the grave of Tristan and curves over to take root on the grave of Iseult.

Three times it is cut down and three times it grows again, until King Mark commands that it be left alone. Iseult is depicted as very beautiful, gifted (among other things, she has great skill in healing wounds), shrewd, and something of a sorceress. In James Joyce's *Finnegans Wake* (1939), the wife and daughter of Earwicker represent the two Iseults of Tristan.

Isherwood, Christopher [William Bradshaw] (1904–   ). English novelist, short-story writer, and playwright. He was a member of the talented group of left-wing young writers of the 1930's that included W. H. Auden, C. Day-Lewis, and Stephen Spender. Living in Germany during Hitler's rise to power, Isherwood brilliantly described the social corruption and disintegration in his *Berlin Stories*: MR. NORRIS CHANGES TRAINS, *Sally Bowles* (1937), and *Goodbye to Berlin* (1939). He collaborated with W. H. Auden on the verse plays THE DOG BENEATH THE SKIN, THE ASCENT OF F6, and *On the Frontier* (1938), a political melodrama. He traveled to China with Auden and collaborated on *Journey to a War* (1939), about the war between Japan and China. At the outbreak of the European war he, like Auden, emigrated to the U.S. Auden abandoned Marxism for earnest Christianity; Isherwood abandoned it to become a disciple of Aldous Huxley in the study of Eastern religions and yoga. Among Isherwood's other publications are the novels *All the Conspirators* (1928), *The Memorial* (1932), *Prater Violet* (1945), *The World in the Evening* (1954), *Down There on a Visit* (1962), and *A Single Man* (1964). He has also translated Baudelaire's *Intimate Journals*.

Ishmael. In the Old Testament, the son of Abraham and HAGAR. In general, the name refers to any outcast from society because of the prophecy: "And he will be a wild man; his hand will be against every man, and every man's hand against him" (Gen. 16:12). After the birth of Isaac, Ishmael was cast out of Abraham's household, married, and settled at Paran; the Arab people were descended from his 12 sons.

Herman Melville gave the name Ishmael to the narrator of MOBY DICK.

Ishtar. The Babylonian goddess of love and war. Known to the Canaanites as Astarte, to the Israelites as Ashtoreth, to the Arabs as the god Athtar, she developed from the Sumerian goddess INANNA, and was the most widely worshiped of all the deities of the Near and Middle East. According to one version of the myth, she was the daughter of Sin (the moon) and sister of Shamash (the sun); according to another, the daughter of Anu, the lord of heaven; in both, she was identified with the planet Venus. Though the goddess of erotic love, she was often warlike and, at best, had a remarkably irritable disposition. Her worship involved ritual prostitution, which was severely condemned by the Hebrew prophets. She may have been "the queen of heaven" mentioned by Jeremiah; Solomon built a temple to her.

Of the many myths in which she figured, the most famous tells of her love for Tammuz, a young fertility god. In some unexplained way, her love caused his death. She mourned him extravagantly—her lamentations were ritually commemorated yearly when the summer sun dried up the vegetation—and finally descended into the underworld to bring back her lover. At each of the seven gates through which she passed, she was divested of one of her ornaments or pieces of clothing, until she stood naked before her terrible sister ERESHKIGAL, goddess of the underworld. She was imprisoned there, and the gods were powerless to help her, until EA fashioned a hermaphroditic creature called Asushu-Namir and sent it armed with magic spells against Ereshkigal. These were successful, and, after Asushu-Namir had poured over her "the water of life," Ishtar returned to earth, taking Tammuz with her. Ishtar's love for Tammuz and her struggle for him with the goddess of the underworld obviously influenced the myth of Aphrodite's rivalry with Persephone over ADONIS.

As Tammuz discovered, the love of Ishtar was a mixed blessing. In the *Epic of* GILGAMESH, the hero resists her advances and, employing many unflattering epithets, reminds her that her other lovers have regretted their good fortune, many being turned (literally or figuratively) into beasts. In her fury at this rude treatment, Ishtar induces her father Anu to send the bull of heaven against Gilgamesh, but he and Enkidu kill it. It is for this crime that Enkidu dies.

Isis. The principal goddess of ancient Egypt, forming with her husband-brother Osiris and son Horus the major triad of deities. As the patron saint of mariners in Alexandria, she was often identified with the moon; the cow was sacred to her, its horns representing the crescent moon which, in Egypt, appears lying on its back. Her chief temples were at Amydos, Busiris, and Philae. She is represented as a queen, her head being surmounted by horns and the solar disk or by the double crown.

The later Greeks and Romans also identified her with the goddess of nature and Apuleius, in the *Golden Ass* (second century A.D.), describes her as "the universal mother nature." Representations of Isis suckling Horus were possible prototypes of the Madonna and Child.

Milton, in *Paradise Lost* (1667) places Isis among the fallen angels. In the *Faerie Queene* (1596), Spenser used the legend of Isis and Osiris to symbolize English equity and justice.

to lift the veil of Isis. To pierce to the heart of a great mystery. Proclus mentions a statue of Isis, which bore the inscription, "I am that which is, has been, and shall be. My veil no one has lifted. The fruit I bore was the Sun."

Islam. The religion of MUHAMMAD, whose adherents are called Muslims, Moslems, Musulmans, Mohammedans. The word means *resignation* or *submission to the will of God.* MUSLIMS believe every child is born in Islam and would continue in the true faith if not led astray.

Islam emphasizes five duties: (1) bearing witness that there is but one God and one prophet, Muhammad; (2) reciting daily prayers; (3) giving appointed and legal alms; (4) observing the RAMADAN, a month's fast; (5) making a pilgrimage to Mecca at least once in a lifetime. See HADJI; KORAN.

Island of the Seven Cities. A kind of mythical Utopia. There seven bishops, who quitted Spain during the dominion of the Moors, founded seven cities. The legend says that many have visited the island, but no one has ever left it.

Islands of the Blessed. A mythical abode of dead heroes, called by the Greeks Happy Islands, and by the Romans Fortunate Islands. They are imaginary islands somewhere in the West, where the favorites of the gods are conveyed at death, and dwell in everlasting joy.

Isla y Rojo, José Francisco de (1703–1781). Spanish Jesuit and satirist. His best-known work is the *Historia del famoso predicador fray Gerundio de Campazas, alias Zotes* (1758), a satire aimed at bombastic and pedantic religious oratory. It was banned in Spain by the Inquisition, and the second part did not appear until after the expulsion of the Jesuits from Spain in 1767. Isla also wrote *Triunfo del amor y de la lealtad, o Día grande de Navarra* (1746), a satirical treatment of a celebration in Pamplona upon the accession of Ferdinand VI.

Isle of Dogs, The (1597). A lost play by Thomas NASHE and Ben JONSON. It was so scornfully satiric that it resulted in the imprisonment of Jonson and in the temporary closing of the theatres.

Isle Sonante, L' (*Fr.,* "Ringing Island"). The title of the first edition (1562) of 16 chapters of what is now known as Book V of Rabelais' GARGANTUA AND PANTAGRUEL. Ringing Island, which is the first of several islands visited by Pantagruel and his friends, is inhabited by variously colored birds named cardinjays, priestjays, etc., and one popejay, "unique in his species." Birds of passage who had migrated to the island from Nobreadland and Alltoomany, they pass their time in sumptuous living, warbling to the ringing of bells. The episode of these lucky folk who enjoy paradise "both in this world and the next" is a transparent satire on the luxurious living of the Roman Catholic clergy, who thus lured into their ranks many social outcasts and poverty-stricken people.

Ismene. In Greek legend, daughter of Oedipus and Jocasta. Antigone was buried alive by the order of King Creon, for burying her brother Polynices, slain in combat by his brother Eteocles. Although she had actually been too timid to do so, Ismene declared that she had aided her sister, and requested to be allowed to share the same punishment. The episode occurs in Sophocles' ANTIGONE.

Ismeno. In the GERUSALEMME LIBERATA of Tasso, an enchanter who advises and aids the infidel forces against the Crusaders attacking Jerusalem. At one point, he brings the Arab chieftain Solimano to the battle by transporting him in a cloud. Later he enchants a forest near the Christian camp so that the Crusaders cannot build any more war machines. This spell is broken by Rinaldo.

Isocrates (Isokrates) (436–338 B.C.). An Attic orator, a pupil of SOCRATES. He founded a school and taught some of the greatest future statesmen, orators, and philosophers. When Philip of Macedon conquered Greece, he committed suicide. Of his orations, 21 have been preserved.

Isolde. See ISEULT.

Isolt. See ISEULT.

Israel (*Heb.,* "contender with God"). In the Old Testament, it is the name given to Jacob after he wrestled with the angel of the Lord (Gen. 32:28). Thus, it is also the name given to the Jewish nation descended from him, frequently referred to as the *Children of Israel.*

Israel Potter: or, Fifty Years of Exile (1855). A novel by Herman MELVILLE. The book is based on Henry Trumbull's biography, *Life and Remarkable Adventures of Israel Potter* (1824). In search of freedom and adventure, Israel becomes involved in the battle of Bunker Hill. He meets three Americans: Benjamin Franklin, who robs him while masquerading as a friend; John Paul Jones, who genuinely befriends him; and Ethan Allen, who possesses America's most admirable characteristics. Israel's personality is a mixture of the virtues and faults of all three men. An archetypal American, he is taken prisoner by the English, exiled for 50 years, and returns home to die. Melville suggests, at the end of this satirical novel, that the best hope for America is in her pioneering West.

Israfil, Israfel, or Uriel. The Muslim angel of music, possessed of the most melodious voice of all God's creatures. It is he who, on Judgment Day, is to sound the last trump of resurrection. Along with Gabriel and Michael, he was one of the three angels, according to the Koran, who warned Abraham of Sodom's destruction.

Israfel is the title of one of Edgar Allan Poe's poems (1831), and also of Hervey Allen's biography of Poe.

Issa. See KOBAYASHI ISSA.

Istar. See ISHTAR.

Isthmian games. Games consisting of chariot races, running, wrestling, boxing, and other sports. They were held by the ancient Greeks in the Isthmus of Corinth every alternate spring, the first and third of each Olympiad. They were instituted, according to the myth, in honor of MELICERTES.

Isumbras, Sir. See Sir ISENBRAS.

italic. A style of type. *Italic type* or *italics* (the type in which the letters, instead of being erect, as in roman, slope upward from left to right, *thus*) was first used by Aldo Manuzio in printing the Aldine classics. It was called by him cursive, a running hand (from Lat. *curro,* I run). Vergil was the first author printed in this type (1501).

It Can't Happen Here (1935). A novel by Sinclair LEWIS. It presents a fancied fascist dictatorship in the U.S., set up by Berzelius Windrip, a New England demagogue who is elected to the presidency. Doremus Jessup, a Vermont editor, fights Windrip, is arrested, escapes, and joins an underground movement in Canada headed by Walt Trowbridge, Windrip's opponent in the election.

Ithuriel. In Milton's PARADISE LOST, an angel who, with Zephon, is commissioned by Gabriel to search for Satan after the latter has effected his entrance into Paradise. He is armed with a spear, the slightest touch of which exposes deceit.

It Is Never Too Late to Mend (1853). A novel by Charles READE. This fictional study of the discovery of gold in Australia and the British convict system is notable for the character of Isaac Levi, one of the first serious attempts to portray the Jew favorably in fiction.

Iturbide, Agustín de (1783–1824). Mexican soldier and emperor. After fighting against Hidalgo and Morelos in the Spanish army, Iturbide joined the rebel forces and contributed to the final victory over Spain in 1821. Exploiting the confusion that followed the separation from Spain, Iturbide, the self-styled father of Mexican independence, seized power and had himself proclaimed emperor in 1822. During his brief reign as Agustin I, he was harassed by financial difficulties, by disgruntled generals, and by republican critics. He was deposed in 1823, and when he attempted to return to power the following year, he was captured and shot.

Iudushka. Nickname of Porfiri Golovlyov in Mikhail Saltykov's novel THE GOLOVLYOV FAMILY. His nickname means "Little Judas" and he is referred to as a bloodsucker. He lives up to his reputation as he takes over the family estates from his despotic mother and weakling brothers. He is regarded as a supreme portrayal of unctuous heartlessness.

Iulus. See ASCANIUS.

Ivan IV or Ivan the Terrible (1530–1584). Czar of Russia (1533–1584). Ivan engaged in a power struggle throughout his reign with the nobility (the boyars). During this time he consolidated the Muscovite state, the core of the future Russian empire, and gained an undying reputation for ferocious cruelty toward his enemies—a predilection which alternated with bouts of sensuality and piety. His squabbles with the boyars induced him to set up his own private state within the Muscovite state. Ivan's realm, called the *Oprichnina,* had its own courts, administration, and army. The rest of the country, called the *Zemshchina,* was ostensibly ruled by a prince appointed by Ivan, although the puppet ruler's power was slight.

Ivan's stormy career has provided the basis for many literary and dramatic works by Russian authors, as well as a two-part film by Sergei Eisenstein. Ivan's own literary remains consist of several letters in an acrimonious correspondence with Prince Andrei Mikhailovich Kurbski, who fled to Lithuania when the Czar began his reign of terror in Russia.

Ivanhoe (1819). A novel by Sir Walter SCOTT. The action occurs in the period following the Norman Conquest. The titular hero is Wilfred, knight of Ivanhoe, the son of Cedric the Saxon, in love with his father's ward Rowena. Cedric, however, wishes her to marry Athelstane, who is descended from the Saxon royal line and may restore the Saxon supremacy. The real heroine is REBECCA the Jewess, daughter of the wealthy Isaac of York, and a person of much more character and charm than the mild Rowena. Yet Ivanhoe finally rejects her in favor of Rowena. Richard the Lion-heart in the guise of the Black Knight and Robin Hood as LOCKSLEY play prominent roles, and the novel is further emblazoned with a colorful entourage of chivalric knights and fair ladies. The frenzied variety of the action, with the pageantry of a tournament and a great flame-engulfed castle, makes this the most enthralling of Scott's works. See Brian de BOIS-GUILBERT; Reginald FRONT DE BOEUF; and ULRICA.

Ivanov, Vsevolod Vyacheslavovich (1895–   ). Russian novelist and short-story writer. Ivanov ran away from home while in his teens and worked at a variety of jobs, including that of a circus clown and as a fakir and dervish. His first story was printed in a Siberian newspaper and attracted the attention of Maksim Gorki, who helped and encouraged the young writer. After the civil war, in which he fought first for the Whites and then for the Reds, Ivanov went to Petersburg and joined the SERAPION BROTHERS. His novels, *Colored Winds (Tzvetnye* *vetra;* 1922) and *Blue Sands* (*Golubye peski;* 1923), and his stories, such as *Partisans* (*Partizany;* 1921) and *Armored Train No. 14–69* (*Bronepoyezd No. 14–69;* 1922), are exotic in both theme and treatment, written in the ornate prose style popular in the 1920's. The inherent primitivism that Ivanov depicts as a constant factor in human behavior eventually displeased Soviet critics, who felt he should deal more with life's social aspects. Ivanov then toned down the highly colored prose of his earlier work and made his stories more conventional, with some loss of vigor and excitement. His later work includes an autobiographical novel, *The Adventures of a Fakir* (*Pokhozhdeniya fakira;* 1935), and a war novel *The Taking of Berlin* (*Vzyatiye Berlina;* 1945).

Ivanov, Vyacheslav Ivanovich (1866–1949). Russian poet. A classical scholar, Ivanov was the leader of the St. Petersburg branch of SYMBOLISTS from 1905 to 1911, when he moved to Moscow. His earlier poetry was a compound of classical references and archaic Slavic diction, with an admixture of Nietzschean philosophy. His later *Roman Sonnets* (*Rimskiye sonety*), written just before World War II, dispense with ornateness and archaism, achieving powerful effects in simple, direct lines. Ivanov's study of Dostoevski (1932) examines the novelist's work as creations of myth. Ivanov emigrated in 1924 and settled in Italy. He died in Rome, after becoming a Roman Catholic convert.

Ives, Charles [Edward] (1874–1954). American composer and businessman. The income from his insurance firm, Ives & Myrick, supported his musical experiments. In his works, which include symphonies, and choral and chamber music, he anticipated modern techniques of later composers. His *Sonata No. 2* (subtitled *Concord, Mass., 1840–1860*) has four movements, labeled: *Emerson, Hawthorne, The Alcotts, Thoreau.* The inspiration of these transcendentalists he explains in *Essays Before a Sonata* (1920). Ives' work has only recently received public attention.

Ives, James Merritt. See CURRIER AND IVES.

ivory gate. See DREAMS, GATES OF.

Ivy Day in the Committee Room. A short story in James Joyce's DUBLINERS (1914). It is an account of a conversation between a group of party political workers on the anniversary of the birth of Charles Stewart Parnell. The disunity, corruption, and pettiness of these small politicians is contrasted with the idealism of Parnell, whom these characters hypocritically idolize.

Ixion. In Greek mythology, a Lapith king. He tried to seduce Hera, but Zeus shaped a cloud in her likeness and he lay with it. Zeus bound him to a fiery wheel that perpetually rolls through the sky. The phantom, later called Nephele, bore Centaurus, ancestor of the centaurs.

Iyangar, Venkatesa (1891–). Kannada novelist, short-story writer and essayist, known affectionately in India as "Masti." Eleven volumes of his stories have been collected under the title *Sanna Kathegalu:* they show charm, humor, wit, compassion, and great narrative fluency.

Iyengar, K. R. Srinivasa (1908–). Indian critic writing in English; head of the department of English in Andhra University. His major work has been the assessment and publicizing of Indian creative writing in English. His main study is *Indian Writing in English* (1962).

J

Jabberwocky. A well-known mock-heroic ballad by Lewis Carroll, found in THROUGH THE LOOKING-GLASS. It contains a number of words coined by the author himself, including PORTMANTEAU WORDS such as slithy, a compound of lithe and slimy, mimsy, a compound of flimsy and miserable, etc. The Jabberwock is a species of dragon.

J'accuse (I accuse). The title of Emile ZOLA's famous open letter addressed to President Faure of France (first appearing in the newspaper *Aurore*, January 13, 1898), in denunciation of the Dreyfus affair. Zola used the phrase *"j'accuse"* several times in the letter, addressing himself to the injustices perpetrated by the war department. After a year of exile in England, Zola returned to France, a hero for the part he had played in this national crisis. See Alfred DREYFUS.

Jack and Jill. A well-known nursery rhyme. It is said to be a relic of a Norse myth, accounting for the dark patches in the moon. The two children are supposed to have been kidnaped by the moon while drawing water, and they are still to be seen with the bucket hanging from a pole resting on their shoulders.

Jack and the Beanstalk. A nursery tale. It is found among a wide variety of races from Icelanders to Zulus. Jack is a very poor lad, sent by his mother to sell a cow, which he parts with to a butcher for a few beans. His mother, in her rage, throws the beans away, but one of them grows during the night as high as the heavens. Jack climbs the stalk, and, by the direction of a fairy, comes to a giant's castle, where he begs food and rest. This he does thrice, and in his three visits steals the giant's red hen, which lays golden eggs, his money bags, and his harp. As he runs off with the last treasure, the harp cries out, "Master! master!" which wakes the giant, who runs after Jack. But the nimble lad cuts the beanstalk with an axe, and the giant is killed in his fall. As we know it, this story is of Teutonic origin. According to a frequently advanced theory, the "beanstalk" is the ash, Yggdrasil, of the *Eddas,* the giant is All-Father, whose three treasures are the wind, the rain, and the red hen which lays golden eggs (the sun). Jack typifies Man, who avails himself of these treasures and becomes rich.

Jack Ketch. See John KETCH.

Jacks, Lawrence Pearsall (1860-1955). English philosopher and Unitarian minister. He wrote books about Smokeover, an imaginary industrial city, and such works as *The Revolt Against Mechanism* (1934).

Jackson, Andrew (1767-1845). 7th president of the U.S. (1829-1837), sometimes known as "Old Hickory." Jackson fought in the American Revolu-

tion at the age of 13, was imprisoned by the British, and later became a backwoods lawyer in what is now Tennessee. In 1791 he married Mrs. Rachel Robards in the erroneous belief that she had obtained a divorce from her husband. Although they were remarried immediately after the divorce was granted in 1793, Jackson's enemies used the scandal as a political weapon until Mrs. Jackson's death in 1828. From 1798 to 1804 he was a judge of the Tennessee supreme court. Commissioned a major general in the U.S. army during the War of 1812, Jackson defeated the British at New Orleans (1814), an exploit that won him a national reputation. In 1818, as leader of an expedition to quell Indian depredations near the Georgia border, he entered Spanish-held East Florida and executed two British subjects. Although there were diplomatic repercussions, Jackson was not punished.

He was narrowly defeated for the presidency by John Quincy ADAMS in 1824 but was elected in 1828 after a campaign that portrayed Jackson as a symbol of the common man. During his first term he introduced the "spoils system" on a large scale and relied heavily on a KITCHEN CABINET of unofficial advisers. At a Jefferson's Day dinner in 1830, he chagrined supporters of states' rights by proposing a toast to "Our Union: It must be preserved," to which Vice President John CALHOUN replied, "The Union, next to our liberty, most dear." Jackson broke definitively with Calhoun the following year, partly as a result of a quarrel over the social status of Margaret EATON, wife of the secretary of war. (See NULLIFICATION.) Jackson's opposition to the 2d Bank of the U.S., which he attacked as an organ of monopoly and privilege, was the main issue of the 1832 campaign. After his re-election, Jackson had federal funds withdrawn from the bank and deposited in state institutions that were known as pet banks. This policy contributed to the growing financial disorder which culminated in the Panic of 1837. By that time Jackson's successor, Martin Van Buren, had been inaugurated, and the ex-president had retired to The Hermitage, his estate near Nashville. Perhaps the most significant aspect of Jackson's administration was his expansion of presidential power.

Jackson, Charles [Reginald] (1903–   ). American novelist and short-story writer. Jackson is best known for THE LOST WEEKEND, his first novel, a vivid report on the life of an alcoholic. His subsequent novels showed a continued preoccupation with pathological states of mind: *The Fall of Valor* (1946) has a homosexual theme, and *The Outer Edges* (1948) tells of the murder of two children by a sexual degenerate. *The Sunnier Side* (1950) and

Earthly Creatures (1953) are collections of short stories.

Jackson, Helen [Maria Fiske] Hunt (1830–1885). American poet, novelist, and essayist. She is best known for her novel RAMONA. Her sympathetic attitude toward the Indians in the novel had earlier manifested itself in the tract, *A Century of Dishonor* (1881). *Mercy Philbrick's Choice* (1876) is a novel supposedly dealing with the life of Emily Dickinson, who was a friend of the author.

Jackson, Holbrook (1874–1948). English literary scholar and editor. He is best known for his study of *The Eighteen Nineties* (1913).

Jackson, Shirley (1919–1965). American novelist and short-story writer. Her most famous tale, THE LOTTERY deals with a ritualized lottery in a small American town. It is not until the final lines of the story that death by stoning is revealed as the prize of the lottery. In a similar way, many of her stories and all her novels deal with the fantastic and the terrifying. *Hangsaman* (1951) shows a sensitive girl's flight into fantasy while attending a progressive girls' school. By way of contrast, *Life Among the Savages* (1953) and *Raising Demons* (1957) are autobiographical books describing with much humor the life of a middle-class intellectual family in a small New England town. Miss Jackson's other novels include *The Bird's Nest* (1954), *The Sundial* (1958), *The Haunting of Hill House* (1959), and *We Have Always Lived in the Castle* (1962).

Jackson, Thomas Jonathan. Known as "Stonewall" Jackson (1824–1863). American general. Considered one of the ablest Confederate generals in the Civil War, Jackson played an important role in both of the battles at BULL RUN and conducted a brilliant campaign in the Shenandoah Valley (1862), defeating the Union forces at Front Royal and Winchester. He died a few days after being accidentally wounded by his own men at CHANCELLORSVILLE. The words he supposedly said as he lay dying, "Let us cross the river and rest in the shade of trees," have inspired several poems and suggested the title of Ernest Hemingway's *Across the River and into the Trees* (1950). John Greenleaf Whittier paid tribute to Jackson after his death in BARBARA FRIETCHIE, based on an apocryphal incident.

Jack the Ripper. Popular name of an unknown London criminal to whom were attributed a number of gruesome murders (1888–1889).

Jacob. A biblical patriarch of the book of Genesis, whose 12 sons were the founders of the 12 tribes of ISRAEL. As a young man, he purchased the birthright of his brother Esau for a mess of pottage and, by impersonating him, secured from his blind father ISAAC the blessing intended for Esau (see REBEKAH). To win Rachel's hand, he served her father Laban for seven years, but was then given her less attractive sister Leah instead; whereupon he served another seven years, which "seemed to him but a short while so great was the love he bore her." Jacob is famed for the shrewdness with which he accumulated wealth while in Laban's service (Gen. 24:34). For his later life, see BENJAMIN; JOSEPH.

Jacob's ladder. The ladder seen by Jacob in a vision (Gen. 28:12). *Jacob* is a slang name for a ladder; and steep and high flights of steps going up cliffs are often so called.

Jacob, Max (1876–1944). French poet, prose writer, painter. A friend of Guillaume Apollinaire and his circle, he was writing poetry concerned with "nocturnal nightmares" and "day hallucinations" before the official beginning of Surrealism. Most famous are his early poems in prose, *Le Cornet à Dés* (1917), and verse, *Le Laboratoire Central* (1921). Other works include *La Défense de Tartuffe* (1919), reflecting his conversion to Catholicism; *Les Pénitents en maillot rose* (1925); and *Derniers Poèmes* (1945).

Jacobean. Pertaining to the reign of James I of England (James VI of Scotland), 1603–1625. With the accession of James I, a national spirit that had begun to make itself felt as early as 1600 (see ELIZABETHAN) became more pronounced. The dour and pedantic Scot who acceded to the throne had none of the symbolic value of his predecessor, "Good Queen Bess." The nation grew increasingly factious, particularly on the religious question. In 1603 the GUNPOWDER PLOT, an attempt by a group of Roman Catholics to blow up Parliament, increased the animosity. On the intellectual plane the new discoveries in science and astronomy made it increasingly clear that the beautifully ordered universe of PTOLEMY, the large world of which man was the microcosm, was a pleasant fiction that would have to be traded in for the more realistic but less comforting world of COPERNICUS. Skepticism and doubt, together with an acute self-consciousness, became the dominant note, which SHAKESPEARE—who strode both Elizabethan and Jacobean ages like a Colossus—sounded in HAMLET (1601) and in MEASURE FOR MEASURE (1604–1605).

In prose the new mood was reflected in the reaction against the rhetorical, elaborate Ciceronianism of the Elizabethans. The new prose style, modeled after SENECA and TACITUS, was a more concise and flexible instrument, better suited to the new prose form, the essay. The essay, which had been developed by Montaigne, was imported and perfected by Francis BACON, whose aphoristic style established the dominant tone of that form. But the prevailing mood was better represented by Robert Burton's massive ANATOMY OF MELANCHOLY, a detailed treatment of the affliction that characterized the age. Independently of these currents the Jacobean age also witnessed one of the greatest achievements of English prose: the King James or Authorized Version of the BIBLE.

The poetry of the Jacobean age can be characterized in terms of the two poets who dominated it, Ben JONSON and John DONNE. The poetry of Jonson and his followers was generally derived from classical models and attempted to bring to English poetry the classical virtues of restraint, form, lucidity, and decorum. The cavalier poets later in the century looked to Jonson's poetry as their chief English model. From John Donne, however, derives the more important strain of metaphysical poetry. In metaphysical poetry the Jacobean reaction against the Elizabethan qualities of generous, rich profusion and abounding optimism is most clearly focused. In drama, "Jacobean melancholy" invaded both comedy and tragedy. In the comic area it produced vivid, scathing satire of human rapacity in such plays as Ben Jonson's VOLPONE and THE ALCHEMIST and in John MARSTON's THE MALCONTENT. In tragedy it resulted in some of the most memorable studies of evil in the history of drama. Webster's THE WHITE DEVIL and THE DUCHESS OF MALFI, Tourneur's THE REVENGER'S TRAGEDY, Ford's 'TIS PITY SHE'S A WHORE, Middleton and Rowley's *The Changeling* focus with an almost savage intensity on human, specifically sexual, corruption. Jacobean dramatists, heavily patronized by the pleasure-loving court, were called upon to create elaborate masques in the splendid settings of Inigo JONES as well as the courtly pastoral drama associated with BEAUMONT AND FLETCHER. Finally, it was in the Jacobean age that Shakespeare's greatest work was produced. The Jacobean element in Shakespeare is reflected in his refusal after 1600 to return to the charming simplicity of the early comedies or to the patriotic fervor of the histories. His mature work, whether the tragedies or the later "romances," never loses sight of the existence of evil as an operative force in life.

Jacobi, Friedrich Heinrich (1743–1819). German novelist and popular philosopher who stressed intuition and faith as opposed to rationalism. His thought is related to that of Hamann and Herder, and in his early career is close to the STURM UND DRANG movement. The concept of NIHILISM is his invention, but not his creed. His best-known novel is *Aus Eduard Allwills Papieren* (*From the Papers of Edward Allwill*, last version 1792).

Jacobins. (1) Name given the Dominican friars in France because in Paris they first established themselves (1219) in the Rue St. Jacques.

(2) A political club, originally called the *Club Breton*, formed by liberal members of the National ASSEMBLY at Versailles (1789). On their removal to Paris, they met in the hall of an ex-convent of the Jacobins (hence their name). Although only moderately democratic in the beginning, they became increasingly radical and were a prime force in the Revolution. Many of their more moderate members broke off and formed their own clubs, notably the FEUILLANTS. Among the best-known Jacobins are MIRABEAU, ROBESPIERRE, DANTON, and MARAT. The term "Jacobin" has come to denote a violent radical.

Jacobites. The partisans of JAMES II and, after William III superseded him, the partisans of James's heirs. They maintained the indefeasible right of the house of Stuart to the throne and engaged in two fruitless rebellions: first to enthrone James's son ("the Old PRETENDER"), and later, his grandson (Bonnie Prince Charlie, or "the Young Pretender"). The Jacobites remained a powerful and disturbing political influence for generations. See the FIFTEEN; the FORTY-FIVE; WARMING-PANS.

Jacobowsky and the Colonel (*Jacobowsky und der Oberst*, 1944). A satirical comedy by Franz WERFEL in which an anti-Semitic Polish colonel is led from behind the Nazi lines by a clever Jew.

Jacobs, William Wymark (1863–1943). English story writer. His comic tales about sailors and rustics were collected in *Snug Harbor* (1931). *The Monkey's Paw* is a powerful horror story.

Jacobsen, Jens Peter (1847–1885). Danish poet and novelist. Jacobsen began his career as a student of botany and zoology; he introduced the scientific theories of Darwin to Denmark. His body of creative work is small and was all produced after he retired to his native Thisted as a tubercular patient in 1873. Naturalistic in his subject matter, Jacobsen writes in a careful, precise style. The novel *Fru Marie Grubbe* (1876) is a psychological study; *Niels Lynne* (1880) portrays an atheist in the modern world. His stories, noted for their skillful use of language, were published as *Mogens og andre Noveller* (*Mogens and Other Stories*, 1882).

Jacob's Room (1922). A novel by Virginia WOOLF, her first original and distinguished work. The life story, character, and friends of Jacob Flanders are presented in a series of separate scenes and moments. There are numerous little descriptions of scenes and people that do not enter into his life at all—such as an old woman selling matches and an irrelevant conversation in another room—but help to provide a complete, rounded world. The story of this sensitive, promising young man carries him from his childhood, through college at Cambridge, love affairs in London, and travels in Greece, to his death in the war. At the end, instead of describing his death, Virginia Woolf describes his empty room.

Jacopo della Quercia (1367–1438). Italian sculptor. One of the first of the great Renaissance sculptors, Jacopo is noted for his luxuriant style, revealed in the reliefs surrounding the doors of the Church of S. Petronio at Bologna, and for the expressive power of his other efforts in low relief. He influenced such painters as MASACCIO and such fellow sculptors as Michelangelo.

Jacopone da Todi (c. 1230–1306). Italian poet. After 10 years of penance following his wife's death in 1268, he became a Franciscan monk. His hymns reveal a fervent mysticism, and he is possibly the author of the *Stabat Mater Dolorosa*.

Jacquard, Joseph Marie (1752–1834). French inventor. Jacquard produced a loom (1801) that revolutionized the technique of inwoven designs. He was later awarded a pension and elected to the Legion of Honor (1819).

Jacquerie, La (1358). An unsuccessful insurrection of the French peasants of Ile-de-France, provoked by their oppression under the noble class while King Jean II was in captivity in England. Acts of great violence and cruelty were committed first by the peasantry, who had sworn to kill every nobleman in France, and then by Charles the Bad of Navarre and his nobles in their suppression of the revolt and their reprisals. The name *Jacquerie* came from the 14th-century use of *Jacques* as a generic name for the peasant, connoting the humiliation of serfdom.

Jacques, Pauvre. See PAUVRE JACQUES.

Jacques le fataliste (1796). A novel by Denis DIDEROT. It was possibly Laurence Sterne's remark, "Digressions, incontestably, are the sunshine; they are the life, the soul of reading," that inspired Diderot to write this, his last important work and longest novel. The story, intentionally disorderly in structure, is a burlesque recitation of Jacques' love affairs, as told to his master, but this framework in itself is of practically no importance since it is interrupted constantly by digressions and stories within stories; in which the characters comment on their own tales, and even the reader is constantly brought into the narrative. Some of the interpolated stories are well known, for example, the tale of Mme. de la Pommeraye who exacts vengeance from her faithless lover, or the tale of the immoral Father Hudson, in which evil triumphs. In this complex work, Diderot is concerned with the problems of the novel as a literary medium to depict reality, with the philosophic problem of determinism versus fatalism, and with defining a mature attitude toward life.

Jade Emperor. The chief god of the triad of popular Taoism.

Jael. See SISERA.

Jagannath. See JUGGERNAUT.

Jaggers, Mr. In Charles Dickens' GREAT EXPECTATIONS, the lawyer who is Pip's legal guardian and Miss Havisham's man of business.

Jahannam or **Jehennam.** The name of the Muslim Hell, or the first of its seven divisions. The word is the same as the Hebrew GEHENNA.

Jalna. See MAZO DE LA ROCHE.

Jaloux, Edmond (1878–1949). French novelist and critic. His novels are delicately realistic accounts of the inner life of restless souls, such as *Le Reste est silence* (1909), *L'Incertaine* (1918), and *La Chute d'Icare* (1936).

James I (1566–1625). Stuart king of England (1603–1625). The son of Mary Queen of Scots and Lord Darnley, he ruled effectively in Scotland as James VI for 20 years before the death of Elizabeth when he succeeded to the throne of England. There his awkwardness, pedantry, and Scottish accent were against him; his insistence on divine right and attempts to keep peace with Spain created a popular resentment which helped bring on the English Civil War. James was called "the English Solomon" and "the Wisest Fool in Christendom" on account of his impractical learning and literary ambitions. His most famous work was *Daemonologie* (1599), a treatise denouncing witches, but it was his *Essays of a Prentice in the Divine Art of Poesy* (1584), a critical treatise, and *Poetical Exercises at Vacant Hours* (1591) which led English poets to hope that he might become their patron; however, he is known to have assisted only Ben Jonson. He also wrote a well-known *Counterblaste to Tobacco* (1604), refuting the alleged virtues of the plant.

James II (1633–1701). Stuart king of England (1685–1688). The son of Charles I, he became a Roman Catholic, and succeeded to the throne after the death of his brother Charles II. Convinced that James planned to rule as absolute monarch and to restore Catholicism to England, seven representatives of the property-owning classes offered the throne to William of Orange, the king's Protestant son-in-law. After William had landed at Torbay in Devon (1688), James, finding himself without military and popular support, fled to France, where he was cordially received by Louis XIV. In an attempt to recover his throne, he landed in Ireland (1689), but was decisively defeated at the battle of the Boyne (1690). See GLORIOUS REVOLUTION.

James, Henry [Jr.] (1843–1916). American novelist, short-story writer, and man of letters. A major figure in the history of the novel, James is celebrated as a master craftsman who brought his great art and impeccable technique to bear in the development of abiding moral themes: the relationship between innocence and experience, especially as exemplified in the confrontation of American and European civilizations; the dilemma of the artist in an alien society; the achievement of self-knowledge through psychological and moral perception. With an approach to the art of fiction that resembled the research of the careful historian, James admitted into his stories and novels only that which could be represented as the perception or experience of his characters. With this approach to the problem of "point of view" in the novel, James achieved reality and unity, and it is perhaps in this respect that he had the strongest effect on subsequent writers.

James came from a distinguished family: his grandfather was one of the first millionaires in America; his father, the Swedenborgian Henry James, Sr., was a writer and lecturer in the fields of philosophy and theology; his brother was the psychologist William JAMES. Thus, the novelist grew up in an atmosphere that encouraged his becoming what he thought all novelists should be: "one on whom nothing is lost."

James entered Harvard Law School in 1862, but withdrew at the end of a year. Always a scribbler, he wanted to write seriously, and in 1864 his first story, *A Tragedy of Error,* appeared in the *North American Review;* he soon caught the attention of William Dean Howells who, as editor of the *Atlantic Monthly,* helped and encouraged James; in 1871 James's first novel, *Watch and Ward,* was published serially in the *Atlantic.* Between 1864 and 1871 he wrote a number of stories and astute reviews for both the *Atlantic* and the *Nation.* It was during this period, too, that he made his first independent trip to Europe. (He had spent much of his youth in Europe, as had his three brothers and sister, traveling there with his family and attending various schools.) The trip marked the beginning of his fascination with the theme of the American in Europe. During his second European trip (1872–1874) he wrote his best story to date: *A Madonna of the Future,* the story of an artist who never manages to paint the perfect madonna.

In 1875, after much thought, James decided to make his home abroad, settling first in Paris—where he knew Maupassant, Flaubert, and Turgenev—and finally in England (1876) where he spent the rest of his life. The 1870's, in England, saw the first real blossoming of James's talent. THE PASSIONATE PILGRIM AND OTHER STORIES appeared in 1875, followed in rapid succession by RODERICK HUDSON, THE AMERICAN, THE EUROPEANS, DAISY MILLER, and *Confidence* (1879). The major theme running throughout this work—the international confrontation of European and American civilizations—is posed clearly and unambiguously at this early stage: Christopher Newman in *The American* is basically innocent and naïve as he comes into contact with sophisticated and evil De Bellegardes. In his later work, James was to see his theme in a more complex light: the innocently unaware may themselves be the cause of evil in others.

In 1879, James published *Hawthorne,* a book in which James pays tribute to Hawthorne as a writer who accomplished much despite the cultural aridity of his surroundings. WASHINGTON SQUARE, set in the New York of James's childhood, was published a year later. The climax of this early period is THE PORTRAIT OF A LADY, considered by many to be not only James's finest but one of the finest novels in English. The 1880's also saw the publication of THE BOSTONIANS, THE PRINCESS CASAMASSIMA, and THE ASPERN PAPERS. The publication of THE TRAGIC MUSE, for many, marks the beginning of the more complex prose style generally associated with James. An interesting study of an actress, it preludes James's excursion into playwriting during the 1890's. The plays were all more or less unsuccessful, and few would claim much for them, but the effect of them on his fiction was marked. His stories and novels of the late 90's show a radical concern with experiment and with the adaptation of dramatic technique to fiction; this was the beginning of James's later style of involved sentences in which every thought and image is qualified, and the sentence is itself presented as a work of art. WHAT MAISIE KNEW, THE TURN OF THE SCREW, THE AWKWARD AGE, and THE SACRED FOUNT are all products of these experiments.

With the turn of the century, James entered into his last and perhaps his greatest period, publishing in rapid succession three long and complex novels: THE WINGS OF THE DOVE, THE AMBASSADORS, THE GOLDEN BOWL. Difficult as many have found them, the novels mark the pinnacle of James's art. This period also saw the publication of such famous short stories as *The Beast in the Jungle* (1903), a story of a man who waits for a special fate only to find that his fate was to be the man "to whom nothing was to have happened"; *The Birthplace* (1903), the story of a couple who become caretakers at a Shakespeare-like birthplace; and *The Jolly Corner* (1908), a complicated tale of a man who meets his alter ego as a ghost.

In 1904, James came to the U.S. and toured the country, producing on his return to England THE AMERICAN SCENE. The major effort of these years, however, went into the task of writing the critical prefaces and making, where needed, the revisions for the reissue of his works in the New York edition (1907-1909), a venture that ultimately ran to 26 volumes. The prefaces, important comments on his work and craft, were later republished as *The Art of the Novel* (1934), edited by R. P. Blackmur. After his brother William's death in 1910, James turned to another major undertaking, the writing of three autobiographical volumes: *A Small Boy and Others* (1913), *Notes of a Son and Brother* (1914), and the unfinished *The Middle Years* (1917). Two novels were left incomplete at his death in 1916: *The Sense of the Past* and *The Ivory Tower*, both published in 1917. James became a British subject in 1915 as a measure of support for the British cause in World War I. See SPOILS OF POYNTON, THE.

James, Jesse [Woodson] (1847-1882). American bandit. After riding with Quantrill's guerrillas during the Civil War, Jesse and his brother Frank committed daring railroad and bank robberies in the Middle West during the 1870's, becoming popular heroes. When a large reward was offered for their capture, Robert Ford, a member of the James gang, earned it by shooting Jesse in the back. His murder was narrated in an anonymous ballad, *Jesse James*.

James, The General Epistle of. A New Testament book. It is a letter to the entire Christian Church. The date and authorship of this letter are not known. Traditionally it has been ascribed to James, the first bishop of Jerusalem and the brother of Jesus; this would date the work before A.D. 62 when James was martyred. Others feel that the epistle was written about the year 90 by an unknown church father. The writer reminds his readers of their moral obligations as Christians and calls for not only a faith in Christ but for Christian action in life as well.

James, William (1842-1910). American philosopher, physiologist, psychologist, and teacher. The son of Henry James, Sr., and the brother of Henry James, he began to teach at Harvard in 1872. A gifted writer, he produced works on theology, psychology, ethics, and metaphysics, coining such phrases as "the bitch goddess success." He was distinctly American in the concepts he advanced, and his approach to metaphysics was frankly commonsensical. He objected to the pure and highly "logical" but unreal systems of Idealist metaphysicians. Emphasizing the role of the nature of the knower in the character and validity of knowledge, he insisted that any view of the world is a compromise between the objectively given and the personally desired. He gave a series of lectures on PRAGMATISM at the Lowell Institute and later at Columbia University that was published as *Pragmatism* (1907) and *The Meaning of Truth* (1909). Turning away from abstractions, verbal solutions, fixed principles, and pretended absolutes, he looked for concreteness and facts, action and power. He argued that "the ultimate test for us of what a truth means is the conduct it dictates or inspires." The same attitude characterizes *The Varieties of Religious Experience* (1902), which contends that any article of religious faith is "true" when it provides emotional satisfaction. *The Principles of Psychology* (1890, 1892) shows James as a keen observer of sense data; one chapter, devoted to "The Stream of Thought," advances the concept of the STREAM OF CONSCIOUSNESS, later an important and revolutionary fictional technique. In other books, James discusses *The Will to Believe* (1897), *Human Immortality* (1898), *The Sentiment of Rationality* (1905), and *A Pluralistic Universe* (1919). See Charles Sanders PEIRCE.

Jameson, [Margaret] Storm (1897-   ). English novelist who often sets her stories in Yorkshire. *The Lovely Ship, The Voyage Home,* and *A Richer Dust* (1927-1931) comprise a trilogy about a shipbuilding family. Her other books include *The Hidden River* (1955), *A Cup of Tea for Mr. Thorgill* (1957), and *The Road from the Monument* (1962).

Jameson Raid (1895-1896). A raid on Johannesburg, South Africa. It was led by the Englishman Sir Leander Starr Jameson (1853-1917). It was an attempt to overthrow the Boer government during the troubles between the Boers and English in the gold mines. Jameson was captured and handed over to the British for trial, but was released shortly and later became prime minister of Cape Colony (1904-1908). See BOER WAR.

James the Greater, St. One of the 12 apostles of Jesus and the patron saint of Spain. He was the brother of John and a son of Zebedee. Legend states that, after his missionary journey to Spain and his subsequent death in Palestine, his body was placed in a boat with sails set, and that next day it reached the Spanish coast; at Padron, near Compostela, they used to show a huge stone as the veritable boat. According to another legend, it was the relics of St. James that were miraculously conveyed to Spain in a ship of marble from Jerusalem. A knight saw the ship sailing into port, his horse took fright, and plunged with its rider into the sea. The knight saved himself by "boarding the marble vessel," but his clothes were found to be entirely covered with scallop shells. The saint's body was discovered in 840 by divine revelation to Bishop Theodomirus, and a church was built at Compostela as a shrine for the relics. St. James is commemorated on July 25, and is represented in art sometimes with the sword by which he was beheaded and sometimes attired as a pilgrim, with his cloak covered with shells. He is also known as Santiago, a variation of St. James (Span., *San Diego*).

James the Less, St. One of the 12 apostles of Jesus. His attribute as a saint is a fuller's club, in allusion to the instrument by which he was put to death after having been thrown from the summit of the temple at Jerusalem in A.D. 62.

Jamestown. The first permanent English settlement in the New World, founded (1607) on the site of the abandoned Spanish settlement of San Miguel, and named for King James I. It was the capital of Virginia until 1698. The first settlers suffered great hardships, especially during the starving years of 1609–1610, which also brought forth the leadership of John Smith. Jamestown was burned down during Bacon's Rebellion (1676). Before its restoration in modern times, the only surviving relics were the tower of the church and a number of tombs.

Jammes, Francis (1868–1938). French poet and novelist. His pastoral elegies describe his native region of the Pyrénées with sensuous and sentimental simplicity. The poems of *De l'angélus de l'aube à l'angélus du soir* (1897) were written during the time of his friendship with André GIDE, as were *Le Triomphe de la vie* (1902) and the novel *Le Roman du lièvre* (1903). Then he drew closer to Paul Claudel and was converted to Catholicism in 1905, after which his poems were more religiously inspired, such as *Clairières dans le ciel* (1906) and *Les Géorgiques chrétiennes* (3 vols., 1911–1912). Among his novels are *M. le curé d'Ozeron* (1918); *Le Poète rustique* (1920), modeled on himself; and *Cloches pour deux mariages* (1924).

Janaka. In Hindu legend, the foster father of Sita. He was the king of Mithila and discovered Sita

Jamestown: contemporary woodcut of Capt. Smith's capture.

when he was ploughing the land; he is praised in the *Ramayana* for his extraordinary performances of charity and penance.

Jane Eyre (1847). A novel by Charlotte BRONTË. In both heroine and hero the author introduced types new to English fiction. Jane Eyre is a shy, intense little orphan, never for a moment, neither in her unhappy school days nor her subsequent career as a governess, displaying those qualities of superficial beauty and charm that had marked the conventional heroine. Jane's lover, Edward Rochester, to whose ward she is governess, is a strange, violent man, bereft of conventional courtesy, a law unto himself. Rochester's moodiness derives from the fact that he is married to an insane wife, whose existence, long kept secret, is revealed on the very day of his projected marriage to Jane. Years afterward the lovers are reunited.

Jane Seymour (1509?–1537). Third wife of HENRY VIII of England, mother of Edward VI. A lady in waiting to Catherine of Aragon and then to Anne Boleyn, Jane caught the fancy of the king in 1535. The following year Anne Boleyn was executed, and less than two weeks after her death Henry and Jane were privately married. She gave birth to Henry's first son in 1537, an event that was met with great public rejoicing, but she died 12 days later.

Jane Shore. See Jane SHORE.

Janice Meredith (1899). An historical novel by Paul Leicester FORD. It takes place during the American Revolution, and is the story of a Tory's patriotic daughter, who falls in love with a bond-servant named Charles Fownes. He is later revealed to be John Brereton, a colonel in the Continental army.

Janissaries or **Janizaries** (Turk., *yenitscheri,* new corps). A celebrated militia of the Ottoman empire, raised by Orchan in 1326, originally, and for some centuries, compulsorily recruited from the Christian subjects of the Sultan. It was blessed by Hadji Bektash, a saint, who cut off a sleeve of his fur mantle and gave it to the captain. The captain put the sleeve on his head, and from this circumstance arose the fur cap worn by these foot guards. In 1826, having become too formidable a threat to the state, they were abolished after a massacre in which many thousands of the Janissaries perished.

Jannings, Emil (1887–1950). Swiss-born actor of German-American parentage. He began his stage career with Max Reinhardt at the Deutsches Theater in Berlin, and made his screen debut in 1916 in Lubitsch films. From 1926 to 1929 he enjoyed enormous success in Hollywood, and in 1932 he returned to the stage. He is especially remembered for his portrayals in the German films *The Last Laugh* and *The Blue Angel*, with Marlene Deitrich.

Jansen, Cornelius. See JANSENISM.

Jansenism. The doctrines of the sect of Roman Catholics known as Jansenists, derived from the teachings of Cornelius Jansen (1585–1638), professor of exegesis at Louvain and later the bishop of Ypres. An opponent of the Jesuits, Jansen advocated reforms based, he claimed, upon the teachings of Augustine. Posthumously published in *Augustin* (1640), his tenets included irresistible grace, original sin, and "the utter helplessness of natural man to turn to God." The Jansenists' declaration of man's personal relationship with God resembled Calvinist doctrine and influenced the thinking of both Racine and Pascal. Louis XIV opposed the movement, whose influence was felt at court, in society, and in French letters (see PORT-ROYAL), and the Jansenists were finally put down by Pope Clement XI in his bull *Unigenitus* (1713).

Januarius, St. (Ital., San **Gennaro**; ?272-?305). Patron saint of Naples. A bishop of Benevento, martyred during the Diocletian persecution, he is commemorated on September 19. His head and two vials of his blood are preserved in the cathedral at Naples, where the congealed blood is said to bubble and liquefy three times a year: on the Saturday before the first Sunday in May, on September 19, and on December 16. It is also said that this occurs whenever the head is brought near to the vials.

January and May. See MERCHANT'S TALE.

Janus. One of the most ancient of Roman deities. Originally the god of light who opened the sky at daybreak and closed it at sunset, in time he came to preside over all beginnings and endings, all entrances and exits. He is often represented as having two faces, one in front and one behind, one to see into the future and one to see into the past. Doors (*ianuae*) were under his protection. The first month after the winter solstice, January, was sacred to him, and since 153 B.C. the first day of Janus' month has marked the beginning of the year. His principal temple was near the Roman forum. The doors of this temple were kept open in time of war and locked in time of peace. From the time of the earliest kings to the time of Augustus, these doors were closed only four times, twice during the latter's reign.

Japanese literature. The first literary productions date to the Nara period (710-794), which was marked by the wholesale importation of Chinese cultural elements. Native Japanese poetry is represented by the MAN'YŌSHŪ, a collection of pre-Nara and Nara poems, many of which reflect indigenous Japanese concepts. In this period the first histories, based on the Chinese model, were composed and much emphasis was laid on the study of Buddhist scriptures. The Heian period (794-1185) saw a great literary flowering, marked by the novels and diaries of women writers. Although Chinese literature, particularly poetry, continued to exert considerable influence, new, purely Japanese tendencies came to the fore. The TALE OF GENJI by MURASAKI SHIKIBU, a celebrated court lady, is regarded as the greatest single piece of Japanese literature; it has continued to influence the writers of Japan even to the present century. Diaries, some of them amusingly irreverent accounts of court life (PILLOW-BOOK OF SEI SHONAGON), feature the writings of this age. The succeeding Kamakura period (1185-1333) was a time of warfare and natural disaster. Its literature is colored by a pessimistic resignation, partly Buddhist inspired, to the uncertain and transitory nature of life during this era (ACCOUNT OF MY HUT). Tales of military valor, originally the transmitted stories of ballad singers, were written down and became a permanent part of the literature (TALES OF THE HEIKE). Military unrest and natural calamities continued during the Muromachi period (1333-1600), although the country was unified for the first time. It was in this age that NO drama evolved, under the sponsorship of the great warlords. The Tokugawa period (1600-1868),

which saw Japan at peace after centuries of almost constant warfare, was an age of many new literary departures. The Tokugawa family, imposing a rigid feudal hierarchy based on Neo-Confucian thought and ethics, set a firm and inflexible code of behavior for its subjects. Studies of the Chinese classics were encouraged and Buddhism, although the official religion, was severely regulated. Nevertheless, the merchant class, which was formally placed at the lowest of social levels, was responsible for a great new literary flowering. The merchants, because of inherent weaknesses in the feudal system, gained great wealth and power, which was reflected in the writings of the time. A new society developed, known as the floating world (*ukiyo*), which centered around the entertainment districts, the gay quarters, and the theaters. With it came this new literature: the stories of IHARA SAIKAKU, detailing the life of shopkeepers, courtesans, and humble people, and the puppet plays (JORURI) and KABUKI of CHIKAMATSU MONZAEMON, which attained great popularity and are still performed. In art the *ukiyoe* wood-block prints portray graphically the life depicted in the literature. Poetry saw the rise of HAIKU under the direction of MATSUO BASHŌ, reflecting a more sensitive approach to life and nature. With the arrival of the Americans and Europeans in the mid-19th century the Tokugawa regime began to collapse, and in 1868 the Imperial Court was returned to prominence with the Meiji Restoration. A great wave of Western influences swept Japan: imitation of the Occident influenced all phases of life; the literary scene was no exception. Vast numbers of Western works were translated and imitated, various European literary and artistic movements had their vogues. Nevertheless works representative of the Japanese tradition continued to appear, especially in the pre-World War II period, when nationalistic sentiments encouraged such a trend. In the postwar period American influence has been strong and much Western material in all fields has appeared in Japanese. Throughout the 20th century there have been many novelists of exceptional talent and originality; a number of their works have appeared in English translation. Japan is a country of great literary productivity which accounts for its being the second greatest (after Russia) publisher of books in the world.

Japhet or **Japheth.** A name for IAPETUS, introduced by Milton in PARADISE LOST. He was also one of the sons of Noah and, according to legend, the father of Histion from whom descended the French, Italian, German, and British peoples.

Jaquenetta. A blowsy peasant wench who is wooed in histrionic style by Don Adriano de ARMADO in Shakespeare's LOVE'S LABOUR'S LOST.

Jaques. In Shakespeare's As YOU LIKE IT, a lord, attendant on the banished duke in the forest of Arden. A philosophical idler, cynical, melancholy, and contemplative, he has little to do with the plot, but his musings furnish some of Shakespeare's most frequently quoted lines, notably from the speech on "the Seven Ages of Man":

> All the world's a stage,
> And all the men and women merely players:
> They have their exits and their entrances;
> And one man in his time plays many parts,
> His acts being seven ages.

Jaques-Dalcroze, Emile (1865–1950). Swiss composer and inventor of eurhythmics. Eurhythmics coordinates bodily movement with music systematically to develop the physical experience of music, especially rhythm. This system has influenced modern dance. Jaques-Dalcroze founded the Institut Jaques-Dalcroze in Geneva, wrote folklike compositions and several expository and pedagogical works, among them *Rhythm, Music and Education* (1922).

Jardin des Plantes. Familiar name for what was originally the *Jardin du Roi* (1635), and is now the *Muséum d'Histoire Naturelle* (1794) in Paris. At first the site served as the royal garden for medicinal herbs; today the *Jardin des Plantes,* equipped with classrooms, laboratories, and museums, is a center of experimental scientific study.

Jarley, Mrs. In Charles Dickens' OLD CURIOSITY SHOP, a kindhearted woman, mistress of a traveling wax-work exhibition. She is kind to Little Nell and employs her as a decoy duck to "Jarley's unrivalled collection."

Jarndyce, Mr. See BLEAK HOUSE.

Jarnés [Millán], Benjamín (1888–1949). Spanish novelist. The elaborate style of his work, which often strays to the borders of poetry, is apparent in his best-known novels: *Mosém Pedro* (1924); *Vida de San Alejo* (*Saint Alexis,* 1928), an interesting biography; and *Castelar, hombre del Sinai* (1935).

Jarrell, Randall (1914–1965). American poet, novelist, and critic. Jarrell served in the Air Force during the Second World War, and a considerable portion of his poetry deals with the war. Among his collections of verse are *Blood for a Stranger* (1942), *Little Friend, Little Friend* (1945), *Losses* (1948), *The Seven-League Crutches* (1951), and *Selected Poems* (1955). Some of his critical essays have been collected in *Poetry and the Age* (1953) and *A Sad Heart at the Supermarket* (1962). *Pictures from an Institution* (1954) is a novel satirizing life at a women's college.

Jarry, Alfred [-Henry] (1873–1907). French dramatist and novelist. Jarry is most famous for his epic burlesque UBU ROI (1896) and its sequels, and for the novel *Le Surmâle* (1902). Both works are considered major precursors of surrealism. Although the coarseness of his language was deliberately shocking, Jarry's humor was often metaphysical in nature. He would, for example, give a logical demonstration in lucid style of an absurd proposition.

Jason (Iason). In Greek mythology, the son (christened Diomedes) of Aeson. He led the ARGONAUTS to recover the GOLDEN FLEECE. Saved by his mother from Aeson's brother Pelias, who had seized the throne of Iolcus, he was reared by CHIRON. When he returned to claim the throne, he was sent to capture the Fleece. Thanks to the aid of Medea, he succeeded, killed Pelias, and became king of Ephyre (Corinth). Later, when he divorced Medea to marry Glauce, she killed her two children by Jason and escaped to Athens. Jason lost favor with the gods and wandered as an outcast until his old age, when the prow of his old vessel, the Argo, fell on him and killed him.

Jaspers, Karl (1883–   ). German philosopher. In 1913 he became an unsalaried lecturer on psychology at Heidelberg; he was made a full professor of philosophy in 1921. The Nazi regime secured his dismissal in 1937, but he was reinstated in 1945. Since 1949 he has lectured at the University of Basel. Jaspers is one of the founders of existentialism. From the beginning his interest in psychiatry has provided the particulars for his search for a "perennial philosophy." His concern in this direction distinguishes him from his fellow-existentialists. He is less iconoclastic than other modern philosophers, such as Sartre. Although his system is rigorously logical, it acknowledges a transcendental power with which man seeks to communicate. Among his works are *Psychology of World Conceptions* (*Psychologie der Weltanschauungen;* 1919), *Man in the Modern Age* (1933), *On Truth* (*Von der Wahrheit;* 1947), *The Question of German Guilt* (1947), *The Perennial Scope of Philosophy* (1949), and *Tragedy Is Not Enough* (1953).

Jatayu. In Hindu legend, the eagle-king of birds. In the *Ramayana* he dies trying to save Sita from the clutches of Ravana. He is a symbol of unswerving loyalty and self-sacrifice.

Jaurès, Jean Léon (1859–1914). French socialist leader. Jaurès defended Captain Dreyfus in his newspaper *La Petite République.* With Briand, he founded (1904) and edited the daily *L'Humanité.* Jaurès was elected several times to membership in the Chamber of Deputies; in that capacity he expounded his socialist convictions eloquently. *Histoire socialiste collective* (1879–1900), a history of France from the Socialist perspective, was written under his direction. In 1914, at the outbreak of World War I, Jaurès was assassinated by a French chauvinist.

Java Head (1919). A novel by Joseph HERGESHEIMER. In his examination of the American past, Hergesheimer turned to the China trade that helped make New England rich. Gerrit Ammidon, the son of a famous Salem shipowner and retired captain, whose home is called Java Head, brings back from the Orient a Chinese wife, Taou Yuen, of aristocratic family. But she is received with kindness only by the wife of her husband's brother, and in addition arouses passion in a dissolute neighbor. Lured into a room she commits suicide by taking opium in order to escape him. In the end, the bereaved husband marries a girl he had once been fond of and sails back to the Orient.

Javert. In Victor Hugo's LES MISÉRABLES, the relentless pursuer of Jean Valjean. An officer of the police, Javert is the personification of the law's inexorability. He pursues the ex-convict Jean Valjean relentlessly, but finally commits suicide rather than arrest his prey.

Jay, John (1745–1829). American diplomat, jurist, and public official. After serving in the Continental Congress and as joint commissioner in making peace with Great Britain, he was secretary of foreign affairs under the Confederation. Upon the adoption of the Constitution, which he defended as one of the authors of THE FEDERALIST papers, he became chief justice (1789–1795) of the Supreme Court. In 1794 he was made special envoy to Great Britain to settle differences that had arisen over British failure to comply with the Treaty of 1783. The resulting treaty, known in the U.S. as Jay's Treaty, provided for British evacuation of the Northwest Territory and set up machinery for settling other grievances, though it was silent about British violations of American neutral rights during the Anglo-French war. As Jay had foreseen, the treaty was extremely unpopular; he was denounced in the press and burned in effigy.

jazz. Syncopated music of American Negro and possibly African origin that, in the 20th century, grew out of the dance and folk music of the American Negro and out of elements derived from Protestant hymns and march tunes. Among the predecessors of jazz are work songs, SPIRITUALS, ragtime, and blues (which has continued to be the main vocal form of jazz). Different jazz styles are identified with the successive decades of this century: hot jazz, or Dixieland, in the twenties; swing in the thirties; bebop in the forties; cool and progressive jazz in the fifties.

The extraordinary vitality of jazz, particularly in its rhythms, has extended its popularity throughout the world. It has influenced literature and other arts both implicitly and explicitly, for jazz also often connotes certain attitudes on the part of its listeners and performers; e.g., a freedom of behavior and feeling of exclusiveness that have interested writers since the twenties. Among the earliest of these writers were F. Scott Fitzgerald, John Dos Passos, and James T. Farrell. A resurgence of interest in the people associated with jazz has accompanied the rise of beat writing.

Some poets, both beat and otherwise, have imitated the rhythms of jazz, especially BLUES. Among them are Langston Hughes, Vachel Lindsay, Gregory Corso, Allen Ginsberg, and Gary Snyder. See George GERSHWIN; Aaron COPLAND.

Jazz Age. A term used to designate the period of the 1920's in the U.S. At that time the apparent emotional abandon of jazz seemed best to express the spirit of determined unconventionality, gaiety, and dissipation of the American boom era that followed World War I. Such dances as the "Black Bottom" and "Charleston" went hand in hand with "speakeasies," "petting parties," and the bobbed hair, short skirts, and new freedom of behavior of the "flapper." F. Scott Fitzgerald was one of the first to use this term by titling one of his works *Tales from the Jazz Age* (1922). Other writers of this period include John Dos Passos and James T. Farrell.

J.B. (1958). A verse drama by Archibald MacLeish. Based on the biblical story of Job, it is noted for its circus-tent setting and play-within-a-play structure. In contrast with Job, *J.B.* shows modern man in a universe whose laws he cannot understand; while the Voice from the Whirlwind offers an answer which is irrelevant to the human problem of how to live, the play simply affirms man's capacity to "endure and Love."

Jean Barois (1913). A long novel, written almost entirely in dialogue, by Roger MARTIN DU GARD. Its hero decides that conscience compels him to leave the church, and though he finds few answers to problems of morality and conscience in agnosticism, he remains a free-thinker until his old age, when he returns to the church, more through fear of death than out of conviction. The novel deals in part with the Dreyfus affair and with its shattering effect upon French intellectual life.

Jean Christophe (1904–1912, 10 vols.). A novel series by Romain ROLLAND. The hero, Jean Christophe Kraft, is a German-born musician who travels through France and Germany, observing and criticizing contemporary civilization. A satire on modern society, the massive work is also a sensitive analysis of the artist's isolated position in his world. Rolland, speaking through his musician hero, proposes that the purpose of art is to express moral truth and thus to combat the disintegration of values.

Jean de Meun[g]. Pen name of **Jean Clopinel** (c. 1250–c. 1305). French poet and scholar. His continuation of the ROMANCE OF THE ROSE satirizes most existing institutions of his day and makes Nature the standard for all moral and social judgments in a series of lucidly reasoned arguments.

Jean des Entommeures, Frère. See FRIAR JOHN.

Jean Jacques. The given name of Jean Jacques ROUSSEAU, by which he is often called.

Jeanne d'Arc. See JOAN OF ARC.

Jeanneret, Charles Edouard. See LE CORBUSIER.

Jean Paul. See Jean Paul Friedrich RICHTER.

Jean Santeuil (1952). An unfinished novel, written 1895–1899, by Marcel PROUST. It is largely an adapted version of his own life until 1895. Many of the characters and incidents are prototypes of those in his major work, *Remembrance of Things Past* (1913–1927), though none of the names are the same.

Jedermann. See EVERYMAN.

Jeeves. The perfect English valet. He appears in many stories by P. G. WODEHOUSE.

Jeffers, Robinson (1887–1962). American poet. He is known for his concern with the introversion of modern culture; his belief in extreme individualism, tending toward a Nietzschean adulation of the hero; his attraction to strong, primitive types; and his quasi-mystical preoccupation with sexual abnormality. The son of a minister, educated in the classics from early childhood, Jeffers based many of his narrative poems on biblical and classical sources. After two romantic volumes, *Flagons and Apples* (1912) and *Californians* (1916), he wrote TAMAR, AND OTHER POEMS. This volume, which caused the recognition of his unusual dramatic power, included among its contents THE TOWER BEYOND TRAGEDY. The title poem of ROAN STALLION, TAMAR, AND OTHER POEMS, his next collection, was based on a Monterey incident in which a man was killed by his own horse. Jeffers used the incident to contrast the primitive sexuality of the stallion with the degenerate lusts of man.

The Women at Point Sur (1927) deals with a minister who tries to found a new religion but is driven mad by his conflicting desires. The title poem of CAWDOR, AND OTHER POEMS is based on Greek mythology; DEAR JUDAS, AND OTHER POEMS is biblical. *Descent to the Dead* (1931) contains *At the Fall of an Age*, a dramatic poem dealing with the execution of Helen by Polyxo 20 years after the fall of Troy. THURSO'S LANDING reveals, perhaps more than any other of Jeffers' poems, his abhorrence of modern civilization. His many other volumes include *Give Your Heart to the Hawks and Other Poems* (1933), reiterating his idea that man must go beyond humanity if he is to survive; *Solstice and Other Poems* (1935), containing an early use of the Medea story, to which Jeffers returned in *Medea* (1946); *Such Counsels You Gave to Me and Other Poems* (1937), *Selected Poetry* (1938); *Be Angry at the Sun* (1941); *The Double Axe* (1948); and *Hungerfield, and Other Poems* (1954).

Jefferson, Thomas (1743–1826). Third president of the U.S. (1801–1809). A graduate of the College of William and Mary, Jefferson was admitted to the bar in 1767 and sat in the Virginia House of Burgesses from 1769 to 1775. As a delegate to the Continental Congress (1775–1776), he drafted the DECLARATION OF INDEPENDENCE. While he was a member of the Virginia House of Delegates (1776–1779), he supported the abolition of primogeniture and entail, the establishment of religious freedom, and the separation of church and state. After serving as wartime governor of Virginia and as a member of congress, he succeeded Franklin as minister to France, where he published his *Notes on Virginia* (1784–1785), still considered a valuable source of information about the natural history of Virginia as well as about 18th-century political and social life. He was named secretary of state under Washington, but resigned in 1793 as a result of long-standing political and personal differences with Alexander Hamilton and his supporters. Jefferson's championship of states' rights and agrarian interests distinguished him and his followers from the Hamiltonians and resulted in the emergence of the Democratic-Republican Party, of which Jefferson was the leader. He was the presidential candidate of the new party in 1796, but ran second to John ADAMS, the Federalist nominee, and, in accordance with the practice then followed, became vice president. In 1798, Jefferson and James Madison prepared the Virginia and Kentucky Resolutions in reply to the Federalists' ALIEN AND SEDITION ACTS.

In the election of 1800, Jefferson tied with Aaron Burr in electoral votes and was chosen president by the House of Representatives with the support of Hamilton, who considered Jefferson the lesser of two evils. Important events of his administration were the Tripolitan War, the LOUISIANA PURCHASE, and the short-lived Embargo Act, designed to preserve American neutrality rights.

After 40 years of public service, Jefferson retired permanently to his home at MONTICELLO in 1809, devoting much of his time to the creation of a university for Virginia. He was reconciled with his old political opponent, John Adams, and the two men, from 1811 to their deaths, carried on a voluminous correspondence, which is one of the most interesting in American letters. Perhaps the most versatile of the founding fathers, he is remembered for his faith in the capacity of the people to govern themselves through representative institutions. On his tombstone at Monticello is the inscription he ordered: "Author of the Declaration of American Independence, of the Statute of Virginia for religious freedom, and Father of the University of Virginia." His other writings include *A Summary View of the Rights of British America* (1774), *A Manual of Parliamentary Practice* (1801), and *Life of Captain [Meriwether] Lewis* (1817).

Jeffreys, George. 1st Baron **Jeffreys of Wem** (1648–1689). Welsh-born English jurist. As chief justice and lord chancellor of England, he supported the efforts of James II to rule as an absolute monarch. His conduct at the trials known as the BLOODY ASSIZES, over which he presided, made his name a byword for injustice and brutality. When James was overthrown, Jeffreys was imprisoned and died in the Tower of London.

Jeffries, Richard (1848–1887). English writer and novelist. He wrote *Gamekeeper* (1877) and *Red Deer* (1884), two collections of sketches, and the novels *Wood Magic* (1881) and *Bevis* (1882). These books are distinguished by their close and poetic observation of nature, particularly animal life.

Jehovah. In the Bible, the Christian version of the word used for the name of God, the Almighty, the Supreme Being in the Hebrew Scriptures. It is a transliteration of the four Hebrew letters *Y, H, W, H,* which form the incommunicable name of God. These four letters are called the tetragram. Since the Jews consider the name of God too sacred to be pronounced, the tetragram is read aloud as Adonai or Elohim, when encountered in the Scripture. The original form and pronunciation of the tetragram has been lost over the centuries; there is evidence that it may have been Yahwe or Yave, but certainly not Jehovah.

Jehu. In the Old Testament, the son of Nimshi, who overthrew the Ahab dynasty and took over the throne. He put to death King Joram, son of Ahab, the evil queen mother, Jezebel, and all the prophets of Baal. A *jehu* is a humorous appellation for a coachman, in reference to the swift chariot which Jehu drove (II Kings 9:20).

Jekyll, Dr. See STRANGE CASE OF DR. JEKYLL AND MR. HYDE, THE.

Jellyby, Mrs. In Charles Dickens' BLEAK HOUSE, an enthusiastic, unthinking philanthropist who forgets that charity should begin at home. She would do anything for the poor fan-makers and flower girls of distant Borrioboola-Gha, but shamefully neglects her own children and would send away a poor beggar dying of starvation on her doorstep.

Jenkins, Winifred. In Tobias Smollett's novel HUMPHREY CLINKER, Miss Tabitha Bramble's illiterate maid. An earlier Mrs. MALAPROP, she exhausts the possibilities of humor in English misspelling.

Jenkins' Ear, War of. The popular name of a war between England and Spain (1739–1741) declared by Sir Robert Walpole when the English mariner Robert Jenkins declared that a Spanish captain, upon boarding his vessel, had cut off his ear. The conflict was absorbed in the War of the Austrian Succession.

Jenkinson, Ephraim. A sharp old swindler in Oliver Goldsmith's novel THE VICAR OF WAKEFIELD. He sells the vicar's son Moses a pair of green spectacles for the money with which Moses was supposed to have purchased a harness horse. His eventual reformation saves the Primrose family from ruin.

Jenner, Edward (1749–1823). English physician and discoverer of vaccination. His best known work is *An Inquiry into the Causes and Effects of the Variolae Vaccinae* (1798). He first performed public vaccination on his own son in 1796, but it was not until 1853 that the practice was made compulsory in England.

Jennie Gerhardt (1911). A novel by Theodore DREISER. Jennie's harsh German father forces her to leave home when he discovers that she is pregnant; an Ohio senator had promised to marry her but died before he could carry out his intention. She becomes the mistress of the scion of a wealthy family, Lester Kane, who is finally forced by his family to give her up. He marries in his own class, becomes ill, and **is**

nursed by Jennie. When he dies she steals in to his funeral, afraid to speak to his family. Jennie's daughter dies, and she is left to face life alone, but with the characteristic acceptance she has shown all along.

Jennifer Lorn (1923). A novel by Elinor WYLIE. Her first novel, it deals with 18th-century England and India at the time of Warren Hastings. It is a satiric study of a pompous aristocrat, seen through the eyes of his wife. The title is a pun: Jenny forlorn.

Jenseits von Gut und Böse. See BEYOND GOOD AND EVIL.

Jensen, Johannes Vilhelm (1873–1950). Danish novelist, poet, and essayist. Jensen attained literary prominence with the publication of *Himmerlandsfolk (Himmerland Tales,* 1898), stories of his native Jutland. *Kongens Fald (The Fall of the King,* 3 vols., 1900–1901), his first successful novel, paints a vivid and appreciative although sometimes critical portrait of Denmark and her people. Philosophically committed to Darwinism, Jensen published *Den Lange Rejse (The Long Journey,* 6 vols., 1908–1922), an evolutionary study of the Cimbrians, i.e., the Teutonic race, which moves from the baboon stage of the preglacial age to the time of Christopher Columbus. In his novels and even in his lyric verse, Jensen expressed his Darwinist convictions. From 1906 to 1940 eight volumes of *Myter (Myths)* appeared, containing poetic and subtle stories and essays. He was awarded the Nobel prize for literature in 1944.

Jensen, Thit Marie Kirstine (1876–1957). Danish novelist, sister of Johannes Jensen. Her early novels, among them *Martyrium* (1905), *Hemskoen* (1911), *Gerd* (1918), *Den erotiske Hamsta* (1919), and *Af Blod er du kommet* (1928), portray peasant life and express vigorous feminist convictions. Later she turned from present reform to Denmark's past, producing such fine historical novels as *Valdemar Atterdag* (2 vols., 1940), *Drotten* (2 vols., 1943), and *Rigets Arving* (2 vols., 1946).

Jephthah's daughter. The only daughter of Jephthah, judge of Israel. She went to greet him on his return home from victory over the Ammonites, unaware that he had vowed to offer up to Jehovah the first thing that met him. Her story is told in *Judges.*

Jeremiah. An Old Testament book. The prophet Jeremiah, who gave his name to the book, lived in Jerusalem during the time of the fall of this city to the Babylonians. With the destruction of the city and the temple, the emphasis in Jeremiah turns from the nation to the individual. The root of the prophet's religion is in his own heart, rather than a temple building. Matthew reports that Jesus was thought to be the returned Jeremiah.

Jeremy (1919). A semiautobiographical novel by Hugh WALPOLE about the daily life of a small boy. *Jeremy and Hamlet* (1923) and *Jeremy at Crale* (1927) are sequels.

Jericho. One of the oldest inhabited sites in Palestine, perhaps the oldest in the world. Mesolithic flints associated with fortifications are traceable to the ninth millennium B.C., a "proto-Neolithic" culture predates the eighth. Jericho was the first city conquered by the Israelites under Joshua after they crossed the Jordan into their Promised Land.

Jeroboam. In the Old Testament, the son of Nebat who "made Israel to sin" (I Kings 15:34).

Under his leadership, 10 tribes revolted against REHOBOAM, the son of Solomon, and set up a separate northern state with Jeroboam as king. Because of the idol worship he initiated, his name has become a byword for wickedness. A very large wine bottle or flagon is called a *jeroboam,* in allusion to his power and strength.

Jerome, St. (full Latin name, **Sophronius Eusebius Hieronymus;** c. 340–420). One of the fathers of the Western Church and translator of the Latin version of the Bible known as the VULGATE. He is generally represented as an aged man in a cardinal's dress, writing or studying, with a lion seated beside him. Legend has it that while St. Jerome was lecturing one day, a lion entered the schoolroom and lifted up one of its paws. All the disciples fled, but Jerome, seeing that the paw was injured, drew a thorn from it and dressed the wound. The lion, out of gratitude, showed a wish to stay with its benefactor.

Jerome, Jerome K[lapka] (1859–1927). English novelist and playwright, best known as a humorist. His works include *Three Men in a Boat* (1889), a novel, and *The Passing of the Third Floor Back* (1908), a modern morality play set in a boarding house.

Jerusalem. A city in Palestine. It is a holy city for Christians, Jews, and Muslims. A Canaanite city long before the arrival of the Israelites, Jerusalem was captured by David (c. 1,000 B.C.) who made it his capital city. David's son Solomon built his famous temple in Jerusalem, but after his death the city began to decline in importance. Under Solomon's son, Rehoboam, the city was sacked by the Egyptians (920 B.C.). A weak city, it remained fairly secure for two centuries until the Assyrians began to invade Judah in the middle of the eighth century. Most of the kingdom was lost in ransom, but the city itself was spared until 586 B.C., when it fell to the Babylonians, who destroyed it almost completely.

More than a century later (c. 420) Jerusalem was rebuilt under Nehemiah. The city was captured again by Alexander the Great in 332 B.C. After a period of domination by the Seleucid kings of Antioch, the revolt of the MACCABEES restored rule of the city to the Jews.

Jerusalem became a Roman city in 46 B.C. under Herod who rebuilt it on a grand scale. Revolts in A.D. 66–70 and 132–135 saw the city leveled again. Under Byzantine control for five centuries, it fell to the Muslims in 638.

Modern Jerusalem is a city divided between the Jews and Arabs who fought bitterly for it when the state of Israel was created in 1948.

Jerusalem. A long, mystical poem (1804) by William BLAKE in which he presents his theory that the world of imagination is a world of eternity after death.

Jerusalem (1901–1902). A collection of stories by Selma LAGERLÖF, dealing with an old peasant family, the Ingmars of Ingmarson, and their devotion to the family farm in Sweden. The title refers to a pilgrimage to Jerusalem, for which the land is finally sold at auction by one member of the family. Another Ingmar, however, renounces his fiancée and marries a rich woman in order to save the farm.

Jerusalén Conquistada (1609). A historical epic by Lope de VEGA. Although the theme is the unsuccessful attempt of Richard the Lion-Hearted to capture Jerusalem from the Saracens, it contains much legendary and nonhistorical material, such as the participation of Alfonso VIII of Spain in this crusade.

Jerusalem Delivered. See GERUSALEMME LIBERATA.

Jesse. In the Old Testament, the father of David. A *Jesse tree* is a genealogical tree, usually represented as a vine or as a large brass candlestick with many branches, tracing the lineage of the house of David from Jesse to Jesus, it having been prophesied that the Messiah would be a "rod out of the stem of Jesse." (Isa. 11:1.) Jesse is himself sometimes represented in a recumbent position with the vine rising out of his loins. A stained-glass window showing Jesse and the tree tracing the ancestry from him to Jesus is called a *Jesse window.*

Jesse, F[ryniwyd] Tennyson (18?–1958). English novelist, dramatist, journalist, and criminologist. Her best novel was *The Lacquer Lady* (1929). She described a number of cases for the *Notable British Trials* series.

Jessel, Miss. See TURN OF THE SCREW, THE.

Jessica. The rebellious daughter of Shylock in Shakespeare's MERCHANT OF VENICE. "Wise, fair, and true," she elopes with Lorenzo, but is practical enough to take with her a portion of her father's treasure.

jester. See FOOL.

Jesuit Martyrs of North America. Eight French missionaries whom the Indians martyred in the 17th century in New York and Canada: the priests Isaac Jogues, Jean de Brébeuf, Noël Chabanel, Anthony Daniel, Charles Garnier, Gabriel Lalemant, and the laymen René Goupil and John Lalande. All eight were canonized by Pope Pius XI in 1930 and celebrated in an epic poem, *Brébeuf and his Brethren,* by the Canadian poet Edwin John Pratt (1883–   ).

Jesuits. A name applied to members of the Society or Company of Jesus, founded in 1534 by St. Ignatius of LOYOLA. From the first six disciples made by Ignatius, four of whom were Spaniards, the order had grown to over 1000 at the time of his death in 1556. Jesuits were particularly active in three fields: education, missionary endeavor in non-Catholic lands, and the development of deeper spiritual life.

The order was founded to combat the Reformation and to propagate the Roman Catholic faith among the heathen, but through its discipline, organization, and methods of secrecy it soon acquired such political power that it came into conflict with both the civil and religious authorities. It was driven from England in 1579, from France in 1594, from Venice in 1607, from Spain in 1767, from Naples in 1768; in 1773 it was suppressed by Pope Clement XIV, but was revived in 1814.

Owing to the casuistical principles maintained by many of the leaders of the older organization and attributed to the order as a whole, the name *Jesuit* acquired a very opprobrious signification both in Protestant and Roman Catholic countries. A *Jesuit* or *Jesuitical person* came to connote a deceiver or prevaricator.

Jesus or **Jesus Christ** (Heb. "the Messiah"), or **Christ Jesus.** Known also as **Jesus of Nazareth.** Born between 4 and 6 B.C. and crucified about A.D. 28.

One of the world's major religious figures, he is regarded by his followers as the Messiah predicted by the Old Testament prophets (Isa. 9: 2–6). The events of his life are recorded in the four Gospels of the New Testament. His genealogy is traced through David to Abraham.

Miraculous events occurred at his birth, but little is known of his youth and young manhood. He was born and lived in a time of distress and oppression. After his baptism by John the Baptist, he gathered 12 disciples (see APOSTLES) and began to teach his message of God's redeeming love for all mankind, the necessity of repentance, and the duty of the individual to God and to other men. Through his doctrine of salvation for mankind and his extraordinary healing powers, he had a large following among the common people. He became suspect with the authorities, both Roman and Jewish, because of his popularity and his attacks on the hypocrisy of the privileged. He foretold the advent of a new Kingdom of God, which the priests regarded as blasphemy and the Romans as sedition.

After his ministry in Galilee, he went to Jerusalem for the observation of Passover. There, after the Last Supper, JUDAS ISCARIOT, one of the disciples, betrayed him to the authorities. He was arrested by the Roman soldiery, tried, and crucified. His followers believe that after three days he rose from the dead and later ascended to heaven to assume his rightful place with God.

The Christian Church was founded by the followers of Jesus, after his death. He is viewed as the word of God made flesh (John 1:14), the divine Incarnation that became fully human to redeem mankind. Through a series of Church councils, the nature of Jesus' exact relation to the Godhead was defined in the concept of the TRINITY, the three-person union of Father, Son, and Holy Spirit.

Jeune Alcidiane, La. See Marin le Roy GOMBERVILLE.

Jeune fille Violaine, La. See TIDINGS BROUGHT TO MARY, THE.

Jeune Parque, La (**The Youngest of the Fates,** 1917). A long poem by Paul VALÉRY. Written in a free-flowing version of classical rhymed Alexandrine couplets, it takes the form of a dramatic monologue. The young speaker is a maiden; she is simultaneously fearful of and fascinated by the desire awakening within her, for the violation of her self that will mark the beginning of her participation in the life process and her responsibility for new life.

Jevons, William Stanley (1835–1882). English economist and logician. He was a pioneer in the application of statistics to economics. Among his numerous books are *Pure Logic* (1864), *Theory of Political Economy* (1878), and *The State in Relation to Labour* (1882).

Jewett, Sarah Orne (1849–1909). American novelist and short-story writer. Her familiarity with her native Maine countryside enabled her to become one of the most successful of the local-color writers. Miss Jewett's pictures of New England life were described as "poetic realism" by Edward Garnett. *Deephaven* (1877), a collection of sketches of life in rural Maine, was her first successful book. Her masterpiece, THE COUNTRY OF THE POINTED FIRS, a series of episodes taking place in a Maine seaport town, is considered a minor classic.

Jew, the Wandering. See WANDERING JEW, THE.

Jew of Malta, The (probably performed in 1589; quarto of 1633, first extant edition). A romantic tragedy by Christopher MARLOWE. *The Jew of Malta* is essentially a dramatic portrait of one man, Barabas. At first the Jewish merchant, counting his "infinite riches in a little room," shares the longing for some extraordinary power and the ability to express his desire in stirring poetry that characterize other Marlovian heroes. He is a man of some dignity, unjustly persecuted by hypocritical Christians. But during the course of the play he degenerates from a human being who commands sympathy into a caricature of the grasping, greedy Jew dominated by his desire for gold. Barabas murders his daughter and an entire nunnery with poisoned porridge, performs other atrocities, and dies in an absurdly grotesque manner by falling into a bubbling caldron.

Jezebel. In the Old Testament, the wife of AHAB, who married him before he became king of Israel. After establishing the Phoenician worship of Baal at her husband's court, she was put to death at the order of JEHU.

A painted jezebel refers to a flaunting woman of bold spirit but loose morals (see II Kings 19:30).

John Masefield's poetic drama *King's Daughter* (1923) is based on the story of Jezebel and Jehu.

Jibanananda Das (1899–1954). Bengali poet. He was born in East Pakistan. Considered to be the finest exponent of "pure poetry" in India, he taught English literature in a college in Calcutta. Of his published volumes, the finest is *Banalata Sen,* translated into English in 1962.

Jiménez, Juan Ramón (1881–1958). Spanish poet. His work, which has had the greatest impact upon contemporary Spanish poetry, brought Jiménez the Nobel Prize for literature in 1956. Educated at Seville, the poet resided in Madrid for some years before the civil war sent him into exile. His earlier volumes are lyrical, full of delicate metaphors, and stress folk motifs; these include *Ninfeas* (1900), *Baladas de primavera* (1910), and the more traditional, spiritual work, *Sonetos espirituales* (1917). The last-mentioned year also marks the publication of *Diario de un poeta recién casado* (1917), the poet's first venture into the field of "pure poetry." It is characterized, as is his later work, by a striving for simplicity, free verse, intense concentration, and condensation of form. Perhaps his best-known work is the prose poem *Platero y yo* (1917), which relates the wanderings of the poet and his poetical donkey through Andalusia. Jiménez's poetry may be surveyed in the anthology of his own selection, *Tercera antología poética* (1942).

Jimson, Gulley. The passionate, comic artist hero of Joyce Cary's novel THE HORSE'S MOUTH.

Jingle, Alfred. In Charles Dickens' PICKWICK PAPERS, a strolling actor who imposes for a time on the members of the Pickwick Club. He is discovered to be a scoundrel and an imposter.

jingo. A word from the meaningless jargon of the 17th century conjurers. Probably it was substituted for God, in the same way as are *gosh, golly,* and the like. In Motteux' translation of Rabelais (1694), where the original reads *par Dieu* (Bk. iv. lvi), the English rendering is "By jingo." There is a possibility that the word is Basque *Jinko* or *Jainko,* God, and was introduced by sailors.

The later meaning of the word, a blustering so-called patriot who is itching to go to war on the slightest provocation, or a chauvinist, is taken from a music-hall song by G. W. Hunt, which was popular in 1878 when the country was supposed to be on the verge of intervening in the Russo-Turkish War on behalf of the Turks:

We don't want to fight; but, by Jingo, if we do,
We've got the ships, we've got the men, and got the money too.

The Russophobes became known as the *Jingoes,* and such policy has been labeled *Jingoism* ever since.

jinn or **genii** (singular, *jinnee*). Demons of Muslim legend thought to have been created from fire 2000 years before Adam was made of clay. Fable holds that they were governed by a race of kings named Suleyman, one of whom built the pyramids. Living chiefly in Mount KAF, they assume the forms of serpents, dogs, cats, monsters, or even human beings and become invisible at will. Evil jinn are hideously ugly, while the good are exquisitely beautiful. See AFREET; EBLIS; GIAN BEN GIAN.

Jinnistan. The Arabian fairyland.

Jo. In Charles Dickens' BLEAK HOUSE, a poor little outcast living in one of London's decaying tenements. The child wanders about from place to place until he finally dies of want and neglect. He is one of Dickens' most poignant characters.

Joad, C[yril] E[dwin] M[itchinson] (1891–1953). English philosopher. Many of his books are of a popularizing nature; among them are *Essays in Common Sense Philosophy* (1919), *Great Philosophies of the World* (1931), and *Guide to Modern Thought* (1933).

Joad family. The central characters in John Steinbeck's novel THE GRAPES OF WRATH. Escaping from the dust bowl of Oklahoma during the depths of the depression, they migrate to California as fruit pickers.

Joan, Pope. A mythical female pope, fabled in the Middle Ages to have succeeded Leo IV (855). The vulgar tale is that Joan conceived a violent passion for the monk Folda and in order to get admission to him assumed the monastic habit. Being clever and popular, she was elected pope, but was discovered through giving birth to a child during the enthronement.

Joan La Pucelle. Shakespeare's name for JOAN OF ARC, whom he depicts in HENRY VI: PART I as "a vile fiend and shameless courtezan."

Joanna or **Joan the Mad.** Also known as **Juana la Loca** (1497–1555). Spanish queen. The daughter of Ferdinand and Isabella, she married (1496) Philip the Fair of Flanders, whose infidelities probably aggravated her mental disorder. By him she bore the future Charles V. Although she inherited the crown of Castile upon the death of Isabella in 1504, the death of Philip (1506) increased her derangement, and Ferdinand sent her to live in seclusion in Tordesillas, while he became regent of Castile. At the time it was widely rumored that she was sane and was merely the victim of her family's machinations.

Joan of Arc. *Fr.* **Jeanne d'Arc** or **Darc.** Later known as the **Maid of Orleans,** *Fr.* **La Pucelle** (1412–1431). French heroine. A deeply religious peasant girl of the village of Domrémy, she began at 13 to have visions in which she identified the voices of St. Michael, St. Catherine, and St. Margaret. Henry VI of England had been crowned king of France in 1422, and when the English began their siege of Orleans in 1428, Joan become convinced that the saints had chosen her to repulse the English and conduct the French Dauphin to be crowned at the Reims cathedral. She finally convinced the Dauphin of her mission and, in male attire, led the French troops to victory at Orleans and elsewhere (May and June, 1429) and stood beside Charles VII at his coronation in July. But then she was not given sufficient troops, and her military campaign began to fail; she was taken prisoner in May, 1430, by the Burgundians, who sold her to their English allies six months later.

They did not want the English to execute her, however, until they could defame her in the eyes of the French peasants and troops, who regarded her as a saint. So she was turned over to the French ecclesiastical courts, the weak Charles not daring to interfere, and was tried on 12 charges of sorcery, wantonness in cutting her hair and wearing men's clothes, and blasphemous pride in regarding herself as responsible directly to God rather than to the Church. Worn out by the examination and condemned to the stake, she finally signed a recantation of her alleged sins; her sentence was commuted to life imprisonment. But in the next few days she resumed male attire and repudiated her recantation, so she was handed over to a secular English court and burned at the stake (May 30, 1431). After confused legal proceedings to shift the blame for her death, Joan was officially declared innocent in 1456; she was canonized as a saint in 1920.

The official records of her trial give the best account of the historical Joan. In literature she is treated variously as a witch, as in Shakespeare's *Henry VI,* reflecting contemporary English sentiment; with skepticism toward the mystic aura surrounding her belief in her voices, as in Voltaire's *La Pucelle* (1738, pub. 1755); or with complete acceptance of the supernatural element, making her a romantic heroine, as in Schiller's tragedy *Die Jungfrau von Orleans* (1801). Famous accounts of her life include the one in Michelet's *History of France* (1838–1867), Mark Twain's *Personal Recollections of Joan of Arc* (1896), and Anatole France's *Life of Joan of Arc* (1908). More recent plays about her include G. B. Shaw's *Saint Joan* (1923) and Jean Anouilh's *L'Alouette* (1953; translated by Christopher Fry as *The Lark,* 1955).

Job. An Old Testament book. The greatest poetic drama in the Old Testament, it is one of the most philosophically involved books in the Bible. The unknown, undated author deals with the problem of undeserved suffering and God's justice in the framework of an antique folk legend. Job and his friends discuss the question of whether suffering is always the punishment for sin and conversely whether sin is always punished.

The Lord, confident of Job's faith, permitted Satan to test him; thereupon, his wealth vanished, his children died and he was smitten with boils. Yet, despite his wife's advice to "curse God and die," he remained steadfast, and his faith was rewarded. (See ELIHU.)

In the Koran, Job's wife is said to have been either Rahmeh, daughter of Ephraim, son of Joseph, or Makhir, daughter of Manasses; and the tradition is recorded that Job, at the command of God, struck the earth with his foot from the dunghill where he lay, and instantly there welled up a spring of water with which his wife washed his sores and they were miraculously healed.

Job's comforter. One who intends to sympathize with you in your grief, but says that you brought it on yourself, thus in reality adding weight to your sorrow.

Job's post. A bringer of bad news.

Jocasta (Iokaste). See OEDIPUS.

Jocelyn (1836). A narrative poem by Alphonse LAMARTINE. The hero is a priest. As a lad he finds refuge from war in an Alpine cave, where he lives with another boy, who turns out to be a girl named Laurence. Although he loves her, he remains true to his priestly vows and leaves her for a life of self-denying devotion.

Jochumsson, Matthías (1835–1920). Icelandic poet and playwright. Although he founded modern drama in Iceland, he is most famous as a fine lyric poet. Elegaic, religious, and nature poems appear in the collections *Ljóomoeli* (1884) and *Grettisljóo* (1897).

Jōdo Buddhism. See AMIDISM.

Joel. An Old Testament book named for its author. A very approximate date of 350 B.C. has been assigned to the writing. The central event is a devastating plague of locusts, described in terms of an apocalyptic vision. The return of God's love is foretold and with it the wealth of the land.

Joe Miller's Jests. A book of jokes compiled by John Mottley in 1739. He named it for Joseph Miller (1684–1738), a popular comedian of the day who could neither read nor write. The term Joe Miller has become synonymous with a stale joke.

John (1167–1216). King of England (1199–1216). The youngest son of Henry II and ELEANOR OF AQUITAINE, he was nicknamed "Lackland," because he had not shared in the division of Henry's territory; he was probably Henry's favorite son, however, and his subsequent rebellion against his father broke the old king's heart. John succeeded to the throne upon the death of his childless brother Richard I, successfully thwarting the claim of his nephew Arthur of Brittany. As a result of John's famous quarrel with Pope Innocent III over the selection of Stephen LANGTON as archbishop of Canterbury, England was laid under an interdict and the king was declared deposed; in 1213, however, John submitted to the pope, going so far as to make England a fief of the papacy. The following year John invaded France in an attempt to regain the provinces of Normandy, Anjou, and Touraine, which he had previously lost, but he was decisively defeated by Philip II of France at the battle of Bouvines. Meanwhile, John's arbitrary practices had aroused the ire of the English nobles, who compelled him to sign the MAGNA CARTA in 1215. He is the subject of KING JOHN, a play by Shakespeare, and is a character in Scott's *Ivanhoe* (1820).

John, St., also St. **John the Evangelist** or **the Divine.** One of the twelve, frequently called "the

Joe Miller's *JESTS:*

OR, THE

WITS

VADE-MECUM.

BEING

A Collection of the moſt Brilliant JESTS; the Politeſt REPARTEES; the moſt Elegant BONS MOTS, and moſt pleaſant ſhort Stories in the *Engliſh* Language.

Firſt carefully collected in the Company, and many of them tranſcribed from the Mouth of the Facetious GENTLEMAN, whoſe Name they bear; and now ſet forth and publiſhed by his lamentable Friend and former Companion, *Elijah Jenkins, Esq;*

Moſt Humbly INSCRIBED

To thoſe CHOICE-SPIRITS *of the* AGE,

Captain BODENS, Mr. ALEXANDER POPE, Mr. Profeſſor LACY, Mr. Orator HENLEY, and JOB BAKER, the Kettle-Drummer.

LONDON:

Printed and Sold by T. READ, in *Dogwell-Court, White-Fryars, Fleet-Street.* MDCCXXXIX.

(Price One Shilling.)

Title page of *Joe Miller's Jests* (1739).

beloved disciple," since he is referred to as "that disciple whom Jesus loved" in the narrative of the Gospel of St. John. He was one of the sons of Zebedee and brother of St. James the Great. His day is December 27, and he is usually represented bearing a chalice from which a serpent issues, in allusion to his driving the poison from a cup presented him to drink. Tradition says that he took the Virgin Mary to Ephesus after the Crucifixion, but there is no evidence to support this. Most scholars now agree that while John was an influential leader of the early church, he was not the author of the fourth Gospel, the *Epistles of John,* or *The Revelation of St. John.* All of these works date after A.D. 80; Papias, a second century Christian writer, reports that John was killed in Palestine before A.D. 70.

John, Don. In Shakespeare's MUCH ADO ABOUT NOTHING, the jealous and vindictive bastard brother of Don Pedro, prince of Arragon. His plot against Claudio and Hero nearly succeeds, but he is finally undone and punished.

John, The Epistles of. Three short books of the New Testament. They are letters addressed to all Christians. The first two warn against the false teachings that had been filtering into the Church, with a special condemnation of Gnostic ideas. The third shows concern for an ambitious, arrogant young church official with whom the writer intends to deal personally. All three are held to be the work of one man, an elder of the church in Ephesus, named John (not to be confused with the apostle). Stylistic similarities plus an agreement in outlook indicate that this man was also the author of the fourth Gospel.

John, The Gospel According to St. The 4th book of the New Testament. The most spiritual of the accounts of Jesus' life, its emphasis is more on interpreting the meaning of his life and death than in recording the events. See JOHN, THE EPISTLES OF.

John Brown's Body (1928). A epic poem by Stephen Vincent BENÉT. A narrative of the Civil War, it opens with a prelude on the introduction of slavery, which is followed by a description of John Brown and his raid on Harpers Ferry. The poem, which considers both sides of the conflict with sympathy, includes sketches of famous participants, battles, the hardships of those on the home front, etc.

John Bull. The English nation personified, or the typical Englishman. Represented as a bluff, kindhearted, bull-headed farmer, the character originated in John ARBUTHNOT's political satire *The History of John Bull,* which was first published in 1712 as *Law is a Bottomless Pit.* In Arbuthnot's work "John Bull" is the Englishman, the Frenchman is termed "Lewis BABOON," and the Dutchman "Nicholas FROG." See Lord STRUTT. In the early years of the 19th century there was a scurrilous journal of this name, and in 1906 the name was adopted for a British weekly edited by Horatio Bottomley.

John Bull's Other Island (1904). A play by George Bernard SHAW. It was written at the request of William Butler Yeats for the Irish Literary Theatre, the group that later became the Abbey Theatre, Dublin. As might be expected the play deals with the conflict between the Irish and the English over home rule. The preface, written after the play, is strictly political, but the drama is subtle, having neither hero nor villain. The Irishman, Larry Doyle, is sensitive, imaginative, and more mature than his English friend Tom Broadbent. Broadbent's life is more straightforward, simpler than Doyle's; he is practical, adaptable, less bothered by thinking or feeling.

The conflict between the two men is in their characteristics, not their personalities. By the end of the play Tom has assumed all of Larry's ties with his birthplace in Ireland: his girl, his Parliamentary candidacy, even control of his property. This happens, not through conniving—Tom is too honest—but through Larry's reticence and Tom's blunt ambition.

John Dory. A popular ballad of the 14th century, often referred to in later literature. John Dory was a French pirate who was taken prisoner by the English.

John Gabriel Borkman (1896). A play by Henrik IBSEN. The story of a man who sacrificed love for ambition, *John Gabriel Borkman* expresses Ibsen's belief that the only unforgivable sin is "to murder the love-life in a human soul." As a young man, Borkman dreamed of power and broke his engagement to Ella Rentheim because Hinkel, the man whose help he needed to succeed, wanted to marry her. Borkman then married Ella's sister, but Ella persistently refused Hinkel's proposals. Finally Hinkel exposed Borkman's misappropriation of the bank's money, and Borkman was sent to jail. The action of the play concerns the meeting, after many years, of Ella and Borkman, and the attempts of Ella, Borkman, and Mrs. Borkman to influence young Erhart Borkman to choose his duty to his relatives, rather than his right to live for his own happiness.

John Gilpin (1782). A humorous ballad by William Cowper; its full title is *The Diverting History of John Gilpin, Showing How He Went further than He Intended and Came Safe Home Again.* Gilpin's wife says to him, "Though we have been married twenty years, we have taken no holiday"; and at her advice the well-to-do linen draper agrees to make a family party, and dine at the Bell, at Edmonton. Mrs. Gilpin, her sister, and four children go in the chaise, and Gilpin promises to follow on horseback. The horse begins to trot, and then to gallop, and John, a bad rider, flies through Edmondton, and never stops till he reaches Ware. Here he heads his horse back towards Edmondton, but is unable to stop until he reaches his original starting place in London. The model for John Gilpin was a Mr. Beyer, of Paternoster Row, who died in 1791.

John Halifax, Gentleman (1856). A novel by Dinah Maria Mulock Craik. It is a moralistic tale concerning an orphan who by perseverance and fortitude establishes himself in life and marries the heroine, Ursula March.

John Hancock. See John Hancock.

John Henry (1931). A novel by Roark Bradford. See John Henry.

John Marr and Other Sailors (1888). A collection of 25 poems by Herman Melville. Marr and other sailors invoke the spirits of their long-dead shipmates. The poems are chiefly nostalgic in mood.

Johnny Appleseed. See Johnny Appleseed.

John of Gaunt. Duke of **Lancaster** (1340–1399). English noble. The fourth son of Edward III and the father of Henry Bolingbroke (later Henry IV), he was the founder of the house of Lancaster and, during his lifetime, one of the most powerful figures in England. In Shakespeare's Richard II, he is an English nationalist who, upon his deathbed, utters one of literature's most moving expressions of patriotism:

> This royal throne of kings, this scepter'd isle,
> This earth of majesty, this seat of Mars,
> This other Eden, demi-paradise,
> This fortress built by Nature for herself
> Against infection and the hand of war,
> This happy breed of men, this little world,
> This precious stone set in the silver sea,
> Which serves it in the office of a wall,
> Or as a moat defensive to a house,
> Against the envy of less happier lands;
> This blessed plot, this earth, this realm,
> this England . . .

John of the Cross, St. Also known as San Juan de la Cruz. Religious name of **Juan de Yepes y Alvarez** (1542–1591). Spanish mystic and poet. Known as the "ecstatic Doctor," he became a Carmelite in 1563 and took an active part in Saint Teresa's

efforts to reform the order. He was canonized in 1726.

In his verse he blended his religious ardor and his gift for rich poetic imagery to produce what has been called "the supreme expression of Spanish mysticism." His best-known poems include *Noche oscura del alma, Llama de amor viva,* and the *canciones* of *La subida al Monte Carmelo.*

John o'Groat's House. Popularly considered the most northerly point in Great Britain. Originally, a building is said to have occupied this site, which is on the coast of Caithness, in Northern Scotland, near Duncansby Head; it had an eight-sided room with a door in each side and an octagonal table within. The story is that it was built by John o'Groat (or Jan Groot) who came from Holland with his two brothers in the reign of James IV of Scotland. They purchased lands, and in time the o'Groats increased, so that there came to be eight families of that name. They met regularly once a year in the house built by the founder, but on one occasion a question of precedency arose, and John o'Groat promised them the next time they came he would contrive to satisfy them all. Accordingly he built his eight-sided room, and the building became so noted that ever after the place has borne the name, *John o'Groat's House.*

Johns, Orrick (1887–1946). American poet and editor. Johns was a radical in politics and in poetry; *Second Avenue,* which won the *Lyric Year* poetry prize (1912), had a deliberate social concern. His poetry was collected in *Asphalt* (1917), *Black Branches* (1920), and *Wild Plum* (1926). He also wrote *Time of Our Lives: The Story of My Father and Myself* (1937).

Johnson, Andrew (1808–1875). 17th president of the U.S. (1865–1869). A self-educated ex-tailor, Johnson served as governor of Tennessee and as a member of the House of Representatives. Elected to the U.S. Senate in 1856, he was the only senator from any of the 11 seceded states who remained loyal to the Union when the Civil War broke out. He was Abraham Lincoln's running mate in 1864 and succeeded to the presidency after Lincoln's assassination. When Johnson attempted to carry out Lincoln's conciliatory policies toward the defeated South, he clashed with radical Republicans who demanded a harsher Reconstruction program under Congressional supervision. In 1868 he dismissed Secretary of War Edwin Stanton in defiance of the Tenure of Office Act (1867), which forbade the removal, without Senate approval, of officials whose appointments had been confirmed by the Senate. As a result, Johnson was impeached by the House of Representatives, but in the Senate trial was acquitted by a single vote, a two-thirds majority being needed for conviction.

Johnson, Esther (1681–1728). Lifelong friend of Jonathan Swift, immortalized by him as "Stella" in Journal to Stella. Their friendship began in 1689 in the home of Swift's patron, Sir William Temple (she may have been Temple's natural daughter), when Swift became her tutor, and they remained close friends until her death. There is unconvincing evidence that they were secretly married in 1716.

Johnson, James Weldon (1871–1938). American poet and lawyer. The first Negro admitted to the Florida bar since Reconstruction days, Johnson was a vigorous spokesman for his race. He edited *The*

Book of Negro Poetry (1922) and several collections of spirituals. He is also known for *God's Trombones* (1927), a collection of seven sermons in free verse. Among his other books are *The Autobiography of an Ex-Colored Man,* a novel (1912); *Fifty Years and Other Poems* (1917); *Black Manhattan* (1930); *Along This Way* (1933), his autobiography; and *Selected Poems* (1936).

Johnson, Lionel [Pigot] (1867-1902). English poet and critic. Johnson was a classicist, disciple of Walter Pater, and member of the RHYMERS' CLUB. He wrote *Poems* (1895) and *Post Liminium* (1911), a book of essays.

Johnson, Lyndon B[aines] (1908-). 36th president of the U.S. (1963-). After graduating from Southwest State Teachers College in San Marcos, Texas, in 1930, Johnson taught in the Houston public schools before going to Washington as secretary to a member of Congress. There he attracted the attention of President Roosevelt, who named him Texas state director of the National Youth Administration in 1935; Johnson was himself elected to the House in 1937 and served until 1948 when he won a seat in the U.S. Senate, defeating his rival by only 84 votes. As leader of the Democratic majority in the Senate from 1955 to 1961, Johnson became known as a superb legislative strategist who often won Democratic support for the policies of a Republican administration. After an unsuccessful bid for the Democratic presidential nomination in 1960, Johnson accepted the vice-presidential nomination on the ticket headed by John F. Kennedy and succeeded to the presidency after Kennedy's assassination in 1963.

Johnson, Pamela Hansford (1912-). English novelist and literary critic, wife of C. P. SNOW. Among her books are *This Bed Thy Center* (1935), *Six Proust Reconstructions* (1958), *The Humbler Creation* (1960), and *An Error of Judgement* (1962).

Johnson, Robert Underwood (1853-1937). American poet, editor, and public official. Johnson was editor of *Century Magazine* (1909-1913) and helped to establish the Hall of Fame at New York University; he was its director from 1919 to 1937. He helped to secure better copyright protection for authors, and served as ambassador to Italy (1920-1921). A volume of *Poems* was published in 1902, and enlarged in later editions; Johnson's memoirs are called *Remembered Yesterdays* (1923).

Johnson, Samuel (1696-1772). American philosopher, theologian, and teacher. The first native disciple of the 18th-century movement of rationalism, he is considered one of the most important thinkers of early America. His works include *An Introduction to the Study of Philosophy* (1731), *A System of Morality* (1746), and *Elementa Philosophica* (1752), which was printed by Benjamin Franklin. Johnson also served as the first president (1753-1763) of King's College (now Columbia University).

Johnson, Samuel. Known as **Dr. Johnson** (1709-1784). English lexicographer, essayist, poet, and moralist, the major literary figure in the second half of the 18th century; he was referred to as the GREAT CHAM OF LITERATURE. After being a schoolmaster and a bookseller for six years in Lichfield, the town of his birth, he left for London in 1737, with his tragedy *Irene* under his arm, and remained there permanently.

He was employed by Edward Cave, the founder of THE GENTLEMAN'S MAGAZINE, and contributed regularly essays, poems, Latin verses, and reports on Parliamentary debates to that publication. In 1738 he published his poem *London* which was compared favorably with the maturer works of Pope; in 1749, *Irene* was produced and indifferently received, and in the same year appeared *The Vanity of Human Wishes,* a poem marked with the pessimism that pervaded his life.

Meanwhile, he was earning renown as a prose moralist, notably with his periodical essays THE RAMBLER and THE IDLER, and later with his philosophical romance RASSELAS, which, though not distinguished for its action, is a cogent presentation of Johnson's moral views and his abiding theme: the vanity of human wishes and the impossibility of human happiness in an imperfect world. His literary style, often referred to as "Johnsonese," is severely balanced, Latinate, and pithy.

The monumental DICTIONARY OF THE ENGLISH LANGUAGE (1755) secured his reputation as a scholar and, though faulty, it was highly useful. His edition of Shakespeare (1765), historical and interpretative in approach, greatly stimulated Shakespearean scholarship. His *Preface to Shakespeare* is sometimes considered one of his finest pieces of prose. In defending Shakespeare for not following the "rules," he makes a good case for imaginative truth while attacking the classical unities: "The objection arising from the impossibility of passing the first hour at Alexandria, and the next at Rome, supposes, that when the play opens, the spectator really imagines himself at Alexandria, and believes that his walk to the theatre has been a voyage to Egypt, and that he lives in the days of Anthony and Cleopatra. Surely he that imagines this may imagine more."

His last years were spent in the society of other great men. Of this facet of Johnson's career—that of conversationalist—we have BOSWELL'S LIFE OF SAMUEL JOHNSON, LL.D., to inform us. In person slovenly, in manner abrupt and even rude, driven by fears of insanity and damnation, suffering from hypochondria, he yet emerges from Boswell's *Life* as a man of essential kindness, generosity, and sociability. He had married (1734) a woman 20 years his senior to whom he was devoted; her death (1752) may have caused him to seek more and more the society of men with whom he could indulge his fondness for conversation. In 1764 the LITERARY CLUB was founded, and here Johnson found an outlet for conversation; he cultivated the art consciously and even admitted that he sometimes talked for the sake of victory.

In 1773, at the age of 64, he was prodded into taking a walking tour of the Hebrides with Boswell. His account of it, *A Journey to the Western Isles of Scotland* (1775), is overshadowed by Boswell's *The Journal of a Tour of the Hebrides with Samuel Johnson, LL.D.* which is the more lively for having Johnson as its subject. His last published work, in 10 volumes, is the biographical and critical LIVES OF THE POETS. See Hester Lynch THRALE.

Johnson Over Jordan (1939). A play about time by J. B. PRIESTLEY. Johnson, an aviator in an accident, re-experiences events from his past life.

Johnston, Mary (1870-1936). American historical novelist. She is known as the author of some of the best of the historical romances that were so popular at the beginning of the 20th century. Her second novel, To HAVE AND TO HOLD, which is still read, was her most successful. It was followed by *Audrey* (1909). Most of her books are set in Virginia, *The Long Roll* (1911) and *Cease Firing* (1912) describing the Civil War from the Confederate point of view. Miss Johnston later became interested in mysticism, feminism, and socialism, and these found their way into such books as *Silver Cross* (1922).

John the Baptist, St. Patron saint of missionaries. He is so regarded because he was sent "to prepare the way of the Lord." He baptized Jesus in the river Jordan. John the Baptist was a fearless denouncer of the sins of his contemporaries who was thrown into prison and later beheaded because he opposed Herod's act of making away with his brother to secure his brother's wife Herodias. For the use of this story in drama and opera, see SALOME.

Joinville, Jean de (1224-1317). French chronicler. As royal seneschal he accompanied Louis XI on his first crusade (1248-1252); his *Histoire de saint Louis* (1305-1309) is a colorful first-person narrative of the events of the crusade and of his friendship with the king.

Jolas, Eugene (1894-1952). American editor and founder of the experimental magazine TRANSITION. Born in Union City, N.J., Jolas spent his childhood in Lorraine. While still a youth, he returned to the U.S., worked on various newspapers, and became passionately interested in the contemporary avant-garde. He then went to Paris, where in 1927 he founded his famous magazine. A brilliant editor, trilingual from childhood, Jolas gave encouragement to numerous important writers in the 20's and 30's. His anthology *Transition Workshop* (1949) contains representative selections of the work he published and encouraged.

Jolliet or **Joliet, Louis** (1645-1700). Canadian-born French explorer. Though intended for the priesthood, Jolliet became a merchant and is remembered for his trips through the Mississippi Valley and the regions of the Gulf of St. Lawrence and Hudson Bay. See Jacques MARQUETTE.

Jolly Beggars, The (1785, pub. 1799). A poem by Robert BURNS written in the form of a cantata with recitative. It presents a series of songs by a group of beggars who tell variously of their sorrows, their wretchedness, their cynicism and disillusionments, and their scorn for the church and the nobility. The setting of the poem is "Poosie Nansie's" disreputable inn at Mauchline. (See also THE HOLY FAIR.) It is considered by many critics to be Burns's most accomplished work.

Jolly Roger. See BLACK FLAG.

Jolyon. A character in John Galsworthy's THE FORSYTE SAGA. Young Jolyon is the most sensitive member of the Forsyte family. He marries Soames Forsyte's former wife, Irene.

Jonah. In the Old Testament, the prophet said to have been swallowed by a mammoth fish, and the Old Testament book bearing his name. Instructed by Jehovah to preach in the great but wicked city of Nineveh, he willfully took ship in another direction. When a storm arose, the sailors, after casting lots, threw Jonah into the sea to appease the Deity. He was swallowed by a whale in whose belly he lived for three days until "the great fish" deposited him on dry land. He then went to Nineveh where he was the cause of widespread repentance.

Jonathan. See DAVID.

Jonathan Wild, the Great. *The Life of Mr. Jonathan Wild* (1743). A novel by Henry FIELDING. Jonathan WILD was a famous highwayman and receiver of stolen goods (1682-1725), but his life has little relation to this ironic satire on tyranny and political innocence. Wild is meant to be an ironic representation of Sir Robert Walpole.

Jones, David (1895-   ). Anglo-Welsh water-color painter and writer. He has written IN PARENTHESIS, *The Anathemata* (1954), a long fragmented fusion of prose and poetry about the history of Britain, and *Epoch and Artist; Selected Writings* (1959).

Jones, Sir Henry Arthur (1851-1929). English playwright. Influenced by Ibsen, his plays deal with social relationships and social problems. Among his works are *Breaking a Butterfly* (1885), *Saints and Sinners* (1891), MICHAEL AND HIS LOST ANGEL, and *Mrs. Dane's Defense* (1900).

Jones, Inigo (1573-1652). English architect. He is also well known for his designs of sets, costumes, and stage machinery for court MASQUES written by Jonson, Heywood, and Davenant. These designs were of unprecedented elaborateness and ingenuity and had considerable influence upon later theater design. The elegance and grace of his architectural work, which was based on classical Renaissance elements, earned him the title of "the English Palladio." Among the buildings still in existence are the Banqueting Hall at Whitehall and the Queen's House at Greenwich.

Jones, James (1921-   ). American novelist. Born in Robinson, Ill., Jones joined the U.S. army, which provided the material for his massive and forceful first novel, FROM HERE TO ETERNITY, that established his reputation. The book, which won a National Book Award, aroused a critical storm, many

Inigo Jones's design for Whitehall Palace (London).

deploring the lurid language and shocking incidents, others admiring its vitality and force. His second novel, *Some Came Running* (1957), is concerned with the vagaries, mostly sexual, of small-town life. *The Pistol* (1959), a novella, and *The Thin Red Line* (1962), a full-length novel, are both concerned with the military.

Jones, John Paul (1747–1792). Scottish-born American naval officer, famed for his exploits in the Revolution. In a naval engagement off the coast of England (1779), Jones captured the British warship *Serapis,* although his own vessel, the BONHOMME RICHARD, was sunk. In response to a British demand for surrender during the battle, Jones is said to have replied: "I have not yet begun to fight!" He is the model for the hero of Cooper's novel *The Pilot* (1823) and a prominent character in Winston Churchill's *Richard Carvel* (1899).

Jones, Robert Edmond (1887–1954). American stage designer. Known for the sets he did for some of the most notable theatrical productions of the first half of the 20th century, he frequently worked with experimental troupes, among them the Washington Square Players, the Provincetown Players, the Greenwich Village Theater, and the Theatre Guild. He also was the author of *The Dramatic Imagination* (1941).

Jones, Lady Roderick. See Enid BAGNOLD.

jongleurs. Medieval entertainers, including acrobats, jugglers, and exhibitors of animals as well as musicians and reciters of poetry. They entertained at the courts of the nobility, and also in public places, especially near the shrines and churches along the routes of pilgrimages. It was the jongleurs who sang the CHANSONS DE GESTE, FABLIAUX, and other romances and lyrics written by the TROUVÈRES, although sometimes a jongleur was also a trouvère: that is, he would be both poet and singer-musician. Jongleurs permanently employed by a court were called *ménestrels,* or minstrels, and the security they enjoyed allowed them to devote more time to literary composition, so that by the 14th century there was considerably more specialization of function between composers and performers.

Jonson, Ben (1573–1637). English dramatist and poet. His father having died a month before his birth, Jonson was raised as the stepson of a bricklayer, and briefly entered this trade after leaving school. Though considered the most learned of the Elizabethan dramatists, his formal education seems to have been limited to his years at the Westminster School, where he was sent at the expense of its master, William Camden. He spent a short time as a soldier in the Netherlands, returned to England and, some time not later than 1592, married. During the next six years he probably existed as an actor and dramatic hack-writer, reworking old plays. His first original play, EVERY MAN IN HIS HUMOUR, was performed in 1598, with Shakespeare as a member of the cast. A comedy that already gives evidence of Jonson's brilliant gift for caricature and comic realism, it presents a group of assorted characters, each dominated—almost possessed—by one overriding characteristic, or HUMOR. Later in 1598 Jonson killed a man in a duel, and was imprisoned and charged with manslaughter. While in prison he was converted to Catholicism, to which he adhered for 12 years. He

narrowly escaped execution, but was released by benefit of clergy, forfeiting his property and receiving a brand on his left thumb. This incident, however, seemed to have few untoward effects on him, and the following year a sequel to his first play, called *Every Man Out of His Humour,* was produced at the Globe Theater. Less coherent in plot, and containing more blatant caricatures, it assailed the morals and foibles of the age, and contained (in response to John MARSTON's satiric portrait of him in HISTRIOMASTIX) veiled attacks on some of his fellow playwrights. *Cynthia's Revels,* which followed in 1600, was a flinging down of the gauntlet in the now-raging WAR OF THE THEATERS between Jonson, Marston, and Thomas DEKKER. Marston and Dekker retaliated with plays satirizing Jonson, and Jonson came back into the fray with *The Poetaster* (1601). Dekker answered with *Satiromastix, or The Untrussing of the Humorous Poet* in 1602, but Jonson did not take up the stage aspects of the war again. He turned to tragedy, writing the play *Richard Crookbacke* and SEJANUS HIS FALL, the latter performed at the Globe in 1603. A classical tragedy dealing with the attempt of the upstart Sejanus to overthrow the Emperor Tiberius, it lacks the verve and color of his comedies and the depth of characterization and psychological insight requisite for tragedy. Jonson only essayed one more tragedy, *Catiline* (1611), also based on classical models.

After the accession of James I in 1603 Jonson turned most of his energies to writing MASQUES for the new court, working for a time with the architect Inigo JONES on sets and stage effects. He developed the antimasque, a satiric or grotesque interlude juxtaposed against the imaginative and usually lighthearted content of the rest of the work. His quarrel with his fellow playwrights was evidently patched up, for in 1604 he collaborated with Dekker on *The King's Entertainment* and with Marston and George Chapman on *Eastward Ho* in 1605. When Marston and Chapman were imprisoned because James I found some parts of the play unflattering to the Scots, Jonson voluntarily joined them.

Though his masques far outnumber his plays during the Jacobean period, the five comedies he then wrote are the crowning pieces of his dramatic career: VOLPONE, OR THE FOX (performed 1605 or 1606, printed 1607); EPICENE, OR THE SILENT WOMAN (performed 1609; printed 1610); THE ALCHEMIST (1610); BARTHOLOMEW FAIR (1614); and *The Devil is an Ass* (1616). Colorful, crowded canvases filled with all manner of contemporary English types, these comedies satirize hypocrisy and greed, exploiters and gulls, rogues and fools; and as Jonson points out in the title of the last piece, the devil himself is a mere piker compared to humankind and its capacity for mischief.

In 1616 Jonson published the first folio edition of his collected works. Two years later he went on an extended holiday to Scotland, where he visited with the Scotch poet William Drummond. From this visit came Drummond's recollections of their *Conversations at Hawthornden,* a source of many of Jonson's opinions and an implicit portrait of the man as seen through the eyes of his friend.

The plays of Jonson's last period never reached the heights he had achieved before, though he remained until the end of his life the greatest figure of the English stage, the acknowledged leader of the gatherings of men of letters at the MERMAID TAVERN. His last plays include *The Staple of News* (1625); *The Magnetic Lady* (1632); and *Tale of a Tub* (1633). The lovely pastoral drama *The Sad Shepherd* (printed 1641), was left uncompleted at the time of his death.

A classicist who took the Roman writers for his models, a humanist who would engraft classical control and purity on English forms, and a moralist to whom the drama was a means of instruction and of criticism, Jonson both reflects the temper of his age and anticipates the more rock-ribbed classicism of the Augustan period. His poetry, notable for its balance, its control, its unadorned simplicity that is not without lyricism, prefigured the later lyrics of the 17th-century Cavalier poets, the "sons of Ben." Among his *Epigrams,* published in the first folio of 1616, are the two well-known poems mourning the deaths of his first daughter and his seven-year-old son; *The Forrest,* also in the first folio, contains the famous *To Celia,* beginning "Drink to me, only, with thine eyes." The second folio, published in 1640, contains *Underwoods,* a collection of miscellaneous poems.

Jormungard. See MIDGARD SERPENT.

Jorrocks. A famous amateur sportsman, a Cockney grocer passionately interested in the hunt, created by Robert Smith SURTEES. He appeared in *Jorrocks' Jaunts and Jollities, the Hunting, Shooting, Racing, Driving, Sailing, Eating, Eccentric and Extravagant Exploits of that Renowned Sporting Citizen, Mr. John Jorrocks of St. Botolph Land and Great Coram Street* (1838), and other books.

jōruri. Japanese puppet theater. Developed during the Tokugawa period (1600–1868), its most important plays were written by CHIKAMATSU MONZAEMON. The dolls are operated by puppet masters visible to the audience. The roles and narrative explanation of the story are rendered by a reciter (*gidayu*). Many of the same plays are used also in the *kabuki* theater.

Josaphat. See BARLAAM.

José, Don. A Spanish officer in Bizet's opera CARMEN, in love with Carmen.

Joseph. An Old Testament hero of the book of Genesis. The younger son and favorite of his father Jacob, he was hated by his 10 older brothers who sold him as a slave to a caravan going to Egypt. There, with his master Potiphar, he rose to a position of responsibility, but was maligned and imprisoned upon his refusal to respond to the advances of POTIPHAR'S WIFE (Gen. 39). In time, he was set free and, as a result of his interpretations of the king's dreams, made prime minister. Pharaoh's dreams of seven lean cattle swallowing up seven fat cattle and seven lean ears of corn devouring seven full ears were said to betoken the coming of famine, and Joseph was therefore installed as food administrator. During the famine, his brothers came to Egypt to buy corn and after a dramatic series of events (see BENJAMIN), Joseph revealed his identity and brought about their migration to Egypt. See JOSEPH AND HIS BROTHERS.

Joseph, St. Husband of the Virgin Mary. He is the patron saint of carpenters, because he was of that craft. In art, Joseph is represented as an aged man with a budding staff in his hand. His day is March 19.

Joseph II (1741–1790). Holy Roman Emperor (1765–1790). The son of Maria Theresa, he was called the revolutionary emperor because of his rigorous policy of social and economic reform within the Austrian dominions, which he ruled after her death in 1780.

Joseph and His Brothers (Joseph und seine Brüder; 1933–1943). A tetralogy of novels by Thomas MANN, based on the biblical story of JOSEPH: *Die Geschichten Jaakobs* (*The Stories of Jacob,* 1933), *Der junge Joseph* (*Young Joseph,* 1934), *Joseph in Ägypten* (*Joseph in Egypt,* 1936), and *Joseph der Ernährer* (*Joseph the Provider,* 1943). In these four thick volumes, Mann has expanded the original story tremendously, but most of the added episodes and digressions contribute not so much to the tale itself as to the characters' depth and symbolic significance. In its over-all attitude, the *Joseph* tetralogy is neither ambiguous like *The Magic Mountain* nor tragic like *Doktor Faustus,* but unqualifiedly redemptive. Joseph's return from the pit into which he is cast by his brothers is symbolically connected with Christ's Resurrection, among other things, and indicates the redemption of man from death, whose realm is dominant in most of Mann's earlier writing.

Joseph Andrews (1742). Hero and shortened title of *The History of the Adventures of Joseph Andrews and of his friend, Mr. Abraham Adams, written in Imitation of the Manner of Cervantes,* a novel by Henry FIELDING. Joseph Andrews, a prudent, brawny, pleasant young man, is intended to be the brother of Samuel Richardson's heroine PAMELA. His widowed employer, Lady BOOBY, dismisses him from his position as footman for refusing her advances, and he flees London to rejoin his own true love, Fanny Goodwill. On hearing the news of his disgrace, Fanny rushes to meet him. Both are set upon by thieves, but are providentially rescued by Parson ADAMS, and the three return to their parish, where Joseph and Fanny, after comic-opera reversals and discoveries, are married in triumph. The time of the novel is coincident with *Pamela,* which it parodies and transcends. See Mrs. SLIPSLOP; Parson Oliver TRULLIBER.

Joseph of Arimathea. The rich Jew, probably a member of the Sanhedrin, who believed in Jesus but was afraid to confess it, and after the Crucifixion begged the body of Jesus and deposited it in his own tomb (Matt. 27:57–60). Legend relates that he was imprisoned for years, during which time he was kept alive miraculously by the Holy GRAIL, and that on his release by Vespasian, about A.D. 63, he brought to Britain the Grail and the spear with which Longinus wounded Jesus, and there founded the abbey of GLASTONBURY, beginning the conversion of Britain.

The origin of these legends is to be found in a group of apocryphal writings of which the *Evangelium Nicodemi* is the chief one. These were worked upon at Glastonbury between the 8th and 11th centuries, and were further embellished by Robert de Boron in the 13th century; the latter version was used by Malory in his *Morte d'Arthur* (c. 1469).

George Moore introduces Joseph of Arimathea into his novel *The Brook Kerith* (1915).

Josephson, Matthew (1899–   ). American editor and biographer. Along with many other young writers, Josephson became an expatriate during the 1920's. He helped to found and edit a number of little magazines, including *Secession*, *Broom*, and *transition;* he later served as assistant editor of the *New Republic*. Among his numerous biographies and books on business and politics are *Zola and His Time* (1928), *Jean-Jacques Rousseau* (1932), *The Robber Barons* (1934), *The President Makers* (1940), and *Life Among the Surrealists* (1962).

Josephus, Flavius. Original name, **Joseph ben Matthias** (A.D. 37–?95). Jewish historian and general. Imbued with deep admiration for Rome and its institutions, he managed in his later years to live in the sunshine of the favor of the emperors Vespasian and Titus. This was after the defeat of his people in their revolt (A.D. 66) against the Romans in Jerusalem, in which he had taken an active part. Among his writings are *History of the Jewish War* (7 books in Aramaic and Greek) and *Antiquities of the Jews* (in 20 books).

Joshi, Gaurishankar Govardhandas. Pen name **Dhumketu** (1892–   ). Indian novelist and dramatist in Gujerati, one of the Indian languages. He wrote more than 50 books in a wide range of styles, among them the famous *Jivan-rang* (*Life's Colors*), an autobiography.

Joshua. In the Old Testament, the successor of Moses and the name given to the 6th book of the Old Testament. Forty years before leading the Israelites into the Promised Land, he had been one of the 12 spies who reported favorably on Canaan; he was thus one of the two Israelites whom Jehovah permitted to enter it. He was a valiant fighter who gradually conquered the land. One of his most striking exploits was his commanding the sun to stand still (Josh. 10:12–13). See CALEB.

Josiah Allen's Wife. The pen name of Marietta HOLLEY.

Josquin. Full name **Josquin des Prés** (c. 1440–1521). The most celebrated French composer of his day. Josquin began and ended his life in Burgundy (now Belgium), but spent much of his life in Italy, in the service of the Sforza family, and of Popes Innocent VIII and Alexander VI. He wrote secular *chansons* in French, but his most important works are his masses, and above all, his motets. Their style humanized the mechanical compositional practices of the 15th century, and paved the way for the great flowering of polyphony in the 16th century.

Josse. A jeweler in Molière's comedy L'AMOUR MÉDECIN. Lucinde, the young daughter of Sganarelle, pines away, and the anxious father asks his neighbors what they would advise him to do. Josse replies that he would buy the young lady a beautiful piece of jewelry. Sganarelle's answer is, "You are a jeweler, Monsieur Josse (*Vous êtes orfèvre, Monsieur Josse*), and are not disinterested in your advice!"

Jötun[n]heim or **Utgard** (Old Norse, "outer ward"). In Norse mythology, one of the Nine Worlds, the home of the giants, situated at the northernmost edge of the universe. One of the roots of the ash tree Yggdrasill extends into it.

Jotuni, Maria (1880–   ). Finnish novelist, short-story writer, and playwright. She is best known for her plays, which blend humor with psychological insight and are cleverly constructed. *Klaus Lovhikon Herra* (*Klaus, the Master of Lovhikko*, 1941) received a Finnish drama award; other plays include *Miehen Kylkiluu* (1914), *Kultainen vasikka* (1918), and *Kurdin prinssi* (1932).

Jouhandeau, Marcel (1888–   ). Pen name: **Marcel Provence.** French fiction writer, essayist, dramatist. Among the novels that give a bitterly introspective and cynical account of his own married life are *Monsieur Godeau intime* (1926), *Monsieur Godeau marié* (1933), and *Chroniques maritales* (1938). Cruel portraits of his town are painted in *Les Térébinte* (1926), and *Chaminadour* (3 vols., 1934–1941). His short stories include *Astaroth* (1929), *L'Amateur d'imprudence* (1932), and *Elise* (1933).

Jourdain, Monsieur. The title character of Molière's LE BOURGEOIS GENTILHOMME. He is the prototype of the bourgeois who, elevated by sudden wealth to the upper ranks, makes himself ridiculous by his attempts to imitate a gentleman's manners and accomplishments. Much of the fun of the play derives from the awkward figure M. Jourdain cuts as the pupil of dancing and fencing masters and professors of philosophy. One of his remarks is especially noted: he expresses his astonishment that he has been talking prose all his life and that he never knew it till his professor told him.

Journal of a Voyage to Lisbon, The (1755). A prose account of a voyage to Portugal made by Henry FIELDING to recover his health; it is Fielding's last published work.

Journal of the Plague Year, A (1722). A famous account of the epidemic of bubonic plague in England during the summer and fall of 1665 by Daniel DEFOE. It purports to be an eyewitness report by a resident of London named "H. F.," and is remarkable in its convincingness as such, considering the fact that Defoe was only five years old when the plague ravaged London. Some of the details, such as the bell-man ringing his bell and calling, "Bring out your dead," seem more authentic than the original accounts reported in such works as the *Diary of Samuel Pepys*.

Journal to Stella. A private diary kept by Jonathan SWIFT from 1710 to 1713 in the form of letters addressed to "Stella," Swift's name for his friend Esther JOHNSON. *Stella* being the Latin word for *star*, the name was fancifully arrived at from equating this with the Greek word for star, *aster*, and Esther. The journal reveals the author's hopes, anxieties, social life, political intrigues. Baby talk sprinkles the correspondence. See PPT; PRESTO.

Journey's End (1929). A play by Robert Cedric SHERRIFF. It is set in the British trenches of World War I. The three main characters are Stanhope, the once idealistic school-hero of 18-year-old Raleigh who has just come to the front and Osborne, a former teacher. In the course of the play both Osborne and the boy are killed. Stanhope is still alive, but he drinks constantly to calm his shattered nerves and to hide his constant fear.

Journey's End played successfully in England and America.

Journey to the End of the Night (*Voyage au bout de la nuit;* 1932). A novel by Louis Ferdinand CÉLINE, about the driftings of the cynic Ferdinand in World War I and afterward. The work caused a scandal by the coarseness of its language and the violence of its despairing pessimism.

Jouve, Pierre Jean (1887-   ). French poet, novelist, and critic. At first closely associated with the ABBAYE GROUP, influenced by UNANIMISM and Romain Rolland, Jouve wrote stories of the war and poems of pacifist protest against it. His early poetry was collected in *Heures* (1919, 1920) and *Tragiques* (1923). In 1924 he turned to Catholicism and to Freudian psychoanalysis. The resultant energetic mingling of religious and sexual imagery produced his best work: the poems of *Les Noces* (1928); *Le Paradis perdu* (1929); *Sueur de Sang* (1933); *Kyrié* (1938); and the novels *Paulina 1880* (1925); *Le Monde désert* (1926); *Histoires sanglantes* (1931); and *La Scène capitale* (1935).

Jouvet, Louis (1885-1951). French actor, director, and producer. Jouvet worked with Jacques COPEAU in the *Théâtre du Vieux-Colombier* before becoming the director of the *Comédie des Champs-Elysées* in 1924, and establishing his own company at the *Théâtre de l'Athénée* in 1934. In the drama he sought to achieve a blend of the intellect and the fancy, through the skillful use of light to focus upon the inner drama, combined with stylized staging and acting. Plays by Jules Romains, Marcel Archard, and Jean Giraudoux were produced at his theater, as well as imaginative interpretations of Molière.

Jove. Another name for JUPITER.

Jovellanos, Gaspar Melchor de (1744-1811). Spanish statesman, economist, and man of letters. Appointed a magistrate in Seville (1767) and in Madrid (1778), he was banished to his native Asturias in 1790 because of his progressive views. He returned from exile to serve briefly as minister of justice, only to fall from favor again. From 1801 to 1808 he was a prisoner in Majorca. Refusing to collaborate with the Bonapartists, he was a prominent member of the Central Junta and helped convene the *Cortes* of Cadiz.

His finest work is the well-known *Informe sobre la ley agraria* (1794), ostensibly a report on a projected code of agrarian law, but in reality an enlightened program for extensive economic reform. In *Defensa de la Junta Central* (1810), he outlined his moderate political ideas.

Jovellanos also wrote verse in the classical tradition. His best poems are probably his didactic and philosophical satires, notably *A Arnesto, sátira contra la mala educación de la nobleza* and *El estado de España, bajo el gobierno de Godoy*. His play *El delincuente honrado* (1794) introduced lachrymose comedy in the manner of Diderot to Spain. His other works include *Elogio de las bellas artes* (1782), an evaluation of medieval Spanish art, and *Pelayo* (1792), a tragedy.

Jovial Crew, A, or The Merry Beggars (1641). A comedy by Richard BROME. The fears of the wealthy and kindly Squire Oldrents are realized when his two daughters, Rachel and Meriel, along with their sweethearts and Oldrent's trusted steward, Springlove, run off to join a band of roving beggars. However, the girls are soon discomforted and return with the steward, who proves to be the squire's illegitimate son.

Joyce, James (1882-1941). Irish novelist, short story writer, and poet. He is regarded as one of the greatest literary talents of the 20th century, and is known for his revolutionary innovations in the art of the novel. Joyce's technical innovations include an extensive use of the interior monologue (see STREAM OF CONSCIOUSNESS) and other experimental narrative techniques; the use, in FINNEGANS WAKE, of a unique language of invented words, puns, and complex allusions; and the use of a complex network of symbolic parallels drawn from mythology, history, and literature. Joyce is also famous for his detailed rendering of Dublin life, his objective presentation of organic functions, his extraordinary psychological penetration, his robust humor, and his sensitivity to auditory impressions (he had a lifelong passion for vocal music). Before other writers had imitated his techniques and critics had explained his methods, his books were denounced as obscure, unintelligible, nonsensical, and obscene.

Joyce was raised in the kind of environment that might be least expected to produce a revolutionary genius. Son of an ordinary, chronically insolvent civil servant and a conventionally pious mother, and eldest of a family of 10 children, Joyce's youth was marked by poverty and the struggle to maintain solid middle-class respectability. He was educated at a succession of excellent Jesuit schools, where he received a thorough training in Catholic and scholastic doctrines and in several languages. Joyce's rebellion against his family background, against Catholicism, and against Irish nationalism (see THE DAY OF THE RABBLEMENT), are described in his largely autobiographical novel, A PORTRAIT OF THE ARTIST AS A YOUNG MAN. "I will not serve that in which I no longer believe," says the hero, Stephen Dedalus, "whether it call itself my home, my fatherland, or my church: and I will try to express myself in some mode of life or art as freely as I can, using for my defence the only arms I allow myself to use—silence, exile, and cunning." In 1902 the 20-year-old Joyce left Dublin to spend the rest of his life in exile in Paris, Trieste, Rome, and Zurich, with only an occasional brief visit to Ireland. But the world he had rejected remained basic to all his writing. From the short stories in DUBLINERS to *Finnegans Wake,* his subject matter is the city of Dublin, its streets, topography, history, and residents, and, to a somewhat lesser extent, biographical details of his own childhood and youth. The Catholicism he had rebelled against remained so ingrained in him that its doctrines and methods of thought, its symbolism and scholasticism, strongly color all his writings.

Always an admirer of Ibsen, Joyce's earliest publication was an essay on *Ibsen's New Drama* in the *Fortnightly Review* of 1900. He also wrote two collections of poems, CHAMBER MUSIC and *Pomes Penyeach* (1927), and a play, EXILES.

Joyce had a difficult life. In 1904 he ran away to Trieste with Nora Barnacle, an almost entirely uneducated Dublin chambermaid, whom he met on June 16 of that year (the same day on which the action of ULYSSES takes place). On account of his antireligious principles they were not married until many years later. With their two children they wandered about Europe, while Joyce earned an inadequate living teaching languages and doing clerical work; he earned almost nothing from his writings until his last years. His poor eyesight deteriorated until he was almost blind; like Milton, he had to depend in his work on memory and the secretarial help of friends. His books were banned by censors, pirated by publishers, and misunderstood by the public. His much-loved daughter became insane and had to be confined in an institution.

A perfectionist who sought to fill his mature work with a network of complex internal echoes and allusions, Joyce toiled long hours at his writing and repeatedly revised and polished his work. *Ulysses* required seven years to complete (1914–1921), and *Finnegans Wake,* which was known until its publication as *Work in Progress,* took 17 years (1922–1939).

Joyeuse. The name given to Charlemagne's sword in medieval romances.

Joyous Gard (Fr., *La Joyeuse Garde*). In Malory's *Morte d'Arthur* (c. 1469), the castle of Sir Launcelot. It was given to him by King Arthur for defending Queen Guinevere's honor against Sir Mador. It is supposed to have been at or near Berwick-on-Tweed, but the Arthurian topography is very indefinite.

Juana Inés de la Cruz, Sor. Religious name of **Juana Inés de Asbaje y Ramírez** (1651–1695). Mexican poet and dramatist. Sor Juana's love for knowledge, the quality that governed her entire life, first became evident at the age of three when she coaxed her sister's tutor into teaching her how to read. Her intelligence and learning attracted wide attention, and at 14 she became lady-in-waiting to the viceroy's wife. When a panel of 40 scholars and theologians questioned her to determine whether her wisdom came from God, she emerged from the ordeal, as the viceroy reported, like a galleon harried by shallops. Her zeal for study led her to contemplate becoming a nun, though some have maintained, on the basis of the love poetry that she was writing at the time, that a blighted romance was another cause. After a short and unsuccessful stay in a Carmelite convent at the age of 16, she took her final vows in the Order of St. Jerome in 1669. In the convent, Sor Juana continued her studies despite the opposition of some prelates.

Sor Juana's literary production was merely one facet of her intellectual activity. She has described her surprise on learning that not everyone wrote poetry; her own verse, while revealing great technical virtuosity and some gongoristic traits, is on the whole as unaffected and spontaneous as the scientific deductions she made while watching an egg fry or the spinning of a top. Among her most famous poems are the *redondillas,* or quatrains, in which she "rationally describes the irrational effects of love" and those in which she censures men for being critical of qualities in women that they themselves have caused. *Primer sueño,* a long poem modelled on Góngora's *Soledades* (1627), is an analysis of sleep, describing how man's soul is dazzled at night by its vision of the universe and tries unsuccessfully to comprehend its laws. For church holidays she wrote numerous *villancicos,* or carols, and *autos sacramentales,* or one-act religious plays, the most notable of which are *El divino Narciso* (1692) and *El cetro de José* (1692). Her plays include the comedies *Los empeños de una casa,* written between 1680 and 1686, and *Amor es más laberinto,* written in 1688

with Juan de Guevara. Of her extant prose pieces, the best known is the *Respuesta a Sor Filotea* (1691), a rebuttal to clerical criticism, in which she discusses her devotion to learning and her difficulties in overcoming the hardships inflicted on her sex.

Juan de la Cruz, San. See JOHN OF THE CROSS, St.

Juan Manuel, Infante Don (1282–?1349). Spanish statesman and writer. A nephew of Alfonso X, Juan Manuel was an important political figure as well as an outstanding prose writer. His masterpiece is *El Conde Lucanor* or *Libro de Patronio;* completed about 1335, it is a collection of 50 "exemplary tales," some of oriental origin, which illustrate the counsels of Patronio to his pupil, Count Lucanor. His other extant works include *Libro de los estados,* which contains an adaptation of the story of Barlaam and Josaphat, and *Libro del caballero y del escudero,* a treatise on chivalry and encyclopedia of medieval knowledge.

Juárez, Benito (1806–1872). Mexican statesman. A full-blooded Zapotec Indian, Juárez became the leader of *La Reforma,* a liberal, anticlerical movement for political, economic, and social reform. Named president in 1857, he fought the French-supported regime of MAXIMILIAN, whom he defeated in 1867, and ruled Mexico until his death. Though *La Reforma* was at best a qualified success, Juárez occupies a place in Mexican hagiography similar to that held by Lincoln in the U.S.

Juarez und Maximilian (1924). A play by Franz WERFEL. It is about the rising of Mexican patriots to throw off the rule of the Austrian emperor MAXIMILIAN. Werfel concentrates more on the luckless emperor than on the Mexicans, and the play ends with his execution and funeral.

Jubal. In the Old Testament, the son of Lamech and Adah. As "father of all such as handle the harp and organ" (Gen. 4:21), he is said to have invented wind and stringed instruments. George Eliot has a narrative poem of this title (1874).

jubilee. In Jewish history, the year of jubilee was every fiftieth year, which was held sacred in commemoration of the deliverance from Egypt. In this year the fields were allowed to lie fallow, land that had passed out of the possession of those to whom it had originally belonged was restored to them, and all who had been obliged to let themselves out for hire were released from bondage. The year of jubilee was proclaimed with trumpets of ram's horn, and takes its name from Hebrew yobel, "a ram's horn."

Judah. In the Old Testament, the 4th son of Jacob; also, the name of the most powerful of the 12 tribes of Israel. After the death of Solomon, king of Israel, 10 tribes seceded under JEROBOAM, and the remaining kingdom, with its capital at Jerusalem, was known thereafter as Judah.

Judas Iscariot. The disciple who betrayed Jesus. Judas' specific act of betrayal was to cause the arrest of Jesus by the Roman soldiery by identifying him with a kiss in the Garden of Gethsemane. He was paid for this act 30 pieces of silver. Matthew (27:3–10) records that Judas returned the money to the Jewish priests and then hanged himself (see ACELDAMA). The version in Acts (1:16–20) has Judas dying by "falling headlong" after which "he burst asunder . . . and all his bowels gushed out."

Judas is known as one of the blackest villains in history. Dante in the INFERNO places Judas in the mouth of Satan. There are numerous allusions to his crime in figures of speech: a Judas kiss, 30 pieces of silver, and the name itself all signify treachery and deception.

There have also been many attempts to explain the motives of Judas. Early Christians felt that Judas acted as he did for the silver; however, the amount he was paid was not any great fortune, 30 pieces being about the price of one slave. Modern theorists feel that Judas was dissatisfied with Jesus' actions and wanted to force him into a situation where he would have to assert his divine powers and establish a glorious new order on earth. If this was the case it is obvious that Judas had no understanding of Jesus' message or ministry.

Judas Maccabaeus. The Hebrew patriot who gained decisive victories against the Syrians. In 165 B.C., he entered Jerusalem and reconsecrated the Temple; Hanukkah, the Jewish feast of dedication, commemorates this event. See MACCABEES.

Jude, St. One of the 12 disciples, also known as Thaddeus. He is represented in art with a club or staff, and a carpenter's square, in allusion to his trade. His day is October 28. According to tradition, he was shot to death by arrows in Armenia.

Jude, The General Epistle of. A New Testament book. It is a general letter denouncing heretical teaching. The identity of the author is not known definitely. One of Jesus' half brothers was called Jude; some scholars feel that he was also the apostle Jude.

Jude the Obscure (1895). Thomas HARDY's tragic last novel. This story dramatizes the conflict between carnal and spiritual life, tracing Jude Fawley's life from his boyhood aspirations of intellectual achievement to his miserable, early death. His passions entangle him in marriage with Arabella, an insensitive, animalistic woman who gives birth to a son, but then deserts them both. Jude then falls in love with his cousin, Sue Bridehead, an intelligent, sensitive, high-strung girl. She marries the decaying schoolteacher, Phillotson, but, finding him physically repellent, she flees to Jude. They both obtain divorces, but Sue, guilt-ridden over her desertion of her husband, cannot bring herself to take the step of marrying Jude, so they live together and have children, scorned by society. "Because there were too many," the children are killed by Arabella's son, a grotesque boy also named Jude, who subsequently hangs himself. Broken by this tragedy, Sue goes back to Phillotson and Jude returns to Arabella. Soon thereafter Jude dies.

Judges. A book of the Old Testament. An historical account of the tribes of Israel between the times of Joshua and Samuel (c. 1225–1020 B.C.). The Israelites had just invaded Canaan; the book tells of their attempts to subdue the former inhabitants and settle the land. Parts of the book are contemporaneous with the events; the rest are later additions. Judges had its present form by 500 B.C.

Judgment Day. See STUDS LONIGAN.

Judgment of Paris, The. A mythological beauty contest of goddesses. It led to the TROJAN WAR. Angry at not having been invited to the famous wedding of Thetis, Eris, the goddess of discord, threw into the gathering a golden apple bearing the inscription "For

the fairest." It was claimed by Hera, Athene, and Aphrodite. They took it to Paris, a son of Priam, who was then a shepherd on the slopes of Mount Ida. As the handsomest man in the world, he was regarded as an authority. Hera promised him greatness, Athene warlike prowess, and Aphrodite the love of the world's most beautiful woman in return for his vote. He awarded the apple to Aphrodite, and won for his pains the disastrous love of Helen. This famous subject was a favorite with artists both in classical times and the Renaissance.

Judgment of Solomon. See SOLOMON, JUDGMENT OF.

Judith. A legendary Jewish heroine of Bethulia whose story is told in the Apocryphal book bearing her name. To deliver her native city from the onslaught of Holofernes, general of the Assyrian king Nebuchadnezzar, she entered his camp and slew him in his drunken sleep. When she showed the head of Holofernes to her countrymen, they rushed on the invading army and put it to complete rout.

In his tragedy *Judith* (1841), Friedrich HEBBEL deepens the story's psychological complexity by having Judith become intimate with Holofernes before murdering him. Jean GIRAUDOUX adapted the story for his play *Judith* (1931).

judo. See JUJITSU.

Judson, E[dward] Z[ane] C[arroll]. Pen name, **Ned Buntline** (1823–1886). American adventurer and dime novelist. Judson's career was more incredible than any of the 400 dime novels he is said to have written. He was an inveterate duelist, led the Astor Place riots against the English actor Macready, was an organizer of the nativistic Know-Nothing Party, and during the Civil War was dismissed from the Union army for drunkenness.

In the meantime, he was a prolific writer of dime novels, a genre that he is credited with originating. Some he published in a magazine he founded, *Ned Buntline's Own;* later he worked for the publishing firm of Beadle & Adams. On a trip to the West he met William F. Cody and wrote a play, *The Scouts of the Plains* (1872) for him; it was Judson who named the famous scout Buffalo Bill. Judson also wrote hymns and lectured on temperance.

He undoubtedly had an astonishing knack with words and once wrote a novel of more than 600 pages in 62 hours. His dime novels have become collector's items. A few characteristic titles are *Magdalena, The Beautiful Mexican Maid* (1847), *The Black Avenger* (1847), and *Stella Delorme, or, The Comanche's Dream* (1860).

Juggernaut or **Jagannath.** A Hindu deity, literally "Lord of the World." His temple is at Puri, in Orissa, eastern India. Juggernaut is regarded as the remover of sin, and his image is on view three days in the year. The first day is the *Snanayatra,* or the Pilgrimage of the Bath, when the image is washed. Ten days later the image is taken in its chariot to a nearby temple. It was formerly erroneously supposed that on this day, known as the *Rathayatra* or the Journey by Chariot, fanatical devotees threw themselves beneath the wheels of the enormous, decorated chariot, in the hope that they would attain *moksha* or liberation from the cycle of birth and rebirth. Hence, the phrase *the car of Juggernaut* is used of customs, institutions, and traditions beneath which people are ruthlessly and unnecessarily crushed.

jujitsu. Literally "soft art." A Japanese system of self-defense without weapons. It is based entirely on the principle that the opponent's own (superior) strength can be used to defeat him. A *jujitsu* expert is able to nullify his attacker, not by meeting strength with strength, but by using specialized applications of momentum, balance, and leverage to disable or paralyze. *Judo* is a refined, modern version of *jujitsu*. Both are practiced as sports in Japan.

Jukes, The, a Study in Crime, Pauperism, Disease and Heredity (1877). A report of the New York Prison Association by Richard Louis Dugdale (1841–1883). The subjects are the descendants of several sisters who lived in New York toward the end of the 18th century. The study is a sociological companion to fictional studies of the decline and fall of families.

Julia. In Shakespeare's Two GENTLEMEN OF VERONA, the faithful love of Proteus. She follows him to Milan, disguised as a page, forgives him his inconstancy, and finally wins him back.

Julia de Roubigné (1777). A sentimental and theatrical novel by Henry MACKENZIE modeled upon Jean Jacques Rousseau's NOUVELLE HÉLOÏSE. Although she loves Savillon, Julia is forced to marry the count de Montauban. Misunderstanding and groundless jealousy bring tragedy to them all.

Julian, surnamed **the Apostate.** Full Latin name, **Flavius Claudius Julianus** (A.D. 331–363). Roman emperor, nephew of Constantine the Great. Although educated in monastic schools, Julian renounced Christianity when he became emperor (361). He attempted to drive out Christianity and to reinstate a polytheism based on Neoplatonic philosophy. He was, however, killed fighting in Persia before he could carry through his plans.

Julian calendar. See Julius CAESAR.

Julian emperors. A collective name for the Roman emperors Augustus, Tiberius, Caligula, Claudius, and Nero, as members by birth or adoption of the family of Julius Caesar. As a member of the Julia gens, or clan, Julius Caesar traced his ancestry back to Iulus, son of Aeneas; Vergil chose Aeneas as the hero of his great, nationalistic epic, the *Aeneid*, for this reason.

Caesar, a family name of the Julia gens, was assumed as a surname by Augustus as Julius Caesar's adopted son, and from him was handed down to all the Julian emperors either by adoption or by female descent. Though the Caesar family became extinct with the death of Nero, subsequent emperors retained the name Caesar as part of their title. The name survived to the 20th century in the forms of Czar and Kaiser.

Julie ou la Nouvelle Héloïse. See NOUVELLE HÉLOÏSE, JULIE OU LA.

Juliet. The passionate young heroine of Shakespeare's ROMEO AND JULIET. The love of this wildly romantic girl for Romeo, the son of her father's bitterest enemy, brings about her own death and that of her lover. Strong in spirit, she refuses to marry the husband that her family chooses and secretly weds Romeo. Her speeches contain some of Shakespeare's most beautiful and famous poetry:

> O Romeo, Romeo! wherefore art thou Romeo?
> Deny thy father, and refuse thy name;
> Or, if thou wilt not, be but sworn my love,
> And I'll no longer be a Capulet. . . .
>   O! be some other name:
> What's in a name? that which we call a rose
> By any other name would smell as sweet.

(2) In Shakespeare's MEASURE FOR MEASURE, the gentle, loyal betrothed of Claudio. Her pregnancy is the cause of Claudio's imprisonment for immorality.

Julius II, Pope. See DELLA ROVERE.

Julius Caesar (c. 1599). A tragedy by William SHAKESPEARE. It deals with the conspiracy against Julius CAESAR, his assassination, and the defeat of the conspirators by Marc ANTONY and Octavius CAESAR.

The crafty and ambitious CASSIUS, envious of Caesar's political and military triumphs, forms a conspiracy against him. Although BRUTUS, a man of great integrity, loves Caesar, he is persuaded to join the conspiracy by Cassius, who argues that Caesar's power is a threat to Rome's freedom. Ignoring the entreaties of his wife, CALPURNIA, who has dreamed of his death, Caesar goes to the Senate on the Ides of March and is assassinated by the conspirators. When Antony discovers Caesar's body, he feigns friendliness towards the conspirators and asks only that he be allowed to speak at Caesar's funeral. His oration so inflames the people that the assassins are driven out of Rome. Antony, joined by Lepidus and Octavius, engages the conspirators in battle at Philippi. Cassius' rash suicide weakens the army and turns the tide of battle. Brutus is routed and falls on his own sword rather than be taken captive.

Shakespeare's source for the play was Sir Thomas North's translation (1579) of Plutarch's *Lives*.

July Revolution (1830). An uprising (July 27–29) of the people of France against the reactionary Bourbon dynasty. The newspapers, protesting the abolition of freedom of the press, fanned the fires of the insurrection. After some fighting in barricaded streets King Charles X abdicated. The Bourbon-Orléans line then succeeded to the throne in the person of LOUIS PHILIPPE, "the citizen-king."

Jung, Carl Gustav (1875–1961). Swiss psychologist and author. Jung received his M.D. degree from the University of Basel in 1900. He then attended lectures by the pioneer French psychologist Pierre Janet at the Salpêtrière at Paris and worked with Eugen Bleuler, head of the Zurich school of the new depth-psychology. In 1909 he and Sigmund FREUD, the head of the Vienna School, traveled to Clark University in Worcester, Mass., to lecture and receive honorary degrees. He broke with Freud four years later, not because he differed with the master in fundamentals but because Freud could not agree with some of the applications which Jung was beginning to see for psychology. In 1912, Jung had published *Wandlungen und Symbole der Libido* (*Psychology of the Unconscious*, Engl. trans., 1916; revised for the *Collected Works* as Vol. 5, *Symbols of Transformation*), in which he presented several concepts alien to Freudian psychology. For Jung, the term "libido" itself signified a wider area than for Freud. Perhaps the most significant and important departure from orthodox Freudianism was Jung's theory of the collective unconscious advanced in this work. According to this concept, mankind shares a common and inborn unconscious life, not limited to the experience of any one individual, which is expressed in dreams, fantasies, and mythologies in the form of archetypal images and symbols. Among other of Jung's many contributions to psychology are his formulation of introvert and extrovert types (found in *Psychological Types,* 1923), his development of analytical psychology, his use of the association method, and his extensive work on symbology. An 18-volume edition of Jung's collected works is now in preparation by the Bollingen Foundation.

Jung Deutschland (Young Germany). A German literary movement of about 1830–1848. Its name was coined by Ludolf WIENBARG. He and the other important authors in the movement, LAUBE, GUTZKOW, and MUNDT, did not actually constitute a group until their names were linked in a Prussian edict (1835) prohibiting their writings. Their principal desire was to break away from the idealism that had characterized most previous German literature in the 19th century, for they felt that every literary work should take a stand on the real political and social problems of the day. Specifically, they advocated freedom of thought—which was by no means a fact under the oppressive Prussian and Austrian regimes of the time—emancipation of women, and frequently, free love. See Heinrich HEINE; BIEDERMEIER.

Jünger, Ernst (1895–). German novelist and essayist. His works show the influence of existentialism, especially the philosophy of Martin Heidegger. His best-known novel is *Auf den Marmorklippen (On the Marble Cliffs,* 1939).

Jungfrau von Orleans, Die. See MAID OF ORLEANS, THE.

Jungle, The (1906). A novel by Upton SINCLAIR. Seldom has a book been the subject of more widespread discussion than this appallingly grim account of life in the Chicago stockyards. It depicts with vivid and brutal realism the experiences of a Slavic immigrant, Jurgis Rudkus, and his wife, Ona. Jurgis becomes debased and then, in accordance with Sinclair's own creed, turns to socialism as a way out.

Jungle Books, The (1894–1895). A series of animal stories for children in two volumes by Rudyard KIPLING. The central figure is the human MOWGLI, brought up by Mother Wolf and instructed in the lore of the jungle.

Junius Letters. A series of anonymous letters, the authorship of which has never been finally settled, which appeared in Woodfall's *Public Advertiser* in London from January, 1769 to January, 1772. Junius was apparently an ardent Whig partisan of the Grenville faction and a bitter opponent of the administrations of the duke of Grafton and Lord North. His daring address to the king brought a libel suit against his printer, but a London jury refused to convict him. The author himself said, "I am the sole depositary of my secret, and it shall die with me." The letters were probably written by Sir Philip Francis (1740–1818), but many other authors have been suggested.

Junker. A member of the landed aristocracy of Germany, particularly east of the Elbe. The Junkers gained ascendency in Prussia during the early 18th century, when they represented a political philosophy of competent, military oligarchy, but with the development of the German national state in the 19th century, the Junkers became political and social reactionaries. It was not until after World War II that their large estates were redistributed.

Juno. In Roman mythology, the wife of JUPITER and queen of the gods. Like her Greek counterpart, HERA, she was the special protectress of marriage and of women. In Vergil's *Aeneid,* she is represented as the bitter foe of the exiled Trojans.

The Junonian bird was the peacock, dedicated to the goddess-queen.

Juno and the Paycock (1924). A comitragedy by Sean O'CASEY. Again the background of the Irish Civil War of 1922, the action concerns the attempt of Juno Boyle to overcome the triple menace of war, poverty, and drunkenness which result in the destruction of her family. Juno's heroic posture, which is defined in terms of her unillusioned, long-suffering grasp of reality, is contrasted to that of her husband, the "Paycock," a vain, posturing—but extremely funny—weakling who hides from reality behind a bottle and a flow of fine language. The initial production, which starred Sara Allgood as Juno and Barry Fitzgerald as the husband, represented one of the finest triumphs of the ABBEY THEATRE.

junta (Sp.). In Spain, a council or legislative assembly other than the Cortes, which may be summoned either for the whole country, for one of its separate parts, or for some special object only. The most famous is that called together by Napoleon in 1808.

Junto. In English history, a faction of Whigs who exerted great influence during the reigns of William III and Queen Anne. The name was first applied to the advisors of Charles I. The word is a corruption of *junta.*

Jupiter or **Juppiter** (from early Lat., *Diespiter,* "Father of the sky"). The ancient Italian sky-god and the supreme deity of Roman mythology, also known as Jove and corresponding roughly to the Greek ZEUS. He was the special protector of Rome and, as Jupiter Capitolinus—his temple being on the Capitoline hill—presided over the Roman games. He knew and could influence the course of history and made known the future to man by means of signs in the heavens, by the flight of birds, and, most awesomely, by the stroke of his lightning bolt.

Jurgen (1919). A novel by James Branch CABELL. This book, which became a *cause célèbre* and gave the author popular fame, forms part of an elaborate series of novels laid in the imaginary realm called Poictesme. Jurgen, a middle-aged pawnbroker, is married to a nagging wife who suddenly disappears. Jurgen goes in search of her, but actually he is in quest of his own lost youth. By magical dispensation, he finds himself 21 again and sets out on a series of strange adventures, including visits to Heaven and Hell, in which he meets a lost sweetheart and encounters a host of mythical persons. At the end he returns home, finds his wife there, and is glad to be a middle-aged, henpecked husband again.

Jusserand, Jean Jules (1855–1932). French writer, diplomat, and student of English literature and history. He was minister at Washington, D.C. (1902–1925), and the only non-American ever to head the American Historical Society. In 1917 he received the Pulitzer prize in History for his *With Americans of Past and Present Days.*

Justice (1910). A drama of social protest by John GALSWORTHY. A young lawyer's clerk, William Falder, forges a check in order to secure funds to free the woman he loves from her husband's cruelty. He serves a three-year prison sentence; on his release, his struggle to live down his past ends in tragedy. The play's title is ironic. Although Falder is treated justly according to the law, he is in fact treated very inhumanely by his employers, the court, the prison officials, and, on his release, by almost everybody. A basically good man, he is destroyed by society and "justice." Galsworthy's play was influential in the reform of English prison administration.

Justine (1791). A novel by the Marquis de SADE, celebrating a sexually persecuted heroine.

Justine. See ALEXANDRIA QUARTET, THE.

Justinian I. Called **Justinian the Great.** Full Latin name, **Flavius Anicius Justinianus** (483–565). Emperor of the BYZANTINE EMPIRE (527–565) during its most brilliant period. He married THEODORA (525). In 531 he bought a peace treaty with the Persians. In the West his generals Belisarius and Narses destroyed the Vandal kingdom in Africa and defeated the Ostrogoths in Italy, retaking Rome in 536.

Justinian's reign is highlighted by the amount of building that took place in the Empire (Sant' Apollinare in Classe and San Vitale, both in Ravenna, and Santa Sophia in Constantinople) and the code of laws he had published, the *Corpus Juris Civilis,* now called the Justinian Code. This codification is the foundation of the Roman law still used in many European countries.

Just So Stories (1902). Children's animal stories written and illustrated by Rudyard KIPLING, giving amusing and fanciful answers to such questions as why the leopard has spots or the elephant a trunk.

Jutland, Battle of. One of the greatest naval battles in history. It was fought in 1916 off Jutland peninsula between the German and British fleets. It won for England the undisputed control of the North Sea. Curiously it was the British fleet that sustained the heavier casualties.

Juvenal. Full Latin name, **Decimus Junius Juvenalis** (A.D 60?–?140). Satirist of Roman vices under the empire. Of his life little is known, although most early accounts agree that he spent some time in military service and ended his life in exile for having criticized a popular stage performer who was a special favorite of the emperor Domitian. He is the author of 16 satires, divided traditionally into 5 books. In these biting attacks on public manners and morals. Juvenal shows himself to have been a sharp observer of his fellow men. "Whatever men do," he announces in his first satire, "their devotion, their fear, their rage, their pleasure, their joys, their conversations— all these will make up the potpourri of my little work"; and he fulfills his pledge with the bitter gusto of an inspired cynic. Unlike Horace, the other great satirist of Roman letters, Juvenal seldom places himself among the foolish, the corrupt, and the frustrated; and while Horace's satires are conversational in tone and meter, Juvenal's are tight, rhetorical, and finely polished. He excels in sketching memorable vignettes and small portraits etched in vitriol. His satires abound in witty observations and terse proverbs, among which is the motto *mens sana in corpore sano,* "a sound mind in a sound body."

K

K., Joseph. The hero of Kafka's THE TRIAL. His initial, like that of K. in THE CASTLE, is the same as Kafka's. This is an example of the way Kafka often introduces elements of himself into his works behind the mask of a character. See Gregor SAMSA.

ka. In Egyptian mythology, a double that survived after a man's death if a statue of him were made into which it might enter and certain other rites were performed. Such a statue, placed usually near the mummy in the tomb, came to be called a *ka.*

Kaaba (Arabic *kabah,* a square house). The holiest shrine of the Muslims. Located at Mecca, in the center of the Great Mosque, it is said to have been built first by Adam, who received pardon there 200 years after his expulsion from Paradise, and rebuilt by Ishmael and Abraham after the Flood. In the northeast corner is the famous black stone. See HAJAR-AL-ASWAD.

Kabale und Liebe (Love and Intrigue, 1784). A bourgeois tragedy by Friedrich SCHILLER. The theme is the love across social barriers of Luise Miller, a musician's daughter, and Ferdinand von Walther, an aristocrat. Ferdinand's father opposes their love, and following the advice of a jealous schemer at court, unwittingly causes the lovers' death.

Kabir, Humayan (1906–). Indian man of letters. Born in Bengal, he was educated at Calcutta and Oxford universities. From 1958 to 1962 he was minister of scientific research and cultural affairs in the Indian government. He wrote *Men and Rivers* (1942), a novel, and edited *Green and Gold* (1960), an anthology of Bengali writing.

kabuki. Japanese theater. Developed together with *jōruri* during the Tokugawa period (1600–1868), it catered to the tastes of the newly arisen merchant class. Kabuki plays are either historical dramas or domestic works, performed by male actors only. The greatest Kabuki playwright was CHIKAMATSU MONZAEMON, who wrote originally for *jōruri* and whose plays were later rewritten for *kabuki* presentation. *Kabuki* is still performed extensively today.

Kaddish (*Aram.,* "holy"). In Judaism, the prayer recited to hallow the name of God. Since medieval times, it has been repeated by mourners as a declaration of their faith. It is used in the synagogue to close a section of the service.

Kadr, Al. The night on which the Koran was sent down to Muhammad. Al Kadr is supposed to be the seventh of the last ten nights of RAMADAN, or the night between the 23d and 24th days of the month.

Kaf, Mount. In Muslim myth, the huge mountain that served as the chief dwelling place of the JINN. According to legend, the earth was sunk in its middle. Its foundation is the emerald SAKHRAT, the reflection of which gave the azure hue to the sky.

from Kaf to Kaf. From one extremity of the earth to the other. The sun was supposed to rise from one of its eminences and to set on the opposite.

Kaffir (*Arab.,* "infidel"). A term of contempt for non-Muslims, chiefly in Africa. Hence the name came to be applied in the Western languages to either all or some of the Bantu races in Southern Africa, including the Zulus of Natal.

Kafka, Franz (1883–1924). Bohemian writer of Jewish descent. He is known especially for the unique visionary character of his novels, stories, parables, and sketches, all written in German. His thought is related to that of Søren Kierkegaard, and his writings center on the problematic existence of modern man.

Japanese print of a kabuki actor.

In them, a world of absurdity and paradox, of aimlessness and futility, and sometimes of faint hope, is revealed just beneath the surface of the everyday world. Specific problems Kafka explores, mainly through symbolism and allegory, include the utter incomprehensibility of God and the psychological ambivalence of family relationships, especially between father and son. His own strained family life, as well as his intense personal concern with religious problems, undoubtedly contributed much of the material for his work. But despite the atmosphere of human misery and futility that pervades most of his writing, Kafka did not entirely lack comic detachment, and he often shows a fine sense of humor. His style is remarkably precise and lucid, despite the grotesque unreality of the occurrences that it is used to describe, and his stories, in their combination of clarity and unreality, have often been compared to dreams. Less than one quarter of Kafka's entire production consists of finished works, the most famous of which are the stories, *The Judgment* (*Das Urteil;* 1913), THE METAMORPHOSIS, and *In the Penal Colony* (*In der Strafkolonie;* 1919). When he died of tuberculosis, all his unfinished writings, including the three novels, THE TRIAL, THE CASTLE, and AMERIKA, were left in manuscript form with his friend Max Brod with orders that they be burned, but Brod preserved and edited them.

Kahn, Gustave (1859–1936). French poet. A member of the school of SYMBOLISTS, Kahn, with Jules Laforgue, is considered to be the originator of vers libre. Kahn discarded the set line length and introduced such devices as assonance and internal rhyme for rhythmic purposes. His volumes of poetry include *Les palais nomades* (1881), *Chansons d'amant* (1891), *La Pluie et le beau temps* (1895), and *Le Livre d'images* (1897).

Kaikeyi. In the RAMAYANA, the daughter of Kekaya and one of the three chief queens of DASHARATHA, king of Ayodhya.

kailyard (*Scot.,* "kale" or "cabbage patch"). The name of a group of Scottish writers of the 1890's who wrote partly in dialect on humble, homespun topics. They took their name from the line, "There is a bonnie briar bush in our kailyard," which was the motto of the poem *Beside the Bonnie Briar Bush,* written by John Watson (1850–1907) under the pen name Ian Maclaren. Other members of the school beside Maclaren included James M. Barrie and Samuel R. Crockett.

Kaiser, Georg (1878–1945). German playwright. Belonging to the movement of EXPRESSIONISM, his plays turn, not on personal interaction among individualized characters, but rather on conflicts of ideas as exemplified in contrasting human types; often, in fact, his dramatis personae are nameless. His early writing (pre-1914), consisting mainly of satirical comedies in the tradition of such authors as Sternheim and Wedekind, is of no significance, but, with the coming of World War I, he was finally able to give effective expression to a deep longing for human redemption. In FROM MORN TILL MIDNIGHT, he depicts the complete emptiness of modern life, but in *Der Brand im Opernhaus* (*The Fire in the Opera-House,* 1918) he sees a possible solution for the individual in love. He preaches the salvation of peaceful society through individual sacrifice in *Die Bürger*

von Calais (*The Burghers of Calais,* 1914), but he also envisions the possibility of an increasingly deindividualized society leading to ultimate cataclysm in his GAS trilogy. His later works, which follow the same general thematic lines, include *Nebeneinander* (*Side by Side,* 1923), an interesting formal experiment involving three parallel plots; *Lederköpfe* (*Leather Hoods,* 1928), an anti-militaristic piece; *Mississippi* (1930), a religious play in which love is the spark of hope; and *Das Floss der Medusa* (*The Raft of the Medusa,* 1943), a children's tragedy.

Kalb, Johann. Known as **Baron de Kalb** (1721–1780). German army officer. While serving as a major general in the American Revolutionary army, he was mortally wounded at the battle of Camden, S.C.

Kalevala. Finnish national epic. It was compiled from popular songs and oral tradition by the Finnish philologist Elias Lonnrott (1802–1884), who published his first edition of 12,000 verses in 1835, and a second edition, nearly twice as long, in 1849. There is an account of the origin of the world, followed by the adventures of the three sons of Kaleva: the hero WAINAMOINEN, ILMARINEN, and the gallant Lemminkainen. The plot takes them to Pohjola, a dismally cold land to the north, both to fight for the return of the lost SAMPO and to find a bride for Wainamoinen. It was written in unrhymed, alliterative, trochaic verse; and a German translation in the same meter suggested to H. W. Longfellow both the form and the epic style for his *Hiawatha* (1855).

Kali. Hindu goddess. From her Calcutta receives its name, *Kali-ghat,* the steps of Kali, i.e., those by which her worshipers descend from the bank to the river Ganges. As wife of Shiva, she symbolizes the essence of destruction and bloodthirstiness, and the THUGS sacrificed their victims to her. Her naked idol is black and besmeared with blood; she has red eyes, four arms with blood-stained hands, matted hair, huge fanglike teeth, and a protruding tongue that drips with blood. She wears a necklace of skulls, ear rings of corpses, and is girdled with serpents. She is described as "terrible and beautiful, terribly beautiful" by a contemporary Indian poet. She plays a major role in Thomas Mann's "legend of India," *The Transposed Heads* (1940), where she is also Durga and Parvati, her two benign aspects. See SAKTISM.

Kalidasa (3rd century?). Sanskrit dramatist, sometimes referred to as the "Shakespeare of India." He wrote three plays, SHAKUNTALA, *Vikrama and Urvasi, Malaviki and Agnimitra;* two narrative poems, RAGHUVANSHA and *Kumara-sambhava;* and three long lyrics, *Meghaduta* (*The Cloud Messenger*), *Ritusamhara* (*The Cycle of Seasons*), and *Sringara-tilaka.*

Kalilah and Dimnah. See BIDPAI, FABLES OF.

Kallas, Aino Julia Maria (**Krohn**) (1878–1956). Finnish-Estonian novelist. Finnish born, she married an Estonian scientist and wrote in the native language of her new land. Few of her novels have appeared in English; among those translated are *The White Ship* (1924), *Eros the Slayer* (1927), and *The Wolf's Bride* (1930).

Kalyb. The legendary "Lady of the Woods." She is said to have kidnapped St. George from his nurse, brought him up as her own child, and endowed him with gifts. St. George enclosed her in a rock, where she was torn to pieces by spirits.

Kama. Also known as **Kamadeva** or **Kandarpa.** In Hindu mythology, the god of love. His wife is Rati (voluptuousness), his friend the season *vasanta* (spring); he rides on a sparrow, and holds in his hand a bow of flowers and five arrows which stand for the five senses. He was shriveled into cinders by the eye of Shiva, because Kama stirred passion in Shiva who was practicing penance; later Kama was reborn as Pradyumna.

Kamakura. Japanese historical period (1185–1333) following the Heian. The military clans in Eastern Japan gained the ascendency, destroying the power of the imperial court in Kyoto. New forms of Buddhism, notably Amidism and Zen, arose; a literature developed, centering on military chronicles that reflected the uncertainties of a period of incessant warfare and natural disasters. Kamakura is a small city south of Tokyo, where the military government, or shogunate, had its headquarters. A colossal bronze statue of the seated Buddha, known as the *Diabutsu,* is in Kamakura.

Kama-sutra (Sans. *kama,* love; *sutra,* science). A detailed account of the art and technique of Indian erotics by the sage Vatsyayana (first century?).

Kamboja. In ancient Indian history, the territory to the east of Kashmir and beyond the Himalayas.

Kamenev, Lev Borisovich (1883–1936). Russian Communist leader. With Stalin and Zinoviev, he formed the triumvirate ruling Russia after Lenin's death. By 1929, Stalin had taken the upper hand, and in 1936 he purged both his colleagues.

Kami. A god or divinity in SHINTO, the native religion of Japan. The title is also given to *daimyōs* or governors, and is about equal to "lord."

Kamsa. In Hindu mythology, the uncle of KRISHNA. He is Krishna's unremitting enemy.

Kandarpa. See KAMA.

Kandinsky, Wassily (1866–1944). Russian painter. He was a cofounder, with Franz Marc, of the BLAUE REITER, and a pioneer in abstract expressionist painting. In 1910 he rejected representational art and he evolved a style of turbulent, vividly colored abstractions. After 1920 his style gradually became orderly and strict. The works of this later period are limited to brightly colored dots, bundles of straight or broken lines, rectangles, and circular forms, but these shapes are handled with great freedom and inventiveness. From 1922 to 1933, Kandinsky taught at the BAUHAUS, where he did important work in his basic course on the theory of form and published *Punkt und Linie zu Fläche (Point and Line to Plane,* 1926).

Kane, Harnett [Thomas] (1910–   ). American writer. He is best known for *Louisiana Hayride: American Rehearsal for Dictatorship* (1941), the story of the Huey Long administration. In addition to other nonfiction, he has written several popular biographical novels, including *Bride of Fortune* (1948), about the wife of Jefferson Davis; *The Lady of Arlington* (1953), a story based on the life of Mrs. Robert E. Lee; and *The Gallant Mrs. Stonewall* (1957).

Kangaroo (1923). A novel by D. H. LAWRENCE. Set in Australia, it is notable for its vivid account of that country, largely drawn from Lawrence's own experience. The central characters of Richard Lovat Somers and Harriet Somers are closely based on Lawrence and his wife Frieda LAWRENCE. The novel is largely concerned with their difficult marriage relationship, in which the husband keeps trying unsuccessfully to assert his will over his wife. Kangaroo is the nickname of an invented character, Benjamin Cooley, the leader of a political party whose platform is a combination of fascism and Lawrence's own doctrine of "blood-consciousness."

K'ang-hsi. The Chinese era 1662–1722. K'ang-hsi was a period of great literary and scholastic activity.

Kannon. See KUAN-YIN.

Kansas-Nebraska Act (1854). In U.S. history, an act of Congress that provided for the territorial organization of Kansas and Nebraska. The principle of popular sovereignty, which permitted the admission of new states into the Union with or without slavery according to the decision of local governments, was incorporated in the bill, thereby rescinding the MISSOURI COMPROMISE. Because of the popular sovereignty provision, "bleeding Kansas" became a battleground for proslavery and antislavery forces. See John BROWN; Stephen A. DOUGLAS.

Kant, Immanuel (1724–1804). German philosopher. Kant's attempt to define precisely the domain of rational understanding is a landmark in Western thought. On the one hand, he opposed Hume's skepticism, the idea that pure reason is of no real use in understanding the world, and on the other, he challenged enlightenment faith in the unlimited scope of reason. The basic formulation of what is called his critical philosophy is contained in the CRITIQUE OF PURE REASON, the CRITIQUE OF PRACTICAL REASON, and the CRITIQUE OF JUDGMENT. His ideas were used by Schiller as the basis for aesthetic theories and marked the beginning of German idealistic philosophy, which was developed by Fichte, Schelling, and Hegel. The quiet regularity of Kant's everyday life in Königsberg, where he was a university professor (1770–1804), became proverbial. According to an anecdote of Heinrich Heine, the residents of the town set their watches by Kant's daily walks.

Kantemir, Antiokh Dmitryevich (1709–1744). Russian poet. Kantemir helped to form the classic tradition in Russian literature. He is known chiefly for his satires, written in imitation of those of Horace and Boileau. Although he made Russians aware of European classical culture, Kantemir's own work had little direct influence. His prosody, based on the number of syllables in each line of verse, was supplanted by the accentual verse introduced by Mikhail Lomonosov.

Kantor, MacKinlay (1904–   ). American novelist. He is known for his popular historical novels, especially those dealing with the Civil War. *Andersonville* (1955), which won a Pulitzer Prize, is a lengthy and grimly realistic story of the infamous Confederate prison. *Long Remember* (1934) and *Arouse and Beware* (1936) also have Civil War backgrounds, the former centering on the battle of Gettysburg. *The Voice of Bugle Ann* (1935), the story of a hound, became very popular. Kantor also wrote the scenario for the movie *The Best Years of Our Lives* (1947), and many earlier novels. *Spirit Lake* (1961) is an account of the massacre of 30 settlers near Spirit Lake, Iowa, in 1857.

Kanva. In Kalidasa's play, SHAKUNTALA, the foster father of Shakuntala.

Kapital, Das. See CAPITAL.

Kapp Putsch. A revolt in Berlin (1920) staged by army officers seeking to replace the Weimar Republic with an authoritarian state. The *putsch* collapsed when the unions shut off all public utilities.

Karamazinov. In Feodor Dostoevski's THE POSSESSED, a satirical portrait of Ivan TURGENEV, whose aesthetic posing and love of Western culture Dostoevski detested.

Karamazov, Feodor Pavlovich. In Feodor Dostoevski's BROTHERS KARAMAZOV, the father of the Karamazovs. He is a lustful, buffoonish character who thoroughly enjoys his sensual life and the sense of his degradation and only occasionally reveals a contempt for himself because of his unwholesome nature. The shock and disapproval of others only inspires him to further antics. Some of his sensual zest is contained in each of his sons in varying degrees, but none can match him for sheer animalism. He is the model of rampant irrationalism whose favorite mode of expression is the *non sequitur.*

Dmitri Fyodorovich Karamazov. Also known as *Mitya.* The eldest of the Karamazov brothers. Dmitri has inherited more of his father's lustiness than his brothers, but is saved from the old man's depravity by his own innately noble nature. Accused of his father's murder, he refuses to defend himself adequately, because by so doing he would injure the reputation of his ex-fiancée, KATERINA IVANOVNA. The most full-blooded of the characters in the novel, Dmitri is also one of Dostoevski's most successful character creations.

Ivan Fyodorovich Karamazov. Also known as *Vanya.* The intellectual member of the Karamazov family. Ivan is used by Dostoevski to represent the dead end to which he believed rationalism led. Tortured by the injustice and suffering in the world, Ivan "returns the ticket" to God, rejecting salvation from a Being who has allowed such a world to exist. Ivan both pities man's weakness and despises him for being so weak. Both of these attitudes are revealed in his "Legend of the GRAND INQUISITOR," a parable he recites to Alyosha during their most prolonged discussion. Ivan's guilt for wishing for his father's death rends him, culminating in his hallucinatory conversations with a shabby, imaginary Devil who espouses many of Ivan's own ideas in a debased form, much as the bastard Smerdyakov does.

Alexei Fyodorovich Karamazov. Also known as *Alyosha.* The youngest son of Feodor Pavlovich. Alyosha is a novice at the monastery who intends to become a monk, but his mentor, the elder Zosima, orders him to go into the world and serve God there. Although he is a religious mystic, Alyosha is much less removed from normal human concerns than Dostoevski's other famous mystic, Prince Myshkin of THE IDIOT. Despite his evident purity of heart, Alyosha admits to having a streak of the Karamazov sensuality in him. In the novel, he acts as the constant, sorrowful, and patient observer of his tormented father and brothers.

Smerdyakov. The illegitimate son of Feodor Pavlovich, who raped the boy's half-wit mother and later took the bastard into his house as a servant. Smerdyakov is a composite of cheap foppishness and second-rate intellect. He adopts Ivan's nihilistic ideas wholesale, perverts them in his own less fertile brain, and under their influence eventually commits the murder for which Dmitri is blamed.

Karamzin, Nikolai Mikhailovich (1766–1826). Russian writer and historian. He introduced the romanticism of Jean Jacques Rousseau and the romanticism of the early 19th-century English writers into Russian literature. His best-known works are *Letters of a Russian Traveller* (*Pisma russkogo puteshestvennika;* 1790–1791), based on his journey through Europe; *Poor Liza* (*Bednaya Liza;* 1792), a sentimental love story; and the multi-volume *History of the Russian State* (*Istoriya gosudarstva rossiskogo;* 1818–1824). Besides his introduction of new sensibilities and themes into Russian literature, Karamzin is important for his linguistic reforms. He attempted to make literary Russian less heavy in style by introducing French syntax and terms into the language.

Karatayev, Platon. The wise peasant in Count Leo Tolstoi's novel WAR AND PEACE. His message of the goodness of the natural, simple life affects the spiritual development of Pierre Bezukhov, one of the book's main characters.

Karenina, Anna. See ANNA KARENINA.

Karlfeldt, Erik Axel (1864–1931). Swedish poet. Karlfeldt's work is characterized by its purposely archaic style and its basis in folklore and custom, in such collections as *Fridolins visor* (1898), *Fridolins lustgård* (1901), and *Hösthorn* (1927). In 1918 he refused the Nobel prize for literature, arguing that his work was unknown outside of Sweden. The prize was awarded to him posthumously in 1931.

karma (*Sans.,* "action, fate"). In Buddhism and Hinduism, the name given the results of action, especially the cumulative results of a person's deeds in one stage of his existence as controlling his destiny in the next. Among Theosophists the word has a rather wider meaning, viz., the unbroken sequence of cause and effect; each effect being, in its turn, the cause of a subsequent effect.

Karoon or **Karun.** The Arabic form of *Korah* of the Old Testament, who, according to the commentators of the Koran, was the most wealthy and beautiful of the Israelites. It is said that he built a large palace overlaid with gold, with doors of solid gold. He was the Croesus of the Muslims and guarded his wealth in a labyrinth.

Kartaphilos. See CARTAPHILUS.

Karttikeya. Also known as **Skanda** and **Kumara.** The Hindu god of war. He is said to have been born without a mother and to have been adopted by the Pleiads or Krittikas, for which reason he is sometimes called "the son of Krittikas." He rides on a peacock, with a bow in one hand and an arrow in the other.

Kaswa, al. Muhammad's favorite camel. It fell on its knees in adoration when the prophet delivered the last clause of the Koran to the assembled multitude at Mecca. This is one of the dumb creatures admitted into the Muslim paradise.

Katayev, Valentin Petrovich (1897–   ). Russian novelist, short story writer, and playwright. His first important novel was *The Embezzlers* (*Rastratchiki;* 1927), a comic picaresque about two officials who make off with a large sum of money and go through hilarious adventures before being caught.

Another popular comic work of the same period is Katayev's play SQUARING THE CIRCLE (*Kvadratura kruga;* 1928).

In 1932, Katayev published TIME, FORWARD!, one of the better novels depicting the Five-Year Plan in Russia. His next novel, *Lone White Sail* (*Beleyet parus odinoki;* 1936), is set in Odessa, Katayev's birthplace, during the period of the 1905 revolution. The story, obviously autobiographical, deals with the adventures of two young boys in the exotic seaport. The same two boys, grown into manhood, appear in Katayev's novel about wartime partisans in Odessa; *For the Power of the Soviets* (*Za vlast Sovetov;* 1949).

Katerina Ivanovna. In Feodor Dostoevski's THE BROTHERS KARAMAZOV, the former fianceé of Dmitri Karamazov. One of Dostoevski's "infernal woman" characters, Katerina refuses to abandon Dmitri, because of her gratitude to him for helping save her father from disgrace. So tenacious is she that she is described as being in love only with her own virtue. Ivan, the second brother, is in love with her, but their relationship is mainly a harrowing series of sadistic and masochistic scenes. Finally incensed at Dmitri's rejection of her, Katerina is instrumental in bringing about his conviction for his father's murder.

Katharina. The fiery and ungovernable daughter of the bewildered Baptista in Shakespeare's TAMING OF THE SHREW. "Renowned in Padua for her scolding tongue," Katharina is wooed and won in wild and highhanded fashion by the equally high-spirited Petruchio.

Katharine Walton. See PARTISAN, THE.

Kathasaritsagara (*Sans.,* "great ocean of stories"). A collection of stories in Sanskrit consisting of 22,000 verses in 124 chapters. They were written by the Kashmiri poet Somadeva of the 11th century. According to some the work is a recast of the "larger ocean," the *Brihat-kathasaritsagara* of the fifth century.

Käthchen von Heilbronn, Das (pub. 1810). A play by Heinrich von KLEIST. It is Kleist's most romantic work, a kind of dramatized fairy tale. Käthchen, apparently a young commoner, is drawn to the count von Strahl by a mysterious, irresistible love and refuses to leave his side. Her perfect devotion survives through a number of knightly and supernatural adventures, and it is finally discovered that she is the emperor's daughter. She and the count marry in the end.

Katmir or **Kratim.** In the Koran, the dog of the SEVEN SLEEPERS. It spoke with a human voice, and said to the young men who wanted to drive it out of the cave, "I love those who love God. Go to sleep, masters, and I will keep guard." The dog kept guard over them for 309 years, and neither slept nor ate. At death it was taken up into paradise.

He wouldn't give a bone to Katmir, or *he wouldn't throw a bone to the dog of the seven sleepers* is a traditional Arabic reproach, applied to a very niggardly man.

Katsushika Hokusai (1760–1849). Japanese painter and wood-block artist. His highly individual work had considerable influence on Western painting.

Kaufman, George S[imon] (1889–1961). American playwright. The author of numerous popular

From Katsushika Hokusai's *War Between the Han and Ch'u.*

plays and musical comedies, Kaufman worked with a number of well-known writers. His long series of collaborations with Marc CONNELLY included DULCY; *To the Ladies* (1922), a comedy on home life; BEGGAR ON HORSEBACK; and *Merton of the Movies* (1922), a satire on Hollywood. With Moss HART, Kaufman wrote *Once in a Lifetime* (1930), another satire of Hollywood; YOU CAN'T TAKE IT WITH YOU; *I'd Rather Be Right* (1937), a satire on the New Deal; *The American Way* (1939), a paean to democracy; THE MAN WHO CAME TO DINNER; *George Washington Slept Here* (1940), a satire on the city dweller's urge to buy and renovate a house in the country; and other plays.

Kaufman worked with Edna FERBER on several plays: *Minick* (1924), based on one of Miss Ferber's short stories; *The Royal Family* (1927), dealing with a theatrical family resembling the Barrymores; *Dinner at Eight* (1932), an exposé of high society; *The Land Is Bright* (1941); and *Bravo!* (1948). With Morrie Ryskind he wrote the book for the Ira and George GERSHWIN musical OF THEE I SING. With Howard Dietz he collaborated on *The Band Wagon* (1931), with Ring Lardner on *June Moon* (1929), with Alexander Woollcott on *The Dark Tower* (1933), with Nunnally Johnson on *Park Avenue* (1946), and with Leueen MacGrath, his second wife, on *The Small Hours* (1951).

Kautsky, Karl (1854–1938). German Marxist. He denounced the revisionist socialism of Eduard Bernstein and Jean Jaurès, as well as the revolutionary socialism of the Russian Bolsheviks.

Kavanagh (1849). A romance by Henry Wadsworth LONGFELLOW. Mr. Churchill, the local schoolmaster, is unable to see the drama going on around him, while he attempts to be an author. Two girls fall in love with Fairmeadow's new minister, Kavanagh. Alice Archer, a poor girl, must nurse her invalid mother. Cecilia Vaughn, rich and beautiful, wins the minister, who is blind to Alice's love. The two leave Fairmeadow, and Alice wastes away and dies. On the couple's return, Kavanagh and Churchill discuss literature, and the latter must confess that his romance is still unwritten. The book delighted many discerning readers; it is an amusing and romantic vision of a small New England town, in which passions are either satirized or sentimentalized.

Kavanagh, Patrick (1905–). Irish poet. He wrote the long poem *The Great Hunger* (1942), about poor Irish farming people and their hunger both for land and life, and the collection *Come Dance with Kitty Stobling* (1960).

Kaverin, Venyamin. Pen name of **Venyamin Aleksandrovich Zilberg** (1902–). Russian novelist and short-story writer. Kaverin was a member of the SERAPION BROTHERS, in which he joined Lev Luntz in advocating more attention to Western literary methods. His special favorite was Edgar Allan Poe. His early stories, published in the collection *Craftsmen and Apprentices* (*Mastera i podmasterya;* 1923), show an attention to plot that sets them apart from the typical works of the time with their diffuse construction and ornate prose. Kaverin's best early novel is *The Artist Unknown* (*Khudozhnik neizvesten;* 1931), the story of a young artist's problems in finding a place for himself in the new society after the revolution. Another novel with a similar theme, although less complex in its structure, is his *The Fulfillment of Desires* (*Ispolneniye zhelany;* 1934–1935), translated into English as *The Larger View.* Kaverin's next novel, *Two Captains* (*Dva kapitana;* 1939), was an adventure story of Arctic exploration with some detective elements thrown in.

In 1949, Kaverin published the first part of a novel entitled *The Open Book* (*Otkrytaya kniga*), the story of a young girl who becomes a prominent bacteriologist. This fragment was not well received. In 1956, during the relaxed period following Stalin's death, Kaverin issued another part of the novel, a section entitled *Searches and Hopes* (*Poiski i nadezhdy*), which proved to be an outspoken criticism of Soviet scientific bureaucracy and the chauvinistic concern for Russian primacy in all fields, in this particular case, penicillin research. Kaverin was criticized for the story and, along with other writers attacked for their works at the time, he defended his views at a meeting of the Moscow Union of Writers.

Kawabata Yasunari (1899–). Japanese novelist and literary critic. Two of his novels have appeared in English, translated by Edward Seidensticker: *Yukiguni* (*Snow Country*, 1935, 1947); *Sembazuru* (*Thousand Cranes*, 1955).

Kay, Sir. In Arthurian legend, King ARTHUR's seneschal (steward). In the Welsh tale, *Kulhwch and Olwen* (c. 1100), Sir Kay is a great hero—a wound from his sword, no physician might heal. In later tales, such as *Lancelot* (c. 1180) by Chrétien de Troyes and *Le Morte d'Arthur* (c. 1469) of Malory, he becomes the rude and boastful knight whose sharp tongue is always stirring up trouble and who is inept in combat; yet Arthur always defers to him. In *Le Morte d'Arthur,* he is the son of Sir Ector, King Arthur's foster father.

Kaye-Smith, Sheila (1887–1956). English regional novelist. Set in Sussex, her best novels are *Sussex Gorse* (1916) and *Joanna Godden* (1921). Other works include *Mrs. Gailey* (1951) and *Quartet in Heaven* (1952).

Kazantzakis, Nikos (1883–1957). A Greek poet and novelist. Born in Crete, Kazantzakis took a law degree at Athens, then traveled widely for several years. From 1919 to 1947 he held, off and on, a variety of governmental posts. In his first novel, *Toda Raba,* written in 1929, he declared, "I am a mariner of Odysseus with heart of fire but with mind ruthless and clear." This essential ambivalence, the conflict between Dionysus and Apollo, between flesh and spirit, was the fundamental subject of his life and his writings. Zorba, the hero of ZORBA THE GREEK, the novel that established Kazantzakis' reputation in America, was beset by the same conflict; it is central also to his next great novel, THE GREEK PASSION. The author's preoccupation with the dual nature of man found its ultimate expression in his monumental poem, THE ODYSSEY: A MODERN SEQUEL.

Kazantzakis was influenced by philosophies as remote from one another as those of Dante, Lenin, and Buddha. His principal mentors, however, were Nietzsche, whose works he avidly read, and Bergson, under whom he studied in his youth. Like his hero Odysseus, Kazantzakis valued freedom above all other blessings. Yet, he believed that the ultimate good is not freedom, which, in any case, can never be achieved, but the passionate, often tragic *search* for freedom. Though greatly admired by such figures as Albert Schweitzer and Thomas Mann, and repeatedly nominated for the Nobel prize, Kazantzakis' writings became known in America only toward the end of his life.

Kazin, Alfred (1915–). American literary critic. His works of criticism include *On Native Grounds* (1942), *The Inmost Leaf* (1955), and *Contemporaries* (1962). Of his own native grounds in Brooklyn, Kazin wrote an appealing book of memories and reflections, *A Walker in the City* (1951).

Keable, Robert (1887–1927). English novelist and clergyman. *Simon Called Peter* (1921), his portrait of a disillusioned clergyman, was a best seller and perhaps autobiographical in nature.

Kean, Edmund (1787–1833). English actor. He was unrivaled in his day as a tragedian; his greatest successes were Shakespearean roles, notably Othello, Richard III, and Lear. His excessive drinking ruined his career and his health.

Keats, John (1795–1821). English poet. The oldest of four children, Keats was born in London. His father, a livery-stable keeper, died when Keats was eight and his mother six years later. The following year, when he was 15, he was withdrawn from school by his guardian and apprenticed to an apothecary-surgeon. In 1815 he entered a London hospital as a medical student, and though he received his certificate to practice he soon gave up medicine in order to devote himself entirely to poetry. In the autumn of 1816 he gained the acquaintance of the influential editor of the *Examiner,* Leigh HUNT, who published his sonnet *On First Looking into Chapman's Homer* (1816) and through whom he later met Shelley and Wordsworth. The following year saw the publication of his first collection, *The Poems of John Keats*. He then began work on *Endymion* (1818), a long allegory of imagination in search of ideal beauty; the story is based on the Greek myth of the shepherd ENDYMION on Mount Latmos who was loved by Selene, the goddess of the moon. Though Keats may have attached enough hopes to the poem to be troubled by the attacks of unfriendly critics, he was maturing rapidly both as a poet and as a critic of his own work and soon spoke of *Endymion* as "mawkish" and "slipshod." There is little truth in the popular belief, stimulated by Shelley's preface to his elegy ADONAIS, that Keats wasted away and died as a result of the "savage criticism" of *Endymion,* which "produced the most violent effect on his susceptible mind . . . [ending] in the rupture of a blood-vessel in the lungs."

In 1818 Keats had to cut short a walking tour because of a severe sore throat, possibly the first sign of his illness. He then nursed his brother Tom, suffering from tuberculosis, until Tom's death in the beginning of December. He had met Fanny Brawne in September, and he became engaged to her at Christmastime. Between the autumn of 1818 and the summer of 1819, Keats composed his finest poetry. He worked on *Hyperion,* a Miltonic blank-verse epic of the Greek myth of Creation, but left it after a little more than two books had been completed. The story was to deal with the Titan Hyperion, god of the sun, and his overthrow by Apollo, representative of the new generation of gods headed by Zeus.

In January, 1819, he began THE EVE OF ST. AGNES; the story, which he probably got from Boccaccio, is based on the medieval belief that on St. Agnes' Eve a girl who follows certain rituals will see her future husband in her dreams. He wrote LA BELLE DAME SANS MERCI, a haunting and mysterious ballad, and began to compose his great odes—*Ode on Melancholy,* ODE ON A GRECIAN URN, *Ode to Psyche,* ODE TO A NIGHTINGALE—adapting elements of the rhyme-scheme of both Petrarchan and Shakespearean sonnets. Notable for their sensuous imagery and sustained feeling, these odes are among the finest in English.

By summer he was at work on *Lamia,* an allegorical poem based on a story, found in Burton's *Anatomy of Melancholy,* of a youth who met a phantasm in the shape of a lovely woman and went to live with her. At their wedding, the woman was revealed to be a serpent (a lamia), and all her possessions mere illusions which, with her, vanished "in an instant." He began a revision of *Hyperion,* called *The Fall of Hyperion,* and *The Eve of St. Mark,* both of which were left incomplete. By the fall of 1819 his tuberculosis had progressed until he could do little but revise and prepare his poems for publication. This third and final collection, *Lamia, Isabella, The Eve of St. Agnes and Other Poems,* appeared in July of 1820. In February of that year he had suffered his first hemorrhage. Bothered by financial problems, frustrated and unhappy in his unconsummated relationship with Fanny Brawne, he became progressively worse until a doctor warned that another English winter would kill him. In August he refused an in-

vitation from Shelley, whom he knew slightly, to spend the winter at the Shelleys' villa in Italy. He borrowed money and sailed for Italy in September, accompanied by the young painter Joseph Severn, and died in Rome the following February.

Probably the most talented of the English romantic poets, Keats wrote a surprisingly large body of poetry before his early death. Practically all the finished poems of the 1818–1819 group are the work of a mature poet, and a few of them, such as the magnificent *To Autumn,* are among the finest examples of English lyric poetry. His letters are of particular interest not only for their biographical value but for their poetic and philosophic insights. See ISABELLA, OR THE POT OF BASIL.

Keb. See GEB.

Keble, John (1792–1866). Anglican clergyman and poet. Keble's Oxford sermon on *National Apostasy* was considered by Cardinal Newman to be the start of the OXFORD MOVEMENT. He was professor of poetry at Oxford (1831–1841) and author of a popular collection of religious verse, *The Christian Year* (1827), as well as several volumes of sermons and essays.

Keeldar, Shirley. See SHIRLEY.

Kelland, Clarence Budington (1881–1964). American newspaperman and novelist. A reporter early in his career, he later became editor of *The American Boy* and wrote books for juveniles. His fame rests on the title character of his 1921 novel, *Scattergood Baines.* A shrewd, fat Yankee promoter, Baines appeared in a succession of humorous novels and short stories, including *Scattergood Pulls the Strings* (1941). Among Kelland's other books are *Dynasty* (1929), *Archibald the Great* (1943), *No Escape* (1952), and *Monitor Affair* (1960).

Keller, Gottfried (1819–1890). Swiss novelist and poet, writing in German. He is known especially for his ability to combine bourgeois good sense and humor with powerful symbolism and subtle psychological perception. After failing to realize his youthful ambition of becoming a painter, he turned to poetry in 1842. He was involved in the Swiss civil disputes of the time, and a number of his early poems are in the manner of such liberal political poets as Herwegh and Freiligrath. During 1848–1855, he traveled and studied in Germany, completing his first major narrative work, the novel GREEN HENRY, (*Der grüne Heinrich;* first version, 1854; second, 1879–80) which was shortly followed by a collection of stories, *Die* LEUTE VON SELDWYLA. Most of his later years were spent comfortably in Zürich where, during 1861–1876, he was a government official. Outstanding among his later works are the *Sieben Legenden* (*Seven Legends,* 1872), treating the early period of the Christian era. In them, he weaves a delicately ironic web of both Christian and pagan elements, by which he implies his own preference for a secularized view of religion, an idea that reflects the strong influence of Feuerbach.

Keller, Helen [Adams] (1880–   ). American memoirist, essayist, and counselor on international relations for the American Foundation of the Blind. Disease deprived her of sight and hearing at the age of 19 months; cut off from human communication, the child finally learned the relationship between words and things from her devoted teacher, Anne

Sullivan Macy (1866–1936). When she was 10 years old, her "Teacher" helped her learn to speak. Miss Keller graduated from Radcliffe College *cum laude* in 1904. Mrs. Macy remained her companion until her death. Helen Keller has received several honorary degrees from universities all over the world. She wrote *The Story of My Life* in 1902 (reissued, 1947); among her other books are *Optimism* (1903), *The World I Live In* (1908), *Out of the Dark* (1913), *The Open Door* (1957), and *Helen Keller's Teacher: Anne Sullivan Macy* (1955). Several books have been written about Helen Keller; in 1954, a movie called *The Unconquered* was based on her life story. *The Miracle Worker* (1959), a Broadway play and later a movie, dramatized Anne Sullivan Macy's first success in communicating with Helen as a child.

Kelly, George [Edward] (1887–   ). American playwright. He first achieved fame with *The Show-Off* (1924), a satire on American success stories. CRAIG'S WIFE won a Pulitzer Prize. Later plays included *Behold the Bridegroom* (1927) and *The Fatal Weakness* (1946).

Kelmscott Press. A cooperative publishing and printing enterprise established by William MORRIS on his English country estate in 1891. It was noted for the beauty of paper, binding, and typography in the books it published. The *Kelmscott Chaucer* is considered the masterpiece among these. See CHAUCER.

kelpie or **kelpy.** In Scottish folklore, a spirit of the waters in the form of a horse. It was supposed to take delight in the drowning of travelers, but also occasionally to help millers by keeping the mill wheel going at night.

Kemble, Charles (1775–1854). English actor. His noted family of actors included his brother John Philip Kemble (1757–1823) and Sarah SIDDONS. Charles was manager of Covent Garden from 1822. His daughter **Frances Anne** or **Fanny Kemble** (1809–1893) was a popular leading lady who resided alternately in England and the U.S. She wrote several autobiographical books, a play, *The Star of Seville* (1837), and a collection of notes on Shakespeare.

Kemp, Harry [Hibbard] (1883–1960). American writer, poet, and vagabond. *Tramping on Life* (1922) and *More Miles* (1927) are fictional accounts of his vagabond days. His poetry includes *Chanteys and Ballads* (1920) and *The Thresher's Wife* (1914), a narrative poem. *Judas* (1910) is a four-act play.

Kemp, William (fl. c. 1600). English comedian and dancer. He acted in the plays of William Shakespeare and Ben Jonson. He was an important member of Shakespeare's company until 1600, and later traveled widely on the continent. Kemp's *Nine Daies Wonder* is an autobiographical account of his famous morris-dance from London to Norwich.

Kempis, Thomas à. See THOMAS À KEMPIS.

Kempner, Alfred. See Alfred KERR.

Kemp Owyne. A medieval Scottish or English ballad. It deals with the transformation of Isabel into a "loathly lady" by her stepmother's magic and with her deliverance by the fortitude and courage of the knight Kemp Owyne. Kemp is the Scottish word for champion.

Kenelm, St. An English saint, son of Kenwulf, king of Wessex in the early 9th century. He was only seven years old when, by his sister's order, he

Kemps nine daies vvonder.

Performed in a daunce from
London to Norwich.

Containing the pleafure, paines and kinde entertainment
of *William Kemp* betweene *London* and that Citty
in his late Morrice.

Wherein is fomewhat fet downe worth note; to reprooue
the flaunders fpred of him : many things merry,
nothing hurtfull.

Written by himfelfe to fatisfie his friends.

LONDON
Printed by *E. A.* for *Nicholas Ling*, and are to be
folde at his fhop at the weft doore of Saint
Paules Church 1600.

Title page of Kemp's *Nine Daies Wonder* (1600).

was murdered at Clente-in-Cowbage, Gloucestershire. The murder, says Roger of Wendover, was miraculously reported at Rome by a white dove, which alighted on the altar of St. Peter's, bearing in its beak a scroll with these words:

> In Clent cow pasture, under a thorn
> Of head bereft, lies Kenelm king-born.

Kenilworth (1821). A novel by Sir Walter SCOTT, famous for its portrayal of Queen Elizabeth and her court. The other principal characters are Robert Dudley, the earl of Leicester, who entertains ambitions of becoming king-consort, and his beautiful, unhappy wife, Amy Robsart. She suffers neglect, insult, and finally death at his hands. Kenilworth is a magnificent castle near Stratford, now ruined.

Kennan, George (1845–1924). American journalist. The Century Company commissioned him to visit Russia and Siberia, a trip that involved a 5,000-mile trek by dogsled; he was also sent to the front in the Spanish-American and Russo-Japanese wars. From these experiences Kennan published *Siberia and the Exile System* (2 v., 1891), *Campaigning in Cuba* (1899), and several other volumes.

Kennedy, John Fitzgerald (1917–1963). 35th president of the U.S. (1961–1963). The son of Joseph P. Kennedy, Boston financier and former ambassador to England, and the grandson of a popular mayor of Boston, Kennedy was born into an atmosphere of wealth and prominence. After attending the London School of Economics (1935–1936), he entered Harvard University, from which he graduated with honors in 1940. During World War II, Kennedy served as the commander of a PT boat in the South Pacific and was decorated by the navy for the courage and leadership he displayed after his boat was rammed by a Japanese destroyer during a night action in the Solomons.

Kennedy's political career began in 1946 when he was elected to Congress as a representative from Massachusetts. He was re-elected in 1948 and 1950, and in 1952 defeated Henry Cabot Lodge for a seat in the Senate. As a senator, Kennedy quickly became a leader of the moderate liberal wing of the Democratic Party and won prominence as a member of the Senate Foreign Relations Committee and the Select Senate Committee on Improper Labor-Management activities. In 1956 he was a leading contender for the Democratic vice-presidential nomination, and in 1960, after impressive victories in a number of state presidential primaries, he became the Democratic nominee for president, winning the election by a narrow margin over Vice-President Richard Nixon. He was the first Roman Catholic and the youngest man ever to be elected to the presidency.

During his brief administration, Kennedy launched the Peace Corps to aid underdeveloped areas, demanded the withdrawal of Soviet weapons from Cuba, and encouraged the Negro drive for full civil rights. On Nov. 22, 1963, Kennedy was shot to death as he rode in a motorcade in Dallas, Texas. His accused assassin, Lee Harvey Oswald, was himself killed on November 24 by Jack Ruby, a Dallas night club operator, in full view of the nation's television audience.

Kennedy was the author of *Why England Slept* (1940), an analysis of the causes of England's failure to rearm before World War II; *Profiles in Courage* (1956), a Pulitzer Prize-winning collection of essays dealing with congressional leaders who, in historically critical moments, placed conscience over political expediency; and *The Strategy of Peace* (1960), which presented a statement of Kennedy's aims in international affairs.

Kennedy, Margaret (1896–   ). English novelist. Author of the best-selling THE CONSTANT NYMPH, she has also written the novels *Return I Dare Not* (1931), *Troy Chimneys* (1953), and *The Forgotten Smile* (1961).

Kennicott, Carol. See MAIN STREET.

kenning. In Anglo-Saxon poetry, a figure of speech using a descriptive circumlocution in place of the common noun. Examples are "whale-road" or "gannet's bath" for "sea," and "ash-wood" for "spear." *Beowulf* contains a number of excellent examples of kennings.

Kensington Gardens (1722). A mock-heroic descriptive poem by Thomas TICKELL in which Kensington Gardens, then only a few years completed, is peopled with fairies. The gardens are the royal domain of Oberon, and the hero is Albion, son of "Albion's royal blood," who was stolen thence by the fairy Milkah. He later falls in love with Kenna, daughter of Oberon, and after many adventures and a war caused by Oberon's opposition, they are married. Kensington Gardens is a royal park in London, and site of the Great Exhibition of 1851.

Kent, earl of. In Shakespeare's KING LEAR, the honest courtier banished by Lear for interceding on behalf of Cordelia. Under the assumed name of Caius, Kent continues to serve Lear.

Kentigern, St. (c. 510–601). The patron saint of Glasgow, born of royal parents. He is said to have founded the cathedral at Glasgow, where he died. He is represented with his episcopal cross in one hand, and in the other a salmon and a ring, in allusion to the well known legend:

Queen Langoureth had been false to her husband, King Roderich, and had given her lover a ring. The king, aware of the fact, stole upon the knight in sleep, abstracted the ring, threw it into the Clyde, and then asked the queen for it. The queen, in alarm, applied to St. Kentigern, who after praying, went to the Clyde, caught a salmon with the ring in its mouth, handed it to the queen, and was thus the means of restoring peace to the royal couple, and of reforming the repentant queen.

The Glasgow arms include the salmon with the ring in its mouth, and also an oak tree, a bell hanging on one of the branches, and a bird at the top of the tree:

> The tree that never grew,
> The bird that never flew,
> The fish that never swam.
> The bell that never rang.

The oak and bell are in allusion to the story that St. Kentigern hung a bell upon an oak to summon the wild natives to worship.

St. Kentigern is also known as St. Mungo, for *Mungho* (i.e., dearest) was the name by which St. Servan, his first preceptor, called him. His day is January 13.

Kenton, Simon (1755–1836). American soldier and Indian fighter, famous in frontier legends. At one time a scout for Daniel Boone, he fought in the American Revolution and in the War of 1812. See Simon GIRTY.

Kentucky Cardinal, A (1894). A novel by James Lane ALLEN. The hero, Adam Moss, is a nature lover who reluctantly cages a Kentucky cardinal at the capricious demand of his jealous betrothed, Georgianna. To their great remorse, the bird dies, but the two are reconciled. *Aftermath* (1896) is a sequel.

Kentucky Tragedy, the. A murder and suicide which took place in 1825. Anna Cook, a Kentucky girl who had been seduced by Col. Solomon P. Sharp, married an attorney, Jeroboam O. Beauchamp, in 1825. She made her husband take an oath to kill her seducer. Beauchamp stabbed Sharp to death the same year in Frankfort, Ky. He was tried, denied his guilt, but was convicted. The evening before his execution, Anna joined him, and both took laudanum. His wife died, but Beauchamp lived to be hung the next day.

The dramatic possibilities of the crime inspired many works. Beauchamp wrote his own *Confession* (1826). Thomas Holley Chivers treated the theme in his verse drama *Conrad and Eudora* (1834); Poe used it in POLITIAN. Charlotte Mary Barnes wrote a tragedy called *Octavia Bragaldi* (1837); Mary E. MacMichael wrote *The Kentucky Tragedy* (1838); Charles Fenno Hoffman treated the same story in his romance *Greyslaer* (1849). The popular Southern novelist William Gilmore Simms wrote BEAUCHAMPE in 1842. In recent years, two well-known works have been based on the story: Robert Penn Warren's WORLD ENOUGH AND TIME and Joseph Shearing's *To Bed at Noon* (1951).

Kenyon Review, The. A quarterly founded by members of the Kenyon College faculty in 1939. John Crowe RANSOM was the first editor. The magazine stressed close structural criticism and reviews of important new trends in the arts. The advisory board initially included Allen TATE, Mark VAN DOREN, Robert Penn WARREN, and other writers of reputation. In 1951, Ransom edited the anthology *The Kenyon Critics: Studies in Modern Literature from the "Kenyon Review."*

Kepler, Johannes (1571–1630). German astronomer. He helped to establish the validity of the Copernican system by his empirical formulation of the laws of planetary motion. Using the precise data of Tycho BRAHE, he discovered that all planets move in elliptical orbits with the center of the sun as one of the foci, that the speed of a planet is related to its orbital position, and that the speeds of the different planets have a mathematical relationship to one another.

Kerenski, Aleksandr Feodorovich (1881–   ). Russian revolutionary leader. He became the head of the provincial government in 1917 after Czar Nicholas II's abdication. He was overthrown by the Bolsheviks in October, 1917, because of his moderate policies, and fled to Paris.

Kern, Jerome [David] (1885–1945). American composer of musical comedies. The best was undoubtedly SHOW BOAT. Some of his songs, such as *Ol' Man River* and *Smoke Gets in Your Eyes,* are still favorites.

Kerner, Justinus (1786–1862). German poet, writing for the most part in folk-song style. Though a medical doctor, he was especially interested in occult phenomena, and his famous *Die Seherin von Prevorst* (*The Prophetess of Prevorst,* 1829) is the record of his experiences with a visionary, somnambulist peasant woman whom he treated with mesmerism. The poets of Swabian romanticism, including Schwab, Uhland, and Lenau, were frequent guests at his house.

Kerouac, Jack (1922–   ). American novelist and poet. Recognized as one of the leading representatives of the BEAT MOVEMENT, Kerouac writes in a "spontaneous prose" that parallels the long, loose line employed by many of the beat poets. Like the poets he has been sharply criticized for lack of organization and for extolling the amorality of his characters, who seem concerned only with self-gratification. His best-known novels include *On the Road* (1957), *The Subterraneans* (1958), *The Dharma Bums* (1960), and *Big Sur* (1962).

Kerr, Alfred. Pen name of **Alfred Kempner** (1867–1948). German critic. His critical writings, especially on drama, were influential. His works were collected in 1917 under the title *Die Welt im Drama* (*The World in Drama*).

Kerr, Orpheus C. The pen name of Robert Henry Newell, author of the ORPHEUS C. KERR PAPERS.

Kessel, Joseph (1898–   ). Argentinian-born French novelist of Russian parentage. Kessel is best known for *Le Lion* (1958), a novel set in a wild animal reserve in Kenya. His other books include *La Steppe rouge* (1922), short stories of the Russian revolution, and adventure tales of war and aviation, such as *L'Equipage* (1923); *Crossroads* (*Fortune carrée;* 1932); and *Army of Shadows* (*L'Armée des ombres;* 1944).

Kessel, Maurice. See Maurice DRUON.

Kesten, Hermann (1900–   ). German novelist. He is known for his attacks on Nazism in such works as *Die Zwillinge von Nürnberg* (*The Twins of Nürnberg,* 1946).

Ketch, John. Known as **Jack Ketch** (d. 1686). English hangman and executioner, notorious for his barbarity. His name appeared in a ballad as early as 1678, and by 1702 it was associated with the executioner in Punch and Judy puppet-plays, which had recently been introduced from Italy.

Kevin, St. An Irish saint of the 6th century. Legend relates that, like St. Senanus, he retired to an island where he vowed no woman should ever land. Kathleen tracked him to his retirement, but the saint hurled her from a rock, and her ghost never left the place while he lived. A rock at Glendalough (Wicklow) is shown as the bed of St. Kevin. Moore has a poem on this tradition (*Irish Melodies,* iv).

Key, Ellen (1849–1926). Swedish feminist and author. While she was a prominent figure in Sweden, her works, proposing radical social views, gained her fame outside her own country. Her pacifist and feminist sympathies, as well as her broad humanitarian concerns, find expression in *Barnets århundrade* (*The Century of the Child,* 1900), *Kvinnorörelsen* (*The Woman Movement,* 1909), and *Kriget, freden och framtiden* (*War, Peace, and the Future,* 1914).

Key, Francis Scott (1779–1843). American lawyer and author of THE STAR-SPANGLED BANNER.

Keyes, Frances Parkinson (1885–   ). American novelist. Mrs. Keyes has written dozens of books since her first novel, *The Old Gray Homestead* (1919). Her best-known novel, *Dinner at Antoine's* (1948), is a murder mystery set in modern New Orleans a few weeks before Mardi Gras. *The Chess Players* (1961) is a fictional version of the life of the 19th-century American chess master Paul Morphy.

Keyes, Sidney (1922–1943). English poet. He was killed in World War II just as he was beginning to show his originality and talent. *Collected Poems* appeared in 1946.

Keyne, St. A Celtic saint, daughter of Brychan, king of Brecknock in the 5th century. Concerning her well, near Liskeard, Cornwall, it is said that if a bridegroom drinks therefrom before his bride, he will be master of his house, but if the bride gets the first draught, she will rule. Southey has a ballad, *The Well of St. Keyne* (1798), on this tradition. The man leaves his wife at the porch and runs to the well to get the first draught, but when he returns, his wife tells him his labor has been in vain, for she has "taken a bottle to church."

Keynes, John Maynard. 1st baron of **Tilton** (1883–1946). English economist. Originator of the so-called New Economics, Keynes lectured in economics at Cambridge from 1908 until his death, became an editor of the *Economic Journal* in 1912, and wrote such works as *The Economic Consequences* *of Peace* (1919), denouncing as unrealistic the reparations of the treaty of Versailles; *A Tract on Monetary Reform* (1923); *The End of Laissez-Faire* (1926); *A Treatise on Money* (1930); *The General Theory of Employment, Interest, and Money* (1936), his most influential and best-known work; and *How to Pay for the War* (1940). Keynes served on the staff of the Treasury from 1915 to 1919 and was its principal representative at the Paris Peace Conference of 1919. During the 30's he advised wide government expenditure as a counter measure to deflation and depression. Though his suggestions were less followed in Great Britain, they became the foundation of President Roosevelt's recovery program in the U.S. At the close of World War II, Keynes was influential in the planning for the World Bank and for the stabilization of international currency. Though his doctrine of deficit spending has been widely opposed, he was undoubtedly the most brilliant British economist of his time, and his influence is still apparent in British and U.S. government economic planning.

Keyserling, Count **Hermann Alexander** (1880–1946). Estonian social philosopher and mystic of German stock. Deprived of his estates by the Russian Revolution, he founded at Darmstadt the *Schule der Weisheit* (School of Wisdom). His thought was conditioned by contact with many cultures and the direct result of his far-flung travels, which earned him the well-deserved epithet of "the wandering philosopher." His final ideal was a synthesis of the Western notion of doing with the oriental notion of being. His books include *Reisetagebuch eines Philosophen* (1919) or *Travel Diary of a Philosopher* (1925) and THE BOOK OF MARRIAGE.

Kezia. A little girl, the heroine of Katherine MANSFIELD's stories about her childhood in New Zealand.

Khadijah. Muhammad's first wife and, according to the Koran, one of the four perfect women. The other three are Fatima, the prophet's daughter, Mary, daughter of Imran, and Asia, wife of the Pharaoh drowned in the Red Sea.

khedive. The title, from 1867 to 1914, of the ruler of Egypt, as viceroy of the sultan of Turkey. The word is Turkish, derived from Persian, and means a prince or viceroy.

Khepera. An Egyptian solar deity represented by the beetle.

Khlebnikov, Velemir Vladimirovich (1885–1922). Russian poet. One of the originators of FUTURISM in Russia, Khlebnikov was an inventive poet whose searchings for new poetic techniques helped revivify Russian poetry. His fellow futurist Vladimir Mayakovski described him as "the Columbus of new poetic continents now settled and cultivated by us." Khlebnikov, who had a love for old Slavic culture, replaced his original first name, Viktor, with the more archaic name Velemir.

Khnemu. An Egyptian ram-headed deity, worshiped especially in the region of the 5 cataracts of the Nile.

Khodasevich, Vladislav Felitzyanovich (1886–1939). Russian poet. He began publishing verse in 1908, but most of his best work appeared after the revolution. He emigrated in 1922 and became one of the best Russian *émigré* poets. His best-known collection of poetry is *The Heavy Lyre* (*Tyazhiolaya lira;* 1921).

Khrushchev, Nikita Sergeyevich (1894–   ). Russian leader of the government and Communist Party of the Soviet Union (1953–1964). A factory worker, Khrushchev joined the Communist Party in 1918 and began a rapid rise through the ranks. In 1939 he was elected to the Soviet Union's ruling body, the Politburo (renamed the Presidium in 1952). He was named in 1949 as a secretary of the Communist Party Central Committee. After Stalin's death he became first secretary of the Party, sharing power with Georgi Malenkov, who was chairman of the Council of Ministers (the head of the government). Malenkov resigned in 1955, and Nikolai Bulganin became head of state, to be replaced by Khrushchev in 1958. He was deposed and disgraced in 1964.

Khrushchev's speech at the 20th Congress of the Communist Party in 1956 created a sensation by its violent attacks on the memory of the past dictator Stalin. The de-Stalinization campaign instituted by Khrushchev created a freer atmosphere that was quickly reflected in Soviet literature. In spite of this new atmosphere, named "the thaw" from the title of a novel by Ilya Ehrenburg, Khrushchev has kept a watchful eye on the work of Soviet writers and has several times personally admonished them to maintain the correct spirit of loyalty to the Party and state. This has been an insistent demand, even though the degree of freedom of Soviet writers has increased measurably since the Stalin era.

Ki. In Sumerian mythology, the primeval earth goddess. Born of Nammu, the sea, she bore the air-god Enlil by her brother-consort An, with whom she was originally joined as one. Enlil separated them, An becoming the upper sky. In religion she was supplanted by such younger counterparts as NINTU.

Kiblah or **Keblah.** The point of adoration toward which Muslims turn when they worship; i.e., the direction of the KAABA at Mecca. In mosques, the direction is shown by the *mihrab,* or hole in the interior wall.

Kid, The (1947). A poem by Conrad AIKEN. It deals with the legendary William Blackstone who is said to have greeted Boston's first settlers on what is now Boston Common. His later wanderings and other American heroes are also described.

Kidd, William. Known as **Captain Kidd** (1645?–1701). Scottish-born English pirate. Kidd was originally an affluent ship owner and sea captain who saw service against French privateers during King William's War and was later engaged by the British government to suppress piracy in the Indian Ocean. By 1799 a combination of circumstances, including a mutinous crew, had induced Kidd to turn to piracy; he captured several vessels and was declared a pirate by British authorities. Informed that he would be pardoned, he landed at Boston and was promptly arrested. He was sent to England, tried, and hanged at Execution Dock in London.

After his death, Kidd became a legendary figure in both England and the U.S. He became the hero of many ballads, his ghost was seen on several occasions, and numerous attempts were made to unearth a fabulous treasure which he supposedly buried in various points ranging from Oak Island, Nova Scotia to Gardiner's Island, N.Y. Cooper referred to Kidd in several works, notably *The Water Witch* (1830), a novel. The influence of the Kidd legend is also evident in Poe's short story *The Gold Bug* (1843), and Stevenson's novel *Treasure Island* (1883).

Kidnapped (1886). A historical novel by Robert Louis STEVENSON. It deals with the adventures of David Balfour, the young hero, and Alan BRECK, a Jacobite who is considered one of Stevenson's most interesting and best-drawn characters. A sequel, *Catriona,* was published in 1893.

Kielland, Alexander Lange (1849–1907). Norwegian novelist, short-story writer, and playwright. Although his own background was wealthy and aristocratic, Kielland's writing was spurred by a strong sense of social protest. In *Arbeidsfolk* (1881) he criticizes the bureaucracy, and in *Sankt Hans Fest* (1887) he denounces the clergy. *Garman og Worse* (1880) and *Skipper Worse* (1882) are tempered by childhood memory and display a clear beauty of style.

Kieran, John [Francis] (1892–   ). American newspaperman. An excellent sports columnist and authority on Shakespeare and bird life, he is best known for his prodigious memory which he displayed on the radio quiz show "Information Please." Kieran has written several books on his specialties, the most recent being *Natural History of New York City* (1959).

Kierkegaard, Søren Aabye (1813–1855). Danish philosopher. The early years of his life were dark and cheerless, his home a lonely, gloomy place. Kierkegaard published his first philosophical works under pseudonyms. In contrast to Hegel's objective philosophy, he proposed, in such works as *Stadier paa Livets Vej* (*Stages on Life's Way*, 1845) and *Gjentagelsen* (*Repetition*, 1843), a system based on faith, knowledge, thought, and reality. In *Enten Eller* (*Either-Or*, 1843), he discusses the razor-edge decision made by man's free will, which determines his personal relation to God. In 1846, events in his private life led him to experience a deeper commitment to Christianity and to attack with new vigor orthodox, organized religion. For Kierkegaard the relation with God must be a lonely, agonizing experience of a man's inner solitude. During his lifetime he was not recognized in Denmark as a genius; a rebel against secure bourgeois morality, he was mocked and reviled for his unorthodox views and for the strange, ungainly figure he cut on the cheerful streets of Copenhagen. The 20th-century revival of Kierkegaard was initiated by the German philosophers Heidegger and Jaspers, and furthered by members of the French existentialist movement, notably Sartre and Camus.

Kikuchi Kan (1888–1948). Japanese popular writer of prodigious output. Author of numerous short stories, novels, plays, and magazine serials. See *Madman on the Roof* (1923) translated by Y. T. Isasaki and G. Hughes.

Killers, The (1927). A short story by Ernest HEMINGWAY. One of Hemingway's most famous works, this story has as its protagonist Nick Adams, the same figure who appears in many of the stories of IN OUR TIME. Two city gunmen enter a small-town lunchroom to inquire about Ole Andreson, an ex-prizefighter, whom they announce they are going to kill for having double-crossed them. Nick, a customer in the lunchroom, goes to warn Andreson in his rooming-house, but Andreson, knowing that there is no final escape for him, refuses to help himself. The story does not really deal with urban gangsters; its focus is on Nick and the effect on him of the acceptance of violence.

Killigrew, Thomas (1612–1683). English dramatist and theater manager. A favorite of Charles II, he wrote several plays, including the licentious tragicomedy *The Parson's Wedding* (1640). He is also remembered as the founder of the first Theatre Royal (1663) in Drury Lane.

Kilmansegg, Miss. The heroine of Thomas HOOD's satirical poem *Miss Kilmansegg and her Golden Leg* (1828). She is an heiress of great expectations who has an artificial leg of solid gold.

Kilmer, [Alfred] Joyce (1886–1918). American poet. He is remembered chiefly for his poem *Trees,* which was published first in *Poetry* in August, 1913, won its author national fame, and became the title poem of *Trees and Other Poems* (1914). Kilmer had earlier published a collection, *Summer of Love* (1911), and published another one later, *Main Street and Other Poems* (1917). He was killed in France during World War I. His wife, Aline Kilmer (1888–1941), was also a poet and published several collections, including *Candles That Burn* (1919) and *The Poor King's Daughter and Other Poems* (1925).

Kim (1901). A novel of Indian life by Rudyard KIPLING. The hero, an Irish boy named Kimball O'Hara, is an orphan shifting for himself in Lahore. He attaches himself to a holy man, an old lama from Tibet who is on a quest for the mystic River of the Arrows, and together the pair roam about India. By accident Kim is recognized by his father's Irish regiment and much against his wishes is sent to school. During the long vacations he still tramps with his beloved lama. His intimate knowledge of India makes him a valuable asset to the English Secret Service, in which he wins renown while still a boy. The book abounds in brilliant descriptions of Indian scenes.

King, Clarence (1842–1901). American geologist and author. King presented to Congress a plan for the survey of the Cordilleran ranges from eastern Colorado to the California boundary. He was placed in charge of the approved project, and, leading a corps of geologists, was the first to explore and describe the Yosemite Valley, an area of about 100 miles in width. The monumental *Report of the Geological Exploration of the Fortieth Parallel* (1870–1878), one of the finest of government publications, included the results of the survey. King, a gifted writer, also published a volume called *Mountaineering in the Sierra Nevada* (1872; rev. ed., 1902); appearing first in *The Atlantic Monthly,* the book includes scientific description as well as vivid narrative. In 1871, King met Henry Adams, with whom he traveled and whose work he greatly influenced. Once considered by many an ideal American, King suffered financial loss during the business depression in 1893. During 1894, he suffered a nervous breakdown and remained in Bloomingdale Asylum for several months. He died of tuberculosis, alone and uncared for, in an Arizona tavern.

King, Edward. See LYCIDAS.

King, Henry (1592–1669). English poet and churchman, bishop of Chichester. An intimate friend of Donne and possibly his first editor, he was also close to Ben Jonson and Izaak Walton. King wrote two volumes of verse: *Psalmes of David Turned into Meter* (1651) and *Poems, Elegies, Paradoxes and Sonnets* (1657).

King Arthur and the Emperor Lucius. See MORTE D'ARTHUR, LE.

King Cole. See COLE, KING.

King Horn. See HORN, KING.

Kingis Quair (1424, pub. 1783). A long poem by James I of Scotland. Written while the king was a prisoner in England, it laments his fortune and celebrates a beautiful woman, Lady Jane Beaufort, whom he married. *Quair* is an older form of *quire*, "booklet." In modern times, Maurice Hewlett has written a novel called *The Queen's Quair* and James Leslie a trilogy called *A Scots Quair.*

King James Bible. See BIBLE, ENGLISH VERSIONS.

King John, The Life and Death of (c. 1595). A historical play by William SHAKESPEARE. The action concerns the efforts of the weak and despicable King JOHN to fend off the royal claims of Arthur, duke of Brittany, who is supported by the king of France. In spite of the able support of Philip FAULCONBRIDGE, John alienates the English nobility and runs disastrously afoul of the pope. In the end he is poisoned, and his son, Henry III, becomes king. An earlier play, *The Troublesome Reign of King John* (pub. 1591), was once attributed to Shakespeare.

Kinglake, Alexander William (1809–1891). English historian. He described a tour of the Near East in *Eothen, or Traces of Travel Brought Home from the East* (1844), considered a classic English travel book. His *Invasion of the Crimea* (1863–1887) is a detailed account of the Crimean War.

King Lear (c. 1605). A tragedy by William SHAKESPEARE. Seeking peace in his old age, the weary Lear, king of Britain, resolves to divide his kingdom among his three daughters GONERIL, REGAN, and CORDELIA, but first he requires that they make declarations of their love for him. The first two, crafty and insincere, profess their love in the most grandiloquent terms and are each rewarded, in turn, by the bestowal of a third of the kingdom. Cordelia, the youngest and favorite, then disappoints Lear by stating that she loves him according to her bond "nor more, nor less." Rage blinds him to the deeper, truer love of Cordelia, and he divides the portion designed for her between her sisters. Thus undowered, she is taken by the king of FRANCE for his wife. Lear now begins to suffer for his foolish vanity. It quickly becomes clear, as he spends a month first with one and then the other, that Goneril and Regan are grasping hypocrites and that they are bent on humiliating Lear. Goneril refuses to put up his entire retinue and demands that he reduce it to 25; Regan puts Lear's servant, the faithful earl of KENT, in the stocks. In a famous scene, Lear goes out upon the heath in a raging storm and raves with the agony of madness. Cordelia, learning from Kent of her father's condition, brings an army from France to Britain's shores. Goneril and Regan unite against this threat. Cordelia sends attendants out after her father, and they are happily reunited in a tent in the French camp. In the battle that follows, Cordelia's army is defeated and they are taken prisoner. Goneril poisons Regan for love of EDMUND, the evil bastard son of GLOUCESTER; then stabs herself.

By an order countermanded too late, Cordelia is hanged in prison and Lear, broken-hearted, dies soon after. A subplot, paralleling the main plot, involves Gloucester, who allows the jealous Edmund to turn him against his real son, EDGAR, who loves him. See duke of ALBANY; duke of CORNWALL; OSWALD; Lear's FOOL; LEIR, KING.

King Lent. An anglicism for Carêmeprenant, the ruler of Tapinois, or Sneaks, Island in Rabelais' GARGANTUA AND PANTAGRUEL. His body and limbs resemble inanimate objects, so that his feet suggest guitars and his skin is like a gabardine jacket. He personifies the Lenten customs of fasting and penitence which Rabelais thought unnatural.

Kingmaker. Epithet for Richard Neville, earl of Warwick (1420–1471). He was so called because, when he sided with Henry VI, Henry was the king, but when he sided with Edward IV, Henry was deposed and Edward crowned king. He was killed at the battle of Barnet.

King of Misrule. See LORD OF MISRULE.

King of the Wood. Lat., *Rex Nemorensis.* The priest of Diana who must pluck the golden bough (as Aeneas did before his descent into the underworld) and then slay his predecessor in a duel before entering on his office at Aricia on the shores of a lake (now Lago di Nemi) in the Alban Mountains, where the goddess had a sacred grove. A discussion of this myth is the opening passage in, and explains the title of, Sir James G. Frazer's THE GOLDEN BOUGH.

King Philip (died 1676). Name given by English settlers to Metacomet, the son of Massasoit and chief of the Wampanoag tribe. During King Philip's War (1675–76), the most important Indian uprising in New England, Wampanoag, Narragansett, and Nipmuck warriors made sudden raids on frontier settlements; many towns were destroyed and captives taken, including the famous Mrs. Mary ROWLANDSON. Although the Indians were initially successful, the movement collapsed after Philip's death. See also Benjamin TOMPSON.

Kings, The First Book and The Second Book of. Two books of the Old Testament. Together these books—originally one—relate the history of Israel from the last years of David to the Babylonian Exile. They record the glories of Solomon's reign (c. 960 B.C.) and the decline of the Southern Kingdom, which followed, ending with the destruction of the temple in Jerusalem in 586 B.C.

king's evil. Scrofula. It was so called from a notion that prevailed from the reign of Edward the Confessor to that of Queen Anne that it could be cured by the royal touch. The Jacobites considered that the power did not descend to William III and Anne because the divine hereditary right was not fully possessed by them, but an office for such healing remained in the Prayer Book till 1719. Prince Charles Edward, when he claimed to be prince of Wales, touched a female child for the disease in 1745; but the last person touched in England was Dr. Johnson, in 1712, when only 30 months old, by Queen Anne.

The French kings laid claim to the same divine power from the time of Clovis (A.D. 481). On Easter Sunday, 1686, Louis XIV touched 1,600 persons, using these words: *le Roi te touche, Dieu te guérisse.*

Kingsley, Rev. Charles (1819–1875). English clergyman, novelist, and poet. Kingsley was much involved in the social reform movements of his time, having been strongly influenced by Carlyle. His earliest novels, ALTON LOCKE and *Yeast* (1851), deal with CHRISTIAN SOCIALISM, a movement with which he was associated. His best-known books are the historical romances HYPATIA, WESTWARD HO!, and HEREWARD THE WAKE, and his fairy tale THE WATER BABIES. A review of his in *Macmillan's Magazine* led to the famous church controversy with Cardinal Newman, which moved the latter to publish his *Apologia Pro Vita Sua.* See MUSCULAR CHRISTIANITY.

Kingsley, Henry (1830–1876). English novelist and journalist, brother of Charles KINGSLEY. His best-known works are the romantic novels *Geoffrey Hamlyn* (1859) and *Ravenshoe* (1862). He wrote several other novels, of which *The Hillyars and the Burtons* (1865) and *Mademoiselle Mathilde* (1868) are worthy of note, and a number of short stories, essays, and children's books.

Kingsley, Sidney (1906–   ). American actor and playwright. He is the author of the Pulitzer Prize-winning drama MEN IN WHITE and of the popular DEAD END. Later plays include *The Patriots* (1942), written with his wife, Madge Evans Kingsley, and *Darkness at Noon* (1951), an adaptation from the book by Arthur Koestler.

King, the Greatest Alcalde, The. See MEJOR ALCALDE EL REY, EL.

Kingu. A Bablyonian demigod. He was a general and consort of Tiamat, in the WAR OF THE GODS. After her defeat, Marduk killed him and fashioned man out of his blood and bones.

King William's War (1689–1697). A war waged by Great Britain and its American colonies against France and its Indian allies. It was the American phase of the war between the Grand Alliance and Louis XIV and was concluded by the Peace of Ryswick.

Kinsmen, The. See SCOUT, THE.

Kipling, Rudyard (1865–1936). English novelist, poet, and short story writer. Born in India of English parents, he was taken to England at the age of six and spent six unhappy years there, later described in *Baa Baa, Black Sheep.* In 1878 he entered the United Services College in North Devon, and his experiences there later served as the basis for STALKY AND CO. Kipling returned to India at the age of 17 where his father had secured him a post at the *Civil and Military Gazette* of Lahore; the collection of verses *Departmental Ditties* (1886) and the collection of stories PLAIN TALES FROM THE HILLS were originally written for the *Gazette.* The stories that he produced as editor, during his last two years in India, of the Allahabad *Pioneer* were collected into *The Phantom Rickshaw* (1889).

Kipling returned to England via Japan and America, writing letters during the trip that were to form *From Sea to Sea* (1899). Once in London, he enjoyed spectacular success: all his Indian volumes were republished, and he followed up quickly with LIFE'S HANDICAP, THE LIGHT THAT FAILED, and BARRACK-ROOM BALLADS, the collection of poems that included GUNGA DIN, FUZZY WUZZY, *Danny Deever,* and MANDALAY. He wrote *The Naulahka* (1892) in collaboration with Charles Wolcott Balestier, whose sister Caroline he married in the same year. They settled in Vermont, and during the next five years

Kipling published *Many Inventions* (1893), THE JUNGLE BOOK (1894), *The Second Jungle Book* (1895), *The Seven Seas* (1896), and *Captains Courageous* (1897). After bitterly quarreling with his brother-in-law Beatty, Kipling returned to England. Except for a brief visit to New York in 1899, when his daughter died of pneumonia and he almost died of the same disease, Kipling never returned to the U.S., and spoke of it with bitterness despite the fact that, with the exception of Mark Twain, no other author had been so popular there as Kipling. In the years between 1897 and 1914, he published *The Day's Work* (1898), *Stalky and Co.* (1899), KIM, JUST SO STORIES, the only book that Kipling himself illustrated, *The Five Nations* (1903), *Traffics and Discoveries* (1904), *Puck of Pook's Hill* (1906), *Actions and Reactions* (1909), *Rewards and Fairies* (1909), *A Diversity of Creatures* (1917), *The Irish Guards in the Great War* (1923), a memorial to his only son John, fallen in battle, *Debits and Credits* (1926), *Limits and Renewals* (1932), and *Something of Myself* (1937), an autobiography left unfinished at his death.

Kipling was one of the first English poets to exploit the Cockney dialect. While his life-long glorification of imperialism has antagonized some critics and caused them to miss his more poetic side, it has had no effect on his popularity. See RECESSIONAL; SOLDIERS THREE; WEE WILLIE WINKIE; MAN WHO WOULD BE KING, THE.

Kipps (1905). A novel by H. G. WELLS. Arthur Kipps is a draper's apprentice who suddenly acquires wealth and makes comic efforts to fit into his new social world. Eventually he marries a housemaid and settles down to a happy, simple life.

Kirby, William. See GOLDEN DOG, THE.

Kirchhoff, Gustav Robert (1824–1887). German physicist. With Robert Bunsen, he developed the method of spectrum analysis and explained the FRAUNHOFER LINES.

Kirilov, Alexei Nilich. In Feodor Dostoevski's THE POSSESSED, a fanatically rebellious atheist who resolves to commit suicide, asserting man's freedom from his terrible fate—death. The idea has been implanted in the half-mad Kirilov by STAVROGIN. The revolutionary Pyotr VERKHOVENSKI tries to persuade Kirilov to leave a suicide note confessing to the murder of SHATOV, who has been killed by Verkhovenski's group.

Kirkland, Caroline [Matilda Stansbury]. Pen name, **Mrs. Mary Clavers** (1801–1864). American writer. Mrs. Kirkland, who traveled to the West with her missionary husband expressed her disillusionment with the crudeness of pioneer life in three books of semifictional narrative: *A New Home—Who'll Follow* (1839), *Forest Life* (1842), and *Western Clearings* (1845).

Kirkland, Joseph (1830–1894). American novelist. The son of Caroline KIRKLAND, he was one of the earliest exponents of realism. Kirkland was known for his frank and powerful studies of life in the Middle West. His best novel, *Zury, The Meanest Man in Spring County* (1887), was taken from his own grim youthful experience.

Kirkrapine. See FAERIE QUEENE, THE.

Kirkup, James (1923–   ). English poet, novelist, and playwright. Among his collections of poetry are *The Cosmic Shape* (1947), *A Spring Journey* (1954), and *The Prodigal Son* (1959). *The Love of Others* (1962) is a novel, and *Upon This Rock* (1955) is a play.

Kirov, Sergei Mironovich (1886–1934). Russian revolutionary leader. One of Stalin's chief aides and a member of the praesidium (1930–1934), Kirov was the Communist Party's secretary for the Leningrad area whose assassination in 1934 set off the purges of 1936–1937.

Kirsanov, Pavel Petrovich. In Ivan Turgenev's novel FATHERS AND CHILDREN, the chief antagonist of the nihilist BAZAROV. Pavel Petrovich, who defends the aristocratic way of life against the iconoclastic young radical, is called by Bazarov "an archaic phenomenon" and an "idiot."

Kirshon, Vladimir Mikhailovich (1902–1938). Russian dramatist. His plays, which champion the Soviet world against all forms of intervention and counterrevolution, include *Konstantin Terekhin* (*Rust*, 1927) and *Khleb* (*Bread*, 1930).

Kishar. See ANSHAR.

kismet (from Turk., *qismat*, portion, lot). Fate; the fulfilment of destiny.

Kissbreech, Lord. An anglicism for Seigneur de Baisecul, the plaintiff in the great lawsuit against Lord SUCKFIST in Rabelais' GARGANTUA AND PANTAGRUEL.

Kiss Me Kate (1948). A musical comedy with libretto by Bella and Samuel SPEWACK and music by Cole PORTER. Based on Shakespeare's *The Taming of the Shrew*, it contains some of Porter's best-known songs and is often considered his best musical.

Kit-cat Club. A club formed in the beginning of the 18th century by the leading Whigs of the day, whose meetings were held in the house of Christopher Catt, a pastrycook. Catt's mutton pies, which were eaten at the club, were also called *kit-cats*, and probably gave the club its name. The publisher Jacob Tonson was secretary, and the members included Richard Steele, Joseph Addison, William Congreve, Samuel Garth, John Vanbrugh, Robert Walpole, and William Pulteney. Their portraits by Sir Godfrey Kneller were reduced to three-quarter length in order to accommodate them to the size of the clubroom wainscot. Hence, a three-quarter portrait is still called a *kit-cat*.

kitchen cabinet. A name applied to President Andrew Jackson's informal advisers (1829–1833). The name was used in a derogatory manner by Jackson's political opponents, with particular reference to Francis P. Blair and Amos Kendall, both of whom were connected with the pro-Jackson newspaper *The Globe*.

Kitely. In Ben Jonson's EVERY MAN IN HIS HUMOUR, a rich elderly merchant. He is convinced that his young wife has made him a cuckold. His "horns i' the mind are worse than o' the head." Ironically, his wife is equally suspicious of his activities.

Kithara. See GREEK MUSIC.

Kittredge, George Lyman (1860–1941). American teacher and scholar. Kittredge, who taught at Harvard University from 1888 to 1936, was known as a great Shakespearean authority. Among his important works were *The Language of Chaucer's "Troilus"* (1894), *English and Scottish Popular Ballads* (1904), with H. C. Sargent; *Chaucer and His*

Poetry (1915); *Sir Thomas Malory* (1925); *Witchcraft in Old and New England* (1929); and an edition of *The Complete Works of Shakespeare* (1936).

Kivi, Aleksis. Pen name of A. Stenvall (1834–1872). Finnish novelist, playwright, and poet. Regarded as his country's greatest 19th-century writer, Kivi found inspiration for his best work in the country life of Finland. In *Kullervo* (1864) he dramatized an episode from the *Kalevala*, while in the comedy *Nummisuutarit* (*Shoemakers of the Heath*, 1864) and in the novel *Seitsemän Veljestä* (*Seven Brothers*, 1870) he depicted Finnish peasant life with a realism and humor that have never been matched by any other writer. He is also noted for his numerous collections of lyric verse.

Kjartan. In the LAXDALE SAGA, a young Icelander in love with the strong-willed heroine Gudrun. When he returns home from the Danish court and learns Gudrun has married his cousin Bolli, he takes a wife of his own, Hrefna. During the ensuing feud between the two couples, Kjartan continues to love Gudrun and defend her even when she is in the wrong.

Klaboterman. The kobold of the phantom ship, CARMILHAN.

Klabund. Pen name of **Alfred Henschke** (1890–1928). German poet, playwright, and novelist. He was a versatile writer with expressionistic leanings and wide cultural interests. His novels include *Pjotr* (*Peter the Great*, 1923), *Borgia* (1928) and *Rasputin* (1929).

Klaus or **Claus, Peter.** German legendary hero, the prototype of RIP VAN WINKLE. Klaus is a goatherd of Sittendorf who is led into a deep dell, where he finds 12 knights silently playing skittles. He drinks of their wine and is overpowered with sleep. When he awakens, he is amazed at the height of the grass; and upon discovering how strange his village seems, he realizes he has been asleep for 20 years.

Klee, Paul (1879–1940). Swiss painter. Generally considered one of the great masters of modern painting, Klee spent much of his life in Germany; he joined the BLAUE REITER group in 1912 and taught at the BAUHAUS from 1920 to 1929. Interested in the abstract meaning of pictorial representation, he was a highly original metaphysical painter, who by his playful line and subtle use of color created an art of great whimsy and spontaneity.

Kleist, Ewald von (1715–1759). German poet and grand-uncle of Heinrich von Kleist. He is most famous for his long philosophical lyric *Der Frühling* (*The Spring*, 1749) and for his heroic *Ode an die preussische Armee* (*Ode to the Prussian Army*, 1757).

Kleist, Heinrich von (1777–1811). German dramatist and novella writer, considered by many the greatest of all German authors in both genres. As a young man, he was induced by his family to undertake a career in the Prussian army, but in 1799 he resigned his commission and began an intensive study of mathematics and philosophy in hopes of perfecting his mind and gaining intellectual control over his destiny. In 1801, however, after reading Kant, his faith in the perfectability of knowledge was shattered, and for the first time he turned decisively to a career in writing. During 1801–1802 he worked on two plays, *Robert Guiskard* and *Die Familie Schroffenstein* (*The Schroffenstein Family*, pub. 1803), a tragedy of errors influenced by Shakespeare's *Romeo and*

Juliet. Though he never carried the latter beyond a fragmentary stage, he felt that it would be his *magnum opus,* and parts of it were highly praised by Wieland; but in 1803, in a fit of despair, he destroyed the manuscript, and the fragment of it that he published in 1808 consisted only of some 500 lines restored from memory. The year 1803, however, also saw the completion of his great comedy THE BROKEN JUG. He then spent three years as a government official in Königsberg. But in 1807 he went to Dresden where, with his friend Adam Müller (1779–1829), he founded the periodical *Phöbus* (1808) in which his greatest novella, MICHAEL KOHLHAAS, appeared. By 1809 he had also completed several more plays: an adaptation of Molière's *Amphitryon,* DAS KÄTHCHEN VON HEILBRONN, and PENTHESILEA.

Around 1808, along with the growing anti-Napoleonic movement in Germany, Kleist's interests became more patriotic. In 1810, again with Müller, he began editing the *Berliner Abendblätter (Berlin Evening News)* in which he took a firm stand against Napoleon; and in the same year he completed his last play, the strongly patriotic PRINZ FRIEDRICH VON HOMBURG. But in 1811, after his newspaper had been closed by the government, after all hope had faded of a successful German uprising against Napoleon in the near future, and in despair about his lack of literary recognition, he took his own life.

In form, Kleist's dramas show the clear influence of Schiller's classicism; but Kleist's characters, unlike Schiller's, have no clearly defined structure of moral principles and personal standards upon which to base their actions. They tend more to vacillate unpredictably among various attitudes, to show more the nervousness and insecurity of the modern individual. Some theoretical background to Kleist's dramatic style may be found in his essay *Über das Marionettentheater (On the Puppet-Theater,* 1810), in which he suggested that man's self-consciousness hinders his freedom of action, that man cannot act purely and simply in accordance with conscious ideas or standards.

Kline, Franz (1910–1962). American painter. A creator of abstract paintings, he built tension and movement by means of deliberate, wide brush strokes in his large black and white canvases.

Klinger, Friedrich Maximilian (1752–1831). German dramatist of the STURM UND DRANG, which took its name from the title of his play of 1776. His works are noted for boldness of expression and freedom of form. Goethe helped him through Giessen university.

Klingsor or **Klingshor.** An evil magician in medieval German legend. His small role in Wolfram von Eschenbach's *Parzival* (13th century) is greatly expanded in Wagner's opera PARSIFAL. He also appears in the stories of the WARTBURG singing contest.

Klondike. A region in the Yukon Territory of Canada, famous for its gold mines. See Robert William SERVICE.

Klopstock, Friedrich Gottlieb (1724–1803). German poet in the movement of irrationalism. In his preference for classical forms, especially the elegy and ode, and in his virtually total rejection of rhyme, he was consciously attempting to develop for the German language a classical perfection of its own that would place it on a par with Greek and Latin. His

major work is a religious epic in hexameters, *Der Messias (The Messiah,* 1773; final version, 1800), which shows the influence of Milton and pietism. He was deeply patriotic and hoped to be remembered as a prophet of his country's future greatness. This side of him appears in much of his lyric and in his dramatic trilogy (1769–1787) celebrating Hermann, the Germanic hero who defeated the Romans in the first century. His most famous prose work, *Die Deutsche Gelehrtenrepublik (The German Republic of Letters,* 1774) proposes the outlines of a utopian state in Germany, and parallels the poet's more practical efforts toward the founding of a German Academy. See BODMER; GOTTINGER HAIN.

Klotho. See the FATES.

Knaben Wunderhorn, Des (*The Boy's Wonderhorn;* vol. 1, 1805; vol. 2, 1808; vol. 3, 1818). A collection of folk songs edited by Clemens BRENTANO and Achim von ARNIM, named for the first song in it. As opposed to Herder's earlier cosmopolitan collection of *Volkslieder (Folk Songs,* 1778–1779), the *Wunderhorn* contains only German songs and was intended to draw attention specifically to the German folk spirit. It is not, however, a scholarly work, for Brentano and Arnim frequently made their own changes in the material they collected.

Knecht, Josef. The hero of Hesse's MAGISTER LUDI. Though he rises to the position of master in the hierarchy of the glass-bead game, the fact that his name in German means servant is a central indication of the book's pervasive irony. Even as he dominates the game, he is dominated by it.

Kneller, Sir Godfrey (1649?–1723). German-born English portrait painter. Highly successful, he served English kings from Charles II to George I.

Knickerbocker, Diedrich. A character invented by Washington IRVING.

Knickerbocker's History of New York. See HISTORY OF NEW YORK FROM THE BEGINNING OF THE WORLD TO THE END OF THE DUTCH DYNASTY, A; Washington IRVING.

Knight, Eric (1897–1943). Anglo-American writer. Knight's best-known tales are laid in Yorkshire, particularly *The Flying Yorkshireman* (1937), in which he created the character of Sam Small. His other works include the popular juvenile *Lassie Come Home* (1940), the novel *This Above All* (1941), and the short-story collection *Sam Small Flies Again* (1942).

Knight, G[eorge] Wilson (1897–   ). English literary critic. His studies of Shakespeare's plays were controversial and influential; in them he treats the plays as poems expressing cosmic ideas through patterns of imagery. Among his books are *The Wheel of Fire* (1930), *The Shakespearean Tempest* (1932), *The Mutual Flame* (1955), and *The Golden Labyrinth* (1962).

Knight, Sarah Kemble. Known as **Madam Knight** (1666–1727). American schoolteacher. She is known for the diary in which she recorded observations and impressions of a journey made on horseback from Boston to New York in the winter of 1704–1705. Published in 1825, her *Journal* is a firsthand source of information on the transportation, housing, manners, and speech of early 18th-century New England.

Knightly, Mr. See EMMA.

Knight of the Burning Pestle, The (c. 1607). A comedy by Francis Beaumont. (See BEAUMONT AND FLETCHER.) A performance of a play called *The London Merchant* is interrupted by a grocer who insists upon interspersing it with scenes from his own concoction, *The Knight of the Burning Pestle*, with his apprentice Ralph in the leading role. In the hilarious potpourri that follows, hackneyed sentimental scenes from bourgeois romance are laced with scenes from the grocer's effort, a parody of chivalric romance with Ralph cast as a kind of Don Quixote. The whole thing is continuously interrupted with comments by the grocer and his wife.

Knight of the Garter. See GARTER, ORDER OF THE.

Knights, The (Hippeis). A comedy by Aristophanes. Because of its political topicality, this play is less interesting to modern audiences than some others by Aristophanes. It is remarkable, however, for the freedom with which the playwright is able to attack the powerful Athenian demagogue CLEON and for the fact that it was awarded a first prize.

Knight's Gambit (1939). A book of interrelated stories by William FAULKNER. Dealing with the various inhabitants of YOKNAPATAWPHA COUNTY, *Knight's Gambit* is a collection of detective stories in which Gavin STEVENS, the county attorney, ferrets out the real culprits and saves the innocent. The book is ingenious and skillfully narrated; perhaps the best story is *Monk*, which deals with an idiot who is imprisoned for a murder he did not commit and who finally is incited to kill the warden who has befriended him.

Knights of Labor. A pioneer U.S. labor organization. Founded as a secret league in Philadelphia in 1869, it aimed at the regulation of wages, of the degree of skill to be exacted from workmen, and of the length of a day's work, as well as attempting to control strikes. The league decided when a strike was to take place and when the workmen of the union might resume work.

Knights of Malta. First called "Knights of St. John of Jerusalem," otherwise "Knights of Rhodes," the most celebrated religious military order of the Middle Ages.

Knight's Tale, The. One of the CANTERBURY TALES of Geoffrey CHAUCER, a chivalric romance adapted from Boccaccio's *Teseida*. Theseus of Athens defeats Creon at Thebes, and the royal Theban cousins Palamon and Arcite are imprisoned in a tower. They see Emily, sister of Theseus' wife Hippolyta, walking in a garden; both fall in love with her. Arcite is released and banished from the territory, but he returns and works disguised as a court servant. Palamon escapes from prison, also determined to win Emily; the cousins meet by accident and determine to fight the next day in knightly regalia for the right to love her. Theseus interrupts the battle and orders that in a year the combatants will each bring 100 knights to a tourney. Emily prays to Diana that both warriors will forget their quarrel and desert her, but her prayer is rejected. Palamon prays to Venus that he may win his beloved, while Arcite prays to Mars that he may triumph in the battle. Accordingly, Saturn arranges that Arcite be victorious in the joust, but be thrown by his horse as he rides toward Emily. Dying, he yields Emily to Palamon,

and after a suitable time the two are happily married.

Knoblock, Edward (1874–1945). British playwright, scenarist, and novelist. His works include *Kismet* (1911), *Milestones* (with Arnold Bennett; 1921), and *Grand Hotel* (from the novel by Vicki Baum).

Knowles, James Sheridan (1784–1862). Irish-born English playwright and actor. He wrote both verse tragedies, such as *Caius Gracchus* (1815) and *Virginius* (1820), and comedies, such as *The Hunchback* (1832) and *The Love-Chase* (1837).

Know-Nothing party. In U.S. history, a popular name for the American party, which reached its greatest influence in 1854–1855. Its program called for the exclusion of Catholics and foreigners from public office and for other nativist measures. It was originally a secret society whose members answered questions with "I don't know." The party split over the slavery issue and faded after the election of 1856.

Knox, John (1505–1572). Scottish reformer and founder of Presbyterianism. He was twice at Geneva in personal contact with Calvin (1554, 1556–1558). He published six tracts dealing with religion in Scotland; the best known are his *Blasts of the Trumpet Against the Monstrous Regiment of Women* (1st and 2nd, 1558). They were not meant for Queen Elizabeth but offended her deeply. Knox preached throughout Scotland against Mary Queen of Scots, whom he simply called "Jezebel," and against Catholicism in general.

Knut. See CANUTE.

kōan (Ch. *Kung-an*). In ZEN Buddhism, the problem or case to be meditated upon. Frequently paradoxical, and usually concerned with the sayings and actions of Chinese CH'AN (Zen) masters, it is one of the methods used for training in Japanese Rinzai Zen. A *kōan* is always studied under the guidance of a Zen master. There are some 1,700 *kōans*.

Kobayashi Issa (1763–1827). Japanese *haiku* poet. He is noted for the humorous and simple treatment of his subjects. He was a prolific writer of both poetry and prose.

Kober, Arthur (1900–   ). Polish-born American writer and playwright. Kober is noted for his dialect stories set in the Bronx or Hollywood. These appeared in the *New Yorker* and were later reissued in several books, the best known being *Having Wonderful Time* (1937), the story of a group of vacationers in the Berkshires who try to improve themselves culturally. It became a play (1937) and was later made into a successful musical called *Wish You Were Here* (1952).

kobold. In German folklore a mischievous house spirit, similar to Robin Goodfellow or the Scottish Brownie. It is also a gnome who works in the mines and forests.

Koch, Martin (1882–1940). Swedish journalist and author. A pioneer in the Swedish proletarian novel, Koch describes the strike of 1909 and the struggles of laborers in his naturalistic novel *Arbetare* (*Workers*, 1912). His concern with social problems appeared again in *Guds vackra värld* (*God's Lovely World*, 2 vols., 1916), a treatment of crime.

Koch, Robert (1843–1910). German physician, one of the pioneers of modern bacteriology. He discovered the anthrax and tuberculosis bacilli and did research on cholera, malaria, and other diseases. He was awarded the Nobel Prize for medicine in 1905.

Koel or **Kokila.** An Indian bird often mentioned in imaginative writing. The poignance of the koel's song is supposed to convey the sad sweetness of frustrated or alienated love. In Sanskrit it is called the *parabhrita,* "brought up by another," because the female koel leaves her eggs in the nest of a crow, where they are hatched.

Koestler, Arthur (1905–   ). Hungarian novelist and essayist. Bilingual from childhood, Koestler became a German-language journalist and a writer of popular articles on science. In 1926 he left Europe for Palestine, and remained in the Near East for some time. His life from his childhood until the end of this period is described in the first volume of his autobiography, *Arrow in the Blue* (1952). In 1931 he became a member of the Communist Party. While covering the Spanish Civil War for an English newspaper, he was captured by the Fascists early in 1937 and spent three months in prison under sentence of death before being released through British intervention. His war and prison experiences he recorded in *Spanish Testament* (1938) and in the shorter *Dialogue with Death* (1942). *The Invisible Writing* (1954), the second volume of his autobiography, deals with the seven-year period of his membership in the Communist Party. At the beginning of the Second World War he was arrested in France as a refugee and sent to the detention camp at Le Vernet, about which he wrote in *Scum of the Earth* (1941). He was released in 1940, and after the end of the war became a British subject.

Among his nonfiction works are *The Yogi and the Commissar* (1945), essays; *Promise and Fulfillment* (1949), a report of the fighting between the Jews and the Arabs after the partition of Palestine; *Insight and Outlook* (1949); *The Trail of the Dinosaur* (1955); *Reflections on Hanging* (1957), which helped end capital punishment, except in special cases, in England; and *The Lotus and the Robot* (1961), an examination of Eastern and Western thought. He is perhaps best known for his novel *Darkness at Noon* (1941), based on the Moscow trials during the 1930's. His other novels include *The Gladiators* (1939), based on Spartacus and the slave revolt; *Arrival and Departure* (1943); *Thieves in the Night* (1946), a story of Jewish settlers of Palestine in the 1930's; and *The Age of Longing* (1951).

Kohlhaas, Michael. See MICHAEL KOHLHAAS.

Kokoschka, Oskar (1886–   ). Austrian painter and playwright. Known as an exponent of EXPRESSIONISM, he is primarily significant as a painter. His plays, however, with their tendency to depict extreme human agony in almost abstract terms and with their use of an ecstatic and compressed diction, contributed considerably to the development of expressionist dramatic style. The best known are *Mörder, Hoffnung der Frauen* (*Murderer, Hope of Women,* 1907), *Hiob* (*Job,* 1917), and *Orpheus and Eurydice* (1918).

Kolchak, Aleksandr Vasilyevich (1874–1920). Russian admiral. The leader of the anti-Bolshevik forces in the Far East during the civil war in Russia, he advanced far into western Russia before having to retreat. He was captured and executed by the Bolsheviks.

Komsomol. The youth organization of the Soviet Communist Party.

Königsmarke, The Long Finne: A Story of the New World (1823). A novel by James Kirke PAULDING. An amusing satire, the book tells of the trials of a Finnish immigrant in the Delaware colony of New Sweden.

Koo, V[i] K[yuin] Wellington (1887–   ). Chinese statesman. He represented his country on the Council of the League of Nations (1932–1934); was ambassador to France (1936–1941); ambassador to England (1941–1946); ambassador to the U.S. (1946–1956). "Wellington" became part of his name through sound association with the original Wei-chün.

Kopit, Arthur (1937–   ). American playwright. His plays, often distinguished by their dark humor, by their mixing of realistic and antirealistic elements, and by the longest titles in theatrical history—except, perhaps, for those of the Restoration—have caused certain critics to classify him among the playwrights of the absurd. His works include *On the Runway of Life You Never Know What's Coming off Next* (1958); *Oh Dad, Poor Dad, Mama's Hung You in the Closet and I'm Feeling So Sad* (1960); *The Day the Whores Came out to Play Tennis* (1963); and *Mhil'daiim* (1963).

Korah. An Old Testament Levite, his name signifying "ice." He led a rebellion against Moses and Aaron for which he was swallowed by the earth (Num. 16; 26:9–11). His descendants, the Korahites, were temple musicians.

Koran. The ISLAM Bible, the sacred book of the Muslims. In Arabic, the word means reading, from *quran;* the variant form, *Alcoran,* has a prefixed article. Written in the purest Arabic, it is considered the Word of God, the uncreated and eternal truth revealed to Muhammad by the angel Gabriel. The tradition that the text should be transmitted orally had to be broken under the third Caliph, Othman, when the best Koran reciters had fallen in battle. There are 114 *Suras* or chapters in the Koran, unnumbered but individually named. Historically, the subject matter is of Jewish, and to a lesser extent, of Christian origin.

Kore. See PERSEPHONE.

Korneichuk, Alexander Evdokimovich (1905–   ). Russian dramatist. Noted for their use of Ukrainian themes and their strong nationalistic and militaristic devotion to the Soviet regime, his plays include *On the Ukrainian Steppes* (1941), a sequel, *Guerillas on the Ukrainian Steppes* (1942), *The Front* (1942), *The Sinking of the Squadron* (1934), *Truth* (1937) and *Mr. Perkins' Mission to the Land of the Bolsheviks* (1944). He has won three Stalin Prizes.

Körner, Theodor (1791–1813). German patriotic poet who died in the wars of liberation against Napoleon (1813–1815). His best-known collection is *Leier und Schwert* (*Lyre and Sword,* 1814).

Kornilov, Lavr Georgyevich (1870–1918). Russian general. The commander of the troops in Petrograd after the revolution (1917), he attempted to overthrow the Kerenski regime, and afterwards fought against the Bolsheviks in the civil war until his death.

Korobochka. A dull-witted woman landowner in Nikolai Gogol's DEAD SOULS. Her fear that Chichikov, the swindler-protagonist of the novel, may be cheating her in their strange business deal is instrumental in exposing Chichikov.

Korolenko, Vladimir Galaktionovich (1853–1921). Russian writer and political radical. He was instrumental in helping the young Maksim Gorki get his start in literature. Korolenko, who was exiled to Siberia for six years by the Czarist government, was also opposed to the Bolshevik regime, an attitude he forcefully expressed in letters to Anatol Lunacharski, the future commissar of education. Korolenko's best works are *Makar's Dream* (*Son makara;* 1885), a short story depicting the death of a Siberian native; *Tongueless* (*Bez yazyka;* 1895), a humorous story of three non-English speaking peasants in America; and *The History of My Contemporary* (*Istoriya moego sovremennika;* 1910–1922), an autobiographical work.

korrigans. Nine fays of Breton folklore. They can predict future events, assume any shape they like, move as quickly as thought from place to place, and cure diseases or wounds. They are not more than two feet high, have long flowing hair, which they are fond of combing, dress only in a white veil, and are excellent singers. Their favorite haunt is beside some fountain. They flee at the sound of a bell or benediction, and their breath is most deadly.

Korzybski, Alfred [Habdank] [Count] (1879–1950). Polish-born American semanticist. Korzybski came to the U.S. in about 1915. He founded what he called "general semantics," an approach to semantics that rejects the Aristotelian language structure, with its *is* of identity, as tending to confuse words with the things for which they stand, to see propositions as either "right" or "wrong," and to limit severely the levels of abstraction. Among his writings is *Science and Sanity: An Introduction to Non-Aristotelian Systems and General Semantics* (1933). With other general semanticists, he often expressed his views in *ETC., A Review of General Semantics.*

Koshar-wa-Khasis. Divine artisan of the Canaanite pantheon. In THE POEMS OF BAAL and THE POEM OF AQHAT, he fashions weapons and palaces for the gods. In this respect he is clearly parallel with the Greek HEPHAESTUS. His Phoenician counterpart seems to be Chusor.

Koskenniemi, Veikko Antero. Pen name of V. A. Forsnäs (1885–1962). Finnish poet. A university professor and scholar, he is known for his skill as a lyric poet. Careful artistry and subdued melancholy characterize the poems of *Runoja* (1906) and *Sydän ja Kuolema* (1919) and the ballads of *Kurkiaura* (1930).

Kotzebue, August von (1761–1819). German dramatist. His *Sämtliche dramatische Werke* (*Complete Dramatic Works,* 1827 ff.) fill 44 volumes, but though he was popular in his time, none of his plays is today considered any more than oversentimentalized melodrama. He was ridiculed by the poets of German romanticism, and his reactionary political writings led to his murder by a university student.

Koussevitzky, Sergey Alexandrovitch (1874–1951). Russian-born conductor. He began his career as a performer on the double-bass, first conducted publicly in Berlin (1908), and came to the U.S. to conduct the Boston Symphony Orchestra (1924–1949).

He directed the Berkshire Music Festival at Tanglewood and championed modern music.

Krafft-Ebing, Baron Richard von (1840–1902). German neurologist. His *Psychopathia Sexualis* (1886) is a famous collection of psychiatric case histories.

Kramm, Joseph (1908–). American playwright. He is best known for *The Shrike* (1952), a play about a man who tries to commit suicide to escape an overpossessive wife. It won a Pulitzer Prize.

Krapp's Last Tape (1958). A one-act play by Samuel BECKETT. Its one character, Krapp, an old man, plays back tapes of monologues he recorded when young and ridicules the passions and ambitions of his youth and middle years, which have come to nothing. In the light of his broken-down old age, hope and optimism seem absurd, and we are made aware of the futility and meaninglessness of life.

Kreisler, Fritz (1875–1962). Austrian-born violin virtuoso and composer. His colorful career includes an amusing hoax by which he convinced the public that many of his own works were written by Baroque or Classical composers. He wrote some memoirs: *Four Weeks in the Trenches: The War Story of a Violinist* (1915) about his experiences in the Austrian army.

Kremlin. A walled section of Moscow, containing cathedrals and palaces dating back to the 15th century. There are 20 towers of various sizes and architectural styles. The largest building, the Great Kremlin Palace, is now used for sessions of the Supreme Soviet, the Soviet Union's governing body. Until Peter the Great moved the capital to St. Petersburg in 1712, the Kremlin was the residence of the Czars. After the revolution it became the seat of government and a symbol of Soviet power.

Kretzer, Max (1854–1941). German novelist. He is known only for his early works, which show affinities with the movement of naturalism, especially *Die Betrogenen* (*The Betrayed Ones,* 1882), *Die Verkommenen* (*The Fallen Ones,* 1883), and *Meister Timpe* (*Master Timpe,* 1888). All these novels stress the needs of the proletariat and reflect Kretzer's socialist sympathies.

Kriemhild. Heroine of the NIBELUNGENLIED, known as **Gudrun** in the VÖLSUNGA SAGA and **Gutrune** in Wagner's RING DES NIBELUNGEN.

Krishna (*Sansk.,* "the black one"). One of the greatest of the Hindu deities. The god of fire, lightning, storms, the heavens, and the sun, he is usually regarded as the eighth *avatar* of VISHNU. One legend relates that Kamsa, the demon-king of Mathura, committed great ravages so that Brahma prayed to Vishnu to relieve the world of this distress. Vishnu plucked off two hairs, one white, the other black, and promised they would revenge the wrongs of the demon-king. The black hair became Krishna.

Another legend says that Krishna was the son of Vasudeva and Devaki. When he was born among the Yadava tribe at Mathura, between Delhi and Agra, his uncle King Kamsa, who had been warned by a prophecy that this nephew would slay him, sought to kill Krishna, who was, however, smuggled away. He was brought up by shepherds, and later he killed his uncle and became king of the Yadavas. He is often represented playing on his divine flute and attracting the *gopis* or cowherdesses to dance the *rasa-lila* around him in the moonlight. To Arjuna on the battlefield (see Bhagavadgita), he becomes a provider of divine consolation and inspiration. See Mahabharata.

Kriss Kringle. The Pennsylvania Dutch Santa Claus. On Christmas Eve, arrayed in a fur cap and strange apparel, he goes to the bedroom of each good child, where he leaves a present in the stocking that is hung up in expectation of his visit. The word is a dialectal variant of High German *Christkindle*, "the little Christ child," and has undergone such radical changes because it is no longer associated with either of its component parts.

Kristin Lavransdatter (1920–1922). A trilogy of historical novels by Sigrid Undset. Re-creating a woman's life in the devout Catholic Norway of the 13th and 14th centuries, this great romance appeared in successive volumes: *The Bridal Wreath* (*Kransen;* 1920), *The Mistress of Husaby* (*Husfrue;* 1921), and *The Cross* (*Korset;* 1922).

Kröger, Tonio. See Tonio Kröger.

Kronos. See Cronos.

Krook. In Charles Dickens' Bleak House, proprietor of a rag-and-bone warehouse where everything seems to be bought and nothing sold. He is a grasping drunkard who eventually dies of spontaneous combustion.

Kropotkin, Prince Piotr Alekseyevich (1842–1921). Russian social philosopher and geographer. A leading theorist of anarchism, Kropotkin took part during the 1870's in the revolutionary movement against the Czarist government. To escape arrest, he emigrated to Europe and settled in England (1876). He returned to Russia in 1917, but was no friendlier to the Bolsheviks than he had been to the Czars. His most famous book, *Zapiski revolyutzionera* (*Memoirs of a Revolutionist,* 1899), describes the social ferment in Russia during the reign of Alexander II.

Krull, Felix. See Confessions of Felix Krull: Confidence Man.

Krupp. A German family in control of the corporation that built and managed the greatest ordnance works in modern Germany. The firm was founded in 1811 by Friedrich Krupp (1787–1826) as a steel mill, and expanded rapidly under Alfred Krupp (1812–1887). Bertha Krupp (1886–1957), who controlled the firm during World War I, gave her name to the long-range gun, Big Bertha. After World War II, production shifted to peacetime machinery. Alfred Krupp von Bohlen und Halbach (1907–   ) is now the sole owner.

Krutch, Joseph Wood (1893–   ). American critic, essayist, and teacher. Krutch was a drama critic for *The Nation* for many years, as well as an English professor at Columbia University and elsewhere. His critical works include *Edgar Allan Poe: A Study of Genius* (1926), one of the first psychoanalytical interpretations of literature; *Five Masters, a Study in the Mutations of the Novel* (1929); and *The American Drama Since 1918* (1939; revised in 1957). His essays are collected in *The Modern Temper* (1929), *The Measure of Man* (1954), and *Human Nature and the Human Condition* (1959), in which he discussed the need for humanistic values in a mechanized so-

ciety. *The Desert Year* (1952) and *The Best of Two Worlds* (1953) deal with natural history.

Krylov, Ivan Andreyevich (1769–1844). Russian fabulist. In his early career both dramatist and journalist, Krylov published his collections of fables from 1809 on. They have become classics in Russian literature and were translated into English by the British historian Sir Bernard Pares in 1927.

Kshatriya. See caste.

Kuan-yin (Sans. *Avalokiteśvara;* Jap. *Kannon*). Chinese Buddhist deity, the Bodhisattva of Mercy. She is much represented in painting and sculpture and the object of popular veneration.

Kubera or **Kuvera.** In Hindu mythology, the god of wealth. He was the half-brother of Ravana, the demon-king of Ceylon.

Kublai Khan (1216–1294). Mongol emperor of China after 1259 and grandson of Genghis Khan. He established his court at what is now Peking (1264) and founded the Yuan dynasty, which ended in 1368. His kingdom, finally extending as far as Russia, flourished under his patronage of commerce and culture. His reign was vividly described by Marco Polo, and the splendor of his court inspired S. T. Coleridge's poem Kubla Khan.

Kubla Khan (1797). An unfinished poem by Samuel Taylor Coleridge. According to Coleridge, the poem was composed in an opium-induced sleep; when he awoke he immediately began to set it down, but was interrupted by a visitor, and when he returned to his task, he found that the rest of the poem had vanished from his memory. A precursor, to some extent, of both symbolism and surrealism, the poem is considered one of his best. See Xanadu.

Kūkai (774–835). Japanese priest, founder of Shingon Buddhism. The most literate scholar of his time, he was influential in the introduction of Chinese learning to Japan. His command of the Chinese language and the diversity of his writings marks him as one of the major literary figures of the early Heian period (794–1185). He is known posthumously as Kōbō Daishi.

Ku Klux Klan. A name given to two American secret societies. The original Ku Klux Klan was formed about 1866, in Pulaski, Tenn.; an organization for ex-Confederates, it was dedicated to Southern white political supremacy. It developed into a secret society whose purpose was frightening Negroes into submission. In April, 1867, the Grand Wizard or Cyclops of the Pulaski group, Nathan Bedford Forrest, called a convention of delegates to Nashville. At

Poster of the Klan dealing with carpetbaggers (1869).

this convention the Klan declared its principles, which were to protect the weak and aid the enforcement of the Constitution. Two years later, Forrest disbanded the group when it proved to be an instrument of violence. In 1870 and 1871, Congress passed the Ku Klux Klan acts, to deal with offenders.

In 1915, a new Ku Klux Klan was organized on a nationwide basis in Georgia. Its avowed aims were to maintain "pure Americanism" and white supremacy; it attacked Negroes, Catholics, Jews, as well as such ideas as birth control, Darwinism, pacifism, and the repeal of prohibition. In the early 20's, the Klan was reputed to have a membership of 5 million throughout the U.S. After its terroristic activities were exposed in newspapers after 1923, it began to splinter and decline; it still exists, but in a limited form.

Many novelists have written about the Klan, both favorably and unfavorably. In Thomas Nelson Page's Red Rock, the hero is a Klan leader. A clergyman, Thomas Dixon, Jr., made the Klan the subject of several novels, including the sensational *Clansman* (1905); this novel, the basis of the motion picture *The Birth of a Nation* (1915), is credited with reviving interest in the society. Two anti-Klan novels are Howard Fast's *Freedom Road* (1944) and Ward Greene's *King Cobra* (1940).

The name of the society is taken from the Greek word *kuklos*, meaning band or circle; it is often referred to with the abbreviation K. K. K.

kulak. A wealthy Russian peasant. The name, derived from the word for "fist," was used derogatorily by Soviet authorities who exterminated the class in the 1920's to make way for the collectivization of agriculture.

Kulhwch and Olwen (c. 1100). One of the tales in the Welsh Mabinogion. This prose narrative is especially important, being perhaps the earliest, full-fledged Arthurian romance. Kulhwch, the hero, gains the help of Arthur and his followers in accomplishing the hard tasks set by the giant Ysbaddaden, whose beautiful daughter Olwen he seeks to win.

Kulturkampf (*Ger.*, cultural battle). The struggle between Bismarck and the Roman Catholic church in the 1870's. Considering the church a threat to national unity, Bismarck imposed laws restricting Catholic worship and education, expelled the Jesuits, and forced many bishops into exile.

Kumara. See Karttikeya.

Kumarbi. In Hurrian mythology, the supreme god. Kumarbi is probably best known for his role in the Hittite myth of the Stone Monster. After nine years as vizier of the sky god Anu, Kumarbi revolted. He won the ensuing battle by emasculating Anu with his teeth, but was soon alarmed to discover that Anu's two children were growing inside him. After a good deal of trial and error, Kumarbi managed to give birth to them. The second of these children promptly overthrew Kumarbi and replaced his true father, Anu, on the throne. On the advice of the lord of the sea, Kumarbi now impregnated a mountain, which, in due course, labored mightily and brought forth a baby made of stone. The delighted Kumarbi named the infant Ullikummi and arranged to have it placed on the right shoulder of Upelluri, the giant who held up earth and heaven, standing in the midst of the ocean. The stone child grew most remarkably,

and soon his immense size threatened to topple heaven itself. Neither the might of the gods nor the wiles of Ishtar could prevail against it. Finally, Ea, the god of wisdom, severed his legs at the ankles with a magic knife, and the stone monster fell into the sea. Thus ended Kumarbi's revolt.

Kunitz, Stanley J[asspon] (1905-   ). American poet and editor. Though his work is not widely known, Kunitz is regarded as one of the better American metaphysical poets. His first volume of poetry was *Intellectual Things* (1930); *Passport to the War* appeared in 1944. His *Selected Poems, 1928-1958* (1958) was awarded a Pulitzer Prize. With Howard Haycraft he has edited a number of biographical dictionaries of authors, including *British Authors of the Nineteenth Century* (1936), *American Authors: 1600-1900* (1938), *Twentieth Century Authors* (1942), and *British Authors before 1800* (1952).

Künstlerroman (*Ger.*, artist novel). A type of novel popular in German romanticism. It is basically a Bildungsroman (novel of education) in which the hero finally becomes an artist or poet, and thus the form reflects a characteristic romantic interest in the growth of the artist as a person. The most important examples are Tieck's *Franz Sternbalds Wanderungen* (*Franz Sternbald's Wanderings*, 1798) and Novalis' *Heinrich von Ofterdingen* (1802). In later literature, Joyce's *A Portrait of the Artist as a Young Man* (1916) is such an artist novel.

Kuomintang. The three parts of this Chinese term mean *nation, people,* and *party.* The Kuomintang is the nationalist, republican party that was organized chiefly by Dr. Sun Yat-sen and gained control of most of China in 1926-1927. After years of civil war, the communists finally gained control of the mainland (1949) and the Kuomintang, under Chiang Kai-shek, was forced to Taiwan, which it now governs.

Kuprin, Aleksandr Ivanovich (1870-1938). Russian novelist and short-story writer. Kuprin left Russia during the civil war, but returned two years before his death. His work covers a wide range of subjects. Best known are the short novel *Poyedinok* (*The Duel,* 1905), a story of army life in a provincial garrison; *Yama* (*The Pit,* 1915), an account of a Russian brothel; *V tzirke* (*The Circus Wrestlers,* 1905); *Shtabs-kapitan Rybnikov* (*Captain Rybnikov,* 1906), a spy story; and *Granatovyi braslet* (*The Bracelet of Garnets,* 1911), a sentimental love story.

Kur. The Sumerian underworld and the dragon-like lord thereof. He carried off Ereshkigal and fought with Enki, who pursued him. He was destroyed in two other myths by Ninurta and Inanna, respectively. Obviously related to many other dragons slain by heroes of Semitic mythology, he also seems to have had some of the characteristics of the Greek Hades.

Kurma. See Vishnu.

Kürnberger, Ferdinand (1821-1879). German novelist. He is most famous for his *Der Amerika-Müde* (*Tired of America,* 1855), which treats the life of Nikolaus Lenau.

Kurosawa Akira (1910-   ). Japanese film director. A large number of his films have been successfully shown in the West. *Rashōmon* won first prize at the Venice Film Festival (1951).

Kurtz. See HEART OF DARKNESS.

Kuru. In Hindu mythology, a legendary monarch. From him are descended the Kauravas and Pandavas, whose contests form the subject of the epic, the *Mahabharata.* He was a prince of the lunar race, reigning over the country around Delhi.

Kurusu Saburo (1888–1954). Japanese diplomat. He was special envoy to the U.S. (Nov.–Dec., 1941) during negotiations cut short by the attack on Pearl Harbor.

Kuvera. See KUBERA.

Kyd, Thomas (1557?–1594). English dramatist. A scrivener by profession, Kyd became the author of the most popular drama of his day with his Senecan revenge-play THE SPANISH TRAGEDY (produced between 1584 and 1589). He may have written a lost play on Hamlet, and is thought to have worked on parts of Shakespeare's *Titus Andronicus* and *Henry VI. Arden of Feversham* is sometimes attributed to him, as is the anonymously published *Soliman and Perseda* (written c. 1588). In 1593 he was sharing a room with Christopher Marlowe, and was arrested with him for atheism and heresy. Possibly suffering from his imprisonment and disgrace, he died the following year.

Kyoto. Old capital of Japan (794–1868), formerly known as Heian. It was the site of the imperial court until moved to Tokyo in the Meiji period (1868–1912). Famous as a cultural and sight-seeing center, it has numerous Shinto shrines, Buddhist temples, objects of art, and places of scenic beauty.

Kyrie eleison (Gr., "Lord have mercy"). Originally an invocation to the Greek sungod. This petition is the first fixed chant in most Western Eucharistic liturgies, and is also used in the liturgies of the Eastern churches.

L

Laban. In the Old Testament, the uncle of JA-COB and father of Leah and Rachel. Jacob served him for 14 years in order to marry Rachel.

labarum. The standard borne before the Roman emperors. It consisted of a gilded spear with an eagle on the top. From a cross-staff hung a splendid purple streamer, with a gold fringe, adorned with precious stones. CONSTANTINE THE GREAT added Christian symbols to the Roman military symbols at the time of his vision and subsequent conversion to Christianity.

Labé, Louise (1524?–1566?). French poet. Celebrated for her talent and beauty, she was one of the best-known of the school of French poets centered at Lyons. In the elegies and sonnets included in her *Oeuvres* (1555), she expressed in a direct, intense style the torments of a passionate nature which had been profoundly marked by an unhappy love. The wife of a wealthy rope-maker, she was sometimes called *la belle cordière*.

Labe, Queen. The Circe of the Arabians, who, by her enchantments, transformed men into horses and other brute beasts. She is introduced into the *Arabian Nights* when Beder, a prince of Persia, marries her, defeats her plots against him, and turns her into a mare. Restored to her proper shape by her mother, she turns Beder into an owl, but the prince ultimately regains his own form.

Labiche, Eugène [Marin] (1815–1888). French playwright. Responding to the Second Empire's demand for farcical comedy, Labiche wrote a long series of popular plays including *Un Chapeau de paille d'Italie* (1851) and *La Poudre aux yeux* (1862). The delightful *Le Voyage de M. Perrichon* (1860)—perhaps his best-known comedy—was written in collaboration with Edouard Martin.

labors of Hercules. See HERACLES.

La Bruyère, Jean de (1645–1696). French writer and moralist of the neoclassical period. La Bruyère's sympathies lay with the ancients in their literary battle with the moderns, and, in addition to being conservative, his outlook was deeply misanthropic. His most famous work, *Caractères de Théophraste traduits du grec, avec les caractères ou les Moeurs de ce siècle* (*Characters of Theophrastus Translated from the Greek, with Characters or the Manners of This Century*, 1688), is a piece of social satire in the manner of Theophrastus, combining maxims with character portraits of French social types and individuals of the day.

Labyrinth (Labyrinthos). The palace of Minos in Knossos, the Minoan capital of Crete, said to have been devised by Daedalus. According to the legend, it was a mazelike building in the center of which the MINOTAUR was imprisoned. The word has come to be applied to any structure with many confusing passages. The origin of the word is not known, but it may be connected with *labros,* the double ax constantly used in the religious symbolism of ancient Crete.

Labyrinthine Ways, The. See POWER AND THE GLORY, THE.

La Calprenède, Gauthier de Costes de (1610–1663). French dramatist and novelist. He is best known for his enormous historical romances: *Cassandre* (10 vols., 1642–1645), *Cléopâtre* (12 vols., 1648) and *Pharamond, ou l'histoire de France* (12 vols., 1661–1663). La Calprenède's novels abound in complex plots, detailed descriptions, literary portraits, and Oriental settings.

Lacedaemon (Lakedaimon). An ancient name of Laconia, and of SPARTA, its chief city. (See LACONIC.)

La Chaise, Père François d'Aix de (1624–1709). French Jesuit confessor to Louis XIV. His favorite retreat near Paris later became the site of the cemetery popularly known as the *cimetière du Père-La-chaise.*

Lachaise, Gaston (1882–1935). French-born American sculptor. He is known for his long series of ample, vigorous female figures.

La Chaussée, Pierre Claude Nivelle de (1692–1754). French dramatist, inventor and champion of the COMÉDIE LARMOYANTE (*Fr.,* "sentimental comedy"). His most famous play is *Le Préjugé à la mode* (1735), in which the fashionable attitude of making light of a wife's love is criticized. Many of his other plays, among which are *Mélanide* (1741) and *L'Ecole des mères* (1744), are somewhat moralizing. He was elected to the ACADÉMIE FRANÇAISE in 1736.

Lachesis. See the FATES.

Laclos, Pierre [Ambroise François] Choderlos de (1741–1803). French artillery officer and author of the epistolary novel LES LIAISONS DANGEREUSES. The novel depicts the immorality of his times, particularly corrupt and cynical seducers of innocence. He was a member of the JACOBIN club, became a general, and played an important military role in the French Revolution.

Laconic, Laconian. Pertaining to Laconia or its main city, SPARTA. Hence laconic, sparing of words, as the Spartans were reputed to be.

Lacretelle, Jacques de (1888–   ). French novelist. His books are usually psychological analyses of lonely characters, such as *Silbermann* (1922), about a young Jewish student, and *Les Hauts Ponts* (4 vols., 1932–1935), about a woman's passion for her family estate. Other novels include *Marie Bonifas* (1925) and *A Man's Life (Amour Nuptial;* 1929).

Ladislaw, Will. In George Eliot's MIDDLEMARCH, the gay young artist whom Dorothea Brooke marries after the death of her first husband, the desiccated Mr. Casaubon.

Lady Chatterley's Lover (1928). A novel by D. H. LAWRENCE, presenting the author's mystical theories of sex in the story of Constance, or Connie, the wife of an English aristocrat who runs away with her gamekeeper. Her husband, Sir Clifford, is a physical and emotional cripple. The gamekeeper, MELLORS, is a forthright, individualistic man, uncontaminated by industrial society. Because of the frank language and detailed descriptions of love-making, the book was banned in England and the U.S. as obscene. After historic court cases the ban was lifted in the U.S. in 1959 and in England in 1960.

Lady Day. See ANNUNCIATION, THE DAY OF THE.

Lady Geraldine's Courtship (1844). A poem by Elizabeth Barrett BROWNING. The lady falls in love with a peasant-poet, whom she marries. The poem contained a tribute to the poetry of Robert Browning, which prompted a warm letter from him and their subsequent meeting, romance, and marriage.

Lady Into Fox (1922). A novel by David GARNETT. It is a delicate, solemn fantasy about a man whose wife suddenly turns into a fox—and their consequent marital problems.

Lady Macbeth. See MACBETH.

Lady of Pleasure, The (1635). A comedy by James SHIRLEY. The good Sir Thomas Bornwell becomes increasingly alarmed at the growing extravagances of his wife, Aretina. Pretending to become converted to her spendthrift ways, he turns to gambling and begins paying attention to the beautiful widow, Celestina, Lady Bellamour. Eventually, as he had hoped, Aretina becomes alarmed and returns to modesty and thrift.

Lady of the Aroostook, The (1879). A novel by William Dean HOWELLS. Lydia Blood sails for Europe on the *Aroostook;* a delicate young schoolteacher, she is traveling for her health. The only woman passenger, she attracts the attention of Staniford, who gradually recognizes the nobility of character beneath her village rusticity. Lydia's Venetian relatives are interested only in knowing whether Staniford is socially suitable for her. Although Lydia is free of European social restraints, she reveals her upbringing in her shock at Sunday opera and Venetian immorality.

Lady of the Fountain, The. A medieval Welsh tale from the MABINOGION in which are found King Arthur and his court. This tale has a remarkable parallel in the story YVAIN by Chrétien de Troyes.

Lady of the Lake. In Arthurian legend, an obscure, supernatural figure endowed with magical powers. In Malory's *Morte d'Arthur* (c. 1469), she lives in a castle in the midst of a magical lake, which prevents access to her. She steals LAUNCELOT in his infancy and plunges with him into her home in the lake; hence, Launcelot comes to be called *Lancelot du Lac* (Launcelot of the Lake). When he has grown to manhood, she presents him to King Arthur. It is from the Lady of the Lake that Arthur receives the magical sword EXCALIBUR; he takes it from the mysterious arm extending above the surface of the lake.

She is also known as Nimuë or Vivien, the mistress of MERLIN, whom she ultimately imprisons forever in a tower. The Lady of the Lake appears in later works, notably in Tennyson's *Idylls of the King* (1859–1885) and James Branch Cabell's *Jurgen* (1919).

Lady of the Lake, The (1810). A long narrative poem by Sir Walter SCOTT. It tells of Ellen Douglas, who lives with her father near Loch Katrine, and of the varied fortunes of her suitors in troubled times of border warfare. One of her suitors is the king of Scotland, but she finally chooses the bold Malcolm Graeme.

Lady of the Lamp. See Florence NIGHTINGALE.

Lady or the Tiger?, The (1882). A short story by Frank R. STOCKTON. Stockton originally called the story *The King's Arena* and read it at a party given by a friend. Its reception there was so good that he elaborated it and sent it to the *Century Magazine.* It was the most famous story the magazine ever published; its plot was simple but unique. In a barbaric land a handsome youth is audacious enough to fall in love with the king's daughter and she with him. His offense is discovered, and he is condemned. In a great arena he must walk up to two doors and open one of them; behind one door is a beautiful maiden who would be given to him in marriage; behind the other is a ravenous tiger. The princess learns the secret of the doors and signals the young man to open the door on the right. Who comes out, asked Stockton, the lady or the tiger? Stockton wrote another story supposed to solve the puzzle, *The Discourager of Hesitancy* (1887), but it also cleverly left the query unanswered.

Lady's Not for Burning, The (1949). A play in verse by Christopher FRY.

Lady Windermere's Fan (1892). A comedy of manners by Oscar WILDE. Annoyed at her husband's persistent interest in Mrs. Erlynne, a woman of little reputation, Lady Windermere decides to leave him and run away with Lord Darlington. Mrs. Erlynne, actually Lady Windermere's mother who deserted her husband and daughter years ago for a lover who then left her, finds the note and rushes to Lord Darlington's apartments. Here, without revealing her identity, she persuades Lady Windermere not to take this rash step and succeeds in rushing her off in a carriage just as Lord Darlington appears with Lord Windermere. Lord Windermere immediately notices his wife's fan; Mrs. Erlynne comes forth and generously assumes guilt, saying that she mistook it for her own, thus saving her daughter's reputation at the expense of her own. She succeeds, however, in convincing Lord Augustus Lawton that it was in his interests that she came to Lord Darlington's rooms, and the two marry.

Laelaps. In classical mythology, a powerful dog. It was given by Artemis to Procris who gave it to Cephalus. While pursuing a wild boar it was metamorphosed into a stone. The name, which was originally that of one of Actaeon's fifty dogs, means "the hurricane."

Laelius. See DE AMICITIA.

Laertes. In Shakespeare's HAMLET, the son of Polonius and brother of Ophelia. A well-meaning but impetuous young man, he contrasts with the introspective and indecisive Hamlet, whose death he causes.

Laestrygonians (Laistrygones). A fabulous race of cannibal giants who lived in Sicily. Odysseus sent two of his men to request that he might land, but the king of the place ate one for dinner and the other fled. The Laestrygonians assembled on the coast and threw stones against Odysseus and his crew; they fled with all speed, but many men were lost.

La Farge, Christopher (1897–1956). American poet and novelist. Originally an architect by profession, La Farge published a long narrative poem, *Hoxsie Sells His Acres* (1934), dealing with childhood recollections and followed it in 1939 with *Each to the Other,* a novel in verse about a happy marriage. Among his other works are *Poems and Portraits* (1940); *The Wilsons* (1941), a collection of interrelated short stories; *Mesa Verde* (1945), a play in verse; and *The Sudden Guest* (1946), a novel about the 1938 and 1944 New England hurricanes. La Farge was a grandson of the artist John La Farge, a nephew of Father John La Farge, and a brother of Oliver La Farge.

La Farge, John (1880–1963). American Jesuit leader and writer. He became well known for his dedicated and highly successful work in rural American missions, which led to the founding of the National Catholic Rural Life Conference. Beginning in 1928, he was for many years the director of the Catholic Laymen's Union. From 1942 to 1948 he was first executive editor, then editor-in-chief of the Jesuit weekly *America,* and he continued as an editor for many years thereafter. Known for his contributions to the causes of minority groups, Father La Farge was the author of several books on the Jesuits and on racial problems. His highly praised autobiography, *The Manner Is Ordinary,* appeared in 1953, and he completed *Reflections on Growing Old* just a month before his death. He was an uncle of Oliver and Christopher La Farge.

La Farge, Oliver [Hazard Perry] (1901–1963). American anthropologist and writer. He is best known for his works dealing with the American Indian, especially his notable first novel, LAUGHING BOY. A member of several anthropological expeditions to Arizona, Mexico, and Guatemala, La Farge was particularly interested in the Navaho and throughout his life was an eloquent spokesman and champion for the American Indian. *Tribes and Temples* (1945) is a book on archeology. *Sparks Fly Upward* (1931) and *All the Young Men* (1935) were collections of short stories. *The Eagle in the Egg* (1949) is a novel based upon his experiences as an officer in the army's Air Transport Command. *Raw Material* (1945) is his autobiography. La Farge and his brother, Christopher, were grandsons of the artist John La Farge, and nephews of Father John La Farge.

Lafayette, Marquis de. Marie Joseph Paul Yves Roch Gilbert du Motier (1757–1834). French statesman and general, known as "the Hero of the Worlds." He served (1777–1781) the American cause during the Revolutionary War as a major general in Washington's army. On furlough in France from 1778 to 1780, he did much to cement Franco-American relations. Active in French politics, he advocated moderation during the French Revolution. He was forced to flee to Austrian lines in 1792 after failing in his attempted *coup d'état* against the revolutionary government in Paris, and returned to Paris in 1799. He did not engage in politics during the Napoleonic era, but after the Bourbon Restoration (1815–1830) he was one of the leaders of the liberal opposition. It was he who persuaded the leaders of the 1830 revolution to accept Louis Philippe as their monarch, saying the famous words: "Take him, he will make the best of republics." At Lafayette's suggestion, Louis Philippe appeared on the balcony of the Hôtel de Ville, wrapped in the TRICOLOR. Lafayette lived to regret his decision, becoming quite disappointed in the July Monarchy.

La Fayette, Comtesse de. Born Marie Madeleine Pioche de La Vergne (1634–1693). French novelist. Although Comtesse de La Fayette borrowed the format of her early work *Zayde* from de Scudéry, her novels *La Princesse de Montpensier* (1662) and LA PRINCESSE DE CLÈVES (1678) are unmarred by the sentimentality and extravagance that characterize the works of her predecessor. With these simply and soberly written romances, melancholy in mood, Comtesse de La Fayette originated the French novel of character.

Lafcadio's Adventures (Les Caves du Vatican; 1914). A satirical farce by André GIDE. Also known in translation as *The Vatican Swindle,* the book caricatures various types in society by means of the three brothers-in-law and their many relations who comprise its major characters. The plot concerns the confusion resulting from a swindler's scheme to extort money by falsely reporting that the pope has been kidnapped and organizing a conspiracy to liberate him. The interest of the book, however, focuses on the apparently unmotivated murder of one of the brothers by Lafcadio, a bastard relative.

Lafeu. In Shakespeare's ALL'S WELL THAT ENDS WELL, an old French lord sent to conduct Bertram to the royal court on the king of France's invitation.

Lafitte or **Laffitte, Jean** (1780?–?1826). French pirate and smuggler. Lafitte seems to have reached the neighborhood of New Orleans around 1809 as the head of a band of smugglers and privateers. During the War of 1812 he offered his services to Andrew Jackson and took part in the battle of New Orleans. Later he returned to his freebooting in Texas.

The subject of many legends, he was the hero of *Lafitte, The Pirate of the Gulf* (1836), a best-selling romance by Joseph Holt Ingraham. He also appears in Hervey Allen's *Anthony Adverse* (1933). Lord Byron, in a note to *The Corsair* (1815), suggested some likenesses between his hero and Lafitte.

La Follette, Robert M[arion] (1855–1925). American statesman. An opponent of Republican Party regulars in his native Wisconsin, La Follette was elected district attorney of Dane County in 1880 and served in Congress from 1885 to 1891. In 1900 he won the GOP gubernatorial nomination by acclamation and after his election, instituted an extensive reform program that included opposition to political bosses, establishment of the direct primary, and regulation of the railroads. In the U.S. Senate (1906–1925), he continued his battle against the "interests." As leader of the newly formed Progressive Party, he sought the 1912 presidential nomination but lost it to Theodore Roosevelt. He opposed President Wilson's foreign policy and argued against U.S. entry into the League of Nations. In 1924 he won nearly five million votes as the presidential candidate of the Progressives.

His son, Robert M. La Follette, Jr. (1895–1953), was appointed to the elder La Follette's Senate seat in 1925 and served until 1946 when he was defeated by Joseph R. McCarthy.

La Fontaine, Jean de (1621–1695). French author. A prolific writer of comedies, lyrics, elegies, ballads, and licentious tales, La Fontaine is remembered primarily for his FABLES CHOISIES, MISES EN VERS and his CONTES ET NOUVELLES EN VERS. Despite disputes with the French Academy, police condemnation of his *Contes,* and royal disfavor, La Fontaine was little distracted from his work and remained in the eyes of the world a vagabond, dreamer, and lover of pleasure, drifting happily from one patron to another throughout his highly productive literary career.

Laforet, Carmen (1921–   ). Spanish novelist. Her first work, *Nada* (1945), won great acclaim in Spain. This is a simple tale centering about the experiences of a young girl who settles in Barcelona after completing her education. Her more recent works include *La isla y los demonios* (1952), set in the Canary Islands, and *La mujer nueva* (1955), which relates the fall and spiritual regeneration of an adulterous woman.

Laforgue, Jules (1860–1887). French poet. Laforgue, with Gustave Kahn, is considered to have invented vers libre, as free verse is known in the 20th-century. Associated with the SYMBOLISTS, his volumes of poetry include *Les Complaintes* (1885), *L'Imitation de Notre-Dame la lune* (1886), and *Le Concile féerique* (1886). *Moralités Légendaires* (1887) is a collection, published posthumously, of satires upon old tales. Laforgue exerted considerable influence upon the form, rhythm, attitude, and subject matter of T. S. Eliot's early poetry.

Lagado. In Jonathan Swift's GULLIVER'S TRAVELS, the capital of Balnibarbi, the continent neighboring LAPUTA. Lagado is celebrated for its Academy of Projectors, where scholars spend their time in such useless projects as extracting sunbeams from cucumbers and converting ice into gunpowder.

Lagerkvist, Pär (1891–   ). Swedish novelist, playwright, and poet. Lagerkvist is a moralist without a system of belief; profoundly humanistic, he probes the human mind and heart with agonized honesty. During the troubled decade of the 1930's, he spoke out against tyranny, Nazism, and totalitarianism. He published *Brödeln* (*The Hangman;* 1933) to show the evil of violence. His best-known novels are *Dvärgen* (*The Dwarf;* 1945), BARABBAS, and *The Sibyl* (1956). He was awarded the Nobel Prize for literature in 1951.

Lagerlöf, Selma (1858–1940). Swedish novelist and short-story writer. Uncomfortable with the literary realism current in her day, Selma Lagerlöf returned to the past for her stories and wrote in a romantic, imaginative manner. Her best known works are the novels GÖSTA BERLINGS SAGA and JERUSALEM. *Nils Holgerssons underbara resa genom Sverige* (*The Wonderful Adventures of Nils;* 1906–1907) and *Further Adventures of Nils* (1911), are fanciful accounts of a young boy's adventures as he travels over Sweden on the back of a wild goose. In 1909, Selma Lagerlöf received the Nobel prize for literature.

Lagrange, Joseph Louis (1736–1813). French-Italian mathematician. He received great acclaim during his lifetime, and was highly honored by Frederick the Great, Louis XVI, and Napoleon.

La Guardia, Fiorello H. Known as **the Little Flower** (1882–1947). American political leader. From 1901 to 1906 LaGuardia worked for the U.S. consular service in Europe and from 1907 to 1910 was an interpreter on Ellis Island in New York harbor. Elected to Congress in 1916, he resigned to become an air force officer during World War I, then returned to the House, where he served from 1923 to 1933. In 1933 he was elected mayor of New York on an anti-Tammany reform ticket. During his three terms as mayor, La Guardia conducted an energetic, incorruptible administration; sponsored an ambitious public-works program; and secured the adoption of a new city charter. In 1941–1942 he headed the U.S. Office of Civilian Defense and in 1946 was director of the UN Rehabilitation and Reconstruction Administration.

Lahamu. See LAHMU.

Lahar. The Sumerian god of cattle.

Lahmu and **Lahamu.** A Babylonian god and goddess. Born of the union of fresh water (Apsu) and salt water (Tiamat), they in turn were the parents of Anshar, a sky-god, and Kishar, an earth-goddess.

La Hogue, Battle of. The successful naval operations of the English and Dutch fleets against the French off the coast of Normandy (May 19 to 23, 1692). La Hogue itself is a harbor which served as the base of Louis XIV's attempted invasion of England.

lai. (1) A verse form in medieval French verse, composed of three-line units rhymed *aab.*

(2) also **lay.** A short narrative poem using the material of the medieval romances or the *fabliaux,* of the type written by MARIE DE FRANCE. These *lais* are not to be confused with the *Lais* (or *legs,* meaning legacies) written by François VILLON.

Laing, Alexander [Kinnan] (1903–   ). American poet and teacher. He is author of several volumes of verse, including *Fool's Errand* (1928) and *The Flowering Thorn* (1933), and of a discourse on poetry, *Wine and Physic* (1934). A teacher at Dartmouth, he has written an epic of the clipper-ship era, *The Sea Witch* (1933), and a prose work dealing with the same subject matter, *Clippership Men* (1945). Laing has also edited horror stories. With R. A. Lattimore, he published *American Sail, a Pictorial History* (1961).

Laïs. Name of two celebrated Greek HETAERAE or courtesans. The earlier was the most beautiful woman of Corinth, who lived at the time of the Peloponnesian War. The beauty of Laïs the Second so excited the jealousy of the Thessalonian women that they pricked her to death with their bodkins. She was the contemporary and rival of Phryne and sat to Apelles as a model. Demosthenes claims that she sold her favors for 10,000 Attic drachmae.

laissez-faire (*Fr.,* "let do," that is, "let people and things alone"). The principal tenet of laissez-faire is that problems should be allowed to work themselves out without planning or regulation. It is, specifically, the principle of noninterference by government in commercial affairs. The phrase comes from the motto of the PHYSIOCRATS, a school of French economists of the mid-18th century: *Laissez faire, laissez passer* (let do, let pass). The physiocrats wished to have all customs duties abolished and demanded free circulation for their goods, thus anticipating the later free traders. Jean Claude Marie Vincent de Gournay (1712–1759) is generally credited with being the author of the motto. Adam SMITH was the principal exponent of laissez-faire theories in England, from where they later spread to the United States. As embodied in the writings of Smith, the principle has become one of the bulwarks of capitalist economics.

Laius (Laios). See OEDIPUS.

Lake poets, also called **Lake school.** A name applied to a group of poets in the 19th century, including Wordsworth, Coleridge, and Shelley, making reference to their residences in the Lake District of England (Westmoreland, Cumberland, Lancashire). The name was first used as an epithet of derision by the *Edinburgh Review,* but has long since lost its disparaging connotations.

Lakmé (1883). A romantic opera by the French composer Léo DELIBES. The libretto by Gondinet and Gille is based on Loti's novel *The Marriage of Loti* (1880), and is Oriental in character. It contains the famous "Bell Song."

Laksmi or Lakshmi. One of the consorts of the Hindu god Vishnu, and mother of Kama, the god of young love. She is goddess of beauty, wealth, and pleasure, and the *Ramayana* describes her as springing, like Venus, from the foam of the sea.

Lal, P. (1929–   ). Indian poet writing in English. He has published *The Art of the Essay* (1952); *The Parrot's Death and Other Poems* (1960); *Love's the First* (1962), poems; and adaptations of six *Great Sanskrit Plays* (1963).

Lall, Anand (1911–   ). Indian novelist writing in English. He was consul-general of India in New York, 1951–1954. He wrote *The House at Adampur* (1956), a study of the decaying Indian *zamindari* class, and *Seasons of Jupiter* (1960).

Lallans. A Scottish dialect used by some modern Scottish poets. It is a synthetic language, made up of the dialects of the Scottish lowlands and elements from the Scottish literary language of the past. See SCOTTISH RENAISSANCE.

Lalla Rookh (1817). A series of four Oriental tales in verse held together by a story in prose, by Thomas MOORE. The narrative tells of Lalla Rookh, daughter of the emperor of Delhi who, on a journey to meet her betrothed, is entertained by the young Persian poet Feramorz; he relates four tales of romance and she falls in love with him. Ultimately she discovers that he is her betrothed.

The four tales he entertained her with are:

(1) *The Veiled Prophet of Khorassan* in which the chief figure is the prophet Hakem ben Haschem who wears a silver gauze veil "to dim the lustre of his face" or rather to hide its extreme ugliness.

(2) *Paradise and the Peri,* about a Peri who is told she will be readmitted to heaven if she brings the gift most dear to the Almighty. After a number of unavailing offerings she brings a guilty old man, who weeps repentantly. The Peri offers the Repentant Tear and the gates of Heaven fly open.

(3) *The Fire Worshippers,* about Hafed, the fire worshiper, who, when betrayed to the Muslims,

throws himself in the sacred fire and is burned to death.

(4) *The Light of the Harem,* about Nourmahal, who regains the love of her husband, the Mogul Emperor Jehangir, by means of a magic spell.

lama. A Buddhist monk or priest in Tibet. Prior to 1959, when he was forced to flee from the Chinese, the Dalai Lama had been both the temporal and spiritual leader of the Tibetans. Ruling from the Potala, a huge palace-lamasery in Lhasa, the Dalai Lama is considered a reincarnation of Avalokitesvara, the ancestor of the Tibetan race.

Lamarck, Chevalier **de. Jean Baptiste Pierre Antoine de Monet** (1744–1829). French naturalist. Lamarck advocated views on organic evolution which are sometimes mistakenly interpreted as representing Darwinism in a preparatory stage. In his *Philosophie zoologique* (1809), he held that an organism reacts to a new or changing environment by fitting developments; he did not hold, as did Darwin, that a new or changing environment permits the survival of the accidentally fittest. Lamarck also introduced new principles in the classification of animals and originated the term *vertebrate* and *invertebrate*. See Charles Robert DARWIN.

Lamartine, Alphonse Marie Louis de (1790–1869). French poet, writer, and statesman. Lamartine's work is marked by a preoccupation with nature, religion, and love, all subjectively presented (see ROMANTICISM). He is regarded as the first truly romantic poet in French literature. Among his published volumes are *Les Premières méditations* (1820), *Les Nouvelles méditations* (1823), and *Les Harmonies poétiques et religieuses* (1830). His narrative poems include *Jocelyn* (1836), dealing with a priest's love, and *La Chute d'un ange* (1838). A liberal in his beliefs, Lamartine tended toward radical republicanism in politics. Serving as a deputy for several years, he distinguished himself as an orator. A leader in the Revolution of 1848, he became the virtual chief of the provisional government, but fell from power upon the coup d'état of Napoleon III (1852).

lamasery. A Buddhist monastery (or convent) of Tibet or Mongolia, presided over by a LAMA, who corresponds to a Christian abbot.

Lamassu. In Babylonian religion, one of a race of semidivine beings. The Lamassus were visualized as colossal bulls or lions with human heads. Statues of them flanked the entrances of palaces and public buildings.

lamb. In Christian art and imagery, Jesus is often symbolically represented as a lamb, in allusion to John 1:29, "Behold the Lamb of God, which taketh away the sins of the world." The reference is to his sacrificial act for the redemption of the sins of all men.

Lamb, Lady Caroline (1785–1828). English novelist, the wife of William Lamb (later 2d Viscount Melbourne, prime minister to Queen Victoria). She is better known for her nine-months' intrigue with Lord Byron than for any of her novels. She was neurotic and demanding, and Byron soon tired of her. She took revenge in an anonymous novel, *Glenarvon* (1816), which contains a caricature of the poet. After Byron's death she gave way to conduct of such impropriety that Melbourne was forced to separate from her.

Lamb, Charles. Pen name **Elia** (1775–1834). English essayist of the romantic period, a schoolmate of Coleridge and friend of other figures of English romanticism. He attempted work in the fields of drama and poetry, but was most successful in the personal essay. His writings in this form are known for their humor, whimsy, and faint overtones of pathos. He was also a perceptive critic with a special sympathy for the work of Elizabethan and early 17th-century writers: a sympathy that is reflected in his own vivacious, idiosyncratic style.

His essays are contained in the two series entitled *Essays of Elia*, which appeared in *The London Magazine* from 1820 to 1823 and from 1824 to 1825, being collected and published in 1823 and 1833, respectively. Outstanding single essays are: A DISSERTATION ON ROAST PIG; *A Chapter on Ears; Mrs. Battle's Opinions on Whist;* DREAM CHILDREN; and *The Superannuated Man.* Other works of Lamb are *The Tale of Rosamund Gray and Old Blind Margaret* (1798), a prose narrative; *John Woodvil* (1802), a dramatic tragedy; *Tales from Shakespeare* (1807), adaptations for children written in collaboration with his sister, Mary Lamb; *The Adventures of Ulysses* (1808), another book for children; *Specimens of English Dramatic*

Caricature of Charles Lamb.

Scratched on Copper from Life in 1825 by his friend Brook Pulham.

Poets Contemporary with Shakespeare (1808); *Album Verses* (1830), poetry.

Though he was much loved for his personal sweetness and good humor, Lamb's life was marked by frustration and sorrow. Because of a stammer, he was unable to qualify for a university position and went to work as an accountant for the East India Company, where he stayed until 1825. There was a strain of insanity in the family, and Mary Lamb had several attacks of madness, during one of which she killed her mother. Lamb, who himself suffered from alcoholism and stayed for a while in a sanatorium, took care of her.

Lamb, Harold [Albert] (1892–1962). American writer. Lamb is known for his vivid and popular historical studies and biographies: *Genghis Khan* (1927), *Tamerlane* (1928), *The Crusades* (2 vols., 1930, 1931), *The March of Muscovy: Ivan the Terrible* (1948), *Constantinople: Birth of an Empire* (1957), and many others. As these titles indicate, Lamb was primarily interested in Asia and the Near East.

Lamber, Juliette. See Juliette ADAM.

Lambert, Marquise **Anne-Thérèse de** (1647–1733). French writer. Famed for her salon, which was reputed to exercise influence in the appointment of members to the French Academy and where aristocracy and men of letters freely mixed, the marquise de Lambert expressed her high moral principles in two instructive works: *Avis d'une mère à son fils* (*A Mother's Advice to her Son;* 1726) and *Avis à sa fille* (*Advice to her Daughter;* 1728).

Lamentations of Jeremiah, The. An Old Testament book. It is ascribed to the prophet Jeremiah, but is probably the work of various authors. It is comprised of five poems, the first four of which are alphabetical acrostics. The book's theme is that suffering is the result of sin.

Lamerok, Sir. In Arthurian legend, one of the knights of the Round Table. In Malory's *Le Morte d'Arthur* (c. 1469), he is the son of King PELLINORE. He becomes the lover of Queen MARGAWSE and her son Sir Gawain kills him.

La Mettrie, Julien Offroy de (1709–1751). French physician and philosopher, the most notorious materialist of his day. His most famous work, *L'Homme machine* (1747), shows how thought depends on matter, not on God or the soul, and that though man is a machine, he is too complicated ever to be completely understood.

lamia. A female phantom. Her name was used by the Greeks and Romans as a bugbear to children. She was a Libyan queen beloved by Zeus, but robbed of her offspring by the jealous Hera. In consequence she vowed vengeance against all children, whom she delighted to entice and devour.

Witches in Middle Ages were called lamioe, and Keats's poem *Lamia* (1820), which relates how a bride when recognized returns to her original serpent form, represents one of the many superstitions connected with the race. Keats's story came (through Burton) from Philostratus' *De Vita Apollonii*, Bk. iv. In Burton's rendering, the sage Apollonius, on the wedding night

found her out to be a serpent, a lamia. . . . When she saw herself descried, she wept, and desired Apollonius to be silent, but he would not be moved, and thereupon she, plate, house, and all that was in it, vanished in an instant; many thousands took notice of this fact, for it was done in the midst of Greece. *Anatomy of Melancholy*, Pt. iii. sect. ii, memb. i, subsect. i

Lammas. Elements of the word are "loaf" and "mass." Formerly a harvest festival, *Lammas Day* falls on August 1.

Lamming, George (1927–). West Indian writer. *In the Castle of My Skin* (1953) is an evocation of village life in his childhood home of Barbados.

Lamont, Corliss (1902–). American writer and teacher. The son of a millionaire banker, Thomas W. Lamont, he taught courses in philosophy and Russian civilization at Cornell, Columbia, and Harvard. Politically a leftist, Lamont has expressed his views in a book called *You Might Like Socialism* (1939), and in several pamphlets, including *The Myth of Soviet Aggression* (1953), *Challenge to McCarthy* (1954), and *The Congressional Inquisition* (1954). Among his other books are *Issues of Immortality* (1932), *Russia Day by Day* (1933), *The Independent Mind* (1951), and *The Illusion of Immortality* (1935; rev. 1950, 1959).

Lampedusa, Giuseppe di. See LEOPARD, THE.

Lamplighter, The (1854). A novel by Maria Susanna Cummins (1827–1866), originally published anonymously. The author's first book, it was an immediate success; sentimental and materialistic, it was typical of the best-selling women's novels of the time. Gerty, the heroine, is brought up in squalid surroundings, from which she is rescued by a kindly old lamplighter, Trueman Flint. She finds a playmate named Willie, and is taken into the home of Emily Graham, a rich blind girl, when Flint dies. There Gerty learns that her father is really Emily's brother, who ran away from home when he accidentally blinded his sister. Finally, she marries Willie, who has become wealthy and successful. The fantastic sales of *The Lamplighter* puzzled Nathaniel Hawthorne, who complained that the America of his time was "wholly given over to a d—d mob of scribbling women."

lampoon (F. *lampon*, from the refrain *lampons,* let's drink, in 17th-century French satirical drinking songs). A malicious, often scurrilous satirical piece, in prose or poetry, attacking an individual's character or appearance. The lampoon flourished in 17th- and 18th-century England. It fell into disuse as a result of a revulsion of public feeling, as well as of modern libel laws. The term is still in use, however, both as noun and verb, for any piece of pointed mockery of an individual or institution. A generalized use is seen in the name of the Harvard University humor magazine, *The Harvard Lampoon*.

Lancastrian. A member or supporter of the English royal house of Lancaster during the Wars of the Roses.

Lancelot, Sir. See LAUNCELOT.

Landino, Cristoforo (1469–1527). Florentine teacher and critic. Connected with the circle of Lorenzo de' Medici, he gave lectures on poetry and rhetoric and wrote the commentary for a 1481 edition of Dante that included some designs by Botticelli. His most famous critical work is the *Disputationes Camaldulenses,* which consists of discussions on literary subjects supposedly held at the monastery of Camaldoli in 1468.

Landino, Francesco (1325–1397). Italian composer, poet, and organist. The most important composer of 14th-century Italy, Landino was renowned for singing to his own organ accompaniment, musical settings of his own poems. He won a laurel crown at a tournament in Venice in 1364; Petrarch was on the jury.

Land of Nod. See NOD, LAND OF.

Land of Promise. See PROMISED LAND.

Landon, Letitia Elizabeth (1802–1838). English poet and novelist. Her sentimental poems, usually signed L.E.L., were a popular feature of annuals during the third and fourth decades of the century. She also wrote several novels, including *Esther Churchill* (1837).

Landor, Walter Savage (1775–1864). English poet, literary critic, and prose writer. Landor is best remembered for his interest in the classics and for the severity and intellectual coldness of his lyrics, many of which were written in direct imitation of Greek and Latin models. Among his works are *Gebir* (1797), an Oriental tale in blank verse; *Count Julian* (1812), a tragedy; *Imaginary Conversations* (1824–1853), a series of discussions between historical figures on a variety of subjects; *Citations and Examination of William Shakespeare* (1834), literary criticism; *Pericles and Aspasia* (1836), imaginary letters; *Poemata et Inscriptiones* (1847), Latin verse; *The Hellenics* (1847), poems on Greek subjects; *Last Fruit Off an Old Tree* (1853); *Antony and Octavius* (1856), dramatic dialogues; *Heroic Idyls* (1863). *Rose Aylmer* is his best known lyric.

In his youth, Landor was influenced by the revolutionary atmosphere of the time and was forced to leave Oxford because of his opinions. In 1808 he went off with a regiment he had raised to fight Napoleon in Spain. He tried to institute humanitarian reform on his estate in Wales but failed, and for a number of years lived in Italy. His poetry was never popular in his own time.

land o' the leal. The land of the faithful or blessed. It is a Scotticism for a hypothetical land of happiness, loyalty, and virtue; hence, the equivalent of heaven.

Landseer, Sir Edwin Henry (1802–1873). A famous English animal painter. He drew Sir Walter Scott's dogs with the poet in their midst. His paintings owe their popularity largely to the etchings made of them by his brother Thomas Landseer (1795–1880).

Land's End. The most westerly point in England. Called Bolerium in ancient geography, Land's End is on the southwest coast of Cornwall, and consists of granite cliffs, 60 to 100 feet high.

Lang, Andrew (1844–1912). Scottish scholar and man of letters. In a controversy with Max Müller he held that literary mythology is the outgrowth of anonymous folklore. He wrote several books of graceful verse, collaborated with Samuel Henry Butcher on a well-known prose translation of the *Odyssey* (1879), and edited numerous volumes of fairy tales.

Lang, Fritz (1890–). German motion-picture director and producer. Among his notable films are *Destiny* (1921), *Dr. Mabuse* (1922), and *M* (1931).

Langbehn, Julius (1851–1907). German popular philosopher, opposed to materialism and rationalism. His *Rembrandt als Erzieher* (*Rembrandt as Educator,* 1890), published anonymously, was a best-seller.

Langer, Susanne K. (1895–   ). American philosopher and teacher. Mrs. Langer's interest in the symbol-making function of the mind led her into aesthetics and to her book *Philosophy in a New Key: A Study in the Symbolism of Reason, Rite, and Art* (1942). It was influenced by the work of the German philosopher Ernest Cassirer, whose *Language and Myth* she translated in 1946. *Feeling and Form; A Theory of Art* appeared in 1953; 10 of Mrs. Langer's lectures on philosophy and aesthetics were printed in *Problems of Art* (1957).

Langland or **Langley, William.** See under PIERS PLOWMAN.

Langner, Lawrence (1890–1962). Welsh-born American playwright and producer. Langner came to the U.S. in 1914 and shortly thereafter organized the Washington Square Players; the group performed several of his early plays, including *Another Way Out* (1916), a popular one-act drama. Out of the Washington Square Players grew the Theatre Guild, of which Langner was the founder and, after 1919, the director. He also founded the American Shakespeare Festival Theatre and Academy of Stratford, Conn. In addition to adapting foreign plays for the American stage, Langner collaborated with his wife, Armina Marshall, on several successful plays. *Pursuit of Happiness* (1934) deals with a Hessian soldier involved in the old American custom of bundling. The Langners also conducted their own summer theater in Westport, N.Y., until 1959. Langner's *G.B.S. and the Lunatic* (1963) describes the business relationship between the Theatre Guild and George Bernard Shaw.

Langton, Stephen (c. 1150–1228). English prelate, statesman, and scholar, Archbishop of Canterbury (after 1207). King John refused to recognize his appointment until 1213, and Langton became the leader of the barons in their struggle against John, representing them with his signature on the MAGNA CARTA.

Langtry, Lily. Born **Emily Charlotte Le Breton** (1852–1929). English actress, known as the "Jersey Lily," famous for her great beauty. She went on the stage in 1881 in the role of Kate Hardcastle in Goldsmith's *She Stoops to Conquer.*

langue d'oc and **langue d'oïl.** The two groups of medieval Romance dialects that emerged from Vulgar Latin in Gaul, named after the word for "yes" in each group. The *langue d'oc* was spoken in the region of southern France and northern Italy known as Provence. The *langue d'oïl* was spoken in France north of a line running approximately from the mouth of the Gironde River east to the Alps; it was the ancestor of standard modern French (in which *oïl* became *oui*).

Lanier, Sidney (1842–1881). American poet. After graduating from Oglethorpe University in his native Georgia in 1860, Lanier enlisted in the Confederate army and, in 1864, was captured and imprisoned for four months at Point Lookout, Md. He emerged from the war afflicted with the tuberculosis that remained with him for the rest of his short life. Prevented by economic necessity from devoting himself to literature, Lanier worked at odd jobs after the war. In 1873 he settled in Baltimore, becoming first flutist with the Peabody Symphony Orchestra.

Considered one of the most accomplished poets of the American South in the latter half of the 19th century, he tried to achieve in his work the auditory effect of music and experimented with varying metrical patterns and unusual imagery. Much of his poetry shows an affinity with that of the Pre-Raphaelites and Swinburne. His best-known poems include *The Symphony* (1875), a denunciation of industrialism designed to illustrate the close relationship between poetry and music; THE MARSHES OF GLYNN; and *The Song of the Chattahoochee* (1883), notable for its successful combination of alliteration, onomatopoeia, and melody. Lanier also wrote *Tiger Lilies* (1867), a novel based on his Civil War experiences, and three works of criticism, *The Science of English Verse* (1880), *The English Novel* (1883), and *Shakespeare and His Forerunners* (1902).

Lanigan, George Thomas (1845–1886). Canadian-born American journalist and humorous poet. He sometimes published under the pseudonym of G. Washington Aesop. Lanigan worked on the New York *World* from 1874 to 1883 and published two volumes, *Canadian Ballads* (1864) and *Fables* (1878). He is chiefly remembered for his poem *Threnody for the Ahkoond of Swat* (1878), which was inspired by an item in the London *Times*. One of Lanigan's best sayings was that he dreamed of the day "when the singular verb shall lie down with the plural noun, and a little conjunction shall lead them."

Lantern Land. The land of literary charlatans, pedantic graduates in arts, doctors, professors, prelates, and so on. They were ridiculed as "Lanterns" by Rabelais (with a side allusion to the divines assembled in conference at the Council of Trent) in his *Gargantua and Pantagruel.*

Laocoön (Laokoön). In Greek mythology, a Trojan priest who, having offended the gods, was strangled by sea serpents. In Vergil's *Aeneid,* he draws down the anger of Athena by warning the Trojans not to accept the Trojan horse and by hurling his javelin into the hollow flank of the wooden statue dedicated to her. She sends two huge sea snakes to the shore where Laocoön, assisted by his two sons, is sacrificing to Poseidon. The monsters choke the three to death.

The famous group of sculpture representing these three in their death agony, now in the Vatican, was discovered in 1506, on the Esquiline Hill in Rome. It is a single block of marble, and is attributed to Agesandrus, Athenodorus, and Polydorus of the school of Rhodes in the second century B.C. The discovery lent tremendous impetus to the renascence of interest in the classical period and had great impact on the art world.

In a famous treatise on the limits of poetry and the plastic arts (1766), Lessing uses this group as the peg on which to hang his dissertation, called *Laocoön.*

Laocoön, or On the Limits of Painting and Poetry (Laokoon, oder Über die Grenzen der Malerei und Poesie; 1766). An essay by Gotthold Ephraim LESSING. It seeks to dispute the idea that art criticism and literary criticism may be based on the same principles. The fundamental point is that a painting exists in space and all its parts are perceived simultaneously, whereas a work of literature exists in time and its parts are perceived one after another. On this basis, Lessing develops an extensive theory of the respective domains of painting and poetry, in which he challenges some of Winckelmann's ideas. Lessing uses the statue "Laocoön" as one of his central examples.

Laodamia. In classic myth, the wife of PROTESILAUS, who was slain before Troy.

Laodicean. One indifferent to religion, caring little or nothing about the matter. The reference is to Revelation 3:14–18 where the Christians of the city of Laodicea are "lukewarm."

Laomedon. In classic myth, a king of Troy, the father of Priam. He is remembered chiefly for his ingratitude in refusing to give the rewards he had promised to Apollo for pasturing his flocks on Mount Ida, to Poseidon for building the walls of Troy, and to Heracles for rescuing his daughter Hesione from the sea-monster sent by Poseidon. Heracles slew him and all his sons but Priam in revenge.

Lao Tzu. Legendary Chinese sage, supposedly contemporary with Confucius (6th century B.C.) and regarded as the founder of TAOISM. Lao Tzu is also the name of the basic text of the Taoist religion; it is more commonly known as the TAO TE CHING.

Lapiths (Lapithai). A Thessalian tribe. They were neighbors of the CENTAURS, with whom they had a famous battle. The Lapiths invited the Centaurs to the wedding of their king Pirithous to Hippodamia. Under the influence of wine, the Centaurs tried to carry off the Lapith women, including even the bride, but were roundly defeated. During the battle, an invulnerable Lapith leader named Caeneus was driven into the ground by the Centaurs, since he could not be killed. This Caeneus had been a girl until, upon being violated by Poseidon and granted a boon, she chose to become a man and invulnerable. The battle of Centaurs and Lapiths was a favorite subject for Greek artists. It appeared on the PARTHENON, the Theseum at Athens, and the temple of Apollo at Basso, as well as on numberless vases.

Laplace, Marquis **Pierre Simon de** (1749–1827). French astronomer and mathematician. Laplace made discoveries in celestial mechanics and set forth a nebular hypothesis of cosmogony (*Exposition du système du monde;* 1796) which is essentially similar to that advanced by Immanuel Kant.

Laputa. The flying island which Gulliver visits in Jonathan Swift's GULLIVER'S TRAVELS. It is largely inhabited by abstract philosophers. In this third voyage, technical knowledge is extensively satirized. Laputans, in their preoccupation with the theoretical and with innovation in technical methods, are ill equipped for living in society. Swift regarded Laputan ingenuity as misplaced. See LAGADO; GLUBDUBDRIB.

Lara. See CORSAIR, THE.

Lara, Cantar de los siete infantes de. A lost Spanish epic, or *cantar de gesta,* parts of which are preserved in the *Crónica general* of Alfonso X and in the *Crónica de 1344.* Menéndez Pidal used these fragments as the basis for his reconstruction, *La leyenda de los infantes de Lara* (1896).

The legend deals with the seven sons of Gonzalo Gustios, lord of Salas, or Lara. Gonzalo González, youngest of the brothers, incurs the enmity of his aunt, Doña Lambra, by killing her cousin, Alvar Sánchez, at a tournament celebrating her marriage to Ruy Velázquez. As a result, a bloody vendetta ensues. Spurred by his wife, Ruy Velázquez asks Almanzor, military governor of Córdoba, to kill Gonzalo Gustios, but the magnanimous Moor merely holds him captive. Meanwhile, as a result of Velázquez' machinations, the sons and their old tutor, Nuño Salido, are killed while fighting against the Moors. They are later avenged by their half-brother, Mudarra, the offspring of their father's union with a Moorish slave.

This legend has formed the basis of many later works, notably Juan de la Cueva's *Tragedia de los siete infantes de Lara,* Lope de Vega's *El bastardo Mudarra,* and the romantic epic *El moro expósito* (1834) by Angel Saavedra, duque de Rivas.

La Ramée, Pierre. Known as **Petrus Ramus** (1515–1572). French philosopher, grammarian, and mathematician. He is known for his opposition to Aristotelian logic, which he attacked in his *Dialectique* (1555). He was a victim of the MASSACRE OF ST. BARTHOLOMEW.

Larbaud, Valery (1881–1957). French poet, fiction writer, critic. His *Poèmes par un riche amateur* (1908) and especially the *Journal d'A. O. Barnabooth* (1913) are lyrical reflections upon his many travels and express his yearning for some unattainable absolute. He was a close friend of James Joyce, and helped to launch *Ulysses* in 1922.

Lardner, Ring[gold Wilmer] (1885–1933). American humorist and short-story writer. He is known for his bitterly humorous and satirical stories and sketches of 20th-century American life, told in the language of baseball players, boxers, songwriters, stockbrokers, stenographers, chorus girls, etc. Lardner's first important work was YOU KNOW ME AL, letters of a baseball player which first appeared in the *Saturday Evening Post.* Previously, he had published a collection of verse, *Bib Ballads* (1915), and a long series of books followed, including HOW TO WRITE SHORT STORIES; *The Love Nest and Other Stories* (1926), a collection that includes the famous story *Haircut; The Story of a Wonder Man* (1927), a satirical autobiography; and *June Moon* (1929), a play written with George S. Kaufman, satirizing the song writers of Tin Pan Alley.

lares. Household gods of the ancient Romans, usually referred to in the singular (lar), there being one lar to a household. The lares were protective, and were usually deified ancestors or heroes. The *lar familiaris* was the spirit of the founder of the house who, never leaving, accompanied his descendants in all their changes. See PENATES.

Lark, The (L'Alouette; 1953). A play by Jean ANOUILH about JOAN OF ARC. It was translated into English by Christopher Fry.

Larkin, Philip [Arthur] (1922–). English poet and novelist. He has been a leader in the English antiromantic movement of the 1950's. *The Less Deceived* (1955) is a collection of witty poems. *Jill* (1946) and *A Girl in Winter* (1947) are novels.

La Rochefoucauld, Duc François de (1613–1680). French writer. In his *Mémoires* (1662), La Rochefoucauld records his political activities, describing his efforts to destroy the power of Cardinal Richelieu over the royal family and his participation in the battle of the FRONDE. After 1652 he abandoned politics for a sheltered intellectual life. The *Maximes* (*Maxims*, 1665) are concise and biting observations upon society and human nature, illustrating his conviction that self-interest is the spring of human conduct and that men delude themselves in pretending to virtue or disinterested behavior.

Larra [y Sánchez de Castro], Mariano José de. Known as *Fígaro* (1809–1837). Spanish journalist, literary critic, and author. The penetrating intelligence of this thoroughly romantic spirit brought him fame through his articles concerning Spanish regional life. These appeared in the 14 issues of the biting and satiric magazine *El pobrecito hablador* (1832–1833), which Larra edited and wrote himself. His reputation established, he went on to become one of the leading journalists of the period. His novel *El doncel de don Enrique el Doliente* (1834) and the drama *Macías* (1834) deal with the tragic loves of a minstrel who figures in Spanish literature as one of the authors who contributed to the *Cancionero de Baena*, an anonymous collection of medieval Spanish lyrics.

Larsen, Wolf. See SEA WOLF, THE.

Lars Porsena. See Lars PORSENA.

larvae. A name among the ancient Romans for malignant spirits and ghosts. The larva, or ghost, of the emperor Caligula was often seen (according to Suetonius) in his palace.

La Salle, Sieur de. Robert Cavelier (1643–1687). French explorer in North America. La Salle descended the Mississippi River to the Gulf of Mexico (1682), claiming the entire valley for France. He named the region Louisiana after the French king Louis XIV.

Lasca, Il. See Anton Francesco GRAZZINI.

Lascaris, Constantine (1434–1501). Greek scholar and teacher in Italy during the Renaissance. After teaching at Milan and Naples, he settled at Messina, where his school drew such northerners as Bembo for Greek studies. His Greek grammar was very popular in Italy and throughout Europe at the time.

Lascaris, John (1445–1535). Greek scholar in Italy during the Renaissance. He lectured at Florence and published there the first edition of the Planudean Anthology, part of the *Greek Anthology* as the entire collection was later called.

Las Casas, Bartolomé de (1474–1566). Spanish-born Dominican missionary and historian. He came to Santo Domingo in 1502 and was the first priest ordained in the New World (1510). In 1514, Las Casas suddenly became aware of the injustice with which the Indians were being treated in America, and subsequently devoted himself entirely to promoting their welfare, usually with the support of the crown, but against the bitter opposition of the Spanish settlers. *Brevísima relación de la destrucción de las Indias* (1552), his vivid, but probably exaggerated, account of Indian sufferings, was instrumental in fostering the long-lived "black legend," which denigrated the colonial policies of Spain in America. His major work, *Historia general de las Indias* (1875), is an important source for the early period of colonization in Latin America.

Laski, Harold J[oseph] (1893–1950). English political scientist. A convinced Marxist but not a Communist, he was an authority on American politics, history, and law.

Laski, Marghanita (1915–   ). English novelist and critic. She is the author of *Little Boy Lost* (1949), about an orphan, and *The Victorian Chaise Longue* (1954), a tale of the supernatural. Among her other works are *The Offshore Island* (1959), a play, and *Ecstasy: A Study of Some Secular and Religious Experiences* (1961).

Lassalle, Ferdinand (1825–1864). German socialist. His program of state socialism, or cooperation between worker and government, was criticized by Marx. His life is the source of George Meredith's novel *The Tragic Comedians* (1880).

Lassus, Orlandus de. Also **Orlando di Lasso.** Original name **Roland Delattre** (1530–1594). Flemish composer and choirmaster. Though, with Palestrina, he represents the apogee of 16th century polyphonic composition for voices, he also understood and composed for the instruments of his day. He left over 1,250 compositions at his death, including Italian canzoni, French chansons, secular madrigals, sacred motets, psalm-settings and masses.

Last Days of Pompeii, The (1834). A historical novel by Edward BULWER-LYTTON. The young Greek lovers, Glaucus and Ione, are thwarted in their intentions by Ione's rancorous guardian. The eruption of Vesuvius fortuitously allows them to escape to happiness.

Last Leaf, The (1907). A short story by O. HENRY. None of O. Henry's tales is more characteristic of his technique and sentiment than this account of a girl who lies, desperately ill of pneumonia, in a Greenwich Village apartment and makes up her mind to die as soon as the last leaf of five drops off the vine outside her window. One leaf hangs on, and she recovers—but there is a typical O. Henry twist to the ending.

Last of the Barons, The (1843). A historical novel by Edward BULWER-LYTTON dealing with the Wars of the Roses. The hero is Richard Neville, earl of Warwick, known as the Kingmaker. The novel traces his downfall. Sybil Warner and her father Adam Warner are important characters.

Last of the Just, The. See André SCHWARZ-BART.

Last of the Mohicans, The (1826). A novel by James Fenimore COOPER, the second of THE LEATHER-STOCKING TALES. The plot revolves around the efforts of Alice and Cora Munro to join their father, the British commander at Fort William Henry, near Lake Champlain. Their course is blocked by Magua, leader of a group of Hurons, who are leagued with the French against the British in the war. The schemes of Magua, an evil Indian, are frustrated by Uncas, the last of the Mohicans, his father, Chingachgook, and their friend, Natty BUMPPO. The rhythm of the book is set by a series of thrilling attacks, captures, flights, and rescues. The climax is the escape by suicide of the ill-fated lovers, Cora and Uncas.

Last Puritan, The (1936). A novel by George SANTAYANA. Subtitled *A Memoir in the Form of a Novel*, the book is a study of Oliver Alden, descendant of an old and wealthy New England family, who comprises in himself the Puritan characteristics of austerity, single-mindedness, gravity, and conscientious, scrupulous devotion to purpose. He is out of place in the civilization of the 20th century; as a friend of his in the novel says, "In Oliver Puritanism worked itself out to its logical end. He convinced himself, on Puritan grounds, that it was wrong to be a Puritan. . . . He thought it his clear duty to give Puritanism up, but couldn't." Oliver is presented in the prologue of the novel supposedly as a former student of the author at Harvard University and one of the young men killed during World War I. (Santayana later stated that he was partly based on W. Cameron Forbes.) In style, subject matter, and approach, *The Last Puritan* recalls the novels of Henry James.

Last Rose of Summer, 'Tis the. The title and first line of a song, generally known from the second act of the opera *Martha* (1847) by Flotow. It was written (1813) by Thomas Moore to the tune of an old air.

Last Supper. The last meal shared by Jesus and his 12 apostles. They celebrated the PASSOVER, then Jesus gave his followers bread and wine, thus instituting the sacrament of the Eucharist, also known as the Lord's Supper, and Holy Communion. The original occasion has been the subject of many works of art, the most famous of which is a fresco by Leonardo da Vinci in the refectory of Santa Maria delle Grazie, Milan. It shows the consternation of the disciples when Jesus told them that he would be betrayed that night.

Last Time I Saw Paris, The (1942). A book of reminiscences by Elliot PAUL. After the Germans took Paris in World War II, Paul set down in carefully interwoven episodes this nostalgic remembrance of Paris. The title was taken from a popular song of the 1940's. In *Springtime in Paris* (1950), Paul told of revisiting Paris.

Late George Apley, The (1937). A novel by John P. MARQUAND. Subtitled *A Novel in the form of a Memoir*, the story is told by Horatio Willing, a staid and polished annotator, who manages to satirize himself as he recounts the life of the recently deceased George Apley, a conventional, tradition-bound, but somewhat pathetic Bostonian. A highly successful book, it was awarded a Pulitzer Prize and later dramatized (1946) by its author and George S. Kaufman.

Lateran. See SAINT JOHN LATERAN.

Lathrop, George Parsons (1851–1898). American poet, biographer, and editor. Lathrop founded the American Copyright League in 1883, was editor of the Boston *Sunday Courier*, and associate editor of the *Atlantic Monthly*. In 1871, he married Rose Hawthorne LATHROP, and five years later wrote a *Study of Nathaniel Hawthorne* (1876), her father. He also published several collections of verse, among them *Rose and Roof-Tree* (1875) and *Dreams and Days* (1892).

Lathrop, Rose Hawthorne [Mother Mary Alphonsa] (1851–1926). American poet, memoirist, humanitarian. The second daughter of Nathaniel Hawthorne, she married George Parsons LATHROP in 1871. The marriage was unhappy, and Lathrop became a heavy drinker. In 1891, both husband and wife were converted to Roman Catholicism; working together, they established the Catholic Summer School of America and wrote a history of the Order

of the Sisters of Visitation, published as *A Story of Courage* (1894). In 1895, the Lathrops separated permanently. Mrs. Lathrop began to work in a hospital, and after her husband's death was received into the Dominican order as Mary Alphonsa. In 1901, she bought a home in Westchester County, N.Y., which she named Rosary Hill Home, and devoted the rest of her life to the care of incurable cases of cancer. In 1897 she published her *Memories of Hawthorne*.

Latimer, Hugh (1485?–1555). English bishop and Protestant martyr. Latimer was made bishop of Worcester in 1535, but resigned because he felt unable to accept the Act of the Six Articles of 1539. On the accession of Mary he was committed to the Tower, and was burned at the stake for heresy in 1555.

Latini, Brunetto (c. 1220–c. 1294). Italian philosopher and scholar, Dante's teacher. He wrote a didactic poem, the *Tesoretto*, in rhymed couplets of seven-syllable verse. His major work, the prose *Livre du Trésor* (c. 1265), was written in French and soon translated into Italian as *Tesoro* by Bono Giamboni; it is an encyclopedic "treasure book" of medieval scholastic knowledge.

Latin Quarter (*Fr.* **le Quartier Latin**). The University quarter of Paris on the left bank of the Seine. For centuries it has been a center for artists, writers, students, intellectuals, and Bohemians of all varieties and from many lands.

Latinus. The legendary king of the Latini, the ancient inhabitants of Latium. According to Vergil's AENEID, Latinus had been advised by an oracle to give his daughter, LAVINIA, in marriage to a stranger. Accordingly, he offers her to Aeneas, but Turnus, king of Rutuli, declares that she is betrothed to him. The contest between Aeneas and Turnus is settled by single combat, in which Aeneas is victorious.

Latitudinarians. Members of the liberal faction of the Church of England in the time of Charles II. They opposed the doctrinal rigidity of both the High Church and the Puritans. The term came to be applied to those persons who attach little importance to dogma and what are called orthodox doctrines.

Latmos, Mount. The mountain where ENDYMION pastured his flocks when Selene, goddess of the moon, fell in love with him.

La Tour du Pin, Patrice de (1911–   ). French poet. After the youthful lyrics of *La Quête de Joie* (1933), he collected the succeeding volumes into *Une Somme de Poésie* (1946), a long and allusive work interspersed with prose speculations which give it a mythological and philosophical unity. The development of the adolescent concerned only with himself into an adult involved with the fraternity of men provides subject and pattern for the work. *Le Second Jeu* (1959) stresses again that the man is born only through the death of the child, and leads La Tour du Pin to the third stage, the Christian confrontation with the mystery of God.

Latzko, Andreas (1876–   ). A Hungarian writer. His best-known book, *Men in War* (1917), is a war novel of pacifist tendencies.

Laube, Heinrich (1806–1884). German novelist and dramatist. His most famous work is the novel *Das junge Europa* (*Young Europe*, 1838 ff.), which attempts to define a unifying connection between the

Jung Deutschland (*Young Germany*) movement of which he was a representative and the other liberal young movements in Europe at the time, such as La Jeune France and Giovane Italia.

Laud, William (1573-1645). English prelate. The son of a clothier, he rose to the rank of archbishop of Canterbury (1633) and became one of the foremost supporters of Charles I, representing absolutism in both Church and State. His attempts to impose High Church conformity in Scotland and England aroused the bitter opposition of the Puritans. Impeached for treason by the Long Parliament (1640), he was condemned and beheaded.

lauda. Religious songs popular in Italy during the medieval and early Renaissance periods. These used the BALLATA form and were composed for lay confraternities. The outstanding early master of *lauda* was Jacopone da Todi (1230-1306). As the form developed in his hands and in those of his successors, it became increasingly dramatic, with dialogue, action, and setting assuming dominance. As such, it became the Italian equivalent of the mystery play, called the SACRA RAPPRESENTAZIONE (sacred representation). Though plays of this type dwindled in popularity in the later Renaissance, they left their influence on the secular and neoclassical drama, which replaced them in popularity. During the Renaissance, some *lauda* were still written, but not for large religious organizations; usually they were conceived as texts for musical setting, to be performed by individual artists or as part of religious services.

Laughing Boy (1929). A novel by Oliver LA FARGE. Centering around the ill-fated love of Laughing Boy for Slim Girl, it is noted for its sensitive and accurate depiction of Navaho culture and psychology. La Farge's first novel, it was awarded a Pulitzer Prize.

Laughing Philosopher, The. See DEMOCRITUS.

Launce. In Shakespeare's TWO GENTLEMEN OF VERONA, the clownish servant of Proteus. Launce is especially famous for his remarks to his dog Crab, "the sourest-natured dog that lives."

Launcelot, Sir. In ARTHURIAN LEGEND, the most famous of the knights of the Round Table. In the

Launcelot at a tournament. From a
French romance (1513).

early Welsh legends of King Arthur, he does not appear, but almost seems a French innovation since we first find him figuring importantly in the 12th-century *Lancelot, or the Knight of the Cart* by Chrétien de Troyes. He comes to full growth, however, in Malory's *Morte d'Arthur* (c. 1469), as do so many of the other Arthurian characters.

In most versions he is the son of King Ban of Benwick, and his full title is Sir Launcelot du Lac (see LADY OF THE LAKE). In almost all versions in which he appears, he is the champion and lover of Queen GUINEVERE and the favorite of King Arthur. In Malory's version, he begets Sir GALAHAD by ELAINE, when he is deceived into believing that she is Guinevere, and he is then driven to madness for a long period by the jealousy of Guinevere. Most of his exploits are in the name of the queen, one way or another, and sometimes they take the form of rescuing her, as, for example, from being burnt at the stake. He is finally exiled by King Arthur who afterwards comes to war with him at Benwick. In a combat with Sir GAWAIN, Launcelot mortally wounds that knight; then, going back to England, he finds King Arthur dead, the Round Table dissolved, and Queen Guinevere become a nun. He himself becomes a monk and dies not long after Guinevere. Launcelot is a major figure in Tennyson's *Idylls of the King* (1859-1885) and in the narrative poem *Lancelot* by Edwin Arlington Robinson. See JOYOUS GARD.

Launcelot Greaves, The Adventures of Sir (1760). A rambling, satiric novel by Tobias SMOLLETT. It is an attempt to adapt DON QUIXOTE to the 18th century by creating a benevolent reformer so disinterested as to seem mad. The hero, Sir Launcelot Greaves, is a well-bred and noble-minded young English squire of the George II period, half-crazed by love. He sets out, attended by Captain CROWE, to detect fraud and to right the wrongs of the world. After sundry adventures which give the author opportunity for satiric treatment of English life, he is welcomed back by his faithful love Aurelia Darnel. The novel was among the first serialized in English.

Laura. The beloved of PETRARCH and the subject of his collection of lyrics called *Rime* (verses) or *Canzoniere* (song book). The poet says he first saw her in the church of St. Claire at Avignon on April 6, 1327, fell in love, and was inspired to write poetry. Her death, on the same date 21 years later, resulted in a profound spiritual crisis with which the poet struggled for the remainder of his life. Who Laura actually was is still a controversial matter. It was formerly thought that she was a certain Laure de Noves of Avignon, born in 1308, wedded to Hugues de Sede and the mother of 11 children, who died in the great plague of 1348. Modern scholars reject this identification in favor of the idea that Laura is a poetic fiction, a symbol of the poet's aspirations as well as a focal point of his psychological conflicts. In the poems, Petrarch frequently puns on the name because of its resemblance to the Italian words for *air* and *laurel* (hence, inspiration and fame). The name has been used by poets ever since, in love poems addressed to a similar idealized lady. Robert Tofte entitled his 1597 collection of love lyrics *Laura*; Lord Byron used the name for the Venetian lady who marries *Beppo* in the poem of the same name; and Schiller wrote a series of poems to Laura.

laureate. See POETS LAUREATE.

Laurence, Friar. The wise and kindly Franciscan friar in Shakespeare's ROMEO AND JULIET who marries the young lovers. He hopes that the alliance will end the feud between the Montagues and Capulets.

Laurent, Jacques. Pen names: Jacques Laurent-Cely, Cécil Saint-Laurent, Albéric Varenne (1919–). French novelist and historian. The risqué popular novels he has published as Saint-Laurent, such as *Caroline chérie* (1947) and *Clotilde* (1957), are better known than his more serious *Les Corps tranquilles* (1948) and *Le Petit Canard* (1954).

Laurie, Annie (1682–1764). The subject of a Scottish song (c. 1700). A daughter of Sir Robert Laurie of Maxwellton, Dumfriesshire, she married Alexander Ferguson. The song was written by the man she rejected, William Douglas. It was revised and set to music by Lady John Scott (1855).

Lauriers sont coupés, Les (We'll to the Woods No More, 1888). A novel by Edouard DUJARDIN. It is considered the first example in fiction of an intended interior monologue (see STREAM OF CONSCIOUSNESS). Daniel Prince, a young Frenchman, is in love with an actress, Léah d'Arsay, and pretends to himself to be satisfied with a merely "Platonic" relationship, although he actually wishes to make her his mistress. She allows him to believe that she is about to grant him her favors, but after she has secured a sum of money from him she skillfully puts him off. He therefore resolves never to see her again.

The story is told through the thoughts and impressions of the hero as he walks in the street, meets friends, sits in a restaurant, rides in a carriage, and visits Léah. James Joyce is said to have read this book about 1901 and to have been partly influenced by it while writing *Ulysses*. Dujardin himself claimed to have been influenced in his technique by Richard Wagner's device of the musical *Leitmotiv*, by the dramatic monologue of Robert Browning, and by the psychological monologue of Dostoevski.

Lautréamont, Le Comte de. Pen name of Isidore Lucien Ducasse (1846–1870). French poet. Born in Montevideo, Uruguay, Lautréamont came to Paris in 1867. In 1868 he published his first work, *Les Chants de Maldoror*. His poetry, marked by despair, violence, and savagery, possesses the quality of a surrealist nightmare.

Lautrec. See Henri de TOULOUSE-LAUTREC.

Laval, Pierre (1883–1945). French politician. A member of the Chamber of Deputies (from 1914) and premier (1931–1936), Laval is remembered for his policy of collaboration with the Germans during the Occupation. He was ousted as vice-premier of the Vichy government by Pétain (Dec., 1940) but reinstated through German pressure as administrative chief of state. At the end of the war, Laval was tried by a French court for high treason and executed by a firing squad.

Lavater, Johann Kaspar (1741–1801). Swiss divine and poet. In his *Physiognomische Fragmente zur Beförderung der Menschenkenntnis und Menschenliebe* (*Physiognomical Fragments for the Promotion of Knowledge and Love of Man*, 1775 ff.), on which Goethe collaborated, he founded the study of "physiognomy." See PHRENOLOGY.

Lavengro: The Scholar, Gypsy, Priest (1851).

A novel by George BORROW. Mingling autobiography with fiction, the author relates the wanderings of a youg man who is interested in philology and becomes intimate with a family of gypsies. His adventures are resumed in the sequel, *The Romany Rye* (1857). The name Lavengro, which means philologist in the language of the gypsies, was applied to Borrow in his youth.

Lavinia. (1) In Vergil's AENEID, the daughter of LATINUS. She is betrothed to Turnus, king of the Rutuli. When Aeneas lands in Italy, Latinus makes an alliance with the Trojan hero and promises to give him Lavinia as his wife. After Aeneas defeats the angry Turnus, he marries Lavinia and becomes by her the ancestor of Romulus, the mythical founder of Rome. The ancient city of Lavinium near Rome was said to have been built by Aeneas and named after her.

(2) In Shakespeare's TITUS ANDRONICUS, the daughter of Titus. Described as "gracious Lavinia, Rome's rich ornament," she is abducted and married to her betrothed, Bassanius, to prevent her forced marriage to his brother Saturninus. Later the evil sons of the vengeful Tamora slay Bassanius, rape Lavinia, and cut off her tongue and hands.

Lavoisier, Antoine Laurent (1743–1794). French chemist. Lavoisier, who discovered oxygen and the composition of air (at the same time as Priestley), is one of the founders of modern chemistry. He is best known for his theory of the indestructibility of matter. His reforms in chemical nomenclature are the basis of the system still in use. In 1794, he was guillotined by the Revolutionists.

Lavransdatter, Kristin. See KRISTIN LAVRANSDATTER.

Law, John. See MISSISSIPPI BUBBLE.

Law, William (1686–1761). English devotional writer who was influenced in later life by the philosophy of the German mystic Jakob Böhme. He is the author of the *Serious Call to a Devout and Holy Life* (1729), which strongly influenced the Evangelical revival in England, and is especially remembered for his attack on Bernard Mandeville's *Fable of the Bees* (1723). In 1740, Law became the spiritual advisor to Edward Gibbon's aunt, as well as to John and Charles Wesley.

Lawless, Emily (1845–1913). Irish novelist and poet. Her best-known works are the novels *Hurrish* (1886) and *Grania* (1892). *With the Wild Geese* (1902), a volume of poems, is also noteworthy.

Lawrence, St. The patron saint of curriers. He was broiled to death on a gridiron. He was deacon to Sextus I and was charged with the care of the poor, the orphans, and the widows. In the persecution of Valerian (258), being summoned to deliver up the treasures of the church, he produced the poor under his charge and said to the praetor, "These are the church's treasures." He is generally represented as holding a gridiron, and is commemorated on August 10.

The phrase *lazy as Lawrence* is said to take its origin from the story that when being roasted over a slow fire he asked to be turned, "for," said he, "that side is quite done." This expression of Christian fortitude was interpreted by his torturers as evidence of the height of laziness, the martyr being too indolent even to wriggle.

Lawrence, D[avid] H[erbert] (1885–1930). English novelist, short-story writer, poet, and essayist. He is known for his frequently misunderstood but basically idealistic ideas about sexual relations, and for his interest in primitive religions and nature mysticism. Lawrence regarded sex, the primitive subconscious, and nature as cures for what he considered modern man's maladjustment to industrial society. His philosophy, life history, and prejudices are inextricably involved in his writings; many of his views are expressed in WOMEN IN LOVE and LADY CHATTERLEY'S LOVER. SONS AND LOVERS is a partly autobiographical novel which deals with the author's boyhood and adolescence as the son of a coal miner. Lawrence struggled to become a teacher, then an established member of London's literary society, but he never ceased to rebel against Anglo-Saxon puritanism, social conventions, and mediocrity. He was attracted to the Nietzschean idea of the superman, and expressed his idea of the hero in his novels KANGAROO and THE PLUMED SERPENT.

Lawrence's work, of great volume and variety, is uneven in literary value. At its best it is marked by intensity of feeling, psychological insight, vivid evocation of events, places, and particularly nature. A controversial figure, he is regarded by some critics as the greatest of modern English novelists; most concede that he is a major writer in spite of his overfondness for preaching, his obscurantism, and his ranting attacks on the people and institutions he regarded as his enemies. Lawrence's other novels are The White Peacock (1911), The Trespasser (1912), THE RAINBOW, The Lost Girl (1920), Aaron's Rod (1922), and The Boy in the Bush (1924), in collaboration with M. L. Skinner. Among his short novels are St. Mawr (1925), THE MAN WHO DIED, and The Virgin and the Gipsy (1930). Lawrence's short stories, which do not have the faults of his novels, are widely admired. Among them are THE PRUSSIAN OFFICER, THE CAPTAIN'S DOLL, Sun, The Fox, THE WOMAN WHO RODE AWAY, The Man Who Loved Islands, THE ROCKING-HORSE WINNER, and THINGS. His early fiction tends to be fairly conventional and realistic while his later work is more immersed in the subconscious and rich in symbolism. Some of his later short stories, however, are taut and naturalistic.

Lawrence's first published works were poems (see MIRIAM). He began by writing in the school of imagism. His best-known poems are in free verse, about the individual, inner nature of animals and plants: Fish, Snake, Mountain Lion, and Bavarian Gentians are among them. Birds, Beasts and Flowers (1923) is a well-known collection. Look! We Have Come Through (1917) is a collection of poems about his relationship with his wife, Frieda von Richthofen LAWRENCE. Pansies (1929) is a collection of didactic, satiric, and iconoclastic poems, which was seized as immoral by the English authorities on its first publication.

Lawrence's fine, vivid collections of travel sketches are Twilight in Italy (1916), Sea and Sardinia (1921), Mornings in Mexico (1927), and Etruscan Places (1927). His most influential book of criticism is Studies in Classical American Literature (1923), which contains brilliant, eccentric insights into American writers from Benjamin Franklin to Walt Whitman. Psychoanalysis and the Unconscious (1921) and Fantasia of the Unconscious (1922) are statements of his philosophy. He wrote a great many colloquial, iconoclastic essays, including Pornography and Obscenity (1930), Reflections on the Death of a Porcupine (1934), and Democracy (1936). He also wrote Movements in European History (1921), under the pen name of Lawrence H. Davidson, and a few unsuccessful plays. His interesting Letters were edited by Aldous Huxley (1932).

Even after Lawrence established himself in London literary circles—he was a close friend of Aldous Huxley (see POINT COUNTER POINT), and of Katherine Mansfield and J. Middleton Murry—he still had many troubles. He suffered from tuberculosis, saw his books banned as obscene, and was persecuted during World War I for his supposed pro-German sympathies. Disgusted by England, he left it to travel with his wife, but he was continually disappointed in his quest for a homeland and congenial associates. At one time or another, Lawrence lived in Italy, Germany, Ceylon, Australia, New Zealand, Tahiti, the French Riviera, Mexico, and the southwestern part of the United States. In Taos, New Mex., an artists' colony, he once dreamed of setting up an ideal social community. (See Mabel Dodge LUHAN.) At the end of his life he was extravagantly admired by several women who called him "Lorenzo," regarded themselves as his disciples, and engaged in jealous quarrels over his attentions. After Lawrence's death a number of people who had known him published books and memoirs about him, both unfriendly and adulatory, often attacking each other. Among these remembrances were those of J. Middleton Murry, Catherine CARSWELL, Mabel Dodge Luhan, Dorothy BRETT, Richard ALDINGTON, E. T. (see MIRIAM), and his wife.

Lawrence, Frieda von Richthofen (1879–1956). Aristocratic German wife of D. H. LAWRENCE. She was married to Professor Ernest Weekley, an English philologist, and had three children when she met Lawrence and eloped with him in 1912. Lawrence described their stormy, happy marriage in his writings, especially in the collection of poems Look! We Have Come Through and in the novels WOMEN IN LOVE and KANGAROO. She wrote Not I, But the Wind . . . (1934), a memoir of her husband. Her brother, Manfred von Richthofen, was a celebrated German aviator during World War I.

Lawrence, James (1781–1813). American naval officer. During the War of 1812 he commanded the Chesapeake in an engagement (June 1, 1813) with the British frigate Shannon near Boston harbor. Mortally wounded, Lawrence is said to have shouted, "Don't give up the ship!" The British captured the Chesapeake, but Lawrence's last words became a popular slogan in the U.S. navy.

Lawrence, Josephine (1897?–   ). American newspaperwoman and novelist. She writes of the common problems faced by average people in such books as Head of the Family (1932), If I Have Four Apples (1935), No Stone Unturned (1941), The Web of Time (1953), All Our Tomorrows (1959), and Hearts Do Not Break (1960).

Lawrence, T[homas] E[dward]. Known as Lawrence of Arabia (1888–1935). English soldier, archaeologist, and author. He is famous for his activities in arousing and directing a successful rebellion of the Arabs against the Turks during World War I, for his account of his exploits in *Seven Pillars of Wisdom* (1926), and for his enigmatic personality. During the war he became an almost legendary figure in the Middle East; after the war, he received a number of honors and was offered, but refused, the Victoria Cross and a knighthood. He retired from public life to write the *Seven Pillars of Wisdom,* an abridgement of it called *The Revolt in the Desert* (1927), and a prose translation of Homer's *Odyssey* (1932). Meanwhile he sought still more obscurity by joining the Air Force as a private under the name of Shaw. His journal from this period was published as *The Mint* (1955). There has been much interest in, and controversy about, Lawrence's psychological motivations. B. H. Liddell-Hart, Robert Graves, and Richard ALDINGTON are among those who have written about him.

Lawrence, Sir Thomas (1769–1830). English portrait painter. A child prodigy, he succeeded Sir Joshua REYNOLDS as principal painter to the king in 1792. He was the graceful and romantic portraitist of the most brilliant society of England, and after his reputation spread to the continent, he painted the European princes and the heroes of the Napoleonic wars.

Lawrence of Arabia. See T. E. LAWRENCE.

Lawson, John Howard (1895–   ). American playwright. He is known for his experiments in expressionism in the 1920's and his later plays expressing proletarian sympathies. *Processional* (1925), set in a West Virginian town during a coal strike, is perhaps the best known of his plays influenced by the expressionist movement. *Loud Speaker* (1927), on American politics, *The International* (1928), dealing with a worldwide revolution of the proletariat, and *Marching Song* (1937), dealing with a sit-down strike, are all examples of his proletarian plays. Among his books is *Film in the Bottle of Ideas* (1953).

Laxdale Saga. An Icelandic saga of the early Middle Ages, dealing chiefly with the wilful, selfish, and much-married Gudrun who falls in love with Kjartan. While Kjartan is at the court of King Olaf, his cousin Bolli tells Gudrun that Kjartan has become friendly with Olaf's sister Ingebjorg. Vindictively, Gudrun marries Bolli; when Kjartan returns to Iceland and hears of the marriage, he marries Hrefna, also vindictively. He gives to Hrefna an ornate coif, which Ingebjorg had originally sent with him as a gift for Gudrun, and this causes Gudrun to precipitate a feud between the two families by having the coif stolen. There follows a series of raids and battles in which Kjartan is eventually killed through the machinations of the woman who really loved him and whom he loved.

Laxness, Halldór [Kiljan] (1902–   ). Icelandic poet, novelist, and playwright. One of the great figures in modern Icelandic literature, Laxness, who was awarded the Nobel Prize for literature in 1955, passed through several spiritual stages during the course of his literary career. A world traveler, he discovered expressionism in Germany, surrealism in France, and was converted to Catholicism in Luxembourg. The novels *Undir Helgahnúk* (*Under the Holy Mountain,* 1924) and *Verjarinn mikli frá Kasmír* (*The Great Weaver from Kashmir,* 1927) portray the spiritual turmoil of Laxness and the discontent

that led him to the church. He turned to Communism during a visit to the U.S.; when he returned to Iceland in 1930, he published *Alpýðubókin* (*The Book of the People*), a collection of essays expressing his new Communist views. Laxness' finest work, however, appears in the three novels set in an Icelandic fishing village: *Salka Valka* (1936), *Sjálfstoett fólk* (*Independent People,* 2 vols., 1934–1935), and *Ljós heimsins* (*The Light of the World,* 4 vols., 1937–1940). These novels are a rich blend of social criticism, vivid lyricism, and a turbulent, highly exciting prose style. The simple village girl, the sturdy farmer, and the victimized poet who contains an inextinguishable spark of life emerge as symbols from the grand canvas of the work. His *Paradise Reclaimed* was published in 1962.

lay. See LAI.

Layamon. See BRUT, THE.

Lay of the Last Minstrel (1805). A narrative poem by Sir Walter SCOTT. Lady Margaret of Branksome Hall, "the flower of Teviot," is beloved by Baron Henry of Cranstown, but a deadly feud exists between the two families. The poem celebrates the martial prowess and amorous success of the baron.

Lays of Ancient Rome (1842). A series of ballads by Thomas Babington MACAULAY. The chief ballads are *Horatius* (see HORATIUS COCLES), THE BATTLE OF THE LAKE REGILLUS, and *Virginia*.

Layton, Irving (1912–   ). Romanian-born Canadian poet. Layton's family settled in Montreal in 1913. He studied agriculture, served in the Royal Canadian Air Force, and was an editor of *Preview,* an experimental literary magazine published in the 1940's. He is known for his poems of rebellious protest against the social inequalities he saw both in the countryside and the city; often he purposely shocked readers with harsh, "unpoetic" images. His works include *Here and Now* (1945), *In the Midst of My Fever* (1954), *The Bull Calf and Other Poems* (1956), and *The Swinging Flesh* (1961).

Lazarillo de Tormes, La vida de (1554). A PICARESQUE novel by an anonymous author, sometimes identified with Diego HURTADO DE MENDOZA. Divided into seven chapters or *tratados,* it is the autobiography of the wily Lázaro, who describes his experiences with the various masters whom he served: the blind man, the miserly priest, the proud but hungry squire, the mendicant friar, the seller of indulgences. He ends his career as town-crier of Toledo. Written with vigorous realism and irony, *Lazarillo* was enormously popular and inspired several sequels. It is considered the greatest Spanish work in this genre.

Lazarus. (1) In the New Testament, a character in one of Christ's parables who begged daily at the gate of the rich man Dives (Luke 16:19).

(2) Another better-known Lazarus of the New Testament is the brother of Mary and Martha of Bethany, whom Jesus raised from the dead after four days (John 11:12).

Lazarus, Emma (1849–1887). American poet and translator. She translated Heine's poems and published a novel, *Alide: An Episode in Goethe's Life* (1874). This early work, flowery and romantic, would not have won her a reputation. In 1882, however, her indignation was kindled by the Russian pogroms; she set out to defend and glorify the Jewish people. *Songs of a Semite* (1882) includes her best poem, *Dance to Death*. Her sonnet *The New Colossus* (1883) is inscribed on the pedestal of the Statue of LIBERTY. *By the Waters of Babylon* (1887) showed the influence of Whitman.

Lazarus Laughed (1927). A drama by Eugene O'NEILL. It deals with Lazarus after his resurrection by Jesus. The man to whom new life has been given goes about preaching a new religion of love and eternal life, symbolized by laughter. He eventually goes to Rome and causes a sensation there, finally being stabbed by Caligula in the great amphitheater of the city but affirming until the last his belief in the triumph of life. Seven masked choruses, symbolizing varying periods of life, are used in this play.

le, la, l'. For titles beginning with these words, see following words.

Leacock, Stephen (1869–1944). Canadian humorist and political scientist. His satirically humorous short stories and essays were very popular; among them are *Nonsense Novels* (1911), *Moonbeams from the Larger Lunacy* (1915), and *The Garden of Folly* (1924). He also wrote standard works on political science, and studies of Mark Twain (1932) and Charles Dickens (1933).

League of Nations. A league to promote international cooperation and peace, formed after World War I. Its headquarters were at Geneva, Switzerland. Its members were the signatories of the treaty of VERSAILLES on behalf of the Allies, with certain other states, including Germany and the U.S.S.R. Although it was created largely through the exertions of President Woodrow WILSON, the U.S. Senate refused to ratify the treaty of Versailles, and thus the U.S. was never a member of the league.

During the 1920's the league was able to settle a few minor disputes between nations, and its contributions in the fields of refugee rehabilitation, public health, and international labor problems were considerable, but it had no power to enforce its policies in cases of war waged by important nations. It failed especially to be effective at the invasion of Ethiopia by Italy (1935), of Manchuria by Japan (1931), and also during the Civil War in Spain (1936–1939). Several members, including Italy, Japan, and Germany, resigned from the league in the late 1930's. It was formally dissolved on April 18, 1946, its material and moral heritage being taken over by the UNITED NATIONS.

Leah. In the Old Testament, the daughter of Laban and sister of Rachel. She became one of the wives of JACOB.

Léandre. (1) In Molière's *Les Fourberies de Scapin* (*Rogueries of Scapin*, 1671), the son of Géronte. During the absence of his father, he falls in love with Zerbinette, whom he supposes to be a young gypsy but who is in reality the stolen daughter of Argante, his father's friend. SCAPIN raises the money to ransom the girl from the gypsies and Léandre marries her.

(2) In Molière's LE MÉDECIN MALGRÉ LUI, the lover of Lucinde.

leaning tower. The campanile of the cathedral of Pisa, Italy. About 180 feet in height, it began to lean during its construction in the 12th century, and this condition has worsened until it is now about 17 feet out of plumb.

Lear, Edward (1812–1888). English painter and writer. He is known for his LIMERICKS and nonsense verse, marked by absurd humor, whimsy, and fantasy. These are inimitable in their kind, and perennial classics of English humorous verse. *The Owl and the Pussycat* (1871) is his best-known of verses. His books include *A Book of Nonsense* (1846), *Nonsense Songs, Stories, Botany, and Alphabets* (1871), *More Nonsense Songs* (1872), and *Laughable Lyrics* (1877). Lear was also the author of interesting illustrated travel books, such as a *Journal of a Landscape Painter in Greece and Albania* (1852) and so prominent a painter of landscape and animals that he once gave drawing lessons to Queen Victoria.

Learchus (Learchos). See INO.

Leatherstocking Tales, The. A series of five novels by James Fenimore COOPER. The novels appeared in the following sequence: THE PIONEERS (1823), THE LAST OF THE MOHICANS (1826), THE PRAIRIE (1827), THE PATHFINDER (1840), and THE DEERSLAYER (1841). The series follows the career of Natty BUMPPO from his youth (*Deerslayer*) to his death (*The Prairie*). An abridgement of the five novels was made by Allan Nevins in a single volume called *The Leatherstocking Saga* (1954).

Leaves of Grass. A collection of poems by Walt WHITMAN. First published in 1855, it was revised and augmented every few years until the poet's death in 1892. The first edition, unsigned, contained only 12 untitled poems. The first and longest was later called SONG OF MYSELF. In 1855 the poems were preceded by a preface declaring Whitman's poetic credo. "The United States themselves," he said, "are essentially the greatest poem." The country's genius is the common people; the poet must be "commensurate" with the people and "incarnate" the spirit and geography of the States. Echoing *Walden* (1854), Whitman praises simplicity. A great poem, he says, is for "all degrees and complexions and all departments and sects." The poem's form was to be organic; it must grow out of the demands of its subject.

The book, radical in form and content, takes its title from the themes of fertility, universality, and cyclical life. Critics have noted the influence of Shakespeare and the Hebraic poetry of the Bible.

As he revised and added to the original edition, Whitman arranged the poems in a significant autobiographical order. In the final poems, the poet, though dead, survives in his work. In 1881, the permanent order of the volume was established; all later work was assigned to an annex. The final or "death-bed" edition was issued in 1892.

Leavis, F[rank] R[aymond] (1895–   ). English literary critic. One of the CAMBRIDGE CRITICS, he edited the influential magazine *Scrutiny* (1932–1953). Making it his business to maintain standards in English literature and criticism, Leavis wrote controversial essays attacking what he considered mediocre and dilettante work. Above all, he required literature to have moral value and to be concerned with the health of society. He found the qualities he admired in the novelists George Eliot and D. H. Lawrence, and praised them extravagantly. Leavis' criticism was very influential in England. His chief works are *New Bearings in English Poetry* (1932), *Revaluations* (1936), *The Great Tradition: George Eliot, James, and Conrad* (1948), *The Common Pursuit* (1952), and *D. H. Lawrence, Novelist* (1955). Much of the material in these books first appeared in *Scrutiny*, which served as a vehicle for the ideas of Leavis and of other Cambridge critics who shared some of his principles.

Le Beau. In Shakespeare's As You Like It, a garrulous French courtier, "his mouth full of news," attending on Duke Frederick.

lebensraum. See Karl HAUSHOFER.

Lebyadkin, Marya Timofeyevna. In Feodor Dostoevski's novel The Possessed, the crippled half-wit Stavrogin has married for obscure and perverse reasons that are not clarified. She is portrayed in the tradition of the Russian "holy **fool**" and, along with Shatov, is the vehicle for the expression of many of Dostoevski's own religious ideas.

Lebyadkin, Captain. The comical and unscrupulous brother of Marya Timofeyevna, Stavrogin's half-wit wife. He calls himself a retired army captain, although doubt is cast on the truth of this by the narrator. Lebyadkin, who callously mistreats his sister, continually tries to extort money from Stavrogin for her support. He is murdered along with Marya at the end of the novel.

Le Charlier, Jean. See Jean GERSON.

Leconte de Lisle, Charles Marie René (1818–1894). French poet, leader of the PARNASSIANS. A dislike for the excessive subjectivity and exaggerated emotionalism of the romantic writers caused him to write poetry that was objective in content and austere in style. Leconte de Lisle gave voice to dark pessimism, and his hatred for the ugly industrial civilization in which he lived led him to seek his subjects in the past or in strange, distant places. His works include *Poèmes antiques* (1852), *Poèmes barbares* (1862), *Histoire populaire du Christianisme* (1871), *Poèmes tragiques* (1884), and *Derniers Poèmes* (1895). His drama *L'Apollonide* (1888) and the verse tragedy *Les Erinnyes* (1889) are also well known.

Lecoq, Monsieur. A brilliant French detective created by Emile GABORIAU. Monsieur Lecoq appears in several novels: *Monsieur Lecoq* (1869), *L'Affaire Lerouge* (1866) and *Le Dossier no. 113* (1867). He is one of the first of the famous detectives of literature and a precursor of Sherlock Holmes.

Le Corbusier. Real name, **Charles Edouard Jeanneret** (1887–   ). Swiss-born French architect and painter. He is known for his contributions to functionalism. Among these are the corner window, the glass façade, the use of ferroconcrete in buildings, and the elevated traffic ramp. Le Corbusier is an innovator in city planning. His suggested plans for Algiers and St. Dié are no less influential than his planning, undertaken in 1951, of the new town of Chandigarh for the Indian government. He is the author of *Towards a New Architecture* (1923). Among his best-known works are the Radiant City of Marseilles (1946–1952) and the chapel at Ronchamp (1955). As a painter, Le Corbusier demands of art a total submission to its architectural setting. About 1918, with Amédée Ozenfant, he developed purism with the idea of preventing cubism from becoming a mere decorative ornament. He adopted the machine as an object of absolute perfection and rejected every accidental detail in his rigorous compositions. Yet at no time did Le Corbusier condemn lyricism, but rather sought rules, both in painting

and architecture, proper to the creation of a setting that would satisfy the very nature of man as he conceives it, with its need for light, order, and joy.

Lecouvreur, Adrienne (1692–1730). French actress. The greatest tragedienne of her day on the French stage, Lecouvreur substituted unaffected delivery for the then current bombastic, declamatory style of tragic acting. The church's refusal to grant her burial in consecrated soil provoked an anticlerical scandal and aroused Voltaire to compose an elegy on her death. Lecouvreur is the subject of a play by Scribe and Legouvé and of an opera by Cilèa, both based on the unfounded tradition that she was poisoned by a rival in love.

Lectern, The. See LUTRIN, LE.

Leda. In Greek mythology, the wife of Tyndareus. She was the mother by Zeus (who is fabled to have come to her in the shape of a swan) of two eggs, from one of which came Castor and Clytemnestra, and from the other Polydeuces and Helen. There are, however, many versions of their birth. The subject of Leda and the Swan has been a favorite with artists; Paul Veronese, Correggio, and Michelangelo have all left paintings of it.

Ledoux, Louis V[ernon] (1880–1948). American poet and critic. Head of the firm of Ledoux & Co., chemists and assayers, Ledoux wrote such volumes of verse as *Songs from the Silent Land* (1905), *The Soul's Progress and Other Poems* (1906), and *The Shadow of Aetna* (1914). Following one of his main interests, he wrote *The Art of Japan* (1927) and *Japanese Prints of the Primitive Period* (1942).

Ledwidge, Francis (1891–1917). Irish nature poet. He wrote *Songs of the Field* (1914) and *Songs of Peace* (1916). He was killed in World War I.

Lee, Ann (1736–1784). English mystic and founder of the American Shaker society in Watervliet, N.Y. (1776). She claimed the power of discerning spirits and working miracles. She was known to her followers as "Ann the Word" or "Mother Ann" since they were convinced that she was the manifestation of the female counterpart of Christ.

Lee, Henry. Known as **Light-Horse Harry Lee** (1756–1818). American soldier and statesman. The father of Robert E. Lee, he was a brilliant cavalry commander in the Revolutionary War and received his nickname because of his quick movements in the field. His eulogy of Washington (1799) contains the famous words: "First in war, first in peace, and first in the hearts of his countrymen."

Lee, Laurie (1914–   ). English poet. The author of simple lyrics, mostly about nature, he has written *The Bloom of Candles* (1947) and *A Rose for Winter* (1955). *Cider with Rosie* (1959) is an autobiography.

Lee, Lorelei. The heroine of Anita Loos's novel Gentlemen Prefer Blondes. Not very bright but an enterprising young lady, she is a remarkably successful "gold-digger."

Lee, Manfred B. See Ellery QUEEN.

Lee, Nathaniel (c. 1653–1692). English dramatist. His bloody and extravagant tragedies, extremely popular in his time, include *The Rival Queens, or The Death of Alexander the Great* (1677); *Mithridates, King of Pontus* (1678); and *Caesar Borgia* (1680). He also collaborated with Dryden.

Lee, Robert E[dward] (1807–1870). American soldier. The son of Henry Lee, he was graduated from West Point in 1829, fought in the Mexican War, and commanded the marine detachment that quelled John Brown's abortive insurrection in 1859. Although Lee favored preservation of the Union, loyalty to his native Virginia, where his family had long been prominent, led him to refuse field command of the U.S. army in 1861 and to accept command of the state's forces. Named commander of the Army of Northern Virginia in 1862, he thwarted McClellan's Peninsula Campaign against Richmond in the Seven Days' Battles (1862), suffered a technical defeat at ANTIETAM, and won engagements at Fredericksburg and CHANCELLORSVILLE. His defeat at GETTYSBURG began the attrition of Confederate strength that compelled him to surrender to Grant at Appomattox Courthouse on April 9, 1865. After the war, Lee became president of Washington College in Virginia, which was later renamed Washington and Lee University in his honor. An excellent strategist and leader of men, Lee is admired in both North and South for his courage and chivalry.

Lee, Vernon. Pen name of **Violet Paget** (1856–1935). English novelist, essayist, and writer on aesthetics, politics, and Italian art and life. *Euphorion* (1884) is a study of Renaissance art.

Leech, Margaret (1893–   ). American writer. Her works in the field of American history and biography are known for their careful research and readable style. For *Reveille in Washington* (1941), an account of life in the capital during the Civil War, she received a Pulitzer Prize. Her other books include *Anthony Comstock, Roundsman of the Lord*, written with Heywood Broun (1927), and *In the Days of McKinley* (1959), another Pulitzer Prize winner.

Leech-gatherer, The. See RESOLUTION AND INDEPENDENCE.

Le Fanu, Joseph Sheridan (1814–1873). Irish novelist, journalist, and balladeer. He is known for his mystery novel *Uncle Silas* (1864), and his tales of the supernatural, the best of which is *The House by the Churchyard* (1863). His work compares favorably with that of Poe and Wilkie Collins. He was a distant relative of the 18th-century playwright Sheridan.

Lefèvre d'Etaples, Jacques. See Jacques Lefèvre d'ETAPLES.

left, right, center. Names applied to political positions. In the amphitheater where the French National Assembly of 1789 convened, the nobles still commanded sufficient respect to be given places of honor to the *right* of the president. The radicals moved naturally as far away from them to the *left* as they could. The moderates found themselves squeezed in between in the *center*. Hence the political connotations of these terms. Carlyle, in *The French Revolution* (1847), was one of the first to speak in English of "the extreme Left." Such derivatives as *leftist, leftism,* and the like, did not come into general use until after the Russian Revolution (c. 1920).

Legalist School. Chinese political philosophy of the 4th and 3d centuries B.C. Largely based on the teachings of the HAN FEI TZU, it called for harsh and expedient means for gaining political and mili-

tary control. Its teachings were adopted during the Ch'in Dynasty.

Le Gallienne, Eva (1899–   ). English-born American actress, director, and producer. The daughter of the English writer Richard Le Gallienne, she founded (1926), directed, and acted in the Civic Repertory Theater in New York, and was cofounder of the American Repertory Theatre (1946). She is noted for her continuing interest in repertory theater in the U.S. In addition, she has translated many of Ibsen's plays and has written an autobiography *At 33* (1934), continued in *With a Quiet Heart* (1953).

Legenda Aurea. See GOLDEN LEGEND.

Legend of Good Women, The (c. 1386). Unfinished poem by Geoffrey CHAUCER, of over 2700 lines in decasyllabic couplets. In the prologue, which contains the best poetry, the poet describes his delight at wandering through the meadows on a May morning, especially celebrating the daisy. He falls asleep and dreams that the god of Love, attended by Queen Alceste, appears and berates him for having translated the *Romance of the Rose* and written *Troilus and Criseyde,* thereby discouraging men from the service of COURTLY LOVE. Alceste intercedes, pointing out Chaucer's exaltation of love in other works, and suggests that he be allowed to redeem himself by writing a collection of 20 lives of women who have served Love truly and well. There follow nine short narratives, modeled on stories by Vergil and Ovid, about women who suffered or died because they were faithful in love and (except for the first two stories) because men were treacherous: Cleopatra; Thisbe; Dido; Hypsipyle and Medea, both betrayed by Jason; Lucrece; Ariadne; Philomela; Phyllis, betrayed by Demophon; Hypermnestra.

Legend of Montrose, The (1819). A novel by Sir Walter SCOTT, dealing with the struggle between the Royalists and the Parliamentarians in the time of Charles I. Interwoven with this are the amorous quandaries of the heroine, Annot Lyle.

Legend of Sleepy Hollow, The (1819). A tale by Washington IRVING, collected in his SKETCH BOOK OF GEOFFREY CRAYON, GENT. The story takes place at Sleepy Hollow, now Tarrytown, N.Y. ICHABOD CRANE, the local schoolmaster, courts Katrina Van Tassel. The affair is interrupted when Crane's rival, Brom Bones, masquerades as a headless horseman, and scares the schoolmaster out of town.

Legends of the Alhambra, The (1832; enlarged, 1852). A group of tales and sketches on Spanish subjects by Washington IRVING. The book grew out of Irving's sojourn in Spain as a member of the U.S. Embassy, in 1826. The legends deal with the clashes between Spaniard and Moor. Irving, an admirer of Moorish civilization, invests the tales with glamour and mystery.

Léger, Aléxis St.-Léger. See St.-John PERSE.

Léger, Fernand (1881–1955). French artist whose paintings, murals, tapestries, mosaics and stained glass windows exercised a profound influence upon his time. In 1917 he began to construct his compositions from mechanical elements such as radiators, railway wheels, or cogs; human figures were themselves treated as machines. Léger's art gradually became more human, achieving a liveliness, and gaiety, while retaining its monumental quality. His construction workers, mechanics, divers, or picnickers were constructed in bright flat colors increasingly dissociated from his strong and direct drawing but full of movement and power.

Legion of Honor (Légion d'honneur). A French order of distinction and reward instituted by Napoleon Bonaparte in 1802 for either military or civil merit. The order has continued to exist in France during the 19th and 20th centuries.

Legree, Simon. The overseer in Harriet Beecher Stowe's Uncle Tom's Cabin. He flogs Uncle Tom, causing his death, when the latter refuses to reveal the hiding places of two runaway women slaves. His name has become a synonym for a brutal taskmaster.

Lehár, Franz (1870–1948). Hungarian composer of operettas. He wrote The Merry Widow; *The Count of Luxemburg* (1909); and others.

Lehmann, John (1907–   ). English editor, brother of Rosamond Lehmann. He edited the influential left-wing magazine *New Writing* and its successor from 1936 to 1950 (publishing the work of Auden and other left-wing poets), and edited *The London Magazine* from 1954. His autobiographies are *The Whispering Gallery* (1955) and *I Am My Brother* (1960).

Lehmann, Lotte (1888–   ). German-born concert and operatic soprano. She is especially famed for her interpretation of German lieder. She wrote a novel, *Orplied mein Land* (1937; translated, *Eternal Flight*, 1938), and two autobiographies: *Anfang und Aufsteig* (1937; translated, *Midway in My Song*, 1938) and *My Many Lives* (1948).

Lehmann, Rosamond (1903–   ). English novelist. She is the daughter of L. C. Lehmann, long on the staff of *Punch*, and sister of John Lehmann and of Beatrix Lehmann, an actress. *Dusty Answer* (1927) is about the emotions of a young girl growing up, especially during her years at college. *Invitation to the Waltz* (1932) describes the experiences of a girl at her first elegant party. *The Ballad and the Source* (1945) is an experimental novel in which the most violent events that afflict three generations of a tragically doomed family are narrated by a 14-year-old girl in the order in which she hears about them. She also wrote *A Note in Music* (1930), and *The Echoing Grove* (1953). A writer of grace and sensibility, her work may be compared with that of Virginia Woolf and Elizabeth Bowen.

Leibniz or **Leibnitz, Gottfried Wilhelm** (1646–1716). German philosopher. A major figure in the German enlightenment, he believed in a pre-established harmony, created by God, of matter and spirit. His statement that "this is the best of all possible worlds" was ridiculed by Voltaire in Candide for its supposedly irresponsible optimism; actually, however, Leibniz meant his statement in a metaphysical sense and did not intend it to be directly applied to everyday life. In his *Monadologie* (1714), Leibniz maintains that the divine order of the universe is reflected in each of its parts, the smallest unit being the monad. The happiness of man is in striving for harmony with God, the original creator of harmony. Leibniz formulated the calculus in 1676, independently of Newton.

Leicester, earl of. See Robert Dudley, earl of Leicester.

Leiden des jungen Werthers, Die. See Sorrows of Young Werther, The.

Leif Ericson. See Leif Ericson.

Leigh, Augusta. See Anne Isabella Milbanke.

Leino, Eino. Pen name of **Armas Eino Leopold Lönnbohm** (1879–1926). Finnish poet, playwright, and novelist. Considered the outstanding lyric poet of modern Finland, Leino published many collections of highly subjective verse. In such works as *Ajan Aalloilta* (*The Waves of Time,* 1899) and *Helkavirsia* (*Helga Hymns,* 1903), he gave expression to the feelings of his people and to his own intense emotional life.

Leipzig, battle of. Also called the **battle of the nations** (October 16–18, 1813). A famous battle where the French under Napoleon Bonaparte were badly defeated by the allied forces of Prussia, Austria, Sweden, and Russia.

Leir, King. A central figure in a tale in the History of the Kings of Britain by Geoffrey of Monmouth. His story is much the same as that found in Shakespeare's great tragedy King Lear: Leir divides his kingdom among his three daughters; he rejects Cordelia, and is subsequently rejected by Goneril and Regan. In this tale, however, the king goes to France to enlist the aid of Cordelia, reconquers Britain, and, when he dies, is buried under the river Soar. For his tragedy, Shakespeare seems to have made use of the version of Leir's story found in Holinshed's *Chronicles.*

leitmotiv or **leitmotif** (*Ger.,* "leading motive"). In the Wagnerian music drama, a theme consistently reappearing with the reappearance of a given character, problem, emotion, or thought. The term has also been applied to a corresponding device in literature. Thomas Mann has used the leitmotiv technique in conscious emulation of Wagner. For instance, in *The Magic Mountain,* each appearance of Settembrini is accompanied by the same brief description of his clothes.

Leland, Charles Godfrey. See Hans Breitmann.

Lélia (1833). A novel by George Sand. The highly romantic tale describes the tragically misdirected feelings of love that motivate the various characters. These include Lélia, the lovely heroine; her sister Pulchérie, a prostitute; Sténio, an idealistic young poet; and Magnus, a priest who becomes insane.

Lely, Sir Peter. Originally **Pieter Van der Faes** (1618–1680). Dutch-born English portrait painter. He migrated to England in 1641, where his studio became a school that introduced Dutch technique to the artistically isolated English.

Lemaître, [François Elie] Jules (1853–1914). French writer and critic. Lemaître served as drama critic for the *Journal des Débats* and was noted for his lively impressionistic articles, refreshing for the spontaneity of their reactions. His essays and reviews were published in the 7-volume series *Contemporains* (1855–1899), the 8th volume appearing posthumously in 1918, and in his 10-volume *Impressions de Théâtre* (1888–1898) whose 11th volume also appeared posthumously (1920).

Lemnos. The island where Hephaestus fell when Zeus flung him out of heaven. One myth connected with Lemnos tells how the women of the island, in revenge for their ill-treatment, murdered all the men. The Argonauts found the place an "Adamless Eden." They were received with great favor by the women; as a result of their few months' stay the island was repopulated, and the queen, Hypsipyle, became the mother of twins by Jason.

Lemon, Mark (1809–1870). English playwright, editor. Author of some 60 plays, numerous novels, essays, and children's books, Lemon is remembered as one of the founders and first editor (1841–1870), of *Punch*, the English magazine of humor and satire, whose tone and popularity he did much to establish.

Le Morte d'Arthur. See MORTE D'ARTHUR, LE.

Lemoyne, Jean Baptiste. See Sieur de BIENVILLE.

Lemprière, John (1765–1824). English classical scholar who compiled the reference work *Bibliotheca Classica, or Classical Dictionary* (1788), dealing with classical history and mythology.

lemures. The name given by the Romans to the spirits of the dead, especially specters which wandered about at nighttime to terrify men.

Lemuria. The name given to a lost land that supposedly connected Madagascar with India and Sumatra in prehistoric times.

Lenau, Nikolaus. Name at birth: **Edler von Strehlenau Niembsch** (1802–1850). Hungarian-born Austrian poet. His lyrics are marked by a striking exactness of imagery and an occasionally morbid personal intensity that reflects the instability of his temperament. He wrote two religious epics pleading for tolerance, *Savonarola* (1837) and *Die Albigenser* (*The Albigensians*, 1842), and an epic-dramatic *Faust* (1836). In 1832 he came to the U.S., hoping to begin a new, idyllic existence, but returned disappointed to Germany in 1833, and in 1844 he went mad. See Ferdinand KÜRNBERGER.

Lenclos, Anne. Known as **Ninon de Lenclos** (1620–1705). French lady of fashion. Famous for her wit and beauty, she conducted a dazzling salon and numbered among her lovers the most distinguished men of the day. In the novel *Clélie*, her friend Madeleine de Scudéry drew a portrait of her under the name Clarisse.

Lenin, Nikolai. Pseudonym of **Vladimir Ilyich Ulyanov** (1870–1924). Russian Communist leader. Lenin, who led the BOLSHEVIKS to power in 1917, was born in Simbirsk (now called Ulyanovsk in his honor), the son of a provincial schoolmaster. His elder brother Alexander was executed in 1887 for an attempt on the life of Czar ALEXANDER III. Lenin, who studied at the universities of Kazan and St. Petersburg where he became a profound student of Marxism, entered revolutionary activity in the 1890's. Much of his time was spent in Siberian exile or abroad. In 1903 he became a leader of the Bolshevik faction of the Social Democratic Party, having been largely responsible for the schism that split the party, the other faction being known as the Mensheviks. Lenin's drive and astuteness as a practical revolutionary led the Bolsheviks to power in the *coup d'état* of October (November by the Western calendar) of 1917. He became the head of the Soviet state and retained the post until his death. Like his colleague Trotsky, Lenin had a background of bourgeois culture and apparently was little interested in the manipulation of cultural life of the kind that took place in the Soviet Union under Stalin. His giant mausoleum in Red Square, Moscow, is a national shrine to the Russians.

Lennox. In Shakespeare's MACBETH, a Scottish noble. He informs Macbeth of Macduff's flight to England.

Lenore (1774). A ballad in folk style by Gottfried August BÜRGER, in which a soldier appears after death to his sweetheart and carries her with him on horseback to the graveyard where a macabre marriage is celebrated by departed spirits.

Lenormand, Henri René (1882–1951). French dramatist. His plays, influenced by Freudian theory, show the psychological conflicts of men at the mercy of the forces of nature. *Time is a Dream* (*Le Temps est un songe;* 1919), *Failures* (*Les Ratés;* 1920), *The Dream Doctor* (*Le Mangeur de rêves;* 1922) and *Man and His Phantoms* (*L'Homme et ses fantômes;* 1924) are among his better known works.

Lenz, Jakob Michael Reinhold (1751–1792). German dramatist of the STURM UND DRANG, admirer of Goethe. His plays, which are distinguished by a revolutionary realism and looseness of form, include *Der neue Menoza* (*The New Menoza,* 1774) and *Die Soldaten* (*The Soldiers,* 1776).

Leo X, Pope. See MEDICI.

Leo XIII. Original name: **Gioacchino Pecci** (1810–1903). Pope (1878–1903), and Italian poet. His encyclical *Rerum Novarum* (1891), urging reform in favor of the working classes, is significant for its liberal approach. He wrote poetry in Italian and Latin and in 1832 was admitted to the ARCADIAN ACADEMY, whose bicentenary (1890) he later celebrated in a long poem praising Metastasio, Parini, and Alfieri. Also noted is his ode written on New Year's Eve, 1900, in which he calls for spiritual renewal and the avoidance of war in the coming century.

Leodegraunce, King. See ROUND TABLE.

León [y Román], Ricardo (1877–1943). Spanish novelist. His works of popular fiction include *Casta de hidalgos* (*A Son of the Hidalgos,* 1908), a descriptive narrative, and *El amor de los amores* (*The Wisdom of Sorrow,* 1910), a study in mysticism.

Leonard, William Ellery (1876–1944). American poet and educator. He is best known for the sonnet sequence, *Two Lives* (1925), which forms an autobiographical account of Leonard and his first wife. He also published several volumes of verse, including *A Man Against Time* (1945), *The Vaunt of Man and Other Poems* (1912), and *The Lynching Bee and Other Poems* (1920). *The Locomotive God* (1927) is his autobiography. A student of Lucretius, Leonard translated his poems (1916), wrote a study of his life and poetry (1942), and helped edit the Latin text.

Leonardo da Vinci (1452–1519). Italian painter, sculptor, architect, engineer, scientist, poet, and musician. A universal genius and one of the greatest intellects in the history of mankind, Leonardo was born at Vinci, near Florence, and became in 1466 an apprentice to VERROCCHIO. The latter's *Baptism of Christ* contains an angel and landscape features probably executed by his pupil, who was already his superior. In 1482, he went to Milan where he worked for Lodovico Sforza as an engineer as well as a designer of costumes and scenery for court entertainments. He also made sketches for churches, painted the murals and ceiling pictures of the Sforza castle, and worked on problems of irrigation and central

Leonardo da Vinci: sketches for war machines.

heating. In 1502, he served for a time as military engineer to Caesar Borgia. An offer from the French king, Francis I, took him to France in 1516, where he stayed until his death. Misfortune and Leonardo's own habit of endlessly experimenting with pigments have left few of his paintings to posterity. The best known are *The Adoration of the Magi* in the Uffizi; *The Madonna in the Grotto* (c. 1495) and *Mona Lisa* (also called LA GIOCONDA, 1503), both in the Louvre; and the LAST SUPPER (1495–?1498) in the Milan church of S. Maria delle Grazie. *The Battle of Anghiari*, done in 1505 at Florence in competition with Michelangelo, survives only in drafts. His style in painting is characterized by the use of *sfumato*, or blurring of outlines. the mysterious effects of chiaroscuro, the clarity of composition, and the over-all tone of serenity. In sculpture, only sketches remain of the destroyed equestrian statue of Francesco Sforza and of the unfinished one of the *condottiere* Trivulzio. He left no architectural works, but his sketches for buildings and even whole cities were influential for his contemporaries. As engineer and scientist, Leonardo was led by his avid curiosity to speculate about and experiment with various mechanical devices, including guns and cannon, flying machines, parachutes, hydraulic works, submarines, and spiral staircases. In his notebooks, there are some 5,000 pages of sketches and comments that reveal his concern with anatomy, botany, and mathematics, including mechanical perspective drawings, studies of people and animals, caricatures, plant studies and landscapes. He left also a treatise on painting, *Trattato della pittura* (1489–1518), which has been extracted from the notebooks. Here he espoused again his favorite motif: fidelity to nature, which must be observed directly, not through abstractions or Aristotle or Galen. It was this attention to things themselves which produced the paradox of Leonardo's life, for he accomplished hardly a fraction of his schemes, so overwhelmed was he by the need to investigate and know everything. But even his most tentative ideas and experiments were years ahead of his time and simply beyond the capacities of his contemporaries.

Leonato. In Shakespeare's MUCH ADO ABOUT NOTHING, the governor of Messina, father of Hero and uncle of Beatrice. He joins with Don Pedro in bringing Beatrice and Benedick together and later forgives Claudio for having doubted Hero's virtue.

Leoncavallo, Ruggiero (1858–1919). Italian operatic composer and librettist. He is best known for *I Pagliacci* (1892).

Leone. In the ORLANDO FURIOSO of Ariosto, a Greek prince, and prospective husband of Bradamante. His rival, Ruggiero, wins Bradamante by defeating her in a duel, but he is wearing Leone's armor! Finally, Leone gives up to Ruggiero his right to wed Bradamante.

Leonidas. A Spartan king and hero (fl. early 5th century B.C.). He resisted the Persians at Thermopylae with only three hundred Spartans and was slain with all his forces at the pass.

Leonov, Leonid Maksimovich (1899–   ). Russian novelist, dramatist, and short-story writer. Leonov fought with the Red Army during the civil war. He published some short stories during the early 1920's, but first attracted attention in 1924 with a long story, *The End of a Petty Man* (*Konetz melkogo cheloveka*). The story, dealing with the acceptance of the revolution by a member of the old generation, foreshadowed a theme Leonov and others were to take up often in later works. Leonov's first novel, *The Badgers* (*Barsuki;* 1925), dealt with the conflict between the city and countryside during the civil war. The conflict is personified in two brothers, one of whom leaves the village for the city and eventually comes back at the head of an armed force sent to quell a revolt led by his brother. Leonov's second novel, considered by some critics as his best work, is THE THIEF, which is set in the period of the New Economic Policy in Russia.

Leonov's other novels are *Soviet River* (*Sot;* 1930), *Skutarevski* (1932), *Road to the Ocean* (*Doroga na okean;* 1935), and *Russian Forest* (*Russki les;* 1953). His best-known plays include *The Orchards of Polovchansk* (*Polovchanskiye sady;* 1936), *Nashestviye* (*Invasion;* 1942), and *Lyonushka* (1943). One of his best wartime works was the short novel *The Taking of Velikoshumsk* (*Vzyatiye velikoshumska*, 1944), describing a Red Army offensive in the Ukraine.

Leonov is noted as one of the foremost stylists of Soviet prose. His rich and exuberant language and his predilection for complex intrigues in his stories have caused critics to cite him as a follower of Dostoevski, although this influence is only plainly evident in his novel *The Thief.*

Leontes. In Shakespeare's WINTER'S TALE, the king of Sicilia, husband of Hermione and father of Perdita. Consumed with blind, unreasoning jealousy, he accuses his wife of adultery and tries to poison his friend Polixenes. When he finally realizes his folly, he is stricken with remorse.

Leopard, The (Il Gattopardo, 1956). An historical novel by Giuseppe Tomasi, prince of Lampedusa (1896–1957), Sicilian novelist. It describes the impact of Garibaldi's invasion of Sicily and the subsequent unification of Italy on a proud, aristocratic Sicilian family devoted to the Bourbon kings. The novel is celebrated for its refined, poetic style.

Leopardi, Count **Giacomo** (1798–1837). Italian poet. A self-taught prodigy, afflicted by physical deformity and spinal disease, he distinguished himself at an early age with the lyrical beauty and intense melancholy of his poetry. All his writings express belief in a cosmic nature that is unalterably hostile to man and the chief obstacle to human happiness. This pessimism provides the connective motif in the various collections of his verse: *Canzoni* (1824), *Versi* (1826), and *Canti* (1836). It is treated philosophically in the brief dialogue-essays *Le Operette Morali* (1824) and the miscellany of aphorisms *Pensieri* (1834–1837).

Leopardi described himself as an ardent patriot and a confirmed classicist, but he revealed romantic tendencies in asserting that imagination rather than reason is the true source of poetic inspiration.

Lepanto, battle of (Oct. 7, 1571). A naval engagement in the gulf of Corinth, fought between the forces of the Ottoman Empire and those of a Holy League comprising Spain, Venice, and the papacy. Under the leadership of Don John of Austria, the Christians overwhelmingly defeated the Turks, ending their naval domination of the Mediterranean. CERVANTES took part in the battle and was wounded in the left hand.

Lepidus, Marcus Aemilius (d. 13 B.C.). A member, with Octavius and Mark Antony, of the Second TRIUMVIRATE (43–33 B.C.). He was forced by Octavius into retirement.

Leporello. In Mozart's opera DON GIOVANNI, the valet of Don Giovanni.

leprechaun. An elflike creature in Irish folklore, often associated with shoemaking and the guarding of hidden treasure. He is usually characterized by small stature, supernatural qualities, and a puckish sense of humor. Modern treatment of the leprechaun may be found in James Stephens' fantasy *The Crock of Gold* (1912) and in William Butler Yeats's *Fairy and Folk Tales* (1888).

Lermontov, Mikhail Yurievich (1814–1841). Russian poet and novelist. In his work and his life he was the outstanding example of the influence of Byronic romanticism on Russian literature. His reputation as a poet in the 19th century was exceeded only by Pushkin's. Many of Lermontov's works are set in the Caucasus, where he was exiled for a poem denouncing court circles after Pushkin's death. He returned to St. Petersburg later, was exiled again for dueling, and was killed in a duel in the Caucasus. A few months before, he had described a death similar to his own in a short poem *Son* (*A Dream*). His most famous poems are *Angel*, *Demon*, *Mtsyri* (*The Novice*), and *Zaveshchaniye* (*The Testament*). Lermontov's only completed novel, A HERO OF OUR TIME, was important in the development of the Russian novel, marking a transition from the earlier form of a cycle of stories to the traditional novel form of the later 19th century. It consists of five stories, centering around the romantic hero Pechorin, which are presented out of their chronological sequence for purposes of suspense and retardation of the narrative, just as later novelists were to do. Lermontov's psychological analysis of the hero and realistic treatment of the secondary characters, also, anticipate the work of the great 19th-century Russian realists.

Lernean hydra. See HYDRA.

Lesage or **Le Sage, Alain René** (1668–1747). French novelist and dramatist. His early works are translations of Spanish authors, such as Rojas, Lope de Vega, Calderón, and others; these works caused no comment. His first original work, *Crispin, rival de son maître* (1707), a comedy, made him a repu-

tation. It was soon followed by the novel *Le Diable boiteux* (1709), an imitation and enlargement of Luis Vélez de Guevara's *El Diablo cojuelo* (1641). AsMODEUS, as this novel is sometimes called in English translation, is an unrelated series of satirical tableaux, more descriptive than moralistic, of life in 18th-century France. His next play *Turcaret, ou le Financier* (1708) is a bitter satire on money and financiers, and caused a great scandal. After this comedy, Lesage wrote some 100 farces or comedies of manners, often interspersed with popular airs, for the Théâtre de la Foire. His masterpiece, *Histoire de* GIL BLAS DE SANTILLANE (definitive ed. 1747), is considered by some critics to be the first novel of manners. Lesage wrote three other picaresque novels, *Don Guzman d'Alfarache* (1732), *Estevanille Gonzalès* (1734), and LE BACHELIER DE SALAMANQUE (1736), and some inferior minor works of fiction. Celebrated for his animated style, and for his vivid and dramatic presentation of human foibles and absurdities, he had a marked influence on Fielding, Smollett, and Sterne, the English novelists.

Lesbian. Pertaining to Lesbos, one of the islands of the Greek Archipelago. It pertains also to Sappho, the famous poetess of Lesbos, and to the practices of female homosexuality (Lesbianism) attributed to her.

Lesbino. In the GERUSALEMME LIBERATA of Tasso, the youthful page of Solimano, the leader of the Arab forces pitted against the Crusaders. The lad is killed by the knight Argillano, whom the bereaved Solimano then kills in revenge.

Lescaut, Manon. See MANON LESCAUT.

Leskov, Nikolai Semionovich (1831–1895). Russian novelist and short-story writer. Leskov, whose parents died when he was 17, supported himself as a civil servant, estate manager, and journalist in various provincial towns, until at the age of 30, he became a journalist in St. Petersburg. His first large literary work, the novel *Nekuda* (*No Way Out*, 1864), won little critical acclaim. The radical critics held sway over literature at the time and Leskov had displeased the radicals with some of his journalistic articles. His next novel, *Na Nozhakh* (*At Daggers Drawn*, 1870–1871), depicted young radicals in a manner that enraged the radical camp still more. Leskov was disinclined to placate the critics, even though their influence was able to delay his recognition as a major writer. He eventually attained this recognition with the general reading public for the humor and raciness of his stories and for his remarkable prose, which is full of puns, colloquial expressions, folk etymologies, and neologisms. Many of his most popular stories are set in the milieu of the clergy and Old Believers, which Leskov had had ample time to observe during his early years in the provinces. Leskov was one of the early masters of the narrative technique termed *skaz* by Russian critics: the re-creation in prose of indigenous oral narration, by reproducing the speech mannerisms, cadence, and vocabulary of a fictional narrator. Leskov often placed the *skaz* narration in the framework of the story by having the recorder of the story meet a character who relates the tale in his own words.

Leskov's most popular works include the novel *Soboryane* (*Cathedral Folk*, 1872), and the tales *Zapechatlionni angel* (*The Sealed Angel*, 1873), *Ocharovanni strannik* (*The Enchanted Wanderer*,

1874), *Melochi arkhiyereiskoi zhizni* (*Details of Episcopal Life*, 1880), and *Skaz o tul'skom kosom levshe i o stal'noi blokhe* (*The Left-handed Smith of Tula and the Steel Flea*, 1882).

Les Misérables. See MISÉRABLES, LES.

Lespinasse, Julie Jeanne Eléonore de (1732–1776). French letter-writer. She was the companion and protégée, from 1754 to 1763, of the blind Mme du DEFFAND. Together, they conducted for a time a sparkling literary salon; later, her own salon became a center for the *Encyclopédistes* (see ENCYCLOPÉDIE). She was a friend of d'Alembert, the marquis de Mora, and the comte de Guibert. To this latter are addressed her passionate love letters, *Lettres de Mlle de Lespinasse*, with their constant theme, *Je ne fais qu'aimer, je ne sais qu'aimer* (Fr., "I do nothing but love, I can do nothing but love"). The letters were published by Guibert's widow in 1809.

Lesseps, Vicomte **Ferdinand Marie de** (1805–1894). French diplomat and engineer. The original conceiver of the Suez Canal, de Lesseps received a concession from Said Pasha, viceroy of Egypt in 1854. He completed the canal in 10 years (1859–1869). De Lesseps was also, unfortunately, president of a French company that began work on cutting through the isthmus of Panama (1881–1888). The scheme collapsed and de Lesseps was condemned for misappropriation of funds, although his sentence was never carried out.

Lessing, Doris [May] (1919–). English novelist, short-story writer, and essayist, born and for many years resident in Southern Rhodesia. Her intense commitment to socialism and to other causes is reflected in her work. She began a series of novels about *Martha Quest* in 1952. *The Grass is Singing* (1950) and *This Was the Old Chief's Country* (1951) are set in Africa. *In Pursuit of the English* (1960) is a sociological essay. *The Golden Notebook* (1962) is an ambitious experimental novel about a modern "liberated" woman.

Lessing, Gotthold Ephraim (1729–1781). German dramatist, aesthetician, and critic, a strong advocate of religious tolerance. His thought has roots in the enlightenment but is not cramped by a too strict rationalism. Perhaps more than any other, he was responsible for the emergence of German drama as a significant contribution to world theater; in his critical work *Hamburgische Dramaturgie* (*Hamburg Dramaturgy*, 1767–1768), he attacked the formalism of neo-classicism and called for a drama in which the form springs from the dramatist's vision of life. Among his more general works on aesthetics are the *Briefe, die neueste Literatur betreffend* (*Letters, Concerning the Most Recent Literature*, a periodical with Christoph Nicolai, 1759–1765), which includes a Faust fragment and a classic attack on Johann Gottsched; LAOCOÖN, OR ON THE LIMITS OF PAINTING AND POETRY; and *Wie die Alten den Tod gebildet* (*How the Ancients Represented Death*, 1769). Late in his life, he wrote a number of tracts on theological subjects, the best known of which is *Erziehung des Menschengeschlechts* (*Education of the Human Race*, 1780). His most famous dramas are *Miss Sara Sampson* (1755), MINNA VON BARNHELM, EMILIA GALOTTI, and NATHAN THE WISE.

Les Six. A group of French composers: Darius MILHAUD, Arthur HONEGGER, Francis POULENC, Georges Auric (1899–), Louis Durey (1888–), and Germaine Tailleferre (1892–). A music critic coined this soubriquet in comparing these composers with "THE FIVE" Russians. Although they joined Erik SATIE, their mentor, and Jean COCTEAU, their spokesman, in decrying the pretentiousness of Romanticism and admiring the directness of popular music, they seldom met, and developed different musical styles. They collaborated without Durey on Cocteau's ballet *Les Mariés de la Tour Eiffel* (1921).

L'Estrange, Sir **Roger** (1616–1704). English journalist, political pamphleteer, and translator. In 1663 he became surveyor of printing presses and licenser of the press and established *The Public Intelligencer* and *The News*, both of which ceased publication in 1666. He later edited the *Observator*, in which he attacked the Whigs. His best-known translation is *The Fables of Aesop* (1692).

Lethe (Gr. *letho, latheo, lanthano*, to cause persons not to know). In Greek mythology, one of the rivers of Hades. The souls of all the dead are obliged to taste its water, that they may forget everything said and done when alive. See STYX.

Leto. In Greek mythology, a daughter of the Titans Coeus and Phoebe and mother by Zeus of Apollo and Artemis.

Leto, Pomponio (1428–1498). Italian scholar. He was prominent during the Renaissance as the leader of a group of Humanists and men of letters who formed one of the first modern academies at Rome.

Letter, The. See CASUARINA TREE, THE.

Letters from an American Farmer (1782). A group of essays by CRÈVECŒUR, under the pseudonym of J. Hector St. John. They deal with farm life on the American frontier in the 18th century, sometimes idealizing it in the tradition of Jean Jacques Rousseau, yet depicting realistically the hard unpleasant facts of the social life and customs in the American colonies. Crèvecœur sees America as a refuge for the persecuted and oppressed peoples of the world.

Letters of Unknown Men. See EPISTOLAE OBSCURORUM VIRORUM.

Letters on the Study of History (1752). A political and philosophical treatise by Henry ST. JOHN, Viscount Bolingbroke, setting forth the concept that "history is philosophy teaching by examples." St. John proclaims a new Tory position which, in effect, is no different from the Whig doctrines of the Revolution of 1688.

Lettres de Mon Moulin (Letters from My Windmill, 1866). A collection of short stories by Alphonse DAUDET depicting country life in Provence with skill and sympathy.

Lettres provinciales. See Blaise PASCAL.

Leucadia's Rock. A promontory, the south extremity of the island Leucas or Leucadia in the Ionian Sea. According to legend, SAPPHO leapt from this rock when she found her love for Phaon unrequited. At the annual festival of Apollo, a criminal was hurled from Leucadia's Rock into the sea; but birds of various sorts were attached to him in order to break his fall, and if he was not killed, he was set free.

Leucippus (Leukippos; fl. 450 B.C.). A Greek philosopher. His atomist theory held that all matter is composed of an irreducible and unchanging set of atoms. Always in motion, the atoms circulate in a void, and link to form an unlimited number of worlds. See DEMOCRITUS.

Leucothea (Leukothea). See INO.

Leute von Seldwyla, Die (The People of Seldwyla; vol. 1, 1856; vol. 2, 1874). A collection of humorous novellas by Gottfried KELLER, all set in the fictional Swiss town of Seldwyla. The two best-known ones are *Kleider machen Leute* (*Clothes Make the Man*), about a man who is taken for a Polish nobleman and, with an eye to his personal advantage, continues the pose, and *Spiegel, das Kätzchen* (lit., Spiegel, the Little Cat, trans. as *The Fat of the Cat*), about a down-and-out cat who sells his cat-fat to a magician without fully realizing that in order to relinquish his fat, he must be killed.

Leutnant Gustl (1901). A short novel by Arthur SCHNITZLER. An early experiment in the technique of stream-of-consciousness, this story probes deeply into the mind of a young officer whose traditionally based values are put to a severe test by the prospect of a duel.

Levana (from Lat., *levare*, "to raise up"). In Roman mythology the goddess who watched over newborn infants. It was in her name that the father accepted the infant as his legitimate offspring; he did this by the ritual of lifting the child from the ground and raising it aloft. In *Suspiria de Profundis* (1845), Thomas De Quincey writes of an opium dream in which he beheld the goddess.

Levelers or **Levellers.** In English history, a group of ultrarepublicans during the Civil War, who wanted to give all men the right to vote and to end class distinctions. John LILBURNE was one of the leaders of the sect, which was active from 1647 to 1649, when it was suppressed by Cromwell's troops.

In Irish history, an illegal association of 18th-century agrarian agitators, also called WHITEBOYS.

Lever, Charles James (1806–1872). Irish novelist. His early novels, reminiscent of student and military life, are his best, and include THE CONFESSIONS OF HARRY LORRIQUER, *Charles O'Malley* (1841), and *Tom Burke of Ours* (1843). These books are highly anecdotal, notable for their swift and witty narrative and comic secondary characters. In his day, Lever was an extremely popular writer.

Leverkühn, Adrian. The hero of Thomas Mann's novel DOKTOR FAUSTUS. He is a contemporary composer, and in several places Mann has used actual music of Arnold Schoenberg to describe the fictional works of his protagonist. In order to achieve a breakthrough into the most sublime realms of art, Leverkühn, like the legendary FAUST, makes a pact with the powers of evil. Like Faust, he himself is utterly destroyed by the forces he has set in motion, but the magnificence of his music remains as a monument. The name *Leverkühn* suggests "one who lives boldly."

Leverrier, Urbain Jean Joseph (1811–1877). French astronomer. Leverrier determined mathematically, on the basis of previously observed irregularities in the motion of the planet Uranus, the existence and exact position of another planet. Galle, a German astronomer, discovered the planet (1846) and named it Neptune. The same discovery was made independently by the English astronomer J. C. Adams.

Leverson, Ada (1865–1936). English novelist. She is well known for her literary friendships; she befriended Oscar Wilde during his trial. Her urbane, witty novels are in the manner of Wilde; *The Limit* (1911) is a typical work.

Levertov, Denise (1923–   ). English-born American poet. Of Welsh and Jewish parentage, Miss Levertov married an American and came with him to the U.S. in 1948. Recognized as one of the most accomplished of the younger poets, she shows the influence of William Carlos Williams and Wallace Stevens and writes poetry that is lyrical, graceful, and of colloquial simplicity. Her collections include *Overland to the Islands* (1958), *With Eyes at the Back of Our Heads* (1959), and *The Jacob's Ladder* (1961).

Levi (1). In the Old Testament, one of the sons of the patriarch Jacob. The tribe of his descendants are known as Levites, the priestly tribe of the Israelites (Deut. 21:5).

(2) In the New Testament, a name for Matthew.

Levi, Carlo (1902–   ). Italian writer. He is especially noted for his book CHRIST STOPPED AT EBOLI. Other books include *Le Parole Sono Pietre* (1955), a study of Sicily, and *Il Futuro Ha Un Cuore Antico* (1956), a study of Soviet Russia. His novel *The Watch* (*L'Orologio*; 1950) is set in the turbulent period following World War II. *La Doppia Notte dei Tigli* (tr. 1962 as *The Linden Trees*) records his impressions of a visit to Germany, a nation split both by artificial borders and its sense of guilt for the past while enjoying prosperity.

leviathan. A word from the Hebrew, meaning literally "that which gathers itself together in folds," and given in the Bible to a mythical sea serpent (Job 41:1; Isa. 27:1; Ps. 104:26). The name is also applied to the whale and the crocodile, and by extension it has come to mean something vast and formidable of its kind.

Leviathan, or the Matter, Form, and Power of a Commonwealth, Ecclesiastical and Civil (1651). A treatise on the origin and ends of government by Thomas HOBBES. This work, a defense of secular monarchy, written while the Puritan Commonwealth ruled England, contains Hobbes's famous theory of the sovereign state.

Hobbes, following the trend of his time, tended to regard politics as a branch of physical science, a kind of social physics. Comparing the motion of physical bodies to human behavior, he argued that just as physical things, when left to themselves, pursued their own direction, so individuals, when uncontrolled, naturally followed their own direction, their private self-interest. Thus, in his view, the first principle of human behavior was egoism, or self-interest, and it was this egoism that was the root of all social conflict. He believed that social peace could only be achieved within a stable government which had an absolute authority over its subjects and its institutions. Since the attainment of all desirable social ends was hindered by the "war of all against all," it was necessary that men agree among themselves, upon the basis of a social contract, to accept a common and absolute power that would protect them from themselves and from each other, keep the peace, and allow thereby a moderate satisfaction of human desires.

Levin, Konstantin. See ANNA KARENINA.

Levin, Meyer (1905–   ). American journalist and writer of fiction. He is known for his studies of American Jewish life, especially in the city of Chicago. His first novel *Reporter* (1929) was based on his own experiences as a Chicago newspaperman. *The Golden Mountain* (1932) contains stories of the Chassidim, a remarkable sect of medieval Jewish mystics. *The Old Bunch* (1937) is a novel about 11 boys and 8 girls of Jewish parentage, all graduating from the same Chicago high school in 1921. More recent books are *My Father's House* (1947); *Compulsion* (1956), a fictional study of the Leopold-Loeb case; *Eva* (1959), the story of a Jewish girl in flight from the Nazis during World War II, and *The Fanatic* (1964).

Levine, Jack (1915–   ). American painter. He is known for his satirical portraits and mordant social commentaries.

Leviticus. A book of the Old Testament. It was written about 475 B.C. and records the religious and ceremonial law of the Jews in the period after the rebuilding of the temple in 516 B.C. In an effort to give the book greater authority, the author ascribes it to Moses. It is the basic compendium of Jewish law.

Levy, Benn [Wolfe] (1900–   ). English playwright. His works include *Mrs. Moonlight* (1928), *Art and Mrs. Bottle, Springtime for Henry* (1931), and *Topaze* (from the French of Marcel Pagnol).

Lewes, George Henry (1817–1878). English scientific writer and critic. Lewes is better known for his connection with the novelist George ELIOT than for his own work; the two lived together as man and wife from 1854 (Lewes being separated from his first wife), and he discovered and fostered her talent. He was the first editor of the *Fortnightly Review* (1865–1866). His plays and novels were never successful; his works on marine biology, physiology, and psychology (fields in which he did original scientific work) are dated; but his *Biographical History of Philosophy* (1845–1846), *Life of Goethe* (1855), and *Actors and the Art of Acting* (1875) retain some interest.

Lewis, Alun (1915–1944). Welsh poet, killed in World War II. *Ha! Ha! Amongst the Trumpets* (1945) is a posthumous collection of verse.

Lewis, Cecil Day. See Cecil DAY-LEWIS.

Lewis, C[live] S[taples] (1898–1963). English novelist, literary critic, and writer of essays on Christian theological and moral problems. Lewis wrote science fiction in the form of interplanetary fantasies which are really Christian allegories of good and evil: *Out of the Silent Planet* (1938), *Perelandra* (1943), and *That Hideous Strength* (1945). *The Problem of Pain* (1940) and THE SCREWTAPE LETTERS (1942) were widely read works of Christian apologetics. Among his important books of literary criticism are *The Allegory of Love* (1936), a study of the medieval courtly tradition; *Preface to Paradise Lost* (1942); and *An Experiment in Criticism* (1961).

Lewis, D[ominic] B[evan] Wyndham (1894–   ). Welsh-born English humorist, essayist, and biographer. Lewis is perhaps best known as a whimsical, chatty essayist in the manner of Chesterton. His humorous works include *A London Farrago* (1922), *At the Green Goose* (1923), *At the Sign of the Blue Moon* (1924), and *On Straw and Other Conceits* (1927). He also edited with Charles Lee an anthology of bad verse, *The Stuffed Owl* (1930), and conducted a humor column for the London *News Chronicle* under the name Timothy Shy, which he used as co-author with Ronald Searle of *The Terror of St. Trinian's* (1954).

In addition, Lewis has written several scholarly and colorful biographies, including *François Villon* (1928), *King Spider* (1930), *Emperor of the West* (1932; U.S. title, *Charles of Europe*), *Ronsard* (1944), *The Hooded Hawk* (1946; republished as *James Boswell*, 1952), *Doctor Rabelais* (1957), and *Molière: The Comic Mask* (1959). Despite the similarity in names, he is not related to novelist and painter Wyndham Lewis.

Lewis, Matthew Gregory (1775–1818). English novelist and dramatist, author of the famous GOTHIC NOVEL *Ambrosio, or* THE MONK, for which he was known as "Monk Lewis." A lover of poetry, Lewis collaborated with Sir Walter Scott and Robert Southey in a collection of verse, *Tales of Wonder* (1801). Lewis' contributions included some of the earliest translations of the German romantics Goethe and Herder. He was a successful dramatist and a liberal who did his best to alleviate the condition of the slaves on his Jamaica plantation, where he died. See ALONZO THE BRAVE.

Lewis, [Harry] Sinclair (1885–1951). American novelist. Born in Sauk Centre, Minn., Lewis was an awkward, lonely boy, something of a dreamer. After his graduation from Yale in 1908, he spent several years in newspaper and editorial work. His first novel, *Hike and the Aeroplane* (1912), was a story for boys. He achieved moderate success with his early novels, and two of them—*Our Mr. Wrenn: The Romantic Adventures of a Gentle Man* (1914) and *The Job: An American Novel* (1917)—contain hints of the satire and realism that were to be characteristic of his best work.

According to Mark Schorer, Lewis' biographer, the appearance of MAIN STREET in 1920 was "the most sensational event in 20th-century American publishing history." Although there were some howls of outrage, in general both the critics and the public were delighted with Lewis' devastating portrayal of the smugness and provincialism of the American small town, as typified by Gopher Prairie, the novel's mythical locale. Lewis next directed his barbs at the American businessman in BABBITT, in many ways an extension of *Main Street*. In ARROWSMITH, often considered his best work, he attacked the venality and pettiness that impede the search for scientific truth. Although Lewis was awarded a Pulitzer Prize for *Arrowsmith*, he promptly refused to accept it, because the terms of the award state that it is to be given, not for literary merit, but for the best presentation of "the wholesome atmosphere of American Life." Other successes of this period were ELMER GANTRY and DODSWORTH.

Lewis was awarded the Nobel Prize in 1930, the first American to win such an honor. But his work declined in the 1930's, and he tended to make peace with the attitudes he had earlier satirized. *Ann Vickers* (1933) traces the career of a neurotic woman who starts as a social worker and ends as the mistress of a politician. *The Prodigal Parents* (1938) presents rebellious children in an unsympathetic light. Perhaps the most vigorous of Lewis' work in the 30's was

IT CAN'T HAPPEN HERE, a warning about the possibility of fascism in the U.S. Among his later novels are *Cass Timberlane* (1945), the story of an older man's love for his young and unsuitable wife; *Kingsblood Royal* (1947), about racial prejudice; and *The God-Seeker* (1949), about a missionary in Minnesota in the 1840's.

There is much disguised biography in Lewis' work, and many suggestions of Lewis himself in his characters. A romancer as well as a realist and satirist, he loved the Babbitts and Main Streets of America even as he deplored them.

Lewis, [Percy] Wyndham (1882–1957). English novelist, essayist, and vorticist painter. A vitriolic satirist, Wyndham Lewis wrote the notable satiric novels TARR, THE APES OF GOD, and the trilogy THE HUMAN AGE. His largest output consisted of essays written to express his near-fascist political views and his literary opinions. Trained as an artist, Lewis first attracted attention, before World War I, as the leader of the school of painting known as VORTICISM. In association with Ezra Pound, he edited the little magazine BLAST (1914–1915). With Pound, T. S. Eliot, and James Joyce, he sympathized with a French-inspired movement to reject "romanticism" and return to "classicism." The four were sometimes called "the men of 1914." *Blasting and Bombardiering* (1937) is an autobiography about Lewis' experiences in action in the second half of the war. Lewis' sympathy with fascism came to a peak in the years between the wars; at the outbreak of World War II he emigrated to Canada, describing his experience, in fictional form, in *Self-Condemned* (1954). *Rotting Hill* (1951) is a novel purporting to demonstrate the decay of England under postwar socialism. In 1949 Lewis began to go blind.

Among Lewis' other works are poems (1933); *The Wild Body* (1927), a collection of short stories; the novels *Snooty Baronet* (1932), *The Revenge for Love* (1937), and *The Red Priest* (1956); and the autobiography *Rude Assignment* (1950). Some of his political and literary tracts are *The Art of Being Ruled* (1926), TIME AND WESTERN MAN, *The Lion and the Fox: the role of hero in the plays of Shakespeare* (1927), *Hitler* (1931), *Men Without Art* (1934), and *The Demon of Progress in the Arts* (1954).

In his heyday in the 1920's Wyndham Lewis was thought as original and exciting as James Joyce. Since then he has been neglected.

Lewis and Clark Expedition (1804–1806). An expedition across the U.S. to the Pacific Ocean led by Meriwether Lewis (1774–1809) and William Clark (1770–1838). Starting out from St. Louis in the spring of 1804, the party of 23 soldiers, three interpreters, and one slave ascended the Missouri River, spent the winter among the Mandan Indians of North Dakota, and descended the Columbia River to the Pacific late in 1805. The expedition showed that an overland route to the Pacific was feasible and provided scientific data about the previously unexplored region. *The Original Journals of the Lewis and Clark Expedition* were edited by R. G. Thwaites in 1904–1905. See SACAJAWEA.

Lewisohn, Ludwig (1883–1955). German-born American editor, teacher, critic, and writer. Lewisohn, who came to America as a boy, became an authority on German literature and translated works of Hauptmann, Rilke, and others. Some of his critical works are *The Modern Drama* (1915), *The Spirit of Modern German Literature* (1916), *The Story of American Literature* (1937), and *Goethe* (2 vols., 1949). He treated the problems of Jews in *The American Jew* (1950) and other volumes. This subject also found its way into his fiction; among his novels are *The Island Within* (1928), *The Last Days of Shylock* (1931), *Anniversary* (1948), and *In a Summer Season* (1955). He also published memoirs in *Up Stream* (1922) and *Mid-Channel: An American Chronicle* (1929).

Lexington. A town in Massachusetts, site of the first engagement of the American Revolution (April 19, 1775). General Gage sent 700 men to destroy the American supply depot at Concord, 21 miles from Boston. At Lexington, 5 miles from Concord, the troops ran into 70 armed minutemen, forewarned by Paul Revere, who forced them to withdraw. Moving on to Concord, the British were turned back at the Concord bridge and shot at from behind walls and trees. They retreated to Boston under fire of gathering swarms of minutemen. Estimates of the casualties vary.

Ley, Robert (1890–1945). German Nazi, noted for his extreme anti-Semitism. As head of the Labor Front (1933–1945), he mobilized German war industry and supervised the slave labor camps. He committed suicide after his capture by the Allies.

Lhasa. The capital of Tibet and sacred city of Tibetan Buddhists. Its chief buildings are monasteries, some of which are 1,200 years old, and the Potala, palace of the Dalai Lama. Prior to Chinese occupation, Lhasa was the goal of religious pilgrims from all over the Himalayan plateau. Not open to Westerners until the British forced entry in 1904, Lhasa is still known as the Forbidden City. In 1959 the Dalai Lama fled to India to escape the Chinese who had assumed control of Tibet in 1951.

L'Hermite, François. Known as **Tristan l'Hermite** (1602–1655). French author and playwright. The popularity of his tragedy *La Mariane* (1636) rivaled that of *Le Cid,* and *La Mort de Sénèque* (*The Death of Seneca,* 1644) is the finest French tragedy on a classical theme outside of Corneille's and Racine's. The comedy *Le Parasite* (1654) introduced to the French stage the stock parasitic figure of Latin comedy, and the autobiographical novel *Le Page Disgracié* (*The Disgraced Page,* 1642–1643) recounts episodes from the author's erratic youth.

L'Hospital or **L'Hôpital, Michel de** (1505–1573). Chancellor of France (1560–1568) and the most celebrated French orator of his century. His speeches urging religious tolerance and justice during the religious wars are notable for their simplicity and honesty. The complete *Œuvres* of L'Hospital were published in 1824–1825.

Liaisons dangereuses, Les (1782). An epistolary novel by Pierre Choderlos de LACLOS. The novel deals with the corruption of innocence and virtue by Valmont, a libertine, and his equally vicious and immoral mistress, Mme de Merteuil, for their own amusement. It is essentially a study of the fascination and power of evil, and one is struck by the absence of frivolity and sentimentality in this work;

the battle of the sexes is depicted with utter seriousness and humorlessness. The style is Racinian in its brilliance, lucidity, and precision, diabolical in its impassivity.

Liar, The. See MENTEUR, LE.

Libellus Merlini. See MERLIN.

Liber. An Italian god of wine, later identified with the Greek DIONYSUS, known in Rome as BACCHUS. He and his feminine counterpart, Libera, were honored at the festival of the *Liberalia* on March 17.

liberal arts. In the Middle Ages, the seven branches of learning: grammar, logic, rhetoric, arithmetic, geometry, music, and astronomy. In modern times, the liberal arts include the languages, sciences, philosophy, history, and related subjects. The term is a translation of Latin *artes liberales,* so called because their pursuit was the privilege of the freemen who were called *liberi.* See QUADRIVIUM.

Libertins (Libertines). A sect of French freethinkers and skeptics of the 17th and 18th centuries, precursors of VOLTAIRE and the encyclopedists. Advocates of total freedom of thought and conscience, the *Libertins* questioned the doctrines and morality of all received religion and were continually accused of atheism and immorality. The greatest religious thinkers of the day, including Bossuet and Pascal, denounced their views, and ultimately the *Libertins'* own poor conduct discredited their very name.

Liberty, Statue of. A colossal statue, *Liberty Enlightening the World,* which stands on Liberty (formerly Bedloe's) Island, at the entrance to New York harbor. Dedicated in 1886, it was a gift of the French people, and commemorates the alliance between the two nations during the American Revolution. Of bronze, it stands 152 feet high on a pedestal almost 150 feet high, and represents a woman, draped, holding a lighted torch in her upraised hand. It is the work of Frédéric Auguste Bartholdi (1834–1904). On its base is carved a sonnet, *The New Colossus,* by Emma Lazarus, which ends with the lines:

> Give me your tired, your poor,
> Your huddled masses yearning to breathe free,
> The wretched refuse of your teeming shore,
> Send these, the homeless, tempest-tost, to me
> I lift my lamp beside the golden door!

Liberty Bell. The bell in Independence Hall, Philadelphia, which was rung when the Continental Congress adopted the Declaration of Independence. First cast in London (1752) with the inscription, "Proclaim Liberty throughout all the Land unto all the Inhabitants Thereof," it was recast in Philadelphia (1753) with the same legend, and cracked in 1835 when it was tolled for the death of John Marshall.

liberty cap. A symbol of freedom. When a slave was manumitted by the Romans, a small Phrygian cap, usually of red felt, called *pileus,* was placed on his head; he was termed *libertinus* (a freedman), and his name was registered in the city tribes. When Saturninus, in 100 B.C., possessed himself of the Roman Capitol, he hoisted a similar cap on the top of his spear, to indicate that all slaves who joined his standard should be free; Marius employed the same symbol against Sulla; and, when Caesar was mur-

dered, the conspirators marched forth in a body with a cap elevated on a spear, in token of liberty. In the French Revolution, the cap of liberty (BONNET ROUGE) was adopted by the revolutionists as an emblem of their freedom from royal authority.

Libethra. The place in Greece where the nightingales sing most sweetly. It is there that the Muses buried the fragments of ORPHEUS' body.

Library, The. See APOLLODORUS.

Library of Alexandria. See ALEXANDRIAN LIBRARY.

Libro de buen amor, El. See Juan RUIZ.

Libya. The name given by the Greeks to Africa in general. The Romans used the word sometimes as synonymous with Africa, sometimes for that section on the Mediterranean which included Carthage.

Libya was also a goddess whom the Greeks identified as a daughter of the Egyptian king Epaphos and mother of Belus and Agenor.

Licenciado Vidriera, El. One of the tales in Cervantes' NOVELAS EJEMPLARES. It is really a collection of aphorisms, uttered by a demented law student who believes that he is made of glass but who, like Don Quixote, displays amazing insight and perspicacity.

Lichas. In Greek mythology, the friend of HERACLES who brought him Deianira's fatal tunic. He was thrown into the sea by Heracles.

Li-chi. See BOOK OF RITES.

lictor. In ancient Rome, an officer attending a magistrate. A dictator, for example, had 20 lictors, a consul 12, a praetor 6, and so on. The lictor bore the FASCES as the insignia of his office. He cleared the way, enforced respect for his superior, and arrested offenders and executed condemned criminals.

Liddell, Alice. See Henry George LIDDELL.

Liddell, Henry George (1811–1898). English classical scholar and dean of Christ Church (1855–1891). He is the author, with Robert Scott, of the standard *Greek Lexicon* (1843; last revised 1925). He also wrote a *History of Ancient Rome* (1855). His daughter Alice Liddell was the original Alice, the child for whom Lewis Carroll wrote his famous *Alice's Adventures in Wonderland* and *Through the Looking-Glass.*

Lidia. In the ORLANDO FURIOSO of Ariosto, a princess of Lidia whose spirit is encountered by Astolfo in his journey through Hell. There among those sinners who are being punished for treating their lovers cruelly in life, she tells Astolfo her story, revealing her cruelty to her suitor Alceste.

Lido. A reef and sandbank outside the lagoon of Venice, famous as a fashionable bathing resort on the Adriatic.

Lie, Jonas [Lauritz Idemil] (1833–1909). Norwegian novelist, playwright, and poet. Financial difficulties caused Lie, always fascinated by literature, to begin his professional literary career. In 1870 he published *Den Fremsynte;* both this first novel and later volumes of stories, *Trold* (1891–1892), mingle realistic with fantastic elements. His studies of family life in the middle classes—among them *Lodsen og hans Hustru* (1874), *Familjen paa Gilje* (1883), and *Kommandørens Døtre* (1886)—are his finest work.

Lie, Trygve (1896–   ). Norwegian statesman and secretary-general of the United Nations (1946–1953). Formerly Norwegian minister for foreign affairs (1940; 1941–1945), Lie served in the cabinet as minister of justice (1935–1939) and minister of commerce (1939–1940).

Liebelei. See LIGHT O' LOVE.

Liebknecht, Karl (1871–1919). Socialist leader in the German Reichstag, son of Wilhelm LIEB-KNECHT. As a member of the SPARTACIST PARTY, he opposed the war policies of the government and supported the Russian Bolsheviks. The proletarian revolt that he organized with Rosa Luxemburg in 1919 was suppressed by the provisional government, and he was shot.

Liebknecht, Wilhelm (1826–1900). German so-cialist and associate of August Bebel. He helped to found the German Social Democratic Party in 1869.

Lied von Bernadette, Das. See SONG OF BERNA-DETTE, THE.

Lien Chi Altangi. Narrator and central figure of Oliver Goldsmith's epistolary novel THE CITIZEN OF THE WORLD, a Chinese who, for all his philosophy, cannot help being surprised by the follies of Gold-smith's England. He also prophesies the successful revolution of the American colonies and the rise of Russia.

Lif. See VALI.

Life and Death of Mr. Badman, The (1680). An allegorical dialogue by John BUNYAN, in which Mr. Wiseman tells of the vicious life and habits and the eventual death of Mr. Badman, using his story to point out the folly of wickedness.

Life Is a Dream. See VIDA ES SUEÑO, LA.

Life of Galileo, The (Leben des Galilei; 1938–1939). A play by Bertolt BRECHT. Written in the style of the EPIC THEATER, it concerns Galileo's con-flict with the church. Brecht deliberately makes Gali-leo a very unheroic figure, always ready to com-promise his principles when pressure is put on him. The play is not so obviously tendentious as most of Brecht's later works, but there are several anachro-nisms in which Marxist doctrine is propounded.

Life of Samuel Johnson, LL.D., The (1791). A biography by James BOSWELL, generally considered the greatest in the English language. Boswell met Dr. Samuel JOHNSON in 1763 in London and visited him periodically from that time, spending a great deal of time with him in the three years before Johnson's death. Boswell's method is of particular note: occa-sionally he made notes on the spot during Johnson's conversation; more often, however, from the habit of a lifetime, he made notes in his copious journals nightly on the events and conversation of the day, and for this, he had a prodigious memory to serve him. He questioned Johnson himself, prodding him into talk, and questioned Johnson's friends; after Johnson died, he was in constant quest of letters and anec-dotes. He was greatly aided in his task by Edmund MALONE, who went over the last draft of the manu-script. Boswell's aim and achievement was complete-ness; no detail was too small for him, and on this very point Dr. Johnson remarked to him: "There is nothing, Sir, too little for so little a creature as man." Boswell's achievement is twofold: first he was able, from his scrupulously accurate memory, to record faithfully the brilliance and wit of Dr. Johnson's conversation; second, he had the artistry to transform a painstaking, almost scholarly profusion of detail into a perceptive, lifelike portrait. The result is a

Illustration for *The Life and Death of Mr. Badman* (1680).

study in depth of a complex and fascinating man who was the prime moving force in the literary world of his time. Although Boswell's *Life* is indisputably the finest of the many biographies of Johnson, Sir John Hawkins's *Life* (1787) is a better source for young Johnson, and Hester Lynch THRALE saw more of Johnson's intimate, domestic side.

Life on the Mississippi (1883). An autobio-graphical account by Mark TWAIN. The book de-scribes the apprenticeship of a river pilot, and the excitement of life on the river. The second half of the book was added seven years after the first part was published; it records Twain's revisit to the river in 1882.

Life's Handicap, Being Stories of Mine Own People (1891). A volume of short stories of India, including THE MAN WHO WAS, by Rudyard KIPLING.

Life with Father (1935). A collection of sketches by Clarence DAY. In them the author recalls with delightful humor the not-always-easy life with his eccentric and domineering father. In spite of the elder Day's tyrannizing, however, his very feminine wife nearly always managed to get her way. The book was dramatized in 1939 by Howard LINDSAY and

Russel CROUSE and achieved the longest unbroken run of any American play. The second book of sketches, *Life with Mother* (1936), was dramatized by the same playwrights but had only a moderately successful run.

Life with Mother. See LIFE WITH FATHER.

Lifthrasir. See VALI.

Ligea (Ligeia). In classical myth, one of the three SIRENS.

Ligeia (1838). A tale by Edgar Allan POE. Ligeia, the narrator's mysterious dark-haired wife, dies after a lingering illness. He later remarries, though he does not love his fair Rowena. In the lavishly furnished English abbey to which they move, Rowena dies. The narrator, affected by opium, sees signs of life return to the corpse. Finally she rises; the Lady Rowena has been transformed into Ligeia.

Light-Horse Harry Lee. See Henry LEE.

Light in August (1932). A novel by William FAULKNER. The book reiterates the author's concern with a society that classifies men according to race, creed, and origin. Joe CHRISTMAS, the central character and victim, appears to be white but is really part Negro; he has an affair with Joanna Burden, a spinster whom the townsfolk of Jefferson regard with suspicion because of her New England background. Joe eventually kills her and sets fire to her house; he is captured, castrated, and killed by the outraged townspeople, to whom his victim has become a symbol of the innocent white woman attacked and killed by a Negro. Other important characters are Lena GROVE, who comes to Jefferson far advanced in pregnancy, expecting to find the lover who has deserted her, and Gail Hightower, the minister who ignores his wife and loses his church because of his fanatic devotion to the past.

Lightnin' (1918). A play by Winchell SMITH and Frank BACON. Its 1,291 performances set a record for its day. Bacon himself played the leading role of Lightnin' Bill Jones, owner of a hotel which lies half in Nevada and half in California. An amusing liar, Lightnin' has numerous troubles, but manages entertainingly to solve them all.

Light o' Love (Liebelei; 1894). A play by Arthur SCHNITZLER. It is a more serious treatment of the erotic themes that Schnitzler had stated earlier in *Anatol* (1891). The naïve young heroine Christine commits suicide when she learns that her lover has died dueling over another woman.

Light that Failed, The (1890). A novel by Rudyard KIPLING. Through his experience as an illustrator in the Sudan, the hero, Dick Heldar, wins both professional success and a firm friend in the war correspondent Torpenhow. He is in love with his foster sister Maisie, now also an artist, but Maisie is shallow and selfish and does not appreciate his devotion. Dick gradually goes blind from a sword cut received in the Sudan, working courageously against time on his painting, *Melancholia*. Although Maisie is summoned by Torpenhow, she heartlessly leaves Dick to his fate, and he carries out his plan of dying at the front. In a later edition a happy ending is provided.

Li Hung-chang (1823–1901). Chinese statesman; long the major force in foreign policy, after the emperor. Visited Europe and U.S. (1898). Commis-

sioned to restore peace after the BOXER uprising (1900). Often referred to as "the Bismarck of Asia."

Lilburne, John (1614?–1657). English political agitator and Puritan pamphleteer, noted for his rancorous temper. He was imprisoned several times for printing unlicensed books and for verbal attacks on persons of authority. See LEVELERS.

Liliencron, Detlev von (1844–1909). German poet. All his youth was spent as an officer in the Prussian army, in which he served through three wars, and his army experiences form the background for his first and most important volume of poems, *Adjutantenritte (An Adjutant's Rides,* 1884). In this book, he emphasizes a subjective but realistic treatment of the individual experience, as opposed to the emphasis on formal polish and generalized experience in such authors as Heyse and Geibel. These characteristics made his writing important in the budding movements of NATURALISM and IMPRESSIONISM.

Liliom (1909). A play by Ferenc MOLNÁR. It was produced in New York in 1921. The hero is a disreputable but fascinating side-show barker. One act shows him before the judges of the other world; another, on earth again with a single chance to redeem himself. The play was made into the musical play *Carousel* (1944), by Richard Rodgers and Oscar Hammerstein.

Lilith. In Talmudic tradition, a demon, probably of Babylonian origin, said to haunt wildernesses in stormy weather and be especially dangerous to children and pregnant women. She is referred to as "the screech-owl" (Isa. 34:14), and as "the night monster" in the Revised Version. Hebrew legend holds that she was created simultaneously with Adam and was his first wife, but, refusing to be considered his inferior, she left him and was expelled from Eden to a region of the air. In Arabic mythology, she married the Devil and became the mother of evil spirits. Superstitious Jews put four coins in the chambers occupied by their wives inscribed with the names of Adam and Eve and the words, "Avaunt thee, Lilith!" Goethe introduced her in his *Faust* (1790–1833), and Dante Gabriel Rossetti in his *Eden Bower* (1870) made the serpent the instrument of Lilith's vengeance against Adam.

Lillibulero or **Lilliburlero.** A political song, popular during the English revolution of 1688 and still the most savagely thunderous of British marching songs. The music is by Henry Purcell. The text by Thomas Wharton (c. 1686) satirizes James II and the Catholics, using the refrain "Lillibulero bullen a la" which is said to have been used as a watchword by the Irish Catholics in their massacre of the Protestants (1641). The song was included by Bishop Percy in his *Reliques.*

Lilliput. The country of Gulliver's first voyage in GULLIVER'S TRAVELS by Jonathan Swift. The Lilliputians are about $\frac{1}{12}$ human size, and Gulliver is a giant among them. At first he falls in with their views, takes an interest in their disputes, helps them, and accepts their honors to him as real praise; he is soon disillusioned when the little creatures grudge him food and propose binding him lest he fend for himself. Their smallness is not merely a matter of stature; the pettiness of their lives is used by Swift to mirror the pettiness of human beings. See BIG-

ENDIANS; BLEFESCU; LOW HEELS AND HIGH HEELS; QUINBUS FLESTRIN.

Lillo, George (1693–1739). English dramatist. He is remembered chiefly for the sentimental bourgeois tragedy THE LONDON MERCHANT.

Lilly, William (1602–1681). English astrologer. He issued a series of prophetic pamphlets and almanacs from 1644 to 1680 and wrote *Christian Astrology* (1647). As Sidrophel he is satirized in Samuel Butler's *Hudibras* (1663–1678).

lily. A flower of innumerable varieties. There is a tradition that the lily sprang from the repentant tears of Eve as she went forth from Paradise. In Christian art, the lily is an emblem of chastity, innocence, and purity. In pictures of the Annunciation, Gabriel is sometimes represented as carrying a lily branch, while a vase containing a lily stands before the Virgin, who is kneeling in prayer. St. Joseph holds a lily branch in his hand, indicating that his wife Mary was a virgin.

lily of France. The *fleur-de-lis* (*Fr.,* "flower of the lily"; the iris). It is an emblem of France. The device of Clovis was three black toads, but the story goes that an aged hermit of Joye-en-valle saw a miraculous light stream one night into his cell, and an angel appeared to him holding an azure shield of wonderful beauty, emblazoned with three gold lilies that shone like stars, which the hermit was commanded to give to Queen Clotilde. She gave it to her royal husband, whose arms were everywhere victorious, and the device was thereupon adopted as the emblem of France. Tasso, in his *Jerusalem Delivered*, terms the French *gigli d'oro* (golden lilies). It is said the people were commonly called *Liliarts*, and the kingdom *Lilium* in the time of Philippe le Bel, Charles VIII, and Louis XII.

limbo (Lat., **limbus**, "border, edge"). The abode of souls that through no fault of their own are debarred from heaven. It is particularly identified with the souls of righteous men that lived before the coming of Christ and with the souls of unbaptized infants. Believed to be located near the region of hell, it is the setting for the first stage of the journey in Dante's *Commedia*. The word has come to refer more generally to the condition of being lost or confined to a state of neglect or oblivion.

limbus of the moon. A legendary land. On the moon was treasured everything wasted on earth; misspent time and wealth, broken vows, unanswered prayers, fruitless tears, abortive attempts, unfulfilled desires and intentions. In Ariosto's *Orlando Furioso*, Astolpho found on his visit to the moon that bribes were hung on gold and silver hooks; princes' favors were kept in bellows; wasted talent was kept in vases, each marked with the proper name. Pope describes the place in *The Rape of the Lock* (canto v). Pope tells us that when the Lock disappeared:

> Some thought it mounted to the lunar sphere,
> Since all things lost on earth are treasured there,
> There heroes' wits are kept in pond'rous vases,
> And beaux' in snuff-boxes and tweezer-cases.
> There broken vows and death-bed alms are found
> And lovers' hearts with ends of ribbon bound,
> The courtier's promises, and sick man's prayers.
> The smiles of harlots, and the tears of heirs
> Cages for gnats, and chains to yoke a flea,
> Dried butterflies, and tomes of casuistry.

Hence the phrase, *the limbus of the moon.*

Limehouse. Violent and vitriolic abuse of one's political opponents; so called out of compliment to an oratorical display by Mr. Lloyd George at Limehouse, London, on July 30, 1909, when he poured forth scorn and abuse on dukes, landlords, financial magnates, etc., many of whom, in the course of later events, became his best friends. It is also the name of London's Chinatown.

limerick. A humorous, usually epigrammatic piece of verse in five lines of mixed iambic and anapestic meter, lines 1, 2, and 5 in trimeter and 3 and 4 in dimeter, rhyming a-a-b-b-a. The form, the origins of which are uncertain, was popularized by Edward LEAR in his *Book of Nonsense* (1846). Following Lear's practice, the first line of most limericks ends in a place name, usually the place of origin or residence of the protagonist of the verse. The last line, in most of Lear's limericks, repeated the place name instead of furnishing another rhyme upon it, but most modern limericks end with a rhyme word instead of a repetition. The subject of the typical limerick is likely to be somewhat ribald and puns and plays on words are often included. The limerick has a wide oral circulation and, being a truly popular form of verse, is often of anonymous authorship. The following is an example:

> There once was a man from Nantucket
> Who kept all his cash in a bucket;
> But his daughter named Nan
> Ran away with a man,
> And as for the bucket, Nantucket.

Linacre, Thomas (1460?–1524). English physician and classical scholar, one of the earliest representatives of British humanism. He was physician to Henry VIII and one of the founders of the College of Physicians in London (1518). Among his students were Sir Thomas More and Erasmus. He was the author of *Rudimenta Grammatica* (1523), a Latin grammar; a Latin translation of Galen; and various medical works.

Lincoln, Abraham (1809–1865). 16th president of the U.S. (1861–1865). Born in a log cabin in Hardin (now Larue) County, Ky., Lincoln lost his mother, Nancy Hanks Lincoln, in 1818, while the family was living in Indiana. In 1831 he settled in New Salem, Ill., where he studied law and worked as a store-keeper, postmaster, and surveyor; in 1838 he was admitted to the bar. From 1834 to 1841 he served in the state legislature as a Whig and supporter of Henry Clay. While Lincoln was living in New Salem, he met Ann Rutledge (1816–1835), to whom he became engaged and who died in 1835; their romance has inspired many legends for which there is little concrete evidence. The truth about Lincoln's relationship to Mary Todd, whom he married in 1842, has also been distorted, largely as a result of the writings of William HERNDON, Lincoln's law partner, who disliked Mrs. Lincoln intensely.

After serving one term (1847–1849) in Congress, where he voiced his opposition to the Mexican War, Lincoln returned to his flourishing law practice in Illinois. Stirred to renewed political activity by the sectional agitation of 1854, Lincoln soon aligned himself with the newly formed Republican Party and ran for the U.S. Senate against Stephen A. DOUGLAS in 1858; although Lincoln lost the election, his famous debates with Douglas won him national prominence. In 1860 he won the Republican presidential nomination over such rivals as William SEWARD largely because of his conservative record on the slavery question, but the Southern states seceded from the Union soon after his election. His first Inaugural address was conciliatory: he emphasized the indissolubility of the Union, but promised not to interfere with slavery where it already existed. During the Civil War, which began with the Confederate attack on Fort SUMTER, Lincoln did not hesitate to use his extensive powers as commander-in-chief, and although Northern Democrats and members of his own party often assailed his war policies, he handled his opponents with aplomb. In the election of 1864 he easily defeated George B. McCLELLAN, who had often tried his patience in the early days of the war. In his second Inaugural address, he asked the nation "to finish the work we are in . . . with malice toward none, with charity toward all." Just after Lee's surrender, Lincoln was shot by John Wilkes BOOTH and died the following day.

Now transformed into a major American folk hero, Lincoln has been the subject of numerous literary works. Among the best-known poems about him are Walt Whitman's O CAPTAIN! MY CAPTAIN! and WHEN LILACS LAST IN THE DOORYARD BLOOM'D. He is a character in many novels and stories, notably Henry Ward Beecher's *Norwood* (1867), Edward Eggleston's *The Graysons* (1888), and Winston Churchill's THE CRISIS. His early life is the subject of Robert E. Sherwood's play ABE LINCOLN IN ILLINOIS. Edgar Lee Masters wrote a hostile biography, *Lincoln the Man* (1931), while another poet, Carl Sandburg, offered a vivid portrayal in the six volumes of ABRAHAM LINCOLN. See Mary Todd LINCOLN; GETTYSBURG ADDRESS; EMANCIPATION PROCLAMATION.

Lincoln, Mary Todd (1818–1882). Wife of Abraham LINCOLN. Descended of a distinguished Kentucky family, Mary Todd was courted by Lincoln when she moved to Springfield, Ill., in 1839 to live with her sister, Mrs. Ninian W. Edwards, who was the daughter-in-law of the state governor. There is no contemporary evidence for the story that the wedding was scheduled for Jan. 1, 1841, and that the groom failed to appear; some emotional crisis in Lincoln's life, however, probably did lead him to delay the marriage, which took place in 1842. Despite the testimony of William HERNDON, Lincoln's law partner, the Lincolns' married life was probably happy, though some difficulties arose after his election to the presidency, when Mrs. Lincoln was accused of extravagance and disloyalty to the Union cause. Her mind weakened by her husband's assassination and by the loss of three of her four sons, she was adjudged insane in 1875 but declared competent the following year.

Lind, Johanna Maria. Known as **Jenny Lind** or Madame **Jenny Lind-Goldschmidt** (1820–1887). Swedish coloratura soprano, called "the Swedish Nightingale." She made her début as Agatha in *Der Freischütz* (1838). She was introduced to the U.S. by P. T. Barnum (1850–1852). She married (1852) Otto Goldschmidt, a German-born composer and pianist, and toured the continent. A resident of England during her last years, she was professor of singing at the Royal College of Music (1883–1886).

Lindbergh, Anne Morrow (1906–   ). American writer. The wife of Charles A. LINDBERGH, she has described their flights together in *North to the Orient* (1935) and *Listen! The Wind* (1938). Her controversial essay, *The Wave of the Future* (1940), was influenced by her husband's isolationism and was regarded by some as an apologia for fascism. She also wrote *Gift from the Sea* (1955), essays especially addressed to women; *The Unicorn and Other Poems* (1956); and *Dearly Beloved* (1962).

Lindbergh, Charles A[ugustus] (1902–   ). American aviator. Lindbergh is best known for his solo flight across the Atlantic on May 20–21, 1927, the first in history. With Fitzhugh Green he wrote an account of the flight called *We* (1927); the title refers to Lindbergh and his plane, *The Spirit of St. Louis*. In 1929 he married Anne Morrow, the daughter of the U.S. ambassador to Mexico, Dwight Morrow. The tragic kidnaping and death of their infant son, Charles, Jr., in March, 1932, resulted in the passing of "Lindbergh laws" which make interstate kidnaping a federal offense. The Lindberghs moved to Europe in 1935, where he worked with Alexis Carrel on the mechanical heart. In the years immediately preceding World War II, Lindbergh was an advocate of American neutrality. He wrote *Of Flight and Life* (1948) and an autobiography, *The Spirit of St. Louis* (1953), which was awarded a Pulitzer Prize. See Anne Morrow LINDBERGH.

Lindsay, Howard (1889–   ). American actor, director, producer, and playwright. In collaboration with Russel CROUSE, he dramatized LIFE WITH FATHER, in which he and his wife played the leading roles for five years. Also with Crouse, he wrote *State of the Union* (1945), which won a Pulitzer Prize, and produced *Arsenic and Old Lace* (1941). Lindsay also worked with Damon Runyon on *A Slight Case of Murder* (1935); with Irving Berlin on *Call Me Madam* (1950); and with Richard Rodgers and Oscar Hammerstein on *The Sound of Music* (1959).

Lindsay, Jack (1900–   ). Australian poet, novelist, and classical scholar. His Marxist, mass-declamation poems were popular in England in the leftist 1930's. Most of his novels are historical, about ancient Greece and Rome, such as *Caesar is Dead* (1935). His other works are polemical writings on Russia and Marxism, literary criticism, translations from Greek and Latin, and the history *Byzantium into Europe* (1952). He was the son of Norman Lindsay.

Lindsay, [Alfred William] Norman (1879–   ). Australian artist and novelist. Lindsay, the son of a physician, turned to art at an early age, and worked later for a Melbourne paper. His pen drawings hang in English galleries. A novel, *Red Heap* (1913), was censored in Australia but well received in America under the title *Every Woman's Son*. His talent for satire and plot are discernible in *The Cautious Amorist* (1934) and *Age of Consent* (1938). He has been described by critics as a "true humorist," while his writing has the "gauntness of Australia." Other works include *A Curate in Bohemia* (1913), *The Magic Pudding* (1919), *Pam in the Parlor* (1934), *Halfway to Anyway* (1947), and *Dust or Polish* (1950).

Lindsay, [Nicholas] Vachel (1879–1931). American poet. Known for the dramatic and auditory effects of his poetry, he read from the lecture platform with theatrical gestures and intonation in an effort to make a love of poetry public property. His own work dealt in the main with American subjects and heroes, patriotism, and a mystic faith in the earth and nature. The crusading spirit was strong in Lindsay, and for a time he lectured for the Anti-Saloon League in the winter; in the summer (1912) he walked from Illinois to New Mexico, exchanging for meals the poems collected in *Rhymes to Be Traded for Bread* (1912). In the following year he published one of his best-known poems, GENERAL WILLIAM BOOTH ENTERS INTO HEAVEN. THE CONGO and THE SANTE FE TRAIL were published in 1914. Among others of his more famous single poems are *A Gospel of Beauty* (1908), *A Net to Snare the Moonlight* (1913), *The Eagle That Is Forgotten* (1913), *Abraham Lincoln Walks at Midnight* (1914), *The Chinese Nightingale* (1917), *The Ghost of the Buffaloes* (1917), and IN PRAISE OF JOHNNY APPLESEED. *The Golden Book of Springfield* (1920) is a prose work giving a Utopian picture of his native city. His other books include *Adventures While Preaching the Gospel of Beauty* (1914), *The Art of the Moving Picture* (1915), *The Golden Whales of California and Other Rhymes in the American Language* (1920), *The Candle in the Cabin* (1926), *Every Soul Is a Circus* (1929). His *Selected Poems* (1931) were edited by Hazelton Spencer.

As his poetic powers failed, Lindsay became weary and disillusioned. In 1931 he committed suicide by drinking poison.

Lingard, Captain. As a young man, the hero of Joseph Conrad's THE RESCUE; in later life, in AN OUTCAST OF THE ISLANDS and ALMAYER'S FOLLY, a powerful white trader who takes Almayer and Willems for protégés.

linguistic philosophy. See LOGICAL POSITIVISM.

Linklater, Eric (1899–   ). Scottish novelist. He writes witty novels of travel, fantasy, and satire. He is best known for *Juan in America* (1931). Among his other books are *Roll of Honour* (1961) and *Husband of Delilah* (1962).

Linnaeus, Carolus. The latinized name of the great Swedish botanist **Carl von Linné** (1707–1778). In his *Systema Naturae* (1735), he outlined what was largely adopted as the *Linnaean classification* or *system* of plants. It is also known as the *sexual system*. It differs from Jussieu's system (1789), by which it was superseded, in that it made no attempt to show the relationship of species and genera. Hence the name *artificial system* as opposed to Jussieu's *natural system*. Linnaeus' *Species Plantarum* (1753) is considered the foundation of modern botanical nomenclature.

Linné, Carl von. See Carolus LINNAEUS.

Lins do Rego, José (1901–1957). Brazilian novelist. In the sensitive, realistic novels of his "sugarcane cycle" (*Ciclo da Cana-de-Açúcar*), Lins do Rego depicted the decline of the patriarchal society that revolved around the sugar plantations of northeastern Brazil. The works usually included in the cycle are *Menino de Engenho* (1932), *Doidinho* (1933), *Banguê* (1934), *O Moleque Ricardo* (1935), and *Usina* (1936). In *Pedra Bonita* (1938) and other novels, he portrayed aspects of rural life in the arid portions of this same region.

Lin Yu-t'ang (in English usually **Yutang**) (1895–   ). Chinese teacher, translator, editor, and writer. Lin attended Harvard Graduate School, after which he returned to China to teach. He founded and wrote for several English and Chinese periodicals and edited textbooks. He is chancellor of Nanyang University, Singapore, and head of the Arts and Letters Division of UNESCO. Lin has written several books interpreting China and her people; among these are *My Country and My People* (1935), *A History of the Press and Public Opinion in China* (1936), *The Wisdom of Confucius* (1938), and *The Chinese Way of Life* (1959). He has written and translated short stories, among them *Famous Chinese Short Stories* (1952) and *Widow, Nun and Courtesan* (1951). Among his other books are *A Leaf in the Storm* (1941); *Between Tears and Laughter* (1943); and an anthology, *The Wisdom of China and India* (1942). His most recent works are *The Importance of Understanding* (1960) and *The Red Peony* (1962).

lion. The "king of beasts." This animal figures perhaps more than any other in legend, symbolism, and heraldry. In religious art, the lion is an emblem of the Resurrection. According to tradition, the lion's whelp is born dead, and remains so for three days, when the father breathes on it and it receives life. Another tradition is that the lion is the only animal of the cat tribe born with its eyes open, and it is said that it sleeps with its eyes open.

St. Mark the Evangelist is symbolized by a lion because he begins his gospel with the scenes of St. John the Baptist and Christ in the wilderness. The device of Venice is the winged Lion of St. Mark. St. Jerome befriended lions. (See ANDROCLES, HERACLES, and UNA for legends of lions.)

Ever since 1164, when it was adopted as a device by Philip I, duke of Flanders, the lion has figured largely, and in an amazing variety of positions, as a heraldic emblem.

Lion Gate. The gate leading from the ancient Greek city of Mycenae in Argolis to the acropolis. It is about 10 feet high and wide, has monolithic jambs and a huge lintel. Above the lintel is a great slab with a relief of two affronted rampant lions which account for the name. It was built in the Mycenaean era (1400–1100 B.C.).

Lipchitz, Jacques (1891–   ). Russian-born French sculptor. Established in New York since 1941, he has composed powerful figures, notably of bulls, in which the play of light on rough surfaces and on large masses contributes to a great feeling of movement; he has also done monumental semihuman standing columns of interpenetrating circular forms and shafts.

Li Po or **Li Tai Po** or **Li Tai Peh** (c. 701–c. 762). Chinese poet, considered one of the greatest. Fond of wine, fencing, and adventure, he traveled widely, then retired to the mountains as one of the Six Idlers of the Bamboo Streams. Admired by the emperor for his learning and his poetry, he was brought to the royal court, but palace intrigue and his part in the rebellion of An Lu-shan (775–776), forced him to leave and resume his wanderings. Imperial orders, however, allowed him to obtain free wine, and he formed another group of companions called the Eight Immortals of the Wine Cup. According to legend he drowned one night trying to embrace the reflection of the moon near his boat. His poems are passionate lyrics about wine and love, rich in delicate, imaginative imagery of natural beauty. See Arthur Waley, *The Poetry and Career of Li Po* (1950).

Lippi, Fra Lippo or **Filippo** (1406–1469). Italian painter. A Florentine monk of the Carmelite order, he painted religious easel paintings and frescoes in a style stressing charm, imaginative detail, and sinuous outline. He was influenced primarily by Masaccio, Fra Angelico, and Donatello, and in turn was the teacher of Botticelli. Among his best-known works are *The Madonna with Saints* and the *Virgin and Child with Saints and Angels*. His restlessness as a monk, which caused him to leave his monastery, inspired Browning's famous poem FRA LIPPO LIPPI. His son **Filippino** (1475–1504), who studied with his father's pupil Botticelli, also became famous as a painter of religious scenes. His masterpieces include the *Madonna Appearing to Saint Bernard,* the *Madonna and Child with Angels,* the *Allegory of Music,* and the frescoes of the Strozzi Chapel in the Florentine church of S. Maria Novella. He also finished the frescoes left incomplete by Masaccio in the Brancacci Chapel of the Carmine.

Lippmann, Walter (1889–). American journalist. After aiding in the preparations for the peace conference after World War I and holding important editorial positions on the *New Republic* and New York *World*, Lippmann became famous for the thoughtful and reasoned political comments of his influential newspaper column, which he began to write in 1931 for the New York *Herald Tribune*. He has lucidly set forth his social philosophy in several influential volumes, including *Public Opinion* (1922), *A Preface to Morals* (1929), *The Good Society* (1937), and *The Public Philosophy* (1955).

Lippold, Richard (1915–). American sculptor. He is known for constructions of metal plates and wires, such as the hanging *Orpheus and Apollo* in the New York Lincoln Center Philharmonic Hall.

Lismahago, Captain. In Tobias Smollett's novel HUMPHREY CLINKER, an eccentric, superannuated veteran officer of the Indian wars who marries Miss Tabitha BRAMBLE. He is a forbidding Scotsman, singular in dress and in manners, conceited, disputatious, and rude. Though most tenacious in argument, he can yield to Miss Tabitha, whom he wishes to conciliate.

Lissauer, Ernst. See HYMN OF HATE.

Liszt, Franz (1811–1886). Hungarian composer and virtuoso pianist. A child prodigy, he first performed in public at the age of nine. He studied in Vienna under Czerny and Salieri, in Paris under Reicha. He lived at Geneva (1835–1839) with the Comtesse d'Agoult, by whom he had three children, one of whom was Cosima, who later married Richard Wagner. Liszt was court Kapellmeister at Weimar from 1848 to 1859. In 1865 he entered the Franciscan order at Rome (1865) and was thenceforth known as the Abbé Liszt. He died at Bayreuth (1886) in the midst of a Wagner festival. He was outstanding as a piano teacher as well as a performer.

Much of his music, especially from the last 20 years of his life, is marked by daring innovations in form and harmonic relations, which have fascinated and influenced composers ever since, even though he had no true disciples or imitators. His works include the *Faust Symphony* (1853–1861), the *Dante Symphony* (1856); twelve symphonic poems, including *Les Préludes* (after Lamartine), two piano concertos; much piano music, notably the *Années de Pèlerinage* and the 20 Hungarian Rhapsodies (1851–1886); two oratorios, several masses, and other church music; songs, and organ pieces.

Literary Club, The. A group founded by Sir Joshua REYNOLDS and Samuel JOHNSON in 1764 under the simpler title of "The Club." They met weekly for conversation at The Turk's Head Tavern in Gerrard Street, Soho, until 1783, when the tavern was converted to a private dwelling. They continued at various meeting-places until the end of the century. The members included Edmund Burke, Thomas Percy, James Boswell, Edward Gibbon, David Garrick, Oliver Goldsmith, and Adam Smith, among other famous 18th-century figures.

Litigants, The. See PLAIDEURS, LES.

Little, Henry. The inventor-hero of Charles Reade's PUT YOURSELF IN HIS PLACE.

Little, Thomas. Pseudonym under which Thomas MOORE's *Poetical Works* of 1801 were published. Moore is called by this name in Byron's *English Bards and Scotch Reviewers*.

Little Clay Cart, The or **The Toy Cart** (Sans., *Mrichchhakatika*). A Sanskrit comedy ascribed to King Shudraka and variously assigned to the 3rd to 10th centuries. The hero is Charudatta, an impoverished Brahmin merchant, the heroine the lovely courtesan Vasantasena. The villain of the play, Sansthanaka, the king's brother-in-law, smothers Vasantasena in a remote garden and accuses Charudatta of the crime, but Vasantasena recovers and appears just in time to save her lover from execution. An important subplot is concerned with a successful conspiracy to overthrow the reigning monarch. Goethe paraphrased the drama in his poem *Der Gott und die Bayadere,* and it was made the basis of a popular ballet *Le Dieu et la bayadère* which was staged throughout Europe about the year 1830. The drama itself was produced in New York by the Neighborhood Playhouse players in 1924–1925.

Little Corporal. An epithet applied to Napoleon Bonaparte after the battle of Lodi in 1796. Bonaparte stood barely five feet two inches in height.

Little Dorrit (1855–1857). A novel by Charles DICKENS. William Dorrit, with his three children Edward, Fanny, and Amy (who is Little Dorrit), lives in prison where he is confined for debt. Little Dorrit was born in the prison, spends most of her life there, and ultimately, chooses to be married there. The three children try to make a living outside the prison and bring back their earnings each night. Little Dorrit does her part by sewing for Mrs. Clennam. Suddenly, her father comes into a fortune and the whole family becomes as pretentious and despicable as they were formerly objects of compassion. Only Little Dorrit remains unchanged with her father's changing fortune, retaining her sweet and generous disposition. She grows to love Arthur Clennam, middle-aged son of Mrs. Clennam, who has recently returned from India; he helps to free her father from prison. In Arthur's struggle with the civil service's CIRCUMLOCUTION OFFICE, Dickens levels an attack on bureaucracy. Arthur is sent to prison for debt and Little Dorrit labors to help him. Their love ends happily, and they are married in Marshalsea prison. This novel is one of Dickens' strongest attacks on bureaucratic inefficiency and the practice of imprisonment for debt.

Among the many memorable characters in the book are the soft-hearted Meagles family; the BARNACLES; and Mr. and Mrs. PLORNISH. See MARSHALSEA.

Little Em'ly. See PEGGOTTY.

Little-Endians. See BIG-ENDIANS.

Little Entente. See ENTENTE.

Little Eva. A character in Harriet Beecher Stowe's UNCLE TOM'S CABIN.

Little Foxes, The (1939.) A play by Lillian HELLMAN. In telling the story of the Hubbard family, it depicts unfavorably the rise of industrialism in the South and condemns the new breed of Southerners as rapacious and ruthless—like "the little foxes who spoil the vines" of the biblical verse. *Another Part of the Forest* (1946) deals with an earlier stage in the Hubbards' career.

Little Gidding. The home of an Anglican lay religious community in England in the 17th century. It was composed of the family and friends of Nicholas FERRAR, who was intimate with the poets George Herbert and Richard Crashaw. It is the setting for the novel *John Inglesant,* by J. H. Shorthouse, and for T. S. Eliot's poem *Little Gidding* (see FOUR QUARTETS). The community was dispersed by the Parliamentarians in 1647, during the Civil War.

Little John. A chief follower of ROBIN HOOD in the English Robin Hood ballad cycle. He was a big stalwart fellow, first named John Little (or John Nailor), who encountered Robin Hood and gave him a sound thrashing, after which he was rechristened, Robin standing as godfather. He appears in Scott's novel *The Talisman* (1825).

Little Lord Fauntleroy. A story for children by Frances Hodgson BURNETT (1886), illustrated by Reginald Birch. The seven-year-old hero, Cedric Errol, is the son of a disinherited English father and an American mother. His title of Lord Fauntleroy he would normally inherit from his grandfather, an English earl, who has, however, never forgiven the boy's father for marrying an American. On the death of the father the boy is summoned to England, leaving his mother, whom he calls "Dearest," in the poverty-stricken quarters where they have been living in New York. He so completely wins the hearts of his English relatives that they are soon persuaded to extend to "Dearest" a cordial welcome. Little Lord Fauntleroy is a striking figure, dressed in black velvet with lace collar and yellow curls, and his name passed into common usage as referring either to a certain type of children's clothes or to a beautiful but pampered and effeminate small boy.

little magazines. A name applied to small, noncommercial, usually short-lived periodicals whose aim is to promote avant-garde writing. These magazines, frequently the only means of expression available to young, unknown experimental writers, have provided a meeting-ground for writers and thereby sometimes formed the nucleus of new literary movements. They were a major factor in the literary revolution of 1910-1920.

The little magazine form goes back to the mid-19th century with the Transcendentalist magazine THE DIAL (1840-1844), *The Philistine* (1895-1915), and

The Mirror (1893-1920) in America, and *The Germ* (1850) and *The Yellow Book* (1894-1897) in England. Between 1910 and 1920 little magazines began to appear in abundance: *The Blue Review* (England, 1911), POETRY (1912), *Blast* (England, 1914), THE LITTLE REVIEW (1914), *Bruno's Weekly* (1915), THE SEVEN ARTS (1916), *The Dial* (1917). During the 1920's a number of magazines were published by American expatriates in London and Paris: *The Criterion* (London, 1922), TRANSITION (Paris, 1927), *Exile* (Paris and Chicago, 1927), *Broom* (Rome, then London, then New York, 1921-1924), *Secession* (Vienna, Berlin, New York, 1922-1924). The most important American little magazines during this period were *The Double Dealer* (1921), *The Fugitive* (1922), and *The Chicago Literary Times* (1923).

The late 20's and 30's saw a shift in emphasis away from the more purely literary little magazines toward two new forms: the politico-literary journal, such as the *New Masses* (1926), which was dominant during the 30's, and the quarterly review, such as the *Prairie Schooner* (1927), which became important in the late 30's and have continued to be widely influential critical and usually academic journals. New magazines in the 30's and 40's included *The Harkness Hoot* (1930), *Story* (1931), THE PARTISAN REVIEW (1934), *New Directions in Prose and Poetry* (1936), THE KENYON REVIEW (1939), *Furioso* (1939), *Accent* (1940), *Chimera* (1942), *Quarterly Review of Literature* (1943), *Hudson Review* (1948), and *Cronos* (1947). In reaction against the quarterlies, which were no longer avant-garde and were critical more than creative, a new group of little magazines appeared during the 50's, many of them with titles borrowed from now-defunct magazines of the twenties: *The Dial, The Seven Arts, Transatlantic Review, Contact.* Practically all the major writers of the 20th century had their early work published in little magazines: Sherwood Anderson, Van Wyck Brooks, Hart Crane, E. E. Cummings, John Dos Passos, Theodore Dreiser, T. S. Eliot, William Faulkner, Robert Frost, Ernest Hemingway, James Joyce, D. H. Lawrence, Marianne Moore, Eugene O'Neill, Katherine Anne Porter, Ezra Pound, Gertrude Stein, Dylan Thomas, William Carlos Williams, Edmund Wilson, and others. Critical studies of the little magazines include F. J. Hoffman's *The Little Magazine* (1946).

Little Minister, The (1891). A novel by J. M. BARRIE. The hero, Gavin Dishart, is a young preacher in the Scottish village of Thrums. He struggles in vain against his love for the irresistible gypsy, Babbie, and marries her on impulse. The parish is scandalized. The two are separated, but after many vicissitudes, the Little Minister regains both his prestige and his bride.

Little Nell. See OLD CURIOSITY SHOP, THE.

Little Orphant Annie (1885). A poem in Hoosier dialect by James Whitcomb RILEY. Orphant Annie tells hair-raising tales about the goblins, and is finally carried off by them. A comic strip by Harold Gray is called *Little Orphan Annie.*

Littlepage Manuscripts, The (1845-1846). A series of three novels by James Fenimore COOPER: SATANSTOE, *The Chainbearer,* and THE REDSKINS. Presumably related by several generations of Littlepage men, the novels deal with the antirent controversy and its historical background. In this now forgotten issue, the tenants of the New York patroons, suffering hardships, refused to pay rent. Cooper defended the landlords' rights, insisting that the tenants had enjoyed years of advantages in the bargain. Cooper saw, in this controversy, a crisis in American democracy; if contracts could be broken by mob rule, democracy would turn to anarchy.

The three novels become progressively weaker, as Cooper's political principles outweigh those of his art. The trilogy marks the end of his most creative period.

Little Red Riding-Hood. A nursery tale. It comes to us from *Le Petit Chaperon Rouge* (1697) of Charles PERRAULT (in his CONTES DE MA MÈRE L'OYE), though with slight alterations the story is common to France, Germany, and Sweden and probably originated in Italy. A little girl bringing a present to her grandmother is devoured by a wolf who has disguised himself in the old lady's ruffled nightcap. The brothers GRIMM added a happy ending to the tale: a huntsman slits open the wolf and restores the child and her grandmother to life.

Little Review, The (1914–1929). An American literary periodical. It was published, first in Chicago, later in New York and Paris, under the editorship of Margaret Anderson, and championed all the 20th-century experimental movements, publishing the work of outstanding English, American, and European writers of the period. When James Joyce's *Ulysses* appeared in installments (1918–1921), four issues were confiscated and burned by the Post Office.

Little Shepherd of Kingdom Come, The (1903). A novel by John Fox, Jr. The highly sentimental story deals with Chad Buford, a shepherd of doubtful parentage who, before going to fight in the Civil War, comes to live for a while at the Cumberland Mountain settlement which is used in the book's title. The novel was dramatized by Eugene Walter in 1916.

Little Tragedies (*Malen'kiye tragedi*; 1830). Four short dramatic works in blank verse by Aleksandr PUSHKIN. The short dramas, which Pushkin referred to as "essays of dramatic investigation," are studies of character in four varied situations. *The Stone Guest* (*Kamyenni gost'*) is a re-telling of the Don Juan legend. *Mozart and Salieri* (*Motzart i Sal'yeri*) depicts Salieri's jealousy of Mozart's artistic genius and his legendary poisoning of Mozart. *The Covetous Knight* (*Skupoi rytzar'*) is a study of the effects of avarice. *The Feast during the Plague* (*Pir vo vremya chumy*), translated from the English drama *City of the Plague* by John Wilson, shows the evil effects on human behavior of imminent death. All four of the small dramas are regarded as being among Pushkin's most powerful poetic work.

Little Women, or Meg, Jo, Beth, and Amy (1868, 1869). A widely read story for young people by Louisa May ALCOTT. The heroine is Jo March, the tomboyish and literary member of the family, who retires to the attic when "genius burns." Meg, her older, pretty sister, marries a young tutor, John Brooke, and reappears in the sequel, *Little Men* (1871), with her twins, Daisy and Demi. Gentle, music-loving Beth dies young. The fashionable and artistic Amy finally marries Laurie, a high-spirited boy who had long been Jo's boon companion, but who failed to persuade her to marry him. Jo herself becomes the wife of a kindly old German professor, Mr. Bhaer; in *Little Men*, she and the professor turn their home into a school for boys. *Jo's Boys* (1886) is a second sequel.

Litvinov. The hero of Ivan Turgenev's novel SMOKE, who allows his former lover, Irina, to disrupt his love affair with Tanya.

Lives of the Poets, The (1779–1781). A collection of biographical and critical essays on 52 English poets from Cowley to Johnson's contemporaries by Samuel JOHNSON. It is noted for its approach; Johnson was interested in establishing a causal relationship between the artist's life and his art:

> To judge rightly of an author we must transport ourselves to his time, and examine what were the wants of his contemporaries, and what were his means of supplying them.—*Life of Dryden*

His criticism was vigorous and articulate. He considered Dryden, Pope, Swift, and Addison the most important authors of the Restoration and Queen Anne periods. Some of his critical opinion has been discredited with the perspective of time; the romantics deplored his failure to appreciate the odes of Thomas Gray and Milton's work, and his attack on metaphysical poetry, in the *Life of Cowley*, is not compatible with the modern view. However, Johnson's *Lives* remains an achievement beyond the "correctness" of its critical evaluations.

Livingstone, David (1813–1873). Scottish-born English missionary and explorer in Africa. After working in a cotton mill from the age of 10, he went to college in 1837, received a medical degree in 1840, and left England for South Africa as a medical missionary. He discovered Lake Ngami (1849), Zambesi River (1851), the Victoria Falls of the Zambesi (1855), and Lake Nyasa (1859). On his return to England (1864) he published *Narrative of an Expedition to the Zanzibar and Its Tributaries* (1865). Appointed British consul in central Africa, he went back with the express purpose of wiping out slave trade and determining the watershed of the Nyasa-Tanganyika region. Exhausted and near death, he spent some months in Ujiji; in 1871 an expedition was sent out under Sir Henry M. Stanley (1841–1904) to find Livingstone and their famous encounter began with Stanley's anticlimactic, "Dr. Livingstone, I presume?" Livingstone died in a village on the south shore. His body was taken to England and buried in Westminster Abbey. His journals for the years 1866 to 1873 were published as *Last Journals of David Livingstone in Central Africa* (1873). Livingstone's example was followed by many missionaries and his influence was considerable in reducing slave trade.

Livius Andronicus (fl. 3d century B.C.). Founder of Roman epic poetry and drama. He was a Greek slave who, after being freed by his master Livius, whose name he adopted, introduced both comedies and tragedies in Latin on Greek models for performance in Rome. He also made a Latin translation of Homer's *Odyssey* which was used for centuries in Roman schools. His importance is due to the fact that he gave the Romans their first contact with Greek literature in translation.

Livre de mon ami, Le. See Anatole FRANCE.

Livy. Full Latin name, **Titus Livius** (59 B.C.–A.D. 17). Roman historian. His *Ab Urbe Condita Libri,* the history of Rome from the founding of the city, was written in 142 books of which only about 36 have been preserved. We have, however, summaries of all but two of the missing books; these outlines, written by an unknown scholar of the fourth century, give an indication of the vast scope of the work which extended from the mythological beginnings of Rome down to A.D. 9. Though Livy's research must have been voluminous, it was unscholarly; his information is often inaccurate, and his facts are sometimes self-contradictory. But scientific history was not his primary objective. He wished to hold up to his countrymen the great panorama of their past, to recall to them the glories of their ancestors, and to urge them to abandon the decadent ways they had. In this sense his aim was similar to that of Vergil in his *Aeneid.* Livy's style is one of polished rhetorical brilliance; the speeches which he puts in the mouths of historical personages are masterful, both as oratory and as character analysis.

A native of Patavium (Padua), Livy began his great work about 26 B.C., but did not publish his first 21 books until A.D. 14. Excerpts were, however, in circulation much earlier, for Asinius Pollio, who died in A.D. 4, had occasion to criticize Livy's "patavinitas." This was apparently a reference to his provincial, Paduan manner of expression, evidence of which scholars have not been able to detect in Livy's prose.

Liza of Lambeth (1897). The first novel of W. Somerset MAUGHAM. It depicts the life and loves of Liza, a girl of the London slums. Written in the tradition of naturalism, it is filled with minute descriptions of poverty, violence, and physical and psychological illness. The novel was considered shocking when it was first published.

Llareggub or Llaregyb. See UNDER MILK WOOD.

Llewellyn, Richard. Pen name of **Richard David Vivian Llewellyn Lloyd** (1907–   ), Welsh novelist. Llewellyn wrote the very popular Welsh novel How GREEN WAS MY VALLEY. His other books include *None But the Lonely Heart* (1943), *A Few Flowers for Shiner* (1950), *The Flame of Hercules* (1957), *Chez Pavan* (1959), and *Up, Into the Singing Mountain* (1961).

Lloyd George, David (1863–1945). British statesman of Welsh descent. Succeeded Asquith as prime minister (1916–1922) and directed British policies during World War I and in the negotiation of peace terms. Instituted negotiations resulting in the establishment of the Irish Free State. Author of *War Memoirs* (6 vols., 1933–1936) and *The Truth About the Peace Treaty* (2 vols., 1938). Created Earl Lloyd-George of Dufor (1945). See LIMEHOUSE.

Lloyd's of London. An association of underwriters, merchants, shipowners, and brokers. The company deals principally with ocean-borne commerce, marine insurance, and the publication of shipping intelligence, but it has a worldwide reputation of being willing to insure almost anyone against almost anything. The company is so called because the society was founded, in 1688, at a coffee house kept in Lombard Street by one Edward Lloyd. In 1774, the offices, or *Lloyd's Rooms,* were moved to the Royal Exchange, where they still are.

Lloyd's books. Two enormous ledgerlike volumes, placed on desks at the entrance (right and left) of Lloyd's Rooms. They give the principal arrivals, and all losses by wrecks, fire, or other accidents at sea.

Lloyd's List. A periodical, in which the shipping news received at Lloyd's Rooms is published. It has been issued regularly since 1726, and as a daily since 1800.

Lloyd's Register. A register of ships, English and foreign, published yearly.

Lludd and Llefelys. See MABINOGION, THE.

local color. In reference to literature, the concrete details of natural scenery, architecture, language, local custom and tradition, used by authors to lend a sense of authenticity to their work. Local color writing flourished in the U.S. during the post-bellum 19th century. Native manners and dialect were frequently exploited for humorous effect. Among the outstanding local colorists of the Far West were Bret Harte and Joaquin Miller; New England scenes and characters were delicately recorded by Sarah Orne Jewett and Rose Terry Cooke. In the Middle West, Edward Eggleston and John Hay employed local color, while Hamlin Garland and Edgar Lee Masters, under the influence of the new realism, presented their devastating studies of local life. The South was nostalgically or accurately portrayed by George Washington Cable, Lafcadio Hearn, Charles Egbert Craddock, Joel Chandler Harris, Thomas Nelson Page, and Grace Elizabeth King.

Local color writing in the United States may be traced back as far as James Fenimore Cooper's SATANSTOE, Washington Irving's Knickerbocker's HISTORY OF NEW YORK, Charles Brockden Brown's WIELAND, and Nathaniel Hawthorne's THE SCARLET LETTER. Among the 20th-century American writers whose work local detail enriches are William Faulkner, Ellen Glasgow, J. P. Marquand, O. Henry, Edith Wharton, James T. Farrell, John Steinbeck, and Sherwood Anderson.

In Great Britain, writers who employ local color to a significant degree include J. M. Synge, Sean O'Casey, Thomas Hardy, Arnold Bennett, A. E. Housman, and Winifred Holtby. In the novels and stories of James Joyce, the atmosphere of Dublin is vividly evoked. In France, Guy de Maupassant reveals the details of life in Normandy; Alphonse Daudet, Frédéric Mistral, and Jean Giono have written of Provence.

Locarno Pact or **Treaty.** A series of five treaties between Germany and Belgium, France, Great Britain, Italy, Poland, and Czechoslovakia (October 1925). They were negotiated at Locarno in Switzerland with the purpose of guaranteeing peace and the existing territorial boundaries.

Lochiel. The title of the head of the clan Cameron. The hero of Thomas CAMPBELL's poem *Lochiel's Warning* (1802) is Donald Cameron, known as the Gentle Lochiel. He was one of the Young PRETENDER's stanchest adherents, and escaped to France with him after Culloden (1746). He took service in the French army, but died two years later.

Lochinvar. A young Highlander, hero of a ballad in Scott's MARMION. Being in love with a lady already committed to an unenviable marriage, he persuades her to dance one last dance, during which he swings her into his saddle, and makes off with her before the bridegroom and his servants can recover from their astonishment.

Locke, David Ross. See Petroleum Vesuvius NASBY.

Locke, John (1632–1704). English philosopher. Educated at Christ Church, Oxford, Locke was a lecturer in Greek, rhetoric, and philosophy at that university and apparently practiced medicine, though he never received a medical degree. He became confidential secretary to the earl of SHAFTESBURY, who was one of the proprietors of Carolina, and wrote a well-known constitution for the colony in 1669. Suspected of complicity in Shaftesbury's plots against the government, Locke was forced to leave England and lived in the Netherlands from 1684 to 1689. After the accession of William and Mary, he was appointed commissioner of appeals.

Locke's most famous work is AN ESSAY CONCERNING HUMAN UNDERSTANDING, an inquiry into the nature of knowledge. His *Two Treatises on Government* (1690), written in defense of the Glorious Revolution, exerted enormous influence on British and American political thought. The Declaration of Independence, in particular, echoes his contention that government rests on popular consent and that rebellion is permissible when government subverts the ends—the protection of life, liberty, and property—for which it is established. Locke also wrote *Some Thoughts Concerning Education* (1693), *The Reasonableness of Christianity* (1695), and four *Letters on Toleration* (1689–1692, 1765).

Locke, William J[ohn] (1863–1930). English popular novelist, author of the best-selling novel THE BELOVED VAGABOND. He also wrote *The Morals of Marcus Ordeyne* (1905), *The Glory of Clementina Wing* (1911), and *The Great Pandolfo* (1925).

Locker-Lampson, Frederick. Before 1885, **Frederick Locker** (1821–1895). English poet. He was noted for his light verse and elegant *vers de société*. He was the author of *London Lyrics* (1857), and editor of *Lyra Elegantiarum* (1867), an anthology of light verse. Lampson was the maiden name of his second wife.

Lockhart, John Gibson (1794–1854). Scottish editor and writer. He published the sketches of Edinburgh life *Peter's Letters to his Kinsfolk* (1819), under the pseudonym Peter Morris, and translated *Ancient Spanish Ballads* (1823). At the age of 23 he wrote for *Blackwood's Magazine* a series of four articles, signed "Z," dealing with the supposed COCKNEY SCHOOL of poetry and excoriating Leigh Hunt and John Keats. Though the ruffianly tone of these articles is abusive and though to later generations many of Lockhart's adverse judgments seem as vicious as they are obtuse, especially in their confusion of enmity with criticism, Lockhart enjoys a high reputation in English letters, his life of his father-in-law Sir Walter Scott (7 vols., 1837–1838) ranking second only to Boswell's *Johnson* among the great biographies in the language. Lockhart also published a biography of Robert Burns (1828).

Lockit. See BEGGAR'S OPERA, THE; THREEPENNY OPERA, THE.

Locksley. In Scott's IVANHOE, a name assumed by Robin Hood, who appears as an archer at the tournament. It is said to have been the name of the village where the outlaw was born.

Locksley Hall (1842). A poem by Alfred TENNYSON. The hero takes a last look at Locksley Hall, the remote seaside mansion where he spent his youth. Here he fell in love with his cousin Amy, who, yielding to social and parental pressure, married a rich "clown." Though disgusted by the weakness of women and the mercenary corruption of the age—he even considers exiling himself to some tropic island—his youthful belief in progress and in the high destiny of Europe reasserts itself. In 1886 Tennyson published *Locksley Hall Sixty Years After*, a sequel.

Lockyer, Sir Joseph Norman (1836–1920). British astronomer. He initiated (1866) the spectroscopic observation of sunspots. He investigated the chemistry of the sun, and, in 1868, determined the presence in its atmosphere of an unknown element to which the name helium was given (from Greek *helios*, "the sun")—a name that it has kept although helium was later discovered to exist also in the earth's atmosphere.

Loco-Focos. The radical urban wing of the Democratic party in New York in the mid-1830's. They favored the abolition of monopolies and advocated "hard" (as opposed to paper) money. They derived their name from a Tammany Hall meeting in 1835 at which the Democratic regulars nominated a ticket, ignoring the protests of the radicals, and turned out the lights in order to evict them. The radicals then obtained candles, which they lit with the new self-igniting matches called loco-focos, and proceeded to select their own candidates.

Locrine. In Geoffrey of Monmouth's HISTORY OF THE KINGS OF BRITAIN, king of England and son of BRUTE. His love for Estrildis, daughter of a German king, causes his jealous wife Gwendolen to raise arms against him. Locrine is slain, and Gwendolen, assuming power, drowns Estrildis and her daughter SABRINA. According to Geoffrey, England (Loegria) received its name from him.

Locusta. One who murders those she professes to nurse or take care of. The original Locusta was a professional poisoner living in Rome about A.D. 54. She poisoned the emperor Claudius at Agrippina's bidding and was hired by Nero to poison Britannicus. She was put to death under the emperor Galba.

Lodge, Thomas (1558?–1625). English poet, playwright, and prose writer. The son of the Lord Mayor of London, Lodge was educated at Oxford and became one of the group in London known as the UNIVERSITY WITS. Considered by some to be the best of the imitators of LYLY and the Euphuistic style (see EUPHUISM), Lodge wrote several prose romances, the first of which was *The Delectable History of Forbonius and Pisceria* (1584). During a voyage to the Canary Islands he wrote *Rosalynde, Euphues' Golden Legacie* (printed 1590), his most famous work. Based to some extent on the medieval tale of Gamelyn, it provided Shakespeare with the plot for As YOU LIKE IT. Lodge's poetry includes *Scillaes Metamorphosis, Enterlaced with the Unfortunate Love of Glaucus* (1589; reissued as *Glaucus and Scilla*). As the first example of a classical story given romantic treatment in verse, it may have influenced Shakespeare's VENUS AND ADONIS. *Phillis,* a sonnet sequence, was published with the narrative poem *The Complaint of Elstred* in 1593. *A Fig for Momus* (1595), based on the satires of Horace, is one of the earliest English verse satires.

THE

Lamentable Tragedie of

Locrine, the eldest sonne of King *Brutus,* discoursing the warres of the *Britaines,* and *Hunnes,*
with their discomfiture:

The Britaines *victorie with their Accidents, and the
death of* Albanact. *No lesse pleasant then
profitable.*

Newly set foorth, ouerseene and corrected,
By *VV. S.*

LONDON
Printed by Thomas Creede.
1 5 9 5.

Title page of *Locrine*. Possibly by George Peele,
it was mistakenly included in the Shakespeare
Third Folio.

Only two of Lodge's plays have survived: *A Looking
Glass for London and England,* written with Robert
GREENE in about 1590, published in 1594; and *The
Wounds of Civil War,* produced c. 1587, published
1594. Some critics believe Lodge may have had a
hand in Part II of Shakespeare's HENRY VI and in
KING JOHN. In the latter part of his life Lodge became a physician, and his writings after that time
are confined to more serious and edifying subjects,
such as a *Treatise on the Plague* (1603) and a translation of Seneca.

Lodi, League of (1454). A 25-year nonaggres-
sion pact signed by the major states of Italy. Negotiated by the Venetians, it is regarded as the first
triumph of modern diplomacy.

Lodovico. In Shakespeare's OTHELLO, kinsman
to Brabantio, father of Desdemona.

Lofting, Hugh (1886-1947). English-born American writer, author and illustrator of children's books.
Lofting created the amiable and fantastic Dr. Dolittle,
the title character of several popular and imaginative
works such as *The Story of Dr. Dolittle* (1920), *The
Voyages of Dr. Dolittle* (1922), and *Dr. Dolittle's
Garden* (1927).

Loftus, Cissie. Stage name of **Marie Cecilia
McCarthy** (1876-1943). Scottish actress. She starred
on the stage and in early motion pictures. She was
famous for her sparkling impersonations of other
stage and screen stars.

Log, King. A king who rules in peace and quiet-
ness, but never makes his power felt. It is an allusion
to the fable of the frogs who asked for a king. Jupiter
first threw them down a log of wood, but they
grumbled at so spiritless a king. He then sent them
a stork, which devoured them eagerly.

logical positivism. A leading school of 20th-cen-
tury philosophy. Logical positivists believe man's
thoughts, ideas, and concepts are dependent on his
command of language, so they approach truth and
logic through a study of language. The school had
its origin in Vienna but it is now centered at Oxford
in England. It was much influenced by the writings
of Ludwig WITTGENSTEIN. Logical positivism is also
known as linguistic philosophy and its exponents are
often called the Oxford philosophers. A. J. AYER is
a leading English member of the school. Linguistic
philosophy has profoundly influenced literary criticism in England. See CAMBRIDGE CRITICS.

Logistilla. In the ORLANDO FURIOSO of Ariosto,
the sister of the witch Alcina. Herself a symbol of
reason and virtue, she teaches Ruggiero to ride the
Hippogriff and gives Astolfo a book that enables him
to break enchantments, and a horn whose sound has a
shattering impact on all who hear it.

Lohengrin. A son of Percival or Parsifal in German legend, the Knight of the Swan. He appears at
the close of Wolfram von Eschenbach's *Parzival* (c.
1210), and in other German romances, where he is
the deliverer of Elsa, a princess of Brabant, who has
been dispossessed by Telramund and Ortrud. He
arrives at Antwerp in a skiff drawn by a swan,
champions Elsa, and becomes her husband on the sole
condition that she shall not ask his name or lineage.
She is prevailed upon to do so on the marriage night,
and he, by his vows to the Grail, is obliged to disclose
his identity, but at the same time disappear. The swan
returns for him, and he goes, but not before re-
transforming the swan into Elsa's brother Gottfried,
who, by the wiles of the sorceress Ortrud, had been
obliged to assume that form. Richard Wagner has an
opera based on the subject, composed (words and
music) in 1847.

Lohenstein, Daniel Caspar von (1635-1683).
German dramatist, poet, and novelist of the late
baroque period. Like the poems of Hofmann von
Hofmannswaldau, his plays are rich and sensual in
language and imagery. Unlike Gryphius, who often
gives his heroes a martyr's death, Lohenstein's tragedies frequently end in suicide—showing less of an
attempt to remain within Christian teachings. His
most famous tragedies are *Cleopatra* (1661), *Ibrahim
Sultan* (1673), and *Sophonisbe* (1680). His historical
novel *Arminius* (1689) reveals many parallels with
the actual political situation of the time and embodies
the author's own views.

Loki. In Scandinavian mythology, the Satanic
Aesir god of strife and evil who fathered the 3 monsters with the giantess Angerboda: the Midgard serpent, Fenris, and Hel. As enemy of the good gods,
he artfully contrived the death of BALDER. He was
finally bound to a rock by 10 chains and tortured by

drops of venom from a serpent overhead. One legend holds that he will remain captive until the Twilight of the Gods, when he will break his bonds. Another story says that he was freed at RAGNAROK when he and Heimdall slew each other.

Lokman. A fabulous personage, the supposed author of a collection of Arabic fables. The name is based on Lugman, the title of the 31st Sura of the Koran, in which it is stated, "We gave to Lugman wisdom." Like Aesop, he is said to have been a slave, noted for his ugliness.

Lollards. A name given, sometimes disparagingly, to members of the 14th-century English movement in England associated with John Wyclif and his demands for ecclesiastical reform. The Lollards held that the Church in England had become so encrusted with false doctrine as to be virtually useless and that the only true way of life was one based on the Bible. They particularly objected to the wealth and power of the clergy and advocated that the Church practice the poverty exemplified by Christ in the Gospels. The Lollards' rise into prominence during the latter half of the 14th century can best be understood in the historical context of the times: while the great mass of the people were plagued by warfare, pestilence, and poverty, the English clergy by skillful abuse of ecclesiastical prerogatives had amassed enormous power, wealth, and property. The Lollards reached the height of their strength in the decade following Wyclif's death: in 1395, it was said that one out of every two Englishman was a Lollard. Under the house of Lancaster in the 15th century, they were more and more sternly repressed and, waning in numbers, responded to their loss of strength by ever-increasing fanaticism. In part their decline was due to a loss of leadership; in the 16th century, to all practical intents and purposes, the Lollards had ceased to exist. Though it cannot be claimed that the Lollards sparked the English Reformation, the movement bore important fruit: the placing of the clergy under lay jurisdiction, the curbing of clerical abuses (especially in the form of the reduction in ecclesiastic holdings and possessions), and the insistence that the Bible through translation into the vernacular be made available to the reason of common men and women are all due, directly or indirectly, to the legacy left by the Lollards.

Lomax, John Avery (1872-1948). American folklorist and collector of folk songs. These he published in numerous books. His work has been continued by his son **Alan Lomax** (1915-), who has collected thousands of American and European folk songs by means of phonograph recordings, many of which are in the Library of Congress; some are also available on commercial recordings.

Lombard. A banker or money-lender. They are so called because the first English bankers were from Lombardy, and set up in Lombard Street (London), in the Middle Ages. The name Lombard is a contraction of Longobards. Among the richest of these Longobard merchants was the celebrated Medici family, from whose armorial bearings the pawnbrokers' insignia of three golden balls may have been derived (see St. NICHOLAS). The Lombard bankers exercised a monopoly in pawnbroking until the reign of Elizabeth I.

Lombard, Peter (c. 1100-c. 1164). Italian scholastic theologian. He studied Aristotelian philosophy under Pierre ABÉLARD, then himself became a teacher at Paris. He is often called Master of the Sentences (Lat., "Magister Sententiarum") because of his compilation of the *Sententiarum Libri Quatuor (Four Books of Sentences)*. These volumes contain quotations from the authorities on doctrinal questions, with objections and replies also from "the sayings of the fathers." The fourth volume, concerning the nature of the sacraments, was especially important at the time; the whole work became a theological textbook and inspired innumerable commentaries.

Lomonosov, Mikhail Vasilyevich (1711-1765). Russian scholar and poet. He is considered the founder of modern literary Russian and the first to introduce what became standard Russian prosody. The son of a fisherman, Lomonosov became one of the most versatile and brilliant Russians of his time. He made valuable contributions in chemistry, mathematics, grammar, and rhetoric. He formed modern literary Russian by establishing a working relationship between the Old Church Slavonic language and the Russian vernacular, producing a literary language that rivals any other for richness and flexibility. Realizing that the old-style syllabic versification, based on the number of syllables in a line, was not fitted for Russian, Lomonosov introduced a system based on accents—alternating stressed and unstressed syllables. This system became the standard one used by the great classic Russian poets. Not until the early 20th century were new methods of versification introduced into Russian by Aleksandr Blok.

London, Jack. Real name, **John Griffith London** (1876-1916). American writer. Born in San Francisco, an illegitimate child, London was for a time the highest-paid and best-known writer in America. Brought up in dire poverty, he had already been at the age of 20, a hobo, a sailor, and a Klondike adventurer. Largely self-educated, he was influenced by the ideas of Darwin, Marx, and Nietzsche, and his work is marked by sympathy with the poor; prophecies of world revolution and a future socialist state; emphasis upon the primitive, the powerful, the cruel; and a predilection for the violent, usually embodied in an animal or a superman.

Going to the Klondike in 1897, London began writing stories of his Alaskan experiences for various magazines. These were collected in *The Son of the Wolf* (1900). His first novel, *A Daughter of the Snows* (1902), stresses his belief in Anglo-Saxon superiority, seen often in his later books. In 1903 came his most popular and enduring book, THE CALL OF THE WILD, the story of the dog Buck; WHITE FANG was a sequel. THE SEA-WOLF, again based on his own experiences, is an attempt to portray the Nietzschean superman. *The Game* (1905) is a novelette about a prizefighter, engaged to be married, who dies in his last fight. *Before Adam* (1906) describes the experiences of mankind in the far distant past; THE IRON HEEL turns to the future. MARTIN EDEN is a partly autobiographical novel in which the hero commits suicide, just as London was ultimately to do. *John Barleycorn* (1913), a tract against drinking, is also autobiographical. THE VALLEY OF THE MOON shows London's faith in socialism. *The Star Rover* (1915) describes trances experienced by a man in prison.

Best Short Stories of Jack London (1945) and *Tales*

of Adventure (1956) are selections of his stories. Leonard D. Abbott made a collection of London's *Essays of Revolt* (1926), and Philip S. Foner has edited *Jack London: American Rebel* (1947), a collection of his socialist writings.

London Merchant, The (1731). A bourgeois tragedy by George LILLO. It depicts the seduction of George Barnwell by the villainous Sarah Millwood and his subsequent crimes and degradation. The play, which was highly popular in its time, is chiefly remembered as an extreme example of sentimentality and bathos.

Loneliness of the Long Distance Runner, The (1959). A long short story by Alan SILLITOE. A boy who is sent to reform school for robbing a bakery narrates his own story. The corrupt society that has made him a delinquent is incidentally analyzed. The boy scores a triumph over the warden of the reformatory and the Establishment in general by deliberately losing in a long-distance race against another school.

Long, Gabrielle Margaret Vere (1886–1952). Prolific English novelist who wrote under 6 or 10 pen names. As Marjorie Bowen she wrote historical romances, such as *The Viper of Milan* (1906). As Joseph Shearing she wrote historical novels usually based on actual criminal cases, such as *Lucile Cléry: A Woman of Intrigue* (1932).

Long, Huey [Pierce] (1893–1935). American politician. Perhaps the most notorious as well as the most successful of American demagogues, Long began his career as a traveling salesman and later studied at Tulane University, completing the three-year law course in seven months. Having served as railroad commissioner of Louisiana, he was elected governor in 1928 and consolidated his power by placing his followers in strategic positions. After the failure of an attempt to remove him from office (1929), he was elected to the U.S. Senate in 1930 and, retaining the governorship until 1932, made himself master of the state; he provided Louisiana with good schools and highways during his term as governor, built a new state capitol at Baton Rouge, and helped the state university. In 1934 he announced a Share-Our-Wealth program to provide financial security for every American. After declaring himself a candidate for the presidency, he was assassinated on the steps of the state capital by Dr. Carl A. Weiss, who was killed by Long's bodyguards.

Long's career inspired several novels, including Hamilton Basso's *Sun in Capricorn* (1942) and John Dos Passos' *Number One* (1943). Although Robert Penn Warren has denied that the character of Willie Stark in his ALL THE KING's MEN should be identified with Long, the similarity is striking.

Longaville. In Shakespeare's LOVE's LABOUR's LOST, one of the three young lords who join Ferdinand, king of Navarre, in an oath of celibacy and study. He becomes enamored of Maria.

Long Day's Journey into Night (1956). A play by Eugene O'NEILL. An autobiographical drama, it was apparently written before July 22, 1941, when O'Neill presented the manuscript to Carlotta, his third wife. It deals with the Tyrone family: the father, mother, and two sons. The only other character is Cathleen, a servant girl. The father is a celebrated actor; the older son is a drunkard and ne'er-do-well.

A harrowing domestic tragedy, the play offers a clear insight into the character of O'Neill himself.

Longest Journey, The (1907). A novel by E. M. FORSTER. Its main character is Rickie Elliot, a student at Cambridge University. Lame, an orphan, and weak-willed, he neglects his good friend, Stewart Ansell, to marry Agnes Pembroke. Agnes, a shallow girl, with her brother influences Rickie to cheat his half brother, Stephen Wonham. Rickie finally redeems himself when he loses his life in saving Stephen's. The novel is notable for its picture of the intellectual and social life of Cambridge students.

Longfellow, Henry Wadsworth (1807–1882). American poet, translator, romancer, and college professor. Longfellow is two poets: one, the popular schoolroom image of the wise but harmless old man who wrote A PSALM OF LIFE, THE CHILDREN's HOUR, and THE VILLAGE BLACKSMITH; and the other, the serious but limited poet who wrote MEZZO CAMMIN and was the subject of a recent study by the critic Newton Arvin.

Descended from old New England families, Longfellow went to Bowdoin College in Maine and then to Europe to study languages. On his return, he became professor of languages at Bowdoin and married Mary Potter. Dissatisfied with life in Maine, he turned to reminiscences. The result was his first book, the Irvingesque series of travel sketches *Outre-Mer: A Pilgrimage Beyond the Sea* (1835). After another trip to Europe, he accepted the chair of modern languages at Harvard, succeeding George Ticknor. His wife had died in Rotterdam on the European trip.

At home, Longfellow wrote HYPERION, a romance in which he modeled his heroine on Frances Appleton, whom he had met in Europe. In the same year, he published his first volume of poems, VOICES OF THE NIGHT, and three years later, his second, *Ballads and Other Poems* (1842). In 1843, after another trip to Europe, he married Frances Appleton. Her father gave the pair, as a wedding present, the beautiful Cambridge mansion, Craigie House. Longfellow lived in the house for the rest of his life, and it is now dedicated to his memory.

Increasingly interested in narrative forms, he produced a series that helped to establish a native mythology: EVANGELINE, THE GOLDEN LEGEND, HIAWATHA, THE COURTSHIP OF MILES STANDISH, and TALES OF A WAYSIDE INN. To these he added a long prose romance of curious charm, KAVANAGH.

In 1861, at the height of his fame, Mrs. Longfellow died. The poet's shock and sorrow prevented his working for several years. He finally finished his translation of *The Divine Comedy* (1865–1867) and his religious poem, *Christus* (1872). In his last years he added to his volumes, expanding earlier editions, and writing a number of sonnets.

His poetry and values have been subject to great reversals in critical opinion. Never profound or powerfully original, he did have a sound lyric sense and an effective understanding of European culture. His work, however, is rooted in literature, rather than life; there is always a feeling of aloofness in his lines. Longfellow's immense popularity did a great deal to develop audiences for poetry in America. See ARSENAL AT SPRINGFIELD, THE; BUILDING OF THE SHIP, THE; MY LOST YOUTH; WRECK OF THE HESPERUS, THE.

Longinus. See ON THE SUBLIME.

Longinus, or Longius. The traditional name of the Roman soldier who stabbed Jesus with a spear at the crucifixion.

Longinus, Cassius (c. 220–273). Greek rhetorician and philosopher. A Neo-Platonist and the teacher of PORPHYRY, he is not to be confused with the unknown author of the treatise, ON THE SUBLIME. Longinus taught at Athens, and counseled Queen ZENOBIA at Palmyra. He was executed by Aurelian for his loyalty to the queen.

Long Parliament. In English history, the Parliament that assembled in November, 1640, after the dissolution of the Short Parliament. The Long Parliament impeached the earl of STRAFFORD, passed the GRAND REMONSTRANCE and, after the final rupture with CHARLES I in 1642, conducted the CIVIL WAR against the king's forces. In 1648, the members who were willing to come to terms with Charles were ousted during PRIDE'S PURGE. The remaining members constituted the RUMP PARLIAMENT, which was forcibly dissolved by Oliver Cromwell in 1653 but was twice recalled in 1659. Early in 1660, after the Rump assembled and was joined by the members expelled in 1648, the Long Parliament declared itself dissolved.

Longstreet, Augustus Baldwin (1790–1870). American lawyer, clergyman, editor, writer, and college president. Longstreet, in addition to many activities, founded and edited the *States Rights Sentinel* in Atlanta in 1834, and wrote a classic of regional humor, GEORGIA SCENES. Later he wrote a series of short stories and a novel, *Master William Mitten* (1864).

Longus (4th or 5th century A.D.). Greek writer, supposed author of DAPHNIS AND CHLOË.

Long Valley, The (1938). A collection of 13 stories by John STEINBECK. They deal with the life of people in the Salinas Valley in California, especially in relation to the migrants who have come into the valley. Best known of the tales is *The Red Pony,* separately printed in 1945.

Lonigan, Studs. See STUDS LONIGAN.

Lonsdale, Frederick (1881–1954). British playwright. He is best known for his sophisticated comedies such as *The Last of Mrs. Cheyney* (1925).

Look Back in Anger (1957). A play in 3 acts by John OSBORNE, one of England's Angry Young Men. Tied down by his working-class origins, Jimmy Porter turns his resentment against English class values on his upper-class wife, Alison. Although he has brought her down to his own level of poverty, it gradually becomes apparent that only by breaking her spirit can he revenge himself for the injustices he has suffered, but Alison remains impassive in the face of his insults and cruelty. When a childhood friend, Helena, learns that Alison is pregnant, she persuades her to leave Jimmy. Helena then becomes his mistress and scapegoat, but because she is incapable of real suffering he can take no pleasure in her. When Alison comes back in complete despair after having lost her baby, Jimmy is able to show her his love, and they are finally united in their mutual degradation and pain.

Look Homeward, Angel: A Story of the Buried Life (1929). A novel by Thomas WOLFE. It describes the childhood and youth of Eugene GANT in the town of Altamont, state of Catawba (said to be Asheville, N.C.), as he grows up, becomes aware of the relations among his family, meets the eccentric people of the town, goes to college, discovers literature and ideas, has his first love affairs, and at last sets out alone on a mystic and romantic pilgrimage. OF TIME AND THE RIVER is a sequel.

Looking Backward: 2000–1887 (1888). A utopian novel by Edward BELLAMY. The author describes a collectivist Boston society in the year 2000. Its hero transported into the future, the book advocates the peaceful evolution of society until it reaches the point of state socialism. The book was extremely popular; numerous other writers adopted Bellamy's plot and characters to qualify or attack his theme, and the book led to the forming of a Nationalist Party to advocate his principles.

Loos, Anita (1893–   ). American humorous writer. Her famous light satire GENTLEMEN PREFER BLONDES inspired a play (1925), a sequel, *But Gentlemen Marry Brunettes* (1928), a musical comedy (1949), a movie (1953), and the title of her autobiography, *This Brunette Prefers Work* (1956). Miss Loos is also the author of the play *Happy Birthday* (1946) and numerous film scenarios.

Lope de Vega. See Lope Félix de VEGA CARPIO.

López de Ayala [y Herrera], Adelardo (1828–1879). Spanish statesman and dramatist. He is best known abroad as an exponent of the moral tendency that infused 19th-century Spanish drama, in spite of the fact that he attained the rank of prime minister of the Spanish government. His plays include *El tanto por ciento* (1861), dealing with wealth and honor in love, and *Consuelo* (1870). His delicate and lyrical sonnets have also added to his reputation.

López de Ayala, Pero or **Pedro.** Also known as **the Chancellor** or **el Canciller Ayala** (1332–1407). Spanish statesman, poet, and historian. His chronicles of the reigns of Peter the Cruel, Henry II, John I, and Henry III are distinguished by their dramatic style and psychological penetration. As a poet he is best known for *Rimado del Palacio,* a miscellaneous compilation containing religious verse as well as realistic satire on contemporary society. He also wrote a treatise on falconry and translations of the works of Boethius, St. Isidore, and Boccaccio.

López de Mendoza, Iñigo. See marqués de SANTILLANA.

López Velarde, Ramón (1888–1921). Mexican poet. A disciple of Leopoldo Lugones, López Velarde wrote about love, religion, and his homeland in a style characterized by the use of eccentric, unexpected words and images. The poems in *La sangre devota* (1916) and *Zozobra* (1919) deal with the spiritual and carnal aspects of love, showing the poet's final disenchantment and dismay at his failure to satisfy either his physical appetites or the demands of his soul. *La suave patria,* his best-known poem, which appears in *El son del corazón* (1932), is an ironic but tender tribute to his native province.

López y Fuentes, Gregorio (1895–   ). Mexican novelist. His best-known novel is *El indio* (1935), in which he reveals the injustices inflicted upon Mexico's Indians in the early decades of the 20th century and realistically describes tribal customs and institutions.

Lorca, Federico García. See Federico GARCÍA LORCA.

Lord Jim (1900). A novel by Joseph CONRAD. It is about a man's lifelong efforts to atone for an act of instinctive cowardice. The young Jim is one of the officers of the *Patna* who frantically take to the boats when their ship appears to be sinking—leaving their passengers, eight hundred Muslim pilgrims, to apparently certain death. But the ship survives and is towed to port, and Jim becomes a wandering outcast. Eventually he wins a measure of satisfaction and self-respect from a busy, useful life among the natives of Patusan, who put complete confidence in *Tuan* Jim (Lord Jim). His life comes to its second crisis when a group of white men whom he has befriended betray his trust by murdering Dain Waris, his best friend, the son of the old chief Doramin. In spite of the pleas of the native girl he loves, Jim immediately gives himself up to native justice and is killed by Doramin. He wins back his lost honor and triumphs in death. The story is told obliquely, through Marlow's account of his own experiences and stories and letters from his friends.

Lord of Burleigh, The (1842). A ballad by Alfred, Lord TENNYSON. In the guise of a village painter the noble-born hero courts and wins a simple country maiden; but, when he takes her home to his castle, she feels out of place and pines away and dies.

Lord of Misrule. Sometimes **King,** or **Abbot of Misrule.** An official appointed to oversee the horse-play of Christmas festivities during the 15th and 16th centuries. In Scotland he was called the Abbot of Unreason; in France, *L'abbé de Liesse* (jollity). At Oxford and Cambridge one of the Masters of Arts superintended both the Christmas and Candlemas sports, for which he was allowed a fee of 40s. A similar "lord" was appointed by the lord mayor of London, the sheriffs and the chief nobility. These mock dignitaries often had other officers under them, and were furnished with hobby-horses, dragons, and musicians. Polydore Vergil says the Feast of Misrule was derived from the Saturnalia, the disorderly Roman festival held in December.

Lord of the Flies (1955). A novel by William GOLDING about a group of boys stranded on a paradisal island after a plane crash. In spite of the efforts of a few leaders to form an organized society, the group reverts to primitive religious rites and ritual murder. Children's adventure stories and anthropology are powerfully combined with Eden and original sin.

Lord Ormont and His Aminta (1894). A novel by George MEREDITH. It is based on the career of the earl of Peterborough, who rendered distinguished service at Valencia but in later life nourished resentment against the government, which had recalled him for high-handedness in 1707. He married Anastasia Robinson, the singer, but made no public acknowledgment of the marriage for many years. In the novel the names are changed, and the heroine, Aminta, remedies her equivocal position by eloping with Matthew Weyburn and opening a school in the Alps.

Lord Ullin's Daughter (1809). A ballad by Thomas CAMPBELL. Lord Ullin's daughter elopes with the Chief of Ulva's Isle, and is pursued by her father with a party of retainers. The lovers reach a ferry, and promise to give the boatman "a silver pound" to row them across the Lochgyle. The waters are very rough, and the father reaches the shore just in time to see the boat capsize, and his daughter drowned.

Lorelei or **Lurlei.** The name of a rock cliff that juts into the Rhine near Bingen and is known as a danger to shipping. Clemens Brentano, in his ballad "Lore Lay" (included in the novel *Godwi,* 1800–1801), was the first to associate the rock with a woman of the same name; and the poem is so convincingly folklike in style that Brentano's invention came to be regarded as a genuine folk legend. But Brentano's Lore Lay is only a woman, and it was not until Heinrich HEINE's famous poem *Die Lorelei* (1827) that the now-popular idea of a siren sitting atop the rock and luring ships to their destruction by her singing was actually created.

Lorenzetti, Ambrogio (1265?–1348) and **Pietro** (fl. 1306–1348). Italian painters of the early Sienese school. Ambrogio is noted for his allegorical fresco *The Effects of Good Government* and for his paintings of religious subjects. His brother Pietro is noted for his *Deposition* fresco and for the *Madonna and Child with Saints* in the church of St. Francis at Assisi.

Lorenzo. In Shakespeare's MERCHANT OF VENICE, the impractical but honest young man with whom Jessica, the daughter of Shylock, elopes.

Lorenzo. The name by which D. H. LAWRENCE was known to his admirers and disciples.

Loretto, the house of. Santa Casa, the reputed house of the Virgin Mary at Nazareth. It was miraculously translated to Fiume in Dalmatia in 1291, thence to Recanati in 1294, and finally to a plot of land belonging to a certain Lady Lauretta, near Ancona, Italy, around which the town of Loretto sprang up. The chapel contains bas-reliefs showing incidents in the life of the Virgin, and a rough image traditionally held to have been carved by St. Luke. See Richard CRASHAW.

Lorimer, George Horace (1867–1937). American editor (1899–1936) of the *Saturday Evening Post.* Lorimer also wrote two "inspirational" books, advocating rugged individualism: *Letters from a Self-Made Merchant to His Son* (1902) and *Old Gorgon Graham* (1904).

Lorna Doone, a Romance of Exmoor (1869). A historical novel by R. D. BLACKMORE set in 17th-century Devonshire at the time of the rebellion of the duke of MONMOUTH. The young hero, John Ridd, falls into the hands of the Doones, an outlaw clan. He is saved by Lorna Doone, a mere child, and when he comes of age, he sets out to find her again. Because the Doones killed his father he hates them, but protects Lorna against them, and finally, learning that she is the kidnaped daughter of a Scottish nobleman, marries her.

Lorrain, Claude. Originally, **Claude Gellée** or **Gelée** (1600–1682). French landscape painter. At the age of 27, Claude Lorrain established himself permanently in Rome, where he studied the surrounding countryside and the varying aspects it assumed with the passage of the day. Acknowledged a master during his lifetime, he permanently influenced the art of landscape painting. His calm and poetic, idyllic scenes are known for their golden light.

Los de abajo (The Underdogs, 1916). A novel by Mariano AZUELA. Ignored for years after its first appearance in a Spanish-language El Paso newspaper, *Los de abajo* is now generally regarded as the best of the many novels inspired by the Mexican Revolution. Written in a spare, colloquial style, the novel consists of a series of sharply etched vignettes that recount the career of Demetrio Macías, the leader of a band of ignorant, often bestial, peasants. Through Macías, Azuela brilliantly re-creates the blind, apparently futile struggle of the nameless masses who took up arms for a cause they did not understand and, swept along by the turbulence of the revolution, continued fighting because they did not know how to stop.

Lost Chord, The (1858). A once popular poem by Adelaide Anne Procter (1825–1864), daughter of Bryan Waller PROCTER. She wrote it under the pseudonym of Mary Berwick; it begins "Seated one day at the organ . . ." and was set to music by Sir Arthur Sullivan.

Lost Colony of Roanoke. See ROANOKE ISLAND.

lost generation. A term used to refer to the generation of men and women who came to maturity during World War I (1914–1918); specifically it refers to their experiences in the war itself, to the social dislocations following it, and to their rootlessness and disillusionment. Gertrude Stein is said to have coined the term in a conversation with Ernest Hemingway, whose early novels are considered to typify the attitudes and behavior of the lost generation. *The Lost Generation* (1931) by Malcolm Cowley dealt with the subject.

Lost Lady, A (1923). A novel by Willa CATHER. The "lost lady" of the title is Marian Forrester, the charming young wife of a rugged pioneer and railroad-builder. She is seen, with a naïveté that becomes the most delicate irony and revelation, through the eyes of Niel Herbert, an adoring young boy. Her husband's death leaves Marian in financial difficulties, and she becomes the mistress of Ivy Peters, an aggressive businessman of the new generation. After Peters marries and moves into the Forrester mansion with his wife, she disappears and is heard of again only by rumor as the wife of a wealthy Englishman in South America.

Lost Weekend, The (1944). A novel by Charles JACKSON. It is a realistic study of an alcoholic who first resists, then succumbs to his passion for liquor. On a five-day "lost weekend" much of his life flashes before him. The title has become a catchword for a drunken fling of major proportions.

Lot. In the Old Testament, the son of Haran and nephew of Abraham, who accompanied his uncle to Canaan and divided the land with him. Lot was one of the inhabitants of the wicked city of SODOM and escaped by the intervention of an angel, just before the city was destroyed by fire and brimstone, but Lot's wife was turned into a pillar of salt for ignoring the warning not to look back at the city (Gen. 19:26).

Lot, King. In Arthurian romance, king of Orkney and one of the kings subdued by Arthur. In Malory's *Morte d'Arthur* (c. 1469), he is the husband of MARGAWSE and father of the knights Gawain, Aggravaine, Gaheris, and Gareth.

Lothair. A novel by Benjamin DISRAELI (1870). The hero, Lothair, is a young English nobleman who, upon coming of age, inherits a great fortune. The plot centers about the struggle of the Anglican Church, the Church of Rome, and the revolutionary societies of Italy to secure his money and support. One of the most interesting characters of the book is the witty Lord St. Aldegonde. A primary cause for the popularity of the book was the interest taken by the English public in identifying the persons of prominence who appeared in it as characters only slightly disguised.

Loti, Pierre. Pen name of **Louis Marie Julien Viaud** (1850–1923). French novelist. His career as a naval officer sent him to distant places, providing him with the exotic backgrounds for many of his novels, which were sentimental in theme and luxurious in setting. *Aziyadé* (1879) is set in Constantinople, *Le Mariage de Loti* (1880) in Tahiti, and *Madame Chrysanthème* (1888) in Japan. In his sensuous and impressionistic style, Loti gave voice to a persistent melancholy. Although his travel romances first brought him fame, it was the publication of his three novels of Breton life—*Mon Frère Yves* (1883), PÊCHEUR D'ISLANDE, and *Matelot* (1893)—that won him enduring acclaim.

Lotis. See LOTUS.

Lotte in Weimar. See BELOVED RETURNS, THE.

Lottery, The (1949). A short story by Shirley JACKSON. This quietly told tale describes an annual lottery held since time immemorial in a small American town. Only in the final lines of the story does it become apparent that the winner is to be stoned by the other townspeople.

Lotto, Lorenzo (1480–1556). Italian painter. A leading figure of the Venetian Renaissance, he painted religious themes and secular portraits in his native Loreto, in Venice, and in other northern cities. His best-known works—*Portrait of Andrea Odoni, Virgin and Child with Saints and Angels, The Maiden's Dream*—reveal a style recognizable by the alabaster texture given to flesh by the manipulation of light and shade. *The Maiden's Dream,* an enigmatic allegory, best reveals his characteristic tone—sad, almost sinister.

lotus. A name of many plants. To the Egyptians, it was various species of water-lily, to the Hindus and Chinese the Nelumbo (a water-bean, *Nymphaeaceae speciosum*), their sacred lotus, and to the Greeks *Zizyphus Lotus,* a North African shrub of the natural order *Rhamneae,* the fruit of which was used for food.

According to Muhammad a lotus tree stands in the seventh heaven, on the right hand of the throne of God, and the Egyptians pictured God sitting on a lotus above the watery mud.

The lotus is a symbolic flower in Indian religion and literature. Brahma sits on a lotus and is himself born out of the lotus in Vishnu's navel. The Buddha is always depicted seated on a lotus; the Tibetan prayer chant is *Om mani padme hum* (I salute the jewel in the lotus). Growing in stagnant village ponds, the flower stands for the emergence into light from the darkness and sensuality of the phenomenal world; the leaves, unaffected by water, symbolize the *atman* (self) unpolluted by the attractions of the *gunas* (senses); and the daytime opening and nighttime closing of the flower suggest the timeless day and night of Brahma in the context of Hindu metaphysical belief.

The classic myth is that Lotis, a daughter of Poseidon, fleeing from Priapus was changed into a tree, which was called Lotus after her. Another story goes that Dryope of Oechalia was one day carrying her infant son, when she plucked a lotus flower for his amusement, and was instantaneously transformed into a lotus.

Lotus-eaters or **Lotophagi.** In Homeric legend, a people who ate the lotus-tree. The effect of this was to make them forget their friends and homes, and to lose all desire of returning to their native country, their only wish being to live in idleness in Lotus-land (ODYSSEY, ix).

Hence, a lotus-eater is one living in ease and luxury. Tennyson wrote one of his best-known poems on this subject.

Lotus Sūtra. (Sans. *Saddharma-pundarīka;* Ch. *Fahua ching;* Jap. *Hokke kyō*). Buddhist *sūtra* of great popularity in China and Japan. The *T'ient'ai* (Jap. *Tendai*) and *Nichiren* sects base their teachings on this work.

Loubet, Emile (1838–1929). French statesman and president of France (1899–1906). Loubet, with other liberals, sought revision of the Dreyfus case.

Louis XIV. Called **Louis the Great, le Roi Soleil** (the Sun King), and **le Grand Monarque** (1638–1715). King of France (1643–1715). The greatest autocratic monarch that France has ever known, he left his country bankrupt through his wars, conquests, and extravagances. His reign was marked by his lavish patronage of art, literature, and women, and coincided with the greatest flowering of French civilization to date. Louis secretly married Mme de MAINTENON, the last of his many mistresses, after the death of his first wife, Marie Thérèse of Spain.

Louis XVI (1754–1793). King of France. He married MARIE ANTOINETTE in 1770, and in 1774, on the death of his grandfather Louis XV, he began his reign; he was deprived of his powers by the Legislative ASSEMBLY in 1792 and was beheaded in 1793. See BAKER; VÉTO, M. ET MME.

Louis XVII. See DAUPHIN.

Louis, Pierre. See Pierre LOUŸS.

Louise. See Gustave CHARPENTIER.

Louise, the Glee-maiden. A prominent character in Scott's FAIR MAID OF PERTH. Enamored of Prince James of Scotland, she flings herself from a precipice at his death.

Louisiana Purchase (1803). The acquisition of Louisiana from France during the consulship of Napoleon by the U.S. for approximately $15 million. Alarmed by the threat implicit in Spain's retrocession of Louisiana to France in 1800, President Jefferson appointed James Monroe to purchase New Orleans and West Florida from the French. Napoleon, however, had abandoned his projects for a French empire in the New World and offered to sell the whole of Louisiana instead. The purchase of Louisiana, a vaguely defined tract of some 828,000 square miles lying between the Mississippi River and the Rocky Mountains, more than doubled the area of the U.S.

Louis Philippe (1773–1850). King of France (1830–1848). A son of Philippe Egalité, he was the first elected king of France. At the insistence of Thiers and Lafayette, Louis Philippe was elected constitutional monarch after the deposition of Charles X (see JULY REVOLUTION). A partisan of the Revolution in his youth, and democratic in the first years of his reign, he became, more and more, a typical Bourbon and absolutist. He himself abdicated the throne after the revolution of February, 1848, and died in exile at Claremont, England.

Lounsbury, Thomas Raynesford (1838–1915). American scholar and educator. A professor of English literature at Yale, he wrote a *History of the English Language* (1879), *Life of James Fenimore Cooper* (1882), and edited Chaucer's minor poems and the works of Charles Dudley Warner. A student of Early and Middle English, he was one of the original members of the American Academy of Arts and Letters, and a fellow of the American Academy of Arts and Sciences.

Loup Garou. See WERWOLF.

Lourdes. See BERNADETTE OF LOURDES.

Louÿs, Pierre. Pen name of **Pierre Louis** (1870–1925). French poet and novelist. A close friend of André Gide and Paul Valéry, he still remained primarily a disciple of the Parnassian school of José-Maria de Hérédia, whose daughter he married in 1899. *Astarte* (1891) is a collection of Hellenistic poetry; *Aphrodite* (1896) is a novel of Alexandrian manners. Although much of his fiction, such as the short story *Les Aventures du roi Pausole* (1901), was intended to shock conventional morality, Louÿs was essentially a worshiper of form and beauty, and a moralist. His other works include *La femme et le pantin* (1898), *Le Crépuscule des Nymphes* (1925), *Psyché* (1927), and *Poésies* (1927).

Love and Intrigue. See KABALE UND LIEBE.

Love and Mr. Lewisham (1900). A semi-autobiographical novel by H. G. WELLS. Mr. Lewisham is a rather comical young English science teacher and, later, college student. He reluctantly gives up his schemes for an ambitious scientific, literary, and political career when he falls in love and marries ordinary, domestic Ethel. The teaching and college background are like Wells's own; after an unsuccessful first marriage he always feared domestic confinement.

Loved One, The (1948). A novel by Evelyn WAUGH. It is a very funny, biting satire on American life, especially Hollywood mortuary practices, and on the more universal themes of love and death. The hero finally cremates the heroine in a dogs' cemetery.

love feast. A meal or banquet in token of brotherly love and friendship. It is often used as a synonym for the agape, or common meal, shared by early Christians, which originally always preceded the Lord's Supper.

Love for Love (1695). A comedy by William CONGREVE. The extravagant Valentine agrees to relinquish his inheritance to his sea-faring brother Ben if his father, Sir Sampson Legend, will pay his debts. Valentine's attempts to regain his inheritance are unsuccessful until the resourcefulness of his devoted Angelica extricates him from his predicament. Among the well-known lesser characters are Prue, Angelica's rustic cousin, and Jeremy, Valentine's enterprising servant.

Lovelace, Richard (1618-1658). English poet. One of the CAVALIER POETS, Lovelace was known for his grace, his handsome appearance, and his aristocratic gallantry. A passionate Royalist, he was imprisoned twice by Parliament during the Civil War and ruined himself supporting Charles I. He died in a London slum in great poverty.

Lovelace's poetry is very uneven: a large proportion of it is lifeless, extravagant, and labored, but he wrote a few lyrics whose nobility and grace equal anything of the period. Such are To ALTHEA FROM PRISON; To Lucasta, Going Beyond the Seas (1649); and To LUCASTA, GOING TO THE WARS.

Lovelace, Robert. The principal male character in Samuel Richardson's novel CLARISSA HARLOWE. He is a polished libertine who is kind and considerate to all who acknowledge his power, but ruthless (to himself and to Clarissa) in his search for proven affection. He is killed in a duel by Colonel Morden, Clarissa's cousin.

Love Me Little, Love Me Long (1859). A novel by Charles READE. It is concerned with the successful wooing of Lucy Fountain, the heroine, by David Dodd, a seaman completely at home on shipboard but extremely ill at ease on land. In a sequel, *Hard Cash* (1864), David's struggles to bring home a large sum of money result in his losing his mind, and as "Silly Billy Thompson" he escapes from a burning lunatic asylum to a frigate and lives through a series of exciting adventures before fate restores to him his reason, his wife, his exuberant daughter Julia, and his bank account of "hard cash." This novel was written as an exposure of conditions in the private lunatic asylums of England and as such aroused much discussion.

Lover, Samuel (1797-1868). Irish novelist, painter, and song writer. A successful portrait artist, Lover later turned to writing on Irish themes. His novel *Rory O'More* (1839) was avidly received, as was HANDY ANDY, an entertaining story of a singularly inept Irishman. His sympathetic portrayal of the Irish peasantry and his popular songs and ballads helped to herald the dawning of Irish Nationalism.

Lover's Complaint, A. An anonymous poem. It was attributed to William SHAKESPEARE on the basis of its inclusion in the first edition of the *Sonnets of Shakespeare* in 1609. The poem, which is somewhat wooden and stilted in its manner, is not generally regarded as a legitimate item in the Shakespearean canon.

Love's Labour's Lost (c. 1594). A comedy by William SHAKESPEARE. FERDINAND, king of Navarre, and his friends, Berowne or BIRON, Longaville, and Dumain, take an oath to eschew the company of women and devote themselves to study for three years. The charming princess of France arrives with her three vivacious ladies, Rosaline, Maria, and Katherine, on a diplomatic mission and, because of Ferdinand's vow, is housed in a pavilion outside the city gates. Despite their oath, the four gentlemen fall in love with the four ladies: Ferdinand with the princess, Biron with Rosaline, Longaville with Maria, and Dumain with Katherine. Discovering each other's perfidy, the gentlemen acknowledge love's power and decide to pursue the ladies, who gently mock them for their conceits. Learning that the king

Title page of *Love's Labour's Lost*. It is the first title page to bear Shakespeare's name (1598).

of France has died, the ladies are obliged to leave, but they assign various penances to the four suitors and promise to return to them in a year.

The play cannot be attributed to any early source, and the plot, which is based on current court life, is presumed to be of Shakespeare's invention. See HOLOFERNES.

Loves of the Angels (1822). The stories of the love of three angels for mortal women, in verse, by Thomas MOORE. The stories are founded on Eastern and rabbinical tales.

Love Song of J. Alfred Prufrock, The (1915). A poem by T. S. ELIOT. Said to have been written when Eliot was still an undergraduate at Harvard, it was first published in *Poetry* magazine after he had settled in England. Through the person of the poem's narrator, J. Alfred Prufrock, Eliot explores a kind of death in life and suggests the spiritual decay of his society. Prufrock, a middle-aged man of anonymous respectability, differs from those around him only in his greater degree of self-awareness and suffering. Conscious of the sterility of his world, he longs to make some significant gesture, but lacking the necessary will and passion, puts the matter off in introspection. The poem ends on a note of hopelessness. Completely paralyzed by social habit and a sense of his own futility, Prufrock will never escape and is finally identified with his surroundings.

Love, the Doctor. See AMOUR MÉDECIN, L'.

Loving (1945). A novel by Henry GREEN. Set in an Irish castle during World War II, it is a picture of the lives of the owners and their many servants. On this level, the book is a light, witty social comedy. Each of the characters loves some person or idea, and the different kinds of love are revealed by an ironical juxtaposition of scenes. The central characters are Raunce, the butler, and Edith, a maid, both of whom grow mature as their love develops. This love is emphasized by various recurrent symbols, like an imaginary cave of fairy gold. The gold is later replaced by a valuable ring whose loss and recovery is a focal point of the plot and a touchstone for the attitudes of the various characters.

Lowell, Amy [Lawrence] (1874-1925). American poet, critic, and biographer. A member of an old and distinguished New England family, Amy Lowell became a serious student of poetic forms. She is known for her association with and leadership in the imagist movement, in accordance with which she wrote numerous poems in free verse and "polyphonic prose." Her first book was *A Dome of Many-Coloured Glass* (1912). A year after its publication she met Ezra Pound and others in the imagist movement in England and subsequently became the leader of the movement in this country. Although Pound complained that she converted IMAGISM into "Amygism" she did much to sponsor imagist poets and edited a number of imagist anthologies. Celebrated as a personality as well as an artist, she was eccentric in behavior, keeping a large troupe of dogs, smoking large black cigars, and using language of extreme frankness. One of her best single poems is *Lilacs* (1925); several others are familar to readers of anthologies, notably *Patterns.* Among her books of poetry are SWORD-BLADES AND POPPY SEED, *Men, Women, and Ghosts* (1916), *Can Grande's Castle* (1918), and *What's O'Clock* (1925). Among her critical works are *Six French Poets* (1915), A CRITICAL FABLE, and a two-volume biography of Keats (1925). Her *Complete Poetical Works* (1955) were edited by Louis Untermeyer.

Lowell, James Russell (1819-1891). American poet, editor, critic, and diplomat. Although he was born into a distinguished Brahmin New England family, Lowell favored democratic ideas, attacked slavery, and was an early admirer of Lincoln. Trained for the law, he turned instead to journalism; he contributed to *The Dial,* and founded a short-lived magazine, *The Pioneer.*

In 1844, Lowell married Maria White, poet and firm abolitionist. Four years later, he published THE BIGLOW PAPERS, First Series, which brought him to the notice of the literary world. The dialogue between Hosea Biglow, the Yankee farmer, and his friends was especially important for its use of authentic New England dialect. The interest in language was to remain with Lowell throughout his career. In the same year, his long poem, THE VISION OF SIR LAUNFAL, was published; long a favorite among schoolchildren, it is far from his most significant work. Lowell's satirical, often accurate, always amusing A FABLE FOR CRITICS was also published during this important literary year.

His reputation established, Lowell became a leader of what is now called the popular, conservative school of American letters. After travel abroad, he succeeded Longfellow to the chair of modern languages at Harvard, and in 1857 was appointed as the first editor of *The Atlantic Monthly.* In 1861, he became co-editor with Charles Eliot Norton of the *North American Review.*

Lowell's active public life included the positions of minister to Spain and to England; in both countries he was an able spokesman for democracy. See COMMEMORATION ODE.

Lowell, Robert [Traill Spence], Jr. (1917-   ). American poet. One of the Lowell family of Boston, he is considered a leading poet of his generation. Many of his poems are set in New England, and several of them deal with his ancestors. His conversion to Catholicism in 1940 is reflected in many of the poems in his first collection, *Land of Unlikeness* (1944). A number of poems in this privately printed book were included in *Lord Weary's Castle* (1946), for which he was awarded the Pulitzer Prize. His poetry is complex and intense, occasionally ironic, and is marked by a strong sense of rhythm. *The Mills of the Kavanaughs,* of which the title poem is a dramatic narrative set in Maine, appeared in 1951. *Life Studies* (1959) is an autobiographical piece in prose and verse; *The Old Glory* (1964), a verse drama.

Lower Depths, The (*Na dne;* 1902). A drama by Maksim GORKI. The best known of Gorki's works, it is set among the derelicts of a sleazy flophouse. The theme of the play is the problem of whether to live without illusions and on one's own strength or to shield oneself from the pain of life by accepting a romanticized view of things. These choices are supported by the thief Satin and the wandering pilgrim Luka. A highly similar theme was used by U.S. playwright Eugene O'Neill in his drama, *The Iceman Cometh.*

Lowes, John Livingston (1867-1945). American teacher and scholar. Lowes taught at several universities before he joined the Harvard faculty (1918-1939). Among his works are *Convention and Revolt in Poetry* (1919), an account of action and reaction in the history of poetry; *The Road to Xanadu* (1927), an examination of the sources of Coleridge's *Kubla Khan* and *The Ancient Mariner;* two books on Chaucer; and two collections of essays, *Of Reading Books and Other Essays* (1930) and *Essays in Appreciation* (1936).

Low Heels and High Heels. Two great political factions in the LILLIPUT of Jonathan Swift's GULLIVER'S TRAVELS who are also called the Tramecksan and Slamecksan. The High Heels are the Tories, and the Low Heels are the Radicals. The king is a Tramecksan, the heir-apparent a Slamecksan.

Lowndes, Mrs. Belloc. Pen name of **Marie Adelaide Lowndes,** born **Belloc** (1868-1947). English novelist. The sister of Hilaire Belloc, she wrote historical and mystery novels, including *The Lodger* (1913), a murder story based on the crimes of Jack the Ripper.

Lowry, Malcolm (1909-1957). English novelist and traveler. He wrote *Ultramarine* (1933), a sea story in experimental, impressionistic style; UNDER THE VOLCANO, a psychological, symbolical novel about Europeans living in Mexico; *Hear Us O Lord* *from Heaven Thy Dwelling Place* (1961), a collection of novellas and short stories; and *Selected Poems* (1962).

Loyola, St. Ignatius of (1491-1556). The founder of the Society of Jesus (the order of JESUITS). He is depicted in art with the sacred monogram I.H.S. on his breast, or as contemplating it, surrounded by glory in the skies, in allusion to his claim that he had a miraculous knowledge of the mystery of the Trinity vouchsafed to him. He was a son of the Spanish ducal house of Loyola, and after being severely wounded at the siege of Pampeluna (Pamplona) (1521) he left the army and dedicated himself to the service of the Virgin. His Order of the Society of Jesus, which he projected in 1534, was confirmed by Paul III in 1540. His *Spiritual Exercises* (*Exercitia;* 1548), a manual of devotions and prayer, is considered a remarkable treatise on applied psychology as an inducement to mystic vision.

Lubbock, Percy (1879-). English literary critic. He is best known for his book *The Craft of Fiction* (1921).

Lucan. Full Latin name, **Marcus Annaeus Lucanus** (A.D. 39-65). Roman poet and prose writer. He wrote the *Pharsalia,* an epic in 10 books on the civil war between Caesar and Pompey. No other work of his is extant. He was, like Brutus and Cassius before him, an aristocrat and a rebel; like them, he regretted the lost republic and hated the regime of the Caesars. He joined PISO's CONSPIRACY against Nero, was denounced and, like Seneca, was ordered to commit suicide. He was only 25 when he took his own life.

Lucan enjoyed a great vogue during the Middle Ages, but of late has been more criticized than praised for his exaggerated treatment of the war between Caesar and Pompey.

Lucas, E[dward] V[errall] (1868-1938). English novelist, poet, essayist, and man of letters. He wrote numerous essays in the manner of Charles Lamb, on whose work he became an authority. Among his collected essays is *Adventures and Misgivings* (1938). He was also a prolific writer of novels, such as *Over Bemerton's* (1908) and *The Barker's Clock* (1931); travel books, such as *A Wanderer in London* (1906) and *French Leaves* (1931); biographies, such as *The Life of Charles Lamb* (1905); poetry; and art criticism.

Lucas, F[rank] L[aurence] (1894-). English writer and literary critic. He is the author of such works as *Decline and Fall of the Romantic Ideal* (1936) and *The Greatest Problem and Other Essays* (1960).

Luce, Clare Boothe (1903-). American playwright and wife of Henry Luce, the publisher. Although she has written a novel, *Stuffed Shirts* (1931), under the name of Clare Boothe Brokaw, her literary reputation rests on her plays. Among them are *The Women* (1937), an antifeminine play set on Park Ave.; *Kiss the Boys Good-bye* (1938), a satire set in Hollywood; and *Margin for Error* (1939), an anti-Nazi mystery melodrama. She also wrote *Europe in the Spring* (1940), observations on her travel abroad at the time of Germany's invasion of France and the Low Countries.

Mrs. Luce became more and more interested in politics and served two terms in Congress (1943-1947). She later became U.S. ambassador to Italy (1953-1956).

Luce, Henry R[obinson] (1898-1967). American editor and publisher. With Briton Hadden, Luce founded TIME, the weekly news magazine, in 1923. *Fortune,* a monthly for businessmen, followed in 1930, and *Life,* the weekly picture magazine, appeared in 1936. Luce, who is married to author and diplomat Clare Boothe Luce, also publishes *Sports Illustrated, Architectural Forum,* and *House and Home.*

Lucentio. In Shakespeare's TAMING OF THE SHREW, a young man who comes to Padua to "deck his fortune with his virtuous deeds." He is immediately smitten with Bianca and resorts to a number of tricks in order to win her hand.

Lucia di Lammermoor (1835). An opera by Gaetano DONIZETTI. It is based on Sir Walter Scott's *Bride of Lammermoor.* In the opera Lucy Ashton is Lucia, Arthur Bucklaw is Arturo, and Edgar of Ravenswood is Edgardo. Bucklaw does not recover from the wound given him by his bride, as he does in the novel, and Edgardo, instead of being swallowed up in the quicksands, kills himself. The opera contains a celebrated "Mad Scene" for Lucia, and a popular "Sextet."

Lucian. The chief character in THE GOLDEN ASS of Apuleius. His behavior when changed into an ass, which he remains throughout most of the book, satirizes the follies and vices of the age.

Lucian (Loukianos, c. 120-200). A Greek satirist. He was the most brilliant wit of Greek letters under the Roman empire. A free-thinker, he was often referred to in his own time as the blasphemer and later compared with Swift and Voltaire. He wrote rhetorical, critical, and biographical works, romances, dialogues, poems, and other works. His *Voracious History,* a mock narrative of travel, is the archetype of such books as Swift's *Gulliver's Travels.* His *Dialogues of the Dead* have been called brilliant satires of the living. He is regarded as the inventor of the satirical dialogue. His novel, *Lucius, or The Ass* may have been based on a work by Lucius of Patrae that also served as a model for Apuleius' *The Golden Ass.*

Luciana. The meek and gentle sister of the shrewish Adriana in Shakespeare's COMEDY OF ERRORS. She is wooed by Antipholus of Syracuse.

Lucifer. The morning star. The Hebrew name for it was figuratively applied by Isaiah to Nebuchadnezzar, the proud but ruined king of Babylon; "Take up this proverb against the King of Babylon, and say ... How art thou fallen, from heaven, O Lucifer, son of the morning!" (Isa. 14:4,12). It was later claimed that SATAN, before he was driven from heaven for his pride, was called Lucifer. In Marlowe's *Doctor Faustus* and Dante's *Inferno* Lucifer is the ruler of hell. In Milton's *Paradise Lost,* Lucifer is called Satan after his fall.

Lucifer, Lawrence. The narrator in Lawrence Durrell's novel THE BLACK BOOK.

Lucifera, Queen. See FAERIE QUEENE, THE.

Lucile (1860). A narrative poem by Owen MEREDITH. The heroine is beloved by two bitter rivals, an English lord and a French duke. She loves the former, but misunderstandings keep them apart. Many years later the lord's son and the duke's niece fall in love, are separated by the old rivalry, but are reunited through the efforts of Lucile, who has become a nursing nun.

Lucilius. In Shakespeare's JULIUS CAESAR, a friend of Cassius and Brutus. Captured by the enemy at Philippi, he pretends to be Brutus, but Antony, recognizing him, asks that he be treated with kindness for he would like to count such a man among his friends.

Lucina. In Roman mythology, a goddess of childbirth. She was sometimes identified with JUNO.

Lucinde. (1) The heroine of Molière's comedy L'AMOUR MÉDECIN. She is the daughter of Sganarelle. As she has lost her spirit and appetite, her father sends for four physicians, who all differ as to the nature of the malady and the remedy to be applied. Lisette, her waiting woman, sends in the meantime for Clitandre, the lover of Lucinde, who comes disguised as a doctor. He tells Sganarelle that the disease of the young lady must be reached through the imagination and prescribes a mock marriage. As his assistant is in reality a notary, the marriage turns out to be a real one, and Lucinde, who has been pining because her father disapproved of her beloved, is cured.

(2) The heroine of Molière's LE MÉDECIN MALGRÉ LUI. Géronte, her father, wants her to marry Horace, but as she is in love with Léandre she pretends to have lost the power of articulate speech, to avoid a marriage which she abhors. Sganarelle, the woodcutter, is introduced as a doctor specialising in dumb cases, and soon he sees the state of affairs. He takes with him Léandre as an apothecary; the young lady receives a perfect cure, an elopement.

Lucius Apuleius. See APULEIUS, LUCIUS.

Luck of Roaring Camp, The (1868). A short story by Bret HARTE. This is a sentimental tale of gold-rush miners and their false toughness. Dying, Cherokee Sal, a prostitute who frequents the mining camps, gives birth to a child the miners adopt and name Thomas Luck. The following year the camp is destroyed in a flood, and one of the miners, Kentuck, dies holding the infant in his arms. The story established Harte's fame after its first printing in his magazine, *The Overland Monthly.*

Lucky Jim (1954). A best-selling novel by Kingsley AMIS. The title is ironic, since the story is about the comic misfortunes of Jim Dixon, a young, lower-middle-class instructor at an English university. The book satirizes the academic "racket" and cultural pretensions. See ANGRY YOUNG MEN.

Lucrece. See LUCRETIA.

Lucretia. In Roman legend, the daughter of Spurius Lucretius, prefect of Rome, and wife of Tarquinius Collatinus. She was dishonored by Sextus, the son of the king Tarquinius Superbus. Having avowed her dishonor in the presence of her father, her husband, and their friends Junius BRUTUS and Valerius, she stabbed herself. The outcome was an insurrection which changed the magistracy of kings to that of CONSULS. The story of Lucretia has been dramatized in French by Antoine Vincent Arnault in his tragedy *Lucrèce* (1792) and by François Ponsard in 1843; in Italian by Alfieri in *Brutus;* in English by Thomas Heywood in *The Rape of Lucrece* (1630), by Nathaniel Lee in *Lucius Junius Brutus* (17th century), and by John H. Payne in *Brutus or The Fall*

of *Tarquin* (1820). Shakespeare selected the same subject for his poem *The Rape of Lucrece* (1594).

Lucretius. Full Latin name, **Titus Lucretius Carus** (98?–55 B.C.). Roman poet. He was the author of the unfinished *De Rerum Natura* (*On the Nature of Things*), a didactic poem in six books, setting forth in outline a complete science of the universe based on the philosophies of DEMOCRITUS and EPICURUS. The purpose of the work was to prove, by investigating the nature of the world in which man lives, that all things—including man—operate according to their own laws and are not in any way influenced by supernatural powers. Lucretius hoped thereby to free himself and all men from the yoke of religious superstition and the fear of death. The poem is arranged as follows:

Book I. All things are made up of eternal atoms which move through infinite space.

Book II. The entire world of material substances is produced through the joining together of these atoms.

Book III. The mind and the spirit are also an arrangement of atoms, in this case exceedingly more subtle. At death the individual soul is dispersed as its imperishable atoms fly apart.

Book IV. Sensation, perception, and thought are all produced by the images which are emitted by external surfaces.

Book V. The world, as we know it, was created by a fortuitous concourse of atoms.

Book VI. All natural phenomena can be explained according to this atomic theory.

De Rerum Natura is the only large-scale poem written in dactylic hexameter which has come down to us from the period of the Roman republic and is, with the possible exception of Vergil's *Aeneid,* the most ambitious poem written in Latin. Its scientific and philosophical argumentation often rises to magnificent heights of emotional power, intensified by an eloquent simplicity of diction and by the great passion of the poet's conviction. Lucretius was prevented by his suicide from completing the final draft of the poem; Cicero was said to have prepared the manuscript for publication.

Tennyson's dramatic monologue *Lucretius* repeats the legend that the poet committed suicide in a fit of insanity induced by a love potion given him by his wife.

Lucullus (110–57 B.C.). A wealthy Roman noted for his banquets and self-indulgence. On one occasion, when a superb supper had been prepared, being asked who were to be his guests, he replied, "Lucullus will sup tonight with Lucullus."

Lucy, St. Patron saint for those afflicted in the eyes. She is supposed to have lived in Syracuse and to have suffered martyrdom there about 303. One legend relates that a nobleman wanted to marry her for the beauty of her eyes, so she tore them out and gave them to him, saying, "Now let me live to God." Hence she is represented in art carrying a palm branch and a platter with two eyes on it. Her day is December 13.

Lud. One of the kings in the HISTORY OF THE KINGS OF BRITAIN by Geoffrey of Monmouth. According to Geoffrey, London (Kaerlud) received its name from Lud. He was buried near what is still known as *Ludgate.*

Lud's Town. London, so called from King Lud.

Ludendorff, Erich (1865-1937). Quartermaster-General in the German High Command (1916-1918). He was more powerful than either Hindenburg or Kaiser Wilhelm II during the last years of World War I. Acknowledging German defeat, he ordered the formation of a constitutional government to negotiate with the Allies. Later, he supported HITLER, then deserted him. See BEER-HALL PUTSCH.

Ludwig, Otto (1813-1865). German novelist and playwright who popularized the term poetic realism as a description of the realistic trend in German literature of his time. His own works, realistic in style, include the novel Zwischen Himmel und Erde (Between Heaven and Earth, 1856), about the tragic conflict of two brothers both in love with the same woman; Der Erbförster (The Forester, 1850), a domestic tragedy; and Die Makkabäer (1854), a play in verse about the revolt of the Maccabees.

Luftwaffe (Ger., "air weapon"). The air force of Nazi Germany, organized by Hermann GOERING.

Lug. In the Gaelic mythological cycle, a hero of the people called the TUATHA DÉ DANANN. Later, he becomes an important god for the Sons of Mil, who are said to be the first Celts in Ireland. See BALOR.

Lugnasad. August 1, one of the 4 great feast days of the ancient Celtic year. See SAMAIN; BELTINE; IMBOLC.

Lugné-Poë, Aurélien-François (1869-1940). Actor and producer. An actor at the Théâtre d'Art of Paul FORT, he later became director of the theater (1893) and called it Théâtre de l'oeuvre. Lugné-Poë encouraged new dramatic talent: Crommelynck, Sarment, Salacrou, and Marcel Achard were first played in his theater. The avant-garde Théâtre de l'oeuvre, begun as a symbolist theater, sought to return poetry and an atmosphere of mystery to the French stage.

Lugones, Leopoldo (1874-1938). Argentine poet. The outstanding exponent of MODERNISM in Argentina, Lugones was a close friend of Rubén Darío, whom he resembled in verbal virtuosity and ingenuity. In his first books of poetry—Las montañas de oro (1897), Los crepúsculos del jardín (1905), and Lunario sentimental (1909)—he revealed a penchant for startling but beautiful imagery and rhythmical experimentation. His return to poetic orthodoxy was signaled by his Odas seculares (1910), written to commemorate the centenary of Argentine independence. In this and later works, including Romancero (1924) and Poemas solariegos (1928), he expressed his ardent love of country in a style that became progressively less personal and more realistic. His prose writings include La guerra gaucha (1905), poetic accounts of episodes in Argentina's war for independence, and Las fuerzas extrañas (1906), fantastic short stories.

Luhan, Mabel Dodge (1879-1962). American patroness of the arts and memoirist. Famous for her salons in Italy and New York in the early 20th century, she cultivated close associations with Max Eastman, D. H. Lawrence, John Reed, Gertrude Stein, and Carl Van Vechten. She told of their lives and hers in a four-volume autobiography, Intimate Memories (1933-1937). She had three husbands before she married a Pueblo Indian and settled down in Taos, N.M., where she was a vital force behind the art colony there. She also wrote Lorenzo in Taos (1932) about her relationship with Lawrence.

Lu Hsun (1881-1936) Pseudonym of Chou Shu-jen. Chinese short-story writer, essayist, and educator. A leader in the movement to overthrow the Ch'ing government and an ardent reformer, he is idolized by the communists. Many of his stories have been translated into English by Chi-chen Wang, in Ah Q and others (1941).

Luke, St. Patron saint of painters and physicians, author of the Gospel of St. Luke and the Acts of the Apostles in the New Testament. Tradition says he painted a portrait of the Virgin Mary; Col. iv. 14 states that he was a physician.

Luke, The Gospel According to St. The 3rd book of the New Testament. One of the SYNOPTIC GOSPELS, it was the third account of the life of Jesus to be written, the author using Mark and Matthew as sources, as well as other documents now lost. It has high literary merit and a strong humanitarian appeal. The author is almost certainly the Greek physician who was a traveling companion of Paul and the author of The Acts of the Apostles.

Lully, Jean Baptiste or Giovanni Battista Lulli (1632-1687). Florentine-born French composer. Known as the originator of French opera, he was appointed court superintendent of music by Louis XIV in 1653, and received his French naturalization patent in 1661. Out of the music that he composed for court entertainments, notably the ballets of Benserade and the comédie-ballets of Molière, he developed French opera with its characteristic accompanied recitatives, dramatic scoring, and balletic interludes. In 1672, Lully founded the Académie Royale de Musique, which later became the Paris Opéra, and for which he composed 20 or more operas and ballets to librettos by QUINAULT. Reflecting the fashion of the day in their choice of classical subjects (Alceste, 1674; Proserpine, 1680), these works held the stage for almost a century.

Lunsford, Sir Thomas (c. 1610-c. 1653). English jailer and long-time governor of the Tower of London. He was noted for his vindictive temper. Samuel Butler mentions him in Hudibras.

Lunt, Alfred (1893-). American actor. With his wife, Lynn FONTANNE, he has appeared on stage in The Guardsman, Elizabeth the Queen, The Taming of the Shrew, Idiot's Delight, Amphitryon 38, The Sea Gull, and The Visit of the Old Lady.

Luntz, Lev Natanovich (1901-1924). Russian playwright and critic. An active member of the SERAPION BROTHERS, Luntz was especially insistent on Russian writers looking to the West for their methods, particularly for ways of handling plot. He advised Russian writers to pay attention to such authors as Conan Doyle and Rider Haggard. Besides his work publicizing the viewpoint of the Serapion Brothers, Luntz also wrote four plays: The Outlaw (Vne zakon; 1921), The Apes are Coming (Obezyany idut; 1921), Bertrand de Born (1922), and The City of Truth (Gorod pravdy; 1923-1924).

Lun-yü. See ANALECTS.

Lupercalia. In ancient Rome, an annual festival, held on February 15, probably in honor of FAUNUS, worshipped under the name of Lupercal. The worshippers gathered at a grotto on the Palatine where Romulus and Remus were supposed to have been suckled by the wolf (lupus). It was a festival of expiation and purification, and goats and a dog were sacrificed. Youths smeared with sacrificial blood ran round the Palatine carrying thongs of goat's hide (*februa*); women struck by them were supposedly made fertile. The ceremony survived into Christian times; it was suppressed A.D. 494.

Lurcanio. The brother of Ariodante in a tale from the ORLANDO FURIOSO of Ariosto. He charges Ginevra, the heroine, with having caused the suicide of his brother, in despair over her alleged unfaithfulness. As a result, she is doomed until rescued by Rinaldo and the returned Ariodante, who had survived.

Luria (1846). A poetic drama, written in Elizabethan style, by Robert BROWNING. The titular hero, a noble Moor, leads the army of Florence to victory against the Pisans, but the Florentines distrust him and summon him to trial. Overwhelmed by their ingratitude, he ends his life with poison. The poem is based on a historical character of the 15th century.

Lurlei. See LORELEI.

Lusíadas, Os (The Lusiads, 1572). An epic poem by Luis de CAMÕES. It relates the illustrious actions of the Lusians, or Portuguese, of all ages, but deals principally with the exploits of Vasco da GAMA and his comrades in their "discovery of India." Gama sailed three times to India. It is the first of these voyages (1497) which is the theme of the epic, but its wealth of episode, the constant introduction of mythological "machinery," and the intervention of Bacchus, Venus, and other deities make it far more than the mere chronicle of a voyage. Bacchus is the guardian power of the Muslims, and Venus, or Divine Love, of the Lusians. The fleet first sails to Mozambique, then to Quiloa, then to Melinda in Africa, where the adventurers are hospitably received and provided with a pilot to conduct them to India. In the Indian Ocean, Bacchus tries to destroy the fleet, but the "silver star of Divine Love" calms the sea, and Gama arrives in India safely.

Interwoven in the poem are episodes based on notable events in Portuguese history, such as the death of Inés Castro and the victory of Aljubarrota.

Lusitania. (1) The ancient name for Portugal (2) A British transatlantic liner torpedoed without warning by a German submarine off the coast of Ireland on May 7, 1915. She sank in 18 minutes with a loss of 1198 lives, including 124 Americans. Indignation over this act contributed to U.S. entry into World War I.

Lustra (1916). A collection of poems by Ezra POUND. The title, from the Latin, refers to the offerings made by Roman censors "for the sins of the whole people." Pound also issued a collection called *Lustra of Ezra Pound* (1917), an extension of the earlier volume, containing *Near Perigord*.

Lutetia (from Lat. *lutum,* mud). The ancient name of Paris, which, in Roman times, was merely a collection of mud hovels. Caesar called it *Lutetia Parisiorum* (the mud town of the Parisii), from which comes the present name Paris.

Luther, Martin (1483–1546). German religious reformer. He was an Augustinian monk and the professor of biblical exegesis at Wittenberg where, in 1517, he posted his critique of the Roman Catholic Church's practices, the NINETY-FIVE THESES which are usually regarded as the original document of the REFORMATION. From then on, he was the center of a

Title page of St. John Fisher's sermon against Luther (preached 1521). Fisher was later beheaded by Henry VIII.

violent religious upheaval in Germany where—among the humanists, for example—there had already been a great deal of feeling against Rome. The most important of Luther's later contributions to the controversy were his pamphlets *An den Christlichen Adel deutscher Nation (Address to the Christian Nobility of the German Nation,* 1520) and *Von der Freiheit eines Christenmenschen (On Christian Liberty,* 1520). His principal contention was that man is justified by faith alone, and not by works. On the basis of this idea of a personal faith, he favored the abolition of many church rituals and challenged the supreme authority of the pope. He was excommunicated in 1520 and appeared before the Diet of Worms in 1521, where he took a firm stand upon his views and was put under the ban of the Holy Roman Empire. The elector of Saxony, however, undertook to protect him; and in a safe retreat, Luther began his translation of the Bible into German (New Testament, 1522; Old Testament, 1534). His other works include the *Sendbrief von Dolmetschen (Letter on Translation,* 1530), defending his rendering of the Bible, and 40 *Kirchenlieder (Church-Songs,* 1524), among which is the famous hymn *Ein feste Burg ist unser Gott (A mighty fortress is our God).* His *Tischreden (Table-Talk)* is a valuable source of detail about his personality and beliefs. See Philipp MELANCHTHON; Ulrich von HUTTEN; Thomas MURNER.

Lutrin, Le (The Lectern, cantos 1-4, 1674; cantos 5-6, 1683). A mock-heroic poem by Nicolas BOILEAU.

It satirizes a dispute between the treasurer and the choirmaster of the Sainte-Chapelle over the positioning of a choir lectern. The treasurer triumphs, but the poem ends with a reconciliation. Boileau not only lampoons clerical pomposity and pettiness with merciless irony, but manages, by contriving a battle in a bookshop, to comment satirically upon the literary feud between the ancients and the moderns. (See QUERELLE DES ANCIENS ET DES MODERNES.)

Luxemburg, Rosa (1870–1919). German socialist. She was killed with Karl LIEBKNECHT by the provisional government, because of her leading position in the SPARTACIST PARTY revolt of 1919.

Luzán Claramunt de Suelves y Gurrea, Ignacio de (1702–1754). Spanish scholar and critic. A bilingual academician, he is known for his championship of the neoclassic cause in Spanish literature. His ideas are contained in the treatise *Poética, o reglas de la poesía en general y de sus principales especies* (1737), which advocated a didactic poetry and adherence to the three unities in the drama. He also gained fame as a result of his Latin compendium of Descartes' ideas.

Lycaon (Lykaon). In classical mythology, a king of Arcadia. Desirous of testing the divine knowledge of Zeus, he served human flesh on his table, for which the god changed him into a wolf. His daughter, Callisto, was changed into the constellation Bear, whence this is sometimes called *Lycaonis Arctos*.

Lyceum (Lykeion). A grove and gymnasium on the banks of the Ilissus, in Attica. ARISTOTLE taught philosophy there as he paced the walks. The name is sometimes used to stand for Aristotle's philosophic school.

Lycidas (1637). An elegiac poem by John MILTON, commemorating the death of Edward King (1612–1637), a Cambridge schoolmate who was drowned in the Irish Sea. The title is taken from the name of a shepherd in Vergil's third *Bucolic*. One of the most famous English elegies, *Lycidas* is not only concerned with King's untimely death, but attempts to deal with a world in which the good die young and false priests and poets prevail. Milton's solution is partly that of the Christian—ultimately God's justice will win out on earth; meanwhile virtue is rewarded in heaven—and partly that of the dedicated humanist poet—true genius is interconnected and immortal and enjoys a special relationship to, and survival in, the powers and beauties of the natural world. *Lycidas* has the strength and majesty of Milton's mature poetry and is consciously a poem of self-renewal and dedication to great work ahead.

Lycurgus (Lykourgos). A legendary legislator of Sparta. He is referred to by Herodotus and Xenophon, but nothing certain is known about him. His reforms are dated, as a result of archaeological evidence, at 600 B.C. Lycurgus is credited with transforming the Spartans from an art- and luxury-loving people into the stern and disciplined state-directed citizens of the sixth century.

Lycus (Lykos). See AMPHION.

Lydgate, Dr. See MIDDLEMARCH.

Lydgate, John (c. 1360–c. 1451). English poet and priest. Lydgate studied in both English and European universities, and was ordained as a priest in 1397. He was a close friend of the son of CHAUCER,

and knew the elder poet, whose influence is obvious in much of Lydgate's work. An amazingly versatile and prolific writer, he is one of the few poets of merit in the 150-year period between the death of Chaucer and the beginnings of the Elizabethan period. However, though his work was esteemed only less than that of Chaucer during the 16th century, his prolixity and medieval attitudes make him little read today. Among his numerous works are two allegorical poems, the *Complaint of the Black Night* and the *Temple of Glass;* the *Troy Book* (1412–20), based on the *Historia Troiana* of Guido delle Colonne; *The Story of Thebes* (1420–22); *The Pilgrimage of Man* (c. 1424), a translation of a work by Guillaume de Deguileville; and the FALLS OF PRINCES (1430–38), based on a French prose version of Boccaccio's *De Casibus Virorum Illustrum*.

Lydian mode. See GREEK MUSIC.

Lyly, John (1554?–1606). English prose writer, poet, and dramatist. Lyly gained a reputation as a wit at Oxford, and took M.A. degrees both at Oxford and Cambridge. He went to London, where he became one of the UNIVERSITY WITS, and tried to gain a place at court. Though associated with the court for a number of years, he never gained the position of

Title page of Lyly's *Campaspe* (1584).

Master of Revels for which he had hoped. He came under the patronage of Edward Vere, earl of Oxford, and wrote the first part of his most famous work, *Euphues, the Anatomy of Wit* (1579), for which he was immediately acclaimed. The following year he published the second part of this work, called *Euphues and his England*. The balanced, elegant, and highly artificial style of these pieces was very possibly Lyly's own invention. It was widely imitated for many years, notably by Robert GREENE and Thomas LODGE, and has come to be known as Euphuistic (see EUPHUISM; EUPHUES).

Lyly succeeded in becoming the vice-master of the acting company of the Children of St. Paul's, for whom he wrote plays to be presented at court. Of the eight plays he wrote for the Children the best known are *Alexander and Campaspe* (1584; reissued as *Campaspe*, 1591); *Endimion* (1591); and *Midas* (1592). He took his plots from Greek and Roman classic literature and transformed them into charming, ornate allegories of court flirtations and intrigues and the political affairs of the time, and refined and intellectualized comedy from its former and cruder state. All but one of his plays (*The Woman of the Moon*, 1597) were written in Euphuistic prose.

Lyly was involved on the side of the bishops in the Martin MARPRELATE CONTROVERSY, although only one pamphlet thought to be his has survived. Called *Pappe with an Hatchet* (1589), it was answered by Gabriel HARVEY in *Advertisement for Papp-Hatchet and Martin Marprelate*, which was appended to his *Pierce's Supererogation*.

Lynceus (Lynkeus). One of the ARGONAUTS and brother of Idas. He was so sharp-sighted that he could see through the earth, and distinguished objects nine miles off. He and his brother were killed in a fight with their fellow Argonauts, Castor and Polydeuces.

Lynch, Benito (1885?-1951). Argentine novelist. Lynch is best known for his depiction of the Argentine gaucho and for the homely fidelity with which he described rural life in Argentina. (See GAUCHO LITERATURE.) His books include *Los caranchos de La Florida* (1916), which relates the conflict between the domineering master of La Florida ranch and his impetuous son; *El inglés de los güesos* (1924), a love story of an English scientist and a gaucho girl; and *El romance de un gaucho* (1930), which is written entirely in gaucho idiom.

Lynd, Robert (1879-1949). Anglo-Irish essayist and journalist. He wrote essays in the manner of Charles Lamb; among his collections are *Books and Authors* (1922) and *In Defence of Pink* (1939). His wife, Sylvia Lynd (1888-1952), was a poet and novelist.

Lyonnesse. A legendary land in medieval romance. It was located near Land's End, off the coast of England; at present, it is submerged "full forty fathoms under water." King Arthur came from this mythical country, and the battle of Lyonnesse was the final conflict between Arthur and Sir Mordred.

Lyons, Eugene (1898-   ). Russian-born American journalist. At one time warmly sympathetic to Soviet Russia, Lyons became disillusioned and vigorously attacked the regime in articles and books, including *The Red Decade* (1941). He was editor of *American Mercury* (1939-1944) before becoming a senior editor for *Reader's Digest*.

lyre. See GREEK MUSIC.

Lyrical Ballads (1798). A volume of poems by Samuel Taylor COLERIDGE and William WORDSWORTH; a second edition was published in 1800, and a third in 1802. It was the first important publication of the poetry of the romantic period in English literature, and is considered one of the landmarks of literature. Wordsworth's contributions were his poems of country scenes and people, written in plain language and style, and his *Tintern Abbey*. Coleridge's principal contribution was *The Rime of the Ancient Mariner*. The second edition of *Lyrical Ballads* contains a preface by Wordsworth explaining his theory that poetry should be drawn from the everyday life and speech of men; this preface came to be considered the manifesto of English ROMANTICISM.

Lysander. In Shakespeare's MIDSUMMER NIGHT'S DREAM, a young Athenian in love with Hermia. He escapes with her into the woods in order to prevent her marriage to Demetrius.

Lysander (Lysandros, died 395 B.C.). Spartan naval and military commander. He defeated the Athenians at Aegospotami in 405 B.C., thus ending the PELOPONNESIAN WAR.

Lysistrata (c. 415 B.C.). The title and heroine of a comedy by ARISTOPHANES. It deals with an effective women's peace organization. In the 21st year of the Peloponnesian War, Lysistrata persuades the wives of Athens and Sparta to shut themselves up away from their husbands until peace shall be concluded. She has the satisfaction of dictating the terms.

Lyttelton, George. Baron Lyttelton (1709-1773). English author and statesman who was in the forefront of the opposition to Sir Robert Walpole. His works include *Letters from a Persian in England* (1735), an imitation of Montesquieu's *Lettres Persanes;* and *Dialogues of the Dead* (1760).

Lytton, Edward George Earle Lytton Bulwer-. See Edward George Earle Lytton BULWER-LYTTON.

Lytton, Edward Robert Lytton Bulwer-. See Owen MEREDITH.